THE NEW INTERPRETER'S BIBLE
COMMENTARY

In Ten Volumes

Editorial Board

The credentials listed here reflect the positions held at the time of the original publication.

THE NEW INTERPRETER'S™ BIBLE
COMMENTARY

VOLUME NINE

Acts
Introduction to Epistolary Literature
Romans
1 & 2 Corinthians
Galatians

ABINGDON PRESS
Nashville

THE NEW INTERPRETER'S BIBLE COMMMENTARY
VOLUME IX

Copyright © 2015 by Abingdon Press

This volume is a compilation of the following previously published material:
The New Interpreter's® Bible in Twelve Volumes, Volume X (Acts, Introduction to Epistolary Literature, Romans, 1 Corinthians), Copyright © 2002 by Abingdon Press.
The New Interpreter's® Bible in Twelve Volumes, Volume XI (2 Corinthians, Galatians), Copyright © 2000 by Abingdon Press.

This book is printed on acid-free paper.

Library of Congress Cataloging-in-Publication Data has been requested.

ISBN 978-1-4267-3585-1

19 20 21 22 23 24—10 9 8 7

MANUFACTURED IN THE UNITED STATES OF AMERICA

CONTRIBUTORS

ROBERT W. WALL
Professor of Biblical Studies
Department of Religion
Seattle Pacific University
Seattle, Washington
(Free Methodist Church of North America)
Acts, Introduction to Epistolary Literature

N. T. WRIGHT
Canon Theologian
Westminster Abbey
London, England
(The Church of England)
Romans

J. PAUL SAMPLEY
Professor of New Testament and Christian
Origins
The School of Theology and The Graduate
Division
Boston University
Boston, Massachusetts
(The United Methodist Church)
1 & 2 Corinthians

RICHARD B. HAYS
Professor of New Testament
The Divinity School
Duke University
Durham, North Carolina
(The United Methodist Church)
Galatians

* *The credentials listed here reflect the positions held at the time of the original publication.*

CONTENTS

VOLUME IX

THE ACTS OF THE APOSTLES

INTRODUCTION, COMMENTARY, AND REFLECTIONS
BY
ROBERT W. WALL

THE ACTS OF THE
APOSTLES

INTRODUCTION

The Acts of the Apostles is one of the most exciting and challenging books in the Christian Bible. Here we find a highly evocative story of the church's beginnings that traces its dramatic growth from sacred Jerusalem to imperial Rome. Because of its continuing importance in shaping the identity of today's church, Acts demands our most careful reading and thoughtful interpretation.

The importance of Acts for Christian formation is belied, however, by its sparse use in the church's lectionary, which assigns but a few of its most colorful episodes from the early chapters for use during the seven weeks leading from Easter to Pentecost. While liturgical practice reflects the book's keen stress on the Lord's resurrection and God's Spirit, I will argue for a much thicker portfolio of lessons, drawn from the entire narrative and included throughout the year, to enhance the teaching ministry of the church.

In order to draw fully upon the resources brought forward from the book of Acts, especially in this postmodern era of Bible study when methodological imperialism has been replaced by methodological pluralism, the student of Scripture should examine every biblical text in the light of different interpretive interests and cultural sensibilities. What follows seeks to introduce readers to this methodological pluralism by considering various topics from the book's origins to its inclusion within the NT canon. Layers of the text's full meaning are found at each of four different locations where interpreters pause for instruction in guiding the church's reflection upon God's Word for today. The critical admission of a text's multivalency, or variety of meaning, need not imply that the meaning is relative to an individual interpreter. What must finally regulate a faithful reading of Acts at every location—whether "behind the text" or "in the text" or "in front of the text"—are those core convictions of Christian confession and those distinctive practices that mark out Christian κοινωνία (*koinōnia*, "community"). When every element of Scripture study aims at theological understanding, the community of interpreters moves toward obedience to the divine will.

ACTS AS CONVERSATION: READING ACTS AS HISTORY

The Acts of the Apostles began its life as the written conversation between a storyteller (Luke) and his story's first reader (Theophilus). Modern commentaries on Acts are generally interested in reconstructing the circumstances of this correspondence as the most direct angle of vision to the text's intended meaning. To learn about the personal identities of the narrator and the first readers, their location, the circumstances that occasioned the writing of the book, and its date and communicative intention is not the disinterested pursuit of historians. Attending to such queries can make today's interpreters more aware of the book's continuing relevance and religious authority. To be sure, the historian's interest in the narrative of Acts does not necessarily supply us with accurate historical information about the origins of Christianity or of the narrator's purpose in telling his story. Such a presumption would be anachronistic, for Luke's task is to interpret and grant theological significance to past events rather than to describe them objectively or with factual precision suitable for his modern readers.[1]

Acts is an anonymous book. Even though the traditions of the ancient church assert that the evangelist Luke wrote both the Third Gospel and Acts—and there is no hard evidence to deny his authorship—knowing his identity or even that he was a sometimes traveling companion of Paul adds hardly anything to our understanding of his narrative. We can, perhaps, sketch the basic features of the nameless author of this narrative: He was an educated and well-traveled Greek who may well have converted to Judaism years before he became a Christian missionary; perhaps he was even an associate of Paul.[2] As a matter of literary fact, however, this narrator does not insinuate himself into his story, nor does he even bother to identify himself when joining Paul's company during the apostle's European mission (16:10-17; 20:5-16; 21:1-18; 27:1–28:16). Some modern scholars have come to base their historical judgment of Luke's authorship and the reliability of his story about Paul on these so-called we passages and the perceived intimacy they reflect between the narrator and the apostle.[3] The ambivalence of current opinion over both the reliability of Luke's sources and his authorship of Acts reflects the indeterminacy of these matters. In any case, the anonymity of Acts indicates that the narrator's focus is on the story rather than on his own identity.

The date and provenance of Acts, while important for determining its original social location, also cannot be determined with precision. Even if a date for Luke's Gospel from the mid-80s is likely and the narrative unity of Luke and Acts is presumed, this critical conclusion does not guarantee that Acts came from the same time and place as the Gospel. The argument that the same narrator must have written Acts with his Gospel depends largely on the claims that both the Gospel of Luke and Acts share (1) common language, (2) consistent theology, and (3) an ignorance of a second-century corpus of Pauline letters. Each of these claims, however, has been challenged; each is at day's end indeterminate.[4]

Once again the reader's sense of the time and place of Acts must arise from a close reading of the narrative. Luke probably wrote at a time when stressing the church's Jewish roots was necessary for both theological and political reasons. On the one hand, Rome should allow the church the same political freedoms it allowed Judaism; on the other hand, believers should retain their Jewish Scriptures and practices in order to be fully Christian. This later emphasis would have been especially pertinent if the theological tendency of Luke's church was toward supersessionism or some other theological expression that reflected the general failure of the

---

1. See J. Green, "Internal Repetition in Luke-Acts," in *History, Literature and Society in the Book of Acts*, ed. B. Witherington (Cambridge: Cambridge University Press, 1996) 283-99.

2. For this line of evidence, see A. Culpepper, "The Gospel of Luke," in *The New Interpreter's Bible Commentary*, 10 vols. (Nashville: Abingdon, 2015) 8:4-8.

3. For a positive assessment of the relationship between the Paul of Acts and the historical Paul, see M. Hengel and A. Schwemer, *Paul Between Damascus and Antioch* (Louisville: Westminster John Knox, 1997) 1-23.

4. See R. Maddox, *The Purpose of Luke-Acts* (Edinburgh: T. & T. Clark, 1982) 6-9. D. Trobisch, *Paul's Letter Collection* (Minneapolis: Fortress, 1994), has argued that Paul (or a close associate) placed a collection of his letters into circulation at Ephesus, perhaps as early as the mid-60s. Whether Luke knew of a collection of Paul's letters in any case cannot be so easily dismissed if allusions to (rather than citations of) them are credible evidence. The Commentary will argue at several points on the second half of Acts that Luke may well be alluding to one or more Pauline letters (e.g., Romans; 1–2 Corinthians) and not simply to common Pauline traditions used in both Acts and certain (esp. later/deutero-) Pauline correspondence (e.g., Ephesians; 1–2 Timothy). See also W. Walker, "Acts and the Pauline Corpus Reconsidered," *JSNT* 24 (1985) 3-23, who argues that Luke surely knew a collection of Paul's letters, was influenced by them, but had none open before him when writing Acts. This later conclusion is now revised in W. Walker, "Acts and the Pauline Corpus Revisited," in *Essays in Honor of Joseph B. Tyson*, ed. R. Thompson and T. Phillips (Macon: Mercer University Press, 1998) 77-86.

church's mission to the Jews of the diaspora.[5] This would explain Luke's principal concern regarding the health of the church's Jewish legacy.

Perhaps we can discern more about the world behind Acts by considering the first reader, Theophilus (see 1:1; Luke 1:3), who is otherwise unknown to us. Evidently Theophilus is a new, although socially prominent, believer. Some have speculated that his name, which in Greek means "dear to God," is Luke's clever metaphor for every new Christian seeking theological instruction. However, it is more likely that Theophilus is a wealthy patron who has provided funds to enable Luke to write a detailed narrative of the church's beginnings for public consumption. Both his Greek name and his apparent spiritual immaturity (see Luke 1:4), especially when considered with the writer's honorific appellation "most excellent Theophilus" (Luke 1:3), suggest that Luke's first reader was an affluent Greek, perhaps a God-fearer before converting to Jesus,[6] who desires a useful story to confirm his faith in the face of mounting confusions and challenges. It is reasonable for us to imagine that he found the transition from one symbolic world to another profoundly difficult.

While the narrative unity between the Gospel and Acts links Luke's story of Jesus to the events that follow his departure, the commentary will treat Acts as an independent biblical writing with its own literary, theological, and canonical integrity. While not disconnected from the purpose of his Gospel, Luke's reasons for writing a second book may be inferred from the distinctive theological emphases in Acts. Powell usefully summarizes these emphases in six categories: irenic, polemical, apologetic, evangelistic, pastoral, and theological.[7] His index catalogs those historical contingencies at the end of the first century that occasioned and helped shape this narrative as edifying communication from Luke for Theophilus.

(1) Acts was written to consolidate disparate faith communions. Luke's *irenic* spirit is no doubt an idealized feature of his theological vision. At the same time, his ecumenicity is never divorced from the hard pragmatics of the first church's mission in the world (see 6:1-7; 11:1-18; 14:27–15:29). A religious movement that lacks solidarity within its diverse membership will be ineffective in advancing its claims. Moreover, in the wider Roman culture, riddled with conflict and controversy of all kinds, a community of shared goods (material and spiritual) would embody evidence for the transforming power of God's saving grace. Surely the historical referent of this narrative theme is intended to compel Theophilus to locate himself within a community that practices reconciliation as the way of God.

(2) Acts was written as a *polemic* against idolatry. Scholars have long argued that Luke wrote Acts to challenge certain heretical forms of Christianity or even formative Judaism. That is doubtful. Rather, Luke responds positively to the concerns voiced by James at the Jerusalem Council over the "gentilizing" of the church (see 15:20-21, 28-29; see also the Commentary on 15:13–28:28). Agreeing with Paul's epistolary advice to the Corinthians (see 1 Corinthians 8–10), Luke's narrative sounds a cautionary note. Adding uncircumcised, uncatechized Gentiles to the church's rolls while the church's mission carries the Word of God farther and farther from the holy city may very well incline a pragmatic leadership (perhaps including Theophilus) to accommodate pagan religious practices and secular values that will corrupt its Jewish heritage.

(3) Acts was written as an *apologia* for Christianity. Read as a narrative about people, Luke's portrayal of Christian leaders underscores the authority and importance of their traditions for the future of the church. This is especially true of Paul, whose standing within the ancient church was contested into the second century. Luke does not locate Paul's religious authority in his apostolicity (see 1:21-22), as he does in his letters (e.g., Galatians 1–2). Rather, Paul's importance for the church is guaranteed by his prophetic vocation and performance (see 20:17-35).

Read as a political narrative, Luke's ambivalent depiction of Rome (and of Paul's Roman citizenship) in Acts may intend to define citizen Theophilus's relations with a non-Christian Roman

---

5. Any attempt to "update" religious conviction in the light of present contingencies is a kind of supersessionism—e.g., Judaism's efforts in rereading its Scriptures to take into account the destruction of the Temple/priesthood and its result in moving early Judaism toward its rabbinical expression is a kind of supersessionism. For this reason, R. Gordon, *Hebrews* (Sheffield: Sheffield Academic, 2000) 27-28, compares favorably the supersessionism evident in the Letter to the Hebrews with respect to the Scriptures with that taking place in contemporary Judaism.

6. Cf. J. Nolland, *Luke 1–9*, WBC (Dallas: Word, 1989) xxxii-xxxiii.

7. M. Powell, *What Are They Saying About Acts?* (New York: Paulist, 1991) 13-19.

world. While it is possible for a strong believer to be a good citizen (e.g., Paul), loyalty to the gospel or the church's missionary vocation must never be compromised by the obligations of citizenship.[8] Paul's defense speeches (see Acts 22–26; 28) are not concerned with his relationship to Rome; his *apologia* in Acts is funded by a rehearsal of his Jewish background and practices, along with a description of his prophetic vocation as a teacher of Israel. For this reason, neither repentant nor unrepentant Israel should have a problem with him or with the Christian congregations he has founded. Such a defense would be especially crucial if Theophilus belongs, as seems likely, to a congregation founded by Paul's mission. The Paul of Acts embraces his Roman and Tarsain citizenship without apology, and so should Theophilus when appropriate; the more important commitment, however, is to the church's Jewish roots. The Pauline legacy shapes a future that is closer to Israel than to Rome.

(4) Acts was written as a tool of the church's evangelistic *mission*. Clearly the literary theme that follows the triumph of the Word of God from Jerusalem to Rome testifies to the power and necessity of the proclaimed gospel. The prophetic boldness and effectiveness of the church's mission, superintended by God's Spirit, expresses this same theme. If the missionary episodes are read as indicating normative patterns of outreach for subsequent generations of Christians, then Acts may have been written for Theophilus to invigorate his congregation's missionary vocation or to teach him how to convert others in continuity with the missionaries of the earliest church.

The natural shift of the church's geographical epicenter from Jerusalem to Rome following the fall of Jerusalem would have instigated different concerns from those earlier between the Gentile mission and the Jewish church (see 11:1-18; 15:13-29; 21:17-26). The pressures on Luke's first readers would have been most keenly felt from the pervasive paganism of Roman cities. His response to this new missionary situation, however, is reactionary rather than progressive. When Paul finally arrives in Rome, he does not carry God's Word to its pagan population but first establishes his Jewish credentials (see 28:17-22) in order to convert religious Jews to Jesus (28:23-25). Luke does not perceive paganism as the church's principal threat; rather, the church's outreach is substantially weakened by the loss of its connection with the core beliefs and practices of repentant Israel.

(5) Acts was written to deepen the fragile faith of new believers such as Theophilus. Luke's *pastoral* intent for writing this narrative may have been to characterize Christian discipleship in response to his patron's particular struggles, with implications for all who share Theophilus's social status within the church. This motive underlies several narrative themes. For example, Acts provides a basic chronology of the religious roots of Christianity that may have enabled Theophilus and other new believers to locate themselves within space and time as participants of a real historical movement.[9] More important, Acts' distinct emphasis on the community of goods and description of well-known role models, such as Barnabas, may well have commended to affluent believers like Theophilus the sharing of their wealth with the community's poor as a Christian practice (see 2:42-47; 4:32-37; 11:27-30). This and other distinctive resurrection practices envisage a counterculture that may have proved a difficult life-style for the empire's rich and famous. That is, Acts was written to encourage members of urban congregations, such as Theophilus, to spearhead the redistribution of wealth as the guiding principle of the church's welfare program (cf. 1 Timothy 5–6). Further, the content and narrative significance of the speeches in Acts may have reassured the well-educated Theophilus that the gospel has intellectual integrity (see 17:22-31).

(6) Acts was written in response to a *theological* crisis. It is only a slight exaggeration to say that every NT book is occasioned by a theological crisis—a confusion over or misappropriation of some core conviction of God's Word that threatens to subvert the audience's Christian formation and witness. Several important interpreters of Acts have considered the occasion of Luke's

8. This ambivalence is reflected in competing assessments of the church's relationship with Rome in Acts. P. Walaskay, *"And So We Came to Rome": The Political Perspective of Acts*, SNTSMS 49 (Cambridge: Cambridge University Press, 1983), argues that Acts defends Rome to the church, while R. Cassidy, *Society and Politics in the Acts of the Apostles* (Maryknoll, N.Y.: Orbis, 1987), argues that the church is a counterculture that brooks no political allegiance with Rome.

9. See B. Witherington, *The Acts of the Apostles: A Socio-Rhetorical Commentary* (Grand Rapids: Eerdmans, 1998) 77-97, for a full discussion of Acts' chronology.

narrative from this angle of vision. For example, H. Conzelmann famously opined that Acts was written to correct the apocalyptic eschatology of a church troubled by an internal conflict over end-time fanaticism and doubt. For this reason, Luke edited out most eschatological speculation from his sources and creatively shaped a narrative that emphasizes mission and church growth in a "real" world.[10]

The theological crisis that occasioned the writing of Acts, however, is similar to that of Paul's Letter to the Romans; it concerns whether "there is any unrighteousness on God's part" (Rom 9:14) with respect to unbelieving Israel (Romans 9–11).[11] The rousing success of Paul's urban mission in the diaspora among God-fearing Gentiles, coupled with his relative lack of success among Jews who remained divided in their response to the risen Jesus (see 28:16-28), may have prompted some Jewish believers to wonder whether the church's mission actually subverted God's promise to restore historic Israel: "Has Israel stumbled so as to fall?" (Rom 11:11). The church's missionary reports, combined with the destruction of the Jerusalem Temple, the placing of Palestine to direct Roman rule by Roman governors, and the virtual cessation of the Jerusalem church by end of the first century, provided the necessary warrants for some believers in Luke's church to argue that the relevant symbols of covenant renewal between God and a "true" Israel no longer should include the traditional expressions of Jewish identity and holiness. These believers may have even appealed to Jesus' prediction of Jerusalem's destruction by Rome as the just desserts of Israel's rejection of him as Messiah (see 6:14; cf. Matt 24:1-2; Luke 19:41-48). The worrisome consequence was the attenuation of the church's Jewish legacy, without which the church could not be the church.

We should note that Luke's response in Acts is different from Paul's in Romans; Paul wrote a generation earlier when this internal threat was not so keenly felt. While both contend that only a remnant within Israel ever repented of sin and turned to God in faith (Rom 9:6-29), Paul is clearly dissatisfied with a divided Israel as a permanent solution. He, therefore, posits the full restoration of historic Israel at the return of Jesus following the Gentile mission (see Rom 11:25-36).[12] Acts does not register so sharp a dichotomy between the Jewish rejection of the gospel and the Gentiles' embrace of it as found in Romans (see Rom 11:11-24). Rather, Luke is resigned to a divided Israel as a permanent feature of God's plan of salvation (see 3:19-23). The promise of a faithful God to restore Israel has *already* been realized in the church's mission to the entire household of Israel (Acts 2–8). For Luke, unlike for Paul, the return of Christ inaugurates a season of "universal restoration" (3:21); and for him, unlike for Paul, the promise of Israel's "refreshment" has already been fulfilled among repentant Jews (see 3:19-20). In the meantime, the pattern of God's faithfulness to Israel agrees with (rather than reverses) biblical prophecy: Israel is restored first and only when repentant Gentiles are "grafted in their place to share the rich root of the olive tree" (Rom 11:17).

This same difference is also reflected by the principal opponents of Paul's Gentile mission within the church. In the Pauline letters, Paul is opposed by "Judaizers"—Jewish Christians who stipulated that all Gentile converts must also be catechized and circumcised according to the traditions of the Judaizers' ancestral religion. As a working symbol of his opposition to this "Judaizing" movement within the church, he refused to circumcise Titus, a Greek convert (see Acts 15:1-2; cf. Gal 2:1-10). When Luke wrote Acts, however, the principal internal threat to the church's faith were "Gentilizers" who threatened to erase anything Jewish from the church's core identity. To mark this different context, Luke tells the story of Paul's circumcision of Timothy, who symbolizes the mission's resistance to the gentilizing of the church's Jewish legacy (see 16:1-5; cf. 15:19-21, 28-29; 21:25). Surely Luke was right to worry; the attenuation of the church's Jewish legacy led to Marcionism in the next generation and has cultivated the anti-Semitism that continues to debilitate our own.

---

10. H. Conzelmann, *The Acts of the Apostles*, trans. J. Limburg et al., ed. E. J. Epp and C. R. Matthews, Hermeneia (Philadelphia: Fortress, 1987) xlv-xlvii.

11. See R. Wall, "Israel and the Gentile Mission According to Acts and Paul: A Canonical Approach," in *Witness to the Gospel: The Theology of the Book of Acts*, ed. I. Howard Marshall and D. Peterson (Grand Rapids: Eerdmans, 1998) 437-58.

12. See C. Hill, "Romans," *Oxford Bible Commentary* (Oxford: Oxford University Press, 2001).

ACTS AS COMPOSITION: READING ACTS AS LITERATURE

The principal interest of those interpreters who approach Acts as a composition is to construct the literary world within the text rather than to reconstruct the ancient world behind it. Some "in-the-text" readings of Acts are vitally interested with historical questions too—with those first-century exigencies and communicative intentions that contributed to the narrator's choice of literary genre and narrative aim. Other literary explorations into Acts detach the literary text from these historical moorings in order to consider its intertextuality, linguistics, or creative storytelling in ways that treat Acts' historical context as largely irrelevant to the theological points it scores.

For the majority of interpreters of Acts, the most important literary query concerns its *genre:* Is Acts a history, a biography, a novel, an apologia, or a variety of literature without ancient parallel?[13] The stakes in answering this question are large, since what one concludes about a book's genre influences what one concludes about its overarching purpose—that is, function follows literary form. The literary critic typically begins with the recognition that Acts is the second of two volumes whose interpretation requires a prior decision about its narrative unity with Luke's Gospel. Until recently most commentators have simply affirmed the unity of Luke and Acts and extended this unity to a common genre. In this case, the genre of "Luke-Acts" is introduced by the preface to Luke's Gospel (1:1-4), which is then alluded to in the preface to Acts (1:1-2). That is, Acts is the second volume of a continuous *diēgēsis*—a historical narrative of some sort—about "the things fulfilled among us" (Luke 1:1).

At the very least, however, this consensus must now be qualified in several ways. Simply put, Acts is not a gospel. Luke's Gospel is more like ancient biographical literature that tells the story of a person's life and career. This biography is "gospel" because it tells the life story of the Savior from conception to ascension. Acts, on the other hand, sketches the origins of a religious movement, itself full of miracles and magic but without telling the story of only one heroic character. Moreover, the narrative of this second volume is deliberately set within a chronological and geographical framework similar to historical monographs produced in antiquity (see 1:8). Acts is hardly "secular" history, since its narrator structures the progress of this movement as a commentary on biblical prophecy. Read from this literary perspective, the story of the successive missions of various prophets-like-Jesus who carry the Word of God from Jerusalem to Rome and from Jew to Gentile has been scripted by God according to Israel's Scriptures (see 2:14-21; 15:13-21; 28:25-28).

A number of studies have demonstrated that Acts is best read as a genre of ancient *historiography*, itself quite fluid in form and function. Luke's narrative is a selective account of what happened—a "history" shaped and signified according to his personal theological beliefs and pastoral purposes (see above, "Acts as Conversation"). History, whether ancient or modern, is almost always written with a language and within a framework that reflects the historian's discrete perspective on the meaning of events. In the case of Acts, then, Luke selects and arranges a series of events that he narrates for his reader(s) in order to give meaning to the church's mission and message as a history that accords with God's redemptive plans for Israel and the nations.

Since Luke was not himself an eyewitness to much of what he recounts and interprets, he depended upon sources for his relevant information.[14] The content and nature of these sources, whether oral or written; their identity; and Luke's reception and handling of them are all matters of considered and continuing speculation. Dibelius's verdict that Acts is largely the creative work of its author, whose access to reliable material was limited at best, has keenly influenced the modern discussion.[15] On this view, for example, the speeches of Acts are not based on notes taken by auditors but are Luke's literary creations. Even the "we" passages of Acts are not the accounts of an eyewitness but reflect the rhetorical artistry of a narrator who inserts himself into

13. Cf. M. Parsons and R. Pervo, *Rethinking the Unity of Luke and Acts* (Minneapolis: Fortress, 1993). See also Witherington, *The Acts of the Apostles*, 2-39, for a careful review of Parsons and Pervo's work. The editorial tendency of many modern commentary series to assign both Luke and Acts to the same scholar reifies the assumption that common authorship presumes a common theological conception.

14. For a competent review of Luke's use of various sources when writing Acts, see J. A. Fitzmyer, *The Acts of the Apostles*, AB 31 (Garden City, N.Y.: Doubleday, 1998) 80-90. I will take up more specific problems with Luke's sources when apropos to the discussion of specific texts.

15. M. Dibelius, *Studies in the Acts of the Apostles*, ed. H. Greek (New York: Scribner's, 1956).

the narrative world in order to influence the reader's impressions of what is read (see 16:10-16). This older view has been substantially revised by new appreciation for the artistry of ancient historiographers, whose representations of a real event cohere not only with other literary elements of their composition but also with available information about that event as recalled by reliable (and often firsthand) witnesses. Many scholars, therefore, are inclined to accept Luke as one of Paul's team whose memory (or personal diaries) is the principal (but not the only) source he draws upon when shaping his story of Paul's mission and trials. While it remains another matter to assess the historical credibility of what is written in the first person or the nature of Luke's personal relationship with Paul, the narrator's presence as "credible witness" to events narrated in several passages has a measured rhetorical effect on the reader. Luke must have realized this, or else he would have surely erased every trace of himself from Acts. Instead, he chooses to address certain reservations about Paul or the results of his mission by placing himself unobtrusively in the story to help relieve the suspicions about a controversial Paul.[16]

In this light, another important interest of literary criticism is to determine how the various elements of Luke's story form a coherent plotline: How does Acts work as a narrative?[17] Simply stated, the plot of Acts unfolds in support of Luke's theological aim. On the one hand, he designs his story according to a specific geographical and chronological framework. The action begins in Jerusalem before moving beyond the holy city into the neighboring provinces of Samaria and Judea before moving into the nations and peoples beyond Palestine (see the Overview to Acts 9–28). Many have found this geographical outline indexed by Jesus' programmatic prophecy in Acts 1:8. In addition, Acts traces the key events with brief glimpses of the most important leaders of earliest Christianity to establish a general chronology of the church's origins. On the other hand, this historical conception provides the framework for two grand thematic movements ("conversion" and "consecration"), each scripted by extended citations of Scripture (see 2:17-21; 15:16-18) that narrate how the redemptive purposes of God are realized through the church's mission (see "Acts as Theology," below).

Among the many narrative elements that make up the plot of Acts, the speeches are especially important.[18] They make up roughly one-third of the composition and often signal programmatic movements in the plot while providing summaries of the narrator's core theological commitments. The speeches of Acts typically provoke further responses to the gospel that move the story's action from setting to setting in a "logical" manner. As such they supply an interpretive matrix by which the narrative's aim is made clearer. The most important and often debated of these speeches serve missionary ends. Peter's Pentecost sermon (see 2:14-41), the inaugural sermon of Paul's mission to the nations at Pisidian Antioch (see 13:16-41), and Paul's sharply stated Socratic retort at the Athenian Aeropagus (see 17:22-31) are good examples of missionary discourse that serve the narrator's programmatic concerns. Other speeches shaped according to the conventions of different rhetorical genre are important to the plotline of Acts. For example, Stephen's apologia as a prophet-like-Jesus stipulates the nature of the prophetic vocation that details the conflict between Christian preaching and Jewish tradition (see 7:1-53). Paul's so-called farewell speech defines the sort of person who best serves an orderly succession of future leaders in the fledgling church his mission has founded (see 20:18-35). Finally, the various defense speeches of the Paul of Acts at the book's end (see 22:1-21; 24:10-21; 26:2-23; 28:17-20) serve to defend his spiritual authority within emergent Christianity and within the Christian biblical canon of the Pauline letters that follow.

Even though reflecting different rhetorical conventions to serve different narrative settings, the speeches of Acts draw from a common pool of images and ideas.[19] The result is a profound

---

16. Cf. S. Porter, *The Paul of Acts*, WUNT 115 (Tübingen: Mohr Siebeck, 1999) 10-66, who argues that the use of "we" in Acts cues the reader to an independent and continuous Pauline source (which may be, but probably is not, Luke) whose favorable view of Paul was of special usefulness in advancing the narrator's apologetic interests.

17. For good examples of reading Acts as narrative, see R. Tannehill, *The Narrative Unity of Luke-Acts*, vol. 2 (Minneapolis: Fortress, 1990); F. S. Spencer, *Acts*, Readings: A New Biblical Commentary (Sheffield: Sheffield Academic, 1997).

18. See M. Soards, *The Speeches in Acts: Their Content, Context, and Concerns* (Louisville: Westminster/John Knox, 1994).

19. I will consider the implications of the rhetorical shaping of the speeches of Acts in some detail when commenting upon specific passages. For a useful introduction to this literary element, especially as it relates to ancient models of public speaking, see the relevant essays gathered together in *The Book of Acts in Its First Century Setting*, vol. 1, ed. B. Winter and A. Clarke (Grand Rapids: Eerdmans, 1993).

sense of continuity both in the *content* of Christian proclamation from the risen Jesus (see 1:3) to the imprisoned Paul (see 28:30-31) and in the *vocation* of Christian preachers inspired by the Holy Spirit to perform competently, faithfully, and boldly all the tasks of the prophet-like-Jesus. Thus every speech in Acts—whether missionary, apologetic, or edifying—is centered by the non-negotiable content of God's saving word. Jesus performs signs and wonders as God's Messiah; he then suffers and is crucified; and finally he is resurrected and exalted by God to confirm that "there is no other name under heaven by which we must be saved" (4:12). To show that this messianic "event" conforms to the script of God's salvation, proofs from prophecy are layered into the speeches. Eyewitness testimony, whether of the risen Jesus (e.g., 2:32; 26:8, 15-16, 26), of personal experience of God's presence (e.g., 15:7-11, 12), or of an exemplary life (e.g., 20:18-21), complements Scripture's witness. Religious experience is glossed by Scripture's interpretation to prove the trustworthiness of the Gospel's claims about the Lord's messiahship and the faithfulness of God to promises of redemption. Other narrative elements, such as Luke's summaries (see 2:42-47; 4:32-35) and interludes (see 6:1-7), perform roles within Acts similar to the speeches. These elements underwrite the most important literary themes and provide a retrospective on previous events in preparation for the future.

Luke's use of repetition is another important literary convention of his narrative. For instance, the triadic telling of important episodes underscores their value in the narrative world (e.g., Paul's call, 9:9-19; Cornelius's conversion, 10:1-44). In addition, the repeated uses of prophetic catchwords (e.g., παρρησία *parrēsia*, "boldness") and phrases (e.g., σημεῖα καὶ τέρατα *sēmeia kai terata*, "signs and wonders" or ἔσχατος τῆς γῆς *eschatos tēs gēs*, "end of the earth"), of kerygmatic motifs (e.g., ἄφεσις *aphesis*, "forgiveness" or βασιλεία τοῦ θεοῦ *basileia tou theou*, "kingdom of God"), of literary themes (e.g., ἅπαντα κοινά *hapanta koina*, community of goods) and narrative actions (e.g., mixed response to the gospel or mass conversions) are important for several reasons. The entire range of meaning unfolds by each repetition of a word or literary theme in new compositional settings. More important, the *intratextuality* within Acts invites a more reflexive or unified reading of the story. Through repeated words or images the reader is reminded of earlier episodes or texts that are then recalled and brought into a mutually informing dialogue with the current text or episode. For example, in the testimony that God did "signs and wonders" among the Gentiles (15:12), the reader recognizes that the use of "signs and wonders" recalls Joel's prediction concerning the last days (Joel 2:19). In this way, the reader recovers the theological subtext of Paul's (and Peter's) testimony: God's promise of salvation is extended to include everyone, Jew and now Gentile, who repents and turns to the Lord Jesus in faith. Luke's use of repetition forges a literary coherence that aims disparate pieces of the narrative toward a common theological purpose.

Similar to the phenomenon of intratextuality within Acts, the *intertextuality* between Acts and antecedent sacred tradition supports and adds an inherent depth of understanding to Luke's narrative aim.[20] Even a cursory reading of Acts reflects Luke's routine use of sacred tradition, both biblical (LXX) and kerygmatic. He needs only to mention a familiar biblical phrase or employ a familiar prophetic typology (e.g., God's judgment of unrepentant Israel) to evoke other biblical texts and stories where that phrase is used or follows a typological pattern. Sometimes these texts are actually cited (e.g., 2:17-21), but more often Scripture is echoed by reference to common words or narrative elements (e.g., people, places, events). The "diverse components of the biblical anthology share a common worldview, [where] innumerable strands link together the constitutive units [to form] a literary and ideological entity."[21] The anticipated result of finding these citations or hearing those echoes of an earlier text when reading another is to link these two texts together as partners in a reflexive, mutually informing conversation—hence, the label "intertextuality." Significantly, the cited or echoed text recalls not only a particular story or idea but also a history of reception (both within and external to Scripture) that adds still

---

20. See R. Wall, "Intertextuality, Biblical," in *Dictionary of New Testament Background*, ed. C. Evans and S. Porter (Downers Grove: InterVarsity, 2000) 541-51.

21. S. Talmon, "Emendation of Biblical Texts on the Basis of Ugaritic Parallels," in *Studies in the Bible*, ed. S. Japhet (Jerusalem: Magnes, 1986) 279.

additional layers of information to the interpretive matrix. The result is that the reader is able to discern a fuller, richer meaning.[22]

While Luke's rereading of his sacred tradition is also shaped by the currents of his Greco-Roman world, his use of Scripture in Acts is essentially Jewish. Thus he employs tradition in a way consonant with the church's Jewish heritage. The idea of Scripture that lies behind its appropriation in Acts is that the cited or echoed text is produced by the Spirit of God. This same Spirit leads interpreters to render Scripture's divinely intended meaning in public proclamation (17:3). In this way, Scripture (or Jesus tradition) is rightly used to supply evidence that "these things that have happened among us" follow God's prophesied plan for Israel's promised restoration. That is, Luke does not use Scripture in defense of the faith ("proof from prophecy") but as integral to his story's theological meaning. This particular quality of Lukan composition is similar to Jewish midrashic literature.[23] Modern interpreters, alert to the principles of Jewish exegesis, will recognize, for example, that Luke's composition of Peter's Pentecost sermon is midrash-like: the citation of a relevant biblical text (Joel's prophecy, Joel 2:28-32 [LXX 3:1-5]) is followed by commentary on its contemporary meaning (see Joel 2:14-21, 22-41) and the inclusion of biblical commentaries (*midrashim*) on Pss 16:8-11 and 110:1. Luke's use of catchwords and phrases from biblical texts throughout his narrative suggests a sustained and reflexive dialogue with Israel's Scriptures—that is, between his text and the biblical text—that is characteristic of midrashic literature. The intent is to lead us into a fuller and more contemporary understanding of God's Word.[24]

No introduction to the literary fabric of Acts is complete without mentioning the artistry of Luke's storytelling. His effective use of romance[25] and dramatic episodes involving divine speech and action,[26] his use of local color to add realism to the most crucial episodes of Paul's mission (27:1–28:10), and the lively wit he brings to his storytelling (20:7-12), sometimes to mock the early church's competition (see 19:28-34), all contribute to a well-told story that entertains as well as edifies.

Finally, this commentary will often call attention to the complex textual history of Acts.[27] R. Brown comments that "Acts has a textual problem more acute than that of any other NT book."[28] In addition to the standard set of textual variants, the ancient Greek manuscripts of Acts include a distinctive group best exemplified by the bilingual (Latin and Greek) Codex Bezae (D), known as "the Western text of Acts."[29] One must decide whether this Western text or another prominent family of manuscripts, the so-called Alexandrian text of Acts, most nearly represents the Acts written by Luke and thus the narrative used for this study. The majority of textual scholars believe that the most distinctive features of the Western text are scribal interpolations added long after Luke's death; for this reason such scholars prefer to use the Alexandrian text as the basis of modern translations (including both the NIV and the NRSV).

Some scholars, however, have proposed that both texts of Acts were put into circulation roughly at the beginning of the canonical process toward the end of the second century, when Luke's reasons for writing Acts were replaced or qualified by still other concerns of the emerging church catholic. Significantly, the Western text of Acts, which expands Luke's narrative (more than the speeches) to reflect the theological tendencies of this church, betrays its concern to distinguish Christianity from Judaism as two discrete religious and theological options. In doing

---

22. According to R. Hays, *Echoes of Scripture in the Letters of Paul* (New Haven: Yale University Press, 1989) 18-19, the critical task of finding echoing predecessors prevents a version of intertextuality that is purely literary and of the present moment.

23. For Luke's narrative style as midrash-like, see C. A. Evans and J. A. Sanders, *Luke and Scripture: The Function of Sacred Tradition in Luke-Acts* (Minneapolis: Fortress, 1993), 1-13.

24. Cf. D. Boyarin, *Intertextuality and the Reading of Midrash* (Bloomington: Indiana University Press, 1990) 1-21; M. Fishbane, *The Garments of Torah* (Bloomington: Indiana University Press, 1989) 16-18.

25. See R. Pervo, *Profit with Delight* (Philadelphia: Fortress, 1987); D. Edwards, *Religion and Power* (New York: Oxford, 1996).

26. See J. Thomas, *The Devil, Disease and Deliverance*, JPTSS 5 (Sheffield: Sheffield Academic, 1998); H. Kee, *Medicine, Miracle and Magic in the NT Times*, SNTSMS 55 (Cambridge: Cambridge University Press, 1986).

27. See C. K. Barrett, *A Critical and Exegetical Commentary on the Acts of the Apostles*, 2 vols., ICC (Edinburgh: T. & T. Clark, 1994, 1998) 1:2-29. The most important textual problems will be considered in the footnotes to this commentary.

28. R. Brown, *An Introduction to the New Testament* (New York: Doubleday, 1997) 327. For a full account of the history of this textual problem, see W. Strange, *The Problem of the Text of Acts*, SNTSMS 71 (Cambridge: Cambridge University Press, 1992).

29. See E. Epp, *The Theological Tendency of Codex Bezae Cantabrigiensis in Acts*, SNTSMS 3 (Cambridge: Cambridge University Press, 1966). The most balanced discussion of how this version of Acts compares with the other principal Greek text of Acts, the so-called Alexandrian text, is P. Head, "Acts and the Problem of Its Texts," in Winter and Clarke, *The Book of Acts in Its First Century Setting*, 1:415-44.

so, this popular version of Acts became an "anti-Judaic" narrative. The hostility of unrepentant Jews and their leaders is intensified in the text, while the institutions and traditions of Judaism are diminished in importance. A large number of "Western" variants contribute to this negative impression; thus, in Epp's words, "the Jews come out rather poorly in the D-text."[30] Further, Western scribes added narrative materials to enhance Paul's already powerful profile. Not only are his deeds made even more spectacular and his character more virtuous, but also he is routinely protected by the Holy Spirit against the evil machinations of his Jewish opponents, who are powerless against him in any case. While these later interpolations may well reflect an early scribal commentary on Luke's Acts in the service of the canonical process,[31] they helped to foster a supersessionist theology and anti-Semitic prejudice within the church that remains to this day. For the contemporary church, reading the story of Paul in Acts in the light of Luke's original theological agenda may provide a necessary corrective to this dark side of the canonical project.

ACTS AS CONFESSION: READING ACTS AS THEOLOGY

The decisions one makes about reading Acts as literature influences one's reading of Acts as a theological narrative.[32] Biblical narrative envisages the narrator's confession of faith—his core Christian beliefs—in narrative form. B. Gaventa's salient point is worth keeping in mind: "Luke's theology is intricately and irreversibly bound up with the story he tells and cannot be separated from it. An attempt to do justice to the theology of Acts must struggle to reclaim the character of Acts as a narrative."[33] At the same time, the theology of Acts contributes to a fuller biblical theology that monitors and molds the church's confession of faith according to its rule of faith.[34] For this reason, reading Acts as theology is an important project for any interpreter whose faith seeks theological understanding.

The theological substructure of Luke's narrative world is an antecedent "master" story about what God has done to bring salvation to the world according to the Scriptures. The inner logic of this foundational narrative and the substance of its core themes are introduced into Acts by the story of the first Pentecostal outpouring of the Holy Spirit (2:1-47) and are then developed within the rest of Acts by subsequent stories of the church's mission and speeches of a succession of prophets-like-Jesus. That is, the theological coherence of Acts is not found in a system of propositions about God or the way of God's salvation, but in the integral elements of a Christian story about how God's redemptive promises, prophesied by Scripture, are fulfilled. The following outline of this master story is intended only to orient the reader to the principal elements of a more theological reading of Acts.

(1) *God, the only God, has a plan of salvation disclosed in Israel's Scriptures.* God's sovereign presence and God's saving activities, according to Acts, are inextricably linked to God's redemptive plan (see 2:23; 13:36; 20:27). While God is not a character in the narrative, the narrated events occur as a "divine necessity" ($\delta\epsilon\tilde{\iota}$ *dei*; see 1:16; 3:18; 5:38; 13:27; 27:24), whether they result in great successes or puzzling tragedies. The narrative world of Acts is underwritten by a faithful God who works through an empowered church to fulfill promises made both to Israel and to all "the families of the earth" (3:25).

God promises to restore repentant Israel first of all (1:6). For this reason the church's mission begins in the holy city among devout Jews from "every nation under heaven" (see 2:5-11) and religious status (2:10*b*; 6:1-7; 8:4-25, 26-40). God is Israel's God, and God's salvation is promised to the "people" ($\lambda\alpha\acuteo\varsigma$ *laos*) of Israel and is first experienced by repentant Jews before

30. Cf. Epp, *The Theological Tendency of Codex Bezae Cantabrigiensis in Acts*, 166.

31. Cf. B. Childs, *Introduction to the Old Testament as Scripture* (Philadelphia: Fortress, 1979) 84-106.

32. In organizing the theological conception of Luke's Gospel, Culpepper, *Luke*, 13-30, considers a range of "christological emphases" before treating a "compendium" of the gospel's most important theological themes. I would advise readers to peruse Culpepper's considered discussion of the theology of Luke's Gospel in conjunction with my outline of the theology of Luke's book Acts. The reader should keep in mind, however, that while various themes of Luke's Gospel do recur in Acts, the theological unity between them is much more dynamic. Luke's "confession of faith" in Acts adapts itself to a different historical setting and genre of literature; but his faith, reflected in the story he narrates, has also developed in consideration of new theological concerns facing his church. The theology of Acts is not redundant and makes its own distinctive contribution to a NT theology.

33. B. R. Gaventa, "Toward a Theology of Acts: Reading and Rereading," *Int.* 42 (1988) 150.

34. See R. Wall, "The 'Rule of Faith' in Theological Hermeneutics," in *Between Two Horizons*, ed. J. Green and M. Turner (Grand Rapids: Eerdmans, 2000) 88-107.

moving out to include believers from every nation (chaps. 1–8; see esp. 3:17-26).[35] When the Word of God is finally carried beyond Palestine to the nations, the foundation of every new congregation is the church's Jewish legacy (15:19-21, 28-29; see also chaps. 16–28). Indeed, Israel's God is the sovereign Creator of all things (see 4:24) who alone determines the destiny of every nation (see 14:15-17; 17:22-31). It is this God who promised Abraham that all the nations would be blessed (see 3:25-26; cf. 7:5). For this reason the terms and aim of God's Word are never circumscribed by nationalistic or ethnocentric commitments, nor can any one sacred place domesticate a transcendent God or a people's covenant with such a God (see 7:44-50). The universal scope of God's salvation is predicated on the success of the church's mission among repentant Jews whose vocation is as "light to the nations to the end of the earth" (see 13:44-47). Repentant Gentiles who are added to the church membership rolls share in blessings promised to Israel, not because unrepentant Israel rejected the gospel but because a remnant of repentant Jews within Israel accepted its assertion that the resurrected Jesus is the Messiah of God.

The God of Acts orchestrates Christian history. The surety of God's redemptive purpose is central to the theology of Acts. Good planning not only envisions the prospect of what a people might become but also implements and actively brings its purpose to realization in people's lives. Thus the God who makes promises also keeps them by carefully choreographing the events that accomplish redemption in the history of the repentant community. God's Spirit is poured out on this community as a gift of salvation, and, just as critically in Acts, the Spirit enables and directs members of the community in missionary activity according to God's plan.

This divine plan is revealed by the Scriptures of Israel, especially its prophetic texts and typologies. Jervell has famously asserted that "Luke is the fundamentalist within the New Testament,"[36] because Luke believes that Scripture vocalizes the intentions of God and predicts the history of God's salvation. God's Spirit and Israel's Scriptures are two parts of an integral whole in Acts. The Spirit can guide the church's mission and make its message effective only when witness is grounded in the wisdom of Scripture as rightly interpreted by Spirit-inspired prophets-like-Jesus (see 2:4; also, e.g., Peter, 4:8; Stephen, 6:3, 10; Philip, 8:4-6, 11-13; Paul, 13:4-12; James, 15:28). The conflict within Israel is essentially over which community is custodian of the christological interpretation of Scripture (see 17:2-3). In this sense, Scripture not only is interpreted by the Spirit-filled community in the light of the risen Jesus but also interprets and authorizes the community's mission in the Spirit's power and message about the Lord's resurrection.

(2) *According to prophecy's script, Jesus of Nazareth is God's Messiah, the only Savior, who realizes God's redemptive purpose as attested by his prophetic ministry and resurrection.*[37] The redemptive partnership between God, who takes complete responsibility for creation's promised restoration, and Jesus, who ushers its fulfillment into history, is at the epicenter of the theological conception of Acts. Jesus is God's Messiah, whose divine appointment as the world's Savior is at God's direction and according to God's plan as disclosed in Scripture (see 2:22-23, 36; 10:34-43). God alone can attest to Jesus' redemptive role and does so by the powerful deeds and persuasive word that God effects through him (see 2:22; 10:38). God's ultimate confirmation of Jesus' messiahship is disclosed in God's resurrection of him (see 2:36). God has made Jesus reigning Lord (2:36; cf. 1:9-11; 5:30-31); all must call upon his name for their salvation (see 2:21; 4:12).

God's faithful response to Jesus is reciprocal of Jesus' costly faithfulness to God, indicated by his suffering. The narrative of Jesus enshrined in the missionary speeches of Acts echoes both

---

35. This summary follows the lead of J. Jervell, whose "theology of Acts" is found in several of his publications, especially *The Theology of the Acts of the Apostles* (Cambridge: Cambridge University Press, 1996). I disagree, however, with his description that repentant Gentiles *in every case* are found in the synagogue where their Jewish sensibilities have been cultivated prior to hearing the Christian gospel proclaimed. However, there are instances of pagans responding to the gospel in Acts (e.g., 14:8-9). Moreover, the point of Paul's proclamation to the pagans of Lystra (14:15-17) and Athens (16:22-33) is that God, the only God, is the God of every nation who desires to forgive everyone who calls upon the Lord for salvation.

36. Jervell, *The Theology of the Acts of the Apostles*, 61. Jervell contends that this "fundamentalism" extends from Luke's idea of Scripture's absolute authority and the validity of its teaching to his pervasive use of Scripture in support of his narrative's plotline.

37. See C. F. D. Moule, "The Christology of Acts," in *Studies in Luke-Acts*, ed. L. Keck and L. Martyn (Philadelphia: Fortress, 1980) 159-85, who argues that the developing christology the careful reader notes when moving from Luke's Gospel to Acts is integral to a realistic narrative that reflects changes in the church's confession of Christ in a post-Easter setting. Thus, e.g., the frequency of "Lordship" language in Acts (see 2:36) and the description of Jesus as the heavenly recipient of the church's petitions (see 7:59-60) is possible only *after* the events of the Gospel narrative are in "the past of Jesus."

Jesus tradition and Scripture to render the Lord's suffering and death as faithful to God's redemptive purpose (see 5:30; 10:39). In this sense, God's resurrection of Jesus is more than a vindication of his messiahship; it is also symbolic of Christian mission and discipleship that demands bold obedience to God's divine purpose in order to participate in its forward movement to the end of earth and time (see 14:22).

The kerymatic Jesus of Acts reflects a fairly robust christology. While the terms of the church's proclamation emphasize his suffering and resurrection, details of Jesus' entire messianic career are included (1:22; 10:37-38), as is his parousia, when he will come to restore (3:19-21) and judge (17:30-31) all humanity (10:42). Luke's profile is consistent with the Gospel's story about Jesus and clearly assumes his readers' familiarity with it (1:1). Luke's theology of the cross is more prophetic than salvific. That is, rather than emphasizing Jesus' death as a sacrifice for sin (= Pauline), Acts interprets the crucifixion as symbolic of unrepentant Israel's obduracy about Jesus' mission (3:22; cf. 7:37).

The question may well be asked, then, In what sense is the Jesus of Acts the Savior of the world? The profile given above suggests various activities at different stages of his messianic career: in his past as the prophetic carrier of God's saving word (see 3:22; 7:37); during his present as exalted Lord with divine authority to save all who call upon him (see 2:21; cf. 7:56, 60); and in his future as returning agent of God's final restoration and judgment of all people (see 3:20-21; 17:31). The departure of the living Jesus at the beginning of Acts is a condition for a mission that continues what he has begun to do and say (see 1:1-2, 9-11). His bodily absence, however, does not mean that his redemptive influence is effectively in the past or that he is experienced as exalted Savior only in the words of the proclaimed gospel. The emphasis on the Lord's resurrection in Acts underwrites his living presence and active participation in the church's mission.[38] Thus, while Jesus does not dwell within the believer or the community "in him" (as in Pauline thought), he does exist beyond the church's kerygma. For instance, he reappears in visionary guise at strategic moments in the church's mission to disclose God's purpose for particular people (especially Paul) and places (see 7:55; 9:3-6, 10-16; 23:11), and the mere mention of his name revitalizes those who come into its power (see 4:8-12). It is incorrect, therefore, to speak of Jesus as a passive figure during the church's present mission. While God's Spirit has replaced God's Messiah as the principal agent of salvation during "these last days" (see 2:17-19), the exalted Lord continues as a sometimes participant in the church's mission.

(3) *All who earnestly repent and call upon the living Jesus will be saved, the Jew first and also the Gentile.* All who hear the gospel, whether Jewish or Gentile, are divided into two groups: the repentant and the unrepentant (see "Acts as Conversation," above). Indeed, the common identifying mark of all who belong to Jesus is their positive response to the saving call of God issued in the proclamation of the gospel and their reception of the Holy Spirit (see 15:7-11). Likewise, the spiritual crisis facing Israel (most especially) and the nations is their ignorance of the gospel: People cannot convert to the light if they continue to live in darkness. The prophet's imperative is grounded in this practical reality (see 3:17; 13:27; 17:30).

Converting to Jesus means calling him "Lord" (see 2:21) and confessing that he is the promised Savior God has sent forth into the world to rescue us from our enemies and—especially—to forgive our sins (see 2:38; 3:19; 5:31; 13:38-39; 15:9) and so to liberate us from eternal death (see 13:46). But salvation also involves healing the sick (see 3:7-8; 4:8-12; 28:7-9), illuminating the ignorant (see 3:17; 13:27; 17:30), rescuing the vulnerable from political threat (see 12:4-11; 16:30-31) and material poverty/hunger (see 4:33-34), guarding against demonic powers (see 5:16; 16:16-18; 19:11-20; 26:17-18), and protecting from natural catastrophe (see 27:21-26, 31-44). Each expression of saving grace heralds God's commitment to keep the biblical promise of a "universal restoration" (see 3:21).

At the same time, each act of divine benefaction responds to a deliberate act of faith commensurate with need. Repentance is an intellectual reorientation—a change of one's mind—away from any ordering of one's life that opposes the reign of God and toward the truth claims of God's Word. The repentant Jews who asked Peter following Pentecost, "What shall we do?"

38. Cf. R. O'Toole, *The Unity of Luke's Theology*, GNS 9 (Wilmington, Del.: Glazier, 1984) 38-61.

vocalize the decisive question that is implied throughout Acts in different narrative settings: How shall a needy people respond to the gospel's invitation to enter into a new life with God? The answer comes in a series of imperatives: listen (2:22; 7:2; 8:6; 13:7, 16; 15:13; 19:10; 28:28); believe (3:16; 8:12-13, 37; 11:17, 21; 13:12; 14:23; 15:11; 18:8); be baptized (2:41; 8:38; 9:18; 16:15, 33; 19:1-5); turn to God (3:19; 9:35; 11:21; 20:21; 26:20); request instruction (8:31; 9:5; 10:30-33; 24:24; 26:17-18); show hospitality to strangers (16:15, 33-34; 28:7-10). Indeed, there are some who will respond more eagerly to the Word of God because of conscientious study (17:11) or faithfulness to Jewish training (15:21), both of which indicate readiness to receive God's truth.

The clear impression left by this glossary of salvation is its all-encompassing holistic nature. God's grace saves people from disease, disaster, demons, death, and destitution; and it also forgives people of sin. This penetration of divine grace into human life symbolizes the biblical conception of salvation—one that reroutes a broken and battered creation back toward the original intentions of its Creator, beginning with Israel's restoration (3:19-21).

(4) *Those who repent and belong to the Lord Jesus Christ receive the Holy Spirit and are initiated into a community of goods.* The third person of the Holy Trinity is disclosed at Pentecost as the Spirit of prophecy who empowers persons to bear a persuasive and insightful witness to the risen Jesus (see 2:4). As the reader of Acts should expect, this is not very different from the idea of God's Spirit in Israel's Scriptures.[39] However, the powerful influence of the Holy Spirit in Acts extends to all believers and reflects the characteristics of a personal deity. The Spirit speaks (8:29; 10:19; 13:2) and guides (13:4; 15:28; 16:6-7), and people can lie to (5:3), test (5:9), and resist (7:51) God's Spirit. The Spirit is not external to those it influences (cf. 11:15) but is "poured out" to "fill up" (2:4; 4:8, 31; 6:3, 5; 7:55; 9:17; 11:24; 13:9) those it empowers for ministry.

The Holy Spirit enables the Lord's successors to continue to do and say what he began during his messianic career (1:1-8). That is, the Spirit's presence within the community of believers provides the essential resource for obeying its missionary vocation (1:8; 2:1-4, 17-21). As Jervell notes, "the church does not lead and guide itself: God does through the Spirit."[40] In particular, the Spirit funds the religious authority of a succession of prophetic leaders (8:14-19) who interpret the prophecies of Scripture (2:4), speak the Word of God persuasively (4:8) and boldly (4:29-31; 9:27, 29; 19:8; 28:31; cf. 18:26), and perform mighty signs and wonders (5:12-16; 8:13; 14:3). All of these activities are in continuity with Jesus and the OT prophets before him.

Peter's programmatic reference to the "gift of the Holy Spirit" at Pentecost (2:38) is important in two ways for filling out Luke's idea of the Spirit. First, the Spirit of prophecy is also the transforming Spirit of God, whose work is especially realized in the resurrection practices of the repentant community.[41] Second, salvation is marked out within history by a concrete experience of the Spirit's reception (see 8:14-17, 39-40; 9:17; 10:43-44; 19:5-6). Neither the protocol nor the experience of being filled with the Spirit follows a common pattern, and the narrator stresses different literary themes in each episode. Nevertheless, it is clear from Acts that God's salvation and the reception of God's Spirit are integral elements of any real experience of God's benefaction, to which the community bears witness in the manner of its life together (see 2:47).

The church of Acts is a community of goods. Its united witness to the Messiah's resurrection is not only proclaimed but is also embodied in its common life under the aegis of the Holy Spirit. The community's "resurrection practice" includes four discrete elements: economic, spiritual, religious, and social. As economic κοινωνία (*koinōnia*), the community reorders its possessions according to the principle of Jubilee (see Luke 4:16-18) so that its generosity toward the needy reciprocates God's generosity in the gift of salvation (see 2:44-45; 4:32–5:11; 6:1-6; 11:27-30). Likewise, the gift of God's salvation is embodied as the gift of God's Spirit. As with material possessions, the Holy Spirit is the common property of an inclusive community, so that its Pentecostal coming upon repentant Jews is repeated on repentant Samaritans (see 8:14-16) and Gentiles

---

39. See R. Stronstad, *The Charismatic Theology of St. Luke* (Peabody, Mass.: Hendrickson, 1984), and *The Prophethood of All Believers*, JPTSS 16 (Sheffield: Sheffield Academic, 1999); cf. Jervell, *The Theology of the Acts of the Apostles*, 43-54.
40. Jervell, *The Theology of the Acts of the Apostles*, 51.
41. See M. Turner, *Power from on High: The Spirit in Israel's Restoration and Witness in Luke-Acts*, JPTSS 9 (Sheffield: Sheffield Academic, 1996).

(see 10:44; cf. 11:17; 15:9). Living boldly under its powerful influence is a second resurrection practice of those who follow Jesus. The religious dimension of the community's solidarity is expressed most profoundly by a prohibition: Abstain from things polluted by idols (15:20; see also 15:29; 21:25). The concern of Acts is not so much the inward, spiritual purification of individual believers but the political purity of a community's identity. The sin of idolatry undermines Scripture's legacy as that which gives shape to a people's worship of and allegiance to God (see 7:38-44). Those who practice idolatry—who substitute alternative deities for worship of Israel's God, the only God—demonstrate their ignorance of God's redemptive purpose (14:14-18; 17:22, 24-29; 19:26). A prophetic community is a counterculture to the surrounding order. A sociology of external conflict requires all the more a sociology of internal unity. This is possible to maintain only by a carefully managed protocol of conciliation that forges unity between its disparate groups (see 6:1-6; 14:27–15:29). The solidarity of believers is emphatic within Acts: Believers are "together" when at worship and in mission.

The religious authority of the community's leadership team receives particular stress in Acts even as it does in the so-called Pastoral Letters of the Pauline corpus (1–2 Timothy and Titus). The emphasis is not on ecclesiastical orders so that a succession of male leaders is placed at the top of an institutional hierarchy/patriarchy. Rather, the religious authority of the Lord's successors is practical, prophetic, and personal. Further, it is ever adaptable to the changing landscape of the church's mission, for no one model of leadership is found in Acts. Yet Peter (4:32–5:16), Priscilla (18:1-28), and Paul (20:18-35) are surely the principal prophetic exemplars of Acts.[42] In particular, the similarities between Luke's portraits of the apostle Peter in the first half of Acts and the missionary Paul in the second half suggest that God grants spiritual authority predicated by a common prophetic vocation that is commissioned by and in continuity with the risen Lord. Moreover, the confirmation of this authority is by persuasive word and powerful deeds that are enabled by the Holy Spirit rather than by individual talent or education (see 4:13). Both Peter and Paul stand out as individuals. The moral value of their personal portraits in Acts should not be underestimated. Each embodies characteristics that are critical to the future leaders of the church: Their courageous and costly obedience to their calling, stewardship of possessions, theological perspicuity, religious observance, and personal piety are marks of the faithful disciple (see 20:18-35).

There are also real differences between the Twelve, represented by Peter, and their successors, represented by Stephen, Philip, James, and Paul. Although the matter remains contested among scholars of Acts, I want to emphasize the special significance of the Twelve—and Peter in particular—within the economy of God's salvation. They are close friends of the historical and resurrected Jesus and thus warrant being considered his apostolic successors (see 1:3-11, 21-22); and their commission to prophetic ministry and spiritual authority are glossed by Jesus' earlier prophecy that they would act as regents and judges of Israel (see chaps. 3–5; cf. Luke 22:29-30). Their inspired ministry is the medium through which the kingdom is restored to repentant Israel. Further, every decisive movement in the church's mission to the end of the earth is initiated or confirmed by apostolic authorization. While the Paul of Acts embodies most fully the vocation of repentant Israel as light to the nations, it is the Peter of Acts who both inaugurates (10:1–11:18) and confirms it (15:6-11). The continuity between Peter and Paul can function as an important element of Luke's apologia for Paul precisely because of Peter's key role in God's plan of salvation.

(5) *The community's resurrection hope during the last days is for the return of Jesus and the promised season of universal restoration he will fulfill.* Acts is a narrative about "the last days" (see 2:17; 3:19-26); in fact, every element of this "master story" is ultimately understood against an eschatological horizon. This theological conception may come as a surprise to those who note that while Acts opens in a resounding eschatological key (see 1:6-8, 10-11), the remaining narrative rarely sounds another futuristic note (see 3:19-21; cf. 7:31; 10:42; 17:30-31). Nowhere is there a discourse on the future as found everywhere else in the NT. Of course, Luke presumes a prior reading of his Gospel and knowledge of its prediction of the Lord's return, confirmed at

---

42. Cf. L. T. Johnson, *The Acts of the Apostles*, SP 5 (Collegeville, Minn.: Liturgical, 1992) 12-14.

Jesus' ascension. Further, Peter's reference to a future "time of universal restoration" (3:21) and Paul's prophecy of endtime judgment (see 17:31) point to God's cosmic triumph at the Lord's return to earth. Although scholars continue to debate the meaning of these texts, the narrator's theology is not shaped by a concern to correct some mistaken eschatology—for example, a perceived delay in Christ's return or an apocalyptic faction within his church. The focus of Luke's eschatology in both his Gospel and Acts is God's commitment to promises made according to Scripture. Therefore, the primary theological problem addressed by the book is *theodicy*, the vindication of God's justice.

Acts envisages both the Lord's return (1:10-11) and the outpouring of the Holy Spirit (2:17) as eschatological events. The central theme in Luke's reckoning of this eschatological moment, however, is neither a detailed chronology nor the apocalyptic cast of the future (see 1:7); rather, his emphasis shifts to the historical means by which God's people will make their way under the aegis of the Spirit from Pentecost to parousia. The narrative framework of the church's movement toward God's ordained future consists of two integral motifs: the church's Spirit-led mission from Jerusalem to Rome, the principal cities of two symbolic worlds that represent all people for all time, and an interpretive strategy that warrants each episode of this mission as fulfilling the promises of Israel's Scripture. The historic reality that confirms God's faithfulness is that a portion of Israel is restored (see 2:40; 3:19-23; cf. Rom 9:1-29). Despite the recurrent hostility of unrepentant Jews and Gentiles, this restored Israel, led first by the apostles and ultimately personified by the Paul of Acts, becomes "a light to the nations" from Jerusalem to Rome (see 3:25-26; 13:47; cf. 1:6-8).

The mode by which the Lord bids the covenant community to journey from Pentecost to parousia is to bear powerful witness to his resurrection (see 1:8). Scripture's promise of a restored Israel is not realized within "national" Israel—as many Jews anticipated—but within a remnant of repentant Jews (see 3:23) whom God calls out of Israel through the church's mission (see 2:37-41). Indeed, the church's mission to the whole household of Israel has already carried the Word of God to every group within the household of Israel (see 2:5-11): Hebrews and Hellenists (Acts 2–7), Samaritans and proselytes (Acts 8), those inside and those outside of the holy land. The conflict and mixed results that this mission has provoked fulfill Scripture's prophecies (see 28:25-27), and Paul personifies the prophesied vocation of repentant Israel in his mission as "light to the nations" (see 13:47; see also chaps. 9–28).

The church's hope in God's coming triumph is expressed through daily proclamation of God's faithfulness, in continuity with the risen Messiah and the prophetic community that succeeded him in this ministry of the Word. The ending of Acts (28:30-31), which summarizes Paul's mission in Rome, serves to facilitate the transition from the book's narrative world to the readers' real worlds. The book bids its audience to move ever forward to God's coming triumph by engaging in Spirit-enabled witness in the world.

ACTS AS CANON

Approaching Acts in search of the Word of God requires more than a rigorous analysis of the book's social world, literary artistry, and theological conception. For the most part, modern interpreters concentrate on reconstructing the book's point of origin, whether in historical, literary, or theological categories. From their perspective, Acts is typically read as the second volume of Luke's continuous narrative. This narrative is shaped by his pastoral intentions, composed with ancient literary, rhetorical, and historiographical conventions and informed by his theological convictions to serve in the Christian formation of his first readers and the church. This critical construction, however, is often based on scholarly conjecture and runs the risk of freezing *the* meaning of Acts in an ancient world far removed from that of its current readers.

Even on historical grounds, Acts followed a separate and more difficult course into the biblical canon from the one taken by the Third Gospel. Those who formed the church's Scriptures for future generations of believers evidently did not think it necessary or even profitable to read Luke and Acts together. More likely, the pre-canonical Acts circulated with different collections of letters, both catholic and Pauline. For this reason, by the time the canonical process had concluded a few centuries later, the canonical Acts had its own peculiar function within the biblical canon, different from that of the Third Gospel. The importance of its role *as Scripture* thereby underwrites a particular approach to the study of Acts and its distinctive deposit to the biblical witness.

Reading the Book of Acts as Scripture. In the Commentary to follow, the central critical question raised is, *What do Luke's reasons for writing Acts have to do with the church's reasons for reading Acts as Scripture?* Any interpreter must try to bridge these two hermeneutical horizons. However, they are in constant flux due both to new insights about Luke's world and his writing and to changes in the time and location of his various interpreters. In particular, this text's movement from personal "conversation" to the church's "canon" sharply resets the interpreter's angle of vision toward Acts.[43] Several implications of this shift should be briefly noted:

(1) Reading Acts as Scripture recognizes the importance of different literary relationships within the New Testament. The intracanonical relationships between Acts and the four Gospels and between Acts and the two collections of letters (especially Pauline) that follow it are elevated in importance within canonical context. The "canon logic" envisaged by the arrangement of the different parts within the NT whole, and sometimes even of individual writings within these canonical parts, stipulates important markers in guiding the reader's approach to the NT. According to this arrangement, then, the fourfold gospel (not just Luke's Gospel) is perceived as prerequisite reading for the study of Acts, and the study of Acts under the gospel's light is prerequisite reading for the study of the letters that follow. The implications of this "canon logic" will be teased out in the Commentary.

(2) These new intracanonical relationships forged by the canonical process are also valuable when assessing the distinctive importance of the theology of Acts within the NT. No longer does the biblical theologian consider the thematic interests of Acts only in terms of their congruence with those found in Luke's Gospel. Rather, the theological contribution Acts makes to *biblical* theology is now measured as an indispensable part of an integral whole. Put in different words, upon consideration of the various theologies that make up the NT's entire theological conception, the interpreter is now pressed to imagine what a biblical witness to God might lack if it did not include Acts. What distorted idea of the church's faith, its religious or social identity, or of its vocation in the world might result from a conversation with a body of sacred writings that did not include this book? What thin reading of the Pauline letters would result if the interpreter failed to prepare by first reading the story of the canonical Paul of Acts? Simply put, reading Acts within its biblical setting reminds us that any theological understanding lacking the witness of Acts will distort Christian faith and life.

(3) The Paul of Acts is valued more keenly from this canonical perspective than when his role is reduced to a cameo appearance in the modern quest of the historical Paul. At stake in following the story of the Paul of Acts is not so much the historical accuracy of Luke's portrait—even though this is currently being reconsidered—or even the important questions about his credibility within earliest Christianity. The most important issues from a canonical angle of vision are theological ones: What does the Paul of Acts have to say about the future of the church? How does Paul's story in Acts orient its readers to the implied author of the Pauline letters that follow and the Pauline witness they enshrine (see the Overview to 15:13–28:28)?

(4) The church's conflict with the synagogue at the end of the canonical process was no doubt different from Luke's assessment when he wrote Acts (see "Acts as Conversation," above). What began as an intramural "Jewish problem" had become a "Judaism problem" by the end of the second century. Keen competition had developed between two "world religions," a problem made all the more prickly by their common history and theological conception. The scribal emendations to the Western version of Acts, with a more negative characterization of unrepentant Israel, may well reflect the canonizing community's heightened sensitivity to its relationship with Judaism and its sense of the canon's function to clearly delineate the church's identity (see "Acts as Composition," above). In a different sense, the portrait of Israel found

---

43. See R. Wall, "Canonical Context and Canonical Conversations," in Green and Turner, *Between Two Horizons*, 165-82.

in Acts clarifies the difference between Christianity and Judaism in christological rather than nationalistic or ethnocentric terms. Thus Acts subverts any "Christian" prejudice against Jews on ethnic grounds (= anti-Semitism) or on the mistaken presumption that God has either re-neged on promises made to historic Israel according to the Scriptures or has replaced Jews with Christians in the economy of salvation (= supersessionism). God's faithfulness to Israel remains inviolate; therefore, today's church must become more—not less—Jewish in order to be fully Christian in its worship and witness.

(5) The "primitivism" of Acts simply reflects the ecclesial experience of the earliest church, which fashioned itself after the diaspora synagogues and other voluntary organizations of the Roman world. Worship consisted of prayer meetings and teaching, with Christian fellowship centered in the homes of believers. The sociology of the church dramatically changed during the canonical process; these loosely confederated house congregations became in time participants of an emerging church catholic. For this reason, the ongoing interest in the images and ideas of "church" in Acts should focus on emulating its missionary vocation and prophetic message, its resurrection practices, and the nature of its spiritual leadership—important claims on any con-gregation in every age—rather than on replicating outward forms of governance and worship or other time-conditioned practices.

(6) In this regard, reading Acts as Scripture seeks to insinuate its narrative world into the changing "real" worlds of current readers. New layers of meaning hitherto hidden are discov-ered whenever sacred texts are allowed to penetrate and interpret the world of their interpret-ers. For example, contemporary readers will more easily discern the relevance of the Ethopian eunuch's story (8:26-40) for reflecting upon the relationship between the church and its homo-sexual membership or more readily recognize the example of Priscilla in chap. 18 (as well as other women in Acts) as a role model for prophetic ministry in congregations that once were reluctant to encourage women in ministry. The vivid snapshots of the community of goods or repeated episodes that depict Paul's relations with Rome may challenge today's congregations to a more prophetic understanding of church as counterculture. Read as Scripture, Acts provides an important element of a wider "canonical context" in which the faithful community gathers to reflect on those issues that either undermine or underscore God's presence in today's world.

(7) Finally, reading Acts as Scripture cultivates a fresh sense of sacred time and space. The church continues to live in "the last days," betwixt Pentecost and parousia, when the Spirit of God empowers Christ's disciples to bear witness to the resurrection throughout the world in anticipation of God's coming triumph and creation's final restoration (see 3:20-21). The book of Acts has continuing authority to form a church that proclaims God's word and embodies a witness to its truth, heralding that coming day.

Reading the Book of Acts Within Scripture. If Acts is approached as a narrative written for and relevant to only its first readers, then the book's current readers will find little of value for their own Christian formation. Perhaps it was precisely a concern for subsequent readers of sacred texts that guided the canonical process that produced the NT in its present form. For example, in its canonical setting the book of Acts is detached from Luke's Gospel, which is now read as one of a set of four. If Acts is read in its current canonical placement rather than as the second volume of Luke-Acts, then the reader will naturally reflect upon its narrative as continu-ing the story of Jesus presented by the four Gospels. The reader's understanding of "all that Jesus began to do and teach" will be greatly expanded and enriched by a fourfold presentation.

The book of Acts acquired two properties during the process of canonical development that continue to help readers envisage its distinctive role within the NT: (1) its title, "The Acts of the Apostles," and (2) its placement as a bridge between the Gospels, on one side, and the two collections of letters, Pauline and catholic, on the other. Most people begin reading a book by considering its title, for a book's subject matter is typically indicated by its title and/or its sub-title. Consider the curious title of this book, "The Acts of the Apostles." Commentators routinely adjure that Luke's story is inappropriately titled. The book is about the activity of the Holy Spirit, they claim, rather than that of the apostles. Or, if read as Luke-Acts, the "mighty acts" of Acts are best understood as the continuation of Luke's historical narrative about Jesus. Against this conjecture, the effect of recognizing the superscription of Acts as a canonical property is to call attention to a new set of orienting concerns for readers of Acts as Scripture.[44]

Canonically, the two halves of the title each function to signal a key concept about the role of the apostles in Acts. First, the literary genre of πράξεις (*praxeis*, "acts")[45] tells stories of people, real or imagined, who are divinely favored to act in powerful ways on behalf of their community or nation. Such an aretology, or "folk" story, also functions as social commentary, since supernatural powers are given to heroes as evidence of their special status (and by extension, the special status of those communities or nations they helped to found). Their mighty deeds are not of their own making but testify to divine favor, and anyone who links his or her destiny to these heroic characters is assured of divine favor.

In the case of the book of Acts, the canonical process recognized the importance of Jesus' successors, whose persuasive words and powerful deeds founded the church and formed its rule of faith. The second half of the title—"of the apostles"—identifies those heroes of the faith whose special status and divinely ordained destiny ensures the salvation of all who submit to their spiritual authority (chaps. 4–5; 20:18-35). While it may seem theologically prudent to think of these characters as merely the means of the Holy Spirit's work, the effect of the canonical title is to shift the reader's interest from the Spirit's baptism to those prophetic successors of the Lord whom the Spirit fills for ministry. This concern to attach the church to its apostolic forebears reflects the sociology of the emergent "one holy catholic and apostolic church." This church's claims of special status in the economy of God's order were contested by rivals both within the church (Gnosticism, Montanism) and outside it (formative Judaism).[46] The book of Acts reminds its confessing readers that the church's sacred memories of the Lord's apostolic successors (including Paul) exemplify a vocation, character, message, and faith that all Christians must imitate in demonstrating their obedience to God.

The strategic placement of Acts between the Gospels and the letters suggests the transitional role it performs within the NT. The narrative of Acts continues and concludes the authorized biography of Jesus while introducing the Bible's readers to the apostolic writings that follow. Acts functions as a bridge connecting Gospels and letters in a logical relationship that mirrors the ultimate aim of the NT: to nurture Christian discipleship after the pattern of Jesus.

Acts can first of all be read as "commentary" on Jesus' story narrated in the four Gospels. Not only does the story Acts tells offer substantial proof of Jesus' resurrection as Lord and Messiah (cf. Acts 2:36), but it also issues Scripture's response to the theological crisis occasioned by his bodily absence from the Christian community (see John 13:31–14:31). Those disciples who follow after the exalted Lord are to continue in the power of the Holy Spirit to do and to say what Jesus began (see Acts 1:1-2). In this regard, the importance of retaining the final shape of the NT rather than combining Luke and Acts as a single narrative is indicated by the significant roles performed by Peter and the Holy Spirit in Acts where Jesus is absent—roles for which Luke's Gospel does not adequately prepare the reader of Acts. Peter's rehabilitation at the end of John (John 21:15-17) as well as the teaching about the Spirit's post-Easter role by John's Jesus (John 14–16) signify the important role that John's Gospel performs in preparing the reader for the story of Acts. Moreover, what it means to be a "witness" of the risen Jesus (Acts 1:8) is more fully understood by the biblical reader in the context of John's Gospel (John 15:26-27; cf. Luke 24:48).

The relationship between Acts and the following two collections of letters is more difficult for the interpreter to order. The conventions of epistolary literature are different from those of narrative literature and thus the differences between Acts and the letters are readily discernible. For example, Luke's portrait of Paul is sometimes at odds with Paul's self-understanding or missionary itinerary as given in his letters. Further, Luke does not quote any of Paul's letters. Reading

44. See R. Wall, "The Acts of the Apostles in the Context of the New Testament Canon," *BTB* 18 (1988) 15-23.

45. See Fitzmyer, *The Acts of the Apostles*, 47-49.

46. Some scholars use the expression "early catholicism" when referring to an emergent Christianity whose principal concern was to delineate the theological boundaries of the faith—by means of a "rule of faith"—to regulate Christian preaching and preserve the core beliefs of the apostolic traditions from their internal and external religious rivals. See E. Käsemann, "Paul and Early Catholicism," in *New Testament Questions of Today* (Philadelphia: Fortress, 1969) 236-51.

Acts as Scripture, however, compels a dialogue between the Paul of Acts and the Pauline letters of the NT. [47] The potential gains of this perspective may be illustrated when considering the canonical "seam" that connects the final passage in Acts, which portrays a missionary Paul in Rome (see 28:17-31), to the opening text of the first Pauline letter, that to the Romans, which introduces biblical readers to a missionary-minded apostle who is eager "to proclaim the gospel to you also who are in Rome" (Rom 1:15). [48] The interplay between the ending of Acts and the beginning of Romans underscores the primary concern of Luke's Paul, who is not found in a secluded study writing dense Christian theology but on city streets or in living rooms of rented apartments relating the Christian gospel to life in practical and persuasive ways.

Perhaps the most important role Acts performs within the NT is to proffer biographical introductions to the implied authors of the letters that follow. In canonical context, such biographies serve a theological purpose by orienting readers to the religious and moral authority of apostolic authors as trustworthy carriers of the word of God. While the historical accuracy of Luke's narrative of Paul and other leaders of earliest Christianity may be challenged, the rhetorical and ethical power of these figures confirms and commends the importance of their letters. The salient issue is not whether Acts fails as a historical record but that it succeeds as a theological resource, contributing to the church's understanding of its vocation and identity in the world.

In this regard, Acts provides an angle of vision into the Pauline and catholic epistolary collections that follow. [49] For instance, the relations among Peter, John, James, and Paul and their respective missions, as depicted in Acts, suggest how the interpreter arranges the intracanonical dialogue between those NT writings attached to each leader. Similarities and dissimilarities in emphasis and theological conception found when comparing the catholic and Pauline letters may actually correspond to the manner by which Acts narrates the negotiations on theological convictions and social conventions between different missions (e.g., Acts 2:42-47; 9:15-16; 11:1-18; 12:17; 15:12-29; 21:17-26). The modern discussion has emphasized how a narrator committed to the practical requirements of an "early catholic" church softens the disagreements between the leaders of earliest Christianity. But what is often overlooked is that the church collected and eventually canonized a Pauline corpus whose principal letters are often polemical and potentially divisive. The question is never raised as to why these Pauline letters were included in the canon of an "early catholic" church if the aim was to shape theological uniformity. Might it not be the case that the church recognized the importance of Acts in introducing the apostolic writings not so much to smooth their disagreeable edges as to interpret them?

Indeed, perhaps the canonical role Acts best performs is to explain rather than to temper the diversity found in the two collections of biblical letters. According to Acts, the church that claims its continuity with the first apostles tolerates a rich pluralism even as the apostles did, not without controversy and confusion. What was achieved at the Jerusalem Council is a kind of theological understanding rather than a theological consensus. The divine revelation given to the apostles, according to Acts, forms a pluralizing monotheism that in turn informs two distinct missions and appropriate proclamations, Jewish and Gentile (see Gal 2:7-10). Thus, sharply put, Acts interprets the two collections of letters in a more sectarian fashion: The Pauline corpus reflects the gospel of a Gentile mission, while the catholic collection reflects the gospel(s) of a Jewish mission. However, rather than causing division within the church, such a theological diversity is now perceived as normative and necessary for the work of the One who calls both Jews and Gentiles to be the people of God. As a context for theological reflection, Acts forces us to interpret the letters in the light of two guiding principles. First, we should expect to find kerygmatic diversity as we move from the Pauline to the catholic letters. Second, we should expect such a diversity to be useful in forming a single people of God. Against a critical hermeneutics that tends to select a "canon within the canon" from among the various possibilities,

---

47. For a comprehensive listing and analysis of the intertextual echoes of Pauline letters in Acts, see D. Wenham, "Acts and the Pauline Corpus," in Winter and Clarke, *The Book of Acts in Its First Century Setting: Ancient Literary Setting*, 215-58.

48. See R. Wall, "Romans 1-1-15: An Introduction to the Pauline Corpus of the New Testament," in *The New Testament as Canon*, ed. R. Wall and E. Lemcio, JSNTSup 76 (Sheffield: *JSOT*, 1992) 142-60.

49. See R. Wall, "Introduction to Epistolary Literature," in this volume.

the Bible's own recommendation is for an interpretive strategy characterized by a mutually il-luminating and self-correcting conversation among biblical theologies.

Finally, the dominant theological commitments of Acts guide theological reflection upon the letters. The point is not that a theology of Acts determines or even anticipates the various theologies found in the letters. Rather, Acts shapes a particular perspective, a practical concern, an abiding interest that influences the interpretation of the letters. For example, if according to Acts the church's vocation is to continue what Jesus began to do and to say, then a subsequent reading of the letters should bring to sharper focus the identity and praxis of a missionary people who respond to the Lord's demand to be his witness to the ends of the earth. This same perspective holds true of the catholic epistles, where believers constitute a community of "resident aliens" whose vocation is a costly faithfulness to God rather than that of the missionary witness to a needy world found in the Pauline letters. How does the catholicity of Acts deepen our understanding of God's people as a community of "resident aliens"? The canonical approach presumes that the connection is complementary rather than adversarial. In this case, the Pauline church, which may be inclined to accommodate itself to the mainstream of the world in order to more effectively spread the gospel (see 1 Cor 9:12*b*-23), is reminded by the catholic witness that it must take care not to be corrupted by the values and behaviors of that world (see Jas 1:27). That is, the synergism effected by the dominant theological commitments of Acts suggests that the diverse theologies ingredient in the biblical canon compose a dynamic, self-correcting system, preventing theological distortion.[50]

50. For a defense of this interpretive strategy and illustrations of its usefulness for reading across the NT canon, see Wall and Lemcio, *The New Testament as Canon.*

BIBLIOGRAPHY

Commentaries:

Barrett, C. K. *A Critical and Exegetical Commentary on the Acts of the Apostles.* 2 vols. ICC. Edinburgh: T. & T. Clark, 1994–98. The standard technical commentary on the Greek text in the English language. Offers valuable insight on the philology, grammar, transmission and translation, and history of interpreting Acts. Both volumes include comprehensive introductions with bibliographies covering every aspect of Acts criticism.

Bruce, F. F. *The Acts of the Apostles.* Rev. ed. NICNT. Grand Rapids: Eerdmans, 1988. An informed and helpful exposition of Acts that defends the historical accuracy of Luke's narrative.

Dunn, J. D. G. *The Acts of the Apostles.* Valley Forge, Pa.: Trinity, 1996. A highly readable commentary on the narrative plotline of Acts; written for preachers and teachers.

Fitzmyer, J. A. *The Acts of the Apostles.* AB 31. Garden City, N.Y.: Doubleday, 1998. This sparse commentary on Acts, which presumes information found in Fitzmyer's commentary on Luke's Gospel in the same series, contains informed summaries of introductory matters and current bibliographies of value to students. Fitzmyer's translation of Acts is highly recommended.

Haenchen, E. *The Acts of the Apostles.* Philadelphia: Westminster, 1971. Haenchen's masterful commentary reflects the interests and traditions of modern German scholarship. Alhough he is skeptical of the historical value of Acts, his commentary is rich with insight; and most recent interpreters use it as the starting point for their own studies.

Jervell, J. *Die Apostelgeschichte.* KEK 3. Göttingen: Vandenhoeck & Ruprecht, 1998. Innovative and controversial, Jervell's commentary (which replaces Haenchen's in the KEK series) defends the Jewish character of Acts against the critical consensus that Luke's story reflects a Gentile (and largely anti-Jewish) perspective.

Johnson, L. T. *The Acts of the Apostles.* SP 5. Collegeville, Minn.: Liturgical, 1992. Theologically profound and written in lively prose; integrates technical fluency with practical insight. Johnson's understanding of how Luke's prophetic theology informs the telling of his story is highly recommended for both preacher and scholar.

Kee, H. C. *To Every Nation Under Heaven: The Acts of the Apostles*. NTC. Valley Forge, Pa.: Trinity, 1997. A nontechnical commentary that seeks to understand Acts in the context of Luke's social and political world; several illuminating excurses on various topics are included throughout, and Kee concludes with a topical bibliography of recent research.

Spencer, F. S. *Acts*. Readings: A New Biblical Commentary. Sheffield: Sheffield Academic, 1997. An excellent nontechnical commentary that highlights Luke's evocative narrative style. Especially useful for those interested in reading Acts as literature.

Tannehill, R. C. *The Acts of the Apostles*. Vol. 2 of *The Narrative Unity of Luke-Acts: A Literary Interpretation*. Minneapolis: Fortress, 1990. The second volume of Tannehill's influential study of Luke's narrative argues that Acts continues the plotline of the Gospel to underwrite Luke's distinctive account of God's redemptive plan.

Witherington, B. *The Acts of the Apostles: A Socio-Rhetorical Commentary*. Grand Rapids: Eerdmans, 1998. Considers a massive amount of secondary literature in order to comment on a wide range of pertinent issues, often summarizing his research in judicious excurses and nontechnical appendixes that are well worth consulting.

Specialized Studies:

Cassidy, R. J. *Society and Politics in the Acts of the Apostles*. Maryknoll, N.Y.: Orbis, 1987. This provocative collection of short studies analyzes various social and political controversies provoked by the community's ministry within and beyond Palestine. Contends that Luke's characterization of the church as opposed to the political and social world of the day continues from and is warranted by the prophetic Jesus of his Gospel.

Evans, C. A., and J. A. Sanders. *Luke and Scripture: The Function of Sacred Tradition in Luke-Acts*. Minneapolis: Fortress, 1993. Contends that Luke-Acts is a narrative commentary on select portions of Israel's Scriptures that are either cited or alluded to in order to underwrite the claim that Jesus is the Christ of God according to biblical promise.

Hill, C. C. *Hellenists and Hebrews: Reappraising Division within the Earliest Church*. Minneapolis: Fortress, 1992. Responding to the modern consensus that the earliest church was deeply divided by competing theological commitments concerning Temple and Torah purity, Hill argues that first-century Judaism and Christianity were much too variegated and fluid to allow for simple cataloging of traditions.

Jervell, J. *The Theology of the Acts of the Apostles*. NTT. Cambridge: Cambridge University Press, 1996. This more accessible companion volume to Jervell's commentary (see above) summarizes the themes of a theology of Acts.

Marshall, I. H., and D. Peterson, eds. *Witness to the Gospel: The Theology of Acts*. Grand Rapids: Eerdmans, 1998. Treats the main theological themes of Acts from a variety of methodological perspectives and in an expository style that intends to clarify the meaning of the *text* of Acts.

Martin, C. J. "The Acts of the Apostles." In *Searching the Scriptures: A Feminist Commentary*. Vol. 2. Edited by E. Schüssler Fiorenza. London: SCM, 1995. Martin's illuminating "womanist" readings of select passages in Acts are combined with an introduction that surveys Luke's characterization of women.

Parsons, M., and R. Pervo. *Rethinking the Unity of Luke and Acts*. Minneapolis: Fortress, 1990. A fresh introduction to a vexing issue of Lukan scholarship.

Porter, S. E. *The Paul of Acts*. WUNT 115. Tübingen: Mohr Sebeck, 1999. First sifts through and evaluates recent scholarship on the role Paul performs in Acts and his relationship to Luke and the Holy Spirit then seeks to interpret the relationship between Luke's Paul and the portrait of Paul found in his letters.

Powell, M. A. *What Are They Saying About Acts?* New York: Paulist, 1991. Reviews and synthesizes scholarly opinion concerning the unity of Luke-Acts, the distinctive literary makeup and core theological themes of Acts, and the history of its interpretation in both the church and the scholarly guild.

Soards, M. L. *The Speeches in Acts: Their Content, Context, and Concerns.* Louisville: Westminster/ John Knox, 1994. Written in response to M. Dibelius's programmatic form-critical analysis of Acts; examines the literary structure and narrative role of every speech in Acts in the light of an oral culture shaped by Greco-Roman rhetorical conventions.

Winter, B. W., and A. Clarke, eds. *The Book of Acts in Its First Century Setting.* 6 vols. Grand Rapids: Eerdmans, 1993–. This series seeks to reconstruct the cultural and historical context of Acts. An indispensable resource for any student who seeks to interpret Acts guided by knowledge of the ancient world behind the text.

OUTLINE OF ACTS

ACTS 1:1-2

THE PROLOGUE

COMMENTARY

In antiquity prefatory sentences aroused interest and put readers on notice what to expect in the story that follows; the first sentence of Acts is such a sentence.[51] The narrator begins in the conventional way of second volumes: Luke addresses his reader, Theophilus, in the first person by sharply summarizing the content of his first volume.[52] Theophilus's identity and role in the production of Acts remain indeterminate, although likely the name refers to an actual person rather than to a symbolic audience (see Introduction, "Acts as Conversation").

Acts lacks, however, the narrator's conventional summary of the second volume. Luke is content to review what he has already written and Theophilus has read: the gospel story of what "Jesus began to do and to teach." In doing so, he introduces Acts within a wider narrative that infers a working "intertext" between Luke's Gospel and Acts, the first influencing and expanding the meaning of the second. The introduction includes a caveat: The reader who attempts to follow the plotline of Acts without benefit of "the first book" will have missed much that is utterly essential for reading the second volume. The story of Jesus' messianic career is the narrative subtext of Acts; the stories must be read together as a whole greater than the sum of its two integral parts (see Introduction, "Acts as Canon").

Verse 2 emits three signals that alert the reader to the importance of the events that will soon follow. First, the awkward reference to the Lord's ascension, which at first seems unnecessary here, actually helps to introduce the succession of the apostles to Jesus' ministry (see also 1:3-14). As the concluding event of his earthly ministry, the ascension of the risen Jesus inaugurates the ministry of his apostles, who will continue to do and teach what he has begun (see 1:9-11). But this passing reference to the Lord's departure also frames the religious crisis it occasions: Will the new age of God's promised salvation, which dawned with the Messiah, continue to unfold in his absence?

Second, although his Gospel lacks detail in this regard, Luke understands that all Jesus did as God's Messiah is "through the Holy Spirit." The Holy Spirit is "the Spirit of prophecy" who calls forth, empowers, and authorizes the Messiah's prophetic ministry and will ensure continuity in his absence. The Lord's instructions to his apostles are given "through the Holy Spirit," since only by the Spirit's power and direction will they fulfill their vocation as prophets-like-Jesus (see 1:8; cf. Luke 24:46-49).

Third, Luke finally mentions "the apostles whom Jesus had chosen" who will continue to do and to speak what the Lord has begun.[53] The title ἀπόστολος (*apostolos*, "apostle") derives from the verb ἀποστέλλω (*apostellō*, "to send"), denoting someone who is "sent out" with something important to give another—in this case, with a word of salvation to proclaim and mighty works to perform in Jesus' name. The images conjured up by this concept are similar to those associated with OT stories of the commissioning of God's prophets. Indeed, apostles bear a

---

51. There is no end to the various ways commentators divide the preface to Acts from its main story. I separate 1:1-2 from the rest of Acts for special consideration as Luke's *literary* introduction to his second book, which he then begins with the story of apostolic succession in 1:3-14.

52. See L. C. A. Alexander, *The Preface to Luke's Gospel: Literary Convention and Social Context in Luke 1.1-4 and Acts 1.1*, SNTSMS 78 (Cambridge: Cambridge University Press, 1993).

53. The phrase "whom [Jesus] had chosen" presumes the reader knows something of Luke's earlier narrative of the selection process by which Jesus "elected" the Twelve (Luke 6:12-16). Critical in the Gospel account is that Jesus first prayed to God—on the mountain and all night—to learn precisely God's will in this matter. Prayer is an important narrative thematic in Luke's Gospel and Acts and functions as a theological metaphor for God's sovereign control over those events that fulfill God's promised salvation.

striking family resemblance to OT prophets in both their vocation and their suffering.[54] The

reference to their selection by Jesus recalls that he chose them with God's provident help (see Luke 6:13) and gave them special responsibilities and a privileged status within a restored Israel (see Luke 22:30), detailed now in this second book.

54. Agnew's review of discussion of the concept of apostleship commends an understanding based on an OT description of the prophetic vocation. See F. H. Agnew, "The Origin of the NT Apostle-Concept," *JBL* 105 (1986) 75-96.

REFLECTIONS

1. "I wrote about all that Jesus began to do and to teach" (1:1 NIV). The clear signal emitted by that declaration is that what Jesus began, his successors will continue, not in dutiful practice but in sincere devotion to the sublime truth disclosed in that messianic life. The purpose of Acts is to tell a story that bids its living readers to continue what Christ began in their own time and hence to the end of history. The apostles continued the Messiah's mission without repeating its unique importance in the economy of God's salvation. However, the pattern of his life and work shapes the direction of theirs as prophets-like-Jesus. This core conviction of Luke's is made evident in the literary shaping of Acts.

2. "Giving instructions through the Holy Spirit to the apostles whom he had chosen" (1:2 NRSV). The catchphrases "through the Holy Spirit" and "the apostles whom Jesus had chosen" introduce the key elements of this continuity. The Spirit and the apostles are both the appointed successors of God's Messiah, and through their sacred partnership, divine and human, the promised salvation of God continues to be fulfilled in history. This is the first mention of the Spirit's agency in Acts and cues the reader both to Jesus' imminent departure and the coming of the Spirit at Pentecost, when both the need for continuity and its means will be disclosed. It is important to note that the Spirit is introduced in connection with the Lord's instruction. This is the "Spirit of prophecy" whose prominent role in the OT is maintained in Acts—the instrument by whom prophets are raised up, commissioned, instructed, and inspired to carry God's word to God's people. In Acts, the Lord's apostolic successors, and their successors in turn, are God's Spirit-filled prophets, the principal interpreters of Scripture and of the course of salvation's history scripted by biblical prophecy.

What are the marks of Spirit-filled prophets today? Surely those, whether well known or anonymous, who help the community experience God's love, know God's Word, and discern God's will are the successors of the earliest believers. At times their activities may be grand events; more often, leadership is exercised in the everyday faith and practice of the community.

ACTS 1:3–2:13

PREPARING TO CONTINUE THE MINISTRY OF JESUS

ACTS 1:3-14, THE APOSTOLIC SUCCESSION

COMMENTARY

The prefatory sentence of Acts is followed by a brief summary of what Jesus does and says over the forty days between his resurrection and ascension (1:3). Luke recapitulates the conclusion to Jesus' messianic mission according to Luke's Gospel (cf. Luke 24:36-53), recalling in particular those memories that will be elaborated in this second book. Here are the Lord's final instructions to his apostles that function as his "last will and testament" and lend authority to the future work of his chosen successors.[55]

The central moment of the narrative is the prophecy of the coming of God's Spirit (1:4-5), whose arrival in the holy city portends the restoration of Israel (1:6) and empowers the mission of the church (1:7-8). According to Acts, the hope of Israel's restoration and the mission of the church are integral features of "the last days" of salvation's history soon to be inaugurated by God during Pentecost (see 2:1-4). The departure of the glorified Jesus into the heavens (1:9-11) concludes the first stage of his messianic mission and creates the circumstance that requires an apostolic succession. But the succession from Messiah to his apostles is not without problems. The messianic community left behind gathers for prayer (1:14) to wait for God to act on the Lord's promise of the Spirit. Yet we note that it includes only *eleven* apostles (1:13). How will God's salvation go forward without the requisite twelve "to sit on thrones judging the twelve tribes of Israel" (Luke 22:30)?

1:3-8. The brevity of v. 3 presumes that the reader of Acts will be familiar with the

Gospel account of Jesus' resurrection and his teaching about the reign of God. The idiom of Luke's summary, however, is provocative. The term he uses for the living Lord's "many convincing proofs" (τεκμήριον *tekmērion*) is found only here in the NT. In ancient rhetoric this same word is used of the hard evidence that convinces the skeptic or confirms the authority of the apologist. Used here in Acts, the Lord's "proofs" confirm his resurrection, perhaps for those disciples who still doubt it (cf. Matt 28:17), and underwrite the propriety of his instructions (1:2) that prepare his followers for their mission soon to be at hand.

The resurrection of Jesus is a theme of enormous importance for Acts. It testifies to Jesus' faithfulness to God and confirms him as Lord and Christ (see 2:36). The authority of Jesus is deeply rooted in his faithfulness to God as God's servant and his relationship with God as God's Son. Jesus not only understands God's redemptive plans but interprets Scripture's disclosure of those plans faithfully. His "suffering" is the signature of the Lord's costly obedience, which is requisite of Messiah's faithful service to God, as the resurrected Jesus himself points out (Luke 24:26).

Unlike the Gospel narrative, in which the details of Jesus' Easter appearances are recounted in the course of a very long and exciting day, Acts simply says that Jesus "appeared" to his disciples over an extended period of "forty days" (1:3). Some interpreters think Luke's reference to forty days is his rhetorical marker that extends the compressed last day of the Gospel's Jesus to a more leisurely forty days in Acts. Others think Luke adds "forty days" to fill out the chronology

55. Fitzmyer, *The Acts of the Apostles*, 199.

from Easter to Ascension, and then finally on to Pentecost some ten days later. Various OT writings, which Luke knew, refer to forty days/years as a period of preparation during which God fully instructs people for their future work (e.g., Exod 24:12-18; 34:28; 1 Kgs 19:8). In Luke's Gospel the Spirit leads Jesus into the wilderness for forty days of testing (Luke 4:1-13). The reference to "forty days," then, probably symbolizes an extended period of preparation and examination for the difficult work ahead.[56]

The Lord first instructs his apostolic successors about the "kingdom of God," which is the central idiom of Jesus' preaching ministry, according to Luke's Gospel. While not as prominent in the speeches of Acts, it is used here and at the book's end as a literary inclusio (see 28:31). The reader is put on notice that the triumph of God's reign is the subtext of the narrative sandwiched between. However, nowhere does Acts supply a normative definition of God's "kingdom." Elements of a definition are perhaps best inferred from its uses in the fourfold gospel and from the images and ideas of Luke's theological perspective in Acts. For example, Luke's narrative is centered upon God, who alone reigns and who, as the divine choreographer of history, is not detached from this history but is powerfully present to heal and restore those who trust God. In this context God promises to bless all nations through the mission of a restored Israel (see 1:8).

Jesus' second instruction is "not to leave Jerusalem" (1:4a). According to Luke's narrative map, all roads leading into God's salvation are to or from Jerusalem. It is a city built with the bricks of prophecy, and the fate of all creation depends on what happens there. This has already proved true for the Messiah, for whom Jerusalem was the city of his destiny and now is the site of his imminent departure (cf. Luke 9:51). So, too, will it be for his successors, since Jerusalem is the point of their departure into the world, carrying the word of the Lord forth to the "ends of the earth" (1:8; cf. Luke 24:47).

The third and climactic instruction is to "wait for the promise of the Father" (1:4b), which is "you will be baptized with the Holy Spirit" (1:5). John the Baptist's prophecy

of the Messiah's Spirit-filling, unfulfilled in the Gospel, is now recalled and prophesied again by Jesus. The Lord calls the Spirit "the promise of the Father" because the Spirit is God's Spirit, who continues to mediate God's word before, through, and after Christ (2:33). There is continuity between the prophetic ministry of Jesus and his apostolic successors because each is baptized into the realm of this same Spirit of prophecy who empowers an effective ministry of word and living witness.[57] Jesus' response to the provocative question posed by his apostles (1:6) indicates that the role of the Holy Spirit in Acts is more functional than soteriological: Initiation into the realm of the Spirit enables the believers to bring an effective witness of the risen Jesus to the world (1:7-8). Unlike the Pauline emphasis on the Spirit's mediation of God's salvation-creating grace, then, the images and ideas of the Spirit's role are almost always tied to the apostles' mission or to the authority of their leadership. The kind of interpretive myopia that privileges the Pauline idea to the exclusion of Acts, or the reverse, is corrected within canonical context where these different emphases are brought into a mutually enriching relationship. The Pauline conception of the "spiritual life," which emphasizes the Spirit's role in enabling believers to live in new ways, is complemented by Acts' conception of the Spirit as the invigorating source of the community's witness in the world.

Luke follows Jesus' instruction with the apostles' question: "Lord, is this the time when you will restore the kingdom [of God] to Israel?" (1:6). All that has happened since the Lord's passion has convinced them of God's triumph. However, Jesus had not yet engaged in those messianic actions that would redeem Israel (cf. Luke 24:21). Was the arrival of the promised Spirit Israel's redemptive moment? Recalling that their minds had been opened by the resurrected Lord to understand the meaning of Scripture (cf. Luke 24:44-45) and that they have just spent the past forty days learning about the kingdom of God from him (see 1:3), we should presume that the apostles are correct in drawing the implication they do from Jesus' prophecy of the Spirit's outpouring: The Spirit signals the fulfillment of Scripture's prophecy of Israel's restoration

56. C. H. Talbert, *Reading Acts* (New York: Crossroad, 1997) 23-24.

57. See Stronstad, *The Prophethood of All Believers.*

(cf. Isa 32:14-20).[58] Jesus' vague response to their query is nothing like "an indirect denial that it is Israel to whom the Kingdom will be given."[59] Nor does it point to "the rule of God over human hearts,"[60] since Acts steadfastly refuses to substitute a distinctively Christian or spiritualized meaning for the more traditional Jewish hope of Israel's restoration.[61] The apparent intention of Jesus' answer is not to set aside the implicit connection between Pentecost and the promise of Israel's restoration but rather to clarify the terms of its fulfillment at Pentecost.

Jesus' final instruction is prefaced by the claim that God's plan to restore Israel does not become the special knowledge of insiders: "It is not for you to know" (1:7). Many scholars suppose that this stern word responds to the painful disappointments experienced within the ancient church over unrealized predictions of Christ's return. Some speculate that Luke has in mind Christian prophets who claimed personal insight into the "times and periods" of endtime events and had gathered a cult-like and divisive congregation around themselves. I doubt this. Jesus does not respond to speculation surrounding what is "not yet" but insists that his disciples engage in a mission "right now." He points out that the disciples are not waiting for the Spirit within some apocalyptic time zone, where saving events come from heaven and erupt into human history in the "twinkling of an eye." The apostles are to wait for a different redemptive reality. Jesus defines in a paradigmatic way the relationship between the Spirit's outpouring and Israel's restoration. He prophesies that "you will receive power when the Holy Spirit has come upon you" (1:8)—a prediction that echoes Isaiah's prophecy of the pouring out of the Spirit to renew Israel's eternal covenant with God (so Isa 32:15). While Jesus thereby agrees with the theological subtext of the apostles' query—the Spirit's outpouring does indeed signal the season of Israel's restoration—he applies it to their vocation: God's reign will be reestablished among God's people not by some apocalypse from heaven but by a mission on earth.

The word Luke uses for "power" is δύναμις (*dynamis*), which denotes a robust force at work in demonstrative ways for all to see and feel. Such a "power" comes with the Spirit of prophecy. The Spirit does not confer a political authority upon the apostles but rather new competencies that enable them to perform the tasks given them, whether through their inspired words, their miraculous works, or their leadership within the community's common life (see 2:42-47; 4:32-35). For this reason, the Lord stipulates emphatically that this power will reside upon "you" (= apostles) to enable the apostles to "be my witnesses." They are to continue "all that Jesus began to do and teach" (1:1).

When Jesus turns the expectation of Israel's restoration from an indeterminate chronology to the means of its realization within the church's missionary history, the theological subtext of Acts is established. He then provides a geographical index to underwrite this history's eventual progress. The plotline of Acts follows this same index, beginning "in Jerusalem [Acts 2–7], in all Judea and Samaria [Acts 8], and to the end of the earth [Acts 9–28]."[62] The Spirit's outpouring empowers a global mission as the divinely intended means by which God's covenant with a repentant Israel is renewed and Israel is called as "a light to the nations" so that repentant Gentiles also can share in the blessings of Israel's salvation (see 3:19-26; 13:44-47; cf. Luke 2:32).

1:9-11. The two accounts of Jesus' ascension here and in Luke 24:51 are unique in the NT. Jesus' ascension further validates his resurrection (see 1:3) and vindicates the claim that he is God's Messiah (see 2:21, 36). Unlike others who are resuscitated to life (e.g., Lazarus), Jesus is brought back to life never again to die. The Gospels report only

---

58. For the importance of the Spirit of prophecy in Israel's restoration theology, see Turner, *Power from on High*.

59. Maddox, *The Purpose of Luke-Acts*, 106.

60. Johnson, *The Acts of the Apostles*, 29.

61. Jervell, *The Theology of the Acts of the Apostles*, 18-43.

62. Significantly, the final phrase (ἕως ἐσχάτου τῆς γῆς *heōs eschatou tēs gēs*) is singular, "the *end* of the earth," and probably echoes Isa 49:6 and its prophecy of Israel's identity as a "light to the nations" (see Acts 13:47). See J. Dupont, *The Salvation of the Gentiles* (New York: Paulist, 1979) 17-19. Others, such as Conzelmann, *The Acts of the Apostles*, 7, find the phrase's referent, quite possibly Rome, in the narrative itself and, therefore, view the phrase as another element of the story's inclusio: Even as Jesus teaches the "kingdom of God" to his apostles at Acts' beginning (1:3) for their mission to the "end of the earth," so also Paul continues his teaching of the "kingdom of God" at the "end of the earth" (Rome) at its conclusion (28:31). In this sense, Jesus' commission is ultimately carried out (and on) by Paul; indeed, the commission is an essential feature of the story's Pauline apologia. R. C. Tannehill, *The Acts of the Apostles*, vol. 2 of *The Narrative Unity of Luke-Acts*, 102-12, argues, however, that the Ethiopian eunuch (8:26-39) represents those at the "end of the earth," formally bringing to conclusion the narrative of the Lord's apostolic successors indexed by Acts 1:8 and preparing the reader for the story of Paul beginning in Acts 9.

the discovery of an empty tomb followed by various post-resurrection epiphanies of the risen Jesus; but there are no witnesses to the resurrection itself. Perhaps for this reason, the verbs Luke employs in Acts stress the availability of the ascension to eyewitnesses: they "were watching" until he was "out of their sight" (1:9), continuing to "gaze" (1:10) while two men asked them why they were "looking."

In Jewish literature the biblical story of Elijah's dramatic departure in a fiery chariot (2 Kgs 2:11) is followed by the apocalyptic retelling of Enoch's ascension in whirlwinds to the very "end of the heavens" (*1 Enoch* 39:3-4) and also by Philo's description of Moses' ascension to God while still proclaiming God's word.[63] Luke's story of the ascension glosses this important Jewish tradition of exalting God's prophets: Jesus is the prophet-like-Moses Messiah (cf. Deut 18:15-22), powerful in word and work (cf. Luke 24:19; Acts 7:22), whom God sent to announce the arrival of God's salvation and to broker it on behalf of the world.[64]

The ascension also provides the implied religious motive for the apostles' testimony to Jesus (1:8). While they are not eyewitnesses to his resurrection, the apostles are eyewitnesses to his ascension, lending credibility to their proclamation that he is alive. Significantly, the "cloud" (νεφέλη *nephelē*) that carries Jesus heavenward (1:9) recalls the use of a "cloud" to symbolize God's faithful presence among the liberated people in the OT story of Israel's exodus (see Exod 16:10; 19:9; 24:15-18).[65] If Luke adds *nephelē* to make this allusion, he also implies that the apostolic proclamation about the living Jesus further confirms God's commitment to fulfill promises made to Israel (see 1:6-8).

The "two men in white robes" redirect our line of vision from the past of Jesus to his future with the words "this Jesus . . . will come in the same way" (1:11). Their eschatological commentary on Jesus' ascension makes two different, although complementary, points. Their words cultivate the

haunting awareness of Jesus' bodily absence from his disciples. In its canonical setting, the theological crisis occasioned by the Lord's departure is addressed in a farewell speech of John's Jesus (John 14–16), when he tells his followers that his departure results in the "coming of the Counselor to you" (John 16:7) to "bear witness to me" (John 15:26) and to "teach you all things and bring to remembrance what I have said to you" (John 14:26). By this exhortation, Jesus encourages the disciples to find their way in the world without him and to shoulder the tasks of the messianic movement he had begun. Jesus' departure is the formal condition of their succession, even as it is the material condition of the Spirit's empowerment. In fact, the Lord's instructions given over the past forty days (Acts 1:3) become sheer nonsense without his bodily departure.

Yet, the eschatological horizon of the church's mission is the Lord's return from heaven to complete his messianic vocation (see John 14:3). The church's mission, which continues the past of Jesus, is motivated by the hope of his future (see 3:19-21; 10:42). Much has been made of the lack of clear references to Christ's return in the speeches of Acts. Certainly this lack is all the more remarkable when these speeches are compared to the frequency of references to the second coming found in the letters and gospel traditions. While Luke diminishes the "not yet" of Jesus in favor of the "right now" of the church's mission, this narrative opening that asserts "this Jesus . . . will come" frames the entire story with future expectation (see Introduction, "Acts as Confession").

Most interpreters claim that the two "men" symbolize the Torah's requirement that two witnesses must confirm the veracity of an alleged event (see Deut 19:15). Given the integral connection of ascension and resurrection, the reader should assume that these "men" are the same two who also appeared to the women in the empty tomb to confirm his prediction of execution and resurrection (Luke 24:4-7). Perhaps we should also take them as angelic witnesses to heaven's confirmation of the living Jesus, as Cleopas did (Luke 24:23). Earlier in the Gospel, however, Elijah and Moses—both of whom ascended into heaven, according to well known Jewish

63. Philo *Life of Moses* 2:291.

64. For this see M. Parsons, *The Departure of Jesus in Luke-Acts*, JSNTSup 21 (Sheffield: *JSOT*, 1987), who views the ascension as a literary device that helps the reader from Gospel into Acts, its sequel. The function of this hinge-narrative is to form impressions of the triumph of the risen Jesus, which is the christological subtext for reading Acts.

65. Fitzmyer, *The Acts of the Apostles*, 209-10.

legends—appear at the Son's transfiguration and speak of his "departure" from Jerusalem (see Luke 9:30-31). The echoes of familiar traditions about Elijah and Moses that reverberate throughout Acts provide good reason to think that the identity of the "two men" is not angelic but "Jesus'" prophetic predecessors who ascended, Moses and Elijah.[66] In either case, they provide "official" testimony to the Lord's importance that will fund the apostles' proclamation about him.

1:12-14. With the departure of the Messiah and his "official" succession to them now complete, the apostles are left to wait for the promised Spirit to empower their mission. Whether they are able to continue what their Lord began depends on their faithfulness to God. Luke is careful to depict them as observant Jews who journey only "a sabbath's day" from Jerusalem (cf. Exod 16:27-30).[67] They are also faithful to Jesus who instructed them to wait in Jerusalem for the Spirit's outpouring (1:4), and they "constantly devoted themselves to prayer" (1:14). Typically in Luke's narrative world, true believers gather together for prayer to wait upon God to act at critical moments of their history (cf. 1:24-25; 4:24-30; 6:6; 8:15; 9:11; 12:12; 13:3;

14:23; 16:25; 20:36; 28:8). This prayerful waiting upon the Lord not only characterizes the church of Acts; it also underscores the implicit importance of Pentecost when God will deliver them the Holy Spirit as promised.

The community's constituency is noteworthy. The listing of apostles (1:13) is a literary convention of succession narratives and is expected here: These are the names of those who form the community's leadership and will provide the messianic community's leadership in the Messiah's absence. Only eleven apostles are named, members of an incomplete apostolic circle. This narrative detail explains the purpose of the subsequent account of Judas's demise (see 1:15-20a) and his replacement's selection (1:20b-26). The inclusion of "certain women, including Mary the mother of Jesus" recalls the importance of various women in Jesus' ministry (cf. Luke 8:1-3; 24:1-11; John 4; 11) and makes clear that women will continue to play a significant role in the church's mission to the end of the earth (see Acts 18). Finally, Luke's curious reference to Jesus' "brothers" has led some commentators to find here a metaphor for all other disciples that make up the messianic community at Pentecost. It is more likely, given the central importance of the resurrection in the opening of Acts, that this final phrase alludes to the Lord's Easter day appearances to members of his own family (James, Jude) according to tradition (cf. 1 Cor 15:7).

---

66. Johnson, *The Acts of the Apostles*, 31.
67. Luke locates Mt. Olivet in Bethany (Luke 19:29), a suburb of Jerusalem that John's Gospel reports is two miles from the city center (John 11:18), well beyond the limit prescribed for a sabbath's walk. If we use the same map as Josephus, we find Mt. Olivet in the Kidron ravine on the city's southeastern edge and well within the distance allowed for the "Sabbath day's journey" stipulated in Acts.

REFLECTIONS

1. "They were looking intently up into the sky as he was going" (1:10 NIV). Jesus gathers his followers after Easter to prepare them for their future without him. The initial spiritual crisis concerns their discipleship and whether they can follow after Jesus without seeing or hearing him, drawing strength from his physical presence among them. The same remains true today: How can we live as earnest disciples of a now-departed Lord? Jesus prepared his followers to continue in the pattern of ministry that he had begun. According to Acts, discipleship is defined in terms of an active witness to the risen Jesus rather than a deeply affecting relationship with him. While any biblical definition of discipleship must include those prophetic tasks in continuity with what Jesus did and said, Acts' overemphasis in the life of the church can replace the centrality of an abiding relationship with the living Jesus that ultimately saps the spiritual energy believers draw from him. We live in an activist's age in which participation in good deeds is keenly encouraged, even demanded of the "committed person." For this reason the biblical interpreter must take care to bring together the "task discipleship" of Acts with teaching of a more contemplative pattern of discipleship from, for example, John's Gospel (John 14–17), where God's Spirit is given to cultivate an intimate relationship with the living Jesus.

2. "After his suffering . . . he appeared to them during forty days" (1:3 NRSV). Jesus' curriculum in preparing his followers to continue his mission concerns "the many proofs" of his resurrection and instruction about "the kingdom of God" (1:3). What must be noted first is that the Lord consecrates a period of time to prepare his followers *fully* for their future ministry, symbolized by the number "forty." Their witness will be guided and empowered by the Spirit (1:8), but they are thoroughly briefed by Jesus to understand *accurately* what they have seen and its theological significance. The Holy Spirit does not work in an intellectual vacuum; nor is Christian witness effective if it merely testifies to the experience of God's salvation without being able to interpret meaning for all of life. Impoverishment of theological understanding in the church diminishes the community's influence on its surrounding culture.

3. "He presented himself alive to them by many convincing proofs" (1:3 NRSV). The gospel that is preached and embodied in life is not funded by fictions or theological abstractions but is predicated on various proofs—the hard evidence—that Jesus appears to real people as really alive. From the fourfold gospel tradition, the interpreter can list what these proofs are: He "appeared" to them over several days to share table fellowship with them and show them his wounded hands and feet; he interpreted Scripture for them and commissioned them for ministry; and he made promises to them that were realized in their transformed lives. The horizon of Christian life and practice is fashioned by the credibility of Jesus' resurrection and by the continuing experience of the living Jesus. The Gospel stories of Easter tell us of the apostles' initial confusion and incredulity at the report of the Lord's resurrection. This period of preparation therefore engenders their confidence that what they will announce to others is true; and also confirms their spiritual authority to do so. And at its very essence, this time of preparation presumes that those who know that Jesus lives will want to tell others the good news.

4. He "spoke [to them] about the kingdom of God" (1:3 NIV). Any reflection on the Lord's goodness to his disciples must include this season of preparation, making clear to them what to expect and how to best use their time without him. He does not leave them to discover these practical truths on their own. Therefore, in addition to this robust portfolio of experiences with the living Jesus, he schools them to teach the kingdom of God, now informed by his passion and resurrection, and to recognize or discern its disclosure during the course of their mission. The kingdom of God is ordered by God's benevolent presence and redemptive purposes. Although God rarely appears as a character in Acts, God's plan for human history controls the plotline of the story.

5. "Wait in Jerusalem for the promise of the Father" (see 1:4). After instructing the apostles, Jesus directs them to wait for the Father to send them the promised Spirit. Waiting for this dynamic future to unfold involves a measure of uncertainty and urgency. What makes it possible for them to hope for tomorrow's best is God's past faithfulness to Jesus. His resurrection and ascension are reflections of God's faithfulness both to him and to promises made to Israel because of him. Our capacity to wait expectantly for God to act according to "the promise" is cultivated by memory of the record of God's faithfulness in the history of others.

6. Waiting for God to act is also a community's project. Waiting with others is an act of solidarity with friends. The apostles do not scatter and go their separate ways to await a private Spirit-filling or a personal experience of divine faithfulness. They "were joined together" in a specific place to await God's action on them all.

7. "They all joined together constantly in prayer" (1:14 NIV). Waiting on the Lord to act is not a passive inactivity: They waited by praying (1:14) and studying Scripture together (1:15-22). Prayers are not offered to solicit God's benefaction, which they have already experienced, nor to ensure that God would fulfill what is promised them. Praying together publicly demonstrates the importance of their spiritual unity and resolve in accomplishing their missionary vocation as Jesus prophesied it and as God will continue to clarify it to them. As is often the case in Acts, however, prayer precedes doing the tasks given by the Spirit's power. Experiencing the living Jesus and knowing thoroughly the content of the Gospel is not sufficient for effective ministry. The community will have nothing to say that matters without God's full participation in all that they do. The substance of what we proclaim and live as good news must first of all be grounded in a community that is given over to constant prayer and worship.

8. "But you will receive power when the Holy Spirit has come upon you" (1:8 NRSV). This passage introduces the Holy Spirit as the "Father's promise" and the receptacle of "power" that enables the progress of the gospel to go forward from sacred Jerusalem to profane Rome. The Spirit's role within the faith community is central to Acts, but it is carefully circumscribed. This Spirit is the "Spirit of prophecy," poured out upon God's people, according to Scripture's promise, in order to enable them to perform the various tasks of mission. The church routinely neglects teaching believers that they live in the realm and under the influence of a more mission-minded Spirit whose presence empowers an effective, responsible witness for Jesus in the world. The Christianity shaped by Acts is neither quiet or passive but aggressive, assertive, challenging, and countercultural in calling upon everyone everywhere to repent and turn to Jesus in faith. However, the interpreter must aim at a balanced theology of the Spirit that includes Paul's teaching of its transforming spiritual and moral effect in the individual believer's life.

9. "'Lord, is this the time when you will restore the kingdom to Israel?'" (1:6 NRSV). With minds opened by Jesus to understand the witness of Scripture to the salvation of Israel, the disciples ask Jesus whether God's promise of the Spirit is coordinate with God's promise to restore the kingdom to Israel (1:6). Jesus is instructive both in what he says and in what he does not say in response (1:7-8). He does not reprove the apostles for they are right in making this connection: Pentecost has *everything* to do with God's fidelity to the biblical promises made to the Jews. Nowhere does Jesus suggest that God's promise to restore "real" Israel has been reclaimed and given to the church as a spiritual or "true" Israel. Christianity has not superseded Israel in the plan of God's salvation so that God's future now belongs to the church. Jesus rather indicates to his apostles that the fulfillment of God's promise to revitalize Israel is not a matter of "when" (1:7) but "how" (1:8): God's concern for what happens at the "end of the earth" or at its very center in Jerusalem is evinced by the church's *mission*. The Gentile mission is *not* the result of Jewish rejection. It is God's idea from the very beginning according to biblical prophecy, and it is made possible only because of God's prior saving work among repentant Jews mediated by the church's *Jewish* mission.

10. So much of this passage involves believers' "coming together" in order to learn, to wait upon God, to pray in preparation to witness in Jesus' name by the Spirit's power. This fairly extensive collocation of images and ideas formulates a particular understanding of the church's identity and vocation: The church of Acts is a missionary community called together by God's Messiah and sent out into the world by the power of God's Spirit to interpret the importance of Jesus' resurrection for all people everywhere. Of course, the various resources of our canonical heritage teach us that to be the church we should seek a complement of witnesses. Thus the witness of the Confessing Church in Nazi Germany and that of Martin Luther King, Jr., in a racially divided United States speak to the importance and power of Jesus' resurrection in modern life. The distinctive contribution Acts makes to our understanding of mission is that the risen Lord bids and fills us with the Spirit to witness to him publicly and boldly in all that we do and say.

11. "This same Jesus . . . will come back in the same way you have seen him go into heaven" (1:11 NIV). The seventh and final Sunday of Easter is Ascension Sunday, and this passage is its principal lection. What do we really believe when we confess together the good news that Jesus "ascended into heaven"? Simply put, it is our affirmation that Jesus is *still* alive and *presently* metes out the Spirit's power for ministry (2:33) and God's grace for forgiveness (5:31) until he returns for "the restoration of all things" (3:21). In addition the ascension story in Acts (unlike Luke's Gospel) is directly tied to the forty days required by Jesus to prepare his apostles for their succession to his ministry. They are now "on the clock"—a formidable challenge, but one realistically envisaged by the promised Spirit.

12. Just as Acts is preeminently a theological book, so also the first images of God presented in the book are particularly important. No matter how vague or incomplete they are, these initial impressions of God in the opening paragraphs of Acts shape how its readers interpret God's subsequent appearances in its narrative world. God is faithful to Jesus (1:3, 9-11). God makes promises to Israel and plans to keep them (1:4-6). God's people gather to worship and pray to God, confident that God will act as promised (1:12-14). Perhaps keener than any other image, however, is that the God of Acts has a redemptive purpose to accomplish and a plan already worked out according to the promises of Scripture. The missionary vocation of the apostles, and by implication of the community they lead, is a task-centered one: The community will be enabled by God's Spirit to witness to God's Messiah—to preach persuasively and teach boldly, to interpret Scripture after the mind of God, and to perform miracles to awaken people to the benevolence of God's rule (1:8).

ACTS 1:15-26, AND THEN THERE WERE TWELVE

COMMENTARY

Symbols are important to biblical stories because they provide theological markers for their readers. There is hardly a more important numerical symbol in Scripture than twelve. Simply put, the number twelve stands for Israel as God's people. The significance of twelve apostles is elevated in Acts because Luke's Jesus had placed the prospect of Israel's restoration in the hands of his apostolic successors (see Luke 22:28-30; see also Acts 1:6-8). In this sense the restoration of the Apostolate to Twelve symbolizes (and is a necessary condition of) Israel's restoration. The stories of Judas's demise (1:15-20a) and Matthias's selection to replace him (1:20b-26), so laden with theological import and interpretive problems, are related here to explain how God acts to restore the Twelve. The group's return to its full complement heralds the apostles' inspired roles as agents of God's plan to restore the "twelve tribes of Israel." Moreover, the stories symbolize a divided Israel (see Luke 2:34-35) and therefore also the pattern of Israel's restoration. Even as Judas represents unrepentant Israel who rejects Messiah and is therefore rejected by God (see 13:44-47), Matthias, who unlike Judas is a "witness with us to his resurrection" (1:22b), represents a repentant Israel in whose life God's reign is present through the gift of the Spirit.

1:15-20a. The problem facing the interpreter of Judas's demise according to Acts has been framed and freighted in two ways.

The NT reader approaches it with Matthew's version already in mind (see Matt 27:3-10). Matthew's Judas is paradigmatic of the unrepentant disciple and contrasted to Peter who is rehabilitated because of his earnest repentance (see Matt 26:57-75; John 21:15-17). Upon closer reading, however, many discrepancies are noted between the Matthean and Acts' versions, not only in detail but in theological motivation as well.[68] Imaginative harmonies of Judas's death have been created in response to these discrepancies and then put forward as "authorized"—ironically, to preserve the authority of the very Scripture they displace! At the very least, the interpreter should take care to understand each account of Judas's death within its particular context. The different meanings should then be cobbled together as integral parts of a fuller, more textured understanding of Judas's death (see below).

Those who have read both Matthew's and Luke's Gospels before Acts may be puzzled as to why Luke delays telling this story rather than including it in his Gospel. However, Luke's placement of the story in the introductory material of Acts envisages its strategic role. Luke understands that Judas's betrayal has greater theological significance than the spiritual failure of a particular disciple; indeed, Judas's failure and demise appear to pose a real threat to the destiny of the messianic community itself. This seems especially true if Luke composes Acts to address a question concerning God's faithfulness in keeping promises made to Israel, for God's fidelity will be embodied in the apostles' future career as the Lord's successors (see 1:3-8). Jesus himself prophesied that the Twelve would rule over the "twelve tribes of Israel" in his absence (Luke 22:28-30). In this light, then, the reader of Acts realizes that Judas's demise fractures the Twelve and thereby undermines God's future plans: They are currently only the "eleven" and the divine plans cannot go forward (see 1:13).[69] If God's plans have gone awry because of Judas's defection—an

apostle that God had chosen (see 1:2)—we may be inclined to ask further about God's faithfulness or to question whether God really has sovereign control over salvation's history. By this story, Luke rescues God from embarrassment!

Quite apart from any symbolic significance that the reference to "one hundred and twenty persons" (= a multiple of twelve) may suggest (1:15), Peter may have convened these believers as an official body to hear relevant testimony leading to an important decision or action. Peter's first speech in Acts provides testimony in two parts (1:16-20a and 1:20b-22) necessary to render a verdict in favor of God. He prefaces his remarks with two claims of Scripture's authority as the context in which such deliberation takes place. Peter begins his speech by asserting that "the scripture had [δεῖ *dei*] to be fulfilled." Luke characteristically uses the "*dei* of divine necessity" to mark out certain events as ordained by God (see Luke 22:37; 24:26, 44; Acts 3:21; 17:3); and Scripture is cited or alluded to as an independent testimony that these events are, indeed, written into the divine script by biblical prophecy as elements of God's plan of salvation. Computed by this redemptive calculus, then, Peter will logically contend that both Judas's death and the selection of Matthias are prophesied by Scripture (see 1:20) and must be viewed by the community as "necessary" for the realization of God's purposes and even included in the script of God's salvation—even though by public perception these events have an awkward feel and accidental look.

Indeed, Peter claims "the Holy Spirit spoke long ago through David concerning Judas." That is, the Spirit's production of biblical prophecy through inspired prophets such as David[70] and the recovery of its contemporary meaning by inspired interpreters such as Peter ensure that the divinely intended meaning of Scripture is transmitted to the faith community. This careful staging of Peter's comments about Judas's death and the importance of selecting a replacement, justified by his reading of Scripture, presume that the production and interpretation of Scripture are by

---

68. Read in terms of Matthew's theological conception, the contrasting responses of remorseful Peter and an equally remorseful Judas to their betrayal of Jesus illustrates the nature of spiritual conflict: Peter is penitent because he failed Jesus (26:75), whereas Judas's remorse is evoked by a private sense of guilt (27:4) that turns him inward rather than back to Jesus and the community for forgiveness (see Matt 18:20-22).

69. See J. Jervell, *Luke and the People of God* (Minneapolis: Augsburg, 1972) 75-112, esp. 88-96.

70. In Acts, David is "the prophet par excellence, the central figure in Scripture" according to J. Jervell, *The Unknown Paul: Essays on Luke-Acts and Early Christian History* (Minneapolis: Augsburg, 1984) 126.

the same Spirit of God and therefore espouse a single truth: Judas's accidental death and Matthias's selection by chance are executed according to divine purpose.

Peter explains that Judas "was numbered among us and was allotted a share in this ministry" (1:17). The verbs used place Judas under the provident care of a sovereign God, note the happy beginning of a tragic story, and make clearer that his defection from "this ministry" is by his choice and not God's. The parenthetical description of Judas's death in vv. 18-19[71] examines his spiritual failure and casts blame on him, thereby justifying God's rejection of Judas as the one who betrayed the Messiah and reneged on his portion of the apostolic ministry—all for the "reward of his wickedness" (1:18). In sharp contrast to Matthew, Peter does not claim a remorseful Judas returned the money; here Judas chooses instead to purchase "a field" (= a "small farm"), perhaps to buy his way into a higher social class. Judas's choice of money over Messiah is paradigmatic of spiritual failure in Acts. In contrast to the exercise of spiritual authority and maturity within the community of goods, exemplified by the glad sharing of material wealth with others (see 2:42-47; 4:32-35), Judas's rejection of Jesus and defection from his apostolic duties is embodied in his use of ill-begotten money for a personal end. This act supplies ample proof of his alienation from God.[72] Noteworthy is Peter's use of Ps 69:25 (Ps 68:26 LXX), which is prophetic of Judas's *land* and not his death: "Let his homestead become desolate, and let there be no one to live in it" (1:20a).[73] Luke employs the symbolism of property to underscore that the money paid Judas ultimately bought land used to bury the dead rather than land used

to house the living. Likewise, the person who chooses money over Messiah actually makes a choice for death rather than for life.

The vivid description of Judas's death is also shaped for its theological effect: "he burst open in the middle and all his bowels gushed out" (1:18). Luke shapes his story after familiar Jewish (and secular) death stories of the wicked in which the more wicked the deed the more graphic and inopportune the death (see Acts 12:20-23; see also Josh 7; 2 Sam 20:4-13; 2 Macc 9:5-6).[74] Moreover, the burst "bowels" (σπλάγχνον *splanchnon*) of Judas may allude to famous exemplars of his opposites in Luke's Gospel: the "good Samaritan" who is "moved by pity" (σπλαγχνίζομαι *splanchnizomai*, Luke 10:33) to care for the wounded stranger and the caring father who is "filled with compassion" (*splanchnizomai*, Luke 15:20) when welcoming his prodigal son home. This Lukan intertext cultivates the reader's impression of Judas as a tragic symbol of religious disaffection whose self-absorption wins out over mercy.

Finally, the discrepant versions of Judas's fate found in Matt 27:3-10 and Acts 1:18-20 are actually complementary within a canonical whole. Rather than viewing them as contradictory and in need of some kind of exegetical arbitration, the interpreter should think of them as the discrete yet collateral interpretations of Judas's death that the church has included within its Scriptures to be read together and reflexively. In this way the very differences found in one text frame a fresh angle of vision into the other text, allowing the interpreter to detect hitherto hidden layers of meaning. For example, commentators on Acts routinely fail to find an implicit contrast between Peter and Judas (as noted above). With Matthew's sharpened contrast in mind, the reader approaches Peter's speech about Judas's demise quite differently: The living Jesus has fullest effect in a restored Peter who has now succeeded him as

---

71. Since punctuation marks are not used in the Greek text, the writer must revert to syntactical markers to introduce a narrative parenthesis. Luke uses the transitional phrase οὗτος μὲν οὖν (*houtos men oun*, "Now this man") in 1:18 to signal this to the reader.

72. According to L. Johnson's literary analysis, *The Literary Function of Possessions in Luke-Acts*, SBLDS 39 (Missoula, Mont.: Scholars Press, 1977) esp. 173-222, Luke's view of the use and misuse of possessions constitutes an important theological symbol in the narrative world of Acts. The pattern of divine judgment and future blessing is routinely linked to money. Possessions symbolize the condition of a person's relations with God and neighbor. The roots of such a motif are deeply set in the prophetic tradition of Israel's Scriptures and in contemporary Greek philosophy (Stoic, Cynic) that valued the sharing of possessions as a public expression of friendship.

73. H. C. Kee, *To Every Nation Under Heaven: The Acts of the Apostles*, NTC (Valley Forge, Pa.: Trinity, 1997) 40, suggests that blood spilled on land renders it impure and off limits to the observant Jew, analogous to the woman whose loss of blood at childbirth requires that she go through a period of purification in order to be restored to the community (see Leviticus 12).

74. The Acts account may echo the well-known legend of Antiochus's fatal illness (2 Macc 9:1-12; 1 Macc 6:1-16). In 2 Maccabees, a theological lesson is drawn from the manner of a person's death, whether the death of a righteous martyr or of a wicked foe. In the case of wicked Antiochus, his "bowels" (σπλάγχνον *splanchnon*) become painfully infected—"justly so" because he had tortured the "bowels" of observant Jews who refused to compromise their community's devotion to God (2 Macc 6:9). The connection to Judas's death is clear enough; the reader now is able to see a similar lesson in the Acts narrative of Judas's death.

Israel's primary interpreter of Scripture.[75] Given Matthew's description of the contrasting responses of Peter and Judas to their betrayal of the Lord, Peter's speech may also fulfill Jesus' prediction that Peter's betrayal would yield a greater faith, one that would enable him to lead the messianic community (see Luke 22:31-34). In this way, the contrasting destinies of Judas and Peter that Matthew introduces at the moment of their common failure are lifted up in the opening of Acts to underscore the continuity of all that Jesus had begun.

1:20b-26. Part two of Peter's speech (1:20*b*-22) outlines the requirements of the qualified replacement for Judas with an aim of restoring the apostolic circle according to God's prophesied plan.[76] The "*dei* of divine necessity" (1:21) stipulates two credentials: The successful candidate will (1) "have accompanied us all the time that the Lord Jesus went in and out among us, beginning from the baptism of John until the day when he was taken up from us;" and will (2) "become a witness with us to his resurrection." Peter's job description contrasts with the prior failure of Judas: The successful candidate must be a "witness with us," unlike Judas, who was an apostate from the apostolic circle; and this candidate must have

"accompanied us all the time—until the day he was taken from us," unlike Judas, whose death occurred prior to the Lord's passion and ascension.

Neither of the two candidates, Justus and Matthias, is ever again mentioned in the NT. The importance of this story has nothing to do with the two people involved; it illustrates the theological principle that the God who "knows everyone's heart" (1:24) controls the course of salvation's history. Equally important is the conviction that God collaborates with others in the progress of salvation toward its ordained end. Thus the community is a full partner in the decision-making process: First they petition God to make the tough decision (1:24-25) and then they cast lots as the means by which God's decision is made known (1:26). As with Judas's demise, which those outside the community would surely classify as an accidental death or bad luck, outsiders would think the casting of lots brings Matthias good fortune. The faith community knows differently, since lot casting was a traditional and widespread practice for disclosing God's will (see Josh 19:1-40; Jonah 1:7-8). Moreover, God's will is discerned by a community whose decision process values Scripture (1:20), a close relationship with Jesus (1:21-22), and prayerful petition (1:24-25). The concluding phrase that Matthias "was added to the eleven apostles" suggests that a vote was taken to ratify God's evident choice.

---

75. Tannehill, *The Acts of the Apostles*, 2:20.

76. Johnson, *The Acts of the Apostles*, 36, notes that Luke's use of Ps 109:8, "Let another take his position as overseer," works well here only because the LXX renders the Hebrew word פקדה (*pequdâ*) by the Greek ἐπισκοπή (*episkopē*), a word that designates an office of ecclesial leadership as in Acts 20:28 (cf. 1 Tim 3:11).

REFLECTIONS

1. "So one of the men who have accompanied us during all the time that the Lord Jesus went in and out among us" (1:21 NRSV). The twelve apostolic successors to Jesus are colleagues of Jesus and witnesses of what he did and said from beginning to end (1:21-22). This close and comprehensive knowledge of Jesus ensures the reliability of what is said about him to others in his absence. From the ancient church forward the comprehensiveness, consistency, and integrity of the Rule of Faith (*regula fidei*), which measures every claim that is called "Christian," is predicated on its source: We have received our confession from the apostles who were taught it by Jesus. Thus, for Irenaeus, the church's rule of faith predates Scripture (and every other canonical text) and is funded by the precious memories of Jesus that were received from his apostles,[77] and then preserved and passed on to the "one holy, catholic and *apostolic* church" through a succession of its canonical episcopate.[78] The authority of Scripture's teaching or the theological perspicuity of its interpretation is warranted by analogy to this Rule of Faith, which has its origins in leaders who knew Jesus personally and intimately.

---

77. Irenaeus *Against Heresies* 1.10.1.
78. Irenaeus *Against Heresies* 3.3.3.

2. "The Scripture had to be fulfilled" (1:16 NIV). This "δεῖ [*dei*] of divine necessity" is a literary theme of importance in Acts. Luke employs it to make certain readers understand that this or that event is a necessary bit or piece of God's plan of salvation according to Scripture. Judas's demise and Matthias's selection to replace him in the circle of the Twelve are the first instances of this use of *dei* in Acts (1:16, 21); both accord with God's plans and redemptive purposes. But how is this so? Judas was "chosen" by Jesus (1:2) in consultation with a sovereign God (cf. Luke 6:13). How is it possible that someone handpicked to lead the people of God as a member of the apostolic circle then dies in accordance with God's scripted plans? God's selection is never coercive but collaborative. Tasks are given with the requisite resources to accomplish them. The emphasis on character in Acts, however, leads the reader to presume that God's instructions are provisional and must be obeyed to be implemented. God's sovereignty is never at the expense of human freedom. Thus, even though Judas's "accidental" death and Matthias's "lucky" selection are in some sense God's actions and accord with biblical prophecy, God can act only because of freely made human choices.

3. "The lot fell on Matthias; and he was added to the eleven apostles" (1:26 NRSV). Various models for selecting leaders are found in Scripture. In this case, Matthias's selection follows a protocol of discernment by which a game of chance is used to complement corporate prayer in discerning God's will. In his letters, Paul claims to hold the gift of apostleship (Rom 1:5) by virtue of his Damascus road calling (Gal 1:11-17; see also Acts 9:10-19) and witness of the living Jesus (1 Cor 15:7-8; see also Acts 9:3-9). Paul's résumé is similar to that of the Old Testament prophets, who were also called by God through visionary episodes. This is still different from the protocol used for selecting the seven (see 6:1-7) or for "appointing" congregational elders (see 14:23). According to Pauline instruction, found in 1 Timothy 3 and Titus 1, the "overseer/ elder" is identified by scrutinizing the sort of person he is rather than according to his acquaintance with the historical (= Matthias) or resurrected (= Paul) Jesus. It should be noted that the requirements for apostleship given in Acts 1:21-22 would disqualify even the Paul of Acts who did not accompany the Twelve "during all the time that the Lord Jesus went in and out among us" (1:21). Different situations require different processes for selecting a congregation's leaders. In every case, however, some institutional means for discerning God's will is established to ensure that those selected are of God's choosing rather than of our own.

ACTS 2:1-13, PENTECOST: THE SPIRIT OF PROPHECY FALLS UPON THE COMMUNITY

COMMENTARY

The succession from the now-departed Messiah to the Twelve is made complete with the arrival of God's promised Spirit. First John the Baptist (in Luke 3:16) and then the risen Jesus (in Acts 1:4-5) predicted this high moment in the church's history (see 1:6-8). Not surprisingly, then, this passage is structured to reflect Jesus' earlier prophecy: The reception of God's Spirit (2:1-4) enables the community to carry an inspired word about God's risen Messiah to the entire household of Israel (2:5-13).[79]

2:1-4. No episode narrated in Acts has received more attention than this one. Such scrutiny is deserved for several reasons: the

79. Barrett, *A Critical and Exegetical Commentary on the Acts of the Apostles*, 108, suggests that Luke's purpose in this narrative is concentrated on the universalism of Jesus' commission. Even though occurring in Jerusalem and observed only by Jews, the coming of the Spirit effectively transforms the community into a "universal society in which a universal communication is possible."

importance Jesus gives the Spirit's role in his final instructions to the apostles (see 1:4-8), the passage's highly evocative description,[80] the way certain faith traditions and religious movements have drawn on this passage to warrant their religious experience and theological contribution, and the fact that this text frames and informs the church's observance of its Pentecost season when believers gather together in heightened expectation of being renewed and reborn by the power of God's Spirit. Yet, the attraction to Pentecost is also surprising. Luke alone among biblical writers has the Spirit's arrival as his "great theme," without which "there would be no story to tell."[81] To be sure, John's Gospel makes passing reference to the risen Jesus bestowing the Holy Spirit upon his disciples (20:22) and Paul draws upon a tradition about the Lord's appearance to five hundred at one time (1 Cor 15:6), perhaps in the form of his "life-giving Spirit" (1 Cor 15:45). But neither witness seems to know the particular tradition Luke uses in composing his story of the coming of God's Spirit.[82] The reader is doubly surprised, then, to find the account of so important an event so "slender and spare."[83] Perhaps its telescoping to a scant four verses intends to move the reader more quickly to the story of the Spirit's powerful effect in the community's mission to Israel (see 2:5-13), which is more central to Luke's theological program.

According to the opening phrase of this passage, the entire community is baptized into the realm of the Spirit "when the day of Pentecost had come."[84] This is evidently the particular day for which the community had been instructed to "wait" (see 1:4). The word for "Pentecost" (lit., "fiftieth day") was used by Diaspora Jews for a day-long harvest festival more commonly known as the "Feast of Weeks" (*Shavuot*) and scheduled fifty days following Passover (Exod 23:16; 34:22; Lev 23:15-21; Num 28:26; Deut 16:9-12). Luke's staging of the Spirit's outpouring and miracle of tongues may be explained in part by the subsequent "list of nations" (2:9-10), since Pentecost was one of three pilgrimage feasts when the entire household of Israel gathered in Jerusalem to celebrate the goodness of God toward the nation (cf. 2:11).

Some interpreters of this passage have heard echoes of Scripture's narrative of the Sinai theophany and the giving of Torah (Exod 19:16-19; Deut 5:4-5); on this basis they claim its typological significance for Luke's theology of the Holy Spirit. The Sinai typology contains two key elements: the giving of the Torah occurred roughly fifty days after Passover (so Exod 19:1) as an act of covenant renewal, and the Torah-based covenant renewal of Israel was mediated through Moses. Whereas Jewish interpreters vest Pentecost with the importance of the Torah of Moses for Israel's future with God, Christian interpreters posit that a new dispensation has dawned when the Holy Spirit through the Messiah mediates a new covenant with repentant Israel (see Jer 31:31-34; Rom 8:2). Both interpretations of Pentecost, however, are now contested. The specific question is whether the symbolism that links Pentecost and Sinai was available to Luke when he wrote Acts. Most scholars have concluded that Israel's commemoration of the gift of Torah during Pentecost reflects a later rabbinical practice, appearing in Jewish writings only after Luke wrote Acts.[85] Still,

---

80. According to Conzelmann, *The Acts of the Apostles*, 15, "Luke has fashioned [the Pentecost narrative] into its present form as an episode with a burlesque impact."

81. J. D. G. Dunn, *The Acts of the Apostles* (Valley Forge, Pa.: Trinity, 1996) 22.

82. Barrett, *A Critical and Exegetical Commentary on the Acts of the Apostles*, 108, notes that this is especially problematic when considering Paul, for whom the Spirit's role in the community's life is of special significance. However, G. Lüdemann, *Early Christianity According to the Traditions in Acts* (Minneapolis: Fortress, 1989) 42-43, contends that these three NT accounts may well reflect elements of a common tradition that link christophany with the giving of the Spirit. Two other factors suggest an even fuller memory reflected by the "Pentecost" stories of John and Acts (and perhaps even known to Paul). The timing of the promised Spirit in both narratives falls after and points to the exaltation of Jesus—in John immediately following his resurrection and in Acts soon after his ascension. Further, in both cases the gift of the Spirit climaxes succession narratives, when the Spirit empowers the community to continue the Lord's work—in John to forgive sin (John 20:23; cf. 16:8-9) and in Acts to do and teach what Jesus began (Acts 1:1).

83. So Johnson, *The Acts of the Apostles*, 45.

84. Luke leaves unattended the evident tension between the apostolic provenance of the Lord's (and his Father's!) original promise of the Spirit according to 1:4-5 and the corporate realization of this promise according to 2:1-4. Clearly more than the Twelve are gathered together, and all are given the ability by the Spirit to proclaim the good news of God's deeds of power in different languages. This same tension is unresolved in Acts criticism. Some scholars, such as Fitzmyer, speak only of the apostles as baptized with the Spirit; others, such as Stronstad, *The Prophethood of All Believers*, press for a more communitarian baptism.

85. The best summary of the evidence for this position is provided by Barrett, *A Critical and Exegetical Commentary on the Acts of the Apostles*, 111-12. Yet even his review omits important countervailing evidence. For example, while he is correct in setting aside the reference to the "Feast of Weeks" in *Jub.* 6:17-21 as referring to the Noahic rather than the Mosaic covenant, *Jub.* 1:1 nevertheless suggests that God's covenant with Noah is glossed by God's covenant with Moses at Sinai. See Talbert, *Reading Acts*, 40.

both *Jubilees* and Philo imply this connection between Pentecost and Sinai, if only vaguely so. Further, Luke uses familiar OT symbols of theophany, similar to Moses' experience on Sinai (e.g., fire, sound, speech), to describe the Spirit's outpouring at Pentecost; and elsewhere in Acts he makes reference to Moses and the Exodus when defending the importance of Jesus' messiahship for the renewal of Israel's covenant with God (see 3:19-24; 7:35-38). So Luke's careful staging of this event on a particular day may reflect his own theological innovation.[86]

In any case, the inbreaking of heaven into human affairs is a salient feature of Luke's narrative world. The reader of Acts is hardly surprised, then, that the promised Spirit arrives from heaven with special effects, sounding like a "violent wind" and appearing like "tongues of fire." Significantly, the community's reception of God's Spirit is perceptible; and the Lord's prophecy is fulfilled beyond doubt. The church's mission can and must begin. This passage does not claim the Holy Spirit *is* a "wind" or *is* a "fire"; rather, the Spirit is compared to the sound wind makes (cf. Gen 1:2)[87] and to the flames fire produces (cf. Exod 3:2; Ps 104:4). The narrator's intent is to create a vivid impression of the Spirit's presence among the community of the Lord's disciples as its distinguishing mark.[88]

The image of "tongues of fire" (γλῶσσαι ὡσεὶ πυρός *glōssai hōsei pyros*) heralds the gift of speaking in foreign languages (2:4) as the Spirit enables the community, especially the apostles, to testify publicly to Israel. This connection of Spirit and proclamation does not yet concern the content of the message but rather the powerful and persuasive manner by which the gospel is boldly preached (see 2:29; 4:13; 9:27-28; 14:3). J. Levison has argued, however, that "fire" (πῦρ *pyr*) was frequently used in contemporary Jewish (e.g., Philo, Pseudo-Philo) and Greco-Roman popular writings (e.g., Quintillian, Plutarch) as

a metaphor for the physiological experiences of prophetic inspiration (i.e., inflammation and agitation in combination) that occurred when the spirit of prophecy awakened and elevated the prophet's ability to think, reason, and speak.[89] That is, Luke's symbolism of the Spirit's fiery presence not only signifies the power to speak the word of God effectively but also to think about God in fresh and "inspired" ways.

In this regard, Levison's study also illumines how we should take the prophetic idiom "filled with the Holy Spirit" (2:4). While certainly reflecting Luke's insistence that God guides the witnessing community through the Holy Spirit, we can no longer limit the meaning of Spirit baptism to prophetic demeanor—to the boldness or even the persuasive rhetoric of the community's (and especially their apostles') missionary proclamation. The Spirit also gives extraordinary insight to those it fills. The prophet who is filled with the Spirit of prophecy is able to set aside the processes of human intellect, such as conjecture and guesswork, and replace them with "true" knowledge of a divinely inspired intellect.[90] The practical result, according to Philo, is that the Spirit-filled prophet is given an enriched capacity to exegete Scripture—to interpret the biblical word after the mind of God.[91] Surely Luke understands the baptism or "filling" by the Spirit in this way. Thus, the Spirit is the power by which the Scriptures are written through the inspired prophets of old (1:16; 4:25; 28:25); and these same biblical words inspired by the Spirit are rendered accurately and with keen insight into the human (and especially Israel's) condition by the power of this same Spirit. Acts does not depict the Spirit's filling, then, in a manner that is disconnected from Scripture.[92] Charismatic (i.e., inspired) utterance is deeply rooted in charismatic exegesis.

---

86. Johnson, *The Acts of the Apostles*, 46.

87. The depiction of the Spirit as "wind" may well recall the creation story to posit yet another typological rendering of the baptism with the Spirit—namely, that the creative power of the Spirit results in the birth of a new creation or even new life. This subtext could very well be intended by John 20:22, referring to Jesus' "breathing" upon the disciples (so alluding to the creation of human life in Gen 2:7), especially given the theological importance of the "new creation" motif in John's Gospel. In this case, the "fire" symbolism in Acts 2:3 could infer the cleansing purification of the old, fallen order brought by the Spirit at Pentecost. Nonetheless, I doubt this meaning is present in Acts, where the coming of the Spirit is so keenly linked to the community's vocation as witness to Jesus.

88. Jervell, *The Theology of the Acts of the Apostles*, 45.

89. J. R. Levison, *The Spirit in First Century Judaism*, AGAJU 29 (Leiden: Brill, 1997) 114-21, 245-46.

90. Levison, *The Spirit in First Century Judaism*, 168-89.

91. Levison, *The Spirit in First Century Judaism*, 190-211.

92. The actual phrase "baptism with the Spirit" is nowhere used in Scripture. Luke uses the verb "baptize" (βαπτίζω *baptizō*) with "Spirit" (πνεῦμα *pneuma*) in only Acts 1:5; 11:16; and probably in 9:18; and interchangeably with "fill" (πίμπλημι *pimplēmi*) in Acts 2:4; 4:8, 31; 9:17; 13:9) as the idiom of the Spirit's enabling those chosen by God to do the tasks of the prophet-like-Jesus. My use of "baptism with the Spirit" is a nontechnical reference to the prophecy of Jesus (1:8) that his witnesses will receive (i.e., be "baptized into" or "filled" with) the Spirit, which will enable them to do the tasks given them by God: persuasive preaching to nonbelievers, edifying teaching of believers, inspired interpretation of Scripture, miraculous "signs and wonders," and the like. Throughout this commentary, I understand the gift of the Spirit primarily (although not exclusively) in functional or missional terms.

Although concentrated in the apostles (following OT teaching), this Spirit of prophecy is neither the private property of an enlightened few nor a transitory presence. This Spirit belongs to a people of God as their shared, permanent property. Luke makes this point clearer by repetition: "they were all together" in a "whole house where all were sitting," when the Spirit came to rest on "each of them" so that "all of them were filled."[93] The power of the Spirit in this case evinces an extraordinary ability for them to "speak in other languages"—that is, in foreign languages unknown to them.[94] This "gift of tongues" should not be confused with the spiritual gift of *glossolalia* that concerns Paul in 1 Corinthians 12–14. The relevant issue at stake is not the source or the linguistic structure of this gift, whether "of men or of angels" (1 Cor 13:1); nor does Luke's use of "other" (ἑτέρα *hetera*) distinguish this from subsequent episodes of extraordinary speeches in Acts (e.g., 10:45-46; 19:6).[95] The key difference is between competing purposes. According to Pauline teaching, the gifts of the Spirit are used to empower Christian ministry to other believers for the purpose of Christian formation. Thus the Pauline meaning of *glossolalia* denotes a special language given to a few believers by the Spirit (so 1 Cor 12:14-30) to edify the entire congregation (so 1 Cor 14:5)—a purpose quite different from that of Luke.

2:5-13. The crowd of "devout Jews" (2:5) hears "this sound" (2:6), whose source is "Galileans" (2:7)—notorious for their lack of linguistic talent—"speaking in the native language of each" (2:6, 8, 11) about "God's

deeds of power" (2:11).[96] This is the first of over fifty references to the "Jews" in Acts and has paradigmatic value for the reader.[97] Jews occupy the center stage of Luke's narrative world; for this reason, we must be alert to the nuances of his usage here. In particular, they are "devout" Jews. The church's proclamation of the mighty acts of God begins with faithful Jews. Significantly, the catalogue of nations (2:9-11)[98] indicates that these Jews constitute an international assembly. Luke's hyperbole captures this nicely: "every nation under heaven" (2:5). In effect, the entire household of Israel, including "both Jews and proselytes"[99] (2:10), is present to hear

93. The implicit contrast in Acts between the evident importance of particular Spirit-filled apostles, who are inspired to preach, interpret Scripture, perform miracles and lead the church, and rank-and-file believers who are also Spirit-filled but not central to the church's mission has led Turner to distinguish between the transforming power of the Spirit, which is experienced by all believers, and the more functional empowerment of the Spirit, which is experienced only by the prophets-like-Jesus (e.g., Peter, Stephen, Paul). See Turner, *Power from on High*, 314-427.

94. Many interpreters, ancient and modern, find in this miracle of *glossolalia* an allusion to the OT story of Babel in Gen 11:1-9, where the division of speech is the hallmark of human creation's rebellion against the Creator. Here the use of multiple languages by a cohesive community to present a coherent message is the hallmark of the Creator's initiative to reverse Babel's curse. The emphasis of 2:5-13, however, is upon the *hearing* of (see 2:6, 8, 11) rather than the *speaking* of different languages (see 2:4). In fact, the Babel typology might be more effectively understood if the real miracle envisaged by this story is rather one of hearing a *single* language of the Spirit but in multiple declensions. Nevertheless, the Commentary on 2:5-13 unfolds from my analysis of 2:4, which stipulates that the miracle of Pentecost is the enabling of these Spirit-filled Galileans to speak in multiple languages.

95. So Fitzmyer, *The Acts of the Apostles*, 239.

96. The language of "power" may refer specifically to Pentecost and the power of the Spirit that now transforms the community, or more generally to the "power" that enables the community to proclaim a word about the redemptive acts of God in Jesus. I take it that this latter meaning is intended here: the power of the Pentecostal Spirit enables proclamation.

97. See the helpful excursus on "'The Jews' in Acts" in Kee, *To Every Nation Under Heaven*, 45-47. See also Jervell, *The Theology of the Acts of the Apostles*, 18-54; J. Jervell, *Die Apostelgeschichte*, KEK 3 (Göttingen: Vandenhoeck & Ruprecht, 1998) 92-93, where Jervell asserts that in Acts God's people and God's promises for them always refer to the entire household of Israel. In this sense, the church of Acts *is* Israel. Unlike Jervell, Kee (with most other interpreters) divides references to Jews into two semantic fields, roughly according to the two parts of Acts. In the book's first half (chaps. 1–15), concluding with the Jerusalem Council, "the Jews" refer to those committed to Israel's Torah and Jewish religious traditions as the very foundation for maintaining good relations with God as well as working relations with the wider society. In the book's second half (chaps. 16–28), which follows missionary Paul to the "end of the earth" (Rome), "the Jews" are more narrowly circumscribed as the ruling elite of "official" Israel and are generally hostile to "the sect of the Nazarenes" (24:5). Jervell, *The Theology of the Acts of the Apostles*, 34-43, rightly deduces that both groups are players, for good and ill, in resolving (or not) the central crisis facing the Jewish people, which is the division *within* Israel between messianic and non-messianic Jews. In this sense, then, Israel has not rejected the gospel that the Messiah has come as the risen Jesus of Nazareth; rather, Jews are divided over the issue and this theological conflict plots the action of Acts.

98. The so-called list of nations is routinely identified as a critical problem by modern interpreters. See, e.g., E. Haenchen, *The Acts of the Apostles* (Philadelphia: Westminster, 1971) 172-75; Conzelmann, *The Acts of the Apostles*, 14-15. For example, the inclusion of "Judea" (2:9) seems strange since they would speak (roughly) the same language as the Galileans. Further, the list includes various "ancient" nations no longer in existence when Luke wrote Acts (e.g., Parthians, Elamites), and the Cretans or Arabians are better understood as groups rather than nations. But Luke knew all of this! The narrative function of the list is theological, defining the inclusive boundaries of the household of Israel for whom the promise of restoration is now going forth from the community of the Spirit.

99. The word for "proselyte" (προσήλυτος *proselytos*) refers to "one who has come over," or the Gentile who has converted to Judaism. Scot McKnight, *A Light Among the Gentiles: Jewish Missionary Activity in the Second Temple Period* (Minneapolis: Fortress, 1991), has demonstrated that while Gentiles converted to Judaism during the Second Temple period, there was no organized Jewish mission to the Gentiles. Contra Fitzmyer, *The Acts of the Apostles*, 243. Since there was no Jewish mission to the Gentiles, these converts were first "God seekers" who were attracted to Jewish faith because of its teachings and way of life. This is an important group of Jews in Acts, perhaps because Luke was a proselyte before becoming a believer. In any case, the concerns raised about Paul's Gentile mission, which is the first organized Jewish mission to the Gentiles, according to Acts, are concerns about *how* (and not *that*) Gentiles convert. These are concerns settled at the Jerusalem Council (Acts 15:13-21). Perhaps the reference to "proselytes" in 2:10 hints at Paul's mission to the outsiders and the Gentile constituency of a restored Israel. See also R. Zehnle, *Peter's Pentecost Discourse Tradition and Lukan Reinterpretation in Peter's Speeches of Acts 2 and 3*, SBLMS 15 (Nashville: Abingdon, 1971).

this inspired witness to God's faithfulness to Israel.[100]

Moreover, these Jews are "bewildered" (2:6), "amazed and astonished" (2:7), and "perplexed" (2:12) by what they hear. The present crisis facing Israel is their divided house: Some have the promised Spirit but others do not and therefore remain ignorant

of Scripture's confirmation that Jesus is God's Messiah (see 2:14-36; 3:17-24). Their amazement also reflects their spiritual predicament: Who will show them the way? The short-term consequence of their ignorance is to write off the importance of what they have heard as a case of inebriation: "They are filled with new wine" (2:13). Their confusion leads Peter to interpret the divine audition they have witnessed while dispelling their ignorance about the Messiah, for it is the task of the prophet-like-Jesus to show Israel the way of the Lord.

---

100. Those who comment that this catalog of nations implies a universal mission, which ultimately will conclude in Rome (Acts 28; see also 2:10), are doubtless correct. Jesus' commission (1:8) has already provided the reader with such a geographical index and its implication for the church's missionary endeavor. However, it is more critical that the catalog of nations depicts the extent of a restored Israel, which will consist of Jews and proselytes from every nation.

REFLECTIONS

1. "When the day of Pentecost had come" (2:1 NRSV). The Spirit arrives in Jerusalem on the day of Pentecost as the fulfillment of prophecy and as the answer to the community's expectant prayers; it is a clear sign of God's faithfulness. Earlier Jesus told his apostles that God has "marked" the crucial dates of salvation's history (see 1:7). The entire household of Israel had gathered in the holy city on Pentecost to celebrate God's provident care. The gift of the Holy Spirit is another concrete example of God's goodness to Israel, and it models God's faithfulness in keeping divine promises.

2. The Pentecost experience of God's Spirit is repeated in Acts; its images are routinely recalled to interpret subsequent outpourings of God's Spirit as the constant testimony to God's continuing faithfulness (8:17; 10:44–11:18; 19:1-6). While a special moment in salvation's history, this Pentecostal outpouring of the purifying, empowering Spirit upon God's people is not a unique event from a time long ago. Luke's narrative of this wondrous action symbolizes the powerful and effective nature of God's ongoing presence among those who follow after God's Messiah.

3. "They were all together in one place" (2:1 NIV and NRSV). God's Spirit is poured out upon a community of believers. The Holy Spirit is not a "personal" gift from God that each believer privatizes—"you can have your Spirit if I can have mine." This same Spirit of one God "appeared among them—on each of them" as the distinguishing mark of a *people* belonging to God. The restoration of Israel is the work of this Spirit sent by God as promised (see 1:6), which is why the first auditors of the miracle of tongues were "devout Jews from every nation" (2:5).

4. "And at this sound the crowd gathered" (2:6 NRSV). The church has always tended toward *bitarianism*, worshiping the Father and the Son while regarding the Spirit as a marginal member of the Holy Trinity. The Holy Spirit is kept to the interior region of individual devotion and only under special circumstances makes a public appearance in the form of odd religious experiences that frighten away the uninitiated. However, it is clear from this story that the arrival of the Holy Spirit is anything but private and hidden from view, nor does it prompt folks to run from its illuminating power. The Spirit's arrival is a noisy affair with special effects that draws an interested public "from every nation" to the community in amazement.

5. "All of them were filled with the Holy Spirit and began to speak in other languages" (2:4 NRSV). The presence of the Holy Spirit in the community's life is indicated first of all by the miracle of speaking in unknown foreign languages. In explaining why this is so, the interpreter should begin with the obvious: The miracle occasions proclamation, which is central to the community's vocation as a witness to the risen Messiah (1:8). The dramatic speech is neither ecstatic nor unintelligible; it is language that communicates to others "the wonders of God" (2:11). Moreover, this miracle of speech is not just good rhetoric but the result of the Spirit's "filling" that issues in elevated insight. The community is filled with the Spirit to express the wonders of God in intelligible and intelligent tongues.

6. "Are not all these who are speaking Galileans?" (2:7 NRSV). The Jewish auditors, amazed and perplexed, recognize the community's familiar Galilean dialect. The language of the Spirit is not communicated with perfect or heavenly diction, free from the marks of human identity; it is the language of particular human groups, spoken in their idiom. God works in collaboration with real people—people who are filled with the Spirit to work on God's behalf in their own world.

7. Preaching during the season of Pentecost should take its principal cues from Luke's story of the first Pentecost. Yet John's narrative of the Spirit's arrival provides another angle of vision into the meaning of Pentecost (see John 20:19-23). While the plotline of the church's liturgical life follows Luke's theological instincts and separates Easter from Pentecost, John's Gospel combines them. It is still Easter and John's Jesus has not yet departed "for his Father's house" when he presents himself to the community of his disciples. They receive from their Lord his benediction of peace and the gift of the Holy Spirit. There is theological value in John's perspective because it resists any attempt to detach the resurrection of Jesus from the mission of his disciples whose motive derives from Easter. For this reason John's story of the Spirit's arrival is read and preached during both Easter and Pentecost seasons. At the same time John leaves vague what the Spirit's role is in the mission of the church. Acts sharpens the reader's understanding by clearly connecting the outpouring of the Spirit with the dynamic power that enables the church to give effective witness to the living Jesus.

8. The story of the Spirit's arrival in John's Gospel recalls Jesus' farewell discourse (John 14–17), where the Holy Spirit is introduced as teacher and comforter of the disciples in the Lord's absence. While these ideas are introduced in terms of cultivating an "abiding" relationship between disciples and Lord (rather than empowerment for world mission), the reader of Acts is better prepared to understand the ultimate importance of the Spirit's arrival at Pentecost having first read John's Gospel.

ACTS 2:14–15:12

PART ONE: A NARRATIVE OF CONVERSION

OVERVIEW

Peter's initial response to his mocking audience is to quote a prophecy from Joel 2:28-32 (3:1-5 LXX; Acts 2:17-21) to prove that the outpouring of the Spirit is the inaugural event of Israel's "last days" during which "everyone who calls upon the name of the Lord will be saved." This theological insight also frames what comes next in the narrative.[101] Parallel with Acts' geographical structure (1:8), Luke leads his readers to the Jerusalem Council by telling stories of different people in ever-changing geographical settings who all call upon the Lord's name and are saved.[102] These converts form a variegated community that witnesses to God's faithfulness in keeping promises made. When read reflexively with Joel's prophecy, Acts' constant repetition of the prophecy's catchphrases (e.g., "signs and wonders") and concepts (e.g., Spirit baptism/filling, inspired prophets, conversion) expands the full significance of the Spirit's outpouring at Pentecost.

Luke's narrative commentary on Joel's prophecy is, then, a narrative of conversion, marked out and enclosed by two parallel verses, Acts 2:22 and 15:12. According to 2:22, Peter addresses the Jews in Jerusalem about "Jesus of Nazareth, a man attested to you by God with [1] deeds of power, wonders, and signs [2] that God did [3] through him [4] among you [Israel]." By the time the narrator informs readers in 15:12 that another assembly of devout Jews gathered once again in Jerusalem and "listened to Barnabas and Paul as they told of all the [1] signs and wonders [2] that God had done [3] through them [4] among the Gentiles," the shift from Peter to Paul and from Jews to Gentiles corresponds to a fuller understanding of Joel's prophecy provided by the intervening chapters. Beginning in Jerusalem (Acts 2–7), then beyond the holy city into the surrounding provinces of Samaria and Judea (Acts 8) before leaving Palestine for "the ends of the earth" (Acts 13–14), Spirit-filled prophets-like-Jesus proclaim the word of God to Jews first and then to Gentiles. In each geographical region of the gospel's progress, hidden contours of the prophecy's messianic meaning are exposed to endorse Luke's belief that the promised blessings of God (= forgiveness, eternal life, gift of the Spirit) extend to everyone who does truly repent and believe the gospel about the living Jesus.

The church's intramural conflict that surfaces in Antioch (15:1-2) and Jerusalem (15:4-5; cf. 11:1-18) reflects the contested nature of God's universal salvation within the household of Israel. The pivotal testimonies presented before the assembly of elders in Jerusalem (15:6-11, 12) consolidates the normative meaning of salvation. When opponents to Paul's mission in Antioch insist that uncircumcised Gentiles "cannot be saved" (15:1), no new argument comes forth to refute their claim: the whole narrative supplies implicit evidence that requires no

---

101. See S. Walton, "Where Does the Beginning of Acts End?" in *The Unity of Luke-Acts*, ed. J. Verheyden, BETL 142 (Leuven: Leuven University Press, 1999) 447-67. After reviewing six different proposals for delimiting the preface to Acts from Acts "proper," Walton uses a complex linguistic analysis of Lukan vocabulary to argue that Acts 1–2 marks the beginning of Acts, primarily due to the perceived role these two chapters perform within Luke-Acts (as "bridge" between Luke's stories of Jesus and church) and within Acts (as "overture," where the principal themes of Acts are introduced). He admits, however, that the boundary between the beginning of Acts and the rest of the book is kept "fuzzy" by Luke as an implicit exhortation for his readers to keep the whole narrative pointing ever forward to the "end of the earth."

102. In Barrett's words, "there can be little doubt—that it was Luke's intention in these opening chapters (Acts 1–14) to describe a decisive step by which the faith of a group of Jews, and the Gospel that had been committed to them, were communicated to men who were of a different religious and racial background." See Barrett, *A Critical and Exegetical Commentary on the Acts of the Apostles*, 1:49.

additional comment. Peter summarizes the past and concludes that "we believe that we shall be saved through the grace of the Lord Jesus, just as [Gentiles] will" (15:11). The adumbrations of Peter's clear statement of divine grace have already appeared throughout the intervening narrative.

If Acts is written to defend the faithfulness of God toward historic Israel, the first half of the narrative offers Luke's preliminary response. The movement of the gospel from Jerusalem to the nations is scripted by Scripture's prophecy and therefore accords with God's purposes. Prophecy's fulfillment symbolizes divine faithfulness. Moreover, repentant Israel's mission to the nations, inaugurated by Peter and spearheaded by Paul, does not require the "Judaizing" of uncircumcised Gentile converts. Whatever protests had been voiced in this regard, whether in Antioch or in Jerusalem, have now been silenced. The problem that remains is whether the church will become so thoroughly "Gentilized" that the church's Jewish legacy will be truncated or abandoned, which would be a tacit denial of God's faithfulness to historic Israel. This version of the problem of theodicy shapes the plotline of the second half of Acts (see 15:13-29).

ACTS 2:14-41, PETER'S PENTECOST PROCLAMATION

COMMENTARY

Almost a third of the book of Acts consists of speeches. Although different in many ways, most of these speeches seek to convince their auditors of the gospel's central claims: God's resurrection of Jesus confirms him as Messiah and through him God has acted faithfully to the biblical promise to save the world from sin and death. The speeches are "missionary speeches," the principal expression of the church's obedience to Jesus' commission (1:8); and they are Luke's compositions, although most reflect his use of reliable sources. When reading a speech from Peter or Paul, then, the reader should not infer that the narrator has transcribed it verbatim. Rather, every speech functions as an element of Luke's narrative world and serves to make sense of his narrative aim.[103]

Peter's sermon plays a paradigmatic role within Acts. From the opening of the book, the reader is made alert to the narrative's redemptive calculus: A Spirit-empowered witness to the risen Jesus is the means by which God's purposes are realized. The departure of Jesus has made witness to him necessary, while the Pentecostal baptism with the Spirit has made it possible. In this setting the attentive reader recognizes that Peter's speech is exemplary of the community's witness and is made possible by the filling of the Spirit. Only the inspired prophet can recover the plan of God's salvation from Scripture, according to which Jesus dies (2:22, 25-28) and is raised again (2:23, 34-35) to confirm him as Messiah and Lord (2:36). He is the "Lord" on whose name everyone must call in order to be saved (2:21). The Spirit of God empowers persuasive speeches for specific audiences and not ecstatic events that convince no one in particular. Persuasive preaching is not a matter of being "filled [μεστόω *mestoō*] with new wine" (2:13) but being "filled [πίμπλημι *pimplēmi*] with the Holy Spirit" (2:4).

Like other speeches in Acts that address a Jewish audience, Peter's Pentecost sermon is Jewish midrash (or commentary) on Scripture. He begins by echoing the preceding prophecy and then goes on to provide a persuasive

103. The extent to which these speeches are the product of Luke's creative imagination remains contested. In this case, the historical problem is whether Luke's composition of Peter's sermon is in line with what the real Peter actually taught. Dibelius considers the speeches of Acts as Lukan literary creations, there only to advance Luke's theological agenda without any interest in an historical referent. See M. Dibelius, "The Speeches in Acts and Ancient Historiography," in *Studies in the Acts of the Apostles* (London: SCM, 1956) 138-85. While there are no historical conventions to follow when composing stories of real people or events that include speeches, Witherington notes that if Luke is accepted as a "careful historian in the mold of Thucydides and Polybius," then we may expect his speeches to be accurate summaries of the major points that were spoken. See Witherington, *The Acts of the Apostles,* 117. On balance, the speeches of Acts report substantial historical information, gleaned from reliable sources, that are then reshaped and positioned into Acts to serve Luke's rhetorical and theological purposes. See Johnson, *The Acts of the Apostles,* 5-9.

commentary on its messianic meaning (2:22-40) in order to address the present crisis—namely, ignorance of the importance of the present moment in salvation's history (i.e., Messiah has come and gone; God's Spirit has come to replace him).[104] The miracle of *xenolalia* (speaking foreign languages; see 2:12) has confused these devout Jews, producing a mocking retort (2:13-15) rather than a faithful response (cf. 2:41).

The speeches of Acts are also composed with attention to well-regarded Greco-Roman rules of persuasive speaking, rules that regulate what is said in terms of the particular audience addressed, the specific crisis that occasions the speech, and the subject matter.[105] Accordingly, Peter's speech reaches its climax in 2:36 in a stylized manner that seems logical, even necessary because of the evidence he marshals: scriptural testimony from David plus the testimony of eyewitnesses to the Lord's signs and wonders (2:22), his resurrection (2:31-32), and his exaltation (2:36).[106] Peter is not careless with evidence but carefully crafts it into a persuasive speech that deals with the immediate crisis of Israel's skepticism. For this reason, he is able to lead some into faith. One implication of the rhetorical shaping of this speech is that faith (2:41) is the *logical* response to Peter's persuasive speech. John Wesley called gospel preaching an "awakening experience." Good preaching compels people to deeper reflection and courageous action, and under the aegis of the Spirit can even transform scoffers into believers.

We should also note the importance of this narrative within the New Testament.

O. Cullmann argues that the portrait of Peter in Acts introduces the NT reader to his spiritual authority and that his speeches introduce his theological conception.[107] For all the critical attention that concentrates on the relationship between the Paul of Acts and the Pauline letters, Cullmann's study reminds the interpreter that the rehabilitated Peter of Acts provides the NT's introduction to the implied "voice" of the Petrine letters as well. While Peter's authorship of the Petrine letters is disputed, these images of his spiritual authority in Acts cultivate a keen impression of the canonical authority of their implied author. As an introduction to a distinctively Petrine theological conception within the NT, Peter's identification of Jesus as Isaiah's suffering Servant (3:13, 26; 4:27, 30) introduces the reader to the most important christological vocabulary of 1 Peter (1 Pet 2:21-25). A reflexive reading may also bring together the apocalyptic eschatology of 2 Peter 3 with Peter's programmatic teaching about the future of God's salvation in Acts 3:21-26, the one expanding the central ideas of the other (see the Commentary on 3:1–4:4).[108]

2:14-15. Peter heads the apostolic Twelve and so continues the Messiah's magisterial office (see 1:15-20).[109] His address boldly circumscribes his audience: "Fellow Jews (or Judeans) and all those living in Jerusalem; let this be known to you (who) listen to what I say." Israel's ignorance about their Messiah, which has provoked derision rather than confession, will be reversed only if they listen well to the prophet's message. Careful "listening" is an important literary theme in Acts and sometimes functions as a narrative marker, preparing the reader for an important moment in the story's plotline (see 15:13; 28:28). In this case, Luke employs an unusual Septuagintal term for "listen" (ἐνωτίζομαι *enōtizomai*) that literally means "let me place it [= the word of God] into your ears" (cf. Exod 15:26). In his Gospel, Luke uses a similar expression at a critical point when Jesus tells his audience in Nazareth that "today" the prophet's promise of good news

104. Dodd's interpretation, which now must be put forward only in a highly qualified manner, is that Peter's sermon not only reflects the theological commitments of the Jerusalem mission at its very beginning but is quintessentially Christian, providing a broad outline for NT theology and Christian proclamation (or *kerygma*). See C. H. Dodd, *The Apostolic Preaching and Its Developments* (New York: Harper and Bros., 1937) 21.

105. B. Mack's comment about the inadequacy of this sermon's evidence to convince anyone but the faithful readers of Acts (and by implication *not* the sophisticated nonbeliever) points out, if unwittingly, the rhetorical importance of audience. See B. Mack, *Rhetoric and the New Testament*, GBS (Minneapolis: Fortress, 1990) 91-92. That is, a good speech "works" because it addresses particular auditors at a particular moment in time about a relevant issue at hand; and it can do so because of appeals to accepted authority. Peter's sermon thus would not convince Mack's implied audience of secular intellectuals—who are not, in fact, the audience for this speech.

106. Witherington's rhetorical analysis of Acts is helpful at this point. He regards the main speech (2:14-36) as a kind of "forensic rhetoric" by which Peter refutes the charge that the apostles are drunks. A second speech of "deliberative rhetoric" follows (2:37-40), by which Peter responds to his audience's remorse (2:37) by encouraging them to take a particular course of action leading to their salvation (2:38-40). See Witherington, *The Acts of the Apostles*, 138.

107. O. Cullmann, *Peter: Disciple-Apostles-Martyr* (London: SCM, 1953) 33-69.

108. See R. W. Wall, "The Canonical Function of 2 Peter," *BibInt* 9 (2001) 64-81.

109. Lüdemann, *Early Christianity According to the Traditions in Acts*, 49, admits that Peter played a leading role from the beginning and would have probably been the one to give such a speech.

for the poor would be fulfilled among those "with ears" (ἐν ὠσίν *en ōsin*, 4:21).

The immediate point Peter must make defends the community's Pentecostal experience against the charge that it must result from a round of drunken debauchery. Evidently in popular culture "nine o'clock in the morning" was an hour inhabited only by those who intend no good.[110] Using a retort (2:15) dripping with comic irony Peter corrects their misunderstanding before moving on to address his audience as their teacher by interpreting the Scriptures in order to interpret the Pentecostal experience.

2:16-21. Peter explains that what the household of Israel has experienced has been prophesied by Joel as the "outpouring of the Spirit" that inaugurates "the last days" of salvation's history when "everyone who calls upon the name of the Lord will be saved." Peter quotes from the Greek version (LXX) of Joel 3:1-5. The Greek rendering allows Luke's Peter to use this text in support of his kerygmatic claim that Jesus is "Lord." When the prophet claims that "everyone who calls upon the name of the Lord [κύριος *kyrios*] shall be saved" (2:21), *kyrios* translates here the Hebrew word for God[111] and therefore allows Peter to argue that this "Lord" is the risen Jesus (so 2:36). Israel must call upon Jesus for the salvation they anticipate will come with God's messianic ruler.[112]

2:16-17a. Peter "rewrites" Joel's prophecy in still other ways to adapt it more precisely to this Pentecostal setting. Two important changes are made in the opening line: He substitutes "in the last days" (ἐν ταῖς ἐσχάταις ἡμέραις *en tais eschatais hēmerais*) for "after these things" (μετὰ ταῦτα *meta tauta*),[113] and he then adds the phrase "God

declares" (λέγει ὁ θεός *legei ho theos*) to clarify the earlier prophetic formula (2:16). Especially when read within its wider NT context, the catchphrase "in the last days" (cf. 1 Tim 3:1; Heb 1:2; Jas 5:3; 2 Pet 3:3) locates the outpouring of the Spirit against a new eschatological horizon. Simply put, Pentecost initiates Israel into a new epoch—"the last days"—of God's salvation history, when things said and done by Jesus' successors take on added urgency, not of an imminent apocalypse in the case of Acts but rather of a mission to restore God's kingdom to Israel (see 1:6-8).

The addition of "God declares" to the biblical citation underscores the premise of all prophetic texts in Acts: Events that fulfill biblical prophecy are in God's script of salvation.[114] The intensification of this very emphasis stands behind Luke's addition of the phrase "and they shall prophesy" (προφητεύσουσι *prophēteusousi*) to 2:18. The community's forward movement toward God's eschatological horizon of a restored Israel is fundamentally a *prophetic* movement, a movement of empowered and illumined proclamation (2:18); and Pentecost is fundamentally the pouring out of the Spirit of prophecy as the distinguishing mark of that movement.

2:17b-18. Much has been made in recent years of the inclusiveness of this prophetic community and rightly so: "I will pour out my Spirit on *all* flesh" (2:17). The entire membership receives God's Spirit and will speak like prophets (2:18). Peter adds "my" (μοῦ *mou*) here to the LXX, which is especially suggestive of the grand reversal wrought at Pentecost, when even household slaves are transformed into "my servants" (δοῦλος μου *doulos mou*) and given important prophetic tasks to perform. This revolutionary feature of the eschatological community Joel depicts anticipates subsequent episodes in Acts that will draw out its fuller meaning.

2:19-20. The special effects that accompany the outpouring of Spirit are also noteworthy. In their original prophetic setting, these dramatic occurrences signal the imminent arrival of the "Day of the Lord" in judgment of the nations that treated Israel shamefully. Not so in Acts. In this new setting, the "signs

---

110. See Conzelmann, *The Acts of the Apostles*, 19, followed by many others. However, the point may be simply that to be drunk at such an early hour is a sign of shiftless debauchery.

111. *Kyrios* is the referent used most frequently in Acts for Jesus; it is also the only title used for both Jesus and God. I suspect this indicates that Luke regarded Jesus and God as co-collaborators in the salvation of reconstituted Israel. In that the Spirit is the "Father's promise" and is sent forth according to God's timing (1:4-7), Jesus' messianic mission, now followed by the community of his successors, is redemptive work that is subordinate to God's provident care for Israel.

112. Haenchen, *The Acts of the Apostles*, 179n5.

113. The transmission of the text of Acts is corrupted at this point. *B* (Vaticanus), one of the earliest witnesses to Acts, reads μετα ταυτα (*meta tauta*, "after this") and so returns the text back to the sense of its LXX original. Most critics, especially those who conclude that Peter's Pentecost speech is largely Luke's composition, prefer the majority reading "in the last days," since its eschatological horizon better frames Luke's theological agenda in Acts.

114. For this interpretation see Johnson, *The Acts of the Apostles*, 49, 54.

and wonders" (σημεῖα καὶ τέρατα *semeia kai terata*) mark the presence and progress of the Spirit who prepares the way for the church's missionary work (see 2:43; 4:16, 22, 30; 5:12; 6:8; 8:6, 13; 14:3; 15:12).[115] In this context, then, "the coming of the Lord's great and glorious day" no longer conjures up images of God's imminent retribution but instead that of Pentecost, with its promise of empowered witness and God's salvation.[116]

2:21. Typically, the most important phrase of a quoted text is the last one read, which lingers in the auditor's ear; "everyone who calls upon the name of the Lord shall be saved" (2:21) is such a phrase. Its full meaning is the interpretive project of the first half of Acts (see the Overview above). By the time the reader arrives at the depiction of the Jerusalem Council in Acts 15 the meaning of Joel's prophecy of Israel's salvation will be understood differently than it had been by the prophecy's original Judean audience or even those Jewish pilgrims who heard Peter's recitation on Pentecost. Then, on the other side of Paul's mission to the Gentiles, the meaning of Joel's "everyone" will have been embellished to include every repentant Jew and Gentile (see the Overview above). The adumbration of "salvation" through the first half of Acts will clearly indicate that at the epicenter of Luke's theological conception of Israel's restoration is a God who forgives every person who names Jesus as their Lord and confesses him as God's Messiah (see 2:38; cf. 4:12; 7:25; 13:23, 26, 47; 15:11).[117]

Frankly, Acts is much clearer in addressing the questions, "What must one do to get saved?" and "Who does the saving?" than the corollary "What happens when one gets saved?" The near context of the prophecy emphasizes forgiveness from sins for those who repent and believe, complemented by the repentant believer's initiation into life with God's Spirit (see 2:38-39). Insofar as the community of goods exhibits a distinctive social life, we are also led to believe that salvation results in a new way of living one with another (see 2:42-47). As we will find in the story that follows, however, divine forgiveness and human healing form an integral whole in Acts: to be saved from sins means to be healed from sickness (see 3:1-8; 4:9-12; 14:8-10). While this connection can be and has been pressed in dangerous directions, the theological note sounded by the various healing and prison-escape episodes in Acts makes clear the close relationship in Luke's mind between the Lord's spiritual and physical rescue from internal and external threat. Even as his conception of God's salvation is international in scope it is also holistic in consequence.

2:22-36. Peter's commentary on the quoted Scripture (midrash) is in two parts, linked together by his stunned audience's pertinent question, "What should we do?" (2:37). The first part (2:22-36) appeals to his Jewish auditors (2:22*a*) to listen and consider his witness to "Jesus of Nazareth" (2:23-24)[118] in the light of the substantial evidence put forward from his eyewitness reflection (2:22*b*) and from Scripture (2:25-35) in support of the gospel's claim that "God has made this Jesus whom you crucified both Lord and Messiah" (2:36).[119] It is imperative that we follow Peter's speech to its christological climax as a midrash on Joel's prophecy that seeks to clarify the relevance of the Spirit's outpouring at Pentecost for this Jewish audience.

---

115. Johnson, *The Acts of the Apostles*, 50, notes that "signs and wonders" is associated with the prophetic role that Moses performed during the exodus. Since Luke routinely portrays Jesus as the "prophet-like-Moses" in both his Gospel and in Acts (3:22; 7:36-37), Johnson is inclined to find the purpose of this catchphrase in the Pentecost speech rather than in its association with the "signs and wonders" Jesus performs according to 2:22. I take it that the succession theme of Acts, and the role Pentecost plays in its development, would allow the reader to make the interpretive move from the "signs and wonders" of prophetic Jesus to his Spirit-filled successors.

116. Notably, Luke edits out Joel's prophecy of God's judgment of the nations in order to underscore Pentecost as a redemptive event. At the same time, Luke's Peter turns his Jewish audience back to Joel's judgment theme in concluding his speech in 2:40: "Save yourselves from this corrupt generation." Clearly, the reference to "save yourselves" picks up Joel's salvation idiom and renders it more closely to his original meaning, which was an exhortation for faithful Israel to turn to God during a season of international calamity when God would destroy the nations, including unfaithful Israel—"the crooked generation" in Peter's words (cf. Deut 32:5)—while protecting and restoring the fortunes of the faithful nation.

117. Although he undervalues the prophetic aspect of the community's mission, Marshall is especially clear on this point: The witness of the prophetic community to the Messiah is for the world's salvation. See I. H. Marshall, *The Acts of the Apostles*, NTG (Sheffield: *JSOT*, 1992) 47-63. See also Witherington's apt summary of this narrative theme, *The Acts of the Apostles*, 143-44.

118. According to Conzelmann, the community's preaching (*kerygma*) or formal confessions about Jesus include his name, his pre-crucifixion works, his death, and his resurrection, all of which are elements present in this speech. See Conzelmann, *The Acts of the Apostles*, 20. Behind this speech, then, the careful reader already discovers the later (Pauline?) notion of saving faith, which is to accept the beliefs of Christian proclamation as true.

119. The well-known charge of anti-Semitism posited against 2:36—that Jews killed Jesus—is substantially qualified in near context by 2:23, "you crucified—by the hands of those outside the law." This earlier detail recalls and glosses the gospel story of Jesus' crucifixion, itself a Roman and not Jewish form of political execution. The Jewish decision to execute Jesus was possible only through the agency of pagan Roman authority.

2:22-24. This observation seems evident from the opening line, where testimony to the "signs and wonders" of Jesus picks up Luke's rewriting of Joel's prophecy about the "signs and wonders" of the Spirit (2:19). If the interpreter considers this intertext rhetorically, Peter is simply asking his auditors to remember and apply what some in his audience first heard and saw performed by Jesus the Nazarene—what "you know" to be his divine authorization (2:22*b*)—to this most recent episode of Pentecostal "signs and wonders," which must be assumed as divinely accredited as well. But the implied theological claim is much more telling than its rhetorical intent: what Jesus began did not end with his crucifixion but continues in his absence under the aegis of God's Spirit in the life and mission of this community. This implied claim is what is good news! Joel's prophecy of Pentecost is really a prophecy about a season of salvation that has already begun with Messiah (see 1:1) and continues on as the prospect of this community's transformed life (see 2:42-47) and empowered mission (see 1:8).

The appeal to God's "definite plan and foreknowledge" (2:23) does not envisage a predestinarian notion of divine providence but Luke's logical deduction from his idea of Scripture. That is, if the Jesus event and the Spirit's outpouring both follow the biblical script of God's salvation, then God must have known about both in advance of their occurrence. In this regard, then, the biblical texts from the LXX psalter that Peter quotes (Pss 18:4-6 [17:4-6 LXX] = 2:24; 16:8-11 [15:8-11 LXX] = 2:25-28; 132:11 [132:11 LXX] = 2:30; 110:1 [109:1 LXX] = 2:34-35) supplies additional biblical testimony in support of the community's claim that the Jesus event in all its tragic and glorious aspects is intended by God as messianic.

2:25-33. Peter's clever rereading of these psalms assumes first that King David is a type of the coming Messiah and, therefore, a principal participant in Israel's future plans (2:25*a*).[120] Peter also claims that David is God's prophet (2:30; cf. 1:16, 20) with keen

insight into the future of Israel and the identity of the Messiah (cf. Acts 4:25; 13:33-36). He finally claims that David is Israel's "patriarch" (2:29 NIV), obligating the household of Israel to give proper respect to David's voice.[121] This last point is made with considerable irony, since every ancestor or patriarch, although important to Israel's history, remained dead, as their famous tombs memorialized.[122] The Messiah, on the other hand, gets resurrected and stays alive (2:31-33)!

2:34-36. The readers of Acts will recognize the powerful logic of Peter's point that while Israel's great king-prophet-patriarch David "did not ascend into the heavens" (2:34), Jesus did (see 1:10-11). As midrash, however, Peter's chain of citations from the biblical psalter funds his christological commentary on God's intended meaning of Joel's prophecy that salvation comes to those who call on the "Lord" (see 2:21). For this reason his appeal to the "my Lord" of Ps 110:1 (109:1 LXX), well used elsewhere in the NT to support christological claims (cf., Mark 12:36; 14:62; 16:19; Luke 20:42; Rom 8:34; 1 Cor 15:25; Eph 1:20; Col 3:1; Heb 1:3, 13; 8:1; 10:12),[123] supports his climactic point that God has made the risen Jesus to rule over Israel as its "Lord" (2:36). David's "Lord" is this risen Lord Jesus of Joel's prophecy on whose name everyone must call for their salvation from sin and death (see 2:21).

2:37-40. The crowd understands the implications of Peter's dramatic claim that the crucified Jesus of Nazareth is, in fact, the risen Christ of God. Luke tells us "they were cut to the heart." Perhaps the crowd's emotional response is simply recognition of their own guilt in the matter of Jesus' death.[124] In any case, Peter concludes his sermon by calling these enlightened auditors to conversion.

2:37. The crowd's question, "What shall we do?" is more than rhetorical; it makes a sincere request for instruction that will lead to forgiveness and restoration. As such, the theological subtext of their question of Peter

---

120. See Jervell, *Die Apostelgeschichte*, 147-48. We know by an earlier text (see 1:16, 20) that what David says is actually the voice of the Holy Spirit and that what is spoken by the Holy Spirit must be fulfilled. This feature of Peter's speech is deeply rooted in Luke's conception of Scripture and the prophetic role to recover God's intended or eschatological meaning from the biblical text.

121. Peter bestows on David the title of patriarch to ensure his audience's respect for David's prophecy of Jesus. See Haenchen, *The Acts of the Apostles*, 182; Jervell, *Die Apostelgeschichte*, 147.

122. For David's tomb, see Josephus *The Jewish War* 1:61. See also Fitzmyer, *The Acts of the Apostles*, 257.

123. For the NT use of Ps 110:1 LXX as Christian apoligia, see M. Black, "The Christological Use of the Old Testament in the New Testament," *NTS* 18 (1971-72) 6-11. See also Barrett, *A Critical and Exegetical Commentary on the Acts of the Apostles*, 150-51.

124. So Haenchen, *The Acts of the Apostles*, 183.

is this: Will God forgive and restore them even if they do repent of their participation in Messiah's death? The reader rightly raises this question in light of Judas's demise since God apparently refused him a second chance (see 1:16-20; cf. 5:1-10). Why did Peter continue beyond v. 36 and its implicit indictment of Israel's guilt in rejecting the Messiah? In canonical context, the reader imagines that this rehabilitated Peter knows from personal experience that God gives betrayers second chances (see 1:15-20; cf. John 21:15-17). The outpouring of God's Spirit at Pentecost is God's second chance to Israel. If the Jesus and Spirit events are scripted by God as the climactic pieces of the plan to restore Israel, Peter cannot now turn his back on these Jews who want to know what to do in response.

2:38a. Peter stipulates the basis by which his audience may be saved (2:38a) and anticipates the results of their salvation (2:38b-40). In doing so he demands nothing different from what John the Baptist did prior to Easter and Pentecost (cf. Luke 3:10 with Acts 2:37). Of course, the subtext of Peter's response is that Easter and Pentecost have since occurred; they provide spiritual resources for Israel's conversion that were not present to John the Baptist. While Peter's speech at this point echoes John's redemptive protocol— "repent and be baptized"—the theological implications of Peter's invitation are substantially different.

In shaping Peter's evangelical appeal, Luke emphasizes a repentant response to the gospel message (cf. "repent" [μετανοέω *metanoeō*] in Luke 10:13; 11:32; 13:3, 5; 15:7, 10; 16:30; 17:3, 4; Acts 3:19; 8:22; 17:30; 26:20; and "repentance" [μετάνοια *metanoia*] in Luke 3:3, 8; 5:32; 15:7; 24:47; Acts 5:31; 11:18; 13:24; 19:4; 20:21; 26:20). Jesus earlier predicted that his successors would preach "repentance in his name" (cf. Luke 24:47). Literally, "to repent" denotes a radical change of mind. Spiritual reform is possible only with an intellectual reorientation—how one thinks and what angle of vision one takes when looking at the "real world." After all, the wrong-headed response of Israel to Jesus can only be explained by their ignorance of him—ignorance now dispelled by Peter's sermon and Israel's witness to the outpouring of God's Spirit. Significantly, "repent" is

plural in form, which indicates that Peter's demand is addressed to the entire household of Israel; the second demand, "be baptized," is stipulated only of those individual Jews who convert. The baptism of converts makes personal what should be true of all Israel. The interpreter should observe the tension in Acts between national and individual repentance. The promise of Israel's restoration obtains only to those baptized *individuals* within Israel who repent and turn to Christ in faith. These converts are those who constitute a repentant (= restored) Israel in whose history the promised blessings of God will be realized.

The significance of a rite of baptism probably stems from John the Baptist's mission, and its symbolism is brought forward with new and greater meaning by command of Jesus (cf. Matt 28:19; Mark 16:16). Christian baptism remains a rite of initiation into a new life under a different Lord with membership in a community of common faith in him and a new future with God. As the central symbol of this new orientation, the convert is baptized "in the name of Jesus Christ" (see 2:21). No believer goes unbaptized in Acts simply because no believer exists outside of the Messiah's community into which every new believer is initiated. Yet, in this narrative setting Peter issues his demand for baptism *because* of Pentecost and the community's experience of the baptism with the Spirit. Baptism, then, is initiation into a community that lives within the powerful realm of God's Spirit. Sharply put, Christian baptism assumes Spirit baptism in Acts and the readiness of the converted for the work of witness.[125]

2:38b-40. Repentance and Christian baptism result in the "forgiveness of your sins" (ἄφεσις τῶν ἁμαρτιῶν ὑμῶν *aphesis tōn hamartiōn hymōn*) and "the gift of the Holy Spirit" (ἡ δωρεά τοῦ ἁγίου πνεύματος *hē dōrea tou hagiou pneumatos* 2:38b). The word for "forgiveness" (*aphesis*) means "pardon," and in Acts it typically is combined with "sins." Forgiveness of financial debts is one connotation of this phrase and perhaps reflects the sociology of salvation, so that believers are members of a community of goods where those pardoned of sin pardon the debts of others (see 2:42-47; cf.

125. Dunn, *The Acts of the Apostles*, 32-33.

Luke 11:1-13).[126] The second phrase, "gift of the Holy Spirit," is exceptional. Peter does not have in mind the role the Spirit performs in a charismatic congregation (1 Corinthians 12–14), where according to Paul the Spirit supplies different spiritual gifts that enable each believer to edify the faith of the others. The Spirit of Acts is not an intrinsic member of the community as "Lord" (*kyrios*; cf. 2 Cor 3:17), nor often the agent of the community's transformed existence as God's new creation (cf. Gal 5:16-26). Again, the Spirit of Acts is more like the Spirit of OT prophecy who fills believers with an explosive power that enables them to perform the church's missionary vocation.

The principal difficulty in the history of the interpretation of this text is whether Christian baptism is a condition for or a consequence of the "forgiveness of your sins" and thus the reception of the "gift of the Holy Spirit." The problem turns on the causal use of the preposition εἰς (*eis*): "for [*eis*] the forgiveness of your sins." However, Barrett reminds us that Luke does not use this preposition consistently, nor does he place much value on it in any case.[127] Moreover, Acts evinces a variety of grammatical formulas when speaking of God's forgiveness and baptism together (see 8:16; 10:44; 19:5; cf. 8:38-39; 18:26). Peter's formulation of these different demands therefore is not technical and in no way establishes a theological norm.

More important, baptism "in the name of Jesus Christ" (ἐπὶ τῷ ὀνόματι Ἰησοῦ Χριστοῦ *epi tō onomati Iēsou Christou*) and "forgiveness of sins" are joined by Peter to embellish the meaning of Joel's prophecy, which concludes by linking "the name of Jesus Christ" with salvation.[128] The saving power of the "name" is hardly magical but is rather a metaphor for Joel's announcement of salvation, which has arrived from God in the form of forgiveness because of Jesus. For this reason, Christian baptism after Pentecost initiates the repentant believers into a new spiritual reality that John the Baptist could only predict (so Luke 3:16) but in which

neither he nor his baptized followers could participate, even though their sins were forgiven (cf. Luke 3:3). In addition, the Baptist's exhortation to do "works in keeping with repentance" is glossed in this new setting as those missionary tasks that pertain to the community's vocation.

The referent of Israel's "promise" (ἡ ἐπαγγελία *hē epangelia*, 2:39) is Israel's restoration (see 1:6). The phrase "for all who are far away" (πᾶς ὁ εἰς μακράν *pas ho eis makran*) in this setting is a faint echo of Isaiah's promise that "the wind [Spirit?] of the Lord" (57:19) will bring exiled Jews back to Israel to become members of the restored community. If intentional, the intertextual echo intensifies Peter's address to those of his audience from the diaspora, perhaps anticipating Paul's mission to the diaspora.[129] The interplay between Joel's promise of salvation to "everyone who calls upon the name of the Lord" and Peter's exhortation that God's promise belongs to "everyone whom the Lord our God calls to him" (ὅσους ἂν προσκαλέσηται κύριος ὁ Θεός ἡμῶν *hosous an proskalesētai kyrios ho theos hēmōn*) reminds the reader of the reciprocal nature of salvation: God calls everyone into the blessings of salvation (forgiveness, Spirit), which then are experienced by everyone who calls upon the Lord.

Peter's haunting words to "save yourselves from this crooked generation" (2:40) round off his midrash on Joel's prophecy. The repentant Jews who save themselves realize Joel's promise that those who call upon the Lord will be saved. The effect of its iteration is to sound a warning to all those Jews who refuse to repent: They will not participate in the blessings of a restored Israel. Rather, they belong to "this crooked generation" (ἡ γενεὰ τῆς σκολιᾶς ταύτης *hē genea tēs skolias tautēs*), a phrase that echoes a memorable lyric from Moses' farewell song (Deut 32:5), in which God's faithfulness to Israel is contrasted with the faithlessness of "this crooked generation" of unrepentant Jews (see Acts 7:35-43).

2:41. The purpose of Luke's numerical summary of Peter's first evangelistic

---

126. See S. Ringe, *Jesus, Liberation, and the Biblical Jubilee: Images for Ethics and Christology*, OBT 19 (Philadelphia: Fortress, 1985).

127. Barrett, *A Critical and Exegetical Commentary on the Acts of the Apostles*, 1:154.

128. See J. Roloff, *Die Apostelgeschichte* (Göttingen: Vandenhoeck & Ruprecht, 1981) 61.

129. It is highly unlikely that this phrase hints at the future Gentile mission. Luke's narrative theme is to give all of Israel a second chance to be restored to God. See R. Denova, *The Things Accomplished Among Us*, JSNTSup 141 (Sheffield: Sheffield Academic, 1997) 155-77.

preaching is to make a good impression on the reader rather than to provide readers with an accurate count of new converts.[130] Prior to Pentecost, the community's membership stood at one hundred and twenty (1:15); and now it stands at over three thousand—a

vigorous growth spurt that commends the gospel's truth. Peter's persuasive powers, granted him by the Spirit of prophecy, are significant, which commends his spiritual authority as the community's leader and anticipates his coming conflict with those in authority over "official" Israel. Finally, the growth of the community implies that it will enjoy a strong public presence in Jerusalem and will be noticed by outsiders (2:47).[131]

130. Haenchen, *The Acts of the Apostles*, 188-89, and others following him have called attention to the practical and political problems that a mass conversion would have created for this fledgling movement. Witherington, *The Acts of the Apostles*, 156, rightly cautions against dismissing Luke's poll as unlikely, when evidence exists that makes it possible. The question remains as to what is the function of Luke's summaries, such as this one, within Acts. See Witherington's discussion, *The Acts of the Apostles*, 157-59.

131. G. Schneider, *Die Apostelgeschichte*, 2 vols., HTK (Freiburg am Breisgau: Herder, 1981–82) 1:279.

REFLECTIONS

1. "This is what was spoken through the prophet Joel" (2:16 NRSV). Jacob Jervell calls Luke the "Fundamentalist within the New Testament."[132] That is, Luke believes that all Scripture is divinely given and therefore binding upon human life and religious faith. At the center of Israel's Scriptures are the prophecies of God's salvation that "script" Luke's narrative of Israel's restoration and its mission to the nations. Given this perspective, it is appropriate that Peter should appeal to Joel's prophecy to explain the outpouring of God's Spirit. Scripture and Spirit are the indispensable instruments by which the way of salvation is marked out for the church to trod. The Spirit not only inspires Scripture but also inspires its proper interpretation. This interpretation of Scripture, mediated by the successors to Jesus, is inviting and invigorating of salvation. Scripture functions as canonical context within which we comprehend the grand truth that "God has made Jesus Lord and Christ." However, only the repentant are ushered into understanding by the Spirit.

2. Joel's prophecy shapes the church's mission in Acts. God's Spirit, the Spirit of prophecy, has been poured out to inaugurate "the last days" of salvation's history— those days that are urgent harbinger of "the Lord's great and glorious [= terrifying] day" (2:20), a future day of "universal restoration" (3:21). These are no longer days of waiting but days set apart for mission. God's Spirit is poured out upon the community's entire membership in order to prophesy, see visions, and dream dreams (2:17-18). As the meaning of Joel's prophecy unfolds in the narrative world of Acts, these prophetic activities (or others like them) clarify and direct the church's overarching vocation of giving witness to the risen Jesus. Following the passage from Joel, the shape of this witness includes two primary tasks: the mediation of God's "wonders" or "portents" and "signs" (2:19) and the proclamation of God's word that issues an invitation to "everyone who calls on the name of the Lord shall be saved" (2:21 NRSV). Without this prophetic awareness, the ministry of the church is corrupted by self-interest and its presence in the world ceases to matter.

3. The speeches in Acts are not abstract, homiletically crafted sermons featuring an attention-grabbing introduction and a tear-jerking conclusion. They are typically responses to theological challenges, sometimes made by those who mock, as here, and sometimes made by those ignorant of truth but earnest to find it. Not surprisingly, then, the speeches of Acts center upon God. The rhetor's logic is truly *theological*. Evidence is claimed from religious experience and sacred texts; however, the essential points

132. Jervell, *The Theology of the Acts of the Apostles*, 61.

always concern God's eternal plans and purposes and are rooted in a firm conviction about God's faithful benevolence to all.

4. "They were cut to the heart and asked, 'What must we do?' " (see 2:37). What should we make of this account of the crowd's response to Peter's speech? Every dissonant voice is removed; initial scorn is quickly turned to vital interest. Peter never stumbles, his voice never breaks; the crowd never raises objections to his interpretation of Scripture or his witness to the risen Jesus. Their question of Peter "what should we do?" does not seem peculiar or out of place. It aptly frames a universal and timeless search for relevant answers to the ultimate questions of life, and Peter's message to these devout Jews speaks to their questions—that is, to their life with God. The question, "What should we do?" continues to express concern for "the relevant" or "the real" in life. The church's response should not be to offer the gospel with apology but to do so with the confidence that we are presenting the words of eternal life.

5. "Repent, and be baptized, every one of you, in the name of Jesus" (2:38 NRSV). Peter is asked by his audience to relate the practical relevance of the gospel proclamation just given. He offers no helpful hints on living a more fulfilling life, no useful projects to work on, no feel-good platitudes; rather, he calls people to conversion. Further, he does not require a particular mode of baptism according to an exact liturgical formulation. What is important is his demand that they turn from competing beliefs and values toward Jesus in faith that God has made him Lord and Savior—in short, that they repent.

6. Repentance is the internal and intellectual act of exchanging old beliefs for new ones. In Acts the Evangelist's call to conversion comes only after careful attention is paid to evidence. For example, in Luke's narrative of Paul's mission expressions for serious study of Scripture strengthen the perception that turning to God in faith is not an irrational act (e.g., 17:2-3). Bringing the non-believer into the faith often requires critical investigation of texts and careful study of the Christian religion. Moreover, this turning to God unfolds over time. Peter's call to conversion is placed alongside a passage that summarizes the religious practices of the community of converts. These activities, such as study and worship, nurture faith and facilitate the catechesis of the newly repentant. Those congregations that are active in the work of evangelism must also develop an infrastructure that fully initiates the baptized believer into the faith tradition. Many converts are lost to the faith for the lack of attention to a *process* of repentance that includes participation in committed fellowship with other believers who attend to "the apostles' teaching" and to daily prayers (see 2:42-47).

ACTS 2:42-47, THE COMMUNITY OF THE UNCOMMON LIFE

COMMENTARY

The early chapters of Acts include several important summaries of the community's life and mission in Jerusalem (see 4:32–5:16; 6:1-7). These "snapshots" are touched up and colorized by Luke—some say considerably so[133]—to form a portfolio of biblical images

paradigmatic of the church's corporate witness. While evangelism is certainly one

traditions (see B. Capper, "The Palestinian Cultural Context of Earliest Christian Community of Goods," in *The Book of Acts in Its Palestinian Setting*, ed. R. Bauckham [Grand Rapids: Eerdmans, 1995] 323-56). Most scholars (including Capper) agree that Luke's portrait of this first Christian congregation is "obviously idealized" (Johnson, *The Acts of the Apostles*, 61) but that Luke also intends to leave impressions of the community's common life. In sum, there is no good reason to think Luke's narrative summaries are figments of his creative imagination, written only for his readers' religious edification or moral instruction.

133. The critical problem with this text (and with all of Luke's so-called narrative summaries) is whether it is Luke's utopian fiction (see Haenchen, *The Acts of the Apostles*, 193-96) or reports based upon reliable

effect of their life together (see 2:47), the primary purpose of their common life is to nurture Christian community.[134]

2:42. Luke writes stories to instruct his readers about normative matters of the faith rather than merely to set the historical record straight.[135] The Christian norm reflected in this text, and others like it in Acts, is that believers who share a common geographical address are also to share a common religious life. The chief characteristics of this common life are listed in v. 42 and elaborated in the following verses: "apostles" teaching (v. 43, ἡ διδαχὴ τῶν ἀποστόλων *hē didachē tōn apostolōn*), fellowship (v. 44, κοινωνία *koinōnia*), the breaking of bread (vv. 45-46, ἡ κλάσις τοῦ ἄρτου *hē klasis tou artou*), and prayer (v. 47a, προσευχή *proseuchē*).[136] These same characteristics are repeated throughout Acts as the hallmarks of an ever-expanding people of God (2:47b).[137]

2:43. That the believers in Jerusalem should "devote themselves to the apostles' teaching" is not surprising, for the apostles are not only the principal successors to Jesus but also the principal depositories of the Spirit's power. The "many wonders and signs" (πολλά τέρατα καὶ σημεῖα *polla terata kai sēmeia*) they perform bear witness to their spiritual authority. This phrase recalls Joel's prophecy (2:19) of the outpouring of the Spirit to mark them out as important participants in a new epoch of salvation's history. In fact, they are the heirs of Jesus' authority, which he earlier demonstrated by the "wonders and signs that God did through him among you" (2:22; cf. Luke 9:1-2; 24:19). The effect of their authority within the community is confirmed both by adherence to their instruction but also by

the "awe (that) came upon everyone." "Awe" translates φόβος (*phobos*; lit., "fear"), which Luke routinely uses to summarize even the outsider's response to God's activity (cf. Luke 2:9; 8:37; Acts 19:17). The performance of these same "signs and wonders" of Jesus is the evident result of their baptism with God's Spirit that enables them to do and teach in continuity with their Lord (cf. 1:1-2). In fact, 2:43 glosses 2:19 as well, indicating the "signs and wonders" of the Spirit will continue in the community's life through the presence of the apostles.

2:44. "Fellowship" (*koinōnia*) is used only here in Acts, but for Paul it is an important idiom of the community that is initiated into newness of life in partnership with the Spirit (cf. 2 Cor 13:13; Phil 2:1). In this case, however, God's gift of the Spirit to the community suggests a transforming presence that unites the different believers into a common *koinōnia*.[138] In elaboration, Luke uses a well-known phrase from Greek philosophy indicating friendship: "all things in common." A fellowship of believers shares more than common beliefs and core values; they display a profound regard for one another's spiritual and physical well-being as a community of friends. The Jewish community at Qumran, for example, tied its rituals of purification to this same ideal of friendship[139] in a manner recalling 1 Peter's exhortation that the "purification of souls" issuing from Jesus' passion should form a community of friends (cf. 1 Pet 1:19-22).

2:45-46. The formation of believers into a community of goods is an important theme in Acts. Popular sentiment may well have led Luke to emphasize more traditional elements of public piety—the contented soul of Stoic thought or the civility of Platonic theory. While no doubt Luke knew these popular Greco-Roman notions of true friendship,[140] his ideals are more deeply rooted in the prophetic typology of Jubilee (cf. Lev 25:10)— Isaiah's "favorable year of the Lord" (Isa 61:2a; cf. Luke 4:19)—that had previously shaped his Gospel narratives of Jesus' ministry among the poor (see, e.g., Luke 4:16-21;

134. This community of goods is characteristic of great religious renewals when spiritual enthusiasm generates a robust common life and communal practices, of both an ordinary (e.g., eating together) and a religious (e.g., worshiping together) kind. See Dunn, *The Acts of the Apostles*, 34-35.

135. F. Horn argues that this summary and the one found in 4:32-37 serve Luke's paraenetic and pragmatic interests for maintaining a distinctive form of Christian fellowship (*koinōnia*). What the reader finds in these summaries, then, are the most important topics of catechesis not only for the first converts but for all other converts as well. See F. Horn, *Glaube und Handeln in der Theologie des Lukas*, GTA 26 (Göttingen: Vandenhoeck & Ruprecht, 1983) 36-49.

136. Jeremias argues that the four are given in a liturgical sequence proper to the order of Christian worship in the ancient church and represent the earliest tradition Luke draws upon for his summary. See J. Jeremias, *The Eucharistic Words of Jesus* (Philadelphia: Fortress, 1977) 118-21.

137. The opening phrase of 2:42, "they devoted themselves" (ἦσαν προσκαρτεροῦντες *ēsan proskarterountes*), literally means that they "held fast to" or "persevered in" these disciplines enumerated. The sense is of enduring practices.

138. See R. Wall, "Community (NT)" in *The Anchor Bible Dictionary*, 6 vols. (Garden City, N.Y.: Doubleday, 1992) 1:1103-10.

139. Johnson, *The Acts of the Apostles*, 58-59.

140. Tannehill, *The Acts of the Apostles*, 2:45; Johnson, *The Acts of the Apostles*, 62.

6:20-36; 12:22-34; 15:1–16:31; 17:20–18:4; 19:1-10). According to this biblical pattern, the redistribution of proceeds from sold property reflects the social character of God's kingdom, where all share equally in the good gifts of God.[141] The community of goods of Acts is indicative of those economic practices of the restored Israel of God.

Luke's reference to temple observance is not a bid to take it over for Christian worship or to advance the church's claim that it is the "true Israel."[142] Rather, his point is that worship is a resurrection practice of repentant Israel. The reference to the joyful practice of "breaking bread at home" ($\kappa\lambda\omega\nu\tau\acute{\epsilon}\varsigma$ . . . $\kappa\alpha\tau$' $o\mathring{\iota}\kappa o\nu$ $\acute{\alpha}\rho\tau o\nu$ *klōntes . . . kat' oikon arton*), the perfect evidence of life in the Spirit, should not be interpreted as a Christian sacrament (i.e., the Lord's supper)[143] or some other

distinctly Christian discipline.[144] Rather, Luke recalls the practice of devout Jewish families who following temple worship would share meals together as symbolic of their social and spiritual solidarity.[145] The decisions the community makes about "bread"—how to sell it, distribute it to those with needs, and share it without rank or rankle—manifests the effect of the Spirit in its common life.

2:47. The community's worship is characterized by the people's praise of God (2:47*a*; see also 3:8). The community has no material needs, no intramural conflicts, no broken hearts for which to petition God for tender mercy. This will come soon enough. At the beginning of its mission there are only success stories and a community of friends filled with gladness. The reader's lingering impression of the daily rhythm of this community of the uncommon life is that it is both growing "day by day" and worshiping in the Temple "day by day." Indeed, the formation and practices of this community of goods testify to God's commitment to Israel's restoration.

---

141. See R. North, *Sociology of the Biblical Jubilee*, AnBib 4 (Rome: Pontifical Biblical Institute, 1954) 225-31, who argues that Luke's appropriation of the Jubilee typology found in Isaiah's prophecy is messianic and "improves" upon the OT ideal by mapping the kind of life, individual and corporate, that has arrived because of Jesus.

142. So Conzelmann, *The Acts of the Apostles*, 24.

143. Fitzmyer, *The Acts of the Apostles*, 271, with others.

144. Johnson, *The Acts of the Apostles*, 59; Roloff, *Die Apostelgeschichte*, 67.

145. Jervell, *Die Apostelgeschichte*, 157.

REFLECTIONS

1. "All who believed were together and had all things in common" (2:44 NRSV). At the beginning of his Gospel, Luke uses an Isaianic prophecy about "the favorable year of the Lord" to introduce the principal themes of Jesus' anointed ministry (Luke 4:16-18). In particular, Jesus' actions among the poor and powerless in identifying with their marginal status within Israel and announcing their deliverance are taken as the fulfillment of this prophecy of the Lord's Jubilee (Luke 4:21). Jesus' teaching about sharing possessions envisages the social character of God's kingdom, where the conditions of the least, lame, lost, and last are transformed. God's grace does not privilege the rich and famous; God's liberating love extends to everyone who calls on the name of the Lord for salvation. However, this Jubilee is possible only *because* of the empty tomb and only *after* Pentecost. The community of converts formed on the Day of Pentecost is a repentant Israel to whom the kingdom of God has been restored. God's kingdom reflects solidarity and mutuality rather than a class system; therefore, believers live together and have "all things in common."

2. Teaching, fellowship, sharing goods, and prayers are the religious practices of repentant Israel. Each is a concrete expression of forgiveness of sins and the reception of the Spirit; each is made possible only because of conversion, and together they make possible the convert's continued formation toward maturity. This is so because these practices are much too demanding to implement without the habits of a repentant mind and purified heart. They are also too demanding for the individual believer; therefore, the initial images of conversion in Acts are those of a community and of shared practices and goods.

3. These are religious practices that envisage a steady and lasting obedience. The popular conception of a Pentecostal outpouring of the Holy Spirit or of a great revival featuring many conversion experiences is of religious phenomena characterized by fleeting spiritual intensity. The religious practices of the converted in Acts suggest a different enthusiasm, one that is more disciplined and holistic. The spiritual authority of the Twelve, exercised by their teaching and miracle working, is coupled with corporate worship and prayer. The traditional Jewish routines of temple observance are paired with meetings in believers' homes. The Acts' model of Christian community is one of common worship, common practice, common good, and common witness.

4. "They would sell their possessions and goods and distribute the proceeds to all" (2:45 NRSV). The most distinctive practice of the community's common life is the sharing of goods. It should be noted that Luke is not interested in the production of goods but rather that these goods already possessed are now shared with other believers. In an economic culture shaped by individual acquisitiveness, this resurrection practice seems idealistic and even scandalous. All the institutions and mythologies of the present order teach us to value *private* property as the principal motive of hard work, invention, and national wealth. Yet, for Luke the kingdom of God *is* the real world; there can be no economic policy more prudent, therefore, than one that cultivates a community of goods in which class divisions are dismantled under the aegis of the Holy Spirit. Why should this be so? Social inequity of any sort fosters no good thing. It is impossible (and finally impractical) to achieve a lasting unity, no matter how important the cause, if inequality persists. This is precisely why Luke is so keen to press the inclusiveness of God's salvation.

ACTS 3:1–8:3, "YOU SHALL BE MY WITNESSES IN JERUSALEM": THE JERUSALEM MISSION

OVERVIEW

This narrative unit reflects the increasing demands placed on the apostles and their fierce rivalry with the priesthood of "official" Judaism for the affections of "the people" (4:5-22; 5:17-39; 6:8–8:3). But there is also intramural conflict within the faith community over the distribution of goods (4:32–5:16; 6:1-2). With each new conflict, external or internal, the apostles are forced to discern afresh the ways of Israel's God and to call the emerging church back to worship and to reliance on the spiritual resources God has made available to them (4:23-31; 5:40-42; 6:3-7). God's faithfulness to Israel and the spiritual authority of these prophets-like-Jesus who rule over a restored Israel are the predominant themes of Luke's narrative of the Jerusalem mission. Both are easily detected in the cycle of the stories told. Each episode consists of four elements, closely following the plotline of the paradigmatic events of the earlier Pentecost drama:

(1) God initiates mission by acting in powerful and public ways (3:1-8; 4:5-12; 5:17-23; 6:8-10; cf. 2:1-11) to compel those living in Jerusalem to deal with the nature of God's rule and the meaning of God's promise to restore that rule in Israel (see 1:6).

(2) The crowds who witness these mighty acts of God are ignorant of their significance for Israel (3:17); thus, the people are puzzled—even scornful—and typically mistaken in their perceptions. Their bewilderment about the miracles they witness and the opposition of their own religious leaders toward the Jesus movement prompts more information (3:9-11; 4:13-18; 5:24-28; 6:11–7:1; cf. 2:12-13).

(3) Beginning with and framed by Peter's programmatic sermon on Pentecost, the apostolic proclamation of the gospel is the centerpiece of the church's mission. The authority of the Spirit-filled apostles is demonstrated by their keen ability to respond to questions the crowd raises, questions displaying the crowd's misunderstanding of God's salvation and the character of God's reign in Israel (3:12-26; 4:19-20; 5:29-32; 7:2-53; cf. 2:14-40). Each sermon appeals to Scripture and religious experience to contribute yet another element to the church's *kerygma*, or gospel. Some of the speeches of Acts are spare (see 4:19-20) and presume the reader's recollection of earlier sermons, while others such as Stephen's masterpiece are more full-bodied and self-standing (see 7:2-53).

(4) The final element of this literary pattern of mission turns the story back to the crowd and describes a variety of responses provoked by the proclamation of the gospel (4:1-4, 21-31; 5:33-42; 7:54–8:3; cf. 2:41). The results are mixed. The community's prophetic leaders are arrested and thrown into prison; Stephen is executed; the rank-and-file are persecuted. The word of God is disagreeable to some, especially those priests in charge of "official Judaism," who are annoyed by the movement's popular appeal and alarmed by what it asserts (4:1-2). At the same time, thousands believe (including some priests;

6:7) and the movement continues to grow and gain in influence among the people of God. Conflict is the theme of this narrative.

Two fascinating interludes (4:32–5:16; 6:1-7; cf. 2:42-47), or "summaries," are strategically placed within this narrative to add depth to Luke's profile of the Jerusalem community. Their principal role is to remind the reader that repentant Jews are beneficiaries of God's promise to bless a restored Israel; it is here and only here that the gift of the Spirit is experienced "day by day." But these blessings come at a price: There are intramural conflicts that challenge the very practices that organize the community's common life (2:42) and, therefore, its public witness (2:47). Central to its common life is the resurrection practice of sharing goods (4:32-35; cf. 2:45-46), which is first threatened by the deception of Ananias and Sapphira (5:1-11) and then by an unequal redistribution of food among the growing community's most marginal membership (6:1). This threat precipitated two others: a breakdown in Christian fellowship ("the Hellenists complained against the Hebrews," 6:1; cf. 2:44) and the frustration of the apostles' prophetic vocation ("it is not right that we should neglect the word of God to wait on tables," 6:2; cf. 2:43). Significantly, regular worship is the one resurrection practice that the worshiping community does *not* neglect.

Acts 3:1–4:4, Story One: The Apostles Heal the Lame of Israel

COMMENTARY

The first story of the Jerusalem mission begins abruptly. The literary pattern and images recall the earlier story of Pentecost, suggesting that the two should be read together reflexively, the one expanding the meaning of the other. The first panel (3:1-8) portrays the devout Peter and John on their way to the Temple for evening prayers (see 2:46-47). A beggar asks them for money but they have none to give since their possessions are now the shared property of the community (see 2:45). But as practitioners of "signs and wonders" (see 2:43), they respond to the

beggar's request for money by healing him "in the name of Jesus Christ of Nazareth." The lame man—now healed—leaps up and walks into the Temple in praise of God (see 2:47a) to pray with the apostles. His healing provokes puzzlement among those who see him walking (3:9-11). Instead of mocking the apostles as before (see 2:12-13), the crowd rushes to Peter and John for their commentary on this mighty act of God. Peter's explanatory speech in response reveals the depth of their ignorance about God's redemptive plans for Israel (3:12-17). This healing in Jesus' name is evidence that Scripture's prophecy of God's refreshing forgiveness is fulfilled (3:18-20; cf. 2:38) and is a harbinger of the Messiah's return for a season of universal restoration, fulfilled first in Israel through him (3:21-26). The final panel concludes this missionary drama with images of a divided Israel (4:1-4). On the one hand, unrepentant Sadducees arrest Peter and John; on the other hand, Luke's last word is that "many of those who heard the word believed" (4:4; cf. 2:41). This happy report is what the reader carries into the next story of Acts.

3:1-8. While John now accompanies Peter to the Temple for "evening" prayers (actually in mid-afternoon) and daily sacrifice,[146] he is given a limited speaking role in Acts (see 4:19-20). Luke includes him to make a theological rather than historical point: The two most important apostles are depicted here as colleagues and pious Jews, unimpeachable witnesses to the miracle about to occur.[147] The object of the miracle is a beggar they encounter on the incline leading up to the Temple. His résumé is carefully drafted by Luke to depict someone in need of a savior: He is "a man" who has been "lame from birth" and was "daily carried by people" and placed "at the temple gate called 'the Beautiful Gate,'" where he asked for alms from those entering the temple" (3:2). Since the combination of temple prayers and alms-giving characterizes Jewish piety, beggars are found outside the Temple at three o'clock in the afternoon, for those headed for evening prayers are the most likely to give alms to the poor.

L. T. Johnson reminds us that the narrated details of the beggar's existence are hardly arbitrary for another reason: They recall similar accounts both of Jesus before them (e.g., Luke 5:17-26) and of the biblical prophets before

Jesus (e.g., 1 Kgs 17:17-24; 2 Kgs 4:32-37).[148] In this case, the healing of a lame beggar in public view of other devout Jews is surely controversial. According to current Jewish practice his physical condition marks him as an "outsider" to the temple community (cf. Lev 21:17-20; mSabb. 6:8). By contrast, his healing and entrance into the Temple for prayer symbolize the dawning of a messianic epoch when the conditions of "the poor, the maimed, the lame, the blind" are reversed so that they too can participate in the blessings of God's kingdom (cf. Luke 7:22). Scripture's special concern for the last and least of Israel (see Lev 25; Deut 24:10-22; Isa 58:6-7; 61:1-2), then, is a piece of God's bold promise that the boundaries of Israel will one day be redrawn to include repentant beggars and the restored lame as constituents of the covenant community.

The precise location of the Beautiful Gate in the Temple's courtyard remains debated among scholars.[149] Luke's chief concern, in any case, is to describe the daily routine by which the lame beggar is placed *outside* this temple gate and thus to contrast it with that of those Jews entering the Temple for prayer and with the man's eventual entrance following his healing. This crucial narrative detail suggests that the lame man was excluded from the Temple and all it symbolized in Israel under the current temple leadership. Conflict with Jewish authority is inevitable, and it explains the movement of the plotline toward the second story of this narrative cycle (see 4:5-31).

Luke makes much in this story of Peter's eye contact (cf. 3:4-5). Why does Peter "look intently" at the lame man (3:4) and command him to "look at us," which naturally compels the mans to "fix his attention" on the apostles? The demonstration of divine mercy is always a personal concern: Peter's line of sight is set squarely upon a particular individual whose brokenness is in need of repair (cf. Luke 10:32-34). The beggar's obedience to Peter's demand is prompted by his

---

146. The sacrifice is called "Tamid" and is a continual offering of supplicants made in demonstration of their devotion to God (cf. Exod 29:38-42; Ezek 46:13-15). The Ezekiel reference is especially revealing, since Tamid is featured as part of the sacrificial practice of the eschatological Temple. Perhaps the time of daily prayers is added by Luke to evoke another symbol of "the last days" that Pentecost has inaugurated.

147. Many scholars think that Luke adds John here and elsewhere in Acts (4:13, 19; 8:14; cf. Luke 22:8) to make clear the plurality of the apostolate (so 2:42) and to supply the story with a necessary second witness to confirm what is said and done in witness to the name of Jesus. See O. Bauernfeind, *Die Apostelgeschichte*, THKTT 5 (Leipzig: Deichert, 1939) 60. Bruce considers them as leaders of the apostolate by their "special association with the Lord," which would give this story added weight with a Christian readership. See F. F. Bruce, *The Acts of the Apostles*, rev. ed., NICNT (Grand Rapids: Eerdmans, 1988) 135.

148. Johnson, *The Acts of the Apostles*, 71-72. The striking parallels between this story and the later story of Paul's healing miracle in Lystra (14:8-18) draws a similar conclusion: Paul continues the prophetic ministry of Peter and John before him. A feature of Luke's telling of miracle stories that is important for his theological program is the contribution others make to those who receive God's mercy. Similar to the friends who dropped the paralytic man through the roof for Jesus to heal (Luke 5:18-19 and par.), the lame beggar "was being carried" by others and placed by them in a setting where he would be healed (Acts 3:2).

149. See Fitzmyer, *The Acts of the Apostles*, 277 for the alternatives. See also Haenchen, *The Acts of the Apostles*, 198n12.

business savvy (3:5*b*): He wants money from them. His ignorance of their spiritual authority characterizes all who first hear the gospel, whether they are devout Jews or destitute beggars. Given Luke's interest in the outcast, perhaps it is not surprising that an outsider helps mark out the path that leads into God's salvation. The man adheres to the apostles' demand and once healed joins them in the Temple to praise God (3:8; cf. 3:11).

Luke's description of the man's healing symbolizes one who finds salvation. First is Luke's vivid narration: "he stood and began to walk . . . walking, leaping" (3:8). The reality that healing happened is confirmed. Luke is also careful to establish the theological implications of healing: "he . . . entered the temple with them . . . and praised God" (3:8). The restored man is now a member of a restored Israel whose new identity is "with them" (σὺν αὐτοῖς *syn autois*, "the apostles"; see 2:42-43) and whose worship of God is characterized by prayers of praise and Temple fellowship (see 2:46-47). This story also demonstrates Luke's use of possessions to contrast what the apostles do not have (money) and the miracle-working power they do have: The power to heal the sick in "the name of Jesus Christ of Nazareth."[150] It will be this power that is put on trial in the next story of this Jerusalem cycle (see 4:5-31).

3:9-11. The man who is restored both to health and to Israel "clings" (κρατέω *krateō*) to Peter and John (3:11), thereby intimately identifying with them as his healers and with the movement they are authorized by God to lead.[151] They have become the center of all the people's attention—and for good reason. Luke is careful to provide the reader with a "police report" of precisely what the crowd

witnessed, which confirms the details of the prior account (3:9-10*a*). It is noteworthy that Luke twice refers to this crowd of witnesses as "all the people" (3:9, 11). Rather than a story-teller's hyperbole, Luke's repetition of this phrase indicates its theological purchase. Luke's uses "people" (λαός *laos*) to recall OT references to Israel as a people belonging to God. As with "all" who witnessed the "signs and wonders" of Pentecost (cf. 2:12), this second congregation of devout Jews represent the whole house of Israel for whom God has promised renewal and restoration (see below).[152]

The intention of Luke's elaborate description of the crowd's response to the healing miracle is almost certainly indicated by the ironical phrase, "filled with wonder and amazement [ἐπλήσθησαν θάμβους καὶ ἐκστάσεως *eplēsthēsan thambous kai ekstaseōs*]" (3:10*b*). The verb, a favorite of Luke's, recalls his earlier story of Pentecost when Peter and John and the other believers were "filled [*eplēsthēsan*] with the Holy Spirit" (2:4). Israel's persistent unbelief is indicated by the implicit contrast between the Pentecost experience and their "filling": They are "filled with wonder" rather than with the Holy Spirit.

Luke's striking choice of ἔκστασις (*ekstasis*) for "amazement," which figures into subsequent stories of those confused by the implications of the Spirit's "signs and wonders" (cf. 8:9, 11, 13; 10:45), nicely captures the crowd's spiritual ambivalence. They have had a powerful, ecstatic experience that has transported them from the ordinary into an encounter with God. Such experiences typically provoke theological reflection that requires a change of mind. As before, the reader is led to ask: How will this Israel respond to its encounter with God?

3:12-26. Actually the stakes may have reached a critical stage for these Jews. In Luke's narrative world, God anoints and then sends prophet Peter to "all the people" to give them a second chance to repent and turn to God in faith. If they rebuff the prophet's word a second time, God will send them into exile and delay the fulfillment of their

---

150. Johnson puts it this way: "possessions are being used simply as a negative foil, to point out the enormity of what the Apostles did possess, the power to heal in the Name of Jesus." See L. Johnson, *The Literary Function of Possessions in Luke-Acts*, SBLDS 39 (Missoula, Mont.: Scholars Press, 1977) 190-91.

151. The addition of "Solomon's Portico" (3:11) to the scene's description is problematical. According to Josephus (*Antiquities of the Jews* 15.396-401; *The Jewish War* 5:184-85), the portico was a shelter primarily for Greek visitors to the holy city and, therefore, was built outside the Temple, although its precise location remains uncertain. Yet Luke's narrative places Peter and John, along with the healed man, inside the Temple for prayers (3:8). To resolve this disagreement, the Western text (D) provides a different topology, placing the portico outside the Beautiful Gate, where the apostles and the man had since retreated—which Bruce, *The Acts of the Apostles*, 138, considers historically correct. Whether or not Luke's knowledge of the Temple is suspect, as some think, the purpose of his reference may be to recall an important site of Christian witness, as is clear from 5:12. What is important to his narrative world is that Solomon's Portico is a Christian "shrine" remembered for apostolic "signs and wonders" and witnessing and for the conversions that resulted.

152. Jervell, *Die Apostelgeschichte*, 163.

restoration.[153] If this story is read as structurally and thematically parallel to his Pentecost narrative and if Luke's emphasis on "all the people" relates this crowd to the Israelites Peter addressed on the day of Pentecost, then the implication is that these are those Jews who refused his earlier invitation of salvation and this speech may well be their second chance to respond favorably. Clearly Peter's second speech to them, which provides the additional testimony of the healed man, is more sharply worded and the call to conversion is more urgently proffered. The question asked earlier of the stunned crowd at Pentecost (see 2:37) is even more pressing now: How will this Israel respond to Peter's second sermon, based on its second hearing of the gospel message?

The circumstances of Peter's second sermon to Israel are similar to those of his first (see 2:14-40): The whole household of Israel—"all the people"—has witnessed God's mighty work and has congregated around Peter for his commentary on their experience.[154] This sermon, too, is a missionary speech in two parts about the importance of the resurrection of Jesus (3:12-16) that intends to convert its auditors to him as their Lord and God's Christ (3:17-26).[155]

3:12. The purposeful interplay between these first two missionary speeches in Acts is indicated by the repetition of Peter's opening

address, "Men of Israel" (cf. 2:22). The reader of this speech knows to have the Pentecost speech in mind when reflecting on what is now proclaimed. Yet, the differences between the addresses make for a fuller understanding of the gospel. For example, Peter's judgments of Israel's guilt in Jesus' execution are much more harshly drawn than before (3:13-15; cf. 2:23). He also makes explicit the charge of Israel's ignorance (3:17), which has led to their wickedness (3:26) and away from God's purposes as articulated in the promise to Abraham (3:25). This sharp condemnation compels keener attention to Peter's interpretation of Scripture (midrash) and makes more urgent its reception. If the whole Pentecost narrative is more idealistic and pastoral in tone, this speech is more polemical and prophetic. This is Israel's second chance; the urgency of Peter's appeal underscores their theological crisis.

Peter's sermon is prompted again by misunderstanding, although certainly more good-hearted than before. His audience does not mock what they have just witnessed (cf. 2:13-15) and their honest mistake concerns the nature of Peter's spiritual authority in effecting the man's cure (3:12b). Peter and John *do* exercise enormous power as God's chosen prophets and their piety is well documented by the preceding narrative. Peter is concerned that the crowd understand that these are not attributes apostles themselves have cultivated over time, qualities that can manipulate a sovereign God's prerogative. Peter's cautionary note reminds the reader that healing is "in the name of Jesus Christ of Nazareth" (3:6b) and is mediated by the saving power vested in and released by that name according to Scripture (cf. 2:21; 4:7-12). This theme persists into the next story, where Peter's audience consists of Israel's rulers, who are also guilty of "ignorance" (3:17) but whose response is more cynical and political than that of rank-and-file Jews.

3:13-16. Peter's correction concerning the protocol of the prophet's exercise of power leads naturally and immediately to Christian *kerygma*:[156] To understand the meaning of

153. Johnson, *The Acts of the Apostles*, 13, contends that such second visits are an important narrative theme of Acts and supply one element of its "prophetic structure." According to Johnson, the account of Moses (Acts 7:22-50) in Stephen's speech is patterned after Luke's story of Jesus and provides an exposition of the theme that the prophet is sent to save Israel, but out of ignorance the people reject him. The prophet returns to offer salvation to the same people a second time. If the people reject the prophet again, they will be sent into exile. While my reading of Peter's second sermon follows Johnson's lead in general, several differences should be noted. Peter's Jewish audience is the entire household of Israel, including Jews of the diaspora. Further, the decision of Jews in a synagogue of a particular city (e.g., Jerusalem, Pisidian Antioch) does not determine the fate of all Israel, but only that of those particular Jews who hear the prophetic word and refuse to obey its demands. Finally, this "second visitation" theme is joined by another—namely, the "divided house of Israel." The restoration of repentant Israel unfolds over time in response to the prophetic word in various locations, sometimes proclaimed in two visits (see 13:44), even as does the harsh exclusion of unrepentant Israel (3:23; cf. 13:45-47).

154. Luke's shaping of the traditions of this second sermon, as with the first, reflect his own linguistic choices and theological intentions. Again, the interpreter should read this text as the recounting of an event, the memories of which have been preserved and transmitted to Luke but whose significance is his to tell.

155. These two parts are rhetorically similar to Peter's Pentecost speech, combining "judicial" (or "explanation," 3:12-16) with "deliberative" (or "appeal," 3:17-26) conventions. See Soards, *The Speeches in Acts*, 40-44, for analysis and alternate outlines. In this second speech, however, Peter combines traditions differently than he did on Pentecost; he uses *kerygma* rather than proof from prophecy to address the problem of Israel's rejection of the Messiah (cf. 2:22-36), while his missionary appeal is to Israel's Scripture rather than to the Christian *kerygma* (cf. 2:38-40).

156. Fitzmyer, *The Acts of the Apostles*, 282, lists the kerygmatic elements of this speech as follows: (1) miracle is the work of Israel's faithful God (3:13ab), not powerful and pious prophets (3:12b); (2) miracle witnesses to Jesus and thus to the ignorance of Israel about him (3:13c-19); (3) Israel's restoration is predicated on Jesus' resurrection (3:20-21), which is (4) proved by biblical prophecy (3:22-26).

the miracle (3:16) is to come to grips with who Jesus is (3:13-15). The entire sermon is framed by Abraham's promise of universal salvation (3:13, 25) and, therefore, by Israel's role toward that redemptive end. The traditional appeal to "the God of our ancestors" expresses Peter's confidence in God's faithfulness to aid Israel in fulfilling that role.[157] Indeed, God has acted faithfully toward Israel in Jesus, God's glorified "servant" (δοῦλος [doulos]; 3:13, 26).[158] While the precise meaning of Jesus' identification as God's servant is unclear (see below), the reference to Jesus no doubt reminds the audience that the healing miracle was done in his name. That Jesus is "glorified" (δοξάζω doxazō) probably alludes to his resurrection and ascension[159] and envisages his vindication as God's faithful "servant."[160]

Peter quickly moves to clarify Israel's guilt for rejecting Jesus, which is more sharply and elaborately stated here than in his first sermon. Notice five new details Peter adds to his legal brief against Israel (see 3:13c-15b; cf. 2:23): Even though Jesus is (1) "the Holy and Righteous One," (2) they handed him over to Pilate (3) when Pilate wanted him released; (4) they exchanged him for a murderer, (5) which occasioned the execution of "the Author of life." The reference to Pilate's role in Jesus' trial and death is generally consistent with its synoptic narration (see Luke 23:1-25

and par.; cf. Acts 4:27; 13:28). With a prior reading of the gospel narrative in mind, however, the reader knows that pagan Pilate had little interest in intramural Jewish conflict and therefore in the final disposition of Jesus. He cedes Jesus to his Jewish opponents for political reasons. In any case, Peter's point is less to depict Rome's passive stance toward Jesus and more to depict unrepentant Israel's active participation in bringing about his execution.

Twice Peter mentions that Israel "rejected" Jesus (3:13-14), using the verb ἀρνέομαι (arneomai), which means "to deny" or "to disown" someone. Peter presumes that Jesus belongs to Israel in some special way and that Israel betrayed that relationship by participating in his execution. The two titles of Jesus used here in rapid succession— "the Holy and Righteous One [ὁ ἅγιος καὶ ὁ δίκαιος ho hagios kai ho dikaios]" (3:14) and "the Author of life [ὁ ἀρχηγὸς τῆς ζωῆς ho archēgos tēs zōēs]" (3:15)—draw upon important OT/Gospel terms to define the nature of that relationship and therefore also the enormity of Israel's treason. The first title follows from Peter's reference to Jesus as God's glorified servant by recalling the Roman centurion's ironic commentary on the death of Jesus, whom he asserts is "innocent" (or "righteous," ho dikaios, Luke 23:47). In the Gospel setting, as here, ho dikaios alludes to Isaiah's depiction of the suffering servant as ho dikaios (Isa 53:11 LXX) and so as having divine authority to bear Israel's sins. In this sense, Peter interprets Jesus' passion as the expression of his faithful service for Israel, which Israel then rejected—and so too the salvation that attends it.

The latter title is repeated in Acts 5:31 for the glorified Jesus.[161] This speech contrasts Israel's action of taking life with Jesus' action of authoring life, and perhaps also with God's bringing Jesus back to life (3:15). Thereby Israel demonstrates its robust ignorance of God's purposes by removing the very source of its promised life! On Pentecost, Peter marshals proofs from biblical prophecy to commend his eyewitness of the risen Jesus. He

157. D. L. Bock, *Proclamation* from *Prophecy and Pattern: Lukan Old Testament Christology* (Sheffield, 1987), 187-88. Bock argues that the precise formula of Peter's appeal in 3:13a intentionally recalls the same confession used in Exod 3:6, 15 in the famous exchange between God and Moses. There God commends Israel's confidence in the exodus event due to God's prior faithfulness to their ancestors. A similar justification project is in view here, where Peter's use of the traditional formula of Israel's confidence is posited for the resurrection where God has acted faithfully in Christ to restore Israel.

158. There is an intriguing connection between Peter's use of God's "servant" (paῖ" *pais*) in this sermon (3:13, 26) and the important and clear allusions to Isaiah's "suffering servant" in 1 Peter 2 (in this case with reference to household). See O. Cullmann, "Jesus serviteur de Dieu," *Dieu vivant: perspectives religieuses et philosophiques* 16 (1950) 17-34. Both texts allude to Isaiah's prophecy of God's servant (Isa 52:13), who suffers as Israel or on Israel's behalf. Bruce, *The Acts of the Apostles*, 139-40, suggests that this connection between Peter's speech and 1 Peter's use of servant indicates the historical accuracy of Luke's narrative, while others, such as J. Jeremias, *TDNT*, 5:677-717, are more reserved and allow that both Acts 3 and 1 Peter 2 reflect a very early christology stemming from Peter himself, although in the case of Acts without the redemptive value it has in 1 Peter. In my view, the combination of "servant" and "the Holy and Righteous One" in this speech almost certainly alludes to Isaiah 53's Suffering Servant, perhaps not to forward a theology of the cross but to relate servant Jesus and Israel together in a redemptive way.

159. So Haenchen, *The Acts of the Apostles*, 205.

160. Most scholars still think that "servant" is not used as a messianic title in the NT. See M. D. Hooker, *Jesus and the Servant* (London: SPCK, 1959). Even if this view is right, that the Messiah is exalted by God and worshiped by the church as Lord because of his faithful service to God seems clear enough from the NT (e.g., Phil 2:5-11; Revelation 5).

161. The meaning of *archēgos* is unclear. Most accept the translation "author" and yet question how this translation fits easily with Luke's strong views of God's sovereign and provident control of salvation's history, expressed in the opening of Peter's Pentecost sermon. For this reason, Bauernfeind, *Die Apostelgeschichte*, 63-64, understands by the expression that Jesus is *Lebensführer*, "leader into life," to make the evident contrast between life and death more vivid.

makes the same claim as before that "we are witnesses" (3:16; see also 2:32), but here Peter speaks of Israel's rejection of Jesus rather than of the resurrection.

Peter's response to the misunderstanding of his prophetic powers (3:16; cf. 3:12a) uses the crucial phrase "by faith in his name" (ἐπὶ τῇ πίστει τοῦ ὀνόματος αὐτοῦ *epi tē pistei tou onomatos autou*), which brings together the objective reality of the man's "perfect health" with the subjective faith "that is through Jesus."[162] The reference to "the name" that "made the man strong" recalls the circumstances of the healing miracles (see 3:6) and the promise of Joel's prophecy that those who call upon the *name* of the Lord will be saved (= healed). In this larger sense, healing heralds the fulfillment of prophecy and provides additional evidence of God's faithfulness.

3:17. By pointing to the Lord's authority, Peter has set the stage for his appeal to his auditors to repent and believe in order to become members of a "healed" Israel. He begins graciously by excusing their treachery: "I know that you acted in ignorance as did also your rulers" (3:17). With these words Luke succinctly sets forth the theological crisis facing a devout but divided household: They are "ignorant" (ἄγνοια *agnoia*, 7:25; 13:37; 17:30; cf. Luke 19:44; 23:34; Acts 7:60). In particular, Israel is divided over Jesus because of its ignorance of Scripture that would indicate his messianic identity and mission. Peter adds "as did also your rulers" (3:17b) as a prophet's emphasis, since the ignorance of leaders transfers to the people they lead. The leaders' obduracy will become increasingly clear as the narrative of the community's Jerusalem mission depicts the conflict between the apostolic leaders of restored Israel and the priestly leaders of "official" Israel. Of course, the reader of Acts is well aware that the Spirit has filled the apostles and has thereby elevated their intellectual abilities to discern Scripture's meaning. They alone are enabled to know God's intended meaning in Scripture and to make clear God's redemptive purposes for Israel. In a word, they are Israel's rightful

spiritual leaders during these last days of salvation's progress to its consummation.

3:18-21. Peter now reissues his call to conversion: "repent therefore and turn to God"[163] (3:19a; see 2:38). Repentance embraces a different interpretation of Scripture—the one that Peter has just provided his auditors.[164] The primary purpose of repentance is "so that your sins are wiped out" (cf. Isa 43:25), which will then usher repentant Israel into "times of refreshing" and trigger the return of Messiah (3:20) from heaven (cf. 1:11) to inaugurate "the time of universal restoration" (3:21).[165] Peter's argument stakes out the enormous purchase of Israel's repentance, since the restoration of Israel is the pre-condition that leads to God's universal blessing.

The eschatology of Luke is predicated on God's faithfulness to the promises "announced long ago through his holy prophets" to Israel (3:21).[166] He does not have in mind a detailed timetable of specific dates when this or that event will happen (cf. 1:7). The reader knows only that "the last days" of salvation's history have been inaugurated by the suffering of God's Messiah (3:18) and the Spirit's arrival at Pentecost (see 2:17-21), and that Jesus will return at the consummation of history (see 1:11). Between these two eschatological markers unfolds the Spirit-enabled mission of

---

162. It remains unclear whether the lame man's faith was required and, therefore, preceded his healing or whether the apostles' faith "in the name of Jesus Christ of Nazareth" resulted in the man's healing and then his faith. The logic of the earlier healing story suggests the latter: It is "*the apostles'* faith in his name" that "has made this man strong—and has given him perfect health." While the power to heal resides in Jesus, Peter claims that the requisite faith in Jesus that heals resides in the apostles (see 3:12a).

163. Dunn, *The Acts of the Apostles*, 46, contends with others that Luke combines the imperatives μετανοήσατε *metanoēsate* ("repent") with ἐπιστρέψατε *epistrepsate* ("to turn") to clarify the experience of conversion called for by the gospel. On the one hand, the gospel requires a "change of mind" (in what one believes about God); but on the other hand, it also requires a radical change of direction (in how one lives for God). The logic of conversion, which moves from changing what one thinks or believes about God to changing the way one lives with others, is already implied by the Pentecost narrative. There the 3,000 who converted (2:41) formed a community whose common life enjoyed favor with all (2:42-47).

164. According to Jervell the theme of Israel's repentance in Acts can only be understood in continuity with Luke's Gospel, where Jesus' mission was to begin a process of healing a divided Israel. See esp. Jervell, "The Divided People of God," in *Luke and the People of God*, 41-74.

165. Although the two phrases Luke uses in 3:20-21 of eschatological "seasons"—"the times of refreshing" and "the time of universal restoration"—are clearly related, they do not refer to the same saving season but to a *sequence* of saving seasons. Fitzmyer, *The Acts of the Apostles*, 288, contends, correctly, that the temporal word καιροί (*kairoi*) that Luke uses in "the times of refreshing" denotes the *beginning* of a season, whereas his use of χρόνος (*chronos*) in the second phrase denotes "the duration of it." Luke is commenting on conversion as the initiation into the first of "the last days" of salvation's history which will conclude at the parousia in the cosmic triumph of God's reign.

166. The "must" in the phrase "[Jesus] *must* remain in heaven" translates the Greek particle δεῖ (*dei*), which functions in Acts as a catchword of prophetic fulfillment. Luke has already used it in the Gospel's prediction of Jesus' passion (Luke 9:22; 17:25) and in the report of its fulfillment (Luke 22:27; 24:7, 44). As the critical eschatological elements of this same divine purpose, Jesus "must" remain in heaven and "must" return to earth to inaugurate God's restoration of all creation, because this is what "all the biblical prophets" predict according to apostolic (i.e., Spirit inspired) interpretation.

the Lord's successors as his witness to Israel and the nations to the end of the earth and history.

The present text sharpens the Messiah's future horizon and its importance as the religious motive of the church's mission in Jerusalem and beyond. The Lord's return to earth to complete his messianic mission is heralded by "times of refreshing that come from the presence of the Lord" (3:20). This first reference to a season of redemption refers to the present blessings of repentant Jews, which are both spiritual (see 2:38) and material (see 2:42-47). This, too, is the immediate objective of the church's vocation: to reestablish God's presence—"the kingdom" (see 1:6)—within the community of a restored Israel during the "last days" of salvation's history (see 2:17).

According to Peter, these days of mission culminate in God's dispatch of the glorified Messiah, Jesus, "who must remain in heaven until the time of universal restoration." The phrase "time of universal restoration" (NRSV) translates χρόνων ἀποκαταστάσεως πάντων (*chronōn apokatastaseōs pantōn*) to recall and gloss the apostles' decisive question that begins Acts: "Lord, is this the time [*chronos*] when you will restore [ἀποκαθιστάνεις *apokathistaneis*] the kingdom to Israel?" (see 1:6). Peter now extends the scope of God's plan for restoring Israel to include creation and in doing so underscores the universal importance of Israel's repentance.

Luke emphasizes that God's promise of "refreshing times" for a repentant Israel has already been fulfilled and is the necessary precondition for the Lord's coming triumph and creation's restoration. In fact, the church's mission to the "families of the earth" as agent of God's faithfulness to Abraham's promise (3:25) is also preconditioned on Israel's repentance (3:26).[167]

Peter's earlier reference to the man's "perfect health" (3:16) is expanded in its significance as the eschatological metaphor of creation's perfection in the coming age. That is, the healed man is the herald of a broken and battered creation's being made whole again. While Peter's kerygmatic announcement of Messiah's return and creation's restoration is the last we hear of it in Luke's narrative, he provides the three broad movements of God's future plans: (1) These "last days" consist of a mission to heal Israel, which will result in a divided household; (2) God's promise of "refreshing times" will nevertheless be fulfilled among repentant Jews who will carry the gospel to the Gentiles so they too can share in Israel's blessings; and (3) then the Day of the Lord will come, which will inaugurate "the time of universal restoration."

3:22-23. Peter's eschatological program for repentant Israel is sharpened by combining the promise of "a prophet-like-Moses" (3:22-23*a*; cf. Deut 18:15-19 LXX) with a levitical warning of excommunication for those who are unprepared for the Day of Atonement (3:23*b*; Lev 23:29). Although not widely attested during the Second Temple period, the deuteronomic expectation of a prophet to succeed Moses does find currency in an important Qumran text.[168] Peter follows this same interpretive line by claiming that God has "raised up" Jesus (3:26; cf. 2:36) as indication that a Moses prophet has been "raised up for you." The significance of Peter's identification of Messiah with the prophetic ministry of Moses is that each discloses God's word for Israel. Whether or not one "listens to that prophet"[169] determines one's membership in the covenant community where the refreshing presence of God may be experienced. Put negatively, those who refuse to listen to God's prophetic word are "utterly rooted out of the people [λαός *laos*]" (3:23) and excluded from the experience of God's refreshing grace. During these "last days" of salvation's history, Israel remains divided over this apostolic word about Jesus; however, God's redemptive purpose moves inexorably toward the coming age by the witness of repentant Jews.

3:24-26. The division within Israel between those who heed (or not) the

---

167. According to Paul, the completion of the Gentile mission is the necessary precondition for the Lord's return, at which time "all Israel will be saved" (cf. Rom 11:25-27) and creation repaired (cf. 8:18-25). Of course, the Evangelist knows what the apostle did not know when writing Romans: Paul would not complete his mission to the nations and would not live to see Jesus return.

168. *4QTestim* 7/4Q175.5-8. It should be pointed out that unlike traditional Judaism this "prophet-like-Moses" figured prominently in Samaritan religion, which some suggest is Luke's source for what becomes the foundation of his Moses christology. See C. C. Hill, *Hellenists and Hebrews: Reappraising Division Within the Earliest Church* (Minneapolis: Fortress, 1992) 87.

169. Johnson, *The Acts of the Apostles*, 70, notes that Luke's rewriting of the LXX text suggests that the verb "listens" (ἀκούω *akouō*) connotes obedience and is better translated "obeys."

prophet's call to conversion implies an essential internal characteristic of Israel prior to the Messiah's return. The reader of Acts should anticipate still other expressions of a divided house and should not be distracted by them. Clearly God's present blessing of faithful Jews—this "time of refreshing" (3:20)—is sufficient evidence that God has faithfully kept the promise to restore Israel, and on this basis the gospel's advance to "all the families of the earth" is also anticipated but awaits Paul's mission to bring "light to the nations" for its fuller narration. At this early moment in the church's mission, however, Peter can only iterate the premise of God's redemptive plan (3:24) that the things that are happening (e.g., the healing of the lame outsider) herald the realization of what God has foretold through "all the prophets" (cf. 3:18).

Samuel, who is the first prophet following Moses by Peter's counting, and all "those (biblical prophets) after him predicted these days"—that is, "the last days" beginning at Pentecost (cf. 2:17). This leads to an expansion of previous themes in reverse order. The future prospect of "universal restoration" (3:21) is now interpreted in the terms of God's promise to Abraham (3:25) that "in your descendants [lit., "seed" = Jews] all the families [= Gentiles] of the earth shall be blessed" (cf. Gen 22:18)—a promise whose fulfillment requires, then, the conversion of these very Jews since they are "the descendants of the prophets" (3:25). Perhaps for this reason Peter's final note repeats the present prospect of Israel's "refreshing" (3:20) for which Messiah was sent "first to you, to bless you by turning each of you from your wicked ways" (3:26; see 3:19).

Throughout this passage, Luke carefully and creatively adapts his language to order and commend his view of salvation history. He shifts the terminology in 3:20-21 from "times/time" (καιροί/χρόνος *kairoi/chronos*) to "these days" (αὗται ἡμέραι *hautai hēmerai*), thus recalling the earlier reference to Joel's prophecy of the "last days" (2:17). This shift returns the auditors and readers from future speculation to the present moment in order to address their situation in light of Scripture: What is the meaning of this man's healing? How can one enjoy God's promised blessing? What or who is the ground

of repentance? Moreover, Luke changes the contextual sense of ἐνευλογηθήσονται (*eneulogēthēsontai*, "will bless themselves") in Gen 22:18 (LXX) from a middle to a passive voice—"will be blessed"—to underscore God's future act of blessing the "nations." Finally, he substitutes "families" (πατριαί *patriai*) for "nations" (ἔθνη *ethnē*) without changing the universal sense of the promised salvation that will come in some unknown future. In Luke's presentation, then, Peter's appeal has mostly to do with his hearers' participation in current blessing, beginning with their sins being "wiped out" (3:19) and "turning from your wicked ways" (3:26), as the focal moment in the larger plan.

4:1-4. Luke frequently tells stories of interrupted speeches or actions (e.g., 2:37; 7:54; 8:39-40; 10:44; 17:32; 22:22; 26:24). This literary device often introduces important elements into the story—a leading question, a principal player, a theological problem.[170] The interrupted speech also serves to connect consecutive episodes as logically related. Thus when the Sadducees (4:1-3), who will become the movement's most hostile opponents, interrupt Peter's speech, the stage is set for Peter's defense of the gospel before a hostile tribunal consisting largely of Sadducees (4:5-31).

Three groups are mentioned as approaching John and Peter while Peter concludes his speech (3:12-26): "the priests, the captain of the temple, and the Sadducees."[171] The first two represent the Temple, the central symbol of "official" Israel; it is in their responsibility to protect the Temple's interests, especially matters of ritual purity. This is the first reference to Sadducees in Acts; while demonized in the Gospels and here, not much is actually known about them or the nature of their authority in Jerusalem.[172] In the ancient world behind Luke's story, the Sadducees

---

170. See Conzelmann, *The Acts of the Apostles*, 22.

171. Some early MSS (B, C) read instead "chief-priests" (ἀρχιερεῖς *archiereis*), which would be consistent with Luke's identification of both Jesus' hostile opponents in the Gospel and the apostles' opponents in the next story in Acts (see 4:23). "Priests" (ἱερεῖς *hiereis*) is the preferred term here because it is the more difficult to explain and thus presumed to be earlier.

172. Fitzmyer, *The Acts of the Apostles*, 297-98. The name "Sadducees" is related to the Hebrew word for "righteous" and the OT "Zadok," the name of an Aaronid priest (2 Sam 2:17; Ezek 40:46). Sadducees are thought to be contemporary descendants of Zadok and the Zadokite priesthood, keenly influenced by Hellenistic culture and philosophy and quite sophisticated—perhaps the reason why they were so impressed by the speech of "uneducated and ordinary men" (4:13).

were probably devout laity from wealthy (mainly priestly) Jerusalem families who were close to the political and financial institutions of Judean culture but who were without any direct power over temple protocol.[173] Within Luke's narrative world of Acts, however, Sadducees are portrayed as "flat characters" with flawed personae and incorrect theology. In fact, they represent the Jewish group most responsible for a divided Israel—in particular, for unrepentant Israel's resistance to the church's testimony to the word in Jerusalem. In effect, the negative depictions of the church's opposition are neatly summarized in verses 2-3: The opponents are "annoyed" (διαπονέομαι *diaponeomai*) because of the people's welcome response to the apostles' proclamation "that in Jesus there is the resurrection of the dead,"[174] and for this reason

"they arrested [the apostles]." Putting prophets into prison is commonplace in Acts; this is the first of several conflicts that result in arrest and incarceration.

In contrast to the response of the temple establishment, five thousand who heard the word believed (4:4; see 2:41). Luke frequently uses "the word" (ὁ λόγος *ho logos*) in Acts for the Christian *kerygma*, or gospel. The movement of the word through Acts is sometimes surprising (see 8:4) and always expansive, whether from Jew to Gentile or from Jerusalem to the "end of the earth." To "believe" (πιστεύω *pisteuō*) in this word is Luke's shorthand for obeying the gospel imperatives to "repent and turn to God" by believing in what the apostles proclaim about the risen Jesus and in how they support their christological claims by Scripture (see 3:19; cf. Matt 4:17 and par.).

173. See Roloff, *Die Apostelgeschichte*, 80-81.

174. This is Luke's succinct, but difficult, summary of the gospel. The point and problem of Luke's phrase is that the apostles nowhere claim that "in [or by] Jesus" the dead are raised but rather that he is raised from the dead. See Barrett, *A Critical and Exegetical Commentary on the Acts of the Apostles*, 219-20. The Sadducees did not possess a robust notion of a restored Israel or believe in the "resurrection from the dead" (see 23:8). Their Bible contained only the Torah, and not the prophecies (such as Isaiah) that script God's plan of salvation, according to Luke. They expressed their hope

for Israel's salvation in terms of temple observance by which Israel's covenant purity with God is faithfully maintained. Luke's phrase reflects, rather, the core belief of the Pharisees, who understood Israel's hope in terms of the endtime resurrection of the dead; and it envisages the intramural conflict within religious Israel between these two groups (see 23:6-10). The eventual triumph and spread of the Pharisees' influence and the concurrent demise of the Sadducees in post-70 CE Judaism, certainly known to Luke when he wrote Acts, lend tacit support that the church's proclamation of the risen Jesus is the hope of Israel.

REFLECTIONS

1. "In the name of Jesus Christ of Nazareth, walk" (3:6 NIV). Peter's command is not the incantation of a magician, as though healing powers were released by the mere mention of a sacred "name," but a believer's confession of the continuing authority of the living Jesus. In the Gospels, Jesus admonished his followers for having "little faith" (cf. Matt 6:30; 8:26) since the proper exercise of trusting God is a powerful force, strong enough to "move mountains" (cf. Matt 17:20; 1 Cor 13:2). Peter's words to the crippled beggar are words that issue in new life precisely because they are words of profound confidence in the present authority of Jesus to heal the lame and save the lost.

2. "He stood and began to walk, and he entered the temple with them" (3:8 NRSV). In his farewell speech, Jesus commissions his apostles to a Spirit empowered witness (1:8); the implied result of their witness is the restoration of God's reign to repentant Israel (1:6). The Lord's interplay between vocation and restoration provides the reader with the interpretive key for understanding why Luke features healing miracles in Acts and narrates them with a similar resonance (5:14-16; 9:32-34; 36-41; 14:8-10; 16:16-18; 19:11-12; 20:7-13; 28:7-9). The healing of crippled beggars "in the name of Jesus Christ of Nazareth" in order to restore them physically also restores them to membership within the restored Israel of God. The beggar's entrance into the Temple to the shouts of holy praise symbolizes a *religious* restoration, since he is now restored to a community of faith and able to worship God with them.

3. "And they recognized him as the one who used to sit and ask for alms . . . and they were filled with wonder and amazement at what had happened to him" (3:10 NRSV). Healing is the principal "sign and wonder" performed by God's Spirit through the prophets-like-Jesus of Acts. Healing miracles are "enacted parables" of the manner or experience of God's saving grace. For this reason, Luke sometimes uses the verb "to save" for "to heal" (see Luke 7:50; 8:36, 48, 50; Acts 4:9; 14:9). This is not because sin precipitates in bodily infirmity under the curse of God. God's redemptive intention is to liberate people from whatever debilitates them and prevents them from enjoying the good things created for them. The interpreter of Acts sometimes makes the distinction between spiritual sickness (= sin), from which one is healed by the salve of divine forgiveness, and physical sickness (= lameness), from which one is healed by God's miracle-working power. The one is more public and spectacular but no more exceptional than the other. They are two sides of a common coin, minted by grace and received in faith.

4. God "glorified his servant Jesus, whom you handed over and rejected in the presence of Pilate" (3:13 NRSV). Luke makes the execution of Jesus the primary symbol of unrepentant Israel, even as believing that Jesus is God's Messiah is the primary mark of repentant Israel. Peter's presentation of the gospel highlights the ultimate importance of choosing for Jesus, since to reject him is to reject all the blessings of grace that God metes out to us because of him. When unrepentant Israel turns to Pilate—a disinterested, cynical ruler who represents a pagan power—from an interested God, they freely choose death rather than life. Their bad choice represents every bad choice people make when rejecting the words of eternal life in favor of competitors that are disinterested in our future with God.

5. "I know that you acted in ignorance, as did your leaders" (3:17 NIV). In the first century of the new millennium, most religious people are theologically and biblically illiterate. They believe in God, but they are not clear as to why they believe. At the same time, because of secular culture's pervasive awareness of and profound interest in God, the popular media routinely feature stories on religious beliefs, miracles and angels, and the universal importance of Jesus. How can the church contribute to the wider discussion—that is, how can the church respond to awareness and interest in things spiritual—if believers are ignorant of their own faith?

6. Jesus "must remain in heaven until the time of universal restoration" (3:21 NRSV). Modern interpreters of Acts often point out that the book's emphasis on the church's present mission has the effect of diminishing the sense of eschatological intensity. Salvation is today and only the expectation of God's universal judgment is delayed to the end of history (see 10:42; 17:31). The future is "fixed" in God's mind and therefore removed as a principal concern of ours. While the surface level of the narrative does stess the church's present mission, the future of God's salvation provides a theme of enormous importance for the theological "superstructure" of Luke's story. Indeed, salvation history provides the "authorial motive" that explains the direction the story takes from beginning to end. Peter's speech in particular suggests that the church's mission is coordinated with salvation's future. Thus the mission is first to Jews (3:17-19, 26) whose repentance are so "your sins may be wiped out" (3:19 NRSV) and "times of refreshing may come" (3:20 NRSV). The restoration of repentant Israel in these last days (3:24) is the condition for a Gentile mission (3:25), the completion of which will trigger the return of the glorified Jesus at the end of history (cf. 1:11) for "the time of universal restoration" (3:21; cf. Rom 11:25-26). Genuine mission activity is always part of the larger and longer plan of God's salvation.

7. "So they arrested them and put them in custody until the next day" (4:3 NRSV). Institutional authority is always concerned with deviant voices and movements. Those in elected or established positions of power act in self-interest to protect the interests of those they represent. However, we should guard against the facile collapse of private and public morality. Good people are sometimes caught doing bad things—things that are against their own moral code—for the good of those that employ or elect them.[175] The Sadducees are the antagonists of Luke's narrative world whose exercise of authoritarian (and some might even say "responsible") leadership is repressive and sometimes even murderous. These horrific public actions should not lead us to make negative judgments about the Judaism they represent. To do so is a source of the anti-Semitism that has shaped the destructive relations between Jews and Christians for two millennia.

175. See R. Niebuhr, *Moral Man and Immoral Society* (New York: Macmillan, 1983).

Acts 4:5-31, Story Two: The Apostles vs. the Sanhedrin, Round One

COMMENTARY

Peter and John are arrested because they testify to Jesus, by whom, they claim, there is "the resurrection of the dead" (4:1-3). They are detained overnight, perhaps to give the authorities opportunity to build their case against the apostles, since so many devout Jews in Jerusalem have come to believe "the word" they proclaim (4:4). But the new political reality is this: The apostles are under arrest (4:3) and the movement they lead is under attack by hostile forces with the political power and financial resources to threaten the Jerusalem mission. Thus Luke shapes this narrative of the apostles' defense against the charges leveled against them to underscore those divine actions that safeguard the mission and are responsible for its continuing success.

By following the literary pattern of Luke's Jerusalem story cycle, the reader is aided in understanding his theological purpose. Once again Luke's narrative is severely gapped and its full meaning depends upon a prior reading of all that has preceded it (see the Overview for 2:14–15:12). With this in mind, then, the first panel (4:5-12) recounts how Peter and John are asked by a council of Jerusalem's "rulers" (4:5; cf. 3:17) to explain the "the power of the name" that has apparently healed the crippled beggar (see 3:1-8). Peter does so in the power of the Holy Spirit (4:8; cf. 2:4; 1:8). The narrative's second panel (4:13-20) briefly tells of the outsiders' reaction; as with

Peter's other audiences, "they are amazed" (4:13; cf. 2:12; 3:9-11). Their puzzlement at Peter's rhetorical ability is only deepened by the presence of the healed man standing before them, whom they admit is "a notable sign [= evidence] . . . we cannot deny" (4:16; see also 3:1-8). But their amazement shows their profound ignorance (cf. 3:17) of what they observe but fail to comprehend. In turn, they suppose they can squelch the "power of the name" and silence the apostles' witness to it. In response, then, John and Peter add a firm judicial statement (4:19-20) as epilogue to their earlier speech (cf. 4:9-12). The summary of their speech clarifies both the imperative and the motive of their witness to Jesus and makes clear why silencing or subverting the word is impossibile. The final panel of this story (4:21-31) testifies again to a divided Israel. The leaders of unrepentant Israel threaten the apostles (4:21*a*) but will not punish them because of their popular support (4:21*b*-22). The apostles' spiritual authority is aptly envisaged in their benediction that seeks God's "bold" grace to lead all the peoples of Israel (4:24-30). By these responses Luke clarifies the challenges and choices that are occasioned by the apostles' ministry of the word (4:31).

4:5-12. Not much is known about the legality of the case that is brought against Peter and John or of the tribunal that hears it. As with many trials depicted in Acts, this one has the informality of a pre-trial hearing when judges and lawyers gather to determine whether there is sufficient evidence to prosecute. This assembly of different "rulers, elders, and scribes" (4:5) makes up the Jerusalem law-court that Luke later identifies by its technical name, "the Sanhedrin" (4:15; cf. 5:21, 27, 34, 41; 6:12, 15; 22:30; 23:1-28; 24:20). Their collective authority in Jerusalem is made cohesive by the high priest, whom Luke identifies as "Annas" (4:6),[176] and its membership is based on their family pedigree (priests), social prominence (elders), and education (scribes). Court opinions were rendered by those most interested and knowledgeable in the issues being debated. For example, legal matters relating to ethical issues (*halakhah*) were routinely deferred to the Pharisees in attendance, even though Sadducees maintained control over most other matters (as well as over the majority of the Sanhedrin's seventy-one members).[177] In every case, however, a vital relationship to the Temple and its politics was central to membership and participation. Thus, the arresting group (4:1) exercised influence upon the Sanhedrin and their concerns eventuated this pre-trial hearing.[178]

The council poses the relevant question: "By what power or by what name did you do this?" (4:7). But the antecedent of "this" (τοῦτο *touto*) is intentionally unclear and may indicate a trick question. On the one hand, "this" could refer to Peter's healing of the man (3:1-8); on the other hand, "this" could refer to Peter's "teaching the people" in and around the Temple (3:12-26) that had resulted in much controversy and many converts (4:1-4). In the narrative context, the question regarding "this" refers to a name rather than to a magical power—to "the name of Jesus Christ" by whom the man is healed in fulfillment of Joel's prophecy (see 3:6; cf. 2:21).

Peter is "filled with the Holy Spirit" (4:8*a*; see 2:4)[179] to give a persuasive and powerful response to whatever accusation is implied by the council's question. In fact, the following speech (4:9-12) is actually a compressed rehearsal of what has already been proclaimed by Peter both on Pentecost (2:22-40) and at Solomon's Portico (3:12-26): the Spirit inspires Peter to define the "this" of the council's leading question in kerygmatic terms. Before he presents his christological evidence, however, he interprets what occurred as a "good deed" (εὐεργεσία *euergesia*) done to a sick man who is now healed, realizing correctly that the primary purpose of this hearing is to examine the hard evidence of a purported healing (4:9).[180] The healed man himself has already been placed on exhibit (see 4:14) and the purity of Peter's motive is irreproachable—healing is "a good deed done to someone" (4:9), the sort performed by any law-abiding, civil-minded Jew.[181] The true focus of Peter's opening statement is indicated by his word for "healed": σώζω (*sōzō*), which means "saved." Throughout Acts this verb has the double sense of "to heal" and "to save." It echoes the salvation theme of Joel's prophecy (see 2:21), which theme has already been glossed by its previous soundings (see 2:40, 47). The subtext of Peter's explanation, then, is theological rather than legal, and his primary evidence is biblical, not "scientific."

Peter's speech is addressed to the very "rulers" he earlier accused of acting in ignorance regarding Scripture's prophecies about Jesus (see 3:17-18). While he does not actually demand their repentance in this case (cf. 3:19), the sharpened contrast between "Jesus . . . whom you crucified" and "Jesus

176. Annas was actually high priest emeritus, since he held the office only until 15 CE; he was succeeded eventually (in 17 CE) by his son-in-law Caiaphas, whom Luke also mentions. Caiaphas was probably the high priest when this event took place.

177. This may explain why the Pharisee Gamaliel, even though a member of the minority party, is asked to give the "majority opinion" in the Sanhedrin's closing argument against the apostles (Acts 5:33-42).

178. The NRSV translation of the ambiguous Greek αὐτοὺς (*autous*, lit., "them") as "prisoners" (4:7; the NIV translates it "Peter and John") seems to stretch the textual and historical evidence. With the semi-circular courtroom in mind, the KJV translation gets it right: "And when they had set them in the midst. . . ."

179. Does this second reference in Acts to the Spirit's filling suggest that the power of Spirit baptism that came with Pentecost is temporary? Jervell is no doubt right when saying that "the speech is understood here to result from the Spirit's miracle-working power." See Jervell, *Die Apostelgeschichte*, 178. At moments such as this one in Israel's history, the Spirit of God has enabled the prophets of God to speak with power and insight in order to set Israel on the way of righteousness. The Spirit does not withdraw from the apostles after this speech is finished; that is clear by the "signs and wonders" they continue to perform (5:12). Dunn suggests that this phrase envisages "an occasional 'topping up' of a Spirit once bestowed at Pentecost." See Dunn, *The Acts of the Apostles*, 52-53.

180. Both translations obscure the juridical aspect of this pre-trial hearing by translating ἀνακρίνω (*anakrinō*, "called to account," NIV; "questioned," NRSV) instead of its more literal sense, "critically examined."

181. The term *euergesia* denotes benefaction, which agrees with Luke's general understanding of saving grace. The use of the Greek word for "save" (*sōzō*) for "healing" already commends a more theological accounting of the miracle event.

... whom God raised from the dead" (4:10) makes clear that these rulers are not aligned with God's purposes. The unstated implication is that they must "repent and turn to God so that their sins may be wiped out" (3:19).[182] Peter appeals to Ps 118:22 (Ps 117:22 LXX) for proof that their conflict has a divine purpose (see 4:11). Luke cites this same text in his Gospel's parable of the vineyard (Luke 20:17; cf. 1 Pet 2:4, 7) in a collocation of texts gathered around the catchword "stone" (ὁ λίθος *ho lithos*) to warn these same leaders that to reject Jesus is to reject the "cornerstone" of Israel's promised salvation. The intertext forged with Acts implies this same warning. However, in this post-resurrection setting where "the stone" is clearly a messianic metaphor of Jesus, the rulers of "official" Israel can no longer be excused for their ignorance (see 3:17). This is their second chance, and to reject the apostolic word is to forfeit their participation in Israel's promised blessings (see 3:12-26; 7:35-42).

The final line of Peter's speech, awkwardly but emphatically stated, offers another synthesis of Luke's theology of salvation with echoes of Joel's prophecy: "There is salvation in no one else, for no other *name* under heaven is given by which *we must be saved* [= healed]" (4:12, italics added). Peter deflects attention from apostolic authority or the miracle to the christological meaning of this redemptive moment. The statement's subtext is easily discerned by the repetition of catchwords from Joel's prophecy ("name," ὄνομα *onoma*; "save," *sōzō*; "heaven," οὐρανός *ouranos*), which is here combined with Luke's δεῖ (*dei*, "must") of divine necessity to confirm that Israel's Scripture testifies to the universal importance of Peter's kerygmatic claims (see 1:16). In this sense, the redemptive significance of the healed man is once again extended beyond the rulers of Jerusalem and "all the people" of Israel to include humankind (see 3:25).

4:13-18. What will be the rulers' response to the gospel? Will they repent and turn to God for forgiveness of their sins or remain unrepentant and therefore excluded from the "season of refreshing" that has come with Pentecost (see 3:19-21)? The reader should not be surprised that their initial reaction to Peter's "bold" proclamation is "amazement"

(4:13).[183] Nor should we be surprised that their amazement is rooted in mistaken identity (cf. 2:13-15; 3:9-12): They are impressed with the rhetorical ability of "uneducated and ordinary men,"[184] which we know "is due to the work of the Spirit." The rulers fail to recognize that Peter is an inspired prophet-like-Jesus and that the "filling with the Holy Spirit" (4:8) had elevated his intellectual and rhetorical abilities without benefit of theological training or academic schooling (see 2:4).

Therefore, the council debates the wrong things even though asking the right questions. They have heard and seen the evidence but can offer no countervailing opinion (4:14): "a notable sign has been done through them; we cannot deny it" (4:16b).[185] Rather than repent in faith, they retire into "executive session" where they "discussed the matter with one another" (4:15)! Their discussion finally turns on a political solution, ironically stipulated by Luke's prophetic idiom: "let us warn them to speak no more *in this name* [ἐπί τῷ ὀνόματι τούτῳ *epi tō onomati toutō*]" (4:17, italics added). The council's strict ban, motivated by the perceived interests of the city, actually restates and legitimizes Joel's "in the name" formula (2:21): The apostles have won the argument! By failing to recognize them as prophets who carry an inspired word from God to proclaim to Jerusalem, the council seeks to separate the merit of the "good deed" performed "in this name" from its kerygmatic commentary (4:18).[186] In doing

---

182. G. Krodel, *Acts*, ACNT (Minneapolis: Augsburg, 1986) 110.

183. The glossary of terms Luke uses to describe Peter's speech and the rulers' reaction in 4:13 almost always is used to narrate this sort of encounter between the proclaimed word of God and its Jewish auditors. For example, Luke employs the term παρρησία (*parrēsia*, "boldness") in its various forms to describe the manner of prophetic or inspired proclamation (2:29; 4:29, 31; 9:27-28; 13:46; 18:26; 19:28; 26:26; 28:31), which is possible because of Spirit baptism. Likewise, we anticipate the initial reaction of devout but unbelieving Jews to such bold preaching will be θαυμάζω (*thaumazō*, "amazement"; 2:7; 3:12; 7:31; 13:41). That is, they recognize the numinous because of their loyalty to Israel's God and Scriptures, but they fail to "get it" and so are amazed instead of repentant. These qualities reflect Greco-Roman notions of powerful and persuasive public speaking.

184. These terms are probably not to be taken literally as though Peter were unschooled and could not write or read. They simply recognize the profound difference in social class between those sitting in judgment and the apostles.

185. The helplessness of the Sanhedrin's situation is made more apparent by Luke's use of σημεῖον (*sēmeion*, sign") as the idiom of "proof from (Joel's) prophecy" (2:19; cf. Acts 2:22, 43; 4:22, 30; 5:12; 15:12). The profound conflict to which these rulers of "official" Israel are party is between spiritual and political realities, between what God reveals and the city's "mean streets" require of them.

186. Witherington notes that nothing is said in 4:17-18 about preventing the apostles from performing healing miracles, which the council assumes they have power to do. See Witherington, *The Acts of the Apostles*, 196. This implicit separation of healing miracle from gospel proclamation not only clarifies the antecedent of the ambiguous "this" in the council's opening question (4:7)—the real issue at stake *is* kerygmatic—but the nature of their theological "ignorance" as well.

so, the rulers seek to keep Israel ignorant of the very means by which "all the people" (see 3:9-11) and "also your rulers" (see 3:17) are guided into a season of refreshment (see 3:19).

4:19-20. The apostles famously defy the council's verdict rather than their prophetic commission.[187] Soards calls their response an "epilogue" to Peter's previous speech, continuing its final, firm statement (4:12), and therefore judicial and kerygmatic in substance.[188] "To listen" translates the Greek ἀκούω (*akouō*), which also connotes obedience in Acts. That is, John and Peter's decision is to obey God's command rather than the council's. In narrative context this command must surely refer to their prophetic vocation, issued by the risen Jesus (see 1:8), which is "to speak about what we have seen and heard" (4:20).[189] From the beginning, the community's mission has been to bear witness to Jesus' resurrection and its redemptive significance for Israel. The "signs and wonders" that outsiders have also witnessed simply supply the platform for their inspired proclamation of the gospel. The subtext of this epilogue, however, includes a political criticism of the council's ability to lead Israel: Its members are unable to speak for God because they are unable to understand (*akouō*, "listen") the proclamation of God's word or the meaning of the healed man. There is considerable irony, then, in Peter's exhortation to these judges that they "must judge" (κρίνω *krinō*) for themselves, since to do so would lead to self-condemnation.[190]

4:21-31. The concluding panel of this episode is shaped by Luke's assessment of the council's paltry reaction to Peter's bold comment (4:21-22), which contrasts sharply with the apostles' prayerful response (4:23-31). In fact, Luke's shaping of their prayer of thanksgiving (4:24c-30) functions as an important theological commentary that deepens the reader's understanding of Peter's speech before the council, especially its dramatic epilogue.

4:21-23. Luke provides the motive of the council's timid decision: They responded "because of the people" (διὰ τὸν λαόν *dia ton laon*; 4:21; cf. Luke 20:19; Matt 21:26). The reason why the apostles go unpunished, then, is not due to the council's devotion to the law, which might have constrained them;[191] their repeated threats and their evident desire to teach them a lesson they would not soon forget are frustrated "because of the people," all of whom are praising God. The reader is now in a position to return to 3:17 for a more wakeful reading of Luke's phrasing "I know that [all] you [people] acted in ignorance, *as did your rulers*" (italics added). The contrasting responses drawn here between Jerusalem's rulers and the "people" of whom they are fearful (cf. 4:25, 27) makes clear that the rulers remain ignorant and therefore fail to "repent and turn to God" (3:19). Not only is there a deep division between the people and their religious rulers, which will make it politically difficult for them to lead; there is also a deep theological division between the rulers and God, which will make it impossible for them to guide Israel through the latter days into the promised season of refreshment. That is, the members of the Sanhedrin, no matter how dedicated they are to Torah and Temple, are unable to bridge the division between repentant and unrepentant Israel; and it is due time for the Twelve to mount Israel's thrones to shepherd all the people of Israel (cf. Luke 22:30).[192] For this reason, Johnson contends—rightly, in my view—that the destination of the apostles' return "to their friends"[193] to report the council's verdict is the apostolate rather than the entire community. These are matters that concern the identity of Israel's leaders and therefore the apostolic circle.[194]

4:24-30. Luke's reshaping of his biblical traditions and of this apostolic memory nicely captures the mood and circumstances of the

---

187. Luke's educated first readers would have known Plato's famous account of Socrates' trial and his courageous (and civil) response to his Athenian jury: "I will obey the god rather than you—and never cease from the practice and teaching of philosophy." Plato *Apology* 29d. Examples of such courage in similar settings are easily found in Jewish writings as well (e.g., Dan 3:16-18; 2 Macc 7:2; Josephus *Antiquities of the Jews* 17.158-59).

188. Soards, *The Speeches in Acts*, 47.

189. See P. Anderson, *The Christology of the Fourth Gospel* (Valley Forge, Pa.: Trinity, 1996) 274-77, who persuasively argues that 4:20 reflects the "seeing and hearing" idiom of John's Jesus and preserves the central motifs of the Johannine "witness motif" (cf. John 3:32; 1 John 1:1-3). More interesting to the readers of Acts is Anderson's conclusion that Luke has preserved a memory of Peter's retort (in 4:19) and then also of John's (in 4:20).

190. Jervell, *Die Apostelgeschichte*, 181. See also Schneider, *Die Apostelgeschichte*, 1:351-52.

191. So Dunn, *The Acts of the Apostles*, 55.

192. See Jervell, *Luke and the People of God*, 75-112.

193. This phrase translates πρὸς τοὺς ἰδίους (*pros tous idious*, "to their own") and is unclear. Does "friends" refer to all members of the community or to apostolic colleagues? The NIV's "to their own people" is clearer but mistaken in meaning.

194. Johnson, *The Acts of the Apostles*, 90.

moment (cf. 2:42, 46-47a).[195] The apostles' benedictory recognizes the importance of their spiritual authority and prophetic vocation (see 4:29). As with other speeches in Jewish settings, this one too is a collection of biblical interpretations (midrashim) on alluded and cited biblical texts that interpret the apostles' conflict with the rulers of "official" Israel and make clear God's intended meaning for all of Israel. The principal text that supplies the canonical context for the apostles' prayer is Ps 2:1-2, cited verbatim in vv. 25b-26. In its biblical setting, Psalm 2 celebrates the enthronement of Israel's king (= David) as God's son, yet the competition is already at work to plot his overthrow—a setting roughly analogous to the one facing the apostles.[196] It is introduced in Acts by an address to and ascription of God as "Sovereign Lord" (Δέσποτα *Despota*), the Creator of all things (4:24b; cf. 14:15; 17:24), and indicates that the prayer is deeply rooted in a belief in God's provident care over creation and God's plan to restore it (see 3:21; cf. 4:30). David is again introduced as a prophet of God whose words cited from the psalm are words of the Holy Spirit that carry divine authority (4:25a; see 1:16; cf. 2:25-27, 30-31).[197]

The following prayer offers an inspired interpretation of their apostolic/prophetic vocation in terms of the earlier conflict between Jerusalem's leaders, apostolic and priestly. The relevant meaning of their midrash-prayer is in its petition (4:29-30) that is introduced by a new salutation, "And now, Lord" (4:29a). Their petition is for a continuation of the Spirit's power "to speak your word with all boldness"—the very attribute recognized by the Sanhedrin (cf. 4:13)—and for a continuation of the Spirit's "signs and wonders" (4:30) according to Joel's prophecy (cf. 2:19; see 2:22). In simple terms, Luke's shaping of the apostles' petition enshrines the principal theme of his narrative: Apostolic successors live boldly within their vocation where the resources of the Holy Spirit will empower them to continue to do and to teach what the Lord Jesus had begun (1:1).

4:31. The Lord God's response to the apostles' petition for power is immediate, dramatic, and confirming: "they were filled with the Holy Spirit and spoke the word of God with boldness" (4:31; see 2:1-4).[198]

195. Marshall, *The Acts of the Apostles*, 103-4.

196. Although there is no evidence of a messianic reading of this psalm prior to Jesus, a christological midrash of this point would surely find here a prophecy of Israel's rejection of Jesus—a principal topic of Peter's speeches to this point in Acts.

197. The word order of this formula has been corrupted, making it difficult to understand. See Barrett, *A Critical and Exegetical Commentary on the Acts of the Apostles*, 244-45; Fitzmyer, *The Acts of the Apostles*, 308-9. The meaning of παῖς (*pais*), translated "servant" and applied here to David, was earlier applied to Jesus (3:13, 26) and could mean "child/son"

in reference to his royal status as Israel's king and ancestor to Messiah, God's "child/Son." This latter meaning makes sense in the light of the intended function of Psalm 2 to install the king of Israel as God's son and ruler in God's place over God's people. The continuity between David and Jesus, both God's servant-son, underscores the implied meaning of this difficult phrase: The Holy Spirit inspired David to write this psalm and now inspires the apostles of Jesus to render it.

198. Commentators debate the composition of the recipients of the Holy Spirit in this text. E.g., Stronstad, *The Prophethood of All Believers*, 55-59, 73-75, argues that it must include every believer (now numbering in the thousands) and locates "the place where they were gathered" as the Temple. However, if the petition is made by the apostles to embolden their prophetic ministry, then the theophany that responds to their prayer is restricted to them.

REFLECTIONS

1. "Then filled with the Holy Spirit, Peter said to them . . . and when they realized he was an uneducated and ordinary man, they were amazed" (see 4:8, 13). Jesus warned his disciples to expect the very crisis that Peter and John here encounter: "When they bring you before the synagogues, the rulers, and the authorities, do not worry about how you are to defend yourselves or what you are to say; for the Holy Spirit will teach you at that very hour what you ought to say" (Luke 12:11-12). One of the cultural affectations that has always influenced the religious politics of the church is the value placed upon the educated person and informed opinion. Typically those who aspire to positions of spiritual authority in the life of the church must spend years being properly trained. No one should deny the importance of education in the production of a thoughtful, competent Christian leadership. Yet this story in Acts reminds us that spiritual authority is primarily the result of the Spirit's work in human life and is therefore subject to spiritual disciplines that make us more available to the Spirit's filling. Peter was an ordinary man who did extraordinary things to influence thousands of people because he was "filled with the Holy Spirit." While talent and a fine education are worthy attributes of a Christian leader, there is simply no substitute for the spiritually mature believer whose leadership reflects the rule of the Spirit in her life.

2. "There is salvation in no one else" (4:12 NRSV). While the hallmark of the theological conception of Acts is its universalism, whereby the blessings of God's salvation are extended to all people, there is but a single route that leads into life with God. This is sometimes taken as an offense in a day of cultural pluralism that commends diversity and variety. The monotheism of biblical religion is only elevated and intensified by the theocentrism of Acts: God, the only God, has a single plan according to which no one except Jesus can mediate salvation to all people. Today's challenge is to interpret the exclusivity of this way to divine blessing in an idiom that is relevant to all people, no matter what else might characterize them as individuals.

3. They "commanded them not to speak or teach at all in the name of Jesus" (4:18 NIV). All of us know from hard experience the foolishness of the children's saying that "sticks and stones may break my bones but words never harm me." Words carry enormous power to do good and evil. They hold sway over us, and all appreciate the political wisdom that whoever controls the "words" influences what goes on in the townsquare and marketplace. The struggle for people/power in Jerusalem between the apostles and the Sanhedrin is over the right to speak and the content of what is said. The most precious civil right of a liberal democracy is the right to free speech, which allows the prophet to afflict the comfortable without fear of reprisal and give equal right to the priest to comfort the afflicted without fear of ridicule. Tragically, this is often not the case within the church. A pundit once remarked that the church is the only army that kills its wounded. The community of believers transformed by God's grace should exemplify the kind of tolerance that will allow thoughtful opinion to be voiced, if only then to be challenged by the prophets among us.

4. "When they had prayed, the place in which they were gathered together was shaken" (4:31 NRSV). In response to the official efforts to repress their preaching ministry, the apostles prayed together for ability "to speak your word with great boldness" (4:28). Their prayer (4:24-30) is exemplary of how to petition God when under pressure to silence the gospel. The interpreter should take note first of the effective interplay between worship and witness. The two form an integral whole in Acts and mark out together the community's identity and vocation: Vital witness is not possible without fervent worship. In their prayer the apostles first invoke God's presence (4:24-28). In this confession of who God is and what God has done a particular idea of God emerges that is appropriate for the difficult situation they find themselves in. God is the Creator who is sovereign over and in control of all things. While this does not prevent the "nations to rage" or frustrate the conspiracy against the Messiah, it does mean that God's redemptive plan will finally succeed. Further, this confident trust in God's ultimate triumph issues in a petition for a bold and aggressive witness even in the presence of threats (4:29-30). If the church is too timid of what others may think and does not ask God for enough "boldness" for ministry, it must have timid convictions about who God is, what God has done, and what God will do.

Acts 4:32–5:16, Interlude: "One Holy and Apostolic Church"

COMMENTARY

The apostolic leaders have now been singled out by the religious authorities of Jerusalem for special attention. Their spiritual authority and prophetic practices have disturbed and challenged those with power in the holy city (4:1-2), resulting in the arrest of Peter and John (4:3) and a hearing before the Sanhedrin court (4:5-20). The controversies and conflict provoked by the church's Jerusalem mission will only increase as the narrative unfolds, even though the reader knows that God favors, and God's Spirit empowers, the apostolic leadership team. Although the battle lines are just now drawn, we already know the eventual outcome (see 4:31). Luke pauses in his story to continue his keen interest in the Jerusalem community's inner life and especially its communal practice of sharing its possessions with one another. Similar to his first narrative summary (see 2:42-47),[199] this interlude looks back to retrieve important images of what the church should look like in every age. The reader of Acts is reminded that the church's internal witness is centered by the sharing of goods, even as its external witness is centered by the proclamation of the gospel. Both activities attract favorable attention from "the people," for they publicly demonstrate the church's common life and shared purpose under the aegis of the Holy Spirit.

Luke's second description of the Jerusalem church's common life (4:32-35) is rounded off by contrasting examples of the community's most distinctive internal practice (4:36–5:11): the redistribution of proceeds from the sale of possessions. These proceeds are "laid at the apostles' feet" (4:35, 37; 5:2) in acknowledgment of their spiritual authority and then redistributed to other members according to their financial situation so that

"there was not a needy person among them" (4:34*a*). Barnabas is an exemplar of this practice (4:36-37), while Ananias and Sapphira are negative examples whose tragic deaths underscore the vital importance of this practice as social marker and spiritual barometer for this community (5:1-11).

This interlude concludes by shifting attention once again from the post-resurrection practices of the faith community to its apostles, whose performance of "signs and wonders" (see 2:19) not only reconfirms God's favorable response to their petition for power (see 4:29-30) but also reconfirms, despite recent internal setbacks and increasing external tension, that the mission they lead continues forward under the direction and power of the Holy Spirit.

4:32-35. Luke uses a well-known rhetorical device called chiasmus[200] to summarize the Jerusalem community's internal life in a way that locates the center of its theological gravity. The apostles' magisterial office leads Luke's first summary (see 2:42-43). He begins this second summary by paying special attention to the church's distinctive practice of sharing goods (see 2:44-45) and so brackets the entire unit with the assertion that this community of believers is "of one heart and soul" (καρδία καὶ ψυχὴ μία *kardia kai psychē mia*)—they live together as loving neighbors[201]—as indicated by repudiation

199. See the Commentary on 2:42-47. The ongoing critical problem is whether these summaries are Luke's creations, and essentially "edifying fictions," or idealized, theologized portraits of what actually occurred in earliest Christianity. In the particular example of Barnabas (4:36-37), who became an important figure in earliest Christianity, Luke's narrative almost certainly reworks a personal tradition that is historically accurate and relevant. The subsequent, contrasting case of Ananias and Sapphira (5:1-10) is more difficult to assess. See Conzelmann, *The Acts of the Apostles*, 37. However, the authority of Peter and the importance of the rule of common goods form a historical nucleus.

200. The term "chiasmus" derives from the Greek letter χ, which looks like an "X" and indicates that the focus of a reader's attention should be placed at that point where "X marks the spot." As a rhetorical device, then, a chiasmus orders the details of a particular narrative unit into an inverted parallelism (ABB´A´), but then places a distinctive element of the story at its center (or "vertex")—that is, its focal point. Typically, the elements the narrator locates at the beginning and end of the unit (A//A´) its overall importance and establish a meaningful interplay with the detail the reader finds at the unit's vertex (C). In this case, the community's social solidarity, indicated by its sharing of goods (4:32//4:35*b*) is the result of appropriating God's grace and results in the abolition of the poverty that offends God (4:33*b*-44). (Letters in parentheses refer to elements in this passage's chiastic pattern.)

201. Luke is drawing on popular Greek literature for these images, in which the intimacy of close friendship was often characterized as sharing "one heart and soul" and also personal possessions. The combination of "heart and soul" also finds currency in the OT, notably in the *Shema* (Deut 6:5), to characterize Israel's love for God, which Jesus then applies to neighborly love (Luke 10:27)—even extending to strangers and enemies (Luke 10:29-37). While the Greek ideal included the practical necessity of reciprocity, Luke's description in continuity with the Lord's instruction indicates that there is no thought of payback: Sharing is a spiritual convention that is obligated out of love for God.

of private ownership and by sharing of goods (A = 4:32), redistributing them according to financial need (A´= 4:35b).

In this narrative setting, where the question of who should lead Israel has been placed squarely before the reader, Luke logically continues to point us to the spiritual authority of the Twelve. Renewed in the Spirit's power (see 4:29-31), the apostles witness "to the resurrection of the Lord Jesus" (see 1:8; cf. 4:2) "with great power [δύναμις *dynamis*]" (B = 4:33a). Indeed, now even the radical economic practices of the community are subject to the apostles' authority: "they laid [the proceeds of what was sold] at the apostles' feet"[202] (B´ = 4:34b-35a).

The resurrection practice of holding everything in common, which enjoys favorable public reputation (see 2:47), is now used as evidence of the apostles' increasing grip on the inner life and destiny of all believers. The repetition of "power" in Acts signals their competency to be prophets-like-Jesus, the medium of God's word in the world. Their power does not derive from their education or social status; it is mediated only "in the name of Jesus" (so 4:7). The function of their "great power" is to bear witness to the risen Jesus (so 1:8) and, therefore, serves only the redemptive purposes of God in continuity with Jesus (so 2:22) according to the Scriptures (cf. 2:19). Given the meaning of "power" supplied by this narrative setting, the reader resists the temptation to think of the apostles as deities and the gifts placed at their feet the equivalent of votive offerings deposited at the feet of religious shrines by pagan worshipers. They are prophets baptized with the Holy Spirit to bear powerful and effective witness of the Sovereign Creator (cf. 4:24), first to the whole house of Israel.

Luke's theological commentary on the community's internal practices is inserted at the center of this vignette to give it principal importance (4:33b-34a). At this point in Acts Luke significantly turns his earlier reference that the community enjoyed the "favor [χάρις *charis*] with all the people" (see 2:47a) toward God's favor: "and [God's] great grace [*charis*] was upon them all" (4:33b; cf.

Exod 3:21; 33:12-13).[203] The interplay between these two texts fills out Luke's theology of grace: The effective power of God's grace "upon" the assembly of believers enables it to produce those public behaviors that cultivate good will and interest (i.e., civic "favor") among outsiders. Jerusalem's rulers, otherwise upset with the apostles' teaching, did not resent the "good deed" of healing the lame man (see 4:9, 16-17).

More critically, Luke insinuates God's grace upon the community's social life so that "there was not a needy person among them." The practice of landowners selling their property and giving the proceeds over to the apostles for redistribution embodies a sociology of divine grace (4:34b). This summary recalls an element of what Jesus began to teach at Nazareth (cf. Luke 4:16-30). Different words for "favor" are repeated in that narrative to draw attention to Isaiah's promise of eschatological blessing to the poor: The promise of the Lord's "favorable year" for the poor (cf. 4:18-19; Isa 61:1-2a) is already underway among those who "hear" (or believe) the Messiah's prophetic announcement of its arrival (cf. 4:21). Before the Nazarenes turn against Jesus, they confirm the truth of his prophetic commentary as words about God's grace (4:22). The people's ironical response to the Lord's announcement is now recalled by the reader of Acts: The gift of the Holy Spirit given at Pentecost effectively mediates God's "great grace upon them all" that reforms and reshapes them into a community of goods.

4:36-37. An early exemplar of this practice is Barnabas. He is evidently influenced by God's "great grace" to sell a field and give the proceeds over to the apostles' for redistribution (4:37). But first Luke provides three salient features of Barnabas's résumé to aid a fuller understanding of his action. How so? Barnabas is a Levite. Members of the Levitical household were to be dedicated to the Lord

202. The practice of placing goods at the apostles' feet, no doubt an element of early Christian liturgy, is a nonverbal way of demonstrating submission to another of higher authority.

203. Luke's expression "grace *upon* [ἐπί *epi*] them all" (4:33b, italics added) is similar to Paul's conception of divine grace in that it denotes "the active favour of God" (Barrett, *A Critical and Exegetical Commentary on the Acts of the Apostles*, 254) and is the by-product of the Holy Spirit's work within the community. There is an important difference between Luke and Paul as well. Luke's idea of divine grace probably does not refer to the personal transformation of believers "in Christ" as in Pauline thought. Note that Luke's phrase is not "grace *in* them all" but rather "grace *upon* them all." This phrase suggests that grace functions more like an "impulse" or influence that God has "upon" the entire community to move believers in God's direction. This idea is much closer to the OT idea of God's Spirit or even the more contemporary Jewish idea of a "יצר [*yēṣir*, "impulse"] of righteousness."

and Israel's spiritual well-being rather than to the stewardship or cultivation of the promised land (Deut 12:12; Josh 14:3-4; cf. Josh 21). Even though the historical record tells us this stipulation was rarely practiced in Jewish history,[204] the inclusion of this detail in the story to illustrate the benefaction of landowners is ironical and may well deepen Luke's sense that an economic reversal has begun with Jesus and Pentecost.

Barnabas is "a native of Cyprus." That is, he is a diaspora Jew, who has become a member of the Jerusalem community. The point certainly continues from Pentecost, when many converts were from the diaspora. However, this feature of his résumé will become more important in Acts when Barnabas defends and then teams with Paul in their mission to the diaspora. Barnabas's submission to the Twelve (4:37) is harbinger of his important role as mediator between Paul and the apostles of the Jerusalem church. If Paul is something of a "loose cannon" and always suspect, Barnabas is not and adds credibility to Paul's witness in Jerusalem.

Barnabas is called Joseph, "to whom the apostles gave the name Barnabas (which means 'son of encouragement')."[205] This action echoes biblical stories of name changes, including Peter's own from "Barjona" (cf. Matt 16:17-19). Typically names change with vocational changes and indicate God's favor, as does Barnabas's obedience to the rule of this community of goods (see 4:33b-34). That the apostles changed Joseph's name underscores once again their religious authority; and thereby, Luke shows that these are social conventions of the apostolic church.

5:1-11. The story of Ananias and Sapphira survives in ignominy.[206] Luke finds it useful as a negative example of community life: If Barnabas's actions embody God's favor, then Ananias and Sapphira's actions embody God's disfavor. But does Barnabas's good example imply that the redistribution of goods is voluntary or obligatory? Can God's efficacious grace be resisted and if so what are the consequences? Finally, what is the relationship between God's grace and the community's practice? The answers to these important questions are forthcoming in this story.

5:1-2. Ananias and Barnabas belong to the same social class: They are landowners and believers who sell their property according to the community's practice of common goods and bring the proceeds to the apostles for redistribution (5:1-2). Unlike Barnabas (cf. 4:37) and subversive of the community's common practice (see 4:34b), Ananias "kept back some of the proceeds" (5:2) with his wife's consent (5:1) and knowledge (5:2). Aware that a sin has been committed, the reader may want to know whether there exists in this community a protocol for restoring a sinful believer to fellowship (cf. Matt 18:15-17). Luke's narrative returns only "blanks": we are told nothing of what transpired between verses 2 and 3, how Peter came to know what was in Ananias's "heart" (5:3; cf. 4:32) or whether Ananias was given a chance to repent and be restored (as was Simon the Samaritan, for instance; cf. 8:18-24). Luke's interests are focused on the nature of Ananias's deception and his tragic end—and on what this may teach us about the working of divine grace within the faith community.

5:3-6. Peter's rebuke of Ananias carries the weight of a death sentence (cf. 5:5), and it introduces two new elements into the story. Assuming his prophetic perspicuity, the rebuke first of all expresses God's assessment of Ananias's action:[207] His sin is prompted by Satan's filling of "his heart"[208] (5:3) rather than by the Spirit's "filling" (see 2:4), exemplified by Barnabas's generosity. The cosmic struggle between Satan and Spirit

---

204. See Josephus *Life* 68-83.

205. Luke's parenthetical comment is problematic, since the meaning of the second part of his Aramaic name, *nabas*, does not mean "consolation"; the name literally means "Son (*Bar*) of Nebo (*nabas*)" (see Isa 46:1). I take it that Luke knew as much and that the purpose of his parenthetical comment is to stipulate the *motive* of the name change (i.e., its connotative meaning) rather than its literal meaning.

206. Fitzmyer, *The Acts of the Apostles*, 317, says that this story is "the main incident in Acts that raises questions about the historical value of the Lucan narrative as a whole." Because it relates to the community's practice of redistributing goods, the story's essential plotline seems likely; although composed as an "edifying tale," it nevertheless tells of a known couple and something that happened to them. Without question, Luke reworks the story delivered him by his Jerusalem sources, whatever its form and substance, to fit well into his narrative and illustrate his theological conception.

207. This is not to say that Peter is a "divine man" who can read hearts; the narrative does not indicate how he came to know Ananias's motives and is not important to the story. Peter is an inspired prophet whose analysis is "of God." See Fitzmyer, *The Acts of the Apostles*, 322-23.

208. The "heart" symbolizes one's internal decision-making apparatus. When "Satan," who personifies evil in Luke's narrative world (Luke 10:18; 11:18; 13:16; 22:3, 31; Acts 26:18), enters the believer's heart the result will be to turn that person toward apostasy and treachery. This reference to "heart" probably cues the earlier reference to the community's "one heart" (4:32): Ananias's action was not in solidarity with other believers; however, the presumption of this story is that he is a full member of the faith community.

has its historical precipitate in Ananias's decision to depart from the community's practice, to remove himself out from "under" God's "great grace" (χάρις μεγάλη *charis megalē* 4:33*b*), and to deceive the apostles and therefore the Spirit.[209]

Moreover, Ananias is deceived because he remains ignorant of the participatory nature of God's "great grace." Peter tells him that the believer retains ownership of property and the personal freedom to do with it what he wants. Thus, if surrendered to the apostles, it is by voluntary action and the result of a individual choice rather than by apostolic coercion (5:4).[210] Ananias is not charged with failure to sell his property or to place the proceeds at the apostles' feet (cf. 5:1-2) but with deception. His act undermines the accord of the community of goods and the authority of the apostles.[211]

A further question from Peter reveals that Ananias is also engaged in a theological deception: "How is it that you have contrived this deed in your heart?" (5:4). His deception of the community (and its Spirit) is finally not Satan's handiwork but the result of a decision that Ananias himself makes by resisting the influence of God's "great grace" (4:33*b*), without which such promises are impossible to keep.[212] The practices of the common life cannot be obeyed out of a sense of duty or as a requirement of saving grace; compliance results as the believer freely responds to the prompting of God's grace.

In hearing Peter's verdict, Ananias dropped dead and was buried, and "great fear seized all who heard of it" (5:5; see 2:43). The reader must presume his is not an accidental or coincidental death. Rather, Peter's words are a death sentence, and Ananias is removed from the community of goods.[213]

5:7-11. The second new element follows the first: Three hours after Ananias's death, his unwitting wife, Sapphira, comes before the apostle (5:7). She, too, receives his rebuke (5:9; cf. 5:3-4), and she also dies upon hearing it and is buried "beside her husband" (5:10; cf. 5:6). The second act concludes on the same note: "Great fear seized the whole church and all who heard about these events" (5:11; cf. 5:5). Critically, the flow of this parallelism is interrupted, however, by Peter's initial query of her: "Tell me, is this the price you and Ananias got for the land?" (5:8). The reader knows that even though Sapphira entered "not knowing" what had happened to her husband (5:7), she did know his deception fully (cf. 5:2). That is, Peter exposes her as Ananias's accomplice. Yet, at another level, Peter's question invites Sapphira's repentance and restoration. Had she not lied in response, Peter's judgment would not have been rendered. Again, his questioning of Sapphira underscores the importance of the believer's choices in determining the outcome of God's provident care of God's people.

5:12-16. The final pericope of Luke's interlude concentrates the reader's attention even more keenly on the Twelve, their prophetic powers, and their growing influence among "the people" of God that now stretches beyond the city limits of Jerusalem (5:16). Luke is preparing the reader for the next story of the church's Jerusalem mission when the apostles' authority comes under attack again.

Much of this summary is familiar to the reader of Acts: The theological implication of the phrase "signs and wonders" (5:12) is deduced by its earlier uses (see 2:22, 43; 4:16, 22, 30) as the continuing realization of Joel's prophecy about the Spirit's outpouring in "the last days" of Israel's history (see 2:19). The apostles, through whom the Spirit's "signs and wonders" are performed in Jerusalem, are God's endtime prophets who are called and empowered to gather Israel together for the day of their salvation. While their prophetic ministry to this point in

---

209. The parallelism between Luke's stories of Ananias and Judas (see 1:16-20) is often noted by commentators: Both are insiders who are cursed by God because of actions taken against the community for love of money—in Judas's case, to betray God's Messiah, and in Ananias's case to lie to God's Spirit. Of course, the shift of referent to the Spirit in Luke's narrative of Ananias's deception makes sense only after Pentecost.

210. The community of goods is often compared to the Essene community at Qumran. Luke's narrative, however, makes clear an important difference between the two: The Essenes required the surrender of all property upon admission to membership as an element of their vow to deny the world; the Jerusalem community did not require compliance to the rule of common goods for membership. Evidently, this was a choice that each made in counsel with the Holy Spirit.

211. Johnson, *The Acts of the Apostles*, 88.

212. Why Ananias resists God's grace is not stated. Luke's use of possessions as a narrative theme suggests that he is deeply concerned to spell out the spiritual pitfalls of trying to juggle the secular socioeconomic values with a vital piety. Therefore, the interpreter may reasonably assume that Ananias falls victim to theological deception and resists the influence of God's grace because of his undue acquisitiveness.

213. Witherington, *The Acts of the Apostles*, 216, constructs a plausible historical explanation. Ananias suffers a fatal heart attack resulting from being publicly unmasked and shamed by Peter's words.

Acts has focused on their inspired interpretation of Scripture and powerful proclamation of the word, here Luke adds a more detailed summary of their healing ministry that brings them more completely into continuity with the Lord Jesus, who similarly healed and cast out the demons of those who came to him from surrounding towns (5:15-16; cf. Luke 4:40-41 and par.). Despite the disapproval of the rulers of "official" Israel (see 4:5-31), their prophetic ministry evidently continues with increasing success "among the people" (5:12; cf. 4:17). Indeed, Luke tells us that "more and more believed in the Lord" (5:14; cf. 2:41; 4:4). These numinous images are used to persuade us of the Twelve's enormous and compelling powers. Indeed, they are so astounding—even extending to Peter's shadow (5:15)![214]—and intimidating that "the rest" of the people are too afraid to believe

and "dared not join" (5:13) the congregation gathered at the Temple's Solomon's Portico for worship (see 3:11). Why does Luke add this puzzling reference to "the rest" (τὰ λοιπά *ta loipa*) who "dared not join" (οὐδεὶς ἐτόλμα κολλᾶσθαι *oudeis etolma kollasthai*) the remnant community for worship (5:13a)?[215] Unlike the hostile rulers of Jerusalem these nonbelieving Jews "held the apostles in high regard" (5:13b). Despite the apostles' great success and growing public acclaim, "the rest" of Israel did not join the faithful remnant at Solomon's Portico because they had not yet called upon the name of the Lord and were not yet saved.

214. The referent behind "Peter's shadow" is uncertain and is perhaps closest to the gospel's story of the woman touching Jesus' garment as he walked by (Luke 8:43 and par.) or Greek myths of "divine men." While no doubt hyperbolic, the reader cannot miss Luke's point: Peter radiates the power of God for the purpose of witness and (now) leadership.

215. Haenchen, *The Acts of the Apostles*, 242, admits that the exegete is "helpless" in determining the meaning of Luke's phrase "the rest who dared not join." Conzelmann, *The Acts of the Apostles*, 39, blames Luke for a "clumsy" narrative. In any case, it is doubtful that "the rest" refers to those believers who are not apostles. So R. Pesch, *Die Apostelgeschichte*, 2 vols., EKKNT 5 (Zurich: Benziger, 1986) 1:206; Johnson, *The Acts of the Apostles*, 95), since they are contrasted with "all" the believers of 5:12. With Barrett and others, then, it seems best to understand "the rest" as nonbelievers. See Barrett, *A Critical and Exegetical Commentary on the Acts of the Apostles*, 274. Perhaps Luke has in mind the implied distinction in the OT prophetic writings between a faithful remnant within Israel and "the rest" (or unfaithful) Israel (e.g., Isa 11:11; 37:31-32; Jer 6:9; 44:7, 12-13, 28).

REFLECTIONS

1. "With great power the apostles gave their testimony to the resurrection of the Lord Jesus" (4:33a NRSV). Acts 4:32-35 is read on the Second Sunday of Easter with John's account of the Spirit's arrival—the so-called Johannine Pentecost (cf. John 20:19-31). This Gospel lesson includes the poignant and important exchange between Jesus and Thomas, who demands and is given the hard evidence of the Lord's resurrection. Their conversation together on the evening of the first Easter concludes with Jesus' pronouncement of blessing on those who believe without seeing him in the flesh. The earlier arrival of the Spirit helps the interpreter understand what Jesus implies: The Spirit's life within the community of disciples in the Lord's absence will help shape and fortify relationships between them that will cultivate faith and bring others to faith. A vital and vigorous faith in the living Jesus can only be formed within a community of the Spirit. This lesson from the Gospel is the pretext for this lesson from Acts. The powerful images collected together in this passage—among the most radical in Scripture related to our possessions—are interpreted under the light of Easter and Pentecost. Indeed, the formation of a community of goods is a *realistic* prospect only because God's transforming benevolence symbolized by the resurrection is now realized wherever the Holy Spirit resides.

2. "There was not a needy person among them" (4:34 NRSV). Possessions are an important symbol of power. How possessions are used provide important social markers about the nature of human relations within particular groups, whether families or churches. The value we place on private ownership, not only on what we purchase but the motives for acquiring particular brands or models, is an expression of our inmost and utmost loyalties. Few biblical books are as important as Acts in providing the church with teaching and exemplars about the proper use of our wealth. Other books, such as James, are important in helping their faithful readers form proper attitudes and responses while struggling with the poverty and powerlessness of a socially marginal existence. This is not the case with Acts, whose implied audience has wealth to share with others and whose poverty is more spiritual than social. Both the positive (Barnabas) and negative (Ananias and Sapphira) examples have wealth; moreover, their stories pay little attention to the effects of their generosity or greed upon the community's poor. The importance of this passage and others like it in Acts (see the Reflections at 2:42-47), then, is to provide its readers with principles and illustrations that encourage the formation of a community of goods that exemplifies friendship and spiritual maturity by the manner it handles its wealth.

3. "Those who believed were of one heart and soul" (4:32 NRSV). The first principle the community of goods follows is one of perspective. A way of thinking is decisive to a way of doing. This is especially true of human relationships, which is why in Matthew's Sermon on the Mount Jesus ratchets up the manner of a "righteous" life by giving equal moral weight to the way the disciple thinks of another (see Matt 5:21-48). Luke begins his summary of the community's life together with this familiar description of friendship among Greek moral philosophers. "All is shared between friends," Aristotle taught. Congregational solidarity evinces more than shared beliefs; to share "one heart and soul" implies a level of intimacy with and commitment to others that blurs the boundaries of personal rights or private property. A community of goods is a community full of friends. It is important, therefore, to cultivate a way of thinking about other believers as precious friends, as "soulmates." To the extent we come to value others and what they need more than we do our possessions and what we want, we will come to think of what we own as "common property."

4. "As many as owned lands or houses sold them and brought the proceeds of what was sold. They laid it at the apostles' feet, and it was distributed to each as any had need" (4:34b-35 NRSV). The proper exercise of spiritual authority is crucial in the formation of a community of friends. It is difficult to mobilize a people to "practice resurrection" in their common life without having competent leaders who instruct and exemplify the principles that warrant such a practice. The apostles lead by example in a manner that inspires trust and reverence and prompts the believers to submit to them for the good of the whole. They are also the distribution center of the community's life; they are in a position to know all who have need and they have the maturity to discern what an equitable distribution of goods entails. What would it mean in our own time for Christian leaders to invigorate and inspire the church by their teaching and example to act against the grain of an acquisitive and materialistic culture?

5. "And great grace was upon them all" (4:33b NRSV). The act of laying proceeds at the apostles' feet not only symbolizes submission to their religious authority over the community's life; it also symbolizes a self-emptying spirituality that follows the pattern of Jesus' suffering for the salvation of others. One does not just do generosity; new habits of mind and spirit must be developed before new religious practices occur. The problem with the Greek pattern of friendship according to which all things were shared between kindred spirits is that human will left to itself rarely accommodates such an ideal. The experience of God's transforming grace—God's "great grace"—enables believers to work in partnership with God through dispossession of their self-interest.

6. "Tell me whether you and your husband sold the land for such and such a price" (5:8 NRSV). J. Polhill remarks that the teacher of this hard passage "must not pass (it) off—as an adjunct to Luke's ideal portrait of the church. If the incident makes us feel uncomfortable, it should. It deals with money—and the pitfalls of wealth."[216] Peter's

---

216. J. P. Polhill, *The Acts of the Apostles* (Nashville: Broadman, 1992) 162.

question to Sapphira cuts to the heart of the lessons learned in this story. The community of goods must first of all be a community of friends. The religious practice of generosity envisages a new and elevated way of seeing other believers that is possible only by reliance upon the grace of God. Peter gives Sapphira the chance to retreat from her earlier conspiracy with her husband to choose greed over grace. Her marital relationship with Ananias is the most intimate friendship possible between human beings; the interpreter must imagine how difficult it is to choose against one's spouse. Yet her apostasy is precisely that she chose in favor of him rather than God, breaking the circle of friendship that joined their community in "one heart and soul."

7. "But the people held them in high esteem" (5:13 NRSV). What is it that nonbelievers—"the people"—recognized about the apostles? Clearly they offered a charismatic leadership in a different key from that sounded by other leaders in Jerusalem. But new patterns of leadership, as with most fads, wear quickly. Luke's profile of the apostles in this passage concentrates on two enduring attributes that galvanize a public's attention. First, they were power brokers: Acts displaying God's resurrection power were "done among the people through the apostles" (5:12a) and "they were all cured" (5:16b). The exercise of these "signs and wonders" is not for self-promotion, which was evidently of little concern to the apostles. They mediated God's power to make *others* whole. Second, they were found in Solomon's Portico at the Temple (5:12b; see 3:11) doing what was forbidden by those in charge of public propriety. Later Peter will tell the Sanhedrin simply and modestly that "we must obey God rather than human authority" (see 5:29). The courage of one's core convictions is the substance of which heroes are made. This was certainly true in Luke's world; it is true in our own day as well. Thus, while the people largely ignore the council's authority (cf. 5:41-42), Peter's presence evokes the fear of God (5:11).

Acts 5:17-42, Story Three: The Apostles vs. the Sanhedrin, Round Two

COMMENTARY

The plotline and logic of the third story of Luke's Jerusalem cycle unfolds according to its missionary pattern: (1) The opening episode (5:17-23) tells of God's wondrous intervention on behalf of the imprisoned apostles, (2) whose unexplained escape "perplexes" their hostile captors (5:24-28). (3) The result is to mistake the motive and content of the apostles' teaching ministry in Jerusalem, which leads to Peter's kerygmatic clarification (5:29-32). (4) Peter's gospel proclamation occasions both increased conflict between the opposing leaders of a divided Israel (5:33-40) and the joyful obedience of the apostles (5:41-42).

The elements of this narrative unit are broadly reminiscent of Luke's second story (see 4:5-31), which suggests that they were written to be read together as mutually

interpreting narratives of apostolic vocation and authority.[217] Yet Luke introduces new themes into this account, two of which are noteworthy in expanding our understanding of the apostles' prophetic vocation and spiritual authority. The "angel of the Lord" (ἄγγελος κυρίου *angelos kyriou*) makes its first appearance in Acts (5:19; cf. 7:30, 35, 38; 8:26; 10:3; 12:7-11, 23; 27:23). Although a few commentators suggest that a Hellenistic motif supplies a working model for the angel's role

217. Such literary doublets are characteristic of Luke's narrative art—e.g., the broad parallelism between the story of Pentecost in Acts and the subsequent story of Peter and John's healing of the lame man. The modern discussion of Lukan doublets puzzles over whether there is a single historical referent behind them or whether there are sufficient differences in detail and sources to warrant the conclusion that these stories are of two different events. See Fitzmyer, *The Acts of the Apostles*, 332. Whatever one's conclusion is on this point, it seems evident that Luke's intention is for his readers to read similar stories reflexively, the details of the one filling in the narrative gaps and thickening the meaning of the other.

in Acts,[218] angelic intervention is also a common literary theme of biblical narrative. Angels are not merely agents of divine power who are able to reorder historical circumstances according to God's plans; they also deliver messages that disclose the theological particulars of God's word. These narrated angelic activities insinuate God's provident control into events that seem out of control or to be threatening God's redemptive plans.

The other new feature of this story is Gamaliel's speech (5:34-40). The protocol that allows for his speech and reaction to it provides an important perspective on the Sanhedrin. But Gamaliel speaks as a Pharisee. Depending on whether the reader perceives the motive of his speech to be ironic or supportive of the apostles' mission, Luke's subtext may intend to set the political programs and intentions of the Sadducean and Pharisaic parties at odds for future reference (see 22:30–23:10). The reader could suppose at the outset of this story that the Pharisees, whose core beliefs (Messiah, resurrection, restored Israel, a coming new order, spirit world) are similar to those already proclaimed by Peter and later by Paul, would naturally be more supportive of the apostles' teaching ministry than the Sadducees; this story may confirm such a suspicion.[219] In any case, the profile of the Pharisees in Acts, where some become believers (15:5) and Paul professes loyalty to his Pharisaic roots (23:6-9; 26:5), is in sharp contrast to that of the Gospels, where Pharisees unite with other religious and political groups in opposition to Jesus (see Matt 22:23–23:39; cf. Luke 13:31).[220]

5:17-23. There is good reason for the high priest, the chief justice of the Sanhedrin and leader of "the sect of the Sadducees"[221] (5:17), to be upset with the apostles. Earlier this same council had demanded their silence (cf. 4:21), perhaps even implying their acquiescence to the Sadducees' political authority in Jerusalem. Their demand went unheeded. In fact, the incorrigible apostles petitioned God for even greater prophetic boldness (cf. 4:24-30), with dramatic results evident in both internal (4:31–5:11) and external (5:12-16) venues. Sharply put, the people feared the apostles and were attracted to their message in increasing numbers, while the Sadducees were "filled with jealousy"[222] (5:17). The result is as we might anticipate: they arrest the apostles, not only Peter and John as before, and lock them all up in "the public prison" (τήρησις δημοσία *tērēsis dēmosia* 5:18).[223]

Luke's clipped narrative of the angel's jailhouse intervention includes the two essential components of divine assistance: the liberating act and the commanding word (cf. Gen 16:7-11; 22:10-18; 31:11-13; Exod 3:2-6).[224] Under the cover of night, an angel is dispatched by Jesus to free his apostles from jail.[225] The "prison escape" is a literary theme that symbolizes the futile attempt to subvert the redemptive purposes of God by silencing God's prophetic word. In this setting, where those attached to the Temple are responsible for their arrest, the apostles are instructed to continue their ministry "in the temple." They and not the Sanhedrin elders are the legitimate leaders of Israel; they are the ones who are called and empowered by God to teach the people. The liberation of the apostles to preach the gospel "in the temple" makes clear the triumph of "the whole message about this life" they proclaim over all other

---

218. E.g., Johnson, *The Acts of the Apostles*, 97, mentions Euripides' tale of Bacchus liberating a group of his persecuted followers from prison. See also Euripides *Bacchae* 346-640.

219. Kee, *To Every Nation Under Heaven*, 83-84, reminds us that the Pharisees were hardly the "pious nitpickers" or rigid legalists of popular distain, but were rather devout believers who sought to live life in conformity with the Law of Moses as Scripture taught it ("written law") and as they interpreted it ("oral law"). They often met in informal groups for Bible study and prayer, and demanded rigorous attention to religious and moral purity in obedience to God.

220. See Tannehill, *The Acts of the Apostles*, 2:67.

221. Even though the word "sect" (αἵρεσις *hairesis*) is the root of "heresy," and may denote this in Paul's judicial although ironical use in 24:14 (cf. 24:5), its meaning here is political and refers to a party (so also 15:5). See Conzelmann, *The Acts of the Apostles*, 41.

222. "Jealousy" translates ζῆλος (*zēlos*), a term that typically appears in contemporary catalogues of moral vices. While some interpreters want to give it a religious meaning—a zeal for the truth (see Barrett, *A Critical and Exegetical Commentary on the Acts of the Apostles*, 283)—Luke's use of it in Acts is clearly a negative judgment on the moral character of those to whom it is assigned (cf. 13:45). This observation is made more important by Luke's connection of character with one's ability to discern truth. Johnson, *The Acts of the Apostles*, 98, notes that "envy" is often the chief motive for murder in Hellenistic moral philosophy, which may explain the Sanhedrin's murderous reaction to Peter's speech in 5:33.

223. The phrase "the public prison" has two plausible meanings, and scholars are divided as to which is best here. Both the NIV and the NRSV take *dēmosia* as an adjective, "public," modifying "prison"; but others take *dēmosia* as an adverb to emphasize the more public or demonstrative nature of the arrest. See Haenchen, *The Acts of the Apostles*, 249.

224. Dunn is puzzled by Luke's matter-of-fact and abbreviated narrative of this episode, when compared to the later and more fulsome parallel story of Peter's prison escape (12:6-11; cf. 16:23-24). He suggests that the jailbreak of 5:17-18 was the bold work of a sympathizer on the prison staff, whose role in the church's retelling of the story was likened to the "angel of the Lord." See Dunn, *The Acts of the Apostles*, 67-68.

225. The phrase "of the Lord" translates the genitive noun *kyriou* (Jesus; 2:36) and denotes here the source from which the "angel" (*angelos*) derives rather than the angelic appearance of the exalted Lord Jesus.

alternatives.[226] Obedient to the angel's (= the Lord's) instruction, the apostles return to the Temple "at daybreak and went on with their teaching"[227] (5:21a).

The following panel paints a somewhat sarcastic portrait of the high priest and his Sadducean entourage (cf. 5:17). They arrive prepared to indict their prisoners (5:21b), only to find them missing (5:22) without reasonable explanation (5:23; the literary intent is the rough equivalent of "rubbing it in"). The Sadducees, who convened this assembly to demonstrate their confidence and authority, are shamed before their judicial and cultural peers.[228] Indeed, at the very moment of their humiliation, the apostles are teaching the people of Jerusalem in the Temple—the one place the Sadducees presumed to have control!

5:24-28. The central character of this brief episode is "the captain of the temple" (5:24, 26). He is responsible for the safeguard of the prisoners and is especially affected by the apostles' disappearance. He is "perplexed," no doubt because he worries what will become of his career and the future of those he serves and who serve him. The reader of Acts, however, is familiar with this response to the activity of God. In fact, the very word that translates "perplexed" (διαπορέω *diaporeō*) is used earlier by Luke to describe the response of pious Jews to the miraculous speech at Pentecost (see 2:12). There as here, perplexity is the response of an eyewitness who lacks understanding to interpret the theological significance of a miracle for the future of Israel.

When the captain and his assistants receive the report that the prisoners "are standing in the temple and teaching the people" according to the angel's instruction, their initial response is as it should be: Police are duty-bound to retrieve their prisoners and bring them to "stand before the council." But

Luke's description suggests anything but the ordinary! What seems strange, even comical, is that the captain takes extraordinary precaution "because they were afraid of being stoned by the people" (5:26). Surely their fear is another indication of the apostles' popular support in Jerusalem. However, the precise nature of their fear—"of being stoned" by pious Jews—indicates that the support for the apostles is *religious* in nature. Execution by stoning, while illegal in Roman provinces, might be carried out on the sly by devout Jews on any other Jew suspected of blasphemy. This emotional response of the temple police to the apostles is further evidence that at the popular level religious authority in Jerusalem has shifted to the apostles; the Sanhedrin has every reason to be concerned.

This new political reality is the subtext of the high priest's scolding of the apostles: "We ordered you to stop teaching in this name" (5:28). They have disobeyed the Council's ban (see 4:18) in obedience to God's command with the result of increased power and widespread popularity—such that even now the opponents fear for their lives! The high priest's accusation reflects his theological obduracy as well and underscores the real reason for the shift of religious power in Jerusalem. His comment that the apostles "are determined to bring this man's blood *upon us*"[229] (5:28, italics added) not only reflects the arrogance of his institutional authority but also the mistaken presumption that the actions of the apostles are politically motivated. However, the apostles teach because it is their prophetic vocation to do so; and they teach in the temple's courtyard because they are instructed to do so by the "angel of the Lord."

5:29-32. As in the prior stories of Acts, Peter is prompted to speak out to correct mistakes made by perplexed nonbelievers (see 2:13; 3:11; 4:13-17). Luke adds "and the apostles" to Peter's answer, not because all of them spoke in unison but because they stood united in agreement with what Peter said, acknowledging his apostolic authority for saying it. In this setting, the mistake

226. "This life" probably recalls Peter's earlier title for Jesus, "Author of life" (ἀρχηγός τῆς ζωῆς *archēgos tēs zoēs*; see 3:15) and indicates "the new life offered by Jesus," which is similar in meaning to Paul's subsequent phrase "message of this salvation" in 13:26. The angel's reference to "people" (ὁ λαός *ho laos*) refers to the "people of Israel," who are the first recipients of this good news (see 3:17). See Barrett, *A Critical and Exegetical Commentary on the Acts of the Apostles*, 284.

227. Josephus *Antiquities of the Jews* 18.29 tells us that while the gates to the Temple remained open through the night, faithful Jews began their day of worship "at daybreak." Luke no doubt adds this small detail to his narrative to emphasize the piety of the apostles and their spiritual authority to lead faithful Israel.

228. See Haenchen, *The Acts of the Apostles*, 250-51.

229. The antecedent of "upon us" (ἐφ᾽ ἡμᾶς *eph᾽ hēmas*) is unclear, since in earlier teaching Peter blamed the Jewish people generally (see 2:23; 3:13) but notably their rulers as well (3:17). Almost certainly in this comment, however, the high priest has only the Sanhedrin in mind. See Barrett, *A Critical and Exegetical Commentary on the Acts of the Apostles*, 288.

made by the high priest is to assume that he is the political target of an opposition party led by these apostles: They were teaching in the Temple to provoke a popular uprising against Sanhedrin (or Sadducean) authority in order to replace the council with the Apostolate as the center of religious (and political) authority in Jerusalem.[230] Peter's famous and provocative reply attempts to make clear the true motive: "We must obey God rather than men [i.e., the men—no women!—seated on the Sanhedrin]!" (5:29; see 4:19-20; cf. Num 22:38). Even though it is a more sharply stated version of what was said before to the Council, Peter's reply is puzzling because it does not directly respond to the high priest's accusation, as one might expect of a judicial retort. It is more puzzling because on face value Peter's statement is tautological in a Jewish setting: The high priest, a dedicated monotheist, would surely not disagree with Peter's claim, nor with Peter's assumption that it is biblically based. Peter's opening comment reminds the council that the principal concern of religious leadership is theological, not political or institutional or personal.[231] Indeed, Gamaliel's exhortation that follows (see 5:33-39) provides additional commentary on Peter's assertion and essentially agrees with it.

What follows in Peter's speech, however, commends a missionary motive: In a wonderfully concise way, Peter preaches the gospel to the council![232] By repeating "God," Luke shapes this speech to provide a normative definition of obedience "to God rather than men." Simply put, to obey God means to confirm as true the claims of the Christian gospel. This seems so because "the God of our ancestors raised up Jesus" (5:30) and "exalted him . . . that he might give repentance to Israel"

(5:31) and give the Holy Spirit "to those who obey [God]" (5:32). From beginning to end, the claims of the apostles about Israel's restoration are framed by God's decisive and determinative action. The claims are in continuity with Israel's traditions and interests—the God who restores Israel through Jesus is the same "God of our ancestors." To "obey God" rather than human authority is to obey the demands of this gospel to repent and be baptized (see 2:38).

These claims are stated here in outline much like a confession of faith, since Peter has already addressed each point in earlier speeches (see 2:22-40; 3:12-26; 4:8-12, 19-20). Yet, this speech is more prophetic and provocative than those that have come before. Peter's reference to Jesus' death— "whom you had killed by hanging him on a tree"—is graphic in a way the earlier speeches were not. The verb translated as "you had killed" (διεχειρίσασθε *diecheirisasthe*; cf. 26:21) is a judicial charge of premeditated murder made in a courtroom, a charge made only slightly less severe by reversing the order of Jesus' death and resurrection. That is, the Sanhedrin's decision about Jesus was not God's and therefore—fortunately for them—not final or permanent. Peter also calls Jesus' crucifixion a lynching—"you had [him] killed by hanging him on a tree" (5:30). The phrase clearly alludes to the prescription found in Deut 21:22-23 about the burial of Israel's worst criminals who are cursed by God.[233] Used in this speech before a council that had condemned Jesus to death, the intertextual echo deepens the enormity of their previous error: Rather than Israel's traitor cursed by God, Jesus is Israel's "Leader and Savior" (ἀρχηγός καὶ σωτήρ *archēgos kai sōtēr*) exalted by God (5:31; cf. 2:36).

This is the first time the title "Savior" (*sōtēr*) is used for Jesus in Acts (cf. Luke 2:11; Acts 13:23). Its importance for Luke is indicated not only by the appended "that he might give repentance to Israel and forgiveness of sins" (5:31; see 2:38) but also by recalling Joel's prophecy that salvation comes to those

230. Haenchen, *The Acts of the Apostles*, 251, thinks the high priest may also be worried that the apostles are calling upon God to punish the Sanhedrin for their role in the execution of Jesus, which would certainly be in keeping with their role as Israel's judges (cf. Luke 22:30) and consistent with the narrator's explanation of Judas's demise (see 1:16-19).

231. Haenchen, *The Acts of the Apostles*, 251, rightly adds that Peter's response "stands as an example to all readers of how the Apostles bear witness before the authorities, whose guilt in the death of Jesus they fearlessly expose."

232. Peter's speech serves as Luke's summary of Peter's prior kerygmatic speeches to his Jewish audiences. He emphasizes here as before the Jewish rejection of Jesus, and his resulting death, resurrection, and ascension as the enactment of God's plan for restoring Israel. Luke uses these speeches to ameliorate the ignorance of the Jewish people and their rulers (3:17), which will lead to their repentance and conversion (3:19) and finally to their prophesied role as healing agent in God's repair of all creation (3:20).

233. Fitzmyer, *The Acts of the Apostles*, 337, refers to a citation of the Deuteronomy text in the Temple Scroll of Qumran (11QT 64:7-12) that reserves death by "hanging on a tree" for those found guilty of treason against the people of Israel. If Luke is aware of this use of Deut 21:23, the irony of Peter's statement is deepened significantly, especially if the council has in mind to charge the apostles with treason. In fact, it is the council that has acted against God's best interests for the people of Israel.

who "call upon the name of the Lord" (see 2:21; cf. 2:38).[234] We are reminded again that God must be obeyed because the kerygmatic claims that map Israel's repentance accord with the prophecies of Israel's Scripture.

Peter's speech concludes by claiming, "we are witnesses to these things," which connects his summary of the gospel with the apostolic vocation as commissioned by this same Jesus (see 1:8) and with various speeches since (see 2:32; 3:15; 4:33). The familiar connection of apostolic testimony with the Holy Spirit glosses Peter's opening statement that the apostles obey God rather than Sanhedrin, not only because their testimony is also centered on God's redemptive activity but also because it is inspired by God's Spirit. Peter's appeal to the Spirit as given by God "to those who obey God" (5:32) authorizes both what the apostles teach and the results of their teaching, since the verb "has given" (ἔδωκεν *edōken*) recalls the giving of the Spirit at Pentecost (see 2:38). More provocatively, however, Peter may well be suggesting that without the gift of the Holy Spirit, the Sanhedrin lacks the spiritual resources to understand the claims he has just made.

5:33-42. The final panel of this story describes the Council's reaction to Peter's speech. At first its membership is "enraged and wanted to kill [the apostles]" (5:33; see 5:17). Not only were the apostles insubordinate by refusing to obey the Sanhedrin's ban against their public teaching, but Peter's speech effectively exposed the illegitimacy of their claim to lead God's people. The Temple and all that it symbolizes—including the religious authority of the Sadducees—has been given over to the apostles for their teaching ministry (see 5:20). This excludes the Council not only from political power but also from participation in the restored Israel and its blessings!

It is left to Rabban Gamaliel to bring peace. Not much is known about this Gamaliel, the purported teacher of Paul (so Acts 22:3), other than what Luke gives us in 5:34: He was "a Pharisee in the council—a teacher of

the law and respected by all the people."[235] More critically, the motive of his speech remains unclear. Its plain intent appears to be conciliatory and supportive of Luke's theological emphasis on God's sovereignty, expressed aptly by Peter's earlier retort "we must obey God rather than men"—and this is how most scholars take it.[236] If we are to assume from 5:33 that the threat to kill the apostles is real, even though unlikely given their popularity, then Gamaliel's persuasive speech may well have had a conciliatory intention.

L. T. Johnson, however, has challenged this consensus in a penetrating analysis of Gamaliel's "little speech."[237] According to Johnson, the first readers of Luke-Acts recall that a malevolent Gamaliel had previously participated in various damning decisions resulting in Jesus' death, to which Peter has just referred, and the flogging of his apostles. Peter excuses no one sitting on the Sanhedrin from these previous crimes (5:30-31); and, Johnson contends, neither should the reader. Further, the historical examples of Theudas (5:36) and Judas (5:37) that Gamaliel uses to argue his case have the rhetorical effect of "reducing Jesus to the status of those 'would-be' prophets and kings."[238] Johnson finds Gamaliel's advice, therefore, disingenuous. He is a leading example of the hypocrisy of the Pharisees who aspire to prudence but who then refuse to obey the word of God (Matt 23:13-29; Luke 11:44).[239] The reader also may wonder why the high priest, a Sadducee, would allow Gamaliel, a Pharisee, to

---

234. Jesus' dying and rising gives Israel "the opportunity" for repentance; God does not restore Israel independent of its repentance. See Conzelmann, *The Acts of the Apostles*, 42. Further, Luke assumes the necessity of Peter's kerygmatic proclamation; the opportunity to convert to Jesus does not present itself outside of the apostolic mission.

235. It was said of Gamaliel upon his death that "when Rabban Gamaliel the Elder died, the glory of the law ceased, and purity and abstinence died" (*m.Sotah* 9:15); see also Fitzmyer, *The Acts of the Apostles*, 339.

236. See Witherington, *The Acts of the Apostles*, 233-35, for a summary of this consensus.

237. Johnson, *The Acts of the Apostles*, 99-103.

238. Johnson, *The Acts of the Apostles*, 103. Johnson notes that the verbal ideas Luke uses echo both the prophetic ministry and resurrection of Jesus in a way that discredits him. Thus, Theudas "rose up—but was killed"; and then Judas "rose up—and also perished." I would add that the order in both Luke's references to these insurrectionists is first to their "rising up" and then to their death, which follows the order of Peter's speech (see 5:30-31) as if to mock his kerygmatic claims for Jesus. The notorious critical problem raised about Luke's misdating of Theudas's popular uprising—it actually took place in the mid-40s according to Josephus, about ten years after Gamaliel's speech!—and reversing its order with the earlier one led by Judas falls within the literary conventions of ancient historiography and does not finally subvert the point he has Gamaliel make in this speech. See Dunn, *The Acts of the Apostles*, 73. Bruce's solution that Gamaliel may be referring to a different Theudas seems like special pleading. See Bruce, *The Acts of the Apostles*, 176.

239. Luke's use of "plan" (ἡ βουλή *hē boulē*) in 5:38 ironically echoes its earlier uses in 2:23 and 4:28 of God's plan disclosed in the death and resurrection of Jesus (cf. Luke 7:29). That is, Gamaliel speaks of the apostolic mission as "this plan," which the faithful reader understands as God's plan but which Gamaliel thinks is of human derivation.

address the Council on a non-halakic case unless he anticipated his support. If Johnson's interpretation is accepted, the necessary conclusion is that unrepentant Gamaliel expects the apostles to fail and his verdict is a cynical one: "if it is of God, you will not be able to overthrow them—in that case you may even be found fighting against God" (5:39a). That the council is "convinced" by a disingenuous Gamaliel only indicates the depth of their obduracy (5:39b)![240]

And so the apostles are released—but not before they are "flogged—and ordered not to speak in the name of Jesus" (5:40; cf. 4:18). Their joyful response to suffering is in stark contrast to the Council's response to them and expands their profile as prophets of God and leaders of restored Israel, who

are "worthy to suffer dishonor for the sake of the name" (5:41).[241] Whether in the Temple or in the households (see 2:46) the apostles continue to live within their prophetic vocation "to teach and proclaim Jesus as the Messiah" (5:42). These concluding words have a "rounding off effect" on the reader.[242] Not only has Luke supplied a succinct summary of Peter's missionary speeches in Acts (5:29-32); here he describes the practical results of obeying God rather than humans. The community's priestly opposition, while continuing to wield judicial authority, can do nothing to deter the apostles from continuing to proclaim "the name of Jesus." At the end of this day, the conflict between these two groups of leaders dissolves in favor of the apostles.

---

240. Luke's use of a language of "power" to conclude Gamaliel's speech ("you will not be able to overthrow [δύναμαι *dynamai*, lit., 'to have power'] them") reflects God's ultimate control over human affairs but also echoes the apostles' appropriation of the Spirit's "power" (δύναμις *dynamis*) in service of God (see 1:8). While Gamaliel believes in God's sovereign power, he is evidently unconvinced that God's power and authority—God's *dynamis*—are vested in either Jesus or his apostles.

241. The pattern of suffering as a result of proclaiming the word of the Lord is distinctively Lukan. It will be a decisive motive in shaping the plotline of his story of Paul's mission (see 9:15-16) and generally reflects Luke's understanding of prophetic ministry according to his Scriptures (cf. Luke 11:45-52).

242. Dunn, *The Acts of the Apostles*, 73-74; cf. Jervell, *Die Apostelgeschichte*, 212-13.

REFLECTIONS

1. "During the night an angel of the Lord opened the prison doors [and] brought them out" (5:19 NRSV). There are three jailbreak stories in Acts (cf. 12:6-11; 16:25-34). Every narrative "triad" in Acts sends a signal to the reader of its theological importance. The primary meaning of the apostles' heavenly deliverance from prison is clear: In spite of public appearances to the contrary, God remains in firm control over the particulars of the church's mission and intends to safeguard the apostles against all foes. No one or no thing can intrude upon the forward movement of the gospel according to God's plan of salvation. Three other details of this brief episode nuance this theological principle. The prison symbolizes hostility against God's redemptive plan; it is the location of spiritual warfare between good and evil. The angel's command to "Go and stand in the temple and tell the people the words of life" is a call to a provocative boldness, which takes center stage in the very place of the apostles' opponents, the priestly establishment. There is no break to a safehouse but to battle. The second detail is the befuddlement of the captors whose confusion is testimony both to God's liberating presence and to their ignorance of God's presence. These are the "Keystone Kops" of Acts; their role is to exemplify the incompetence of God's opposition. Finally, the apostles willingly make themselves available for re-arrest. This has nothing to do with their respect—or lack thereof—for civil authority and everything to do with their sublime confidence in God's provident care.

2. "We must obey God rather than any human authority" (5:29 NRSV). Peter's heroic retort to the high priest is Scripture's leading justification for civil disobedience. The interpreter must take care, however, to use it in full awareness of its near and wider canonical context. In Acts, Peter's response is toward a particular kind of political authority, carefully drawn by the narrator. Hostile, unrepentant, tyrannical, envious, clearly unfit to lead the people, who seem to recognize what the narrator does! In our worlds, political authority is rarely so sharply drawn, and a response like Peter's is rarely so glibly made. Such defiance is possible only with several qualifications. In Acts, Peter's comment introduces kerygma, gospel. That is, his expression of civil disobedience does not serve political but rather missionary ends. He does not define himself or his religious authority in terms of protest but as a witness to God's salvation of Israel. He is not the leader of a movement of protest but a movement of God.

In wider canonical context, the interpreter should note the variety of ways in which Scripture defines the relationship between church and state. For example, Paul in Romans speaks with respect (and possibility with irony?) of how civil (= Roman) authority is divinely sanctioned to serve the good purposes of God in the world. Peace is maintained; troublemakers are locked up; good neighbors are rewarded. In a word, the church supports civil authority to make it possible for the church to be the church (cf. Rom 13:1-10). Yet, the book of Revelation speaks with apocalyptic cynicism of a political "Babylon" that is ruled by an unholy trinity, where the people of God are persecuted and even martyred because of their courageous opposition. In this biblical context, the church stands opposed to a civil authority whose self-interest is contrary to the purposes of God (cf. Revelation 13; 17–18). Within the New Testament, Acts takes a stand between these two extremes to help maintain their self-correcting interplay. Scripture seems to suggest that the uneasy relationship between the church as counter-culture and the state as custodian of cultural order will remain uneasy.

3. "If it is from God, you will not be able to stop these men" (5:39 NIV). Gamaliel's cautionary note, however motivated, sounds a practical perspective for judging religious claims. The truth of God embodied in the church's witness in the world should look, act, and sound peculiar to the outsider. There is nothing stranger than the God of Scripture! This may be especially the case of truth that demands one's repentance. The thoughtful person will take longer to test the gospel's claims, for the risks and costs of trusting them are much greater. At the same time, it seems that the apostles recognize the problem with Gamaliel's "wait and see" argument. His pragmatic test could lead to the kind of inactive determinism that waits for God to triumph at the end of the day. There are challenges the church must face squarely. To wait and see is to allow evil its momentary victory in this person's or that group's life. Wait in confidence of God's coming triumph, yes—but "wait and *act*," as did the apostles who left their court appearance to continue their prophetic vocation (5:42).

4. "They rejoiced that they were considered worthy to suffer dishonor for the sake of the name" (5:41 NRSV). The prophetic vocation is a call to share in the suffering of Jesus. The Lord predicted that his disciples would suffer and pronounced God's blessing to those persecuted because of him (cf. Luke 6:22-23). Suffering is the "downward" way of discipleship and is a hard concept to embrace (let alone embody) for those in the "upward" middle class, who enjoy a relatively secure and comfortable life-style. Stories like this one have produced an extraordinary amount of guilt in believers who do not suffer at the hands of oppressive foes—perhaps even a sanctified masochism that substitutes self-inflicted suffering for the suffering envisaged here. In adapting this text to the contemporary church, the interpreter should note that suffering is the result of ministry not masochism. Peter does seek to suffer; he seeks to obey God and to execute the tasks God has given him with grace and courage. His joy is not in his suffering but in his service. The costs of Peter's discipleship are peculiar to his prophetic tasks, spiritual authority, and special role as the Lord's apostolic successor in salvation's history. However, what he models for all believers in every situation is the nonnegotiable importance of serving the interests of God whatever the cost, wherever the occasion.

Acts 6:1-7, Interlude: Resolving Conflict Within the Community of Goods

COMMENTARY

Interludes generally help make transitions from one story to the next. Accordingly, Luke uses this episode to introduce elements that trigger a sequence of events bringing the Jerusalem mission to conclusion and so beginning the next stage of the church's mission, beyond the holy city (see 8:4-40; cf. 1:8).[243] Interludes also underwrite previous points. For example, this passage concerns the distinctive practice of sharing goods so that "there was not a needy person among them" (4:34*a*), indicating to all the presence of God's "great grace upon" the community (4:33*b*; cf. 2:47). New procedures are introduced into the community due to its vigorous growth and the problem of supply and demand that growth has created. One group in particular—the widows from among "the Hellenists" (οἱ Ἑλληνισταί *hoi Hellēnistai*)— is adversely affected, and their neglect is blamed on "the Hebrews" (οἱ Ἑβραῖοι *hoi Hebraioi*). The circumstances that have given rise to this accusation are unstated, and Luke's interest seems more practical than political—that is, he is concerned with the ineffective infrastructure that has resulted in unmet needs within the community of goods.

The apostles understand the nature of the problem and have a strategy for its effective resolution. However, they curiously use this intramural conflict to remind the community that their vocation is to be prophets-like-Jesus rather than waiters on tables[244] (6:2). The present threat to the widows' welfare, therefore, is defined in two ways: On the one hand, the most needy members of the community are being neglected; on the other hand, the

apostles find themselves spending more time in administrative matters than in the ministry of the word to which they are called (6:4; see 1:8). To resolve this vocational conflict the apostles gather "the whole community of disciples" to recommend "seven from among yourselves" who will assume responsibility for food distribution (6:3). These seven are commissioned by the Twelve (6:6), and so "the word of God continued to spread" and new converts were added to the church (6:7).[245]

6:1-2. While Luke has emphasized the resurrection practice of sharing goods with the needy, the personal tragedies of Judas (see 1:6-20) and then Ananias and Sapphira (see 5:1-11) have prepared the reader to recognize that the community's witness is threatened by the problems that believers have with their possessions. Heretofore, when problems arise the offending parties are simply "excommunicated" (see 5:1-11) without indicating how these problems could be resolved more constructively. The importance of this episode in Acts, then, is to introduce a pattern for resolving congregational conflict, which is then repeated as a strategic element of the church's mission (see 11:1-18; 14:27–15:29; 21:17-26).

At its root this conflict envisages the economic disparity between members that threatens any rapidly growing community no matter how cohesive they are in mind and practice: "the disciples were increasing in number" and so their "widows were being neglected in the daily distribution" (6:1). Rapid growth imperils the performance of the biblical injunction to take special care to meet the material requirements of the community's most vulnerable members—widows, orphans, resident aliens, the destitute, and the powerless (cf. Lev 19; 25; Deut 16:11;

---

243. See E. Richard, *Acts 6:1–8:4: The Author's Method of Composition*, SBLDS 41 (Missoula, Mont.: Scholars Press, 1978).

244. The interpreter should note that Luke's use of διακονέω/διακονία (*diakoneō/diakonia*, "to wait (on tables/distribution") in this passage follows its plotline. The failure is stated as a breakdown in the daily *diakonia* ('distribution') of food (6:1). Luke's subsequent use of the verbal form *diakoneō* (6:2) assesses this conflict: food is not being "distributed" to the needy. Finally, the repetition of *diakonia* in 6:4 introduces the resolution of this conflict: the apostles are no longer diverted by administrative tasks and are now fully engaged in their *diakonia* ("ministry") of the word. Significantly, both food "distribution" and the "ministry" of the word are a *diakonia*.

245. Barrett, *A Critical and Exegetical Commentary on the Acts of the Apostles*, 1:305.

Mal 3:5; 1 Tim 5:3-16; Jas 1:22–2:17).[246] The prophets make clear that the treatment of its poor and powerless effectively gauges Israel's relationship with God (Mal 3:5; Zech 7:10) and heralds repentant Israel's renewed covenant with God (Isa 47:8). For this reason, the Hellenists were right to lodge their complaint.

Despite the story's importance within the narrative, the reader may still puzzle over several of its details. The first is to identify "the Hellenists" and the source of their grievance with "the Hebrews." The interpreter must avoid the kind of pigeonholing that places each group into a rigidly defined social class or ideological camp; there is little basis in the text, or behind it, for doing so.[247] The reader should presume that the Hellenists and Hebrews "were of one heart and soul" (see 4:32) and *in principle* shared equally in the blessings of a restored Israel. The present complaint stems from the realization that one group *in practice* has not yet fully participated in the community of goods according to its rule of faith (see 4:32-35).

The terms "the Hellenists" and "the Hebrews" are used together only in this passage, and their wider currency in contemporary Jewish literature is of little help in understanding their use in Acts. Luke's use of the adjective form of "Hebrew" (Ἑβραῖος *Hebraios*) suggests that these terms refer to a spoken language. Paul, for example, sometimes speaks in "Hebrew" to his Palestinian audiences (Acts 21:40; 22:2; 26:14). The division inferred here, then, is between language groups rather than theological outlooks: "The Hellenists" speak mostly Greek,

"the Hebrews" speak mostly Aramaic, and the language barrier between them may explain in part why the practice of food distribution was impeded.

But different languages often involve other, more subtle differences. Just as diaspora Jews have been an important constituency of Israel in Acts since Pentecost (see 2:5-11), so also Luke's "Hellenists" may be Jews who have come to Jerusalem from the diaspora and have settled in ethnic enclaves throughout Jerusalem, where they maintain their own cultural conventions. Many became believers (see 2:41) and perhaps since Pentecost had even established Greek-speaking congregations in their neighborhoods while recognizing the religious authority of the Twelve.[248] If this construction of the story behind the story is accurate, their "complaint"[249] against the Hebrews may well reflect other, more cultural barriers that now divide different congregations within the Jerusalem church.

Another important and somewhat puzzling feature of this passage is its turn toward a second team of seven leaders, two of whom (Stephen, Philip) are given prophetic tasks to perform similar to those of the powerful Twelve. The previous narrative has settled the public debate over Israel's leadership in favor of the apostles (see 5:40-42) whose authority within the faith community is unrivaled (see 4:32–5:16). Their prominence is predicated on two important roles effectively performed. The first is their prophetic ministry of the word and mediation of the Spirit's "signs and wonders." Their second role, however, is to redistribute goods to the community's needy. They now rank their prophetic tasks ahead of their administrative role[250] and are even willing to share their spiritual authority—which the redistribution of goods

246. Johnson, *The Acts of the Apostles*, 105-6. The Hellenist "widows" of Acts combine two welfare classes: they are widows and resident aliens, without family or national support. If by "Hellenist" Luke means those who speak mostly Greek in a Semitic culture, their inability to speak the native language would push these widows to Jerusalem's social and economic fringe. Because of the conflict between the temple elites and the Twelve, the welfare system operated by the Temple might also have been placed outside the grasp of these poorest of the poor. See Haenchen, *The Acts of the Apostles*, 260-61.

247. The most important study of this issue is by Hill, *Hellenists and Hebrews*. Hill's thesis is that the old consensus that divided these groups by competing theological commitments concerning Temple and especially Torah purity is mistaken. First-century Judaism is simply too complex and fluid a religious phenomenon for an easy cataloging of its various subgroups; and Jewish Christianity reflects the pluriform Judaism that mothered it. There is no evidence from the NT that Luke's depiction of intramural strife in Acts is deeply rooted in age-old prejudices against "the Hellenists" who were therefore singled out for mistreatment in Jerusalem. Contra Dunn, *The Acts of the Apostles*, 82. At least according to Acts, "official" Judaism's persecution of the community's leaders is not selective: the Twelve, who were from among "the Hebrews," are opposed (4:5) by the same antagonists who later oppose Stephen, who came from among "the Hellenists" (6:12; 7:1).

248. Conzelmann, *The Acts of the Apostles*, 45, suspects that preferences in everyday language extended to worship and Scripture; so that "the Hellenists" read the Septuagint (rather than the Hebrew Scriptures) and prayed publicly in Greek. His point seems right; and since everyday language is decisive in shaping a general cultural orientation, differences of other kinds may well be implied by Luke's term. See Kee, *To Every Nation Under Heaven*, 88; Dunn, *The Acts of the Apostles*, 81-82.

249. Johnson, *The Acts of the Apostles*, 105, contends that "slighted" better translates παραθεωρέω (*paratheōreō*) in this passage because it better judges the nature of discrimination in this case than the more pejorative "complained."

250. Luke uses the phrase "preaching the word of God" in 6:2 of the apostles' principal activity, which certainly is consistent with his portrait of them to this point in Acts. In 6:4, however, he adds prayer to "the ministry of the word," perhaps recalling their effective petition in 4:24-30 and its connection with "bold" preaching. In Luke's mind, these two prophetic actions of praying and preaching are inseparably linked.

symbolizes (see 4:32–5:16)—with other members of the wider community. Before this crisis the Twelve acted only in collaboration with the Holy Spirit; now, the community's growth and ethnic diversity prompts the realization that their performance standards have not been met. Their mature recognition signals the redistribution of their authority to others within the community. Ironically, then, the selection of the seven will substantially qualify the reader's understanding the Twelve: Although they continue to do and teach what Jesus began, their authority to do so now extends to different leaders of the next generation and from a different constituency of believers.

A final interpretive puzzle is the identity and purpose of those who belong to "the whole community of disciples" (6:2, 5).[251] This text is the first to mention "disciples" in Acts.[252] In the Gospels, of course, a "disciple" is a follower or student of Jesus, and the same is true here. Luke introduces this term into Acts, however, in connection with the Hellenists' complaint, and for this reason "disciples" probably refers to the Greek-speaking believers in Jerusalem, many of whom are new to the faith (6:1). The impression made by the translations of this text is that the Twelve "called together/gathered" the "whole/all" the "disciples"—now well into the thousands—for a discussion of the problem. More likely, this "community of disciples" refers to a much smaller representative "group" of Hellenists who are more mature in the faith and have been given responsibility for the care of their constituents.

6:3-6. The charge given to this advisory group is to "select from among yourselves seven men" (6:3). The number seven is not arbitrary but reflects the Jewish practice of choosing seven members to provide oversight to local congregations (cf. Exod 18:21; Num 27:18-19 LXX). Nor is the process of selecting leadership an arbitrary one. The verb ἐπισκέπτομαι (*episkeptomai*, "select")

is from a word family used of critical and prudent judgments; this decision is made only after careful deliberation by mature believers.

The community is asked to investigate potential leaders on the basis of three personal attributes, which differ from those used for selecting the Twelve (see 1:21-22) but are deemed most important in meeting the urgent demands of this appointment: "good standing, full of the Spirit and of wisdom" (6:3). Each attribute is important for "waiting on tables" and also foreshadows the seven's talent in providing competent oversight within the church. The participle translated "good standing" (μαρτυρούμένος *martyroumenos*) suggests a good reputation that is based upon the favorable "testimony" of others; it is a crucial feature of leading others (cf. Acts 15:14, 36). The combination of "full" (πλήρης *plērēs*) with "Spirit" (πνεῦμα *pneuma*) denotes evidence of a candidate's mature faith (so 2:38) and implies the capacity for prophetic ministry (so 2:4; cf. 6:5; cf. Num 11:16-17). The final characteristic, "wisdom," may refer to organizational talent; but in combination with the Holy Spirit it suggests spiritual authority. Seven from among the Hellenists meet these criteria and are selected. Luke provides the reader with a list of their Greek names, highlighting for future reference the appointments of Stephen ("a man full of faith and the Holy Spirit"; 6:5)[253] and Philip (see Acts 8). The presence of "Nicolaus, a proselyte of Antioch" among the seven indicates a diversity that extends across the entire household of Israel (see 2:11); it also is a harbinger of the church's Antiochene mission to that city's large population of Hellenists (see 11:20).

The apostolic vocation is here defined as devotion "to prayer and to serving the word" (6:4). Luke uses "word" (λόγος *logos*) as a catchword for the full range of the prophet's tasks—the keen interpretation of Scripture, the persuasive proclamation of the gospel, and the performance of the Spirit's "signs and wonders" that provide the eschatological

251. "Community" translates πλῆθος (*plethos*), which denotes a particular subgroup within the community—one that is assembled for deliberation and decision making. Some commentators contend that the reference to "disciples" (μαθητής *mathētēs*) belongs to Luke's primary source and that he simply retains this reference without added meaning or import. This, however, is unlikely given Luke's intentional shaping of his traditions to tell his story and forward his theological vision, and given the repeated use of "disciples" from this point on in Acts.

252. The Western text of Acts, followed by the KJV, substitutes "disciples" for "believers" in 1:15.

253. Luke's introduction of Stephen into the narrative uses the same verb ("they chose [ἐκλέγομαι *eklegomai*] Stephen") used earlier in Acts of the apostles (see 1:2). The implied meaning of this phrase is that his principal vocation is *not* to wait on tables but to join the line of prophets in continuity with Jesus and his apostolic successors to preach the gospel (6:10) and do "signs and wonders" (6:8) in witness to God's reign. Luke also adds "full of faith" (πλήρης πίστεως *plērēs pisteōs*) to Stephen's attributes for ministry, a characteristic phrase that denotes faithfulness to God.

setting for biblical interpretation and evangelistic preaching according to Acts (see 4:31; 6:7; cf. 8:4, 14; 11:1; 12:24; 13:48; 19:20). The petition of apostolic prayers seeks greater power from God to make certain these various prophetic tasks will be boldly and effectively executed (see 4:23-30).

Commentators have made much of the Twelve's gesture of "laying their hands on" the seven Hellenists who "stand before" them (6:6).[254] This service of installation indicates their religious authority to govern the community's internal life and sanction its decisions. The reader of biblical texts also recognizes that this gesture often signals a succession of authority from one leader to the next (cf. Num 27:18, 23; Deut 34:9). Ironically, only the apostles have the authority to transfer their power to others, and here they do so to preserve the most distinctive practice of the community of goods and in order to safeguard their prophetic vocation.

6:7. Luke encloses this interlude with an optimistic note: "The number of disciples increased greatly in Jerusalem" (see 6:1). The reader is thereby assured that the present problem has been effectively handled so that the Jerusalem mission moves ever forward (see 2:41, 47; 4:4; 5:14).

This latest notice of the community's success is especially noteworthy for two curious phrases. First, "the word of God continued to spread" personifies the apostles' proclamation of the gospel, shifting the reader's focus from the power and authority of those who preach it (the apostles) to the power and authority of what is preached (the word of God). By leaving open the identity of the prophetic carrier of the word the reader is made even more alert to the diminishing attention Acts will pay to the story of the Twelve and to the progress of the word of God to the end of earth—no matter who proclaims it.

Second, the verse claims that "a great many of the priests became obedient to the faith."[255] Given the apostles' past grievances with the priestly establishment of Jerusalem, this phrase initially strikes the reader as confirming once for all the reversal of religious leadership within Israel (see 5:17-42). Closer attention to the historical referent, however, suggests otherwise. Haenchen estimates that upwards of 18,000 priests were living in Jerusalem at the time, most with minimal responsibilities in their service of the Temple and, held in low public esteem, with little or no income.[256] Their attraction to the Jesus movement indicates that the ministry of the apostles proffers nothing that is offensive to traditional Jewish sensibilities; however, they may have been drawn to the community by the availability of food. This too implies the favorable result of the community's welfare program that is now administered by the seven.

---

254. Some take the antecedent of v. 6 to be the advisory committee mentioned in v. 5, which may lead the reader to suppose that this committee joined the Twelve to lay hands on and consecrate the seven for their sacred task (cf. Num 8:10). See Barrett, *A Critical and Exegetical Commentary on the Acts of the Apostles*, 315-16. My sense of the wider context leads me to understand that it was the Twelve who laid their hands on the seven as a function of their apostolic authority—although not without first "pleasing" the advisory group from the Hellenists (see 6:5).

255. Some commentators find Paul's influence in Luke's phrase "obedient to the faith" (ὑπήκουον τῇ πίστει *hypēkouon tē pistei*). Paul's parallel phrase is "for an obedience of faith" (εἰς ὑπακοὴν πίστεως *eis hypakoēn pisteōs*; Rom 1:5; 16:26) and reflects the central claim of his Gentile mission: The sinner's profession of trust that "Jesus is Lord" saves (10:9). In the context of Acts, Luke's phrase "obedient to the faith" envisages a response to "the word of God" that requires the new convert to "repent" and be "baptized" into the community of goods.

256. Haenchen, *The Acts of the Apostles*, 264. Josephus claims that some priests without means even starved to death during famine. See also Josephus *Antiquities of the Jews* 20.181.

REFLECTIONS

1. "The Hellenists complained . . . because their widows were being neglected in the daily distribution of food" (6:1 NRSV). Disputes within the fellowship of believers are especially painful, because close friends often find themselves on different sides of an issue and upset with each other for that reason. Nevertheless complaints must be voiced with civility to initiate the community's practice of reconciliation. The most important internal conflicts to settle are those that go to the heart of a community's identity; these are the most passionately contested because more is at stake. In this passage, the practice of distributing food among the Jerusalem community's most needy and vulnerable members—its displaced widows—has apparently broken down.

Besides the prior concern for the welfare of its membership, the congregation's public identity for sharing goods according to need is being challenged. The vocation of the church is to extend that witness to the entire household of Israel (see 2:1-13). The scope of God's promise to restore all of Israel is threatened by this apparent division along ethnic and language lines. The church's witness to the holy city is subverted as a result of this internal crisis. The protocol followed, which both addresses the problem and preserves the prophetic vocation, is a biblical model to guide conflict resolution in today's church, in particular conflict issuing from ethnic, class, or gender divisions.

2. "And the twelve called together the whole community of the disciples" (6:2a NRSV). The first step in resolving this internal conflict is to bring together all those involved and include them as parties to a remedy. The implied subtext of this account in Acts is that all are members of a cohesive congregation whose regular experience is serving God together with "one heart and soul" (see 4:32). There is the presumption of solidarity—of shared faith and abiding friendship—that provides the groundwork for this meeting. The "community of disciples" convened are the most mature representatives of the parties involved. This is not a "town hall" meeting that gives voice to any and every grievance. Instead, the Twelve solicit a representative assembly of members who have registered the crisis and have their collective finger on the pulse of the problem at issue.

3. "It is not right that we should neglect the word of God in order to wait on tables" (6:2b NRSV). As is often the case, at the nub of the conflict is a failure of leadership. Almost certainly there is more to the complaint of the Hellenists than that the increasing demands of a growing community have outpaced the ability of the apostles to exercise their spiritual authority in the distribution of goods. Growth requires change, and change comes slowly to any culture, but especially to a religious movement that is indebted to past memories and ancestral traditions, preserved and transmitted to others. To change with the times is a function of an agile leadership team. The practical failure of apostolic leadership to administrate effectively the community's food bank occasions the next triumph of their leadership: They received a report from the leaders and recognized their inability to preach and do all the bookkeeping at the same time. It is time to redefine the job description of an apostle. Others outside of the circle of the Twelve need to share in their religious authority for the good of their common life and witness. The Twelve clearly recognize the importance of a congregation's infrastructure for maintaining its spiritual and physical health as a community of goods. A staff of competent people is selected to wait on tables so that the welfare of the most needy believers is attended. Once settled, the outreach ministry of the church continues to flourish (see 6:7).

One should also note that the Twelve recognize that the "real" problem of their leadership is that they are unable to live within their vocation because of their increasing administrative duties (see also 6:4). The pastor and the congregation should ever be alert to those crises occasioned when the administrative demands of running a church eat into the time one must devote in preparing for those tasks to which the pastor is called—most especially the ministry of the word.

4. "Select from among yourselves seven men" (6:3 NRSV). When an organization such as a church or university opens a search to find strong candidates to fill a vacancy, a list of qualifications and special talents is drawn up that envisions the job to be done. If a congregation requires a strong preacher, the search committee catalogs the attributes of good preaching to guide them in finding and evaluating possible candidates. Today's orientation toward work emphasizes the required tasks or expected activities of the vacated post. This is as it must be in the current job market. However, in Acts the emphasis is on *character* not task, whether a person is of "good standing, full of the Spirit and of wisdom." Luke's bias reflects his Greek intellectual culture, which championed the notion that habitual virtue—the sort of person one is—is the most important credential when considering people for leadership positions. This emphasis is found in the so-called "Pastoral Letters" of the New Testament (1–2 Timothy, Titus), where instructions for appointing congregational leaders concern exclusively whether one is known as a person of moral character and mature faith.

5. "The word of God continued to spread; the number of the disciples increased greatly" (6:7 NRSV). Within the fourfold Gospel tradition, a similar interplay between the community's outreach and "in-reach" is found. For example, the Synoptic Gospels define the love commandment in terms of caring for the "enemy" (cf. Matt 5:43-48 and par.) and the Lord's parting commission instructs his disciples to go out into the nations with the gospel in witness to nonbelievers (cf. Matt 28:18-20 and par.). The Fourth Gospel defines the love command in terms of caring for other disciples (cf. John 13:34) and the Lord's parting admonition to Peter is for him to take care of other believers (cf. John 21:15-17). How does the interpreter engage these different emphases as parts of a coherent, constructive whole? Luke's summary of the results of resolving the intramural squabble between the Hellenists and Hebrews of the Jerusalem community may give us a clue. With unity restored through careful attention to the welfare of all believers first of all (John's concern), the community's outreach ministry flourishes and its membership rolls increase, especially among those who earlier had felt marginalized (synoptic concern)! Congregational leaders would do well to build and fund an infrastructure that maintains the spiritual and material care of the entire congregation as the foundation and condition for an effective outreach program.

Acts 6:8–8:3, Story Four: Stephen, a Prophet Mighty in Word and Deed

COMMENTARY

The final episode of Luke's Jerusalem cycle features Stephen of the seven rather than Peter of the Twelve. The earlier interlude signals this narrative shift to the charismatic Stephen, who succeeds Peter to lead another constituency of disciples and continue what the Messiah "began to do and teach" among them (1:1).

Luke shapes his story of Stephen according to the literary pattern of this cycle of missionary stories (see the Overview to 3:1–8:3).[257]

257. The debate over the reliability of Luke's sources and the extent to which he edits them continues unabated. The literary parallelism between the events leading up to Stephen's speech (6:8–7:1) with those that follow it (7:54–8:3) lead some to conclude that Luke received his information about Stephen from a single source but then thoroughly reshaped it for his own theological purposes (Dibelius, Haenchen, Conzelmann, Lüdemann). Others emphasize the reliability of this single source and conclude that Luke does not modify it much in interest of historical accuracy that reflects the importance of Stephen's martyrdom for earliest Christianity (Bruce, Marshall, Witherington). The truth is probably found somewhere between. While allowing that Luke exercised considerable freedom in shaping his story to suit his narrative aim, it seems likely that the memory of Stephen's martyrdom is precisely the sort that would have been preserved and transmitted, not only for its moral value but also because it witnesses to a decisive turning point in the relations between Christianity and Judaism (Fitzmyer, Johnson, Jervell, Barrett, Kee, Soards).

(1) The first narrative panel profiles a powerful Stephen, whose résumé indicates that he is a prophet-like-Jesus who provokes public scrutiny (6:8-10). (2) The official response to his ministry, however, is ever more hostile (6:11-15). Added to the coalition of Jewish opponents to Jesus and his apostolic successors—the elders, scribes, and Sanhedrin—is a more aggressive and malevolent contingent from the diaspora's "synagogue of Freedmen." This group of Hellenists agitates unrest and sets up "false witnesses" against Stephen, one of their own. (3) Like Peter, Stephen responds to this mistake in a speech. His speech (7:1-53) is the longest in Acts and counts among the most significant for understanding the theological contribution the book makes to Christian faith. It is a stunning retort to his opponents, who falsely claim that he opposes "Moses and God" (6:11), the two central characters of his biblical retelling of Israel's history. (4) The story's

final panel depicts a variety of responses to Stephen's speech (7:54–8:3). His martyrdom envisages the prophet's exemplary response to the truth of God's Word even as his executioners' hostile response to that Word confirms the accuracy of Stephen's characterization of unrepentant Israel.

6:8-10. Luke alerts his readers to Stephen's spiritual authority: "Stephen [is] a man full of faith and the Holy Spirit" (6:5)—he is a prophet-like-Jesus among his peers. Stephen's persona is filled out by the present text, which adds that he is "full of grace and power" (v. 8) with competence to defend the word of God "with wisdom and the Spirit" (v. 10) and to perform "great wonders and signs among the people" (v. 8).[258] This profile is surprising given Stephen's recent selection to assume the administrative duties of the Twelve (see 6:4). Clearly the Spirit has now marked him out also for a ministry of the word that will continue what Jesus (see Luke 2:40, 52) and his apostolic successors (see Acts 5:12) had begun in Jerusalem.[259] Toward this end, Luke's repetition of the catchphrase "signs and wonders" recalls Joel's prophecy of the last days (see 2:17-21; cf. 2:22, 43; 4:16, 30; 5:12) and enables the reader to discern Stephen's true vocation. Both his wonders and his inspired words are prophetic instruments used in service of an effective witness to the resurrected Lord. Such an inspired ministry specializes in the spoken word; it is finally what the prophet says to the people that provokes a protest from unrepentant Jews. They "argued with Stephen" (6:9) but could not withstand the combination of wisdom and Spirit "with which he spoke" (6:10).[260]

Stephen's opponents "belonged to the so-called synagogue of the Freedmen" (v. 9).[261] The reference to "synagogue" is neither to a particular building nor a local institution but to a religious movement within diaspora Judaism, which included vast regions of the Roman Empire, including Asia and Africa.[262] The word that is translated "Freedmen" is Λιβερτῖνος (*Libertinos*), a transliteration of the Latin word for "former slaves" (*libertinus*). A few of these "freedmen" became Roman citizens with influence in the political arena related to Judaism. Apparently a substantial number had settled in Jerusalem out of a sense of religious devotion and had founded a local chapter, or "synagogue," of this religious movement.[263]

This is Luke's first reference to the movement, and its appearance here implies its connection with "the disciples" from among "the Hellenists" (6:1), who now are led by Stephen and are enjoying great success in the Greek-speaking neighborhoods of Jerusalem (6:7). This latest round of conflict suggests that there are rival factions among "the Hellenists" that parallel the standing rivalry among "the Hebrews" between the Sanhedrin and the Twelve.[264]

6:11-15. Since fair debate fails Stephen's opponents, they resort to dirty tricks to subvert his influence. They do so by underhanded rabble-rousing, which pegs them as unfit representatives of diaspora Jews. The accusations they level against Stephen are three: (1) He speaks "blasphemous words against Moses and God" (6:11); (2) he "never stops saying things against this holy place and the law" (6:13); and (3) he claims that "Jesus of Nazareth will destroy this place and change the customs of Moses" (6:14).

6:11-12. The initial charge is both surprising and revealing. It is surprising because "blasphemy against Moses" is not illegal, and yet the opponents mention it before charging him with blaspheming God, which is illegal. Luke's phrasing of this twofold accusation

---

258. Luke's phrase "among the people [λαός *laos*]" (6:8; see also 2:12; 3:9-12; 5:12) places Stephen's ministry among and for Israel as the "people of God." See Jervell, *Die Apostelgeschichte*, 224-25. I would sharpen the focus of this biblical idiom within this passage so that the "people" are from "among the Hellenists" (see 6:1) who have not yet become Christian "disciples" (see 6:1, 7).

259. The Western text of Acts amends v. 8 by adding "in the name of Jesus Christ" and v. 10 by adding "with all boldness [παρρησία *parrēsia*] so that they were refuted by him, unable to deal with the truth ἀλήθεια *alētheia*]." Both emendations forge greater agreement between Luke's portrait of Stephen's ministry and the prophetic "boldness" of the apostles' ministry.

260. Jesus predicted that his witnesses would be characterized by "words and wisdom that none of your opponents will be able to withstand" (Luke 21:15). This prophecy is here fulfilled by Stephen. The point is that it no longer matters whether Stephen's ministry is authorized by the apostles by the laying on of hands; it is sanctioned by prophecy of the Lord.

261. Barrett calls attention to the repetition of the article (τήν . . . τήν *tēn . . . tēn*) in 6:9 and suggests that two different groups of diaspora Jews are in view; the first are members of a "synagogue of Freedmen" as distinguished from a second who are unattached to this particular assembly but join them against Stephen. See Barrett, *A Critical and Exegetical Commentary on the Acts of the Apostles*, 323.

262. Kee, *To Every Nation Under Heaven*, 317n3.

263. See Fitzmyer, *The Acts of the Apostles*, 356-58.

264. So Pesch, *Die Apostelgeschichte*, 237, who says that "jealousy" remains the primary motive of the Jewish opposition to the church.

may intend to put the reader on notice that the substance of the legal case against Stephen is bogus.

By posting a previous concern for what Stephen teaches about Moses, his opponents prepare the reader for two "legitimate" allegations that they place before the council for judicial deliberation, which concern "the customs that Moses handed on to us" (6:14). The real issue at stake, then, is over Mosaic prescriptions concerning the sanctity of the Temple rather than the orthodoxy of Stephen's theology. In any case, Stephen will defend his loyalty to both "Moses and God" as the two principal characters in his provocative recital of Israel's history that follows (see 7:2-53).

Luke shapes his story of Stephen's trial to parallel the story of Jesus' trial. Thus the freedmen's charge of blasphemy alludes to a similar accusation leveled against Jesus (see Matt 26:65; Mark 14:57-58).[265] The deceit of Jesus' accusers is similar to that of Stephen's as well: While "falsely" accusing Stephen of breaking the law that prohibits blasphemy against God (Lev 24:11-26), they break the law that forbids bringing false witness against another (Exod 20:16).[266] Luke's literary interplay implies that Stephen is a prophet-like-Jesus whose vocation is to bring the Word of God to Israel but whose destiny is rejection and death (see Luke 45–52).

6:13. His accusers bring Stephen before a tribunal, which had already threatened and flogged the apostles without just cause, in order to hear the claims of "false" witnesses. The chances of Stephen's receiving a fair hearing are nil to none! Both accusations heard by the Sanhedrin delimit the earlier charge that Stephen blasphemes against Israel's Mosaic traditions. In the first offense, his accusers claim that Stephen teaches against "this holy place and the law" (6:13). Since the Temple and the Torah form an integral pair of Mosaic

traditions, what is actually alleged is that Stephen's teaching about the role of the Temple in God's salvation cuts against the grain of traditional Jewish practice as legislated by scribal "oral torah" (traditional *halakhah*).[267]

6:14. But the real climax of the court case against Stephen is scored by the second "false" accusation: "we heard him say that this Jesus of Nazareth will destroy this place." Significantly, this is the first negative appraisal of Jesus' suffering found in Acts and is proffered by these opponents of the church's mission. To this point we have heard only from Peter, who accuses unrepentant Israel of participating with Rome in the Messiah's death. The charge against Stephen not only implies a rejection of the church's gospel but also represents a considered political opinion that both the Jewish charge against Jesus for blasphemy and his subsequent Roman execution are legitimate consequences of his teaching against the Temple and Torah. In this regard, N. T. Wright has argued that Jesus' actions in the Temple were motivated by the conviction that his messianic role and authority for Israel had replaced both Temple and Torah as the central symbols of a Jewish way of life and faith. According to Stephen's Jesus, then, God's promise to purify and then restore an eschatological Israel does not include the Temple at all but is, rather, fulfilled through Jesus' messianic activity alone.[268]

Perhaps Luke's emphasis on the Temple as the principal location of apostolic proclamation and subversive authority in Jerusalem continues this element of the Lord's apologia

---

265. Luke's version of Jesus' trial does not include the testimony of false witnesses. Dunn explains this omission as characteristic of Luke's narrative strategy, which delays certain gospel stories to Acts, where they perform a more important role than in the gospel tradition. This explanation presumes without hard evidence that Luke knew he would write Acts when composing his Gospel. If that is the case, this element of Jesus' trial may have been delayed to the present episode in order to underscore the history of an unrepentant Israel, who persists in rejecting God's offer of salvation at every stage of its history. See Dunn, *The Acts of the Apostles*, 88. See also Johnson, *The Acts of the Apostles*, 112.

266. This characterization of witnesses as "false" is a narrative device, since the council could not have known this at the time (see below).

267. Fitzmyer, *The Acts of the Apostles*, 359. Among Pharisees a distinction was made between written Torah and oral Torah—what Josephus called "ancestral rules" (*The Jewish War* 7.10.2), the Mishnah labels "sayings of the fathers," or what Luke referred to as "the customs that Moses handed down" (6:14). This "oral torah" is based on case study and reflects the pious attempts of Pharisaic scholars to adapt written Torah to their congregational setting. Of course, there was no unanimity within Pharisaic Judaism over these matters. Other devout diaspora Jews were living in Jerusalem at the time of Stephen who were not believers and yet probably would have sided with him against the temple hierarchy in order to elevate practical "piety" over temple protocol (see 8:2).

268. N. T. Wright, *Jesus and the Victory of God* (Minneapolis: Augsburg Fortress, 1996) 405-27. The inference drawn from Jesus' *actions* within the Temple about what his *teaching* against the Temple might include is difficult to ascertain. Luke's Jesus predicts the Temple's destruction (Luke 21:6) but at the hands of pagans (21:24) and John's Jesus cryptically replies to the request for a sign: "Destroy this temple and in three days I will raise it up" (2:19). Jesus does not say "*I* will destroy this temple and *I* will rebuild it in three days." Perhaps in the ears of priestly loyalists to temple purity and scribes equally loyal to torah purity, Jesus' words were misconstrued—especially since he routinely pronounced the forgiveness of the unforgivable. Likewise, nowhere does Jesus teach against the law; indeed, he demands that his disciples obey all of it. However, his interpretation and practice of the law challenge and even change its current status within Israel—a point that was offensive to his scribal conversation partners.

(see 3:11; 5:12, 20-21). Those who oppose the church's witness, such as these freedmen, seek to maintain the centrality of the Temple to Israel's national identity and destiny. While their actions certainly intend to counteract Stephen's growing influence among their compatriots in the holy city, the various allusions to the story of Jesus suggest that their hostility toward Stephen is rooted in a historical memory of Jesus' troubling actions in the Temple (see John 2:13-22 and par.) and his prediction of its destruction (see Luke 21:20-24 and par.).[269]

If Stephen's proclamation of Jesus included, if only implicitly, a denial of the Temple's centrality in Israel's future relations with God, in what sense is this second accusation against Stephen false? Are these witnesses "false" because they never really heard him say what they allege? Is the substance of their accusations "false" because Stephen never said or practiced what they allege? Or are they "false" witnesses from the narrator's perspective because they claim that Stephen is blasphemous when he is not? This latter option seems best. Stephen's subsequent speech does not criticize either the Temple or Torah but an unrepentant Israel whose zeal for the Temple prevents them from believing that Jesus is the Messiah.[270] In continuity with the teaching and actions of Jesus, then, Stephen denies the Temple its pivotal role in "the last days" of salvation's history, when Israel's purification and restoration will result from turning to God's Messiah rather than by observing the practices of temple purity (see 3:17-23; cf. 7:44-50). While these allegations against Stephen may have misstated what he actually said about Jesus' troubled relations

with the temple leadership and are in this limited sense "false," they accurately summarize the essence of Stephen's position, which the unrepentant Sanhedrin and freedmen would deem "false."

6:15. Stephen's transfiguration before his accusers, who "saw that his face was like the face of an angel," echoes the OT story of Moses' descent from Mt. Sinai, tablets in hand, when "his face shone because he had been talking with God" (Exod 34:29 LXX; cf. Matt 17:2; 2 Cor 3:10). This intertextual echo glosses Stephen's trial with the irony that it is Stephen, accused of blasphemy against Moses, and not the Sanhedrin, who is Israel's authorized interpreter of Moses. Stephen's speech that follows should be read not as a defense but as this prophet's inspired midrash on the biblical traditions of Moses for "the last days." Stephen, then, is hardly critical of Torah; he is, rather, an interpreter of these same "living oracles" (7:38), which can lead those who listen to the Messiah.[271]

7:1-53. Barrett claims that Stephen's is "the most important speech in Acts";[272] and many agree with this verdict. Johnson, for example, claims that "it provides the reader with the key to understanding everything that had happened in [Luke's] story of Jesus and the apostles up to this point."[273] But it is also the most perplexing and difficult speech of Acts to analyze, as the history of its interpretation surely attests.[274]

Speeches in Acts typically respond to a theological mistake. Stephen's is no exception: The question, "Are these things so?" is asked by a hostile court in consideration of "false" testimony (see above). On the face of it, however, Stephen's speech is hardly an apologia in either form or motive; nowhere does he *directly* respond to the charges brought against him. Nor is his speech kerygmatic, since nowhere does he draw together biblical passages in support of the church's

269. The Temple had been destroyed by the Romans well before Luke wrote Acts, and the public debate about building its replacement as an eschatological sign was a lively one within diaspora Judaism. The historical subtext of the present passage sounds an unwritten note of Stephen's vindication. It may explain why Luke uses the future tense in stating the charge that Jesus "will destroy this place" (6:14) when, in fact, Jesus' prediction has already come true. But it also presumes a specifically Christian (or messianic) opinion about the building of a "third" Temple and an explanation about why Israel had been defeated by a pagan power and its Temple destroyed. See C. Giblin, *The Destruction of Jerusalem According to Luke's Gospel*, AnBib 107 (Rome: Pontifical Biblical Institute, 1985).

270. As Hill points out, Stephen does not actually criticize the "institution of the temple" but rather Jewish unbelief that resulted in the Temple's destruction. See Hill, *Hellenists and Hebrews*, 69. If Acts 6:1–8:3 is dated *after* the Temple's destruction, Luke's probable intent is to draw an analogy between Israel's rejection of Moses and its dire consequences (see 7:35-50; cf 3:22-23) and Israel's rejection of Jesus and its implied tragic consequence, the destruction of the Temple. See C. C. Hill, "Acts 6:1–8:4: Division or Diversity," in Witherington, *History, Literature, and Society in the Book of Acts*, 129-53.

271. Tannehill, *The Acts of the Apostles*, 2:85-87, notes how Stephen constructs his history of unrepentant Israel by quoting Moses ten times.

272. Barrett, *A Critical and Exegetical Commentary on the Acts of the Apostles*, 334.

273. Johnson, *The Acts of the Apostles*, 137.

274. The secondary literature on Stephen's speech is vast, reflecting the variety of critical issues at stake. See Fitzmyer, *The Acts of the Apostles*, 386-88, for a working bibliography. Haenchen admits that "experts have cudgeled their brains" in trying to sort these issues out. See Haenchen, *The Acts of the Apostles*, 286. For a summary of these scholarly debates, see Soards, *The Speeches in Acts*, 58-70; Witherington, *The Acts of the Apostles*, 259-64.

proclamation that the risen Jesus is God's promised Messiah. Rather, he tells a story of unrepentant Israel. Johnson reminds us that similar prophetic recitals of Israel's history were commonplace within biblical and contemporary Jewish literature. The manner of the storyteller's retelling of that sacred history—what is included or omitted and in what sequence—presents a particular line of vision into Israel's faith and destiny.[275] Apart from its brevity, the principal literary convention that distinguishes this historiography from secular counterparts (e.g., Herodotus, Thucydides, Josephus) is its biblical diction and citation: Stephen's speech is midrashic—that is, he retells Israel's history by recalling a selection of biblical stories that carry his theological freight—a prophet's exposure of Israel's need for repentance and restoration.[276] He only indirectly responds to the charges leveled against him as an element of this theological perspective, and the central themes of his speech are those of a pious Jew who would never blaspheme God or Moses (see 6:11).[277] The following summary should help to orient readers to Stephen's story.

(1) *God is the principal subject of Israel's story, and God's provident care throughout Israel's history is its main predicate.*[278] God has persistently acted in the history of "our ancestors" to reverse evil with good, to make and keep promises, and to see (7:34), hear (7:34), appear (7:2), speak, (7:3, 6, 33) and come down (7:34) to rescue (7:10, 34) Israel from despair and death. This is the God who judges those who oppress Israel (7:7) and who turns from an unfaithful Israel in sorrow (7:42). No fair-minded assembly of Jewish jurists could seriously entertain the

freedmen's original accusation that Stephen blasphemed against God.[279]

(2) *God grants wisdom, special insight, and "signs and wonders" to those chosen and called by God to lead the repentant Israel (7:10, 22, 36).* The liberators of Israel are prophets of God. Even before Israel was Israel, God raised up prophets, such as Joseph, who suffered at the hands of hostile authorities; and when Israel became Israel, God chose and empowered prophets-like-Moses (and Jesus) to deliver God's word to an Israel that routinely misunderstood and denounced them. In fact, while "the pharaohs" recognized their prophetic gifts (7:11, 22), these servants of God were rejected within Israel. Stephen's ministry and martyrdom are exemplary of these prophetic leaders of God's people.

(3) *Unrepentant Israel is a "stiff-necked people" (7:51).* As a pattern expressive of God's persistent concern for Israel and its persistent disregard for God's saving word, God sends the prophetic carrier of God's saving word twice to Israel (7:12-13, 35-36). An ignorant Israel fails to obey the first time and will listen to him only upon his return—but only with short-term results.[280] Whereas the community that shares goods lives together (most of the time) with "one heart and soul," disobedient Israel is a divided people; this makes it impossible to hear the word of God (7:9, 26, 39-41). The execution of Stephen is this Israel's second rejection of God's prophet, and so the word will depart Jerusalem for another place.[281]

(4) *The Lord God's activity on behalf of Israel is not bounded by a particular place of worship or time of salvation.* Clearly the distinction between "true" and "false" worship is an important theme of Stephen's speech; "true" worship of a transcendent God can never be domesticated into cultic

---

275. Johnson, *The Acts of the Apostles*, 120.

276. Luke's quotation or allusions of Scripture are in line with his use of Scripture elsewhere in Acts. He does not distort the theological intent of the cited/echoed biblical (LXX) text but interprets its current meaning to fit into his narrative. The impression that lingers after this speech is that Stephen's verdict of those who accuse him is also God's verdict as scripted and sanctioned by the Scriptures.

277. Soards, *The Speeches in Acts*, 58, notes that the speech, although incomplete, is a kind of judicial rhetoric called "counteraccusation." The defendant does not offer countervailing evidence to overturn an indictment or even seek acquittal on some other grounds. Rather, the defendant takes the offensive to indict his accusers as the guilty party. Naturally, since the accusers generally hold judicial power and the indicted defendant has none, the audience should not expect the defendant to be acquitted, and Stephen isn't.

278. Krodel claims that the opening phrase of Stephen's speech, which invokes God as "God of glory," introduces divine transcendence as the organizing theme of the speech, which for this reason is enclosed by Stephen's final vision of "the glory of God" (7:55). See Krodel, *Acts*, 140.

279. See Dunn, *The Acts of the Apostles*, 92.

280. According to Johnson's "two visitation" hypothesis, the Gospel story of Luke's Jesus tells of God's messianic prophet sent forth a first time to save Israel. Because of their ignorance, Israel rejects him and he is forced into exile (i.e., his ascension). Acts narrates the "second visitation" and second offering of God's salvation to Israel. In Acts, however, Jesus' role is resumed by his Spirit-filled successors—substitutes for the glorified Jesus and armed with his Spirit's "signs and wonders" and inspired word. In hearing the word of God proclaimed a second time, Israel can no longer plead ignorance. Israel will no longer be excused as Peter accused them earlier in Acts (3:17). The stakes are elevated for Israel: If they reject the prophet's second offer of salvation, they and not he will be sent into exile. See Johnson, *The Acts of the Apostles*, 13.

281. Johnson, *The Acts of the Apostles*, 136.

prescription, to handmade artifacts, or to an institutionalized protocol.[282] The vital texture of his speech is provided by the perpetual motion that marks Israel's relations with God: It moves constantly from place to place, from land to land, while God's promise given to Abraham, reissued by the prophets to this constantly changing environment, remains the fixed constant. Against those who accuse him, then, Stephen's concluding point about the tent *cum* Temple is not to criticize the Temple as a sacred site for worshiping God but only the Sanhedrin's temple politics, which divide the house of Israel and blind the people of God to the truth about Jesus.

In his concluding words, Stephen clearly understands that there is a christological component to temple politics. The resurrection of Jesus has confirmed him as God's Messiah and the central symbol of Jewish faith and life—not the Temple, not the Torah, not any institution of Jewish national life or religious cult. But temple politics are a politics of power. The subtext of Stephen's accusation of official Israel's "stiff-necked" leadership is to challenge their presumption that a transcendent God, the only God, can be contained within a sacred place or particular parcel of land and regulated by a powerful group of self-appointed people. The God of Stephen's speech is constantly on the move from heaven to earth, and upon earth from place to place, making surprising choices at every turn in fulfilling the promise of salvation.

7:1-16. The "Patriarchal" Epoch of God's Promise. Stephen begins his story of Israel's history with God's promise to Abraham (vv. 2-8). Peter's earlier speech provides initial commentary on Abraham's promise both to lay claim on God's ultimate intent to bless "all the families of the earth" and to condition this universal salvation upon Israel's repentance (see 3:19-26). Stephen's rehearsal of God's promise to Abraham reflects a similar theme in that the promise is not realized during the patriarch's lifetime but points to its future fulfillment for "his descendants after him" (vv. 6-7). He depicts a wandering Abraham as following God's directions from place to place (vv. 3-4; cf. Gen 11:31–12:5), even being removed from the promised land, of which "God did not give him any of it . . .

not even a foot's length" (v. 5; cf. Gen 15:7; 22:17; Deut 2:5).[283] Stephen also depicts this future posterity of promise as "resident aliens in a country not their own, and they will be enslaved and mistreated for four hundred years" (v. 6; cf. Gen 15:13; see 3:25). But he does not indicate that their eventual experience of divine blessing reverses these social misfortunes; rather, the essential characteristic of blessing is that "they will worship me in this place" (v. 7; cf. Gen 15:14; Exod 3:12 LXX).[284] Stephen's reference to Abraham as "our ancestor" (7:2; cf. 7:11-12, 19, 38, 44-45), coupled with his striking phrase "covenant of circumcision" (7:8; cf. Genesis 17), reflects his position on the point currently debated "within family": Israel's principal identifying mark is neither its fertile land nor its sacred sites but its covenant relationship with God.[285]

Consistent with his interpretive key, Stephen's account of Joseph portrays him as a type of prophet (vv. 9-16) whose story typifies all prophets, including Jesus and now Stephen. The "patriarchs" are "jealous" (ζηλόω *zēloō*) of Joseph and sell him into slavery (v. 9; cf. Genesis 37). But God rescues him and enables him to "win favor and to show wisdom" with the pagan pharaoh (v. 10; cf. Genesis 41). This same prophetic pattern of reversal was introduced earlier in Acts when the Sadducees were "filled with jealousy" (ζῆλος *zēlos*) because of the popularity of the apostles (5:17), provoking their arrest and their miraculous rescue (5:18-19). Moreover, that a pagan ruler discerns Joseph's prophetic gifts when Israel's patriarchs do not is another kind of reversal that will be prominent in Luke's story of Paul, when Rome safeguards

---

282. Witherington, *The Acts of the Apostles,* 271.

283. The Genesis narrative indicates that God promises Abraham "this land as your inheritance" (Gen 15:7). Luke presumes that God's promise was not realized by Abraham (Deut 2:5) and believes that it has only recently been realized for Abraham's progeny since the resurrection of Jesus (so Acts 3:25-26; cf. Romans 9–11; Gal 3:15-20).

284. Luke rewrites Gen 15:13-14 LXX by editing out its final phrase "with vast possessions" and substituting a modified phrase from Exod 3:12 that substitutes τόπος οὗτος (*topos houtos,* "this place [= Canaan]") for τόπος ὅρος (*topos oros,* "this mountain [= Sinai]"). The effect is to hear that God's purpose for Israel (and for all creation) is to "worship me in this place." While "this place" might anticipate Jerusalem's Temple, Luke is well aware that this Temple has long since been destroyed according to the Lord's prediction. The center of sacred worship has now shifted from a particular place to a particular person.

285. Note at the same time that Stephen adds "in which *you* are now living" (7:4) to the biblical allusion to Judea/Jerusalem. While he locates himself among God's people, Stephen at the same time distances himself from the "land" and "place" of God's promise in keeping with the central theme of his speech.

him from malevolent Jewish opposition (see 18:12-17).

Stephen's attribution of Joseph's "wisdom" and his success at winning the pharaoh's "favor" recalls Luke's description of him as "full of grace" (6:8) and "wisdom" (6:10). Joseph is a biblical exemplar whom Stephen follows. As with Joseph, Stephen's destiny is in the hands of God. Joseph is enabled by God's Spirit to deliver his brothers from death (cf. Gen 41:38-39); likewise, Stephen's mission is to deliver "his brothers and fathers" (v. 2) from death. Yet, unlike Joseph's brothers, who finally respond to him on their second visit to Egypt (v. 13), God's saving grace is not mediated through this prophet-like-Jesus because Stephen's brothers refuse to heed his word. In the context of God's promise to Abraham, these seemingly unrelated experiences of Joseph and his brothers prepare Israel "for the fulfillment of the promise that God had made to Abraham" (v. 17).

Stephen's inclusion of a burial story (vv. 15-16) is puzzling, especially since its details disagree with Scripture.[286] Apparently Luke has taken bits and pieces from different biblical texts to feature Samaritan Shechem, a region scorned by Stephen's orthodox Jewish audience because Shechem is associated with Mt. Gerizim, the most sacred site of Samaritan religion and the chief competitor to the temple site in Jerusalem (v. 16; cf. Gen 33:18-20). Its reference here functions as another piece of his larger contention that true worship of God is not relegated to a single place, which is a form of idolatry. Characteristic of his narrative style, Luke may also mention Samaria to prepare his readers for the following account of Philip's highly provocative Samaritan mission as the legitimate concern of Israel's God (see 8:4-25).[287]

7:17-43. The "Mosaic" Epoch of God's Prophet. The second, longest, and most important section of Stephen's speech focuses on Moses as another exemplary prophet of God. Indeed, Moses is the prototype of the anticipated Messiah whom God will raise up to deliver God's people from death to lead

them into newness of life (v. 37). This messianic prophet-like-Moses is, of course, Jesus (see 3:22-23).[288] Thus Stephen's account of Moses authorizes his gospel proclamation that Jesus is God's Messiah and at the same time provides his defense against the charge that he speaks "blasphemous words against Moses" (see 6:11).

7:17-22. Stephen's opening assertion places this episode of Israel's history within the broader movement of God's plan to save Abraham's international progeny: Moses was born at a time "for the fulfillment of the promise God had made to Abraham" (v. 17; see also v. 5). Moses was born at a time of political crisis as well, when God's prediction of Israel's oppression (v. 6) was being realized under the rule of "another king who had not known Joseph" (vv. 18-19; cf. Exod 1:8). God's recognition of Moses' "beauty"[289] (v. 20*a*; cf. Exod 2:2 LXX) and Egypt's appraisal of his "wisdom" and "powerful words and deeds" (vv. 20*b*-22; see also 6:8, 10) confirm him as to the prophet's manner born.[290]

7:23-29. Stephen's résumé of the second forty years of Moses' life follows this same prophetic typos and is coincidental of Luke's important two-visitation motif (see 3:17-23).[291] Stephen recounts the intent of Moses' first visit to the Israelites (v. 23) as a failed attempt to fulfill God's promise. Even though Moses was the one through whom God would "rescue" Israel (v. 25*a*), "they did not understand" (v. 25*b*; see also v. 12; 3:17).[292] The Israelite who ironically accused Moses of

---

286. Krodel, *Acts*, 143-44. However, the Genesis accounts of patriarchal burials are confusing and have led to different speculations about locations of burial sites. See Barrett, *A Critical and Exegetical Commentary on the Acts of the Apostles*, 350-51.

287. Marshall, *The Acts of the Apostles*, 139. His solution seems more likely if Luke views Samaritans as "the lost tribes" of Israel.

288. For development of the "prophet-like-Moses" theme in Luke-Acts, see the various studies by D. Moessner, especially his programmatic essay, "The Christ Must Suffer," *NovT* 28 (1986) 220-56. Moessner cautions the interpreter that Luke's typological use of Moses neither elevates Moses to messianic level nor diminishes Jesus' role in Israel as analogous to Moses. Jesus' fulfillment as the prophet-like-Moses is unique and final; there can be for Luke no messianic predecessor or successor.

289. Although Kee, *To Every Nation Under Heaven*, 319, translates ἀστεῖος (*asteios*) as "well-pleasing" and proleptic of Moses' obedience to God, the tradition of Moses' physical attractiveness is widespread in Jewish literature (see Heb 11:23).

290. Stephen's phrase "powerful in words and deeds" is the same one used of Jesus by his disciples in Luke 24:19 (cf. Acts 2:22) and is similar to Luke's description of Stephen in Acts 6:8. There is no support for this description of Moses either in the exodus narrative, which makes the opposite point (Exod 4:10), or in Jewish tradition. The phrase is Luke's, and its motive is typological: Moses is the proto-prophet-like-Jesus after whom Peter and now Stephen are modeled.

291. See Johnson, *The Acts of the Apostles*, 13, although the two visits of the prophet determine the destiny only of those repentant or unrepentant Jews in that particular location.

292. Stephen's comment that Moses first failed due to Israel's ignorance (7:25) is not in either the biblical narrative or any extant Jewish commentary on Exodus. His midrash reflects Luke's hand in adapting the biblical story to his "two visitation" typology, according to which the people of Israel are given another chance to repent and turn to God for salvation because of their leaders' ignorance (see 3:17; 7:12).

being "a ruler and a judge over us" (v. 27) got it right, but then "pushed him aside" and thus frustrated God's initiative to reconcile a divided Israel (v. 26; cf. Exod 2:14).[293] Because of Israel's obduracy, Moses was sent into exile in the land of Midian (vv. 28-29).

7:30-34. The recounting of the final forty years of Moses' life includes a second visitation and its tragic aftermath and is more critical to the overall aim of Stephen's speech (vv. 30-43). Exiled Moses is called back to Israel by divine revelation to rescue an afflicted people (v. 34; cf. Exod 3:7-10).[294] Luke's telling of Moses' theophany at the burning bush concentrates on the Lord's statement that "the place where you are standing is holy ground" (v. 33; cf. Exod 3:5-6). Johnson comments that once again Stephen's speech relativizes the importance of a particular "holy place" (= temple site in Jerusalem; see also 6:13), since any place where God presides among God's people through the Holy Spirit is holy.[295]

7:35-40. God dispatches Moses on his second visit to Israel. Stephen frames his retelling of this visit by mentioning the poor results of the first visit: "It was this Moses whom they rejected—whom God now sends as both ruler and liberator" (v. 35).[296] This depiction of Moses, reminiscent of Peter's earlier proclamation of the gospel about Jesus (3:13-15; cf. 3:22), is combined with the familiar catchphrase "wonders and signs" (see 2:19, 22, 43; 4:30; 5:12; 6:8) to draw a close family resemblance among Moses, Jesus, and his prophetic successors. Prophets are all called by God and are imbued by the power of the Holy Spirit to proclaim God's word and perform mighty deeds that make clear God's intention to fulfill the promise to Sarah and Abraham.

The comparison between Moses and Jesus in the literature of the ancient church emphasizes how much Jesus outdistances Moses (cf. Heb 3:1-6).[297] Here, however, and in Peter's earlier speech (see 3:22), Moses is considered the prophet par excellence because he predicted the one who would fulfill Abraham's promise to be a messianic "prophet-like-me" (v. 37).[298] Notably, Stephen employs the Moses typology without including his role as a lawgiver, since Moses "received living oracles to give to us" that evidently remain in effect (v. 38). The importance attached to the OT story of Moses is vocational: The Messiah will be "like *me*" in ministry and result. Thus the pattern of Israel's response to Moses' prophetic ministry is insinuated into Messiah's career: "Our ancestors were unwilling to obey Moses" (v. 39*a*; cf. Exod 16:3) and "in their hearts turned back to Egypt" in spiritual disaffection (v. 39*b*; cf. Num 14:2-3 LXX; Ezek 20:8), claiming ignorance (to Aaron) that "we do not know what happened to him" (v. 40). Roughly the same response characterizes a subsequent generation's response to God's Messiah, Jesus.

7:41-43. Stephen next describes the spiritual treachery that resulted because Israel rejected Moses' mission: "They made a calf, offered a sacrifice to the idol, and reveled in the works of their hands" (v. 41; cf. Exod 32:4-6).[299] Even though his second visitation had produced a saving result (v. 36), Israel's disaffection with God soon after and their desire to return to Egypt and offer sacrifice to idols committed them to a slavery of a different sort: "God turned away from them and handed them over to worship the host of heaven" (v. 42*a*; cf. Rom 1:24, 26, 28), captive to the consequences of their choice to live without God's grace and power.[300]

Stephen's quotation from the prophecy of Amos (Amos 5:25-27 LXX) to conclude his telling of the Moses story makes "the most astonishing jump in the speech."[301] Luke

293. Stephen's assessment that Moses' act is motivated by reconciliation reflects Luke's assessment that the principal theological crisis facing Israel is its divided house (Luke 2:34). As with Moses' failed effort to reconcile divided Israelites, the Messiah's attempt to bring peace to Israel was also rebuffed, because "they did not understand" (see 3:17).

294. Stephen cites and alludes to several fragments from Exod 3:7-10, combining them in a more succinct version to emphasize God's sovereign initiative in calling Moses to rescue Israel. The repetition of "this Moses/one" in the following verses recalls "Come now, I will send you to Egypt" (7:34*b*) and underscores his mission according to divine necessity. The implication is that this is true of the Messiah's mission as well, since he is the prophet-like-Moses.

295. Johnson, *The Acts of the Apostles*, 128.

296. The vocabulary used of Moses' two visitations recycles the kerygmatic language used in 3:13-15. In doing so Luke draws an implicit parallel between Moses and Jesus, thereby aiming the reader ahead to the prophecy about the "prophet-like-Moses" fulfilled by Jesus. In Peter's speech this same proof from prophecy is used (3:22) as to indicate the fulfillment of Abraham's promise (3:25).

297. See M. Simon, *St. Stephen and the Hellenists* (London: Longmans, Green, 1958) 60-62.

298. Jervell, *Die Apostelgeschichte*, 240.

299. The sin of the golden calf is viewed within Judaism as Israel's archetypal sin—a kind of "original sin."

300. The phrase "host of heaven" (ἡ στρατιὰ τοῦ οὐρανοῦ *hē stratia tou ouranou*) derives from 1 Kgs 22:19//Jer 7:18 and probably denotes astral powers. Luke shapes his account of Israel's spiritual failure in the wilderness by describing a religion composed of handmade idols and human calculations, neither of which leads a people into communion with God.

301. Dunn, *The Acts of the Apostles*, 96.

inserts the phrase "to worship" (προσκυνεῖν *proskynein* v. 43c) into the prophecy and changes Damascus to "Babylon" (v. 43d) to correct its history and make clear Scripture's lesson: If Israel rejects the prophet's second offering of God's salvation, it is the people and not the prophet of whom God says, "Therefore I will send you into exile" (v. 43d).[302]

7:44-50. The "Temple" Epoch of God's Presence. At last Stephen considers the Temple directly, moving with great rapidity from the "tent of testimony in the wilderness" (v. 44; cf. Exod 27:21) to Solomon, "who built a house [temple] for God" (v. 47; cf. 1 Kgs 5:1–7:51). He uses the regular Septuagint term for the tabernacle (ἡ σκηνή *hē skēnē*), which indicates its role within Israel is as a "testimony" (μαρτύριον *martyrion*) or witness to the "God of glory"—the same prophetic role the apostles, and now Stephen, have assumed within Israel (see 1:8, 22; 2:32; 3:15; 5:32; 10:39, 41). Stephen's choice of "tent" instead of "Temple" envisages God's direct control over its construction and its easy movement in the wilderness journey from place to sacred place so that one particular site is unimportant. By contrast, Solomon's (and certainly Herod's) Temple was not built according to God's pattern and instruction and could not be easily moved in any case! The glossary of worship terminology Stephen employs—"land," "tent," "worship," "God," "our ancestors"—shifts the definition of worship from the routines of a permanent structure to the dynamic presence of a transcendent God. Stephen's ironic wordplay concludes that any definition of Israel's worship that fails to emphasize worshiping God (= "the tent of testimony") runs the risk of substituting a "*tent* for Moloch" for the "dwelling place for the *house* of Jacob" (v. 46, italics added; cf. Ps 131:5 LXX).[303]

Stephen's contrast between Solomon, who builds a "house for God" (v. 47), and a God

who "does not dwell in houses made with human hands" (7:48) is the very nub of the prophet's criticism of his accusers (see 17:24-25).[304] Read in the context of Acts, his intent is *not* to criticize the Temple per se, since it continues to function as a worship center for the faith community (see 2:46; 3:8; 5:12).[305] Nor does Stephen demonize Solomon (or even Herod) for building a Temple to worship God; in fact, Solomon merely realizes his pious father's heartfelt petition when building the Temple (v. 47; cf. 2 Sam 7:2-7). Stephen's implied criticism is rather of any theological claim that domesticates God's transcendence, whether this obtains to the legalisms of observing an oral Torah or following a priestly protocol for purification. That is, God does not inhabit "houses" bound by space and time, since "the prophet says 'Heaven is my throne, and the earth is my footstool'" (7:49).[306]

Stephen's use of Isa 66:1 LXX to conclude his retelling of the Temple's history repeats earlier references to Israel's idolatry in the wilderness, when "our ancestors" built an idol sacrifice by "the works of their hands" (v. 41; cf. "made with human hands," v. 48) and turned from God "to worship the host of heaven" (v. 42; cf. "heaven is my throne," v. 49). This intertext clarifies the primary subtext of Stephen's speech, which does not polemicize against religious institutions (Temple, Torah) but against an unrepentant people who persist in refusing to believe the word of God's prophets (see v. 39)—Moses, Messiah, his apostolic successors, and now Stephen.[307]

7:51-53. The Prophet-Like-Jesus Indicts Unrepentant Israel. The charges against Stephen are without merit: He blasphemes neither Moses nor God. His charge against his accusers, however, is more serious and has merit. They are in danger of repeating Israel's wilderness sin and are thereby perilously close to being sent into spiritual

---

302. Moloch and Rephan (7:43a) are deities to whom the Israelites offered sacrifices in the wilderness. Moloch is a Babylonian deity; Stephen's reference to "tent of Moloch" stipulates that Israel's Babylonian exile resulted from idolatry. See Johnson, *The Acts of the Apostles*, 132. The threat posed by idolatry will become an important motif in the narrative of Paul's mission and the formation of Christian congregations in pagan environs (see 15:20-21).

303. There is a significant textual problem with the NRSV's "the tent of Jacob," as indicated by the different translation found in the NIV, "the God of Jacob." For arguments in support of the NRSV reading, see B. Metzger, *A Textual Commentary on the Greek New Testament*, (Stuttgart: Deutsche Bibelgesellschaft, 1994) 351-53; for arguments in support of the NIV reading, see Johnson, *The Acts of the Apostles*, 132-33.

304. 7:48 begins with ἀλλά (*alla*) to signal such a contrast between 7:47 (Solomon's Temple) and 7:48-50, which claims that God dwells in heaven.

305. Contra Dunn, *The Acts of the Apostles*, 97, along with others.

306. Mark 14:58 also substitutes "house" for "temple." The use of the plural "houses" reflects Christian tradition and, as used here, perhaps refers to all temples, pagan and Jewish. See Evans and Sanders, *Luke and Scripture*, 197n102.

307. Evans, *Luke and Scripture*, 197-99, rightly adds that the "people" Stephen attacked were the temple hierarchy, who sought to place God in the Temple and then define the terms of Israel's worship of God. This subverts the sovereignty of God and constitutes idolatry.

exile. Stephen accuses them of four evils: (1) They are "stiff-necked" (σκληροτράχηλος *sklērotrachēlos*; this term repeats an angry Lord's condemnation of disobedient Israel in Exod 33:3, 5), (2) "uncircumcised of heart and ears,"[308] (3) "forever opposing the Holy Spirit" (echoing Isa 63:10, which remembers Israel's rebellion in the wilderness) and so (4) behave "just as *your* ancestors used to do"[309] (v. 51, italics added). These accusations provide court evidence for his stinging indictment: "You are the ones that received the law as ordained by angels and yet you have not kept it" (v. 53).[310]

The real issue at stake in marking out a people belonging to God is neither temple nor torah purity but obedience to God's command. In this regard, Stephen's shocking condemnation of his accusers as "betrayers and murderers" of "the Righteous One" (v. 52) brands them as law breakers and unable to live up to their own standard of covenant loyalty. His use of ὁ δίκαιος (*ho dikaios*, "the Righteous One") recalls the story of Jesus' death, when the centurion confessed Jesus as *dikaios* ("an innocent man," Luke 23:47). The reader of Acts knows to fill in the gaps of Stephen's accusation with details of Luke's story of Jesus' execution as an innocent man; the gospel tradition provides the evidence in support of Stephen's judgment that those who put him to death were "murderers" and therefore law breakers. But its use here is articular—*the* Righteous One—and so recalls Peter's title for Jesus (an allusion to Isaiah's suffering servant), "the Righteous One" (see

3:14; cf. Isa 53:11).[311] Of course, the word of God's prophet that unrepentant Israel rejects concerns the salvation brokered by Jesus. The harsh implication is that the priestly establishment has forged temple practices and manipulated torah observance into a kind of idolatry that keeps Israel in a spiritual wilderness without Jesus, the true medium of sacred worship.

7:54–8:3. The contrasting responses to Stephen's speech are anticipated: The prophet's criticism of opponents inevitably provokes rage and death. Stephen's martyrdom confirms what Acts has only hinted at in the earlier suffering of the apostles: Prophets-like-Jesus will share in the passion of the suffering servant. The evident importance Luke attaches to Stephen's death may also reflect a common secular sensibility that self-sacrifice legitimates the truth of one's witness. Thus in his death Stephen exemplifies Christian discipleship. He is killed because of the shocking things he says about God's relations with an unrepentant Israel.

Stephen's death also marks a radical turning point in the Acts narrative of the church's mission. Clearly things are different now: "That day a severe persecution began" (8:1*b*). The church's mission is largely finished in the holy city because of Stephen's death. Never again will Acts narrate an evangelistic effort in Jerusalem, and the holy city will now become home to all kinds of forces that are opposed to God's plan of salvation. To be sure the Twelve (and presumably disciples from "the Hebrews") still live there (8:1*b*). But soon their ranks will dwindle through martyrdom and its threat (cf. Acts 12). And James will later report to Paul that mass conversions among the Jews still take place in Palestine (see 21:20). But the narrative's movement of mission from Stephen's martyrdom forward will push away from Jerusalem and toward Rome. Something has happened in God's relations with Jerusalem's Jews as a result of Stephen's death. Perhaps his speech represents the prophet's second visitation; perhaps his rejection and execution have sent these unrepentant Jews into spiritual exile and they

308. The charge of being "uncircumcised in heart" reverses the deuteronomic definition of covenant renewal when "God will circumcise your heart" (Deut 30:6; cf. Rom 2:29). The phrase recalls Jeremiah's judgment of unfaithful Israel as having "ears that are uncircumcised/they cannot listen [= obey]" (Jer 6:10). Surely his accusation recalls Stephen's earlier retelling of God's promise to Abraham, when "the covenant of circumcision" (7:8) indicated God's commitment to fulfill the promise within the history of the covenant/circumcised people (7:17). In effect, then, the refusal to believe Jesus imperils one's membership in the covenant community.

309. To signal the rhetorical shift from defense to accusation, Stephen turns from a recital of traditions received from "*our* ancestor(s)" (ὁ πατὴρ ἡμῶν *ho patēr hēmōn*; 7:2, 11, 15, 17, 19, 38-39, 44-45) to an accusation that his auditors belong to a history of spiritual failure written and handed down by "*your* ancestors" (οἱ πατέρες ἡμῶν *hoi pateres hēmōn*), a Jewish tradition to which Stephen/Jesus does not belong.

310. The reference to "angels" continues an interesting *leitmotif* of Stephen's speech introduced in his retelling of Moses' story. In two different places—at his calling (7:30, 35) and at his giving of the Torah (7:38)—angels communicate the word of the Lord to Moses. While Luke may well be continuing here the practice of the Septuagint to substitute "angel" as a euphemism for God's personal name, the usage probably carries theological freight within Luke's narrative world, in which angels typically mediate between heaven and earth as brokers of divine transcendence. This symbolic value is elevated in Stephen's contrast between God's heavenly habitation (7:49) and God's alleged habitation in the Jerusalem Temple.

311. The reference to Jesus as "Righteous One" recalls the cluster of titles for Jesus in Peter's second missionary speech (see 3:13-16) on the basis of which Peter demands Israel's repentance. While Stephen's appeal to Jesus lacks kerygmatic details, in the context of Acts Peter's earlier speech forms the intertext with 7:52 and fills in these missing details.

now must await the return of the Messiah for their own return. Yet there is also the prospect of rebirth and renewal in death. And so it is that Stephen's death serves to spread the gospel to other regions where the experience of the Spirit's signs and wonders and the hearing of the gospel will add others to the restored Israel of God.

The narrative of Stephen's martyrdom also introduces us to Saul, who will become in time the featured character of Acts and his mission its central topic. Luke introduces Saul to the reader at a theologically significant point: immediately before Stephen's death and his extraordinary petition for the Lord's forgiveness of those complicit in his murder. The deep logic of Saul's commission as a witness to the risen Jesus is not his background in diaspora Judaism, his membership in its Pharisaic party, his rabbinical education, or his Roman citizenship—all of which are important details of his biographical sketch in Acts and his vocation as a teacher of Israel. His conversion to Jesus and calling as a prophet-like-Jesus are explained by Luke in gospel terms: Saul is a forgiven man. By his own testimony, Stephen's martyrdom was a significant feature of Saul's conversion (cf. 22:20), not only as a benchmark of his own theological reversal but also as the foreshadowing of divine forgiveness and his restoration to faithful Israel.

7:54. The reader must eavesdrop on several conversations that fashion this story. The loudest is between Stephen and the mob that will kill him. Nowhere in Acts is the contrast between those who disobey and those who obey God's will more sharply drawn. The effect on the reader is to experience more concretely Stephen's biblical retelling of Israel's story as a history of disobedience. This somber effect is intensified by constant echoes of both OT and gospel traditions, reminding us that the harsh response to Stephen's prophetic ministry is characteristic of God's people.

The "these things" heard by Stephen's accusers are words critical of disobedient people and not of Temple or Torah. Their initial response is as expected: "They became enraged [lit., "their hearts were ripped open"] and ground their teeth at Stephen." The rage of a judicial body was first experienced by

Peter in 5:33 in response to a kerygmatic summary of the gospel (see 5:29-32). The angry reaction against Stephen is like Peter's before him: Disobedience to God is measured by a people's response to the gospel and not by maintaining temple or torah purity. The phrase "ground their teeth" (ἔβρυχον τοὺς ὀδόντας *ebrychon tous odontas*) is used in the psalter of the angry response of the wicked against God's servant (Pss 35:16; 37:12; 112:10; cf. Job 16:9) and in Matthew's Gospel of those excluded from the kingdom of heaven (Matt 8:12; 13:42, 50; 22:13; 24:51; 25:30). The testimony of the biblical witness glosses this expression of righteous indignation as evidence of the accusers' guilt and their status as outsiders of God's kingdom.

7:55-56. Stephen's response is Spirit-filled and exemplary: He accepts his fate as the prophets of God had before him (cf. 2 Chr 24:21). The phrase "filled with the Holy Spirit" (v. 55) designates him as one who is enabled by the Spirit to give bold and powerful witness to the risen Messiah (see 2:4; 4:8, 31; 6:5, 8). In this case, the Spirit elevates Stephen's prophetic consciousness to envision "the glory of God" (v. 55) and "the Son of Man standing at the right hand of God" (v. 56). His vision confirms his faithful testimony and prepares him for a martyr's death. Thus in seeing "the glory of God" Stephen is linked with Abraham, to whom "the God of glory" also appeared with promise of divine blessing (see 7:2). He is further associated with the death and rising of Jesus, whom Peter claimed was "glorified" by the God of this same Abraham (see 3:13), and also with his return "in a cloud with great glory" (Luke 21:27; cf. Acts 1:11). Good company, indeed!

Stephen is enabled by the Spirit of prophecy to envision "the Son of Man *standing*" (ἵστημι *histēmi*; v. 56, italics added).[312] While several interpretations seek to explain the posture of the exalted Son of Man,[313] the

312. In both Acts and the Gospels, this "Son of Man" refers to Jesus. Contra Haenchen, *The Acts of the Apostles*, 295. As a title for Jesus, this is the only example of its use outside of the Gospels and Revelation (1:13; 14:14).

313. Barrett, *A Critical and Exegetical Commentary on the Acts of the Apostles*, 384-85, helpfully catalogs the various interpretations of "standing." He thinks it is an idiom of Christ's parousia: Jesus stands in preparation to come for Stephen in the same manner that he will come for all believers at the end of time. If so, "standing" envisages the Lord's readiness to return to complete his messianic task (see 1:11; 3:20).

juridical cast of this setting suggests that Jesus now stands before heaven's jury to give convincing testimony in support of his servant Stephen.[314]

7:57-58. The council does not have a compelling capital case against Stephen, for he has not blasphemed Moses or God. But now they think their case has been made by Stephen's "blasphemous" claim that the Spirit had led him through heaven's portal and to the very throneroom of God.[315] In blind passion the mob "with a loud shout all rushed together against him" (v. 57). Luke combines the vivid expression "they covered their ears" with "uncircumcised in ears" (7:51) to form a vivid couplet expressive of the accusers' obdurate solidarity in opposition to God's word.[316] No formal verdict is rendered; their murderous response is an act of rage—in effect, a lynching.

There is a profound depth of irony in Luke's formulation of Stephen's execution: They "dragged him out of the city and began to stone him" (v. 58*a*). In their fit of rage, the mob maintains their pious decorum and takes him "out of the city," according to Torah's proscription (cf. Lev 24:11-13; Num 15:35) against murdering an innocent person, laying their coats at the feet of Saul (7:58*b*) in accordance with rabbinical *halakhah*.[317]

7:59-60. And so Stephen dies in imitation of Jesus: He prays, "Receive my spirit"[318] (cf. Luke 23:46), and cries out, "Do not hold this sin against them"[319] (cf. Luke 23:34), and died (cf. Luke 23:46). Unlike Jesus, however, the object of Stephen's petitions is the glorified "Lord Jesus" himself, the one whom the martyr worships.

8:1-3. Luke's transitional narrative features Saul. Luke upgrades Saul's passive

witness to Stephen's execution to the status of one who "approves of their killing him" (v. 1). Saul also assumes a more aggressive role in "ravaging the church by entering house after house; dragging off men and women and putting them in prison" (v. 3).[320] The apostles, along with other Hebrews, are momentarily exempt from this localized persecution because Saul's persecution follows the lead of Stephen's execution and probably concerns only disciples among the Hellenists.[321]

These initial snapshots of Saul in Acts provide a critical background for reading Luke's story of his conversion and calling in Acts 9 and then of his subsequent career as a Christian missionary. Saul's earnest opposition to the church is of a kind with those who executed Stephen, and his malevolent evolution from passive bystander (7:58) to leading enemy of the church (8:3) will be stopped by his breathtaking transformation into a leader of the church's mission.

Sandwiched between narrative summaries of Saul's dreadful persecution of Hellenist Jewish believers (8:1*b*, 3) are two comments that move the reader forward in Acts. First, the church is "scattered throughout the countryside of Judea and Samaria" (8:1*b*). Will they advance the gospel beyond Jerusalem, as prophesied by the Lord (see Acts 1:8)? Second, "devout men buried Stephen and made loud lamentation over him" (8:2). Luke's vague description of "devout men" has led some to think that they are not believers but are either pious Jews interested in maintaining torah purity[322] or Jewish sympathizers who shared Stephen's opposition to the

---

314. Witherington, *The Acts of the Apostles*, 275.

315. Barrett, *A Critical and Exegetical Commentary on the Acts of the Apostles*, 383.

316. Johnson, *The Acts of the Apostles*, 140.

317. See *m.Sanh.* 6:1–7:10. Mishnaic rules governing such things as the execution of a blasphemer come from a later period; it may well be anachronistic to read them into Luke's narrative. On the other hand, many of these regulations recall case studies extended back to the Second Temple period, perhaps including the protocol followed here in Luke's narrative of Stephen's death.

318. Haenchen, *The Acts of the Apostles*, 296, says that Luke fashions these words after a short Jewish evening prayer based upon Ps 31:5 to commend pious Stephen's "spirit" to the Lord.

319. Stephen's petition that God forgive *him* reverses what we would usually expect from a condemned man. His petition for forgiveness of the sins of others reflects his personal righteousness in two ways: by the implication that he has no sins to forgive and by the depth of his mercy in forgiving those who falsely and illegally execute him.

320. The purpose and nature of Saul's persecution remain contested. What is on firm historical ground is that such a persecution took place and that it was precipitated by Stephen's death. What is also clear from contemporary Jewish literature from the Maccabean period is that a zeal for torah purity could lead to harsh demonstrations against those perceived as violating God's covenant with Israel. In this historical light, the reader of Acts is better able to understand that Saul's persecution of other diaspora Jews in Jerusalem is prompted by his own zeal for torah purity (see Phil 3:6) and by the perception that this messianic movement led by Stephen had transgressed the bounds of faithful Israel as measured by torah regulation of temple practices and prerogatives.

321. See Hill, *Hellenists and Hebrews*, 32-40, who thinks it unrealistic to suppose that business returned to normal following Stephen's death. Passions among the Hellenists within the church would have been every bit as fierce as those that precipitated their leader's execution—especially if their numbers were as large as 6:1, 7 suggests. Paul's severe persecution may well have been a court-sanctioned strategy to maintain peace in the Greek-speaking enclaves of Jerusalem (see Acts 22:4-5). See also Witherington, *The Acts of the Apostles*, 278.

322. See Schneider, *Die Apostelgeschichte*, 479. Jervell, *Die Apostelgeschichte*, 255, thinks this is the first reference to "God-fearers" and foreshadows the conversion of Cornelius (similar to Pesch and Roloff).

temple hierarchy. Johnson is probably correct that this comment echoes the Gospels' tradition about Joseph of Arimathea (see Luke 23:50; John 19:38-42); he also suggests that "a good and righteous" remnant still remains outside repentant Israel.[323]

323. See Johnson, *The Acts of the Apostles*, 141.

REFLECTIONS

1. "For we have heard him say that this Jesus of Nazareth . . ." (6:14 NIV). The growing hostility provoked by Stephen's ministry is due to his likeness to Jesus. Similar to Luke's description of Jesus, Stephen is portrayed as a prophet full of "wisdom and Spirit," capable of performing "great wonders and signs." He continues what Jesus had begun to say and to do (see 1:1). The accusations brought against him are also similar in kind and are made by common opponents. Both Jesus and Stephen died as martyrs, ever obedient to God, whose chief concern in the end was the forgiveness of those responsible for their deaths. Stephen is like Jesus in character and conduct, and he is lionized by the church as exemplary of a Christlike obedience to the redemptive purposes of God. But Stephen is not the Messiah. The church's confession of Jesus as Savior and Lord underlines his unique role and status in the economy of God's salvation. To imitate the risen Jesus is not to assume for oneself his messianic calling or his heavenly status: "Salvation is found in no one else, for there is no other name under heaven given to men by which we must be saved" (4:12 NIV).

2. "The time drew near for the fulfillment of the promise that God had made to Abraham" (7:17 NRSV). Great sermons often mark turning points in the book of Acts as they do in the life of congregations. In Acts they are precipitous of either transformed lives or hostile actions because of the ideas they introduce about the nature and manner of God's salvation. This speech by Stephen marks such a moment, largely because of the two important ideas he presses for. The first is that the history of God's salvation, marked out by a recital of Old Testament events, pivots on the promise of God to Abraham. The surety of Israel's future is predicated on divine promise, not on political negotiation. The second is that God's salvation is brokered by prophets-like-Moses, who are marked out within Israel by their liberating works and living words. The good future promised is determined by Israel's response to the provocative ministry of God's inspired prophets. As the history of God's salvation continues into our day, this prophetic calculus for realizing the promises of God in the church's life remains the same. Who are the prophets-like-Jesus among us? And what is our response to their provocative words and powerful deeds?

3. "Make gods for us who will lead the way for us" (7:40*a* NRSV). When any congregation of a faithful God refuses to listen to honest warnings of their spiritual laxity, they inevitably turn away from the one true God to idols they have fabricated to validate their selfish values. In response to his accusers, who claim that he challenges the religious "customs" of Moses, Stephen considers the prophetic vocation of Moses as exemplary of faithful Israel. The Word of God not only offers people God's forgiveness and healing, but it also engages them in self-criticism. While the primary task of the prophet-like-Moses is to mediate God's gracious rescue of people from death (in its various forms), the prophet also is called to mediate God's indictment of a people's obduracy and ungratefulness. Israel's rejection of Moses and then Stephen illustrate how difficult it is for God's people to hear harsh and honest words that call us to repentance.

4. "The Most High does not dwell in houses made with human hands" (7:48 NRSV). One of the most provocative themes of Stephen's biting criticism of official Israel's religious practices is the exhaltation of a particular sacred place (i.e., the Temple in Jerusalem), a particular priesthood, and a particular protocol of purity as the medium of God's active presence among God's people. This theme continues for the rest of Acts. When James expresses anxiety about the relations between repentant Gentiles and Jews in the diaspora (see 15:20-21, 29), he reflects a similar sentiment to the one challenged by Stephen: Can spiritual formation take place outside those practices and institutions the church (or Judaism) has established for this purpose? Jesus' criticism of the Temple as the central symbol of Jewish faith, followed now by Stephen, is deeply rooted in Christianity's core conviction that we are a people gathered together and marked out by our faith in a person. Jesus Christ sanctifies the place—any place— where the congregation gathers for worship and instruction.

5. "While they were stoning him, Stephen prayed" (7:59 NIV). The manner of Stephen's death is exemplary of his costly obedience. His inspired vision of the exalted Lord, glossed by his faithful confession and earnest prayers at the very moment of his martyrdom, expresses a genuine piety. Yet the most compelling evidence of the depth of Stephen's spiritual life is the content of his prayers. Similar to Jesus' dying words, Stephen prays for the forgiveness of his enemies at the very moment of their apparent triumph over him and his witness. He does not ridicule his executioners, nor does he express regret for his untimely death. He prays for their salvation: It is what and for whom he prays, and not that he prays, that gives his death its most profound meaning.

Included among Stephen's enemies is Saul. Prayers that petition God for the forgiveness of another are important for Luke: They make second chances for spiritual renewal possible (cf. 1 John 5:14-16). Paul's later, seemingly passing reference to Stephen in his apologia (22:20) is laden with this realization: The earnest prayer of Saul's religious opponent supplies the context for his own calling to be, as Stephen was, a prophet-like-Jesus. For whom does the church pray today? And what is the concern of our intercession?

ACTS 8:4-40, "AND IN ALL JUDEA AND SAMARIA": PHILIP'S MISSION TO OUTCASTS BEYOND JERUSALEM

OVERVIEW

This passage narrates the beginnings of the church's mission beyond Jerusalem, thereby fulfilling Jesus' prophecy of Acts 1:8.[324] The holy city remains in the reader's rear view mirror—always in sight but now left behind: "all except the apostles were scattered throughout the countryside of Judea and Samaria" (8:1b). This passage also tells the story of Philip, another charismatic prophet-like-Jesus and one of the seven (see 6:5) who has evidently succeeded Stephen as leader of the persecuted Hellenists.[325] It is principally through his prophetic ministry that the word of God goes forward into these new

324. Dunn, *The Acts of the Apostles*, 102, claims that the initial expansion into Judea began in 5:16, but clearly "the towns around Jerusalem" refers to the suburbs of Jerusalem and are still within its city limits. On the other hand, Tannehill, *The Acts of the Apostles*, 2:108-9, sees the conversion of the eunuch (8:26-39), who comes to Jerusalem from Ethiopia (mythology's "end of the earth") as the fulfillment of Jesus' prophecy that the gospel would spread to the "end of the earth." In this sense, then, the conversion of the eunuch sounds a transitional note in the church's international mission and prepares the reader for the activities of Paul the evangelist. However, this, too, is an unlikely reading, since Jesus' prophecy in Acts 1:8 concerns the *geography* (not the biography) of mission—i.e., Philip's conversion of the eunuch is the first such episode *on Judean soil*.

325. The secondary literature on Philip is slender. See F. S. Spencer, *The Portrait of Philip in Acts*, JSNTSS 67 (Sheffield: *JSOT*, 1992); Spencer, *Acts*, 84-94. Pesch, *Die Apostelgeschichte*, 288, suggests that this is not the Hellenist Philip of the seven but the Hebrew Philip of the Twelve (see 1:13). Indeed, as Fitzmyer, *The Acts of the Apostles*, 410, argues, Luke considers it a "divine necessity" for each discrete stage of the church's mission to be initiated by one of the Lord's apostolic successors. But the textual evidence strongly argues that this is deacon Philip.

territories and continues to flourish there (see 21:7-14).[326]

Despite the strategic importance of Philip's mission, Acts relates only two episodes. Their combined role within Acts is much debated, although it seems more like a transition or interlude that moves the reader from one significant moment (Stephen) to the next (Paul) by nuance rather than by bold and substantive contribution. In fact, the literary shaping of Luke's account of the Samaritan mission (8:4-25) recalls the pattern of the first interlude of Acts (see 4:32–5:16): (1) The passage begins with a summary of Philip's mission to underscore its continuity with the Jerusalem apostolate (cf. 8:4-8//4:32-35). (2) This summary is followed by the story of that curious figure, Simon the Great, whose contrasting responses to the powerful word of God illustrate the theme of its continuity beyond Jerusalem (see 8:9-19//4:36–5:11). (3) The interlude concludes with another vividly rendered portrait of apostolic authority (cf. 8:20-25//5:12-16). In this sense, then, the story of Philip's Samaritan mission gathers together in a compressed way the most important literary themes of Acts thus far, moving them beyond Jerusalem into a new territory in preparation for the dramatic stories of Saul's commission to carry the word beyond Israel (see 9:15) and Peter's conversion of an uncircumcised Gentile (see 10:1–11:18).[327]

The role of the second story (8:26-40), Philip's conversion of an Ethiopian eunuch, is more difficult to assess. Once again, the reader finds a critical clue in its literary pattern, which Luke shapes as a chiasmus to bring to clearer focus the eunuch's pertinent question, "About whom, may I ask you, does the prophet say this?" (8:34), and thereby also his idea of Scripture (see 1:16). The eunuch's question reflects what he presumes about the Isaianic prophecy he ruminates upon—that is, Scripture is prophetic of God's plan of salvation: "About whom, may I ask you, *does the prophet say this*?" He also believes that

biblical prophecy can make sense of people, places, events, and protocols that are the variegated bits and pieces of this redemptive plan: "*About whom*, may I ask you, does the prophet say this?" But he finally recognizes that biblical prophecies require prophetic interpreters to recover their meaning: "About whom, *may I ask you*, does the prophet say this?" The Ethiopian has already admitted his dependence upon "someone [who] guides me" (8:31a). The eunuch's question of Philip is appropriate, and this second story of Philip's mission rounds off his prophetic résumé. In addition to the gospel that he proclaims and the signs and wonders that he performs, Philip is enabled by the Spirit to read sacred texts after the mind of God (see 2:4; 8:35).

Of equal importance are the surprising converts that are added to the church's rolls. Samaritans and Ethiopian eunuchs are marginal Jews, more removed from Israel's promised blessings than their geographical separation from Jerusalem suggests. While Samaritans are not proto-Gentiles,[328] they are "the lost sheep of Israel"[329] and religious renegades as well as racially "impure" according to more traditional Jews. While the second convert is a pious pilgrim, his geographical origin and sexual condition disclose a religious status that is far removed from the epicenter of Jewish life and faith.[330] In fact, the subtitle of this section—"the outcasts of Israel"—comes from Isa 56:8, a prophecy echoed in Luke's story of the Ethiopian eunuch (see 8:27). According to this prophecy, God will gather the entire household of Israel, including both "foreigners" and "eunuchs," for worship in celebration of God's faithfulness to

---

326. If Luke was Paul's traveling companion and visited Philip in Caesarea with him, it could be that he first heard these stories directly from Philip (21:8-10). If Luke did not know Paul or travel with him, then this narrative is more likely composed freestyle to advance his theological interests. As with most speculations about Luke's sources, the truth is probably somewhere between: Luke had and used reliable sources but shaped his story to advance his own theological perspective.

327. For the connection between Philip and the later portrait of Peter in Acts, see Spencer, *The Portrait of Philip in Acts*, 103-22.

328. Luke seems to locate Samaritans and this Ethiopian eunuch within historic Israel in 11:19 when he summarizes Philip's mission: "They spoke the word to no one except Jews."

329. See Jervell, "The Lost Sheep of the House of Israel," in *Luke and the People of God*, 113-32.

330. The precise religious identity of the eunuch is a critical problem of long standing, since it determines his role within the story. Is he a Gentile, a God-fearer, a Jewish proselyte, a diaspora Jew, or a representative of all God "seekers"? Barrett, *A Critical and Exegetical Commentary on the Acts of the Apostles*, 425-26, summarizes the various options and contends (with others) that the eunuch is the first Gentile convert. However, his portrait in Acts is certainly not that of a pagan Gentile, since he is linked to the Temple and to Scripture. Nor is he (at least in Luke's mind) a God-fearing Gentile like Cornelius, since Peter later claims him to be the first Gentile convert (Acts 15:7). Fitzmyer, *The Acts of the Apostles*, 410, concludes that the eunuch is a Jewish proselyte—a Gentile who has converted to Judaism; but this is not his distinguishing mark within Acts, since other proselytes had come to the faith (see 2:10; 6:5). He represents the most marginal groups within the household of Israel, since he is a sexually castrated Jew, considered impure and, therefore, forbidden from participating in Jewish fellowship.

God's people. Philip's mission in Samaria and his conversion of the eunuch do *not* initiate the church's mission beyond Israel; they are, rather, the climactic episodes in Luke's narrative of Israel's restoration that began with Jesus' messianic mission to Israel.

Finally, this narrative of mission is shaped by a biblical conception of salvation's progress, which begins within Israel as a divine necessity before moving out to the nations (cf. Isa 2:3). By the time we reach Luke's concluding summary of Philip's mission (see 8:40), Acts will have recounted conversions from the various groups that constitute the *whole* household of Israel—resident Jews from Jerusalem to pilgrims from the most distant regions of the diaspora, pious Jews most devoted to their religious heritage to those most detached from it. Why? To prepare the reader for the Lord's shocking commission of another Jewish convert who will carry the word of God beyond Israel as "a light to the nations" (see 9:15).

Acts 8:4-25, Philip's Mission to the "Outcasts of Israel": The Samaritans

COMMENTARY

There was considerable antipathy between Samaritans and Judean Jews in the first century.[331] Samaritans were widely viewed by traditional Jews as racially "impure," religiously "heterodox," and politically treacherous—the gatekeepers of the Roman occupation in Palestine headquartered in Samarian Caesarea. Even though they worshiped the same God and followed a version of the same torah, Samaritans were outcasts within the household of Israel because the location of their temple was on a different mountain and in a different holy place. Most religious Samaritans were dedicated messianists, who hoped for the coming of the *Taheb*, the restorer of Samaritan fortunes, according to Deut 18:15. The Jesus of the Synoptic Gospels avoids traveling in Samaria altogether, although Luke's Jesus does rebuke his disciples for asking him to be like Elijah and call down heaven's fire to purge a rogue Samaria (cf. Luke 9:51-56). However, the story of Jesus' Samaritan mission found in John 4:1-42 prepares readers for Philip's Samaritan mission in the following ways:[332]

(1) John's story of Jesus' sojourn in Samaria is introduced by, "Jesus had to [ἔδει *edei*] go through Samaria" (John 4:4). The geographical necessity of Jesus' detour envisages its theological necessity: Jesus went through Samaria as part of God's redemptive plan.[333] In continuity with John's Jesus, then, this account of Philip's Samaritan mission is governed by divine purpose (see 1:8).

(2) Jesus' encounter with the Samaritan woman underscores its "shock value." The woman is surprised that Jesus would speak to her (John 4:9), not only because it violates long-standing social conventions that arrange male/female relations by a particular etiquette but also because it offends traditional religious beliefs that have long divided observant Jews from Samaritans. The Gospel's subtext, which is now worked out more fully in this story of Philip's mission, is that God's "living water" is for the Samaritans too (John 4:10, 13-14).

(3) Jesus' response to the woman's remark concerning the popular currents that locate

331. Literature on this issue is divided. On the one hand, Samaritans are considered a Jewish problem, and as such their origins, history, beliefs, social status, and religious practices are all evaluated within the context of Jewish history. See A. Crown, ed., *The Samaritans* (Tübingen: J. C. B. Mohr [Paul Siebeck], 1989). On the other hand, Samaritans are considered a Christian problem, and their role in Acts is considered from the angle of Samaritan Christianity, whose influence on Luke is seen through his emphasis on themes linked to Samaritan beliefs—e.g., the messianic prophet-like-Moses, God's preferential option for the social outcast. See Hill, *Hellenists and Hebrews*, 95-99.

332. The following is an example of a "canonical conversation" that takes place *between* biblical texts rather than in the actual ancient world *behind* the text. Whether the historical Jesus ever conducted a Samaritan mission is not the principal interest of this conversation. If the reader follows a sequential (i.e., ideal) reading of Scripture, he or she would have already considered Jesus' provocative use of the "good Samaritans" in Luke 10:29-37 and 17:11-19 and then Jesus' Samaritan mission in John 4 before taking up Acts 8. The "canonical" task is to discern whether this prior reading of the Gospels informs and gives direction to the interpretation of Acts 8.

333. See G. R. O'Day, "John, Introduction, Commentary, and Reflections," in *NIBC*, 8:480.

the center of worship in different parts of Palestine (John 4:20-24) illumines the literary relationship that places this passage following the story of Stephen's dispute with the temple hierarchy over the right "place" of sacred worship. Both Stephen and John's Jesus direct our attention to a God who is worshiped in "spirit and truth" rather than upon a particular mountain and at a certain site.[334]

(4) At the same time Jesus reminds the Samaritan that God's salvation comes from "the Jews" (John 4:22b); the redemptive protocol insists that a Samaritan mission follow a Jerusalem mission. The woman's climactic confession that "I know the Messiah is coming" (John 4:25) recognizes that his saving word is prophetic (cf. John 4:19) of her own hope in a coming Messiah (John 4:25).

(5) The Lord's extraordinary confession that "I Am" the Messiah (John 4:26) discloses his true identity as "the Savior of the world" (John 4:42) to this outcast and provides the christological subtext of Philip's distinctive proclamation of "the Messiah" to the Samaritans (Acts 8:5). Even as the experience of God's salvation that comes in the name of this "Savior of the world" dissolves the social and economic barriers in the community of goods, so now in the Samaritan and Judean missions of Philip long-standing religious barriers begin to crumble as well.

(6) More extraordinary still is that the Samaritan woman, now a convert, becomes a witness to Jesus (John 4:39-42). She is Philip's predecessor in Samaria, and her personal testimony of Jesus leads others into a shared experience with him. Yet this new faith is rooted in a personal encounter with Jesus (John 4:40-41) rather than public testimony about him (John 4:42). The confidence that these new Samaritan believers share the same experience of Jesus with those that come before is supported in Acts by the literary theme of succession: Philip is a prophet-like-Jesus vested with power by the Spirit to continue what Jesus began to say and do as Savior of the world.

8:4-8. The various panels of this episode are enclosed by Luke's characteristic use of the Greek phrase οἱ μὲν οὖν (*hoi men oun*, "Now those," v. 4; "Now after," v. 25), which indicates that his plotline has turned in a new direction.[335] This catchphrase begins the story by introducing a doublet that summarizes the church's Samaritan mission: "Those scattered [in Samaria; v. 1b] preached [εὐαγγελίζω *euangelizō*] the word" (v. 4), and "Philip went to the city of Samaria and proclaimed [κηρύσσω *kēryssō*] the Messiah" (v. 5). The people of the city listen carefully ("with one accord") to what Philip says and watch closely what he does. Earlier missionary speeches fill in the gaps of what Philip proclaims and provide meaning of the "signs" he performs (v. 6; see also 2:19). The impression is clear: Philip is a prophet-like-Jesus who has come to Samaria to announce the arrival of God's salvation.

Yet, Philip proclaims a word in a different idiom for the citizens of a different city. A new stage of Christian mission is symbolized by a new sign: the exorcism of unclean spirits (v. 7), which recalls Jesus' ministry of exorcism as an expression of God's triumphant kingdom (cf. Luke 11:14-26). The Samaritans' "joyful" experience of God's salvation (v. 8) is also noted for the first time in Acts and is another symbol of the gospel's arrival in a new territory.[336] Philip's success topples the wall of enmity between Samaritans and Jews, and Stephen's puzzling reference to the tombs of Samarian "shechem" (see 7:16) finally makes sense: The patriarchs buried here found an Israel that includes "the lost tribes of Israel" (= Samaritans).

8:9-13. To illustrate this new day, Luke recruits one of the most interesting characters of Acts, Simon the Great.[337] Carefully selected

---

334. This Lukan collocation of two episodes from Philip's mission concerns groups viewed as marginal in relation to the Jerusalem Temple. Not only are Samaritans considered religious rogues because of the location of their "temple," but also the eunuch is prohibited by Torah from entering the Temple (see Deut 23). The Temple subtext plotted by Luke's narrative of the Jerusalem mission is brought forward—although more implicitly—into this next stage of mission.

335. See Krodel, *Acts*, 160-61; Barrett, *A Critical and Exegetical Commentary on the Acts of the Apostles*, 400.

336. Luke introduces "proclaimed the Messiah" (ἐκήρυσσεν τὸν Χριστόν *ekēryssen ton Christon*), an important verb for gospel preaching, in this narrative summary and will repeat it in describing Saul's first and final preaching ministries in Acts (9:20; 28:31) and in Peter's mission to Cornelius to define the essential task of the Gentile mission (10:37, 42). The experience of "joy" (χαρά *chara*) is introduced into Acts here as well and is subsequently used in 13:52 and 15:3 (cf. 20:24) to summarize the experience of Paul's Gentile converts.

337. His alias, Simon the Magician (Simon Magus), is never used by Luke and is the creation of later church theologians who demonized Simon and attached his name to all kinds of heresies and subversive activities—a reputation that Simon the Great has been unable to shake. Compared to his apocryphal profile, Luke's Simon is a rather benign fellow whose character functions to illustrate the transforming power of God's saving grace as well as the dangers of immature faith.

elements from his legendary biography are recalled by Luke in a brief narrative flashback: Previously Simon had "practiced magic" and "amazed Samaritans" of every kind, who "listened eagerly to him" and called him "Power of God" (δύναμις τοῦ θεοῦ *dynamis tou theou*) or simply "Great" (μέγας *megas* v. 9).[338] This résumé echoes Luke's portrait of the crowd who responds to Philip by "listening eagerly" (vv. 6, 11) to the gospel he proclaims. In this way, Luke links Simon and Philip as two brokers of a power that attracts people to them. Unlike Simon's case, however, the source of Philip's prophetic power is the Holy Spirit and its motive is redemptive rather than political. This contrast is implicit in Luke's use of the adversative δέ (*de*, "But," v. 12). The Samaritans "believed Philip"[339] and were "baptized" (v. 12; see 1:3; 2:38; 3:6-11; cf. 20:25; 28:31). Whatever rivalry existed between Simon and Philip is now over: "Even Simon himself believed and was baptized" (v. 13*a*). This Simon whom the Samaritans "followed" everywhere (v. 11) now "follows Philip everywhere" (v. 13*a*)!

But Luke alerts the reader to a spiritual problem on the near horizon: "Simon was amazed at the signs and great miracles that took place" (v. 13*b*). This expression is characteristic in Acts of the *unbeliever's* response to their experience of God's mighty deeds through the Holy Spirit and typically comes *prior to* repentance. In his case the redemptive protocol is reversed: His amazement at the Spirit's "signs" comes after his conversion and not as a precondition of it. He seems more impressed by the spectacular than by the spiritual. This response to the Spirit's "signs and wonders" reflects Simon's theological mistake.

8:14-17. The plot thickens when Philip's role is assumed by the Jerusalem apostles, Peter and John. Their house call on this newly formed Samaritan congregation is an exercise of their spiritual authority and should take no one by surprise. To read a sinister motive into their Samaritan mission is simply unwarranted; they are clearly putting their apostolic powers to use in solidarity with Philip's mission.

The expression of their apostolic leadership within the church is a different expression of a familiar practice: Peter and John redistribute the Holy Spirit among believers in need of its spiritual powers, analogous to their redistribution of goods to the community's needy (see 4:32-35; cf. 2:44-45). The Samaritan believers had not yet been baptized with the Holy Spirit, even though they already have been "baptized in the name of the Lord Jesus" (8:16). Luke does not explain the delay between these two baptisms, and their relationship remains quite fluid in Acts in any case (see 2:38-41; 10:44-48; 19:1-6). We can only infer from Jesus' promise of Spirit baptism that believers are unable to participate fully in the community's missionary vocation without receiving the gift of the Holy Spirit (see 1:4-8). The aim of the apostles' mission in Samaria, then, is precisely as before: to form a religious community that shares all things in equal measure including their missionary vocation. Even their liturgical acts of "prayer" (v. 15; see also 6:4) and "laying their hands on them" (v. 17; see also 6:6) recall the role they performed when commissioning the seven to heal the growing rift between the "Hellenists" and "Hebrews" within the community of goods.

8:18-19. Nevertheless, the narrative's spotlight remains on Simon. "Now when Simon saw" (v. 18) shifts the story's action quickly back to him for his reaction to the apostles' actions. Nothing in the text indicates that Simon has been excluded from the Spirit's empowerment, but his political ambition solicits a different species of "power" that would qualify him to lead the community—an authority to rule that Jesus had given only to his apostolic successors (see 1:2). The word translated "power" (ἐξουσία *exousia*, v. 19) denotes the legal authority of decision making.[340] Simon offers money to purchase for himself a share of the apostles'

---

338. Although their precise meaning remains debated, the names Luke gives to Simon suggest his deification. Luke follows Scripture and consigns "magic" to the demonic realm (e.g., Acts 13:10; 19:13-20). Magicians exercise real power and have real influence over people, but magic's form and result are spiritually oppressive and physically debilitating. Hence, exorcism demonstrates God's reign precisely because of its liberating effect in the demoniac who is freed from oppressive or physical ailment (see Luke 11:14-26). See R. W. Wall, "The 'Finger of God': Deuteronomy 9:10 and Luke 11:20," *NTS* 33 (1987) 144-50.

339. While the phrase "believed Philip" is exceptional, since Luke typically has either God or Jesus as the object of the convert's trust (see 5:14; 9:42; 10:43//11:17; 16:31-34), it undoubtedly is elliptical and means something similar to his earlier phrase, where converts "accepted Peter's message and were baptized" (see 2:41).

340. See W. Foerster, "ἐξουσία" *TDNT* 2:566-74.

exousia, with all the rights and privileges that obtain to their appointment as rulers over the restored Israel of God. His theological miscalculation is again symbolized by his offering of money in exchange for something he could possess and manipulate for himself in complete disregard for the community of goods (see 5:1-10).[341]

8:20-24. Simon's spiritual failure is sharply pointed out by Peter, who exclaims, "May your money perish with you!" (v. 20).[342] The direction and purpose of God's Spirit (v. 20; see also 2:38) are divine prerogatives (see 1:2).[343] Spencer contends the implied subject of Peter's severe rebuke is not Simon's salvation but Peter's honor.[344] That is, Peter regards Simon's spiritual insolence as degrading of his apostolic rule—the mistaken presumption that membership in the Apostolate can be purchased by someone who is so obviously unqualified (see 1:21-22). The subtext of Peter's retort and Simon's prompt acquiescence is recognition of the apostle's ultimate authority on earth to determine the terms of any believer's participation in God's salvation (cf. Matt 16:19). Thus again

the practical objective of Peter's exercise of apostolic authority is to save people from the consequences of their sins, as in his earlier speech that associates Israel's ignorance (see 3:17) with its wickedness (see 3:26) and prompts his exhortation to "repent and turn to God so that your sins may be wiped out" (see 3:19). Read in this light, Peter's rebuke of Simon is considerably less severe than his earlier condemnation of Ananias, and the prognosis of Simon's restoration is more favorable. The apostle tacitly excuses Simon for being ignorant (or theologically immature), and the reader more clearly understands the motive of his exhortation that Simon "pray to the Lord" (v. 22). Peter evidently holds out hope for God's forgiveness and Simon's restoration (cf. v. 23).

8:25. The story that begins with Philip preaching the gospel as he departs Jerusalem with other persecuted believers (see 8:4) here concludes with the apostles retracing his evangelistic mission by preaching their way back to Jerusalem. The inclusio that frames this episode by a common phrase (οἱ μὲν οὖν *hoi men oun*) indicates the continuity between the church's missions in and beyond Jerusalem and relates the differences between them.[345] The different tasks performed in Samaria (e.g., the exorcism of demons), the proclamation of the gospel in a new idiom (e.g., preaching the Messiah or the kingdom of God), and even the time lapse between water and Spirit baptisms all aim at the same redemptive reality: the restoration of the whole house of Israel (see the Overview above).

341. Johnson, *The Literary Function of Possessions in Luke-Acts*, 216. For the parallelism in narrative details and theological significance between this story and Luke's earlier story of Ananias and Sapphira (see 5:1-11), see Johnson's fuller discussion in *The Literary Function of Possessions in Luke-Acts*, 213-17.
342. So Haenchen, *The Acts of the Apostles*, 304, who nicely captures the threat Simon's lust for power poses to his eternal salvation.
343. Several allusions clarify Peter's intention in rebuking Simon. His assertion that Simon has "no part [μερίς *meris*] or share [κλῆρος *klēros*] in this [gift]" (8:21a) recalls the story of Judas, who forsakes his "part" (*klēros*) of apostolic ministry by failing Jesus for money (1:17)—the same "part" that Matthias then plays in replacing him (1:25). Ironically, Simon offers money to gain the apostolic "part" of the mission that Judas lost for money. The next phrase, "your heart is not right before God," echoes Ps 78:37 and its teaching that one who repents will be restored to God. The OT intertexts of "gall of bitterness" (see Deut 29:18; Heb 12:15-17) and "chains of wickedness" (see Isa 58:6) harshly condemn the practice of idolatry, and here one might infer that Peter's holds little hope for Simon's restoration. See Barrett, *A Critical and Exegetical Commentary on the Acts of the Apostles*, 417. These biblical intertexts supply Peter's rebuke with a kind of prophetic undercurrent that makes his appeal to Simon to repent more urgent.
344. Spencer, *Acts*, 88-89.

345. F. S. Spencer, "The Ethiopian Eunuch and his Bible," *BTB* 22 (1992) 155-65, argues that 8:25 better forms an inclusio with 8:40, framing the story of his evangelistic tour of Judea and conversion of the eunuch as a nice complement to the story of his Samaritan mission, which is circumscribed by political bounds and social conventions of a particular Samaritan city.

REFLECTIONS

1. "Those who were scattered went from place to place, proclaiming the word" (8:4 NRSV). Persecution does not stop proclamation. In fact, Luke's story of Philip employs many images of traveling and references to geography to create a vivid impression that the word of God is on the move beyond Jerusalem in productive ways. This passage also indicates and illustrates the three "big ideas" of Christian proclamation: Philip preached the good news about (1) *the kingdom of God* (8:12), (2) *the resurrection of Jesus Christ* (8:4-5, 12), and (3) *the gift of the Holy Spirit* (8:15-17). The complement of gospel preaching and miraculous "signs" has a galvanizing effect on those who "listened eagerly" to Philip (8:6). The fact that a program of religious repression fails to stop the word from spreading says something about both the character of those faithful witnesses who are scattered and the intention of a faithful God whose commitment to humanity's salvation cannot be subverted.

2. "Simon . . . followed Philip everywhere, astonished by the great signs and miracles he saw" (8:13 NIV). The Samaritan Simon of Acts is a compelling figure. Later theologians who wrongly identify him as the prototype of every Christian heretic rightly recognize that at the root of Simon's spiritual failure is a temptation every new believer must resist. From his conversion, he is attracted to the spectacular. He covets the religious authority that would allow him to broker the power of the Spirit. He knows from personal experience that the one with hold on the reins of the spectacular can control the entire community (see 8:9-10). Thus Simon does not follow Philip for instruction in the faith, as the Ethiopian eunuch later would (below); rather, he is attracted to Philip and then to Peter because of the miracles they perform by the power of the Spirit. While miracles are a frequent phenomenon in Luke's story world, the spectacular is always a means to draw people to hear the word of God.

Acts 8:26-40, Philip's Mission to the "Outcasts of Israel": The Eunuch from Ethiopia

COMMENTARY

Acts combines the narrative of Philip's urban mission in Samaria with the memorable story of his encounter with an Ethiopian eunuch. As a religious person the Ethiopian symbolizes what the Samaritan Simon is not: He is spiritual pilgrim from a distant land who is earnestly seeking to understand Scripture's prophecies of God's salvation. This eunuch shares the same status as the Samaritan, however, for he too is on the margins of mainstream Israel, excluded by law from full participation in the covenant community (see Deut 23:2 LXX; Lev 21:17-21). The unwritten conflict plotted by this story, then, is that this pious proselyte, who seeks to know God's purposes more fully, has been excluded from the very religious community whose resources would illumine his quest (see the Overview to 8:4-40).

The resolution of this conflict puts Luke's well-known concern for God's preferential option of the poor and powerless in sharper focus. The crisis facing the eunuch is not so much his social standing—he is after all an "official" with solid political connections—as his spiritual standing with God. Nor is his spiritual poverty the consequence of his own lack of earnest dedication to find God—as is true of Simon. Rather it is his forbidden castration and perhaps his nationality, not his piety or his practices, which have compromised his religious standing. The essential task of the prophet, then, is to clarify membership requirements of those belonging to God, sometimes in ways that redraw Israel's boundaries to include the excluded ones. The Ethiopian eunuch symbolizes the eschatological horizon of the Israel in the last days that is now taking form because of Jesus under the aegis of the Holy Spirit.

The key in recovering this point from the present passage is its chiastic literary pattern. The reader finds it stated in the form of "the right question" at the intersection of and framed by an inverted parallelism. The commentary on this passage will try to pay attention to the clues provided by this pattern:[346]

346. See Krodel, *Acts*, 167. Talbert, *Reading Acts*, 90-93, uses a similar strategy to reach a similar conclusion but through a different rhetorical design.

A (vv. 26-27a): Philip "got up and went" from Samaria south to Gaza

  B (vv. 27b-28): the Ethiopian eunuch worships and reads Scripture (Isaiah 56)

    C (vv. 29-30a): Philip "runs" according to the Spirit's command

      D (vv. 30b-31): the eunuch queries prophet Philip

        E (vv. 32-33): Scripture (Isa 53:7-8) quoted

          F (v. 34): "About whom is the prophet talking?"

        E´ (v. 35): Scripture is interpreted by Philip

      D´ (vv. 36-38) the eunuch queries prophet Philip

    C´ (v. 39a): Philip snatched away by the Spirit

  B´ (v. 39b): the eunuch rejoices

A´ (v. 40): Philip passes through "all the towns" from Gaza north to Samaria

8:26-33. The elements of the first line of the chiasmus (A-E) introduce the principal players of this conversion drama—the Ethiopian eunuch and Philip. The encounter between the God-seeker and the prophet, complete with angelic visitations and chariot riding, are familiar to the OT reader of Elijah's story cycle (see 1 Kings 17–2 Kings 3). Luke's Jesus alludes to just such an encounter during his inaugural mission in Nazareth (see Luke 4:26-27). In addition, many commentators have noted the parallels between this story and Luke's story of Jesus' exchange with his two disciples on the Road to Emmaus (Luke 24).[347] These stories from the Gospels provide additional texture to this story of the eunuch's conversion, where Philip is a prophet-like-Jesus whose words and deeds continue to lead the church's mission "from place to place" (8:4) beyond Jerusalem.

Instead of preaching in a particular "city of Samaria," Philip is on the road; he is up north and needs to take a southbound route to Gaza—"the road that goes down from Jerusalem to Gaza." The narrator's aside that this is "a wilderness road" (8:26) is puzzling because the road is not a desert route. The reader is left to wonder what this detail

contributes to the story. Spencer suggests that it relocates the prophet and the eunuch in a "liminal zone off the beaten path of regular traffic," where serious theological reflection and personal transformation are more likely.[348] Perhaps. In any case, the presence of both "the angel of the Lord" (8:26; see 5:19) and "the Spirit" (8:29), who give Philip directions,[349] make clear the divine necessity of his encounter with the Ethiopian. The images of heaven's intervention in earth's work could hardly be clearer.

The eunuch's religious résumé is even more interesting and detailed. As with Philip, the narrator carefully locates him on Judea's map: "he had come to Jerusalem to worship" (v. 27b) and "was returning home" (v. 28a). He was evidently a proselyte from the diaspora who had recently made a hard pilgrimage as a mark of his profound religious devotion, since the farther one journeys the more devotion one exhibits. The reference to "worship" in Jerusalem is provocative since eunuchs were forbidden to enter the Temple for worship (see 3:8). By juxtaposing "eunuch" and "worship" the narrator perhaps imagines that the Ethiopian's recent "worship experience" has triggered a theological crisis over his future in the household of Israel. His social class— "a court official of Queen Candace in charge of her treasury" (v. 27a)—only intensifies the impression that he is spiritually hungry and not materially impoverished.

The final feature of the eunuch's profile is that "he was reading the prophet Isaiah" (v. 28b). Perhaps he dwells on Isaiah because of its hopeful references about Ethiopia's participation in the blessings of God (Isa 18:1; 45:15). The quoted prophecy from Isa 53:7-8 (see Acts 8:32-33) provides the prophetic intertext necessary for interpreting the *second* half of this story (see 8:35-40). However, the Ethiopian man's personal biography echoes a second Isaianic prophecy (Isa 56:3-8; cf. Ps 67:32), one that provides an important subtext that illumines the initial encounter between prophet and convert (i.e., 8:26-33). According to this echoed prophecy, God

347. For a summary, see Witherington, *The Acts of the Apostles,* 292.

348. Spencer, *Acts,* 90-91. While, perhaps, another indication that Luke's geographical knowledge of Palestine is poor, this could be yet another example of Luke's use of geography to cue a theological interest in his story.

349. On the interchangeability of "Spirit" and "angel" in contemporary Jewish literature, see J. Levison, "The Prophetic Spirit as an Angel According to Philo," *HTR* 88 (1995) 189-207.

promises to "gather the outcasts of Israel" (Isa 56:8), including those "eunuchs and foreigners" (Isa 56:3-4; cf. 39:7) who "keep the Sabbath and do not profane it" (Isa 56:6) and come to "my holy mountain//my house of prayer" (Isa 56:7), and to grant them a future with God. This Ethiopian eunuch who "has come to Jerusalem to worship" (v. 27) represents both these disenfranchised, disinherited groups of an exiled Israel as the choice recipient of God's promise.

Philip joins the Ethiopian eunuch by instruction of the Spirit of prophecy (vv. 29-30*a*), and Philip's abrupt question is appropriate to his prophetic vocation: "Do you understand what you are reading?" (v. 30*b*). At one level, such a question asked by a stranger of a literate man seems condescending and offensive. Philip's question, however, presumes that Scripture is more than a literary text, for this man is "reading the prophet Isaiah," who conveys information about God's plan of salvation. Moreover, the man's earnest piety suggests a likely interest in the text's theological meaning; thus, his retort is also apropos: "How can I unless someone guides me?" (v. 31).[350] His subsequent invitation that Philip "sit beside him" implies spiritual discernment that recognizes this stranger as his theological mentor who is authorized by God to comment on this biblical prophecy.

The cited prophecy is from Isaiah 53, whose history within Christianity commends its profound influence in shaping our core convictions about Jesus' death.[351] Its function in Acts, however, is to define more clearly why an Ethiopian eunuch should be interested in the Christian gospel. Luke quotes the prophecy verbatim from the Septuagint. At first glance, we note that only that portion of the prophecy that speaks of the servant's

"humiliation" ($\tau\alpha\pi\epsilon\acute{\iota}\nu\omega\sigma\iota\varsigma$ *tapeinōsis*, v. 33) is mentioned. If the Servant's humiliation denotes social ostracism, the eunuch's situation is interpreted by Isaiah's suffering Servant because he too is a social outcast. Further, Johnson notes that this quotation departs from its Hebrew source in several important ways. The most dramatic and important deviation is found in the final phrase "for his life is taken from the earth" (8:33; the NIV translation, which renders the tense of the clause $\H{o}\tau\iota$ [*hoti*] in the past ["for his life *was taken* ($\H{o}\tau\iota$ $\alpha\H{\iota}\rho\epsilon\tau\alpha\iota$ *hoti airetai*) from earth"], is unwarranted).[352] While the Hebrew text claims that the servant is "cut off [גזר *gzr*] from the earth" (i.e., he dies), the Septuagint translation oddly renders *gzr* as "lifted up" ($\alpha\H{\iota}\rho\omega$ *airō*) from the earth." This verbal shift allows Luke to interpret the Servant's humiliation as the means to his exaltation—he is "lifted up from earth" into heaven (see 1:9-11). If Luke takes this phrase to refer to the vindication (or "lifting up") of the humiliated Servant, then perhaps the reader should suppose that the eunuch's identification with the humiliated Servant might lead him to hope for a different future than the one consigned him by official Israel.

8:34. Found at the center of the chiasmus (see the Overview to 8:4-40) is the eunuch's question, which keys a redemptive encounter: "About whom, may I ask, does the prophet say this, about himself or about someone else?" Of three possible interpretations, he omits the nationalistic one most common in his day: faithful Israel. But naturally an outcast and foreigner is unlikely to include an interpretation, no matter how popular, that excludes him. Some contemporary sectarian movements within Judaism were interpreting this prophecy as pointing to God's eschatological prophet whom Isaiah "himself" represents. Given the response to Stephen's accusation that Israel persecutes and murders its prophets (see 7:52), including the "Righteous One" (see 7:53; cf. Isa 53:11), this second reading is entirely plausible.[353] But apparently the eunuch holds out for a "someone else" with whom the outcasts and aliens of Israel might more closely identify and then join in God's coming triumph.

350. The eunuch's question is awkwardly stated and "corrected" by later scribes. Luke's intent is hardly to express the eunuch's slow wit, but his self-awareness that his prospects for understanding this Scripture are conditioned on the aid of a talented/inspired interpreter. See Haenchen, *The Acts of the Apostles*, 312. Barrett, *A Critical and Exegetical Commentary on the Acts of the Apostles*, 428, however, claims that the eunuch's Greek reflects his rhetorical elegance and literacy.

351. Isaiah 53 is rarely cited but often echoed in NT passages of Jesus' suffering (Matt 8:17; Luke 22:37; John 12:38; Rom 10:16; 1 Pet 2:21-25; Rev 14:5). Whether these intertextual echoes support later Christian use of Isaiah 53 as a prophecy of Jesus' atonement remains contested. See Hooker, *Jesus and the Servant*, 113-14, who claims that Luke cites only Isa 53:7-8 in Acts 8 and, therefore, avoids any soteriological implication. See also M. Parsons, "Isaiah 53 and Acts 8," in *Jesus and the Suffering Servant: Isaiah 53 and Christian Origins*, ed. W. Bellinger and W. Farmer (Harrisburg, Pa.: Trinity, 1998) 104-24, who argues for a soteriological meaning in Luke's use in Acts 8.

352. Johnson, *The Acts of the Apostles*, 156.

353. See J. Jeremias, $\pi\alpha\H{\iota}\varsigma$ $\theta\epsilon\omicron\H{\upsilon}$ *TDNT*, 5:684-89. But note Barrett's important criticisms, *A Critical and Exegetical Commentary on the Acts of the Apostles*, 1:430-31.

8:35-40. The eunuch's conversion, recounted by the second line of this chiasmus (E[prime]-A[prime]), issues from the prophet's inspired response to his climactic question. "Then Philip began to speak" (v. 35*a*) translates a biblical expression for divinely inspired speech (ἀνοίξας ... τὸ στόμα αὐτοῦ *anoixas ... to stoma autou*; lit., "opening his mouth"; see 10:34; Exod 4:12; Ezek 3:27). In an encounter that is so evidently superintended by the Spirit, we are not surprised that Philip's answer is not his to give but God's. Luke's characteristic summary of Philip's response— "the good news about Jesus" (v. 35*b*)—is filled out by details from the other missionary speeches of Acts.

The conversion of the eunuch is recounted elliptically by his request to be baptized (v. 37), which presumes his public confession of faith "in the name of the Lord Jesus" (v. 16; see also 2:21, 38-41).[354] In the prior story of the Samaritan mission, water and Spirit baptism are discrete but integral media of divine grace (see 8:12-13, 16-17). Perhaps to preserve this pattern of Philip's mission a few scribes rewrote v. 39 this way: "When they came up out of the water, the Spirit fell upon the eunuch, but an angel carried Philip away." In any case, water baptism initiates new believers into the realm of the Spirit of prophecy whose filling empowers them for Christian ministry; conversion makes one dependent upon God's Spirit to perform the tasks of God's work. The evident and direct participation of the Spirit in this final panel of the story lends support to the importance of this theme in Acts. The reader is left to presume, then, that when Philip and the eunuch go their separate ways they both engage in Christian mission.

The text tells us nothing of what becomes of the Ethiopian.[355] However, we are told that the Spirit deposits Philip in Azotus, where he resumes his mission by going from place to place (see 8:4), to the north up the coastline to Caesarea (8:40), where he establishes a family ministry of lasting importance (see 21:8-10).[356] The Spirit's action is reminiscent of the prophets Elijah (1 Kgs 18:12; 2 Kgs 2:16) and Ezekiel (Ezek 11:24), whose experiences with this same Spirit of prophecy effected compliance to God's plans. It is likewise here in Acts: Philip is "snatched up" and relocated to a place where God wanted him to resume his evangelical mission according to the Lord's commission (see 1:8).

354. A few late MSS, agreeing with patristic commentary, add a v. 37 to make clear the protocol of Christian conversion, which requires a profession of faith as the condition of baptism. Both the NIV and the NRSV omit this verse for text-critical reasons, since the vast majority of MSS do not include it. In any case, this inference of faith is made without scribal assistance on the basis of Acts 2:38-41; 8:12-13.

355. There is no evidence of a first-century Ethiopian church, although Irenaeus claims—no doubt on the basis of a much earlier tradition—that the eunuch was responsible for the evangelization of Ethiopia. See Irenaeus *Against Heresies* 3.12.8-10.

356. Luke's narrative is consistent with his Scripture: The Spirit sometimes "snatches up" and moves prophets from place to place to facilitate the plans of God (see 2 Kgs 2:16; Ezek 11:24).

REFLECTIONS

"How can I understand Scripture unless someone guides me?" (see 8:31). The Ethiopian eunuch is a double outcast within Israel, twice rejected by those in control of religious sentiment because of where he lives and because he has been castrated: his sexuality has excluded him from the assembly of God and his distance from the holy city makes for a difficult pilgrimage. Similar concerns continue to be impediments today for those from society's margins who seek after God. The way of the eunuch's salvation establishes a pattern of catechesis for the convert who must travel some distance to secure God's salvation. If the emphasis of Luke's story of Samaritan conversion is placed on reception of the Spirit, then the emphasis of his story of the eunuch's conversion is placed on reception of the Scripture. The two are decisively and strategically intertwined in Acts as the principal media of God's word and thus of the believer's theological formation. Certainly the images of the Spirit's detailed guidance of Philip in this narrative—giving him direction, inspiring his interpretation, transporting him from place to place—symbolize God's active presence in enabling the church's mission in the world, especially among those whom our religious traditions marginalize.

In each case those placed outside the borders of official religion turn to the prophet-like-Jesus to access these powerful resources of Spirit and Scripture. The Spirit is distributed through the apostles to the Samaritan believers, and then the Scriptures are interpreted by the evangelist for the Ethiopian proselyte. For all the current debate about the authority of Scripture in the contemporary church, of equal importance in Luke's story world is the authority of Scripture's interpreter. The eunuch, who evidently understood the importance of Scripture in his search for God, recognized as well the importance of one who could interpret its meaning for him. Philip's authority to do so has already been evinced by his continuing obedience to God's calling.

Scriptures point us to God. The climax of Luke's story of the eunuch's conversion is Philip's response to his critical question of Scripture's referent: "About whom . . . does the prophet say this?" (8:34 NRSV). Philip then "proclaimed to him the good news about Jesus." When the Christian teacher is invited to mentor someone seeking to find God, she should do so by interpreting Scripture in theological terms.

ACTS 9:1–15:12, "TO THE END OF THE EARTH": PAUL'S MISSION AS "LIGHT FOR THE NATIONS"

OVERVIEW

No conversion to Jesus is more renowned than Saul's (alias Paul). Luke's account in Acts follows a carefully constructed sequence of events according to which Saul is introduced as a minor player at Stephen's execution (see 7:58). Although Luke relativizes Saul's participation in this treachery through Stephen's petition for divine forgiveness (see 7:59-60), Saul's solidarity with the church's opponents in Jerusalem is immediately evident by his persecution of the very community that Stephen once led (see 8:1-3). Therefore, when his story resumes in Acts, the reader is left to puzzle over how the Lord will cash Stephen's promissory note. Meanwhile, much has happened beyond Jerusalem since Stephen's martyrdom and Saul's purge of the holy city. In fact, Philip's successful mission has extended the gospel's influence north toward Syria (see 8:26-27a, 40), which explains why there are disciples in Syrian Damascus with a zealous Saul still in pursuit of them (see 9:1-2).

Philip's mission completed the evangelization of those marginal groups that constitute the whole household of a restored Israel (see 8:4-25, 26-40). Under the impress of Scripture's prophecy that salvation will spread from "the Jew first and then to the Greek [or non-Jew]" (cf. Rom 1:16; see Acts 3:25-26), now this narrative turns toward non-Jews. In the peculiar economy of God's salvation, the Lord responds to Stephen's petition for Saul's forgiveness by commissioning him as carrier of God's word "to the Jew first and then to the [Gentile]." Given the strategic role that Saul plays in Acts, Luke pays considerable attention to his conversion and commission. As with other pivotal moments in the church's mission, Luke narrates this dramatic episode three times (cf. 9:1-31; 22:3-16; 26:4-23), as he does the subsequent conversion story of the Roman centurion Cornelius (cf. 9:32–11:18; 15:6-11). The literary combination of these two conversion stories of a Jewish missionary and a Gentile convert provide a critical subtext for the remainder of Acts. Saul is called and empowered to carry the word of God to the Jew first and especially to "God-fearing" Gentiles, like Cornelius.

Even though Paul will spearhead the last stage of the church's mission, it begins with Peter (see Acts 9:32–10:48). The plotline of Acts unfolds according to a succession of prophetic leaders. Their continuity in ever-changing situations ensures the solidarity of the community's life and the integrity of its witness across space and time. The word Saul will proclaim about the resurrected Jesus is the very word Peter, Stephen, and Philip have proclaimed before him in an unbroken line of testimony to the faithfulness of God. In this light the stories of Peter's involvement in the conversion of Cornelius and of his escape from prison (see Acts 12:1-21) are elements of a "succession narrative" that authorizes Saul to continue the sacred role performed by the Twelve and the seven before him for another generation and in another place.

Luke orchestrates his composition of Saul's mission in several movements. He preaches God's gospel boldly and persuasively, interprets Israel's Scriptures properly and cogently, does miraculous "signs and wonders," wins arguments, and gets into conflict with unrepentant Jews and suffers because of it (see 9:16). Saul is now Paul (see Acts 13:9); his urban mission is centered in the city's synagogue where he encounters other devout Jews from the diaspora and more receptive God-fearing Gentiles (Acts 13:13–14:28). Paul's programmatic success among non-Jews extends even to pagans (Acts 14:8-10); however, he will find most of his Gentile converts in the diaspora synagogues where "Moses is read every sabbath" (15:21). His founding of this mission church provokes conflict among traditional Jews, even those within the church (see 14:27–15:5; cf. 11:1-2). In prayerful consideration of personal testimony and biblical prophecy, however, the elders of the Jewish church resolve to support Paul's mission to the nations while expecting him to maintain his commitment to the church's Jewish legacy (see Acts 15:6-29; cf. 11:3-18).

Following this Jerusalem Council, Paul never deviates from his prophetic vocation or from the pattern of mission established during his first evangelistic effort in Asia. He continues to extend the influence of the Word of God to the most important provinces and urban centers of the Roman Empire. His secular work as a "tentmaker" in Corinth would come to symbolize his sacred work

that Amos prophesied: to repair and rebuild "the tent of David" (cf. Acts 15:16-18). His second mission westward to Macedonia (cf. Acts 15:30–17:15) and then southward to Greece (17:16–18:17) includes Athens, the intellectual center of Paul's world (see Acts 17:16-34), and Corinth, among its wealthiest (see Acts 18:1-17). Luke's narrative of his third mission (see Acts 18:18–21:16) considers Paul's evangelistic work in a single city, Ephesus, which would become a pivotal center in the succession of Paul's mission to the diaspora (see Acts 20:17-38).

When Paul finally returns to the holy city as a religious pilgrim (Acts 20:16), he faces increasing hostilities both within the church (see Acts 21:16-26) and within Judaism (see Acts 21:27-31; cf. 20:22-23; 21:11-14). Yet Rome, not Jerusalem, is the city of Paul's destiny; it is there at the mythic "end of the earth" that Paul fulfills Jesus' prophecy-commission (see 1:8) and God's ultimate plan for his life (see 19:21; 23:11; 27:24). His mission to Rome, however, is delayed (and ironically triggered) by his arrest in Jerusalem (see Acts 21:32-36) and the protracted legal case brought against him by the leadership of unrepentant Israel (see Acts 21:37–26:32). Even though Paul, a Roman citizen, ends formal litigation against him by appealing to the Caesar (cf. Acts 25:6-12), he arrives in Rome only after surviving the perils of a stormy sea (Acts 27) and a poisonous snake (Acts 28:1-10). Finally in Rome and still under house arrest, Paul resumes his missionary work in defense of his prophetic vocation and according to the biblical script of God's salvation (Acts 28:11-31).

Acts was placed before the Pauline letters during the canonical process to provide the church catholic with Scripture's own introduction to the Pauline letters. From this point forward, Acts forges impressions of Paul's vocation and authority, his prophetic persona, and his missionary purpose that provide a line of sight into the biblical letters that follow. By encountering the Paul of Acts as a central character in Luke's narrative, readers acquire a different although complementary perspective of the canonical Paul, one that is productive of a more faithful reading of his letters as Scripture (see Introduction, "Acts as Canon").

Acts 9:1-31, The Conversion and Commissioning of Saul

COMMENTARY

The literary importance and theological complexity of Saul's (= Paul's) Damascus road encounter with the risen Jesus is indicated by the fact that it is recounted three times, here in the narrator's voice and twice again in Paul's voice (see 22:3-16; 26:4-23). The primary problem facing the interpreter of Luke's narrative triad is not how best to harmonize or explain its discrepant details, but how its repetition more fully defines the prophetic vocation of the Paul of Acts.[357] It is impossible either to deny or to overestimate the transforming effect Jesus' visitation had on him and on his understanding of God's relations with faithful Israel.[358] Yet, Saul's repentance and radical turn toward Jesus is only one element of a literary pattern that climaxes with his prophetic calling and baptism with the Spirit. Acts is more interested in Saul's calling than in his conversion, since it provides the impetus of his mission and the foundation of his future authority in the church.[359]

This passage is framed by an inclusio of characteristic irony: Even as Saul's persecution of the church (see 8:1-3) occasions Philip's mission beyond Jerusalem (see 8:4-40), so his conversion and departure brings a fresh season of shalom among believers living in the region (9:31; cf. 8:40). Enclosed between is the riveting drama of Saul's own "great reversal." On his way to persecute the Syrian church (9:1-2), he encounters the living Jesus, who converts him (9:3-9) and prophesies his prophetic ministry (9:10-18). An obedient

Saul takes two painful steps toward his destiny, the first in Damascus (9:19-25) and the second in Jerusalem (9:26-30), where he preaches the gospel and suffers in fulfillment of Jesus' prophecy (9:15-16).[360]

9:1-2. Saul's zealous persecution of the church has taken him from Jerusalem to Damascus, where he desires to continue and extend his hostilities among "any who belonged to the Way (9:2).[361] Evidently his efforts in this regard continue to be supported by those same religious elites who opposed and executed Stephen. The historical circumstances for his solicitation of letters of support from the high priest (probably Caiaphas) remain uncertain; however, their "legitimate" interest in Saul's mission in the synagogues of Damascus suggests that the membership of "the way" consists of devout Jewish believers, probably Hellenists, who have attached themselves to congregations of other diaspora Jews in that city.[362] Saul's mission is to "bind" believers and return them to Jerusalem for a religious inquisition, perhaps one patterned after Stephen's (see 6:11-14).

9:3-9. This passage recounts Saul's conversion to Jesus.[363] The day begins with Saul "approaching Damascus" (9:3) as a take-charge zealot who is "breathing threats and

---

357. See Witherington, *The Acts of the Apostles*, 305-15, for a detailed analysis of these discrepancies and possible explanations for them. See also Jervell, *Die Apostelgeschichte*, 288-93, who pays close attention to the sources behind Luke's triadic narrative of Paul's mission statement.

358. The idea of Paul's "conversion" is important to reconsider in the light of K. Stendahl, "The Apostle Paul and the Introspective Conscience of the West," *HTR* 56 (1963) 199-215. While there was a radical and fundamental change in Paul's zeal (he stops persecuting the church and starts preaching about Jesus), it is not a conversion from Judaism to Christianity. The Paul of Acts remains an observant Jew and continues to live within his vocation as a teacher of Israel. See Jervell, *The Unknown Paul*, 71-72; A. Segal, *Paul the Convert* (New Haven: Yale University Press, 1990).

359. Paul himself regards this appearance of the risen Jesus as confirmation of his apostolic authority within the church—and he is the "last" to be so confirmed (1 Cor 15:8; cf. Gal 1:11-16). While the Saul of Acts does not qualify for membership in the apostolate (see 1:21-22) and is nowhere called an apostle (cf. 13:1-3), his prophetic vocation assigns an equal measure of authority to him, since all prophets-like-Jesus are granted similar tasks, powers, and responsibilities.

360. Luke's narrative of Paul's conversion agrees with Paul's letters at every main point: the location, the visionary event, the effects, and the overarching importance of his calling. While the terms for Paul's mission are given to Ananias rather than to Paul (Acts 9:15), his Spirit-filling confirms that divine authority has been given him to enable this mission.

361. Luke's use of "the way" (ὁ ὁδός *ho hodos*) in Acts (19:9, 23; 22:4; 24:22) as a title for the church is distinctive within the NT. There is little doubt of its currency in earliest Christianity, especially among its Jewish opponents. Luke may use it here ironically, however, because of its theological resonance. According to the OT, "way" is a catchword for living in conformity with Moses (Exod 18:20; 32:8; Deut 26:17; Pss 1:1, 6 LXX; 118:1, 29) or to God (Isa 40:3). The term usually implies that such obedience is freely chosen (esp. the proverbial use of "way"; Prov 3:17; 10:17) and that the consequences of such are a choice justly dispensed. In Acts, the articular "way" circumscribes the church as a messianic sect within Judaism (so 24:14) that is marked out by a distinctive way believers live together and by its beliefs about Jesus. See Fitzmyer, *The Acts of the Apostles*, 423-24.

362. Damascus was an important Syrian city about 135 miles to the north of Jerusalem. It was known for its former glory and for its role as strategic commercial center for the Roman Empire. Several important trade routes passed through Damascus, including the "Great North Road" on which Saul was traveling. Josephus reports in *The Jewish War* 2.20.2 that Damascus was home to a large population of Jews.

363. Spencer, *Acts*, 95-96, notes that Luke's repeated use of "bind" (δέω *deō*) in 9:2, 14, 21 to describe Saul's intended plan nicely captures the irony of his situation: He intends to "bind" believers, but it is he who is incapacitated and led by other believers to safety and service.

murder against the disciples of the Lord" (9:1).[364] By day's end, however, he is "led by hand into Damascus" (9:8), blind and utterly dependent upon others for food and drink (9:9). What occurs in the meantime is the stuff of legend: Saul the persecutor becomes Paul the prophet-like-Jesus. Here and in the other stories of his conversion in Acts, his personal encounter with the living Jesus is emphasized (see 1 Cor 9:1; 15:8).

The sudden appearance of "a light from heaven" (φώς ἐκ τοῦ οὐρανοῦ *phōs ek tou ouranou* 9:3; cf. 22:6, 9) that is "brighter than the noon-day sun" (26:13; cf. 2 Cor 4:4-6) and that "flashed around him" (cf. 22:6; 26:13) are the special effects of a theophany when God meets a prophet (cf. Exod 19:16; Ezek 1:4, 7, 13, 28; Dan 10:6).[365] Similar to the prophet Ezekiel's response to his vision of God's glory (Ezek 1:28), Saul "fell to the ground" (9:4) in anticipation of hearing God speak to him. In this case, the "light" (φώς *phōs* he sees is of the exalted Jesus, shrouded in the glory of God (cf. 7:55).

This epiphany is a divine audition (cf. Exod 3:4-10; Gen 31:11-13; see 2:5-13): Saul "heard a voice" (9:4*b*), and what he hears converts him to Jesus. The Lord's intent is evidently not to frighten him into obedience but to reveal a plan of action. The primary purpose of visionary episodes in Acts is not to convert non-believers—gospel preaching performs this role—but to commission prophets to missionary tasks (see 10:9-16; 16:6-10). Saul does not recognize the "voice" (φωνή *phōnē*) he hears, and asks, "Who are you, Lord?" (9:5*a*). His ironical use of "Lord" (κύριος *kyrios*) is not yet a confession of faith in Jesus but the honest query of a devout Jew who understands the significance of his experience from reading Scripture.[366] For this reason, Saul is absolutely attentive to what is said next: "I am Jesus, whom you are persecuting" (9:5*b*).

Saul's brief exchange with Jesus validates what will become the central claim of his gospel: God made the crucified Jesus alive as Messiah and Lord (see 26:8; cf. 2:36). Jesus could keep his retort brief because his very appearance exposes the ignorance that prompts Saul's mission to Damascus. Jesus is not another dead pretender to the messianic throne but is alive and is Christ indeed. What real choice does Saul have other than to embrace his future? The Lord's use of personal names and his direct appeal to Saul underscores the "personal character of the early Christian belief in the resurrection."[367] The living Jesus recruits him personally into the faith and then commissions him for ministry.[368]

The imperative of their encounter is introduced by the intensive "But" (ἀλλά *alla*, 9:6), which usually links contrasting statements. In this case, it makes more emphatic the purpose of this christophany: to send Paul on a mission. "Get up and enter the city and you will be told what you are to do" (9:6; cf. 22:10; 26:14). "He who a moment ago was so powerful has now become utterly powerless. But it is not the weakness of Saul so much as the power of Christ that Luke is concerned to show."[369]

Witnesses of this drama are in shock because they hear the living Jesus without seeing him (cf. 9:7; 22:9; 26:13; Deut 4:12; Dan 10:7).[370] Aware that something has happened to the posse's leader, they can only lead him into town. Saul's "blind obedience" to Jesus' imperative is indicated by a fast— "for three days . . . he neither ate nor drank" (9:9). On the one hand, Saul's condition is physical confirmation that a vision occurred, shocked him into blindness, and took away his appetite for food. On the other hand, "three days" of abstinence nicely symbolizes Saul's conversion to the *resurrected* Jesus. When he begins to eat again (see 9:19) and receives his sight (see 9:18), he will have been given time to begin an intense spiritual

364. For historical background on Luke's strategic use of "disciples," see Kee, *To Every Nation Under Heaven*, 118-20.

365. B. Gaventa strategically links the "light" that blinds Paul with his subsequent mission as a "light to the nations" (εἰς φῶς ἐθνῶν *eis phōs ethnōn*) as the organizing image of Luke's story; *From Darkness to Light: Aspects of Conversion in the New Testament*, OBT (Philadelphia: Fortress, 1986) 52-95.

366. I am convinced that Luke shapes this narrative in the light of the Exodus story of Moses' commissioning. Jesus' address, "Saul, Saul," echoes the angel's address, "Moses, Moses" (Exod 3:4); and Jesus' response to Saul's query, "I am Jesus [ἐγώ εἰμι Ἰησοῦς *egō eimi Iēsous*]," echoes God's response to Moses' similar question, "I am I AM [*egō eimi*]" (Exod 3:13-14). The logic of Luke's intertext reflects the importance of Moses in Acts as prototypical prophet-like-Jesus (see Acts 7:23-43).

367. Johnson, *The Acts of the Apostles*, 163.

368. S. Kim, *The Origin of Paul's Gospel*, WUNT 2/4 (Tübingen: J. C. B. Mohr, 1984) 51-66, contends that Paul receives the essential terms of his gospel in this brief exchange and the following commissioning statement. Contra Conzelmann, *The Acts of the Apostles*, 71.

369. Haenchen, *The Acts of the Apostles*, 322.

370. The three accounts of Paul's conversion disagree on this detail but agree in meaning "to reserve the appearance (of Jesus) to Paul alone." See Haenchen, *The Acts of the Apostles*, 71.

journey that will fortify him for the work ahead—though he once was blind, now he sees (cf. John 9:25).[371]

9:10-19a. The next narrative panel concerns what Saul is to do; it is for this reason that Jesus bids him go into Damascus (see 9:6). Coincidental to Saul's vision of his healing (v. 12), the Lord appears to Ananias[372] in a second vision (vv. 10-16).[373] Like Saul, he is a devout Jew (cf. 22:12); however, he is numbered among the believers Saul seeks to harm. Ironically, it is now Ananias who seeks out Saul to heal him and deliver the initial instructions of a new life (vv. 17-18).

Ananias's initial response to the Lord's bidding is the prompt reply, "Here I am, Lord" (v. 10)—reminiscent of Samuel's (1 Sam 3:4, 10) and Abraham's (Gen 22:1-2) obedience to God's call. The Lord reveals Saul's name to Ananias and provides him with a specific address where he might be found.[374] Luke also provides an important biographical detail: Saul is "a man from Tarsus" (9:11)—a Jew of the diaspora.

Ananias's caveat in vv. 13-14 does not indicate spiritual failure or a concern for personal well-being. Rather, Luke adds it to prompt readers to take special note of the radical turn of events that has just occurred with Saul's conversion (see 10:14-15). Since healing symbolizes salvation in Acts (see 3:1-8), his dismay evinces the "hard rationalist's" case against the fact of Saul's conversion and by implication therefore confirms its legitimacy.[375]

The climax of this narrative is the Lord's prophecy of Saul's forthcoming mission, which indexes the plotline of his mission in Acts and provides a glossary of its key terms that are repeated in his later speeches (13:46-47; 20:18-35; 22:14-15; 26:16-18).[376] Moreover, the Lord's reference to Saul as one "chosen" (ἐκλογή *eklogē*) for a task repeats the terms used for the work of the Twelve (see 1:2) and the seven (see 6:5) as instruments of salvation. This repetition emphasizes that the tasks the Lord gives to Saul "to bring my name before Gentiles and kings and before the people of Israel" (9:15) continue the church's witness to God's salvation.

Significantly, for the first time in Acts the international scope of the church's witness is clarified in terms of Saul's future mission. The order of "Gentiles and kings"[377] before "people of Israel" reverses the typical pattern of his urban mission, which usually begins in the synagogue and often on the Sabbath. In any case, Acts never depicts Paul aiming the gospel only at Gentiles or Jews; his mission is international in scope because God has promised to bless "all the families of the earth" (see 2:21; 3:25). The order here is probably for rhetorical effect to cue the narrative's turn toward a mission that will include non-Jews.

The second part of the Lord's programmatic prophecy of Saul's mission connects his witness to personal suffering, contining this important literary theme. Saul's suffering is stipulated here as a divine necessity: "I will show him how much he must [δεῖ *dei*] suffer" (v. 16; see 1:16, 22; 3:21; 4:12). This suffering places Saul in continuity with the Messiah and his apostolic successors, and it shapes the way Acts tells his story. The *dei*—the "must" of divine necessity of Saul's suffering— reminds us that suffering is not incidental to salvation but in the prophet's case is instrumental in realizing God's promises according to the Scriptures (cf. 1 Pet 1:10-12). The

371. Fitzmyer, *The Acts of the Apostles*, 426, allows that the meaning is primarily spiritual so that this is a fast in preparation for Christian baptism. However, see Johnson, *The Acts of the Apostles*, 164.

372. The repetition of the name "Ananias" in Acts may indicate that the reader should take these "Christian" stories together as mutually glossing commentaries on the meaning of the name, "God is merciful." The first Ananias is a disciple who does not obey God's word and is shamed, whereas the second Ananias is a disciple who obeys the Lord's word and is honored (22:12). The purpose of the interplay is to remind the reader that God's merciful response is conditioned upon the disciple's obedient response to God's word.

373. The literary convention of a "double vision" is a familiar feature of ancient stories. Luke uses visions in Acts to clarify God's call and a "double vision" to underscore God's control over the various details of the call—in this case, Saul's call. See C. Hedrick, "Paul's Conversion/Call," *JBL* 100 (1981) 415-32.

374. Luke's careful attention to detail in describing Ananias's vision reflects his use of a source carefully maintained and transmitted, in part because of the names and places it contains. Judas and Ananias are probably known to the first readers and Judas's home on Straight Street may well have housed an important synagogue of Jewish believers.

375. Bauernfeind, *Die Apostelgeschichte*, 134, points out that Ananias's reluctance rightly reflects the ambiguity of Saul's situation—that Saul exists in a kind of "no man's land" between his conversion on the one hand and his triumphant mission on the other. Ananias's response to the Lord is noteworthy because it introduces "saints" (ἅγιοι *hagioi*) into Acts (cf. 9:32, 41; 26:10). It is used of Jerusalem's believers in Acts and

has a similar referent in the Pauline letters (Rom 15:26; 1 Cor 16:1; 2 Cor 8:4; cf. Eph 2:19), which may indicate a semitechnical use in the Pauline mission. See Barrett, *A Critical and Exegetical Commentary on the Acts of the Apostles*, 1:455.

376. See Tannehill, *The Acts of the Apostles*, 2:118-20.

377. The prophecy that Paul would carry Christ's name to a plurality of "kings" is fulfilled in his speech to King Agrippa (cf. 25:23–26:29) and in anticipation of his audience with the Roman Caesar (cf. 27:24). Fitzmyer's argument, *The Acts of the Apostles*, 429, for combining "Gentiles and kings" as a discrete audience different from Paul's second audience, "the people of Israel," seems correct. The punctuation of this phrase is better rendered "before Gentiles and kings, and before the people of Israel."

repetition of "my name" (ὄνομά μου *onoma mou*) in both parts of this commissioning prophecy recalls Joel's prophecy that in the last days "everyone who calls upon the *name* of the Lord will be saved" (italics added; see 2:21).

The report of Ananias's mission rounds off this initial account of Saul's calling as a prophet-like-Jesus. His initial gesture of "laying his hands on Saul" (v. 17*b*) obeys the Lord's instruction (v. 12). Yet when read in context of Acts (see 6:6) in combination with his "Christian" greeting, "Brother Saul" (see 1:15) and the extraordinary exhortation for Saul "to be filled with the Holy Spirit" (v. 17*c*), Ananias's gesture connotes the community's confirmation of his salvation and vocation. Luke's idiom is pregnant with implicit information about Saul's destiny: The immediate restoration of Saul's sight (v. 18)[378] and his filling/baptism with the Holy Spirit symbolize God's confirmation of his salvation (cf. 2:21) and prophetic vocation (cf. 1:8).[379] His turn to action is indicated by ending his fast (9:19*a*).

9:19b-25. With his return to normalcy, Saul "began to proclaim Jesus in the synagogues" (v. 20). Luke's repeated use of "immediately" (εὐθέως *eutheōs*, vv. 18, 20) leaves the impression of urgency.[380] We are not told, however, by whom or by what curriculum Saul is catechized to preach Jesus, which leaves the impression that this initial and urgent mission is prompted by his recent experience of the living Jesus (cf. Gal 1:11-17).[381] Although more details are provided later in Acts, Luke uses the narrative gaps effectively to underscore the importance of Saul's conversion.

---

378. The phrase "something like scales fell from his eyes" is probably contemporary medical parlance for the natural process of healing momentary blindness caused by a "bright light." See Haenchen, *The Acts of the Apostles,* 325.

379. Paul never mentions his baptism in his letters. The reference here is likely to his baptism with the Spirit (cf. 1 Cor 12:13). Luke's literary intention is to form a promise-fulfillment parallelism between Ananias's words (i.e., promise, 9:17) and the report (i.e., fulfillment, 9:18). The further implication of this literary conclusion is a theological claim: Paul's baptism is a baptism with the Spirit rather than a rite of initiation into the Damascus community. The point of this story is Paul's calling to prophetic ministry, which the filling/baptism with the Spirit enables and confirms.

380. Paul writes that he came back to Damascus only after spending an indeterminate length of time in Arabia (cf. Gal 1:17). There have been various proposals to explain (or not) this chronological discrepancy. From a literary perspective, one can imagine that Luke had access to a fuller Pauline chronology from his source but telescopes his account to enhance the impression of the urgency of Paul's mission.

381. Hengel and Schwemer, *Paul Between Damascus and Antioch,* 43-47, finds agreement between Luke's telling of this episode and Paul's autobiography of his post-conversion experiences in Galatians 1, especially in maintaining Paul's independence from apostolic authorization to preach the gospel.

Further, the location of his Damascus mission—"in the synagogues"—and the substance of what he says there—"Jesus is the Son of God" (v. 20; cf. Gal 1:16)—are compressed details of a pattern of ministry that will be expanded in considerable detail later in Acts. Moreover, his gospel proclamation is typically accompanied by a rigorous exegesis of Scripture that "amazes" (ἐξίστημι *existēmi*) and "confounds" (συγχέω *syncheō*) his opponents (so vv. 21-22), and the results are often hostile. Saul will proclaim that Jesus is God's Messiah, and unrepentant Israel will protest it. While his opposition often plots to get rid of him (cf. 14:19-20; 23:12-15), he inevitably escapes with the aid of others (sometimes heavenly) in order to continue the work for which he is called (so vv. 23-25).

The content of what Saul proclaims—that "Jesus is the Son of God"—is more difficult to explain. The interpreter should expect that these first words from a newly converted Saul are programmatic of any future missionary speech where the implications of this messianic title are developed in detail. Yet what is found instead is silence: this is the title's only kerygmatic use in Acts, even though it is routinely used both in the Gospels and in the Pauline letters (cf. Luke 1:32-35; 22:67-71; Rom 1:3; Gal 1:16; 2:20).[382] Because Paul's only other use of it in Acts is as part of a biblical citation (see 13:33; cf. Ps 2:7) to warrant his claim that Jesus is the Davidic Messiah (see 13:22-23), its use here should be viewed as synonymous with the epithet of v. 22 that "Jesus was the Messiah."[383]

Neither the fact that gospel preaching provokes a divided Israel beyond Jerusalem—the Jews of Damascus "plotted to kill Saul" (v. 23)—or that Saul escapes them to preach another day is surprising.[384] Johnson points out that even the incredulity of Saul's auditors is expressed in words that Paul himself uses to explain his preconversion mission (cf. Gal 1:13, 23).[385] Yet the irony of this incident is envisaged by the reversal of his status within Israel. This episode began with him on the road to Damascus "breathing threats and

---

382. Dunn, *The Acts of the Apostles,* 124-25, reviews the various historical constructions of the meaning of "Son of God" in earliest Christianity and its propriety for this particular setting in Acts.

383. See Haenchen, *The Acts of the Apostles,* 331.

384. The reference to "his disciples" (9:25) denotes something akin to "his colleagues."

385. Johnson, *The Acts of the Apostles,* 171.

murder against the disciples" on behalf of official Israel (v. 1) and now concludes with his former religious cohort seeking his death.[386] The persecutor has become the persecuted, fulfilling the Lord's prophecy that Saul would suffer for his name (see v. 16).

9:26-30. The persecuted Saul now heads south from Damascus to Jerusalem. The conflict experienced in the public square of Damascus now moves indoors where the church hesitates to embrace their new brother: "Saul attempted to join the disciples—they were afraid and did not believe that he was a disciple" (v. 26). Their suspicion is reasonable: Enemies do not become fast friends overnight! More important for Acts, the conflict is a harbinger of the profound difficulty the Jerusalem church will have with Paul's mission, whether to the Gentiles (so 15:4-5) or to the Jews (so 21:17-21). Intramural conflict over the nature of God's salvation, especially over acceptance of its revolutionary shape, is an important theme in Acts.

Barnabas, known to the readers of Acts for his generous spirit (see 4:36-37), intervenes and rehearses the evidence of Saul's conversion and prophetic calling (v. 27). The consecutive καί (*kai*, "So," v. 28) suggests that Barnabas's intercession is effective and the Twelve confirm Saul's conversion and calling. Their official confirmation allows Saul to take a second missionary step in Jerusalem,[387] which results in a showdown with nonbelieving "Hellenists" (v. 29; see 6:1, 9-14) who attempt to kill him as they earlier had Stephen. We are left to imagine that their conflict with Saul is for similar reasons: His "bold speaking in the name of the Lord"[388] asserts

the redemptive purchase of Jesus against a manner of purity that derives from temple routines or Torah observance. Of course, Saul was once a zealot among them and now has reversed his position. Such great reversals are certain to be noticed by friends and foes alike for their public appeal. Unlike Stephen, Saul escapes the Hellenists with a little help from his friends (9:30).[389]

9:31. This verse is another narrative summary and eases the transition to the "next stage" of the church's mission. Here we learn that the church founded by Philip's mission (see Acts 8) has entered into a period of "peace and build up"[390]—perhaps now because Saul is "off to Tarsus" (9:30)!

The reference to Galilee (the only time in Acts) is striking because it contrasts so sharply with the Gospel's geography of Jesus' Galilean mission. Perhaps Luke adds this detail to remind his readers that the church's mission is moving *from* Galilee and beyond the perimeter of the Lord's messianic mission toward still other territories. The phrase "comfort of the Holy Spirit" in connection with the "peace" and "fear" of the Palestinian church recalls the discourse on the Spirit by John's Jesus, who prophesied the coming of God's Παράκλητος (*Paraklētos*), the Holy Spirit, to comfort the disciples in his absence (John 14:26). The comforting Spirit is the medium of God's peace, so there is no cause for fear of others (John 14:27). According to the Johannine text, the disciples' fear that threatens their relationship with the Lord is precipitated by those "who will put you out of the synagogues" (John 16:1-2). Readers of Acts who are familiar with John's Gospel add a layer of meaning to this narrative summary: The church experiences peace and stability by "fearing the Lord" rather than the synagogue's opposition and by "the comfort of the Holy Spirit" that the Lord has given them.

386. There may very well have been a coalition of religious and political factions that ganged up on Paul in Damascus. See V. Furnish, *II Corinthians,* AB (Garden City, N.Y.: Doubleday, 1984) 521-23, 540-42. Paul mentions only the Nabatean faction (2 Cor 11:32-33) and Luke only the Jewish faction to serve their respective rhetorical and theological interests. In Acts, Luke makes "the Jews" Saul's foes because he is keen to demonstrate that the conflict is theological and internal to Judaism. He features it at the beginning of Paul's ministry as programmatic of the species of suffering that he will experience during his career as a prophet-like-Jesus.

387. The apparent contradiction with Paul's own contention that he was unknown to the Judean church (Gal 1:22) is resolved by Luke's careful placement of Paul within the city limits of Jerusalem without any reference to a wider ministry. See Haenchen, *The Acts of the Apostles,* 332.

388. Luke's use of "bold" (παρρησιάζομαι *parrēsiazomai*), speaking of Paul, is strategic in Acts because it links the power of his public speaking with the apostle's earlier petition for "boldness" (παρρησία *parrēsia*) in 4:29 and the Spirit's subsequent filling to effect an ever bolder preaching (4:31). The reader presumes that Paul's Spirit-filling (9:17-18) has a similar result—a presumption borne out by Luke's repetitive use of *parrēsiazomai* in Acts with reference to Paul's rhetorical effectiveness (13:46; 14:3; 18:26; 19:8; 26:26; 28:31).

389. For the meaning of the articular "the believers" (οἱ ἀδελφοί *hoi adelphoi*) in Acts, see Kee, *To Every Nation Under Heaven,* 123.

390. "Peace" (εἰρήνη *eirēnē*) is an important result of God's salvation and marks the people belonging to God, according to Luke (cf. Luke 1:79; 2:14; 10:5-6; 12:51; 19:38, 42; Acts 10:36; 24:2). Likewise, the word for "build up" (οἰκοδομέω *oikodomeō*) will be featured in the second half of Acts with reference to Amos's prophecy of the rebuilding of the house of Israel (see 15:16-18). Its use here probably refers to Christian nurture, as in the Pauline letters.

REFLECTIONS

1. "The reply came, 'I am Jesus, whom you are persecuting. But get up and enter the city, and you will be told what you are to do.'" (9:5*b*-6 NRSV). The story of Saul's/ Paul's conversion and calling forms an important subtext of Acts. For generations readers have formed their impressions of conversion on the basis of this story or have read their own experiences of conversion into this text. Scholars continue to debate whether interpreters should universalize the relevance and manner of Paul's conversion experience; almost certainly Luke recognized the distinctive importance of what happened to Paul on his way to Damascus and even in his story is careful to restrict those who saw the same "light" or heard the "voice" as Paul. Perhaps the highly personal cast of their exchange and of Paul's experience indicates that the pattern of Christian conversion is neither preformed nor universal: God finds people in a variety of ways.

Three elements of Paul's experience form the core of the story's different versions in Acts. First, Paul is converted to Jesus and not from one religion to another. There is no repudiation of his Jewish heritage when he turns to the Lord: Paul remains a pious Jew and a teacher of Israel. Nor is Paul led toward Jesus by the persuasive sermon of a talented preacher or the Christian nurture of loving parents. His change of mind is about Jesus and the realization that he is alive, not dead. The idea and experience of conversion in Acts concerns a coming to the Messiah in the confidence that God sent him into the world to rescue everyone from all that kills. That he is living confirms that he is God's promised salvation (see Luke 2:29-32). Second, Paul is changed— not immediately but over time—because of his encounter with the living Jesus. The "before-and-after" graphic is striking: Paul heads for Damascus with authority and purpose, but he is led by hand into the city helpless and blind. This one-time enemy of the church becomes its great champion. This persecutor of Jesus is then persecuted for proclaiming him. Personal transformation is the mark of genuine conversion; in some, like Paul, the changes are more dramatic and public. Finally, conversion is the means to a missionary end. Paul is converted for a calling. This pattern of Paul's salvation is typical of Acts: Personal transformation never collapses into sanctified self-absorption. Rather, conversion prepares the believer for performance of concrete tasks in the service of God.

2. "I will show him how much he must suffer for my name" (9:16 NIV); "Saul talked and debated with the Hellenists, but they tried to kill him" (see 9:29). Paul is called to preach the gospel to all people because God desires the salvation of all people. Yet as good as this theological sentiment feels, there are some who are determined to define God's salvation on more limited terms and to fight those who disagree with them. The Lord's prediction that Paul would suffer for proclaiming his name is not a condition of his calling but a consequence of his faithful exercise of it. Paul's fiercest opponents do not deny the integrity of his faith nor do they campaign in earnest against his personhood. Rather, they object to what he says about Jesus.

3. "All who heard [Saul] were amazed and said, 'Is not this the man who made havoc in Jerusalem among those who invoked this name?'" (9:21 NRSV). There are two dangers the church must guard against when regarding Christian conversion. On the one hand, believers should not presume that authentic Christianity is always characterized by conversion experiences resulting in radical personal transformation. Strong evangelism programs coupled with revivalist preaching often display this orientation toward dramatic transformation. However, many traditions teach that the child of faith gradually grows into Christian maturity, not through the giant leaps of conversion experiences but through the small steps fostered by a nurturing congregation. Many Christians cannot remember a time when they were not believers. On the other hand, believers should not diminish or ignore the resources God has given the church to transform people. Acts reminds its readers time and again that "we ignore the phenomenon of conversion at the peril of losing the church."[391] I am a Methodist with deep roots in the revivalist heritage of Wesleyan Holiness Christianity; while growing up I was "born again" and "purified" many times! The marvel of Luke's narrative is that both orientations are held together as integral elements of a mutually informing whole. Clearly Paul is converted to Jesus and his personal life is transformed as a result. This much is confirmed by his letters (see 1 Cor 15:3-11; Gal 1:11-19). Luke, however, is careful to place him within a faith community that confirms his salvation and safeguards his prophetic vocation.

Acts complements Paul's rehearsal of his conversion by reminding us that Christian discipleship is far too demanding for the individual. Only within a caring community will the believer find those resources and relationships that forge an enduring faith.

391. W. Willimon, *Acts* (Atlanta: John Knox, 1988) 104.

Acts 9:32–11:18, Back to the Future: Peter's Prophetic Ministry Beyond Jerusalem

COMMENTARY

Acts weaves together different narrative strands of the church's mission to the end of the earth. If Peter's story is the warp of Acts, then Paul's is its weft. Both men are prophets-like-Jesus who execute their commissioned tasks in different places with similar authority and effectiveness. As Saul departs to prepare for his future mission (see 9:30-31), the narrative resumes Peter's story, describing his mission beyond Jerusalem that also prepares for Saul's future endeavors.

Although a case can be made that Philip is forerunner to this stage of Peter's ministry,[392] the religious authority of the apostolic Twelve continues as an important theme in Acts. Peter and not Philip is the principal link between the risen Jesus and the messianic movement beyond Jerusalem that bears his name,[393] and the conversion of Cornelius, the first uncircumcised Gentile admitted into the faith, is considered his prerogative. This claim leads to two brief observations. First, new snapshots of Peter are added to his portraiture to commend his personal charisma, which is actually *increasing* and in no way has been attenuated by Saul's arrival on the

scene. Peter restores the paralytic Aeneas in Lydda (9:33-35; see 3:1-8) and the deceased Tabitha/Dorcas in Joppa (9:36-42) in a manner reminiscent of Jesus (cf. Luke 5:17-26) and the prophets before him (cf. 1 Kgs 17:17-24; 2 Kgs 4:19-27). These healings reestablish and even enhance Peter's spiritual authority, underwriting his mission to convert Cornelius's household and then to bear witness to the Spirit's "Gentile Pentecost" (cf. 10:44). The latter event confirms God's plan to allow uncircumcised but repentant Gentiles to experience the blessings of Israel's salvation (see 10:44; 11:15-18; 15:8-11) and defines the terms of Paul's future mission to the Gentiles.

Second, the theological subtext of Peter's mission to Cornelius is framed by Luke's allusion to the story of Jonah.[394] As with the OT prophet who reluctantly received a call to take the word of God from Joppa to Gentile Nineveh (cf. Jonah 1:3), Peter is commissioned by the same God to carry the gospel from this same Joppa (see Acts 10:23; cf. 9:36, 43) to the home of Gentile Cornelius. Perhaps recollection of Peter's Aramaic name, Simon bar Jonah (Matt 16:17), led Luke to see Jonah's story repeated in Peter's. In any

392. So Spencer, *The Portrait of Philip in Acts*.

393. Dunn, *The Acts of the Apostles*, 133, notes that Luke's Gospel avoids using Jesus tradition that considers clean and unclean foods and people (Gentiles), delaying it to Luke's narrative of the Gentile mission in Acts where these social boundaries are more properly considered.

394. See R. W. Wall, "Peter, 'Son of Jonah': The Conversion of Cornelius in the Context of Canon," *JSNT* 29 (1987) 79-90.

case, both prophets withdraw initial protests to their commissions only after God reveals more clearly the divine intention of their missions—after Jonah spends three days and nights in the belly of the great fish (Jonah 2:1) and after Peter hears a divine audition three times (Acts 10:15-16). Jonah's mission results in the repentance of Gentile Ninevites unto life (Jonah 3:1-10), to which the repentance and baptism of Cornelius's household corresponds (Acts 10:43, 47-48). The salvation of repentant Gentiles provokes a hostile response from "traditional" Israel (Jonah 4:1; see also Acts 11:1-2; cf. Acts 10:14), which then God refutes (Jonah 4:2-11; Acts 11:17-18; cf. Acts 15:13-21). Jonah's God is Peter's God; "the Gentile mission is from the beginning seen not as the work of men, even if they are Apostles, but of God (11:18)."[395]

9:32-35. The Plain of Sharon runs along the Mediterranean coastline from the twin cities, Lydda and Joppa, northward to Samarian Caesarea.[396] Peter is there, following in Philip's footprints (see 8:40), moving "here and there among all the believers" (v. 32; see 8:4). In Lydda, he finds himself in a situation similar to the early days of his Jerusalem mission when he healed the beggar (see 3:1-8): "Aeneas who had been bedridden for eight years, for he had been paralyzed" (v. 33). As before, Peter heals faithful Aeneas by invoking the name of Jesus: "Jesus Christ heals you" (v. 34; cf. 3:6; also, 10:38; 28:8).[397] In this instance, Peter removes himself as a broker of the Lord's healing grace and asserts that the Lord heals Aeneas.

The use of Aeneas's personal name—a Greek name for a diaspora Jew—roots the story in historical memory and reflects the expectation that God's salvation is experienced individually. The motive of the curious instruction to "get up and make your

bed" is not the same as that of the frustrated parent of a lazy child; rather, Peter's instruction seeks confirmation by some responsible action that a healing has taken place. The effect of God's healing grace is both immediate and public, with the result that "all the residents . . . turned to the Lord" (v. 35).[398] As earlier with Jesus, Peter connects the truth of the gospel with the healing of a paralytic; but unlike Jesus, Peter's ministry is among the "saints" where healing does not incite controversy (see Luke 5:17-26).

9:36-42. This second healing story takes place in Joppa (modern Jaffa) and is linked to Peter's first healing by the geographical proximity of these twin cities (v. 38*a*). The situation in Joppa, however, is considerably more urgent: Another believer, Tabitha (= Dorcas),[399] "became ill and died" (v. 37*a*). For this reason, her congregation sends two witnesses of her demise to Peter with the extraordinary appeal to "come to us without delay" (v. 38*b*). Peter's widespread reputation as a healer, coupled with biblical accounts of dramatic healings that Luke's narrative echoes (cf. 1 Kgs 17:17-24; 2 Kgs 4:32-37), have cultivated an optimism of grace that believes even a dead woman already prepared for burial—"they had washed her and laid her out"[400]—can be resuscitated by the apostle.

There is even more at stake in Tabitha's restoration than in Aeneas's case, as the details of her public profile make clear. She is renowned for "good works and charity." The widows of her congregation cry out to Peter, showing him the clothes she had made for them (v. 39*b*).[401] Her loss is keenly felt because of the community's responsibility for the welfare of its needy widows (see 6:1-2).

395. S. Wilson, *The Gentile and the Gentile Mission in Luke-Acts,* SNTMS 23 (Cambridge: Cambridge University Press, 1973) 177.

396. This region, known for its lush grazing areas (Isa 65:10), was an important commercial and political site during the Roman governance of Palestine; it would have been a natural area for Philip and then Peter to evangelize. Luke's repeated reference of "all the saints" (9:32) and "all the residents" (9:35), which encloses this first healing story, suggests that Peter's ministry takes place in a well-populated area.

397. The tense of the verbal idea of "Jesus Christ heals [ἰᾶται *iatai*] you" is debated, whether it is an aorist present or perfect (ἴαται *iatai*) and whether in the indicative or subjunctive mood. Barrett, *A Critical and Exegetical Commentary on the Acts of the Apostles,* 481, weighs the various options and decides in favor of an aorist present indicative, which intensifies the reality of a particular moment in time: Jesus Christ heals you *right now.*

398. With characteristic hyperbole Luke reminds the reader of the evangelical purpose of this current demonstration of Peter's apostolic powers. The residents of the Sharon valley are Jews since they "turned to the Lord [Jesus]" rather than to God. See Haenchen, *The Acts of the Apostles,* 338.

399. Luke uses the feminine form for "disciple" (μαθήτρια *mathētria*)—the only time it is used in the NT. The double naming of Tabitha, her Aramaic name, and the summary of her personal profile "she was devoted to good works and acts of charity" (9:36*b*) indicate her substantial reputation in the church. We learn nothing, however, about her marital or social status from this narrative.

400. The fact that Luke does *not* mention that her body was "anointed" with burial salts as expected may well indicate the community's confidence in her imminent resuscitation.

401. The middle voice of the participle "showed" (ἐπιδεικνύμεναι *epideiknymenai*) indicates that the widows are actually wearing clothes made for them by Dorcas, who distributes them among the most needy of the community in keeping with the principle of the community of goods (see 4:32-35).

Her healing bears additional witness to the importance of the community of goods. Yet the spotlight remains on Peter, who "sends them all out of the room" (v. 40). Perhaps the reader has reason to wonder how he will respond to the weeping widows, given the earlier failure of the Twelve to respond adequately to the welfare of Hellenist widows. In his ministry beyond Jerusalem, Peter's response is more direct and empathetic: He hears the widows' lamentation, he prays, and then he resuscitates Tabitha (vv. 40-41).

Peter's command, "Tabitha, get up" (ἀνάστηθι *anastēthi*), and the narrator's refrain, "he presented her to them alive," recall the resurrection of Jesus (see 1:3). This refrain also glosses Peter's similar command of Aeneas (see v. 34*b*) and thus we now suppose that his earlier claim that "Jesus Christ heals you" (see v. 34*a*) is implied here as well. That is, Peter's prophetic role is to announce the availability of the Lord's healing power among those who believe (cf. Luke 8:49-56). Peter's power to heal is not an exercise of magic but a function of his close communion with the Lord of glory. Once again, the action of "helping her up" (v. 41) and returning her to the "saints and widows" confirms the resuscitation. And again as a result of this healing, "many people believed the Lord" (v. 42*b*; see also v. 35). Although the catalytic character of "signs and wonders" is characteristic of Acts, Luke's summaries of conversions are characteristically gapped and should be filled out with additional details culled from similar missionary episodes. In this way, the reader knows that the inference of every conversion is that people "turn to the Lord" (v. 35) and "believe in the Lord" (v. 42) in response to the proclamation of the gospel.

9:43. The impression left by this verse is one of a pause in preparation for the next episode. Two details are important in this regard. First, Peter "stayed in Joppa." The repetition of the city in the following story of Cornelius's conversion (10:6, 17, 32) commends the importance of "Joppa" to the story's meaning: Peter's location connects his prophetic mission and Jonah's, who also departed from Joppa on his fateful mission to Nineveh (see above). Second, Peter stays "with a certain Simon, a tanner." The symbolic importance of kosher purity in Luke's Cornelius story

(see 10:14) is introduced here by reference to Simon's trade, since a tanner carries the odors and blood of animals that would make him "unclean."[402]

10:1-8. The taxonomy of God's universal salvation reaches a watershed moment with the introduction of God-fearing Roman Cornelius. The brief sketch of his résumé, completed by subsequent reports of close associates (see 10:22) and then by Cornelius himself (see 10:31), places him in Caesarea and identifies him as a ranking "centurion" attached to the "Italian Cohort" (v. 1).[403] Cornelius is the first person with Roman authority named in Acts. Religiously, he is "a devout man, who feared God—gave alms generously—and prayed constantly to God" (v. 2; cf. 10:22, 31). Although Luke attaches considerable importance to God-fearing Gentiles in Acts, we have no standard definition or precise classification of "God-fearing" from the ancient world.[404] Allowing for a technical difference between the non-Jewish believer who has completed the prescribed rite of initiation into Judaism ("proselyte"; cf. 6:5) and the non-Jewish seeker who is simply interested in the beliefs and practices of Judaism ("God-fearer"; see v. 2), references to the actual practices of Gentile proselytes (cf. 13:43) are roughly the same as of God-fearers in Acts. In any case, Luke's emphasis is on Cornelius's character rather than on his political or religious status—and implicitly on the causal relationship between his character and conversion. Thereby his piety is a "memorial before God"[405] (v. 4; cf. 10:31) and showing him to be the sort of pious Gentile that has favor with God.

God responds to Cornelius's prayers with a vision. The missionary function of visions

402. Some scholars think this connection is too clever for Luke's readers if not for Luke. Others suggest that this negative reaction to a tanner's work stems from the casuistry of later rabbis and is probably not yet in Luke's social world. See J. McConnachie, "Simon a Tanner" (Acts ix.43; x.6, 32), *ExpT* 36 (1924-25) 90.

403. A centurion was a noncommissioned officer who commanded one hundred soldiers; he was probably a Roman citizen. A "cohort" of soldiers typically numbers six hundred (one-tenth of a legion)—although this is contested by historians of the Roman army, as is the location, date, and precise role of the "Italian Cohort." See Fitzmyer, *The Acts of the Apostles*, 449.

404. The scholarly literature on the status of Gentile God-fearers is extensive. For good summaries of the social and religious worlds of God-fearers see Witherington, *The Acts of the Apostles*, 341-44; Kee, *To Every Nation Under Heaven*, 133-36.

405. This striking phrase alludes to OT offerings made to God whose fragrance ascends to God's "nostrils"—an anthropomorphism of divine pleasure (cf. Lev 2:2, 9, 16; 5:12; 6:15). While the content of Cornelius's prayers is unknown, it is reasonable to infer that the angelic vision is a response to prayer.

in Acts is to locate a person in the right place at the right time in order to receive God's benefaction. In this light, the soldier is given marching orders to follow into salvation: "send men to Joppa" for a certain man who is staying in a particular house (vv. 5-6). Obedience to God's bidding is the hallmark of readiness to receive God's grace. Cornelius obeys God according to his own military conventions: He "called . . . a devout soldier from the ranks" whose experience is most like Cornelius's (see v. 2) and would therefore be best able to represent his interests to Peter, which he evidently does (v. 8).

References to the time of day are always theologically laden in this book: The pious Cornelius had a vision "one afternoon at about three o'clock" (v. 3; see also 3:1). This was a time of day set aside for religious observance among the faithful of Israel—in the middle of the afternoon for all to see. Once again a "double vision" is employed in Acts to get two people on God's page. Before both Saul and Ananias had separate visions about the same future (see 9:11-12); and here again Cornelius and "a certain Simon who is called Peter" will also have visionary experiences of the same future—God's future. Cornelius's response to the angel is the same as Saul's to Jesus—"What is it, Lord?" (v. 4; see also 9:5)—and for the same reason: He lacks understanding, which the vision then supplies.

10:9-16. "About noon the next day," as the caravan travels to Joppa, Peter has gone to a rooftop in Joppa to pray.[406] Luke adds that the apostle prays while hungry, an appropriate context for a vision about food. Peter's hunger is a function of his piety, since prayer likely is joined with a fast to underwrite his devotion to God. Peter's piety in turn might then explain both his "trance" (ἔκστασις *ekstasis*), which occasions prophetic ecstasy, and his subsequent hesitancy to kill and eat unclean foods.

The general role of visions in Acts is to clarify God's redemptive plan with regard to specific places and people. "This is the moment

when new religions or sects are born—when what has hitherto been taken for granted as a fundamental and defining principle is called into question, and the question is heard as the voice of God."[407] In Peter's case a picnic blanket is envisaged, spread with various species of animals (vv. 11-12) without distinguishing clean from unclean.[408] Characteristically, what he sees is accompanied by what he hears: the Lord's instruction for him to "get up, kill and eat" (v. 13) the animals without proper attention to their kosher preparation (cf. Leviticus 11). Peter's negative response—"By no means, Lord"—should be anticipated by his Jewish piety (v. 14).[409] The subsequent repetition of this divine audition makes Peter's proper response clear: What was formerly "profane and unclean" is now clean and no longer profane. The second repetition of the divine audition (v. 15) explains the first and provides the essential message of the vision. Peter does not require the third audition, which serves a symbolic rather than an epistemic role.

The exchange between God and Peter only indirectly concerns traditions regarding clean and unclean foods, even though this is surely what prompts him to "puzzle greatly" and ponder the meaning of his vision (vv. 17, 19*a*).[410] Comprehension unfolds only with additional information:[411] Peter's vision concerns his mission to fulfill God's purpose that unclean (= uncircumcised) Gentiles will also share Israel's blessings (see vv. 42-43).

10:17-23a. Several coincidental incidents occur that gradually illumine Peter's understanding of his vision. Cornelius's emissaries arrive from Caesarea and ask to see Peter (vv. 17-18). The clever literary interplay between

---

406. While not a fixed time of daily prayer for the pious Jew, Peter's noontime prayer may very well be part of a fast since it is associated with his hunger. Some later MSS read "three o'clock" instead of "noon" but this is clearly a scribal accommodation to the earlier reference to Cornelius's prayer and is in any case a better known time for demonstrations of Jewish piety (see 3:1).

407. Dunn, *The Acts of the Apostles*, 138.

408. Reptiles (cf. Lev 11:29-38) and birds (cf. Lev 11:13-19) are especially unclean for a pious Jew.

409. The phrase "by no means" translates the adverb μηδαμῶς *mēdamōs* and is found only here (and in Peter's retelling of this incident in 11:8) in the NT. The intensity of Peter's response is expressed by the addition of "never" (οὐδέποτε *oudepote*; lit., "at no time") and the pairing of "profane or unclean" (κοινὸν καὶ ἀκάθαρτον *koinon kai akatharton*)—synonyms for the unlawful taken from both Jewish ("unclean") and Greek ("profane") religious vocabularies.

410. The word for "puzzle" (διαπορέω *diaporeō*) is used only by Luke in the NT and typically of an inward response to divine revelation, whether in reference to nonbelievers (see Acts 2:12; 5:24; cf. Luke 9:7) or believers (cf. Luke 24:4). All have the inherent ability to perceive the importance of what they see or hear, even though without understanding.

411. Peter's failure to "get" his vision is not the result of hardened resistance or spiritual obduracy (as perhaps is true with Jonah) but reflects the sheer difficulty of deciphering the symbols of God's message. Contra Dunn, *The Acts of the Apostles*, 138. Peter needs more information; and when he receives it, he understands.

two "Simons"—Simon the tanner (v. 17) at whose house "Simon who was called Peter" (v. 18) is staying—may intend to create the impression of confusion (related to Peter's understanding of the vision) that is then resolved by the Spirit's intervention (v. 19).

The Spirit's word to Peter serves both theological and practical ends: "Look, three men are searching for you" (10:19b). Peter is evidently lost in his meditation on the meaning of his vision and does not hear the three men knocking and calling for him from the gate. The Spirit's intervention to facilitate their meeting makes us expect that those who stand at the door knocking will somehow aid Peter in deciphering his vision. Further, its instruction for Peter to "go with them—for I have sent them" (v. 20) indicates that the message these men bring him accords with divine purpose.

Peter's question, "Why have you come?" (v. 21), seems to challenge the Spirit's earlier instruction, "Go with them without hesitation" (v. 20). The phrase translated "without hesitation" (μηδὲν διακρινόμενος *mēden diakrinomenos*) means to act without pausing to doubt its merit.[412] Peter's question, perhaps, functions as a literary prompt that occasions yet another sounding of God's reasons for saving Cornelius. The three messengers assert that "he is a righteous and God-fearing man, who is respected by all the Jewish people" and that he was "directed by a holy angel" to listen to what Peter says (v. 22). These details comprise both a confirmation and an expansion of Luke's earlier résumé (see vv. 1-4) and reflect an independent appraisal of Cornelius's fitness to receive God's salvation. Cornelius is described for Jewish Peter's benefit as a "righteous man" (replacing the earlier "devout man"), as though he lived his life according to Torah's precept.[413]

Significantly, Peter learns that they were "directed" by a "holy angel" with the tacit promise that Peter would go to Cornelius's home where a Gentile would listen

to what the prophet would say to him. The verb χρηματίζω (*chrēmatizō*), translated "directed" (NRSV) or even more timidly as "told" (NIV), is a much stronger term that denotes a revelatory word from God (see Matt 2:12, 22; Luke 2:26; Heb 8:5; 11:7). For this reason, Peter is responsive to what his visitors tell him; indeed, the demonstration of his hospitality toward them—he "invited them in and gave them lodging" (v. 23)—is characteristic of one who is responsive to God's Word.[414] The reader must presume that Peter now understands the intent of his vision and has accepted the prospect of a Gentile mission as a feature of God's plan of salvation (see 10:28-29).

10:23b-33. This panel of Luke's story takes place "the next day," when Peter departs for Caesarea. He is joined by "some of the [Jewish] believers from Joppa" (v. 23b) who will later attest to Cornelius's conversion (see v. 45; 11:12). Cornelius has already been prepared for Peter's visit and "had called together his relatives and close friends" (v. 24) of his extended household.[415]

For all his religious devotion Cornelius is not yet a believer and still makes theological mistakes: "Cornelius, falling at Peter's feet, worshiped him" (10:25).[416] Given the importance the angel has attached to Peter, Cornelius's response seems reasonable since it proffers homage to someone heaven has authorized to mediate the blessings of eternal life. Peter, however, has consistently refused to exercise his religious authority in a self-centered manner and always has subordinated it to the will and purposes of God (see 3:12; 9:40). Cornelius's honest mistake, then, is in supposing that Peter is in some sense directly responsible for his salvation; Peter's role, however, is to proclaim salvation, not to dispense it. His response testifies

---

412. Barrett, *A Critical and Exegetical Commentary on the Acts of the Apostles*, 511. It is noteworthy that Luke uses this same verb in Peter's review of this incident before the Jerusalem Council (15:9). In this later use, however, it is used of God, who "makes no distinction" (οὐθὲν διέκρινεν *outhen diekrinen*) between Jews and Gentiles. The later glosses the earlier use so that the reader understands that the Spirit tells Peter to go "without hesitation" to a Gentile because God "makes no distinction" between Jew and non-Jew.

413. Fitzmyer, *The Acts of the Apostles*, 457.

414. Johnson, *The Acts of the Apostles*, 185.

415. In Acts the "household" is an important location for the experience of God's saving power, as the use of οἶκος/οἰκία (*oikos/oikia*, "house") shows (see 2:2, 46; 5:42; 9:17; 10:22; 11:12-14; 16:31-32; 18:7-8; 20:20). A range of important literary themes in Acts are centered in the house, such as goods, hospitality, friendship, and worship. The reader should be alert, then, to the social fabric of salvation that is indicated by repeated references to the household, as here in the story of Cornelius's conversion where members of his extended household—including clients and friends—are not only witnesses to his salvation but participants in it.

416. The word "worship" (προσκυνέω *proskyneō*) denotes either homage given a deity or the profound respect one demonstrates toward an emissary sent by God. Peter's response suggests that Cornelius presumes that Peter is worthy of worship that is due God alone.

to this subordinate role in Cornelius's salvation: "Stand up; I am only a mortal" (10:26; cf. 14:14-15).

In all modesty, then, Peter's opening missionary address testifies to his own recent "conversion" (see 10:22-23*a*): "God has shown me that I should not call anyone profane or unclean" (10:28*b*; see 10:14-15). In fact, the process of divine disclosure began with Peter's missionary efforts beyond Jerusalem among marginal Jews (see 8:25; 9:32-42, 43). These missionary efforts beyond Jerusalem are now directed to those beyond Israel.[417] The temporal framework supplied by the narrative itself indicates that Peter's understanding of his Gentile mission unfolds over several days of visions (see 10:30), internal reflection (see 10:17, 19), and the reports of others (see 10:22). What God finally "shows" him is the subtext of this unusual house call, since an observant Jew deems it "unlawful to visit a Gentile" (10:28*a*)[418] and especially "without objection" (10:29*a*).

Peter's question, "May I ask why you sent for me?" (10:29*b*), and Cornelius's response (10:30-33) appear redundant (see 10:4-6, 22) and an unnecessary preface to the proclamation of the gospel. Such restatements are characteristic of Luke's narrative style, however, and are employed to elucidate and clarify important literary themes. For example, Cornelius's commentary on this occasion emphasizes God's faithfulness more than his own religious résumé: "God has heard—and remembered"[419] (10:31; cf. 10:4*b*). Cornelius's goodwill (and earlier homage) toward Peter and submission to his spiritual authority are now explained by his desire to "listen to all that the Lord has commanded you to say" (10:33).

10:34-43. Peter and Cornelius share a premonition that a religious revolution is about to commence in Israel. For this reason, Peter's gospel presentation is not defensive but *epideictic* (= edifying) in tone and christological in substance.[420] Its chiastic shape (ABCB´A´) funnels its auditors to the speech's core kerygmatic elements (see 10:38-42*a*) to underline the continuity between his proclamation to Jew and now to Gentile.[421]

10:34-35 (A). Luke's opening formula, "Then Peter began to speak" (lit., "Peter then opened his mouth"; see 8:35) is a literary convention indicating that the speech is inspired prophecy. The full implication of his mission has now been made clear to him: "I now realize how true it is that God shows no partiality" between Jew and Gentile (v. 34*b*; see also vv. 28-29). Peter's lesson is about God and not the scope of his mission. Surely he knows from Israel's Scriptures that God is not a respecter of persons (cf. Deut 10:17; cf. Ps 81:2 LXX; Lev 19:15; 2 Chr 19:7); however, this conviction has acquired new dimensions of meaning in the light of recent events. Moreover, the biblical principle of divine impartiality comes with a critical aspect: Although God does not discriminate by ethnic group or nationality, God does indeed single out those "in every nation . . . who fear him and do what is right" (v. 35).[422] Cornelius is a Roman exemplar of this theological principle (see 10:4-6, 31).[423]

10:36-37 (B). Peter's brief geographic review of the Messiah's career also argues for the fairness of God, although not without considerable irony.[424] Perhaps this element of

---

417. The word translated "Gentile" in 10:28 is ἀλλόφυλος (*allophylos*); it is used only here in the NT but often as a pejorative in the LXX. The term denotes people of different or mixed ethnic grounds other than Jewish; its sense is not religious but racial.

418. Some scholars pose considerable problems with Peter's initial address to his Gentile audience since they claim his visitation of Gentiles is not unprecedented. Observant Jews did cultivate friendships and have social relations with non-Jews, especially in the diaspora. See Haenchen, *The Acts of the Apostles*, 350; Josephus *The Jewish War* 2.463. However, Peter's idiom is not relational but cultic. He merely restates the teaching of rabbis that it is ritually unclean for a "clean" (i.e., observant) Jew to enter the home of an "unclean" (i.e., non-observant) Gentile. See Fitzmyer, *The Acts of the Apostles*, 457, 461. Cornelius is not a proselyte Jew or yet a believer. He is, therefore, "unclean" from Peter's perspective as an observant Jew.

419. Johnson, *The Acts of the Apostles*, 190-91, argues that the choice of "remember" intentionally recalls the OT idiom of God's covenant faithfulness, when God "remembers" Israel and blesses them. In this setting, then, God's act of remembering Cornelius is a response of God's faithfulness to the promise made to Abraham that Gentiles would share in Israel's blessings—rather than a per se response to Cornelius because of deeds he had done.

420. Peter's speeches in Acts follow a common literary pattern consisting of an opening address that connects with the audience (vv. 34-35), christological kerygma (vv. 36-41), scriptural proofs (v. 43), and a summons to repent (v. 42).

421. The chiastic pattern is as follows: A = 10:34-5 (God is not partial); A´ = 10:43*b* (God forgives all who believe); B = 10:36*a* (God sent the gospel to Israel first); B´ = 10:43*a* (God sends the gospel to Gentiles); C = 10:36*b*-37 (Jesus is Lord of all); C´] = 10:42*b* (Jesus is judge of all); and D = 10:38-42*a* (the gospel message: Jesus sent forth as Messiah).

422. The phrase "what is right [δικαιοσύνη *dikaiosynē*]" refers to practices that conform to God's law; Barrett, *A Critical and Exegetical Commentary on the Acts of the Apostles*, 1:520-21. Peter thereby allows that an uncircumcised Gentile like Cornelius can become a member of the covenant community, even though not a proselyte, because his life is characteristic of the faithful Jew.

423. The meaning of the predicate "God accepts" (NIV; NRSV, "is acceptable to God") is unclear. Has God already "accepted" Cornelius because of his acts of piety as a God-fearer (so NIV)? Or has his righteousness more simply made him "acceptable" to be saved (so NRSV)? The latter translation seems best here since salvation in Acts is impossible apart from a hearing of the gospel and a believing response to its kerygmatic claims (see 2:38).

424. For the difficult text critical, grammatical, and interpretative issues regarding 10:36-38, see Barrett, *A Critical and Exegetical Commentary on the Acts of the Apostles*, 521-25; Schneider, *Die Apostelgeschichte*, 2:76-77.

Peter's speech responds to an unstated problem concerning the perceived partiality of Jesus' mission, which was only to Jews. His response is to claim that the biblical promise of peace is made first to Israel; therefore, the Messiah is sent first to Israel (v. 36) with a "message [ῥῆμα *rhēma*, "event"][425] spread throughout Judea, beginning with Galilee" (v. 37). Nevertheless, the implicit universal importance of Jesus' mission to Israel is ironically captured by Peter's parenthetical confession that "[Jesus Christ] is Lord of all" (v. 36).

10:38-42a (C). Peter brings his gospel to climax with a summary of "the message [ὁ λόγος *ho logos*] God sent to the people [lit., "children"] of Israel," of which "we are witnesses" (v. 39). Its familiar content in this rhetorical setting is yet another way to articulate the biblical principle of divine impartiality. Peter emphasizes not only the basis of Jesus' prophetic ministry ("with the Holy Spirit and with power")[426] but also its public venue and the dramatic manner by which "he went about doing good and healing all who were oppressed by the devil, for God was with him" (v. 38). For this reason, his reputation for good works is already known by this Gentile audience (see "you know the message," v. 36). Moreover, Jesus has reliable "witnesses [μάρτυρες *martyres*] to all that he did both in Judea and Jerusalem" (v. 39; see also 1:21-22; 2:22-24; 3:13-15; 4:40; 5:30) and following his resurrection (vv. 40-41; see also 2:32). That is, the details of the Messiah's career—how and what he did—were not hidden from public view and now allow for the impartial dissemination of God's message to non-Jews.

Because these apostolic witnesses "were chosen by God" (v. 41; see 1:2) as the special audience to whom the risen Jesus appeared and with whom he "ate and drank" (see Luke 24:30-31, 41-43; John 21:12-13), the sense is that God operates from a predetermined plan with the relationship between the

Messiah and his apostles at its center.[427] The implied point again is to underline the inherent authority of the apostles as witnesses and colleagues of the risen Jesus, and that through their ministry God's plan of salvation goes forward.

10:42b-43a (B'). Peter's witness to the resurrected Jesus presumes a special relationship with him and a privileged knowledge of him, which obligates him "to testify" (διαμαρτύρασθαι *diamartyrasthai*; see 2:40; 8:25) to the Jewish "people" (see 2:47; 3:23; 10:2) after the pattern established by the Messiah's mission and biblical prophecy. It is noteworthy that Peter introduces Jesus' future role as Israel's "judge of the living and the dead" to a Gentile audience (cf. 17:29-31), which is, perhaps, another symbol of the principle of divine impartiality.

10:43b (A'). Scripture's witness is added to Peter's testimony to complete his presentation of the gospel. Peter's appeal to Scripture makes sense only because Cornelius is God-fearing and would recognize the authority of Israel's Scriptures. There is no specific citation given; Peter's appeal to "all the prophets" is to the whole tenor of Scripture (cf. 3:18, 24; 7:42; 26:22; 28:23). All Scripture testifies to God's promise of salvation, which has been fulfilled in the Christ event, so that "*everyone* who believes in him receives forgiveness of sins through his *name*" (italics added). This final refrain echoes Joel's prophecy (see 2:21), which joins Jonah's prophecy as the implied biblical witnesses to the theological truth of Peter's proclamation to Cornelius. The Pauline phrase "believes in him" is found only here in Acts (cf. 13:39), which may cue the narrative's turn toward Paul's mission to the nations but here is still more clearly bound to the familiar themes of Peter's earlier preaching—"forgiveness of sins" (see 2:38; 3:18-19) and "through his name" (e.g., 2:38; 3:6; 4:10).

10:44-48. Although Acts mentions twice that Peter's speech is interrupted (v. 44*a*; see also 11:15), nothing important is left out and it stands as a complete presentation of

---

425. In this case *rhēma* is probably better rendered as "event" (i.e., the Christ event) as in Luke 2:15. See Haenchen, *The Acts of the Apostles*, 352.

426. Dunn, *The Acts of the Apostles*, 142-43, notes three OT allusions that together provide a prophetic co-text to clarify Luke's intended meaning for 10:36-38: Ps 107:20 ("he sent out his word and healed [the people of Israel]"); Isa 52:7 ("those who preach peace [to the people of Israel]"); and Isa 61:1 ("The Spirit of the Lord is upon [Jesus of Nazareth] because he has anointed [him] to preach good news [to the people of Israel]"; cf Luke 4:18). Thus Peter's rehearsal of Jesus' messianic mission (the "Christ event") is understood as the concrete fulfillment of God's *biblical* promise to Israel.

427. The word translated "chosen" (προχειροτονέω *procheirotoneō*) is used only here in the NT, although it is similar to the word used in 3:20 for God's "choosing" of Jesus as Messiah (προχειρίζομαι *procheirizomai*). This vocabulary not only confirms that Peter's (= the Twelve's) ministry is a sign of God's provident care of the Jewish people, but that it also follows a carefully prearranged (*pro*) script that inspires the audience's confidence in its completion.

the gospel. It is probably best to understand this "interrupted speech," then, as a literary convention employed earlier (cf. 2:37) and later (cf. 17:32; 22:22; 23:7; 26:24) for rhetorical effect—in this instance to showcase two important theological convictions. First, the Holy Spirit insinuates itself into Peter's preaching as a demonstration that God takes the lead in fulfilling the prophesied plan of salvation; in effect, God's Spirit intrudes upon Peter's ministry to illustrate a point he has just made about the testimony of prophets (see v. 43)!

More critical, however, is a second core conviction: God's Spirit interrupts Peter to empower *his* witness to the history of God's salvation, another theme of this speech (see v. 39). Peter's subsequent witness to this "Gentile Pentecost" will both complete the task God has given him and revolutionize how he thinks of Gentile admission into the covenant community. Indeed, from this moment forward whenever Peter is asked to interpret the status of uncircumcised Gentiles within the church or in relationship to Jews/Jerusalem, his final appeal will not be to his vision but to Cornelius's reception of the gift of the Holy Spirit. Peter is a witness not only to the historical Jesus (and so his apostle) but also to the initial outpouring of the Holy Spirit at Pentecost and its subsequent outpourings in Samaria and now upon the household of Cornelius, an uncircumcised Roman Gentile. Only Peter is in a position to recognize the strong family resemblance between them and to draw its soteriological significance from what he has observed (see 11:15). Perhaps for this reason Luke shapes his account of the Gentile Pentecost after the sequence of events of Israel's Pentecost narrated in Acts 2: (1) "The Holy Spirit fell upon all who heard the word" (v. 44//2:4); (2) "the circumcised believers . . . were astounded . . . for they heard them speaking in tongues and extolling God" (vv. 45-46//2:11-12); (3) "Then Peter said, 'Can anyone withhold the water for baptizing these people who have received the Holy Spirit just as we have?' " (v. 47//2:38); and (4) they were "baptized in the name of Jesus Christ" (v. 48*a*//2:41).

This literary interplay within Acts between the Jerusalem and the Gentile "Pentecosts" guarantees an appropriate response to Peter's rhetorical question, "Can anyone withhold the water for baptizing these people?" (v. 47). The logical response must be a resounding no. There is nothing that should exclude these repentant Gentiles from their initiation into the faith community. The reader of Acts recalls, however, that the Spirit's outpouring had earlier "amazed" Jewish pilgrims in the holy city who out of ignorance mistook "God's deeds of power" for human folly (see 2:11-12). In a similar way, the "astonishment" of those "circumcised believers" who witnessed "that the gift of the Holy Spirit had been poured out even on the Gentiles" (v. 45) alerts the reader that other repentant Jews may not be prepared to readily embrace the revolution that Peter's mission to Cornelius has begun. Thus, even though the apostle "ordered them to be baptized" (v. 48*a*), there is hint of trouble brewing back home in the Jerusalem church (see 11:2). The question remains why the Spirit's baptism of Cornelius should have amazed Peter's Jewish cohort. Because of the church's prior experience with the Spirit's outpouring in both Jerusalem and Samaria, it is doubtful that their astonishment obtains to the phenomena of "speaking in tongues and extolling God" (v. 46). Moreover, they would have heard reports from both Peter and Cornelius of their coincidental "double vision" as testimony that God intends to include "unclean" Gentiles in the church. The surprising element of this incident of Spirit baptism must be that repentant Gentiles share the same gift of the Holy Spirit equally with repentant Jews—in Peter's words "these people who have received the Holy Spirit *just as we have*" (v. 47, italics added). The conclusion the Peter of Acts draws from their common religious experience is that uncircumcised believers belong as fully to the messianic community as do these stunned "circumcised believers."

11:1-17. With every case of repetition, especially when it is of whole episodes as here, we must be on the lookout for changes in setting, in details, or in literary design that uncover the full importance that episode carries within the whole narrative. In this second telling of Cornelius's conversion, Peter is compelled to provide testimony to a council of church leaders in Jerusalem (vv. 1-3). Evidently, some believers are upset by reports that "Gentiles had also accepted the word of

God" (v. 1; cf. 8:14). Peter's careful rehearsal of Cornelius's conversion (vv. 4-14) does not seek to defend his own actions but the actions of God, who has saved an "unclean" Roman Gentile (vv. 15-18; see also 15:6-11).

11:1-3. The report of the favorable reception of the word by Gentiles was well received by Peter's apostolic colleagues who "praised God" (v. 18). Luke implies a division exists in the Judean church between "the apostles and the believers" and "the circumcised believers" (cf. 10:45) who "criticized" (διακρινόμενος *diakrinomenos*) Peter's actions in converting Cornelius (11:2; see 10:20). Ironically, their criticism of Peter echoes his own hesitancy to obey the directive of his divine audition to eat non-kosher foods (see 10:13-16) and then his anxiety over the "legality" of visiting a non-kosher household (see 10:28). Peter's earlier anxiety is now reflected by leading members of the Jewish church who worry that table fellowship with unclean Gentiles will defile them as well. Only time will tell whether their anxiety over the intermingling of clean and unclean people will also dissolve upon consideration of their common gift of the Holy Spirit.

The first Jerusalem assembly to consider controversies provoked by the Gentile mission is now convened, and will continue at a second Jerusalem assembly (15:4-5) that concludes the first part of Acts (see the Overview to 2:14–15:12). The irony of the present story is nicely captured by Luke's clever repetition of *diakrinō*, first of the Spirit's injunction for Peter to hear out Cornelius's emissaries and accompany them "without hestitation" (*diakrinō*, 10:20) and now here of Peter's opponents in Jerusalem who "criticize" (*diakrinō*, 11:2) him for doing so. If the anxiety of conservative Jews is that they will become as Gentiles by sharing table fellowship with them, then their salve for this anxiety is that the Gentile convert must become as a Jew by following their purity laws. The real danger is to trivialize their anxiety and criticize these Jewish believers as "legalists" or worse. Their concern for purity is in reality a concern for the community's solidarity. This is after all a community of friends that has distinguished itself in Jerusalem's public life by living together with "one heart and soul" (see 4:32). Now, however, the currency of the community's solidarity is no longer merely sharing goods; the community's new currency minted by the Gentile Pentecost is the sharing of the same spiritual food, "the gift of the Holy Spirit," which purifies *everyone* who calls upon the risen "Lord of all." That is, while the stated anxiety is table fellowship, the implied and real anxiety is over sharing the Holy Spirit with unholy Gentiles. The tendency to embody the pattern of God's salvation, which privileges Jews (see 10:37-39), in the social practices of the faith community as symbolized by table fellowship is subverted by the shared experience of the Holy Spirit.

11:4-14. Peter's response to their question about his alleged table fellowship with Gentiles is characterized as an "explanation" (ἐκτίθημαι *ektithēmai*, v. 4). His primary motive is to set forth the chronological order of events in a straightforward fashion, and he does so in the first person as the principal witness to these events.

The summary of the double vision follows closely its initial narration in 10:9-33; there are, however, two substantial additions that gloss the earlier story. The first is Peter's reference to "these six brothers also accompanied me, and we entered the man's house" (v. 12). Even though it remains unclear from the earlier account whether these "circumcised believers" agreed with Peter's actions (see 10:45-48), he has now made them witnesses to confirm Peter's report as trustworthy. Clever politics indeed! The second and far more important change comes with Peter's retelling of Cornelius's report concerning what the angel had told him (see 10:31-32) in the light of what ultimately transpired. Cornelius mentioned nothing of an angelic promise that Peter's message would be the means "by which you and your entire household will be saved" (v. 14).

The angel's emphasis on *salvation* adds three new elements to the Cornelius tradition. (1) The prior concern that Gentiles follow Israel's purity code is redefined to invite reflection on God's "code" by which Gentiles participate in the blessings of Israel's salvation. (2) Peter's shift to the soteriological implications of Cornelius's conversion prepares us for a second Jerusalem council when Peter will refer to Cornelius's conversion and Spirit baptism (see 15:6-11) as paradigmatic of the conversion of uncircumcised Gentiles and their solidarity with Jewish believers (cf. 15:4-5). Peter concludes with the Paul-like assertion that "we believe that we [Jews] will be saved through the grace of the Lord Jesus, just as they [Gentiles] will" (15:11; cf. Eph 2:8-9). (3) The phrasing of Peter's "you will be saved" (σωθήσῃ *sōthēsē*) recalls the final phrase of Joel's paradigmatic prophecy that everyone—now including God-fearing uncircumcised Gentiles—who believes in the Lord Jesus "will be saved" (σωθήσεται *sōthēsetai*, 2:21). This intertext glosses Peter's previous climactic claim that "all the prophets [Jonah and now Joel] testify about him that everyone who believes in him receives forgiveness of sins through his name" (10:43).

11:15-17. Peter's explanation emphasizes Cornelius's experience of Spirit baptism (see 10:44-48). Clearly this has become for him the hermeneutic key to understanding God's plan to save "unclean" Gentiles like Cornelius. He does not mention his speech; Peter's witness is not to a kerygma but to a religious experience. His use of a traditional saying, "John baptized with water, but you will be baptized with the Holy Spirit" (v. 16; cf. Luke 3:16), recalls the Lord's instruction of his apostolic successors at the beginning of Acts (see 1:5). However, neither Cornelius nor any member of his household engage in ministry following their Spirit baptism (cf. 1:8). The Gentile Pentecost presumes a different religious motive and effect that is redemptive and not vocational. In this regard, Peter asserts that "God gave them the same *gift* that he gave us when we believed in the Lord Jesus Christ" (v. 17, italics added; cf. 11:15*b*), which echoes his conviction that repentance occasions receiving the "*gift* of the Holy Spirit" (2:38, italics added) and initiation into the community of goods (see 2:42-47). The implied point is that repentant Gentiles are initiated into a community of goods that shares God's gift of the Holy Spirit with repentant Jews.

11:18. The Jewish believers' response to Peter's report and stunning conclusion is silence (v. 18*a*): Their initial objection (see 11:3) is considered an irrelevancy by their Apostle, who has skillfully turned the occasion into a theological platform to sound a programmatic note about Israel's mission to the Gentiles. The importance of the council's judgment that "God has granted even the Gentiles the repentance unto life" (v. 18*b*), which otherwise sounds redundant, is gleaned from two "repentance" texts found earlier in Acts and echoed here to "thicken" the importance of repentant Gentiles. In concluding his speech to Cornelius, Peter appeals to "all the prophets" for proof that "forgiveness of sins" is granted to "everyone who believes in Jesus" (10:43). In the light of the pairing of "repentance" with the reception of both "forgiveness of sins" and "the gift of the Spirit" in 2:38, the council's verdict is that the requirements and results of Gentile and Jewish repentance are the same. The full implication of their conclusion will be cashed out when this same council reconvenes to consider whether the repentant Gentiles of Paul's congregations in the diaspora should practice circumcision (see 14:27–15:29).

The second text alluded to is 5:30-32, where Peter famously addresses the Sanhedrin with the affirmation that "we must obey God rather than men" (5:29). Peter goes on to explain that his obedience to God is predicated on "the *God* of our ancestors [who] raised Jesus" (5:30, italics added) in order to "grant *repentance* to Israel and the forgiveness of sins" (5:31, italics added) and to give the Holy Spirit "to those who obey God" (5:32). That is, according to Peter, God's plan to bless a repentant Israel is signaled by the reception of the Holy Spirit. In concluding this first Jerusalem Council, then, those elders assembled agree that this fresh outpouring of the Spirit must mean that God has "*granted* even the Gentiles the *repentance* unto life" (italics added). Behind this verdict lies the critical recognition that Cornelius's repentance and Spirit baptism are not at odds with Jewish tradition but actually *agree* with it. In fact, the success of Peter's earlier mission to repentant Israel is the prior condition of his current success with repentant Cornelius. This raw belief stands now only in theory; its practical outworking will bring to surface other concerns that Paul, not Peter, will consider and respond to.

Reflections

1. "Peter knelt down and prayed—Tabitha opened her eyes, and seeing Peter, she sat up" (see 9:40). In a single year I lost two dear colleagues to terminal illness. Both had requested prayers for healing, and earnestly, repeatedly we gathered together as believers and friends to petition God on their behalf. The practice of our prayers reflected a type of Christian realism that recognizes and depends upon God's transcendent love as our final hope. But our friends died anyway. Some of us were tempted to shrug it off, supposing our prayers did not work once again. Luke's account of Peter's healing ministry, repeated in Acts for emphasis, provides a biblical setting that helps us reflect upon "unanswered prayers." How is this true when Peter's prayers were answered? But this is the essential truth of our faith: God does heal the sick whether by medicine or miracle. More remarkably a gracious God intervenes to heal the least and last among us—widows such as Tabitha. There is something arresting about these stories of healings in Acts and the parallels found in the Gospels and the prophets. Peter says only "rise up." Nothing more is necessary but his simple claim on God's resurrection power. What confidence—but then Peter had seen the crucified Jesus alive!

What is sometimes missed in reading these healing stories, however, are the wider, more public consequences of being sick and of being healed. For example, Tabitha's sickness provided the occasion for renewing Peter's relations with the widows of the community, who themselves gathered for mutual consolation and to display the handiwork of their sick sister. There is more at stake in sickness than the miraculous cure of the one. It affords a grieving community the chance to express gratitude for someone else, to worship and weep together, to find a measure of God's comforting presence among them. In this case God does heal Tabitha. But once again Luke's story does not end with her but with others: "This became known throughout Joppa, and many believed in the Lord" (9:42 NRSV).

When I reflect upon the death of my friends, I cannot help feeling their haunting absence. Yet, I continue to seek God's help to look through a wider angle of vision that allows me to see other consequences of their sickness and death, consequences reflecting the evidence of God's active mercy. And I have, praise be to God.

2. "Cornelius, your prayers and alms have ascended as a memorial before God" (see 10:4). Luke's telling and retelling of Cornelius's conversion and the inauguration of the church's mission to the Gentiles (= nations) is shaped by an ancient conflict between the synagogue and church. Today's reader is alerted to importance of that tension by a world profoundly influenced by the tragedy of the Jewish Holocaust. While there are vast differences between the two, both are born by an intolerance conceived in ignorance and cultivated by nationalistic zeal. The conflict between the two as portrayed in Acts has its origins in God's "surprising" salvation of uncircumcised Gentiles who are granted the same religious status and Spirit given to repentant Jews. Luke's explanation of God's gracious decision is multifaceted and seeks to dispel the impression that the conversion of repentant Gentiles is a surprise. To do so, he characteristically appeals to the non-negotiable evidence supplied by Scripture (e.g., Jonah) and religious experience (e.g., visions, the Gentile Pentecost) according to the sound interpretation of the inspired prophet (= Peter). In this case, Jewish ignorance (and so intolerance) of repentant Gentiles who are saved because of God's benefaction is dispelled by relevant prophecy properly interpreted (see 10:43).

In the case of Cornelius, however, repeated references to his pious character suggest another reason (see 10:2, 4, 22, 30): He is saved because of the sort of person he is. An uncircumcised Gentile? Yes. A military commander of the despised Roman army? Yes again. Yet, God finds him anyway because he first made himself known to God by his prayers and gifts to the poor. The point is not that God saves Gentiles such as

Cornelius because he is a pious person; rather, it is his pious acts that prove his spiritual competence to repent. Perhaps his attachment to Israel, if only as a God-fearer, has helped form him into such a person who is responsive to God's word. In any case, Luke's insistence throughout Acts on the importance of an outsider's good character is instructive for today's church. Although some unbelievers are simply unable to repent by their fundamental lack of spiritual goods, there are many others who come under the influence of the church's public witness even though they are not members of any congregation. This *indirect* witness to the culture at large by caring deeds and prophetic word may help form the sorts of persons who, like Cornelius, are responsive to the gospel's invitation to turn to God in faith.

3. "God has shown me that I should not call anyone profane or unclean" (10:28 NRSV). God's pastoral project is to bring us into an understanding of God's will so that we may better collaborate with God in the work of salvation. The conversion of Cornelius takes Peter by surprise but not because God decides at the last moment to save an uncircumcised Gentile. In fact, the universal embrace of divine love was promised to Abraham and prophesied by Scripture long before Cornelius was saved. Yet, for all his spiritual authority, Peter still did not "get it"; his religious parochialism prompted him to divide people into "clean" (repentant Jews) and "unclean" (uncircumcised Gentiles). God's redemptive purpose for Gentiles could not be realized unless the apostle changed his mind.

The theological crisis envisaged by this story, then, is the issue of by what manner an earnest believer like Peter learns God's will in order to obey it and serve God's redemptive interests. Even though Peter's case is exceptional, it also exemplifies two important elements in finding God's will for our lives. First, we learn of God's will from God rather than from our own resources: "God has shown me." The Lord is not a passive bystander or a disinterested partner but is committed to a process of disclosure by which God's will is made known to us. In fact, the urgency of this matter is indicated by the repetition of Peter's vision, which discloses something new to him about God's redemptive will that he otherwise could not have known on his own. Second, we typically learn God's will over time through a series of "aha" experiences. Peter's vision initially left him baffled. Peter's understanding of his Gentile mission unfolds as a result of "double visions" (see 10:30), internal reflection (see 10:17, 19), through the reports of others (see 10:22), and by Cornelius's hospitable reception of him and his word. Peter turned to Scripture for confirmation and clarification only after he learned by these multiple experiences over several days that God's forgiveness is offered to all people without partiality.

We live in a society that promises instant reward for self-sufficient people who know with certainty the way forward. These cultural values collide with the practical aim of Christian faith to know and act upon God's will. The process of getting on the same page with God is frequently confusing, profoundly dependent upon others and often takes a considerable time. But God will tell us the page number!

4. "I truly understand that God shows no partiality" (10:34 NRSV). The biblical idea that God has chosen a particular people as object of special regard cultivates the dangerous suspicion that God did not therefore choose others. Those believers who think themselves among God's "elect" are often inclined on this theological basis to think that God has not chosen anyone else who disagrees with their beliefs or customs. We pin labels on our disagreeable opponents to disenfranchise them: they are "liberal" or "conservative" or "homosexual" or "Jewish" or "Lutheran" or "female" or "laity" or "black" or "divorced." Yet, what has become crystal clear to Peter is that to do so is not the prerogative of pious Israel or anyone else: It is God alone who judges the living and the dead (10:42). One of the most surprising features of Acts is the diversity of people God calls to be included among God's people—all of whom are symbolized by uncircumcised Cornelius.

5. "If then God gave them the same gift that he gave us . . . who was I that I could hinder God?" (11:17 NRSV). There is little room for the importance of religious experience in the Christian congregation that views Scripture as the only source of divine revelation. In fact, some faith traditions dismiss human experience of God's truth as inherently flawed by human depravity. Such a theological perspective is at odds with Acts, where God's word often takes the form of a surprising phenomenon rather than a biblical text. In fact, when testimony of God's new direction is asked for in Acts, the prophet-like-Jesus typically cites a saving event before a sacred text. Scripture is reread by experience. For all our proper attention to careful Bible study, God's prodding is sometimes felt within us or first observed in the bustle of life around us. Often our opinion is reversed for the Lord's sake by our existential encounters with the Holy Spirit in the mess and muck of ordinary living.

Acts 11:19–12:25, The Succession of the Twelve

COMMENTARY

To this point in Acts, "the gospel road has been paved to the Gentiles, but the traffic remains sparse."[428] Coincidental to Jerusalem's confirmation of Peter's Gentile mission in Caesarea, however, a new mission among Gentiles has also begun in Syrian Antioch.[429] Not many details of its origins are provided;[430] evidently it is the unexpected result of the scattering of believers that followed Stephen's death (11:19; see 8:4). In addition to the missions led by Philip and Peter, nameless others from Cyprus and Cyrene have continued the gospel's northward progress to Syrian Antioch, where they had successfully evangelized Gentiles, "proclaiming the Lord Jesus" to them as well as to Jews (11:20-21). Following the protocol established in

response to Philip's Samaritan mission, the Jerusalem church dispatches Barnabas to bear witness to God's work in Antioch and to aid in the pastoral work there (11:22-23; cf. 8:14-25). The remarkable growth of this congregation soon required additional support staff, and so he departs for Tarsus to find Saul and bring him to Antioch—and back into his future (11:25-26*a*). Their team ministry lasted a year, at the end of which the Antiochene believers were "for the first time called 'Christians' " (11:26*b*).

The passage that follows looks at first to be a collocation of three seemingly unrelated episodes. The first recounts the prophet Agabus's prediction of a Judean famine and the Antiochene congregation's hospitable response to the church there (11:27-30). The final episode contrasts the community's feeding program with that of King Herod (12:20-24). These contrasting responses to material need enclose the second episode, the angel's dramatic rescue of Peter from Herod's prison (12:1-17). Luke shapes this story with constant allusions to the concluding story of the exalted Jesus in the Gospels in order to confirm Peter's religious authority a final time and prepare the way for his succession to both James (12:17) and Paul (12:25).[431]

11:19-26. The expression "now those who were scattered because of the persecution" picks up the unwoven threads of 8:4

428. Spencer, *Acts*, 119.
429. The church in Antioch is second in importance within Luke's narrative world, surpassed only by the "mother church" in Jerusalem. For this reason, the reader of Acts should have in mind relevant information about this city. Founded in the third century BCE by Seleucus I as the capital city of his Assyrian Empire, Antioch was a large cosmopolitan city of great importance to the Roman Empire—the third largest in population and prosperity after Rome and Alexandria. In Luke's day, it was designated the capital city of Roman Syria and home to many political and commercial interests. Nearby were shrines to various pagan deities as well. Its strategic importance in Acts, however, is due to its pivotal role in the Jewish diaspora. Proselyte Jews were abundant in the city (so Josephus *The Jewish War* 7.45), which also enjoyed favorable relations with the Herodian family and so with Israel. All these historical details provide the raw material for an illuminating backdrop against which the outline of its cityscape in Acts is made more apparent.
430. The question of Luke's sources for "the Antioch Chronicles," as Witherington, *The Acts of the Apostles*, 366-72, titles his discussion of Acts 11:19–15:35, remains indeterminate and problematic. Most are willing to admit that Luke depended upon some "Antiochene source" that had preserved the essential details of its founding and of Paul's involvement in its mission to the Diaspora. That is, this story is not a fiction. Few remain as convinced as Witherington, however, that Luke's "Antiochene source" is none other than Paul and thus reliably transmitted to Luke.

431. See R. W. Wall, "Successors to 'the Twelve' According to Acts 12:1-17," *CBQ* 53 (1991) 628-43.

to weave an account of the missionary activities of unnamed fugitives from the Jerusalem church. They have extended Philip's Samaritan and Peter's Caesarian missions into Syrian Antioch. The double reference to Cyprus (11:19-20) and then to the Cypriot Barnabas (see 4:36; 11:22) foreshadows the importance of Cyprus in Paul's first mission (cf. 13:4) and subsequently his split with Barnabas, who returns to Cyprus following the Jerusalem Council to some unwritten future (cf. 15:39). Presumably the importance of Cyprus in Acts, which had been Barnabas's address before his conversion to Christ and participation in the Jerusalem community, is due to its large colony of diaspora Jews. This fact may also explain why missionaries from Cyprus and Cyrene "spoke the word to no one except Jews" (11:19).[432] In any case, the prophetic stipulation to move the word of God from "the Jew first and then to the Greek" is maintained in Antioch, since after bringing the gospel to the Jews they "began to speak to Greeks also" (11:20).[433]

The expression "the hand of the Lord" (11:21) recalls the petition of the apostles for God to "stretch out your hand" to perform mighty signs and wonders in fulfillment of Joel's prophecy (see Acts 2:19) and confirmation of their prophetic authority in Jerusalem (see 4:30-31). That earlier prayer continues to be answered by God in fresh ways and in new places. In this setting, the "Lord" (κύριος *kyrios*) refers to the exalted Jesus as the medium of divine power and mercy, who not only is the object of Christian proclamation (11:20) but also assists the mission in Antioch so that "a great number became believers and turned to the Lord" (11:21; see 2:41; 4:4; 6:7). The Lord Jesus' powerful presence and active participation confirms the legitimacy of this work and the importance of its future.

When Jerusalem hears of the founding of this new mission, they dispatch one of their own—Barnabas—not to assess or confirm what had taken place but to collaborate with the missionaries already at work (see 8:14-25). The decision to send Barnabas to Antioch as Jerusalem's emissary makes sense for two reasons: (1) He is from the same Cypriot community that produced the founders and unnamed leaders of this Antiochene congregation (so 4:36; 11:21), and (2) his spiritual authority is practically demonstrated by his earnest submission to the community's apostolic leadership when sharing his possessions with the needy of the community of goods (see 4:36-37). He also ably defended Saul's conversion and calling before its leadership council (see 9:27). In the present text, Barnabas's positive profile is expanded by his characterization as "a good man, full of the Holy Spirit and faith" (11:24; see 6:5, 8; 7:55; cf. Luke 23:50), all familiar features of the prophet-like-Jesus, whose authority is concentrated on the task of testifying to the risen Jesus as Messiah.

Barnabas is a prophet-like-Jesus, cut from the same cloth as Stephen (11:24*a*; see 6:5). Thus the Spirit enables him to "see the grace of God" resting upon these new believers and to "exhort them all to remain faithful to the Lord with steadfast devotion" (11:23).[434] The important phrase "grace of God" (χάρις τοῦ θεου *charis tou theou*) denotes God's public and demonstrative benefaction on an entire community of believers (see 2:47; 4:33; cf. 14:26). In context of Acts, "grace" (*charis*) refers to a divine blessing promised Israel that arrives with the Messiah and is now poured out through the Holy Spirit. This benefaction is first visited on a restored Israel (2:47; 4:33) and then on believing Gentiles (so 10:44-46; cf. 15:8-11) as here in Antioch (cf. 14:3, 26). The responsibility of prophet Barnabas's presence in Antioch is to bear Israel's second witness that the saving grace of God now extends to Gentiles, who also experience the salvation God promised first to Israel. Further, Barnabas is restored as Israel's herald that its ordained role in these last days of salvation's history as "light to the nations" has begun.

While previous clues in Acts have shaped the reader's anticipation of Barnabas's successful ministry in Antioch, where "a great many people were brought to the Lord" (11:24*b*)

---

432. Hill contends that they preached the gospel only to Jews because the church's Gentile mission had not yet "officially" begun. Further, the first Gentile converts in Antioch were doubtless similar to God-fearing Cornelius and were connected to the synagogues there. See Hill, *Hellenists and Hebrews*, 137-38.

433. The text-critical problem of whether to read "Greeks" (Ἑλληνάς *Hellēnas*) or "Hellenists" (Ἑλληνιστάς *Hellēnistas*) is similar to 6:1, where "Hellenists" is preferred. In this case, "Greeks" is preferred due to context. Fitzmyer, *The Acts of the Apostles*, 476, speaks for many scholars in saying "in this situation the reading 'Hellenists' makes little sense."

434. Luke employs wordplay to show that Barnabas's persona is ideally suited for the Antiochene setting, since his name means "son of encouragement" (παράκλησις *paraklēsis*; see 4:36) and here he "exhorted [παρεκάλει *parekalei*] them to be faithful to the Lord" (11:23).

under his ministry, what happens next is full of irony: "Barnabas went to Tarsus to look for Saul, and . . . brought him to Antioch" (11:25-26a). His patronage does not take us by complete surprise, however, since earlier Barnabas had "brought Saul to the apostles" (so 9:27) and probably was among those who encouraged him to return to Tarsus for further preparation (cf. 9:30). Here it appears that he acts on his own without the approval of either Antioch or Jerusalem. But from the imagined perspective of the Antiochene parishioners, who knew nothing of what transpired on the Damascus road, their pastor's bold initiative must have seemed shocking: This Saul was the primary reason why they had "scattered because of the persecution." Their implied forgiveness and later their generosity to the endangered Judean church disclose character fashioned by the "grace of God."

In any case, the result is stated in pregnant terms: "and in Antioch the disciples were first called 'Christians'" (11:26c).[435] Why does Luke add this aside to an otherwise sparse account of the formation of this important congregation? While the origins of the designation "Christian" may well be the outsider's pejorative for the disciple of Christ, its connotation in this narrative setting is more neutral: It simply recognizes the *differences* between the Antioch and Jerusalem congregations. Surely there is a sociological difference between the Antiochene congregation, constituted by a mixture of Jewish and non-Jewish believers from various places, and the Jerusalem congregation, which continues to symbolize the restoration of the whole household of historic Israel and is constituted by Jews only (see 21:17-26). Perhaps more important, a theological difference is also implied, since the formation of this congregation is the result of instruction: "for an

entire year [i.e., for a long time] they met with the church and taught a great many people" (11:26b). Could Luke's use of "Christians" as the name of a new congregation of believers signal future battles within the church over the *ordo salutis* ("order of salvation") that the Jerusalem Council is convened to resolve? I think so.

11:27-30. The story of the Antiochene relief effort to Judea introduces two classes of officers within the church: the Christian prophet, represented by Agabus, whom we will meet again in Acts 21,[436] and the elders of the Judean church, who apparently have replaced the seven with the administrative duty of food distribution within the community of goods (v. 30). Important features of their leadership are symbolized by Agabus, who, although apparently attached to a local congregation, is an itinerant charismatic enabled by the Holy Spirit to predict the future. The purpose of his ministry is similar to other prophetic figures who populate Luke's narrative world, such as Barnabas and Saul, whose prophetic tasks include the encouragement and instruction of believers. The special talents of Christian prophets are always tied to missionary tasks in Acts and are used as part and parcel of the church's vocation to bear witness to the risen Messiah. For this reason, Agabus's inspired ability to see into the future is not tied to self-promotion but serves the well-being of the community of goods.

Agabus came with other prophets "from Jerusalem to Antioch" (v. 27). Their mission helps to define the relationship between repentant Jews (= Jerusalem) and Gentiles (= Antioch), who share the messianic blessings equally. Appropriately, images of shared goods symbolize their partnership. The peril of being without food in a social world where a hand-to-mouth existence is the norm underscores the practical importance of sharing goods;[437] and no doubt this resurrection practice continues within a community pastored by Barnabas, who himself is an exemplar of

---

435. See Fitzmyer, *The Acts of the Apostles*, 477. The Western text of Acts expands 11:25 by adding "[Barnabas] found [Saul] and exhorted him to come with him to Antioch," thereby stressing not only the independence of Barnabas's decision to recruit Saul as his co-worker, but also Saul's decision to share in his Antiochene ministry. Johnson suggests that this independence stands behind the concluding note that these Antiochene "disciples were for the first time called 'Christians,'" which indicates agitation rather than solidarity within the church. See Johnson, *The Acts of the Apostles*, 204. Conzelmann is typical of those who suppose the historical referent behind the word "Christians" in 11:26 is a political (and hostile) reality: Rome had come to recognize that believers constituted a religious organization and as such were accountable to Roman law and prosecution. See Conzelmann, *The Acts of the Apostles*, 88-89. However, the literary shaping of this account seems rather to underscore Antiochene Christianity's independence from Jerusalem, a result of Pauline teaching.

436. For a discussion of Christian prophets and prophecy, see Stronstad, *The Prophethood of All Believers*; D. Hill, *New Testament Prophecy* (London: Marshall, Morgan & Scott, 1979) esp. 94-109. See also the collection edited by J. Panagopoulos, *Prophethic Vocation in the New Testament and Today*, NovTestSup 45 (Leiden: Brill, 1977).

437. See B. Winter, "Acts and Food Shortages," in Winter and Clarke, *The Book of Acts in Its First Century Setting*, 2:59-78.

sharing goods with the community's needy (see 4:36-37).[438]

Within the wider narrative setting of Acts, then, the prediction of Agabus sounds a fuller note: The future he predicts occasions a spiritual test for this new congregation of believers in Antioch. Will they be participants in a community of goods, whose solidarity with God and each other is exemplified by sharing their food with needy believers? The short answer is a resounding yes. In doing so, these Antiochene disciples follow the pattern of other collections mentioned in Pauline letters (see Rom 15:25-31; 1 Cor 16:1-4; 2 Corinthians 8–9; Gal 2:10) as well as in Acts (see 24:17).[439] Once a need within the community of goods is made known—in this case by a prophet's prediction of famine—a collection is gathered "according to their ability" (v. 29; cf. 4:35)[440] and is sent to the needy—in this case "to the believers living in Judea"—by congregational representatives—in this case "to the elders by Barnabas and Saul" (v. 30),[441] who will return to Antioch when their mission is complete (12:25). Thus the Antiochene congregation supplies additional testimony that the Lord's "great grace was upon them all" (see 4:33) and that they could be counted among those believers who "were of one heart and soul" (see 4:32).

In shaping this story Luke is careful to locate the fulfillment of Agabus's prophecy within secular history: "A severe famine over all the world . . . took place during the reign of Claudius" (v. 28). Such concrete reporting is a literary convention of the historian; and the measure of his report, whether ancient or modern, is whether he gets it right. The reliability of Luke's history has been repeatedly challenged by modern Acts criticism, and this episode is another case in point.[442] Here the stakes are a bit higher for a *theological* reason, since the famine in question is predicted by an inspired prophet. The nub of the historical problem is not whether a famine occurred during the reign of Caesar Claudius, which is supported by reliable secular historians;[443] rather, it is the scope of the famine, whether it was "over all the world." If taken as objective reporting, Luke is surely mistaken, since famines are regional in scope. Johnson contends, however, that the word οἰκουμένη (*oikoumenē*, "world") better connotes "empire," and so this phrase could be rendered, "over all the empire."[444] If that is the case, the reader is still left to wonder why this famine had bypassed Antioch. Other scholars simply suggest the phrase is a metaphor for a "widespread" famine and thus a reliable report.

12:1-17. Once again the community's apostolic leadership is threatened in Jerusalem by the violent repression of political rivals—in this case King Herod, who had executed the apostle James and now arrested Peter (vv. 1-5*a*). The "hand of the Lord" is felt not only in a season of blessing and renewal (cf. 11:21) but also in this season of suffering and political reprisal, for Peter is rescued by the "angel of the Lord" (vv. 5*b*-11) in response to the community's earnest prayer. Peter's "great escape" is fitting conclusion to his prophetic ministry in Acts, and when he departs on the sly for another place (v. 17*b*)—to the great frustration of Herod (vv. 18-19)—his leadership in Jerusalem is transferred and continued by James the brother of Jesus (vv. 12-17*a*) and Saul (v. 25).

---

438. Johnson commends the importance of this distribution of goods as carried out by Barnabas in the company of Saul, who has had no previous experience with such a practice. Indeed, even as the succession of spiritual authority from the Twelve to the seven is indicated by food distribution ("wait on tables," διακονέω *diakoneō*, 6:2) among needy widows (see 6:1-7), so again here the succession of spiritual authority to Saul/Paul is symbolized by food distribution ("relief," διακονία *diakonia*, 11:29). See Johnson, *The Literary Function of Possessions in Luke-Acts*, 217-20.

439. The interpreter should recognize the critical problem of reconciling Luke's report of a Gentile collection for the Jewish church and Paul's own report of a similar collection. It is unlikely that Acts 11:27-30 should be read by the light of Gal 2:10 (contra Witherington, *The Acts of the Apostles*, 375-76), since Paul's Jerusalem visit, mentioned in Gal 2:1, "is undoubtedly the same as the visit for the 'Council' in Acts 15:4." Fitzmyer, *The Acts of the Apostles*, 480.

440. This phrase translates καθὼς εὐπορεῖτό τις (*kathōs euporeito tis*; lit., "just as each is able") and recalls the phrase from 4:35 that distribution of goods was made "to each according to their need" (καθότι ἄν τις χρείαν εἶχεν *kathoti an tis chreian eichen*). The interplay between these two texts completes the calculus of giving, so that the offering of "each according to their ability" (11:29) is redistributed to "each as they have need" (4:35).

441. This is the first instance in Acts of "elders" (πρεσβύτεροι *presbyteroi*) used for the leadership team of Christian (although Jewish) congregations (cf. 14:23; 15:2, 4, 6, 22-23; 16:4; 20:17; 21:18). The role of the Judean elders is probably similar to the "elders" of Jewish synagogues; however, in this instance the elders have taken on the role of food distribution—a responsibility of the seven before their scattering from Judea with other Hellenists at the time of the "great persecution" (see 8:1-3). See R. A. Campbell, *The Elders* (Edinburgh: T. & T. Clark, 1994).

442. See S. Joubert, *Paul as Benefactor*, WUNT 124 (Tübingen: Mohr Siebeck, 2000) 91-93, who argues that a collection gathered and delivered by Paul prior to the Jerusalem Council (Acts 15; Galatians 2) would surely have been factored into its proceedings. The lack of clear reference to a collection by either Luke or Paul (but see Gal 2:10), however, is strong evidence against this conclusion.

443. See Fitzmyer, *The Acts of the Apostles*, 481-82; R. Riesner, *Paul's Early Period: Chronology, Mission Strategy, Theology*, trans. Doug Scott (Grand Rapids: Eerdmans, 1998) 128-30, who catalogs several regional famines throughout the empire based on these sources.

444. Johnson, *The Acts of the Apostles*, 205-6, 208.

Stories of God's rescue operations are familiar to the reader of Acts.[445] In every case the forces of evil are pitted against the forces of good, with good prevailing by divine intervention. Luke's interest in such stories is to make clear the religious authority of the one rescued, which is not only indicated by God's intervention on his behalf or by the redemptive consequences of his miraculous escape but also by the literary shaping of the story itself. Characteristic of Luke's typological handling of the traditions of heroic individuals, Peter's escape takes on even greater significance by consistent and clear allusions to the story of Jesus' death and exaltation. Surely this episode supplies final proof that he is a prophet-like-Jesus par excellence whose memory continues to shape the faith and mission of the messianic community he helped to found.

12:1-4. To this point in Acts, the apostles of Jerusalem are keenly favored by the "people" of Israel and resisted only by the council—the "official" religious authority in the holy city. The reputation of the apostolate throughout Palestine has most recently attracted the malicious attention of Herod Agrippa I, client of Caesar Gaius and the principal political authority of the region. He is the third in a succession of kings named Herod to "[lay] violent hands upon some who belonged to the church" (v. 1): Herod the Great (see Luke 1:5) was followed by Herod Antipas (see Luke 23:7-15; Acts 4:27), whose exile in 39 CE led to King Herod Agrippa I's expanded domain over most of Palestine.[446] According to Josephus, his reign was characterized by violence and caprice,[447] which is vividly captured by the account of his death in Acts (see vv. 20-22). Perhaps this is sufficient evidence to fill in the historical gap left by the narrative, which tells the reader nothing of Herod's motive for this most recent attack upon the Judean church. Nor does Luke make clear why the apostle James is beheaded and the apostle Peter spared; presumably the church prayed for the release of

both. The brief mention of James' martyrdom indicates the depth of difficulty Peter finds himself when Herod "proceeded to arrest Peter also" (v. 3). More important, however, James is not replaced as Judas was before him (see 1:15-26), and so the circle of the Twelve seems broken beyond repair with their rule at an end in Jerusalem. The succession of their spiritual authority appears necessary, since the Jerusalem mission must continue on under new leadership (= James the brother of Jesus) as Acts makes clear (see 15:4-29; 21:17-26).

Herod "had seized [Peter] . . . put him in prison and handed him over to four squads of soldiers to guard him" (v. 4) because "it pleased the Jews" that James was beheaded. Decapitation is the most severe form of execution and usually reserved for "murderers and a city's apostates,"[448] which James was not. We presume that his execution was warranted for illegitimate reasons similar to Stephen, and that the city's secular authority (= Herod) has now come to agree with its religious authority (= Sanhedrin) that the Jesus movement is detrimental to Israel.[449]

The circumstances of Peter's arrest and apparent fate, therefore, are similar to those that faced Jesus, especially given Herod's political motive for arresting Peter (cf. Luke 23:10-12). This parallelism extends to the timing of Peter's arrest "during the festival of Unleavened Bread" (v. 3; cf. Luke 22:1) and the ironic concern of his "pious" enemies to maintain the purity of Passover out of concern for what the "people" might think (cf. 12:4; Luke 23:1-5, 17).[450]

12:5-11. The transitional phrase μὲν οὖν (*men oun*; lit., "So therefore") marks the beginning of the climactic scene of this drama. In stark contrast to the hostile action of a powerful tyrant against its apostolic leadership, the "church prayed fervently to God for [Peter]" (v. 5; see also 1:14, 24; 2:42; 4:24-30). The narrator makes certain that the reader understands the extent of the evidence against Peter's possible escape: He is bound with two chains and sleeps between two

---

445. Johnson, *The Acts of the Apostles*, 217, points out that similar stories are found in Hellenistic fiction as well, where they are used to illustrate virtuous character and divine favor.

446. Following the lead of J. Darr, Spencer contends that Luke-Acts forms a "composite Herodian profile" to cast the quintessential "villain" of the story, whose violent demise (see 12:20-22) is the just recompense of a fair-minded God. See Spencer, *Acts*, 123-25, 120-29.

447. Josephus *Antiquities of the Jews* 18.250-56; 19.6.1-4, 292-316.

448. *mSanh.* 9.1.

449. See Bruce, *The Acts of the Apostles*, 281-83.

450. See Fitzmyer, *The Acts of the Apostles*, 487. Luke's reference to "the people" probably continues his thematic interest in the reactions of rank-and-file Jews to the community's apostolic leadership. Cf. Johnson, *The Acts of the Apostles*, 216-17; Hill, "Acts 6:1–8:4," in Witherington, *History, Literature, and Society in the Book of Acts*, 135-36.

soldiers, with additional guards stationed at every exit to prevent escape the "very night" before he is scheduled to suffer a fate similar to that of James (v. 6). That is, his situation is hopeless; there remains only heaven's help. On cue "an angel of the Lord appeared—in the cell" (v. 7a). In elaborate detail, equal to that describing the jailhouse security system, the narrative rehearses the angel's rescue operation: first comes the "tap" on Peter's side to awaken him (v. 7b), followed by a series of commands—get up, get dressed, get going (vv. 7c-8).

The angel must still negotiate the prison's hallways, and do so with Peter still in his post-epiphany daze. They first pass the guards and then go through the prison's "iron gate" (πύλη pulē), which was miraculously open to them, and into the city and to freedom (v. 10). The reference to the iron gate is especially important to the story, not only because it symbolizes Herod's misbegotten initiative to subvert God's purposes and the community's prayers but also because it forms a wordplay with the "outer gate" (πυλών pulōn) that leads into the home where the community had gathered to pray for Peter's release (vv. 13-14). Going in through one gate and then out another marks out not only Peter's escape route but also the triumph of God over the community's enemies. Still, Peter "did not realize that what was happening with the angel's help was real; he thought he was seeing a vision" (v. 9). This dream-like state during his escape explains why he "came to himself"; finally realizing that the "light shone in [his] cell" (v. 7a) meant that "the Lord has . . . rescued me" (v. 11a; see also 9:3).[451]

Acts offers no explanation of what exactly "the Jewish people" (ὁ λαός ὁ Ἰουδαῖος ho laos ho Ioudaios) had expected in Peter's case, although his execution is surely implied. There is no evidence in the text to assign malicious motive to the Jewish people or to suppose that they are "unrepentant" Jews who are Peter's religious adversaries. It is possible to read the phrase as quite benign and in terms of v. 4, where the "people" (laos)

expect Herod to "bring Peter out" to them after Passover. If malicious motive is intended, then Peter's once vigorous public popularity in Jerusalem has fallen on hard times indeed (see vv. 18-19).

12:12-17a. After Peter recovers his sense and sensibility, he "went to the house of Mary . . . where many had gathered and were praying" (v. 12). These are characteristic features of the faith community in Acts: Believers have gathered in the home of another believer for prayer (see 1:14; 2:45-46; 5:42). The reader supposes that the subject of their petition is Peter's safety (see v. 4), even though they are as yet unaware that their prayers have been answered.

For the first time, the meetinghouse is specified by its owner—Mary, the mother of John Mark, who will have an important if ambiguous role in Acts (13:5, 13; 15:37-39). She is apparently an independent woman and is sufficiently wealthy to employ a maidservant. Luke's interest in "leading women" is well known, and this episode is another case in point. What is of greater interest to Luke, however, is the role performed by her servant Rhoda, whose voice is the first heard from a Christian woman in Acts. In attending to her household chores, she discovers Peter alive and well. In a manner reminiscent of risen Jesus' encounter with his unwitting disciples, Peter's verbal encounter with Rhoda produces her "recognition" (cf. Luke 24:31) and joyful report that he is alive (cf. Matt 28:8). But her good news of Peter's safety evokes a response of incredulity in other believers (cf. Luke 24:10-11, 41). Meanwhile Peter is left standing at the door, while his friends imagine that the voice Rhoda has heard actually belongs to his guardian angel (12:15)![452] To their mutual credit Peter persists in his knocking and Rhoda to her story, until at long last "they opened the gate, saw him and were amazed [ἐξίστημι existēmi]" (v. 16). Amazement is typically the result of a mistake (see 3:10)—in this case, of mistaking Peter for his guardian angel, which Peter corrects by rehearsing "how the Lord had brought him out of the

---

451. Given the Passover setting of this story, Luke's use of the verb "rescue" (ἐξαιρέω exaireō) is intentional and ironical, recalling God's rescue of Israel from Egyptian bondage (Exod 18:10), which was also led by the angel of the Lord (so Exod 14:19; Num 20:16; cf. Dan 3:28). See Wall, "Successors to 'the Twelve' According to Acts 12:1-17," 637; S. Garrett, "Exodus from Bondage: Luke 9:31 and Acts 12:1-24," *CBQ* 52 (1990) 656-80.

452. Conzelmann, *The Acts of the Apostles*, 95, notes that Judaism regarded the guardian angel as a "celestial double" who could imitate a person's appearance and voice—in this case, the voice of Peter. The entire scene is rich comedy and only adds to the theological claim that stands behind the story: A sovereign God acts powerfully to reverse misfortune, even to the joyful surprise of God's people.

prison" (v. 17a). His testimony alludes to the Lord's appearance before stunned disciples with persuasive proofs of his resurrection (cf. Luke 24:28-43; see also Acts 1:3).

12:17b. The story of the living Peter's exodus from certain death had not yet been told to "James and the brothers." The abrupt introduction of James into the narrative, typical of Luke's storytelling strategy, both presumes that the reader knows him to be "James the brother of the Lord" and leader of the Jewish church and hints at the importance of his future role in Acts.[453] The introduction of James into the narrative world of Acts is the complement of Peter's departure from it. Although Peter will make an important cameo appearance during the proceedings of the Jerusalem Synod (cf. 15:6-11), his role in the history of God's salvation has already been served when "he left and went [ἐπορεύθη *eporeuthē*] to another place."[454] This echoing of Jesus' "going [πορευομένου *poreuomenou*] . . . toward heaven" (see 1:10) at his ascension, which necessitates his apostolic succession, adds a layer of meaning to the concluding moment of Peter's mission in Jerusalem. The implied meaning is that the reins of spiritual authority have been transferred from Peter to James.

12:18-19. A new day dawns, and the prized prisoner is nowhere to be found: The soldiers attached to Herod "searched for Peter and could not find him"—naturally, since they were looking for him in the wrong city! The bewilderment of the prison guards echoes their response to an earlier escape in 5:22-26 and fills in the gaps of this story. Indeed, the captain of the guard had wondered in the aftermath of that earlier escape "what would come of this escape" (see 5:24); and the apostles did not hide nor did they resist re-arrest since they knew "the people" of Israel were on their side and feared they might turn violent against the temple guard (see 5:26). On this occasion, as the story turns back to King Herod, the reader realizes that the atmosphere in Jerusalem has changed dramatically since Acts 5. The circle of the Twelve, broken by Herod, has not been restored and those left evidently do not enjoy the same level of public respect from "the people" as before (see vv. 4, 11). Further, the apostles' more benign religious opposition in Jerusalem has now been replaced by the graceless political tyranny of Herod, who "examined the guards and ordered them to be put to death."[455] Moreover, Herod's departure from Jerusalem for Caesarea immediately after Passover "to stay" at the capital of the Roman occupation of Palestine is indicative of his true loyalties.

12:20-22. While Herod's tyranny has already made him God's foe and destined him for harsh judgment, the final evidence is his response to a community's request for food. Nowhere is the reader made aware of the reason why "Herod was angry with the people of Tyre and Sidon" (v. 20a). The motive of Herod's anger is unimportant to the telling of this story; rather, the issue is his vile personality and inhospitable response to the desperate delegation from neighboring Syrian cities, which heap evidence upon evidence of his opposition to God's purposes in the world and supports the justice soon meted out to him. On the one hand, the more obvious act of Agrippa's rebellion against God's reign is his crude spectacle of self-aggrandizement that coerced the pitiable Phoenician delegation to worship and listen to him "on an appointed day."[456] On the other hand, a more subtle contrast is made that anticipates Herod's demise. Those emissaries that came to Herod through his chamberlain, Blastus, to negotiate a peace settlement were from Tyre and Sidon, free cities located on the Phoenician coastline. The ultimate purpose of this entreaty is for food distribution, since "their country depended upon the king's country for food" (v. 20b).

---

453. R. Bauckham, "James and the Jerusalem Church," in Winter and Clarke, *The Book of Acts in Its First Century Setting*, 4:427-50, argues that 12:17 is glossed by 11:30: Even as Peter's spiritual authority is transferred to James at this moment, so also this accords with a change already underway in the governance of the church from apostolic to elder rule.

454. The precise location of the "another place" where Peter ended is unknown, as is the role he assumed there. Ancient tradition tells us that Peter went to Rome and established a faith community there prior to Paul's arrival.

455. The Greek is more ambiguous than either the NIV or the NRSV allows. The verb translated "execute/put to death" is ἀπάγω (*apagō*), a legal term that usually denotes "to make an arrest." The Western text substitutes the verb ἀποκτείνω (*apokteinō*, "to execute"). Given Luke's literary intent to cast Herod in a bad light, when added to his reputedly violent persona and the intolerance in the Roman world of a soldier's dereliction of duty, the present translation of the passage is certainly plausible.

456. Despite chronological differences, Josephus's account of the early death of Herod Agrippa I, in *Antiquities of the Jews* 19.343-53, is similar to Luke's. See also Barrett, *A Critical and Exegetical Commentary on the Acts of the Apostles*, 589-92.

The reader should note that the Phoenician delegation came to Herod from the same region visited by the missionaries mentioned in 11:19 who later founded the congregation in Antioch (see 11:19-26). In effect, they are an unwitting witness to the vast differences between the secular and sacred as evinced by contrasting practices of food distribution. Unlike arrogant Herod's petulant response to the Phoenicians, the elders of the Antiochene church hospitably received the prophetic delegation from Jerusalem and responded immediately to Agabus's prophecy of a famine with an offering of food (see 11:27-30; cf. 12:25). The intent of this narrative interplay is not to engage in culture criticism—to portray the pretentious Herod as representative of society's rich and famous who typically exploit the weak and powerless and force them to submit to self-deification. The issue at stake is a theological one, consistent with all of Acts, that God posits spiritual authority in the community that gives all glory to God alone (see 3:12-13; 4:24; 10:25-26) and that is enabled to respond to its own needy with graceful benefaction (see 2:42-47; 4:32-35).

12:23-25. Two integral events summarize the fallout from Peter's escape "to another place." The death of a vile antagonist is commonplace in the happy endings of world literature—the more horrible the villain's death the more satisfying the story's ending. It is not surprising to the reader of Acts that Herod is "struck down" in horrific fashion. Luke's account is enhanced by his reference to an angel of death that carries out God's death sentence against Herod and by the "worms" that eat his flesh, which both allude to biblical stories of holy terror. In the first case, the angel of the Lord who earlier had tapped Peter to rescue him from Herod's death sentence now executes God's judgment by tapping Herod

for death. The angel's activities throughout the chapter recall the first Passover when the heavenly "destroyer" delivered a deathblow against another king-like-Herod (cf. Exod 12:12, 23, 29) that occasioned Israel's exodus from the Pharaoh's death sentence. Likewise, Peter departs on his exodus from Jerusalem to another city (see 12:11; cf. Exod 14:19). Finally, the mode of Herod's demise—his flesh "was eaten by worms"[457]—reminds one of the Maccabean description of the gruesome death of Antiochus IV Epiphanes (2 Macc 9:9); it also recalls Isaiah's exhortation that in the light of the permanence of God's faithfulness, God's people should not fear the attacks of their foes since "the worm will eat them like wool" (Isa 51:8). Such is the fate of God's foes.

In contrast to Herod's death, "the word of God continued to advance and gain adherents" (v. 24; see also 6:7). This summary underscores the plotline of Acts: the word of God flourishes in the face of hostile opposition in its unalterable advance to the end of the earth. Moreover, in contrast to the failure of Herod's approach to food distribution, "Barnabas and Saul returned from Jerusalem"[458] having completed their relief mission in service of the Judean church and according to the sacred practice of the community of goods (v. 25; see also 11:27-30). The successful completion of their mission complements the advance of the gospel in the region and serves on this basis to validate Paul's mission that is soon to commence.

457. The Western text of Acts embellishes the story of Herod's death by recasting it as a torture scene, so that the worms attack his body while he is still alive.

458. The difference in translation of the prepositional phrase "from [ἐξ *ex* or ἀπό *apo*] Jerusalem" or "to [εἰς *eis*] Jerusalem" reflects its corrupted status in the Greek MSS of Acts. The NIV, which accepts *ex* on contextual rather than textual grounds, is preferred in this case; while *eis* is the best attested rendering, it does not make sense of the plotline.

REFLECTIONS

1. "News of this came to the ears of the church in Jerusalem, and they sent Barnabas to Antioch" (11:22 NRSV). I belong to a church that has long valued ecclesiastical "connectionalism." While this means different things to different congregations, at its core is an abiding commitment of each congregation toward the well-being of others. When the church's mission moved beyond Jerusalem into new neighborhoods where marginal Jews and uncircumcised Gentiles were evangelized, its leaders realized that certain safeguards were needed to protect the gospel's sacred deposit from contamination. For this reason Peter and John are earlier sent to Samaria and Barnabas to Antioch. Certain theological norms, religious experiences and ecclesial practices—church "tradition"—are maintained to ensure solidarity of Christian fellowship and witness even between diverse congregations founded in different geographical locations. Even though Jerusalem retains a certain level of authority over Antioch, because it is still home to the Lord's apostolic successors, the generosity of the Antiochene congregation toward the Jerusalem church in its time of need reflects the dynamic and caring mutuality between congregations connected to each other by a common faith and witness. Simply because one fellowship is larger and richer or is perceived to have more mature communicants than another does not imply that it will dictate the terms of the other's life. Connectionalism is not coercive; it is caring toward the end of forming a faith founded on the gospel.

2. "About that time King Herod laid violent hands upon some who belonged to the church" (12:1 NRSV). The theme of the church's repression is important in Acts. The contemporary reader is tempted to read these stories of Herod's rampage in a detached way, especially if we live in a liberal democracy that values religious freedom. Yet even in North America religious sentiment is openly ridiculed at times, and modest public expressions of a thoughtful Christian faith are often arrogantly dismissed. What should be the church's response to such a culture?

Luke's story of Peter's "great escape" is full of symbols of transcendence: the rescuing angel, the community's earnest prayers, the Jewish celebration of Passover, even the gruesome details of Herod's demise. The church's response to any attempt to repress its public witness ought not be vengeful or prickly, nor ought it to be passive. There is nothing passive about praying for deliverance from our enemies and for their salvation. Prayer is a defiant act because it recognizes that the purpose of a sovereign God will win out in the end: "thy kingdom come, thy will be done on earth as it is in heaven." Prayer presumes a position of confident trust, believing that the God of the exodus has the power to release the captive and to reverse bad news to good. For all the silly arrogance of a malevolent Herod who seeks to stamp the church's leaders underfoot and bring glory to himself, Peter escapes while Herod dies. When it seems God's plan has been overtaken by enemies and/or events, we pray in faith for God's deliverance anyway. This story assures its readers that God hears our prayers and renders the final verdict: "the word of God continued to advance and gain adherents" (12:24).

Acts 13:1–14:26, Paul's Mission to the Nations

COMMENTARY

Luke's story of Paul's first mission is bracketed by Antioch, where he and Barnabas are commissioned for missionary service (13:1-4*a*; see 9:15-21) and where they then report "all that God had done through them" (14:21-26). Antioch has replaced Jerusalem as the center of the church's mission, and Paul (see 13:9) and Barnabas have replaced Peter and John[459]

as the principal pair of prophetic witnesses to Jesus.

Between their departure from and return to Antioch, Paul and Barnabas are sent out under the aegis and at the behest of the Holy Spirit (13:2, 4*a*) to do "the work to which [God has] called them" (see 13:2; 14:26). They travel together to several important cities of Roman Asia (modern-day Turkey), including Cyprian Paphos (13:4-12), Pisidian

459. Although Barnabas is a more robust character than John in Acts, his pairing with Paul serves a similar rhetorical role: Barnabas is to Paul as John is to Peter—his "silent partner" in their missionary outreach. Some have speculated that their religious authority is indexed by the order of their names, with Barnabas placed first as the leader of their mission. As such, e.g., it is speculated that he speaks for both when they appear before the church (e.g., in 15:12). The text is silent on this issue, however; in any case, Luke's story is now Paul's story, as earlier it was Peter's story.

Antioch (13:13-52), Lycaonian Iconium (14:1-7), and Lystra (14:8-20). This new missionary endeavor is marked by old practices and priorities: Paul proclaims the word of God (see 13:5, 7, 16-41, 44; 14:3, 7, 25) and performs prophetic "signs and wonders" (14:3; see 2:17-21; cf. 13:11; 14:8-10; 15:12) in the synagogues of urban centers (13:5, 14; 14:1) to mixed audiences (13:6-7, 42-48; 14:1-5, 27) and suffers because of it (cf. 13:50; 14:5, 19). While Paul shares in the suffering of Jesus (see 9:16), he also shares in the successes of the church's earlier missions. His evangelistic efforts in Asia typically result in many conversions among both Jews and Gentiles and in the founding of congregations similar to his sponsoring church in Syrian Antioch. On the way, he preaches the gospel, rebukes another practitioner of magic (Elymas; cf. Simon in Acts 8), converts a sympathetic Roman official (Sergius Paulus; cf. Cornelius in Acts 10), and commands the crippled to walk (cf. the lame man of Acts 3:1-8; 9:32-35). In each case, Paul replicates the actions of his prophetic predecessors. And like Peter (see 8:25), at the end of their mission Paul and Barnabas retrace their footsteps to encourage new converts and to testify to the grace of God at work in the believers (cf. 14:21-26).

At the same time, a more radical dimension in both scope and effect characterizes Paul's missionary work. For example, Paul's religious authority is mistaken by pagans as divine in the shadow of their temple to Zeus (cf. 14:8-13) for doing precisely what Peter had done before him in the shadow of the Jerusalem Temple (see 3:1-8). Israel's mission as "light to the nations" is being realized through his mission, and different cultural symbols are being overturned as a result. Paul's climactic call to conversion in the synagogue at Pisidian Antioch (13:38-41), then, introduces a distinctive element to the gospel about Jesus: Forgiveness from sin comes through belief in Messiah Jesus rather than through Mosaic law (cf. 15:11). This idea so unsettles some devout Jews that they provoke Paul to clarify repentant Israel's prophesied mission as "light to the nations" (see 13:44-48)—a mission that he himself personifies in Acts.

The narrative of Paul's first mission has a "primacy effect" on its reader.[460] The impression that lingers on for the rest of Acts is that Paul is a central figure in God's plan of salvation, whose personal authority is envisaged by his résumé as a devout teacher of Israel, a virtuous man, a persuasive orator, and a person with recognized religious and social standing. This portraiture is different from that found in his letters, where his disinclination to speak of his apostolic charism reflects differences of literary genre and purpose. Also missing from Acts are accounts of Paul's controversies with other church leaders, although the narrator sometimes presumes these controversies as the narrative subtext that Acts itself seeks to answer.[461] The function of Paul's portrait in Acts within the NT, however, is to form a powerful impression of Paul's inspired persona that insinuates itself into his NT letters, resulting in a more attentive, trusting hearing of the word of God that is mediated there (see Introduction, "Acts as Canon"; see also the Overview to 15:13–28:28).

13:1-4a. Chapter 13 begins with a catalog of the leaders and their offices "in the church at Antioch," which signals a turning point in the narrative to the mission God has given this congregation. I doubt that this reference to Antioch's "prophets and teachers" indicates a departure from the organization of the Jewish church,[462] since the Twelve and Seven also engaged in teaching and prophetic ministry. If anything, it establishes the identity of those within the congregation who act as conduits for the Holy Spirit to make clear God's will for the congregation. More interesting is the cultural and social range of the leadership as evinced by the roll of names (see 11:19-20): "A Levite from Cyprus, a black man, a North

460. So Tannehill, who understands 13:1-12 as a commissioning story that establishes the future concerns of God—the reader's orienting concerns—from the outset of Paul's mission. Further, commissions define the terms of mission and have a "primacy effect" upon the one sent out. Following the lead of B. Hubbard, Tannehill identifies seven elements in biblical narratives of commission: (1) introduction, (2) confrontation, (3) reaction, (4) commission, (5) protest, (6) reassurance, and (7) conclusion. See R. C. Tannehill, "Gospels and Narrative Literature," in *NIBC*, 7:10-11. If the reader recalls the story of Saul's conversion from Acts 9:1-21 as co-text with this one, then Luke presents the reader with a full sense of what lies ahead for Paul in Acts.

461. The omission of any direct reference to Paul's letter writing in Acts is much less a problem than it once was in Acts criticism, for two reasons: (1) There are clear allusions to Pauline letters in Acts, and (2) it now seems possible that a collection of Paul's letters was placed in circulation—perhaps even by Paul himself—before the turn of the first century. It is simply inconceivable that Luke would not have known and read these letters, and therefore used them as a secondary source when writing Acts.

462. So Dunn, *The Acts of the Apostles*, 172-73.

African from Cyrene, a boyhood friend of Herod Antipas and a Pharisee educated under Gamaliel were acknowledged to be spiritual dynamos."[463]

In addition to sharing goods with the Jerusalem community (see 11:27-30), the resurrection practices of the Antiochene community also include "fasting and praying" (v. 3; see also 1:24; 6:6; 8:15; 12:12), which indicate their disciplined devotion to the Lord and capacity to discern his will (cf. 10:30; 14:23; Matt 6:5, 16; Luke 2:37). It is not surprising, then, that God's will is disclosed to them through the Holy Spirit: "Set apart for me Barnabas and Saul for the work to which I have called them" (v. 2). The verb ἀφορίζω (*aphorizō*, "set apart") denotes the separation of clean from unclean, typically for service or sacrifice to God (see Exod 13:12; 19:12, 23; Lev 13:4-5; Ezek 45:1-4). Luke's use of it in the commissioning of Barnabas and Saul sounds an important intertextual echo of two Pauline texts that describe the apostle's calling: Rom 1:1 and Gal 1:15. Paul's use of this verb in these texts recalls the biblical prophets whose commissioning is similar to his own (cf. Isa 49:1; Jer 1:5; *As. Mos.* 1:14; 1 Tim 1:12-16). Naturally, he also associates his missionary tasks with the prophet's vocation (cf. Rom 1:1-5; Gal 1:15-16). In the LXX this same verb is used for Israel's being "called" out of unclean nations to make a consecrated witness to God's salvation, even to the "ends of the earth" (Isa 52:10-11; cf. Lev 20:26). Both of these biblical connotations are combined in the present text where the Spirit of God calls Paul to a work among "unclean" nations (cf. Gal 1:15).[464]

The liturgy of commissioning, when church leaders "laid their hands on" Saul and Barnabas (v. 3), is used earlier in Acts 6:6 to symbolize apostolic authority. In this setting the Christian prophets and teachers of Antioch transmit the authority and benefaction of the Spirit to Barnabas and Saul in "sending them off." The reader should note that Paul's apostolic status in Acts (see 14:4, 14) is carefully qualified in deference to and distinction from the Twelve. While the Paul of Acts cannot claim apostolic status, since

that is predicated on a personal relationship with the historical Jesus (see 1:21-22), he is "sent out by the Holy Spirit" (v. 4*a*)[465] and according to the prophecy of the resurrected Lord (see 9:15-16). Moreover, his religious authority is well established by the conclusion of his mission through the execution of those same tasks that other Spirit-filled prophets-like-Jesus have performed before him: inspired interpretation, persuasive preaching, and the performance of "signs and wonders" that result in mass conversions.

13:4b-12. One must have a map at hand when reading Acts, since geography serves Luke's theological purpose. In this instance, the expedition party leaves Antioch and stops first on the island of Cyprus, where they arrive at Salamis, the principal port city on Cyprus's east coast and a logical place to begin their island campaign. They then cross the island to Paphos, the principal port on the west coast and the provincial capital, which is the logical place to conclude and climax their campaign. Barnabas and Saul proclaim "the word of God in the Jewish synagogues" (v. 5; see 6:9),[466] and they are joined by John Mark as their "helper" (see 12:12, 25). He soon returns to Jerusalem (v. 13), however and becomes party in the later split between Barnabas and Paul (see 15:37-39).

Their mission to Paphos leads Saul and Barnabas to meet with the Roman proconsul stationed there, Sergius Paulus (46–48 CE), whom Luke describes as "an intelligent man."[467] Human virtue and receptivity of the divine word are often paired in Acts (see 17:11), even as are malicious character and spiritual failure. For example, the missionaries also encounter a "magician and Jewish false prophet, named Bar-Jesus" (v. 6),[468] who

463. Krodel, *Acts*, 226.

464. See R. Wall, "Power and Purity in the Acts of the Apostles," *WTJ* 34 (1999) 64-82.

465. Luke does not use the more familiar "sending" verb ἀποστέλλω (*apostellō*), which would have called attention to the noun "apostle," but the rather unusual verb ἐκπέμπω (*ekpempō*, "send out"; cf. 17:10) to emphasize that this new mission was undertaken by *direct* instruction of the Spirit (rather than by the leadership of a local church). See Barrett, *A Critical and Exegetical Commentary on the Acts of the Apostles*, 1:610.

466. While "Jewish synagogues" may seem like a redundancy, the Greek word for "synagogue" (συναγωγή *synagōgē*) denotes a place for assembly and was used for other voluntary organizations in the Roman world. Luke's linguistic precision at this point reflects his theological precision: Paul's identity and mission are centered by the symbols of his Jewish world.

467. Luke uses the proper Greek title for a "proconsul" (ἀνθύπατος *anthypatos*; cf. 18:12) for the Roman official in charge of the island's governing senate, located in Paphos.

468. The combination of "magician" with "Jewish false prophet" may well envisage Luke's attempt to dissociate Christianity from a popular criticism of Judaism (and therefore Christianity) as a nonrational superstition.

is likely an adviser to the proconsul. If Sergius is a type of Gentile convert, then Bar-Jesus is a type of Jewish opponent. Contrary to Sergius' intelligence, this false prophet is an "enemy of all righteousness [δικαιοσύνη *dikaiosynē*; cf. Luke 1:75; Matt 5:20] full of all deceit [δόλος *dolos*; cf. Deut 27:24 LXX; Rom 1:29; 1 Thess 2:3] and villainy [ῥᾳδιουργία *rhadiourgia*; cf. Acts 18:14]"—a catalog of vices suggesting that the principal motive of Jewish opposition is moral rather than theological. Sharply put, Bar-Jesus fears that Paul might intrude on his political relationship with Sergius Paulus and subvert his political influence.

His motive is not unlike that of Simon the Great, who offered to purchase the "political" authority of Peter and John when he encountered them during Philip's Samaritan crusade (see 8:19). In both episodes, the presence of missionaries is considered an invasion of the magician's territory, where he enjoys power and status.[469] As before, the magician's opposition occasions a sure demonstration of religious authority.[470] In this case, when the opposition is less benign, Saul "discerns the spirits," demonizes Bar-Jesus, and then as the authorized medium of "the hand of the Lord" (v. 11; see 11:21) blinds him. Saul's rhetorical question "will you not stop making crooked the straight paths of the Lord?" (v. 10*b*) combines phrases from different prophecies (Prov 10:9; Isa 40:3-4; 59:8; Hos 14:9; cf. Luke 3:4-5; see also Acts 8:21) to supply the biblical subtext of his curse: The false prophet seeks to make crooked what the true prophet of God makes straight.[471] Perhaps the magician's temporary blindness is a metaphor of the failure he and others like him have in blinding people to the course of God's salvation.

Significantly, at this moment of spiritual warfare, when Saul is "filled with the Holy Spirit" (v. 9; see also 4:8), Luke changes Saul's name to Paul and, for rhetorical effect, Bar-Jesus' name to Elymas. In both cases, Jewish names (Saul/Bar-Jesus) are exchanged for Gentile names (Paul/Elymas) to underscore the conversion of the Roman man Sergius Paulus. In this sense, name changes cue both the Gentile mission and the nature of the Jewish opposition to it. That is, Elymas (= unrepentant Jews) tries "to turn [Sergius Paulus] away from the faith" (v. 8) and so exposes himself as an "enemy of all righteousness, full of all deceit and villainy" (v. 10*a*). His blindness (v. 11*b*), the result of Paul's punitive word (vv. 10-11*a*), combined with Sergius Paulus's conversion, in response to Paul's prophetic word (v. 12), clearly indicates Paul's authority and predicts his mission's ultimate success.[472]

13:13-15. From Cyprus, "Paul and his companions," which now include John Mark, set sail to the Asian coast of provincial Pamphylia, where they travel inland about eight miles to Perga (v. 13*a*). No journal is kept of their campaign there; the reader is expected to fill in this entry with details inferred from earlier mission stories. What is most noteworthy about this stop, however, is that John "left them and returned to Jerusalem" (v. 13*b*; see also v. 6) and his mother's house (see 12:12). No reason for his departure is given. Perhaps the first readers of Acts knew the reason and Luke was being polite in not mentioning it. Bruce speculates that Paul had displaced his cousin Barnabas as the mission's chief leader and Luke cues this change by mentioning Mark's departure.[473]

Following the pattern of Jesus before him (cf. Luke 4:1-30), Paul and Barnabas "went into the synagogue" (at Pisidian Antioch)[474]

469. Spencer's treatment of this story illumines the importance of its social cues, which extend from Roman/visible to cosmic/invisible worlds. See Spencer, *Acts*, 138-43.

470. Johnson, *The Acts of the Apostles*, 226, sees the parallelism between this story and the story of Jesus' temptation following the outpouring of the Spirit on him at his baptism/commission. If Jesus' temptation proves that he has the mettle to be Messiah, Paul's quick defeat of Elymas, who evidently is the devil's agent (see 13:10), makes a similar point: Paul has the mettle to be a prophet-like-Jesus with the religious authority to carry the word of God to the end of the earth.

471. Tannehill argues that the intertextual echo is of John the Baptist's statement in Luke 3:4-5, which launches a "renewal movement based upon repentance and release of sins." This movement now continues with Paul's mission under the aegis of the glorified Messiah. See Tannehill, *The Acts of the Apostles*, 2:163.

472. I doubt that the conversion of Sergius Paulus begins Luke's apologia for a variety of "early catholic" Christianity that accommodates Roman rule, as is suggested by Haenchen, *The Acts of the Apostles*, 403-4, following others. Luke's portrait of Rome's relationship to Paul's mission is ambiguous at best, typically presenting it as utterly secular and self-interested.

473. Bruce, *The Acts of the Apostles*, 300. Johnson, *The Acts of the Apostles*, 229, finds a layer of possible meaning in the use of the verb ἀποχωρέω (*apochoreō*, "to leave") in Jer 46:5 LXX, where it implies a cowardly retreat, or in 3 Macc 2:33, where it connotes apostasy. Paul evidently finds John Mark inadequate for the missionary task, whatever the reason (Acts 15:38-39).

474. Pisidian Antioch in Paul's day was a flourishing Roman colony located in central provincial Asia (modern Turkey). It was well known as home to powerful relatives of Caesar Tiberias and Herod, as well as to members of the Antiochene dynasty that had founded the city centuries earlier. For this reason, perhaps, Antioch had become a leading center of the imperial cult in Roman Asia. See S. Mitchell and M. Waelkens, *Pisidian Antioch* (London: Duckworth, 1998).

to worship God (v. 14) following the defeat of the evil one. The reference to the "reading of the law and the prophets" refers to the most essential moment during Jewish worship when lessons from the Torah (reading from the law of Moses) and the *Haftorah* (a related reading from the biblical prophecies) are recited, typically followed by a teacher's midrash—an interpretation of the recited Scriptures that seeks to explain both its contemporary relevance (*dĕrash*) and plain meaning (*pĕshāt*) for the congregation. What is extraordinary about this scene is not that Paul worshiped with other pious Jews on sabbath, for this is his religious habit. Rather, it is that "the synagogue rulers" invited him to offer the morning's midrash or homily on the biblical lessons (13:15). Actually, "word of exhortation" (λόγος τῆς παρακλήσεως *logos tēs paraklēseōs*) is a technical term in Jewish homiletics for an edifying homily concerning God's saving acts in the history of Israel.[475]

13:16-41. Paul will provide them a "word of exhortation" in vv. 17-25, perhaps even alluding to the morning's lessons—which Luke does not actually cite[476]—before expanding his exhortation to include Christian proclamation (vv. 26-37), an invitation to repent (vv. 38-39), and a warning of why his audience must do so (vv. 40-41). Commentators favorably compare the importance and rhetorical brilliance of Paul's speech with Peter's Pentecost address (see 2:22-40) and Stephen's speech (see 7:1-53). Besides numerous parallels in rhetorical design, literary detail, and theological substance, the paradigmatic role of each within Acts is similar. As Paul stands to speak and makes the rhetor's gesture for the congregation to quiet down (v. 16*a*) and "listen" (v. 16*b*), the reader of Acts also comes to the alert, knowing that his first speech is paradigmatic of every other speech Paul will give in Acts.

---

475. The "word of exhortation" might be what the Mishnah later calls a "priestly blessing," which follows the biblical recitations and concludes the worship service. See Fitzmyer, *The Acts of the Apostles*, 510; Barrett, *A Critical and Exegetical Commentary on the Acts of the Apostles*, 1:628-29; J. Bowker, "Speeches in Acts," *NTS* (1967-68) 96-111. What is more puzzling is why Paul is invited to encourage a congregation that he does not know. Luke's literary aim, however, is to show Paul engaging in his primary missionary activity—synagogue preaching—and to set forth in this inaugural speech an account of God's salvation that coheres with the theological aims of his narrative.

476. From his careful analysis of allusions in the speech with attention to contemporary Jewish hermeneutics, Bowker, "Speeches in Acts," 101-10, speculates that the Torah reading includes Deut 4:25-46 with 2 Sam 7:6-16 as the *Haftorah* reading.

13:16. The congregation of the diaspora synagogue is different from those addressed during the church's Palestinian mission. Paul addresses not only "Israelites" (Ἄνδρες Ἰσραηλῖται *Andres Israēlitai*; lit., "men," "brothers," 2:22; 7:2; cf. 13:16*b*) but now also "others who fear God" (οἱ φοβούμενοι τὸν θεόν *hoi phoboumenoi ton theon* also in v. 26)—pious Gentiles such as Cornelius.[477]

13:17-25. The first section of Paul's speech retells Scripture's narrative of salvation's history in a manner similar to Stephen's speech (see 7:1-53). Paul, however, draws out Jesus' connection to the Davidic dynasty as royal Messiah rather than Stephen's primary emphasis on Jesus as the messianic prophet-like-Moses. Because Stephen has already said what must be said to the reader about Moses and the exodus, the Paul of Acts says few words in moving "this people Israel" from their divine election (v. 17*a*; see also 7:2-16) and exodus from Egypt (v. 17*b*; see also 7:17-34) through the wilderness (v. 18; see also 7:35-44) and into "their land as an inheritance for about four hundred fifty years" (vv. 19-20*a*; see also 7:45-50).

Although Paul pays careful attention to the various time periods of God's provident care of Israel's destiny, as did Stephen, he slows his pace at the mention of "the prophet Samuel" and the people's request made to him for a national king (vv. 20*b*-21*a*; cf. 1 Sam 8:5-9, 19-22). The climax of Paul's rehearsal of salvation's history is the founding of Israel's monarchy, for it is from Israel's kingly lineage that the Messiah will come: This prophet-like-Moses of Stephen's speech is also the messianic king-like-David. Paul's claim is rooted in the most traditional expression of Israel's expectation of a national savior, which Paul now asserts is realized in Jesus according to Scripture's testimony (v. 23). That is, the biblical story of David's ascendancy to Israel's throne (cf. 1 Samuel 10–16), when Saul is "removed" as Israel's unfaithful king and David is "made [ἐγείρω *egeirō*; lit., "raised up"] their king" (v. 22*a*; see also v. 30), is the biblical *typos* of God's "raising up" Jesus as Israel's messianic ruler (see 2:25-36). He

---

477. Barrett, *A Critical and Exegetical Commentary on the Acts of the Apostles*, 630-31, takes "others who fear God" as referring to Gentile proselytes rather than mere Jewish sympathizers.

is this prophesied Savior from David's royal household.

Because Scripture provides "testimony" (εἶπεν μαρτυρήσας *eipen martyrēsas*; see 10:43) of David's triumph, since God "found David" (cf. Ps 88:21) to be "a man after my heart, who will carry out all my wishes" (cf. 1 Sam 13:14; Isa 44:28), this typology supports Jesus' triumph as Israel's Messiah.[478] For this reason, Paul's segue to his proclamation about Jesus alludes to Scripture's promise of a Davidic heir to rule an eternal kingdom (v. 23; cf. 2 Sam 7:12-14). Jesus is this "posterity" (lit., "seed," see 2:30) who is destined to be Israel's "Savior" (see 5:31; cf. Luke 2:11) according to what God "promised" David (see 2:29-32; 3:21-25; 7:46-47)—that is, an eternal kingdom (cf. 2 Sam 22:51). According to Acts, however, this promised kingdom has already been realized within a repentant Israel (see 1:6) and is marked out by the presence of God's Spirit, who is also the "Father's promise" (see 1:4). The flashback to John the Baptist is apropos of Paul's reference of divine promise because John the Baptist had predicted the promised Spirit's arrival with the Messiah (see 1:5). Paul's mention of his message when heard with these various intertextual echoes underscores the immediate relevance of the "repentance to all the people of Israel," including these members of this diaspora synagogue (cf. Luke 3:17, 23; John 1:20-21). John the Baptist also joins King David as a more contemporary prophetic witness to Paul's gospel about Jesus (cf. Luke 16:16).

13:26-37. The second section of Paul's speech reiterates his opening address to the devout Jews and God-fearers in attendance (see v. 16*b*), but now as recipients of "the message of this salvation" (v. 26). If his message concerns Jesus, who is "Savior" (so v. 23), then what is said about him pertains to God's salvation, which Joel's prophecy links with calling upon the name of that Savior (see 2:21). When Paul repeats the church's proclamation about Jesus' death and resurrection (vv. 27-30; see 2:22-24; 3:13-17), he adapts his message to a sabbath setting in a Jewish synagogue of the diaspora, where Israel's Scriptures are read and interpreted. So Paul

clarifies that the Savior's rejection was by "the residents of Jerusalem and their leaders" (v. 27*a*), who were ignorant of "the words of the prophets that are read every sabbath" (v. 27*b*; see also v. 15; 3:17; 4:8, 26; cf. 15:21).

Paul stresses Jesus' innocence (v. 28), pointing out that "the words of the prophets" stipulate that "[Pilate, the Jerusalemites, and their leaders] had carried out everything that was written about him" (v. 29*a*; see 4:25-28). The gospel subtext expands the redemptive irony of the Christ-event: The malevolent killing of an innocent person triggers God's benevolent plan in raising Jesus from the dead, thereby reversing such evil for good. The elaboration of Jerusalem's guilt is new in Acts and no doubt intends to recall the earlier story of the Jerusalem church and the obduracy of the city's religious leaders in rejecting the proclamation of the Lord's apostolic successors. The narrative logic of this emphasis is "to open the way to a 'second chance' for these dwellers in the Diaspora."[479]

Paul marshals support for his gospel both from Israel's Scriptures and from those eyewitnesses who encounter the living Jesus and are "witnesses to the people [λαός *laos*]" (v. 31; see also 1:8, 21-22; 10:41), proving "that what God promised to our ancestors he has fulfilled for us" (vv. 32*b*-33*a*; see also vv. 27, 29; cf. 2:25-36). The subtext of Paul's message is ironical because he was an agent of the very Jerusalem leadership he now condemns for rejecting the gospel's witness to the risen Jesus. His complicated midrash of Scripture brings into conversation three texts about David—two from the psalter (Pss 2:7; 16:10 [15:10 LXX] and another from Isaiah's prophecy (Isa 55:3). Together they supply the principal warrant for his proclamation that Jesus' resurrection is proof that he is the prophesied Davidic Messiah. The first prophecy, "written in the second psalm" (v. 33; cf. Ps 2:7), reiterates the promise made to "our ancestors" that is now fulfilled "for us, their children" (vv. 32-33; cf. Rom 1:4; Heb 1:5): Jesus' resurrection discloses that he is the Messiah (cf. 2:36). Paul offers no further reflection on the meaning of the cited psalm but assumes that this text would not make sense of a dead Jesus but only of one who "no more [returns to] corruption" (v. 34*a*). Isaiah's

478. Johnson, *The Acts of the Apostles*, 232-38, argues that in shaping this speech Luke uses a rabbinical exegetical technique called *gezerah shewa* by which different biblical texts are combined by common words or figures, such as David.

479. Johnson, *The Acts of the Apostles*, 238.

promise that God "will give [δώσεις *dōseis*] you the holy [ὅσιος *hosios*] promises made to David" (v. 34; cf. Isa 55:3) is then interpreted by a second Davidic psalm, which draws the inference about the living Jesus who does not "return to corruption" and must be the referent of David's promise that God did "not let *dōseis* your Holy One [ὁ ὅσιος *ho hosios*] experience corruption" (v. 35; cf. Ps 15:10 LXX). Surely David could not be its referent, since he "died, was laid beside his ancestors, and experienced corruption" (cf. 1 Kgs 2:10 LXX; see also Acts 2:27-31).

13:38-41. Paul begins the final section of his speech with his third appeal for "my brothers" to listen to his message (see vv. 16 *b*, 26). This is his "altar call" (the *peroratio*)—a missionary's appeal for his or her auditors to convert to Jesus as Savior in order to be initiated into a new life with God. Haenchen contends that the critical phrase "through him everyone who believes is justified" is Luke's attempt to reproduce Pauline theology—or at least that portion of Pauline theology still accepted by Luke and his church.[480] However, this definition of God's salvation is more typical of Paul's speeches in Acts than of his NT letters. In particular, the proclamation of "forgiveness of sins" (v. 38) is an implicit call to repent and turn to the risen Jesus as Savior, which is a distinctive theological emphasis of Luke-Acts (see 2:38; 10:43; cf. Luke 24:47). The vague reference to "the law of Moses" (13:39) strikes a note more loudly sounded in the earlier Stephen story (see 6:11, 14; 7:20, 53) and subsequent Jerusalem Council than in Pauline thought;[481] and, most important, the reference to "everyone who believes" (v. 39) cues Joel's prophecy as its theological referent in Acts (see 2:21; 10:43; however, see Rom 10:11-13). The point is that Luke shapes the *peroratio* of Paul's programmatic

speech to confirm the theological sensibilities of *his* Paul, in continuity with *his* Jesus and the apostolic successors. In doing so Luke confirms Paul's religious authority and the trustworthiness of his message.

The caveat that concludes Paul's inaugural speech agrees broadly with the language and spirit of the prophecy in LXX Habakkuk.[482] The prophecy warns Judah to "believe" rather than "scoff" when the prophet "tells you" (ἐκδιηγέομαι *ekdiēgeomai*, "to report"; see 15:3) of God's "work." Paul uses the prophecy here to warn Jews in the Diaspora to believe his "report" of God's work (= gospel) or forfeit the promised blessing of eternal life (see vv. 44-46). By "reporting" the details of God's "work" through Messiah Jesus, Paul continues Habakkuk's prophetic ministry of announcing God's work to Israel. In this essential way, then, Luke's Paul uses Habakkuk to underscore the urgency of his "report" about God's work (= gospel) among them.

Although on balance the original meaning of the prophecy is not distorted, a close reading evinces slight modifications to update its meaning for Acts. Luke's most important addition is of a second ἔργον (*ergon*, "work"). This repetition emphasizes the importance of Paul's missionary "work" entrusted to him by the Holy Spirit (see v. 2), which is confirmed by the mission's success (see 14:26). The entire narrative of this inaugural mission is thereby enclosed by repeated reference to Barnabas and Paul's missionary "work" (13:2–14:26), which is to proclaim and mediate God's "work" of grace (14:26). The Habakkuk prophecy stands at the center of this inclusio to remind the reader of the peril of "scoffing" and "never believing" the prophet's warning; indeed, unrepentant Jews will refuse the prophet's message (v. 45), proving them "unworthy of eternal life" (v. 46).

13:42-43. The congregation's initial response is cautiously positive: Barnabas and Paul are invited to preach again in the synagogue the following sabbath (v. 42), while many "Jews and devout converts to Judaism" who heard him "followed Paul and Barnabas" and encouraged them "to continue in the grace of God" (v. 43). Luke does not provide precise definitions of each group within

480. Haenchen, *The Acts of the Apostles*, 412.

481. The Protestant interpreter should not be too quick to contrast the two statements about "believes is justified" (NIV; NRSV, "believes is set free") and "law of Moses" in terms of Paul's distinctive contrast between the faith of/in Jesus and works of law, especially found in Romans (3:21-26; 9:28–10:13) and Galatians (2:11-16; 3:21-24; cf. Titus 3:4-7). See Conzelmann, *The Acts of the Apostles*, 106. The meaning of Luke's reference to "the law of Moses" is unclear. He almost certainly is not suggesting that Torah observance subverts God's plan of salvation, nor is he introducing a "theology of the law"; rather, the "law of Moses" is mentioned in passing as performing a different role in the economy of God's salvation than that of the Savior; the law is Israel's "sign" that they are God's people. See Jervell, "The Law in Luke-Acts," in *Luke and the People of God*, 133-51; and *Die Apostelgeschichte*, KEK 3 (Göttingen: Vandenhoeck & Ruprecht, 1998) 360-61.

482. See R. W. Wall, "The Function of LXX Habakkuk 1:5 in the Book of Acts," *BBR* 10 (2000) 247-58.

the synagogue. For example, even though the combination of "devout" (σεβόμενος *sebomenos*) with "convert" (προσήλυτος *prosēlytos*) is unique within Acts, it is not clear whether these Jewish proselytes are different from those "who fear God" mentioned earlier (vv. 16*b*, 26). In this context, however, they are likely viewed as recent converts to Christ who have now come to "follow" the truth of Paul's message—a situation perhaps similar to Luke's own experience.[483] If this is not the case their exhortation for Paul and Barnabas "to continue in the grace of God" makes little sense, since in Acts the "grace of God" always refers to the concrete experience of divine faithfulness among those who repent (see 2:47; 4:33).

13:44-47. The next week, Paul and Barnabas return to the synagogue. Word of Paul's earlier sermon has filtered out into the Jewish community and so "almost the whole city gathered to hear the word of the Lord" (v. 44). The purpose of Luke's characteristic hyperbole is to create an impression of Paul's rhetorical powers in keeping with his religious authority; he also wants to explain why Paul's Jewish opponents "were filled with jealousy" (v. 45). They sense that Paul is their principal rival as teacher of the Jewish community of their city.

Their reaction recalls Elymas's earlier response to Paul, which is paradigmatic of all Jewish opposition during Paul's mission (see vv. 8-10). His "deceit and villainy" when seeking to subvert Paul's influence in Paphos resulted in blindness—a metaphor of his spiritual blindness. The real offense felt by local Jewish opponents to Paul's message, whether in the court of Sergius Paulus or in the synagogue of Pisidian Antioch, is not in what is said but in the influence exerted upon those "many Jews and devout converts" (v. 43) who had responded favorably to the word and now "followed Paul and Barnabas." Change is never easy, and any substantial change in

what a community believes or values has wide-ranging social repercussions that are felt by the elites of the "old order."[484]

Yet the reaction of Paul's Jewish opposition in Pisidian Antioch also reflects their spiritual obduracy and anticipates the indictment that Paul and Barnabas issue them: "since you reject [ἀπωθέομαι *apōtheomai*] it [the word of God] and judge [κρίνω *krinō*] yourselves to be unworthy of eternal life" (v. 46). That they condemn their opponents "boldly" (παρρησιάζομαι *parrēsiazomai*) suggests that they do so in the power of God's Spirit (see 4:29). Paul's denunciation echoes his earlier use of *krinō* in describing Jerusalem's ignorant rejection of Jesus ("condemning him," v. 27) by which God's redemptive purposes are realized. The same irony stands behind the Jewish rejection of Paul's synagogical preaching, since it leads to his Gentile mission. Further, Stephen had said that the word of God brought to the people by Moses was twice "pushed aside" (*apōtheomai*) by unrepentant Israel (see 7:27, 39), resulting in their idolatry and exile. Not only does their rejection of Paul's message a second time accomplish God's redemptive purposes among the Gentiles; it also marks Paul's Jewish opponents out as an unrepentant Israel who are "exiled" from the prospect of "eternal life."[485] These who "pushed aside" the "word of the Lord" proclaimed by this prophet-like-Jesus are themselves "pushed aside" from the coming age. A harsh verdict indeed!

This passage has performed an important, if sometimes notorious, role in the history of Acts criticism. On its basis, many have argued that Paul's Gentile mission is both occasioned and justified by Jewish rejection of his gospel, or that Paul's words express "a divorce between the gospel and Judaism."[486] Such general statements, however, typically fail to note that "many Jews" and proselytes are converted to Jesus (v. 43) and that Paul does not cease his mission to the synagogue in any case (see 14:1). The scope of his denunciation is local and pertains only to those Jews of Pisidian Antioch who have twice rejected

483. Contra Witherington, *The Acts of the Apostles*, 414, who, along with other commentators, assumes that no one in Paul's audience has yet been converted. But see I. Levinskaya, *The Book of Acts in Its Diaspora Setting*, in Winter and Clarke, *The Book of Acts in First Century Setting*, 5:19-49. Her essential argument is that the combination of *prosēlytos*, ("convert") with *sebomenos* ("devout"; lit., "worshiping"), found only in 13:43, refers to a special group of God-fearing Gentiles who have become "Jewish" in outlook and religious observance. Moreover, she thinks that in combination "Jews and devout proselytes" form a discrete group within the synagogue that has *already* converted to Christianity and for this reason are now "followers" of Paul.

484. Dunn, *The Acts of the Apostles*, 183-84.

485. The phrase "eternal life" (ἡ αἰωνία ζωή *hē aiōnia zōē*) is a synonym of "salvation" (σωτηρία *sōtēria*; see 13:38-39) and occurs only here in Acts (cf. Luke 10:25; 18:18, 30). It is, however, well used in first-century Judaism of life with God in the coming new creation. See 4Q181 1.4-6.

486. Haenchen, *The Acts of the Apostles*, 417; cf. Conzelmann, *The Acts of the Apostles*, 145.

the gospel (cf. 18:3; 28:28). According to Scripture's prophesied pattern Paul carries the Word of God to the Jews first, and then a second time if necessary; those who are still unrepentant are justly condemned by God (see 3:17-26; 10:34-43).[487] Moreover, Paul's "turning to the Gentiles" in Pisidian Antioch personifies the missionary vocation of repentant Israel. His statement, a defining moment in Acts, is ironical of divine sovereignty, since an episode of conflict both clarifies and accomplishes God's redemptive purposes rather than subverts them (see 13:27-30). Paul's turn toward the city's Gentiles, no doubt a practical move given the Jewish opposition there, satisfies Scripture's command that faithful Israel "be a light for the Gentiles, so that you may bring salvation to the ends of the earth" (13:47; see 1:8; 9:15-16; 26:23; cf. Is 49:6; Luke 2:32).

In this light, note should be taken of the formula that introduces Isaiah's prophecy, "I have set you [ἐντέλλομαι *entellomai*] to be a light [φώς *phōs*] for the Gentiles [= nations]." The word *entellomai* is a term of vocation (see 1:2), and Isaiah's original sense of it, carried over to Acts, is of faithful Israel's purpose in the world. While Paul appeals to Isaiah to justify his mission to the Gentiles, he does so ironically since he personifies the missionary identity of repentant Israel. The biblical metaphor of "light" refers to the theological illumination occasioned by the hearing of "the word of the Lord" (see 26:23; 13:44, 48-49). In Acts this proclaimed word is informed by memories of the risen Jesus and the prophet's inspired interpretation of Scripture. The matrix of important terms supplied by Isaiah's prophecy not only delineates the biblical justification of Paul's mission to the Gentiles but also will provide the subtext of his defense before Israel (see 22:21): He personifies the vocation of repentant Israel according to Scripture. This citation also picks up Simeon's prophecy of Jesus' messianic mission (cf. Luke 2:32), and the phrase "ends of the earth" recalls Jesus' commission that his apostles be his witnesses "to the end of the earth" (1:8). In fact, it will be Paul who will bear primary responsibility of bearing Jesus' witness to the "end of the earth" (= Rome; see 28:16-31). In this sense, Paul's urban mission continues the

witness of Messiah and his apostolic successors to God's salvation. While God's salvation is a theme of his earlier sermon (see 13:26), its use here in a missionary text surely recalls Joel's prophecy that the blessings of salvation are extended to "everyone who calls upon the name of the Lord" (see 2:21).

13:48-49. Upon hearing Paul's response to his Jewish opposition, the Gentiles "were glad and praised the word of the Lord." The reader rightly assumes that these Gentiles are from Antioch and attached to its synagogue as either God fearers (vv. 16, 26) or devout proselytes (v. 43). Further, Luke's division of people is not primarily along ethnic lines; thus here it might seem to indicate that the Gentiles' happy response is inherently antisemitic. No more did all "the Gentiles" believe than did all "the Jews" reject the gospel. Luke typically divides audiences along religious lines according to their different responses to God's promises. In this sense, then, the Gentiles of Antioch rejoice simply and rightly because Paul has come to them carrying the word of the Lord in fulfillment of Scripture's prophecy that eschatological Israel would invite the nations to share in the blessings of its salvation.[488]

The repetition of the phrase "word of the Lord/God" (ὁ λόγος τοῦ κυρίου/θεοῦ *ho logos tou kyriou/theou* vv. 44, 46, 48-49; see also vv. 5, 7; 4:31; 6:7; 8:25; 11:1; 12:24), culminating in a summary of its triumph "through the region" (v. 49), concentrates the reader's focus upon the message of salvation rather than on its prophetic messenger or on the ethnicity of his auditors; the message is the locus of God's visitation among the Gentiles and the legitimate cause of their joy. It is this saving word that calls *everyone* to repentance and trust, and not the ethnicity of the community's constituency (see 13:46); and so "as many as had been destined [passive, ἦσαν τεταγμένοι *ēsan tetagmenoi*] for eternal life became believers [ἐπίστευσαν *episteusan*]."

Barrett says about this hard text that it stands "as unqualified a statement of absolute predestination as is found anywhere in

488. Whether diaspora Judaism was a missionary religion or whether Paul was the first Jew to launch an active mission to the Gentiles as Acts suggests remains a lively debate. E.g., McKnight, *A Light Among the Gentiles*, argues that diaspora Judaism was not a missionary religion and that the Acts portrait of Paul's controversial diaspora mission to the Gentiles is historically likely.

the NT."[489] Two characteristics of salvation, consistently and constantly employed by Luke, qualify every definition of salvation found in Acts: The plan and history of God's salvation are mapped by the prophecies of Scripture; and everyone who experiences salvation's blessings does so because he or she has turned to God in faith (see Introduction, "Acts as Confession"). The joy of the Antiochene Gentiles springs from Paul's inspired interpretation of Scripture that locates them in God's plan of salvation.[490] Their faithful response to the word of the Lord results in eternal life (rather than in condemnation or in nothing at all). Moreover, this inclusive salvation is the exclusive experience of all those who believe—whether Jew or Greek. The joy of these particular Gentiles, then, presumes they have believed the truth of the word of the Lord that Paul has delivered to them; and in accordance with the divine purpose they are made worthy of eternal life.[491]

13:50-52. The negative reaction toward Paul and Barnabas from a coalition of leading Jews and "devout women of high standing and the leading men of the city" is not surprising. The adjective σεβομέναι (*sebomenai*, "devout"), suggesting that the women were Jewish proselytes (see v. 43), combined with "the Jews" who instigated the protest, indicates that hostilities toward the Christian missionaries originated from within the synagogue and were motivated because of the leaders' "jealousy" (see v. 45).

Reference to the "persecution [διωγμός *diōgmos*] against Paul and Barnabas," however, reminds us of the theological context of Acts.[492] Jesus' prophecy of Paul's mission, which insinuates itself into the narrative pattern in Acts, defines both its universal scope (9:15) and Paul's suffering (9:16). Both Luke's social world and his theological conception shape a narrative, then, that elevates suffering as the consequence of mission—the collision

of obedient proclamation and unrepentant hearts—but also as the mark of a new horizon. They "shook the dust off their feet in protest against them" and traveled down the road to Iconium. Theirs is not a fearful flight without fight, but one of prophetic protest and severance from a contaminated place (cf. Luke 9:4; 10:11).

The happy prospect of new converts now stands before Paul and Barnabas in Iconium, even though the haunting tragedy of a rejected salvation lay behind them in Antioch. It is not because of their departure that "the disciples were filled with joy and with the Holy Spirit"; rather, these are the marks of salvation and the founding of a new community of "disciples" (see 2:38; 4:31; 8:38; 10:44-46).[493] Thus, even though the missionaries have departed for another city, in their absence the Holy Spirit remains behind in Antioch to enable the disciples to advance the word of the Lord there (see 2:4) and to cultivate joy in their community.

14:1-7. Iconium, Lystra, and Derbe are neighboring cities in the Roman province of Galatia, roughly ninety miles southeast from Antioch on the Via Sebaste, the main roadway connecting the most important Roman cities of the area. Paul's missionary pattern repeats itself in this Lycaonian district; the narrative of this mission has severe gaps and requires the reader to recall details from earlier stories. As before Paul and Barnabas "went into the Jewish synagogue and spoke" (v. 1*a*; see also 13:5, 14). Luke writes that they spoke "in such a way" (οὕτως *houtōs*) to cue readers to fill in the narrative at this point with details ascribed to Paul's ministry at Pisidian Antioch (see 13:16-47).[494] The immediate result is the same as well: "A great number of Jews and Greeks became believers" (v. 1*b*; see 13:43), again testifying to the universal cast of Paul's mission and message.

As before, "unbelieving Jews stirred up the Gentiles and poisoned their minds" (v. 2; see also 13:10, 44-45, 50). Characteristically

---

489. Barrett, *A Critical and Exegetical Commentary on the Acts of the Apostles,* 1:658. The NIV preserves the absolute sense of Luke's statement.

490. Marshall, *The Acts of the Apostles,* 231.

491. Cf. Haenchen, *The Acts of the Apostles,* 414, who argues that the word ὅσοι (*hosoi,* "as many as") indicates that not all Gentiles believed, which makes sense of the later conflict among other Gentile women and men (see 13:50). The "predestination" of Gentiles for salvation is thereby qualified by the faith of individuals freely given.

492. The Western text of Acts adds "a great tribulation and" before "persecution" to intensify the conflict and to recall the earlier use of "tribulation" (θλῖψις *thlipsis*) in 11:19, where the Antioch mission was first established as a consequence of the founding members "tribulation."

493. Dunn, *The Acts of the Apostles,* 185, draws the unwarranted inference from the Lukan summary in 13:52 that the joyful experience of Spirit filling is exclusively felt among Gentiles (see 13:43) and is now possible because of the departure of Paul and Barnabas from Antioch.

494. Barrett, *A Critical and Exegetical Commentary on the Acts of the Apostles,* 1:668.

in Acts, the household of Israel is divided by the proclamation of the gospel (v. 4; see also 4:1-4; cf. Luke 2:34) between those who repent and believe (14:1) and those who do not (v. 2). In this case, the counterattack is fueled by some unspecified anti-Christian propaganda that "poisoned [κακόω *kakoō*; lit., "made evil"] their minds," a phrase that recalls Stephen's use of Exod 2:22 to characterize Egypt's reign of terror over Israel (see 7:6, 19)—in the present case, however, in reference to an intellectual rather than physical repression. Indeed, according to Acts the battle waged for the gospel is often for the mind, whether to overcome the ignorance that keeps people's minds numb to the truth (see 3:17) or to correct wrongheaded interpretations of the prophet's wisdom (see 6:8-10). The reader again should presume that the unstated motive of their "villainy" (see 13:10) is "jealousy" (see 13:45) over the growing influence of Paul and Barnabas, including the duo's interpretation of Israel's Scriptures.[495]

Perhaps because of the threat this opposition posed for the new converts, "they remained [in Iconium] for a long time" (v. 3a)—narrative logic made clear by the use of the conjunction μὲν οὖν (*men oun*; lit., "so therefore") to link vv. 2-3. "Bold" (= inspired; see 4:29-31) proclamation of the "word of grace" and performance of "signs and wonders," all the tried and trusted tools, catalog their prophetic activity (see 2:19, 22, 43; 4:13, 16, 29-30; 5:12; 6:8; 9:27-28). This fresh outpouring of God's Spirit on pagan turf provides evidence that the prospect of salvation has arrived in another region, for the prophecy of Joel is fulfilled here too (see 2:17-21). In this particular Lukan formulation, however, the exalted Lord confirms their religious authority, as God had confirmed his (see 2:22) and the mission of the Twelve (see 2:43). Luke's subsequent use of "apostles," when dividing the assembly into rival factions (14:4), does not suggest Paul's/Barnabas's authority is due to the apostolic office

but rather that it is evinced in the performance of their prophetic tasks.[496]

The escalation of tensions in Iconium that required Paul and Barnabas to make a mad dash for Lystra, Derbe, and "the surrounding country" (14:6) sounds a familiar note in Acts (see 13:50-51). As before in Antioch, the opposition party has united Jews and Gentiles against their mission (cf. Luke 23:6-12). In this case, however, the intent is not mere expulsion motivated by a sense of civic duty; the opponents seek "to mistreat them and to stone them" (14:5; see 14:19). The combination of infinitives makes certain we do not mistake their vile behavior as the result of Jewish legal procedure, where stoning is meted out to blasphemers. The conflict over Paul is political, having to do with the exercise of power, and not theological, having to do with spiritual formation (see 13:44-45). In any case, the "good news" is irrepressible, and persecution only occasions its proclamation is still another urban venue (14:7).[497]

14:8-20a. The preceding paragraph had the feel of a missionary report, providing a general, mostly positive summary of Paul's mission in the Lycaonian district. The present passage complements this summary by narrating a specific incident in Lystra. The obvious literary parallelism between this healing story and Peter's healing of the lame man in Jerusalem (see 3:1-8) suggests a similar narrative role, which is to underscore that Paul's religious authority in the Diaspora is commensurate to Peter's authority in Palestine.[498]

---

495. The Western text of Acts fills in the narrative gap to sharpen the conflict between Jewish leaders and Christian missionaries by substituting "the rulers of the Jewish synagogue and the leaders of the synagogues began persecuting the righteous" for the opening more ambiguous phrase, "The unbelieving Jews."

496. The curious reference to Paul and Barnabas as "apostles" is certainly non-titular, since neither meets the qualifications for membership in the apostolate established by 1:21-22. I doubt that Luke uses an Antiochene source here in which the term "the apostles" refers to commissioning by a local (= Antiochene) congregation, which "sent out" (apostles) Paul and Barnabas as missionaries. Indeed, Acts makes clear that Paul and Barnabas were sent out by the Holy Spirit and not by a local church (see 13:1-3). The best alternative is that "the apostles" is a term of continuity, which reminds the readers that the mission and message of Paul and Barnabas are grounded in the same religious authority and practices as were those of their prophetic (= apostolic) predecessors. See Barrett, *A Critical and Exegetical Commentary on the Acts of the Apostles,* 1:671-72; Spencer, *Acts,* 149.

497. Once again the Western text of Acts makes more explicit the popular success of their mission by adding to 14:7 "Every person in the entire crowd was astounded by their teaching."

498. The precise linguistic connections between these two Lukan stories suggest their intentional pairing within Acts: The recipients of God's healing grace are both "crippled from birth" (3:2//14:8); the agents of healing "look intently" at the lame men immediately before healing them (3:5//14:9); both healed men provide the same public evidence of the miracle—"leaping up and walking" (3:8//14:10); both healing miracles take place in the shadow of temple gates (3:2//14:13); both healing miracles illustrate saving faith (3:16//14:9)—in the first case of the apostles and in this case of the lame man; and both are subsequently interpreted in succinct missionary speeches that make clear the connection of faith and the healing/saving power/grace of God (4:8-12//14:15-17).

Moreover, the repetition of "apostles" at the climax of this story (v. 14; see also v. 4) may well point to this narrative intention. The persistence of Paul's concern for his legitimate apostolic authority, reflected by his letters (e.g., 2 Corinthians 11–12; Galatians 1–2), discloses the contested status of his authority during his lifetime. The issue at stake does not appear to be a fractious rivalry with Peter; rather, what matters is whether Paul possesses an authoritative (and independent) witness to Jesus and whether such a witness requires a personal relationship with him (see 1:21-22; cf. 22:15; 26:16). In the case of the Twelve, their physical proximity to the historical Jesus is supplemented by his prophecy of their reign over a restored Israel (cf. Luke 22:29-30)—a gospel tradition that Acts elevates in importance (see 1:1-14). If Paul's religious authority—and his persona, his teaching, and the pattern and results of his urban mission—is second-guessed for the future of Luke's church, then the Evangelist is rightly interested in clarifying and confirming it. If something like this problem occasioned the writing of Acts (see Introduction, "Acts as Conversation"), then the purpose of this story is to account for Paul's authority on grounds other than "apostleship" that nonetheless legitimize his continuing importance for the church.

The literary template Luke earlier followed in narrating Peter's healing of the lame man in Jerusalem is employed here as well. By comparing the two stories in common sequence, the reader more easily detects both similarities and also the real differences in Paul's exercise of his religious authority. Accordingly, the church's mission proceeds from a public demonstration of God's benevolent rule: God's healing power is mediated first through Peter and here through Paul (see 3:1-8). Thus, "looking intently and seeing that [the lame man] had faith to be healed [σωθῆναι *sōthēnai*]" (v. 9*b*; see 3:4), Paul heals the man. Unlike the lame man Peter healed, however, this man's faith *precedes* his healing. This important difference makes clear the healed man had first "listened to Paul as he was speaking" (v. 9*a*), and thereby his faith is awakened by what Paul says— that is, by the gospel he proclaims. What is finally awakened in the man's heart results

in his salvation symbolized by his healing (see 13:23; cf. 3:16): "And the man sprang up and began to walk" (v. 10; see also 3:8*a*), but not to enter into the nearby temple to worship God as before (see 3:8*b*) since the temple of Lystra belongs to Zeus. The demonstration of Paul's authority, then, is related to his prophetic vocation of preaching the Word of God.

The reader anticipates that those who witness this healing miracle will react in amazement (see v. 11; see also 3:9-10) and that their amazement exposes a theological mistake that the prophet-like-Jesus must correct (see 3:11). In this pagan setting, the crowd mistakes Paul and the silent Barnabas for deities: "Barnabas they called Zeus, and Paul they called Hermes, because he was the chief speaker" (v. 12). So powerful is this misguided impression of Paul that the priest of Zeus "brought oxen and garlands to the gates," ready to offer an appropriate sacrifice to them on behalf of the people (see v. 13). This comedy stands in stark contrast to the hostility of temple priests in Jerusalem toward Peter and reflects a vastly different theological sensibility from that of the observant Jew, who would never think to idolize a human being.[499] Ironically, only in this pagan setting at Lystra is it possible to reach "a highpoint in the demonstration of apostolic [sic] powers"[500]—or at least in the public's "appreciation" of them.

The public deification of Paul in the shadow of the temple of Zeus at Lystra sets the stage for a prophet's gesture and speech that clarify the nature of his religious authority. First, Paul and Barnabas "tore their clothes and rushed out into the crowd" (v. 14). This gesture typically reflects inward grief (cf. Gen 37:29-34) and is used in the Gospels to signal a perceived "blasphemy" (cf. Matt 26:65// Mark 14:63; see also Acts 22:23). Here it carries these same connotations as a public protest against pagan enthusiasm that is considered blasphemous by faithful Jews, who are

---

499. Commentators have made much of the literary allusions to Ovid's well-known myth told in *Metamorphoses* 8.617-725 of the elderly couple who wined and dined Zeus and Hermes—who were disguised as humans—without knowing their true identities and were rewarded for their hospitality with appointments as priests of the Phrygian temple of Zeus. See Haenchen, *The Acts of the Apostles*, 432-34. While the myth doubtless contributed to the final shape of Luke's story, his aim is less to explain the crowd's response and more to clarify Paul's religious authority.

500. Haenchen, *The Acts of the Apostles*, 433.

represented here by Paul and Barnabas. The attribution of Barnabas and Paul's authority as "apostles" (v. 14), already expressed by their prophetic actions, is theocentric rather than egocentric or institutional.

Paul's speech underscores this point. He asserts three traditional Jewish beliefs (see 17:22-31): (1) He and Barnabas "are mortals [ὁμοιοπαθής *homoiopathēs*] just like you,"[501] and so as mortals they "bring you good news" (v. 15a; see also 10:26). (2) The subject of the good news is "the living God, who made the heaven and the earth and sea and all that is in them" (v. 15c, cf. 17:24-25; Exod 20:11), and its predicate is "that you should turn from these worthless things to the living God" (v. 15b). Although framed in a different idiom, presumably apropos to this pagan audience, the deep logic of Paul's message is the same as all other missionary speeches in Acts: Repent of your ignorance and turn to God (see 3:17-19a; 17:30-31). (3) This "living God" has graciously maintained a "witness" to the nations, even though they have routinely rejected God in ignorance "to follow their own ways" (vv. 16-17a; cf. 2:28; 3:17; 13:27; 17:26-31; Psalm 1 LXX; see esp. Rom 1:18-31). God's good deeds are adumbrated as the "rains" that produce fruitful harvests of "food" that reproduce heart-felt "joy" (v. 17b). Paul's striking contention that these activities do not leave the nations "without a witness [μαρτύρος *martyros*]" to God's ordinary goodness recall the earlier uses in Acts of witnesses to God's good news (see 1:8; 2:43; 3:15; 5:32; 10:39-41; 13:31; cf. 7:44). If this brief speech offers a correction to the theological mistake made by ignorant pagans, its implied force is this: God's prior witness to the nations consists of nature's good works; but the Creator's divine goodness is now climaxed in a mission that brings the good news of salvation (= healing) to them. The aim of their witness is not hearts gladdened by a full stomach occasioned by a bountiful harvest but hearts gladdened by the Holy Spirit occasioned by forgiveness (see 13:52).

The crowd's responses to Paul all along have been curious. It is as though only the healed man listened to anything he said and

is saved as the result. The act of deifying Paul and Barnabas surely cut against the grain of everything Paul had said initially; and now his clarifying speech has concluded and the pagans are still "scarcely restrained . . . from offering sacrifice to them" (v. 18; see also v. 13)—obviously they are still ignorant! Where are Paul's powers of persuasion when he really needs them? For all the local color that enriches this story, there is this note of realism: Not every Gentile audience is won over by Paul's rhetorical brilliance. Those in Lystra are not, perhaps due to the sheer depth of their theological ignorance.

The Jewish problem with Paul is not so benign. Their resistance to his witness in the diaspora has escalated to the point of violence. Evidently their new strategy is to follow Paul wherever he goes—in this case to pagan Lystra from Jewish Antioch (see 13:50) and Iconium (see 14:5)—and attempt to "[win] over the crowds" (14:19a). No reason is given why the once exuberant crowds at Lystra were so quickly turned against Paul: Was it something said but unrecorded? Or did he finally convince them he was a mere mortal after all? In any case, his Jewish opposition evidently succeeds: The crowds "stoned Paul and dragged him out of the city, supposing he was dead" (14:19b; see also 14:5). But they were wrong about Paul again; he is alive and so "got up and went into the city," from where he left with Barnabas for Derbe (14:20).

Luke's poignant imagery makes a subtle point concerning Paul's religious authority, a point revealed in the narrative gaps. Paul but *not* Barnabas is persecuted and then surrounded by the disciples. Luke has eyes for Paul only. Johnson rightly says Luke's portrayal of Paul's recovery from attack is not about his "irresistible power so much as his indefatigable faith and loyalty. Paul does not return to the city in triumph to best his opponents in a contest of wonders." He returns in the company of friends who have turned to Jesus because of his ministry.[502] This scene nicely captures another dimension of Paul's religious authority: He is able to build a network of supporters whose aid makes it possible to sustain his mission (cf. 14:22, 27-28).

14:20b-23. The importance of the final two paragraphs of the narrative of Paul's first

---

501. *Homoiopatheis* denotes "with the same [*homoi*] nature *pathos*" and extends to emotional and psychological characteristics shared by all humans. "Fully human" may be another way of translating this word—"we are fully human just like you."

502. Johnson, *The Acts of the Apostles*, 256.

mission has less to do with Paul himself and more to do with the protocol he followed in establishing Christian congregations in the diaspora—a social location that connotes separation and struggle. The plotline of this passage is the retracing of previous steps back to Antioch (vv. 20*b*-21) to strengthen and encourage new converts along the way (v. 22; see also 11:23; 13:43), while entrusting their spiritual leaders to the Lord through acts of prayer and fasting (v. 23). The aim of Paul's pastoral visit is to keep Christians "Christian" in an environment hostile to the faith—a hostility that Paul himself has recently experienced firsthand, in accordance with Jesus' prophecy (see 9:16).

For this reason Paul's message to them interprets their shared struggle: "We must [δεῖ *dei*] go through [διά *dia*] many hardships [θλῖψις *thlipsis*] to enter the kingdom of God" (v. 22; cf. Luke 18:24-25). The word *thlipsis* ("hardships," "persecutions") is used earlier in Acts to recall the circumstances that led to the founding of the Antiochene parish (see 11:19; cf. 8:1-3), the mother church of Paul's mission. Its use here implies that these new converts belong to a community whose roots and reputation are of faithful suffering. More critically, this use of *dei* reminds one of Paul's synagogue preaching of the Lord's messianic affliction (see 13:27-30; cf. Luke 24:46) and the prophecy of his own mission (see 9:16). In context, then, the suffering of faithful believers is an element of God's plan of salvation and even the gateway (*dia*) through which salvation is entered (cf. 1 Pet 1:10-12). Although this idea of the divine necessity (*dei*) of entering God's kingdom "through many persecutions" helped to shape the cult of martyrs during the century following Luke, it is not so in Acts: God's kingdom has arrived with Christ and the kingdom has already been restored to a repentant Israel. Paul's mission as light to the nations bids Gentiles to share in Israel's blessings—right now, right here.

The appointment of elders (πρεσβύτεροι *presbyteroi*) "in each church" was attended to by prayer and fasting. Paul and Barnabas had also been sent out by the prayer and fasting of a congregation's leaders (see 13:1, 3); now they take responsibility for the selection of leaders for the congregations their mission had founded (cf. 20:17; 2 Cor 8:19;

Titus 1:5). The interpreter makes a mistake to think this practice reflects a situation later than Paul—that Luke takes for granted the polity of his day, reflected, for example, in the Pauline Pastorals.[503] In fact, Luke's earlier reference to the "elders" of the Judean congregations (see 11:30) does not suggest novelty but compatibility and continuity between the Gentile and Jewish churches.

14:24-26. Barnabas and Paul return to Syrian Antioch (v. 26*a*), "preaching the word" along the way (v. 25), to conclude their mission where it had originated and where their congregational support lay (see 13:1, 3). With this passage Luke encloses his account of Paul's inaugural mission, using two important phrases—touch points for his entire account, by which we can review the "work" that Paul and Barnabas have been authorized to perform (see 13:2).

The first phrase is that "they had been commended [= "committed," NIV; παραδίδωμι *paradidōmi*] to the grace of God" (14:26*b*). Luke's choice of verbs is revealing, since in his Bible (the Septuagint) *paradidōmi* carries the negative connotation of being delivered to one's enemies with nasty results (cf. 27:1). He may intend to remind his readers of Paul's suffering provoked by his "work." At the same time, the surety of God's providence is given expression here, since Paul is routinely delivered from his enemies by "the grace of God" (cf. 15:40). At the outset of the story he and Barnabas were sent on their way "by the Holy Spirit" (13:2, 4), which is now replaced by a confessional idiom, "the grace of God." The pairing of God's Spirit and grace in this inclusio makes theological sense in Acts, where "the grace of God" often denotes the "graces" of prophetic ministry (preaching, performance of miraculous signs) that are executed by the inspiration of the Spirit, including in this narrative (see 13:43; 14:3). The second phrase, "for the work that they had completed," repeats "work" (see 13:2; cf. 13:41) as the primary catchword of Luke's

---

503. The standard treatment of this notion that the rule of elders over local congregations reflects the polity of the post-Pauline church is H. von Campenhausen, *Ecclesiastical Authority and Spiritual Power in the Church of the First Three Centuries*, trans. J. A. Baker (Stanford: Stanford University Press, 1969). This thesis is simply assumed by most modern commentators; however, the structure for governing the local congregation found in 14:23 (cf. 20:17) and in the Pauline use of "elders/bishops" (1 Timothy 3; 5; and Titus 1) is quite simple and draws its model from the governing structures of the diaspora synagogue (see 11:30) or other voluntary organizations of the Roman world.

inclusio. We are reminded that the work done is divinely authorized and enjoys the favor of God. That it has been "completed" validates God's choice (see 12:25).

REFLECTIONS

1. "Then after fasting and praying they laid their hands on them and sent them off" (13:3 NRSV). The readers of Acts have an advantage over Paul: By eavesdropping on the Lord's prophecy to Ananias, they know something of Paul's future missionary task (see 9:15-16). The practical problem this text addresses is the manner by which Paul himself comes to discern his prophetic calling. Today's church would do well to follow a similar protocol of discernment when commissioning its workers for Christian ministry. What is clear from this text is that spiritual discernment is not a private matter. Paul and Barnabas are "sent off" by the "hands"—a personal touch—of the particular congregation that knows and cares for them. The disclosure that they are given missionary tasks to perform comes to this congregation's leadership from the Holy Spirit. For this reason, a positive discernment of God's clear direction is possible only when the congregation is actively engaged in spiritual practices—worship, fasting, prayer. The Spirit does not communicate with God's people by religious osmosis.

Luke's placement of Paul's encounter with the con artist Elymas (= Bar-Jesus) is strategic in this regard, for in context it confirms the congregation's discernment of Paul's calling. Elymas claims the capacity to divine truth by the power of his spirit; on this basis he seeks to influence the Roman Sergius Paulus. When competing claims of truth are placed on the table, how does one "test the spirits" to discriminate between the true and false prophet? We should follow the lead of an "intelligent" outsider, Sergius, who first gave thoughtful hearing to the "word of God" and then observed the results of the contest between the two prophets, which the Spirit-filled Paul clearly won. The coherence of the message complemented by the powerful consequences of the messenger's work confirmed Paul's calling as a true prophet.

2. "They were filled with jealousy and talked abusively against what Paul was saying" (13:45 NIV). How should the church respond to those who make it their public business to reject the gospel? Paul's message is powerfully preached but typically enjoys mixed results. While many who hear Paul's gospel respond by turning to God in faith, many others do not. Ancient narratives are full of action, but they rarely provide reasons for the actions that are taken. In this passage, however, Luke tells us that certain Jews in Pisidian Antioch viewed Paul as their rival and contended against his gospel to retain their political status within the synagogue—a status they share with powerful Gentiles who are attached to the synagogue (13:50). Still other Gentile auditors of Paul's preaching who are attached to the Zeus temple rather than the synagogue also reject the Word of God, but more out of ignorance than rivalry. In each case Paul challenges those who reject his mission by interpreting the eternal consequences for doing so (13:44-47) or by correcting the underlying reasons for his opponents' wrongheaded response (14:15-17). More important, however, Paul is irrepressible; he boldly continues to do what he is called to do in spite of his public rejection, moving from location to location while seeking out those more responsive to the gospel for special attention (13:47; 14:21-26). While the church should expect opposition to the gospel, whether for political reasons or out of blind ignorance, its response is to be ever agile, willing and able to move to new places in order to minister to different groups who are responsive to its witness to God's good news.

3. "After they preached the good news to that city and had made many disciples, they returned to Lystra, then on to Iconium and Antioch" (see 14:21). Paul is an urban missionary. According to Acts, the church's mission is primarily concentrated in important cities, first in Palestine and then beginning with Paul, across the Roman Empire. Why? In part the reasons are sociological and practical: A wide range of people from different cultures and with diverse backgrounds congregated in cities because of their religious, financial, and political resources. Simply put, Paul evangelized cities because that is where concentrations of people were found. However, urban ministry also expresses the purpose of God to save all people. The city in Acts is a religious symbol of God's universal salvation. Nothing can be farther from Luke's theological point than for a congregation to gather in isolation from its surroundings without any interest in reaching out to diverse populations or institutions. The vocation of the urban congregation as exemplified by Paul is to bear witness to the risen Jesus to everyone from the least and last to the rich and famous. God wants us all to hear and receive the good news of salvation.

Acts 14:27–15:5, The Jerusalem Council: Report and Reaction to Paul's Mission

COMMENTARY

Even if Luke's account of the Jerusalem Council is not the watershed event of his book as many hold, it undoubtedly remains a storm center of modern Acts criticism.[504] Surely Haenchen is still right when commenting shortly after the Second World War that "nearly every scholar has hacked his own way through the jungle of problems, and often it was done in a thoroughly violent fashion."[505] Many simply point to the story's placement in the middle of Luke's narrative as symbolic of its centrality to his theological conception.[506] After all, they claim, here the Paul of Acts shucks off all associations with the Jerusalem church and points the gospel toward Rome as the new epicenter of God's symbolic universe.[507]

I am not convinced. The role this story performs in Acts is not paradigmatic; instead, it is similar to that of a narrative summary that reviews the past rather than introducing something new. That is, this passage provides a literary moratorium in the middle of the story where the reader can take pause to reflect upon the importance of earlier decisions made or actions taken in preparation for

what lies ahead. For this purpose, then, the narrator of Acts convenes his central characters a final time to render "official" decisions that confirm the direction and character of God's salvation ever since Pentecost.

Two intramural conflicts over different, but related, matters—one in Antioch (14:27–15:2) and then another in Jerusalem (15:4-5)—occasion the second gathering of an assembly of church elders (see 11:1-18) to assess God's redemptive plans in light of mission reports (15:6-12) and biblical teaching (15:13-21). The result is a pastoral letter sent from Jerusalem to Antioch that lists general agreements made for the sake of Christian unity (15:22-29). But does their deliberation change the direction of the church's mission or its theological basis? Does James introduce a new pattern of salvation by which faith rather than Torah observance saves? No. The Judean protest in Antioch for a different pattern of salvation is glossed by Peter's citation of Joel's prophecy at Pentecost. This rehearsal stipulates a redemptive pattern from the beginning of these "last days" that emphasizes calling upon Jesus as Lord in order to save non-believers from sin and initiate them into a community of goods ruled over by the Spirit of God (see 2:17-21, 38). Although Luke does not tell us why the "question" carried by the Antiochene delegation to Jerusalem for deliberation (15:2) is set aside in

---

504. See Witherington, *The Acts of the Apostles*, 439-50, for a judicious introduction to the modern history of this scholarly debate. Also noteworthy is Haenchen's discussion of whether to identify this Jerusalem Council with the one mentioned by Paul in Galatians 2. See Haenchen, *The Acts of the Apostles*, 461-72.
505. Haenchen, *The Acts of the Apostles*, 455.
506. See Marshall, *The Acts of the Apostles*, 242.
507. See Conzelmann, *The Acts of the Apostles*, 121-22.

Jerusalem (15:4-5), the reader presumes that such a question is finally considered irrelevant, given the course of salvation to this point in Acts and the unauthorized nature of the protest movement in Antioch (see 15:24).

The conflict in Jerusalem provoked by Pharisaic believers, while more constructive, is *halakhic* in nature, having to do with ethical norms for daily life (see the Commentary on 15:4-5). The objection to Paul's Gentile mission frames a "case study" regarding the appropriate practices of Gentile converts within the church. The issue here is not whether Israel's salvation should be shared with uncircumcised Gentile converts—a decision already affirmed at the first Jerusalem meeting following the conversion of Cornelius (see 11:1-18).[508] Even though Paul and Barnabas were not in attendance at that first meeting, the repercussions of the earlier decision are evident in their inaugural mission, when God-fearers and pagans alike came to faith in Christ (see 13:42-52; 14:8-10).

And what about Jerusalem, the location of this assembly? Is Haenchen correct that "up to Chapter 15 all roads lead to Jerusalem" and afterward to Rome? Do the council proceedings mark a geographical if not an ecclesiastical turning point?[509] No again. In fact, God's salvation has traveled on roads leading out of Jerusalem since Acts 8. Moreover, the association of the Jerusalem Twelve with various missions beyond the holy city is collaborative; there is no sense that missions led by other prophets-like-Jesus must be subordinate to Jerusalem's prerogatives for legitimacy (see 8:4-40). This is certainly true of the Antiochene mission, whose independence from Jerusalem is symbolized both by the effect of Paul's teaching at Antioch, which distinguishes believers there as "Christians" for the first time (see 11:25-26), and by the congregation's food offering for the Judean church (see 11:27-30). Moreover, the circle of the Jerusalem Apostolate has already been broken and was never repaired, leading to a succession of authority to other leaders (see

12:1-19; cf. 6:1-7). While it is true that Peter and Barnabas appear no more in Acts, the church continues its mission to the Jews in Palestine (see Acts 21:20-21).

The practical purpose of this and other meetings in Jerusalem, then, is an exercise not of religious authority but of corporate solidarity in fulfilling the church's vocation in the world. Paul makes no paradigmatic speech or symbolic gesture in this story, even though Peter makes a cameo appearance (see 15:6-11). He even continues to share the stage with Barnabas, who otherwise has been his silent partner (15:4, 12). The verdict James renders provides Scripture's validation to what God has already authorized and Paul has already realized (see 15:13-21); James offers nothing really new to the reader of Acts, even though he shifts the gravity of the debate from the practice of circumcision to the purity concerns of table fellowship (see 15:19-21). His rhetorical role is to clarify and confirm what the reader already knows, and his decision or the subsequent "decree" does not change Paul's message or the pattern of his mission. The Paul of Acts is more polite than the Paul of Galatians, but he is just as resolved in his prophetic identity and missionary vocation. Thus, the reader of Acts is no more or no less confident of Paul's authority after Acts 15 than before, where the value of Paul's prophetic agency in the history of God's salvation is already made evident by the Lord's prophecy (see 9:15-16) and its fulfillment during Paul's first mission. All that is left to tell in Acts is the story of *how* Paul gets to "the end of the earth"; whether he will do so is never in doubt, before or after Jerusalem. Acts 15 is more a rest stop than a gateway toward that end.

Passing reference was made earlier to the troublesome relationship between Acts 15 and Galatians 2. Without minimizing the complexity or importance of the issues at stake, I suspect that most disagreements are in details that are responsibly explained as the literary reflection of Luke and Paul's different pastoral interests, historical perspectives, and theological commitments. These inform compositions of different genres written for different audiences. Fair-minded scholars acknowledge real disagreements between Acts and any Pauline letter, but to privilege either

---

508. P. J. Achtemeier, *The Quest for Unity in the New Testament Church: A Study in Paul and Acts* (Philadelphia: Fortress, 1987) 49-55, suggests that Paul's version of the Jerusalem Council in Galatians 2 is actually closer to Acts 11:1-18 than to Acts 15:1-29. Not only are Paul's stated concerns closer to the issues provoked by Cornelius's conversion, but also the leadership of the Jerusalem church is still apostolic and has not yet been succeeded by James, which is clearly the case in Acts 15.

509. Haenchen, *The Acts of the Apostles*, 461.

text is theologically and historically tendentious. In fact, when proper consideration is given the conciliatory bent of Luke and the polemics of Paul, the substance and ethos of their reports of a Jerusalem meeting are quite complementary. Both reports underscore the independence and authority of Paul's mission, and both agree that its results accord with God's redemptive purposes.

Among several insoluble disagreements between the two, the most serious is whether an "apostolic decree" (see 15:22-29) was ever issued. Paul never mentions an "official" decree in Galatians, and he claims that the Jerusalem accord promptly dissolves during the infamous "incident at Antioch" (Gal 2:11-14). Besides attempting to resolve various chronological issues, the interpreter should resist using the phrase "apostolic decree" to characterize the results of this meeting. Luke's account does not indicate that the accord reached in Jerusalem is then mandated upon rank-and-file believers in Antioch. The impression cultivated—especially with the invocation of the Spirit's partnership (see 15:28)—is that the publication of the council's agreements function like a pastoral exhortation and that they are joyfully embraced by other believers as such (see 15:31). How does this square with the more polemical tone and substance of Gal 2:11-14? Surely Paul would not have easily embraced the specific terms of the pastoral exhortation as stipulated in Acts 15:20-21, 29. Holmberg is probably right when suggesting that Luke conflates two different episodes—the council and the writing of the pastoral exhortation—as an integral whole, when in fact the Antioch incident that Paul speaks of in Gal 2:11-14 probably happened sometime between the two.[510]

14:27-28. This passage describes the initial report Paul and Barnabas make of their missionary adventure in the diaspora; they do so in Antioch, their home congregation. In solidarity with them, "they called the church together" to hear their mission report of "all that God had done with them," the theological substance of which is that "God had opened a door of faith to the Gentiles." Salvation is God's activity; and God's Spirit enables a working partnership with

prophets-like-Jesus such as Paul and Barnabas, "with whom" God works in the world as witnesses to God's Messiah.

The use of the metaphor "door of faith" (θύρα πίστεως *thyra pisteōs*) nicely captures the thematic interest in faith—faith in the truth proclaimed as the word of the Lord is requisite for sharing in the messianic blessings promised by God (see 13:39, 48; 14:22, 23). "Door" suggests a divine openness to or opportunity given Gentiles to participate in the blessings God had promised Jews (cf. 1 Cor 16:9; 2 Cor 2:12; Col 4:3). The door is opened to repentant Gentiles not because of unrepentant Israel but because of a repentant, restored Israel, which is now able to lay hold of its prophesied vocation, embodied in Paul and Barnabas, to be "a light for the Gentiles" (13:47). This is an upbeat report, with mention made of the conflict that followed Paul from town to town. The reader's mind is concentrated upon what God has done in partnership with these prophets-like-Jesus to save repentant Gentiles.

15:1-2. The Jerusalem Council concerns conflict resolution—a more difficult project because there are actually two conflicts within two different congregations that need resolution. The first intramural conflict takes place in Syrian Antioch, where Paul's mission report has apparently provoked protest from "certain individuals came down from Judea" (v. 1*a*). Their protest concerns the conversion of uncircumcised Gentiles, whether circumcision is necessary for their salvation: "Unless you are circumcised according to the custom of Moses, you cannot be saved" (v. 1*b*).

Among a range of possible responses to Pauline preaching within the Jewish church, theirs is a more conservative expression.[511] The subtext of their protest is a long-standing Jewish tradition that the rite of circumcision is central to the public identity of a covenant people (see Genesis 17). Thus, for example, when the Syrians attempted to suppress the practice of circumcision two centuries before, presumably for political reasons, Israel revolted under its Maccabean leadership (1 Macc 1:60-61) to assert circumcision as a national priority (1 Macc 2:46). To define

---

510. B. Holmberg, *Paul and Power*, ConBNTS 11 (Lund: CWK Gleerup, 1978) 11-34, provides the best discussion of the critical problems.

511. These opponents of Paul, frequently noted in his letters (e.g., Rom 16:17-20; Gal 2:11-14; Phil 3:2, 18-19), are sometimes called "Judaizers." Luke portrays them as an extreme and unauthorized (see Acts 15:24) expression of the Jewish church's opposition to Paul's mission.

one's Jewish identity on some other terms is tantamount to apostasy and grounds for exclusion from the covenant community (1 Macc 1:11-15). Naturally, then, circumcision was expected of every proselyte who expected to share in Israel's blessings according to the promise God made Abraham (see 3:25-26). Beyond Palestine in the diaspora, however, the literal observance of this initiatory rite was not always practiced. Paul's appeal—written a few decades before Acts—to the deuteronomic injunction of a spiritualized circumcision in Rom 2:29 (see also Deut 10:16; Jer 4:4; 9:25 LXX) may reflect the prevailing teaching of more liberal diaspora communities that did not require their proselytes to undergo the physically painful rite of circumcision. The rite of initiation was reduced to a symbolic exercise, more a matter of the heart than of the flesh.

This spiritualizing of the rite of circumcision may well have upset the more traditional Jews from Judea who believed that the apostasy of Maccabean Syria is revisiting Paul's mission and the believers in Syrian Antioch. The first Jerusalem Council, however, had already given tacit approval of the conversion of uncircumcised Cornelius (see 11:18). For this reason the protest movement in Antioch is made up of renegade rigorists who act "without portfolio" from their religious leaders in Jerusalem (see 15:24). Nonetheless, they have insinuated themselves into the mixed congregation in Antioch as custodians of Jewish tradition. The readers of Acts know they are wrong on the issue, since at Pentecost Peter cites the prophet Joel to establish that God's pattern of salvation includes everyone who "calls upon the name of the Lord" in faith—the very theological point developed from that moment forward in the narrative.

The result of their presence in Antioch is "no small dissension and debate." The congregation's constructive response is the formation of a delegation "to discuss this question with the apostles and elders" of Jerusalem (v. 2). Since these "certain individuals" from Judea are members of the Jerusalem church and are under the spiritual authority of its leaders, the decision is left for those leaders to make—not as an exercise in ecclesiastical authority but as an act of corporate solidarity.

15:3. The repeated pattern of a mission report (14:27-28//15:4) followed by contentious reaction (15:1-2//15:5) encloses and therefore highlights this oft-neglected travelogue sandwiched between. The careful design of Luke's account of the intramural dissension that occasioned this second Jerusalem assembly would seem to indicate the pivotal role of this verse.[512]

The reader is simply told that on the way from Antioch to Jerusalem the appointed delegation "reported [ἐϰδιηγέομαι *ekdiēgeomai*] the conversion of the Gentiles." The implication is that their primary concern is not the dust-up back home—perhaps even that they dismiss the "question" about circumcision raised in Antioch by the Judean believers. Upon closer reading, however, the reader's attention is drawn not to the implied subject matter of the report, which we already know (see 14:27-28), but to the act of "reporting" it. Luke's use of an exceptional verb for "reporting" (*ekdiēgeomai*) is striking. It is used only here and in Acts 13:41 within the NT. This fact suggests that Luke echoes Acts 13:41 in order to recall Paul's prophetic warning and the resulting dissension among *unrepentant* Jews (see 13:44-47) his ministry in Pisidian Antioch occasioned as a context for reading the present story of dissension among *repentant* Jews. His earlier warning is recalled as the subtext of the subsequent gathering of the Jerusalem Council: To scoff at Paul's mission report runs the risk of divine judgment. The sense of urgency that pervades this meeting, then, is not whether traditional Jews embrace Paul's mission to the nations, nor even whether the purity and practices of uncircumcised Gentile believers will subvert the church's social solidarity or its Jewish legacy. The implied threat lies not with Paul's mission but with the obduracy of certain Jewish believers whose protests of Paul's mission threaten *their* membership within the restored Israel of God.

15:4-5. The pattern of mission report/reaction repeats itself in Jerusalem, although in softened tones. Paul and Barnabas are welcomed by the whole "church," which hears their mission report of "all that God had done with them" (v. 4//14:27-28). What

512. See Wall, "The Function of LXX Habakkuk 1:5 in the Book of Acts," 247-58.

is surprising here is that the floor is then given to Pharisees, who are evidently members of the Jewish church that has already welcomed Paul and Barnabas. Moreover, their opinion is not dismissed by the church leadership as marginal but is taken seriously, in marked contrast to the earlier protest in Antioch that apparently had been dismissed as unwarranted.

The Pharisees are concerned that believers live within carefully prescribed social and theological boundaries (= *halakhah*), especially when sharing table fellowship with impure sinners. Their earnest commitment in relating biblical teaching to the practices of true religion reflects a larger commitment to the community's purity before a Holy God and within a profane world (cf. Jas 1:27). Their angle of vision toward Gentile circumcision is slanted differently than Paul's opponents in Syrian Antioch, where the issue at stake obtains to the salvation of uncircumcised Gentiles. The Pharisees in the Jerusalem church are not troublemakers; they rightly press for an "official" interpretation regarding the religious *practices* of repentant Gentiles according to Israel's Scriptures, whether they should include the rite of circumcision. The question raised about uncircumcised but repentant Gentiles is not about their forgiveness; the text implies the Pharisees were part of the congregation's hospitable response to the Antioch delegation's arrival in Jerusalem (v. 4; cf. v. 24). The issue at stake has shifted, then, from soteriology to sociology—that is, to seeking clarification whether the practice of circumcision should remain the leading symbol of the proselyte's fellowship with repentant Jews within the whole church. The Pharisees' assertion that "it is necessary [δεῖ *dei*] for them to be circumcised" is introduced by the familiar Lukan idiom of "divine necessity," which in turn frames the "case study" the council now convenes to consider: *Does the practice of circumcising repentant Gentiles in "the last days" of salvation's history accord with God's will?* (See Reflections at 15:6-12.)

Acts 15:6-12, The Jerusalem Council: Evidence That Demands a Verdict

COMMENTARY

Part one of Acts—a "narrative of conversion"—concludes in a setting vaguely reminiscent of a courtroom drama in which a jury of peers, consisting of "apostles and elders," gathers "to consider this matter [λόγος *logos*]" (v. 6). The case brought by certain Pharisaic members of the Jerusalem church is whether circumcision is a "divine necessity" for Gentile converts (see vv. 4-5). The evidence considered includes relevant testimony from Peter, who rehearses the story of Cornelius's conversion (see vv. 7-11), and then from Barnabas and Paul, who summarize for a third time what "God had done through them among the Gentiles" (v. 12; see also v. 4; 14:27; cf. 2:22). Their combined witness to the nature of Gentile conversion will provide the raw material for James's commentary on a prophecy from Amos (see vv. 13-21).

15:6. Those who brought the case to public hearing are now excused for an "executive session" of the church's "apostles and elders" (cf. 6:1-2; 11:1-2). Too much has been made of the politics of this assembly, whether Luke's passing reference to "apostles and elders" says anything about a succession of leadership within the Jerusalem community from the apostles to its elders. In fact, the succession to new leadership within Jerusalem has already taken place (see 11:27–12:25). The apostle Peter, who no longer resides in Jerusalem (see 12:17), is present to provide testimony; it is elder James who interprets the evidence in settling the case before the council. Their activity is "to consider" (ἰδεῖν περί *idein peri*; lit., "to look into") this matter, which suggests that they have convened as a rabbinic lawcourt to deliberate over an issue of *halakhah*.[513]

513. Barrett, *A Critical and Exegetical Commentary on the Acts of the Apostles*, 2:713.

15:7-11. Peter's portrait in Acts stands behind his testimony. Here is the friend of Jesus, his principal apostolic successor, whose powerful prophetic ministry had congregated a restored Israel in fulfillment of biblical prophecy. Here is the Peter whose miraculous escape from prison merely adds the climactic entry to the *vita* of his life's work. Here is the legendary prophet-like-Jesus par excellence whose witness is unimpeachable. He alone—not James or Paul—has the authority to supply the terms of Israel's future identity.

It is now commonplace to say that Luke's shaping of Peter's testimony is "Luke being Pauline."[514] Luke's unfolding portrait of Peter in Acts, however, should reflect the latter's theological development, especially in light of his own diverse missionary experiences and the growing influence of Paul upon the future of the church. To think that Luke composed Peter's testimony to impersonate Paul, presuming that the historical Peter remained unaffected by what was happening around him, is a highly dubious conjecture. Even so, the deep logic of Peter's speech and the idiom of his testimony are Pauline, and in fact they follow closely the argument found in Paul's Letter to the Romans. The careful reader will note, for instance, the following similarities: (1) Peter's claim that God chose him to carry "the message of the good news" to the Gentiles, along with the pairing of their hearing and believing, loudly echoes Paul's own description of his apostolic vocation (v. 7*b*; cf. Rom 1:5); (2) his reference to God's investigation of the human heart (v. 8; cf. Rom 8:27), (3) without partiality (v. 9*b*; cf. Rom 2:11; 3:22) (4) according to a person's faith (v. 9*a*; cf. Rom 10:8-10); and (5) his contrast between the impossibility of carrying out all the law's demands (v. 10; cf. Rom 2:25-27) and the universal need for God's grace (v. 11), which nicely formulates a familiar Pauline teaching (13:38-39; cf. Rom 3:21-26; also Eph 2:5-8).

15:7-9. Peter reprises his decisive testimony at the first Jerusalem Council (see 11:4-17) by concentrating on God's prerogatives: "God made a choice [ἐκλέγομαι *eklegomai*] among you" (v. 7; cf. 11:5-14), "[God] testified to them by giving them the Holy Spirit"

(v. 8; cf. 11:15), "[God] made no distinction between them [= Gentiles] and us [= Jews]" (v. 9; cf. 11:12, 17). God's will is publicly disclosed in the conversion of Cornelius, the circumstances of which have already been ratified by an earlier council in praise of God that "God has given even to the Gentiles the repentance that leads to life" (11:18). End of debate.

Peter's assertion that the church's mission to uncircumcised Gentiles is God's "choice" recalls other uses of *eklegomai* in Acts for initiatives that fulfill God's redemptive purposes (see 1:2, 24-25; 6:5; 13:17). In combination with the phrase "the message [*logos*] of the good news," which occurs only here in the NT (cf. 20:24), Peter underscores that the hearing and believing of the preached gospel are the principal means by which the divine purpose is achieved.[515]

Peter's mention of the reception of the Holy Spirit as divine confirmation (v. 8) perhaps alludes to the curious timing of the Gentile Pentecost, when the Spirit fell upon Cornelius before Peter had chance to finish his gospel presentation (see 10:44). No outward gesture of belief or conversion experience is noted by the narrative; God, "who knows the human heart . . . [gave] them the Holy Spirit" as testimony to what God found there. That this gift of salvation is predicated on inward trust and not on some public confession or rite may very well insinuate a standard of "divine necessity" into this hearing that meets the Pharisees' implied requirement (see v. 5)—not that of circumcision, a public rite of initiation, but rather a heartfelt response to the gospel that only God need detect.

The final and most important element of Peter's theological reflection repeats in sharper fashion his earlier claim that "God has made no distinction [οὐθὲν διέκρινεν *outhen diekrinen*] between them [= Gentiles] and us [= Jews]" (see 10:34; 11:17; cf. Rom 2:11; 3:22; 10:12; Gal 2:6; Col 3:25//Eph 6:9). Significantly, his repetition of διακρίνω (*diakrinō*) recalls the ambivalence of Peter's initial struggle to understand his calling to uncircumcised Cornelius, when the Spirit instructed him to do so "without hesitation" (μηδὲν διακρινόμενος *mēden diakrinomenos*, 10:20) and then also "by circumcised

514. Ludemann, *Early Christianity According to the Traditions in Acts*, 167.

515. See Johnson, *The Acts of the Apostles*, 262-63.

believers" in Jerusalem who reacted to the report that Peter enjoyed table fellowship with Cornelius with criticism (διεκρίνοντο *diekrinonto*, 11:2). This string of textual connections rehearses the difficult history of the present debate but also reminds the reader of God's "judgment" that repentant Gentiles, even though uncircumcised, will share in the blessings of Israel's salvation.

This leads Peter to conclude climactically that God has cleansed the hearts of Gentiles by faith rather than by ritual purification, whether symbolized by circumcision or table fellowship (so 15:9). This emphasis again responds to the Pharisees who are rightly concerned with the purity (and perhaps parity) of uncircumcised Gentiles within the faith community but who want to define the issues at stake in traditional terms.

15:10-11. Peter's rhetorical question, "Why are you putting God to the test?" (v. 10), calls the council back to the relevant issue at stake: whether the circumcision of Gentiles is a necessary practice of Christian community. Peter's rhetoric should not be taken as polemical; this is a juridical hearing among colleagues who have to this point not even hinted at leaning one way or another. In context, then, the idea of testing God refers to the Apostle's just rendered theological judgments as establishing a norm for discerning God's will. To set aside his witness to God's activity is to subvert God's redemptive purpose since Pentecost.

Peter now prods the council in a manner that echoes Paul's definition of "the true Jew" in Romans (see Rom 2:25-29). Recalling Paul's argument helps to clarify the Lukan Peter's argument for the reader. Paul stipulates as a general principle the meaninglessness of circumcision as an initiation ritual if the observant Jew cannot then meet the legal obligations of the covenant community into which he is initiated: Such a Jew in effect becomes "uncircumcised" (see Rom 2:25) and is no better in God's view than the uncircumcised Gentile whose moral accomplishment is roughly the same (see Rom 2:26-27). The disciple's identity, whether Jew or Greek, must be predicated on grounds other than Torah purity; it must be evinced by a new life in the Spirit who circumcises the believer's heart and enables her to live in a transformed

manner (see Rom 2:28-29). Paul's argument is neither novel nor revolutionary. He draws upon the Torah's own argument to warrant his claims: True circumcision is a matter of the heart (see Lev 26:41; Deut 10:16; 30:6; Jer 4:4; 9:26; Ezek 44:7-9). No doubt the eschatological horizon of this teaching is Jeremiah's prophecy of a "new covenant," when the restored Israel would live in covenant with God through a transformed (and therefore obedient) heart (so Jer 31:33). This eschatological horizon has been brought into view for everyone who repents because of Jesus. God's promise to Israel, then, is not revoked, and Israel's truest identity can now be realized because of the Messiah (see Romans 9–11).

Peter's conclusion addresses the purity of a Jewish social identity within an inclusive faith community. If Torah purity demands utter blamelessness and this state is impossible to attain, then the Pharisees' concern is misplaced even if sincere. More to his (and Paul's) point is that such a perspective actually subverts a Jewish identity marked by trusting a faithful God to "save [us] through the grace of the Lord Jesus" (v. 11).

15:12. Often overlooked in Luke's narrative of the Jerusalem Council, this verse functions strategically with Acts 2:22 to enclose Luke's narrative commentary of Joel's prophecy of the "last days" cited by Peter at Pentecost (see the Overview to 2:14–15:12). The assembly's "silence" is not due so much to their unspoken agreement with Peter's words but rather is a rhetorical device to direct the reader's attention to what is said next and to listen more carefully "to Barnabas and Paul as they told of all the signs and wonders that God had done through them among the Gentiles." Their final mission report of what "God had done" highlights the theme of Peter's speech that God's election of Peter to carry the gospel to the Gentiles and God's testimony to their salvation in the "Gentile Pentecost" is now consummated by the prophetic work done through Paul and Barnabas among the Gentiles (Acts 13–14).

With testimonies from Peter (vv. 6-11; cf. 11:1-18) and from Barnabas and Paul (v. 12; cf. 14:27-28; 15:3-4), Luke's "narrative of conversion" concludes and the full meaning of Joel's prophecy is clarified: God has poured out the Holy Spirit upon witnesses to carry God's word into the whole world, to the Jew first and then to the Gentile. All who repent and call upon the Lord Jesus in faith are saved from their sins and receive the gift of the Spirit in equal measure. The primary theological subtext of this first half of Acts is whether God is faithful to the biblical promise of a restored Israel (1:6; 3:19-20). The short answer is yes. According to Acts 2:22–15:12, the Spirit's repeated outpouring testifies to God's continuing faithfulness to Israel, not so much by its transforming presence as by its empowering agency that enables a people's

compelling witness to the risen Messiah. The church's Spirit-filled mission goes first to the entire house of Israel to call out a community of repentant Jews for a "season of refreshment" (Acts 2–9). This same Spirit then empowers this community to fulfill God's call as "a light to the nations," beginning with Peter (Acts 10–12) and more fully personified in Paul (Acts 13–14). God's salvation of the Jew first and then the Gentile through common prophetic witness with shared blessings envisages the stunning impartiality of God's faithfulness (10:34-48).

REFLECTIONS

"Paul and Barnabas and some of the others were appointed to go up to Jerusalem to discuss this question with the apostles and the elders" (15:2 NRSV). L. Johnson characterizes the Jerusalem Council as a "theological process" because the decisions made there determine how the church understands itself as a people belonging to God.[516] It is a long and reflective process characterized by sharp and sometimes heated conflict within the church. The importance of theological controversy for initiating a process of discernment is a literary theme of importance in Acts; yet, it sounds a dissonant note for most readers, who have been encouraged to agree with their leaders and conform to their religious traditions. In such situations, appeals are typically made to biblical texts that extol the importance of Christian unity to support uniformity. If agreement is not possible, the disgruntled are advised either to remain silent or to leave the congregation to find or form another. Especially within the Protestant church, church shopping and schisms are responses of first resort when theological debates are not resolved amicably. Tragically, some leave never again to return to a community of faith.

While sharp disagreement between believers is always hard and must be confronted and resolved in every case, the passionate exchange of different opinions is a crucial element of any process by which a faithful people seek to understand the will of God. Reform and renewal are sometimes the Spirit-led results of open protest and debate between earnest believers of the same congregation. Indeed, Acts considers this prospect with considerable optimism! The practical problem, however, is that the leaders of most congregations lack expertise or effective models to guide a congregation through intramural conflict toward a constructive end. Moreover, those on different sides of an issue often lack the kind of civility that resists demanding too much change at once. In my experience, this is especially true of the "liberal" who demands that the "conservative" change quickly and more completely than is practically possible.

If a more civil debate is welcomed, the relevant question is, What are the "rules of engagement" to guide participants toward a formative end? The following observations may be helpful in this regard.[517]

(1) The congregation should acknowledge that open disagreement between earnest believers is formative of Christian theological understanding. Constructive disagreements are finally *not* between believers over issues of power and personality but about God over issues of theological formation. Sometimes the most important pastoral task

---

516. L. Johnson, *Decision Making in the Church* (Philadelphia: Fortress, 1983) 86-87.
517. My profound thanks are due Professor Richard B. Steele for his incisive (and private) comments on an earlier draft of this reflection.

---

is to help members of the congregation distinguish between the *motives* that prompt their disagreement. Purposeful debate of the sort that should be encouraged is aimed at settling issues about who God is and how God acts in our midst. Disagreeable believers who debate issues out of pride, peevishness, or personal ambition allow their disagreements to destroy congregations and make reconciliation, which is God's work, impossible.

(2) Present disagreements between believers typically have a long prehistory. For instance, the strife in Antioch that prompted the convening of the Jerusalem Council began much earlier with the conversion and Spirit baptism of the uncircumcised Gentile, Cornelius. Then Paul's mission beyond Palestine and the congregations he founded there press the theological boundaries of the accord subsequently reached between Peter and the elders of the Jewish church. Reading the story of the Jerusalem Council in its narrative context reminds the reader that conflict resolution should include the "long view" of a particular issue, where its entire prehistory informs its present debate. To do so relativizes and contextualizes our disagreements by bringing other voices from different venues to the same table; the result often diminishes their animosity.

(3) The primary evidence offered is personal testimony, and personal testimony is largely shaped by one's experiences of God. First Peter (15:7-11) and then Barnabas and Paul (15:12) testify to the entire assembly what God has done through them; their audience keeps silent and listens carefully to their stories (15:12-13). Open and formative debate between earnest believers within a congregational setting is largely narrative in shape, existential in substance, and practical in aim. Public testimony is never a monologue intended to draw attention to the speaker. Rather, personal testimony is illustrative of a community's witness and serves to shape its identity and future direction.

(4) The primary authorization offered is scriptural. While public testimony of personal experience is decisive, it cannot settle debates between believers. God's will is made known finally by God's word. According to Acts, the teacher's faithful interpretation of Scripture and the leading of the Holy Spirit are intertwined. When James writes down his exhortation for the believers of Antioch and asserts that it agrees with what "seemed good to the Holy Spirit" (15:28), he recalls his reading of Scripture as the authoritative commentary on the personal testimony just heard. The congregation discerns the Spirit's direction when its teachers use Scripture to both warrant and explain their experience of God.

(5) James's interpretation of Scripture envisages something of a compromise solution that accepts the personal testimony of the missionaries to the Gentiles on the one hand and seeks to maintain the church's Jewish heritage on the other. It is often necessary for decision makers to forge careful compromises between two competing positions to preserve Christian unity, whenever each person or party makes a valuable contribution. It must be said that James does not bring both sides of the issue together as a political accommodation in which both sides make grudging concessions and wind up equally unhappy; he offers a theological affirmation of each as a critical part of a more robust whole. This result is characteristic of *good* theology: to propose constructive solutions that enable the church to go forward.

(6) The verdict that James renders is not only a compromise but it is also a corrective. That is, James not only recognizes that God has acted through both Peter and Paul to call Gentiles into the covenant community but he also realizes the dangers of allowing uncircumcised Gentiles into a community whose heritage is Jewish. Good theology facilitates new ways of thinking about God when new situations require it; however, good theology is ever alert to the danger of discarding the non-negotiable "old" for the "new." While James says "no" to the Pharisaic believers, he also sounds the cautionary note to the missionaries to guard against facile cultural compromise that renders

"Moses" irrelevant. Yes, Paul should continue to evangelize uncircumcised Gentiles, but he should search them out in places where Jewish traditions have helped to shape their religious sensibilities.

(7) While the community's leaders are convened as the "official" council to receive "this question" (15:2) or hear that protest (15:5) between believers, they communicate their decisions and offer appropriate exhortations and other resources to the entire church (15:22-29). Even disagreements between two individuals may spread to the entire congregation; therefore, their settlements should be communicated in all civility to everyone affected to guide future decisions.

(8) Present disagreements between believers typically have a long posthistory. Paul's bumpy relations with the Jewish church are not settled by the Jerusalem Council. Controversies continue to swirl around his mission as he extends the reach of the word of God in new settings. An ongoing review of James's decisive exhortation is required in order to update God's will for the present community of believers (see 21:25). Perhaps this is the final exam whether or not the community has properly discerned God's will: Does the settlement of a momentary disagreement between believers result in an understanding of God that influences the future of the entire congregation in positive ways?

ACTS 15:13–28:28

PART TWO: A NARRATIVE OF CONSECRATION

OVERVIEW

The literary structure of Part Two of Acts is similar to that of Part One: James, Peter's successor, cites (15:16-18; cf. 2:17-21) and then interprets (15:19-21; cf. 2:22-36) Scripture's prophecy (specifically, Amos) of restored Israel, which supplies the theological substructure for the second half of Luke's narrative. The brackets of this narrative unit are again indicated by repetition of a catchword—in this case, "listen." Just as James bids his audience to "listen to me" (15:13), so also Paul concludes his haunting indictment of unrepentant Israel by predicting that God will include repentant Gentiles to share in Israel's salvation because "they will listen" to God's Word (28:28). The narrative within this inclusio recovers an expanded understanding of Amos's prophecy that in turn makes the reader ever more alert to what is at stake in "listening" to God's Word. Further, the Amos prophecy continues the narrative theme introduced by Joel and developed to this point in Acts: God's rebuilding of Israel will find a place for "all the Gentiles who are *called* by my *name*" (15:17, author's trans.; cf. 2:21; 3:19-26). In particular the repetition of the "call" upon the Savior's "name" confirms God's promise to bless "all the families of earth" is now being fulfilled through the church's mission.

James's use of a different name for Peter signals a shift of thematic emphasis in Acts, much as the change from Saul to Paul had earlier cued a turn in plotline toward Rome (see 13:9): "*Simeon* has related how God first looked favorably on the Gentiles" (15:14).[518]

In fact, James's commentary on biblical prophecy introduces new words and themes by which the reader can better track God's salvation to "the end of the earth." In particular, "rebuild" (ἀνοικοδομέω *anoikodomeō*; lit., "housing") is a restoration metaphor recalled again and again in the stories of various "households" (οἰκία *oikia*) and "houses" (οἶκος *oikos*) that provide a strategic locus of Paul's urban mission. Even the reference to a Davidic "tent" (σκηνή *skēnē*; NRSV, "dwelling") resonates with Paul the "tent-maker" (σκηνοποιός *skēnopoios*, 18:3) who is Israel's brightest "light" in God's new housing project.

More significant, James no longer appears interested in the original question of whether converted Gentiles should be circumcised according to Mosaic teaching. The matter of *halakhah* (teaching on legal matters) he now introduces concerns the purity of diaspora Christian congregations where uncircumcised Gentiles and repentant Jews worship together, with a potentially deleterious effect upon the authority of the Jewish legacy they share (15:19-21, 29; cf. 21:25). The vital issue of Gentile purity for James is not the same as for Peter, who claims that uncircumcised Gentiles were purified of heart by their faith in Christ (see 15:9). The relevant issue for James is ecclesiological—and more sociological than spiritual (see the Commentary on

---

518. There is no textual evidence to support the NIV's "Simon"; this translation simply recognizes the logic that James is apparently responding to Peter (and therefore to "Simon") and not to someone else named "Simeon." R. Riesner has rehabilitated an ancient interpretation (Chrysostom's) that James is not referring to Simon Peter but to the Simeon of Luke's Gospel,

whose *Nunc Dimittis* prophecy (Luke 2:29-32) predicts that the salvation that comes with Jesus will extend "as a light to the nations." James is simply announcing here the fulfillment of Simeon's prophecy on the basis of the evidence just heard from Simon Peter. See R. Riesner, "James's Speech (Acts 15:13-21), Simeon's Hymn (Luke 2:29-32), and Luke's Sources," in *Jesus of Nazareth: Lord and Christ*, ed. J. Green and M. Turner (Grand Rapids: Eerdmans, 1994) 263-78. The case for viewing the *Nunc Dimittis* as the intertextual allusion of James's "Simeon" would be strengthened by extending the text to include Simeon's prophecy of a divided Israel in Luke 2:34-35, which is evidently fulfilled because of the Gentile mission as well.

15:19-21).[519] If the implied question raised by Jewish believers about the salvation (15:1) and solidarity (15:5) of uncircumcised Gentiles is whether repentant Gentiles should "become like Jews," then the thematic shift signaled by James's use of the Semitic form of Peter's name addresses the same question in reverse, whether repentant Jews (= "Simeon") should "become like Gentiles."

That this is an interpretive key for the second half of Acts is made clear when Paul returns to Jerusalem following his farewell tour through Roman Asia (Acts 21:17-26). While James is no longer concerned with the religious practices of uncircumcised Gentile converts, he is distressed over reports that Paul's urban mission has subverted important religious traditions among Jewish converts who live in a pervasively pagan culture: "You tell them not to circumcise their children or observe the [Mosaic] customs" (21:21). The relevant issue, then, turns on whether Paul's mission "gentilizes" repentant Jews. In response, Paul defends his mission in the manner of an observant Jew: He purifies himself for temple worship (see 21:24-26) and then appeals to his purity (24:18) to claim that his Jewish opponents have found no "impurity" (ἀδίκημα *adikēma*) in him (24:20; cf. 18:14). One subtext of his defense, then, is that his mission among "impure" Gentiles in no way imperils the "purity" of repentant Jews.

Luke is probably responding to the attenuation of the Jewish foundations of Christianity within his own church (see Introduction, "Acts as Conversation"). His conciliatory response to this rather thorny theological crisis cannot disguise the tension within the early church, or the anxiety felt by Jewish believers at the sudden influx of Gentiles into their fellowship or at the movement of the gospel farther and farther away from the holy city. In fact, Luke's interest in protecting the Jewish heritage of Christian faith is not wholly expected and must be viewed as somewhat radical given the evidence. Even as God does not require uncircumcised Gentile converts to follow conventional Jewish practices (i.e., circumcision) for Christian fellowship with Jewish believers, neither does God require repentant Jews to forsake their ancestral traditions out of loyalty to the Messiah. *The spiritual crisis as Luke sees it is the possible loss of a distinctively Jewish memory without which the church cannot be the church.*

In shaping the second half of his story as a response to this theological challenge, Luke composes accounts of three additional Pauline missions. It is here in Acts that he occasionally places himself within the narrative world—as eyewitness and reporter on Paul's newsbeat. The literary net effect of the "we" passages is to make his account more direct and reliable (see Introduction, "Acts as Composition").[520] The first mission follows the aftermath of the Jerusalem Council (15:22-35) and extends the scope of Paul's urban mission beyond Roman Asia into Macedonia and Greece (15:36–18:17). The second narrative block is centered on Paul's Ephesian mission and includes panels of his "farewell tour" that ends in Jerusalem, once again before an assembly of church elders led by James (18:18–21:26). Significantly, this narrative is enclosed by acts of ritual purification that characterize Paul as an exemplar of holiness within traditional Judaism (18:18-21; 21:26). Paul's final mission is to Rome, the city of his destiny. His route there is circuitous and strategic: He is arrested in Jerusalem and put on "trial" (21:27–26:32), but he appeals to the Caesar to hear his case and journeys to Rome by ship with much intrigue but without a verdict yet rendered (27:1–28:16). His great adventure concludes in Rome, where he awaits his court appearance by engaging in prophetic ministry that, as we might anticipate, divides the house of Israel according to Scripture (28:17-28). Luke's second book then concludes with a curious summary, noting only that Paul's mission continues on but

519. The particular *halakhic* matter James has in mind when commenting upon the Amos prophecy is the levitical concern for the effect of "the practices of the nations" upon Jewish purity or when "resident aliens" mingle with faithful Jews (Leviticus 17–18). See R. Bauckham, "James and the Gentiles (Acts 15:13-21)," in Witherington, *History, Literature, and Society in the Book of Acts.*

520. The debate continues whether the narrator's use of "we" is purely literary and used to create an impression upon the reader or is drawn from the personal memory (perhaps even written in a diary) of an eyewitness. An aspect of the critical problem is the lack of precise "we" parallels in contemporary literature or historiography that could be used for comparison with Luke's Acts. Most commentators fall somewhere between, supposing that Luke actually was a participant in the "we" passages of Acts but that he places himself in the narrative for rhetorical or literary (rather than purely historical) ends. See Witherington, *The Acts of the Apostles*, 480-86; Barrett, *A Critical and Exegetical Commentary on the Acts of the Apostles*, 2:xxv-xxx. Johnson adjures that "the presence of these first-person passages seems to have little impact on the development or meaning of the story." See Johnson, *The Acts of the Apostles*, 297.

without any indication of what the Emperor decides (28:30-31). Perhaps this is only the beginning of the story![521]

The second half of Acts is a story of *consecration*, a word that derives from the Latin root for "sacred." Consecration denotes the act of separating someone or something for a sacred purpose. While Paul exemplifies consecrated service to God, the very idea of consecration evokes a constellation of images, ideas, and claims about purity staked out by James's commentary on Amos. Israel's "consecration" among the nations is publicly expressed by practicing those purity laws and national traditions that cultivate a distinctively Jewish ethos. Does Paul's mission to the nations contaminate this ethos? The Jewishness of Paul's profile in the second half of Acts, both in his religious practices and his missionary protocol, indicates that his witness to the risen Messiah does not displace his ancestral heritage but reshapes it in new and sometimes unconventional ways. Luke makes clear that neither Paul nor his mission sponsors the attenuation or contamination of Israel's social identity. In fact, there is reason to think that his mission to the nations worked hard to safeguard the church's Jewish legacy in those cultural settings where its future was anything but certain (see 16:11-40).

From a canonical perspective, the second half of Acts points the Bible's readers forward to the Pauline letters. The stories of Paul's urban missions in the great Roman cities of his day—Philippi, Thessalonica, Corinth, Ephesus, Rome—prepare readers for the related Pauline letters that follow in the NT. Although the intracanonical relationship between Acts and the Pauline letters is laden with important historical questions,

this commentary will continue to ask what these stories of Paul's mission in Acts contribute to our reading of Paul's letters *today*, as his legacy passes to his *living* readers (see Introduction, "Acts as Canon").

My interpretive interest in this relationship between Acts and the NT letters is both rhetorical and theological. At a rhetorical level, great narratives such as Acts have the capacity to evoke powerful impressions that influence how we approach related, more discursive literature such as Pauline letters. Acts tells us something of the canonical Paul's persona, his circumstances, his vocation, and his religious motives, that enables the interpreter of his letters to fill in gaps imaginatively and in agreement with Pauline tradition. Acts is also a theological narrative that offers its own witness to God's gospel. While the contrast between the Jewish cast of Luke's Paul and the essentially Gentile cast of Paul's letters has long been recognized as a critical problem; in combination the two writings envisage the prophetic protocol that Acts sponsors. In particular, the founding of different congregations according to Acts is at its roots a Jewish enterprise: It begins in the synagogue with Jewish and Gentile converts who are attached to the synagogue. Even when Paul is forced to leave the confines of the synagogue to maintain the Christian character of his urban mission, he does not leave behind the congregation's Jewish practices or constituency (e.g., see 18:5-8). Even though the recipients of Paul's letters (e.g., 1–2 Corinthians) are primarily Gentile, their future with God is predicated on their congregation's Jewish roots—the very point that Acts illumines by its narrative emphasis. The connection between Acts and the Pauline letters suggests, then, that "to the Jew first, then the Greek" is an ecclesial calculus every bit as much as it is a prophetic protocol.

521. For this possibility, see L. Alexander, "Reading Luke-Acts from Back to Front," in Verheyden, *The Unity of Luke-Acts*, 420-46.

ACTS 15:13-35, THE JERUSALEM COUNCIL: THE VERDICT OF JAMES

COMMENTARY

The inaugural event of the second half of Acts is actually the concluding event of the

Jerusalem Council: the speech of James. Having heard all the relevant evidence from the mission field, the new leader of the Jerusalem church is prepared to render a verdict. The specific issue before the council is whether Gentile converts should be circumcised as a religious practice required by Torah (see 15:5). The theological method used by James considers first the religious experience testified to by Peter (see 15:6-11) as well as by Barnabas and Paul (see 15:12). Their combined missionary experiences appear to confirm God's intention to call out of all nations "a people for his name" (15:13-15). Such experiences of conversion, however, must finally be "read" by Scripture. Thus James turns from religious experience to Israel's Scripture, citing a prophecy from Amos that provides a context in which the testimony presented to the council might be considered a theological norm (15:16-18).

Earlier James referred to Peter by his Aramaic name, "Simeon" (15:14), to signal a change of direction (see the Overview). Neither his rehearsal of the available evidence nor his appeal to biblical prophecy give the reader any indication of what that new direction might be. His commentary on Amos, however, does (15:19-21). The question that had occasioned the council's deliberation is no longer of interest to James or anyone else since it seems clear that uncircumcised Gentiles (such as Cornelius) share equally in the blessings of Israel's salvation. The matter of *halakhah* that concerns James is instead the potentially deleterious effects that Gentile converts may have on repentant Jews with whom they share congregational life, and whether a "gentilizing" of the mission in the diaspora may even lead to the attenuation of the church's Jewish legacy. James's commentary on Amos is inscribed as a pastoral "exhortation" and sent to the Antiochene congregation (15:22-29). Their joyful response (15:30-31) cues the continuation of Paul and Barnabas's mission in Syrian Antioch (15:32-35).

15:13-14. Only the passing reference to James, when Peter departs Jerusalem following his miraculous escape from prison (see 12:17), provides the reader with any hint of the important role James will play in the second half of Acts. Here and later in Acts 21, he stands as the teaching authority of the Jewish church. His discernment of God's will proves decisive in settling the present conflict and for anticipating the potential problem of mixing uncircumcised and circumcised believers in the Christian congregations of the diaspora.

James addresses the council only "after they finished speaking"—that is, following the testimonies of Peter (see 5:6-11) and of Barnabas and Paul (v. 12), and in due consideration of them. Following his appeal for a reasoned "listening," James summarizes the previous testimony: "Simeon has related how God looked favorably on the Gentiles" (v. 14; see the Overview). His understanding of the evidence includes: (1) "God first," which echoes Peter's earlier temporal location "in the early days" (v. 14; see also v. 7) to place God's redemptive action within space and time, where God's will is more easy to detect. (2) That God "looked favorably on" (ἐπισκέπτομαι *episkeptomai*) repeats a verb used in Stephen's speech of God's visitation through Moses to deliver the Israelites from Egyptian oppression (see 7:23; cf. 6:3). The James of Acts admits, then, that Peter is a prophet-like-Moses through whom God's grace has delivered an uncircumcised Gentile from death to eternal life. (3) James's concluding expression, "a people [λαός *laos*] for his name" (15:14), recalls important literary themes in Acts. The term for "people" is an OT idiom for Israel that Luke typically uses in Acts of Jews. Here the term is used for Gentiles, not because they are included into a spiritual or "true" Israel but because they share in equal measure the blessings of Israel's salvation from a God who is impartial (see 10:34-43).[522]

15:15-18. While the church's religious experience establishes a theological precedent, it must agree with and be explained by "the words of the prophets" (v. 15). This introductory formula of a prophetic citation reflects Luke's idea of Scripture: Prophecy scripts salvation and necessarily lends its support for and clarification of its progress (see Introduction, "Acts as Confession"). The use of plural "prophets" is perplexing since only Amos is mentioned. Upon closer reading, however, we find a pastiche of fragments mostly from Amos 9:11-12 LXX, but also

522. Jervell, *Die Apostelgeschichte*, 394; however, see Johnson, *The Acts of the Apostles*, 264. Bauckham, "James and the Gentiles," 169, contends that it is likely that this phrase alludes to Zech 2:11: "many nations shall join themselves to the Lord on that day, and shall be my people."

including a bit from Jeremiah and another piece from Isaiah. More likely this is a consensual prophecy in which the testimony of "all the prophets" is implied even though a single prophetic witness is mentioned (see 3:24; 10:43).

The prophecy quoted and James's interpretation of it mark a storm center of Acts criticism. There are two related problems with which the interpreter must contend. The first problem concerns the significant differences between the Greek (LXX) translation of this Amos prophecy and its Hebrew (MT) version, which differences allow James to adapt Scripture to comment on the potential "gentilizing" of repentant Jews in the diaspora (see vv. 19-21). Additional changes are made to the LXX citation, two of which are important to mention.

(1) Luke substitutes "after this" (μετὰ ταῦτα *meta tauta*) for "on that day" (ἐν τῇ ἡμέρα *en tē hēmera*) to begin the citation (v. 16; cf. Amos 9:11). The editorial effect is that this prophecy responds to the timing of the earlier prophecy from Joel about "these last days" (see 2:17), insinuating that Israel's restoration, predicted by Joel, has now been fulfilled "after this"—that is, after the church's mission to Jews (Acts 2–8) and Gentiles (Acts 9–14).

(2) According to Amos 9:12 MT, the promise of Israel's restoration is coupled with the promise that Israel would reclaim the lands of Edom and all the other nations as well. According to Amos 9:12 LXX, to which the James of Acts appeals, the promise of Israel's restoration makes it possible that "all other peoples may seek the Lord" (v. 17).[523] James is thereby able to confirm that the testimonies of Peter, Barnabas, and Paul agree with the prophesied plan of God: Following Israel's restoration, now realized, God will allow "all other peoples" (i.e., uncircumcised Gentiles) to share in Israel's blessings (i.e., forgiveness of sins, gift of the Spirit, eternal life) without first becoming proselytes.

The second problem concerns what role this prophecy performs within Acts. R. Bauckham has observed that the cited text is similar to other prophecies (Isa 45:21; Jer 12:16;

Zech 2:11-15) that predict the rebuilding of an eschatological temple—the rebuilt "tent of David" (15:16)—that would signal and be a gathering point for the conversion of the nations. The story of Stephen has already reminded us that the Lord's symbolic actions within the Jerusalem Temple and prediction of its destruction transvaluate the role the Jerusalem Temple will play in Israel's future purification (see 6:13-14). The Messiah is the sole agent of Israel's rebuilding project. Amos's promise of a rebuilt "tent of David" is fulfilled by this Davidic Messiah; and the prospect of Israel's eschatological purification and the conversion of "all other peoples" have been transferred to him (see 3:19-20).[524]

The real worry of the Jewish church over Paul's mission to the nations, however, concerns those religious practices from which James exhorts repentant Gentiles to abstain (vv. 20, 29)—practices that are linked to pagan temples. If God's grace has been extended to "all other peoples," even those with a background in pagan religion who have not been properly catechized by Jewish teachers, they are obliged to embrace the "rules of polite company" set out in Leviticus 17–18, which delineates the respectful conduct of "resident aliens" living among the holy "house of Israel" (see below). The thematic interplay between this prophecy from Amos concerning the salvation of the nations and the Levitical injunctions against their "abominations" among Jews (cf. Lev 18:24-30) provides the biblical context for Luke's subsequent narrative of Paul's mission. Indeed, his mission among the pagans carries the considerable risk that repentant Gentiles, set free from the requirements of Jewish proselytism, will retain their former religious practices—idols, sexual immorality, food regulations—that will defile believing Jews who are members of their congregations (see below).[525]

15:19-21. James begins his commentary on the Amos prophecy with, "I have reached the decision." This is not a personal opinion but a reasoned judgment from someone with authority to render a verdict on behalf of the

523. The differences in translation are easily explained by the similar sounding words: "Edom" (אֱדוֹם *ʾĕdôm*) is mistaken for "peoples/men" (אָדָם *ʾādām*) and the Hebrew word for "possess" (יָרֵשׁ *yāraš*) is mistaken for "seek" (דָּרֵשׁ *dā raš*).

524. Cf. J. Dupont, "Je rebátirai la cabane de David qui est tombée [Ac 15,16 = Am 9,11]," in *Glaube und Eschatologie*, E. Grässer and O. Merk (Tübingen: Mohr, 1985) 19-32. Bauckham, "James and the Gentiles," 164-66.

525. Bauckham, "James and the Gentiles," 154-84.

council. The "therefore" (διό *dio*) presumes his judgment that "we should not trouble those Gentiles who are turning to God" (v. 19) is based upon the preceding evidence of personal testimony (vv. 13-14; cf. vv. 6-12) and Scripture (vv. 15-18). The force of the word translated "trouble" (παρενοχλέω *parenochleō*) denotes pestering someone against the person's will. Read in light of Peter's earlier admonition that requiring circumcision of converted Gentiles puts God "to the test" (see v. 10), James may assume that to do so unduly "pesters" God against God's will. His *halakhah* is as straightforward as the evidence allows: God's intention is to purify the hearts of non-proselyte Gentiles.

But there is a proviso: James is unwilling to grant them *carte blanche*. The intent of his comment that "we should write to them" (v. 20) is debated by scholars, whether what is written serves as a pastoral "exhortation" to guide behavior or as an administrative "decree" to regulate behavior. If the reader takes this as Antioch's happy response, then he or she should perceive James's judgment as hortatory and pastoral (see v. 31).[526] Further, it is doubtful that the Jerusalem church is any longer in a position to demand Antioch's compliance to a "decree" (see 11:19-30).

The strong adversative conjunction ἀλλά (*alla*, "But") cues the shift in the gravity of James's concern from "Judaizing" repentant Gentiles to "gentilizing" repentant Jews. The importance of v. 20 within Acts should not be underestimated and requires the interpreter's most careful attention. As with some other significant matters in Acts, there are three versions of James's proviso that differ slightly in nuance (see also v. 29; 21:25). In this first instance, James encourages repentant Gentiles to abstain from four impurities observant Jews associated with the pagan world: (1) idolatry, (2) sexual immorality, and (3) eating either food with blood or (4) strangled food[527]—religious practices that are all associated with temple feasts.[528]

In this regard, then, to abstain from "things polluted by idols" refers to the food offered in pagan temples, which is contaminated by contact with idol worship (cf. Mal 1:7). The second behavior, "fornication" (πορνεία *porneia*), has broad moral currency in Greco-Roman moral thought but probably refers to temple prostitution in this setting and may well anticipate issues at stake in Paul's later missions in both Corinth and Ephesus, which were well-known centers of this pagan religious practice. The final two impurities from which to abstain concern food laws: Do not eat food with "blood"[529] or "strangled food." The levitical injunctions regarding table fellowship extend not only to certain kinds of foods but also to food preparation, both of which were routinely broken during pagan feast days.

The biblical context for understanding the importance of these injunctions against pagan religious practices is Leviticus 17–18, a text from Moses that is "read aloud every sabbath in the synagogues" (Acts 15:21).[530] This text legislates the behaviors of "resident aliens" living in the holy land among Jews and sounds a cautionary note about possible effects of "aliens who sojourn in your midst" whose practices may defile and subvert the people's covenant relationship with God. The exhortation to avoid "the practices of the nations" is deeply rooted in the prophet's keen awareness that Israel's single-minded loyalty to God (and so its future) can be imperiled by the manner of a people's worship or fellowship in a heterogeneous culture.[531] This same concern is here adapted by James to guide the behaviors of converted Gentiles who share Christian fellowship with repentant Jews in the urban synagogues of the diaspora (cf. 15:21). In effect, James implies that Jews should treat uncircumcised Gentiles who otherwise share the same sacred space as "resident aliens." James offers guidelines to ensure that Christian fellowship in the mixed congregations of Paul's urban mission will nurture faith rather than contaminate it.[532] The lack of sensitivity

---

526. It is likely that this pastoral letter is Luke's primary source for his narrative of James's speech. If so, then his impressions of its purpose and effect given in 15:31 are instructive for how we understand the motive of Luke's James in rendering his oral judgment. See Bauckham, "James and the Gentiles," 178-84.

527. In all 3 versions of this list, the Western version of Acts omits "strangled food" and adds the Golden Rule, perhaps to contemporize the list for a later time.

528. Witherington, *The Acts of the Apostles*, 462.

529. Although Barrett, *A Critical and Exegetical Commentary on the Acts of the Apostles*, 2:733, thinks "blood" refers to murder and is a prohibition against bloodshed rather than to animal blood left on eaten meat.

530. So Bauckham, "James and the Gentiles"; cf. Barrett, *A Critical and Exegetical Commentary on the Acts of the Apostles*, 2:734-35; Johnson, *The Acts of the Apostles*, 273.

531. See G. Wenham, *Leviticus*, NICOT (Grand Rapids: Eerdmans, 1979) 240-61.

532. S. G. Wilson, *Luke and the Law*, SNTSMS 50 (Cambridge: Cambridge University Press, 1983) 68-102.

to the church's Jewish legacy would surely have an adverse effect on a congregation's Jewish membership (cf. Romans 14; 1 Corinthians 8–10).

It may also be true that in Acts the only good Gentile is a "God-fearing" one—one who is attached to the synagogue. It is noteworthy that most Gentile converts are those whom Paul finds in the synagogue; moreover, the only reported failure from his first mission is at Lystra among the Zeus worshipers there (see 14:8-18). Even within the narrative world of Acts clear religious distinctions are made between Gentiles that indicate a preference for God-fearers as more ready to embrace the gospel and to live in appropriate ways with their Jewish sisters and brothers. Perhaps the missionary subtext of James's *halakhah* is that uncircumcised Gentiles attached to synagogues where Moses is preached every sabbath are to be privileged. If so, then certainly the Paul of Acts seems to agree, since he finds most of his Gentile converts in the urban synagogues of the Diaspora.

Upon an initial reading, the interpreter may wonder how James's interest in table fellowship within the Christian synagogues of the diaspora relates to the biblical prophecy just cited. Is it part of his midrash on this Scripture or a pastoral exhortation detached from Scripture? If the Gentile believers in the church are the Gentiles of the prophecy, whose salvation is then confirmed by prophecy (Amos), then his exhortation for them to remain pure according to Moses (Leviticus 17–18) should not be viewed as odd. The same Scripture that claims them for God also obligates their civility.[533]

15:22-23a. The foregoing commentary on biblical prophecy is offered by James alone, even though it expresses a wider concern within the Jewish church. The consensus reached by "the apostles and the elders, with the consent of the whole church" has to do with the dissemination of the council's verdict. They "choose" and "send" a delegation of men to the Antiochene church "with the following letter," presumably to publish for believers there. This delegation of witnesses includes another fascinating list of names, which serves to bring all of Acts around the

contents of this letter. "Judas called Barsabbas," who shares the same name as a candidate for Judas's replacement (see 1:23), serves as a rhetorical link to the mission to the Jews narrated in the early chapters of Acts; mention of "Paul and Barnabas" and their initial mission to the nations brings "the narrative of conversion" to this midpoint; and "Silas" will play an important role as Paul's colleague during his forthcoming Macedonian mission (cf. 18:5). Silas and Judas are called "prophets" (15:32), apparently because the Spirit empowers them to engage in the prophetic tasks by which believers are "strengthened."[534]

15:23b-29. The literary convention of communicating an earlier decision by letter is similar to the "double vision" (see 9:10-18; 10:1-16) in that the letter reads back into the previous narrative and fills in gaps with added detail. The result in Acts is a more fully nuanced account of important moments that clarify God's purposes and the motives of those with whom God participates in the church's prophetic mission.

The members of the delegation are introduced and given credentials apropos to an important task: They are of one mind (v. 25a), beloved (v. 25b), "who have risked their lives" for the Lord's sake (v. 26), with the personal integrity to confirm orally the validity of what is written (v. 27). More important, however, what is written and carried to Antioch "has seemed good to the Holy Spirit" (v. 28). The content of James's reading of Scripture agrees with the intentions of its author, the Holy Spirit (see 1:16). Any interpretation of Scripture that is on target must enjoy a consensus that includes God's Spirit. The implied response to such an interpretation is obedience.

All this leads to the second iteration of the material in v. 20. The only differences in this statement of the "essentials" of ecclesial (= synagogal) solidarity are minor: The order of terms here places "fornication" last, and εἰδωλόθυτων (*eidōlothytōn*, "sacrificed to idols") replaces the phrase τῶν ἀλισγημάτων τῶν εἰδώλων (*tōn alisgēmatōn tōn eidōlōn*, "polluted by idols"), making more explicit the specific religious practice that would be

---

533. Cf. Bauckham, "James and the Gentiles (Acts 15:13-21)," 177-78.

534. The Western version of Acts adds "filled by the Holy Spirit" to 15:32 to make this Lukan point more clearly.

considered a social pollutant if carried into a Christian synagogue.

The exhortation "if you keep yourselves from these, you will do well" (v. 29*b*) underscores the importance of reciprocity in any covenant relationship. Its conditionality commends the importance of human accountability to God's purposes, discerned by James from Scripture. This is not a pointless formality—a polite way of saying good-bye to friends. There will be other disputes within emergent Christianity that will require turning back to James's reading of Amos for support and clarity in moving the word of God forward. In opening "a door of faith for the Gentiles" (14:27), a set of other concerns has also been let in that will require constant cooperation between the faith community and the Holy Spirit.

15:30-35. Reading the letter occasioned rejoicing at the exhortation (15:31) among the community's membership. The word "strengthen" (ἐπιστηρίζω *epistērizō*) denotes fortifying believers to resist threats to their faith, usually through instruction and comfort (Luke 22:32; Rom 1:11; 1 Thess 3:2, 13; 1 Pet 5:10). This text is paradigmatic of follow-up ministry, where mature leadership stands alongside rank-and-file believers in working through the implications of new teaching. Luke's note of "peace" at the return of Silas and Judas to the elders and apostles of the Jerusalem church is his familiar idealism that always serves a larger theological purpose: The intention of James's speech is Christian solidarity for the sake of the gospel.[535] This optimistic panel concludes with Paul and Barnabas together in ministry where it all began for them—"in Antioch . . . they taught and proclaimed the word of the Lord" (v. 35; see 11:25-26; cf. 4:31; 6:7)—and nicely rounds off this important narrative.

535. Some MSS add "Silas decided to stay there" and edit Silas out of v. 33 to keep him in Antioch with Paul until their departure in 15:40.

REFLECTIONS

1. "After they finished speaking, James replied, 'My brothers, listen to me'" (15:13 NRSV). One of the most important roles that Acts performs within the New Testament is to provide its readers with "authorized" introductions of important people linked to the letters that follow (and to the interpretive traditions they envisage). Among these people is James. Details regarding the James of Acts provide an angle of vision toward the Letter of James and its implied author. When making sense of what Luke's James says at the Jerusalem Council, the interpreter should have the Letter of James open for reflexive reading. Thus, for example, the continuing importance James posits on the Moses tradition for repentant Jews (see 21:20-21) as well as for repentant Gentiles (15:21) prepares the reader for the texts and subtexts of the epistolary James where high value is posited on Torah purity as a distinctive mark of the faith community (see Jas 1:22–2:13). Moreover, his concern for the "gentilizing" (Paulinzing?) of the Jewish heritage in the diaspora church (15:20, 29) may shape an important perspective on the letter's teaching about "faith and works" (2:14-26). For every Pauline claim that our faith in the faithfulness of Jesus saves us for eternal life, there must be a complementary Jamesian claim that our faithfulness to Jesus maintains our membership in the covenant community.[536]

2. "Abstain . . . from things polluted by idols" (15:20 NRSV; cf. 15:29). L. T. Johnson notes that with the exhortation of James, "Luke has given fundamental and programmatic expression to the nature of Christianity as a people of faith."[537] At the very least, James recognizes that a convert to the faith must give up various practices. While the community welcomes all who truly repent—as God welcomes them—there are limits to what the community marks out as "Christian." The subtext of James's

536. For these arguments and their practical implications, see R. Wall, *The Community of the Wise: The Letter of James*, New Testament in Context (Valley Forge: Trinity, 1997).
537. Johnson, *The Acts of the Apostles*, 280.

exhortation is the fear that as the church's mission carries the gospel farther and farther from the Holy Land, the social world in which the church must bear witness and worship will become increasingly pluralistic and secular. The reader of Acts will recognize this concern for the contaminating effect of idolatry registered by Paul also (1 Cor 10:14), in a passage that delineates an acceptable accommodation of a pluralizing and pagan culture without a correspondent compromising of the gospel's core beliefs and values (cf. 1 Cor 10:1-22). Paul alerts his readers to two present and integral dangers in a cultural setting "polluted by idols." Whether the believer is aware of it or not, the symbols (if no longer the practices) of "idol worship" have a profound effect in shaping one's loyalties and how one engages the culture for Christ's sake. Paul further contends that a jealous God will judge those whose witness is polluted by their worship of idols.

In today's culture believers no longer contend for Christ in a world dominated by pagan shrines or temples. Nonetheless, the polluting effect of idolatry continues, as witnessed in the unprincipled acquisition of wealth or in triumphal nationalism—and "temples" to these idols are found in our city's marketplaces and town squares. Whatever holds primary value in place of God is an idol, and related institutions function as its temples. Along with this understanding, the interpreter may translate James's remarks on purity, sexual and ritual, as symbolic of a discipleship that is ever alert to those competing interests that sully our daily walk with the Lord and our neighbors.

3. "[Moses] has been read aloud every sabbath in the synagogues" (15:21 NRSV). If the "essence" of Christianity is insufficiently Jewish, one's interpretation and application of Scripture for daily living will tend to marginalize those ideas and ideals that are Jewish in character. The practical result of listening to Moses according to James is that people will be prepared for a right hearing of the gospel. In other words, those who are most likely to respond to the gospel and grow in God's grace are those attached to a congregation where the truth of Torah is embraced in faith and its core values embodied in human relations. The casual dismissal of this essential Jewish concern for fear that it somehow shapes a legalistic approach to the faith subverts the church's identity and its mission in the world. Time and again I have heard non-Christians tell me that they have decided against the faith because of the hypocrisy they see in the Christians they know. At the same time, believers tell me that they have decided in favor of Jesus while living or working or even worshiping alongside Christians, due to the coherence of their gospel witness with the integrity of their lives.

ACTS 15:36–16:10, INTERLUDE: PAUL BEYOND ROMAN ASIA

COMMENTARY

With the conclusion of the Jerusalem Council, the narrator is now prepared to focus exclusively on Paul and his mission to bring "light to the nations." The present passage moves the reader quickly through several important events, which prepares the way for Paul to join different colleagues on a new mission field along the other shoreline of the Aegean Sea. The "interlude" has a twofold function in Acts. An interlude moves the reader from episode to episode in a "logical" manner, accounting for transitions in places and personnel.[538] In this instance, Silas replaces Barnabas as Paul's missionary colleague, and together they return to former venues, "strengthening the churches" (see 15:36-41; cf. 14:21-26). While traveling in the region of Lystra and Iconium (see Acts 14:7, 21-22), Paul adds Timothy to his

---

538. Fitzmyer, *The Acts of the Apostles,* 570, for instance, says that Luke begins the second half of Acts with this passage.

team (see 16:1-5). Timothy personifies the issues just addressed in Jerusalem, at least as James finally understands it (see 15:20-21); therefore, he becomes a test case of its resolution: Paul circumcises him "because of the Jews" (cf. Gal 2:3). Significantly, there is also a transition in places. Although his mission in Roman Asia enjoys considerable success (see 16:5), Paul is called to Macedonia (16:6-10), where he breaks new ground for the Word of the Lord.

Interludes also summarize common theological themes that link different narrative units as the bits and pieces of a narrative whole. What is true in Jerusalem at Pentecost continues in the synagogues of Macedonia, where prophetic ministry results in converts added to the membership rolls of local congregations (see 16:5; see also 2:41; 4:4; 5:14; 6:7; 14:21-23). Especially important is the intervention of the Holy Spirit (see 16:6-8) and an auditory vision to make clear the plans of God for Paul (see 16:9). The role of visions is not to convert the non-believer but to commission prophets-like-Jesus; likewise, the Spirit in Acts is the divine agent not so much of personal transformation but of prophetic power. The first instance of the narrator's use of first person plural occurs in this passage (see 16:10). Although inconsistently used and occurring only in the second half of Acts, such language allows the narrator to participate in some of the events he narrates; along with Silas and Timothy, he is another of Paul's traveling companions (see Introduction, "Acts as Composition").

15:36-41. The close working relationship between Paul and Barnabas is an important theme in Acts to this point. It was Barnabas who supported the newly converted Saul when others did not trust him (see 9:27) and who later went to Tarsus and sought out Saul to help him with his fledgling church at Antioch (see 11:25-26). Barnabas was Paul's colleague in the first mission to the nations (see chaps. 13–14) and stood with him when giving testimony to the Jerusalem Council of its success (see 15:12). Therefore, it comes as a stunning surprise when the successful team is split apart.

The historical referent behind the story in Acts remains indeterminate. Paul mentions Barnabas's failure of nerve in his reference to the infamous Antioch spat with Peter (cf. Gal 2:11-14) but in a way that contends for his religious independence and theological perspicuity more than his alienation from others. Luke mentions none of this. In Acts, the estrangement between these two colleagues concerns the failure of nerve of someone else, John Mark.

This episode begins with good resolve: "'Let us return and visit the believers in every city where we proclaimed the word of the Lord and see how they are doing'" (v. 36; cf. 14:21-23). The impression is that Barnabas and Paul intend to continue their mission now that the council has settled the controversies that the mission provoked. It is Paul's initiative to do so and his suggestion to Barnabas neatly summarizes their earlier mission together: an urban mission in which the "word" was proclaimed by prophets-like-Jesus with conversions the result.

Barnabas wants to take John Mark along (v. 37). His motive is unknown and left to the reader's imagination. Perhaps it is for family reasons, since John Mark is Barnabas's cousin (cf. Col 4:10) or because John Mark's mother is the apostle Peter's patron (see Acts 12:12) or because Barnabas, who is generous of heart (see 4:36-37), is himself a patron of second chances. We simply do not know. What Luke does tell us, however, is that Paul will have none of it and his reasons are sound: John Mark "had deserted them in Pamphylia and had not accompanied them in the work" (v. 38; cf. 13:13). Paul's reasons are both theological and practical. The defection from community life and vocation carries the connotation of apostasy. For someone to quit on a mission field previously delineated by the Spirit's instruction (13:1-4a), and without good excuse, is tantamount to spiritual defection. Paul disqualifies John Mark for two reasons: He lacks field experience—he is not a witness to "all the signs and wonders that God had done through them among the Gentiles" (v. 12)—and he is a defector, an apostate from a mission the Spirit had sanctioned.[539] Barnabas's "sharp disagreement" with Paul and his subsequent decision to take John Mark on an independent (and unsanctioned) mission to Cyprus (15:39) must finally be viewed as

539. Cf. Johnson, *The Acts of the Apostles*, 288.

casting an unfavorable light upon Barnabas's otherwise idealized profile in Acts. Luke is too polite to say anything more; however, the word he selects for "sharp disagreement" (παροξυσμός *paroxysmos*) denotes a passionate, even bitter, exchange. Words were said that made this partnership impossible to continue. The reader should note that Luke takes Paul's side (for reasons mentioned above) and drops both Barnabas and John Mark from the narrative.

In Luke's narrative world, mission is usually in pairs (cf. Luke 10:1). For this reason Paul replaces Barnabas with Silas, who is commended by the believers "to the grace of the Lord" (15:40; cf. 14:26). Luke has already introduced Silas, who is called a "prophet" (15:32) and, therefore, qualifies for missionary work. Significantly, with this change of partners comes a change of plans. Rather than return to the cities of his first mission, Paul joins Silas in Syria and Cilicia, where Silas is already at work "strengthening the churches" (see vv. 22-23). Nothing more is added to this summary. However, the implied motive for Paul's actions is that he wants to strengthen his relationship with Silas for the work ahead and does so on the latter's turf—in his comfort zone—before continuing on to Derbe and Lystra as originally planned.

16:1-5. The second part of this narrative interlude throws a spotlight on Timothy, whom Paul wanted to accompany him. Timothy proves to be a good find and in due course becomes one of the most important leaders of the Pauline church. He is mentioned with affection in several Pauline letters; and he is, of course, the implied recipient of 1–2 Timothy—two of the so-called Pastoral letters and among the most important resources in Scripture for organizing and nurturing a congregation of believers. For this reason, his mention in Acts takes on added importance.

Timothy is the personification of the diversity found in the Christian synagogues of the diaspora and embodies Paul's solution to the theological crisis James addresses at the Jerusalem Council (see 15:19-21, 28-29). He is an uncircumcised believer, the "son of a Jewish woman, who was a believer" and a Greek father (v. 1). This profile is confirmed in 2 Timothy, which reports that he learned "the sacred writings" (i.e., the Septuagint) during

his childhood (so 3:15), presumably from his faithful mother (Lois) and grandmother (Eunice; see 1:5). Moses was preached to him from his "earliest times" every sabbath (see 15:21).

Even though his Jewish identity is guaranteed through his mother, Timothy is the product of a mixed marriage and his birthright is imperiled for this reason; indeed, he has Jewish ancestry but is not yet circumcised! The ambivalence among repentant Jews of the diaspora, symbolized by Timothy, is precisely the subtext of James's earlier verdict rendered at the Jerusalem Council (see 15:19-21). What makes this case pertinent is that Timothy's Jewish identity has not been cultivated at home "for they all knew that his father was a Greek" (v. 3). The sense of this phrase is that Timothy's Gentile father had prevented his circumcision;[540] his religious identity had been "gentilized" in a mixed home and neighborhood.

Paul's circumcision of Timothy "because of the Jews who were in those places" (v. 3) must be understood, then, as an accommodation to James.[541] This seems especially important given Luke's reference to Paul delivering "the decisions that had been reached by the apostles and elders who were in Jerusalem" from town to town (v. 4). His motive is not to make Timothy into an honest Jew, nor is he responding to Timothy's lack of circumcision from his Pharisaic background as a peril to his salvation as a Jew.[542] An exemplary Paul circumcises Timothy to restore his Jewish identity in order to maintain good working relations between faithful Jews and Gentiles in the churches he founded. This religious motive agrees with James and will serve us again when he accuses Paul of preventing the circumcision of Jewish children (see 21:21). From Luke's perspective, Paul is as

540. Johnson, *The Acts of the Apostles*, 284, 289.

541. Whether the historical Paul would have circumcised Timothy remains contested. The relevant issue is not whether Paul *could* have circumcised Timothy, since circumcision could be performed by any Jew. See Conzelmann, *The Acts of the Apostles*, 125. The difficulty is in understanding Paul's religious motive for doing so. Lüdemann, *Early Christianity According to the Traditions in Acts*, 176, appeals to Paul's missionary principle of accommodation in becoming a "Jew in order to win Jews" (1 Cor 9:19). That is, circumcision may have been necessary if Timothy was to accompany Paul in a mission that went first to the synagogue to preach the gospel.

542. M. Hengel, *Earliest Christianity* (London: SCM, 1986) 64, thinks it likely that Timothy would have been viewed as a Jewish apostate by other Jews rather than merely as an outsider like his father. In this sense, Paul's action rehabilitated Timothy's favorable status within Jewish society.

committed as James is to keeping the Jewish heritage of Christian faith alive and well. To confirm this fact, he notes that "the churches were strengthened in the faith and increased in numbers daily" (v. 5; see also 2:41; 6:7).

16:6-10. The story of Paul's turn toward Europe begins with a summary of his travels. The Holy Spirit is responsible for the plotline of the church's mission, leading sometimes by divine speech and at other times by heavenly vision. In this case, the Spirit directs Paul by blocking doors in Asia rather than by opening them. Luke's earlier use of the verb κωλύω (*kōlyō*, "forbidden/kept from") in Acts (8:36; 10:47; 11:17) makes the positive point that God's redemptive plans, worked out in the church's mission, cannot be frustrated (see 11:17)—Gamaliel's ironic point made in different words (see 5:38-39). Yet here God frustrates Paul's plans, which he had announced to Barnabas (15:36) and begun to accomplish with Silas and Timothy's help. Perhaps there is in this text a faint echo of the circumstances of Peter's mission to Cornelius, which also began with resistance to God's plans for the Gentiles and were also challenged and overturned by visionary revelation.

The repetition of "Spirit" (πνεῦμα *pneuma*) is striking and reconfirms a theological conviction central to Acts: The Spirit guides as well as empowers the church's witness. This is the only occurrence of the expression "Spirit of Jesus" in Acts and probably cues the reader's recollection of Jesus' active role in Paul's conversion and commission (see Acts 9:1-20). There, Ananias received a vision of the Lord's prophecy of Paul's future mission and suffering (see 9:15-16). That earlier visionary appearance of Jesus supplies a subtext to this reference to the Spirit of Jesus" and prepares the reader for the following account of Paul's night vision of a certain Macedonian man.

Visions call prophets to mission. In Paul's vision, "there stood a man of Macedonia pleading with him and saying, 'Come over to Macedonia and help us'" (v. 9). Paul's epiphany is of a human and not a heavenly figure. His actions of standing and begging stress the human urgency of the situation, thereby qualifying the prior emphasis on the Spirit's control of Paul's mission by showing the importance of people's receptivity to the gospel. God does not produce faith in people as though the church is an "imperial juggernaut streaming its way to the ends of the earth."[543] Luke's use of βοηθέω (*boētheō*, "help") is almost prayer-like and recalls the invocative language of petitions for help in the psalter (e.g., Pss 5:2; 9:35; 12:1; 17:2; 18:6; 36:40; see also Acts 21:28; Heb 2:18; 4:16). The proclamation of the good news is in response to the urgent plea for help.

Paul's response is immediate: "We *immediately* tried to cross over to Macedonia, being *convinced* that God had called us to *proclaim* the good news to them" (v. 10, italics added). The rest of Acts hinges on this text. Luke joins Paul's mission to underscore its dramatic importance. Significantly, "vocation" words used here recall a similar matrix of vocation words used following Paul's Damascus road epiphany (see 9:18-22) and again at his Antiochene recommissioning (see 13:1-4*a*): Paul "immediately" responds to his calling by proclaiming the gospel and seeking to "convince" his auditors that Jesus is the Messiah. In both of these earlier texts, Paul's mission is superintended by the Holy Spirit. A reflexive reading of these three commissioning stories alerts the reader of this passage to the implied subtext—namely, that the "Spirit of Jesus," who had earlier closed the door to Asia, had now opened another for Paul to go to the people of Macedonia.

543. Spencer, *Acts*, 162.

REFLECTIONS

1. "Paul wanted Timothy to accompany him; and he took him and had him circumcised because of the Jews" (16:3 NRSV). If Barnabas is no longer a suitable colleague for Paul, then Timothy is. Clearly he meets the job description's minimum requirements: He is a "disciple" (16:1) who is "well spoken of by the believers" (16:2). But the details of Luke's description of Timothy would suggest that Paul is more interested that he is the progeny of a "mixed" marriage than in his religious credentials. Timothy is the right person for the work ahead because his ethnic mix envisages the very mixture of Paul's mission. As the church extends into new territories, new missionaries are added to the team to meet the new challenges that will be encountered. Although Acts underlines the importance of certain personal characteristics for those given tasks to perform in service of God's plan of salvation, there remains this pragmatic feature of the effective leader. Paul wanted Timothy as a traveling companion not because of his professional résumé but because he personifies and presumably has a grasp of the tensions between "being Greek" and "being Jewish" that will characterize the Pauline church. When choosing the right people to staff our ministries, congregations must consider issues of character and skill. However, the congregation should also search outside the "professional boxes" of religious culture to find those gifted leaders with instincts and personal histories that seem well suited for the tasks at hand.

2. "Come over to Macedonia and help us" (16:9 NRSV). Luke reports that the Spirit of Jesus both prevented Paul from going in one direction and allowed him to advance in another. Routinely in Acts the Spirit intervenes—we are not always told how—to guide, assist, and inspire the prophets-like-Jesus. In one sense these are images of divine sovereignty—the active presence of a faithful God to ensure that the plan of salvation is realized. In another sense, these are images of divine concern—the active presence of a caring God to move these prophetic agents of salvation to the places where grace is most needed. Paul's commitment to safeguard the faith of new congregations is a complement of this understanding of God's caring presence among us, helping us enter into and enjoy a strong relationship with God.

ACTS 16:11-40, PAUL'S MISSION TO THE PHILIPPIANS

COMMENTARY

Even though Paul's urban mission remains centered in the synagogues of the diaspora, his turn toward the great cities of Europe reflects changes of cultural scenery and of missionary strategy. Compared to his mission in Roman Asia (see Acts 13–14), for example, Macedonia has a much smaller Jewish population and therefore a more pronounced pagan ethos. Paul's encounter with a clairvoyant slave girl in Philippi, whose unscrupulous handlers have influence over the city's rulers, is an evocative symbol of this region's spiritual state. Moreover, Paul had to leave the city to worship Israel's God, and he found that this same girl was the only "witness" within the city limits to the "Most High God"—empowered by "a spirit of divination" rather than by the Holy Spirit![544] At

the end of his mission, the only "houses" that God rebuilt in Philippi are those belonging to Christian converts—first Lydia's and then the jailer's; in fact, Luke's story is enclosed by references to Lydia's "household" congregation (16:15, 40) and centered by the conversion of the jailer's "household" (16:30-34). The reader is reminded, not without considerable irony, of Amos's prophecy of God's housing project among the nations (see 15:16-18): The absence of a Jewish testimony to the "Most High God" in pagan Philippi is finally supplied by repentant Gentiles.

The plotline of this passage begins where most of Paul's efforts do: on a sabbath in a place of prayer with attentive God-fearing Gentiles in attendance (16:11-15). But this place is not an urban synagogue but an informal setting at a riverside outside the city limits, where the most responsive in a group of religious women is a Gentile merchant, Lydia. Paul's mission receives harsher

544. There is no archival or archaeological evidence of a Jewish congregation in Philippi in Paul's day. See P. Pilhofer, *Philippi*, WUNT 87 (Tübingen: Mohr [Siebeck], 1995). M. Bockmuehl, *Philippians*, BNTC (London: Black, 1997) 6-8, argues that the religious threat Paul envisages in his letter is from pagan "folk" or indigenous religions.

treatment within the city limits, where he encounters the possessed slave girl (16:16-18; cf. 13:6-12) whose healing provokes a sharp legal challenge (16:19-24). As with the apostles before them (see 5:17-18; cf. 12:4-11), Paul and Silas are miraculously liberated from their shackles—in this case, by a timely earthquake rather than by heaven's angel (16:25-26; see 5:19; cf. 4:31).[545] Unlike the Twelve, however, Silas and Paul remain in prison much to the surprise of the jailer who awakened to opened prison gates and the expectation of a nighttime jailbreak (16:27; see 5:20-26). This occasions the famous missionary exchange between the terrified jailer, who asks his ambiguous question, "What must I do to be saved?" Paul's retort, "Believe on the Lord Jesus, and you will be saved," results in the conversion of a second household of Gentiles (16:28-34). Paul and Silas are released from prison the next day (16:35-36), but rather than depart with grateful acquiescence, citizen Paul excoriates the city's magistrates for their abuse of Roman justice (16:37-38) before making a pastoral house call on Lydia's congregation and then leaving for another city (16:39-40).

The cache of common themes between this story and Paul's Letter to the Philippians commends its role within the NT as the letter's "canonical context." Paul's poignant reflection on his imprisonment and suffering in Philippians (Phil 1:12-14), especially in light of the Lord's humility (Phil 2:6-8), is provided a narrative context by the Acts account, even though it was not written at Philippi. In this regard, the detailed description of the legal apparatus leading to Paul's imprisonment may provide a set of images that enable a more powerful reading of Philippians 1. Paul's preaching of the gospel during his imprisonment is vividly portrayed in Acts, where he sings praises and witnesses to the other prisoners and the jailer. The opposition of pagan religion to Paul's teaching, perhaps even of the Roman imperial cult (Phil 2:9-11), that Paul indicates in his letter (Phil 2:15) is made more clear by Luke's unflattering portrait of Philippi. The significant christological teaching found in this letter (e.g., Phil 2:5-11) is framed by Paul's exhortation

to "believe in the Lord Jesus and you will be saved" (Acts 16:31). In particular, this kerygmatic summary from the Paul of Acts captures nicely the central point Paul makes in Philippians against the potential threat of "the dogs" (Phil 3:2-4a) who boast of their nationality and ritual purity as the true marks of covenant renewal (Phil 3:4b-6) rather than of their faith in Christ (Phil 3:7-11). Finally, the poignant images of hospitality, which frame and center this story, may well help the interpreter of Philippians recover the important epistolary theme of the congregation's financial support of and partnership (κοινωνία koinōnia) with him in the ministry of the gospel (Phil 4:14-17; cf. 2 Cor 11:9). An element of that congregational partnership is the full participation of men and women in Paul's mission there (Phil 4:2-3), which may explain Luke's shaping of this story about the conversion of a woman and a man and their respective households.

16:11-15. A traveling itinerary (vv. 11-12) assures the reader that Paul arrives in Macedonia in response to his vision of the Macedonian man (vv. 8-10). Whatever reluctance Paul may have felt in leaving Roman Asia for Macedonia prior to his vision (see vv. 6-7) was probably not due to a difference in cultures or languages, since people on both sides of the Aegean Sea were thoroughly influenced by Greek culture and literature. The team's base of operations is Philippi, "a leading city of the district of Macedonia and a Roman colony."[546]

The plotline of the activities that follow is initially shaped by two encounters with two very different working women. The first is "a certain woman named Lydia" (v. 14). According to literary pattern, Paul meets Lydia on a sabbath in a makeshift synagogue—in this case located outside of town (v. 13) as a "place of prayer"—that he frequented while staying in Philippi (v. 16). Evidently there is no synagogue in the city. The term "place

---

545. For comparison of prison stories in Acts, see Pilhofer, *Philippi*, 167-69.

546. Luke's introduction of Philippi is awkward and its transmission corrupted. The two most likely readings are provided by the NIV, which has Philippi as "the leading city of that district of Macedonia," and the NRSV, which more ambiguously notes that Philippi is "a leading city." While Philippi was an important Roman colony with the privileged status of *ius italicum* (a Roman legal status exempting the colony from various taxes) it was *not* the leading city of its district; Amphipolis was. The NRSV follows the critical text more precisely, and its rendering (and implied meaning) is preferred: Philippi is one of four "leading" cities that made up Roman Macedonia. Luke emphasizes its importance in order to underscore its programmatic importance for Paul's European mission.

of prayer" (προσευχή *proseuchē*) is synonymous with "synagogue," even though in this case the term designates a marginal location *outside* the city gates and *beside* a small river on the southern edge of town. The more informal setting allows rabbi Paul to sit with Gentile women gathered there, which may indicate the city lacks a quorum of ten Jewish males to congregate an assembly of Jews for worship.[547] That Paul only supposed this was a place of prayer may well symbolize the insignificance of a Jewish presence within the city, more than a lack of familiarity with the cityscape—since he had arrived days earlier. All these narrative details contextualize the anti-Semitic slur of the slave girl's owners (16:20).

Paul's posture toward these religious women may indicate the beginning of a worship service, with Paul acting as guest liturgist and rabbi. Lydia is among the women before whom he sits and speaks; her profile is sufficient to indicate the importance of her conversion for the wider Philippian mission (see v. 40). One of the implied conclusions of James's paradigmatic commentary on Amos is that God-fearing Gentiles attached to synagogues are preferred converts (see 15:20-21). The details of her spiritual biography are therefore similar to God-fearing Cornelius:[548] she is a "worshiper of God, [who] was listening to us" (v. 14; cf. 10:1-8). Although Luke is ambiguous about her religious identity, it is more likely that she is a Gentile attracted to the synagogue than that she is a Jew, since his earlier use of similar wording in Acts 13:43 describes Gentile seekers who are attached to the local synagogue. Also, her personal name, "Lydia," is Greek rather than Jewish; she is named after an ancient city well known for the fabrics she sells. Her attention to Paul's message because "the Lord opened her heart" may well be the result of her good character, reflected in her hospitable reception of Paul (v. 15). The connection between hospitality—sharing goods with others—and responsiveness to the word of God is an important literary theme in both Luke and Acts (cf. Luke 24:29-31).[549] This is another indication of her

spiritual authority as first convert and leader of the church in Philippi.

Several details of Lydia's professional résumé indicate her success: She owns her own business and her own home.[550] She is a "dealer in purple cloth" from Thyatira, a city well known for its textile industry (v. 14; cf. Rev 2:18-29). Purple clothing was destined for the rich and royal in the Roman world, where it symbolized power and influence. A merchant in purple cloth, then, is someone who rubbed shoulders daily with society's rich and famous. Luke's use of Lydia's personal name in his story may well indicate her social prominence.[551] In his narrative world, however, even the socially prominent are spiritually impoverished without Jesus; Lydia's eager response to the gospel is another illustration of this reality.

16:16-18. Paul's exorcism of the divining slave girl recalls a similar encounter found in Mark's Gospel (Mark 1:21-26; cf. Luke 4:41). At the beginning of his messianic mission, Jesus enters the synagogue at Capernaum to worship God. Among those in attendance is a demoniac who alone among the worshipers knows Jesus' messianic identity. Jesus' authority and, ironically, the truth of the gospel he proclaims are aptly demonstrated when he expels the demon from the worshiping community. Similar points are made by this episode in Acts. There is also the sense that the slave girl unwittingly has thrown down a gauntlet of sorts to Paul. His spiritual authority as a prophet-like-Jesus is thereby confirmed by this exorcism: Paul's Holy Spirit is greater than the unholy spirit who speaks through the girl. Moreover, her public divination that Paul and Silas are "slaves of the Most High God, who proclaim to you a way of salvation" (v. 17), which goes on "for several days," ironically introduces the kerygmatic theme that Paul's conversion of the Philippian jailer will later illustrate (see vv. 30-31). The term "Most High God" is also used in worship of Zeus, to whom her own handlers may be attached and she their "slave" as well.

547. Bruce, *The Acts of the Apostles,* 358-59.
548. See Spencer, *Acts,* 164-65, for details of their comparison.
549. See Johnson, *The Acts of the Apostles,* 297.

550. No husband is mentioned, which may indicate that she is a single (divorced, widowed) woman or, if married, that her husband is not a believer.
551. Witherington, *The Acts of the Apostles,* 491-92; however, see Spencer, *Acts,* 165, who follows Reimer's argument that Lydia's location within Philippian society is more marginal than most scholars assume. See I. Reimer's, *Women in the Acts of the Apostles: A Feminist Liberation Perspective* (Minneapolis: Fortress, 1995) 102-9.

Paul, of course, is "slave" to the Most High God of Israel (see 7:48), and his exorcism of the girl's spirit is a demonstration of God's authority over Zeus and all other pagan gods of the Philippian pantheon. This demonstration clears the way for a fuller expression of Paul's prophetic authority and gospel when he leads the jailer's household into the "way of salvation" (see 4:12; also 2:28; 9:2).

The species of the girl's unholy spirit is literally "a pythian spirit" and recalls the Greek Πυθῶν (*Pythōn*) myth of the dragon that guarded the Delphi oracle at Mt. Parnassus and was killed by Apollo. In Luke's day, its name and legend were attached to someone with clairvoyant powers or, perhaps, to the trickery of a ventriloquist.[552] The powers or trickery of this slave girl are apparently extraordinary or the Philippian public extremely gullible, since she "brought her owners a great deal of money by fortune-telling" (v. 16).

The formula Paul uses to expel the spirit from the slave girl recalls Peter's command for healing "in the name of Jesus Christ" (see 3:6, 16; 4:10). Then as here the prophet's use of "the name" to heal and make people whole again is not magical but confessional: Paul's rebuke of the spirit expresses his surety of God's triumph over evil. While an exercise of his spiritual authority, it is also symbolic of his kerygmatic claim that the risen Jesus is Messiah and Lord. This exorcism itself, then, aptly illustrates what Paul will later proclaim to the jailer, fulfilling the slave girl's own prophecy: The Most High God saves the lost.

16:19-23. The dispossession of "property" is an important literary theme in Acts, typically serving as a barometer of relations with God. Evident exploitation of another for profit is especially condemning, not only of the girl's owners but of the religious climate of Philippi that would support their religious profit-taking. The animus toward religious charlatans, especially those who exploited human "property" to satisfy their greed, is often expressed in Greco-Roman literature as well. The greedy owners' immediate response to the healing of their slave girl, then, is hardly happy: "They seized Paul and

Silas and dragged them into the marketplace before the authorities" (16:19). Their motive for doing so is clearly financial; they saw that their profits "went out with the demon"![553]

The juridical terms used by Luke in this passage indicate that a lawsuit is brought against Paul for this loss of income. The "marketplace" (ἀγορά *agora*) is the city's secular synagogue where people assemble to conduct various transactions, including legal ones. The greedy owners follow a precise protocol in bringing their claims to the court: They go first to the "authorities," who are responsible for public order, and turn Paul and Silas over to the local "magistrates," who are responsible for settling civil claims. Perhaps realizing that loss of income due to the loss of a pythian spirit would not work well in a public court, the clever owners bring a more mean-spirited yet appealing accusation before the magistrates in two parts: "They are Jews and are advocating customs that are not lawful for us" (16:20-21). The initial charge appeals to Roman anti-Semitism and is propagandistic without legal merit. The clear intent is to incite prejudice against Jews in a pagan marketplace, and it is this appeal that sparks the crowd's hostilities against Paul.

Their second charge appeals to the legal "principle of incompatibility" according to which it is considered unlawful within the premises of a Roman colony to proselytize converts to a non-Roman cult.[554] This charge is also without merit since by Paul's day the principle was no longer followed in legal practice. Further, there is every indication that Paul recruited converts *outside* the city limits at the place of prayer and therefore was not in violation of this law in any case—unless the slave girl's exorcism in Jesus' name is considered an act of proselytizing her.

It is significant that Paul's religious practices, which Luke carefully links to the place of prayer, are recognized as "Jewish" and in sharp contrast with the Roman customs of Philippi (v. 21). In fact, the mob reaction against Paul, obviously incited by their anti-Semitic sentiments, makes this point all the more clear. Once again Luke portrays Paul as an exemplar of James's primary concern

552. Barrett, *A Critical and Exegetical Commentary on the Acts of the Apostles*, 2:785; however, see Conzelmann, *The Acts of the Apostles*, 131.

553. Johnson, *The Acts of the Apostles*, 295.
554. Barrett, *A Critical and Exegetical Commentary on the Acts of the Apostles*, 2:790.

for Jewish purity on pagan turf; Paul has not contaminated himself by accommodating to Gentile forms of religious observance. Paul is no "gentilized" Jew (see 15:20-21).

There is no indication of a court verdict, unless the violent crowd is considered a jury of sorts and their attack on Paul and Silas constitutes an indictment of guilt. Without being granted any opportunity to defend their actions,[555] Paul and Silas are stripped and beaten with rods by the order of the court, the standard Roman legal procedure (v. 22). They are then thrown into prison and are securely guarded (v. 23). These injudicious actions, however, will come back to haunt the magistrates by story's end (see vv. 35-40).

16:24-34. The next scene introduces the city's jailer, who will play a complementary role to Lydia's in this drama. As its plotline unfolds he will personify the power of God's grace that Paul proclaims. He appears as a functionary of civil authority who "following these instructions" puts Paul and Silas in solitary confinement, their feet fastened "in the stocks" (v. 24). These images of harsh treatment and loneliness serve two purposes. They recall the Lord's prophecy that Paul would "suffer for the sake of my name" (9:16). Paul is imprisoned because he exorcized the girl's divining spirit "in the name of Jesus Christ" (see v. 18).

The jailer's actions also stage the miracle that follows: Surely there is no escape at "midnight" from "the innermost cell" when one's feet are "in the stocks."[556] The prison itself symbolizes a place where the cosmic and invisible battle between God and evil (or Zeus) is being waged. Paul and Silas are doing what exemplary believers must do when waiting for God to act: They are "praying and singing hymns to God" (v. 25; cf. 1:14). While observing their witness, the attention of their co-prisoners is directed to the source of liberating power; indeed, "that the other prisoners heard them proves—that the earthquake is God's answer."[557]

The earthquake strikes suddenly and opens the prison doors and unfastens the prisoners' chains (v. 26), but no one leaves.

Luke does not give the reason for this unexpected response to God's intervention; however, had Paul and Silas left no one would have prevented the jailer from taking his life. The earthquake has also awakened him, but why he should consider taking his life prior to a check of the innermost cell is the stuff of legend! Nor is it clear in any case why he should resort to such a dramatic solution to his problem, unless living is a fate worse than death (see 12:17).

More likely, the jailer's decision to take his own life is due to his religious conviction. Especially since earthquakes were thought to be acts of divine intervention, he may have thought it was an act of judgment from which his salvation is unlikely. The jailer's response to Paul's saving call makes perfect sense against this backdrop. Initially, he "fell down trembling [ἔντρομος *entromos*] before Paul and Silas" (v. 29; see also 10:25). This jailer is scared because he has "seen" his fate and it is not good. The question he poses of his prisoners, whom he now recognizes as agents of divine power, is utterly pragmatic: "Sirs, what must I do to be saved?" (v. 30). That is, he wants to know whether or not his life can be spared by Paul's God.

The jailer's story parallels Paul's own story, which is the subtext of the gospel he now presents: "Believe on the Lord Jesus, and you will be saved, you and your household" (v. 31; cf. 1 Tim 1:12-14). This firm connection of belief and salvation is central to Luke's account of Paul's gospel (see 14:9; 15:11; cf. Rom 10:9), and it provides a succinct formulation of the "way of salvation" called for by the slave girl's oracle (see 16:17). The repetition of "household" (οἶκος *oikos*) both in Paul's gospel presentation and then again in Luke's following summary (16:32) recalls the images of "re-housed" Israel from Amos's prophecy to remind the reader that God has granted Gentiles a share of Israel's blessings (see 15:13-19). What is different about this second conversion story in Philippi, and yet complementary to Lydia's, is that the jailer is not a God-fearer attached to a local synagogue; he is a pagan attached to the city prison, a symbol of opposition to the church's mission. The referent of Amos's prophecy concerning "all the Gentiles over whom my name has been called" (15:17) is thereby expanded to

---

555. This is no doubt the case because to this point Paul and Silas are unwelcome and Jewish "foreigners" without local rights. See Witherington, *The Acts of the Apostles*, 497.

556. Conzelmann, *The Acts of the Apostles*, 132.

557. Haenchen, *The Acts of the Apostles*, 497.

include even those pagan converts God calls out of spiritually desolate places that are full of evil spirits, moral rogues, and anti-Semitic sentiments.

First a woman, now a man, and the households of both evince the universal scope of God's saving work. As before in Lydia's case (see v. 15), confirmation of the jailer's salvation is demonstrated by his hospitality toward Paul and Silas. In this case, "he took them and washed their wounds . . . and brought them up into the house and set food before them" (vv. 33-34). With the festive meal, Luke adds that the "entire household rejoiced that he had become a believer in God." The combination of meal and joy strongly implies their celebration gathered around holy Eucharist, when Jesus' suffering is remembered as an act of redemption. The faithful reader likewise sees in Paul's suffering for the sake of Jesus' name a means of grace that brings the jailer and his family into the way of salvation.

16:35-40. The account of the jailer's salvation is sandwiched between episodes that tell of Paul and Silas's legal problems. The present passage continues from 16:23, describing events the morning after the great earthquake. Paul and Silas are back in jail. "The police" (οἱ ῥαβδοῦχοι *hoi rhabdouchoi*) are now involved as delegates of the court who carry messages from the magistrates to the jailer on prison-related matters. Their message in this case is highly compressed, since Luke is not interested in what prompts their decision to "let those men go" (v. 35)—even though we can imagine why.[558] Paul's response, however, reflects the honor/shame culture of his world. He does not want the magistrates to brush the crumbs of their shameful behavior under the carpet of public scrutiny, and so he lists the grievances that resulted in his humiliation: public flogging, condemnation, and incarceration of innocent Roman citizens, without benefit of trial or defense attorneys (16:37). Imprisoning and

flogging a Roman citizen without benefit of a trial is illegal; to do so publicly is a criminal act worthy of execution. No wonder the magistrates "were afraid when they heard that they were Roman citizens" (v. 38).

The stunning new piece of information that Paul and Silas are both Roman citizens requires a rereading of Acts in two important ways. If Paul's suffering is not due to political questions about his Roman citizenship, then it must be due to his religious identity. In this sense, the anti-Semitism of the slaveowners, motivated by greed, is true to public form. Beyond Palestine and the Jewish synagogues of Roman cities, Paul suffers for being Jewish. Moreover, Acts tells us what the Letters do not: Paul is a Roman citizen, with all the rights and privileges due him. Even though the interpreter may set aside the historicity of Luke's claim,[559] Paul's citizenship is an important, although typically ironic, feature of his apologia in Acts. In this regard, Paul's acceptance of Philippi's official apology (see v. 39) symbolizes his general attitude toward Rome in Acts. His point is that Rome is unable to subvert the work of God's salvation in the world; and even this great empire must come hat in hand to the prophets of the Most High God.

Paul and Silas depart the city only after having gone to Lydia's home to encourage "the brothers and sisters there" (v. 40). Luke's nice literary touch effectively encloses the narrative of the Philippian mission by mentioning hospitable Lydia's faithfulness to the Lord (see v. 15). The sequence of their departure from the city following their visit to the Christian congregation gathered in Lydia's home is deliberate and important—that is, her home lies *within* city limits. In absence of a quorum of male Jews to establish an urban synagogue (see vv. 13-14), believers now gather in the home of a God-fearing Gentile woman in witness to the gospel.

---

558. The Western version of Acts explains how the magistrates reconvened in the *agora* to reflect upon the previous evening's earthquake, determined it had something to do with Paul and Silas, and decided to release them to appease the gods.

559. For an evaluation of Paul's claim of Roman citizenship, see A. Sherwin-White, *The Roman Citizenship*, 2nd ed. (Oxford: Clarendon, 1973). See also Fitzmyer, *The Acts of the Apostles*, 144-45; Lüdemann, *Early Christianity According to the Traditions in Acts*, 240-41.

REFLECTIONS

1. "A certain woman named Lydia, a worshiper of God, was listening to us" (16:14*a*). Much has been written about Luke's view of women. Although largely oriented toward males (e.g., the prophets-like-Jesus of Acts are all males, with the possible exception of Priscilla and the daughters of Philip), Luke's narrative world is still a location where females are given greater prominence and independence in comparison to his social world. Lydia is a literary example of a theological conviction: God's saving grace dismantles various social barriers that cultivate strife between people. Mutuality is the watchword of a community of goods! Upon closer reflection, the case of Lydia is especially invigorating as an example of the church's counterculture. She makes her entrance into Acts as a religious person without permission of or reference to her husband. The first place mentioned is not her home but a "place of prayer," and when she does mention her home it is by self-reference: It is "my" home. The impression is given that she is self-sufficient, a successful businesswoman with a decent income whose hospitality demonstrates her fine character. In all these ways, Luke has Lydia play the role of an ideal convert. His depiction of the easy relations between a male religious leader and a female outsider symbolizes a counterculture that remains impressive even for our modern liberal democracies. Indeed, it is her home that becomes the spiritual center for the entire city, and the story's presumption is that she becomes its spiritual leader. Yet Luke's principal point is not sociological but theological: Lydia is saved because "the Lord opened her heart to listen eagerly" (16:14*b*). For all her evident social accomplishment, she had a spiritual need satisfied by hearing God's word.

2. "What must I do to be saved?" (16:30 NIV and NRSV). Luke's marvelous telling of the Philippian jailer's improbable conversion is useful for reflection on the nature of Christian conversion. Paul and Silas's worshipful response to their jailhouse suffering and their refusal to escape strikes most readers as odd if not humorous. These missionaries are incorrigible! But is not this Luke's point? Typically, conversions are the by-product of the trenchant faithfulness of others, when believers are ever alert to the need and prospect of salvation. The polyvalence of the jailer's cry for help is also instructive. Luke resists the divorce between bodily and religious species of salvation: The God who saves the jailer from the executioner's sword is the same God who forgives him and his household of their sins. In fact, conversion often occurs at the intersection of the two wants, when the need for healing or physical rescue occasions the need to hear the gospel appeal, "Believe on the Lord Jesus, and you will be saved" (16:31 NRSV). Note also that an extended protocol of conversion suggests a way of salvation beyond gospel preaching that includes Christian instruction (16:32), baptism (16:33), and caring fellowship (16:34). These are all sacraments of grace that initiate new believers more fully into their life with God.

3. "They were afraid when they heard that they were Roman citizens" (16:38 NRSV). For the first time Paul appeals to his Romans citizenship, and he does so strategically. In many ways the Paul of Acts personifies the church's sometimes messy but potentially useful relations with the secular state, and this story narrates a case in point. The reader should first ask why Paul delayed insisting on his rights as a Roman citizenship until *after* his experiences of police brutality and illegal incarceration? Paul's strategic acceptance of their apology (16:39) suggests a reversal of power that has become an important political matter only *after* the households of faith have been established in Philippi. The proper role of civil authority is not to dictate terms so that the church becomes yet another institution of its power. Rather civil authority is now obliged to safeguard the deposit of faith in their city as an institution of divine power (cf. Rom 13:1-7). Luke's portrait of Rome in Acts is of the *inability* of secular authority to subvert the work of God's salvation in the world.

ACTS 17:1-15, CONFLICT AND CONVERSION AMONG DIASPORA JEWS

COMMENTARY

Acts next follows Paul's travel itinerary along the Via Egnatia from Philippi to Thessalonica, the most important city of Macedonia. The related narratives of his mission there (17:1-9) and then down the road in Beroea (17:10-15) are shaped by a familiar pattern: Paul begins his crusade in the city's synagogue (17:1, 10b) where he worships according to Jewish "custom" on successive sabbaths (17:2) and expounds the Scriptures to those in attendance (17:2-3, 11). Even though some Jews are convinced by Paul's teaching and are converted (17:4, 12), his argument from Scripture that Jesus is the Messiah divides the house of Israel. Other Jews do not repent and turn against Paul and his converts (17:5-6a, 13), bringing legal action against them (17:6b-9). Although he enjoys success among devout Gentiles attached to the local synagogue (17:4), this hostile response forces Paul and Silas to leave town "immediately" for the next venue of ministry (17:10a, 14-15).

The specific charges leveled against Paul repeat in different circumstances what earlier had taken place in Philippi (see 16:19-23). The involvement of the Roman legal system in his destiny will be a featured narrative element during the second half of Acts. The accusations brought to the city officials of Thessalonica by Paul's Jewish opponents are similar to those brought earlier to Philippi's rulers and magistrates by his pagan opponents. In both cases, Paul is accused of disturbing the peace in a way that goes against Roman political conventions. It should not surprise us that Paul's Philippian opponents would appeal to Rome in a jingoistic idiom and with materialistic intent—they are pagans. That Paul's *Jewish* opponents would bring similar charges to civil authority, however, is surprising. Perhaps Luke considers this an instance of James's anxiety about the "gentilizing" of repentant Jews—but with irony, since his worries are realized in *unrepentant* Jews

whose legal maneuver evinces a thoroughly secular approach.

This story prepares the NT reader for the Thessalonian correspondence of the Pauline corpus that follows. On the one hand, "we find the highest degree of correspondence between Luke's narrative and the information given by Paul's letters."[560] Paul's sketch of his suffering and opposition in Thessalonica (1 Thess 2:1–3:2) follows the plotline of Luke's story. On the other hand, Luke's shaping of his story supports his own theological interests, which include not only the Jewish element of Paul's religious practices, his spiritual authority, and his mission, but also the character of the "devout Gentiles" attracted to Paul's preaching—in this case, prominent women. These are not unrelated to the themes of Paul's Thessalonians letters, especially their common concern that Paul's religious authority is deeply rooted in his heroic suffering. Further, the thematic connection between character and receptivity to the gospel, nicely illustrated in the story of Paul's Beroean mission (see 17:11), is envisaged in 1 Thessalonians, where Pauline paraenesis functions to describe a manner of life that both pleases God (cf. 1 Thess 4) and establishes a congregation firmly in the faith (cf. 1 Thess 3).

17:1-4. Amphipolis and Apollonia are cities along the main Roman road through the region, the Via Egnatia. Nothing more is said of them in Acts, which has led some scholars to speculate that Paul made no missionary effort in these cities, perhaps because they had no synagogue.[561] In any case, Paul no doubt had included Thessalonica in his itinerary because of its importance to the region, and he found "a synagogue of the Jews" there (17:1).

---

560. Johnson, *The Acts of the Apostles*, 308.
561. Cf. Barrett, *A Critical and Exegetical Commentary on the Acts of the Apostles*, 2:809.

An exemplar of repentant Israel, Paul "went in [the synagogue] on three sabbath days" (v. 2). His growing reputation among the Jewish communities in the diaspora is due to his authoritative Bible teaching. This feature of Paul's mission is nicely captured by this text, where he is said to perform a sequence of tasks apropos of a trained exegete of Scripture: "from the scriptures" (γραφαί *graphai*; see 1:16), he "argued" (διαλέγομαι *dialegomai*), "explained" (διανοίγω *dianoigō*), and "proved" (παρατίθημι *paratithēmi*). The first task should not be viewed as argumentative but as that of the scholar who carefully sifts textual evidence is mounting a persuasive case. The second task refers to the interpretive act of recovering Scripture's contemporary meaning for its present readers. In the gospel this same word is used of the Lord's instruction following his resurrection, when he "opened" their minds to the messianic meaning of Scripture (cf. Luke 24:32, 45). The final task envisages the interpreter as a host who sets the table in preparation for a common meal. Here, then, Paul gathers together the fruit of his study and research, together with appropriate illustrations, to feed his congregation the gospel truth that "it was necessary [δεῖ *dei*] for the Messiah to suffer and to rise from the dead" (v. 3). We can fill in the kerygmatic gaps from earlier speeches in Acts; and we know the theological import of *dei*, which claims that the gospel agrees with Scripture's script of God's salvation (see 1:16; 3:18; cf. 2:22-23). Even so, Fitzmyer's observation bears repeating: These notions of a suffering and resurrected Messiah (rather than Israel) are foreign to the "plain" teaching of the OT, and it is this radical cast of Paul's argument from Scripture that explains the conflict and controversy he provokes among Thessalonica's Jews.[562]

In any case, Paul's proclamation that the Jesus who suffered is the living Messiah "persuaded" (πείθω *peithō*; see 5:36-37; 13:43) a few Jews into the faith, and they "joined" (προσκληράομαι *prosklēraomai*; lit., "cast their lot with") the Christian mission in their city. Presumably these Jewish converts include Jason and those meeting in his house (see 17:6). In addition to these repentant Jews, characteristically mentioned first by Luke, are "a great many of the devout Greeks and not a few of the leading women" (17:4). Probably nothing is indicated by Luke's separation of "devout" Gentiles from the important women who also converted; they are all attached to the synagogue. The impression of Jewish influence in high places of Thessalonian culture now extends to Paul's mission (see 13:50).[563]

17:5-9. "The Jews" (see 12:3; 13:45; 14:2) who reacted against Paul's teaching ministry did so in disagreement with his messianic reading of Scripture (see above), not because of Paul's growing influence in the city's synagogue (v. 5*a*; see also 5:17; 13:45; cf. 7:9). They hired some "ruffians" to form a mob in the agora that would "set the city in an uproar" (v. 5*b*), which thereby allows them to falsely accuse Paul and Silas of "turning the world upside down" (v. 6). Paul's opponents routinely use this tactic, using the riot they instigate as evidence against the church's mission. In this case, Paul's opponents wanted to bring him and Silas before the δῆμος (*dēmos*, "citizens' assembly") but could not locate them; and so they took their mischief to "Jason's house" (v. 5*c*) and "dragged Jason and some believers" before the city authorities to accuse Jason of having "entertained them as guests" (v. 7*a*), thereby bringing the virtue of hospitality to trial.

The "city authorities" (πολιτάρχαι *politarchai*) are local magistrates who formed the city's administrative council and whose tasks are similar to those of the Philippian "magistrates" (see 16:20). One of their principal duties is to make certain that proper respect and due loyalty are given to Caesar. For this reason the only politically relevant accusation leveled against Paul and Silas is the third, which claims that they say that there is "another king named Jesus" (v. 7*b*)—high treason against the empire and disrespect toward Caesar. Such a charge foreshadows Paul's Roman trial, when he will be accused of sedition by reason of preaching the gospel that Jesus is the Messiah (see 24:5). The legal challenge before this court is not whether Paul preaches that Jesus is the Davidic

---

562. Fitzmyer, *The Acts of the Apostles*, 594.

563. In noting the contrasting responses between the "leading women" at Pisidian Antioch and here, Tannehill observes that Luke's literary tendency is to use common patterns in varying ways to give some sense of the varied results of Paul's mission. See Tannehill, *The Acts of the Apostles*, 2:208.

Messiah who rules as Lord over an invisible, cosmic kingdom; clearly he does (see 13:21-23; cf. Luke 1:33; 23:2-3). The relevant issue is whether Christian missionaries are free to do so in a secular empire where the only legitimate ruler is Caesar—a religious vigilance maintained under threat of social unrest (v. 5*a*).

Paul's Jewish opponents are disingenuous since their criticism of him is motivated by theological disagreement rather than political loyalty. For this reason, Rome does not take their court appearances and legal accusations seriously. More often than not, civic authority rightly recognizes this is a religious conflict and properly locates it within Jewish community. While the court is "thrown into turmoil" (v. 8),[564] it nevertheless releases Jason and the other believers in receipt of bail money (v. 9) and refuses to give in to the will of the mob.

17:10-12. Realizing the imminent danger to Paul and Silas in Thessalonica, the believers send them by night to Beroea, a major city about fifty miles southwest of Thessalonica in the foothills of the Olympian mountains and the regional center of the imperial religion (v. 10*a*). The narrative is compressed, and so nothing more is known of Paul's activities upon arrival; the plotline moves him quickly into the synagogue (v. 10*b*), where Paul finds Jews "of more noble character [εὐγενέστεροι *eugenesteroi*] than the Thessalonians" (v. 11). Luke's comparative judgment of character, perhaps grounded in local knowledge,[565] explains the Beroean's responsiveness to the gospel: They took to Paul's teaching "eagerly" and studied with him every day.

Paul's Bible study in Beroea is a function of his prophetic vocation and is realized in synagogue study that follows the same sequence of interpretive tasks as in Thessalonica with the same christological aim: to call Jews to repent and turn to Jesus as God's Messiah (see 17:2-3). The new word introduced here, ἀνακρίνω (*anakrinō*, "examine"), is a legal term used nowhere else in the NT for the study of Scripture. Luke uses it here for Paul's appeal to Israel's Scriptures as a legal "witness" to warrant his gospel's claims about Jesus. That is, his claims about Jesus are not the by-product of an imaginative reading of Scripture. Rather, they are judicious and give competent testimony by which a fair verdict may be rendered by his auditors; indeed, "many of them therefore believed" (v. 12).[566]

17:13-15. Perhaps for this reason, when "the Jews of Thessalonica" hear of Paul's success in Beroea, they arrive "to stir up and incite the crowds" (v. 13; see also vv. 5-9). Because the Thessalonian *politarchai* (or city authorities; see 17:6, 8) have no civic jurisdiction in Beroea, the Thessalonians cannot bring their legal brief with them; their mischief is localized and ad hoc. In fact, Luke mentions that Silas and Timothy remain in Beroea, perhaps because they are free to do so and the pastoral need there is great (v. 14).[567] Once again, however, Paul is scurried away in haste toward the coast for his safety (17:14) before being brought overland to Athens (17:15)—a journey of over two hundred miles from Beroea.

---

564. The NRSV's translation of ταράσσω (*tarassō*, "disturbed") fails to pick up its primary connotation of being confused by different reports, which is better captured by the NIV. See Fitzmyer, *The Acts of the Apostles*, 597.

565. So Witherington, *The Acts of the Apostles*, 509.

566. The Western text significantly modifies Luke's expansive description of both Jewish and women conversions: Some Jews "believed while others did not; and from the Greeks and people of high standing, many men and women became believers."

567. Lüdemann, *Early Christianity According to the Traditions in Acts*, 188, argues that Paul's reference to Timothy in 1 Thess 3:2 assumes that he becomes Paul's colleague during his Athenian mission and was only then sent back to Thessalonica before finally joining him in Corinth. Acts seems to place Timothy in Beroea/Thessalonica prior to Athens. For this reason, Lüdemann claims that Luke's information is inaccurate. More likely, as Barrett, *A Critical and Exegetical Commentary on the Acts of the Apostles*, 2:820, points out, Timothy has been a "silent partner" since Lystra (see 16:1-3) and only now is entrusted with an important task. For this reason, Johnson, *The Acts of the Apostles*, 308, concludes that "the narrative corresponds exceptionally well with the information contained in 1 Thess 3:1-2."

REFLECTIONS

1. Paul "argued with them from the scriptures, explaining and proving that it was necessary for the Messiah to suffer" (17:2-3*a* NRSV). Few passages in Acts so clearly express the importance of Scripture in Christian preaching. In Thessalonica on successive sabbaths Paul argued and explained and proved the core claims of his gospel from the Scriptures, while the Jews of Beroea "examined the scriptures every day" with him

(17:11). This pattern of proof from prophecy, which assumes that belief in Scripture's Messiah will lead the reasonable person to choose for Jesus, is a distinctive feature of Luke's apologia. Elsewhere in the New Testament, Scripture is merely cited as fulfilled by Jesus. According to Acts, however, Scripture supplies the working "script" that sets out the terms of God's salvation, which its inspired interpreters then relate logically both to Jesus and to their missionary experiences that are made necessary by divine ordination. In Luke's sense, biblical prophecy provides an authoritative context within which a messianic community gathers together to reflect on the redemptive importance of Jesus' death and resurrection. For the Jewish Paul of Acts, the Hebrew Bible is not some sacred text that can be bent at will but Israel's special witness to God's plan of salvation. That plan reaches its climax in the suffering and resurrection of Jesus (= the gospel) and continues to be disclosed in the church's mission (= Acts).

This story provides, however, two important qualifications to what has become for some believers the typical pattern of Christian apologetics—that is, the defense and/or proof of Christian belief. First, Paul's audiences in Thessalonica and Beroea consist of Bible-believing Jews. There are no pagans at his Bible studies. In this sense, then, his proof from prophecy arguments and the *theo*logic he presumes make sense only for those who agree that Scripture is the inspired medium of God's Word. For those who deny the authority of Scripture, Paul's argument that prophecy provides reason to believe that Jesus is the Messiah is without rational basis. Second, the response to Paul's apologia among Bible-believing Jews is mixed. That is, the controversy within the synagogue turned on competing conceptions of the "gospel" to which Scripture aims its interpreters. Not every religious person who accepts the authority of Scripture will interpret its theological meaning and practical relevance in the same way. The conflict between Paul and his opponents is not over his view or use of Scripture, which is thoroughly Jewish; rather, the unrepentant Jews who challenge Paul do so because they reject his belief that the risen Jesus is God's Messiah by whom God's biblical promises are approached and interpreted.

Believers are simply mistaken when they think that the contest for souls is settled by the battle for the Bible. Winning agreement over the precise terms of Scripture's authority is no guarantee for a right understanding of or a faithful response to gospel truth. While proof-from-prophecy provides an additional reason to consider the gospel message more carefully, it is finally the proclamation of the gospel and its embodiment in the community's life together that draw all people toward Christ in faith.

2. "The Bereans were of more noble character than the Thessalonians, for they received the message with great eagerness" (17:11 NIV). Is everyone who hears the gospel on equal footing to respond to its truth in faith? Evidently Luke would answer no. The inherent inequality between people, however, is not a matter of divine predestination according to which some are elect for salvation while others are not. Rather some are better able to receive the message of salvation with greater eagerness because of their more "noble character." This "nobility" is not a genetic disposition or an "accident of birth." But surely there are certain environments of family life, relationships, and even culture, as well as various personal habits of mind and heart, that nurture and shape the sort of person who is interested in the things of God. While salvation is surely the work of a faithful God in combination with an obedient church, every choice for Jesus is freely made by those who are moved to respond to the gospel. Luke's additional factor in this redemptive calculus is that some people are more responsive simply because of who they are.

ACTS 17:16-34, PAUL'S ATHENIAN MISSION

COMMENTARY

The conflict plotted by this story is immediately introduced upon Paul's arrival in Athens: He sees idols everywhere and is distressed (17:16). The plot thickens when Paul characteristically visits the city's synagogue and then also the *agora*, arguing with those he finds in both places (17:17). The philosophers among Paul's auditors in the *agora* fail to fully grasp what he proclaims to them and so they make two errors of judgment: They question his spiritual authority, calling him a "babbler," and they confuse the content of what he proclaims about Jesus and his resurrection (17:18). Their misunderstanding leads them to bring Paul to the Areopagus where he is asked by the city's intellectuals to explain his "new teaching" (17:19-21). Paul does so in a speech of uncommon power that both legitimizes his spiritual authority (17:22-23) and examines the claim that he teaches "foreign deities" (ξενία δαιμόνια *xenia daimonia*, 17:24-29), then he turns to his "new teaching" about Jesus and the resurrection (17:30-31). Characteristically, his call to conversion results in a divided house (17:32-34).

Fitzmyer and others claim that this is "the most important episode" of Luke's narrative of Paul's second mission.[568] The episode is important not because it evinces some missionary innovation or exposes a new angle of vision into Paul's message. In fact, Luke has already supplied a précis of Paul's important speech earlier at Lystra (see 14:15-17) and the pattern of Paul's missionary activity in Athens rings familiar.[569] The importance of this episode in Acts is rather due almost

entirely to the *city* Athens.[570] Although a bit tattered by comparison to the golden age of Pericles and Socrates, Athens was still a great university town and symbolized the "high culture" where important ideas have value and are carefully considered by the intellectually curious. It is here that the Paul of Acts delivers one of his three major missionary speeches and the only one to non-believers.

The theological subtext of Paul's "Mars Hill" apologia is his distress over the city's pervasive idolatry (cf. 17:16). Great learning has not eliminated false religion from Athens, but neither has the city's synagogue, which apparently exerts little influence on the beliefs of its citizens (cf. 17:17). In wider context, Paul's distress over idolatry recalls James's earlier admonition concerning Gentile converts "polluted by idols" as a potential source of confusion for repentant Jews in the diaspora (see 15:20). James was worried that the Pauline mission might accommodate the religious practices of pagan temples; the present passage expands this concern to include the thought and practice of an entire city, for Paul finds "the *city* was full of idols" (17:16, italics added). The emotional response to what he sees and the terms of his subsequent speech indicate agreement with James's exhortation, though on a grander scale.

The principal critical problem facing the interpreter is whether the portrayal of Paul's portrait and especially his speech as a philosopher-like-Socrates is Luke's invention, or whether Luke reliably preserves Paul's visit and speech in Athens. Those who argue that Luke has rendered an "authentic" Paul refer to 1 Thessalonians 3:1, where he mentions an Athenian visit. They then add that Paul does or says nothing in Athens that disagrees with anything he writes in his NT letters. In fact, the substance of his speech, if not its idiom, is

---

568. Fitzmyer, *The Acts of the Apostles*, 600, 613-17. The scholarly literature on this passage is voluminous and comes from biblical scholars and theologians, ancient and modern—probably more than on any other passage in Acts.

569. Tannehill, *The Acts of the Apostles*, 2:211-12, carefully relates the various bits and pieces of this story with other stories in Acts, showing they are all of a single textured cloth. In this light, Schubert claims that when considered along with all other missionary speeches in Acts, Paul's Areopagus speech is the final and climactic element in Luke's exposition of God's plan to save all humanity. "The Place of the Areopagus Speech in the Composition of Acts," in *Transitions in Biblical Scholarship*, ed. J. Rylaarsdam (Chicago: University of Chicago Press, 1968) 260-61. Similarly, Tannehill, *The Acts of the Apostles*, 2:215, considers the speech paradigmatic of the gospel's encounter with secular culture.

570. Athens was a "free city" located in Roman Achaia. Most of the great public buildings from its days as capital city of Grecian Attica were destroyed during the Persian wars (480s BCE), and its population had dwindled to between 5,000 and 10,000 when Paul visited. Although Haenchen says that Athens "lived on its great past," Cicero and other intellectuals of the day spoke well of Athens as a place of great learning, and this tradition seems to have been its essential cultural identity when Luke wrote Acts. See Haenchen, *The Acts of the Apostles*, 517.

confirmed in general terms by Romans 1:18-32 (cf. 1 Thess 1:9-10).[571] Further, his actions and speech seem to reflect a well practiced Jewish response to contemporary secular philosophy in the Diaspora.[572] If not an eyewitness to Paul's mission, Luke certainly draws upon reliable Pauline sources when shaping this story.[573]

While Paul's objection to idolatry and the theological conception of his speech in Athens are consistent with Pauline tradition found in the letters, the critic must still respond to the question whether the historical Paul would be drawn into an intellectual sparring match with Athenian philosophers. Most scholars say probably not. Paul seemed to have little use for such discussions, nor were "such negative themes the basis and prime content of his message."[574] Moreover, the apocalyptic cast of his missionary message in the letters shapes an ecclesiology that did not compel him to spend his time in becoming "relevant" to the surrounding culture. This passage is rather an expression of Luke's authorial intentions; it reflects the narrator's "idealized version of what ought to have happened, so marvelously wrought that for its readers it provides the emblem of what possibly could happen."[575]

17:16-17. Upon arriving in Athens, Paul is "deeply distressed to see that the city was full of idols." Although these "idols" were often valued as great works of art, Paul's response to them is one of Jewish outrage. "Deeply" translates the phrase τὸ πνεῦμα αὐτοῦ ἐν αὐτῷ (*to pneuma autou en autō* lit., "his spirit within him") and refers to his inner life—his mind and soul. Evidently what is shocking to Paul is the sheer number of idols he finds in Athens. The word translated "full of idols" (κατείδωλος *kateidōlos*) is found only here in the NT and conjures up the image of a forest of idols. Although Athens has a Jewish synagogue, we infer that the misunderstanding of

Paul's proclamation of Jesus in the *agora* (see 17:18) is due to an ignorance of Jewish history and religion, which have proved unimpressive to the citizens.

Following his missionary pattern, Paul "argues [διαλέγομαι *dialegomai*] in the synagogue with the Jews and the devout persons" (17:17; see 17:2, 10). In this cultural setting, Luke's word-choice "to argue" is strategic, recalling the memory of Socrates who often engaged ordinary citizens in the marketplace (*agora*) in philosophical debate. Earlier accounts of Paul's synagogal arguments allow the reader to fill in the gaps of this text; the assumption is that his arguments with Jews in the synagogue now spill over into the marketplace. Paul thereby performs the role of Socrates in this story, even though public debate with "those who happened by" has been a feature of his European mission since Philippi (see 16:19).

17:18. Among those in the *agora* are "Epicurean and Stoic philosophers" who debated [συμβάλλω *symballō*] with him. The style of discourse is indicated by Luke's choice of *symballō*, a favorite term of his, which denotes a collegial exchange toward a constructive end (see 4:15; 18:27; 20:14; cf. Luke 2:19; 14:31). The impression made, then, is that Paul is engaged in an honest, not hostile exchange with his "scholarly peers." They include members of divergent schools of thought, although both were interested in practical rather than theoretical discourse—the rhetorical bent of Luke's missionary Paul as well. In any case, their practical orientation toward intellectual discourse would certainly have included religion and in ways reflected in Paul's later speech to them. For example, Epicureans were materialists and believed that human life exists by natural chance. Avoidance of pain and suffering is the true aim of this life and not religious devotion, since a personal, provident god—a god who could make a practical difference in the outcome of a happy life—simply does not exist. Significantly, Epicureans were harsh critics of idolatry as well; their primary criticism of Athenian folk religion was that offering sacrifice to gods who are neither personal nor provident may be "religious" but it is also non-rational: Impersonal deities cannot produce personal happiness. Stoics, on the other

571. Cf. Dunn, *The Acts of the Apostles*, 231-32; Witherington, *The Acts of the Apostles*, 425-26; Porter, *The Paul of Acts*, 141-49. Cf. Maddox, *The Purpose of Luke-Acts*, 83-84, who rightly cautions against a facile analysis of Rom 1:18-32 and Paul's Areopagus speech.

572. Haenchen, *The Acts of the Apostles*, 522-23.

573. Dibelius's famous verdict that this speech "is absolutely foreign to Paul's theology" has been overturned by recent scholarship, but it still influences current discussion of Luke's Pauline sources. See Dibelius, "The Speeches in Acts and Ancient Historiography," 71-72.

574. Barrett, *A Critical and Exegetical Commentary on the Acts of the Apostles*, 2:826.

575. Cf. Johnson, *The Acts of the Apostles*, 318-19.

hand, were hard rationalists, guided by their analytical observations and careful reasoning. They sought to live in harmony with the cosmos. Stoics believed in the solidarity of the human race and in a deity in whom "we live and move and have our being" (17:28), because, conversely, the deity is in all things, not transcendent, as is the Most High God.

The initial impression made on the audience overhearing their debate on "practical reason" is that Paul's proclamation of the risen Jesus is ill-conceived and intellectually impoverished—he is a "babbler" (σπερμόλογος *spermologos*; lit., "seed picker") of old ideas that are no longer relevant or important. This mocking term challenges Paul's spiritual authority to contend for a superior account of practical divinity.

The second and quite different challenge is that Paul lobbies for "foreign deities" (*xenia daimonia*; see 16:21).[576] The earlier allusion to Socrates as a public philosopher is now made clear by Luke: Like Socrates, Paul is charged with propagating strange gods in Athens. Johnson argues that the allusion to Socrates is especially strategic since his response to his accusers was widely recognized by contemporary philosophers as "the model for philosophical integrity."[577] In any case, Paul is a philosopher-like-Socrates who contends that Jesus is Messiah.

17:19-21. Paul's place in the marketplace of ideas has been challenged in the two ways most damning of the ancient philosopher: he is an incompetent "seed-picker" who traffics in strange religion. The best place to respond to such an accusation is the Areopagus of Athens, and that is where Paul is taken. The meaning of ἐπιλαμβάνομαι *epilambanomai* ("took"), however, is ambiguous: It can mean either "to arrest" (to take into police custody) or "to accompany" (to take along with) to the "Areopagus" (lit., "Mars" Hill).[578] Whether his speech there should read as a legal defense, a scholarly discussion, or something

of both largely depends on how one understands "the Aeropagus" (17:22).

The "Areopagus" (ὁ Ἄρειος Πάγος *ho areios pagos*) is the name given to an elevated, open-air site just to the west of the acropolis in Athens. The Areopagus also denotes the equivalent of a city assembly or council that would hear public debates and render verdicts. In this sense the Areopagus enjoys a role and authority similar to all the other councils of Acts. In this light, then, Paul may well have been taken into custody to determine whether he has sufficient "intellectual" authority to bring his "strange teaching" into Athens.

His prosecutors and judges in this case are more intellectually curious than hostile.[579] The charges against Paul are restated with more civility than before and appear to reflect keen interest in learning something new from Paul: "May we know what this new teaching is that you are presenting?" (17:19). The potentially dangerous charge of teaching "foreign deities" has been dropped and replaced by the famous Athenian curiosity in the latest fad (τι καινότερον *ti kainoteron*; lit., something new," 17:21). While their interest in Paul's message is promising, the council's disappointing response to his speech (see 17:32-34) reflects the narrator's irony. Luke's parenthetical comment about Athenian curiosity suggests that it both occasions Paul's speech and explains why his call to conversion is then rejected: The curious might find a definitive claim for ultimate truth unsettling.

17:22-31. The broad structure and content of Paul's Areopagus speech are similar to what is heard earlier at Lystra, where he championed "the living God who made the heaven, the earth and sea and all that is in them" and asserted its predicate "that you should turn from these worthless things to the living God" (14:15). But we are in Athens, not Lystra; and here before the Areopagus, Paul is asked to defend this new religion he is proclaiming throughout the city.

R. Garland recently has demonstrated that three claims were necessary to establish a new religion in Athens: (1) the sponsor must claim to represent a deity; (2) he must

---

576. R. Bultmann argued that upon first hearing Paul's proclamation, the Athenians mistook his claim of "resurrection" as a female fertility goddess (the Greek word for resurrection is the feminine noun, *anastasis*) paired with his male god, "Jesus"—hence the plural, "foreign deities," refers to "Jesus and Anastasis." See R. Bultmann, *Theology of the New Testament,* trans. K. Grobel (London: SCM 1952) 1:77. See also Tannehill, *The Acts of the Apostles,* 2:214. Paul's speech, then, is occasioned by a theological mistake.

577. Johnson, *The Acts of the Apostles,* 313.

578. Ares is the Greek god of war usually referred to by his Latinized name, Mars.

579. This explains in part why Soards refers to the rhetorical situation of Paul's speech as "judicial" while Paul's rhetorical motive is "deliberative." See Soards, *The Speeches in Acts,* 96.

provide evidence that this deity is eager to reside in Athens; and (3) the deity's residence in Athens must benefit Athenians as a mark of its goodwill.[580] In this light, Paul's Areopagus speech may be read as an *apologia* (however subversive!) in response to these three criteria.[581] Accordingly, Paul introduces himself as an authorized herald (22-23) of a living deity whose transcendent residence above the earth requires no Athenian residence, priesthood or religious practices (24-29). Paul's deity does not therefore seek formal induction into the Athenian Pantheon—of this the Areogapus need not worry; rather, his God seeks to judge and save all repentant Athenians as disclosed in the Lord's resurrection—and of this they need worry (30-31)!

17:22-23. Characteristically Luke cues the speech by dramatic gesture: "Paul stood in front of the Areopagus" and addressed his auditors directly by name, "Athenians." Paul clarifies his motive by responding to the earlier charge that he is a "seed picker" (*spermologos*)—a babbler of secondhand ideas and therefore without scholarly credentials in the scholar's *agora* where Socrates once taught. The scholar's most important talent is the capacity to make careful observations. Paul's first words intend to cultivate the impression that he is a skilled practitioner of the scholar's trade who "went through the city" and "looked carefully at objects of your worship," concluding that the Athenians are "extremely religious [δεισιδαιμονέστερος *deisidaimonesteros*] in every way." The superlative *deisidaimonesteros* could mean that they are very superstitious or, more likely, that they are keenly pious—a characteristic of the educated person in the ancient world. Paul's opening words thereby intend to elicit a positive impression (rhetoricians regarded such an opening of a discourse as the *captitio benevolentiae*). They also help to cue his religious motive: He intends to address them as a religious audience in a religious idiom about religious matters in anticipation of a religious response (i.e., conversion). While doing so he challenges the perception that he lacks the scholar's talent, which would disqualify him from the marketplace of important ideas.

Paul is also accused of being "a proclaimer [καταγγελεύς *katangeleus*] of foreign divinities" (17:18)—or as the council more politely rephrases it, for presenting a "new teaching" that "sounds strange to us" (17:19-20). In reporting his most important observation from his tour of Athens, Paul notes an altar's inscription "To an unknown God" Ἄγνωστος Θεός *Agnōstos Theos*). Paul is being ironical by providing evidence of his audience's superlative piety: You are so religious that you even worship gods you do not know! Paul's implied point is made clear by his subsequent claim that they live during "times of human ignorance" (see 17:30) when what is unknown about god is the hallmark of the intellectual's religious devotion. With this stunning observation of the non-rational cast of Athenian religion, Paul has positioned himself to declare boldly the purpose of his speech (and mission) before the Areopagus: This God whom you worship in ignorance, "I proclaim [*katangellō*] to you."

While his Athenian auditors could not have known the powerful resonance of Paul's assertion, readers of Acts will detect in his use of *katangellō* a richly textured meaning. This verb is repeatedly used for the church's prophetic witness, when the good news is proclaimed for conversion (see 3:24; 4:2; 13:5, 38; 15:36; 16:17; 17:3). In the guise of a philosopher-like-Socrates, Paul discloses his true vocation as a prophet-like-Jesus;[582] and as such a prophet he defends his spiritual authority as the inspired medium of God's word, which exposes the ignorance of these learned people and bids them to repent and turn to the one true God for salvation.

17:24-25. Paul begins the main body of his speech with a series of theologically dense statements. Most scholars detect a prophet's *theo*logic in his sequence, not unlike a Jewish confession of faith in the idiom of Greek philosophy. Axiomatic and essential to this logic is that God is one God: Paul's God is "the God" (ὁ θεός *ho theos*, 17:24), the definitive divinity, and is neither dependent upon another nor is divided by another. God does not depend upon Paul's claim that God has

580. R. Garland, *Introducing New Gods: The Politics of Athenian Religion* (London: Duckworth, 1992) 18-19.

581. Cf. B. Winter, "On Introducing Gods to Athens: An Alternative Reading of Acts 17:18-20," *TynBull* 47.1 (1996) 71-90, esp. 84-87.

582. Haenchen, *The Acts of the Apostles*, 521, notes that Paul's declaration of his intention shows that he introduces no new god but rather discloses one already known as "unknown," thereby distinguishing himself from Socrates, who was accused of introducing brand-new gods into Athens' religious culture.

a "right" to exist in Athens. God is God and transcends such requirements.

It follows that God "made the world [κόσμος *kosmos*] and everything in it" (17:24a; see 4:24; 14:15; cf. Isa 42:5; Gen 1:1-23; Exod 20:11) without aid of another and is therefore "Lord of heaven and earth" (17:24b; cf. Luke 10:21). These first two assertions are logically related since the Creator God justifiably takes responsibility for what is created—a conclusion that appeals to the Stoics, whose belief in humanity's solidarity is predicated on a God who is the source for all of life (see 17:18). The deduction that Paul draws from this formulation of divine sovereignty is that no creature of the natural *kosmos* is capable of domesticating the Creator. This is, after all, a God who "does not live in shrines made by human hands" (17:24c)—the very point Stephen made about the Jerusalem Temple (see 7:48; cf. Isa 57:15-16). What is true for the Jews of Jerusalem is true for the intellectuals of Athens! Nor does God require the worshiper's religious gifts "as though [God] needed anything" (17:25a; cf. Amos 5:12-23)—a conclusion that appeals to the Epicureans, whose functional atheism is predicated on a belief that such a God would need nothing from anyone (see 17:18). God is rather a gracious Benefactor who "gives to all mortals life and breath and all things" (17:25b; cf. Isa 42:5; Gen 2:7). This same assessment of God's goodness is envisaged in Peter's earlier theological assertion that Israel's God, the only God, freely dispenses the gifts of salvation to all who repent and believe without prejudice (see 10:34).

17:26-28a. On the foundation of these more general claims of God's benevolent lordship over all things, Paul narrows his focus to God's relations with human creation to make his most dramatic theological assertions. Even as Paul contends that from one God everything derives, so now he argues that from one human stock (i.e., Eve/Adam) many races/nations descend "to inhabit the whole earth" (17:26; cf. Gen 1:24-25; Rom 5:12-14). This pairing of one God with one species implies that the "many" who physically descend from common parents (some manuscripts read "from one blood") share an inherent religious sensibility, whether this God is recognized or not.[583] The

initial implication Paul draws from his argument is that God allots "the times . . . and the boundaries" that circumscribe human existence (17:26). While Paul's comment is laden with contemporary philosophical and theological speculation, the point he makes is practical and straightforward: God who makes human life has a plan for it. He would be accused of muddled thinking to contend that a provident Lord who takes great care in making and sustaining human creation, then would abandon us to find our own way in a *kosmos* without coherent pattern or purpose (see 14:16-17).[584]

In this regard, the second implication Paul draws is axiomatic of biblical faith: God's intent for ordering human life with purpose and precision is "so that humans would search for God and perhaps grope for him and find him" (17:27a). God creates an environment that allows close participation with humanity in their history so that God "is not far from each one of us" (17:27b; cf. Rom 10:8; Ps 145:18). In setting forth this theological claim, Paul prepares the audience for his ultimate move to Christian proclamation, where he will proclaim that the Creator God makes just such a world to deliver them all from divine judgment.

Paul's appeal to appropriate evidence is central to all speeches in Acts. For this audience of learned non-believers, Paul draws upon Greek poetry to confirm his theological point: "In him [ἐν αὐτῷ *en autō*] we live and move and have our being" (17:28a; cf. Titus 1:12).[585] Although the Stoics in his audience may well have taken this poetic source as confirmation of their pantheism that God is near us because we are in him, the Paul of Acts almost certainly would have understood *en autō* as instrumental: Human existence depends upon God, "*by whom* we live and move and have our being."[586]

---

583. Cf. Fitzmyer, *The Acts of the Apostles*, 609 for a discussion of the difficult syntax and various translations of the awkward phrase that "From one [ancestor] God made all nations to inhabit the whole earth." He translates the phrase, "From one [stock] God made the whole human race inhabit the whole earth."

584. Conzelmann, *The Acts of the Apostles*, 142-44.

585. The anonymous citation of sources is a convention of ancient rhetoric, whether of secular poets or biblical prophets. The audience would almost certainly know their identity and recognize the authority of their words. Although a growing number of scholars think that Luke composed the first poetic citation, most scholars believe that it comes from a Stoic philosopher. There is a consensus from Clement forward that the second citation is from the Stoic philosopher Aratus, c. 310 BCE, *Phenomena* 5.

586. So Johnson, *The Acts of the Apostles*, 316; Witherington, *The Acts of the Apostles*, 529; cf. K. Lake and H. J. Cadbury, *The Acts of the Apostles*, vol. 4 of The Beginnings of Christianity, ed. F. J. Foakes Jackson and K. Lake (Grand Rapids: Baker, 1979).

17:28b-29. Paul's second citation from a philosopher-poet uses "offspring," a term whose meaning he exploits: "Since we are God's *offspring*, we ought not to think that the deity is . . . an image formed by the art and imagination of mortals" (17:29). In its wider narrative setting, Paul's commentary on Athenian idolatry adds a layer of meaning to James's earlier condemnation of the "pollutions of idols" as an expression of his principal concern to preserve the church's Jewish identity (see 15:20). At the same time, it prepares the reader for Luke's forthcoming account of Demetrius's polemic against Paul during his Ephesian campaign (cf. 19:23-27). Paul's contribution to both episodes is to expose the faulty logic of religious devotion whose chief symbols—shrines, idols, foods offered to gods, pagan rituals—are inconsistent to the inherent character of God's relations with humankind. God must be worshiped in accordance with who God is; and religious practices must reflect humanity's kinship with God. The substitution of inanimate materials for a God who is transcendent and animate makes no sense.

17:30-31. In a sharply stated conclusion Paul wonderfully captures the essence of the biblical conception of a God who is at once transcendent yet personal, sovereign and fully engaged in human life. He thereby exposes the logical flaw of Athenian religion, suggesting that the inward distress he experienced when observing the pervasiveness of Athenian idolatry was both spiritual and intellectual in origin. Idolatry evinces "times of human ignorance [ἄγνοια *agnoia*]," recalling Peter's criticism of pious Jews whose continued "ignorance" (*agnoia*; see 3:17) about Jesus subverted the prospect of their repentance for the forgiveness of sins and participation in Israel's "times of refreshing" (3:19). Paul tells his audience, much like Peter before him, that a benevolent God "overlooks" ignorance and has brought a prophet to them with the word of God (17:30; see 3:17). The theological subtext of Peter's earlier warning, however, is God's faithfulness to the promise of Israel's restoration, whereas the subtext of Paul's speech is the universality of God's salvation. The terms used in his missionary appeal——"times of ignorance," "repent," "day of judgment"—are glossed by

this universality to include those of the Athenian Areopagus. When the similar appeals of Peter and Paul are combined, one arrives at a theological conception not unlike Paul's argument in Romans 1:18–3:26 for the universal need of salvation and a Savior. To this the Paul of Acts may well add that the ultimate reason any person—whether religious Jew or secular intellectual—fails to repent and turn to God in faith is attachment to cultural idols and an ignorance of God's gospel.

The warrant for turning to God and away from idolatry is that God "will have the world [οἰκουμένη *oikoumenē*] judged in righteousness" (17:31; cf. Amos 5:18; Pss 9:8; 67:4; 96:13; 99:9). Paul's turn to the future is yet another feature of his gospel appeal that follows the deep logic of Peter's second missionary speech (see 3:17-26). Paul's emphasis, however, is on universal judgment rather than "the time of universal restoration" (see 3:21). Envisaged by both prophetic speeches is universality concentrated on the Lord's return both to judge (= purify) and to restore the *oikoumenē*—the inhabited world (see 11:28; 17:6; cf. Luke 21:26). The righteousness of this judgment implies that the criterion used will be fairly employed and there will be no need for an Areopagus to intervene on the final "day of judgment" to render a verdict about the fairness, legitimacy, or authority of God's judgment about people.

What is left unstated is the content of that eschatological criterion by which a "righteous" or evenhanded verdict will be rendered. The reader of Acts will draw the unstated implication from the exhortation to repent that the criterion is whether people repent of the "pollutions of idols" and turn to the living God in faith. Paul is more interested to press for the urgency of the matter. This day of universal judgment (and restoration, 3:21) is assured by the resurrection of "a man whom God has appointed" (i.e., Messiah; see 2:22-24, 36).

17:32-34. The response to Paul's exhortation to repent on the basis of the resurrection is mixed, as the reader of Acts would expect. Clearly the resurrection remains a "strange teaching" to the Athenian scoffers (17:32*a*), even though now wrapped up in a robust common ground of theological and philosophical ideas. That these ideas are generally accepted and found stimulating may well be indicated by the response of others who say, " 'We will hear you again about this' " (17:32*b*). Significantly, Paul is not mocked nor disabused of his authority to argue his case; even though the response is not great, he "left them" a free man (17:33). Luke notes two converts:

Dionysius, a member of the Areopagus, and Damaris. Although this mission report shows only modest gains, Luke wants to assure the reader that the foundations for an Athenian parish are of highest quality.[587]

587. The Western version of Acts adds that Damaris is a "respected" woman, which implies her social prominence.

REFLECTIONS

1. "What does this babbler want to say?" (17:18 NRSV). Luke's story re-imagines Paul for a "post-Pauline" venue, where his letters are read in response to a similar "culture war" in which the gospel is challenged by cities "full of idols" and where the church is asked to respond to the important questions of secular intellectuals. In this regard, we should take care to consider the continuing relevance of the initial objections to Paul's proclamation of Jesus and the resurrection. The first objection questions his spiritual authority in the Athenian marketplace: he is only a "babbler" of secondhand religious propaganda. Paul's response lays claim to the prophet's inspired powers to "see" and to "proclaim" God's truth (see 17:22*b*-23). It is on this basis that the church reads his letters with confidence that their teaching carries sufficient intellectual insight to engage the thinking public.

The skeptics also question whether he teaches "foreign deities," which contain irrelevant or incomprehensible subject matter. His speech makes clear that belief in his God is reasonable and practical, while exposing the fraud of a society's idols. Confident that Paul's judgment extends to his letters, their reader approaches these writings as sacred witness to a God who is neither "foreign" to outsiders nor tolerant of their various idolatries. Simply put, Paul's Mars Hill speech in Acts reminds students of his NT letters that the church intends their teaching to have universal appeal. Luke does not "invent" this encounter between Paul and the secular intellectuals of his day; he composes a story that is faithful to both Athenian secular culture and to Pauline tradition. For this reason his story has paradigmatic value for the church's continuing teaching of the Pauline letters.

2. "So that they would search for God and perhaps grope for him and find him" (17:27 NRSV). Does Paul's speech to the Athenians offer contemporary readers a model for engaging the secular intellectuals of our day? Many think so. While different language and ideas are required to contemporize Paul's message, his core ideas about religious culture and God remain relevant and important. This prospect challenges two assumptions still prevalent about the gospel. On the one hand, by playing the role of Socrates in a university town Paul challenges the anti-intellectualism among believers today who are deeply suspicious of secular "learning." On the other hand, believers should not be intimidated by those pundits who characterize the Christian gospel as unintelligible superstition or as an equal among many religious options. Especially in our day when ideologies once considered on the margins for lack of evidence and common sense have become mainstream, the gospel thoughtfully presented has never sounded more attractive to those earnestly searching for ultimate answers.

The rhetorical design of Paul's speech is noteworthy because of its comprehensiveness and internal coherence. Each statement by turns calls his auditors for a conversion of sorts; and every "small" conversion leads them step-by-step toward the risen Christ. Paul's opening observations about idolatry call for an admission that even pagans seek spiritual satisfaction, although "groping" in ignorance. While we should admit that some skeptics reject out of hand the very idea of a spiritual reality, most do give expression to their spiritual yearning by their adherence to the values and core convictions of one or another "ism"—scientism, materialism, individualism, nationalism, naturalism, humanism, and so on. A commitment to any of these worldviews shapes loyalties and informs decisions. Following Paul's pattern, then, the initial moment in conversion is a people's recognition that they order their lives according to some ultimate loyalty, staking their futures on something or someone in which they believe. In this sense, all people are religious. Such an agreement about religious pluralism marks the beginning point of a conversation that narrows the choices to Christ.

Admission of God's knowability comes next, followed by a robust summary of what then can be known about God: God is Creator, Sustainer, Sovereign, Benefactor, Judge. We should also take note that while Paul does not cite Scripture and uses language suitable for this academic setting and secular audience, the content of his theological summary is thoroughly biblical. True to the core biblical idea, then, God is transcendent yet personal, vastly superior to some detached deity that consigns humankind to the vicissitudes of fortune. God is not some provincial deity, the God of a few; nor is God unmoved and unconcerned about the struggles of real people in particular places. God is truly worthy of worship.

Yet Paul regards philosophical speculation as the means to a missionary end. Although the church cannot preach the risen Jesus without a comprehensive profile of the biblical God persuasively presented, neither can the church be content to construct new and more relevant models of God for popular consumption without also calling for repentance and faith in Christ. Thus, Paul's speech concludes with a call to repentance that is predicated on the meaning of Christ's resurrection, God's ultimate judgment of sin and death.

To agree with this concluding claim is not a matter of theological proofs but of personal faith. Even those who may have agreed with everything Paul has said to this point about God will find a final decision in favor of his gospel profoundly difficult to make. Those Athenians who scornfully interrupt Paul at the very moment he turns his speech toward the resurrection of Jesus and God's coming triumph are indicative of the scandal of faith (cf. 1 Cor 1:18-25). I doubt that the real difficulty with the gospel is finally one of knowledge: there is no lack of evidence or intellectual integrity in Paul's presentation. The problem provoked by Paul's appeal to the resurrection is a more practical one, since it calls for a complete reordering of what one thinks and how one lives. The confession that the living Jesus is the only Messiah and the one Lord (see 2:36) means that all other competing loyalties and practices must be set aside in order to begin a new life with him. Most in Athens are unable to do this, and secular intellectuals today face a similar challenge when they encounter the gospel.

ACTS 18:1-17, PAUL'S CORINTHIAN MISSION

COMMENTARY

In shaping his account of Paul's mission to Corinth,[588] Luke provides several new details of the everyday conditions of the missionary's life. For example, we find out that Paul works by day in the leather shop of Priscilla and Aquila to sustain himself financially (18:2-3).

---

588. The city of Corinth is fifty miles west of Athens and is its rival in reputation. While not Athens's equal as a cultural center, ancient Corinth was the capital city of Roman Achaia and a leading commercial center overlooking two ports, which allowed for easy access to the Aegean and Ionian seas and beyond. The many important civic and religious buildings surrounding the city's *agora* were known throughout the world, as was the city's reputation for sexual perversion. Ancient Corinth (or Roman "Neocorinth") is an important archaeological site today. The literature that describes various archaeological expeditions is extensive; for bibliography and abstract of these findings, see Fitzmyer, *The Acts of the Apostles*, 623-24, 631-32.

While Paul's mission is still centered in the city's Jewish synagogue where he teaches, there is indication of a transition to another venue—namely, a "household" of Gentiles attached to the synagogue (18:4-8). Paul's previous visits to important European cities were short term, due either to political pressure or lack of success. He spends a longer period of time in Corinth to establish a congregation of believers there (18:11). Earlier hints of Rome's benign attitude toward Paul's mission are realized in Corinth as Achaia's proconsul Gallio intervenes to rule that Paul's message and church planting activity falls within Judaism's protected boundaries. Thus, the conflict between him and unrepentant Jews is a Jewish and not a Roman affair (18:12-17).

Paul's Corinthian mission, however, is carefully circumscribed by familiar patterns found elsewhere in Acts. He continues his sabbath routine of worshiping in the city synagogue where he argues that Jesus is Messiah (18:4). He faces Jewish resistance to his message there (18:5-6a) but still enjoys modest success among other Jews (18:8) as well as with God-fearing Gentiles attached to the synagogue (18:6b-7). There is no mission in Acts without suffering (18:9), nor one that is not superintended by a provident Sovereign (18:10).

The disassociation of Paul's mission from the Jewish synagogue and its new association with "the house [οἰχία *oikia*] of a man named Titius Justus, a worshiper of God" (18:7) once again echoes the Amos prophecy of a "re-housed" Israel and its interpretation by James (see 15:16-21). The passing reference to Paul's trade as a "tentmaker" (σκηνοποιός *skēnopoios*; 18:3) may well echo Amos's critical catchphrase of Israel's restoration, "the tent (*skēnē*) of David" (see 15:16), since it is Paul the tentmaker who best personifies the restored Israel's vocation as a "light to the nations." In particular, however, these intratextual echoes recall James's understanding of the real theological crisis provoked by Paul's mission, which is not the Judaizing of repentant Gentiles but the "gentilizing" of repentant Jews in the Diaspora synagogues (see 15:19-21, 28-29).

In this regard, the present story alerts the reader to the deepening rift between Paul and his Jewish opponents who sharply disagree with his *Christian* proclamation that Jesus is Messiah. Gallio's benign neutrality makes him the perfect referee of this conflict, for it is really an intramural debate between religious Jews over a messianic interpretation of Israel's Scriptures. Paul's departure from the synagogue for Titius's house may well indicate something of a solution in maintaining the fragile accommodation of his Christian beliefs with his Jewish practices, which is the hallmark of his mission in Acts (cf. 1 Cor 9:16-23). Indeed, the participants in this new house congregation—Paul, Silas, Timothy, Priscilla and Aquila (cf. 1 Cor 16:19), Titius, Crispus (cf. 1 Cor 1:14), Sosthenes (cf. 1 Cor 1:1)—are all former members of the Corinthian synagogue who follow Paul's example and would presumably want to preserve Jewish traditions in this new setting. Reading the text by the light of the Jerusalem Council adds an additional layer of meaning to this movement: Leaving the synagogue may afford the best chance of preserving what is Jewish for the future church.

Finally, this story provides a canonical context for studying Paul's Corinthian letters. On the face of it, it lacks mention of several important themes found in the letters; this is perhaps due to the generic differences between Luke's narrative and Pauline letters that are written as rejoinders to the practical problems of a divided church more pagan than Jewish in religious background. A number of these problems result from the socioeconomic diversity within an urban church that made creating Christian solidarity in witness and fellowship difficult. Moreover, Paul's defense of his religious authority weaves together his apostolic office, charismatic power, and exemplary persona into a seamless whole, whereas the authority of the Paul of Acts derives from his prophetic vocation. Nevertheless, this account of his founding of the Corinthian church in Acts prepares the reader of 1–2 Corinthians by providing the following important impressions of his work there.[589]

(1) The present passage narrates the origins of Corinthian Christianity and adds details to Paul's own more allusive account

---

589. Johnson, *The Acts of the Apostles*, 324, contends that the agreements between Acts and the Corinthian correspondence confirm the reliability of the Acts account while the disagreements between them suggest that Luke did not use the letters as sources when writing his narrative.

in 1 Corinthians 3–4. In this regard, Paul's enigmatic references to his colleague Apollos in 1 Corinthians (1:12; 3:5-9; 4:6-13) may be illumined against the background of his story in Acts (see 18:24-28). Even though some modern interpreters of 1 Corinthians suppose a bitter rivalry existed between them (cf. 1 Cor 1:12), there is no evidence of such rivalry and Paul seems to make the contrary point: Where we expect to find a power struggle between two gifted men, we discover a commitment to each other and to the missionary tasks each is given.[590] Paul's point in 1 Corinthians is confirmed by Acts; however, Luke contrasts Paul's spiritual authority to the individual talent of Apollos, whose powerful gifts are not due to his Spirit baptism but to his Alexandrian education (cf. 1 Cor 4:13).

(2) The impression that Paul's mission took place in a milieu of conflict (18:6-7, 9-10) is also evident in the Corinthian letters (cf. 1 Cor 1:10-17). Two kinds of conflict are envisaged. The first is more implicit and obtains to Paul's troubled relationship with the congregation. If at the heart of Paul's troubles in Corinth is the rejection of his religious authority (cf. 1 Cor 4:1-21; 9:1-27; 2 Cor 10-13), then the story of the church's founding in Acts may function as an apologia to underscore his foundational importance for the church's future.

(3) The second conflict concerns various problems that Paul responds to especially in 1 Corinthians, including sexual practices (chaps. 5–7) and foods sacrificed to idols (chaps. 8–10). The reader may well wonder how a congregation founded by Jews (= Acts) had evolved some four or five years later (= 1–2 Corinthians) into a congregation that is largely pagan in background and without keen awareness of the gospel's debt to the church's Jewish heritage. Paul's declaration that "from now on I will go to the Gentiles" (18:6) may help explain this sociological phenomenon. More important, however, the lack of a Jewish touchstone opens the church's witness to contamination from the very practices that were of concern to James and his Jewish church: eating food "polluted by idols" and sexual immorality (15:20, 29; 21:25). The purpose of the canonical conversation

between Acts and 1 Corinthians is simply to remind the reader of the vital importance to resist the "gentilizing" of the church's Jewish legacy in order to be the church.

(4) Among the topics of contention within the Corinthian community, central is the conviction of Christ's lordship over any other lordship, political or religious. Cultural predilections and social norms have been voided by the Lord's death and resurrection and replaced by the community's relationship with him in a way that regulates every dimension of human existence (1 Cor 7:22-24; 8:5-6; 12:2-3). Is not this the subtext of the charges against Paul heard by Gallio? The litigious Jews ironically are guilty of a religious lawlessness (see 18:12-17) according to which they reject the word of God (see 18:11).

18:1-3. Luke's reference to Caesar Claudius's edict for "all Jews to leave Rome" (18:2) is an important chronological marker in Acts. Most place the date at 49 CE, following the Roman historian Suetonius, who chronicled Claudius's career and wrote that his expulsion of Jews from Rome was "because of their constant disturbances at the instigation of *Chrestus* (= Christ)."[591] While it is unlikely that he would expel Rome's entire Jewish community, then numbering about 40,000 people, it is likely that those sent packing would include the most active participants in these "disturbances," and some of those were probably believers.[592] Aquila and Priscilla were evidently among them, arriving in Corinth around 50 CE, probably as mature believers, suggesting the presence of a Christian community in both Corinth and Rome before Paul's arrival in each city.

Paul's reasons for searching out Aquila and Priscilla were twofold: They shared both the same faith and the same trade: "by trade they were tentmakers" (18:3). The social setting of Acts layers this phrase with important nuances. Paul was a member of a trade guild, which provided a context of financial support and friendship. R. Hock has argued that Paul's

590. Cf. R. Hays, *First Corinthians*, IBC (Louisville: John Knox, 1997) 67-73.

591. Suetonius *Claudius* 25.4. This edict was rescinded upon the accession of the next emperor, Nero, in 54 CE, which dates Paul's Corinthian mission sometime in the early 50s CE.

592. Cf. R. Brändle and E. Stegemann, "The Formation of the First 'Christian Congregations' in Rome," in *Judaism and Christianity in First Century Rome*, ed. K. Donfried and P. Richardson (Grand Rapids: Eerdmans, 2000) 125-26. For a helpful discussion of Rome's attitude toward the Jews, see Witherington, *Acts*, 539-44.

trade would have occupied him through most of the day. At least in those cities where he remained a considerable amount of time, such as Corinth, he no doubt spent more hours in his workshop than in the city's *agora* preaching the gospel.[593] The lack of social esteem given to the city's working class would have been sharply qualified by Paul's own Jewish sensibilities, since working creatively with one's hands to pay the bills is an important value of the teacher of Israel (cf. 1 Cor 4:12; 1 Thess 2:9; 2 Thess 3:6-8).

18:4-5. If Paul's weekly schedule included a long day working alongside Priscilla and Aquila in their tentmaking shop, then they worshiped alongside each other every sabbath when Paul "would argue in the synagogue and would try to convince Jews and Greeks" (18:4).[594] The reader can recover relevant details of Paul's sabbath ministry from earlier episodes to fill in the gaps of this summary (see 13:14-47; 17:2-3, 10-11, 17).

With the arrival of Silas and Timothy from Macedonia (see 17:15; cf. 1 Cor 16:10-11; 2 Cor 1:19), Paul "was occupied with proclaiming of the word . . . that the Messiah was Jesus" (18:5). Paul's experiment with bivocationalism has apparently ended; his occupation has shifted from tentmaking to evangelism, perhaps facilitated by funds brought by Silas and Timothy from the Macedonian congregations (cf. Phil 4:15; 2 Cor 11:9).[595] This text repeats the core content of his synagogue discussions to the Jews and God-fearing Greeks every sabbath, which has become the central feature of his daily teaching in the city.

18:6-8. For a second time Paul's frustration with unrepentant Jews who "opposed and reviled him" is recounted (18:6*a*). Paul's prophetic gesture—"he shook the dust from his clothes" (see 13:51; cf. Neh 5:13)—signals their apostasy in rejecting the word of God.[596] If Paul's transition to full-time ministry is a variation of Luke's "second visitation"

prophetic motif (see 7:35),[597] Paul's gesture and declaration of intention that follows render God's verdict on the spiritual failure of Corinthian Jews. They have been given every opportunity to hear Paul's message in full and in repetition, and their continuing opposition to him confirms their unwillingness to repent, disqualifying them from participating in the blessings of Israel's restoration (see 13:44-47).

His fierce rebuke that "Your blood be on your own heads" is an intertextual echo of Ezek 33:4, where Jewish "blood" flows because they do not heed God's warning proclaimed through the prophet. Paul's earlier denunciation of unrepentant Jews at Pisidian Antioch used a similar prophecy from Habakkuk to warn hostile Jews that to deny his teaching that Jesus is God's Messiah would result in the loss of eternal life (see 13:46). The message of that earlier incident is implied in this one.

Paul's declaration that "from now on I will go to the Gentiles" should be understood in context. On the one hand, Paul is turning from those Jews who continue to reject his message and revile him to those who are more responsive. The declaration is a statement of fact rather than of resolve; indeed, God-fearing Gentiles in Corinth have been more responsive to the gospel. Luke's Acts is interested in stipulating *that* it is so not *why* it is so. On the other hand, Paul does not turn from Corinthian Jews in general since he enjoys some stunning successes, including two "officials of the synagogue," Crispus (18:8) and Sosthenes (18:17).

The failure of Paul's mission to the Jews of the Corinthian synagogue precipitates moving the location of his teaching ministry to a different house, one in the shadow of the synagogue (see 6:9).[598] This fledgling congregation met in the home of Titius Justus, whose home is the second noted in Acts (Lydia's in the first) where believers meet for worship. However, the congregants of Titus's house church are not only Gentiles formerly attached to the synagogue; the Jewish leader Crispus "became a believer in the Lord together with

593. R. Hock, *The Social Context of Paul's Ministry: Teaching and Apostleship* (Philadelphia: Fortress, 1980).

594. The Western version depicts a subversive Paul who "inserted" the name of the Lord Jesus into the Scripture lessons, probably as substitute for "Lord," when reading and teaching them. The variant also implies that Greeks in attendance were Paul's principal audience, again reflecting its anti-Semitic bias.

595. Conzelmann, *The Acts of the Apostles*, 152; Dunn, *The Acts of the Apostles*, 242.

596. Cf. Haenchen, *The Acts of the Apostles*, 535.

597. Johnson, *The Acts of the Apostles*, 13.

598. Luke's proximity of Titius's house "next door to the synagogue" (18:8) symbolizes the congregation's continuity with the religious practices of the synagogue—more likely since the distance of houses to meeting places allowed members of the synagogue to observe sabbath *halakhah* (see 1:12).

all his household [οἶκος *oikos*]," along with many other Corinthians (18:8). Although the text does not identify these Corinthians, they are probably attached to the synagogue and join Crispus upon hearing of his conversion.

This transition from synagogue to house must also be understood in terms of the concerns raised by James at the Jerusalem Council. Whatever confidence James has that a diaspora congregation of mixed constituency will retain its Jewish heritage is predicated on a mission that is synagogue-based, since there Moses will be preached every Sabbath (see 15:21). God-fearing Gentiles, who are attached to the synagogue and hear Moses preached, will more likely understand how they should live among their Jewish brothers and sisters. The relocation of Paul's mission from synagogue to house may well imperil the sabbath reading of Moses and thus make more likely the "gentilizing" of Christian faith. The pervasiveness of the Jewish character of this Corinthian house, however, where its first members are Jewish and its location is in close proximity to the synagogue, ensures that Moses will be read there. The implication that the transition from synagogue to household church will not necessarily jeopardize its Jewish heritage is strengthened by Stephen's speech that criticized the reification of a particular place as inherently sacred. The crucial issue in this new dispensation of salvation's history is not where the faith community worships but who is worshiped.

18:9-11. The visions of Acts prophesy the church's mission; the opening formula "One night the Lord [= Jesus] said to Paul in a vision" (18:9), then, is anticipatory of the story's plotline. The antagonism of certain Jews toward Paul's mission (see 18:6) will continue (see 18:12; 9:16). In this context of escalating tensions Jesus does not say to Paul "do not be afraid" because he would intervene to end Paul's mission and inaugurate more halcyon days. Rather, he promises physical protection so that Paul may continue to speak and grow the church in Corinth. Jesus' comment that "there are many in this city who are my people [λαός *laos*])" (18:10) again is prophetic of future conversions not only from among the Jews (= Sosthenes, 18:17), who are the people (*laos*) of God (see 4:10, et al.), but also from among the Gentiles as the continuing

fulfillment of Amos's prophecy that God would call out "a people" (*laos*; 15:14) from the Gentiles (see 15:17). Drawing strength from the Lord's exhortation, Paul stays on in Corinth for "a year and six months," during which he continues his prophetic ministry of "teaching the word of God among them" (18:11; see 4:31).

18:12-17. The conflict implied and protection promised in the Lord's vision to Paul is here fulfilled in a remarkable manner, and providing additional insight in how Luke's shaping of Acts instructs his readers about the nature of God's sovereignty (see Introduction, "Acts as Confession"). The central character of this episode is the Achaian proconsul Gallio (52 CE), the political name of Seneca's older brother and member of his influential Roman family. Achaia is the most important region of Roman Greece and therefore the importance of Gallio's pedigree is enhanced by the location of his post.

At the elevated center of the city's *agora* is the "tribunal" (βῆμα *bēma*) where public pronouncements are heard and important court cases settled. This is where Paul's Jewish opponents bring him, apparently so Gallio can dispose of their legal grievances against this rogue teacher of Israel. Their accusations are similar to those brought by Hellenist Jews against Stephen before another tribunal (6:13-14; cf. 16:20-21) and therefore probably should be glossed by that earlier indictment. In this Roman setting, however, Paul is charged with breaking Roman (not Jewish) law in Corinth (not Jerusalem). The legal presumption is that Judaism is an approved religion of the empire and that what Paul taught was outside of religious boundaries approved by "official" Israel. In this limited sense, then, Paul's proclamation that Jesus is God's Messiah and Israel's Savior is "contrary to the [Roman] law" (18:13).

Gallio intervenes before Paul can speak— a literary convention of Luke to add drama and importance to what comes next—and renders a legal verdict, which is paradigmatic for every Roman verdict from this point forward in Acts. His speech asserts crucial judgments about Paul's mission in the Diaspora. The first is that the relevant legal "matter" of the Jewish complaint against Paul does not pertain to a "crime [ἀδίκημα *adikēma*] or serious villainy" (18:14).[599] Gallio's reference to *adikēma* is more than a reference to an important Hellenistic *topos* for criminal vice; it also denotes religious impurity. The irony of his commentary on Paul's legal innocence is that it helps to render Luke's judgment about Paul's theological innocence, which is the real motive of the complaint against him. In this sense, Gallio infers that Paul is "Torah pure" and for this reason his case should be tossed out of a *Jewish* courtroom even as it is dismissed from his Roman court.

This implied sense is made explicit by Gallio's second judgment: This "matter" concerns "words [= resurrection] and names [= Messiah, Jesus] and your own law [= Israel's Scripture], see to it yourselves" (18:15). Gallio nicely expresses a central point of Luke's apologia: Paul's mission and message take place *within* the purview of Israel's traditions and destiny, not outside of them. The disputes provoked are deeply religious in nature, pertaining to Paul's messianic reading of Scripture that proves Jesus is Messiah (see 18:4-5). Gallio's refusal to make a judgment confirms that such a conflict falls in a "legal" category over which Roman law and therefore a Roman court has no jurisdiction.

Gallio's brusque dismissal of the case[600] will come to symbolize Rome's prudent if sometimes heavy-handed neutrality toward Paul's mission. Some scholars have argued, against the evidence supplied by his Acts, that Luke intends to rehabilitate Rome's

relationship with the church as an element of his "catholicizing" theology that seeks conciliation of relevant parties. Luke's depiction of Rome's relationship to Paul's mission in Acts, however, is rather more realistic than this and suggests that Rome's political aloofness evinces a more benign rejection of the gospel in favor of the empire's sovereignty and security.

The final scene of this episode is bizarre but perhaps illustrates Rome's disposition toward Paul's mission (see 18:17). There is no indication in the narrative of what prompts the Jewish retaliation against Sosthenes or of whether his involvement in the case is pro or con; nor are we told who the attackers are. It could be the response of embarrassed litigants taking out their legal failure on "the official of the synagogue," who may have replaced Cristus following his conversion and forced the issue against Paul as a first (and now failed) act of his administration. Or it could be, as many suppose, that Sosthenes is also a recent convert who personifies the growing anxiety of Paul's Jewish opponents in Corinth. If so, to attack him is to attack the undesirable effect of the Christian mission on members of their synagogue.

In any case, another purpose of Luke's conclusion is to portray the mocking disinterest of Gallio (= Rome) in bad light. Gallio's casual arrogance nicely captures Luke's understanding of God's hold over the unfolding of salvation to the end of the earth and harkens back to the Lord's exhortation in Paul's dream-vision. Simply put, God's will is done. But the way it gets done is often messy and the agents of God's will are sometimes unsavory people.

---

599. The grammatical construction of Gallio's declaration is a "first-class conditional," which states something as a matter-of-fact.

600. The NIV translation of ἀπελαύνω (*apelaunō*, "eject") captures the sense of the text better than the NRSV. Gallio's frustration in hearing an irrelevant case is reflected in literally tossing the case (and litigants!) from the courtroom.

REFLECTIONS

1. "Because Paul was a tentmaker as they were, he stayed and worked with them" (18:3 NIV). While Paul did not consider manual labor essential to his missionary strategy, his bivocationalism is nonetheless exemplary of a Jewish ethic that fully integrates one's work with one's life and service before God and neighbor (cf. 1 Thess 2:9; 4:11-12; 2 Thess 3:12). Not only is it practical for Paul to work his trade to support himself while growing a church in Corinth—especially if many converts came from the working-class poor (cf. 1 Cor 1:26)—but to work his prophetic calling "free of charge" may have been illustrative of a gospel about God's grace. Yet Paul's ability to work two jobs becomes impossible as the congregation grows. Clearly his preference is to devote himself fully to his spiritual calling and thus as soon as the congregation is able to support him and Silas and Timothy arrive to help him, Paul leaves his trade and "devoted himself exclusively to preaching" (8:5 NIV). Paul's bivocationalism is a useful pattern for clergy of new congregations to follow in our contemporary situation. However, congregations should carefully consider whether bivocationalism should be a permanent arrangement or whether they should support a full-time ministry as soon as they are able.

2. "Then he left the synagogue and went to the house of a man name Titius Justus . . . and many of the Corinthians who heard Paul became believers and were baptized" (18:7-8 NRSV). The Christian congregation in Corinth moves from the local synagogue to a neighbor's home. The primary motive for doing so is not a matter of convenience or one of planting a new congregation among those outside the synagogue. Instead, Paul is prompted to leave the synagogue in order to maintain theological purity. If the "sacred" is not circumscribed by where the faith community worships but by who they worship, as Luke maintains throughout Acts, the departure of believers from one congregation for another should be precipitated only by substantial theological disagreements that cannot be resolved—and then only as a last resort (see 14:27–15:5).

ACTS 18:18-23, INTERLUDE: PAUL'S PILGRIMAGE FROM CORINTH TO ANTIOCH

COMMENTARY

Paul's follow-up ministry among those congregations founded during earlier campaigns is an important feature of his overall missionary strategy. In the present passage that recounts various bits from Paul's itinerary following the end of his Corinthian mission (18:18), he returns to the Jerusalem church (18:22a) and then Antioch (18:22b) before "strengthening all the disciples" throughout the region of his first missionary tour (18:23). Only with the prophet's "second visitation" does he consider his work there complete.[601]

The primary function of narrative interludes in Acts is to move the reader from stage to stage—or from city (Corinth) to city (Ephesus), as is the purpose of the present text. Yet there is always a sense of continuity that coordinates Paul's mission in different cities. Thus his strategy of initiating his urban mission in the synagogue continues. In this case, he stops briefly in Ephesus but long enough to enter a synagogue and discuss Scripture's messianic meaning with the Jews he finds there (18:19), a harbinger of his future mission in that great city.

18:18. Acts tells us nothing of the actual circumstances that prompted Paul to conclude his Corinthian mission and sail for Roman Syria—to Jerusalem and Antioch (see vv. 22-23). Nor are we told why Priscilla and Aquila would close their tentmaking business in Corinth to accompany him. The fact that they stayed there "for a considerable time" indicates that a measure of peace resulted because of the Gallio verdict, allowing establishment of the church there.

The circumstances of Paul's voyage to Jerusalem, however, are implied by his religious practices that remain in the foreground of Luke's narrative. In this case, reference is made to Paul's ritual haircut to fulfill a vow he had made. In fact, he refuses to stay on in Ephesus, even though the response to him there is hospitable, and presses forward to Jerusalem because of the obligations of his vow. The importance of Paul's vow is more fully appreciated by recalling the concerns expressed in concluding the Jerusalem Council (see 15:20-21). Paul's pilgrimage to Jerusalem is prompted neither by his high regard for the "mother church" nor by a ministry

601. Cf. Tannehill, *The Acts of the Apostles*, 2:230.

of reconciliation within his own Antiochene congregation, which is still hurting over his split from Barnabas. His haircut, rather, symbolizes a pious Jew's vow to maintain the purity of his consecrated relations with God.

Although only a passing reference in Acts, Paul's vow is probably that of a Nazirite (lit., "consecrated one") described in Num 6:1-21. If that is the case, then his ritual haircut symbolizes his dedicated service for God and within Israel (Num 6:9, 18; *m. Nazir* 1.1-9.5). Although usually done in Jerusalem, it was sometimes allowed outside of the holy city if the consecrated servant then made a pilgrimage to the Jerusalem Temple for priestly confirmation.[602] The imperfect tense of the verb "to vow" (εἶχεν *eichen*; lit., "was taking a vow") may indicate that his haircut initiates a particular period that would end several months later (see 21:26). In Acts, vow taking is another indication that Paul's ministry among uncircumcised Gentiles has not contaminated his loyalty to the ancestral traditions of his Jewish faith nor his vocation as a teacher of Israel (see also 21:22-26).[603]

18:19-21. Luke deposits "Priscilla and Aquila"[604] in Ephesus[605] to await their encounter with Apollos (see 18:24-28), while Paul "went into the synagogue and had a discussion [διαλέγομαι *dialegomai*; see 17:2-3] with the Jews." Once again, the reader is expected to fill in the gaps with earlier narrative details of Paul's synagogue mission. In this case, the response to his messianic interpretation of Scripture reflects interest, which implies a request for the prophet's second visitation (see 7:35-40; 13:42-43). Although Paul is ambivalent in his response to their invitation (cf. 18:21), since his current intent is vow-keeping rather than gospel preaching, the reader is soon to learn that his promise is

kept when he returns to Ephesus. Evidently, an Ephesian mission is God's will (see 19:1; cf. Rom 1:10; 1 Cor 4:19; Heb 6:3; Jas 4:15).

18:22. The principal issue for the interpreter is whether Luke has Paul "going up" to Jerusalem before "going down" to Antioch, for the words "to Jerusalem" are not found in the Greek text.[606] In an interlude whose most important detail is Paul's haircut and vow taking in preparation for a pilgrimage to the holy city, the reader should probably assume that Paul's return to Caesarea included a trip to Jerusalem. Johnson argues that Luke uses the verbs ἀναβαίνω/καταβαίνω (*anabainō/ katabainō*, "going up/down") elsewhere in Acts to keep contact with Jerusalem and have a similar connotation here.[607] In paying respects to the church leadership, Paul has previously responded in good faith to the council's pastoral exhortation to Antiochene believers. He has rigorously resisted any practice that might "gentilize" his Jewish heritage or the congregations his mission has founded. Paul's visit in Antioch symbolizes his mission's solidarity with Jerusalem.

18:23. The catchphrase "strengthening all the disciples," which concludes this interlude, is a narrative boundary marker that cues the reader that one mission is complete, with all its obligations, and that Paul will soon venture into another (see 14:22; 20:1-3).[608] The itinerancy of missionary Paul, who "went from place to place through the region of Galatia and Phrygia," is characteristic of pastoral Paul's keenly felt motive to root new converts in teaching. This follow-up circuit to previous fields of service is an important feature of his overall mission strategy. Dunn suggests that we should understand this cultivation of the Aegean church as background for the collection of an offering for the poor and hungry believers of Palestine whom the letters mention (cf. Rom 15:25; 2 Corinthians 8–9), which may have been sparked by Paul's recent visit to Jerusalem and Antioch.[609] (See Reflections at 18:24–19:7.)

---

602. Witherington, *The Acts of the Apostles*, 557.

603. Cf. B. Levine, *Numbers 1–20*, AB 4 (New York: Doubleday, 1993) 229-35, who notes the heroic dimension of naziritism in OT narratives, especially of Israel's Judges (e.g., Deborah, Samson, Samuel). This resonance is probably intended by Luke to gloss Paul's behavior throughout his European mission.

604. Some think the reversal of the names here and in 18:26 to "Priscilla and Aquila" (see 18:2) indicates Priscilla's role as lead teacher, who is given credit for Apollos's theological rehabilitation according to 18:24-28. See Dunn, *The Acts of the Apostles*, 247.

605. Ephesus is the provincial capital of Roman Asia and a city of enormous wealth and culture. The diaspora community of Jews was especially strong there, since they were granted citizenship without prejudice. Many successful archaeological expeditions have made more precise the knowledge of the city behind the biblical story of Paul's mission there. For bibliography and discussion of the literature that describes these findings and their relevance as an interpretive tool for Acts 19–20, see Fitzmyer, *The Acts of the Apostles*, 634-35.

606. The Western version of 18:21 adds the note that Paul must leave in order to "spend the coming feast in Jerusalem," which clarifies the verse's ambiguous reference to "this church."

607. Johnson, *The Acts of the Apostles*, 330. Dunn, *The Acts of the Apostles*, 247, however, suggests Luke remains silent of any such visit because of Paul's unpopularity in Jerusalem—as Paul will find out in no uncertain terms upon a later visit in Acts 21.

608. Polhill, *The Acts of the Apostles*, 390-91.

609. Dunn, *The Acts of the Apostles*, 248.

ACTS 18:24–19:7, INTERLUDE: PAUL RETURNS TO EPHESUS

COMMENTARY

The next two stories in Acts take place in Ephesus and are related by their common interest in the continuing prominence of "John's baptism" among those with deficient knowledge of the gospel and incomplete experience of the Holy Spirit. By these stories of Apollos (18:24-28) and the Ephesian "disciples" (19:1-7), the reader is apprised of yet another element in the purview of Paul's mission: It includes the theological integration of marginal believers—those who know some of the truth but not all of it or who have experienced some of God's blessings but not to the full extent promised. In both instances, these believers are catechized and initiated into the fold of Christian fellowship to whom the Scriptures and the Spirit belong.

Apollos's remediation prepares him to contribute to Paul's ongoing Corinthian mission. Moreover, Priscilla and Aquila assume responsibility for his education in the absence of Paul. Both details of Apollos's story in Acts suggest that Paul's mission strategy is collaborative; he routinely enlists gifted colleagues to help him along the way. Priscilla and Aquila enjoy extraordinary freedom in preparing Ephesus for Paul's arrival, while at the same time Timothy and Silas are given responsibility over the Macedonian congregations. Luke's interest in the origin and positive outcome of Apollos's teaching ministry is especially noteworthy, given his future importance to the Achaian church, as Paul notes in 1 Corinthians 3–4 (see also Acts 18:1-17).

This interlude also confirms the theological fluidity within earliest Christianity, which is personified by Apollos and the Ephesian twelve, who represent all those believers (including Theophilus) whose faith is formed by an inchoate presentation of the gospel. The mentoring ministry of Priscilla and Aquila becomes paradigmatic of the church's response to this critical problem within a religious movement whose growth has far outstripped its educational resources (cf. 6:1-7).

Even though the boundary marker of this passage concerns the Holy Spirit, the subsequent story of Paul's Ephesian mission testifies to the primary cultural threats to the church's theological purity, including syncretism and magic (19:11-20) and pagan religion (19:23-41). Simply put, then, the story of Paul's Ephesian mission testifies to the importance of forming Christian faith in ways that more clearly distinguish its beliefs and practices from those of other religious options.

18:24-26. While Paul is revisiting the circuit of earlier missions (see v. 23), significant ministry is taking place elsewhere in Ephesus, where he had earlier left Priscilla and Aquila (see v. 19). This narrative vignette concerns their recruitment of Apollos to help Paul in Corinth, where he had planted a vigorous Christian congregation (see vv. 1-17). Apollos's credentials to teach are impressive: He is a Jew from Alexandria, a man who is good with words, and he has a "thorough knowledge of the Scriptures."

Acts tells us nothing about the church of Alexandria in Egypt—its origins, teaching, or practices. Yet Alexandria was second in influence only to Rome. It was not only a leading center of commerce and learning with a renowned library, but it also housed one of the most important communities of diaspora Jews in the Roman Empire. The great Jewish scholar Philo lived in Alexandria, and Apollos may well have been taught by him.[610] In fact, the unusual predicate adjective λόγιος (*logios*, "eloquent") expresses a characteristic of the educated person, since training in rhetoric was an essential part of education in Greco-Roman society.

In Acts, however, the prophet's rhetorical competence results from Spirit filling (see 4:8) and is explicitly disconnected from

---

610. From the ancient church forward, some scholars claimed that Apollos is the author of the anonymous NT letter "To the Hebrews" because it echoes the writings of Philo, employs a hellenized (= Alexandrian) exegesis of Scripture, is similar in theological conception to Paul, and reflects an intellectual rigor that corresponds to the profile of Apollos in Acts. Others, including myself, are not convinced, mostly because the echoes of Philo are faint and the letter's theological similarity to Paul is vague.

learning (see 4:13). Luke's reference to Apollos's eloquence, then, must be considered an ironic feature of his résumé since he had not yet received the Spirit of prophecy (see v. 28). This same irony extends to his thorough knowledge of the Scriptures. Although Apollos knows Scripture well, without the filling of the Holy Spirit he is unable to interpret Scripture in the elevated ways of the prophet-like-Jesus (see 2:4; 6:10).

Apollos arrives in Ephesus "with burning enthusiasm and taught accurately [ἀκριβῶς *akribōs*] the things concerning Jesus" (v. 25). Luke's clipped comment that Apollos "knew only the baptism of John" (v. 25) cues us that the source of his "burning enthusiasm" (ζέων τῶ πνεύματι *zeōn tō pneumati*) is not the Holy Spirit; rather, this is a feature of his rhetorical eloquence: He speaks with a lively (ζέων *zeōn*) spirit (πνεῦμα *pneuma*) and so has attracted a following at Ephesus. If Apollos has experienced only John's baptism (whatever that may entail) but not yet the Holy Spirit's (and all this entails according to Acts), the content of his teaching may be suspect. Apollos does not seem to fail in his religious (= Jewish) practice; and while his knowledge of the "way of the Lord" (cf. Luke 3:4) is "accurate" (18:25), the relevant issue probably concerns an inadequate doctrine of the Spirit. The connection of Apollos's story with the twelve disciples of Ephesus (see 19:1-7) would seem to support this conjecture (see above).[611] The implication is that Apollos has been initiated into Christian discipleship by John's baptism and that he has learned only the first lessons of Jesus, perhaps only to the time of John the Baptist's martyrdom before the cross and the empty tomb.

In any case, Priscilla and Aquila "took him aside and explained the Way of God to him more accurately" (v. 26). That his information about Jesus is incomplete is indicated by Luke's use of the comparative form of ἀκριβῶς (*akribōs*). While he knows "the way of the Lord" (ἡ ὁδός τοῦ κυρίου *hē hodos tou kyriou*), he does not know "the Way of God [= "The Way"; ἡ ὁδός τοῦ θεοῦ *hē hodos tou theou*]." "The Way" is used elsewhere in Acts only in Pauline narratives (9:2; 19:9; 22:4;

24:14, 22), which suggests it is an idiom of Luke's Pauline source and is defined by the content of Paul's gospel. If so, then Apollos's problem is that he has not yet received the Pauline seal of approval, which Priscilla and Aquila now provide him.

18:27-28. The results of Priscilla and Aquila's mentoring are immediate: "The believers [in Ephesus] encouraged [προτρέπτομαι *protreptomai*] him and wrote to the disciples [in Achaia] to welcome him" (v. 27). Evidently, this congregation, whose faith is cultivated by Priscilla and Aquila's teaching, recognizes Apollos's vocation and gifts. Their favorable impression of him is signaled by Luke's use of *protreptomai*, which connotes the confirmation of a newly instructed teacher, and by the writing of a letter of introduction, an act of friendship and support.

Upon his arrival, Apollos "greatly helped" in the catechesis of new believers and "powerfully refuted [διακατελέγχομαι *diakatelenchomai*] the Jews in public" from the Scriptures, now more fully understood. The repetition of Paul's teaching in the synagogue that "Jesus is Messiah" (see 17:2-3) would suggest that Apollos's own instruction is complete and that he has been brought into agreement with Paul's christological interpretation of Israel's Scriptures. Moreover, the powerful refutation of opponents suggests Apollos's filling with the Spirit of prophecy. The location of his public ministry in Corinth (see 19:1), however, is neither the synagogue, since Paul left it for Titius's house (see 18:6), nor the courtroom, since Gallio has closed its door (see 18:12-17). Therefore, he must be contesting unrepentant Jews in the town square. There his "eloquence" coupled with his elevated understanding of Scriptures ("showing by the scriptures") has funded teaching that "powerfully refuted" the unrepentant Jews who contest the gospel's claims.

19:1-7. The disciples whom Paul found upon his arrival in Ephesus are similar in theological defect to Apollos: They know John's baptism but not the Spirit's.[612] It remains unlikely that their theological similarity is due to their personal acquaintance in Ephesus, however, since these "disciples" apparently did not attend a synagogue (cf. 18:26; 19:2).

---

611. Cf. Spencer, *Acts, Readings*, 183-84, who pairs Apollos as Paul's "forerunner" much like the Baptist is to Jesus and Philip is to Peter. However, see Turner, *Power from on High*, 388-97.

612. Cf. Barrett, *A Critical and Exegetical Commentary on the Acts of the Apostles*, 2:892-95.

Nothing is known of the lessons Priscilla and Aquila may have used for instructing Apollos about "the Way of God"; presumably their curriculum was based on what was learned from Paul. This inference also suggests that his response to the twelve of Ephesus would be similar to the unwritten instruction given earlier to Apollos by Priscilla and Aquila.

19:1-4. Luke refers to Paul's conversation partners without qualifying them as "disciples" (μαθηταί *mathētai*), a term otherwise used only of believers in Acts. Here it suggests that they are untrained students in search of a master teacher.[613] Their ignorance of the Holy Spirit (v. 2*b*) has placed them outside of Christian fellowship: they evidently have not yet found the synagogue where Priscilla and Aquila teach, since their subsequent responses to Paul suggest they worship God outside of the synagogue where Moses and Messiah are preached.

Paul's initial and decisive question presumes their Christian faith: "Did you receive the Holy Spirit when you became believers?" (v. 2*a*). The narrative does not indicate what prompts Paul's question or why he presumes that they are believers. Paul's query recognizes that they lack the mark of the Spirit's presence and that their theological education, therefore, is incomplete; that they "have not even heard that there is a Holy Spirit" (v. 2*b*) only sharpens Paul's interrogations. Has Luke shaped their response to underscore the theological problem? Probably so, since they would have surely learned about the Holy Spirit from this prophet who predicted that the Messiah would baptize his followers with the Holy Spirit! What they seem to lack, then, is both a more robust knowledge of the Spirit formed by an *experience* of its filling and the theological claims that are adumbrated in Acts.

A second round of questions and answers detects this root problem. As with Apollos before them, these initiates "into John's baptism" had not yet received the Spirit of prophecy (v. 3; see also 18:25). Paul insinuates his own theology into John by asserting that he taught his initiates "to believe in the one who was to come after him" (v. 4). Nowhere in the Gospels does John the Baptist ever say this; Luke's Paul infers the next logical stage of John's proclamation, since the Lord's resurrection merely confirms his prophecy that he is the Messiah and the agent of forgiveness for those baptized in his name (v. 5; see also 2:21; 13:38-39).[614] Paul's commentary on John's testimony of Jesus does however recall John the Baptist's final appearance with Jesus before his imprisonment, when the Lord makes a comparison between his own importance and John's, concluding with a dramatic warning that "whoever believes in the Son has eternal life; whoever disobeys the Son will not see life, but must endure God's wrath" (John 3:36). Read in canonical context, Paul's summary of John's teaching about the Messiah's baptism implies these same consequences in exhorting John's current disciples "to believe in the one who was to come after him" (v. 4; see also 13:44-47; 19:9).

19:5-7. With these clipped exchanges, the catechesis of John the Baptist's former students is complete, and so "they were baptized in the name of the Lord Jesus" (v. 5), and "the Holy Spirit came upon them" (v. 6). Again, we should not presume a formal relationship between Christian baptism and the reception of the Holy Spirit.[615] Nor should we privilege this text over others in establishing a particular baptismal liturgy ("Paul had laid his hands on them") or evidence of the Spirit's reception ("and they spoke in tongues and prophesied," v. 6). In Luke's narrative of Paul's mission, Christian baptism is sometimes mentioned without reference to the Spirit's reception (see 16:15, 33; 18:8). Elsewhere in Acts the outpouring of the Spirit of prophecy falls prior to baptism (see 9:17-18; 10:47-48), or after baptism as here (see 2:1-4; 8:12-16, 38-39), or even at the same time as baptism (see 2:38-41). And the arrival of God's Spirit does not ensure in every case the capacity to speak in tongues *and* to prophesy (cf. 2:1-11; 8:16-17, 38-39; 10:46).[616]

---

613. The root meaning of "disciple" (μαθητής *mathētēs*) is "student," a primary connotation of Luke's use of the word here. The Ephesian twelve are itinerant "theologues" searching for a mentor to replace John; they find him in Paul.

614. Haenchen, *The Acts of the Apostles*, 553.

615. This is Scripture's only narrative of the "rebaptism" of believers, and the "rebaptism" of Apollos is implied by the parallelism of his story and this one.

616. Luke's reference to the twelve's capacity to prophesy must be considered remarkable by any interpretation. It will not do simply to read this capacity to speak in tongues and prophesy in the light of 1 Corinthians 12–14 as instances of "gifts of the Spirit," for in Acts these gifts fund the church's witness to Jesus rather than the formation of the Christian community, as in Paul.

The close parallelism between this case and the earlier story of the Samaritans' reception of the Spirit (see 8:14-24) clarifies the story's subtext: to authorize the Pauline mission. Unlike Simon the Great, who coveted but could not acquire Peter's apostolic "authority" to lay hands on believers as the medium for the Spirit's reception (see 8:17-19), Paul has been granted this authority. This clarification of Paul's spiritual authority cues the reader of Acts to the ensuing account of the Ephesian mission, where his prophetic powers reach their zenith.

REFLECTIONS

1. "When Priscilla and Aquila heard [Apollos], they took him aside and explained the Way of God to him more accurately" (18:26 NRSV). For all his evident gifts, Apollos is an immature teacher. He knows Scripture well, but he lacks full understanding of what he is teaching. Priscilla and Aquila tutor their protégé to maturity. A congregation's theological formation depends on its teachers; misguided teaching can result in incorrect beliefs that divert believers from the Way of God. For this reason no pastoral activity is more critical to the spiritual health of a congregation than overseeing those who instruct the flock concerning the things of God. Following the pattern of Priscilla and Aquila, mentoring young teachers includes three steps: Those mature in the faith observe the new teacher firsthand in a classroom setting, assessing the content of what is being taught to make certain it agrees with the congregation's faith statement. If there is need for remediation, mentors should schedule time outside the classroom for instruction. Finally, church leaders should make certain the person resumes teaching with the full support and encouragement of the congregation (18:27-28).

2. This story of Priscilla's ministry introduces and frames those famous passages within the Pauline collection that instruct Christian women to submit as good wives and mothers (1 Cor 7:34-35; Eph 5:21-24), to remain silent as good students (1 Cor 14:34; 1 Tim 2:9-12), and to circumscribe their prophetic ministry with head coverings to symbolize patriarchal claims on their lives (1 Cor 11:2-10). The relevant relationships of Christian women—to Pauline tradition, to familial obligations and the workplace, and to the local congregation and its male teachers—are subtexts of Priscilla's story. Pauline teaching about women is often obscure, but the portrait of Priscilla in Acts 18 produces a fresh angle of vision for the troublesome epistolary texts that follow. Moreover, her story coheres with the gospel witness to Jesus' relationships with his female disciples—and with Paul's statement that there is neither male nor female, for all are one in Christ (Gal 3:28). Christian women can form equal partnerships with their husbands in the workplace (18:2) and the local congregation (18:26), even taking the lead in these efforts (18:18). And female teachers can instruct men in the way of the Lord (18:26). Women in ministry produce a more robust performance of God's Word in the world (18:27-28).

ACTS 19:8-41, PAUL'S EPHESIAN MISSION

COMMENTARY

The narrative of Paul's final mission as a free man is important mostly for a canonical reason. Unlike Paul's Athenian mission, whose importance in Acts is due to the city's significance, or the paradigmatic importance of his first Asian mission with Barnabas or the European mission in Philippi, this story concentrates the reader's attention on Paul's work, on his religious authority, and ultimately on his stunning success as a Christian missionary and teacher. Ephesus was a great city and strategically situated within the Roman Empire; and in due time its church would become the center of Pauline Christianity. Yet this story is not about Ephesus or the founding of its church; it is about Paul's authoritative persona and destiny (see 19:21-22). Like Peter before him, Paul's prophetic vocation and personal status within God's redemptive program cannot be imitated by the likes of Sceva's sons, nor can they be easily trivialized, as Demetrius discovers without Paul needing to say a word in his defense (see 19:30-31)!

Compressed summaries (19:8-10, 17-20), interspersed with vivid vignettes (19:11-16) lead us to Paul's climactic confrontation with local merchants (19:23-41) to draw a "picture which stood before the eyes of the sub-apostolic Church of that Paul whom the early Church recognized and honoured and who down to Augustine and Luther stood before the Paul of the letters."[617] Perhaps this more universal Paul whom we find in Ephesus is apropos to the Pauline letter of Ephesians, which has few features of the typical occasional letter and appears to be an encyclical letter written for the post-Pauline church. This led E. Goodspeed, for example, to hypothesize that the writing of Acts occasioned the writing of Ephesians by the same author, who was motivated to provide ongoing generations of Christian readers both a biography (Acts) and a theological introduction (the Letter to the Ephesians) to the Pauline tradition.[618] This historical thesis is now dismissed for lack of evidence. However, it serves to underscore the ongoing relevance of the Paul of Acts for the summary of Pauline teaching in Ephesians; and it testifies to the universal truth of his gospel and the continuing efficacy of God's gospel to each new generation of believers. The Paul of Acts will make this clear enough in his farewell speech to the elders of the Ephesian church (see 20:17-35). Nowhere in Acts is the importance of listening and following Paul as personal exemplar and theological mentor more forcefully depicted than in this story.

19:8-10. In this passage, Luke summarizes the general pattern of Paul's mission since arriving in Ephesus: Following prophetic convention, he returns to the synagogue (see 18:19-21) where over a period of "three months" he speaks "boldly" (see 4:29-31) and "argues" (see 17:2-3, 17; 18:4) persuasively "for the kingdom of God" (v. 8). The added reference to the "kingdom of God" recalls the central theme of the Lord's teaching ministry and is used in Acts to express the continuity between what he "began to say" according to the "first book" (see 1:1) and the ministry of his apostolic successors (see 1:3). Paul is their successor within the restored Israel both in prophetic ministry and spiritual authority (see 14:22; 28:31). Simply put, the word of God that Paul is teaching in the synagogues of the diaspora is in agreement with the word of God taught by the Lord and his apostolic successors; Paul's message and mentoring are utterly trustworthy.

In Acts, the proclamation of God's kingdom is linked to Israel's restoration (1:6); therefore, the synagogue at Ephesus is the appropriate diaspora setting to announce the good news that the Lord has acted faithfully to restore God's kingdom to Israel. As expected, however, the prophet's proclamation of God's gospel divides the house of Israel between repentant (= restored) and unrepentant Jews. On the one hand, "some stubbornly [σκληρύνω *sklērynō*] refused to believe [ἀπειθέω *apeitheō*] and spoke evil of the Way before the congregation" (v. 9*a*; see also 7:51; 13:45; 14:2; 18:6). The use of *sklērynō* in this context recalls the exodus story and the hardening of Pharaoh's heart after he stubbornly failed to respond to God's Word, brought to him by Moses (Exod 13:15). As a biblical motif, the hardened heart not only symbolizes the steadfast refusal to repent but also the loss of divine blessings that results. The irony of drawing on an important OT theme for Israel's unbelief and refusal to turn back to God to characterize the Jewish opposition only intensifies the conflict provoked within the Jewish diaspora by Paul's mission. The level of hostility is indicated in passing by the "evil" (κακολογέω *kakologeō*) that some spoke publicly against the Way of God (see 18:26).[619]

---

617. Haenchen, *The Acts of the Apostles*, 558.
618. E. Goodspeed, *The Meaning of Ephesians* (Chicago: Chicago University Press, 1933).

619. "The Way" not only refers to the distinctive beliefs of these Jewish messianists but also to their social solidarity—a way of living together as a community of goods. See Cassidy, *Society and Politics in the Acts of the Apostles*, 95. The "evil," perhaps, might be slandering the social values of a community of goods, not just public disagreement with a Pauline interpretation of Scripture.

On the other hand, the rejection of the gospel on Paul's second visit to the synagogue (see 18:19-21) signals the conclusion of the prophet's mission to the unrepentant Jews of this city; and so he leaves their synagogue, students in tow, for "the lecture hall [σχολή *scholē*] of Tyrannus" (v. 9*b*).[620] Their departure repeats what had earlier taken place in Corinth (see 18:6-7), a move made necessary by opposition to Paul's gospel but one that in no way undercuts the Jewish heritage of the faith. In this case, the believers who accompanied Paul are called "disciples" (μαθηταί *mathētai*) and the new venue is not a member's home but a *scholē*, a term that once meant "leisure" but came to mean "school" because of the leisure time required for students to gather for learning. Nothing is known of this Tyrannus, whether he is the owner of the building or one after whom the hall is named.[621] In any case, Tyrannus Hall is the place in Ephesus where Paul's "disciples" gathered to learn from their trusted theological mentor.[622]

Luke concludes this summary by indicating Paul's length of stay in Ephesus, two years, rather than the number of converts; however, when combined with other time periods noted in this narrative (vv. 8, 22), Paul's time in Ephesus totals a period of roughly three years (see Acts 20:31). By almost any criterion, this is an extraordinarily productive season in Paul's ministry (cf. 1 Cor 16:9) and helps to explain why Ephesus became the base of his continuing influence within earliest Christianity. This is even implied by Luke's hyperbolic "all the residents of Asia, both Jews and Greeks, heard the word of the Lord" (v. 10; see also 4:4, 31; 6:7; 8:4; 12:24; 13:5; 16:32; 18:11).

19:11-12. Paul's depiction as an Ephesian miracle worker should not be viewed as extraordinary. The city of Ephesus was itself a center of the magic arts in the ancient world. Some citizens considered their books of magic sacred scripture and paraphernalia for mediating miraculous power as commonplace. The resolution of any confusion

between miracle (which God does) and magic (which magicians do) is an important biblical theme and a subtext of this passage. More important, Luke's comment that "God did extraordinary miracles through Paul" must be read ironically, since the miracles Paul performs in Ephesus parallel stories of healing and exorcism miracles found in the Gospels (e.g., Mark 6:53-56 and pars.) and elsewhere in Acts (see 5:12-16). The implication is that Paul is a prophet-like-Jesus in vocation and authority.

The text is careful to qualify Paul's miracle-working activity as the action of God: "*God did extraordinary miracles through* [διά *dia*] Paul" (lit., "through the hands of Paul," v. 11, italics added; cf. 2 Cor 12:12; see also 1 Cor 1:22-23). Neither the NRSV nor the NIV is sufficiently literal to convey the sense that God's healing power is mediated by the direct touch of Paul's *hands*. This more complete image of intimate touch envisages the collaboration between God and the prophet who is the authorized medium of God's power, symbolized by laying his hands directly upon the sick or possessed person (see 3:7; 5:12; 9:17, 41; 14:3; cf. 6:6; 8:17; 13:3). Moreover, Paul evidently uses the healing formula "in the name of the Lord Jesus" (see 4:5-12) since it is this that the sons of Sceva imitate (see 19:13).

The transmission of God's healing power through Paul's hands extends also to "handkerchiefs or aprons that had touched his skin" (v. 12). There is no difference whether Paul lays hands upon the sick or is touched by them: It is Paul's persona through whom God works to heal the sick. Surely these items are the very paraphernalia used in magic shows and reflect long-standing Ephesian superstitions that magic dispensed by the paranormally gifted (or demonically enabled) make sick people whole. Critically, then, this story is placed following the summary of Paul's teaching mission, where he dispenses the "word of the Lord" to all who hear before he dispenses the Lord's healing power to all who are sick. The effect of Luke's shaping of these stories is to demythologize Paul's reputation as a magic man, as though his personal powers are due his own paranormal talent rather than God's working through him. This is a fantastic image; however, it is less due to the

620. Cf. Johnson, *The Acts of the Apostles*, 339, esp. 13 for review of his "two visitation" literary theme and why it applies here.

621. Marshall, *The Acts of the Apostles*, 309, suggests that Luke "drops" this name into the narrative to honor a believer who may well have rented the hall to Paul at an affordable rate to encourage his mission.

622. The Western version of Acts adds "from eleven AM until four PM," the routine workday in the life of an ancient philosopher-educator.

hagiography of a legendary Paul and more due to Luke's intent to distinguish between human magic and divine miracle. The implication is that the Pauline "word of the Lord" is safeguarded by God's extraordinary power according to God's redemptive purposes.

19:13-16. The story of the seven sons of Sceva is strange and has caused commentators a great deal of difficulty.[623] It almost certainly alludes to the earlier story of Simon the Great, who wanted to remain competitive with the apostles in Samaria and sought to purchase their religious authority for himself (see 8:9-24). Simon was merely chastised by Peter for his foolish simony (from whose name this term derives), but the reader is made more fully aware that apostolic authority cannot be imitated by those not chosen by the Lord to rule over Israel. With characteristic wit, Luke has a demon make this same apologia in support of Paul to the sons of Sceva, who come away in far worse shape than did Simon: "Jesus I know, and Paul I know, but who are you?" (v. 15).

The reputation of Paul's healing powers had evidently spread throughout the religious community in Ephesus, and "some itinerant Jewish exorcists" attempt to invoke the name of Jesus to liberate the possessed without having a personal relationship with him. Jesus apparently allows this practice among outsiders (see Luke 9:49-50; cf. Matt 7:21-23), since its effect is not opposed to the salvation he brings or to the religious practices of his Jewish faith. Josephus mentions exorcism as a Jewish practice and even commends it as a mark of Jewish identity.[624] The issue at stake, however, is not the Jewish practice of exorcism or even that it is practiced by outsiders in the name of Jesus. The issue is that it is practiced in imitation of this prophet-like-Jesus— the formula they use is "the Jesus whom Paul proclaims." Because Paul's miracle work is closely connected to his proclamation of the word of the Lord, which presumably is not true of these Jewish exorcists, their practice threatens to subvert his mission in Ephesus and, therefore, must be stopped.

The identification of the Jewish exorcists with the "seven sons of a Jewish high priest named Sceva" is problematical, since we know nothing of a high priest by that name.[625] Luke seems intent only to give a measure of realism to the current crisis by finding pretenders to Paul's religious authority in Ephesus, since members of priestly families would likely be familiar with the "rules" governing the practice of exorcism. In this regard, the refusal of the "evil spirit" to respond to any of Sceva's sons is not a matter of their ignorance of liturgical formulae; they do not appear to lack technical expertise. What they lack is Paul's *authority* over demons. The use of two different verbs in the demon's witty response commends this conclusion: "Jesus I know [γινώσκω *ginōskō*], and Paul I know [ἐπίσταμαι *epistamai*], but who are you?" (v. 15). The distinction the spirit makes between two ways of knowing, which "recognizes" (*ginōskō*) the Lord's ultimate authority and "experiences firsthand" (*epistamai*) Paul's authority to evoke Jesus' name for exorcism (see 16:18), subverts any religious authority the sons of Sceva may presume to have.[626] The evil spirit's combination of Jesus and Paul "permits the Christians to make a complete break with magic."[627]

But why does Paul allow the demon to have its way with the seven sons? The spirit's mastery over the sons of a priest remains a vivid image of their personal failure to be like Paul. Yet Luke's unexpected use of the prophetic catchword "house" (οἶκος *oikos*)—the place from which Sceva's sons fled "naked and wounded"—recalls Amos's prophecy of a "re-housed" Israel (see Amos 9:11-15; 15:16-21, 28-29) to add an additional layer of meaning to this story. In response to the worries of James about the gentilizing of Jewish practices (= exorcism), Luke again posits the problem among unrepentant Jews—in this case, the Jewish exorcists who come from a priestly family—rather than in the Pauline mission.

19:17. The public relations fallout from this episode has an immediate effect: "All residents of Ephesus . . . [were] awestruck [ἐπέπεσεν φόβος *epepesen phobos*; lit., "fear fell"]; and the name of the Lord Jesus

---

623. Cf. Haenchen, *The Acts of the Apostles*, 565.
624. Josephus *Antiquities of the Jews* 8:42-49.

625. The Western version of Acts erases "high," changing their father's status to that of a mere "priest." Less dramatic solutions are no less satisfying. See Witherington, *The Acts of the Apostles*, 580-81; Fitzmyer, *The Acts of the Apostles*, 650-51.
626. Cf. Barrett, *A Critical and Exegetical Commentary on the Acts of the Apostles*, 2:910.
627. Haenchen, *The Acts of the Apostles*, 565.

was praised." The thematic response of fear in Acts typically indicates the public recognition of God's visitation (see 2:43), sometimes to judge (see 5:5, 11) but always to make clear the reality of God's reign (see 4:16; 9:12). Likewise, the people's recognition of the prophet's authority through his wondrous acts is expressed not with praise of the prophet but with praise of God, who is the source and basis of his power.

19:18-20. The demythologization of magic in Ephesus leads to spiritual renewal: "Many of those who became believers confessed and disclosed their [magic] practices" (v. 18). The repentance of *believers* (rather than sinners) is rare within Scripture. The sense of this text is that certain believers have continued to indulge in practicing magic after their conversion to Jesus. The result of Paul's ministry, however, is the completion of their initiation into Jesus' Lordship. In this sense, then, Luke continues to gloss James's Jerusalem exhortation to put aside the "pollutions of idols," which magic practice surely is. Based on this text, James has reason to be concerned that those converted from pagan backgrounds may well continue their former religious practices; yet, at the same time he has reason to trust in Paul's authority to turn believers from these contaminates to what enriches faith.

Luke adds a vivid image of the conclusion of magic and superstition in the Ephesian church as Paul watches "fifty thousand silver coins" worth of magic books tossed into a public bonfire and incinerated. This is an enormous expense, probably equal to fifty thousand days' wages, and symbolizes the resolve to turn from magic to miracle, from pagan writings to Israel's Scriptures, from demonic charlatans to Paul. The dispossession of demonic property also symbolizes the inability of believers to appropriate God's power as another commodity; God's power is made available only through a relationship with the Lord. To this end, then, "the word of the Lord grew mightily and prevailed [ἰσχύω *ischyō*]" in Ephesus (v. 20; see also 4:4; 14:25; 16:6; 17:11). Earlier, *ischyō* is used to express Stephen's victory over his religious rivals in Jerusalem (see 6:10) and in the near context of the demoniac's mauling of Sceva's sons (see v. 16). These prophets-like-Jesus

prevail against their opponents and so authorize the word they proclaim as true, the life they live as exemplary, and the mission they lead as approved by God.

19:21-22. This transitional text foreshadows the plotline for the rest of Acts and for this reason performs an important role within the narrative. With the elimination of various impediments (i.e., confusion about John's baptism, magic, demon possession, sickness, pretenders to Paul's authority), a mature community in Ephesus is now formed and Paul begins to make travel plans to return to Macedonia and Achaia before going "on to Jerusalem" (v. 21*a*). These plans are commensurate with his missionary strategy of returning to those churches planted during earlier missions to fortify converts' spiritual resolve and theological understanding (see 14:21-23; 18:23; 20:2). Paul's priestly tasks, as much as his prophetic tasks, are an exercise of his religious authority within the church. Toward this end, then, he plans to follow the same route he paved according to Acts 16–18. The reader suspects that his plans to visit the holy city reflect his commitments to his ancestral religion, and he will travel there as a pious pilgrim (see 20:1).[628]

What is unexpected is Paul's resolve that he "must [δεῖ *dei*] also see Rome" (v. 21*b*). The shift within the overarching geographical structure of Paul's mission in Acts from Palestine (Antioch/Jerusalem) to Rome is here noted for the first time. While Paul himself tells us that he desired to see Rome (Rom 1:10; 15:24), Luke's use of the "*dei* of divine necessity" implies that his travel plans include Rome because God has disclosed it to him as the city of his destiny—in what manner Acts does not tell us. In fact, Paul leaves Ephesus for Macedonia in relative calm (see 20:1); he is not forced to leave as is more typically the case.[629]

An element of Paul's collaboration with God, however, is careful planning. In this

---

628. Drawing on Paul's letters (2 Cor 8:1-2; 9:2-4), some commentators contend that Paul's motive for including Jerusalem is to deliver the collection from Macedonian and Achaian congregations to the poor of the Judean church. The Jewish cast of Paul's profile in Acts, however, suggests rather that Paul prepares to travel to Jerusalem as a pious pilgrim to celebrate Pentecost.

629. Paul however mentions facing fierce opposition in Asia/Ephesus in 1 Cor 15:32 (cf. 2 Cor 1:8-10). In shaping his story of a triumphant Paul, Luke has edited out any clear sense of suffering or conflict—even though Acts 20:3 may allude to growing animosity among the Jews of Ephesus that prevented him from traveling overland to Antioch.

case he dispatches "two of his helpers, Timothy and Erastus, to Macedonia, while he stayed for some time longer in Asia [= Ephesus]" (v. 22). Paul's colleague Erastus is dropped into the narrative at this point, never to be mentioned again. He impresses us as yet another of Paul's associates who travels ahead with Timothy to prepare the way of the prophet-like-Jesus.

19:23-41. The portrayal of Paul's spiritual authority in Acts would not be complete without a controversy over property. Indeed, the dispossession of property is an important barometer of the disciple's relations with God and symbolic of the possession of authority within the community (see 4:32–5:11). While Paul's ministry in Ephesus enjoys extraordinary success—so great, in fact, that the city's merchants claim that Paul's mission has had an adverse effect upon the wealthy and prominent Artemis cult—the pagan opposition to him is nevertheless pervasive and well organized. In general terms, the story of their opposition to Paul follows the plotline of his earlier controversy in Philippi. The leader of the opposition party in Ephesus is the silversmith Demetrius (vv. 23-24; cf. 16:16b), whose arguments against Paul (vv. 25-27) echo those made by the handlers of the clairvoyant girl in Philippi (16:20-21): Paul has turned people away from traditional religion, and he is bad for business. These accusations lead to mob riot and confusion (vv. 28-32; cf. 16:22), which is only intensified by the crowd's anti-Semitism (vv. 33-34; cf. 16:20). In the present passage, the city chancellor intervenes rather than God (vv. 35-41; cf. 16:25-26; 18:12-16); however, the result is the same: The charges against Paul are dismissed, and his opposition is silenced (cf. 16:35-40).

The literary function of this parallelism between Luke's narratives of Paul's Philippian and Ephesian missions is to enclose and concentrate this phase of his work on controversy with pagans (rather than with unrepentant Jews) who are more concerned to maintain their profit margins than to hear the word of God's prophet. In this contest between God and Mammon, God's word always prevails. The disturbing anti-Semitic theme found in both stories is characteristic of pagan culture and not unique to Paul's mission.

19:23-24. As Paul made travel plans to revisit other congregations on his way to Jerusalem and then Rome, "no little [οὐκ ὀλίγος *ouk oligos*] disturbance broke out concerning the Way" (v. 23). The ringleader of this controversy is "a man named Demetrius, a silversmith who made silver shrines of Artemis, brought no little [*ouk oligos*] business to the artisans" (v. 24). The repeated use of litotes (a literary device to express understatement) makes it clear that the disturbance is due to business rather than to religious devotion. The phrase "no little disturbance" expresses publicly the Way's threat to "no little business." This wholesaler of devotional goods has suffered a financial downturn because of Paul's Ephesian mission! The effect conversion may have on Demetrius's business is made explicit in the earlier account of burning expensive books (see v. 19): Conversion demands a complete rejection of one's pagan past, including the destruction of religious paraphernalia—magic books along with the silver shrines that Demetrius manufactured to support the Artemis cult in Ephesus.

The Artemis cult is well known from ancient literature and modern archaeological expeditions.[630] The temple of Artemis in Ephesus was considered among the seven wonders of the ancient world and was a financial center for all of Roman Asia (hence, Demetrius's worry). Its temple functionaries provided relief to the poor and shelter for the refugee. The stature of Artemis in the pagan pantheon was due in large part to the splendor of the Ephesian temple and the practices and celebrations connected with it. In Greek religion, Artemis (= Diana in Roman religion) was Apollo's sister, the virgin goddess and defender of chastity, the huntress goddess and champion of fertility. In local religion, these various associations were integrated with still others (especially with the Great Mother of Anatolian mythology), and Artemis worship took on an indigenous character in Ephesus: It was a civil religion, and the rhythm of city life revolved around the temple and its festivals. To subvert the worship of Artemis the Great was to threaten the city's culture, its way of life, both economic and social, shaped by its routines and calendar.

---

630. For a bibliography and abstract of these expeditions, see Fitzmyer, *The Acts of the Apostles*, 657-58.

19:25-27. Demetrius organizes a protest movement among members of his silversmith guild (v. 25a), forming a cohesive group of workers in opposition to a common threat: the Way. His speech appeals to common knowledge or experience and makes clear the threat and, therefore, the reasons for the people's protest. As we would expect, his principal anxiety is "that we get our wealth [εὐπορία *euporia*] from this business" (v. 25b). Luke's vocabulary for wealth is varied. The word Demetrius uses here for "wealth" denotes a more holistic conception than mere financial gain; it includes one's sense of well-being. In the light of what he goes on to say, the use of this word is ironical and implies that while he has other concerns in life, including religious devotion, his perspective toward all of life is at base a materialistic one.

Demetrius again appeals to what his colleagues "see and hear"—to common knowledge—to claim that "Paul has persuaded and drawn away [μεθίστημι *methistēmi*] a considerable number of people" (v. 26a). This statement simply reports what the reader knows from the earlier account of Paul's Ephesian mission: It has been a rousing success. However, the statement testifies as well to what the narrator has not said: A large number of Paul's converts come from the Artemis cult. The word *methistēmi* denotes the kind of religious seduction that makes people turn away from their cults. (Of course, this is very bad for Demetrius's business!) His summary of Paul's message that "gods made with hands are not gods" (v. 26b) echoes Paul's Areopagus speech in Athens (see 17:24-27; cf. 7:48) and recalls from that speech his polemic against idolatry on both practical (idols are not personal) and theological (God is "the God") grounds.

In his final statement, Demetrius strings together a series of infinitives that globalize his previous claims, and he ties them to the main idea that there is danger to "all Asia and the world": "not only [for] this trade of ours— but also [for] the temple of the great goddess Artemis" (v. 27). The Artemis cult was widespread; pilgrims traveled from all corners of the empire to purchase silver shrines from craftsmen and to worship in her Ephesian temple. With the loss of Artemis's global esteem would come the loss of Demetrius's

importance and income. While Demetrius may be guilty of using highly charged rhetoric and exaggerated claims of Paul's threat to incite this group of local merchants, his statement measures reality accurately. The convincing logic of Paul's message against idolatry, when coupled with his powerful persona, has shifted the center of religious authority in Ephesus from the temple of Artemis toward the lecture hall of Tyrannus.

There is a sense, however, that the interpreter's principal interest in Demetrius's commentary on Paul's universal influence should be neither historical (Was history's Paul really this influential?) nor redactional (Was Luke's Paul really this influential?) but canonical (Is Scripture's Paul really this influential?). The effect of his repeated claim that the "whole of Asia" is persuaded by Paul's teaching (v. 26) and that he has deprived "all Asia and the world" of Artemis' devotion (v. 27), especially when considered with other similar statements in this narrative (see vv. 10, 17), is to internationalize the influence of Pauline teaching. Indeed, the teaching of his letters is universally persuasive and will result in a turning from idols every place where they are read.

19:28-31. Demetrius's speech has its intended effect: His audience becomes "enraged," and they cry out on cue, "Great is Artemis of the Ephesians" (v. 28). Their acclamation is in the form of a confession that well expresses both their devotion to her and their astonishment that the great Artemis cult could be under attack.[631]

The Western version of Acts adds that the Ephesians' rage carried them "into the street," which makes possible the story's logic that what began as a small labor protest resulted in a city that was filled with confusion (v. 29a). Among the details of "local color" included in this episode is the reference to the theater in Ephesus, which accommodated 24,000 people and was often used for assemblies. It is not clear why in their confusion the crowd would drag with them "Gaius and Aristarchus, Macedonians who were Paul's travel companions" (v. 29b; cf. 20:4), unless to remind the reader that this present dust-up

---

631. Cf. Haenchen, *The Acts of the Apostles*, 573. On Luke's use of the literary conventions of Hellenistic novels, see Johnson, *The Acts of the Apostles*, 348-49.

threatens Paul's travel plans to carry the Word of God with Gaius and Aristarchus to Rome via Macedonia and Jerusalem (see vv. 21-22). Perhaps it is his concern for their safety that prompts Paul's wish "to go into the crowd"; the disciples had such a reciprocal concern for his safety that they "would not let him" (v. 30)—a decision supported by friendly provincial "officials" (v. 31).[632] The keen impression these vivid images of chaos and a mob riot create indicates a threat to the gospel far worse than reasoned debate.

19:32-34. The repeated description of the city's "confusion" (v. 32) perhaps explains what happens next. Haenchen refers to this passage as "an old *crux interpretum*."[633] The interpretive problems are twofold: What motivates "the Jews" to push Alexander forward "to make a defense before the people"? And what prompts Luke to include this detail in his narrative? He does not provide clear answers, nor does he tell us anything about Alexander. The implication is that the crowd's confusion exists at several levels, including religious. The Jews push Alexander forward to clarify the status of "official" Judaism within Ephesus—perhaps in relationship to the Artemis cult. From other stories in Acts, the reader might be able to recover the gist of what Alexander would have said if given half a chance by the angry mob: Surely at the center of his defense would be Judaism's status as a *religio licita* ("officially recognized religion") in the empire (see 18:12-17). In addition to this general defense, most commentators suspect that Alexander's apologia would not have given support to this protest movement against Paul or attempted to distinguish Judaism from "the Way," even though Paul had long since disassociated himself from the synagogue. For both these implied reasons he is shouted down.

And he is shouted down *as a Jew:* "But when they recognized that he was a Jew, for about two hours all shouted in unison 'Great is Artemis of the Ephesians'" (v. 34). The undertone of this dramatic scene is fiercely anti-Semitic (see 16:20; 18:17). For this

reason, Luke's motive is sometimes questioned: Did he add this to the story to embarrass "the Jews"? His motive, however, is very different. Within a pagan setting, the distinction the synagogue may have made between its teaching and Paul's would have been heard with the same neutrality displayed by Gallio in Corinth (see 18:12-16) or by the handlers of the slave girl in Philippi (16:20). These pagans readily understand (although with derision) what Paul's Jewish opponents fail to admit: He is a messianic Jew who shares with them the same religious practices and sacred traditions. When compared to Paul's pronounced Jewish profile within Acts, these occurrences of anti-Semitism in the narrative of Paul's mission are heavily ironic. There is a tragic contour to Luke's meaning here: While all Jews share together a fundamental opposition to the symbols of Artemis worship, pagan cult members who are polluted by idols nevertheless see this theological solidarity more clearly than do Jews.

19:35-41. As before in Corinth when Gallio intervened on Paul's behalf and argued against his opponents, again "the town clerk" (γραμματεύς *grammateus*; lit., "scribe") quiets and addresses the angry crowd in defense of Paul (v. 35*a*). A *grammateus* was a bureaucrat, the chief city official who kept accurate records for the city and acted as a liaison with Rome. For this reason he has a good feel for the legalities of both Paul's case and a lynch mob and is the right person to "quiet" the current situation. His speech is an example of deliberative rhetoric in which he persuades his auditors to see Paul from his perspective. Significantly, his ability to move the crowd is not a function of his status in Ephesian politics but of the reasonableness of his appeal to them.

The town clerk makes three legal statements that warrant his admonition to "be quiet and do nothing rash" against Paul and his colleagues. (1) They are neither temple robbers nor blasphemers—that is, they have done nothing against the Artemis cult that would constitute hard legal evidence against them (v. 37). (2) The mob has acted inappropriately in dragging Gaius and Aristarchus, with Paul, to the theater. There is a legal protocol in place to handle all complaints: If Demetrius and his guild have a complaint,

---

632. Luke's reference to "officials of the province" ('Ασιάρχοι *Asiarchoi*) who are friends of Paul is remarkable. On the one hand, it supports an important missionary theme of Acts that Paul's mission has friends in high places. On the other hand, these provincial rulers exercised their civic responsibility to maintain devotion to the official Roman cults, including that of Artemis.

633. Haenchen, *The Acts of the Apostles*, 574.

the courts are open with proconsuls available to hear cases, "let them bring charges there [i.e., rather than here]" (v. 38). This is a compressed statement that implies that papers must be filed (perhaps with the town clerk) before a court appearance is scheduled. (3) Finally, the town clerk moves to defer whatever accusations might be brought against Paul to "the regular assembly [i.e., and not to this one, which is an irregular assembly without judicial portfolio]" (v. 39). The clerk's case, which began with a religious appeal, concludes with a legal verdict that is a more modest version of the one rendered by Gallio (see 18:12-16). If Paul is guilty of neither sacrilege (v. 37) nor criminal behavior (vv. 38, 40), and if this is simply a matter of contested religious claims between the Artemis cult (vv. 35-36) and followers of the Way, then let the case be settled in a religious context. There is no legal case, but there is a religious case; and clearly the Paul of Acts has won that one.

The clerk's argument for prudent behavior follows the logic of another scribe, Gamaliel, before a very different courtroom (see 5:35-39). His appeal to do nothing rash is grounded in religious absolutes: Since the Artemis shrine "fell from heaven,"[634] and Ephesus is "the temple keeper" (v. 35), the gods must be for us, and Paul can do nothing that subverts true believers or the Artemis shrine. The translations of the phrase "cannot be denied" (ἀναντίρρητος . . . δέον *anantirrētos . . . deon*; lit., "necessarily undeniable") disguise Luke's striking use of δεῖ (*dei*), which elsewhere in Acts speaks of the divine necessity of an event because it agrees with biblical prophecy. In this case, the clerk's appeal allows for Paul's departure and moves him a step closer to Rome, the city of his destiny (see vv. 21-22).

---

634. Greco-Roman literature mentions several objects "fallen from heaven": Pseudo-Apollodorus *Bibliotheca 3.12.3*; Appian *Hannibal* 56; Herodian 1.11.1; Pausanias 3.12.4. Euripides, in his *Iphegenia at Tauris* 15-88, 1381-85, specifically mentions such an object's being in the temple of Artemis in Taurica. Presumably these objects were meteorites that were venerated as objects sent by the gods to show divine favor. See also Fitzmyer, *The Acts of the Apostles*, 661.

REFLECTIONS

1. "A number of those who practiced magic collected their books and burned them publicly" (19:19 NRSV). Various stories that distinguish between magic and miracle are featured in Acts (see 5:12-16; 8:14-24; 13:6-12; 14:8-18). The casual observer might note there are real similarities between the magician and prophet that only lead to public confusion concerning the claims of the gospel: Both brokered power, predicted futures, and influenced people by incantation of names or by human touch. Today similar comparisons are sometimes made between well-known televangelists with healing ministries or prosperity gospels and "shamans" of the occult. In part, these comparisons persist in popular culture because the distinction made in Acts is not always made clear in the church. The Jewish exorcists who attempt to use the name of Jesus magically are mocked in Luke's story in stark contrast to the reverence reserved for the name of Jesus preached by Paul. Why? Because their practice of magic is detached from a personal relationship with Jesus; it is the precise incantation of mere words to defeat the devil, motivated finally by self-interest, and it does not work.

Do we make it clear in our teaching that the promise of God's salvation-creation power is predicated on our dependence upon Jesus and not ourselves and that it enables us to serve God's purposes and not our own? The life-changing power of the gospel is concrete and demonstrative; but its transforming effect in the believer's life aims its recipient at God rather than at a material result that serves our selfish wants. The miraculous power brokered by Paul is not a commodity dispensed to manipulate the direction of human life; rather, it is the mark of his spiritual authority that serves the missionary purposes of his prophetic vocation. In this sense, the public book burning ceremony in Ephesus is not due to the ineffectiveness of these expensive books; no doubt these books are the source of powerful magic. The burning of "magic books" (or their contemporary parallels, such as diet, therapy, self-help books) is, rather, the believer's divestment of an alternate source of power and influence that detracts from the gospel message and the Spirit's power and thereby subverts our eternal relationship with the Lord.

2. "There is danger not only that our trade will lose its good name, but also that the temple of the great goddess Artemis will be discredited" (19:27 NIV). Demetrius views Paul as a threat because his message and its powerful effect endanger his profit margin. Hardly prompted by crass materialism, however, the protest movement he organizes against the Way is informed by a perspective that links religion and money. Demetrius is honest in his grievances but mistaken in his core beliefs.

The church will not be the church if its principal concerns are with the economic "bottom line" and with the "big business" of being a successful institution. Rather, the church's principal concerns/core beliefs are to center on the formation of a community of goods whose vocation is to cultivate together a single-minded and profound devotion of God.

ACTS 20:1-16, PAUL'S PILGRIMAGE TO JERUSALEM

COMMENTARY

Under the shadow of Acts 19:20-21 and with new assurances of the Way's triumph in Ephesus, Paul resumes his preparations to extend the scope of his European mission to include Rome, the city of his destiny. With growing awareness of the struggles that await him during his journey to "the end of the earth," he sets out for Jerusalem as a Jewish pilgrim to worship God on the holy day of Pentecost (see 20:16). In this collocation of three stories, details of Paul's travel itinerary and chronology are combined to help the reader follow his progress. Mention of his colleagues and others along the way form a community of witnesses who are able to mark the pilgrim's path to the holy city. Among these is the narrator, who rejoins Paul's entourage to add another voice to the journey (see 20:5).

Scholars have long noted the vague parallelism between Paul's and the Lord's final journey to Jerusalem and posit this as another proof of his solidarity with God's Messiah, whose suffering in the holy city resulted in the salvation of Israel and the nations.[635] While the literary structure and allusions found in this passage may support that reading, its theological connection is more dubious (see below). Two parallel passages that provide Paul's travel plans for Jerusalem, complete with careful chronological markers and details of his religious intent (20:1-6, 13-16), enclose another of Luke's dramatic typological stories (20:7-12), this one of a young man named Eutychus who falls from the third story of an apartment building in Troas and then is "raised from the dead" on the "first day of the week." The rhetorical effect of this triad is to convince the reader that Paul's travel plans for Jerusalem and finally Rome (see 19:21-22) are motivated by his desire to serve God's redemptive plans and purposes.

20:1-6. Paul's decision to leave Ephesus had already been made before the turmoil provoked by the guild of silversmiths; it was made in response to God's will rather than to escape personal attack (see 19:21-22). For this reason his departure from the city takes place during relative calm, "after the uproar had ceased" (v. 1a). Before bidding farewell, Paul characteristically sends for the disciples, encourages (παρακαλέσας *parakalesas*) them, and leaves for Macedonia (v. 1b; see also 14:22; 15:32; 16:40). Luke's repeated use of the participle *parakalesas* in Acts recalls earlier uses, inviting the inference that

635. The parallelism is as follows: (1) like Jesus before him, Paul announces his intentions to travel to Jerusalem (19:21; cf. Luke 9:31); (2) he sends delegates before him in pairs (19:22; 20:4; cf. Luke 10:1); (3) unrepentant Jews plot against his life (20:3; cf. Matt 12:14; 26:4); (4) he goes forward despite this threat (20:6, 16, see 20:22-23; cf. Luke 9:51; 13:22; 17:11); (5) he enters the Holy City a final time (21:15-17; cf. Luke 19:28).

Paul's ongoing encouragement includes additional teaching now made evident by a prophecy of coming tribulation that would require a mature faith and theological understanding to endure (see 14:22). The reader is not told the route Paul takes from Ephesus to Macedonia, but only that "he had gone through those regions and had given the believers much encouragement [*parakalesas*]" before arriving in Greece (v. 2), where he stayed for three months (v. 3*a*; cf. 1 Cor 16:5-6).

During his stay in Greece, Paul learns of another Jewish plot against him (see 9:24; cf. 23:30). He had originally planned "to set sail for Syria," which would have put him in Jerusalem more quickly—perhaps to celebrate Passover (see v. 6). To throw his enemies off track (cf. 23:12-24), Paul changes his plans for a sea voyage and instead retraces his overland route through Macedonia (v. 3).[636]

A list of seven traveling companions is provided but without any description of their responsibilities toward Paul and his mission (v. 4)[637] other than as an advance team sent to Troas (in Asia) to make preparations for Paul's future visit. The narrator plans to join them there (v. 5). Perhaps the intended impression is that together they represent Paul's various mission fields, often in pairs, and provide witness to his past efforts.

Following the detour through Macedonia, Paul is further delayed in Philippi in order that he and the narrator can celebrate "days of Unleavened Bread" (Passover; see Luke 22:1) before joining the others in Troas (v. 6). Evidently, the plot against his life, which required him to take this detour, also made it impossible to reach Jerusalem in time to observe Passover with other pilgrims. Yet this reference to a Philippian Passover is striking for several reasons. At the surface level of the narrative, the chronological detail anchors Paul's final journey to Jerusalem in historical time: He has seven weeks to make

Jerusalem by Pentecost (see v. 16). We also recognize that this passing reference contributes to Luke's portrait of a Jewish Paul who religiously integrates the practices of his ancestral faith with the belief that the living Jesus is God's Messiah. There is then in his observance of Passover tacit allusion to James's concern that Paul's mission to the nations maintain the church's Jewish identity whenever and wherever it is threatened by potential pagan pollutants (see 15:20-21).

In this regard the location of Paul's observance of Passover—in Philippi—must be recognized as theologically significant. Acts demonizes Philippi as a lawless city, full of anti-Semitic bias and without an urban synagogue before Paul arrived (see 16:11-34). By the time he left town under police escort, he had established a "house" of worship *within* city limits composed of converted God-fearing Gentiles (see 16:35-40). If any congregation of the Pauline church is a prime candidate for setting aside its Jewish heritage or being contaminated by the "pollutions of idols," it surely would have been this one. And yet here is Paul the pious Jew in Philippi celebrating Passover with a congregation of God-fearing Gentile believers!

20:7-12. Paul arrives with Luke in Troas, where they stay a week (20:6b). On "the first day of the week" he met with a congregation there to "break bread" and to "hold a discussion with them" (v. 7). Mention of this Sunday is the first reference in the NT of observing a Christian sabbath (cf. 1 Cor 16:2; Rev 1:10), no doubt as a continuing memorial to the Lord's resurrection (cf. Luke 24:1). In fact, images of the resurrection are found throughout this story, which should be read as a typological narrative for this reason. That is, Paul's pilgrimage to Jerusalem and mission to Rome are motivated by his vocation to proclaim that Jesus is alive, and the present episode typifies this core conviction.

This congregation probably followed traditional sabbath rules and so began worship on Saturday evening after sunset into Sunday's dawn (see v. 11).[638] The practice of "breaking bread" refers to a common meal rather than to the Lord's supper and is symbolic of their social and spiritual solidarity (see 2:45-46).[639]

636. The Western text of Acts adds to 20:3: "The Spirit said to him to go through Macedonia."

637. Several modern commentators speculate on the basis of Pauline letters (cf. Rom 15:25-27; 1 Cor 16:1-2; 2 Cor 9:4) that those listed here are actually collection agents who have been assigned the task of delivering an offering from Macedonian and Achaian congregations to Jerusalem. Acts makes no mention of this offering during the entire travel narrative, however, and only mentions such a "gift" vaguely and in passing in 24:17 as a small bit of Paul's defense speech—and there perhaps in reference to 11:27-30. See Haenchen, *The Acts of the Apostles*, 378-79. Johnson, *The Acts of the Apostles*, 357, notes that those listed might be members of a so-called "Pauline School" who are engaged in preserving and transmitting Pauline teaching.

638. Fitzmyer, *The Acts of the Apostles*, 668-69.

639. Cf. Conzelmann, *The Acts of the Apostles*, 169, who says that in its original form this was a secular story with a popular comic touch meant to provide rhetorical relief rather than "ritual exactitude."

Such meals were opportunities to gather together for community prayer and to hear inspired teaching (see 2:42). Paul's "discussion [διαλέγομαι *dialegomai*] with them" is the central activity of worship, even as it was during his synagogue ministry (see 17:2, 17; 18:4; 19:8). The implication from Luke's earlier uses of *dialegomai* is that Paul is engaged in a Bible study, interpreting the Scriptures to show that the risen Jesus is God's Messiah (see 17:3). Because of time constraints on a pilgrim's journey—Paul wants to make it to Jerusalem in time for Pentecost—he "continued speaking until midnight" (v. 7*b*) in an upstairs meeting room with "many lamps" (v. 8). These circumstances are added to explain what happens next in the story: A long speech in a stuffy room well past bedtime makes falling asleep plausible. These same details, however, also allude to the gospel story in which Jesus met with his disciples in the upper room to break bread in preparation for what takes place on the first day of the week (see Matt 26:20-29; Mark 14:17-25; Luke 22:14-38).

With careful staging, then, we are introduced to the other main character of this tragicomedy, "a young man named Eutychus [= Lucky]" (v. 9*a*). He is precariously seated on the sill of an open window, where he dozes off and falls three stories to the ground below, to be "picked up dead" (v. 9*b*). In dramatic fashion reminiscent of Jesus (cf. Mark 5:40), Peter (see 9:40-41), and other prophets before him (cf. 1 Kgs 17:21-22; 2 Kgs 4:34-35), Paul resuscitates Eutychus and announces to the others, "Do not be alarmed, for his life is in him" (v. 10). Several commentators have noted Paul's matter-of-fact tone and the way he hastens back upstairs to resume his conversation without fuss or fanfare (v. 11); these commentators suggest that his pronouncement makes a diagnosis rather than declares a healing miracle.[640] Paul's life-saving action, which appears as a mere hiccup during his teaching ministry, would seem to indicate that the two actions—teaching and

miracle-working—form a coherent whole to express a common resurrection theme.[641]

20:13-16. Paul continues his pilgrimage to Jerusalem by traveling from Troas to Miletus. He travels the first leg by land to Assos, where he meets his companions, who have arrived by boat.[642] Together they continue by sea to Miletus with stops between in Mitylene, Chios, and Samos. These Aegean ports-of-call were roughly a day's sailing apart, a standard route to take into the Miletus port. Luke's travel summary, written in the first person, concludes by reconfirming Paul's religious motive for his journey to Jerusalem: "He was eager to be in Jerusalem . . . on the day of Pentecost" (v. 16; see also 2:1). His decision to bypass Ephesus is for lack of time rather than for lack of security—although one wonders why then he should wait in Miletus for the Ephesian elders to come and bid farewell to him there unless he had reason to be concerned for his safety in Ephesus (cf. 2 Cor 1:8-10).

The pairing of Paul's observance of Passover in Philippi and his eagerness to arrive in Jerusalem to celebrate Pentecost make clear the motive for his hurried travel. There is no indication whatsoever in Acts that Luke has suppressed the "real" reason for Paul's journey—delivery of the Macedonian collection. The narrator shapes a story that depicts this prophet-like-Jesus as a practicing Jew (see v. 6). For this repentant Jew, however, the celebration of Israel's Pentecost has taken on even deeper significance as a festival for remembering that God has poured out the Holy Spirit upon God's people to empower their witness to the risen Messiah to the "end of the earth." Paul's urgency to reach Jerusalem "by the day of Pentecost" is now qualified by his prophetic vocation to carry God's word to Rome (see 19:21-22). The pilgrim's pace is set by God's plan as well as Judaism's liturgical year.

---

641. The hagiographic tendency of the Western version is exemplified here by adding to 20:12 the note that Paul himself brought the boy and gave them to him alive: "When they were saying goodbye, Paul took the boy away alive; and they were not a little comforted!" While the scribes want to make certain that Paul gets credit for the miracle, they subvert Luke's intentions of portraying his power as typical of his normal prophetic routines.

642. Luke does not explain Paul's travel itinerary. Fitzmyer's suggestion that he travels by land to Assos rather than by sea for reasons of safety does not square with the persona of the Paul of Acts. See Fitzmyer, *The Acts of the Apostles*, 671.

640. Cf. Haenchen, *The Acts of the Apostles*, 586.

REFLECTIONS

Then Paul "went upstairs again, broke bread and ate" (20:11 NIV). The wonderful story of Paul's resuscitation of "lucky" Eutychus illustrates the good news of Jesus' resurrection. The episode is part of a journey narrative that depicts Paul on his way to Jerusalem, stopping along his pilgrim's way to "encourage" and say his fond farewells to various congregations of disciples (see 20:1-2). Central to his ministry of encouragement is Christian fellowship (= "breaking bread") and intensive instruction. The ministries of Word and table are the twin hallmarks of authentic *koinōnia*, without which the church cannot be the church in the world. The Benedictine Rule, which posits great value on a community's hospitality—its table fellowship—recognizes the practical truth that the Word is better received and understood in an atmosphere of congeniality and acceptance. In this special sense, Word and Table are integral parts of a formative whole.

Amid his ministry of encouragement and in continuity with other prophets before him, Paul brokers God's life-giving power in raising Eutychus from the dead. Luke does not want the reader to dwell on the miracle, however, and so Paul resumes his ministry of the Word without pause. In one sense, this is so because there is no real dichotomy between miracle and message. Paul makes so little of this miracle because the hallmark of Christian community is not the miraculous but the message of the risen Jesus. In a religious culture that is drawn toward the spectacular, the community of believers must be ever diligent to congregate around the gospel for instruction. The Word is the thing!

ACTS 20:17-38, PAUL'S SPEECH OF SUCCESSION

COMMENTARY

Paul's speech to the Ephesian elders at Miletus brings to fitting conclusion his controversial mission to the city of Ephesus. Because it is his only speech addressed to believers, it carries paradigmatic value for the readers of Acts. We may insinuate what Paul says to the Ephesian elders into other stories in which Paul makes pastoral house calls to organize and encourage fledgling Christian congregations. His sermon topics concerning Christian leadership and character, in which he is exemplary, are particularly relevant themes of Paul's ongoing mentoring ministry.

S. Walton has noted the centrality of the Miletus discourse to the ongoing debate over whether Luke used any of Paul's letters when writing Acts.[643] In contrast to Paul's missionary speeches or legal briefs, this one addresses a pastoral setting similar to his letters, many of which convey similar concerns and interests.[644] For this reason an analysis of this speech may prove to have special importance in understanding the relationship between the Paul of Acts and the Pauline letters.[645] All the speeches of Acts are composed by Luke, and this one in particular is a piece of his finished portrait of Paul; however, its topics and theological conception are substantially Pauline,[646] so much so that C. Hemer thinks it possible to consider it Luke's précis of Paul's actual words, of which

643. S. Walton, *Leadership and Lifestyle*, SNTSMS 108 (Cambridge: Cambridge University Press, 2000). In what follows in this paragraph, I am dependent on Walton's fine study and my private conversations with him.

644. This intracanonical relationship is especially true of the so-called Pastoral Epistles (1–2 Timothy and Titus) in which the canonical Paul addresses a similar problem facing the Paul of Acts in Miletus: the continuation of the Pauline legacy in a post-Pauline setting through his appointed delegates.

645. See Witherington, *The Acts of the Apostles*, 610, for a listing of linguistic parallels between this passage and the Pauline letters.

646. Cf. Porter, *Paul of Acts*, 115-18.

Luke was an auditor.[647] While the majority of modern commentators remain uncertain about whether Luke witnessed this event or had direct access to any of his letters, they concur that he at the very least used Pauline sources to compose a speech that substantially agrees with the Pauline letters in its portrait of Paul and presentation of his message.[648] What must be added to this conclusion, however, is that Luke conveys an idealized representation of a canonical Paul whose Miletus message he intends to function as formative of Christian mission well into the future.[649]

The question of the speech's literary genre is also pertinent to any discussion of its wider role within the NT canon. There is virtual unanimity among commentators that this is Paul's farewell speech, serving to publish his "last will and testament" to a gathering of close associates and friends.[650] There is one problem with this consensus: Paul does not die in Acts. For this reason, I am inclined to consider this speech more narrowly as a "speech of succession," occasioned by Paul's departure from Ephesus when it is appropriate to charge newly appointed leaders to continue his work in his absence. In this sense, it functions within Acts in a manner similar to the opening narrative, where details of the apostolic succession of Jesus are given (see 1:3-14; also 12:1-17; cf. Luke 22:14-38; 24:36-53).[651] In that earlier story, Jesus prepares his apostles for their future ministry in light of his departure (1) by reviewing and interpreting his past suffering, proofs of his resurrection (cf. 20:7-12), and his message of God's kingdom (see 1:3); (2) against the

horizon of his future ascension/departure from them (1:2); (3) and in retrospect of John's promise of the Spirit (1:4-5), (4) the Lord charges his apostles to bring a Spirit-empowered witness of him to restore Israel as a light to the nations (1:6-8). (5) The succession is completed with Jesus' departure into the heavens (1:9-11). The purpose of Jesus' final speech to his apostles is not to bid them farewell but to commission them for a future mission that continues what he has begun to do and to say as Messiah (see 1:1).[652]

If the interpreter considers Paul's Miletus speech and departure as roughly analogous in form and function to the Lord's final speech to his apostles, then the following sketch of topics emerges (see below):[653] (1) Paul rehearses his past ministry, relating his suffering and testimony (20:18b-20) (2) against the horizon of his future departure from them (20:21-25) and (3) in retrospect of his ministry among them (20:26-27). (4) Paul then charges the Ephesian elders to care for the church of God (20:28-35). (5) The succession is completed with Paul's departure from them (20:36-38). Paul's purpose is pastoral preparation; his aim is to equip his successors to continue what he has begun to do and say in Ephesus, knowing that his departure from the city and its Christian congregation is now final (20:25).

These various literary and redactional conclusions point to the value of this speech in framing an approach to Paul's epistolary witness. What the Paul of Acts says to his successors in Asia forms a rhetorical ethos that cultivates the living reader's confidence in his exemplary persona and trustworthy instruction and has lasting importance for the church catholic in every generation. By extension, then, if the Paul of Acts has lasting importance as the spiritual exemplar and theological mentor of God's people, then the Pauline letters supply his theological primer and personal testimony to their living readers who are confident of his lasting importance in their Christian formation. In this regard, the themes of his speech suggest touch-points with his letters that help to fashion a coherent

---

647. C. Hemer, "The Speeches in Acts: I. The Ephesian Elders at Miletus," *TynBul* 40 (1989) 77-85. Hemer argues against Haenchen, *The Acts of the Apostles*, 596-97, who contends that the "we" passages of Acts constitute a literary device to strengthen Luke's apology for Paul, of which this speech is a crucial element, and are therefore not based upon an auditor's historical memory.

648. Cf. Lüdemann, *Early Christianity According to the Traditions in Acts*, 226-30, who does not think the setting/speech is historically based. More cautious in this regard is Barrett, *A Critical and Exegetical Commentary on the Acts of the Apostles*, 2:963-66, who notes that Luke's agreements with Pauline tradition are especially evident with those found in the Pastoral Epistles (particularly 2 Timothy) and probably depend upon similar if not the same Pauline sources. However, see Walton, *Leadership and Lifestyle*, 193, for whom "it can be unhelpful to group the Pastorals together in an undifferentiated way" and for whom the parallels even with 2 Timothy are mostly vague and not as close as Barrett, *A Critical and Exegetical Commentary on the Acts of the Apostles*, 195-98, thinks.

649. Cf. B. Childs, *The New Testament as Canon* (Philadelphia: Fortress, 1984) 225-27.

650. Cf. Walton, *Leadership and Lifestyle*, 61-65, for a summary and evaluation of the literary conventions of the "farewell speech" in both Jewish and Greco-Roman contexts.

651. For gospel parallels, see Walton, *Leadership and Lifestyle*, 100-117.

652. The eschatological horizon is different between Jesus and his prophet, since the expectation is that he will return to earth to complete his messianic mission (see 1:10-11; 3:21) whereas there is no expectation of Paul's return to Ephesus (however, cf. 1 Tim 1:3; 2 Tim 1:15-18).

653. For a summary and analysis of the different proposals concerning this speech's rhetorical design, see Walton, *Leadership and Lifestyle*, 66-75.

theological understanding of their collective witness to "the whole counsel of God"—for example, faithful and humble leadership, costly suffering of consecrated service to God, congregational welfare over personal gain, threats against the church.[654]

Paul's discourse also concerns those who are responsible for transmitting and interpreting his legacy to others in his absence. His previous mission in Ephesus laid a foundation, and his gospel defined its theological boundaries; yet, this deposit of God's grace is under constant threat, and spiritual vigilance is required of those who are custodians of it. These Pauline inheritors are charged to imitate their mentor's faithfulness no matter the cost, without which his precious legacy has no future. By extension, if the Pauline letters are the textual precipitate of Paul's legacy, then their future in the church is predicated on faithful interpreters who firmly embrace Paul's testimony to God's grace and imitate his faithful service to God's calling. The responsibility of interpreting Paul for the next generation of believers is no longer a matter of casting lots or of holding ecclesial office, but of good character and orthodox belief in faithful imitation of Paul.

20:17-18a. This brief introduction to the speech sets its stage and tone: Paul "sent a message" (μεταχαλέω *metakaleō*) to Ephesus asking that the "elders [πρεσβύτεροι *presbyteroi*] of the church" meet with him in Miletus. Luke assumes that a council of elders leads in the formation of Christian congregations from the very beginning of the mission to the nations (see 11:30; 14:23; 15:6; 16:4). The use of *metakaleō* suggests that this is a meeting according to God's plans, which gives it an air of importance (see 10:32).

20:18b-27. The first half of Paul's speech to the Ephesian elders concentrates their attention on his legacy. It is enclosed by an apologia of his past ministry at Ephesus, which he characterizes as faithful both to his prophetic calling (vv. 18*b*-21) and to his congregants (vv. 26-27). Sandwiched between is a prophecy of his future suffering in Jerusalem (vv. 22-24) and an assertion on this basis that he will not return to Ephesus (v. 25).

20:18b-21. In a single Greek sentence, the Paul of Acts defends his Asian mission,

centered in Ephesus, in two integral movements. The first appeals to the entire body of evidence of "how I lived among you" (cf. 1 Thess 2:1-2; 5:10-11; Phil 4:15)—a life characterized by humble service to the Lord and by costly endurance of "the plots of the Jews" (v. 19; cf. 2 Cor 1:3-11). While testimony of his "humility"[655] reflects Paul's commentary on his inward affections (cf. 2 Cor 10:1; 11:7; 1 Thess 2:6), the appeal to consider his suffering, which resulted from various plots against him, is more empirical and invites his auditors to evaluate the hard evidence in his favor. The reader too can participate in this review by recalling the narrative of his Ephesian mission in consideration of Paul's struggles there (see 19:8-10; 20:3; cf. 20:33-34).

The second broad movement concerns the disposition of his pastoral obligations to the Ephesian church. Paul's description of prophetic tasks performed is exemplary of Christian leadership for the church's future; he will later recall these same images as characteristic of ministry that continues his legacy in his absence. He asserts that in general he "did not shrink from doing anything helpful." On the one hand, Paul does not shrink from his calling to teach the congregations ("house to house"; see 15:16-17; cf. Rom 16:5; Phlm 21) his mission has founded—unlike Judas, for example, whose betrayal of Jesus was a repudiation of his divine appointment to care for the messianic community (1:16*b*-17). On the other hand, Paul does not shrink from the message he publicly proclaims "to Jews and Greeks about repentance toward God and faith toward our Lord Jesus" (v. 21; cf. Rom 10:8-13). Not only is there a practical apostasy that Paul avoids in his regular ministry among believing households; there is also a theological apostasy that Paul avoids in defending the truth claims of the gospel, which he summarizes by the Lukan catchwords "repentance" and "faith."

---

654. Walton, *Leadership and Lifestyle*, 140-98.

655. The importance of "humility" in Paul's retrospective is intensified by its rarity. It is used only here in Acts, infrequently in the NT, and not at all in the LXX. Significantly, its NT use is mostly Pauline and posited in the virtue catalogues of Ephesians (4:2) and Colossians (2:18, 23; 3:12)—writings whose Pauline traditions are closely associated with those used by Luke. Walton, *Leadership and Lifestyle*, 75-76, suggests "humility" has Christian currency as a "coin word" of the earliest church and expresses an affection prompted by the Spirit that is at odds with well-known vices, such as excessive personal ambition or a sense of rivalry.

20:22-24. The shift from apologia (retrospect) to prophecy (prospect) is signaled by the appearance of the phrase καὶ νῦν ἰδοὺ (*kai nyn idou*, "And now I . . ."). Even as Paul's faithfulness is made evident by his costly devotion to the tasks of the prophet-like-Jesus, he is also faithful or "captive/compelled" (v. 22) to/by what the "Holy Spirit testifies to me in every city that imprisonment and persecutions are waiting for me" (v. 23). Details of a particular revelation from the Spirit to Paul are not mentioned. In fact, he claims that he does not know what will happen to him in Jerusalem (cf. Rom 15:30-32). Commentators have long noted the parallelism between Paul's prophecy and the Lord's prediction of his passion in Jerusalem. While this is certainly characteristic of Luke's typological shaping of his narrative and perhaps is a subtext of this part of Paul's speech, the prophecy is still much too vague to assert that Paul's final Jerusalem visit is of a type with the Lord's. Paul did not die there, nor does he know what will happen to him there.

That he should expect suffering to await him in Jerusalem is no different from what he expects in every city, since the Lord prophesied that his mission would result in Paul's suffering for his sake (see 9:15-16). This is the inevitable effect according to Acts of preaching a message that he characterizes as "the good news of God's grace" (see 15:7-11). Further, it seems more likely that the compelling motive of Paul's journey to Jerusalem is as a religious pilgrim in keeping with his observance of Jewish practices (see v. 16) and not as a Christian martyr. While he can claim that he does not count his life of any value (v. 24a; cf. 2 Cor 4:7–5:10; 6:4-10; Phil 1:19-26), the revelation to which he refers must be the vision in the Spirit that indicates that Rome is the city of his destiny (see 19:21). Only Paul and the readers of Acts know that it will be Rome, with a layover in Jerusalem, where Paul will "finish my course and the ministry that I received from the Lord Jesus" (v. 24b; cf. 1 Cor 9:24; Phil 3:8-13).

20:25. For these reasons, Paul's statement of departure does not predict a Jerusalem "passion." His emphatic assertion that none of them will ever see his face again must be understood in terms of his earlier vision of a new mission field in Rome, which therefore requires his departure from and a succession of his leadership in Asia. That his farewell concerns the Roman mission and not a Jerusalem passion is indicated by repetition of the central task of his prophetic vocation in Ephesus—"proclaiming the kingdom" (see 19:8)—and recalls Jesus' paradigmatic prophecy about the inspired witness of his successors that includes teaching about God's kingdom (see 1:3, 6; 14:22; 28:23, 31; cf. 1 Cor 6:9-11; 1 Thess 2:12; Col 1:13) at the "end of the earth" (see 1:8).

20:26-27. Paul concludes his personal reminiscence by again declaring that he did not shrink from his prophetic obligations in proclaiming the gospel in Ephesus (see v. 20). The striking declaration that he "is not responsible for the blood of any of you" (v. 26; cf. 1 Thess 2:10) recalls his earlier indictment of unrepentant Jews in Corinth (see 18:6), which presumed that they no longer could excuse their rejection of God's gospel on grounds of their ignorance of its claims and Scripture's warrants. Paul's preaching ministry has clarified God's script of salvation's history and so to refuse his message is to refuse God's invitation. In this new setting in which Paul addresses believers the issue is not the salvation of his auditors but their assumption of Paul's mission in Ephesus. Whether or not the foundation he has laid in that city continues to be built upon is no longer in his hands; his departure signals the official beginning of their own ministry in his absence.

The addition of a final summary of Paul's gospel, "the whole purpose [βουλή *boulē*] of God" (v. 27; cf. Eph 1:11), delineates the theological boundaries of this ecclesial foundation. Elsewhere in Acts *boulē* denotes God's sovereign purpose that is worked out in the Messiah's mission (see 2:22-23) and now in the church's mission under the aegis of the Holy Spirit (see 4:28; 5:38; 13:36; cf. Gal 1:4; Eph 1:9, 11). There is no Pauline teaching that deviates from God's *boulē*; therefore, Pauline teaching is "canonical" in congregations founded by him. The implication is that *God* views any deviation from his catechesis as apostasy and subversive of God's scripted plans for salvation's progress into the future of Ephesus.

20:28-35. The second half of Paul's speech shifts from a description of his past and prophecy of his future to consideration of his succession in Ephesus by the elders of the church. He charges the elders (here called ἐπίσκοποι [*episkopoi*, "overseers"] without change of meaning) with their ministry in ever-vigilant expectation of coming dangers (vv. 28-31). He goes on to exhort them to follow his and the Lord's example of leadership within a community of goods that cares for the poor (vv. 32-35).

20:28-31. Paul's rehearsal of the dangers that will face the elders following his departure is enclosed by his charge for them to "keep watch [προσέχω *prosechō*] over yourselves and over all the flock" (v. 28; see also 5:35 b) and to "be alert" (γρηγορέω *grēgoreō*) to his pastoral example (v. 31). The image of a shepherd watching over his flock is a familiar biblical metaphor of the leader's provident care over Israel (cf. Exod 10:28; Deut 4:9; Ezek 14:11-12; Jer 23:2; Hos 5:1; Mic 5:4; John 10:11-16; 21:17) of which the Paul of Acts is exemplary. He presumes their competence to do so because "the Holy Spirit has made you overseers," which not only suggests the mediation of the Spirit's power for ministry (see 1:8) but also the Spirit's authorizing "mark" in their lives that others have recognized (see 6:3-4).

While the role of elders to pastor "the church of God" seems clear enough, it is confused by the following relative clause "he bought [περιποιέω *peripoieō*] with his own blood [διὰ τοῦ αἵματος τοῦ ἰδίου *dia tou haimatos tou idiou*]," which is obscure both in plain meaning and in its purpose in the speech.[656] That God acquires (*peripoieō*) a people by saving them from destruction is a biblical idea and probably Paul's meaning here (cf. Ps 74:2). But that God did so by means of God's own blood is very difficult to understand theologically. A few commentators think that ἴδιος (*idios*) connotes here a term of endearment for a near relative, or "one's own" (= one's own Son, so the NRSV). Others suggest that Luke combines fragments from two Pauline formulae about "the church

of God" and "Christ purchases the church for God by his blood" but in a jumbled way. He may have been grammatically careless at this point because of his lack of theological interest in the efficacy of Christ's blood in saving people from their sins. Even if Acts does include a theology of the cross elsewhere, it is clearly not of the robust variety found in the Pauline letters.[657] In any case, the general sense of Paul's vague phrase is that the church has extraordinary value for God and for this reason the elders must take their calling with utmost seriousness.

The ethos shaped by the inclusio of Paul's charge to pastoral action is of a countercultural community whose beliefs and practices are set against the social norm—which is certainly in line with the preceding narrative of his controversial Ephesian mission. Paul recognizes that his departure will occasion a serious challenge to the purity of that ethos. Two potential dangers are noted: False teachers will come as "savage wolves" from the outside (v. 29) and "from your own group" inside the flock of God (v. 30). The catchphrase echoes the Lord's reference to "savage wolves" (Matt 7:15; 10:16; Luke 10:3; John 10:12), which connotes "false prophets" within Israel—teachers of Israel who reject the messianic word. The phrase has a similar meaning in Paul's speech, except that now it is his proclamation about God's kingdom that establishes a rule of faith that measures doctrinal purity within the church: The "savage wolf" is any teacher who distorts the truth of Pauline teaching (see 13:10; cf. Phil 2:15).

Paul's warning of false teaching within the church is unusual in Acts. The repetition and variety of references to Paul's teaching in this speech underscore the importance of theological purity in maintaining and transmitting the Pauline legacy to the next generation of believers. Further, Paul calls upon the memory of the elders to remember "that for three years I did not cease night or day to warn everyone with tears" (v. 30; cf. 2 Cor 2:4). Luke's characteristic use of hyperbole again underscores the value of Paul's personal example, which also carries canonical status within the ongoing community.

---

656. The NRSV's "the church of God that he obtained with the blood of his own Son" follows a later (and less theologically difficult) textual tradition, probably borrowing Paul's own words in Rom 8:32. The NIV is preferred simply because it follows the most essential of all text-critical rules; preference is given to the most difficult rendering as more original.

657. Cf. Barrett, *A Critical and Exegetical Commentary on the Acts of the Apostles,* 2:976-77.

225

20:32-35. A rhetorical shift from warning to encouragement is once again marked by the καὶ νῦν (*kai nyn*, "and now")—"and now" Paul's concern for an effective succession is made more apparent to his auditors. These final lines of the speech combine blessing (v. 32) and exhortation (vv. 33-35) similar to the benedictions of Pauline letters. The main thread of Paul's speech remains fixed on his "message" (λόγος *logos*) of God's grace (see v. 24; see also 14:3; 5:32). The edifying connection of Paul's gospel with the "building up" (οἰκοδομέω *oikodomeō*) of his successors (cf. Rom 14:19; 15:2; 1 Cor 3:9; 8:1; 10:23; 14:3-5, 12, 17, 26; 2 Cor 10:8; 12:19; 13:10; 1 Thess 5:11) for their future "inheritance" (cf. Rom 15:16; 1 Cor 6:9-11; Gal 3:18; 4:30; 5:21; Titus 3:7) reflects Pauline themes expressed in Lukan vocabulary.

In the context of Acts, however, the use of *oikodomeō* to encourage the spiritual formation ("build up") of elders glosses the earlier use of ἀνοικοδομέω (*anoikodomeō*) in Amos's prophecy of a "rebuilt" Israel (see 15:16) to remind the reader that God continues to fulfill the promise of a restored Israel's mission to the nations (see 15:17-18) even in Paul's absence through the ministry of spiritually restored elders. In this regard, Paul's concluding admonitions reflect the concerns expressed by James concerning whether the mixing of uncircumcised Gentiles with repentant Jews in the synagogues of the diaspora will result in the attenuation of the Jewish legacy within the church (see 15:20-21, 29). Even though Acts has carefully depicted Paul and, therefore, his legacy as Jewish, the reader should note the implied connection between his final exhortations and the cautionary notes sounded earlier by James regarding the social solidarity of the community. If the principal concerns of James, however, are to maintain this sense of solidarity by abstaining from the pollutants of pagan religion, Paul's concerns are more ethical and echo the social practices of the community of goods (see 2:42-47) within an acquisitive culture such as Ephesus (see 19:25b-27): The dispossession rather than "coveting" of property is the measure of one's spiritual authority

(v. 33; see 4:32-35);[658] and working with one's hands to earn one's keep (v. 34; see also 18:3) is motivated by the evident need "to support the weak" (v. 35). As with the content of what is taught, these moral norms are in imitation of Paul and obedient to the Lord's command, "It is more blessed to give than to receive."[659] The purpose of appealing to Jesus is to underscore the practical truth that the community's solidarity is only as strong as its commitment to its own "weak" (see 4:32-35; 6:1-7). Finally it is not because of his example but because of the command of Jesus that Paul can also say that "we must [δεῖ *dei*]"—a divine necessity—help the poor and the powerless. This practice remains the social mark of the community of goods in whose life the kingdom of God has been restored by God's grace.

20:36-38. This concluding panel casts a poignant image of a fond farewell. The sheer weight of emotive terms Luke layers into this scene—"much weeping," "embraced Paul and kissed him," "grieving especially because . . . they would not see him again"—highlights the theme of Paul's departure from Ephesus in the speech itself (vv. 25, 29) and all that is staked out because of it. It is a mistake to conclude, however, that since Luke writes from a perspective after Paul's death he must, therefore, be writing *about* Paul's death. As has been argued earlier, the Paul of Acts addresses the importance of an orderly succession of ministry in Ephesus that is occasioned by Paul's departure for a new mission elsewhere (= Rome; see 19:21) and not by his so-called passion in Jerusalem. The finality of Paul's farewell, when "they brought him to the ship," simply makes more urgent the elders' (and the reader's) compliance with his instructions.

---

658. Paul considers "coveting" (ἐπιθυμέω *epithymeō*) Adam's original sin (cf. Rom 7:7-12) and thus appropriate to use in this closing exhortation. While his own teaching regarding the dangers of wealth is not nearly as clear as Luke's, the Corinthian correspondence is replete with his protest against those who would use their wealth to marginalize "weaker" believers (cf. 1 Cor 1:27; 8:11-12; 9:11-22; 2 Cor 7:2; 11:7-11).

659. This wisdom saying is not found in the gospel tradition (cf. Sir 4:31; *Did.* 1:5; 4:5; Luke 1:45), although it reflects the Lord's teaching (see Luke 6:35-38 and par.).

REFLECTIONS

"Keep watch over yourselves and over all the flock, of which the Holy Spirit has made you overseers" (20:28 NRSV). There are few biblical passages more instructive of the role and character of church leaders than this one. Both in what he assumes and by what he says, Paul supplies the church of every age with the essential role model and curriculum for a course in leadership training. In describing his own trials and temptations, Paul insinuates himself into his successors' minds as their prophetic exemplar: They, too, will encounter similar attacks both within and outside the congregation and must deal with them as he has. Paul assumes in his absence the continuing presence of the Holy Spirit in the congregation—the Spirit who both calls and, therefore, enables its leaders to survive these attacks and to flourish as a result.

The primary marks of the Christian leader correspond to the primary problems Paul anticipates will always threaten the Christian leader: purity, possessions, power. The peculiar definition of each envisages the nature of the countercultural community that these people have been called to lead. Those who are called by God and nurtured by God's Spirit to lead a people belonging to God should neither be trained nor be measured by secular standards of leadership. Thus, for example, the quotient of one's *purity* is measured by faithful ministry of the word of God (20:20). Especially in the Pastoral Epistles, congregational leaders are instructed to teach "sound (or "healthy") doctrine" to others, ever alert to avoid theological error and to squelch its dissemination from other sources (cf. 1 Tim 1:3-7, 10-11; 4:6-10; 2 Tim 1:8-14; 2:2; 3:1-9; Titus 1:9-11). The effectiveness of the gospel to initiate people into life with God is subverted by theological compromise. Beware of the "wolves" within and without the congregation who might threaten the purity of our rule of apostolic faith (cf. 20:29-30).

The messianic career of Jesus is the subtext of Paul's speech: He is the model the Paul of Acts follows (cf. 20:24), who in turn bids the Ephesian elders to follow his example (20:31). Strategically, then, he concludes by quoting Jesus as saying, "It is more blessed to give than to receive" (20:35). Perhaps of greater practical importance to Paul than doctrinal purity is how leaders use their *possessions* (cf. 1 Tim 6:3-10, 17-19). No interpreter of Acts denies the importance of intelligent and articulate preaching (see 19:16-34); yet, Luke knows that the world will consider such preaching specious if the church says one thing and lives another. The abstract truth of a word about God's grace is tested in the real world by whether or not the handling of our goods is also gracious rather than greedy. The motive of Christian ministry must never be monetary and momentary. Those put in charge of the spiritual formation of believers must not covet their possessions (20:33); indeed, they are to make money to redistribute it among the poor (20:34-35). In the simplicity of one's lifestyle and the sharing of one's goods the truth of God's generosity toward us all is made more concrete.

The third mark of the Christian leader according to Paul is how that person handles personal *power*. Most of us can rehearse with regret the moral failure of various Christian leaders. The media sometimes gloat in telling of these failures as though it impugns the integrity of the church's witness in the world. Perhaps it does. All too often these failures are prompted by an "arrogance of power" when those placed in positions of influence have used their high standing to coerce others to do their bidding. The leader who imitates Paul's example is drawn to ministry by the Holy Spirit to serve the redemptive interests of God and the needs of God's flock. The prophetic leader of a countercultural community is one who serves others and sets aside as unseemly the ambitious acquisition of power or pretension of self-importance. The disturbing effect Jesus had on the power brokers of his world was due to the presence of God in places where life was being shaped by norms and values contrary to God's kingdom. The kingdom preaching of the incorrigible Paul had a similar effect on the rich and famous of his day (cf. 20:22-25). So it is in our day that the mark of competent leadership is the disturbing effect a faithful life will have on those whose definition of power places personal ambition over justice and grace as God has defined it in Jesus.

ACTS 21:1-16, PAUL'S JOURNEY INTO JERUSALEM

COMMENTARY

Pilgrim Paul is determined to reach Jerusalem in time to celebrate Pentecost (see 20:16), and the present passage follows him into the holy city (21:15-16). Luke's shaping of this entire pilgrimage narrative (20:1–21:16), while reminiscent of the Lord's final journey into Jerusalem, is hardly the prelude to Paul's "passion" as many commentators contend.[660] While Paul anticipates his suffering (see 20:22-23)—a prospect that is subsequently confirmed by "witnesses in every city" (see 20:23; 21:4, 10-11)—he does not die there; in any case, Rome and not Jerusalem is the city of his destiny (see 19:21). Moreover, the principal parallel between the Lord's final journey to Jerusalem and Paul's is that both end up and suffer in the holy city because both are inspired prophets who obey God's will rather than their own (21:14; see 11:18; 18:21; cf. Luke 22:42). The rhetorical effect of this parallelism reminds the reader that Paul suffers not because of what he says about himself but because of what he says about Jesus.

All the elements of a travel narrative are reflected in this passage. It is framed by Paul's itinerary from Miletus to Jerusalem. There is a sense that the emotional scenes with different congregations (21:3-6, 13-14; see also 20:36-38) transform his pilgrimage into a "farewell tour," since Paul will not visit these mission fields again. He even makes pastoral calls on congregations in Tyre and Caesarea that his mission did not establish in order to demonstrate his solidarity with those whom he had earlier persecuted (see 8:1-3).[661]

Along the way Luke reports various incidents in the first person, such as Agabus's prophecy (21:10-12; see also 11:27-28), and drops important names into the story, such as Philip (21:8-9; see also 8:4-40), to add vivid color to an otherwise conventional travelogue.[662] This final stage of Paul's pilgrimage is also shaped by Luke's theological interest in portraying the spiritual authority of Paul as one called to serve God's redemptive interests as a prophet-like-Jesus. In particular, his responses to repeated prophecies of his forthcoming suffering (21:4) and captivity (21:10-11) underscore his determined obedience to God.

21:1-6. With the resumption of his more conventional travel narrative, Luke places himself back into the story: "*We* had parted . . . set sail . . . [and] came" to the standard portages that take sea travelers from Miletus on "a ship bound for Phoenicia" (vv. 1-2), landing in Tyre "to unload its cargo there" (v. 3), including Paul and his entourage (v. 4). That they had to "look up" (ἀνευρίσκω *aneuriskō*; lit., "discover") the disciples (v. 4a) living in Tyre suggests that Paul did not evangelize this region and does not know the exact locations of its congregations. He is nevertheless determined to seek them out, knowing they are somewhere nearby since he had earlier visited them briefly with Barnabas to report the happy news of Gentile conversions (see 15:3).

During his weeklong visit, the disciples warned Paul through the Spirit "not to go on

660. E.g., Dunn, *The Acts of the Apostles*, 277-78.
661. Spencer, *The Portrait of Philip in Acts*, 258-60, suggests that these visits in Palestine are implicitly "works of repentance" since it was Paul who had previously persecuted believers there.

662. These elements of local color, coupled with the first-person narration, has led historians to conclude that Luke draws upon accurate sources in writing this travel narrative. See Lüdemann, *Early Christianity According to the Traditions in Acts*, 439-40. The reader should note that the narrator takes the side of those who oppose Paul's trip to Jerusalem for reasons of personal safety (see 21:12), which indicates a more direct connection with this story than with other "we" passages in Acts.

to Jerusalem" (v. 4*b*). Glossed by Paul's earlier reference to such testimonies of the Holy Spirit (see 20:23), the interpreter presumes that other prophets have received advanced warning that he would suffer in Jerusalem; for this reason his friends urge him to stay away from the city. This advice was gladly received elsewhere by those who felt the currents of public opinion turning against Paul and so quickly hustled him out of town and to safety. Why not here? Because Paul has received word from the Spirit of his future suffering in Jerusalem (see 20:22-24) as a "necessary" circumstance of his final mission to Rome (see 19:21). With this confidence, then, "when our days there were ended, we left and proceeded on our journey" (v. 5*a*).

The fond farewell to Paul at Tyre is similar to the one he had experienced in Miletus, and for a similar reason: They will not see him again. The manner of his farewell also reflects the religious motive of his journey: "We knelt down on the beach and prayed" (v. 5*b*), since through prayer a community of believers receives divine direction and benefaction (see 1:14). The emphasis on Paul's corporate escort is enforced by reference to entire families who kneel together on the beach for public prayers. It must be said that Paul is traveling to Jerusalem not to suffer, although he will, and not only as a pilgrim intent to celebrate Pentecost as a messianic Jew; he makes the pilgrimage in service of God knowing that it is "necessary" for him to do so (see 19:21; 20:24).

21:7-9. The role of repetition in biblical narrative is to recall and engage earlier episodes in meaningful conversation. Much has happened since Philip founded the Samaritan church and settled in Caesarea to raise a family, including "four unmarried daughters who had the gift of prophecy" (20:8-9; see also 8:40).[663] In particular, Luke's careful titling of Philip as both "evangelist" (εὐαγγελιστής *euangelistēs*; see 8:4, 12, 40) and "one of the seven" and a companion of Stephen (see 6:3-6) recalls the chain of circumstances following Stephen's death that led Paul (= Saul)

to persecute Philip and commit other Hellenist believers to prison (see 8:1-3). It was Paul who ultimately drove them beyond Jerusalem and to Caesarea to plant and cultivate these very congregations he now visits. Paul's personal reversal takes an ironic twist when he stays with Philip, shortly before making his return to Jerusalem to be persecuted and imprisoned himself as a Hellenist believer! Johnson notes that "by enmeshing Paul with [Philip], Luke reminds the reader that Paul and the narrative are completing a full circle. His trip to Jerusalem is not simply a trip to a geographical place but a return to a narrative 'place' that is, for Paul, filled with the memories and possibilities of conflict."[664] In fact, Paul will soon face hostile Jews similar to those who brought Stephen to trial (see 6:9-10), and the accusations they will level against Paul are like those brought against Stephen (see 21:28; 6:11-14). Knowing this, the reader of these stories leading to Paul's arrest cannot help but note their profound irony.

21:10-14. The dramatic reappearance of "a prophet named Agabus" in Acts sounds a warning to the reader: His role is to predict future crises in the holy city. Earlier he came from Jerusalem to forecast a famine (see 11:27-30); in this case he both enacts and pronounces a warning to Paul: "The Jews will bind [him] and will hand him over to the Gentiles" (v. 11; cf. Luke 9:22, 44; 18:31-33; 24:7). Agabus, who "bound his own feet and hands" with Paul's belt (v. 11), presents himself in the manner of an OT prophet whose symbolic actions personify and make vivid his message from God (cf. Isa 20:2; Jer 13:1-7; Ezek 4:1-17).[665]

Paul learns two important details about his future suffering from Agabus: Jewish opposition will instigate his suffering (see 21:27-32), and his suffering will result from being "bound" (imprisoned; see vv. 33-36) and "handed over (prosecuted; cf. Luke 9:44; 18:32) to the Gentiles" (the Roman court; see 24:1-21; cf. 28:17). Agabus offers no

663. The reference to Philip's daughters is curious because they perform no immediate role in the narrative. They may be persons known to Luke's first readers, added here to commemorate Philip's historic meeting with Paul. In any case, it serves to remind readers that Joel's prophecy of inspired "daughters" who will prophesy during "the last days" (see 2:17) is fulfilled.

664. Johnson, *The Acts of the Apostles*, 371.

665. Agabus's symbolic enactment of his prophecy is the only such incident in the NT. Moreover, the introductory formula he uses—"Thus says the Holy Spirit"—is unique, although it surely corresponds to the common OT prophetic formulation "Thus says the Lord." In my judgment this account reflects Luke's perspective that the Christian prophet is inspired by the Spirit to know the word and will of God, whether in interpreting Scripture (see 2:4) or through prophetic ecstasy (see 10:19).

extended clarification on the details of his prophecy; however, Luke's narrative of Paul's arrest and trials will provide these details soon enough. The Tyrian believers (with Luke!) who misread the prophecy of Paul's suffering as an implied warning for him not to continue his pilgrimage (see v. 4) are now joined by the believers here (again with Luke): "When we heard [Agabus's prophecy], we and the people there urged him not to go up to Jerusalem" (v. 12). Perhaps their response alludes to the disciples of Jesus' story who refuse to believe Jesus' prediction that their journey to Jerusalem would end in his suffering and death.

Acts delays Paul's heartfelt response to his friends to this point in the story—immediately before entering Jerusalem. The reader knows that Paul alone possesses the correct motive of Agabus's prophecy, which is not to warn him away from Jerusalem but to quicken his resolve to go on into Jerusalem, and so from there to Rome. Agabus has authority to receive and deliver God's revelation, and others to interpret it according to their own lights. Only Paul, however, possesses additional revelation that enables him to interpret its normative meaning; and the reader of Acts knows from the Lord's prophecy of Paul's mission that he would suffer for it (see 9:16).

Luke shapes his story of Paul to reflect his spiritual authority for the church, which is reflected both by his firm correction of interpreted prophecies concerning his future suffering and by his affectionate responses to his friends. Luke portrays him as a sympathetic pastor who cares deeply for his flock (see 20:31): "What are you doing, weeping and breaking my heart?" (v. 13). Through their sincere entreaties and Paul's emotional response, however, his resolve "to be bound [and] even to die in Jerusalem" (v. 13; cf. Rom 15:30-32) becomes all the more apparent to everyone. Again, as with Jesus before him, his motive is that "the Lord's will be done" (v. 14; see 11:18; 18:21; cf. Luke 22:42).

21:15-16. Paul's authority is recognized by the whole church and they gather around him in common support as he "started to go up to Jerusalem" (v. 15). He is joined in his ascent into the holy city by "disciples from Caesarea" who delivered Paul to the home of Mnason of Cyprus, "an early disciple" and perhaps one who could recall the suffering caused by Saul's persecution of the church.[666]

---

666. The Western version expands the text's geography in order to clarify its chronology and smooth the awkward transition from 21:16 to 21:17. In this later reading, Mnason lived in a village about two days' journey outside of Jerusalem, where Jesus spent the night.

REFLECTIONS

"The Lord's will be done" (21:14 NIV and NRSV). Nowhere in Acts is the literary theme of suffering more clearly brought into focus than here. The Lord had earlier prophesied that Paul would suffer for his name's sake (see 9:16). Certainly Paul has already suffered persecution and public humiliation. Yet here the repetition of predictions of Paul's future suffering in Jerusalem (20:22-23; 21:4, 11) underlines the high cost of his calling. The narrative's keen emphasis on Paul's suffering is not a reflection of Lukan hagiography. What honor is due Paul is not because he suffered heroically, and he is not depicted a masochist who takes unnatural delight in his suffering. He does not heed the church's exhortation to avoid the suffering predicted by the Spirit because the Spirit also directed him to go to Jerusalem (see 19:21; 20:22). The suffering that awaits him there is one consequence (or cost) of his obedience to the Lord's call.

Suffering for Jesus is not by itself a mark of superlative devotion; nor should it ever be the motive of Christian discipleship. Believers through the ages have sometimes confused their suffering with spiritual maturity. The two are not the same, nor are they necessarily related. The cost of discipleship is not always persecution or prison. In Paul's case it is; however, he is exemplary not because he suffered but because he chose to obey the Lord's will at any cost.

ACTS 21:17-26, PAUL MEETS WITH JAMES

COMMENTARY

With this passage Luke begins the final section of Acts. The plotline follows the adventures of Paul, who survives legal problems with hostile Jews and ambivalent Roman courts in Jerusalem (21:17–26:32), and then with nature during a stormy sea voyage and with a poisonous serpent (27:1–28:10), before safely arriving as a prisoner in the city of his destiny (28:11-31). Through it all a faithful God safeguards Paul to Rome as promised (cf. 19:21; 23:11; 27:24), "for he is an instrument whom I have chosen to bring my name before Gentiles and kings" (9:15) at the "end of the earth" (1:8).

On the day following his safe arrival in the holy city, Paul visits James along with other leaders of the Jerusalem church (21:17-19). The topic of their conversation resumes the concerns James had earlier expressed at the Jerusalem Council: whether Paul's mission to the nations would result in contaminating the church's Jewish legacy (see 15:20-21, 28-9). There now are rumors in circulation that James's worst fears have been realized. Jerusalem believers who zealously maintain Jewish practices (21:20) have heard reports from unidentified sources that Paul teaches "Jews living among the Gentiles to forsake Moses, and that you tell them not to circumcise their children or observe the customs" (21:21). A strategy of reconciliation is devised that allows Paul to respond to these fears: He will join with other repentant Jews in Jerusalem to purify themselves in the rite of the Nazaritic vow (see 21:22-23) in order to demonstrate that he observes and guards the law (21:24); this Paul does (21:26). Since Paul arrives in Jerusalem as a pilgrim to celebrate Pentecost (see 20:16), his easy accommodation of a purification ritual is not due to church politics but to its agreement with his religious practices as a devout Jew.

Luke's shaping of the story of Paul's final visit to Jerusalem in response to this theological crisis raises serious critical problems for the interpreter. For example, Luke has edited out any reference to Paul's Jerusalem collection (cf. 24:17). The issue is not simply his silence on the topic, when Paul makes it a critical feature of his urban mission and his relationship to the Jewish church. The more knotty problem is that the epistolary Paul makes the Jerusalem collection a condition of his Roman visitation (cf. Rom 15:22-31), which otherwise squares with Luke's narrative plotline that follows Paul's movements from Jerusalem to Rome. Why not then mention the Jerusalem collection, since it fits nicely into Luke's narrative plotline?

It is unlikely that this most recent meeting reflects poor relations between the Jerusalem church and Paul's mission; it may be nothing more than a literary convention of Luke's storytelling, which routinely plays down the role or even silences secondary figures in order to play up the role of his central characters. The theological crisis that Paul addresses in his letters is whether Gentile converts, who are not Jewish proselytes, are nonetheless initiated into their new life with God through trusting in Jesus alone. He only rarely has occasion to address the practices of repentant Jews or the internal problems facing Jewish-Gentile congregations in the diaspora (however, see Romans 14; 1 Corinthians 8–10). Even relevant autobiographical details are rhetorically designed to illustrate the larger theological lessons learned from his mission to the nations. In Acts, these concerns have already been resolved at the Jerusalem Council, and Luke's plotline has moved on to consider another worry—namely, whether Paul's mission occasions the gentilizing of repentant Jews (rather than the Judaizing of repentant Gentiles). Luke's narrative of Paul's mission since the Jerusalem Council has adequately addressed this worry.

Yet, Luke's newest concern since Paul's Miletus speech is whether a *Pauline* legacy has any future in the church (see 20:18-35). Insofar as Luke portrays Paul as an observant Jew, the reader of Acts must insist that the legacy of Paul is not only distinctively Christian but decidedly Jewish. Because this Jewish argot is almost entirely lacking in his letters, the contribution made by the Paul of

Acts to Scripture's Pauline witness is to place him among Jews even as his letters place him among Gentiles. Yet some interpreters continue to wonder whether the Paul who wrote Galatians would ever have accommodated the Jewish church's suggestion that he observe a temple rite and Mosaic law (cf. Gal 2:19-21). One can easily imagine, however, that the missionary Paul who wrote 1 Corinthians could easily adapt his "principle of accommodation" to reconcile troubled relations between discordant believers in the manner narrated by this passage (cf. 1 Cor 9:19-21).

21:17-20a. Despite Paul's fears to the contrary (see Rom 15:31), he is warmly greeted by James in a spirit of generous hospitality; "and all the elders were present" (vv. 17-18; see also 15:4, 6, 22-23). This should be perceived not as foreboding but as a literary cue that the same board of church leaders who received the report of Barnabas and Paul's first mission to the nations has reconvened to hear Paul's report of his second mission. Paul rehearsed with them "one by one the things that God had done among the Gentiles through his ministry [διακονία *diakonia*]" (v. 19; see also 15:12; cf. 2:22)—things that the reader of Acts has already considered from 16:6 to this point.

The use of *diakonia* repeats a catchword of Paul's Miletus speech to the leaders of his church and recalls his abiding interest that he "may finish my course and the ministry [*diakonia*] that I received from the Lord Jesus" (20:24). This linguistic link suggests two implied reasons for Paul's visit with James: He is there to say farewell, since he already knows that Rome is his appointed destination, and he is there for confirmation from the leaders of the Jewish church of the importance of what "God had done among the Gentiles through his ministry." Their response confirms that this Pauline legacy accords with God's will: "When they heard [Paul's report], they praised God" (v. 20*a*; see also 4:21; 11:18).

21:20b-21. The mood of this friendly meeting quickly changes from confirmation of Paul's mission among the Gentiles to concern over his mission among the Jews (see 15:20-21). His prior testimony seems unaware of this concern since he reports nothing of his

successes among repentant Jews. The effect is to take Paul by surprise as though this information is "entirely new."[667] But, of course, this has been Luke's subtext all along!

Luke sharply draws the contrast between James and Paul for rhetorical effect. On the one hand, James reports that "many thousands" (lit., "many myriads") of repentant Jews "are all zealous [ζηλωτής *zēlōtēs*]) for the law [Torah]" (21:20*b*).[668] Luke's characteristic hyperbole makes the impression keener: The Jewish Christian community in Judea is vibrant and strong, and their strength is tied to their identity as observant Jews.[669] The adjective *zēlōtēs* characterizes these Jewish converts as "traditional," people for whom a public identity as a consecrated people belonging to God is marked by their dedicated adherence to the Torah (cf. Exod 20:4-5; Deut 4:23-24; 5:8-9; 6:14-15; Nah 1:2). Ironically, before his conversion Paul depicts his devotion to these same traditions in similar terms: He performed his ancestral traditions with "zeal," so that a consecrated life is a Torah-observant one (cf. Gal 1:14; Phil 3:6; see Acts 22:3).

This religious ethos and the Jewish identity it cultivates forge a stamp of covenant loyalty similar to the Pharisaic believers who sought clarification on the practices of uncircumcised Gentiles at the Jerusalem Council (15:5). Given the cautions of James in response (see 15:20-21, 29), we are not surprised when he becomes agitated upon hearing rumors that Paul teaches "Jews living among the Gentiles to forsake [ἀποστασίαν διδάσκεις ἀπό *apostasian didaskeis apo*; lit., "teaching apostasy against"] Moses . . . not to circumcise their children or observe the customs [ἔθος *ethos*]" (v. 21; see also 15:21; cf. 20:20, 27). The problem raised is not a soteriological matter but a sociological one. The use of *ethos* refers to those religious practices or routines within which a distinctively Jewish life is formed. From Acts 16:3 forward, the reader of Acts knows full well that these unfavorable reports are a canard. Not only is Paul an exemplary Jew who finds the vast majority of

667. Haenchen, *The Acts of the Apostles*, 608.

668. The Western version omits "among the Jews," no doubt a reflection of its anti-Semitism. However, the resulting text makes little sense.

669. See, however, Jervell, *Die Apostelgeschichte*, 524-25, who rightly cautions that Luke's hyperbole must not at the same time underestimate the vigor and success of the mission to traditional Jews in Judea as though such a mission has been superseded in Acts by Paul's mission to the nations.

his Gentile converts in the synagogues where Moses is preached every sabbath (see 15:21), but he is careful to safeguard a Jewish *ethos* against the intrusion of magic, materialism, or pagan religion—even on those occasions when believers have been forced out of their synagogues to form indigenous "household" congregations.

21:22-24. The proposed strategy begins with a realistic appraisal of "what then is to be done" (v. 22*a*). Paul's presence in Jerusalem cannot be kept secret from these zealous believers: "They will certainly hear that you have come" (v. 22*b*). The present crisis cannot be evaded and appropriate action is required. For this reason the church's leadership takes neither side, nor is there time for a measured deliberation over the relevant issues at stake. Paul's spirit of conciliation is not a matter of ceding to those with greater authority or to Jerusalem's supervisory prerogatives over his mission. The autonomy of Paul's mission and his spiritual authority is beyond dispute. Rather, his willingness to accommodate himself to the circumstances of the Jerusalem congregation demonstrates his agreement with James's worry about the gentilizing of the church's Jewish legacy.

Because Paul is, indeed, a Jew who observes and guards the law (v. 24*b*), the agreed course of action is viewed as an appropriate and practical response to the current rumors. The "rite of purification" called for is roughly patterned after the OT "law of the Nazirites" (cf. Num 6:1-21) and is similar in character and purpose to the vow Paul made earlier in Cenchraea (see 18:18). The Hebrew meaning of Nazirite is "consecrated one" and refers to the laity of a congregation who are set apart for service to God. Obedience to this law symbolizes one's disciplined devotion to God and the effects such a life has on the entire community. None of the three primary vows made by the Nazirite is mentioned in the text,[670] and only the ritual of shaving one's hair after completing the pledged period is indicated (cf. Num 6:13-21). For reasons of cost and ease this ritual of termination was the rule most consistently observed

in completing this vow. Nor were Nazirite vows considered acts of purification per se, or together as a "rite of purification."[671] Rather, such vow-keeping symbolizes the purity of those who make such a commitment.[672]

Pilgrim Paul is inclined for religious, if not also for political, reasons to join with "four men who are under a vow" (v. 23) and to shoulder their expenses while doing so—this, too, is a resurrection practice of the community of goods. Quite apart from the Nazirite's offering of shorn hair, the "rite of purification" requires a sacrifice that exacts a considerable financial cost from the supplicant. Might this be an allusion to Paul's collection hitherto unmentioned in Acts? Probably not, and the reader knows nothing of Paul's personal financial resources. The focus of the story is on his implied willingness to make a sacrifice within a faith community whose distinctive public identity is in part the sharing of goods with their needy (see 2:42-47; 4:32-35; 6:1-2). Moreover, Paul's compliance indicates his spiritual authority, since the dispossession of wealth envisages the possession of God's Spirit.

21:25. Some commentators find James's reiteration of his pastoral exhortation to Antioch (see 15:29; also see 15:20) superfluous here: The reader of Acts knows well that the current crisis is not about Paul's mission among uncircumcised Gentiles but rather about his mission among repentant Jews.[673] That the exhortation is repeated here may simply reflect Luke's use of a different source or the use of a new setting where James is speaking more widely to Paul's traveling companions (including Luke) who were not present at either the Jerusalem Council or the Antiochene reading of its verdict. As I have argued, however, this repetition of James's verdict provides a narrative prompt for a review of Paul's mission in Acts: At no time

---

670. That is, abstinence from wine, not cutting one's hair, and avoiding contact with anything dead. It should also be noted that the law of the Nazirites applies equally to men and women (cf. Num 6:2), and so Luke's specification that "four *men* are under a vow" (21:23, italics added) is required.

671. See Barrett, *A Critical and Exegetical Commentary on the Acts of the Apostles,* 2:1010-13, for the various possible explanations of this interpretive problem. Note also this same problem obtains to 21:26 where "days of purification" are mentioned. In brief, the critical problem is that the law of the Nazirites is not a per se rite of purification. A week-long period of purification and sacrifice is required of the Nazirite only after touching something dead (cf. Num 6:10-11).

672. Cf. Levine, *Numbers 1–20,* 229-35, who notes the heroic dimension of naziritism in OT narratives, especially of Israel's Judges (e.g., Deborah, Samson, Samuel). Luke probably intended such resonances between the judges of the OT and the Paul of Acts.

673. The Western version of Acts clarifies this by adding that Gentile believers have nothing but good things to say concerning Paul's catechesis of them. The issue is thereby more narrowly considered as a "Jewish" problem with Paul's mission.

has Paul allowed the "pollutions of idols" to contaminate a Jewish identity in the congregations of the diaspora church.

21:26. Paul complies with the request: "The next day he took the men and purified himself along with them." Although the grammar of the text does not require that all five Nazirites concluded the period of their vow at the same time, they all followed biblical protocol. The sacrifice would include cutting the hair of each man to indicate that the period of consecration had been completed according to Mosaic law. Paul has passed this test of faithfulness to the practices of his ancestral religion for all to see: "He entered the temple with them, making public the completion of the days of purification." When this hard evidence of Paul's piety and teamwork is ignored and even misconstrued, the blame must shift from him to his critics.

REFLECTIONS

1. "They have been told about you that you teach all the Jews among the Gentiles to forsake Moses, and that you tell them not to circumcise their children or observe the customs" (21:21 NRSV). The continuing concerns voiced about Paul by other Jewish believers in Jerusalem concern his commitment to their common religious heritage. Moses and circumcision are deeply felt religious symbols; they are observed as formative of a community's loyalties, responses, and religious zeal. To subvert them is to derail the community's progress into the future of God. Thus for these believers the past of Israel defines the present of the church. Earlier their pastor James had voiced concern that the intermingling of multiple identities, Jewish and pagan, is a practical problem that might split loyalties and confuse people (see 15:20-21, 29). The Jews of Jerusalem now have reason to be concerned about their identity and whether what Paul has wrought "among the Gentiles" will jeopardize it. Of course, the readers of Acts know Jerusalem need not worry about Paul's mission. He has steadfastly protected the church's Jewish heritage as more and more Gentiles are added to its membership rolls.

The subtext of this passage, however, is Paul's identity as a prophet-like-Jesus. The prophet's task is not to replace the old with something new, but to recover and reform the old as God's unchanging word for a new day. The very idea that Paul had compromised his Jewish heritage or subverted its transmission to a new generation of children challenges his prophetic vocation. Thus Paul's actions to prove the reports false also defend an important ingredient of his prophetic task.

When we speak of the church as a counterculture or a prophetic community and look to Acts for authoritative models, central to what we find in the reading of Acts is the high value placed on Jewish tradition. To be the church means to recover and continue to reform the sacred traditions of Israel for a new day.

2. "What then is to be done?" (21:22 NRSV). The practical lesson learned from this passage is the importance of a review protocol to ensure the church's forward progress. The church often makes the mistake of implementing a new policy without including specific guidelines for future review and evaluation. Years earlier as the result of two Jerusalem assemblies, the church agreed to accept uncircumcised Gentiles as full members (cf. 11:1-18; 14:27–15:29). But James expressed his reservations regarding Paul's mission to the nations. He feared that the presence of converted pagans in an assembly of Jewish believers would compromise their Jewish identity (see above). Clearly these reservations remain (21:25), but they have been rewritten in Jewish terms (21:21). A strategy is devised that would ameliorate anxiety: Paul would demonstrate his commitment to his Jewish tradition and the formation of repentant Jews by completing with others the rite of Nazirite purification (21:26).

Taken as a whole, this passage establishes a pattern of review that a congregation could institute to measure the long-term effectiveness of some policy or program. (1)

An overview of positive results is presented by relevant leaders to the church's board of elders in a setting of worship and praise to God (21:17-20a). What are the evidences of God's activity mediated through this policy or that program? (2) The elders may then present reports of concern from members who believe the policy or program imperils the church's witness and life (21:20b-21). (3) Rather than taking these reports at face value, the elders devise a test of the merits of any negative report (21:22-25). (4) The test is then implemented and its results publicly observed to determine whether the result commends the continuation of the policy or program (21:26).

ACTS 21:27-39, PAUL'S "ARREST"

COMMENTARY

The Paul of Acts has the remarkable capacity to incite strong emotions of both friendship and opposition. The present text is a case of the latter. It seems that for all its good intentions, the "Nazaritic strategy" misfired even before it was fully completed (21:27a). But did it? The conspiracy against Paul's mission hatched by hostile Jews in Asia (see 20:3) had extended its reach to Jerusalem where they "had seen [Paul] in the temple [and] stirred up the whole crowd [and] seized him" (21:27b). Paul's performance of a ritual of purity evidently has had no positive effect on these outsiders whose antagonism in any case does not concern the religious practices of the Jewish Paul of Acts. This is the solution to an intramural conflict between Paul and "zealous" *repentant* Jews and does not refer to unrepentant Jews. Nowhere in Acts is Paul accused by his Jewish opponents of impugning the traditions or practices of Israel. The Jewish opposition against Paul's mission in the diaspora is due entirely to his interpretation of the Jewish Scriptures that the risen Jesus is God's Messiah.

For this reason, the reader must consider the charges brought against Paul by "the Jews from Asia" as unfounded and disingenuous (21:28-29). Nevertheless with characteristic hyperbole and local color, Luke dramatically describes the riot that ensues (21:30-36). Stirred by passion and prejudice, the crowd drags Paul from the temple and tries to kill him. Roman soldiers intervene to rescue him from the lynch mob. In his interrogation of Paul (21:37-38), the Roman tribune reflects the general ignorance about him in the holy city. Paul's retort to the tribune (21:39) sets the stage for his first great apologia that follows.

21:27-29. The reader should not be surprised to find "Jews from Asia" at the Jerusalem Temple within eyesight of Paul, since they are all there as Jewish pilgrims to celebrate Pentecost (see 2:5-9; 20:16). Paul's Asian opponents are probably from Ephesus, where the synagogue's opposition toward Paul's teaching ministry is especially keen (see 19:8-10; 20:3, 19). This is reflected in their violent reaction to seeing Paul in the Temple: They "stirred up the whole crowd . . . [and] seized [lit., "laid hands on"] him" (v. 27); and then they shout for additional help in apprehending him (v. 28a). Passions peak during religious festivals! A mob of opponents who act in a non-rational and unprofitable manner is a thematic element of Luke's narrative (e.g., 6:1-7; 11:1-18; 14:27–15:21).

What is somewhat more surprising is the first allegation that Paul "is teaching everyone everywhere against our people, our law, and this place" (v. 28b). This is patently untrue; and we have heard it all before in any case, not only as gossip circulating among "zealous" believers that Paul teaches "all the Jews living among the Gentiles to forsake Moses" (see v. 21) but also as "false" testimony in the prosecution of Stephen that he (and Jesus before him) taught against "this holy place and the law" (see 6:13).[674] The second charge is more serious and new: He "has defiled this

---

674. Hill, *Hellenists and Hebrews,* 58, suggests the possibility that Paul's faithfulness and not Stephen's (or perhaps even Jesus') is the more relevant issue for Luke and therefore he reads the accusations leveled against Paul back into the Stephen story. This presumes that the parallelism between his two accounts is not coincidental but redactional.

holy place" (v. 28c) by bringing an unclean Gentile into the Temple. Gentiles were not allowed into the inner courts of the Temple beyond the "Court of the Gentiles" upon penalty of death—a point of law still enforced by the Roman occupation. Stone slabs inscribed in both Latin and Greek with warnings to this effect were posted throughout the temple courtyard.[675] But the evidence against Paul is circumstantial: They had earlier seen him walking the streets of downtown Jerusalem with one of his Gentile companions, Trophimus the Ephesian (see 20:4). On the basis of this sighting, his accusers infer that he must have continued his tour by taking Trophimus with him into the inner courts of the Temple—an unthinkable act for the Paul of Acts!

21:30-36. Luke exaggerates the crowd's violent reaction to these accusations, but the rhetorical effect explains why the "tribune of the cohort" was thereby alerted. The crowd "seized Paul and dragged him out of the temple" (v. 30) with the temple police shutting the doors behind them,[676] not because Paul's alleged desecration had made the Temple unclean for everyone but because they intended "to kill him" (v. 31)—an act that would have defiled the Temple if carried out within the inner courts.[677] The "tribune of the cohort" (v. 31),[678] later named as Claudius Lysias (see 23:26), understood well the psychology of a mob riot, that things could quickly get out of control. Therefore, "he immediately took soldiers and centurions and ran down to them . . . [and] they stopped beating Paul" (21:32) for fear that they would be arrested.

What happens next supplies the details that fulfill Agabus's prophecy: The Roman tribune arrests Paul and orders him "to be bound with two chains" (v. 33; see also 21:11, 13; cf. 22:29). Paul is in Roman hands from the outset for safekeeping. The term "inquired" (πυνθάνομαι *pynthanomai*; lit., "began to interrogate") reflects the tribune's

uncertainty or ambivalence about Paul's guilt. He continues to question Paul about "who he was and what he had done," but he conveys a calming and more reasonable perspective toward him that personifies Rome's posture toward Paul throughout his imprisonment.

Lysias's persona stands in stark contrast to that of the crowd, which shouts "one thing, some another" (v. 34a)—an atmosphere of confusion that prevents the more rational Lysias from "learn[ing] the facts [lit., "knowing with surety"]." The uproar over Paul is just too loud and intense (v. 34b; see 17:5; 20:1; cf. 24:18). Such scenes are commonplace in Acts and always subvert a setting where Paul's reasoned arguments from Scripture are heard and considered, if not always in faith. Ironically, peace is found in the barracks of pagan soldiers rather than in a synagogue of pious Jews![679] There are stairsteps leading up from the temple area to the barracks that slowed the escort's progress and so again Rome safeguarded Paul from the angry mob: The soldiers carried Paul up the steps (21:35) to the shouts of "Away with him! [= Kill him!]" (v. 36; cf. Luke 23:18; John 19:15) that continues to reverberate through the narrative of Paul's trials (cf. 22:22; 28:19).

21:37-39. Finally away from the rabble-rousing mob, Lysias can now hear what Paul says and observe the manner by which he speaks. The results transform their legal relationship. Paul uses Greek to make a request: "May I say something to you?" (v. 37). The tribune is surprised that Paul addresses him in Greek, not because it is rare for a Jew to speak Greek; bilingualism was commonplace in Paul's Palestine. He seems surprised that Paul speaks with a particular inflection of Greek, different from those who come to Palestine from North Africa (see 2:7-8). That is, the tribune knows now by his Greek dialect that Paul is not from Egypt and therefore cannot be "the Egyptian who recently stirred up a revolt and led the four thousand assassins out into the wilderness" (v. 38).[680] His use of

675. So Fitzmyer, *The Acts of the Apostles*, 698.

676. Probably the inner gates, restricted to purified Jews, rather than the outer gates, open to all pilgrims. So Marshall, *The Acts of the Apostles*, 348.

677. Haenchen, *The Acts of the Apostles*, 616.

678. A Roman cohort of soldiers consisted of at least 760 infantrymen and 240 cavalrymen. Roughly ten centuries are stationed with a cohort, each one with responsibility for 100 soldiers. The "tribune" (= commandant) of this cohort is garrisoned at the northwest corner of the temple area in the Fortress Antonia with stairway access to where the riot is taking place. The response time would have been short and fits the details of Luke's narrative.

679. The barracks in question were the soldiers' quarters at the nearby Fortress Antonia. See Josephus *Antiquities of the Jews* 15.11.4. 403-9. See also Johnson, *The Acts of the Apostles*, 382.

680. Josephus speaks of this same Egyptian revolutionary, who came to Jerusalem during the time of Procurator Felix as a messianic figure and predicted the destruction of the Temple. Apparently thousands were killed in the riot that ensued but the Egyptian escaped with several thousand followers—Josephus claims thirty thousand but Luke's figure is more accurate. See Josephus *Antiquities of the Jews* 20.8.6.169-72.

οὐκ ἄρα (*ouk ara*, "Then you are not . . .") to introduce a rhetorical question implies that Lysias first thought Paul is this wanted assassin; were it so this would have marked a military coup for him! Alas, Paul is but "a Jew, from Tarsus" (v. 39), which perhaps explains his diction as well as his ethnicity and citizenship.[681]

Paul's biographical sketch reveals important information about who he is, which will dictate how Lysias must handle his legal case. Its literary construction, for example, combines nationality, city of origin, and statement of citizenship (= passport), reflecting a rhetorical form learned from his classical education—perhaps in Tarsus, a center of Greek culture and rhetoric.[682] Paul is an educated man. Significantly, he is a Jewish man as well,

not only confirming Lysias's verdict that Paul is not the Egyptian fugitive but also implying that the real conflict the soldiers rescued him from is religious rather than political in nature. Moreover, for a Jew to be "a citizen of an important city" other than Rome is no idle boast. Typically, this would have implied that Paul is a member of a prominent family or held deed to substantial real estate holdings in the region of Tarsus.

It is on this personal basis that Paul makes his polite request known to this tribune: "I beg you, let me speak to the people [= the people of God]." His request to address this audience of religious Jews, coupled with his identity as a Jew from Tarsus, discloses the religious motive of his defense. The Paul of Acts surely knows there will be no miraculous escape from the chains that now bind him, since it fulfills prophecy; his speech does not intend to set him free but to interpret his imprisonment as an act of his faithfulness to God and for Israel.[683]

---

681. Witherington, *The Acts of the Apostles*, 662, argues that Paul's response to Lysias's rhetorical question is more than a legal definition of his persona; it is also a rebuttal that seeks to restore his personal dignity in response to what he took to be a racial slur or deprecating perception that he was this Egyptian renegade.

682. For a description of Tarsus and its importance in the Roman world, especially as Athens's complement well known for its excellent schools, see Hengel and Schwemer, *Paul Between Damascus and Antioch*, 158-67.

683. For this argument worked out in detail, see Tannehill, *The Acts of the Apostles*, 2:268-84.

REFLECTIONS

The tribune "ordered that Paul be taken into the barracks" (21:34 NIV). Many interpreters of Acts suggest that the relationship between Lysias and Paul personifies the ideal relationship between the secular state and the church. On the one hand, Lysias's perspective toward Paul is completely free of religious interest. He has no apparent interest in the gospel or in Paul as a prophet-like-Jesus. His interrogation of Paul is calculated to determine whether he is a threat to the state's interests in Palestine, and he evaluates Paul's innocence according to Roman law. Lysias's preoccupation is Rome, not God; and perhaps this is as it should be. On the other hand, Lysias protects Paul against a threat to his life. More important, he recognizes this threat as provoked by religious rather than political disagreements, and he allows Paul the freedom to explain himself on this basis. While Lysias's Rome is no liberal democracy, his decisions about Paul exemplify an understanding of the separation between state and church that tolerates, even safeguards religious freedom.

In making this point, however, the teacher of this passage should be careful not to sacralize the state. The decisions Lysias makes personify a state concerned for a secular version of peace without any concern whether its decisions agree with God's purposes. According to Luke's model, the sovereign God, the only God, can collaborate with any pagan state interested in legal justice and concerned to safeguard the church's witness to the gospel. At the same time, this same model keenly discourages revolutionary violence as legitimate means for ensuring that God's will is done on earth as it is in heaven.

In the biblical context, one finds competing models of the relationship between the state and the church. These differing models should be pressed into service to bring "checks and balances" to any discussion of this literary theme in Acts. For example, the book of Revelation characterizes the church's relationship to the state in negative terms: "Babylon" is an evil order ruled over by the unholy trinity and demands that the faithful children of God submit to their corrupting demands or be martyred (Revelation 12–13). At the very least, the congregation's teachers should guard against any interpretation of Scripture that regards civil order as "Christian" whether by nature or in purpose.

ACTS 21:40–23:35, PAUL DEFENDS HIMSELF BEFORE JEWS IN JERUSALEM

COMMENTARY

This passage narrates the first of four episodes in which Paul defends himself in Palestine against accusations brought against him by his Jewish opponents (21:40–26:30). Luke's shaping of these four episodes forms a whole that nicely coheres around certain big ideas and vivid images that the reader should keep in mind. For example, this is a section of Acts that is more speech than story; and these speeches are typically forensic (apologia) in form and function and, therefore, are different from the missionary speeches heard to this point in Acts.[684] Perhaps the most obvious characteristic of these speeches is their Jewishness. In part this reflects Paul's effort to respond to his opponents' accusation that he is guilty of teaching against Israel's ancestral traditions. Even though his Jewish opponents attempt to ratchet up their charge to expose a political consequence (= sedition), the Roman judges who hear their case against Paul follow Gallio's earlier example (see 18:12-16) and never adjudicate its legal merit. While disinterested in the theological quotient of Paul's message or even the fact that it evidently divides the house of Israel, Rome at least comprehends that nothing he has done or said is punishable under Roman law. Surely Paul pays attention to this more political accusation, but in things said and done "off the record" rather than in his

speeches, in which the topics are Jewish not Roman and the motives religious not secular. Indeed, the singular contention of his apologia is that he has acted in conformity with God's purposes for God's people.

Paul's enduring commitment to Israel is easily observed by consideration of the internal dynamic between the basic components of his first (see 22:3-21) and the final (see 26:1-23) speeches that frame Luke's narrative of Paul's legal difficulties. In both these bracketing texts Paul begins with a brief autobiographical sketch that emphasizes his Jewish background and personal identity (22:3-5; 26:4-11) before settling on different rehearsals of his Damascus road experience and calling (22:6-16; 26:12-18; see 9:1-19a). His encounter with Jesus defines his prophetic vocation as a "light to the nations" (22:17-21; 26:19-23; cf. 13:47). Yet the house of Israel, divided over whether Jesus is the Messiah, remains divided about Paul (see 22:22-23).

What role does the defense of the Paul of Acts perform within the NT canon? In particular, how does this narrative aim form the interpreter's angle of vision toward the canonical Paul and into the Pauline letters of the NT? Without doubt Luke shapes the entire narrative of Paul's trials, and in particular his apologia, to portray him as someone who is a personal exemplar of Jewish piety and a redemptive agent of Israel's God. Paul has spiritual power, and he is an inspired interpreter of God's word—the equal of Peter and John before him and of his contemporary James. At the end of the day, Luke is disinterested in Rome's verdict on Paul and so concludes Acts without legal closure. Nothing is

---

684. The basic rhetorical structure of a Greek-styled *apologia* begins with an exordium in which the speaker commends his credentials to his audience in order to win the right to be heard; next is the *narratio*, or an edited narrative of relevant events, that delimits the "case study"; with the case before the audience, the speaker provides the *probatio*, or standard proofs—eyewitnesses, textual support, revelatory events—that might be brought forward as testimony; and the speech concludes with the *refutatio*, in which the speaker brings to focus everything said in direct response to the accusations brought forward.

written of Paul's meeting with the Emperor because Luke is fundamentally *disinterested* in what Rome thinks. Luke's interest is rather posited in Paul's status as an interpreter and carrier of God's word for God's people, which has importance for the future of the church.

In this regard, Paul emerges from his legal entanglements as a principled defender of Israel's faith whose teachings are in essential continuity with the purposes of God for Israel according to Israel's Scriptures. More important, it is on this profoundly Jewish ground that Paul now can define and defend his vocation as prophetic witness to the nations. The real meaning of his Damascus road vision and his vocation is that the God of Israel has called Paul to carry God's transforming word about God's Messiah to the nations so that all people might participate in the blessings promised first to the Jews. By rooting this claim in the Scriptures the Paul of Acts is portrayed as a defender of a truly Jewish religion. In this sense, then, it is not Paul who must change how he reads Scripture, but rather it is unrepentant Israel who must revise its hermeneutic—its "official" story of God's restoration of Israel—in the light of the gospel that Paul proclaims.[685]

The plotline of the present passage, which narrates Paul's defense before the Jews of Jerusalem, includes two speeches, the first to the people (22:1-21) and the second to the Sanhedrin (23:1-6), with a variety of responses from both Jewish audiences (22:22-23; 23:7-9) and from the Roman tribune Claudius Lysias (22:24-30; 23:10) following each. The dramatic interplay of these encounters sets the stage for the plot against Paul's life (23:12-22), which is sandwiched between a christophany repeating that Rome is his destiny (23:11) and his escape from harm's way in Jerusalem to Caesarea (23:23-35), the venue of his Roman trial, which follows.

21:40–22:21. In his exchange with Lysias, Paul identifies himself as a Jew from Tarsus, which is also how he begins his speech to Jerusalem's Jews. He climaxes his apologia by claiming that God commissioned him to go "far away to the Gentiles" (22:21). The interplay between his Jewish identity (22:3-5) and his Gentile commission, with its echo of Jeremiah and Isaiah's commissions (22:6-11), frame this first speech, which includes important roles performed by the devout disciple Ananias (22:12-16) and by the Temple, the erstwhile symbol of religious Israel (22:17-20). For the Paul of Acts, the public symbol of a restored Israel in the last days of salvation's history is its vocation as light to the nations.

21:40–22:2. Paul quieted his audience first with a hand gesture (21:40) and then by addressing them in Hebrew (22:2). The use of language again plays a strategic role in Luke's story, as Paul shifts from the Greek used to gain the attention of his Roman captor (21:37-38) to Hebrew in order to win the sympathy of a Jewish audience. His opening line to them (his exordium) identifies his speech as a "self-defense" (an apologia). In an oral culture, as Paul's surely was, auditors would be accustomed to hearing orators speak and could follow the form and related function of their speeches. An apologia spoken in the vernacular would certainly have been apropos to Paul's situation in addressing a hostile crowd. Moreover, the use of Hebrew would have appealed to the crowd's nationalistic and ethnic passions, which would have registered at fever pitch during the feast of Pentecost (see chaps. 5–11).

22:3-5. In presenting his Jewish credentials Paul broadly sketches a *vita* similar to the one he had submitted to Lysias (see 21:39): "I am a Jew, born in Tarsus in Cilicia."[686] He again emphasizes that he is a Jew of the diaspora—a relevant detail, since his principal antagonists are also Jews from the diaspora. In exchange for any reference to his citizenship, which may have disenfranchised him

---

685. One cannot help noting Paul's ambivalence in maintaining his Jewish identity with his Christian message—Dunn's image is of a "shuttlecock batted back and forth between the two spheres—of his twofold identity and double loyalty." See Dunn, *The Acts of the Apostles*, 292. Perhaps it is this that explains his name change from "Saul" to "Paul" (see 13:9); it is a Lukan metaphor for the tensions inherent within Paul, who is Jewish and Christian, from Jerusalem and Tarsus, who is citizen of Rome and Tarsus while a loyal Israelite, and speaks as prophet-like-Jesus and philosopher-like-Socrates.

686. The construction of this Greek sentence is awkward and has led commentators to debate how to punctuate it, with implications for constructing a Pauline biography. Most follow the present translations and place a comma after "Gamaliel," which distinguishes between Tarsus as Paul's ancestral home and Jerusalem as the place of his education. See A. du Toit, "The Tale of Two Cities," *NTS* 46 (2000) 375-402. It is entirely possible, however, to follow Luke's use of three participles as three discrete stages of Paul's life and so place commas after "in this city" and "law." In this case, then, Jerusalem would have been Paul's ancestral home, where he was brought up as a child and educated as a youth before moving to Tarsus—where he evidently had close family connections (see 21:39)—after completing his education and initiation into the teachers of the Pharisaic party. See Barrett, *A Critical and Exegetical Commentary on the Acts of the Apostles*, 2:1034-36.

from "the people," he speaks of a childhood during which he was "brought up in this city" and educated "at the feet of Gamaliel . . . according to our ancestral law, being zealous for God" (v. 3). These details of Paul's education are classically Pharisaic. It is hardly possible to have been initiated into the Pharisaic elite (cf. Phil 3:5-6; see also Acts 23:6) without spending a considerable apprenticeship in the holy city. Gamaliel (the Elder) is probably the same teacher Luke mentions earlier in Acts as a respected member of the Sanhedrin (see 5:34); he lived in Jerusalem at the time and was one of the foremost teachers within the Pharisaic party. To sit "at the feet" of a great teacher denotes Paul's initiation from an early age (probably at age five) into the rigorous regimen of Jewish learning (lasting at least until his Bar Mitzvah at age thirteen).

He finally characterizes his devotion to his studies with two catchwords associated with the demands of the Pharisaic school: "educated strictly" (ἀκρίβεια *akribeia*) and "zealous" (ζηλωτής *zēlōtēs*) for God. The first is used by Josephus to describe the distinctive concern of the Pharisees for precision in their interpretation and observance of the "ancestral laws."[687] In this light, the auditor may well have expected Paul to speak of his "zeal for the law" (see 21:20; cf. Gal 1:14) instead of his "zeal for God" (cf. Rom 10:2). This slight shift of emphasis from torah to God may well stand as a gentle rebuke of those whose devotion to Jewish "tradition" prevents them from hearing the truth of God's gospel. At the same time, Paul's reference to "God" may intend to provide the antecedent for his next claim that he "persecuted this Way" (v. 4; see also 9:1-2; 8:1-3; cf. 19:9, 23; 22:19): Paul did so out of his devotion to God rather than to a particular interpretation of the torah.

22:6-11. The three accounts of Paul's conversion and calling in Acts are broadly similar in that each describes his crusade against believers, his trip to Damascus for the purpose of imprisoning believers there, his epiphany of the living Jesus when approaching Damascus, and his entry into Damascus a changed man. The repetition of the same incident in a single composition makes it unnecessary to rehearse all its details; this version glosses the earlier one in Acts 9, and together these accounts prepare the reader for

Paul's second retelling (= third version) of his conversion story, found in Acts 26. This particular retelling of his persecution of the church with clear allusions to Stephen's case (see 22:20) repeats what the reader of Acts already knows, although in this setting the irony is unmistakable. His claims may be slightly exaggerated to cultivate the impression of his devotion to God, since nowhere in Acts do we read that Paul's actions resulted in the death of any believer, rather just in the suffering and dispersion of some (see 8:1-4). In any case, to persecute "up to the point of death" with the consent of the council of elders would have been illegal in Roman Palestine. Especially important to note is that Paul recruits this council, along with the high priest and "the [Jewish] brothers in Damascus" (22:5) as witnesses to the integrity of his Jewish pedigree.

Paul's firsthand account of his encounter with Jesus differs very little from the first narrative of this event (see 9:3-6; cf. 26:12-18). He adds the time, "about noon," which makes the account more realistic,[688] and intensifies the "great" light that "shone about" him (v. 6). Moreover, in this retelling, the Lord identifies himself more fully as "Jesus of Nazareth" (v. 8; see also 2:22; 3:6; 4:10; 6:14; 26:9), which may intend not only to locate Jesus in Palestine for his Jewish audience but also to convey an ironic allusion to the circumstances of Paul's arrest when completing his Nazirite vow, for the Greek text has "Nazorean" rather than "Nazareth."

The most obvious deviation from the narrator's account in chap. 9 is that "those who were with me saw the light but did not hear the voice of the one who was speaking to me" (22:9; see 9:7; cf. 26:13). The reason for this change is not as obvious to the interpreter, but its significance in any case must be minor. The exchange between a blinded Paul and Jesus, lacking in the first version, is here added to indicate more clearly that Paul conceives of his conversion to the living Jesus in terms of his vocation—"What am I to *do*, Lord?"—which Jesus tells him will be clarified once he gets up and goes to Damascus (22:10).[689]

---

688. So Haenchen, *The Acts of the Apostles*, 625.
689. Johnson takes δόξα (*doxa*), translated "brightness/brilliance" (22:11), more literally as "glory" to reflect what he regards as Luke's intention to connect this event with the presence of God in the world. See Johnson, *The Acts of the Apostles*, 389. This makes better sense of the provocative use of "Lord" (22:10) when speaking of Jesus and of Paul's calling before a hostile Jewish audience (cf. 2 Cor 4:6).

687. Josephus *Life* 191.

22:12-16. Paul's retelling of his conversion is strategically sandwiched between his Jewish *vita* (vv. 3-5) and this expanded account of Ananias's role in his commissioning. Ananias is a "devout man according to the law and well spoken of by all the Jews" (v. 12; see also 9:10), who is recruited as a relevant witness to Paul's own religious credentials before an audience of other pious Jews. Note again the use of language—Ananias calls Paul by his Aramaic name, "Saul" (v. 13), to intensify the claim made: He is a religious Jew. Ananias has no role in Paul's second version in Acts 26, where Paul addresses an audience of secular Jews and Roman leaders.

According to this version, Ananias, who first received the Lord's prophecy of Paul's mission (see 9:15-16), now reports to Paul the substance of what he is to do. The effect of telescoping the details of Paul's healing to the simple phrase "regain your sight" (v. 13; see also 9:17-18) is to posit the auditor's attention on Ananias and his witness to Jesus' prophecy of Paul's future mission. The interplay between these two texts within Acts is made more striking since Ananias restates the Lord's prophecy in a biblical idiom: "the God of our ancestors" (see 3:13; 5:30; 7:32; 13:23) has "chosen" him to know God's will (see 13:22; 21:14) and "to see the Righteous One" (see 3:14; 7:52; cf. Luke 23:47). This combination of biblical phrases, which is asserted by a pious Jew, anchors Paul's commission to "witness to all the world" (22:15) in Jewish tradition.[690] Moreover, Paul's contested interpretation of Scripture is predicated on "what you have seen and heard," thereby making the connection between his conversion to Jesus and his commission to proclaim God's word all the more clear (cf. 1 Cor 15:1-11).

Ananias's exhortation to "get up, be baptized, and have your sins washed away, calling on his name" (v. 16; see also 2:38; 3:19) rounds out the sparse earlier account where we are told that Paul is encouraged to "be filled [= baptized] with the Holy Spirit" (see 9:18-19). The interplay supplies the full logic of Christian baptism. Baptism initiates the converted Paul—the one who calls upon the Lord's name (see 2:21; 9:14)—into the covenant community on the basis of God's forgiveness of his sins (see 2:38); and it is within the context of this community's life and vocation that the Holy Spirit empowers this prophet-like-Jesus to perform the tasks that accord with God's will.[691]

22:17-21. The final incident in Paul's retelling of his Damascus road calling takes the reader by surprise: Paul does not mention his Jewish opposition (see 9:23-25), and he reveals that Jesus commissioned his mission during a *second* christophany while Paul was praying in the Temple (v. 21),[692] where Jesus (rather than the "disciples") also alerted him to the Jewish threat against him and urged him to leave Jerusalem immediately (v. 18; see also 9:29-30).

Paul's version of this episode is consistent with Luke's portrait of him in Acts. Although clearly ambivalent toward the Temple as a symbol of faithful Israel, Luke employs it here as a crucial element of an apologia that proves Paul's purity: A person praying in the Temple is an unlikely candidate to desecrate it. In addition, there are certain allusions to Isaiah's temple vision (cf. Isa 6:1-10), during which he is called a prophet of God and told that Israel will resist his message,[693] both of which parallel Paul's own experiences with Jesus.[694] Echoes of Jeremiah's theophany that commissioned him a "prophet to the nations" (cf. Jer 1:5; Gal 1:15) further alert the reader to the prophetic subtext of Paul's narrative of his temple vision: Paul is a prophet-like-Jesus who stands in the line of Israel's prophets.

---

691. Cf. J. D. G. Dunn, *Baptism in the Holy Spirit* (London: SCM, 1970) 73-78.

692. Lüdemann, *Early Christianity According to the Traditions in Acts*, 238-40, asserts that "Paul's vision in the temple is certainly unhistorical" because Paul claims he was called to be the apostle to the nations near Damascus in Gal 1:15 and because it is so evidently Lukan in language and purpose within this Acts setting.

693. The continuing literary theme of Israel's rejection in Acts is again carefully circumscribed by Luke: In Paul's apologia it is used ironically of Paul's own theological reversal—once a rejecter of Jesus, now rejected because of him. However, the prophecy of Israel's division over the Messiah is carefully placed alongside Paul's own Jewish credentials to make certain the reader understands Isaiah's prophecy is not anti-Israel, as though Christianity were destined by God to be a Gentile religion, but is a prophecy about unrepentant Israel realized during Paul's mission.

694. Paul and Isaiah are called to their prophetic vocations by a temple vision (cf. Isa 6:1//Acts 22:17); both try to excuse themselves because neither views himself as able to do the tasks involved (cf. Isa 6:5//Acts 22:19-20); and both are "sent" and both "go" at the Lord's command (cf. Isa 6:8-10//Acts 22:21). Moreover, the prophetic connection to Paul's mission to the nations is found in Jeremiah's theophanic calling as prophet to the nations (cf. Jer 1:15//Acts 22:21; Gal 1:15). See O. Betz, "Die Vision des Paulus in Temple von Jerusalem," in *Verborum Veritas* (Wuppertal: Rolf Brockhaus, 1970) 113-23.

690. The use of "witness" (μάρτυς *martys*) is rarely used of anyone except the Twelve and often in connection to their prophetic ministry (see 1:8, 22; 2:32; 3:15; 5:32; 10:39, 41; cf. 13:31). Luke's use of it here almost certainly recalls the earlier stories of the apostles as inspired witnesses to the risen Jesus, thereby connecting their "witness" with Paul's.

Paul's reference to "the blood of your witness Stephen" (v. 20) demonstrates the extent of his "great reversal." Paul recalls the earlier story of Stephen's martyrdom, not as a prediction of his own martyrdom but as a symbol of his own conversion. The pairing of Paul's witness to the living Jesus and the dying Stephen funds his gospel as the light "to the Gentiles/nations [ἔθνη *ethnē*)]" (v. 21; see also 13:47; cf. Isa 49:6; Luke 2:29-35; Rom 11:13; Gal 2:7).[695] Paul delays his divinely sanctioned commission until the end of the speech to underscore the universal scope of God's word and the salvation it promises: The good news for Gentiles is that they now can share in Israel's promised blessings according to the prophets. Paul's climactic assertion that he is called to carry the word of God "far away to the Gentiles [nations]" (v. 21) not only sanctions his urban mission to distant places but underscores for his Jewish audience that his mission embodies the vocation of a faithful Israel according to the prophets (= Isaiah).

22:22-23. There is no good reason why the crowd should react as violently as it does: A pious Paul infers from personal experience and allusions to Scripture's prophecy that the limits of Israel's promised blessings should be extended to include repentant Gentiles (see 3:21-26).[696] But the polemical cast of Luke's story precludes reasoned debate; the church's opponents in Acts are rarely if ever reasonable! Thus, an angry mob interrupts Paul before he can provide formal proof (peroratio) of his innocence.[697] Their vitriolic shouts—"he should not be allowed to live" (v. 22)—and hostile gestures—"throwing off their cloaks" (see 14:14) and "tossing dust into the air" (v. 23; see also 13:51)—seek to silence Paul, perhaps in preparation for stoning him.[698] These actions are symbols of an unthinking, unrepentant Israel's obduracy

and the hard possibility that not all of Israel will repent (see 1:11; cf. Luke 4:22-30; Rom 11:25-32). The reasons why any Jew should resent the inclusion of repentant Gentiles in the blessings of Israel's salvation are less clear (see the Commentary on 23:12-22).

22:24-29. The actions of the tribune suggest that he is confused as well. As a pagan outsider, he fails to pick up the controversy provoked by Paul's testimony. He sees only the mob's hostile and loud reaction and knows that Paul is guilty of something bad. Thus he resorts to an "examination by flogging"—a military routine for extracting useful information from a prisoner in an unsettled case.[699] The soldiers "stretched him out to flog him" (v. 25a) in prospect of a brutal, sometimes fatal beating. Paul is prompted by their treatment to identify himself at last as a Roman citizen to the supervisory centurion: "Is it legal for you to flog a Roman citizen who is uncondemned [ἀκατάκριτος *akatakritos*]?" (v. 25b; see also 16:37). The weighty word here is *akatakritos*, which carries two legal connotations, either of which is damning. In this quasi-legal setting, Paul could mean either that the tribune is about to mete out an unjust punishment or that his anticipated flogging is premature or arbitrary, since a "proper" investigation has not yet been conducted according to Roman law. Perhaps Paul is purposefully vague in his polite but pointed question of the centurion in order to elicit precisely the response he received.

Lysias had earlier expressed surprise when Paul reported that he was a citizen of Tarsus (see 21:39). Imagine his shock when informed that "this man is a Roman citizen" (v. 26)! If a citizen's prestige and standing are determined by the city of his citizenship, few honors were more important in Paul's Mediterranean world than Roman citizenship.[700] Evidently Paul's citizenship is inherited, whereas Lysias's is purchased at great cost (v. 28). Citizen Lysias surely understood that among the most important rights of Roman citizenship is that of a fair public trial for a

---

695. This formulation of Paul's commission recalls Simeon's prophecy of a universal salvation (cf. Luke 2:29-32) and a divided house of Israel (cf. Luke 2:33-35). In this sense, the hostile response to Paul's declaration is viewed within Luke's narrative as another fulfillment of Simeon's prophecy.

696. D. Boyarin, *A Radical Jew* (Berkeley: University of California Press, 1994) 228-60, argues, however, that Paul's universalism "poses a significant challenge to Jewish notions of identity," primarily because it subverts Jewish ethnic particularity envisaged not only by its monotheism but by its "cultural specificities."

697. Speeches are routinely interrupted in Acts (see 10:44; 18:14; 23:7; 26:24), and as a literary device they aid the reader in detecting the speech's climactic point, which is scored exactly when the auditors interrupt the speaker! In this case, the Jerusalem Jews interrupt Paul when he implies that Gentiles will share in Israel's salvation. In fact, however, interrupted speeches are already complete.

698. Cf. Haenchen, *The Acts of the Apostles*, 633.

699. See Witherington, *The Acts of the Apostles*, 676-77, for illustrations of various Roman scourges, any one of which was used to flog Paul. Flogging was legalized torture and was used in Roman Palestine to extract testimony from an accused party, typically an alien, slave, or someone from the lower classes, and only when legal briefs could not resolve a case. In this sense, then, flogging is a reflection of the tribune's indecision.

700. See J. Neyrey, "Luke's Social Location of Paul," in Witherington, *History, Literature, and Society in the Book of Acts*, 276-78.

citizen accused of any crime. In Paul's case, there is no evidence of a crime—indeed, accusations, once scrutinized, turn out to be religious rather than civil in nature. For this reason, Lysias is rightly afraid of the consequences of breaking Roman law at this point (v. 29; see also 16:38-39), an offense that does not respect one's status and could result in his loss of face and high position. His fear of public embarrassment may help to explain why from this moment forward he is more restrained in his handling of Paul's legal case.

22:30. This transitional text reflects a more cautious Lysias intent on determining the legitimacy of the accusations leveled against Paul by his Jewish antagonists. He first releases him and then convenes the Sanhedrin by his civil authority (or that of the current Roman procurator in Palestine). Paul is the latest prophet-like-Jesus to follow the Lord in appearing before this council (cf. Luke 22:66; see 4:15; 5:21; 6:12). Paul does so, however, as a pious Pharisee and a solid Roman citizen with the protective support of the empire and the theological support of the Pharisees on the council. It will make a difference: Paul does not die in Jerusalem.

23:1-10. The story of Paul's informal hearing before Jerusalem's Sanhedrin is as strange as it is strategic. The meeting is arranged by Lysias to understand more clearly the religious nature of the Jewish protest against Paul's mission to the nations; it is another venue for his ongoing interrogation of Paul. By this time, Lysias understands that the issues are "nationalistic" (= Jewish) and that he has no real reason to retain Paul as a prisoner. One might even suppose that Lysias has taken an interest in Paul and that this hearing is more for his personal edification than for determining Paul's legal standing.

For this reason the intemperate proceedings are difficult for a rational outsider such as Lysias to follow. The rules of jurisprudence certainly seem different before this council than before a Roman tribunal! Why would the high priest Ananias take offense at Paul's declaration of his "clear conscience" (v. 1) and then respond with physical abuse rather than reasoned rebuttal (v. 2)? What is the meaning of Paul's prophecy and name-calling in retaliation (v. 3)? And why should Paul cede his high moral ground so quickly, especially with

a disingenuous comment (vv. 4-5)? Paul's attempt to explain the reason for his trial (v. 6) only provokes old rivalries, and the meeting degenerates into a shouting match over Paul's religious legitimacy. Roman Lysias is left on the sidelines scratching his head over the legal politics of these Palestinian Jews (vv. 7-9). In any case, this utterly fruitless hearing ends as it began with Paul held in protective custody (v. 10).

Yet, the reader of Acts will recognize what Lysias does not: Paul's claim of Pharisaic orthodoxy (v. 6), and the division within the Sanhedrin that follows (vv. 7-9) envisages Israel's theological crisis. Israel is divided over the issue of a resurrected Messiah and therefore its national "hope" is never fully realized during these "last days" of salvation's history.

23:1. Paul begins his self-defense in good faith. His first statement begins with the salutation, "Brothers" (see v. 6; 1:16), which intends to stage his remarks for an audience of religious peers. For this reason, he asserts the constancy of his good reputation before God. Paul's appeal to the moral norm of a "clear conscience" may well be considered provocative in this Jewish setting since it is an idea not found in the OT but one known among Hellenist moral philosophers of the day (cf. Rom 2:15; 1 Corinthians 8–10; 2 Cor 11:12; 2 Tim 1:3).[701] Its meaning, however, is plain enough: Paul asserts that the internal motivation for all his practices is zeal to perform God's will. Haenchen wonders whether this includes Paul's behaviors prior to his conversion, such as his participation in Stephen's execution or the persecution of the church (see, e.g., 7:58; 8:1-3; 9:1; 22:4).[702] But Paul's claim obtains to his "conscience before God" and not his behaviors per se.

23:2-5. The motive for Ananias's order for members of his entourage standing next to Paul "to strike him on the mouth" (v. 2; cf. John 18:22), presumably in response to what he has just said, is unclear and unreasonable in any case.[703] More certain is the intent of Paul's prophecy that "God will strike you,

701. For a full discussion of "clear conscience," see R. Wall, "Conscience," in *The Anchor Bible Dictionary*, 1:1128-30.

702. Haenchen, *The Acts of the Apostles*, 637.

703. Ananias was high priest from 47 to 58 CE and probably at the height of his popularity when Paul stood before him in Jerusalem. He is remembered for his volatility and his wealth—and for his assassination because of pro-Roman policies in 66 CE. See Josephus *The Jewish War* 2:426-29, 441-42. See also Fitzmyer, *The Acts of the Apostles*, 717.

you whitewashed wall!" (v. 3). On the face of it, his curse responds to the illegality of Ananias's attack upon him. With biting irony, then, Paul deigns to rebuke this high priest for judging him "according to the law" and yet acting against him "in violation of the law"—probably alluding to Lev 19:15, which condemns the punishment of the powerless innocent.

Adding texture to this surface meaning, Paul's prophecy of Ananias's demise echoes Deut 28:22 and so locates it in a biblical setting where God's curses are listed "on account of the evil of your deeds, because you have forsaken me" (Deut 28:20). An angry Paul, therefore, interprets the council's peremptory strike against him as evidence that it rejects his mission and message and, therefore, Israel's God. The other intertextual echo is of Ezek 13:10 (cf. Matt 23:27), recalling the prophet's condemnation of the hypocrisy of Israel's leaders by calling them builders of a weak wall that is obscured by a veneer of white paint. That is, Ananias's rejection of Paul's prophetic ministry among the Jews incriminates not only the high priest but also all of unrepentant Israel, who blindly follow his spiritual leadership.

Trading biblical allusions, supporters of Ananias's prerogatives as president of the Sanhedrin scold Paul for insulting "God's high priest" (v. 4), which Paul accepts by citing Torah's injunction that "you shall not speak evil of a leader of your people" (v. 5*b*; cf. Exod 22:27). He is after all Torah observant, and his appeal to the alluded Scripture warrants a public apology. But how is the reader to understand Paul's remark, "I did not realize that he was high priest"? Surely he knows Ananias is the high priest and evidently understands the council well enough to exploit its internal dynamic (see v. 6)! Johnson's solution seems right that Paul's remark is ironical and intends to be read as a "prophetic criticism of the chief priest, whose behavior makes him 'unrecognizable'" since it did not accord with his spiritual status and religious function within Israel.[704] If Johnson's point is taken, then Luke's portrait of the Sanhedrin in Acts continues to reflect its remarkable inability to pick up the irony of prophetic criticism (see 5:38-40).

23:6. At this point in these hearings, which already have collapsed, Paul attempts a "diversionary tactic," similar to that employed by Greek rhetors when public debates were not going their way,[705] that mixes the Sanhedrin's volatile chemistry of Pharisees and Sadducees who are political rivals for the religious affections of the Jewish people. Significantly, Paul for the first time publicly identifies himself as "a Pharisee, a son of Pharisees," although earlier he claimed that he observed the law strictly (22:3; see also 26:5; cf. Phil 3:5)—characteristic of the Pharisee—and was trained by the Pharisee scholar Gamaliel (22:3). During the course of his legal difficulties, Luke completes Paul's public profile for benefit of the reader: He is educated in Jerusalem, a citizen of Tarsus and Rome, and a member of the Pharisee party.[706]

The reason for doing so is theological, not political.[707] We should not think that Paul's rhetorical tactic is a clever maneuver to save his life, even though it does. Rather, its principal purpose is to single out the most critical element of his interpretation of Scripture in order to place it strategically within the framework of "official" Judaism: "I am on trial concerning the hope of the resurrection of the dead."[708] The theological tradition of his Pharisaism, adapted to the church's belief in the resurrected Jesus, is the essence of the Jewish heritage of the church, without which the church cannot be the church.[709] While distinctive in their attitudes and performance of the torah, it is finally the Pharisees' *theological* distinction from the Sadducees that is most important: the "hope" that a faithful God would fulfill the biblical promise of a "resurrected" (= restored) Israel and that God's eternal reign would commence

704. Johnson, *The Acts of the Apostles*, 397.

705. G. Kennedy, *New Testament Interpretation Through Rhetorical Criticism* (Chapel Hill: University of North Carolina Press, 1984) 135.

706. The apparent contradiction between this statement and Paul's epistolary claim that he *was* a Pharisee but is no longer (Phil 3:5) has been explained both as a reflection of Luke's theological interest to portray a Jewish Paul or as Paul's rhetorical interest to portray the "dogs" of Philippi in unfavorable light; the truth is probably someplace in between.

707. By Luke's day, however, only the Pharisees had survived the tragedy of Rome's destruction of Jerusalem; they were the dominant religious elite in the diaspora that ensued. The Sadducees were no more because the various institutions they controlled were no more after 70 CE.

708. Paul's confession is a hendiadys, a literary device in which two or more terms are joined by the conjunctive "and" so that no term is subordinate to the other(s). Thus, "hope" and "resurrection of the dead" refer to the same idea: Israel's hope is its future resurrection from the dead (Dan 12:2-3; cf. 2 Macc 7; Isa 26:19).

709. Jervell, *Die Apostelgeschichte*, 555-56, points out that by this logic the Pharisaism of Paul is also the Pharisaism of Christ.

within its history (see 1:6). It is into this same theological soil that the Christian gospel is planted. Paul and the other inspired missionaries of Acts therefore proclaim the gospel that God's resurrection of Messiah Jesus is an act of divine faithfulness, first for the Jews and then also for the nations.

23:7-9. Luke's brief summary of the "dissension between the Pharisees and the Sadducees" illustrates in microcosm the realization of Simeon's prophecy of a divided Israel over God's gospel of the resurrected Messiah (cf. Luke 2:35). Israel's division is finally over different conceptions of its future with God. On the one hand, "Sadducees say there is no resurrection" (v. 8a). The theological purchase of adding "angel or spirit" is not immediately clear. There is little evidence that Sadducees denied the existence of angels and spirits, nor is it realistic since they were conservative torah-literalists and torah recognizes both angels and spirits; however, this exclusion "entirely corresponds to their this-worldly religion."[710] Fitzmyer suggests that both terms are appositive to the resurrection, specifying modes of it:[711] in the resurrection, Israel will become like angels (cf. Matt 22:30), or the resurrected "physical" (= historical) Israel will be in some sense a "spiritual" Israel (cf. 1 Cor 15:44).

On the other hand, since "Pharisees acknowledge all three" (v. 8b), the Sanhedrin Pharisees must at least admit the plausibility of Paul's earlier testimony of a christophany (see 22:7-11)[712] and allow the possibility that there is "nothing wrong with this man" (v. 9)—nor, the reader presumes, with his message of the resurrected Messiah. Of course, these erstwhile supporters of Paul are yet nonbelievers, so what Paul clearly reports as a vision of the living Jesus the Pharisees allow might be a "spirit or an angel."

23:10. From Rome's perspective nothing is settled, nor is it entirely possible to turn to the Sanhedrin for help in explaining its theological disagreements with the Way. From the reader's perspective the leadership team of official Israel is in shambles, forever fighting among itself and without competence or patience to debate the merits of a case. The Sanhedrin is no better than a common mob (see 21:29-30); both "become violent" and threaten to "tear Paul to pieces" because of their theological differences, and so the tribune in both cases must intervene and safeguard Paul back to the soldiers' barracks at the Fortress Antonia (see 21:34; 22:24).

23:11. Paul's vision in the Jerusalem prison is the second of a Lukan triad (see also 19:21; 27:24), indicating that Rome is the city of his destiny: "You must [δεῖ *dei*] bear witness also in Rome." The repeated use of *dei* makes it clear to the reader that Paul's future includes a mission to Rome as a "divine necessity" and that no evil can subvert what God has planned. This point is highlighted by timing, since each revelation comes to Paul at a moment of personal suffering, when it is not at all certain that the historical circumstances he finds himself in will allow God's will to be done. The intent of each vision, then, is to encourage God's servant—"Keep up your courage"—and to assert that the plans of a sovereign God will be executed, as unlikely as it may seem at the moment. The interplay between Paul's personal courage and God's transcendent sovereignty stands at the center of Luke's theological conception and shapes the plotline for the rest of Acts.[713]

23:12-22. This scene of conspiratorial intrigue tells of Paul's transfer from protective custody in Jerusalem under the Roman tribune Claudius Lysias to Caesarea, the setting of his formal trial before the Roman governor of Palestine, Antonius Felix. Paul's situation in Jerusalem has become ever more tenuous as a group of forty Jews consecrate themselves to carry out an assassination plot against him, evidently with the blessing of certain Sadducees on the Sanhedrin (vv. 12-15).

While certain that the assassination plot will never succeed because of the Lord's prophecy that Paul "must" see Rome (v. 11), the reader may still wonder what provokes this intense hatred of Paul among Jews. The

---

710. Haenchen, *The Acts of the Apostles*, 638.

711. Fitzmyer, *The Acts of the Apostles*, 719.

712. The KJV, which follows the *textus receptus*, supplies the conclusion "let us not fight against God" to the implied conditional "if a spirit or angel has spoken to him." In doing so the scribes make allusion to another Sanhedrin Pharisee, Gamaliel's, earlier commentary on the Twelve's ministry in Jerusalem that "if [the apostles' ministry/teaching] is of God, you will not be able to overthrow them—in that case you may even be found fighting against God" (5:39 NRSV).

713. Cf. Talbert, *Reading Acts*, 203-15, who contends that 23:11 leads the entire "thought-unit" that concludes with Agrippa's verdict of Paul's innocence, though his appeal to Caesar must also be honored (26:32). The subtext of Paul's various legal steps toward Rome is that "the plan of God cannot be blocked."

narrator, who is concerned only to describe the tension between them, does not explain the motives of Paul's antagonists. Their hostility toward him is evidently not with a "Jewish" Paul: His practices and pedigree are traditional. While the reader is aware that Paul's mission to the Gentiles fulfills biblical prophecy (see 13:47), it nevertheless threatens a variety of working definitions of Israel and Israel's salvation that are tied explicitly to nationalistic and ethnocentric fervor felt throughout Palestine at the time. To these Jews who plot against him, Paul is a traitor (see 21:28) and must be executed as such. Even within the church there is a deeply felt concern that Paul's mission to the nations threatens Israel's identity as God's people (see 21:21). This concern is surely exacerbated by the departure of Pauline-led congregations from various urban synagogues into self-standing house churches (see 18:7; 19:9), where Jewish leaders can no longer exercise their traditional leadership over the theological formation and social identity of these new believers.

There is also the sense that Paul's message about Jesus threatens Israel in a similar manner. Not only does his interpretation from Scripture to support the Lord's resurrection provoke long-standing tensions between the Pharisees and the Sadducees (see v. 6), his claim of the Lord's messiahship also provokes antagonism between messianists and non-messianists within religious Israel. The gospel about Jesus divides Israel. Because the plotline of Luke's narrative so closely follows Paul, the reader is easily more persuaded to think that Paul's troubles are due to his own "unconventional" practices or "controversial" profile. But Luke's account of Paul's testimony is at odds with this conclusion: He is a pious Jew and a solid citizen. I suggest that whatever parallelism the reader notes between Luke's story of Paul and Jesus' final journey to and passion in Jerusalem may well intend to draw attention to Jesus and not to an element of Luke's Pauline apologia: Paul is in trouble because of what he proclaims of the resurrected Jesus and for a restored Israel.

23:12-15. Acts provides very little information about either the identity or motivation of the forty Jews who joined together "in a conspiracy and bound themselves by an oath . . . until they had killed Paul" (vv. 12-13). Lysias's earlier reference to the sicarii or assassins (see 21:38) alerts the reader to the general unrest in Palestine where such violent activism was a familiar marker on the political landscape. Whatever the precise motive behind this deadly plot against Paul, it is surely religious fanaticism—indicated by their solemn oath and fast from food and drink—that drives the plotters. These are devout Jews who are dedicated to their murderous mission out of zeal to serve God and Israel. Luke no doubt intends the reader to contrast the aims of their vow with those of the Nazirite vow earlier completed by Paul and members of the Jewish church (see 21:26).

Their plan requires the cooperation of certain "chief priests and elders" (v. 14), probably among the council's Sadducean membership only, given the earlier reluctance of the council's Pharisees to condemn Paul (see v. 9). They are to request that Lysias bring Paul from the barracks of Antonia Fortress to the courtroom of the Sanhedrin, where council members would question Paul to gain "more accurate information [διαγινώσκω *diaginōskō*]" about his case (v. 15 NIV). Since *diaginōskō* is a technical term for questioning a witness to settle a case, the request would be in keeping with the tribune's wishes, even though Lysias may well have hesitated, given his earlier experience with the Sanhedrin! The assassination attempt would take place during Paul's transit from the barracks to the courtroom.

23:16-22. Paul's nephew, a "young man" (νεανίας *neanias*, v. 17) in his twenties, overhears rumors of the ambush and gains access to Paul (perhaps as a relative) to warn him about the danger (v. 16). The severely compressed staging of Paul's escape, which tells nothing of the circumstances that allow his nephew to learn of the plans for this "secret" conspiracy, is indicative of a narrator who wants his reader to be interested only in the safety of his central character. In that regard, this passage contains elements of the literary theme of God protecting the imprisoned servant from bodily harm by liberating intervention. The liberating agent in this case is neither angelic nor natural phenomena but a family member. The loyalty of family members who come to the rescue of another, however, is a familiar convention of ancient literature and one that is glossed by Paul's earlier reference to his family's Jerusalem residence (see 22:3).[714]

The nephew's retelling of the plot for the tribune's benefit (vv. 20-21) confirms what the reader was earlier told in a Jewish setting (see v. 15). The prompt and pliant responses, first of the centurion (vv. 17-18) and then of Lysias, envisage the nature of Paul's relations with Rome in contrast to his Jewish opposition, making the reader more sympathetic to Luke's depiction of a Rome wary of Israel's intramural squabbles. That an unnamed young man should alert an important Roman tribune that "the Jews" intend to dupe the official, and then challenge him not to be persuaded by them (v. 21) enhances Rome's popular appeal while cultivating a healthy distrust of Paul's enemies, symbolized by the secrecy of Lysias's liaison with the nephew (v. 22). Sharply put, Paul has more status in secular society as a Roman citizen than in Israel as an observant Jew and prophetic carrier of God's word. This is not to claim that Rome's perspective on Paul and his mission is favorable; rather, it is simply to assert that the Rome of Acts is more obedient to its constitutional law than unrepentant Israel of Acts is to its biblical law.

23:23-35. The "Jerusalem" phase of Paul's trials concludes with a change of venue from Antipatris (v. 31) to Caesarea (v. 33), where Paul will be formally tried before Governor Felix (v. 35). This is accomplished by accompaniment of a large escort of four hundred and seventy troops at a late and unexpected hour (vv. 23-25). The impression made by this clandestine military operation is that Paul's safety as a Roman citizen is of paramount concern, as evidenced by the official letter sent by Tribune Lysias to Governor Felix (vv. 26-30). In his letter, which functions as an important element of Paul's whole apologia, Lysias at last gives his verdict of Paul's innocence and so provides the narrator's summary of this initial phase of Paul's legal problems. His letter also makes clear that Rome's interest in Paul is self-centered and not theological. For this reason, no real change in Paul's situation takes place, and so upon reading Lysias's letter, Felix orders that

Paul be kept imprisoned to await the next phase of his trials (vv. 31-35).

23:23-25. A detachment of roughly half of those under Lysias's command in Jerusalem are assigned to safeguard Paul's transfer to Felix. Some have regarded these as inflated numbers that reflect a convention of Luke's storytelling: God's plans for Paul are being safeguarded by Rome as well. If, however, Paul is a solid citizen and an innocent man under a death threat, then the tribune would naturally want to take extra precautions in guaranteeing Paul's safe arrival into the jurisdiction of another official (= Felix). The tribune's reputation as a soldier is at stake. Luke's subsequent comment that the bulk of these troops returned to Jerusalem after taking Paul to Antipatris (vv. 31-32), about forty-five miles northwest of Jerusalem and out of harm's way, makes sound military sense and seems to confirm the story's reliability.

23:26-30. Claudius Felix was the co-procurator of Roman Palestine and "governor" of Judea (52–60 CE). The Roman historian Tacitus says of Felix, a freedman with considerable influence on the emperor: "With all cruelty and lust [he] wielded the power of a king, with the mentality of a slave."[715] Perhaps for this reason Lysias's letter is carefully crafted to state the legal facts as he (and the reader) have ultimately come to understand them. His letter is an example of *litterae dimissoriae* (notice to a higher court) sent by a Roman provincial official (Claudius Lysias) and addressed to his superior ("his Excellency the governor Felix") to appeal a legal case ("This man was seized by the Jews . . . but when I had learned").[716] The facts are as the reader knows them to be: Paul is a Roman citizen who was accused and interrogated by other Jews for indiscretions outside the bounds of Roman jurisprudence; he was taken into protective custody because of a death threat and is now sent to a higher authority for legal review.

Lysias's epistolary narrative generally agrees with Luke's, but it also reflects careful editing to enhance his position with Rome. For example, the reader knows the incriminating

---

714. Johnson, *The Acts of the Apostles*, 404.

715. Tacitus *Histories* 5.9. See also Fitzmyer, *The Acts of the Apostles*, 727. Felix married well and often; however, he was also an anti-Semite with particular animus against Jewish zealots, whom he treated so brutally that he was dismissed as Roman procurator in 60 CE.

716. Fitzmyer, *The Acts of the Apostles*, 726.

circumstances by which Lysais learned that Paul was a Roman citizen and, therefore, "rescued him"; yet, he takes full credit in his letter without indicating his blunders along the way. We also learn from this letter that Paul's legal troubles are not yet over: "I sent [Paul] to you at once, ordering his accusers to state before you what they have against him" (v. 30). This concluding statement of Lysias's intentions sets the stage for what follows in chap. 24 and for the reiteration of unrepentant Israel's case against Paul brought forward by their prosecuting attorney, Tertullus (see 24:5-6). Finally, Lysias's letter provides Felix with Rome's legal perspective by which he should interpret these accusations: "I found that [Paul] was accused concerning questions of their law, but was charged with nothing deserving death or imprisonment" (v. 29). The reader is even more convinced that God's plans for a Pauline mission in Rome will have found willing but unwitting collaborators in the various pagan officials of Roman Palestine.

23:31-35. Upon arrival in Caesarea (23:33) and reading of Lysias's *litterae dimissoriae* (v. 34*a*), Felix holds a preliminary hearing to clarify the issue of jurisdiction (v. 34*b*). Although he had the option of referring Paul back to Tarsus and to the regional legate, Felix chose not to for reasons that Luke does not specify. Witherington speculates that he kept Paul's case in Caesarea because of his relations with the Cilician-Syrian legate and to make traveling plans more convenient for the plaintiffs.[717]

Paul is kept under guard in Herod's *praetorium* (= "headquarters") during his trial. The *praetorium* was a multipurpose building, serving both as the official residence of the region and as a venue for the governor to render justice. Paul is still a Roman prisoner, unjustly disposed, but he is guarded by Rome in a safe and comfortable place.

717. Witherington, *The Acts of the Apostles,* 702.

REFLECTIONS

1. "Listen to the defense that I now make before you" (22:1 NRSV). The series of speeches Paul makes in this portion of Acts to defend himself against charges of criminal activity may well provide a pattern for the believer's apologia, even if in less stressful circumstances. The rhetorical function of each part of this first defense speech, its narrative setting, and the ethos it cultivates within Luke's narrative world envisage important features of an effective Christian apologetic. In general terms, the motive of Paul's apologia is to defend his mission and message as the will of God. While the subtext of his speech is therefore theological, its details are biographical. Paul offers his story as sufficient evidence that his mission and message are coordinate with God's redemptive purposes for repentant Israel according to the Scriptures. In this regard, his familial background (22:3-5), his personal experience (22:6-11), and the testimony of relevant others (pious Ananias) in support of his prophetic vocation (22:12-16) coupled with his own testimony (22:17-21) contend for Paul's understanding of his conversion to Jesus and his calling to the nations. Characteristic of all his speeches in Acts, Paul employs the cultural idiom of his audience when presenting his case. Thus, he defends his conversion and mission to a Jewish audience in their official language as a Jewish insider who adheres to the core symbols of Jewish faith. The language, form, and idiom of his apologia are adapted to changing audiences and settings, always to defend the terms of his mission.

If as Christian apologists we pattern our presentations after that of Paul, we will not be primarily interested in converting others: No appeal for repentance is given, no offer of salvation is made in the text. The purpose of a believer's apologia is to defend his or her own experience of God in the idiom of the audience as a particular expression of the manner and purpose of God's presence in the world. In this sense, the material of Christian apologetics does not consist mainly of various viable evidences (historical, archaeological, scientific, linguistic, biblical, cultural, and so on) marshaled to "prove" the truth claims of the gospel; it rather consists mainly of stories that tell of personal experiences of Christian conversions and vocation. The explicit intent of these spiritual biographies, especially in hostile settings, is not to convince and convert the rational non-believer to Jesus; rather, it is to explain clearly one's own faith in the idiom of non-believers—to give them good reason for the "hope that is in [us]" (1 Pet 3:15).

2. "Up to this point they listened to [Paul], but then they shouted, 'Away with such a fellow from the earth! For he should not be allowed to live!'" (22:22 NRSV). What is the reader of Acts to make of the passionate and violent responses within Israel to Paul's declaration that God's Messiah has called him to go to the unclean Gentiles (see 22:21)? Why do pious people conspire together to kill God's prophet? In part, the hostile response to Paul is due to the parochialism of his opponents, who define God's salvation in nationalistic terms. Had Paul claimed the Lord sent him with a word for Israel alone, his Jewish auditors may have continued to listen to him. Had he included the purification requirements of the Sadducees in his message of the resurrected Messiah, the Sanhedrin may have united behind him instead of dividing because of him. The danger of the gospel is that it makes particular and absolute claims about who God is, what God does, and to whom God belongs; and these claims sometimes challenge our current beliefs and traditional sensibilities. Paul's Jewish opponents disagree with his sense of vocation, as they also disagree with his interpretation of Scripture, because these are particular expressions of an absolute truth that imperil their own social requirements and religious beliefs. It is hard for any of us, no matter how spiritual-minded and earnest we are, to embrace a version of "the truth" that includes those we exclude and grants access to God's liberating grace via a different route than the one we have taken.

3. "When Paul noticed that some were Sadducees and others were Pharisees, he called out in the council, 'Brothers, I am a Pharisee, a son of Pharisees. I am on trial concerning the hope of the resurrection of the dead'" (23:6 NRSV). The reader of Luke's story of Paul's legal troubles cannot help but admire how clever Paul is. He is not only an effective orator but he also manages and manipulates the legal proceedings to his advantage. He inserts new information about himself at opportune moments, as he did when allowing that he is a Roman citizen at the very moment when Lysias is about to torture him (see 22:25). When standing before the Sanhedrin, he again rescues himself from a difficult situation by craftily turning his interrogation into a shouting match between the council's competing political parties. In manipulating the legal proceedings to his benefit by persuasive rhetoric and crowd control, Paul exemplifies what Jesus admonished all his disciples to be in the midst of wolves: "Be wise as serpents and innocent as doves" (Matt 10:16 NRSV).

ACTS 24:1-27, PAUL'S ROMAN TRIAL IN CAESAREA

COMMENTARY

The second phase of the legal proceedings against Paul takes place before the Roman Procurator Felix in Caesarea, the provincial capital of Roman Palestine. Moreover, for the only time in Acts Paul is actually prosecuted. Both prosecutorial and defense speeches, and the legal protocol that organizes the plotline of this passage, follow standard Roman judicial procedures and the rhetorical conventions of professional orators (= lawyers).[718] Accordingly, the prosecution schedules its trial against the accused (24:1; see 23:35); the prosecuting attorney (Tertullus) presents the charges (24:2-8); the defendant (Paul) then responds (24:10-21); after that the case is remanded to the judge, who either renders a verdict or postpones it indefinitely (24:22-27). The result of this carefully crafted scene is a more precise understanding of the "legal" issues that separate Paul and the Way from official Judaism.

Tertullus accuses Paul of four illegalities: He is a pest, an agitator, the ringleader of a Jewish "sect," and one who tried to defile the Temple. What is lacking in these allegations is any clear mention of Paul's mission to the Gentiles, and for obvious reasons: Paul's agitation "among all Jews throughout the world" is theological, and this present conflict is Jewish and religious and not Roman and political. Thus, at the heart of Paul's rebuttal of the charges (24:11-13) and counter accusation (24:18b-21) is his "confession" of the Way's continuity with Jewish belief (24:14-15) and behavior (24:16-18a).

The reader of Acts has heard all of this before in different words and settings. If any doubt lingers in the reader's mind concerning the spiritual authority of Paul and his lasting importance for the whole church, it should end with his apologia before Felix. He is no criminal, no maverick, no madman, no seller of snake oil, no intellectual lightweight or religious mediocrity; the Paul of Acts is a prophet of God whose personal intentions are above reproach, whose confession of faith is thoroughly orthodox, whose religious and social practices are blameless, and whose proclamation is rightly concentrated on Israel's hope in the resurrection of the dead. These are the very prejudgments of Paul that interpreters of the Pauline letters brings with them as they glean meaning from them for the church.

24:1-2a. The constituency of the Jewish delegation that arrives from Jerusalem to prosecute official Judaism's case against Paul is important to determine in advance of the trial. Acts includes only "the high priest Ananias . . . with some elders" along with the "attorney" (ῥήτωρ *rhētōr*) Tertullus who may not even be Jewish.[719] Given the council's evident division along party lines on the question of Paul's purity (see 23:9) and the implied purpose of Ananias's appearance in Caesarea to broker his influence, it seems plausible that the elders he brought with him were Sadducees. The Pharisaic cast of Paul's "confession" (24:14-18a) and his concluding assertion (24:21), even though expressed as quintessentially Jewish, contains an implicit polemical edge. Moreover, the Jerusalem delegation includes no Jew from the diaspora who may have been able to rebut Paul's statement that "some Jews from Asia" had falsely accused him (24:19). The impression made on the reader is that this legal team came to Caesarea without a carefully crafted brief, having only "five days" to prepare for trial against the more clever and innocent Paul.

24:2b-4. Tertullus's opening remarks (the exordium) conform to the rhetorical conventions of a legal argument in the ancient world. On the face of it, his shameless use of flattery intends to establish good rapport with Felix so that he will be more favorably disposed to his case against Paul. More important, however, Tertullus's description of Felix's contribution to Jewish well-being is carefully contrived to relate directly to his allegations against Paul. That is, he wishes to convey the sentiment, however true,[720] that Felix is able to render an appropriate verdict in this case as aptly demonstrated by his administrative talent and personal "foresight" (πρόνοια *pronoia*)— a virtue that denotes one's "innate benevolence" toward citizens.[721] These virtues of peacemaking and providence make him keenly alert to the problems "all the Jews" have with Paul. For example, the statement

---

718. For an analysis of these forensic speeches in their ancient setting, see B. Winter, "Official Proceedings and Forensic Speeches in Acts 24–26," in Winter and Clarke, *The Book of Acts in Its First Century Setting*, 1:305-36, who observes that Luke's narrative "is a cameo of some of the complexities of criminal litigation in the first century" (335).

719. The argument that Tertullus is Jewish rests on his use of first person when listing Judaism's charges against Paul (see 24:5-6). But this may reflect only the attorney's professional obligation to identify with his clients. On the other hand, his impersonal reference to "all the Jews" might indicate that he is a Gentile, and his apparent distinction from "the Jews who joined in the charge" (24:9) might as well. The name "Tertullus" is not Jewish, and his training as a professional orator and knowledge of Roman law would necessarily have been secular.

720. Luke would have known the historian's negative verdict that Felix was a poor governor, and his use of *captatio benevolentiae*, using compliments for rhetorical effect, is ironic then of *God's* providence. The NRSV shifts "most excellent Felix" from v. 3 to the beginning of the speech in v. 2 ("Your Excellency").

721. Winter, "Official Proceedings and Forensic Speeches in Acts 24–26," 316.

that "because of [Felix] we have long enjoyed peace" (v. 2) implies that he will consider viable the charge that Paul is a pest and agitator who disturbs the public order. It is for this reason that Tertullus can claim that his Sadducean clients "welcome this [case/judge] in every way and everywhere with utmost gratitude" (v. 3)—as well they might, given their political alliance with Roman authority in Palestine.

Since brevity is a rhetorical virtue, Tertullus wants "to detain [Felix] no further" and promises to proceed with "brief" remarks. His request that Felix listen with "customary graciousness" conveys the desire for a fair and reasoned hearing of legal matters, perhaps even to render his case with a "non-legalist interpretation."[722] This appeal may well indicate in advance that Tertullus is clever enough to realize that the case against Paul is sparse.

24:5-8. The four accusations Tertullus levels against Paul iterate the allegations of the "Jews from Asia" (see 21:28). The most important of these in this Roman setting is that of sedition: Paul is "an agitator [κινοῦντα στάσεις *kinounta staseis*; lit., "stirring up discord"] among all the Jews [πᾶσιν τοῖς Ἰουδαιοῖς *pasin tois Ioudaiois*] throughout the world [κατὰ τὴν οἰκουμένην *kata tēn oikoumenēn*]"[723] (v. 5; see also 17:6-7;18:12). This phrase echoes the Jewish church's charge that Paul is teaching "all the Jews living among the Gentiles to forsake Moses" (see 21:21). From this intratext the reader more precisely understands the Jewish concern with Paul and the controversy his mission provokes: Paul's mission and message threaten to contaminate the identity of Israel as God's people in the world. One may think as well that when Tertullus speaks of "all the Jews throughout the world" he includes both repentant and unrepentant Jews in Israel's common concern with the effect of Paul's mission "among Jews."

This "was the right charge to bring against an opponent in criminal proceedings."[724] Paul

is portrayed as a subversive who threatens the Pax Romana. The failure to bring Paul's opponents from diaspora Judaism in support of this critical charge must be considered a serious weakness in the prosecution's case, as Paul himself implies (see 24:19). It should be said, however, that the prosecutor's intent is only to interest Felix in the case so that he will seek out appropriate witnesses to interrogate in arriving at a fair verdict.

From the narrator's perspective the third charge, that Paul is "ringleader of the sect of the Nazarenes,"[725] is weighty for a different reason. The meaning of "sect" (αἵρεσις *hairesis*) is intentionally vague since Tertullus employs it here in a pejorative sense as an element of Paul's rabble-rousing, but Luke uses this same term earlier in Acts for the Sadducean (see 5:17) and Pharisaic (see 15:5) "parties." In this more positive sense, *hairesis* denotes a particular interpretive tradition within a wider, more inclusive religious order or philosophical school. This meaning is implied in Paul's retort to the charge when he defends "the Way" (= "sect of the Nazarenes") as a messianic movement *within* Judaism, similar to the Pharisaic and Sadducean parties, and not outside its theological, moral, or traditional boundaries (see 24:14-18).

From the perspective of the Sadducean delegation from Jerusalem, the final accusation is most condemning of Paul's spiritual authority: "He even tried to profane [βεβηλόω *bebēloō*] the temple, and so we seized him" (v. 6). The reader knows how flawed this charge is, and given its tepid expression when compared with its more forceful sounding during the Jerusalem riots (see 21:28) Tertullus would seem to agree: There is simply no evidence that would convict Paul of this sacrilege; in fact, Paul will later claim that his religious practices in the Temple purified him (see v. 18)! The relationship between this Pharisaic prophet-like-Jesus and the Temple, considered realistically, is ambivalent at best: Is he so different from Stephen in his desire to shift the epicenter of Israel's symbolic universe from the Temple to the risen Messiah? But the issue is a legal one and,

---

722. Barrett, *A Critical and Exegetical Commentary on the Acts of the Apostles*, 2:1096.

723. Johnson, *The Acts of the Apostles*, 411, translates *oikoumenē* as "empire." Barrett, *A Critical and Exegetical Commentary on the Acts of the Apostles*, 2:1097, adds that the intent of the charge is to extend Jerusalem's grievance against Paul to be found in every part of the empire where there exists a Jewish community.

724. Winter, "Official Proceedings and Forensic Speeches in Acts 24–26," 320.

725. The term "sect of the Nazarenes" derives from "Jesus from Nazareth" (see 2:22; 6:14; 22:8); however, it resonates in biting irony with its Hebrew root נזר (*nzr*, "to dedicate" or "to consecrate") to recall that it is Paul who performs the law of the Nazirites (see 21:26). See Barrett, *A Critical and Exegetical Commentary on the Acts of the Apostles*, 2:1098.

based on the evidence the narrative supplies, Paul is innocent of this charge. In fact, the second half of Tertullus's accusation that the Jews "seized him" is a falsehood. The word κρατέω (*krateō*), weakly translated "seize," is a legal term for "arrest." Yet the reader knows that Paul's was no legal seizure by the temple police or Roman soldiers but an illegal beating by a mob.[726]

The peroratio, which calls on Felix to interrogate Paul "concerning everything of which we accuse him" (v. 8), concludes the prosecution's case. It is revealing that Felix refuses to question Paul at this juncture of the trial, as was customary during this species of legal procedure, and chooses to examine Paul in private and outside the bounds of the trial (= Roman law).

24:9. "The Jews" who "joined [συνεπιτίθημι *synepitithēmi*] the charge" represent those who support the charges Tertullus has articulated, including the high priest and his Sadducean entourage. Their support of Tertullus against Paul is expected: He is a Pharisee who asserts, "it is about the resurrection of the dead that I am on trial" (v. 21). The military term *synepitithēmi* denotes a unified and strategic attack against an enemy. Paul is public enemy number one of priestly Israel.

24:10. Luke's précis of Paul's apologia conforms to the rhetorical conventions of the ancient world, even though his exordium is more restrained than that of Tertullus. He, too, expresses a rhetor's confidence in Felix's expertise to judge the affairs of "this [Jewish] nation." In particular, Acts confirms that Felix is able to negotiate between the theological claims of Paul's messianic "Way" and Tertullus's official Judaism to render a fair verdict in this case (see vv. 22-23), perhaps because his wife, Drusilla, possesses a keen understanding of Israel's religious culture (see v. 24).

24:11-13. The main body of Paul's speech consists of three proofs of his innocence in response to the four charges made by Tertullus. The first accusation is that Paul "is a pestilent fellow," guilty of sedition (see v. 5). But the Paul of Acts comes to the holy city "to worship in Jerusalem"; he is a pilgrim who intends to celebrate Pentecost

with other pious Jews (see 20:16). Moreover, examination of the public record, including his notice to the temple priests that he had completed the Nazaritic vows (see 21:26), would show that he could have been in Jerusalem for no more than twelve days—hardly sufficient time to organize a rebellion against Judaism![727]

Paul rebuts Tertullus's claim that he is a "pest" by countering that "they cannot prove [παρίστημι *paristēmi*]" that he disputed with or stirred up anyone in the Temple, synagogues, or city. The legal term *paristēmi* suggests that without sufficient evidence Paul's accusers have no basis for their charge of sedition that Felix could then assess. What the prosecution itself has asked the judge to do (v. 8) is impossible.

24:14-16. Paul's second proof responds to the accusation that he is the ringleader of a religious sect. Rather than protest the charge, he cleverly "admits" (ὁμολογέω *homologeō*) his association with the "sect [party] of the Nazarenes" (v. 5). Johnson calls Paul's legal maneuver a "breathtaking turn" when after a series of denials he makes a public confession of his allegiance to the beliefs and practices of this sect.[728] While the legal term *homologeō* denotes admission of guilt, Paul's use of it connotes a confession of faith: Paul confesses that he worships "the God of our ancestors" (v. 14*a*; see also 22:3). The clause is placed in an emphatic position in this text and underscores Paul's complete loyalty to the God of the OT. He has invented no new God (= God of Israel; cf. 17:23-31); rather, he participates in a new "Way," or path, that gains access to God's saving mercies through God's risen Messiah (see 24:21).

Paul's worship of Israel's ancestral God is proved by his belief in "everything laid down according to the law or written in the prophets"—Israel's Scriptures (v. 14*b*; cf. Luke 24:44-45). Moreover, his traditional (= Pharisaic) faith is demonstrated by his theology of hope: "There will be a resurrection of both the righteous and the unrighteous" (v. 15; see also 3:20-21; 23:6; cf. Dan 12:1-3; Rev 20:11-15). His assertion that his Sadducean opponents confess belief in "this same hope" when they do not (see 23:7-8) must

---

726. Some MSS insert vv. 6*b*-8*a* here, as noted by the NRSV and the NIV.

727. See Haenchen, *The Acts of the Apostles*, 652.
728. Johnson, *The Acts of the Apostles*, 412.

be understood as an element of Paul's rhetoric that plays off the ambiguity of the word "sect" (*hairesis*), which is much like our contemporary use of "cult" and can mean either religious heresy or party. The Way is not a Jewish "sect" in the sense of an alleged heresy because it shares common ground with the faith traditions of its opponents; it must be another religious "party" within Judaism.

The move from "confession of faith" to refutation of the claim that he profaned the Temple (see v. 6) is an easy one: Paul pledges, "I strive [ἀσκέω *askeō*] to have a clear [ἀπρόσκοπος *aproskopos*] conscience toward God and all people" (v. 16, author's trans.). The athletic term *askeō* is used of rigorous training in preparation for a contest and is widely used for academic or moral training, as here: Paul's disciplined devotion to Israel's God and to those religious practices or disciplines—such as temple purity—that cultivate a close relationship with God. More directly, the aim of his religious discipline is a morality that is "clear," which translates *aproskopos*, a term connoting a healthy or stable conscience (for "conscience," see 23:1). Tertullus's accusation goes to Paul's *intent* to "profane" the Temple (see v. 6); however, a person with Paul's internal spiritual goods could never intentionally subvert a religious practice (temple purity) that aims at a closer relationship with Israel's God.

24:17-20. The third proof frames the other two by explaining more deliberately Paul's commendable reasons for coming to Jerusalem—reasons that Rome would have endorsed and even encouraged. He does not indicate what calendar he is using in commenting that it has been "several years" since last visiting Jerusalem (cf. 18:22). I take it that he means many years have passed since he last made the trip as a Jewish pilgrim "to bring alms to my nation and to offer sacrifices" (v. 17). In doing so, Paul was *inside* the Temple, completing "the rite of purification" (see 21:26) and thereby could not have created a public disturbance (v. 18). The reader knows from Luke's account of this rite that Paul would have logged his time in the Temple and Felix would have had access to this official record for confirmation of his claims.

Paul's parenthetical note that his original accusers (see 21:27-28) are unavailable for

Felix's interrogation is a strategic maneuver of legal defense. Sherwin-White points out that Paul's comment is in reality a "sound technical objection" since "Roman law was very strong against accusers who abandoned their charges."[729] Therefore, while Paul's larger point is that he was "inside the temple" for legitimate reasons, his proof is made even more substantive by noting the absence of those who had initially brought the charge and incited the riot that triggered Paul's legal problems.

In his final proof, the Paul of Acts makes his most important although indirect claim of innocence: He is without "crime" (ἀδίκημα *adikēma*, v. 20). As a legal term, *adikēma* underwrites his claim of innocence (see 18:14); however, it carries the connotation of religious purity as well. That is, Paul has done nothing that would have rendered him religiously impure. The entire Jerusalem ordeal has been a spiritual test of Paul's own purity in belief and practice and, indeed, of the purity of the messianic movement he represents. He has ably proved the purity of both.

24:21. The speech's peroratio, or conclusion, skillfully draws attention to the *theological* subtext of Tertullus's political charges. Paul's apologia rests on the validity of a theological claim that is distinctively Jewish in cast (so v. 15)—namely, "the resurrection of the dead" (see 23:6). The reader may well gloss Paul's closing statement by his comments to the Corinthians that "if Christ has not been raised, then our preaching is in vain and your faith is in vain" (1 Cor 15:14). His mission and message, and the controversies that swirl around each, are reduced to this single claim, which if not true render every accusation and legal consideration moot.

24:22-23. The reader should assume that the narrator's explanatory comment that "Felix was rather well informed about the Way" (v. 22) implies the official's essential agreement with Paul's definition of the church's beliefs and practices (see vv. 14-16) and that it must be considered a religious "party" within normative Judaism rather than a renegade movement on its margins. The historical referent to which Luke's comment points the reader is not so much that

729. A. N. Sherwin-White, *Roman Society and Roman Law in the New Testament* (Oxford: Clarendon, 1963) 52.

Felix possesses an accurate understanding of Christianity. Rather, Paul assumes his competence in his captatio, opening compliments (see v. 10)—married as he was to a Jewess (see v. 24)—and therefore will his ability to recognize the orthodoxy of Paul's confession of faith. A postponement is called for, which indicates that Felix does not intend to keep his promise to "decide the case" when the accusers arrived.

24:24-26. When Paul's powerful defense apparently prompted a brief postponement of the trial, the reader is left with hope that Felix's verdict will be favorable. The real reason and extended duration of the postponement reflects Luke's ambivalence toward pagan Rome's participation in God's plans for the church's (= Paul's) mission in the world. Although there is reason to think Felix is interested in what Paul "teaches concerning faith in Christ Jesus" (v. 24), "at the same time he hoped that money would be given him by Paul" (v. 26).

Luke's repeated references to time—here to "some days later"—creates the impression that a familiar legal protocol is followed in adjudicating Paul's case. Felix's continuing interrogation of Paul was now off-the-record and in the company of "his wife Drusilla, who was Jewish." She is the youngest daughter of Herod Agrippa I (see 12:1-4, 19-23) and sister of King Agrippa II (see 25:13). While her devotion to Jewish faith is unknown, Luke's reference that she is Jewish explains why she is interested in hearing Paul's "Jewish" gospel. The reader is reminded of the Jewish shape of Paul's "confession of faith" (see vv. 14-16); this is confirmed again by Drusilla's presence at this informal hearing—it is not a legal hearing but a hearing of the gospel.

The subject matter of Paul's message concerning "faith in Christ Jesus" is "righteousness [δικαιοσύνη *dikaiosynē*],[730] self-control [ἐγκράτεια *enkrateia*] and the judgment [κρίμα *krima*] to come" (v. 25). In context these topics are not Paul's lectures on a virtuous Roman administration of the sort Seneca might give Felix; rather, these are the catchwords of the Pauline gospel, glossed by his NT letters, and they expand his earlier confession of faith in Israel's ancestral God.[731] In this regard, the sequence of terms is important to consider and reflects the deep logic of his gospel. The revelation of God's "rightwising" grace (*dikaiosynē*) inaugurates a new era in salvation's history that promises forgiveness and eternal life to those who have faith in Christ Jesus (cf. Rom 3:21-26; 9:30; 10:13; Gal 3:21-22; Phil 3:8-11; Titus 3:4-7). The term translated "self-control" (*enkrateia*), otherwise known as a moral virtue, is cataloged among the Spirit's "fruit" (cf. Gal 5:23) and is a public hallmark of saving trust in God's grace. While God's future *krima* is mentioned only here in Acts, it is an important theme of Romans where the fairness of God's endtime verdict is emphasized (Rom 2:1-11; 5:16; 11:33; 13:11-14).

The interpreter should resist speculating that the source of Felix's frightened dismissal of Paul is Felix's guilty conscience (for one reason or another), pricked by Paul's teachings concerning God's coming judgment. More likely the source of his guilt is his greed. The capacity of persons to respond to God is measured by their proper use of money. Felix kept Paul in custody in the hope that "money would be given him by Paul" (v. 26). While "becoming frightened" (ἔμφοβος *emphobos*) may well indicate that Felix is alert to the hard truth about God (see 10:4; 22:9; cf. Luke 24:5, 37), his greed envisages the character of someone unable to respond to God's word in faith.

Felix's interrogation of Paul continues for two years not in search of salvation but as an illegal means of acquiring money.[732]

Here again the narrative portrays Paul as a person of financial means. Earlier James asked Paul to cover the costs of expensive sacrifices offered by four brothers (21:24); Lysias's reaction to Paul's biographical sketch suggests that his Cilician and Roman citizenships envisage personal or familial wealth (21:39; 22:27-28); and Paul's testimony to his traditional piety, which required him to

---

730. The NIV's translation of *dikaiosynē* as "righteousness," which is a catchword of Jewish theology denoting God's covenant renewing ("rightwising") action (cf. Rom 3:21-26; 9:30 10:13), is preferred to the NRSV's "justice," a catchword of Hellenistic moral philosophy denoting human fairness.

731. Commentators have interpreted this Pauline (= Lukan) triad in a variety of ways. Representative are (1) Haenchen, *The Acts of the Apostles*, 660-61, who takes the three as the "central themes in the post-apostolic preaching." (2) Johnson, *The Acts of the Apostles*, 419, who understands the triad as "a sort of ethical translation of 'messianic faith' for Gentile ears." And (3) Witherington, *The Acts of the Apostles*, 715, who takes the terms as a rebuke of Felix's sexual lust for Drusilla, a beautiful woman by all accounts, which resulted in her divorce of Azizus.

732. Accepting money from prisoners in exchange for their freedom was illegal under Roman law. See Haenchen, *The Acts of the Apostles*, 661.

bring alms to Jerusalem as part of his pilgrimage, implies that he had money to devote to Israel's coffers (24:17). This unfolding portrait of Paul's ample funds is not an allusion to his Gentile collection but to personal resources that he willingly shares with others as the mark of his spiritual authority within the church (see 4:32-35).

24:27. Felix's role in Acts ends in ignominy. Luke's take on him is similar to that of secular historians: Felix was a malcontent, better known for greed than for competent leadership. This text reflects another feature of Roman law, which placed a two-year term limit on the detention of a Roman citizen without an official verdict being rendered.[733] Paul should have been released; however, Felix left him in prison, "since he wanted to grant the Jews a favor." What this "favor" is, Luke does not say.[734] The presumption of

this passage, made clear by the next phase of Paul's trials, is that Felix turned his case over to his successor, Porcius Festus, as a delaying tactic, perhaps to give "the Jews" (see 24:1) more time to build a more persuasive case against Paul. Their time to do so will soon run out.

Little is known of Festus because his term of office was short. Josephus characterizes him as a competent leader who worked hard to reestablish good relations with the Jews and bring a lasting peace to the region. Festus's early death prevented him from realizing his ambitious dreams.[735] His role in God's purposes for Paul are more important, for he is the procurator who hears the prophet's appeal to Caesar (see 25:6-12) and, in agreement with Herod Agrippa II, takes responsibility for delivering Paul to the city of his destiny (see 26:30-32).

733. Fitzmyer, *The Acts of the Apostles*, 740.

734. Johnson, *The Acts of the Apostles*, 419, notes that Josephus reports a delegation of Jewish leaders from Palestine traveled to Rome to present the Emperor with various "injustices to the Jews" for which Felix is

responsible. Felix is in trouble with Rome and this "favor" may be his futile attempt to win some points with his Jewish opposition so that Rome would go easier with him. See Josephus *Antiquities of the Jews* 20.182.

735. See. J. B. Green, "Festus, Porcius," *ABD* 2:794-95.

REFLECTIONS

"Felix left Paul in prison" (24:27 NRSV). The tragic subtext of Acts is how frequently people make decisions against God out of greater concern for their financial situation, political status, or some other momentary accommodation. Felix is a case in point. He sat under Paul's instruction "concerning faith in Christ Jesus" (24:24 NRSV). Paul is literally his captive audience as they discuss the ultimate issues of human existence—"righteousness, self-control, and the judgment to come" (24:25). Even though Paul's message alarms him and he realizes the charges against Paul are false, Felix postpones the "not guilty" verdict to retain custody of Paul in order to extort money from his Jewish enemies. It is his greed and not his ignorance that keeps Felix from the faith.

ACTS 25:1-12, PAUL APPEALS TO CAESAR

COMMENTARY

Nero's appointment of Porcius Festus around 60 CE as procurator of Judea signals an important shift in the politics of the region. Festus is a cunning man, full of energy, whose administration is characterized by fairness toward the Jews, especially when compared

to his greedy predecessor. Unfortunately, there is not a corresponding change for the good among Jerusalem's priestly elite. Two years later, the elites of official Israel continue to plot an assassination attempt against Paul, now with Festus as their intended dupe (25:1-5; see also 23:12-22). This persistence in conspiracy implies the ongoing importance of the imprisoned Paul to regional politics. The reader of Acts is right to wonder why. On the one hand, Paul is granted freedom to receive visitors in Caesarea (see 24:23), implying that he continues to be involved in the business of the Way through the mediation of close colleagues (e.g., Timothy, Silas). On the other hand, Paul's continuing influence in Palestine may well imply that he does in fact have the support of the Jerusalem church. Contemporary Acts criticism has interpreted Luke's silence on the role of the Judean or Caesarean churches as a lack of support. However, the intense concern of the religious establishment in Jerusalem regarding Paul's influence in Palestine during his two years of enforced exile, to the extent that these pious men would use subterfuge to murder him (25:2-3), can be explained only if the Jerusalem church continued to champion his mission.

No doubt Festus has heard from Felix of the failed conspiracy against Paul and knows something of the Jewish case against him as well. He is, therefore, duly cautious in his responses and actions in dealing with the Jewish leadership team in Jerusalem. After all, his prisoner is a Roman citizen in good standing, which he has also no doubt learned from Felix (see 25:12), and the legal case against him failed to convince his predecessor of Paul's guilt. Even so, Festus listens to the ad hoc case against Paul and to his rebuttal (25:6-8) before tendering Paul the choice, "Do you wish to go up to Jerusalem and be tried there before me on these charges?" (25:9).

Although biblical narrative is wont to provide the reader with information concerning the inner motivations of its characters, we simply do not know what "favor" Festus thought he was granting "the Jews" by asking Paul such a question. He is a clever politician and he makes a strategic decision as a new ruler over an intractable region. Perhaps he believes that Paul would not leave Jerusalem alive. But the reader is also unclear as to why Paul chose this particular moment to make his appeal to the Roman Caesar. Is he afraid for his personal safety in Palestine, and thus this is his ticket out to the safety of Rome (doubtful)? Or is he prompted by his sense of judicial propriety that the allegation

of sedition against Rome should be evaluated by the emperor (perhaps)? Or is he motivated by his faithfulness to his prophetic vocation to "bear witness also in Rome" (23:11). Probably the latter. Luke does not tell his readers the reason for Paul's appeal and is concerned only to narrate the result: "I am appealing to the emperor's tribunal" (25:10); "To the emperor you will go" (25:12). In any case, the interpreter is simply mistaken if concluding that this legal maneuver backfired in light of Agrippa's concluding verdict (see 26:32): Paul's decision triggers a series of events that results in his mission to Rome according to God's plan, and in some significant sense it is therefore essential to the plotline of Acts.[736]

25:1-3. Festus hits the ground running: "Three days" after arriving in the provincial capital, he departs on an official visit of Jerusalem, his region's other principal city, where he meets with "the high priests and the leaders of the Jews" (v. 2). The promptness of his visitation may well be an indicator of the political urgency of Paul's case. Felix had left Palestine an unstable province and a breeding ground for terrorist activity. No doubt Paul is portrayed by his Jewish opponents in inflammatory terms, since they think his mission to the nations threatens to corrode Israel's theological beliefs and social practices (see 21:21, 28; 22:21-23; 24:5-6).

The change of designation from religious "elders" (πρεσβύτεροι *presbyteroi*; see 24:1) to political "leaders" (πρῶτοι *prōtoi*) connotes a wider spectrum of leadership and may indicate a broader, better-organized attack against Paul. Festus meets with the economic, political, religious elites to deal with the "Paul problem." The positive implication is that his message is pervasive and touches every institution of Jewish life. The plural "high priests" here is unusual but probably reflects the continuing role that retired high priests play in the city's religious and political culture.[737]

---

736. Commentators continue to draw parallels between the Lukan stories of Paul and Jesus, and in this case their Roman trials (cf. Luke 23). See, e.g., Barrett, *A Critical and Exegetical Commentary on the Acts of the Apostles*, 2:1122. While the same narrator is responsible for both narratives and some linguistic parallelism is sure to exist for this reason, what is clearly important to him is that neither Jesus nor Paul is guilty of the crimes alleged and that Rome does not release either prophet.

737. According to Josephus *Antiquities of the Jews* 20.179 the high priest during Festus's short regime was Ishmael ben Phiabi. Even the contentious and unpopular former high priest Ananias (see Acts 23:2) remains influential, primarily because of his landholdings and family wealth.

Luke states the business of their private meeting sharply: They "gave Festus a report against [ἐμφάνιζω κατά *emphanizō kata*]" Paul. The repetition of *emphanizō kata*, which was also used in 24:1, indicates the resumption of the Jewish case against Paul. The impression is that the change of procurators in Caesarea prompts a renewed effort to destroy Paul and the influence of his message about the risen Jesus. With this motive in mind, they "appealed to him and requested . . . a favor": Transfer Paul to Jerusalem for a new trial (v. 3). This is the second of three times that Paul's Jewish opponents request a favor of a Roman ruler (see v. 9; see also 24:27). Such Lukan triads frame important elements in the plotline of his narrative. Since the "favor" requested is to place Paul in harm's way, this motif intends to depict his Jewish opposition in bad light and draw attention to their immoral behavior, provoked by the sharp theological differences they have with Paul. The ambush they plan is similar to the one earlier proposed by the forty hasidim (would-be Jewish assassins; see 23:12-15), except that Paul now would be traveling from Caesarea to Jerusalem.

25:4-5. Festus is not, however, a witting participant in the plot to ambush and kill Paul. Initially, he insists on his prerogatives as Roman procurator. The provincial seat of his administrative and judicial power is Caesarea, not Jerusalem; therefore, "come with me and press charges against the man there" (v. 5). If Festus has an inkling of the murderous motive behind the Jewish leaders' request, he has no intention of being their dupe. In a compromise, however, he does tacitly agree to reopen Paul's case, to see if "there is anything wrong [ἄτοπος *atopos*; lit., "out of place"] about the man."

25:6-8. And so it is in Caesarea, upon his βῆμα (*bēma*, "seat"),[738] with the leaders of the anti-Paul movement surrounding him, that Festus orders Paul to be brought for interrogation (v. 6). The narrator leaves the reader of Acts to fill in the details of this hearing, including the "many serious charges" against Paul (v. 7; see also 21:21, 28; 24:5-6) and the details of Paul's *apologia* (v. 8; see also 23:6;

24:10-21). The final element of Luke's summary of Paul's defense is new and interesting, however: "I have in no way committed an offense . . . against the emperor" (v. 8). The effect of Luke's shaping of Paul's response is twofold. Clearly it prepares the reader for the climax of the story; namely, Paul's appeal to Caesar, thereby erasing his case from Festus's docket and rendering this venue irrelevant. Yet it also seems true from the previous trial before Felix—as well as from Paul's various court hearings during his mission in the diaspora (see 16:21; 17:7)—that Paul is well aware from personal experience that the most serious charge against him is that of sedition. It is left to Paul, then, to clarify the prosecution's case against him!

25:9. A further compromise is now proposed by Festus. In immediate context, the requested favor of a change of venue is no mere legal maneuver. While it is certainly true that a Jerusalem trial, preferably conducted by the Sanhedrin, would be the most favorable legal option for Paul's opponents, their main intent is murder and not a change of court venue or trial judge. The Jews would be more than happy to accept Festus as judge, which he evidently requires ("be tried before me"), as long as the case is transferred to Jerusalem. Their plan is for Paul to miss his court appearance there, no matter who is presiding (see v. 3)!

Haenchen assails the historical reliability of Luke's account, which he finds "incomprehensible." In his mind, a verdict would have probably been rendered immediately following Paul's defense speech.[739] But Roloff is surely right to question Festus's integrity when asking Paul to decide between Jerusalem and Caesarea; he understands the implications for himself and for Paul very well, and chooses to ignore them for reasons of political expedience.[740] Festus's duplicity is characteristic of his role in Acts; as representative of Rome, he contributes to the overall negative portrait of Rome's relationship to Paul and his mission. While Roman law safeguards Paul to Rome under the constant threat of unrepentant Jews, and so is an unwitting collaborator with God in achieving God's purpose for Paul, Roman leaders are presented as untrustworthy and self-interested.

---

738. The *bēma* is variously translated and understood by commentators. It refers to a portable rostrum or raised platform placed so that the judge can sit over the crowd to render a verdict in dramatic fashion. See Josephus *The Jewish War* 2:172; see also Acts 18:12.

739. Haenchen, *The Acts of the Apostles*, 669.
740. Roloff, *Die Apostelgeschichte*, 343.

25:10-12. For this reason, Paul's response to Festus's question must be considered a sharp rebuke in character with his prophetic vocation: "This is where I should be tried . . . as you very well know" (v. 10). His charge against Festus, rooted in moral ground, is made more convincing by Paul's willingness to pay the death penalty if his crimes justify it under Roman law; his own sense of fairness commands the very same of Festus. Both translations of Paul's last statement before making his appeal—"no one can turn me over to them" (NRSV) and "no one has the right to hand me over to them" (NIV)—miss the important wordplay between the Jewish request of Festus for a "favor" (v. 3, χάρις *charis*) and Paul's challenge to him that he cannot "turn/hand over" (χαρίζομαι *charizomai*) an innocent man to his enemies. Luke shapes Paul's retort to echo the triad of requested "favors" (vv. 3, 9; see also 24:7) in order to condemn Festus's political expedience: The prophet-like-Jesus does not play Rome's games!

The most crucial right of Paul's Roman citizenship allows him to demand a fair trial before Caesar.[741] More critically, Paul

recognizes that the most important legal challenge to his innocence is that of sedition against the empire and that the emperor is the appropriate judge in this case (see above). He also must realize after two years of imprisonment that he is the ball in an ongoing game of "political football" played out between the Roman procurator and the leaders of his Jewish opposition. Paul's sharp retort to Festus's lame question would seem to indicate that he does not trust Festus to call the end to this game. It is, perhaps, a frustrated citizen, then, who concludes, contrary to the procurator's suggestion to change the trial site, "I appeal to the emperor" (v. 11). The legal wrangling stops here; Paul will soon be on his way to Rome according to divine purpose (see 23:11).

The unnamed Caesar to whom Paul appeals is probably Nero (54–68 CE). Festus would have known, informally from Felix and officially from the records kept of previous interrogations and defense speeches, that Paul is a solid citizen. Although Luke mentions no sigh of relief, Festus must have felt the burden of a "no-win" situation lifted from his administration. For this reason, his conference with his advisors must have been relatively brief, perhaps only to precisely formulate his response: "You have appealed to the emperor; to the emperor you will go" (25:12).

---

741. Cf. Sherwin-White, *Roman Society and Roman Law in the New Testament*, 144-47. See also J. Lentz, *Luke's Portrait of Paul*, SNTSMS 77 (Cambridge: Cambridge University Press, 1993) 139-70, who argues that the appeal to Caesar serves Luke's rhetorical interests in characterizing Paul's high social class and civic reputation, and as such the growing status of Christianity within Luke's Roman world. Paul's appeal to Nero raises many questions. See also Fitzmyer, *The Acts of the Apostles*, 746, for a summary and working bibliography.

REFLECTIONS

"This is where I should be tried" (25:10 NRSV). The narrative climax of Paul's trials is his direct appeal to the Caesar for justice (25:11). Yet, this exercise of Roman citizenship seems a strange action for this bold prophet-like-Jesus to take. On the one hand, the interpreter is tempted to argue that Paul's appeal is a prudent act: a change of venue (Rome) and magistrate (emperor), which is Paul's civil right to demand, will allow him to overcome Festus's moral failure. Upon closer reflection, however, the interpreter realizes that Paul's initiative is prompted by his awareness that the Lord plans for him to go to Rome (see 23:11). Thus his assertion that he "should" be tried in Rome is a theological claim and not a legal maneuver: Rome is the city of Paul's destiny because it is in the script of God's plan of salvation.

The precise relationship between the provident concerns of a sovereign God and the careful and clever choices that central characters like Paul make is not always clear in Acts. What does seem clear, however, is that the collaboration between the two—a faithful God and God's faithful servants—is a necessary feature of God's intention to fulfill the biblical promises of salvation. Thus Paul's appeal triggers a chain of events both political (so Acts 26) and natural (so Acts 27) that takes him into Rome, where once again he personifies God's faithfulness to Israel in securing the salvation of the nations to the end of the earth (see 28:23-28, 30-31). Our story becomes like Paul's when our personal decisions are weighted with divine importance—when the actions we choose to take or the words we decide to speak allow us to participate effectively in accomplishing God's plans.

ACTS 25:13-27, INTERLUDE: FESTUS TWICE REVIEWS PAUL'S CASE

COMMENTARY

The narrator has created a confidential conversation between the Roman procurator Festus and the Palestinian ruler King Agrippa and his sister Queen Bernice[742] (25:13-22), to which he adds the *précis* of a public speech (25:23-27), in order to summarize the Roman proceedings against Paul. Agrippa and Bernice, along with their sister Drusilla (see 24:24), are members of the same notorious Herodian family whose reign during the days of Jesus (cf. Matt 2; Mark 6; Luke 23) and his apostolic successors (see Acts 12) was notorious for its bloody and brutal repression of the faith community's witness to God. The reader is right to wonder whether this family's infamy will carry over to Paul's case.

This passage uses two literary conventions of Luke's narrative style: the interlude and the double speech. The double speech functions like the double vision (e.g., 9:10-17; 10:1-16) or the follow-up letter in Acts (e.g., 15:22-29; 23:26-30) to emphasize themes that carry important theological freight. In this instance, Festus recognizes Paul's innocence of any seditious activity against Rome (see 25:25); he knows that the real issue at stake turns on a theological claim about the resurrection rather than a legal charge against Paul (see 25:18-19). At the same time, these two different versions provide different perspectives on the same events. In his second speech, Festus improves both his role in the judicial proceeding to this point (see 25:14*b*-17) and

his political standing in Palestine by asking Agrippa and Bernice to interrogate Paul and enlighten him in this matter (see 25:20-21), presumably to aid him in writing his official report to Rome (see 25:26). Rome's take on Paul is one of persistent theological ignorance and political self-interest, which in combination ironically safeguards him from the treachery of his Jewish opponents.

25:13-14a. The meeting of King Agrippa and Bernice with their new colleague Festus is an act of political solidarity between Roman rulers and pro-Roman interests in the Holy Land. Because of their different backgrounds—Festus is a pagan and Agrippa and Bernice are secular Jews—Festus quickly turns to them for help in settling the long-standing "Paul problem." It is hardly conceivable that Agrippa and Bernice would not have heard of Paul from the very same "chief priests and the leaders of the Jews" who reported to Festus, since Agrippa was Roman curator of the Temple and titular head of its priestly establishment. It is reasonable, therefore, that "Festus laid Paul's case before the king" (v. 14*a*), even though Luke does not indicate that Paul is the primary reason for this summit.

25:14b-21. Festus's initial rehearsal of Paul's case follows the plotline of Luke's script (see vv. 1-12), adding new details to reflect his judicial talent. The reference to inheriting prisoner Paul from Felix is not an implicit rebuke of his predecessor but an implicit request for help to understand the case's religious nuances. Festus also fills in gaps of what took place in his Jerusalem meeting with "the leaders of the Jews" (see v. 2); nothing is mentioned, however, about their request for a change of venue (see v. 20). Evidently, the

---

742. Bernice and Agrippa were the children of Herod Agrippa I; they lived together following the death of her husband. Although she had a reputation for piety, rumors spread of an incestuous relationship between the two. They did little to end the gossip and their relationship continued until Titus conquered Palestine and took Bernice as his Jewish mistress (only later to abandon her due to anti-Semitic sentiment in Rome when he became Caesar). Whether this is a historical subtext of the present story is impossible to determine, although it might explain their ambivalent responses to Paul.

leaders, now identified as "the chief priests and the elders" (i.e., the Sanhedrin), had initially wanted Festus to bring a guilty verdict against Paul without a trial: "They asked for a sentence against him" (v. 15). Festus states the conflict between Roman and Jewish judicial protocol with high moral tone: "It was not the custom [*ethos*] of the Romans to hand over anyone before the accused . . . had been given opportunity to make a defense [apologia] against the charge" (v. 16). No mention is made of Paul's Roman citizenship, which guarantees his right to a fair trial; nor is provision of the details of Paul's apologia necessary, since these are in mind already. Emphasis is placed as it should be on Festus, who is protector of the Roman constitution and therefore acts with due dispatch: "I lost no time . . . and ordered [Paul] be brought" (v. 17). Law and order are the hallmarks of Festus's regime!

Festus's rehearsal makes Luke's point: There is no evidence to support the Jewish case against Paul, in particular the charge of sedition to which Festus could render Rome's verdict (see 25:18). He rightly concludes that "they had certain points of disagreement with him about their own religion [δεισιδαιμονία *deisidaimonia*; lit., "superstition"]" (v. 19*a*) devolving into an intramural squabble over contested claims "about a certain Jesus."

The Roman pagan's negative caricature of Paul's gospel of the living Jesus as "their own superstition" (see 18:14-15), coupled with his apparent lack of knowledge "about a certain Jesus," explains why he seeks Agrippa's advice and why he has not yet rendered a verdict. Luke's intent is not yet to characterize Agrippa but rather Festus as an outsider[743] whose negative reading of the gospel remains unchanged in Acts. This is hardly Haenchen's "rehabilitated Festus,"[744] whose queries of the more knowledgeable Agrippa and Bernice are supposedly motivated by a leading citizen's desire to do right by Rome. When Festus persists in his obduracy and is finally dismissed by Paul as a parody of self-promotion (see 26:24-29), the reader cannot maintain a positive view of Festus. In fact, his hypocrisy

is revealed when he tells Agrippa and Bernice that his motive for raising the prospect of a Jerusalem venue for Paul's trial is that he "was at a loss how to investigate these questions" (25:20). We know better (see 25:9). The generally negative portrayal of Felix and Festus, both of whom act like Gallio in Acts, only intensifies what must be the central irony for Luke: These pagan outsiders grasp what his Jewish opponents do not admit— that the much disputed mission of Paul to the Gentiles/nations falls within the bounds of a Jewish ethos ("*their own* religion") and has everything to do with the much disputed message of Paul that the resurrected Jesus is God's Messiah (see 25:19).

25:22-23. The staging of Paul's "show trial" before King Agrippa and Queen Bernice is dramatic and carefully crafted. The pomp that testifies to the importance of Paul's speech to Agrippa makes more vivid that with this speech Paul fulfills Jesus' prophecy that he will "carry my name before kings" (see 9:15). The procession of (probably five) military commanders and civic leaders into the "audience hall" of Herod's praetorium in Caesarea is but a prelude to Paul's climactic entrance (see 25:23). The interpreter should take special note of Luke's careful use of time throughout this portion of Acts; it is as though he is narrating the chronology of the trials of Paul as their "official" court recorder.

25:24-27. Festus's second speech publicly reviews Paul's case in broad currents for a secular venue. Once again Festus declares Paul's innocence, without even providing a summary of the prosecution's case against him: "He has done nothing deserving death" (v. 25; see also v. 18; 24:5). Festus's request for Agrippa's involvement is surely politically motivated and reflects the insecurity of a new administration. He wishes to please his Jewish constituents by finding Paul guilty but cannot do so under Roman law; he must, therefore, depend on Agrippa either to find some guilt in Paul (not likely) or to be the one to declare him innocent and take the political heat for doing so upon himself. Since Festus already has indicated to Agrippa that the alleged "crime" against Paul is heresy—which only those more knowledgeable in Jewish theology could judge (i.e., the Sanhedrin, Bernice) and which is irrelevant in this secular setting

---

743. So Johnson, *The Acts of the Apostles*, 426, who claims that Festus uses a pejorative "superstition" (*deisidaimonia*) because he considers Agrippa a secular Jew and "as much an outsider to these disputes as himself."

744. Haenchen, *The Acts of the Apostles*, 674-75.

in any case—his primary political goal is for Agrippa to declare Paul innocent, which he eventually does (see 26:31-32).

Festus's use of hyperbole when describing the scope of controversy, saying that "this man about whom the whole Jewish community petitioned me, both in Jerusalem and here" (v. 24a), intensifies the Jewish cast of the problem. The reader will know that in private conversation Festus had made it clear to Agrippa that only "the chief priests and the elders" had petitioned him for a guilty verdict (see v. 15). Perhaps they did so on behalf of the Jewish people and Festus took their claim at face value. If this is true, then his hyperbole simply reflects his ignorance of the Jewish problem with Paul. His expressed sentiment is certainly at odds with Acts, which has more carefully circumscribed Paul's Jewish antagonists in terms both religious—they are *unrepentant* Jews—and sociological—they are only the (often Sadducean) *leaders* of the "people" who do not speak for all the people. In this sense, Jesus and his apostolic successors provoked the very same opposition previously, and for the same reasons.

Festus's concluding remarks are interesting for two reasons. Once again Luke contrasts the rational outsider (= Festus), to whom "it seems to me unreasonable [ἄλογος *alogos*; lit., "illogical"] to send a prisoner without indicating the charges against him" (v. 27), and the various Jewish mobs (including the Sanhedrin) who have been "shouting that [Paul] ought not to live any longer" (v. 24b) without any evident interest in the arguments made in Paul's (and his gospel's) favor. The rational thing to do in Paul's case is to examine him and then write up a report of the findings of fact (v. 26; see also 21:34; 22:30). Since Paul has already been declared innocent and his appeal to Caesar put into the record, this public examination is not another trial to determine his guilt or innocence but a public examination or "hearing" that should lead to a clarification of the truth of the matter. It is from this angle of vision—a rational investigation into the facts surrounding the case of an innocent man—that the reader should consider Paul's final and most important apologia in Acts. (See Reflections at 26:1-32.)

ACTS 26:1-32, PAUL DEFENDS HIMSELF BEFORE KING AGRIPPA AND BERNICE

COMMENTARY

If Paul's appeal to Caesar is the climax of the Acts narrative of his trial, this final apologia before Agrippa, Bernice, Festus, and their political and military entourage is its denouement. There is no longer need to rebut the charges of his Jewish opponents; there is need only to define the religious movement that Paul embodies. Luke's elaborate staging of this speech point the reader to this programmatic purpose. Festus asserts that this trial intends to "examine" Paul in order that legal brief can be written for the emperor (see 25:26-27). Paul need not present himself before Agrippa as a defendant who must prove his innocence in the face of charges leveled against him. Those days in court have ended with his appeal to Caesar. Therefore, while the form of Paul's speech is forensic (see 26:2, 24), its function is not to defend

his political innocence per se (however, see 26:21) but to define his prophetic vocation as the personification of the very messianic movement he now represents.

The audience of Roman delegates is important to note in this regard. Powerful and privileged people, well educated and aristocratic in bearing, Paul's auditors are people of the Roman Empire. Agrippa and Bernice are Jews to be sure; but they are pro-Roman Jews, well connected with the power elites of imperial Rome. Governor Festus personifies in his rational self-interest and religious skepticism the enlightened pagan of the Greco-Roman world. Even though this hearing takes place in Palestine, then, Paul's audience represents the interests of the Roman Empire and thus the mission field for Paul's gospel. Reference to the legal charges against Paul have been dropped from his apologia because his Jewish opponents are no longer relevant; the future of the word of the Lord belongs to the world inhabited by the likes of Festus and Agrippa.[745]

The principal ideas in this speech are familiar to the reader of Acts, and their repetition underlines the most important elements of Paul's religious authority in the book. Once again Paul sketches his Jewish credentials for a new audience (26:4-8; see also 21:39; 22:3; 23:6; 24:14-16): he is a Pharisee, a vigorous defender of the Jewish faith, ever faithful to Israel's Scriptures rightly interpreted (so 26:22-23). He again describes in detail his persecution of "the saints" (26:9-11; see 22:4-5), his dramatic conversion to Jesus (using fresh word pictures; 26:12-15; see 22:6-11), and his subsequent commission to bear witness to his resurrection to the nations (26:16-18; see 22:17-21). It is now Jesus who commissions him to his prophetic ministry, and its recital illustrates his obedience (26:19-20) according to the Scriptures (26:22). Within the framework of this testimony, then, the opposition of those unrepentant Jews that led to his arrest hardly needs to be mentioned (26:21), for the Lord has promised to rescue him from "from your people and from the Gentiles" (26:17).

In concluding his speech, Paul integrates the two different issues that have agitated controversy about him: His mission to the Gentiles (see 22:21, 22-24) and his message of the resurrected Messiah (see 23:6, 7-10; also 24:14-16, 21; 25:19). He finally claims that according to "the prophets and Moses" the rejected Messiah is resurrected by God to "proclaim light [φῶς phōs] both to our people [ὁ λαός ho laos] and to the Gentiles [ἔθνη ethnē]" (26:23). The reader hears an echo of Paul's earlier reference to his mission, "so that they [ho laos/ethnē, 26:17] may turn from darkness to light [phōs]" (26:18). The "light" that illumines darkness is the core proclamation of Paul's gospel, "that they [= ho laos/ethnē] may receive forgiveness of sins and a place among those who are sanctified by faith in [Jesus]" (26:18). Moreover,

reverberations are heard of Isaiah's prophecy of the Servant's (= Israel's) vocation as "a light [phōs] to the nations,/that my salvation may reach to the end of the earth" (Isa 49:6)—a prophecy whose fulfillment begins with God's Messiah (cf. Luke 2:32) and continues in the mission of Paul (see 13:47). The defense of the Paul of Acts finally turns on this claim. It is not what Rome or even Israel may think of his mission or message, for the status of Paul's religious authority in the world is determined by what God thinks. God's favorable verdict on Paul's service is therefore not rendered in terms of his political innocence (26:30-32) but rather by the salvation of those who are prospective beneficiaries of divine grace "to the end of the earth," represented here by this Roman governor and Jewish king (26:24-29).

26:1. Luke structures the exchange between Agrippa and Paul according to ancient rhetorical form: The expert adjudicator (= Agrippa) takes over the proceedings and gives the rhetor (= Paul) permission to speak.[746] Paul makes a familiar hand gesture (see 13:16; 19:33; 21:40)—despite his shackles (see 26:29)—and "began to defend [ἀπολογέομαι apologeomai] himself."[747] Because Festus has already indicated that the charges against Paul do not carry any guilt from a Roman perspective and are essentially religious in kind, Paul's defense is religious in substance as well. In fact, he does not defend himself directly against his opponents' allegations but defines himself in terms of his heavenly calling and the results of his mission among Jews and Gentiles. It is by obeying Israel's God that Paul defends himself against the accusation that he has transgressed Israel's traditions.

The positive tone established by Agrippa should be noted as well. He does not say "I give you permission" to establish a power or hostile relationship between himself and Paul. Rather more graciously, he gives Paul the freedom to state his case autobiographically—to speak *about* and not merely "for yourself"—and to him personally.[748]

745. Being members of the Herodian family, both Agrippa and Bernice would have been regarded Jewish by both Paul and Luke. However, with Josephus, *Antiquities of the Jews* 14.15.2, Herodians were *hēmiioudaios*, "half Jewish." That is, they were half Roman or "Roman Jews" in their split allegiance and bifurcated perspective toward Israel. See Fitzmyer, *The Acts of the Apostles*, 756.

746. See Winter, "Official Proceedings and Forensic Speeches in Acts 24–26," 327-31, who concludes that both Paul and Luke understood and carefully followed the rules of conventional rhetoric, which "regulate" how Acts narrates the case in favor of Paul and his appeal to Caesar.

747. The Western version elevates Paul's piety and importance by adding "confidently, having received the consolation of the Holy Spirit."

748. Cf. Witherington, *The Acts of the Apostles*, 738, who also notes that for this reason Luke does not refer to Agrippa as "Herod," a name synonymous with Christian oppression.

26:2-3. The *exordium*, or introduction, of Paul's speech briefly expresses his good fortune (*captatio benevolentiae*, or compliments for rhetorical effect) that he makes his defense before Agrippa, not because of his royal rank but because he is an expert "with all the customs [ethos] and controversies of the Jews" (26:3; see 26:10*b*). Paul addresses Agrippa personally, "King Agrippa," as though in a conversation between just the two of them. According to rhetorical rules, it is necessary for Paul to first indicate the judicial competence of his judge and to tie Agrippa's expertise directly to the very essence of his defense. Thus, when Paul repeatedly addresses Agrippa personally (26:2, 7, 13, 19), the reader presumes it is because of Agrippa's familiarity "with all the customs and controversies of the Jews."

The elegance of phrasing of Paul's opening address is perhaps best illustrated by the interplay between two unusual but similar-sounding words that enclose it: "I consider myself fortunate [μακάριος *makarios*] and therefore beg of you to listen to me patiently [μακροθύμως *makrothymōs*]." The rhetor's intent is made clear by this wordplay: Paul's plea for a favorable hearing is predicated on his good fortune in having Agrippa as his judge.

26:4-18. In conformity to the rhetor's rules, the substance of Paul's defense once again consists of a narrative (*narratio*) of his Jewish upbringing (4-8) and the circumstances (9-11) surrounding his conversion *as a Jew* to Jesus (12-15) and his calling *as a Jew* by Jesus (16-18). His autobiography is centered by two admittedly controversial claims: First, "I stand here on trial on account of my hope in the promise made by God to our ancestors" (26:6*a*); and, second, this hope is that "God raises the dead" (26:8; see 23:6).

26:4-5. Paul signals the transition to the *narratio* by the introductory formula μὲν οὖν (*men oun*; lit., "Now then . . ."; neither the NIV nor the NRSV picks this up). The repetition of the temporal phrases "from my youth" and "from the beginning" defines the extent of his Jewish "way of life" (see 22:3). No mention is made of Tarsus; rather, the location of his Jewish life has been "in Jerusalem" and "among my own people." Thus, those Jews from Jerusalem who now oppose him could

easily be asked by Agrippa to lend witness to Paul's claim that he has lived a robust Jewish life in full public view—as his Jewish opponents "have known for a long time" (v. 5*a*).

Perhaps more important to his self-defense is that this thoroughly Jewish upbringing was Pharisaic in kind: "I have belonged to the strictest sect [αἵρεσις *hairesis*] of our religion [θρησκεία *thrēskeia*] and lived as a Pharisee (v. 5*b*). The various subtexts of Paul's text alert the reader to a fuller meaning of his religious location. His reference to the Pharisees as a *hairesis* reminds the reader of the charge leveled earlier by Tertullus against Paul that he is "a ringleader of the sect [*hairesis*] of the Nazarenes" (24:5). The implicit claim here is that he is not the member of a heretical sectarian movement within Judaism but of a legitimate "party" of pious messianists. Paul's use of the rare superlative "strictest" (ἀκριβεστάτης *akribestatēs*), which denotes the precise or accurate interpretation of biblical law characteristic of the Pharisees, only intensifies the impression of his orthodoxy. The use of *thrēskeia*, which denotes formal or recognized religious observance, instead of Festus's more cynical term for "religion" (δεισιδαιμονία *deisidaimonia*), which denotes "superstition" (see 25:19), locates Paul within the bounds of Jewish orthodoxy—a subtle point meant for Agrippa due to his expert's knowledge of a Jewish ethos.

The aorist tense of the verb "I have lived" (ἔζησα *ezēsa*) is constative and retrospective; that is, it views the action as a whole to that point, without noting the duration of time. However, Paul is vague as to *which* point. Jervell rightly insists that the logic of Paul's apologia requires Agrippa to accept that Paul's Pharisaic "way of life"—his piety and core beliefs—carry over to his Christian way of life (see 23:6).[749] One can hardly imagine Paul's speech a "defense" against Jewish accusations, however implicit, before an expert in Jewish ethos, however personal, if this logic were somehow otherwise. Paul's argument is not to show how "Christian" his former Judaism was, but rather to show how Jewish his current Christianity is.

749. Jervell, *Die Apostelgeschichte*, 591, although some point out that Paul's adherence to purity laws governing table fellowship in mixed company is too lax to claim for his present life a "strict" adherence to Pharisaic practices. Cf. Witherington, *The Acts of the Apostles*, 740.

26:6-8. For this reason, the καὶ νῦν *kai nyn* ("And now") should not be taken as a formula of contrast but of the unbroken continuity (= "And") between Paul's Pharisaic Judaism and his current (= "now") messianic Christianity. For him, the essential definition of true religion concerns "my hope [ἐλπίς *elpis*] in the promise [ἐπαγγελία *epangelia*] made by God to our ancestors" (26:6) and those religious practices that cultivate this hope by "[earnest] worship day and night" (26:7). Although not explicitly stated, the reader of Acts understands from earlier texts that Paul's reference to *elpis* is to the "hope of the resurrection" (see 23:6; 24:15; 25:19), which then explains his cryptic question, "Why is it thought incredible by any of you that God raises the dead?" (26:8). Such an expression of perplexity is deeply rooted in Pharisaism's theology of hope for the resurrection of faithful Israel to eternal life, without which every other religious belief and practice is held to in vain (cf. 1 Cor 15:12-19).

Actually, the more important term of Paul's statement—at least in Acts—is *epangelia*, which recalls God's fulfilled "promise" of the Spirit's outpouring (1:4; 2:33, 39) and of the Messiah's deliverance (13:23, 32) according to Israel's Scriptures. God's realized promises of both the Messiah and the Spirit, however, are carefully related in Acts to God's umbrella promise of a restored Israel (see 1:4-8). The centrality of Paul's belief in the resurrection and of its experience in the Spirit, the content both of what God has promised repentant Israel and of what worshiping Israel hopes, is at the center of the Christian gospel from the beginning. From Pentecost forward, prophets-like-Jesus have proclaimed a gospel that integrates these two resurrections of a Spirit-filled Israel and Spirit-giving Messiah. Indeed, the fact of the resurrected One signifies that Israel's hope of its own end-time resurrection has already been realized (see 3:19-22; 5:28-32).

The Greek text marks a shift in implied audience from a single person, King Agrippa, to a plural "you" (ὑμεῖς *hymeis*) to make Paul's pointed question ironical, "Why is it thought incredible by any of you that God raises the dead?" (26:8). On the face of it, Paul's apologia for the resurrection appeals to human reason to evaluate the concept of deity by a supernatural power that only the gods possess: Any deity who cannot raise the dead—or transform human existence—is not a deity worth worshiping. Yet some of his Roman auditors would no doubt find this "hope in the resurrection" the core belief of a "superstitious" religion (see 17:22; 25:19). For this reason, Paul's comment may be directed to those *not* in attendance: unrepentant Jews, especially from the party of Pharisees, who share with him the ancestral hope in a resurrected Israel but who have rejected its fulfillment in the resurrected Jesus.

26:9-11. Luke again uses μὲν οὖν (*men oun*, "Indeed") to introduce the next period of Paul's narratio. The reader is already familiar with this "before Jesus" stage of his story from earlier texts (see 8:1-3; 9:1-2; 22:4-5). Several features of this iteration, however, deserve attention. Most critically, the opening *men oun* suggests continuity between his beliefs as a Pharisee (vv. 6-8) and his persecution of the church (vv. 9-11). More specifically, Paul's ferocity against believers exemplifies the incredulity of unrepentant Pharisees that Jesus is God's Messiah and Israel's Lord. Ironically, *he* is one who has thought it incredible "that God raises the dead [= Jesus]," and therefore "was convinced that I ought to do many things against the name of Jesus of Nazareth" (v. 9). At issue is *not* Paul's skepticism regarding resurrection. Rather, the presumed nationalism and ethnocentrism of his Jewish faith, cultivated by a Jewish education and membership in Pharisaism, had fashioned a variety of hope posited in the nation's end-time resurrection; and so the very idea of a resurrected Messiah in the past (rather than a resurrected Israel in the future) seemed to him "incredible." His is a very different sort of skepticism from that which characterizes the secular or pagan intellectual, for whom the very idea of a "resurrection" may seem incredible. Paul did not believe in resurrected messiahs and, therefore, thought it his religious duty to squelch this new messianic movement.

The use of "the name [ὄνομα *onoma*] of Jesus of Nazareth" once again recalls the movement of the word of the Lord in Jerusalem from the very beginning. The inspired proclamation of the word witnesses to "the name of Jesus" (4:18-19), so that "by the name of Jesus Christ of Nazareth" (4:10) and "by no other name" (see 4:12) the supplicant is saved from sins (see 2:21, 38) and healed from sickness (see 3:4, 16). The "name of Jesus" stands in Acts as a metaphor for true religion because in witness to that name the hope of a restored Israel is realized. Thus, the "many things" that Paul did "against the name" refers to his efforts to subvert the movement of the word in and beyond Jerusalem.

These efforts are enumerated in a single sentence that details "what I did in Jerusalem; with authority received from the chief priests" (26:10; see 9:2, 14; 22:5). This catalog of atrocities against "the saints" (see 9:13) confirms the standing impression of Paul's antagonism against the gospel on the other side of the Damascus road, here intensified: "I was so furiously enraged at them" (26:11). According to Paul's testimony, he: (1) "locked up many of the saints" (see 8:3; 9:13); (2) "cast my vote against them"; (3) "tried to force them to blaspheme" (see 22:5); and (4) "pursued them even to foreign cities [i.e., beyond Jerusalem]" (vv. 10-11; see also 9:1-2).

Several features of this description of Paul's hostilities are new and self-incriminating and deserve further discussion. Most important in this regard is the second: "I also cast my vote [κατήνεγκα ψῆφον *katēnenka psēphon*; lit., "to cast a voting pebble") against them when they were being condemned [ἀναιρέω *anaireō*]" (v. 10*b*). Judicial bodies routinely used pebbles when deciding verdicts and so "to cast a pebble" came to refer to the vote itself; in turn, the vote cast revealed one's truest values and core beliefs. To cast a condemning vote in this instance means to vote for the death penalty against believers: Paul's opposition to the faith is thus confirmed. Acts mentions only Stephen and the apostle James as martyrs; however, this text suggests there were others. While doubtless Luke feels no compulsion to tell the story of every Christian martyr in Acts, it is most likely that Paul's comment here is a metaphor for his intense opposition to the messianic movement in Jerusalem. Further, it is unlikely that he was a voting member of the Sanhedrin and would have had a vote to cast, although some think it possible that he was a clerk or associate

of Pharisees who were and therefore participated in some indirect way in any voting that actually took place.[750] Again, however, Luke is probably using the image of a "voting pebble" as a metaphor for Paul's cooperation with malevolent forces in Jerusalem (see 7:58).

Also new is the claim that Paul punished them "often in the synagogues . . . to force them to blaspheme" (v. 11*a*). There is no reference to believers attending synagogues in Jerusalem, even though this perhaps could be implied from the story of Stephen's arrest (see 6:8-12; cf. 2 Cor 11:24). Yet in his earlier testimony Paul did mention that he arrested and brought believers to Jerusalem for punishment (see 22:5). The new elements in Paul's rehearsal of his opposition to the Hellenists are his attempts (evidently failed)[751] to get believers to utter publicly "anathema Jesus" or some other specifically anti-Christian slogan. Paul's opposition to believers in and around Jerusalem, then, demonstrates his profound devotion to the orthodoxy of official Judaism.

26:12-15. Paul's public testimony is centered by his Damascus road experience, which has shaped his identity as a prophet-like-Jesus. By this point in Acts the broad details of this experience are familiar: when traveling to persecute believers in Damascus "with the authority and commission of the chief priests" (v. 12; see also 9:1-2; 22:5), he "saw a light from heaven, brighter than the sun, shining around me and my companions" (v. 13; see also 9:3; 22:6). The intensity of the brightness is here emphasized, and Paul now includes his traveling companions as witnesses to his experience: The great light surrounded them (cf. 22:9) and "we all had fallen to the ground" (v. 14*a*; cf. 9:7; 22:7).

Keeping with Luke's thematic interest in the use of language, Paul notes the dialect of the divine audition: "I heard a voice saying to me in the Hebrew (lit., "Hebrew dialect"; i.e., "Aramaic") language" (v. 14*b*). While metaphorical of the participatory nature of God's saving activity in the world, Paul's addition of this detail in his apologia to a Roman audience stresses the essentially Jewish cast of his story

750. Cf. Witherington, *The Acts of the Apostles*, 742.
751. See Barrett, *A Critical and Exegetical Commentary on the Acts of the Apostles*, 2:1156.

and mission. The ensuing dialogue between Jesus and Paul is as before, except the addition of the famous although cryptic aphorism, "It is hard [σκληρός *sklēros*] for you to kick against the goads [κέντρον *kentron*]" (v. 14c). A *kentron* is a stick with a sharpened point used as a variety of cattle prod to goad an animal in the right direction. For Paul to "kick against the goads" is to resist God's goading. The addition of *sklēros*, which is an OT metaphor for "hardening" one's resolve against God's will (cf. Exod 6:9), adds an additional layer of meaning to his implied response to the Lord's probing question, "Saul, Saul, why are you persecuting me?" Paul's persecution of Jesus indicates his stubborn refusal to obey God's redemptive plan, which includes him. Because God's plan does include Paul, it is fruitless for him to persecute Jesus.

26:16-18. God's plan for Paul is now disclosed. There is no mention of Paul's blindness and the witness of pious Ananias to Paul's conversion is replaced by that of Paul's traveling companions. Luke shapes this final apologia to emphasize Paul's prophetic calling and in doing so brings to the fore several elements of his portrait in Acts. Jesus "appears" to Paul "to appoint [προχειρίζομαι *procheirizomai*] you to serve [ὑπηρέτης *hypēretēs*] and testify [μάρτυς *martys*] (v. 16a). The purpose of this unmediated visitation is to call Paul to a task in continuity with that of the Messiah whom God "appointed" and sent to restore Israel and the entire world (see 3:19-21). Paul's tasks are also in continuity with those of the Lord's apostolic successors who are chosen (see 1:2) and given the Spirit in order to "be my witnesses" (*martyres*; see 1:8). The Paul of Acts is not appointed to an apostolic office but to be a "servant" of the word (cf. Luke 1:2). The use of *hypēretēs* almost certainly alludes to Isaiah's Servant in whose role Paul is depicted (see the Commentary on 26:18).

The content of this word of the Lord involves the things in which you have seen me and . . . those in which I will appear to you" (v. 16b; see also 22:15).[752] This testimony agrees with Paul's autobiography according to which "the revelation of Jesus

Christ" supplied him with the core beliefs of his gospel (cf. Gal 1:12-16). Paul implies that the Lord promised additional appearances to enhance and direct his witness. In Acts, surely this must refer to Paul's other epiphanies, most notably the Lord's disclosure that Paul "must bear witness also in Rome"[753] (see 23:11; cf. 27:23-24). That is, Paul's vocation is supplied with both a word about the living Jesus and a city of destiny in which to proclaim it.

Jesus also promises to "rescue [ἐξαιρέω *exaireō*] you from your people and from the Gentiles [lit., "nations")—to whom I am sending you" (26:17). The intriguing features of this segment of Paul's commissioning revelation are twofold: First, the prospect of the Lord's "rescue" (*exaireō*), which is an important element of the exodus typology used both in Acts (7:10, 34; 12:11; 23:27) and in OT narrative (cf. Exod 3:8; 18:4; Ps 38:40 LXX; see also Jer 1:8,19): God rescues those that God has chosen, whether Israel from Egyptian oppression or Paul from his opponents, so that God's promises are realized. Second, even more important is Paul's note of universal opposition to his message of universal salvation. The interpreter simply cannot sustain an argument that Acts casts only "the Jews" in the "bad guys" role. Paul's comment is an effective summary of the rejection theme, which recounts how unrepentant Gentiles along with unrepentant Jews seek to subvert the progress of the word of the Lord to the end of the earth and how God "rescued" Paul from their evil machinations (see 13:44-45; 14:2, 19; 16:7, 9, 19-24; 17:5-9, 13, 32; 18:6, 12-13; 19:9, 22-24; 22:7; 23:11).

The universal scope of Paul's mission is indicated even though it is possible that "to whom" (εἰς οὕς *eis hous*) in v. 17 refers only to the Gentiles. Earlier, Paul's claim that his mission among the Gentiles was undertaken in obedience to God's command had incensed the Jerusalem Jews (see 22:21-23). Perhaps Paul wants now to explain and expand that earlier controversy to Agrippa. In any case,

---

752. The NIV's "as a servant and as a witness" is more literal than the NRSV, which paraphrases the nouns *hypēretēs* and *martys* by using verbs.

753. The Greek of this phrase is convoluted and for this reason its transmission is corrupted. Its plain meaning is more plainly stated in 22:15: Paul is to bear witness to "what you have seen and heard." The problem is with the direct object με (*me*, "me"), whether to retain it (as do both translations) or not. The textual and internal evidence is equally divided. In my judgment, the NIV translation offers the best compromise: retain *me* but of its fuller sense that Paul's witness is "of me"—i.e., of the living Jesus he met on the Damascus Road.

I think it best to take the antecedent of *eis hous* as inclusive of "the people and the Gentiles."

The religious aim of Paul's witness is set forth in a sequence of pregnant phrases that summarizes his understanding of the conversion experience.[754] The structure of 26:18 is supplied by three infinitives, "to open," "to turn," and "to receive," all of which are dependent upon the concluding action of the preceding verse, "to whom I am sending you." Simply put, God sends Paul to the nations in order "to open" them to the truth of the gospel, "to turn" them from ignorance to the light of God's gospel, with the result that they are able "to receive" forgiveness and eternal life from God.

The idiom and ideas of this important text echo Isaiah's prophecy of the Servant's calling (cf. Isa 42:6-7) and constitute of the most powerful statements of conversion in Scripture. The original sounding of Isaiah's prophecy is introduced by the Creator's declaration of the Spirit's gift (cf. 42:5), so that the Servant's calling as "a light to the nations" (cf. 42:6) "to open the eyes that are blind" (cf. 42:7) presumes the Spirit's enablement. The spiritual calculus of Isaiah's definition of Israel's calling is also the logic of Paul's self-understanding. That is, his mission to the nations and the divine forgiveness that results are impossibilities without the Spirit's inspiration.

Moreover, the Paul of Acts is a prophet-like-Jesus (cf. Luke 4:14-21) who receives the mantle of Isaiah's Servant by commission of the resurrected Lord and continues to do and say what Jesus revealed to him as the personification of Isaiah's Servant Israel. Unlike Luke's Jesus, however, whose messianic mission extended only to the Jews, Paul's mission to the nations more fully realizes Isaiah's prophecy of a faithful Israel's service to God: Paul is a witness to "the people and the Gentiles" and opens all their eyes to the truth of God. He summarizes, then, the unstated justification for the plotline of Luke's Acts: Paul's Damascus road commissioning and the commencement of his mission as light to the nations (Acts 9–28) take place when God's promise of Israel's restoration had been fulfilled through the church's mission to the

whole house of Israel (Acts 1–8; see 3:19-26). The timing of Paul's encounter with the living Jesus in the plotline of Acts is the effect of the formation of a repentant Israel under the leadership of the Twelve.

What follows is a description of the universal experience of all who convert from darkness (= ignorance/Satan) to light (= gospel/God) through "faith in [Jesus]" (see 2:21; 11:17; 13:38-39; 15:9-11; 20:20-21). They all share in the blessings God promised to a restored Israel: God's forgiveness (see 2:38; 5:31; 10:43; 13:38) and a thorough cleansing of sins (see 3:18-19; 20:32; cf. 15:8-11; Rom 15:16; 1 Cor 6:11).

26:19-20. The speech's *confirmatio* testifies to Paul's obedience to the Lord's visionary commission, using litotes (deliberate understatement)—"I was not disobedient"—to make the character of his response more emphatic. Paul traces his obedience by the geography of his mission, narrated by Acts and easily confirmed by its readers: "first to those in Damascus [see 9:20-22] . . . then in Jerusalem [see 9:28-29], and also to the Gentiles [vv. 13-20]." The added phrase, "and throughout the countryside of Judea," is difficult not only because of its awkward grammar (stated in the accusative case rather than in the dative as the others) but more so because nowhere does Acts indicate a Pauline mission "throughout the countryside of Judea." The shift of case is exceptional but not unknown where the phrase in the accusative bounds those items enumerated in the dative; thus, Paul's preaching "throughout the countryside of Judea" merely encompasses in general those particular missions in Damascus and Jerusalem. The latter problem is amplified, however, by Paul's claim that he was "still unknown by sight to the churches of Judea" (Gal 1:22), although he also claimed to have preached the gospel in Illyricum (cf. Rom 15:19). Different solutions have been suggested; however, the grammatical solution also settles the historical conflict if the reader takes the phrase "throughout the countryside of Judea" as iterative of Paul's Damascus and Jerusalem missions in order to demonstrate that Paul's is a Jewish missionary who goes first to the Jews before reaching out to the Gentiles.[755]

---

754. For this theme in Acts, see Gaventa, *From Darkness to Light,* 52-95.

755. Cf. Barrett, *A Critical and Exegetical Commentary on the Acts of the Apostles,* 2:1163-64.

Paul repeats in different words the content of his evangelical declaration to the Jews and Gentiles (see 26:18), that "they should repent and turn to God"; but he then adds the ethical imperative "and do deeds consistent with repentance" (v. 20). Although Paul implies that two discrete responses to the gospel are required for salvation, he does not clarify the exact relationship between the sinner's turn toward God for forgiveness and the believer's works that are consistent with repentance. He has already stipulated that repentance is by faith in Jesus (v. 18), and that a thorough spiritual cleansing will result; this formulation implies that works follow from repentance. The question remains whether the forgiven believer can live a manner of life that is contrary to God's will. Clearly this is impossible for the epistolary Paul, for whom good works are the natural yield of saving faith (cf. Rom 6:1-11; Eph 2:8-10). For him there is but a single response that is required, and that is the sinner's faith in the crucified Christ's sacrifice for sin (cf. Rom 3:21-26). Repentance and "deeds consistent with repentance" constitute a seamless, mutually inclusive response to God's grace, and not two related but separate responses, as Luke's Paul implies.

26:21. The *refutatio* rebuts the original charge brought against Paul that he profaned the Temple and provides Agrippa with an apt synopsis of what has been described in detail in 21:27–25:12. According to the design of his apologia, however, Paul can now claim that his arrest is the result of his responsiveness to the Lord's calling and follows Scripture's imperative (see v. 22)—the polar opposite of what his Jewish opponents allege!

26:22-23. Any defense speech that follows the rhetorical rules of the day includes a plea for divine help, "for which the use of the verb [τυγχάνω] *tynchanō* ("help") is standard."[756] Paul's concluding *peroratio* implies that God's help has kept him safe as promised and "so I stand here" (i.e., "I am alive and well"). More important, however, God has kept him safe for this moment when he bears witness "to both small and great" (see v. 29) that Scripture's promise of salvation has been fulfilled in the Christ event. With good reason, R. O'Toole contends that this text is "the

christological climax of Paul's defense" if not of all Luke-Acts.[757] Nowhere in Acts is there a clearer expression that the gospel's theological substructure is a narrative of fulfillment: The Messiah's suffering and resurrection are fulfilled in the life of Jesus according to the prophesied pattern of "the prophets and Moses" (see 13:15; 24:14; also 2:16; 3:18, 21-25; 7:52; 10:43; 13:27, 40; 15:15, 32; 28:23; cf. Luke 24:44-48). The ultimate importance of this point is recognized by Agrippa, who subsequently takes it up with Paul for fuller discussion (see 26:27-28).[758]

This striking summary of Paul's testimony deserves careful attention. Earlier in the speech he asserted that Israel's national hope rests on God's promise to resurrect the dead (see 26:6-8). The more controversial calculus of Paul's apologia is that Israel's hope in the resurrection must surely be related to God's resurrection of Jesus: the promise of Israel's restoration is already being realized from the empty tomb forward. It is in this specific sense that Paul can now claim that his own testimony "to both small and great" is thoroughly Jewish and follows the redemptive script of the Jewish Scriptures—"the prophets and Moses."

The strategic repetition of "Moses" in this formula (instead of the more familiar "the law") probably intends to recall other references to "Moses" in Acts so to "thicken" the meaning of Paul's appeal to Moses in his defense. The "Moses" of Acts not only denotes the biblical torah (see 15:21); he is also the type of and a prophet of Jesus. Taken together, then, all Scripture, inclusive of the books of Moses, testifies to and confirms the Christ event to which Paul himself publicly testifies. It does so because Jesus fulfills the promise that God "will raise up for you" a prophet-like-Moses (see 3:22-23; 7:37). The prophetic pattern of Moses, in which Jesus and now Paul follow, establishes the kerygmatic core of Christian proclamation: "that the Messiah must suffer [and] . . . rise from

756. Winter, "Official Proceedings and Forensic Speeches in Acts 24–26," 330; cf. Bruce, *The Acts of the Apostles*, 504.

757. Cf. R. O'Toole, *The Christological Climax of Paul's Defense*, AnBib 78 (Rome: Pontifical Biblical Institute, 1978) 101-22.

758. The grammar of this text suggests that Paul proposes discussion topics rather than that he proclaims religious beliefs. The key phrases of the gospel summary are introduced by the Greek particle εἰ (*ei*), picked up in the translations as "must" (NRSV) or "would" (NIV), which by in ancient rhetoric introduces points of debate. Agrippa follows Paul's rhetorical cue and takes up these propositions for further dialogue.

the dead." Rejection leads to vindication according to "the prophets and Moses."

What stands out more clearly as a result of Paul's mission is Israel's identity as a light to the nations (Isa 49:6-7; see 13:47; cf. Luke 2:32). Already grounded in biblical prophecy, Paul now claims that the Messiah is not only the "first to rise from the dead" to establish Israel's hope but is also the first to "proclaim light to our people and to the Gentiles" to establish Israel's vocation (cf. 2 Tim 1:10). His implied defense is that because his own identity follows from God's Messiah who fulfills Jewish Scriptures, he must therefore be considered an exemplary Jew.

26:24-29. Luke often uses the interrupted speech—a speech that actually has been completed—as a rhetorical device to underline the last thing said (see 10:44). The last element of Paul's speech is not the core beliefs of the Christian kerygma—the Lord's passion and his resurrection—but rather the Lord's universal mission that he now emulates. The reader already realizes the challenge that his mission represents for Jewish notions of identity (see 22:21-23); Festus's outburst recognizes that Paul's mission to the nations challenges Roman (or secular) notions of identity as well, but for very different reasons. If the universalism of Paul's mission subverts the particularity of a Jewish identity, whose religious beliefs and practices stress Israel's special relationship with the one and only Creator God, then his messianism subverts also the relativism of Rome's ethos, which tolerates the diverse and multiple identities of its different subjects. Not only does Jesus' resurrection fulfill Israel's hope according to its Scriptures, but his present and future significance is cosmic in scope (see 3:19-21).

The persona of the Festus of Acts is that of a person of rational self-interest. His judgments of Paul's "great learning" ($\pi o\lambda\lambda\grave{\alpha}$ $\gamma\rho\acute{\alpha}\mu\mu\alpha\tau\alpha$ *polla grammata*) and even of his "insanity" ($\mu\alpha\nu\acute{\iota}\alpha$ *mania*) are measurements of the human mind. He correctly realizes that if Paul is right in his concluding words, then the Roman way of life he personifies and champions has come to an end with Jesus. Paul's retort is in kind and appeals to precisely what Festus values: "What I am saying [$\grave{\alpha}\pi o\phi\theta\acute{\epsilon}\gamma\gamma o\mu\alpha\iota$ *apophthengomai*] is true [$\grave{\alpha}\lambda\acute{\eta}\theta\epsilon\iota\alpha$ *alētheia*] and reasonable [$\sigma\omega\phi\rho o\sigma\acute{\upsilon}\nu\eta$ *sōphrosynē*]" (v. 25).[759] His initial response goes to the genre of his speech: *apophthengomai* denotes divinely inspired speech—the speech of a prophet (see 2:4, 14). Thus, his "great learning" (*polla grammata*) derives from inspired insight into the meaning of Scripture that enables him to detect the gospel's *alētheia* (cf. 2 Cor 6:7; 11:10; Gal 2:5, 14). Hardly insane, what he says is *sōphrosynē*, a word that denotes intellectual sobriety.[760]

Paul's continual personal appeal to Agrippa throughout his apologia reaches its climax with this final exchange between them. Paul had invited dialogue when summarizing his gospel message and the divine sanction of its universal application (see v. 23). While Festus fully understands the implication of what Paul says for a Roman ethos, its Jewish cast makes it an awkward fit and more suitable for Agrippa, even though the latter is a secular Jew. His familiarity with "these things" (= Jewish Scriptures) allows Paul to "speak freely" ($\pi\alpha\rho\rho\eta\sigma\iota\acute{\alpha}\zeta o\mu\alpha\iota$ *parrēsiazomai*; lit., "boldly"). The repetition of *parrēsiazomai* cues its earlier use in Acts as characteristic of the prophet-like-Jesus who is inspired by the Spirit to proclaim the gospel (see 4:29-31). It is precisely at this moment that Paul's apologia turns into a missionary speech: To "speak freely" to Agrippa is to proclaim the word of the Lord to him.

Paul contributes two elements that frame his earlier kerygmatic claims regarding the dying and rising of the Messiah and his ministry as God's light to Jews and Gentiles. These claims are a matter of the historical record: "none of these things has escaped his notice, for this was not done in a corner" (v. 26). The apologetic purpose of this litotes is emphatically to point out that the gospel's subject matter is experiential, and it can be tested whether "true and reasonable" by any "sane" person. Christian religion is neither private nor internal; as a faith consonant with Scripture's definition, its claims are worked out within history for all to see.

---

759. The NRSV plausibly translates this phrase as a hendiadys: What is "true" and "reasonable" constitutes the "sober truth."

760. The two genitives that delimit Paul's prophetic speech—what he "says"—set forth what is said ("true" is an objective genitive) and how it is said ("reasonable" is a subjective genitive). See Barrett, *A Critical and Exegetical Commentary on the Acts of the Apostles,* 2:1168.

Paul's query about Agrippa's belief in the prophets (v. 27) evinces his theological purpose. The subtext of the question, of course, is that Paul's messianic interpretation of the prophets recognizes that God's promises of Israel's restoration and of an international participation in its blessings are fulfilled in the ministry, suffering, and resurrection of Jesus. He is asking Agrippa whether he believes this gospel, not whether he knows the relevant prophecies. Agrippa is quick to recognize Paul's intent: "Are you so quickly persuading me to become [ποιέω *poieō*] a Christian?" (v. 28). What is more difficult for the interpreter to discern is how seriously Agrippa takes Paul's evangelistic query. The meaning here of the verb *poieō*, which literally means "to make/perform," is unclear. Is Agrippa on the verge of "making" a Christian conversion? Perhaps. However, many commentators now understand the exchange between Agrippa and Paul to be more witty than sober.[761] Especially when considered in light of Paul's punning response, perhaps all Agrippa is asking is whether he could "perform the role" of a Christian, presumably to demonstrate both his good sense and his identity with his Jewish subjects. But to "perform a role" is not to "become" a true believer.

Paul seems to sense Agrippa's lack of resolve and puns his line in reference to "these chains"—the metaphor of Paul's commitment to the gospel. That is, Paul prays that Agrippa, indeed, "perform the role" of a believer, but not that of a bit part and rather with the firm authentic dedication exemplified by his own example: "I pray God—all who are listening to me today may become what I am [i.e., perform my role]" (v. 29).

26:30-32. Paul has the last word in his final apologia; its exhortation is not unlike his final words to the elders of Ephesus at Miletus (see 20:35). That both unbelieving and believing leaders should follow Paul's example underwrites the universalism of his spiritual authority. It is also noteworthy that Luke narrates the ad hoc review of Paul's hearing between the king, the governor, Bernice, and "those who had been sitting with them" in a way that echoes the Jewish Sanhedrin's conference following Peter's powerful testimony earlier in Acts (see 4:15-18; cf. 5:33-40). Rome's more favorable verdict toward Paul, which confirms his innocence, contributes to the general impression that Rome is the city of his destiny. There is a sense in which neither Agrippa nor Festus has authority to determine that "this man could have been set free if he had not appealed to the emperor" (26:32). Rather, it is by authority of a sovereign God that Paul will appear before Caesar in Rome (see 23:11; 27:24). And so it is that Paul's legal entanglements end, not with a bang but with a whimper. All these various decisions fund the larger script that the word of the Lord will be carried by the anointed prophet as a "light to the nations, that my salvation may reach to the end of the earth" (Isa 49:6; see 13:47).

761. E.g., Johnson, *The Acts of the Apostles*, 439-40.

REFLECTIONS

1. "Why is it thought incredible by any of you that God raises the dead?" (26:8 NRSV). When people object to the idea or fact of the resurrection, we should ask them what sort of god is it that would make hope in the resurrection unreasonable. If there is no personal and powerful God, then the conversation ends there. Paul's incredulity that anyone might regard his Easter faith as specious, however, reflects a profoundly biblical faith. From his perspective, the resurrection makes perfect sense: What other way would a life-giving God demonstrate fidelity to the promise of new life, free from the threat of death? And what other evidence makes sense of his own conversion and calling?

For others the first Easter dawned a scandalous surprise. Even the women who came to the tomb did so out of loyalty for their fallen friend. They had witnessed his execution; and they had seen his body wrapped in burial cloth and placed in a grave, sealed with a stone. Jesus of Nazareth was dead indeed. Luke captures the women's

Easter surprise: "They did not find the body" (Luke 24:3). They found the tombstone rolled away, disclosing in the grave's emptiness the cornerstone of our faith. Jesus of Nazareth is risen; God has made him Lord and Christ (see 2:36). The subtext of Acts is that without God's resurrection power Christianity would have fizzled out; our faith stands or it falls with the truth of the resurrection.

Yet, none of the New Testament writers recount the resurrection itself; they are more concerned with what results from the resurrection. The importance of Easter is envisioned by the core theological convictions of the church that are clustered around the empty tomb. We cannot glibly dismiss Jesus as another "great teacher" or "moral exemplar." The resurrection stamps him as the authoritative teacher of God's truth, so that to know him is to know God in a more personal way. The resurrection illumines his life as the incarnation of God's demand perfectly obeyed, so that to follow him is to love God and neighbor in life-giving ways. Nor can we talk about the scandal of Jesus' death as a "bad Friday" on which one more innocent man was killed by powerful leaders made blind and jealous by their self-centered ambition. The innocent one crucified on that Roman cross is none other than the Son of God, and his atoning death results in "a ransom for many" (Mark 10:45).

By God's salvation-creating grace, what began as a "bad Friday" is transformed into the church's Good Friday: In the risen Jesus, God has declared the forgiveness of our sins; our hope in God's forgiveness is not groundless. Hidden in God's resurrection of the living Lord is the promise that "he will come again to judge the living and the dead." This familiar confession of our hope, so mysterious and modest, expresses the church's profound confidence: Despite the persistence of sin and the presence of suffering, God's triumph over the evil one through the risen Christ will surely have its day.

God's resurrection of Jesus also provides incisive commentary on a right understanding of ourselves, both during the present moment and into the future. A student of mine, already the graduate of a fine university just eight years before, had enrolled for classes at my university to acquire another degree and additional skills for a second career. When I congratulated him on his desire for more education, he responded with a shrug that he had become obsolete in the marketplace. The work force no longer needed his skills and he was replaced. His story is a symbol of our contemporary "hi-tech" culture, in which we are made to feel quickly dispensable and are easily forgotten. Our individual identities are reduced to numbers stored in a computer; only rarely does our work survive as a lasting contribution, and few remember our names after we leave. The pressures and secular perceptions of our everyday world shove each of us toward oblivion. But Paul writes that by faith we participate with Christ in the results of his death and resurrection, which constitute a "new life" (Rom 6:4).

God's resurrection of Jesus is bodily and historical; likewise, God's good purposes are embodied in our own particular histories, made new by God's empowering love. On the one hand, the death of Jesus' body says "no" to the spiritual sin and natural decay that destroys the various "bodies" in which we participate—personal, familial, ecclesial, and social. Yet, on the other hand, the resurrection of Jesus' body says yes to God's life-giving power: Through the redeemed community, God can bring those decaying bodies back to life. Further, God remembered Jesus when others rejected him and God brought him back to life as indispensable humanity. Likewise, God remembers us "while we still were sinners" (Rom 5:8) and restores our true humanity (Rom 8:28-30). By God's grace, our character is transformed with Christ from bad news into good (Col 3:1-11), resulting in the revitalization of our relationships with others (Col 3:12–4:6). We are risen indeed (Eph 2:5-6)! Finally, then, the resurrection envisages the "hope of Israel"—the promise of a new creation, purged of decay and death, where a community's ordinary experience is of God's shalom (cf. 1 Cor 15:35-49).

When the risen Jesus met his former disciples, they recognized him by name (John 20:16; Luke 24:35) and were reunited with him. Likewise, at Christ's triumphant return, God will not reduce our unique individuality but will restore it completely. Because we retain our individuality, those loved ones now missed will be remembered. Those lost in this life will be found in the next, for the resurrection is about reunion too: on that first Easter, Christ with God, so that on the last Easter, us with Christ and each with one another. The resurrection is a powerful symbol that God's design for creation is purposeful. The suffering, evil, and futility all around us today is challenged by the hope of tomorrow—a hope warranted by the resurrection.

2. "Festus exclaimed, 'You are out of your mind, Paul! Too much learning is driving you insane!'" (26:24 NRSV). Paul's perceived insanity is noteworthy by its coherence! His final speech on Palestinian soil claims two familiar moments in his life that give shape to his Christian identity—his conversion and his calling. Yet he also insists that his Christian identity is shaped by the intellectual traditions of Israel. Paul is not converted from guilt and misery or called to a journey toward self-fulfillment. He is no guru of New Age spirituality but a devout Jew whose experiences of conversion to the resurrected Messiah and calling to a prophetic ministry are consistent with the Scriptures of Israel properly understood. These holistic claims of mind and heart, of written text and living context, are the constants of a personal testimony whose coherence does not change with shifts of audience and circumstance.

Would Paul's apologia before a sophisticated audience of rich and influential leaders sound a responsive note today? Perhaps not: Most might repeat Festus's harsh verdict. Today's society is cultivated by a scientific sophistry, convinced that all claims to universal truth must be assessed by empirical investigation. The principal disposition toward anything religious, especially if revivalist in tone, is one of deep suspicion of its intellectual integrity. Central to Paul's testimony, whether to religious Jews or sophisticated pagans, is that his conversion and calling is not his doing but the living Lord's: As Willimon has noted, "Most of the traffic on the bridge between us and God is moving toward us."[762] The subtext of Paul's testimony is that a reasonable yet radical leap of faith is required to grab hold of the theocentricity of the Christian gospel. At the end of the day, Festus and then Agrippa (26:28) remain unconvinced, not because they lacked solid evidence but because they lacked faith in a faithful God who forgives and transforms human life, both now and forevermore.

762. Willimon, *Acts*, 180.

ACTS 27:1-12, SETTING SAIL FOR ROME

COMMENTARY

The last two chapters of Acts narrate Paul's dramatic journey to the city of his destiny (27:1–28:16), concluding with his mission in Rome (28:17-31). The present passage narrates the first stage of Paul's voyage to Rome; it is slowly paced, reflective of the calm before a storm. The reader is introduced to Paul's traveling companions (27:1), and a travel itinerary is provided that follows their progress from Adramyttium to Fair Havens (27:2-8). Repeated references to various delays and difficult sailing (cf. 27:3-4, 6-8) alert the attentive reader to the dangerous prospect that an experienced Paul forewarns: The delays have pushed the timetable of this voyage beyond a safe point; to continue will endanger the ship and its cargo (27:9-10). Unfortunately, the Roman soldier put in charge of this expedition votes with the majority against Paul's advice and they set sail for Cretan Phoenix against poor odds (27:11-12).

Throughout it all Paul is still a prisoner of Rome, not due to his guilt but as a safeguard for his self-appointed audience before the Caesar (see 25:10-12). In truth, Rome's political institutions—its law court, military, and provincial administration—are but the public instruments of God's sovereign purpose for Paul who will arrive safely in Rome to proclaim the word of God as a "divine necessity" (see 23:11; 26:17).

27:1. The narrator resumes telling his story in the first person (see 16:10). Although the first person telling of a sea voyage or shipwreck is a literary convention of ancient fiction,[763] the differences between his story in Acts and those "parallels" found in Greek novels point in another direction; namely, the narrator places himself in the story to serve as a reliable witness to Paul's heroics.[764] In this sense, Paul's responses during a stormy sea complement his earlier defense speeches to provide the reader with an even more robust portrait of his spiritual authority as a prophet-like-Jesus. Indeed, his calming effort with lives at stake is far different from that of the frightened Jonah, another prophet at the mercy of a tempestuous sea. That prophet Jonah imperiled his traveling companions while prophet Paul delivered saving grace even to his military escort symbolizes their contrasting relations with God and God's purposes: Whereas Jonah is on the run from God's calling, Paul is obedient to it. Clearly, the Paul of Acts is an experienced traveler;[765] but surely this risky feature of his ministry only evinces his single-minded interest in serving God's will (see 20:27; cf. 2 Cor 11:25-26). Moreover, in this concluding story of Paul's travels, his authority is exhibited among Gentiles who are not connected with any synagogue.

The narrator's intention is also shown by his intimate knowledge of a Mediterranean sea voyage. The reader rightly wonders why Luke takes such care in narrating this journey when he mentions more important events only in passing. I doubt his primary reason is either to follow literary convention or to liven up an otherwise slowly paced narrative. Rather, the detailed references found in this chapter to nautical terminology, complete with documentation of weather patterns and ports of call, provide the details of a realistic drama in which Paul's prophetic vocation is more fully exemplified in relation to Gentiles.

While the narrator and Aristarchus (see 19:29; 20:4; cf. Phlm 24) accompany Paul to Italy for unstated reasons, they are clearly distinguished from Paul and "some other prisoners" who are turned over to a "centurion of the Augustan Cohort, named Julius" for safekeeping (v. 1; however, see Col 4:10).[766] Perhaps Paul is allowed traveling companions because of his status as a Roman citizen or perhaps even because of his notoriety in Palestine. Not much is known about Paul's military escort. The title "Augustan Cohort" is honorific and was probably formed from auxiliary troops in Palestine who were now returning to Rome and were given this tour as extra duty. The personal name of the centurion is given—"Julius"—not because of his importance to the story but as a feature of realistic storytelling.

27:2-8. With the passenger list complete, the ship is ready to embark for Rome. From Luke's itinerary, it would appear this is the first of two boats. The ferry boarded in the Asian port city of Adramyttium regularly serves only the "ports along the coast of Asia" (v. 2), and is not seaworthy for the more demanding voyage on open sea to Rome. Julius must locate and book passage on another boat that will take his ship's cargo to Rome (so v. 6). However, a series of other delays and difficulties will put him well behind schedule and lead him into stormy waters ahead. For example, he "kindly" (φιλανθρώπως *philanthrōpōs*) allows Paul to visit friends in Sidon—a privilege that reflects either Paul's good relations with Rome or his social status (so 24:23) but which nevertheless causes delay in an already tight schedule.

The primary obstacle they face to a safe journey, however, is unfavorable weather: In both boats, even though sailing under the lee of Cyprus and the lee of Crete, "the winds were against us" (vv. 4, 7). The islands did nothing to protect them from severe winds, which initially forced the boat to move more slowly northward up the coastline from

763. Luke's editorial decision to include, shape, and integrate certain stories like this one suggests his familiarity with the classical literary canon, including epics such as Homer's *Odyssey* and Virgil's *Aeneid*, which tell tales of sea storms and shipwrecks. See Pervo, *Profit with Delight*; V. Robbins "By Land and By Sea," in *Perspectives on Luke-Acts*, ed. C. Talbert (Edinburgh: T. & T. Clark, 1978) 215-42; Johnson, *The Acts of the Apostles*, 450-52; Talbert, *Reading Acts*, 215-25; however, see also Porter's cautionary note in Porter, *The Paul of Acts*, 12-24.

764. Cf. C. Hemer, *The Book of Acts in the Setting of Hellenistic History*, WUNT 49 (Tübingen: Mohr Siebeck, 1989) 308-34.

765. Cf. Haenchen, *The Acts of the Apostles*, 702-3.

766. The Western version makes clear that the timing of this transfer occurred when "the governor (= Festus) decided to send him to Caesar."

Cyprus to Lycian Myra instead of westward toward the open sea and Rome. In Myra their Aegean ship is exchanged for a larger Alexandrian ship headed for Rome; however, the natural forces are still against them and so their sailing proceeds "slowly for a number of days" before they arrive at their next port "off Cnidus with difficulty." Through repeated references to the severe headwinds and the sheer difficulty of their sailing, Luke makes the impression of a slowly paced voyage. Fair Havens, where they finally find safe harbor after "a number of days" at sea, is still a long distance from Rome.

27:9-10. In context, Paul's warning should not be understood as a prophecy but as prudent advice illustrative of his exemplary persona; that is, his prediction is fair warning that reflects the sound wisdom of a seasoned sea traveler. He understands that because "much time had been lost" and because "the Fast" (= Day of Atonement) had already been observed (in late September or early October), the Mediterranean shipping lanes to Rome are closed for the winter. The careful reader should not overlook that Paul's method of counting time is Jewish rather than secular: The Day of Atonement, Israel's only national fast, is the traditional means of marking Jewish time and is used by observant Jews when dating journeys and events.

Paul's dire forewarning comes true only in part, which further suggests that the narrator does not intend his readers to take it as a prophecy. While it is true that by continuing there "will be with danger and much heavy loss," only the ship and its cargo will be lost; no person will die.

27:11-12. Paul's authority to make such a forecast presumes his good relations with Julius. But Julius, not Paul, is in charge of this voyage; therefore, it is his choice whether or not to heed this prisoner's sound advice. He seems to make a good decision based upon good reasons and majority opinion. He listens to Paul and agrees that it would be a foolish try to sail for Rome; the prospect of making Rome on schedule is no longer tenable. He disagrees with Paul, however, that they should remain in Fair Havens. In fact, Fair Havens "was not suitable for spending the winter"; his more prudent concern, then, is to find a port where his crew and cargo, and those passengers entrusted to his care, can winter safely and comfortably. Phoenix is his intended destination.[767] After consulting the ship's captain, presumably about the prospects of making Phoenix, and the ship's owner, presumably about issues of financial liability, the decision is made to set sail "on the chance that somehow they could reach Phoenix" (27:12).

767. The precise location of Phoenix is disputed. Hemer, *The Book of Acts in the Setting of Hellenistic History*, 139-41, places it close to Cape Mouros on the southern coast of Crete and less than fifty miles from Fair Havens. The implication is that the harbor at Fair Havens did not protect ships from the winter's winds, which swept in from the southeast, whereas the harbor at Phoenix, which faced "southwest and northwest," protected its ships from these strong southeast winds.

REFLECTIONS

"But the centurion paid more attention to the pilot and to the owner of the ship than to what Paul said" (27:11 NRSV). From the narrative's perspective, of course, Paul's opinion should be trusted over all others! In this case, however, Paul's expertise is due to his experience in sailing the Mediterranean Sea: There are a dozen references in Acts to voyages Paul undertakes. His opinion in this ordinary matter, then, is not due to his spiritual authority, as though God inspires insight into weather patterns in the same manner God inspires an authoritative reading of Scripture! The church often makes the mistake of thinking that one's spiritual maturity transfers to all matters of life, or, conversely, that the person who builds a successful business will be able to build strong believers as a congregational leader. The special kind of expertise that enables one to lead a congregation of believers is indicated by one's spiritual maturity and graces, even as the expertise to read weather patterns is cultivated by one's relevant experience at sea.

ACTS 27:13-26, STORMY WEATHER

COMMENTARY

The action of the second stage of Paul's sea odyssey is determined by "a violent wind, called the northeaster" that seized his ship and drove it from the coastline out into a stormy sea (27:13-15). Now adrift and at considerable risk, the ship's vigilant crew executes a sequence of emergency actions intended to ensure the ship's structural integrity and its ability to fight the wind's forceful drift toward the Libyan sandbanks, where the ship would be pounded to destruction (27:16-20). At the nadir of their physical and emotional exhaustion, when "all hope of our being saved was at last abandoned," Paul delivers a prophetic word from "the God to whom I belong and whom I worship" that assures them all of God's favor, their eventual safety, and Paul's personal destiny (27:21-26).

27:13-15. Some knowledge of the southern coastline of Crete is necessary to understand the peril facing the ship's crew when traveling from Fair Havens to Phoenix for the winter. The moderate southwest winds that pick up when clearing the harbor are ideal for sailing to the west, and they allow the boat's crew to tack toward the shoreline under the leeward protection of the island's land mass. The gentle south winds are mentioned perhaps to explain why the majority of the ship's crew is seduced into leaving Fair Havens for safer harbor. However when the ship rounds Cape Matala just eight miles down the coast, it is left exposed to much stronger wind called "the northeaster" that even experienced mariners feared; if seized by these winds nothing could prevent their ship from being pushed away from the island's natural protection and out into a dangerous and tempestuous sea.

The narrator's seafaring jargon creates a picture that those who knew the vicissitudes of the Mediterranean Sea or who had read stories of sea voyages would readily have recognized as a hopeless situation. The fatalism of Luke's report is a familiar *leitmotif* of ancient literature: Once a ship is taken hold of by gale force winds its crew can do nothing but "give way to it [= furl the ship's sails] and [be] driven" out to sea where, lives and cargo are imperiled (v. 15). The desperation of the sailors is genuine when natural forces beyond their control overwhelm their skill and experience.

27:16-20. The emergency protocol followed by the sailors is precipitated by the situation in which they find themselves. Fortunately, they are able to drift behind a wind hedge provided by a small island, Cauda (modern-day Gaudes), which buys them a brief moment to carry out necessary "measures" (= lit., "helps") in preparation for their inevitable battle with the northeaster (v. 16). They attach the "lifeboat" to the hull; they wrap heavy ropes around the ship to undergird its structural integrity; and the anchor is lowered to produce additional drag in the hope of keeping the ship from the hazardous "sandbars of Syrtis" in the Gulf of Sidra, where it would be pounded to pieces (v. 17).

After two days of safeguarding the ship from the destructive powers of the violent storm, the crew is forced on the third day to take even more extreme measures to save their lives: They throw cargo overboard (v. 18), and then as a last resort throw "the ship's tackle [σκευή *skeuē*] overboard" (v. 19; cf. Jonah 1:5).[768] Luke's use of a genitive absolute, "neither sun nor stars," and litotes (understatement), "no small tempest raged on," coupled with an imperfect main verb, "all hope of our being saved [σώζω *sōzō*] was at last abandoned [περιηρεῖτο *periēreito*]" (v. 20) graphically describes an impossible situation that is getting worse. Paul and his companions are literally in the same boat: lost at sea, without necessary gear, without sun or stars for guidance, and without a favorable weather forecast.

---

768. The meaning of σκεῦος (*skeuos*, "anchor")/*skeuē*, "tackle") is uncertain but probably refers to the ship's tacking gear. More critically, the repetition of *skeuos* recalls its use in Jonah's story when similar emergency measures are taken by the ship's crew to lighten the boat in the face of a tempestuous sea. In canonical context this intertext prepares the reader for the contrasting portraits of two prophets, Jonah and Paul, and the different ways they respond to a dire situation as representational of differing responses to God's calling (see 27:21-26).

27:21-26. Once again Paul intervenes when all seems lost. Luke's use of *sōzō* ("save") to describe the hopelessness of the situation acquires a greater depth of meaning in Acts where salvation from harm's way or from serious illness is due to God's grace, typically mediated by God's prophet.[769] In this sense, the loss of any hope of rescue experienced by those on Paul's boat is an appropriate stage for the prophet to pronounce hope for a reversal of fortune when God's saving grace triumphs over elements that provoke human despair. This is precisely what Paul now does.

His brief speech is a mixture of different elements. He chides, encourages, reports and prophesies—all to encourage his companions to hope in the plan of God. Initially, Paul chides those in charge for their decision to dismiss his warning and leave Fair Havens (v. 21), which has now proven a manifestly poor judgment. The point of Paul's comment is not to engage in a round of "I told you so." Rather, his initial comment echoes his earlier forecast (see vv. 10-12) to form an ironical reminder of his personal authority in the present situation and so to prepare the reader for his following exhortation. Indeed, given this reminder, Paul's listeners are readied to hear him and heed what he says next about their (and his) future.

And what Paul tells his dispirited audience is stunning news indeed. In a setting where everyone is sapped of hope and strength, Paul exhorts his co-travelers "to keep up your courage" (v. 22; see also vv. 25, 36). Their capacity to act courageously, which seems unrealistic under the present circumstances, is prompted by a vision that proffers a different future from the one presently anticipated. Angels populate Luke's narrative world and often serve important roles as the bearers of God's messages, which typically predict, as in this case, God's saving actions (see 5:19; 7:26; 10:3; 12:7; cf. Luke 1:26; 2:9-13; 22:43). Paul need not explain or justify his angelic visitation to his pagan auditors, since divine messengers are a shared feature of their religious mythologies.[770] For their benefit, however, he does identify this particular

angel as the agent of "the God to whom I belong and whom I worship" (v. 23).

His theological confession echoes Jonah's explanation, given to an earlier crew of pagan sailors during a voyage to another center of political and military power, of why his disobedience to God's calling has caused a sea storm that now imperils their lives: "I worship the Lord, the God of heaven, who made the sea and the dry land" (Jonah 1:9). Paul's affirmation presumes, with Jonah's, the Creator's sovereign control over the course of nature as much as over the course of salvation. Unlike Jonah, however, the angel's visitation and the promise of God's salvation is the consequence of Paul's obedience to his prophetic calling. Thus his assurances of their deliverance from death, even though the cargo is lost (27:22) and the ship is grounded (v. 26), are predicated on Paul's faithfulness to God.[771]

For the third time in Acts Paul is told in different words that Rome is the city of his destiny: "Paul, you must [δεῖ *dei*] stand before the emperor" (v. 24; see also 19:21; 23:11). Once again, God's future plans for a Roman mission are disclosed to Paul during a time of personal suffering and have the practical effect of bringing comfort to him. The difference in this case is that Paul also comforts his companions with the news of his divinely ordained future: They will be rescued at sea because of their association with a prophet-like-Jesus who has been called to mediate God's saving grace to others. In fact, this speech is framed by repetition of the "*dei* of divine necessity": Paul "must [*dei*] stand before Caesar" (v. 24) and the ship "will have to [*dei*] run aground on some island" (v. 26). The rest of Luke's story tells how this divine purpose is ultimately realized—an important point to remember when interpreting the behavior of both sailors (see vv. 30-32) and soldiers (see v. 42).

Finally, the reader should note that the repetition of Paul's exhortation to have courage is now joined by his pious expression of "faith in God that it will be exactly as I have been told" (v. 25). The significance of his personal affirmation becomes clear in that others onboard remain largely unaffected by Paul's

---

769. Witherington, *The Acts of the Apostles*, 767; cf. Tannehill, *The Acts of the Apostles*, 2:336-40.
770. Cf. Haenchen, *The Acts of the Apostles*, 705.

771. For this reason, Miles and Trompf contend that this sea story continues Paul's apologia. See G. Miles and G. Trompf, "Luke and Antiphon," *HTR* 69 (1976) 259-67.

speech and have a more realistic appraisal of their present peril. Surely Luke has shaped Paul's brief speech, then, to make the ironical point more emphatic that it is *Paul's* trust in God alone—"for *I* have faith in God"—that saves his companions, in spite of their lack of trust.

REFLECTIONS

" 'God has granted safety to all those who are sailing with [me].' So keep up your courage, men, for I have faith in God that it will be exactly as I have been told" (27:24-25 NRSV). One of the most intriguing theological elements of this story is Paul's relationship with his pagan traveling companions. While Paul's religious authority certainly extends to other believers in Luke's narrative world, here it also extends to non-believers. Their safe passage depends upon their relationship with him and their heeding his practical instructions (see 27:33-35). Paul's concern to keep them within the bounds of his authority (see 27:31) suggests that he assumes responsibility for their physical (if not for their spiritual) salvation. As such he personifies the scope of God's provident care over all people, but especially the role the church must perform as the agent of God's salvation. The faith in God's grace that prompts the church to petition God for the salvation of others (= "So keep up your courage, men") is legitimized not only by what God has promised in the Scriptures (= "it will be exactly as I have been told") but also by our confidence that God keeps precisely what God has promised (= "for I have faith in God").

ACTS 27:27-44, SURVIVING THE SHIPWRECK

COMMENTARY

In two weeks' time Paul's ship has drifted westward from Crete to Malta.[772] Suspecting that land is near, the crew takes repeated soundings of the seabed for fear that the ship might run aground in the shallows (27:27-29). When certain sailors try to escape by lifeboat, leaving the ship in the hands of inexperienced soldiers, Paul detects their subterfuge and alerts the centurion who detains the sailors and cuts the lifeboat adrift to prevent their escape (27:30-32). The motive behind Paul's action, glossed by his earlier prophecy (see 27:21-26), is not his fear that without skilled sailors the ship would otherwise be wrecked with inevitable loss of lives and cargo: According to his prophecy, the ship and cargo have been slated for destruction but lives have not. Consistent with his other actions, Paul's report to the centurion is prompted by his prophetic calling as agent of God's salvation; his concern is for the sailors whose departure from the ship (and from his presence) would almost certainly result in their death.

At daybreak on that fateful day, Paul gathers all two hundred seventy-six persons onboard his ship for breakfast, perhaps with Eucharistic overtones commensurate with Paul's prophetic vocation (see 27:35), which is necessary in any case for their emotional and physical survival (27:33-38). A strategy is quickly devised and final preparations made for a beach landing. However, their desperate plans quickly fall to ruin as the ship is caught on a sandbar and breaks apart (27:39-41). This time renegade soldiers rather than sailors threaten to subvert Paul's prophecy by killing the prisoners, but the centurion

772. A modern calculation of Luke's chronology of Paul's voyage confirms its accuracy: This type of boat set adrift in the face of a gale force northeaster would take about two weeks to travel from Crete to Malta. See J. Smith, *The Voyage and Shipwreck of St. Paul*, 4th ed., rev. W. Smith (London: Longmans & Green, 1880) 124-27.

thwarts them again and so ensures that all are brought safely to land, as Paul had predicted (27:42-44).

27:27-29. The Sea of Adria, where they now find themselves, is bounded most closely by Sicily to the north. In the dead of night and in the midst of chaotic circumstances, the experienced crew rightly realizes that "they were nearing land" (v. 27), perhaps because they could hear the crashing of breakers on Malta's Point Koura. The various "soundings" they take by using a weighted line confirm they are drifting toward shore—from "twenty fathoms [120 feet]" to "fifteen fathoms [90 feet]" (v. 28). While land is a symbol of hope, a refuge from a stormy sea, the sailors also realize with terror that without adequate tackle their defenseless ship will "run on the rocks [= cliffs]" and be pounded to destruction. Luke records their final approach with a note of fatalism: After dropping four drift anchors from the stern (rather than the bow) to keep the ship from turning broadside into the strong waves, they "prayed for day to come" (v. 29).

27:30-32. Most commentators agree that skilled sailors would know best the futility of their present situation and the best means for escaping it.[773] Under pretense of dropping additional anchors from the bow, then, some of the crew "lowered the boat [= dinghy] into the sea" to clear the inevitable wreck (v. 30). Paul alerts the centurion of their subterfuge (v. 31), and the officer orders his soldiers to cut off their only means of escape (v. 32).

Any explanation of Paul's comment to the centurion, "Unless these men stay in this ship, you cannot be saved," must emphasize his prophetic vocation, both in the terms of his earlier prophecy (see vv. 21-26) and by his role as agent of God's saving grace. In this light, Paul's worry is surely not the safety of the ship, since its destruction is a "divine necessity" (see v. 26); nor is he hopeful that the weather will improve to elevate the chance of an orderly disembarkation by lifeboat. He has also prophesied that there will be no loss of life (see v. 22), but that this outcome will be due to God's provident care and not the efforts of a skilled crew (see

v. 23). Paul's prophetic concern is for the salvation of the sailors, since safety is promised only to those who remain connected to his destiny (see v. 25). Therefore, to "stay in the ship," though doomed, is to stay within the protective hedge that surrounds the prophet of God and God's plans for him in Rome. The eschatological horizon of Paul's remark to the centurion is not an improved weather forecast but the prospect of his Roman mission, which has been confirmed a third time on board this ship (see v. 24). To escape the ship is to become detached from Paul who is the medium of God's saving grace. Paul's singular worry is for those separated from him, for this means that "you cannot be saved" by God. What appears to be their "lifeboat" is, in fact, its opposite!

The Roman centurion and the soldiers under his command set the dinghy free and remove the only means of escaping a doomed ship. Theirs is not a capricious act; rather, ironically, it is the only means of securing the sailors to the destiny of Paul who alone can broker their salvation from the stormy sea.

27:33-38. God's promise of salvation for the ship's passengers is sealed with a meal. The time is now daybreak when Paul encourages "all of them to take some food" (v. 33). His constant interventions during this crisis display his calm spirit and judicious concern for his traveling companions. By this point in the story he has proved his character under fire and has cultivated the trust of all who now listen to him and follow his instructions: "then all of them were encouraged and took food for themselves" (v. 36).

Commentators, ancient and modern, have noted several linguistic links between Paul's instructions to eat (v. 34) and the sequence, "he took bread; and giving thanks [εὐχαρίστησεν *eucharistēsen*] to God in the presence of all, he broke it and began to eat" (v. 35), and the institution of the Lord's supper.[774] Indeed, Paul urges them to eat their food, "for it will help you survive [σωτηρία *sōtēria*]" (v. 34): This is a meal for their salvation.[775] These connections should not be

---

773. Johnson, *The Acts of the Apostles*, 454, notes several parallels in ancient literature both of the untrustworthiness of sailors and of desperate attempts to flee doomed ships by lifeboat during raging sea storms.

774. Cf. Walaskay, *"And So We Came to Rome,"* 236-38.

775. Although *sōtēria* in this setting denotes "survival" and is rightly translated as such by NIV/NRSV, Luke does not sharply distinguish between physical (= healing/survival) and spiritual (= forgiveness) forms of being saved, salvation in its various forms is always and in every case the work of God.

taken literally since Paul would not have celebrated the Eucharist with pagans (cf. 1 Cor 11:17-26) and are in any case the actions of a pious Jew. Yet, almost certainly Luke shapes this poignant moment as typological of the "last supper" in which God's sustaining grace is dispensed to communicants by the authority of God's appointed servant. In this sense, the intent of this respite is once again to illustrate Paul's spiritual authority among pagans (in addition to Luke and Aristarchus), not only because of his competent leadership in a crisis but also because he is the source of salvation for those who follow his instruction. As Johnson notes, the importance of Paul's gesture to distribute the blessed food "in the presence of all" (v. 35) is to "present an example for them, one which in fact they imitate," for those who imitate Paul are saved (cf. 20:31-35; 1 Cor 4:16; 11:1; Phil 3:17; 4:9; 1 Thess 1:6; 2 Thess 3:7-9; 2 Tim 1:13).[776]

Having eaten this meal for their salvation, the "two hundred and seventy-six persons in the ship" (v. 37) rid themselves of an extra weight by "throwing the wheat into the sea" (v. 38), thus adding to the buoyancy of the ship and allowing the waves to carry it as close to the shoreline as possible. In all likelihood, this final emergency measure is only now possible because the storm's violence has subsided enough to allow the bottom hatches to be opened and the grain shoots to be operative. These images, narrated and implied, suggest the necessary collaboration between people and God whose aim is to save them.

27:39-41. In this same sense, a prudent strategy is devised to beach the ship safely (v. 39) and measures are taken to make shore: "they cast off the anchors [on either side of the stern] . . . loosened the ropes that tied the steering-oars [= rudder] . . . then hoisting the foresail to the wind, they made for the beach" (v. 40). The purpose of this combination of mariner maneuvers is to exploit their location with respect to visible land and the natural force of the wind, while at the same time regaining maximum "hand-control" of the ship's direction. Alas, they do not make shore and run aground on a patch of "reef"—literally, "a place of two seas" or a sandbar that splits the sea into two breakers. Held fast by gravity, the ship and its crew are defenseless against the pounding sea and the stern breaks apart—but without loss of life. The practical problem remaining is how to reach land without a lifeboat (see v. 32).

27:42-44. There also remains a military problem, however remote: The prisoners would need to be secured, since their escape could exact severe penalties on soldiers responsible for their custody (see 12:19; 16:27). The escort's plan is to kill the prisoners (v. 42); however, this plan is flawed in two important ways. First, it is based upon the implausible premise that any passenger could "swim away and escape" through rough seas and on foreign land, which is in any case a self-contained island. Second, as with the sailors' earlier plot to flee ship by its lifeboat, a plan to kill prisoners would subvert God's plan to save all on board the ship. Remarkably, it is not Paul who intervenes in this case to save the soldiers from their actions but Julius, who "wishing to save [διασώζω diasōzō] Paul" frustrates the inopportune plans of his soldiers (27:43). Whatever his motive, Julius acts as a pagan agent of divine purpose by whom all those traveling with Paul are saved (see 27:22-26).[777] This then is the final twist of a well-told story narrated with dramatic irony: Julius's action results in the survival of everyone, who are all "brought safely to land" (27:44) not because he is able to stop his men from carrying out their plan but because by protecting Paul he ensures the fulfillment of his prophecy.

---

776. Johnson, *The Acts of the Apostles*, 455.

777. On the role of non-believers in realizing God's redemptive program, see Tannehill, *The Acts of the Apostles*, 2:340.

REFLECTIONS

"But the centurion, wishing to save Paul, kept them from carrying out their plan" (27:43 NRSV). One feature of Luke's conception of God's sovereignty that is reflected in this story is the use of different kinds of agents to broker God's promised salvation.

Luke's world is populated by prophets and angels who follow God's instructions in delivering God's word, which when followed by others realize promised blessings. What is more surprising, perhaps, is that God also uses the unsuspecting as agents of God's salvation. The Roman centurion, Julius, is a case in point. First in cutting the dinghy free (27:32) and then in keeping his soldiers from executing their prisoners, Julius kept all onboard ship within the hedge of Paul's protection and allows God's promise of their safety to be fulfilled. Julius is prompted to take these actions not out of some confidence in God's promise but because of his friendship with Paul and his concern for Paul's safety (see 27:3). The practical lesson of his example is that sometimes non-believers unwittingly collaborate with God in working out God's salvation for the sake of believers for whom they care. Our friendship with non-believers cultivates personal loyalties that sometimes prompt decisions and actions that God can use as the means to a redemptive end.

ACTS 28:1-16, "AND SO WE CAME TO ROME"

COMMENTARY

Paul and his co-travelers have washed ashore on the island of Melita (= Malta), where they will spend the winter. They arrive cold and wet from the sea in need of immediate warmth and long-term restoration, for they are weary survivors of a traumatic experience. Surviving a stormy sea and shipwreck, Paul also shrugs off a viper's bite (28:3-5) in further demonstration that God is protecting him for Rome (28:6; see 27:24). Even the island's "natives" recognize Paul as God's man (28:1-6) and the inspired medium of divine powers dispensed for both great and small (28:7-10). Their continuing hospitality toward Paul and the others (28:2, 7, 10) indicates a people who by nature are receptive to the truth of God's Word (28:8-9; see also 17:11). Ironically, Luke's positive judgment of a superstitious and primitive people (28:6) not only underscores the universalism of God's reign but exposes as well the obduracy of the gospel's more learned and sophisticated opponents.

Paul's journey to Rome resumes "after three months" on Malta. The details of his itinerary follow the famous Appian Way; the favorable wind conditions (28:11-13) combine with the graciousness of other believers on land in bringing Paul to Rome under God's provident care (28:14-16).

28:1-2. When the survivors reach the shore on bits and pieces of their wrecked ship, they learn that they have landed safely on the small island of Malta, about sixty miles south of Sicily. Because the island is a Roman colony and its harbor a strategic stop on shipping lanes leading to Rome, the Maltese were not unfamiliar with the language and customs of their unexpected visitors from Palestine and Rome.[778] Luke, however, calls their hosts "natives" (βάρβαροι *barbaroi*)—that is, they were religious barbarians who held to superstitions about God—the "Gentiles" referred to in the Pauline letters who do not know the law and have only their conscience to guide them (cf. Rom 2:12-16).[779] His effective use of litotes underlines their moral character in implicit contrast to their theological ignorance: their hospitable response is an "unusual kindness" (28:2; lit., "no usual kindness").

778. Cf. Witherington, *The Acts of the Apostles*, 775-76.

779. Other commentators contend that the *barbaroi* refer to uneducated islanders who could speak only in their "native" Punic language. See, e.g., Haenchen, *The Acts of the Apostles*, 713; Barrett, *A Critical and Exegetical Commentary on the Acts of the Apostles*, 2:1220-21; Dunn, *The Acts of the Apostles*, 346. This connotation, however, seems unlikely in Acts since communication between the islanders and survivors is indicated. Moreover, archaeological evidence supports the impression of a bilingual culture on first-century Malta. The only barbarism indicated by Luke's story is theological: The Maltese are much too quick to leap from the mistaken conclusion that Paul is an immoral man (28:4) to another that he is an "immortal man" (28:6).

Hospitality without discrimination is among the most highly regarded virtues of the ancient world. Initially the kindness of the islanders takes the form of building a bonfire on the beach to dry out and warm up all their stranded guests: "they kindled a fire and welcomed all of us around it." In the narrative world of Acts, hospitality is vested with theological importance. Not only does a people's benefaction toward others symbolize their "receptivity to God's visitation" (see 10:24; 15:4; 16:11-15; 20:6; 21:4);[780] it also evinces the good character necessary to recognize the truth of God's word when they see it demonstrated or hear it proclaimed. Although nowhere does Luke write that Paul proclaimed the word of God during his three-month stay in Malta, the interpreter easily fills this narrative gap in light of inferences drawn from other stories of Paul in Acts—or does the reader really believe that the Paul of Acts would remain silent about the risen Messiah? The "honors" his hospitable hosts give him at his departure confirm his importance to them (28:10).

28:3-6. As Paul pitches in to help build the fire, a poisonous viper is chased from its home by the heat and bites his hand. The initial interpretation of the natives regarding Paul, whom they now know only as a Roman prisoner and lucky survivor, reflects the logic of the *barbaroi*'s superstitious worldview: He must be guilty of the crime he has committed after all. The reference to "justice" (ἡ Δίκη *hē Dikē*) does not denote the philosophical notion of fair play but rather an avenging "Justice" of ancient mythology that personifies those cosmic fates that dispense a person's ultimate reward or punishment for deeds done. Evidently, surviving the shipwreck is an insufficient sign of Paul's innocence; Lady Justice who has withheld her final verdict until now "has not allowed him to live" (v. 4).

Given this judgment, Paul does the unexpected: "He, however, shook off the creature into the fire and suffered no harm" (v. 5). This dramatic incident recalls the Gospel text in which the risen Jesus promises miraculous "signs" that would confirm the truth of the proclaimed gospel (Mark 16:20), among them, "they will pick up snakes in their hands" without harm (Mark 16:18;

cf. Luke 10:18-19). In this new setting, the truth about Paul is disclosed to them: When he is unharmed by the viper's poison, the *barbaroi* recognize it as a "sign" that "he was a god" (v. 6; also see 14:8-13). While their primitive theology does not allow them to fully comprehend what they have seen, their verdict about Paul invites the Christian reader to draw the obvious conclusion: Paul is indeed a divinely inspired man of God's own choosing and a carrier of God's word to the whole creation (cf. Mark 16:15) whom God is safeguarding for the ministry that awaits him in Rome.

28:7-10. Luke includes a snapshot of Paul's three-day visit at the estate of Publius, "the leading man of the island" (v. 7). Paul's relations with city officials is an important dimension of his mission; there is a sense in which the response of civic leaders to Paul helps to determine the response of an entire city to his prophetic ministry. Here Publius's benefaction toward Paul and his companions under difficult circumstances (v. 7) commends the entire region under his care to Paul's healing power (vv. 8-9). This healing ministry, here expressed in combination with prayer and the laying on of hands (v. 8),[781] is an important feature of Paul's prophetic ministry in Acts (see 14:8-10; 19:11-12; 20:9-10) and continues what the Lord had begun in demonstration of the triumph of God's reign (cf. Luke 4:38-44). For this reason, beginning with Jesus (cf. Luke 7:20-23) and continuing in the ministry of his successors before Paul (see 3:12-16; 6:7-8; 9:36-42), the wonders of healing ministry typically complement the gospel proclamation of God's fulfilled promises (see 14:9; 19:20; 20:11).

The vigorous response of the islanders to Paul's healing of Publius's father, who had been "seized" by a fever (v. 9; cf. Mark 1:29-34 and par.), combines with their earlier recognition of him as vested with divine authority (see v. 6) and explains why they "bestowed many honors on us . . . and put on board all the provisions we needed" (v. 10). Such a response may simply be a token

---

780. Johnson, *The Acts of the Apostles*, 461.

781. Laying hands on the sick is a practice unknown in the OT and rabbinic literature; it may well have originated in the Messiah's mission as symbolic of his divine authority (see Luke 4:40). The striking juxtaposition of a medical phrase, "sick in bed with fever and dysentery," with a gesture that signifies spiritual authority indicates that the "healing is accomplished not by medical means but by prayer and laying on of hands." Haenchen, *The Acts of the Apostles*, 714.

gesture for all that Paul had done for the Maltese. However, the giving of possessions to the prophet is symbolic of the presence of divine grace (see 4:32-35); and we may infer from this that Paul's unexpected adventure in Malta had resulted in the salvation of these "natives" who now live together as a community of goods under the aegis of the Holy Spirit.

28:11-13. With characteristic detail, Luke charts the course from Malta to Puteoli in Italy with ports of call at Sicilian Syracuse and Rhegium on the toe of Italy in between; in Puteoli they are able to pick up the Appian Way to take into Rome. The curious addition that the Alexandrian ship Julius hired to take his contingent to Italy had "the Twin Brothers as its figurehead" may serve as an ironic recollection of the full sweep of Paul's sea odyssey. The twins Castor and Pollux, "the sons of Zeus," were astral deities venerated as saviors from stormy seas. Of course, the readers of Acts understand that they are not responsible for Paul's safety; rather, it is "the God to whom I belong and whom I worship" (27:23) who has safeguarded him and his traveling entourage for their appointed ministry to "bring salvation to the end of the earth" (see 13:47; 1:8).

28:14-16. Paul is not the founder of the Roman church; other evangelists and believers had already cultivated this spiritual ground in preparation for his mission (cf. Rom 15:18-29).[782] Similar to the narrative of Paul's pilgrimage to Jerusalem when he visited congregations founded by other evangelists along the way (see 21:1-17), he is greeted by believers from "as far as the Forum of Appius [= 40 miles from Rome] and Three Taverns [= 30 miles from Rome]" (v. 15) who "invited [Paul] to stay with them for seven days" (v. 14) and then accompanied him into the city (v. 16). This evocative image of a church's festive welcome depicts Paul as an important person

and is evocative of Jesus' entrance into the city of his destiny on Palm Sunday. The stage is set for an important ministry in this leading city of Paul's world.

Luke's spotlight again shines exclusively on Paul. The reader presumes, however, that Julius and his soldiers, as well as the ship's other prisoners, accommodated Paul's desire to spend time with believers in the Roman precinct before moving into his rented flat in Rome to await his appointment with the emperor. Perhaps this explains why the Paul of Acts arrives in Rome *twice*, the first time with the terse sentence, "And so we came to Rome [εἰς τὴν Ῥώμην *eis tēn Rhōmēn*]" (v. 14*b*), and again when "we came into Rome [εἰς Ῥώμη *eis Rōmē*]" (v. 16*a*). The reference to "the soldier who was guarding him" (v. 16*b*) may indicate that new arrangements had been made by Julius upon first arriving in Rome (v. 14*b*), separating Paul from his military escort and the other prisoners while granting him considerable freedom to meet with other believers for pastoral ministry (v. 15), before he took permanent residence in Rome (v. 16*a*; see also v. 30). No doubt these official allowances granted Paul reflect on his political innocence and good character; and yet the lack of attention given him in Rome—only a single ordinary soldier now watches over him—may be preparing the reader for the surprising news that Paul is a relative unknown in Rome (see v. 21).

Luke's passing comment that when Paul met with the others he "thanked God and took courage [θάρσος *tharsos*]" (v. 15) explains why Luke's plotline is so fixed upon Paul: He is an exemplar of the man of God whose ministry within a community of faith is directed toward God in thankful worship and toward others, from whom he now draws courage for the important mission that awaits him. The verbal form of *tharsos* was earlier used in the Lord's visionary exhortation for Paul to "keep up your courage [θαρσέω *tharseō*] for you must witness also in Rome" (see 23:11). The courage necessary for prophetic ministry is not a virtue that one cultivates by self-discipline or by self-confidence but by submission to the Lord.

---

782. Many scholars have attempted to reconstruct the origins of Christianity in Rome. For recent efforts, see K. Donfried, ed. *The Romans Debate* (Minneapolis: Augsbury, 1977; rev. ed. London: T & T Clark, 1991). Luke refers to Priscilla and Aquila, Jewish believers who are forced from Rome and settle in Corinth where they meet and work with Paul (Acts 18). This may well indicate the Jewish origins of Roman Christianity and give insight into the ambivalent responses of Jewish leaders to Paul's presence in Rome (see 28:17-28).

REFLECTIONS

"After this happened, the rest of the people on the island who had diseases also came and were cured" (28:9 NRSV). The conjunction of vivid images of hospitality and healing in this passage with the characterization of the Maltese as *barbaroi* underscores an important element of Luke's critique of religious culture: Those most open to God's word are often those without a sophisticated theology. While their theological illiteracy prevents them from precisely assessing the prophet's predicament and power (28:4-6), the Maltese finally do recognize his innocence and the authority given him by God. Their hospitality toward Paul (28:2, 7, 10) indicates that even *barbaroi* can be the sort of persons who are responsive to God's healing power and saving word. The church makes a mistake by presuming that the least, last, and lost among us do not have the spiritual capacity to detect the presence of God in the world. Indeed, they often are the most willing to position themselves before God's word in order to be found by God's grace.

ACTS 28:17-28, PAUL'S MISSION IN ROME

COMMENTARY

The Paul of Acts at long last has reached Rome, the city of his destiny. That his story concludes in this city and not in Jerusalem supplies an important geographical element in Luke's theological framework. Within the symbolic universe of Luke's Jewish readers, Rome represents "the end of the earth," the most distant point on the circumference of a sacred compass whose epicenter is Jerusalem (see 2:5-11; cf. *Ps. Sol. 8:16*).[783] The Lord's orienting prophecy that the church's mission would progress from the holy city to the "end of the earth" is now fulfilled through Paul's mission in Rome (see 1:8; 13:47; cf. Isa 49:6). This concluding episode, then, is a "framing device" that brings closure to a narrative whose geographical framework is provided by this prophecy.[784]

Although his legal appeal to the emperor provides the circumstance of Paul's visit (see 25:12), he is in Rome to preach the word of God. The present passage should be read from this angle of vision and as a narrative piece within the whole of Acts (see 1:8; 9:15; 13:47; 19:21; 23:11; 27:24). In fact, only passing mention of Paul's appeal to Caesar is made (28:19*a*); he is not here as a citizen of Rome with legal problems to settle but as a prophet-like-Jesus with a gospel to proclaim (cf. 28:20, 23). The parallelism of plotline and portraiture of Paul's final mission in Rome and his first mission at Pisidian Antioch (see 13:13-47) underscores the consistency of his urban mission, according to which Paul meets first with the Jews of Rome (28:17-20). As a prisoner, he no longer has freedom of movement and cannot go to a Roman synagogue for worship and instruction as was his custom, so he invites the "local leaders of the Jews" to his flat for introductions—in reality a rehearsal of his previous apologia with the added assurance that he is in Rome as a friend of Israel (see 28:19). This initial meeting ends on a hopeful note with the promise of a continuing conversation (28:21-22). True to the pattern of his interaction with other Jewish audiences, Paul is invited to address this contingent of Roman Jews in increased numbers for a second time (see 13:42-44). The subject matter of this second speech shifts attention from a personal defense of his prophetic vocation to a proclamation of the word of God (28:23). The response to his missionary message is as expected in context of Acts: Some believe, others do not. As usual there is conflict within Israel over the

---

783. From a non-Jewish perspective, Rome is at the *center* of the earth, not on its margins, from which all roads radiate out. See Alexander, "Reading Luke-Acts From Back to Front," 426-27.

784. Cf. Parsons, *The Departure of Jesus in Luke-Acts,* 156-59.

kerygmatic claim that Jesus is God's Messiah (28:24-25; see also 2:12-13; 4:1-4; 5:12-17; 6:8-15; 9:21-25; 13:42-47; 14:1-2; 15:4-29; 17:1-15; 18:12-17; 19:8-10; 21:17–26:29; cf. Luke 2:34). But this conflict agrees with biblical prophecy, which foretells national Israel's obduracy to the gospel (28:26-27; see also 13:46). By contrast, God-fearing Gentiles "will listen" to the word of the Lord (28:28; see also 13:47).

28:17-20. Paul finds a flourishing Jewish community in Rome, founded long before during the first days of the Republic. A dozen or more Roman synagogues were spiritual homes to many thousands of Jews living in various neighborhoods throughout the city.[785] The reader should assume that Luke's reference to "the local leaders of the Jews," then, refers to an alliance of important leaders from these synagogues who kept in close contact with each other and with other Jewish leaders across the empire (see v. 21). Their solidarity was especially important when securing basic rights assured by the emperor in the face of widespread antisemitic activities. Their dedication to this supervisory role is indicated by the prompt response to Paul's request for a meeting.

Paul's addresses his audience as "brothers" (ἄνδρες ἀδελφοί *andres adelphoi*), a formula used throughout Acts to introduce speeches shaped for Jewish audiences who at least on paper share a significant common ground of beliefs and values (see 2:29; 3:17; 7:2; 13:26, 38; 22:1; 23:1, 6). What he says to them rehearses what has already been said during his trials and therefore functions as a summary of the previous narrative:

(1) "I [have] done nothing against our people [λαός *laos* = Israel; see 2:47] or the customs [ἔθοι *ethoi*] of our ancestors" (28:17*a*; see 21:21, 28; 22:3; 23:6; 24:12-16; 25:8; 26:4-8). Even though Mosaic *ethoi* cannot save (see 15:1; cf. 13:38-39), their performance helps to shape the public identity of a people belonging to God. In this sense, Paul again asserts that the ethos of the church is Jewish.

(2) "Yet I was arrested in Jerusalem and handed over to the Romans . . . [who having] examined me . . . wanted to release me" (28:17*b*-18*a*; see 21:33; 24:2-21; 25:6-12;

26:2-29). Paul explains that he does not wear "this chain" because of criminal behavior worthy of the death penalty (so 28:18*b*; see 22:24; 23:28; 25:18; 26:31-32), and that the legitimacy of this verdict was proved by careful examination (cf. 24:8).

(3) "When the Jews objected . . . I had no charge to bring against my nation [ἔθνος *ethnos*]) (v. 19; see also 22:3; 23:6; 24:14; 26:4-5). Paul roundly and routinely denies any antipathy toward Israel, always locating himself within its faith tradition and religious culture. Paul's summary implicitly contrasts Rome's legal verdict of innocence (v. 18) and the Jewish objection that rejects Paul's messianic reading of Scripture for theological reasons. In any case, he reminds his audience, probably for rhetorical effect in an anti-Semitic cultural setting, that he has come to Rome as a Jewish prisoner rather than as a prosecutor opposed to Jewish interests. His personal ethos is shaped out of deep loyalty to his Jewish *ethnos*.

(4) "It is for the sake of the hope of Israel that I am bound with this chain" (v. 20; see also 23:6; 24:15; 26:6-7). Paul's highly evocative phrase, "the hope of Israel," is glossed by its earlier uses in Acts as a symbol of God's promise of Israel's restoration now fulfilled by Messiah Jesus, the Pentecost of God's Spirit, and the successes of the church's Jewish mission and finally of Paul's mission to bring the gospel's light to the nations. Paul's constant apologia is that his status as a Roman prisoner is due to his obedience to a prophetic vocation that is thoroughly Jewish in character.

28:21-22. With characteristic irony, the narrator shapes the Jewish response to Paul's apologia to agree with his subtext: The Jewish problem is not with the prophetic messenger but with his message about Jesus. The lack of hostility toward Paul, which sharply contrasts with the Jerusalem Jews, is quite beside Luke's point and is historically suspect in any case.[786] The claim that Roman Jewry has "no letters from Judea" about Paul, nor intends the inception of any legal proceeding against him in Rome (v. 21), is due to their ignorance of "this sect [αἵρεσις *hairesis*] we know that everywhere . . . is spoken against" (v. 22). Luke's repetition of *hairesis* recalls the earlier confusion during Paul's Roman trial in Caesarea over whether he leads a Jewish

---

785. Cf. Fitzmyer, *The Acts of the Apostles*, 792.

"party" or a heretical movement (see 24:5, 14; 26:5). When combined with an apparent willingness to listen to Paul's views— "we would like to hear from you what you think"—the impression is that the leaders are simply confused about this messianic movement and desire clarity in the matter. Curiously, they do not ask Paul to clarify the relations between the believers already found in and around Rome (see vv. 15-16) and the Jews represented by these leaders; this question would seem reasonable given that Paul's arrival in Rome follows Claudius's expulsion of messianic Jews—such as Aquila and Priscilla—from the city (see 18:1-2). Perhaps they are merely interested in hearing from Paul a more conciliatory version of this controversial sect. Consistent with his pattern of prophetic ministry,[787] Luke depicts this first visit as responding to the ignorance of Jews who need yet another opportunity to "hear from you what you think."

28:23. The purpose of the prophet's second visitation of Jews in a particular place is to repeat God's offer of salvation so that they are without excuse (see 13:42-44; 7:35). The care with which Paul engages in this prophetic task is indicated by references to time: "they set a day to meet with him," and after assembling in Paul's flat, he examines the evidence "from morning until evening." The imperfect tense of ἐξετίθετο (*exetitheto*, "explain"), found only here in the NT, is inceptive and indicates that Paul began to teach in the morning and continued teaching throughout the day.

The topics of Paul's testimony are the two constants of persuasive gospel preaching from the beginning of Jesus' ministry (Luke 4:43; Acts 1:3) to the conclusion of Paul's: the "kingdom of God" (see 28:31; cf. Luke 9:2; 10:9-11), which God promises to restore to Israel (see 1:6); and Messiah Jesus, through whom God's promise of a restored Israel is realized in full.[788] The mention of this core promise and its fulfillment summarizes Paul's entire gospel; it also frames his biblical hermeneutic according to which "both the law and the prophets" testify to the gospel's truth

(see 24:14-15; 26:22-23; cf. Luke 24:25-27, 44-46). In bringing this testimony to Rome, then, Paul realizes the Lord's commitment to him envisaged in Jerusalem (see 23:11) and fulfills Jesus' prophecy to his apostolic successors that witness to him would be made at the "end of the earth" (see 1:8).

28:24-25a. Luke uses a well-known formula of conflict to describe the division within Israel provoked by his interpretation of Scripture: "some were convinced [πείθω *peithō*] by what he had said, while others refused to believe" (28:24; see 13:42-47; 17:1-5; 18:4; 19:8-10; cf. 26:28). Luke uses *peithō* elsewhere in missionary settings as a synonym for repentance (see 13:43; 17:4; 18:4); there are some who are "convinced" by Paul's interpretation of "the law of Moses and the prophets" about Jesus and repent, while still others "refuse to believe" (see 19:8-9; 23:6-9).[789] What happens in Paul's lodgings is entirely consistent with what has happened in every place the gospel has been proclaimed since the beginning of Jesus' story: The gospel of God is presented first to the Jews with clarity and conviction but with mixed results. Yet we should not suppose that Paul's mission to the Jews of Rome is a complete failure, or that the Jewish rejection of the gospel explains his success among Gentiles. The plain meaning of this text is that some Jews are convinced by Paul and become believers; and their response to his ministry in Rome is hardly hostile in any case.

28:25b-27. Paul's parting shot—a citation from Isaiah's prophecy (Isa 6:9-10 LXX)—has been understood by many modern interpreters as a sign of resignation with which Paul washes his hands of a future mission to Israel. However, while the Paul of the letters anticipated a national turning to the Messiah (cf. Rom 11:26) and is clearly frustrated when this does not immediately occur (cf. Rom 9:1-5), the Lukan Paul's appeal to Isaiah is explanatory of what he has experienced firsthand now and before (see 13:44-47; 18:5-7): Not every Jew who hears the gospel believes its central claim that the risen Jesus is the promised Messiah. The tragic reality, foretold at the Lord's birth, is that the word of God

786. Cf. Barrett, *A Critical and Exegetical Commentary on the Acts of the Apostles*, 2:1241-42.

787. See Johnson, *The Acts of the Apostles*, 12-14, 473-74.

788. Cf. Barrett, *A Critical and Exegetical Commentary on the Acts of the Apostles*, 2:1243.

789. Cf. Jervell, *Die Apostelgeschichte*, 625-27, 630; Witherington, *The Acts of the Apostles*, 801-2; R. Bradley, *Luke-Acts and the Jews*, SBLMS 33 (Atlanta: Scholar's Press, 1987) 74-75.

about him will divide Israel into a responsive remnant for salvation and an obdurate opposition for spiritual exile (cf. Luke 2:34). The plotline of the biblical Gospels and Acts follows the fulfillment of this prophecy.[790]

In its original setting, Isaiah's prophecy of Israel's spiritual dullness (Isa 6:9-10) is featured in his commissioning as a prophet of God (cf. Isa 6:6-8). While the prophet of God is called to "go and say to this people [= Israel]" (28:26), his expectation should be of Israel's obduracy rather than of a nation's renewal: "they will listen, but never understand/look, but never perceive." Significantly, the LXX version of the prophecy that Luke uses renders the verbs describing Israel's dullness as aorist indicatives rather than as the imperatives found in the Hebrew text: "For this people's mind has grown dull [rather than "Make the mind of this people dull"] . . . ears are hard of hearing [rather than "stop their ears"] . . . close their eyes [rather than "shut their eyes"]." The rhetorical effect of this change of verbal mood is to diagnose Israel's spiritual sickness as the result of its deliberate decision to reject God's word—rather than of God's preordination or the prophet's provocation of spiritual failure. Thus the prospect of God's promised restoration of the entire nation— "and I would heal them" (28:27)—is subverted by unrepentant Jews who "refuse to believe" God's saving word (see 3:19-23).

Paul's adaptation of Isaiah's prophecy to this new missionary setting follows the lead of the Gospels (cf. Matt 13:14-15//Mark 4:12//Luke 8:10//John 12:39-40) where Jesus appeals to this prophecy to explain why some in Israel fail to understand his teaching. The Gospels give this prophecy prominent position, as Acts does here, because in the hands of Christian interpreters Isaiah provides a useful apologia to a vexing question: Why does the Christian gospel fail to convince the majority of religious Jews? The force of this question is felt even more keenly in Acts, since its narrative of the church's mission begins amidst great optimism in Jerusalem with mass conversions of devout Jews. Although James can still report to Paul that "many thousands" of Jews continue to convert to the Lord in Palestine (see 21:20), the

fruit of Paul's mission to the Jews is considerably less bountiful. In response to this concern, Luke delays his use of Isaiah's prophecy to give its message greater import as his story's conclusion. The word of God convincingly presented by the prophet does not deafen, blind, or dull Israel's reception of God's promises; those Jews who "refuse to believe" have no one to blame but themselves (cf. Rom 11:7-8).[791] Indeed, the subtext of Paul's use of the prophecy is that Israel's ambivalence toward Jesus is a piece of God's scripted salvation: On this side of the Messiah's return to earth for creation's restoration (see 3:20-21; 1:10-11), Israel will remain divided over Jesus (see 3:22-23).

The same can be said of all the nations, of course; however, God's salvation belongs first of all to a faithful Israel. For this reason Jewish rejection is considered a more serious theological crisis than the obduracy of Gentiles: While all believers from every nation share God's salvation and Spirit equally (see 10:34-35; 11:18; 15:7-11), the salvation of the nations is predicated on the restoration of repentant Israel (see 3:19-26).[792] A prophetic calculus that presumes Gentiles "will listen" because repentant Jews do so first explains why Luke attaches such importance to Paul's loyalty to his Jewish heritage (see 28:17-20) and also to the Jews who were "convinced" by Paul's gospel (see 28:23-24). The more positive response of Jews to Jesus meets the necessary precondition for his mission to go forward in Rome not only to those Gentiles who "will listen" (see 28:28) but also to "all who came to him" (28:30).

In this regard, we should give special note to the formula Paul uses to introduce the prophetic citation: "The Holy Spirit was right in saying to your ancestors through the prophet Isaiah" (28:25b). Luke uses the reference to the Holy Spirit to qualify the authority of the written word: When properly interpreted by an inspired prophet (such as Peter or Paul), the sacred text becomes the authorized conduit by which the living *vox Dei* (voice of God) is heard, thereby establishing the norm

---

790. Cf. D. Tiede, *Prophecy and History in Luke-Acts* (Philadelphia: Fortress, 1980).

791. Cf. Johnson, *The Acts of the Apostles*, 476.

792. For Isaiah's nationalistic interest in Israel's salvation as integral to a universal hope in the salvation of the nations, see D. van Winkle, "The Relationship of the Nations to Yahweh and to Israel in Isaiah xl-lv," *VT* 35 (1985) 446-58. Van Winkle asserts that the restoration of God's rule in Israel is the eschatological signal to all the nations of earth that blessings promised them have drawn nigh and are received from God through Israel. I suspect something like this belief is a theological subtext of Paul's citation of Isaiah in this setting.

for contemporary auditors in a particular setting (see 1:16; 4:25). In a similar fashion, Paul's shift from "our people or the customs of our ancestors" (28:17) to "your ancestors" is a rhetorical device that allows him to focus the inspired meaning of the cited text on those Jews who have rejected his presentation of the gospel. That is, the Holy Spirit speaks through the biblical text a word from the living God for those among Paul's departing guests who "refuse to believe."

For this reason, Paul's retort does not argue for a more permanent or inclusive "Jewish rejection of the gospel." When Paul responds twice before to the obduracy of Jewish opponents (see 13:46-47; 18:5-6), his manifest intent is not to forgo future missionary efforts among the Jews in other places. This is true to the end of his story, where he meets and presents the gospel first to Roman Jews before inviting other interested guests to his Bible study. Dunn is therefore correct in arguing that the Paul of Acts "would have understood Isaiah as indicating the course (and frustrations) of Paul's mission to his own and Isaiah's people, not as calling on him to end it in dismissive denunciation."[793] In fact, although the prophet's words are harsh, there is no evidence of personal animosity between Paul and his departing guests. At most this text provides a realistic interpretation of why an inspired teacher of Israel should expect failure when attempting to convince the entire congregation of Israel about Jesus. To say more than this or to impute other motives to Paul's use of Isaiah is to claim more than the text allows.

28:28. What is the connection between the mixed response of the Jews to Paul's message, Isaiah's prophecy of unrepentant Israel's obduracy, and Paul's prophecy that Gentiles "will listen" to him? This is the third time in Acts where the topics of Jewish rejection and Gentile acceptance of the gospel are combined (see 13:46-47; 18:5-6). Such Lukan triads are narrative constructions that assure the reader of the lasting importance of these themes; but the precise logic that combines them is not at all certain. Many commentators think that Luke shapes this final scene in light of a growing realization that the church's mission to the Jews in the Diaspora had failed and the main focus of its ministry should now be

directed toward non-Jews. Luke's narrative, however, does not evince such a motive. At face value, Paul's statement that salvation "has been sent to the Gentiles" and his prediction that Gentiles "will listen" assert two additional facts that are well established by the narrative from the conversion of Cornelius forward. Even as Acts makes clear that not every Jew is unresponsive to Paul, it is equally clear that not every Gentile will listen to him. He has in fact found the most responsive Gentiles in Jewish synagogues: Those who listen most keenly to the word of God are those who have left behind the idolatries of pagan religion in exchange for those sacred places where a Jewish ethos is cultivated by the teaching of Moses (see 15:20-21). The purpose of combining the themes of Jewish rejection and Gentile acceptance in Acts is to underwrite this central irony in the plan of God's salvation: *Even when devout Jews refuse to believe the word of God persuasively presented, Gentiles whose spiritual sensibility is forged in their midst are more apt to listen.*

Finally, then, the correspondence between the themes of this present passage and those that have shaped the past ministry of Paul in Acts orients the reader toward a similar future. The ending of Acts portrays an unchanged and incorrigible Paul who welcomes all to his home in Rome to hear his "bold and unhindered" proclamation of the very same gospel he has always preached (see 28:30-31). Perhaps the point that should linger on in the reader's mind is not about Paul, or Jewish rejection, or that Gentiles will listen to the gospel, but rather about the assurance of this prophet-like-Jesus: Even though the proclamation of the word of God will provoke different responses in those who hear it, the inherent trustworthiness of its claims determines the triumphant progress of God's salvation to the end of time. Others will take this gospel up and preach it as boldly as Paul; some will listen while others will refuse its claims. This reality was true in the past of the church and so it will be true in the church's future, until the Lord comes back to earth in the same way he departed to inaugurate the season of universal restoration.[794]

793. Dunn, *The Acts of the Apostles*, 355.

794. The Western version adds an additional verse that repeats the sentiment of 28:25: "When he had said this, the Jews went out debating vigorously among themselves" (28:29). The rhetorical effects of this addition are to enclose 28:26-28 more clearly as Paul's commentary on the conflict his gospel has provoked within Israel and to clearly demarcate 28:30-31 as the ending of Acts.

REFLECTIONS

"This salvation of God has been sent to the Gentiles; they will listen" (28:28 NRSV). Paul's final declaration in Acts continues to haunt the church. Interpreters ancient and modern have inferred an antisemitic motive and supersessionist theology from it: Israel's rejection of the gospel in Rome is final and justifies Paul's Gentile mission and explains its success. One of the interpretive keys of this commentary is to challenge this reading of Acts.

Frankly, Luke offers his readers little to explain the mixed results of Paul's mission to the Jews or why the church has become by his day a Gentile institution. Clearly this result does not reflect either God's longing or Paul's effort. The Paul of Acts routinely presents himself as Jewish and conforms his religious practices to Israel's. He can claim with integrity at the end of the day to seek only "the hope of Israel" (28:20). His pattern also remains constant, whether free or captive: He meets with religious Jews in Rome for worship and instruction, and so they are the first to hear his testimony from their Scriptures that God's kingdom has visited them in Jesus, their promised Messiah. Why some Jews take Paul's testimony to heart while most others do not remains a mystery to those of us who believe. At the very least, the interpreter of Acts must identify with Paul's final struggle to ground his vocation in the traditions of Israel while trying to understand why all of Israel did not happily embrace his good news. This same struggle was central to Jesus' messianic career.

Nonetheless, Acts stands as an important biblical text for reflecting upon the ongoing relationship between the church and synagogue. According to Luke's reading of Scripture's prophecy, God's plan for restoring historic Israel has always divided the "people" into those who repent and those who do not (28:25-27). The mixed response to Paul's teaching in Rome is indicative of Israel's response to the preaching of God's word beginning with Moses (see 7:35) and continuing throughout Israel's history to include the Messiah (Gospel) and his successors (Acts). God has not forsaken *repentant* Israel and relentlessly offers unrepentant Israel second chances (see 7:39; 13:44-45). The word has gone first to Israel as promised (see 3:25-26), and the mission to the nations is possible only because the church's mission to the Jews has succeeded (Acts 1-8; see 13:47). Moreover, as promised God has forgiven all in Israel who repent and turn to the Lord, restoring their covenant and leading them into a season of refreshment under the aegis of the Holy Spirit (see 3:19). Likewise, Paul's claim that "Gentiles will listen" must be glossed by the rest of Acts: Clearly not all Gentiles "listen" to the gospel (see 19:23-27). Those who do and repent are typically those attached to the prophet who teaches Moses (see 28:10; 28:23) or to the synagogue where Moses is read (see 15:21). Even though enjoying a greater measure of success among Gentiles, the Paul of Acts does not register resignation but rather persistence in trying another city and synagogue where he sometimes enjoys greater success among the Jews (see 17:11; cf. 21:20).

These same concerns are also reflected in Paul's letter to the Romans. Even though he tends to spiritualize the biblical idea of Israel in Romans (cf. 2:28-29; 9:6-12), Paul concludes the principal part of his letter by claiming that historic Israel will be restored when the Gentile mission is completed and the Messiah returns to earth to complete his mission (cf. Rom 11:25-27). This remarkable vision of Israel's future restoration not only complements Luke's understanding of Paul's mission but helps the interpreter of Acts put together the story's beginning and ending. The promise of Jesus' return (see 1:9-11) glosses Paul's response to the ambivalence of Roman Jews by adding an eschatological subtext: After all the nations are finished "listening" to the gospel according to God's timetable (see 1:7; cf. Rom 11:25) and the Messiah returns to broker God's cosmic triumph over the powers of darkness, then all Israel will understand and turn for God to heal them (see 28:27).

When the conclusion to Acts is read in this wider narrative context, especially with the Romans co-text, the interpreter may well appreciate Paul's optimism in "welcoming all [Jews and Gentiles alike] who came to him" (28:30) to hear the gospel of a faithful God and God's risen Messiah (see 28:31). Nothing has changed since Paul.

ACTS 28:30-31

THE ENDING OF ACTS

COMMENTARY

The final sentence of Acts is clear enough: Paul spends two years in Rome confined to his lodgings but entertaining all who visit him without legal restraint. He boldly preaches the "kingdom of God" to all his guests and teaches them about the Lord Jesus Christ. Although this portrait of Paul coheres with the rest of Acts, the passage pricks the interpreter's curiosity because it concludes Acts without saying anything of Paul's meeting with the Roman emperor—the "official" reason why he is a prisoner in Rome. Many have speculated that Luke does not include this information because he did not know the details of what happened to Paul. Yet this hardly seems possible, since Acts was probably composed after Paul's legal difficulties were resolved. Others claim that Luke knew the outcome of Paul's case but intended to produce a trilogy of earliest Christianity that he never completed. Some speculate that he considered this biographical detail either anticlimactic (e.g., the statute of limitations ran out after two years and he was released to no great fanfare) or too tragic (e.g., he was martyred) to fit the plotline of Paul's heroic story in Acts. Some modern scholars have even speculated that an early version of Acts circulated with a longer ending that included details of Paul's trial and alleged martyrdom, but then subsequent editors of Acts erased this ending because of embarrassing testimony raised in court against Paul or more likely against the Jewish or Roman churches that had failed to support him during his time of need.[795] Still others, myself included, find no problem with Luke's ending because it portrays Paul engaged in the routines of his prophetic vocation in the divinely ordained city of his destiny. The faithful Paul

of Acts has never been much concerned about the politics of Rome, nor does he think to defend his good citizenship. When he does appeal to Rome, it is in service of his mission. In this sense, Luke may well suppose that whatever the Emperor may have decided in Paul's case is irrelevant. The silence of Acts on any of these matters, however, precludes a final solution.

28:30-31. The pertinent interests of the interpreter of Acts as Scripture do not concern an imagined *Urtext*, or missing information, that may contribute to an impression of Luke's "unfinished business." Rather, the interpreter's principal concern is to make sense of this passage and its role in summarizing Paul's Roman mission and also in concluding the whole book of Acts. In this regard, the terms used of both the messenger (v. 30) and his message (v. 31) are highly evocative of other episodes in Acts and effectively bring a sense of closure to its reading. Perhaps the most important impression made by this repetition of important terms in Acts is one of permanence and continuity. No matter what has transpired since the beginning of his mission, these final images depict an exemplary Paul steadfastly obedient to his prophetic calling: He "welcomed all who came to him, proclaiming [κηρύσσω *kēryssō*] the kingdom of God and teaching [διδάσκω *didaskō*] about the Lord Jesus Christ with all boldness [παρρησία *parrēsia*] and without hindrance." Mention is made of the central theme of gospel preaching since Jesus, "the kingdom of God." Paul's own summary of his ministry at Miletus already had contained this (see 20:25; cf. 19:8; 28:23), even as the Lord had earlier instructed his apostolic successors concerning the reign of God in preparing them to bear witness to him (see 1:3, 6; 10:42; cf. Luke 24:47; 9:2). From beginning to end, the preoccupation of the prophets-like-Jesus is to preach the kingdom of God. Likewise,

---

795. For various hypotheses, see Conzelmann, *The Acts of the Apostles*, 228; Wilson, *The Gentiles and the Gentile Mission in Luke-Acts*, 233-36; and Witherington, *The Acts of the Apostles*, 807-12.

teaching about Jesus remains a constant of the church's missionary praxis, beginning with the Twelve (4:2, 18; 5:21) and continuing with Paul's ministry (11:26) to the end (28:31; see also 20:20). These two practices of preaching about God's kingdom, restored to a faithful Israel (see 1:6), and teaching about God's Messiah enclose the whole of Acts to remind its readers of the church's ongoing vocation. God's saving purpose for all people cannot be known otherwise.

Two other important themes emphasize the *where* and the *how* of Paul's ministry in Rome and deepen the reader's sense of closure to Acts. The hospitable Paul welcomed his religious clients into his own lodging and spoke to them concerning the word of God "with all boldness." Hospitality and makeshift meeting places for worship and Bible instruction are important themes in the second half of Acts (see 16:15, 31-34; 17:5; 18:7-8; 19:9; 20:20), not only in dispelling James's anxiety over the future of a distinctively Jewish ethos in the Pauline church (see 15:20-21) but also in showing the manner by which Amos's prophecy of God's "re-housing" Israel is fulfilled through Paul's mission to the nations (see 15:16-17). The use of *parrēsia* ("boldness") recalls how the apostles prayed for the Holy Spirit's inspiration to empower a more effective proclamation of the gospel (see 4:29-31). It is this holy boldness of prophets-like-Jesus, cultivated by living in the Spirit, which enlivens a courageous communication of the gospel (see also 2:29; 9:27-28; 13:46; 14:3; 18:26; 19:8; 22:26).

According to Luke, Paul spent two years in Rome, where he lived "at his own expense and welcomed all who came to him." Paul's freedom of movement is curtailed by his house arrest. However, his freedom to entertain guests probably reflects the ambiguity of his legal status (he is not guilty of any crime or perceived as a troublemaker by Rome) or perhaps the early years of Nero's reign (early 60s) when the Roman emperor was considerably less hostile toward Jews and Christians than later in his regime.[796] Much has been made of the reference to the duration of Paul's stay—"two whole years." Why include such a specific detail in a narrative

summary? Many suppose that Luke's reference to a finite period of time suggests termination of some sort, whether Paul's release or his death.[797] However, in Acts similar references are included in summaries of Paul's urban missions to convey the impression of his commitment to a particular work under difficult circumstances (see 18:11); and I suspect Luke has this apologetic intent in mind.

Among the important characteristics of Paul's persona is his handling of finances: "He lived—at his own expense." Consistent with his Pharisaism, Luke's Jewish Paul works at a trade to support himself (see 18:3). Additionally, he may have family resources to draw upon (see 21:39; 22:3) sufficient to allow him to cover the expenses of those with whom he completed vows and sacrifices of purification (see 21:24, 26). Here he takes care of his rent, and the emphatic construction of the phrase underlines the importance Luke places on Paul's doing so. That Paul's lease is for two years and is not open-ended may well indicate a lack of permanence,[798] but for what reason is left unclear (see above). In my mind, the principal point is not of Paul's impermanence but of his rented quarters, which nicely serves as a substitute for a local synagogue where the word of God is taught to any who come for as long as the prophet remains in Rome (see 7:44-50).

More important, Paul "welcomed all [πᾶς *pas*] who came to him." The Western version of Acts rightly adds the appositional phrase, "all Jews and Gentiles," to *pas*. Prisoner Paul continues to live within his vocation to extend the gospel of God to all people (see 9:15) in the realization of Joel's prophecy that "everyone [*pas*] who calls upon the name of the Lord will be saved" (2:21).

The two features of Paul's prophetic ministry are "preaching the kingdom of God" and "teaching about the Lord Jesus Christ" (see above). These two tasks are boldly executed by inspiration of the Spirit of prophecy (see 4:13, 29-31) "and without hindrance" (ἀκωλύτως *akolytōs*). Luke places *akolytōs*

---

796. Cf. Barrett, *A Critical and Exegetical Commentary on the Acts of the Apostles*, 2:1249-50.

797. Cf. Hemer, *The Book of Acts in the Setting of Hellenistic History*, 383-87.

798. The phrase ἐν ἰδίῳ μισθώματι (*en idiō misthōmati*, "at his own expense") does not actually mention a home (οἶκος/οἰκία *oikos/oikia*), which would connote a private residence. However, Luke has already mentioned Paul's ξενία (*xenia*, "lodgings," 28:23) and need not do so here. Most now take this phrase as connoting that Paul rented (rather than purchased) his Roman *xenia*. See Witherington, *The Acts of the Apostles*, 812-13.

in the emphatic position at the end of his book not merely to characterize Paul's imprisonment as allowing him considerable personal freedom but also to characterize the unhindered and unstoppable spread of God's gospel according to God's purposes (cf. 2 Tim 2:8-13).

The final sentence of Acts is a summary, not a climax: Paul is simply being Paul in Rome. Its overall importance to Luke's narrative, therefore, is not to contribute new information but to facilitate a transition with a deep impression of the story's continuity from beginning to end. Typically Luke's summaries make literary transitions to move readers along from one episode to the next.

In the case of an ending, however, there is no next stage in the telling of Luke's story. What then? Perhaps he would have his last words stage a transition from the narrative world of Acts to the considerably more complicated worlds of his readers. If that is the case, then these parting images of Paul linger on in the reader's imagination to stimulate further reflection on what it means to continue what this exemplary prophet-like-Jesus "began to do and to say" in Rome (cf. 1:1). While times and places will continue to change around us, the church's prophetic calling in "proclaiming the kingdom of God and teaching about the Lord Jesus Christ with all boldness" remains constant.

REFLECTIONS

Paul "welcomed all who came to him, proclaiming the kingdom of God . . . with all boldness" (28:30-31 NRSV). The final sentence of Acts is a summary, not a climax. Paul is simply being Paul, ever faithful to his prophetic vocation. But this is Luke's point. His conclusion does not intend to contribute new information to his biography of Paul or to frustrate his readers by leaving out important information. The ending to Acts does what good endings to excellent stories must always do: facilitate a transition that moves readers from the narrative world to their own considerably more complicated real worlds. These parting images of Paul linger on in our collective imagination to stimulate further reflection on what it means to continue what Paul began to do and to say in Rome. We are his successors. While times and places will continue to change, the church's prophetic calling is to "proclaim the kingdom of God and teach about the Lord Jesus Christ with all boldness." The church must simply be the church.

INTRODUCTION TO EPISTOLARY LITERATURE

ROBERT W. WALL

This article intends neither to offer a succinct summary of each NT letter's subject matter nor to survey solutions to the various critical problems each poses; these are tasks of the individual commentaries that follow. Rather, the primary purpose is to introduce readers to the "orienting concerns" that are essential for studying and reflecting upon the NT epistolary texts as Scripture. Given the literary and theological diversity of these texts, and the complex and variegated history of their interpretation, this introduction will necessarily be selective. If my intent is served, however, both the theological subject matter of the NT letters as a whole and those interpretive strategies employed to seek and find this instruction will be brought into clearer focus.

After a *general introduction* to the letters, I will lay out a rough map of sorts, employing a familiar typology to chart three essential "worlds" that will orient readers to the Bible's epistolary literature: *behind-the-text* (the world of authors and their first audiences), *within-the-text* (the world of compositions) and *in-front-of-the-text* (the world of the audience for whom the text is Scripture).[1] These

worlds are not discrete locations; rather, there is considerable overlap among them. Further, the plurality of interpretive locations reflects the current intellectual climate of biblical studies, in which modernity's dominant commitment to historical models has given way to a much wider range of methodologies that together can better discern the text's full meaning. An integrated approach to the letters, combining rather than dividing historical, literary, and theological information, may better serve the primary work of Scripture's performance within the faith community: to lead readers into a deeper understanding of the gospel of God.

GENERAL INTRODUCTION

The NT canon includes twenty-one letters gathered in two collections, Pauline (Romans through Philemon) and non-Pauline (Hebrews through Jude), that are strategically sandwiched between the books of Acts and Revelation. Both collections are often divided and grouped according to certain judgments about their points of origin, content, or current influence—judgments that remain contested. For this reason the rubrics employed

---

1. See, e.g., D. Barr, *The New Testament Story: An Introduction*, 2nd ed. (Belmont, Calif.. Wadsworth, 1995) 2-18; I. B. Green and M. Turner, "NT Commentary and Systematic Theology: Strangers or Friends?" in *Between Two Horizons* (Grand Rapids, MI: Eerdmans, 2000) 1-22.

during the history of their interpretation enjoy only moderate success as explanatory constructs and sometimes even dampen the distinctive contribution each letter makes to the whole canon.

In particular, while the entire Pauline collection concerns the ministry and message of the apostle Paul, its letters are often divided into those that are "genuine" (written by Paul) and those that are "disputed" (thought to have been written after Paul's death but in the manner of his "genuine" letters). This division is intended to distinguish the theology of the "real" Paul from that of his followers. Some scholars think that an imprisoned Paul (when and where are disputed) wrote or transcribed the "prison letters" (Ephesians, Philippians, Colossians, 2 Timothy, Philemon). The themes of the "Pastoral Epistles" (1–2 Timothy and Titus, which are usually studied together and are listed among the "disputed" letters) concern the characteristics of Christian leaders as well as the organization of Christian congregations (even though 2 Timothy differs in significant ways in this regard from 1 Timothy and Titus). Still another group of Paul's letters, whose greater length and influence are deemed "major" (Romans through Galatians), is occasionally separated from the shorter letters (Ephesians through Philemon). The influence of the shorter letters is sometimes perceived as less significant in forming the church's theological understanding—a view that seems to persist among some Protestant communions.

Although scholars sometimes rearrange the thirteen Pauline letters to follow a chronological scheme, the final form of the modern NT follows the Latin Vulgate so that letters written to congregations (Romans through 2 Thessalonians) precede those written to individuals (1 Timothy through Philemon). Within each group, letters are arranged by decreasing length, even though Ephesians is slightly longer than Galatians (which may well account for its priority in early canon lists; e.g., Chester Beatty papyri from c. 200 CE and the Muratorian canon list from c. 190 CE). It should be noted, however, that the early church arranged the Pauline corpus in different sequences and often included Hebrews.[2] Sometimes these letters were arranged according to theological importance.

For example, Marcion placed Galatians first among Paul's letters, since he thought its teaching best supported his own contention that the influence of the OT (and its theology) ended with Christ. Typically, Romans is placed first in the Pauline corpus not only because of its length but also because it presumes to offer its readers the best theological introduction to the writings of Paul, a status surely justified by its history and use within the church.

Unlike the Pauline letters, which are named after those being addressed, all the letters that make up the second collection (except Hebrews) are named after their supposed authors. The placement of each within the NT once again follows their decreasing length. As with the Pauline corpus, however, other sequences are found in the early and medieval churches, perhaps indicating the estimation of their relative theological importance for the purpose of Christian formation. In the canon lists of the Roman church (e.g., those of Carthage, 397 CE) and Augustine, the Petrine correspondence is placed first, which may reflect the primacy of Peter's memory and his teaching. The present form, James–Peter–John, follows Paul's list in Gal 2:9.

The writings of this second collection are even more difficult to organize into groups of common denominators than are the Pauline letters because their literary diversity is more pronounced and their theological traditions more diverse. The rubric "non-Pauline" is used in reference to those letters that do not claim residence within the Pauline domain—no matter what others may claim for them. More important, "non-Pauline" intends to orient the reader to the presence of two discrete collections of letters and then to the reflexive relationship between them as integral epistolary parts within the biblical whole. In most cases, seven of these letters (James through Jude) are listed under the ancient rubric "catholic," or more recently "general," because it is thought they were originally encyclical epistles that circulated among geographically dispersed and ethnically mixed congregations. Missing from this and other catalogs is Hebrews, which is typically left orphaned without either a Pauline or a

2. B. Metzger, *The Canon of the New Testament* (Oxford: Clarendon, 1987) 297-99.

catholic home. Perhaps its placement within the letter canon between the Pauline and the catholic letters is strategic: Being neither and yet having elements of both, Hebrews is an effective bridge, reminding readers of the interdependent character of these two collections of letters.

A. Deissmann's well-known distinction between the "epistle," compositions of public art intended for a wide audience, and the "letter," occasional correspondence intended for private and confidential reading, supports the Pauline/catholic distinction. That is, the catholic collection is composed of epistles written as artful homilies for a general readership, whereas the Pauline letters were written for and first read by particular congregations or individuals.[3] Upon closer analysis, however, this distinction does not seem appropriate for the catholic epistles, since nowhere do James, Jude, and 2 Peter (or Hebrews) claim to address a general audience; and 3 John addresses an individual. Moreover, 1 John and James (and Hebrews) only approximate literary epistles. Nor can it be said that all these epistles are known by their author, for those from "John" (and Hebrews) are anonymous.

Despite the difficulty of forming neat and convenient groups, these letters all share a common purpose: to combine theological instruction and moral exhortation toward particular practical and pastoral ends. Each addresses the spiritual struggles and theological controversies that face ordinary believers seeking a more mature witness to their faith in Jesus Christ, often within hostile social settings. Each reflects its own particular historical occasion and theological situation, where the gospel of God is adapted to the life of God's people. Each is deeply rooted in particular interpretive traditions judged acceptable by the early church as apostolic and divinely inspired. For this reason, "catholic" is sometimes also used to classify the subject matter of these letters as applicable to every Christian congregation; they were even called the *epistulae canonicae* in the West because their divine inspiration (and so canonicity) was recognized by "all the churches."[4] However, this

sense of universal significance is true of every biblical writing whose canonical status is due in part to its perceived usefulness in the spiritual formation of every generation and congregation of believers.

THE WORLD BEHIND THE LETTERS: CONVERSATIONS IN HISTORICAL CONTEXT

No letter began its life as a biblical writing, read by the whole church for theological understanding. Every letter was at first a pastor-teacher's written response to believers whose particular sociohistorical circumstances provoked a spiritual crisis that required theological explanation and practical resolution. The letters of the NT are occasional literature, then. That is, in every case writers adapted their core theological convictions to a particular audience's historical situation in ways that enabled their writing to be, in C. Beker's apt phrase, "a word on target."[5] Therefore, current interpreters, far removed from the social world that helped to shape the letter's subject matter, are obligated to narrow the gap by gathering and using as much historical, political, and socioeconomic information regarding the original setting as possible. The epistolary text becomes a "window" through which its ancient author and first readers/auditors (authorial audience) are viewed more clearly, their worlds and traditions more fully understood, and the events implied by the text better known.

The result is a "thickened" description of the letter's subject matter that can facilitate its present performance as the church's Scripture. Within the community of faith, rarely if ever does an interest in the "world behind the letters" marginalize the theological aspect of the text itself so that we view it merely as a historical resource. Rather, we use the tools of historical criticism to understand better the biblical text as a witness to God's revelation

---

3. A. Deissmann, *Light from the Ancient East*, trans. L. R. M Strachan, 2nd ed. (London: Hodder & Stoughton, 1928).

4. So J. Fitzmyer, "Introduction to the NT Epistles," *NJBC* (Englewood Cliffs, N.J.: Prentice Hall, 1990) 771.

5. Beker has argued that Paul is not a systematic theologian but an interpreter of the Christian gospel who adapts the unchanging convictions of his faith ("coherence") to the ever-changing "contingencies" of his audiences. According to him, then, Paul's interpretive activity seeks to make the "abiding Word of the gospel a word on target." See C. Beker, "Recasting Pauline Theology" in *Pauline Theology*, ed. J. Bassler (Minneapolis: Fortress, 1991) 1:15.

within history, within circumstances in which letters are heard or read as a "word on target." The interpreter approaches these ancient texts with historical sensitivity, then, to understand more precisely their meaning at the point of origin.

Since most NT letters deal with the concrete problems of specific communities, the letters themselves are the clearest line of sight into their social world. This methodological claim does not exclude non-biblical resources, literary or otherwise, whether from the early Roman Empire or from early Judaism. Rather, it insists only that we move outward from the epistolary literature itself to all other sources when reconstructing the world behind the letters.

THE PAULINE COLLECTION

The most important conversation partner in the Pauline correspondence is the author. To be sure, an interpreter's decisions regarding Pauline authorship depend on prior decisions about sources. Which of the letters that claim Pauline authorship were actually written by Paul? To what extent should we trust the historical veracity of Luke's portrait of Paul in Acts? And what of the apocryphal Paul of early Christian memory and legend, which many scholars think so idealizes Paul's memory and theological trajectory that both are badly distorted? Even the autobiographical portions of the authentic letters, which many suppose offer us the best window onto the historical Paul, serve primarily an apologetical (i.e., rhetorical) purpose. Other matters, such as those related to the authorial address and the date and place of origin of a particular letter, are all part of the historical matrix that help to settle the question of Pauline authorship. We leave these decisions and discussions to the commentators on the individual letters.

On balance, however, few figures from antiquity are better known than Paul. As N. Dahl has noted, "in his letters, Paul himself comes to life."[6] Current readers of his letters have sufficient raw material to sketch a basic chronology of Paul's life and mission. This

historical project has a direct bearing upon the interpretation of the Pauline letters, especially when trying to date and place them in some historical sequence or social location. The construction of a Pauline chronology helps the interpreter to assess the development of Paul's theological conception; the subject matter of Paul's message is no longer presented as a static and systematic whole. Instead, on the basis of a chronology of his ministry and letters, the development of the most important theological themes of Pauline preaching (e.g., the promise and fulfillment of God's salvation, the results of Christ's death and resurrection, the life and witness of the church) and of the central theological controversies of his Gentile mission (e.g., election, law, theodicy, Israel) can be traced through the sequence of letters. Paul's theology was a work in process.[7]

The Book of Acts and the Chronology of the Pauline Collection. What is known about Paul comes to us from three sources: (1) the autobiographical portions of his letters, (2) his "authorized" biography found in the book of Acts, and (3) his "unauthorized" biography found in such apocryphal writings as *The Acts of Paul* and *Thecla*. These sources are not of equal value to Paul's chronologists. Accepting the historian's rule of favoring primary (or direct) over secondary (or mediated) evidence, preference is always granted to what Paul says about himself in his letters, even though the book of Acts contributes necessary information to fill out his epistolary portrait. Most scholars hold that Paul's portrait in Acts is the literary invention of the narrator, whose principal interests are theological and not historical. The apocryphal story of Paul is still farther removed from the historical Paul, deriving in part from the canonical Acts and in part from legend, and is thus deemed either redundant or useless as a historical resource.[8]

---

6. N. Dahl, *Studies in Paul* (Minneapolis: Augsburg, 1977) 6.

7. Trobisch has argued that Paul edited and published his own letter collection (consisting of Romans, 1–2 Corinthians, and Galatians) for his client-friends. See D. Trobisch, *Paul's Letter Collection: Tracing the Origins* (Minneapolis: Fortress, 1994). Paul's purpose was to supply them with a literary testament shortly before his death that would respond in a normative way to a variety of controversies generated by his Gentile mission. Trobisch's provocative thesis suggests that it was Paul (and not Marcion) who first devised a "Christian canon" by which his other writings were understood and that there is a literary and theological unity to these four letters, concentrated by a set of core themes, that fixes and stabilizes the meaning of the entire corpus.

8. See D. R. MacDonald, *The Legend and the Apostle* (Philadelphia: Westminster, 1983).

The most crucial task facing the chronologist is the correlation of datable events mentioned in Paul's letters or his story in Acts. Sharply stated, the primary problem is that the chronology of Paul's life according to Paul's letters differs at significant points from the chronology of Paul's life according to Acts. Further, the difficulty facing the chronologist is exacerbated by the lack of any clear reference to Paul's letters in the book of Acts. Acknowledging this disparity, a growing number of scholars now follow the lead of J. Knox and try to reconstruct Paul's life using only his writings, admitting into evidence information from Acts only when it is absolutely necessary for a coherent chronology and does not contradict Paul's testimony.[9]

Yet this position is not without problems. Paul surely colors his own story with rhetorical and theological intent; and there is a growing appreciation for the historical integrity of the second half of Acts, which narrates Paul's movements from the Jerusalem Council (Acts 15) to Rome (Acts 28; Paul tells us virtually nothing about the first stage of his missionary activity [Acts 9–14],[10] and none of his letters can be dated with any probability from this period in any case). Even if the pattern of Paul's mission according to Acts 15–28 serves the narrator's literary and theological interests, his story contains reliable information.[11] Therefore, most chronologists continue to work between Paul's letters and Acts to calculate the pivotal dates of his mission and letters.[12] The following provides a tentative chronology of Paul's life, with supporting textual evidence:

9. See J. Knox, *Chapters in a Life of Paul*, rev. ed. (Altanta: Mercer University Press, 1987); R. Jewett, *Chronology of Paul's Life* (Philadelphia: Fortress, 1979); G. Luedemann, *Paul, Apostle to the Gentiles: Studies in Chronology* (Philadelphia: Fortress, 1984).

10. See M. Hengel and A. Schwemer, *Paul Between Damascus and Antioch* (London: SCM, 1997).

11. See F. F. Bruce, *Paul: Apostle of the Heart Set Free* (Grand Rapids: Eerdmans, 1977); W. W. Gasque, *A History of the Interpretation of the Acts of the Apostles* (Peabody, Mass.: Hendrickson, 1989); C. Hemer, *The Book of Acts in the Setting of Hellenistic History*, WUNT 49 (Tübingen: JCB Mohr, 1989).

12. A complicating factor in this historical project is the profound difficulty of dating the most pivotal of these events with precision. For instance, Luedemann accepts the Claudius decree, which expelled Jews from Rome and is mentioned in Acts 18:2, as a chronological marker for Paul's Corinthian mission (and so dates his letters written from Corinth accordingly). However, he dates this decree from 41 CE rather than from the commonly accepted date of 49 CE. As a result, he dates Paul's Macedonian mission, which antedates the Jerusalem Council, and the Thessalonian correspondence, which was written from Corinth, in the early 40s. Even those who accept Luedemann's reconstruction of Paul's Macedonian mission from its narrative in Acts 18 and references in 1–2 Thessalonians and yet reject Luedemann's dating of Claudius's decree will, therefore, locate the Thessalonian correspondence several years later.

CE	
33	Paul's conversion/call near Damascus (Gal 1:17; Acts 9:1-22 [22:6-21; 26:12-18])
35	First journey to Jerusalem (Gal 1:18-20; Acts 9:26-29)
47–48	Mission from Antioch to Asia (Phil 4:15; Acts 13–14)
48	Second journey to Jerusalem: the Jerusalem Council (Gal 2:1-10; Acts 15:1-12)
49	Macedonian mission from Galatia to Athens (1 Cor 16:1; 2 Cor 11:9; Gal 4:13; 1 Thess 2:2, 3:1; Phil 4:15-16; Acts 16:6–17:34)
49–52	Claudius's decree (Acts 18:2); Corinthian mission (2 Cor 1:19; 11:7-9; 1 Thess 3:6; Acts 18:1-11)
50	**Paul writes 1–2 Thessalonians**
53–56	Ephesian Mission (1 Cor 16:1-8; Acts 19)
53	**Paul writes Galatians**
54	**Paul writes 1 Corinthians**
55	**Paul writes Philippians and Philemon**
55–56	**Paul writes 2 Corinthians**
56	Paul's "painful" return to Corinth (2 Cor 13:2; cf. 10:11; 12:21; 2:13)
57	Third visit to Corinth (2 Cor 13:1; Acts 20:1-3)
57	**Paul writes Romans**
57	Third journey to Jerusalem (Rom 15:22-27; Acts 21:15–23:30)
57–59	Imprisonment and legal "trial" in Caesarea (Acts 23:31–26:21)
58	**Paul writes Colossians (and Ephesians?)**
60–62	Arrival and imprisonment in Rome (Acts 28:15-31)
62–?	Paul's Mission in Spain (Rom 15:22-24); Paul Writes to Timothy and Titus?

The NT says nothing about Paul's death. Acts concludes without mentioning the outcome of Paul's meeting with Caesar, but Paul does mention his intent to continue the mission in Illyricum (Rom 15:19) and then to Spain, following a visit to Rome (Rom 15:22-24, 28). Most scholars suppose that the narrator of Acts knew that Paul was executed in Rome (Acts 20:22-24) but realized that mentioning it would have undermined his literary purpose to portray Paul as the triumphant successor to Jesus and the Twelve. If, however, Paul was in fact released and allowed to continue his mission in Spain until his death, then we are provided a possible provenance for his final letters to his young colleagues in distant Asia, Timothy and Titus.

Paul and Judaism. Most reconstructions of Paul's life mention his youth in Tarsus of Cilicia, his Roman citizenship, his education in Jerusalem, and his career within Judaism. This biography is especially dependent upon Acts, where he is portrayed as a Pharisaic Jew and Roman citizen from Tarsus (22:3) who persecutes the first followers of Jesus for religious reasons (8:1-3), but who is forgiven (7:60) by them and then commissioned (9:15-16) by this same Jesus as a prophetic "teacher of Israel." Yet, Paul touches only briefly on these elements from his early life, and the references serve his writings' rhetorical design (Gal 1:11-15; Phil 3:2-11; cf. Rom 9:1-5). Nevertheless, these elements may well provide important clues in orienting us to his letters.

For example, we know that Tarsus, where Paul was apparently born and raised in diaspora Judaism, was an impressive center of Hellenistic culture and mystery religions. There, Paul could easily have picked up his understanding of moral philosophy and rhetoric as well as pagan religion, which then informs his letters and frames his message. Especially for those interpreters who explore the meaning of Paul's writings against the backdrop of Greco-Roman moral and religious culture, this feature of his early life is crucial.[13]

Paul himself points us in another direction: to his life within Judaism as "a Hebrew, born to Hebrews, and as to Torah, a Pharisee"

(Phil 3:5). This identity marker reflects the formative influence of Judaism on both his religious understanding that Christianity is the fulfillment of Judaism and his missionary belief that God's elect people include Gentiles, who are also called out of the world as heirs of God's promised salvation.

Certainly Paul's background in diaspora Judaism may have contributed important symbols to his understanding of the gospel.[14] Two brief examples must suffice to illustrate this influence:

1. Paul's Bible was the Septuagint (LXX), the Greek translation of the Hebrew Scriptures used in diaspora Judaism. While true to the spirit of Jewish faith, the process of translating Scripture interprets its meaning for a new readership, infusing relevant tendencies of that readership's world into the text. The grand themes of the Jewish faith, then, were refined and even redrawn by the LXX in an effort to communicate to its Hellenistic audience. For instance, the resonances of νόμος (*nomos*), the Greek word for "law" that translates the Hebrew תורה (*tôrâ*, "instruction"), broadens the concept's meaning within diaspora Judaism. Thus, while the Jews of the diaspora looked to the teaching of the *nomos* to settle issues of religious and moral identity (= *torah*), they also understood the law in a more abstract and philosophical way as constituting a cosmic rule, instituted by the Creator, by which all of creation is patterned. Paul's use of "law" in his letters is multiform and reflects the variegated uses of this word in Hellenistic literature.

2. Paul's willingness to cross cultural lines in preaching the gospel (1 Corinthians 9), and all the tensions he notes in doing so (Romans 12), may well have been shaped within diaspora Judaism. Many have noted that the Jews of the diaspora were caught between two very different worlds. The dominant world was non-Jewish and syncretistic, inviting compromise and assimilation. The Jews were a minority called by God to remain separate and distinctive as a witness to truth. Conflict was inevitable for those Jews trying to live in a non-Jewish world that rewarded conformity

13. On the influence of Paul's Jewish upbringing upon his life and thought, see J. Neyrey, *Paul, In Other Words* (Louisville: Westminster, 1990).

14. In elaboration of this point, see the interesting debate on Paul's relationship with first-century Judaism: E. P. Sanders, *Paul and Palestinian Judaism* (Philadelphia: Fortress, 1977); J. D. G. Dunn, *Jesus, Paul and the Law* (Louisville: Westminster, 1990); and N. T. Wright, *The Climax of the Covenant* (Edinburgh: T. & T. Clark, 1991).

and punished deviance. The fact that Paul was a Roman citizen from birth suggests that his family was skilled in moving between both worlds—a skill, according to Acts and his letters, that Paul learned well.

In any case, the Jewishness of Paul's theological understanding is not really altered by his conversion to Christ. The deeper logic of Paul's theology is neither shaped by Greco-Roman religious culture nor created through some profound innovation on his part. He remains Israel-oriented, a committed monotheist; he utterly rejects the dualism of his pagan culture. Further, he retains a vital interest in the doctrine of divine election, even retaining its sociological importance as a primary marker for the community's public identity. Indeed, these very interests, which are the most important to his Jewish world, are at the center of the controversies provoked during his Gentile mission.

Why, then, did his message provoke so much confusion and commotion, especially within his Jewish audience? Primarily because Paul was a "christological monotheist."[15] That is, he reworked the core symbols of his Jewish world, including its "foundational story," which celebrated God's creation, God's promised salvation, and God's Israel and *torah*, in radically christological terms. Because of Christ, the confession of monotheistic faith had now been expanded to "one God, one Lord" (1 Cor 8:6); and the social marker of God's Israel was the public confession that Jesus is Lord (Rom 10:9). Those who belong to the Lord Jesus are the very same members of eschatological Israel whom God will vindicate on the future "Day of the Lord" (= resurrection from the dead).

Central to this symbolic world is Israel's Scripture, which both nurtures and justifies Paul's theological understanding. The critical issue in this regard is how Scripture functioned in the writing of Paul's letters. In his use of *midrash* and *catenae* (or connected series) of Scripture to interpret his message, Paul shared the exegetical strategies of other first-century Jewish interpreters. At an even deeper level, Paul's letters may be read as "intertexts," as texts written in intended (and reflexive) conversation with earlier Scripture.

Images or words that link Christian letters with OT Scripture frame a theological setting that discloses additional layers of Paul's strategy: to confirm that Gentiles are also members of the elect community prefigured by Israel's Scriptures.[16]

Besides his penultimate commitment to God's election of Israel at the beginning of salvation's history and his ultimate concern for God's vindication of righteous Israel at the consummation of salvation's history, still other elements of Paul's teaching can be traced back to his own Pharisaic heritage. Perhaps because Pharisaism was a lay movement, engaged in all matters of the town square and marketplace, Paul's practical account of Christian faith extends God's rule and grace to every part of the community's life. Even though his rejection of the "laws of purity" seems anti-Pharisaic, his teaching about eating in 1 Corinthians 8–11 and Romans 14, especially as it relates to church order, is deeply rooted in the social world of Pharisaism. On the one hand, the pattern of Christian fellowship, as demonstrated by how and what believers eat together, is the social marker of their solidarity as a people belonging to Christ. On the other hand, the same social patterns that control the community's eating habits distinguish it from other religious communities/options. As with Pharisaic Judaism, Pauline Christianity places a religious value on meals, eating habits, and foods—a value that when not observed can cause divisions within the community and that when observed can divide those inside the community from those outside.

Paul and Jesus. These two are the most prominent figures of the NT world; thus Paul's lack of contact with the historical Jesus remains an awkward feature of his résumé. Paul seemed aware of this omission (1 Cor 15:8-11; 9:1), even defensive about it (Gal 1:11-16). On this basis, Luke's defense of Paul's authority and mission in Acts tacitly admits that Paul lacked the credentials of the original apostolic successors to Jesus (see Acts 1:21-22).

The relationship between Jesus and Paul is the subject of an old debate.[17] There are

---

15. So N. T. Wright, "Putting Paul Together Again," in Bassler, *Pauline Theology*, 1:206.

16. See R. Hays, *The Echoes of Scripture in the Letters of Paul* (New Haven: Yale University Press, 1989).

17. For a fine historical survey of this debate, see J. Barclay, "Jesus and Paul," in *Dictionary of Paul and His Letters*, ed. G Hawthorne et al. (Downers Grove, Ill.: InterVarsity, 1993) 492-98.

still a few who appeal to the lack of contact as evidence for a fundamental discontinuity between the two, especially regarding the ongoing role of the law within the faith community. Some even speculate as to whether Jesus or Paul is the true founder of Christianity. To be sure, generic and thematic differences between the biblical Gospels and the letters contribute to this impression of discontinuity. On the surface, it seems that Paul lacked a vital interest in the details of Jesus' life. For example, although he paid heed to the dominical message, only twice does he actually cite sayings of Jesus (1 Cor 7:10-11; 9:14); on other occasions Paul alludes to his sayings (Rom 12:14, 17; 13:7; 14:12-14; 16:19; 1 Cor 11:23-25; 13:2; 1 Thess 4:2, 15; 5:2, 13, 15), often in support of his own instruction or apostolic authority. To be sure, the parables and proverbs of Jesus, so rooted in the agrarian life of rural Palestine, would have little relevance for those living in the cities of Paul's mission. However, even in those letters where Paul might have appealed to the memory of Jesus for support, he failed to do so. His teaching included a more "vertical christology," concentrated on the moment of Jesus' death and resurrection as the climax of salvation's history. As for the other great events of the Messiah's earthly ministry, there is a deafening silence.[18]

Paul's lack of personal contact with Jesus of Nazareth and the lack of crucial details from the "life of Jesus" in his letters prompt the critical issue raised by Paul in Galatians: To what extent is there continuity between the message of Jesus and his immediate successors and the message of Paul? According to Pauline autobiography, continuity exists by virtue of his personal revelation of Jesus (christophany), both "to" him on the Damascus road (Gal 1:12; cf. 2 Cor 4:6; 5:16) and "in" him by some religious experience (Gal 1:16). S. Kim takes this feature of Paul's autobiography to mean that his personal experience of Jesus on the Damascus road, along with subsequent charismatic episodes,

was a primary source of Paul's christological understanding as well as of his central claim that God's saving activity results in human transformation.[19]

There is little explicit evidence from his letters that Paul was familiar with the Gospels or even with pre-Gospel stories of Jesus, the Lord's Supper (1 Cor 10:16-17 [cf. Matt 26:27]; 11:23-26 [cf. Luke 22:14-20]), and perhaps the synoptic apocalypse (1 Thess 2:16; 4:15; 2 Thess 2:2) being important exceptions. More likely, Paul was a beneficiary of early Christian traditions or memories of Jesus' ministry from "ear" and eyewitnesses, traditions that he received from believers throughout Palestine (Jerusalem, Antioch, Syria). He sometimes mentioned these sacred traditions to his readers (1 Cor 11:2, 23; 15:1, 3; cf. Rom 6:17; 1 Thess 2:13; 2 Thess 2:15; 3:6; 1 Tim 6:3). In still other passages (e.g., Rom 3:25), Jesus tradition from the Jewish church in particular was more implicit. More critically, Paul's message was informed by the thematics of messianic monotheism, grounded in the hope that God's promise to Abraham was now fulfilled and experienced for those who trusted in the redemptive results of Jesus' messianic death. Although he modified tradition about Jesus in order to recenter the significance of the Christ-event upon the cross, the grand themes of Paul's gospel are those of the Messiah. The biblical Gospels and Pauline letters are different parts of the same theological universe.

Paul and His Mission. Most of Paul's autobiographical statements defend his apostolic status and describe the costs of his missionary work (e.g., Rom 1:1-15; 1 Corinthians 9; 2 Cor 1:12–2:17; 7:5-16; 11–12; Phil 1:12-26; 3:1-14; 1 Thessalonians 1–3). Indeed, this self-understanding obligates the interpreter to understand Paul's letters as "missionary-minded," written for newly formed congregations of converts whose faith and witness he was committed to maintaining and nurturing. Given this understanding, in recent years much has been made of the social and cultural contexts of Paul's missionary work, located as it was in several

---

18. Wenham contends that Paul knew a great deal about Jesus and had access to collections of his sayings and stories. See D. Wenham, *Paul: Follower of Jesus or Founder of Christianity?* (Grand Rapids: Eerdmans, 1995). Wenham concludes that Paul adapted the tradition implicitly and creatively in his letters in order to preserve it, not to alter or "remythologize" it. The historical-critical problem in this regard is hermeneutical—that is, a determination of how Paul represented Jesus tradition in his own voice and in a new idiom for a different audience.

19. S. Kim, *The Origin of Paul's Gospel* (Grand Rapids: Eerdmans, 1982). See also A. Segal, *Paul the Convert* (New Haven: Yale University Press, 1990).

important urban centers of the early Roman Empire. There Paul's message of God's grace found a ready audience among social groups constituted by the urban poor and powerless, who perhaps responded more out of psychological than spiritual need.[20]

In this light, scholars analyze the themes of the Pauline letters as intended for a readership formed from alienated and displaced city people. They were written to aid new converts in discriminating between the morality and life-style of a true Israel, and that belonging to "this evil age." Paul's letters to the Corinthians and the Thessalonians, in particular, can be read as primarily concerned with these sorts of issues. A sociohistorical approach makes the interpreter more sensitive to those themes that address moral or religious conflict with the surrounding pagan culture or with the social institutions of urban life. For example, D. Meeks contends that the typical member of an urban congregation founded by the Pauline mission was an artisan or trader, perhaps because Paul was an artisan.[21] R. Jewett suggests that the artisan membership of the Thessalonian congregation was primarily poor, in keeping with Paul's description of the Macedonian church in 2 Cor 8:2-4. It appears that these believers lived a hand-to-mouth existence, dependent on the sometimes fickle benefaction of their wealthy patrons. Against this social background, the modern reader of the Thessalonian correspondence can better understand Paul's admonition to "work" (1 Thess 4:9-12; 2 Thess 3:6-13) as the measure of a life pleasing to God and appreciate his concluding exhortation to depend on the steadfast benefaction of their Lord (1 Thess 5:24; 2 Thess 3:5, 16).[22]

The Apostle Paul and His Readers. A final element critical to Pauline autobiography defends his role and authority as a legitimate apostle (1 Cor 15:1-11; Galatians 1–2). Since this epistolary element conforms to the conventions of Greco-Roman rhetoric, we suppose Paul's intent was to posture himself

and his correspondence before his reading/hearing audience: He and, therefore, what he says have religious authority for those being addressed. Yet, the subject matter of his letter and the spiritual crisis it addressed cohere as well to the definition of this relationship between the apostle and his audience.

In recent years, those interested in constructing a critical biography of Paul have turned to other questions, primarily concerning the internal life and organization of his congregations and their interaction with their surrounding social environment and with Paul, their apostle.[23] For this work, the letters provide primary information, whether to describe the characteristics of these interactions or to analyze them using the methods of social science. To be familiar with these social contingencies is to better understand the setting in which the Pauline voice was first heard as witness to the gospel of God.

THE NON-PAULINE COLLECTION

The eight "conversations" found in the second collection of letters (Hebrews through Jude) are sufficiently different from one another to preclude any general treatment of those historical features that may group these letters into a discrete and coherent collection. Nonetheless, these conversations were shaped by the same larger circumstances that fashioned the Pauline correspondence: the political and social institutions of the Roman Empire; the moral and philosophical thematics of Hellenistic culture; and the core theological convictions of Judaism, informed and interpreted by its Torah.

These letters, however, are grouped around a single feature of their social world that may well orient the interpreter to the distinctive subject matter of the non-Pauline letters in toto. While both collections can be read as different responses to the theological problem of theodicy, the non-Pauline letters locate the roots of this crisis in a sociological rather than a missiological setting. The primary marks of this readership were

20. For this point, see W. Meeks, *The First Urban Christians: The Social World of the Apostle Paul* (New Haven: Yale University Press, 1983); A. Malherbe, *Social Aspects of Early Christianity*, 2nd ed. (Philadelphia: Fortress, 1983) 1-28.

21. See Meeks, *The First Urban Christians*. See also R. Hock, *The Social Context of Paul's Ministry: Tentmaking and Apostleship* (Philadelphia: Fortress, 1980).

22. R. Jewett, *The Thessalonian Correspondence*, FFNT (Philadelphia: Fortress, 1986).

23. See G. Theissen, *The Social Setting of Pauline Christianity* (Philadelphia: Fortress, 1982); B. Holmberg, *Paul and Power* (Philadelphia: Fortress, 1980), both with special interest in the congregations at Corinth.

its poverty (James),[24] its social dislocation (Hebrews), and its alienation (1 Peter)[25] within a hostile environment. The readers of the general epistles suffered because they had been marginalized as a direct result of their faith (Hebrews, 2 Peter, Jude) or because the norms and values of their faith conflicted with those of the persons in charge of the present world order (James, 1 Peter). Although the conflict in the Johannine epistles is internal to the faith community, the dissidents who have left the congregation are sharply castigated as "antichrists" and "deceivers" (1 John 2:18-29; 4:1-4), "who have gone out into the world" (2 John 7). Rather than being received hospitably into one's home (3 John), they are to be shunned as evil (2 John 10-11). In turn, the spiritual test occasioned by suffering required the maintenance of community solidarity during seasons of suffering and social conflict. The marks of God's Israel, then, were not primarily their beliefs, as was true of the Pauline collection, but their behaviors in response to economic poverty and sociopolitical powerlessness.

The theological foundation of their response was, as with Paul, a particular understanding of divine election. However, in the case of the non-Pauline collection, election was redefined not in terms of being Gentile converts but in terms of being socially marginal: God has called out the "poor" (Jas 2:5), the "pilgrim" (Hebrews 11), the "alien and stranger" (1 Pet 1:2; 2:9), the religious sectarians (1 John) of this world, for salvation. The diverse audiences of this collection together formed a community of outcasts for whom the realization of God's promise of socioeconomic and political reversal lay still in the future, in a different world order where the last and the least will be first and fulfilled. The problem of theodicy was concentrated on the apparent contradiction of the community's dual citizenship, which forced it to ask: "Which reign is real, God's or Caesar's?" Surviving the present age in right relationship with God in order to get to the next was the religious project; the community's final, not initial, justification by God was its theological aim.

The distinctive theological accents of this collection interpret the Christian community's struggle to remain faithful to their sacred traditions on many fronts when faithlessness was the more natural response. The keenest stress, then, is on an exemplary (not crucified) Christ—a stress well suited for a collection more ethical than theological in tone. God's will is embodied in Christ's faithfulness (Heb 12:1-4; Jas 2:1; 1 Pet 2:21-25; 1 John 3:11-17; 4:7-21). Further, the terms of Christ's obedient life both legitimate and illustrate the paraenetic traditions used by these writers to give concrete direction to their audiences. The moral exhortations transform the ambiguity of the current crisis into order and tradition (2 Peter/Jude). The eschatological consequences of the community's defection from the truth are envisaged in the warnings and exhortations to view Jesus as the prophetic exemplar of piety. Thus to follow or imitate him during the trials and tribulations of spiritual testing will result in the future blessings of God's promised salvation (Heb 12:25-29; Jas 2:1-13; 1 Pet 3:13-19; 2 Pet 2:17-22; 1 John 3:19-24; Jude 19-20).

Finally, the writings of the non-Pauline collection fashion the social world of a pilgrim people. Suffering and oppression represent those hardships that all pilgrims must bear on their way to the "shrine." Especially in Hebrews, much of this articulates a code of conduct that prepares a people for a pilgrimage: to break from existing ties in the world outside of Christ, to launch out on a journey toward the heavenly shrine, so to enter into the full blessing promised there by God.[26] A pilgrim stands at a distance from the norms and values by which the non-believing world lives. There is an intense desire to obey God steadfastly as a condition of enduring the journey through human existence and entering into eternal life, the chief blessing awaiting the pilgrim people at their heavenly shrine. Every decision and every action prepares for and promotes that pilgrimage to the heavenly end (Heb 10:32–12:29; Jas 1:2-4, 12; 1 Pet 1:1, 6-9; 2:11-12; 2 Pet 1:4-11).

24. So P. Maynard-Reid, *Poverty and Wealth in James* (Maryknoll, N.Y.: Orbis, 1985).

25. So J. Elliott, *A Home for the Homeless* (Philadelphia: Fortress, 1981).

26. For the "pilgrim" motif in Hebrews, see W. Johnsson, *Hebrews*, KPG (Atlanta: John Knox, 1980).

THE WORLD WITHIN THE LETTERS: COMPOSITIONS IN LITERARY CONTEXT

Any responsible interpretation of Scripture demands consideration of the diverse literary genres and rhetorical conventions that characterize its various writings. The full meaning of any letter is not determined solely by the reconstructed history behind the text but also by the literary structure of the composition itself. The discussion of this point will concentrate on two related elements: the literary genre and the rhetorical design of the NT letter. Biblical authors crafted and communicated meaning by using conventional or recognized patterns of speech.

Written correspondence and oral conversation are closely related activities, although their similarity can be exaggerated.[27] Not only do letters convey what the writer might say in person, but also ancient letters were written to be read aloud to an audience (see Eph 3:2-4; Rev 1:3). The oral audience of antiquity was attuned to a speech that affects the ear. As a result, letter writers crafted literary compositions for auditors by using the same techniques of public orators, who steered their audiences and shaped their common histories for their own persuasive purposes. For example, oral communication tends to be sequential, with each new idea introduced and understood by what precedes it. The integral connection of each part of the literary whole is maintained by the repetition of catchwords (or digressions), which not only underscores the composition's unity but also draws the audience to its central point. Today's audience, constituted by silent readers rather than auditors, is more familiar with other kinds of literary markers: computer fonts and typefaces, paragraph indentations, and creative punctuation, all of which organize our reading of a written text. However, an ancient audience heard a text read and organized its subject matter according to repeated words and phrases.

Literary critics usually classify NT letters according to types of oral discourse: sermons or homilies (Hebrews, 1 John),

pastoral exhortation (James, 1 Peter), classroom instruction (Romans, Ephesians), and the like. Although the message is not its medium, it certainly is true that the author's message would be lost were not his or her ideas reconstituted in a language and presented in a literary form that connected with the intended readership. In this sense, then, biblical letters are sufficiently ambiguous or elastic in meaning that their current readers, who live in far different circumstances from those to whom they were written, can still appreciate them as resources for their own theological understanding. Yet, historical questions must still be addressed. The ancient world of literature treasured the act and art of letter writing. The genre and rhetorical artistry current in the literary culture of biblical writers would naturally have informed their decisions about the medium or mode of letter writing.

Two different methods were used in writing letters. One could either write a letter personally or have it written by a skilled scribe. Several of Paul's letters hint at the use of a secretary. The secretary would not be responsible for the subject matter but would do most of the writing. For instance, most epistolary addresses name more than Paul as sender; some scholars think that Sosthenes (1 Cor 1:1) and Silvanus (1 Thess 1:1; 2 Thess 1:1) served as Paul's secretaries. The benediction to 1 Peter mentions Silvanus as its scribe (1 Pet 5:12). References to a personal signature (Gal 6:11; 2 Thess 3:17; Col 4:18) or greeting (1 Cor 16:21) may well imply that the rest was dictated; Rom 16:22 actually names Tertius as "the writer of this letter" (although a few scholars still question whether Romans 16 belongs to the "authentic" Romans letter).[28] Shorter letters, such as Philemon, were probably written by Paul alone (Phlm 19); however, longer letters, such as Romans and the Corinthian correspondence, may have required secretarial assistance. Paul's employment of different scribes to help with his correspondence may well explain the literary and linguistic differences scholars have observed between his letters.

---

27. D. E. Aune, *The New Testament in Its Literary Environment*, LEC (Philadelphia: Westminster, 1987) 159.

28. For a defense of the integrity of Romans, see H. Gamble, *The Textual History of the Letter to the Romans*, SD 42 (Grand Rapids: Eerdmans, 1977).

Letters were sometimes written as literary substitutes for personal (or even "official") visits.[29] They were often written as a practical matter, because authors could not visit their congregations, even though some communities needed apostolic attention. For example, Paul's stated preference was to address a spiritual crisis directly and in person (see Rom 1:9-12), but he was not always able to do so because of imprisonment or missionary obligations. To maintain his ministry and authority in the life of a particular congregation, Paul wrote and sent letters as vehicles of his theological instruction, pastoral care, and moral counsel. These same letters, which were subsequently preserved, collected, and canonized, continue to perform a similar role and to exercise a similar authority today. That is, the letters of the NT are the authorized substitutes for apostolic personae and powers. By reading these letters, the audience of contemporary believers continues to "hear" apostolic "voices" and benefit from their instruction. In this way, the community of faith develops under the aegis of the Spirit into the "one holy catholic and apostolic church."

This theological conviction cues a final literary point: The NT letters were written as if their authors were actually speaking to their audiences. There is nothing artificial or contrived about the epistolary literature of the NT; its expected purpose was to instruct and to persuade its readers, and its intended aim was to enable those readers to make decisions that conformed to the faith. The interpreter must approach these writings as literary art, crafted according to the conventions of the ancient world, whose aim was theological understanding.

THE LETTER GENRE: THE PAULINE COLLECTION

A literary genre is a conventional pattern of written speech that intends to facilitate communication from its author to an audience living in a particular social setting. The epistolary literature of the NT comprises several genres of ancient literature.[30] During the last two centuries, archaeologists have unearthed a treasure trove of Greco-Roman papyri (including Jewish) and clay tablets of the ancient Near East. Included in these finds are thousands of letters that exhibit many of the same literary structures, conventions, and functions as the letters of the NT. Although the NT letters resist formal classification, they exhibit no real literary innovation.[31] Their authors were not literati but pastors who employed the standard epistolary conventions of their day; these writers sought to communicate specific messages, not to create an innovative literary genre.

The modern interpreter approaches the letter genre in terms of its overall literary structure, the rhetorical role of its every part, and the anticipated effect each convention exacts upon the audience. For example, how should the interpreter approach the Pauline letters as a literary genre? The letters unfold according to the simple structure of the integral parts, each of which has a specific role to perform in the effective communication of his gospel:

(1) *Greeting*. In accordance with the conventions of his literary world, Paul begins his letters by introducing himself (and cosenders or secretaries) before greeting his audience with a salutation. The purpose of such prescripts was similar to that of modern business cards, a convention of today's professional world. Business cards make introductions and help to establish relationships with potential clients. Likewise, Paul greets his readers (or auditors) in order to establish a more intimate relationship with them, thereby providing a positive setting for reading (or listening to) his message and then responding accordingly.

In Paul's letters, however, variations of this opening formula carry important theological freight. Paul intends to frame a rhetorical relationship with his first audience through the phrases he uses to introduce himself, to describe his audience, and to fashion his salutation. This relationship is usually grounded in his apostolic charisma, so that his message is received as instructive if not also normative

---

29. See R. Funk, "The Apostolic *Parousia:* Form and Significance," in *Christian History and Interpretation,* ed. W. Farmer, C. F. D. Moule, and R. R. Neibuhr (Cambridge: Cambridge University Press, 1967) 249-68.

30. For a survey, see Aune, *The New Testament in Its Literary Environment,* 158-82.

31. For details of this conclusion, see Aune, *The New Testament in Its Literary Environment,* 183-225.

for life and faith. Sharply put, the Pauline writings of the NT are not personal letters; they are formal "apostolic" briefs, meant to be read to the entire congregation as a word to heed and to follow.

Paul's standard salutation combines χάρις (*charis*, "grace"), an innovation on the Hellenistic salutation χαῖρε (*chaire*, "greetings"), and εἰρήνη (*eirēnē*, "peace"), the greeting found in most Jewish letters. The rhetorical effect of the salutation is twofold: It addresses the audience as beneficiaries of God's universal salvation and prefaces the subject matter of the letter by the essential promise of Paul's gospel—that salvation is entered into by "grace" and "peace" with God is the result (so Rom 5:1-2).

(2) *Thanksgiving.* The second part of a Pauline letter expresses thanksgiving for the spiritual formation of the audience. In giving thanks, Paul continues the convention of Hellenistic and Jewish letter writers who offered thanks for blessings received. There are notable exceptions to this convention, however, within the Pauline corpus. In Galatians, for instance, Paul substitutes stern rebuke for expected blessing with striking effect (Gal 1:6-9); and in 2 Corinthians, a letter to another difficult congregation, Paul offers a benediction for divine comfort where one would expect to find thanksgiving for his audience (2 Cor 1:3-7)! Since there is no specific addressee, the encyclical letter Ephesians (as with 1 Peter) offers thanksgiving to God in the form of a Jewish *berakah*, a liturgical prayer of thanksgiving. Personal letters to well-known colleagues (1 Timothy, Titus) need not include formal thanksgiving, which is implicit in the intimate relationship between author and reader and may not serve the hortatory character of the correspondence in any case.

In most Greco-Roman letters, divine blessings were perceived as deliverance from some physical calamity or economic ruin.[32] The phraseology of the Pauline thanksgivings is quite different, echoing rather the biblical psalms. For instance, the tone of Paul's thanksgiving is worshipful, often fashioned as a prayer that perhaps could serve as a call to worship for a public reading of his letter. Paul's thanksgiving is much like a pastor's invocation at the beginning of a worship service, exalted in language and full of important theological themes that will be taken up again in the following sermon. Long sentences are often used by Paul to evoke a sense of sustained conversation with God (e.g., 1 Cor 1:4-8; Col 1:3-8, 9-11). Only in this spiritual setting can Paul's letter be heard for edification.

Important theological themes supply the substance of Pauline thanksgiving, typically articulating God's saving action in Christ. Rhetorically, these themes bring the audience immediately to the core convictions of Paul's gospel and establish the foundation for the message that follows. Paul is careful to state the practical benefits of accepting these theological convictions. Here, in the most formal and worshipful section of his letter, Paul remains a pastor seeking to nurture his flock. He does not compose his letters from a scholar's study but from that of a pastor; the concerns of his flock press upon his heart and mind. Interpreters of Pauline writings must recognize them as missionary and pastoral in motivation.

The Pauline thanksgiving often includes a prayer for the audience's spiritual formation. Paul projects an intimate, caring attitude toward his auditors. Rhetorically, this prayer fosters a positive, constructive relationship between author and audience. The prayer is also intercessory and often hints at the crisis at hand—that is, at the vital theme of the letter. The words and phrases are not "devotional musings," detached from the main body of Paul's letter. Quite deliberately, they form the basis for what Paul will say to his readers. The prayers in Pauline thanksgivings petition God to resolve the audience's spiritual crisis that has occasioned the writing of the letter.

(3) *Main Body.* Paul next addresses the difficulties that have prompted the writing of the letter, often beginning with a transitional formula or even with a statement of a thesis (e.g., Rom 1:16-18). While the most important and longest part of his letters, the main body remains resistant to formal analysis. Generally, the style of the main body depends on the audience's social location and the circumstances that occasion the letter. Typically,

---

32. The best discussion of Pauline thanksgivings is P. T. O'Brien, *Introductory Thanksgivings in the Letters of Paul,* NovTSup 49 (Leiden: Brill, 1977).

Paul is interested in defending or clarifying his gospel and mission, and he uses those literary devices that help to make his case.

For example, much of the main body of Romans is fashioned as a diatribe, a Greco-Roman literary genre used by philosophers in teaching their students.[33] This kind of formal literature belongs to the classroom, where the teacher imagines himself in a debate with an opponent, who raises questions or makes objections that allow the teacher to argue (and win) his case. Paul addresses his Roman readers, then, as a teacher introducing his students to the grand themes of his gospel. Yet, Paul's self-understanding as a teacher is more deeply rooted in his Pharisaic culture. Recent scholars have made much of Paul's use of Scripture in his letters, in which *midrashim*, or interpretations of biblical texts (whether cited or "echoed"), are incorporated into Paul's arguments both to justify a point and to clarify his intended meaning.[34]

Many other literary genres are also used in the Pauline collection to advance the apostle's message and mission. These include autobiography (e.g., 1 Thess 1:2–3:13; Gal 1:10–2:21; 2 Cor 1:12–2:17; 7:5-16; 10:7–12:13; Col 1:23–2:3); vice and virtue lists (e.g., Rom 1:29-31; 1 Cor 6:9-10; Gal 5:19-23; Col 3:5-9, 12-13; Eph 4:2-3; 1 Tim 1:9-10); household codes (Col 3:18–4:1; Eph 5:21–6:9); and portions of early Christian or Jewish hymns and creeds (e.g., Phil 2:6-11; Col 1:15-20; 1 Tim 3:16).

Most interpreters note that the main body of a Pauline letter reflects the interplay of two integral parts of Pauline preaching: the indicatives of theological instruction (*kerygma*) and the imperatives of moral exhortation (*paraenesis*). Paul's use of common moral traditions found in both Scripture and Greco-Roman philosophy is not arbitrary; indeed, it is a remarkable innovation of his letter genre. While the subject matter of his moral instruction was well-known and widely accepted in his cultural world, he adapted it to the crisis at hand to fashion an exhortation that is "a word on target." More critically, the interplay

between theology and ethics accords with the deeper logic of Paul's gospel. This deeper logic claims that the acceptance of right beliefs, or what he refers to as "the obedience of faith" (Rom 1:5; 16:26), yields right behaviors as the result of participating by faith in Christ's death and resurrection (Col 1:9-10). Believers become in life what they have already become in Christ (so Rom 6:1-12). The internal structure of the main body of the Pauline letter, then, envisages this deeper logic; moral exhortation is adapted not only to his audience's particular situation but also to his gospel.

(4) *Benediction.* Letter writers in the ancient world usually added various greetings, specific instructions, and general exhortations to their readers in the benediction. Paul is no different, although he baptizes these literary conventions by adding the distinctive phrases of his Christian ministry. The Pauline benediction includes personal news (e.g., Rom 15:14-23), general exhortation (e.g., 1 Thess 5:12-28), more specific advice or greetings to individuals (e.g., 1 Cor 16:1-24), a recap of the letter (e.g., Rom 16:17-20; Gal 6:15-16), and a signature like that of modern letters (e.g., Gal 6:11; 2 Thess 3:17), all concluding with a benediction (his "good-bye"), typically a doxology (e.g., 2 Cor 13:13) or prayer (e.g., Rom 16:25-27) that extends the benefaction of divine grace upon his audience.

Except for the occasional "recap," the benediction falls outside the letter's main body, where he addresses the audience's spiritual crisis in a more direct fashion. Paul's concern is for the general well-being of Christian congregations, regardless of the more particular problems of the moment. Benedictions also provide us with a window onto the complex and collaborative character of Paul's mission and early Christian congregational life.

THE RHETORICAL DESIGN OF THE NT LETTER

Not only were NT letters composed according to a variety of contemporary literary genres, but some were deliberately composed according to the ancient rules of rhetoric. Aristotle defined *rhetoric* as the public art of discovering

33. For this point, see S. Stowers, *Letter Writing in Greco-Roman Antiquity*, LEC (Philadelphia: Westminster, 1986); for the form and function of the "main body" in Pauline letters, see J. White, *The Form and Function of the Body of the Greek Letter*, SBLDS 2 (Missoula, Mont.: Scholars Press, 1972).

34. See, for example, Hays, *The Echoes of Scripture in the Letters of Paul.*

the best possible means of persuasion on any subject matter of importance.[35] As so defined, rhetoric is hardly glib or idle conversation. Rather, antiquity understood rhetoric as the disciplined act of speaking about the pertinent issues of the public square, which combined compelling arguments with studied conclusions in a way that informed the audience and prompted its civil action. When a NT letter is approached in terms of its rhetorical art, then what is said can no longer be separated from how it is said, since both contribute to the fuller meaning of the text.

There is, of course, a rhetorical aspect to literary genre. Each part and every convention of a Pauline letter, for example, performs a persuasive role in the conversation between its author and his audience that intends to effect not only increased understanding of the theological crisis that occasioned the letter but also proper response to the writer's admonitions. Thus the rhetorical analysis of a NT letter seeks to combine an interest in how each part fits together in its overall literary design according to the rules of ancient rhetorical theory with the flow and aim of the author's argument. The anticipated result for exegesis is a keener sense of how the content and even language of the text helps to produce a particular response from a community of its readers (or auditors).

According to G. Kennedy's influential studies of ancient rhetoric, the design of a literary composition depends on the kind of response sought.[36] Rhetoricians term "epideictic" those compositions that intend to persuade readers to change their understanding of the world—somewhat comparable to what the gospel calls "repentance"—and "deliberative" those compositions that iterate and reinforce beliefs and values already embraced—akin to what the gospel calls "faith." These are judgments an audience makes about itself. In his letters, Paul sometimes calls for a verdict about his own ministry or apostolic charisma—that is, for a judicial decision by the audience regarding the author's credentials (e.g., 2 Corinthians 10–12; Galatians 1–2).

H. D. Betz's analysis of Galatians as a composition shaped by the rules of judicial rhetoric illustrates this approach to the literary structure of a letter.[37] According to the rules of this type of persuasive speech, Paul begins his correspondence with (1) a *superscriptio* or "prescript" (Gal 1:1-5), in which he first identifies the charges brought against him by laying out the contrast: "neither from human commission nor from human authorities, but through Jesus Christ and God the Father" (Gal 1:1; cf. Gal 1:11-12). The body of his letter begins with (2) a *stasis*, or sharp transitional statement of why the letter is necessary (1:6-10), immediately followed by the extended (3) *narratio* (Gal 1:11–2:14), an autobiography that supplies the audience with all the necessary information (the "facts" of the matter) to make an informed choice. The critical (4) *propositio* (Gal 2:15-21) suggests a common ground, but then sets forth the "proposition" to be proved (2:19-21). The (5) *probatio*, or "proof," follows (Gal 3:1–4:31), which justifies Paul's proposal. This proof consists of several different kinds of evidences: experiential (Gal 3:1-5; 4:12-20), biblical (Gal 3:6-14, 19-25; 4:21-31), legal (Gal 3:15-18), and historical (from Christian tradition, Gal 3:26–4:11).

Paul concludes the main body of his argument with (6) an *exhortatio*, in which the countervailing position of his opponents is refuted in a series of exhortations that both warn and encourage the Galatian believers (Gal 5:1–6:10). Recent literary critics, more concerned with praxis than with aesthetics, are especially drawn to this feature of Pauline (and non-Pauline) rhetoric, which draws the audience's attention to the consequences of their choices. That is, in refuting his opponents in the Galatian churches, Paul is less concerned about the internal logic of his case and more concerned about the success of his arguments in securing a particular kind of communal ethos among his readers.

A (7) *peroratio*, or "postscript," concludes the entire composition (Gal 6:11-18); here

---

35. Aristotle *Rhetoric* 1.1.

36. G. Kennedy, *New Testament Interpretation Through Rhetorical Criticism* (Chapel Hill: University of North Carolina Press, 1984). See also his important survey, *Classical Rhetoric and Its Christian and Secular Tradition from Ancient to Modern Times* (Chapel Hill: University of North Carolina Press, 1980).

37. Betz's work has been criticized by some for trying to "pour" Galatians into a preconceived cast of judicial rhetoric, esp. the nonautobiographical sections of the book (chaps. 3–6). Longenecker, for example, contends that Paul's composition evinces a more creative and synthetic literary art that combines rhetorical conventions with those of Jewish letters and personal innovation. See R. Longenecker, *Galatians*, WBC (Dallas: Word, 1990) clx-cxlii, for a summary of criticisms against Betz and his own suggestions on the rhetorical design of Galatians.

the main points of the debate are summarized and sharpened. This final statement, which contrasts his opponents (Gal 6:12-13) with Paul (6:14-15), suggests that the letter could also be read as a more deliberative discourse in which Paul is seeking to persuade his readers to make a right decision about their beliefs. In most of the Pauline letters, however, these two styles of rhetoric—judicial and deliberative—coexist: What one thinks about Paul and his mission is decisive in one's decision about the faith. Paul seems to recognize well the most important point of rhetorical discourse: The decisions made about the message and the messenger are inseparable.[38]

THE WORLD IN FRONT OF THE LETTERS: CONFESSIONS IN CANONICAL CONTEXT

The NT letters are more than the literary art of particular authors or mere artifacts of ancient history. These same writings belong to the Christian Bible, and their primary purpose in this biblical canon is to inform the theological understanding of believers who hear and read Scripture as "the word of the Lord." This final section, then, will consider the importance of the epistolary writings of the NT from a third perspective, complementary to the other two. This perspective recognizes their canonical authority as part of the church's Scripture and their theological affirmation as part of the church's normative witness to God. Together, these writings form a "cloud of witnesses" that continues to supply their current readers (the "canonical audience") with authorized testimonies to the word of God, revealed in Jesus of Nazareth, and thereby help to define and maintain Christian life and faith "to the end of the age." From its composition by different authors and editors to its canonization as one discrete part of the Christian Bible, and throughout the history of its interpretation and application by

the church catholic, the letter canon serves the theological aim of transmitting a normative and empowering interpretation of God's gospel to each generation of the canonical audience. A "text-centered" interpretation of Scripture is ultimately a theological approach by which the faithful seek to understand what it means to be God's people today.

This orienting concern for Scripture's theological (rather than historical or literary) referentiality and for its ecclesial (rather than authorial or rhetorical) intent supplies the final and most critical interpretive clues for readers of the NT letters. When reading a biblical writing as Scripture, the interpreter must determine meaning in terms of the church's intent to enrich our faith in God and to nurture our understanding of God's gospel. In this sense, the canon and creed of God's people give shape and structure to the world "in front of" Scripture. Faithful readers do not lie prostrate under Scripture in mindless devotion, nor do they stand above Scripture in intellectual arrogance; rather, they bow "in front of" Scripture in order to grasp what may be seen of God's mystery and what may be heard of God's Word. In a world centered by faith in the mercies of God, Scripture is trusted and treasured; its principal readers, members of the faith community, undertake interpretation as a sacred activity performed in obedience to the faith. These core convictions, imbued by experiences of Scripture's empowering effects upon life and faith, forge the faithful interpreter's approach to the meaning of the NT letters for life and faith.

READING THE LETTERS AS SCRIPTURE

The dramatic rise of scholarly interest in the NT canon in recent years has two focal points: the historical and the hermeneutical. Historians of the biblical canon are primarily interested in its formation within early Christianity, whether as a theological construct or as a literary collection. Although these historians sometimes recognize and consider substantial theological issues, they give most of their attention to the chronological development of the canon and to the ideological

---

38. Significant studies emphasizing the interpretive importance of the rhetorical design of specific non-Pauline letters include H. Attridge, *Hebrews*, Hermeneia (Philadelphia: Fortress, 1989); T. Cargal, *Restoring the Diaspora: Discursive Structure and Purpose in the Epistle of James*, SBLDS 144 (Atlanta: Scholars Press, 1993); and D. Watson, *Invention, Arrangement and Style: Rhetorical Criticism of Jude and 2 Peter*, SBLDS 104 (Atlanta: Scholars Press, 1988).

concerns that guided the canonizing process. For example, such scholars typically discuss the relationship between a book's authorship and its canonization in terms of how attribution of authorship influenced the reception of a particular book, both within the earliest church and later into the biblical canon.

The key interpretive issue for the church rests less upon these historical projects and more upon a theological idea: Scripture is the church's *canon* or "rule of faith." Scripture's role as the church's rule of faith presumes its trustworthy witness to him whose incarnation ultimately norms the community's faith. Only in this christological sense can one say that Scripture supplies both the subject matter for the church's theological reflection and the theological boundaries or context within which Christian theology and ethics take shape.

This conviction regarding the contributions of Scripture combines two integral beliefs: Scripture is both a "canonical collection" of sacred writings and a sacred collection of "canonical writings." In the first case, when Scripture's final literary form is privileged as a "canonical collection" (*norma normata*, or "that which *becomes* the rule")—the result of the canonical process that includes and arranges certain writings—the interpretive emphasis is on a specific and limited body of sacred writings. This emphasis not only values the Bible's subject matter for theological reflection and confession, but also discerns the very ordering of Scripture's subunits as the privileged, permanent expression of an intentioned, dynamic interaction between the faithful and their written rule of faith. Such an approach into the meaning of the biblical letters is less interested in the reconstructed history behind a particular letter or in the environs that gave that text its literary and rhetorical shape. These historical and literary interests are retained, but they are located in a later period of the letters' life when the Christian Bible took its final literary shape.[39]

While various historical constructions of the canonical process have been proposed, no one is entirely clear why the various writings eventually stabilized into the Christian Bible. Certainly, one possible reason is rhetorical

or even aesthetic: Over time, different communions of believers came to recognize that particular arrangements of books were more persuasive articulations of the Word of God and performed in more useful ways within that community's life and worship. Indeed, diverse arrangements of books and collections (or "canon lists") may well suggest that different theological values were held among the numerous faith communions of the early church. Eventually, use and disuse narrowed this diversity of arrangements, and a specific form of biblical literature triumphed because it facilitated or better served its intended role as Scripture for the faith community. The theological principle suggested by the canonical process is this: The final shape of the Christian Scriptures best combines and relates its subject matter to serve the church as the literary location where theological understanding is well founded and soundly framed.

In the second case, emphasis is placed on its ongoing religious function (*norma normans*, or "that which *is* the rule") in the act of interpretation that enables biblical texts to function authoritatively in shaping the theology and guiding the praxis of the church.[40] The idea of a "canonical process" is not defined by a specific historical moment or literary product as before. Rather, it draws on the entire history of the Bible's interpretation, whenever the faith community draws upon its Scriptures to "norm" its faith and life. Beginning even before biblical texts were written and continuing today, faithful interpreters contemporize the meaning of their Scriptures so that the faith community might better understand what it means to be God's people.

This canonical function antedates and explains the canonical form, even as the final form facilitates those functions the faith community intended for its canon. In the ongoing act of interpretation, biblical texts "become" canonical when different interpreters pick up the same text again and again to "comfort the afflicted or afflict the comfortable." In the hands of faithful interpreters, past and present, Scripture acquires multiple

---

39. The most influential studies of this approach to biblical studies come from B. Childs, *Introduction to the Old Testament as Scripture* (Philadelphia: Fortress, 1979), and *The New Testament as Canon* (Philadelphia: Fortress, 1984).

40. Sanders understands the canonical process as orchestrated by the "hermeneutics of adaptation." See the important collection of his pioneering studies in J. A. Sanders, *From Sacred Story to Sacred Text* (Philadelphia: Fortress, 1987). For a synthesis of Childs and Sanders into another model of "canonical criticism," see R. Wall and E. Lemcio, *The New Testament as Canon*, JSNTSup 76 (Sheffield: JSOT, 1992).

meanings with the theological aim of forming a people who worship and bear witness to the one true God. In this sense the history of the Bible's formation and interpretation settled more than its final literary shape as the church's written rule of faith. The history also evinced a type of hermeneutics that contemporizes the theological quotient of biblical teaching to give it an authoritative voice for today's community whose worship and witness is again undermined by similar theological crises. What gets picked up again and again and reread over and over by God's people are these same writings that interpret the believer's spiritual testing and resolve it in a way that strengthens faith and transforms life.

The reconstructed meaning of epistolary conversations between ancient writers and their first readers, occasioned by particular sociohistorical circumstances, is now relativized and universalized within Scripture. The letters of the NT are read as *biblical* confessions that bear witness to God's ongoing relationship with current readers, rather than simply as ancient conversations between authors and first audiences. They are preserved and transmitted as Scripture precisely because they promise and demonstrate the practical authority to "norm" Christian faith and guide the life of every believer who struggles to remain faithful to God in ever-changing settings. Under the aegis of God's Spirit, these epistolary compositions, formed by the literary and rhetorical conventions of the ancient world (see above), continue to communicate the gospel and persuade a people to embrace it more fully.

What follows considers the practical importance of these observations: Two properties of the canonical process, evident in the final form and placement of the letters within the NT, are Scripture's own markers that orient the canonical audience to the epistolary literature of the NT as God's Word for today.

THE FINAL FORM OF SCRIPTURE'S MULTIPLE-LETTER CANON

The two collections of letters, pluriformed in literary shape and theological substance, raise problems and possibilities similar to those facing the interpreter of the fourfold gospel of the NT. While the multiplicity of gospels has long been a topic of scholarly investigation and comment, few have considered the relationship between the NT's two corpora of letters a matter of hermeneutical value. What possible relationship does the non-Pauline collection have with the Pauline? At the very least, the sum of all their various theologies constitutes Scripture's whole epistolary witness to God. Yet, different communions privilege different witnesses, each following a "canon within the canon" in turn. For example, the Pauline collection has served Protestant believers as the primary context for theological reflection and moral guidance. This preferential option for the Pauline witness has led some to a reductionism that either reinterprets the non-Pauline letters in Pauline terms or neglects them entirely. For example, Luther at first decanonized the book of James because it seemed to communicate a gospel contrary to the one found in Galatians and Romans. Many still read James through a Pauline filter as a way to preserve its authority. Theological coherence is maintained, then, but at a cost: James is read as a "Pauline" book, distorting or denying its distinctive message.

The witness of the full canon of letters, however, is that diverse theologies are gathered together to form a community of meaning that includes the Pauline and the non-Pauline. Moreover, there is a sense in which this epistolary whole is actually better focused by disagreement than by agreement. That is, the collection's witness to the truth is better forged by the mutual criticism of its contributors, making the whole greater than the sum of its parts. Through contrasting the theologies of Paul and James, the letter canon becomes more robust than if the contributions of James were simply added to what Paul has already brought to the table. The full effect is more like the vibrant sound produced by a complement of different and sometimes dissonant voices. The critical point is that the recognition of the complementary, reflexive relationship between these two collections is absolutely strategic in their interpretation; one cannot be read in isolation from the other lest the canonical purpose of both be diminished. More specifically, the theological substance of the second collection of letters actually extends and enhances the theological setting for reading the first. These epistolary writings, whose names and sequence recall the faith of the "pillars" of the Jewish mission (Gal 2:7-9), provide an authorized apparatus of various checks and balances that prevent the distortion and finally deepen the church's understanding of the Pauline letters—and so of the full gospel.

A common christological formula in the *intracanonical* conversation between Pauline and non-Pauline collections illustrates this point. According to the non-Pauline book of James, the faith community is exhorted to embrace "the faith of our Lord Jesus Christ" (Jas 2:1). This formulation is similar in phraseology to Paul's claim that the coming age of God's salvation has already been inaugurated because of Christ's own faithfulness to God's redemptive will, which is most significantly expressed in Gal 3:22 ("by the faith of Jesus Christ"), Rom 3:22 ("through the faith of Jesus Christ"), and Rom 3:26 ("the one who has the faith of Jesus"; but also in Gal 2:16; Eph 3:12; Phil 1:27; 3:9; Col 2:12; and 2 Thess 2:13).

These crucial phrases are variously translated, of course, depending on how one understands the genitive Ιησοῦ Χριστοῦ (*Iēsou Christou*). In fact, most scholars, ancient and modern, have understood this genitive construction to be "objective": The genitive noun (*Iēsou Christou*) is the recipient or object of the action implied by the verbal noun to which it stands related (πίστις *pistis*, "faith"). Virtually every modern translation of Paul's claim, therefore, is rendered, "through/by faith in Jesus Christ." Especially since the publication of R. B. Hays's influential monograph on the Pauline formula in Gal 3:22,[41] however, an increasing number of scholars understand the Pauline phrase as a "subjective" genitive: The genitive noun is the subject of the action implied by the verbal noun. Thus this phrase gives expression to the personal faith of Jesus in God—"the faith of Jesus Christ"—because of which the salvation-creating grace of God now resides in the community of Jesus' disciples. In the light of this reading, the Pauline confession of the faithfulness of Jesus is taken to underscore the singular significance of his messianic death: God's salvation-creating power was publicly disclosed in the death of Jesus, whose "act of obedient self-giving on the cross became the means by which the 'promise' of God was fulfilled."[42] The object of Jesus' faith is the faithful God, who promises to bring forth life from death.

Likewise, it makes better sense of James to understand the relevant phrase's genitive construction as subjective: To "hold to the faith of the Lord Jesus Christ" (2:1) is to follow his example by not discriminating against the poor (Jas 2:2-4), who are the elect of God and heirs of God's coming kingdom (Jas 2:5). In both texts, then, the "faith of Jesus Christ" expresses his personal faith, which is embodied in his faithful actions, whether on the cross (Paul) or in his ministry among the poor (James). In each case, Jesus' faithfulness to God's will lays claim to his lordship and is exemplary for his eschatological community.

Yet, James uses the formula for a different reason and with a different meaning. Most significant, the nature of Christ's faithfulness serves a moral rather than a soteriological interest. According to James, God's will is summed up in the "royal law" that calls the community to love its (poor and powerless) neighbors (Jas 2:8). Jesus is the messianic exemplar of faithfulness to God's law (Jas 2:8-10), which prohibits playing favorites with the rich and promises life to those who care for the poor neighbor (Jas 2:12-13). There is no messianic death in James; rather, the *life* of Jesus bears witness to God's coming triumph and to the ultimate vindication of true and pure religion by caring for the needs of those in distress (Jas 1:27).

These two different ways of understanding the "faith of Jesus Christ" reflect different theologies, both normative for Christian faith. Given an interest in the complementary and reflexive character of their *intracanonical* relationship, the interpreter is obligated to consider these different conceptions of the "faith of Jesus Christ" together. At the very least, one is compelled by the witness of James to consider the significance of the exemplary life of Jesus, and particularly his

---

41. R. B. Hays, *The Faith of Jesus Christ*, SBLDS 56 (Chico, Calif.: Scholars Press, 1983).

42. Hays, *The Faith of Jesus Christ*, 175.

treatment of the poor, as having messianic value. The resulting balance between Jesus' life and his passion brings the NT letters into greater congruity with the NT Gospels, whose narratives all make this same point. This emphasis on the utterly faithful life of Jesus corrects a tendency in Pauline hermeneutics to concentrate on Christ's death and resurrection as singularly important. Further, the profoundly ethical nature of Jesus' faithfulness helps to form an ethical Christianity that not only is more aware of social injustice but also is obligated to reject it.

On the other hand, the faith community that places emphasis exclusively on the ethical competence of Jesus' life denies the necessity of divine grace as that which both purifies the faith community and empowers its obedient and worshipful response to God. Again, what is lost is the essentially collaborative character of biblical faith, which joins God's response of grace to a needy humanity with humanity's response of obedience to a gracious God. In this case, the "faith alone" of the Pauline witness is replaced by the "works alone" of James. A christology that bears witness to both Paul and James as two discrete, yet complementary, parts of a whole looks to Christ as prototypical of the faith and faithfulness that characterize Christian faith.

THE PLACEMENT OF THE LETTERS WITHIN SCRIPTURE

Not only is it important for the interpreter to approach the two collections of letters as partners engaged in a complementary and reflexive conversation, but it is also important to consider the *intracanonical* relationships between the letters and the other parts of the canonical whole. Both the placement and the titles of NT writings are properties of the canonical process; each is suggestive of the writings' respective roles within the canon and, therefore, properly orient (or reorient) the interpreter to the NT's subject matter.[43]

Quite apart from authorial intentions or the rhetorical design of individual letters, then, the final literary design of the NT canon suggests that particular units of the NT

canon (Gospel, Acts, letter, Apocalypse) have particular roles to perform within the whole. In particular, the sequence of these units within the NT envisages an intentional rhetorical pattern—or "canon-logic," to use A. Outler's[44] phrase—that more effectively orients the readership to the NT's pluriform witness to God and to God's Christ. By this internal logic, readers perceive that each part of the NT has a specific role to perform, which in turn explains the rich diversity of theology, literature, and language that presents Scripture's subject matter and facilitates the performance of Scripture in nurturing the faith community's theological understanding. For example, the Gospel is placed first within the NT because its narrative of the person and work of the Messiah, when taken as a fourfold whole, provides the canonical audience with a theological and moral foundation and focal point for all that follows. And the Apocalypse is placed last because it offers a visionary conclusion to Scripture's story of God.[45]

Along with the final placement of writings and collections within the biblical canon, sometimes the title provided for the various units by the canonizing community brings to clearer focus the particular contribution of that unit to a more robust understanding of God. For example, titles were provided for anonymous compositions to locate them within authoritative traditions (e.g., the four Gospels). In the case of 1 John (and Hebrews in some translations), the title included the word "epistle," even though it follows the homily rather than the letter in literary form and original function. The intent of the added superscription is not to classify its literary genre but to clarify its function within Scripture, which approximates that of a literary letter: to instruct and encourage its faithful readers who seek theological understanding.

The titles and arrangement of writings within the NT are the results of the canonizing stage of Scripture. They shed additional light on how these compositions and collections, written centuries earlier for congregations and religious crises long since settled,

43. See Wall and Lemcio, *The New Testament as Canon*, 161-207.

44. A. Outler, "The Logic of Canon-making and the Tasks of Canon-criticism," in *Texts and Testaments*, W. March, ed. (San Antonio, TX: Trinity University Press, 1980) 263-76.

45. For this point, see Wall and Lemcio, *The New Testament as Canon*, 274-98.

may continue to bear witness to God and to God's Christ for an unknown future readership. The importance of any one biblical voice for theological understanding or ethical praxis is focused or qualified by its relationship to the other voices that constitute the whole canonical chorus. Extending this metaphor, one may even suppose that these various voices, before heard only individually or in smaller groups, became more impressive, invigorating, and even "canonical" for faith only when combined with other voices to sing their counterpunctal harmonies as the full chorus.

The Gospels and the Letters. The interpreter's interest in the relationship between the Jesus of the Gospels and the Jesus of the letters within the world of Scripture differs from that in the relationship within either historical or literary contexts. On the one hand, the difficulties of reconstructing the relationship between the historical Paul and the pre-gospel Jesus traditions of earliest Christianity are well known (see above); equally so are the difficulties of relating narrative (Gospels) and epistolary literature. On the other hand, the canonical approach to the relationship between the Gospels and the letters is guided by theological convictions envisaged by the NT's own canon-logic. In particular, the two collections of letters, written to instruct and encourage faith communities, follow the Gospels, written as narrative interpretations of Jesus' earthly life and messianic ministry. That is, even as faith communities, constituted by the current disciples of Jesus, seek to "follow after" the teaching and example of their Lord, so, too, do the letters "follow after" the Gospels in the NT canon.[46] The very order of NT collections supplies the interpreter with a visual aid that sharpens this crucial concern: The theological aim of biblical letters is to inform and thereby fashion their readers into a people whose life and faith are patterned after the Jesus of the Gospels.

This approach suggests that there is a theology for the entire letter canon that coheres around an integrated set of beliefs, a set that is not propositional but narrative in shape. That is, the narrative of the biblical Jesus provides the readers of the letters with a narrative substructure that puts all the pieces back together again. If most interpreters agree that the letters seek to relate gospel to life, then the subject matter of that gospel, within the canonical context, is provided by the fourfold gospel tradition. In this case, this coherent center of the letters (and all NT literature) is not defined by the reconstructed life of the historical Jesus but by the kerygmatic story of God's actions through Jesus told by the Gospels. This latter story is the presupposition for all the practical advice given and theological claims made by the NT letters.

Acts and the Letters. By this same canon-logic, the final placement of Acts immediately prior to the letters alerts readers to the strategic importance of Acts in providing an introduction to the letters that follow.[47] The ancient church recognized the importance of this role; a version of Acts typically circulated with early collections of the Pauline and non-Pauline letters. The production and transmission of sacred texts in antiquity was limited by size and cost; thus smaller portions of the modern NT circulated independently, in service not only of the church's budget but also of its theological agenda. In the East, for example, Acts was combined with a collection of non-Pauline letters to form a smaller, more portable manuscript called the "Apostolos,"[48] apparently in memory of Jesus' apostolic successors whose stories are told in Acts and whose names are attached to the catholic epistles.[49] In the West, the Pauline corpus was added to the collection to prove Paul's apostolic character and to vindicate the right of his letters to share canonical status with the Gospels.[50] The authors of both collections of letters are introduced and authorized by Acts; and Acts' story of the church's mission to "the end of the earth" becomes a theological

---

46. So P. Achtemeier, "Epilogue: The New Testament Becomes Normative," in H. C. Kee, *Understanding the New Testament*, 4th ed. (New York: Prentice-Hall, 1983) 367-86.

47. See R. W. Wall, "Acts," in *The New Interpreter's Bible Commentary*, 10 vols. (Nashville: Abingdon, 2015) 9:19-21.

48. K. Aland and B. Aland, *The Text of the New Testament* (Grand Rapids: Eerdmans, 1987) 49-50.

49. Trobisch, *Paul's Letter Collection*, 10.

50. See Metzger, *The Canon of the New Testament*, 257-58. E. Goodspeed, now followed by others, hypothesized that an early canon of Paul's letters, mentioned in 2 Pet 3:15-16, was produced and in circulation by the end of the first century. Goodspeed speculated that the production of this proto-canon was prompted by the publication of the book of Acts, whose story of Paul rekindled interest in his literary work. There is no evidence to support Goodspeed's thesis; it rests on the perception that a literary relationship exists between the book of Acts and the letters of Paul. In my view, such a perception became possible only later during the canonical stage of the NT, when the book of Acts and the letters were bound together for the first time in the great uncials of the ancient church.

primer for its readers, making them more alert to the theological subject matter of the letters that follow. Three points will help to clarify these suggestions.

First, Acts offers biographical introductions to the authors of the letters. In the canonical context, such biographies serve a theological purpose by orienting readers to the authority (religious and moral) of apostolic authors as trustworthy carriers of the word of God. This is true even though the historical accuracy of Acts' portrait of Paul and the other leaders of earliest Christianity is still keenly debated (see above). Indeed, from Scripture's perspective Acts offers its readers a theological (rather than a chronological or historical) introduction to the letters that follow. The rhetorical and moral powers of these leaders of earliest Christianity confirm and commend the importance of the letters they wrote or that stand in their apostolic traditions.

The unstoppable expansion of Christianity into the pagan world through apostolic preaching, which Acts narrates with profound optimism, underscores the anticipated result of reading and embracing what these same agents of the divine word have written. Again, the issue is not that Acts fails as a historical resource; rather, its narrative succeeds as a resource that facilitates the theological aim of the epistolary literature. In Acts' case, the *writer's* intention to defend Paul and his Gentile mission, which especially shapes the second half of his narrative, serves well the overarching *canonical* intention to introduce Paul's letter collection as theologically normative, whether or not the author had read the letters in advance of writing Acts.

Second, Acts offers readers a narrative backdrop against which they can better understand the diverse theologies that make up both collections of letters, whether those linked with Paul and his Gentile mission or those linked with the "pillars" of the Jewish mission (so Gal 2:9). Acts retains, approves, and deepens the appreciation of the theological diversity found within this epistolary witness (see Acts 15:1-21).

Modern discussions have emphasized how the "catholicizing" narrator of Acts softens the disagreements between the leaders of earliest Christianity. What is often overlooked in making this point is that the church eventually collected and canonized a Pauline corpus whose principal letters were often polemical and potentially divisive. The question is never raised as to why these letters were included in the canon of a catholic church if the aim was to shape theological uniformity. Might it not be the case that the canonizing process looked to Acts not to smooth Paul's polemical edges but to interpret them?

According to Acts, the church that claims continuity with the first apostles tolerates a theological pluralism even as the apostles did, although not without controversy and confusion. The Jerusalem synod described in Acts 15 achieves a kind of theological understanding rather than a theological consensus (see Acts 15:19-21). According to Acts, the divine revelation given to the apostles forms a "pluralizing monotheism,"[51] which in turn informs two discrete missions and appropriate proclamations, Jewish and Gentile (so Gal 2:7-10). Sharply put, Acts interprets the two collections of letters in a more sectarian fashion: The Pauline corpus reflects the gospel of the Gentile mission, while the non-Pauline collection reflects the gospel(s) of the Jewish mission. However, rather than causing division within the church, such theological diversity is now perceived as normative and necessary for the work of a God who calls both Jews and Gentiles to be the people of God.

As a context for theological reflection, Acts forces us to interpret the letters in the light of two guiding principles. First, we should expect to find theological diversity as we move from Pauline to non-Pauline letters. Second, we should expect such a diversity to be useful in forming a single people for God. Against a critical hermeneutics that tends to select a "canon within the canon" from among the various possibilities, the Bible's own recommendation is for an interpretive strategy characterized by a mutually informing and self-correcting conversation between biblical theologies.

Third, the core theological commitments of Acts guide theological reflection upon the letters. The point is not that a theology of Acts determines or even anticipates the

---

51. See J. A. Sanders, *Canon and Community* (Philadelphia: Fortress, 1984) 46-68.

theological subject matter of the letters but that Acts shapes a particular perspective, an abiding practical interest that influences the interpretation of the letters. For example, one may contend that the primary theological interest of Acts is the missionary advancement of the word of God to the "end of the earth" under the aegis of the Spirit. This missionary concern then functions in theological reflection as an implicit way of thinking about and organizing the subject matter of the letters that follow. That is, a reading of the letters under the light of Acts will bring to sharper focus the identity and praxis of a missionary people who respond to the Lord's demand to be God's witness to the end of the earth. Whether or not the authorial intent of the Pauline letters is missiological, their intent in canonical context becomes missiological because the Pauline letters are interpreted in the light of the missionary Paul of Acts.

The theological orientation to the letters provided by Acts holds even for the non-Pauline letters. The audiences of the non-Pauline letters are addressed in terms of their marginal social status rather than their missionary vocation. How does the missionary perspective of Acts, then, finally inform and deepen the understanding of God's people as a faith community, the outcasts from the cultural order? In part, the response is to read the non-Pauline and Pauline letters together for a fuller understanding of mission. On the one hand, the mission of the church requires accommodation in order to spread the gospel (1 Cor 9:12b-23); on the other hand, the mission of the church must take care not to be corrupted by the values and behaviors of the world outside of Christ (Jas 1:27). This more prophetic (and complete) definition of mission, which goes out into the world yet remains unconformed to it, is confirmed by Matthew's Jesus: "I am sending you out like sheep into the midst of wolves; so be wise as serpents and innocent as doves" (Matt 10:16).

The Letters and the Apocalypse. The strategic relationship between the letters and the book of Revelation within the NT is made evident to the interpreter by the similarity of their literary structure and theological function. While its literary conventions are mainly apocalyptic (Rev 1:1) and its message is prophetic (Rev 1:3), the Apocalypse is composed by its author as an encyclical epistle, similar in form to Ephesians or 1 Peter, and written for the theological instruction of "the seven congregations of Asia" (Rev 1:4), whose communicants are at very different places of their spiritual journey (Revelation 2–3). The placement of the Apocalypse at the end of the Christian Bible envisages its role as the conclusion to Scripture's story of God. God's final triumph over death has already begun through the messianic Lamb (Revelation 5; 19–21), by whom all creation will be purified and then restored to its original intent, which is to worship God and to rule with God forever (Rev 5:9-10; 21:22-27).

Of course, the congregation's response to this great confession of Christian faith depends on its spiritual maturity. If the communicants refuse to repent of their theological immaturity or moral impurity and become "overcomers" (Rev 2:7, 11, 17, 26; 3:5, 12, 21), then the message of God's coming triumph is heard with apocalyptic terror (Rev 3:14-22). However, this same message is heard by the mature and faithful, especially in a context of suffering and spiritual testing (Rev 2:8-11; 12–13), with profound hope for their eschatological vindication (Rev 14:1-5). And these same options do not change through space and time, for "the Lord God Almighty was and is and is to come" (Rev 4:8). No less than did its first auditors, contemporary congregations approach the book of Revelation as Scripture to read and reflect upon its message of God's coming triumph, either to repent or to hope because of their fidelity to the "eternal gospel" (Rev 14:6).

This orientation to the truth of the "eternal gospel," nurtured by the Apocalypse, infuses the interpretation of the NT letters with greater power and urgency, "for the time is near" (Rev 1:3; 22:10). This is the case not because the subject matter of the letters is more finely nuanced by the canonical interplay between epistle and Apocalypse but because the principal incentive and purpose of biblical interpretation are now understood more clearly than before. The church's interpretation of the NT letters aims at obedience to their inspired instruction—obedience now excited afresh by the Apocalypse's wondrous vision of the sovereign creator's sense of justice and the slain Lamb's conquering mercy.

BIBLIOGRAPHY

Childs, Brevard S. *The New Testament as Canon.* Philadelphia: Fortress, 1984.

Donelson, Lewis R. *From Hebrews to Revelation: A Theological Introduction.* Louisville: Westminster/John Knox, 2000.

Doty, William G. *Letters in Primitive Christianity.* GBS. Philadelphia: Fortress, 1973.

Dunn, James D. G. *The Theology of Paul the Apostle.* Grand Rapids: Eerdmans, 1998.

Fitzmyer, Joseph, S.J. *Paul and His Theology.* 2nd ed. Englewood Cliffs, N.J.: Prentice Hall, 1989.

Hengel, Martin. *Judaism and Hellenism: Studies in Their Encounter in Palestine During the Early Hellenistic Period.* 2nd ed. Minneapolis: Fortress, 1991.

McDonald, Lee M. *The Formation of the Christian Biblical Canon.* Rev. ed. Peabody, Mass.: Hendrickson, 1995.

McNamara, Martin. *Palestinian Judaism and the New Testament.* GNS 4. Wilmington, Del.: Glazier, 1983.

Meade, David G. *Pseudonymity and Canon: An Investigation into the Relationship of Authorship and Authority in Jewish and Earliest Christian Tradition.* Grand Rapids: Eerdmans, 1986.

Neyrey, Jerome. *Paul, In Other Words: A Cultural Reading of His Letters.* Louisville: Westminster, 1990.

Stambaugh, John E., and David L Balch. *The New Testament in Its Social Environment.* LEC. Philadelphia: Westminster, 1986.

Stowers, Stanley. *Letter Writing in Greco-Roman Antiquity.* LEC. Philadelphia: Westminster, 1986.

Wall, Robert. W. "Reading the New Testament in Canonical Context." In *Hearing the New Testament: Strategies for Interpretation.* Edited by Joel B. Green. Grand Rapids: Eerdmans, 1995.

Wall, Robert W., and Eugene E. Lemcio, *The New Testament as Canon.* JSNTSup 76. Sheffield: JSOT, 1992.

THE LETTER TO THE ROMANS

INTRODUCTION, COMMENTARY, AND REFLECTIONS
BY
N. T. WRIGHT

THE LETTER TO THE

ROMANS

INTRODUCTION

R omans is neither a systematic theology nor a summary of Paul's lifework, but it is by common consent his masterpiece. It dwarfs most of his other writings, an Alpine peak towering over hills and villages. Not all onlookers have viewed it in the same light or from the same angle, and their snapshots and paintings of it are sometimes remarkably unalike. Not all climbers have taken the same route up its sheer sides, and there is frequent disagreement on the best approach. What nobody doubts is that we are here dealing with a work of massive substance, presenting a formidable intellectual challenge while offering a breathtaking theological and spiritual vision.

Perhaps not surprisingly, it remains the case that anyone who claims to understand Romans fully is, almost by definition, mistaken. It is common to list saints and Christian leaders whose lives have been changed by reading this letter; the catalog could be balanced by a similar number who have radically misunderstood it. Troublingly, the lists would overlap. Having studied this letter intensively for much of my adult life, I, of course, believe that my current opinions on its historical and theological meaning, though humble, are accurate. But the example of others, and the memory of my own past changes of mind, leave me under no illusions as to the provisional nature of my conclusions.

Equally, anyone who claimed to have read all the commentaries (let alone all the other secondary literature) on Romans would be lying. Likewise, anyone who tried to refer to it all, let alone enter into debate with it all, would produce an unreadable book. I am indebted to far more colleagues, ancient and modern, than can be mentioned in the footnotes or bibliography; but the purposes of this series are better served by exposition of the view to which the author has come, with occasional debates with other major interpretations, than by endless listing of and interaction with the many alternative readings that have been put forward. At the end of almost every sentence the reader should imagine an invisible footnote: "For more information, alternative views, and secondary literature, see the recent commentaries." Though in my earlier work I studied and interacted with interpreters from many generations, I have here deliberately tried to engage in debate the more recent writers, not least the two major Roman Catholic commentaries of Fitzmyer and Byrne and the two major Protestant ones of Dunn and Moo.[1]

It has become customary to approach a biblical book by asking when, where, why, and by whom it was written and then, as a second stage, what it actually says. Some of these initial questions, fortunately, are not controversial in the case of Romans; nobody doubts that Paul wrote it in the middle to late 50s of the first century, from Corinth or somewhere nearby, while planning his final voyage to Jerusalem with the intention of going on thereafter to Rome and thence to Spain. But the remaining question, "Why?" has proved remarkably difficult. Romans stands as a reminder that "why" and "what" are more organically related than we have sometimes liked to think. Theories about why Paul wanted to write this letter to this church at this moment must remain in constant dialogue with the complex discussion of what the letter itself actually says. As in other disciplines, the greatest strengths of a hypothesis or theory are to make sense of the data, to do so within an appropriately simple overall design, and to shed light on other areas of cognate research. These large aims are in view in what follows.

THE SHAPE AND THEME OF ROMANS

It is no good picking out a few favorite lines from Romans and hoping from them to understand the whole book. One might as well try to get the feel of a Beethoven symphony by humming over half a dozen bars from different movements. Romans is, indeed, a symphonic composition: Themes are stated and developed (often in counterpoint with each other), recapitulated in different keys, anticipated in previous movements and echoed in subsequent ones. Although the demands of a commentary mean that headings will be offered for its different sections, we should not thereby be misled into supposing that each paragraph is simply "about" one particular topic. That is not how Paul wrote, at least not here. He was far more likely, in individual sentences, paragraphs, and sections, to state a point in a condensed fashion and then steadily to unpack it, in the manner of someone unfolding a map stage by stage so that each new piece offers both a fresh vision and a sense of having been contained within what had gone before. At almost no point in this letter does he offer detached reflections on isolated "topics" (13:1-7 is perhaps an exception, which is one reason, though not the main one, why some have suggested that it may be an interpolation). Although Romans, written within the general Hellenistic culture of the Greco-Roman world, shares some rhetorical features with other letters of the time and place, it is impossible either to pigeonhole it within a particular genre or to use such possible parallels to infer what the letter is about independent of full-scale consideration of its argument. We must follow the sequence of thought, the inner logic, of the whole work.

The easiest thing to determine about Romans is its basic shape. Its four sections emerge clearly: chaps. 1–4, 5–8, 9–11, and 12–16. From time to time, impressed by the way in which chap. 5 draws out and in a way completes the thought of chaps. 1–4, some writers have suggested that the key break occurs between chaps. 5 and 6 rather than between 4 and 5;[2] but most are now content with the outline suggested, not least since it is clear that the opening of chap. 5 states in summary form the themes that are then developed through to the end of chap. 8. In any case, to note the divisions is not to say that Paul is doing more than rounding off one train of thought before proceeding to a closely cognate, and logically consecutive, idea. As we shall see, the most abrupt and decisive breaks—those at the ends of chaps. 8 and 11—by no means indicate that he is now going to write "about" something else altogether. Attempts to impose a formal structure on the letter are either trivial (e.g., pointing out that the opening of chap. 1 functions as the "Greeting" and 15:14–16:27 as the "Conclusion") or tendentious (e.g., suggesting that 1:18–11:36 is the "body of the letter," thereby implying that chaps. 12–16 are a mere exhortatory postscript—a view challenged in the commentary).

1. Joseph A. Fitzmyer, *Romans*, AB 33 (Garden City, N.Y.: Doubleday, 1993); Brendan Byrne, *Romans*, SP 6 (Collegeville, Minn.: Liturgical, 1996); James D. G. Dunn, *Romans 1–8*, WBC 38A (Dallas: Word, 1988); James D. G. Dunn, *Romans 9–16*, 38B (Dallas: Word, 1988); Douglas J. Moo, *The Epistle to the Romans*, NICNT (Grand Rapids: Eerdmans, 1996).

2. See Ulrich Wilckens, *Der Brief an die Römer*, 3 vols., EKK 6 (Zurich: Benziger, 1978–82) 1:93.

In fact, to see how the different parts of the letter hang together and to understand why Paul wanted to say just this at just this moment to these people, the most important thing to do is to grasp the main theme of the letter and to see why it was important to first-century Jews in general, to Paul in particular, and to him in this setting most specifically.

"God's Righteousness." It is not difficult to discover the main theme of the letter. "God's gospel unveils God's righteousness": That, in effect, is Paul's own summary in 1:16-17, and the letter does, indeed, unpack this dense statement. Unfortunately, though, even this apparently simple sentence is controversial, and we must clarify what is meant and justify, at least preliminarily, the decision to treat the passage, and the letter, in this way. As often in Paul's writings, to understand one key phrase we need to draw on a range of evidence and pick our way through a minefield of arguments. Before we can even address the question of why Paul wrote this particular letter, we must examine the broader question of why a Jew like him would be concerned with this overarching issue.

"God's Righteousness" in Paul's Judaism: Covenant, Lawcourt, Apocalyptic. The phrase "the righteousness of God" (δικαιοσύνη θεοῦ *dikaiosynē theou*) summed up sharply and conveniently, for a first-century Jew such as Paul, the expectation that the God of Israel, often referred to in the Hebrew Scriptures by the name YHWH, would be faithful to the promises made to the patriarchs. Many Jews of Paul's day saw Israel's story, including the biblical story but bringing it up to their own day, as a story still in search of a conclusion—a conclusion to be determined by the faithfulness of their God. As long as Israel remained under the rule of pagans, the great promises made by this God to the patriarchs, and through the prophets, had still not been fulfilled.

Thus, although the Babylonian exile had obviously come to a literal end some centuries before, the promises made at the time—promises of a glorious restoration of the nation, the Temple, and the whole Jewish way of life—were widely regarded as still awaiting complete fulfillment (see the Commentary on 9:6–10:21).[3] Loyal Jews living under the various post-Babylonian powers (Persia, Greece, Egypt, Syria, and finally Rome) continued to tell the whole story of Israel in terms of promises made to the patriarchs; of an early golden age under David and Solomon; of rebellion, decline, and exile; of a long period of waiting for restoration; and of the eventual new day of liberation that would dawn in God's good time. They believed that YHWH had entered into covenant with them to do all this; paradoxically, the exile was itself, as Jeremiah, Daniel, and others had insisted, part of the covenant, since it was the result of Israel's disobedience. But their God would remain loyal to the covenant, and this loyalty would result in the great day of liberation coming to birth at last.[4] The phrase that captures this whole train of thought, occurring in various forms in the Scriptures and post-biblical writings, is "God's righteousness," in the sense of God's loyalty to the covenant with Israel (see, e.g., Ps 33:4; Isaiah 40–55; Jer 32:41; Lam 3:23; Hos 2:20). The overtones of the phrase thus bring its semantic range very near to another great biblical theme, that of God's sure and steadfast covenant love for Israel—a point of considerable importance for understanding Romans, as we shall see.

Never leaving behind this covenantal meaning, the word "righteousness" is also shaped by the Second Temple Jewish setting of the lawcourt. In the lawcourt as envisaged in the OT, all cases were considered "civil" rather than "criminal"; accuser and defendant pleaded their causes before a judge. "Righteousness" was the status of the successful party when the case had been decided; "acquitted" does not quite catch this, since that term applies only to the successful defendant, whereas if the accusation was upheld the accuser would be "righteous." "Vindicated" is thus more appropriate. The word is not basically to do with morality or behavior, but

---

3. This is still controversial, in my view needlessly. See N. T. Wright, *The New Testament and the People of God*, vol. 1 of *Christian Origins and the Question of God* (Minneapolis: Fortress, 1992) 268-71; and *Jesus and the Victory of God*, vol. 2 of *Christian Origins and the Question of God* (London: SPCK, 1996) xvii-xviii, with reference to the massive evidence in Second Temple Judaism. See also N. T. Wright, "In Grateful Dialogue: A Response," in *Jesus and the Restoration of Israel*, ed. C. C. Newman (Downers Grove, Ill.: InterVarsity, 1999) 253-61; and J. M. Scott, ed., *Exile: Old Testament, Jewish, and Christian Conceptions* (Leiden: Brill, 1997). Even if it is not accepted that most of his contemporaries would have agreed, I would still contend that this is demonstrably Paul's own point of view. Another Pauline passage that makes excellent sense on this reading is Gal 3:10-14, on which see N. T. Wright, *The Climax of the Covenant: Christ and the Law in Pauline Theology* (Minneapolis: Fortress, 1991) chap. 7; and S. J. Hafemann, "Paul and the Exile of Israel in Galatians 3–4," in Scott, *Exile*, 329-71.

4. This sequence of thought is clearly visible in passages like Ezra 9 and Daniel 9. See Wright, *The New Testament and the People of God*, chaps. 9–10.

rather with status in the eyes of the court—even though, once someone had been vindicated, the word "righteous" would thus as it were work backward, coming to denote not only the legal status at the end of the trial but also the behavior that had occasioned this status.[5]

The word "righteousness" applied not only to the accuser or defendant; it also denoted the appropriate activity of the judge. His duty was clear: to be impartial, to uphold the law, to punish wrongdoing, and to defend those who, like the orphan and the widow, had nobody else to defend them. Thus the "righteousness" of the judge, on the one hand, and of the parties in the case, on the other hand, are very different things. Neither has anything directly to do with the general moral behavior or virtue of the persons concerned.

Covenant and lawcourt are far more closely linked than often imagined. Behind both categories there stands a fundamental Jewish self-perception, which, if we grasp it, will enable us to understand things Paul holds together in many passages in Romans, but which interpreters have consistently separated. Through many and various expressions of covenant theology in the biblical and post-biblical periods, a theme emerges that, though by no means central in all Second Temple Judaism, has a claim to represent a deep-rooted and biblical viewpoint. It can be stated thus: The covenant between God and Israel was established in the first place in order to deal with the problem of the world as a whole. Or, as one rabbi put it, God decided to make Adam first, knowing that if he went to the bad God would send Abraham to sort things out.[6] The covenant, in other words, was established so that the creator God could rescue the creation from evil, corruption, and disintegration and in particular could rescue humans from sin and death.

In biblical thought, sin and evil are seen in terms of injustice—that is, of a fracturing of the social and human fabric. What is required, therefore, is that justice be done, not so much in the punitive sense that phrase often carries (though punishment comes into it), but in the fuller sense of setting to rights that which is out of joint, restoring things as they should be. Insofar, then, as God's covenant with Israel was designed, at the large scale, to address the problem of human sin and the failure of creation as a whole to be what its creator had intended it to be, the covenant was the means of bringing God's justice to the whole world. Since "justice" and "righteousness" (δικαιοσύνη *dikaiosynē*) and their cognates, translate the same Hebrew and Greek originals, we discover that God's righteousness, seen in terms of covenant faithfulness and through the image of the lawcourt, was to be the instrument of putting the world to rights—of what we might call cosmic restorative justice.

The images of covenant and lawcourt thus draw together, within one complex range of imagery, a familiar Second Temple perception of the Jews' own story in relation to the rest of the world. Many Jewish writings of this period tell the story of Israel and the pagan nations in terms of a great cosmic lawsuit: When the psalmists beg God to vindicate them against their adversaries, they are expressing a characteristic standpoint (e.g., Psalm 143). The pagan nations are oppressing Israel; whether they are thought of as accusers and Israel as a defendant or whether Israel is accusing the pagans of wrong-doing is unimportant. YHWH is not simply Israel's God, but the creator of the whole world and its judge; as such, YHWH is under an obligation to set things right, not least to vindicate the oppressed. True, there are some biblical passages in which YHWH is Israel's adversary at law; but, although Paul recognizes this as a theoretical and problematic possibility (see the Commentary on 3:5), his argument sticks to the more usual conception. YHWH is the judge; the nations that make war upon Israel are to be tried and condemned; Israel is to be vindicated. This scene is classically portrayed in the seventh chapter of the book of Daniel.

It takes only a little reflection, and a little acquaintance with the Jewish history and literature of Paul's period, to see that a tension or conflict could arise between the covenantal and lawcourt meanings of "righteousness." YHWH was supposed to come to Israel's rescue because of the covenant obligations between them; but YHWH was also the judge in the cosmic court, committed to judging justly between Israel and the nations and to establishing an appropriately

---

5. A good example of this can be seen in Genesis 38:26, when Judah acknowledges that his daughter-in-law Tamar is in the right and he is in the wrong. This states a legal position; only secondarily, and by implication, does it comment on the morality of their respective behavior.

6. *Gen. Rab.* 14:6.

just rule over the whole world. Is Israel also guilty? What will YHWH do then?[7] That was a puzzle for many Jews in Paul's world, and we may suppose it had been so for Paul as well; as a zealous Pharisee (his own self-description; see Gal 1:13-14; Phil 3:6), he must have longed to see God's righteousness revealed against wicked pagans and renegade Jews alike, vindicating covenant-faithful Jews like him. Although recent scholars have emphasized that there is no evidence for the pre-Christian Paul suffering from a bad or troubled conscience in the post-Augustinian sense, we must insist that there is every reason to suppose that he agonized over the fate of Israel, longing for YHWH to act decisively in history, but uncomfortably aware that if this were to happen many Jews would face condemnation along with Gentiles.

All this brings into view a final dimension of the phrase "God's righteousness." Precisely because the term evoked covenant loyalty, on the one hand, and commitment to putting the whole world to rights, on the other, it was perhaps inevitable that Jews who longed for all this to happen would come to describe it in what we now call "apocalyptic" language. We need to be clear, however, what we mean by this. In common with many scholars, I use the term "apocalyptic" to denote not so much a state of mind or a set of beliefs about the future, but a way of writing that uses highly charged and coded metaphors to invest space-time reality with its cosmic or theological significance. "The stars will not give their light, and the sun and the moon will be darkened" (Isa 13:10); what Isaiah had in mind was the destruction of Babylon. Four beasts will emerge from the sea; what Daniel had in mind was the rise of great empires. "One like a son of man will come to the Ancient of Days"; what Daniel had in mind was "the saints of the most high" receiving the kingdom (Daniel 7). Even so, "God's righteousness will be revealed" was a coded way of saying that God would at last act within history to vindicate Israel. The word for "is revealed" in Rom 1:17 is ἀποκαλύπτεται (*apokalyptetai*), suggesting precisely, within the first-century Jewish world, the final unveiling within history of the secret plan that Israel's God had all along been hatching.

However, just because apocalyptic language was not designed to denote literal cosmic events (the collapse of the space-time universe, for instance), that does not mean that first-century Jews did not suppose that their God would act suddenly and swiftly to bring about these long-delayed purposes. On the contrary, as the night grew darker, as pagan power increased, and as disloyalty within Israel itself became more rife, Jews like Paul must have prayed and longed for actual space-time events that would demonstrate beyond any doubt that Israel's God was the creator and judge of all the world. Through God's actions on behalf of Israel, the world would see the truth for which it had longed, the justice for which it had striven. Since this expectation of a radically new event breaking into history is in any case what some mean by "apocalyptic," we can assert that "God's righteousness" is to be understood within a framework of thought in which "covenant," "lawcourt," and "apocalyptic" language and thought forms are joined together in mutual compatibility.

"God's Righteousness" as Paul's Christian Question. Paul's world of thought was a variation on the Second Temple Jewish worldview. However much his encounter with the risen Jesus on the road to Damascus challenged and changed him, and however much he saw himself as "the apostle to the Gentiles," he still thought like a Jew and, most important, regarded his own Jewishness as significant (see the Commentary on 11:1-6). He quickly came to regard the events of Jesus' death and resurrection as the apocalyptic moment for which he and others had longed, and he rethought his previous way of viewing the story of Israel and the world as a result.

This can be seen precisely in Paul's vocation to be "the apostle to the Gentiles," a theme of considerable significance for Romans. Paul did not take the message of Jesus the Messiah to the Gentiles out of mere frustration that his fellow Jews had refused it, as a kind of displacement activity, but rather out of the conviction that, if God's purposes for Israel had indeed now been fulfilled, it was time for the Gentiles to come in. As becomes increasingly clear, his Gentile mission was an eschatological activity—that is, a task to be undertaken once God had acted climactically

---

7. This question, and the question of "God's righteousness" that it raises, is a major theme of the book known as 4 Ezra, written after the destruction of the Temple in 70 CE. See B. W. Longenecker, *Eschatology and the Covenant: A Comparison of 4 Ezra and Romans 1–11* (Sheffield: JSOT, 1991).

and decisively within history. It was a key feature of the new age that had now dawned, part of Paul's sense that God's future had arrived in the present, in the person and achievement of Jesus and the power of the Spirit. Although Paul clearly believed that there was a further and final event still to come, which he describes variously at different points in his writings, the great promised "end" had already begun to happen (see particularly 1 Cor 15:20-28).

This, of course, forced him to reconsider what it was that Israel's God had promised. If this was how the promises had been fulfilled, had God suffered a change of mind? Or had Israel misunderstood God's intentions? Jesus' death and resurrection, seen as the messianic events through which Israel's God had brought the covenant story to its unexpected climax, functioned for Paul not unlike the way the fall of Jerusalem functioned for the author of 4 Ezra: as the catalyst for a serious rethinking of God's promises and intentions, God's covenant faithfulness. Paul's point, to which he stuck like a leech throughout his different debates, was that Israel's God had been true to the covenant and the promises. Paul resisted all tendencies to move toward what would later be called Marcionism.[8]

This notion emerges particularly in Paul's view of the Torah, the Jewish law, which will be touched on a good deal in the commentary. Paul's fundamental insights here, which have earned him much criticism from his fellow Jews from that day to this, are (1) to uncouple the Mosaic law from the Abrahamic covenant and thus (2) to regard the Abrahamic covenant as fulfilled "apart from the law" (3:21); (3) to see the Torah as applying to Jews and Jews only, and hence not being relevant to the eschatological period when the Gentiles were coming in to God's people; (4) to see the Torah as intensifying the problem of Adam's sin for those who were "under the Torah," and thus as something from which its adherents needed to be freed; and (5) to claim, nevertheless, that the Torah had been given by God, had performed the paradoxical tasks assigned to it, and was now strangely fulfilled in the creation of the new people of God in Christ and by the Spirit. Romans makes a substantial contribution to this complex but coherent picture.

Paul thus stuck to, and argued at length for, a view of what God had done in Jesus the Messiah according to which these events were to be seen as the fulfillment of what God had promised to the patriarchs. It was, of course, a sudden and surprising fulfillment, overturning cherished expectations, breaking in unexpectedly upon the worldview that Paul himself had cherished. Recent debates have highlighted the need to stress both the continuity, in Paul's mind, between his gospel and that which had gone before in Judaism and the discontinuity, the sense of radical newness, of a divine purpose suddenly and shockingly unveiled. To soft-pedal either of these strong points is to miss the inner tension and dynamic of Paul's thought. It is, in particular, to miss the peculiar force and glory of the letter to the Romans.

"God's Righteousness" as the Theme of Romans. Romans has suffered for centuries from being made to produce vital statements on questions it was not written to answer. All that has been said so far by way of historical and theological introduction will seem strange to those traditions of reading the letter that assume its central question to be that of Martin Luther: "How can I find a gracious God?" If we start there, as many commentaries will reveal, Paul's discussion of Israel and its Torah either takes second place or, worse, is relegated to a more abstract and generalized discussion of the sin and salvation of humans in general, in which the question of Israel's fate is essentially a side issue.[9] Within such a reading, it has been common to highlight the doctrine of "justification by faith," in which humans must realize their inability to make themselves "righteous" and must instead trust God's action in Christ, because of which they will be reckoned as "righteous" despite not having obeyed "the law"—that is, a general or universal moral code.

This "righteousness," the status now enjoyed by God's people in Christ, is described in Phil 3:9 as "a righteousness from God [ἡ ἐκ θεοῦ δικαιοσύνη *hē ek theou dikaiosynē*]," from which many have suggested that this status, too, is what is referred to in Rom 1:17 and elsewhere as

---

8. Marcion was a 2nd cent. CE Roman heretic who taught that the God of the Jews was a different god from that revealed in Jesus.

9. See C. H. Dodd, *The Epistle of Paul to the Romans*, 2nd ed. (London: Fontana, 1959) esp. 161-63. For a recent commentary in the Reformation tradition, see P. Stuhlmacher, *Paul's Letter to the Romans: A Commentary*, trans. S. J. Hafemann (Louisville: Westminster John Knox, 1994).

the *dikaiosynē theou*, "the righteousness of God."[10] Although etymologically possible, this is historically very unlikely. When the latter phrase occurs in biblical and post-biblical Jewish texts, it always refers to God's own righteousness, not to the status people have from God; and Jewish discussions of "God's righteousness" in this sense show close parallels with Paul's arguments in Romans (obvious passages include Deut 33:21; Judg 5:11; 1 Sam 12:7; Neh 9:8; Pss 45:4; 72:1-4; 103:6; Isaiah 40–55 [e.g., 41:10; 45:13; 46:12-13]; Dan 9:7-9, 14, 16; Mic 6:5; Wis 5:18; *Ps Sol.* 1:10-15; 2 Bar 44:4; 78:5; 4 Ezra 7:17-25; 8:36; 10:16; 14:32; *TDan* 6:10; 1QS 10:25-6; 11:12; 1QM 4:6). I believe the detailed exegesis will bear out this interpretation.

In particular, the flow of thought through the letter as a whole makes far more sense if we understand the statement of the theme in 1:17 as being about God and God's covenant faithfulness and justice, rather than simply about "justification."[11] It brings into focus chapters 9–11, not as an appendix to a more general treatment of sin and salvation, but as the intended major climax of the whole letter; and it allows for the significance of 15:1-13 as a final summing up of the subject. Within this larger theme, there is still all the room required for that which other readings have traditionally seen as the major subject—namely, the justification and salvation of individual human beings. But in this letter at least (remembering again that this is not, after all, a systematic theology but a letter addressed to a particular situation), these vital and highly important topics are held within a larger discussion. Paul's aim, it seems, is to explain to the Roman church what God has been up to and where they might belong on the map of these purposes.

Accustomed as we are to translating *dikaiosynē* as "righteousness," we should recognize from this account that the other obvious meaning of the word, "justice," is not far away. The sense of covenant faithfulness and the sense of things being put to rights, held apart within both the Reformation and the Enlightenment as "theology and ethics" or "salvation and politics," were not far removed in the mind of a Jew like Paul. Just as the Messiah was destined to be Lord of the world, so also, and for the same reasons, God's covenant with Israel had always been intended as the means of putting God's world to rights.[12] When, therefore, God's righteousness was unveiled, the effect would be precisely that the world would receive justice—that rich, restorative, much-to-be-longed-for justice of which the psalmists had spoken with such feeling (e.g., Pss 67:4; 82:8). Even a quick skim through Romans ought to reveal that this is indeed what Paul was talking about, though of course full justification of the point awaits the detail of the commentary.

But we need to remind ourselves to whom Paul's great letter was sent. Looming up behind the various discussions of why Romans was written is an issue not usually noticed. Paul was coming to Rome with the gospel message of Jesus the Jewish Messiah, the Lord of the world, claiming that, through this message, God's justice was unveiled once and for all. Rome prided itself on being, as it were, the capital of justice, the source from which justice would flow throughout the world. The Roman goddess Iustitia, like the Caesar cult itself, was a comparative novelty in Paul's world; the temple to Iustitia was established on January 8, 13 CE, and Iustitia was among the virtues celebrated by Augustus's famous *clipeus virtutis*, the golden shield set up in the Senate house and inscribed with the emperor's virtues (27 BCE). So close is the link between the new imperial regime and the virtue Iustitia that this goddess sometimes acquires the title "Augusta."[13] So, without losing any of its deep-rooted Jewish meanings of the covenant faithfulness of the creator God, Paul's declaration that the gospel of King Jesus reveals God's *dikaiosynē* must also be read as a deliberate challenge to the imperial pretension. If it is justice you want, he implies, you will find it, but not in the εὐαγγέλιον (*euangelion*) that announces

---

10. For a classic statement of this, see C. E. B. Cranfield, *A Critical and Exegetical Commentary on the Epistle to the Romans*, ICC, 2 vols. (Edinburgh: T. & T. Clark, 1975) 91-99.

11. Statistically, the word "God" (θεός *theos*) occurs with far more frequency in Romans (once every 46 words) than any other Pauline work. See L. L. Morris, "The Theme of Romans," in *Apostolic History and the Gospel: Biblical and Historical Essays presented to F. F. Bruce on his 60th Birthday*, ed. W. W. Gasque and R. P. Martin (Exeter: Paternoster, 1970) 249-63. Paul's other letters are also, of course, "about" God, but Romans makes God and God's justice, love, and reliability its major themes.

12. I have explored this theme in various places, e.g., Wright, *The Climax of the Covenant*, 21-26; *The New Testament and the People of God*, chap. 9.

13. On *Iustitia*, the Roman equivalent of *dikē*, see, e.g., Ovid *Letters from the Black Sea* 3.6.25; the *Acts of Augustus* chap. 34.

Caesar as Lord, but in the *euangelion* of Jesus.[14] The rest of Romans will show that this meaning is indeed in Paul's mind at point after point.

Nor is this meaning an indication that Paul is, as it were, shuttling to and fro between "Jewish" and "Gentile" contexts of meaning. Part of the whole point, for him, of the Jewish claim to be the covenant people of God was that the divine purpose for the whole creation would be revealed through Israel. In other words, when God at last fulfilled the covenant, the Gentile world would see, unveiled, what its own life was about. Applied to Rome, this meant that the very Jewish, very biblically based, revelation of the divine righteousness/justice was necessarily at the same time the revelation of the true Iustitia, that which really did accomplish what Caesar's Iustitia had claimed to do—namely, the putting to rights of the entire creation. We have only to think for a moment of Isaiah 40–55 to see how similar the train of thought is: Israel's God will reveal righteousness and salvation, confronting pagan empire as the sovereign creator and rescuing the covenant people in the process. All this, too, will emerge at various points throughout the letter and the commentary.

We may, therefore, offer the following highly compressed summary account of the flow of thought in the letter, which gradually unpacks the summary statement of the introduction (1:1-17).

Chapters 1–4: God's gospel unveils the fact that in the Messiah, Jesus of Nazareth, the God of Israel has been true to the covenant established with Abraham and has thereby brought saving order to the whole world. In the face of a world in rebellion and a chosen people unfaithful to their commission, God has, through the surrogate faithfulness of Jesus the Messiah, created a worldwide—that is, a Jewish and Gentile—family for Abraham, marked out by the covenant sign of faith.

Chapters 5–8: God has thereby done what the covenant was set up to do: to address and solve the problem expressed in biblical terms as the sin of Adam. In the Messiah, Jesus, God has done for this new people what was done for Israel of old in fulfillment of the promise to Abraham: Redeemed from the Egypt of enslavement to sin, they are led through the wilderness of the present life by the Spirit (not by the Torah), and they look forward to the inheritance, which will consist of the entire redeemed creation. This is how the creator will finally put the whole world to rights. All this is the result of God's astonishing, unchanging, self-giving covenant love expressed completely and finally in the death of Jesus.

Chapters 9–11: This section highlights the peculiar tragedy of the gospel's revelation of God's righteousness—namely, the ironic failure of Israel to believe in the Messiah. This, too, however, turns out to be held within the strange purposes of God, whereby Israel's fall, acting out on a grand scale the death of Jesus, is the means by which salvation can extend to the whole world. This cannot mean that Jews themselves are thereby forever debarred from participating in the covenant blessing; Paul himself is a counter-example, and God desires that even now, by recognizing that it is indeed their promised blessings that the Gentiles are enjoying, more of Paul's fellow Jews will come to share in new covenant membership. Gentile Christians, therefore, are warned severely against anti-Jewish arrogance. The section ends with a paean of praise for the strange but glorious purposes of God.

Chapters 12–16: The community that is created by this gospel must live as the true, renewed humanity, in its internal and external life. In particular, it must reflect God's intention that Jew and Gentile come together as one worshiping body in Christ. Paul's own plans are bent to this end, and his greetings to different groups in the Roman church may indicate his desire to bring together disparate groups in common worship and mission.

Such a summary, which of course depends at every point on the commentary for explanation and justification, nevertheless enables us to ask, in conclusion: How then may we understand the letter's situation, and how does the shape and detailed content of the letter address it?

---

14. This point, though it was developed independently, has close analogies with the argument of Neil Elliott, *Liberating Paul: The Justice of God and the Politics of the Apostle* (Maryknoll, N.Y.: Orbis, 1994) 190-92. See also Dieter Georgi, *Theocracy in Paul's Praxis and Theology* (Minneapolis: Fortress, 1991) chap. 4, excerpted in Richard A. Horsely, ed., *Paul and Empire: Religion and Power in Roman Imperial Society* (Harrisburg, Pa.: Trinity, 1997) 148-57. See further Richard A. Horsely, ed., *Paul and Politics: Ekklesia, Israel, Imperium, Interpretation: Essays in Honor of Krister Stendahl* (Harrisburg, Pa.: Trinity, 2000) chaps. 1, 10.

THE HISTORICAL OCCASION FOR ROMANS

The letter appears to have two main "situational" aims that surface in the great climactic passages 11:11-32 and 15:7-13. Each has in view the relationship between Jews and Gentiles; the former, however, addresses Christian Gentiles who are faced with non-Christian Jews, and the latter addresses a community in which Christian Gentiles and Christian Jews find themselves in uneasy coexistence. Although the details remain unclear, it is certain that a large proportion of Rome's substantial Jewish population had to leave the city in the late 40s CE following rioting that may have resulted from early Christian preaching among the Jewish community in Rome.[15] The expulsion edict came from the Emperor Claudius, after whose death in 54 the new emperor, Nero, rescinded his decrees, making it possible for the expelled Jews to return. This historical sequence produces a situation into which Romans fits like a glove.

Consider, on the one hand, the position of Gentile Christians vis-à-vis non-Christian Jews. The Roman anti-Jewish sentiment, for which there is abundant evidence in late antiquity, would create a context in which many Romans would be glad to see the Jews gone and sorry to see them return.[16] How easy, then, would it be for the Gentile Christians who remained in Rome through the early 50s to imagine that God had somehow endorsed, at the theological level, what Caesar had enacted at the political level and that God had in fact written the hated Jews out of the covenant altogether. How easy, also, when the Jews returned to take up their property and positions in society, to suppose that, though the new faith would spread to include other Gentiles, there was no point in attempting to win over any more Jews.

But Paul was coming to Rome with a gospel that was "God's power for salvation to the Jew first and also to the Greek" (1:16). If the Roman church were to accept his gospel, and indeed to support him in his missionary intention to go on from Rome to Spain, it was vital for them to realize that, even as the apostle to the Gentiles, he remained under obligation to his fellow Jews as well. Paul's travel plans in chap. 15 are thus woven into the same picture: Having been undermined by the apparent failure of his earlier home base in Antioch to support him in his practice of incorporating believing Gentiles into the same social structure as believing Jews (see Gal 2:11-21), he was determined that in the western Mediterranean he was going to make things clear from the start.

Consider, on the other hand, the position of Christian Jews and Christian Gentiles in relation to them. Paul will have known of some Jewish Christians who had returned to Rome and who, alongside Gentile cobelievers, would now be facing the difficult question of how to live together as one family with those who cherished very different cultural traditions, not least food taboos. Paul knows that this will not be solved overnight and stresses instead a doctrine of *adiaphora*: There are some practical things over which Christians can legitimately disagree, and they should not impair common worship. Underneath it all is Paul's desire that the Scriptures should be fulfilled: "Rejoice, you Gentiles, with God's people!" (15:10, quoting Deut 32:43).

Romans 9–11 and 12–16 thus are explicable in terms of the double situation of the Roman church and Paul's agendas in addressing them. Why, then, does he write chaps. 1–8? Are they just an extended introduction, before Paul reaches his real point?

By no means. If he is to address the deep-rooted problems of the interrelationship between Jews and Gentiles within God's purposes, Paul must go down to those deep roots themselves, to the foundations of Jewish and Christian thinking: to creation and fall, covenant and Torah, to Israel's covenant failure and God's covenant faithfulness. He must show how the death and resurrection of Jesus, the basic announcement of "the gospel," are God's solution to the complex problems of Israel and the world and how these events have called into existence a people,

---

15. See Wright, *The New Testament and the People of God*, 354-55; W. Wiefel, "The Jewish Community in Ancient Rome and the Origins of Roman Christianity," in *The Romans Debate*, rev. ed., ed. K. P. Donfried (Peabody, Mass.: Hendrikson, 1991) 85-101. Some scholars remain doubtful about whether the Jews were really expelled. See P. Achtemeier, "Unsearchable Judgments and Inscrutable Ways: Reflections of the Discussion of Romans," in *Pauline Theology*, vol. IV, ed. E. E. Johnson and D. M. Hay, SBLSS 4 (Atlanta: Scholars Press, 1997) 3-21; S. Mason, " 'For I Am Not Ashamed of the Gospel' (Romans 1:16): The Gospel and the First Readers of Romans," in *Gospel in Paul: Studies on Corinthians, Galatians, and Romans for Richard N. Longenecker*, ed. L. A. Jervis and P. Richardson, JSNTSup 108 (Sheffield: Sheffield Academic, 1994) 254-87.

16. See Menahem Stern, *Greek and Latin Authors on Jews and Judaism*, 3 vols. (Jerusalem: Israel Academy of Sciences and Humanities, 1974). On the Jewish community in Rome see H. J. Leon, *The Jews of Ancient Rome*, rev. ed. (Peabody, Mass.: Hendrikson, 1995).

composed of Jew and Gentile alike, led by God's Spirit and defined not by Torah but by faith, in whom all the promises of God have come true. Only so can his hearers sense the poignant tragedy of Israel's situation in Romans 9 and so move toward the main thrust of the letter. Only so can they appreciate the subtle logic of the argument that he then mounts. And only so can they be equipped for the larger questions that hover in the background—questions of the relation of Jesus' new empire with that of Caesar, of the justice of God facing the justice of Rome.

At the same time, the chapters in which he lays the foundation for his specific arguments can stand almost on their own as a statement of what God has done in the Messiah for the whole world. Here we must be careful. Romans is a tightly knit, coherent whole with an inner logic that affects every word and sentence. But the arguments of chaps. 1–4, on the one hand, and chaps. 5–8, on the other, have their own integrity. This is perhaps particularly true of chaps. 5–8, with their christological refrains tolling like a great bell at the end of almost every section. Here, if anywhere, Paul is clearly making Jesus the lens through which one may see the saving plan of God working its way out. At the same time, one must quickly add that it is precisely this section, for just this reason, that sets up the argument of chaps. 9–11. It is not simply that, having written chaps. 1–8, he finds he has to go on to 9–11; it is just as much that, because he wants to write chaps. 9-11, he finds he must write 1–8 in this way. Thus in key passages in Romans 1–8, Paul seems deliberately to set up problems and questions that he then leaves hanging in the air, only to resume them in chaps. 9–11 (the most obvious place where this occurs is 3:1-8, on which, see the commentary).

There are, of course, many other matters often covered in an introduction to a biblical book. But these are the things of most value for the intended readers of this series to understand before proceeding further. Others will be covered at the appropriate points in the commentary itself.

BIBLIOGRAPHY

Commentaries:

Bryan, Christopher. *A Preface to Romans: Notes on the Epistle in Its Literary and Cultural Setting.* Oxford: Oxford University Press, 2000. Brief and helpful; copious reference to frequently overlooked ancient literature; interesting and original ideas and practical comments.

Byrne, Brendan. *Romans.* SP 6. Collegeville, Minn.: Liturgical, 1996. Deep scholarship; a light and wise touch; fresh insights.

Cranfield, C. E. B. *A Critical and Exegetical Commentary on the Epistle to the Romans.* ICC. 2 vols. Edinburgh: T. & T. Clark, 1975, 1979. Already a classic. A model of lucid, wide-ranging and judicious exegesis; a major contribution not just to Romans but to NT theology as a whole.

Dunn, James D. G. *Romans 1–8 and Romans 9–16.* WBC 38A and 38B. Dallas: Word, 1988. No stone left unturned; some of the details that crawl out from underneath (innumerable secondary discussions in the unfootnoted text) may be more than the ordinary reader wants. A major representative of the so-called new perspective on Paul.

Fitzmyer, Joseph A. *Romans.* AB 33. Garden City, N.Y.: Doubleday, 1993. Thorough on bibliography and background details, not always reliable (though often very stimulating) on theological judgments. With Byrne, the most important Roman Catholic commentary of recent years.

Käsemann, Ernst. *Commentary on Romans.* Translated by Geoffrey W. Bromiley. London: SCM, 1980. Possibly the most important book on Paul since the Second World War. Rigorous in exegesis, robustly Protestant in theology, bracing in application. Not for the beginner, but exhilarating for those ready for a challenge.

Moo, Douglas J. *The Epistle to the Romans.* NICNT. Grand Rapids: Eerdmans, 1996. The most thorough and learned of recent Protestant expositions. Solidly evangelical but not afraid to find his own way through interpretative dilemmas.

Studies on Romans:

Donfried, Karl P. *The Romans Debate*. Rev. ed. Peabody, Mass.: Hendrickson, 1991. Useful collection of 23 important essays on the background, occasion, and content of Romans.

Dunn, James D. G. *The Theology of Paul the Apostle*. Grand Rapids: Eerdmans, 1998. Full, detailed, thoroughly annotated, but clear and readable. Modeled in outline on Romans: at one level, a traditional presentation of topics in Paul; at another, many important fresh interpretations (e.g., on "works of the law") for which Dunn has become famous.

Hay, David M., and E. Elizabeth Johnson, eds. *Pauline Theology*. Vol. III: *Romans*. Minneapolis: Fortress, 1991. Papers from the SBL Pauline Theology seminar, including several important discussions.

Hays, Richard B. *Echoes of Scripture in the Letters of Paul*. New Haven: Yale University Press, 1989. Seminal monograph, already something of a classic. Explores Paul's complex use of Israel's scriptures; a one-line quotation can evoke a whole biblical passage or context, thereby revealing deeper meanings in Paul.

Horsley, Richard A., ed. *Paul and Empire: Religion and Power in Roman Imperial Society*. Harrisburg, Pa.: Trinity Press International, 1997. Essays, with important introductions by the editor, highlighting the Roman imperial context (including ideology and emperor cult), whose significance for understanding Paul is only now beginning to be felt.

Sanders, E. P. *Paul, the Law, and the Jewish People*. Philadelphia: Fortress, 1983. Sequel to the same author's *Paul and Palestinian Judaism* (Philadelphia: Fortress, 1977), which marked a watershed in Pauline studies. Detailed discussions of key texts, including several from Romans.

Wagner, J. Ross. *Heralds of the Good News: Isaiah and Paul "In Concert" in the Letter to the Romans*. NovTSup 101. Leiden: Brill, 2002. Isaiah was one of Paul's most important biblical sources; this book discusses what he did with it. Full of patient and wise scholarship on the meaning of the letter.

Wright, N. T. *The Climax of the Covenant: Christ and the Law in Pauline Theology*. Edinburgh: T. & T. Clark; Minneapolis: Fortress, 1991. Detailed discussion of key texts on christology and the law, including several on Romans.

_____. *The New Testament and the People of God*. Vol. 1 of *Christian Origins and the Question of God*. London: SPCK; Minneapolis: Fortress, 1992. Early Christianity within its historical and theological settings.

OUTLINE OF ROMANS

ROMANS 1:1–4:25

THE FAITHFULNESS OF GOD

OVERVIEW

The letter's main subjects are laid out in the first four chapters. The introduction (1:1-17) offers a dense statement of the theme: In the gospel announcement of the risen Jesus as Messiah and Lord, the one true God has unveiled covenant faithfulness and justice, God's own faithfulness and justice, for the benefit of all who believe. Paul then launches into a description of the world that has worshiped other gods and has reaped a harvest of dehumanization, moral deterioration, and condemnation (1:18–3:20). Though the spearhead of this attack (1:18–2:16) corresponds to regular Jewish polemic against the pagan world, Paul sharpens it up with specifically Christian notes, and he hints that Israel itself is included in the general indictment. He turns in 2:17-29 specifically to his own people, the Jews; while endorsing their claim to be the people chosen by God to bring light to the world, their own prophets indicate that they have failed in this vocation and are in danger of relinquishing their special status.

This raises acutely these questions (3:1-9): What is the point of being part of God's chosen people in the first place? How is God righteous in the whole sequence of events? Putting off these questions for the moment with very brief answers, Paul stresses both the faithlessness of Israel and the abiding faithfulness of God. But to place the issue beyond doubt he mounts a list of biblical passages (3:10-18) that all point one way: The Jews have joined the Gentiles in the dock, with nothing to say in their defense. All are equally guilty before the impartial judge.

This conclusion poses a classic question within the world of Second Temple Judaism. What happens when God's intended covenant faithfulness appears to be in conflict with the demands of impartial justice—when

the double meaning of "the righteousness of God" seems to contradict itself? Paul's answer is emphatic (3:21–4:25): In Jesus the Messiah, God has been true both to the covenant with Abraham and to the demands of justice. As a result, there is now a Jew-plus-Gentile people of God, the true children of Abraham, marked out by faith rather than works of Torah.

All this has come about "through the faithfulness of Jesus the Messiah" (3:22). Jesus has accomplished—to put it another way, God has accomplished through Jesus—what Israel failed to accomplish. God's own covenant faithfulness is thus unveiled at last, an event to which the law and prophets pointed but that they could not bring about. The "faithfulness" of the Messiah, the subject matter of the gospel itself, denotes specifically his death, seen as the culmination of his whole "obedience." This faithful obedience (or obedient faithfulness) was the means of dealing with sin and hence of creating a forgiven people. The badge of membership in the renewed people of God is faith, not works of the Torah, which would have restricted apparent membership to Jews and proselytes and would in any case have condemned everyone (since all alike are sinful). However, since the gospel of Jesus thus creates a single family for the one God of Jews and Gentiles alike, the Torah itself, in which confession of this one God is central, is strangely fulfilled.

All this has come about in fulfillment of the covenant with Abraham (4:1-25). Abraham is the father, not just of Jews, but of all who believe. In a lengthy exposition of Genesis 15 (the chapter in which God made the initial covenant with Abraham), Paul demonstrates that the promises to the patriarch were not conditioned by works (Rom 4:2-8), by circumcision (Rom 4:9-12), or by Torah (Rom 4:13-15). God has now created, through faith, the single family promised in the first place (Rom 4:16-17), consisting of believing Jews and believing Gentiles. In a closing peroration (Rom 4:18-25), Paul echoes his indictment of pagan humanity in 1:18-32 and shows by implication how the problem has been undone. Abraham's faith is the characteristic mark of genuine, God-honoring humanity. This new family, called into being by the gospel, is marked out by faith in the God who raised Jesus from the dead (Rom 4:23-25; for Paul's view that the gospel was already, in a sense, preached to Abraham himself, see Gal 3:8).

The first main statement of Paul's thesis is thus complete. The gospel of Jesus the Messiah unveils the righteousness, the covenant faithfulness, the justice of God in such a way as to bring into being the single family promised to Abraham, characterized by faith in this Jesus. Paul has constructed this argument in such a way as to prepare carefully for the points he wishes to address in chaps. 9–11 and 12–16. To develop these lines of thought, however, and to address the questions connected with them, he needs to lay still deeper foundations. Chapters 1–4, by also leading naturally into chaps. 5–8, point to where those foundations are to be found.

ROMANS 1:1-17, OPENING STATEMENT OF THEME: GOD'S GOSPEL AND GOD'S RIGHTEOUSNESS

Romans 1:1-7, God's Gospel and Paul's Ministry

COMMENTARY

Paul introduces himself in terms of his vocation and defines that vocation in terms of the gospel. The opening seven verses of the letter move swiftly from Paul to the gospel, back to Paul and his ministry, and out into the world, which includes the Roman Christians. As usual, he introduces, within the formal structure of a letter opening, the themes that will occupy him in what is to come.

1:1-2. Paul announces himself with the word that, above all others in his world, carried overtones of social degradation. Slaves had no rights, no property, and no prospects; they were simply there to do what they were told. Modifying this to "servant," as though Paul were a free agent who happened to have a job as a cleaner or butler, misses the point. Paul will claim no social standing in his approach to the greatest imperial capital his world had ever known.

Slave though he be, however, his master is the King before whom other kings should quail, and he can thus hold up his head not on his own account but on that of "king Jesus." By transliterating Χριστός (*Christos*)

rather than translating it, most English versions of Paul have encouraged the view that the word had already become a proper name for Paul. This, however, is misleading: Paul's careful and differentiated usage of "Christ," "Jesus," and for that matter "Lord" leads to the conclusion that he intended each word to carry its own set of overtones.[17] And the overtones of "Christ"—i.e., "Messiah"—are, as we shall presently see, clearly royal: The Messiah is the anointed king of Israel who in Scripture was supposed to be the ruler of all other earthly monarchs (see, e.g., Pss 72:8-11; 89:27; Isa 11:1-4). It is because Paul is the slave announcing the king that he can call his message "gospel" (see below).[18]

Paul's two further self-designations, building on the slave-of-the-king status, are both significant for this letter. First, he is "called apostle" or "apostle by God's call" (NEB). "Call" in Paul's writings usually refers, not to

17. See Wright, *The Climax of the Covenant*, 41-49.
18. The counterimperial overtones are well brought out by M. J. Brown, "Paul's Use of Δοῦλος Χριστοῦ Ἰησοῦ in Romans 1:1," *JBL* 120 (2001) 723-37.

the specific vocation of which a Christian may gradually become aware, but to the moment when the gospel message of Jesus first makes its saving impact on him or her. Here, in the light of Gal 1:15-16, the two ideas seem to be run together: Paul's "conversion" was also his "vocation" to be the apostle to the nations. There is a further consonance between the words; elsewhere Paul seems to define what he means by "apostle" in terms of those who had actually seen the risen Jesus (1 Cor 9:1), alluding not least to his own moment of seeing Jesus on the Damascus road. For him, conversion and calling were both contained in the one event.

In parallel with this vocation, Paul has been marked off from others, including (it seems) from other apostles, others who had seen the risen Jesus. The word translated "set apart" (ἀφορίζω *aphorizō*) indicates God's intention: If a slave is a piece of property, the owner has set this piece apart from other uses and focused it on one in particular, the service of "the gospel." "Set apart" may also reflect, with wry irony, the self-description of a Pharisee who had considered himself "separated" from the common herd of ordinary Jews. If Paul is in any sense a Christian Pharisee, it is because he has now been separated out as a slave, given a particular commission by which he is defined from now on.

"The gospel of God" is thus at the heart of Paul's self-definition and self-understanding. The word "gospel" (εὐαγγέλιον *euangelion*) referred in early Christianity to the proclamation about Jesus before it was used to denote particular books; Paul uses the term to denote the message, or announcement, that he was making around the Mediterranean world. In Paul's Jewish world, the word looked back to Isa 40:9 and 52:7, where a messenger was to bring to Jerusalem the good news of Babylon's defeat, the end of Israel's exile, and the personal return of YHWH to Zion. In the pagan world Paul addressed, the same Greek word referred to the announcement of the accession or the birthday of a ruler or emperor. Here already we find Paul at the interface of his two worlds. His message about Jesus was both the fulfillment of prophecy, as v. 2 indicates, and the announcement of one whose rule posed a challenge to all other

rulers.[19] Though the word "gospel" itself occurs infrequently in Romans, it is truly part of the main theme, since its content, Jesus Christ, forms the substructure of the entire train of thought.

The gospel is not, strictly speaking, Paul's own property (though he refers to it as "my gospel" in 2:16); it is God's. As noted in the Introduction, the word "God" occurs far more times, proportionately, in Romans than in Paul's other writings. This letter is about the way in which, through the lens of the gospel, the covenant plan and purpose of the one true God have been unveiled before the world. Paul's view of God remained deeply Jewish; he believed that the one God of Abraham, Isaac, and Jacob, the creator of the world, had now brought world history to its climax in Jesus. Paul is urging the Roman Christians to understand this purpose, and their own place within it, so that they can then live and work appropriately and, indeed, support Paul's apostolic task as well. The fact that the gospel is God's means that Paul is entrusted with an awesome responsibility. He is like one in charge of distributing royal bounty.

1:3a. The gospel is a message about God's Son. This is another key phrase that, although it occurs quite seldom in the letter, naturally takes center stage. Paul, in fact, lived at a moment of transition in the history of this phrase and helped it on its way to subsequent development. In the OT, "son of God" can refer to angels (Gen 6:2; Job 1:6; 2:1; 38:7; Dan 3:25; cf. Dan 3:28; Song of Three 26). But its better known referents are Israel, adopted as God's child explicitly at the time of the exodus and looking back to that moment in order to plead for subsequent deliverance (Exod 4:22; Jer 31:9; Hos 11:1; 13:13; Mal 1:6); and the king, adopted as YHWH's first-born son—the seed of David who is also the son of God (1 Sam 7:14 [quoted with this sense in 4Q174 10-13; cf. 4Q246 2:1]; 1 Chr 17:13; Pss 2:7; 89:26-27).[20] These two senses belong together, since in some Jewish thought the Davidic king represents Israel, so that what is true of him is true of the people. To belong to Israel, in a passage that seems to

19. See N. T. Wright, "Gospel and Theology in Galatians," in Jervis and Richardson, *Gospel in Paul,* 222-39.

20. In view of this it is extraordinary that Fitzmyer can deny the existence of an OT background for the idea. See Fitzmyer, *Romans,* 235.

have become proverbial, is to be "in David" or "in the son of Jesse" (1 Sam 19:43–20:2; cf. 1 Kgs 12:16; 2 Chr 10:16). The natural meaning of the phrase "God's gospel concerning his son," therefore, is "God's announcement, in fulfillment of prophecy, of the royal enthronement of the Messiah, Israel's anointed king, the lord of the world."

There is a huge difference between all this and the much later Christian usage in which "son of God" comes to be a simple predication of Jesus' divinity. We should not allow this difference, however, to obscure the fact that already in Paul, at least as early as Gal 4:1-7, we find the phrase used in a way that, while still rooted in this Jewish tradition of Israel/kingship, now draws on other Jewish imagery, such as God's sending of Wisdom, to make the point that the "son" is one sent into the world not only as a messenger but also as the personal expression of God's love and purpose. As we shall see later in Romans, the arguments work only if we postulate a fundamental identity between "the son" and God's own very self—alongside, of course, the differentiation inherent in the father/son division. This raises further questions to which Paul provides no answers, only hints. But it does suggest that the earliest Christian incarnational theology known to us remained deeply rooted in Jewish tradition, however much it was saying things no one had said before.

1:3b-4. The "son" is then described in a complex double statement concerning Jesus' human descent, on the one hand, and the meaning of his resurrection, on the other. Like many of Paul's more formulaic passages, this passage has generated speculation that we are here dealing with that hypothetical entity the "pre-Pauline formula," which Paul has quoted, quite possibly adapting or modifying it as he did so, in order not least to establish his credentials with an audience to whom the formula would have been familiar.[21] It is, of course, quite possible that Paul might use formulae known to his readers but not otherwise to us, and the present passage might indeed be a case in point. But it must be stressed, here and elsewhere, that

the reason why Paul quoted things, if he did, was that they expressed exactly what he intended to say at the time. As we shall see throughout this commentary, the christology of 1:3-4 is by no means an isolated statement attached loosely to the front of the letter but not relevant to its contents. It is the careful, weighted, programmatic statement of what will turn out to be Paul's subtext throughout the whole epistle (see also 9:5; and 15:12, the final scriptural quotation of the main body of the letter).

In particular, the "discovery" of pre-Pauline fragments such as this has sometimes been employed as a way of distancing Paul from the precise emphases of the passage. Often this is done to make him appear less "Jewish" than the statement seems to be (see the Commentary on 3:24-26). In the present case, it is pointed out that Paul nowhere else refers to Jesus' Davidic sonship; it is often assumed (less often argued) that Paul had moved away from Jewish messianic ideas altogether.[22] Themes are more important than words; once we understand how messianic ideas functioned for Paul we discover them throughout his writings. In particular, as we shall see in its proper place, his incorporative christology ("in Christ" and similar expressions) is best explained in terms of the Messiah's role of summing up his people in himself. There is also a persistent tendency in traditional Pauline scholarship to play down Jewish messianic ideas on the grounds that this makes Paul's theology more political. One could equally well argue the other way: Because Paul's theology, and for that matter his life, was so obviously political, in senses to be explored in the commentary, it is scarcely surprising that we discover Jewish messianic ideas at the center of his writings.[23]

Whether or not Paul wrote vv. 3-4 from scratch himself (and we must guard against assuming that a writer such as Paul was

---

21. See Fitzmyer, *Romans*, 229-300; Moo, *The Epistle to the Romans*, 44-46. Among earlier literature, see J. D. G. Dunn, "Jesus—Flesh and Spirit: An Exposition of Romans 1.3-4," *JTS* 24 (1973) 40-68.

22. E.g., J. A. Fitzmyer, *The Letter to Philemon*, AB 34C (New York: Doubleday, 2000) 99. I have argued elsewhere, and here reemphasize, that this is a mistake. If 2 Timothy is by Paul, we can count 2:8 as another instance. If it is not, we might speculate that 2:8 was a pre-2 Timothy formula, in which case its hypothetical author could, of course, have been Paul himself. See Wright, *The Climax of the Covenant* part one, esp. chaps. 2 and 3.

23. On the political side of Paul's work, see Neil Elliott, *Liberating Paul: The Justice of God and the Politics of the Apostle* (Maryknoll, N.Y.: Orbis, 1994); Horsley, *Paul and Empire; Paul and Politics: Ekklesia, Israel, Imperium, Interpretation: Essays in Honor of Krister Stendahl* (Harrisburg, Pa.: Trinity, 2000). From a different angle, see B. Blumenfeld, *The Political Paul: Justice, Democracy and Kingship in a Hellenistic Framework*, JSNTSup 210 (Sheffield: Sheffield Academic, 2001).

incapable of dictating an apparently formulaic statement off the top of his head, especially as he had had countless occasions to sum up his message orally before a wide variety of audiences), the passage as it stands offers a striking statement of that messianic view of Jesus that we shall discover at the heart of the letter. God's son, declares Paul, was born of the seed of David and marked out as "son of God" by the resurrection. As it stands, shorn of extra explanatory (but also, to us, confusing) clauses and granted what has been said about the meaning of "God's son" in Jewish tradition, this is a reasonably straightforward two-part statement of Jesus' Messiahship.[24] (1) Jesus was born of David's line;[25] (2) the resurrection declared to the world that he really was the Messiah and had been so all along.[26] This, indeed, was almost certainly where Paul's Christian thinking began: with the recognition, at or shortly after his Damascus road experience, that the Jesus he had thought to be a false Messiah was after all the true one (cf. Gal 1:16; Acts 9:20, 22, where it is clear that "son of God" and "Messiah" are virtually interchangeable).[27]

To the first phrase Paul adds "according to the flesh," intending, of course, to clarify the sense of Jesus' Davidic descent, but also thereby opening a can of worms for the interpreter. Earlier readers, still reflected in the NIV, took the double statement as expressing Jesus' "humanity," on the one hand, and his "divinity," on the other, and thus read "according to the flesh" as referring to his "human nature." But "flesh" (σάρξ *sarx*) is never simply "human nature" for Paul; nor is it simply a reference to physical humanness as opposed to nonphysical aspects, such as soul or spirit. It is always human nature

seen *as* corruptible, decaying, dying, on the one hand, and/or rebelling, deceiving, and sinning, on the other. "Flesh" always carries negative overtones somewhere on this scale, whereas for Paul being human was not something negative, but good and God-given and to be reaffirmed in the resurrection. In any case, Paul has given no hint at this stage in the letter that he intends "son of God" to be taken in an explicitly "divine" sense. Since Messiahship (which in the Jewish world, of course, carried no overtones of "divinity") is the main theme of the passage, we should be careful not to overexegete it in the light of other, fuller Pauline statements—or, indeed, of later Christian tradition.

Others have seen "according to the flesh" as Paul's way of hinting that, while Jesus was indeed of the seed of David, this was not the most significant thing about him. In other words, this was Paul's way of distancing himself from Jewish messianic beliefs in order to hurry on to the more important point about Jesus' divine sonship. This, too, is misleading for the reasons already given. The whole point of Paul's gospel is that Jesus, precisely as Israel's Messiah, is now Lord of the world. That belief informs and undergirds much of this letter.

This relationship between 1:3-4 and the rest of Romans indicates what Paul means by adding "according to the flesh" and "according to the spirit." Jesus the Messiah is the one in whom God's people find their identity and salvation; he has come where they are in order to rescue them (more fully stated in 8:3-4; cf. Gal 4:4-5). His human, "fleshly" (in Paul's sense) identity is the place where he does for Adamic humanity that which Adamic humanity could not do for itself. Verse 3 thus looks ahead to 5:12-21 and all the elements of chaps. 6–8 that follow from it. It is also evoked by 9:5, which, as we shall see, restates a very similar two-part christology, making it the ground plan of the argument of chaps. 9–11: Jesus is Israel's Messiah according to the flesh and is also (now at last explicitly) "God over all, blessed for ever."

Although, therefore, "according to the flesh" carries negative connotations, Paul is not denying or playing down Jesus' physical Davidic descent and Jewish Messiahship. They are part of God's saving plan. But, as

---

24. Although there are no biblical texts that explicitly predict the resurrection of the Messiah ("resurrection," when it developed as a belief in the post-biblical period, was thought of as happening to all God's people simultaneously), it is possible that some at least read one of the key "son of God" passages, 2 Sam 7:12 ("I will raise up your seed after you"; cf. 1 Kings 8:20), in this sense, not least because of the LXX's καὶ ἀναστήσω τὸ σπέρμα σου (*kai anastēsō to sperma sou*, "and I will resurrect your seed").

25. "Born" is a better translation for γενομένου (*genomenou*) than "descended." Paul reveals no awareness of Jesus' supposed virginal conception and hence offers no answer to the question raised by Matthew and Luke as to how such a belief is compatible with Jesus' Davidic pedigree.

26. "Declared to be" is not misleading, but the word ὁρίζω (*horizō*) really means "marked out as."

27. On the meanings Paul gave to, and deduced from, his experience of meeting the risen Jesus, see Martin Hengel and Anna Maria Schwemer, *Paul Between Damascus and Antioch: The Unknown Years* (London: SCM, 1997) 101-5; R. N. Longenecker, ed., *The Road from Damascus: The Impact of Paul's Conversion on his Life, Thought and Ministry* (Grand Rapids: Eerdmans, 1997).

Paul knew, Jesus' public career and horrible fate had been very different from that expected of a Messiah. We know of several other messianic movements in first-century Judaism, and none of them looked like this— though many of them ended up equally horribly and were thereby shown up as false, as non-messianic.[28]

One still frequently meets the suggestion that the pre-Christian Paul rejected Jesus' Messiahship for purely theological reasons— e.g., that Jesus had been crucified and was, therefore, according to Deuteronomy, cursed by God. This proposal comes from a milieu where "history of ideas" has ousted history itself. A crucified Messiah was a failed Messiah; no first-century Jew would have needed theological exegesis of a particular text in order to make that point. The Messiah had a task: to rebuild or cleanse the Temple, to defeat the pagans, to rescue Israel and bring God's justice to the world. Anyone who died without accomplishing these things, particularly one who attacked the Temple and died at the hands of the pagans he should have been defeating, leaving Israel unredeemed and the world still unjust, was obviously not the true Messiah. This is why it took something utterly extraordinary to make anyone suppose that Jesus was in fact the Messiah. Paul is clear: It was the resurrection that marked Jesus out as "son of God" (v. 4). The resurrection reversed the verdict that all thoughtful first-century Jews would have passed on Jesus at the time of his crucifixion. If such a Messiah could not be fitted in to existing conceptions of what Israel's God was supposed to be doing, that was too bad. The existing conceptions would have to be rethought around him. That, indeed, was the intellectual dimension of Paul's lifework.

Jesus was declared to be son of God "in power." This phrase seems to refer both to the power of God that raised Jesus from the dead (see 1 Cor 6:14; 15:24, 43; 2 Cor 13:4; Eph 1:19-20; Phil 3:10) and that thereby declared his identity as Messiah, and to the powerful nature of his sonship, through which he confronts all the powers of the world, up to and including death itself, with the news of

a different and more effective type of power altogether. Paul, of course, sees this same power at work now, by the Spirit, through the proclamation of the gospel and in the lives of those who are "in the Messiah" (see, e.g., 1:16; 11:23; 15:13; 1 Cor 1:24; 2:4-5).

Balancing "according to the flesh" in v. 3 is "according to the spirit of holiness" in v. 4. This apparent semitism ("Spirit of holiness" for "Holy Spirit") is unique, lending some further weight to the suggestion of a pre-Pauline formula—which would, nevertheless, thereby include the characteristically Pauline flesh/spirit antithesis. It is just conceivable that Paul intends to mark, by this phrase, the difference between the Spirit by whom Jesus was raised from the dead and the Spirit, now to be known as the Spirit of Jesus, who dwells in the hearts of believers. Even though these are ultimately the same Spirit, there are two different stages of operation. The point is that, for Paul, God raised Jesus from the dead by the power of the Spirit (see 8:11), in line with scriptural promises that attributed to the breath, wind, or Spirit of God the promised new life on the other side of death, and more particularly the new hope for exiled and desolate Israel (Ezek 37:5, 9-10, 14; Joel 3:1-5; the same Hebrew word [רוח *rûaḥ*] stands for "breath," "wind," and "spirit"; so too with the Greek πνεῦμα [*pneuma*]). This formulation, therefore, provides further grounding for Paul's coming description of God's rescue, in the Messiah, of the old, fleshly humanity and God's constitution, in the Messiah, of the new humanity, "who walk not according to the flesh but according to the spirit" (8:4). This contrast has nothing to do with that dualism that denies or downgrades human physicality. The spirit was, after all, responsible in Paul's view for Jesus' bodily resurrection. Rather, it has to do with the direction of a person's life, in both senses: the question of who is directing it and the question of which route it is taking.

The spirit thus marked out Jesus as son of God "by the resurrection of the dead." The word "dead" is plural in the Greek. The NIV reads "his resurrection," which obscures the point; for Paul the Jew, "the resurrection" was something that would happen at the end, when all God's people would be raised to life together. What had happened to Jesus, Paul

28 On other messianic and similar movements, see Wright, *The New Testament and the People of God*, 307-20; and *Jesus and the Victory of God*, 481-86.

believed, was the bringing forward into the present of this general resurrection, in one particular case, which still belonged organically to, and anticipated, the total "resurrection of the dead" (cf. 1 Cor 15:20-22; and see the Commentary on 6:9). This is important for understanding Paul in general and Romans in particular: Paul saw the event of Easter as the start and foretaste of God's long-promised new age, "the age to come" that he and many other Jews had been expecting.[29] The resurrection told Paul not only who Jesus was (the Messiah), but also what time it was (the start of the "age to come").

Paul's initial summary of the gospel is rounded off with Jesus' full Pauline title: "Jesus, Messiah, our Lord." "Jesus" for Paul regularly refers to the human being, Jesus of Nazareth, now risen and exalted but still the same human Jesus. When Paul writes "Christ," he still means "Messiah," the one in whom Israel's destiny is summed up and brought to proper fulfillment; the word is on its way to being a name (denoting Jesus but no longer connoting Messiahship), but it has not reached that point in Paul. "Lord" expresses both the exalted humanity of Jesus, including his superior position to all other "lords" in the world, and the sometimes explicit ascription of divinity. This is seen most clearly when Paul, speaking of Jesus, quotes passages from the LXX where "Lord" (κύριος *kyrios*) stands, as he well knew, for "YHWH," the divine name (e.g., Rom 10:13). The possessive pronoun "our" is not a way of limiting the sphere of Jesus' lordship, but of giving explicit allegiance to the one who is, for Paul, lord of the whole world, supreme over all others.

This, then, is Paul's shorthand summary of "the gospel of God." Despite the unusual diction of these verses, their meaning is not only consonant with his theological views of Jesus but is closely tied to the letter's developing line of thought. Note that for Paul "the gospel" is not a system of salvation, a message first and foremost about how human beings get saved. It is an announcement about Jesus, the Messiah, the Lord.[30]

1:5. The shorthand summary complete, Paul returns to his introduction of himself and his vocation. Through this Jesus, Paul has received "grace and apostleship" (possibly a hendiadys—two words used to express one idea—meaning, "the grace of apostleship") with a particular purpose: to call the ἔθνη (*ethnē*, "nations"), the Gentiles, into covenant relationship with the one God of Israel so that the name of Jesus might be glorified throughout the world (cf. Mal 1:5, 14).

The shorthand expression he uses to describe this relationship is "the obedience of faith." It is possible that by this dense phrase he means, as in the NIV, "the obedience that comes from faith," but it is much more likely that he means "the obedience which consists in faith."[31] "Obedience" is a more prominent theme in Romans than elsewhere in the NT (elsewhere in Paul only in 2 Cor 7:15; 10:5-6; Phlm 21). It serves as a shorthand both for the total work of Jesus the Messiah, over against that of Adam (5:19), and as the sphere or realm into which, or under the rule of which, Christians come through baptism (6:12-17). Paul can again use it as a summary of that which he seeks to bring about among the nations (15:18; cf. 16:19) and in a concluding formula that closely echoes this opening one (16:26; on the textual status of this verse see the Commentary on 16:25-27).

What overtones should we hear in this dense phrase? "Obedience" in Greek is ὑπακοή (*hypakoē*, a compound from the verb ἀκούω *akouō*, "hear"). Regularly in the LXX it translates שָׁמַע (*šama'*), which carries not only the meaning "hear and obey," but also the connotation, emphasized in the regular Jewish daily prayer, of personal covenant obligations: "Hear, O Israel, YHWH our God, YHWH is one; and you shall love YHWH your God" (Deut 6:4-5). To bring the nations into "obedience" would therefore mean to bring them into the family of this one God. The fact that Paul refers explicitly to the *Shema* prayer at the very point when he is saying just this (3:29-30) is a further indication that this train of thought is in his mind, albeit here expressed in very compact form.

Of course, the actual notion of "obedience"—doing what one is told—is itself

---

29. On which see Wright, *The New Testament and the People of God*, 299-300, with other references there.

30. Moo's insistence, *Romans*, 51, that "the gospel cannot be understood without reference to the person of Christ," while true, implies that "the gospel" itself is something other than the proclamation of Jesus as Lord.

31. Cranfield, *A Critical and Exegetical Commentary on the Epistle to the Romans*, 66, sets out various options. See also Moo, *Romans*, 51-53.

important. Generations of theologians have worried whether this emphasis on obedience, so early in a letter supposedly about "justification by faith alone," does not suggest the priority of good moral works rather than pure faith.[32] Such anxiety misses the point. When Paul thinks of Jesus as Lord, he thinks of himself as a slave and of the world as being called to obedience to Jesus' lordship. His apostolic commission is not to offer people a new religious option, but to summon them to allegiance to Jesus, which will mean abandoning other loyalties. The gospel issues a command, an imperial summons; the appropriate response is obedience.

The "obedience" Paul seeks to evoke when he announces the gospel is thus not a list of moral good works but faith. Faith, as Paul explains later (10:9), consists in confessing Jesus as Lord (thereby renouncing other lords) and in believing that God raised Jesus from the dead (thereby abandoning other worldviews in which such things did or could not happen, or not to Jesus; cf. too 4:23-25). This faith is actually the human faithfulness that answers to God's faithfulness. As we will discover in chap. 3, that is why this "faith" is the only appropriate badge of membership within God's true, renewed people. Despite the anxieties of some, therefore, that Paul is undermining his own doctrine of "justification by faith" before he has even stated it, v. 5 really does look ahead to Paul's exposition of justification, even though it places that theme in a rather different context from that which some expositors have assumed.

1:6-7. Paul has now drawn a miniature map of God's purpose, revealed in Jesus the Messiah, proclaimed in the apostolic gospel.

To this he adds a pointer: "you are here."[33] The church in Rome, predominantly Gentile, though now once again including some Jews (see the Introduction), is included among those who have given allegiance, "the obedience which consists in faith," to the gospel of Jesus. They are, therefore, literally "called of Jesus Christ." As the translations (e.g., the NIV) suggest, this can be expanded as "called to belong to Jesus Christ," but we should not thereby place the emphasis on "belong" at the expense of "called." For Paul, the "call" was God's powerful word, creating new life—creating, indeed, the response it sought, as a word of love is always capable of doing. And it is to the love of God that Paul now appeals, not for the last time: "God's beloved in Rome," he labels the church, "called to be saints." Both of these phrases, while carrying their own echoes of love and holiness, look back inevitably to the status of God's people in the past, the people whom Paul sees as now renewed and expanded so as to include believing Gentiles as well as Jews.

The greeting that follows, after this densely packed introduction of Paul and his gospel, is straightforward, though this should not deceive us into treating it lightly. "Grace" and "peace" are two of Paul's greatest words for God's gift in the Messiah. The former reaches out to those currently in rebellion; the latter gives them the central covenant blessing. And, consonant with the gospel itself, Paul couples "the Lord Jesus Messiah" with "God our Father" as the source of these gifts. The latter phrase, too, is clearly rooted in the OT, indicating that Paul is claiming for himself and his readers the status of Israel before God—indicating, too, in the light of the gospel, that the people of God are to be seen as siblings of the firstborn son (8:29). (See Reflections at 1:16-17.)

32. This anxiety has left its mark in the NIV and in Fitzmyer's translation "commitment." See Fitzmyer, *Romans*, 237.

33. The words "in Rome" in 1:7, and also in 1:15, are missing in a few MSS, no doubt because the letter was copied and circulated to a wider audience at an early date.

Romans 1:8-15, Paul's Desire to Come to Rome

COMMENTARY

This section actually runs on without a break into the next one (vv. 16-17). Since, however, the latter forms such a crucial summary of the whole letter, it will be better to treat it separately.

As usual, Paul follows his introduction with a report of the prayer he offers for the recipients. The formal style does not indicate mere formality. Paul's writing is set in the context of an ongoing ministry of prayer, and if he had to choose between praying and writing, he would have regarded prayer as more important. Here he reports his regular thanksgivings for the faith of the Roman church and his unceasing prayer that he might be able to visit them. This passes naturally into a further statement of his own apostolic vocation, amplifying what has already been said in vv. 1, 5 and explaining further his desire to come to Rome. This in turn leads to his summary of the letter's thesis in vv. 16-17.

1:8-12. Hyperbole it may be, but it is still no mean thing to say that the faith of the Roman church was proclaimed "in all the world." Presumably this means that travelers known to Paul, not least Jewish Christians who had had to leave Rome under Claudius, were reporting the arrival in the capital of this strange new sect, neither ethnically Jewish (all the Christians in Rome for five years being Gentiles) nor pagan. There is unlikely to be a particular reason why he stresses their "faith" here, rather than, say, obedience (as in 16:19) or love (as in Col 1:8). What matters is that they are an authentic Christian congregation, for whom Paul thanks God through Jesus the Messiah (another formula that is hardly a formality). Paul often speaks of his "unceasing" prayers, referring probably to his keeping of regular times of prayer each day, though not excluding the sense of being "in prayer" at all times, standing in the presence of God with the churches on his heart and mind.

He calls God to witness to this in a somewhat strange phrase (v. 9). Although regularly translated as "whom I serve with my spirit by announcing the gospel" (it is unclear why the NIV has "whole heart" for "spirit"), the verb in question ($\lambda\alpha\tau\rho\epsilon\acute{u}\omega$ *latreuō*), when it has a divine being as its object, regularly means "worship." The thought is not so much that Paul performs service for God by announcing the gospel, but that Paul *worships* God in his spirit (cf. Phil 3:3; there may be an implied contrast with the temple cult, with its geographical focus and physical activity), and that he does so "in the gospel" (the literal translation), either in the sense that his announcing of the gospel constitutes in itself an act of worship or in the sense that he worships the God he sees revealed in "the gospel of his son" (i.e., as in v. 3, the gospel concerning the son of God).

Paul's primary request, in these constant prayers, has not been so much for the growth in Christian character of the Roman church, as we might have expected, but that he will be able, in God's good time, to visit them. However, the ultimate purpose remains similar: He hopes to be able to impart "some spiritual gift" to strengthen them. Speculation about what he had in mind in this cryptic phrase should be quickly put to rest by v. 12, which may be intended to preempt any suggestion that the Roman church, founded by someone other than Paul, was lacking anything basic in its status as a Christian community. Paul's hope is simply for the mutual encouragement that comes from meeting and sharing in fellowship with others who have the same faith (Paul expands this further in 15:14-29).

1:13-15. "I do not want you to be unaware." Paul's slightly heavy-handed double negative indicates caution. This springs, we may guess, from his anxiety about building on someone else's foundation (cf. 15:20). He is facing the implicit question, "Why would you, a pioneer evangelist, want to come to a place where a church already exists?" To this his answer is twofold, in both cases presenting a personal appeal.[34]

First, he has been eager to come for a long time, so that he can "reap some harvest among you, as among the other nations" (v. 13). Since there were at this time probably not more than a few dozen, or at most a couple of hundred, Christians in a city of roughly a million, this would not indicate a lack of confidence in the Roman church's own evangelistic performance or prospects. Anyway, so far his eagerness has come to nothing. "I have been prevented" may indicate a sense that God has not permitted it or perhaps that Satan has hindered it, or even both. (The Corinthian correspondence indicates well enough how Paul's plans could be thwarted; see, e.g., 2 Cor 1:15-19.) Either way, he remains undeterred.

Second, Paul's commission places him under obligation, not just to God, but to all

---

34. It is noteworthy that he here, unusually in Romans, addresses them as ἀδελφοί (*adelphoi*). The Greek word would be understood to embrace both genders (brothers and sisters); "siblings" performs this function, but is sufficiently rare in common usage to be inappropriate. "Family" is perhaps our best equivalent. "Friends," though a common alternative today, is inadequate, not least in our world of casual friendships, to express the intimacy and mutual belonging that *adelphoi* would carry for Paul and his readers.

categories of non-Jewish humanity, Greeks and barbarians, wise and foolish (v. 14). He does not mean that they have done something for him for which he owes them a return, but simply that God has entrusted him with a message for them; until he has discharged this commission he is still, in that sense, in their debt, retaining in his possession something that properly belongs to them. Thus,

even though there may already be a church in Rome, his sense of obligation includes that city also (v. 15). This double reason is presented as a personal desire and obligation, appealing to the Roman Christians as fellow Christians, members of the same family (cf. Gal 4:12-20 for a similarly personal appeal). (See Reflections at 1:16-17.)

Romans 1:16-17, The Gospel Unveils God's Righteousness

COMMENTARY

This brings us to the great statement of the letter's theme, which is noted in the Introduction. Paul offers it as the further explanation of his desire to come to Rome and announce the gospel there. It consists of an opening statement and two successive explanations, backed up with a scriptural quotation. This style of arguing, with clauses linked by the word "for" (γάρ *gar*), is characteristic of many passages in Romans and elsewhere. Frequently the final explanatory clause expresses the deepest thing Paul wishes to say: A is so because B; B is so because C; C is so because D; and D is thus the foundation of the whole sequence. This is undoubtedly the pattern here.[35]

1:16. Just as King Herod looms over much of the Gospel narratives, so also Caesar, the Roman emperor, looms unmentioned over several passages in Paul's works. Caesar was the current lord of the world, whose position was by implication challenged and threatened by the Jewish Messiah, who claimed the same role. To come to Rome with the gospel of Jesus, to announce someone else's accession to the world's throne, therefore, was to put on a red coat and walk into a field with a potentially angry bull. (This proposal might seem to be in tension with 13:1-7, but see the commentary there).

Paul is determined not to shrink from this calling; he is "not ashamed of the gospel."

There may be a hint here of the tradition of Jesus' words to the disciples about people being ashamed of him (Mark 8:38 and par.). The explanation (*gar*) for Paul's not being ashamed is not simply that he is a brazen optimist, marching cheerfully toward danger while sensible people are fleeing in the opposite direction. The explanation is that the gospel, this message about Jesus that he has outlined in vv. 3-4, is itself God's power. It not merely "possesses" God's power or "is accompanied by" God's power but simply *is* God's power. Paul has discovered in practice, in city after city, that announcing the good news—that there is one God who now claims the world as his own through the crucified and risen Jesus—is in itself powerful and that the power is all God's (cf. 1 Cor 2:4-5; 1 Thess 1:5).

Paul, as so often, has expressed this point in such a way as to evoke a biblical tradition. "In thee, O Lord, do I put my trust," says the psalmist; "let me never be ashamed, deliver me in thy righteousness" (Ps 71:1-2; cf. Pss 31:1-3; 143:1; Psalm 71 continues to emphasize the same theme in vv. 15-16, 19, 24, by which time it is the psalmist's opponents who are "ashamed," while he continues to speak of God's righteousness). "Shame" in such a context is what God's people feel when their enemies are triumphing; it is what Israel (and many other peoples) felt in Paul's day, suffering at the hands of Rome. The gospel, and the power it carries, enables Paul to share the position of the psalmist, celebrating God's

35. The NIV omits the first "for" at the start of v. 16; the NRSV, the second one. Paul is eager to preach in Rome, *for* he is not ashamed, *for* the gospel is God's power, *for* in it God's righteousness is unveiled, *as it is written.* Paul's little connecting words regularly indicate the way his mind is working.

righteousness and so remaining unashamed in the face of enemies and gainsayers.[36]

The power unleashed within the gospel message is "for salvation." "Salvation" is another of those "Christian" technical terms, like "son of God," for which most readers today assume a particular meaning that is actually a much later development. Paul's readers had not had the dubious benefit of expositions of "salvation" that focused simply on the state of post-mortem bliss enjoyed by the redeemed in a more or less disembodied "heaven." Of course, Paul's view of God's saving purposes included, as we shall see, the belief that death itself was now a defeated enemy; his doctrine of salvation was in that sense ultimate, not merely penultimate. It had to do, not merely with rescue from evils in the present life, but with rescue from ultimate destruction. But the context of meaning remained Jewish, and in that setting "salvation" had far more to do with the rescue of Israel from pagan oppression, from Egypt or Babylon or, now, Rome, than with "life after death." Insofar as Romans 5–8 expound Paul's theology of "salvation," it is of the utmost importance to note that the climax of that passage is the redemption of creation itself. If we are right to hear all these overtones, we will also hear in this word, in the present context, a mention of that benefit that Caesar was supposed to give to his loyal followers. As in Phil 3:20-21, Jesus turns out to be the reality of which Caesar is the parody. Just as there is only one "lord of the world," so also in the last analysis there is only one "savior."[37]

The salvation in question is "for everyone who believes." Paul will explain the significance of Christian faith in chap. 3, and further explanation will be deferred to that point. Here as there, however, part of the point of faith is that it is open to all, "to the Jew first and also to the Greek." Paul has expressed this in such a way as to insist both upon the temporal primacy of the Jew within the purposes of God ("to the Jew first," corresponding to the Messiah's mission to "the circumcised" in 15:8) and the absolute equality of status now granted to the non-Jew ("Greek"

here is a way of saying "Gentile").[38] If faith is a major theme in Romans, so is the equality under the gospel of what, from the Jewish point of view, are the two great divisions of humankind. These themes, as we shall see, are inseparable. Every word, every phrase in the second half of v. 16 supports the first half; that is to say, the whole clause governed by the second "for" in the verse ("for it is God's power to salvation for all believers, Jew first but equally Greek") explains why Paul is not ashamed of the gospel.

1:17. The third "for," undergirding the other two, goes to the heart of the matter, explaining in turn every aspect of v. 16*b*. In the gospel, God's righteousness is unveiled. This revelation happens, not just in the events referred to in the gospel, true though that is, but in the very announcement of the gospel. The death and resurrection of Jesus the Messiah form the initial disclosure of God's righteousness, the major apocalpytic event that burst upon an unsuspecting world and an uncomprehending Israel; now the apocalypse happens again, every time the message about Jesus is announced, as God's righteousness is unveiled before another audience.

The gospel message about Jesus, in other words, opens people's eyes to see for the first time that *this was what God had been up to all along.* It enables Jews to see how the promises they had cherished had been fulfilled, quite otherwise than they had expected. It enables Gentiles to see that there is one true God, the God of Israel, the creator; that this God has purposed to set the world to rights at last; and that this God has now in principle accomplished that purpose. And when we say "enables to see," we should not think merely of propositions commanding intellectual assent. Paul believed that the announcement of the gospel wielded a power that overcame the unseen forces, inside people and around them, that prevented them from responding in obedient belief and allegiance (see 2 Cor 4:1-6).

It is important to note that the NIV translation ("a righteousness from God is revealed") presupposes what I argued in the Introduction to be the wrong understanding of the phrase. Instead of God's own righteousness,

---

36. See R. B. Hays, *Echoes of Scripture in the Letters of Paul* (New Haven: Yale University Press, 1989) 38-39, suggesting other parallels, e.g., Isa 50:7-8.

37. See N. T. Wright, "Paul's Gospel and Caesar's Empire," in Horsely, *Paul and Politics,* 160-83.

38. See esp. Cranfield, *A Critical and Exegetical Commentary on the Epistle to the Romans,* 90-91.

it suggests that Paul is referring here to the status that Christians have as a result of God's justifying action. Although this is a possible meaning of the Greek, there is no warrant for it in Paul's Jewish background; it makes the reading of 3:21-26 very problematic; and it effectively splits off other sections of Romans, notably chaps. 9–11, from the early chapters, since in 9–11 the questions Paul is addressing are precisely those summarized in Jewish literature by the notion of God's own righteousness.

God's righteousness is revealed "through faith to faith" (NRSV). By itself this is too dense and cryptic for a modern reader to be certain of its meaning. As it stands, the phrase could mean "by faith from first to last" (NIV) or one of a number of other options.[39] But in the light of 3:21-22 and other passages, its most natural meaning is "from God's faithfulness to human faithfulness."[40] When God's action in fulfillment of the covenant is unveiled, it is because God is faithful to what has been promised; when it is received, it is received by that human faith that answers to the revelation of God in Jesus Christ, that human faith that is also faith*fulness* to the call of God in Jesus the Messiah.

Paul finishes the summary statement by quoting Hab 2:4, "the righteous shall live by faith." This innocent-looking quotation has generated enormous discussions. These have to do with the apparent shifts in meaning between the original Hebrew text ("the righteous shall live by his faithfulness"), the LXX ("the righteous shall live by my faithfulness"), and Paul's own quotation ("the righteous shall live by faith[fulness]"), and also with two particular questions: Does "by faith" modify "live" or "righteous" and where, therefore, does the emphasis fall—"the righteous shall live *by faith*" or "the one who by faith is righteous *shall have life*"? And how does Paul intend the quotation to support what has gone before? All these matters, obviously, interlock.[41]

We should avoid a minimalist solution on the last question. Some have suggested that Paul merely ransacked his mental concordance for passages in which "righteousness" and "faith" occurred side by side, came up with this passage and Gen 15:6, and proceeded to quote them in Romans 1 and 4 (and in Galatians 3) without regard for their original context and meaning. His general use of Scripture and the particular sense of this passage and of Galatians 3 indicate otherwise. We need to inquire as to the wider context of the original sentence and the echoes Paul may have intended alert readers to hear.[42]

The original passage in Habakkuk belongs within a book full of woe and puzzlement. The Chaldeans are marching against Israel; all seems lost. What is Israel's God up to in allowing it? This is, once more, the question of the righteousness, or justice, of God (this alone should warn us off the idea that Paul was quoting at random a verse that merely happened to contain his two catchwords). By way of answer, the prophet is given a vision, but it is a vision for the future, to be revealed at a later date (Hab 2:3). At the moment God's true people, the righteous within a sinful nation, "will live by faith." "Faith" here, whether the human faith, as in the Hebrew text, or God's faithfulness, as in the LXX, is the key feature of the interim period.

What does this mean in practice for the prophet? It means believing that God will eventually punish the idolatrous and violent nation (2:5-20), that God will remember mercy in the midst of wrath and bring salvation to Israel (3:2-19). This thematic parallel with Rom 1:18–3:20 and 3:21–4:25 is striking and continues to suggest that Paul does, indeed, have the larger context from Habakkuk in mind. Faced with pagan idolatry and arrogance, the devout first-century Jew longed for God's righteousness to break forth, bringing wrath on the nations and salvation for Israel.[43] Paul, however, has seen God's purpose unveiled in the gospel and believes, like the prophet, that this vision is the key

---

39. See, e.g., Schelkle who, following Augustine, sees 1:17 as describing a transference from faith in the law to faith in the gospel. For Cranfield, *Romans*, 99-100, the phrase is a rhetorical way of saying "completely by faith." See also Moo, *Romans*, 76.

40. ἐκ πίστεως . . .εἰς πίστιν (*ek pisteōs . . . eis pistin*) in 1:17 corresponds quite closely to διὰ . . . πίστεως εἰς πάντας τοὺς πιστεύοντας (*dia pisteōs . . . eis pantas tous pisteuontas*) in 3:22 (see also Gal 3:22). For this interpretation, see Dunn, *Romans 1–8*.

41. On these questions see the detailed analysis of Rikki E. Watts, " 'For I Am Not Ashamed of the Gospel': Romans 1:16-17 and Habbakuk 2:4," in *Romans and the People of God: Essays in Honor of Gordon D. Fee on the Occasion of His 65th Birthday*, ed. S. K. Soderlund and N. T. Wright (Grand Rapids: Eerdmans, 1999) 3-15.

42. On such echoes, deliberate or otherwise, see above all Hays, *Echoes of Scripture in the Letters of Paul*, 39-41. Moo, *Romans*, 77-78, seems to miss the thematic connections between Habakkuk and what Paul is here talking about.

43. On the use of Hab 2:4 in this context in Second Temple Judaism, see A. Strobel, *Untersuchungen zum eschatologischen Verzögerungsproblem, auf Grund der spätjüdisch-urchristlichen Geschichte von Habakuk 2,2 ff.*, NovTSup 2 (Leiden: Brill, 1961).

to understanding all that will now take place. This solution to the problem of first-century Israel produces a second-order problem: Much of ethnic Israel is failing to believe the gospel, while Gentiles are coming in in droves. Paul will deal with that in due course. For the moment he contents himself with the cryptic, but evocative, quotation. He is not ashamed of the gospel, because it is God's power to salvation for all believers; because, faced with a world in idolatry and ruin, God's righteousness is revealed in the gospel, a matter of divine faithfulness reaching down and calling out the response of human faithfulness. In this setting, "the righteous shall live by faithfulness"; whether divine or human or both, Paul does not need to say. The sentence remains cryptic until we reach 3:21–4:25.

Part of the strength of this exegesis of v. 17 is the sense it makes of the transition to v. 18, which has long been a puzzle to students of Paul's flow of thought. But before moving to the next section of the letter, a word is needed about the road we have traveled thus far.

Romans has been thought of for centuries as the letter in which Paul expounds his doctrine of "justification by faith." This half-truth has opened up some aspects of the letter and concealed others. As will become clear, the theological content of this substantial opening section contains "justification by faith" within it by implication, but this is not the stated theme of the letter. The theme is, to repeat once more, the revelation of God's righteousness, God's covenant faithfulness, God's justice, in and through the gospel proclamation of the crucified and risen Messiah. Like the two opening themes of a classical sonata, Paul's summary of "the gospel" in 1:3-4 and his summary of "God's righteousness" in 1:16-17 will do further business with each other as the work progresses, and their contrapuntal interweaving will support other tunes, other harmonic progressions. But this letter has announced itself as a treatment, not so much of humans, their plight and their rescue (though all of that has its proper place), but of God—God's gospel, God's righteousness. We will not understand Romans unless we grasp this from the outset and remember it throughout.

REFLECTIONS

1. Despite the many surface differences between Paul's world and ours, we, too, live in an age where the question of God's righteousness, God's justice, weighs heavy upon us. The wars and atrocities of the twentieth century have left major questions in the air: How can a good God allow such things? Where was God in Auschwitz? Where is God in Rwanda? In the Balkans? Where was God on September 11, 2001? It is now the world as a whole, not simply the Jewish people, that cries out for redemption, that recognizes increasingly the folly and dehumanization of idolatry, and that asks Habakkuk's questions of "Why?" and "How long?"

Our own setting, therefore, enables us to appropriate Paul's discussion of God's righteousness, here and throughout the letter, with a sense of the coming together of "covenant faithfulness" and "justice." If God is the creator of the world, and has promised to bring all things into justice, peace, and harmony, then the cosmos as a whole, and the human race within it, is called to believe in this justice and the faithfulness that will bring it about. The church's ministry to the world in our generation includes, and perhaps even focuses upon, this task: to unveil God's righteousness once more through the gospel of Jesus, the Jewish Messiah, knowing that as this happens the power of God for salvation is unleashed, so that where there is faith the blessings of God's future may be brought forward into the present.

2. "The gospel," in Paul's terminology, was not primarily a message about sinful human beings and how they attained justification and salvation. We can, of course, use words however we wish, but if we are to understand and appropriate Paul we will do well to use his words in his way. For him, "the gospel" was the sovereign message, from none other than God, concerning Jesus the Messiah, God's unique son. This message was not simply the offer of a new reordering of one's private spiritual interiority, a new clearing up of a morally dysfunctional life via forgiveness for the past and new moral energy for the present. It was not simply a new vocation to live for God and for others in the world. It was, rather, news about God and about Jesus; news that this Jesus had become the spearhead of God's "age to come"; news that, within this new age, the principalities and powers, including earthly rulers, the powers of darkness, and sin and death themselves had been defeated and were now summoned to allegiance. "The gospel" was a command requiring obedience, much more than an invitation seeking a response.

Always the command comes out of the blue, unexpected and in many ways unwelcome. Paul's contemporary Jews neither expected nor wanted a crucified Messiah. Paul's contemporary Gentiles neither expected nor wanted to worship and serve a Jewish figure, still less a Jewish failure (cf. 1 Cor 1:18–2:5). Our own contemporaries, long schooled to regard the climax of world history as having occurred in Western Europe in the eighteenth century (giving birth, of course, to modern North America), neither expect nor want to hear that the true climax in fact occurred in Palestine in the first century CE. They will urge counterexamples: Surely the world has not in fact improved (did Paul say it had or would?); surely Christianity has been responsible for many great evils (in part, yes, though often demonstrably when in rebellion against the gospel itself); surely we now know that Christianity is untrue (actually, no, we don't). These objections must be taken seriously; yet they may also be smoke screens to hide the fact that the grandiose claims of "modernity" are now themselves looking increasingly threadbare. The command of the gospel is a summons to give the allegiance of body and mind, heart and soul, to Jesus; and its basis is neither more nor less than the event that constituted him in Paul's eyes as Messiah and Lord—namely, his resurrection. And it is in the proclamation of this gospel, and its acceptance in faith, that people begin to glimpse a great curtain being drawn aside and the covenant faithfulness and justice of God displayed to view. Faced with that sight, it is impossible to remain a mere spectator.

3. Paul's self-portrait and personal introduction in these verses is both stark and subtle. Content to be defined simply by the gospel—think how much of his personal history and background he could have mentioned here, as he prepares to visit the senior city of the empire, but chooses not to—he presents himself as a slave bearing a commission from royalty. At the same time, he will not simply barge in upon the Roman church, relying on his God-given commission to give him the necessary status. He will pray for them, thank God for them, and in that context think into their possible anxieties about his coming and meet them with a personal appeal. Conscious of the biblical story, stretching ahead into his own time and catching him up within it (see the Commentary on 9:6–10:21), he is also very aware of the human stories with which his own personal story must intertwine. His prayer functions not least as a way of ensuring, so far as he can, that these stories will work together in harmony.

4. Already in these opening verses we find a major theme that creates huge problems in our world, and for practicing Christians. How, we ask, can the gospel message be for both Jew and non-Jew? We stand appalled at the incalculable crimes committed against Jews in our supposedly civilized world. Many feel, understandably, that for Christians to say any word to Jews about the gospel of Jesus Christ is now inappropriate. I have wrestled with these questions elsewhere and will revisit them more than once in what follows.[44] But it is impossible to suppose that Paul, for whom Jesus' Messiahship was the central content of the gospel and for whom the Jewish question

---

44. See N. T. Wright, *For All God's Worth* (Grand Rapids: Eerdmans, 1997) chap. 13.

of God's righteousness had in principle been addressed and solved precisely by Jesus' messianic death and resurrection, would have been content to keep this gospel only for non-Jews. Time was when the nuances of justification by faith aroused passions around the world; these days it tends to be the political overtones of the gospel that make people angry. But these issues cannot be easily either solved or wished away, and Romans remains one of the great stimuli and sourcebooks for dealing with them.

ROMANS 1:18–3:20, THE CHALLENGE FOR GOD'S RIGHTEOUSNESS: GENTILES AND JEWS ALIKE UNDER GOD'S WRATH, GUILTY OF IDOLATRY AND WICKEDNESS

OVERVIEW

The first major section of the letter is a courtroom scene. It opens with the sentence being passed; it moves back to explain the grounds for the verdict, highlights the problems the judge has had to cope with in hearing the case, and concludes with the guilty parties in the dock, with nothing to say in their defense.

Romans 1:18–3:20, in other words, is all about God's righteousness, both in the sense that God is the judge in the cosmic lawcourt and in the sense that God is in covenant with Israel, the covenant that causes the peculiar problems when Israel, too, is found guilty in God's sight. The whole section serves as a further explanation of 1:16-17; hence the γάρ (*gar*, "for") that links 1:18 to the previous passage (omitted in the NIV). In particular, 1:18–3:20 explains why the gospel is God's saving power for *all* who believe: because God's wrath is revealed against *all* ungodliness and wickedness (1:18), and it turns out that "all sinned, and came short of God's glory" (3:23, summing up 1:18–3:20). Apart from the gospel, there is no alternative route to salvation.

The section, though, is not simply about "the human plight." It is about God's own problem and gives a preliminary statement of God's way of dealing with it. God created humans to bear the divine image within the creation and called Israel to shine the divine light into the dark world. Faced with human rebellion and Jewish faithlessness, will God abandon these projects? This section repeatedly emphasizes that God will remain faithful, though it does not yet explain how—except that God's wrath means precisely the determination not to give evil the last word, to root out from the good creation all that defaces and destroys it. Already, therefore, we find ourselves looking ahead both to the end of chap. 8, with the renewal of humans and of creation, and to the end of chap. 11, when "all Israel shall be saved." It is because the creator God remains implacably opposed to all the forces of evil that there is hope. The revelation of wrath is itself, however paradoxically, part of the good news (see the Commentary on 2:16). As in Habakkuk, quoted in v. 17, the whole world is in turmoil, but God remains sovereign. This prepares the way for the solution: As in Habakkuk once more, God's people are defined, at this moment of crisis, in terms of faithfulness. The portion of the letter that begins with 1:18 does indeed explain and unpack what is implicit in the dense statement of 1:16-17.

Two elements of Paul's strategy throughout the section are worthy of note. First, he draws extensively on traditional Jewish critiques of the pagan world. This section, particularly the first long paragraph, echoes Wisdom 12–16, which, under the guise of describing the wickedness of the Canaanites and Egyptians at the time of the exodus, launches a polemic against paganism in general, describing it in terms of idolatry and the consequent fracturing of human society. Paul agrees with this assessment of paganism, but he goes further, and by doing so effectively undercuts Wisdom's eventual point. Wisdom argued that the Israelites, rebellious in the wilderness, escaped with punishments that served as a warning and a reminder of God's law (Wis 16:5-6, 10-11). Paul will not have it. The Jews, he declares, are just as guilty as the pagans; all alike end up in the dock (Rom 3:19-20).

Second, he argues his case by a process of gradual unfolding. At first sight, 1:18-32 seems to be directed solely against the Gentiles; but, as we shall see, at two points in particular he alludes to scriptural passages that suggest that Israel, too, has behaved in a pagan manner and will receive the appropriate reward. Then in 2:1-16 he seems to be aiming at the tradition of pagan moralism; but, not least with Wisdom in mind, it is reasonable to suppose that he is also thinking of the virtuous Jew (including his own pre-Christian self, of course), looking with disdain on the ungodly and dissolute pagan world. So when he turns explicitly to the boast of Israel in 2:17, only to deconstruct it from Scripture itself, he is bringing into the open what has already been hinted. From then on the section focuses almost entirely on Israel: Israel failing in covenant obligations (2:17-24); Israel being upstaged by a new covenant family, which includes Gentiles (2:25-29); Israel joining the pagans in the dock (3:1-20).

A good deal of the material in 1:18–3:20 looks ahead to later passages in the letter. The devastation of humanness brought about by idolatry, described in chap. 1, is reversed through the gospel, as chaps. 4, 6, 8, and 12 bear witness. The covenant purposes of God for Israel, to which Israel was unfaithful, are fulfilled in the faithful Messiah (3:21-26; 5:12-21, and throughout). The exodus, the subtext of the Wisdom passage upon which Paul draws in 1:18-32, forms the subtext, too, of Paul's exposition of the new people of God in Christ in chaps. 5–8. Above all, the problem of God's righteousness, highlighted in the dense little argument of 3:1-8, looks ahead to the whole theme of chaps. 9–11, where Paul will draw on another image from Wisdom: the potter and the clay (Wis 15:7; cf. Wis 12:12; Rom 9:19-22). The present section, then, is far from being a mere exposé of human sinfulness. Within the architecture of the whole letter, it begins the construction of several great arches, which, having reached their various peaks in reference to Jesus the Messiah, come back to earth in the specific conclusions of the different stages of the argument.

Romans 1:18-32, Idolatry and Dehumanized Behavior Resulting in God's Wrath

COMMENTARY

After the lofty and evocative introduction, the body of the letter begins with energy, verve, and passion. With so many cross threads of thought going to and fro, it is best to begin by seeing it as a whole.

The thought moves from an explanation and denunciation of idolatry to an explanation and denunciation of the fracturing of human life that results from it. Paul saw no reason to dissent from the Jewish insight that regarded "sin"—living in a less-than-fully-human fashion, missing the mark as regards God's intention for his human creatures—as the result of worshiping something other than the creator.[45] And, again with Jewish tradition, he regarded idolatry itself as culpable and thus as worthy of appropriate punishment, since the creation was full of the signs of the creator's hand. Over the whole sorry picture, therefore, stand the bracketing statements: The wrath of God is revealed (1:18); they know God's decree that those who do such things deserve to die (1:32).

The connecting threads of the paragraph appear in the thrice-repeated "God gave them

---

45. ἁμαρτία (*hamartia*), Paul's regular word for "sin," does not appear in chap. 1; but when Paul uses it later to summarize the human condition, he is clearly referring back to this passage among others.

up" (vv. 24, 26, 28). In each, Paul spotlights some aspect of human corruption and degradation that results from a failure in worship. The first is a general statement; the second, a specific comment about the fracturing of gender roles. The third is general again and gives rise to the climax of the paragraph, a sprawling, squirming catalog of vices that demonstrates in equal measure Paul's disgust at dehumanized behavior and his rhetorical skill in describing it.

1:18-23. The opening section, which leads up to the first of these hammer blows ("God gave them up"), introduces us to a major theme within Paul's indictment of the human race. The problem is not just wrong behavior, but wrong thought patterns—the latter, indeed, being the cause of the former. Humans suppress the truth (v. 18); they refuse to acknowledge what they in fact know (v. 21*a*); their reasoning becomes futile, their heart darkened (v. 21*b*); claiming to be wise, they become fools (v. 22). This theme echoes through the rest of the chapter (vv. 25, 28, 32) and anticipates the problem highlighted in 7:7-25, where the "wretched person" knows what ought to be done but cannot do it. Equally, it points on to 12:1-2, where the "renewal of the mind," enabling one to think clearly about what God approves, is the key to presenting the body in God's service.

1:18. God's wrath, a prominent theme throughout Scripture, was a major problem for an older liberal theology, which struggled, rightly enough, to avoid any suggestion of God as a malevolent despot, hurling thunderbolts at those who broke arbitrary laws.[46] The tide has turned now, and the great wickednesses of the twentieth century have reminded us that unless God remains implacably opposed to the evil that distorts and defaces creation, not least humanity, God is not a good God. Paul's whole theology, not least the expression of it in Romans, is grounded in the robust and scripturally rooted view that the creator is neither a tyrannical despot nor an indulgent, *laissez-faire* absentee landlord, nor yet, for that matter, the mere inner or spiritual dimension of all that is. God is the creator and lover of the world. This God has a passionate concern for creation, and humans in particular, that will tolerate nothing less than the best for them.

The result is "wrath"—not just a settled attitude of hostility toward idolatry and immorality, but actions that follow from such an attitude when the one to whom it belongs is the sovereign creator. The content of this wrath is not merely the process (described in the rest of the chapter) of God's "giving people up" to the result of their own folly. That, rather, is simply the anticipation of the final judgment itself, the "death" spoken of in 1:32 and the ultimate judgment described in 2:5-6, 9. The two are, of course, organically connected. Present moral degradation (and physical, too, in many cases) anticipates the ultimate degrading of humanness in death itself.

This wrath is revealed "from heaven," in the present time. As with all of Paul's "apocalyptic" theology, the "end" expected by Second Temple Jews had split into two; the end had in one sense happened, but in another sense was yet to happen fully (see esp. 1 Cor 15:12-28). Thus, although the wrath is still to be revealed in the future (2:5), the last day has in some sense been brought forward into the present. Granted the rest of Paul's thinking about how future and present fit together, this can only mean that something in the events concerning Jesus has unveiled the wrath of God in a new way. Paul's point is not that the moral corruption of the pagan world provides a fresh revelation of God's wrath. Pagans have always behaved like that, at least when seen from Paul's Jewish standpoint. He must mean that, in some way or another, the fact of Jesus has drawn back the veil on the wrath to come.

How has this happened? The answer is provided in 2:16. God, writes Paul, will judge the secrets of humans, *according to my gospel, through the Messiah, Jesus.* Drawing on the Jewish tradition that the Messiah would be the judge of the whole world, Paul sees that his gospel involves the announcement that God has fixed a day on which the world will be called to account; that the agent of this divinely appointed judgment will be none other than Jesus himself; and that the proof of the matter is to be found in Jesus' resurrection (see Acts 17:31; other links between Romans 1 and Acts 17 are noted below).

---

46. The classic statement of this position may be found in Dodd, *The Epistle of Paul to the Romans*, 47-50.

This explains the train of thought that leads Paul into 1:18. The same gospel message that functions as God's saving power (1:3-4, 16) also names the judge through whom the world will be brought to account and confirms his appointment to that role. From then on nothing can be the same again. A new moment of world history has come to birth. Between the resurrection and the final judgment, the world, whether it acknowledges it or not, lives before the unveiled gaze of the judge.

But it does not, of course, acknowledge the fact. Paul's basic charge (like so many of his introductory sentences, it contains the rest of the passage in a nutshell) is that humans, in their ungodliness and injustice, suppress the truth, and do so precisely by means of that injustice. The word rendered "wickedness" in the NRSV and the NIV is ἀδικία (*adikia*), not just general evil but injustice, the crucial symptom of the world's out-of-jointness. This human injustice contrasts sharply with God's justice (v. 17); Paul's language is too tightly integrated to allow for loose translation here. The truth is dangerous—so rebellious humans suppress it, hide it away, try to prevent its leaking out. Not only in war is truth an early casualty.

1:19-21. Characteristically, Paul fills out his initial statement with three layers of explanation. God's self-revelation has displayed what can be known; this revelation takes place in the created order, rendering all without excuse; humans have refused to honor God in the appropriate way.

These verses have had to bear the weight of debates about "natural theology" (the question of whether, and to what extent, the truth of God is accessible through the created order without the aid of special revelation).[47] As with some other doctrines that have wandered to and fro seeking biblical support, this one has fastened upon certain brief passages, in this case the present one and a few others (notably Acts 17:22-31, which has other affinities with this passage in Romans), none

of which offers a full-dress exposition of the matter, but only an allusion on the way to making some other point. Nevertheless, however brief the statement, Paul clearly does believe that when humans look at creation they are aware, at some level, of the power and divinity of the creator. The problem, of course, is that this knowledge does not save those who possess it, but only renders them guilty. Paul does not say that saving knowledge of God may be had through observing the creation; nor, however, does he say that there is nothing that can be known of God that way. Indeed, granted his belief in the renewal of the human mind by grace, we must assume that in his view the Christian can indeed discern the truth of God by observing creation. But that is not his point here. In fact, like several of his Jewish contemporaries, he believes—consonant with the Jewish belief that the world was made by a good creator—that signs of the creator are visible within this world (see, e.g., Wis 13:5).[48] But these never permit humans to gain over the creator the kind of power that comes with knowledge. On the contrary, they are simply enough to ensure that when humans rebel—as they do—they are manifestly guilty.

The appropriate response to the divine self-revelation in creation would have been worship and thanksgiving. Instead, however, human thought became futile and foolish, and human hearts (not "minds" as NRSV, though the two ideas are not far apart in Paul) became darkened. This unfolding of the dense v. 18*b* prepares the way for vv. 22, 24-25 and above all vv. 28 and 32.

1:22-23. The result of the refusal to know God through creation is the false boast of humans and the corruption of the worshiping instinct into idolatry. Here Paul is deliberately, though covertly, retelling the story of Genesis 3, on the one hand, and of Israel in the wilderness, on the other.

Talk of God the creator has prepared the way for the first of these. When, in Genesis 3, the serpent tempts Eve, what is on offer is fruit that will, supposedly, make humans wise

47. See the discussion in Fitzmyer, *Romans*, 273. The question of natural theology was tightly intertwined, for German theologians in the first half of the twentieth century, with the ideology of the Third Reich and with the massive protest against it of Karl Barth. That is why, for instance, Käsemann assumes that Paul's eschatology and christology would militate against anything like the natural theology found in some Hellenistic Judaism. See Ernst Käsemann, *Commentary on Romans*, trans. Geoffrey W. Bromiley (London: SCM, 1980) 41.

48. See also Letter of Aristeas 132; 2 Bar 54:17-22; Philo *On Rewards and Punishments* 43; and, in non-Jewish sources, Pseudo-Aristotle *De Mundo* [*On the Universe*] 399ab; Epictetus *Discourses* 1.6.19. The essay by G. Bornkamm, *Early Christian Experience* (London: SCM 1969) chap. 3, remains important.

(Gen 3:6). The primal sin was a matter of obeying instructions, or at least suggestions, not from the creator in whose image humans were made, but from an agent within creation itself. Instead of recognizing wisdom as an attribute of the creator, to be gained by worshiping and serving that God, humans boasted in a wisdom that consisted in supposed independence. But this wisdom consisted in the greatest folly possible—namely, giving allegiance instead to images of humans and also of birds, animals, and reptiles.

This "exchange" of God's glory for an idol echoes Ps 106:20, which speaks of Israel in the wilderness swapping the living God for the golden calf. Here Paul corrects the implicit narrative of the Wisdom of Solomon, written most likely not long before his own day, by referring back to Scripture: In Wisdom, Israel in the wilderness may commit sins, but it will receive only a mild, correcting rebuke. In general, the people stand out from the pagan Egyptians. For Paul, as for the psalmist, Israel rejected the covenant God and fell away into copying the pagans (see further the Commentary on 7:9-11; 9:15-16).[49] This not only anticipates the explicit turn in the argument at 2:17, but it also looks ahead to 7:7-12, where once again the narratives of Adam and Israel are woven together.

The first part of Paul's basic charge is now complete. The human race, called to worship and reflect the image of the creator, has turned to idolatry—and has sought to dignify it by claiming it as the true wisdom. The results follow swiftly.

1:24-27. "God gave them up." This repeated phrase carries scriptural echoes from Ps 81:12. This psalm is itself a hymnic telling of the exodus narrative, warning of idolatry, bemoaning the fact that Israel has not heeded the warning, and appealing for the people to return to YHWH. Thus, again, Paul's surface text describes paganism, but the subtext quietly includes Israel in the indictment. The result, for pagan and Jew alike, is that the creator allows all to reap what they have sown. The punishment not only fits the crime, but

directly results from it as well: Those who worship images of their fellow creatures must not be surprised if their own bodies are dishonored as a result of the lusts (NRSV) or desires (NIV) of their hearts (ἐπιθυμία [epithymia] need not have a negative sense, but here and elsewhere in Romans it certainly does; cf. 6:12; 7:7-8; 13:9; 13:14). This condition is further evidence of Paul's general charge, focused in a new way in v. 25: Humans have swapped God's truth for a lie and have given allegiance to that which is not God. Paul, unusually, pauses to express his own allegiance to "the creator, who is blessed for ever. Amen" in this typically Jewish word of praise.

The exchange of truth for a lie results in the second "God gave them up." After the general comment about dishonoring of bodies, Paul now describes particular "lusts of shame"—that is (so NRSV), passions that degrade human beings, making them less than the full humans they were meant to be. Paul notes homosexual practice, both female and male, adding the comment that those who do these things receive in their own persons the reward of their error (the NIV's "perversion" is perhaps too exact a word, since the Greek indicates a more general wandering off course). Out of the many things Paul could have highlighted in the pagan world, he has chosen same-sex erotic practices, not simply because Jews regarded homosexual practice as a classic example of pagan vice, but more particularly because it corresponds, in his view, to what humans in general have done in swapping God's truth for a lie.[50]

The underlying logic seems to be as follows. Those who worship the true God are, as Paul says elsewhere, renewed according to the divine image (Col 3:10). When this worship is exchanged for the worship of other gods, the result will be that this humanness, this image-bearing quality, is correspondingly distorted. Paul may suppose that in Genesis 1 it is male and female together that compose the image of God; or he may simply be taking it for granted that heterosexual intercourse is obviously the creator's intention for genital activity. Either way, his point is

---

49. Several Jewish traditions regarded the golden calf incident as a critical turn in Jewish history. These are cataloged in Samuel Vollenweider, *Freiheit als neue Schöpfung,* FRLANT (Göttingen: Vandenhoeck & Ruprecht, 1989) 258. See also S. J. Hafemann, *Paul, Moses and the History of Israel: The Letter/Spirit Contrast and the Argument from Scripture in 2 Corinthians 3* (Peabody, Mass.: Hendrikson 1995) 227-31.

50. On what follows see the thorough treatment in R. A. J. Gagnon, *The Bible and Homosexual Practice: Texts and Hermeneutics* (Nashville: Abingdon, 2001) 229-303; and R. B. Hays, *The Moral Vision of the New Testament* (San Francisco: Harper, 1996) 379-406.

that homosexual behavior is a distortion of the creator's design and that such practices are evidence, not of the intention of any specific individual to indulge in such practice for its own sake, but of the tendency within an entire society for humanness to fracture when gods other than the true one are being worshiped. The point is: Exchange your God for an idol, and you will exchange your genuine humanness for a distorted version, which will do you no good. What particular physical ailments Paul believed resulted from homosexual practice is not clear, but the last line of v. 27 is in any case an aside, rather than a main plank in the argument.

1:28-32. The remaining five verses, all one sentence in the Greek, fill in the picture with strokes as broad and general as the previous two verses were specific and focused. The third "God gave them up" is again a close punishment-and-crime analysis: They did not see fit to have true knowledge of God, so God gave them up to an unfit mind (neither the NRSV nor the NIV retains the wordplay that encapsulates Paul's point). And the unfit mind becomes the source of inappropriate deeds; Paul's view of sin, once more, is not that it is the breaking of arbitrary divine rules but that it is subhuman or nonhuman behavior, deeds that are unfitting for humans to perform. Such people are full, Paul says twice, of all kinds of evil; like jugs filled to overflowing with noxious liquids, they are brimful of wickedness, ready to spill over at any moment. Paul's catalog of vices, arranged for maximum rhetorical effect, reads better in Greek than in any possible English version, ending with four resounding words: ἀσυνέτους (*asynetous*), ἀσυνθέτους (*asynthetous*), ἀστόργους (*astorgous*), and ἀνελεήμονας (*aneleēmonas*). The NIV comes closest to the verbal effect: "senseless," "faithless," "heartless," "ruthless." Paul's main concern has not been to provide an exhaustive or logically ordered list of all the ways in which idolatry defaces human behavior. His intention, rather, is to paint a picture in the richest verbal colors and patterns that he can.

The final comment (v. 32) is the most devastating. They know God's just decree (for δικαίωμα *dikaiōma* see the Commentary on 8:4)—namely, that those who do such things deserve to die. Paul is again appealing to something that, in theory at least, the whole human race is aware of. He cannot mean that all humans have heard of a law that prescribes the death penalty for certain specific types of behavior. Rather, he asserts that humans in general have an innate awareness that certain types of behavior are inherently dehumanizing, to their practitioners as well as to their victims. Those who behave in these ways are destroying themselves, and at a deep level they are aware of the fact.

Nevertheless, they not only do these things but also applaud (NRSV) those who practice them. It is one thing to live a self-destructive life-style, recognizing it for what it is, grieving over it, and urging others to avoid it if they can. It is another, more sinister, thing to call evil good and good evil. Once light and darkness have been renamed, the process of dehumanization is complete and may well prove irreversible.

REFLECTIONS

1. One still meets, from time to time, the belief that there is nothing really wrong with the human race. It is unhealthy, we are told, or perhaps morbid to dwell on sin or always to be drawing attention to it; it is pathological to approve of punishment, still less retribution. It is bordering on blasphemy to suppose that God would ever be wrathful.

Romans holds these notions up to the light and exposes the counterfeit theology they contain. There is such a thing as human wickedness, and if God does not oppose it relentlessly, then God stands accused of conniving at destructive and dehumanizing practices. The generation that has known both mid-century totalitarianism and late-century apartheid and "ethnic cleansing" should be in no doubt of systemic injustice, rooted in the reality of wickedness deep within the human heart. Within such settings, "embrace" (a gentle liberal toleration of different viewpoints) is not enough; there must also be "exclusion," the making and implementing of judgments that risk pronouncing a "no" as well as a "yes." Finding the appropriate coexistence of those two is an urgent task for our day.[51]

2. Our generation has seen the resurgence, in the Western world, of various forms of paganism. The worship of blood and soil, and the symbols that evoke them, was characteristic of the Nazi movement and remains all too familiar within the tribal and geographical disputes that still disfigure our planet. The worship of Mammon, granting absolute sovereignty to "economic forces," whatever the human cost, is endemic in much contemporary culture of both East and West. Eros, the god of sexual love, claims millions of devotees who genuinely believe they are bound to obey its every dictate, however many times its grandiose promises prove hollow. Mars, the god of war, is worshiped by many, tolerated by many more, and still wreaks havoc. And serious nature worship is on the increase, as the old "god" of eighteenth-century Deism has disappeared from view, leaving a vacuum to be filled by the "forces" within the created order, producing various kinds of pantheism.

We cannot, then, dismiss Paul's analysis of idolatry as relevant only to his own age. In some cases we can easily see how such idolatry leads to dehumanized and dehumanizing behavior—when, for instance, worship of Mammon by the few leads to widespread poverty for the many and when, faced with the call to remit large-scale and unpayable international debt, many in positions of power and financial security kick and scream rather than give up a single dollar of "owed" interest. Paul's thesis that dehumanizing behavior is rooted in the worship of idols deserves full contemporary exploration.

3. Paul's comment about homosexual behavior is deeply controversial today. Attempts have been made to mitigate its force by saying (for instance) that he is only referring to a deliberate swapping from heterosexual to homosexual practice, not to what in recent years has been regarded as an innate homosexual condition, or that he was only concerned with practices directly related to idolatrous cults. As in some other matters, it would be wrong to press 1:26-27 for a full analysis of same-sex desires or practices; but equally it is wrong to minimalize or marginalize what Paul teaches here. He is not saying, as in an individualistic culture he is inevitably read as saying, that individuals who are aware of same-sex erotic tendencies or who engage in the practices that result have themselves been worshiping idols. He is not proposing a case-by-case analysis. Rather, his argument is that the existence of homosexual practice in a culture is a sign that that culture as a whole has been worshiping idols and that its God-given male-and-female order is being fractured as a result.[52]

We cannot isolate these verses from Paul's larger argument, both in this paragraph and in Romans as a whole. From this it is clear that he regards homosexual practice as a dangerous distortion of God's intention. It is quite logical to say that we disagree with Paul or that in the light of our greater knowledge of human psychology we need to reassess the matter. That can be argued either way. What we cannot do is to sideline this passage as irrelevant to Christian ethical discourse, or for that matter to the argument of Romans, or to pretend that it means something other than what it says. It is, of course, important to remind ourselves also that Romans 1 is followed at once by Romans 2, with its emphatic warning against a moral superiority complex. As the argument goes on its way, Paul's most damning condemnation is reserved, not for those who engage in what he sees as dehumanizing practices, but for those who adopt

---

51. See Miroslav Volf, *Exclusion and Embrace: A Theological Exploration of Identity, Otherness, and Reconciliation* (Nashville: Abingdon, 1996).

52. Much fuller treatments of this topic can be found in the works of Gagnon, *The Bible and Homosexual Practice*, and Hays, *The Moral Vision of the New Testament*.

---

a posture of innate moral virtue while themselves failing in their most basic vocation, to be the light of the world.

4. Paul's concern with truth, and with the tendency of humans to deceive themselves about it, addresses precisely the clash in contemporary culture between modernity and postmodernity. The Western Enlightenment bequeathed an intellectual climate in which it was assumed that "truth" could be known "objectively," by scientific and similar observation. Clear and hard thought, it was supposed, would probe into and lay bare the secrets of all subjects. Suspicion about this has been aroused in recent years as post-modern thinkers have pointed out, following Friedrich Nietzsche, that claims to truth are often covert claims to power. The old Roman legal question, *cui bono?* "who stood to gain by this?" formerly restricted to criminal deeds, is now asked of every human action and statement.

Paul's warnings about the ways in which humans distort the truth and come to believe and approve lies remind us of the postmodern critique. There is such a thing as a darkened heart, a mind made foolish or futile through idolatry. The practice of injustice does indeed "suppress the truth" (1:18). However, postmodernity proves too much. Not only does it, quite appropriately, self-destruct. (How do we know that the postmodern claim about knowledge is itself true? Might not it, too, be subjective posturing?) It runs the risk of ruling out what Paul emphatically claims, that despite all suspicion there is such a thing as truth, and it can be known. However, since for Paul the truth is ultimately not something objective, discovered by observation and reason alone, but something personal, given in encounter with the living God, the debates of recent centuries are transcended within a Christian epistemology. Though modernists may sneer and postmodernists gnash their teeth at the very thought, there is in Paul's book such a thing as a mind renewed by the Spirit, and he is so bold as to suggest, in Romans and elsewhere, that this is attainable in Christ (see, e.g., 1 Cor 2:14-16).

Romans 2:1-16, God's Impartial Judgment Leaves No Room for Moral Superiority

COMMENTARY

The scene is set for final judgment. The judge is impartial; the truth will out; the world will be put to rights at last. This typically Jewish depiction of the last great assize is now transposed into a Christian key: The judgment will be "through the Messiah, Jesus" (2:16). What is more, God's impartiality means that Jews and Gentiles will be judged alike.

This paragraph, completing Paul's depiction of "the revelation of God's wrath" (1:18), appears to be addressed to anyone who, faced with the vices mentioned in chap. 1, tries to adopt a superior posture. There were, after all, many pagan moralists in Paul's world, not least in Rome itself, who disdained the behavior Paul condemns just as much as he did and who regarded their philosophy as raising them above it. The question, though, of who Paul is really talking to here is complex. This is a problem we shall meet again.

Paul adopts, here and elsewhere, the prose style known as diatribe, familiar enough from classical works of the same period, such as those of the philosopher Epictetus (and not to be confused with our contemporary meaning of the word, "bitter and abusive speech; ironical or satirical criticism").[53] In this style, the writer engages in debate with imaginary opponents, putting them on the spot, asking them rhetorical questions, answering their supposed objections. Paul had had plenty of experience of real debate and knew which arguments might come up; but he does not,

---

53. *Merriam-Webster's Collegiate Dictionary*, 10th edn., 321.

we must assume, expect his real opponents, non-Christian pagans or Jews, to be reading this letter. He therefore creates a double audience: the real one (the Christians in Rome) and the fictitious one (the hypothetical opponent).[54]

This is not designed simply to enable the Roman church to listen in on his debates and so be better equipped for similar ones themselves, though that might be important too. The point is that he wants them to think the argument through with him, to see why these things must be so and not otherwise; and the fiction of a hypothetical interlocutor enables him to do this. In particular, since part of his aim is to show that the justice of God upstages all the justice that the pagan world had to offer, he is prepared, not least in this paragraph, to use technical terms known in Stoic philosophy, taking (as he says in 2 Cor 10:5) every thought captive to obey Christ (see the Commentary on 2:14).

So far so good; but, as with chapter 1, Paul here has in mind not only pagan moralists but also Jews. This does not become explicit until 2:17 (there, too, it is a literary fiction; Paul does not expect the letter to be read by non-Christian Jews). But, just as the scriptural echoes in chapter 1 indicated that Israel shared in the idolatry and immorality of the Gentile world, so the repeated emphasis on "the Jew first and also the Greek" in 2:9-10, and the emphasis on those under the law and those outside the law being treated the same in 2:12-15, make better sense if, behind the screen of "whoever you are" in v. 1, Paul envisages as his hypothetical listener not just a pagan moralist but a moralizing Jew.

To understand this section of Romans, then, we must envisage Paul intending his Christian audience in Rome to listen in on a conversation between himself and imaginary Jewish interlocutors whom he is addressing, for the moment, as if they were pagan moralists. The multiple resonances and echoes that this complex scenario sets up go some way to explaining why the text is sometimes dense and difficult. They also prepare us for later stages of the letter, in which similar many-sided writing plays a critical part.

The thrust of 2:1-16 is that God's judgment, when it arrives, will leave all without excuse. To make this point, Paul sketches one of the fullest descriptions of the final judgment in all early Christian writing. He emphasizes that the judgment is indeed unveiled through the gospel; this may come as a surprise to modern readers, for whom "the gospel" has come to mean salvation from judgment, but for Paul "the gospel" is the announcement of Jesus as Messiah, and according to one strand of tradition the Messiah was expected to be the judge at the last day.[55] In addition, as the psalmists never tire of repeating, judgment—the putting of things to rights at last—is itself good news for those (the majority of the human race past and present) who suffer injustice and oppression. Long exegetical tradition has schooled us to read this part of Romans as simply about individuals being shown up as sinners. This is indeed one element in Paul's argument, but it falls within his larger theme: the good news that, in Jesus the Messiah, the one God of Jews and Gentiles is finally setting the whole world to rights.

This is by no means simply bad news for all humans. To the surprise, again, of those whose traditional readings of the letter lead them to expect that Paul will here simply declare that all are sinners, so that justification can be by faith alone apart from works of the law, he announces on the contrary that at the last assize justification will be on the basis of works (v. 6), and that there will not only be tribulation and wrath for all wrongdoers, but glory, honor, immortality, eternal life, and peace for all who seek for these things in the appropriate way (vv. 7, 10).

As well as a description of the last judgment itself, Paul offers a classic apocalyptic view of the period leading up to that moment (2:4-5). Again both drawing on and interacting with the book of Wisdom, he describes God as being extremely patient, holding back from summary judgment to give people a chance to repent—but thereby inevitably

54. On the diatribe, see S. K. Stowers, *The Diatribe and Paul's Letter to the Romans*, SBLDS 57 (Chico, Calif.: Scholars Press, 1981); "Diatribe," in *Greco-Roman Literature and the New Testament*, ed. D. E. Aune (Atlanta: Scholars Press, 1988) 71-84; and *A Rereading of Romans: Justice, Jews, and Gentiles* (New Haven: Yale University Press, 1994).

55. The tradition goes back to, e.g., Psalms 2; 72; Isa 11:1-10; in Paul's day esp. *Ps. Sol.* 17-18. This is part of the wider belief that the Messiah will be God's agent in putting the world to rights. See the material surveyed in Wright, *The New Testament and the People of God*, 307-20.

storing up all the more wrath for the hard-hearted, who still refuse to do so.

2:1-3. The "therefore" at the start is puzzling, since the person addressed is *ex hypothesi* not guilty of the charge at the end of 1:32.[56] They at least have not called evil good and good evil. Perhaps the underlying thought is that, by standing in judgment on others while being guilty of similar offenses (in a way yet to be explored), they have been similarly deceitful, holding up their own behavior as an example when it should in fact have been condemned.

Verse 2 is sometimes taken, as in the NRSV, as a quotation from the hypothetical interlocutor, to which Paul then responds. This is not impossible. Paul almost certainly does this sort of thing in 1 Cor 6:12-13; 8:1, 4, and in the latter two verses he introduces the phrase, as here, with "we know that." The problem with all such theories, though, is the difficulty of proving that Paul intended it and that the readers would have understood. Here the strength of the proposal is that v. 3 seems to be picking up what is said in v. 2 and tossing it back, expanding v. 1 ("you who condemn") into "you who condemn those *who do such things*," which is what, according to the theory, the interlocutor has just done. In this case, the sequence of thought runs: "You are without excuse when you condemn others, since you are doing the same things. Yes, you will no doubt say that 'God judges those who do such things'; but when *you* judge 'those who do such things', do you really suppose that you will escape that same judgment?"

This train of thought is possible, maybe even plausible. But even in this case Paul does not dissent from the thought of v. 2; and in several other passages "we know that" introduces, not a remark from an interlocutor, but something that Paul can take for granted as common ground between himself and his hearers. It may well be, then, that v. 2 is simply Paul's preliminary move, before repeating and amplifying in v. 3 the warning of v. 1: Remember, God's judgment is in accordance with truth! In other words, there is no hiding place at the last assize.

2:4-6. One who presumes to stand as judge over others, whether a pagan moralist or a Jewish critic of the pagan world, may be presuming the stance outlined in Wisdom and elsewhere: God is kind and forbearing, at least toward Israel, so that Israel's sins appear as mere peccadilloes, regrettable no doubt but not serious like those of the pagans (see Wis 11:9-10; 15:1-6; 16:5-12; 18:20-25). Thus, while Paul's thought echoes that of Wisdom to the extent of seeing God mercifully allowing a space for people to repent (Wis 11:23), he urges that all need to avail themselves of this chance and that not to do so means despising God's patience and storing up wrath for the final day.

On that day God will indeed render to each according to works. Paul quotes more or less exactly from Ps 62:12 (61:13 LXX) and Prov 24:12, both of which, in context, offer warnings against pride. The psalm, which ends with the phrase quoted here, sees God's just judgment according to works as an expression of God's power and mercy. This deep-rooted Jewish tradition is not denied by Paul, but rather celebrated. If one of the purposes of the letter is to show that God's justice upstages that of Caesar and Rome, we could expect nothing less. We must reserve for a later point the important question of how this final judgment according to works, described as "justification" in v. 13, relates to the "justification by faith" spoken of in chap. 3 and elsewhere.

2:7-11. Paul now expands what it will mean that God judges according to works. He describes the contrasts in the sequence *a, b; b, a*: the godly and the wicked, the wicked and the godly. The first contrast, in vv. 7-8, sketches out the underlying attitude of the two classes; the second, in vv. 9-10, emphasizes their final state and insists that Jew and Gentile will be judged fairly and impartially.

The attitude of the two groups is not described in moralistic terms. Paul does not, as a rabbi might have done, produce a list of things that will qualify or disqualify for "the age to come." Rather, the one group, by "patience in well doing," *seeks for* glory, honor and immortality. Paul does not say that they earn them or grasp them; merely that they are seeking them.[57] The other group,

---

56. F. Godet, *Commentary on Paul's Epistle to the Romans*, 2 vols. (Edinburgh: T. & T. Clark, 1880–81) 190, holds that Paul's argument runs thus: If to sin while approving of the sin is criminal, is it not more inexcusable still to condemn the sin of others while joining in it?

57. T. Zahn, *Der Brief des Paulus an die Römer ausgelegt*, 3rd ed. (Leipzig: Deichert, 1925), understands glory, honor, and immortality to be the objects of "give": "to those who seek eternal life, He will give glory and honor and immortality." Although this is possible, given the syntax, it is unlikely.

seeking their own selfish gain,[58] does "not obey the truth, but obey injustice" (again the word is ἀδικία [*adikia*], more specific than "wickedness" or "evil"). The first group is defined in terms of that for which they seek and the means by which that quest is pursued; the second, in terms of that which is obeyed and not obeyed. We are left to fill in the gaps and to presume that the former do obey the truth and that the latter do not patiently seek for glory. What we are not encouraged to do is to draw up a checklist of things done and not done, to weigh them against one another and thereby to arrive at the final verdict. This suggests that Paul is being careful not to endorse the merit-measuring schemes that, despite not being at the covenantal heart of Judaism, nevertheless played some role in discussions of final judgment.

Paul then sums up the two attitudes in terms of the most general moral language (vv. 9-10): The one group works evil; the other does what is good (cf. 12:9). This time the contrast is between the two final states: tribulation and distress, on the one hand, glory and honor and peace (finding that which they had sought, in other words), on the other hand. And the great emphasis here, which colors the reading of the whole chapter, is on the universality of the judgment. Condemnation and glory will alike come "to the Jew first and also, equally, to the Greek" (the "equally" is implied by Paul's careful Greek construction, just as in 1:16).

The impartiality of God as judge is known, though not a major theme, in Jewish tradition.[59] Of course, when Jews thought reflectively, rather than urgently, on God's justice, impartiality was seen to be a vital element in it. But this is where the problem outlined in the Introduction comes into view: What happens when God's impartiality as the cosmic judge appears to conflict with the covenant promises made with Israel, to which God might also be supposed to be bound? How,

so to speak, does God's lawcourt justice work together with God's covenant justice? The answer will be revealed in 3:21–4:25. For the moment, like a rich but unresolved musical sequence, Paul's argument makes its striking point, that God has no favorites, and passes on.

2:12-13. The whole of vv. 12-16 explains further what is involved in vv. 7-11.[60] God will judge Jew and Greek alike, in complete impartiality, *for* those without the law and those within the law will be judged justly. Paul may well be responding to an implicit Jewish interjection: "We at least have Torah; that sets us apart from the Gentiles." Here we meet for the first time a crucial point, without which much of Romans remains incomprehensible: "Those apart from the law" means quite simply "Gentiles," and "those under the law" (literally "those in the law") means "Jews." "The law," here and more or less throughout Romans, means "the Jewish law," the Torah given to Moses on Mount Sinai, the law that defines and directs Israel, enabling them (supposedly) to be God's people. Gentiles were not "under the law," unless of course they became proselytes, voluntarily submitting to the Jewish code and becoming members, of a sort, within Israel.[61]

The point of v. 12, then, is once more the justice with which the condemnation will be meted out. God will not use the Jewish law to condemn Gentile sinners, but will use it to condemn Jewish sinners. The force of v. 13 is further to undergird God's impartiality; it cannot be the case that mere possession of Torah, hearing it read in synagogue, will carry validity with God. Torah was meant to be obeyed, not merely listened to. This is the beginning of a great theme that recurs frequently in Romans: Possession of Torah had become, in much Jewish thought, a badge of privilege, a talisman, a sign that Israel was inalienably God's people. No, says Paul. What counts is doing Torah. It will take him eight or ten more chapters to explain finally what he means by "doing" Torah, and we must follow the argument through to understand

---

58. The word ἐριθεία (*eritheia*) is rare, but probably means something like this. Its only attested use before Paul (cf. Gal 5:20; 2 Cor 12:20; Phil 1:17; 2:3) is Aristotle, *Politics* 5.3. See also Jas 3:14, 16. See esp. Moo, *The Epistle to the Romans*, 138n. 14.

59. E.g., Sir 35:15[12], with a similar phrase, reflecting, as does Paul's rare word (found only here, Col 3:25, and, in the plural, Jas 2:1; cf. similar terms in Acts 10:34; Jas 2:9), the Hebrew idiom of "receiving someone's face." On the theme, see above all J. M. Bassler, *Divine Impartiality: Paul and a Theological Axiom*, SBLDS 59 (Chico, Calif.: Scholars Press, 1982); and "Divine Impartiality in Paul's Letter to the Romans," NovT 26 (1984) 43-58.

60. Both the NRSV and the NIV, unfortunately, omit the γάρ (*gar*, "for") that links v. 12 to what precedes.

61. Virtually every book on Paul, and every commentary on at least Romans and Galatians, takes a position on the meaning of "law." An important recent collection of essays is J. D. G. Dunn, ed., *Paul and the Mosaic Law*, WUNT 89 (Tübingen: Mohr-Siebeck, 1996).

him at that point (see on 8:1-4; 10:5-11). For the moment, he is content to assert the point: Israel's ethnic privilege, backed up by possession of Torah, will be of no avail at the final judgment if Israel has not kept Torah. Justification, at the last, will be on the basis of performance, not possession.

2:14-15. These verses, or part of them, are sometimes considered an aside, letting the main thrust of the paragraph jump from v. 13 straight to the conclusion in v. 16 (so NIV; KJV includes v. 13, too, in the bracket). This once more ignores the γάρ (*gar,* "for") that introduces the passage. Paul intends to explain something he has just said, and there is no need to suppose that the thought of v. 15 cannot run on into v. 16 just as well, if not better, than that of v. 12 or v. 13.

But how do vv. 14-15 explain vv. 12-13? By providing an example of doers of the Torah who are not hearers of it; people, in other words, who perform what Torah requires even though, not being Jews, they have not sat in the synagogue and heard it read. Their thoughts may be confused on the last day, but they will show that "the work of the Torah" had been written on their hearts.

Who are these Gentile law-keepers? There are three basic ways in which scholars have taken these passages.[62] Some have said, in the light of the conclusion of the larger argument in 3:19-20, that this is a purely hypothetical category. Paul is indicating that, when God judges the secrets of all hearts, *if* there should be any who succeeded in doing good, they would indeed reap the appropriate reward; but he is holding up a mirage that will disappear when the argument is complete. There may, in other words, be Gentiles who fulfill part of the law, but in the end this will count for nothing. Others have taken the opposite line and seen 2:1-16 as evidence that Paul does not after all hold that all humans are sinners. He is aware, they say, that in both the Jewish and the pagan world there are some humans who really do that which God intends, who avoid vice and practice virtue, and who will be suitably rewarded in the end.[63]

Both of these positions are difficult to maintain. The first has Paul leading his readers far further up the garden path than the demands of a rhetorical strategy would suggest. The second falls foul of Paul's emphasis on the universality of human sin, in the overarching theme stated in 1:18 and concluded in 3:20. (A further option—that the passage does not really represent Paul's thought, but is either a synagogue homily thrown in here for some reason or is a train of thought that Paul should have assimilated more fully to his own mature views—is I believe a counsel of despair.)[64] The third way through is that, just as in chapter 1 Paul was hinting at Jews sharing in the judgment that would fall on pagans, a theme waiting to be explored more fully in due course, so here he is hinting at a theme he will explore later in the letter, namely that the people in question are *Christian* Gentiles (vv. 14-15)—indeed, Christian Jews and Gentiles alike (vv. 7, 10).[65] There are problems with this reading, too, but they are not so insuperable as sometimes supposed.[66]

Throughout the section so far Paul has been saying things that cry out for further explanation, which he will provide as the letter moves forward. He is at this point sketching a scene, not filling in all the details. But by the end of chap. 2 he has revealed a little more (see on 2:25-29 below); the picture will be colored in fully in 8:1-11; 10:5-11; and 13:8-10. Paul's view, to anticipate the later argument, is that those who are in Christ, who are indwelt by the Spirit, do in fact "do the law," even though, in the case of Gentiles, they have never heard it. The law, in Paul's view, pointed to that fullness of life and obedience to God which comes about in the Messiah; those who attain that fullness of life and obedience are therefore "doing the Torah" in the senses that, to Paul, really matter. He is well aware that this is paradoxical, but well aware also that to say anything else would be to imply, which he never does, either that the Torah was a bad thing, now

62. See K. Snodgrass, "Justification by Grace to the Doers: An Analysis of the Place of Romans 2 in the Theology of Paul," *NTS* 32 (1986) 72-93.

63. See Dodd, *The Epistle of Paul to the Romans,* 61-62; H. Räisänen, *Paul and the Law* (Philadelphia: Fortress, 1983) 107; E. P. Sanders, *Paul, the Law, and the Jewish People* (Philadelphia: Fortress, 1983) 123-35.

64. See Sanders, *Paul, the Law, and the Jewish People,* 123-35.

65. See N. T. Wright, "The Law in Romans 2," in Dunn, *Paul and the Mosaic Law,* 131-50. See also Cranfield, *A Critical and Exegetical Commentary on the Epistle to the Romans,* 159-63; S. J. Gathercole, "A Law unto Themselves: The Gentiles in Romans 2.14-15 Revisited," *JSNT* 85 (2002) 27-49.

66. See esp. the critiques of Käsemann, *Commentary on Romans,* 62-66; Ulrich Wilckens, *Der Brief an die Römer,* 3 vols., EKK 6 (Zurich: Benziger, 1978–82) 1:133-37, 142-46; Moo, *Romans,* 148-52.

happily left behind, or that Gentile Christians are second-class citizens in the kingdom of the Messiah. He will have it both ways; they are not under the Torah, but at the same time they are essentially doing what Torah really wanted.

The main problem with taking vv. 14-15 to refer to Gentile Christians is the word φύσει (*physei*) in v. 14, translated "by nature" in the NIV and "instinctively" in the NRSV. It is commonly thought both that this modifies the verb "do," and that Paul here echoes Stoic thought about a "natural law."[67] Neither of these is as secure as it might appear.

Physei comes in the middle of the clause: ὅταν γὰρ ἔθνη τὰ μὴ νόμον ἔχοντα <u>φύσει</u> τὰ τοῦ νόμου ποιῶσιν (*hotan gar ethnē ta mē nomon echonta <u>physei</u> ta tou nomou poiōsin*, "for when nations not having Torah by nature do the things of Torah"). "By nature" could, grammatically, go either way, in Greek as in that English translation. It could modify "having Torah" instead of "doing the things of Torah." (One might have expected, if Paul was going to say the first of these, that *physei* would come between τά [*ta*] and μή [*mē*], τὰ φύσει μὴ νόμον ἔχοντα [*ta physei mē nomon echonta*], but that is by no means certain; hypothetical reconstructions of what Paul might have said remain insecure.) Paul's point would then be the obvious one: that Gentiles do not, by nature—that is, by origin and parentage—possess the Torah. This is exactly the sense that Paul gives to φύσις (*physis*) thirteen verses later when, making an almost identical point, he describes Gentile Christians as ἡ ἐκ φύσεως ἀκροβυστία τὸν νόμον τελοῦσα (*hē ek physeōs akrobystia ton nomon telousa*, "the by-nature uncircumcision that fulfills the Torah"). "Nature" cannot here refer to something that is common, innate, to all humans. Jews, too, are born uncircumcised; that is, in that sense, their "natural" state. It must refer to Gentile humanity as opposed to Jewish (cf. Gal 2:15). I suggest that this is so for 2:14 as well.

If it is insisted that the Stoic echoes of "natural law" are so strong in this passage as virtually to force the reading "do by nature what the law requires," I still maintain, for the reasons given earlier, that the people Paul has in mind must be Gentile Christians. In

that case, however, he would be providing a polemical twist of his own to the phrase "by nature." I doubt, frankly, whether Paul would suppose that any pagan could actually fulfill the Torah "by nature" in that sense. What he would be saying, with one eye on a Stoic interlocutor, would be, in effect, "You vaunt your celebrated 'natural law,' and think you can obey it. I will show you some people who have a different sort of law in their 'natures'— because, as I shall show, their 'natures' have been renewed in Christ and by the Spirit."[68]

Further evidence in favor of this overall interpretation is provided by v. 15a. To have the work of the law "written on the heart" is one of the promises of the new covenant in Jer 31:33 (see also Jer 32:40; cf. the "new heart" in Ezek 36:26). Paul clearly believed, and elaborated this at various points, that the covenant had been renewed, according to this promise, through Jesus, and that this renewal was being implemented by the Spirit in those who were "in Christ." This phrase is a further indication that he has Christian Gentiles in mind. Their conscience bears witness to this; nothing here, or in Paul's other references to "conscience," implies that he accords this faculty the status of offering direct revelation of moral truth, and indeed he envisages, in 1 Corinthians 8, persons who have "weak" consciences and need to be treated accordingly.[69] Here the thought is simply that the Gentile Christians who, living in the Spirit, are in fact fulfilling the Torah, are aware deep within their own hearts that they are right with God.

Why then do their thoughts become confused as they approach the judgment, as the end of v. 15 indicates? Perhaps because their situation, being outside the Torah and yet fulfilling it from the heart, leaves them with questions that may produce a moment of panic in even the most settled believer. Perhaps because, as Paul has said in v. 7, they have not *earned* glory, honor, and immortality, merely sought it; they know it remains

---

67. For careful discussion, see Käsemann, *Romans*, 62-66.

68. See esp. Stowers, *A Rereading of Romans*, 109-18. See also T. Engberg-Pedersen, *Paul and the Stoics* (Edinburgh: T. & T. Clark, 2000) 359: Paul knows perfectly well that he is using terms that are familiar from non-Jewish philosophy and is able to use them for his own purposes without either needing to be technically "correct" or to feel himself moving in a totally alien environment. Philosophical treatments of "law" and "nature," and "being a law to oneself," include, e.g., Aristotle *Rhetoric* 1.15.3-8; *Nicomachean Ethics* 4.8.8-10; Hermogenes "On Ideas" 1.221; Dio Chrysostom *Discourses* 36:23.

69. See Eckstein, *Syneidesis*, 170-79.

a gift, however much it will turn out to be in accordance with the life they have in fact lived. Perhaps because the doctrine of assurance, which is indeed Pauline and is based securely in Romans, especially chaps. 5–8, leaves room, as it did in Paul himself, for times of "fightings without and fears within" (2 Cor 7:5), for times of utter despair (2 Cor 1:8). Perhaps because, as the hymn writer puts it, "they who fain would serve thee best are conscious most of wrong within."[70] Paul is clear, though, about the outcome.

2:16. On the day of judgment—Paul has reserved this climactic statement for the end of the argument, picking up the scriptural theme of "the day of YHWH"—God will judge the secrets of human hearts. Nothing will then escape scrutiny. God will be seen to be just. And this judgment, as we have already noted, will be "through the Messiah, Jesus." God's justice will be revealed, fulfilling scriptural promises and putting all other justice (Caesar's included) to shame. Why so? Not least precisely because this revelation will expose and assess the secrets of all human hearts. Just as Jews cannot hide from the judgment by pleading their Jewishness, so no human can hide from the judgment by relying on outward appearances and covering up the secrets of the heart.

70. H. Twells, "At even, ere the sun was set."

REFLECTIONS

1. It is important not to jump too quickly into a blanket condemnation of moralism. Our culture has a strong inbuilt prejudice against moralizing. We much prefer either a laissez-faire tolerance or the street-level existentialism that reduces all morals to "do what you feel like as long as you don't hurt anyone." We are thus all too eager to read Romans 2 as a denunciation of moralism and then to feel self-righteous because we are not self-righteous. This is to miss Paul's point.

He clearly believed that morals mattered to society and to persons and was not frightened to state what those morals were and how disregarding them brought disaster. Of course, he set all this in a different context from that of either Judaism or the pagan moralists (and from that of contemporary secular or postmodern moralists, for that matter), but he did not object to people holding or propagating high moral standards. What he did object to was doing so while failing to practice what one preached. It is interesting to note that his great contemporary Seneca was criticized, both in his lifetime and after his death, for preaching one standard and living another. Seneca responded, somewhat lamely, that it is the duty of moralists to hold out the highest conceivable standard even if it turns out to be impossible for themselves. For Paul this would have been nonsense. What he objected to, here at least, was the hypocrisy of denouncing faults while secretly practicing them oneself.

2. This is a problem familiar from psychology. We project aspects of our character—the aspects of which we are ashamed and perhaps even ignorant—on to other people and then blame them angrily for the very same things. This happens, notoriously, between parents and children. It also occurs, for instance, when journalists (the main source of moralizing in our society), whose own lives might not always bear public scrutiny, take delight in exposing, in the rich and famous, failings of which they themselves may be privately guilty. Behind Paul's specific argument here there stands an assumption, spelled out in other places, that the Christian should be so open to the searchlight of the Spirit that the dark corners of his or her life and inner motivations are increasingly spotlighted and dealt with. Only then will an authentic holding forth of standards of behavior be possible. Only then will one be able gently and firmly to articulate a standard and to denounce evil.

3. Belief in a final just judgment remains excellent news for millions in our world, as it was in Paul's. Of course, when this belief is downgraded into vague hopes for a better life hereafter and vague warnings about possible unpleasant consequences of wrongdoing (or for that matter when it is artificially pumped up into shrill hell-fire denunciations and casual self-satisfied salvation-assurance), the clarity of the Christian view of future judgment is lost, and with it both the moral imperative and the true hope of the oppressed. Indeed, as Marx pointed out, projecting hope for a better life forward into the future can then be used by oppressors to keep their subjects, if not happy, at least not rebellious. But that is a parody, a caricature, of Paul's teaching. There is indeed a promise that wrongs will be put to rights, offering a strong and sure hope that can sustain those who suffer oppression and injustice. But in Jesus the Messiah this hope has come forward into the present. Those who give allegiance to Jesus, so far from being agents of oppression by reinforcing a vague future hope and hence a passivity about the present, are charged with realizing God's justice in the present time in all ways possible.

4. It still needs saying, though it remains difficult to say, that the creator of the world has no "favored nation clause." No one, no culture, no nation, no ethnic group, can say "because we are x, y, or z, God will be gracious to us come what may." In a world of increasing ethnic and tribal tensions, often exacerbated by different religious affiliations (including, alas, different supposedly Christian affiliations; one cannot but think of Northern Ireland), this message needs to be heard afresh.

5. The most disturbing application of this passage is surely to the world of professing Christians. Paul seems to take it for granted that Christians will not be in the position of his imaginary interlocutor; but we are sadly familiar with those who preach or profess allegiance to Jesus as Messiah and Lord but do not practice it. Romans 2 can serve as a second-order reminder of the folly and danger of thus presuming on God's kindness and forbearance. To name the name of Jesus is, as 2:16 makes clear, to invoke the one to whom all, especially his own, will give account.

Romans 2:17-29, The Direct Challenge to "the Jew"

COMMENTARY

We now arrive at the point to which the whole section has been building up. Israel, resting on God's special vocation, has not fulfilled that vocation, and must face the challenge from those who, though not ethnically Jewish, are now inheriting Israel's role in God's purposes.

In addressing "the Jew" Paul was, of course, talking to his own former self. More; he was aware, as 9:1-5 will make clear, of deep personal grief, witnessing "his flesh" in rebellion against the gospel message of the Jewish Messiah, Jesus. All that now follows must be seen in this light.

We should beware of the natural tendency, within our individualistic culture, to assume that when Paul uses the second-person singular ("If *you*, singular, call yourself a Jew") he is referring to a typical *individual*. Just as in

chap. 7 his rhetorical use of "I" arguably indicates the nation as a whole, so here his "you" focuses and makes dramatic that which is said of the whole Jewish people. Paul is not for a moment suggesting anything so absurd as that all Jews steal, commit adultery, rob temples, and so forth. His point is rather that the national boast of ethnic Israel, that of being the creator's chosen people, is falsified if theft, adultery, and so forth are found within the nation. The presence of misbehavior within ethnic Israel renders void the national, ethnic boast; it prevents Israel from fulfilling its calling to be the light of the world.

The passage, then, is not simply part of a long demonstration that all humans are sinful. That is indeed one of the major thrusts of the section 1:18–3:20, but within that overarching purpose these verses introduce a quite different idea. Faced with a general denunciation of the pagan world, many educated Jews—including, presumably, Paul himself in his pre-Christian life—would say that this is of course true of pagans, but that God has chosen Israel as the light to the nations and has given Israel the Torah so that it can fulfill this role. Israel is the solution to the world's plight (see, among countless possible examples, 2 Bar 48:20-24). The problem he is outlining at this point in the argument, and to which he will offer a solution in the section beginning at 3:21, is not simply that all are sinful and in need of salvation, but that the bearers of the solution have become part of the problem. Israel, called to be the light of the world, has become part of the darkness. How then can God's covenant plan be fulfilled? The problem of Israel is thus also a problem for God. It is, in fact, a further dimension of the problem of God's righteousness. Only if we appreciate this will the transition from chapter 2 to chapter 3 make any sense.

Paul's turn to "the Jew" in 2:17 has some analogies with the rhetorical ploy of Amos, denouncing the surrounding nations before turning to Judah (Amos 2:4) and particularly the northern kingdom, Israel (Amos 2:6). But this is not the whole truth of this passage. For a start, as we have seen, Paul has had Israel in mind all along, hinting darkly in chap. 1 that his fellow Jews were as guilty of idolatry as were the pagans, strongly suggesting in 2:1-16 that their would-be superiority was no better than that of the pagan moralists. But his point now is not so much to bring out into the open a charge that they are sinful like the rest. He will rub that in in the middle of chap. 3 (and say it again, from another angle, in 7:7-25). The point here is that Israel *should* have been—had been called to be—the divine answer to the world's problem; and that, instead, Israel is itself fatally compromised with the very same problem. Israel's sinfulness is at the heart of the charge, but the charge itself is that the doctor, instead of healing the sick, has become infected with the disease.

The ethnic boast of "the Jew" is thereby called into question. How can a nation that so manifestly fails to be the light of the world claim to be keeping Torah? In the second paragraph of this section (2:25-29), Paul advances a stronger and more detailed form of the argument he made in 2:13-15. Supposing, he says, there exists a people, not sharing Israel's ethnic privileges, in whom the purposes of God as expressed in Torah are coming to fulfillment. Will they not thereby upstage ethnic Israel? Yes, he declares, such people are members of the renewed covenant. That is what being "a Jew" is all about.

Thus, just as Paul built into his exposition of human sin (1:18-32) elements that hinted at what was to come, so now, in the same way, he is building in to his statement of the complex problem of sin—human sin and the failure of Israel to be the solution-bearer—hints of the solution. This, too, challenges normal simplistic views of the construction of Romans. We can only fully understand 2:26-29, dense and proleptic as it is, with help from elsewhere; but when we grasp its meaning we see why Paul has included it here. Not only is the existence of a parallel company of non-ethnic "Jews" and uncircumcised "circumcision" a direct, albeit oxymoronic, challenge to Israel's ethnic boast; it sharpens up the question Paul must raise at the start of chap. 3 if the solution, when he finally unveils it in 3:21 and thereafter, is to make the full sense he intends. If God has called this parallel company of "Jews" into existence, what is the point of being a Jew, the point of there being an "Israel," in the first place? What is God up to?

2:17. Paul's introduction is designed as a challenge: You claim the name "Jew," but are you true to it?[71] Do you know what it really involves? Certainly a Jew such as Saul of Tarsus would be ready enough with the answer, beginning with "reliance on Torah," "boasting in God," and quite possibly the vocation to be "the light of the world."

The first two of these need more nuance. The word translated "rely" principally means "rest on"; it is a matter of finding security and comfort, not a matter of using the Torah as a ladder of good works, up which to climb to a position of moral superiority or a self-earned salvation. The attitude Paul describes would say: "God gave Israel the Torah; our

---

71. It may have been a typical motif of the diatribe style to have upbraided one's opponents for not living consistently with the teaching they espouse. See Moo, *Romans*, 157; Stowers, *The Diatribe and Paul's Letter to the Romans*, 112.

possession of it is the rock on which we stand; it is what makes us Jews God's special people."

The attitude to God is much the same. The NIV's "brag about your relationship to God" sounds as though "the Jew" is telling people about a marvelous personal friendship between him or herself and the true God; but this is not Paul's meaning. (The word "relationship" is responsible for too many fudged arguments in contemporary theology.) The NRSV's "boast of your relation to God" is a little better, but the word "relation" still sounds, in our culture, as though it is referring to a "personal relationship" in the sense of two persons engaged in active friendship. Neither expression catches the depth of the Greek, which simply and literally means "boast in God"; the point is the Jewish claim, supported throughout the Hebrew Scriptures, that the creator of the world is Israel's God, and vice versa.

The word "boast" is difficult, too. In contemporary English it is almost always negative, whereas Paul is not only capable of using it in a positive sense (e.g., 5:11), but is here both reporting and commending the attitude of "the Jew" as good and God-given. "Celebrate" would bring out the point: "the Jew" celebrates the fact of election, of being God's chosen people. Neither here nor in the verses to come does Paul regard these claims with contempt, or try to undermine them. The Torah really was given to mark out Israel as God's people. God really was "their God." Paul does not for a moment reject the specialness of Israel. At this stage in the letter, he simply questions whether those making the claim have forfeited the right to do so.

2:18-20. This basic picture is filled out with more of "the Jew's" self-description. Verse 18 states two ways in which Torah enables the Jew to attain true moral knowledge, as a result of which (vv. 19-20) Israel should be in a position to instruct the nations, again because of Torah. This prepares the way for the charge in vv. 21-23, which consists of four moral challenges and a question about Torah, backed up with a quote from the prophets. In this paragraph Paul is concentrating on Torah, in the following one on circumcision; these are the badges that marked out Jews from their pagan neighbors.

Possession of Torah should enable "the Jew" to know God's will and "distinguish things that differ" (v. 18), in other words, to make moral judgments, determining what is best (NRSV) or approving what is superior (NIV; the NEB, for once, comes closest to the literal meaning with "you are aware of moral distinctions"). The point is that Torah's instruction enables the Jew to see to the heart of moral issues. As a result (vv. 19-20), Israel is in theory the light of the nations, the world's moral teacher, because in Torah Israel really does possess "the embodiment of knowledge and truth." The term μόρφωσις (*morphōsis*, translated here "embodiment") means "the outward manifestation"; Paul is acknowledging, and endorsing, a remarkably high, almost incarnational, view of Torah, which should be kept in mind during subsequent discussions.

2:21-22. Granted your possession of this lofty privilege, Paul enquires, what have you done with it? Remembering that the "you" in question is not "every Jewish individual," but "Israel as a whole," the answer must be: Israel has squandered its inheritance. Like the biblical prophets, one of whom he will presently quote, Paul charges Israel with infidelity (see also Ps 50:16-20 and the other passages quoted in 3:10-18). The first question serves as a heading for the others: Teacher of others, will you not teach yourself? Theft and adultery exist in Israel, both literally in many cases and spiritually wherever people "rob God" (Mal 3:8) or are unfaithful to him, as a bride to her husband (e.g., Hos 2:2-13).

The charge of temple robbery is, at first blush, more surprising, both because it seems a less obvious offense than theft or adultery and because it seems even less likely that many Jews were involved in such a practice. The best explanation is, once again, that Paul is not so interested in demonstrating that "all Jews are sinners" (as we have seen, his argument scarcely proves this point), as in showing up Israel's failure to be the light of the world. One is unlikely to demonstrate to the watching pagan world that there is a better way to be human by stealing from pagan temples. This practice, though probably not widespread, was not unknown. Some Jews had evidently used the scriptural polemic against idols to argue that, since idols have no real existence, things given to them are nobody's property, and hence may be taken with impunity.[72] Paul's point is that the practice exists and brings discredit on Israel precisely among the people to whom "the Jew" is supposed to be acting as the light of the world. This charge shows once more (a) that his concern here is with Israel as a whole, rather than every individual within it and (b) that his point about Israel as a whole is not simply Jewish sin, important though that is, as the fact that this sin results in the failure of Israel to be God's light to the Gentile world.

2:23-24. This opens up the substance of the charge. The real problem is Israel's failure to bring God worldwide honor. That was the purpose for which Torah had been given. What Israel has done with Torah has instead brought dishonor: The pagan nations scorn the true God on the basis of the behavior of the covenant people. Breaking Torah nullifies boasting in Torah. Israel, in fact, is in the state spoken of by Isaiah in 52:5. Exile has come because of Israel's sin (the pagan behavior among YHWH's own people that caused YHWH's displeasure), because the pagan nations, looking at Israel, now blaspheme Israel's God. The same theme appears in other prophetic passages, notably Ezek 36:20-23, a passage that (as we shall see) Paul almost certainly has in mind as well.

As usual, Paul evokes with a single quotation a whole world of scriptural resonance. His point throughout the paragraph is something that few Jews in his day would have contested: that Israel as a whole is not living up to what YHWH would desire and that Israel's continued subservience to the pagan nations, which had begun with the Babylonian captivity, was a sign that the great promised redemption had not yet arrived. In other words, Israel's "exile" was still continuing, not in a geographical, but in a theological, spiritual, and moral sense. The prophecies of Isaiah, Ezekiel, and others had not yet been fulfilled. As the book of Daniel had emphasized, the seventy years of exile had become seventy

weeks of years (Introduction, 398 [and footnote 3]). And the very point to which Paul draws attention, in both Isaiah and Ezekiel, is the point at which YHWH declares that, now that the pagans are blaspheming, and the very name of God is dishonored among them, it is time to act. Isaiah goes on at once to speak of the herald who announces good news to Zion (52:7, quoted by Paul in 10:15); Ezekiel goes on at once to speak of covenant renewal, involving a change of heart and the gift of a new spirit through which God's people will at last keep the statutes of the law. Paul, with these larger contexts in mind, has called up the one element of the prophetic critique that makes his present point—that Israel has failed in bringing honor to God's name among the nations—and also hints at the renewal of the covenant and the gift of the Spirit.

2:25-29. He comes at this latter point by introducing, in parallel with the point about Torah, the question of circumcision. This was not seen in Judaism as a quasi-moral "good work," or as a "ritual" designed to earn God's favor, but as a key badge of Jewish identity, marking out the Jew from the pagan world around. Bringing circumcision and Torah together, Paul declares that the former only means what it is supposed to where Torah is kept; and, once again, Torah has been broken. The badge therefore tells a lie. But if the prophecies of Ezekiel and others about covenant renewal seem to be coming true elsewhere—if there are people with new hearts, new spirits, who are keeping the ordinances of Torah—then, whether they are circumcised or not, they will by their very existence show up the brokenness, the invalidity, of the covenant membership of those who still, despite their circumcision, break Torah.

Paul's description of this parallel "Jewishness," this new sort of "circumcision," is replete with overtones of "new covenant" passages both in scripture and elsewhere in his writings. The problems that this causes, for Paul and for contemporary readers, will emerge later in the letter, together with the solutions Paul proposes (see the Commentary on 3:27-31; 8:1-11; 10:1-13).

2:25. The initial statement, out of which the rest emerges, is sharp. Circumcision is of value (this will be raised again in 3:1) for one who keeps Torah. In other words, keeping

---

72. Deut 7:25-26 and Josephus *Antiquities of the Jews* 4.287 show that the temptation existed; Josephus *Against Apion* 1.310-11 reports a pagan slander against Jews that the name Jerusalem was a pun on the word for "temple robbery" because the Jews who settled it had done so much of it; Acts 19:37 shows that the charge was likely to be levied against Jews in the pagan world. For rabbinic material, see H. L. Strack and P. Billerbeck, *Kommentar Zum Neuen Testament aus Talmud und Midrash,* 6 vols. (Munich: C. H. Becksche, 1922–61) 3:113-15.

Torah is basic, and without it circumcision becomes an empty sign, a meaningless talisman (cf. 1 Cor 7:19, which puts the point even more strikingly: Neither circumcision nor uncircumcision matters, since what matters is keeping God's commands! Paul must have known that this was paradoxical to the point of being funny, since the command to circumcise loomed so large in Judaism and in the written Torah itself). Indeed, to break Torah means not just that circumcision is meaningless, but that it "becomes uncircumcision"; in other words, it works in reverse, marking you out as *not* a member of God's people. It becomes a badge of exclusion rather than of inclusion (cf. Gal 5:2-6, albeit with reference to ex-pagans). Paul will have more to say on this topic (which was, of course, central in the Galatian controversy) in chap. 4.

2:26-27. Paul now explicitly introduces a category of people that is central to his thought and that will occupy him for much of the letter. These are people who, though uncircumcised, "keep the decrees of Torah." The words he uses are, in effect, an abbreviated version of Ezek 36:27, carrying other biblical echoes as well (notably Deut 30:16 [φυλάσσεσθαι τὰ δικαιώματα *phylassesthai ta dikaiōmata*, the same root words as here]; cf. Lev 18:5; both these passages recur in Rom 10:5-11, which develops the present thought; see the Commentary on 10:1-21). Of these people Paul declares that their uncircumcision will count as circumcision; in other words, that God will recognize their physically Gentile state, paradoxically, as the badge of their membership in Israel. As though this were not scandalous enough, Paul goes on to state that these persons, law-keeping though "naturally" uncircumcised through their Gentile origins,[73] will judge those who, despite having the "letter of the law" and physical circumcision, nevertheless transgress the law.

By referring to the law as "the letter" Paul has carefully introduced the category that will enable him to contrast two types of covenant membership in the climactic verses that now follow.

2:28-29. By way of explanation (γάρ *gar*, "for"; as in the NRSV; unwarrantedly omitted by the NIV), Paul sets out two types of "Jew." The section began with "the Jew" that claims that name, and that calls Torah and God to witness it. Paul now transfers the name, and the validation, to a different group. In the previous verses he has referred to Gentiles who, though uncircumcised, keep the law's regulations; he can only mean Gentile Christians, since this passage, explaining what has gone before, is clearly about membership in the new, or renewed, covenant. But the primary category he is describing is not restricted to Gentiles; Paul explains the narrower point (vv. 26-27) by setting out a broader one. He most certainly regarded himself, and his fellow Jewish Christians, as part of the same new covenant people of God.

The contrast he makes is between that which is open, visible, and obvious, and that which is secret. This boils down, more or less, to the "outward/inward" distinction (NRSV, NIV, and most others), but we should beware of importing into Paul a Platonic either/or that is foreign to him. His sentences are clipped and dense at this point, and paraphrase is almost inevitable; literally, what he says is, "For the one in visibility is not a Jew, nor is the one in visibility (in the flesh) circumcision; but the one in secret is a Jew, and circumcision is of the heart, in the spirit not the letter." We should note that he does not say, as the NEB and others do, the "true" Jew, the "true" circumcision. His point is more stark. The name "Jew," and the attribute "circumcision," belong to the secret/ heart/ spirit people, not to the visibility/flesh/ letter people (cf. Phil 3:3, where a closely accurate translation might be "the 'circumcision' means us"). It is as shocking as that. As if to emphasize that he really means it, Paul will at once go on to challenge himself on the point and to think through what follows.

In referring to the secret/heart/spirit people, Paul clearly means to designate those in whom the gospel of the Messiah has done its work. The promises of God through Deuteronomy 30, Ezekiel 36, and elsewhere have come true. God has done, in Jesus and the Spirit, what he had promised; the result is the

---

73. The verb here for "keep" (NRSV) or "obey" (NIV) is τελειόω (*teleioō*, "fulfill," cognate with τέλος *telos*, "end" or "goal," on which see 10:4, with the commentary there). To refer to the uncircumcision as "physical" is slightly misleading. By "naturally" Paul means, as we saw in reference to 2:14, "in that they are Gentiles." All males are "naturally uncircumcised" in the sense that they are born that way.

creation of the people of the new covenant. Paul's clearest statement of this point may be found in 2 Cor 3:1-6, where the letter/spirit contrast is again prominent.[74] There are several other passages in which a similar theological understanding may be discerned, not least Romans 8 and 10. Resistance to finding the notion of "covenant" in Paul has proved remarkably strong, not least among those for whom the center of Paul's thought is the radical newness of God's action in Christ; but once it is appreciated that Paul's covenant theology is precisely about the radically new and unexpected, even shocking, way in which God has fulfilled the promises of Ezekiel and elsewhere, and that "covenant" and "apocalyptic," so far from being antithetical categories, belong closely together in Second Temple Judaism and in Paul himself, the problem should fade away.[75]

The paragraph carries a typically Pauline sting in the tail. This new covenant people, the ones who fulfill Torah whether or not they are circumcised, the ones who carry the covenant marks on their hearts rather than in their flesh—this people show that they have the right to the name "Jew" because "their praise is not from humans, but from God." Paul is alluding to, rather than making, a pun that would be obvious to an educated Jew;

in Hebrew the word "Judah" means "praise." They receive the name "Jew," in other words, from God, as a gift of grace. These are the ones who can now "celebrate in God" (2:17), as he will declare in 5:11.

Paul has introduced this brief description of the new covenant people into his argument without full explanation. Within 2:17-29, its primary purpose is simply to highlight the failure of Israel to be the covenant people of the creator God, the light of the dark world. As so often, however, Paul's tantalizing asides serve other purposes as well; here he has introduced one of the major themes of the letter, to be elaborated more fully in due course and has done so not least in order to raise the questions that he will glance at in chap. 3 and then return to more fully in chaps. 9–11. In fact, 2:26-29 stands to 3:1-8 much as 5–8 stands to 9–11. Paul's thought in this letter moves in a great expanding upward spiral; when we reach chap. 8, we shall be able to look down from a greater height and see this dense little statement more or less exactly beneath us.

Like many other things in chap. 2, this passage must wait for further elaboration in subsequent chapters. In addition to the questions Paul asks at once at the start of chap. 3, the reader, ancient or modern, wants to know: In what sense do these people "fulfill the Torah," or "keep the ordinances of the law"? Here, as so often, the exegete needs patience, which is itself, after all, one of the fruits of the Spirit.

---

74. See Wright, *The Climax of the Covenant,* chap. 9.

75. This comment is in dialogue with, among others, the remarkable work of J. L. Martyn, *Galatians,* AB 33A (New York: Doubleday, 1997), and *Theological Issues in the Letters of Paul* (Nashville: Abingdon, 1997) esp. chap. 7.

REFLECTIONS

1. The alarming conclusions of the previous paragraph are further reinforced. Who today sets themselves up as teachers of the foolish, guides to the blind? At one level, of course, politicians and journalists—who, routinely enough in many cases, show by their own behavior that they have not taken their own advice. At a different level altogether, there are some Jews, particularly some idealistic Zionists, who cling to the belief that the modern state of Israel is supposed at last to be the light to the nations. If that were so, it would not take a particularly cynical reading of contemporary Middle Eastern social and political realities to say that things are very far from where they should be. Indeed, a good many Jews, including many who themselves live in Israel, would heartily agree. One does not have to be unsympathetic with the ambiguous plight of that state to recognize the problem; indeed, the more sympathy, the more agonizing over the way things are.

But at another level altogether, a Christian reader cannot escape the acute discomfort of saying that the church, in both its local, denominational and international manifestations, stands equally under the condemnation of a passage like this. Those who read the Sermon on the Mount in the course of regular worship hear themselves now called to be the light of the world, and to embody, in secret as well as in public, the generous love of the creator God. There are many churches, of course, where the gospel is lived out in its full transforming reality. But equally there are many that must hang their heads in shame at the question, You who would teach others, can you not teach yourself?

This question arises particularly in the question of Christian unity. Part of the point of Paul's gospel is that there is one God, who, therefore, desires one people (see on 3:30). Paul fought against splitting the church along ethnic or cultural lines; Christian denominations often reflect precisely these splits, using dogmatic differences as a cloak for continuing tribal identity. Sometimes this becomes openly scandalous, as in Northern Ireland or the Balkans. But as long as those who name the name of Jesus Christ cannot at least share the Eucharist, cannot in some cases even pray together, the name of God will continue to be blasphemed among pagans.

2. The claim that those who belong to the new covenant, in the Messiah and by the Spirit, are now entitled to the name "Jew" was deeply controversial in Paul's day and has again become so in the twentieth century. Until we reach Romans 9–11 we cannot attempt a full treatment of the subject; but we must note again both that Paul's writing about "the Jew" was writing about himself, and that when he spoke of the failure of his own people he did so with tears.

These concessions will not, of course, mollify those for whom any claim by Christians, including Jewish Christians, to be the people of the renewed covenant is downright offensive. The offense comes at at least three levels. First, many Jews in today's world, all too aware of centuries of persecution by soi-disant Christians, are highly sensitive to the early Christian claim that the events concerning Jesus were the fulfillment of prophecy, the unveiling of the "righteousness of God"—and in particular, of course, to the claim that Jesus of Nazareth was and is Israel's promised Messiah. To make such claims, it has again been urged in our day, is itself an act of anti-Judaism, perhaps even now of anti-Semitism (the former a rejection of Judaism as a way of life, the latter a rejection of a particular race, with overtones of nineteenth- and twentieth-century racial theories).[76]

Second, many Christians have thought long and hard about the meaning of the ghastly events in Europe in the first half of the twentieth century and have arrived at a firm conviction that the massacre of six million Jews in the Nazi "final solution" was the result of, among other things, an emphasis on claims such as those made by Paul in this passage. The moral imperative seems then inevitable: The church must back off from all such claims and should at the most express its faith in terms of a way of spirituality, based on the Jew Jesus of Nazareth, which many non-Jews have found life-giving. A corollary has sometimes been mooted: Paul is to be rejected as a paganizer of the Jewish message of Jesus.[77]

Third, a position that many consider "modern," but which is rooted, at least in its current expressions, in the eighteenth-century Enlightenment. According to this, all religions are inadequate approximations to truth, and, despite what many of them say, none has exclusive rights to it. The appropriate stance is therefore mutual tolerance. This is, of course, a covert way of saying, among other things, that (at least) Judaism, Islam, and Christianity are all actually misleading, since all of them make, at the very heart, claims that the others are bound to deny if they are not to lose their very identity. Nevertheless, this secularized agenda has seeped into both Jewish and Christian

---

76. The classic statement of this position is that of Rosemary R. Ruether, *Faith and Fratricide: The Theological Roots of Anti-Semitism* (New York: Seabury, 1974).

77. See particularly Hyam Maccoby, *The Mythmaker: Paul and the Invention of Christianity* (London: Weidenfeld and Nicolson, 1986); *Paul and Hellenism* (Philadelphia: Trinity, 1991).

circles, often coupled with the laudable desire for humility and mutual respect, sometimes using that as a pretext for a highly arrogant liberalism that challenges all truth claims while pressing its own with remarkable intolerance.

Two points only can be made at this stage. First, Paul's own position was that of a Christian Jew. He regarded this as natural and normal, indeed the most appropriate thing possible. Though his own vocation was to declare to the pagan world the Jewish gospel message (that the one God of the whole world, the God of Abraham, Isaac and Jacob, the God who gave the Torah, had now unveiled in Jesus the final stage of the plan to bring justice and healing to the world), he knew, and insisted in this letter, that the gospel remained "for the Jew first," however much it was also "and equally to the Greek." Any suggestion that Paul would have countenanced a split, a twin-track salvation-history, in which Jews should remain Jews and Gentiles might become Christians is without the slightest foundation in his thought or writings (see the Commentary on 9:1–11:36).[78]

Second, there is a curious anomaly within the Christian position outlined above. On the one hand, we are urged to reject non-Jewish styles of Christianity, to recover the Jewish roots of our faith, and to cherish and nourish such echoes of Jewish ways, Jewish rituals, Jewish understandings, as we can. Christian versions of Seder meals have become common. This, it seems to me, is a healthy corrective to the many ways in which Christians so easily slip into non-Jewish modes of thought, taking their color and agenda instead from the pagan world around. On the other hand, the same people who urge this agenda regularly also press upon the church the need to renounce all claim to be "the Jew," "the circumcision." "Supersession" is the magic word here, or perhaps we should say the demon-word. It is wheeled out again and again, implying that in such a view the church has taken Israel's place in God's plan, leaving no room any longer for non-Christian Israel, Israel (in Paul's phrase) "according to the flesh."

This double position is grossly inconsistent. The more we examine the Jewish roots of the Christian faith, the more we are bound to discover that all the early Christians known to us defined themselves with joy as God's Israel, living in and seeking to share the blessings of the messianic age that had dawned with Jesus, the new age for the whole world that began when Jesus rose from the dead. This is hardly supersessionism, unless we were to charge Isaiah, Ezekiel, Deuteronomy even, and figures like John the Baptist, and indeed the Essenes, with that crime as well. Making the totally Jewish claim that God will renew, or has renewed, the covenant, throwing its membership open far and wide, was unpopular when the prophets did it, when Jesus did it, when Paul did it. There is no easy answer to the large-scale question underneath this discussion. If there were, Paul would have given it, rather than mounting the massive argument we find in chaps. 9–11. But let us at least talk sense, however humbly, in wrestling with it.

---

78. Against Lloyd Gaston, *Paul and the Torah* (Vancouver: University of British Columbia Press, 1987); John G. Gager, *The Origins of Anti-Semitism* (Oxford: Oxford University Press, 1983).

Romans 3:1-8, Israel's Faithlessness and God's Faithfulness

COMMENTARY

The force of this section is only grasped when two things are appreciated: the "symphonic" structure of the letter (see Introduction), in which themes are hinted at in advance of their full statement, and the underlying subject of God's faithfulness to the covenant and Israel's vocation to an answering faithfulness through which God's purpose for the world will be accomplished. Paul is concerned here not so much with the sinfulness of all Jews, important though that is, as with Israel's failure to carry out the divine commission, to be the means of the world's salvation. The thought remains dense and sometimes elliptical, but the clear point emerges: God remains faithful to the covenant plan even though Israel has failed in the covenant task.

Israel's failure puts God into an apparently awkward position. Will not the divine righteousness at one level generate unrighteousness at another? Paul rebuts these charges briefly without actually answering them fully; he will return to them in due course.[79] For the moment his aim is to assert the continuing faithfulness of God, despite Israel's failure; this then clears the ground for the point (which many have assumed was the only one in the entire section) that Jews have joined Gentiles in the dock, guilty as charged.

3:1-2. What then of Israel? The question is natural in view of the end of chap. 2. If God is capable of calling "Jews" from among the uncircumcised, what was the point of being Jewish, or being circumcised, in the first place? Paul, given the chance to offer a radically Marcionite answer (e.g., "None whatever!"), has no intention of doing so. The God revealed in Jesus Christ, as he will make clear in the next two chapters, remains the God of Abraham, the covenant God. His answer gives the clue to his real concern throughout the paragraph. The Jews were *entrusted* with God's oracles. (Paul says "in the first place," but never gets round to saying "in the second place." Until, that is, chap. 9.)

"The oracles" τὰ λόγια (*ta logia*) is an unusual phrase, found only here in Paul (it is used for the "oracles" of the prophet Balaam in Num 24:4, 16 and often for words spoken by God to Israel; e.g., Deut 33:9 and frequently in Psalm 119; in the NT, see Acts 7:38; Heb 5:12; 1 Pet 4:11). In its pagan usage it often referred to oracles in the technical sense: short utterances given, supposedly under inspiration, at shrines such as Delphi. A ruler would send emissaries to an oracular shrine, who would return entrusted with the (often cryptic) words of the deity, not for

themselves but for their master. In addition, the priest or priestess at the shrine would themselves be "entrusted" by the god with the message for the recipient. This explains well enough the sense of Paul's comment. The Jews were "entrusted" with messages for the world; not simply with Torah itself, but, through their living under Torah, with words of instruction, of life and light, for the Gentile world. They were to be God's messengers. The fact that this theme is so evident in the present paragraph is further proof of the reading of 2:17-29 proposed above.

3:3. Paul's basic answer is the central point of the paragraph. Israel's faithlessness cannot nullify God's faithfulness. He expresses this as a question, but the Greek construction demonstrates that he clearly expects the answer "No." We should note, despite the NIV's translation "What if some did not have faith?," that Paul is not so concerned with whether they "had faith" in the sense of "Christian faith," a personal trust in the God who raises the dead, but rather with their faithfulness—faithfulness (that is) to the commission to be God's messenger people. The Greek word πίστις (*pistis*), used here for the first time in the body of the letter (i.e., since 1:17), is much broader than the English "faith," particularly in some of its theological developments, and encompasses the meanings "trustworthiness" and "loyalty" as well as what we have come to think of as its more "religious" meanings (personal trust in, and knowledge of, God and belief in true statements about God). It is clearly the broader meaning that is on view here, both in its negative form, applied to Israel (unfaithfulness, untrustworthiness) and in its positive form, applied to God (faithfulness, reliability). The πίστις θεοῦ (*pistis theou*), "God's trustworthiness," is thus clearly one aspect of, one way of referring to, the δικαιοσύνη θεοῦ (*dikaiosynē theou*), "God's righteousness." God's covenant always envisaged Israel's being faithful to the commission to be the light of the world; Israel's untrustworthiness does not abolish God's trustworthiness. It merely sharpens up the question: What will God do now?

3:4. To back up the point, Paul quotes Ps 51:4 [50:6 LXX], the great prayer of repentance ascribed to David after his adultery

79. All the questions in this section are rhetorical, made by imaginary objectors. Paul does not wish to press them on his own account. The NIV flags this up in v. 7 by adding "someone might argue."

with Bathsheba.[80] The verse indicates the abject sorrow of the penitent, acknowledging that when God condemns this sin there will be no question about the rightness of the verdict. God's words are true, even if all human words prove false. It is interesting to observe that when Paul alludes to or mentions David, here and in 4:6-8, it is in connection with sin and forgiveness.[81] The psalm goes on, of course, to speak of the new heart that God will create within the penitent and the gift of the Holy Spirit—"new covenant" themes, in other words, that tie in, via Ezekiel 36, with the close of chap. 2. The verse Paul quotes stresses that sinful humanity, and sinful Israel, can have no claim on God.

3:5-6. This raises an apparent problem, caused perhaps by the language of the psalm as much as anything else. It might seem as though God were acting as judge and executioner in a case where the two parties at law were Israel and—God's own self! This would constitute flagrant injustice; how could the party on trial also judge the case fairly? But Paul is quick to point out that God is not actually at law with Israel; God is the cosmic judge, who must bring justice to the whole world. Some scriptural passages do speak of God having a lawsuit against Israel, but the more fundamental truth is that God is the judge.[82]

3:7-8. The same objection is now put from another angle, returning to the truth/falsehood antithesis of v. 4. This is not so much a legal dilemma, but an apparent absurdity at a less formal level.

Paul slips into the first-person singular ("my falsehood," "why am I condemned?"). This does not mean that he is thinking of himself as an individual, nor simply that he is personalizing the argument for the sake of rhetorical impact. He is in effect anticipating the rhetorical move of 7:7-25 (see the commentary at that point), where the "I" is a way of talking about Israel while not seeming to

stand over against "his kinsmen according to the flesh." The fact that he moves back to treating Jews in general in v. 9 strongly supports this reading. The question is then, if Israel's falsehood means that God's truthfulness shines out all the more brightly, why should God object? Surely "I" should not then be condemned—in other words, surely God cannot actually endorse what was said in 2:17-29, not least 2:27? The deepest charge against Israel in 2:17-24, after all, was that God's name was being blasphemed because of Israel's disobedience to Torah. Very well, if God's glory is enhanced by this process, surely God will now be pleased? Why should "I" then be condemned as though "I" were a ἁμαρτωλός (hamartōlos), a "sinner," a mere pagan, one of the lesser breeds outside the Torah?[83] (This question again reflects the charge Paul has been mounting throughout the previous paragraphs: The condemnation incurred by the pagans falls on Israel as well.)

Paul does not deign to answer this question, but instead amplifies it by referring to a still more blatant attack on the integrity of his theology. Some, he says, have been slandering him (lit., "blaspheming" him; but the word had a more general sense); some are reporting him as saying "let us do evil that good may come."[84] In other words, the "evil" of Israel's failure has brought the "good" of the gospel—a point one can understand people thinking on the basis of, say, Rom 11:11-15—so why not apply the principle more generally?

Paul's only comment on this is the heavily ironic one: Here at least is someone whose condemnation is manifestly just. If nothing else about God's judgment is certain, it is thoroughly deserved by people who can say such a thing—either in general, or as a caricature of Paul's teaching.

Why has Paul allowed himself even to note these problems, providing so much puzzlement for subsequent readers, without giving answers? Part of the answer, as we

---

80. On this, see Hays, *Echoes of Scripture in the Letters of Paul*, 48-50.

81. See 4QMMT C26. On other parallels with 4QMMT see esp. the Commentary on 10:5-8.

82. There may be here an analogy with the book of Job. Job, assuming that he and God are adversaries at law, declares his innocence; Job's comforters, making the same assumption, declare Job guilty. In fact, Job's adversary is Satan; God remains the judge and in the end clears Job's name. God and Job can both be in the right simultaneously. The parallel is not exact, but the analogy holds to this extent: God appears unjust to those who assume that God is a party in the lawsuit, rather than the judge.

83. For the usage, see Gal 2:15. A *hamartōlos*, from the Jewish point of view, was one who, without having the benefit of Torah, sinned as it were in the dark. When a Jew sinned the result was παράβασις (*parabasis*, "transgression"), breaking a known commandment. See the Commentary on 5:13-14.

84. The Greek could mean that there are two different groups making similar accusations, the former in a more slanderous fashion (reflected in the NIV). But the NRSV may be right to take the sentence as a hendiadys, a single point expressed in two parallel ways.

hinted earlier, is that he had to acknowledge them after what he had said in 2:25-29 (and indeed 2:13-15). But a further and deeper reason, which will emerge in 3:21-26, is that the gospel itself reveals God's righteousness, precisely that righteousness that is called into question in the ways outlined so briefly here.

The fuller answer, though, comes in chaps. 9–11, where the same questions recur:

3:1, "What is the point of being a Jew?" corresponds to 9:1-5 as a whole;

3:3, "Has Israel's failure impugned the faithfulness of God to the words previously issued?" corresponds to 9:6, "It is not as though God's word had failed";

3:5, "Is God then unjust?" corresponds to 9:14, "Is there injustice with God?";

3:7, "Why am I still condemned?" corresponds to 9:19, "Why does God still find fault?"

3:9, as we shall see below, corresponds in all sorts of ways to 9:30–10:21. In addition, the narrative logic of chap. 3, in which the failure of Israel leads to the fresh revelation of God's righteousness (3:21-26), corresponds closely to the narrative logic of the whole of 9–11, focused particularly on 10:1-4.

We should also note that in 7:7-25 we find a much fuller presentation of Israel's failure and of the strange way in which the Torah was involved in it, which develops the thought of 2:17-29 and prepares the way for chaps. 9–11. There, too, the first-order problem is not "legalism" so much as law*breaking*. The second-order problem there is the plight of Israel, called to be under Torah and yet discovering that it condemns rather than giving life—again, not too far from 2:17-29, and ending with a cry of frustration that bears some relation to the (admittedly more cynical) questions of 3:7-8. There, too, the statement of the problem in 7:7-25 prepares the ground for the statement of the solution in 8:1-11, just as the present passage prepares for 3:21–4:25, both "solutions" hinging on the death of Jesus. All in all, then, the present paragraph is thoroughly integrated into the rest of the letter.

All this indicates how Paul's mind works as he paints on this grand theological canvas, and how vital it is, if we are to grasp his full picture, to look to other places where the same theme is treated. At the same time, we must remember the role of the passage in its own context. Paul is doing much more than rehearsing the same argument two or three times, in more detail perhaps, just for the sake of it. So what role does the rapid listing of questions in 3:1-8 play within 1:18–3:20, the section within which it belongs?

The paragraph forms a vital part of three things that are going on simultaneously here. First, it is part of the specific theme of universal human sinfulness (see below on 3:19-20). If Jews are to be included in this indictment—the basic problem being not that they are legalists or moralists, but that their boast is undercut by their own lawbreaking—this raises questions that must be addressed, or at least noted, before the conclusion can be drawn (3:10-20). Thus the sequence of thought runs: 2:17-29, initial accusation against Israel; 3:1-8, weighty theological objections to such an accusation (if it is true, what does that do to your wider theology?); 3:9-20, confirming the truth of the initial accusation.

Second, the paragraph belongs also with the second-order charge that Paul levels against Israel: that, commissioned to be God's messenger people, the light of the world, it was disloyal to God and failed in the commission. Since the commission was God's answer to the problem of idolatry and dissolution (1:18-32), the problem might now seem insoluble. Paul here asserts that God will remain faithful; in other words, that despite Israel's failure the problem of universal sin will be addressed and dealt with.

Third, therefore, and overarching both of these, the paragraph is part of the larger theme of God's righteousness revealed in the gospel. The character of God is a major theme here; within vv. 2-7 alone Paul deals with God's oracles, God's faithfulness, God's truth (twice), God's justice, God's wrath, God's judgment, and God's glory. He has already argued in 1:18–2:29 that the gospel reveals God's impartial judgment, enabling one to understand present moral chaos as an anticipation of the coming wrath. Objections to this are noted in 3:1-8 (it seems to impugn God's character), and they are answered in such a way as to prepare for the description of the unveiling of

God's righteousness (3:21–4:25). If God is to be true to character, if the promises are to be fulfilled, what is needed is a faithful Israelite who will act on behalf of, and in the place of, faithless Israel. Paul will argue in 3:21-26 that God has provided exactly that.

First, however, the lawcourt scene must be rounded off. The Gentile world has long since been arraigned and found guilty. Paul will now insist that all Jews belong in the dock as well, with nothing to say in their own defense. (See Reflections at 3:9-20.)

Romans 3:9-20, Torah Puts Jews in the Dock Alongside Gentiles

COMMENTARY

"Whatever Torah says, it speaks to those under the law" (lit., "in the law," 3:19). This is the clue to the present paragraph, with its string of scriptural quotations. Having already argued for the universality of Gentile sin and guilt, Paul now needs to emphasize that the Jews must be seen in the dock alongside the pagans. This has been where his argument has been going for some while, but 2:17-29 and 3:1-9 are not just part of the indictment; they are aimed at answering potential objections, at getting rid of excuses, before the final word is spoken.

The biblical quotations come from Israel's Scriptures and are themselves indictments, not of pagans, but of Jews. Scripture itself, in other words, bears witness against those to whom it was entrusted, leaving the whole world accountable to God (cf. 10:19-21). Paul sums up the problem in terms of the impossibility of anyone being justified by Torah, since all Torah can now do is to point to sin. This will enable him to move at once to demonstrate how the revelation of God's righteousness in the gospel has dealt with precisely this problem.

3:9. The words of v. 9 could, as they stand, bear several different meanings. Once the train of thought of the chapter as a whole is grasped, however, the options are reduced effectively to one.[85] Paul has been arguing

that the privileges of the Jews are real, even though they have been squandered; he has answered his own question of v. 1 with "much in every way." This verse asks a different question: So, then, are we Jews in a better position, in absolute terms? Are we still, in J. B. Phillips's translation, "a march ahead" of everyone else? Since the answer is filled out not only in the second half of v. 9 but also in vv. 10-20 as a whole, we can deduce that it almost certainly should be "no, not at all."[86]

Paul now begins a lawcourt metaphor, which he will develop further in vv. 19-20. He has already laid a charge, like a plaintiff in a case; a charge against both Jews and Greeks ("Greeks" here, as usual, is a metonym for "Gentiles in general"), alleging that they are both "under sin" (NIV, taking the text exactly), i.e., "under the power of sin" (NRSV). By "already charged" he is referring back, obviously, to the argument that began in 1:18. He has not, however, mentioned the word ἁμαρτία (*hamartia*, "sin") up to this point and has only used the cognate verb ἁμαρτάνω (*hamartanō*) in 2:12, first of Gentiles and then of Jews (see also ἁμαρτωλός *hamartōlos* in 3:7). Clearly Paul regards "laying a charge of being under (the power of) sin" as an accurate summary of all that he has said so far. This introduces us to another major theme in the letter, that of "sin" as a personified force and of the slavery of humankind to this force.

In Paul's usage, "sin" refers not just to individual human acts of "sin," of missing the mark (the basic meaning of the word) as regards the divine intention for full human

---

85. The word translated "Are we any better?" (NIV) or "Are we any better off?" (NRSV, which is to be preferred, since the word refers to position and status, not moral behavior) could also mean "Are we any worse off?"; the answer, "No, not at all" (NRSV), could mean "Not completely" or "Not entirely." The translation is further complicated because the question mark we assume after the opening words Τί οὖν (*Ti oun*, "What then?") could belong instead after the next word, προεχόμεθα (*proechometha*), producing a single question, "In what way, then, are we better/worse off?" But most agree that the meaning in the NRSV is correct. For different options, see Cranfield, *A Critical and Exegetical Commentary on the Epistle to the Romans*, 188-91; Fitzmyer, *Romans*, 330-31; Byrne, *Romans*, 119-20.

86. Against Cranfield, *Romans*, 190, who argues cautiously for "not in every respect."

flourishing and fulfillment. "Sin" takes on a malevolent life of its own, exercising power over persons and communities. It is almost as though by "sin" Paul is referring to what in some other parts of the Bible is meant by "Satan" (though Paul can use that language too; e.g., 16:20); this is particularly striking in 7:7-25. By analyzing the human plight in this way he is able to introduce the notion of enslavement to sin (e.g., 6:20) and thereby to clear the way for his own version of the story of the exodus: for Pharaoh, read "sin"; for Passover and Red Sea, read the death and resurrection of Jesus; for the arrival at Sinai and the giving of Torah, read the Spirit; for inheriting the promised land, read the renewal of all creation. This sequence of thought, as we shall see, determines a good deal of the shape of Romans 5–8. In the present chapter this is anticipated in the dense description of the death of Jesus in 3:24-26 (on which see below).

3:10-18. Paul arranges his string of biblical quotations quite carefully.[87] He opens with the general charge that no one is "righteous," anticipating the conclusion in v. 20. The rest of the description is framed by charges of impiety: Nobody understands, or seeks after God (v. 11); nobody keeps the fear of God before their eyes (v. 18). Within this, he draws up a comprehensive charge of going astray (v. 12), wicked speech (vv. 13-14), and violent behavior (vv. 15-17).

As always with Paul's biblical quotations, it is worth checking the contexts to see whether he might have intended wider reference than simply the words quoted.[88] After the opening line, which corresponds both to Eccl 7:20 and Ps 14:1, Paul quotes at length from Ps 14:53, which ends with a prayer that God would deliver Israel out of captivity. He then moves to Ps 5:9, the denunciation of those whose throat is an open sepulcher and who deceive with their tongue; the previous verse prays that YHWH would lead the psalmist "in your righteousness." Continuing in vv. 13-14 the theme of the wickedness of the mouth and tongue, Ps 140:3 adds to Paul's list of charges that the unrighteous

have adders' poison under their lips, and Ps 10:7 that their mouths are full of cursing and bitterness. Both psalms beseech YHWH that he would act at last, to judge the wicked and establish the kingdom for ever. All of these wider themes, clearly, fit within the overall subject matter of Romans 1–3.

We then move in v. 15 to Isa 59:7-8, the complaint that the wicked are swift to shed blood, bring ruin and destruction, and do not know the way of peace. Of all the chapters in the Hebrew Scriptures, this is the one that most strikingly depicts YHWH discovering that there is no righteousness to be had in the world, and so putting on the clothes of righteousness and salvation to rescue the covenant people and judge their adversaries (59:16-18). The chapter ends with YHWH coming to Zion as redeemer—a passage Paul will quote in 11:26—and establishing the divine covenant with Israel, putting the divine spirit within them. Psalm 36:2, the final quotation ("there is no fear of God before their eyes"), moves on to a paean of praise of God's mercy and faithfulness (36:5), God's righteousness and judgments (v. 6), and ends with a prayer for God's mercy and righteousness to abide with Israel and for the wicked to be judged at last (36:10-12).

This is too much for coincidence. What looked at first like a repetitious list of biblical quotations, apparently laboring the point that all are deeply wicked, turns out to be a subtle sequence of thought, linking in at virtually every point with the themes from Paul's surrounding argument. The surface meaning of the text is clear, that all who are "under the law" are condemned as sinners; but the subtext is saying all the time, "Yes; and in precisely this situation God will act, because of the divine righteousness, to judge the world, to rescue the helpless, to establish the covenant." Had Paul been a composer, we may suspect that he would not only have written strong, clear tunes; he would also have been a master of harmony, counterpoint, and orchestration.

3:19. To conclude the matter, Paul returns to lawcourt imagery. The Torah (here taken as the whole of the Jewish scriptures, not merely as the first five books) addresses those "in the law," so that every mouth may be stopped and the whole world be accountable

---

87. L. E. Keck, "The Function of Romans 3:10-18—Observations and Suggestions," in *God's Christ and His People: Studies in Honor of Nils Alstrup Dahl*, ed. J. Jervell and W. A. Meeks (Oslo: Universitetsforlaget, 1977) 141-57, suggests that this may actually be a pre-Pauline composition.

88. See Hays, *Echoes of Scripture in the Letters of Paul*, 50-52.

to God. The stopping of the mouth, by placing a hand over it, was a conventional sign to indicate that one had no more to say in one's own defense; if an obviously guilty defendant continued to speak, the court might of course order that his mouth be stopped for him (cf. Acts 23:2; the NIV's and NRSV's "silenced" describes the effect, but loses the forensic significance of the physical stopping of the mouth). The term ὑπόδικος (hypodikos, "accountable") probably carries a negative sense; not just "answerable" (which might imply that a good answer could be forthcoming), but "guilty and punishable." This is confirmed by the "because" at the start of the next verse, explaining as it does why the only evidence that can be produced is evidence of sin. The case has been heard; the defendants have no more to say; they stand in the dock awaiting the verdict, which can only go one way.

3:20. The διότι (dioti) that opens v. 20 certainly means "for" (NRSV) or "because," not "therefore."[89] This verse offers the logical ground for 3:19, not the other way around. The Torah speaks to those under the Torah, says Paul, with the result that every mouth is stopped, because (v. 20a) nobody will be justified by works of Torah, because (v. 20b) through Torah comes knowledge of sin.[90] To remove all doubt, turn the sequence the other way around: Torah brings knowledge of sin, therefore no one will be justified by "works of Torah," therefore when Torah speaks it leaves those "under Torah" without any defense. Paul has, no doubt, left this point (about the role of Torah in the process) until last in order that he may then state the new point of 3:21 with maximum rhetorical effect.

This verse is one of those points in a Pauline argument where each phrase needs to be weighed with particular care.

To begin with the subject of the sentence: "No human being" (NRSV) and "no one" (NIV) do not capture the nuance of Paul's phrase. In alluding to Ps 143:2 [142:2 LXX], it is striking that he says, literally, "all flesh [πᾶσα σάρξ pasa sarx] shall not be justified."[91] "Flesh," as we saw at 1:3, is a heavily loaded term for Paul. It designates, not so much ordinary physicality as opposed to non-material existence, but rather humankind seen as physically corruptible and morally rebellious, heading for death in both senses. It can also carry the sense of Jewish "flesh," sharing the problem of "fleshly" humanity, with the "fleshly" badge of circumcision only serving to emphasize this identification. That, indeed, is an important part of the argument of Galatians. Although, therefore, Paul's "all flesh" here means the whole of humanity, it is strikingly appropriate, within his wider theology, that he should use it when insisting that the Jews must join the Gentiles as guilty defendants before the judgment seat of God.

Though Paul is not quoting the psalm verbatim, he clearly intends to refer to it. Once more he seems to have the wider scriptural context in mind.[92] Psalm 143 is a prayer invoking the faithfulness and righteousness of YHWH (Ps 143:1), pleading for deliverance, not on the basis of any merit (since, as v. 2 says, no one living is righteous before God), but simply for the sake of God's name and God's righteousness (v. 11). Though the surface level of Paul's argument demands that he quote v. 2, the underlying theme of the whole section now drawing to a close, and of that about to begin, is the righteousness of God. God, being righteous, must judge the wicked; but those who are not righteous themselves may nevertheless cast themselves on God's righteousness to find deliverance.

What, then, does Paul mean, "by works of the law shall no flesh be justified before God"? How does this relate to 2:13, where "the doers of the law" shall be justified?

The question can only be answered fully in relation to the many other passages where Paul speaks of "works of the law." But a preliminary answer may be given here, to be filled out as the commentary progresses and with additional sidelong glances at Galatians.

89. Thus the NIV, showing remarkable disregard for Paul's connecting links. The penalty for this is to be forced to alter the next connective as well: γάρ (gar), introducing the last part of the verse, means "for," not "rather," as in the NIV.

90. The NIV's "through the law we become conscious of sin" adds a first-person plural where Paul leaves the matter abstract. This sentence, which sounds like a restatement of the Lutheran view of the "preaching of the law," reflects Paul's meaning only if we remember that "we" would have to mean "those under the law" (see the Commentary on 7:7-12). In addition, "becoming conscious of sin" is not quite the same as having "knowledge of sin" (see 7:7).

91. The LXX has πᾶς ζῶν (pas zōn, "every living thing"). Paul quotes the same verse, with the same alteration, in Gal 2:16. "All flesh" (pasa sarx) takes the mind to Isa 40:5-6.

92. See Hays, Echoes of Scripture in the Letters of Paul, 51-53; Richard B. Hays, "Psalm 143 and the Logic of Romans 3," JBL 99 (1980) 107-15.

Justification, in this passage, is clearly a lawcourt term. We may remind ourselves that the Greek words "justify" (δικαιόω *dikaioō*) and "justification" (δικαίωσις *dikaiōsis*) belong to the same root as "righteous" (δίκαιος *dikaios*) and "righteousness" (δικαιοσύνη *dikaiosynē*). Attempts to clarify this in English by choosing one of the two roots and forcing it through ("just, justice" rather than "righteous, righteousness"; "rightwise, rightwising" rather than "justify," "justification") bring other problems and have not commanded general assent. As noted in the Introduction, when Paul uses this language he has three interlocking spheres of reference in mind. The language most naturally belongs in the lawcourt;[93] the overarching concept in Paul's mind is God's covenant with Israel, the covenant through which (as though in a cosmic lawcourt) the world will be put to rights. And the critical turn in the argument is eschatological: Paul's affirmation that the final lawcourt scene has been brought forward into the present, that the divine "righteousness" has been disclosed already in Jesus the Messiah.

Put simply, then, Paul's point here is that the verdict of the court, i.e., of God, cannot be that those who have "works of Torah" on their record will receive the verdict "righteous." We remind ourselves again that he is not speaking of Gentiles here, but of Jews; we already know, from 1:18–2:16, that Gentiles will not be justified as they stand. "The Jew" of 2:17 will come into court, metaphorically speaking, and "rest in the Torah," producing "works of Torah"; these, it will be claimed, demonstrate that he or she is indeed a member of Israel, part of God's covenant people. No, says Paul. To cite one's possession of Torah as support will not do. Torah will simply remind you that you are a sinner like the Gentiles. That was the point of the hints in 1:18–2:16 and of the direct charge in 2:17-29–not, as is sometimes said, that the Jews are "legalists," but that they have broken the law they were given. And transgression of Torah shows that Jews, like Gentiles, are "under the power of sin" (3:9). To appeal to Torah is like calling a defense witness who

endorses what the prosecution has been saying all along. (This is the point that Paul will develop, via such apparent throwaway lines as 5:20, in 7:7-25; cf. too 1 Cor 15:56.)

What then are these "works of Torah"? How does this indictment against those who have "works of Torah" on their record square with what Paul says about himself in Phil 3:6, that concerning "righteousness in Torah" he had become "blameless"? How does it fit with wider, non-Christian evidence for Jewish beliefs about Torah in Paul's day?

The only pre-Christian Jewish text we possess that uses the phrase "works of Torah" is a recently published Dead Sea Scroll, the already well-known 4QMMT.[94] "We have indeed sent you," writes the author to his readers, "this selection of works of the Torah according to our decision, for your welfare and the welfare of your people."[95] However, this cannot be used as a template for Paul's meaning of the phrase itself, since the "works" spoken of there are (a) post-biblical rulings concerning temple purity, aimed at (b) defining one group of Jews over against others. It is clear from Romans and Galatians, as we shall see, that when Paul speaks of "works of the law" he is thinking rather of (a) biblical rules that (b) defined Jews (and proselytes) over against pagans. The phrase is, after all, quite general, and we may suppose that it had a wider currency than just Paul and Qumran, even though only they out of our surviving literature use it, and that infrequently.

The main positive thing that this Qumran text contributes to the present discussion, though, is a sense of how "works of the Torah" could function within the language of justification. The third and final section of MMT tells the story of Israel, from the

---

93. Paul is assuming, of course, the ancient Jewish lawcourt, not a modern one, as Seifrid accuses me of proposing. See M. A. Seifrid, *Christ Our Righteousness: Paul's Theology of Justification* (Downers Grove: InterVarsity, 2000) 59.

94. MMT (an acronym for the Hebrew words meaning "a selection of works of Torah," which, coming in line C27 of the scroll, appear to sum up the text's main thrust) is reconstructed from six Qumran fragments, none of them complete (4Q394-399). It seems to be a letter, written in the mid-second century BCE, from the leader of the Qumran group to the head of a larger group, of which the Qumran sect was once a part. For the text, translations, and preliminary discussions, see Elisha Qimron and John Strugnell, *Qumran Cave 4 V: Miqs.at Ma'ase Ha-Torah. Discoveries in the Judaean Desert X* (Oxford: Clarendon, 1994); Vermes, *The Complete Dead Sea Scrolls in English* (Harmondsworth: Penguin, 1997) 220-28; Michael Wise, Martin Abegg, Jr., and Edward Cook, *The Dead Sea Scrolls: A New Translation* (San Francisco: Harper, 1996) 358-64; Florentino García Martínez, *The Dead Sea Scrolls Translated: The Qumran Texts in English* (Leiden: Brill, 1994) 77-85. On the relation between MMT and Paul, see also the Commentary on 10:5-8. Despite Vermes (493), it now appears that the other reference sometimes suggested, 4Q174, frag. 1, 1:7, reads "works of thanksgiving" (מעשי תודה *ma'asê-tôdâ*) rather than "works of the law" (מעשי תורה *ma'asê-tôrâh*).

95. MMT C26-27, author's trans.

promises and warnings of Deuteronomy up to the writer's own day. Deuteronomy 30 promised a historical sequence: covenantal blessing, curse, then blessing again. The initial blessing and curse, says the text, came upon Israel in the time of the monarchy, with the curse being, more or less, the exile. Now, however, the second blessing promised by the same text has come upon Israel, precisely in the life of the sect, the secretly inaugurated new covenant people, yet to be finally and publicly vindicated. The members of the sect are already marked out as the eschatological Israel, ahead of the time when they will be vindicated as such. The thing that marks them out in the present is precisely the specific "works of the Torah" that the text urges upon its readers—the detailed post-biblical regulations deemed necessary by the sect. These "works of Torah," then, were the sign that the future verdict (God's vindication of the sect) was anticipated in the present; the sect could be confident now of their membership in the renewed covenant, the community of fresh blessing, the "returned-from-exile" people spoken of in Deuteronomy 30. When we widen the horizon from the sectarian "works" mentioned in the scroll to the more fundamental biblical "works" Paul has in mind, the position he is opposing can be stated thus: "works of Torah" are the sign, in the present, of that membership in Israel, God's covenant people, which will be vindicated in the future when the long-awaited "righteousness of God" is finally unveiled in action.

It is vital to keep our balance at this point. One of the great gains of the last quarter of a century in Pauline scholarship has been to recognize that Paul's contemporaries—and Paul himself prior to his conversion—were not "legalists," if by that we mean that they were attempting to earn favor with God, to earn grace as it were, by the performance of law-prescribed works.[96] Paul's fellow Jews were not proto-Pelagians, attempting to pull

themselves up by their moral shoelaces. They were, rather, responding out of gratitude to the God who had chosen and called Israel to be the covenant people and who had given Israel the law both as the sign of that covenant membership and as the means of making it real. Paul's critique is not that the Torah was a bad thing that the Jews should not have followed, nor that their Torah-observance was done in order to stake a claim on God that God had not already granted in the covenant. His point, rather, was that all who attempted to legitimate their covenant status by appealing to possession of Torah would find that the Torah itself accused them of sin. If "the Jew" appealed to Torah to say "This shows that I am different from the Gentiles," Torah itself, according to Paul, would say "No, it doesn't; it shows that you are the same as the Gentiles."

The "works" that were regarded in Paul's day as particularly demonstrating covenant membership were, of course, those things that marked out the Jews from their pagan neighbors, not least in the diaspora: the sabbath, the food laws, and circumcision. A strong case can therefore be made for seeing "works of the law," in Romans and Galatians, as highlighting these elements in particular.[97] This case rests on the larger thrust of Paul's argument, in which "the Jew" is appealing not to perfect performance of every last commandment, but to possession of Torah as the badge of being God's special people. Special they are, but also sinning; and sin means that the specialness is of no ultimate avail.

Why, then, could Paul say of himself, in Phil 3:6, that concerning "righteousness under the law" he was "found blameless"? Presumably he meant that, as a good Jew, he regularly used the means of forgiveness and purification that were on offer in the Temple and the sacrificial cult and took part in the great fasts and feasts through which the devout Jew was assured of God's forgiveness and favor. Thus at any moment he was a Jew in good standing; not that he had always done what Torah prescribed (we must not suppose the pre-Christian Paul to have been so ignorant of his own motivation and behavior), but that he had always repented and sought God's

---

96. This so-called new perspective, associated principally with E. P. Sanders, *Paul and Palestinian Judaism* (London: SCM, 1977), has now not only taken on a life and literature of its own but has generated a growth industry of opposing publications. See, e.g., R. H. Gundry, "Grace, Works, and Staying Saved in Paul," *Biblica* 66 (1985) 1-38; C. H. Talbert, "Paul, Judaism, and the Revisionists," *CBQ* 63 (2001) 1-22; D. A. Carson, P. T. O'Brien, and M. A. Seifrid, *Justification and Variegated Nomism* (Grand Rapids: Baker Academic), whose first volume, *The Complexities of Second Temple Judaism*, appeared just as this commentary went to press.

97. This is argued especially by Dunn in various works. See Dunn, *Romans 1-8*, 153-60, and the other refs. there.

forgiveness through the appropriate methods. Torah, he might have said, can show me that I am a sinner and can also show me the way of forgiveness. We must assume that someone who followed this path would consider themselves "blameless according to the law."

Further discussion of this point must be postponed until we arrive at 7:7-25, since that passage needs to be factored into the argument in various ways. But one major difference between what Paul says in Philippians and what he says in Romans 3 is that in the present passage his primary concern is not to analyze every single individual and to demonstrate somehow that he or she really is sinful, but rather to show that possession of Torah itself cannot sustain the claim that "the Jew" is automatically in covenant with God, automatically a cut above the Gentiles. And, in referring to those (like his own former self) who are "under the law," he looks at them in their totality, sin included. Just as Israel cannot be affirmed in the present as the inalienable covenant people of God because of the presence, within Israel, of various kinds of sin that demonstrate the failure of the national vocation (2:17-24), so no Jews, however blameless in terms of current status, can be affirmed as they stand as complete and adequate human beings, since all alike commit sin. If God is the righteous judge, God cannot allow particular members of that nation to escape the judgment they incur just as do all Gentiles.

If, however, God is truly "righteous" in the widest senses, including that of keeping the covenant promises made long ago, how then can that "righteousness" be put into operation without contradicting itself? This question was raised extremely sharply for Paul's near-contemporaries by the fall of Jerusalem in 70 CE. For Paul, it had already been raised, and answered, by the events concerning Jesus of Nazareth. Paul is now in a position to address this question, one of the most fundamental that he and his contemporaries were ever to face.

REFLECTIONS

1. Before we "translate" or "apply" these severe and often dense verses to our own day, we must consider the relevance of their own unique meaning in Paul's own time. Part of the burden of eschatology—part of the problem, that is, of believing in a God who (though always active within the world in various ways) acted uniquely and decisively at one moment in history, and part of the problem of living on the basis of that one-off action—is that one is committed to getting inside that historical situation in all its differentness to our own day, to understanding what it was that God was up to then. Preachers of the gospel cannot escape the task of being ancient historians. The alternative is shallow anachronism.

Paul insists that God will be just and faithful, despite the faithlessness of the particular humans to whom the divine oracles had been entrusted. In the post-Enlightenment world, ironically, the goodness and justice of God are often called into account precisely because of the suggestion that God might act in a particular and decisive way, in one place and time rather than at another. The rhetoric of the last two hundred years has been in favor of broad general truths, timeless and abstract religious or ethical norms or guidelines. Projecting our hard-won (and often deeply ambiguous) democracy onto the heavens, we demand that all humans should have the same vote and voice. How, we ask, can a unique act of God be fair?

This question is, at one level, a manifestation of the old discussion, associated with Barth and others, as to whether Christianity is a "religion" or rather a "revelation." In these debates, however, it was often assumed that the Jews followed a "religion," and were indeed the archetypical manifestation of *homo religiosus*, religious humanity. (This is a major theme in the great commentary of Ernst Käsemann.) We have learned, painfully enough, the danger of such caricatured generalizations. What Saul of Tarsus and his contemporaries were longing for, in any case, was a revelation, an unveiling, the fresh action of their God within history. That was how wrongs would be put right, how justice would come at last. The irony of our changing points of view, the transformation of assumptions between Paul's day and ours, is that this idea of a specific and decisive act of God, in one place and time beyond all others, is itself now felt to be wrong or unjust. We here reach basic questions of worldview, and choices have to be made. The whole New Testament witnesses to a unique act of God, such as Saul of Tarsus had expected, but at a different level, of a totally different kind. Yes, says Paul the Apostle, God has acted in history to unveil that faithfulness of which Scripture spoke. But no, the action was not what Israel, Saul of Tarsus included, had expected.

The "modern" objection to the idea of God's acting decisively and uniquely is based, it seems, on a false impression about what such actions mean. If the main purpose of divine revelation were to convey information to humans, or to give a set of rules to be kept, then it would seem unfair and arbitrary to give these to some and then to judge the others despite their disadvantage. If the main purpose was to straighten out a few design faults in creation, to perform "miracles" that helped certain people out of insoluble or life-threatening situations, this too would seem grossly unfair; why would a good God, capable of doing this sort of thing, not do it at other times, when faced (for instance) with the chance to prevent genocide?

These are, however, by no means the only possible models of divine action in the world. All analogies are imperfect; but we can conceive of other, perhaps better, ways of looking at the question. An architect has to produce a single blueprint at one time and place, so that the building may be constructed for the benefit of all. A medical researcher has to produce medications at one time and place, so that all may eventually be cured. A gardener has to plant a fruit tree in one place and at one time, so that there may be fruit for all. God, in the Jewish thought that Paul reflects, needed to act decisively at one time and in one place, so that there might be salvation for all. We should not allow the rhetoric of modernity to rob us of the glory of the gospel: a God with muddy boots and dirty hands, busy at the center of the mess so that all may be cleaned up and sorted out.

2. The question of the point of being Jewish, once its own unique dimensions have been grasped, broadens out in our own day to the question of the point of being human. This has been asked in the twentieth century over and over, as philosophers, writers, and artists, as well as theologians, have reflected on the horrors of our "civilized" world, producing ever more cunning machines for making war but still unable to invent one that will make peace. Just as the Jewish vocation was to bring God's light to the Gentiles, so the human vocation was to reflect God's image into the world. Manifest human failure to do this could lead to the equivalent, for this question, of the Marcionite rejection of Judaism as a whole, i.e., a denial of the entire God-given human vocation. This, indeed, is what we find in some New Age thinking today, with humans being regarded as simply part of the world's problem, rather than potential contributors to the solution.

But Paul would be as adamant on this point as he is on his own topic: Let God be true, though everyone should prove false. God has created humans to reflect the divine image in worship and service, and God will be true to that promise. "The righteousness of God" can be called upon to fulfill the purpose of creation, not just of Israel. How this will happen, Paul will work out from 3:21 through to the end of chap. 8. To claim that it will happen is the equivalent, for these questions, of Paul's brief and clipped responses in 3:1-8. That it has already happened is the burden of his song in 3:21–4:25, summed up in 5:12-21: God has provided an obedient human being, in whom the original purpose of Genesis 1 has at last been fulfilled (see also 1 Cor 15:20-28; Phil 3:20-21; and, further afield, the whole argument of Heb 2:5-10).

3. The charge of universal human sinfulness is of course as controversial today as ever. Nobody, almost by definition, likes the humiliation of recognizing their sinful condition (or, if they do, we may raise questions about their balance of mind). Just as much psychology tacitly avoids the category of "evil," preferring to see varieties of human behavior in less threatening terms, so many Christians, eager for the great acceptance, the astonishing welcome, of the gospel, use this as a reason for denying human sinfulness. But, of course, if humans are not deeply sinful the gospel is no longer astonishing; indeed, it is not good news at all, since there was no problem to which it was the shocking, startling answer. Tragically, just as those who do not understand history are condemned to repeat it, so those who turn a blind eye to wickedness are always in danger of perpetrating it. If there is no disease, why worry about precautions, let alone cure? If the human race is morally sound (no doubt with a few glitches here and there), we should eat, drink, and be merry, for tomorrow we shall live. Oddly enough, at the same time as postmodernity is urging us to be suspicious of every action, every word, and every motive, the imperative it sanctions—to be true to oneself, even though "oneself" may be constantly changing—is itself deeply suspect. Tyrants, bullies, extortioners, adulterers, and murderers are all being true to themselves. And those who look at such activities and thank God that they are not like that need once more to go deeper (2:1-16), to examine the secrets of their own hearts.

4. There is much to learn from the way in which Paul has pulled together the awful catalog of sin in 3:10-18. Under the surface-level indictment there is hope, precisely because this wickedness is shown up by the righteousness of God, which can then be appealed to for mercy. How easy it is for preachers either to denounce wickedness in a dualistic fashion, or to abstain from such denunciations because they sound too depressing, too dismissive. Paul's denunciations, for those with ears to hear, are always hinting at the solution. His robust faith in God's forgiving faithfulness enables him to call a spade a spade.

5. The dismissal of "works of the law" as the means of justification has all kinds of overtones. Paul's fundamental meaning is that no Jew can use possession of the Torah, and performance of its key symbolic "works" of ethnic demarcation, as demonstration in the present time that they belong to the eschatological people of God, the people who will inherit the age to come. Torah is incapable of performing this function: When appealed to, it reminds its possessors of their own sin.

This Israel-specific and context-specific argument and meaning, vital though it is, must send off warning signals in other spheres as well. To the Roman moralist of Paul's day, it might have said that clear thought and noble intention were not enough; the clearer the thought, the nobler the intention, the more this clarity and nobility would condemn the actual behavior. To an anxious monk of the early sixteenth century, fretting about his own justification, Paul's words rang other bells. Performance of Christian duties is not enough. Despite the Reformation, the message had still not been heard by the devout John Wesley, until a fresh hearing of Luther's commentary on Galatians caused light to dawn. In the post-Enlightenment period, many, including many Christians, have assumed that "the law," here and elsewhere, refers to the Kantian idea of a categorical moral imperative suspended over all humans, and have preached this "law" to make people recognize their guilt, in order then to declare the gospel to them.

These are important overtones of Paul's statement here, but they are not its fundamental note. If we play an overtone, thinking it to be a fundamental, we shall set off new and different sets of overtones, which will not then harmonize with Paul's original sound. Sadly, this has occurred again and again, not least within the Reformation tradition, which, eager for the universal relevance and the essential *pro me* (i.e., "for me") of the gospel, and regarding Israel mainly as a classic example of the wrong way of approaching God or "religion," has created a would-be "Pauline" theology in which half of what Paul was most eager to say in Romans has been screened out. Provided, however, one is careful to tell again the unique story of Israel and Jesus, not as an example of something else but as the fundamental truth of the gospel, many of the things the Reformers wanted to insist on can be retained and, indeed, enhanced.

ROMANS 3:21–4:25, GOD'S FAITHFULNESS TO THE COVENANT

OVERVIEW

It should now be clear that the great theme Paul will unveil in the new section is "the righteousness of God," meaning by that the faithfulness of God to the promises long ago announced to Israel. That divine faithfulness, which seemed to be called into question by Israel's failure to be the light for the Gentiles, is now revealed through the faithful Israelite, Jesus the Messiah. The plan has not failed; rather, it is focused on, and accomplished through, one person. Through him, God has kept the promise made to Abraham.

Paul is therefore speaking, without using the word, of the covenant. This biblical term, found occasionally in Paul, is in my view a useful and appropriate shorthand for drawing attention to the fact that in this section, as in Galatians 3, Paul is evoking one chapter in particular, namely Genesis 15. In that chapter, God established the covenant with Abraham, promising both that he would have countless descendants and that his seed would attain their inheritance by passing through slavery to freedom (Gen 15:5, 13-16). Referring to Paul's "covenantal" theology at this point, as I and others have sometimes done, means simply this: Paul intends to affirm that what God has done in Jesus the Messiah is the fulfillment of the promises to Abraham. This, indeed, is the answer, or at least the initial answer, to the string of questions in 3:1-8. Despite the unwarranted suspicions of those who assume that to refer to the covenant is to flatten out the contours of Paul's telling of the story of God, Israel, and the world, to reduce the sharp impact of the crucifixion, or to capitulate to a particular type of Reformed

theology, this proposal passes the most important test of all: It makes excellent sense of the relevant texts, as we shall now see.[98]

The place of Abraham in the argument of the present section, and its partial parallel in Galatians 3, is therefore far more than as an "example" of someone who was justified by faith, as is still commonly supposed.[99] Paul is doing something much more large-scale, much more intricately crafted, than merely "stating a doctrine" in 3:21-31 and then "offering a proof from scripture" in chap. 4. He has not merely introduced Abraham because his opponents, real or imagined, would have made Abraham a strong part of their own argument. Nor is Abraham's faith the sole or central feature of chap. 4; indeed, by making it so, as we shall see, commentators have introduced puzzles into the exegesis that disappear once the larger theme is grasped.

The proposals cited here as inadequate have entered the exegesis of Romans not least because many readers have come to the text with questions other than Paul's. In particular, the broad questions of human sin and of justification by faith have dominated the discussion, so that Paul's own much more specific questions in Romans, not least those of the coming together of Jew and Gentile in Christian faith, and of the fulfillment of the Abrahamic promises, have been marginalized, to the detriment of exegesis and, in my view, of the life of the church.

98. For the debate, see, e.g., Wright, *The Climax of the Covenant*; Hays, *Echoes of Scripture in the Letters of Paul*. On the other side, see, J. L. Martyn, *Theological Issues in the Letters of Paul* (Nashville: Abingdon, 1997).

99. See Fitzmyer, *Romans*, 369.

Exegesis has been hampered in particular by a misunderstanding of δικαιοσύνη θεοῦ (*dikaiosynē theou*, "the righteousness of God") in 3:21-26 (on "righteousness" language, see the Introduction). Once the wider context (of 3:1-8, on the one hand, and 4:1-25, on the other) is appreciated, and the specific argument of 3:21-26 itself fully grasped, it is quite impossible that this phrase should mean, as NIV, "a righteousness from God," that is, the righteous status that believers enjoy as a gift from God and in God's presence. Paul does indeed hold that those who believe the gospel are reckoned "righteous" (e.g., 3:26, 28), and he can speak of this as "a righteous status *from* God" (ἡ ἐκ θεοῦ δικαιοσύνη *hē ek theou dikaiosynē*, Phil 3:9). But this status, which Paul describes in that significantly different way, is not the same thing as God's own righteousness. It results from the revelation of that righteousness, of God's salvific covenant faithfulness; the present passage is, in fact, the fullest statement of this. If we wish to press for an alternative to the technical term "righteousness," with all its attendant puzzles and possibilities for misunderstanding, perhaps the best current option is that of the NJB: "God's saving justice."

Paul declares (3:21) that the Torah and the prophets bear witness to this saving justice. What was it, then, that they said, to which God has now been faithful?

The main subject Paul expounds in this section is God's creation of a single worldwide family, composed of believing Jews and believing Gentiles alike. Since the main thing standing in the way of this achievement is human sin, the central focus of the paragraph describing how God has done it is the way God has dealt with sin through the death of Jesus. "Justification," in its Pauline contexts, regularly includes both aspects: the rescue of sinners from their sin, and the creation of the worldwide family of forgiven sinners. The universal scope of this eschatological Abrahamic family is emphasized in the "all" of 3:23 and the sustained arguments of 3:27-30; 4:9-12; 4:13-15; and 4:16-17. It is not so much that Paul, wanting to emphasize "faith," shows incidentally that it happens to bring together the different ethnic groups; rather, he wants to emphasize the coming together of Jew and Gentile in Christ and, therefore, demonstrates

that this aim is achieved through faith. God's aim in calling Abraham in the first place was to put the world to rights. Only through the creation of a single forgiven family, comprising Gentiles as well as Jews, can that purpose be fulfilled.

Once this is grasped, several problems can be seen in their proper light. Despite what is sometimes supposed, for instance, Paul does not intend to offer here (i.e., specifically in 3:24-26) a full "doctrine of atonement." He is rather summing up a much larger train of thought, which we can observe at various points in his letters, in order to use this whole train of thought within his present argument. Romans has frequently been pulled out of shape by the insistence that it should provide full information at each point on the "topic" that dogmatic theology has been expecting at this point in the argument. Only when we allow Paul to develop his own trains of thought in his own way will we avoid doing violence to the text.

Recognizing the centrality of the Jew/Gentile question in the present argument explains Paul's running sub-theme that appears in the phrase "apart from the law" (3:21). Despite the fact that Torah and prophets bear witness to God's faithfulness, Torah itself not only sustained the division between Jew and Gentile, now overcome in Christ; it also condemned those "under the law" by showing them up as sinners. Both these themes are present in 3:21–4:25 (e.g., 3:27; 4:13-17).

Paul emphasizes throughout this section that this single worldwide family is "justified" in the present time. Thinking within the same overall frame of thought as 4QMMT, he looks ahead to the future time when God will finally make all things new and will reveal once and for all who his own people are. He has already spoken of this in 2:1-16; failure to factor that passage properly into the argument has led to the ignoring of the eschatological dimension of his teaching on justification. The whole point is this: The verdict "righteous," to be issued in the future on the basis of the totality of the life led, is brought forward into the present. But, whereas MMT regarded the performance of certain specific post-biblical purity regulations as the present defining badge of those whose future justification is thereby assured, Paul regarded faith, specifically faith in the God who raised Jesus from the dead, as this badge (see 4:24-25; 10:8-10).

Justification in the present is possible, Paul argues, because the grace of God deals with the sins of the people through the death of Jesus. The people in question are, therefore, a forgiven family (4:5-8). The covenant with Abraham existed all along to deal with the problem of Adamic humanity; the echoes of the latter in 3:23, which sums up so much of 1:18–3:20, and the anticipation here of 5:12-21, indicate clearly enough that this is what Paul has in mind.[100] God's faithfulness, when met with answering human faithfulness, creates the genuine humanity that idolatry so cruelly distorts (4:18-22, reflecting and reversing 1:18-25). And Paul also hints at the wider purpose he believes God had in view in the original creation: The promise to Abraham and his seed was that they should inherit (not the land, but) the world (4:13; cf. 8:18-25).

God has, then, been faithful in Jesus the Messiah to the promises made to Abraham, to the covenant established with the Jewish people and, through them, with humankind and the entire creation. The short, straightforward way of saying this is: "God's righteousness has been unveiled." Chapters 5–8 will show how the revealing of this righteousness works for the wider circles of humankind and creation as a whole, laying the foundations for Paul's arguments in chaps. 9–11 and 12–16. And this divine righteousness, Paul declares, has been revealed in and through the Messiah, Jesus, for the benefit of all who believe.

The dense and unusual language of 3:24-26 is best explained on the premise that Paul is here briefly summarizing an argument he could in principle have spelled out far more fully, and to which he also alludes in many other places both in Romans and elsewhere. I regard this as preferable to the proposal, which has been adopted by several scholars, that the passage contains a pre-Pauline formula that Paul is here adapting.[101] Though the

language is dense and formulaic, this is not itself an indication that Paul is quoting from a source. When the theory proposes, as it does in some forms, that he is using a formulation in which "God's righteousness" meant God's faithfulness to the covenant, but that Paul himself was broadening this into a different sense of "righteousness," we may suspect that the real motivation for the "discovery" of the formula was to protect Paul from such a "Jewish-Christian" idea.

The text, though difficult, can in fact be read adequately without recourse to this hypothesis, as I hope to show.[102]

Paul's purpose in 3:21-26 is not, then, to give a full "doctrine of atonement," a complete account of how God dealt with the sins of the world through the death of Jesus. Rather, as one part of his argument that on the cross the righteousness of God was unveiled, he is content to state, not completely *how*, but simply *that* this had been accomplished. Fuller statements elsewhere indicate that for Paul the resurrection of Jesus was also significant in God's dealing with sins (e.g., 1 Cor 15:17). Had crucifixion been the end of Jesus' story, no one would ever have ascribed saving significance to the event. The resurrection casts a retrospective coloring over the crucifixion, revealing it to be the decisive, heaven-sent saving act of God. That is presumably why when Paul spells out the nature of Christian faith in 4:24-25, he describes it as faith "in the God who raised Jesus from the dead, who was put to death for our trespasses and raised for our justification."

Jesus' achievement is thus to have done what Israel should have done but failed to do (see 3:2-3). He has been the light of the world, the one through whom God's saving purpose has been revealed. Through him God has at last dealt with the sin of the world, the purpose for which the covenant was made. Although the statement of this is already compact, Paul can summarize this, too, in shorthand form: "the faithfulness of Jesus the Messiah" (3:22). This notion has become something of a storm center in recent debate, and all we can do here is to

100. See Wright, *The Climax of Covenant*, 21-26; Wright, *The New Testament and the People of God*, 251-52.

101. See Käsemann, *Commentary on Romans*, 95-100; Stuhlmacher, *Paul's Letter to the Romans*, 58-59; the summary in Fitzmyer, *Romans*, 342-43.

102. For shrewd criticism of the theory, see Moo, *The Epistle to the Romans*, 220-21, 240; and, in more detail, D. A. Campbell, *The Rhetoric of Righteousness in Romans 3.21-26*, JSNTSup 65 (Sheffield: Sheffield Academic, 1992) 37-57.

summarize what seems to me the correct way forward.[103]

When Paul summarizes the present train of thought in 5:12-21, he uses the term "obedience," and means something very similar to what he says here. The Messiah's "obedience unto death" (cf. Phil 2:6-8) is the critical act—an act of Jesus, and also in Paul's eyes an act of God—through which sins are dealt with, justification is assured, and the worldwide covenant family is brought into being. In making this point it is important to be clear what is not being said. Paul is not speaking of Jesus' "faith" either in the sense of the things Jesus believed, or Jesus' exemplary trust in God, or Jesus' religious experience. Nor is he suggesting that Jesus' "obedience" was somehow meritorious, so that by it he earned "righteousness" on behalf of others. That is an ingenious and far-reaching way of making Paul's language fit into a theological scheme very different from his own.[104] Rather, he is highlighting Jesus' faithful obedience, or perhaps we should say Jesus' obedient faithfulness, to the saving plan marked out for Israel, the plan by which God would save the world. On the cross Jesus accomplished what God had always intended the covenant to achieve. Where Israel as a whole had been faithless, he was faithful: 3:22 answers to 3:2-3.

Jesus' faithfulness unto death is here, as in some other Pauline passages, described in sacrificial terms (for the details, see the comments below). This is one of the trickiest passages in Paul in terms of precise nuances, but the context appears to be that reappropriation of the Levitical sacrificial language, particularly from the Day of Atonement scene in Leviticus 16, which we also find in, for instance, the Maccabaean literature

(4 Macc 17:22).[105] There, as here, the setting is (1) the great wrath that hangs over Israel (and, in this case, the world), because of sin; (2) the death of the martyrs as somehow dealing with that wrath on behalf of God's people; and (3) the liberation from wrath that comes as a result. And, like the Maccabaean passage, this one arguably carries overtones also of that other great reworking of Levitical themes, the fourth Servant Song of Isaiah (Isa 52:13–53:12). Jesus is, for Paul, more than a mere martyr, but not less. Paul is here drawing together several rich biblical and post-biblical strands of thought to make the point that Jesus, in his death, completely fulfilled the saving plan of God. Through his death, sin and its results have been dealt with. Wrath has been turned away from God's people.

It is Jesus' death, therefore, that reveals God's righteousness. The puzzles of 3:1-8 are hereby resolved, at least in preliminary form. God has been faithful to the promises, while remaining impartially the God of Jews and Gentiles alike; God has dealt with sin as it merited and now rescues those who cast themselves on the divine mercy. This act of grateful trust in the God who raised Jesus is the characteristic Christian "faith," which plays such a large role in Paul's thought; it is the "obedience of faith," the proper response to grace that God always sought. Though faith has an affective content (being aware of God's presence and love), a propositional content (believing that Jesus is Lord and that God raised him from the dead), and an actively trusting content (casting oneself on God's mercy), we should not ignore the meaning the word has in the same passage when applied to Jesus: faithfulness. Paul does not so easily distinguish, as we do, between believing in God and being loyal to God. Notice how closely verbal confession and belief in the heart are linked in 10:9-10.

This faith then becomes the badge that identifies, in the present time, the members of the people of God. This is the meaning of Paul's doctrine of "justification by faith." The verdict of the last day has been brought forward into the present in Jesus the Messiah; in raising him from the dead, God declared that

---

103. The Greek πίστις (*pistis*) can mean "faith" or "faithfulness," "trust" or "trustworthiness." On the whole subject, see esp. L. T. Johnson, "Rom 3:21-26 and the Faith of Jesus," *CBQ* 44 (1982) 77-90; R. B. Hays, *The Faith of Jesus Christ: An Investigation of the Narrative Substructure of Galatians 3:1–4:11*, 2nd ed., SBLDS 56 (Grand Rapids: Eerdmans, 2001); S. K. Williams "Again Pistis Christou," *CBQ* 49 (1987) 431-47; M. D. Hooker, "ΠΙΣΤΙΣ ΧΡΙΣΤΟΥ," *NTS* 35 (1989) 321-42; and the debate between Hays and Dunn in *SBL 1991 Seminar Papers*, ed. E. H. Lovering (Atlanta: Scholars Press) 714-44. Fitzmyer, *Romans*, 345, and Moo, *Romans*, 225, both reject the proposal of Hays and others, while Christopher Bryan, *A Preface to Romans: Notes on the Epistle in Its Literary and Cultural Setting* (Oxford: Oxford University Press, 2000) 108-10, accepts it.

104. For discussion of this viewpoint, frequent within Reformed theology, see Moo, *Romans*, 225; R. N. Longenecker, "The Obedience of Christ in the Theology of the Early Church," in *Reconciliation and Hope: New Testament Essays on Atonement and Eschatology Presented to L. L. Morris on his 60th Birthday*, ed. R. Banks (Exeter: Paternoster, 1974) 142-52.

105. See Wright, *The New Testament and the People of God*, 276-77.

in him had been constituted the true, forgiven worldwide family. Justification, in Paul, is not the process or event whereby someone becomes, or grows as, a Christian; it is the declaration that someone is, in the present, a member of the people of God. This is inevitably controversial, but is I believe borne out by careful study of the relevant texts.[106] We may remind ourselves of the triple layer of meaning in Paul's "righteousness" language: The covenantal declaration, seen through the metaphorical and vital lens of the lawcourt, is

put into operation eschatologically. The verdict to be announced in the future has been brought forward into the present. Those who believe the gospel are declared to be "in the right."

Christian faith is thus the appropriate badge of membership in God's renewed people. It is accessible to all, not, like the Torah, restricted to Jews only. It perfectly expresses both that self-abandonment that refuses to claim anything as of itself, but simply casts itself on God's mercy, and, paradoxically, that genuine humanness that honors God, trusts God's power to raise the dead, and so truly worships the true God and is remade as a true human being in God's likeness. That is the point, made finally in 4:18-22, toward which the present discussion is moving.

---

106. On the way in which confusion then arises through subsequent Christian theology using the term in a significantly different sense to that of Paul, see A. E. McGrath, *Iustitia Dei: A History of the Christian Doctrine of Justification*, 2 vols. (Cambridge: James Clark, 1986) 1:2-3; N. T. Wright, *What St. Paul Really Said: Was Paul of Tarsus the Real Founder of Christianity?* (Grand Rapids: Eerdmans, 1997) chap. 7. See, e.g., Gal 2:15-21, where the question of justification is not "how to become a Christian" but "whether Jewish Christians and Gentile Christians can share table fellowship."

Romans 3:21-26, God's Righteousness Revealed Through the Faithfulness of Jesus

COMMENTARY

3:21-22a. "But now"—commentators and preachers love to roll this vintage Pauline phrase around the palate. Expressing both logical and temporal transition, it carries all the flavor of Paul's inexhaustible excitement at what God had done in Jesus the Messiah. It was, after all, news: not a new religion, nor a new ethic, but an event through which the world, Paul himself, and the situation described in 3:19-20 had been changed forever. It was the new wine that had burst the old bottles once and for all.

The paragraph thus begun—not the only time when a couple of words hint at the entire coming train of thought—continues with a summary statement of the revelation of God's righteousness. The initial mention is flanked by carefully balanced statements about the Torah, and gives rise to the fuller proposition: God's righteousness is revealed through the faithfulness of Jesus the Messiah and is for the benefit of all who believe.

The Torah has been the main theme of vv. 19-20. The first thing Paul must now do, to emphasize the newness of the good news, is to stress that this revelation has taken place

"apart from Torah." This performs two functions. Most obviously, it is Torah that has pronounced the Jews guilty, standing them in the dock alongside the pagans; if there is a new word from God, this is good news for the Jews. Less immediately obvious, but vital for Paul's developing argument, it is Torah that has erected a barrier against Gentiles; if there is a new word from God, it may be good news for Gentiles also. This double meaning, of course, corresponds negatively to Paul's emphatic and repeated statement, "to the Jew first and also the Greek" (1:16; 2:9-10).

The revelation is, however, "witnessed to by the Torah and the Prophets." Paul could no doubt have added "and the Writings," the third division of the Hebrew Bible, containing among other things the psalms, from which he will shortly quote; but the phrase "the law and the prophets" was a regular way of summarizing the whole Jewish scripture (cf. Matt 5:17; 7:12). It is vital to Paul that the fresh revelation takes place "apart from Torah," but it is equally vital that, new though it is, it is the very thing that God promised beforehand (1:2; cf. 15:7-13, the final theological summary of the whole letter). This is not just a matter of being able to "prove" the gospel from ancient authoritative scriptures. It signals the continuity and reliability of God's purpose, which is part of the meaning of God's covenant faithfulness itself.

"The righteousness of God is revealed" (not here and in v. 22 a righteousness "from" God, as in the NIV); in other words, that for which the prophets (particularly Isaiah) and the psalmists longed had come to pass. God had unveiled the covenant plan, had drawn back the curtain on the grand design; and this had been done, not in the sense merely of communicating information, but in action, as had always been promised. "Revelation" here means more than just the passing on of knowledge, important though that is as well; it means the unveiling of God through a historical event. Though it would not be strictly accurate, it would not be a very great hyperbole to say that, for Paul, "the righteousness of God" was one of the titles of Jesus the Messiah himself. God's saving justice walked around Galilee, announced the kingdom, died on a cross, and rose again. God's plan of salvation had always required a faithful Israelite to fulfill it. Now, at last, God had provided one.

This righteousness, this world-righting covenant faithfulness, has been revealed "through the faithfulness of Jesus the Messiah." Though the phrase could mean "through faith in Jesus the Messiah," the entire argument of the section strongly suggests that it is Jesus' own πίστις (*pistis*) that is spoken of and that the word here means "faithfulness," not "faith" (see the NRSV note and the secondary literature referred to in the Overview). This is not to say that Jesus himself was "justified by faith."[107] Nor does Paul envisage him, as does Hebrews, as the "pioneer" of Christian faith, the first one to believe in the way that Christians now believe (Heb 12:1-3). Nor is his "faith" a kind of meritorious work, an "active obedience" to be then accredited to those who belong to him. To be sure, Paul would have agreed that Jesus believed in the one he called Abba, Father, and that this faith sustained him in total obedience; but this is not the point he is making here. The point here is that Jesus has

offered to God, at last, the faithfulness Israel had denied (3:2-3).

A further reason why πίστις Ἰησοῦ Χριστοῦ (*pistis Iēsou Christou*) here is likely to refer to Jesus' own faithfulness is that, if taken instead to refer to the faith Christians have "in" Jesus, the next phrase ("for all who believe") becomes almost entirely redundant, adding only the (admittedly important) "all." The train of thought is clearer if we read it as "through the faithfulness of Jesus the Messiah, for the benefit of all who believe." This then corresponds closely to the reading suggested above for 1:17: from God's faithfulness to answering human faith. (It is also very close to Gal 3:22, where similar discussions have taken place.)

The paragraph's opening statement, then, declares that God's long-awaited faithfulness has been newly disclosed in the events concerning Jesus the Messiah. His faithfulness completed the role marked out for Israel and did so for the benefit of all, Jew and Gentile alike.

3:22b-24. The explanation, and with it the drawing out of further meaning in the opening statement, focuses on the universality of both plight and solution. "For there is no distinction" (the NIV, as often, omits "for"); Jew and Gentile, as we have seen, are in the dock together. Verse 23 sums up 1:18–3:20, but with a new emphasis: Human rebellion led to the loss of the glory of God (cf. 1:23). "For all sinned"—the tense is aorist, indicating a single moment, despite the almost universal perfect tense ("all have sinned") in the translations (the JB is a solitary exception, but the NJB has reversed this decision, going back to the perfect). Paul seems again to be thinking of Adam, hiding under the argument as in 1:18-25 and 7:7-12, emerging into daylight only in 5:12-21. This is confirmed by the next clause, "and they come short of God's glory." Here the tense is present, the continuing result of a past event. In Jewish literature of the period, losing God's glory is closely associated with the fall of Adam, just as the sense of regaining Adam's glory is one of the key features of the expected redemption.[108]

Paul does not at once announce that the glory has been restored, that humans are as it were re-humanized in the Messiah

107. As is argued by A. T. Hanson, *Studies in Paul's Technique and Theology* (London: SPCK, 1974) 39-51.

108. On loss of glory, see *Gen. Rab.* 12:6; *Life of Adam and Eve* 21:6. On regaining it, see 1QS 4:23; CD 3:20; 4QpPs37 3:1-2.

he will come to that in chap. 5). Instead, he announces the necessary step toward it: They are "justified" (cf. 8:30: those God justified, God glorified). Only the KJV keeps the participle of the Greek ("being justified"), which perhaps indicates that vv. 22b-23 are partly parenthetical (referring back to the point already made at length in 1:18–3:20), and that in Paul's mind v. 24 continues the main theme of the paragraph, begun in vv. 21-22a and now to be developed in detail.[109] This also explains, what Paul will repeat in v. 26, who the subject of this participle is; it is scarcely the "all" of v. 23 (except insofar as "all" here emphasizes "Jew and Gentile alike"), but rather the "all who believe" of vv. 22, 26, 28-30.

This "justification" takes place in the present time, rather than in the future as in 2:1-11. This particular "justification" is the surprising anticipation of the final verdict spoken of in that passage, and carries both the law-court meaning that we would expect from the sustained metaphor of 3:9, 19-20, and the covenantal meaning that we would expect from 2:17–3:8—these two being, as we have already explained, dovetailed together in Paul. It is God's declaration that those who believe are in the right; their sins have been dealt with; they are God's true covenant people, God's renewed humanity. This astonishing declaration needs explaining. How can the righteous judge, spoken of at the start of the chapter, make such an announcement about those who a moment ago were standing in the dock, guilty and without defense?

Paul offers three explanations, of which the third is then developed further. This justification happens "freely"; it is neither deserved nor paid for, but is pure gift.[110] More particularly, it is "by God's grace"—the first mention of "grace" since the introduction (1:5, 7), but another theme that is now going to dominate, particularly in chapters 5 and 6. "Grace" is one of Paul's most potent shorthand terms, carrying in its beautiful simplicity the entire story of God's love, active in Christ and the Spirit to do for humans what they could never

do for themselves. This, indeed, is what he at once explains in the present passage, with the last phrase of v. 24: "through the redemption that is in the Messiah, Jesus." About this there are three vital things to grasp.

The first thing to notice is that what happened in the Messiah was the gift of God's grace. Paul has no conception, as in some medieval paintings and their accompanying theology (some of which has lingered on to this day), of a stern Father-figure on a throne with the Son pleading with him, against (as it were) his better judgment, to exercise clemency. Rather, what takes place in Jesus and supremely on the cross is all from God's side. As Paul will insist in 5:6-10, the death of Jesus reveals the love of God. God does not, so to speak, have to be persuaded that Jesus' death makes a good enough case for sinners to be justified. It was God who initiated the movement in the first place.

The second point is the meaning of "redemption." At one level, this is a metaphor from the slave-market, but it is much more besides. As with the lawcourt setting of "justification," the obvious first level of metaphor is only the front door to the many-storied home of Paul's allusive writing. "Redemption" was, to be sure, a word with overtones of slaves being bought back, finding their freedom; but Israel could scarcely hear the word without thinking of Egypt, of Passover, of the Red Sea, the wilderness wanderings, and the promised land. Paul has already hinted that the whole human race languishes in the Egypt of sin (3:9—a point he will develop more explicitly in chapter 6); what such people need is a new exodus, the cosmic equivalent of what God did for Israel long ago. As we shall see, the exodus provides a key subtext, a hidden but very powerful metanarrative, for a good deal of the rest of the letter, particularly chapters 5-8.[111]

"Redemption," in other words, is not simply one term among others, a metaphor chosen at random as another bit of street-level color for the meaning of Jesus' death. It stands at the head of the dense statement that follows, evoking a whole world of thought, offering a biblical lens through which to view

109. See the helpful discussions in Cranfield, *A Critical and Exegetical Commentary on the Epistle to the Romans*, 205; Moo, *The Epistle to the Romans*, 227.

110. δωρεάν (*dōrean*) is rare in the NT but is cognate with δωρεά (*dōrea*, "gift" or "bounty"), which Paul uses as one way of referring back to this whole train of thought in 5:15, 17.

111. See N. T. Wright, "New Exodus, New Inheritance: The Narrative Substructure of Romans 3–8," in Soderlund and Wright, *Romans and the People of God*, 26-35.

what Paul is about to say. In particular, we may notice again that in Genesis 15, the passage Paul will expound in chap. 4, God promised Abraham, as the focal point of the covenant, that his seed would dwell as slaves in a foreign land and would be rescued at the proper time (Gen 15:13-16). "The redemption that is in Christ Jesus" is thus the complete fulfillment of God's covenant promise to Abraham. This is how God's covenant faithfulness is unveiled (3:21, 26; the "redemption" of the individual is linked with "the righteousness of God" in, e.g., Ps 71:19, 23-24).

Third, this redemption happens "in the Messiah, Jesus." This is where Paul makes explicit the compressed point of 3:22, that when Jesus acts in faithfulness and obedience he does so as the Messiah, Israel's representative, the one "in whom" Israel is summed up. We shall have more to say about "in Christ" when discussing chaps. 6–8; for the moment we notice that Paul's messianic christology is explicit here, at the point where he is stating how the world has been brought from guilt to grace. What the world needed (3:2) was a faithful Israelite, to carry out God's saving purpose. God has now provided one. And, because Israel itself has joined the rest of the world in the dock, this Messiah is also God's Israel *for* Israel. All have become disobedient, that mercy might be shown to all (11:32).

3:25-26. Every word and phrase in these two verses has been the subject of intense scholarly debate. It is vital to keep our bearings and remind ourselves, before examining the trees, of the shape of the forest. Paul's overall point is clearly that Jesus' death demonstrates God's righteousness, being the reason why sinners are now justified. But why has he said it like this? And what extra overtones and nuances are hereby built in to the overall argument of Romans, to be developed and picked up elsewhere?

It will not do to detach all or part of these verses, declare them a pre-Pauline fragment, and so relativize their force within the current argument. It is by no means impossible that Paul was making use, in what is after all a highly charged and densely packed statement, of phrases already familiar in early Christianity. But, here of all places, he is very unlikely to have allowed himself to say something he did not mean; and, once we have grasped the

meaning of "God's righteousness" in 3:21, it should be clear that the repeated emphasis of the same point in 3:25, 26 is not (as some have said) an intrusion from a "Jewish Christian" context in which God's covenant faithfulness was important, but which Paul himself has all but left behind (see the Overview). For Paul, we must not tire of repeating, God's covenant faithfulness did not mean a reaffirmation of a supposed "favored nation clause"; nor did it mean that salvation-history proceeded in a smooth developmental line. Rather, it meant that God was fulfilling the promise to Abraham that he would have a faithful family composed of Jews and Gentiles alike. We are right, then, to see these verses as expressing the heart of that which Paul began to say in 3:21.[112]

We are right, also, to interpret this dense statement of the meaning of Jesus' death in the light of the other statements in subsequent passages. We should neither press one or two words here to say more than they do, nor forbid the recognition, by reference to other passages in the letter, of a larger world of thought in the light of which the present statement makes the sense Paul intends (cf., e.g., 4:24-5; 5:6-10, 15-21; 8:3-4; we could also, of course, appeal to other letters—notably Galatians—but it is important to keep the argument here as tight as possible).

We may remind ourselves again that the covenant was put in place precisely to deal with sin. Abraham was called so that through his family God might undo the problem of Adam—the problem (in other words) Paul has set out extensively in 1:18–3:20. This is exactly the sequence of that larger logic in which 3:21–4:25 replies to the preceding section. If, then, God has been faithful to the covenant, it must be clear that sins have indeed been dealt with. This is a matter not simply of lawcourt "justice," but of covenant theology; the latter includes the former and must not be played off against it. God's creation of a new Jew-plus-Gentile family was the aim; forgiveness of sins the necessary means.

---

112. The NIV reveals the weakness of its mistranslation of 3:21 ("a righteousness from God," repeated at 3:22) when at 3:25-26 it is forced to translate the same word with "justice" and to acknowledge that the justice in question is God's. This simply deconstructs the tight logic of 3:21-26. Moo, *Romans*, 219, 240, reveals the same problem as the NIV.

Hence the double statement about the demonstration of God's righteousness in 3:25 b-26, which we may take first in order to give ourselves maximum purchase on the difficult 3:25 a. God has put Jesus forward (see below) in order to display, to prove, to demonstrate that covenant faithfulness, that saving justice, which would otherwise be called into question (3:1-8).[113] In particular, God had passed over, that is, left unpunished, acts of sin committed in former times. God, it seems (Paul here takes this for granted), had been forbearing, patient, unwilling to foreclose on the human race in general or Israel in particular. Paul had emphasized this in 2:3-6, where the same word is used, and he now refers back to that point.[114] The first question at issue, then—the aspect of God's righteousness that might seem to have been called into question and is now demonstrated after all—is God's proper dealing with sins— i.e., punishment. Whatever Paul is saying in the first half of v. 25, it must be such as to lead to the conclusion that now, at last, God has punished sins as they deserved.

The second half of the double statement, which occupies v. 26, repeats almost verbatim the phrase about demonstrating God's righteousness (or covenant faithfulness, or saving justice), but this time takes it in a different direction. First, Paul adds "in the present time"; this is cognate with the "but now" at the start of the paragraph and emphasizes both that the past problem has reached a present conclusion and that the future verdict has been brought forward into the present time. One does not now have to wait for a future judgment to see the covenant people of God manifested (nor, as Paul will stress in vv. 27-30, can one see this through works of Torah). They are revealed in the present time by God's action in Christ.

This means that God is now seen to be "just, and the justifier." God, as both the covenant God and the "righteous judge" of the lawcourt metaphor, displays "righteousness," not simply through dealing with sins as they

deserved, but also, in his summing up of the case, through finding in favor of this category of people. We must remind ourselves again that this declaration, this decision of the judge, is what constitutes these people as "righteous." The word is primarily forensic/covenantal and only secondarily (what we would call) "ethical." God's justifying activity is the declaration that this people are "in the right," in other words, announcing the verdict in their favor. Calling them "righteous," as one must on this basis, should not be misunderstood to mean that God has after all recognized that they possess ethical characteristics that have commended themselves, caused their sins to be overlooked, and persuaded the judge that they deserved a favorable verdict. To say that they are "righteous" means that the judge has found in their favor; or, translating back into covenantal categories, that the covenant God has declared them to be the covenant people.

The point, anyway, is that the display of God's righteousness in the death of Jesus is the basis for God's justifying declaration of this category of people.[115] As we come closer to the hardest part of the passage, v. 25 a, we notice at this stage that Paul clearly intends that clause to prepare the way for this statement of God's justifying declaration. Whatever precisely Paul intends to say, it must have to do with the means by which the righteous God could, without compromising that righteousness, find in favor of the ungodly (4:5).

Paul's final description (v. 26 b) of the object of God's justifying declaration is very elliptical: τὸν ἐκ πίστεως Ἰησοῦ (*ton ek pisteōs Iēsou*, "the one"; lit., "out of the faith[fulness] of Jesus"). (We may compare the condensed descriptions in 2:29.) Here the referent is not in doubt; the person concerned is a Christian. But is "of Jesus" an objective or subjective genitive? In other words, is Paul referring to

---

113. ἔνδειξις (*endeixis*, "demonstration" or "proof") makes more emphatic the general πεφανέρωται (*pephanerōtai*, "is manifested," 3:21) and ἀποκαλύπτεται (*apokalyptetai*, "is revealed," 1:16), stressing particularly the divine answer to the possible charge of ἀδικία (*adikia*, "unrighteousness," 3:3-5).

114. The phrase ἐν τῇ ἀνοχῇ τοῦ θεοῦ (*en tē anochē tou theou*, "in the forbearance of God") opens v. 26 in the Greek editions, but the English versions rightly treat it as part of the unit of thought at the end of 3:25.

115. The meaning of καί (*kai*) in 3:26 is contested. (1) If rendered "and," it implies that Paul is making two statements: (a) that God is just and (b) that God justifies the Jesus-faith people. (2) If translated "even" or "namely," Paul would be saying that God's justice in this case consists in God's justifying activity (so most commentators). If translated "even though," he would be emphasizing that God's punitive justice is satisfied by Christ's death so that now sinners can be justified (see Moo, *Romans*, 242). Although the theological arguments against the last of these (e.g., Fitzmyer, *Romans*, 353; Byrne, *Romans*, 134) are not strong, the wider meaning of δικαιοσύνη θεοῦ (*dikaiosynē theou*) elsewhere in the passage suggests that the first is more likely.

the Christian's "faith in Jesus" (as NIV), or, as in v. 22, to Jesus' own "faith(fulness)"?[116]

It could in principle be the former. Paul has already referred to Christian faith in 3:22 (and perhaps in 3:25a, on which see below). He is about to mount an argument in 3:27-31 in which the faith of Christians is central. But he normally speaks of the object of Christian faith not as Jesus, but as God—as, for example, in the striking phrase in 4:24, "those who believe in the God who raised Jesus from the dead." Granted the importance of Jesus' faithfulness in the argument of this passage, stated proleptically in 3:22 (see above), it is more likely that what he means here, stated still in condensed form, is that God justifies the one whose status rests on the faithful death of Jesus. Even there, of course, the notion of the believer's own faith is not absent, since it is this faith that precipitates God's announcement of the verdict in the present time. But the basis for this faith is precisely the faithfulness of Jesus seen as the manifestation of the covenant faithfulness of God.

We must now return to the opening words of v. 25, whose meaning we have seen to be constrained by vv. 25b-26. Somehow, what Paul says here is designed to explain how it is that God has now dealt with sins on the one hand and declared "the one out of the faithfulness of Jesus" to be in the right on the other.

The initial surprise, granted that such language has not made its way into Romans until now, is that v. 25a is heavily sacrificial in content. God "put Jesus forth," says Paul, using a quite rare verb many of whose LXX uses are to do with the shewbread in the Temple (cf. Exod 29:23; 40:4, 23; Lev 24:8; 2 Macc 1:8). Jesus was put forth as a ἱλαστήριον (hilastērion)—a term whose precise translation focuses the problem of the clause but is undoubtedly cultic in context. And this was effective "through his blood," again a clear sacrificial reference. How does this work? What is Paul's train of thought? Why does he here refer to Jesus' death in sacrificial terms?

How does sacrificial language come together with the overarching exposition of the righteousness of God? And how does the sacrifice of Jesus mean that sins have now been dealt with, creating a "righteous" people and leaving God's righteousness unimpeachable?

The language Paul uses goes back to Leviticus. In Lev 16:2 the *hilastērion* was the "mercy-seat," the lid on top of the ark of the covenant, the place where God appeared in the cloud to meet with Israel (cf. Exod 25:17-22; 31:7; 35:12; 37:6-9 [38:5-8 LXX]; Num 7:89; Amos 9:1). In this chapter, which prescribes the ritual for the Day of Atonement, the "mercy-seat" has a crucial role: It is the place where Aaron is to sprinkle the blood of the bullock and goat of the sin-offering (vv. 14-15), having first lit the incense to create a cloud around the mercy-seat, so that he may not die from being in the presence of God (v. 13). The sprinkling of the blood is to make atonement for the holy place, because of the Israelites' uncleannesses, transgressions, and sins (v. 16). The LXX verb for "make atonement for" (ἐξιλάσκεται *exilasketai*) is from the same root as *hilastērion*.

Paul's other references to Jesus' death indicate that sacrificial ideas, though not his only grid of reference, were not far from his mind when he thought of the cross. In particular, elsewhere in Romans he refers to the crucifixion in terms of the sin-offering, in a context that makes it clear that he intends this precise reference to be heard (8:3, on which see below). But he does not elsewhere refer explicitly to the great Day of Atonement. He does not, for example, develop the idea of Jesus as sacrifice, or indeed as priest, in the way we find in the Letter to the Hebrews. However, on a broader canvas it is a natural Second Temple Jewish perception to see God's faithfulness to Israel (and Israel's answering loyalty to God) expressed through the temple cult and to see God's righteousness expressed in the face of Israel's sins through the sacrifices in general and the Day of Atonement in particular. To put it another way, if Israel is in trouble because of sin, the Day of Atonement will put things to rights.[117] To that extent, what Paul has done is simply to declare that God has done the same thing

---

116. The NRSV's note "who has the faith of Jesus" takes the genitive as subjective but implies that Paul's point would thereby be that Jesus' own "faith" is somehow either the model for Christian faith or even its substance (as though Jesus' own faith were somehow infused into the believer). It seems far more likely that, if the subjective genitive is the right reading, that πίστις (*pistis*) here means "faithfulness." In any case, to render *ton ek pisteōs* as "who has the faith" seems to strain the meaning of the Greek almost intolerably.

117. See Wright, *The New Testament and the People of God*, 272-79.

on a once-for-all, grand scale; he is, in that sense, alluding to Jesus as the place where the holy God and sinful Israel meet, in such a way that Israel, rather than being judged, receives atonement.

But this does not plumb the full depths of what Paul is saying here. In particular, it does not provide an explanation of the intimate connection Paul is assuming between a human death and this sacrificial language; nor between this sacrificial death and God's dealing with Israel's sins such as would justify the immediate conclusion of v. 25 *b*; nor between this whole complex of thought and "the righteousness of God." What other contexts of meaning were available to a Second Temple Jew that might explain all this?

The most obvious answer can be found in the stories of the Maccabaean martyrs. Whatever actually happened in the torrid years of Syrian oppression in the 160s BCE, the story as it was told in Paul's day sometimes interpreted the martyrs' deaths in sacrificial terms. Second Maccabees clearly regards the suffering of the martyrs as bound up with God's special purposes for Israel. Other nations, says the author, go unpunished, in the patience of God, until finally they reach the full measure of their sins; but Israel's punishment is brought forward, being visited on the righteous, in order that God's mercy may remain with Israel (2 Macc 6:12-16). Though this is not exactly Paul's meaning, there is close similarity with the thought he expresses in 2:3-6 and in the mention of God's patience in the present verse. It is in this setting that the youngest of the seven famous martyred brothers declares that their suffering will soon bring an end to the wrath of the Almighty that had justly fallen upon the whole nation (2 Macc 7:38, the climax of the speech). The writer of 4 Maccabees is even more explicit: As Eleazar is being martyred, he prays that the punishment he and the others are enduring may suffice for the nation, that his blood may be their purification, and that his life may be received in exchange for theirs (4 Macc 6:28-29). Their death, says the writer, purified the land; they became as a "ransom" (ἀντίψυχον *antipsychon*) for the sin of the nation. Through their blood, and through their death seen as a *hilastērion*

(NRSV, "atoning sacrifice"), divine providence has preserved Israel.[118]

It was, then, thinkable in Paul's period that the suffering of the righteous Jew might in some way atone, as a sacrifice did, for Israel. These Maccabaean passages, in fact, belong within a larger world of thought for which there is no space here.[119] But even this does not completely explain how Paul's whole sequence of logic fits together. The Second Temple trains of thought that enabled some writers to construe martyrdom in terms of sacrificial and other redemptive actions went back, in the biblical tradition, to passages in the book of Daniel, such as 11:35 and 12:1-10, where imagery from the temple cult is applied to human suffering. And behind Daniel itself, clearly alluded to there and in much other literature familiar in Paul's day, stands Isaiah, particularly chaps. 40–55.[120] Although the attempt to read Paul, and particularly Romans, in the light of these chapters has been controversial, the argument so far shows that there is a good deal to be said for such an allusion as at least part of the explanation of the present passage.

The major point to be made here is that in Isaiah 40–55 we have a sustained exposition of the righteousness of God, focused more and more tightly on a suffering figure who represents Israel and fulfills YHWH's purpose of being a light to the nations and whose sufferings and death are finally seen in explicitly sacrificial terms.[121] We have, that is, exactly that combination of elements that we have observed, and that are otherwise puzzling in exactly that combination, in Rom 3:21-26. In other words, the sacrifical language of 3:25, used in connection with the violent death of a righteous Jew at the hands of pagans, makes sense within the context of the current martyr stories; but those martyr stories themselves send us back, by various routes, to Isaiah 40–55; and when we get

118. 17:22; an alternative reading of the passage takes *hilastērion* as adjectival, qualifying θάνατος (*thanatos*), "a propitiatory death." so H. G. R. Liddell, R. Scott, H. S. Jones, *A Greek-English Lexicon*, 9th ed. (Oxford: Oxford University Press, 1996), apparently omitting the τοῦ (*tou*) that in Rahlfs' ed. of the LXX stands before θανάτου (*thanatou*). See A. Rahlfs, *Septuaginta* (Stuttgart: Deutsche Bibelgesellschaft, 1979).

119. Fuller details in Wright, *Jesus and the Victory of God*, 576-84.

120. See Wright, *Jesus and the Victory of God*, 584, 588-91, with other refs. there to both primary and secondary literature.

121. For "the righteousness of God" in Isaiah 40–55, see 46:13; 51:5-6, 8. The idea of God's covenant faithfulness, through which Israel is redeemed and creation itself is renewed, is central to the whole section, both when the phrase occurs and when it is assumed.

there we find just those themes that we find in Romans 3.

Neither in the fourth servant song (Isa 52:13–53:12) nor at other key points in the prophet do we find the same sacrificial language that Paul uses in 3:25. However, what we do find is that the language and thought of Isa 52:13–53:12 crop up at key points in Paul's subsequent argument, leaving us in little doubt (unless we are arguably far too stringent in what we will allow as an allusion) that Paul did indeed have this passage in mind. Thus in 4:25, summing up the entire train of thought from 3:21, Paul uses the verb παρεδόθη (*paredothē*, "he was given up"), which occurs twice in Isa 53:12, with the active form ("the Lord gave him up") in 53:6; in both cases this happened "for our sins," as in 4:25.[122] And when in 5:15, 19 Paul speaks of Jesus' act of obedience availing to justify "the many," this is a clear allusion to Isa 53:11-12 (some also see a reference to Isa 53:5 in Rom 5:1). Further afield, Paul quotes Isa 52:15 in Rom 15:21 and Isa 53:1 in Rom 10:16.

The significance of Isaiah 40–55 here lies in its ability to tie together and explain what otherwise is inexplicable, namely why Paul should imagine that the death of Jesus, described in sacrificial terms, should be supposed not only to reveal the righteousness of God but also to deal properly, i.e. punitively, with sins. The idea of punishment as part of atonement is itself deeply controversial; horrified rejection of the mere suggestion has led on the part of some to an unwillingness to discern any reference to Isaiah 40–55 in Paul.[123] But it is exactly this idea that Paul states, clearly and unambiguously, in 8:3, when he says that God "condemned sin in the flesh"—i.e., the flesh of Jesus.

All this may be of help when it comes to the precise meaning of *hilastērion*. By itself, as we saw, it meant "mercy-seat," the focal point of the great ritual of the Day of Atonement; and, thence, the place and/or the means of dealing both with wrath (or

punishment) and with sin.[124] Dealing with wrath or punishment is propitiation; with sin, expiation. You propitiate a person who is angry; you expiate a sin, crime, or stain on your character. Vehement rejection of the former idea in many quarters has led some to insist that only "expiation" is in view here. But the fact remains that in 1:18–3:20 Paul has declared that the wrath of God is revealed against all ungodliness and wickedness and that despite God's forbearance this will finally be meted out; that in 5:8, and in the whole promise of 8:1-30, those who are Christ's are rescued from wrath; and that the passage in which the reason for the change is stated is 3:25-26, where we find that God, though in forbearance allowing sins to go unpunished for a while, has now revealed that righteousness, that saving justice, that causes people to be declared "righteous" even though they were sinners.

The lexical history of the word *hilastērion* is sufficiently flexible to admit of particular nuances in different contexts. Paul's context here demands that the word not only retain its sacrificial overtones (the place and means of atonement), but that it carry the note of propitiation of divine wrath—with, of course, the corollary that sins are expiated. It should go without saying that this in no way implies, what the start of the verse has already ruled out, that God is an angry malevolent tyrant who demands someone's death, or someone's blood, and is indifferent as to whose it is. The point Paul is making, carried by the word *hilastērion*, is that Jesus' death was God's answer both to the plight of the world and to the problems outlined in 3:1-8—the problems, that is, for God's own justice, truth, and faithfulness. To the objection, that sacrifices in Leviticus and other biblical texts do not seem to be propitiatory, the response must be that, as we have seen, by Paul's time sacrificial language was used in exactly this way, precisely of the righteous Israelites whose deaths somehow exhausted the divine wrath that was otherwise suspended over Israel. To see Jesus as the place where atonement is made (the narrow, focused meaning of the word) and hence

---

122. Paul uses παράπτωμα (*paraptōma*, "trespass"), not ἁμαρτία (*hamartia*, "sin") as in LXX Isa 53:5, 12, but the allusion is clear nonetheless. *Paraptōma* never occurs in LXX Isaiah.

123. The hasty rejection of such a train of thought as hopelessly Anselmic is seen, for instance, in Fitzmyer, *Romans*, 353.

124. For the mass of details, see Cranfield, *A Critical and Exegetical Commentary on the Epistle to the Romans*, 214-18; Moo, *The Epistle to the Romans*, 231-36. Bryan, *A Preface to Romans*, 112, argues, against Cranfield, that the meaning "mercy-seat" can indeed make sense here. See also Stuhlmacher, *Paul's Letter to the Romans*, 58-59.

as the means by which atonement is made (in the broader context of the echoes set up by the word, and the entire passage) is exactly what is needed at this point in the passage.

There remain the two phrases by which *hilastērion* is qualified: "through faith" and "by means of his blood." These are most likely intended as independent modifiers of the noun, rather than the former modifying the latter ("through faith in his blood," as though the blood of Jesus were itself the object of faith). In addition, the reading we have cautiously recommended for "faith" in 3:22 and 3:26, i.e., the faithfulness of Jesus, his obedience to the divine saving plan, inclines one to the possibility—it can hardly be stronger—that this is Paul's meaning here as well. Jesus' faithfulness was the means by which the act of atonement was accomplished, by which there took place that meeting between God and the whole world of which the mercy-seat was the advance symbol. Furthermore, just as the mercy-seat fulfilled its function when sprinkled with sacrificial blood, so Paul sees the blood of Jesus as actually instrumental in bringing about that meeting of grace and helplessness, of forgiveness and sin, that occurred on the cross. Once again, the sacrificial imagery points beyond the cult to the reality of God's self-giving act in Jesus.

I suggest, therefore, that Paul has here condensed, in typical manner, three trains of thought into a single statement, to which he will then refer back, explaining himself more fully as he does so. First, the righteousness of God is revealed in God's giving of Jesus as the faithful Israelite, through whom the covenant plan to save the world from sin will be put into operation at last, despite universal failure. Second, Jesus' faithfulness was precisely faithfulness unto death, a death understood in such sacrificial terms as would evoke not only the Day of Atonement but also the self-giving of the martyrs and, behind and greater than that, the sacrificial suffering of the Servant. Third, Jesus' self-giving faithfulness to death, seen as the act of God, not of humans operating toward God, had the effect of turning away the divine wrath that otherwise hung over not only Israel but also the whole world. Thus is God's righteousness revealed in the gospel events of Jesus' death and resurrection: God has been true to the covenant, has dealt properly with sin, has come to the rescue of the helpless and has done so with due impartiality between Jew and Gentile. Although Jesus' death is the means by which God's righteousness is revealed, and that righteousness is the main subject of the section, Paul does not supply a more extensive treatment of Calvary. But what he says here is one of the key foundations for what he will go on to argue. In order to expound his major themes, he needs a firm basis in what subsequent writers would call atonement-theology. This passage has now provided it.

REFLECTIONS

1. The most important point for all subsequent Christian generations to grasp from this dense but explosive paragraph is that the righteousness—the saving justice, the covenant faithfulness—of the creator God was unveiled once and for all in the death of Jesus, the Jewish Messiah. This claim appears counter-intuitive in the contemporary world, the usual reason given being the fact that the world, and often enough the church, does not look as if Jesus' death has made a dramatic difference to them. Justice has not come to the world. Regularly, therefore, the meaning of Jesus' death has been reduced to that of an example, albeit the supreme one, of the love of God—a general truth that happened to be exemplified in one specific instance, rather than an event through which the world became a different place. Or it has been used to construct a particular kind of "atonement theology" that rescues souls out of the world while leaving this-worldly injustice unaffected. Either way, theology and exegesis have retreated from Paul's vision of God's justice unveiled on the cross.

There are, in fact, other agendas that press upon the contemporary world and insist that nothing significant can actually have happened when Jesus died. The Renaissance world saw itself as the new beginning—the revival of the best of the past, to be sure, but the new start through which everything would now be different. Whoever invented the idea of the "Middle Ages," thereby designating their own age as the start of the new period, was not only one of the most powerful figures in the history of ideas, but also the perpetrator of the belief that the real change in history had not come about in the first century of the common era, but at some much more recent time. The Enlightenment swapped the idea that history had turned its critical corner in Palestine in the first century for the belief that the moment had happened instead in Western Europe in the eighteenth century. The tacit assumption of this point of view is the deeper reason why the Pauline claim sounds simply incredible to so many. It offers a rival eschatology to that by which our culture has lived.

The claim makes the sense it does, of course, within a broadly Jewish, i.e., biblical, worldview. It was first-century Jews like Paul who were expecting their God, the creator and covenant God, to act in history in such a way that the world might recognize the divine power and faithfulness. However, precisely because this Jewish/biblical worldview posited a God who was the creator of the whole cosmos and who intended to address all humans, neither the worldview nor the Pauline claim could ever be conceived as mere private opinions. They were for all, and if they remained meaningless for all they might be thought to have failed. Hence Paul's Gentile mission, which is in view already in 3:23-24: Jew and Gentile alike sinned, but Jew and Gentile alike are now declared to be God's people as a free gift. The revelation of God's righteousness is an event of cosmic significance.

The task of teaching Christian people to think and live on the basis of a unique event that happened in the first century, but that was the turning point of cosmic history, is therefore, hard though it may seem, one of the most Pauline tasks facing a preacher and teacher today. The resurrection (vital, though unmentioned, in the logic of this paragraph) is, of course, the event that anchors this eschatological belief; if Christ is not raised, as Paul says elsewhere (1 Cor 15:17), faith is futile and we are still in our sins. In other words, if the resurrection has not happened, God's new world has not begun. We could still use Jesus as an example, his teaching as a wonderful and teasing challenge. But none of Romans would make any sense.

2. God's covenant faithfulness, that saving justice of which Paul speaks, demands further exploration. The loyalty of God to promises made, the unbreakable commitment to working through Israel even when Israel became faithless, is a theme not sufficiently remarked on or thought through. But only in this light can we grasp the full meaning of Jesus' Messiahship. Only thus can we comprehend his taking on of Israel's vocation to be God's faithful partner in the project for which Abraham had originally been called.

The wider dimension at which this hints is God's faithfulness to the human project itself, and indeed to the whole cosmos. To this we shall return in chapters 5 and 8, and in the wider reflections on chapters 9–11. Because Paul eventually opens up these other dimensions, we do well to remind ourselves here that the present paragraph, though its prime focus is on how God was true to the promises made to Israel and through Israel for the world, points beyond itself to the promises and commands given by God to all humankind. The challenge is then to work out how the cross of Jesus unveils, in a decisive action, those promises as well; and how to live on the basis of the belief that it does so.

3. Within that, of course, the paragraph states in sharp and concise form the extraordinary and still earth-shattering proposition that the creator God has acted to provide the deeply costly remedy for the plight that hangs over all humankind. Not to be deeply moved by this is to fail to listen. "Freely . . . by God's grace . . . God set him forth . . . that God might be savingly just, and the justifier." God's initiative, energy, and commitment to carrying through the project of the justification of sinners is at the heart of Paul's message and is the true source of all genuine Christian devotion. Verses 24-26 could stand as a heading over one gospel passage after another, as though to say, "This is what this story is all about."

4. Within that again, these verses highlight one aspect of Paul's complex portrait of Jesus: his faithfulness. Given a vocation, he was true to it, though it cost him everything. This is not said in order to be an example, to make us feel guilty once more about our own faithfulness, our half-heartedness in pursuing our own tasks, though no doubt this may be an accidental side effect. It is a matter for awe and gratitude. Paul does not here note the way in which this action of Jesus impinges on each believer personally, but those with ears to hear will detect, just below the surface of the paragraph, his words in Galatians: The son of God loved me and gave himself for me (Gal 2:20). It is this utter faithfulness, seen as an act of love, that will sustain the whole argument of Romans from this point to the end of the letter; and it can also sustain the believer and the Christian community through all the trials that beset them. It is significant that at the point where Paul says exactly this, his normal mode of speaking about "the love of God" slips, and he speaks instead of "the love of the Messiah" (8:35). It is that kind of subtle change that tells us where his heart really is.

Romans 3:27-31, One God, One Faith, One People

COMMENTARY

The connection of this paragraph to what precedes, and the internal logic within it, have both sometimes seemed difficult.[125] This is largely due to the interpretation, within the Reformation tradition and elsewhere, that treats "justification" as meaning "how someone becomes a Christian," "law" as a general moral code rather than the Jewish Torah, and "boasting" as the activity of "legalists" who, having kept whatever moral code they may be aware of, believe that they have thereby established a claim upon God, have somehow "earned" their status of "righteousness," their designation as "righteous." Within this, Paul's contrast of "works of law" and "faith" becomes more a matter of method than content: "Works" have to do with achievement, and "faith" is the abandoning of one's own efforts and trust in God instead. Paul is thus supposed to be standing alongside Augustine in his battle against Pelagius, alongside Luther

in his fight against Rome. Further, though this is not always noticed, Paul is often aligned thereby with the Enlightenment in its elevation of abstract truth against this-worldly reality ("faith" as a "spiritual" matter, "works" as having to do with material things); with the Romantic movement in its elevation of feeling over outward reality, ritual, and so on; and with twentieth-century existentialism in its insistence on being true to one's inner motivations rather than being constrained from outside. Not for nothing could Rudolf Bultmann read Heidegger into the New Testament and claim to be a good Lutheran.

It is important to say that the battles of Augustine and Luther were not entirely mistaken. Paul's whole thought is characterized by the free grace of God, and any suggestion that humans, whether Jewish or Gentile, might somehow put God in their debt, might perhaps earn their good standing within God's people, would be anathema to him. This, however, is not the issue he was

125. See Cranfield, *Romans*, 218.

facing. Contemporary studies of first-century Judaism indicate that Paul's contemporaries did not think like Pelagius or Erasmus; they were not bent on earning their justification, or their salvation, from scratch by performing the "works of the law." The overarching context of the covenant embraced all Jewish law-keeping; the most detailed exploration of what living by Torah involved must be seen as falling within the category of response to grace, rather than the attempt to merit it.[126] In any case, whether or not we allow this point, we find that some of Paul's key arguments, when taken to refer to the problem that Luther thought Paul was talking about, simply do not work. The exegesis does not come away clean. The present paragraph is a case in point (see the Commentary on chap. 4; 9:30–10:13). The proof of the theories must lie, ultimately, in the coherence of the exegesis. Much of Galatians could be called as further evidence.

The link between 3:21-26 and 3:27-31, made initially by the "therefore" at the start of v. 27 ("then," NIV, NRSV), indicates that Paul is now drawing the conclusion he has always had in mind from the brief and dense statement of the revelation of God's righteousness in Jesus' messianic faithfulness unto death. He is returning, in fact, to the question he raised in 2:17-24, that of the "boasting" of "the Jew" (see the Commentary on 2:17). The point here is that Paul is now ruling out the "boast" whereby "the Jew" maintained a status above that of the Gentiles. Paul is not addressing the more general "boast" of the moral legalist whose system of salvation is one of self-effort, but the ethnic pride of Israel according to the flesh, supported as it was by the possession of the Torah and the performance of those "works" that set Israel apart from the pagans.

This explains the crucial turn in the paragraph. If the statements of vv. 27-28 are not true, this would mean that God is the God of Jews only, not of Gentiles also. The point of the whole paragraph, not just vv. 29-30, is that, because there is one God—the central Jewish belief, of course—there must ultimately be one people of God; and, therefore, that people must be marked out by something other than the Jewish law, which would have left a high fence down the middle of the church, with Jewish Christians on one side and Gentile Christians on the other. That, again, is the main thrust of chap. 4, to which the paragraph points in several particulars, and also of Galatians 2–3, with which the present paragraph has many points of overlap.

3:27. Boasting is excluded. It is always risky to guess at how onomatopoeia might have worked in an ancient language, but the verb ἐξεκλείσθη (*exekleisthē*) has, to my ear at least, the ring of a door being slammed shut. The revelation of God's righteousness in Jesus' death shuts out once for all any suggestion that there might be a special status, a "favored nation clause," for ethnic Israel. God's righteousness, in other words, has not been revealed, as had been expected, in some great victory whereby Israel overcame her enemies and obtained national liberation. It came about through the Messiah's dying at the hands of the pagans, as the great act of atonement needed not only by Israel but also by the whole world. This is why a crucified Messiah is "a scandal to Jews" (1 Cor 1:23) and why Paul can speak of his having been "crucified with the Messiah" (Gal 2:19). A crucified Messiah is either an impossibility (as Paul would have said before his conversion) or it must spell the end of Israel's ethnic "boast." This, of course, will be followed up in a good deal more detail in chaps. 9–11.

The means of boasting's exclusion is then stated compactly. Israel's status depended on the gift and performance of Torah; how is the new arrangement undergirded? What sort of Torah sustains it? The Torah characterized by "works"? No; the Torah characterized by "faith." It is, of course, controversial to take νόμος (*nomos*) here as "Torah" throughout; a long tradition, represented by NIV, has taken it as "principle"—which then causes the mistranslation of τῶν ἔργων (*tōn ergōn*; lit., "of works") as "on [the principle] of observing the law." Paul's point is more subtle and is once again so dense here that we need to call on the fuller statements later in the letter (in this case 8:1-6; 9:30–10:13) to come to our help.[127]

---

126. This is what Sanders has famously called "covenantal nomism." See particularly Sanders, *Paul and Palestinian Judaism.*

127. On the debate, see Moo, *Romans,* 247-50 (taking the usual line that "law" means "principle"); see Cranfield, *Romans,* 219-20, whom I follow with slight modifications.

He is already beginning that line of thought that, in 7:7-25, will see Torah cleared of blame, though itself helpless in the cause of justification or salvation, and that, in chap. 10, will see him describe Christian faith as that which really fulfills Torah, even where the believers, if they are Gentiles, have never heard it. Paul has already hinted at this line of thought in 2:25-29: "uncircumcised people who keep the law's decrees" is an oxymoron, unless Paul is thinking of a deeper "keeping of Torah," a "fulfillment" of Torah (2:27, τὸν νόμον τελοῦσα *ton nomon telousa*) that takes place not in the letter and the outward works that define Jew from Gentile, but in the heart (see also 1 Cor 7:19).

Paul is thus distinguishing, not for the last time in the letter, between the Torah seen in two different ways. On the one hand, there is "the Torah of works"—this is Torah seen as that which defines Israel over against the nations, witnessed by the performance of the works that Torah prescribes—not only sabbath, food-laws and circumcision, though these are the obvious things that, sociologically speaking, give substance to the theologically based separation.[128] On the other hand, there is the new category Paul is forging here: "the Torah of faith," in a sense yet to be explained (like many things in chap. 3), gives the indication of where the true, renewed people of God are to be found. He is unwilling, it seems, to give up the belief that the God-given Torah defines the people of God. What he has done is to deny that performing "the works of Torah," the things that define Israel ethnically, is the appropriate mode of use for Torah. Rather, the Torah is to be fulfilled through faith; in other words, where someone believes the gospel, there Torah is in fact being fulfilled, even though in a surprising way (on this whole topic, see the Commentary on 9:30–10:13).

3:28. Paul now explains the antithesis between "the law of works" and "the law of faith" by declaring that a person is "justified by faith apart from works of the law." This, interestingly in view of the history of interpretation, is not itself a conclusion for which he has so far argued in the present letter (despite the KJV's "we conclude" and the NEB's "for our argument is"); it is a further belief that he

is simply stating, as part of his present actual argument that Jewish boasting ("we possess Torah, therefore we are inalienably God's people") is excluded by the revelation of God's covenant faithfulness. The actual argument for justification by faith comes in the next chapter. The word for "we hold" (NRSV) or "we maintain" (NIV) is in fact λογιζόμεθα (*logizometha*): "we reckon," "we calculate." Paul is reporting on a calculation that has taken place, not in the present passage, but elsewhere, which he will shortly unveil.

The greatest problem facing the contemporary reader in understanding what Paul means by "a person is justified" is that centuries of usage of the English word "justify," and of its Latin root and its French and German equivalents, have assumed that "to be justified" meant much the same as "to be converted," "to be born again," "to become a Christian."[129] The further debates that have occurred have often taken their starting-point from there, distinguishing for instance between the beginning of the the process of becoming a Christian and the continuation of that to the end. The question of an *ordo salutis*, the sequence of events that takes a person from outright unbelief through to final salvation, has been hugely influential in some circles, and I recognize that my insistence on letting Paul say what he means by his own key terms does violence to many such well-loved frameworks of thought.[130] This is not, by the way, a matter of the so-called "new perspective" on Paul, though insights from Sanders, Dunn and others, critically sifted and factored in where appropriated, must make their contribution. It is a matter of exegesis; and when we exegete Paul we find that when he talks about what later theology denotes as "conversion" and "regeneration" he speaks of God's "call" through which, by the work of the Spirit, people come to faith. "Those God called, God justified; those God

---

128. On the symbols of Jewish identity, see Wright, *The New Testament and the People of God*, 224-41.

129. On the history of the doctrine of justification, see Alister E. McGrath, *Iustitia Dei: A History of the Christian Doctrine of Justification*, 2 vols. (Cambridge: Cambridge University Press, 1986). McGrath rightly notes (1:2-3) that the usage of the term "justification" in Christian theology does not correspond exactly to the more precise Pauline meaning; he does not draw out all the ways in which this has vitiated the exegetical endeavors of those theologians who have sought to ground their views in Paul. See Wright, *What St. Paul Really Said*, chap. 7.

130. I have in mind Mark A. Seifrid, *Justification by Faith: The Origin and Development of a Central Pauline Theme*, NovTSup 68 (Leiden: Brill, 1992); and *Christ Our Righteousness: Paul's Theology of Justification* (Downers Grove: InterVarsity, 2000).

justified, God also glorified": Rom 8:30 is Paul's clearest *ordo salutis*, and we will not go far wrong if we stick to it.

Of course, what Paul means by "justification" is closely linked to the question of how people who start off as sinners end up being glorified; but the word "justify" and its cognates do not refer to the event of "conversion" or the process of Christian living, for which he uses other language (see, for instance, 1 Thess 1:5; 2:13). They refer to God's declaration that certain persons are members of the covenant people, that their sins have been dealt with. Nor is it true—as anxious opponents of the "new perspective" are wont to say—that I am here simply reverting to the old either/or made famous by Wrede and Schweitzer, that Paul only talks about justification and the law in order to address a particular problem in the church. When we understand the place of Israel within his vision of God's purposes for the world, the relation of Jew and Gentile can never be an incidental side-issue.

Anyway, Paul's point in the present passage is quite simply that what now marks out the covenant people of God, in the light of the revelation of God's righteousness in Jesus, is not the works of Torah that demarcate ethnic Israel, but "the law of faith," the faith that, however paradoxically, is in fact the true fulfilling of Torah. There is no problem in adding the word "alone" to the word "faith"—a tradition that goes way back beyond Luther, at least to Aquinas—as long as we recognize what it means: not that a person is "converted" by faith alone without moral effort (that is true, but it is not the truth that Paul is stressing here), nor that God's grace is always prior to human response (that is equally true, and equally not Paul's emphasis here), but that the badge of membership in God's people, the badge that enables all alike to stand on the same, flat ground at the foot of the cross, is faith.

That this is his meaning is at once demonstrated in the following verse. That those who insist on other meanings are not following his train of thought is demonstrated by the trouble they have with it.[131]

3:29-30a. If justification were through "works of Torah," God would be shown to be the God only of Jews; whereas in fact God is the God of Gentiles also, because God is one. If justification were through Torah, God's impartiality would be impugned (2:11), and the whole fabric of the δικαιοσύνη θεοῦ (*dikaiosynē theou*), the justice and faithfulness of God, would start to unravel. Here we are at the characteristic point of tension in all Paul's thought: God's faithfulness to the covenant with the Jewish patriarch, Abraham, and his descendants, can only be fulfilled through the creation of a worldwide, Jew-plus-Gentile, family. The whole question of "Paul and the Law" can only be comprehended within this framework. What Israel has always been tempted to forget, from Paul's point of view, is that the God who made the covenant with Abraham is the creator of the whole world and that the covenant was put in place precisely in order that through Israel God might address the whole world (cf. 2:17-24; 3:2).

To prove the point, Paul quotes the most fundamental Jewish confession of faith, the *Shema*: "since God is one."[132] That which defines Israel at the deepest level, the belief in and commitment to the one God of heaven and earth, itself points to the conclusion that this one God must ultimately create a single family not only of Jews but also of Gentiles.[133] The *Shema* is itself the ultimate summary of Torah (as Jesus also believed, Mark 12:29), and this summary points away from the possession of Torah and the use of it as a national badge, toward a different sort of fulfillment altogether. The very word שְׁמַע (*šāma'*) itself, meaning "hear (and obey)," a meaning picked up in the Greek compound ὑπακούω (*hypakouō*, "obey [as a result of hearing]"), points to Paul's concept of ὑπακοή πίστεως (*hypakoē pisteōs*), "the obedience of faith" (1:5; 16:26), signaling the way in which the "faith" of which Paul spoke was, for him, the true "obedience" the Torah sought, responding of course to the "faithfulness," the

---

131. The NIV's omission of ἤ (*ē* "or") at the start of the verse is a symptom of the (classical Protestant) misunderstanding that runs through its translation of the whole of 3:21-31. Fitzmyer's translation "but" (*Romans*, 359) indicates the same misunderstanding, as does Barrett's suggestion that this is a different point to the previous verse. See C. K. Barrett, *A Commentary on the Epistle to the Romans* (London: A. & C. Black, 1957) 83.

132. The *Shema*, the Jewish daily prayer to this day, begins with the words of Deut 6:4: "Hear, O Israel, YHWH our God, YHWH is one." The NIV's "since there is only one God" fails to catch both the stark emphasis of the Greek and the echoes of Deuteronomy 6.

133. For the similar (and similarly dense) argument of Gal 3:15-22, see Wright, *The Climax of the Covenant*, chap. 8. Paul makes a different, though related, use of the *Shema* in 1 Cor 8:6, on which see Wright, *The Climax of the Covenant*, chap. 6. See also the Commentary on Rom 5:5; 8:28.

"obedience," of the Messiah through which God's faithfulness was revealed. God is one, and therefore recognizes as the true covenant family all those who offer this "obedience" to the gospel, whatever their ethnic origin.

3:30b. Paul now explicitly draws the conclusion: God will justify circumcised and uncircumcised alike, on the basis of faith. That is, God will declare that wherever this faith is found, the believer is a true member of the covenant family. Only faith can have this role, not because faith is a superior type of religious experience to anything else, nor because faith is an easier substitute for "works," putting it within the range of the morally incompetent (it is remarkable how many people still suppose that this is what Paul was talking about),[134] but because faith—this faith, to be defined in 4:18-25 and 10:9—is the appropriate human stance of humility and trust before the creator and covenant God, the stance that, only possible through grace, truly reveals the heart in which new covenant membership has been inscribed by the Spirit (2:29; cf. 1 Cor 12:3; Eph 2:8-10).

Paul makes the slightest of distinctions in phraseology, suggesting that the circumcised are justified "on the grounds of" faith and the uncircumcised "through" faith (the NRSV and the NIV both have "the same" faith, perhaps bringing out the fact that the second occurrence of "faith" has the definite article in the Greek). If Paul intends any difference, it is that the circumcised are already, in a sense, within the covenant and now need to be declared true covenant members on the basis of faith, while the uncircumcised, being outside the covenant, need to come in through the doorway marked "faith." The distinction only applies to their starting-point, not to their destination or to the badge that demonstrates that they have arrived there.

3:31. The density of Paul's argument has led some of his readers to miss the hints he has been throwing out at various points about the way in which, in this new covenant dispensation, the Torah is in fact fulfilled. What has been most striking, following 2:12-15, 17-20, 26-27; 3:19-20 (in all of which Paul is clearly affirming Torah as God's law and its

verdict as true), is the way in which, beginning with 3:21 "apart from Torah," he has now declared that "the works of Torah" cannot be the badge of membership in God's people. Being an ethnic Jew, with Torah to prove it, does not establish a special inalienable status; being circumcised is neither here nor there when it comes to justification. The natural question that must follow is: Have we then abandoned the affirmation of Torah stated up to 3:20? Do we then abolish the Torah, make it null and void, through faith? (The NIV and the NRSV, by translating "this faith," again bring out the force of the definite article.)

This is just the question some readers of Paul are waiting for. Those who follow an ultra-Protestant reading, in which "the law" refers to the legalistic, moralistic, or ritualistic practices designed, at least in the eyes of their opponents, to establish a claim on God, and those who follow an ultra-liberal (or ultra-Romantic) reading of Paul, in which "the law" refers to any moral code imposed on human beings from without—and who have therefore celebrated the victory, respectively, of low-church piety on the one hand and spontaneity on the other—will naturally want to answer "Yes!" to this question. They will perhaps feel that Paul's own answer ("On the contrary! We uphold the law") is illogical, that it represents the old Pharisee peeping out from his hiding.[135] Or they will water it down to merely "Well, I can prove the point from scripture; watch me expound the Abraham story in the next chapter." But that is to miss the inner logic and subtlety of Paul's actual argument.

Likewise, those in the Reformed tradition who are deeply concerned for the continuity of the new covenant with the old, for the abiding validity of the Old Testament, for the rejection of all that even smells of Marcion, will find that, while their sensitivities are much closer to Paul's, their emphasis, too, is not quite his, or not at this point.[136] His

---

134. E.g., the telltale aside of W. Sanday and A. C. Headlam, *A Critical and Exegetical Commentary on the Epistle to the Romans*, 5th ed., ICC (Edinburgh: T. & T. Clark, 1902) 283, suggesting that faith is "much easier." Would they still say that at the start of the twenty-first century?

135. John A. T. Robinson, *Wrestling with Romans* (Philadelphia: Westminster, 1979) 51, describes revealingly how C. H. Dodd, arriving at 3:31*b* during the course of the NEB translation project, exclaimed, "What rubbish!" Käsemann, *Commentary on Romans*, 104, declares that the verse is "incomprehensible" as a conclusion to chap. 3 and that it only makes sense as a transition to chap. 4—i.e., as saying, "I can prove this from scripture."

136. See Cranfield, *A Critical and Exegetical Commentary on the Epistle to the Romans*, 223-24.

answer is completely genuine. We "establish" (so NASB) Torah; that is perhaps better than "uphold" (NRSV, NIV, REB). Paul is indeed concerned that what God said in the past is shown to be right and true; he will argue the point in detail in 7:7–8:11 and 9–11. But at the moment he is doing two rather different things. First, he is drawing out the significance of having the *Shema* itself as a pointer to the Jew-plus-Gentile quality of the new family (and, behind this, of the paradoxical "fulfillment of the Torah" spoken of in 2:25-9, referring to those in whose hearts the Spirit has been at work). Second, he is pointing ahead, as so often at this stage of the letter, to the dark and deep arguments yet to come, in which, through the fulfillment of God's overall purpose in Christ and by the Spirit, even

Torah, with all its negative side fully allowed for, will be seen to have accomplished its strange vocation.

The rhetorical force of the paragraph, and of 3:21-31 as a whole, is thus to say that God has unveiled in Jesus the Messiah, and supremely in his death, that covenant faithfulness, that saving justice, through which the outstanding problem of sin and wrath has been dealt with, so that now a new covenant family emerges, consisting of Jews and Gentiles alike, characterized by the faith that answers to the faithfulness of the Messiah.

This is offered as a summary statement; Paul now proceeds to the detailed argument (not merely "proof from scripture") to back it up. What was the covenant with Abraham all about in the first place?

REFLECTIONS

1. It was one thing for Paul, looking back at his own life "under Torah," to declare that possession of Torah, and the accomplishment of its "works," was not the way by which the people of God were demarcated. It is quite another, after a checkered history, for Christians to declare the same thing as though nothing dangerous or subversive were being said. We must never forget that Paul's gospel remained "to the Jew first and also to the Greek." He never for a moment implied that Jews were not just as much the objects of God's love and grace; indeed, the crowning passage of this letter mounts a long argument to exactly this end. It is easy for Christians who live in areas where there is little or no visible Jewish presence to make "the Jews" a soft target, repeating the slogans of former theological polemics without realizing how damaging, taken out of context, such things can be, using this straw figure as a way of attacking their own opponents without imagining that there might be some real Jews listening in on the conversation, for whom this would be deeply offensive.

Of course, we must quickly say, Paul's gospel was offensive, not only to Gentiles (who often did not take kindly to being told that there was now another lord of the world, and a Jewish one at that), but also to Jews, for whom the idea of a crucified Messiah was a contradiction in terms, while the idea that God might now admit Gentiles into the covenant family on equal terms was close to unthinkable. Contemporary Western culture, in which being inoffensive has become the supreme virtue, hops from one foot to another to avoid saying anything that anyone might take exception to, forgetting that, according to the prophet, God's word is like a hammer that breaks rock in pieces. Often, of course, it is not actually Jews who are most offended by Christian claims, but rather those post-Enlightenment thinkers for whom any idea of God acting, choosing, doing specific things, appears undemocratic, not in keeping with the spirit of our age. Mainstream Judaism, and for that matter mainstream Islam, is just as offensive to this mood as mainstream Christianity.

In particular, there is no avoiding the Pauline insistence that in Christ there is "neither Jew nor Greek." One can understand why it is that, for instance in Palestine/Israel today, there are some churches where only Arab Christians worship, and others where only Jewish Christians worship; just as one can understand why there are some churches that are black only (or, indeed, white only), not by law but by choice, in multiracial communities on both sides of the Atlantic and elsewhere. But one must insist, on the basis of Romans 3, that all such situations, understandable though they may be, are regrettable and fraught with danger. Such communities are always likely to forget the truth Paul insisted on in the present passage: that the only thing uniting Christians is their faith in the God made known in Jesus Christ. To suggest by one's social or cultural behavior that the one God has any kind of "favored nation clause" is to fly in the face of the revelation of God's righteousness in the gospel. In this context, the concept of a "national church," or "state church," needs very careful thought (the writer speaks as a member of the established Church of England) if it is not to overthrow the gospel itself.

2. This applies not only to churches but also to communities and nations. The post-colonial world in Africa and elsewhere has seen the resurgence of tribalism; the post-immigration world in Europe has seen the resurgence of racism; the post-Cold War world of the Balkans has seen the resurgence of enthocentric nationalism. A British writer looking at Northern Ireland, where the two militant sides are still often referred to as "Catholic" and "Protestant" (now rightly being replaced by "Republican" and "Unionist"), can only hang his head in sorrow. The church's witness, so often compromised in these situations by the easy assumption that the Christian God was on the side, shall we say, of the Orthodox Serbs against the Bosnian Muslims—or the Croatian Catholics!—must shine out again, precisely with the message of Romans and Galatians, that in Christ there is neither Jew nor Greek, and if so then certainly neither Catholic nor Protestant.[137]

3. This latter hard lesson—Romans, after all, has been seen for many generations as the bastion of "Protestant" theology—is of course reinforced once we realize what Paul's teaching on "justification" actually is. The Protestant polemic of half a millennium has been directed against the "religion" of Catholicism, and by extension against any teaching or practice that seems to suggest a desire to "earn" justification, favor with God, or even salvation, by the correct performance of religious or sacramental duty. It must be said, sadly, that one does indeed still find, not only in some popular expressions of Roman Catholicism but also in many Protestant churches and writings, the idea that at the last the reason why God will be merciful to humans, if that will indeed be the case, is that the humans in question have performed certain deeds that will outweigh their undoubted misdeeds. The notion of free forgiveness, of

> Nothing in my hand I bring;
> Simply to thy cross I cling;

is so vast, so shocking, so radically life-changing, that many seem to prefer, when all is said and done, a simple religion of good deeds and bad. Let it be said as clearly as possible that, though this is not basically what Paul is writing about, he would have had only one thing to say about it: It stinks.

Nevertheless, the Protestant polemic has gained more targets as it has gone on, and they have less and less to do with any questions that Paul would have recognized as relevant. The Enlightenment, by rehabilitating the dualism of the spiritual and the physical, aligned quite closely with the dualism of reason and contingent historical reality, was able to introduce within Protestantism the sense that anything to do with physical objects or behavior was somehow "worldly" as opposed to "godly," thus compounding the original Reformation protest against the theology of "works-righteousness" with a subtly different protest against Christian belief having anything to do with the present

---

137. On this whole topic see M. Volf, *Exclusion and Embrace: A Theological Exploration of Identity, Otherness, and Reconciliation* (Nashville: Abingdon, 1996).

world. It is that separation, of course, against which liberation theology has made a necessary, albeit sometimes perhaps a misguided, protest.

The effect on the church's worship has also been dramatic, producing a low-church mentality in which, despite all the verbal protestations about the priority of grace, the unworthiness of the worshipers, the offer of free forgiveness and the Spirit's inspiration of all that is performed in faith, any suggestion of liturgical movement, gestures, objects, robes, or even the fact of liturgy itself, can be rejected as constituting a compromise of the gospel, a collapse back into a human-centered religion, a kind of legalism, rather than a living relationship. This attitude, frankly, owes nothing to Paul, however much it claims him as its patron saint. Of course, all worship activities can come to be regarded as "things we do to earn God's favor." But that is just as true of the still and silent Quaker meeting, of the informal (and yet often secretly formal) charismatic prayer meeting, of the unscripted, yet totally predictable, public prayers in some "free" churches, as it is of the full Orthodox or Roman Catholic liturgy. It is time to recognize these debates, important though they may be, as having little or nothing to do with what Paul is talking about in his rejection of "justification by works."

And there is more. The Romantic movement, seeking, after the sterility of eighteenth-century Rationalism, to recapture a sense of integration with the natural world, and awe and wonder when faced with it, encouraged the belief that the only "authentic" way for humans to do anything was to act as it were spontaneously, allowing things deeply felt and known to come forth as from a hidden spring. Poetic inspiration, as practiced by the Lakeland poets, became a kind of model; the suggestion that one might have to work at a poem, to cross things out and try different words here and there, seemed shoddy, second-rate, indicative of a less-than-complete inspiration.

This view would not be maintained by many writers or philosophers today; but it has left its legacy in the Christian churches in the form of the desire for spontaneity, for freedom from rules and hence also from liturgies. (I doubt whether Luther, at least, would have recognized this movement as a legitimate extension of his theology.) And this, too, is often supposed to have something to do with "justification by faith apart from works." There is of course great value in the stumbling prayer that comes from the heart as against the beautifully phrased prayer read from a book while the heart is busy elsewhere. But many, perhaps most, of the greatest spiritual guides would regard this as a quite false antithesis. Often somebody else's words will act as lightning conductors, enabling one's belief in, and sense of, God's presence to go down to the very center of one's being. The drama of the eucharistic liturgy is the reenactment of the story of Israel, focused on Jesus and supremely on his death; to break up its lines, to avoid any sense of drama in case it became a new "works-righteousness," can itself be an act of human-centered arrogance, declaring one's independence from the very gospel events themselves. Some forms of Christianity still use Paul's words, filtered through the Reformation, the Enlightenment, and the Romantic movements, to justify practices, or the lack of them, in a way that has everything to do with personal, social, and cultural preferences and prejudices and nothing whatever to do with Paul.

Indeed, at a deeper level, Paul's positive point in this paragraph cuts against many such attitudes, bound up as they are with cultural differences (e.g., Northern European or Mediterranean cultures, with their various transatlantic offshoots). A good deal of polemic that disguises itself with theological language is in fact the determination to preserve one particular cultural way of doing things; and that itself is ruled out by Paul's whole argument. When we arrive at 14:1–15:13, the final great climax of the letter, we will discover that justification by faith, as expounded in chap. 3, is designed to result in "fellowship by faith," in which different cultures, different ways of doing things, respect and celebrate one another's practices within the fellowship of the one Lord, worshiping the one God. How the church may learn to distinguish that which is of the essence of the gospel, to be preserved at all costs, from that which is part of a local culture, and hence a matter of theological indifference, is of course a well-known and exceedingly difficult problem. To put it another way, one of the main challenges facing the Western church in the twenty-first century is how to preserve the celebration of different cultures from degeneration into a mere postmodern smorgasbord of options in which everything, including morality and theology, are up for negotiation. But for Paul it was precisely part of the essence of the gospel, of the revelation of God's impartial saving justice in Jesus, that Jews and Greeks belonged together in God's family and should learn to work that out in practice. And if that division could be overcome, how much more those that still divide Christians in our own day.

Romans 4:1-25, The Covenant Family of Abraham

OVERVIEW

Once we recognize the main subject of the section (3:21–4:25) and its place within Paul's larger argument, we find that chapter 4 itself comes into its own. It is not simply, as it has so often been labeled, a "proof from scripture," or even an "example," of Paul's "thesis" of justification by faith in 3:21-31 (for the idea that Paul simply ransacked his mental concordance for texts about "righteousness" and "faith" and came up with Hab 2:4 and Gen 15:6, see the Commentary on 1:17). The chapter is, in fact, a full-dress exposition of the covenant God made with Abraham in Genesis 15, showing at every point how God always intended and promised that the covenant family of Abraham would include Gentiles as well as Jews.[138] Irrespective of what we might say about a systematic presentation of Paul's ideas, in his present argument this is the main topic, to which "justification by faith" makes a vital contribution, rather than the other way round.

The three main points in the argument concern works (vv. 2-8), circumcision (vv. 9-12), and the law (vv. 13-15). In the second and third cases obviously, and in the first case arguably, the discussion does not concern the question normally supposed, of how someone becomes a Christian (and whether religious ritual, "works of the law" in that sense, has anything to do with it), but rather the question, does Abraham's family consist just of Jews, or also of Gentiles? To answer this

question, Paul quotes or refers to Gen 15:6 in vv. 3, 9-12, 13, 18-22, 23, arguing in detail for its meaning in its own context and for the relation of that meaning to surrounding passages in Genesis, particularly chap. 17.

This strongly supports one particular reading of v. 1, and with it the whole argument. The question Paul faces here is whether covenant membership means, after all, coming to belong to the physical family of Abraham (the question, of course, at stake in Galatians). This reading also means that the climax of the chapter can properly be located in vv. 16-17, where the remark about Abraham being the father of many nations, so far from being a parenthesis as sometimes suggested, is in fact the answer to the question of v. 1, the decisive point in the whole sequence of thought. Abraham is indeed the "father" of the covenant people of God, but he is not the father "according to the flesh." He is the father of all, Gentile and Jew alike, who believe in the God who raised Jesus.

Genesis 15:6 ("Abram believed God, and it was reckoned to him as righteousness"), which ties the chapter tightly together, is one of only two passages in the Hebrew Scriptures that speak of something being "reckoned as righteousness" to someone (the other is Ps 106:31 [105:31 LXX], referring to Phineas; see also 4QMMT C 31, on which see below). It is not a usual phrase in classical Greek, either.[139] The Hebrew of Gen 15:6 has no word corresponding to "as" in the regular

---

138. At this stage of the Genesis story, Abraham is still called Abram. Paul's regular title for the patriarch is Ἀβραάμ (Abraam), which corresponds to the longer form. I will follow Paul in using the longer name, although strictly it is anachronistic at this point.

139. H. G. R. Liddell, R. Scott, H. S. Jones, A Greek-English Lexicon, 9th ed. (Oxford: Oxford University Press, 1996) cite only Xenophon Cyropaedia 3.1.33.

translation, but simply says ויחשבה לו צדקה (*wayyaḥšĕbehā lô ṣĕdāqâ*, "he reckoned it to him righteousness").[140] The LXX is as Paul quotes it. Paul does not, of course, leave the phrase cryptic; his frequent repetitions and paraphrases of it throughout the chapter give us a clear idea of what he takes it to mean. It is about trusting the God who justifies the ungodly (v. 5) and can be explained by a psalm passage about the forgiveness of sins (vv. 6-8). When the original phrase says "he reckoned it to him," the "it" is clearly Abraham's faith (v. 9); and the resulting status Abraham enjoys can then be described as "the righteousness of faith" (v. 11), in a passage where "righteousness" is directly equivalent to "covenant" in the original Genesis passage. This "faith" can then be imitated, and those who share it will also have "righteousness" reckoned to them (vv. 11, 24). Verses 18-21 describe how, having received the promise of Gen 15:5, Abraham came to believe despite all the contrary factors; this offers a remarkable midrashic account, almost psychological in content. The conclusion of the chapter demonstrates that all those who share Abraham's faith will have "righteousness" reckoned to them on this basis, so that Paul can go on at once to say "Being then justified by faith" in 5:1.

Paul is arguing, then, that Abraham's faith is the sole badge of membership in God's people, and that therefore all those who share it are "justified." He offers a description of this faith, showing, on the one hand, that it is the stance of true humanity before the creator God, reversing the rebellious and idolatrous stance of 1:18-25, and, on the other, that it is the same faith that Christians demonstrate when they believe in the God who raised Jesus from the dead. This enables him to round off Romans 1–4 with a pregnant christological formula that sums up everything he has said so far. Jesus' death has dealt with the sin described in the first three chapters; his resurrection, by demonstrating that he was indeed God's faithful one, God's "son" (1:4) and that, therefore, his death was God's victory over sin, establishes justification. And, by there alluding to Isaiah 53, Paul is able to make again the point that, though often ignored by commentators, runs most of the way through Romans 1–4: Jesus has done what Israel was called to do. His faithfulness, his obedience (as Paul will refer to it in 5:12-21) reveals the covenant faithfulness, the saving justice, of God. This perfectly prepares the way both for the development of the argument in 5–8 and for its new and decisive turn in 9–11.

A comment is necessary about why Paul goes to all the trouble of this complex argument about Abraham and his family. It has long been assumed, by those who think of Paul as opposing "Judaism," that he would not have brought Abraham into his argument (here, in chap. 9, and in Galatians 3–4) had he not been forced to do so by hypothetical "opponents." Were there, some ask, "Judaizers" or Jewish sympathizers among the Roman church, to address whom Paul felt obliged to bring Abraham into the picture? Or was he deliberately snatching the best argument away from potential opponents?[141]

These suggestions may have some secondary part to play. Paul may have been aware, in writing these passages, of people (the so-called "Judaizers," perhaps) who would appeal to Genesis in favor of a theology and practice that enshrined Jewish ethnicity as a necessary, perhaps even a sufficient, condition of membership in the people of God. We have no independent evidence for this, however; and the suggestion that Paul would not otherwise have brought Abraham into the argument strikes me as the thin end of a Marcionite wedge. Paul's whole theme in Romans is the faithfulness of God to the covenant, the divine saving justice by which the world is both condemned and rescued. Here, not as an aside, a semi-apologetic or semi-polemical exegetical footnote, but as his own choice of passage and topic, he presents the story of Abraham to show that, in Jesus Christ, God has done what had been promised from the beginning and has thereby created the family whose defining mark is faith in God the life-giver.

---

140. The LXX clarifies the sense by adding "to" before the last word. The near parallel in Ps 106:31 [105:31 LXX] has the "to" in the Hebrew as well as the Greek.

141. E.g., Käsemann, *Commentary on Romans*, 105.

Romans 4:1-8, Believing the Promise

COMMENTARY

4:1. "What then shall we say? Have we found Abraham to be our forefather according to the flesh?" This is not, of course, what any of the commentaries or translations say, but it has a strong claim to represent Paul's mind.[142] Three reasons stand out. First, it introduces the chapter Paul is writing, as opposed to the one that many think he should have written; in other words, a chapter about the scope and nature of Abraham's family, rather than a chapter about "justification by faith" as a doctrine about how people become Christians. This, as we shall see, results in the straightforward solution of at least one major exegetical problem. Second, it recognizes that when Paul introduces an argument with τί οὖν ἐροῦμεν *ti oun eroumen*, "what then shall we say?" this phrase is frequently complete in itself, requiring a question mark at once. (There is, of course, no punctuation in the earliest MSS.) Obvious examples are 6:1; 7:7; see also τί οὖν (*ti oun*) in 3:9. Third, it avoids at a stroke the awkwardness of sense, and hence of translation, in the usual readings (of which the NRSV and the NIV are typical) in which Abraham is the subject of εὑρηκέναι *heurēkenai*, "to have found," rather than the object as in the reading proposed; since it is not clear what "to have found" could possibly mean in this context, the sense of the verb has to be stretched as in the NRSV ("was gained by") and NIV ("discovered"), neither of which lead in to what Paul is actually going to say.[143] The proposal, then, is that Paul raises in v. 1 a possible conclusion that could be drawn from what has been said so far, in order to argue against it.

At this point, however, I diverge from the meaning Hays gives to his own proposed reading. He suggests that Paul wants to say "Have we *Jews* normally considered Abraham to be our forefather only according to the flesh?" I suggest, rather, that the whole of Romans 4 hinges on the question, whether 3:21-31 means that we *Christians*, Jews and Gentiles alike, now find that we are to be members of the fleshly family of Abraham (note how the word "find" suddenly makes perfect sense).[144] In other words (Paul is proposing this as a hypothetical question), if in Christ God has been true to the covenant with Abraham, might that not mean, as the Galatians had been led to believe, that members of the Christ-family in fact belong to Abraham's fleshly family? When we read Romans 4 as the answer to this question, it gains in coherence and force.[145]

4:2. Verses 2-8 are regularly appealed to by those who still argue that Paul was after all attacking a theology of self-help legalism, in which "righteousness" is earned by moral effort. By themselves these verses might indeed bear that sense. But within the present argument they are much better understood as a further metaphorical expansion, rather than the inner substance, of Paul's point.

Paul's main argument is that "works" (i.e., of Torah) were not the reason for Abraham's justification; and the idea of "working" is then expanded metaphorically in vv. 4-5 into the idea of doing a job for which one earns wages. The critical connection is established with "for" at the start of v. 2 ("in fact" in the NIV is a loose way of making the same point) and depends on the link between "works of Torah" and "Jews only" that Paul had established in the immediately preceding verses. It is ethnic Jews who possess Torah; so if Abraham were the forefather of an ethnic

---

142. See esp. Richard B. Hays, " 'Have We Found Abraham to Be Our Forefather According to the Flesh?' A Reconsideration of Rom 4:1," *NovT* 27 (1985) 76-98. See also Hays, *Echoes of Scripture in the Letters of Paul*, 54-55. The suggestion goes back at least to J. A. Bain, "Romans iv. 1," *Expository Times* 5 (1893–94) 430. It is not clear that subsequent commentators (e.g. Byrne, Fitzmyer, Moo, Bryan) have recognized the force or point of Hays's proposal; the same is true of S. K. Stowers, *A Rereading of Romans: Justice, Jews, and Gentiles* (New Haven: Yale University Press, 1994) 234, 242, who unlike them claims to follow it.

143. *Abraam* is indeclinable in Greek, and hence its grammatical role in the sentence is unclear until defined from elsewhere.

144. R. B. Hays, "Adam, Israel, Christ," in *Pauline Theology Volume III: Romans*, ed. D. M. Hay and E. E. Johnson (Minneapolis: Fortress, 1995) 81, has graciously accepted my amendment of his proposal.

145. Bain took "according to the flesh" to modify "to have found" and, therefore, assumed that Paul was asking the question, "Have we, by our fleshly efforts, found Abraham to be our forefather?" In other words, have we attained membership in Abraham's family by performing works of the law? Fitzmyer's objection to this (Fitzmyer, *Romans*, 371) in no way damages the reading I am proposing; Fitzmyer does not seem to have noticed that the meaning proposed by Hays is quite different from that of Bain. Stowers, claiming to agree with Hays, is actually agreeing with something more like Bain's reading.

family only, this family would be defined by Torah, and hence defined visibly by Torah's "works." Thus (v. 2*a*) if Abraham was reckoned to be in covenant with God (i.e., was justified) on the basis of works of Torah, he and his family would be able to "boast," in the way that Paul described in 2:17-20 and then firmly excluded in 3:27-30. Verse 2*a*, in other words, explains the question of v. 1, as follows: If Abraham's covenant membership was indeed defined in terms of "works of Torah" (v. 2*a*), then he and his family would be able to sustain an ethnic boast, and so (v. 1) any Gentiles wishing to belong to this family would then have to consider themselves ethnic Jews—would, in other words, need to become proselytes, with the males among them becoming circumcised.

Paul's response, to be filled out as usual in what follows, is brusque: "but not before (lit., "toward") God," i.e., "not as far as God is concerned." Verse 2*b* is thus Paul's initial reaction to the suggestion, rather than part of the "if . . . then" clause of the earlier part of the verse.[146] This now forces Paul into saying what *is* true "before God," to cut the ground from under any potential ethnic boast, and to establish once and for all the non-ethnic nature of Abraham's true family, on the basis of the original covenant itself.

4:3. By way of explanation (γάρ *gar*, omitted in NIV), Paul quotes Gen 15:6: Abraham believed God, and it was reckoned to him as "righteousness." The word "reckoned" is a bookkeeping metaphor, indicating either the placing of something in a column of figures to be added up or the result of the addition itself; so NIV's "credited" is helpful. The Greek construction of the whole phrase, however ("to credit something *to* someone *unto* something"), is rare, and the precise meaning Paul intends must be sought principally in the Genesis account itself on the one hand and in the rest of Romans 4 on the other (Ps 106:31 and MMT C 31 largely restate the problem).

Genesis 15 opens with Abraham's puzzlement. YHWH has made great promises to him, but he has no children. Who then will inherit after him? Back comes the promise: God will give Abraham a family as numerous as the stars in heaven. This promise is what

Abraham "believed," at which the writer comments that God "reckoned" it (presumably, Abraham's believing of the promise) "to him (as) righteousness." The passage goes on at once to speak of God's further promise, echoing that in chapter 12, to give Abraham the land of Canaan as his inheritance. Abraham asks how he may know that he will inherit it. God commands him to prepare a covenant ceremony, which then takes place, in which God solemnly tells him that his seed will languish as slaves in a foreign country, but that God will bring them out and give them the land. The whole chapter, of which the covenant ceremony forms the climax, is thus all about Abraham's promised seed and the route by which they will come to their assured inheritance. Within this context, the key statement of 15:6, cryptic and almost unparalleled as it is, appears to be proleptic, referring forward to the covenant ceremony about to take place. Its overall meaning must then be something like: "God counted Abraham's faith as constituting covenant membership"; or "Abraham's believing the promise was seen by God as the sign that Abraham was 'in the right,' was to be upheld."

There are thus three levels of meaning in the dense phrase as Paul quotes it in 4:3.

The most obvious metaphorical level is the bookkeeping one ("reckoned"). God made an entry in Abraham's ledger, writing "faith," or more specifically "faith in this promise," in the column marked "righteousness" (i.e., "covenant membership").

The second level is the lawcourt one, which is clearly in Paul's mind through the way he develops the idea. God, as the judge, declares that Abraham's faith in this promise is the sign that he is in the right in some hypothetical lawcourt. We should be careful not to assume, as normal English usage of "righteousness" might lead us to do, that (a) "righteousness" means "moral goodness," and that (b) "faith" is then either a form of, or a substitute for, such moral goodness. When Abraham's faith is "counted as righteousness," it means that this faith is the sure sign that his acquittal or vindication has already taken place. Both of these meanings, the bookkeeping one and the lawcourt one, are metaphors.

146. So Cranfield, *A Critical and Exegetical Commentary on the Epistle to the Romans*, 228; Moo, *The Epistle to the Romans*, 260.

The third and deepest level of meaning is the one that dominates the chapter: the covenant and membership within it (on "righteousness" and "covenant," see the Commentary on 4:11). Abraham's faith was the sure sign that he was in partnership with God; and God sealed this with the covenant ceremony and the detailed promises about Abraham's seed and their inheritance. Both these themes play an important role in later parts of the chapter and the letter.

We must, then, resist the easy temptation to misunderstand Paul's quotation from Genesis in either of two misleading ways. First, Paul does not mean that God was looking for a particular type of moral goodness (referred to as "righteousness") that would earn people membership in the covenant, and that, failing to find this, was prepared to accept faith as a substitute.[147] Faith, for Paul, is not a "substitute" qualification because *it is not a qualification at all*; nor is "righteousness" the same thing as moral goodness. "Righteousness," when applied to humans, is, at bottom, the status of being a member of the covenant; "faith" is the badge, the sign, that reveals that status because it is its key symptom. Once that is grasped, the way is open not just for the rest of Paul's argument in the present passage to unfold smoothly, but also for the nuances carried by faith and the law later in the letter to be understood clearly.

4:4-5. By way of showing what he means in 4:3, Paul develops the bookkeeping metaphor in the direction of employment and wage-earning. This is the only time he uses this metaphorical field in all his discussions of justification, and we should not allow this unique and brief sidelight to become the dominant note, as it has in much post-Reformation discussion. Verse 4 indicates the metaphorical situation that might have obtained if Abraham had after all been justified by works; v. 5, by contrast, shows the true position. Through this contrast, Paul is able to build into his developing picture two further important elements: God's declaration of justification is a matter of grace (v. 4), and it has to do with God's justifying the *ungodly* (v. 5).

The danger in a contemporary reading of the contrast is to suppose that v. 5 is a straightforward reversal of v. 4: Workers get paid not by grace but by debt, but believers get paid not by debt but by grace. This then smuggles back again the possibility that faith is something for which one gets paid, a substitute or alternative work, even if payment is *ex gratia* (the fact that we use that Latin phrase for an uncontracted payment shows how easily the language slips). The two sentences are not in fact balanced, partly because Paul pulls himself out of the bookkeeping metaphor halfway through v. 5 and returns to his main points, the lawcourt and the covenant. What Paul says in v. 5 not only contrasts with v. 4 ("working" and "not working"), but also deconstructs the whole frame of thought: The alternative to "working" is to "trust the one who justifies the ungodly."

This description of God is striking for three reasons. First, nothing so far has prepared us for the description of Abraham himself as "ungodly." In the Genesis story he has already obeyed God's call (chap. 12) and, though moments of apparent disobedience are part and parcel of the story (calling Sarah his sister rather than his wife, Gen 12:10-20; 20:1-18), he appears for the most part to be worshiping and obeying God. Does Paul mean, then, that though Abraham was not ungodly, the God in whom he believed was nevertheless the one who justifies the ungodly? Probably not. The links between v. 5 and what precedes strongly imply that Abraham is still in mind. Paul is presumably thinking of Abraham's whole history, from his background in pagan Ur through to YHWH's call and the establishing of the covenant. Jewish tradition knew of Abraham's background in idolatry and tended to regard him as the first one to protest against this and to worship the one true God instead.[148] Paul does not entirely dissent from this tradition. As he will show in the rest of the chapter, Abraham is thus the forefather quite specifically of Gentiles who come to faith, not merely of Jews. This is, in fact, the beginning of a daring theme: that Abraham is actually *more like* believing Gentiles than he is like believing Jews.

Second, God's action in justifying the ungodly is, of course, exactly what, according to Scripture, a just judge should not do.

---

147. E.g., J. A. Ziesler, "Paul and Arboriculture: Romans 11:17-24," *JSNT* 24 (1985) 124.

148. See L. Ginzberg, *The Legends of the Jews*, 7 vols. (Baltimore: Johns Hopkins University Press, 1998) 1:186-217.

Exodus 23:7 declares, in words Paul echoes, οὐ δικαιώσεις τὸν ἀσεβῆ (*ou dikaiōseis ton asebē*), "you shall not justify the ungodly"; and Proverbs 17:15, with different phraseology but the same intent, declares that those who justify the unjust, or condemn the righteous, are alike an abomination (cf. too Deut 16:19; 27:25; Prov 17:26; Ezek 22:12; Susanna 53). Paul's striking phrase simply overthrows this in the case of God; the only possible grounds for this are the revelation of God's impartial saving justice spoken of in 3:21-26. The death of Jesus has explained why it is that God was right to pass over former sins. That which was unjust in the human lawcourt is now contained within a higher justice, reminding us again that, just as the bookkeeping metaphor is not Paul's basic point, so the lawcourt metaphor too does not reach to the heart of what he is saying. What matters is the covenant, established by God with Abraham while he was still "ungodly," and now extended by sheer grace to any and all who, despite their ungodliness, trust in this God. The covenant was always intended to be God's means of putting the world to rights; the key moment in this promised accomplishment comes when, because of the unveiling of God's righteousness in the death of Jesus, God not only can but must declare the ungodly to be set right, to be within the covenant. Paul is here preparing for the climax of the chapter, in which he defines faith as belief in "the God who raised Jesus our Lord from the dead" (4:24). Throughout the passage, in fact, Paul is wrestling not simply with the question of Abraham's faith, but with the question of God's character and identity. He insists on seeing these in the light both of Abraham and the covenant and of the events concerning Jesus.

Third, the word "ungodly" takes us right back to the start of Paul's description of human idolatry and wickedness in 1:18: The wrath of God is revealed against all ungodliness and injustice of those who suppress the truth through injustice. That Paul intends this reference back, demonstrating how, within the Abraham story, one can see God's proposed solution for the problem of 1:18–3:20, will become clear in vv. 18-22.

One who believes in this God, therefore, will discover that this "faith" will be regarded,

not as a meritorious spiritual act (how could that be, for the "ungodly"?), but as the badge of covenant membership given by God in sheer grace. And already the answer to the opening question of v. 1 is starting to emerge: We (Jewish and Gentile Christians alike) have not found Abraham to be our father according to the flesh, but according to God's promise (see the same contrast in 9:8).

4:6-8. Paul now calls a second witness. At one level the choice of David may be determined by the key word "reckon" in Ps 32:2 [31:2 LXX]. At another, it may be that the multiple references to sin enable him, as in v. 5, to cast an eye back again to 1:18–3:20. But it is interesting to note that David is mentioned as a forgiven sinner and thereby takes a place not merely as an example but as part of covenantal history, in one Second Temple Jewish text.[149] There, however, David is described as having been "one of the pious," and it is clear that his forgiveness is seen as stemming from his observance of Torah; the implication is, if you keep Torah you, too, will be forgiven many sins. For Paul, however, it is just a matter of God not "reckoning" sins; nothing in the psalm, or in Paul's quotation from or comment on it, implies that David had been able to claim forgiveness on any grounds whatever. It was free and undeserved. David "pronounces the blessing on the person to whom God reckons righteousness apart from works" (v. 6). This gives us a further important unpacking of "reckoning righteousness"; the psalm does go on to speak of the forgiven as "the righteous" (32:11; an important indication that "the righteous" does not, there either, mean "the morally perfect"), and Paul can assume that "reckoning righteousness apart from works" and "not reckoning sin against someone" are equivalents. The covenant, we must always remind ourselves, was there to deal with sin; when God forgives sin, or reckons someone within the covenant, these are functionally equivalent. They draw attention to different aspects of the same event.

Paul has now laid the foundation for the specific point he wants to make, namely that Gentiles are welcome in the covenant family on the basis of faith and faith alone,

149. 4QMMT (C 25-26).

without having any of the badges of Jewish membership—and, indeed, that there is an appropriateness, a natural relation as it were, between them and Abraham, precisely because of the condition he was in at the time when the covenant was established. He was then uncircumcised; he did not then possess the Torah. (See Reflections at 4:23-25.)

Romans 4:9-15, Not by Circumcision, Not by Torah

COMMENTARY

4:9-12. Paul now repeats, in sharper form, the question of 4:1, in order to address it head-on in the light of verses 2-6. Does all that has been said about Abraham and David apply only to Jews, i.e., to the circumcised? Should Gentile Christians, in other words, be required to become circumcised if they want to inherit the Abrahamic covenant blessings, not least forgiveness of sins? In addressing this question, Paul builds on 2:25-29 and 3:30, the previous mentions of circumcision. Is what he said there about the new family, composed of uncircumcised and circumcised alike, contradicted by the story of Abraham and the terms of the original covenant? Certainly not. Beginning again from Gen 15:6, Paul is able to show (v. 10, which by its question and answer ensures that the reader cannot miss the point) that, since Abraham was not circumcised until Genesis 17, his "reckoning righteous" took place before he was circumcised; in other words, that in Genesis 15 he was an uncircumcised member of the covenant.

The stress of the paragraph thus falls not so much on the method or timing of Abraham's justification, important though that is, but on what follows from it: that uncircumcised believers are every bit as "justified" as Abraham was (v. 11b). Indeed, vv. 11b-12 seem to imply almost that uncircumcised believers are the more obvious children of Abraham and that it is circumcised ones who come in on their coattails—and even then, Paul underlines, not on the basis of their circumcision, but on the basis of their following in the footsteps of Abraham's "uncircumcised faith" (v. 12b). In this passage, therefore, for the rhetorical purposes of stressing the free and glad welcome that grace gives to Gentiles who believe the gospel, Paul is almost reversing the sequence of 1:16, saying, "To the Gentile believer first and foremost—and also,

equally, to the Jewish believer." So far from it being necessary, in other words (still answering v. 1), for Gentile believers to "discover" Abraham as their physical father—that is, for them to get circumcised—it is necessary for Jewish people to "discover" Abraham to be their uncircumcised father—that is, to share his faith. Paul does not go on to say that they should therefore remove the marks of their circumcision, since for him that would now be irrelevant (cf. 1 Cor 7:18-20). But his argument means that their circumcision is completely beside the point as regards covenant membership.

In case of any suggestion (as in 3:1) that circumcision is therefore a bad thing, Paul gives it a place of honor in v. 11a. It was a "sign or seal" of the "righteousness" that was Abraham's on the basis of the faith he had while still uncircumcised. Paul does not say here, as he does in Galatians 3, that the covenant of circumcision with Abraham's ethnic family, and for that matter the territorial covenant concerning one piece of land, was designed by God as a temporary staging-post on the way to the time when, with the coming of the Messiah and the universal availability of Abrahamic faith, all nations and all lands would be claimed by God's grace.[150] But his thought here is not far off. By designating circumcision as a sign or seal of Abraham's status of faith-demarcated righteousness, Paul reclaims it rather than renouncing it: Faith is the indication of covenant membership, and circumcision was supposed to be a pointer to that status and, apparently, to that mode of indication. The implication is that to use circumcision as a pointer to a status "according to the flesh" is to abuse the sign. This too is, then, part of Paul's developing answer to the question of v. 1.

150. See Wright, *The Climax of the Covenant,* chap. 8.

We should note, in particular, that Paul's effortless rewording of Gen 17:11 indicates clearly, what we have argued all along, that for him a primary meaning of "righteousness" was "covenant membership." God says in Genesis that circumcision is "a sign of the covenant"; Paul says it was "a sign of righteousness." He can hardly mean this as a radical alteration or correction, but rather as an explanation.[151] The whole chapter (Genesis 15) is about the covenant that God made with Abraham, and Paul is spending his whole chapter expounding it; if he had wanted to avoid covenant theology he went about it in a strange way. Rather, we should see here powerful confirmation of the covenantal reading of "righteousness" language in 1:17 and 3:21-31. "He received the sign of circumcision as a seal of the covenant membership marked by the faith he had while still uncircumcised."[152]

There may be a hint here, also, that Paul is thinking of baptism as the Christian version of circumcision—a pointer to the covenant status people have in Christ, by the Spirit, and whose badge is Christian faith. He seldom uses the word "sign" or "seal," but the few occurrences of the latter root are mostly found in probably baptismal contexts (2 Cor 1:22; Eph 1:13; 4:30), and in the one passage where baptism and circumcision are brought together it is clear that, for Paul, baptism in some ways at least plays the same role within the establishment of the Christian covenant people that circumcision played within the Jewish family, i.e., that of marking out the covenant people with the sign that spoke of their unique identity (Col 2:11-12). If this is a correct understanding, it prepares the way for the developed statement of chapter 6, where we shall pursue the point further (see also on v. 13 below).

So far, then, the argument is developing step by step. First step: Does the faith family have to regard Abraham as its physical father? No. Abraham was justified freely, by grace, without works, as was the sinful David; and this faith was faith precisely in the God who justifies the "ungodly," i.e., the Gentile idolaters, the outsiders. Second step: Abraham was justified while uncircumcised, establishing the pattern for other uncircumcised

people also to be justified. "That righteousness might be reckoned to them also" in v. 11*b* ("also" reflects the καί [*kai*, "also" or "even"] that in some good MSS stands before αὐτοῖς [*autois*, "them"]; the NRSV and the NIV assume its omission) anticipates the conclusion of the chapter's argument: "that we too will have righteousness reckoned to us, we who believe in the God who raised Jesus" (v. 24). Paul is not, then, using Abraham primarily as an example, but as the basis of his argument about who God is and who God's people are. He is still, we must remind ourselves, expounding God's covenant faithfulness.

4:13-15. These verses do not introduce a new topic; they explain what has just been said (the NIV yet again omits the *gar*, "for"). This is a further indication that Paul is not simply going through a list of three items, "works," "circumcision," and "Torah," but is rather mounting a sustained and developing argument about the extent of Abraham's promised family. He has now reached the point he has had in mind ever since the χωρὶς νόμου (*chōris nomou*) of 3:21: Torah itself cannot be the boundary marker of the covenant family (the NIV, keeping the generalized "law" throughout these verses, is in danger of obscuring Paul's focus on the Jewish law as Israel's boundary marker; the NRSV rightly keeps the definite article ["the law"] throughout). He introduces this here as the further explanation of why circumcision is neither necessary nor sufficient for membership in this family. That would absolutize Torah as the badge of membership; but Paul has already shown that Torah simply condemns those who possess it. Torah brings wrath (4:15*a*, referring back to 3:19-20, and behind that 2:12*b*); if the divine promise is to be fulfilled, it must be in a realm apart from Torah (4:15*b*, referring back to 3:21). That is the thrust of these verses.

Into this dense statement, though, Paul has built hints of other points to be developed as his argument progresses. First, he reads the geographical promises of Genesis 15 in terms of God's intention that Abraham's "seed" would inherit, not one territory merely, but the whole cosmos. Paul is here close to one strand in Second Temple Jewish thought that developed the idea of Gen 12:3; 18:18; and 22:18 (all nations being blessed in Abraham) through the prophetic promises

151. Against, e.g., Käsemann, *Commentary on Romans*, 114-15; Fitzmyer, *Romans*, 381.
152. For later Jewish texts referring to circumcision as a "seal" see Moo, *Romans*, 268-69.

of Isa 11:10-14; 42:1, 6; 49:6; 54:3; 65:16; Jer 4:2; Zech 9:10 (Israel as a light to the nations, the ruler of the nations, etc.), and the psalmic visions of Ps 72:8-11 (the Messiah's worldwide dominion; cf. Exod 23:31; 1 Kgs 4:21, 24) to the post-biblical thought of Sir 44:21 (which brings together Gen 12:3 and Ps 72:8) and *Jub.* 19:21 (where Jacob's family is spoken of as Abraham's had been). One destination of this line of thought is 2 Bar 14:13; 51:3, where the promised inheritance is a new world entirely, distinct from the present one; as we shall see, this is not Paul's view (see the Commentary on 8:18-27). Paul remains distinct from the other post-biblical developments too. Whereas in Sirach and Jubilees the thought, as in Psalm 72, is of a geographical expansion through which Israel, still based in the promised land, and still identified ethnically, rules an increasing area until it has brought the rest of the world into subjection, in Paul's thought ethnic, national Israel will not rule the world. God will rule the world, and will do so through Jesus the Jewish Messiah, in such a way as to bring all nations equally into God's family (see 9:5; 10:13). Paul's development of the "inheritance" theme, so important in Genesis 15 and elsewhere in the Pentateuch, here takes a decisive turn that looks ahead to 8:12-30.[153]

The point of v. 13, then, that this inheritance, promised repeatedly in Genesis, was not to be made over to Abraham's seed ("descendants" [NRSV] and "offspring" [NIV] are accurate enough, but "seed" is such an evocative biblical term, and one that Paul exploits so interestingly elsewhere, that it seems worthwhile retaining it) on the basis of Torah. This is then explained (*gar*) in v. 14. In Galatians 3:17-18 Paul argues a nearly identical point, but with a different line of thought, corresponding more to that which he has just used in the present passage in relation to circumcision: The Torah, coming later than the promise, cannot be allowed to annul it. This time he uses a different strategy but to the same end: If "those from the Torah," in other words ethnic Jews, were to be the heirs, then nobody at all would inherit. This would make faith useless (that of Abraham, we must

suppose, and that of anyone trying to copy him) and would nullify the promise, since God would ultimately be giving Abraham neither a seed nor an inheritance.

Why? Paul's explanation for this cryptic conclusion, given in v. 15*a*, is terse: the law works wrath. Putting this shorthand statement together with that in 3:19-20, we arrive at the composite that explains them both. (a) Torah shows up sin within ethnic Israel; (b) sin invokes wrath. Therefore (c) if the inheritance were confined to ethnic Israel, (d) nobody at all would inherit. Those outside would be kept there; those inside would be subject to God's wrath.[154] This does not cast a slur upon Torah; Torah is simply doing its job, and Paul affirms that it is right to do so. He does not yet address the question, raised by the similar argument in Galatians, as to why God would give the Torah (Gal 3:19); he will deal with it fully in chap. 7, having allowed the problem to build up further through similar hints in chaps. 5 and 6.

The other cryptic hint given here of the wider theological scheme invoked is in 15*b*: "Where there is no law, there is no transgression." In view of his entire earlier argument, Paul can scarcely mean by this that Gentiles, being outside the Torah, are guiltless; there is, presumably, still sin, the miscellaneous missing of God's intended target for human beings, but there is no explicit disobedience to a known commandment (NRSV, "violation"; see the Commentary on 5:14). The point, however, is that (a) Abraham, not possessing the Torah, was not in this technical sense a "transgressor"; (b) Gentiles can inherit the promises made to Abraham without finding Torah standing in their way; they are not transgressors.[155]

This prepares us for the climax of the chapter. The covenant is fulfilled in the creation of a worldwide family marked out by Abraham-like faith. (See Reflections at 4:23-25.)

153. See N. T. Wright, "New Exodus, New Inheritance. the Narrative Substructure of Romans 3–8," in Sunderlund and Wright, *Romans and the People of God*, 26-35.

154. Again, Paul makes a similar point in Galatians with a different argument: in 3:15-22 he urges that God promised Abraham a single "seed," i.e., family, and that since the Torah would divide the world into two (Jews and Gentiles) it cannot be allowed to stand against the promise. See Wright, *The Climax of Covenant*, chap. 8.

155. This appears at variance with Gal 3:10-14, which assumes that the Torah does put some kind of a roadblock between promise and fulfillment, which it takes the death of Jesus to deal with. See Wright, *The Climax of Covenant*, chap. 7.

Romans 4:16-17, The Whole Family, According to the Promise

COMMENTARY

Paul now gives the full answer to the question he asked in v. 1. This is the significance of the introductory Διὰ τοῦτο (*Dia touto*): "Thus it comes about that . . ." (cf. 5:12; 2 Cor 4:1; Paul can, of course, use the phrase in many other less climactic contexts, e.g., 1:26; 13:6). The main sentence has neither verbs, subjects nor objects, not least because Paul is hurrying on to what he most wants to say in the whole chapter: literally, "Therefore by faith, so that by grace, so that the promise might be valid for *all* the seed, not only for the one from the Torah but also for the one from the faith of Abraham."[156] The universal availability of the promise is Paul's main thrust, and he backs it up at once with the explanation that answers v. 1: Abraham is the father of all of us, as it is written, "I have made you the father of many nations."

This in turn is backed up with the great statement of the other main theme of the chapter, the character of the God in whom Abraham believed. Just as Paul answered his own hypothetical suggestion in v. 2 with the brusque remark "but not before God," so now the statement of what is in fact the case is backed up with "in the presence of the God in whom he believed, the one who gives life to the dead and calls into existence things that do not exist."

Faith, grace and promise, then, are vital to this chapter, but they are not its main subjects. The main subjects are Abraham, his family, and his God. This is what we should expect if the overall subject of the larger section is indeed the revelation of God's covenant faithfulness and the creation of a Jew-plus-Gentile family. The present verses have often been read exactly the other way round, resulting in the bracketing, by the NRSV, of the key statement in vv. 16b-17a (the KJV and the JB simply bracket 4:17a; the RSV begins its parenthesis after "to all his descendants"). When

exegesis comes out smoothly it shows that we are approaching the text from the right angle; when it comes out awkwardly, with phrases and sentences that do not fit, we should take it as a sign that the chapter is being forced in the wrong direction. Romans 4 is not a "proof from scripture" of "justification by faith," into which Paul has inserted some remarks about the fatherhood of Abraham and the character of God; it is an exposition of the covenant God and the way in which the covenant promises to Abraham were fulfilled, with justification and faith playing their part within that overall argument. Verse 17b does indeed seem a bit abrupt, immediately after the biblical quotation; but putting v. 17a in a bracket, with or without part of v. 16, does nothing to ease the suddenness of the change of topic. The abruptness, however, corresponds closely to the opening of v. 16, where Paul is virtually writing in shorthand, and to the suddenness of 4:2b ("but not before God!" which is making the same point as v. 17b ("in the presence of the God in whom he believed"). Once we grasp this, vv. 16-17, instead of seeming awkward and broken up, appear to sum up neatly the argument of the chapter so far.

In particular, the passage makes explicit something about the character of God as revealed (albeit to Paul's Christian hindsight) in Genesis 15, something Paul will then use brilliantly to bring his discourse round to where he wants it to be at the end of the chapter. God is the God who gives life to the dead—something the pagan gods did not even claim to do—and calls into existence things that do not exist. This is, of course, a characteristically Jewish view of the one true God, the creator and lifegiver (cf. Wis 16:13; Tob 13:2; 2 Bar 48:8; belief in God's giving life to the dead is expressed in the second of the Eighteen Benedictions, part of daily Jewish prayer); and it corresponds, within the present argument, to the

156. We may fill out the clipped and cryptic opening words of 4:16 easily enough, as do the NRSV (13 words for Paul's 5) and the NIV (12): All is by faith, so that all may be according to grace.

description of God in v. 5 as "the God who justifies the ungodly."

Within this overall statement, there is one slightly puzzling note. In v. 16 he speaks of "the whole seed"—all Abraham's multi-ethnic family, in other words[157]—as consisting of (literally) "not the one from the Torah only but also the one from the faith of Abraham." Taken by itself, this might imply that Jews who kept Torah formed one part of the family, while the other part consisted of Gentiles who, though not having Torah, shared Abraham's faith. This possibility is ruled out by everything Paul has said from 3:19 to the present point. "The one from the Torah" is simply here a shorthand for "the Jew"; and Paul has already insisted in 4:12 that Jewish ancestry, signaled by circumcision, is only of any value if the person concerned follows in the steps of Abraham's faith (cf. 2:25-29; 10:1-13; 11:23). This should alert us to the interesting overtones of the double description of God at the end of v. 17: God is the one who gives life to the dead and calls into existence the things that do not exist (so NRSV; the NIV, closer to the Greek, has "calls things that are not as though they were"). This may perhaps correspond to the double road into justification hinted at in 3:30. When God brings a Gentile to faith, this is a creation out of nothing; the person had no previous covenant membership of any sort. "Call" is, after all, a strange word to use of creation, but it is one of Paul's regular ways of speaking about the effect of the gospel on someone's life (see, e.g., 9:24, in a similar context). When God brings a Jew to share the faith of Abraham, this is more like a life out of death, a renewal of covenant membership after the threat of being cut off (cf. 2:25-29; 11:11-16, esp. 11:15, on which see the Commentary on 11:12-32).

Verses 16-17 form a striking and original argument that belongs recognizably within Second Temple Judaism but which cuts across the line of thought we might expect. Paul's emphasis contrasts with that of Sir 44:19-21 (NRSV):

Abraham was the great father of a multitude of
    nations,
    and no one has been found like him in glory.
He kept the law of the Most High,
    and entered into a covenant with him;
he certified the covenant in his flesh,
    and when he was tested he proved faithful.
Therefore the Lord assured him with an oath
    that the nations would be blessed through
        his offspring;
that he would make him as numerous as the
        dust of the earth,
    and exalt his offspring like the stars,
and give them an inheritance from sea to sea
    and from the Euphrates to the ends of the
earth.

Here, Torah and circumcision are the central features, along with Abraham's near-sacrifice of Isaac (Genesis 22, which is absent from Romans 4).[158] Sirach also highlights Abraham's faith(fulness) (εὑρέθη πιϛστος *heurethē pistos*, "he was found faithful," 44:20), but this does not have the sense of "believing the promise" that Paul has drawn out. The two belong on the same map; but Paul's new construal, his new way of telling the story, grows directly out of what he now believes about God because of the events concerning Jesus, resulting in the establishment of the Jew-plus-Gentile family with faith as its central demarcating feature.

Abraham's faith is what Paul now analyzes as he draws together the threads, not only of this chapter but of the letter so far. (See Reflections at 4:23-25.)

---

157. For "seed" as "family," see Wright, *The Climax of Covenant*, 162-68, comparing the present passage with Gal 3:15-18. See also the Commentary on 9:6-8.

158. Some have cited Gen 22:17-18 as a parallel to 4:13, but the verse is equally explicable in reference to Gen 12:3; 18:18; in other words, there is nothing specific to Genesis 22. A more likely reference to that chapter is found in Rom 8:32 (see below).

Romans 4:18-22, The God Who Gives Life to the Dead

COMMENTARY

The revelation of God's character to Abraham called forth, Paul now argues, a specific form of faith. Abraham's faith was not just a general religious belief, an awareness of "the other" or of a *mysterium tremendum*. It was a trust in specific promises that the true God had made, which, if fulfilled, would show this God to be what Paul has described in v. 17*b*: the lifegiver, the creator out of nothing.

Paul's fulsome description of Abraham's faith and what it involves, which corresponds to nothing in previous Jewish expansions of the biblical text, seems to be designed with two things in mind. In vv. 18-22 he demonstrates that when Abraham believed this promise he was exemplifying what it meant to be truly human, in contrast to the human disintegration in 1:18–3:20. In vv. 23-25, which conclude the chapter and section, he shows that this type of faith is the same as that which Christians demonstrate when believing that God raised Jesus from the dead. This, he argues, is why Christians, whether Jews or Gentiles, share the faith of Abraham and consequently share the justification spoken of in Gen 15:6.

The theme of the unity and equality of believing Jews and believing Gentiles now fades from view. Paul concentrates instead on the nature of the faith that unites them, and on the certainty of the justification that follows. Are justification and faith then after all the main themes of chap. 4? By no means. Paul has finished in vv. 16-17 the main argument that began with 4:1; he now returns to the overall argument not only of 3:21–4:25 but of 1:18–4:25. He is rounding off the larger section of which 3:21–4:25 was the second main part. He therefore widens the horizon of chapter 4, to speak more directly of the true God, the nature of faith in the true God, and the way in which this faith is the hallmark of genuine humanness as opposed to the corrupt variety.

He thus also points forward to chapters 5–8. There, in order in turn to lay a platform for the specific arguments of 9–11 and 12–16, he leaves the discussion of the Jew-plus-Gentile nature of the family out of explicit consideration for the moment, focusing instead on the way in which the story of Israel has reached its climax, and its true recapitulation, in Christ and the Spirit.

4:18-19. Paul returns to Genesis 15, this time to the verse that precedes his key phrase: God showed Abraham the stars, and declared, "So shall your seed be" (Gen 15:5). This was the promise that Abraham believed. Paul has linked this with the quotation from Gen 17:5 already referred to in v. 17, "I have made you the father of many nations"; he assumes that having offspring like the stars of heaven and being the father of many nations amount to the same thing. Abraham believed this promise, he says, "Hoping against hope" (so NRSV, using a well-known English idiom that more or less matches Paul's slightly more complex phrase)—in other words, persevering in hope when all reasonable expectation ("hope" in a more neutral sense) would have urged that it was impossible. He faced the fact of his own physical condition,[159] and that of Sarah, without any weakening in his faith. Paul draws a veil over the various episodes such as Abraham's passing Sarah off as his sister and the whole matter of Hagar and Ishmael (Sarah: Gen 12:10-20, and particularly 20:1-18, which occurs between the promise concerning Isaac [18:1-15] and his birth [21:1-7]; Hagar: Gen 16:1-16). The feature of this faith to which Paul draws attention is its persistence in hoping for new life when Abraham's and Sarah's bodies were, in terms of potential childbearing, as good as dead because of their age. This builds on 4:17 and looks directly forward to 4:24-25.

4:20-21. Paul now describes Abraham's faith in lavish detail. He shows that Abraham was exactly unlike the human condition described in 1:18-32. Paul is rounding off the larger argument. This, in principle, is how humanity is restored.[160] We may tabulate this as follows:

---

159. Some puzzled early scribes, thinking further to highlight Abraham's faith, added "not" before the verb "considered," implying that Abraham simply ignored his own physical condition. Not so: Paul's point is that Abraham took it fully into account, and still believed and hoped. The NIV ("he faced the fact") splendidly catches the force of this.

160. For more detail, see E. Adams, "Abraham's Faith and Gentile Disobedience: Textual Links Between Romans 1 and 4," *JSNT* 65 (1997) 47-66.

4:17 Abraham believed in God the lifegiver, the creator	1:20, 25 God the creator, ignored by humans
4:19 Abraham's body as good as dead, yet he believed in God's promise of new life	1:24 Human bodies dishonored because of idolatry
4:20 Abraham gave glory to God	1:21 Humans did not glorify God as God
4:21 Abraham recognized God's power	1:20 Humans knew about God's power but did not worship
4:19 Abraham and Sarah given power to conceive	1:26-27 The dishonoring of bodies by females and males turning away from one another.

To this may be added the overall point, that Abraham in this passage worshiped, trusted, and believed the true God and so was given power to be fruitful and to obtain the promised inheritance, whereas human beings in chap. 1 turned away from the true God to idols and so were given over to dishonor, unfruitfulness and corruption. The stress on Abraham's faith/faithfulness also contrasts powerfully with the faithless Israel described in 2:17–3:20, notably at 3:3. Abraham was given grace to be in faithful covenant relation with the true God and thereby to embody and exhibit, initially in his faith and subsequently in his fruitfulness, the marks of genuine humanity. The whole thrust of 4:20-21 is the God-centeredness and God-honoringness of Abraham's faith, worshiping and relying totally on the faithful, lifegiving creator God. This stands in close relation to what Paul had said in 3:21-22, where God's covenant faithfulness is unveiled for the benefit of those who believe.

4:22. Therefore, declares Paul, Abraham's faith was "reckoned to him unto righteousness." The word "therefore" could, if we were not careful, send shock waves back through Paul's previous argument. Is he really saying, after all his language about grace, that this type of faith was so special, so virtuous, so remarkable, that Abraham was rewarded for his faith by having it "reckoned as righteousness"? Is Abraham then the one conspicuous exception, prior to Jesus Christ, to the general rule laid down in 1:18–3:20, that "none is righteous, no not one"? Why, if so, did the full redemption have to wait for two thousand more years? Why did it not happen then and there, with Abraham himself?

Paul does not address these questions, which arise for us when we determine to give Abraham his full place in Pauline theology rather than being shunted into a siding as a mere polemically useful "example." But it is clear that Paul did *not* think that Abraham's faith was meritorious, something to boast about; rather, it was his response to grace (vv. 2, 4, 16, corresponding to 3:24), the grace that had called him in the first place and that now addressed him with lifegiving promises. When, therefore, Paul says that the reason Abraham's faith was "reckoned as righteousness" was because it was this sort of faith, he does not mean that Abraham earned special favor by having a special sort of faith. He means that precisely this sort of faith, evoked by sheer grace, is evidence of that redemption and renewal of humanity as a result of which there appears evidence of a human life back on track, turned from idolatry to the worship of the true God, from disbelief to faith and from corruption to fruitfulness. Faith is the sign of life; life is the gift of God. Justification is God's declaration that where this sign of life appears, the person in whom it appears is within the covenant.

Romans 4:23-25, The Meaning of Christian Faith

COMMENTARY

There remains but one task for Paul, and the first section of the letter is complete. He has not talked specifically about "us" (i.e. himself and his audience) since 1:5-15. Insofar as he has been addressing anyone, it has been the hypothetical debating partner within the "diatribe" style; for the rest, the argument has remained at a general level. Now at last he places his readers on the carefully drawn map; from here the next four chapters will develop, in which "we," and "our" status before God, are a major theme. This is a vital clue to the relation between chaps. 1–4 and 5–8, to the transition between them, and to the way in which both sections together lay the foundation for the second half of the letter, which contains the more particular things Paul wants to say to the Roman church.

4:23. As often, Paul declares that a biblical passage had, in God's intention, a wider meaning than simply its historical reference (see, e.g., 1 Cor 9:9-10; 10:11; and above all Rom 15:4, on which see the Commentary on 15:1-13). This is not arbitrary or fanciful. Precisely because of the covenantal way Paul reads scripture, he insists that what was said and done by way of foundation determines the shape of the whole building. What God said in scripture ("it was written" is a way of saying that scripture says what God intended) opens out to include all those who share Abraham's faith—which, not surprisingly, granted the full explanation of this faith in 4:17-21, is seen as faith in God the lifegiver. Abraham's faith was evoked by the word that spoke to him of his great family, even though he was as good as dead; Christian faith is called forth by the word of the gospel, which speaks of the resurrection of Jesus from the dead (1:4) and the disclosure thereby that he was and is Israel's Messiah, the Lord of the world.

4:24. Christian faith is thus, for Paul, irrevocably resurrection-shaped. Like Abraham's faith, it is by no means simply a general religious awareness or trust in a remote or distant supernatural being, but gains its form, as well as its content, from the revelation of God's covenant faithfulness in the events concerning Jesus (see 10:6-13, and the Commentary thereon). "Faith," for Paul, is never a thing in itself, but is always defined, as Rom 4:16-22 makes clear, in relation to the God in whom trust is placed. The purpose of a window is not to cover one wall of the house with glass, but to let light in and to let the inhabitants see out.

Paul is careful, therefore, to speak of Christian faith as "believing in the God who raised Jesus our Lord from the dead." God, not Jesus, is the primary object of Christian faith (one of many reasons why πίστις Χριστοῦ [*pistis Christou*], "the faith of Christ," is more likely to mean the faithfulness of Jesus himself than the faith people put in Jesus). This description of God is important for Romans, being echoed at another memorable point, 8:11; for Paul it is axiomatic that the resurrection took place by God's initiative and power (see, e.g., 10:9; 1 Cor 6:14; 15:15; 2 Cor 4:14; 13:4; Gal 1:1. 2 Cor 4:14 is very close to the present phrase and to 8:11), so that the meaning of the event is the meaning God intends (1:4), namely, that Jesus is thereby marked out as God's Son, the Messiah, Israel's representative, the one in whom God's promises of redemption have finally come true. Confessing that Jesus is Lord, therefore, and that God raised him from the dead (10:9), means sharing the faith of Abraham; and that faith, as Paul has now argued, is the one and only badge of membership in Abraham's family. Paul does not in this passage spell out the implication, but the rest of the chapter, along with 3:27-30, should still be echoing in the mind. Because there is only one badge of membership, all those who share this faith are members of God's redeemed and forgiven people, no matter what their ancestry. Paul is not making a substantially new point at this stage in the chapter. Rather, he is for the first time putting himself and his readers on the map he has drawn. It is the map of the Abrahamic family, created by the revelation of God's righteousness in Jesus the Messiah, the family in which the distinction between Jew and Gentile, maintained by Torah in particular, is set aside once for all, the family whose sole identifying badge is Christian faith.

Remarkably enough, this verse is the first mention of Jesus' resurrection since the programmatic and formulaic 1:4.[161] But, as we have seen at various points, the rest of the argument would be incomprehensible without it. For neither the first nor the last time, Paul reveals at the very conclusion of an argument something that has been foundational to it all along. Thousands of other young Jews were crucified by the Roman authorities in the first century; several would-be Messiahs were killed one way or another. What distinguishes Jesus from the rest, quite apart from his teaching and actions (which would scarcely by themselves have sustained the sort of movement that Christianity rapidly became), was obviously the resurrection. It is what gives the crucifixion the remarkable meaning it has, enabling Paul to say, by way of a closing christological summary (this, too, anticipates the careful writing of chaps. 5–8), that Jesus was "given up because of our trespasses and raised because of our justification" (for the resurrection as giving meaning to the cross, see 1 Cor 15:17-18).

The point of this verse, then, is that those who believe the gospel of Jesus, which involves believing in the God who raised Jesus from the dead, are thereby sharing Abraham's faith, and will, like him, be reckoned "righteous" in the senses already outlined. Paul has now shown how the bald assertions of 3:27-30 are grounded in the original covenant and promise, thus explaining the λογιζόμεθα (*logizometha*) of 3:28: When Paul said "we reckon," "we figure it out," he was referring not so much to the argument he had already sketched in 3:21-26 as to the full picture he was intending to draw in chap. 4. Having stated in 3:28 the result of the calculation, he has now shown his detailed working.

4:25. All this has been accomplished, of course, through Jesus himself. Paul lays bare, in conclusion, the foundation of the whole structure. This was where God's righteousness, God's covenant faithfulness, God's saving justice, was displayed. Jesus "was given up for our transgressions and raised for our justification."[162]

This pregnant formulation may well have been stated in this or a similar way by Paul himself and/or by other early Christians, many times before.[163] But if it was in that sense pre-Pauline, or at least pre-Romans, Paul has used it here because it sums up exactly what he has been saying, under the general heading of 1:3-4, throughout the letter so far. (It is not, in other words, a non-Pauline formula, quoted here for merely phatic purposes, i.e. to make a pleasing Christian noise unrelated to what has gone before.) Paul has spent the best part of three chapters demonstrating that all human beings were "under the power of sin" (3:9); very well, Jesus was "given up because of our trespasses" (3:24-26, in other words, answers exactly to the problem of 1:18–3:20.) Paul has spent the last thirty or so verses arguing that because of the revelation of God's righteousness in Jesus the Messiah all who believe are justified; very well, Jesus "was raised for our justification." This is another way of saying that the lifegiving God, in whom Abraham believed and was justified, gave life to Jesus, in whom we believe and are justified. This much is at once clear. But there are other questions lurking beneath the surface.

To begin with, Paul seems to be quoting, or at least deliberately alluding to, Isa 53:5, 12 (see the Commentary on 3:24-26; see also the Commentary on 5:18-19).[164] This should not come as a surprise. Isaiah 40–55 is one of the central scriptural passages in which the righteousness of the creator God is said to be revealed, both to confound the pagan nations and their gods and to rescue sinful and wayward Israel from its sin and exile, and in which this task is accomplished supremely through the death and resurrection of "the

---

161. It is also only the tenth time—and this is the 116th verse of the letter!—that the name "Jesus" has occurred in Romans (1:1, 4, 6, 7, 8; 2:16; 3:22, 24, 26; and now this passage) and only the fifth in the 99 verses since the introduction. Without Jesus, there would be nothing to say; this alerts us to the way in which Paul by no means always puts the most important parts of the logical structure of his thought into the actual rhetorical flow of a particular letter.

162. This and 5:18 are the only two occurrences of the term "justification" (δικαίωσις *dikaiōsis*) in the NT—surprisingly, granted its use as a technical term in Christian theology and the regular appeal made to Paul, and Romans in particular, on the topic. It is rare in classical Greek; in the LXX only at Lev 24:22; in Symmachus, at Ps 34[35]:23.

163. On the possibility that this is a pre-Pauline formulation, see P. Stuhlmacher, "Jesus' Resurrection and the View of Righteousness in the Pre-Pauline Mission Congregation," in *Reconciliation, Law and Righteousness: Essays in Biblical Theology* (Philadelphia: Fortress, 1986) 55-56.

164. In particular, the strange word παρεδόθη (*paredothē*, "he was given up" or "he was handed over"), not of itself the most natural word to use for the death of Jesus, is the word used in Isa 53:5 and twice in 53:12. These verses in Isaiah use the word ἁμαρτία (*hamartia*) for "sin," rather than παράπτωμα (*paraptōma*; lit., "transgression") as here.

servant of the Lord." Once we recognize the large themes that tie together Romans and the central section of Isaiah, there ought to be no problem in recognizing that when Paul alludes to one central verse in this passage in Isaiah he intends a reference to the whole. Just as 4:25 expresses for the first time the theological point that turns out to have been foundational for the whole preceding passage, so it is reasonable to suggest that Isaiah 40–55 has been implicit throughout as well.[165]

This strongly implies that, though the death of Jesus has only been mentioned so far in 3:22-26 (taking references to Jesus' "faithfulness" to include a reference to his death), it has remained basic to the whole theology of justification, and of the non-ethnic covenant family, which Paul has expounded from 3:27 through to 4:24. This, again, should not surprise us. To see the cross as the basis of the coming together of Jews and Gentiles is certainly Pauline. The cross is central to the whole argument of Gal 2:11–4:11, with its exposition of Abraham's single family, justified by faith (see also Eph 2:11-22). This prepares us for the repeated emphasis on Jesus' death in chaps. 5–8. Paul is not changing course there, but drawing out what is latent in the present section.

But what, more precisely, does the present verse say about the meaning and effect of Jesus' death and resurrection? He was handed over, says Paul, "because of" our trespasses and was raised up "because of" our justification. The word in each case is διά (dia), which, when governing the accusative (as here), indicates the reason why something happens, that "on account of which" something occurs.

The first half of the verse is fairly clear. "Our trespasses" were the reason or cause for Jesus' "handing over"; as in Isaiah, he was so identified with "us" that he suffered the fate we deserved. What then of the second half of the verse? It is much harder to envisage, let alone establish, a causal connection in Paul's mind by which "our justification" could have been the cause of Jesus' resurrection, as would be required if the two halves of the

verse were as closely parallel in logic as they are in literary form. The nearest Paul comes to saying something like that is 1 Cor 15:17-18: If the Messiah has not been raised, your faith is futile and you are still in your sins. Seen from that point of view, the resurrection demonstrates that Jesus' death accomplished the forgiveness and justification of God's people; one might almost say, in those terms, that the accomplishment of justification was the "cause" of the resurrection.[166] But this seems, frankly, a strange and roundabout way of saying it, and Paul has not prepared us in Romans (or Galatians) for any such statement thus far. It seems to me more likely that two other meanings come together at this point.

First, the servant of Isaiah 53 is raised to new life after his vicarious death (53:10b-12); his task then, as God's righteous one, is "to make many righteous" (v. 11, alluded to in Rom 5:18-19). Carrying this meaning into Romans 4, as the allusion invites us to do, would suggest that Jesus' resurrection took place "because of our justification" in the sense of "because God intended thereby to justify us."[167] This is not exactly parallel in meaning to "because of our trespasses" in the first half of the verse, unless, of course, Paul there means "he was handed over because God intended thereby to deal with our trespasses." But it is not necessary to insist on a strict parallelism of content; Paul uses the matching form to cover, by way of a shorthand summary, the two topics that have occupied him throughout the last four chapters.

This is supported, second, by the one previous mention of the resurrection in the letter (1:4). There God declares, by raising Jesus, that he really was and is God's Son, the Messiah. The resurrection unveils to the surprised world, Israel included, that this was after all the age-old saving plan of the creator God. In particular it declares, as in a lawcourt, that God has vindicated Jesus. Jesus is shown to be in the right. His life and death were the true faithfulness for which God had created Israel in the first place. Thus, if faithful Jesus is demonstrated to be Messiah by the resurrection, the resurrection also declares in

---

165. On Paul's use of Isaiah, see F. Wilk, *Die Bedeutung des Jesajabuches für Paulus*, FRLANT (Göttingen: Vandenhoek und Ruprecht, 1998); J. Ross Wagner, *Heralds of the Good News: Paul and Isaiah "In Concert" in the Letter to the Romans*, NovTSup 101 (Leiden: Brill, 2002).

166. This is, more or less, the account given by F. Godet, *Commentary on St. Paul's Epistle to the Romans*, 2 vols. (Edinburgh: T. & T. Clark, 1880–81) 1:311-12.

167. So most commentators, e.g., Dunn, *Romans 1–8*, 225; Moo, *The Epistle to the Romans*, 289.

principle that all those who belong to Jesus, all those who respond in faith to God's faithfulness revealed in him, are themselves part of the true covenant family promised to Abraham. In other words, the resurrection of Jesus can at this level be seen as the declaration of justification. And this can perfectly well be expressed as "He was raised because of our justification."

Romans 4 thus leads us to a high rock looking back over the landscape we have covered. From the same vantage point, looking ahead, we can glimpse the route we are now to take.

First, the view backward. The events concerning Jesus the Messiah, and the gospel message in which these events are announced, unveil the covenant faithfulness, the saving justice, of the creator God; because in these events the promises made to Abraham have at last been accomplished. These promises were designed to redeem the world, by creating a worldwide family in whom the grim entail of human sin and its consequences (present corruption, future wrath) would be dealt with. This has now been achieved through the sacrificial death and the resurrection of the Messiah, Jesus. Through Jesus' faithfulness, God has thus fulfilled the purpose for which the people of Israel were called into being in the first place and marked out with circumcision and Torah. Torah, however, cannot be the boundary marker of covenant membership, since it inevitably points to Israel's sin. God's creation of the non-ethnic covenant family is therefore an act of supreme grace, modeled on the way in which grace came to Abraham to begin with, bringing forgiveness of sins and present justification to all, Jew and Gentile alike, who believe in "the God who raised Jesus."

Every line in this argument, every turn in the thought, will be vital for the specific points that Paul wants to make to the church in Rome in chapters 9–11 and 12–16. From our vantage point we can see, in the distance, the outline of these passages.

In 9–11, Paul wrestles with the problem of Jewish unbelief and tells again the story of Israel, from Abraham to the Messiah and on into the future. He explains how God has in fact been faithful to the promises and how, within that framework and without smuggling in favoritism by the back door, God has not written off the Jewish people. The point of the section is found in chapter 11, where Paul warns the largely Gentile church in Rome not to despise the non-Christian Jews, who are still the objects of God's saving love and purposes.

Then, in 12–16, Paul sets out the parameters for the church to live as the renewed humanity within a pagan society. The key is again the unity, across traditional barriers, of all who believe in the God revealed in Jesus (14:1–15:13). The latter passage closes, dramatically, with the quotation of Isa 11:10, which speaks of the Messiah and his resurrection as the means by which the Gentiles will be brought under the rule of the God of Israel (Paul uses a version of Isaiah that makes this point more clearly than most translations of the prophet indicate). Paul thereby completes a huge circle with 1:3-5. The mission and unity of the church, grounded in a covenantal understanding of what the one true God accomplished in Jesus the Messiah, are the thrusts of the last two sections.

This is not the only view, however, that we gain from the end of chapter 4. As we saw when examining Paul's gospel and the way it reveals God's justice, this message offers an implicit challenge to the world Paul and his readers inhabited—the world in which Caesar ruled supreme, in which his justice had rescued the world from chaos and had established a single empire embracing all nations. Paul is not ashamed of the gospel of Jesus, because in it God's saving justice, his covenant faithfulness, is revealed. The living God thereby upstages Caesar.

What about the landscape in between our vantage point at the end of chap. 4 and the two great sections 9–11 and 12–16? How do chaps. 5–8 grow out of 1–4 and pave the way for what is to follow? This is perhaps the central question about the thought structure of Romans. It would be artificial to answer it in any other way than by introducing chaps. 5–8, which is the next exegetical task.

REFLECTIONS

1. The most important reflection to arise from Romans 4 is the non-negotiable task of persuading those who believe in Jesus as Messiah and Lord to see themselves as the children of Abraham (and indeed of Sarah). Abraham is not merely an example of a biblical character who happened to be "justified by faith"; he is, declares Paul, "the father of us all." To this picture 1 Pet 3:6, and by implication Gal 4:28-31 and Heb 11:11-12, adds that Sarah is our mother. The Pauline picture of the people of God is inescapably rooted in the history of Israel from Genesis 12 onward.

This has immediate implications. First, the Christian is committed to a rigorously non-Marcionite view of the Jewish scriptures, the history to which they bear witness, and above all the God of whom they speak. The God revealed in Jesus the Messiah is the God of Abraham; the meaning of the death and resurrection of Jesus is the meaning those events acquire when seen as the fulfillment of the promises made by this God. Christian living is characterized by faith in this God, by loyalty to the project of this God for creation, by the renewing, healing, and sanctifying power of the Spirit of this God (see chap. 8). Christians read the story of Abraham and Sarah, of Isaac and Rebekah, and of Jacob, Leah, and Rachel as their own story, as an earlier act in the great drama that reached its climax in the Messiah, Jesus (cf. 9:4-5), and has now opened up to embrace the whole world.[168] Paul struggled to persuade his Gentile converts to see themselves this way, rather than to imagine that they belonged to a new group (certainly not a new "religion"!) lately sprung up from nowhere. Largely Gentile churches in our own day need to engage in the same struggle.

Second, however, the Christian is committed to believing that this family of Abraham is not defined in terms of the Jewish law. This inevitably appears a contradiction in terms to those who, for whatever reason of personal involvement or study, know from the inside the way in which devout non-Christian Jews have thought of themselves, their traditions, and above all their Torah, from that day to this. Paul, as himself a supremely devout Jew, faced exactly this problem and made every effort to convince his readers that this surprising turn of events was in fact what had been promised and intended all along. This is the main argument of the present chapter, and indeed of Galatians 3, and it bears repeating frequently, not least in Jewish-Christian discussions. It is most revealing to compare the two quite different traditions of reading Genesis 15 in, say, Paul and the rabbinic midrashim.

The questions raised by this in our own day are not addressed in this chapter. We defer, therefore, to Romans 9–11 the matter of the continuing relationship between those who see themselves as the children of Abraham defined by faith in the lifegiving God revealed in Jesus and those who see themselves as the children of Abraham defined by the possession and keeping of the Mosaic Torah.

2. Within the family given by God to Abraham, there is no room for sub-definitions. It is hard to live in community on the basis of nothing more nor less than belief in the God who raised Jesus. Humans naturally gravitate toward communities of similar background, personality, speech, or indeed social position or bank balance; Christians are no exception. Within Western society, particularly in urban areas, this leads to choosing one's Christian fellowship and church membership for reasons that Paul would have regarded as irrelevant, possibly damaging. This in turn leads to the suspicion that others, whose faith is in fact every bit as well founded, are somehow less Christian, or maybe not even Christian at all, because of their different social or cultural idioms. Every effort must be made to overcome this. Once Paul had shown that the barrier between Jew and Gentile had been overcome in Jesus, and that God had wonderfully

---

168. On the different "acts" of the biblical story, see Wright, *The New Testament and the People of God*, 139-43.

achieved the worldwide community promised originally to Abraham, there was no excuse, and there remains no excuse, for thinking that one's own culture is so deeply important, even important to the gospel, that it must not be compromised by fellowship with others who do things differently.

3. Within this, Christians must embody in their church life the truth articulated in 4:4-8: the fact that the family promised by God to Abraham is a family of forgiven sinners, rescued by grace alone from the personal and communal disintegration that results from idolatry and sin. The God we worship is the God who justifies the ungodly, not the pious. There is, no doubt, a danger in setting up a social or even a theological inverted snobbery, of imagining that because we are socially inferior, or poor, or casual rather than devout in worship, or even that we are morally careless rather than legalistic, that this in turn somehow establishes us, rather than the devout, as the true people of God. This, indeed, is the implication, and sometimes more than the implication, of some writing on Paul and Romans, in which the problem Paul is addressing is the problem of "religion" and the apparent human attempt to use religious practices as a means of earning God's favor.[169] But if piety will not earn God's favor, nor will impiety; if religion will not do, nor will irreligion; if moralism will not qualify us, nor will immoralism.

When this bit of ivy, which easily winds itself around church life, has been uprooted—it is not, after all, what Paul is talking about—the tree is free to use its energy for proper growth. And the point at which we need to grow continually is in making real, to ourselves and one another, and particularly in the way we structure our corporate life, the fact that we believe in, and celebrate, the God who justifies the ungodly. Forgiveness remains one of the most astonishing gifts, and the church should be the place where people are regularly astonished by it.

4. Romans 4 urges us to examine the way in which true faith reflects, and feeds on, the character of God, and the way in which it leads to the rehabilitation of the true image-bearingness of human beings. Abraham's faith, analyzed in detail in vv. 18-21, is focused on, and gains its character from, the true God at every turn. It looks fully at the human and worldly situation, filled as it is with death and decay; it acknowledges that this is the state we are in; and it also looks steadfastly at the God who raises the dead and creates out of nothing. Worshiping this God (4:20), and acknowledging that this God has the power to deliver on promises of new life in the place of death, is fundamental to Christian faith. It is also the reversal and undoing of that idolatry outlined in 1:18-25, and therefore cannot but issue in a life that undoes and reverses the consequent behavior spoken of in 1:26-31. Paul does not develop this further here, but those who want to live with the meaning of Romans 4 cannot avoid looking further, not just to chap. 6, but also to chap. 12, where he holds out a model of remade humanity in which the faith spoken of in chap. 4 has its full effect in transforming mind, character, and behavior.

5. The centrality of faith in God's raising of Jesus from the dead emerges with peculiar clarity from this chapter. In Western liberalism it has often been thought quite acceptable, sometimes even desirable, sometimes actually mandatory, that one should disbelieve in the resurrection of Jesus. There is much misinformation on this topic. It is often assumed that people who believe in Jesus' bodily resurrection hold a pre-scientific worldview without knowledge of the real facts of the world. To this mentality Paul's statement in v. 19 is especially relevant. It was not the case that Abraham was living in a fool's paradise, refusing to face the facts about himself. On the contrary, he looked them in the face and went on believing in the God who raises the dead. It will not do to declare that we modern persons now "know" that no such thing as bodily

---

169. See esp. Käsemann's repeated talk of *homo religiosus* as the real target of Paul's polemic.

resurrection occurs. It does not help to cite the fact that in all cases observable to us dead people have in fact stayed dead. The testimony of the early church was precisely that, though of course all other humans remained as dead as Abraham's and Sarah's bodies (in terms of their childbearing possibilities), in this particular case the creator God had acted in a decisive, striking and as yet unique way, to give to Jesus a new bodily life—not merely a resuscitation into the same sort of bodily existence as before, but a new dimension of bodily existence. There is, no doubt, room for endless discussion about what form precisely Jesus' resurrection took and how best we might speak of it in subsequent generations. But there is no room, as far as Paul is concerned, for that impossible hybrid, a Christian who does not in any sense believe in the resurrection of Jesus.

ROMANS 5:1–8:39

GOD'S PEOPLE IN CHRIST AS THE TRUE HUMANITY

OVERVIEW

Romans 5–8 is a majestic statement of some of Paul's greatest themes. The love of God embodied in Jesus' death; the hope, even during suffering, enjoyed by God's justifed people; Jesus' reversal of Adam's sin and its effects; Christian freedom from sin, the law and death itself; the life-giving leading of the Spirit. Parts of this section are sure to feature in anyone's selection of favorite biblical passages. Countless Christians, faced with life's greatest trials, have found strength and joy in Paul's closing words: "Neither height nor depth nor any other creature shall be able to separate us from the love of God in Christ Jesus our Lord" (8:39).

At the same time, these chapters contain some of Paul's densest and most difficult writing. The Adam/Christ contrast of 5:12-21 is cryptic and elliptical: trying to read its Greek after the measured sentences of 5:1-11 is like turning from Rembrandt to Picasso. Chapter 7 has produced dozens of conflicting interpretations: it has been both hailed as a profound analysis of the human condition and dismissed as a tortured and self-contradictory rambling. The description of cosmic liberation (8:19-22) is seen by some as a great climax, by others as an irrelevant aside. The section offers, in short, just what every Pauline exegete really wants: good, strong themes to enjoy, knotty problems to puzzle over.

Not everyone has agreed that 5–8 constitute a discrete section. Some have suggested that 1:18–5:11, or even 1:18–5:21, should be seen as the real first main section of the letter, with 5:12 or 6:1 starting the new symphonic movement. Paul's argument does indeed run on without a break here, unlike the deep breath between chaps. 8 and 9 or between chaps. 11 and 12. The two main paragraphs of chap. 5 (vv. 1-11, 12-21) sum up what has gone before as well as setting out material to be further explored (e.g., 5:9 looks back to 3:24-26 and to the "wrath" of 1:18; 5:12-21 refers back to the implicit "Adam" theme in 1:18-25; 5:20 picks up 2:17-24 and 3:19-20). The chapter and paragraph divisions of Romans are of course a late invention. If Romans had concluded with personal greetings after 5:21, some might feel let down, but nobody would suggest that 5:1-21 belonged to a different world of thought from chaps. 1–4.

Nevertheless, the subject matter of 5:1-11 and 5:12-21 contains so many differences from that of chaps. 1–4 that most exegetes have concluded, rightly in my view, that they belong more naturally with what follows than with what precedes. Paul here speaks of God's love, not (principally) God's righteousness. Abraham is not mentioned, nor (apart from 5:1-2) is faith (see also 6:8; this is not part of a discussion of "faith" per se, but refers to a particular thing that Christians believe). The whole "Jew-plus-Gentile" theme, strikingly, is never mentioned; the law is again a major theme, but "works of the law" is not. Jesus, hardly mentioned in 1:18–4:25, is everywhere. Equally telling, Paul says a good deal in chaps. 5–8 about "we" and "you," whereas in the preceding section he has not spoken of "us" until the very last verses, and the earlier "you" passages are rhetorical, addressing imaginary interlocutors, whereas here he is speaking to his own actual audience.

There is a marked contrast of style. Instead of expounding passages of Scripture, Paul develops his own line of thought, alluding to Scripture frequently, and indeed retelling one of Scripture's greatest stories, but without regular quotation or exposition of specific passages. And instead of the diatribe style and its rapid-fire verbal tennis match, addressed to imaginary debating partners, we have a sustained line of thought, addressed to "my family" (ἀδελφοί *adelphoi*; lit., "brothers," 7:1, 4; 8:12; some translations, anxious about the gender-specific "brothers," replace it with "friends," but for Paul the family identity and consequent unity of God's people is paramount), building from one point to the next with an extraordinary integration of complex thought (Paul uses elements of the previous rhetorical style in, e.g., 6:1-3, 15-16; 7:7, 13—in other words, to turn particular corners in the argument, rather than to develop particular points).

This sequence of thought is opened up initially with four paragraphs of very similar length (5:1-11, 12-21; 6:1-11, 12-23), each rounded off with a christological formula that is not just added on for effect but sums up the paragraph. This then gives rise to two larger expositions. The first concerns the law: this is introduced in 7:1-6 and developed in 7:7–8:11. While completing this subject, 8:1-11 simultaneously introduces the second theme, that of the Spirit and of Christian and cosmic hope (8:1-30). Paul then returns to the topics with which the section began (8:31-39 repeats the themes of 5:1-11, with all the rhetorical stops pulled out), concluding once more with an emphatic christological summary.

Romans 5–8, then, is a carefully crafted unit. Here, more than anywhere else in Paul's surviving writing, we have a sense of a piece that might well have been composed earlier. Some have even argued that it is just that and that its placing between Romans 1–4 and 9–11 is, in effect, the combining of two quite different writings.[170] However, even if we suppose that Paul has thought it all through ahead of time and perhaps already committed some or all of it to writing (but would he really have left the grammar of 5:12-21 like that?), we are still faced with the question: why did he insert it here? When we add

that chaps. 5–8 grow naturally out of 1–4 and prepare the way for both 9–11 and 12–16, we realize that the problem is not solved by the surgeon's knife. We must enquire further how the actual train of thought of these chapters develops the larger argument that Paul is actually mounting in the letter—as opposed, unfortunately, to the argument that various traditions, both Christian and scholarly, have assumed that he is mounting. It is easy here to analyze the trees and ignore the forest. We here offer a preliminary solution, to be filled in as the exegesis progresses.

Romans 5–8 has played a vital role in mainstream Protestant readings of Romans. If chaps. 1–4 are held to be about "justification by faith," this section, starting from this point (5:1), is about something that follows from justification. Since the Reformers' exposition of justification regularly led to the question of Christian behavior, often framed in some such way as in 6:1 or 6:15, and since the word "sanctification" occurs twice in chap. 6 (vv. 19, 22), some concluded that chaps. 1–4 were "about" "justification," and chaps. 5–8 were "about" "sanctification." However, though there is indeed a sequence of thought from justification to something else in these chapters, this particular reading is unlikely to be accurate. The scarcity of the word "sanctification," and the fact that when Paul sums up the argument in 8:30 the final line reads "those he justified, them he also *glorified*," point in a rather different direction. If 1–4 is in any sense "about" justification, we might expect 5–8 to be "about" glorification.[171]

This is strikingly confirmed by the last phrase of 5:2, which completes the introductory sentence (5:1-2), and by the argument of 8:18-25, which has a good claim to be the point toward which the rest is moving. Of course, "glorification" here serves as a shorthand for the entire Christian hope, to which Paul can equally well refer by such phrases as "eternal life" (e.g., 2:7); but the point seems to be, throughout, that what God has done in Jesus the Messiah, and what God is already doing through the Spirit, guarantees that all those who believe the gospel, and are thus "justified by faith," can be assured of their

170. See Robin Scroggs, "Paul as Rhetorician: Two Homilies in Romans 1–11," in *Jews, Greeks and Christians: Religious Cultures in Late Antiquity: Essays in Honour of William David Davies*, ed. Robert Hamerton-Kelly and Robin Scroggs, Studies in Judaism in Late Antiquity 21(Leiden: Brill, 1976) 71-98. This is discussed, together with several other similar suggestions, by Leander E. Keck, "What Makes Romans Tick?" in Hay and Johnson, *Pauline Theology Volume III*, 3-29.

171. I place "about" in quotation marks because it is always unwise, in Romans, to imply that a given section has one topic and only one. The writing is more complex and symphonic than that.

final hope. They will be delivered from wrath (5:9), in other words, "saved."[172] They will be given the new bodies of resurrection life that will correspond to that of Jesus (8:11). And, since "glory" is another way of speaking of the presence of God, dwelling in the wilderness tabernacle or the Jerusalem Temple, the line of thought that runs from 5:2 ("we celebrate the hope of God's glory") to 8:30 ("those he justified, them he also glorified") involves specifically the indwelling of God, by the Spirit. The whole passage thus emphasizes that what God did decisively in Jesus the Messiah is now to be implemented through the Spirit. Paul points to ways in which the Christian's present status and future hope determine life in the the present, but the real theme is the secure future. All is guaranteed by the unshakable love of God—which is in turn demonstrated in the death of Jesus (5:6-10; 8:31-39). This is the argument that emerges most obviously from the surface of chaps. 5–8.

Beneath the surface, however, and poking out like the tips of a huge iceberg at various key points, there runs a different theme, not so often noticed. A word is necessary about the detection of apparently submerged themes. For centuries nobody minded when exegetes declared that Romans 1–4 was "about" justification and 5–8 "about" sanctification. These were regular topics in the systematic theology that sustained many churches and preachers; it seemed reasonable that Paul should develop his argument along such lines, and some sense could be made of the text on that basis (with little exceptions like 7:7-25; 8:18-25). The fact that Paul nowhere said that this was how he was dividing his material, and that so far as we know "justification" and "sanctification" did not function in his mind (or anyone else's in the first century) in the same way as they did in the church, did not seem to matter. But when people today propose alternative underlying themes, even when they are far more plausible within the mind of a Second Temple Jew, they are often howled down. "How can you be sure?" they are asked. "Why does Paul not say it more openly if that's what he meant?"

The argument for all such interpretations is cumulative. It consists of a hypothesis that one obtains not deductively (starting with the material before us and seeing what we can deduce from it), but by induction (moving from the particular to the general) or abduction (moving from data to larger theory).[173] As in much scientific procedure, the aim is to postulate a framework that, when examined, may turn out to explain the data before us better, with more complete satisfaction, than the alternatives.[174] Like all serious readings of literary texts, such a proposal is to be verified, or as it may be falsified, not by the knock-down arguments of pseudo-scientific "proof," nor by the largely irrelevant question as to whether Paul's first audience would have seen the point at first hearing,[175] but by the overall sense that results. There are times when the answer to the objection, "But I don't see that in the text," is "Try looking through the telescope the right way round," or perhaps, "Try looking at the forest, not just the trees."

In case it seems that I protests too much, let me propose the reading of chaps. 5–8 of which I have become convinced and that, as I shall attempt to show, allows fully both for the integrity and distinction of these chapters as a section in their own right and for their careful integration with the four chapters that precede them and the eight that follow—in other words, for the advancement of the overall argument of the letter. Paul, I suggest, is telling the story of the people of the Messiah in terms of the new exodus. Jesus' people are the liberated people, on their way home to their promised land.[176]

---

172. It is curious that Fitzmyer, *Romans*, 393, supposes "salvation" to be the topic of Romans 1–4, now left behind. The only mention of the idea (even then, not the key words) in 1:18–4:25 is in 2:7, 10, which look forward precisely to chaps. 5–8.

173. On "abduction," the least known of these, see C. S. Peirce, *Collected Papers* (Cambridge, Mass.: Harvard University Press, 1958) 7:89-164.

174. For further discussion of method, see Wright, *The New Testament and the People of God*, chaps. 2–5.

175. This will be addressed in due course. Most major pieces of writing, and for that matter music and art, reveal their depths gradually. This is not a matter of bad communication but of the impossibility of instantaneously communicating truths that function at many levels simultaneously.

176. A detailed account of the proposal is found in N. T. Wright, "New Exodus, New Inheritance: The Narrative Substructure of Romans 3–8," in Sunderlund and Wright, *Romans and the People of God* 26-35. Though I go some way beyond either, I have learned much from Frank Thielman, "The Story of Israel and the Theology of Romans 5–8," in Hay and Johnson, *Pauline Theology, Volume III*, 169-95, and Sylvia C. Keesmaat, *Paul and His Story: (Re)Interpreting the Exodus Tradition*, JNSTSup (Sheffield: Sheffield Academic, 1999). An earlier statement of one part of the proposal is found in Ignace de la Potterie, "Le chrétien conduit par l'Esprit dans son cheminement eschatologique (Rom 8,14)," in *The Law of the Spirit in Rom 7 and 8*, ed. L. de Lorenzi (Rome: St Paul's Abbey, 1976) 209-41.

The theme of "new exodus" is a major topic in Second Temple Judaism. It is a central way by which Jews in Paul's day expressed, symbolized, and narrated their hopes for the future–for the time when, as the prophets had foretold, their God would repeat, on their behalf, the great acts whereby their forebears were liberated from Egypt (e.g., Isa 11:11; 35:3-10; 51:9-11; 52:4-6; Jer 16:14-15; 23:7-8; Ezek 20:33-38; Hos 2:14-23). One biblical passage in particular stands out as carrying the themes of Romans 1–11 as a whole:

The days are surely coming, says YHWH, when I will raise up for David a righteous Branch, and he shall reign as king and deal wisely, and shall execute justice and righteousness in the land. In his days Judah will be saved and Israel will live in safety. And this is the name by which he will be called: "YHWH is our righteousness."

Therefore, the days are surely coming, says YHWH, when it shall no longer be said, "As YHWH lives who brought the people of Israel up out of the land of Egypt," but "As YHWH lives who brought out and led the offspring of the house of Israel out of the land of the north and out of all the lands where I had driven them." Then they shall live in their own land. (Jer 23:5-8)

The Messiah, the righteousness of God, and the new exodus. Allowing for Paul's new perspective, whereby the promise of the land has been redefined into the promise of inheriting the whole cosmos (4:13; 8:18-25), the pattern is exact. Paul, like many other Second Temple Jews, longed for the day when God would fulfill the promises made to Abraham by bringing Israel back from exile, repeating what had been done at the exodus. Only this time, through the work of the Messiah, it would be on a different scale. This time the whole cosmos would be involved. This would be the revelation of the righteousness of God before the whole world. Paul's mind has already been moving in this way in chaps. 2 and 4; now he will develop the picture far more extensively. If he is talking about salvation, he is talking about the new exodus.[177]

The case for this reading of chaps. 5–8 can be seen to good advantage by working backward from its most obvious point, Rom 8:12-25. Paul speaks of those who are led by the Spirit of God being God's children (8:14); the phrase is very similar to that of Deut 14:1, looking back (as do all such ascriptions of divine parentage) to Exod 4:22 (see also Isa 1:2; Hos 1:10; Sir 1:10). The contrast between "the spirit of slavery" and "the spirit of adoption" (8:15) can well be construed as the contrast between Israel in Egypt and Israel journeying through the wilderness; Paul's appeal is that his readers should not think, as Israel sometimes did, of going back to slavery rather than on to full freedom. And the crowning point of the paragraph is that God's children are also "heirs." Paul's word here (κληρονόμοι klēronomoi) employs the root that occurs dozens of times in the LXX, not least in Deuteronomy, usually standing for the Hebrew roots ירשׁ (yrš) or נחל (nḥl), in reference to the promised land, or part of it, as the "inheritance" God's people would acquire when the wilderness wandering was complete. For Paul, as we saw in Rom 4:13, the promise to Abraham concerning one particular piece of land has been transformed into a promise concerning "the world" (ὁ κόσμος ho kosmos) or, as here, "creation" (ἡ κτίσις hē ktisis).

This answers to the deepest level of the problem outlined in 1:18-32. God fulfills the promise to Abraham by redeeming the human race; when the human race is redeemed, the whole creation will be set free. Paul applies to creation as a whole the same exodus language he uses of God's people in chap. 6 and elsewhere: creation itself "will be set free from its slavery to corruption, into the freedom of the glory of the children of God" (8:21). The argument is based upon a retelling of the exodus story, in which not only God's people but also the whole creation are set free from "Egypt"—that is, sin, decay, and death. God's redeemed people are given the "glory" that humans lost at the fall (3:23), receiving "the world" as their inheritance.[178] God's creation

---

177. Paul uses salvation terms (from the roots σωτηρία sōtēria; σώζω sōzō; and their cognates) in Rom 5:9-10; 8:24 in such a way as to make it clear that this is another way of talking about the "glorification" and the "eternal life" that has already been mentioned, on which see below.

178. See also Matt 5:5, which uses γῆ (gē, "land") as the object of "shall inherit." This is ambiguous. It could refer either to the land of Israel (as in Deut 4:38) or the whole world. Cf. Acts 1:8, where "to the ends of the earth" (NRSV) translates ἕως ἐσχάτου τῆς γῆς (heōs eschatou tēs gēs), which could technically mean "to the ends of the land [i.e., of Israel]," but in the light of Acts as a whole seems to mean "to the ends of the world."

currently shares the futility and corruption of the human race; when humans are set free, creation will be liberated as well.

Within the argument of Romans, the motif of slavery and freedom goes back at least to "redemption" in 3:24, but is highlighted especially in chap. 6. In 6:16, Paul personifies "sin" and "death" as the slavemasters who have kept the human race captive, and "obedience" and "righteousness" as the new owners under whom humans find freedom. He then continues the metaphor, recognizing its limitations (6:19a), through to the end of the chapter, and builds it in to the theme of the next section (7:6, 25). This, clearly, is anticipating the "exodus" passage about slavery and freedom in chap. 8. But 6:16-23 is the development of the earlier part of the chapter, where the key event is baptism, uniting the Christian with the Messiah in his death and resurrection. Baptism, it appears, is the event through which, by means of this uniting, those enslaved to sin and death are now set free. But baptism, elsewhere in Paul, becomes a symbolic reminder of the crossing of the Red Sea (1 Cor 10:2—a passage in which Paul is urging his readers to think of themselves as in the same position as the wilderness generation, set free from Egypt and on the way home to their inheritance).[179] My proposal is that the journey that ends in chap. 8 with the glorious inheritance began in chap. 6 with the new covenant version of the crossing of the Red Sea, the event through which the slaves are set free.

This gives a new narrative coherence to the central section of 5–8—namely, 7:1–8:11. It is not just that Paul must now address, head on, the problem of the law to which he has referred several times (3:19-20; 4:15; 5:20; 6:14). Paul, unfortunately for his interpreters, is aware of no obligation to explain all the puzzling one-liners scattered throughout his writings. He is writing a letter, after all, not a doctoral dissertation. The deeper reason for writing chap. 7 is that he is following the storyline. After the Red Sea, and before the journey to the promised inheritance, comes Mt. Sinai and the giving of the Torah.

Using the exodus-story in this way carries, of course, a certain ambiguity. Paul does not think in terms of a simple typology whereby a pattern repeats itself over and over, but of a continuing narrative in which the new sequence, for all it repeats the old and gains its meaning from that repetition, also in some senses replaces the old and even undermines it. This ambiguity comes to its head in the parallel between the law and the Spirit: Torah itself has become part of the problem, part of the thing from which one needs to be set free. Paul's task in chap. 7 is then to exonerate Torah from blame, while demonstrating that only in Christ and the Spirit can its underlying intention—to give life—be realized. As an abstract theological proposition, this has always seemed difficult to maintain, and this difficulty has been produced as the reason for Paul's dense and problematic argument. When seen within the context of an overarching narrative in which the events of the exodus are recapitulated in Christ and by the Spirit, in which the promises of the law and the prophets are fulfilled "apart from the law," it makes considerably more sense, and leads naturally into the passage we have already drawn attention to as the most obvious "new exodus" allusion (8:12-25).

At the head of this whole sequence of thought stands 5:12-21, where the Messiah is set in parallel, and also sharp contrast, with Adam. Adam, of course, was the one to whom, in Scripture, the whole creation was given as his inheritance. His "glory" consisted not least in his rule over the rest of God's world. The result of the fall was that the inheritance and the glory were lost; this is the picture Paul drew in 1:18-32, and summed up in 3:23. Now, in the Messiah, inheritance and glory are given back to the human race. They are to become truly human at last. Romans 5:12-21 functions as a programmatic statement, awaiting the fuller explanation of 8:12-30.

The story is more complicated than that, of course, because Israel was itself called to be the people through whom this should happen. The failure of Israel, expounded in 2:17–3:20 and presupposed here, has left a double task to be performed. The Messiah has not only reversed the fall of Adam; he has accomplished the redemptive work of Israel. His "obedience," which means almost exactly the same as his "faithfulness" (3:22),

179. See R. B. Hays, "The Conversion of the Imagination: Scripture and Eschatology in 1 Corinthians," *NTS* 45 (1999) 391-412.

has accomplished that for which God called Israel in the first place. Torah was not, then, the means of redemption, but rather a further part of the problem, a further twist of the knife; and God has dealt with that as well. Verses 12-21, summing up where the argument of the letter has got to so far, plant the seeds that will bear fruit for the rest of 5–8.

The theme of 5:1-11 is clear, introducing the line of thought that will be summed up at the end of chap. 8: those who are justified are also glorified, because of the love of God effective through the death of Jesus. It is the move from faith to hope; from the one-off work of the Messiah to the inaugurated, but not yet consummated, work of the Spirit. This is Paul's other great theme, here and in 5–8 as a whole: those who are on this pilgrimage know the presence of the living God, not now in the pillar of cloud and fire, but in the Holy Spirit, who pours the love of God into their hearts, so that "reconciliation" (5:10-11) is not merely a fact but an experienced fact.

What contribution, then, does Romans 5–8 make toward the developing argument of the letter as a whole?

At one level, it functions as the natural sequel to 1–4. The argument for the assurance of salvation—the argument, that is, on the surface of the text—answers to one of the main strands of thought in the opening chapters. All sinned, came short of God's glory, and faced wrath. Despite what is commonly thought, 3:21–4:25 is not Paul's main answer to this problem, but rather the groundwork for the answer. The full answer comes in 5–8: there we are told that those in Christ will escape the wrath and inherit God's glory. There it is explained that those who are justified are also glorified. There Paul shows how the human race is renewed, to bear God's image afresh in Christ (8:29).

Chapters 5–8 are also where the achievement of Jesus, supremely in his vicarious messianic death, is set out most fully. The dense and cryptic statement in 3:24-26, vital though it is, points ahead to the fuller statement in 5:6-11 and 5:15-21, which are then developed in key summaries throughout the following chapters (6:3-11; 7:4; 8:3; 8:31-39). Throughout it is clear that the death of Jesus, seen here as the ground of Christian hope and

Christian life, functions as such because it is first the ground of justification. Once more, 5–8 completes the train of thought in 1–4.

The theme of assurance, and of the salvation of the human race in Christ, is given power and depth by the latent exodus-narrative. When, in Genesis 15, God promised Abraham a family, the promise was explained in terms of the exodus. Now, developing the larger vision that Paul discovered in the Abrahamic promise, the human race as a whole has its exodus: its rescue from the slavery of sin and death, the indwelling presence of God by the Spirit, the present journey through the wilderness, and the hope of the final inheritance. As in 1 Corinthians, one of Paul's aims, particularly when writing to a largely Gentile church, is to implant in their worldview the scriptural narrative through which they will discover their own place on the map of God's purposes.[180] The gospel unveils the righteousness (that is, the covenant faithfulness) of God; God's people in Christ must learn to tell the story of that faithfulness and to live within it. Again, Romans 5–8 completes a strand within chaps. 1–4.

The theme of "Jew first and also Greek," so prominent in 1–4, may be absent from the text of 5–8, but it is not forgotten or left behind. What Paul says in 5–8 he says to, and of, the church as a whole. But only his Jewish and proselyte readers had been "under the law." The freedom from the law that looms so large in the middle of this section (7:1–8:11; anticipated in 5:20-21 and 6:14-15) and that gives rise to Paul's central statement of the death of Jesus, the indwelling of the Spirit, and the promise of resurrection (8:1-11), belongs to the story of how Israel's history reached its climax in the Messiah, and did so for the benefit of the whole world. In each case, however, the completion of one line of thought raises a further question. If salvation is assured because of Jesus' messianic death and the work of the Spirit, what about the people to whom the promises were first made? If God has accomplished the true exodus, what about the people of the original exodus? How can their story be truly told in the light of the full unveiling of God's righteousness in Jesus the Messiah?

180. See Hays, "The Conversion of the Imagination: Scripture and Eschatology in 1 Corinthians."

The opening of Romans 9 indicates that Paul is raising exactly these questions in exactly this way. The problem addressed in Romans 9–11, therefore, is introduced precisely as the dark side of the new exodus. Furthermore, Paul's account of Israel's privileges in 9:4-5 lists the very things that throughout chaps. 1–8 have been attributed, through Christ and the Spirit, to the wider family of Abraham described in chaps. 4–8. In other words, the first eight chapters of the letter raise particular questions about God's faithfulness to ethnic Israel that must be addressed for the sake of completeness.

But it would be a mistake to see chaps. 9–11, or for that matter chaps. 12–16, simply as necessary outworkings of an inner logic latent within 1–8. That would be to collapse back once more into regarding Romans 1–8 as "the things Paul really wants to say" and 9–16 as "the things he is now forced to deal with because of what he has said." Without sliding into the opposite mistake (supposing that chaps. 9–11 and/or 12–16 are the "really important" parts, and chaps. 1–8 a mere preliminary), it is vital to see that one of the reasons Paul has set his argument out like this is precisely so that he can move forward from here to address the major issues that face the church in Rome. We postpone more detailed examination of this point to the introduction to chaps. 9–11.

It is possible, in other words, to read Romans 5–8 without reference to what has gone before or what comes after. It stands as one of the most central and majestic statements of all that Paul most passionately believes and articulately expounds. But to take it out of its context is like looking at a tree without considering its roots or its fruits. What Paul says here grows out of chaps. 1–4 and is designed to bear fruit in chaps. 9–11 and 12–16.

ROMANS 5:1-11, FROM FAITH TO HOPE

OVERVIEW

The first paragraph of the new section states and develops the theme that overarches the next four chapters: those whom God justified, God also glorified. In typical fashion, this is stated densely to start with (5:1-2). It is then developed with two new elements, suffering and the Spirit (5:3-5), explained and grounded (in the death of the Messiah) (5:6-9), and finally further explained and celebrated (5:10-11). As usual, Paul's successive explanations do not add new points to the opening summary, but rather explore what is contained by implication within it.

The theme is that of inaugurated eschatology. God has accomplished the justification of sinners; God will therefore complete the task, saving those already justified from the coming wrath (cf. Phil 1:6: when God begins a work, God will complete it). God's decisive disclosure of covenant faithfulness in the death of the Messiah (3:21–4:25) is now expressed in equally covenantal language, that of God's love (5:8). The argument is simple: if God loved sinners enough for the Son to die for them, God will surely complete what was begun at such cost. Those who have left Egypt will be brought to Canaan, even though suffering awaits them on the journey. Part of Christian assurance is learning to tell this story and to understand its inner logic.

The three tenses of salvation (as they are sometimes called) are thus unveiled. Paul presupposes and builds on his exposition of justification by faith in 3:21–4:25, though in 5:9-10 he will reveal its further depths: being "justified by (Christ's) blood" is functionally equivalent to "being reconciled to God through Jesus' death." This is the past tense of God's action in the Messiah. The future tense is supplied by the word "salvation" (5:9-10); this means "rescue from the coming wrath" (5:9; cf. 1 Thess 1:10) through Jesus' life. The present tense, held between these two, consists of peace, celebration, suffering, hope, love, reconciliation and (once more) celebration.

Paul is not, then, describing a mere formal or legal transaction. The whole paragraph is suffused with the personal relationship between the justified person and the God revealed in Jesus. It is a relationship of love on both sides, in which reconciliation has replaced enmity (5:5, 10). This intimacy comes about through the gift of God's Spirit, the presence of God with the newly constituted community and within the redeemed person, not least in their present wilderness sufferings. Verses 1-11 thus reveals something that had all along been at the heart of chaps. 1–4, though often hidden underneath Paul's legal imagery and the long tradition of its forensic interpretation: all that God said to Abraham, all that God accomplished in the Messiah, was done out of love, and designed to call out an answering love. The intimacy and ecstasy of 5:1-11 are a necessary further dimension of the doctrine of justification by faith.

Romans 5:1-5, Peace, Patience, and Hope

COMMENTARY

5:1-2. Justification results in peace with God, in access to God's loving favor, and thereby, unstoppably, to the hope of glory. Thus Paul opens the paragraph and section with a characteristically dense statement of the past event, the present result, and the future promise. The whole thing is built on what has gone before: "therefore," as often, provides a key transition.

The emphasis of v. 1 falls on "we have peace." Many good manuscripts read ἐχῶμεν (*echōmen*, "let us have peace," imperative), rather than ἔχομεν (*echomcn*, "we have peace," indicative), and some scholars have made a case for this reading.[181] The argument for the indicative, though, is strong: (a) the two main verbs of the second verse are in the indicative (the second could be either, but the first seems determinative); (b) the difference between a long and a short "o" was not very marked in the pronunciation of Greek when the manuscript was being copied and perhaps redictated; (c) "peace" at the start of the paragraph relates closely to "reconciliation" at its end, and reconciliation is there spoken of not as something to be striven for, but something "we have received."

God's justice has led to peace: the echoes of the world Paul was addressing are strong. Augustus Caesar had established the Roman *Pax*, founded on *Iustitia*.[182] His successors, enjoying among their titles "Lord" and "Savior," maintained the powerful imperial myth not least through the imperial cult. Paul is revealing to his Roman audience a different justice, a different peace, in virtue of a different Lord and a different God: the God of Abraham, the world's creator, who has now established peace "through our Lord Jesus Christ." This peace, the first characteristic Paul mentions of the present tense of salvation, includes the deeply personal reconciliation between each believer and the true God, but can hardly stop there; already Paul is sowing the seeds for that communal peace he longs to see come about in the whole Roman church (14:1–15:14; see esp. 14:17, 19), the work, indeed, of "the God of peace" (15:33; 16:20). It is this peace, embracing alike each person and the whole community, that reveals to the wider world the existence and nature of the alternative empire, set up through the true Lord, the Messiah. In one short verse Paul manages to articulate both the heart of Christian personal experience and the politically subversive nature of Christian loyalty.

By way of explaining this peace, Paul uses the language of the cult: we have obtained, he says, "access" to grace, the same root being used as the regular verb for approaching the altar with a sacrifice.[183] "Grace" is here

181. Fitzmyer, *Romans*, 395, lists Kuss, Lagrange, and Sanday and Headlam as taking this view. See the judicious discussion in Moo, *The Epistle to the Romans*, 295-96.

182. For this whole theme, see esp. D. Georgi, *Theocracy in Paul's Praxis and Theology* (Minneapolis: Fortress, 1991) 79-104; reprinted in Horsley, *Paul and Empire*, 148-57.

183. Dunn, *Romans 1–8*, 248, casts doubt on this and suggests instead the idea of approaching the emperor's throne room. This is possible as well, but προσάγω (*prosagō*, "to bring near") occurs very frequently in cultic contexts in the LXX. It is true that the verb is used of bringing the sacrifice, not the worshiper, into God's presence (so Moo, *Romans*, 300-301), but this is hardly an objection in the light of 12:1 and 15:16.

clearly a shorthand, not so much for God's action on behalf of undeserving sinners, but for the sphere of God's continuing love. The metaphor envisages grace as a room into which Jesus has ushered all who believe,[184] a room where they now "stand," a place characterized by the presence and sustaining love of God. Just as the Temple symbolized and actualized Israel's meeting with the gracious God, so now Jesus has effected such a meeting between this God and all who approach by faith.

The result of past justification and the present status of grace is the future hope: "we celebrate the hope of the glory of God." The NRSV's "boast" keeps the same English word that the Greek had in 2:17 and 3:27; the NIV, understandably regarding "boast" as purely negative, replaces it here with "rejoice."[185] Part of the difficulty is that we think of "boasting" as self-advertisement, (which we, unlike the world of Paul's day, find distasteful), whereas Paul's Greek has a larger significance: it has to do with the grounds for confidence when facing both present and future. Hence, "celebrate": this brings together the two senses of joy and confidence. What could not be attained through Torah—namely, a secure confidence in being God's people—on offer through Jesus Christ (see the Commentary on 8:3-4).

The content of the hope is "glory." This is an advance statement of the theme developed in 8:18, 21, 30 (cf. Col 1:27). Adam's lost glory (3:23) is regained in the Messiah: not simply dazzling beauty, but the status and task of being God's vicegerent over creation. That this is what Paul has in mind becomes clear in 8:18-27, where the revelation of God's children and their glory leads to the liberation of the whole created order. When humans are restored to be as they were intended to be, then the whole of creation will be renewed under their lordship. At the same time, the cultic context, and the mention of the Spirit at the end of the next sentence, suggests that Paul has in mind also the glory of God dwelling in the Temple: God's glorious presence, at work already in the hearts of believers, will one day flood their whole being. This, too, is

borne out by the development of the subject in chap. 8. This is the hope that supplies confidence and joy.

5:3-5. Paul now approaches the same result from a different angle. Present Christian existence is not simply a matter of peace with God, but also, paradoxically, of suffering. This suffering, though, is to be understood as part of a larger story that again ends with hope. This time, instead of characterizing the hope by "glory," Paul speaks of the indwelling Spirit, who elsewhere, not least in the climax to chaps. 5–8, is the one who guarantees the future hope for the suffering people (8:12-30). In early Christian thought, as at Qumran, the Spirit is a sign of the in-breaking new age.

So, then, we celebrate our sufferings; a typically counterintuitive Pauline comment, in our day as in his own, where suffering was more likely to be regarded as a sign of the gods' displeasure. Paul tells a different story: Suffering produces patience (the NRSV's "endurance" and the NIV's "perseverance" both bring out aspects of the same idea, which is not so much of pressing ahead in adversity as simply staying put without dismay). The point of this is not simply that patience is a virtue worth cultivating, but that out of patience grows "character"—a difficult word, since, although "a person of character" implies good character, we can also speak in English of "a bad character." The Greek has the overtone of "tried and tested," what we mean when we speak of someone as "firm as a rock." This, too, is valued not so much as a virtue in its own right but because from it springs hope. On the surface, there is no obvious logic in this. The Stoicism popular in Paul's day valued patience under suffering and prized a tried and tested character, but came up with little or no hope as a result. Within Paul's narrative world, however, there was plenty of point: the long journey through the wilderness leads to the promised land. In addition, Paul had personal evidence, from his own life and that of friends and colleagues, to back up the story and theology. When the patience is Christian patience, and the tried and tested character a Christian character, the result is neither shallow optimism nor settled fatalism, but hope.

184. Some MSS, followed by the NRSV mg., omit "by faith." Whether or not it stood in the original text, it certainly says what Paul meant.

185. See Bryan, *A Preface to Romans,* 121n. 3, on the importance of recognizing such "hooks" to what has gone before.

This hope does not make us ashamed. "Does not disappoint us" may well express part of the true understanding: this hope will not let us down. It will be fulfilled. In that case, the evidence he offers (the love of God in our hearts by the Spirit) functions the same way as in 8:23. It is the firstfruits and guarantee of God's ultimate saving work (see 2 Cor 1:22; 5:5; see also the Commentary on 10:11-13, where "not put to shame" is functionally equivalent to "saved"). But it is possible, not least in view of the present tense Paul chooses, that by "not ashamed" he means, rather, that the Christian's present condition, living in hope, is nothing to be ashamed of (cf. 1:16). Though Christian living is often paradoxical and deeply painful, one can hold up one's head, because the present experience of the Spirit fills the heart with love. This reading fits well with 8:24-28, where the thought of the section is coming full circle, and where Paul again wants to explain that unfulfilled hope is nothing to be ashamed of.

In this connection, it is worth giving serious consideration to the minority understanding of "the love of God" in v. 5.[186] The phrase could mean either God's love for us (subjective genitive) or our love for God (objective genitive); the NRSV and the NIV in different ways foreclose on the ambiguity, settling for the former. This is in line with most interpreters, who, rightly noting that God's love for sinners is the major theme in vv. 6-10, assume that "the love of God" in v. 5 has this meaning too. Theological reasoning has also played a part, preferring to see hope as grounded on something about God (and indeed noticing that this is the logic of vv. 6-10) rather than something about ourselves.[187]

Nevertheless, the Spirit's work, to which Paul is here ascribing the pouring out of this love in the heart, is precisely within the innermost beings of believers, and as we have seen this is frequently referred to as the sign, foretaste and guarantee of eventual salvation. (This in no way compromises justification by grace through faith; rather, as with everything in Paul's descriptions of present Christian life, it is the result and outworking of that.) And the parallel passage in 8:24-28 indicates that Paul is well capable of speaking, precisely at this point in the argument, of "those who love God," just as in 1 Cor 2:9; 8:3, the latter in an explicit invoking of the *Shema*, the Jewish daily prayer ("Hear, O Israel: YHWH our God, YHWH is one; and you shall love YHWH your God," Deut 6:4-5.) A further argument for taking "the love of God" to mean our love for God is this: Why would Paul suggest that God's love for us was poured out into, and thus thereafter located in, our *hearts?*[188]

It is then possible, and preferable, to read "the love of God" in 5:5 as a similar allusion to the *Shema*, and to take it therefore as the objective genitive: our love for God. This then links up with two previous programmatic passages in the letter: 1:5, where Paul speaks of "the obedience of faith" as the result of the gospel, and 3:30, where the monotheism of the *Shema* undergirds justification itself. If this is right, 5:5 is tied closely to the exposition of the worldwide family of Abraham in chap. 4: the *Shema* is now fulfilled by all those who love the God revealed in Jesus the Messiah. This fits well with several other passages in the letter (e.g., 2:25-29; 8:4-9; 10:6-11), and provides a striking reason for not being ashamed to be living in hope, which is after all what the present passage is about. To find in one's heart a Spirit-given love for God is itself more than consolation. To realize that this love fulfils the central command of Torah is to discover oneself to be a member of the renewed people of God.

---

186. The word for "love," here and in 5:8; 8:35, 39, is ἀγάπη (*agapē*). As is well known, this word attained a new lease of life in early Christianity, quickly becoming used to denote the self-giving love of God in Jesus Christ, and the answering love, for God and one another, of those grasped by the gospel.

187. E.g., Moo, *Romans*, 304-5; but cf. Bryan, *A Preface to Romans*, 123, who holds the subjective view but distances himself from some of the arguments used against the objective one.

188. This was first put to me by the late G. B. Caird, and was the point that convinced him to change his mind to the objective genitive.

Romans 5:6-11, The Death of the Messiah and the Love of God

COMMENTARY

The compact introduction over, Paul settles to a more leisurely description of how the death of Jesus, by revealing God's love for sinners and by accomplishing their justification, assures those who are justified that they will be saved at the last. This is the larger explanation ($\gamma\acute{\alpha}\rho$ *gar*, v. 6) for the whole statement of vv. 1-5, rather than for one particular part of it. It is, equally clearly, part of the overarching theme of the whole section, since Paul returns to the same point in 8:31-39.

5:6-8. The outline argument is straightforward, the details occasionally tricky. Verse 6 states the basic premise, v. 7 comments on it, and v. 8 draws the conclusion. The Messiah died for the ungodly; people do not normally die even for worthy people; the Messiah's death is thus the measure of God's extraordinary love. Verse 6 emphasizes the unworthiness of the recipients of God's generosity: we were still weak, still actually ungodly.[189] This links in, deliberately no doubt, with the description of God "justifying the ungodly" in 4:5, and prepares for the third member of the sequence in v. 8: when we were still "sinners."

God's love appeared on the scene "at the right time." Paul does not refer, we may suppose, to a particular chronological scheme (though such things were reasonably common among educated Jews looking for the coming of God's kingdom).[190] Nor is he suggesting that the Messiah's death had happened at a moment of particular weakness or sinfulness on the part of Israel and the world. (Was the human race "weaker" in the first century than before?) Rather, with hindsight, he recognized, as in Gal 4:4, that "the time had fully come" (cf. Tob 14:5). He believed that God had brought to fulfilment a plan that, though opaque before, was now open to view.

The main contrast Paul is making in what follows is between worthy people, for whom one would still be unlikely to die, and unworthy people, for whom God gave the Messiah. But v. 7 also contains a contrast between two types of worthy people: a "righteous" person, for whom, he says, one would scarcely die, and "the good person" for whom, he says, one might even brave death.[191] Commentators have sometimes tried to portray the "righteous" here as the cold, legally correct person, in order to contrast such qualities with a warmer, more appealing goodness. But the positive overtones of the word "righteous" in Paul hardly allow for the distinction necessary if the verse is to express that meaning. One possible explanation might be that "the good man" (the word has the definite article, unlike "righteous" earlier in the verse) could actually be an allusion to Jesus himself: Paul, knowing that martyrdom was always possible (e.g., Phil 1:20-21; 2:17), might intend to say here what he says in 8:36 ("for your sake we are being killed all day long"). This is hardly provable, and may seem fanciful; but it deserves considering. The conventional, and perhaps safest, approach is to suggest that "the good man" refers to someone's benefactor.[192]

Such a death would still require huge courage and dedication. The qualification added in v. 7*b* has not damaged the basic contrast: what God did, freely and gladly, demonstrates a love far beyond anything human love can attain. We were, after all, not merely weak or ungodly, but actually sinners: Paul includes himself, and his fellow Jews, in a word that technically described "those outside the law," the pagans who, not possessing the law, were inevitably sinful (cf. Gal 2:15, where the word is used in this technical sense). That was our

---

189. The repeated "still" ($\check{\epsilon}\tau\iota$ *eti*) is hard to bring out in English, and neither the NRSV nor the NIV succeeds. Some MSS omit, and some alter, the second occurrence of the word; presumably it was felt odd even in the original.

190. See Roger T. Beckwith, *Calendar and Chronology, Jewish and Christian: Biblical, Intertestamental and Patristic Studies*, AGJU 33 (Leiden: Brill, 1996).

191. The phrase τοῦ ἀγαθοῦ (*tou agathou*) could be either masc. ("the good man") or neut. ("the good thing"); most understand the former, though "the good" in the sense of "the public good" is not impossible.

192. See Cranfield, *A Critical and Exegetical Commentary on the Epistle to the Romans*, 264-65; full discussion in A. D. Clarke, "The Good and the Just in Romans 5:7," *TyndBul* 41 (1990) 128-42.

condition, Paul says, when "the Messiah died for us"—a basic statement of primitive Christian belief (cf. 4:25; 1 Cor 15:3). The "for" in "for us" is not explained, though what follows fills it out somewhat, and the frequent references to Jesus' messianic death on behalf of others in the chapters that follow develop the thought in various directions.

5:9-10. The love of God seen in action in the death of the Messiah is then the basis for a standard type of argument, the "how much more": If God has done the difficult thing, how much more will the easy thing now be done.[193] God has already done the unthinkable; how much more will God do something relatively obvious! Paul opens up this thought in two stages, first (v. 9) offering a conclusion in terms of justification and salvation, and then (v. 10) explaining it in terms of God's reconciling love. This, too, like so much in the present paragraph, is picked up at the end of the section (8:32).

The first stage indicates that Paul is still consciously addressing the problem stated in 1:18–3:20. "The wrath" hangs over the human race (the NRSV and the NIV both specify that the wrath is God's; this is true, but Paul does not say so here). Paul thinks in terms of a coming day of wrath, not simply the individual fate of unbelievers after death (cf. 2:5, 16). Those already justified by Jesus' sacrificial death, he says, will be rescued from this coming wrath ("by his blood," picking up 3:25, clearly refers to Jesus' death as a sacrifice; see the Commentary on 5:2; the only other Pauline references to the blood of Jesus are 1 Cor 10:16; 11:25, 27; Eph 1:7; 2:13; Col 1:20). This is the negative side of the promise whose positive side is "sharing the glory of God" (5:2). (Just to be clear: "salvation" describes the future of God's people in terms of their rescue from a terrible fate; "glorification" in terms of the status they will enjoy; "resurrection" in terms of their new embodiment the other side of death; "justification," when applied to the future as in 2:13, in terms of their acquittal in the final Assize. In each case the event is the same, the connotation different.) Hope for this rescue is securely based, Paul says, expanding 5:8,

because God has already effected reconciliation when we were not just weak, ungodly, or sinful, but actually God's enemies (cf. 2 Cor 5:18-19; Eph 2:16; Col 1:19-22). The fact that this deeply personal notion is offered in explanation of, rather than in addition to, the mention of justification in the first half of v. 9 indicates that the meaning and effect of justification is to bring humans into the forgiven, reconciled family of God.

Upon whose side was the enmity? At one level, clearly, on ours; we were, says Paul, "god-haters" (1:30), though this word would hardly apply to many pious Jews, or even to the Gentile "god-fearers" who probably made up a significant proportion of the Roman converts. Objectively, though, Paul sees all humans as being at enmity with God through sin. Reconciliation is, after all, effected from God's side, by the initiative of love. However, Paul has just mentioned the wrath, which (as in 1:18 and 2:5-11) clearly means God's wrath. This wrath stood over against us, and God's love has saved us from it. We should not, I think, cut the knot and suggest that the enmity was on our side only. God's settled and sorrowful opposition to all that is evil included enmity against sinners. The fact that God's rescuing love has found a way of deliverance and reconciliation is part of the wonder of the gospel.

Paul here elaborates the christological basis of both reconciliation and salvation. We are reconciled, he says, through the death of God's son. This is the first mention of Jesus' divine sonship since the programmatic 1:3-4, and looks on to 8:3 and 8:32 in particular. Paul uses the title sparingly—not, it seems, from any reluctance, but rather to save it for the really weighty statements. Though "son of God" is still a messianic title for Paul, the logic of this whole passage, in which Jesus' death reveals God's reconciling love, demands that he express some identity between Jesus and God, and this is Paul's chosen way of doing just that. As in 8:3 and Gal 4:4, Jesus as "son of God" is the one sent from God to accomplish that which God alone must perform.

As in 4:25, Paul here sees the cross accomplishing one task, and the resurrection, or at least the risen life of the Messiah, accomplishing another. However, whereas in 4:25 the resurrection was associated with justification,

---

193. Commentators regularly point out the rabbinic model of argument on which this is based; but to argue *a minori ad maius* is common to many systems of logic.

he here assigns reconciliation (in parallel with justification in v. 9) to the cross, and salvation to Jesus' "life."[194] Presumably we should not make too hard and fast a distinction between the effect of the cross and the effect of the resurrection; for Paul the cross was always the death of the one whom the resurrection proved to be the Messiah, and the resurrection was always the raising of the crucified one. There is, however, a particular point here: being saved *in* the life of the son of God looks ahead to chap. 6, where it is precisely "in Christ" that the baptized are brought to new life, indeed, to eternal life (NRSV "by" and NIV "through" both obscure this link).

5:11. The final point of the paragraph is perhaps less expected: we celebrate, we boast, in God! The NIV's "rejoice," though true, does not catch either the echo of 2:17 or the note of real triumph that goes with the reversal of that passage: that which was impossible under the Torah, a boasting in God that reflected pride of race and culture, is strangely possible under the gospel. The

gospel has already reduced all human boasting to nothing (3:27-30; cf. 1 Cor 1:29-31); the Christian status and hope may look foolish in the world's eyes, and is clung to in the teeth of suffering (5:3-5); but when looking at "our Lord, Jesus, the Messiah," and celebrating the reconciliation with God that he has effected, the Christian can say, with the psalmist, "this God is our God, for ever and ever; he will be our guide unto death" (Ps 48:14). Or, indeed, with Paul at the climax of the present section: "if God is for us, who can be against us?" (8:31). The non-Christian Jew of Paul's day would no doubt be as offended by this as the relativist in our own (the pagan of Paul's day, and of our own, would no doubt scoff); but Paul reflects the clear and universal early Christian claim. Those who believe in Jesus the Messiah are the true people of the creator God, the God of Abraham. That is what it means to "boast in God," to celebrate the reconciliation between the creator and those who bear the creator's image. The paragraph ends, as do most in this section, with a christological summary: We boast in God through our Lord, Jesus the Messiah. Other lords, Paul implies, should take note.

194. This is the first mention of "salvation" in the letter; "salvation" and "justification" are not the same thing in Paul's mind, however much they are confused in popular parlance.

REFLECTIONS

1. The deeply personal reconciliation between the creator God and the human race in and through Jesus the Messiah can hardly be explored too often, or too thoroughly. It is the theme that lies at the heart of the Christian experience and claim, the point at which believing certain things *about* God is swallowed up in personal knowledge *of* God. To be sure, it is easy to be deceived at this point, not least through the arrogance that quickly and conveniently forgets that our knowledge and love of God are but the reflex of God's knowledge and love of us (1 Cor 8:2-3). It is easy to imagine that one is knowing the living God when in fact one is worshiping, and deriving spurious comfort from, an idol of one's own imagining. That is why, as in the present paragraph, it is vital to keep Jesus, and the cross and resurrection, at the center of the picture, and to invoke the Holy Spirit through whom God's love floods our hearts.

This knowledge and love of the true God is evoked and sustained most chiefly, as here, through meditation on the death of Jesus. Again, it is possible to get things out of focus at this point, to concentrate morbidly on Jesus' suffering in the same frame of mind that lures people to drool over some great natural or human disaster. But the abuse does not detract from the reality. The Gospel writers tell the story of Jesus' last days and hours in lavish detail; those who allow themselves to be caught up within that story will discover its life-changing power. Here the entire narrative is boiled down to a single sentence: God's love is demonstrated in that, while we were yet sinners, the Messiah died for us. Those whose first thought is to analyze that statement in terms of theological or literary derivations do more damage to it, even if their analysis is accurate, than one who knows no Greek but whose heart is strangely warmed in reading it. Paul is often criticized for being too logical or lawcourt-minded. That may be true of some of his interpreters. For Paul himself, the language of the lawcourt was a powerful metaphor, but the language of love spoke literal truth.

2. The logic of divine love is here pressed into service as part of the argument for assurance. It is ironic that, when many Western Christians are flirting with universalism, there is simultaneously an underemphasis on the eternal security of all Christian believers. It is almost as though we are trying to say that everyone else may well be saved but that we cannot be too sure about ourselves. This may, no doubt, express a proper reaction against triumphalist arrogance, but nothing is gained by ignoring Paul's central argument, here and throughout Romans 5–8: believing and baptized Christians are assured that, by the indwelling Spirit, they will be brought to resurrection life at the last. Paul was well aware, as his other letters show, of the problems of professing Christians whose behavior seemed to make a mockery of their faith (1 Corinthians wrestles with this problem on almost every page). But one of his greatest, most securely grounded, most sustained arguments is precisely this: Those whom God justified, God also glorified. To fail to grasp this, and be grasped by it, is to miss not only the heart of Paul, but, Paul would say, the heart of God.

3. Celebrating one's suffering sounds depressingly morbid. Western Christians easily imbibe from our culture an inclination to regard not only the pursuit but also the attainment of happiness as an inalienable right, and if suffering strikes we look either to technology to solve it or to the lawyers to apportion the blame. Paul is unspecific here about which sufferings he means (he is more explicit in 8:35), but his approach is steady and realistic: suffering produces patience, and patience produces a tried and tested character. Neither of these qualities is much in evidence—or indeed highly prized—in contemporary Western society, which wants everything at once and wants to be free to change character according to the mood of the moment. As a result, we should not be surprised that we are in many respects a society without hope. Those who believe in Jesus the Messiah are called to model communities, familes and personal lives in which the sequence of faith, peace, suffering, patience, character and hope is lived out, sustained by the Holy Spirit's work of enabling us to know God's love and to love God in return.

4. The political challenge implicit in this passage should be pondered and drawn out. God has established the true peace, so different from the *pax Romana*, on the foundation of true justice, so different from the Roman *Iustitia*, and has done so through the Lord Jesus, so different from the lord Caesar. This challenge, of course, had more than a little to do with the sufferings Paul endured. The church as a whole has yet to take seriously the question of how to translate its allegiance to this Lord, who established divine justice and peace through his own death, rather than through the death of those who stood in his way, into action in the world. Comparatively little attention has been given to the question, How might God's reconciling action in Christ become the ground and model for the reconciliation of human enemies? Too often those who have focused attention on the saving death of Jesus have concentrated exclusively on its relevance for final salvation and current spiritual growth, while those who have wanted to make the gospel politically relevant have ignored Paul's theology of Jesus' death. Fresh integration is called for if we are to hear and live Paul's many-sided gospel in a new century and millennium.

ROMANS 5:12-21, FROM ADAM TO THE MESSIAH

COMMENTARY

The next paragraph is as terse and cryptic as the previous one was flowing and lucid. Like an artist in a hurry, Paul paints with a few large, sweeping strokes on a giant canvas, creating an overall picture without many details. It is the picture, in bold, stark outline, of his whole argument to this point; and it may help if we think of him, then, in chaps. 6–8, standing in front of this picture to talk us through the next sequence, pointing back at the extraordinary painting to show us where his different themes belong and how they fit together. As we have seen, the overall argument of 5–8 is outlined in 5:1-11, so that in summing up where he has now got to Paul is not, as it were, making the first in a sequence of logically ordered points, but rather setting up the grid on which all that follows will be plotted.

The paragraph outlines the way in which the creator and covenant God has successfully dealt with the problem of human sin and death. The hypothesis that saw Adam hiding under the argument of 1:18-25 and in isolated statements such as 3:23 is vindicated by Paul's summarizing here where he has got to, not (as has sometimes been thought) adding a fresh point or simply providing an illustration. The opening διὰ τοῦτο (*dia touto*) should

thus be read not simply as "therefore," but "so it comes about that": not a new point to be deduced, but a summary, a conclusion that can be drawn because of what has been said briefly, in advance, in 5:1-11. We have seen, in miniature, that the death of Jesus, the great act of obedient covenant faithfulness, has dealt with sin, that God's love revealed on the cross will certainly bring to salvation those who are justified, and that the Spirit has been given to pour the love of God into the hearts of believers, transforming them so that they become God's true humanity. This enables us to line up the problem outlined in 1:18–3:20 (sin and death) with the solution articulated in 3:21–5:11 (justification and life) and draw the conclusions. That is what Paul does here.

The shape of the argument needs clarifying. The main point Paul is making is begun in v. 12, but broken off to allow for two different sorts of explanation and modification (vv. 13-14, 15-17). He then returns to his main statement in v. 18, further explained and restated in v. 19. Verse 20 adds a further complication, showing how the law fits within the Adam-Christ picture; v. 21 restates the point of vv. 18-19 allowing for this further dimension. Thus the shape of the paragraph is like this:

> 5:12: opening statement, awaiting completion: just as sin entered and brought death
> 5:13-14: first explanatory "aside": sin and death between Adam and Moses
> 5:15-17: second explanatory "aside": the imbalances between sin and grace
> (5:15: first imbalance; 5:16-17: second imbalance, with explanation)
> 5:18: initial completion of opening statement: just as the trespass, so the act of righteousness
> 5:19: explanation and filling out of v. 18: disobedience and obedience
> 5:20: where the Law belongs on this map: intensifying the problem, but grace deals with this too
> 5:21: triumphant conclusion: the kingdom of grace triumphs over the kingdom of sin

Within this, Paul introduces a theme almost unique in his writings, but very important within early Christianity: the clash of the kingdoms. Five out of the nine occurrences in his writings of βασιλεύω (*basileuō*, "to rule as a king," "to reign") come in these verses;

one of the others, picking up this passage, is at 6:12.[195] Paul does not speak here of the kingdom of Satan, but instead personifies "sin"

---

195. The other three are 1 Cor 4:8 (twice), which belong with the occurrence in Rom 5:17, and 15:25, which speaks of the messianic reign of Jesus.

and "death," speaking of each as "reigning" (5:14, 17a, 21a). He does not speak here, either, of the reign of God, or even of Jesus; rather, as in the admittedly ironic 1 Cor 4:8, he speaks of believers as reigning (5:17b), and then finally of the reign of grace itself (5:21b). The last, clearly, is a personification, a periphrasis for God. This theme of kingly rule, coming so soon after the grand statement of justice, peace, and lordship (5:1), cannot but be seen as a further indication of Paul's overall mission: to announce the kingdom of God in the face of all the principalities and powers of the world, not least those of Rome itself (cf. 8:38-39 and the pregnant conclusion of Acts 28:30-31).

The other themes work in groups. Sin and death obviously belong together, and are joined by trespass,[196] disobedience, and condemnation. On the other side are grace, righteousness, free gift (χάρισμα *charisma*), gift (δωρεά *dōrea* or δώρημα *dōrēma*), act of righteousness/justification/acquittal (δικαίωμα *dikaiōma*, δικαίωσις *dikaiōsis*, and δικαιοσύνη *dikaiosynē*). There are no doubt fine distinctions between these terms, but there is also broad overlap and flexibility; we may assume that part of Paul's reason for choosing different words, in some cases at least, is to avoid repetition. To grasp the main thrust of the argument, it helps to see these two groups as solid blocks, from which Paul can draw the particular nuance he wants at any given point.

The substance of the paragraph is the parallel, and contrast, between Adam and the Messiah. Paul alludes more briefly to this in 1 Cor 15:21-22, and develops the theme in one direction in 15:45-49. The context of his thinking is the fairly widespread Second Temple Jewish belief not merely about Adam as the progenitor of the human race, and indeed the fountainhead of human sin (e.g., Wis 2:23-24; 2 Bar 17:3; 23:4; 48:42; 54:15 [but cf. 54:19]; 4 Ezra 3:7; 3:21; 7:118), but about Israel, or the righteous within Israel, as the new humanity, the inheritors of "all the glory of Adam." This theme is particularly prominent in the Qumran scrolls.[197] Adam, in

other words, points forward to God's ultimate intention for the human race; reflection on Adam gives a particular shape to eschatological hope. In particular, as will be important in Romans 8, Adam's sovereignty over creation will be given to the true Adam at the end. This lies at the heart of Paul's view of Jesus' lordship (e.g., 1 Cor 15:27, quoting Ps 8:7), and also of the kingly rule of Jesus' people (5:17). This paragraph, then, demonstrates that, by fulfilling the covenant promises to Abraham, the creator God has addressed and dealt with the problem of Adam; a new humanity has come into being for whom sin and death have been conquered. "The age to come" has arrived in the present with the death and resurrection of the Messiah; those who belong to the Messiah already share in its benefits. That which Israel, or groups within Israel, thought to gain has been appropriately attained by the true Israelite, the Messiah, the obedient one. He now shares this status with all his people.

The balance between Adam and Christ, which is the main point of the paragraph, is not absolute. Verses 15-17 insert two notes of imbalance, where Paul insists that the act of Christ, and its results, far outweighs what was done, and lost, by Adam. Christ did not begin where Adam began: His task, which was actually Israel's task, the vocation outlined (but not acted upon) in 2:17-24 and 3:2, was to take the weight of the human catastrophe upon himself and deal with it. Nor was the result a mere restoration of where Adam was before: in Christ the human project, begun in Adam but never completed, has been brought to its intended goal. In both cases Christ has done what Israel was called to do.

What then of Israel itself? Would Israel not say that the Torah was given in order to enable it to escape the entail of Adam's sin? Paul takes a very different line. Following his earlier statements in 2:25-29; 3:19-20; and 4:15a, he sees the Torah entering the picture with apparently disastrous consequences (5:20). God has, however, dealt with this too. Through Jesus Christ the righteousness of God, which is revealed apart from Torah, has become the means whereby grace can usher in the age to come (5:21, with an oblique echo of 3:21). The main statements of the paragraph, holding the subsidiary and

---

196. "Sin" is simply wrongdoing, whether or not the sinner is aware of it; "trespass" or "transgression" is disobedience to a known command.

197. E.g., 1QS 4.22-21; CD 3.20; 1QH 4.15 [= 17.15 in, e.g., Vermes]; 4Q171 3.1-2. See also Wright, "New Exodus, New Inheritance," 34n. 13.

explanatory additions in place, thus come in vv. 12, 18, and 21 (see the outline on p. 523).

The "obedience" of Jesus is thus the means by which God's faithfulness to the covenant has been effected. This theme, picking up the "faithfulness" of Jesus in chap. 3, awakens echoes both linguistic and theological from Isaiah 53, which were already hinted at in 4:25. As in Phil 2:6-11, Paul has drawn together his view of Jesus as the true Adam and the true Israel. Both themes are focused on Jesus' obedient death, seen as the act of grace by which the true God is revealed.[198]

This paragraph is not only the thematic statement out of which chaps. 6–8 are quarried; it provides, too, the groundwork for chaps. 9–11 and 12–16. Paul's basic thesis about Israel according to the flesh is that they, too, are "in Adam." This, worked out in agonizing detail in 7:1-25, is then thought through in 9:6–10:21: Israel recapitulates Adam's trespass (5:20; 7:7-11; 9:32; 11:11-12). But God has dealt with the sin of Adam, and has also dealt with that of Israel; there is therefore life and hope for Israel, too, not because Paul has smuggled in a renewed nationalism after all, but because he believes in the victory of grace. Israel, even "according to the flesh," remains the people of the Messiah (9:5); thus their "casting away" means "reconciliation for the world" (11:15, echoing 5:10). Key elements of the discussion thus grow from the thematic statements in chap. 5.

The great appeal of chaps. 12–16 is for unity in the church: "We, the many, are one body in Christ." This is worked out through the argument of 14:1–15:13 in particular. Here, working backward, we find the clue to the way in which 5:12-21 draws out the theme so prominent in 1:16–4:25—namely, the coming together of Jews and Gentiles in fulfillment of the promise to Abraham. This subject, so far from being ignored between chaps. 4 and 9, should actually be seen as highlighted in 5:12-21, through Paul's repeated emphasis on "one man . . . for many/all." "Many" and "all," in the light of the whole thrust of 1:18–4:25, must clearly be seen as meaning "Jew and Gentile alike." The problem was universal; the solution is universal. Torah's entry into the picture

(5:20) did not create a race apart; rather, it exacerbated the problem. The solution is the same for all: grace, working through God's covenant faithfulness, resulting in the life of the age to come, through Jesus, Israel's Messiah, the Lord of the world, appropriated by faith; God's love, responded to with answering love inspired by the Spirit. The appeal for the unity of the church in the letter's closing chapters (see especially 15:7-13) is firmly rooted in this same crucial paragraph. With this, we are ready for the details of the text.

5:12. Paul begins the great comparison between Adam and Christ, but breaks it off halfway through, to insert two explanations. On the face of it, v. 12 seems fairly straightforward, granted the story of Adam and Eve in Genesis 2–3 and its interpretation in the Judaism of Paul's day. Given a commandment, to break which meant death, the unhappy pair broke it and (eventually) died. Sin and death, here personified, continue as "characters" in Paul's narrative through to chap. 8. In terms of his overall argument for assurance, they are the forces that must be defeated if the Christian is to be sure of eternal life. In terms of his underlying new-exodus story, sin and death play the role of Pharaoh: Paul imagines them as alien powers, given access to God's world through the action of Adam. Once in, they had come to stay; staying, they seized royal power. Linked together as cause and effect, they now stride through their usurped domain, wreaking misery, decay, and corruption wherever they go. No one is exempt from their commanding authority.

Straightforward in some ways this may be. But it has created huge problems of interpretation for subsequent readers, not least those eager to press Paul for solutions to problems he was not addressing. In part these are historical problems, or at least problems about whether the history really matters: Did sin really enter the world through one man? Was death really a stranger in the world until the first Homo sapiens "worshiped and served the creature rather than the creator"? And—a question that has exercised theologians for most of the years since Paul wrote these words—in what sense did "all sin" when Adam sinned? These are questions more of interpretation than of of exegesis, but unless they are addressed they threaten to derail the

198. See Wright, *The Climax of the Covenant,* chap. 4.

contemporary reader before the paragraph has even properly begun. Since this passage constitutes the driving heart of the letter, it is vital to stay on the track.

Paul clearly believed that there had been a single first pair, whose male, Adam, had been given a commandment and had broken it. Paul was, we may be sure, aware of what we would call mythical or metaphorical dimensions to the story, but he would not have regarded these as throwing doubt on the existence, and primal sin, of the first historical pair. Our knowledge of early anthropology is of course sketchy, to put it mildly. Each time another very early skull is dug up the newspapers exclaim over the discovery of the first human beings; we have consigned Adam and Eve entirely to the world of mythology, but we are still looking for their replacements. What "sin" would have meant in the early dawn of the human race it is impossible to say; but the turning away from open and obedient relationship with the loving creator, and the turning instead toward that which, though beautiful and enticing, is not God, is such a many-sided phenomenon that it is not hard to envisage it at any stage of anthropoid development. The general popular belief that the early stories of Genesis were straightforwardly disproved by Charles Darwin is of course nonsense, however many times it is reinforced in contemporary myth-making. Things are just not that simple, in biblical theology or science.

One potentially helpful way of understanding the entry of death into the world through the first human sin is to see "death" here as more than simply the natural decay and corruption of all the created order. The good creation was nevertheless transient: evening and morning, the decay and new life of autumn and spring, pointed on to a future, a purpose, which Genesis implies it was the job of the human race to bring about. All that lived in God's original world would decay and perish, but "death" in that sense carried no sting. The primal pair were, however, threatened with a different sort of thing altogether: a "death" that would result from sin, and involve expulsion from the garden (Gen 2:17). This death is a darker force, opposed to creation itself, unmaking that which was good, always threatening to drag the world back toward chaos. Thus, when humans

turned away in sin from the creator as the one whose image they were called to bear, what might have been a natural sleep acquired a sense of shame and threat. The corruption of this darker "death" corresponded all too closely to, and seemed to be occasioned by, that turning away from the source of life, and that turning instead toward lifeless objects, which later generations would call idolatry.

The final clause in the verse is deeply controversial. Most interpreters take the opening phrase (ἐφ' ᾧ *eph' hō'*) to mean "inasmuch as," or simply "because"; death spread to all, "because" all sinned. The question is, does the verb refer to actual sins committed by all people (as in the "many sins" of v. 16), or to the primal act of Adam seen as the time when "all sinned"? Since the verb is aorist, as the NIV rightly sees ("because all sinned"), not perfect, as the NRSV implies ("because all have sinned"), it might seem better to take it as a reference to Adam, even while it is clear from 1:18–3:20 that Paul believes that all humans have committed actual sin. However, the fact that that earlier argument can be summed up with an aorist at 3:23 ("all sinned, and came short of God's glory") may indicate that too much weight should not be placed on the tense. What matters is that all human sin can now be lumped together into one. "All sinned."

Faced with this dilemma, some scholars emphasize the responsibility of each individual, while others, not least those anxious to maintain Paul's parallel between Adam and Christ, emphasize the primal sin as somehow involving all subsequent humanity (it is not necessary, to hold this view, to espouse along with it any particular theory of the mode by which sin is then transmitted). Others, maintaining a delicate balance between these alternatives (the former unlikely, the latter unwelcome), suggest that this is a shorthand way of saying that when humans actually sin, as they all do, they are not merely imitating the primal sin but acting from within a human nature, and indeed within a world, radically conditioned by that prior disobedience.

Fitzmyer has recently challenged the reading of *eph' hō* as "because," and proposed instead "with the result that."[199] This

---

199. J. A. Fitzmyer, "The Consecutive Meaning of ἐφ' ᾧ in Romans 5.12," *NTS* 39/3 (1993) 321-39, and in his commentary (*Romans*, 413-17), where details of other views are set out.

does not, he suggests, remove the sense of causality between Adam's sin and those of his descendants, but it allows for a "secondary causality," and so personal responsibility, between individual sins and individual death. The problem in this, it seems to me, is that it makes the last clause of the verse relate, not to its immediate predecessor ("and so death spread to all"), with which it seems naturally to belong because of the repeated "all," but to the first verb of the sentence ("sin entered the world"). Otherwise Paul would be saying that death spread to all, with the result that all sinned—the opposite of what he actually says throughout, which is that sin causes death.[200] Fitzmyer's proposal must, I think, be regarded as at best not proven. Paul's meaning must in any case be both that an entail of sinfulness has spread throughout the human race from its first beginnings and that each individual has contributed their own share to it. Paul offers no further clue as to how the first of these actually works or how the two interrelate.

5:13-14. Paul said "just as" in v. 12, but there is no corresponding "so." As most translations see, we must insert a dash or bracket at the end of v. 12; v. 13 breaks in to the train of thought, and not until v. 18 is it begun again and finally completed. Paul is here addressing a perceived problem, concerning the generations between Adam and Moses—that is, those who lived before the coming of the law. How did they know what was sinful and what was not? This might seem a rather abstruse problem; the patriarchal generations, after all, seem to have known that there was such a thing as good and evil, even though they did not always abide by it. But the underlying problem may well be that if Paul were to tie sin too closely to the Torah, he would not only have a theoretical difficulty with the period between Adam and Moses, but would also run into a more pressing problem about the status of Gentiles "without the Torah" (cf. 2:14).

What Paul needs to explain here is that sin did indeed spread to all people, including those who might at first sight (from a Jewish point of view in which sin meant breaking Torah) have seemed to be without sin. His explanation is simple: sin must have been

there (5:13a) because death was there, ruling like a king (5:14a). He acknowledges (5:13b) that sin is not reckoned up, not logged in any register, in the absence of the law. (We might note that, although it would be easy to take "law" here in a more general sense than the Mosaic Torah, the context makes it quite clear that Torah is what Paul has in mind; a good lesson to learn for the reading of the following chapters.) As a result, the subjects over whom death ruled, though sinners, were not the same type of sinners as Adam had been, that is, sinners against a specific known commandment. They did not, he says, sin "in the likeness of the trespass of Adam." "Trespass" ("transgression," NRSV) means, as we saw, sinning against a commandment (NIV, "sin by breaking a command," is a paraphrase designed to bring this point out).

This is important for what it implies as well as what it denies. It denies that the generations between Adam and Moses, being lawless, were also sinless. But it also implies that those who come after Moses, and who do have Torah, do in fact imitate Adam. This will be further stated in 5:20, echoed in 6:14-15, and will become a major theme in chap. 7.

Adam, he says, is "a type of the one who was coming." This is one of only two places where Paul uses "type" in this technical sense (the other being 1 Cor 10:6; see also 1 Cor 10:11). The thought is of a die or stamp that leaves its impression in wax: Paul's meaning seems to be that Adam prefigured the Messiah in certain respects (other candidates for "the coming one" are sometimes suggested, but it is virtually certain that Paul intended to refer to Jesus), notably in this, that he founded a family that would bear his characteristics. Thus we may hear another hint of the coming argument. Sinning "according to the likeness of the trespass of Adam" is balanced by God's plan to bring Christians "to conform to the image of his son" (8:29). The middle term in this story is supplied, evocatively in this context, by 8:3: "God sent his own son in the likeness of sinful flesh."

Paul has thus clarified a problem that might have come back to haunt him. But he is still not ready to resume the train of thought begun in v. 12. Before he can set out the parallel between Adam and Christ,

200. So rightly Byrne, *Romans*, 183.

he needs to head off the idea that they are *merely* or *solely* parallel.

5:15-17. "But not 'as the trespass, so also the grace-gift.' " That is a more literal rendering of the opening line of this difficult subsection. It is not simply, as with the NRSV and the NIV, that Paul is denying *similarity* between the gift and the trespass; he is denying that there is a *balance* between them. The gift far outweighs the trespass; Christ has not merely restored that which Adam lost, but has gone far beyond. The remainder of v. 15 explains, somewhat complicatedly, what Paul means. The many died because of the trespass of the one (Adam); but God's grace, and the grace-gift through the one (Jesus), abounded for the many. The imbalance here seems to be between the simple progression from sin to death and the astonishing reversal whereby, faced with the result of Adam's sin, God's grace has flourished in what had seemed a hopeless situation. The two sequences are, in other words, out of all proportion to each other: in the one case, sin bred death because that is what sin does; in the other, the gift of grace is nothing short of new creation, creation not merely out of nothing but out of anti-creation, out of death itself.

A second imbalance is then presented in v. 16, with one of Paul's most tortuous shorthand sentences: literally, "and not 'as through the one man sinning, the gift.' " Again, despite the NRSV, the NIV, and others, Paul is denying not merely similarity, but balance, this time in terms of the judicial result of the process and in particular of the conditions in which it took place. The key contrast he wishes to draw is between the one sin, which brought the sentence of condemnation, and the gift that, *after many trespasses*, brought the verdict "righteous."[201] In other words, God's action in the Messiah did not start where Adam's started, and, as it were, merely get things right this time. God's action in the Messiah began at the point where Adam's ended—with many sins, and many sinners. The result in each case is hardly comparable; condemnation and acquittal may seem equal and opposite, but only from the point of view that they are the two alternative results from

a trial. In terms of what they actually mean for the people concerned they are different sorts of things: the one a denial and ending of life itself, the other an affirmation, opening up new possibilities.

Paul offers in v. 17 a further explanation of the imbalance between Adam and Christ, this time in terms of the two "reigns." But it is not, as we might have expected, "death" or "sin" on the one hand, and "God" on the other. It is the reign of death, far outweighed by the reign of—believers! Those who were pronounced dead under the haughty and usurping kingdom of death are themselves to be the rulers in God's new world. Paul describes believers in a roundabout and telling fashion: they are "those who receive the abundance of grace and of the gift of righteousness." Paul has spoken of "the many" on both sides of the equation (v. 15) and will do so again (v. 19); he will speak of "all humans," on both sides, in v. 18. Here, however, he presents a significant modification: it is those who "receive this gift" who will reign in life in God's kingdom (cf. 1 Cor 4:8). The rest of Paul's theology, not least in Romans, makes it clear that he is thinking of those who believe the gospel of Jesus the Messiah.

They will reign, he says, "in life." This refers, we assume, both to the resurrection state in which their final rule will take place and to the "life" of the age to come, over which they will exercise dominion. Paul seems to have got from apocalyptic tradition the belief that God's final rule would be exercised through God's people. When the Ancient of Days takes the throne, the sovereignty is given to "the people of the saints of the Most High" (Dan 7:27). Here, as throughout the passage, Paul is thinking in terms of the promised blessings that Israel hoped for in the age to come being achieved by the Messiah and shared with his people. (This, of course, is what makes 9:1-5 so poignant.)

5:18-19. Paul is ready at last to resume his argument where he broke it off at 5:12. The opening phrase (ἄρα οὖν *ara oun*) is resumptive as well as consequential: "so, then," not simply "therefore." The key sentence, however, in which Paul at last says what he has been waiting to say for five verses, possesses neither subject, verb, nor object in either half. Literally it reads "as through the trespass

---

201. The term *dikaiōma*, usually "decree" or "righteous deed" here has the sense, according to BDAG, of *dikaiōsis*, "justification," "vindication," or "acquittal." Perhaps the form Paul used brings with it the sense of this verdict as an action of the judge.

of the one unto all people unto condemnation, so also through the righteous act of the one unto all people unto acquittal of life."[202] There may be good theology behind this odd grammar: Paul is talking about an entire story over which he sees the creator God presiding. His non-use of subjects and verbs may have an air of reverence, as well as a positively Tacitean density.

The balance he is asserting, after all the imbalances of the previous verses, lies in the universality. Adam brings condemnation for all; Christ, justification for all. Our minds instantly raise the question of numerically universal salvation, but this is not in Paul's mind. His universalism is of the sort that holds to Christ as the way for all. "Condemnation" and "judgment" have been important themes in the letter since the second chapter; Paul here, as usual, refers to the final coming judgment, the time when there will be wrath for some and life for others (2:5-11). The theme remains central in the coming chapters, reaching its dramatic climax in 8:1 ("there is therefore now no condemnation for those in Christ Jesus") and 8:33-34 ("it is God who justifies; who will condemn?"). By referring to Jesus' messianic action on the cross (this, of course, is what the second half of the comparison in each verse has been about) in terms of an "act of righteousness" or "act of acquittal" (the word is δικαίωμα *dikaiōma*, as in v. 16), Paul again draws on the thought of 3:21-26 and 5:9-10. Christ's *dikaiōma* in the middle of history leads to God's *dikaiōsis* on the last day. What was accomplished on the cross will be effective at the final judgment.

As so often, Paul at once explains himself further (γάρ *gar*), and in doing so elaborates his meaning. This time, in v. 19, it is in terms of disobedience and obedience. With audible overtones of Isa 53:11, he declares that, as Adam's disobedience gave "the many" the status of being "sinners" (see the Commentary on 5:8) so Christ's obedience has given "the many" the status of being "righteous." Jesus, whisper the Isaianic echoes, is the servant of YHWH, whose obedient death has accomplished YHWH's saving purpose. He

has "established" or "set up" his people with a new status.

To be a "sinner" is, to be sure, more than a mere status. It involves committing actual sins. But it is the status that interests Paul here. Likewise, to be "righteous," as will be apparent in the next chapter, is more than simply status, but again it is the status that matters here. Justification, rooted in the cross and anticipating the verdict of the last day, gives people a new status, ahead of the performance of appropriate deeds.

What does Paul suppose the Messiah was obedient to? A long tradition within one strand of Reformation thought has supposed that Paul was here referring to Jesus' perfect obedience to the law.[203] In this view, Christ's "active obedience" and his "passive obedience" work together. His active obedience acquires "righteousness," which is then "reckoned" to those "in Christ"; his passive obedience, culminating in the cross, deals with his people's sins. Powerful though this thought is, and influential though it has been (even in liturgy, where "the merits and death of Christ" are sometimes mentioned in this double sense), it is almost certainly not what Paul has in mind here. The Isaianic servant, to whom reference is being made, was obedient to the saving purpose of YHWH, the plan marked out for Israel from the beginning but that, through Israel's disobedience, only the servant, as an individual, can now accomplish. The "obedience" of the Messiah in 5:19 therefore corresponds closely to the "faithfulness" of the Messiah in 3:22. It refers to his obedience to God's commission (as in 3:2), to the plan to bring salvation to the world, rather than his amassing a treasury of merit through Torah obedience. Obedience to the law would be beside the point; the law has a different, and much darker, function in the argument than is often supposed. That, indeed, is the subject of the next verse.

5:20-21. If a devout Second Temple Jew were telling the story of Adam and the Messiah—from, we may assume, a pre-messianic point of view—the Torah would be bound to play a large and positive part in the narrative. As Paul says in 2:17-20, reflecting the attitude he himself would have had before

---

202. The words "of the one" in each case (ἐνός *henos*, a single word in Greek) could, instead, be an adjective modifying the noun, "through the one trespass" and "through the one righteous act." But this is less likely.

203. See Longenecker, "The Obedience of Christ in the Theology of the Early Church," 142-52.

his conversion, the Torah provides the form of knowledge and truth. It is the thing that, above all, enables Israel to escape the entail of Adam's sin, to be different from the pagan world around. Not so, he says here. When Torah came in, its effect—apparently its deliberate effect—was "to increase the trespass."

Each part of this sentence is tricky. The word that describes the law's entrance is παρεισέρχομαι (*pareiserchomai*, "came in alongside").[204] The result was that the trespass increased; was this also the intention, or just the unintended result? The NRSV opts for result; the NIV for purpose. Though the latter seems harder (why would God, giving the Torah, *intend* trespass to increase?) it is almost certainly correct; this half-verse anticipates the whole argument of 7:7-25, and there it is clear that both the law itself and the effect it had were somehow, mysteriously, intended by the giver.

The clue is to link "the trespass" with its previous occurrences in the passage, where the trespass is of course Adam's. The Torah, so far from delivering its possessors from the entail of Adam's sin, actually appears to exacerbate it for them. This is more or less, after all, what Paul already said in 3:19-20. To sin outside the law is still to sin; Paul has made that clear in 5:13-14; but to sin under the law—in other words, to transgress, to break a known commandment—is to make the problem worse. Think of sin as a small color transparency; the law puts a bright light behind it and a large screen in front of it. That is what Paul means by "increase the trespass." Just as in 2:17-24, which follows on from 1:18-32, Adam's sin is writ large in Israel. Paul is stating the theme that will dominate chap. 7.

At the moment, though, he is still painting the canvas with broad brush strokes, and he sweeps on: the problem of Adam's sin was magnified by the Torah, but God has done what Torah could not. Grace has superabounded where sin abounded—that is, in Israel itself, where the full effects of Torah's magnification of Adam's sin were felt. The superabundance of grace in Israel is presumably a further reference to the messianic work, and particularly the messianic death, in which Jesus offered to Israel's God the faithful obedience that Israel had not. In Christ, God has come to where the Torah has magnified sin, and has dealt with it. This points ahead to 8:3-4.

All this leads to the full and climactic statement of the Adam-Christ balance in v. 21. When we stand back and look at the two kingdoms, they are those of sin on the one hand and grace on the other; and if "grace" is a periphrastic (or indirect) personification for "God," we may suppose that "sin" is an indirect way of saying "Satan." Paul is once again summarizing the whole train of thought of 1:18–5:11, and doing so in a way that will launch the next phase of the letter's argument: the reign of sin is matched, and outmatched, by the reign of grace, and sin's entail of death is beaten by the entail of life that follows from grace, working through "righteousness" (not "justification," as in the NRSV). Give these words their full Pauline value, and the sequence of thought becomes clear, despite the fact that the verse is packed with technical terms. Grace (the sovereign, loving purpose of God) is ruling through covenant faithfulness (God's accomplishment in Christ of that which had been promised to Abraham), and the result is the ushering in of the age to come, "eternal life," or, better, the life of the coming age.[205] And all has happened, of course, "through Jesus the Messiah, our Lord." The outstretched arms of the crucified one, embodying the love of the creator God, provide the ultimate balance of the paragraph, the place where the kingdom of sin did its worst and the kingdom of grace its triumphant best.

---

204. Paul uses it in Gal 2:4 of false brethren secretly sneaking in; though the word need not have a negative connotation, it certainly could carry one. The NIV "was added" seems to reflect Gal 3:19, which is after all similar in topic.

205. The phrase "eternal life," the natural one for translators to choose, is nevertheless potentially misleading if it conveys the idea of an endless disembodied bliss, rather than the far more this-worldly meaning of "the life of the age to come," which sits better with the eschatological vision of, e.g., Rom 8:18-27.

REFLECTIONS

1. The overwhelming impression left by these verses is the superabundance of grace. However much theologians and preachers know this with their heads, and can explain it as a theory, it remains strange and surprising that it should actually be true, that it should be the central characteristic of the world in which we—even theologians and preachers!—are called to live. Surrounded as we are day by day with so many signs and symbols of sin and death, and living in a culture that has reinvented a secularized version of the doctrine of Original Sin under the guise of the hermeneutic of suspicion (see below), all our instincts tell us that life is hard, cruel and unfair. If there are signs of life and hope, they tend to be those we make for ourselves. Our culture thus oscillates between despair and self-salvation.

Into this world the news of grace, of the undeserved gift of abundant life, bursts again and again, in the message of Jesus, offering a radical alternative, an entirely different way of construing reality, a new way of conceiving our whole experience of the world and indeed of God. At every point where the seeds of wickedness have been planted, bearing deadly fruits of all kinds, there the grace of God has been planted alongside, a vibrant plant that will take over the soil and produce a life-giving harvest. Of course, it takes faith to believe this and act on it; precisely the faith that believes that God raised Jesus from the dead, and that therefore his cross was indeed "the free gift following many trespasses," "the one man's obedience." But once the world has been glimpsed in this light, everything is different, not least Christian mission and the prayer that accompanies it.

2. At the center of the picture, and always worth further exploration and meditation, is the achievement of Jesus himself. Though the word "cross" is not mentioned, and though Jesus' own death is not spoken of explicitly, we should not miss the fact that in this passage we have one of Paul's fullest statements of what in shorthand we call atonement theology. People often try to glean a full theology of the cross from 3:21-26, where Paul is writing about several things at once and drawing on a dense statement of the meaning of Jesus' death in order to do so. We would do better to see that passage, together with the further statements of 4:25 and 5:6-10, as leading the eye up to the present argument, which is admittedly still terse and clipped. This is the high mountain ridge from which we look back to the earlier statements, and on to subsequent ones (6:3-11; 7:4; 8:3-4, 31-39).

Central to Paul's understanding of the cross, therefore, is the belief that it is the free gift of God to a wicked and corrupt world. This point, stressed again and again in these verses, was and is offensive to those who want to make their own unaided way through life, or who suppose that nothing much is wrong with the world or the human race, or indeed themselves. Free grace is obviously correlated, here more than anywhere else, with a radical view of human wickedness and the threat posed by death. For those who want to remain independent, being ruled by grace appears almost as much of a threat as being ruled by sin and death. But this is, of course, absurd. Grace is undeserved love in powerful action; and love seeks the well-being, the flourishing, of the beloved, not their extinction or diminution. To look love in the face and see only a threat is the self-imposed nemesis of the hermeneutic of suspicion.

But this free gift is offered through the obedience, the faithfulness, of Jesus himself. Here, as in Phil 2:6-8, Paul sees the voluntary death of Jesus as the messianic act *par excellence*, the triumphant accomplishment of that covenant plan for which Israel was called in the first place, the completion of the purpose for which God called Abraham. Not for Paul the currently fashionable idea that Jesus had not intended to die but that the church—Paul himself included!—used theological hindsight to impose upon that death a meaning Jesus himself had never envisaged. Paul's allusions in this passage to the fourth servant song, highlighting his own reference to Jesus' obedience, tell the story of one who knowingly went to the place where Israel's sin and shame, and the world's sin and shame, were heaped up together, and took the full weight on himself. How this could be, theologically speaking, is hinted at in 5:20, and will be explored further in the explosive 8:3-4.

3. Paul's personification of sin and death, and his highlighting of these forces as the deepest problem of humans and of the world, will win him few friends among those for whom sin is merely an outdated neurosis and death an unfortunate problem that the medical profession has not yet solved. One might have thought that the twentieth century, which elevated sin to a technological level previously unimagined, and meted out violent death to more people, more efficiently, than ever before, would have been only too glad to embrace Paul's analysis of the problem, and eager to rediscover his solution. But, as so often, the patient is fearful of hearing the true diagnosis, not least because the treatment may be humiliating. Fancy having to admit, thinks the late modern Western skeptic, that one had been wrong all along, that those boring and out-of-touch Christians had had the answers! No: we will die as we have lived, in ironic agnosticism, worshiping Heisenberg's Uncertainty Principle, maintaining consistency (even in our inconsistency!) rather than embracing salvation.

Part of the problem, of course, is that traditional Christianity has frequently operated with a truncated view of sin, limiting it to personal, and particularly sexual, immorality. These things matter enormously, of course, but there are other dimensions, of which the last century has seen so many examples, which are often untouched by traditional preaching. Equally, those preachers who have focused attention on structural evil within our world, on systematic and politically enshrined injustice, have often left the home base of Pauline theology in order to do so, not realising that there were resources there from which to launch not only critique but also promise and hope. This passage invites us to explore a reintegrated view of sin and death, rebellion and consequent dehumanization, as the major problem of humankind, and thereby to offer diagnoses of our world's ills that go to the roots of the problem and prepare the way for the cure.

4. As a culture, the Western world of the late twentieth century has seen the growth, and the application on a wide scale, of the hermeneutic of suspicion. Every text, every artefact, every piece of popular culture, is interrogated: whose perspective does it represent? Who is it oppressing? Who is implicitly marginalized by it? This process, fueled by the great liberationist movements, not least that of women and (in the United States) of African Americans, has pinpointed many evils, and awakened consciences to many real abuses. But left to itself it functions as the secular shadow of that kind of sub-Christian teaching where the doctrine of original sin was well known but that of free grace was somehow forgotten. It produces, in other words, a gloomy, guilty mind-set, where people feel ashamed of being what they inalienably are, and apologize for innocent actions. When we meet this in an individual, we advise them to see a psychiatrist. Someone who is always apologizing, always overeager to confess their sins, needs pastoral help. But we are well on the way to creating the social or corporate equivalent; that is perhaps what neo-moralism was bound to do. It also produces, as a reflex, a "victim culture" in which those who are, or feel, "oppressed" or "marginalized" become blameless, and any criticism of them is categorized as further oppression.

This naive new morality, a crude attempt at re-erecting ethical frameworks in the wake of the perceived failure of secularism's amorality, would do well to rediscover the Pauline doctrine of which it is the parody. A true analysis of sin, structural and personal, should lead to a true discovery of grace, again both structural and personal. Applying the Pauline doctrine of grace to the larger questions faced in our culture would mean rediscovering, beyond proper and necessary suspicion, that there is such a thing as trust, and that healthy societies, as well as individuals, thrive on it.

ROMANS 6:1-23, BAPTISM AND FREEDOM

Overview

The question Paul now faces is, Where do Christians live on the map of 5:12-21?

This is not quite the same question as theologians and commentators have been eager to discover at this point, namely: granted justification by grace through faith, what is the place of ethics, and of moral effort, in the Christian life? This latter question is, in fact, contained within the former, but we must not, in our eagerness for relevance, ignore Paul's actual argument. The question of 6:1, and even that of 6:15, is not, despite frequent assertions, exactly the same as that which Paul cites, and scornfully dismisses, in 3:8 ("Let us do evil that good may come"). Verse 1 is primarily about *status*, not behavior, as is apparent from the argument about status that follows in 6:2-11 (behavior is included as well, and is highlighted in 6:12-14, but it is not the primary focus). And 6:15, while clearly about behavior, introduces an important argument about the two kinds of "slavery": Paul is still concerned to get his hearers thinking about where they are within the framework of chap. 5, as is evident from the way in which the conclusion (6:23) directly echoes 5:21.

Paul's question is this: Do Christians find themselves now in the Adam solidarity or in the Christ solidarity? Do they still live under the reign of sin and death, or do they live under the reign of grace and righteousness? Since God's grace reaches down to the kingdom of sin to rescue those who are there, must Christians regard themselves as still being in that dark sphere in order that grace may do its proper work? And must they then live in the manner appropriate to that old kingdom?

To this question there can be only one answer, but the manner in which Paul gives it is revealing. Christians, he says, have left the old solidarity, and belong to the new; they must behave accordingly. The transfer is effected by dying and rising with the Messiah. And the event in which this dying and rising is accomplished is baptism.

This comes as a shock to many a good Protestant reader, accustomed to regard baptism simply as an outward expression of a believer's faith, and anxious about any suggestion that the act itself, or indeed any outward act, might actually change the way things are in the spiritual realm. (This anxiety has at least as much to do with the legacy of the Enlightenment, of Romanticism, and of Existentialism, as with the theology of the sixteenth century, let alone of the first; but that is too remote a topic for now.) The words "sacramentalism," "ritualism," and even "magical," spring naturally to mind, and are not dispelled by those writers, like Albert Schweitzer, who have been eager to assert the significance, in Paul, of physical baptism as the key event in which sinners are brought into the kingdom.[206] It is in this context that the older debates, as to whether Paul was here dependent on, or at least alluding to, the mystery religions and their initiatory practices, comes into play; the massive scholarship that has been brought to bear on this issue has now returned a negative verdict.[207] At the opposite extreme, some have suggested that Paul is not here primarily referring to the actual event of water baptism, but only using the language as a metaphor for Christian beginnings, conversion and initiation, in general.[208] As most commentators have agreed, this is unlikely. First-century Christian beginnings included water-baptism; the discussion in vv. 4-5 seems to allude to the physical rite; Paul's readers would naturally understand the passage in a literal sense. We are back with the question: what did Paul mean by baptism, and why does he suddenly introduce it here?

The most obvious explanation, and one that fills the present chapter with fresh

---

206. Albert Schweitzer, *The Mysticism of Paul the Apostle* (New York: Seabury, 1968).

207. See above all A. J. M. Wedderburn, *Baptism and Resurrection: Studies in Pauline Theology Against Its Graeco-Roman Background*, WUNT (Tübingen: Mohr, 1987). Dunn, *Romans 1–8*, 309-11, offers a helpful summary of the debate.

208. Dunn, *Romans 1–8*, 311-12, 327-29, referring to his own earlier work, though careful now to stress that this does not exclude a reference to the physical act.

meaning both in itself and in its relation to its surrounding context, is that Paul understood baptism in terms of the new exodus. Paul had already made this link, strikingly, in 1 Cor 10:2, speaking of the wilderness generation ("our fathers"), being "baptized into Moses in the cloud and in the sea." There he brings out the parallel between their "sacramental" experience and that of Christians, the new-exodus people, and stresses the ethical obligations that lie upon Christians as a result. As we saw in introducing chaps. 5–8, the long argument that is launched by 5:12-21 includes, toward its climax, a passage (8:12-27) in which Christians are characterized as the new wilderness generation, on their way home to the promised land, accompanied by the presence of God through the Spirit. The roots of this full statement are found here in chap. 6.

From a historical point of view this meaning is not just comprehensible, but compelling. The baptism of John is best explained as a new-exodus movement, along with other similar movements that gathered people in the wilderness and looked for signs of salvation. There is every reason to suppose both that Jesus himself saw John's baptism as the starting-point for his own work, not just chronologically but thematically, and that the earliest church likewise looked back not just to Jesus but to Jesus as the leader of the movement that had begun with John's baptism.[209] Christianity was a new-exodus movement from the beginning; baptism in the earliest church, we must assume, retained this character and overtone. Moreover, the death of Jesus at Passover time, and the meal he shared with his followers on the night he was betrayed, so interwove the theme of new exodus with the fact of Jesus' death that the two became inextricable. "The redemption" had occurred, not now when Moses led the children of Israel out of Egypt, but when Jesus died as Israel's Messiah and rose again. The movement that had begun symbolically with John at the Jordan came of age at Easter. And already Jesus himself, whose mission and vocation seem to have been given focus and direction in his own baptism by John, had used baptism as a metaphor for his own

coming ordeal (Mark 10:38; Luke 12:50). We may suppose that the earliest Christian assumption about baptism was that it was *both* a dramatic symbol of the new exodus *and* a sign of Jesus' death.

This is further confirmed both by the parallel between the present sequence of thought and Col 1:13-14, and by the sense this reading makes of the rest of chap. 6. God, says Paul in Colossians,[210] "has delivered us from the power of darkness and transferred us into the kingdom of his beloved son, in whom we have redemption, the forgiveness of sins." This, as has often been pointed out, is exodus language.[211] Similarly, in our present passage, 5:21 sets up the two kingdoms, and chap. 6 argues that Christians have been liberated from the first to belong to the second. A main theme of the rest of the passage is that of the rescue of the slaves: Verse 6 speaks of no longer being enslaved to sin, v. 9 of death no longer being one's master, vv. 12-14 of sin no longer reigning over one. The whole discussion of vv. 16-23 hinges on the notion of slavery recently abandoned and freedom newly found. It simply will not do to say, concerning an argument written by a first-century Jew who has expounded the promises to Abraham two chapters before and will herald the entry into the promised land two chapters later, that this is merely a slave-market illustration taken from the Hellenistic world. It cries out to be interpreted in terms of the exodus. And when we find that the key event through which slavery is abandoned and freedom is gained consists of passing through the water, re-enacting the death of Jesus, which was already interpreted in terms of Passover imagery, the case can be closed. Exodus is not a distant echo here. It is a main theme.

We may reckon, then, that when Paul says "do you not know" in v. 3, introducing his statement about baptism and Jesus' death, this is not a rhetorical trick but a genuine assumption. Baptism would not have been seen as a miscellaneous cleansing rite, or a generalized sign of initiation, but as that which brought people into the historical narrative of the new exodus. The master-narrative

---

209. See Wright, *Jesus and the Victory of God*, chap. 5.

210. I assume Colossians to be by Paul; if not, it is certainly by someone close to Paul's own mind.
211. See Wright, *The Climax of the Covenant*, 109; J. D. G. Dunn, *The Epistles to the Colossians and to Philemon*, NIGTC (Grand Rapids: Eerdmans, 1996) 80-81.

had been enacted when Israel's history was focused on the Messiah and his death and resurrection. The life-stories of individual people, Jews and Greeks alike, needed then to be brought within this larger narrative by the appropriate symbolic means. Just as faith in the God who raised Jesus was common for all, Jew and Gentile alike, so baptism in the name of Jesus had to be undergone by all. It constituted the new people as the single new-exodus people of the one God (cf. Gal 3:26-29). Since what was at stake was the renewal of the people of God, and indeed of the whole creation (8:18-30), the event that brought together the individual life-story and the larger story of God, Israel and Jesus would itself be tangible and physical. That event, clearly, was baptism.

The community into which the baptized person came was the family, the people, of the Messiah. I have argued in detail elsewhere that Paul's incorporative language about Jesus hinges on his understanding of messiahship; the Messiah represents his people, so that what is true of him becomes true of them. The present chapter, indeed, is one of the classic passages on this theme (others include Galatians 3). Paul, it seems, could use the word Χριστός (*Christos*) not only to refer specifically to Jesus himself as Messiah, but to the whole company of the messianic people.[212] That is why, whereas he regularly says "*through* Jesus Christ," referring to that which God has done by the agency of the human being Jesus of Nazareth, who is the Messiah and Lord, he regularly says "*in* Christ Jesus." This is not a mere stylistic variant, but a key indication that he is using the words with a sense of precision. If by *Christos* he means, along with a reference to Jesus himself, "the messianic people; the people who belong to the story of the new exodus," his language in the present chapter becomes clear. People join this family through baptism; that is, they are baptized *into Christ* (v. 3). That which is true of the Messiah is therefore now true of them; that is, what happened to him happens to them *with him*, as in the famous string of words beginning with σύν (*syn*, "with," vv. 4-8). Their status and condition now, therefore, is that they are *in Christ* (v. 11),

so that his having died to sin and being alive to God is true of them also. This is the logic of incorporative Messiahship, and hence of baptism.

One of the great gains of this approach to Romans 6 is that we can move away once and for all from seeing chaps. 6–8, or even 5–8, as expressing a different kind of theology, or even a different train of thought, from chaps. 1–4. As we noted in the introduction, the promises made by God to Abraham in Genesis 15 envisaged the exodus. Paul, expounding those promises in Romans 4, sees them fulfilled in the creation of a Jew-plus-Gentile family through the death and resurrection of Jesus, and envisages them looking forward to the time when Abraham's family will inherit the world (4:13). What more appropriate way of describing the manner of that family's coming together than through the event that evokes the exodus? More particularly, the keynote of chaps. 1–4 is "God's righteousness," which is alluded to in 5:21 as the means through which grace has come to reign through Jesus Christ. Now, in chap. 6, "righteousness" becomes a periphrastic (or indirect) way of referring to God (vv. 13, 16, 18, 19, 20; the periphrasis gives way to literal statement in v. 22). God's covenant faithfulness is the overarching characteristic of the sphere into which the Christian comes through baptism.

Nor is there any conflict between "baptism" as a physical act (a "ritual," in the loaded sense that is still sometimes used) and "faith" as an interior event—or between either of these and the flooding of the heart by the Spirit of which Paul speaks in 5:5. As a first-century Jew, Paul was happily innocent of the dualistic either/or that keeps such things apart in some contemporary Christian thinking. He was well aware of the problems that arose when baptized persons, regularly attending the eucharist, gave the lie to these symbols by the way they were living; he addresses this problem in 1 Corinthians. Yet he never draws back from his strong view of either baptism or the eucharist, never lapses back into treating them as secondary. Indeed, in the present passage one might actually say that he is urging faith on the basis of baptism: since you have been baptized, he writes, work out that what is true of Christ is true

212. Wright, *The Climax of the Covenant*, chaps. 2–3, 8.

of you (v. 11). The point here is not to set out a systematic *ordo salutis* in which different things happen to the Christian, outwardly and inwardly, in a particular sequence, but to expound that which is true of the baptized and believing Christian in such a way as to make it clear that one's basic status now is with Christ rather than with Adam, in the kingdom of grace rather than the kingdom of sin and death.

Into this sequence of thought, as with 5:20 within 5:12-21, comes the law (6:14-15). It looks at first like an odd *non sequitur*, since the law has not been mentioned in the chapter until this point: sin shall not have dominion over you, Paul says (v. 14), because you are "not under law but under grace." Place the whole discussion in the context of the end of chap. 5, however, and the problem disappears. The law has come in to the Adam/Christ dialectic on the side of Adam. If baptism brings you out of the Adam-sphere,

it also brings you out of the law-sphere. Paul is arguing on a knife-edge here, since his exodus theme might have suggested that the freed slaves now needed, as at Sinai, to embrace the Torah as their way of life. He will address that question in the next chapter. For the moment he is content to explore more thoroughly the inner meaning of slavery and freedom in relation to the human condition in general (vv. 15-23). Only when this is done will he at last turn his full attention to the question: what then do we say about the law?

Chapter 6 falls naturally into two main sections, introduced by the questions of v. 1 and v. 15. Verses 12-14 form a small paragraph that applies, and rams home, the lesson of vv. 1-11, as well as preparing the way for the second half of the chapter. The NIV's breaking of the first half of the chapter—vv. 1-4, 5-7, 8-10, 11-14—is idiosyncratic and ignores the way in which Paul builds carefully up to v. 11.

Romans 6:1-11, Dying and Rising with the Messiah

COMMENTARY

6:1-2. As so often, the tight-packed introduction contains all that is to come. The regular rhetorical opening, familiar from earlier in the letter (e.g., 3:1; 4:1), enquires what conclusion might be drawn from what has just been said, and suggests a possibility that is then firmly rebutted. The apparent logic of the question comes from 5:20-21, where Paul spoke of sin "abounding" and grace "superabounding." The question is primarily about status, with behavior included but not the sole or main topic; the NIV's "shall we go on sinning" has jumped the gun somewhat, looking ahead to vv. 12-14 rather than to the primary answer found in vv. 3-11. The NRSV's "shall we continue in sin" sounds to a contemporary ear as though it means much the same thing as the NIV, but the Greek has the definite emphasis of remaining in a place, in a status. Of course, to "remain in sin," in English and for that matter in Greek, will mean to go on committing sin, but Paul is interested here in where one *is* first and foremost; it is like saying "shall we remain in France," with the assumption that if one does

one will continue to speak French. At the end of chap. 5, "sin" was a dark ruling power, not primarily a style of conduct. In those terms, Paul's whole argument is that one has been moved out of one country into another; and that *therefore* (v. 12) it is no longer appropriate to go on speaking the same language. If the logic of the question were to be upheld, one should regard oneself as forever in the kingdom of sin and death, since that is where God's grace has reached to in Christ. This is not a question Paul expected the Roman church to raise—the device is here rhetorical—but that it had been raised many times in his regular preaching and teaching there is no reason to doubt.

The question is clearly wrongheaded. With the familiar μὴ γένοιτο (*mē genoito*, "let it not be so!"), Paul states his basic answer: We are those who died to sin, so how can we live in it any longer? Without the rest of the paragraph it might be difficult to see exactly what he meant by this, so we may proceed at once to his fuller explanation, noting only that his statement about "we" is slightly stronger than the translations make out. "We are the kind of people who . . ." would be better: "we are people whose main characteristic is precisely that we have died to sin."

6:3. Without the wider context it is not immediately clear, when Paul says "do you not know" (cf. 7:1), whether this is actually a new piece of information, imparted with a transparent rhetorical flourish, or something he genuinely expects his audience to be aware of. It has been argued earlier that in this instance he assumes they will know this meaning of baptism, at least in its basic form: those who are baptized into the Messiah, Jesus, are baptized into his death. Jesus himself had spoken of his death as a "baptism"; and that meaning is held in place by the larger new-exodus meaning of baptism from the time of John onward, seen through the early community's awareness of Jesus' death as linked to, and interpreted by means of, the events of Passover. We have no reason to suppose that baptism was ever a merely arbitrary entry rite, with a purpose (to mark out those who belonged) but without any meaning of its own. Like many other things in early Christianity, we have little access to early thinking on this topic, and we are heavily dependent on Paul, as our earliest source, for help. Though his fertile theological mind no doubt developed and expanded the earliest understandings more than a little, we should not question that at this point he is reflecting something that was widely known and believed in the early church.

The key word is of course "into": baptism is *into* the Messiah, and hence *into* his death. Like King David in the scriptures, the Messiah could be thought of as one "in whom" those who belonged to him were summed up. "We have ten shares in the king," said the men of Israel, "and in David also we have more than you" (2 Sam 19:43). When rebellion is sounded, it is precisely this solidarity that will be broken: "We have no portion in David, no share in the son of Jesse!" (2 Sam 20:1; 1 Kgs 12:16). What matters for Paul is the opposite movement, coming "into" the king, the Messiah; and that is effected in baptism. The point is that if the Messiah is Jesus of Nazareth, the crucified and risen one, then belonging to the messianic people means being characterized by cross and resurrection, by dying and rising.

This is at the heart of that dense (and deeply personal) passage Gal 2:15-21, which contains many parallels to the present argument.

6:4-5. What then does it mean to be "baptized into the Messiah's death"? Paul now explains this further, and draws the preliminary conclusion to back up his original statement of v. 2. Baptism involves being "co-buried" with the Messiah; Paul employs a rare word (only here and Col 2:12 in the NT), the first in a string of *syn-* compounds, to bring out the significance that what happened to the Messiah must be regarded as having happened to those who are "in him" by baptism. The prefix *syn-* means "with," and the verb here means "co-buried"—that is, "were buried with." Those who are "in" the Messiah died with him, were buried with him. It is possible, indeed likely, that the symbolism of baptism, with the candidate being plunged under the water, naturally suggested burial to Paul; unless we assume that this is his meaning, it is not clear why he should highlight Jesus' burial rather than simply his death. That seems to be the explanation, too, for "the likeness of his death" in v. 5 (see below). But, if this visible parallel was in his mind, it was as an offshoot of a connection already established between Jesus' death and baptism, rather than its original cause.

This opens the way for the main theme of the rest of the paragraph. The Messiah's resurrection means that those who are "in the Messiah" now stand, and must walk, on resurrection ground. Some have disputed whether Paul here speaks of Christians already being raised with Christ, or whether that is an idea belonging only to Colossians and Ephesians within the larger Pauline corpus; but there should be no doubt. The whole point of the argument is that Christians no longer belong in the world of death; Paul does not here suppose that one should wait until the final bodily resurrection (8:11) before beginning to "walk in newness of life," and this "walk" is based on a present status, not merely anticipating the future reality.[213] The argument of these verses is not simply that one has died to sin and hence must not live in it anymore, but that one is already "alive to God in Christ

213. So Fitzmyer, *Romans*, 435. For the debate, see the judicious remarks of Moo, *The Epistle to the Romans*, 371n. 97.

Jesus" (v. 11) and must now live accordingly. We must allow the past tense of "glorified" in 8:30 to have its full weight (see the Commentary on 8:18-30).

This is the second point at which the programmatic statement of 1:3-4 starts to come into its own (the first being 4:24-5). From here on it will become a dominant note. The resurrection of the Messiah from among the dead is the reason why his death had any salvific meaning at all.[214] Here, and throughout chaps. 6–8, it is the ground for the hope not only of Christians but of the whole created order. Neither here nor in Colossians and Ephesians does Paul offer either an unrealized or a completely realized eschatology: the baptized are in one sense already raised, and must behave accordingly, while in another sense they are still to be raised in the future. Paul emphasizes the parts of this complex truth he needs in different contexts, and we should not play his various statements off against one another. As all theologians know, it is impossible to say everything one believes in every sentence one writes, and there are always some readers who insist on imagining that what one has left out on this occasion one does not believe.

Paul adds, apparently unnecessarily in terms of his ongoing argument, that Jesus was raised "through the glory of the Father." This is to be linked with 4:24; there, too, as in 8:11, it is the Father by whose agency Jesus was raised. Why, then, does Paul speak of God's "glory" as the agent in this event? In the light of 4:20, and further off 1:21, it appears that to recognize "the glory of God" at work in the resurrection of Jesus is part of the attitude of faith in which sin and corruption are replaced with obedience and life (see the Commentary on 4:20; see also John 11:40). The point at issue here, though, is that those who have been buried with the Messiah must reckon that, as he has been raised, they too are called to "walk" with a new quality of life. "Walk" as a metaphor for human conduct is rabbinic (הלכה halākāh, "walking," hence "conduct"; from הלך hālak, "walk"); this is the conduct that will follow from the status, but it is the

status that Paul is emphasizing. A further clue may be found here as to why Paul ascribes Jesus' resurrection to the agency of God's glory: the "glorification" that is God's gift to all the justified consists not merely in their final resurrection (cf. 8:11, 17, and 29-30), but in that which anticipates the resurrection in the present, namely, the practice of holiness of which Paul speaks both here and in 8:12-17 (see also Col 3:1-4, where exactly the same connections are made).

He offers a further explanation in v. 5, which literally reads: "for if we have been united with him in the likeness of his death, we shall also be of his resurrection." For the full English sense we must supply, as the translations do, a repetition of the first verb: "we shall also be [united with him in the likeness] of his resurrection." The word for "been united" comes from a root which means "grown together," and this, together with the word "likeness" (ὁμοίωμα homoiōma), has occasioned much debate on Paul's precise nuance. The NRSV simply says "united in a death like his," which is not quite as strong as Paul's Greek; the NIV omits the idea of "likeness" altogether. It seems to me preferable to suppose that Paul is continuing to regard baptism as in some way a re-enactment of Jesus' death, a making real for the individual of the once-for-all event of Calvary (compare again Gal 2:19-20). This would explain the unusual phrase "grown together": in baptism, the existence of the Christian is, as it were, intertwined with that of the Messiah, like two young trees whose trunks grow around one another.

The main point, however, is in the second half of the verse. Granted the identity with the Messiah's death, however we fine-tune our statement of it; the result is that the baptized will share the likeness of his resurrection also. It is just possible that Paul may have in mind the early Christian practice, reflected elsewhere in the NT, of the newly baptized being clothed in white, symbolizing their commitment to holiness of life (e.g., Col 3:12-15). This, again, would make baptism a visible prefiguring of the point at issue. But we do not have to suppose this to make sense of the verse, which looks at three results simultaneously: the ultimate future, in which the Christian is assured of resurrection (cf.

8:11); the present status, where the Christian stands on resurrection ground; and the present behavior, which must reflect present status and anticipate the future ontological reality (see Col 3:1-4). We must, therefore, take the second half of v. 5 as indicating present status and behavior, not simply the future resurrection.[215]

6:6-7. Paul explains further, arriving as he does so at the central statement of the paragraph. "Knowing this"—again, one may question whether Paul expected his hearers to know this already—that "our old person was co-crucified" (another *syn-* compound, paralleled in Gal 2:19). To understand Paul's meaning we must go back again to 5:12-21. The "old self" (ὁ παλαιὸς ἡμῶν ἄνθρωπος *ho palaios hēmōn anthrōpos*), which used to be translated "our old man," denotes, not some particular part of the human person, but rather the whole person, the entire self, *seen as someone "in Adam."* Call this "the old Adam," perhaps, but that phrase, too, has too many associations with an older pietism in which this "old Adam" still lingered on somewhere in the background, causing trouble from time to time; and Paul's point is precisely that in baptism the old Adamic solidarity is decisively broken. The "old self," whole and entire, is put to death once and for all. This does not mean that the Christian cannot sin; but Paul's sharp point should be felt before caveats and nuances are allowed to dull it. In baptism the whole person leaves the Adam-world for good, leaves it by death, a final one-way journey.

The purpose of this—the divine purpose, one must assume Paul means—is "so that the body of sin might be abolished" (the NIV's "rendered powerless" is a possible meaning of the Greek, but Paul's intention seems to be to insist that this "body of sin" should be destroyed, not simply left to one side without power), "so that we should no longer be under the lordship of sin." We are still within the world of 5:21, the world of the two realms, sin and grace. Paul underlines the location of Christians on that map, emphasizing which of the two countries they now live in and (more to the point) which of the two overlords now

rightfully claim their allegiance. "The body of sin" could have meant the whole human being, seen as the entity that "sin" has made its own. ("Body," as often in Paul, means not "physical body," but something more like our word "person," including the physical aspect but also hinting at the "personality" that goes with it.) This would make good sense, were it not for the fact that it would then approximate very closely to the meaning of "the old self," and since the abolition of "the body of sin" is the result of the crucifixion of "the old self" they cannot be identical. It is probably better to take "body" in the wider sense of "solidarity": "the old self was crucified with Christ, so that the solidarity of sin might be broken, and we should no longer be enslaved to sin." As in 5:21, the sovereign rule of sin has been decisively challenged by grace, the grace operative in Jesus' obedient death and resurrection. When that grace enfolds the baptismal candidate, entwining the Jesus-story and the Jesus-reality with theirs, the communal solidarity that sin has created, generating the sense and the fact of helplessness as humans go along with all that sin suggests, is broken, and they are free to live under a different lordship.

Paul explains yet further with a cryptic aside (v. 7): the one who has died is freed from sin. That, at least, is what he clearly means; but the verb he uses, puzzlingly to us, is δεδικαίωται (*dedikaiōtai,* "has been justified"). Many commentators conclude that Paul is here invoking a well-known rabbinic principle about death paying all debts. I agree with Cranfield that this is unlikely, since Paul nowhere suggests that physical death settles all accounts in God's sight. Verse 7 is not, then, a general principle invoked to explain the more specific point of v. 6, but a comment about the one who has been co-crucified with Christ; such a one has been "justified from"—that is, cleared from—their sin.[216] Once more, we may compare Gal 2:19-20: "I through the law died to the law." Why, then, "justified," rather than "freed"? The answer must be that, unlike most of his recent readers, Paul is able to keep the lawcourt metaphor still running in his mind even while expounding baptism and the Christian's

---

215. The verb ("we shall be") is thus a logical future, following the "if" at the start of the verse. See Fitzmyer, *Romans,* 435, against, e.g., Dunn, *Romans 1–8,* 318. See the Commentary on 6:8.

216. Cranfield, *A Critical and Exegetical Commentary on the Epistle to the Romans,* 310-11.

solidarity in Christ. The Christian's freedom from sin comes through God's judicial decision. And this judicial decision is embodied in baptism.

6:8. Having reached the heart of his analysis in v. 6, Paul now builds toward the conclusion in v. 11. As usual, a terse preliminary statement (v. 8) is then filled out (vv. 9-10), before the conclusion is drawn (v. 11). The preliminary statement is this: "If we co-died with the Messiah, we believe that we shall also co-live with him" (συζάω *syzaō* "co-live" is another συν- [*syn-*] compound). This "shall," like the future in v. 5, is best taken as the logical future after "if." It obviously has a future referent as well in the eventual resurrection life, but it cannot support the conclusion of v. 11 unless it refers to the present time.

6:9-10. "We know" (this time we can be sure that Paul's hearers did know this, at least in principle) "that the Messiah, raised from the dead, will never die again." Jesus' resurrection was not a mere resuscitation, like those of Jairus's daughter, the widow's son at Nain, or Lazarus (Mark 5:21-34 and par.; Luke 7:11-17; John 11:1-44). It is basic to all early Christian thinking on the resurrection (Paul is, of course, our chief witness, but what he says tallies well with the strange stories in the Gospels) that what happened at Easter involved the *transformation*, not merely the revival or resuscitation, of Jesus' body, so that it entered upon a new mode of physical existence, which Paul saw as the beginning and sign of the renewal of all creation (see particularly 1 Cor 15:50-57; Phil 3:20-21). The transforming of Christians' bodies at their resurrection is modeled, in Paul's thought, on the transformation of Jesus' body at his. Transformation, new creation, had already happened within God's world, and would in the end happen on a grand scale. Paul once again insists that what happened to the Messiah happened also to those "in him." He cannot emphasize strongly enough that the rule of sin and death has been decisively broken, and that Christians are no longer subject to it. "Death has no longer any sovereignty over him"; Paul is still working out the implications of 5:21, and urging his readers to do so too.

The balanced explanation of v. 10 has rhetorical force that should not be overpressed for theological precision. The Messiah did not die "to sin" in the same sense that he now lives "to God." Paul's meaning is that the Messiah came under the rule, the sovereignty, of sin and death; not that he himself sinned, but that he came, as Paul says in 8:3, "in the likeness of sinful flesh." "To die to sin" meant, for the Messiah, that he died under its weight, but that in doing so he came out from its domain. And this happened ἐφάπαξ (*ephapax*), once and for all. There is no room here for the idea that the Messiah, or more especially his people, still live with a foot in both camps, or with one foot in the grave and the other by the empty tomb. Jesus, the Messiah, died once and once only, and was thereafter finished with death. If Paul had wanted to say (as some cautious interpreters, aware of the danger of a shallow perfectionism, have wanted him to say) that Christians have not completely "died to sin," that the old Adam still lingers on in some way, he has chosen an extremely misleading way of saying it.[217]

"In that he lives, he lives to God"; in other words, the life Jesus now lives he lives in God's domain, the realm of grace and righteousness. Paul has told Jesus' story in terms of the two spheres of existence in 5:12-21—which is somewhat ironic, since he himself represented the second of the spheres—in order that, through the identity of the Messiah and his people that is now established, he might demonstrate the true status of those "in Christ."

6:11. The key word here is "reckon," the same root as in 4:3 and elsewhere, and with the same bookkeeping metaphor in mind. Do the sum, he says; add it up and see what it comes to. The Messiah has died, once for all, and been raised; you are, by baptism, in the Messiah; therefore, you, too, have died, once for all, and been raised. The "reckoning" in question is to take place in the believing thought-processes of the Christian. The NRSV's "consider" is fine, provided it is taken in a strong sense and not allowed to become more vague ("reflect on this"); the NIV's "count yourselves" is an attempt to keep

---

217. To insist on this was one of the achievements of D. Martyn Lloyd-Jones in his remarkable series of published sermons on Romans. See Lloyd-Jones, *Romans: An Exposition of Chapter 6: The New Man* (London: Banner of Truth, 1972).

the bookkeeping metaphor alive. The point is not, as in some schemes of piety, that the "reckoning" *achieves* the result of dying to sin and coming alive to God, any more than someone adding up a column of figures creates the result out of nothing; it opens the eyes of mind and heart to *recognize* what is in fact true. It is here that one might almost say that Paul appeals for faith on the basis of baptism. Those who have received the sign of the new exodus in the Messiah are urged to think through, and to believe, what has in fact happened to them.

The point is this: on the map of 5:21, the Christian belongs in the second half, the kingdom of grace and righteousness, not in the first half, the kingdom of sin and death. Paul is well aware that sin remains powerful and attractive for the most well-trained Christian, and that physical death awaits all except those for whom the Lord's return comes first (see 1 Cor 9:26-7; 15:51-52). He is speaking of a different level of reality. If someone challenged him and said that sin and death were just as powerful to them as they had been before their coming to faith, he would reply that they had not yet considered the seriousness of their baptism; just as if someone claimed that, now they had been baptized, evil had no attraction whatever for them, he would no doubt reply that they had not yet considered the seriousness of sin. From his whole corpus of writings, we know that Paul was a realist, about himself, about his fellow Christians, about suffering, pain, depression, fear and death itself. These were not enemies he took lightly. But his entire argument in this chapter so far, which anticipates that of 8:31-39, is that the Christian, facing these enemies, stands already on resurrection ground. This is ultimately a truth about the Christian's Lord, the Messiah, but because of baptism it becomes a truth about the Christian himself or herself. "Reckon yourselves," calculate yourselves, count yourselves, "dead to sin and alive to God in the Messiah, Jesus." This is the full answer to the question of v. 1.

Romans 6:12-14, The End of Sin's Reign

COMMENTARY

The three verses that follow are a genuine bridge from one half of the chapter to the other. They follow, obviously, as imperatives that bring the indicative of vv. 2-11 into practical reality; but they also set the terms for the discussion of slavery and freedom that is to come. They, like the rest of the chapter, still belong within, and explore, the world of 5:12-21, and vv. 20-21 in particular.

6:12. If the reign of sin has been broken in Christ, and if the Christian truly lives in Christ, then sin has no business continuing to rule his or her life. And it is now the Christian's responsibility to make sure that this is so. If it is asked, as well it might be, what chance sin has got to rule, if the Christian has died to it, Paul's implicit answer here has to do with the sphere over which sin, though no longer enthroned, can exercise powerful attraction: the "mortal body." The Christian still possesses a body—that is, a whole person—which will die and, indeed, in terms of ethics, must be "put to death" (8:13), since it still has desires that must not be obeyed. This "mortal body" is not far from what Paul means by "the flesh," which will be discussed in due course; it is one of his ways of indicating the continuing ambiguity of the life of the Christian, an ambiguity that in no way takes back the trenchant and definite statements made in vv. 2-11. The idea of "obedience," which, of course, belongs with the idea of being ruled by a sovereign, looks back to 5:21 and on to vv. 16-17; that of the bodily desires (ἐπιθυμίαι *epithymiai*) to 7:7-8.

6:13. The same appeal is now put positively, in terms of "presenting" or "offering" oneself obediently to a master—a theme that will recur frequently in the next few verses. The verb translated "present" can have sacrificial overtones, as indeed in the similar context in 12:1, but here it seems more general. The choice is stark, though Paul does not express it as an exact balance. Do not, he says, present your *members* to sin, but present your *selves* to God. Still on the map of

5:21, Paul is working within the logic of 6:1-11: it is now technically impossible for the Christian to present his own or her own *self* to sin, since the self has died with Christ and been raised "in order to live to God." What is possible—all too possible, alas—is for the Christian to present his or her *members*, the varied parts of personality, mind, or body (what some have misleadingly termed the "old Adam"), to sin.

Paul's argument here is that this is illogical. To present one's members to sin is to be out of tune with the reality of what a baptized Christian is, one who has been brought from death to life (drawing on v. 11). In spelling out the two possible courses of action, he sets the terms for the discussion of slavery that begins with v. 16: instead of sin/death and grace/righteousness, as in 5:21, it is now sin/unrighteousness and God/righteousness. Paul will now, for a few verses, actually use "righteousness" as a metonym for the whole God-side of the picture, and hence even as a metaphor for God. He will add other terms as well, without changing the basic antithesis. For the moment he allows the argument of vv. 2-11 to issue in a clear appeal, reinforced with a promise in the next verse.

6:14. Sin, he says, will not have dominion over you.[218] The reason is clear; you have transferred your abode, your status. You no longer live within the sin/death solidarity, but within the grace/righteousness/life solidarity. Sin, therefore, as a power, a force to be reckoned with, may still be at large in the world, but it has no authority over the Christian. This may seem counterintuitive, but it is precisely for this reason that Romans 6 is a call to that characteristically Pauline combination of faith and clear thinking. For the moment he undergirds the claim about being quit of sin's dominion by the initially unexpected explanation: "for you are not under law but under grace."

---

218. The word "have dominion" is not, despite the NRSV, the same as in v. 12. Here it is from κυριεύω (*kyrieuō*, "exercise lordship"; in v. 12 it is from βασιλεύω *basileuō*, "exercise kingship"). The difference is slight; cf. the NIV's "reign" (v. 12) and "be master" (v. 14).

If he had said "for you are not under sin and death but under grace and righteousness," we might have been less surprised. But clearly Paul is working toward a different point, parallel in some ways with the question of 6:1, which is now to be addressed in the second half of the chapter. Like a composer suddenly modulating into a new symphonic development, Paul turns the argument in a subtly different direction, toward the role of the law. This itself belongs within the passage (5:20-21) that has been the basis for chap. 6 so far. The terms are set in 5:20: The law came in alongside, so that the trespass might abound, but where sin abounded, grace superabounded. Paul has restated the antithesis of 6:1-13 in terms not of 5:21 but of 5:20, in order both to ward off possible misunderstandings that might arise and to prepare for his treatment of the law in chap. 7.

The idea of being "not under the law," which occurs already in Gal 3:23 and 5:18, belongs closely with Paul's previous negative statements about Torah. God's righteousness is revealed "apart from the law" (3:21); justification is by faith "apart from works of the law" (3:28); it was "not through the law" that the promise came to Abraham and his seed that he would inherit the world (4:13), because "the law works wrath" (4:15). Romans 5:20 has hardly explained this negative point, though it has sharpened it up; the law stands on the Adam-side of the equation. It is sometimes said that Galatians has a negative view of the law, and Romans a positive one. This is a very inadequate way of describing the problem, as the evidence already demonstrates. In the present context Paul's point is plain: those who belong to Christ, who have died and been raised in baptism, do not live in the Adam solidarity, *and hence do not live under the law.* This is exactly what we find in Gal 2:19: "I through the law died to the law, that I might live to God." The implication is striking. When we set the theological explanation of 6:14*b* alongside 6:14*a*, Paul is saying that, if one did live under the law, sin *would* indeed have dominion. That will take all of chap. 7 to explain.

Romans 6:15-23, Slavery and Freedom

COMMENTARY

6:15. Having examined the possible drastic consequences of embracing 5:21 the wrong way, Paul now turns to the possible drastic consequences of embracing 5:21 in the light of 5:20: supposing one is no longer under law, does that mean one is now a sinner? This question, like that of 6:1, is not confined to committing actual acts of sin. As the parallel in Gal 2:17 demonstrates, part of the point is that to come out from the sphere of Torah, for a Jew, meant that one was joining the "sinners," the ἁμαρτωλοί (*hamartōloi*), the lesser breeds without the law. "Shall we then be 'sinners?' "

As Paul's answer indicates, however, this time the emphasis is far more on actual behavior and far less on status, important though that remains. Once again the terms of his argument are the two spheres in which humans can belong, and the thrust is on the appropriateness of certain types of behavior for those in the God/grace/righteousness sphere.

6:16. As usual, he sets up the categories in an introductory sentence. "Do you not know"—this time he is invoking a general, fairly obvious, principle of human life, not a piece of Christian teaching—"that you are slaves of the one to whom you give yourselves in obedience?" The choice is between two obediences; but in Paul's eagerness to state this he allows "obedience" to do duty both for the activity itself and for the one to whom it is offered: "whether to sin [which leads to death] or to obedience [which leads to righteousness]." The "obedience" to which one offers obedience is, of course, a periphrasis (or circumlocution); behind it stands the obedience of Christ in 5:19, enabling the word and concept to function as another synecdoche for the entire grace/righteousness sphere. This explains, though it hardly excuses, the unclarity. Paul's point is that all human existence takes place in slavery, to one slavemaster or the other; his problem is that he wants to say as well that serving God in Christ is true freedom. That is why he apologizes for the language in v. 19. The two

slaveries are not equal and opposite; the difference between the slavemasters produces a totally different sort of life for those who obey them.

6:17-19a. Paul places his readers within the diagram of the two slaveries, casting the sentence into the form of a prayer of thanksgiving (cf. 7:25; 1 Cor 15:57, and elsewhere). They were in the Adam solidarity; now they are in the Christ solidarity (again, the transition is definite, and cannot be watered down). He makes the point twice, from different angles. First, they were slaves of sin, but now have become obedient to Christian teaching; second, they were set free from sin, and have become enslaved to righteousness. It is the latter point, with all its latent absurdity in terms of "slavery" to the very thing that sets one most truly free, that draws from him the comment "I am speaking in human terms, because of the weakness of your flesh" (v. 19*a*); in other words, I am using a very basic illustration, to bring the point down to a level that anyone can understand.

The first of the contrasts, that in v. 17, has surprised many readers. Why does Paul not simply say "you have become obedient to grace," or indeed "to righteousness"? Why has he developed the second half of the sentence in this unexpected way: "you have become obedient from the heart to the pattern of teaching to which you were committed"?

Commentators went through a phase, two generations ago, of questioning whether this whole clause might be a later addition to Paul's text.[219] This had more to do with wanting Paul to conform to a particular theological framework than with a serious attempt to read Romans. The "pattern of teaching" to which he is referring may well be a basic Christian confession. This could even be the baptismal confession itself, since the affirmation that Jesus is Lord, and that God raised him from the dead (cf. 10:9), is so clearly

---

219. Bultmann led the way on this. See the discussions in the commentaries, and esp. R. A. J. Gagnon, "Heart of Wax and a Teaching That Stamps: ΤΥΠΟΣ ΔΙΔΑΧΗΣ (Rom 6:17b) Once More," *JBL* 112 (1993) 667-87, at 671-73.

germane to what he is saying at this very point. Indeed, had he said "you were slaves of sin, but now you are under the lordship of the Messiah," no one would have questioned the verse. Dunn's suggestion, that by "the pattern of teaching" Paul is referring to Jesus Christ himself, nearly amounts to the same thing, but the phraseology of the verse points more to a particular teaching, such as we find in baptismal contexts in other letters (e.g., Col 3:1-17), than to the person of Jesus himself. What is more, instead of speaking of the teaching being given to them, he says that they were "handed over" to the teaching; something about the passivity of baptism may be reflected here, as the candidate submits to the dying and rising of the Messiah and acknowledges his lordship. This would then fit with the fresh meaning proposed by Gagnon on the basis of parallels in Hellenistic Judaism: "the imprint stamped by teaching, to which (imprint) you were handed over."[220]

The point, anyway, is that having been slaves of sin Christians have now been transformed, so that they have become obedient to this new pattern "from the heart." Though this precise phrase is unique in Paul, it fits well with his emphasis on the heart in, e.g., 2:29; 5:5; 10:8-9. This is usually connected closely to the new covenant work of the Spirit, transforming the heart from the dark condition described in 1:21 to the renewal and illumination described in 2 Cor 3:2-3; 4:5 (the NIV's "wholeheartedly" is slightly misleading; Paul's emphasis is not on how much of the heart is put into obedience, but on the fact that it comes from the heart as opposed to being mere outward conformity; cf. 2:25-29). This is the point Paul will pick up in 7:6.

The result can be stated simply though paradoxically (v. 18): liberated from sin, you were enslaved to righteousness. "Righteousness" here is not so much "virtue" or moral goodness, but rather (as Paul will eventually make clear) a periphrasis for "God"; it is the divine righteousness, revealed in the death and resurrection of the Messiah (3:21-6), the righteousness through which grace has operated (5:21). It would in any case be odd, in

view of the whole chapter, to think of Christians being enslaved to "virtue," a quality they are to exhibit and even possess, rather than in some sense to God. Since Paul's basic point throughout is the exodus motif of the freeing of the slaves, he is well aware that suggesting an alternative slavery is in principle odd, and is only introduced to make the point of the alternative allegiance more sharply; he uses this human illustration, he says, (literally) "because of the weakness of your flesh." Whereas elsewhere such a phrase might refer to moral disability, it here simply denotes potential slowness of understanding. How Paul knew they would possess this "weakness of the flesh," and how he imagined this remark would not be provocative, we can only guess.

6:19b. By way of explaining vv. 17-18 (γάρ *gar*, omitted by the NIV), Paul restates the command of v. 13, with minor variations. It is not clear how much a command can actually explain something, but it requires little elaboration to see how Paul's logic works. He is explaining the balance of the two "slaveries," and hence further unpacking the paradox of being "liberated" into a different "slavery": *just as* you once presented your members as slaves to uncleanness, *so now* present your members as slaves to righteousness. "Uncleanness" was part of the problem in 1:24, and is now one of the things at which the Christian must look back, as the Israelites looked back at the fleshpots of Egypt. Paul expands the category of the former slavery: "and to lawlessness unto lawlessness," perhaps meaning "from one degree of lawlessness to another." This word, in this context, has nothing to do with the theological category of being "not under the law"; it merely refers to wild and uncontrolled behavior.

The challenge comes in the balance of "so now" with "as then." The energy and initiative that were put into uncleanness and lawlessness must now be put into the "slavery" to righteousness, which leads to "sanctification."

Here for the first time we meet the word that for so long was regarded as stating the topic of this entire section (chaps. 5–8). It is clearly important, but not that important. Its primary meaning, in any case, is focused not so much on ethical qualities as on that

220. Gagnon, "Heart of Wax and a Teaching That Stamps," 687. Gagnon agrees that his analysis says nothing one way or the other about a possible set pattern of early Christian teaching; I think the two ideas fit together rather well.

which is necessary for a person to approach the presence of God; this has clear and demanding behavioral consequences, but the main emphasis takes us back to v. 11: "alive to God." (The NIV's "holiness" is therefore slightly misleading—unless one takes that term, too, in its strict sense, referring not just to behavior but to access into God's presence.) "Slaves to righteousness unto sanctification" is thus God-oriented all through. Christians owe allegiance to the God whose covenant faithfulness rescued them in Christ; the result of this allegiance is that they become fit, through the obedience that wells up from the heart, for the presence of this same God. Paul is here unpacking further what was said so densely in 5:1-2.

6:20-22. By way of yet further explanation, he introduces a new element, which simultaneously brings the chapter back to its starting point at 5:21 (grace reigning through righteousness to eternal life) and points forward into the new topic of chap. 7 (the "fruit" borne by the two ways of life; cf. 7:4-5; this link is obscured by the NRSV's translation of the same word here as "advantage" and the NIV's "benefit"). What, he asks, was the result of the previous slavery? It carried a certain "freedom": free from God and God's righteousness. But the old slavery was a plant that bore a particular fruit, and the fruit was shame, leading to death. The new slavery, however, which Paul at last describes explicitly as slavery "to God," produces the fruit of sanctification, which leads to the life of the age to come. We are back on familiar territory.

There is a problem about the punctuation of v. 21: Does the phrase "in regard to the things of which you are now ashamed" go with "what fruit did you have" or with "their goal is death"? The NRSV and the NIV take the former route. The NEB and the REB follow the Nestle-Aland Greek text in the latter, which is probably to be preferred because of the γάρ (*gar*), significantly untranslated in the NRSV and the NIV, at the end of the last clause ("things that now make you ashamed, *for* their end is death," REB). The thought is the mirror of that in 5:5*a:* hope does not make us ashamed, because it truly leads to life; sin produces shame, because it leads to death. Here "shame" is not simply associated

with the feelings of disgrace or humiliation that belong to the deeds of sin themselves, but with the fact that conduct of that type leads to the human disintegration of death (cf. 1:32). The contrast is with the new slavery, slavery to God, which brings Christians into "sanctification," qualifying them for access to God's presence, and so for the life of the age to come.

6:23. We are, then, back with 5:21, having thoroughly explored the territory it opens up. The two paths of humankind are characterized by sin and death on the one hand, and by God and life on the other. But, as in 5:15-17, they are not balanced exactly. Sin pays wages in proportion to what has been done. God gives generously, beyond all imagining, and the measure of that gift is the death and resurrection of Jesus the Messiah: "the gift of God is eternal life in the Messiah, Jesus our Lord."

In particular, chap. 6 has explored the meaning of 5:12-21 in terms of the human renewal that results from the "new exodus" of baptism. Paul's main concern has not been, at this stage, to offer a detailed agenda for ethical action, though the general commands in chap. 6 are easily strong enough to sustain such a thing. His concern has been to emphasize that when Christians look at the Adam/Christ contrast they should be in no doubt that they belong on the "Christ" side of it. This must, of course, be put into effect by the moral effort of not letting sin reign in the "mortal body"; but this ongoing struggle is not to be thought of in terms of the Christian being some kind of a hybrid, half in Adam and half in Christ. The theology of baptism, both in terms of the "new exodus" and in terms of the dying and rising of the Messiah, prohibits such a thing. That which has happened has happened once and for all.

Paul has thus prepared the way for one of his greatest and most complex arguments. Add the Torah to this Adam/Christ contrast, and what do you get? As 5:20*a* indicated, an increase in "the trespass" (7:7-25). What is God's response? As 5:20*b*-21 stated, the gift of superabundant grace, doing that which the Torah could not (8:1-11). What is the result? The renewal of the covenant, the prophetically promised replacement of the "old letter" by the "new Spirit," resulting in nothing less than resurrection and the renewal of all creation (8:12-30). At the heart of it all stands the sending, the death and the resurrection of the Messiah, God's son, to take on himself the weight of Adamic and Torah-driven trespass, and then to welcome into new life those who through suffering and prayer are led by the Spirit toward the promised inheritance. This is where we see at last what "the obedience of the Messiah," the theological driving heart of 5:12-21, really meant.

REFLECTIONS

1. Romans was not written to provide "a theology of the Christian life," but Paul's larger argument demands that at certain points he write more or less exactly that, and chapter 6 is one of the two clearest examples (the other being chapter 12). Among the principal things it insists on is that being a Christian means living from within a particular story. It is the subversive story of God and the world, focused on Israel and thence on the Messiah, and reaching its climax in the Messiah's death and resurrection. No Christian can ever tell this story too frequently, or know it too well, because it is the story that has shaped him or her in baptism and that must continue to shape thought, life, and prayer thereafter. Otherwise one will be living a lie, allowing sin to continue exercising a sovereignty to which it has no more right.

The exodus story, which stands behind so much of this chapter, remains decisive. Many parts of the Christian church, fortunately, have retained it in their liturgy, particularly at Easter and the renewal of baptismal vows, reflecting an instinct sometimes superior to that of the church's exegetes. The story of coming out of slavery into freedom—with all the new puzzles and responsibilities that freedom brings!—is the story of the gospel, the narrative within which Jesus deliberately framed his own final moments with his followers, the story on which he himself drew to give meaning to his death. And, just as the Jewish people discovered in the exodus story the character of their rescuing God, so the covenant faithfulness of this same God has been fully unveiled in the paschal events of Golgotha and Easter. Learning about the Christian life and learning about the God revealed in Jesus Christ are two sides of the same coin.

2. It is a measure of how deeply this narrative has been woven into the consciousness of Western culture that a great many movements, national, political, social and cultural—including some that have been opposed to each other!—have told their own stories as liberation narratives. This reflects more than simply the influence of the Magna Carta on the subsequent British world and its derivatives; it is the sign of a culture stamped with the word "freedom" at a deeper level than that. The cry for freedom is one we instinctively recognize and want to respond to. At this point the exodus story offers itself as the true story of the human race, and the Christian retelling of this story in terms of the death and resurrection of Jesus Christ must do so as well. This story, if true, cannot simply be one "little story" among others, as though it could take its place happily on the cultural smorgasbord, offering a certain kind of "religious experience," alongside other stories that effectively enslaved humans and led them off to die. Even the postmodern critique that insists that all large metanarratives are instruments of slavery appeals to, and gets its power from, one story that, it assumes, is not: and that story is precisely its own version, filtered through many layers of cultural accretions, of the exodus narrative, the freeing of the slaves from Pharaoh's yoke. The Christian gospel is, at this level, telling the story that all humans know in their bones they want to hear.

3. It is true that in appealing to this story all kinds of things have been said and done that in some way or other distort it, or even threaten to destroy it outright. The magicians of Egypt are also adept at producing miracles to validate their position. At the level of international politics, the word "liberation" has often simply meant that a particular country has been taken over by a different form of virtual political enslavement. At both a personal and a global level, the financial loan that announces it will set you free to do all sorts of undreamed-of things will then enslave you until you have paid it back. In terms of personal morality, the freedom of one person to expand their business empire may well be at the cost of the freedom of their neighbor to remain in business; and the freedom of people to express their sexual potential regularly results both in the diminution of the freedom of others (to put it no more strongly for the moment) and also in their own enslavement to destructive and dehumanizing habits of mind and body. Telling the story of freedom is, by itself, not enough. As Paul seems to have recognized in the second half of chap. 6, freedom from the slavery of sin involves a new kind of "liberated slavery," obedience to the God who loves us and seeks our true freedom, our true humanness. Thus we have discovered, in the political sphere, that freedom from oppressive external regimes is not enough for a struggling country, in Africa or in the Balkans; with freedom come new responsibilities, to oneself and to one's neighbors, and without these one may be worse off than in the original slavery itself.

4. This chapter shines a bright spotlight on the dangerous half-truth, currently fashionable, that "God accepts us as we are." Indeed, the question of 6:1 could be read as raising exactly this question: Will "God's acceptance" do as a complete grounding of Christian ethics? Emphatically not. Grace reaches where humans are, and accepts them as they are, because anything less would result in nobody's being saved. Justification is by grace alone, through faith alone. But grace is always *transformative*. God accepts us where we are, but God does not intend to leave us where we are. That would be precisely to "continue in sin, that grace might abound." Unless we are simply to write Romans 6 out of the canon, the radical inclusivity of the gospel must be matched by the radical exclusivity of Christian holiness. There is such a thing as continuing to let sin reign in one's mortal body, and it will require serious moral effort to combat this tendency. The idea that Christian holiness is to be attained by every person simply doing what comes naturally would actually be funny were it not so prevalent. True freedom is not simply the random, directionless life, but the genuine humanness that reflects the image of God. This is found under the lordship of Christ. And this lordship makes demands that are as testing and difficult as they are actually liberating.

5. The pattern, the motive and the moral power to live in true freedom (in other words, in "slavery" to God) are found in that weaving of our life story together with the death and resurrection of the Messiah that happens in baptism. We are all too aware that thousands, perhaps millions, of the baptized seem to have abandoned the practice of Christian faith and life; but we are nevertheless called to allow the dying and rising of Christ in which we have shared to have its force and way in our own lives. If Jesus and his dying and rising are simply a great example, we remain without hope; who seriously thinks that they can live up to that ideal in their own strength? But if the fact of the messianic events has become part of our own story through the event of baptism, and the prayer and faith that accompany it, and above all the gift of the Holy Spirit of which Paul will shortly say more—then we will indeed be able to make our own the victory of grace, to present our members, and our whole selves, as instruments of God's ongoing purposes.

ROMANS 7:1–8:11, THE LIFE THE LAW COULD NOT GIVE

Overview

The main theme on the surface of Romans 7—and of the first paragraph of Romans 8, which belongs closely with it—is the Jewish Law, the Torah. This conclusion is unwelcome to some, not least because it appears to make the passage irrelevant for those who have never lived "under" the Torah. But Paul is here telling the story of Israel under one particular guise; this is the story that climaxes with the story of Jesus (8:3-4), and the way in which it does so is vital for understanding the basis of Christianity.

Paul is still, in fact, unpacking the last sentences of 5:12-21, and at this point 5:20 in particular: "the law came in alongside, so that the trespass might be filled out; but where sin abounded, grace superabounded." The whole passage is held within the rubric of 5:21: "sin reigned through death, but grace reigns through righteousness to eternal life through Jesus Christ our Lord." The antithesis between the two states, which has already been explored in chap. 6 from the standpoint of baptism and the release of the slaves, is repeated or alluded to several times in the present passage: 7:5-6 serves as an introductory statement; 8:5-10 offers further development, leading toward the conclusion, with echoes of 5:21 still prominent, in 8:10-11. This is where Paul shows, more fully than before, how it is that grace, i.e., God (8:3, 11, "the one who raised the Messiah from the dead") reigns through righteousness (8:10) to eternal life, i.e., resurrection life (8:10-11), through Jesus the Messiah, God's son (8:3-4, 9-11). Here, too, we see a further explication of the programmatic statement of 1:3-4: God's gospel concerns the Son of God, David's descendant "according to the flesh" (cf. 8:3), marked out as Son of God in power by the resurrection (8:10-11). What we have here, in other words, is part of the inner meaning of Paul's gospel, and one of the central passages in the whole letter. The theology of this passage is not to be played off against "justification by faith," either theologically or in terms

of its background in the history of religions. It is part of the continuous, unbroken argument of the whole letter.

In particular, this passage stands at the heart of the great section, chaps. 5–8. If the two very different paragraphs of chap. 5 form a foundation, and chap. 6 an initial platform built on that foundation, 7:1–8:11 must be seen as the main part of the building. It is not the whole; there is a further floor to go on top (8:12-30), and the view from there will be magnificent (8:31-39); but the passage now before us forms the working heart of the section—and, as we shall see, a vital part of Paul's groundwork, also, for the argument of chaps. 9–11.

Romans 7 is not, then, a mere aside, as has sometimes been thought. True, Paul here does finally address the question that has been buzzing like an angry wasp around the edge of the argument so far: what exactly is being said about the law? Ever since 2:17-29; 3:19-21, 27-31; and 4:15 this has been a pressing matter; 5:13-14 and 5:20 sharpened it up, and 6:14-15 merely increased the tension. But it would be wrong to say, as many do, that Paul is therefore simply paying off an old debt, explaining something he should really have explained before. It is just as likely that the hints and suggestions he has already dropped are to be seen as anticipations of the argument he knew he was going to have to make, fragments of a main symphonic theme stated in advance.

What Paul is here doing, as the parallel between 7:5-6 and 2 Cor 3:1-6 should make clear, is setting out *how God has renewed the covenant in Christ and by the Spirit.* "What the Torah could not do, God has done" (8:3). The whole section is, at one level, a vindication of Torah against the imputation that it was identified with sin, or that it was responsible for death. But this vindication, which is also a vindication of the God who gave Torah in the first place, serves the larger purpose, which has been in view since at least

2:17-29, of showing how the *continuity* of God's purposes, clearly seen in 3:21–4:25 and 5:12-21, includes within its purview the *discontinuity* between the dispensation of Torah and the dispensation of the Spirit. Second Corinthians 3, in fact, functions as an oblique but important commentary on this theme, as, of course, does Galatians.[221] Covenant renewal involves, of course, covenant affirmation: to renew something is to affirm it, not to abolish it. Yet renewal also implies the transcending of the old; when, as in this case, the old involves sin and death, renewal is needed to produce righteousness and life (5:21). The logic of 5:20-21 is then worked out as follows: the renewal of the covenant (7:1–8:11) results in the renewal of creation, and of God's people with it (8:12-30).

The passage is therefore an integral part of Paul's argument for assurance. His overarching theme in chaps. 5–8 is that God glorified those whom God justified. What stands in the way of this glorification? Sin and death, of course; but also Torah. "Condemnation," in other words—eschatological condemnation, the final sentence of judgment—still appears to hang over those who have come, by faith, into the Christ-family, the worldwide Abraham-family. It is all very well to demonstrate from Genesis 15 that those who believe the gospel are declared to be God's "righteous" people. But must they not face the final judgment of which 2:1-16 spoke so powerfully? Is there not still a κατάκριμα (*katakrima*), a condemnation, awaiting them on the basis of their present behavior? Romans 7:1–8:11 is designed to show, by way of reply, that "there is therefore now no condemnation for those who are in Christ Jesus" (8:1; for the way in which this verse functions as the "conclusion" of the argument, even though coming at the start of a long final paragraph, see the Commentary on 8:1-11). Paul's analysis of Torah, and now of Christ and the Spirit, shows that the condemnation that might have been supposed to be still future has been dealt with. Those who are in Christ, who are indwelt by the Spirit, can face the future with confidence.

At the same time, as chap. 11 makes clear, Paul is anxious that those who have come out from under Torah, in some sense, should not

turn and despise that God-given dispensation. With an increasing number of commentators, I assume that Paul's audience, though predominantly Gentile, had mostly been either God-fearers or maybe even proselytes before their conversion to the Messiah, Jesus. That is, they had in some sense been "under the law," even though not, for the most part, Jews by birth. To be sure, the significance of Paul's argument in this dense and dramatic passage cannot be confined to its "relevance" to one sub-group of one church at one moment of history. If this is truly how the covenant was renewed, it is of abiding importance for all Christians at all times. If Torah, rightly understood as God's law, poses a threat to God's people, rather than a promise, the threat must be shown to have been dealt with. But, precisely because of the increasingly complex situation in the young church at large, Paul must provide, simultaneously with the argument that one is "not under the law" (precisely because he is not dealing with the Galatians, who were all too eager for the law, but with the Romans, who may have been all too eager to get rid of it!), a *vindication* of Torah against the slurs that it might all too easily incur; 7:1–8:11 accomplishes all these tasks.

The other major theme of chaps. 5–8, which here also reaches its center, is that of the new exodus. 7:7-12 contains several echoes of the story of the children of Israel at Mount Sinai. But that is just one telltale symptom of what is going on. If chap. 6 speaks of the coming through the water by which the slaves are freed, and chap. 8 speaks of the wilderness wanderings, led by the strange presence of God, through which God's people journey toward their promised "inheritance," what we should expect in between is an account of the covenant formed between God and the people, the covenant that in the biblical story took place on Sinai, with the giving of Torah on the one hand and the presence of YHWH, dwelling with Israel in the tabernacle, on the other. That, it seems, is more or less exactly what Paul has written.

With, of course, heavy irony. Torah, the original covenant bond between YHWH and Israel, has now become part of the problem. As 5:20 declared, it has exacerbated the sin of Adam. It cannot, as it stands, constitute Israel as the promised eschatological people of

---

221. See Wright, *The Climax of the Covenant*, chaps. 7–9.

God, the true people of Abraham (see 4:15). The story of the new exodus is thus in tension with the story of the first one, and this tension gives the whole passage its peculiar flavor and its central problem. I can imagine someone objecting to the scheme I have just proposed on the grounds that it appears too complicated, too clever; and the obvious response is that exactly that complexity, exactly that "cleverness," is what we then find in the detail of Romans 7. The "problem of Romans 7," as articulated in its closing summary, is of someone—the celebrated "I," about which more anon—who has been freed and who has not been freed, who appears to be both liberated and still in Egypt. This person serves the law of God with the mind, but with the flesh the law of sin. In terms of chap. 6, this person appears to be on both sides of the either/or that Paul so clearly set out: enslaved to God, enslaved to sin. The exodus both has and has not happened. This is exactly Paul's analysis of the plight of Israel under Torah. In terms of the original exodus, Israel is the free people of God. In terms of the new one, the exodus from sin and death, Israel is still in slavery. The very Torah that spoke of the original freedom reminds Israel daily of that continuing servitude, and its consequences.

Paul's view of Torah here is, however, more subtle still. As I have argued elsewhere, 8:1-11 constitutes among other things the *vindication* of Torah itself.[222] When God does what Torah wanted to do but, through no fault of its own, could not, Torah is affirmed. Torah is not, as in some sub-Pauline theological schemes, a bad thing, to be jettisoned with a sigh of relief; it is a good thing, given by God, no longer the defining boundary-marker of God's people, but given a position of honor. In particular, this passage shows the positive role that Torah has played in the history of salvation, even at the very moment when it might seem most negative. We should not miss the significance, in a Jewish writer like Paul, of the little word ἵνα (*hina*), especially when repeated. "The law came in alongside, *so that* the trespass might abound" (5:20); "sin, *so that* it might appear as sin, was working death in me through the good thing [i.e., the law]" (7:13*b*); "*so that* sin might become

exceedingly sinful through the commandment" (7:13*c*). This is none other than the purpose of God; this is the reason, according to this passage, why Torah was given in the first place.[223] The end of that line of thought comes in 8:3, where Paul affirms that, having heaped up sin into one place, God condemned it all at once. Where sin abounded through Torah, grace superabounded.

At the center of Paul's argument for assurance, therefore, and his exposition of the new exodus, we find one of his clearest statements of the meaning of Jesus' death (8:3-4). To be sure, neither here nor anywhere else does he offer a complete "doctrine of atonement." But, whereas he often refers fleetingly in the course of an argument to Jesus' death, leaving us to fill in the gaps and make assumptions about his total meaning, here the sending and death of God's son (a rare phrase, as we noted earlier, but always decisive when it appears) stands structurally at the apex of the long argument, providing relief for the tension that had built up in chap. 7, and setting the tone for what is to come. "God condemned sin in the flesh"; that is the primary reason why there is now "no condemnation for those who are in the Messiah, Jesus" (8:1). And the means whereby God passed that judicial sentence in that flesh, the flesh of Jesus, was that sin had there been drawn together into one place: "where sin abounded, grace superabounded." What appeared to be the negative work of Torah thus has the deeply positive result: God has dealt with sin once and for all on the cross, and now the life of the Spirit is given to bring the new-exodus people home to their promised inheritance (5:1-5, 6-10; 8:12-30).

It will be clear from all this what answer I give to the question that is often referred to as "the problem of Romans 7." Who is the "I" that dominates 7:7-25?

The first vital move is to rule out any possibility that Paul might here be referring to the "normal Christian." Despite the powerful advocacy of commentators like Cranfield and Dunn—and the present writer knows the force of the argument, since he held it himself for several years before coming to

---

222. Wright, *The Climax of Covenant*, chap. 10.

223. This is confirmed by the parallel in Gal 3:21-2. When Paul says "scripture concluded all under sin," "scripture" is a periphrasis, or indirect reference, for "God."

his present view—we must give full weight to Paul's repeated assertions, throughout 6:1–8:11, that the baptized Christian is not "in sin," not "in the flesh," not "under the law."[224] The whole point of the argument of chap. 6 was to emphasize that the Christian is not "in Adam," but that "the old man" has died with Christ, thus being now, theologically speaking, "dead to sin and alive to God in Christ." The fact that sin could still, however illogically, "reign" in one's mortal body (6:12) does not affect this question of *status*, or the question of being "not under law, but under grace" (6:14-15). The section 6:17-18 could hardly be clearer: you were once slaves of sin, but you are now slaves of righteousness; 6:22 repeats the point. Verses 4-6 of chap. 7 then repeat it again from another point of view: "you died to the law . . . so that you might belong to another"; "when we were in the flesh, the passions of sin, through the law, were at work . . . but now we are set free from the law . . . to be enslaved in the newness of the Spirit, not in the oldness of the letter." It is simply impossible, after this oft-repeated statement, to suppose that Paul will then expound a view of the Christian in which he or she is, after all, "fleshly, sold under sin" (7:14), or that he or she is "enslaved to the law of sin" (7:25). And just in case we had still missed the point, Paul makes it abundantly clear in 8:9: "you are not in the flesh, but in the Spirit."[225]

This is not to say, of course, that normal Christian experience knows nothing of moral struggle and frustration. Part of the problem in the history of exegesis of this passage is precisely that preachers and theologians have read Romans 5–8 as a "theology of the Christian life" and, finding here a portrait of moral struggle that seemed familiar to the sensitive Christian striving after holiness and ever more aware of falling short, assumed that that was what Paul was talking about. Conversely, those who from time to time have taught that it is after all possible for a Spirit-filled Christian to be sinlessly perfect in the present life have spoken eagerly, as part of their theme, about leaving Romans 7 behind and going

on to Romans 8. Romans 7 then becomes a transcript of the "experience," either of the non-Christian, or of the Christian who is still struggling to live a holy life by means of "law" (not usually conceived, in such schemes, as the Torah, but rather as a more general moral law one tries to follow by one's own efforts instead of relying on the Spirit). The debates that these and similar views have occasioned within popular piety are as endless, in their way, as the scholarly debates that have circled around the same passage but with rather different agendas (why one should assume that scholars are not interested in holiness I do not know, but it sometimes appears to be the case, just as pietists are not always interested in what the text actually says). Many of those who have taken a firm stand on the "Christian" reading of 7:14-25 have done so, it appears, out of a desire to rebut the shallow teaching on holiness that the alternative seems to inculcate.[226]

These debates are rendered beside the point when the passage is read in its full context within the ongoing argument of Romans, and with full attention to the meaning of "the law" throughout the passage. "The law" here, to repeat, is the Mosaic law, the Torah, and this is one of Paul's fullest discussions of it. And those who are "under the law" are, basically, Jews, and, by extension, those who attach themselves to Israel, i.e., God-fearers and proselytes.

The "I" of 7:7-25, which on any showing is a remarkable rhetorical feature, may then be approached within Paul's two main controlling narratives: (a) the story of Adam and the Messiah, and (b) the new exodus. Torah intrudes within the first (5:20); Sinai is a key moment in the second. Within these, Paul appears to be speaking of Israel: of Israel under Torah; of Israel at the time when Torah arrived (7:7-12); of Israel continuing to live under Torah thereafter (7:13-25). But he is not thereby speaking of how Israel under Torah would itself analyze the problem. Though in a sense this is Paul's own story, as a Jew who had lived under Torah himself, it is not a transcript of "how it felt at the time."[227] Against

---

224. See Cranfield, *A Critical and Exegetical Commentary on the Epistle to the Romans*, 342-47; Dunn, *Romans 1–8*, 387-99. Moo, *The Epistle to the Romans*, 442-51, provides a careful analysis, taking a similar view to mine.

225. So, rightly, Moo, *Romans*, 448.

226. See J. I. Packer, "The 'Wretched Man' Revisted: Another Look at Romans 7:14-25," in Soderlund and Wright, *Romans and the People of God*, 70-81.

227. Dunn, *Romans 1–8*, 394, is right to reject such a suggestion, but he fails to see the alternative: It may not have felt like this at the time, but this is how Christian hindsight analyzes it theologically.

this idea, and all psychologizing interpretations that have derived from it in the history of research, stands Paul's own statement in Philippians 3: in his pre-Christian life he had been "blameless" in regard to "righteousness under the law." Even granted that he is there making a different point, requiring a positive statement of his pre-Christian position, it is virtually impossible to square that clearly autobiographical passage with a would-be autobiographical reading of Romans 7.[228] The present passage seems, then, to be a Christian theological analysis of what was in fact the case, and indeed what is still the case for those who live "under the law," not a description of how it felt or feels. It is a vivid, rhetorically sharpened way of saying something very similar to what Paul said in 2:17-29: those who embrace Torah find that Torah turns and condemns them. It is not impossible that Paul has in mind at least a sidelong reference to the rabbinic discussion of the two "inclinations," the evil inclination and the good inclination; but his picture of the "I" is not in fact exactly like the rabbinic one, and the passage can in my view be understood without making this a central motif.[229]

The point of the "I," as a rhetorical device, then becomes clear. Though we can learn a certain amount on this topic from considerations of how "autobiographical" language was used in ancient rhetoric, the main thing this teaches us is simply that such language could be used for purposes other than literal descriptions of one's own actual experience.[230] Paul must be allowed to make his own use of the rhetorical possibility. And his motive here is not far to seek. Particularly in view of where his argument will take him in chaps. 9–11, he will not describe the plight of his "kinsfolk according to the flesh" as if this were some foreign or alien concern. This is his own story, and he will feel its theological tension and pain as his own (see 9:1-5;

11:14, referring to non-Christian Jews as ἡ σάρξ μου [*hē sarx mou*, "my flesh"]; see also the Commentary on 3:5, 7). It is a way of not saying "they," of not distancing himself from the problem, from the plight of Israel.

Crucial to most interpretations of the "I" has been the change of tense in the middle of the long "I" passage, the switch (that is) from the past tense in vv. 7-12 to the present in vv. 14-25, with v. 13 as a bridge between them. This has sometimes been explained in terms of Paul first looking at his own previous experience, or perhaps that of someone else, in vv. 7-12, and then turning to describe his own current experience in vv. 14-25. This, though attractive within the non-exegetical schemes of thought mentioned above, is unwarranted when the letter is understood in its own terms. The change of tense has to do, rather, with the change from the description of what happened when Torah first arrived in Israel, the time when Israel recapitulated the sin of Adam (5:20a; 7:9-11), to the description of the ongoing state of those who live under the law, who find themselves caught between the one exodus and the other, freed from Egypt and yet not freed from the "Egypt" of sin and death.

Among the other things the rhetorical "I" enables Paul to accomplish is the analysis of sin under Torah in such a way as to show that the death of Jesus has provided its perfect remedy. The reference to the "sin-offering" in 8:3 (see the notes) exactly suits the context, since that sacrifice was designed to deal with unwilling or unwitting sin, and Paul has so described sin-under-the-law as to make it just that. This explains, at least in part, the lengthy descriptions of moral inability ("that which I do I know not," and so forth) in vv. 15-16, 19-20.

A further explanation for the lengthy description of "life under the law" may perhaps be found—though this can never be more than a likely guess—in the pagan parallels to 7:14-20. In a long tradition from Aristotle to Ovid and beyond, pagan moralists had observed the puzzling fact that even the most morally acute among them could see, and approve, the good, while still continuing to choose and perform evil.[231] Paul's description

228. This was the starting point for Krister Stendahl's epochal essay "The Apostle Paul and the Introspective Conscience of the West." See Stendahl, *Paul Among Jews and Gentiles* (Philadelphia: Fortress, 1976) 78-96.

229. Details in H. L. Strack, *Kommentar zum Neuen Testament aus Talmud und Midrasch*, 6 vols. (Munich: Beck, 1922–61) 4:466-83. See W. D. Davies, *Paul and Rabbinic Judaism: Some Rabbinic Elements in Pauline Theology*, 3rd ed. (Philadelphia: Fortress, 1980) 25-27; J. Marcus, "The Evil Inclination in the Letters of Paul," *IBS* 8 (1986) 8-21. The parallel is rejected as "incomplete" by Dunn, *Romans 1–8*, 391. See also the Qumran doctrine of "two spirits," e.g., 1QS 3:15–4:26.

230. See G. Lyons, *Pauline Autobiography: Toward a New Understanding*, SBLDS 73 (Atlanta: Scholars Press, 1985).

231. For an example roughly contemporary with Paul, see Epictetus *Discourses* 2:26.

is at certain points strikingly reminiscent of this theme, which must have been well known among serious-minded Greeks and Romans. It is probable that Paul is deliberately echoing, or alluding to, this tradition. But why?

Help is at hand in Galatians. In Galatians 5 Paul argued, with polemical intent, that if one put oneself under the law one would simply reside once more in the realm of the "flesh." In other words, becoming Jewish (by getting circumcised and taking on the yoke of Torah) will simply bring you back to the same pagan state as you were in before—exactly the argument of Gal 4:8-11. The parallel between Gal 5:16-18 and Romans 7 is quite close: "the flesh lusts against the Spirit," writes Paul in Gal 5:17, "and the Spirit against the flesh; and these are opposed to each other, *so that you cannot do the things you want.*" And then the punch line: "But if you are led by the Spirit, you are not under the law." Precisely the point of Rom 7:1–8:11.

What happens when we transpose this back into Romans 7? If Paul's point is that Torah increases and exacerbates the plight of humankind "in Adam" (so that, for instance, 2:17-29 places "the Jew" firmly on the map of 1:18–2:16, 3:19-20 re-emphasizes the point, and 5:20 draws it together in a striking summary), what better way of elaborating this insight than by so describing the situation of Israel under Torah as to place Israel by implication fair and square on the map of the puzzled pagan moralist? This is simultaneously, of course, a way of saying that the gospel of Jesus Christ upstages the best in the pagan tradition, too. But Paul's point, I take it, is the other way around: when Israel under Torah—including himself, Paul, in his former life!—does its best, delighting in God's law in the inner person, longing to perform it to perfection, all Israel in fact attains is the same level as—Epictetus, Seneca, and Aristotle himself. "The law came in, so that [Adamic, general-human] trespass might abound." "The flesh," that which Israel shares in common with all humankind, prevents any boast in the Torah. The Torah simply shows up sin (3:19-20).

The consonance of this exposition with what Paul has said about Torah and Israel already in the letter gives supporting weight

to my overall case. And this argument then dovetails nicely with the wider allusions we have observed at regular intervals to key features of Roman culture—the gospel, the justice of God, and the peace of God, all of which challenge and upstage Caesar's equivalent. Without for a moment leaving the home base of Jewish and biblical thought that provides the foundation for all his theology, Paul has directed a typically Jewish challenge to the pagan world. Within that again—also as a typically Jewish move!—he has suggested that those who do not embrace his own construal of Judaism—i.e., allegiance to Jesus as Messiah—are themselves no better than pagans.

All that has been said so far indicates that when Paul is talking about "sin" in this passage—and the word, in one form or another, occurs over twenty times in these thirty-six verses—he means exactly what he means in the letter so far. "Sin" is a power let loose in the world, a deceptive and corrosive parasite that has entwined the whole human race in its tentacles and is slowly choking it to death. And the manifestation of sin is the performance of actions that run counter both to God's purpose for humankind in general (actions that result from idolatry, as in 1:18-32) and of actions that cut across God's law, the Torah, in particular (as in the present passage and, e.g., 6:19). There is no warrant, in other words, for the theory that was popular in Germany in the mid-twentieth century, following the expositions of Kümmel and Bultmann in particular, and is still to be found in some commentaries and expositions: that when Paul here spoke of "sin" he did not mean so much the breaking of God's law *as the attempt to keep it* and so to earn a "status" for oneself independent of God and God's grace.[232] On this view Paul was charging Israel, and all humans who live "under the law" in a sense far wider than simply the Mosaic Torah, with a kind of meta-sin; not the breaking of the law, but pride in keeping it, or in attempting to do so. This theory gained its apparent force from the combination of the Lutheran critique of

---

232. The famous early statement of this was in W. G. Kümmel, *Römer 7 und die Bekehrung des Paulus* (Leipzig: Hinrichs, 1929; repr. Münich: Kaiser, 1974). Bultmann's essay, originally published in 1932, was translated as "Romans 7 and the Anthropology of Paul," in *Existence and Faith: The Shorter Writings of Rudolf Bultmann* (London: Hodder and Stoughton, 1960) 173-85. Perhaps the most powerful modern exposition is that of Käsemann, *Commentary on Romans,* 191-212.

"human works," the attempt by human beings to make themselves righteous, and the existentialist critique of a life lived inauthentically, by human arrogance. But it has little to commend it as exegesis of Romans 7. The problem of the "I" is not that it can perform the law but ought not to try, but that it rightly delights in the law but cannot perform it. Bultmann's exegesis ends up with a negative view of Torah that has little to do with Paul's more subtle exposition.

Little, but perhaps not absolutely nothing. One of the effects of Romans 7, in its analysis of the plight of Israel under Torah, is to ground the further critique of Israel that Paul will mount in chaps. 9–10. There he does indeed describe Israel as "seeking to establish its own righteousness." I shall argue at that point, to be sure, that this sentence, too, cannot be taken in the Bultmannian, and indeed more broadly Lutheran, sense; that it refers, not to human works attempting to establish a moral claim upon God, but to the claim of ethnic Israel to be, permanently and inalienably, the covenant people of God. But Paul does indeed charge Israel here with a kind of meta-sin, albeit not the one Bultmann and others thought. And it is true that this charge looks back, within the spiraling argument of Romans, to the present passage, not least with Paul's assertion that Israel is "ignorant" of God's righteousness (10:3): that which Israel does, Israel does not know, as in 7:15. But the meaning of chap. 10 cannot be read back into chap. 7. Paul is not simply repeating himself. He is making a new point, developed from, but not identical to, the present one.

The present passage is notable for the sudden entry of the Spirit, like a fresh character in a play. There have been isolated hints earlier on (1:4; 2:29; 5:5), but nothing at all by way of exposition. Parallels with other passages where the Spirit plays a leading role might have led us to expect more before now (see the parallel between Romans 4 and Galatians 3, where, in v. 14, the Spirit plays a key role in fulfilling the Abrahamic promises; see also 2 Corinthians 3). It is almost as though Paul has been deliberately holding back in order now to unleash this theme with full impact. 7:6 announces what is to come: we are now slaves, he says, "in the newness of the Spirit, not in the oldness of the letter." Then at last,

in 8:2-11, there are no fewer than eleven references to the Spirit, followed by a further nine in vv. 12-27.[233]

The role Paul here assigns to the Spirit is that of doing what the law could not. Or rather, this is the role Paul gives to Christ and Spirit together; we must not make the mistake, as is sometimes made, of supposing a neat antithesis of either Law/Christ or Law/Spirit. Paul has not simply extracted "the law" from a theological scheme and dropped in "Christ" or "Spirit" instead. Things are richer and more complicated than that. He is not, after all, constructing an abstract soteriology, but telling the story of God and Israel, which reaches its strange, paradoxical, yet deliberate and consistent, climax in the sending of the Messiah and the sending of the Spirit (cf. the close parallel with Gal 4:1-7). He is describing how it is that the covenant with Abraham is fulfilled, and the covenant of the Torah renewed.

The main function he gives to the Spirit in this passage, therefore, is that of *giving life:* the life the Torah promised but could not give (7:10), the life that will consist ultimately of the resurrection of the body (8:11). But this life is not merely future. As in chap. 6, the Christian already stands on resurrection ground; and the status affirmed in 6:4-5, 8-11 is here filled out with practical content, as the Spirit who will give life to the "mortal body" anticipates the resurrection by enabling those "in Christ" to have a new mind-set, to submit truly at last to God's will, even to God's law (!), and to please God in their behavior (8:5-8; cf. 1:21-2, 28; 12:2; the last is especially important). This then gives rise to the exposition of the "wilderness wanderings" of God's renewed people (8:12-27), led by the Spirit who enables them to leave slavery behind and to live as God's children.

The Spirit can thus be spoken of in exodus-language, as having been instrumental in the ultimate liberation of God's people: "the law of the Spirit of life in Christ Jesus has set you free from the law of sin and death" (8:2). That is to say, (a) the Spirit has been located on the outline map provided by 5:21—sin and death ranged against grace, righteousness

233. Depending, in the latter passage, on which references are taken as "Spirit"—i.e., God's Spirit—rather than "spirit"—i.e., the human spirit. For the whole subject see G. Fee, *God's Empowering Presence: The Holy Spirit in the Letters of Paul* (Peabody, Mass.: Hendrikson, 1994).

and life; (b) the Spirit is part of God's way of making grace superabound where sin abounded (5:20b). This is the "exodus" of chap. 6 described now in terms of the analysis of the problem in 7:7-25. Only if we keep a clear eye out for the connections in Paul's ongoing argument will we discover just how tightly woven the texture of Romans actually is, how interconnected all the themes actually are, and hence how consistently Paul is making, and developing, his main point.[234]

What then opens up to our gaze is that Paul has described the sending of the Messiah, and the gift of the Spirit, in language that, precisely within the "new exodus" theme that characterizes so much of Romans 5–8, can be seen in terms of the presence of YHWH with Israel in the wilderness, dwelling in the tabernacle, in the pillar of cloud by day and the pillar of fire by night. The "sending" of the son, as is often enough remarked, belongs within Second Temple Jewish thought in terms of the "sending," or the coming to Israel, of Wisdom, or the Shekinah, or sometimes both together. In Sirach 24 the divine Wisdom comes to dwell in the Temple in Jerusalem, and is simultaneously embodied in the Mosaic Torah (Sir 24:8-12, 23; cf. Wis 9:9-10). We now find that the "indwelling" of the Spirit (8:9, 11) belongs very closely with the same theme. This is "Temple" language, echoing the Jewish belief that the Shekinah "dwelt" within the wilderness tabernacle and then the Temple itself. Whereas, before, the indwelling force was "sin" (7:17-18, 20), now it is the Spirit. In the two other passages where Paul says the same thing he makes the point more explicitly: you, Christians, are therefore God's new Temple (1 Cor 3:16; 2 Cor 6:16). In the latter passage Paul quotes Lev 26:11, and, as in Romans 8, goes on to expound the identity of Christians as God's sons and daughters; in 2 Cor 6:18 this involves a quotation of 2 Sam 7:14, in which the promise to David, that God will build him a house, is democratized to include not only David's son but all Christians. See also 1 Cor 6:19.

The exposition of the Spirit's work in Romans 8, therefore, belongs not only with the theme of assurance but also with that of the new exodus, confirming and filling out the picture we have drawn so far. The people of God, having come out of the Egypt of sin and death, are led through the wilderness by the Son and the Spirit, the new realities to which the old language of Wisdom, Shekinah, and even Torah itself are now seen to point. (So closely are the Son and the Spirit identified in this passage, while still being distinguished in thought, that Paul can speak of the Spirit as "the Messiah's Spirit," 8:9, and of "the Messiah" being "in you," 8:10). Paul has taken some of the central Jewish language about the way in which Israel's God is known in action, saving and leading Israel to the promised inheritance, and has reused it dramatically of Christ and the Spirit. As might be said of the parallel passage in Gal 4:1-11, so we might truly say here: from this point on, if the doctrine of the Trinity had never existed, we might be forced to reinvent it. Paul cannot say anything more exalted than this about the Messiah and the Spirit; but what he has said belongs exactly on the map of Second Temple Jewish language about YHWH, the one God of Israel, and the saving presence and action of this one God.

It only remains to draw attention to the way in which the argument of the present section advances the thought of the letter as a whole. By explaining the renewal of the covenant, the vindication of Torah, and the way in which God gives resurrection life to those in Christ, this passage fills out the argument for assurance, providing the basis for the picture of new creation that follows, and hence for the great celebration at the close of chap. 8. But, precisely because it does this by highlighting the failure of Israel according to the flesh, the failure not because of their own will but because of indwelling sin (the latent "Adam" within Israel, so to speak), it intensifies the problem that must then be dealt with in chaps. 9–11. Or, to put it the other way around (since chaps. 9–11, too, are not to be seen simply as an aside, dealing with an awkward matter that has come up in the course of the letter, but rather as one of the main things Paul wants to say), in order to show what God has been doing with the ethnic family of Abraham, Paul needs first to show in graphic detail how their life under

234. On the notion of Pauline consistency—denial of which has become a knee-jerk reaction in some quarters—see Wright, *The Climax of the Covenant*, 4-7.

Torah has been the means of sin's being magnified—how, in other words, "the law came in so that the trespass might abound." This is the depth-dimension of the problem of Israel that Paul must address. It is not merely that a majority of Jews has not, as it happens, believed the gospel, but rather that the God-given Torah has been part of the problem, part of their stumbling over the stumbling-stone (9:32). Israel's failure as mapped in chap. 7 is the foundation for that further failure of which Paul speaks in 9:30–10:4: Israel has been ignorant of God's righteousness, and has sought to establish its own righteousness. The problem of the church's attitude toward unbelieving Israel cannot be addressed unless this dimension is fully grasped; Paul needs, in other words, to write Romans 7–8 before he can write Romans 9–11. At the same time, the sequence of thought we have observed between 5:20; 7:13; and 8:3—the sequence in which the strange God-given purpose of Torah was to heap up sin precisely in order that it might be dealt with in the "flesh" of the Messiah—stands at the heart of Paul's analysis of Israel's strange fate in 9:14-29, and of the solution he offers in chap. 11.

Romans 7:1–8:11 also stands behind chaps. 12–16, though further in the background. The central argument of that section, presented in 14:1–15:13, is that Christians from all ethnic and cultural backgrounds should accept one another as fellow members of the family. It would be wrong to see 7:1–8:11 as merely a coded way of making this point to one or other particular group within the church, as has sometimes been suggested.[235] But it should be clear that the present passage, in its exposition of the new covenant as doing that which the Torah offered but

could not perform, provides the theological groundwork for what Paul will there say.

The passage 7:1–8:11 is thus part and parcel of Paul's larger argument about the righteousness of God. (With this, indeed, the question of relevance with which this overview began—of how a passage about the Jewish law might be of abiding interest to those who have never lived "under" it—is also answered.) This, Paul is saying, is how God has been faithful to the covenant: to the promises with Abraham, and now, strangely, even to the Torah itself. What God has done "apart from Torah" nevertheless claims, so to speak, the backing of the Torah: "the Torah and the prophets bear witness to it." And what has been done is, of course, done supremely in and through Jesus the Messiah: the death of Jesus in 8:3 is the spelling out of the "righteous act" and the "obedience" of Jesus in 5:18-19, and behind that in 3:24-26. Thus "the gospel of God" (whose content is the Son, born of David's seed according to the flesh, marked out as Son by the Spirit through the resurrection) unveils the righteousness of God. And here all this advances the specific argument: those whom God justified, them God also glorified.

The argument of the passage falls into clear paragraphs. The introduction (7:1-6) leads to the question of whether the law and sin are identical (7:7-12). This produces the second-order question, whether the good law, despite being exonerated from the first charge, is nevertheless the cause of death (7:13-20). This in turn leads to Paul's paradoxical conclusion about the law (7:21-25). Paul can then expound the divine answer (8:1-11), which also, naturally, serves as the foundation of the further exposition of life in the Spirit (8:12-30).

235. See P. Minear, *The Obedience of Faith* (London: SCM, 1971).

Romans 7:1-6, Coming Out from Under the Law

COMMENTARY

7:1. The NRSV and the NIV both omit the first word of the chapter, which in Greek is the single letter ἤ (*ē*, "or"). As usual with Paul's connections, the word matters: he is looking back to 6:14-15. "You are not under the law

. . . or do you not know that the law only rules over someone during their lifetime?" In other words, you could only assume that as a Christian you *were* still under the law if you ignored one of the most basic things about how the law operates. Paul will emphasize in the first six verses of the chapter that a death has indeed occurred that results in the Christian's being "no longer under the law."

We are still working, then, within the picture set out in chap. 6: the death of the "old human" (6:6) because of which the baptized Christian is no longer "in Adam" but rather "in Christ." With this we should recognize, too, that Paul has in mind the further twist in Adamic humanity noted in 5:20. The law intensified the Adamic problem, but grace has dealt with matters at that very point (cf. 1 Cor 15:56-57). Sin will not have dominion over those who were under the law but are now in Christ. They are no longer in the position where the law exacerbated sin; rather, they are the recipients of that grace that has superabounded where sin abounded. This is Paul's subject here.

He is speaking, he says, "to those who know the law." He calls them his family,[236] and seems to want them to identify themselves with him in this argument, just as he is himself identifying with ethnic Israel, Israel under Torah. This, indeed, may be part of the reason why, having spoken of "I" throughout 7:7-25, he suddenly switches to the second-person singular, "you," in 8:2 (on which see the Commentary on 8:1-11). He is addressing them as people who know the law. This could, of course, mean Roman law in general, in which, as in Jewish law, death pays all debts; but in view of the subject matter it is far more likely to mean the Jewish law. When this is put together with the statement in 7:4 that "you [pl.] died to the law," it becomes the more likely that most of his addressees had actually been in some sense "under the law." Since the majority among his readers was probably Gentile, this must mean that they had been either God-fearers or proselytes. (The alternative, that he is here addressing only the Jewish minority within the Roman church, seems unlikely in view of the central role of this passage within the central section of the letter.)

The point at issue, picking up what 6:7 said about sin, is that the law can only rule a person during that person's lifetime. Death brings a person out from under the rule of the law. The commentators find parallels for this in rabbinic and other codes, but the point is so wide and obvious that we do not need to explain it further. That is hardly the case, however, with what follows.

7:2-3. By way of explanation, Paul offers what is sometimes taken as an illustration (the NIV adds "for example," supporting its subheading, "an illustration from marriage"). But what job does Paul intend this picture to do? That depends on how we see it fitting in to the rest of the passage, especially v. 4. It is frequently stated that Paul's argument does not quite work. He seems (it is said) to envisage the "marriage" being between the person concerned ("you") and the law; but then it is the person, not the law, that dies.[237] To put it like this, however, is to miss the extent to which the entire chapter, including the "marriage" scene, grows directly out of 5:20-21 and the whole of chap. 6, and continues to unfold its meaning.

The point of vv. 2-3 is not difficult: the law is the thing that binds the wife to the husband, so that if the husband dies the wife is free, both from the husband and from the law that bound her to him. Thus, while the husband is alive, she will be an adulteress if she goes with someone else, but if the husband dies she is "free from the law" (Paul is already hinting at the direction of this argument, and indeed at its roots in 6:14-15). This does not mean that the law was the "first husband," but that the law bound the woman *to* the "first husband." Thus, if she takes another husband she will not be committing adultery. So far, so good.

7:4. The problem can then be stated succinctly: "you" died, but "you" now belong to another! Paul is not arguing from the detail of the "illustration," seen in the abstract; he is making the point he wanted to make anyway, to which the marriage picture contributes. The latter half of the verse appears to suggest that the Christian is now, in some sense, the "bride" of Jesus the Messiah ("the one who was raised from the dead"), and it adds the extra detail, that this new union will "bear

236. Lit., "brothers." Paul uses this term sparingly in the main argument of Romans (1:13; 8:12; 10:1; 11:25; cf. 12:1; 15:14; 15:30; 16:17), so that its use here and in 7:4 (NRSV, "friends" at 7:4 is an unfortunate flattening down of the intimacy, and rich mutual accountability, of ἀδελφοί adelphoi) seems the more emphatic.

237. See J. A. T. Robinson, *Wrestling with Romans* (Philadelphia: Westminster, 1979) 77-79; H. Räisänen, *Paul and the Law* (Philadelphia: Fortress, 1983) 61.

fruit for God" (for the Christian as the bride of Christ, see 2 Cor 11:2; Eph 5:25-32). This picks up the image of fruitbearing from 6:21-22, but sets it now within a context where its meaning is more precisely *child*bearing.

What then about the first half of the verse? "You died to the law"; the thought is very close to Gal 2:19, "I through the law died to the law" (another use of the "autobiographical" mode of speech, which Paul will presently adopt here). It means "by death, you came out from under the law's domain," as v. 1 implies.

But who is it, then, that has "died"? The previous chapter gives a clear, unambiguous answer, and indeed repeats it seven times: "we died to sin" (6:2); we "were baptized into Christ's death" (6:3), "we were buried with him into death" (6:4), "we were planted with him in the likeness of his death" (6:5), "our old person was co-crucified" (6:6), "we died with Christ" (6:8), "reckon yourselves dead to sin" (6:11). It might seem tedious to list all these, were it not for the fact that chap. 6 is so little invoked to explain 7:4, and that commentators who have referred to 6:6 to do so are frequently waved away by those who insist on treating chap. 7 as though it were an entirely separate discussion. Once we link the law with sin, however (the point of 5:20, which Paul will address in 7:7), "you died to the law" can only have one meaning. "You" in the first half of 7:4 is the "former husband"; "you" in the second half is the "wife." Or, if we prefer, "you" in the first half is the "old human being" of 6:6—the "old Adam," or perhaps better "the person 'in Adam.' " "You" in the second half, at least when the "re-marriage" has occurred, is the person "in Christ." Just as later in the chapter the argument hinges on the double "I," so here it hinges on a double "you."

What then does Paul mean by qualifying "you died to the law" with the phrase "through the body of Christ"? Presumably something close to what he meant in Gal 2:19 by saying "I am crucified with Christ," as the explanation of "I through the law died to the law." Here, again, the proximity to chap. 6 should help. The whole clause appears to be a shorthand way of saying three things simultaneously: (a) the bodily death of Jesus the Messiah is the representative event through which the Messiah's people die "with him" (6:4-11); (b) you are in the Messiah by baptism, and therefore shared that death; (c) your solidarity with the Messiah can be expressed in terms of your membership in his "body." The extent to which this last thought is strongly present (see, for instance, 12:5) is a matter of debate, but not of great importance. What matters is to recognize that the thought is built on the first half of chap. 6, itself an elaboration of chap. 5.

7:5-6. Paul now explains v. 4 with a two-sided description of the old life and the new. This, as is widely recognized, functions as the double heading over the two following sections, 7:7-25 and 8:1-11. It also awakens echoes of the "new covenant" theology of 2 Corinthians 3; this is the means by which Paul, evoking various biblical passages, can affirm the goodness of Torah without affirming its abiding validity as the boundary-marker of God's people.

"When we were in the flesh": this striking formulation tells us once and for all that "flesh" for Paul does not mean simply the physical substance of which humans are made.[238] "The flesh" denotes physicality seen on the one hand as corruptible and on the other as rebellious; it is another way of saying "in Adam," of demarcating that humanity that is characterized by sin and consequently by death. To be "in the flesh" for Paul is to be determined by "flesh" in this sense, i.e., to live under the domain of sin and death, and thus to be in the condition marked by the first half of the various antitheses both of 5:12-21 and of 6:16-23. It does not mean, in our sense, "to be physical," in some Platonic divide between the material and the non-material (see 1 Cor 15:50: "flesh and blood" cannot inherit the kingdom of God—but the resurrected or transformed body can and will; cf. Phil 3:21). It is clear from 8:9 that Christians, even while living ordinary human lives and facing ordinary human suffering and death, are, in Paul's terminology, "not in the flesh, but in the Spirit."

238. The NIV, translating σάρξ (*sarx*) as "the sinful nature," avoids one problem: that most readers of English assume that "flesh" means "physical substance," the stuff of which humans are composed. But it falls into another one, implying either that human nature in general is sinful or that humans have more than one "nature," of which one is "sinful." Its rendering of the verb as "when *we were controlled by* the sinful nature" is further misleading; "controlled by" is not as strong, simple, or morally all-encompassing as "in."

Those "in the flesh" discover that "the passions of sins" are at work in them to bear fruit for death. That much we could have gathered from 5:12-21, and indeed from 1:18–2:16. But Paul adds a vital extra phrase: these passions are "through the law," which both the NRSV and the NIV gloss as "aroused by the law," in the light (no doubt) of 7:9. Paul does not at this point explain what he means, though he shortly will. Here we merely note that, strange though it is to think of the law arousing sinful passions, this is consonant with 6:14-15 and, behind that, with 5:20 yet once more.

"But now we have been released from the law." "But now" awakens echoes of 3:21 and 6:22, introducing the moment of freedom, of redemption. The verb Paul uses is the same as in v. 2 ("she is *released* from the law concerning the husband"). Though the root meaning of the word is "annul," "make ineffective," or "abolish," which might more properly have gone with the law than with the person who is (or has been up until now) "under the law," when used of the person it must mean "discharged" or "released," the force being that they and the law have nothing more now to say to one another. Paul explains this again by reference to "our" death: "having died [to that] in which we were held captive."[239] "Having died" is another reference to the death of the "old human being," as in 6:6; "the thing which held us captive" is the law once more. And the result is, again as in chap. 6, that the old slavery has been exchanged for a new one: we now serve, literally, "in the newness of the Spirit and not in the oldness of the letter" (the word for "serve" is δουλεύω [*douleuō*, "to serve as a slave"], hence making the link with 6:16-22, as explicitly in the NRSV).

The contrast of the old and the new ways of being a slave evokes 2 Cor 3:6, where it is explicitly "new covenant" language: "God has qualified us," says Paul, "to be ministers of a new covenant, not of the letter but of the Spirit; for the letter kills, but the Spirit gives life." This generates the great contrast of 2 Cor 3:7-18, whose multiple overlapping associations with Paul's thought throughout Rom 7:1–8:11 are too numerous and complex to track here.[240] What matters for our present purpose is that, rare though Paul's explicit references to the "covenant" may be, that word can appropriately reflect something absolutely foundational to his thinking: the faithfulness of God to all that had been revealed and promised in the past. This is not undercut by the fact that, because of sin and death, it was necessary for God to do something that seemed totally new in the present. Underneath the radical discontinuity caused by the gospel's breaking in upon Israel and the world, caused indeed by the earth-shattering death of the Messiah, there remains the faithfulness of the creator and covenant God to the promises made to Abraham, and indeed to the implicit though ineffective promise in the law, the promise of new life for a worldwide family, despite the sin and death brought into the world "through the one man" (5:12).

Pauline "covenant theology," then, is not opposed to "apocalyptic" theology, to a sense of the radical inbreaking of God's judgment and salvation in Christ. The covenant provides the fuller context for that. And, as the present passage and 2 Corinthians 3 make clear, the new covenant is designed precisely to take account of the problems inherent in the original covenant. The latter was written in letters on tablets of stone, but the former is to be written on the heart.

We are here very close, too, to Rom 2:29. There Paul distinguishes "the Jew who is one in secret" from one who is so merely "in what is manifest," i.e., outwardly; and he thus contrasts "the circumcision of the heart," which is a matter of the Spirit, with "the letter." This elliptical formulation, on which see the notes, brings together several things simultaneously: the contrast of two groups of people, their characterization as "the Jew" and "the Jew outwardly," circumcision of the heart and circumcision of the flesh, and the letter and the Spirit. The point of all this for Romans 7 is to confirm that here Paul is dealing with "the Jew," living under the "letter" of the Mosaic law, and contrasting this with the Spirit-given

---

239. The KJV's "that being dead in which we were held," implying a reference to the death either of the law or of the old Adam, is based on a hypothetical MS reading introduced by Beza into the Greek *Textus Receptus* (1565), without any existing MS support, on the basis of his guess at Chrysostom's reading. One twelfth-century MS (no. 242) has now been found that supports it.

240. On 2 Corinthians 3, see Wright, *The Climax of the Covenant,* chap. 9.

new life in Christ; and to show that throughout 7:1–8:11 we should keep in mind the discussion in chap. 2, which, demonstrating the inadequacy of the Torah to create and sustain ethnic Israel as God's people, pointed forward to the creation of a new people in whom God's will would be done, described somewhat oxymoronically as "the uncircumcision that keeps the law" (2:26-7). At that stage it was impossible, without more explanation, to see who was being spoken of. The present passage provides that explanation.

A new mode of service, then, has been opened up, a mode to which Torah pointed but which it could not bring to pass. God has renewed the covenant in Christ, and what the Torah could not do has now been done. The new "enslavement"—enslavement to "obedience" (6:16), to the "pattern of teaching" (6:17), to "righteousness" (6:18), to God (6:22)—is one in which the heart is transformed by the Spirit (5:5), in which the whole person is promised new life (8:10-11). This life in the Spirit will dominate chap. 8.

Verses 5-6 introduce the rest of the passage, not least by saying something so outrageously provocative that it must at once raise the question that will lead in to Paul's main argument. If "the passions of sins" are aroused by the law, what are we saying about the law? Is it virtually identical with sin itself?

Romans 7:7-12, The Arrival of the Law: Sin Seizes Its Chance

COMMENTARY

The new paragraph extends, not to v. 13 as in several editions and translations, but to v. 12. The larger unit (vv. 7-25) is clearly subdivided, as can be seen from Paul's careful and logical connectives, into vv. 7-12, 13-20, and 21-25. The first asks, "Is the law sin?" and answers the question by telling the story of the law's arrival on Sinai and Israel's recapitulation of the sin of Adam. This was not the law's fault; the law was the unwilling tool of sin itself. The second, following the sin/death logic that dominates the entire section, asks: "Did this good law, then, cause 'my' death?" The answer again is, No. The point this time is made by telling the story of those who live under the law, emphasizing that it is still sin, not the law—and not the "I," remarkably enough!—that is responsible. The third paragraph draws the conclusion in terms of the the double-sided law, corresponding to the double-sided "I": because of sin, the law cannot give life, and the "I" cannot attain it. This states the problem of the law, and of the "I," in the terms Paul will address in the first paragraph of chap. 8.

7:7a. The opening question faces at last the issue that has been in the background since 2:17-29, more sharply since 5:20, and most urgently since 7:5. If the law stirs up the passions of sins, surely this means that the law and sin are virtually identical?

7:7b-8a. Paul's initial response is to deny the charge ("certainly not!" NIV), and to state again the point that seemed to lead to it ("yet, if it had not been for the law I would not have known sin," NRSV; the NIV, translating ἀλλά [*alla*] as "indeed," misses the force of this: Paul is actually conceding the point that had led to the charge, not yet undergirding his emphatic rebuttal of it; cf. the similar use of *alla* in 7:13, omitted altogether by the NRSV, but correctly translated as "but" in the NIV). But what does it mean "to know sin"? The NIV takes it simply in terms of information, knowing *about* sin: "I would not have known what sin was." The same problem is repeated in the next line, which Paul intends as an explanation (γάρ *gar*): I should not have known covetousness had the law not said "you shall not covet." This time the NRSV joins the NIV: "I would not have known what it is to covet." Yet v. 8 surely indicates something stronger than simply information (cf. 3:20: through the law comes the ἐπίγνωσις ἁμαρτίας [*epignōsis hamartias*, "the knowledge of sin"]). It is not so much that the law gave the "I" information about sin in general, and coveting in particular; the law *produced* coveting, and hence sin. Sin, that is, "seized its opportunity"[241] in the commandment (Paul regularly uses ἡ ἐντολή [*hē entolē,* "the commandment"] in this chapter, more or less as a synonym for "the law," though sometimes with specific reference to the particular commandment just quoted). And, exploiting this opportunity, sin "worked in 'me' all kinds of covetousness."[242] The law, in other words, was the channel not only for knowledge *about* sin but for knowledge *of* sin in the sense that, as a result of the process, "I" knew, from the inside, what sin meant in practice. This still, of course, appears to be an indictment of the law, though Paul is building in to his picture the description of "sin" at work that will result in the law's exoneration four verses later. The law, though weak, was not the source of the problem, merely the unwilling channel.

But what event is Paul describing? The reference to the tenth commandment in v. 7*b* (Exod 20:17; Deut 5:21) might indicate that he was referring to the time when the law was first given on Mount Sinai. Alternatively, many exegetes, taking the "I" literally, have supposed Paul to be referring to his own experience on first becoming aware of the commandments, perhaps at his bar mitzvah, especially if that coincided with the onset of puberty and hence of sexual desire (the tenth commandment, as 4 Maccabees 2 implies, was often taken to refer to sexual desire in particular, while obviously being of wider application). But the larger context in Romans indicates well enough what event Paul is thinking of. 5:20, once again: the law came in, so that the trespass might abound. This is not about Paul himself; it is about the moment in Israel's history, and indeed (5:13-14) in the history of humankind, when the arrival of the law meant that, as at the beginning, humans were faced with a specific command, so that the miscellaneous sin that had existed "from Adam to Moses" (5:14) would again become "trespass," breaking a known law.

That explains, as will become clear in the next three verses, the fact that Paul seems here to be referring also to the "fall" of Genesis 3 (particularly with v. 11: sin "deceived me . . . and killed me," alluding to Gen 3:13; cf. 2 Cor 11:3). We should not attempt to decide between these two (Sinai and Eden): Paul's point is precisely that what happened on Sinai recapitulated what had happened in Eden. Other Jewish exegesis linked the two moments; Paul's view falls well within recognizable Second Temple understandings of the meaning both of covetousness and of the primal sin.[243] What he has done here is so to tell the one story, that of Israel, that echoes of the other, that of Adam, are clearly heard. This is, of course, just what we should expect if he is indeed expanding the programmatic statement in 5:20: "the law came in, so that the trespass might abound."

7:8b-10. Paul's next statement seems to sit uncomfortably with 5:13-14. There, sin was not *counted* apart from the law, but was "in the world" even in the absence of the law, its presence being witnessed by universal death. What then does Paul mean, "apart from the law, sin is dead"? He seems to indicate some kind of potential life for sin beyond simply producing death; when individuals sin and die, sin is not growing, not flourishing in new ways. When, however, the law appears, then sin gains, as we might say, a new lease of life. "I was once alive apart from the law" (for the last phrase, cf. 3:21); this, we must assume, refers within Paul's controlling narrative to Israel in the pre-Mosaic state, corresponding to Adam in the garden before the fateful command had been issued. "But when the commandment arrived," i.e., on Sinai, "sin sprang to life, and I died." There may be an allusion, here and indeed throughout this passage, to the fact that, in the exodus story, the giving of the commandments was the moment when Aaron and the children of Israel made the golden calf—the incident to which some subsequent rabbinic writings looked back with sorrow as the time when Israel imbibed iniquity (see the Commentary on 1:23). Sinai and Genesis 3 still go hand in hand.

---

241. The Greek word here (ἀφορμή *aphormē*) carries the metaphorical sense of "a military base of operations," but it was regularly used in the more general sense of "an opportunity," especially with the verb Paul employs here. See BDAG.

242. In a work roughly contemporary with Paul, 4 Macc 2:5-6, a Jewish writer uses the commandment "you shall not covet" to more or less exactly the opposite effect, arguing that since the law commands this it must be the case that "reason" can overcome the passions.

243. See *bSanh* 38b; 102a; *Exod. Rab.* 21:1; 30:7; 32:1, 7, 11. See the Commentary on 1:23 and 9:15-16; the connections between these passages are important.

The result (v. 10b) is that the commandment that promised life proved to be death for "me" (cf. 4 Ezra 9:33-37: those who received the law and sinned perished; the law, however, does not perish but remains in its glory). The allusion to the tree of life in Genesis is hidden here under the more direct reference to Lev 18:5 (which Paul quotes in Rom 10:5, in a section belonging closely with the present one) and to the covenantal passage in Deut 30:15-20, passages that promise life for those who keep Torah (see Deut 4:1; 6:24; 8:1; cf. Ps Sol 14:1; see also the Commentary on 10:5-11). This is, for Paul, the real irony of Torah, and it points forward to the paradoxical fulfilling of Torah's intention by the Spirit in 8:1-11. Torah intended to give life (Paul personifies Torah, though not as obviously and regularly as he does "sin"), but because of sin all it could give was death.

7:11. By way of explanation, Paul repeats what he had said in v. 8 about sin "taking its opportunity" through the commandment. This time, instead of merely showing that sin produced in "me" all kinds of covetousness, he draws the conclusion: sin deceived me, and so killed me. It is at this point that the disguise of the personified "sin" is close to disappearing: we are clearly talking about the serpent in the garden, though Paul has told the story in such a way as to allow other levels to be heard as well, which, had he been more explicit, might have been drowned out. The preliminary picture is complete: (a) sin and the law are quite distinct; (b) sin has taken over the law, the law that promised life; (c) using it as a base of operations, sin has produced the opposite of that which the law promised. This is of course why "no human being will be justified" in God's sight on the basis of Torah (3:20); it is why the Torah became "a dispensation of death" (2 Cor 3:7-11); it is why, despite the glory of the first exodus and the first covenant, a new exodus and a renewed covenant were necessary. However, this is not the whole story. As will shortly become apparent, through Paul's raising of the necessary second question, even the apparently negative side of Torah has its remarkable and positive purpose in the strange divine plan.

7:12. The Torah, cleared of identity with sin, can be reaffirmed as God's law, holy and just and good. This statement ranks with 3:31b as among those places where Paul most vehemently affirms the goodness of the Torah, rejecting outright the road that would lead, and did lead in the next century, toward Marcionism. This, indeed, in the light of 11:11-32, may be seen as one of Paul's main aims in various parts of Romans: to warn Gentile Christian readers, especially those who had had some connection with Judaism before their conversion and would now be tempted to reject everything to do with it, against such a course. They cannot cut off the branch on which they are sitting, or rather the trunk of the tree of which they are branches (11:16-24). At the present stage of the argument, it is vital that they do not react against the Torah itself (as so many of Paul's subsequent readers, since at least the second century, have been tempted to do), but that they see instead the strange but vital role it has played within the saving purposes of the one God. Romans 7 is poised between 3:1-9 on the one hand and 9:30–10:13 on the other, facing the same question (was God's covenant with Israel simply a mistake?) and giving it the same answer (no, but its purpose was stranger than had been imagined).

Romans 7:13-20, Living Under the Law: Sin Works Death

COMMENTARY

Though v. 13 forms in a sense a bridge between vv. 7-12 and vv. 14-20, it stands naturally at the head of the latter section. It asks, and gives the preliminary answer to, the question that determines the direction and shape of the verses to come. Too little attention has been given to the actual arguments Paul mounts here; the passage is not a string of loosely connected musings, but a carefully structured sequence of thought. Verse 13*a* raises the question, whether the law, now proved to be good, was nevertheless the cause of death; v. 13*b* gives the initial answer, that it was sin, rather than the law, that brought death; this is then further explained (γάρ *gar*) by v. 14 and what follows. Verse 14 can hardly, then, be the start of a new section, as has so often been supposed.[244]

Verses 13-20 then further subdivide. Verses 13-16 are basically about the goodness of the law, despite sin and death in the "I"; vv. 17-20 develop the thought of the paradoxical behavior of the "I" in order to show that it is not really the "I" that is at fault, but once again sin.[245] The "I" here, as I argued in the overview, is to be seen primarily as Israel under Torah, with the point being made that, even under Torah, Israel belongs in the Adam-sphere, the realm of sin and death (5:20; cf. 6:14; 7:5).

7:13a. The question is the natural one, granted that Paul is still thinking in terms of 5:20-21. "Sin reigned in death," and Torah seemed to have exacerbated that rule; 7:5 has repeated the point vividly. But was the good law, now firmly distinguished from "sin," thus responsible for death? Granted that sin was responsible for the initial deceit, using Torah as a base of operations, is Torah then responsible for what happens as a result, i.e., death? Once again Paul answers: of course not! His main object will now be to back up that denial, and in so doing to advance the underlying argument about the power and sinfulness of sin itself, toward the point where it is finally dealt with (8:3).

7:13b. All the blame attaches once more to sin itself. Sin was at work in "me" through the law ("the good thing"); and that work of sin, not of the law itself, produced death. This is the basic explanation that goes behind the dense statement of 7:5, and exonerates Torah from willing complicity in the process. But Paul has here built into this answer a double statement of purpose: it was sin, *so*

that it might appear as sin, working death in me through the law, *so that sin might become exceedingly sinful* through the commandment. This is the key to understanding not only the sequence of thought that leads from here to the decisive statement of 8:3-4 but also, in a measure, Paul's whole mature thinking about the purpose of Torah, or, better, the purpose of God in giving Torah.

We must obviously assume that the repeated ἵνα (*hina*) indicates not the intention and purpose of sin itself, but the intention and purpose of God. This reflects the similar *hina* in 5:20: the Torah came in alongside, *so that the trespass might abound*. But why would God want the trespass to abound? Surely this is counterintuitive?

Not if we understand Paul's point in this passage (and, more compactly, in Gal 3:21-2). God's way of dealing with sin, it appears, is not to hold it at arm's length. It is not a matter of damage limitation, attempting to restrict the operation of sin. Torah, apparently, was not after all given in order that Israel might become a sin-free zone. Rather, God's way with sin takes account of the fact that sin has infected the entire human race, Israel included, and that no law could possibly be given that would deal with the problem. If life could come by the law, then the law would have been the means of covenant membership and hence of life (Gal 3:21*b*; cf. Gal 2:21). If "the commandment which was unto life" (Rom 7:10) really could have given life, God would not have needed to do anything further (8:3-4). No: sin needed dealing with in a more radical way, at the place where it had become resident, that is, at the heart of the human race itself. And it was Torah's peculiar task to draw sin to its height, to let it appear in all its true colors, to be shown up as "exceedingly sinful." Sin must be seen to be sin.

But not only seen. The point of 7:13, coupled with 5:20, is that it looks on to 8:3. God gave Torah in order to draw sin into one place, *in order that it might there be dealt with fully and finally*. Where sin abounded, there grace superabounded; and that latter phrase is, of course, a periphrastic reference to the death of Jesus as the decisive event of obedience through which sin is condemned and the human race freed from its clutches.

---

244. Dunn, *Romans 1–8*, 377, notes the disagreement among German commentators as to where the real division occurs.

245. In Wright, *The Climax of the Covenant*, 218, I suggested that v. 17 functioned both as the conclusion to vv. 13-16 and as the beginning of the new line of thought leading to v. 20. This now seems to me wrong. Verse 16 rounds off the question about the law; νυνὶ δέ (*nyni de*) at the start of v. 17 introduces a new point, which, supported by vv. 18-19, reaches its conclusion in v. 20.

Thus the κατάκριμα (*katakrima*), the "condemnation," of 5:18 is removed (cf. 8:1: there is therefore now no *katakrima* for those in Christ Jesus), precisely because sin itself has been condemned once and for all (8:3). The place where it has been condemned is in the "flesh" of the Messiah, representing the Israel where "sin had abounded," and thereby representing the human race whose Adamic "flesh" was where sin had taken up residence. We shall say more about this at 8:3 itself. But it is vital that we notice already where Paul's thought is moving. The double *hina* of v. 13 points to the understanding of the cross that emerges from the entire argument.

7:14. In order to exonerate Torah, Paul now analyzes further the "I" that is caught up in sin and hence in death. To do this, he contrasts the true nature of Torah with the nature of the human being (and the Jew precisely as a person "in Adam"). Torah is spiritual, he says, but "I" am "fleshly," sold under sin, i.e., a bond-slave to sin. He does not here explain what he means by "spiritual"; this is part of the vindication of Torah, and belongs with 7:12. But in appealing to the basic spirit/flesh contrast that runs through so much of the present section, and which effectively extends and clarifies the Adam/Christ contrast of chap. 5 and the slave/free contrast of chap. 6, he is now placing Torah on the God-side, the Christ-side, of the equation, and placing the "I" on the Adam-side. (We should beware, here as elsewhere in Paul, of supposing that the spirit/flesh contrast had anything very much to do with the contrast of non-physical/physical.)[246]

He does, however, explain a bit more what he means by "of the flesh." The word here (σάρκινος *sarkinos*) is rare, and takes its meaning in Paul not so much from its original lexical force but from the heavy weight of Paul's technical term σάρξ (*sarx*, "flesh," with all its connotations; cf. 1 Cor 3:1, 3; 2 Cor 3:3; 10:4). Paul appears to use both *sarkinos* ("fleshly in *type*") and *sarkikos* ("fleshly in *character*") in both senses. The point he is making is that the "I," the Jew, Israel

"according to the flesh" (cf. 9:5; 11:14; 1 Cor 10:18), belongs within the Adamic solidarity, still held as a slave within the "Egypt" of sin and death; and that the law, in its promise of life, is ontologically as well as morally mismatched with Adamic humanity, Israel included. The problem is not the Torah, but the sort of person "I" am.

7:15. Paul's explanation of "I am fleshly" is an account of the behavior of the "I" (that v. 15 explains v. 14 is clear from the initial γάρ [*gar*, "for"], omitted in both the NRSV and the NIV; these connectives are, as usual, all-important in keeping a grip on Paul's argumentative strategy). The initial clause is the key: "what I do, I do not know." The NRSV and the NIV, perhaps not unnaturally, flatten this out into "I do not understand." The word γινώσκω (*ginōskō*) can indeed mean "understand," and that is part of the meaning here; but the way Paul develops the thought through to 8:3 suggests that he is saying something stronger than that the "I" is intellectually puzzled by its own behavior; he is referring to the actions in question as "sins of *ignorance*." This is further explained (a second *gar*) in the second half of the verse in terms of *unwilling* sin: what "I" do is not what "I" want, but what "I" hate. Here is the paradox of Israel under Torah; seeing what is the right thing to do, delighting in it and wanting to perform it, and yet discovering that what is performed instead is the thing the mind had rejected as hateful. But precisely within this paradox Paul has hinted at part of the solution; ignorant sins, and unwilling sins, are both taken care of within God's atoning plan (see on 8:3).

We must stress, as with 2:17-29, that Paul is not here talking about each individual Jew. He knew himself to have been "blameless in terms of righteousness under the law" (Phil 3:6). He is talking of Israel as a whole. As a nation, Israel delighted in Torah formally and officially (as it were), but was always aware that for the most part Torah was not followed. Israel was not a holy nation, obeying Torah gladly; sin, Adamic life, was evident all through. In the light of his Damascus road experience, and his whole subsequent body of belief, Paul would turn this critique upon himself and his "former life in Judaism" (Gal 1:13), believing that even in his zeal

246. It may be for this reason that the NIV translates σάρκινος (*sarkinos*) simply as "unspiritual." This fails, though, to highlight the link Paul is making, throughout the passage, between the σάρξ (*sarx*) in which sin has taken up residence and the *sarx* of Christ where it is dealt with (8:3), and the "fleshly" nature contrasted with the "spiritual" in 8:5-9. It is perhaps better, with the NRSV, to retain the verbal link, thus clarifying the flow of the argument, and to explain what the key terms do and do not mean.

for Torah, in fact specifically in the actions to which this zeal had led him, he had been missing the way quite radically.[247] This has to do, however, with the next major turn in the argument (9:30–10:4), and is not the primary meaning of the present paragraph. His point here is rather, through the vivid rhetorical "I," to present the plight of Israel-as-a-whole under Torah, seeing Torah's picture of a truly human life, deeply honoring to God, and constantly failing as a people to attain it.

7:16. The conclusion from vv. 13-15 can then be drawn, reinforcing the "certainly not" of 13*a:* If, then, I do the thing I do not wish, I agree that the law is good. In other words, any charges against Torah—that it might have been evil in itself, that it might have caused "my" death—are dropped by the "I." The "I" basically agrees with Torah, and confirms its goodness, even while observing that in its own life it cannot perform the good things Torah prescribes.

7:17-20. The next four verses say nothing about Torah, but concentrate wholly upon the "I" and its own relation with sin. Torah has been exonerated; Paul will presently draw conclusions about it (vv. 21-25), and will then show God's remedy for the whole situation (8:1-11). But for the moment, having thus cleared Torah of complicity in sin and death, he must focus on the "I," and particularly on its "fleshly" state, developing what was said in vv. 14*b*-15 in order to do so. Contrary to much popular opinion, this small section does not portray what is usually meant by the "cloven ego" (this increases the probability that Paul is not here dependent on the rabbinic idea of two "inclinations"; see the Overview). The "I," though frustrated, is actually, like Torah, exonerated, with the blame going (of course) to sin. Paul, having moved the problem off Torah on to the "I," now moves it one stage further, on to sin itself.

7:17."Now, however"; this is a new point, getting to the heart of the problem. "It is no longer I that do it, but sin that dwells in me": a remarkable statement of not just diminished but abrogated responsibility. The "indwelling" of sin is a new idea, introduced for the first and only time in Paul's writings,

perhaps formed on the analogy of the indwelling of the Spirit, which Paul will contrast with this condition in 8:9, 11. Just as blaming sin for death was Paul's means of excusing Torah from complicity, so now sin is blamed for the present "fleshly" state of the "I." The underlying point seems to be not so much that humans in general are not responsible for their evil actions ("it was sin that made me do it"), as that Israel qua Israel is not responsible for the particular sin of breaking Torah. This verse functions, then, as a new proposition, which the next two verses will explain, and which v. 20 will then restate in conclusion.

7:18-19. The idea of being indwelt by sin is now advanced in its negative form, to explain the remarkable statement of v. 17 (*gar*, "for," which links v. 18 to v. 17, is omitted by the NIV). It is sin that dwells within the "I," that is, within its flesh, not "a good thing." Paul may perhaps be alluding to "the good thing"—i.e., the law—as in v. 13, though this remains uncertain.[248] He would then be repeating the contrast between the Torah and the self from v. 14. The point he is pressing, in any case, is that what indwells someone is what gives them power to perform that which otherwise they would want to do but remain incapable of: literally, "for to will lies close to me, but to perform the good, not."[249] Without something "good" "dwelling in me," the "I" cannot bring the good will into reality; again, Paul is preparing the way for the contrast with the Spirit's indwelling, doing what the law could not, in the following chapter. His further explanation in v. 19 is a near-repetition of v. 15*b*, with the addition of "good" and "bad," and the replacement of "the thing I hate" with "the thing I do not want." The effect of all this is to drive a wedge between the "I" that wills, or does not will, certain things, and the "flesh," where sin dwells and where "the good thing" does not dwell.[250] The "I," Israel according to the flesh, is then on the same side, so to speak,

247. See N. T. Wright, "Paul, Arabia and Elijah (Galatians 1:17)," *JBL* 115 (1996) 683-92. In 1 Tim 1:12-16 Paul's persecution of the church is described as constituting him chief among sinners (ἁμαρτωλοί *hamartōloi*); cf. 1 Cor 15:9-11.

248. A couple of ninth-century MSS (F and G) seem to have read it this way, adding "the" before "good" (lit., "for I know that there does not dwell in me, that is, in my flesh, [the] good [thing]").

249. This time it is the NRSV that omits "for." Throughout this passage Paul varies the word he uses for "do" or "perform," variously using κατεργάζομαι (*katergazomai*), πράσσω (*prassō*), and ποιέω (*poieō*); this is almost certainly to avoid repetition, not to introduce subtle shades of meaning between different kinds of "performance" or "accomplishment."

250. The negative goes with the verb: the NRSV's "nothing good dwells within me" and the NIV's "nothing good lives in me" throw the stress in the wrong direction.

as Torah; but, like Torah, it is powerless to prevent sin from doing what it chooses in the flesh, and eventually bringing death.

7:20. The conclusion is then drawn, repeating virtually word for word what was said in v. 17, which opened the subsection: "if, then, this is indeed my state, that I do that which I do not wish, it is no longer I that do it, but sin that dwells in me." It is exceedingly rare that Paul repeats anything in this way, and it gives us pause. Why does he emphasize this point so strongly? Have traditional readings missed something within the dense jungle of chap. 7?

My suggestion is that, as well as being concerned to exonerate Torah from any blame, while nevertheless showing how it has been used within the kingdom of sin and death, Paul is simultaneously anxious to show how the "I," though fleshly and the dwelling-place of sin, is also exonerated, though still subject to sin and death. To remind ourselves what the "I" refers to—Israel according to the flesh, Israel "in Adam," Israel whose "Adamic" condition has been exacerbated by Torah—is to glimpse the solution. Paul is concerned to say that, though all the charges laid at the door of Israel, from 2:17 onward, are true, valid, and indeed grave, *there is nothing wrong with being Israel in itself.* Just as, with 7:5-6, we were back close to Paul's argument in 2:26-9,

so now we are aware of the next question and answer Paul there had to address (3:1-2): What is the advantage of being a Jew? Much in every way. As with 2:17–3:9 and 11:1-32, Paul is determined simultaneously to maintain both the God-givenness of the covenant with Israel, the goodness of being Jewish, and the impossibility of finding eschatological life through that Jewishness alone. At the heart of Paul's exposition of the effect and meaning of Torah, indeed so hidden within it as usually to go unnoticed, we find a key part of Paul's root-and-branch rejection of what would later become Marcionism. Israel itself, the "I" that continues to live under Torah, and continues to discover that it points to sin within Israel and so condemns it to death, is God-given; Israel's delight in Torah (think of Psalm 119!) is a good, not a bad, thing; the problem is simply that that which is wrong with the rest of the human race—namely, indwelling sin—is wrong with Israel too, and Torah can do nothing about it. Here, in the middle of Romans 7, we find a short passage that picks up the theme of the vindication of Israel from early in chap. 3 and anticipates the full-dress statement, as the spiral of argument gradually unwinds, in chap. 11.[251]

---

251. This is in part an answer to the question rightly raised by Hays, "Adam, Israel, Christ," 82.

Romans 7:21-25, Reflecting on the Law: God's Law and Sin's Law

COMMENTARY

7:21. The argument, which as we have seen has been both about the Torah and about the Israel that has lived under Torah, is now brought to its double conclusion. As usual, Paul opens with a broad statement, which is then filled out by a couple of explanatory verses, before he moves to a conclusion—though this time the conclusion is more of an outburst.

"This, then, is what I discover about the law": Paul is here drawing the conclusion from his long argument. This proposal about the meaning of 7:21 can be sharpened up by pointing out that the verb here (εὑρίσκω

heuriskō, "I find") can have the sense, not merely of "come upon by accident," but of "reaching one's findings" as a result of a careful deliberation.[252] One could translate it, "This, then, is my conclusion about the law."

But the real problem here is: What is the "law" that he now refers to? Most commentators and translators, including the NRSV and the NIV, have supposed that what Paul finds is not "the law," but "a law"—a general principle, a theory, a fact of observation, with nothing to do with "the law," the Torah, at

---

252. See BDAG 412.

all: "I find it to be a law," in the sense of "a regular pattern." Such readers have then gone on to suggest that in the remaining verses of the chapter, and in the first few of chap. 8, Paul is as it were playing with the word νόμος (nomos, "law"), using it in a bewildering variety of senses, few if any of which refer in any direct way to Torah.

This must be addressed case by case. But our presupposition, if we are reading Romans with an eye to its overall drift and the careful integrity of its long argument, must be that when Paul says nomos, here of all places at the climax of an argument about Torah, he means what he has meant throughout. Paul is well capable of wordplay; he is no stranger to rhetorical flourishes. But the questions of 7:7 and 7:13 are the questions to which his entire argument has driven him, questions precisely about Torah and its identity and effects; we are in a chapter that began with a complex argument about Torah, which grew directly out of 5:20 and 6:14 where there is no question that nomos meant Torah; and we are now at the point where, with the argument nearly complete, the writer is summing up, drawing the threads together. Are we really to say that at precisely this point he will start twisting and turning and saying "this then is my conclusion—that I find a law"?

"Certainly not!" (μὴ γένοιτο mē genoito), as Paul himself would say. The present verse does indeed introduce the concluding section of the passage, a section in which "the law" remains one of the two principal subjects (the other being the plight of the "I"). And, though this is not always noticed, Paul refers here not to a nomos in general but to the law: εὑρίσκω ἄρα τὸν νόμον (heuriskō ara ton nomon), "this is what I find about the law." The definite article is highly significant. Any first-century reader or hearer, coming fresh through the discussion of 7:1-20, where the subject in almost every verse is ὁ νόμος (ho nomos) in the sense of "the Torah," and then reading heuriskō ara ton nomon, would be bound to understand it as "this, then, is what I find about 'the law'"—"the law," that is, that has been the subject all along. The present verse must be able to stand on its own feet. Paul, it is true, is quite capable of building up gradually to a dense and difficult point, but here, when he is introducing the summing-up of a

long argument, we must assume that what he says would make clear sense.

The initial conclusion picks up from the description of the "I" in vv. 15-16, 17-20, in order to work back from there to what can be concluded about "the law." "This is what I find about the law: it means for me, when I want to do the good, that to me evil lies close at hand." If Paul in 7:7-12 alluded to Adam, hinting strongly (as had already been said in 5:20) that when Torah arrived in Israel, Israel recapitulated Adam's sin, the allusion here, somewhat fainter but still audible for those with ears attuned to echoes not only of Scripture but of Jewish traditions about Scripture, is to Adam's son, Cain.[253] "Sin is lurking in wait for you," said God to Cain, facing him with the choice between good and evil. Cain, choosing evil, committed murder, and found himself a wanderer and a fugitive, bearing forever the memory of his brother's blood.[254] "Wretched man that I am," says the "I" of Romans 7; "who will deliver me from this body of death?" When Torah arrived, Israel acted out Adam's trespass; living in the present under Torah, Israel continues to act out the sad paradox of Cain. Paul will show in chap. 8 how God has addressed this problem, too.

7:22-23. Paul now puts together into a fresh formulation what he has said about Torah on the one hand and about the "I" on the other. This statement obviously anticipates the final conclusion of 7:25b, and must be taken in close conjunction with it.

At this point many commentators have again balked at reading nomos as "Torah" throughout. "The law of God" in v. 22 is clearly the Mosaic law, they say, but surely this phrase itself shows that Paul is then talking about a different law altogether when he says ἕτερον νόμον (heteron nomon, "another law") in v. 23. So too with the formulation "the law of sin" at the end of v. 23, repeated at the close of v. 25. This is clearly a prima facie problem for anyone who wants to interpret nomos as "Torah" right through the passage; yet it is a nettle that must be grasped.

253. The full argument, which depends on the remarkable convergence of many Jewish traditions about Cain with what Paul says in 7:13-25 as a whole, is presented in Wright, *The Climax of the Covenant*, chap. 12.

254. Gen 4:7-16; the LXX of Gen 4:7 is so confused that one should not expect to find verbal parallels; the case is made by the multiple thematic convergence, set out in Wright, *The Climax of the Covenant*, chap 12.

The point to be stressed by way of reply is that these "negative" formulations *simply pick up and spell out what Paul has said about Torah in 5:20; 7:5; and particularly 7:8-11 and 7:13.* We may compare 1 Cor 15:56: "the sting of death is sin, and the strength of sin is Torah"; the fact that Paul goes on at once to say, "Thanks be to God, who gives us the victory through our Lord Jesus Christ" (1 Cor 15:57), paralleling Rom 7:25*a* so closely, indicates well enough that this embodies the same train of thought as we find at the end of Romans 7. Paul has not said anything new here, even though he has said it in a sharp and striking fashion. Precisely by demonstrating that Torah itself is "holy, just and good" (v. 12), while simultaneously explaining how sin "worked death in me" *through* "the good thing" (v. 13), he has already stated the paradox in principle, and now simply displays it in its simplest form. Insofar as the Torah is given by God, and is in itself holy, just and good, it is something rightly to be delighted in. Insofar as Torah has been made into sin's base of operations (vv. 8, 11) it has been taken over by sin, and has become "the law of sin."

Nothing is gained by lessening the force of Paul's paradox, by avoiding the thought that Torah might be its own shadowy *doppelgänger*. This has been, after all, the whole point of the section so far, and indeed the whole point of the paradox inherent not only in 5:20 but as far back as 3:19-21. The attempt to suggest that Paul might mean something else at the climax of his argument, just when he is drawing all the threads together, reminds me of the attempt by nineteenth- and early twentieth-century musical editors to make sixteenth- and seventeenth-century choral music more palatable by removing the false relations that contain not only the harmonic logic but also, frequently, the pathos and tension of the whole piece. After all, if we say that Paul means something other than Torah by some of his uses of *nomos* in this passage, we are already saying that he is writing in a deliberately paradoxical and many-sided way; if we allow this, why not allow that he is actually referring to Torah throughout, albeit highly paradoxically and many-sidedly?

The double Torah then fits the strange double identity of the "I," of Israel under Torah.

The "I" itself, as Paul has been argued in vv. 17-20, is in principle exonerated; but insofar as this "I" is in Adam, is *sarkinos* (v. 14), sin and death are at work within its "members" (v. 23, repeated; cf. 6:13, 19; 7:5, another indication that Paul is making the same point as there). In the present verses Paul expresses this duality in terms of the "mind" on the one hand and the "members" on the other, further explaining the former with the phrase "the inner person" (lit., "the inner human"; the NRSV's "my inmost self" is perhaps a shade too strong). With this "inner being" (NIV) the "I" delights in God's law; Paul may well have in mind the perfectly genuine delight that Israel, even Adamic Israel, finds in the study and contemplation of Torah, as expressed classically in Psalm 19 or 119. "To will [the good] is present with me" (v. 18); this is a reality, and it is not to be denied or mocked, for instance by those who say that "the Jew" was wrong to delight in Torah. The problem here is not "legalism" or "nomism," nor yet *homo religiosus*, but sin: that sin that has taken over Torah, made it a base of operations, and is now—continuing the implicit military metaphor from vv. 8, 11—producing a full-scale war between "another Torah," the Torah as it appears in 5:20 and 7:5, and the holy, just, and good law of God. And in this war the "I" is taken captive, a prisoner of war under the rule of "the Torah of sin." Paul, still exploring the depths of 5:20, is again describing the captivity, the enslavement, the "Egypt" of sin and death, exacerbated by Torah, from which Christ and only Christ can deliver. This, seen with Christian hindsight, is the plight of the "I," of Israel, including the pre-Christian Paul himself, under Torah.

7:24. Paul's famous cry of despair, put into the mouth of the "I," echoes but goes beyond the great tradition not only of the biblical psalms of lament but of subsequent Jewish lamentations such as the Qumran *Hodayot*. "Wretched man that I am": the NRSV, using the well-known phrase, for once allows the gender-specific noun, though ironically the Greek here is ἄνθρωπος (*anthrōpos*, "human being"). This, indeed, is the point: that Israel too is "in Adam," is a human being like all other human beings. Like Cain, bearing about the mark of his brother's death, the "I" finds itself unable to escape from "this body of death," referring perhaps both to its own "fleshly" state but also to the solidarity of sin, of Adamic humanity, with which it is unavoidably bound up (cf. 6:6). The problem is clearly stated: it is not so much sin itself, but the death that results from it. The promise of life held out by the law (with Eden's tantalizing tree of life remembered in the background) appears a mirage. Like a moth trying to fly to the moon, the "I," Israel under Torah, remains frustratedly earthbound. "Sin reigned in death," and Torah merely tightened the noose (5:21, in the light of 5:20); the "I" finds itself enslaved under that regime. "The sting of death is sin, and the power of sin is Torah" (1 Cor 15:56). What the "wretched person" needs is deliverance, and Paul, bringing the passage's rhetoric to its height, cries out for it: "who will deliver me?"

7:25. The full answer is about to be given in chap. 8, and indeed in the passage that, building on chaps. 5–8 as a whole, speaks of the salvation that is still open to ethnic Israel along with the Gentiles (chap. 11). But, as in 1 Cor 15:57, Paul cannot resist anticipating these answers right away, in an expostulation whose sense is clear even if its grammar is oblique. The answer to the question is "God"; "Thanks be to God, [the one who will deliver me] through Jesus the Messiah, our Lord." This verse looks back to 5:21, where "grace" is obviously a periphrasis for "God" (cf. too 6:23), and on to 8:3, where ὁ θεός (*ho theos*, "God") is the emphatic subject of one of the most important sentences in the entire letter. The full triple statement of Jesus' identity— Jesus, the Messiah, our Lord—serves as the weighty christological summary at the end of this stage of the argument, matching those in 4:24-25; 5:11, 21; and 6:23, and pointing toward the christology and consequent soteriology of 8:1-11, 17, 29-30 and supremely 31-39.

Verse 25*b* is not an anticlimax, nor (as used sometimes to be suggested) a dislocated verse, still less a gloss introduced by a later scribe into Paul's argument.[255] The double identity of the "I," and the double identity of Torah, are stated in terms of the double slavery that has ironically characterized the

whole passage. The αὐτὸς ἐγώ (*autos egō*, "I of myself"), apparently ignored by the NRSV, is emphatic, but controversial. It has, inevitably, been pressed into service to support various different readings of the whole passage. By itself, though, it cannot exercise sufficient leverage to determine the meaning of the chapter one way or another. It does, however, fit very well within the line of thought I have been expounding. "I of myself" means, I suggest, "I, Paul, as part of the solidarity of Israel according to the flesh."

We may cautiously use 9:3, the other Pauline occurrence of the same phrase, in support. There Paul expresses his solidarity with his "kinsmen according to the flesh" whom he sees in rebellion against the gospel, in a passage whose deepest point (9:14-23) is as we shall see to be understood very closely together with 7:13-25. He is saying that "I of myself" *could* pray to be accursed, cut off from the Messiah, for their sake. He does not say that this is in fact his prayer; it is what, left to himself as a Jew according to the flesh, he would pray; but that is not who he now is. He is "in the Messiah," by baptism and faith, and cannot and will not change that. He will wrestle with the problem of his "kinsmen according to the flesh" until a better solution, better than merely exchanging his own salvation for theirs, comes to light.

The contrast between the two things that are true of the "I" is made by separating out the "mind" and the "flesh." These are both clearly used in a technical sense; we should once more beware of taking them in terms simply of a nonmaterial thinking capacity on the one hand and physicality on the other. At the same time, we should also beware of trying to understand "mind" univocally in Paul; here it clearly refers to the intention or will spoken of in vv. 15-16, 18-21, and to the "inner person" of 7:22. It goes with the phrase "the law of my mind" in 7:23. It would be a mistake, fatal to the understanding of the whole passage, to insist that it must mean exactly what it does in two of the four other references in Romans, namely 1:28 and 12:2, where the mind is first darkened and then renewed. Clearly the "mind" in the present case, though delighting in God's law, remains powerless to put it into practice, whereas that in 12:2, being renewed by God, is the

---

255. So, rightly, e.g., Fitzmyer, *Romans*, 477, citing various opinions. Käsemann, *Commentary on Romans*, 211, declares that if v. 25*b* is not a gloss everything he has said so far about Paul's major topics will have to be reconsidered.

source of that full transformation in which the person is able to discover in practice what God's will actually is (cf. 8:5-8). The "I" of chap. 7 remains frustrated, rightly delighting in the Torah but finding that the solidarity of Israel with Adam prevents performance and, consequently, bars the way to life. That is the contrast Paul is emphasizing.

The Torah itself, then, simply binds Israel to Adam. Without the death of the "old human," as in 6:6 and 7:2-3, that is what Torah will inevitably do. When this plight is fully understood, however, the remedy can at last be unveiled. When the sickness is properly diagnosed, it can be treated. God has done what Torah could not do—not, of course, to indicate that Torah was bad, or not God-given, but that, through sin and the "flesh," it was weak, and could not give the life it promised.

Romans 8:1-11, God Gives Life Through the Son and the Spirit

COMMENTARY

The first eleven verses of Romans 8 lie at the very heart of Romans 5–8 as a whole. They simultaneously complete the thought of the section that began with 7:1 and begin the majestic sequence that sweeps on through to 8:30. As tightly argued as any piece of Pauline logic, they are at the same time suffused with a sense of exultation, and celebration.

Many regular readers of the Bible will find this passage almost too well known to be any longer audible. As was once said of Shakespeare's *Hamlet*, it is "full of quotations." Liturgies and private prayers have drawn freely on it. Almost every line evokes, and has indeed produced, hundreds of sermons. Johann Sebastian Bach made it the backbone of a whole cantata (*Jesu, meine Freude*). How can we avoid the two equally unhelpful reactions of having heard it all before, on the one hand, and of focusing too narrowly on particular verses, and the theological topics they evoke, on the other? How can we hear the symphony, not just the notes?

The clue is to remind ourselves, not for the first time, that we are still watching the unfolding of the Adam/Christ contrast of 5:12-21, and in particular the exposition of the great statement in the last verse of that seminal passage. "As sin reigned in death" (and we must remind ourselves of the role of the law within that reign, as in 5:20), "so grace also reigned through righteousness to eternal life through Jesus Christ our Lord." From this tight-packed statement, the key contrast for the present passage is that between death and life: "life" is the golden thread that runs through 8:1-11, the gift of God that the law wanted to give but could not, the gift that comes because God's Son has dealt with sin and death and God's life-giving Spirit has replaced sin as the indwelling power within God's people. The promise of resurrection with which the passage concludes is not added for extra effect at the end of the paragraph. It is where the whole argument is leading.

The shape of the paragraph then becomes clear. The opening statement (v. 1) is at once explained, in Paul's usual fashion, first with another dense and cryptic statement (v. 2, linked to v. 1 with *gar*), which is in turn explained (another *gar*) by the complex and powerful statement of vv. 3-4, a sentence that has as good a claim as any to represent the very center of what Paul is saying in Romans 5–8, if not in his whole theology. Verses 1-4 together serve as the platform for the step-by-step argument that explains how precisely it is that God has given the life that the law could not. Verses 5-8 rule out any way to life for those "in the flesh," but declare that the Spirit is the key source of that life. Verses 9-10 apply this to those who are "in Christ" and hence "in the Spirit," those who have the Spirit, or indeed Christ himself, dwelling in them. And verse 11 draws the conclusion: The indwelling Spirit will give new life to the mortal body of the Christian, despite the necessity of physical death.

What has happened, of course, is that the shape of 5:21, still clearly visible in vv. 2, 10, has been filled in with the more detailed content of 7:5-6. "Sin reigned in death" has been expanded, by means of 7:5 and 7:7-25, in terms of two further factors, namely, "the law" and "flesh," and is here summarized in 8:2*b*, 7-8, and the middle phrase of 8:10 ("the body is dead because of sin"). The problem that has thereby been so carefully analyzed is equally carefully dealt with: the death of Jesus and the gift of the Spirit are shown to be exactly what was necessary. "Grace reigned through righteousness to eternal life through Jesus Christ" has been expanded, by means of 7:6, to include the Spirit as the key agent of that reign.

The paragraph thus offers, as its opening statement suggests, the ultimate response to the problem set out in 2:1-16. Final "condemnation" hangs over the heads of all people. All have sinned, and in chapter 2 it was not clear how there could be any who would come into the category Paul held out in 2:7, 10. The hints of 2:13*b*-15*a* were by themselves too oblique to build on; the fuller statement in 2:26-29 can at last be seen for what it is, an advance statement of what Paul can now say clearly. Romans 8:1-11 is focused on those who, whether circumcised or not, submit to God's law in the power of the Spirit, and in whom therefore the positive verdict, the δικαίωμα (*dikaiōma*) of the law is fulfilled. This at last explains how the verdict issued in the *present* on the evidence of faith alone (3:27-30) embodies God's justice, how (in other words) God is right to declare that Abraham's true worldwide family consists of all those who believe in the gospel. As Paul says elsewhere, the one who began a good work will bring it to completion (Phil 1:6). The Spirit who was at work in the coming to faith of those who heard the gospel (1 Thess 1:4-5; 2:13) will continue that work until the final moment of resurrection itself.

This in turn is made possible because the "condemnation" of sin, the real culprit all along, has taken place on the cross. Verse 3 refers back to the theme of Christ's "obedience" in 5:12-21, and stresses that what was done there was the act of God in Christ, not (as it were) the action of Christ upon God. The central sentence of 8:3-4, around which

so many vital subordinate clauses hang like bunches of grapes on a vine, is simply this: "God . . . condemned sin." No clearer statement is found in Paul, or indeed anywhere else in all early Christian literature, of the early Christian belief that what happened on the cross was the judicial punishment of sin. Taken in conjunction with 8:1 and the whole argument of the passage, not to mention the partial parallels in 2 Cor 5:21 and Gal 3:13, it is clear that Paul intends to say that in Jesus' death the condemnation that sin deserved was meted out fully and finally, so that sinners over whose heads that condemnation had hung might be liberated from this threat once and for all.[256] This densely stated but clearly thought out atonement-theology (as it would later be known) is not the main subject of the paragraph. That place belongs to the Spirit's gift of life. But, as John saw equally clearly, the outpouring of the Spirit depends on the prior achievement of the cross (cf. John 7:37-39; 20:19-23).

The paragraph is remarkable, finally, for its dense and many-sided concentration on the work of God. In Jewish thought at this time, the activity of the one God, not least the supremely self-revealing and saving divine activity on behalf of Israel, had been spoken of in many ways. God's Word would go forth to renew Israel and the world. God's Spirit, that breathed on the waters at the beginning, would blow again like a mighty wind, animating the dead bones of God's people. God's Wisdom, the divine agent in creation, would enable humans to live truly human lives, and would be sent by God to live in Israel. God's Law, again at this period sometimes conceived as a pre-existent divine agent, would guide God's people along the path of life. And God's own Presence, God's Glory, would dwell in the Temple in Jerusalem, the source of life and glory for Israel (and, in some readings, for the whole world).[257]

Paul has not expounded these aspects of the character and presence of God in any systematic fashion. But they undergird and explain this whole paragraph. The way

256. On 2 Cor 5:21 see N. T. Wright, "On Becoming the Righteousness of God: 2 Corinthians 5:21," in *Pauline Theology, Volume II*, ed. D. M. Hay (Minneapolis: Fortress, 1993) 200-208.

257. For details, see Wright, *Jesus and the Victory of God*, 629-31; M. J. Borg and N. T. Wright, *The Meaning of Jesus: Two Visions* (San Francisco: Harper, 1999) chap. 10.

to understand the christology of v. 3, for instance, is not simply to study the phrase "Son of God" on its own. Rather, we must observe the way in which the sending of God's Son in this passage, as part of God's doing that which the law could not, belongs, together with the indwelling of the Spirit, as part of Paul's reworking of the Jewish Wisdom theology, and *Shekinah* theology, in which God's character was revealed in the act of bringing salvation to Israel. If the main topic of the paragraph is the gift to God's people of the life the law promised but could not give, the main foundation upon which that topic is built is the saving presence of the one God of Israel in the cross of the Son and the indwelling of the Spirit.

There is thus, we even dare to say, an implicit trinitarianism in this paragraph, which becomes more explicit as chap. 8 unfolds. We glimpse, in other words, how it is that the gospel outlined in 1:3-4 does indeed reveal the δικαιοσύνη θεοῦ (*dikaiosynē theou*, 1:17), thus becoming "God's power unto salvation for all who believe" (1:16). We are still left, of course, with the question as to how this works out "to the Jew first and also to the Greek." Paul's answer to this question, given spectacularly in chaps. 9–11, is constructed with considerable care on the foundations he is laying in the present passage. Here, too, what lies at the heart of it all is a vision of God.

8:1. The opening statement, with its connecting "therefore" (ἄρα *ara*), comes as a shock. How can the analysis of 7:7-25 lead to such a conclusion? "I of myself . . . serve the law of sin; there is therefore now no condemnation!" The answer is that Paul has leapfrogged over the middle premise of his argument. Instead of the normal pattern of a syllogism, *a* plus *b* therefore *c* ("donkeys have crosses on their backs; this animal has a cross on its back; therefore this animal is a donkey"), Paul has created a striking effect by advancing *c* and explaining it with *b:* "I serve God's law with my mind, but sin's law with my flesh; there is *therefore* no condemnation, *because* God has dealt with sin in the flesh, and provided new life for the body." The "now" picks up the "but now" of 3:21; 7:6 (see also 5:9, 11; 6:22), emphasizing the eschatological nature of God's achievement

in Christ and by the Spirit. The verdict of the last day has been brought forward into the present. This is, quite simply, the solid foundation for Christian joy.

The "condemnation" spoken of here is the final judgment that God, the righteous judge, will mete out at the last. It is the necessary reaction of the justice-loving God to all injustice; of the God who created image-bearing human beings to all that defaces and destroys that likeness. Like so much in this part of Romans, it looks back to chap. 5 (here, vv. 16, 18), and behind that to 2:1-16.

The reason why there is now no condemnation is not far to seek. Sin's condemnation has been effected in the cross of God's Son (v. 3), and those who are "in the Messiah, Jesus" discover that what is true of him is now true of them. His death means that, as far as they are concerned, the condemnation that must rightly fall on sin has nothing more to do with them. Thus "in Christ Jesus" at the close of v. 1 offers not just a designation of the people for whom there is no condemnation, but, in compact form, the reason why this is the case.[258]

8:2. Paul's fundamental explanation for v. 1 is God's act of liberation. He has already spoken of this at length in chap. 6 and developed it in 7:1-6. As we have already seen, talk of setting slaves free is exodus language: the present paragraph is describing how those who are in the Messiah, and indwelt by the Spirit, are brought out of the Egypt of sin and death and promised citizenship in the kingdom of life. There is no question but that Paul is referring in this verse to the same composite event that he has been describing in the previous chapters—namely, the messianic (and hence representative) death of Jesus and the gift of the Spirit.

The object of this liberating act is "you," singular.[259] Some MSS, followed indeed by several translations, have "me" rather than "you" (KJV, RSV, NIV, "me"; NEB, NRSV, "you"). But "you" is sufficiently well supported to be

258. Several good MSS add, at the end of v. 1, "who do not walk according to the flesh, but according to the Spirit," thus anticipating the point to be made at the end of v. 4. This was not, as has sometimes been asserted, an attempt by later scribes to undercut the sheer grace of v. 1; nevertheless, the shorter text is certainly to be preferred.

259. Cranfield, *A Critical and Exegetical Commentary on the Epistle to the Romans*, 377, comments, truthfully if nostalgically, on the disappearance of the singular form "thee/thou" from contemporary English, making it almost impossible to convey Paul's sharply personal address.

quite possible, and sufficiently unexpected, after a long paragraph where "I" and "me" are the main focus, to be likely. Why would a scribe alter the expected "me" to "you"? At the same time, Paul is not only addressing each reader as an individual with this striking and joyful message of freedom. He is ensuring that each individual reader, not only those who had in some sense been "under the law" and hence in the precise situation of 7:7-25, would know himself or herself to be included in this joyful news. Like those old portraits whose eyes follow each onlooker around the room, this statement of freedom is aimed at every single hearer of the letter, whoever and wherever they may be.

The liberating action has taken place "in Christ Jesus." Certainty here is impossible, but it is likely that the last phrase belongs with the verb rather than modifying either "law," "Spirit," or "life." Paul is quite capable of writing lengthy strings of mutually modifying nouns and phrases, but I think it more probable that in this instance the NIV and the NEB are correct. The NIV is wrong, though, to change "in" to "through." Paul is always careful about these prepositions; the action has taken place "in the Messiah" so that those who are "in him" may benefit from it. "There is no condemnation for those in Christ, because in Christ God has set you free."

The subject of the verb, and the description of that from which one has been liberated, presents us with a new version of the problem we encountered in 3:27-31 and 7:21-25: can Paul conceivably mean "the law," the Torah, by these uses of *nomos?* This question is linked to that in 7:21-25, since the gaoler from whom "you" are now free is described in almost identical terms here to those of 7:23, 25. As I argued there, so it seems to me compelling here that the "law" in question is not a general principle, "the old vicious circle" as J. B. Phillips renders it, but the Torah itself, seen from one angle, specifically the angle described in 4:15; 5:20; and 7:1-6 (to say nothing of 7:7-25). The situation of all humankind was "under sin and death." Torah, rightly, endorsed this verdict, tightening the grip of Adamic humanness on those who were "under" its sway, and shutting out altogether the "Gentile sinners" (Gal

2:15) who were not. God's act of liberation has broken this stranglehold once and for all.

But Paul does not actually mention God as the subject of the sentence. Can it really be that "the law of the spirit of life" is a further reference to Torah, introducing now a new facet to Torah not visible in chap. 7? Most commentators draw back from this conclusion. I am persuaded, however, that reaction is wrong. When scaling the sheer rock of Paul's thought it is important not to lose one's nerve and settle for an apparently easier path, a seemingly more natural route. The explanation of v. 2, after all, is found in vv. 3-4; and there, as the heart of the chapter so far, we find that the "righteous verdict of the law," the δικαίωμα τοῦ νόμου (*dikaiōma tou nomou*), is now fulfilled "in us who walk . . . according to the Spirit." We then find, by implication, that whereas "the mind of the flesh" does not submit to God's law, the mind of the Spirit actually does (v. 7), and that by the Spirit God will do what the law wanted to do but, through no fault of its own, was unable to do (8:3, 10-11; cf. 7:10). It is not fanciful, then, but strictly in keeping with the thrust of the whole passage, to say that when Paul speaks of "the law of the Spirit of life in Christ Jesus" he is indeed referring to Torah, in a way for which we have only distantly been prepared by 3:27, 31. After all, *ho nomos* in vv. 3, 4, and 7 is clearly Torah. How obscure do we suppose Paul to have been? More will be said on the subject when we arrive at 10:4-8, which plays a similar role in the argument of chaps. 9–11 to that played by 8:1-4 within chaps. 5–8.

It would have been easy to write "for the Spirit of life in Christ Jesus has set you free," but Paul seldom settles for the easy option. He has spent a whole chapter arguing that, despite appearances (and despite many commentators!), the Torah remains God's law, holy and just and good, and that it is not guilty of causing the death that comes to those who embrace it. Now he takes a step further: When God acts in Christ and by the Spirit the Torah is somehow involved as well, somehow present and active. Speaking of Torah, after all, was a thoroughly Jewish way of speaking of God's saving action. Though Paul has spoken with eloquent passion of the way in which Torah locks the door on those who are imprisoned within Adamic humanity, he has never forgotten its promise of life. He can therefore speak, with deliberate but comprehensible paradox, of the law itself as the agent of that which God has accomplished in the Messiah and by the Spirit.

The Torah, then—why, after all, should we be surprised at being surprised by Paul?—is the hidden agent of what God has achieved, which is the life of which the Spirit is the personal giver. This, as we saw, is the main thrust of the paragraph. And it answers the otherwise puzzling question at the start of the next verse.

8:3-4. What was it that the law "could not do"? Some have assumed that Paul meant by this somewhat awkward phrase (lit., "the impossible thing of the law") to refer to law-abiding behavior, as though the main thrust of the paragraph were to fall on (what we would call) the "ethical" passage of vv. 4*b*-8. This then goes with an understanding of τὸ δικαίωμα τοῦ νόμου (*to dikaiōma tou nomou*) in v. 4*a* in which δικαίωμα (*dikaiōma*) would mean "righteous decree" or "requirement" (NRSV) in the sense of moral commands to be obeyed. But (to deal with that problem first) there are two outstanding objections to this reading. First, when *dikaiōma* is used in this sense it is usually plural (e.g., 2:26; elsewhere in the NT, Luke 1:6; Heb 9:1, 10; Rev 15:4; 19:8). Second, in the passage to which the present one looks back, where *dikaiōma* is contrasted with *katakrima*, as here (5:16, 18), the *dikaiōma* is unquestionably God's righteous decree or verdict, not the required behavior of God's people. A similar use appears, in a negative sense, in 1:32. It is highly likely, therefore, that *to dikaiōma tou nomou* here refers to the verdict that the law announces rather than the behavior which it requires. And, in the light of 5:16, 18 and the argument of the present passage, this is clearly (unlike 1:32) the *positive* verdict: "do this and you will live" (cf. on 10:5). That this is the correct reading of 8:4*a*, and with it 8:3*a*, is confirmed by three things: Paul's highlighting of this intention of the law at 7:10; the whole thrust of the argument of 8:1-11 (with 5:21 in the background); and the point about the life-giving Torah in 10:5-11 (see the notes on that passage). What was impossible for the

law? That it should give life. It offered it, but could not deliver.

It could not do so because it was "weak because of the flesh." Despite many commentators and preachers who have been eager to see Paul say negative things about the law, he declares, summing up the argument of chap. 7, that there was nothing wrong with it in itself. The problem lay elsewhere: in the "flesh"—not the physicality of human nature, which was God-given and will be reaffirmed in the resurrection (8:11), but in the present rebellious and corruptible state of humankind, within which sin had made its dwelling (7:18, 20, 23, 25).

The main sentence with which Paul then explains how God has done what the law could not do must then be understood as follows: God condemned sin in the flesh of Jesus, so that the life the law offered could rightly be given to those led by the Spirit. The latter was the long-term purpose of the former, the former the necessary precondition of the latter. Each half of this double statement must now be explored in detail.

God, says Paul, condemned sin. Paul does not, unlike some, say that God condemned Jesus. True, God condemned sin in the flesh of Jesus; but this is some way from saying, as many have, that God desired to punish someone and decided to punish Jesus on everyone else's behalf. Paul's statement is more subtle than that. It is not merely about a judicial exchange, the justice of which might then be questioned (and indeed has been questioned). It is about sentence of death being passed on "sin" itself, sin as a force or power capable of deceiving human beings, taking up residence within them, and so causing their death (7:7-25). To reduce Paul's thinking about the cross to terms of a lawcourt exchange is to diminish and distort it theologically and to truncate it exegetically. For Paul, what was at stake was not simply God's judicial honor, in some Anselmic sense, but the mysterious power called sin, at large and destructive within God's world, needing to be brought to book, to have sentence passed and executed upon it, so that, with its power broken, God could then give the life sin would otherwise prevent. That is what happened on the cross.

For this to be done it was necessary, and Paul here spells this out, that the place where the sentence was executed was indeed the true "likeness of sinful flesh" (the NIV's repeated "sinful man" fails to highlight the link between Paul's expression here and the cognate ones elsewhere in the argument). The difficult word here translated "likeness" (ὁμοίωμα *homoiōma*) is certainly meant to indicate that Jesus' humanity was indeed the genuine article; it is not a cover for a smuggled-in Docetism in which Jesus was not actually human but only seemed to be. Why, then, has Paul not simply said "sending the son in sinful flesh"? Presumably because, though Jesus' humanity was true and genuine, Jesus was himself not guilty of sin—a remarkable fact that appears at various points within early Christian tradition (cf. John 7:18; 8:46; 2 Cor 5:21; Heb 4:15; 7:26; 1 Pet 2:22). For Paul, it would have been axiomatic that sin was not necessary to genuine humanness. Sin was an intruder, not a native inhabitant, of God's good world (5:12). To debate whether Jesus' humanity was therefore "sinful humanity" or "sinless humanity," whether "fallen" or "unfallen," seems to me beside the point. What matters is that it was genuine humanity, not a sham (cf. Phil 2:7, where ἐν ὁμοιώματι ἀνθρώπων [*en homoiōmati anthrōpōn*, "in the likeness of humans"] does not mean "like a human being, but not actually one," but rather "a true human being, bearing the true likeness." Jesus could and did suffer and die, truly and really; he was in principle capable of sinning, but unlike all other humans did not. It was God's design that, in his truly human death, sentence would be meted out on sin once for all.

But how could Jesus' human flesh, and his human death, be the appropriate locus of this judgment? Why, if Jesus was himself in some sense sinless, would it make any sense that sins be condemned in him? I have already suggested that part of the answer lies in the phrase "in Christ Jesus." Because (as the resurrection revealed) Jesus was the Messiah, he represented his whole people; what was true of him was true of them. His death could therefore be counted as theirs. That is the underlying logic, rooted in the biblical picture of Israel's monarchy, that binds the unique event of Calvary to the

status of all those "in Christ" from that day to this.

But the other part of the answer is found in the whole sequence of thought that, begun deep in chap. 7, reaches its climax in this verse. This is the point envisaged by the repeated "in order that" (ἵνα *hina*) of 5:20 and 7:13, the point indeed that must be grasped if the further argument of Romans 9 is to become comprehensible. Once again we are following through the train of thought over which 5:20-21 stands like a gold-lettered heading on a page. The law came in *in order that* the trespass might abound; sin worked death through the law *in order that* it might be shown up as sin, *in order that* sin might be exceedingly sinful. The law caused sin to be heaped up in one place, to flourish and abound in that single location. As many have seen, the "place" implied in 5:20-21 was Israel. As not so many have seen, God's purpose in and through all of this—in giving the Torah with this strange intention—was that sin might be drawn together, heaped up, not just in Israel in general, but *upon Israel's true representative, the Messiah*, in order that it might there be dealt with, be condemned, once and for all. God sent the Son "in the likeness of sinful flesh" to bring this sequence to its appointed climax, that in his death Torah might do the necessary, if apparently negative, work for which it was designed. We are not far, here, from what Paul says in Gal 3:22: Scripture (i.e., God, working through the written law) shut up everything under sin, in order that the promise, effective through the faithful obedience of Jesus the Messiah, might be given to all believers. And now we are not far, either, from the conclusion to the argument of Romans 9–11: God shut up all in disobedience, in order to have mercy upon all (11:32). In the strange plan of God, to deceive and defeat "the rulers of this age" (1 Cor 2:6-8), the personified forces of Sin were lured onto the one field where they were bound to lose the decisive battle. Sin, the real culprit throughout chap. 7, needed to be condemned; on the cross, it was.[260]

260. It is inadequate and misrepresents the whole drift of Paul's argument to suggest, as several have done (e.g., Fitzmyer, *Romans*, 487), that this "condemnation" simply means that sin is now merely disempowered. κατέκρινεν (*katekrinen*) in v. 3 answers directly to κατάκριμα (*katakrima*) in v. 1, and that verse scarcely means "there is no disempowerment."

Paul expands his condensed reference to the cross by adding "and as a sin-offering."[261] The phrase καὶ περὶ ἁμαρτίας (*kai peri hamartias*) can, it is true, mean simply "and to deal with sin" in a more general sense. But this is the regular phrase that, in the LXX, translates the Hebrew terms for the specific sacrifice known as the sin-offering.[262] Why would Paul refer to this sacrifice here in particular? Because in the biblical codes that deal with the whole sacrificial system the sin-offering is designed to deal, not with any and every sin, but with sin that has been committed ignorantly or unwillingly. Either one did something without realizing it was sinful; or, knowing it was sinful, one did it despite intending not to. Without one or other of these saving clauses, of course, any sin would be deliberate, knowing the act to be wrong and intending it none the less. This, known as "sinning with a high hand," is unpardonable; the person who acts thus is to be "cut off from among the people"—that is, put to death (cf. Num 15:30-31).

The sin-offering thus answers exactly, not indeed to any and every sin (that is not what this phrase was designed to do), but to the problem so carefully analyzed in chap. 7. The "I" of 7:15, as we saw, does not "know," and does not "will," the actions committed. The sin in question is precisely, in Jewish terms, sin of ignorance, unwilling sin. When we meet, in the passage where Paul is explaining how God has dealt with the problem of chap. 7, the very phrase the LXX uses regularly to refer to the sin-offering, the sacrifice that deals with this sort of sin, there can be no excuse either for rejecting the sacrificial meaning or for ignoring the tight interlinking of the argument, and its various implications.

In particular, as we shall see when dealing with 10:3, Paul is aware that in the next stage of his argument (i.e., chaps. 9–11) he will need to stress that his kinsfolk according to the flesh are "ignorant of God's righteousness." Here the point of adding "and as a sin-offering" is to emphasize that the death

of Jesus has been the means, not simply of condemning sin in general, but of dealing specifically with the problem set out in the previous chapter, the problem of the "I." Paul's argument from this point on is not focused on the problem of Israel under Torah, but it is important to show, as part of his larger statement, how Israel's peculiar plight has also been taken care of.

I have left to the end of v. 3 what is arguably the most important phrase in the whole verse. If Paul thus sees the death of Jesus as the means whereby the judicial punishment on sin itself was meted out, he blocks off the possible misunderstanding of that (as in much medieval thinking and iconography, and some more recent expressions as well) as the act of a merciful second person of the Trinity placating a hostile first person. The whole action comes from God in the first place, as in 5:6-10. Paul does not use the word "love" at this point, but his dramatic summary of the whole argument in 8:31-39 shows that this is what he has in mind. The condemnation of sin in the flesh of Jesus happened as a result of divine grace, of "God sending his own Son."

The echo of 5:10 here, and behind that of 1:3-4, is obvious, as is the important parallel with Gal 4:4 and the anticipation of 8:32. Without leaving the home base of meaning for "Son of God"—Israel in general, the Messiah in particular (on "Son of God," see the Commentary on 1:3-4; see also Gal 2:20)—and indeed while needing precisely that for his argument to work, Paul has exploited the phrase so that it becomes a way of saying what some Second Temple Judaism said about God's action in the world and Israel through Wisdom, Torah, *Shekinah*, Word, and Spirit: that God had sent, or would send, Wisdom or the others to embody the divine presence, and to be the means of the divinely originated salvation.[263] Here and elsewhere Paul has worked from within the Second Temple Jewish awareness of God's personal action in the world and in Israel. He has exploited the image of "father and son," which already carried the messianic overtones on which his argument depends, to produce genuine and appropriate innovation from within current

---

261. The NIV implies that this is the main purpose of God's sending of the son, with the condemnation of sin being a new idea; but that is not how the Greek works. The NIV does, however, recognize the meaning of *kai peri hamartias* as "and as a sin offering," while the NRSV, with most translations, relegates this to a footnote.

262. E.g., Lev 5:7-8; 6:25 (LXX/Mt 6:18). For full details, and a more complete presentation of the following argument, see Wright, *The Climax of the Covenant,* chap. 11.

263. A classic statement is found in Sirach 24, where Wisdom, sent into the world, becomes *Shekinah,* dwelling in the Temple, and is summed up in the Mosaic Torah.

Jewish language about God. The fact of Jesus himself, the truly human being in whom, as the resurrection revealed, God's saving plan had been put into effect, called forth from Paul the formulation that, while rooted in the pre-Christian soil of Second Temple language about God and God's action, laid the foundations for the developed Trinitarian thought of later theologians (whose main aim, of course, was to retain Jewish-style monotheism while affirming a distinction between Father and Son). The present expression forms the middle term in a crescendo: Starting with 1:3-4 and 5:10, both of which simply refer to Jesus as God's son, 8:3 speaks of God's sending "his own son" (τὸν ἑαυτοῦ υἱόν *ton heautou huion*), and 8:32 speaks of God's not sparing, but handing over "his very own son" (ὅς γε τοῦ ἰδίου υἱοῦ οὐκ ἐφείσατο *hos ge tou idiou huiou ouk epheisato*). The sending and death of the Son of God forms, in fact, one of the key threads that run through the entire letter so far.

Verse 4 then falls into place. The introductory "so that" (the *hina*, as in 5:20 and 7:13, clearly expresses the divine purpose) states God's intention: that the righteous verdict of the law might be fulfilled "in us." The life the Torah intended, indeed longed, to give to God's people is now truly given by the Spirit (for this interpretation, see above). The balance with v. 3 might have led us to expect δικαίωσις (*dikaiōsis*) at this point, but Paul may have chosen δικαίωμα (*dikaiōma*) not least because of its formal balance with the κατάκριμα (*katakrima*) of v. 1, exactly as in 5:16.[264] As argued earlier, the *dikaiōma* could conceivably have referred to the behavior the law commanded rather than the verdict it pronounced. Paul could have said that the intended result of sin's condemnation was that God's renewed people might be able at last to do what the law required (in some sense that does not require either circumcision or observance of the food laws; cf. 2:27; 13:8-10; 14:1-23; 1 Cor 7:19). Yet the singular formulation (ignored by the NIV, which translates "righteous requirements"), taken in conjunction with the larger thrust of the paragraph as a whole, strongly suggests the reference to the law's "righteous decree" of life.

This does not, of course, exclude the former point, since it is precisely by "walking according to the Spirit" that those in Christ "seek for glory, honor and immortality" (2:7). The commandment that was "unto life" brought death because of sin residing in the flesh (7:10); now the same commandment brings life because of the indwelling Spirit. On the "life/death" choice see again Lev 18:5 and Deut 30:15-20, with the discussion below on 10:5-11.

As I pointed out earlier, this in no way compromises present justification by faith. What is spoken of here is the future verdict, that of the last day, the "day" Paul described in 2:1-16. That verdict will correspond to the present one, and will follow from (though not, in that sense, be earned or merited by), the Spirit-led life of which Paul now speaks. Once again Torah is vindicated by God's action. As a detailed analysis of Paul's underlying narrative here will reveal, Torah is the main "character" at this point in the story, and here emerges triumphant.[265]

Those who will find Torah's righteous decree fulfilled in them—those, that is, who will share in the resurrection life (8:10-11)—are those who in the present do not "walk" according to the flesh but according to the Spirit (on "walk" as a Jewish metaphor for conduct [flattened out by the NIV's "live"] see the Commentary on 6:4). Here Paul highlights the Spirit/flesh contrast, already seen in 1:3-4, which will dominate the rest of the paragraph. The "flesh," not in the sense of physicality but in the sense of rebellious and corruptible human nature, is not the sphere of existence in which the Christian lives. Paul is capable of expressing things slightly differently elsewhere, as when, for instance, he speaks in Gal 2:20 of "the life I now live in the flesh," or when he distinguishes in 2 Cor 10:3 between "walking in the flesh," which there simply means "living an ordinary human life" (albeit with the overtones of mortality and decay not far off) and "waging war according to the flesh," which means "adopting the standards of rebellious and corruptible humankind." But in the present passage, as in 7:5 ("when we were in the flesh," implying that this is no longer the case), he brings together "in the flesh" (8:8-9) with

---

264. As BDAG points out.

265. See Wright, *The Climax of the Covenant*, 204-8.

"walking according to the flesh" (8:4) and "being according to the flesh" (8:5), seeing all these expressions as referring to the status and way of life of those without faith, those not baptized, those not in Christ, those not indwelt by the Spirit. "Flesh," then, carries here its fully nuanced negative meaning, not of physicality per se, but of humanity both mortal and rebellious. And part of the point of the passage, as will become clear in chaps. 9–11, is that unbelieving Israel is precisely "in the flesh."

The contrast with "flesh" is "Spirit"; not "spirit," or "on the spiritual level," as though Paul were after all contrasting the merely physical and the merely non-physical. With 1:4 in the background, and the climax of 8:9-11 coming up in the foreground (to say nothing of 8:12-27), he is clearly referring, throughout the present paragraph, to the Holy Spirit. Romans 8 contains one of Paul's greatest expositions of the work of the Spirit, emphasizing constantly the way in which the Spirit's present work anticipates the Spirit's future work of resurrection. In the present passage, it becomes clear that the Spirit "indwells" God's people in Christ, as the *Shekinah* "indwelt" the tabernacle in the wilderness or the Temple in Jerusalem; so we should not be surprised to discover in the following paragraphs that the Spirit takes the role, within the new wilderness wanderings of the liberated people of God, that in the exodus story was taken by the pillar of cloud and fire. Once again Paul, as a theologian in the strict sense (that is, one who thinks and writes about God), is innovating appropriately from within the Second Temple Jewish tradition. The result, as in a more compressed form in Gal 4:4-7, is that the one God of Jewish monotheism now begins to be known in three usually (though not always) distinct ways. Though Paul does not use the language of "person" to distinguish these three ways, he sets up a universe of discourse within which some such development would ultimately appear necessary.

Here the point is simply this: through the action of the Spirit in the present, those who are in Christ are walking on the road that will lead to the resurrection of the body. Indeed, the more we allow for *Shekinah* and Temple overtones in what Paul is saying, the more a further interesting possibility opens up: that Paul is hinting, as he speaks of the resurrection of the body, of the rebuilding of the Temple. In any case, the same Spirit who will raise Christ's people at the last inspires within them in the present a life that is neither corruptible—it will stand at the judgment (cf. 1 Cor 3:10-17)—nor rebellious, but which conforms to God's will for humankind. Torah is thereby vindicated; the problem of Romans 7 is thereby solved; and, as the rest of the chapter will make clear, the whole new creation is thereby brought into view.

8:5-6. The next pair of verses offer a two-stage explanation of why those who walk according to the Spirit inherit life. The logic works like this: (a) The two categories, walking according to the flesh and the Spirit, are each characterized by a certain manner of thinking. (b) Whereas the thinking that goes with the flesh is death, the thinking that goes with the Spirit is "life and peace" (the NEB and the REB have coalesced the two verses, producing a single complex statement instead of a two-stage one). Paul will then develop this contrast in vv. 7-8 and 9-10, using it as the bridge into the climax and conclusion of the paragraph. Both verses begin with *gar*; it seems to me more likely that both independently explain vv. 1-4, rather than that v. 6 is intended to explain something about v. 5. (The NIV omits both connectives; the NRSV, that in v. 6; the NEB, that in v. 5. If a connection between v. 5 and v. 6 is sought, it may be that Paul is meaning "and the reason I highlight the *thinking* of flesh and Spirit is because. . . .") When the verses are taken together, leading to the point about "life and peace" at the end of v. 6, and the flow of thought of the whole paragraph is kept in mind, then the meaning of the connections becomes apparent. Like a pianist needing to keep the coming climax of the movement in mind through a tricky middle section, it is important to sustain the theological rhythm of these verses in their context rather than treating them, as some translations and commentaries have done, as isolated remarks about what it is like to live according to the flesh and the Spirit.

Instead of "walk," Paul merely says "are": "those who *are* according to the flesh." The NIV and the NRSV both say "live," but the

Greek is simply ὄντες (*ontes*), those who "are." In the second half of v. 5 Paul omits both this and the verb for "think," so that 5*b* simply reads "but those according to the Spirit the things of the Spirit." Verse 6 follows swiftly: the thinking of the flesh is death, but the thinking of the Spirit is life and peace (the death/life contrast throughout the passage, with its echoes in 10:5-11, makes it more certain that these verses are about the true fulfillment of Torah). The Greek (τὸ φρόνημα τῆς σαρκός *to phronēma tēs sarkos* and τὸ φρόνημα τοῦ πνεύματος *to phronēma tou pneumatos*) leaves it open as to whether these expressions refer to the thinking, the thought processes, that are characteristic of flesh and Spirit in themselves and are then, as it were, incarnated in human beings, or whether the "of" is objective, as in the NRSV ("to set the mind on the flesh . . . to set the mind on the Spirit"; the NIV breaks the contrast: "the mind of sinful man . . . the mind controlled by the Spirit"). I incline somewhat to the former view: the flesh, personified, "thinks" in a certain way, which then becomes embodied in particular individuals; so too with the Spirit. Certainly the partial parallel in 8:27 suggests this meaning here too.

The reason why Paul highlights the thought-processes, rather than the outward actions, that are characteristic of flesh and Spirit will emerge as the paragraph develops, but we may draw attention to the way in which, as the argument of the letter unfolds, it is the Christian *mind* that must become the initial, and transformative, locus of renewal (12:2, contrasting with 1:22, 28). As frequently in his thinking about how human beings operate, Paul here envisages *thought* as the key to action; not, however, just the process of ideas through the brain, but in the stronger sense of the settled and focused activity and concentration that characterizes the one state or the other.

The important point here, and the reason why these verses help the overall argument forward, is the contrast of "death" and "life and peace" that characterize the two "thinkings." The contrast of death and life is familiar enough in this argument, and has been so since at least chap. 5; but why (apart from the echo of 5:1) add "peace"? It is not simply that

the phrase "life and peace" carries distant covenantal overtones.[266] The evidence Paul is about to adduce for his assertion that walking, or "being," "according to the Spirit" is the guarantee of "life" is precisely that "flesh-thinking" is at enmity with God, whereas "Spirit-thinking" is in tune with God. At least, that is the implication of the next verses, though this time the entire thought involves an ellipsis, which must now be explained if the paragraph is to yield its complete secret.

8:7-8. What follows offers itself as the further explanation of what has gone before. Verse 7 begins with διότι (*dioti*), which (despite the NRSV's idiosyncratic "for this reason") normally means "because" or "for."[267] What Paul intends to say appears to be: (a) flesh-thinking is death, Spirit-thinking is life and peace; (b) *because* flesh-thinking is hostile to God, (c) whereas Spirit-thinking is at peace with God [thus explaining "peace"]; (d) *and* the Spirit is the souce of resurrection life [thus explaining "life"]; (e) and you, therefore, being indwelt by the Spirit in the present, are assured of resurrection life in the future. What he has done, however, is to foreshorten this train of thought simply to (a) (v. 6), (b) (vv. 7-8), and a combination of (d) and (e) (vv. 9-11). For neither the first nor the last time, he has omitted to make explicit the link in the thought (here [c]) that might have clarified things for those attempting to think his thoughts after him—an ironic reflection on a paragraph one of whose central subtopics is "thinking."

Paul does at least explain stage (b) quite fully. Picking up from 5:10, and rounding off hereby the negative line of thought expounded in chap. 7, he explains that flesh-thinking is hostile to God. Interestingly, his further explanation of this (v. 7*b*, introduced with *gar*, omitted by both the NIV and the NRSV), is that flesh-thinking does not submit to God's law, a point that is further explained on the grounds that it cannot. As chap. 7 has made clear, the "flesh" serves "the law of sin"; however much this may, paradoxically, turn out to be the Torah in another

---

266. "Life and peace" describes the covenant between God and Levi in Mal 2:5. See also the "covenant of peace" in Num 25:12; Isa 54:10; Ezek 34:25; 37:26; Sir 45:24. The prophetic passages in particular are full of overtones that are interesting for Romans 8.

267. The only NT examples of the meaning "therefore" given by BDAG are Acts 13:35; 20:26.

role, at this point "the law of God" is clearly a positive thing to which humans ought to submit, not the quasi-demonic thing some Marcionite schemes of thought have imagined. The law in its full God-given glory is, after all, a spiritual thing, so that there is a mismatch between it and the person who is "fleshly, sold under sin" (7:14 and 8:7 thus belong very closely together). The implication, of course (the omitted stage [c] in the argument), is that Spirit-thinking will now fit Torah perfectly; however counterintuitive this may seem in some theological circles, it fits well with Paul's other statements about Christian fulfillment of Torah (e.g., 2:25-9; 10:4-11; 13:8-10; perhaps also 3:27).

Paul's final and most revealing comment about flesh-thinking (v. 8) is that "those who are in the flesh" are incapable of pleasing God.[268] Despite its prominence in various Pauline passages, the idea that one can actually *please* God, or the Lord, is foreign to much thinking and writing on the apostle, perhaps because it suggests to some the thin end of a wedge that will end in works-righteousness. Paul had no such scruples (see, e.g., 12:2; 14:18; 1 Cor 7:32; 2 Cor 5:9; Eph 5:10; 1 Thess 4:1). Those in the flesh cannot please God; but, by strong and clear implication, those in the Spirit can and do.

8:9-11. Paul clearly believes that his readers are "in the Spirit," no longer "in the flesh." The evidence for this is that the Spirit of God dwells in them; the result is that they are assured of final resurrection. Verse 11 thus gives the complete answer to the question of 7:24, the answer anticipated in 7:25*a*.

That much is clear; this is the main thrust of these three verses. But the way in which Paul has said it is complex, and potentially confusing. Three levels of complexity need to be unraveled for clarity to be attained.

First, Paul switches bewilderingly between describing Christians as being "in the Spirit" and describing the Spirit as being "in them." The latter is what Paul wants to emphasize at this point, using the image of "indwelling" that evokes the idea of the *Shekinah*

dwelling in the wilderness tabernacle and the Jerusalem Temple (cf. 1 Cor 3:16; 6:19, etc.). The formulation "in the Spirit" is more of a technical description, formed ad hoc to contrast with "in the flesh"; nowhere else does Paul make this contrast in exactly this way, though there are pointers in this direction in 2:29; 7:6, and he can speak of Christian thoughts, prayers, and actions as taking place "in the Spirit" (e.g., 9:1; 14:17; 15:16; the contrast of "according to the flesh" and "according to the Spirit," as in 8:5, is found again in Gal 4:29). When speaking thus, the "in" seems to denote a basic condition or situation, rather than having precise locative force. Part of the problem in all these formulations is that Paul's picture of the Christian is not simply the mirror-opposite of his picture of the non-Christian. At one level "Spirit" contrasts with "flesh"; at another, "Spirit," as the indwelling power within the person, contrasts with "sin." At another, the Spirit is doing that which the law could not. And so on. We would be wrong therefore to accuse Paul of inconsistency in his terminology. He is carving out language to say what had not been said before. As long as we allow him to explain where he is going he will not mislead.

Second, the terms he uses to denote the indwelling Spirit move in an initially confusing fashion between "the Spirit," "the Spirit of God," "the Spirit of Christ," and then simply "Christ." This, too, we must assume, is the result of Paul hammering out patterns of thought where none had existed previously. For him, the same Spirit is the Spirit of God and of the Messiah—an interesting indication, we note with a sidelong glance, of the status the Messiah already has in his thinking!—and he can move to and fro in his description according to the particular shade or nuance of the actual point being made.

Third, Paul also shuttles to and fro in his description of Jesus the Messiah himself. As elsewhere, he refers to him as "Messiah" not least in order to stress the solidarity between him and his people. He refers to him as "Jesus" when focusing attention on Jesus himself as a specific individual human being. This, too, enables him to impart to his statements particular nuances and subtleties within the clear overall point being made.

---

268. Paul changes the phrase from "those who are *according to* the flesh" in v. 5, apparently treating the two as identical, despite the distinction he maintains in 2 Cor 10:3 and by implication Gal 2:20; in both of these Paul speaks of being "in the flesh," meaning "still living as a human being this side of the grave," while not conducting his life "according to the flesh." In the present passage the distinction is obliterated: "you are not in the flesh," he says in v. 9.

Verse 9, then, introduces the argument that will lead to the triumphant conclusion of v. 11, making the contrast with vv. 7-8: you, he says (the "you" is plural, placing all his readers in the picture) are not in the flesh, but in the Spirit. The evidence for this is precisely that God's Spirit dwells in them. The nuance of the middle clause of v. 9 is hard to catch, since "if" (NIV) appears too doubtful and "since" (NRSV) too certain. The Greek εἴπερ (eiper) hovers in between these two, meaning something like "if after all" or "if, as is indeed the case"; we may compare its use in 3:30 or 8:17. If it contains a shadow of doubt it does so within a basic affirmation. The doubt, however, is raised in the last clause of the verse, which, being introduced by δέ (de) also implies that the middle clause was more of an affirmation than a question: "but if anyone does not possess the Messiah's Spirit, that person does not belong to him." The equivalence of "being in Christ" and "belonging to Christ" is clear in Gal 3:27-29; these are different ways of saying the same thing, denoting the people of God as redefined around the Messiah. Paul does not at this stage of his argument want to raise serious doubts as to whether some of his readers may, after all, be sham Christians; though it is important for later debates to note that, for him, the idea of a Christian who did not possess the Spirit of Christ was a contradiction in terms. Paul's strong incorporative theology of the church is balanced by an equally strong view of the necessity of each individual member of the community being indwelt by the Spirit. The final clause in v. 9 highlights the fact that the Spirit in question is the Spirit of the Messiah. This enables Paul to draw on all that he has said about the Messiah in previous chapters to make the key point of v. 10.

If the Spirit is the Spirit of the Messiah, then the Messiah himself lives in the Christian. Paul, of course, more regularly speaks of the believer being "in Christ"; this is not interchangeable with "Christ in you," which always refers to the indwelling within believers of that divine presence, variably spoken of as Christ or the Spirit, which empowers them in the present and will transform them in the future (see also Gal 2:20; 4:19; Eph 3:17; Col 1:27). Being "in Christ," as we have seen frequently, particularly in 6:1-14, means that

the Messiah's death and resurrection become true of all his people. Because of the indwelling of the Messiah's Spirit, however, this is no longer seen simply as a matter of status, but of actual power.

Paul's way of saying this in the rest of v. 10 may again appear oblique, but will be clear, yet once more, when the background in 5:21 is kept in mind. "The body is dead because of sin"; in other words, even Christians are subject to the laws of decay and death, still living as they do in "the body of humiliation" (Phil 3:21). This is not in itself intended as a description of something that results from Christ being "in you"; the logic is "if Christ is in you, then (though the body is dead) the Spirit is life." Sin has reigned in death, and since sin has indwelt believers prior to their baptism and receiving of the Spirit death must surely follow. But "grace reigns through righteousness to eternal life"; because of God's covenant faithfulness, revealed in the Messiah's saving death and resurrection, the Spirit gives life the other side of death. Artificial schemes for dividing up Romans (and indeed Paul's thought as a whole), designating the first four chapters as lawcourt theology and the next four as incorporative theology, lead to commentators expressing surprise at the use of "righteousness" here, but in the light of 5:21 there should not only be no surprise but no question as to the word's referent. The Spirit, dwelling within Christians, is the lifegiving power; Paul simply says "is life," to make the contrast with "the body is dead" in the previous clause.[269] And this is so because of God's faithfulness to the covenant, God's own righteousness (other alternatives offered to explain this sudden reference to "righteousness" include "righteous behavior," following from v. 4b, and the righteous status Christians have as a result of God's justifying action). We look back here all the way to Abraham, who in chap. 4 believed precisely in the life-giving power of God upon which the covenant depended, the covenant to which God has now been faithful in Jesus the Messiah. Paul's pithy formulation of all this is a sign not of imprecise thought but of rhetorical power as he hastens on to v. 11. This verse is both the goal of the argument that

---

269. "Spirit" here, as in the NRSV and the REB, is more likely than a reference to the human spirit, as still in most translations, including the NIV. See also Wright, *The Climax of the Covenant*, 202; Fee, *God's Empowering Presence*, 500.

began in 7:1 and the foundation of the still greater argument that will take him through to 8:30.

The point of v. 11 is straightforward, and its inner logic can be spelled out as follows: (a) The Spirit dwells in you; (b) the Spirit is the Spirit of the God who raised Jesus; (c) Jesus is the Messiah, and you belong to him; (d) the God who raised Jesus the Messiah will raise all the Messiah's people, you included. Once again, this sequence of thought has been compressed tightly, almost epigrammatically. As in 4:24, summing up the train of thought at that point, God is referred to as "the one who raised Jesus from the dead," repeated here at once with the significant change of "Christ" for "Jesus"; this can only be explained on the basis that "Jesus" is the individual human being and "Christ" the one who royally represents his people, so that what is true of him is true of them. The key assumption Paul makes is that the raising of Jesus is the act of God, as in 6:4; and the conclusion is of course described at much greater length in 1 Corinthians 15. Jesus the Messiah is the firstfruits (cf. too Col 1:18), the first to rise from the dead; all those who belong to him will be raised as he was raised. This final resurrection will, like that of Jesus, be the act of none other than God. In 6:4 Paul said that Jesus was raised by the *glory* of the Father; in 1 Cor 6:14 he says that God raised the Lord, and will also raise us, by the divine *power*; here he says that God will accomplish this by his *Spirit*. A case has recently been made for the strongly attested variant reading, that God will give life to your mortal bodies *because of*, rather than "through," the indwelling Spirit (cf. NRSV margin); but the argument of the chapter seems to me to fit well with the thought that the Spirit is God's agent in the final resurrection, not merely God's reason for accomplishing this great act of new creation.[270]

This, then, is the answer to 7:24*b*, no longer as a bare assertion of faith (as, by itself, is 7:25*a*), but as a tight theological argument. Who will deliver from this body of death? Who, in other words, will give life to the dead? The law, though holy, just and good, cannot do this; God will, through Christ and by the Spirit and will thereby do what the law held out (Lev 18:5; Deut 30:15-20) but could not perform.

At the end of this central passage we may reflect on the nature of Paul's achievement so far. This is the heart of his argument for assurance (those whom God justified, them God also glorified). For the Jew—for Paul himself prior to his conversion—the basis of assurance was membership in the covenant, whose outward badges were circumcision and Torah. The story of the exodus formed the backdrop to the Jewish expectation that the covenant God would once again act within history to deliver Israel. Paul has retold the story of the exodus, the freedom story, demonstrating that the Egypt of sin and death has been decisively defeated through the death of the Messiah, and that the Spirit is now leading God's redeemed people to their promised inheritance. Baptism has marked out God's renewed people; the Spirit is now "the one thing that distinguishes those who are Christ's from those who are not."[271] The sign of the Spirit's work is first and foremost faith (1 Cor 12:3) and indeed faithfulness; and the fruit of the Spirit's work is the final resurrection. Thus is the path from justification to glorification, from "passover" to the "promised land," laid out in this passage. Paul will now develop this picture, drawing on several interlocking images from the exodus story, and widening the angle of vision to include, not just humans, but the whole created order.

---

270. See Fee, *God's Empowering Presence*, 543. The usual reading seems to me more probable in the light of the argument of the passage as a whole. The difference between the two is not, however, enormous.

271. Fee, *God's Empowering Presence*, 553.

REFLECTIONS

1. It is important to see this long and central argument (7:1–8:11) as a whole, before drawing small-scale lessons from its different parts, which by themselves could easily be taken in senses somewhat different from those which the overall context suggests. The passage goes to the heart of the self-identity of the people of God. Israel at its best looked to Torah as the basis of its status as the chosen people of the creator God; Paul has insisted that Torah informs Israel in no uncertain terms that it is instead simply a subset of the people of Adam, in slavery to sin and facing death. Where then can assurance be found? Only in the death of the Messiah and the life-giving presence and power of the Spirit. Insofar as the church remains the people whose family story goes back to Abraham—and Paul would insist that this is a non-negotiable part of being God's people—this story must be told again and again as part of the foundation of who the church is. It is not, in other words, simply a story about how ethnic Israel faced a particular problem and how this problem was overcome—a story that might seem somewhat remote and irrelevant to Christian living in any subsequent century, let alone two millennia later. Like the story of Jesus itself, it is the story of how God's people, the church's forebears, had to pass through the anguish of Romans 7 in order that, through the Messiah and the Spirit, new hope might be born.

2. Within the overarching theme of assurance, the central character in the story of 7:1–8:11 is of course Torah. This is Paul's classic defense of Torah against all the charges that might be, and perhaps were being, laid against it. Torah, he insists, is holy and just and good; it is not responsible either for sin or for death. Indeed, it just goes to show the exceeding wickedness of sin itself that it can as it were make its nest in Torah, twisting Torah so that it becomes a dark and sinister replica of itself, condemning rather than giving life. When God acts in Christ and by the Spirit to give life to those indwelt by the Spirit of Christ, Torah looks on with, as we might say, a sigh of relief and approval: this was, after all, what it had intended all along. It should be clear from this, despite those whom C. E. B. Cranfield memorably called "Marcionites and semi-, crypto-, and unwitting, Marcionites,"[272] that Paul solidly and emphatically reaffirmed the goodness and God-givenness of Torah. Any suggestion that law in general, or the law in particular, were or are shabby, second-rate, primitive, destructive of true religion, and therefore to be abolished, set aside, or treated as irrelevant in the bright new day of a law-free faith, must be ruled out. Paul's theology contains many apparent paradoxes, and this point must be held in careful tension with the next one; but nothing is gained, certainly not in understanding of Paul or attempting to live and work in the light of his writings, by the shallow rejection of Torah.

3. Having said all that, we must also insist, against some current attempts to reinstate or rehabilitate Torah either within the church or (for instance within contemporary Israeli society) in wider social and political contexts, that the Torah is by itself weak. Not only can it not give the life to which it points; it accents, and indeed accentuates, the Adamic condition, the sinful and death-bound position, of those who embrace it. There is always a danger within the church that some Christians, anxious about Marcionism of whatever variety, and eager to insist that the whole Bible is the Word of God, will fail to heed the words of Jesus and Paul and will attempt to live by Torah in matters (for instance) such as the death penalty. There are some Christians today, despite the letter to the Hebrews and indeed the entire temple-based christology and pneumatology of the New Testament, who seem to believe that the rebuilding of the Temple in Jerusalem could still be God's will; equally, there are some who, no doubt with considerable inconsistency (I do not hear them calling for a reappropriation of patriarchal marriage customs, for example), want to see the Jewish law as in some way(s) normative for Christians today. This is to make the mistake of treating revelation in a flat, dehistoricized fashion. As Paul's own writings make abundantly clear, what we find in Scripture is above all a *narrative:* the great story of God and the world, and of God's people as the people of God *for* that world. Torah stands as the headline over that story from the time of Moses to the time of the Messiah (Galatians 3 is the

272. Cranfield, *Romans*, 867.

classic exposition of this); but the story, which started before the giving of Torah, moves on beyond the time when Torah was the determining factor, *and Torah itself celebrates this fact.* To say that its primary role was acted out in an earlier act in the drama than that in which Paul believed himself to be living is not to diminish its God-given role, but rather to celebrate it. To say that it goes on applying equally in the era of Christ and the Spirit is to ignore not only what Jesus and Paul said at several points but, if anything more important, the story Jesus enacted in his life, death, and resurrection, the story Paul took as his starting-point. This is not, of course, to deny what is said in 10:5-11 and 13:8-10 (on which see below).

4. On the day I sat down to write this part of the commentary I received a letter from a parish priest, asking whether the end of Romans 7 might not reflect Paul's sense of standing vis-à-vis his kinsfolk according to the flesh much as Moses had stood in Exodus 33, seeing Israel as a whole in rebellion against God and agonizing over what could be done. This, I believe, reflects a true insight, not so much as exegesis of Romans 7 but as anticipation of Romans 9. As we have had occasion to observe, the argument of Romans proceeds in a series of long spiraling loops, and Romans 7 does indeed provide part of the foundation for what Paul will say in Romans 9, whose introduction evokes exactly the picture, proposed by my correspondent, of Moses standing between God and the rebel people. However, there may be something more to say here as well. In Galatians 1 Paul describes himself as being, in his pre-Christian days, "exceedingly zealous for the traditions of my fathers." We know that this kind of "zeal" could be described as zeal for God (cf. Acts 22:3; Rom 10:2) or for the law (Acts 21:20). When Paul wrote in Romans 7 of delighting in God's law, but observing in his "members" another law bringing about death, I think it is at least worth enquiring whether he had in mind the way in which the zeal for Torah, which he and others had been exhibiting, was not only bringing death to those they opposed but also pulling down death on themselves, driving them closer toward the brink of a war with Rome that they could not possibly win. If this is in any way a valid reflection, it offers a series of concentric circles of application, relating not only to Middle Eastern politics in the twentieth as in the first century, but also to many other areas of conflict around the world, where zeal for ancestral traditions, which may or may not have been good in their way and place, leads to idolatrous behavior that is as destructive for the perpetrators as for the victims. If Romans 7 could help the church to speak more clearly on such issues we should be grateful.

5. Though Paul is not, in Romans 7, writing first and foremost about the plight of the whole human race, but only about that of Israel under Torah, it is nevertheless possible to work outward from what he says to a more general analysis of the puzzle of human moral inability. This, after all, is already hinted at in his (probably deliberate) sidelong allusions to the tradition, from Aristotle to Epictetus and beyond, that spoke of approving the better course but practicing the worse. If the point of Paul's analysis is that Israel is like everyone else only more so, it is perfectly legitimate to reason back from that to what must be true of "everyone else." When we do this we find, consonant with Rom 2:1-16, that even when the human race embraces and affirms some moral code, or even some moral principle, living up to it proves impossible. This does not mean that the code or the principle was wrong or misleading; just that there is a twist within the human race, as it presently finds itself, which distorts the best intentions, and exposes self-interest at the heart of apparent altruism. A glance at political and religious leadership in the Western world (to point the finger only at my own part of the human race) would offer many examples.

Someone is bound to respond to this by saying that the same is true of Christians also. I am bound to agree. Does this not call into question my whole exegesis? Is the passage not after all about Christian existence as well as anyone else's? No. The

Christian is not "under law," and is not "sold under sin." There is a great irony here. In the 1960s many people within the church, as well as outside it, trumpeted loudly that the old moral codes (they often meant the sexual ones, but it applied more widely as well) were no longer relevant, since we now knew that one should live simply by love, not by law. The moral chaos that has resulted, in mainline churches in particular, over the last generation has been pitiful to behold. When people from within that same tradition now say that Christians are no better than anyone else, it seems to me somewhat unfair to hold up as the prime evidence those parts of the church that have exhibited major disloyalty to traditional Christian teaching over many years. Why not look at the many other parts of the worldwide church where Christians today can still be spoken of, as the second-century apologists spoke of their comrades, as people in whom a different way of being human, a way of holiness and joyful self-sacrificial love, was truly being modeled? Yes, it is also true (so I am told) that the greatest saints remain conscious of depths of rebellion and unholiness within them that will not be rooted out until death itself (not even, according to some traditions, until some time after that). But there is such a thing as Christian holiness, however flawed it may still be; and these flaws, and the tensions that result, are not the same as those described in Romans 7.

6. The villain in the drama is Sin. Paul is capable of speaking of Satan, but he does so sparingly (only ten times in the entire Pauline corpus, and only once [16:20] in Romans). But when he speaks of Sin, he means not simply human acts of rebellion or lawbreaking, but a personified force at work in the world and in humans. He speaks of it nineteen times between 7:1 and 8:11, building on the seven occurrences in 5:12-21 and the sixteen in chap. 6. (To get some idea of the scale of this treatment, there are four references in Romans prior to 5:12, two after 8:11, and only seventeen in the whole of the rest of the Paulines.) Writing after a century in which many Western Christians have regarded it as something of a social or even liturgical faux pas to speak of sin, let alone Sin, it is important to stress that our soft-pedaling of the New Testament's analysis of the depths of the human problem has done no service to either the church or the world. Of course, there are healthy and unhealthy ways of speaking about sin. The church has often allowed itself to lapse into a dualism in which certain parts of life are labeled "sinful," in order to create an artificial sphere of "holiness" that is, in fact, no more than an imposed social convention. But to say that there is such a thing as a shallow diagnosis of the human condition is not to deny that there might be a deeper one. Politicians and the media used to pretend that a little more social progress, a little more Western-style democracy in the world, would solve the ills that were still visible. We now know that this was a lie: not only is the world not a significantly better place for having more democracy, but the Western powers themselves have been shown up as riddled with corruption, selfishness masked as public service, and sexual and financial scandals. Cynicism about the political process and those who run it has become endemic. It is time once again to hold out the analysis of human behavior offered in the New Testament. There is such a thing as Sin, which is more than the sum total of human wrongdoing. It is powerful, and this power infects even those with the best intentions. If it could make even the holy Torah its base of operations, how much more the muddled intentions of well-meaning do-gooders.

7. Such an analysis, comes the response, is so gloomy. It will produce a human existence dogged by guilt, paranoia, and self-hatred. Nonsense. With the diagnosis goes the remedy. Not surprisingly, of course, those who dislike the Pauline analysis of sin routinely despise the Pauline remedy—namely, the cross and the Spirit. But this double answer to the problem remains foundational to genuine Christian understanding and indeed, of course, to genuine Christian living. It is, to be sure, a deep mystery that on the cross God "condemned sin" in the flesh of the Messiah. But this stands at the heart of Christianity, offering the way forward through the Red Sea, leaving behind the Egypt of sin and death, and pointing onward to the land of promise. The victory of the cross over the principalities and powers, with sin and death as their chief, provides a solidly grounded freedom from guilt in the present; there is no need for anyone to collapse into that guilty self-absorption, which passes so quickly into self-hatred, which the older liberal denials of sin and guilt were so desperate to avoid. God's love has proved itself stronger than all the powers of darkness. Nor is there any need to fear for the future; the whole point of Romans 8 is to substantiate the great opening shout: there is therefore now no condemnation for those in Christ Jesus. This truth, which always appears surprising even to those who have known it for years, needs constant reiteration in preaching, liturgy, and pastoral counseling. No techniques in these areas can substitute for the truth. But what is needed equally urgently in today's world is the application of these truths to the wider world that has neither diagnosis nor remedy for the huge and horrible problems it faces. Since Paul goes on in Romans to show how God applies the victory of the cross to the liberation of the entire cosmos, is it too much to hope that this victory might have its effect in the realm of human society, government, and law as well as in the hearts and lives of individuals?

8. This brings us to the subject of Christian assurance. Once again, caricatures abound, which put many off the truth itself. Christian assurance is not self-assurance. Some self-assured people happen also to be Christians, and some Christians use their Christian assurance to give off an air of self-assurance; but distortions do not invalidate the reality. In some Christian traditions it has been customary, as a sign of humility, to question whether one can ever know in the present life that one is truly saved, just as in some others it has been customary, as a sign of sound doctrine, to proclaim one's certainty on every occasion. It is perhaps significant that the greatest New Testament step-by-step argument for Christian assurance, of which this passage forms the heart, emerges from the deepest wrestling and struggling. It comes as the answer to the cry of despair that, though Paul places it in the mouth of the Torah-loving Jew, awakens echoes across every continent and in every century. *Who shall deliver me?* God will, through Jesus Christ and by the Spirit. Christian assurance is then built up, as in the argument of 8:1-11, on the basis of what has happened in Jesus the Messiah, and on the solid and unbreakable link between the Messiah and his people, of which faith is the sign, baptism the symbol, and the Spirit the personal guarantee.

9. This passage sees the start of one of Paul's greatest descriptions of the indwelling of the Spirit. "If anyone does not have the Spirit of Christ, that person does not belong to him." There is no such thing in New Testament theology as a Christian who does not have the Spirit dwelling in him or her. Paul will speak in the next passage of some of the signs of that indwelling—which are by no means as narrowly defined, or as obvious, as some teachings have made out. For the moment it must be noted that there can be no split-level Christianity, no division between those who have the Spirit and those who do not. This must challenge both those whose more spectacular manifestations of the Spirit's presence tempt them to despise those with the less spectacular, and those who are in fact unwitting passengers in the church, who think of themselves as Christians but in whose heart and life the Spirit has not taken up residence, and who are still therefore living "according to the flesh," whatever form that may take. Christian assurance is always balanced by warnings against complacency. And, though this is not the main point of the paragraph, we cannot ignore the way in which the presence of the Spirit produces what we would call "ethical" consequences. Reading between the lines of Paul's compressed argument in vv. 5-8, it is clear that a person in whom the Spirit dwells will begin to be at peace with God; they will submit to God's will; they will begin to live in a way that is actually pleasing to God. Paul will spell out later more of what this looks like. He has already spoken of the love for God that the

Spirit inspires in the believer (5:5). For the moment it is important to draw attention to the fact that the presence of the Spirit will make a difference not just to how someone feels, but to how they live.

10. As with Romans as a whole, so with this central passage: it is basically about God. The God of whom Paul speaks here is mysterious, as all true speech about God must acknowledge. The purposes of this God, in which the strange work of Torah described in 7:7-25 finds apparently a central place, are darker and more unexpected than either the devout Jew or the serious pagan, or for that matter most Christians, have allowed for. There is more to learn down this line, as chaps. 9–11 will disclose. But at the same time this one true God is now made known in two complementary and interlocking ways, which call not for intellectual recognition so much as for worship and love. This God has been made known in the sending of the Son, not so that God could remain distant and detached while someone else did the difficult and painful work, but precisely so that God might be personally and intimately present at the point where sin and death had been heaped up to their full height. To imagine for a moment a world in which incarnation and cross had never happened and could never happen—this may be a hard task for a Christian, but it is a salutary one—is to imagine a world in which the rumor of incarnate love would either never be heard or be heard as a dream that was daily defied by waking reality. Without the cross of God's Son, the Scriptures of Israel would indeed speak of a God who embodied covenant love, a God who rescued slaves so that they might be a people of praise for the sake of the world. But it would remain a private story, incredible to the outside world and increasingly puzzling within an embattled and beleaguered Israel. Without the cross, the world at large would continue to believe that might and money were the things that mattered, that sexual pleasure was the highest human good, and that killing people was the way to get things done. Alas, in much of the world, even in much of the would-be Christian world, these things are still implicitly believed. It is time for a genuinely incarnational theology to be let loose again upon the world, so that the rumor may become a report, and the report a life-changing reality. And for that to happen it is vital to grasp as well that the God who sent the Son now sends the Spirit of the Son. A fully Trinitarian theology, calling forth worship, love, and service, is the only possible basis for genuine gospel work that will bring life and hope to the world.

ROMANS 8:12-30, THE INHERITANCE GUARANTEED

OVERVIEW

The stage is now set for the final act of the drama that Paul has been playing out since the start of chap. 5. "Being therefore justified by faith . . . we rejoice in the hope of the glory of God"; we even rejoice in our sufferings, and our hope "does not make us ashamed, because the love of God has been poured out in our hearts through the Holy Spirit who has been given to us" (5:1-5). Spirit; hope; suffering; glory; love: these are the themes, stated in advance at the head of the argument, to which Paul has now worked his way back.

Thus 8:12-30 offers a celebratory description of present Christian existence, rooted in God's past action in Jesus Christ, assured of God's future action for Christ's people and for the whole world, and sustained in the present by the Spirit. It is the conclusion of the argument for Christian assurance, for the belief that those whom God justified God also glorified (8:30). It is also, as we have noted in advance at various places, the moment when the exodus theme, latent under so much of the argument of chaps. 5–8, comes out fully into the open: what God did for Israel at the Red Sea, what God did for Jesus at Easter, God will do not only for those who are in Christ but for the whole created order. This passage is also, therefore, the completion of the basic statement about God's righteousness, God's saving justice, God's covenant faithfulness. The covenant was established in order to put the world to rights; now we see, on the large scale, how this is to happen. God has been faithful not just to the Abrahamic promises but to the whole creation.

As we should expect, God's faithfulness is revealed in the gospel of Jesus Christ. The death and resurrection of Jesus Christ, the Son of God, are the assumed subtext of this entire section, opening out to include the dying and rising, and the adoption as God's sons and daughters, of all those "in Christ." The statement in 8:29 that God's purpose was to make Jesus the firstborn among many siblings is in fact a concise summary of these nineteen verses: "adoption" or "sonship" (the nongender-specific alternatives "siblinghood" and "son-and-daughtership" are out of the question) is a major theme, running through vv. 14, 15, 16, 17, 19, and 21 before being triumphantly summed up in v. 29.

When we put together the themes of new exodus and Christian adoption, as in this passage, they generate the theme of inheritance, which belongs closely in this passage with that of glory. In Paul's scriptural background, the "inheritance" was, of course, the land, promised to Abraham and his family, and promised again to the Israelites after the exile (see, e.g., Gen 15:7; Num 34:2; Isa 57:13; 60:21; Ezek 36:12; cf. Pss 25:13; 37:9). Now, in line with

4:13, it has become the whole world, the whole creation made by the one creator God, itself renewed and redeemed. Part of the meaning of "glory" in this passage—the glory that has been promised to all God's children in Christ—is precisely that they are to receive this inheritance. And this inheritance means that those in Christ are forever indebted to the God who promises and gives this inheritance. This, indeed, is the note on which the passage opens.

But the beating heart of the whole sequence of thought is found in Paul's description of the prayer that the Spirit inspires within God's children (vv. 15-16, 26-27). The "Abba" prayer that echoes Jesus' own prayer, and provides the clearest evidence that one is indeed a child of God, is balanced by the "inarticulate groaning" in which the Spirit calls to the Father from within the hearts of Christians, expressing the longing of all creation for full redemption. In this, too, those in Christ are conformed to the image of the Son (8:29), standing between the pain of the world and the love of God, discovering that their own sufferings, including the ones they cannot begin to comprehend, are somehow themselves becoming the vessels and vehicles of God's redeeming love.

The passage, filled as it thus is with rich themes about the Christians' status, prayer, and future hope, follows a clear line of thought that could be summed up as "debtors to God's grace." We are in debt to God, because, being God's children, we are also God's heirs (8:12-17). We are fellow heirs with Christ, since, sharing his sufferings, we also share his glory (8:17-27; v. 17 is the bridge between the two movements in the long paragraph). God is utterly and unalterably purposed to bring all those in Christ to their glorious Christ-shaped inheritance (8:28-30).

Romans 8:12-17, Led by the Spirit

COMMENTARY

Once again it is important, reading a complex passage like this, not to get bogged down in detail but to keep in mind the overall direction and underlying argument. Paul's point is to draw the conclusion (ἄρα οὖν *ara oun*,

"so then," is a quite emphatic transition) that arises not only from 7:1–8:11, but also from chaps. 5 and 6: the basic truth about Christians is that they are debtors to God, the God who has made them children and heirs. Precisely because this is the argument for assurance, it is framed as an appeal to gratitude.

8:12-13. Following a habit that the reader of Romans is by now used to, Paul never actually finishes the sentence he begins. "We are debtors," he says—but breaks off to say what his readers are *not* indebted to, leaving them to work out from the way the argument proceeds who they are in fact indebted to. Paul works back there quite quickly, using the flesh/spirit contrast of vv. 12-13, repeated here from vv. 5-9, as the springboard to speaking of Christians as God's children and hence heirs; so the basic import of v. 12*a* is not lost. (The NEB flattens out the paragraph opening: "It follows, my friends, that our lower nature has no claim upon us"; the sense of an unresolved harmony, driving the reader forward to the gift and promise of God, is lost.)

First, though, Paul will warn against any going back to the former way of life. Just as in 8:9 he could raise the question as to whether some of his hearers did not in fact possess the Spirit, and hence did not after all belong to the Messiah, so now he warns against continuing to live "according to the flesh." This is not, as some would have it today, a lapse into dualism, a rejection of the God-given body and all its possibilities.[273] It is a recognition that the present body, corruptible and heading for death, is not all it might be and not all it will be in the resurrection, and that to use its possibilities and potentialities as the yardstick for what one ought to be doing is to take orders from that which will turn to dust, and so to come back again under the tyranny of death. "We are indebted, not to the flesh; live that way, and you will die."

The alternative is to see the death-bound inclinations of the present body for what they are, and to anticipate the verdict of the grave by putting them to death here and now. (The NIV rightly interprets the phrase "the deeds of the body" as the *mis*deeds of the body; Paul obviously does not want Christians to do nothing at all—the body, after all, is to be the means of grateful service to God, 12:1.) As

in Col 3:5-11, which explains Paul's meaning in more detail, he sees that there are styles of behavior that, like weeds left to grow unchecked, have the capacity to take over the garden and choke all the flowers. There is only one way with such things: they must be uprooted, killed off. This is, of course, impossible for those who are still "in the flesh"; but those who are led by the Spirit will find that the Spirit's inner agency enables them, if they will, to say "no" to the practices that carry the smell of death with them.

8:14. The γάρ (*gar*) with which v. 14 is linked to what precedes is best understood as explaining not only why this Spirit-led action of killing off "the deeds of the body" leads to life, but also the suppressed statement of that to which, or rather the one to whom, Christians are indebted. "Mortification leads to life because the Spirit that enables it also assures us of our divine adoption"; and also "We are indebted [to God], for, being led by the Spirit, we are God's children [and so God's heirs]." There may also be a further logical connection, depending on the scriptural context, not least the exodus narrative; it is because the people were God's children that holiness was enjoined upon them (see Deut 14:1; cf. Isa 1:2).

It is those who are "led by the Spirit" to whom this status of divine adoption is given. The image here is taken from the wilderness wanderings of Israel, led by the pillar of cloud and fire (Exod 13:21-22; cf. Exod 14:19, 24; 40:38; Num 9:15-23; 10:34; 14:14; Deut 1:33; Neh 9:12, 19; Pss 78:14; 105:39).[274] Those symbols of God's powerful presence are here replaced, as we might have guessed from the "indwelling" theme in 8:9-11, by the Spirit, who now does for God's people that which the tabernacling presence of God did in the wilderness, assuring them of divine adoption and leading them forward to their inheritance. The idea of Christians as God's sons and daughters is rooted in the same exodus narrative, again reapplied in the prophets (Exod 4:22; cf. Isa 1:2; Hos 1:10; 11:1). As in Gal 4:1-7, the God who sends the Son now

---

273. Paul once again moves to and fro between "flesh" and "body," though his regular usage is to treat "flesh" as entirely negative and "body" as the locus both of present possible sin and of present commanded holiness (12:1), and above all as that which will be redeemed in the resurrection (8:11). It is "the *deeds* of the body," not the body itself, that are to be abandoned. "Flesh and blood cannot inherit God's kingdom" (1 Cor 15:50), but the body can and will.

274. De la Potterie, "Le chrétien conduit par l'Esprit dans son cheminement eschatologique (Rom 8,14)," 225, has shown that references to the story of Israel's being "led" through the wilderness are frequently found in conjunction, as here, with the theme of Israel as God's son or of God as Israel's father. See Deut 8:2, 5; 32:6, 12; Isa 63:14-16; Jer 3:14, 19; 31:8-9; Wis 14:3.

sends the Spirit of the Son in order to adopt as sons and daughters all those in whom the Spirit dwells, or (as here, still within the exodus imagery) those who are led by the Spirit.

8:15. The exodus context gives depth, too, to the comment that follows. We did not receive, says Paul, a spirit of slavery; that would lead us back again into fear. In other words, the pillar of cloud and fire is not leading you back to Egypt. Having come to know God, or rather to be known by God, he says in the parallel passage in Gal 4:8-11, how can you embrace what is simply a new form of slavery? No: the Spirit you have received, precisely because it is the Spirit of Jesus, the Son, is the Spirit of sonship, of adoption.

There is a problem of punctuation to be addressed here. The last six words of v. 15 (ἐν ᾧ κράζομεν αββα ὁ πατήρ *en hō krazomen abba ho patēr*) could go with what precedes, as in the KJV ("Ye have received the Spirit of adoption, whereby we cry, Abba, Father"; see also the REB). Although the NIV treats these six words as a separate sentence, they function more in relation to what precedes than to what follows ("And by him we cry, 'Abba, Father' "). Or they could go with what follows, as in the NRSV ("you have received a spirit of adoption. When we cry, 'Abba! Father!' it is that very Spirit bearing witness with our spirit that we are children of God"). The issue is finely balanced, and not very much hangs on it; Paul clearly believes that it is by the Spirit that Christians learn from the heart to call God Father, and he clearly believes also that the Spirit, in doing this, bears witness with us that we are God's children. The NEB is perhaps the most helpful, allowing the thought to flow more seamlessly forward: "a Spirit that makes us sons, enabling us to cry 'Abba! Father!' In that cry the Spirit of God joins with our spirit in testifying. . . ."

More important than the punctuation is Paul's assumption, here and in Gal 4:6, that Christians will find themselves prompted by the Spirit to call God "Father," and to use the Aramaic word that, according to Mark 14:36, Jesus himself used in his prayer in Gethsemane (and, by implication, at other times as well). Paul's addressees were basically Greek speakers, even in Rome, where a sizable portion of the population spoke Greek rather than Latin; but this Aramaic term was clearly known as a regular form of address to God. This may imply that the Lord's Prayer, too, was known in Aramaic, but what matters above all is the sense, which Paul can presume throughout the church of whatever language, that God was known in an intimate, familial relationship for which this term, used by adults as well as children but still tender and personal, was entirely appropriate. It was a way of making one's own all the exodus promises of the Scriptures, of calling upon the God of Abraham, Isaac, and Jacob for deliverance. It was a way, above all, of making Jesus' prayers one's own, and hence of sharing the sonship of Jesus.[275] It was a way of expressing from the heart something at the very center of the gospel: that in Jesus the Messiah, the Son of God, the covenant faithfulness of God had been revealed for the salvation of all who believe (see 1:3-4, 16-17).

8:16. The result of this work of the Spirit, leading through the wilderness and inspiring the cry of "Abba," is that our own human spirit is assured that we are God's children. Throughout the passage some have questioned which uses of "spirit" refer to the Holy Spirit and which to the human spirit that each person has; some, for instance, have seen the human spirit rather than God's Spirit in 8:10, though that is increasingly a rare position. But here, as in 1 Cor 2:11, there is no question. The Spirit's very own self comes alongside our human spirit to bear witness that we are God's children.

8:17. This is the fulcrum about which the whole discourse now pivots. Once Paul has established that all those in Christ and indwelt by the Spirit are "children of God," the end of the argument is in sight: If we are God's children, we are also God's heirs. This is the real reason why he implied that Christians were indebted to God (8:12), and it indicates the substance of the paragraph to come. Paul quickly explains in more detail what it means to be God's heirs: It means that one is a fellow heir with the Messiah. As Christians have shared his prayer, as a symptom of their sharing in his sonship, so they will share also in his inheritance. If he is to be Lord of the world, ruling over it with

275. On sharing the prayer of Jesus see N. T. Wright, "The Lord's Prayer as a Paradigm of Christian Prayer," in *Into God's Presence: Prayer in the New Testament*, ed. R. L. Longenecker (Grand Rapids: Eerdmans, 2001) 132-54.

sovereign and saving love, they are to share that rule, bringing redemption to the world that longs for it (cf. 1 Cor 6:2-3; Paul takes this idea for granted, strange though it may be to us, and assumes that his hearers do so too).

But, as Jesus himself solemnly warned, there is a cost involved (see Mark 8:34-38). The road to the inheritance, the path to glory (the two are now, at last, seen to be more or less synonymous) lies along the road of suffering.

Romans 8:18-30, The Renewal of All Things

COMMENTARY

Paul has now reached the point he mentioned in the introduction to the whole section (5:3-5): suffering is itself a cause of celebration, because it produces patience, character, and a hope that does not leave one ashamed, because the love of God has flooded the heart through the Spirit. So here the present suffering—Paul does not at this point say what this suffering consisted of, but 8:35-39 gives several suggestions—leads to patience and hope (vv. 18, 23-24) for those in whom the love of God is present (8:28). And, just as one might have gathered from the context and layout of chap. 5, and indeed from the careful christological base of the whole argument from that point to this, the aim of it all is that the Christian should be "conformed to the image of God's Son" (8:29); or, as he says in 8:17*b*, "provided that we suffer with him so that we may also be glorified with him." Glory—the splendid reign over the world for which the human race was designed from the beginning, and the splendid form of human existence that will be appropriate for that role—was lost through sin, but regained through the Messiah in his resurrection (cf. 6:4). That which is true of him is, and will be, true of his people, and Paul will now show the route by which they must travel for this to be true of them in fact.

8:18. By way of explanation of his cryptic opening statement in 8:17 (the connective is *gar*, omitted in the NIV and the NRSV), Paul launches the substance of this paragraph with a somewhat expanded declaration of where his calculations about the future have taken him ("I consider" in the NIV and the NRSV translates λογίζομαι [*logizomai*], the same bookkeeping metaphor as was used in 3:28; 6:11). This is not merely a feeling or a private opinion: It is something Paul has thought through. It fits together logically. The

main point, echoing 2 Cor 4:17, is that the glory that is to be revealed will far outweigh the sufferings that have to be endured in the present. The idea that, because Christians are "in Christ," the true life is already present, but hidden, and waiting to be revealed when Christ is finally revealed in glory, is familiar elsewhere in Paul (e.g., Col 3:1-4). Paul's wording here, though, is slightly unexpected: he speaks of "the glory that is to be revealed *toward* us, or *into* us (εἰς ἡμᾶς *eis hēmas*), implying not merely that we are to be shown a vision of glory (as the NRSV implies), nor simply that a glory will appear within us (as the NIV implies), but that the future revelation will bestow glory upon us, from above, as a gift. The way Paul now justifies this opening statement is to describe that future glory, and the present situation of waiting for it, in order to explain both his calculation and the present in-between situation both of creation and of the Christian—and, we might even say, of God.

8:19-21. The first stage of this explanation focuses on something at which Paul has hardly hinted up until now, and hardly mentions anywhere else in his writings, but which he has clearly thought out carefully and intends not just to mention but to highlight at this dramatic stage of the argument. The reason why present suffering cannot compare with the coming glory is because the whole creation is on tiptoe with excitement, waiting for God's children to be revealed as who they really are. Suddenly we have turned a corner. Whereas, up until now, it might have been possible to think that Paul was simply talking about God's salvation in relation to human beings, from here on it is clear that the entire cosmos is in view. Nor is this a strange oddity, bolted on to the outside of his theology, or of the argument of Romans, as though it were simply a bit of undigested Jewish apocalyptic speculation thrown in here for good measure. No: it is part of the revelation of God's righteousness, that covenant faithfulness that always aimed at putting the whole world to rights. This is why, as we saw in 4:13, Paul declared that God's promise to Abraham had the whole world in view.

Paul could hardly express the longing of creation more dramatically. Literally, he writes, "For the eager expectation of the creation eagerly awaits the revelation of the children of God," an obvious pleonasm (use of extra or redundant words for effect) that makes its own point. The whole creation—sun, moon, sea, sky, birds, animals, plants—is longing for the time when God's people will be revealed as God's glorious human agents, set in authority over the world. But why? Why should creation be so eager for this? And how does Paul know such a thing?

He answers by explaining the present state of creation, drawing on Genesis 3 and other Jewish traditions. Creation itself is in bondage, in slavery, and needs to have its own exodus. It has been "subjected to futility," not deliberately (it did not rebel as humankind rebelled), but because God subjected it to corruption and decay, creation's equivalent of slavery in Egypt ("the slavery which consists in corruption," v. 21). God did this precisely in order that creation might point forward to the new world that is to be, in which its beauty and power will be enhanced and its corruptibility and futility will be done away. And, if one dare put it like this, as God sent Jesus to rescue the human race, so God will send Jesus' younger siblings, in the power of the Spirit, to rescue the whole created order, to bring that justice and peace for which the whole creation yearns. (This cannot be reduced to the old liberal Protestant "social gospel"—from which the resurrection, which Paul here presupposes, was usually bracketed out.)

The basis of Paul's belief here must be a combination of two things: the biblical promise of new heavens and new earth (Isa 65:17; 66:22), and the creation story in which human beings, made in God's image, are appointed as God's steward over creation. Putting the picture together, in the light of the observable way in which the created order is out of joint, and the clear biblical

and experiential belief that the human race as a whole is in rebellion against God, Paul, in company with many other Jews, saw the two as intimately related. After the fall, the earth produced thorns and thistles. Humans continued to abuse their environment, so that one of the reasons why God sent Israel into exile, according to the Scriptures, was so that the land could at last enjoy its sabbaths (Lev 26:34-43 [cf. 25:2-5]; 2 Chr 36:21). But the answer to the problem was not (as in some New Age theories) that humans should keep their hands off creation, should perhaps be removed from the planet altogether so as not to spoil it any further. The answer, if the creator is to be true to the original purpose, is for humans to be redeemed, to take their place at last as God's imagebearers, the wise steward they were always meant to be. Paul sees that this purpose has already been accomplished in principle in the resurrection of Jesus, and that it will be accomplished fully when all those in Christ are raised and together set in saving authority over the world (see 1 Cor 15:20-28). That is why, Paul says, creation is now waiting with eager longing.

That for which creation is longing is not, then, that it might be "brought into the glorious freedom of the children of God" (NIV) or might "obtain" the same glorious freedom that those in Christ will have (RSV, NRSV). The closing words of v. 21 (lit., "unto the freedom of the glory of the children of God") could be intended to be run together like that; Greek often expresses adjectival relations through genitives. But here, in the light of the previous verses, the thought seems to be not that creation and Christians will simply all be free and glorious in the same way, together, but that the freedom for which creation longs, and which it will be liberated into, is the freedom *that comes about through the glorification of the children of God.* Paul never says that creation itself will have "glory." It will have freedom *because* God's children have glory; indeed, their glory will consist quite specifically in this, that they will be God's agents in bringing the wise, healing, restorative divine justice to the whole created order.

8:22-27. By way of yet further explanation (*gar*; once again omitted by the NIV and the NRSV), Paul states a broader truth about the way the world is, and about Christians within it. These verses stand at the very heart of his theological description of the Christian life, set within the still-to-be-redeemed world, on the one hand, and held within the powerful love of God, on the other. He draws once more on Jewish tradition, this time the theme of the great tribulation, the great woes, that would come upon the world in order for the new world to be born.[276] This (essentially female) image of the birth pangs of the new age is applied first to the world, then to the church, and then, remarkably enough, to the Spirit. This creates the context within which, as he wants to explain to the Roman church, patience and prayer are the appropriate stance and activity for God's people while awaiting the final redemption. Within Paul's overall argument for assurance, this is vital: he needs to explain why (if all that he has said about Christ and the Spirit is true) things are still so often so painful, and also why Christians can nevertheless be confident of God's final victory and their final redemption.

8:22. He deals first with creation: groaning together and travailing together, which the NIV and the NRSV rightly treat as one large idea, "groaning in labor pains." This is the present state of creation. Part of the point of the image is that the coming new world will involve, not the abolition of the present one, but its transformation: birth (particularly in the culture of Paul's day, both Jewish and pagan) speaks of new life that is at the same time the mother's own life, delighting her, despite the pain of labor, with a fresh fulfillment. This continuity between the present world and the future one is the reason, one may assume, why the present passage has been marginalized in many expositions of Paul and Romans on the part of those for whom a more dualist theology was a working assumption.

8:23. But how will the new world come to birth? Not of its own energy and potentiality, but only through the glorification of God's children (v. 21). That is why, within the groaning creation, the church also groans, longing for its own "adoption": longing, in other words, for the "child" to be born that is its own true self. Here we strike once more

the characteristic note of "now and not yet" that runs right through Paul: we have already received "the spirit of υἱοθεσία [*huiothesia*, "sonship/adoption"]" (v. 15); we are already "children of God" (vv. 16-17); and yet there is a form of this "sonship/adoption" for which we still eagerly long. The link between present and future is made, again as usual, by the Spirit, who is the "first fruits," that part of God's future redeeming power that is brought forward into the present, so that the prayer of the child in the present time (vv. 15-16) truly points on to the future resurrection glory (vv. 11, 17).[277] This idea is closely cognate with the similar statement that the Spirit is the "guarantee," using the metaphor of a down payment, of the full salvation yet to come (e.g., 2 Cor 1:22; 5:5; Eph 1:14). Here "the firstfruits of the Spirit" looks back to 8:4b, 9-11, and 13b-17. Summing up that whole train of thought, Paul can declare, here and in vv. 26-27, that the present "groaning," though at one level a sign of the present not fully redeemed state, is at the same time a sign of the Christian's sure and certain hope.

The "adoption/sonship" of which Paul here speaks—the full and final thing of which the Spirit's work is the beginning and guarantee—is precisely the final redemption of the body, of which Paul has already written decisively in 8:11. "Redemption," mentioned here for the first time since the highly significant 3:24, carries once more the gentle overtones of the exodus theme that underlies so much of the present passage. We ourselves have come out of "Egypt," but our body, which still needs to have its deeds put to death (v. 13), is still awaiting redemption from the slave market (Paul uses the singular "body" rather than the expected plural, as in v. 11, but there seems no particular significance to this change). The body is intended to be glorious, splendid, fashioned after the model of Jesus' own resurrection body, no longer subject to weakness, humiliation, sickness, sin, and death (cf. 1 Cor 15:54; 2 Cor 5:1-5; Phil 3:21). The Christian in the present

---

276. See Wright, *The New Testament and the People of God*, 277-79; *Jesus and the Victory of God*, 577-79.

277. Paul can use the same image of Christ, as the first to be raised from the dead, guaranteeing the harvest to come (1 Cor 15:20-23) or of the first converts in a particular location (e.g., Rom 16:5; 1 Cor 16:15). See also 11:16; 2 Thess 2:13. In Jas 1:18 Christians are seen as the firstfruits of God's new creation, an idea that sits very comfortably alongside Rom 8:22. For the biblical background, see the Commentary on 11:16.

time is but a pale shadow of his or her future self.

8:24-25. "For we were saved in hope." Not in "this hope," as the NIV interprets; that, though true, is not the point Paul is making here, as the further explanation makes clear. The logic of these verses, explaining what has gone before, is as follows: (a) we ourselves groan while awaiting our complete adoption; (b) this is so because we were saved in hope; (c) if we were saved in hope, this must mean that our future salvation is not yet visible; (d) the appropriate Christian stance is therefore patient expectation. Paul's concern is to stress that, while salvation is already a reality for the Christian ("we were saved": the tense is aorist, denoting a one-off event), it carries an inevitable future component. Hope is built in to Christian experience from the start, and remains one of its central characteristics (see 5:2-5; 15:13). But if this is so, Paul is stressing, one cannot expect present Christian living to be anything other than a matter of straining forward for what is yet to come, for what is yet unseen. (See Phil 3:13; 2 Cor 4:18; the present passage makes it clear that the distinction between "seen" and "unseen" things in 2 Corinthians is contrasting present and future, not [in a Platonic fashion] the world of space, time, and matter, on the one hand, and the world of ideas, on the other). One does not anxiously scan the horizon for a boat already in port.

If this is so, the Christian is called to patience. But patience is no mere dispassionate passing of the time. The word Paul uses for "wait" here is ἀπεκδεχόμεθα (*apekdechometha*), the same root that was used in v. 19, where most interpreters recognize a note of eagerness, of excited expectation. The last three words of v. 25 thus have an almost oxymoronic flavor, with the emphasis falling not, as in most English translations, on "with patience" (lit., "through patience," δι' ὑπομονῆς *di' hypomonēs*), but on "eagerly await": if we hope for what we do not yet see, then, with steady patience, we maintain an eager expectation.

Paul has now described the whole creation groaning in labor-pains; he has shown that God's people in Christ share the same struggle and groaning. Where is God in all this? Not, as in so many theological schemes

ancient and modern, standing to one side, or hiding a long way off. God is present in the midst of the pain. God, indeed, is groaning in labor too.

8:26-27. The groaning of the church, in the midst of the groaning world, is sustained and even inspired by the groaning of the Spirit. Paul clearly intends these to be seen in parallel, since he introduces the verse with ὡσαύτως (*hōsautōs*, "in the same way"). The Spirit, he says, helps us in our weakness— or, literally, "The Spirit helps our weakness." He has not spoken of "weakness" before in the present argument, and we must assume that he uses this term to sum up the state he has just described, the state of not yet being fully redeemed. Those who cannot see that for which they eagerly hope need assistance to peer into the darkness ahead and to pray God's future into the present. It is that assistance that the Spirit provides, coming alongside to help (συναντιλαμβάνεται *synantilambanetai*; this is the word Martha used in Luke 10:40 to say what Mary should have been doing for her).

Here, as in vv. 15-16, Spirit-inspired prayer is a key part of the experience of inaugurated eschatology (cf. Zech 12:10, where, in the context of the coming great eschaton, God pours out upon the house of David, and upon Jerusalem, "the spirit of grace and supplication," producing mourning in the midst of the promised glory). It is God's intention that redeemed human beings should be set in authority over the world, should indeed thereby be the agents through whom the cosmos that still groans in travail should be set free. At the moment, however, these human beings are weak, since their own bodies, that part of creation for which they have the most immediate responsibility, are still subject to decay and death. In this condition they do not even know what to pray for, how it is that God will work through them to bring about the redemption of the world. Paul here assumes both that the church is called to the task of intercession and that the church finds this very puzzling—a double truth that most great teachers of prayer from that day to this would endorse. But, just as it is the Spirit's task to inaugurate genuine humanness within the Christian in the form of holiness (vv. 12-14) and the *Abba*-prayer (vv. 15-16), so here it is the Spirit's task to enable genuine humanness, that stance of humbly trusting God and so being set in authority over the world, which is to be anticipated in the life of intercessory prayer.

Many writers, from various standpoints, have suggested that Paul here refers to the gift of *glossolalia*, "speaking in tongues." This is quite possible in terms of Paul's belief about the latter gift and its place within the church, and a strong case can be made out for it.[278] The present writer certainly has no prejudice against finding such a reference here, as some appear to have. Yet I find it strange that Paul, if he wished to refer to speaking in tongues, for which words of the λαλέω (*laleō*) root would be used ("to speak," or, of inanimate things, "to make a noise," "to give forth a sound"; see, e.g., 1 Cor 12:30; 13:1; 14:2), should here use the word ἀλαλήτος (*alalētos*, "speechless" or "voiceless") to describe the practice. It is important to say that, if he is not referring to speaking in tongues, nor is he simply referring to silent prayer such as is commonly practiced in private Christian devotion in the contemporary Western world (in Paul's day most people would have prayed aloud, just as people used to read aloud, even when alone). Rather, he is speaking of an agonizing in prayer, a mixture of lament and longing in which, like a great swell of tide at sea, "too full for sound or foam," the weight of what is taking place has nothing to do with the waves and ripples on the surface. Whether Paul expected all his readers to know this experience in prayer (as he seems to have expected them to know the *Abba*-experience) is difficult to judge. Then as now, perhaps, his words may have come as a challenge to a deeper wrestling with the pain of the world and the church, a struggle in which, like Jacob, Christians might discover that they had after all been wrestling with God as well as with their own weak humanness, and had prevailed.

The point Paul is making, in any case, is that the Spirit's own very self[279] intercedes

within the Christian precisely at the point where he or she, faced with the ruin and misery of the world, finds that there are no words left to express in God's presence the sense of futility (v. 20) and the longing for redemption. It is not (as some early scribes added to the text, followed by the NIV) that the Spirit intercedes "for us"; that misses the point, and makes Paul repeat himself in the following verse. What Paul is saying is that the Spirit, active within the innermost being of the Christian, is doing the very interceding the Christian longs to do, even though the only evidence that can be produced is inarticulate groanings.

The good news about this is that God, the living, transcendent God, is in intimate touch with the Spirit, so that these inarticulate but Spirit-assisted groanings come before God as true prayer, true intercession. To say this, Paul uses another remarkable periphrasis for God (see the Commentary on 8:11; see also the Commentary on 4:24): "the heart-searcher." The Spirit's work (lit., "the mind of the Spirit," as in 8:6), deep within the human heart, is known to the heart-searching God. We may compare 2:16; 1 Cor 4:5; 1 Thess 2:4; since these references (the first two certainly, the third arguably) are to a future judgment at which the heart's secrets will be laid bare, what we have here appears to be yet another example of inaugurated eschatology; God's searching of hearts anticipates the final putting to rights of all things (see also Heb 4:12-13). The Spirit, he says, intercedes for God's people, whom he refers to as "the saints"; he often designates Christians thus, set apart as they are for God, and this is a particularly appropriate context to do so, as God's people are caught up in the inner life of God. The Spirit's intercession is "according to God's will" (lit., "according to God"). This hints at something deeper than merely praying in the way God wants or approves; God's own life, love, and energy are involved in the process. The Christian, precisely at the point of weakness and uncertainty, of inability and struggle, becomes the place at which the triune God is revealed in person.

8:28. Triune? Has not Paul only spoken of the first and third persons of the Trinity? No. The suffering of the church, groaning in longing and prayer for the redemption of the

---

278. See Fee, *God's Empowering Presence*, 575-86, discussing particularly the argument of another notable proponent, Ernst Käsemann.

279. It seems foolish to say "itself," since, though the noun "spirit" is neuter in Greek, the reality Paul refers to is deeply personal. The sustained metaphor of groaning in birth pangs suggests "herself"; but this, though attractive in some ways granted the fact that the word for "spirit" is feminine in Hebrew, Aramaic, and Syriac, might place too much stress on a point that is at best a matter of nuance in Paul's extended metaphor.

world, and of the present body, is the means by which Christians are "conformed to the image of God's son" (v. 29). As usual, Paul has steadily worked his way back to the point at which he began, in this case 8:17*b:* we are fellow heirs with the Messiah, so long as we suffer with him in order that we may be glorified with him. This is the theme that dominates as the paragraph, already one of Paul's most remarkable, draws to its unique and uniquely powerful climax.

Verse 28 does not represent a completely new thought (as is sometimes implied by paragraph divisions in translations, such as the NIV and the NRSV). It is not simply an extra devotional aside about the wonderful workings of providence. It is bound in tightly to the sequence of the argument. The introductory δέ (*de*) is the "but," not of opposition, but of logic; not "I hoped he would come *but* he didn't," but rather "Donkeys like carrots; *but* this is a donkey; therefore let's give him some carrots." The train of thought is, "God knows the mind of the Spirit; *but* we know that God works all things together for good for those who love God; therefore (implicit but vital) God works all things together for good for us, we in whom the Spirit is operating." (This, after all, is where the longer paragraph started, with the Christian being in God's debt [v. 12]). The intercession spoken of in v. 26 will be heard and answered in ways that, though we cannot at present see them or even conceive them, will turn out to be that for which our groaning prayers have been yearning. "All things"—not just the groanings of the previous verses, but the entire range of experiences and events that may face God's people—are taken care of by the creator God who is planning to renew the whole creation, and us along with it.

I have assumed that "God" is the implied subject of "works together." Two other views have been taken. A minority, represented by the NEB, make "the Spirit" the implied subject. The strength of this view is that the Spirit has been a main topic, perhaps the main topic, ever since 8:1, and is the subject of the immediately preceding clause. However, the subject of the previous main sentence is God, not the Spirit; and, with several commentators I regard the sudden and unexplained change of subject at the end of v. 28 (from the Spirit

to God) as a fatal objection to making the Spirit the subject here.[280] A more widely held view is that "all things" are the subject: so, famously, the KJV, "All things work together for good to them that love God." There are considerable problems with this, not least the sheer oddity, for Paul, of giving "all things" such apparent theological priority (even if we understand, as devout readers usually have, a strong theology of providence behind the statement).

The NRSV, echoing the King James, implies in its footnote that to make God the subject is to endorse the variant reading of several good MSS, according to which "God" (ὁ θεός *ho theos*) was to be read after "works together." But this is not strictly the case. Even with the shorter text (which is surely correct; it would be easy to add the word "God" but very odd to omit it), the implied subject must still be that of the previous verse—namely, "the heartsearcher": God. The verse runs on, without any indication of a change of subject, to "those whom [God] foreknew" in v. 29, and indeed to the implied subject of "called according to [God's] purpose" at the end of v. 28. Had Paul not intended "God" as the subject of συνεργεῖ (*synergei*, "works together"), in fact, he really should have specified a *change* of subject to "God" toward the end of the present verse. Paul is, of course, capable of omitting connections, subjects, verbs, and anything else that he hopes will be understood by someone clinging to the tail of his fast-moving argument. But here it seems unlikely.[281]

Paul, then, pulls together the threads of his treatment of the triple groaning of world, church, and Spirit. The whole letter has been about God, God's covenant faithfulness, God's gospel revealed in the Son and the Spirit, and above all—not that this is a separate topic from all those—God's love. The heart of the argument for assurance is the unshakable and sovereign love of God, and the certainty that this love will win out in the end. That, indeed, is the theme that is now emerging as

---

280. Despite the advocacy of Fee, *God's Empowering Presence,* 587-90.

281. It is easier to understand the train of thought in the KJV and the NRSV, because "those who love God" comes at the end of the clause in English, making a smooth transition to "those whom he foreknew" at the start of v. 29. In Greek, however, "to those who love God" comes near the start of the verse, and the accusative case of "God" does not lend itself so easily to the necessary transition to the subject for the following verbs.

the major subject of the end of the chapter. We are debtors, he says, to God, from whom we have received the Spirit of sonship/adoption, and from whom we shall receive the inheritance, the glory, the sonship/adoption in its full form; and the move from present to future is undergirded, made totally secure, by the fact that God works all things together for good to those who . . . now keep the most basic command of Torah.

That most basic command is, of course, the *Shema:* "Hear, O Israel, YHWH our God, YHWH is one; and you shall love YHWH your God." Paul has already alluded to the *Shema* more than once in the letter (1:5; 3:30; 5:5). Now he comes back to it, with a hint of the positive side of the equation of which 8:7-8 was the negative. Those in the flesh do not and cannot submit to God's law; they cannot please God; but those in the Spirit now do that which the law commanded but could not of itself produce. They love God from the heart (cf. 1 Cor 2:9; 8:3). Just as Paul can vary his epithets for God, so here he pulls out a new epithet for the people of God in Christ and by the Spirit: they are the God-lovers, in other words, the true law-keepers, the true Israel.

This epithet, "the God-lovers," is again not a new idea introduced into the passage, but sums up what has been said in vv. 15, 26-27. In v. 15, those who are led by the Spirit are taught to address God in the language of familial love. In vv. 26-27, those who groan as they await their redemption discover that from the depths of their own heart there issues an inarticulate cry of faith, hope, and love to God. This, the work of the Spirit, is what qualifies them to be described in this way in the next verse (of which the clause "to those who love God" is the first substantial part). It is as though Paul had written: "because the Spirit intercedes for God's people, calling from their own hearts with love to God; and for those who thus love God, God works all things together for good."

This same people can also be described with another Israel-epithet: they are those who are now "called according to God's purpose." That purpose—namely, that God would sum up all things in Christ (Col 1:15-20; Eph 1:10); that God would be all in all (1 Cor 15:28); that the whole creation would be liberated into the freedom that goes with the glorification of God's children—this whole purpose was always designed to be fulfilled through the agency of God's image-bearing children, the human race. This purpose has been decisively fulfilled in Jesus Christ (5:12-21), but that which was thereby inaugurated has now to be consummated. Those in Christ are the people through whom God intends to accomplish this task. They, like Israel, are assured that they have been called for a purpose—namely, to show forth the praises of the one true God in all the world (cf. Eph 1:11-12; 1 Pet 2:9). And—this is still the thrust of v. 28—those who find themselves in this category can be assured that the purpose will be fulfilled. God will accomplish it.

8:29-30. In order to show the branches that they are indeed to bear blossom and fruit, Paul demonstrates that the tree is securely planted and well rooted. In order (that is) to complete his argument from justification to glorification—the argument that began with 5:1-2—he goes back behind justification itself to God's purpose and call, and behind that again to God's foreknowledge. God's purpose is the overriding thought of these verses, summing up the line of thought through the whole chapter, but particularly from v. 17: God's plan from the start was to create a Christ-shaped family, a renewed human race modeled on the Son (once again the line of thought from 1:3-4, through 5:6-10, to 8:3 emerges at a crucial point in the argument). Heirs of God, said Paul in v. 17, and *fellow heirs with the Messiah:* fellow children, younger siblings of the Firstborn (see Col 1:15, 18). This would come about through a process of God's adopted children being shaped according to the likeness of the Son. Though this process will only be complete when the body itself is transformed either in resurrection or at the Lord's coming (cf. 1 Cor 15:51-55 with Phil 3:21), it is to begin here and now precisely through the holiness, suffering, and prayer of which Paul has written in the preceding verses (see also 2 Cor 3:18).[282]

This process will bring God's renewed people to the point where they reflect the Son's *image,* just as the Son is the true image of God (2 Cor 4:4; Col 1:15; 3:10). They are,

---

282. On which see Wright, *The Climax of the Covenant,* chap. 9.

that is, to become true, because renewed, human beings. This is the point, at last, to which the long argument beginning with 1:18 was looking forward. The image of God, distorted and fractured through idolatry and immorality, is restored in Jesus the Messiah, the Son of God; and the signs of that restoration are visible in those who, like Abraham, trust in God's life-giving power and so truly worship and give glory to God (4:18-22). But the purpose is never simply that God's people in Christ should resemble him, spectacular and glorious though that promise is. As we saw in vv. 18-21, it is that, as true image-bearers, they might reflect that same image into the world, bringing to creation the healing, freedom, and life for which it longs. To be conformed to the image of God, or of God's Son, is a dynamic, not a static, concept. Reflecting God into the world is a matter of costly vocation.

That, indeed, is the thrust of vv. 28-30, which otherwise can easily degenerate, as the history of interpretation shows, into an abstract theory of personal predestination and salvation. God's purpose for those in Christ is precisely Christ-shaped. They are chosen and called in order to advance God's purpose in and for the world. The five great verbs (foreknown, foreordained, called, justified, glorified), crashing chords at the end of the movement, are all to be understood as Christ-shaped. That which is true of the Messiah is true of his people.

Conformity to the Son means, of course, conformity to his death. This is familiar enough elsewhere in Paul (e.g., Phil 3:10-11, a passage very close to the present one in theme and expression). Here it is the major subject of the unit of thought that, beginning with v. 17, reaches its climax in the present verse. It is by reproducing the likeness of the Messiah, not least in suffering and "groaning," that Paul's apostolic labor went forward; that is the subject of 2 Corinthians, especially chapters 4 and 6, and it is summarized in other passages such as Col 1:24. But it is not merely apostles to whom the privilege of sharing the sufferings of the Messiah is granted. It is, in some measure at least, all Christians. Though the last sections of Romans 8 are often (rightly) thought of as triumphant, it should never be forgotten that

the triumph is announced and celebrated, with irony and paradox, from the midst of circumstances that would be simply unbearable, were it not for faith in God the life-giver, and for the hope and above all the love that accompany this faith.

Thus, in v. 29, Paul is explaining both the general point of v. 28, that God works all things together for good, and the more specific point, what is meant by being "called according to God's purpose." The concept of "foreknowledge" is by no means simply that of God being able to see the future and so to know things in advance as we know things in retrospect (though presumably more accurately). The biblical concept of "knowing" is richer than the mere transfer of information. We might invoke Gal 1:15 as at least a partial explanation. There Paul speaks of God "setting him apart" for a particular purpose, and then "calling" him by grace; the language is reminiscent of various biblical passages, including Jer 1:5, "before I formed you in the womb I knew you; I appointed you a prophet to the nations" (cf. Isa 44:2; 49:1). In Romans, we might compare 1:1, where Paul speaks of his "call" to be an apostle and of being "set apart" for God's gospel, the latter verb (ἀφορίζω *aphorizō*; also used in Gal 1:15) being a compound from the same root as προώρισεν (*proōrisen*, "foreordained") in the present verse. God's "knowing" and "call," however, are not just for prophets and apostles but for all God's people, each in their own vocation and fashion, but all according to the same pattern of Christ. Foreknowledge is a form of love or grace; to speak thus is to speak of God reaching out, in advance of anything the person may do or think, to reveal love and to solicit an answering love, to reveal a particular purpose and to call forth obedience to it.

More particularly, this foreknowledge produces God's foreordaining purpose. The word *proōrisen*, often translated "predestined" here and in v. 30 (the NEB is an exception with "foreordained"), often sends shivers down the spines of readers because of its association with the word "destiny," and the link in much popular thinking between this and "fate" (the NJB makes matters worse on this front by simply translating "destined"). Is Paul after all a determinist, believing in a blind plan that determines everything, so that human freedom, responsibility, obedience, and love itself are after all a sham?

One can easily imagine Paul's own reaction: μὴ γένοιτο (mē genoito, "Certainly not!"). What we have here, rather, is an expression, as in 1:1, of God's action in setting people apart for a particular purpose, a purpose in which their cooperation, their loving response to love, their obedient response to the personal call, is itself all-important. This is not to deny the mystery of grace, the free initiative of God, and the clear divine sovereignty that is after all the major theme of this entire passage, here brought to a glorious climax. But it is to deny the common misconception, based on a two-dimensional rather than a three-dimensional understanding of how God's actions and human actions relate to each other, that sees something done by God as something not done by humans, and vice versa.

One could appeal (scholars often do) to the Hebrew, or the Middle Eastern, mind-set in which paradoxes and apparent antinomies are held together without difficulty (e.g., talk of God's building the new Temple does not mean that there will not be human architects and stonemasons). But there is more to the problem than this. God's actions and human actions are not, as it were, on the same plane. Already in describing the Spirit's work Paul has shown that the groanings that seem to come from the depths of one's own heart are actually the Spirit's groaning within; and that the heartfelt cry of familial love, *Abba*, Father, is itself likewise the result of the Spirit's prompting. Woe betide theology if discussions of grace take their coloring from the mechanistic or technological age where all actions are conceived as though performed by a set of machines. God's foreknowledge and foreordination, setting people apart in advance for particular purposes, are not equal and opposite to human desires, longings, self-questionings, obedience, and above all love. You do not take away from the one by adding to the other. Even the analogy of human love breaks down, since no lover is ever in the position of playing God to the beloved. Yet love, in which love affirms the otherness of the other at precisely the same time as appearing to merge wills, souls, hearts, and bodies into

one, offers some parallels, however oblique, with the workings of divine grace. Christian faith, ultimately irreducible to any analogy, and certainly not reducible to terms simply of "yet another odd paradox," involves wholeheartedly and responsibly answering the call of sovereign love, grace, and commission with a love, gratitude, and obedience that come from the depths of one's own being and are simultaneously experienced as a response to a sovereignty, a compulsion even, to which the closest parallel remains that of the highest love.

The emphasis of vv. 29-30 falls clearly on conformity to Christ; this remains so throughout the dramatic closing words, focused on the four last aorists (pre-shaped, called, justified, glorified). All has been accomplished in Christ: the fore-shaping of Christ's people to be his younger siblings; their call through the gospel that announces his lordship; their justification by faith in the God who raised him from the dead; their glorification, so that they are now already seated in the heavenly places in him (see Eph 2:6, and in the light of that, Eph 1:20-22; Col 3:1-4). There may even be a backward glance to the story of Jesus himself: his incarnation, his baptism, his resurrection, his ascension—though this remains speculative. In any case, the christological basis explains the final aorist, which is otherwise very puzzling, coming as it does after so many futures (8:9-11, 13, 17-18, 23). All these things, including "glorification," have happened already to and in Jesus, the Messiah; and what is true of the Messiah is true of his people.

Pre-shaped; called; justified; glorified—the one link in the chain not already explained in this letter is the second. Paul uses the verb "call" in a more specific sense than some other NT writings (e.g., in the Gospels it simply means the general call to which a variety of answers might be given; e.g., Matt 22:14). For Paul the "call" is what happens when, through the preaching of the gospel (or, in his own case, the revelation of the risen Jesus; but Paul does not suppose this will happen to anyone again), the Spirit works in the heart to produce faith, hope, and love. This "call" is, in the language of an older theology, "effective"; Paul knows that not all hearers of the gospel respond in faith, but when people do he describes the event as their being "called" by God (cf. 1 Thess 1:4-5 with 2 Thess 2:13-14). This will be an important category in chap. 9 (see 9:7, 11, 24-26). Paul can use the word almost synonymously with "conversion"—that is, to describe the moment of coming to faith; though it retains the sense not of a switch in religion (that might happen as well, but it is not the point of this verb) so much as the response to a sovereign command (see 1 Cor 7:15-24; Gal 1:6, 15; Eph 4:4).

Those who respond to the gospel of Jesus Christ with "the obedience of faith"—those, that is, who are "called" in this sense—are declared by God to be part of the new covenant family, the sin-forgiven worldwide people of God, on the basis of this faith alone. "Those whom God called, God also justified"; v. 30*a* thus sums up 3:21–4:25. And those who are justified by faith now rejoice in the hope of the glory of God (5:2, the introductory summary of 5–8); in other words, "those whom God justified, God also glorified" (v. 30*b*, the concluding summary). The detailed argument is done, and the four emphatic aorists of v. 30 are the last four blows of the hammer to ensure that every vital nail in the structure is in place. The steady beat of the verbs within Paul's solemn rhetoric underscores the steady beat of God's unshakable purpose set forth in the Messiah and completed by the Spirit.

It remains to note the way in which, under the general heading of "glorification," Paul's entire future hope for Christians and the world can be spoken of in so many different but overlapping and interlocking ways. To begin with, Paul can speak simply of "life" (8:11) for the mortal body: in other words, resurrection life, the new or transformed physicality that will correspond to the physically renewed body of the risen Jesus (1 Cor 15:50-57). This is what he means, of course, by "eternal life," much misused though that phrase may be in some Christian writing to permit a non-physical interpretation of the final state. But this resurrection life is never something to be enjoyed simply for itself. Those renewed at the last, those who share the glory of the Messiah, will receive an inheritance, which will be the entire world. There they will have tasks to perform, tasks to do with the liberation of creation from the injustice, misery, bondage, corruption, and death that at present characterize it. (This picture, set out briefly in 8:18-22, is what underlies such otherwise peculiar statements as 1 Cor 6:2; cf. Wis 3:5-9; 4:16. On the future work of the redeemed in God's new world, see Rev 21:22–22:5.) This is the "glory" of which Paul speaks. And this is the hope that puts Christians permanently in God's debt.

One final reflection may be in order, to which we shall return in due course. If it is indeed true that Paul saw the gospel, with its revelation of God's saving justice and peace, as the truth of which Caesar's "gospel," and the "justice" and "peace" that flowed from it, were parodies, it may also be the case that he intends, at this end of his argument, to hint at a particular way in which this gospel makes its way in the world, and will eventually take the world over. Caesar's cult was instantiated around the empire by means of images of Caesar himself, soon to be divine, and of his son(s), heir(s), and other family members, themselves all divinities-in-waiting. These images, housed in various places but particularly in temples of the growing Caesar-cult, were there partly in order to be worshiped, and partly in order to remind the local residents whose empire they were living in. Here, at the climax of the argument that God's saving justice and peace are revealed in the gospel of Jesus, the true Lord of the world—at the climax, also, of the passage about the Spirit dwelling within Christians, like the presence of God within the Temple—Paul states that God's purpose is for Christians to be "conformed to the image of God's Son." They are to be image-bearers, forming the Temple of the living God, the people through whom in the present as well as in the future it is to be made known that the God of Abraham is the only God, that Jesus, his Son, is the world's true Lord, and that one day the world will be liberated from its present slaveries, as Israel was from Egypt, to be the true Empire in which justice, peace, and freedom will make their home.

REFLECTIONS

1. The main emphasis of the whole section is on Christian living in terms of being indebted to God's grace. Much has been said and written in the last century about a human "coming of age" that renders unnecessary and undesirable all obligation, all indebtedness, all human dependence. Anything else, we have often been told, leaves us immature as human beings. The pattern of the exodus has even been used to suggest that one ought to escape all overlordship, even including that of God. Theologies that deny this, and that insist, like Paul, on permanent indebtedness to grace, are sometimes vilified as perpetrating a bullying or dominating God. The present passage not only contradicts this, but explains that the condition of permanent indebtedness to God is not a diminution, but rather an enhancement, of full human dignity.

When one considers all that has been said in Romans about "sin" and "the flesh," to protest against grace on the grounds that one ought to be independent, standing on one's own feet, is about as sensible as a drowning person protesting against being thrown a life belt. That is basic to all Paul's theology. But this passage goes further. The biblical theology of humanness that Paul here echoes, endorses, and develops is that of being made in God's image and being remade in the image of God's Son. There can be no greater human dignity than this. To seek for a status independent of this is indeed, on the one hand, to shake one's fist, Prometheus-like, at the creator, and on the other, inevitably, to worship some part of the created order (perhaps even oneself), and so to be remade in the image of that which is enslaved to decay and death. Like human stories in which people try to live without depending on anyone, only finally to be overwhelmed by love and discover a fulfillment, a self-realization, through self-giving and self-abandonment, so the story of grace is one in which humans find themselves by losing themselves, endlessly indebted to the God whose own true self-expression was found in the self-giving love of the Son. Being indebted to grace is like the permanent indebtedness that exists between those who have given themselves freely to one another in lifelong human love: a state of wonder and gratitude in which one's own humanness is enhanced rather than diminished, ennobled rather than belittled.

2. Within this, the wider vista that Paul opens up is the invitation to the Christian to live within the horizon of God's new creation. This great project, the global and cosmic dimension of salvation, has begun with the resurrection of Jesus, and will continue until the whole world is transformed under the just and healing rule of God's children. Though the question of what this will look and feel like, and the question of levels of continuity and discontinuity between the present creation and the new one, are exceedingly difficult to answer, that does not mean that there will not be a reality to which, in retrospect, this language will be seen to have been a true, if inadequate, pointer—much as, with Christian hindsight, the variegated prophecies of the Old Testament can be seen, and are seen in the New Testament, as true pointers to a reality that could not, however, have been fully or adequately described by them alone.

If the Christian is called to live (to use one standard jargon) at the overlap of the old and new creations, this is hardly a matter of passive acceptance of a difficult and tense moment in God's purposes, or of sitting back to await better times when the overlap is done and the new creation fully present. Rather, as the bracing ethical imperatives of 8:12-14 and the call to groaning in prayer in 8:26-27 make clear, the Christian is to embody the tension involved in bringing the new to birth already within the old. The challenge to holiness cannot be put off until some future date; nor can the challenge to bring all things in subjection to the saving rule of God's people, a task that must begin with inarticulate prayer and continue forward from there.

It is under this rubric that all Christian work in the areas of ecology, justice, and aesthetics is to be conceived. If the creation is to be renewed, not abandoned, and if that work has already begun in the resurrection of Jesus, it will not do simply to consign the present creation to acid rain and global warming and wait for Armageddon to destroy it altogether. Christians must be in the forefront of bringing, in the present time, signs and foretastes of God's eventual full healing to bear upon the created order in all its parts and at every level. If the world is to be put to rights, brought under the saving lordship of God's restorative justice, and if that work has already been unveiled proto-typically in Jesus' death and resurrection, it will not do to concentrate on individual justification while allowing wider issues of justice to go unaddressed. Christians must be in the forefront of bringing, in the present time, signs and foretastes of God's heal-ing justice to bear upon the world that is still full of corruption, injustice, oppression, division, suspicion, and war. And if the world is to attain its full beauty and dignity as God's liberated new creation, a beauty and dignity for which the present evidences of God's grandeur within creation are just a foretaste, it will not do to regard beauty, and its creation and conservation, as a pleasant but irrelevant optional extra within a world manipulated by science, exploited by technology, and bought and sold in the economic marketplace. Christians must be in the forefront of bringing, in the present time, signs and foretastes of God's fresh beauty to birth within the world, signs of hope for what the Spirit will yet do:

> And for all this, nature is never spent;
> There lives the dearest freshness deep down things;
> And, though the last lights off the black West went
> Oh, morning, at the brown brink eastward springs—
> Because the Holy Ghost over the bent
> World broods with warm breast and with ah! bright wings.[283]

3. The vocation of the church to live thus in the wrinkle of time that is inaugurated eschatology is focused here on the life of prayer. Paul holds together in this passage the intimate prayer that knows exactly what to call God (i.e., *Abba*) and the groaning prayer that has no idea what to ask for or even what words to use. Prayer itself is a matter of both knowing and not knowing, of security and insecurity, of "having noth-ing yet possessing all things" (2 Cor 6:10). The Spirit is equally and characteristically at work at both extremes, enabling the "now" of glad and assured adoption, of the child/parent relationship with God wherein Christians grow to full human maturity without ever ceasing to be the child of this parent, and enabling also the "not yet" of groaning in travail to be expressed, in the inarticulate depths, in a way that God the heart-searcher knows, hears, and understands. The latter kind of prayer is also, it appears, part of what it means "to love God." The opening of 8:28 relates, after all, quite closely to 8:26-27, for what does it mean to love God but that in the depths of one's own heart and spirit there is a call of love, trust, and hope for which the ultimate explanation is that the Spirit is there at work?

The call to this kind of inarticulate prayer is not, it seems to me, exactly the same thing as the discipline of silence practiced by some who have made long journeys into the realms of prayer and have come back to share their insights with the rest of us. It is not simply contemplation. Nor yet is it contemplation's parody, that stream-of-consciousness prayer in which random musings and daydreams pass before the mind and are vaguely brought into the presence of God. It is, rather, an agony that would come into speech if only it could, part of whose agony indeed is that to bring it to speech, to name the problem and hence to envisage its solution, would be to attain some measure of relief. The problem of evil is not so easily solved. The achievement of the cross and resurrection, and the power of the indwelling Spirit, have not produced that kind of

---

283. G. M. Hopkins, "God's Grandeur."

inaugurated eschatology where everything is now laid out neatly awaiting completion, like a row of beans ripe and ready to be picked. Let no one suppose that Paul's emphasis on what has already happened in Christ leads to that kind of casual ease about the present unredeemedness of the world, or about tasks that lie ahead. However, no one should suppose, either, that the continuing appropriate agony of expectant prayer to which the whole church is now called casts any doubt on that other experience of which the same passage speaks, the *Abba* knowledge of God that is also based on the work of the Messiah and the gift of the Spirit. The two go together in Paul and in Christian experience.

4. Intercession for the world that is groaning in travail is not, then, an optional extra for the Christian. Within this, intercession for the parts of one's own life that are in trouble cannot be discounted either. There is a false humility about some protests against such intercession, discounting it as trivial or self-centered. To the contrary: the groanings of each individual, caught between redemption accomplished in Christ and redemption still awaited (8:23), are all part of the groaning of creation. As long as one does not imagine that the world, and the love of God, revolve around one's own life and concerns—as long, in other words, as one is a mature and adult child of God and not still a spiritual baby—one's own concerns have their proper place, and can indeed be the starting-point for awareness of, and hence prayer about, the wider groanings of the whole cosmos. Just because we must not be self-centered, that does not mean we should ignore the self and its concerns. If we are God's beloved children, our small as well as our great concerns matter.

5. Suffering is a mystery, indeed. It is to be rejected as a final good—as though the Christian were after all to embrace some kind of masochism!—and yet embraced both as a sign of the time at which we live and even as a part of the means whereby redemption comes to the world. There is a terrible danger in this very Pauline theme, which feminism and other recent movements have not been slow to point out: The redemptive value of suffering has all too often been preached by the comfortable to the uncomfortable, by the elderly to the youth going off to war, by masters to slaves, by men to women. Yet the abuse does not invalidate the use, and if *corruptio optimi pessima* is a dire warning to those in danger of corrupting the best it is also a reminder to those who are all too aware of the worst.

At the heart of Paul's picture of the suffering church is the fact that, as he says in 8:10, "the Messiah is in you." If this truth undergirds the hope of future resurrection, it also means that Christian suffering in the present is somehow "messianic," which means it is somehow, in ways that will rightly and inevitably pass our comprehension, redemptive. As we saw in the notes, 2 Corinthians was written not least as an elaboration and defense of this as applied to Paul's apostleship. For millions of Christians in the contemporary world, in places such as China, Pakistan, Indonesia, the Sudan, and elsewhere, daily suffering for the faith is simply part of what being a Christian means. When, in 1998, Westminster Abbey decided to fill the ten vacant niches on the West Front with statues of twentieth-century Christian martyrs, there was no shortage of candidates.[284] For millions of others in comfortable Western churches, such suffering as comes their way often seems incidental to the practice of faith. Yet this too can be transformed, and transformative, if brought through prayer into the divine dialogue spoken of with bated breath in 8:26-27.

6. In a way that is characteristic of Romans 5–8 as a whole, Jesus is seldom mentioned yet everywhere present. "Fellow heirs with the Messiah" (8:17) means being

---

284. The choices were revealing and powerfully evocative both of the worldwide spread of the faith and of the challenge still posed by the gospel to the power of the world, and vice versa: Maximilian Kolbe, Poland (1941); Manche Masemola, South Africa (1928); Janani Luwum, Uganda (1977); Grand Duchess Elizabeth of Russia (1918); Martin Luther King, USA (1969); Oscar Romero, El Salvador (1980); Dietrich Bonhoeffer, Germany (1945); Esther John, Pakistan (1960); Lucian Tapiedi, Papua New Guinea (1942); Wang Zhiming, China (1972).

"conformed to the image of God's Son" (8:29). The pattern of Jesus—his sonship, his kingdom, his suffering, his prayer, his death, and his resurrection—shapes and undergirds the whole paragraph. Paul has certainly not allowed Jesus to become a mere cipher: he remains the assured goal, the inspiration, the companion, the pattern, the older brother. It would not be fanciful to see Gethsemane standing behind 8:18-27, if not in Paul's conscious mind, nevertheless in the strong tradition of the early church reading these words (see Heb 5:7-9). It would be profitable to study the portrait of Jesus as it emerges throughout Romans 5–8, and to reflect on the way in which this picture had already made its way, within less than thirty years, into the imagination and subconscious thought of Paul and the other New Testament writers.

7. The rootedness of the entire discussion in the narrative theology of the exodus enables one to suggest a pattern of Christian reading of the Old Testament that is neither simply historical nor simply typological. On the one hand, it is important that the original events are seen in their own right, as the formative events of the people of Israel. (The question of what precisely happened, and of how "historical" the stories accessible to Paul and to ourselves may actually be, is not our present concern.) On the other hand, as many different strands within Second Temple Judaism bear witness, the exodus story was used as a template for the great expectations that were cherished in the time of Jesus. God would, many believed, accomplish something for which the original exodus would be both the historical starting-point and the pattern. Paul, in company with many other early Christians, believed that this had happened in Jesus' life, death, and resurrection, and in the sending of the Spirit by which the church was enabled to go forward to the promised land of new creation. This suggests a reading of the Old Testament that gives due weight to original meanings and contexts, and to different understandings that were available in the first century, while yet suggesting, as the distinctively Christian meaning, the belief that the new exodus both had happened in Jesus, and was still to happen in the resurrection and the consequent transformation of the whole created order. This, I suggest, reflects part of what Paul, and presumably the rest of the early Christian movement (since he is quoting early common tradition) meant by saying that Jesus' death and resurrection had happened "according to the scriptures" (1 Cor 15:3-4).

ROMANS 8:31-39, NOTHING WILL SEPARATE US FROM GOD'S LOVE

COMMENTARY

Paul's substantial argument in chaps. 5–8 is done. The style as well as the content of 8:28-30 indicates as much. What remains is to celebrate, and to do so in a way that draws together the threads of all that has been said so far—all, that is, in chaps. 1–4 as well as 5–8, which explains the strong presence of justification, as well as glorification, in this concluding passage.

As Paul does so, the theme that emerges with particular strength is that of God's love. This is only the second time in the letter Paul has spoken explicitly of God's love (counting 5:5-8 as a single reference, if 5:5 is read the way most scholars do); yet it now becomes clear that this has been the underlying theme all through. An overemphasis in some quarters on the lawcourt setting of Paul's justification terminology has led some sensitive Christians to feel that the apostle is lacking in the great theme of God's love, so obvious (for instance) in John. This, it turns out, is a false antithesis. Not only is John's Gospel replete with forensic language and imagery, a subject that cannot be pursued here.[285] Paul's whole

---

285. See A. E. Harvey, *Jesus on Trial: A Study in the Fourth Gospel* (London: SPCK, 1976); A. T. Lincoln, *Truth on Trial: The Lawsuit Motif in the Fourth Gospel* (Peabody, Mass.: Hendrikson, 2000).

argument is undergirded by the emphasis on the love of God: the fact that it is the main theme in what is obviously a concluding summary proves as much, and indeed warns against taking lexicographical absence to indicate conceptual absence. The thing may be present when the word is not.

The argument of this paragraph is, in fact, the same as that of 5:6-10: that since God's love has done for Christians all that has been done in Christ, there is no power that can shake that love now, or turn it aside from completing the job. The love of God, enjoyed already in the present, will outlast and defeat all enemies, including death itself; the close links between this passage and 1 Cor 15:20-28 indicate clearly enough where the thought is going. Love is the ultimate assurance, stronger than logic, even the great logic of Romans 5–8; love is not an idea to be worked out, but a fact, an experienced fact, something that cannot be denied any more than one can stop breathing. And if the clouds of present suffering hide the sun for a while, the unshakable evidence of God's love is seen, as Paul had already said in 5:6-10, in Jesus' death. Not much is added here to 5:6-10 in terms of actual argument; this increases the sense we had in that passage (see the notes) that 5:1-11 was a full advance statement of the entire argument of 5–8. What we have now in 8:31-39 is the performative expansion of 5:11: "we celebrate in God through our Lord Jesus the Messiah, through whom we have now received the reconciliation."

The internal theological shaping of the paragraph usually goes unnoticed amid the flurry of ideas, the problems about punctuation, the lists of potential dangers and enemies, and the general tone of celebration. Paul's argument proceeds through a series of rhetorical questions, each of which is followed, not by an answer to the question itself, but by a statement that shows that the answer must be "nobody." The first of these questions and answers is broad, introducing the set; the following three fill out and explain the first. The last two verses, explaining and celebrating the answers just given, round off the whole section of the letter with the appropriate mixture of rhetoric and solemnity. Thus the paragraph works as follows:

(A) First question and answer (introductory): if God is for us, who is against us? Answer: [nobody, because] God, having not spared his Son, will now give us all things (vv. 31-32).

(B) Second question and answer (specific focus on God): Who shall bring a charge against us? Answer: [nobody, because] God is the justifier (v. 33).

(C) Third question and answer (specific focus on Christ): Who shall condemn us? Answer: [nobody, because] Christ died, was raised, and now intercedes (v. 34).

(D) Fourth question and answer (specific focus on the link of love between God and those in Christ): Who shall separate us from God's love? Answer: none of the possible candidates, because as God's faithful people we are victorious "through the one who loved us" (vv. 35-37).

(E) Final explanation, summing up: nothing can separate us from God's love in Christ (vv. 38-39).

There may be the hint of a trinitarian shape to the B-C-D sequence (vv. 33-37), picking up and celebrating the picture of God in the chapter, and indeed the letter, so far. Though the Spirit is not mentioned, the careful structuring of questions and answers may suggest, not least in the light of 8:12-16 and particularly vv. 26-28, that the Spirit is the one through whom God's love enables those in Christ to be "more than conquerors"; or, to put it another way, that over against the list of things that might separate us from God's love, it is the Spirit who joins us to God's love, making it a fact of experience, not merely a theological belief.

Within this structure, furthermore, Paul has created a remarkable web of biblical allusions and echoes, summoning up three passages in particular.[286]

The first, in v. 32, is the story of Abraham and Isaac in Genesis 22. In that passage, Abraham's willingness to sacrifice his only beloved son is the reason given for God's greatest blessings on him; here, God's actual sacrifice of the only Son is the demonstration of a love that will thereafter stop at nothing.

---

286. On which see Hays, *Echoes of Scripture in the Letters of Paul,* 57-63.

The role of the "binding of Isaac" in the Jewish thought of Paul's day has been controversial. Though most of the evidence for this as a major theme is later, and some indeed may have developed as a response to early Christian atonement-theology, it is likely that Paul was familiar with some rabbinic traditions in which Genesis 22 had some role to play, at least in anticipating the events of Passover night and perhaps of the Day of Atonement, in providing theological justification for God's forgiving of Israel's sins and for the liberation from slavery that would follow.[287] Whether Paul is responding to such beliefs, or whether, with his own exposition of Abraham still in mind, he is simply following through his own train of thought, it is difficult to say; but his main point is clear, that God "gave up" the only Son "on our behalf." Remarkably enough, Paul managed to write a whole chapter about Abraham (Romans 4) without mentioning this incident. Now it comes in, not however (as in some of the relevant Jewish traditions) to highlight an achievement of Abraham and Isaac, because of which ethnic Israel would receive blessing or atonement, but to emphasize, almost by contrast, the powerful love of God in going even further than Abraham had done.

The second allusion is to the (so-called) third Servant Song in Isa 50:4-9. Though, of course, much Christian tradition has understood the servant songs in specific relation to Jesus himself, as Paul himself arguably does in Phil 2:6-8, in this reworking it is the church, remarkably enough, that takes on the role of the servant, here standing before hostile adversaries, trusting totally in God, and awaiting vindication (8:33-34). However, it is precisely the church "in Christ" that can take this stance. Paul's point throughout Romans 5–8 is that the identity of the church is discovered in the Messiah. The reference to the Messiah's heavenly intercession in v. 34 may, in fact, be an allusion to Isa 53:12; and the reference to being like sheep for the slaughter within the following quotation (v. 36) may again deliberately echo Isa 53:7.[288] At the same time, declaring that the Messiah is now "at God's right hand" summons up Ps 110:1, one of the most frequently cited passages in early Christian exploration of Jesus' status.[289] Jesus is now sharing the very throne of God; and his place at God's right hand was from early on seen as an encouragement to the suffering church, both because he was interceding on its behalf and because his location provided assurance of eventual vindication (see Mark 12:35-37 and par.; 14:62 and par.; Acts 2:33-34; 7:55-56; Eph 1:20; Col 3:1; Heb 1:3; 8:1; 10:12; 12:2; 1 Pet 3:22; Rev 3:21).

The third biblical reference is an explicit quotation. In v. 36 Paul quotes Ps 44:22 [43:23 LXX]: "for your sake we are being killed all day long; we are reckoned as sheep for slaughter." This psalm, like its longer cousin Psalm 89, begins by celebrating the love of God for Israel seen in terms of great victories over national enemies, all looking back, of course, to the exodus story, leading to the claim that "we have boasted in God continually" (44:8). Then the psalm turns to complaint: everything has gone wrong, the enemies are prevailing and mocking, and Israel is covered with shame (vv. 9-16). However, this is not because of Israel's disloyalty; this time at least, Israel is not guilty of disobedience, of idolatry, of breaking the covenant. God knows the secrets of the heart (v. 21). Rather, it is "for your sake" that "we are being killed all day long, and accounted as sheep for the slaughter." It is precisely by being loyal to YHWH that Israel has pulled down the wrath of the pagan nations upon its own head. Therefore, the psalm concludes: It is time for God to wake up and act, to help and redeem. It is time for God's own covenant faithfulness to be unveiled in action.

There can be little doubt that Paul had the entire context in mind, and intended the alert reader to hear its overtones of faith in the midst of tribulation, of covenant loyalty and covenant hope—in fact, of the major theme of Romans. More particularly, the idea of it being somehow God's purpose that "we are killed all the day long" fits so closely both with the servant allusion in vv. 33-34, and with the christological focus of the whole chapter, that we can go further and suggest that Paul

287. On the Jewish traditions see G. Vermes, *Scripture and Tradition in Judaism* (Leiden: Brill, 1973) 193-227; B. D. Chilton and P. R. Davies, "The Aqedah: A Revised Tradition History," *CBQ* 40 (1978) 514-46; B. D. Chilton, "Isaac and the Second Night: A Consideration," *Biblica* 61 (1980) 78-88. See also Fitzmyer, *Romans*, , 531-32.

288. See Hays, *Echoes of Scripture in the Letters of Paul*, 63: Since the people of God are thereby suffering with Christ, "upon them is the chastisement that makes others whole, and with their stripes is creation healed."

289. See Wright, *Jesus and the Victory of God*, 508n. 116, for details of the extensive sources, both primary and secondary.

is here reflecting again what it means to be "conformed to the image of the Son," and to share the Messiah's sufferings and glory (vv. 17, 29). There may also be the suggestion, lurking in Paul's mind as he himself faces the charge of being a disloyal Jew, that his own sufferings are the result not of infidelity but precisely of fidelity.

By skillful use of this complex web of biblical allusion and quotation, Paul is underscoring his basic contention from 3:21 onward. Those who believe in Jesus the Messiah, who respond with love to God's loving action in his death and with faith to God's raising of him from the dead, are constituted as the renewed Israel of God. They are the true children of Abraham; they are the true servant people; they are the people who claim and sing as their own the psalms of the faithful covenant people. Law, prophets, and writings are thus called in as witnesses to the fact that, in the midst of suffering and oppression, the one God of Israel has, in long-promised redeeming love, reconstituted Israel in and around Jesus the Messiah. All who belong to Jesus are the true people of this one God.

Thus is concluded the thesis of chaps. 5–8. Thus is concluded, too, one part of the argument of 1:18–8:39. And thus is formed once again the great question that takes up the other part, and will lead into some of Paul's densest argumentation: what then about Israel according to the flesh?

8:31. Seven rhetorical questions—four of which are structurally important, as we have seen—make up the bulk of this paragraph. They are proffered not as a challenge to Paul's readers to think up clever answers or counterexamples but as a demonstration of the certainty of his case. As so often, the opening (in this case, the first two questions) functions as an overall statement of what is to come, which is then unpacked in successive stages.

Unlike some other occurrences of an initial "What then shall we say?" (see the Commentary on 3:1; 4:1; 6:1), the opening question is not introducing a possible conclusion that Paul will then deny. Traces of this rhetorical move still remain, however, in the questions that follow, all of which invite hearers to suggest reasons why the security of God's people in Christ might be less than absolute, only for Paul to deny that such reasons could be found. By adding "to these things" (NIV) or "about these things" (NRSV), Paul is rhetorically inviting responses to the argument he has just completed, rather than, as in other "what shall we say?" questions, looking for logical corollaries that might follow.

The opening challenge says it all: "if God is for us, who can be against us?" The statement that "God is for us" is about as basic a way as can be conceived of summing up the revelation of God's saving justice in the gospel. Elsewhere, of course, Paul uses "for us" in one form or another as a basic way of explaining the death of Jesus (see 5:6-8; 14:15; 1 Cor 15:3; 2 Cor 5:14-15, 21; Gal 1:4; 2:20; 3:13; Eph 5:2, 25; 1 Thess 5:10; Titus 2:14). Nowhere else is he so bold as to say simply "God is for us" (it is admittedly conditional, but only as a rhetorical device). "Who is against us?" is clearly expecting the answer "nobody"; but there are plenty of candidates lined up to be considered, once Paul has amplified this basic statement. He is writing, furthermore, not from a comfortable armchair with the world at his feet, but on his way to fulfill a difficult and dangerous mission (delivering the collection to Jerusalem) that might cost him his life for one reason (opposition from Torah-observant Jews), and to begin another perhaps even more dangerous and difficult mission (to Rome, and thence to Spain) that might cost him his life for a different reason (the clash between his gospel and Caesar's kingdom). These, together with the normal hazards of his life as a missionary, and the threats from spiritual as well as human and natural forces, will be noted presently. But Paul stands firm as a Jewish-style monotheist: there is one God, and if this God is on our side, then no force on earth or elsewhere can ultimately stand against us.

8:32. The third question, the rhetorical response to "who is against us," carries the force: "nobody is against us, because of what God has done." God did what even Abraham had not done: Isaac was spared, but Jesus was not (the particular echo is of Gen 22:16, where Abraham is commended, and then richly blessed, because he had not spared his only son; for the significance of this, see the Overview). God's willingness to give up the only Son is cited as the key evidence for God's utter reliability. This fills out, exactly as we would have expected from 5:6-10, what is meant by God's being "for us."

The same passage in chap. 5 explains the rhetorical question that then emerges: "How will God, then, not also give us all things with him?"—i.e., with the only Son. If God has done the hard part, there will be no problem with the easy part. If God has given the most valuable treasure possible, everything else will follow (for "give" Paul here uses the quite rare verb χαρίζομαι [*charizomai*], cognate with χάρις [*charis*, "grace"]). Instead of amplifying the negative aspect of the question of v. 31*b* ("who can be against us?"), Paul moves to the positive: God will give us all things (and therefore no power can stand against us). This way of referring to the final state of blessedness, corresponding to "salvation," "glorification," or "life," picks up from vv. 17-25 the theme of inheritance, of the fact that the world as a whole belongs to the Messiah and hence to those who are his. "All things are yours," says Paul in 1 Cor 3:21-23, anticipating the flourish at the end of the present chapter. You own the world—a statement that can only be made with integrity, perhaps, by one who was facing the perils described in v. 35. The grand, sweeping statements of assurance are balanced with the clear recognition of what is still to be faced within the inaugurated eschatology that dominates the horizon. Once again, 2 Cor 6:10 comes into view: "as having nothing, yet possessing all things."

8:33-36. The next two verses, continuing the sequence of rhetorical questions, have caused problems to interpreters because of uncertainty over punctuation, reflected in the different translations. RSV, for example, treats the second half of v. 33 ("It is God who justifies") as the first half of a sentence, the second being the question in v. 34*a*, "who is to condemn?"; and then translates the rest of v. 34, not as a statement ("It is Christ Jesus who died," NRSV), but as a question: "Is it Christ Jesus [i.e., Is it Christ Jesus who is to condemn?]?" This, indeed, is only one of many possible permutations.[290] But the most likely reading, because it accords best with the rhythm and rhetoric of the whole paragraph,

is to see vv. 33*a* and 34*a* as questions to which vv. 33*b* and 34*b* give oblique answers, as, in their different ways, in the NRSV and the NIV.[291] The answers are oblique because they are not offering candidates by way of reply; they are saying, rather, that because God is the justifier, and because the Messiah has died, was raised, and now intercedes, there can indeed be no one to lay a charge against God's elect, no one to condemn. The passage then flows naturally:

a. Who can be against us? No one; God, after all, did not spare the Son (vv. 31*b*-32).

b. Who will bring a charge? No one; God, after all, is the justifier (v. 33).

c. Who will condemn? No one; Christ Jesus, after all, died, was raised, and intercedes (v. 34).

And this leads to an interesting possibility for v. 35:

d. Who will separate us from Christ's love? (Expected answer: No one; the Spirit, after all, has poured out love for God into our hearts.) Paul's answer, after a list of possible agents of separation, is, however: No, we are more than conquerors through the one who loved us (i.e., presumably God, at work by the Spirit; "through" here means "through the agency of" [διά *dia* with genitive]; a few MSS altered this to "because" [*dia* with accusative]). There may have been a trinitarian sequence in Paul's mind, such as (for instance) we find in 1 Cor 12:4-6 or Gal 4:4-7, but the exuberance of the passage has prevented it from reaching full expression.

Whatever we think about that, with vv. 33-34 we are back in the lawcourt, as in the middle of chap. 3. In 2:1-16 the whole human family faced the judgment of God; in 3:19-20 the whole world was in the dock, with no defense to offer against massive charges. Now we look around for possible accusers, and find none. Any that might appear have to face

---

290. Cf. the NEB with the alternatives noted in its margin. For details of all options, see Cranfield, *A Critical and Exegetical Commentary on the Epistle to the Romans*, 437-38; Moo, *The Epistle to the Romans*, 541.

291. Cranfield, *Romans*, 437-38, argues in favor of the RV's variation, which is to put a colon at the end of v. 33, because of the natural link between v. 33*b* and v. 34*a*, both through the antithesis of "justify" and "condemn" and because of the echo of Isa 50:8. The sense is not seriously different from the one adopted here. The reading taken in RSV—from which the REB is not far in sense—is flawed. God would not be a likely bringer of a charge (God is the judge, not a prosecutor). True, 2:16 envisages Christ as the agent of judgment, so that to propose him as a possible pronouncer of condemnation is not totally unthinkable; but the way all of Paul's questions and answers in this paragraph function tells against this implication (present in J. B. Phillips: "Who is in a position to condemn? Only Christ, and Christ died for us"). See the Overview.

the fact that God, the judge, is the justifier; in other words, that the verdict has already been pronounced by the judge whose righteousness has been fully displayed. And that verdict—that those in the Messiah, marked out by faith, are already to be seen as "righteous," even ahead of the final vindication— is precisely what the lawcourt dimension of "justification" is all about. We should note that at this point Paul is once again speaking of the *final* day of judgment, as in 2:1-16 and 8:1. As he looks ahead to that future moment, he puts his confidence in the *past event* of justification and hence the *present standing* of God's people that results from it, knowing that "those God justified, God also glorified." The logic of justification comes full circle.

Very well, then, if there is no one to bring a charge, is there anyone who might offer a verdict of condemnation? Leaving aside the problem of envisaging a judge other than God—and here the close link between 33*b* and 34*a* comes into play, with the echoes of Isa 50:8—all thought of a negative verdict, even supposing there were any charges to come to trial, must be put out of view by the sight of the Messiah, with the whole sweep of his accomplishment. His death was the condemnation of sin (8:3); his resurrection, the announcement that sin had been dealt with, and hence the achievement of justification (4:24-25; 1 Cor 15:17); his glorification, the glorification of his people (8:17, 29-30). Paul here adds a further element, familiar from the letter to the Hebrews (7:25; 9:24) and the first letter of John (2:1), occurring only here in his writings: the present activity of the Messiah, in his life in the heavenly realm, is to intercede on behalf of those he represents. As the servant songs have already been alluded to in this passage, it is possible that, with Jesus' atoning and justifying death also mentioned, we should detect a reference to the intercessory work of the servant of the Lord in the fourth song, at Isa 53:12.

The thought switches from the lawcourt metaphor to something that is no metaphor but the deepest reality: The love of God, which, shown forth in the Messiah, forms the unbreakable bond between God and the believer. Paul here speaks of the love of the Messiah.[292] This may simply be a telescoped way of saying "the love of God in Christ," as in v. 39; or it may actually be a deliberate reference to the love of the Messiah himself, as in Gal 2:20 ("the Messiah loved me, and gave himself for me"; see also 2 Cor 5:14; Eph 3:19). The question Paul raises is the one that will now take him through to the close of the chapter: who can separate us from this love? As suggested above, it is possible that Paul was thinking of a "Spirit"-response to this question, to follow "God" in v. 33*b* and "Christ" in v. 34*b*. Certainly, if we take the logic of the questions, and think back through all that has been said about the Spirit in chap. 8, this would make excellent sense—just as it would be typical of Paul to interrupt himself and then hurry on to his larger conclusion leaving his readers to fill in the blanks on the way.

The actual answer to the question, in any case, is again, "No one." But there is a formidable list of potential enemies who seem bent on separating believers from God's love, and Paul must list them, place the conflict with them on the map of God's purposes for the chosen people, and declare them beaten. Paul speaks of that which he knows; he had himself faced all these enemies, except perhaps the sword, and he must have known that at any moment this too might come his way, whether judically in a Roman court or casually on the road (cf. 2 Cor 11:23-29).

Facing these foes, as he was to do again in Jerusalem and on the voyage to Rome, he took comfort in the scripturally based knowledge that this was part of the vocation of God's people. Though it seemed that calamity had sent God to sleep, had caused the Almighty to shut up his mercy, yet in fact, as the psalmist affirmed, these sufferings were after all part of the plan. For the people of God, suffering was not just something *from* which God would deliver, but something *as a result of which* God would deliver; this belief, held by some (though apparently not all) Jews of the period,[293] had for Paul and the other early Christians reached its astonishing climax in

292. Two very good MSS, and some lesser ones, say "of God," but the weight of evidence is against this. It would be easy for a scribe to "correct" the text in this way to the more predictable reading, not least in the light of v. 39.

293. Cf. 2 Macc 7:9, 11, where the martyred brothers speak of their deaths as being "for the sake of God's law." See further Wright, *Jesus and the Victory of God*, 579-92.

the death of Jesus, but still obtained as part of the life of the new-covenant people of God. Somehow, as Paul elsewhere affirmed of his own sufferings (2 Cor 4:7-15; Col 1:24), the suffering of Christians was to be taken up into the ongoing purposes of God, not to add to the unique achievement of Jesus the Messiah but to embody it in the world.

If Paul has been thinking implicitly of the Spirit, this would further explain the mode of his answer in v. 37, not indeed to the question of v. 35*a*, but to the problem raised by all the instruments of suffering in v. 35*b*. "In all these things we are more than conquerors"; in other words, we are not only able to win a victory over these enemies, we are able to see them off the field entirely. This is part of the meaning of v. 32*b:* God will "give us all things" with Christ. It goes closely, of course, with the promise in 1 Cor 15:24-28, that God will put all enemies under the feet of the Messiah, the last being death itself. "The one who loved us" is most likely God, though with v. 37 poised between v. 35 and v. 39 it could equally be Christ; but the way in which this love sustains the Christian is through the agency of the Spirit, as in 8:26-27. The present tense does not imply that Paul thinks he, or his readers, are able in the present time to defeat all these enemies and so to maintain a tranquil and trouble-free pursuit of happiness. This is, in other words, a shout not of triumphalism but of exuberant faith, faith in the victory that, as Easter had proved, had already been won on the cross and would finally be won at the moment of complete liberation. "We are more than conquerors," like the claim "God also glorified them," is a past truth about the Messiah, a future truth about all his people, and hence a present reality in faith for those living on the basis of that past and in the hope of that future.

8:38-39. The final γάρ *gar* of this section explains the shout of triumph in terms of the settled conviction (grounded on what Paul knows about the Messiah, Jesus, the Lord of the world and "our Lord") that the one true God has poured out, through this Jesus, love of the most powerful and unbreakable kind. Even justice is not the last word about this God; love is. Of this, Paul is "persuaded" (the literal meaning), in other words, "convinced" (NIV, NRSV; cf. 14:14; 15:14). This is no passing impression, feeling, or imagination. He has thought it through and reached an unshakable conclusion.

In v. 35 Paul listed physical events, threats, and circumstances that might separate one from God's love; now he lists the forces that might stand behind those physical threats. Of these, death itself is the most obvious, at least for a Jew; some parts of the Hellenistic tradition, reflected in some later Christian thinking, saw physical death in a less threatening light, because it valued physical life less highly, but for Paul death remained the last and greatest enemy (1 Cor 15:26). "Life" is presumably not simply included as the natural pair to "death"—this list manages to avoid at least one other natural pair, "principalities and powers" (see Eph 3:10; Col 2:15)—and certainly does not refer to the "life" that is the promise of God and the gift of the Spirit. Rather, it seems to envisage the present life, with all its many delights and problems, as a potential separator between God and the believer. Angels, rulers, and powers—presumably the "rulers" here are heavenly ones, corresponding to the "elements" of Gal 4:3, 9 and Col 2:8, 20, though perhaps their earthly counterparts are not ruled out—might try to break the bond of love between God and the church, but they are a defeated rabble and, though they can make a lot of noise, they can now wield no power at the level required to separate God's people from God's love (cf. Col 2:14-15). Time present and time future, space high and low—the whole world, as we say, of space and time as it stretches out before us—can have no power to break the love God has for those in the Messiah. (Time past is irrelevant; the cross and resurrection have dealt with anything it could do.) The chapter, and the section, end with the characteristic christological summary that demonstrates, not simply Paul's rhetorical skill (cf. 5:11, 21; 6:11, 23; 7:25*a*), but the very height and depth of his entire theology.

We are back with the picture that has been there in Romans from the beginning: God and creation, with the human race poised in between, belonging within the latter but called to reflect the image of the former. Idolatry had reversed God's intended order: humans had worshiped that which was not God, had ceded power to that which, being itself corruptible, could only bring death. Now, in the Messiah, Jesus, humanity has been restored; death has been defeated, and creation itself, so far from being shunned as essentially evil, awaits its redemption. Christian assurance, despite caricatures, is the very opposite of human arrogance; it is the fruit of humble, trusting faith. Those who follow their Messiah into the valley of the shadow of death will find that they need fear no evil. Though they sometimes seem sheep for the slaughter, yet they may trust the Shepherd, whose love will follow them all the days of their life.

REFLECTIONS

1. The security of which Paul has spoken throughout Romans 5–8—the security, that is, of final glorification for all those who are justified by faith—is based firmly on the trinitarian revelation of God in the gospel, reflected at least in part in the shape of the present passage. At a time when the question of God is again central in some quarters at least, it is vital to stress that Paul's theology, agenda, spirituality, faith, and hope are all focused on this very specific God. Not for him a vague Deism, a distant God known only through a thick cloud, a God to whom there could be many routes and of whom there could be many equally valid revelations. Not for him a generalized sense of "the sacred" such as could be encountered with equal validity in all, or at least most, religious traditions. After all, the religious traditions of Paul's day included many that were demonstrably dehumanizing; the most powerful new religion in Turkey during Paul's lifetime was the cult of Caesar himself. The way to the confidence and joy of which Paul here speaks is not through a general or vague sense of religion, or indeed of God, but of the specific and focused belief and trust in this God, Father, Son, and Spirit.

It is noticeable that in the post-Christian world of the modern West this belief has been misunderstood, misrepresented, and then scorned. Trinitarian belief is labeled incomprehensible, a philosopher's dense answer to a question nobody today would ask, and is set aside in favor of either a variation on Deism's distant God, or some kind of pantheism (as in some New Age thinking or a form of panentheism.[294] What we find in Paul, if one may coin the phrase, is instead "eschatological the-enpanism": instead of everything existing "in God," true though that may be in one sense, Paul insists that at the last "God will be all in all" (1 Cor 15:28; cf. Eph 1:15-23; 4:10). What is more, this is something to be *accomplished*, not simply a steady state of affairs. The task began with the call of Israel, reached its climax in the presence of God as a human being within the world of space, time, and matter, and is now to be implemented through the Spirit of this Jesus, until the whole creation is filled with the presence and love of God in a way that at present it is not. The created order is good, but incomplete; God intends to complete it, and thereby to liberate it. To seek for God at the moment within the created order, or to try to think or pray one's way to God solely on the basis of the created order, is at best an invalid form of realized eschatology (only when God is "all in all" will this be possible), and at worst taking the broad road toward idolatry. This is not to say that the creator is not in principle knowable through creation (see 1:19-20); only that to search for a divinity within the created order is out of the question.

It is not surprising, then, that such theological schemes do not produce the kind of assurance of which Paul speaks. Indeed, they often inveigh against it, treating assurance as mere cockiness, self-satisfaction, or spiritual arrogance. It is, of course, perfectly possible for Christians to hold a form of assurance that is guilty of any or all of those things. But once again abuse does not nullify proper use. In particular, we might suggest that a form of Christian assurance that has not actually faced the challenges of vv. 35 and 38-39 may still be at best immature; not that all Christians must face all the

---

294. For the last, see the winsome but to my mind ultimately unconvincing essay of Marcus J. Borg, *The God We Never Knew* (San Francisco: Harper, 1997).

---

problems that some face some of the time, but that all should be committed to the full gospel, which will mean that hostility at either an earthly or a spiritual level will come their way sooner or later. When that happens, nothing short of a trinitarian view of God will supply the assurance that is needed. But when these trials are faced, and this God is known in the midst of them to be reliable, powerful, and above all loving—that is when one may expect to hear the shout of genuine Christian joy.

2. This confidence, this assurance, is kept in place by the Bible. To put it another way, the reading, praying, and singing of Scripture is one of the key ways in which trust in the triune God, and the security of this God's love in Christ, is maintained. Paul, as we saw, here brings together law, prophets, and writings in a web of allusion and echo to which (it seems to me) only the most pedantic of scholars can remain deaf, in order to say in practice what he says explicitly in 15:4: these things were written for our encouragement, "so that through patience and the comfort of the scriptures we might have hope."

For too long scholars have sneered at Paul's use of Scripture, implying that for him it was a blade of grass that could be blown in any direction by any powerful wind. Preachers have taken their cue from this, often saying quite casually that Paul's use of Scripture is simply unprincipled and peculiar; sometimes, indeed, this is used as an excuse for similarly eccentric usage on the part of the expositor. We have seen, however, that his allusions and echoes are not accidental, but fall into a clear pattern. This pattern is completely explicable on the assumption of an overall covenantal reading, in which God's people from Abraham to the Messiah form the advance guard, not of course without paradox and ambiguity, of the people now created in the Messiah and the Spirit. To be sure, there has been a dramatic and decisive explosion in the middle of the sequence, with the Messiah's shameful death and all that went with it. But this, too, Paul insists, was what the covenant God had in mind all along. The people of God in the present are not simply a creation out of nothing; they are, however unexpectedly, the family promised to Abraham. The problems faced by Abraham's family before the Messiah's coming, notably the question of how Israel's God was going to fulfill the covenant and deliver Israel, were problems Paul believed had been answered in Christ. The resurgence of apparently similar problems in the church was to be answered in terms of life in Christ and the victory of the Spirit. God has revealed the divine covenant faithfulness, and the proclamation of the gospel continues to unveil it. The church's task, in its own use of the Scriptures, is to hear both the earlier stages of its own story and the continual resonances, amplified in the echo chamber of the messianic events concerning Jesus, which will inform and guide its own journey through the wilderness. Learning to hear these multiple resonances with the proper blend of imaginative attention and discipline is a major part of Christian teaching and discipleship.

3. This passage offers, for the first time in Romans, a description of the kinds of suffering that Paul and his fellow Christians faced in the first century. Only 2 Corinthians 6 and 11, in fact, go into more detail, though the fact of suffering is everywhere apparent. Not only is there physical affliction to be faced, some from natural causes and some from violent opposition, but there is also the constant threat from supernatural or cosmic forces. Paul does not often speak explicitly about these, but throughout his writings we sense a shadow of danger, threat, and struggle that took these and other forms.

His response, clearly, is very different from that which seeks to attain a higher state of consciousness in which physical pain and suffering are irrelevant and can be ignored. The battle is real; it matters because the physical world is God's world and cannot be played down in favor of a "spiritual" reality. Suffering comes as a result of the gospel, which, by its announcement of Jesus as Lord, challenges all other lordships, many of which, at both the cosmic and the terrestrial levels, will fight in defense. (There are many forms of Christianity on offer today that pose no threat to any principalities and powers, and indeed make a virtue of not confronting anyone with anything. What kind of authenticity can they claim?) Once more, we must not confuse the necessary confrontation between the gospel and the powers of the world with the belligerence of some would-be preachers and evangelists, who are often enough propagating not the gospel itself but a particularly brittle parody of it, which can only be defended by shouting louder. For Paul, the message of the cross and resurrection of Jesus, and his enthronement as Lord of the world, never failed to arouse the wrath of the powers in one way or another. If this message were to catch on, the world would be turned upside down, and a lot of vested interests with it.

Woe betide the church, therefore, if it becomes sidelined into offering an apparently "spiritual" version of "life, liberty, and the pursuit of happiness." A recent book by a best-selling Christian author assures us that "golf, next to marriage and parenthood, can routinely be the greatest of life's learning opportunities," and that "golf can be a wonderful spiritual path of growth toward God."[295] I have no quarrel with golf. No doubt it, like many games, can teach wise players important things about themselves. Golf can also, of course, produce special kinds of suffering, both for those who play and for those who listen afterward. But I think I know what Paul would say to these propositions—and not out of any killjoy spirit, either. The Western church is in danger of becoming so concerned with Christianity as a way to further its own goals of self-advancement that it has forgotten what its siblings in many other countries know day by day, often literally in their (broken) bones; that the gospel confronts the principalities and powers with the news that their time is up, and that the true way to Christian joy lies in discovering in practice that this message is true.

4. The greatest theme of the paragraph is the love of God. This topic is a vast sea to put into a small bottle; far better to swim in it or to set sail upon it. Paul speaks of God's love as the ultimate security. Learning to look at the cross and to see there the strong evidence of how much one is loved is among the most basic and vital Christian disciplines, matched by opening one's heart and life to the tidal wave of that love, displacing all other rivals. The mind is to learn, and the heart is to know in experience, "the love of Christ which passes knowledge" (Eph 3:19). If Christian ministry does nothing but help, encourage, and enable people along these paths, it will have done well.

But God's love is also the ultimate human fulfillment. Much of Romans 5–8 has been about the genuine model of humanness, over against the spurious models offered by sin and the flesh. In a world that is currently lurching from "I think, therefore I am" to "I shop, therefore I am," the challenge to find one's human identity in being loved— *Amor, ergo sum,* I am loved, therefore I am—is central to discovering the genuine way of being human. And when, with or without specific human loves to incarnate it, human beings discover afresh that they are loved and embraced by the God who made heaven and earth, then what is found is a fulfillment that can never be self-centered, a personal enrichment that has nothing to do with self-help programs. Being loved by the true God, we are to become truly human beings in sharing that love. Not to do so is to cast doubt upon which God it was whose love was being felt in the first place.

Once again, the themes of the letter pose a standing challenge to the imperial system of which Paul, himself a Roman citizen, was a critic from within. If it is indeed true, as some have suggested, that already at this period some in Rome thought of the "secret name" of the city as AMOR, "love" ("Roma" spelled backward), it is a further indication of something we would have to stress anyway: that a community founded on, and sustained by, the sovereign love of the creator God is a political threat, not least to anything like a totalitarian system.[296] People who find themselves loved by the Lord

295. M. Scott Peck, *Golf and the Spirit* (New York: Harmony, 1999) 61. He claims that golf teaches humility, *kenosis*, and even grace.
296. Details in D. E. Aune, *Revelation*, 3 vols., WBC 52C (Dallas: Word, 1997) 3:926-27.

of the world tend not to care quite so much as others what happens to them. They care passionately about justice, and many other causes great and small, but in terms of ordinary politics they are often at best seen as mavericks (the compliment that political regimentation pays to freedom of conscience) and at worst as dangerous loose cannons. In Paul's case, believing in *amor Dei*, the Love of God, and finding himself embraced by it, and discovering an answering love in his own heart, made him a highly dangerous citizen within a system that claimed to embody love, perhaps even to be a deity with that name. Citizens within all kinds of systems today need to work out the equivalent in their own terms.

The love of God, finally, offers itself as the key to the truest mode of knowing—knowing about God, knowing about other people, knowing about the world, knowing about oneself. We have learned, often painfully, that when somebody seems to be offering you something for nothing you need to be suspicious of their motives. We have learned that expressions of love are all too often a cover for manipulation and exploitation. God help us, some today even accuse God of these things. We have learned, in other words, the hermeneutic of suspicion, which is a fancy philosophers' way of saying that we have rediscovered the doctrine of original sin by the back door, shortly after the theologians had abandoned it as being historically unfounded, psycho-logically unwarranted, and pastorally unhelpful. What this passage would teach us, however, as one contemporary application of Paul's message about the gospel of Jesus Christ conquering the world of sin and death, the world of which the hermeneutic of suspicion warns but from which it, like the Torah, cannot free us, is that the love of God is the deepest truth in the cosmos, and that to trust this love is to open oneself neither to manipulation nor exploitation but to a richer and fuller humanness—suffer-ing included—than one would ever know, and to a share in the loving liberation and remaking of the cosmos itself. The love of God, in other words, proposes a hermeneu-tic of trust: not a casual or shallow trust of any person or proposition that comes along, but a deep and hard-won trust, a knowing that is born of being loved and of loving in return. There is much that could be said about this, but it is important at least to point out that if we are thus rediscovering the doctrine of sin, we have in Romans the greatest exposition of the victory of the God of love over sin and its consequences. We would do well to apply this to the places in the world, and in our lives, where sin still reigns in death.

We paraphrase, in conclusion, the final two verses of the section. Paul has spoken, and we must speak, of the love of the one true God. This love of God calls across the dark intervals of meaning, reaches into the depths of human despair, embraces those who live in the shadow of death or the overbright light of present life, challenges the rulers of the world and shows them up as a sham, looks at the present with clear faith and at the future with sure hope, overpowers all powers that might get in the way, fills the outer dimensions of the cosmos, and declares to the world that God is God, that Jesus the Messiah is the world's true Lord, and that in him love has won the victory. This powerful, overmastering love grasps Paul, and sustains him in his praying, his preaching, his journeying, his writing, his pastoring, and his suffering, with the strong sense of the presence of the God who had loved him from the beginning and had put that love into action in Jesus. This is the love because of which there is no condemna-tion. This is the love because of which those who are justified are also surely glorified. And this is the love, seen supremely in the death of the Messiah, which reaches out to the whole world with the exodus message, the freedom message, the word of joy and justice, the word of the gospel of Jesus.

ROMANS 9:1–11:36

GOD'S PROMISES AND GOD'S FAITHFULNESS

OVERVIEW

Everything about Romans 9–11 is controversial. Even its place in the letter has been challenged: C. H. Dodd, notoriously, regarded it as an old sermon that Paul happened to have by him. He slipped it in here, Dodd suggested, even though it broke the train of thought, which would otherwise have run on smoothly from chap. 8 to chap. 12.[297] At the other extreme, many have seen this section as the real climax of the letter.[298] Exegesis has attempted to negotiate positions between these two extremes, and there is now a general consensus that the section is extremely important both within the letter and for Paul's wider theology. A good many lines of thought in other letters besides Romans, and indeed in other parts of the New Testament besides Paul, raise the question of which this is the premier discussion: What has God been doing with Israel?

Like almost every part of this letter, 9–11 has suffered from being seen as the classic treatment of certain topics—topics that interpreters have brought to Paul rather than letting him dictate his own terms. Chapter 9 has long been seen as the central NT passage on "predestination," though as we shall see the theological tradition from Augustine to Calvin (and beyond) did not grasp what Paul was actually talking about here. Subsequent debates about how people get saved have used the section to balance the options: In chap. 9 (it has been said) everything flows from divine sovereignty, in chap. 10 everything hinges on human responsibility, and in chap. 11 it turns out that God will in any case have mercy upon all.[299] More broadly, those who have seen Paul's view of God and salvation as being essentially outside space and time have discovered in this passage something that to them seems very strange: a historical "dimension" to salvation. In the light of the interpretation of the first eight chapters, this has the feel of someone who, only knowing Beethoven's symphonies in piano transcription, suddenly discovers a fully orchestrated version of the third movement of his Ninth, and discusses it as a curious sideline rather than being alerted by it to what those transcriptions had been trying to say. It remains, however, the implicit view of a good many readers who have managed, despite Paul's best efforts, to screen out the "Israel" dimension from all that has gone before.[300]

The major topic that has come to the forefront of theological discussion in the second half of the twentieth century, and is obviously much closer to what Paul is really talking about, is the question of the ethnic people Israel. The horrors of Auschwitz have haunted two generations, and we shall not quickly forget what can happen when a culture demonizes an entire people, particularly when that culture professed, in some measure at least, to be Christian. Those of us whose early years were overshadowed by the memory of the Nazi horror are simply incapable of reading texts on relevant subjects—and Romans 9–11 is certainly a relevant subject—without reflecting on the ways in which they relate to what has been a major moral question of modern times.

297. Dodd, *The Epistle of Paul to the Romans,* 161-63.
298. Stendahl, *Paul Among Jews and Gentiles,* 4; Wright, *The Climax of the Covenant,* 234; Fitzmyer, *Romans,* 541.

299. So, ingeniously but inaccurately, G. B. Caird, "Predestination—Romans ix. xi.," *Expository Times* 68 (1956–57) 324-27.
300. See the classic statement of Sanday and Headlam, *A Critical and Exegetical Commentary on the Epistle to the Romans,* 225.

Yet even this reflection may produce distortions. Just as modern Pauline studies have taken account of the fact that, despite Martin Luther, Paul was not after all writing about the pope, so it may be time to pause and reflect that Paul was not after all writing about Adolf Hitler. The controversial revolution in Pauline studies that produced the so-called new perspective of the 1970s shifted attention away from late-medieval soul-searchings and anxieties about salvation, and placed it instead on (in Sanders's phrase) the comparison of patterns of religion.[301] It was a self-consciously post-Holocaust project, aimed not least at reminding Paul's readers of his essential Jewishness. But this should not blind us to the fact that, precisely as a Jewish person, Paul begins this section with grief and sorrow—because he sees his fellow Jews rejecting the gospel of their own Messiah. Paul is not writing a post-Enlightenment treatise about how all religions are basically the same; nor is he writing an essay on the modified version of the same project—namely, how the one God has made two equally valid covenants, one with Jews and the other with Christians.[302] Nor is he writing a postmodern tract about how everybody must tell their own story and find their own way.[303] As we shall see, these chapters remain profoundly Christian—that is, centered on Jesus as Messiah and Lord. Paul does not accomodate himself to our agendas and expectations any more than he did to those of his contemporaries.

But what is he actually saying here? What is his argument, and how does he develop it? And, looking wider, how does this section advance the argument of the letter so far? Is Romans 9–11 peripheral or central to the purpose of the letter? Here we meet once more the question of a distinction between the sequence of thought in a particular letter and the hypothetical logical order of Paul's underlying theology.[304] Part of the difficulty, here as elsewhere, is that Romans has for so long been held to be a statement precisely of Paul's underlying theology, his most fundamental beliefs, that there has always been a tendency to assimilate the actual exegesis of this specific letter to the terms, or sequence, of what the interpreter assumes as rock-bottom Pauline thought. We must beware of this trap, while not ruling out the possibility that Paul has indeed said some things here that serve as the clearest statements of some of his fundamental themes.

It will be particularly important to note the ways in which this section does indeed build on, and develop the argument of, chaps. 1–8, and the ways in which it leads naturally into 12–16. We should note as well, however, that Paul here frequently comes back to topics and questions he handles elsewhere. The letter, we remind ourselves, has not only a linear flow but also something of a spiral shape, in which (for instance) the discussion of the law in 9:30–10:13 looks back to that in 7:1–8:11, and behind that in turn to 2:17-29—and on to some elements of 14:1–15:13.

Two questions dominate these three chapters: the question of unbelieving Israel, and the question of God's faithfulness. The two are, of course, intimately connected: the latter is raised by the former. Israel's refusal (as a whole) to believe the gospel of Jesus raises in its sharpest form the question of whether God has in fact been faithful to his promises. It is somewhat paradoxical that Paul does not spell out these questions themselves; they are, it seems, too huge and obvious. He begins the section by simply addressing them, letting them come to the surface bit by bit. His heartbreaking grief in 9:1-3 speaks eloquently of the first; his opening denial ("God's word cannot have failed!") in 9:6 shows that the second is his primary concern. And when we turn to the end of the section and find the salvation of Israel guaranteed by God's gifts, call, and overall purpose (11:26-32), we can be sure we have correctly identified the double theme.

This double theme comes to focus as the question of God's covenant faithfulness,

301. See the title of his epoch-making book, Sanders, *Paul and Palestinian Judaism*.

302. J. G. Gager, *The Origins of Anti-Semitism: Attitudes Toward Judaism in Pagan and Christian Antiquity* (New York: Oxford University Press, 1983); Gaston, *Paul and the Torah*, esp. 135-50. A fuller list is in Moo, *The Epistle to the Romans*, 549. For more recent critiques of this view see E. E. Johnson, *The Function of Apocalyptic and Wisdom Traditions in Romans 9–11*, SBLDS 109 (Atlanta: Scholars Press, 1989) 176-205; R. Hvalvik, "A 'Sonderweg' for Israel: A Critical Examination of a Current Interpretation of Romans 11.25-27," *JSNT* 38 (1990) 87-107.

303. As seems to be implied in K. Stendahl, *Final Account: Paul's Letter to the Romans* (Minneapolis: Fortress, 1995) chap. 4.

304. This is similar to N. R. Petersen's distinction of "poetic sequence" and "narrative sequence." See N. T. Wright, "Romans and the Theology of Paul," in Hay and Johnson, *Pauline Theology, Volume III*, 32.

the δικαιοσύνη θεοῦ (*dikaiosynē theou*), which is discussed in the Introduction and in relation to such key passages as 1:17 and 3:21-31. In case there is any question of this, the buildup of questions in 9:6, 14, and 19, echoing the questions of 3:1-9, leads Paul's discussion to the central and decisive statement of 10:3: Israel has been ignorant of God's righteousness, and, in seeking to establish a righteousness of its own, has not submitted to God's righteousness. God has done what God always promised, but this does not look like what Israel had come to expect, had come to take for granted as its automatic right. God's righteousness—which means God's faithfulness to the covenant promises, and, beyond that, God's determination that through those promises the world would be put to rights—appears to be called into question by Israel's failure to believe the gospel. The reason why Paul has to write this whole section is that a huge hole has been ripped in the story of God and Israel as he and others had imagined it. We may say, somewhat like Karl Barth, that those eagerly awaiting the divine Yes had heard instead a resounding No. Paul here explores the mystery of how nevertheless this No was the necessary preliminary to an ultimate Yes—albeit a redefined one.

Is the section, then, really after all an "aside," even if a vitally necessary one? Some have suggested so.[305] The problem of Israel's unbelief, they have proposed, is the obvious and major counter-example to Paul's thesis to this point, which is that salvation is assured to all who believe because God can be trusted to keep promises. But this, though certainly true at one level, does not yet plumb the depths of what Paul has been saying in chaps. 1–8 or will now say in chaps. 9–11. The question of Israel—of God's promises to Abraham and of how they are fulfilled—has been central, not peripheral, to the letter all through. The questions of chap. 9 are the questions Paul noted at the start of chap. 3; they were raised by 2:17-29, and are now raised again, more intensively, by chaps. 5–8. This is part of the point of 9:4-5: the privileges of Israel, there enumerated, correspond quite closely, and surely not accidentally, to the things he has

been saying in 5–8. This warrants us in reading 9–11 in the light of 2:28-29, where the question of who counts as a "Jew" is critical, and where the answer is given in the language of covenant renewal—which is now open to all, Jew and Gentile alike.

If these are the questions Paul must face, how does he go about answering them? It is of primary importance in reading Romans 9–11 to realize that its backbone is *a retelling of the story of Israel, from Abraham to (Paul's) present day*. From 9:6 to 10:21, Paul is retelling the great narrative that every Jew knew. His retelling belongs with (though it subverts) other Second Temple retellings of the Jewish story: It is a retelling that speaks to what God had been doing all along, and that leaves Paul in a position to mount the fresh argument of chap. 11. If this is what the story of God and Israel in fact looks like, he is saying, the present position and obligations must be understood accordingly. Only if we fail to see the essential narrative substructure of the section do the biblical references and allusions "distract" us from the point.[306]

The way the story is told is central. There were many retellings of Israel's story current in Paul's world. Obvious examples, themselves important for Romans 9–11, include such different writings as 4 Ezra, Wisdom 10–19, and 4QMMT column C.[307] A word about each will make the point. Fourth Ezra wrestles with the question of God's faithfulness to the covenant with Israel in the face of the disaster of 70 CE.[308] Wisdom reaches back to Adam, like Paul in Romans 5, in order to concentrate on the exodus story, as I have argued that Paul did in Romans 8. The exodus story was told in Wisdom not as a bare historical account, but in order to highlight the strange sovereign ways of God, the potter who molds the clay (15:7)—and particularly as an encouragement to first-century Jews to trust this God for deliverance from the pagan heirs of ancient Egypt. A short, selective version of the story is told in 4QMMT,

---

305. See Bryan, *A Preface to Romans*, 159. Even Moo, *Romans*, 547-52, while affirming that this section is "central," does so because he supposes that Paul is facing opposition and debate on the Jew/Gentile question.

306. Fitzmyer, *Romans*, 542.

307. Obvious NT examples are the speech of Stephen in Acts 7:2-53, whose polemical selection of material and rhetorical force are well known. See B. Witherington, *The Acts of the Apostles: A Socio-Rhetorical Commentary* (Grand Rapids: Eerdmans, 1998) 259-77. See also the shorter speech of Paul in Acts 13:13-41 and the list of heroes in Hebrews 11.

308. See esp. Johnson, *The Function of Apocalyptic and Wisdom Traditions in Romans 9–11*; D. W. Longenecker, *Eschatology and the Covenant: A Comparison of 4 Ezra and Romans 1–11* (Sheffield: Sheffield Academic, 1991).

highlighting the covenant promises of Deuteronomy 29–30, and claiming that the promises of covenant renewal are being fulfilled in those who observe the particular ceremonial practices of the sect (see the Commentary on 10:5-9). Like 4 Ezra, Paul tells Israel's story to vindicate God's faithfulness. Like Wisdom, he recounts the narrative to make points about the way in which God always behaves. Like the author of 4QMMT, he tells the story in order to say: this is where we belong within it. We are the heirs, the new-covenant people promised long ago. His telling, in other words, is exemplary (the story offers examples of how it is with God and Israel), but it is more importantly eschatological (the story is going somewhere and including the present readers within it). Eschatology is the framework within which examples may be understood.

The main thrust of all this, within the present letter, is to arrive at the questions of 11:1 and 11:11 with both feet on firm ground. Paul's aim throughout chap. 11 is to argue from basic principles that God still intends to save ethnic Jews. Why does he need to do this? It seems there is a danger that Gentile Christians in Rome will assume, or even argue, that God has cut unbelieving Jews out of his plan for good, has left them without hope.[309] Paul does not say that Roman Gentile Christians should themselves engage in evangelism among their unbelieving Jewish neighbors. But he declares that part of the point of his own Gentile mission—the primary focus of his work, or so he says here—is to make presently unbelieving Jews jealous, jealous of seeing their privileges now shared by non-Jews, and so to bring them to salvation through faith (11:23).

Why does he need to say this to the Roman church at this stage of its history? He does not say, but three historical answers present themselves, each of which has plausibility and may have combined to give him a sense of urgency. To begin with, Rome had a long tradition of anti-Jewish sentiment.[310] The prominence of some Jews in the imperial court had only increased the sense of many in Rome that this race of foreigners was at best a mixed blessing, at worst an enemy with a dangerous set of beliefs. Gentile Christians in Rome, especially during the period when Jews had been expelled from the capital after the riots in the late 40s, might have found it all too easy to assimilate this popular belief: although Christianity had begun among the Jews, they might suppose, God had now written them off (see the Introduction). Second, the return of considerable numbers of Jews to Rome after Claudius's death in 54 CE—supposing for the moment the truthfulness of the various accounts of expulsion, and the probability of such a return[311]—cannot but have had an impact on the small, young church in Rome. Assuming that the church numbered no more than a few dozen (the argument would still hold if it numbered a thousand, but this is unlikely), it must have seemed threatening for thousands of Jews suddenly to reappear in the capital, for the synagogues to be full again. It would be very easy for the church to demonize them, to regard them as the enemy. Third, by the late 50s there was increasing tension in Judaea and Galilee. The crisis over Gaius's plan to set up his statue in the Temple had passed, but revolutionary fervor had not waned, and successive governors seemed to go out of their way to provoke rebellion. Any Jew hearing news of this would feel involved, even hundreds of miles away across the Mediterranean. Any Gentile Christians in Rome, particularly any groups that were influenced by the two considerations just mentioned, would be eager to distance themselves from any sense of complicity with the impending revolt. Paul himself had declared that God's wrath had come upon the Judaeans at last (1 Thess 2:16); how much more might a Gentile Christian in Rome be eager to assign unbelieving Israel to the scrapheap of history.[312] We only have to think of Marcion, less than a century later, to see how perceptive Paul was in spotting the problems that might arise.[313]

309. Moo, *Romans*, 683-84, doubts whether Roman Gentiles really questioned Jewish salvation. It seems that the whole chapter is designed to argue the point against people whom Paul assumes challenge it.

310. See the mass of material assembled by M. Stern, *Greek and Latin Authors on Jews and Judaism*, 3 vols. (Jerusalem: Israel Academy of Sciences and Humanities, 1976). For a brief survey, see J. C. Waters, *Ethnic Issues in Paul's Letter to the Romans* (Valley Forge, Pa.: Trinity, 1993), chap. 2, esp. 28-55.

311. See Wright, *The New Testament and the People of God*, 354-55; Dunn, *Romans 1–8*, liii; Fitzmyer, *Romans*, 30-36.

312. On 1 Thess 2:16 and its relation to Romans 9–11 see W. D. Davies, *Jewish and Pauline Studies* (London: SPCK, 1984) chap. 7; C. A. Wanamaker, *The Epistles to the Thessalonians: A Commentary on the Greek Text*, NIGTC (Grand Rapids: Eerdmans, 1990) 114-19.

313. On Marcion (d. c. 160 CE) and his significance, see J. J. Clabeaux, "Marcion," in *The Anchor Bible Dictionary*, 6 vols. (Garden City, N. Y.: 1992) 4:514-16.

From this perspective, we may suggest that the retelling of Israel's story in 9:6–10:21 is itself designed not only to suggest a new way of reading Israel's own history but also quietly to undermine the pretensions of Rome itself. Rome, too, told stories of its own history, going back to the brothers Romulus and Remus a thousand years earlier, coming through the long story of the republic and finally arriving at the emperor who was now enthroned as lord of the world.[314] Paul, having declared in 9:5 that Jesus, the Messiah, is "God over all, blessed forever" (see below), returns to the point in 10:12: Jesus is Lord of all, Jew and Gentile alike. Israel's history, climaxing in Jesus, is designed to upstage Roman history, climaxing in Augustus. This helps to create the right atmosphere for chap. 11: This is a Jewish way of construing world history, of telling its story over against the story of pagan empire, and this is the ground that the Christian continues to stand on, the ground that makes it impossible to dismiss unbelieving Jews as forever outside God's ongoing purposes.

Paul's own role and vocation become topics within the story. His mission to the Gentiles is the necessary consequence of the covenant renewal that has taken place in Christ for the benefit of Jew and Gentile alike (10:14-15). The puzzle of its results—continuing Jewish unbelief, while Gentiles flock in—is itself to be understood in terms of the fulfillment of law and prophecy (10:16-21). But that fulfillment itself offers the key to the next stage in God's plan: "jealousy," Israel's jealousy of Gentiles who are inheriting the promises (10:19; 11:11, 14). It is this jealousy, aroused precisely by the success of Paul's work among the Gentiles, that will bring Israel to faith at last (11:14). Paul is himself an example of the fact that Jews can still be saved (11:1-6); he is part of the "remnant," in the sense there explained. But he is not just an example; he is, through his mission and the "jealousy" of his fellow Jews that results, part of the means by which God will save "some of them" (11:13-14). And

all this, we must remember, is held within a discussion introduced by Paul's personal grief (9:1-2), producing an astonishing potential prayer (9:3) and a firm actual one (10:1). He is himself part of the answer to his own prayer, not by becoming "anathema from Christ," as he would have been prepared to be (9:3), but by continuing with his vocation to the Gentiles, so that in looking-glass fashion this may bring Jews back into the family after all. The self-references that emerge from the tightly knit texture of chaps. 9–11 take their place within Paul's self-introduction as we find it in 1:8-17 and 15:14-29.

There remains one underlying introductory question. What can be said about the apparent disjunction between the subject-matter of Romans 5–8 and that of 9–11? Granted that chaps. 1–4, which are, indeed, the ground and basis of chaps. 5–8, have more in common with chaps. 9–11 in terms of subject matter, we are nevertheless left with an obvious break. To look no further, Jesus Christ is mentioned explicitly about twenty-five times in 108 verses in Romans 5–8, with numerous additional references to "he," "him," to the "one man" in whom Adam's trespass is undone, and perhaps above all to "God's son." Yet in chaps. 9–11, after the three mentions in the first five verses, all we are left with is 10:4-13 and the isolated (and textually challenged) 10:17. Even more striking, perhaps, is the vivid presence (eighteen occurrences) of the Spirit in chap. 8, and its total absence, after 9:1, until 14:17 (11:8 is hardly to be construed as a reference to the Holy Spirit; 12:11 probably refers to the human spirit). These indicators have led some, notably the influential scholar Krister Stendahl, to ask whether the entire section is in fact an exposition of a different point of view, a way of salvation in which Jesus Christ plays little or no direct part.[315]

With due deference to Stendahl, whose seminal essay on Paul started many of us thinking in fresh ways a generation ago, I regard this as misleading.[316] Romans 5–8 is a formal, almost stylized step-by-step presentation

---

314. On the ideology of the Augustan Empire see esp. P. Zanker, *The Power of Images in the Age of Augustus*, trans. A. Shapiro (Ann Arbor: University of Michigan Press, 1990); Horsley, *Paul and Empire*, esp. 10-24; and P. A. Brunt *"Laus Imperii,"* in Horsley, *Paul and Empire*, esp. 10-24 and 25-35.

315. Stendahl, *Paul Among Jews and Gentiles*, and *Final Account: Paul's Letter to the Romans* (Minneapolis: Fortress, 1995). Johnson, *The Function of Apocalyptic and Wisdom Traditions in Romans 9–11*, 205, agrees with Stendahl that Paul's argument is "theocentric" rather than christocentric, but insists that "Christology cannot be omitted from the agenda."

316. See K. Stendahl, "The Apostle Paul and the Introspective Conscience of the West," in *Paul Among Jews and Gentiles*, 78-96.

of what God has accomplished in Jesus Christ. But underneath this presentation, as we saw, is the story of Israel, looking back to its beginnings in Abraham, set in the context of God's promise to undo the effects of Adam's fall, and working through exodus, Sinai, and the wilderness wanderings on the way to the inheritance, the new creation promised in Isaiah. The surface story is about Jesus, the deeper dimension is about Israel. In 9–11, I suggest, it is more or less the other way around—though to be sure when Jesus the Messiah appears in 10:4-13 this is not incidental, but, like the "righteousness of God" in 10:3 with which Jesus is closely correlated, as the explicit statement of what is everywhere implicit. The surface story is that of God's people, from Abraham to Paul's own day; but the deeper dimension is the story of the Messiah's people according to the flesh (9:5).

Romans 9:5 stands at the head of chaps. 9–11, in fact, much as 1:3-4 stands at the head of chaps. 1–8 and of the letter as a whole: the opening messianic statement in the light of which everything that follows is to be understood. Israel, Paul is saying, is Messiah-focused. The long story that began with Abraham reached its climax, its goal, its τέλος (*telos*) in him. And Israel is also Messiah-shaped. The pattern of Israel's history (rejection, failure, and exile followed by astonishing covenant renewal) is none other than the pattern of death and resurrection. That is why, when Paul sees God's righteousness unveiled in the Messiah (10:3-4), our minds inevitably go back to 3:21-26, where it was Jesus' death in particular that accomplished God's saving plan. And that is why, when we look ahead to 11:11-16, where Paul is arguing for the restoration, the "receiving back," of Israel, he alludes to key steps in the argument of chap. 5 (see the detailed exposition). He is treating Israel as precisely the Messiah's own people, according to the flesh; his argument is that in Christ, and nowhere else, can we understand what has happened, is happening, and will happen to ethnic Israel.

Hence, crucially for the interpretation of both chaps. 5–8 and 9–11 and of the relationship between the two, the complex discussion of the Torah in 7:1–8:11 turns out to have laid foundations for the equally complex passage 9:30–10:13. The details of this must be explored in their proper place. Suffice it to say here that in this new context we encounter once more Israel's stumble over the God-given Torah, and God's once again doing, through the Messiah, what the Torah always intended, in other words, the fulfillment of the *dikaiosynē theou* (10:3-4). The strange but God-given negative purpose of the Torah (remember the repeated ἵνα [*hina*] of 7:13 and the sequence of thought ending with 8:3) is picked up in the strange but God-given purpose whereby, again through the Torah, Israel trips and stumbles (10:32-33). But God's purpose goes forward to embrace the Gentiles—and Israel itself can in turn be restored. This helps, as we shall see, to explain the harsh predestinarian passages in chap. 9: the double *hina* of 7:13 has become the double ὅπως (*hopōs*) of 9:17. As in 7:1–8:11, so here, the purpose of God through Torah and in Israel was to draw God's history with the world to the single point of the Messiah, in order to deal with sin and death and create a new world the other side. Since this vocation could only be undertaken by the Messiah as an individual, it was necessary that Israel be led along the strange path of being God's people but being called to be cast away—just as the Messiah himself was called to be crucified for the sins of the world. That, it seems, is the logic that underlies 9:6-29 and 11:11-15, and which is focused on the central passage of the whole section: 10:1-13.[317]

If this reading of chaps. 9–11 is correct, and if in particular we are right to see 10:6-13 as an essentially "new covenant" reading of Deuteronomy 30, then we are justified in claiming that the Holy Spirit, though not explicitly mentioned in these chapters, is indeed "underneath" the argument in at least one passage. In 10:9 Paul uses language very close to that of 1 Cor 12:3, where the Spirit is the main subject. In fact, 10:9-13 is close in theme to 2:27-29, where the letter/spirit contrast is crucial. And in the final verse of the section (10:13) Paul quotes from Joel 3:5 LXX, a passage that in its best-known occurrence in the NT (Acts 2:21) was cited on the day of Pentecost as part of the interpretation of the outpouring of the Spirit. Paul has no need to stress the work of the Spirit at this point in his argument; but it is impossible to

---

317. See the important study of C. K. Rowe, "Romans 10:13: What Is the Name of the Lord?" *Horizons in Biblical Theology* 22 (2000) 135-73.

claim that these three chapters present a theology from which Christ and the Spirit have been systematically excluded. This point illustrates, incidentally, a major factor in the exegesis of the section: again and again we can find clues to Paul's meaning in the larger context of the biblical passages he quotes, not least in the light of how those passages were being read in his day.

How do chaps. 9–11 relate to the final chapters of the letter, 12–16? The question is partly answered by realizing that the central passage of that closing section consists of 14:1–15:13, which emphasizes the coming together of different cultures in obedience to the same Lord. That passage is, in that sense, the long-range outworking of the theme we have seen again and again in this letter: the faithfulness of God to Jew and Gentile alike, and their coming together in the Messiah. The main thrust of Romans 11 has to do with the attitude of Christian Gentiles to non-Christian Jews, and the main thrust of Romans 14 and 15 has to do with the mutual attitudes of Christians from different ethnic backgrounds; but the underlying theology is the same. And the historical narrative of God's people in chaps. 9–10 leaves Paul precisely with the sort of community he is addressing in chaps. 12–16: the worldwide, multiethnic people who give allegiance to Abraham's God in and through Jesus the Messiah, called now to live out their lives within the wider pagan world, needing instructions that at one level are closely analogous to those needed by Jews in their diaspora, but at another level have been rethought around the death and resurrection of the Messiah and the consequent fact that the people themselves have been redefined, given new boundary markers, called to a new sort of life.

Chapters 9–11 present, then, a complex and integrated whole, which in turn is closely integrated into the warp and woof of the rest of the letter. Building on the foundations already laid, Paul is developing one of the urgent points he wants to make to the Roman church: that they, more especially the Gentile Christians, should not despise non-Christian Jews or regard them as essentially unsavable. His personal involvement in this topic is passionate; he wears his heart on his sleeve, as he does only rarely elsewhere. (We might compare, e.g., 2 Corinthians, esp. 6:11-13, and Gal 4:12-20.) This is presumably not just because he feels strongly about the subject, but because he is bringing every rhetorical ploy to bear to convince the Roman Christians, more especially the Gentiles among them, to look at the world this way—from the point of view of a thoroughly (though subversively) Jewish telling of the world's story, leading up to the Messiah and now implementing his saving rule.[318] To treat these chapters as marginal to Romans is to misunderstand the whole; the letter will simply not work without them. But this is not merely a literary judgment. To revert to the earlier image: to ignore the fact that we have here a fully orchestrated "salvation history," and to suppose that one can then read the rest of the book as referring to an ahistorical salvation or Christian life, is to remain deaf not just to the structure and flow of the letter but to the subject Paul is dealing with. To imagine that one can bypass these chapters in the interest of a simpler or smoother reading of the letter is to settle, not just for second best here, but for a severely truncated view of everything else as well.

318. On the different types of rhetoric in play in these chapters see Bryan, *A Preface to Romans,* 160.

ROMANS 9:1-5, PAUL'S GRIEF OVER ISRAEL'S FAILURE TO BELIEVE, DESPITE BEING PROMISE BEARER

COMMENTARY

The odd thing about the first five verses of Romans 9 is that Paul never states what the problem actually is. He tells us of his awful grief; he tells us how he would like to pray;

he tells us why the problem is so acute. But the problem itself, like a character in a Beckett play, hovers offstage, a brooding presence, all the more powerful for never being seen directly.

We can, however, accurately infer what he is talking about both from subsequent statements and from the shape of the unfolding argument. In 10:1 he prays for the salvation of his fellow Jews; in 11:1 and 11:11 he asks the critical questions about whether they are to "fall" permanently; and in 11:23 he declares that they can be grafted in again if they do not remain in unbelief. The whole argument implies, in other words, that the problem can be stated as follows: the great majority of Paul's Jewish contemporaries have not believed the gospel of Jesus Christ, and Paul believes that they are therefore, at the moment, excluded from salvation. And this in turn generates a second-order problem, which only comes into view in 11:13 and thereafter: Paul is worried that Gentile Christians in Rome may be happy that Jews should stay forever in that condition.

This packed, tense opening statement is built around the central statement of v. 3, which is a wish or prayer that Paul feels he could express but implies he should not. Verses 1-2 build up to this with a solemn declaration of inconsolable grief; vv. 4-5 explain the enormity of the situation by listing the spectacular privileges of Paul's kinsfolk.[319]

9:1. The shock of the abrupt transition from the exalted heights of chap. 8 to the depths of anguish of 9:2 is made the more acute by the solemn declaration in v. 1. Why Paul needed to make such a powerful affidavit, with its triple emphasis (I'm telling the truth; I'm not lying; my conscience agrees) and its invoking of both Christ and the Spirit, we can only guess; but the guess must surely be that he knew he had an uphill struggle to persuade the Gentile Christians in Rome to concern themselves now, after the last exhilarating chapter, with the plight of Israel according to the flesh. His hearers needed to know that this was not just a rhetorical ploy to gain a little sympathy for a while. It was truly heartfelt. Elements of the solemn opening

words are familiar from other contexts (2 Cor 11:31; Gal 1:20; 1 Tim 2:7), but only here in his writings does he say it so fully: "I'm speaking the truth in Christ." Paul invokes two witnesses to vouch for him: his conscience, and the Holy Spirit. The way he joins the two ("my conscience bears witness in the Holy Spirit") is revealing. Paul can speak of the conscience of the unbeliever (e.g., 2 Cor 4:2), but most of his mentions of conscience are of Christian conscience (frequently, e.g., in 1 Corinthians 8 and 10). Only here, however, does he speak of conscience and the Spirit as working in this close partnership. This gives the strongest possible emphasis to what he is about to say.

9:2. His heart (here, as often, metaphorical for the very center of the personality) is afflicted by grief. He uses two words for this. The first is λύπη (*lupē*), which refers to a state of heart related to something sad outside itself (i.e., "sorrow," "grief"); the second is ὀδύνη (*odynē*), which refers to the state of the heart in itself—"sharp pain," "anguish." The first is "great," the second "unceasing" (presumably intended as a hendiadys: the second is also great, and the first also unceasing). We should remind ourselves that the hearers of the letter would not yet know, at this point, what he was talking about; the effect of this statement would naturally be to excite sympathy and concern. Paul has led them to the point where they may, perhaps, be ready to listen to the topic he must now raise, if only because they have learned to trust him. If he now turns to a matter of such agonizing concern to himself, they should share it as well.

9:3. Paul delays mentioning the people over whom he is grieving until he has expressed the most extraordinary prayer: that he himself might be cut off from the Messiah. Granted the previous eight chapters, and the promises and privileges he has enumerated to date, this prayer is shocking in the extreme.[320] Paul uses the word ἀνάθεμα (*anathema*) to describe the condition he has in mind: not only separated from the Messiah, undoing all that has been poured into the phrase "in

---

319. Calling them his "coreligionists," as Fitzmyer does (*Romans*, 544, 582), is misleading, since it implies that what they had in common was something called "religion," so easily now misunderstood in a post-Enlightenment sense. What Paul says he has in common with them is "flesh" (v. 3).

320. The verb can also mean "wish," as the NIV and the NRSV take it. See Käsemann, *Commentary on Romans*, 258. But the implied parallel with Moses suggests that actual prayer to God is probably in mind. See Cranfield, *A Critical and Exegetical Commentary on the Epistle to the Romans*, 454-57; Moo, *The Epistle to the Romans*, 558; Bryan, *A Preface to Romans*, 159.

Christ" in the previous chapters, but under a solemn religious ban (see 1 Cor 16:22; Gal 1:8-9).[321] The word carries overtones of the curse put on various people in Israelite history, and that seems to be where Paul's mind is; he cannot be unaware of the moment when the greatest prophet of old, Moses himself, stood before God at Sinai and asked that he might himself be blotted out from God's book if only the people as a whole, under condemnation for idolatry when the Torah was first given, might be spared (for the curse, see Num 21:3; Deut 7:26; for Moses' prayer, see Exod 32:30-34, a passage of considerable significance for the argument of Romans 9).

Paul declares that he could pray the same prayer; that he *could* pray it, not necessarily that he *is* doing so, for that would involve him in a direct contradiction of what he has already said in the letter. And it is possible that by describing himself as "I myself" (αὐτὸς ἐγώ *autos egō*) he intends not so much to stress "this really is me, Paul, speaking" but rather to hint, as perhaps in 7:25, that this is what "I, left to myself" might think as opposed to "I, speaking as a man in Christ." But the sentiment is so sharp that, even if he expresses it in such a way as to make it clear that he is not in fact praying like this, the reader is brought up with a shock. What can make this man, this apostle, this towering theologian of the love and justice of God, speak in such a way? The answer comes with rhetorical force: it is on behalf of "my brothers and sisters" (the NRSV's "my own people" retains inclusivity at the cost of the intimacy that ἀδελφοί [*adelphoi*] carries for Paul)—a phrase Paul elsewhere reserves for his siblings in Christ: "my kinsfolk according to the flesh" (cf. 1 Cor 10:18: βλέπετε τὸν Ἰσραὴλ κατὰ σάρκα [*blepete ton Israēl kata sarka*; lit., "consider Israel according to the flesh"]). The referent is obvious: Paul means his fellow Jews. But the way he has described them is once more designed to gain maximum sympathy from the start.

"According to the flesh" is a phrase that carries a variety of overtones, all in some ways negative (on "flesh," see the Commentary on 1:3). Here it serves to distinguish Paul's fellow Jews from his siblings in Christ, both Jewish and Gentile. (It is logically possible that

the phrase here could denote all Paul's fellow Jews, including Christian ones; but the subsequent argument, not least 10:1 and 11:11-14, rules this out.) And it hints at the line of thought that is to come. Paul has shown already how God deals, in Christ, with "the flesh"; the whole of 7:1–8:11 stands behind this phrase, and points to the way in which the present situation will be dealt with in 9:6–10:13. And when, two verses on, he describes the Messiah himself as coming "from them, according to the flesh," we should realize what is going on. His "kinsfolk according to the flesh" are to be understood precisely as "the Messiah's people according to the flesh." That is their privilege, their tragedy, and their hope. The chapters to come will explain each of these.

9:4-5. Paul lists the privileges of his kinsfolk.[322] He does so, at one level, to heighten the immediate rhetorical force, the plea for sympathy: these are the people to whom so much has been given. At another level, the list functions as a point of high irony: most of these privileges are what he has argued in the preceding chapters now belong to those (from whatever race) who are "in the Messiah." Thus, obviously, 8:12-30 has much to say about "sonship" in Christ; chaps. 5 and 8 assure believers that the "glory" lost by Adam (3:23), is guaranteed in Christ; 7:1–8:11 tell the complex story of the "giving of the law," and its strange fulfillment in the Spirit; and chap. 4 spells out the promise to Abraham, the great patriarch. The whole letter, of course, is in one way or another about the Messiah, and 1:3-4 offered an opening statement of the gospel message of which he is the subject, a statement that stands at the head of the whole letter as this statement stands at the head of this section. The force of the list is thus to say: the privileges that now belong to all those in Christ—"not least," Paul might add, "those of you in Rome" (see 1:7, 15)—are actually the privileges God promised to Israel according to the flesh. You Christians have come, as he says explicitly in 11:17 and 15:27, to share in the spiritual blessings of Israel. You must now spare a thought, and a prayer, for their present plight.

---

321. For details on the word see Moo, *Romans*, 557n. 14.

322. Fitzmyer, *Romans*, 543, suggests that the omission of "election" among these privileges is significant; but this is unlikely in view of 11:28.

Three of the privileges he mentions do not so obviously relate to specific earlier parts of the letter, but they are linked by implication. The title "Israelites" itself, which prepares the way for the opening discussion of 9:6, looks back to the many discussions of Israel and its privileges throughout the opening chapters, and especially 2:17–3:9.[323] The "covenants" have not been mentioned specifically before, but it is at least arguable that by this phrase Paul refers, in shorthand as it were, to the relationships God established with Abraham, with Israel through Moses, and with David. These are the subject of chap. 4 (Abraham); 7:1–8:11 (Moses); and 1:3 (taken with 15:12) (David). Finally, Israel's "worship" has not been an explicit topic, but if we were right to see "the obedience of faith" in 1:5 as, among other things, a reference to Israel's central prayer, the *Shema Israel* (see the Commentary on 3:30; 8:28), then the worship that God commanded Israel—the true worship of the true God, as opposed to the idolatry that characterized the Gentile nations (1:18-32)—is at least implicit in much that has gone before.

The point, then, is that God, having called ethnic Israel to be the light of the world, has now shone that light lavishly on the wider world, while Israel seems to have chosen to remain in darkness. Israel, called to be God's messenger to the world (3:1-2), has seen the message successfully delivered while itself failing to give heed to it. The irony and tragedy of this situation is the reason both for Paul's anguish and for this poignant way of expressing it.

The final privilege, though, is the one through which Paul intends to view this problem and bring it to a solution. "From them,[324] according to the flesh, comes the Messiah, who is over all, God blessed for ever. Amen" (NRSV). The word order in the Greek runs thus: "from whom [is] the Messiah, the one according to the flesh, who is over all God blessed for ever, Amen [ὁ Χριστὸς τὸ κατὰ σάρκα ὁ ὢν ἐπὶ πάντων θεὸς εὐλογητὸς εἰς τοὺς αἰῶνας ἀμήν *ho Christos to kata sarka ho ōn epi pantōn theos eulogētos eis tous aiōnas amēn*]."

Word order is one thing; punctuation is another. There is little or no punctuation in the earliest manuscripts, and not much in some of the later ones. This leaves the interpreter of the NT with fascinating puzzles, of which this half-verse is one of the best known. As the various alternative translations in the NRSV and the NIV indicate, there are several possible ways of punctuating, and hence of understanding Paul's intended meaning. In particular, should there be a comma or a full stop after "according to the flesh" (κατὰ σάρκα *kata sarka*)? And should there then be any punctuation after "who is over all" and before "God blessed for ever"? If so, what?

The reason for the puzzle is obvious: does Paul here refer to the Messiah as "God"? Elsewhere, as we have seen, he certainly thinks of Jesus Christ as "son of God" in a divine, not merely messianic, sense (e.g., 1:4; 8:3). Classic passages in other letters celebrate Jesus' divinity within a continuing framework of Jewish monotheism.[325] But this cannot settle, a priori, the question of whether in this passage he refers to him as "God," so apparently baldly, without (for instance) qualifying him as "son" (see 1 Cor 15:28). Within this large question there is a secondary one: Does the phrase "who is over all" (ὁ ὢν ἐπὶ πάντων *ho ōn epi pantōn*) belong with "Christ according to the flesh," which precedes it, or with "God blessed for ever," which follows it? These are the questions that have generated the multiple possibilities evident in the translations, of which the most important are these:[326]

i. from them comes the Messiah according to the flesh, who is over all, God blessed for ever, Amen.

ii. from them comes the Messiah according to the flesh, who is over all. God be blessed for ever, Amen.

iii. from them comes the Messiah according to the flesh. God who is over all be blessed for ever, Amen.

Grammatically the arguments weigh heavily on the side of (i); in other words, on the side of saying that Paul does indeed here

323. Moo, *Romans,* 561, rightly stresses that in chaps. 1–8 Paul regularly speaks of "Jews," but in chaps. 9–11 of "Israel" (exceptions being 9:24; 10:12). But this does not mean that "Israel" in chaps. 9–11 is univocal—as 9:6 signals.

324. Not "theirs," as with the rest of the list. See Moo, *Romans,* 565.

325. On Paul's high christology elsewhere (e.g., 1 Cor 8:6; Phil 2:6-11; Col 1:15-20), see Wright, *The Climax of the Covenant,* chaps. 4–6. Titus 2:13, though normally regarded as non-Pauline, is sometimes also cited in this connection.

326. A further option involves a textual emendation that few today would advocate. See Fitzmyer, *Romans,* 548-49.

ascribe divinity to Christ.[327] Of the various arguments here, perhaps the strongest is that it would be highly unusual for Paul to write an asyndetic doxology—that is, an expression of praise that is not linked to a word in the immediately preceding sentence (see, e.g., 1:25).

More compelling than grammar alone is the consideration of how v. 5, read according to (i) above, makes sense in its wider context. We have already remarked how the complex theological statement of the gospel in 1:3-4 serves as an introduction to the whole letter, especially to chaps. 1–8. In this statement, Jesus is described as both "of the seed of David according to the flesh" and also "son of God in power according to the spirit of holiness." This leads to an emphasis on his universal rule and a call to allegiance. A double statement in which the Messiah's "fleshly" descent is balanced by his universal sovereignty would form a close parallel to this, creating a probability that at least "who is over all" goes with "Christ." This would seem to favor (i) or (ii), but it has to be said that the abrupt final sentence of (ii) is even less likely than the longer but nevertheless "unbalanced" sentence in (iii). In other words, if 9:5 is intended to be the same kind of double statement that we find in 1:3-4, (i) is the most likely reading.

But there are also indications that Paul intended 9:5 to serve in this way—not as a detached christological statement (he was not given to sudden statements of doctrines, however important, in isolation from actual arguments), but as a kind of heading for what is to come. The whole argument of 9–11, as we have suggested, moves toward, and finally affirms, the universal sovereignty of Jesus as Messiah and Lord, with 10:4-13 as

the decisive statement. Though Paul does not there call Jesus θεός (*theos*, "God"), he calls him κύριος (*kyrios*, "Lord"), in one of the many passages where he is quoting from a Septuagint passage in which *kyrios* stood unambiguously for the Tetragrammaton, the sacred name YHWH. "There is no distinction between Jew and Greek; for the same Lord is Lord of all, rich in mercy to all who call upon him; for 'all who call upon the name of the Lord shall be saved' " (10:13, quoting Joel 3:5 LXX; see the Commentary on 10:13). The stress on "all" in this central passage picks up exactly the point of "who is over all" in 9:5, and increases the strong probability that Paul intended the word "God" there to be understood as a predicate of the Messiah. Chapters 9–11 close with the intention of God toward "all" (11:32), and a burst of praise to God (11:33-36) that also echoes the brief "blessed for ever" of 9:5 (cf. 14:5-12).

If we read v. 5 in this way, what force does it add to the opening paragraph as a whole? Just this: that the Messiah who is from Israel's own race, their highest privilege and final hope, is the very embodiment of their sovereign Lord, their covenant God. And it is he whom they have rejected; this is precisely the point Paul makes in 10:21, at the close of the main "story" of chaps. 9 and 10. Just as Israel rejected their God on Mt. Sinai, precipitating Moses into his extraordinary prayer (see above), so now Israel according to the flesh has rejected its God as he came in the flesh, precipitating Paul into his own version of that prayer and his own great, unceasing grief. Israel's highest privilege, when spurned, becomes the cause of Israel's greatest tragedy.

But even that tragedy contains within itself the seeds of hope. Just because the Messiah "according to the flesh" is also "God over all, blessed for ever," and particularly because his "flesh" was the place where God "condemned sin" (8:3), so the strange and sad story of Israel's fate, to which Paul will now turn, is designed to lead on and out into new life. Read this way, 9:5 becomes an exact, if ironic, summary of both parts of the argument that will now unfold.

327. With the NIV and the NRSV, following the KJV and many others, and following also UBS3 and Nestle-Aland27; against the RSV and the NEB. For the detailed arguments see particularly B. M. Metzger, "The Punctuation of Rom 9:5," in *Christ and Spirit in the New Testament: Studies in Honour of Charles Francis Digby Moule*, ed. B. Lindars and S. S. Smalley (Cambridge: Cambridge University Press, 1973) 95-112. Metzger lists eight ways in which the Greek can be punctuated and argues for the one that puts a comma after "flesh" and another one before the final "Amen." Other writings are listed in Fitzmyer, *Romans*, 548-49; Moo, *Romans*, 565-68; Bryan, *A Preface to Romans*, 170-71—all agreeing with Metzger. Commentators agreeing with the RSV and the NEB include Dunn, *Romans 9–16*, 529; Stuhlmacher, *Paul's Letter to the Romans*, 145.

REFLECTIONS

1. Paul's deep, constant, and unresolved grief is a standing rebuke to the shallowness that forbids Christians to grieve on the grounds that all shall be well. Earnest preachers have sometimes read 1 Thess 4:13 as forbidding grief of all sorts, whereas what that passage forbids is grieving of a particular kind ("after the manner of pagans who have no hope"). To hold firmly to the Christian hope is not to pass beyond grief; indeed, not to grieve is not to love, since grief is the form love takes when the beloved is taken away. Paul himself speaks elsewhere (Phil 2:27) of the grief he would have had if Epaphroditus had died ("grief upon grief," he says); no suggestion there of simply "rejoicing that his friend had gone to a better place." As long as death is real, grief is real too. If it is not acknowledged, and expressed appropriately, it can be poisonous.

At the same time, it is vital to learn the lesson that this deep and inconsolable grief can coexist with the joy and celebration that fill the previous four chapters. The many-layered texture of Christian experience has room for both, and more besides. Learning how to live with these different layers, giving each its proper place, is part of Christian maturity; pointing to this task, and helping people to engage in it, is a vital part of Christian ministry. What happens between Romans 5–8 and Romans 9–11 at the level of literature must be facilitated at the level of prayer and Christian self-understanding.

2. The specific grief Paul feels is not, however, for those who have died, but rather for those who have rejected the gospel of Jesus. This calls into question (as do 10:1 and 11:23) any of the easygoing universalistic solutions that have been offered from time to time: Paul really does believe that those who do not believe the gospel are, to put it no stronger, given no promises of sharing in the life of the age to come. Had there been any suggestion that his nonbelieving fellow Jews were on a parallel path to salvation, exercising their rights under a covenant different from that sealed with the blood of the Messiah, his grief would have been neither deep nor unceasing; it would have consisted merely of the frustration of their not at present seeing things from his point of view. This grief is bound to be felt by those who share Paul's theological conviction and who see close family members or friends turning away in deliberate disbelief from the gospel of Jesus.

At the same time, we should note carefully that Paul does not speak of this in terms of himself being superior to them. His grief drives him to feel that it would be better for him to be cast away and for them to be saved in his place, if that could somehow happen. Though he knows it is impossible, his instinct here shows itself, paradoxically perhaps, as a deeply Christian one, formed on the basis that God gave his own son for sinners in the first place (5:8; 8:32), generating a spirituality of self-giving even to the point of wishing to be cut off from the Messiah for the sake of others. If the belief that those who belong to the Messiah are justified and glorified (8:30) is held with total conviction, it issues not in arrogance but in grief over, and in prayer for, those who at present do not share that belief.

3. Here, as throughout 9–11, we face the question of the Christian stance vis-à-vis unbelieving Israel, then and now. We reserve fuller comment on this for later, but we cannot miss at this stage the difference between Paul's stance and two equal and opposite distortions. On the one hand, any church that took Romans 9:1-5 seriously would find it impossible to engage in any of the anti-Jewish, still less the anti-Semitic, rhetoric that has disfigured would-be Christian discourse for many centuries. On the other hand, Paul's position is clearly incompatible with the Enlightenment position that treats all "religions" as equally valid paths to God, or to "the divine," or the local variation on this that sees Judaism and Christianity as parallel though separate "covenants."

The whole point of vv. 4-5 is that what has happened in Jesus the Messiah is indeed the paradoxical fulfillment of God's Israel-shaped promises and purposes. Only if we follow Paul's own argument through the section will we understand his own unique proposal for a way forward from this impasse. But it is already clear that we should not settle for the too-easy solutions that are still propounded in many quarters. Paul demands that we think harder, not settle for comfortable answers.

ROMANS 9:6-29, THE STORY OF ISRAEL, FROM ABRAHAM TO THE EXILE, DISPLAYS GOD'S JUSTICE IN JUDGMENT AND MERCY

COMMENTARY

To see what Paul is doing in the passage that now follows we must recognize that he is telling a single story. Not just any old story, either; this is the story of Israel, from Abraham to the exile and beyond. This passage is the first part of the continuous narrative that runs through to 10:21. It is the story of Israel told in such a way as to bring out some often-overlooked features: the story, both in promise and fulfillment, was always a story of grace, but was simultaneously one of tragic failure, of Israel being narrowed down further and further to a final "remnant." The point of this aspect of the narrative, in Paul's telling of it, is that this, too, was not outside the purpose of God, but was what had been promised all along.

This, after all, is the surface meaning from 9:6 onward. Has Israel failed to believe the gospel? Well, maybe, but it is not as though God's word has failed; for God had always specified one son and not the other, one twin and not the other, one small group while the rest fell away, one tiny remnant while the rest were lost to view, exiled apparently forever (on "exile" as a continuing theme in Second Temple Jewish thought, see the Introduction). What God promised, God has performed. This may not be the way Israel was used to telling its story (though there are affinities here with the prayers in Ezra 9 and Daniel 9), but this narrative has a strong claim, reinforced by numerous quotations and echoes, to be biblical.

Paul is not, then, producing an abstract essay on the way in which God always works with individuals, or for that matter with nations and races. This is specifically the story of Israel, the chosen people; it is the unique story of how the creator has worked with the covenant people, to bring about the purpose for which the covenant was made in the first place. It is the story, in other words, whose climax and goal is the Messiah; that, as we shall see, is the meaning of 10:3-4.

That said, we are in a position at last to understand the vexed question of the predestinarian passages such as 9:13 and especially 9:15-23. It should not need saying, but the compartmentalized ways in which Romans has been read probably require that we should say it anyway: The key to this passage is to be found in its relation to the relevant earlier parts of the letter, particularly 7:1–8:11 (to be understood, as we saw, as an expansion of the compressed statement of 5:20-21). There, the role of the Torah was to draw "sin" on to one place, magnifying it there, making it "exceedingly sinful"—and making those "under Torah" live the puzzled life of people who delighted in Torah but found that it increased the hold that sin and death had on them. This led to the conclusion, in 8:1-4: God has now done what Torah could not, condemning "sin" in the flesh of the representative Messiah, and creating by the Spirit that which the Torah wanted to create, but could not because of the "sinful flesh."

All of this is now presupposed in the unwinding spiral argument of the letter. In the present passage and the one immediately following, the story of Israel is again presented as one of puzzlement and apparent failure, to be resolved through the Messiah and (by implication) the Spirit. Romans 9:30–10:13 is the equivalent passage, at this point in the "spiral," to 7:1–8:11, with the climax of the present passage falling at 10:3-4 as that of the earlier one did at 8:3-4. The multiple resonances between the two passages (and the earlier relevant ones such as 2:17–3:9; 3:21–4:25) are as fascinating and complex as a room full of mirrors, but the main point is this: what the Torah has accomplished in Israel, even though it appears negative, is in fact part of the larger positive purpose that God had for Israel all along, part of what God had in mind in making promises to Abraham in the first place. The mystery of Israel is seen in this: that God called Israel (Abraham and his family) to undo the sin of Adam, but that work was bound to be Christ-shaped, cross-shaped, to involve being cast away that the world might be redeemed. Just as the Torah's effect in 7:7-25 was not simply negative, but served the larger positive purpose of drawing sin (the sin of the whole world!) on to one point so that it could be dealt with there—that is, in the flesh of the Messiah, so here God's purpose in election, designed to narrow Israel down to a single point (the Messiah), had in view the extension of God's saving purpose to the whole world. That something like this has been in Paul's mind all through the letter is apparent from 2:17-29 and 4:13-25. That it is indeed his point here is underlined when, later in the section, he comes to build on it. In 11:11-12 and 11:15 he puts it like this: by their trespass salvation came to the nations; their trespass means riches for the world, their diminution means riches for the Gentiles; their casting away means reconciliation for the world. (Each of those points is a shorthand way of saying what he says extensively in 9:6–10:21, not least in 9:17 and 9:22-23, some of the verses that have been felt to be the most difficult in the whole passage, indeed in the whole letter.)

The passage divides unevenly into three: vv. 6-13, vv. 14-18, and vv. 19-29, the latter of which comprises an argument (vv. 19-24) and scriptural proofs (vv. 25-29). These sections tell the story of Israel's patriarchal foundation (vv. 6-13), then of the exodus (vv. 14-18), and then of God's judgment that led to exile and, through it, to the fulfillment of God's worldwide promise to Abraham (vv.

19-24).[328] In each case Paul shows that what God himself said, through the Torah and the prophets, is what God has done—namely, that Israel was called not to be an ever-expanding empire, but to be the appropriate context for the Messiah's coming and consequent worldwide redemptive rule.

Each section is introduced by either a question or an implied question: Has God's word failed? Is God unjust? and Why does he find fault? These are the main questions that dominate the short but vital section 3:1-9. Verse 6 corresponds to 3:3 ("Does their faithlessness nullify God's fidelity?"), 9:14 to 3:5 ("Is God unjust to exercise wrath?"), and 9:19 to 3:7 ("Why am I still being condemned as a sinner?"). Here again we are aware of the "spiral" pattern within the line of thought of the letter as a whole. These are the questions, already raised by 2:17-29, which Paul mentioned but could not at that stage address. Now, with chaps. 3–8 behind him, he can at last return to them.

Romans 9:6-13 thus tells the story of Abraham, Isaac, and Jacob, in such a way as to say: God always intended that only some of Abraham's descendants would carry forward the saving purpose. This had nothing to do with their respective merits, but only with the divine purpose. Most of Paul's Jewish contemporaries would have been happy with this understanding of the patriarchal narratives; it was his application of the same principle to the subsequent narrative that would have been controversial.

9:6a. This verse opens with the statement that, as we have seen, remains thematic for the whole section to the end of chap. 11: God's word has not failed, indeed it is impossible that it should do so. There is here a thematic echo of Isa 55:11, which in turn looks back to 40:8: God's word accomplishes its purpose (see also Num 23:19; 1 Sam 15:29; Ezek 24:14). Paul will refer to Isaiah 40–55 elsewhere in this section, and this makes it the more likely that he intends some such echo; the story he tells, as does the prophet, is of Israel, God's servant people, being narrowed

---

328. Moo, *Romans*, 569, suggests that vv. 14-24 are an excursus, interrupting the main argument, which consists of vv. 6-13 and 25-29. This ignores the way in which Paul is following, and retelling, the overall biblical narrative of God's dealings with Israel. Instead, Moo allows his discussion to be overshadowed by the anachronistic debates between Calvinism and Arminianism (e.g., Moo, *Romans*, 587-88).

down to a single point through which God will fulfill a worldwide purpose, revealing the divine righteousness to all the nations.

The word for "failed" in 9:6a means, literally, "fall," and though several transferred senses such as "fail" are well attested we should note that Paul uses the language of "stumbling," "tripping up," and "falling" several times later on in the argument. The answer to the implied question is: it is Israel that has stumbled, not God's word. In fact, Israel's stumble has been because of God's own Torah (9:32f.).

9:6b. The exposition of Israel's story begins with a firm dogmatic statement: not all who are from Israel are in fact Israel. There is an "Israel" and an "Israel," just as there is an "I" that delights in Torah and "another I" in 7:21-5; here, as there, the "flesh" is set against the purposes of God. Paul has put down a marker that from this point on the word "Israel" has two referents, just as with the word "Jew" in 2:28-29. Additionally, if that earlier passage is a precedent, the second "Israel" need not be simply a subset of the first, a "true Israel" taken from within the larger group of the physical family. That, to be sure, is what we find in the next verses; but by the time we get to v. 24 the picture has broadened out as it did, proleptically, in 2:29. This double meaning of "Israel" will be crucially important when we reach 11:25-26.[329]

9:7. This verse offers a further explanation, in relation to Abraham. Abraham was, of course, last mentioned in chap. 4, where Paul's point was that his family consists of all, whether Jewish or Gentile, who believe the gospel of Jesus. But for the moment, at the head of the long narrative he will now lay out, his point is simply that a distinction must be made (corresponding to the distinction between "Israel" and "Israel" in v. 6b) between Abraham's "children" and his "seed."

But which is which? Literally the verse reads "nor [is it the case] that seed of Abraham all children." Some (including the NIV) have thought that "seed of Abraham" refers to the larger category—that is, all Abraham's physical offspring, and that "children" refers to

the smaller, the chosen ones. But that seems unlikely.[330] Paul's confirmation of the point with the quotation from Gen 21:12, using "seed" as the positive, more limited category, means that we must read "seed of Abraham" as denoting the "chosen" ones. Abraham, in other words, had two "children," Ishmael and Isaac; but only one, Isaac, was designated "seed." This is strongly backed up by the following verse, where being "reckoned as seed" (NRSV, "descendants"; NIV, "offspring"; both these obscure the link with 9:29, on which see below) means "being part of the elect group, as opposed to merely physical descendants" (see the similar emphasis in 9:29).

The quote from Genesis 21 invokes that whole chapter, in which—as Paul lays out in more detail in Gal 4:21-31—a distinction is made between Abraham's older son Ishmael, born to him by the slave-girl Hagar, and Isaac, born from Sarah. The point Paul is making here is, however, different from that in Galatians. There he was distinguishing between the true family and the false in order to show the spuriousness of his opponents' claims. Here, with an eye to a very different problem—potential Gentile "boasting" against unbelieving Jews—the distinction does not relate to a particular group threatening the church, but rather to the numerous unbelieving Jews over whom, as he has emphasized, he has unceasing sorrow and anguish. He is not content to sit back and casually observe the strange ways of God.

9:8-9. Paul explains with another, closer, echo of Gal 4:21-31. He distinguishes the two groups in terms of "flesh" and "promise": The family divides into "children of flesh" (i.e., children merely of the physical family—remembering the close associations "flesh" gives them with Paul, as in v. 3, and with the Messiah himself, as in v. 5) and "children of promise." This ties in again to the exposition of God's promise to Abraham (4:13-22), to give him an innumerable seed (i.e., family) from "many nations." Here the picture is more focused, though in the light of chaps. 9–11 as a whole we must see the same end in

---

329. Fitzmyer, *Romans*, 560, calls the second "Israel" "the Israel of faith." This may be broadly true to Paul's thinking, but is not a phrase he ever uses.

330. With Moo, *Romans*, 575; Dunn, *Romans 9–16*, 540; against Cranfield, *Romans*, 473; Fitzmyer, *Romans*, 559-60. The NIV's reading turns partly on taking ὅτι (*hoti*), the second word in the verse, to mean "because" rather than "that" as it meant in the previous, and parallel, verse. The NIV then covers its tracks by translating σπέρμα (*sperma*) as "descendants" in v. 7a but as "offspring" thereafter.

view: the family in question will be brought into existence through Isaac. The promise he here quotes from Gen 18:10 (repeated in 18:14) was that Sarah would have a son. This is matriarchal history, not just patriarchal. These were the promises, along with the earlier ones discussed in chap. 4, that Abraham believed; and they referred, not to all his physical descendants, but to the chosen "seed," who was Sarah's child, Isaac. The point here, in case we missed it in the flurry of detail, is that God has done what was promised. The word of God has not failed (the "word" here refers back to 9:6). God promised a son (Genesis 18); then, when time came for a choice (Genesis 21), God reaffirmed the earlier word concerning Isaac.

9:10. The sequence continues in the next generation, only this time the point is more acute. Someone might have responded to the Ishmael/Isaac story by pointing out that the boys had different mothers, or that their characters were quite different. The first objection is ruled out by Paul's introducing the next phase with Rebecca rather than with Isaac; she, the mother of them both by a single father,[331] received the promise concerning Jacob's selection. Paul's thought runs ahead of him here, producing paraphrased translations in both the NIV and the NRSV; from the way he starts the sentence, it looks as though he intends to go straight from mentioning Rebecca to quoting the promise made to her, "The elder will serve the younger." Before he gets there, he inserts three qualifying clauses. The first, occupying the rest of v. 10, explains that her children were from a single father; the second, in v. 11a, explains that at the time of the promise these children were not yet born and so had no moral track record; the third, in vv. 11b-12a, gives the reason for this pre-natal promise—namely, that it emphasizes the sovereign purpose of God. This third explanation is where the weight of the short paragraph lies. This is the lesson Paul wants to take from the story, to use later on in his argument.

9:11-12. The second explanation occupies center stage in this brief telling of the Jacob/Esau story: it cannot be that God's selection

of Jacob had anything to do with Jacob's merits, since the promise was made before he and his brother were born. God's choice has nothing to do with merit observed. Nor (to meet the objection of a later theology) could it have been foreseen, and hence explained in terms of God's knowing how the brothers were going to turn out; Jacob's behavior as a young adult, cheating and twisting this way and that, would scarcely have earned him favor with an impartial deity. The point is, though, that Paul is not here discussing what an abstract, impartial deity would or should have done; he is discussing the long purposes of God for Israel, and through Israel for the world. Central to those purposes is the principle that all must be of grace, "not of works, but of the one who calls."

In the immediate context of Romans 9–11, this phrase sets up a resonance with 11:6, where Paul insists that the remnant that now exists, the group of those Jews who have believed in Jesus, is created by grace, not works. In that context, Paul is ruling out any suggestion that the "remnant" is a small group of Jews who have managed, through obedience to Torah, to avoid the verdict of "disobedience" that had come on everyone else (11:32). If there is a remnant of believing Jews, they can only have come into being by the same route Paul himself took: "I through the law died to the law, that I might live to God" (Gal 2:19). Of course, the phrase "not by works" occurs in many other contexts, not least in Romans, and as we have argued elsewhere its primary emphasis is on the "works of Torah" as the practices that mark out the Jew, the one who knows and (supposedly) does God's will (cf. 2:17-24), from the surrounding pagan world. In the present passage, though the emphasis is on "works" as the doing of good rather than evil, the background in Paul's mind is most likely the regular rabbinic exegesis according to which the patriarchs were already obeying the Torah, even before it was given to Moses. Paul's point, as part of his answer to the question posed by unbelieving Israel, is that God's stated purpose always involved a division within the family. The quotation from Gen 25:23 gives us, finally, the word that was spoken to Rebecca concerning her unborn twins,

---

331. Or possibly "by a single act of intercourse"; the Greek expression κοίτην ἔχουσα (*koitēn echousa*; lit., "having a marriage bed") can refer to the marriage relationship or to an act of intercourse, or indeed simply to a seminal emission. See Moo, *Romans,* 579.

reversing the natural assumption concerning the rights of the firstborn.

9:13. This is supported in turn by the sharp quotation from Mal 1:2-3: "I loved Jacob, but hated Esau." It will not do to flatten this down by suggesting that "hate" here really means "loved somewhat less"; even that would be arbitrary, and would merit the question of v. 14 just the same.[332] The context in Malachi makes it clear what is meant: Esau, the people of Edom, have suffered devastation, and their attempts to rebuild will be thwarted. However, in context this passage of Malachi is not written to provide "Jacob" with a sense of effortless superiority, leading to arrogance. On the contrary, it is meant to undermine such a thing, and to provoke instead a sense of gratitude for the unmerited love of God.

To repeat: Paul's aim throughout this first section (9:6-13) has been to say that God's word has not failed, because he always declared that he would work through Isaac not Ishmael, and through Jacob not Esau, thus setting a pattern that continued through the whole story and on to Paul's own day. This, however, raises for Paul, as it does for contemporary readers, the major question: Has God been unjust? To answer this, Paul continues the story of Israel with its next major moment: the exodus from Egypt.

9:14-18. When faced with a dense and difficult passage like this, one wise course is to examine its roots earlier in the letter. In this case there are at least three relevant passages.

The question of 9:14, as we saw, is parallel to that of 3:5: is God unjust to inflict wrath? There Paul answered abruptly that this could not be so, since God is the world's judge, and as such is bound to punish evil. Here as there, Paul is not talking about people who are, so to speak, morally neutral; he is talking about sinful human beings. The contexts of the quotations from Exod 33:19 and 9:16, in vv. 15 and 17, make this clear. In the first case, God is speaking to Moses about those who sinned by making the golden calf. In the second, God is speaking through Moses to Pharaoh, explaining why, despite his arrogance in opposing God's plan to set Israel free, God has not struck him dead on the spot, but has

allowed him to go on, hardening his heart so that the long-term effect would be the spreading of the news of God's power and reputation.

In both cases, then, the question is not: granted that human beings are a blank slate, what is God writing on that slate? Instead, it is this: Granted that Israel has followed Adam into sin (5:20 and 7:7-25 are the second relevant passages), what will God do with it? The answer Paul gives, continuing his story of Israel from Abraham to the present day, is that God has allowed Israel, like Pharaoh, to stand—that is, he has withheld instant judgment, in order that mercy may spread into the world. This is where the third earlier passage comes into play: God's kindness is meant to lead to repentance (2:4-6), though those who do not avail themselves of the chance will become hardened, to fit them the more thoroughly for the coming judgment. That this is what Paul has in mind is clear from the reprise of the present argument in 11:25-32. As with the previous paragraph, then, it is vital that we see the present statements in the larger context of the narrative Paul is constructing from 9:6 to 10:13 and beyond. What is happening to Israel in the present time serves the purpose of God's covenant intention, to spread the gospel to all the world.

9:14. The question, whether God is guilty of injustice, is essentially the same question as Paul grappled with in chap. 3, that of the δικαιοσύνη θεοῦ (*dikaiosynē theou*). It has to do with God's covenanted obligation to bring salvation to the Gentiles through Israel, and with his simultaneous obligation to deal with sin; both of these are brought into sharp focus by Israel's failure. In 3:21–4:25 Paul addressed the question by declaring that the Messiah, in his faithful death and resurrection, had unveiled God's righteousness in action, for the benefit of all who believe. In the present passage he is working toward a very similar conclusion, which he gives in 9:30–10:13. In 3:5-6 he was content with a brief answer to the charge of God's injustice (God remains judge of the world, and must act accordingly). Here he spells this out in terms of the exodus story.

9:15-16. He begins with a statement of God's sovereignty, not in the abstract

332. Against Bryan, *A Preface to Romans*, 161; Fitzmyer, *Romans*, 563.

but when faced with rebellious Israel. The golden calf incident (Exodus 32) became a byword for Israel's sin, all the worse because it happened at the very moment when God was entering into solemn covenant with his people in the giving of the law and the instructions for making the tabernacle (Exodus 19–20; 24; 25–30; cf. Ps 106:19; Acts 7:41; *Exod. Rab.* 21.1; 30.7; *Pesiq. Rab.* 14.10; *Tg. Neofiti*). In that context, as Moses stood before YHWH and begged forgiveness, offering to take Israel's place in being blotted out of God's book—as Paul had thought to do in v. 3—God had declared that, though severe judgment was bound to fall, some would be spared—namely, the ones God chose. God's purposes, in other words, would continue, though all of Israel be guilty (the very point Paul insisted on in 3:4). The surprise, in other words, is not that some were allowed to fall by the wayside, but that any at all were allowed to continue as God's covenant people, carrying the promises forward to their conclusion. This, in turn, shows that the status of being God's promise-bearing people has in the last analysis nothing to do with whether Israel intends to do what God wants ("human will," NRSV; "man's desire," NIV), or whether Israel expends energy on the task ("exertion," NRSV; "effort," NIV; lit., "running"; for the "running" metaphor, see 1 Cor 9:24-26; Phil 2:16; 3:12-14). What matters, what carries the saving plan forward even though all human agents let God down, is God's own mercy. "Mercy" is in fact a key theme of these chapters, and Paul clearly sees it as such by making it the transition into chap. 12. (The verb ἐλεέω [*eleeō*] and the noun ἔλεος [*eleos*] occur in 9:15-16, 18, 23 and 11:30-31 [twice] and 32; see also 15:9 and Gal 6:16. The verb οἰκτίρω [*oiktirō*] occurs in parallel with *eleō* in 9:15, and the noun οἰκτιρμός [*oiktirmos*], summing up the train of thought of chaps. 9–11, in 12:1.)

9:17-18. The same point is made graphically with another scene from the exodus narrative, that of Moses before Pharaoh. Again Paul first quotes the passage (in this case, Exod 9:16) and then draws the implication. As with Israel after the golden calf, Pharaoh is guilty; God could have punished him at once. God has, instead, "made him to stand," "raised him up" in this sense, rather than

cutting him off instantly.[333] The reason is so that God's power might be displayed in him, and that God's name might be made known in all the world. The moral Paul draws in the next verse shows that he regards God's "making Pharaoh to stand" as the equivalent of "hardening"; Exod 9:16, that is, picks up 9:12 ("the LORD hardened Pharaoh's heart"), itself part of a longer sequence (Exod 4:21; 7:3, 13, 22; 8:15, 32; 9:35; 10:1; 14:8; cf. Deut 2:30; Josh 11:20; Isa 63:17). What God has done to Pharaoh is not arbitrary. Pharaoh has already enslaved God's people and resisted the call to set them free. God has in view not the protracted punishment of Pharaoh for its own sake, but the worldwide proclamation of God's power and name. This is how the language of "hardening" works in at least one strand of Second Temple Jewish thinking. (See the suggestive 2 Macc 6:12-16: God's suspension of judgment means that the pagan nations will thereby reach the full measure of their sins, v. 14; cf. Gen 15:16; Wis 19:4. Israel, meanwhile, though chastened, is eventually granted mercy.) We ought at this point to hear echoes of earlier statements regarding Israel's disobedience (1:18-23; 2:1-11, 17-24), and to detect a line of thought that runs from those passages, through the present one, on to the decisive 11:25-26.

Paul is not, then, using the example of Pharaoh to explain that God has the right to show mercy, or to harden someone's heart, out of mere caprice. Nor is it simply that God has the right to do this sort of thing when someone is standing in the way of the glorious purpose that has been promised. The sense of this passage is gained from its place within the larger story line from 9:6–10:21—that is, as part of the story of Israel itself, told to explain what is now happening to Paul's "kinsfolk according to the flesh." God's action upon Pharaoh was part of the means, not only of rescuing Israel from slavery, but of declaring God's name to the world. In much the same way, as Paul will explain in 11:11-14, God's action at the present time upon Israel "according to the flesh" is part of the means of bringing the gospel to the nations, of declaring God's

---

333. This sense of "raised up" is very different from that of Isa 41:2; 45:13; Hab 1:6; Zech 11:16, sometimes cited as parallels. See Fitzmyer, *Romans*, 567; Moo, *Romans*, 594-95. There the meaning (expressed, in any case, with different Hebrew verbs) is "caused to appear on the stage of history."

name—and, now, the name of the Lord, the name of Jesus Christ!—to the nations (10:9-13). This in turn precipitates the questions of 11:1 and 11, which deal with the problem that remains at the end of it all. Reading this part of Romans is like riding a bicycle: if you stand still for more than a moment, forgetting the onward movement both of the story of 9:6–10:21 and of the letter as a whole, you are liable to lose your balance—or, perhaps, to accuse Paul of losing his.

9:19-24. That, of course, is very tempting at this juncture, and Paul is well aware of it. The question of 9:19 ("Why does he still find fault?") is natural and proper, however much Paul in v. 20 rebukes the creature for answering back to the creator.[334] Paul is dealing, after all, with the topic of God's righteousness; if there is complete disjunction between God's justice and everybody else's, it would be better not to use the term at all.

But here, just when it appears that Paul is going to dig himself even deeper into the hole he seems to have dug in vv. 14-18, we must again notice where he is within the story that began at 9:6. He has begun with the patriarchs; he has continued with the exodus; now he moves to the exile.

There were, perhaps, other options at this point. Some tellings of Israel's story (including one attributed to Paul himself in Acts) moved from the exodus to the establishment of judges and then of the monarchy (Acts 13:17-25). But Paul here waits to mention monarchs until he reaches the king himself in 10:4. Instead, he goes to those passages where Israel, in its own tellings of its own story, knew that God had acted in judgment, to prune the nation right down to a tiny remnant—and he finds, in those same passages, the clue to what God was up to. Once more God's action, evoked in the relevant biblical passages, is to be understood within the larger purposes not only for Israel but through Israel for the world. The setting, again, is not Israel as tabula rasa, but Israel as the sinful, rebellious, idolatrous people to whom God, after years of pleading, threatening, promising, and cajoling, could in the end only respond with devastating judgment. Paul here stands on the same ground as Isaiah, Jeremiah, Daniel,

and the rest, the prophets who interpreted the exile as God's necessary action not only to punish Israel for its long-term infidelity but strangely, through that process, to set forward the ultimate covenant purposes. It is not a matter of echoing this or that passage which speaks, in the abstract as it were, of particular theological doctrines; it is a matter of echoing passages that speak of God's ongoing story with Israel.[335]

The central image of this passage is that of potter and clay. Paul awakens echoes here of two biblical books, and of one written around his own time. The classic passage is Jer 18:6: the prophet watches the potter remold a spoiled vessel into another one, and hears YHWH's word announcing that the same thing will happen to Israel. Israel is acting in the stubbornness of its evil will (18:12), forgetting its God and turning to idols (18:13-17). God therefore claims the right to do with Israel what the potter does with the clay (18:5-11). This is one of Jeremiah's many images of exile and restoration: Israel will be judged severely, but a new covenant will be established the other side of that judgment (Jer 31:31-4; see Rom 2:25-29).

The second passage echoed here is Isa 29:16. The context speaks of God's judgment against an Israel that has become careless, blind in their understanding and hollow in their devotion. Somehow, God will do a new thing, after the time of judgment: God will restore the fortunes of his people. Similar themes recur in Isa 45:9, where God decides to bring Gentiles from far away both to rescue his people and to join them. The image of potter and clay makes the point that Israel has no right to complain if God does such a thing. God is, after all, the creator (45:12). More particularly, the image of potter and clay affirms God's faithfulness to the promises despite full-scale rebellion on Israel's part.[336]

The other echo is of a very different book: the Wisdom of Solomon (there are many other uses of the image in Second Temple Judaism—though most of these, like Lam 4:2, are incidental imagery, not part of a larger implicit narrative; see Sir 33:13; 38:29-30; 1QS 11:22; 1QH 1:21; 3:23-24; 4:29;

---

334. Bryan, *A Preface to Romans*, 91, takes "O man" (NIV) as deliberately scornful.

335. Against Moo, *Romans*, 603.

336. So, rightly, Bryan, *A Preface to Romans*, 162. Bryan's sensitive comments about the intimate relation of potter and clay are worth close attention.

10:3; 12:26, 32; 18:12; *T. Naph.* 2.2, 4). This is one of the Second Temple Jewish books where, as in Paul himself, we find retellings of the story of Israel, particularly of the exodus, drawing out points for those who inherit the story as their own. Paul's account of Pharaoh in the previous verses came close to saying what Wisdom said in its story concerning the Canaanites: God left them unpunished for a while because he was giving them an opportunity to repent, even though he knew they were thoroughly wicked and would never change (12:3-11). In 12:12 Wisdom asks: "For who will say, 'What have you done?' Or will resist your judgment?" And the passage goes on to speak of God's unchallengable righteousness, God's justice as judge of all, God's power and sovereignty as the source of it all, and God's right to judge with mildness and forbearance if he so chooses (12:13-18). Then, in the middle of his denunciation of idolatry, the writer describes the potter who forms from the same clay "both the vessels that serve clean uses and those for contrary uses, making all alike" (15:7). In context, the point is this: those who make idols fail to realize that they are themselves made of the same clay from which they manufacture their false gods (15:8). This then forms part of the denunciation of the Egpytians in particular, the idolaters from whom God rescued Israel. The theme is not identical to Paul's, but the two writings converge in this point: faced with human evil, God has the right both to remake nations and peoples in a new way and to withhold judgment for a while in order that salvation may spread to the rest of the world.

9:19. The question echoes 3:6: why am I still being condemned? God is sovereign; are we not all puppets?

9:20. Paul again refuses to take the easy way out, to assure his readers that humans are free to do what they want. Continuing to reflect on the story of Israel, hopelessly disobedient and provoking its God to wrath and judgment, and ultimately to exile, Paul responds like Isaiah or Jeremiah. Israel has no right of appeal, no right to answer God back. This in turn echoes a more fundamental problem, that of humans as creatures cross-questioning the creator, or humans as sinners arguing with the holy God.

This is the point where, not surprisingly, some have declared that Paul's argument is hopeless. I suspect that Paul would have replied, with Anselm, that post-Enlightenment thought, like many other systems, has not yet considered the seriousness of sin. If Bonhoeffer was right that putting the knowledge of good and evil before the knowledge of God was indeed, and remains, the primal act of human rebellion, then for a human to set up a standard and demand that God keep to it already smacks of such rebellion.[337] And where the humans are themselves among the sinners who have no claim on God except for judgment, their choice is in fact between accepting that judgment at once and accepting instead God's strange purpose in remolding them to carry forward his larger plans. Paul's quotation of Isa 29:16 indicates that this is what he has in mind: the judgment on Israel, following its utter infidelity, will be the prelude to a new beginning, and Israel has no right to complain if this is so.

9:21. Paul then develops the basic potter-and-clay image, without leaving behind its exile-and-restoration overtones, in an echo of Wis 15:7. The potter has the right to make different vessels from the same lump, one for honorable use and one for dishonorable. This verse states the principle that vv. 22-23 will then apply to the particular case of Israel.

9:22-23. Supposing, he says, this is what God had in mind. The force of this two-verse sentence is: "Wouldn't that put the matter in a different light?" To answer this question, though, we have to understand what exactly Paul is saying; and there are two competing ways of doing this. The question hinges on how we read the opening participle (θέλων *thelōn*, "willing"). Is it causal ("because God willed") or concessive ("although God willed")? The NIV ("choosing") and the NRSV ("desiring") seem to take it that Paul means "because": "God wanted to show his wrath and power, and therefore bore with patience." The NJB, however, reads it as concessive: "although all the time he wanted to reveal his retribution and demonstrate his power, [God] has with great patience gone on putting up with those. . . ." And a good

337. D. Bonhoeffer, *Ethics* (London: SCM, 1955) 3-5.

case can be made for this.[338] Within the theological position Paul has sketched out in 2:1-11—echoing several roughly contemporary Jewish writings—it makes good sense to see God as not inflicting wrath, even though it has been richly deserved, but rather creating a breathing space in which there is time to appeal to Israel, and for mercy to spread to more people (see 2 Chr 36:15-16, in the context of Rom 9:11-21 as a whole). Granted, in v. 17 God declares that he wants to display his power through making Pharaoh "stand." This may mean that it is wrong to insist on a straight choice between causal and concessive meanings of "willing." Paul's basic meaning may be "although," but within that there may remain a sense that since this was what God ultimately wanted to do, his long-suffering "bearing with the vessels of wrath" may in fact have been the means whereby, in the longer term, his wrath and power would be displayed all the more clearly.

Paul is saying, then, that the context for God's action is God's right and proper desire to put the world to rights, and to do so swiftly, showing that God, the creator, is also the just judge. This, after all, is what all questions of theodicy seek: the assurance that God is both powerful and just, despite appearances. Verse 22b then explains why those appearances are, in fact, lacking: For the sake of longer-term fulfillment of his wider purposes (we must never forget that this argument continues to 10:12-13 and beyond), God has patiently put up with the Pharaohs of this world, who now alas include much of his own people Israel, as the prophets themselves said over and over again. They are "vessels of wrath," not in the sense of being God's agents to bring wrath on others (as with the identical Greek phrase in Jer 50[27]:25; cf. Isa 13:5; 54:16), but in the sense that they are the appropriate recipients of wrath. As throughout this chapter, Paul is speaking at two levels. He is talking of the pre-exilic generation, with whom God bore patiently despite their persistent idolatry, sending prophet after prophet to them until the only reaction left was the devastating judgment of exile. And he is talking of his own generation, those upon whom, as he said in 1 Thess 2:16, wrath was now coming "to the uttermost." His own generation belong, properly, at the end of the story (10:19-21); but, as with 9:6-13 and 9:14-18, he is looking ahead, noting the pattern of the story, even while retelling its earlier segments.

God, then, has borne with much patience the "vessels of wrath." The theme of God's patience (μακροθυμία *makrothymia*) is another link back to 2:4, and forward thereby to 11:22; 2:4 links God's patience with his kindness (χρηστότης *chrēstotēs*), which is the subject of 11:22.

As in the parable of the sheep and the goats, there is an imbalance between what is said about the "vessels of wrath" and what is said about the "vessels of mercy" (Matt 25:34, 41). The former are "fitted for destruction," leaving it at least ambiguous whether they have done this to themselves by their impenitence or whether God has somehow been involved in the process. The latter, though, have been "prepared for glory" by God himself.[339] And their glory, picking up the theme that runs from 5:2 to 8:30, is God's ultimate objective. Had God simply condemned Israel at once, following its decisive rejection of Jesus as Messiah, there would have been no space either for Jews to repent (beginning, one may suppose, with the disciples themselves!), or for Gentiles to be brought in. Instead, God's patience has served the larger good. God will in the end still display the appropriate wrath and power, but, more important, there will be also displayed "the riches of his glory," the glory, in this case, which God will give to, or share with, the "vessels of glory."

9:24. The grammar at the start of the verse is tricky, because Paul never completes his "what if" sentence of vv. 22-23, but instead moves sideways from the reference to "vessels of mercy." There is no question, though, who Paul has in mind as these "vessels of mercy." It is "we, whom he has called." The language of "call," as in 8:30 and indeed 9:12, is one of his regular ways of describing the process whereby the gospel's sovereign summons evokes the obedience of faith. Paul is preparing the way for the texts

---

338. Similarly the JB. The NEB text has causal, and the margin has concessive. Scholars in favor of the "causal" reading include Barrett, *A Commentary on the Epistle to the Romans*, 189-90; Cranfield, *A Critical and Exegetical Commentary on the Epistle to the Romans*, 493-94; Moo, *The Epistle to the Romans*, 605-6; Bryan, *A Preface to Romans*, 163. For "concessive," see F. J. Leenhardt, *The Epistle to the Romans: A Commentary* (London: Lutterworth, 1961) 258; Fitzmyer, *Romans*, 569.

339. On the imbalance see Bryan, *A Preface to Romans*, 163-64.

from Hosea he is about to quote, in which the idea of "call" is prominent. But the point of the present verse, reached with a sense of triumph after the long journey through the mysteries of Israel's narrative, is that once the exile has done its work, once Israel has gone through the remolding that the potter has the right to accomplish, then the renewed people who emerge, the "vessels of glory," will not be drawn only from Jews, but also from Gentiles. This hugely significant point, which will become a major subject of the next section (9:30–10:21), ties the present telling of the story of Israel to that in 3:21–4:25 (cf. Galatians 3–4). This is how God is keeping his word to Abraham, the word that spoke both of an ongoing selection from within his physical family and also of the worldwide people who would eventually be brought in.

9:25-29. There remain the biblical quotations, two (run together) from Hosea and two from Isaiah. Together they round off the first stage of the argument of 9–11: what God said he would do is what he has in fact done. The echoes of Abraham in all these quotations make it clear that Paul intends to complete here an initial circle of argument from 9:6.

9:25-26. The two quotations from Hosea (2:23 [2:25 LXX] and 1:10 [2:1 LXX]) speak of restoration the other side of judgment. In their original setting they refer to the Israel that has been cast away for infidelity, and has thus become "not my people" and "not beloved." Paul takes these phrases in a wider sense, understanding them to refer to people who had never been within the covenant: Gentiles. And the "call" in question, as we just noted, is not simply a matter of the giving of a name—though in the biblical world name giving was often a sovereign act of character formation. The "call" here is the call of the gospel, through which both Jews and Gentiles are summoned to believing obedience, and hence to a new identity as "sons of God" (9:26). This looks back not only to the theme of "children of God" in 9:8, the children of promise who are "reckoned as 'seed'" (see the Commentary on 9:27-29), but also to the whole theme of sonship in 8:12-30, the theme then drawn together in the reference to υἱοθεσία (*huiothesia*, "sonship") in 9:4. Together, the two Hosea passages speak of the restoration Israel can expect after exile:

it will be a strange reversal of judgment, in which a new word of grace will be spoken to a new people.

9:27-29. To round off the argument that began with God's promise to Abraham, Paul selects two passages from Isaiah that allude in one way or another to that promise and show what God has had to do to accomplish it. In the first passage, Isa 10:22-23, God declares that even if the Abrahamic promise (of descendants as numerous as the sand of the sea) comes true, only "a remnant" will be saved. This also forms a link with the passage from Hos 1:10 (LXX 2:1) quoted immediately before, since that verse begins with the same reference back to Gen 22:17, likening Abraham's promised family to the sand of the sea (see also Gen 13:16; 28:14; 32:12).

When faced with rebellious Israel, in other words, God's first word must be judgment. At the right time, God will act swiftly and decisively (v. 28). Isaiah 10:22 adds the phrase "overflowing in righteousness"; since God's righteousness is Paul's main topic throughout this section the quotation seems designed to strengthen his overall argument. That, presumably, is why several manuscripts have added the phrase, though Paul almost certainly left it unwritten, albeit implied.

At the same time, Isa 10:22 itself is echoed by Isa 28:22, which links us to the crucial passage about the messianic "stone" that Paul will quote from Isa 28:16 in v. 33. The present passage flows directly into the next one, where the Messiah, the one who comes "from them according to the flesh" (9:5), will be seen as the goal of the entire history laid out here. The story Paul has told in vv. 6-29 is the story of what it means for Israel to be the people of the crucified Messiah. Nothing said of Israel in all this passage lies outside that rubric. This is the hidden dimension of God's strange purpose of election: Israel has been called, exactly as in 5:20 and 7:7-25, to be the place where sin gathers itself into one place in order to be dealt with at last. Israel is the people through whom the evil of the world is funneled down on to the representative Messiah. The story of Abraham's family through the exodus and exile to the Messiah himself is a story of the cross casting its shadow ahead of it. The extraordinary things Paul says about God's strange ways with Israel, especially in

9:14-24, all reflect the theology of the cross he stated in 8:3. The judgment on Israel—including its "hardening" in unbelief!—is the result of the divine purpose, that the Messiah would bear, all by himself, the weight of the world's sin and death. This in turn looks on to the conclusion in chap. 11, as we shall see.

Out of the judgment, then, will emerge a "remnant" (v. 27). This remnant will be the "seed" (v. 29)—that is, the true "children of God" promised to Abraham (vv. 7-8). If it had not been for this, Israel would have ended up like Sodom or Gomorrah, the cities of the plain destroyed by God at the very time when he was promising Abraham that Sarah would have a son (Gen 18:16–19:29). The mention of these cities is therefore yet another link to the beginning of the argument in 9:6-9. Paul is working within a dense web of textual echoes, and the cumulative force is not only to declare that God has indeed done what he said he would do but that the pattern of devastating judgment, from which a tiny remnant would escape, is built in from the beginning (cf. Gen 19:29, in which Lot and his family escape from Sodom because "God remembered Abraham"—a foretaste of the exodus [cf. Exod 2:24 with Pss 105:8-9, 42; 106:45], and now of the new exodus that happens in the gospel).

The "remnant," the "holy seed" (cf. Isa 6:13; Ezra 9:2; Mal 2:15), is critical to Paul's argument in chap. 11, and we shall take up the theme there. For the moment we may sum up what he has achieved through this many-layered construction of texts and evocation of contexts.

He has told the story of Israel, from Abraham to the promises of return from exile. At every point the story declares that God intended to affirm, as the true covenant people, not all Abraham's physical family, but only those upon whom he decided to have mercy in order to be faithful to his promises. The background for this is found in chaps. 1–8: all Israel, like all the Gentile world, is guilty of sin, and if God simply left Israel to itself not only would it have ceased to exist long ago but the promises made through Abraham to the whole world would never have come to pass. Hence, at last, Paul has returned to the sequence of thought in 3:1-8, and has spelled out its full implications. Now he can move on in the story to the point that corresponds, at this stage of his argument, to 3:21–4:35 on the one hand and to 8:1-11 on the other. Having explained how God's righteousness requires that he deal properly with sin, he will now explain how that same righteousness, God's faithfulness to the covenant, generates a worldwide family characterized by faith in Jesus as Messiah and Lord and in God's raising of him from the dead.

REFLECTIONS

1. Many readers in our own day will find Paul's argument not only opaque but—at least on the surface—repellent. Our traditions of liberal democracy, not only in Western post-Englightenment civilization but also in many Protestant churches, have made us instinctively recoil against any exercise of sovereign power, even when the one exercising it happens to be the almighty, all-wise, and all-loving creator God. We cherish our freedom, even if we use it to send ourselves or our neighbors to hell (being "free" to deal in heroin, or to perpetrate racist bigotry). Without questioning the value of the liberal democratic tradition, and without pointing out its latent ambiguities and weaknesses, we must insist that the instincts it has engendered have the capacity to cast aspersions on the God of both Jewish and Christian tradition. This, of course, was part of the intention of at least some Enlightenment thinkers. The first step toward appropriating this passage will therefore be, for many, the readiness to think again about who the creator God really is and who we are in his presence.

2. Within that, a second humiliation for us, the heirs of the Enlightenment, is to entertain the thought that the story of Israel is the central story of the true God and the world. This is not a new idea in Romans 9, and it will become more important in chap.

11; but to be grasped by this passage we are bound to see the story Paul tells here as the root of our own story. Romans 9:24 is where for the first time in the section we see the worldwide church, with Jew and Gentile belonging together, the long fulfillment of what God promised Abraham. The humility required of Gentile Christians in admitting that Israel's story is the groundwork, the beginning, of our own story is something that many generations of Christians have refused, with devastating results.

3. We are, however, in a double bind at this point. Paul's necessary language about the failure of ethnic Israel, and God's consequent judgment, "swift and decisive" (9:28), has been used as a stick with which to beat unbelieving Jews from that day to this—with, again, terrible consequences. We shall explore this further when dealing with chap. 11. But for the moment we note the double danger: danger if the church ignores its Jewish roots, danger if the church supposes that, having those Jewish roots, it can look on with anything other than tears and awe at the path God called Israel to tread, the path of being (as he says in 11:15) cast away for the reconciliation of the world. To gloat over Israel as it goes through the story Paul here lays out would be to share the mood of the gloating authorities at the foot of the cross. Israel in this passage is acting out what it means to be the Messiah's people according to the flesh. Those who cherish the death of Jesus Christ, seen in all its Pauline glory as the means of God's dealing with and forgiving their own sin and death, are here summoned to watch in horror and gratitude at the cost of that unique achievement.

The cost is borne by the people who, sometimes knowingly but mostly unknowingly, found themselves called to be members of God's bomb squad, called to take the explosive charge of the world's sin to the waste ground outside the city and there let it be detonated in safety. Paul looks on in tears as most of the team, precisely because they are proud to have this vocation, become unwilling to stand back and allow the crucified Messiah to take the full force of the explosion. By denying that Jesus, the crucified and risen one, is the Messiah, they thereby themselves become caught up in the danger zone. Paul, as we shall see in chap. 11, is anxious that they should leave before it is too late. But he is not sanguine about their chances if they refuse to do so.[340]

4. At a more general level, and once this overall meaning is understood, there are many moments in the passage that can be, and have been, of great comfort to those who find circumstances and obligations overwhelming them. "It isn't a matter of willing, or running, but of God's mercy" (v. 16); that text alone, even without its context, can bring solace to a troubled and anxious heart. That, indeed, is part of the point of expounding God's sovereignty: not to terrify us with the sense of an unknowable and possibly capricious deity, but to assure us that the God of creation, the God we know in Jesus Christ, overflows with mercy, and that even negative judgments have mercy in view all along, if only people will have the humility and faith to find it where it has been placed. To be able to rest in the sovereign mercy of God revealed in Jesus Christ is one of the most valuable aspects of the Christian's calling.

---

340. I cautiously advanced the "bomb squad" illustration in "Romans and the Theology of Paul," in Hay and Johnson, *Pauline Theology, Volume III*, 30-67. R. B. Hays offered criticisms of it in his "Adam, Israel, Christ," 82. I still think it has merit.

ROMANS 9:30–10:21, GOD'S COVENANT FAITHFULNESS REVEALED IN THE MESSIAH

Overview

The second half of Paul's new version of Israel's story brings us from the exile—with the promise of a remnant, and of both Jews and Gentiles called to be God's people—up to the Messiah, and to the renewal of the covenant through him. Through this covenant renewal, the gospel message of Jesus goes out to all the world, though Israel remains recalcitrant. This is the crucial part of the story Paul is telling; it is not an aside or an excursus, but central to the argument of 9–11 as a whole.[341]

This way of reading the passage, like all other possibilities, is bound to be controversial. Yet it is, I believe, solidly based. There are two main points to note, each of which will be amplified in the detailed notes as appropriate.

First, the notorious 10:4 is to be given its full value: τέλος γὰρ νόμου Χριστός (*telos gar nomou Christos*). The Messiah is the . . . end? completion? fulfillment? No: he is the goal of the Torah. The story that Torah tells—the story which Paul has been rehearsing since 9:6—comes to its appointed goal in him, as we might have guessed from 9:5, where already he is the climax and crown of the list of Israel's privileges. This reading of 10:4 holds together the entire larger section, 9:6–10:21; the verse forms a pivot around which the argument moves.

Second, Paul's reading of Deuteronomy 30:12-14 in 10:6-8 belongs with two other Second Temple readings of this passage as a prediction of the true return from exile, the covenant renewal. In both Baruch and 4QMMT we find a similar understanding of the passage, though applied to the authors' own times and groups. Paul is using the same passage to make an equivalent point. Exile, the punishment of Israel's sin, reached its height in the death of the Messiah; now, with

his resurrection and universal lordship (10:9), the new order promised in Deuteronomy 30 has begun, offering a new way of "keeping Torah." Whereas, however, Baruch saw this new way as an invitation to search for the true divine Wisdom, and 4QMMT saw it as a tightening up of purity regulations in the Temple, Paul sees it as faith: confessing Jesus as Lord and believing that God raised him from the dead.

The actual story of Israel, from Abraham to covenant renewal, hinging upon the coming of the Messiah, thus reaches its actual conclusion in 10:13, with Jew and Gentile coming together under the rule of the one Lord (cf. the same conclusion in 15:7-13 and the anticipations in 2:25-29; 3:27-31; 4:13-25). The final part of the chapter (10:14-21) does not add to the narrative line, but explores what has happened at that point. An urgent mission to Gentiles is under way, leading to Gentile inclusion in God's people (10:14-18), while ethnic Israel remains recalcitrant (vv. 19-21). This sets the scene for the fresh discussion of possibilities in chap. 11. Balancing vv. 14-21, at the start of the present section, 9:30-33 does not add a new stage to the story, but sums up where Paul had got to at 9:29, with Gentiles coming in and ethnic Israel tripping up over the "stone." Both parts of this are important. Despite a long tradition of seeing "the failure of Israel" as the main theme, the incoming of Gentiles, via the apostolic mission (9:30; 10:14-18), is just as important.[342]

The discussion in 9:30–10:13 is complicated by the sudden reappearance, four times in 9:30-31, six in 10:3-6, and one final time in 10:10, of the word δικαιοσύνη (*dikaiosynē*), regularly translated "righteousness" (this is assuming that the second occurence in 10:3 is part of the original text; see the Commentary on 10:3). I argued earlier for a particular

---

341. Against Moo, *The Epistle to the Romans*, 618.

342. Against Moo, *The Epistle to the Romans*, 617, and many others, including the NIV's heading for the section ("Israel's Unbelief").

and nuanced understanding of this term, and I regard the coherence that results when this is applied to the present passage as one of the strongest arguments in favor of this understanding. Of course, what strikes one person as coherent may strike another as puzzling, and all such arguments have a necessary circularity about them (reading the word this way makes sense of the passage; reading the passage this way makes sense of the word). However, the circle need not be vicious. Let me briefly rehearse the position, as applied to the present text.

First, *dikaiosynē* here primarily denotes a status that human beings may or may not possess. It is, obviously, a status that Gentiles have come to share but which ethnic Israel as a whole seems, for the moment at least, to have forfeited, though they attempted to establish it, or something like it. The status in question is, however, available through the Messiah, and the badge of it is faith. This explains most of the occurrences in this passage (the four uses in 9:30-31, the second of the three in 10:3, the single ones in 10:4-6 and 10).

At the same time, second, the word also denotes a status that is God's (10:3, the first and third occurrences). It is possible, of course, out of context, to read these as also referring to the status human beings have, marking that status out now as "coming from God" or something similar (see the full discussion, 397-405). But not only do the earlier arguments on δικαιοσύνη θεοῦ (*dikaiosynē theou*) tell heavily in the other direction; the present context does so as well. It will not do to say "since nine out of eleven occurrences refer to a status that humans have, isn't it easier to see the other two that way as well?" Adding "of God" to a word must be allowed to make a difference! The discussion from 9:6 onward, the whole theme that concludes in 11:28-36, is ultimately about God's own character and actions; and, thus far, it has all circled around the question, Has God been faithful to his promises? In doing so, has he been guilty of ἀδικία (*adikia*, "unrighteousness")? This, as we have seen, sends us back to 3:1-8, where the main subject is God's own "righteousness."

Third, the subject matter of chaps. 9–11 indicates strongly that the ongoing theme is the covenant relationship between God and Israel. The word διαθήκη (*diathēkē*) is rare in Paul in general, and in these chapters is only found in 9:4 and 11:27. But the word "covenant" is the simplest shorthand way known to me of referring to that complex of themes that are drawn together frequently in Paul but seldom in such a concentrated fashion as here. Briefly, they comprise God's promises to Abraham; the intention that through Abraham's family God would solve the problem of sin that besets the whole human race; the Torah, with all its ambiguities, as the charter of ethnic Israel, the bond of its relationship with YHWH; and the promise of renewal, of a new mode of being God's people through which exile would be undone, a new way of serving God made possible and actual, with the whole thing being opened up, as originally envisaged, for non-Jews to share. This is what I mean, in these contexts, by "covenant."

All this—it is a story, really, but it includes elements of various sorts—is bound up with the fact that God has been δίκαιος *dikaios*, "righteous." Nor is it simply that God made covenant promises and has now kept them (as one would, in that sense, be "righteous" if one had promised to cut down a tree and had then done so). The notion of God's "righteousness" itself carries "covenantal" meaning. The great majority of occurrences of *dikaiosynē* and its cognates in the LXX reflect an underlying occurrence of צדקה (*ṣĕdāqâ*) and its cognates; and that Hebrew root draws together, not least in books like Isaiah, which Paul drew on extensively, what appear to us as two distinct ideas but that fused together in Jewish thought: legal rectitude or equitableness on the one hand, and covenant on the other.[343]

These two ideas were not sharply distinguished by Paul, because as we have seen he believed that the covenant God made with Abraham was God's appointed means of putting to rights the world in general and the human race in particular. The covenant thus included, as one vital element, God's dealing

---

343. BDAG 247a states somewhat cryptically that "a strict classification of [δικαιοσύνη] in the NT is complicated by freq. interplay of abstract and concrete aspects drawn from OT and Gr-Rom. cultures, in which a sense of equitableness combines with awareness of responsibility within a social context." Quite so: and "awareness of responsibility within a social context," seen in the context of Second Temple Judaism, takes concrete form in the covenant, in the mutual covenant responsibilities of God and Israel in particular, and in the covenant status Israel had, or hoped to have.

with sin and securing forgiveness for sinners. A good deal of chaps. 1–8 is taken up with this one way or another. In the present passage, however, things are different: The word ἁμαρτία (*hamartia*) and its cognates, which occur literally dozens of times in chaps. 3–8, are found precisely once in chaps. 9–11, and that in a biblical quotation, albeit an important one (11:27, quoting Isa 27:9; cf. Jer 31:34). Thus, though in 9:30–10:13 Paul is coming back over territory already familiar from 3:21–4:25 and 7:1–8:11, the spiral of his argument has got to a different point. He can now presuppose God's dealing with sin; here his purpose is to develop the theme that was already bound up within the earlier arguments—namely, the inclusion of Jews and Gentiles together in the single family promised to Abraham.

Though the questions of sin on the one hand and the unity of Jew and Gentile on the other have been held at arm's length in much exegesis and theology, for Paul they are closely intertwined. For him, the whole point of people having their sins forgiven was so that they could then join in the single family who would together and forever sing the praises of the one creator God (15:7-13). This is how, at the level of ethnic structures as well as individual forgiveness and salvation, the world is to be put to rights. And the present section of the letter is where he explains, within the larger story of Israel, and within his overall argument about the faithfulness of God, how that has come about.

Romans 9:30-33, Faith, Works, and the Stumbling Stone

COMMENTARY

The first passage of the section stands back from the detailed story Paul has told so far, and asks: Where have we got to? Without doing more than summarize the previous section, we could answer: Israel has succumbed to judgment, with only a remnant to be rescued from the condemnation of exile; meanwhile, God has used the process described in 9:14-24 as a way of now calling "vessels of glory," not only Jews but also Gentiles. This is more or less exactly what Paul now says, though he adds a new and all-important element to his explanation: the dialectic of law and faith.

9:30. "What then shall we say?" Sometimes when Paul says this he introduces a conclusion that might be drawn, but which he will then reject or drastically modify (see the Commentary on 4:1). It is possible that we should read the rest of the verse in this way: "What then shall we say? Shall we say that Gentiles, not seeking righteousness, have received righteousness? Well, in a sense—but it is a righteousness out of faith." But this may be overly subtle.[344] Paul certainly does want to affirm that Gentiles have attained

"righteousness"; and, as he will explain in 10:6-11, this is in fact the kind of "righteousness" that the Torah always envisaged as God's gift in covenant renewal. The point is that the Gentiles who were not interested in belonging to God's covenant, who were reasonably content with their pagan beliefs and practices, have now received covenant membership, the "being-put-to-rights" status accomplished in the Messiah. But this membership is, of course, marked out not by their keeping of the Jewish Torah—they would have had to "seek" or "strive for" that, and in any case Paul has already declared that nobody will be "put-to-rights" by the Torah (3:20)—but by faith, in the way described in chaps. 3 and 4. That is basic to his argument; he is clarifying, by reference back to what he has said earlier, what he meant in v. 24.[345]

9:31. Israel, however, finds itself in the opposite situation: That which it was, in fact, seeking, it has not in fact found. We expect Paul to say "Israel, pursuing righteousness, did not attain it"; but Paul seldom says just what we expect, and here he adds the twist we would only have anticipated had we

---

344. Though see Fitzmyer, *Romans*, 576-77; Bryan, *A Preface to Romans*, 165, suggesting that vv. 30*b*-31 together form a second question.

345. On "seeking righteousness," see Isa 51:1 in its context; the surrounding material in Isaiah 50–51 is very relevant to Paul's argument (despite Moo, *Romans*, 621).

realized the extent to which his thought here is grounded in 3:21–4:25 and particularly 7:1–8:11. "Israel, pursuing the law, did not attain to the law." Some scholars suggest that Paul is simply unclear, since he "undoubtedly" means that Israel had been pursuing, and did not attain, "righteousness."[346] But, as so often, if we give Paul the benefit of the doubt, and are prepared to revise our expectations, he will not let us down. The thought, in fact, is here not far from 7:21-25: the more Israel clung to the law, the more it found that evil lay close at hand, and that covenant membership could not be had that way. Paul makes this more complicated by adding "of righteousness" to the first mention of "law"; as, again, in chap. 7, he will not imply that the law was not God's law, holy and just and good (the phrase "law of righteousness" occurs in Wis 2:11, but in a very different, and scarcely relevant, context). Covenant membership would indeed have been defined by Torah had that been possible, just as the Torah would have given life had it been capable of doing so, instead of having to work with material that was doomed to die (7:10; cf. Gal 3:21). In that context, as in *Alice Through the Looking Glass*, those who were the most determined to walk toward a particular goal were the ones who never reached it, while those strolling in the opposite direction found themselves arriving at once.

9:32a. Paul's explanation is almost equally paradoxical. The reason Israel did not attain Torah, the covenant charter, is because they were pursuing it, not by faith, but "as though by works"—the implication being "which it never was," or at least "which was an impossible route." Here is the subtlety, so often missed, in Paul's view of the Jewish law. Paul does not suppose that the Jewish law, the

Torah, is bad, shabby, or even second-rate, to be pushed out of the way in favor of something else. The law is God's law, and covenant membership is marked out by attaining to it. The only question is, what counts as "attaining to it"? The full answer to this is given, brilliantly, in 10:6-9, using the "new covenant" passage in Deuteronomy 30. But those who remember what Paul said in 8:1-11, especially 8:4-8, and behind that again in 2:25-29 and 3:27-31, may already have a clue. Strange though it may seem, there is a "keeping of the law" that is open to all, Jew and Gentile alike. This, Paul has already suggested and will shortly argue, is what, so to speak, the Torah really wanted all along. To suppose that it could be fulfilled—to suppose that covenant membership could be secured for all time—simply by the "works of the law," either in the sense of the complete list of commandments, or in the (more normal) sense of the works that marked out the Jews from their pagan neighbors, falls foul of Paul's dictum: by the works of the law shall no flesh be justified (3:20; cf. Gal 2:16). In the present context, it is the second sense of "works" that dominates the horizon. What Israel has sought, and what 9:6-29 has been at pains to deny, is an inalienable identity as God's people for all those who possess Torah, for (that is) ethnic Israel as a whole. Paul, assuming his whole argument to date, declares that this can never be the appropriate fulfillment of, or attainment to, Torah. The God who gave Torah is the God who made promises to Abraham, promises about a worldwide family. Unless we are to suppose (which Paul never does) that Torah was a bad idea that God subsequently abandoned (see the Commentary on 10:4), we must conclude that God always envisaged a kind of Torah-keeping, a kind of law-fulfillment, of a different order from that pursued so vigorously by the zealous Jews of Paul's day, including himself in his earlier days (Gal 1:14; Phil 3:4-6). The subtlety of this is allowed for here not least because Paul does not include a verb in the sentence; we are bound to supply "pursued," but the precise meaning of this is left open, so there is no problem in the idea of "pursued by faith."[347] What this means will become clearer in chapter 10.

346. E.g., Sanders, *Paul, the Law, and the Jewish People*, 42; Fitzmyer, *Romans*, 577-78. The NIV's "a law of righteousness" picks up the fact that Paul does not write a definite article before νόμος (*nomos*, "law"), implying that this might be something other than Torah; and, at the end of the verse, by translating simply "has not attained it," leaves the possibility open that Paul means "attained righteousness," whereas the Greek is very clear in repeating *nomos*. Since this second use is also without the article, but clearly refers to the law just mentioned, it is clear that the absence of the article in the first instance is not as significant as the translation would imply. The NRSV, following the RSV, blatantly turns the first phrase around: "Israel, who did strive for the righteousness that is based on the law." It is possible that this is what Paul meant by διώκων νόμον δικαιοσύνης (*diōkon nomon dikaiosynēs*), but he was perfectly capable of writing διώκων τὴν δικαιοσύνην τὴν ἐν νόμω (*diōkon tēn dikaiosynēn tēn en nomō*) or perhaps ἐκ νόμου (*ek nomou*, cf. Phil 3:6, 9) if that was what he meant. The JB and the NJB both fall into the same trap; the NEB and the REB stick closer to what Paul actually says.

347. See Fitzmyer, *Romans*, 578-79.

9:32b-33. Drawing now on the dark theme he has expounded in vv. 6-29, particularly vv. 14-24, Paul declares that what Israel did, pursuing Torah but not attaining to it, was like a sort of tripping up; and the stone that tripped them up was put there, not by some demon, but by the covenant God himself. We are back once again with the paradox of chap. 7. The law was God's good and holy law, but when it was given sin sprang to life and "I" died (7:9). When Israel continued to live under the law, sin lay close at hand (7:21), creating a "law of sin" (7:23, 25). So, here, God's good law, placed there by God's own self, has tripped up Israel as with a stone put there on purpose. We can only begin to understand this in the light of what has already been said about God's purpose for Israel, and of what will become clear in 11:11-16. God's intention was all along that Israel should be the Messiah's people according to the flesh; that is, that like the Messiah himself they should be cast away that the world might be redeemed.

The Messiah himself provides, so it seems, the final twist to this constantly surprising little paragraph. Paul's double text about the "stone," taken from Isa 28:16 and 8:14, makes use of a motif familiar in several different strands of early Christianity, very likely going back to Jesus' own fresh use of Jewish traditions including Daniel 2.[348] But who or what is the "stone"?

One's initial impression, reading the quotation in its present setting, might be that Paul intends the stumbling-stone to be understood as the law itself. The Torah, it seems, has been at least the proximate cause of Israel's stumble; Paul has just spoken of the correct way to pursue the Torah as being by faith. Hence the marginal translation in the NRSV, "whoever trusts in it," rather than "him."[349] Further reflection, however, suggests two other options. On the one hand, there is God, who according to Isa 8:12-14

is both a sanctuary for those who fear him and a stone of stumbling for those who do not. On the other hand, however, Isa 28:16 is likely to have been understood in a messianic sense; and that, indeed, was how at least some rabbis understood Isa 8:14 too.[350] And, just as in Rom 8:9-11 we detected the theme of the rebuilt Temple, the place where God came to dwell by his Spirit, so in the present passage we would be right to hear at least the overtones of the standard Second Temple idea that the "stone," probably the Messiah, would be the "foundation" of the new "Temple," which would consist of all his followers, the community that would be established around him.[351] Whatever the strength of this resonance—and since the Temple is not mentioned in Romans we cannot easily assess this—we note, as of crucial importance, that the same text that concludes v. 33 recurs in 10:11, where it is clearly Jesus as Messiah who is meant by "him." Nor is this an isolated occurrence: Throughout 10:6-10, which is then summed up in 10:11, the faith in question is faith in, or at least focused upon, the Messiah himself. The positive link between the law and the Messiah in 10:4 (however controversial it may be to put it like this; see below) completes the circle. We conclude that Paul intends the stumbling-stone to be the Messiah himself, the one who is "of them according to the flesh" (9:5). It is through faith in him, or at least through that faith in God which has Jesus' messianic achievements at its cognitional core, that the Torah is attained, as 10:4-11 will explain in detail. Those who "attain . . . by faith," then, will not be put to shame (cf. 1:16; see also the Commentary on 10:13). And since, for Paul, Israel's Messiah according to the flesh is also "God over all" (9:5; see above), we should not be surprised that there are echoes as well, through the reference to Isaiah 8, to God as both the stumbling-stone and the object of faith.

But in what way is the Messiah the stumbling-stone? How has Israel stumbled over him? At one level the answer is obvious,

---

348. See 1 Pet 2:6-8, where the two Isaiah passages are separated, with Ps 118:22 quoted in between; Matt 21:42 and pars.; Acts 4:11-12; Eph 2:20. On Jesus' use (and its Second Temple Jewish context), see Wright, *Jesus and the Victory of God*, 498-500.

349. See also the NJB: "he who relies on this," i.e., on the stone—leaving the interpretative option open. So too the REB: "he who has faith in it." C. K. Barrett argues cautiously for the law as the "stone," though with a christological reference as it were waiting in the wings. See Barrett, "Romans 9.30–10.21: Fall and Reponsibility of Israel," in *Die Israelfrage nach Röm 9–11*, ed. L. de Lorenzi (Rome: St Paul vor den Mauern, 1977) 112. Fitzmyer, *Romans*, 579, proposes the gospel.

350. So *b.Sanh* 38a.

351. Isa 28:16 is quoted in 1QS 8:7-8 in reference to the community. See Wright, *Jesus and the Victory of God*, 499n. 76. See also Matt 16:18, where the notion of building a community on the "rock" belongs with the same strand of thought: B. F. Meyer, *The Aims of Jesus* (London: SCM, 1979) 185-88. The Targum on Isaiah understands the reference in this way; and see 1QS 8:7-8; 1QH 6:26-7.

and leads us back to the lacuna in 9:1-5: ethnic Israel as a whole has failed to believe in the Messiah, because his crucifixion is a scandal to them (1 Cor 1:23; Gal 5:11).[352] This is without a doubt Paul's basic referent. But behind this again lay, as he knew, the rejection by the Judaean leaders of Jesus himself on his last visit to Jerusalem, and his consequent death at the hands of the pagan authorities (see Acts 13:27-9; 1 Thess 2:15). This double answer is bound up in Paul's mind with Israel's attempt to "attain to Torah" by "works"—the attempt, which he will describe further presently, to confine grace to race, to create a covenant status for

Jews and Jews only. Paul sees this attempt in fundamental conflict with Jesus the crucified Messiah, and hence with the whole covenant plan of God that has reached its goal in him. This, too, we should remind ourselves, is not, according to Romans 9, something outside the many-layered purpose of God. Israel stumbled over the stumbling-stone because God "laid it in Zion." The present passage is, after all, part of an argument that "God's word has not failed" (9:6). If Israel is to be "cast away" for the "reconciliation of the world" (11:14), both Torah and Messiah are drawn into that process. The Messiah remains the key to what God has done with Israel; or, to put it another way, Israel remains the Messiah's people according to the flesh.

352. σκάνδαλον (*skandalon*), the word translated "scandal" here, is often translated "stumbling block" (e.g., KJV, RSV, NRSV, NEB, NIV on 1 Cor 1:23); but the metaphor of tripping up is absent from its basic meaning, which is to do with enticing to sin. See BDAG 926.

Romans 10:1-21, God's Righteousness and the Worldwide Mission

COMMENTARY

Romans 10:1-13 must be seen as a whole if its parts are to be properly understood.[353] Too often scholars and preachers have allowed vv. 3-4 to stand almost by themselves; it is revealing that neither the NRSV nor the NIV translates the γάρ (*gar*, "for") that connects v. 5 to what has gone before. In Paul's mind, vv. 5-9 explain and undergird vv. 1-4, so that neither can be understood without the other, nor 1-9 as a whole apart from 10-13. In fact, the whole passage is joined together in such a close chain of explanation (vv. 2, 3, 4, and 5 all link to their predecessors with *gar*; vv. 5-9 then form a unit, the exegetical heart of the passage; then vv. 10, 11, 12a, 12b, and 13 all open with *gar*).[354] This is as tightly linked a chain as any in Paul's writings.

The main theme of the passage is the covenant renewal, and covenant redefinition, that has taken place in the Messiah. God has done what he always promised; and what he had promised, in the crucial Deuteronomy 30, was that after the punishment of exile he

would restore Israel, enabling it to keep the law in a new way. The Israel of Paul's day, his kinsfolk according to the flesh, did not understand this; they did not, in other words, understand the *dikaiosynē theou*, the righteousness of God. They did not understand either how God had been true to the covenant all along, or how he was now doing exactly what he had promised in renewing that covenant and bringing Gentiles into membership, by faith, alongside believing Jews. But the covenant renewal that has taken place in and through Jesus the Messiah, the world's true Lord, is—so Paul argues—the renewal spoken of in Deuteronomy 30. At its heart is faith: faith in this Jesus, faith that is open to all, faith by which all may be saved.

The paragraph, in fact, begins and ends with salvation (vv. 1, 13). This is what covenant renewal in the Messiah has achieved. But we should watch carefully where the emphasis of the paragraph falls. It is easy, in the midst of Paul's enthusiasm for the opening of salvation to the Gentiles, to miss the fact that the paragraph opens with his prayer that Jewish people should be saved. It is, after

353. Against Bryan, *A Preface to Romans*, 159, 175, who divides after v. 10.
354. So, rightly, C. K. Rowe, "Romans 10:13: What Is the Name of the Lord?" *Horizons in Biblical Theology* 22 (2000) 140-41.

all, part of the argument for which 9:1-5 was the curtain raiser. In other words, when he is expounding Deuteronomy 30 in vv. 6-9 he is insisting, along with the general welcome to Gentiles, that faith in the Messiah—faith that Jesus is Lord and that God raised him from the dead—is the way to salvation for all, Jew as well as Greek. This emphasis continues in the following paragraph (vv. 14-21), which Paul exactly summarizes in 11:13-14. He celebrates his own apostleship to the Gentiles in order to provoke his Jewish kinsfolk to jealousy, and so to bring them to salvation. Verse 1 thus states the theme that remains central throughout the rest of the section.[355]

10:1. At the start of chap. 9 Paul expressed a wish, or prayer, which he could imagine himself praying but from which, in fact, he drew back. He knows that such a thought—that he should himself be cut off from the Messiah on behalf of his kinsfolk—is not the way forward. God did not accept that prayer when Moses offered it, and would most likely not do so now. Besides, how would the casting out of an apostle benefit his fellow Jews? If God had acted in the Messiah to renew the covenant and create a way of salvation open to all, the focus of any prayer on their behalf must be that they would attain this salvation by the route God had set up.

That is why, now, he announces the prayer that he is in fact praying: that his fellow Jews may be saved. This is the desire of his heart, the desire that springs out of the grief and pain that reside there (9:2); and this desire turns into prayer. When, therefore, we find him a few verses later speaking enthusiastically of the way by which people come to salvation, and when this is grounded in a biblical passage that speaks of how God restores the fortunes of his people after the punishment of exile, we should conclude that it is the salvation of his fellow Jews that he has primarily in mind. If you confess . . . and believe . . . you will be saved (v. 9); belief and confession lead to salvation (v. 10); all who call upon the Lord's name will be saved (v. 13). This, to be sure, is combined with his new point in 9:24 and 9:30: Gentiles are becoming equal members in God's people. But he knows that is happening anyway. His urgent prayer is that it should happen for Jews as well.

This verse has the effect of curbing any false impressions that might be received from chap. 9. Paul addresses his readers as ἀδελφοί (*adelphoi*, lit. "brothers"), the same word he had used for his kinsfolk in 9:3, though he modified it there by adding "according to the flesh." He wants to draw his largely Gentile audience in Rome (11:13) to share his earnest desire for the salvation of Jews, not to allow them, through a half-understanding of chap. 9, to settle back comfortably and acquiesce in their present plight. This verse already looks forward, then, to the argument of 11:11-32; that passage cannot rightly be understood unless we see it as presupposing what is said here.

10:2. The sense of this verse is straightforward. Paul describes his fellow Jews, and would describe his own former self, as zealous but ignorant. Paul testifies to his kinsfolk that they have "a zeal for God," as he himself had had before his conversion (Acts 22:3; Gal 1:14; Phil 3:6). He can use the word "zeal" both in the specific sense of Jewish "zeal for Torah" or "zeal for God," referring to that burning desire for God's honor, for Torah to be upheld, which had led him to use violence to preserve "the traditions of the fathers," and in the broader sense of any burning energy that made people make much of a person or cause (e.g., 2 Cor 11:2; Gal 4:17).[356] But this zeal is, literally, "not according to knowledge" (the NRSV's "not enlightened" may perhaps import a hint of gnostic superknowledge, but Paul is talking not about private illumination but about what God has revealed in the Messiah). He will explain further in the next verse what it is that they are ignorant of.

But if the sense of v. 2 is clear, what is its connection with v. 1, the connection Paul intends with *gar*, "for" (omitted by the NRSV)? His meaning might be taken to be that they were, so to speak, halfway there; they were at least zealous for God, and it was worth praying that they might complete

---

355. So Rowe, *Horizons in Biblical Theology* 22 139-40.

356. On "zeal" in Judaism see above all M. Hengel, *The Zealots: Investigations into the Jewish Freedom Movement in the Period from Herod I Until 70 a.d.*, trans. D. Smith (Edinburgh: T. & T. Clark, 1989); and Wright, *The New Testament and the People of God*, 170-81. The Jewish background includes Num 25:11, 13; 1 Kgs 19:10, 14; Ps 69:9; 1 Macc 2:26-7, 58; Jdt 9:4. On Paul's different senses of "zeal," see N. T. Wright, *What St Paul Really Said: Was Paul of Tarsus the Real Founder of Christianity?* (Grand Rapids: Eerdmans, 1997) chap. 2. Moo, *The Epistle to the Romans*, 632, is wrong to say that the concept is "uniformly praised" in the NT; he does not mention Gal 1:14 or Phil 3:6, where "zeal" leads to persecuting the church.

the rest of the journey. But this is unlikely. Even supposing that he thought their type of "zeal" would have counted as such, which Phil 3:6-7 would call into question, Paul did not suppose that salvation was a final gift that came to crown a life of unaided human virtue. The more natural connection is to see v. 2 explaining, not the appropriateness of praying for them, but their need of salvation; and the part of v. 2 that explains this is "not according to knowledge." "Salvation is what I'm praying for on their behalf; they need it because, zealous as they are, they remain without vital knowledge."

10:3. Paul now explains (again, with *gar*) what it is they are ignorant of, and what they have been doing as a result. Unfortunately, his meaning has remained obscure because of the different ways in which the phrase *dikaiosynē theou* and its variants have been understood, and we have some tidying up to do before we can proceed.

The NRSV (following the RSV) and the NIV assume that the first occurrence of the phrase denotes the status that God's people have, a status now bestowed upon faith; and that calling this "the righteousness of God" draws attention to the fact that this status comes from God (as opposed, say, to arising from human effort).[357] The assumption is then that the second occurrence refers to the kind of status people attempt to set up for themselves, which in much traditional interpretation has been the status of a "works-righteousness" resulting from keeping the law, or a more general moral effort.

On the basis of the arguments advanced earlier (see the Introduction; Commentary on 1:17; 3:21-26),[358] I propose a different way of reading the verse, which makes more detailed sense in itself and in its relation to the wider context. The most natural way of taking the first and third occurrences of δικαιοσύνη *dikaiosynē* in the verse are to refer to God's own "righteousness"—the quality of equitable covenant faithfulness that has been the main theme of Romans

in general and of 9:6-29 in particular. The second use (τὴν ἰδίαν δικαιοσύνην *tēn idian dikaiosynēn*) refers to the covenant status that Israel according to the flesh had thought to set up for itself.[359] The verse should then be understood, I suggest, as follows: "For, being ignorant of God's righteousness, and seeking to establish a righteousness of their own, they did not submit to God's righteousness."

There is no need, in fact, for each occurrence of "righteousness" to refer to the same thing. On the contrary, the sense is much clearer if they do not. It is true that the status of "righteousness" that believers enjoy is a gift from God; but this is not, here or elsewhere, what the phrase "the righteousness of God" indicates. The final use in the verse is telling: "they did not submit to God's righteousness." This is difficult to square with the idea of "a status that comes from God"; one would "receive" this, not "submit" to it.

How then does the verse, read this way, fit in to the larger sequence of thought? As in 1:17 and 3:21-6, God's righteousness is God's own equitable covenant faithfulness, God's utterly reliable loyalty to the promises to Abraham. And the whole point of 9:6-33 is that this is what it has meant for God to be utterly reliable and loyal to his promise to Abraham. This is what "God's righteousness" looks like in practice. It is not as though the word of God has failed. The problem is that Israel according to the flesh never realized this, never understood what God was doing, in fulfillment of the promise and through the strange Messiah-shaped purpose. "God's righteousness" is a shorthand, here, for the entire sweep of covenantally loyal actions God has undertaken from Abraham to the Messiah. Paul's kinsfolk, like his own earlier self, have remained ignorant of it all, unaware that this was what God was up to and that it was what God had said all along.

As a result, they have not submitted to this covenant history. They have resisted it, like the wicked tenants in Jesus' parable (Mark 12:1-12 and par., culminating in the rejection—and vindication—of the "stone" the builders refused), hoping to claim

357. See Sanday and Headlam, *A Critical and Exegetical Commentary on the Epistle to the Romans*, 283, and many since. The NEB/REB have "God's way of righteousness," as though the phrase referred not so much to a status as to a method or system. The JB follows the RSV, but the NJB, interestingly, has "God's saving justice."

358. See also Fitzmyer, *Romans*, 583, against Cranfield, *A Critical and Exegetical Commentary on the Epistle to the Romans*, 515; A. Nygren, *Commentary on Romans* (Philadelphia: Fortress, 1972) 379.

359. Several good MSS (including A and B) omit δικαιοσύνην *dikaiosynēn* in the latter phrase. It is easier to explain this in terms of scribes tidying up an apparently overly repetitive sentence than it is to explain the addition of what, by the same token, would have seemed to many a redundant occurrence.

the inheritance for their own. They have attempted, in other words, to set up a status of covenant membership in which the principle of 9:6-29 would be quietly set aside; this would be a status for all Jews, and only for Jews. No pruning down to a remnant; no admission of Gentiles (except by becoming full Jews through proselyte initiation). This is the "righteousness" they sought to establish: a status that would be "their own." This does not refer to a status they might have achieved by moral effort, by climbing up a ladder called "works," but to a status that would be theirs and theirs only. Romans 10:3 is a central statement of what Paul principally objects to, on the basis of the gospel, within the Judaism to which he had himself belonged. He does not regard his contemporaries as proto-Pelagians, trying to pull themselves up by their own moral bootstraps in order to be good enough for God and to earn "works-righteousness" of that sort. Rather, they believed that God's covenant with Abraham was their exclusive and inalienable possession, whereas Paul had come to believe that, through the death and resurrection of the Messiah, the long covenant story as set out in the Scriptures had all along had a different shape. Paul is not turning his back on Judaism and its traditions. He is claiming to interpret them in their own terms, through their own Scriptures, and around their own Messiah (9:4-5).

This makes good sense, too, of what follows. Verses 5-9 do not contrast, as has often been thought, moralistic self-help "righteousness" with a simple trust in God. It expounds what Deuteronomy set out as the charter for the new covenant, the return from exile. It is a contrast of eschatology, not of rival and parallel systems of justification or salvation; it is the difference between what was said to Israel in the beginning and what was said by way of invitation to covenant renewal after the exile. And the source of it all is the covenant faithfulness of God as unveiled, in action, in the Messiah. Thus, just as in 3:21-26 the *dikaiosynē theou* was revealed through the gospel of Jesus the Messiah, crucified and risen, so now God's own righteousness, his faithfulness to the covenant, has been unveiled in the Messiah as the resurrected Lord. In both cases, the badge of belonging to the covenant people is, of course, faith.

This, I submit, is the clearest reading of 10:5-9. We shall expound it more fully presently. It strongly supports the understanding of v. 3 that has just been outlined.

To sum up: Paul declares that his fellow Jews are ignorant of God's righteousness, of what God has all along been doing, in faithfulness to God's own word and promise as described in 9:6-29 and now unveiled in the Messiah. Instead, they have sought to establish a covenant membership that would be for Jews and Jews only. As a result, they have not submitted to God's covenant faithfulness, God's decisive action in Jesus the Messiah in fulfillment of the promises. Just as "the mind of the flesh" cannot "submit to God's law" (8:7), so now that same mind cannot and does not submit to God's righteousness—the righteousness to which Torah and prophets bore witness, but which Torah by itself could never produce. We are here, that is, at the point of the spiral of Paul's argument directly above 8:1-11. That should help us to understand the next verse, which presents one of the most famous problems in all of Paul.

10:4. The problem in this short verse does not lie in the meaning of the main theological terms. Law, Christ, righteousness, faith—we have met them all many times before. The problem comes when we put them together, and add at the front the word τέλος (*telos*). Usually translated "end," this word can, like the English "end" itself, mean both "cessation, termination" and "goal, fulfillment." At this point lexicography can offer us options, but exegesis must decide which better fits the flow of thought.

The mainstream opinion, at both scholarly and popular levels, has for many years been the Lutheran or similar understanding, in which "the law" simply leads people into works-righteousness or self-righteousness, into the attempt to achieve their own justification and salvation.[360] If we come to the verse with that assumption, it appears natural to read it, like the NEB, as "Christ ends the law and brings righteousness for everyone

---

360. See Sanday and Headlam, *Romans*, 283-84: "Law as a method or principle of righteousness had been done away with in Christ." See also Dodd, *The Epistle of Paul to the Romans*, 176; Käsemann, *Commentary on Romans*, 282-83. Luther, interestingly, in his *Lectures on Romans*, ed. W. Pauck, LCC 15 (Philadelphia: Westminster, 1961) 288, takes "Christ is the end of the law" as an introduction to what follows, showing that "every word in the Bible points to Christ."

who has faith,"[361] or, with the JB, "But now the Law has come to an end with Christ, and everyone who has faith may be justified."[362] This reading has become extremely common at a popular level, and one is used to hearing it quoted as an excuse for any and every form of antinomianism. At that level, too, it has become a focus of controversy between broadly Lutheran views (seeing the law as a negative force) and Calvinist ones (seeing it as positive). But the broadly Lutheran view has the widest currency.

There are, however, three problems with this, simply at the level of translation of the Greek text, and much larger ones at the level of Paul's thought in the context, in Romans as a whole, and in his other letters. (To oppose the Lutheran view, by the way, is not to say that a Calvinist reading is to be accepted instead. It is after all possible that neither of the great sixteenth-century European Reformers got fully inside Paul's first-century Jewish skin.) We should note before launching into the detail that most early readers of Paul took him to mean "goal," "culmination," or something similar.[363]

The first problem is that the second half of the sentence expresses, grammatically, the result, and probably also the implicit (divine) intention, of the first. It is not a second, different point from the first. Literally translated, the verse reads "For end of law Christ unto righteousness to every believing one." In such a sentence, we assume that "Christ" is the subject, "end of (the) law" is the complement, and that Paul wants us to understand "is." But "unto righteousness to every believer" cannot be a different, second thought. There must be something about Christ's being the end of the law that, in Paul's mind, itself enables or causes "righteousness for all believers." (Nor can "unto righteousness" modify

"law," making the meaning that "Christ is the end of the 'law-unto-righteousness.' ")[364] One can just about imagine such a meaning: if "the end of the law" means "the abolition of Torah," this could conceivably mean "so that now, with Torah out of the way, a different system can come into operation," but it is interesting that those translations that take the verse that way find themselves pushed toward making the second half of the verse a separate thought (NEB, REB, JB). As with 9:30-31, the text itself resists the reading that many have assumed it "must" bear.[365]

The second problem is closely linked with this. Reading *telos* as "termination" tends to push translations into turning the noun "righteousness" into a verb (RSV: "so that everyone who has faith may be justified"; so too NJB). Paul could have written ἵνα δικαιωθήσονται πάντες οἱ πιστεύοντες (*hina dikaiōthēsontai pantes hoi pisteuontes*), "so that all who believe may be justified," and no doubt what he has said is not far from this. But he has chosen to speak, not of an event, but of the status believers now have. He is saying that the Messiah's being the τέλος νόμου *telos nomou* makes that status available. And with 9:31 close behind we can see why, provided we do not lose our exegetical nerve there as well. Israel pursued the νόμον δικαιοσύνης (*nomon dikaiosynēs*), but did not attain to that νόμος (*nomos*); the Messiah is the goal of the *nomos*, resulting in *dikaiosynē* for all who "pursue" it the right way. Israel's pursuit failed because it was undertaken, not by faith, but as though Torah and the status of righteousness it offers were to be attained through works; the Messiah is the goal of the Torah so that there may be righteousness—the righteousness of the "Torah of righteousness"!—for all who have faith. Once we allow Paul to have said what he meant, instead of saying nearly, but not quite, what we expect him to have meant, the passage will come clear.

The third problem with the mainstream reading is Paul's use of the word *telos* and its cognates elsewhere, not least in Romans itself.[366] The only other occurrences of the

361. The REB has changed the verb "ends" back to a noun ("Christ is the end of the law") but still retains the unwarranted addition of an extra verb ("and brings"). The second half of the Greek sentence, though, is the result of the implied verb in the first half, not a second and different thought. The NEB margin is equally unwarranted: "Christ is the end of the law as a way to righteousness for everyone who has faith"; to take εἰς δικαιοσύνην (*eis dikaiosynēn*) with νόμου (*nomou*) in that way is grammatically very harsh.

362. The NJB, however, has changed this to: "But the Law has found its fulfilment in Christ so that all who have faith will be justified." One wonders why, in either case, "but" was preferred to "for" as the connective; but at least a connection was provided, unlike the NIV, which omits γάρ (*gar*) altogether.

363. See esp. R. Badenas, *Christ the End of the Law: Romans 10.4 in Pauline Perspective*, JSNTSup 10 (Sheffield: JSOT, 1985); and the careful discussions of Cranfield, *Romans*, 515-20; and Fitzmyer, *Romans*, 584-85.

364. So, rightly, Moo, *The Epistle to the Romans*, 637.

365. See too the way in which Sanday and Headlam, *Romans*, 284, are forced to say that the *gar* at the start of the verse gives the reason, not for the actual statement of v. 3, but for what was implied—namely, that the Jews were wrong in not submitting to "the divine method."

366. See Badenas, *Christ the End of the Law*, chap. 2.

noun in this letter come in 6:21-22: "the end of those things is death . . . the fruit you have is unto sanctification, and its end is eternal life." By itself, we might be misled into reading the first of these as meaning "termination," but the second makes it clear that what Paul means is "goal." Sanctification leads to, points toward, eternal life, and is consummated and completed thereby. The same is true of the shameful deeds that lead to death. A similar meaning accounts for two of the other Pauline references (2 Cor 11:15; Phil 3:19). Similarly, when Paul declares "then comes the end" in 1 Cor 15:24, he does not simply mean "then everything comes to a full stop," but rather "then comes the moment when everything is accomplished and God is all in all."[367] The other references are either indeterminate or too controversial to be included as evidence.[368] So, too, with Paul's use of the cognate verb τελέω (teleō). Though the verb can mean "bring to an end, finish," Paul's three uses of it all carry the other sense, "accomplish, perform, fulfill." In 2 Cor 12:9 God's power is "accomplished, fulfilled, made perfect" in weakness;[369] in Gal 5:16 he speaks of "accomplishing" the works of the flesh. And in Rom 2:27, at a critical early point in the argument that anticipates both 8:1-11 and the present passage, Paul speaks of "the uncircumcision which fulfills the law [ἡ . . . ἀκροβυστία τὸν νόμον τελοῦσα hē akrobystia ton nomon telousa]." He does not mean "which brings the law to an end," but rather "which completes, fulfills the law"—even though, of course, he has in mind a "fulfillment" that, like the one in 10:6-9, is paradoxical, involving no outward marks of Jewish covenant membership, but instead the inward marks of the spirit through whom the covenant is renewed.

This already points us to the wider context, where again the meaning "conclusion, abrogation" is challenged, and the meaning

"goal, completion" supported. As we have seen, the whole passage from 9:6 onward has been a retelling of the story of Israel, from the promises to Abraham, through exodus and exile, and on toward the long-awaited covenant renewal. This is the story that Torah itself, in its widest sense, tells; this is the story, as 9:31 indicates, of how Israel has pursued "the Torah of righteousness" but has not "attained Torah." It is not that Israel has attained Torah but missed righteousness; that frequent misunderstanding, with its consequent mistranslations (see above), goes with the common, but mistaken, view of 10:4. It is, rather, that Israel has not "attained Torah," because the mode of "works" is not the way whereby one can attain it. Torah, Israel's covenant charter, leads the eye forward along the story line from Abraham all the way to the Messiah, who is the goal of Torah. That is how the story works. It is the narrative logic of the entire section.[370]

Powerful support for this reading of 10:4 is found in 2:27-29; 3:27-31; 8:1-11; and 10:5-13. More details on each are found in the relevant sections of the commentary; here we simply summarize. (Notice how the "termination" reading of *telos* in 10:4 goes with the marginalization of 2:27-29, the misreading of "law" language in 3:27-31, the ignoring of the positive view of the law in 8:1-11, and the non-eschatological reading of 10:5-9; all telltale signs that Paul's theology has been forced on to a Procrustean bed.)

In 2:17-29 not a word is said about the law being a bad thing that needed to be brought to an end. Israel's problem here is that, despite boasting in Torah, it dishonors God by breaking it (v. 23). The solution is not to abrogate Torah, but for God to find a new method whereby people can keep it. There is to be a way of Torah-observance open to uncircumcision (v. 26)—a shocking oxymoron, parallel to 1 Cor 7:19, for those aware, as Paul was, that circumcision was itself commanded in Torah. Such people are described as "the uncircumcision that fulfils Torah" (v. 27). How this happens Paul merely hints. It is a matter of secret identity, the heart, and the Spirit (2:29).

---

367. Against Moo, *Romans*, 638, who cites this as an instance of the meaning "termination."

368. See esp. 2 Cor 3:13, on which see Wright, *The Climax of the Covenant*, 181, esp. n. 25, where I argue that τέλος (*telos*) can be read as "goal" or "final destination," even though the phrase contains the idea of the Torah's dispensation as essentially temporary.

369. BDAG 997 lists this, strangely, as an occurrence of the first meaning, on the grounds that to bring something to an end can also mean to bring it to its consummation or perfection; but, granted that the two meanings do shade into each other, if there is a point in distinguishing them it is because there is a difference between something ceasing to exist or be valid and something finding a fuller, more complete existence and power.

370. This means that Käsemann's argument, *Romans*, 283, against a connection with 9:31-32 misses the point of the larger sequence of thought.

In 3:27 the critical question as to how boasting is excluded is amplified: "By what sort of Torah? A Torah of works?" and the answer comes back, "No; by a Torah of faith" (3:27). This remains cryptic, but pregnant, until the point we have now reached. God's righteousness is revealed "apart from Torah" (χωρὶς νόμου *chōris nomou,* 3:21), but justification by faith is "apart from the works of Torah [χωρὶς ἔργων νόμου *chōris ergōn nomou*]" (3:28). This corresponds exactly to the theme of 9:30–10:4. We do not overthrow the law, says Paul; on the contrary, we uphold it (3:31). So, too, 10:4 does not undermine 3:27-31; on the contrary, it reinforces it.

Romans 7:1–8:11, likewise, does not undermine Torah. It does not suggest that when God acts in Jesus Christ and by the Spirit Torah is abrogated or made to look bad. On the contrary: it is "the mind of the flesh" that cannot submit to God's law (8:7). In Christ and by the Spirit God has at last done what Torah wanted to do but could not do, that is, to give life (7:10; 8:11). This points on to the theme of 10:5-9. In fact, if we wanted to summarize 2:17-29; 3:27-31; and 7:1–8:11, one good way of doing so might be to say: "Christ (and the Spirit) are the goal of Torah, so that all who have faith, all who are in Christ Jesus, may have righteousness and life." In none of these cases, despite the frantic efforts of some exegetes and theologians, would the translation "termination" do justice to what Paul actually says.

I conclude that in 10:4 Paul does not intend to declare the law's abrogation in favor of a different "system," but rather to announce that the Messiah is himself the climax of the long story of God and Israel, the story Torah tells and in which it plays a vital though puzzling part. God's purposes in Torah, purposes both negative and positive, have reached their goal in the Messiah, and the result of that is the accessibility and availability of "righteousness" for *all* who *believe.* Both of those emphasized words are important, underlining the contrast (a) with the restriction of "righteousness" to Jews, and (b) with the badge of covenant membership seen as "works of Torah" in the sense already discussed.

This means, too, that there is an end, a termination, to the period of time that lasts from Moses to the Messiah. That is, of course, a main theme of Gal 3:16-29. But this termination is not like the termination of a journey when the car breaks down halfway and we are left stranded in open country. It is like the termination of a journey when the car has taken us to the very place we wanted to go and can now be rested with its task completed. In that sense, every "goal" implies a "termination" of sorts, but the opposite is emphatically not the case. If I stop writing because the telephone rings, that is not the same as when I stop writing because I have finished the book.[371]

10:5-11. Further proof for this line of interpretation is found in these verses, a difficult but vital passage.[372] At first sight, admittedly, it seems to run the other way: here is Moses telling people to keep the Torah, and here is something called "the righteousness of faith" telling them simply to believe! It has been easy in post-Enlightenment thought to line up Paul with Deuteronomy and against Leviticus; that is what a good deal of particularly Protestant thinking has wanted to do.[373] In fact, however, once we discover what Paul is doing in these verses—and they display one of his more subtle readings of Scripture— we shall see that here, too, somewhat as in 8:1-11, he envisages the fulfillment, not the abrogation, of Torah.

For a start, it would be naive to think that Paul supposed, or imagined his hearers might be tricked into supposing, that Deuteronomy was not a book of Moses just as much as Leviticus was. It would also be out of character for Paul to set up one passage of Scripture against another.[374] But that is only a surface point. More important is the entire context of Deuteronomy 30 (the passage Paul is working

371. Cf. Moo, *Romans,* 641, with Bryan, *A Preface to Romans,* 172. For other "double sense" readings see P. Achtemeier, "Unsearchable Judgments and Inscrutable Ways," 168; Dunn, *Romans 9–16,* 596-98 (though leaning heavily toward "termination" as the primary meaning). Fitzmyer, *Romans,* 584-85, denies that such a double meaning is possible.

372. On which see the suggestive comments of R. B. Hays, *Echoes of cripture in the Letters of Paul,* 73-83. For a stimulating account of the passage see E. M. Humphrey, "Why Bring the Word Down? The Rhetoric of Demonstration and Disclosure in Romans 9:30–10:21," in Soderlund and Wright, *Romans and the People of God,* 129-48.

373. See Sanday and Headlam, *Romans,* 285-86; Dodd, *The Epistle of Paul to the Romans,* 177; Dunn, *Romans 9–16,* 600-602; Moo, *Romans,* 643-50. Among Catholic commentators this view is taken by Fitzmyer, *Romans,* 587-89; Byrne, *Romans,* 317-18.

374. So Bryan, *A Preface to Romans,* 174.

with in vv. 6-8) and the way in which it appears to have functioned in Second Temple Judaism.[375] To draw on this wider world of thought is not "eisegesis," as is sometimes suggested; it is to replace the unspoken assumption that Paul was talking about what modern readers expect him to be talking about with the hard-won historical awareness that he was more likely to be talking about what readers of his day would be expecting. The task facing the interpreter is always to think one's way into a world of thought that Paul would have taken for granted. This is the move that lies at the heart of vv. 5-11 and that, once grasped, makes sense of the entire sequence of thought.[376]

Deuteronomy 30 comes immediately after the chapters in which Moses has held out to the people the covenantal blessings and curses. The curses, it must be said, far outweigh the blessings: Deut 28:1-14 lists the blessings that will follow obedience to Torah, but vv. 15-68 give a far longer list of curses, which are then reinforced in the warnings of 29:18-28. The final and most emphatic curse is exile: Israel will not simply suffer blight, mildew, barrenness, poverty, sickness, and a hundred other evils in the land, but will ultimately be driven off the land itself, scattered among the nations of the earth (28:63-68; 29:22-28; see esp. 29:28[27]: "YHWH uprooted them from their land in his anger, wrath, and indignation, and cast them into another land, as at this day"). It is assumed that all these things will come to pass; Deut 29:4 bewails the fact that Israel has remained hard-hearted, and the curses are bound to follow.

But after they have all happened, and in particular after the exile has done its worst, then there will come a great reversal. Deuteronomy 30 is a prediction of the return from exile, pointing to the spiritual and moral renewal that will make that return possible and appropriate. Israel will return to YHWH with all its heart and soul (30:2, 6). YHWH will turn Israel's captivity around, and regather his people (vv. 3-5). YHWH will

circumcise Israel's heart, to love YHWH, so that Israel may live (v. 6). Blessing will once more follow, if Israel will now be obedient (vv. 8-10). And the central blessing is life itself: God has set life before them (v. 15), the life that results from keeping the commandments (v. 16) as opposed to disobeying and so incurring death (vv. 17-18). Life is what they must choose (v. 19). They must love YHWH, obey his voice, and cleave to him, "for he is your life, and the length of your days" (v. 20). The whole chapter might be entitled, "the new obedience which brings new life."[377]

In the middle of Deuteronomy we find vv. 11-14, the passage Paul quotes in 10:6-8. The commandment is not too hard; it is not far off. You do not need someone to go up to heaven and bring it down, so that you may hear it and do it; you do not need someone to cross the sea and fetch it, so that you may hear it and do it (this language about impossible quests to the deep, or to heaven, has become proverbial in 4 Ezra 4:7-8). "The word is near you; it is in your mouth, and in your heart, so that you may do it" (v. 14). The chapter, in other words, presumes that Israel has been sent into exile and is now going to turn to YHWH from the heart, and proceeds to explain what it really means to "do" the law and so to "live." This life-giving "doing" will be a matter, not of a struggle to obey an apparently impossible law, but of heart and mouth being renewed by God's living "word." It will not be a matter of someone else teaching it to them as from a great distance. Verse 14, significantly, omits even the mention of "hearing" the commandment; it will be inside them, in their mouth and heart. We cannot but think of Jer 31:33-34: In the restoration after the exile, the people will not need to be taught the commandments, because they will be written on their hearts. And this cannot but remind us of Rom 2:25-29, a passage that Paul is about to echo in 10:9-10. It should be clear already that Paul has the context, and overall meaning, of Deuteronomy 30 firmly in mind. This is anything but a clever prooftext taken out of context.

375. The final chapters of Deuteronomy—the conclusion of the Pentateuch—were often read eschatologically at the time. Good examples are Pseudo-Philo 19; *Testament of Moses*; and 4 Ezra (see below), on which see R. J. Bauckham, "Apocalypses," in Carson, *Justification and Variegated Nomism*, 171.

376. This is a response in part to Fitzmyer, *Romans*, 588, who considers Paul's use of Deuteronomy here to be very loose.

377. This was how the chapter was being read in the Second Temple period. See 4 Ezra 7:20-21; Bar 4:1; Sir 17:11. If Paul had wanted to play Leviticus 18 ("do this and find life") off against some other text, he could hardly have chosen a worse one; this is exactly how Deuteronomy 30 was being understood. See the Commentary on 8:5-8.

This should make it clear, too, that Paul's quotation of Lev 18:5 in 10:5 is not set in opposition to Deuteronomy 30. He is not setting up a straw person ("Moses encouraged that stupid and impossible system we know as works-righteousness") in order then to knock it down with a bit of clever but slippery eisegesis of another part of the Pentateuch. Nor, as Barth and some later writers have suggested, was Paul envisaging the Messiah himself as the one who performed the law perfectly and gained life thereby.[378] Lev 18:5 brought together two things, "doing the law" and "living": "the one who does these things shall live by them." This is what the "righteousness which is from the law" declares; that is how Leviticus 18 was heard in Paul's own day.[379] Had Paul really meant that Christ is the termination of the law, we should have expected him to oppose such a view. But he does not suppose that Deuteronomy does any such thing. It offers, he insists, a fresh explanation, granted exile and return, for what "do the law and live" might actually mean.[380] In the original passage, the lines Paul quotes each end with "so that you may do it." Here, as in 2:25-29 and elsewhere, Paul's point is that those who share Christian faith are in fact "doing the law" in the sense that Deuteronomy and Jeremiah intended. Those who believe that Jesus is Lord, and that God raised him from the dead, are the new-covenant people, the returned-from-exile people. The story of Israel in 9:6-29 took us as far as exile, pointing ahead to what might happen beyond (9:24). That story reached its dramatic climax in the Messiah, the one upon whom the curses ultimately fell (Gal 3:13). Now all who believe in the Messiah, whether they be Jew or Gentile, are thereby "fulfilling the law"; they are "doing" it in the sense Deuteronomy 30 intended; and they thereby find "life," as 8:9-11 demonstrated, the life that Torah wanted to give but could not (7:10),

the life that can now be spoken of more specifically as "salvation" (10:9, 10, 13). And that, of course, was all along the point of the paragraph (10:1-13). Paul has prayed for the salvation of his kinsfolk; now, starting with Torah itself, he has shown the way by which that salvation may be found.

Important confirmation of this reading of Deuteronomy 30 is found in one of the final Dead Sea Scrolls to be released, the so-called 4QMMT.[381] Though Pauline scholars have noted that this text speaks of "justification by works of the law," the setting of this within an explicit exegesis of Deuteronomy 30, and thus its fascinating parallel to Romans 10, has not been explored.[382]

The scroll has three sections, A, B, and C; it is C that concerns us, specifically lines 12-32. This passage begins by quoting Deut 30:1-3: when the blessing and the curse have come upon you, then you will take it to heart and return to him with all your heart and with all your soul, "at the end of time" (a significant addition), so that you may live. The text then explains that Deuteronomy is to be read as predicting a three-stage history for Israel: first blessing, then curse, then restoration and renewed blessing. The blessings, it says, came upon Israel in the days of David and Solomon (C 18). The curses then came from the time of Jeroboam son of Nebat, climaxing in the Babylonian captivity (C 18-20). But then, "at the end of days," the return from exile will happen; and this is the time the writer believes Israel is now in. This is the time, then, for making it clear what precisely the Torah now requires, so that when the final end comes "it will be reckoned to you as righteousness" (C 30-31). The practices of Torah in question are those outlined in parts A and B, specifically, regulations for the Temple.

Deuteronomy 30, in other words, is being read as a prediction of the eschatological time when God restores the fortunes of Israel after the exile. This eschatological time, the writer believes, is now coming to pass. Those who,

378. K. Barth, *A Shorter Commentary on Romans* (London: SCM, 1959) 127; followed by Cranfield, *A Critical and Exegetical Commentary on the Epistle to the Romans*, 521-22; Bryan, *A Preface to Romans*, 168. Criticized by Dunn, *Romans 9–16*, 601; JFitzmyer, *Romans*, 587; Moo, *The Epistle to the Romans*, 646-47. The covenantal and narrative reading I am proposing retains the positive sense hoped for by Barth and his followers but within a much more demonstrable Second Temple line of thought.

379. Cf. Sir 17:11; 45:5; Philo *Preliminary Studies* 86-87; *Ps Sol* 14:2. Bryan, *A Preface to Romans*, 175, notes that Lev 18:5 was sometimes used in connection with Gentiles being "righteous." See bBQam 38a; bSanh 59a. See also Moo, *Romans*, 648n. 15.

380. Paul was not, then, quoting it because it was a favorite text of his opponents (against Bryan, *A Preface to Romans*, 175).

381. See note 94, p.460.

382. A start was made by P. Grelot, "Les oeuvres de la Loi (A propos de 4Q394-398)," *RQ* 16 (December 1994) 441-48; Martin Abegg, "Paul, 'Works of the Law,' and MMT," *BAR* (November/December 1994) 52-55, 82; J. D. G. Dunn, "4QMMT and Galatians," *NTS* 43/1 (1997) 147-53; M. Bachmann, "4QMMT und Galaterbrief, מעשי התורה und ΕΡΓΑ ΝΟΜΟΥ," *ZNW* 89 (1998) 91-113 (with copious bibliography, including other works by Bachmann). For a preliminary statement of the present position see N. T. Wright, "Paul and Qumran," *Bible Review* (October 1998) 18, 54.

in the inaugurated eschatology of the present time, observe this "selection of works of the law" (the phrase that, via its Hebrew original, gives the work its modern title),[383] are assured thereby that at the end of time they will be reckoned within God's true people. The structure of this doctrine of justification is identical to Paul's (a future "end," at which some will be vindicated, who are marked out in the present time of inaugurated eschatology by the appropriate indicators), while the content is different. The "works of the law" the writer urges are not the 613 commands in Torah. Nor are they the "works of the law" that Paul warns against, the works (circumcision, food laws, sabbath) that mark out Jews over against their pagan neighbors. Nor, again, are they "works" done to earn a moralistic or proto-Pelagian "righteousness"; they are to demonstrate fidelity to the renewed covenant.[384] They are the particular "works" that will mark out this sect, with its specific practices, over against other Jews. For Paul, the thing that marks out members of the renewed covenant, the people envisaged by Deuteronomy 30, over against all others, Jews and pagans alike, is Christian faith. And the substance and object of that faith—the death and resurrection of the Messiah, and the confession of his universal lordship—is, of course, what determines the difference.

A second striking use of Deuteronomy 30 in Second Temple Judaism is found in Baruch 3, a very different text to 4QMMT and all the more significant as a parallel use of the passage Paul is working with here.[385] The fictive setting of Baruch is the Babylonian exile; the actual setting, it is normally assumed, is in the Jewish diaspora some time in the first or second century BCE.[386] In view of the "continuing exile" theme in much Second Temple thought, however, we may question whether a geographical diaspora situation is required. What matters is that the writer (or compiler) is clearly working with the idea of "exile,"

and is drawing on a wide range of classic biblical texts to do so. Exile is explained, as in Daniel 9—and as in Rom 9:6-33!—with a firm belief in God's righteousness (Bar 1:15; 2:1, 6, 19-23); that is, God has carried out the warnings issued by the prophets, and also in Deuteronomy 28 and 32. In this context, what Israel needs is to learn where wisdom is to be found; here, from 3:9 onward, the writer draws on Proverbs and Job, but the setting of exile-in-need-of-restoration has not been left behind. Wisdom is, in fact, the same thing as Torah (4:1; cf. Sir 24:23), and when Israel seeks God with all its heart, holding wisdom/Torah fast, then Israel will live. In that setting, we should not be surprised that the writer draws on Deuteronomy 30 to encourage his readers to seek wisdom/Torah so as to become the true returned-from-exile people (cf. 3:7 with Deut 30:1; 4:1 with Deut 30:19).

That is the wider context within which the explicit reference to Deut 30:12-13 occurs in 3:29-30: "Who has gone up into heaven, and taken her [i.e., wisdom], and brought her down from the clouds? Who has gone over the sea, and found her, and will buy her for pure gold?" The answer is clear: it is none other than God. "He found the whole way to knowledge, and gave her to his servant Jacob, and to Israel, whom he loved. Afterward she appeared on earth and lived with humankind" (see Sir 24:8-12; Wis 9:9-10). In that context, the writer turns to exhort his kinsfolk to take courage; salvation is at hand. Significantly, much of the rest of the short book, like Romans, is replete with echoes of Isaiah 40–55. God, concludes the book, "will lead Israel with joy, in the light of his glory, with the mercy and righteousness that are with him" (5:9).

The parallel between Rom 10:6-8 and Baruch 3 is frequently noted; the overall narrative context, of exile and return, and the repentance required for the latter, is not. That is why some have been able to suggest that the Baruch passage is not particularly relevant for interpreting Romans.[387] If all it supplies is a parallel use of Deuteronomy 30, and a

383. MMT = מקצת מעשי התורה (miqṣaōt maʿăśê hatôrâ), C 27.

384. I thus agree with J. D. G. Dunn about the place of "works" in Judaism as principally social or covenantal boundary markers, while disagreeing with him about the "works" in MMT being the same as those in view in Galatians.

385. Similar points could be made about 4 Ezra 4:8 (which also alludes to Ps 139:8). Another very different use of Deut 30:11-14 is in the Gospel of Thomas, saying 3. For rabbinic uses see SB 3.279-81.

386. See D. Mendels, "Baruch, Book of," ABD, 1:618-20; A. Salvesen, "Baruch," in The Oxford Bible Commentary, ed. J. Barton and J. Muddiman (Oxford: Oxford University Press, 2001) 699-703.

387. E.g., Moo, Romans, 652-53. A major study of the parallel was that of M. J. Suggs, " 'The Word Is Near You': Romans 10:6-10 within the Purpose of the Letter," in Christian History and Interpretation: Studies Presented to John Knox, ed. W. R. Farmer et al. (Cambridge: Cambridge University Press, 1967) 289-312.

general suggestion that the "Wisdom" sought or propounded by various Jewish writers at the time might be a source for Paul's christology, we might in part agree (cf. Sir 24:5). But it supplies far more than that (though not, we should note, less). Baruch, like 4QMMT, envisages a narrative within which writer and readers find themselves at home: the narrative of exile and restoration.

For all their radical differences of style and content, 4QMMT and Baruch thus reflect a similar understanding of how God is at work in Israel's history, and what is required to be a faithful, true Jew at this moment. Both take Deuteronomy 30 as pointing to what will happen when God restores the fortunes of Israel after exile. MMT sees the intensification of Torah as what is needed; Baruch urges his readers to seek the divine wisdom in which Torah is embodied. Both see this as the way to attain the salvation that God long ago promised would succeed the time of desolation and devastation. Together they create a Second Temple context of meaning within which Paul's fresh understanding, generated by his grasp of the gospel, makes full and rich sense.

With all this in mind—Deuteronomy 30 as a whole, with its emphasis on "doing" and "living," and the eschatological reading of it in two other Second Temple writers—we may offer a preliminary reading of vv. 5-9.

First, it must be noted that the passage, introduced as it is with *gar*, is advanced as the explanation of why the Messiah is the goal of the law for righteousness to all who believe (this explanatory connection is ignored in the NRSV, the NIV, and several other translations). The *gar*, in fact, governs vv. 5-9 as a whole, not simply v. 5. Paul's explanation runs as follows: "For, while Moses does indeed write concerning Torah-righteousness that 'the one who does them shall live in them,' what 'doing' and 'living' come to mean, when God restores Israel after exile, is defined afresh by Deuteronomy 30, not in terms of an impossible demand, but in terms of God's gift of God's own word; and this 'word' is the word of faith, faith that Jesus is Lord and that God raised him from the dead." This, taken as a whole, explains v. 4, and thereby, in turn, explains how salvation is now available for all who share this faith.

In other words, while opening the promise to those of any and every ethnic background, Paul is more specifically showing how his prayer in 10:1 is to be answered. This is how God will restore the fortunes of Israel. Just as MMT urged its readers to make their status in the renewed people of God secure by particular temple regulations, and just as Baruch urged his readers to seek the divine Wisdom, so Paul urges people of every race to discover the risen Lord Jesus as Messiah and find thereby the renewed covenant membership of which Deuteronomy spoke. Verse 5 is not a statement of a legalism that Paul will then sweep aside. The δέ (*de*) that links vv. 5-6 does not indicate a direct antithesis or contradiction, but a modification, a redefinition: "Yes, Moses does write Lev 18:5; *but* its key terms are then further explained in Deuteronomy 30."[388]

But what precisely is Paul making Deuteronomy 30 out to be saying?

He introduces the citation with an allusion to an earlier passage in the same book, Deut 9:4 (cf. too 8:17). This too is significant in itself.[389] "Do not say in your heart," Moses warns Israel, "it is because of my righteousness that YHWH has brought me in to occupy this land." It is a warning, in other words, against exactly that fault that Paul had highlighted in 10:3. The chapter goes on to emphasize the way in which Israel provoked YHWH to anger at Sinai by making the golden calf, and the fact that they only survived because of Moses' intercession. These, as we have already seen, are vital parts of the biblical background Paul has in mind throughout Romans 9. Even in this introductory formula the echoes of what Paul is saying throughout the argument are too strong for us to suppose that he chose the phrase at random. How much more has he chosen, now, to give a fresh and creative reading of Deuteronomy 30.[390]

We have already argued that he, like two near-contemporaries, understands the passage as predicting that renewal of the covenant that he believed to be taking place in the movement to which he belonged—that is, in Paul's case, the messianic movement

---

388. So, rightly, Bryan, *A Preface to Romans*, 168. See also Hays, *Echoes of Scripture in the Letters of Paul*, 76-77.

389. See Hays, *Echoes of Scripture in the Letters of Paul*, 78-79.

390. Against Moo, *Romans*, 651.

of the Lord Jesus. It makes sense, therefore, consistent with his view of Jesus elsewhere, that here he casts Jesus himself in the role that other Jewish thinkers gave to Torah or to Wisdom. Jesus the Messiah is himself God's life-giving, covenant-renewing, community-defining gift to God's people. His "coming down from heaven" and his "coming up from the deep" are the events through which this gift is made available to all. This passage belongs closely with Paul's other expressions of Wisdom christology, such as Col 1:15-20.[391] The emphasis falls on the Messiah as the embodiment of God's own Wisdom, the human being in whom, as in 8:3, God does what Torah could not. And the faith that accepts and celebrates this gift is then the true wisdom, the true Torah-observance, the sign of membership in the renewed covenant. Paul's line-by-line reading of Deut 30:12-14, which has some affinities with the "pesher" exegesis found at Qumran, is not simply a fanciful allegory or metaphor, nor is it "historically outrageous."[392] Like Qumran itself, Paul saw the community he was addressing as the people of the renewed covenant. Like many Second Temple Jews, he understood Deuteronomy to be telling a story, the story in which he himself and his contemporaries were now living, the story of restoration after the curse of exile.

Why then does Paul refer to Deuteronomy 30 as "the righteousness from faith [ἡ ἐκ πίστεως δικαιοσύνη *hē ek pisteōs dikaiosynē*]"? Because this, in the light of the whole argument of the letter so far, and especially 3:21–4:25, serves as a shorthand for his belief that in the Messiah God has at last done what he promised to Abraham, and, as here, what he promised in Deuteronomy 30. He has thereby established the renewed covenant; "righteousness," as a status that people can enjoy, denotes membership in that covenant. And the badge of membership is faith. Paul's exegesis of Deuteronomy 30 thus explains what he means by the Messiah's being the goal of Torah: this covenant renewal, this promised life for those who discover that the word is not far off, but very near to them, this status of being God's people, evidenced

by faith in God's Messiah—this is what Torah envisaged all along, but in and of itself could not perform. The parallels with 7:7–8:11 should be obvious.

10:6-7. The two moments of the Messiah's work that Paul highlights in vv. 6-7 are his "coming down" and his "raising up." There is no problem about the latter; Jesus' resurrection has been a main presupposition of this letter from its very opening (1:4), anchoring the argument at some of its most decisive moments (4:24-25; 8:11, 34; the descent into the abyss echoes Ps 107:26). But what does Paul mean by the Messiah's "coming down from heaven"?

There are two main options. The first is to see this as a reference to his coming from God, the incarnation of God's pre-existent Wisdom. The second is to understand it as his coming from heaven in the parousia.[393] Each has something to be said for it, but in my judgment the balance of probability tilts to the first. It fits with the Wisdom christology of Col 1:15-20; it belongs with Rom 8:3, which as we have seen is anyway close in meaning to the present passage; it prepares the way for the confession κύριος Ἰησοῦς (*kyrios Iēsous*), "Jesus is Lord," in v. 9;[394] it belongs with the double emphasis on Jesus as God's son and David's son in 1:3-4; it goes with the incarnational stress of 9:5, echoed as we saw in 10:11-13. I suggest that Paul intends his fresh reading of Deut 30:11-14 to say: "the covenant has been renewed, following the devastation of exile, through the Messiah's coming from God and his resurrection from the dead. This has meant that God has brought his 'word' near to you, placing it on your lips as you confess Jesus as Lord, writing it on your heart as you believe that he was raised from the dead."

10:8. This, he says, is the "word of faith" that "we preach." For the first time, Paul's apostolic vocation becomes part of the actual argument of chaps. 9–11; this will grow through 10:14-18, and play a crucial role in 11:13-14. From that perspective, we can see

---

391. On which see Wright, *The Climax of the Covenant*, chap. 5. Paul, like Baruch, echoes the wisdom literature at various points here. See, e.g., Prov 30:4; Wis 16:13.

392. Against Hays, *Echoes of Scripture in the Letters of Paul*, 82.

393. Most ancient commentators took it to refer to the incarnation. For details and support, see Cranfield, *A Critical and Exegetical Commentary on the Epistle to the Romans*, 524-25; Fitzmyer, *Romans*, 590; Moo, *The Epistle to the Romans*, 655-56. The second is urged by Käsemann, *Commentary on Romans*, 288; and Dunn, *Romans 9–16*, 605.

394. On the "divine" nature of Jesus' "lordship," see Phil 2:10-11 in the context of the poem of Phil 2:6-11 as a whole; see also Wright, *The Climax of the Covenant*, chap. 4.

what he is saying: his own announcing of Jesus as the risen Lord, summoning people to "the obedience of faith" (1:5), is itself part of the answer to the prayer of 10:1. That is why, in v. 9, he goes on to explain that when faith happens it leads to salvation, that for which he prayed at the start of the chapter.

10:9. Paul then explains this with a remarkable statement, one of the clearest in all his writings, of what precisely Christian faith consists of. It is not, for him, a vague religious awareness, a general sense of the presence of a benevolent deity. It is the confession of Jesus as Lord and the belief that God raised him from the dead.

This, of course, is what undergirds the earlier argument of the letter, as is apparent from 1:3-5 and 4:24-25. Verbal confession of Jesus as Lord was a primitive baptismal formula (see Acts 22:16; 1 Cor 12:3; 2 Cor 4:5; Phil 2:11);[395] it also, from early on, lay at the heart of the confrontation between the kingdom theology of the early church and the ideology of imperial Rome. Jesus' resurrection was, for Paul, the demonstration that he really was the Messiah; his belief in Jesus as the turning-point of Jewish and world history, the bearer of God's purposes, the climax of the story of God's covenant, is unthinkable without it. The resurrection is to be understood, as always in Paul, as the action of God (see 4:24; on the centrality of Jesus' resurrection for Paul, see 1 Thess 4:14; 1 Corinthians 15). And when Paul declares that belief in Jesus' resurrection is located in the heart, he links the argument with 2:28-29 and 5:5 (see also 2:15; 6:17; 8:27); the very core of the personality is where the renewal must take place, and belief in the resurrection is the telltale symptom of that renewal (Paul's fullest statement is 1 Corinthians 15; see also 1 Cor 6:14; 2 Cor 4:14; Gal 1:1). Belief in Jesus' resurrection is thus not an arbitrary dogmatic test, a demonstration that one is prepared to believe something ridiculous on someone else's supposed divine authority. Genuine heart-level belief can only come about, Paul believed, through the action of the Spirit in the gospel. This faith is the sure sign that the gospel has done its work.

10:10. He then explains v. 9 in more detail, separating out "righteousness" and "salvation." He is probably not intending to say that "belief" only goes with "righteousness," or that "confession" only belongs with "salvation"; he may well be saying nearly the same thing from two different angles. However, it is noteworthy that, unlike many people who have thought to summarize his thought, he does not normally speak of "salvation by faith," but rather "righteousness by faith" (as in v. 4, we should note that Paul uses the noun "righteousness," though the NIV and the NRSV turn this into the verb "justified"—as they do in the second half of the verse, turning "salvation" into "saved"). The two are closely correlated but not identical. "Righteousness" denotes the status people have on the basis of faith: a present legal status that anticipates the future verdict of the divine lawcourt, a present covenantal status that anticipates final affirmation of membership in God's people. "Salvation" denotes the actual rescue from sin and death effected in the future by the promised resurrection, and likewise anticipated in the present (so, e.g., 8:24). "Salvation" is not a status but an event, and it is promised to those who have "righteousness" as their status.

The connection of righteousness with faith is clear; the connection of salvation with verbal confession of Jesus as Lord is not so obvious. It may well be that Paul is thinking of "Jesus is Lord" as the baptismal confession, and that, as in Romans 6, he is understanding baptism as the present anticipation of final resurrection—that is, salvation from sin and death. This would make good sense, but, unlike most of the other places where we are able to fill in the gaps in his dense, almost shorthand writing, it is a connection he nowhere makes explicit.

10:11. The final explanation in the present sequence consists of the quotation from Isa 28:16, which returns us to where we were in 9:33. This helps us to appreciate the flow of thought in seeing 10:1-11 as a whole, from the prayer about more Jews being saved, through the exposition of the messianic covenant renewal in which that prayer can be answered, to the affirmation of salvation for all who believe. "The one who believes in him will not be put to shame" (the

---

395. See also Dunn, *Romans 9–16*, 607; Käsemann, *Romans*, 291. On "Lord" see the Commentary on 1:5 and 10:12-13 below.

NIV's "disappointed" is weak and breaks the implied link with 1:16 [see also 5:5], not to mention 9:33; "not put to shame" is clearly intended as equivalent to "saved" in v. 13). Paul has inserted, at the start of the quotation, the little word πᾶς (*pas*, "all"). Everyone who believes in him will be saved. Here there is no question that the "him" is Jesus the Lord, the risen Messiah. But once we have understood Paul's use of Deuteronomy 30, there is no problem, either, in seeing this Jesus as the law's true fulfillment and goal. He is both the stumbling-stone and the object of faith: a scandal to Jews, folly to Greeks, but God's wisdom and power for those who are called, Jew and Greek alike (1 Cor 1:23-24). This universality is the point with which Paul will now round off the paragraph.

10:12-13. "There is no distinction." We are back once more, in the long and unwinding spiral, at a point as it were directly above 3:22-23. There, the fact of there being no distinction between Jew and Greek highlighted the fact that all alike were in sin, and all alike were redeemed and justified by the faithful death of the Messiah and through faith in God's covenant action in him, not some other way. The present passage has no mention either of sin, or of Jesus' death to deal with it. That is now taken for granted, and the argument has moved on round the spiral to consequent topics, already outlined in 3:27-30. Jew and Gentile come together in sharing the common faith in the same Lord (Paul is already looking ahead to chap. 14). And the "Lord" in question, while identified from the earlier verses as Jesus the Messiah, is equally the κύριος (*kyrios*) of the LXX. This is where the breathtaking assertion of 9:5, that the Messiah who belonged to Israel according to the flesh is also "God over all, blessed for ever," shows up at the heart of the argument. This is where christology determines ecclesiology—including where the church stands vis-à-vis the pagan emperor!—as well as soteriology. "The same Lord is Lord of all."[396] That was what Caesar claimed, and it was what Paul claimed for Jesus. At the same time, Paul is picking up, and transforming, a

regular Jewish theme: one God, therefore one people of Israel (cf. Zech 14:9-17).[397] Where, before, "no distinction" was explained by "for all have sinned" (3:23), now it can be explained by "for there is one Lord of all." As in 3:27-30, monotheism undergirds the universality of the gospel—though, as elsewhere in Paul, it is monotheism with Jesus at the heart of it.[398]

Paul does not stop to theorize about this christology, but unless we recognize that this is what he has in mind here we will not have grasped the heart of his argument. Romans 10:12-13 is basically a statement about God, as indeed the whole section of chaps. 9–11 is an argument about God. The idea of God being "rich," already mentioned in 9:23, looks ahead to 11:33. Paul's expression here is dense; literally, it means "being rich toward all."[399] God's own riches are the underlying subject of the section, and it is on that basis that "all who call on the name of the Lord will be saved."[400]

The "all" of Joel 2:32 (LXX 3:5) has cast its shadow before it in Paul's addition to Isa 28:16 in v. 11 and in the repeated "all" of v. 12. The quotation from Joel is a further point at which we are right to hear echoes of God's renewal of the covenant.[401] Joel 2 sits comfortably alongside Deuteronomy 30 as a powerful statement of how God will restore the fortunes of Israel after devastating judgment. When we read the whole chapter there are various echoes of what Paul has already said. The children of Zion are to rejoice in YHWH their God, because of his gift of the early rain for their vindication (εἰς δικαιοσύνην *eis dikaiosynēn*) (2:23). God declares (2:26) that "my people shall never again be put to shame" (οὐ μὴ καταισχυνθῇ ὁ λαός μου *ou mē kataischynthē ho laos mou*), and repeats it with emphasis a verse later (οὐ μὴ καταισχυνθῶσιν οὐκέτι πᾶς ὁ λαός μου εἰς τὸν αἰῶνα *ou mē kataischynthōsin*

---

396. Cf. Acts 10:36. Detailed discussion in C. K. Rowe, "Romans 10:13: What Is the Name of the Lord?" *Horizons in Biblical Theology* 22 (2000) 146 50. Among Second Temple references to Israel's God as "Lord of all," see 1QapGen 20:13; 4Q409 1:6; Josephus *Antiquities of the Jews* 20:90.

397. See Rowe, "Romans 10:13," 147.

398. See Wright, *The Climax of the Covenant*, chaps. 4–6.

399. The NIV ("richly blesses all") and the NRSV ("is generous to all") do not catch the emphasis, which is on the supreme riches that belong to God and are now shared with others. It is possible for a poor person to be generous; Paul's point is (a) that God is not poor but supremely rich and (b) that God shares these riches lavishly.

400. "Call upon the name of YHWH" is a frequent biblical way of designating Israel. See Dunn, *Romans 9–16*, 610-11. For similar formulae in early Christianity, see Acts 2:21; 9:14, 21 (where the phrase is almost a definition of a Christian); 22:16 (a baptismal context); and 1 Cor 1:2; 2 Tim 2:22

401. On the use of Joel here, see Rowe, "Romans 10:13," 152-56.

ouketi pas ho laos mou eis ton aiōna, "all my people shall never, ever, ever again be put to shame"). Joel 2:26-27 is thus extremely close to Isa 28:16, supplying the "all"; perhaps we should regard the scriptural quotation in 10:11 itself as a combination of Isaiah and Joel.

Looming up behind these detailed points, we should not miss the force of v. 13 in relation to the argument of chaps. 9–11 as a whole. If "those who call on the name of the Lord" is a regular biblical designation for "Israel," then v. 13 is an exact functional equivalent of 11:26*a:* "All Israel shall be saved."[402] Verse 13 supplies Paul's initial answer to the problem of 10:1, and suggests the correct way of understanding 11:26*a.*

The Joel passage supplies another strong hint, which we might have guessed from where we are in the "spiral" of Paul's thought, and indeed from the other use to which the same passage is put in the NT. There is here, I suggest, an allusion to the work of the Spirit in renewing the covenant, in restoring the fortunes of God's people (see 2:27-29 and 8:1-11, both of which are thematically close to the present passage; elsewhere in NT see Acts 2:16-21, the day of Pentecost). In Joel 2:28-29, God promises to pour out the divine Spirit on all the members of the community (the "all" is again emphatic). There will be portents in heaven and on earth; and at that time "everyone who calls on the name of the Lord shall be saved, for in Mount Zion and in Jerusalem there shall be those who escape" (LXX ἀνασωζόμενος *anasōzomenos*), "and among the survivors shall be those whom the Lord calls" (καὶ εὐαγγελιζόμενοι οὕς κύριος προσκέκληται *kai euangelizomenoi hous kyrios proskeklētai*, 2:32 [LXX 3:5]). The LXX readings indicate, indeed, that for Paul this text also projects him forward into the next passage, linking with "those who preach the gospel" in Isa 52:7. But the main point to note is that here, in the close hinterland of Paul's thought, we are right to see the Spirit at work, through the preaching of the gospel of Jesus as Lord, to bring people to faith and confession and so to righteousness and salvation. People, we note once more, of all sorts: Jew and Greek, alike and together. This is the initial answer to the prayer of 10:1.

The message of 10:5-13 is so positive and upbeat—God renewing the covenant through the dramatic, even apocalyptic, events concerning Jesus, and throwing open membership to all and sundry—that if Paul had stopped there we would wonder what the problem was. Why the grief of 9:1-5? Why the earnest prayer of 10:1? Surely all that is now needed is for the message of this new covenant, this inbreaking love of God, to be announced, and people everywhere, especially the Jewish people, whose Scriptures were being fulfilled, whose Messiah had now arrived—surely they would all believe it and enjoy the new day that was dawning? Sadly, no. The renewal of the covenant is also the word of judgment, of God's confrontation with human wickedness, including Jewish wickedness (2:17-24). The problem of chaps. 9–11 is that Israel does not want to hear such a scandalous message. Verses 14-21 do indeed take the story forward into the new world that has come into being as a result of the messianic events. But the paradox that cuts right across any sense of a smooth line, of God's purposes going ahead with no problem, comes to the fore in Israel's persistent recalcitrance. The excitement of the apostolic mission and the heartbreak of Israel's refusal come together in the final part (10:14-21) of this section (9:30–10:21), and together set the scene for chap. 11.

10:14-21. The key to this whole part of the chapter is found in 11:13-14: Paul celebrates his apostolic vocation to preach to the Gentiles in order to make his "flesh" jealous and so save some of them. Verses 14-15 explain, in a burst of rhetorical questions, that for the renewed covenant to operate people need to be sent with the news. This puts Paul himself on the map of biblical fulfillment (10:16-18): Isaiah 52–53 spoke of God's coming actions through the Messiah, and of the people who would take the message to the whole world, even though not everyone would listen. But, tragically (10:19-21), Israel according to the flesh remained by and large aloof from it all. They knew from their own prophecies, including Deuteronomy 32, that God would bring Gentiles in to share their blessings; but they have remained unbelieving. This is as close as Paul gets to an explicit statement of the problem that haunts Romans

---

402. So, rightly, Rowe, "Romans 10:13," 156.

9–11 as a whole. The passage is about more than simply "Israel's accountability"; it is about the inclusion of Gentiles so as to make Israel "jealous."

10:14-15. Four questions and a quotation explain the need for the Gentile mission that constitutes Paul's apostolic vocation, and place it on the same map of biblical prophecy that Paul has been sketching for several verses past. The questions—a unique rhetorical device in Paul—take us from the picture we have seen in 10:5-13, of people of all sorts coming to share in the covenant blessings by faith, through to the necessity, and the biblical mandate, of the apostolic mission. For people to "call on the name of the Lord," as Joel says they must, they must first have faith; but this is impossible unless they hear of the Messiah so that they can believe in him. For this, in turn, they need someone to announce him to them; and for that, the announcers need to be "sent" (ἀποσταλῶσιν *apostalōsin*, "apostled"). So far, the argument is simply: if people are to be saved under this new covenant, what has to happen is for God to "send," to commission as "apostles," people to take the message to them. Paul adds Isa 52:7: How beautiful are the feet of the messengers of good news![403] As the following passage seems to indicate, Paul understands the message concerning YHWH's servant in Isaiah 52–53 as the message about Jesus the Messiah. The people who announce the servant-message are therefore the people who now, in his own day, proclaim Jesus. The effect of vv. 14-15 is to say: this is how my own apostolic ministry fits into the large narrative of exile and restoration, of God restoring the covenant in the Messiah and calling both Jews and Gentiles into the renewed community (9:24).

Paul's apostleship was, as he says often enough, aimed at the Gentiles (1:5; 15:18; Gal 1:16; 2:2, 7; cf. Acts 9:15; 15:12; Eph 3:8; 1 Tim 2:7). It was not his primary task to take the message to Jews, though according to Acts he regularly began by speaking in synagogues (suffering the consequences, as he describes in 2 Cor 11:24; cf. Acts 13:5, 14;

14:1; 17:1-2, 10, 17; 18:4, 19; 19:8; see also 28:17, 23). He reports in Gal 2:9 a division of labor: he and his coworkers should go to the Gentiles, leaving Peter and others to go to Jews. When, therefore, he refers to his apostleship here, we may assume he is primarily thinking of speaking to Gentiles. However, as he says in 11:13-14, this is undertaken with one eye over his shoulder to see what effect it will have on his kinsfolk.

It is possible to take another view of this passage: to see vv. 14-18, as well as vv. 19-21, referring to a (largely unsuccessful) mission to Jews.[404] This is a further example of a problem we met earlier in the letter: when does the subject turn to Israel specifically (see chap. 2, where the explicit turn to the Jews in 2:17 corresponds to the explicit statement here)?[405] Here, however, the passage itself does seem to give a clear indication of what Paul has in mind. Not only does 10:19 specify "Israel" for the first time; had that been the subject all along, Paul would most likely have been content, as in vv. 16 and 18, with a simply third-person plural verb, "they. . . ." More important, when he asks whether Israel "knew" (v. 19), the thing Israel did in fact know, highlighted with the quotation from Deut 32:21, is precisely that God would bring in Gentiles to share Israel's privileges, thus making them jealous. The probability, then, is that in vv. 14-18 he is talking about the (partially successful) Gentile mission, and that only with vv. 19-21 does he turn, by contrast, to the (mostly unsuccessful) Jewish mission. The final paragraph of the section thus corresponds to the opening (9:30-33): Gentiles (to their own surprise) are coming in, while Jews are stumbling over the "stone."

10:16-17. In vv. 14-15 Paul has explained the need for his mission to the Gentiles, looking back to his opening statement in 1:5. Now he refers to another element in the same verse: the "obedience of faith." Not everyone, he says, obeyed the gospel ("accepted," NIV, is scarcely a translation of ὑπήκουσαν [*hypēkousan*], but reflects

---

403. Also Nah 1:15 [2:1 LXX]; but the following verse shows it is Isaiah whom Paul has in mind. The word for "messengers" is εὐαγγελιζόμενοι (*euangelizomenoi*, "gospelers"), which echoes Joel 2:32 [3:5 LXX], the verse Paul quoted in 10:13. For the translation "timely" instead of "beautiful," see BDAG 1103; Fitzmyer, *Romans*, 595, 597; Bryan, *A Preface to Romans*, 176.

404. That is presumably the view of the NIV, which heads the section 9:30–10:21 as "Israel's Unbelief" and adds "the Israelites" as the subject of v. 16. The NRSV, starting a new paragraph at v. 18 and introducing v. 19 with "Again I ask" for Paul's ἀλλὰ λέγω (*alla legō*, lit., "but I say"), may imply the same understanding; "they" in v. 18 presumes continuity of subject with the previous verses.

405. Bryan, *A Preface to Romans*, 177, rightly sees v. 19 as the point to which Paul is leading through his exposition of the worldwide mission.

instead the un-Pauline assumption that "the gospel" is something offered on a take-it-or-leave-it basis, rather than an authorized summons from the world's rightful Lord). This is unlikely to be a wry, understated comment on the large-scale failure of Jews to obey the word; that, after all, is the central problem of the entire section, not something to be introduced obliquely in this way. It is far more likely to be a comment on the Gentile mission, in which, though many did believe, many more did not.[406]

Paul's aim here is not so much to face an objection ("But, Paul, if that's how the gospel is meant to work, why doesn't everyone obey it?") but to confirm the chain of events in vv. 14-15 from a second angle, summarized in v. 17. He links this chain to the previous one by quoting a closely adjacent passage of Isaiah to the one just mentioned (i.e., Isa 52:7). "Lord, who believed our report?" (Isa 53:1); this is the prophet's plaintive cry at the start of the main section of the fourth "servant song" (52:13–53:12). Paul sees himself as embodying, in his mission, the prophetic task of announcing the Messiah to the world. The word Isaiah uses for "message" is ἀκοή (akoē). Though this word can also refer to the faculty of hearing, the act of hearing or listening, and the organ with which one hears (i.e., the ear), the meaning here is the thing that is heard: the report or message (see also Gal 3:2, 5; the KJV's "faith cometh by hearing" is thus misleading, as is "act of hearing").[407]

This enables Paul to construct the sequence in v. 17: faith comes from the message, and the message happens through "the word of the Messiah," or perhaps "the word about the Messiah," or perhaps even "the word which is the Messiah."[408] The word for "word" here is ῥῆμα (rhēma), which is rare in Paul; apart from the present passage, it is found only in 2 Cor 12:4; 13:1 (also an OT quotation); and Eph 5:26; 6:17. He much prefers to use λόγος (logos). The chances are that he uses rhēma because his mind has still not left Deut 30:14, quoted in v. 8 (ἐγγύς σου τὸ ῥῆμά ἐστιν engys sou to rhēma estin,

"the word is near you." This, indeed, may be the reason for quoting Ps 18:5 in the next verse, where "their words" (τὰ ῥήματα αὐτῶν ta rhēmata autōn) go out to the end of the earth. The causal chain Paul is establishing is not simply (a) the preached message, (b) the message as heard, and (c) faith; indeed, for there to be a significant difference between the "message" and the "word of Christ," it is likely that the latter phrase denotes something more than "what preachers like me say about the Messiah." When we put v. 17 alongside v. 8, the sequence is clearer: faith comes from the message, and the message occurs through "the word which is near you," the word that has come down from heaven and up from the depths of death, the word that is the Messiah himself, God's self-revelation, God's wisdom, Torah in person. The chain is thus (a) the "word" in this full sense, (b) the preaching of this "word" (i.e., of Jesus as Messiah and Lord), and (c) faith.

10:18. The worldwide "hearing" of the message is now, it seems, undergirded by the grand claim of Ps 19:4 [19:5 MT, LXX]: "their sound went out into all the world, and their words to the ends of the earth." This is offered as the answer to "did they not hear": to restrict this to Jews, when the whole point of the verse is its worldwide universality, is to force a narrow interpretative scheme onto Paul's text.[409] But what precisely Paul means is, at first sight, a puzzle. The verse can scarcely refer to Paul's own apostolic mission, since (a) the psalm refers to the glory of God displayed in the created order and (b) it suggests a universality that neither Paul nor all his fellow apostles together have yet achieved. Option (a) is especially intriguing: If the message were so effectively proclaimed by creation itself, the need for apostles, carefully set out in vv. 14-17, would be undermined. It is possible that Paul means here what he means in Col 1:23, where he speaks of the gospel having been announced to every creature under heaven; this is best taken as a reference to the cosmic message that went out at the resurrection of Jesus, the message that death had been defeated and that the world was now a different place.[410] This

---

406. Against Moo, *The Epistle to the Romans*, 664.

407. Fitzmyer, *Romans*, 598.

408. Many good MSS have "of God," but "of the Messiah" has decisive support and, as the more unusual phrase, is virtually certain to be right. Many scribes, like many modern commentators, will have missed the allusion back to v. 8. Barrett, *A Commentary on the Epistle to the Romans*, 205, has suggested that v. 17 may be a gloss, but most find this implausible.

409. Against Fitzmyer, *Romans*, 599.

410. See N. T. Wright, *The Epistles of Paul to the Colossians and to Philemon: An Introduction and Commentary* (Grand Rapids: Eerdmans, 1986) 84-85.

message still needed Paul as its "minister." There may be something of that here, though the explicit reference to revelation through the created order itself is hardly the same thing, and puts us in mind rather of the revelation mentioned in 1:19-20, a revelation that, though true, proved not enough to save those who received it. It is also possible that, if Paul has the rest of Psalm 19 in mind, he may have taken vv. 1-6, as well as vv. 7-11, as referring to Torah, in which case he could be celebrating the fact that the "word" of Deut 30:14 was now freely available to all, as God always intended. The link between the occurrences of *rhēma* in vv. 8 and 17-18 seems to point in this direction. That seems to me the most likely understanding, though certainty here is perhaps out of reach.[411]

The Gentile world, then, has heard the gospel. Not all have believed; but, as he said in 9:30, Gentiles who were not looking for covenant membership have received it. Meanwhile, Israel, embracing the Torah, which did indeed hold out the status of "righteousness," the prospect of covenant membership, has not attained to that Torah. Instead (and this is what is driving the whole section), Israel has to look on as outsiders come to share the blessings that had been promised, blessings to which they had looked forward for so long. This is the point with which the chapter now closes.

10:19-21. Did Israel not know? "Know" here is preferable to "understand" (NRSV, NIV, and several others; the NEB's "failed to recognize the message" shows that the point has been missed). Not only is it the more basic meaning of the word; the answers Paul gives, quoting from Deuteronomy 32 and Isaiah 65, are not a demonstration that Israel did after all "understand" the gospel, or recognize it for what it was. They are a demonstration that Israel had long ago been warned that Gentiles would be coming in to share, and even apparently to take over, the blessings they had been promised. What Israel could not claim ignorance of, in other words, was not "the gospel," as is sometimes suggested, but the more specific point that Paul had stated first in 9:30-31.[412] This is what the first two quotations are about.

The first is from Deut 32:21. Deuteronomy 32 is the song of Moses, a great, sprawling poem mixing powerful praise to God and scathing indictment of Israel. It is clearly a significant passage for early Christian writers; there are three direct quotations from it in Romans alone, and numerous allusions (in Romans: Deut 32:35 at Rom 12:19; 32:43 at 15:10). The rebellious ways of Israel are detailed in Deut 32:15-18; they ungratefully spurned God after all that had been done for them. In 32:19-25 the judgments that God will visit upon them are listed. According to 32:20, they are "children who do not have faith"; and 32:21 declares that as they have provoked YHWH to jealousy with their idols, beings that are not real gods, so YHWH will make them jealous with "those who are not a people" (perhaps, in Paul's mind, an echo of 9:25-26). Paul clearly takes this as a prophecy of God's call of Gentiles to enjoy Israel's privileges.[413] He will in the next chapter use this key category of "jealousy" as the fulcrum around which to turn his crucial argument.

The second quotation is from Isa 65:1, leading to the third, which is from the following verse. Isaiah, declares Paul, announces the shocking result: "boldly" (NIV) is a reference to the stark, almost horrifying content of what is said, more than to the prophet's state of mind. Again the theme (the continuing answer to the question "did Israel not know?") is the bringing of Gentiles, who were not seeking YHWH or membership in the chosen people, into good standing, just as in 9:30-31. Isaiah 65 comes straight after the long prayer for God to intervene at the time of Israel's devastation (63:15–64:12), a prayer that Paul himself might have been imitating in 10:1. This larger passage has several echoes of Romans 9–10. God is Israel's father, whether or not Abraham acknowledges it (63:16; cf. Rom 9:7-9); God has hardened their heart, making them go astray (63:17; cf. Rom 9:17-18); Israel's righteousness is like an unclean garment (64:6; cf. Rom 9:30-10:3); no one calls on YHWH's name (64:7; cf. Rom 10:13); but nevertheless God is the potter and Israel the clay (64:8; cf. Rom 9:20-23). But God's response is clear (65:1-2):

---

411. See Hays, *Echoes of Scripture in the Letters of Paul*, 175.
412. So Fitzmyer, *Romans*, 595, 599.

413. Sirach 50:25-26 declares that the writer's soul is vexed with two nations, Samaria and Philistia, and also with a third, which is "no nation" namely "the foolish people who dwell at Sichar." On the various rabbinic interpretations of the "non-nations," see SB 3.284-85.

"I was found by those who were not looking for me; I said 'Look, here I am' to a nation that was not calling on my name. Meanwhile, I stretched out my hands all day long to a rebellious people." Paul understands the first verse to refer, as in 9:30, to the Gentiles who are coming in even though they were not expecting or wanting to, and the second to refer, as in 9:31-3, to Israel itself, remaining recalcitrant, "unbelieving and opposing."

The argument has come full circle. Paul has brought the story up to date. From Abraham to exodus, from the exile to the Messiah; and now that the Messiah has come, the new mode of covenant membership, of Torah-observance, of "righteousness," is open, and those who confess Jesus as Lord and believe that God raised him from the dead share not only this status but also the salvation promised as a result. Paul sees Gentiles entering this heritage as he announces the gospel around the world. He is praying that his fellow Jews may enter it too. At the present time, though, he sees the majority of them as Isaiah saw them: unwilling to countenance this fresh revelation from their God. The implied question of 9:1-5, and the prayer of 10:1, are thus left hanging in the air. What will happen next? Having told his version of the story about God and Israel in the past, Paul will now move cautiously to tell a story about God and Israel in the future.

REFLECTIONS

1. The most important thing Paul does in this section is to explain where he, his readers, and the people he is discussing are within God's story with Israel and the world. Learning to think like this—to understand a grand narrative that is larger than ourselves, that may be challenging or even threatening to us—is a major task for those who undertake to live with Scripture. Of course, in our day grand narratives of all sorts have been called into question. They are felt to be hegemonic, attempts to snatch or guard the citadel of power; and, of course, they can be used like that. But the story Paul tells resists all such attempts to deconstruct it. It is the story of how people who had no airs and graces of their own, no thought of being sought by Israel's God, the creator, nevertheless found themselves grasped by the divine call and love as an act of sheer grace. And it is also the story—here Paul is doing some deconstruction of his own—of the shock received by the people who thought the God-and-world story could only be told, and would always be told, with them coming out on top. The climax of their own history was a Messiah who, from their point of view, was as it were an anti-Messiah. The king came, and instead of setting his people free he died their death and invited them to follow him. Only if they do so will they find the fulfillment of their own story: He is, indeed, the true King, the world's true Lord, and will give salvation to all who call on his name.

2. At the level of learning to read the Bible, both the ancient Scriptures of Israel and the strange writings of the early Christians, we are bound to be struck by the sheer demand of a text like this. Isaiah, Leviticus, Deuteronomy, Isaiah again, Joel, Isaiah once more, twice more, a psalm, Deuteronomy again, then Isaiah again: and each text Paul quotes opens up a world, a story, an argument, a celebration, a warning, which needs to be understood as a whole, not simply in the short passage quoted. Paul's mental world is furnished by entire biblical arguments and sequences of thought, and when he quotes or alludes to them he wants the whole passage to resonate. And many of the texts he quotes are themselves caught up, both in their biblical originals and in the ways they were read in Second Temple Judaism, in a complex web of allusion and intertextual echo, creating more meanings, sustaining old stories and inventing new ones, so that we sometimes despair of ever recovering more than a fraction of what was in the mind not only of Paul but of a hypothetical ideal first-century reader.

We should not despair. We may never understand it all, but we can make some significant strides in the right direction. And the lesson we should learn, at the level of method and Christian education, is that (to put it crudely) it is always worth looking up references. Indeed, it is always worth having a Bible with good cross-references; the current fashion for printing Bibles without such aids to inner-biblical reference may save money, but it leaves readers thin on information that could change how they approach the text, and ultimately how they understand and live it.

3. The story Paul tells, of the Messiah as the climax of Israel's history and the strange stumbling of Israel and ingathering of Gentiles, is unique. He does not expect this sequence of events to be played out in other settings and at other times, or in relation to other peoples. The Messiah is not an example of a general pattern in history, still less church history. The protestant tendency to expect a revolution in each generation, and to justify it from the events of the first generation, needs to be held in check by the equally important protestant principle that the death of Jesus Christ was "once for all" (6:10).Yet a shadow from this story may indeed fall across the pages of church history from time to time. There may sometimes be people with apparent privilege who need to see themselves as "ignorant of God's righteousness, and seeking to establish their own." There may be people on the margins who need to be brought in by God's surprising and unimagined grace. And, however unique Paul's apostleship, there needs to be a steady supply of people to be "sent" to announce the message, to tell the world of its rightful Lord. Isaiah's promise of the messengers whose very feet are blessed can be just as true in the twenty-first century as it was in the first.

4. At the heart of the passage is the message of covenant renewal, drawn out of Deuteronomy with breathtaking and yet historically grounded exegesis. The Messiah has brought the long story of Torah to its climax and goal, and all are now summoned to the faith through which Torah finds itself strangely fulfilled, even by those who did not know it (see also 2:25-29). The challenge of this in our own day is that "new covenant" theology is deeply unwelcome to two groups of readers. The first are those for whom any continuity between God's ways with Israel in the past and God's ways now, after Calvary and Easter, is under suspicion for failing to take the cross seriously enough. This charge will not stick in the present context: The cross is woven into the very fabric of Paul's argument throughout chaps. 9–11, as the Messiah's people "according to the flesh" discover what that means in practice. The second group are those who are so concerned to stress (like Paul himself) that God has not finished with Israel according to the flesh that they are anxious about even the talk of renewal. What, they say, was wrong with things as they were? And they are ready to label as oppressive, or otherwise incorrect, any possible answer Paul or anybody today might come up with.

At this point the exegete and theologian have to hold their nerve. Just because there have been substandard versions of the Christian story that have had devastatingly awful consequences for Jews (and others, for that matter), this does not mean that the Christian, not least the serious reader of Paul, must back off from making the central Christian claim, that Jesus of Nazareth was and is Israel's Messiah and the world's true Lord, and that the one God did indeed renew the ancient covenant in and through him. Indeed, as we have remarked before, not to make claims like this is, ironically, to de-Judaize Christianity, leaving the way open for Christians to demonize Jews as "the Other." Paul takes the apparently risky route—but it is the only one available—of trying to teach his readers to think in a Messiah-shaped fashion about God's dealings with the whole world, including Israel, in the belief that this will lead, not to demonization, but to Christians being grateful to the Jewish people (9:4-5) and praying to God on their behalf (10:1). This is not the last word on the subject. The chapter that follows will insist on humility replacing arrogance. But it is certainly one of the first words that needs to be said.

5. The sequence of short questions in 10:14-17 has often, rightly, been seen as pointing to the vocation, which remains in force, to announce the gospel of Jesus throughout the world. Many, reading these words, have had that strange sense of being confronted with a challenge that they dare not ignore. All Christians, reading them, should at least ask themselves, and more important ask God in prayer, whether they are among those who will be "sent" as heralds, enabling women, men, and children in every country and race to hear the good news, so that some at least may come to believe. Paul never promises, any more than the prophets did (think of Isa 53:1, quoted in 10:16; think, too, of Isa 6:9-13), that this will be easy, successful, or popular. Indeed, he normally implies the opposite. But the light that keeps shining through in his writings, the joy that insists on bubbling up to the surface of the toughest argument and the saddest problem, and the sense of purpose that sustains writer and reader through the long and winding discussions, remind us that the surface problems and sufferings, many though they may be, cannot be compared with the glory that will be revealed to us.

ROMANS 11:1-36, THE SALVATION OF "ALL ISRAEL" IN FULFILLMENT OF GOD'S UNBREAKABLE PROMISES

OVERVIEW

The conclusion of the section brings Paul to one of the most majestic sustained arguments in all his writing. Unfortunately it is also one of the most controversial. At the very point where he wants to bring his readers to the mountaintop and show them the glorious view all around, centuries of re-reading and misreading have created a fog in which interpreters wander to and fro, speculating as to what the view might look like if only we were able to see it. And yet the main thrust of the chapter, in itself and in its place within Romans 9–11 as a whole and indeed the epistle as a whole, ought not to be in doubt.

The questions Paul raised at the start of chap. 9 had to do with God and with Israel according to the flesh. The problem he faced is that Israel has, by and large, not believed the gospel of Jesus the Messiah, and that it looks therefore not only as though Paul's kinsfolk are forfeiting salvation but also as though God's own credibility, competence, wisdom, and glory are being called into question. We should not be surprised, then, that this concluding chapter draws together the threads by talking at length, head-on, about God and Israel according to the flesh.

In particular, he seizes upon the motif of "jealousy," introduced by his quotation of Deut 32:21 in 10:19, in order to develop his central point: that the fact of Gentiles coming to share their blessings is designed to make Paul's "flesh" jealous and so bring them to salvation (11:14). The way to that salvation is along the route already mapped out so carefully in 10:1-13, on the basis of Deuteronomy 30. It is faith (11:23), by which Paul continues to mean confession that Jesus is Lord and belief that God raised him from the dead. This reading of 11:11-24, as we shall see, does full justice to the text.

In 11:25-26a, however, Paul declares that, through the strange process of the hardening of Israel and the incoming of Gentiles, "all Israel shall be saved." This has caused readers down the years to believe that what Paul ultimately had in mind was not just the coming to Christian faith, during the course of ongoing history, of more Jews who, like himself, believed the gospel, but the sudden salvation of "Israel according to the flesh" in its entirety, at the very end. Many have puzzled over what exactly this means; many theories have been advanced as to how it might happen. Does he mean all Jews alive at the end, or all Jews of every age? Will this salvation be conditional on a large-scale awakening of Christian faith, or does it occur on some parallel track of divine grace? Will it be the prelude to the parousia (11:26*b* has often been taken to refer to Jesus' "Second Coming") or the result of it? Or what?

These questions have been sharpened in the last hundred years or so by two factors. First, "dispensational" theology, popular in America in particular, has highlighted the belief that, as part of the events leading toward the "millennium," ethnic Israel must return to and be established in the Holy Land, to play a crucial role in the drama that will unfold as ancient prophecies are fulfilled. Romans 11 is seen as a critical text in predicting the eventual salvation that will follow; the internationally recognized state of Israel established in 1947 is seen as the fulfillment of prophecies in the Hebrew Bible and as foreshadowing the fulfillment of Romans 11 itself.[414] Second, the horrible devastation of European Jewry at the hands of the Nazis has led conscience-stricken Christian theologians not only to search out and blame seemingly anti-Jewish texts in the New Testament, but also to highlight the present passage as offering a "two-covenant" alternative to what is seen as "supercessionism," the belief that Christianity has "superseded" or "replaced" Judaism.[415] The popularity of the former views among many large and vigorous churches, and of the latter in influential scholarly circles, has ensured that Romans 11 is firmly fixed in many minds as a prediction that God will act on behalf of "Israel according to the flesh" in a way that bypasses what Paul saw as the normal process of coming to Christian faith. Any attempt to argue for another view is seen by some as an an exegetical equivalent of arguing that the earth is flat. (There are other pressures as well, not least the decline of a belief in "hell" and the popularity of universalism—to which Paul is then supposed to have given support in 11:32.)

Yet to decide on the meaning of a passage first and to do the exegesis afterward is always a recipe for disaster. We have seen all along that Paul's arguments in Romans, particularly in chaps. 9–11, are tightly interwoven both within the letter itself, in the context of his other writings, and in the complex and dense web of scriptural echoes and allusions. Everything he has said so far in the letter, understood both at a surface reading and in its allusive depths, inclines the reader to believe that if Romans 11 envisages ethnic Jews coming to salvation it will be by the same route as Paul himself, that is, through faith in Jesus as Messiah.[416] Consider what he has already said. He has spoken again and again of the renewal of the covenant through the Messiah, Jesus, and by the Spirit. He has made Christian faith—belief that Jesus is Lord, and that God raised him from the dead—central to his argument and pivotal for salvation, urging that this faith, and the "life" that results from it, are what the Jewish law really intended all along. He has argued in great detail that not all Abraham's physical descendants inherit the promises, but that Abraham's family is instead opened up, through faith, to people of every race. He has listed the Messiah as the crowning privilege of ethnic Israel (9:5)—and by the Messiah he obviously means Jesus himself. As we shall see, 11:1-24 is most naturally read as continuing this line of thought, developing strands already there in the argument. Since 11:25 begins with γάρ (*gar*), we should assume that it and v. 26*a* ("and so all Israel will be saved") are an explanation of what has gone before, not a new and radically different point, and if they can be read that way, with a clear line of thought going through to v. 32, the normal canons of exegesis demand that they should be. Unless, of course, Paul has contradicted himself—a possibility that several have seized upon, with variations, as the correct solution.[417] The eventual judgment depends upon the cumulative weight of several exegetical details, and will be argued for step by step.

Paul introduces the two main stages of his argument with key questions in 11:1 and 11:11: "has God forsaken his people?" and

---

414. J. F. Walvoord, *Israel in Prophecy* (Grand Rapids: Zondervan, 1962); J. Fischer, *The Olive Tree Connection: Sharing Messiah with Israel* (Downers Grove: InterVarsity, 1983). The work of the so-called International Christian Embassy in Jerusalem is based on this kind of thinking.

415. On the "two-covenant" proposal of Stendahl, Gager, Gaston and others, see note 302.

416. So Fitzmyer, *Romans*, 620; Moo, *The Epistle to the Romans*, 725-26.

417. See Sanders, *Paul, the Law, and the Jewish People*, 199.

"have they [i.e., ethnic Israel] stumbled so as to fall?" Paul answers each with an emphatic "No!" To put the same point in a positive fashion, we could paraphrase the two questions: "Can any Jews then be saved?" and "Can any more Jews then be saved?"—the answer being an emphatic "Yes!" Verses 11-32 then form one sustained argument, which breaks down into three closely interrelated sections (vv. 11-16, 17-24, 25-32), and leads into the final doxology (11:33-36).

Romans 11:1-10, God Has Not Rejected Israel

COMMENTARY

Paul introduces the two questions that shape this concluding chapter with a solemn λέγω οὖν (*legō oun*), a formula found nowhere else in his extant writings. Elsewhere when he uses λέγω (*legō*), apart from the places where it introduces an explanation of what has just been said (e.g., 1 Cor 7:8), it introduces an emphatic statement (e.g., 12:3; 15:8); here it has a solemn ring to it: "So this is the question I must raise at last. . . ."

The first question examines what might seem a possibility after the sorrowful opening of 9:1-5 and conclusion of 10:19-21. Israel according to the flesh appears to have failed completely. God has done everything possible and no response has been forthcoming. That would generate a "replacement" theology, indeed: God would have "replaced" the Jewish people with Gentiles. But that is certainly not Paul's view. He himself is both an example of a Jew who is now part of the "remnant" spoken of in 9:27, and part of the means by which God will increase the size of that remnant. But this remnant is not a small minority for whom "works-righteousness," in the senses already explored, is after all effective. It is "according to the election of grace," that is, according to the principles enunciated in 9:6-29, the negative side of which is the "hardening" spoken of in that same passage. It is misleading, therefore, to say that the "hardening" is "only partial"; the remnant that now exists, with Paul as its example, does so not by escaping the verdict of judgment but by coming through it to new life (see Gal 2:19-21).[418]

11:1-2a. As often, Paul introduces a new thought by proposing a conclusion that could be drawn from what has been said and then explaining why it is wrong. "Has God rejected his people?" (so NRSV; the NIV is technically correct to make this aorist: "Did God reject his people?" but the sense seems to be that of the NRSV and most translations—i.e., perfect, the present situation that results from a past event). As evidence for his rejection of this proposal, Paul cites his own case.[419] He is a Christian, confessing Jesus as Lord and believing that God raised him from the dead; and he, of course, is a Jew, an Israelite, from the seed of Abraham (the NRSV and the NIV have "descendant," but in view of 9:7-8 it is important to note that Paul says σπέρμα [*sperma*; lit., "seed"]). What is more, he is of the tribe of Benjamin—one of the few tribes left in his day that could trace their ancestry all the way back, being from the southern tribes, who returned after the Babylonian exile (on Paul's sense of his own Jewishness and its privileges, see 2 Cor 11:22; Gal 1:13-14; Phil 3:4-6).

His own example enables him to quote emphatically from 1 Sam 12:22: "God has not rejected his people whom he foreknew" (NRSV; on God's "foreknowledge," see the Commentary on 8:29). The quotation also fits Ps 94:14 [93:14 LXX] quite closely, with only the the verb's tense being different; the context of Ps 94:12-16 offers some suggestive wider links with Paul's argument, but the 1 Samuel reference still appears primary. This passage brings two particular overtones into Paul's context. First, the statement is Samuel's, as part of his promise that he will never stop interceding for Israel, despite their

---

418. Against Fitzmyer, *Romans*, 603.

419. The NEB's translation of μὴ γένοιτο (*mē genoito*) as "I cannot believe it!" reflects Dodd's idea that Paul's logic should have made him give the answer Yes and that only residual national pride made him answer No. See Dodd, *The Epistle of Paul to the Romans*, 68, 184. See also Fitzmyer, *Romans*, 603.

sin and folly. Samuel stands in the tradition of Moses interceding for Israel; Paul has stood in the same tradition in 9:1-5 and 10:1, and the implication here is that he is not only an example of a Jew who has been faithful to the gospel but is also part of the means, through his prayer, of Israel's continuing not-forsakenness. He highlights this praying role, as the next part-verse makes clear (11:2*b*): the link between v. 2*a* and v. 2*b* is Elijah's intercessory task. Second, the Samuel passage is all about God's provision for Israel through the choice of the first king, Saul; and Saul was from the tribe of Benjamin. Paul, whose own Hebrew name was Saul, seems content here to suggest, by implication, that just as God provided for Israel through the choice of the Benjaminite Saul a thousand years ago, so now he has done the same thing.

11:2b-4. Paul more naturally, though, identifies himself with the prophetic tradition than the kingly. In 10:14-17 he appeared like Isaiah, telling the good news of the servant-Messiah. In 9:1-5 and 10:1 he has prayed like Moses, and now (as it appears) like Samuel. But the prophet with whom the young Saul of Tarsus seems to have identified above all, and with whom the converted Paul still felt a strong affinity, was Elijah.[420] Paul's early "zeal" was in the tradition of Elijah's zeal against the prophets of Baal; but now he saw himself in a subsequent part of the story, standing all but alone before God as the true, and persecuted prophet, praying for the people (Paul here uses the verb ἐντυγχάνω [*entygchanō*, "intercede"]; his only other uses of this verb have as their subjects the Spirit [8:27] and the ascended Christ [8:34]). But, like Elijah, he receives the assurance (the word for "the divine reply" or "God's answer" is χρηματισμός [*chrēmatismos*, "oracle"], a word found nowhere else in the NT) that he is not alone: God has created a "remnant" of those who have not bowed the knee to Baal, "leaving" them in the manner spoken of by Isa 1:9, quoted in 9:29.

11:5-6. Who then is this "remnant" in Paul's day, and how do they come to have escaped the fate of the rest of the nation, so graphically portrayed in 9:6–10:21? Can it be that, despite 2:17–3:20; 7:7-25; and

9:6–10:21, there are some ethnic Jews who have succeeded in obeying Torah, attaining "their own righteousness" (10:3), and establishing a status of covenant membership based on their belonging to Abraham's physical family and maintaining its distinctive outward markers? No. These two verses make it clear that this "remnant" (λεῖμμα *leimma*; the only use of this word in the NT) is not a small minority for whom the way of national status actually worked, a tiny group who found that Israel's privileges could after all (in terms of Phil 3:4-7) be counted as "gain" rather than "loss." No: the present "remnant" is "chosen by grace" (NRSV, NIV), literally "in accordance to the election of grace." Paul has already spoken of God's ἐκλογή (*eklogē*, "selection," "choice," 9:11), and will return to it in summing up the chapter and section (11:28). In the present passage he can use the word both for the act of choosing, as here, and the ones so chosen, as in 11:7. This remnant, he emphasizes, is "not according to works," otherwise the whole principle of grace would be violated. This cannot, then, be a small number for whom "works" are after all effective.

Paul's doctrine of the remnant in this passage is thus significantly different from that of some of his contemporaries. The best example of an opposite view comes from Qumran: the sect regarded itself as the small minority who had remained true when all others had fallen away, the diminishing number who were still holding lighted candles as the night got darker and darker.[421] Paul, characteristically, sees it the other way around: those who believe in Jesus, those who are called by God's grace, are the small but increasing number who are awake, and lighting their lamps, before the coming dawn (this is how his metaphor works in 13:11-14 and 1 Thess 5:5-10). And part of the point about this image is that if there are already some who are waking up, the other side of the dark night, then there can be more. If Paul and the other Jewish Christians are a new kind of "remnant," called by God's grace in the gospel of Jesus, there is no reason why others

---

420. See N. T. Wright, "Paul, Arabia and Elijah (Galatians 1:17)," *JBL* 115 (1996) 683-92.

421. For the "remnant" in Qumran see 1QS 8:6; 1QH 6:7-8; 1QpHab 10:13; 4QFlor 1:19; 1Q37 1:3. Fitzmyer, *Romans*, 605, sees the parallel but not the all-important difference between Qumran and Paul at this point.

should not join them. That is the argument of 11:11-16 and beyond.

11:7-10. But for the moment he pauses one more time to describe the state of Israel according to the flesh. This is not a new point, but merely amplifies and underlines what has already been said in 9:25–10:3 and 10:19-21. While "the elect" obtained what Israel as a whole sought, Israel as a whole did not, falling instead into the condemnation already spoken of by (we are not surprised to learn) Deuteronomy and Isaiah.

11:7. It is possible that we should read v. 7 as opening with two questions, the second being answered by Paul's statement about "the elect": "What then? What Israel sought, did it not obtain? Well, the elect obtained it—but the rest were hardened." Whereas in 9:30-31 Paul distinguished between Israel, seeking and pursuing but not obtaining, and believing Gentiles, not seeking but obtaining, here he offers simply a division within Israel itself, the division between "the remnant" and "the rest."

Of "the rest" he says that they have been "hardened." This looks back to and summarizes one strand of 9:14-24. Since it is also a vital move in the decisive statement at 11:25, it is important to understand it clearly. Paul is drawing on the Jewish tradition that runs like this: when God delays outstanding judgment, those who do not use this time of delay to repent and turn back to him will be hardened, so that their final judgment, when it comes, will be seen to be just. This apocalyptic context of "hardening" is vital; ignoring it leads interpreters either into abstract discussions of predestination and reprobation or into the idea of a temporary "hardening," which is then reversed.[422] As the analogy with Pharaoh in 9:17-18 indicates, this "hardening" is not something that comes for a while, during which something else happens, and which is then removed. The "hardening," rather, is what happens during a temporary suspension of the judgment that would otherwise have fallen, to allow time for some to escape. In the case of Pharaoh, the result was the exodus from Egypt, seen as a sign of God's glorious power and the reputation of the divine

name (9:17). In the present case, the result is that there is time not only for the Gentiles to come in (11:11-15), but also for more Jews, like Paul himself, to recognize that the risen Jesus is indeed Israel's Messiah and to serve him in "the obedience of faith."

For those who do not, Paul does not need to invent comments of his own; the Jewish Scriptures themselves declare God's judgment on those within Israel who remain stubborn. Deuteronomy 29, following the long list of the curses that will fall upon disobedience and idolatry, has Moses looking sorrowfully at Israel and seeing nothing but rebellion. Isaiah 29:10, closely related to one of the most-quoted words of judgment from that prophet (i.e., Isa 6:9-10, quoted frequently in the NT: e.g., Matt 13:14-15 and par.; John 12:40; Acts 28:26-27), is taken from the devastating warning in which the saying about the potter and the clay (29:16) forms part of the indictment. These are both, obviously, contexts that have been in Paul's mind for much of the section so far; the quotations from Deuteronomy 29 and Isaiah 29 simply make more explicit what has already been said. It is the Jewish Scriptures themselves that speak of YHWH pouring out a "spirit of stupor" (Deut 29:4 [29:3 LXX]), and making eyes not to see and ears not to hear. Tragic though it is, this is part of what God had said all along, part of what Israel already should have known (10:19). The result is that unbelieving Israel is hardened permanently; that is, there are no promises to be made of a reversal of the "hardening," except in the context of a coming to faith (see 11:23). But this does not mean that any particular individuals are unable to come to faith and so, like Paul, join the increasing "remnant"; on the contrary, some have already done so and many more will follow.[423]

The psalm quotation that follows in vv. 9-10 (Ps 69:22-23 [68:23-24 LXX]) is linked to the combined quotation from Deuteronomy and Isaiah by the reference to eyes that do not see.[424] But there is a closer link still with Paul's overall theme, and this gives us a clear

422. See Moo, *Romans*, 689-90. See also Rom 2:3-7, the language of which Paul picks up later in the present chapter; cf. 2 Macc 6:13-16, discussed in the Commentary on 9:14-18. In the present passage, 11:7 is to be taken closely with 11:25.

423. Moo, *Romans*, 681, seems to get this exactly the wrong way around.

424. A "snare" (παγίς *pagis*) also echoes a curse in Ps 35:8. Paul thus lines up the three elements of the Jewish Scriptures (Law, Prophets, and Writings) to demonstrate that his charge against his fellow Jews is not his own invention but the solemn and sustained witness of their own sacred texts.

indication of what Paul thinks is going on here. Elsewhere in this letter, and frequently in the NT, this psalm is seen as a prediction of the sufferings of the Messiah. (See, e.g., Rom 15:3, quoting Ps 69:9; elsewhere Matt 26:37 and Heb 12:2 quoting Ps 69:20; Matt 27:34, 48 and par. quoting Ps 69:21; John 2:17 quoting Ps 69:9; John 15:25 quoting Ps 69:4; Acts 1:20 quoting Ps 69:25). The judgment that is called down upon impenitent Israel in this passage is not something separate from the central gospel events, the events concerning Jesus. If they are the fulfillment of the sufferings portrayed in the psalm, then those who have mocked and tormented the sufferer have these judgments invoked upon them. How much thought Paul gives to the specifics of the "table" becoming a snare, a trap, a stumbling-block and a delusion it is hard to say; but he did of course hold that the pure table fellowship that excluded Gentiles (cf. Gal 2:11-21) was now done away with in the Messiah, who had himself become a "stumbling-block" to his own kinsfolk (1 Cor 1:23; Gal 5:11). This judgment is simply the other side of the coin of ethnic Israel's rejection of the crucified Messiah. The judgment, moreover, will not be reversed; as long as ethnic Israel refuses to see the crucified one as Messiah and Lord, their eyes will be darkened (v. 10) and their back bent (cf. 2 Cor 3:14-15).[425] Though a case can be made out for understanding διὰ παντός (*dia pantos*) as "continually," the NRSV and the NIV are probable true to Paul's meaning to translate "for ever."[426] As the next passage will make clear, Paul does not suppose that any particular ethnic Jews are subject to this condemnation; there is always room for them to come to faith. The perpetual condemnation, as far as this passage is concerned, lies upon the rejection of the crucified Messiah, not upon this or that person who has acquiesced in that rejection. We should not be surprised at this. Granted all that Paul has argued so far, not least in 3:21–4:25, if God's covenant faithfulness has been revealed in the death of the beloved son, we should not expect the covenant to be effective for any who reject that son, and that death, as the long-awaited unveiling of God's saving plan. But, as we should continually remind ourselves, and as Romans itself insists frequently, it is only when the word of judgment has been fully heard that the word of mercy and grace can sound forth their proper harmony. Judgment must be judgment if grace is to be grace. (See Reflections at 11:33-36.)

425. On which see Wright, *The Climax of the Covenant*, 178-84.

426. Against Cranfield, *A Critical and Exegetical Commentary on the Epistle to the Romans*, 552; Fitzmyer, *Romans*, 607; Bryan, *A Preface to Romans*, 179.

Romans 11:11-32, "All Israel" Will Be Saved

COMMENTARY

The major section of the chapter is a long argument, with (to be sure) pauses and breaks, but essentially to be seen as a single flow of thought. It is sent on its way by the second of the two questions that structure the chapter: Granted that Israel according to the flesh has "stumbled," has this stumble meant a permanent "fall"? Certainly not, Paul replies.

He argues the contrary in three stages. Each stage depends on, and expounds further, ideas already set out both in chaps. 9–11 and in Romans as a whole.

(1) What has happened to Israel has been for the good of the Gentiles, so there is every reason to suppose that Israel itself will become "jealous," and some of Paul's kinsfolk will thereby be saved (11:11b-16). This is the point where Paul picks up language about Adam and Christ from earlier in the letter, notably chap. 5, and applies it to Israel according to the flesh.

(2) Unbelieving Jews are like branches broken off God's cultivated olive tree, while Gentiles are like wild branches grafted in surprisingly; how much more can God graft the natural branches back in "if they do not remain in unbelief" (11:23)? This argument (11:17-24) is aimed specifically against Gentile arrogance, the point to which Paul has been working around: do not, he says,

suppose that you can boast against the branches without yourself becoming at risk.

(3) The mystery of God's dealings with Israel and the Gentiles is thus unveiled. The "hardening" on Israel, and the "coming in" of Gentiles, is God's means of saving "all Israel." The covenant will be fulfilled in the way God always intended, that is, by being renewed through the Messiah for the forgiveness of sins. Whenever Jewish people come to faith in Jesus as Messiah, this is a further sign that God is faithful to the promises made to the patriarchs (11:25-32). The end of this specific argument is thus the end of the whole discussion that began with 9:6. All that remains, balancing the cry of anguish in 9:1-5, is the cry of praise in 11:33-36.

11:11-12. Paul picks up the language of "stumbling" from 9:32-33; the words are different but the idea closely related. Have they, he asks, tripped up in such a way as to fall headlong permanently?[427] Certainly not. He advances his counterargument in two stages, vv. 11*b*-12 and vv. 13-16. Each stage further subdivides; v. 11*b* is the basic statement, with v. 12 as a further conclusion; then vv. 13-14 are his major statement, explained and elaborated by v. 15 and, in turn, v. 16.

Verse 11*b* looks back to 10:19 and on to v. 14. It adds to the discussion an element that appears new but that, it turns out, was hidden in the argument of 9:6–10:21 all along: that Israel's stumble over the stumbling-stone was not just something that happened at the same time as the Gentiles' coming in to faith, to righteousness, and to salvation itself, but was actually part of the *means by which* it happened. We can understand this at one level by saying that Israel's hardening relates to Gentile salvation somewhat as Pharaoh's hardening relates to the exodus (9:17); this, it seems, is what 9:22-24 is all about, and the point is confirmed by the echo in v. 12 of the mention there of God's "riches." Somehow, God's bearing patiently with the "vessels of wrath" is part of the intention to bring these "riches" to the Gentiles. "Through their transgression, salvation has come to the Gentiles."

But if this is so then 10:19 is also in play: this will make ethnic Jews "jealous."[428] The background to this within Romans ought to be clear from 2:17-29—and from the whole sequence of thought that runs from the major statement of Christian identity in chaps. 5–8 into the sorrowful rehearsal of the same privileges in 9:1-5. But, whereas in Deut 32:21, and its quotation in 10:19, this "jealousy" appeared purely negative, it is turned to positive effect in v. 14; and Paul is already preparing the way for this. They (Paul does not use the word "Israel" between vv. 7 and 25) have "transgressed," and the world has been enriched; they have been "diminished," and God's riches have been given to the Gentiles. How much more, then, if they are brought back up to full strength ($\pi\lambda\acute{\eta}\rho\omega\mu\alpha$ *plērōma*)?

Before we explore this "full strength," let us note, so as to be quite clear, what the whole "jealousy" theme presupposes. It assumes (as argued above) that when Gentiles come to Christian faith they do indeed come to share in the blessings God promised to Israel according to the flesh (not, interestingly, the land; see the Commentary on 4:13; 8:18-27; the whole world is now seen as God's holy land, to be redeemed in the new creation). We cannot escape the force of this and retreat into the idea that Gentile Christians have a parallel track to salvation that does not intersect with the Jewish one. Nor, therefore, can we suggest that the way for Jews now to be saved is something radically different from the way Gentiles are saved—by God's grace, through faith in Jesus as Messiah, apart from works of the law.

What then might their "full strength," their complete number, mean? This is the first moment that Paul has suggested an increase in the number of Jews who come to be not merely Abraham's physical descendants but his "seed" in the full sense of 9:7-8. Up until 10:21 the number seemed to be diminishing, whittled down to a remnant. Even in 11:1-10 this "remnant" seemed to consist simply of the small number who, like Paul, had through God's electing grace abandoned the status based on "works" and embraced the messianic faith focused on Jesus. Now for the first time he begins to say that something

---

427. The metaphorical use of πταίω (*ptaiō*) is already found in Deut 7:25. For this use of πίπτω (*piptō*) see Rom 14:4; 1 Cor 10:12.

428. See R. H. Bell, *Provoked to Jealousy: The origin and Purpose of the Jealousy Motif in Romans 9–11*, WUNT, 2nd series, no. 63 (Tübingen: Mohr, 1994).

further may yet happen. Israel according to the flesh has been "diminished"; now it will be brought to fullness.[429] "Fullness" is itself a rare term in Paul, but there is another parallel occurrence close by in 11:25. Other parts of that verse are controversial, but at this point we are on safe ground: by the "fullness of the Gentiles," we may confidently say, Paul means "the total number of those Gentiles who believe the gospel of Jesus." He is well aware that large numbers of Gentiles do not believe it, and never will. The "fullness" will consist of all those who eventually do. There is no reason to suppose that "the fullness" of Israel will mean anything more than this: the complete number of Jews, many more than at present, who likewise come to faith in the gospel.[430]

We should note at this point the way in which vv. 11-12 echo the language and argument of 5:15-21. Paul here describes Israel's "stumble" as a παράπτωμα (*paraptōma*, "trespass"), echoing the key term used six times there in as many verses. What is more, the "trespass" in question forms the first half of a "how much more" argument celebrating the grace of God which overcomes human stumbling. "If, by the trespass of the one, the many died, how much more has God's grace . . . abounded to the many." "If, by the trespass of the one, death reigned . . . how much more will those who receive the gift of righteousness reign in life" (5:15, 17). A moment's thought will show what is going on. This is no accidental allusion. Paul's brief statement in 5:20 ("the law came in so that the trespass might abound"), set out at length in 7:7-25, and developed to its final stage in 9:30-33 where the "stumbling" metaphor is crucial, indicates that through Torah Israel has recapitulated the sin of Adam, has acted it out on a grand scale. But, whereas the trespass of Adam brought sin and death to the world, the "trespass" of Israel has brought salvation and "riches" to the world! How much more, then—this is the force of 11:12—should Israel now receive "fullness." Paul's two simultaneous guiding lights for understanding

Israel according to the flesh are these: Israel, like everyone else, is "in Adam"; but Israel is also, according to the flesh, the Messiah's own people. Verses 11-12 develop the first of these. The following three verses will now develop the second.

11:13-16. Paul moves a little closer toward his rhetorical target, which will come into full view in vv. 17-24 and then, decisively, in v. 25. He is speaking to "you Gentiles." This does not mean that all Christians in Rome were Gentiles (see Introduction). Nor does it necessarily mean that only at this point is he necessarily "turning" to them specifically.[431] Rather, this section of the letter is an argument against Gentile arrogance, against Gentiles falling into the trap of assuming an ethnic superiority, the trap Paul sees the Jews having fallen into (this is hardly, then, just an aside; the REB was right to correct the NEB's "But I have something to say to you Gentiles" to "It is to you Gentiles that I am speaking"). What Paul does not want Gentile Christians to think is that God cannot and will not save any more Jews; that, though there may be a Jewish remnant, Paul himself included, there will not be any more.

After this personal address to one part, perhaps the majority part, of the Roman church, this little argument has three moves:

1. Paul's oblique missionary intent toward his kinsfolk (vv. 13*b*-14): his Gentile ministry is aimed at making "his flesh" jealous and so saving some of them.
2. The explanation (v. 15): like their Messiah, their "casting away" means reconciliation for the world, and their "receiving back" will be like a resurrection.
3. The conclusion: Israel as a whole is "holy," because of the "first fruits" and the "root." This latter image will then open up into the central argument of the passage (vv. 17-24).

11:13-14. Paul's aim is to exploit the "jealousy" of which Deuteronomy 32 had spoken. Knowing, certainly, what a bold and even provocative move this was, he celebrated and "glorified" the ministry he had,

---

429. ἥττημα (*hettēma*), translated "defeat" in the NRSV and "loss" in the NIV, is a rare word (only here and 1 Cor 6:7 in the NT). The cognate verb ἡττάομαι (*hēttaomai*) has a range of meaning, including "to be defeated," "to be inferior," "to be weaker." Since it serves here (like "trespass" earlier in the verse) to sum up the whole sequence of 9:6–10:21 and makes the direct contrast with *plērōma*, a sense of "diminution" seems plausible. See, however, Moo, *Romans*, 688n. 26.

430. Fitzmyer, *Romans*, 611, discusses several possible senses of "fullness."

431. Against Fitzmyer, *Romans*, 608, 612.

his call to be the apostle to the Gentiles (see the Commentary on 1:5; 10:14-17). He was taking to the Gentiles the news that Israel's God, Abraham's God, was welcoming them into the one family now reconstituted around the Messiah (4:1-25). And he was seeking to hold this up before his fellow Jews so as to make them see what was happening and, becoming jealous, long to have a share in the eschatological blessings themselves. No wonder, we think wryly, Paul was beaten in synagogues. Such conduct must have seemed a deliberate and flagrant snub to some of Israel's most cherished assumptions. But he is undaunted. This is the way that some of them will be saved—and again, with this echo of the prayer of 10:1, we should hear also the solid soteriology of 10:9-13 that explains how the prayer will be answered.

To understand the roots of his argument, we should follow the Greek closely in v. 14. He does not say "my own people" (NJB, "the people who are my own blood-relations"; NEB, "the men of my own race"), but "my flesh." This picks up his phrases in 9:3, 5 ("my kinsfolk according to the flesh," and "from them, according to the flesh, is the Messiah"). Equally important, it echoes the whole argument of 7:1–8:11. There Paul, seeing his "flesh" as the place where Adam's sin was being worked out through the Torah itself, grieved over the situation but announced that God would give resurrection life to the "mortal body." Here, echoing Romans 5–8 in various ways, he sees his "flesh" in rebellion against the gospel, following through Adam's "trespass"; and he intends to make this "flesh" jealous, and so provoke it to salvation—by the route, we must assume, that he has sketched in 10:1-13, in other words by faith. He does not expect that all his fellow Jews, or even most of them, will travel this route. Verse 14 has a sober realism about it, parallel to that of 1 Cor 9:22, where the rhetoric cried out for him to say "all" but theology and missionary experience knew he had to say "some" ("I have become all things to all people so that by all means I might save . . . some"; the Greek is briefer [τοῖς πᾶσιν γέγονα πάντα, ἵνα πάντως τινὰς σώσω *tois pasin gegona panta, hina pantōs tinas sōsō*]; the rhetorical pressure to write πάντας [*pantas*] instead of τινάς [*tinas*] was

too strong for some MSS). But even "some" will enable him to answer "no" to the double question of 11:1 and 11:11: God will always be faithful to the promise to Abraham. This is not, then, a contrast with "fullness" in 11:12 and "all Israel" in 11:26.[432] There will always be some of Abraham's physical descendants who are included in the true "seed." That is all that the promise envisaged; that is the whole point of 9:6-29; and God will be true to the promise.

11:15. The explanation sends us back again to chap. 5. Israel truly is the Messiah's people according to the flesh; it was the Messiah's death, his "casting away," that achieved "reconciliation" for the world, and it is his risen life that now provides salvation (5:10; see the Commentary on 11:21 and the parallel there with 8:32). Now, in parallel fashion, the casting away of the Messiah's fleshly kinsfolk has accomplished reconciliation for the world, and their reacceptance will mean "life from the dead."

The idea that the failure, the rebellion, the "casting away" of Israel means reconciliation for the world is clearly a development of what was said in 11:11b-12a. It is a striking way of putting the same point, attributing redemptive, salvific significance to the tragedy that has befallen Israel, a significance that can only be explained on the assumption that Paul is indeed thinking of his own Christology under the argument all along. The "rejection" is indeed, in this sense, God's rejection of Israel, not (as is sometimes suggested) Israel's rejection of God.[433] Israel has acted out the representative death of its Messiah; the Gentiles are the beneficiaries. Paul returns to the same point from yet another angle in 11:30b: You Gentiles received mercy "by their disobedience." He never explains more explicitly what he means, but something like the following can perhaps be said. Paul does not envisage Israel actually "dying" for the sake of the world, as the Messiah himself has done; the Messiah's work is unique, standing over against Jew and Gentile alike. But the "hardening" that has come upon Israel, as in 9:14-24, was the necessary context for the Messiah's death, and as such has become

432. Against Moo, *The Epistle to the Romans*, 692.
433. So Bryan, *A Preface to Romans*, 187. ἀποβολή (*apobolē*) would surely be a strange word to use for the latter idea.

part of the saving plan. That is one of the main points of 9:6–10:21. The "hardening," then, has been the means of suspending the judgment that might otherwise have fallen, creating a breathing space in which Gentiles can be brought in (9:24, 30). In that sense, Israel's "casting away" has been instrumental in the salvation of the Gentiles.

Israel's "receiving back again" (πρόσλημψις *proslēmpsis*, the only occurrence of this word in the NT) must then be explained in terms of vv. 12 and 14. If, after all that has happened, Jews come back into the family, hearing and believing the gospel as in 10:6-13, then, says Paul, the significance of this will be like a kind of resurrection. "Life from the dead" here has sometimes been taken to indicate—anticipating one reading of 11:25-26—that when Israel comes back to faith this will be the signal for, or perhaps the result of, the general resurrection.[434] But v. 15 is introduced as an explanation *gar*, not a new point. Just think, Paul is saying to the Gentile Christians in Rome: once you realize that their "casting away" was like the death of the Messiah, when they are brought back again it will be like a little Easter—and you should celebrate! He is saying what 4:17 had already indicated: Abraham's family will consist of those who are brought back from the dead (i.e., Jewish converts) and those who are created out of nothing (i.e., Gentile converts). The "now" of 11:31 strongly suggests that Paul is not postponing this hoped-for salvation to some distant future.[435]

11:16. This phase of the argument is drawn together, and the ground prepared for the next one, by a further conclusion (for εἰ δέ [*ei de*] as drawing the conclusion, see 8:10-11). The point of this verse is that the whole is sanctifed by the part: the lump by the first fruits, the branches by the root.

The first of these images depends on the sacrificial tradition of the Feast of Weeks, represented in Num 15:20: "Of the first of your dough you shall offer up a cake as a heave offering"; the point being that once the first part of the dough has been offered to God, the entire batch is considered holy, consecrated

and ready for Israel to use.[436] The second image has no particular biblical background, but is introduced by analogy with the first in order to lead to the extended metaphor of the olive tree that then follows. In both images the referent of the second term is clear: the "whole lump" and the "branches" are of course Israel according to the flesh, the Israel that has not as yet recognized its Messiah.[437] But who or what is the first fruits? Who or what is the root?

The answer to these two is not necessarily the same. The argument so far, and some of Paul's other uses of the same image, would lead us to assume that the "first fruits" refers to the "remnant" chosen by grace, including Paul himself (see particularly 16:5; 1 Cor 16:15; 2 Thess 2:13). Some Jews according to the flesh have already been converted; that is, part of the lump of dough has already been offered to God. The rest must therefore be treated as sanctified, not as common or disposable. (By "holy" here Paul clearly does not mean "automatically saved," but rather something like "sanctified by extension" or "by their relationship"; the closest parallel is in 1 Cor 7:14, referring to the non-Christian partner and the children in a mixed marriage.)[438] In other words, Gentile Christians, recognizing the fact of a "remnant" of believing Jews, must regard other Jews as holy by extension.

It is possible to take the image of "root and branches" the same way: the remnant by grace are the root, and the branches are the as yet unbelieving Jews. But it seems harsh, in view of the way Paul develops the picture, to do so. The remnant itself, within Paul's image, consists not of a root that has always been there, nor yet of branches that were never broken off, but of branches that were broken off for a short while and then grafted back in again. Otherwise Paul's protestations about grace in 11:5-6 would be undermined:

---

434. This interpretation goes back to Origen and is favored by, among others, Käsemann, *Commentary on Romans*, 307; Fitzmyer, *Romans*, 613; Moo, *Romans*, 694-96.

435. See Leenhardt, *The Epistle to the Romans*, 284-85.

436. Paul also uses the image of "first fruits" in, e.g. 8:23, (see the note there); 16:5; and elsewhere. For the Jewish context see also, e.g., Philo *Special Laws* 1:131-44.

437. It is striking that the word for "lump" (φύραμα *phyrama*) is the same as in the "potter and clay" illustration in 9:21. The point here is not the same—there the lump was clay, here it is dough—but the two passages are thematically quite close. God can and will refashion the "lump" into something that at present it is not.

438. Though the interpretation of this passage too is a matter of considerable dispute. See A. C. Thiselton, *The First Epistle to the Corinthians: A Commentary on the Greek Text*, NIGTC (Grand Rapids: Eerdmans, 2000) 527-33.

the remnant really would be a permanent part of God's people, a small group for whom ethnic membership and Torah-observance really had proved valid. It is much better to take the "root" as something, or someone, more permanent; suggestions include the patriarchs, the Messiah, even God.[439] Of these I am inclined to prefer the Messiah. It is possible that Paul already has in mind the text that he will use at the climactic and concluding point of the letter's theological exposition, highlighting "the root of Jesse," whose resurrection installs him as the Gentiles' true ruler (15:12, quoting Isa 11:10). But even if that is too far away in the letter to be allowed, the Messiah has been at the center of the argument, either implicitly or explicitly, for much of chaps. 9–11, and it is the messianic pattern of casting away followed by life from the dead that Paul has been thinking through in the preceding verses. The olive tree in the illustration is Israel, the true seed of Abraham, into which wild branches have been grafted but into which, far more easily, natural branches can be regrafted. And the crowning privilege of Israel, the human and historical focus of the nation's long story as God's people, is the Messiah (9:5). It is considerably easier, I think, to see the "root" that "bears" both Gentile and Jewish Christians (11:18) as the Messiah than as the patriarchs.

Does that mean that we would be right to see the Messiah as the first fruits as well, making v. 16a more of a parallel to 1 Cor 15:20, 23? Probably not. The buried reference to the Messiah in 11:15 might sway us in this direction, but it is not necessary to take the two halves of the verse as making exactly the same point in two different ways.[440] If the καί (*kai*) that starts v. 16b is read as "moreover," there is no problem in seeing Paul making a transition at this point to the new picture he is about to draw. Paul of all people is adept at mixing his imagery, and in a dense and allusive argument a transition like this is perfectly comprehensible.

We conclude that 11:11-16 begins the argument that God still wants and intends to save more Jews by lining up Israel according to the flesh with both Adam and the Messiah,

as the argument of chaps. 5–8 might have prepared us for. Israel has acted out both the trespass of Adam and the redemptive "casting away" of the Messiah. Within this, Paul addresses a warning to the Gentile Christians in Rome: even the Gentile mission in which he exults has this as its oblique purpose, to bring more Jews to faith and so to salvation. For Jews to embrace the gospel now, after all they have gone through, would be like resurrection from the dead. They are, after all, the relatives according to the flesh not only of the existing remnant, but of the Messiah himself.

11:17-24. This leads Paul to one of his most famous extended images. Paul is often criticized for his apparent failure to manage such passages; in the present case some have even mocked him for being a city dweller who did not understand horticulture![441] Paul is however well aware that what he is proposing is, in terms of the metaphor he is using, "contrary to nature" (v. 24). A gardener does not normally graft wild branches on to a cultivated stock, but the other way around, directing the energy of the wild plant toward the focused fruitfulness of the cultivated one. There are exceptions to this, noted in ancient literature; we cannot tell whether Paul knew them or not.[442] Most likely he did not: he intends us to understand that what God has done with the olive tree is a miracle of grace, not the sort of thing that people do all the time.

The olive tree in the illustration clearly stands for the people of God, the people stretching back to Abraham and now including both Gentiles and Jews (the main OT reference is Jer 11:16-17: Israel as an olive tree whose branches are broken off in judgment; see also Ps 52:8; Hos 14:6). The Messiah (most probably) is the "root" through whom the tree now gets its life (v. 17), the one who holds the whole thing in place, enabling Gentile members to gain life (v. 18). The force of the illustration is to make the Gentile Christians realize their place within God's saving purposes; they are not the new aristocracy, they are the wild country cousins brought in, to everybody's surprise, to share

439. For patriarchs, see Bryan, *A Preface to Romans*, 188; Moo, *Romans*, 700. Cranfield, *Romans*, 564, takes the first fruits as the Jewish Christian remnant and the root as the patriarchs.

440. Against Bryan, *A Preface to Romans*, 188.

441. Dodd, *The Epistle of Paul to the Romans*, 189.

442. See Columella *On Country Matters* 5:9:16 (contemporary with Paul); Palladius *On Grafting* 53-54 (5th cent. CE). See also Moo, *Romans*, 703n. 33, and the other sources cited there, esp. A. G. Baxter and J. A. Ziesler, "Paul and Arboriculture: Romans 11:17-24," *JSNT* 24 (1985) 25-32.

the inheritance. If that is so, they have no business to give themselves airs over those of the unfortunate original family members who have for the moment been ousted. God is, after all, well capable of bringing them back again. That is the thrust of this passage.

11:17-18. Paul's first main point is: Do not boast. His exclusion of "boasting" in 3:27-30, ruling out any kind of Jewish boast of ethnic superiority based on possession of Torah and performance of its "works," is now balanced by this stern warning to Gentile Christians—a warning that, as the history of Marcionism bears witness, was needed but not heeded.[443] The branches that are broken off are, clearly, Jews who have not believed the gospel; Paul's view of them is not that they are on a parallel track to salvation, but that at the moment they are separated from the parent tree, gaining no life from the root. They are the ones he was grieving over in 9:1-5 and praying for in 10:1. The wild olive branches (i.e., the Gentile Christians), however, have been grafted in, and are sharing the rich oily sap that is the olive's chief glory, and that comes through the root (the NRSV's "the rich root" does not quite convey the force of the phrase, lit., "the root of the richness of the olive," i.e., the root through which the richness comes). This is yet another way of saying what Paul already said in 9:24, 30, and 10:4-13: Gentiles, to their surprise, are inheriting the blessings promised to Israel. But if that is so, they must remember their origin and refrain from crowing over those who have been, for the moment, cut off. They must remember who the Messiah is, and who they themselves are as his utter dependents. They do not support the root, as though Jesus Christ were now the private possession of Gentile Christians. He, Israel's Messiah according to the flesh, supports them. Paul's sudden use of the second person singular throughout vv. 17-24 (contrasting with the plural in vv. 13, 25-32) makes his point all the more sharply.

11:19-21. Paul then envisages a conversation between himself and the newly ingrafted branches. The Gentile branches will declare that other branches were broken off to make room for them—the very point, they might say, that Paul himself has made in 11:11-12 and 15. The "stumble" or "trespass" of Israel has been the occasion of Gentiles coming in. Paul does not disagree; but his point is made sharply by drawing attention to the attendant circumstances both of the breaking off of some branches and the grafting in of others. What counted then, and counts still, is faith: they were broken off because of unbelief, but you stand firm by faith (the NRSV adds "only," which as in 3:28 is a fair explanation though strictly an addition to Paul's text; on the idea of "standing," i.e., remaining firm in a particular status, see 5:2; 14:4). The accusation of unbelief or unfaithfulness (or "untrustworthiness," or "disloyalty," ἀπιστία *apistia*), goes back to 3:3; this was the basic charge leveled against Israel in the beginning of Paul's argument. Abraham is specifically contrasted with this in 4:20: he did not waver in unbelief.

This leads to a more specific warning: Gentile Christians must not just avoid boasting, but must also maintain their faithfulness. They must not permit themselves an attitude of superiority (see the Commentary on 12:3, 16), but must keep humble, in the proper fear of God. Verse 21 explains why, drawing on the fuller picture Paul has in mind that becomes explicit in v. 24: God is quite capable of doing to a Gentile church what he has done to "the natural branches." If they were not spared, perhaps God will not spare Gentiles either.[444] Here, too, there is a strange echo of an earlier passage, 8:32: God did not spare the beloved son. Once again, Paul is thinking of the Jews as the Messiah's people according to the flesh; but this time their fate is held up as a warning to Gentile Christians. This is what happens if you regard yourself as automatically part of God's people, instead of continuing by faith alone. Faith remains the only valid badge of membership; anything else will lead inevitably to "boasting."

What does the threat of being cut off actually mean? After the long argument of 3:21–8:39, it is highly unlikely that Paul would envisage individual Christians being justified

---

443. On Marcion and his movement, see R. J. Hoffman, *Marcion: On the Restitution of Christianity* (Chico, Calif.: American Academy of Religion, 1984).

444. "Perhaps" in the NRSV translates μή πως (*mē pōs*), which is missing in some good MSS but present, and hard to explain as a gloss, in several others. See B. M. Metzger, *A Textual Commentary on the Greek New Testament* (London: United Bible Societies, 1971) 526-27. Without it, the verse reads, as in the NIV, simply, "he will not spare you either." Adding "perhaps" does seem appropriately reverent at this point, though of course the more appropriate it seems the easier it is to explain it as a possible addition.

by faith at one moment, assured of "sharing the glory of God" (5:2; 8:30), and at another moment losing both faith and salvation. On the contrary; his regular view is that when God begins a good work, through the gospel and the spirit, that good work will come to completion (Phil 1:6). What is more likely is that this is a warning to an entire church (as, for instance, in the messages to the churches of Asia in Revelation 2–3). Individual Christians may be muddled or sinful, but they will be saved, even if only, in some cases, "as through fire" (1 Cor 3:15). A church, however, that begins to boast in the way Paul is warning against may not last another generation. The only way forward is through faith; and faith, by its very nature, means dependence on God, rather than confidence in human status, birth, privilege, or merit.

11:22-24. Paul sums up the argument, as is fitting for part of a larger section whose main subject is God, by drawing attention to two balancing attributes of God. These create a setting in which Gentile Christians must learn where they stand, what they risk if they do not remain there, and, particularly, what God can and will do with the Messiah's presently unbelieving kinsfolk according to the flesh. Paul has already spoken of God's "kindness" (χρηστότης *chrestotēs*) in 2:4, in describing how God's patience and forbearance were meant to lead to repentance, and in warning that a hard and impenitent heart that refused God's generosity would lead to wrath. Now, with a not dissimilar point about to emerge (11:25), he is warning that God's blend of justice and mercy, of kindness and severity,[445] has been applied to Israel according to the flesh and will be applied to Gentile churches as well. This is backed up with a reminder of God's "power" (v. 23*b*), echoing the same point earlier in the letter (1:16, 20; 4:21; 9:17, 20).[446]

God's severity is seen in the treatment of those who have "fallen," in other words, Jewish unbelievers. In v. 11 Paul declared that they had not "stumbled so as to fall," but he was there referring to Jewish unbelievers as a whole. Paul does not ignore the fact that some have indeed fallen, nor does he rule out the possibility that some individuals may remain in that condition. He is arguing, though, that God is well capable of grafting them back in to their own olive tree, "if they do not remain in unbelief" (v. 23). As in v. 20, faith and its opposite—and in the light of 10:4-13 "faith" can here only mean explicit faith in Jesus as the risen Lord—are the determining factors. Meanwhile, God's kindness is seen in the astonishing welcome to Gentiles who were neither looking for it nor deserving of it (9:30; 10:20); but they must "remain in God's kindness," in other words, maintain their position simply by trust in God rather than by reliance on their own social, cultural, or ethnic status. If they do not, they in turn can perfectly easily be "cut off." The force of the passage does not lie on the warning about what might happen to arrogant Gentile churches, but on what can perfectly well happen to presently unbelieving Jews: God can graft them back into the olive tree, if they will only follow the path laid down in chap. 10, abandon their present "unbelief," and believe the gospel. Verse 24, explaining how it is that God is capable of grafting them back again, provides a climax to the whole chapter so far, showing incidentally that Paul knew all along how unnatural his horticultural image had been. If God, against all the normal laws of nature and gardening, can cut you out of your natural wild olive and graft you in to a cultivated olive, then the branches that have presently been cut off can certainly be grafted back in again (Paul is aware of the horticultural near-impossibility of regrafting old branches; as in 4:17 and 11:15, what he is describing is a kind of resurrection). The emphasis of the whole chapter so far falls, apparently quite deliberately, on words that stress what Paul had said in 9:1-5: Israel remains God's cultivated olive tree; Jews, even unbelieving ones, belong to it by nature; it is "their own olive tree." That is the point Paul most wants the Gentile Christians in Rome to grasp. It is the point that the following, decisive subsection will then explain fully and finally.

We remind ourselves, arriving at this controversial passage, what Paul at least seems to have intended chaps. 9–11 to be all about. This section is all about Israel, and all about

---

445. ἀποτομία (*apotomia*); its only NT occurrence. Fitzmyer, *Romans*, 616, points out that Paul interestingly does not use the regular words for "mercy" (ἔλεος *eleos*) and "justice" (δικαιοσύνη *dikaiosynē*).

446. Fitzmyer, *Romans*, helpfully links the present passage with 1:16: "Israel's salvation cannot take place apart from the power manifested in the preaching of the gospel of Christ."

God. Israel according to the flesh has failed to believe in the gospel of the Messiah, the gospel that is God's power to salvation to all who believe (1:16), since all who confess Jesus as Lord and believe that God raised him from the dead will be saved (10:6-11). However, God made promises to Abraham and his descendants, and God's word has not failed. That sets up the problem to which, at least in Paul's mind, the present passage is the decisive answer.

Paul continues throughout this section to address Gentile Christians; when he says "you" in vv. 28, 30-31, he refers to them specifically. In those verses (11:28-32) he outlines a scheme of interchange and mutual obligation between Gentile and Jew that looks forward to 15:7-13 (which concludes the letter's theological exposition) and also to 15:27, where the Gentiles have shared in the "spiritual things" of the Jews, and are consequently under an obligation to minister to them in "fleshly things." This interchange is grounded, it seems, in the very plan of God, as Jews and Gentiles play out their unexpected roles, bringing all the human race into "disobedience" in order to have mercy upon all (11:32). ("All," as we noted earlier, cannot here mean "all individuals without distinction," but rather "the whole human race, that is, Jew and Gentile alike.")

11:25-27. Before this summary (vv. 28-32), Paul pulls together his long argument into a succinct statement—too succinct, it seems, for subsequent interpreters, who have continued to puzzle over what precisely he meant. This statement consists of an introduction, with its own explanation ("For I do not want you to be ignorant, brothers and sisters, of this mystery, so that you may not think too highly of yourselves," v. 25*a*; cf. Prov 3:7, a warning against trusting one's own judgment rather than God's); a statement of what has happened to Israel (v. 25*b*); the statement that "all Israel shall be saved" (v. 26*a*); and a composite scriptural quotation (26*b*-27). Each part of this has been variously understood, and the combinations of possibilities are multiple and intricate.[447]

11:25a. The first thing to notice is that Paul at least thinks this passage explains what has already been said. Most translations ignore the opening "for" (few translations represent the *gar* that joins the verse to what precedes it; the NEB, however, does: "For there is a deep truth here"), but Paul is quite capable of starting a new point without that or any other connecting word, and if he wrote it, he meant it. The introduction is somewhat formal ("I do not want you to be ignorant"), a tone Paul adopts when he wants special attention (cf. 1:13; 1 Cor 10:1; 12:1; 2 Cor 1:8; 1 Thess 4:13). He emphasizes once more that the point of saying all this is lest the Gentile Christians become conceited; the phrase he uses here is not easy to translate, as the versions indicate, but the overall sense is clear.[448] So far, there is nothing to indicate that Paul is making a new point, except for one thing: the fact that he speaks of "this mystery."

"This" here clearly looks forward to the "that" (ὅτι *hoti*) later in the verse: "this mystery, namely, the fact that. . . ." Paul does not often speak of "mysteries." But the other uses both in the undoubted letters and in Ephesians and Colossians suggest that he probably intends the word to refer, not to a hidden truth open only to initiates, but to an aspect of the long-range plan and purpose of God that has now been unveiled through the gospel of Jesus the Messiah (see 16:25; 1 Cor 2:1, 7; Eph 1:9; 3:3-9; 6:19; Col 1:26-27; 2:2).[449] Calling what is still to come a "mystery" does not of itself indicate that this is a new point introduced here for the first time, different to what has been said before; that could be the case, as 1 Cor 15:51 indicates, but is by no means necessary. Rather, referring to his summary statement here as a "mystery" simply indicates that it is part of God's previously hidden plan that Paul wants his readers to understand.

11:25b. What, then, has happened to Israel? An attentive reader of 9:6–11:10

---

447. Perhaps the most extreme suggestion is that of C. Plag, *Israels Wege zum Heil. Eine Untersuchung zum Römer 9 bis 11* (Stuttgart: Calwer Verlag, 1969), that 11:25-27 is an extraneous insertion into a text that, without it, would have spoken simply of the continuous conversion of some Jews.

448. The NJB's "to save you from congratulating yourselves on your own good sense" is clearly an overtranslation and perhaps misses the point from the previous verses; they are in danger not of imagining themselves to be clever, but of imagining that God is now inalienably on the side of Gentiles against Jews. See also 12:3, where a similar sense has a broader application.

449. On the background to Paul's use of "mystery," see the useful notes in Fitzmyer, *Romans*, 621; Moo, *The Epistle to the Romans*, 714; Bryan, *A Preface to Romans*, 188-89.

could have answered without difficulty: a hardening has come upon them. Paul has already said this in 11:7, summing up the sequence of thought in 9:14-24. And such a reader could also have said what this means: such a "hardening" is what happens, through the forbearance of God, to those who do not accept the gospel. "Hardening" is what happens when otherwise immediate judgment is postponed but people do not avail themselves of the chance to repent and believe. According to the regular Jewish tradition represented here by 2:1-11, such "hardening" has only two results. Either the person comes to their senses, recognizes God's forbearance, and repents; or they are fitted the more fully for the judgment that will ensue.

To this statement, which acts as a summary of previous material rather than a new point, Paul adds two phrases, both modifying the phrase "a hardening has occurred to Israel." The first phrase is ἀπὸ μέρους (*apo merous*), which often means "in part" but can also mean "for a while"; an example of each is found later in the letter ("in part," 15:15; "for a while," 15:24).[450] We should note that this phrase is normally adverbial, not adjectival, making it probable that it modifies γέγονεν (*gegonen*, "has happened"), rather than πώρωσις (*pōrōsis*, "hardening"). It is unlikely, then, that Paul means "a partial hardening"; even if *apo merous* means "in part," it will mean "has happened in part." The temporal meaning would fit, more or less, with the phrase that follows ("until the fullness of the Gentiles comes in"), in which case it would mean that the "hardening" is temporary in the sense that it postpones judgment but cannot hold it off forever. But it is more likely that, following 11:7, it implies a division between the Israel that is hardened and the Israel that has become the "remnant": "the remnant obtained it, but the rest were hardened." This reminds us that from the very beginning of the discussion Paul made it clear that there were two categories of Abraham's children (9:7-8), and indeed two categories of "Israel" itself: "not all who are of Israel are Israel" (9:6). Paul probably means, then, that a "hardening" has "partly come" upon Israel, in other words, that while

450. Other examples in BDAG 633.

one part of "Israel" now constitutes the "remnant," the other part of "Israel according to the flesh"—the great majority—has been "hardened."

The second modifying phrase indicates how long this "hardening" will last. It is holding back the judgment while the Gentile mission happens, and will be complete when "the fullness of the Gentiles" has come in. As we noted before, Paul does not envisage that all Gentiles everywhere will believe the gospel, any more than they have done so far. He believes, rather, that there is a mode of "completion" (perhaps, when the gospel has been announced to all the nations?) in God's mind. (It is less likely that he imagines God to have a complete mathematical number of future Gentile converts in mind.) Until this has been reached, final judgment will be delayed, leaving those still impenitent in their state of "hardening." And this "hardening," as we saw, leads to judgment, unless those subject to it come to their senses, repent, and believe (2:3-6). Otherwise we are forced to read into the sequence of vv. 25-26 a temporal progression that, as we shall see, is not what Paul has in mind.

11:26a. So far, Paul has still not said anything that goes beyond what we might have deduced from the entire argument to date. But that changes with "and so all Israel shall be saved." This is the sentence— a mere five words in the Greek (καὶ οὕτως πᾶς Ἰσραὴλ σωθήσεται *kai houtōs pas Israēl sōthēsetai*)—around which whole new theories have been built, theories not only of a new theological position but of fresh revelations suddenly received, visions of the end suddenly unveiled, an eschatology of almost Deus ex machina proportions in which God will put everything right and leave the late-modern world, never mind Paul, with no more questions. We should make no mistake: that is the magnitude of what is regularly proposed as the meaning of this half-verse. Whether it is the last-minute large-scale conversion to Christian faith of all Jews living at the time, or even of all Jews of every age; whether it is the eventual salvation of most or even all Jews, irrespective of Christian faith; whether it is the physical and geographical return of Jews to the land of Israel in the twentieth century, and/or their formation to be the leaders of the world after the church has been snatched away to heaven; the combinations and permutations of things that have been taught on the basis of these five words seem endless.[451]

The main positions, though, consist of various answers given to three questions: who is "all Israel," when will its "salvation" occur, and how will it be accomplished? Cranfield lists four options for the first: (a) all the elect, Jews and Gentiles alike; (b) all the elect of the nation of Israel; (c) the whole nation of Israel, including every individual; (d) national Israel as a whole, but not necessarily every individual.[452] The options on the timing are: (a) during the course of present history; (b) immediately before the second coming; (c) at the second coming. The answers to "how" are (a) through the people concerned coming to (Christian) faith; (b) through their own faith, whatever that might be; (c) through some direct divine intervention, perhaps through the agency of Christ at his second coming, which may or may not involve some kind of Christian faith.

To speak personally for a moment. When I began my study of Romans I was strongly committed to answering either (b) or (d) to the first question, either (b) or (c) to the second, and (c) to the third: that is, to understanding Paul to be saying that a very large number from national Israel would be saved at or around the time of the second coming, through the fresh revelation of the gospel that that event would supply. I changed my mind reluctantly, because of what seemed to me strong exegetical arguments; and, though this has put me in a minority even among my friends, let alone among the guild of New Testament scholars, I have seen no reason to change my mind again. I remain convinced that the right answers are (a), (a) and (a): God will save "all Israel"—that is, the whole family of Abraham, Jew and Gentile alike; this will take place during the course of present history; it will happen through their coming to Christian faith.

The principles of sound exegesis include reading short phrases in their contexts. We shall come to vv. 26b-27 presently; that is

part of the puzzle, though as we shall see it strongly supports the view of v. 26a that I shall propose. But we must be clear. The weight of the whole argument of Romans is on the side of the reading I propose. If v. 26a does indeed teach a special kind of salvation for all or most Jews, with or without Christian faith, awaiting them at the end of time, then it is exegetically out of step with the passage before it (11:1-24) and, as we shall see, with the one that follows (11:28-32); it is theologically incompatible with the entire argument of 9:6–10:21; and it undermines what Paul has emphasized again and again in Romans 1–8. If Paul has indeed, while writing the letter, received as some have suggested a fresh revelation to the effect that the whole Jewish race will at the last be saved by some special means, he did the wrong thing by adding it to what he had already written. He would have done better to put the previous eleven chapters on the fire.

In addition, there are more problems with the prevailing view than normally recognized. It is not clear why saving only the final generation of Jews would get God off the hook. That is a bit too reminiscent of some secular utopias that have justified the evils of history by reference to what will happen when progress has finally achieved its goals.[453] But if a large-scale salvation of ethnic Jews is envisaged, that is what we would have to postulate: Paul clearly does not believe that most of his own contemporaries are being or will be saved (if he did, 9:1-5 is a sham and 10:1 a mere formality). Nor is it clear why switching modes of salvation at the last moment would make God look any the less arbitrary; that is exactly what Paul has argued that God has not done up to now.[454]

But there is, fortunately, no pressing reason to move in this direction. We are not forced to suppose that "all Israel" must mean "all Jews, or all living at the time of the end." The phrase "all Israel" is familiar from at least one well-known rabbinic saying, and it is at once followed by a list of exceptions.[455]

451. A good summary of views is in Fitzmyer, *Romans*, 619-20.

452. Cranfield, *A Critical and Exegetical Commentary on the Epistle to the Romans*, 576.

453. See the suggestive essay of R. J. Bauckham, "The Year 2000 and the End of Secular Eschatology," in *Called to One Hope: Perspectives on Life to Come*, ed. J. Colwell (Carlisle: Paternoster, 2000) 249. This is a problem for the view offered by Moo, *Romans*, 722-23, and many others.

454. Against Stendahl, *Paul Among Jews and Gentiles*, 28.

455. *m.Sanh.* 10:1; cf. *T. Benj.* 10:11. The phrase "all Israel" is frequent in the biblical background; see 1 Kgs 12:1; Dan 9:11. Usually it means "the great majority of Jews alive at the time," but in Mal 3:22 it means the whole nation through time.

Indeed, Paul may well be echoing that saying: "All Israel has a share in the age to come"; it would certainly fit with his view of "salvation" to see it as the functional equivalent of the rabbinic "age to come." And, where the rabbis provided exclusion clauses to indicate that not all ethnic Jews did in fact qualify, Paul, in exactly the way we would guess from not only the whole of Romans but also Galatians and Philippians, modifies the phrase more radically. Abraham's true family are "not those of the law only, but all who share Abraham's faith" (4:16); "the Jew is the one in secret" (2:29); "you are all one in the Messiah, Jesus, and, if you belong to the Messiah, you are Abraham's seed, heirs according to promise" (Gal 3:28-9); "it is we who are 'the circumcision,' we who . . . put no confidence in the flesh" (Phil 3:3-4). These are simply the tip of the iceberg. Paul has spent half his writing life telling his readers that Abraham's family, Israel, the Jews, the circumcision, are neither reaffirmed as they stand, nor "superseded" by a superior group, nor "replaced" with someone else—that is what he is arguing against in 11:13-24—but transformed, through the death and resurrection of Israel's own Messiah and the Spirit of Israel's own God, so that Israel is now, as was always promised, both less and more than the physical family of Abraham: less, as in 9:6-13; more, as in 4:13-25.

In particular, 9:6 gives the lie to the constantly repeated assertion that one cannot make "Israel" in 11:26 mean something different from what it means in 11:25.[456] "Not all who are of Israel are in fact Israel"; Paul opened his great argument with a clear signal that he was redefining "Israel," and here the argument comes full circle. Romans 11:25 itself notes that a division has come about within ethnic Israel. Nor does this mean that "all Israel" must simply be a subcategory of ethnic Jews. As we saw in 10:1-13, Paul there announced that he was praying for the salvation of his fellow Jews, and described in detail how such salvation would come about, in accordance with Deuteronomy and Joel: all who call on the name of the Lord will be saved (10:13). That verse, as we noted, is

actually a clear pre-statement of 11:26a: "All (who call on the name of the Lord; i.e., Israel) will be saved." Paul intends that sentence both as the answer to the question of 10:1, the question of salvation for presently unbelieving Jews, and as the indication that God's mode of salvation, held out in Deuteronomy, is one that, as 9:24 had already indicated, would include Gentiles as well. The "all" of 11:26 looks back to the "all" of 10:11-13, and behind that of 4:16 ("all the seed . . . Abraham as the father of all of us"). Paul does not intend to say something radically different in 11:26 from what he has said already. The "mystery" is not a new revelation, standing over against the previous argument. It is the unveiled righteousness of God, of which Paul believed his kinsfolk to be ignorant (10:3).

In particular, of course, 10:13 looks back to 9:5: the Messiah is "God over all." The dramatic theological redefinition in 10:13, whereby "the Lord," which in the original clearly referred to YHWH, now refers to Jesus, undergirds the dramatic redefinition of God's people, whereby "Israel," as in 9:6 and Gal 6:16, now refers to the whole people of God, Gentile and Jew together. When, therefore, at the height of one of his most careful and long, drawn-out arguments, Paul declares with dramatic irony that "all Israel shall be saved," we must stand firm against the irresponsibility that would take the phrase out of its context and insist it must mean something he has carefully ruled out over and over again. However much we might want Paul to have said something else, exegesis will not sustain it.[457]

The phrase "all Israel," then, is best taken as a polemical redefinition, in line with Paul's redefinitions of "Jew" in 2:29, of "circumcision" in 2:29 and Phil 3:3, and of "seed of Abraham" in Romans 4, Galatians 3, and Rom 9:6-9. It belongs with what seems indubitably the correct reading of "the Israel of God" in Gal 6:16.[458]

When, therefore, is this salvation of "all Israel" to take place? The key is the phrase

456. E.g., Cranfield, *Romans*, 576. Good answers to this objection are supplied by J. Jeremias, "Einige vorwiegend sprachliche Beobachtungen zu Röm 11, 25-36," in de Lorenzi *Die Israelfrage nach Röm 9–11*, 199-200, 210.

457. Against both the extreme position (God will save all or most Jews irrespective of Christian faith) and the much more plausible reading (God will save a large number of Jews at the end, through Christian faith) of Fitzmyer, *Romans*, 623-24; Moo, *Romans*, 724-25.

458. See B. Witherington, *Grace in Galatia: A Commentary on St. Paul's Letter to the Galatians* (Edinburgh: T. & T. Clark, 1998) 453; J. L. Martyn, *Galatians*, AB 33A (New York: Doubleday, 1997) 574-77. There has been a considerable shift among scholarly opinion toward this reading of Gal 6:16; we may hope to see a similar shift in relation to Rom 11:26.

καὶ οὕτως (*kai houtōs*), which introduces "all Israel shall be saved." Translating this phrase "and so," as do the NRSV, the NIV, and many others, is technically not incorrect; but it may be misleading if it is supposed that Paul has a temporal sequence in mind, as many commentators have urged and many translations have indicated—in other words, if we imagine that "and so" really means "and then."[459] In English, "so" can mean, effectively, "then," or even "afterward." But the Greek οὕτως (*houtōs*) simply does not bear this sense.[460] It regularly means "thus, in this way, after this fashion, by this means." Often occurring in a pair with καθώς (*kathōs*, "just as . . . even so"), it describes the manner in which, rather than the time at which, something happens. To look no further than the present epistle (though a larger search through the NT would underline the same point), in every other occurrence in Romans *houtōs* obviously means "in this way," and never comes close to meaning "then" or "after that" (1:15; 4:18; 5:12, 15, 18-19, 21; 6:4, 11, 19; 9:20; 10:6; 11:5, 31; 12:5; 15:20; other Pauline instances of *kai houtōs* include 5:12; 1 Cor 7:17, 36; 11:28; Gal 6:2; 1 Thess 4:17; in each of these cases manner, not timing, seems clearly meant). In the present context it must mean "and in this way," or "and that is the way in which." It is the difference between saying "I do all the other chores first, and wait for the right moment, *and then* I go out and work in the garden" (a temporal sequence in which the last clause represents a new point) and "Every day I water the plants, mow the lawn, and sweep up the leaves; *and so* the garden will be at its best for the great day" (an explanatory addition in which the last clause draws attention to the significance of what has been going on all the time).

Does "in this way," then, refer to what Paul has just said ("hardening has come in part on Israel, the Gentiles are being saved—yes, and that is how God is saving 'all Israel' ")?

Or does it refer to what he is about to say ("and this is how God will save 'all Israel': he will do it in the way that scripture indicates")? The former is considerably more likely. Paul can on occasion reverse the normal order of καθώς . . . οὕτως (*kathōs . . . houtōs*, "just as . . . even so"); an obvious example is Phil 3:17 ("mark those who behave οὕτω *houtō* in this way, καθώς *kathōs* just as you have an example"); but mostly he retains the normal order, and we would have to have good extra reason to suppose that on this occasion he reversed it.[461] In addition, the phrase καθώς γέγραπται (*kathōs gegraptai*) is such a standard formula that the apparent sequence *houtōs . . . kathōs* is likely to be a coincidence. The best interpretation of what Paul is saying is this: "A hardening has come upon part of Israel until the fullness of the Gentiles comes in; and *that process is the way in which God will save 'all Israel.'* This is in fulfillment of the scripture. . . ." (On "hardening" see Deut 29:4; Isa 6:9-10; 29:10; 2 Macc 6:12-15; see also the Commentary on 9:14-18.)

11:26b-27. At this point some will no doubt protest. Surely the quotations from Isaiah that now follow are intended by Paul to refer to the parousia? And does not this mean that he is thinking, throughout this passage, of a large-scale last-minute fresh act of salvation, not the steady process of "jealousy," and consequent coming to faith, that he has spoken of throughout chap. 11 so far?

This reading of 11:26*b*-27 has undoubtedly been popular.[462] But it is demonstrably mistaken. Even a glance at the contexts of the passages Paul actually quotes—which is usually, as we have seen, an excellent guide to his meaning—will show that he intends these biblical quotations to describe once more the same process of God's dealing with Israel's (and the world's) sins that he has already described in 9:24-6 and especially 10:6-13, with 2:25-29 and 8:1-11 in the immediate background. These texts, read from the point of view of a Second Temple

---

459. Cf. the NEB's "when that has happened, the whole of Israel will be saved." Among the most explicit is the JB's "and then after this the rest of Israel will be saved as well." Significantly, the NJB has modified this to "and this is how all Israel will be saved." See Fitzmyer, *Romans*, 622-23, against, e.g., Barrett, Käsemann. Moo, *The Epistle to the Romans*, 720, appears to agree, but then smuggles back a temporal sequence that the text does not suggest.

460. See H. G. Liddell et al., eds., *Greek-English Lexicon with a Revised Supplement* (Oxford: Clarendon, 1996).

461. With Fitzmyer, *Romans*, 622-23; against Stuhlmacher, *Paul's Letter to the Romans*. See also the similar οὕτως . . . ὡς (*houtōs . . . hōs*) in 1 Cor 4:1; 9:26 (twice).

462. Käsemann, *Commentary on Romans*, 313-14; Cranfield, *A Critical and Exegetical Commentary on the Epistle to the Romans*, 578; Stuhlmacher, *Paul's Letter to the Romans*, 172. For caution on this point, see Fitzmyer, *Romans*, 624-25.

Jew like Paul, speak of the same events, of exile being undone and sins forgiven, of covenant renewed and the word of faith put in the heart by the Spirit.

The backbone of the scriptural citation comes from Isa 59:20-21. Isaiah 59 opens with a lament for Israel's continuing sinfulness; this includes vv. 7-8, which Paul has quoted as part of his indictment in 3:15-17. Then we read of YHWH himself intervening, wearing righteousness as a breastplate and salvation as a helmet (v. 17). YHWH will bring terrible judgment, so as to be feared by the nations of the earth, from east to west (vv. 18-19). In that context, "a deliverer will come to Zion [or: he will come to Zion as deliverer], and to those in Jacob who turn from transgression." At least, that is the meaning of the MT. The LXX has already altered this to mean "the deliverer will come on behalf of Zion, and will turn ungodliness away from Jacob." Paul has altered this again; the deliverer, he says, shall come out of Zion (ἥξει ἐκ Σιὼν ὁ ῥυόμενος *hēxei ek Siōn ho rhyomenos*). Perhaps he still has Deuteronomy in mind as well, because in 33:2, the beginning of the blessing of Moses, which ends with the salvation of Israel (33:28-29), we find "The Lord comes from Sinai" (Κύριος ἐκ Σινα ἥκει *Kyrios ek Sina hēkei*).[463] So far from pulling the text toward the parousia, he seems rather to be emphasizing the opposite: the redeemer, by whom he must mean Jesus the Messiah, "comes" from Zion into all the world, like YHWH "coming" from Sinai to establish the covenant and give Israel its inheritance. As the Messiah does so, he will banish ungodliness from Jacob. Once again texts that were unambiguously about YHWH in the Scriptures are taken by Paul to refer to Jesus.[464] And once again texts that looked forward to a future event are taken by Paul, not indeed to exclude the many still-future elements of his gospel (see Romans 8 and 1 Corinthians 15),[465] but to highlight the significance of what is already happening through the gospel.

"And this," continues Isaiah, "will be my covenant with them"—at which point Paul switches text, merging seamlessly into Isaiah 27. Had he continued with Isaiah 59, the description of the "covenant," which in context is obviously the covenant renewed after the exile, would tally closely with what he has said throughout the letter so far: "this is my covenant with them, says YHWH: my spirit that is upon you, and my words which I have put in your mouth, shall not depart out of your mouth, or out of the mouth of your seed . . . from now on for ever." This language of covenant renewal, replete with echoes of Joel 2, Ezekiel 36, and Jeremiah 31, also sends us back to Deuteronomy 30, as expounded in 10:6-11. God's Spirit and God's Word, placed by God in the mouths of the people, together renew the covenant. And, to move with Paul to Isa 27:9, with strong overtones of Jer 31:33-34 (38:33-34 LXX),[466] the substance of the covenant is this: God will take away Israel's sins. This is not, then, an alternative "covenant," a way to salvation for Jews and Jews only, irrespective of the entire apocalyptic salvation history Paul has laid out in 9:6–10:21. Nor has it much to do with the "pilgrimage of the nations to Zion," anticipated in some biblical and post-biblical prophecy (e.g., Isa 2:2-3; *Ps. Sol.* 17:26-46). At most, it would be an ironic reversal of that whole idea.[467] This is the same covenant renewal Paul has spoken of again and again in the letter. The hope for Israel according to the flesh lies not in clinging to its privileged status and hoping that, despite everything, God will in the end make a way of salvation other than that revealed in Jesus the Messiah and by the Spirit. Nor does it make any sense to suppose that in the last minute massive numbers of Jews alive at the time will suddenly arrive at Christian faith. What would Gentiles alive at the time say about God's impartiality, one of the major underlying themes of the whole letter? What might they say about God's constancy? No: the hope of salvation lies in the Messiah as the τέλος νόμου (*telos nomou*),

463. On the not dissimilar re-use of Deut 33:2 in 1 Enoch 1:4 see J. J. Collins, *The Apocalyptic Imagination*, 2nd ed. (Grand Rapids: Eerdmans, 1998) 48, with the comments of Bauckham, "Apocalypses," 142n. 24.

464. We do not need to postulate that such a move had already been made in pre-Pauline Judaism: the messianic reading of Isa 59:20 in *bSanh* 98a is interesting but probably irrelevant for Paul.

465. The warning of Hays, "Adam, Israel, Christ," 83, against an over-realized eschatology is well taken, but what exegetes all too often embrace here is an underrealized one.

466. Fitzmyer, *Romans*, 625, says that the present passage is "undoubtedly" a reference to the Jeremianic "new covenant."

467. See Dunn, *Romans 9–16*, 655; Moo, *The Epistle to the Romans*, 684.

the Torah's true goal, and in the renewal that remains available through him. God's salvation must be found where God has accomplished it, revealed it, and proclaimed it.

The combined texts in vv. 26*b*-27, then, undergird, rather than undermine, all that Paul has said so far in chaps. 9–11, and indeed in chaps. 1–8. Verses 25-27 as a whole fit perfectly into the flow of the chapter's argument, instead of sticking out from it like a sore thumb. This, Paul is saying, is how God is saving "all Israel," the people promised long ago to Abraham. God is doing it, not by having two tracks, a Jewish one and a Christian one (what would the "Christian one" mean for Paul if the "Jewish" bits were removed from it?); not by having a "Christian" scheme in the present and then re-inventing a "Jewish" one at the last minute; nor by suddenly relenting and allowing a partial, last-minute version of the "favored nation clause" that had been sternly ruled out up to that point; but by God doing, throughout the period that begins with the Messiah's death and resurrection, what had always been promised in Deuteronomy, Isaiah, and elsewhere. This is probably the implication of the last clause of v. 27: *"Whenever* I take away their sins" (ὅταν ἀφέλωμαι τὰς ἁμαρτίας αὐτῶν *hotan aphelōmai tas hamartias autōn*). That is, God is providing in the present time the path and the means of covenant renewal, of forgiveness, of healing and transformation, of life in and by God's Spirit: the way (in other words) of faith. Paul meant what he said in 11:23, picking up 10:1-13: They can be grafted in again, if they do not remain in unbelief. That rules out any suggestion of a mode of salvation, or a path to salvation, which does not involve the faith spoken of in chap. 10. I therefore conclude that in this passage Paul speaks of the ultimate salvation of all God's people, not only Gentiles but also an increasing number of Jews, a salvation to be brought about through the suspension of judgment (involving the "hardening" of those who do not believe) so that the gospel could spread to the Gentile world, and so by that means ethnic Jews might become "jealous" and so come to believe in their own Messiah.

11:28-32. The conclusion of the argument, like the conclusion of Sibelius's Fifth Symphony, comes in a succession of crashing theological chords, hammer-blows to round off the exposition, development, and climax. We have three typically Pauline statements, the first one with its own explanation, the second one explaining and clarifying the first, and the final one explaining and rounding off the entire sequence.

11:28-29. Paul has now spelled out the balanced view that will enable Gentile Christians to live by faith and without arrogance. He sums it up in v. 28, explaining the second part of it in terms of God's word not having failed (cf. 9:6) in v. 29. In terms of the gospel, he says, "they" (i.e., unbelieving Jews) "are enemies on your account." The NRSV adds the words "of God" after "enemies," but this is a case of protesting too much. Saying "on your account" makes it clear enough that unbelieving Israel is not the enemy of the church, but is rather hostile to the gospel itself, opposing it as a scandal and a nonsense. That, indeed, is the problem that sparks off the entire section, the problem that is heightened because of God's elective purposes and promises (9:11). The idea that unbelieving Israel is "beloved because of the ancestors"—that is, Abraham and Sarah, Isaac and Rebecca, and Jacob (and Leah and Rachel) (9:7-13), certainly does not mean that every Jew from that day to this, or every Jew in some hypothetical final generation, will eventually be saved. It means, rather, that God's own desire, like Paul's, is for them to find salvation in the full and final way it has now been achieved and unveiled. God has not written them off; that is the main point Paul is making. The contrast of "enemies . . . beloved" puts us in mind once more of 5:6-11, which explains yet again how it is that this "beloved" status can itself be the means whereby enmity can be overcome.

Why then does Paul say that they are "beloved because of the ancestors"? Once God has made promises, focused on gifts and callings, these cannot be revoked (v. 29). The word Paul uses here for "gifts" (χαρίσματα *charismata*) is used for "gifts" such as tongues and prophecy in 1 Corinthians 12 and for more general gifts of ministry in Rom 12:6; but Paul has also used it earlier in 5:15-16; 6:23 (see also 1:11) in the sense of the gifts of life, redemption, etc. We are back again to 9:6: God's word has not failed, it cannot fail, and it will not fail. God said that Abraham's family would be the bearers, as well as the recipients, of salvation, and this is what will happen. There will always be ethnic Jews among the "true Jews" of 2:29; there will always be physically circumcised people among the "true circumcision" of Phil 3:3; there will always be some from "Israel according to the flesh" (see the Commentary on 9:1-5, comparing 1 Cor 10:18) among "all Israel." Sin may have abounded through the Torah (5:20), but that was where grace more than abounded; and God will not revoke that grace.

11:30-31. As often, Paul's explanation of an initial compressed statement consists of an expanded version of the same point. In the present case, he retells once more the story of 9:6–10:21, to highlight particular features of it. He does so in two parts, the past (v. 30) and the present (v. 31). You Gentiles, he says (v. 30), were once disobedient to God. Now, however, you have received mercy—all because of their disobedience! He assumes again the connection, never fully spelled out, between Jewish disobedience to the gospel and the coming to faith of Gentiles (see the Commentary on 11:11-16). The point he is stressing is that, under God, the Gentiles depend for their chance at salvation on the "casting away" of Israel according to the flesh. They should no more look down on this Israel, therefore, than they would on the Messiah himself because of his salvific death. This leads naturally to the statement of the present situation (v. 31): in the same way, they have now been disobedient, but this is so that they too may now receive mercy.

What about the extra clause, "by the mercy shown to you"? In the Greek it is much more natural to take it with the verb "they have been disobedient." But the balance of the two verses, and the sense, make it likely that the NRSV and the NIV are correct to take it with "that they may receive mercy." The sense, in fact, is exactly that of 10:19 and 11:13-14: the mercy shown to Gentiles is meant to make unbelieving Jews "jealous," and so bring them to faith and

salvation. If, however, the more likely meaning of the Greek is followed, Paul's sense must be that Jewish disobedience was in some way "caused" by the mercy shown to Gentiles—a new idea to the section, which is in itself unlikely at this moment when he is summing up.[468]

But when does this mercy happen? The word "now," included in the text of both the NRSV and the NIV, is missing in some good MSS. Others, however, have it, and the fact that a few lesser ones read "subsequently" suggests that there was a word at that point that some scribes have seen fit to alter.[469] Even if this "now" were missing, however, the earlier occurrence of the same word in v. 31, together with the hint that this mercy comes about "because of the mercy shown to you," would be enough to tell us what Paul thinks is going on. The mercy that is shown to Israel according to the flesh is not something for which they will have to wait until some putative final day; it is not, therefore, something that can get the church off the hook by postponing a serious reckoning with contemporary Judaism until a conveniently delayed eschaton—as the laissez-faire thought of the Enlightenment might urge.[470] It is available "now"; and Paul's kinsfolk can, he hopes and believes, be provoked into seeking it by being "jealous" of the way in which Israel's privileges are being enjoyed by Gentiles. And this is precisely where the section began (9:1-5).

11:32. The final explanatory statement, as is appropriate, is about God. In an echo of Gal 3:22, Paul declares that God has locked up the whole human race in a prison called "disobedience," in order that what they then receive will be a matter of sheer mercy (for the sense of "mercy on all," see Wis 11:23).

In order to understand and appreciate the point Paul is making, we have to cast our minds back through the long argument of the letter so far. He declared, and demonstrated, that the whole human race was under the power of sin. All were "in Adam," and Israel's

---

468. On the problem, see Bryan, *A Preface to Romans*, 193; Fitzmyer, *Romans*, 627.
469. νῦν (*nyn*): omitted by P46, A and others; included by ℵ, B and the first hand in D. For details see Fitzmyer, *Romans*, 628; Moo, *Romans*, 711, 735.
470. See K. Barth, *Church Dogmatics* 2.2.305.

Torah only bound the nation the more tightly to sin and thence to death. But Israel was nevertheless the bearer of the promise, and the promise would be honored by God even if all humans failed. The Messiah, coming as the faithful Israelite, succeeded where all others had failed; his faithful, obedient death and resurrection accomplished salvation for all who believed. But how could God bring salvation not only to Gentiles—who were so far outside that it was obvious they could only come in by sheer grace and mercy—but also to Jews? How could God prevent it from seeming as though there were, after all, a "favored nation clause"? Paul's answer is that God has imprisoned Israel, too, within "disobedience," so that, if and when Jews according to the flesh come to faith in Jesus as the risen Messiah and Lord, the justification they enjoy, and the salvation they await, will be for them, as much as for Gentiles, a matter of mercy from start to finish. The word of God has not failed. God has been true to the covenant; God's righteousness has been unveiled in the gospel of Jesus the Messiah, "to the Jew first, and also equally to the Greek" (1:17). Verse 32 is the conclusion, not only to chaps. 9–11, but to the whole letter so far. (See Reflections at 11:33-36.)

Romans 11:33-36, Praise to the All-Wise God

COMMENTARY

The concluding doxology emphasizes the sovereignty and inscrutability of God. Paul does not think that God's ways and purposes are now still invisible; they have been revealed in the Messiah. But he does believe that without the revelation granted in the gospel nobody would ever have worked them out. And yet, seen with hindsight, God's way of putting the world to rights, God's way of doing all things from creation to new creation, turns out to be spectacularly right, full of wisdom and insight, of appropriate judgment and overflowing mercy.

This is the longest of Paul's doxologies, almost as long as his two great christological poems (Phil 2:6-11 and Col 1:15-20), and not without echoes of both. It is rooted, as his thought often is, in the Jewish Wisdom tradition (see, e.g., 1 Cor 1:17–2:16; 3:18-23; 8:1-6; cf. 2 Bar 14:8-9; 20:4; 1QH 7:26-33; 10:3-7).[471] What is revealed in the gospel of Jesus is not something other than the wisdom that ancient Jewish sages sought and celebrated, but the very same thing now made known for the salvation of the world.

11:33. Paul's opening words of praise stand on the edge of a cliff, looking down into the fathomless sea of God's riches. Sometimes, in prayer, one gets a glimpse like this, and the vastness, the teeming life, the power, the overall order and beauty, are beyond words. All one can do is point, and that is what this first sentence does. Look, he says, at the riches of God; look at God's wisdom and knowledge. The historical sweep of the divine purpose; the intimate understanding of human motivation; the interlocking of justice and mercy, kindness and severity, that bear patiently with terrible human wickedness and grieve over terrible human loss and tragedy, that yearn for humans to come back to the one in whose image they were made and find true life! All this is contained in these words: riches, wisdom, and knowledge. Paul can only stand in awe. (The NRSV's "riches *and* wisdom *and* knowledge" is more likely than the NIV's "riches *of* wisdom and knowledge.")[472]

But it is not only what God has and is. It is also what God decides and does. God's "judgments," decisions about the world and about humans, cannot be searched out. We humans glimpse them from time to time, we trace small parts of them, but for the most part they are far out of our sight, where they belong. Human arrogance seizes upon this inscrutability as a reason to doubt, to mock, or to question God's wisdom or goodness; the humility proper to faith stands in awe that

471. See E. E. Johnson, *The Function of Apocalyptic and Wisdom Traditions in Romans 9–11*, SBLDS 109 (Atlanta: Scholars Press, 1989) 168-71.

472. See Moo, *Romans*, 741.

the God of all creation is the God of the gospel of Jesus, whose utter trustworthiness was demonstrated once for all in Jesus' resurrection.

11:34-35. At the heart of the hymn of praise Paul places one more double scriptural quotation, partly from his beloved Isaiah and partly from the book of Job, the greatest of biblical wrestlings with the problem of God's justice and human suffering. "Who has known the mind of the Lord?" asks Isaiah (40:13) at the start of his mighty exposition of God's creative power, the power now placed at the service of Israel-in-exile, God's unchangeable might now to be unleashed to bring about the return from exile through the work of the servant. Paul has cast himself in the role of present-day prophet, announcing the Isaianic gospel of the servant (10:14-17); now he celebrates Isaiah's God, the one through whom that gospel is initiated and confirmed. The quotation from Job 41:11 [41:3 LXX] comes from one of the most astonishing biblical statements of the sovereignty of God over all creation. God is in nobody's debt; nobody ever gives God a gift and stands back smug in the knowledge that God must now repay. All is of grace, and only of grace; to think otherwise is not to forget merely some fine-tuned or subtle bit of theology, but rather to forget the meaning of the word "God" itself in the biblical tradition. The God whom Paul has glimpsed in the gospel, whose justice and mercy he has been expounding in this his greatest letter, is vast and mysterious as the sea, near and intimate as breath, decisive and compassionate as a Galilean holy man on his way to a cruel death. The Wisdom tradition, the prophetic tradition, the Pentateuch, the psalms—all are now poured out in justice and mercy, through the gospel of Jesus the Messiah and the power of the Spirit. Let us not imagine that because neither Jesus nor the Spirit are named in vv. 33-36 Paul has forgotten them. If Romans 11 was not built foursquare upon Romans 8 it would not be able to stand upright.[473]

11:36. But stand it does, because the God of whom it speaks is the one from whom, through whom, and to whom are all things.[474] Elsewhere, when Paul uses this language (1 Cor 8:6; Col 1:15-20), he is quite explicit. Jesus the Messiah, the Lord, the Son, is the one "through whom" the one God, the Father, has acted and does act in creation and redemption. The Holy Spirit, the Spirit of the Son, is the one through whom Father and Son act together to renew the covenant with a worldwide family, to bring the "word" very near, on the lips and in the heart. Paul has no need to spell out the detail in this short doxology, because he has already painted it in from so many angles and now just wishes to stand back and gaze in wonder. To this God, he concludes, be glory forever, Amen. Giving glory to God was what humankind failed to do (1:21), which was why humankind itself fell short of that glory (3:23). Abraham, in faith, gave glory to God (4:20), believing that God was indeed able to keep the life-giving promises. Now, in hope, through the gospel of the Messiah, Jesus, the glory is restored (5:2; 8:30); but the glory remains God's, God's to give, God's to be reflected back to God, God's own forever.

In Romans 9–11 Paul belongs in the tradition of the great psalmists. He starts with an urgent problem; he wrestles with it in grief and prayer; he retells the story of Israel, laying out God's acts from of old and in the present. Finally he bursts through to a paean of praise. From this point in the letter we look back and see, as glorious mountain peaks, 4:24-25 and particularly 8:28-30 and 38-39. But where we now stand is higher than them all, so high that some climbers feel dizzy and prefer to return quickly to the lower slopes. Paul is not of such a mind. He will stay and give praise. This, he implies, is what we humans, we Jews, were made for.

---

473. We should not ignore the parallel to v. 34 in 1 Cor 2:16, where "the Lord" is, of course, Jesus; see also 1 Cor 3:21-23. We should at least hold open the posibility that the κύριος (*kyrios*) of v. 34 is the same as that in 10:13.

474. There are similar statements in some Stoic writings (see Dunn, *Romans 9–16*, 701-2), but Paul's thought remains anchored in Judaism.

REFLECTIONS

1. Of the two most urgent matters that concern today's interpreter coming to terms with Romans 11, the first is undoubtedly the way in which Christian readers today can make Paul's argument their own without losing their balance. On the one hand there lies the long, ugly tradition that Paul was doing his best to head off, the tradition of denouncing the Jews and declaring that they are an accursed race. We all know where that leads. On the other hand there lies the overreaction, the eagerness to say that Paul has no critique whatever of Israel according to the flesh, the readiness to pull his text completely out of shape if only we do not (dreaded thought!) have to be so politically ignorant, naive, or simply incorrect as to say that Jesus was and is the promised Messiah and that Paul envisages salvation coming only by the route of confessing him as Lord and believing that God raised him from the dead.

Of course, a solution lies close at hand—a solution that many preachers are only too happy to use on other texts. It is perfectly possible to say that Paul says one thing but that we, today, must believe and live by something else. The discomfort one may feel at abandoning the text as authoritative will be more than made up for by the relieved smiles of the congregation, who no longer need be shocked by attitudes that modern and postmodern thought are eager to label as arrogant, imperialistic, or exclusive—not noticing, of course, that to treat texts in this way is to be guilty, oneself, of all those things. Romans 2:1 has hemeneutical as well as ethical implications. Perhaps one problem underlying at least some post-Holocaust theology is that, being eager to avoid the hard, high, and all-embracing claims of the gospel in other areas of our lives, we are a bit too keen to point out ways in which these claims, when misapplied in the social and political sphere, have done damage, and worse than damage, to peoples and communities.

Yet the challenge of Paul's analysis of the problem of Israel remains, and perhaps only now, two generations after the Nazi Holocaust, can we start to look at it again with the clarity of hindsight not only on the 1930s and 1940s but on that which has been done, with the Holocaust as pretext, in the Middle East over the last fifty years. Christianity and Judaism are, or ought to be, close cousins, yet the very closeness highlights differences as well as similarities, claims made by both that might both be false but that cannot both be true.[475] And if Christians remain loyal to Jesus of Nazareth they cannot evade the challenge of his Messiahship, upon which is based his universal lordship. He is not a private or a tame savior, available on tap, like a favorite beer, for those who want some salvation now and then. If he is not Messiah and Lord, the whole of Christianity is indeed based on a mistake and ought to be abandoned. But what if he is?

If he is, then however much breast-beating remains appropriate for Christians after centuries of arrogance and violence toward Paul's, and Jesus', kinsfolk according to the flesh, there must still be the agony (not the easy acquiescence) that sees them still in rebellion against the gospel; there must still be the prayer (not merely the patronizing acceptance of "otherness") that seeks salvation on their behalf. It is noticeable that at no point in Romans 9–11 does Paul say that he evangelizes Jews directly. He remains the missionary to the Gentiles. We assume that Peter and others still undertake their mission to the Jews (Gal 2:9); but all that Paul will say is that his work with Gentiles is designed to make his kinsfolk jealous and so save some of them. He will pray for them; he will do his own work with one eye on them; he will take a collection, no doubt at considerable personal danger both of misunderstanding and of violence on the road, in order to make his kinsfolk see that Gentiles are sharing their blessings, their common life; and he will tell the Roman church in no uncertain terms not to write them off, not

---

475. See Wright, *The New Testament and the People of God*, 471-76.

to imagine that Jews can no longer be welcomed into the family of the Messiah. That, for Paul, would be the very height of anti-Judaism.

Here, in fact, is the crowning irony of today's attempt to appropriate Romans 9–11. For Paul, anti-Judaism would mean imagining that Jews cannot come to faith in Jesus. For many today, anti-Judaism means supposing that they can and should. There is no easy way through this dilemma. Imagine what it was like for the Prodigal Son, and his older brother, the morning after the party with the fatted calf.[476]

Paul's "solution" is itself challenging and worrying. Jews, we ask, "jealous" of Gentile Christians? The very thought is laughable in much of the modern world. The church has cut such a sorry figure, has seemingly done so much to alienate the older brother, that, for all the internal problems and divisions of contemporary Judaism, there is little reason to suppose that today's Jews look at today's Christians and say to themselves "there they are, enjoying our privileges!" To ask the question, what might the church have to be like for serious-minded Jews even to think like that for one minute, is to raise all sorts of other questions that Romans 9–11 was not written to address. But it is perhaps the right place at which to start reflecting on how those who wish to take Paul seriously might go about doing and being in our own day what he believed himself called to do and be in his own in relation to his beloved kinsfolk, his people "according to the flesh."

As one aspect of this, we can scarcely ignore, as is sometimes done as though they were a category mistake, those who in our own churches are ethnically Jewish but Christian by conviction, baptism, and life. They are Paul's heirs indeed, and need and deserve our prayers for their particular and often painful witness.

2. The second obvious and necessary point is that Paul nowhere gives the slightest indication that ethnic Israel will one day return to their land and set up an independent state, which will in due course become the vehicle of God's blessing to the world. Of course, in his day his kinsfolk were still living in the land and worshiping in the Temple. Most Jews were already in the Diaspora, but many were living in the holy land, and had been for centuries. There was no thought of that awful second exile, of the desolations of 70 CE and 135 CE, of the banishment to which, in the eyes of many, the creation of the modern state of Israel has provided the answer. But even if there had been, there is nothing in Romans or elsewhere in Paul to give any theological support to the latter notion. The roots of the return-to-the-land theology that has become so extraordinarily popular among some churches in our own day are to be sought in the dispensationalist speculations of the nineteenth century, not in the apostolic writings of the first. As far as Paul is concerned, the promise to Abraham and his family was that they would inherit the world (Rom 4:13), the world that would share in the freedom of the glory of God's children (8:18-27). Any attempt to give a Christian gloss to the Middle Eastern political events of 1947 and thereafter is without exegetical foundation.

3. At the heart of Romans 9–11 there lies the humility that recognizes God as God and does not try to second-guess or criticize what God has planned and done. Cynics and skeptics of every age, not only the much-vaunted "humankind come of age" of the Enlightenment, have of course questioned everything, challenged everything, put God in the dock and declared that such a being either does not exist or, if he/she/it does, they disapprove of his/her/its actions. Fearful that every authority is necessarily oppressive, and that every order that does not proceed from within oneself is manipulative, our present-day orthodoxy has left God on the margins, an aid to spiritual well-being for those who feel they need it. But if God is the creator, and we are creatures; if God is holy, and we are sinful—and if these two things are not so, why have we kept company with Paul in the first place?—then there is a proper and grateful humility that

476. See Wright, *For All God's Worth*, chap. 13.

is neither oppressed nor manipulated, a giving glory to God that enhances and does not diminish our true humanness. There is a time to ask the hard questions, and Paul encourages us to do so. There is also a time for recognizing, like Job, that our questions have missed the point, and that God's answers are, for the best of reasons, final.

4. Underneath Paul's repeated warning to the Gentile Christians of Rome we hear a warning that is as important in its different ways in today's church and world as his was at the time. If Paul has criticized his kinsfolk according to the flesh for their "boast," he will also point out to the Gentiles, who in Jewish terms had nothing to boast of, that there is such a thing as inverted "boasting." Most of the "isms" of our time have their reverse side, as different social, cultural, ethnic, gender-based, and agenda-based groups clamber over one another in the anguished quest for the high moral ground. Inverted prejudice, even when completely explicable as defense or natural reaction, as the long scream of the victim, is still prejudice. Where, as in the case of Rome, it may just happen to chime in with a prejudice of long standing in the local culture, it is doubly dangerous.

5. The detailed argument of Romans 9–11 works through the key issue that faced Paul, the issue of unbelieving Jews and of God's faithfulness to the age-old promises. But the same argument could be applied in several other spheres. Starting from the promise to redeem the whole creation (8:18-27), one could ask the equivalent question and work through to a similar answer: has God forgotten the promise to creation? No, the argument would run if we constructed it in parallel to Romans 9–11, because the promise always envisaged death and rebirth. There are already, however, signs of rebirth, of healing and new life; and God intends that there should be more of them. Just as Paul rules out Jewish privilege on the one hand and Gentile rejection of Jews on the other, so a Christian cosmology would rule out the neo-pagan or pantheistic uncritical affirmation of the created order on the one hand and the dualist rejection of it on the other. Just because we are not pantheists there is no reason to suggest that God will not redeem the whole creation. Indeed, the categories of new covenant and redemption developed by Paul in these chapters could well prove valuable in thinking through several similar or related issues.

6. At the heart of many of these issues, as of Romans 9–11 itself, lies the challenge of learning to tell the story. Partly this is a matter of unlearning misleading ways of telling the story of God, the world, Israel, Jesus, and the church. It takes a certain skill to unpack the stories that are implicitly being told, in both church and world, and to make the right adjustments, additions, or deletions to bring them into line with the many-stranded but essentially quite simple story Paul himself is telling. Once that is done, and the story is regularly checked for signs of wear and tear—particularly, for signs that it is becoming self-congratulatory or triumphalistic—it becomes one of the most basic tools of Christian thinking, apologetic, and instruction. Stories, not least the large-scale story from creation to new creation, from covenant to renewed covenant, from Abraham to Moses to the Messiah to final salvation, have their own dynamic. They are bottom-line reality—arguably, if Paul is anything to go by, more bottom-line even than "doctrines." When Paul wants to confront, to comfort, to build up, to worship, his regular way of doing so, admirably displayed in these chapters, is not to offer two or three abstract doctrines. It is to tell the story and invite his readers to make it their own. That remains a prime task of Christian teaching.

ROMANS 12:1–16:27

GOD'S CALL TO WORSHIP, HOLINESS, AND UNITY

OVERVIEW

Paul may be exhilarated by the vision he has laid before us, but he is by no means exhausted. His main argument is not done yet, despite impressions to the contrary.[477] There is, to be sure, a huge turn at this point in both content and (for the most part) style. But the exposition of "the gospel" that began with 1:3-4—the gospel, that is, which announces Jesus the Messiah, whose resurrection demonstrates that he is indeed God's Son and marks him out as the world's true Lord—this exposition continues right through to its closing statement in 15:7-13, one of the most telling theological passages in the letter, which completes the huge circle begun in chapter 1. So, too, the unveiling of God's "righteousness," God's saving justice, through this gospel, is not complete until Paul has shown how the "justified" community lives its life on the basis of its shared belief in Jesus as Lord; until, that is, what we might call the κοινωνία τῆς πίστεως (*koinōnia tēs pisteōs*), the "fellowship of faith," matches and embodies the δικαιοσύνη τῆς πίστεως (*dikaiosynētēs pisteōs*), the "righteousness of faith." And as he does so we discover that one of the major theological themes of chapters 1–11—God's bringing together of Jew and Gentile in the Messiah—now becomes also one of the major practical themes of chaps. 12–16.

But that is only the beginning. Romans 12–16 is the ultimate answer to those who suggest that Paul's "ethics" are not really related to his "theology."[478] Indeed, the way those two terms have sometimes been used implies that belief and behavior are of their very nature completely separate human activities, whereas for Paul they are inextricably interwoven. They are the breath and blood of Christian living, the twin signs of life. Here as elsewhere we should beware of reading back into Paul the disjunctions of much later philosophy, such as that between "is" and "ought," between facts and values. Paul has little time for abstractions like "values," except as they, like every other human thought, are swept up into the revitalized human life that the gospel brings about.

That is indeed the point, and even a glance at the opening of the section (12:1-2) indicates that Paul is stitching the letter together with threads of many colors. It is not just a matter of verbal links and echoes, but of major themes now to be restated, as in a symphony, in a new key perhaps but easily recognizable by all but the tone deaf. God's "mercies" generate an appeal to those who know and have received them. The renewal and harmony of body and mind looks back to the scene of human devastation in chapter 1, to the initial reversal of this in chapter 4, and especially to the promise of restoration, beginning indeed in the present time, in chapter 8. But—in case anyone should think that therefore, despite all that was said above, the argument does indeed skip from chapter 8 to chapter 12—the underlying thrust of these verses is that Christians, Jew and Gentile alike, now offer to the one true God the full and final sacrificial worship in which Israel's worship (cf. 9:4) is made complete. It is, in fact, because of 9–11 that Paul can now explain how it is that all the forward pointers in chaps. 1–8 can now be realized. Ecclesiology—if that is the best word for Paul's rich and nuanced understanding of God's people in the Messiah—provides both context and challenge for "ethics."

---

477. J. Ziesler, *Paul's Letter to the Romans* (Philadelphia: Trinity Press International, 1989) 290.

478. Here I agree strongly with Hays, *The Moral Vision of the New Testament*, esp. 16-59.

So, of course, does eschatology. Romans 12:1-2 draws explicitly on the essentially Second Temple Jewish view that world history divides into two ages, the "present age" and the "age to come," and insists that the two now overlap and that Christians belong in the latter. It is not, then, that the gospel, and the power of the Spirit, simply enable Christians to do somewhat better what other people have tried to do. It is, rather, that the new day has begun to dawn, and that those who belong to the Messiah must live in its light rather than in the darkness of the present world. This indicates, incidentally but helpfully, how this whole section divides up: 12:1-2 points forward to 13:11-14, giving the first two chapters an eschatological framework within which the wide-ranging general instructions of 12:3–13:10 are to be understood (see below), before 14:1–15:13 offer more specific and detailed exposition of a particular issue.[479]

Nor are ecclesiology and eschatology absent from the final division, 15:14–16:27. Paul's travel plans (to go on, via Rome, to Spain), and his request for help (15:14-24), are tightly integrated into his vision of his own vocation as the Apostle to the Gentiles and into the inner meaning and dynamic of the gospel itself (see 1:1-7 with 1:8-15). His present preoccupation—that he is about to go to Jerusalem with a gift of money collected from Gentile churches—belongs with the same understanding (15:25-33). The unusually lengthy closing greetings (16:1-16, 21-23), and the other concluding remarks (16:17-20, 25-27), are likewise not simply tossed off to complete the letter, but make their own point in practical outworking of what has been said already.

It is striking that at several points in this section Paul seems to be echoing the teaching of Jesus himself—something that, notoriously, he does very little.[480] Specific examples will be noted below; none is uncontroversial, but the cumulative effect may be worth pondering. We cannot tell from what sources Paul knew of such material; nor can we tell (since he never here says "as Jesus taught us" or anything like

it) whether the sayings were well enough known that he could appeal to Jesus' authority by implication, or whether they were little enough known at this stage that he would have remained content for the allusions to go unnoticed. I incline to the former view; Paul, I believe, saw Jesus not simply as the crucified and risen Messiah and Lord but also as the one whose teaching articulated the way of life belonging to the new age he came to inaugurate. That this does not reduce Jesus to the status of a mere moral teacher, or cast doubt on the centrality of his death and resurrection, should be obvious.

This point is underscored by another introductory reflection. The pattern of Christian living that Paul sets out here includes the call not to be overcome by evil, but to overcome evil with good (12:21). This challenge, summarizing much of the opening chapter, is then developed further in 15:7-8, where its christological underpinnings become explicit; the pattern of overcoming evil not by revenge but by patient suffering and trust in the justice of God (12:14-21) is one of the most striking themes in early Christianity. The great theological and christological themes may be muted in this section, but we do not have to look very far to see that their lack of explicit mention is a sign, not that they are forgotten, but that they are everywhere presupposed.

To what extent, then, are these chapters "general teaching," the kind of thing Paul would have said to any church in any situation, and to what extent are they specific to the church in Rome? The attempt to tie down the instructions here, particularly those of chapters 14 and 15, to specific groups and situations in the Roman church was given a new boost by the work of Paul Minear a generation ago.[481] There is no agreement on how this works out in detail (or on how much knowledge about groups and parties in Rome Paul might actually have had), but many agree that here at least Paul has a particular aim specific to the Roman church, even if we cannot always be sure who precisely the "strong" and the "weak" may have been and to what extent they represented points of view, or church groups, familiar to Paul from other settings as well (see the Overview

479. See Moo, *The Epistle to the Romans*, 747.

480. See particularly M. Thompson, *Clothed with Christ: The Example and Teaching of Jesus in Romans 12.1–15.13*, JSNTSup (Sheffield: Sheffield Academic, 1991).

481. P. Minear, *The Obedience of Faith: the Purposes of Paul in the Epistle to the Romans* (London: SCM, 1971).

of 14:1–15:13). The view taken here is that chapters 12 and 13 are more general, laying foundations, though not without an eye to the particular situation, and that chapters 14 and 15 are more specific, though not without an eye to other situations (cf. chaps. 14–15 with 1 Corinthians 8–10, for instance) and other related issues. This in turn may help us, as more of the Roman situation comes into view, to understand better why Paul wrote this letter to this church at this moment.[482]

As we have seen, it would be wrong to drive a wedge between chaps. 1–11 and chaps. 12–16, or between two things labeled "Pauline theology" and "Pauline ethics." Paul's theology is always ethical, and his ethics are always theological, even if some of the letters (not all) seem to divide quite neatly into two sections that invite that kind of labeling (the best example is Ephesians 1–6, which is ironic in view of the majority view that it was not written by Paul; obvious counterexamples include the Corinthian and Thessalonian letters). Romans 6 and 8 are hardly nonethical, just as the present section is hardly nontheological. However, it is striking that in the present section some of the key words and themes from chaps. 1–11 are completely absent. The "righteousness"/"justice" word group (δικαιοσύνη *dikaiosynē* and its cognates) simply does not occur. "Faith" is an important theme (12:3, 6; 14:1-2, 23-24), but its meaning has sometimes been thought different from what was discussed in chapters 3–4 and 10. Jesus the Messiah is not highlighted until 13:14, though he is then omnipresent in 14:1–15:13. We should not suppose that he is absent from Paul's mind at any point in 12–13; in fact, as we shall see, the apparently incidental reference to being "in Christ" in 12:5 is probably to be taken as thematic. However, there is no extended discussion of him or his work, and no reference in these first two chapters to either his death or his resurrection. Unlike chaps. 5–8 and 9–11, there is no sense that the underlying biblical references, allusions, and echoes are evoking a larger scriptural narrative; the string of references in 15:7-13, to be sure, points to the eschatological and messianic hope of Israel, but neither there nor elsewhere in the section does Paul attempt to lay out the rest of the grand story. He has already done that, and can presuppose it here. Granted that none of this means a move away from theology toward a detached set of behavioral instructions, what does it signify?

It signifies, I think, that Paul has completed the main structure of the letter and does not need to repeat himself. We have reached the summit of the mountain range, the place from which you can see around in all directions; but the journey must now continue, down the other side, without the strenuous work of climbing, but still with a sense of continuity in our aim and goal. From time to time Paul will refer to the height he has now reached, and perhaps to the path up which he has climbed; but what follows now, with the characteristic "therefore" (οὖν *oun*) of 12:1, is about results, not process.

The last five chapters of Romans divide naturally, then, into two: 12:1–15:13 and 15:14–16:27. The former, which is also the last major section of theological exposition in the letter, subdivides into two segments of nearly identical length: 12:1–13:14 (35 verses) and 14:1–15:13 (36 verses), the first part being more general and the second more specific. In turn 12:1–13:14 divides, though this is more complicated and disputed, into six: 12:1-2 (introduction and foundation); 12:3-13 (unity in the church through each exercising their gifts); 12:14-21 (the church's life, particularly facing those outside); 13:1-7 (responsibility toward authorities); 13:8-10 (the overriding responsibility of love); and 13:11-14 (living in the light of God's dawning day). Of these divisions, the hardest decision is whether to see 12:9-13 as belonging with 12:3-8 (the view taken here), as a separate section in itself, or as introducing 12:14-21; but this is a matter more of tidiness than of content.[483] More interesting is the place of 13:1-7; as we shall see at the relevant point, the section has often been regarded as something of a cuckoo in the nest of Romans, but in fact it goes very closely with the preceding passage, which deals with avoiding vengeance. Chapters 12 and 13, taken together, thus form a circle or chiasm:

482. For the view that Romans 12–13 as well as 14–15 are directed more specifically to the Roman situation see J. Moiser, "Rethinking Romans 12–15," *NTS* 36 (1990) 571-82.

483. The mention of "good and evil" in 12:9, 21 might suggest that 12:9-21 is a single section; but these are such general terms that using them as a structural marker strains the point somewhat. Against Fitzmyer, *Romans*, 658. The word for "evil" is different (πονηρόν *ponēron* in v. 9; κακόν *kakon* in v. 21).

A   12:1-2
  B   12:3-13
    C   12:14-21
    C´   13:1-7
  B´   13:8-10
A´   13:11-14

Romans 12:1-2 set out the Christian's obligation within the dawning "age to come," which joins up with 13:11-14. The appeal for unity and love (12:3-8, 9-13) is matched in turn by 13:8-10. This leaves 12:14–13:7 at the center of the section, dealing from two different angles with the problems of living as citizens of God's kingdom (see Phil 3:20) while also continuing to live in the "present world" with its various challenges.

ROMANS 12:1-2, THE WORSHIP OF BODY AND MIND

COMMENTARY

The opening two verses of the section are as dense as any passage in Paul, and as so often they state concisely a theme that will then be unpacked and explored in various different ways. The key transition word is "therefore": not the only time Paul draws an ethical conclusion in this letter (see, e.g., 6:12; 8:12), but the most obvious moment of transition between the two major parts of the letter (see Overview). But the key word that tells us what sort of material is to come is the opening παρακαλῶ (*parakalō*), the modern Greek word for "please," as in "Please, will you do . . . ?" This is a many-sided word for Paul, ranging from "comfort" to "exhort," and the present instance is clearly closer to the latter; but this is not an empty exhortation, trying by rhetorical force to make people do things they might otherwise not, but an appeal based squarely on what has gone before. The RSV's and the NRSV's "appeal" is therefore preferable to the NIV's and the NJB's "urge," though the latter supplies a force to this opening sentence that should not be softened. (The NEB's and REB's "implore" sounds like a desperate and emotional begging, which is quite inappropriate.)

The ground of the exhortation is "the mercies of God." Paul has spoken of God's "mercy" often enough in the preceding chapters to make it clear that the present appeal is grounded not simply on chaps. 1–8 but on chaps. 9–11 in particular. True, the word he uses here (οἰκτιρμῶν *oiktirmōn*; the plural reflects underlying Hebrew usage) is unusual for Paul (ἔλεος *eleos* is more common, as in 11:31). But its cognate verb has occurred in his quotation of Exod 33:19 at 9:15, and it stands here as a way of summing up "the depth of God's riches and wisdom and knowledge" as invoked in 11:33.

In particular, the opening verse indicates that the foundation of all Christian obedience is that those in Christ, indwelt by the Spirit, are to offer to God the true sacrificial worship to which the cult of the Jerusalem Temple had all along pointed. Romans 12:1 does with temple worship, in other words, what 2:25-29 did with circumcision, just as 15:7-13, at the close of the section and of the letter's great argument, envisages Jew and Gentile alike joining in worship of the true God under the lordship of the Messiah. This can hardly be overemphasized. Paul has spoken of the "worship" that was one of Israel's privileges (9:4); now he makes it clear, as with the other elements in that list, that this worship is now offered by all Christians, Jew and Gentile alike (see also 10:9-13).

This sacrificial worship, though not involving animal sacrifices, is not simply "spiritual" in the sense of "not involving physical sacrifices." Many Jews of Paul's day and before, not to mention the post-70 rabbis, spoke of nonsacrificial forms of worship as the equivalent of the temple cult. This goes back, indeed, to the psalms themselves (Ps 141:2).[484] But here, though this element is

484. For details of later writings see Wright, *The New Testament and the People of God*, 229n. 48.

certainly present, we should not be too eager to press it. Paul envisages the sacrifices in question as being physical, indeed animal; but the animals are human, and they are not to be ritually slaughtered but "presented" to God, still alive. What are to be presented are the "bodies" of Christian worshipers. As we saw earlier, the word "body" enables Paul to look in both directions; at the Christian still living within the world of space, time, and matter, as here, and as living within the multiple pressures and temptations that this places upon us, as in 8:13 where "the deeds of the body" are indeed to be "put to death."[485] Here as there, however, the point of "body" is not that it refers to one part only of the human totality, but that it refers to the complete person seen from one point of view: the point of view in which the human being lives as a physical object within space and time. This whole self is to be "presented"—the word itself carries sacrificial overtones—to God; this implies that we should expect Christian worship to have an emphaticaly bodily character, however much it is also true that worship must be, in Johannine language, "in spirit and in truth" (John 4:23). It must also be stressed that, though the primary worship, the primary "presentation" that Paul envisages, is the obedience of the whole person to the commands that follow, it would be foolish to exclude from this the actual occasions of formal and informal worship when the person is physically present and performs bodily actions in the course of that worship.

These sacrifices are "holy" (the word carries here, as often, both its sense of moral uprightness and its allusion to the temple cult; hence the NJB's "dedicated"), and "well-pleasing to God." (KJV, RSV, NRSV, "acceptable" is possible, but the word is strong and should not be watered down to give the idea that God might just about be prepared to accept these sacrifices.) Paul, unusually, repeats the word "well-pleasing" in the very next verse, making it clear that for him at least what a Christian does, in Christ and by the Spirit, gives actual pleasure to God. This is counterintuitive for many Christians, schooled to insist that nothing we do can commend ourselves

to God. But Paul insists in several passages that Christian worship and obedience, holiness and unity do indeed please God, and if we have articulated his other doctrines (e.g., justification) in such a way as to exclude this notion, we have clearly misrepresented him. (See 14:18; 2 Cor 5:9; Eph 5:10; Phil 4:18; Col 3:20—all the same word as here; see also the use of ἀρέσκω [areskō] in 1 Cor 7:32; 1 Thess 2:4; 4:1; and, most strikingly, Rom 8:8, where "those in the flesh" cannot please God but, it is strongly implied, "those in the Spirit" can and do.) In fact, the alternative to "pleasing God" is not simply living at a morally neutral state, neither pleasing nor displeasing; it may well be "to please oneself" (15:1), or (in a bad sense) "to please other people" (Gal 1:10). If we want to enquire further as to how it can be that a human being, a creature and a sinner, can please the living God, the holy creator, the logic of the letter as a whole, and of Paul's arguments elsewhere, suggests that it might have something to do with being restored in God's image (see 1:18-25 and the Commentary; 8:29; Col 3:10).

Paul describes this complete human worship as "your spiritual worship." The word translated "spiritual" by the NRSV and the NIV is not, however, πνευματικός (pneumatikos), as one might have imagined. It is λογικός (logikos), which as the KJV indicates can mean "reasonable" in the sense of "in accordance with reason." The JB offers a helpful paraphrase in this sense: a worship "that is worthy of thinking beings." In Revelation 4–5, the "beasts," representing creation, worship God totally but unreflectively, and then the twenty-four elders, representing God's people, declare that God is *worthy* of this worship, reflecting on who God is and what God has done. Similarly, Paul may here be insisting, however paradoxical this may sound to ears attuned to later dualisms, that the offering of the *body* is precisely the thing that *thinking* creatures ought to recognize as appropriate. This is more likely than that he is deliberately echoing or aping Stoic ideas in which the λόγος (logos) formed the true inner core of every human; there are distinct echoes, but the Stoic would not have agreed that offering one's body to God was

485. W. Bindemann, *Die Hoffnung der Schöpfung: Römer 8, 18-27 und die Frage einer Theologie der Befreiung von Mensch und Natur,* Neukirchener Studienbücher 14 (Neukirchen-Vluyn: Neukirchen, 1983) 102-3.

the appropriate type of worship.[486] Paul is not highlighting a kind of worship that transcends and therefore need not include the actions of the body itself. This "logical worship," likewise, is more than simply "the worship to which our argument points," though the phrase could mean that as well and it is no doubt true.

12:2. The second sentence does not unpack the first, but stands alongside it as the head of the whole section. In accordance with what he has said all along, Paul sees the new age, long awaited within Judaism, as having broken in to the present age in the Messiah, and understands Christians as living at their point of overlap, needing constantly to reject the pressures of the present age and to be open to the life of the new, the life offered in the Messiah. Here is the interface, for Paul, between what scholars call "eschatology" and "ethics": because you are in fact a member of the age to come, if you are in Christ, new modes and standards of behavior are not only possible but commanded.[487] This new behavior, like the "living sacrifices," is pleasing to God, and Christians should be able to think it out and realize why. Thus, if verse 1 focuses on the body, but with the mind being involved as well (the "reasonable worship"), v. 2 focuses on the renewal of the mind, but the result is that people, being thus transformed, can work out in practice what is the right thing to *do*.[488]

"Don't let the world around you squeeze you into its own mould" was J. B. Phillips's translation of the start of verse 2. It remains memorable, catching the sense of pressure and temptation that "the present age" (Phillips missed the eschatological nuance) constantly provides. This is not a matter of simply resisting pressure from the outside, and discovering the pure unsullied world "within." That is the road to various kinds of gnosticism, the discovery of a hidden spark that, already present, just needs to be uncovered. Rather, as Paul insisted in 1:18-32, the human mind

and heart are, in their natural state, dark and rebellious, full of wickedness and evil. What is required is not for people simply to learn to live authentically, without external pressure, but for them to be renewed, so that what proceeds from the transformed mind does indeed reflect the image of God.[489] The verbs are probably in the present tense, though several manuscripts have aorist instead, reflected in the NIV's implication ("Do not conform any longer") that Paul supposes his hearers to have been conforming to the present age up to now. It is more likely that at this point in the letter he is putting forward a general command rather than a specific and urgent one.[490]

The "mind" is a key category in Paul's vision of renewal (cf. 7:25 and 8:5-8). Instead of the "unfit mind" of 1:28, Paul holds out a vision of a mind renewed, able now at last to think for itself what will please God, instead of being darkened by the deceitfulness of sin (see also the suggestive "we have the mind of the Messiah" in 1 Cor 2:16). The Christian is not meant to rely simply on lists of ethical commands, but to be able to discern (NRSV), to test and approve (NIV), what God's will is—God's will, it seems, primarily for general ethical conduct but also, perhaps, for specific decisions and occasions. Paul's vision of living sacrifice, and mind renewed, generates a picture of Christian behavior in which rules matter but are not the driving force, in which thought and reflection matter but without reducing ethics to purely situational decisions. And once again Paul insists that God's will, when found and followed, is "good, pleasing, and perfect." Fear of the various movements that go under the name "perfectionism" ought not to put us off from reflecting that, with all the ambiguities and perplexities of Christian moral life, there is such a thing as knowing and doing God's will, and that we are commanded to pursue it, as Paul indicates in 1 Cor 3:18-23, humbly but confidently.

486. See Philo *Special Laws*. 1:277; Epictetus *Discourses* 1.16.20-21; 2.9.2. See also A. J. Guerra, *Romans and the Aoplogetic Tradition: The Purpose, Genre and Audience of Paul's Letter*, SNTSMS (Cambridge: Cambridge University Press, 1995) 157-58; T. Engberg-Pedersen, *Paul and the Stoics* (Louisville: Westminster John Knox, 2000) 262-65.

487. See the classic discussion of V. P. Furnish, *Theology and Ethics in Paul* (Nashville: Abingdon, 1968).

488. Some good MSS add "your" with "mind"; whether or not this is original, it is certainly the sense, and the NRSV and the NIV are not misleading when they insert it.

489. The particular words Paul uses (συσχηματίζεσθε *syschēmatizesthe* and μεταμορφοῦσθε *metamorphousthe*, with their root nouns σχῆμα *schēma* and μορφή *morphē*, both of which mean "outward form," "shape") should probably not be pressed for further nuances; in other words, it would not have made much difference if Paul had used συμμορφίζω (*symmorphizō*) and μετασχηματίζω (*metaschēmatizō*), both of which occur in Phil 3:10, 21.

490. So Moo, *Romans*, 755.

REFLECTIONS

1. Paul's transition from chapters 1–11 to 12–16 is a model of integrated theological and practical thinking and writing, and hence a notable standard for those who preach expository or doctrinal sermons. As I have said, we should beware of assuming too readily that the two parts of the letter correspond exactly to what later generations have called "doctrine" and "ethics," and we should note in particular the point at which our perception of these things shades off into the decidedly unbiblical "facts and values" distinction. For Paul, the central facts are the death and resurrection of Jesus the Messiah, the world's true Lord; but if ever facts were value-laden, these are. Genuine humanness, genuine obedient faithfulness to the one God, has appeared on earth, has suffered and been vindicated. Before this fact there are no mere spectators, only subjects and rebels.

2. It is interesting, though, that Paul does not at this stage appeal to the lordship of Jesus as the groundwork of his moral vision. That will come later, in chapters 14 and 15. For the moment he concentrates on the images of new sacrifice and new world, brought about by the work of Jesus. The fact that later in the chapter he seems to draw on or echo the teaching of Jesus should not weaken this observation. He will not turn Jesus into either a schoolmaster to give lessons or a policeman to make sure they are obeyed. The foundation of his ethic is what Jesus *accomplished:* the whole new world, the "age to come" of Jewish expectation, into which the baptized enter and in which they must live by the Spirit. This is where we see how important it is that in chapter 6 the Christian is precisely no longer an "old human being," but instead stands on resurrection ground. Because the resurrection itself took place within continuing earthly history, and is indeed always threatened by "historical" enquiry in the sense of would-be "scientific" historiography that excludes certain things from the start, those who are "risen with the Messiah" in the sense of Col 3:1 (which I argued earlier, despite the normal assumption, is present in Romans 6 as well) are always threatened in their moral behavior by the still-unredeemed world with its assumptions and pressures, its sneers and compromises. But the Christian is not left to struggle alone. When Paul speaks of "the renewal of the mind," he is alluding to the work of God's own self in the person of the Spirit (see again 8:5-9). The Spirit is even now at work to make the new age a reality; and the space-time location where this must happen, as in chapter 8, is none other than the actual bodies of Christians. Inaugurated eschatology begins at home.

3. Verses 1 and 2 offer a fine balance between sacrifice and fulfillment, between an ethic of self-denial and one of self-discovery. Even the self-discovery, however, is the discovery of the *new* self that one is called to become in Christ and by the Spirit, not the uncovering of a hidden truth or inclination that had been present all along. Grace fulfills nature, but only by putting it to death (the living sacrifice) and bringing it to life again (the renewing of the mind). Exactly as in the bracing commands of Jesus himself (e.g., Mark 8:34-38), the path of self-sacrifice is the path of self-fulfillment, as through true, whole-person worship people discover to their surprise that being truly human is not what the present age supposes. Taking up the cross is the way to life, even though believing this is never easy, whether one has been following Jesus for a single day or a lifetime.

4. The other more obvious balance, or, perhaps better, integration, is that of body and mind within Christian obedience. Neither insincere following of an outward code, nor the easy immorality of keeping the mind (supposedly) pure while the body can do what it likes, will suffice in the new age that began with Jesus' resurrection. Behind the body/mind integration of these verses we may hear, once again, the biblical command to love God with heart, mind, soul, and strength: the *Shema*, in fact, to which Paul has alluded before (see 1:5; 3:27-30; 5:5; 8:28) and whose fulfillment is now in sight, as it will be when the present passage is unpacked in 13:8-10.

5. Perhaps the most striking and pastorally relevant feature of these verses is the point already stressed in the comments: that worship and obedience of this sort really does "please God." Centuries of post-Augustine and post-Reformation thought have quite rightly emphasized the free, unmerited grace of God, and the response of faith alone, as the basis of the Christian's standing in Christ, his or her membership in the family whose sins have been dealt with through Jesus' death. But this tradition, precisely in order to avoid the impression of compromise at this central point, has often failed to give due weight to the proper and regular Pauline emphasis that those who are justified in Christ and indwelt by the Spirit can, should, and regularly do "please God," that God is delighted with them not merely because they appear "in Christ" but because of what they are, and are becoming, and are beginning to do. This has nothing whatever to do with justification, and if for a single moment anyone supposed that it did the danger of self-satisfied Pelagianism would again open up before us like a dark pit. It may be difficult to keep one's balance in these matters. But to insist on the unbalanced and unbiblical view that Christians are incapable of pleasing God, in order to avoid the equally unbalanced and unbiblical view that Christians earn God's free grace, is like avoiding railway accidents by staying safely at home. We can never avoid the danger of misunderstandings. Christian living is always a risk. But with Paul as our guide we do not need to be gloomy or defensive about this. He was used to walking tightropes.

ROMANS 12:3-13, UNITY, LOVE, AND COMMUNITY LIVING

COMMENTARY

The present passage has a good deal in common with various other Pauline exhortations to the church to live as a single community, notably 1 Corinthians 12 and Philippians 2. In both cases what really counts is that the community Paul is addressing is to be shaped by the Messiah himself. In particular, in the Messiah Christians are to strive for unity, which will come through the humility in which each thinks soberly about his or her own gifts and role rather than placing too high a value on them. In the present passage, too, we would be right to see the Messiah as the shaping force underneath the argument. We would probably be right to see the reference to the church as being "one body in the Messiah" (12:5) as standing deliberately near the head of the present section (at least 12:1–15:13) much as did the reference to the Messiah being "of their race according to the flesh" in 9:5, and indeed the fuller reference with which the letter itself

opens (1:3-4). Certainly the unity of believers in the Messiah continues to be a recurring theme through to 15:13.

Verses 3-13 divide, as we have said, into 3-8 and 9-13; and vv. 3-8 themselves divide naturally into the introduction (v. 3), the main statement (vv. 4-5), and the immediate application in terms of the use of different gifts (vv. 6-8). These are intended for the whole church, not simply for a "charismatic element" within it.[491]

12:3. The appeal that follows is intended, it seems, to explain (γάρ *gar*, "for") and thereby, in usual Pauline style, to unpack the dense opening of vv. 1-2. "Offer God the true worship; be transformed by having your minds renewed; because you should be thinking as one people in the Messiah."[492] The

491. Against Fitzmyer, *Romans*, 645.
492. Against Moo, *Romans*, 760, whose explanation would require a "therefore" or "and so" rather than a "because."

"for" thus belongs with the whole sequence of thought, not least vv. 4-5, not simply with v. 3 itself. The basic appeal—which Paul addresses emphatically to every single one of his readers—is not just from Paul speaking on his own authority. He makes it because God has equipped him for a particular task, with "the grace given to me." Paul remained conscious—as, given his extraordinary vocation, he needed to—that he attempted the tasks he did because God had appointed him to a specific role, which he refers to in this way elsewhere both in this letter and in his other writings (1:5; 15:15; 1 Cor 3:10; 15:10; Gal 2:9; Eph 3:2, 7-8; cf. Col 1:25). Sometimes this introduces a specific reference to his ministry to the Gentiles (cf. 11:13); and since the appeal in this verse echoes quite closely that of 11:20 and 25, where the respective places and roles of Gentile and Jew are at stake, we may suppose that that thought is not far from his mind. He is, after all, laying foundations here for chaps. 14 and 15, where that mutual relationship is again in view. But for the moment he wants to make the foundation wider and deeper, and so moves to the more general point about all Christians individually learning how to think soberly about themselves.

The appeal itself is couched in quite formal tones, with a repetition of the basic word that is hard to capture in English. "Do not overthink above what you ought to think, but think in wise-thinking ways"; that is more or less it, and as with the emphasis on the mind in 12:2 (cf. 8:5-8) it stresses the role of disciplined thinking as being at the very root of basic Christian living. Here the point is that, just as in 11:25 Gentiles should not think too highly of themselves, so here all Christians should keep guard on their own self-opinion; not, of course, that they should strive for a false or inappropriate humility but that their judgment should be sober and serious.

Paul actually sets up a standard by which one may judge oneself: "the measure of faith" God has apportioned. It is possible that by this he means that every Christian has been given a different "measure of faith," some greater, some less. That would certainly make some sense in the present passage: one should, according to that

interpretation, regard oneself in terms of the amount of faith one has.[493] It might be thought, as well, that this would point on to the discussion of the "strong in faith" and the "weak in faith" in chapters 14–15. But there is more to be said for the rival view: that the "measure of faith" is the same for all. Throughout the letter so far, "faith" is the same for everybody (3:27-30): belief that Jesus is Lord and that God raised him from the dead (10:9; cf. 4:24-25). Paul's point here is not that some should give themselves airs and that others should feel inferior, but that all should exercise their varied gifts on a level one with another. The last mention of "faith," in fact, was in a very similar context: branches were broken off because of unbelief, you only stand fast because of faith, and the branches themselves can be grafted in again if they do not remain in unbelief—so do not think too highly of yourselves! (see 11:19-25). The "measure" here, then, is not a kind of measuring-jug containing different amounts of faith, apportioned to different people, but a measuring-rod, the same for all, called "faith." It is up to each Christian to see where they come against that standard, since it is the only one that matters.[494]

12:4-5. One of Paul's most powerful images for explaining the combined unity and diversity of the church is that of the body; and this, alongside 1 Corinthians 12, is one of the two classic passages on the subject. (In Ephesians and Colossians a subtly different point is made, Christ there being spoken of as the head of the body; see Eph 1:22; 4:15; 5:23; Col 1:18; 2:10, 19.) The present passage differs slightly from 1 Corinthians in that there, having set up the analogy in a very similar way to the present passage, Paul says simply "so also is the Messiah," indicating an identity between the meaning of "the Messiah" (ὁ Χριστός *ho Christos*) and the many "members" who together make up his "body," his complete existence in the world of present space and time (1 Cor 12:12, 27). This needs, and immediately receives in 1 Corinthians, a clear statement of the indwelling Spirit,

493. See Barrett, *A Commentary on the Epistle to the Romans*, 235; Dunn, *Romans 9–16*, 721-22.
494. So Moo, *The Epistle to the Romans*, 761; Fitzmyer, *Romans*, 647. Bryan, *A Preface to Romans*, 197, suggests that the reference is to God's own faithfulness.

which, while being paralleled in various ways in Romans, is not matched in chapter 12. Instead, in Romans 12, Paul keeps the picture one stage removed from apparent total identification: "We, being many, are one body in the Messiah." (It is not clear why the NIV has put "in Christ" at the start of the sentence, distancing it from "body," or why it has translated ἐσμεν [esmen] as "form" rather than simply "are.") In fact, the subtle distinction between 1 Cor 12:12 and Rom 12:5 is more at the level of surface expression, and should not be taken to indicate a shift in underlying meaning; Paul can say similar things elsewhere in 1 Corinthians in a way that indicates that his thought was flexible on this point within a comprehensible framework (see, e.g., 1 Cor 6:15; 10:17). And that framework is, as we have seen several times before in Romans, Paul's belief that, since the resurrection demonstrated Jesus to be the Messiah, he now in that capacity represented his people, summing them up "in" himself, so that what was true of him was now true of them. This is the logic that underlies chapter 6, and the decisive 8:1, as well as the many other "in Christ" passages elsewhere in his writings (see the Commentary on 6:1-23).[495] To be "in Christ," as here, is to be a member of the Messiah's people; to speak of "one body in Christ" is to emphasize the unity of that people despite its obvious diversity.

It is possible that Paul is aware, in using this image, that pagan writers had spoken in similar terms about "the body politic."[496] There may even be a hint, though this should not be pressed on the basis of the present passage, that Paul sees the community of the Messiah's people as an entity over against the great political entity of the time, the state of Rome (see the Commentary on 13:1-7). At the same time, it is noteworthy that, whereas he speaks of the solidarity between the Messiah and ethnic Jews in terms of "flesh" (9:4), something has happened to create a different unity, a different solidarity, which is spoken of instead in terms of "body." Compare Paul's language about "my flesh" in 11:14, the background to which is found in

2 Sam 5:1//1 Chr 11:1, where the tribes of Israel say to David, "We are your bone and flesh" (see also Judg 9:2; 2 Sam 19:12-13). This substitution of terms fits so well with Paul's regular language about the corruptible, dying self ("flesh") and the self that is to be resurrected ("body") that we may well wonder whether he is not suggesting that this new entity, the "one body in Christ" as here or the "body of Christ" as in 1 Corinthians, is as it were the resurrected version of "Israel according to the flesh."

If this is the truth of the united whole, what is true of each one individually? (See the NRSV; the NIV's "each member" does not quite catch the emphasis of the Greek, which is almost "one by one," as though Paul were doing a quick head count, pointing to each person in the room in turn.) They belong to one another. We are so used to the word "member" referring to someone who belongs to a society or club that we are in danger of ignoring the fact that here "members" (μέλη melē) means "parts of the body," and belongs with the extended metaphor (the JB and the NJB bring this out by translating "parts"). In 1 Corinthians 12 Paul spells this out in terms of the metaphor: one is an eye, another a foot, and so on. Here, though the point is substantially the same (the passage, indeed, has the flavor of Paul repeating, more swiftly, something he knows he has said before), he launches straight into a list of gifts.

12:6-8. The gifts listed here, which he refers to as "spiritual gifts" (χαρίσματα charismata), is identical neither with the list in 1 Corinthians 12 nor with the similar lists in, e.g., Eph 4:11, though they overlap. It is difficult to know how much weight to put on the fact that seven "gifts" are listed here (prophecy, ministry, teaching, exhortation, giving, leading, and compassion), perhaps indicating the completeness of God's provision for the work of the church (cf. eight in 1 Cor 12:28, but this omits "interpretation," which is referred to as though it is part of the same list in 1 Cor 12:10, 30; there are five in Eph 4:11, or four if "pastors and teachers" are the same people). The list itself is incomplete in the sense that several categories mentioned elsewhere are missing. Paul does not mention "apostleship," possibly because he does not suppose there to be any "apostles" in Rome

---

495. For details, see Wright, *The Climax of the Covenant*, chaps. 2 and 3.
496. E.g., Plato *Republic* 462c-d; Livy 2:32; Plutarch *Arat* 24:5; *Cor* 6:2-4.

(though see 16:7). Nor does he mention tongues, interpretation, healing, or special words of knowledge, as in 1 Corinthians 12. There is probably not much of significance to be drawn from this; possibly this list is deliberately general, emphasizing "ordinary" rather than "extraordinary" gifts, because Paul does not actually know what special gifts the Christians in Rome may possess.

His main point is that just as God has given him grace for his task (v. 3), so God gives the church grace for its multiple and mutually supportive tasks, and whatever they are they must be exercised to the full extent of one's powers. The NIV supplies the verb for this ("let him use it"), which brings out Paul's intention although, as in the NRSV, there is no corresponding word in the Greek (RSV, "let us use them"; NJB, "let us devote ourselves"). It is possible that Paul intends the participle at the start of v. 6 ("having gifts") simply to modify the main verb of v. 5 ("we are one body in Christ, and individually parts belonging to one another"), and so means the list to imply "and this will mean that the teacher should get on and teach" and the like.

With most of the gifts in the list, the thrust of the commands is obvious: servers should serve, teachers should teach, and so on, with as much energy and skill as they can. This is clear with the second, third, and fourth "gifts," ministry (or "serving," NIV), teaching, and exhortation, where the word describing how one should exercise one's gift is simply the cognate word of the gift itself. The final three (giving, leading, showing compassion) develop the idea slightly (givers should be generous, leaders should be diligent, compassion should be shown cheerfully), and this leads naturally into the more general commands of vv. 9-13.

But what about the strange phrase in v. 6 that explains how "prophecy" should be exercised? Prophecy, it seems, should be exercised "in proportion to faith" (NRSV) or "to his faith" (NIV, supplying the "his"; NEB, "a man's"; REB, "our"; the JB paraphrases: "use [the gift of prophecy] as your faith suggests"; NJB, "we should prophesy as much as our faith tells us"). The implication is that the level or content of the "faith" will vary from prophet to prophet, and that a prophet should

exercise his or her gift to the full extent of that faith. It is possible, however, that as with the "measure of faith" in v. 3 we should understand this as a reference to "the faith" as the same standard for all, so that the point is that prophets should not feel themselves at liberty to say whatever comes into their heads, but rather should speak in conscious accord with the beliefs that make the church what it is. Since this is the only NT passage in which ἀναλογία (*analogia*) occurs, we cannot gauge Paul's meaning from parallels. But its basic meaning concerns proportion within a relationship,[497] and it seems to me more likely that Paul intends to refer to the proportional relationship between the Christian faith as a whole and what individual prophets say, rather than to the proportional relationship between the gift of prophecy and the amount of faith an individual prophet may have.[498]

12:9-13. There then follows a more general list of ways in which individual Christians and groups or churches are to behave, ways almost all of which are concerned with building up the community as a whole (i.e., not simply with the pursuit of individual virtue or holiness as though for its own sake).

12:9. Love stands at the head of the list, as often in Paul (see above all 1 Corinthians 13; and also Gal 5:22). We should assume that this word refers not just to the feelings that Christians have for one another (Paul returns to that in v. 10) but to the practical care for each other that marked the early church (see 1 Thess 4:9-12; it is clear there, however, that the words φιλαδελφία [*philadelphia*] and ἀγάπη [*agapē*] are very close in meaning for Paul, so that we should not drive a wedge between vv. 9-10). There follows a string of participles and adjectives; grammatically these appear to modify the main verb of the opening sentence, even though Paul has left it unexpressed (ἡ ἀγάπη ἀνυπόκριτος *hē agapē anypokritos*; lit., "Love—genuine!"). These are the ways, in other words, in which love will show itself to be the true version rather than a counterfeit, which is all the more interesting in that the list of these ways begins with the most general of moral commands, to loathe what is evil and to cling

497. Cf. BDAG 67, "a state of right relationship involving proportion."
498. Against Cranfield, *A Critical and Exegetical Commentary on the Epistle to the Romans*, 621.

tightly to what is good (both verbs are strong: "hate" [NRSV, NIV] is not forceful enough). This is best explained in terms of 13:10: Love will always do what is good rather than what is evil, since this will be for the good of the other person. Paul presupposes that there is a large area of moral life that does not need spelling out; everyone knows that some things are good and others evil, and at this point there will be a substantial overlap between the Christian community and their neighbors both Jewish and pagan.

12:10-13. The rest of the list consists of lightning sketches of ways to build up the community. There must be real affection; Christians should look up to one another (lit., they should "go first and lead the way in showing honor to one another").[499] They should not (v. 11) be lazy when it comes to diligence and eagerness (this is rather like saying "you mustn't be slow when you're being swift," which seems somewhat obvious, but it appears to correspond to our phrase "not be backward in coming forward"). Their spirits

must be constantly aglow, like the fire that burns in an old-fashioned stove to keep the house warm and to be ready for cooking and similar tasks. And they must regard themselves as servants of the Lord, that is, of Jesus himself.[500] Their life (v. 12) should be a steady stream of rejoicing in hope, remaining patient under suffering, and giving themselves to prayer (again, the word Paul uses is a strong one, indicating an eager and persevering devotion—the sort of attitude that takes trouble over prayer rather than being perfunctory or "when I feel like it"). And (v. 13) they should share with Christians in need, and be eager to be hospitable, to open their home to those who may need to share it. This, again, is not something other than "love," but is part of what Paul and other early Christians meant by that large and all-embracing term.[501]

---

499. See BDAG 869.

500. A few MSS read "serving the time" (καιρῷ *kairō* instead of κυρίω *kyriō*), presumably intending it in a sense something like Col 4:5; but this is almost certainly a corruption. See, however, Byrne, *Romans*, 379, who suggests that it means "make the most of the time remaining."

501. On hospitality, see Heb 13:2. The NRSV's addition of "to strangers" is perhaps an overexplanation: The word φιλοξενία (*philoxenia*) and its cognates can be used for hospitality simply within the Christian community, as in 1 Pet 4:9.

ROMANS 12:14–13:7, THE CHURCH FACING THE OUTSIDE WORLD

OVERVIEW

It has been customary to separate out 13:1-7 from its surroundings, but though it is obviously a separate paragraph it belongs closely with the end of chapter 12. Noting this link helps a certain amount in addressing the problem that, outside the central theological questions of justification, the law, and christology, has probably vexed commentators more than anything else. What did Paul mean by "submitting to the ruling authorities" (13:1), and why did he command it?[502]

Taking 12:14-21 and 13:1-7 as two halves of a statement of Christian responsibility vis-à-vis outsiders gives to the whole of 12–13,

as noted above, a certain symmetry (12:1-2 and 13:11-14 locate Christian living in its wider eschatological framework, insisting on the obedience of bodily life in the present period; 12:3-13 and 13:8-10 expound the obligation of love within the Christian community; now, in the middle, the present two paragraphs deal with the life of the church over against the surrounding world). It is true that some parts of 12:14-21, especially vv. 15-16, could be seen as speaking still of life within the church, but the transition in v. 14 is quite marked, grammatically as well as in content, and it is probably better to see those parts, though no doubt relevant in church life as well, as dealing principally with Christian responsibility toward outsiders. In particular, 12:19-20 forbids vengeance in terms that link closely to the

---

502. I leave out of further consideration the desperate expedient, still adopted by some, of striking 13:1-7 down as a later gloss. See the list in Moo, *Romans*, 791; W. Munro, *Authority in Paul and Peter: The Identification of a Pastoral Stratum in the Pauline Corpus and 1 Peter*, SNTSMS (Cambridge: Cambridge University Press, 1983) 56-67.

description of the rulers' obligations in 13:4, and it seems clear that Paul intends these two passages to be mutually interpretative. There is a balance to be kept between looking outside the Christian community at threatening wolves coming to attack and looking outside at God-given civic authorities whose vocation it is to keep order and peace. If 13:1-7 had been read in this light, some old problems might have been avoided.

Romans 12:14-21, Christian Living Amid (Possibly Hostile) Outsiders

COMMENTARY

12:14. The NRSV and the NIV, and most other translations, are right to treat this as opening a new paragraph (against NEB, REB). Paul switches from the string of participles to a pair of straight imperatives, with a further string of participles dependent on them (imperatives, v. 14; two infinitives, equivalent of imperatives, v. 15; three participles, explaining these, v. 16a; a further imperative, v. 16b; four participles, vv. 17-19a, giving rise to further imperatives, vv. 19-21). Instead of the Christian community taking care of one another, the attention has now shifted to those who would attack and harm them. We do not know of specific persecution in the Roman church during the 50s, but Paul assumes, here as elsewhere, that persecution will come to those who remain loyal to Jesus (1 Thess 2:14; 3:3-4; cf. 2 Tim 3:12). And the appropriate response to it is blessing, not cursing. At this point Paul stands firmly with Jesus and the entire early Christian tradition against all other traditions known to us. The noble stories of the Maccabean martyrs typify the tradition Paul would have received: the seven brothers in 2 Maccabees 7 go to their deaths calling down solemn curses on their persecutors. But in both Jesus' teaching and his own practice there was a strikingly new note: Hostility was to be met with prayer, and violence with blessing (Matt 5:38-48; Luke 6:28-35; 23:34; Acts 7:60; 1 Cor 4:12; 1 Pet 2:20-23; 3:9; Eph 5:1 should probably be considered in this light as well).[503] It is hard to imagine this teaching becoming the norm in the church, as it clearly did from the very start, unless it was firmly rooted in the words and example of Jesus himself

12:15-16. In this context it may be best to read vv. 15-16, not as commands about the internal life of the church, but as suggesting how Christians should live alongside their pagan neighbors. They should not keep themselves aloof; if someone in the next street dies, they should be prepared to sympathize and join the funeral procession, and if someone is celebrating, they should throw their hats in the air as well. It will not do, just because the society around is potentially or actually hostile, to adopt a snooty attitude; much better to know how to establish common ground and to find ways of making friends. "Live in harmony with one another" (v. 16) is literally "thinking the same things toward one another," which sounds like the kind of bracing command Paul can sometimes issue to Christian groups (e.g., Phil 2:2); but here it seems to refer, more generally, to the call to Christians to get alongside their neighbors and fellow citizens ("associating with the lowly," or possibly "taking on menial tasks") instead of hiving off to a ghetto. The final sentence of v. 16 is a strong echo of 11:25 and 12:3; clearly the attitude Paul most wants to head off in the Roman church is superiority, either against non-Christian Jews (11:25), or against fellow-Christians (12:3), or against the wider pagan world (12:16).

12:17-18. Paul reiterates the basic command that runs through this paragraph: one must not repay evil for evil (see 1 Thess 5:15; and, in the background, with further echoes, Prov 20:22). Instead, one must take careful thought, prior to any given situation (this "thinking beforehand," though not implied in the NRSV or the NIV, seems to be present

---

503. On prohibitions of vengeance in Judaism (usually referring only to fellow Jews, not to "enemies") see K. Yinger, "Romans 12:14-21 and Nonretaliation in Second Temple Judaism: Addressing Persecution within the Community," *CBQ* 60 (1998) 74-96.

in the prefix of the participle προνοούμενοι [*pronooumenoi*]), about what will show the watching world that one can hold one's head up, with nothing to be ashamed of. Of course, there will be times when the world will not understand the points at which Christian standards will not permit those who hold them to go along with the ways of the world (cf. Eph 5:11-14; 1 Pet 4:3-5). But there will be many other times, and Christians should be on the lookout for them, when they can join in gladly and show that they, too, act according to the highest moral standards of the surrounding culture. Paul is realistic: he knows that there will be many times when living at peace with every other inhabitant of the street, let alone the city, will be impossible. But he summons Christians to make every effort in that direction.

12:19-20. This sets the scene for the third appeal against retaliation, which this time is explained, albeit somewhat darkly. Do not curse your persecutors (v. 14); do not repay evil for evil (v. 17); now, do not perform acts of vengeance—that is, acts that try to bring justice to bear in your own disputes. (Unusually in mid-paragraph, he addresses his readers as "beloved," perhaps already to indicate a reason why this prohibition is given: God's people are loved by God and must not imagine themselves bereft of his care and hence needing to take matters into their own hands.) The verb ἐκδικέω (*ekdikeō*), as its root suggests, indicates the doing of justice, which Paul is not forbidding; what he prohibits is doing it freelance, in one's own favor—in other words, what we call "vengeance."

Instead, he says, "give place to wrath." Without chapter 13 it might not be clear whether this in fact meant "let your own wrath smolder away quietly," "leave room for God's wrath," or "let the process of moral cause and effect take its course"—though the first one Paul would certainly have ruled out, the second points in the right direction, and the third might not have been foreign to him either. But with 13:4 coming up six verses later, we can be reasonably confident that he means "allow God to do justice—which may well be done through the appointed magistrates." It is impossible to act in one's own case with sufficient impartiality; which is why, as Deuteronomy 32:35 had declared,

God reserves the sole right to judicial punishment (again, this shows why 13:1-7 is necessary, to make the link between God's sole right and the delegated rights of rulers). From this point of view, the traditional translation "vengeance" is misleading; what is meant is judicial punishment, which becomes "vengeance" when offended parties take the law into their own hands. Though Paul is not working here with the larger story of Deuteronomy 32, it is significant that he quotes verse 35 here, as he had quoted verse 21 in 10:19, and will quote verse 43 in 15:10; this was, clearly, a passage upon which he drew consciously and regularly.

In place of private vengeance, Paul recommends a shockingly positive line of action: feed a hungry foe, give drink to a thirsty one. He quotes here from Prov 25:21-22, and the Bible contains one or two striking examples of this practice, notably 1 Kgs 6:20-23, where Elisha commanded the king of Israel not to kill enemies who were supernaturally delivered into his hands, but to give them a banquet. In that instance, the Syrian enemies did not return to invade Israel; in Proverbs, the writer says—and Paul quotes him—that taking this course of action will heap coals of fire on the enemy's head ("and YHWH will reward you," adds Proverbs). At first sight it might look as though the coals of fire were themselves punishment (however metaphorical); but this would hardly qualify as "repaying evil with good," since the vengeful intention would still be uppermost. The "coals of fire" are almost certainly intended as the burning shame of remorse for having treated someone so badly. Though the practice of having penitents carrying a literal tray of hot coals is not widely attested, it is not impossible that it was both the source of the original metaphor in Proverbs and also an allusion that Paul's hearers might pick up.[504] The point is then that treating enemies kindly is not only appropriate behavior in its own right, refusing the vengeance that would usurp God's prerogative; it may also have the effect of turning their hearts.

12:21. Paul sums up the whole paragraph with another possible allusion to the Sermon on the Mount, and to the gospel events

504. See W. Klassen, "Coals of Fire: Sign of Repentance or Revenge?" *NTS* 9 (1962–63) 337-50.

themselves, Jesus' death and resurrection. Yes, there is evil "out there" in the world. But God's people are to meet it in the way that even God met it: with love and generous goodness. The theology of the cross, in fact, can be glimpsed under this apparently detached ethical maxim: when God came to defeat evil, this was not achieved by using an even greater evil, but by using its opposite—namely, the surprising and initially counterintuitive weapons of goodness. To be consumed with vengeful thoughts, or to be led into putting such thoughts into practice, is to keep evil in circulation, whereas the way to overthrow evil, rather than perpetuating it, is to take its force and give back goodness instead. As with the commands of verses 14 and 17, we may question whether someone in Paul's tradition of Torah-based zeal could have come to this position had it not been for the example and teaching of the Messiah himself.

Romans 13:1-7, God's Call to Obedience to the Authorities

COMMENTARY

Theological fashions change, and pressure points move from one exegetical location to another. A previous generation found Romans 9 intolerable, first reading into that chapter a doctrine of absolute predestination to salvation or damnation and then angrily rejecting it. Others have taken a similar view of Rom 1:18-32, hating the very idea of "wrath" as a theologically barbarous concept. Now, after a century in which totalitarian governments have devastated continents, decimated nations, and dehumanized millions of their subjects, it is scarcely surprising that the critical searchlight has swung around and come to rest on the little paragraph now before us. As though by some scapegoating process, these seven verses have been struck out of the canon, vilified, and blamed for untold miseries. They have enabled whole generations of critics to combine their sociopolitical instincts and prejudices with their status as professional exegetes, and to leap-frog over Paul onto what looks like the high moral ground. This is always a deeply satisfying pastime.

But when the sound and fury have died away, we are left wondering what all the fuss was about. Yes, many wicked and powerful governments have appealed to Romans 13 to justify their every move. But have people not done that with words of Jesus himself? If enemies sow weeds in a field of wheat, is the wheat farmer to be blamed? There are many parts of the Bible that can be, and have been, twisted to serve violent and self-serving ends.[505] If we cut them all out, there might be little left. Exegesis, and the determination to live at least with its results, and perhaps even by them, is always a risk, part of the risk of an incarnational religion or faith. Romans 13 is no exception.

This paragraph, I shall suggest, neither needs nor deserves opprobrium. It is not a fully blown "Theology of Church and State"; indeed, as is often pointed out, our post-Enlightenment notion of "State" would have been foreign to Paul. One can hardly blame a writer if, in the course of a letter about something else, a small aside does not contain the full sophisticated and nuanced treatment that subsequent generations might have liked. Paul's point here is essentially quite simple; it fits into the line of thought of Romans 12–13 as a whole; it need not be wished away in an effort to undercut legitimating arguments for totalitarianism, and indeed it needs to be present for the balance of the previous chapter and paragraph to be maintained.

Many theories have been advanced, predictably, as to what Paul was talking about and why. I here list only the major ones.[506] (On the unwarranted suggestion that the entire paragraph is a gloss, see the Overview for 12:14–13:7.)

---

505. See R. P. Carroll, *Wolf in the Sheepfold: The Bible as a Problem for Christianity* (London: SPCK, 1991). For the parable alluded to, see Matt 13:24-43.

506. See E. Käsemann, "Principles of the Interpretation of Romans 13," in *New Testament Questions of Today* (Philadelphia: Fortress, 1969) 196-216.

(1) This passage is a general statement about ruling authorities. It applies to all legitimate authorities all the time. It is based on a general belief in the desire of the creator God for order within all societies.[507]

(2) It is a particular statement about the Roman Empire, based on (a) Paul's belief that it was in some sense God-given, and (b) his experience of sensible magistrates protecting him from persecution, and looking (c) for the safety of the Jewish and/or Christian community in Rome at this historical moment.[508]

(3) It is a very particular statement about the specific moment in the Roman Empire when, with a new, fresh emperor in the throne (Nero's early years were as promising as his later years were terrible), Paul believed there was at least a moment when the church should trust Rome and live content within its world.[509]

(4) It is a statement of something that is now true as a result of the victory of Jesus over the powers of the world in his death and resurrection.[510]

I regard (4) as simply mistaken. Paul does not argue his point on the basis of christology or the gospel. The passage is so close in tone and content to various Jewish writings of the period and before (see below) that there is no reason to suppose that this is a new viewpoint generated by the Christian gospel.

There are further variations within (1), (2), and (3). Maybe Paul intends the paragraph as a general statement (1), but is also influenced by elements of (2) and (3), for instance by the need to distance himself from the groundswell of Jewish resistance against Rome in the Middle East.[511] Maybe he has in mind the particular situation of a tiny Christian group,

including many Jews, in the city from which Jews had been expelled a few years earlier for rioting "at the instigation of Chrestus."[512] Maybe he held view (2) or perhaps (3) at the time of writing, but found that his subsequent experience in Roman prisons led him to a very different view, which emerges in Philippians.[513] Within subsequent interpretation, variants of (2) and (3) have been taken to mean that the passage cannot be insisted upon as relevant for all time.

There may well be elements of particular historical situations visible in the passage; but what Paul actually wrote still looks very much like a general statement about ruling authorities, not a pragmatic assessment of Rome, or the present situation.[514] This is both, so to speak, good and bad news for those who are anxious about the application of the passage to subsequent situations. The more general the passage, the less it can be taken to glorify Rome, and hence to have Paul legitimating the tyranny that within a decade or so had done grievous violence to the church. The more specific the passage (Paul making a positive comment on the Roman Empire), the easier it appears to relativize it and declare it irrelevant to other times and places. However, there is an irony in this specific reading (as in [2] and [3]). By having Paul declare that Rome is a good thing (and thereby having him say nothing much about other rulers and governments), exegesis finds itself unable to see other parts of Paul, and other parts of Romans, as subverting the Roman imperial ideology: Romans 13 is regularly appealed to as an argument against a "counterimperial" reading of the rest of Paul. However, if Paul really did intend it as a general statement, based on God's appointed order in creation (as per [1] above), the less it stands in the way of this counterimperial reading. It would be ironic if, in seeking to avoid a totalitarian reading of this one text, we make it so Rome-specific that it blinds us to the far deeper anti-imperial message of Paul's gospel as a whole.

---

507. This seems to be the position of Sanday and Headlam, *A Critical and Exegetical Commentary on the Epistle to the Romans*, 369-72, though they allow for the possibility of some influence from the specific occasion of the letter. They point out (371) that later NT writings (such as 1 Tim 2:1-2; Titus 3:1; 1 Pet 2:13-17) continue to take the same line despite persecutions.

508. For (a) see B. Blumenfeld, *The Political Paul: Justice, Democracy and Kingship in a Hellenistic Framework*, JNSTSup (Sheffield: Sheffield Academic, 2001) 389-95. For (b), see R. J. Cassidy, *Paul in Chains: Roman Imprisonment and the Letters of St. Paul* (New York: Crossroad, 2001) chap. 3 (though see below). For (c), see N. Elliott, "Romans 13:1-7 in the Context of Imperial Propaganda," in Horsley, *Paul and Empire*, 184-204.

509. See Bryan, *A Preface to Romans*, 205, referring to Tacitus *Annals* 13.51; Suetonius *Nero* 10-18.

510. See Cranfield, *A Critical and Exegetical Commentary on the Epistle to the Romans*, 652-55, summarizing the work of Barth, Cullmann, and others.

511. So M. J. Borg, "A New Context for Romans xiii," *NTS* 19 (1972-73) 205-18.

512. See Wright, *The New Testament and the People of God*, 354.

513. Cassidy, *Paul in Chains*.

514. Against the view that Paul had a rose-colored view of Nero's early years, see Borg, "A New Context for Romans xiii," 381. For the more general point see P. H. Towner, "Romans 13:1-7 and Paul's Missiological Perspective," in Soderlund and Wright, *Romans and the People of God*, 149-69.

The wider context gives good reasons to support (1), even if we want to nuance the question of how Paul's readers would have heard what he was saying. As we have suggested, 13:1-7 goes closely with 12:14-21, which we would be right to assume Paul would have said to any church at any time. Paul is well aware that persecution may come, and even if we date all the prison letters after Romans we are surely not going to say, with 1 Thessalonians and 2 Corinthians behind him (let alone the experiences ascribed to him in Acts), that he had a pragmatically rosy view of authorities in general. Just as in 12:14-21 he seems to have drawn on traditions about the words and actions of Jesus, so there may be a sense here, as in at least one gospel tradition, that even when they are grievously deceived and almost demonic, ruling authorities still have a certain level of divine authorization (see John 19:11; cf. the interesting exchange in Acts 23:1-5).

More especially, the point he stresses throughout 12:14-21 dovetails exactly into what he says in 13:1-7. One must not call down curses on persecutors, nor repay evil with evil, nor seek private retribution; punishment is God's business. Now we see how Paul supposed, in part at least, that God went about that business. Of course, Paul believed in a final judgment (1:32; 2:1-16; 14:10) when all wrongs would be put to rights. But he now articulates, as a central point in 13:1-7, a standard Jewish and then Christian belief: that ruling authorities are what they are because God wants order in the present world. God is not going to allow chaos to reign even in the present evil age. Chaos and anarchy enable the powerful, the rich, and the bullies to come out on top, and they invariably do. God desires that even in the present time, even in the world that has not yet confessed Jesus as Lord, there should be a measure of justice and order. The point can easily be observed by thinking of situations where magistrates and judges are perceived to be failing badly in their duty to keep this order: before too long, vigilante groups and lynch mobs arise, taking "justice" into their own hands. One of the underlying theses that binds 12:14-21 and 13:1-7 together is therefore this: justice is served not by private vengeance but by individuals trusting the authorities to keep wickedness in check. Knowledge that the authorities are there to look after such matters is a strong incentive to forswear freelance attempts at "justice."

This, as I say, looks back to many clear Jewish precedents. Isaiah spoke of pagan rulers accomplishing God's purposes. Jeremiah urged Israel in exile to pray for the welfare of Babylon, because if Babylon was prospering, Israel would as well (Isa 10:5-11; 44:28–45:5; 46:11; Jer 29:4-9; 27:6-11 [God gives Jerusalem into the hand of Nebuchadnezzar]; see also Dan 1:2; 2:21, 37-49; 4:25, 32; 5:18; Ezra 6:10; Prov 8:15-16; Bar 1:11; 1 Macc 7:33). The book of Esther turns on the potentially risky but eventually satisfactory position of Jews under pagan rule. Many Jews in the Second Temple period were happy to see God's hand in the rise, as well as the fall, of great powers, and even though the early hailing of Rome as such a power must have left an extremely bitter taste in later mouths, the principle was established, and articulated in sundry writings of Paul's period: God intends that there should be good and wise rulers, and if rulers know what their business really is they will seek divine wisdom to help them accomplish it (e.g., Wis 6:1-11).[515] Romans 13:1-7 belongs fair and square on this map. It occupies a similar space, ironically enough, to that occupied by the more moderate Pharisees, the Hillelites, who were content for the moment to live and let live (though still believing in the eventual Age to Come and the worldwide rule of the Messiah), rather than the fiercer Shammaites who would have seen such a position as a compromise. From one point of view, if Paul's conversion made him look, on this point, more like a Hillelite than the Shammaite he had been before, that only serves to emphasize how very Jewish, how "natural," a position like this would seem.[516]

But did Paul not believe, and hint at several points in Romans itself, that the gospel and rule of Jesus the Messiah, the world's true Lord, subverted the gospel and rule of Caesar, whose cult was growing fast in precisely the cities (Corinth, Ephesus, and so on) where he

---

515. See also Josephus *The Jewish War* 2.197; *Against Apion* 2.75-77.
516. On Hillel and Shammai, their "schools," and the placing of Paul within this spectrum, see Wright, *The New Testament and the People of God*, 194-203; Wright, *What St. Paul Really Said*, chap. 2.

spent most of his time?[517] Yes; and this is perhaps part of the point. If the gospel of Jesus, God's Son, the King who will rule the nations (1:3-4; 15:12) does indeed reveal God's justice and salvation, which put to shame the similar claims of Caesar (1:16-17; Phil 2:5-11; 3:19-21); if it is true that those who accept this gospel will themselves exercise a royal reign (5:17); and if Paul suspects that his audience in Rome are getting this message— then it is all the more important to make it clear that this does not mean a holy anarchy in the present, an overrealized eschatology in which the rule of Christ has already abolished all earthly governments and magistrates. Precisely because Paul is holding out for the day when all creation will be renewed (8:1-27), when every knee shall bow at the name of Jesus (Phil 2:10-11), it is vital that the excitable little groups of Christians should not take the law into their own hands in advance.[518] In particular (and with events in Palestine in mind), it is important that his readers do not take his covert polemic against the imperial ideology as a coded call to a Christian version of the so-called fourth philosophy.[519] This is where Paul's probable awareness of the riots under Claudius, and the reputation that both Jews and Christians will have gained in Rome because of them, must come into play. God does not intend that Christians should become agents of anarchy, which would replace the tyranny of the officially powerful with the tyranny of the unofficially powerful. The ultimate overthrow of pagan power comes by other means, and Paul has outlined in Romans 5 and 8 what those means are. Rome could cope with ordinary revolutions. Rome could not cope, as history bears witness, with a community owing allegiance to the crucified and risen Messiah as the world's true Lord.

In fact, reading Romans 13 against the backdrop of the extravagant claims made within the burgeoning imperial cult highlights one point in particular. According to Paul (and the Jewish tradition in which he

stands) the rulers are not themselves divine; they are set up by the one God, and they owe this God allegiance. Romans 13 constitutes a severe demotion of arrogant and self-divinizing rulers. It is an undermining of totalitarianism, not a reinforcement of it. By implication, if the rulers themselves are given the task of judging wicked people within their sphere of authority, they themselves will be judged by the God who set them up. Paul does not say this explicitly; but in 13:4 he twice describes the rulers as God's "servants" (διάχονοι *diakonoi*), and if he is capable of pointing out that God's servants in the gospel will be judged on how they have performed, there is every reason to suppose that God's "servants" within the civic community will themselves also face an ultimate tribunal (cf. 1 Cor 3:10-15; 4:1-5, having described himself and Apollos as God's *diakonoi* in 3:5; 2 Cor 5:10). This, however, is not his point at the moment (just as he does not say, in Romans 5–8, what will happen to those who are not "in Christ"), and we must remind ourselves that this is not intended as a full and balanced statement of everything Paul might have wanted to say on the subject. The main thing he wants to get across to the Roman Christians is that, even though they are servants of the Messiah Jesus, the world's rightful Lord, this does not give them carte blanche to ignore the temporary subordinates whose appointed task, whether they know it or not, is to bring at least a measure of God's order and justice to the world. Government and magistrates may be more or less good or bad; but—and this is Paul's basic point—government qua government is intended by God and should in principle command submission from Christian and non-Christian alike.

Reading Rom 13:1-7 in the context of 12:14-21 raises a question, which Paul does not here even touch on: What happens when the "persecutors" (12:14) are the same people as "the governing authorities," and are using their God-given power for that purpose? Since Paul does not raise the question here, we cannot press this passage for a hint of an answer; but we might again compare Acts 23:1-5. Even if this is merely a stylized scene constructed by Luke, it expresses the same balance we might get by reading Romans the way I have suggested, adding Philippians

517. See Horsely, *Paul and Empire*; and Horsely, *Paul and Politics*.

518. I owe this point to Dr David Wenham.

519. This is the point made by Borg in "A New Context for Romans xiii." The "Fourth Philosophy" is Josephus's way of demarcating the Jewish revolutionaries as a separate party alongside the Sadducess, Pharisees, and Essenes.

and the Thessalonian correspondence to the mix, and then returning with the same question. "Paul" in this story declares that God will strike the "whitewashed wall," the judge who is behaving illegally. When confronted with the news that he is addressing God's high priest, he apologizes formally, recognizing that he should not speak evil of a ruler. But he does not retract his charge that the ruler in question has behaved illegally and will be judged for it. A similar pattern emerges when Acts places Paul before pagan magistrates. He will submit to their authority, but he will also remind them of their duty (see Acts 16:19-40; 22:22-29; 25:6-12). We may be right to suspect that Paul could see, not far away, the battle that would come, in which Caesar insisted on an absolute allegiance that left no room for Jesus as Lord. Less than a century later, Polycarp died at the stake because of that; but even he, it seems, held on to a view of magistracy very similar to Paul's.[520]

In particular, Paul always insists on seeing the present in the light of the future. Romans 13:1-7 does not describe a new situation brought into being by the eschatological events concerning Jesus; but the obedience of Christians to earthly magistrates takes place under the sign of ultimate judgment (cf. again 2:1-16). This does not mean, as Paul's own example bears out, that one must be politically and socially quiescent until the great renewal of all things. That is the slur made on the good name of inaugurated eschatology by those who want to insist on the full renewal right away. Preaching and living the gospel must always be announcing and following Jesus, rather than Caesar, as the true Lord. But the eschatological balance must be kept. The church must live as a sign of the coming complete kingdom of Jesus Christ; but since that kingdom is characterized by "righteousness, peace, and joy in the Holy Spirit," it cannot be inaugurated in the present by chaos, violence, and hatred (cf. 14:17). The methods of the Messiah himself (12:14-21) must be used in living out his kingdom within the present world, passing away though it may be.

Romans 13:1-7 is about the running of civic communities, and the duty of Christians toward them. It does not mention or allude to the interactions between different civic communities or nations. It was because of this that later Christians developed a theory of "just war," to argue at a new level that under certain circumstances it may be right to defend the interests of a nation or community, by force if necessary; and it is against that in particular that various pacifist movements have protested. Romans 13 is sometimes called as a witness in this discussion, but its relevance may be doubted (see the Reflections).

13:1. "Every person" (NRSV) is literally "every soul"—a clear enough indication, if such were needed, that by "soul" Paul means more than "the immaterial element within a human being." The word ψυχή (*psychē*) regularly refers, in the New Testament, to the whole human being seen from the point of view of the person's interior life, motivation, and intention. Here it is a way of indicating that every person as an individual must obey this command. The command itself is to "be subject" (NRSV), or "submit" (NIV, NEB/REB); not necessarily "obey" (JB, NJB), though that will usually follow. The point is that one must regard the governing authorities as having a rightful claim on one's submission. The word has echoes of military formation: one must take one's place in the appropriate rank.[521]

But who are the "authorities" to whom one owes this submission? Elsewhere in Paul there are times when the "rulers and authorities," the "principalities and powers," are primarily spiritual beings, shadowy but powerful entities that stand behind the visible and earthly rulers. This seems to be the case in, for instance, Rom 8:38-39. Sometimes it seems as though he intends to refer simultaneously to both earthly and heavenly powers; this is how 1 Cor 2:6-8 is usually read, and how Col 2:14-15 must be read. But here, though it is unlikely that Paul ever made a complete distinction between earthly and heavenly dimensions of civic authority, his primary focus is on the earthly rulers themselves. They are the ones who bear the sword

---

520. Polycarp *Mart. Pol.* 10.2; the whole passage repays study. See also Acts 4:23-31; 1 Pet 3:13-17 within the context of the persecution presupposed by the letter as a whole; and *1 Clement* 60–61.

521. On the difference between "submission," as commanded here, and blind obedience, see Moo, *The Epistle to the Romans*, 797, 807-10.

(v. 4). They are the ones to whom one pays taxes (vv. 6-7).[522]

The problem, of course, at the level of understanding Paul (to postpone for a minute the question of applying him today), is that in 1 Corinthians 2, and again in Col 2:15, Paul declares that the cross of Jesus Christ has defeated the powers. How can he now suggest that one should be subject to them? The answer seems to lie, whether or not Paul wrote Colossians, in the great christological poem in the first chapter of that letter, in which it is affirmed that all things, including all powers and authorities in heaven and on earth, were created in, through, and for Christ, and are also reconciled in, through, and to him.[523] The tension, in other words, is not only between Romans 13 and Colossians 2; it is between Colossians 1 and Colossians 2. And—since Paul seldom sees the need to say everything he could in principle say on a topic every time he brings it up—it is perfectly feasible to propose that Paul in this case was stressing one of the more positive aspects of the "powers." Some have argued, as noted above, that Rom 13:1-7 belongs with Col 1:20: that Paul commands submission to the powers because they have now been reconciled in Christ. But it seems much more likely that he does so in parallel with Col 1:16: he commands submission because they are part of God's good created order. The fact that they are in rebellion does not of itself mean that submission is inappropriate.

Paul, characteristically, gives an explanation for the command: all authority is from God, and (the specific form of the general statement) the actually existing ones have been put there by God. This is not a specific commendation of the Roman Empire as against the ruling systems of other times and places; it is a general point about civic authority. It belongs with mainstream Second Temple Jewish tradition, and has parallels, including one surprising one, in the NT (e.g., Wis 6:3-10; John 19:11).

13:2-4. Paul backs up this initial command and explanation with a short discussion of what happens when people resist the authorities, and of the fact that these results are part of God's appointed order. Resistance incurs "condemnation," or "judgment" (NRSV, NIV) (v. 2), because rulers hold no terrors for those who do good, but only for wrongdoers (v. 3a). Paul could no doubt have given counterexamples from his own recent biography, but his point here concerns God's intended order, not its corruptions. He then turns the point around (vv. 3b-4): if you want to go about your business without fear of the authorities, do what is good, and they will praise you. That is their God-given function. They are "ministers" (*diakonoi*), "stewards" of God for this purpose: their delegated task is to praise good behavior. Conversely, then (v. 4b), if you do evil, you should be afraid, because authority has the right and responsibility to punish. Once again, the authority is God's "steward," this time to administer punitive justice—that is, "wrath"; this is the point at which the authority *must* do what the private individual *may not* do (12:14-21)—a point regularly missed in many popular-level discussions of the judicial role of civic authority.

13:5. This to-and-fro discussion of the appointed role of "authority" and the way in which "you" may encounter it, for good or ill, leads Paul back to reiterate his initial command, now with an extra reason: one must therefore submit, both because the alternative is "wrath" in this sense, and also because, recognizing the God-given role of authority, the educated Christian conscience ought to become disquieted if it finds itself resisting God's "stewards." Paul does not often mention the role of conscience in Christian behavior, but when he does, as here, it appears that this is not because it is marginal in his thinking but because he takes it for granted. The word occurs elsewhere in Rom 2:15; 9:1; most of the other Pauline references occur in 1 Corinthians 8 and 10; see also 2 Cor 5:11.

13:6-7. Conscience, too, prescribes therefore that one must pay taxes.[524] Once again Paul gives the authorities a high status: they

---

522. On the whole question see W. Wink, *Naming the Powers: The Language of Power in the New Testament*, vol. 1 of *The Powers* (Philadelphia: Fortress, 1984) 45-47; C. Morrison, *The Powers That Be: Earthly Rulers and Demonic Powers in Romans 13.1-7* (London· SCM, 1960).

523. On Col 1:15-20 see Wright, *The Climax of the Covenant*, chap. 5.

524. Some in Rome were protesting at this time about taxation. See Tacitus *Annals* 13.50-51. Nero proposed abolishing indirect taxation altogether, but his council restrained him and less sweeping measures were instigated.

are God's λειτουργοί (*leitourgoi*), public servants (in a world where "public service" regularly had cultic overtones at least, sometimes explicit association with religious functions).[525] They must therefore receive what is due to them, whether the material dues of direct and indirect taxes (that is the likely distinction between the two words used here) or the non-material dues of respect and honor. This last point shows once more, not least in relation to Paul's own practice in Acts, what is and is not meant. Paul was always ready to honor the office even while criticizing the present holder. Though of course one hopes that the holder will prove worthy of the office, and one knows that sometimes holders prove so unworthy as to need removing from office, being able to respect the office while at least reserving judgment about the holder is part of social and civic maturity. And, for Paul, being able to say "the existing powers are ordained by God" while living under a system that, as he makes clear elsewhere, was bristling with potential or actual blasphemy and injustice, is part of Christian maturity—a part he urges his Roman readers to make their own.

525. See BDAG 591-92.

REFLECTIONS

1. Romans 13 has attracted so much opprobrium, particularly in the twentieth century where most thinking Westerners developed a more than justified horror of totalitarianism, that to many it seems counterintuitive to do anything but reject it outright. Either Paul did not write it, people say, or he did not mean it like it sounds, or he was just plain wrong. Whatever else you do with this passage, it is implied, you ought not to be caught agreeing with it.

Until, of course, your house is burgled. Or someone you love is murdered. Or you are cheated in business, or even in sport. Then, quite suddenly, you want someone to be in authority. Nobody enjoys the presence of a referee or umpire when they are trying to foul an opponent, or sneak offside; but everybody appeals to them when the other side do it. Actually, we none of us want to live in a world where the bullies get away with it, except when we are planning to do the bullying ourselves.

Libertarian histories of Western culture read the story of the last millennium as one of increasing social and civic freedom. The long march from Magna Carta to universal adult suffrage was not, in fact, as smooth an upward rise to freedom as it is sometimes made out to be. Oppression and systemic injustice still exist within every Western democracy. But since we tell our story as one of dethroning authorities and discovering new freedoms, we are bound to find Romans 13 a surprise, or even a shock. Unless we are actual anarchists, however, we will soon acknowledge explicitly that all societies need some regulation, some ordering, some structure of authority; and we will soon recognize that this ordering is no use unless everyone is, at least in principle, signed up to it or, failing that, able to be coerced into going along with it.

Romans 13:1-7 then issues commands that are so obvious that they only make sense if there might be some reason in the air not to obey the civic authorities. More or less everyone in the ancient world, with the possible exception of Cynic philosophers on the one hand and occasional radical groups like the extreme Shammaite or "zealous" Jews on the other, would have shrugged their shoulders and accepted that some form of civic authority was a necessary part of an ordered world. If a moral or religious teacher took the trouble to explain the rationale for such authorities, and insisted that those who embraced that moral or religious system were bound to obey them, that would be of itself a sign of what we have, in fact, seen both elsewhere in Romans and elsewhere in Paul: that the average Christian might well have supposed that there might be grounds for not doing so. You only put up "No Smoking" signs where people are likely to want to smoke. And, since Paul himself frequently hints at what the grounds for not obeying the authorities might be, we do not need to speculate for long about them. They are the sovereignty and saving justice of the one true God, unveiled in action in the world's true Lord, Jesus the Messiah.

Romans 13, in short, carries a hidden "nevertheless" at its heart. Jesus is Lord; nevertheless, his followers must obey their earthly rulers. This is not because the rulers have somehow, in theory, already submitted to his lordship, but despite the fact that they have not done so. The authorities are part of the present world order, the good and wise structure of God's original creation. Not to submit might look like a noble piece of overrealized eschatology, claiming to belong already to the new world promised when the full day dawns (see 13:11-14); but to make that complete claim ahead of time is in fact to move toward a dualism in which the goodness of the present world, even in its not-yet-redeemed state, is denied. That, in fact, is what millenarian and similar movements have classically done.

2. The authority of the state, however, is strictly limited here by the rubric that stands over the whole paragraph: the rulers exist by God's will and at his pleasure. The book of Daniel is a graphic description of how this works out within a pagan world and how the people of God may find their way through the resultant moral minefield. It is noticeable that even when human rulers become fatally guilty of hubris, and court their own destruction, this does not signal the end of all human rule. Even in the apocalyptic scenario in Daniel 7, the one who eventually sits on a throne dispensing judgment is "one like a son of man." Just as there is a dialectical movement between Daniel 1–6 (the stories of human kings and God's people) and Daniel 7 (the enthronement of the Ancient of Days and the vindication of "one like a son of man," representing God's people), so in Romans 13 the Christian belongs in the tension between the present existence, owing submission to earthly rulers, and the promised future "day." Just because we have become horribly aware of the dangers of brutal, self-serving, self-justifying "governments," it does not follow that there are no errors in the opposite direction.

3. Putting together Rom 12:14-21 and 13:1-7 has the salutary effect of reminding us of one of the most important, if pragmatic, reasons for there being governing authorities. Private vengeance, whether individual or (as in the lynch mob) corporate, is shocking in itself and can easily spiral out of control into vendettas and generations of senseless brutality. Where authorized policing fails, or is felt to be failing, the authority vacuum is quickly filled, and the results are seldom happy. Of course, commanding people to pray for their persecutors, not to repay evil with evil, to live at peace with all, and above all not to avenge themselves, is excellent advice at a purely personal level. People who allow vengeance, however apparently justified, to dominate their motivational life will become eaten up by it. It is a way of allowing the evil that someone has done to you to continue to hold you in its power. Part of the enormous breakthrough achieved by Jesus in his teaching and death is found just here: that to suffer innocently and not to retort or retaliate is to win a far greater victory than can ever be achieved by hitting back. It is to win a victory over evil itself.

4. I write this in the wake of September 11, 2001—a date people will recall for decades, perhaps centuries, and shudder at the memory. Terrorist atrocities against innocent and unarmed civilians, especially on so large a scale, cry out so loudly for punishment that any comment might seem superfluous. Yet in the debates that followed that terrible day Romans 13 was frequently invoked in support of military action by the United States and its allies against other countries; and one of the great problems of Christian moral discourse has been precisely that Romans 13 does not deal with such matters. That is why "Just War" theory was invented, in an attempt to develop the idea of magistracy, of a justice that kept a society in balance, beyond the borders of a particular jurisdiction and into the realms of conflict between nations. The problem with this is, to put it perhaps oversimply, that Romans 13 is dovetailed into an argument against the taking of private vengeance (12:14-21). When punitive and retaliatory action is taken against a nation, or a group within a nation, it becomes difficult to maintain that it is judicial and legitimated by Romans 13. That is not to say that such action is wrong or unjustified, only that this text will not support it. Many have concluded, rightly in my view, that the only way forward is the establishment of a worldwide justice system that will carry moral weight across different cultures and societies. Unfortunately, one of the obstacles to this is precisely the determination of some of the more powerful nations to oppose such a thing, lest they themselves be brought to account for the ways in which they have used, and perhaps abused, their own power. Romans 13 will not help in addressing these issues, then. But the rest of Romans, setting forth God's justice, freedom, and peace over against those of Caesar, could certainly do so.

ROMANS 13:8-10, LOVE FULFILLING THE LAW

COMMENTARY

This little passage on love and the law is clearly a summary of issues that Paul lays out more fully elsewhere (e.g., Galatians 5). It reverts to the theme of 12:3-13, and it may be, as we suggested above, that Paul intends this whole section (chaps. 12–13) as some kind of chiasm (see the Overview on 12:1–16:27). Within this, 13:8-10 plays a similar role within chapters 12–16 as a whole to that played by 1 Corinthians 13 within 1 Corinthians 12–14 as a whole, identifying the characteristic that must be central to all authentic Christian community life.

The thematic difference between this passage and 12:3-13, however, is that there Paul was dealing with life within the Christian community, and here he appears to be advocating a love for neighbors of any and every persuasion. The opening words of v. 8, indeed, if read without a break from what has gone before, look as if they are simply saying "always pay your bills on time"; we must assume that he is still talking about the wider community represented by those who levy taxes and demand respect (v. 7). And this view of a wider community alerts us again to a wider reference within Romans. Just as 12:1-2 looked back to 1:18-32, seeing in Christian worship the reversal of idolatry and dehumanization, so the present passage looks back to 2:17-29 in particular. With 3:27-31; 8:1-8; and 10:5-11 in the background, Paul sketches a brief but telling picture of how the Torah is fulfilled in that love of neighbor which will bring admiration, rather than blasphemy, from the watching world (cf. 2:16-17). Here, in other words, are the "true Jews" (see 2:28-29), those who are bringing God's light and love to the world. This coheres well with the context of Gal 5:14, the other passage where Paul says almost exactly the same thing (see also 1 Corinthians 13, where, though Paul does not mention Torah, the matchless exposition of love and its abiding permanence reminds us of Jewish eulogies of Torah or wisdom; see Sirach 24).

The passage consists, typically, of an opening statement and explanation (v. 8), followed by an extended explanation of the explanation (v. 9), leading to a summary that repeats and reinforces the original explanation (v. 10).

13:8. Although the idea of "debt," immediately after instructions concerning money, using the cognate word ὀφειλάς (*ophelias*, 13:17; "what is due them," NRSV; "what you owe them," NIV), is most naturally taken literally, Paul has twice already in Romans used it as a metaphor, once for his own obligation to bring the gospel to the whole world (1:14) and again to indicate the Christian's obligation to live by the Spirit and not the flesh (8:12). For the sense of obligation we may compare 4:4; 15:1, 27; the root regularly carries both literal and metaphorical meanings in early Christian writings.[526] The

526. See BDAG 743.

context thus breathes life into what might be for him a nearly dead metaphor, giving a particular force to the command to love: This is a debt, owed to everyone, that can never be discharged.

The explanation, in the second half of the verse, should not be misunderstood. Paul does not, of course, mean "Love fulfils the Torah; therefore love is the way to earn righteousness with God." He does not suppose that this was ever the purpose of Torah. Rather, the purpose of Torah was that Israel might be God's light to the world; Israel was "entrusted with God's oracles," but proved unfaithful. Those who are justified by faith "apart from the works of the Torah" (3:28) are now, perfectly logically, instructed to live as the people through whom what the Torah by itself could not do is accomplished (8:3-8; 10:1-11). People who love their neighbors thus "fulfill Torah," both in the immediate sense that they will never do any of the things Torah forbids, and in the wider sense that through them God's way of life will be seen to advantage. The Greek for "the one who loves the neighbor has fulfilled the law" could also be translated "the one who loves has fulfilled the other law" (τὸν ἕτερον νόμον *ton heteron nomon*; cf. τις ἑτέρα ἐντολή *tis hetera entolē*, "any other commandment," in v. 9). This has sometimes been adopted by exegetes with the supposed meaning that love fulfils, not Torah itself, but the "other" law—that is, the one that Jesus gave to replace it. This is very awkward in view of the quotation from the Decalogue that follows immediately; and Paul rarely uses the verb "love" absolutely, without an object. The apparent echo of *heteron nomon* in 7:23 is a pure accident.

13:9-10. Paul explains (γάρ *gar*) what he means by saying that love fulfils Torah. First he simply states that all the commandments are in fact summed up in the command to love (v. 9); then he sums this up to the effect that love does no evil, and draws the conclusion that love is indeed Torah's fulfillment (v. 10).[527] Loving one's neighbor is itself, of course, a command in Torah (Lev 19:18, quoted here), though not part of the Ten Commandments. Paul was not the first to see

it as a summary of the whole law; this is one of several passages in Romans 12–13 where we are right to detect echoes of the teaching of Jesus himself (Matt 22:37-39 and par.; see also Jas 2:8, where this commandment is described as the "kingly law," presumably meaning "the command given by the king," i.e., Jesus; cf. 2 Macc 3:13). The specific commands he lists here consist of four of the last five of the ten (omitting the bearing of false witness, a deficiency that one good MS and a few lesser ones tried to rectify), following the LXX order of Deut 5:17-21 (adultery, murder, theft, coveting) rather than that of Exod 20:13-17 (placing theft before murder).[528] The idea of being able to sum up Torah in a single phrase has a long history in Judaism of which Paul was no doubt well aware.[529]

Though v. 10 opens, unusually, without a verbal connection to what precedes, it is clearly intended as a summary of v. 9. It should not be supposed that the full achievement of "love" consists simply in doing no evil; as Dr. Johnson said, to do no harm is the praise of a stone, not a man. Rather, love, on its way to higher and more positive goals, takes in this negative one in a single stride: If love seeks the highest good of the neighbor, it will certainly do no wrong to him or her. We should notice that Paul leaves no room for the slippery argument whereby sexual malpractice has been routinely justified in the modern world; "love," as the summary of the law, includes the command not to commit adultery, and could never be confused with the "love" that is frequently held to excuse it. One only has to ask the question, whether adultery routinely builds up or breaks down human communities and families, to see the point. Once again, then, the "fulfillment of Torah" does not mean the performance of "good works" designed to put God in one's debt; rather (and perhaps this is why Paul writes v. 8 in this fashion), it is the discharge of one's own debt, to one's neighbor but also to God. This passage takes its place alongside Paul's several earlier statements about the

---

527. Fitzmyer, *Romans*, 677, 679, translating οὖν (*oun*, "therefore") as if it were *gar* ("for"), misses the point that Paul is here arguing for this conclusion, not presupposing it.

528. The MT, in both Exodus and Deuteronomy, has murder, adultery, theft. It is unlikely that we should read into Paul's order any sense that it is Deuteronomy that is fulfilled, rather than Exodus, or that there is particular significance in the omission of bearing false witness.

529. See *T. Iss.* 6; *b. Shabb.* 31a, which ascribes to Hillel the saying, "That which you hate, do not do to your fellows; this is the whole law, the rest is commentary; go and learn it!"

Torah, confirming the positive understanding of it for which we argued earlier, and making it clear once again that ethical obligation is not undermined but reaffirmed by a proper understanding of justification and Christian life.

REFLECTIONS

In the light of the suggestion that this passage belongs to some extent at least with 12:3-13, we may reflect on both together.

1. The obvious centrality of love within early Christian ethics is so well known that we often overlook how striking, almost revolutionary, this was. Judaism, of course, cherished the command to love, but did not highlight it in the same way. Within the pagan world there was far less emphasis on anything that approximates to the early Christian meaning of "love," modeled as it was on Jesus himself. This oversight on the part of contemporary readers goes with the more practical problem that we all give lip service to the idea of love but we do not usually reflect on how to do it. Granted the prevailing context of romanticism and existentialism, it is normally assumed that love will "just happen" as long as people are sincere and do what comes naturally. The moral history of the twentieth century should have given the lie to this, but since it is a convenient thing to believe (giving one the feel of virtue without the need for hard moral work) the belief continues unabated, being propagated by most movies, many novels, and a million shallow sermons. We urgently need moral reflection, at every level of church and society, on what exactly love is, what it means and does not mean, and more especially the steps of moral learning and effort required to attain it. The very fact that this sounds so "inauthentic" ("You mean I've got to pretend?" one can hear people asking) is a measure of how far we have allowed ethical reflection to diverge from early Christianity.

2. Of course, Paul wants love to be "genuine" (ἀνυπόκριτος *anypokritos*, "unhypo-critical"). But here is the strange thing. If you try to treat someone you thoroughly dis-like as though in fact you cared very deeply for them—if you try to think of how it is to live inside their skin and walk in their shoes—then it may well happen that a genuine sympathy arises, and from that real affection, and finally an unhypocritical love. This is, after all, more or less what Paul is commending in 12:19-21. The love of which Paul speaks is tough; not simply in the sense of "tough love" as applied to the difficult task of bringing up children, though that may be true as well, but in the sense that, since it does not spring from the emotions but from the will, love will grit its teeth and act as if the emotions were in place, trusting that they will follow in good time. If we reduce ethics to emotions, we lose not only consistency of behavior but also the very possibil-ity of moral discourse.

3. The unity of the church, highlighted in 12:3-8, remains a goal to be worked for despite the apparent failure of many unity schemes of the period between 1960 and 2000. Here Paul stresses the need for humility and mutual respect between different gifts within a Christian community; when everyone is doing what they are called to do to the utmost of their powers, the whole body is in good health. The ecumenical task may consist not least in the humble recognition, between the different denominations, that we may after all have different callings—overlapping, interlocking, most likely, but perhaps different as well. This is not to minimize doctrinal differences, which still matter; nor is it to connive at the scandalous fragmentation of the body of Christ, or the "one body in Christ" as here. It is to suggest that within the greater unity for which we must work we should be prepared to allow room for the particular tasks, characteristics, and genius of the different "churches" that have grown up over the years, particularly since the Reformation. The ecumenical movements of the twentieth century had a dangerously modernist feel (bringing everything together into one grand and possibly grandiose structure); maybe the ecumenical movements of the twenty-first century, though they must avoid the postmodern trap of easygoing acceptance of all differences, which results in further fragmentation, should work at ways of humbly affirming appropriate differences while learning how to celebrate and share all we hold in common.

4. In particular, the common life of love in the one body should also give rise, as in 13:8-10, to the command of love for the neighboring non-Christian world. This must of course work on a daily basis at the local level, in the street, the theater, the office, the factory. There will always be room for improvement—and for humility, penitence, and fresh starts—at that level. Equally, we should not ignore the bracing call to whole churches, and to communities and even countries that think of themselves as basically Christian, to act toward their neighbors in the global village with that same love, the debt that can never be discharged. One of our major world problems, bringing a myriad other evils in its wake, is precisely financial debts that can never be discharged because the compound interest increases faster than ailing economies can service it. Since the lending countries belong to the part of the world that, rightly or wrongly, is seen as "Christian" (and in some cases sees itself thus), we can scarcely avoid the problem, with all its ironies. "Love does no wrong to a neighbor"; working out what that means personally and collectively, and putting it into practice, is one of the most urgent tasks we currently face.

ROMANS 13:11-14, LIVING BY THE RISING SUN

COMMENTARY

Paul ends the section where he began in 12:1-2, setting the Christian's moral obligations in the context of knowing what the time is: It is almost daybreak. This is a familiar image in early Christian writing, again quite possibly going back to Jesus himself; and Paul has developed it elsewhere (1 Thess 5:1-11; see also Matt 24:42-44; 26:45; Mark 13:33-37; Luke 12:35-46; 21:36; Eph 5:8-16; the idea of staying awake to be about one's Christian tasks is also evident in Eph 6:18). This idea flows consistently from the early Christian belief that with the resurrection of Jesus God's promised new age had dawned, but that full day was yet to come (see above all 1 Cor 15:20-28). Christians therefore live in the interval between the early signs of dawn and the sunrise itself, and their behavior must be appropriate for the day, not the night. There is such a thing as appropriate and good nocturnal behavior, but as with 1 Thess 5:7 Paul takes "night" as a synecdoche (one part standing for the whole) for the types of evil behavior that flourish away from the light. There is also a trace here of the metaphor Paul develops more in 1 Thess 5:8 (and that reaches fuller expression in Eph 6:10-17): What you need, between dawn and full day, are the "weapons of light" (13:12). Finally there is the command to "put on" the Lord Jesus Christ, an idea paralleled both in Galatians (3:27) and in Eph 4:24. This paragraph, in short, though perfectly at home at this point in Romans, bringing the opening exhortation of chaps. 12–13 to an appropriate and sharp conclusion, is also a window on several aspects of Pauline ethics. It should not pass unremarked that this was the passage read by Augustine after hearing children's voices chanting "pick up and read, pick up and read"; it was the final push he needed to make a clean break with his past and devote himself entirely to God.[530]

---

530. Augustine *Confessions* 8.29, trans. H. Chadwick (Oxford: Oxford University Press, 1991) 152-53.

13:11. Paul assumes that his readers will know what "time" it is (the word for "time" here is καιρός [*kairos*], a special moment rather than mere chronological time); as in 12:2, he expects them to be familiar with the idea of the old age, which is passing away, and the new age, which is dawning. (The NIV's "understanding the present time" is a somewhat ponderous way of drawing attention to the significance of what he says.) He expects them to be up before day breaks fully; this theme, with its echoes of the Easter morning stories, resonates through the early Christian sense of new creation, new life bursting through the wintry crust of the old world. It is, he insists, time to wake up.

The reason he gives is that "our salvation" is nearer now than when first we believed. Paul does not say, as many of his interpreters have supposed that he said, that the final end of which he speaks in Romans 8, 1 Corinthians 15, 1 Thessalonians 4–5, and elsewhere, will certainly come within a generation; but he knows that it might well do so, and insists that it is the more urgent that Christians behave already in the manner that will then be appropriate. Though "salvation" can refer to saving events during the present course of history (e.g., Phil 1:19), and Paul can insist in one passage that "the day of salvation" is already present (2 Cor 6:2), here the word has its normal meaning, referring to the final day when God will renew all things in Christ and give all the justified their glorious, risen bodies, and investing that event with its sense of "rescue from disaster" (see Rom 5:9-10; 8:24, 29-30; Phil 3:20-21). The idea of the eschatological moment coming "near," which Paul repeats in the next verse, carries echoes of Jesus' original proclamation, as in Mark 1:15 and parallels: God's kingdom "is near."[531] And now, he says, it is nearer than it was at the time we became believers; this is in one sense obvious, but in another needs saying as a reminder that though to us the passage of time seems to move on without much change we should not forget that the great future moment is steadily coming closer.

13:12. By way of explaining what he means by saying it is time to wake up, he declares that the night is nearly over and the day is breaking, and draws the conclusion in a mixed metaphor: it is time to stop nocturnal activities and put on the "weapons" proper for daylight. (The metaphor is more obviously, and gloriously, mixed in 1 Thessalonians 5, where those who are asleep will go into labor pains, because a thief is breaking into the house, while those who are awake should not get drunk, but should put on their armor.) Though "putting on" is the normal term for clothing or protective armor, the verb anticipates v. 14, where it is "the Lord Jesus Christ" who is "put on." The weapons here are "of light," contrasting with the "works of darkness"; "of light" seems to mean "appropriate for daylight," "the weapons that children of day will need." (The NRSV and the NIV translate ὅπλα [*hopla*] as "armor." The word properly denotes military equipment, not primarily clothing; however, the verb here and in Eph 6:11 is ordinarily used of putting on clothes.)

13:13-14. Paul has in mind, clearly, what in Galatians he calls "the works of the flesh," the things that characterize humanity in rebellion against its creator (Gal 5:19). As is often pointed out, "flesh" here means much more than "physicality"; for "quarreling and jealousy" (NRSV) you need an unquiet spirit as well as a sharp tongue and an envious eye. Nevertheless his main target here is the abuse of the body, one's own and often that of others as well: wild parties, drinking-bouts, sexual immorality and licentiousness. These are characteristic nighttime behaviors in the literal sense that they normally happen after dark, and in Paul's metaphorical sense that they belong with the old age rather than with the new day that is dawning in Christ (see 12:2). We should not forget that "quarreling and jealousy" are put on exactly the same level as immorality; there are many churches where the first four sins are unheard of but the last two run riot.

Instead, Paul commands his readers to "put on the Lord Jesus Christ, and make no provision for the flesh" (NRSV), or, as the NIV rightly interprets, "do not think about how to gratify" the desires that come from the corruptible and rebellious side of human

---

531. ἤγγικεν (*engiken*), as in v. 12; the word in this verse is ἐγγύτερον (*engyteron*). On the meaning of Jesus' proclamation of the "nearness" of the kingdom, see Wright, *Jesus and the Victory of God,* 471-72.

nature. Paul has here returned to the basic commands of 6:12-13 (where, as here in v. 12, he speaks of "weapons," though there it is the parts of the body that are to become "weapons of righteousness") and of 8:12-13. And though his particular expressions shift from passage to passage, his underlying terminology is completely consistent. The "body," which will die but be raised, must already in the present be given to God in service and worship (12:2); the "flesh" will die, and its efforts to drag the Christian down with it must be resisted. There must be no loophole, no secret areas where license is permitted, where the "desires" of the "flesh" are tolerated, let alone encouraged (see 7:4-6).

The ultimate safeguard against the seduction of the "flesh" in this full sense is Jesus himself—the Lord, the Messiah. In Gal 3:27 it is "the Messiah" who is to be "put on"; in Eph 5:24 and Col 3:10 it is "the new human being"; but the imagery of putting on a new suit of clothes, carrying as it may well do overtones of baptism, is used in several different senses and cannot easily be systematized. (In 1 Cor 15:53-4 and 2 Cor 5:3 it is used in relation to the resurrection body; in Col 3:12 it is used of the key Christian virtues; see also the passage about baptism and behavior in Romans 6.) Frequently when Paul uses more than one name or title for Jesus the one he wishes to emphasize is placed first; here, by saying, "put on the Lord Jesus Christ," he seems to be drawing attention to the sovereignty of Jesus, not simply over the believer (who is bound to obey the one whose servant he or she is), but perhaps more particularly over the forces of evil that are ranged against the gospel and those who embrace it. The Lord Jesus Christ thus becomes the personification of "the weapons of light" in v. 12: putting him on like a suit of armor is the best protection against the powers of the present darkness (see Eph 6:12). Paul is addressing those who have already "put on Christ" in baptism (Gal 3:27). The assumption must be that he is urging them, as a regular spiritual discipline, to invoke the presence and power of Jesus as Lord of all things to be their defense against all evil, not least the evil toward which they might be lured by their own "flesh."

REFLECTIONS

1. There are three things this passage highlights as basic to Christian behavior. The first is to know what time one is living at. Though as we have seen there are social and cultural reasons why it seems counterintuitive to say so, the Christian is committed to the belief that the world's new day dawned with Jesus the Messiah, and that ever since his resurrection the world has been caught in the overlap between the old and the new, seen here as the moment just before full dawn when those who know their business are already up and behaving as in the daytime. The mental, moral, emotional, and spiritual effort required to sustain a belief in inaugurated eschatology may at times seem impossible. But the effort must be made. Without it, Christian moral teaching can easily degenerate into apparently baseless, or even pointless, exhortations. Why bother staying awake at midnight?[532]

2. The second basic point is the rejection of "the works of darkness," and the making of no provision for "the desires of the flesh." The balancing point between unbridled hedonism on the one hand and nervous dualism on the other is very delicate, and Christians who react against the excesses of the one position are often in danger of lapsing into the other. It is important to read the present passage with 12:1-2 in mind, recognizing and celebrating the goodness of the body while (as in 8:12-13) rejecting some of the characteristic things that the body gets up to—which are what Paul calls "the works of the flesh." Equally, it is important, in celebrating the goodness

---

532. This is where the metaphor's varied NT uses can become confusing. Paul's regular night/day/staying-awake language is about getting up early and being ready for morning. Sometimes in the Gospels (see references above) it is instead about staying awake late at night so as to be ready if and when the burglar, or the master of the house, arrives unexpectedly.

of the created body, and delighting in the truth articulated in the next chapter, that everything made by God is good (14:14; cf. 1 Cor 10:25-27; 1 Tim 4:4), not to be led astray into thinking that therefore all rules concerning eating, drinking, and sexual practice are now irrelevant, shown up as unnecessary and probably dualistic restrictions on God-given liberty. Far from it. There are many things that must simply be ruled out, cut off without mercy; and drunkenness and sexual immorality (which often go together, of course) are among them. "As the flesh will make its own demands, there is no need to meet it halfway."[533]

3. Third, there is the positive command to "put on the Lord Jesus Christ." Paul never explains what exactly he thinks will constitute obedience to this attractive-sounding but to us opaque command, or to the others like it. Since it is similar to the "putting on Christ" that occurs in baptism (Gal 3:27), we may suppose that he has in mind the spiritual discipline, through daily prayer and meditation, of invoking Jesus himself as Lord (and therefore sovereign over oneself and over all powers that might attack) and savior (and therefore able to rescue one from harm). One of the best ways of doing this, practiced in many Christian traditions, is to meditate on the Gospel narratives about Jesus, placing oneself in the position of one of the onlookers or participants in the story and allowing the presence of Jesus to be felt and known, and with that presence allowing his own struggles against evil, and his call to take up the cross and follow him, to have their full effect. The reading of a gospel passage at a daily or weekly eucharist, followed by the solemn invoking of the risen Lord and feeding on the symbols of his self-giving love, is known in many Christian traditions as an excellent way of steadily obeying this most positive of ethical commands.

533. Fitzmyer, *Romans*, 684.

ROMANS 14:1–15:13, GOD'S CALL TO UNITY OF LIFE AND WORSHIP ACROSS BARRIERS OF CUSTOM AND ETHNIC IDENTITY

OVERVIEW

Romans 14:1–15:13 must be treated as a single section. The final paragraph (15:7-13), it is true, also serves as the concluding paragraph for the major theological exposition not only of chaps. 12–15 but of the letter as a whole. That is part of the effect of 15:12, which echoes the theme of 1:3-5 (Jesus as the risen Messiah, the Lord of the whole world). But, as the repetition of "welcome" in 14:1 and 15:7 indicates, 15:7-13 is a summary and indeed celebration of the point that 14:1 has introduced. These two occurences of προσλαμβάνεσθε (*proslambanesthe*), together with the note that God welcomes someone in 14:3 and that Christ welcomes

"you" in 15:7*b*, are the only occurrences of the word in Paul other than Philemon 17.

This exegetical decision strongly inclines me to a particular view of the subject matter of the whole section. It is remarkable that nowhere between 14:1 and 15:6 does Paul use the words "Jew" and "Gentile," or "circumcised" and "uncircumcised." He discusses the problems faced by the little church in Rome purely in terms of the different opinions that members and groups have on matters of food, drink, and observance of special days. He talks in considerable detail about the need for patience and love rather than straining one another's consciences. He speaks in terms of the "strong" and the "weak"; he sees himself as one of the "strong," but his eventual argument (15:1-6) is that the "strong" should follow the example of the Messiah in not "pleasing themselves."

Thus far, what he says is compatible with several different readings of the situation, and scholarship has duly come up with them. Divisions and subdivisions have been analyzed with great care, but no consensus has been reached.[534] However, when we add 15:7-13, as I believe we must, we suddenly find that Paul speaks of "the circumcision" (v. 8) and "the Gentiles" (v. 9), and then concludes the entire section with a string of scriptural quotations that celebrate the fact that Gentiles are coming to join the people of the one God, under the worldwide rule of Israel's Messiah. At this point we are, of course, back on the same map as in Romans 1–11.

The best reading of this problem, I think, is that the divisions Paul knows to exist within the Roman church have at least a strong element about them of the Jew/Gentile tension that has been underneath so much of the letter. This is by no means to say that "the weak" are Jewish Christians and "the strong" are Gentile Christians.[535] Paul is himself a Jewish Christian who sees himself as one of the "strong"; and, if Galatians is anything to go by, there might well be Gentile Christians whom he would categorize as "weak." Rather, the matters about which disagreement has arisen, threatening to thwart united worship of the one God from people of all sorts, stem not principally from other types of cultural pressures, but from the continuing varied influence of the Jewish law within parts of the Christian community.[536]

This explains why he does not mention Jews and Gentiles until the final summary paragraph. To do so earlier would give the wrong impression; the divisions within the church may well not have lain exactly down the ethnic fault-line, since as we noted there might be both "strong" and "weak" Jewish Christians and both "strong" and "weak" Gentile Christians. In addition, to mention too early in the discussion the fact that there was an element of ethnicity about the whole business would have emphasized the very thing he wanted to avoid, drawing the line more firmly in the sand and polarizing those on either side, rather than doing his best to blur the line that was in danger of being drawn, and to insist that people from either side of it should learn to live together and especially to worship together.

It should not be necessary to labor the point that all the people Paul has in mind here are Christians (unlike chapter 11, where he is speaking of Jewish non-Christians).[537] They all give allegiance to Jesus as Lord, a point he makes pivotal in 14:1-12; they all believe themselves to be sharing in the life of God's kingdom (14:17) and the service of the Messiah (14:18; 15:5, 5-6). They have a duty to one another because they are all brothers and sisters for whom the Messiah died (14:15). This section is not, then, a way of outlining how Christians should live alongside non-Christian Jewish neighbors in Rome. As we might have inferred from the present section of the letter, where chaps. 12–13 have laid a foundation and chaps. 14–15 now build on it, these are instructions for the church.

But we do not know as much about the church as Paul did, or at least thought he did. He assumes much that we cannot even guess. The fact that he writes such a substantial and closely argued section of the letter oriented toward this topic, in the light of the spare and brief comments on several major matters in chaps. 12–13, is a strong indication that he believed he was addressing a real, not a theoretical or merely possible, problem. His basic appeal to "welcome one another" implies that the church was divided into various groups, probably each meeting in a separate

---

534. For details of the relevant discussions, see M. Reasoner, *The Strong and the Weak: Romans 14.1–15.13 in Context*, SNTSMS 103 (Cambridge: Cambridge University Press, 1999). An important alternative view is that of R. J. Karris, "Romans 14:1–15:13 and the Occasion of Romans," in Donfried, *The Romans Debate*, 65-84. Karris argues that Paul did not know the Roman situation, but was generalizing from experience elsewhere (e.g., Corinth).

535. Against Moo, *The Epistle to the Romans*, 829, though many of the points he makes remain important.

536. Horace *Satires* 1:9:71. Horace describes how a fellow poet, Fuscus Aristius, refuses to talk business on a sabbath day for fear of offending the Jews, describing himself, having scruples about such things, as "weaker" (*infirmior*), and saying there are many others like him. This reinforces the point made in relation to Galatians: Those insisting on Jewish regulations might actually be Gentiles, while Jews like Paul and his friends might be sitting loose to them.

537. For the opposite view see Mark D. Nanos, *The Mystery of Romans: The Jewish Context of Paul's Letter* (Minneapolis: Fortress, 1996) esp. chap. 3. It is impossible to do justice here to Nanos's interesting, detailed, but ultimately unsuccessful analysis.

small gathering, a different house, with mutual suspicions or even antipathies. It may well be that the problem had become particularly acute when the capital's Jewish population, expelled five or six years earlier by Claudius, had after Nero's accession returned en masse, including a number of Jewish Christians who had for the time being, like Paul's friends Prisca and Aquila, been forced to live elsewhere (Rom 16:3-5; cf. Acts 18:2-3).[538] We may assume that Prisca and Aquila were themselves "strong" Jewish Christians, like Paul; but the tensions between different groups, in terms of practices that some regarded as mandatory and others as irrelevant, was bound to increase under these circumstances. It is possible that some of the tensions that had emerged in the church in Corinth, due (at an earlier stage) to the personality cults reflected in 1 Corinthians 1–4 and (at a later stage) to the "super-apostles" and/or the "false apostles," whoever they were, mentioned in 2 Corinthians, had arisen in Rome as well (was there, perhaps, a "Peter" party in Rome?). Our comparative uncertainty about the precise details of the Corinthian situation makes it difficult to do more than suggest that parallels might well have existed. We would be safe in assuming that there were several different Christian groups meeting in Rome, involving a spectrum of opinion on these and other debated issues. Paul is determined to address not just some, but all of them, and to use this opportunity to promote their unity.

The tensions we see in this section are therefore similar to those we find in 1 Corinthians 8–10, but with some significant differences. The problem in Corinth seems to have been primarily, in Witherington's choice phrase, the question of venue rather than of menu.[539] Granted that it was legitimate, other things being equal, to eat meat sold in the market even though it had probably been offered to an idol as a sacrifice, it was not legitimate for Christians to go into the idol's temple itself and take part in either the cult, or the meals, or other practices associated with it. This question does not seem to be at issue in Rome; the Christians are not,

it seems, being tempted to visit idol temples, or if they are Paul does not allude to the fact. But the question of whether to eat meat, and the discussion of how to avoid offending the conscience of a fellow Christian, joins the two discussions together. It is not unlike the different discussions of justification, of the promises to Abraham, and so forth, in Romans and Galatians: a different but related situation causes Paul to draw on the same stock of ideas, producing overlap but not identity.

Paul's analysis and treatment of the problem is notable for its initial highlighting of "faith" in 14:1-2, and its return to this in 14:22-23. This raises the question, which an extended discussion like this prompts in any case: what is the relationship of the present passage to the entire letter so far? The mention of "faith" obviously gives more specific focus to this, since "faith" has been a major theme, especially in 3:21–4:25 and 9:30–10:21. At first sight it might seem as though chap. 14 had little to do with these previous passages. This is not because it is about "ethics" rather than "theology"; as we saw in introducing chapters 12–16, this is a distinction we bring to Paul rather than find in him. It is rather that when he speaks of some people being "weak in faith," and of others "believing one can eat anything" (14:1-2), this seems to have nothing to do with the meaning of "faith" in the earlier sections, where it has to do with the confession that Jesus is Lord and the belief that God raised him from the dead (10:9; cf. 4:24-25). Closer investigation, however, suggests otherwise. The first major argument of the section (14:1-12) hinges at every point on the fact that Jesus is Lord and that God raised him from the dead. The word κύριος (*kyrios*; or in one case its cognate verb) occurs no fewer than ten times between v. 4 and v. 11 (the occurrence in v. 11 comes within the quotation of Isa 49:18; see below). The heart of the passage, v. 9, declares that the reason the Messiah died and rose was in order to become Lord of both dead and living; and this gives rise, as in 2:1-16, to a statement of the future judgment of God at which everything will be put to rights. When we put this together—Jesus as the crucified and risen Lord of all, with weak and strong alike together facing the future judgment and working out their

538. Wright, *The New Testament and the People of God*, 354-55.
539. B. W. Witherington, "Not So Idle Thoughts About *Eidolothuton*," *TynBull* 44 (1993) 237-54.

present status in the light of that—we should probably conclude that this is, in fact, another variation on the same theme that Paul was offering in chaps. 3–4 and 9–10 (on the link with 4:20-21 see the Commentary on 14:23). As we might have guessed from Gal 2:11-21, the first time "justification by faith" occurs as a theme in Paul's writings, part of the meaning of this theme itself is the fact that all those who believe in Jesus as the risen Lord should be able to eat together despite cultural and ethnic differences.

This means that we should probably be open to taking "faith" in the passage as meaning something close to its meaning elsewhere in the letter; and this is in fact what we find. Paul does not imply that those who are "weak in the faith" have any less a grasp on the basic content of the faith (Jesus' resurrection and lordship) than the others; only that, like those who have a weak conscience in 1 Corinthians 8, they have not thought through and worked out the full implications of that faith. Paul is constantly hinting that they should do so, but he knows from pastoral practice that people cannot necessarily be hurried on such issues and that, provided they share the basic faith itself, its relative "strength" or "weakness" should not hinder Christian fellowship. The "weak in faith," then, are not people who only accept part of the Christian gospel; they are people whose faith, though real, has not matured to the point where they understand its full implications. Now the real point emerges: "justification by faith" includes "fellowship by faith" as one of its key elements. All those who believe the gospel of Jesus the risen Messiah and Lord belong together in the same family. Romans 14–15 does not contain, after all, something other than Paul's central

theology. It is not simply "practical instructions" that leave the deep and detailed theology of justification and the rest far behind. It is, rather, what justification by faith looks like when it sits down at table in Christian fellowship.[540] And this, as we shall see when we get to 14:9-12, is what ultimately poses a challenge to the surrounding pagan culture itself.

Romans 14:1–15:13 divides up into three segments, which then further subdivide though less obviously. The topic is introduced in 14:1-12 and is given the basic analysis and answer: The weak and the strong must recognize that they have the same Lord, the one who died and rose again to be Lord of all. There will come a judgment at which all will give account, and it is not up to one Christian to pre-empt God's right in advance. Then 14:13-23 focuses on the issue of how to cope in practice, granted that both sides agree not to condemn the other; here, as in 1 Cor 8:7-13, Paul emphasizes the importance of respecting, and not making demands on, one another's consciences. This leads to 15:1-13, which moves in two waves to the great conclusion in which all alike praise the one God. Romans 15:1-6 shows the Messiah leading the way to this united praise, in his "not pleasing himself"; 15:7-13 insists again on the mutual welcome, based on the welcoming ministry of the Messiah, and celebrates with a sudden rush of scriptural citations the coming together in worship of Jews and Gentiles under the rule of this risen Messiah, through whom the one God will supply the present church with hope, through the power of the Holy Spirit.

---

540. On the relation of the various issues in 1 Corinthians 8–10 and the present passage, see N. T. Wright, "One God, One Lord, One People: Incarnational Christology for a Church in a Pagan Environment," *Ex Aud* 7 (1991) 45-58.

Romans 14:1-12, Judging and Being Judged

COMMENTARY

14:1. Without a by-your-leave, Paul launches out from his broad general statement of Christian obligation into a very specific topic, which we must assume had direct relevance to the Roman Christians. There may well have been disputes and dissensions

that had reached Paul's ears. He opens abruptly: "As for the one who is weak as regards faith. . . ." (The singular is important, giving the opening a sharp focus [as against NRSV, which uses plural for the sake of the inclusive pronoun that follows]. NRSV margin suggests that "conviction" is a possible alternative for "faith," but though this is possible it would break the link with earlier parts of the letter.) Paul's command is immediate and to the point: you should welcome such a person. He seems to presuppose that this had not been happening.

Another presupposition emerges at once: Paul assumes that most of those reading or hearing this letter are, like him, "strong" in the sense soon to be developed. The "weak" are perhaps a minority; perhaps not even whole worshiping groups, but individuals within groups. Paul's point is that they must be made welcome, but that this ought not to become an occasion for people to ask them about their particular views and engage them in disputes over matters that are the subject of genuine questioning. (διάκρισις [diakrisis] can have a good sense, "distinguishing," though here it seems to mean "disputes" in a bad sense; likewise, διαλογισμός [dialogismos] can have a positive or neutral sense, "reasoning," or a negative one, "grumbling," "disputing"; the range of meaning of the two words is such that the phrase could mean "disputes about disputes," and perhaps that is more or less what Paul intends to convey.)

14:2-4. The first instance Paul gives contains almost all the elements of the whole first paragraph: (1) naming the disputed area; (2) commanding both sides to back off from passing judgment, on the grounds of God's welcome of the other; (3) warning against "condemning"; (4) invoking the lordship of Jesus, and declaring that Jesus will vindicate either or both parties.

He begins with the issue that, we may well suppose, lay close to the heart of it all. In Antioch, Peter, Barnabas, and others had originally eaten with Gentile Christians, but had separated themselves after "certain persons came from James" (Gal 2:11-14). This is not an identical issue, but it belongs in the same family of disputes, at the center of which lay the centuries-old Jewish taboos regarding food, both what to eat, how to prepare it, and with whom and in what condition to eat it.[541] Like any such deep-rooted cultural

issue, it would emerge in different forms in different situations, but with an underlying family resemblance; and it is not difficult to imagine the context of the present warning. If most Christians in Rome seemed happy to eat non-kosher food, or to eat meat bought in a market when it had almost certainly been originally offered in sacrifice to an idol, there were bound to be some for whom this was unthinkable. It went against everything they had been taught from childhood. If Christianity was an entirely new religion they might be prepared to throw away old beliefs. Part of the point, though, was that in the Messiah God had been faithful to the covenant. The Messiah was the goal of Torah. How then could Torah's forbidding of certain foods be set aside?

These questions are not simple, and Paul could not expect every Christian to come instantly and from the heart to the same conclusion that he and many others had reached: that Torah had indeed been fulfilled but that a new age had thereby been inaugurated that, though it did not deny the goodness and God-givenness of Torah, nevertheless relativized many of its injunctions as relating to the period when God's people were a single nation (see esp. Gal 3:15-29). But already the two poles of the dispute are set up, as in v. 2: one person believes it is permissible to eat everything, while another only eats vegetables. Paul does not say whether the latter position has been taken because kosher meat was unavailable, or because all meat for sale would have been offered to idols. People would know what he was talking about, namely, the kind of scruple that, because of such dangers, reckons it is best to steer clear of meat altogether.

To say that the first person "believes" that everything may be eaten is to say that, in this person's construal of the whole Christian faith, this position is a result of their more fundamental convictions about God and Jesus. The NRSV's "Some people believe in eating anything" is misleading, (a) implying that "eating anything" is the actual object of faith (as though on principle they ate the most peculiar things they could find), whereas Paul surely means that the underlying faith they hold has this as its corollary, and (b) substituting "anything" for "everything," which gives

541. On Jewish food laws see Wright, *The New Testament and the People of God*, 237-41; Wright, *Jesus and the Victory of God*, 396-98.

the phrase almost a contemptuous ring (like "some people think they can get away with anything"). This is not Paul's point. He is simply reporting the fact that some Christians—himself included—have come to the settled conviction that there are no food taboos in the kingdom of God.

Verse 3 issues the basic command and explanation that governs the whole discussion and that Paul will repeat from various angles until the final statement in 15:7. Neither party must pass judgment on the other, because God has welcomed both. Actually, Paul is a little more nuanced than this: the eater must not despise the non-eater. This can hardly be a matter of condemnation, since the non-eater is not doing anything wrong, merely not exercising a right. The attitude Paul is ruling out is like the disdain shown by a motorist who drives as fast as the law allows and looks down on someone who timidly drives at only half that speed. The non-eater, however, may well "condemn" the eater, because from that point of view eating forbidden foods is actually sinful (the NIV more or less doubles the length of the verse by expanding Paul's simple words "the eater" and "the non-eater" into full paraphrases of the two positions). The "welcome" God has already extended to both is a way of summing up the message of 3:21–5:11, as for instance in 5:2: being justified by faith, we have peace with God through our Lord Jesus Christ, through whom we have received access to this grace in which we stand. That this whole strand of thought is not far below the surface will emerge later when Paul, almost casually defining "the kingdom of God" in 14:17, does so in terms that exactly summarize 5:1-5.

In v. 4 he personalizes the point: "Who do you think you are, passing judgment on someone else's household slave?" (the NRSV's concern for inclusivity again blunts the sharp force of the sing. "you" and the sing. "slave"). The point is obvious: it is up to the master to judge the slave. For one slave to look into the next room and pass judgment on another is simply inappropriate; it shows a failure to recognize who's who. Paul expresses this in terms of "standing" and "falling" both as a metaphor for "being vindicated" as opposed to "being condemned" and, perhaps, as a hint of what the Christian "vindication" will

consist in: "being made to stand" is an early Christian way of speaking about "resurrection" (see Eph 5:14; for the metaphorical use, see 11:20; 1 Cor 10:12). When Paul speaks of the Lord (or, since he is using the metaphor of household slaves, the "master" as in the NIV—though this is to obscure the emphasis on Jesus as Lord throughout the passage) being "able" to make the slave "stand," the word for "he is able" is δυνατεῖ (*dynatei*), cognate with words for "power" that Paul often uses in relation to God's accomplishment of the resurrection (see, e.g., Rom 1:4; 1 Cor 6:14). His main point is that the Lord, the master of all the household, is able to vindicate servants who eat meat and servants who do not; but the echoes, as he says this, are of the greater vindication that is promised at the last. Since the paragraph ends with an explicit statement of the final day of judgment, we are right to allow these echoes to be heard, and to understand the present nonjudging life of the community within its eschatological frame of reference.

14:5-6. Paul now adds to the picture a second cause of contention: the observation of special days. The NRSV, translating literally, brings out the interwoven nature of the argument, as "some judge" one day better than another, while "others judge" all alike. The special days are presumably regarded as "more sacred" (NIV) or "holier" (NJB) than the others, but there is no word in the Greek corresponding to this; Paul simply says "one judges a day above a day, another judges every day." It is just possible that Paul has in mind the festival days of the wider pagan world, not least the Roman Empire; but it is far more likely that he is referring to the Jewish festival days, some of which, Acts implies, he himself observed (cf. Acts 20:16; it is, of course, possible to take this as a purely chronological reference). It is interesting, if that is so, that he does not refer to the sabbath explicitly. There is an apparent tension between his open attitude in this passage and his strong condemnation of the Galatians for observing "days, and months, and seasons, and years," the sure sign that by adopting Jewish practices they were, in fact, reverting to another variety of paganism (Gal 4:10). This is the same apparent tension that we find between his open attitude toward circumcision and uncircumcision in 1 Corinthians 7 and his strong condemnation, throughout Galatians, of Gentiles getting circumcised. In both cases the tension is more apparent than real. There seems no question in Romans of erstwhile pagans believing that they had to become full Jews in order to be part of the family of Abraham. The whole emphasis of the letter runs the other way, that the Roman Christians were tempted to look down on non-Christian Jews (chaps. 9–11) and now on Christians who, whether or not because of their Jewish origins, wanted to maintain some of the food taboos and other cultural markers. The "weak" might be condemning the "strong," but the main problem seems to be that the "strong" are looking down on the "weak."

Paul's principle here, which will become more important as the chapter proceeds, is that everyone should be fully convinced in their own mind. He spells out in v. 6 what this will mean: if what is done (observing the day, eating certain foods, or not eating them) is done "to the Lord"—the sign of which, in the case of meals, is the giving of thanks to God—then there should be no cause for complaint.

14:7-9. Paul now explains the argument so far by grounding it in the very heart of the gospel. Verse 7, introduced with γάρ (*gar*, "for"), states the principle, which is then itself explained (*gar* in each case) in turn by vv. 8-9 (this sequence of thought is obscured in the NIV by the inexplicable paragraph break after v. 8). The essential point is that everything Christians do is done, not in relation to themselves alone, but in relation to the Lord. To "live to oneself," the position Paul rules out in v. 7, is to order one's life in relation simply to one's own background, culture, desires, and wishes; these may not be wrong in themselves, but everything must be judged in relation to the Lord himself (see the parallels to this idea in 2 Cor 5:15; Gal 2:19-20). The most basic things we do—living and dying—are done in the presence of the Lord, and for his sake: Whichever of these we do, and by implication everything else we do as well, we belong to the Lord (for the idea of "belonging" to the Lord, see Gal 3:29 ["belonging to the Messiah"] and Rom 8:9; 1 Cor 3:23; 6:19-20; 15:23; 2 Cor 10:7; Gal 5:24). In Rom 14:7-9 we are still,

by implication, in the metaphorical world of masters and servants. But the mention of living and dying brings Paul to the deepest explanation of the whole business: The Messiah died and lived in order to rule as Lord over dead and living alike (v. 9).[542] This "ruling as Lord," clearly, explains the "belonging to the Lord" in v. 8: it is the death and resurrection of Jesus the Messiah that means we now belong to him, and that constitutes him indeed as the Lord of the whole world (1:3-5; 15:12). This proves more than Paul needs to prove for the immediate argument, but it points, as we shall see, to the larger issue that stands behind the entire section. The gospel announcement that Jesus, the crucified and risen Messiah, is the Lord of the whole world is thus appealed to as the reason for unity across the barriers of custom and taboo.

14:10-12. Though the surface argument has developed through the discussion of particular practical matters, and words of command and advice, the underlying sequence of thought has been about God and the Lord. God welcomes all believers (v. 3); the Lord will make them stand (v. 4); the Lord is the one before whom all is done (v. 6), especially when thanks are offered to God (v. 6). The Lord is the one to whom we live or die, to whom we belong, because the Messiah died and rose to become the universal Lord (vv. 8-9). This underlying sequence now reaches its climax in what begins as another rhetorical question about condemning or despising, but is actually a statement of the final judgment, as in 2:1-16 and 2 Cor 5:10, backed up by a passage from Isaiah that was obviously of vital significance to Paul. He has declared in 12:1-2 and 13:11-14 that Christian life is lived in the light of the new age, already breaking in; this is what that eschatological perspective on communal living looks like in practice.

He begins with another question to two imaginary bystanders: "You, there! and, yes, you too!" As in v. 3, one is judging and the other is despising; presumably, again, the weak judging the strong and the

---

542. It is unusual for Paul to say simply "lived" (ἔζησεν *ezēsen*) rather than "lived again" or "was raised." Several mss, reflecting this, have made adjustments accordingly. Presumably Paul has put it like this because he wants to tie in the gospel events very tightly both to our present obligation (v. 8) and to the universal lordship of Christ (v. 9*b*), both expressed in these terms.

strong despising the weak. As they stand there squabbling in Paul's imagination, they are suddenly commanded to look up: there before them is the tribunal, the βῆμα (*bēma*), and it belongs to none other than God.[543] This does not necessarily mean that God the father will do the judging in person; in Acts 25:10 Paul is standing before Caesar's tribunal, but they are in Caesarea, not Rome, and it is the governor Festus who is actually hearing the case. We should probably understand here that Jesus, as the risen Messiah, is the actual judge, even though the court comes under the overall jurisdiction of God the creator. In any case, the point for the present is that all disputes between Christians over inessentials are now irrelevant. It is to God that all must give an account (v. 12).

In between the statement of v. 10 and the conclusion of v. 12, Paul has inserted a quotation from Isa 45:23 ("to me every knee shall bow, and every tongue shall swear to God").[544] This is introduced by "As I live, says YHWH," a phrase that occurs so often in Scripture that it seems pointless to assign it a particular reference, though Isa 49:18 is often cited.[545] This picks up the "lived" of v. 9; in other words, the "living again" of Jesus is the reason why he is thus installed as judge, which in turn is the reason why it would be wrong to collapse κύριος (*kyrios*) here into a general reference to God, rather than retaining it, however paradoxically, as a reference to Jesus as the risen Messiah and, therefore, the judge. (For "resurrection, therefore Messiah," see 1:3-4; 15:12; for "resurrection, therefore judge," see 2:16; Acts 10:42; 17:31; for "Messiah, therefore judge," see Psalms 2; 72; *Pss. Sol.* 17; 2 Tim 4:1.) The main quotation, with Phil 2:10 as a close parallel, is interesting for a number of reasons. First, it brings together (as the whole passage has done), "Lord" (*kyrios*) and "God" (θεός *theos*) in a way that both echoes the LXX usage and indicates how strong and high Paul's underlying

christology is at this point (see the Commentary on 10:13). Second, it emphasizes the universal sovereignty of the God of Israel, exercised in and through the risen Messiah and Lord; this, going way beyond the detail of the present argument, alerts us again to Paul's underlying agenda (see below). Third, Paul is once again linking his argument to the theme of Isaiah 40–55, suggesting that his readers should understand their present position in terms of the overall story of that passage, the unveiling of God's righteousness through the strange work of the Servant. They are the people for whom the promises—and now the responsibilities!—are coming true.

Each Christian, then, must give an account of himself or herself to God. There is no tension in Paul's mind between this and 8:1, where there is no condemnation for those who are in Christ. He has already indicated in 2:1-16 that there will be a coming day when all will be judged; the fact that the Christian believer is assured of a favorable verdict on that day does not make it any less serious, as 1 Cor 3:10-17 indicates well enough. Part of his point is that in the light of the coming judgment we have no business judging one another ahead of the time. There may also be a hint that to condemn or despise a fellow Christian is itself an offense for which one should be rebuked.

In another letter Paul envisages situations where a genuine dispute between believers will have to be settled in at least a quasi-judicial fashion. He instructs the community to appoint fit persons for this purpose, on the grounds that they will themselves one day judge angels (1 Cor 6:1-8). He would rather they did not have disputes with one another at all, but if need be this would be the way to settle them, rather than referring to courts of unbelievers. Once again, there is an apparent tension with the present passage; but we must remind ourselves that Romans 14–15 is not about fraud and similar matters, but about disputes over what Paul (controversially, of course) insists on regarding as inessentials. What is more, by analogy with 13:1-7 we could point out that insofar as such persons are appointed by the community, they are not acting as private individuals.

Underneath the whole argument, as a theme at first almost out of sight but emerging

543. Several MSS, and Polycarp *To the Philadelphians* 6.2, have "Christ," as in 2 Cor 5:10; but the best MSS read "God." Polycarp is in any case quoting freely and probably coalescing this passage and 2 Corinthians 5 in his mind. There are several scenes in Acts involving people (including Paul) appearing before a tribunal: e.g., Acts 18:12, 16-17; 25:6, 10, 17.

544. Paul follows the LXX of the latter passage closely, including the extra "to God" at the end. See the detailed discussion in Wagner, *Heralds of the Good News*, 336-40.

545. For more details, see Wagner, *Heralds of the Good News*, 337-38.

gradually until it becomes clear and central in the closing verses, is Paul's implication that, if Jesus is Lord, Caesar is not. The repeated reference to Jesus as Lord throughout vv. 4-8 opens this theme, not least when it is coupled with reference to household slaves; anyone in Rome would know who the ultimate Master was, with a full household of slaves. This by itself might remain a faint echo. But when we find that the Messiah has died and lived in order to rule as Lord over dead and living alike (v. 9) we begin to see where it is leading; and when we come upon a reference to God's tribunal we realize that God and Caesar are here in explicit competition. When Paul then quotes Isa 45:23, just as in Phil 2:10-11 where the Caesar reference ought certainly to be understood,[546] we are right to see the theme in full daylight. Paul has said much more than he needs for the purpose of explaining that differences of customs are irrelevant when God has welcomed all sides, and that judging one another is inappropriate in view of the coming divine judgment. If he has labored the point to this extent, he has probably done so for a special reason; and the most obvious reason is that he is emphasizing that the kingdom to which those in Christ belong is a kingdom superior to, and destined to replace, that of Caesar. The subsequent

546. Not least because of the link with Phil 3:20-21, where it is explicit. See N. T. Wright, "Paul's Gospel and Caesar's Empire," in Horsley, *Paul and Politics,* 160-83.

similar hints (14:17; 15:12) offer further confirmation.

But why is Paul saying this here, in this context? He is holding out two implications for the potentially divided Roman church. On the positive side, he wants to assure them that they are truly an outpost of the coming great empire of Jesus himself, the world's true Lord. Paul, in Rome as elsewhere in Caesar's territory (including colonies like Philippi and Corinth, and centers of imperial cult like Ephesus), is intent on maintaining communities, united in their loyalty to Jesus as Lord, right under the nose of Caesar, who prided himself on maintaining in the world a unity of peoples under his own rule as Lord. The unity of Christians across traditional barriers is a sign to the principalities and powers that a greater rule than theirs has now begun (see, e.g., Gal 4:1-11; Eph 3:10). Maintaining that unity, then, is not just a matter of preventing squabbles and bad feeling in the church. It is part of essential Christian witness to the one Lord. If the church divides along lines related to ethnic or tribal loyalty, it is still living in the world of Caesar. On the negative side, squabbles over the implications of the gospel could inflame tensions between Jewish and Christian communities in Rome, which could give Caesar an excuse for persecution; memories of the expulsion of the Jews under Claudius were still recent. Differences of cultural practice within the church should not be allowed to give Caesar a chance to exercise his delegated authority in the wrong way.

Romans 14:13-23, Conscience and the Kingdom of God

COMMENTARY

14:13. All right, says Paul in one of his punning moods: if you are so keen on judging things, here is something to judge—how not to trip each other up![547] Verse 13 thus forms a bridge between the two halves of chap. 14,

547. This is completely obscured in the NIV ("stop passing judgment . . . make up your mind") and the NRSV ("resolve instead"). The KJV keeps Paul's verbal flourish ("let us not judge one another . . . but judge this rather"). J. B. Phillips attempts to catch the same echo ("Let us stop turning critical eyes on one another. If we must be critical, let us be critical of our own conduct"), though this implies that the "judging" is always negative, whereas the second "judging" is positive, as in "make a good judgment about this."

introducing the new theme, which is the positive side of Paul's exhortation. It is not simply a matter of giving up passing judgment on, or despising, a fellow Christian; it is a matter of taking positive thought to see how to avoid making life difficult for one another—and particularly how the "strong" can avoid making life difficult for the "weak."

The paragraph divides into two segments, each one unpacking v. 13, with a conclusion (vv. 22-23). In vv. 14-18 Paul warns that even things that are not unclean in themselves become so if someone believes them to be, and that this could mean ruin for someone lured into going against conscience. In vv. 19-23 he tells them to avoid things that make a fellow Christian trip up. These two cover very similar ground from only a slightly different angle.

14:14-18. In v. 14*a*, and then again in v. 20*b*, Paul insists that all foods are "clean." This was a regular early Christian belief, though it must have been hard to hammer out and maintain (see Matt 15:11, 17-20; Mark 7:18-19; Acts 10:15, 28; 11:9; Titus 1:15). Paul says here that he knows this, and has been "persuaded in the Lord Jesus." This cannot mean simply that the belief in the cleanness of all foods is part of the truth of being "in Christ." It seems to mean either that in the course of his service of, and love for, the risen Lord, Jesus had made it clear to Paul that all foods were in fact clean; or that Paul is referring to the traditions of Jesus' own sayings known to us from Matthew and Mark. On balance, and recognizing the ways in which Romans 12–13 as well alludes to (what we think of as) gospel tradition, I think it is more likely that he means the latter. (See 1 Cor 7:10, where the contrast with Rom 14:12 indicates that Paul is aware of having access to some teaching from Jesus himself ["the Lord"], while on other matters he must think things out from scratch under the influence of the Spirit [1 Cor 7:40].)[548]

The exception noted in v. 14*b*, though, is not mentioned in the gospel traditions. The thought that one can make a clean object unclean by regarding it as such is striking, and introduces a main theme of the following verses: the importance of making up one's mind and acting accordingly. Paul would not, of course, take this to the lengths of contemporary existentialism, in which any behavior at all is approved as long as it is done wholeheartedly (it being conveniently ignored that people who commit genocide, acts of terrorism, and the like are often deeply sincere). What he is allowing for, throughout this section, is that genuine Christians grow to maturity at different rates and that during this process one cannot and must not hurry or harry them to accept positions their conscience at the moment cannot allow.

548. See Thompson, *Clothed with Christ*, 185-99.

In particular, one must recognize (v. 15) that actual spiritual harm is caused to people when they are put in this position, and that causing such harm is a failure in the basic Christian virtue of love (13:8-10). The *gar* at the start of v. 15 (omitted in most trans.) indicates that Paul thinks he is explaining something here, but if so it must be v. 13, not v. 14. Indeed, acting in a "strong" way can even, Paul warns here and in 1 Cor 8:10-13, cause a fellow Christian's "destruction," despite the fact that the Messiah died for them. This powerful statement presumably means that one could risk betraying a "weak" person into what was, for them, some form of pagan idolatry, and that this could jeopardize their allegiance to Jesus altogether, putting the "strong" Christian at loggerheads with the Messiah himself, who had given his life for them. Paul then juxtaposes a further command (v. 16); something may be "good" for you, but the weaker Christian may call down a curse on it—and perhaps, the implication may be, on you as well.

This is then explained in vv. 17-18, with one of Paul's rare statements about God's kingdom (other Pauline mentions of the kingdom of God: 1 Cor 4:20; 6:9-10; 15:24, 50; Gal 5:21; Eph 5:5; Col 1:13; 4:11; 1 Thess 2:12; 2 Thess 1:5; 2 Tim 4:1, 18). If, however, we avoid slavish concordance-study, we shall learn to recognize themes even when their technical shorthand is absent; and in this case there is a clear earlier discussion: 5:12-21. This is all about the reign of "grace," and of those who receive it as a gift, over against the reign of sin (see 5:14, 17, 21; cf. 6:12, 14; the key word is βασιλεύω [*basileuō*, "to rule as king"], cognate with βασιλεία [*basileia*, "kingdom"]). It forms one of Paul's central (if highly condensed) statements of the entire Christian worldview and narrative, and plays as we saw a major role in the structure of chaps. 5–8 and hence of the letter as a whole. This of itself might not lead us to postulate a connection between the present passage and chap. 5, were it not that Paul's instant definition of God's kingdom in 14:17 happens to form a tight summary of Rom 5:1-5: God's kingdom does not mean food and drink, but "righteousness, peace, and joy in the Holy Spirit." Here we have not only stumbled upon what seems to be Paul's own summary of an earlier passage in the letter, providing an important linking of the present point right back to the most central theological matters, but also a shorthand account of what he thought "the kingdom of God" was all about. The context, both here and in chap. 5, makes it clear that this definition does not mean that the kingdom is a "spiritual" as opposed to a "worldly" matter: 5:12-21 is all about the rule of sin and the rule of grace, the two powers that compete for every cubic inch of creation and every split second of time. What Paul is emphasizing is a matter of priorities: If Rom 5:1-5 is threatened, whatever is posing the threat must take second place. Since v. 17 explains vv. 15-16 (*gar*), we must take it that Paul's meaning is as follows: you must not cause your fellow Christian to suffer, possibly even to be lost altogether, by what you eat, because Rom 5:1-5 ("justified . . . peace . . . joy . . . Holy Spirit") is the most important thing there is, and food and drink, by comparison, rate nowhere on the same scale.

This is the way to behave, he says in a final explanation of the sequence of thought (*gar* again, v. 18): you are serving the Messiah, the king, and if you do so with his kingdom as your priority (see Matt 6:33) you will be, as 12:2 insisted, "well-pleasing" to God. What is more, other people will recognize and approve what you have done.

14:19-21. Paul then puts a second coat of paint on the same argument. He begins with a summary of the positive aim that one should have in all these things (see too 1 Corinthians 14): peace and mutual upbuilding (v. 19). This leads to a command that covers again the ground of v. 15, but whereas he there stressed the importance of honoring, and not jeopardizing, the Messiah's achievement in his death, he here emphasizes "the work of God," perhaps meaning not simply God's work in that individual but God's work in creating the church as a whole, which should be built up, as the previous verse says, and not destroyed (cf. 1 Cor 3:17).[549] Again repeating the previous segment (v. 20*b*, echoing v. 14), Paul insists that all things are pure.

Whereas before, though, he then declared that food became unclean for someone who believed it so, he here makes the different point: food becomes "evil" (not just "unclean") for someone who eats it in such a way as to cause someone else to stumble. The "strong" are hereby confronted: they are right to consider all foods clean, but they must realize that some food can become unclean even for them. Paul literally says "unclean for the one who eats through stumbling"; this could mean "for the weaker Christian who eats despite the objections of conscience," but the next verse suggests that the meaning normally understood is correct.[550] Verse 21 then supports this: here is something positively right and good that "the strong" can do: to abstain from meat, or wine, or anything else that makes a fellow Christian, a "brother," that is, a member of God's family, to stumble.

14:22-23. Paul concludes with another second-person singular address: "You there!" He returns to the mention of "faith" as in 14:1-2: You must hold the faith you have—that is, the interpretation of faith and its outworking—as a matter between you and God. (Again we note that Paul would not say this about all possible interpretations of Christian faith; had he done so, he would scarcely have needed, for instance, to write the letters to Corinth.) He adds, unusually, a blessing on the one who can make up his or her mind and then have no scruples, no self-judgment, in following it. (Paul never elsewhere coins his own "beatitude" [for the form, see Matt 5:3-11, with its rich Jewish background]; the closest he comes is in the direct quotation of Ps 32:1-2 in Rom 4:7-8.) To "condemn oneself for what one approves" may seem somewhat oxymoronic, and there may be a note of irony here: some people may say, for convenience, that they "approve" of doing something when in fact their conscience will be nagging at them that it was wrong all the time. Or perhaps Paul is rubbing in the point of v. 20: you may sincerely approve it, but you are blessed if, when you go ahead and

---

549. Dr. N. Perrin suggests to me that "the work of God" could be an echo of Exod 32:16, where the tablets of the law are "the work of God," destroyed by Moses because of the people's idolatry.

550. The NRSV ("to make others fall by what you eat") and the NIV ("to eat anything that causes someone else to stumble") are both paraphrases that, while giving the correct meaning, are some way away from Paul's own dense wording. The JB has a similar reading ("if by eating it you make somebody else fall away"), but this has been changed in the NJB to correspond to v. 14: "any kind [of food] can be evil for someone to whom it is an offense to eat it."

eat it, you do not have to judge yourself for thereby causing another Christian to stumble.

The concluding verse of the segment (v. 23) looks back to 14:1: you must welcome the "weak," but not in order to have disputes about disputes. Here Paul uses the cognate verb to the first "dispute" word: ὁ διακρινόμενος (*ho diakrinomenos*, "the one who disputes" or "the one who doubts").[551] In addition, this looks back to a key passage, 4:20-21: Abraham did not "waver" or "doubt" in unbelief (οὐ διεκρίθη τῇ ἀπιστίᾳ *ou diekrithē tē apistia*), but "grew strong in faith" (ἐνεδυναμώθη τῇ πίστει *enedynamōthē tē pistei*), being "fully convinced" (πληροφορηθείς *plērophorētheis*) that God was able to do what God had promised. This concentration of terms that echo the present discussion in a passage leading to 5:1-5, which, as we have seen, is also in Paul's mind here, can hardly be accidental. Though Abraham had good reason in human terms to be "weak," to doubt whether God could give him a child, he believed strongly and without wavering, and this faith became the prototype of Christian faith. The present discussion has not, then, been about something other than basic Christian faith (see the Overview). Paul is seeking to nurture and fortify communities in which that faith—with

that content, faith of that type of full conviction—is the basis of identity and unity.

It is perhaps with Abraham and his type of faith in mind that he makes the sharp distinction that sets such a worryingly high standard for all Christian living. To doubt is not to sin; but to act on something when one has serious doubts about it is to fall under condemnation, because the action does not flow from faith. And—a new point, though we might have expected an explanatory *gar*—everything that is not of faith is sin. In other words, you are either with Abraham or with Adam. You are either living, like Abraham, in unwavering trust in God and God's promises; or you are turning away from God and living by some other means. It may sound harsh, but within the argument it makes perfect sense. The point here is not just that the weak may be convicted of sin if, though doubting, they go ahead and eat, though that is the first and probably the main level of meaning. The further level is that the strong, knowing this, must take care lest, by eating, they entice the weak into stumbling, and so themselves sin against the weak (v. 20; cf. 1 Cor 8:12). This complex little analysis of motives, responsibilities, and results is a copybook exercise in thinking through the delicate demands both of love (13:8-10) and of humility (12:3-8) within the Christian community.

At this point in the letter some MSS add the closing blessing, which we know as 16:25-27 (see the Commentary on 15:33).

---

551. This negative sense of the verb (as opposed to the "neutral" regular meanings of "make a distinction, evaluate, judge") is not attested before the NT, though it appears in classical literature afterward, without dependence. See BDAG 231.

Romans 15:1-13, Mutual Welcome, Based on the Messiah

COMMENTARY

As with the previous paragraph (14:13-23), the present one gives the appearance of saying the same thing from two not very different angles in its own two segments (15:1-6, 7-13). Both parts open with a command relating to the discussion of chap. 14; both continue with a statement of what the Messiah has done; both support and develop this with Scripture; both declare that this supplies "hope"; and both conclude with the united

praise of the one God.[552] Since this passage constitutes the final climax of Romans, we should hardly be surprised at this formal, almost formulaic, repetition. The immediate point may be the practical one about mutual welcome across boundaries of custom and conscience, but the underlying message Paul

---

552. So L. E. Keck, "Christology, Soteriology and the Praise of God (Romans 15:7-13)," in *The Conversation Continues: Studies in Paul and John in Honor of J. Louis Martyn*, ed. R. T. Fortna and B. R. Gaventa (Nashville: Abingdon, 1990) 86.

wants to convey is about the glorifying of God in the united worship of Jew and Gentile together in the Messiah.

This paragraph, in fact, offers a triple conclusion: to 14:1–15:13; to 12:1–15:13; and to the letter as a whole, from its very beginning. In the context of 14:1 onward, it draws together the threads in the summons to the strong to support the weak, so that together they may praise God. Within 12:1 onward, it insists on the same humility ("not thinking of yourselves more highly than you ought") that we find in 12:3-8, and returns to the note of worship and praise with which 12:1 opened: the worship of Israel, God's people, with all the world now joining in. Within the entire letter, the paragraph celebrates the fact that through the gospel of the risen Messiah, the world's true Lord, Jew and Gentile come together in God's single family, demonstrating God's covenant faithfulness.[553] Thus, if we heard strong echoes of 5:1-5, 17, and 21 in chap. 14, we would be right to hear in the present passage strong echoes of chaps. 3–4 and 9–11, to see in the united praise of God the reversal of that human failure and Jewish failure that was spelled out so graphically in 1:18–2:29,[554] and to discover Paul, throughout this passage, returning to the primary theme of the gospel itself—God's gospel, attested in the Scriptures, concerning his Son, whose Davidic Messiahship is declared in his resurrection from the dead. Indeed, as is fitting in such a dense summary, the gospel events themselves, the death and resurrection of the Messiah and his installation as Lord, are told again through Scripture. They are applied to the point in hand, but also allowed to resonate in tune with everything that has gone before (15:3, 8-9, 12).

The first subparagraph (vv. 1-6) approaches the practical point negatively: Don't please yourselves, because the Messiah didn't please himself (15:2-3). The second (vv. 7-13) says the same thing positively: welcome one another, because the Messiah welcomed you (v. 7). Paul's two closing blessings (vv. 5-6, 13) draw together themes from a now familiar source: patience, encouragement, hope, joy, peace, faith, and the power of the Holy Spirit. These blessings are another summary and echo of 5:1-5. For those with ears to hear, Paul is saying: "This is how to obtain in practice the great central blessings I outlined at the heart of the letter. Allow 'justification by faith' to produce 'fellowship by faith,' and you will know the peace, patience, joy, and hope that the Spirit brings."

A major feature of this grand conclusion is Paul's use of the Scriptures. Psalms, Deuteronomy, and finally Isaiah—no surprises about his choice of books, or the themes he draws from them. But here, unusually, he adds a note, as though reflecting on the many-sided exposition of Scripture he has offered in this letter. The Scriptures, he says, were given to us to be the means of patience, encouragement, and hope—in other words, the very things God promises, the very things the Holy Spirit puts powerfully into effect. Scripture, it seems, is a means by which God works in the church; in Pauline language, as well as in later technical theology, it is a means of grace. The present passage exemplifies the principle it thus states: the crescendo of scriptural quotations in vv. 3, 9-12 lead the eye up to the source and ground of Christian faith and hope, the Messiah himself, risen to rule the world. So the letter comes full circle, back to Paul's original self-introduction as the servant of God, the apostle of the Messiah and his gospel. This leads him naturally to 15:14-33, where he sketches in, as the letter moves toward its close, his plans for completing his apostolic task.

15:1-2. Two commands summarize the previous discussion: the strong (including Paul himself) are under obligation to "bear with" (NIV) the weaknesses of the powerless. "The failings of the weak" (NRSV, NIV) is hardly correct; the word translated "failings" is cognate with the word for "weak" (ἀσθενῆς *asthenēs*) throughout the previous discussion, and the word translated "weak" here is ἀδύνατος (*adynatos*), a word Paul elsewhere only uses in 8:3. Paul has not suggested that "weakness" is a "failing"; to pull the text that way is to slant his argument. Better to see, now, a subtly new point: "these 'weaknesses' I have been speaking of—the people who possess them are 'powerless.' They are

553. Moo, *The Epistle to the Romans*, 874, disagrees, noting absent themes. One cannot mention everything explicitly in a few lines; I regard the "absent" topics (justification, grace, etc.) as present by strong implication.

554. See Keck, "Christology, Soteriology, and the Praise of God," 94: "the theme of the universal praise of God is, in Paul's view, much more than a rhetorical flourish. It is the actual material soteriological alternative to the root problem of humanity: not giving praise to God or honoring God."

who they are, and at the moment they can't help it. Thus we who are 'strong' have an obligation to support and help them."[555] This has the advantage that it gives to the main verb of v. 1 the meaning it has elsewhere in Paul: βαστάζειν (*bastazein*) does not normally mean "put up with" in the sense of "be prepared to tolerate," but, more positively, "support, help" (Gal 6:2), or "carry" (Gal 6:5).[556] The meaning then is that the strong must help those who, through their own current powerlessless, have these "weaknesses." They must support and encourage them, not browbeat them with demands for more "strength" than they can presently muster (cf. Acts 20:35 [though the word there is the rare ἀντιλαμβάνομαι *antilambanomai*]).

In doing this, the "strong" must not seek their own advantage, must not "please themselves"; as we saw in 12:2, this is the alternative to "pleasing God," and often "pleasing God" will—despite popular opinion to the contrary—involve precisely not "pleasing oneself." Instead (v. 2), everyone must please his or her neighbor, with a view to their good and to the upbuilding of the community (the NRSV and the NIV both make "upbuilding" relate simply to the individual neighbor, but in Paul the word regularly refers to the building up of the whole community). This is, clearly, what the love spoken of in 12:3-13 and 13:8-10 looks like at street level. It is the principle Paul himself adopts in contentious matters (1 Cor 10:31–11:1, a passage quite close to the present one).

15:3. This principle derives from the Messiah himself. Paul has as many ways of speaking about Jesus' messianic death as he has occasions to mention it. Here he draws on Ps 69:9 (69:10 MT; 68:10 LXX), assuming that this great poem of the suffering and vindication of the righteous Israelite found its ultimate embodiment in Israel's Messiah and his crucifixion.[557] This, he says, shows

that the Messiah "did not please himself"; he assumes, too, that his hearers are familiar with the basic story of Jesus, perhaps with oral traditions of such scenes as Gethsemane in which the Messiah shrank from his fate (Mark 14:32-42 and pars.; see also John 12:27; Heb 5:7-9; Rom 15:3 may also be illuminated by Phil 2:6-8, which, if not written by Paul, is certainly endorsed by him; and 2 Cor 8:9). "Not pleasing himself" is, of course, a remarkable understatement when we consider (as Paul could and did elsewhere) the shame and horror of the cross. But it makes the point Paul needs for the moment, while beginning to sketch for the last time the story of Jesus that will reach its climax in 15:12.

15:4. By way of somewhat oblique explanation (*gar*) of this exegesis of the psalm, Paul states that the Scriptures in general ("whatever was written in former days," NRSV) were written for our instruction, so that through patience and the encouragement of the Scriptures we might have hope. This, as we saw, echoes 5:1-5, ascribing to Scripture what is there effected through the Spirit on the basis of God's work of justification. Granted the theme of chap. 14, and the way in which it seems to be continued in 15:1-2, we might have expected here, on the one hand, a more specific reference to the community being built up through mutual support and readiness to give up one's rights and cultural preferences, and on the other hand a more explicit comment on the Messiah's death in relation to achieving that end. Paul, however, already has his sights on the major themes of his conclusion, and it is in the light of that larger picture that the intermediate goal of united worship will become a reality. The Scriptures, and their multiple interpretation of the Messiah's suffering, give God's people hope; and in that context (vv. 5-6) they will be able to think the same way and to glorify God together. What they need for the present is not simply willingness to do what Paul has said in 14:1–15:2, but patience and encouragement; and that is what Scripture provides (cf. 1 Macc 12:9), especially once they learn to see the story of Israel as devolved onto, and fulfilled by, Jesus the Messiah.[558]

---

555. The NJB's "the susceptibilities of the weaker ones" comes toward this, but still misses the underlying point. See also the NEB/REB: "the tender scruples of the weak."

556. BDAG cites only this reference and Rev 2:3, with Ignatius Polycarp 1:2, for the meaning "bear patiently, put up with." But the Ignatius passage surely means "help" or "support"; and Rev 2:3, which uses the absolute verb without object, can simply mean "enduring" without the somewhat grudging sense of "putting up with" something.

557. For this understanding of the Messiah as the "pray-er" of the psalms, see R. B. Hays, "Christ Prays the Psalms: Paul's Use of an Early Christian Exegetical Convention," in *The Future of Christology: Essays in Honor of Leander E. Keck*, ed. A. J. Malherbe and W. A. Meeks (Minneapolis: Fortress, 1993) 122-36. The other half of the same psalm verse is quoted in reference to Jesus' cleansing of the Temple in John 2:17.

558. The unexpected direction of v. 4 led Keck to propose that it be seen as an interpolation. See L. E. Keck, "Romans 15:4–An Interpolation?" in *Faith and History: Essays in Honor of Paul W. Meyer*, ed. J. T. Carroll et al. (Atlanta: Scholars Press, 1991) 125-36. I agree substantially with Hays's careful rebuttal of this ("Christ Prays the Psalms," 132-34).

15:5-6. Paul turns his thoughts into prayer, the first time he has reported a prayer in relation to the Roman church since 1:9-12, where the theme of mutual comfort was likewise prominent; he is consciously coming full circle. His prayer is that "the God of patience and comfort" will give them a united mind (lit., "to think the same thing among one another according to the Messiah Jesus.").[559] This is Paul's regular appeal, whether or not he thinks a church is actually divided (see Phil 2:2-4, which, in company with 2:5-11, bears close comparison with Rom 14:1–15:13 as a whole). The object of coming to a common mind (ὁμοθυμαδόν *homothymadon*, a word found frequently in the early chapters of Acts (e.g., 1:14; 2:46; 4:24; 5:12; 7:57), is thereby to come to a common worship, literally "with one mouth." The object of this worship, as we might have guessed from the intricate christological dance of the previous chapter, is the God who is now revealed in relation to the Lord: "the God and father of our Lord Jesus the Messiah" (see, e.g., 1 Cor 8:6; 15:28; Phil 2:11; see also the Commentary on 10:13).[560]

15:7. The final paragraph of the letter's theological exposition, like the final paragraph of the great central section chaps. 5–8, transforms into a coda of praise and celebration but without any loss of theological poise. Paul opens with the repeated instruction from 14:1, only this time as a command to any and all parties within the church: welcome one another, therefore (the "therefore," [διό *dio*] picks up the entire previous argument). Here, as in v. 3, the Messiah's action is the crucial basis and model for what the church must now do; again, ὁ Χριστός (*ho Christos*) undoubtedly means "Messiah," and cannot be reduced to a proper name.[561] The Messiah, as he says in the next verse, is the one in and through whom God's promises to the Jewish ancestors are fulfilled; and this short paragraph is framed at its further end also by a celebration of the Messiah's work on behalf of the whole world (v. 12). The final

clause of the verse, "to the glory of God," has in view the glorifying of God in praise and worship that is the subject of the rest of the paragraph. Thus, although the Messiah's welcome is undoubtedly also glorifying to God, this clause goes more directly with the command to welcome one another: "Just as the Messiah welcomed you, so you should welcome one another in order that God may be glorified." The verse forms a typically Pauline paragraph-opening, containing the various elements that will then be developed.

15:8-9a. What is this messianic "welcome"? Paul explains (λέγω γάρ *legō gar*) with a complex statement of what the Messiah accomplished, reminding us of the dense messianic formulations that stand at the head of the letter as a whole (1:3-4) and of chaps. 9–11 (9:5). (There are other echoes of 9:4-5: glory, promises, patriarchs, Messiah [four out of the eight privileges there listed]). There is good reason to suppose that Paul intends here simultaneously to explain the messianic roots of the specific appeal of v. 7, and to sum up the entire letter. This is what he, at least, thinks he has been talking about all the way through.

The heart of the statement rephrases one of Paul's central presuppositions, which has proved difficult for theologians and exegetes alike to come to terms with: it is by bringing Israel's history to its climax that God, through the Messiah, has opened the way of mercy to all the nations. It is not that God has done one thing for Jews, and another thing for Gentiles; God has designed mercy for all (11:28-32), but as 9–11 made clear, the purpose for Israel always had the Gentiles in mind, and the purpose for Gentiles was always that they would come in to the fulfilled, returned-from-exile Israel. This, indeed, is what the scriptural quotations about to be produced are taken by Paul to be saying. Thus vv. 8-9*a* should be read as follows: The Messiah became a servant of the circumcision (i.e., of ethnic Israel) in order to confirm God's truthfulness.[562]

The mention of God's truthfulness sends our minds back to 3:4, 7 ("Let God be true,

559. The NIV's "a spirit of unity among yourselves as you follow Christ Jesus" manages to paraphrase out Paul's sharp meaning at both ends of the clause; Paul is talking about how they are to think, not just feel (as "a spirit" suggests to today's hearers); and "according to the Messiah," granted 15:3 and the whole epistle, is more than simply "following," however high a theology of discipleship we may have.

560. See Wright, *The Climax of the Covenant*, chaps. 2, 4, and 6.

561. So, rightly, Dunn, *Romans 9–16*, 840.

562. Granted Paul's use of Isaiah 40–55, it is not entirely fanciful to see a reference to the Isaianic "servant" here, though the word Paul uses (διάκονος *diakonos*) is very rare in the LXX, where the "servant" is referred to as παῖς (*pais*). This, however, could have been problematic for Paul, since *pais*, which basically means "child," would hardly have done in the present context.

though every human be false . . . if God's truthfulness abounds through my falsehood to his glory, why am I still being condemned as a sinner?" [my translation]), where it is closely correlated with God's faithfulness and righteousness: Paul has the ancient promises in mind once more. But, here as there, these promises were never simply for ethnic Israel; nor were they divided, with one part belonging to Israel and the other to the nations. The promises were both *to* Israel and *through* Israel to the world.[563] This means that we should probably take the next two clauses as both parallel and consequential: the Messiah became a servant (a) to confirm the promises to the patriarchs and (b) so that the Gentiles might glorify God for mercy—but the inclusion of Gentiles is precisely one of the central patriarchal promises Paul highlights, not least in chap. 4.[564] The statement is dense because, as well as summing up the entire exposition of God's righteousness, echoing chapters 3–4 and 9–11 in ways too many and complex to enumerate here, Paul is still conscious of making his final appeal to the community. The Messiah became a servant of the circumcision—so you Gentile Christians should love and serve your Jewish brothers and sisters in the Messiah, and not look down on them; and this was in order that the Gentiles should join with God's ancient people in united praise—so you Jewish Christians should celebrate the fact that you have people of every race joining with you in the messianic community.

The two clauses thus play out the intertwined results of the Messiah's work (while at the same time underscoring the early Christian awareness of the fact that Jesus himself had concentrated his work on ethnic Israel, not in order to exclude Gentiles permanently but because the way to save the world was to complete Israel's destiny; cf. Matt 10:5-6; 15:21-28 and par.; John 4:22-26). "Confirming the promises made to the patriarchs" sums up chaps. 4 and 9, and concisely catches the central meaning of "God's righteousness," the major theme of the letter. Nor was this simply a matter of some unfinished business

on God's part, a few promises left unfulfilled that had to be dealt with if only to avoid the charge of unfaithfulness; these promises encapsulated the single, unalterable divine saving plan for the whole world, and confirming them through the Messiah's servant ministry was the heart of God's intention.

Thus the second, and consequent, result of this ministry, "that the Gentiles might glorify God for mercy," follows both in the logic of the divine plan (and of the messianic achievement) and in the logic of Paul's appeal to the community.[565] This is the doxological correlate of justification by faith: the gathering of Gentiles into the one people of God, not by works of Torah but simply by faith in God's saving action in the Messiah, results in united praise. This, in other words, is where what appear to many exegetes as two different themes in Rom 3:21-31 (God's saving action in Jesus' death resulting in justification by faith, on the one hand, and the coming together of Jew and Gentile on the other) are finally revealed as one and the same. This was what the Messiah's servant work was about all along.

15:9b-11. Paul celebrates the theme of united worship with three biblical quotations, preparing the way for a final quotation (in v. 12) that sums up the entire letter.[566] As Richard Hays has persuasively argued, the opening citation from Ps 18:49 (17:50 LXX), when read in the wider context of that psalm, is intended not simply as a messianic prophecy now fulfilled, but as a statement of the embodiment, in Jesus the Messiah, of the pattern of suffering and vindication through which (as the next verse says) God's salvation and mercy are poured out, not least "upon God's Messiah, to David and his seed for ever" (Ps 17:51 LXX). The citation thus ties in both with the mention of mercy in the earlier part of v. 9 and with the explicitly Davidic statement in v. 12, while itself making the central point that the Messiah himself, understood as the one praying in this psalm, is standing

---

563. There is an echo here of Mic 7:20, which sets up several relevant resonances when read in the context of 7:7-20 as a whole.

564. For a different view, see J. R. Wagner, "The Christ, Servant of Jew and Gentile: A Fresh Approach to Romans 15:8-9," *JBL* 116 (1997) 473-85.

565. The change of subject is grammatically harsh (so Cranfield, *A Critical and Exegetical Commentary on the Epistle to the Romans,* 743), but scarcely impossible for the Paul who, precisely in his dense summaries, was capable of all sorts of shortcuts in his Greek. For the use of ὑπέρ (*hyper*) to give the reason for praise or thanksgiving, see 1 Cor 10:30. See also Wagner, "The Christ, Servant of Jew and Gentile," 479.

566. Keck, "Christology, Soteriology and the Praise of God (Romans 15:7-13)," suggests that Paul has added these verses to an already existing tradition consisting of vv. 8 and 12. This is conceivable, but I do not think it likely.

there, surrounded by Gentiles, singing God's praises.[567]

For the second citation Paul returns to Deuteronomy 32 (cf. Rom 10:19; 12:19). Here the Septuagint comes to his help; the Hebrew text simply says "Praise his people, you nations," but in the LXX of v. 43 this has become "Praise, you nations, with his people," giving Paul not only further grist to his present mill but enabling him thus to tie in this passage with the deuteronomic theme that was so important in chap. 10. He then reverts to the psalter, finding in Ps 117:1 a classic invitation to the whole world to join in the praises of Israel's God. This, after all, was and is the challenge of Jewish monotheism: that the God of Israel was the creator, the God of the whole world, and that therefore the other nations, though presently stuck in idolatry, ought eventually to come to recognize and worship the same God that Israel worshiped. How this would happen remained an almost complete mystery in the ancient Scriptures. It has been Paul's theme throughout Romans that it has now been accomplished through the Messiah and by the Spirit.

15:12-13. It should be no surprise, then, that as his last quotation Paul chooses, with great care, a passage from Isaiah (11:10) that says exactly what he wants to say at the climax of 14:1–15:13 and at the same time completes the circle begun in 1:3-4. The Gentiles will come to hope in the Davidic Messiah, the "root of Jesse" (for "root of Jesse" as a title for the Messiah, see Rev 5:5; 22:16); he is the one who "rises to rule the nations." The echo of 1:4 should leave us in no doubt that Paul intends a reference to Jesus' resurrection. This is what constituted him as Messiah and Lord of the whole world. Once again the wider context of Paul's citation fills in the depths of meaning he has no space to spell out: Isaiah speaks here of God's purpose to renew the whole created order, and to gather the remnant of Israel, together with the Gentile world, into the one community of salvation (Isa 11:1–12:6).[568] The idea of a risen Messiah "ruling the nations" is, further, packed with explosive political implications,

especially in a letter to Rome whose own emperor claimed to rule the nations. Paul, we may suppose, has had this verse of Isaiah in mind throughout the whole letter, waiting to produce it as the final move in his entire argument.

The note that comes through is "hope," as in v. 4. This is not what we might have expected; Paul, we might have supposed, would speak of "love" in concluding a passage about mutual welcome in Christ, or of "joy" in a passage about praise. But we should not suppose that he has been careless at this of all moments, especially since he reinforces the point in v. 13, referring to God as "the God of hope" and praying that his readers may "abound in hope by the power of the Holy Spirit."

Hope was, of course, a major theme of chaps. 5–8, and echoes of that section, and of its summary introduction (5:1-5), abound here. Paul's eye seems to be on the following implied thought: that throughout its struggles to live as one community despite cultural and ethnic differences, what the community needs is precisely that eschatological perspective on their present life that is supplied in 12:2 and 13:11-14: in other words, that in order to be the people they are called to be in the present, they need a constant and lively sense of God's promised and assured future. That, perhaps, is one of the reasons why chaps. 12–13 were shaped as they were, framed by the eschatological hope: they were designed to provide the right basis for an appeal that would itself depend on the hope that one day Jesus Christ would be seen and acknowledged as Lord of all (14:11; 15:12). Thus the line of thought that runs from God's promise-keeping in 15:8 to God's gift of hope in 15:13 ("you can trust this God," Paul is saying; "remember what he's already done in the Messiah!") is what he believes the community should remember as it lives within "the present world," Caesar's world, in the faith that Jesus is already Lord because God raised him from the dead, and that soon every knee will bow at his name.

Hope itself is sustained, then, by the "joy and peace" with which the God of hope will fill the community. Here are the notes we would have expected: "joy" is to be experienced in the glad worship of God, and "peace" is to be known within the combined,

567. See Hays, *Echoes of Scripture in the Letters of Paul*, 70-73; Hays, "Christ Prays the Psalms," 134-35.

568. Partly noted in Hays, *Echoes of Scripture in the Letters of Paul*, 73.

united community (cf. 14:19). And all is sustained by the power of the Spirit, the power that raised Jesus from the dead (8:10-11) and is even now at work among those who form his one body (cf. 1:4, 16; 5:5; 8:1-11, 12-27; 12:3-5; 15:19; 1 Cor 2:4-5; 6:14; 12:12-13; 2 Cor 13:4; Eph 1:19; 3:20; Phil 3:10; Col 1:11; 1 Thess 1:5; 2 Thess 1:11).

REFLECTIONS

1. Paul's appeal for unity in 14:1–15:13 is thus grounded in a solidly if incipiently trinitarian theology, and this emphasizes how important it is, for all work for unity within and between churches, that the theological foundations are laid as deeply as possible. The grand schemes for church unity that characterized much of the twentieth century were often allied, unfortunately, with the kind of theology that sat loose to detail in the hope that people would be able to agree on something a bit simpler. Perhaps in the twenty-first century the churches will come to see that unity is a plant that grows best in the deepest soil, and that by patient shared study of our most central beliefs, not least the exploration of who God really is, as revealed in Jesus the Messiah and by the Spirit, and through the shared worship to which this gives rise, we may discover new ways forward in the ecumenical endeavor.

2. Shared worship, indeed, is central to Paul's vision. He does not say that one should wait to share in worship until all aspects of belief and practice have been hammered out. On the contrary. He sees the mutual welcome, allowing people from very different backgrounds literally to worship together with one voice, as of the essence of the quest for a deeper unity. When we read this alongside Gal 2:11-21, we discover that this is not just a bit of good advice; it grows directly from the doctrine of justification by faith itself. The point of that doctrine is that all who confess Jesus as Lord and believe that God raised him from the dead belong in the same worshiping family, and at the same table. Shared eucharistic fellowship should not be the reward awaiting us at the end of ecumenical negotiations and agreements. It should be a central means by which we travel together along that road.

3. Paul's main point in Romans 14 is that there are some things that appear to divide Christians very deeply in terms of their practice but are, in fact (in the language of later theology), "things indifferent" that should not be allowed to divide them. Most Christians would agree that there are such "indifferent" matters, but the difficulty is that there is no agreement on what those matters are, and on which matters are so centrally important that to disagree on them means dividing the church. Paul clearly believed that there were many things on which it was not a matter of saying "one person believes this, another believes that"; when it was reported that a Corinthian Christian had set up with his father's wife, his reaction was not that he should be welcomed as a weaker believer but that he should be kicked out on the spot (1 Cor 5:1-5; the whole chapter is important, distinguishing as it does between the importance of continuing to have dealings with the pagan world and the importance of breaking off relations with Christians who behave in grossly pagan ways). One may imagine that for some of the "weaker" Christians in Rome the idea of eating meat that had not been certified as kosher, or that had been offered to idols, would seem just as "pagan" and hence evil as sexual immorality; indeed, granted the connection between idol-worship and licentious orgies, one can understand their point of view. But what Paul is doing here is in fact to articulate not only his view that there are some "things indifferent" that should not divide the church but also his view as to what some of the key ones are.

Significantly, they are among the central boundary-markers of Judaism: food and holy days. Romans 14 is in fact an exposition, in other terms, of justification by faith apart from works of Torah. That is why Paul himself is a "strong" Christian, and clearly believes that if and when the "weak" were able to arrive at a deeper maturity in the faith they would come to that position as well. Only when we are prepared to think through divisive issues in the light of this central doctrine will the church be able to distinguish between the things that matter and the things that do not. This plays back into the whole theme of unity. Unity is not itself a "thing indifferent," though many, probably most, Christians today regard it as such ("Some Christians believe we should all get together; others believe this doesn't matter"; can you imagine what Paul would have said to that?).

4. At the heart of the appeal is of course love, as in 12:3-13 and 13:8-10. Love here is not a sentimental reaction, to be provoked simply by seeing a look of hurt or disappointment on someone else's face; it is rooted in the conviction that the Messiah died for the other person, too, and that, being oneself a beneficiary of his self-giving love, one cannot deliberately put a stumbling-block in the way of another beneficiary. The family identity of God's people, in which all are brothers and sisters (in a world where family membership meant a closer tie and obligation than today's Western world imagines possible), meant that taking care of one another, and thinking how to avoid making life difficult for each other, was of prime importance.

5. We should not play down the political significance of this entire passage (see especially the comments on 14:10-12 and 15:12). The present disunity of the worldwide church has multiplied precisely in the historical period when, under the insidious pressure of the Enlightenment, "religion" has been carefully separated off from "politics" and kept in a sealed upper chamber ("what individuals do with their solitude") where it cannot interfere with real life. The churches have often gone along with this, imagining themselves thereby to have attained some kind of freedom. But the price of this "freedom" is that it leaves Caesar enthroned, doubly defended against any attack on the arrogance of empire that might come from the Christian gospel. First, a church that acquiesces in its own marginalization (especially if it calls it "freedom") is never likely even to comment on, let alone to engage with, the ruling powers. Second, a church that all too obviously embodies the social, ethnic, cultural, and political divisions of its surrounding world is no real challenge to the Caesars of this world. It is only when representatives of many nations worship the world's true Lord in unity that Caesar might get the hint that there is after all "another king" (Acts 17:7; cf. Eph 3:10). To settle for comfortable disunity because that way we can "be ourselves" and keep things the way we have always known them is to court disloyalty to the one Lord and failure in the church's mission to challenge the gospel of Caesar with the gospel of Jesus Christ.

6. We should continue to learn how to tell the story of God, the world, Israel, Jesus, and ourselves so as to bring out its full flavor. It is highly significant that when Paul comes to sum up the whole letter in 15:7-13 he does so with a compressed narrative in which all the elements of the longer stories he tells from time to time are present, selected here of course for the particular needs of the argument but nevertheless reminding us of the fuller story he could have told, and does tell elsewhere. As long as we insist on reducing Christianity to slogans and isolated "doctrines" or rules, rather than seeing it primarily as the great story of what the one God has done, through the one Lord, for the one world, we will never understand what Paul is about, or be able to recapture the excitement and many-sidedness of his writing. There has been of late a fashion for "narrative" readings of Paul. It should not be thought that this is simply a fad, a new game to play with old counters. It reflects something close to the heart of Paul's own mind: that when you want to understand who God is, what the gospel is, and what our task in the world now is, the foundation for that understanding is the narrative within which the different elements make themselves at home. Revealingly, the two elements of the narrative that much post-Enlightenment thought has screened out, but that a Pauline telling of the story can never forget, are the Israel dimension and the Caesar dimension. The inalienable Jewish roots of the gospel, and the inevitable confrontation with pagan empire, are both embedded in Paul's narrative here and elsewhere, and only when today's church comes to terms with both will it become truly faithful to Paul's vision.

ROMANS 15:14-33, PAUL'S APOSTOLIC TRAVEL PLANS

COMMENTARY

After the exalted tone and the dense, dynamic content of the writing so far, we might expect a more gentle and pastoral tone in the rest of the chapter, rounding off what Paul wants to say before the closing greetings. We get what we expect, but only up to a point. Paul remains himself, and even when discussing in more relaxed mode his recent apostolic work and his future plans he is still drawing on the same controlling story of God, the Messiah and the world, still appealing to Scripture to explain what he has done and is doing, still teasing readers ancient and modern with compact and allusive prose.

This is in fact one of the longest discussions Paul gives anywhere of how he conceives his apostolic work, and why he has made the decisions he has (the exception to this must be 2 Corinthians as a whole). Coming to a church he had neither founded himself nor previously visited, but where several of his colleagues and coworkers now lived, he was conscious of a need to prepare the ground and explain what he was hoping to achieve. We should perhaps remind ourselves that when we speak of the Roman church in this period we are talking of perhaps a hundred people, more or less, in a city of roughly a million. It was hardly the case that there was no room for fresh work for an apostle and evangelist. However, Paul is keen to stress that his main aim is to use Rome as a base for further work in the western Mediterranean, going all the way to Spain; and this gives us a further clue to the purpose of the letter—namely, that if the Roman church is to support him in this work it is vital that they understand the inner dynamic and perspective of the gospel as he announces it.

The passage divides into two, each part dividing again: (1) Paul's intention to complete his earlier apostolic work by traveling via Rome to Spain (15:14-24); (a) Paul's explanation of his recent apostolic work as the reason for writing the letter (vv. 14-21); (b) his intention now to come to Rome and thence to Spain (vv. 22-24); (2) his forthcoming visit to Jerusalem (vv. 25-33); (a) taking the collection to Jerusalem (vv. 25-29); (b) requesting prayer in relation to that visit (vv. 30-33). Verse 14 picks up where 1:15 had left off: now at last, in the light of everything he has said in between, Paul can explain the reasons for his forthcoming visit.

15:14. It is sometimes suggested that Paul had been writing to Rome in the knowledge that there were serious doctrinal problems in the church—that, for instance, there was no real understanding of justification.[569] There is, though, no reason to suggest that a verse like this one, or its predecessor at 1:8, is not meant seriously. Paul knows several of the Christians in Rome, and is confident that they are not off track, but on the contrary are good-hearted people, well instructed, and able to teach one another (νουθετέω [noutheteō] can imply "warn," "admonish," but here it simply seems to carry its neutral meaning, "instruct"). Paul, in other words, did not need to write to them because they were in bad shape, but because his apostolic vocation demanded that for his new phase of work they should be brought in as partners, and hence needed to understand in detail where he was coming from. This is not to say that there were not potential or actual problems in the Roman church, reflected not

---

569. See M. Black, *Romans*, NCB (London: Oliphants, 1973) 23, 40.

least in 11:11-32 and 14:1–15:13, only that he does not regard these as compromising the basic integrity and maturity of the church as a whole.

15:15-16. Paul's own view of the letter he is now completing is that it is a "reminder." He does, after all, say at various points "You do know, don't you?" and we would probably be wrong to treat all these as merely rhetorical (e.g., 6:3; 7:1). He has put things, he says, with a degree of boldness, a statement no reader of Romans is likely to dispute.[570] Once again, as at 1:5 and 12:3, he invokes his own unique vocation by God's grace, this time to explain what he has been doing in recent years (see too 1 Cor 3:10; 15:10). We who are so familiar with the story of Paul's missionary journeys, whether from Acts (with all its attendant historical problems) or from Paul's letters themselves, may forget that he cut a strange figure in the ancient world, a wandering Jew talking, arguing, suffering, praying, celebrating, making tents, traveling, cajoling, weeping, staying in one place for a day and in another for a year, always talking about God and the Messiah, about Jesus as Lord, about the resurrection of the dead. He was like a wandering philosopher, but without many of the accoutrements and with a very different message. He was like a Jewish apologist, but the communities he founded and the company he kept, not to mention the message he brought, though soaked in Jewish Scripture from start to finish, were not something any Jew had ever dreamed of before, and not something many cared to hear. What was he up to, and why should a self-respecting community in Rome take him seriously?

No doubt many of Paul's friends in Rome could and did speak for him. But his own explanation is striking: he has been a cultic minister of the Messiah with special responsibility for the Gentile world. He has been working in the priestly service of God's gospel. His task has been to ensure that when the sacrificial offerings are brought before God— the sacrificial offerings that consist precisely of the Gentile world itself!—they are pleasing to God because they have been made holy by the Holy Spirit. This sudden rush of sacrificial and cultic imagery can hardly be accidental; it is not, it seems, one metaphor taken at random. Paul is after all on his way to Jerusalem to bring a highly significant, and hence contentious, gift of money (see below); the thought of going up to the Temple, like a Diaspora Jew going on pilgrimage, is clearly in his mind. But he is talking about more than a single trip or a single gift. He is talking about his entire vocation, to gather up the Gentile world and present it as a surprising but appropriate offering before the world's creator and its rightful Lord.

This is not the only time that Paul uses sacrificial and priestly language to describe his apostolic vocation, but it is the fullest and most striking such occurrence (see too Phil 2:16-17). He has already spoken of Christian obedience itself in these terms (12:1-2), and since he has just alluded to 12:3 as well (the grace given him in apostolic vocation) we may take it that he sees this as a fuller statement of the way he himself must fulfill the more general instruction he there summarized.

15:17. This, then, is the claim he makes in the Messiah when it comes to his priestly service "concerning the things of God" (the priestly overtones of the latter phrase [τὰ πρὸς τὸν θεόν *ta pros ton theon*] are underlined by the parallel with Heb 2:17). Though Paul can speak of his only "boast" as being "in the Lord" and in his cross (1 Cor 1:31; cf. 2 Cor 10:17; Gal 6:14), he can in fact, as in the next verse, speak also of "what God [or the Messiah] has done through me," and, in consequence, of his beloved churches as his "boast," his "joy," or his "crown" (1 Thess 2:19-20; 3:9; Phil 2:16; 4:1). It is because of this "boast" that he has felt not only able but obliged to write the letter (the NIV's "glory" avoids the apparent self-claim at the cost of Paul's resonances and underlying meaning).

15:18-19a. He explains this (γάρ *gar*) by speaking of what the Messiah has accomplished through him. He does so through a rather oblique double negative, perhaps indicating a certain self-consciousness: literally "I will not dare to say anything about what the Messiah has not accomplished through me." This may be a way of saying "I wouldn't dare

---

570. ἀπὸ μέρους (*apo merous*) could modify "quite boldly"—i.e., "a certain degree of boldness"; the NRSV and the NIV take it with "wrote," to mean "on some points." It is possible, and perhaps preferable, to see it as modifying "as reminding you." Barrett, *A Commentary on the Epistle to the Romans*, 275, takes it thus, suggesting that Paul means that part of his intention has been to remind, without saying what the other part of his intention was. He is most likely acknowledging that for some hearers it has been more than a reminder.

to tell you any stories that aren't strictly true," or it may mean simply "I have the right to speak of what the Messiah has done through me." He then mentions swiftly the various ways in which this work has been accomplished: word and deed, the power of signs and wonders, and (though this is hardly a separable phenomenon) the power of God's Spirit. We may compare 1 Cor 2:4; 2 Cor 12:12; Gal 3:5; 1 Thess 1:5; and the various scenes in Acts, e.g., 14:8-18. Paul does not often mention this, but he clearly assumes that powerful deeds, particularly healings, were part of his gospel ministry. This is his regular modus operandi; it has led him by strange paths, but his boast is that he has thereby been faithful to his commission.

15:19b-21. The result is an astonishing claim: to have announced the gospel message of the Messiah in a long arc from Jerusalem in the south-east to Illyricum (the Balkan coast opposite Italy on the Adriatic sea) in the northwest. This is surprising, because we have no record, in Acts or in Paul's letters, of a trip that far north. Philippi and Thessalonica are in Macedonia (northern Greece), south of Illyricum. The claim may be hyperbole, despite v. 18, or it may reflect a missionary journey of which we know nothing, which is after all quite likely considering how many holes there are in the Acts account (cf. 2 Cor 11:23-33 with Acts 13–20). What is more, to make Jerusalem his starting-point, though in a sense validated by Gal 2:1-10, conflicts at a surface level with the picture in Acts, where Antioch was the base from which he set out and to which he returned (Acts 13:1-3; 14:26). But the fundamental point is not in doubt, nor should it be seen as less than remarkable. Before Paul began, neither Asia Minor nor Greece had heard of Jesus of Nazareth; by the time he was writing this letter, there were little communities all over that part of Caesar's empire (and it was a very significant part of Caesar's empire, including many centers of the new imperial cult) in which Jesus was being celebrated as the risen Messiah, the world's true Lord. That is in itself an astonishing achievement, and Paul must have known it.

Among his aims, he says (v. 20), is to announce the gospel in places where the Messiah had not been previously named.

Conscious of being a "builder," he did not wish to go to work on someone else's "foundation" (see also 1 Cor 3:10-15; 2 Cor 10:15-16). His use of this metaphor is not uniform; in 1 Cor 3:11 he declares that there is only one possible foundation—Jesus the Messiah—so one might have supposed that it would not matter who else built on it, and indeed in the same passage he sees that other people are building on his own foundation. However, his point here may be influenced by his sense that in coming to Rome he is indeed visiting a church founded by someone else. Whether or not this was Peter, and if so whether Paul was aware of this and so was anxious to avoid any suggestion of conflict between the two of them, following previous disasters (Gal 2:11-21), we cannot easily say.

The point can, once again, be stated in terms of the Isaianic Servant theme that Paul has drawn on earlier in the letter (e.g., 10:15-16).[571] Isaiah 52:13-15 spoke of the servant being announced before nations and kings, startling them with the strange message. Paul has already seen that effect wherever he has gone; but he has also seen people come into glad submission to the Servant, whom he clearly takes here to be the Messiah (the citation serves to explain vv. 19-20).

15:22-24. And so—to Spain! This proposal was bound to come as a surprise. All roads led to Rome, and the church there might well have supposed that once the apostle had reached the great capital he would rest content. But Paul has his eyes on a different target. The prophets in whose works he had steeped himself spoke of the faraway coastlands and islands coming to hear of the one God, of their true Lord (Isa 11:11; 41:1; 42:4, 10; 49:1; 51:5; 60:9; see also Ps 65:5-8). Paul no doubt knows that there are islands and coastlands to be found in quite different directions (going south, for instance, or east to India and beyond), and we have no idea whether he knew of Christian missions going there, or whether he ever dreamed of visiting them himself. What we do know is that, being a Roman citizen, he was able to use his citizenship as a help in traveling within the Roman Empire, and that since Rome was

571. See Wagner, *Heralds of the Good News*, 329-36, noting how appropriate it was to pick a text that spoke of people far away, out of earshot as it were, coming to hear the good news.

itself the capital of much of the world it made sense to go there, following his apparent strategy of taking the gospel to central points and letting it do its work from there. Seemingly the logical next step was to complete the whole circuit of the north side of the Mediterranean Sea. The southern side, too, was a busy center of Roman culture, from Egypt through Libya and Cyrene, including the important province of Africa itself (the prominent tip of contemporary Tunisia, opposite Sicily, centered on Carthage). Perhaps Paul intended to make the return journey from Spain along the southern shore.

We cannot know, and these speculations peter out in frustration. That may well be, actually, what happened to Paul as well. We have no evidence that he ever got farther than Rome, and though later legend did its best to fill in the gaps and have him complete a Spanish mission and return to Rome a second time, there is no compelling reason to accept this.

For the moment he makes four points:

First, this tireless program of activity explains why he has been so long coming to them (cf. 1:13). Elsewhere he can speak of "Satan hindering him" in his desire to visit a church; there is no mention of that here, but rather of fruitful work for the gospel (1 Thess 2:18; cf. the Holy Spirit's hindering in Acts 16:6). He has longed for many years to come to them; now at last the moment has arrived. (Or at least he supposes it has.)

Second, his aims for the eastern Mediterranean have been fulfilled; he no longer has any room for new work. This sounds extraordinary, given the tiny number of Christians we must envisage compared to the population in general; but Paul thinks of himself as a church-planter, and once he has established churches in the major centers of population and culture he has to rely on them to do for themselves the work of continued evangelism in their neighborhoods. So, with Ephesus, Philippi, Thessalonica, Athens possibly, and Corinth established—not without difficulties and anxieties!—he quite genuinely concludes that it is time to move on.

Third, he intends to make them his base for further operations, all the way to Spain. Verse 24 is important for what it does not say; it does not say that Paul intends to stamp

his own apostolic authority on the Roman church, or to take over its leadership in some other way. But he does hope to be refreshed in their company for a while (ἀπὸ μέρους [apo merous] here has its temporal, not partitive, sense; Paul is not saying that he hopes they will refresh some parts of him).

15:25-29. This leads Paul, with a sense of foreboding that emerges at the end of the chapter, to the immediate task in hand. He was not to know, writing this letter, that his trip to Jerusalem would indeed nearly cost him his life, and that it would be a matter of years, not weeks, before he eventually arrived in Rome (see Acts 20–28). All he knows, at the moment, is that he has put his hand to a particular plow, at considerable personal risk and cost, and that he must not turn back. He has been organizing a collection of money, throughout the churches in the Greek world, to take to the poor church in Jerusalem, whom he here refers to simply as "the saints" (vv. 25-26). Galatia, Macedonia, and Achaea have contributed generously to this—we can see that process going on, with painfully tactful hints and suggestions, in 1 Cor 16:1-4, and especially in 2 Corinthians 8 and 9—and now it falls to Paul and his companions to take the money thus raised as a gift to Jerusalem. Paul does not mention the Galatian churches here, but he does in this context in 1 Cor 16:1. (This might conceivably indicate that the Galatian churches had declined to support the venture, but we should be wary of jumping to conclusions on a point like this.) It is likely that this is in long-term fulfillment of the promise recorded in Gal 2:10: the Jerusalem leaders asked Paul and Barnabas that they would "remember the poor," meaning not poor people in general but the little and poor church in Jerusalem itself. We may compare Acts 11:27-30, where the Antioch church sends Paul and Barnabas to Jerusalem with famine relief; the relation of this passage to Galatians is disputed. The Paul of Acts 24:17 refers in one of his Roman hearings to his having brought "alms and offerings to my nation."

The collection was motivated, as Paul insists here, by much more than merely the desire, important in itself, to alleviate poverty. Paul saw it as part of a reciprocal action of Jews and Gentiles, to be understood on the larger map sketched in Romans 3–4; 9–11; and 14:1–15:13. The Gentile Christians, he says, are in debt to the Jewish ones: they have come to share in their spiritual blessings, so it is only right that they should minister to them (the word is λειτουργῆσαι *leitourgēsai*, cognate with Paul's "priestly" language about himself in v. 16) in material (σαρκικός *sarkikos*) things; this is one of the few places where the "spiritual/fleshly" contrast in Paul means more or less what it means in our contemporary parlance. But there is more going on than simply redressing a balance, however important (there are echoes here of the to-and-fro movement of 11:11-32). Paul conceives the collection, it appears, as a vital sign and means the unity between the Jewish Christians in Jerusalem (where tensions with the pagan authorities were rising and fierce zealot nationalism brewing) and the Gentile Christians in the wider world. For Gentiles to give money for Jewish Christians was a sign that the Gentiles regarded them as members of the same family; for Jewish Christians to accept it would be a sign that they in turn accepted the Gentiles as part of their family. The collection was thus designed to accomplish, *mutatis mutandis*, the same thing that Paul had been urging in 14:1–15:13.

This, it seems to me, is preferable to the rival account of Paul's motivation, which suggests that he wanted to use the collection as a means of putting Rom 10:19 and 11:13-14 into operation—that is, to provoke non-Christian Jews to "jealousy" and so save some of them—perhaps even, in some grander theories, to precipitate the great event spoken of (so many think) in 11:25-27.[572] Paul's coming with the collection would thus be a new version of the long-prophesied pilgrimage of the nations to Zion.[573] In company with some others, I see no evidence for that.[574] The "great event" turns out to be a figment of the imagination (see the Commentary on 11:25-27); in the present passage Paul is thinking of the effect on Christian Jews, not on non-Christian

ones. All he says about unbelieving Jews is that he prays to be delivered from them, not that they will suddenly see the light as a result of his labors.

He sees the Jerusalem visit with the collection, however important, as essentially a detour. He has a task to complete, and as soon as it is done he will be on his way to Rome. His language for "completing the task" is strange. The NRSV ("have delivered to them what has been collected") and the NIV ("have made sure that they have received this fruit") struggle with what Paul wrote, which literally translated reads "and have sealed to them this fruit" (cf. NJB, "and have given this harvest into their possession"). The basic import is clear: Paul wants to deliver the money safe and sound. But why put it like this? Some have thought he was referring to a literal "seal"; the money was the fruit of his labor in the Gentile world, and he would deliver it to them under his own seal (so NEB; the REB, however, has backed off from this). He may be envisaging himself as a tenant handing over fruit to the owner; or maybe the "fruit" is his whole work among the Gentiles, which this gift will "seal." Others have suggested that, since sealing is the last act before handing over an article, he simply means "when the matter is complete."[575] In any case, that is the last thing he will do—so far as he knows at present—before coming on, via Rome, to Spain. And (v. 29) he has quiet confidence in God (not in himself) that, when he comes, "the blessing of the Messiah" will accompany him as it always has before.

As with the journey to Spain, we do not know exactly what happened when Paul tried to deliver the money in Jerusalem. Acts, which goes into great detail about that visit, does not mention the money except as part of Paul's speech to Festus (24:17). But the visit, clearly, was anything but a detour. Paul, according to Acts at its most detailed, was beaten up, nearly lynched, put on trial before the high priest, then before successive Roman governors, and kept in prison for two or more years before finally appealing to Caesar, and so getting to Rome courtesy of an armed escort to stand trial in the capital.

---

572. This theory, found in many variations, is associated with J. Munck, *Paul and the Salvation of Mankind* (Atlanta: John Knox, 1959). See also K. F. Nickle, *The Collection: A Study in Paul's Strategy* (Naperville, Ill.: Allenson, 1966) 129-42.

573. See S. McKnight, *A Light Among the Gentiles: Jewish Missionary Activity in the Second Temple Period* (Minneapolis: Fortress, 1991) 47-48, drawing on Isa 2:2-4; 60:6-7, 11; Mic 4:13

574. T. L. Donaldson, *Paul and the Gentiles: Remapping the Apostle's Convictional World* (Minneapolis: Fortress, 1997) 256.

575. See Cranfield, *A Critical and Exegetical Commentary on the Epistle to the Romans*, 774-75, discussing other possibilities as well.

This was not, perhaps, what he had in mind in 15:28; but, being Paul, it seems unlikely that he would have objected in the long run.

15:30-33. Aware of the dangers he faces, he concludes with a request for prayer. The request itself is made with a solemn formality: "through our Lord Jesus the Messiah, and the love of the Spirit." The prayer itself will be a struggle: "wrestle together with me in prayer to God on my behalf," he urges them (the NRSV's "join me in earnest prayer" does not get the force of συναγωνίσασθαί μοι [*synagōnisasthai moi*]; cf. NIV, "join me in my struggle"; NEB/REB, "be my allies in the fight"; see also Col 4:12). He encourages them to a twofold prayer: first, that he will himself be rescued, snatched out of the hands of unbelievers in Judaea (he is under no illusions as to his reputation as a traitor to the nation, the law, and God); second, that his ministry will be acceptable to God's people— that is, to the Christian Jews in Jerusalem. He envisages this as a difficult and dangerous time, and he speaks of coming on to Rome afterward (v. 31) almost as if he were planning a holiday in order to recover from it. He wants to come to them in joy, through God's will, and be refreshed with and by them. It is a touching moment, and we who know how the story continued after this letter was written can only look in awe at the faith and hope of the man who planned and wrote of such things.

The letter's main content is complete. Paul adds (v. 33) a brief blessing—this time invoking "the God of peace"—and moves on to personal greetings.[576]

But not all scribes left it at that. One very early manuscript[577] inserts the concluding doxology we now think of as 16:25-27 at this point, before continuing with what we call 16:1-23 and then concluding abruptly. This interesting detail (not the only oddity in that MS) is actually the tip of the iceberg: Metzger's *Textual Commentary* takes over two pages to describe the complex evidence,

and a further page to evaluate it.[578] Some MSS have the doxology both here and after 14:23; two ninth-century MSS and a derivative fourteenth-century one omit it entirely (though one leaves a space at the end of chap. 14 as though there might be something to insert); one fourteenth-century MS has it here and then stops, omitting chap. 16 itself completely. A large number of good MSS, though, have it where it stands in printed texts today.

Many scholars have regarded 16:25-27 as a post-Pauline addition, but this judgment is reached as much on its content as on its remarkably versatile manuscript location. Since, on the basis of my reading of the rest of the letter, I judge the content to be comfortably Pauline, and since I regard it as likely that Paul would have written a fitting doxology rather than allowed the letter to stop short with a brief blessing such as 15:33 or the spurious 16:24 (see below), I belong to the considerable minority who, on balance, regard the doxology as original, and as originally coming at the end of the letter (see the Commentary on 16:25-27). It is easy to explain the other placings. Scribes faced with a longer than usual list of greetings, involving persons by then unknown, might wish to create a more usable document (i.e., one that could be read out during worship) by bringing the doxology forward. Some of the manuscript displacements are almost certainly due to the influence of the second-century teacher Marcion, who hacked this letter about as he did the rest of (what became) the New Testament, in the interests of producing a text that would validate his particular views (that the God of the Old Testament had nothing in common with the God of Jesus Christ). Some may be due to an early desire, possibly as early as Paul's lifetime, possibly even under Paul's direction, to make copies of this extraordinary letter available to churches other than Rome. T. W. Manson, famously,

---

576. On "the God of peace," see 2 Cor 13:11; Phil 4:9; 1 Thess 5:23; Heb 13:20; cf. 2 Thess 3:16: "the Lord of peace." The range of contexts suggests that this was a frequent early Christian title for God, though the communal peace Paul seeks to inculcate in the present section makes it particularly appropriate here.

577. P[46], dated around 200 CE.

578. B. M. Metzger, *A Textual Commentary on the Greek New Testament* (London: United Bible Societies, 1971) 533-36. Other clear discussions include Cranfield, *Romans*, 5-11; H. Gamble, *The Textual History of the Letter to the Romans: A Study in Textual and Literary Criticism* (Grand Rapids: Eerdmans, 1977); L. Hurtado, "The Doxology at the End of Romans," in *New Testament Textual Criticism: Its Significance for Exegesis. Essays in Honor of Bruce M. Metzger*, ed. E. J. Epp and G. Fee (Oxford: Clarendon, 1981) 185-99; Moo, *The Epistle to the Romans*, 936-37; Fitzmyer, *Romans*, 55-67. Byrne, *Romans*, 461, is wrong to state that there is a "virtually unanimous judgment" that the doxology is post-Pauline.

proposed that chap. 16 was added as a "covering letter" to enable a copy of the letter to Rome, which had stopped at the end of chap. 15, to be sent to a church where he knew far more people than he did in Rome, namely Ephesus.[579]

Educated guesses of this sort have been made, and remain appropriate as ways of explaining the complex MS tradition. But they should not be taken as a solid reason for placing 16:25-27 anywhere other than where it is, still less for deleting it altogether.

579. T. W. Manson, "St. Paul's Letter to the Romans—And Others," in *Studies in the Gospels and Epistles*, ed. M. Black (Manchester: Manchester University Press, 1962) 225-41; reprinted in Donfried, *The Romans Debate*, 3-15.

REFLECTIONS

1. Paul combines a strong belief in divine providence with an equally strong recognition that one may not always, in this life, understand what it is up to. Just as in Philemon he speculates on the possible reason why God allowed Onesimus to leave his master and come to Paul, so here he makes plans with enthusiasm but also with the request for prayer that potential disaster may be averted (see Phlm 15). "Perhaps," he says—a wonderful word for combining a belief in God's overruling mercy with a humility about how much of it we can see. He has seen God do extraordinary things through his preaching of the gospel, and he believes there are more to come; but he knows well enough from previous experience that things seldom turn out exactly as planned, and on one occasion he has had to apologize to a church—or at least explain why an apology was not necessary—because it had looked as though he was changing his plans on a whim (2 Cor 1:15-22). He had Spain in his sights; but with Jerusalem to face before he could turn westward he was not altogether sanguine about the prospects.

That was just as well. According to Acts, Jerusalem was a near-disaster, the trip to Rome happened two years late and under armed guard, and the sea might easily have swallowed Paul and his companions before they ever got to see the Seven Hills. Likewise, we do not know if Paul ever made it to Spain at all, and in the absence of evidence that he did most scholars prefer to play safe and suggest that he probably did not.

If there is a lesson to be drawn from this it is that of Prov 19:21: human minds devise many plans, but it is YHWH's purpose that will be established. Paul would have heartily agreed, even when the human mind in question is that of an apostle guided and equipped by God's Spirit. But this should not lead to a shoulder-shrugging fatalism. On the contrary. One of the most important lessons in Romans 15 might be put thus: God allowed Paul to dream of Spain in order that he might write Romans. No matter that Paul probably never reached Spain. What mattered was that he wrote this letter, which has been far more powerful and influential than any missionary visit, even by Paul himself, could ever have been. Perhaps (that word again) half our great plans, the dreams we dream for our churches and our world, and even for ourselves, are dreams God allows us to dream in order that, on the way there, we may accomplish, almost without realizing it, the crucial thing God intends us to do.

2. Paul cheerfully breaks into "priestly" language when speaking of his evangelistic work, in a way that he does not when speaking of presiding in worship, let alone at the eucharist. The time had not yet come, but was not very far off, when devout Christians would draw on Old Testament typology to speak of such things, and for a while the powerful metaphors could make their own points, as could Paul's. The time would come later, though, when the metaphorical status of such language was forgotten, as a new "priestly" class grew up through whom alone valid worship and teaching could be offered; and the time would then come when a large part of the church overthrew all this in the name of Paul himself. Nor has the world stood still on these matters since the Reformation. Such questions still bedevil the quest for unity Paul himself would so earnestly urge upon us.

But perhaps (once more) the time may come when we shall be able to re-explore Paul's metaphors without the sense of having to revive old factions, restore old policies, or follow an antique drum. Maybe "old men ought to be explorers," and we in the church, creaking and tottering under the weight of unnecessary baggage, could do worse than to arrive where we started and know the place for the first time. Maybe when Protestants rediscover priesthood and Catholics rediscover evangelism then both will rediscover Paul, and the fire and the rose might become one. We can always hope; and, under the rubric of the previous point, working toward that hope might achieve God's ends without us even realizing it.

3. The collection and use of money in the church has always been, and probably will always be, a tense and delicate matter. It is worth pondering how Paul and his companions actually carried the stuff; in the days before paper money, still less international banking and credit transfers, they were taking a huge physical risk, just as in organizing the collection Paul was taking a huge risk to his reputation, as we can see reading between the lines of 2 Corinthians 8 and 9. Paul deemed it worthwhile because he knew that money could be of symbolic as well as practical help. Once someone has given to a cause, they will be far more likely to pray for it. Once somebody has received money from an unexpected source, they will feel themselves far more bonded, more part of the family. Paul had been asked by the Jerusalem apostles to "remember the poor"; they might not approve of half of what he did and said on the mission field, but he was determined never to let them say, "he never kept his promise." The apostolic faithfulness, attempting to bring together Jew and Gentile in one community of love and praise, was meant to mirror the similar faithfulness of God. So with our fund-raising, giving of money, charity work, and indeed famine relief: we have become so sophisticated, so clinical, that we can supply a credit card number from a mobile phone while not taking our eyes off the football game on television. It would not hurt to ask, whenever Romans 15 is read: what are we doing, as a church, as individuals, that will send the symbolic as well as practical message that the church of Jesus Christ is one body, one family, and that if one suffers, all suffer?

ROMANS 16:1-16, COMMENDATION AND GREETINGS

COMMENTARY

Despite the brilliant suggestion of T. W. Manson that Romans 16 was a covering letter to enable Romans also to be sent to Ephesus, most scholars have continued to regard it as part of Paul's original letter, to be sent to Rome along with the rest (see the Commentary on 15:14-33). The fact that Romans contains more personal greetings than the rest of Paul's letters put together alerts us that there may be something special afoot, but this does not increase the chances of chapter 16 being intended for somewhere other than Rome.

Indeed, when Paul writes to churches he knows well there is a remarkable absence of named greetings (1 and 2 Corinthians, Galatians, Philippians, 1 and 2 Thessalonians); there are a few messages from Paul's present companions, but otherwise general greetings to the church, without specification (1 Cor 16:15-18 appears to be a partial exception, but this is a commendation of the three messengers from Corinth to Paul, not a greeting as such). The closest we come is precisely two names in Colossians (4:15, 17)—significantly, another church Paul had neither founded nor visited. We could almost formulate it as a rule: if Paul knows the church, he does not name individuals. Anyone who has had to make a speech or write a letter to a community they know well will understand why. The ice is thin. Mention one, and you must mention all.

This does not by itself explain the very large number of names here, or how Paul knew so many people in Rome.[580] On the latter point, we should take it for granted that there was considerable mobility among the early Christians. Roads were good, travel as easy as it had ever been, and some people, like Phoebe in 16:1, will have been financially independent and able to move about for business or personal reasons.[581] Others, like Prisca and Aquila (v. 3), had been in both Corinth (Acts 18:2) and Ephesus (1 Cor 16:19), having traveled there with Paul (Acts 18:18); but, being originally from Rome, it was understandable that they would have returned there once the coast was clear—that is, after Claudius's death. Nothing is more probable than that they should have stayed in touch with Paul and given him information about the little church in Rome itself, or that several other Christians of his acquaintance had already found their way there.

But why mention so many of them? Here we cannot be sure, but the situation of 14:1–15:13 suggests an obvious answer. In five cases, Paul mentions, along with a name or pair of names, the Christians within a household (16:5a, 10-11, 14-15). He may or may not have wanted to mention all the individual Christians he knew in the city, but he was certainly keen to mention all the household churches he knew: we can only guess which ones might have been "weak" and which "strong," but we can be reasonably sure he was careful to greet them all with equal enthusiasm. All sorts of things can be read into accidental omissions. Paul did not want to arrive at Rome and find that he had caused fresh divisions by appearing to favor one group over another.

16:1-2. In his second letter to Corinth, Paul speaks with heavy irony about needing "letters of recommendation" for or from the church there (2 Cor 3:1-3; cf. Acts 18:27; Col 4:10). They knew him and he knew them. To write a letter at all would be to lie about their relationship. But "letters of recommendation" were vital in the ancient world, where, without electronic communication, anybody could turn up in a town claiming to be somebody else. If today we still need letters of reference for employment or immigration purposes, how much more necessary were they in Paul's world.

The person he commends is Phoebe, whose home is in Cenchreae, the eastern port of Corinth (in the days before the canal, Corinth had two ports, with arrangements to drag ships across the isthmus). The implication is that Phoebe is a businesswoman who is able to travel independently, and for Paul to trust her with a letter like this speaks volumes for the respect in which she was held; so it is no surprise to discover that she is a deacon in the church. Attempts to make διάκονος (*diakonos*) mean something else fail: to call her a "servant of the church," with the NIV, does indeed offer a valid translation of the word, but it merely pushes the problem on a stage, since that would either mean that Phoebe was a paid employee of the church (to do what?) or that there was an order of ministry, otherwise unknown, called "servants." "Minister" (REB) is imprecise, because that word is used for several pastoral offices in today's church; "deaconess" (RSV, JB, NJB) is inaccurate, because it implies that Phoebe belonged to a specific order, of female church workers quite different from "deacons," which would not be invented for another three hundred years.[582] She was in a position of leadership, and Paul respected her as such and expected the Roman church to do so as well. He requests, as people did and still do in such letters, the kind of help that a traveler may need; and adds his commendation on

---

580. A helpful contribution is that of P. Lampe, "The Roman Christians of Romans 16," in Donfried, *The Romans Debate*, 216-30.

581. See L. Casson, *Travel in the Ancient World* (London: Allen & Unwin, 1974).

582. See 1 Tim 3:11, which seems to refer to women who hold diaconal office (see 1 Tim 3:8). Pliny *Letters* 10.96.8 speaks of two serving women "whom they call deacons," *ministrae;* Pliny would naturally use the feminine ending to avoid apparent solecism, and this word should not be pressed to indicate that there was a separate order. Too much should not be made of the masculine form of διάκονος (*diakonos*) either, though, since the fem. form was not available and the word could be used with reference to either gender (cf. 13:4). See further the helpful note in Bryan, *A Preface to Romans*, 184-85. On "deaconesses," see *The Oxford Dictionary of the Christian Church*, 3rd ed. (Oxford: Oxford University Press, 1997) 455-56, with bibliography.

the grounds that she has herself been a benefactor to many, himself included. The word "benefactor" means much more, in Paul's world, than simply "she has been a great help" (NIV): benefaction and patronage were a vital part of the culture, and this makes Phoebe someone to be reckoned with socially and financially as well as simply a sister in the Lord and a leader—of whatever sort—in her local church.[583]

16:3-5a. Prisca and Aquila are known from Acts 18:2, 26; 1 Cor 16:19; and 2 Tim 4:19. Acts calls Prisca "Priscilla." They seem to have been among Paul's closest friends, being, like him, tentmakers. How they had "risked their necks" for him is not known, but clearly they were well known in both Corinth and Ephesus, being capable of setting even someone like Apollos straight in his teaching. They had now returned to Rome, having left because of Claudius's edict. Their house is the first of the "house-churches" Paul mentions.

16:5b-16. The details of the names that follow are mostly of interest only in that they may possibly reflect the ethnic composition of the church, though this is inevitably speculative. Prisca and Aquila were certainly Jews, as were Andronicus, Junia, and Herodion; Mary may have been as well. Paul's comments on the persons concerned, though, are sometimes worth pondering. Epaenetus (v. 5b) was the "first fruits of Asia into the Messiah," which presumably means he was the first to be baptized, the sign of more to come (cf. 1 Cor 16:15, where Stephanas has the same honor in Achaea). Mary (v. 6) has "worked hard for you," perhaps in prayer (cf. Col 4:12-13).

Andronicus and Junia (v. 7) are kinsfolk of Paul (this may mean simply that they are Jewish, or, as the NRSV and the NIV suggest, closer relatives) who had been in prison with him, perhaps in Ephesus; since they had been "in Christ" before Paul himself, that must mean that they had been Christians since very early on, certainly before the gospel

came to Asia Minor or indeed anywhere much outside the Levant. They were therefore themselves traveling Christians, whose journeys had already intersected with Paul's, and they had now arrived in Rome, as they had earlier "arrived in Christ," ahead of him. They are man and woman, perhaps husband and wife or possibly brother and sister.[584] This is the more interesting in that they are "of note among the apostles," presumably meaning that both of them were witnesses of the resurrection (which fits, of course, with their being "in Christ" before Paul). Junia is thus one of the female "apostles," the only one so called; though presumably others, such as Mary Magdalene, were known as such as well. On Paul's meaning of "apostle" as "witness of the resurrection," see 1 Cor 9:1 (cf. Acts 1:22); perhaps the two were among the "five hundred at once" of 1 Cor 15:6.

Ampliatus, Urbanus, Stachys, and Apelles (the last of whom could conceivably be another Jewish member of the list) are greeted briefly (vv. 8-10a). The first three are known to Paul personally, and saying that Apelles is "approved in Christ" perhaps means simply that Paul has heard good things of him though he does not know him personally. The "family" or "household" or Aristobulus (the phrase means simply "those of Aristobulus") is perhaps another house church (v. 10b); it is implied that Aristobulus himself is not a member, though, and perhaps it simply means that a group of believers had grown up within his household.[585] If he was the brother of Herod (see the previous note), it would be natural to mention a "Herodion" in the next breath (v. 11a), presumably a freedman in the service of the household. What relation he is to Paul, or whether (as in v. 7) this simply means that he too is a fellow Jew, we cannot know. The mention of Narcissus (v. 11b) introduces a famous name in mid-century Rome: a freedman who rose to great heights under Claudius, only to incur the jealousy of many Romans and to be forced into suicide

---

583. See BDAG 885; B. W. Winter, *Seek the Welfare of the City: Christians as Benefactors and Citizens* (Grand Rapids: Eerdmans, 1994), though curiously Rom 16:2 does not appear in the index. Other discussion and refs. in Moo, *The Epistle to the Romans*, 916. See esp. R. Jewett, "Paul, Phoebe, and the Spanish Mission," in *The Social World of Formative Christianity and Judaism: Essays in Tribute to Howard Clark Kee*, ed. J. Neusner et al. (Philadelphia: Fortress, 1988) 142-61.

584. The KJV has "Junia," though until recently most other versions read "Junias," the masc. form. See R. S. Cervin, "A Note Regarding the Name 'Junia(s)' in Romans 16.7," *NTS* 40/3 (1994) 464-70, demonstrating that the name is certainly fem., despite the desperate attempts of many earlier lexicographers, some MSS, and some translators to this day, to suggest otherwise.

585. On the identification of this Aristobulus with the brother of Herod Agrippa, see Moo, *Romans*, 925. The name is very rare and the identification quite plausible. This Aristobulus had died in 48/49 CE, but the household might well continue to be known under his name.

after Claudius's death. If this is the same man, as most assume, Christians within his household after his death would have occupied a challenging and dangerous position.

Tryphena and Tryphosa (v. 12*a*) increase the number of women in the list, as does Persis (v. 12*b*); all three hard workers in the Lord. Rufus (v. 13) may perhaps be the son of Simon of Cyrene (Mark 15:21), though it was a common enough name. His mother, who remains unnamed, had been a metaphorical mother to Paul at some stage, though in what place and circumstances we do not know. (One of the tantalizing things about this chapter is that, like watching a sequence of film clips going by too fast to take in, we catch tiny glimpses into the world of early Christianity that could be very revealing if only we could freeze the frame and ask one or two leading questions. There was clearly quite a subculture growing up, but we know very nearly nothing about it.)

Verse 14 greets five more people "and the family with them," presumably another house church (where, we want to ask, would they have been on the map of 14:1–15:13? What would they be thinking by this stage of the letter?). Verse 15 greets five more people, including two male and female pairings; some have speculated that Philologus and Julia were husband and wife, with Nereus and his sister being their children. They, with Olympas, play host to another house-church ("all the saints with them"). Verse 16 commands the church to give one another the greeting that was already in common use, "the kiss of peace" or "the holy kiss" (cf. 1 Cor 16:20; 2 Cor 13:12; 1 Thess 5:26; 1 Pet 5:14; Justin Martyr *Apology* 1:65). Christian fellowship must be embodied. A general greeting from "all the Messiah's churches" concludes the list (v. 16*b*).

What do we learn about the Roman church, or even about the purpose of the letter, from this list? Not very much; but if we are right to see the extraordinary number of names as a sign of Paul's attempt to greet the different parts of the church, perhaps including some groups that were not on good terms with one another, we might speculate on the size of the church as a whole. If there are five groups mentioned here (see above), and if each house-church had between, say, six and twenty members, the total number of Christians in Rome would be somewhere between thirty and a hundred. If the Jewish names were more likely to represent communities that still adhered to some Jewish customs (though, as we saw, this would not be true for Paul himself, nor most likely for Prisca and Aquila, and possibly not for Paul's kinsfolk—which accounts for most of the Jewish names), then we might have a sense of which were the "weak" and which the "strong." I do not think we shall ever be able to tell. It seems just as likely that there were a few "weak" members on the fringe of otherwise "strong" house-churches, needing to be welcomed in, rather than entire communities that were solidly committed to one line of practice. What we do have, then, is a small, vulnerable church, needing to know and trust one another across various boundaries; a church many of whose members were not native to Rome, living most likely in immigrant communities within particular areas; a church in which men and women alike took leadership roles; a church where families and households formed the basis of worshiping communities. There is something both attractive and frightening about this picture: enormous potential, huge risks, a community both lively and vulnerable. This is the community that will now be the first to hear one of the greatest letters in the history of the world.

ROMANS 16:17-20, WATCH OUT FOR DIVISIONS

COMMENTARY

We might now have expected greetings from Paul's companions, and a conclusion, but before that Paul throws in a further sharp word of exhortation. It sounds, actually, as though it had escaped from another letter, though there is no textual evidence to suggest that it originated anywhere but here. Perhaps, as Paul thinks and prays about these small house-churches, he has had a sudden stab of anxiety. Do they, he wonders, need to be warned that there are fierce wolves on the loose, who will not spare the flock (cf. Acts 20:29-31)?

16:17. The opening warning tells them to "watch out for" (NIV) or "keep an eye on" (NRSV) those who cause dissensions and "put obstacles in your way" (NIV), going against the basic Christian teaching that they have received. They are to keep away from them (though how, within a small community, is not clear). This command echoes Paul's disciplinary warnings elsewhere (e.g., 1 Cor 5:9-13). Whatever particular problems Paul may have in mind, his language here does not seem to reflect the questions at stake in 14:1–15:13.

16:18-20. This is then backed up (γάρ *gar,* v. 18) with an explanation of what sort of people these may be. They are not serving "our Lord the Messiah" (one of only two occasions when these two titles occur together in the Pauline literature without the name "Jesus," the other being Col 3:24). Instead, they are serving (literally) "their own bellies," presumably meaning "appetites" in general (so NRSV and NIV). This is standard polemical language in the Jewish world of Paul's day, and normally means that the people concerned appear to be denying or abandoning some central part of the faith or teaching; the general tone makes it difficult to insist that the problem must be the same as that in Phil 3:18-19, where similar language is used.[586] The danger they pose is that they are smooth talkers, deceiving the hearts of those who are too innocent for their own good. Paul is quick to assure his hearers that he is confident of their "obedience," since it is well known to all (cf. 1:8); but it is important that they supplement this with a mature wisdom as outlined in one of Jesus' best-known sayings, being simultaneously shrewd and innocent. See Matt 10:16, "wise as serpents, innocent as doves," the first adjective there

being φρόνιμοι (*phronimoi*) rather than σοφοί (*sophoi*) as here; the second is ἀκέραιοι (*akeraioi*) in both.[587]

Once again (v. 20) Paul concludes a train of thought with a blessing. By contrast with 15:5, 13, and 33, though, we catch a darker tone. He evokes Gen 3:15: the God of peace will see to it that "the satan" will be crushed under your feet (cf. Luke 10:17-19, and behind that Ps 91:13; see also Rev 12:10-11; on "the God of peace," see the Commentary on 15:33). Paul elsewhere sees the new, young church vulnerable to enemy attack; it was part of his theology of new creation that the church was now, like Adam and Eve, open to fresh deceit (2 Cor 11:3). But his earlier exposition of the victory of God in Jesus Christ over the sin of Adam and all its entail (5:12-21) enables him here simply to promise that the victory promised in Genesis will be theirs, and that it will come soon. He adds a brief greeting ("the grace of our Lord Jesus be with you"), which, like the closing doxology, has wandered to and fro in the scribal traditions; some MSS have it as v. 24, which is now regularly omitted in printed editions.

This short interjection, coming between the greetings to friends in Rome and the greetings from friends with Paul, functions rhetorically like the sudden reminder that breaks into a family farewell scene: "Don't forget to water the plants!" "Make sure you take your medicine!" It is clearly heartfelt; Paul knows that troublemakers will surface in any church. There is no reason to suppose that he is thinking specifically of the "Judaizing" problem he faced in Galatians, or whatever cognate problems he was warning against in Phil 3:2-3, 17-19. His concern is to warn against any attempt to pull church members away from the central tenets of the faith, what C. S. Lewis called "mere Christianity." However plausible the persuaders, their underlying attempt to change the ground rules of Christian faith and practice usually becomes clear before too long.

---

586. Bryan, *A Preface to Romans,* 231, with references.

587. The dominical saying may at least "stand in the background" at this point. See Stuhlmacher, *Paul's Letter to the Romans,* 253; so, cautiously, Dunn, *Romans 9–16,* 905; D. Wenham, *Paul: Follower of Jesus or Founder of Christianity?* (Grand Rapids: Eerdmans, 1995) 198. Moo, *Romans,* 932 thinks the allusion "probable."

ROMANS 16:21-24, GREETINGS FROM PAUL'S COLLEAGUES

COMMENTARY

16:21. Timothy is well known to readers of Paul. According to Acts 16:1-3, he is the apostle's hand-picked younger colleague, and we see him either by Paul's side or running his errands at several points in the letters (e.g., 1 Cor 4:17; 16:10; 1 Thess 3:2, 6). Lucius, Jason, and Sosipater are not so well known, but they, like some in Rome, are kinsfolk of Paul's (see the discussion of vv. 7, 11; συγγενεῖς [*syngeneis*] may mean "fellow Jews" or it may imply a closer relation). These are a reminder that, though Paul's grief at his kinsfolk in 9:1-3 was real and deep, some of them at least were alongside him (cf. Col 4:10-11). "Jason" may be the person of that name we meet in Acts 17:5-9; "Sosipater" may be the "Sopater" of Acts 20:4.

16:22. Paul's amanuensis, having toiled thus far anonymously to take down the apostle's spectacular flow of thought, peeps for a moment out of hiding. Tertius is still capable of giving unsuspecting readers a fright by claiming to have "written this letter" (NRSV); the NIV softens the impact by translating "who wrote down this letter," which is, of course, what it means.[588]

---

588. For discussions of scribes, shorthand, etc., at this period, see R. E. Richards, *The Secretary in the Letters of Paul*, WUNT 2.42 (Tübingen: Mohr, 1991) esp. 170-72; A. Millard, *Reading and Writing in the Time of Jesus* (New York: New York University Press, 2000) esp. 168-79.

16:23a. Gaius, in whose house the local church meets, and who is playing host to Paul himself, sends greetings. It is not clear whether he is to be identified with one of the other persons of this name in the New Testament; the most likely is the one in 1 Cor 1:14, a resident of Corinth. If, however, Paul is actually staying at Cenchreae while writing, rather than at Corinth itself, Gaius might be the host of the church where Phoebe (vv. 1-2) is a deacon. This might explain why Paul can say he is host to "all the church," perhaps unlikely in a larger city like Corinth.

16:23b. There is an Erastus known (from an inscription) to have held public office in Corinth at this time, and though identification is never certain this may be the same person, conveying his own greetings.[589] Quartus is not heard of anywhere else; like many others before and since, he has simply been a good though obscure Christian. He stands here for the multitudes of whom we know nothing, but who were lights of the world in their several generations.

16:24. This verse, omitted in what are normally regarded as the best MSS, consists simply of the repetition of the closing words of v. 20, with slight variations. Some of the MSS that include it omit the words from v. 20.

---

589. Details in Moo, *Romans*, 935-36; Bryan, *A Preface to Romans*, 233.

REFLECTIONS

1. To a modern Western eye, the most striking feature in the list of greetings is that nearly half the people named are women. Some of them are taking leading roles in the church. When Paul declared in Gal 3:28 that there is "no 'male and female' " in Christ, just as there is neither Jew nor Greek, slave nor free, he meant it. Some have criticized him for not making as much fuss about gender as about ethnicity, but that is largely a function of the problems he had to address in his church. If this list is anything to go by, he could take for granted something that much of the rest of church history could not.

2. Reading between the lines, we can see Paul taking care to greet several Christian gatherings in Rome that may have taken different positions on the issues he discusses in chaps. 14–15. Being a bridge builder between different Christian groups and opinions is hard and painstaking work; it is as easy to give a wrong impression of favoring one "side" or the other as it is hard to undo that impression once made. Today's church badly needs a new generation of bridge builders who will take the trouble to treat the different groups seriously, not only to greet them by name but, as Paul does here, to honor them for who they are and what they are doing in the Lord. The aim must then be to work with them, with integrity and imagination, to bring them into fellowship and mutual respect one with another. This is not to deny that sometimes a trouble-maker must be rebuked, not courted or soothed; vv. 17-20 make that clear enough. But the point to note is that the work of patiently getting to know different Christians and their contexts is demanding, and church leaders need to give attention to it.

3. The blend of wisdom and innocence commended by both Paul (v. 19) and Jesus (Matt 10:16) is needed as much today as ever. Shrewdness without innocence becomes serpentine; innocence without shrewdness becomes naïveté. The laudable desire to think well of everyone needs to be tempered with the recognition that some are indeed out for their own ends and are merely giving the appearance of friendliness and piety by their skill at smooth talking. Unless this is spotted early on and confronted, trouble is stored up for later, as an untreated sore is allowed to fester.

ROMANS 16:25-27, CONCLUDING DOXOLOGY

COMMENTARY

The manuscript variations in which this closing doxology has been moved to two other places in the letter, causing other dislocations as it goes, have been discussed in the Commentary on 15:33. Hardly any copies omit it altogether, however, and the burden of proof ought to be on those (and there are many) who regard it as a post-Pauline addition. The real trouble is the content. Those who have seen Romans as basically about justification by faith balk at a summary and doxology that do not mention it. Those who regard Ephesians and Colossians as non-Pauline find material here that reminds them of those letters, and declare that therefore this passage, too, cannot be by Paul. When others point out that there are in fact several points of contact between these three verses and the rest of Romans, including some themes that are very important but not so fashionable in traditional interpretations, that then becomes a two-edged sword: precisely, say the critics, and that is because whoever wrote it was trying, cunningly, to give the appearance of summing up the letter. Once an argument gets into that state it becomes like peace negotiations between intractable opponents:

Both sides are dug in, and no advance seems possible.[590]

It is true that Paul does not normally conclude his letters with a doxology like this; but it is also true that Romans, real letter though it be, is not like the other letters. Nowhere else does Paul conclude an argument with a passage like 11:33-36, but we do not for that reason strike out that magnificent paean of praise. Nowhere else does Paul lay out so formal and careful a central statement of the Christian story as he does in chaps. 5–8, replete with closing christological formulae at the end of every stage of the argument; but nobody doubts that Paul deliberately wrote that extended statement at the center of this letter. What is more, the letter is from one point of view about worship, and designed to evoke worship. It is, uniquely in his writings, a book about God (see the Introduction), and one of the running themes is the true response to the true God as opposed to the rejection of this God and the turn to idols (1:5, 18-23;

590. See the very clear analysis of the problem in Moo, *Romans*, 936-37. A helpful recent comment is I. H. Marshall, "Romans 16:25-27—An Apt Conclusion," in Soderlund and Wright, *Romans and the People of God*, 170-84.

2:17-24; 4:20-22; 5:12-21; 11:33-36; 12:1-2; 15:6, 9-13). After a book like this, written by a strongly monotheistic Jew, a doxology is just what we should expect. And Paul is a Jesus-centered monotheist, in the sense explored in 10:9-13; a doxology that remains monotheistic while having Jesus at the middle of it, even at the cost of verbal clarity, is somehow exactly right. An imitator might have tried a bit harder to get the grammar to work (see the Commentary on 16:27).

What is more, Paul did in fact introduce the letter and its major themes with a reference to "God's gospel concerning God's son," attested by holy Scriptures (1:2) and with the law and the prophets bearing witness to it (3:21). This was, he said at the start, the gospel in which God's righteousness was finally "revealed" (ἀποκαλύπτεται *apokalyptetai*, 1:17) or "manifested" (πεφανέρωται *pephanerōtai*, 3:21); so for him to speak, now, of the gospel proclamation as being "according to the revelation [ἀποκάλυψις *apokalypsis*] of the mystery that is now manifested [φανερωθέντος δὲ νῦν *phanerōthentes de nun*]" echoes his wording at central thematic points, though not in a slavish or obvious way. Above all, the result of the gospel, in a phrase often skipped over in exegesis but placed by Paul at the center of his key introduction, is "the obedience of faith among all the nations" (1:5; cf. 15:18). When we meet in this passage a phrase almost identical to that, but not quite (substituting εἰς *eis* for ἐν *en*), it looks as though the same person has expressed things slightly differently, rather than that someone else has been cutting flowers out of Paul's garden and sorting them into a pretty but now rootless arrangement.

16:25a. The doxology is framed by the opening five Greek words and the final seven: To the one who is able to strengthen you . . . to whom be glory forever, amen!" God's "power" has been an important theme in the letter (1:16, 20; 4:21; 9:17, 22; 11:23), and Paul declared at the start that his aim in coming to visit the Christians in Rome was so that he might impart some spiritual gift to strengthen them (1:11). He is coming to Rome confident that the God he proclaims is able to do this, through the preaching of "my" gospel; as in 2:16, this does not mean that Paul has a different gospel from

everybody else, but rather that he has been personally entrusted with it. This gospel consists, at its heart, of the proclamation of Jesus the Messiah.[591]

16:25b-26. This gospel proclamation, the announcement of the royal news of King Jesus, is the unveiling of God's long-kept secret. This chimes in with Ephesians (1:9; 3:3, 9) and Colossians (1:26-27), but is not to be dismissed for that reason; even if those letters were neither Pauline nor from a close associate, whoever wrote them thought that they were expressing Paul's thought. Paul's own apocalyptic language and its specific meaning (1:16-17; 3:21) is well summed up here. In an undoubtedly genuine letter Paul can make the revelation of God's mysteries a main theme (1 Cor 2:1, 7; 4:1; 13:2; 14:2; and esp. 15:51-52), and he has used the same language at a crucial moment in Romans itself (11:25).[592] This mystery, the long-concealed plan of God, has now been unveiled, and is made known to all the nations through the prophetic writings. Readers of Romans may well think of Isaiah and the rest when they hear the phrase "prophetic writings"; those who consider this doxology a later addition may well assume that the meaning is the supposedly apostolic writings, coming from early Christian "prophets." Perhaps Paul himself could have held these ideas together. His own writings, after all, not least Romans itself, are tightly interwoven with biblical prophecy. The revelation has happened according to the command of the eternal God (see the similar language in 1:20). Its purpose, as Paul said from the start, was to bring about the obedience of faith (see the Commentary on 1:5).

All this is designed to explain the significance of the gospel proclamation of Jesus Christ: when this gospel is announced, it enables people of every nation to see that in Jesus the veil has been drawn back on the eternal plan of the eternal God, and to respond in grateful and obedient loyalty and trust. And it is by this gospel that God is able to strengthen the young church, not least

591. The καί (*kai*) cannot here mean "and" as though the proclamation of Jesus were something other than "my gospel"; it is either explicative ("namely") or intensive ("even"). See BDAG, 495-96.

592. This theme, then, is scarcely evidence of a "Marcionite" tendency in the doxology, despite C. K. Barrett, *The Epistle to the Romans*, 2nd ed. (London: A. & C. Black, 1971) 10-11.

through Paul's ministry as he comes to Rome (1:11).

16:27. There remains a twist in the tail. Paul regularly moves with bewildering ease between the one God, conceived in thoroughly Jewish terms, and Jesus the Messiah, the Lord. In Romans itself we have seen a full incarnational theology, set out in 1:3-4 as a theme, developed in 5:6-11 and 8:3-4 in particular, restated in 9:5, developed again, strikingly, in 10:5-13, and then used afresh in 14:1-12. Paul has celebrated the "wisdom" of the one true God in 11:33. Now he puts the whole picture together with more regard for underlying theology than Greek grammar, which often comes off worst, after all, in the bustle and verve of his thinking. The NRSV sticks close to the Greek, with its teasing ambiguity: "To the only wise God, through Jesus Christ, to whom be glory forever! Amen." (The NIV has smoothed this out: "to the only wise God be glory forever through Jesus Christ"; similarly, KJV, RSV, NEB, REB, NJB, and a few [obviously secondary] MSS. The awkwardness of how the Greek actually puts it raises again the question as to whether a careful imitator would have dared to write something like this.)

The question is, To whom does the "to whom" refer? God? Or Jesus Christ? I suspect that Paul's answer would be: Yes. That, of course, is the meaning of "Amen."

REFLECTIONS

The praise of God has been central to this letter, as the formal summing-up in 15:7-13 made clear. It should not surprise us that the letter ends in most MSS with an invocation of the one true and wise God, made known in and through Jesus the Messiah; or that Paul would draw together so many threads of his argument in this way. The ideal reader of Romans, in fact, is one who is prepared to heed a summons to love this one God with mind and heart alike, and who is ready to let that love transform his or her life at every level. If the God of Abraham, Isaac, and Jacob really is the creator, the God of the whole world, and if this God raised Jesus from the dead and thereby announced that he was and is the Messiah, the world's true Lord, then worship—"the *Shema* of faith"; the "living sacrifice"—is the ultimately appropriate response. Because humans are made in the image of this God, such worship renews them in this image, and indeed transforms them to bear the image of God's son, so that he might be the firstborn among many sons and daughters (8:29).

Part of that renewal is the renewal of the mind (12:2). Anyone who has wrestled with Romans will know the challenge of that renewal, and will discover mental muscles, as well as spiritual, that need to be stretched and trained. By summing up so much of the sheer intellectual content of the letter, this doxology challenges readers to turn that mental work, too, into praise, not to rest content with one activity for the study desk and another for the prayer desk.

Ultimately, Paul's vision of the renewed community is of united worship, based on shared faith (15:6, 8-13). The praise that rises to the one God from the renewed community will thus reflect God's righteousness, that covenant faithfulness in which the Jew first, and also equally the Greek, are drawn into the one family. That is how the community will be most truly itself. And if it is to be strengthened for shared worship and living of this quality, what it needs, not merely at the beginning of its life but undergirding it all through, is the gospel, the royal announcement of Jesus Christ. That is what this letter has been all about.

THE FIRST LETTER TO THE CORINTHIANS

INTRODUCTION, COMMENTARY, AND REFLECTIONS
BY
J. PAUL SAMPLEY

THE FIRST LETTER TO THE
CORINTHIANS

INTRODUCTION

Some seventeen years after the death of Jesus Christ, Paul, a Jew who had become a believer about fourteen years earlier, preached the gospel to certain gentiles—and perhaps to a few Jews—in Corinth, and a church was formed.

THE CITY OF CORINTH

Located about forty miles to the south-southwest of Athens on the shoulder of the isthmus linking the Peloponese to the rest of Greece, Corinth is, as important ancient cities needed to be, strategically defensible: It is set back from its two more vulnerable shore towns, Lechaeum on the Bay of Corinth a couple of miles to the north, and Cenchreae on the Saronic Bay about six miles to the east; it backs up against the 1,500-foot elevation of Acrocorinth; and its abundant springs assure an adequate water supply.

In Paul's time, Corinth was a hub commercially and religiously. Corinth was perhaps best known for its artisans' products, such as bronzes, but it also did a thriving business in pottery and earthenware. Religious diversity was ensured by Corinth's location. By portaging the couple of miles across the Corinthian isthmus, shippers of goods between the regions of the eastern Mediterranean basin and Rome could avoid the considerable hazards of storms in the exposed Mediterranean Sea (see Acts 27:2-44). Sailors and travelers brought with them their religions and planted them so successfully in Corinth that modern archaeologists find evidence for most of the more than two dozen temples, altars, and shrines that the mid-second-century Greek chronicler Pausanias described.[1] The archaeological evidence confirms that Greek and Egyptian religious shrines coexisted there along with the Roman imperial cult. In fact, Pausanias records that alongside the forum at Corinth there was even "a temple for all the gods."[2] Also Jews, some

---

1. Jerome Murphy-O'Connor, *St. Paul's Corinth: Texts and Archaeology* (Collegeville, Minn.: Liturgical, 1983) 78 80.
2. Pausanias 2.6–3.1.

like Prisca and Aquila, no doubt expelled by emperors Tiberius (19 CE) and Claudius (49 CE), found Corinth attractive and settled there.

Politically, Corinth enjoyed colony status, the greatest civic honor that could be accorded cities in the empire.[3] Colony status assured a special relation with the Roman Empire in which Roman laws were operative, Latin was the official governmental language (even though the populace spoke Greek and Paul's letters to Corinth are written in Greek), and as noted the imperial cult was established. Under the emperor Claudius (41–54 CE) the senate looked to Corinth even more than to Athens as the lead city of the Roman province of Achaia, and Corinth paid taxes directly to Rome well into the second century.[4] Roman proconsuls, in effect governors, went to the provinces as agents of imperial power; such a person was Gallio, who in 51 CE arrived in Corinth. Paul was haled before Gallio (Acts 18:12-17), and Sosthenes, who in Acts is described as the synagogue leader (ἀρχισυνάγωγος *archisynagōgos*, Acts 18:17), was beaten in Gallio's presence for his association with Paul and the gospel (see 1 Cor 1:1).

Whether justifiably or not, cities sometimes get a reputation, coming to be thought of as having traits, one might even say as having a sort of ethos or personality of their own. So it was with Corinth. Apart from the renowned Isthmian games that were hosted in the area every two years, Corinth was said to have a "generally superficial cultural life,"[5] which may in part ultimately be traced to Julius Caesar's reestablishment of Corinth in 44 BCE and to his populating it, along with emigrants from other parts of the empire, with eager upwardly mobile freedpersons who were unloaded from Rome's burgeoning population.[6] Understandably, the transitory nature of ancient commerce, with sailors relishing life in a city and then moving along, contributed to Corinth's becoming known as "Sin City."

Corinth's reputation for wealth without culture and for the abuse of the poor by the wealthy was so well known that Alciphron, the second- or third-century CE composer of figmentary letters reflecting bygone times, could trade on Corinth's reputation in two of his fictional letters. In one he rejoiced that he was able to escape Corinth for Athens' more friendly setting, and he characterized Corinthians as persons "without grace [or charm] and not the least convivial."[7] In the other letter, he called Corinth "the gateway to the Peloponnesus" and described it as superficially lovely enough, with its great wealth and its location "between two seas," but he found it inhabited by persons whom he once again characterized as lacking charm and grace. In the same letter he calls wealthy people's behavior disgusting, coarse, and objectionable and details the grovelling of the abject, wretched poor for the smallest morsels of food.[8] Paul's letter confirms certain details of Corinth's ethos.

Not only does Corinth have a long-standing ethos, but so does the Corinthian church. *First Clement*, a document written from the church in Rome a full generation after Paul's time, notes that the Corinthian Christians continue to "engage in partisan strife" just as in Paul's time (*1 Clem.* 47.3). Paul's letter will give evidence that the Corinthian reputation, both as a city and as a church, is well deserved.

ESTABLISHMENT OF THE CORINTHIAN CHURCH

Paul probably arrived in Corinth for the first time in 50 CE, shortly after he had established churches in Philippi and Thessalonica, the major cities in the Roman province of Macedonia, to the north of the Aegean Sea. Our best efforts to arrive at such a date depend on a reading of Acts 18:11 and an establishment of when the Roman provincial proconsul Gallio (whose arrival in Corinth is mentioned in Acts 18:12) was appointed. By reasonable effort we can establish

---

3. See Richard E. Oster, "When Men Wore Veils to Worship: the Historical Context of 1 Corinthians 11:4," *NTS* 34 (1988) 489-93, for an excellent weighing of the significance of colony status in Corinth.
4. Victor P. Furnish, *II Corinthians* (Garden City, N.Y.: Doubleday, 1984) 9.
5. Furnish, *II Corinthians*, 13.
6. Strabo 8.6.23.
7. Alciphron Letter 15.2.
8. Alciphron Letter 24.

that Gallio was probably appointed in the summer of 51 CE[9] and that Paul appeared before him shortly thereafter (Acts 18:12). Then, if we measure backward from that time and credit the Acts 18:11 claim that Paul had already stayed in Corinth for a year and a half prior to the time he appeared before Gallio, we deduce sometime early in 50 CE for Paul's arrival and inaugural preaching in Corinth. Furthermore, the note that 1 Corinthians is written from Ephesus (1 Cor 16:8) corroborates Acts' picture in 18:18-19 that, when he left Corinth, Paul went to Ephesus later in the summer of 51 CE after he had been haled before Gallio.

PAUL'S EARLIEST LETTERS TO THE CORINTHIANS AND THE DATE OF 1 CORINTHIANS

Paul wrote the Corinthians a letter that we do not possess but that we learn about in what we call 1 Corinthians (1 Cor 5:9-12; often this lost document is referred to as the "previous letter"); so what the Bible refers to as 1 Corinthians is, in fact, Paul's second letter to them. Attempts have been made to identify 2 Cor 6:14–7:1 as a fragment of the "previous" letter, though that passage may not have been written by Paul and in any case argues that the believers should separate themselves from unbelievers, a notion contradicted in 1 Corinthians not only by the context of 1 Cor 5:9 but also by other places in which Paul clearly supposes that believers and unbelievers relate quite appropriately and openly to one another (1 Cor 7:12-16; 10:27-29; 14:24).

In the "previous" letter, Paul says that he wrote them not to associate with "immoral people," meaning by that not the immoral people of the world, because avoiding them would be an impossibility given their prevalence, but those immoral people who have become part of the believing fellowship (5:11). In part 1 Corinthians is occasioned by some ongoing Corinthian confusion regarding immorality as they had understood it in Paul's earlier—now lost—letter. The establishment of dates for the two letters must be coordinated, beginning with 1 Corinthians and then working backward to some suggestion regarding the lost "previous" letter.

Paul's travel plans mentioned at the end of 1 Corinthians (16:5-9) project a visit to Corinth (see also 1 Cor 4:21) but only after Paul stays in Ephesus until Pentecost (1 Cor 16:8), the Jewish-then-Christian festival that came fifty days after the second day of Passover. Appropriately, Paul's temporal reference has led us to assume that what we call 1 Corinthians was written in late fall or winter, leaving time for the pre-Pentecost, remaining work in Ephesus to which Paul alludes by the metaphor of the "wide door" opened to him there (1 Cor 16:9). But which fall or winter? Depending on the weight one gives Acts' portrait of Paul's work in Caesarea, Jerusalem, Antioch (Acts 18:22), Galatia, and Phrygia (Acts 18:23)—not to mention the time it would have taken to establish his mission in Ephesus to the point at which the "wide door" opened to him there—one may expect that 1 Corinthians was written in the fall or winter a couple of years after Paul left Corinth in late summer of 51. So the earliest reasonable estimate of the date for 1 Corinthians would be late fall or winter of 53–54 CE; at the very latest, one might stretch it to the next winter after that.

The dating of the lost letter mentioned in 1 Cor 5:9, then, would have to be enough prior to 1 Corinthians that Paul would have had occasion to discover that his effort at guidance on the issue of immorality had produced misunderstanding in the church at Corinth, though all we can say for certain is that the "previous" letter was written sometime between late summer of 51—that is, after Paul's departure from Corinth—and the fall or winter of 53 or 54.

THE MAKEUP OF THE CORINTHIAN CHURCH

The congregation at Corinth reflects the socioeconomic and religious makeup of the city. In keeping with the "steep social pyramid"[10] that was typical of that culture, very few believers

---

9. See Murphy-O'Connor's excellent evaluation of the evidence and choice of this date, in *St. Paul's Corinth*, 154-58.
10. Ramsay MacMullen, *Roman Social Relations 50 B.C. to A.D. 284* (New Haven: Yale University Press, 1974) 89.

were rich, and most were poor (1 Cor 1:26). Many persons are named in 1 Corinthians or are connected to Corinth in some other New Testament writing, and we know some things about these people. Some of those who have Latin names were probably of Roman descent: Fortunatus, Quartus, and even Gaius, whose wealth is clear from Paul's description of him in Rom 16:23 as host not only of Paul but also "of the whole church" in Corinth (1 Cor 1:14). Some have Greek names: Stephanas, Achaicus, and Erastus; the latter's status and quite likely his correlate wealth are probably indicated by Paul's identification of him as Corinth's town treasurer (Rom 16:23). Some few were Jews: Aquila and Prisca, mentioned by Paul as sending greetings from Ephesus (1 Cor 16:19), were known to the Corinthians, as may be supposed from Acts 18:2 and from Paul's sweeping claim that "all the churches of the gentiles" were indebted to these two (Rom 16:3); Sosthenes, who is credited by Paul as coauthor of 1 Corinthians and whom Acts says was the leader of the Corinthian synagogue (Acts 18:17); and Apollos, whom Acts identifies as an Alexandrian Jew "well versed in the scriptures" (Acts 8:24) and was an assistant to Paul in inculcating the gospel among the Corinthians (1 Cor 3:6). In 1 Corinthians, there is absolutely no evidence of any strife or even tension in the relation of Jewish believers and gentile believers.

Not surprisingly, when one takes Alciphron's characterization of Corinth into consideration, one finds an indication that wealth and its associated status played a part in some of the struggles between Corinthian believers. Only rich persons adjudicated matters in court (chap. 6); only wealthy persons had homes and staff large enough to host the church and provide for its celebration of the Lord's supper; and only the wealthy could arrive at the dinners early enough to eat the best food and get drunk before the other, less fortunate ones could arrive (1 Cor 11:17-34).

Clearly, most of the Corinthian believers were gentiles. Paul, whose treatment of spiritual gifts seems determined to embrace the entire congregation (see the Commentary on 1 Cor 12:1–14:40), describes the Corinthian believers as former idolaters who *as gentiles* were misled or carried away by devotion to idols (1 Cor 12:2). The Corinthians wrote to Paul about food offered to idols (1 Cor 8:1) because in their pre-faith lives they had been free to partake in the religious festivals as a matter of course. But they are gentiles who have been taught the Scripture and traditions of Israel—surely by Paul and perhaps also by the combined efforts of Prisca, Aquila, Apollos, and Sosthenes. That Paul's churches were strongly gentile cannot be a great surprise because Paul's understanding of his call is focused on the gentiles (Rom 11:13; Gal 2:7), and when he describes his churches to the Romans he calls them "the churches of the gentiles" (Rom 16:4).

Paul successfully resocialized the gentiles who make up most of the Corinthian church into thinking of themselves as a part of the ancient people of God, as members of what he elsewhere calls the Israel of God (Gal 6:16). In fact, Paul writes to the Corinthian gentiles about "gentiles" (τὰ ἔθνη *ta ethnē*) as if the recipients can no longer be counted among those persons (12:2; 5:1; 10:20; see also Eph 2:11; 3:1; 4:17). Paul's Jewish monotheism has become theirs (1 Cor 8:4, 6). Accordingly, they view representations of other supposed deities as "idols" and meat offered in sacrifice to those deities as εἰδωλόθυτος (*eidōlothytos*, "meat offered to an idol");[11] Christ is called "our Paschal lamb" in a context in which leaven is a primary motif, without need of any explanation (5:7); the scriptures of Israel have become theirs in an authoritative fashion (see 10:26; cf. Ps 24:1); the persons in the exodus out of Egypt are unabashedly called "our ancestors" (10:1). Paul expects his readers to understand the Jewish insiders' term ἀκροβυστία (*akrobystia*) as meaning "uncircumcised" (7:18-19); they have adopted Paul's Jewish terminology for at least one day of the week, the sabbath (16:2, μία σαββάτου *mia sabbatou*); and they know the Aramaic, pre-Pauline prayer of the earliest believers, μαράνα θά (*Marana tha*, "Our Lord, come," 16:22).

INTEGRITY AND STRUCTURE OF PAUL'S LETTER

In the past some scholars, seeing the variety of topics and failing to discern links and patterns between them, thought 1 Corinthians was made up of fragments of several letters, but

---

11. Gentiles not so resocialized would have used the term ἱερόθυτος (*hierothytos*), meaning "sacrificed to a divinty." See BAGD, 372.

now most scholars assume, as I do in this commentary, the literary integrity of 1 Corinthians.[12] Even chapter 13, whose links to the material around it are not always explicit, functions as an encomium (see the Commentary) whose praise of love bears on what is written in the chapters on either side of it.

In one sense, the structure of 1 Corinthians is very much like other Pauline letters and, indeed, has much in common with other contemporary epistolography.[13] It opens with a salutation and thanksgiving and, after the body of the letter, closes with greetings and a blessing of the deity. On closer look, however, one sees that the letter is different from all other Pauline letters in some important particulars. Whereas Paul's letters often move toward a climactic appeal (Rom 12:1; Phil 4:2), here the *first* appeal follows directly on the thanksgiving (1:10) and is echoed in 4:16, encasing the opening chapters. Other Pauline letters seem to be dominated by one or two problems or issues that are treated by Paul's weaving them into the fabric of the letter (e.g., Philemon's concern about the runaway slave marks much of that letter; Philippians' concern with the two women's problems has recently been argued to be the main purpose in Paul's writing of that letter),[14] whereas 1 Corinthians has a string of issues or problems that Paul treats sequentially. Further, no other Pauline letter is even partially structured around answering questions that Paul's community has written to him. In 1 Corinthians, though, Paul has received a letter from the Corinthians (7:1) and needs to respond to matters they have raised in writing (see 8:1; 12:1; 16:1). Finally, the chapters that open the letter and only obliquely relate to specific Corinthian problems (chaps. 1–4) are relatively short and appear up front, setting a backdrop against which all the particular issues must be viewed. The commentary will have to inquire whether the string of issues are randomly associated or are linked to one another in some fashion.

PAUL'S RELATION WITH THE CORINTHIANS

Paul's relationship with the Corinthians needs to be addressed in three parts. First, prior to the writing of 1 Corinthians, Paul had known the Corinthian believers for at least three years, having first evangelized there and established the church in early 50 CE, and having lived and worked with them for a year and a half that first time (Acts 18:11). The "previous" lost letter (5:9) is our primary window into what may be known about Paul and the Corinthians before 1 Corinthians. From the reference to the previous letter we may deduce some important information. First, Paul's descriptions of his efforts in that letter indicate that some, perhaps all, of the Corinthians had some confusion about Paul's teaching regarding immoral people and the need to avoid them (1 Cor 5:9-11). From 1 Corinthians it is possible to see that some of the Corinthians, in response to that earlier letter, may have tried to dissociate themselves from "immoral people" (see the question of divorcing unbelievers, 7:12-16) and even from "immorality" in a more general way (see married persons' thinking that they might do well to abstain from sexual intercourse, 7:2-6). Second, Paul's reference to his earlier letter suggests that he and the Corinthians were on good terms, and he readily responds to their confusion.

An additional window onto Paul's relationship with the Corinthians prior to the writing of 1 Corinthians is the letter itself; it makes no specific reference to any preceding event, to any action of Paul, or to any development among the Corinthians that, since the previous letter, has marked a change in Paul's relationship to his Corinthian followers.

First Corinthians gives abundant evidence regarding Paul's relationship to the Corinthians at the time of its composition, but the evidence has been read in a variety of ways that one could readily range along a continuum from an interpretation of 1 Corinthians as depicting Paul and

---

12. Johannes Weiss opened the debate about the integrity of 1 Corinthians, *Der erste Korintherbrief* (Göttingen: Vandenhoeck & Ruprecht, 1910), xl-xliii. Some later scholars followed him. John C. Hurd, *The Origin of 1 Corinthians* (London: SPCK, 1965; repr. Macon, Ga.: Mercer University Press, 1983) 47, is the first modern scholar to review the evidence and make a consistent case for the literary unity of 1 Corinthians. Margaret M. Mitchell, *Paul and the Rhetoric of Reconciliation* (Louisville: Westminster/John Knox, 1991) 2-5, has a good review of literature on this topic and assumes, as this commentary does, the integrity of 1 Corinthians. Hers is the strongest argument yet because she demonstrates the literary integrity of 1 Corinthians as a rhetorical whole.

13. David E. Aune, *The New Testament in Its Literary Environment* (Philadelphia: Westminster, 1987) 158-82.

14. Nils A. Dahl, "Euodia and Syntyche and Paul's Letter to the Philippians," in *The Social World of the First Christians: Essays in Honor of Wayne A. Meeks*, ed. L. M. White and O. L. Yarbrough (Minneapolis: Fortress, 1995) 3-15.

the Corinthians virtually at loggerheads with one another[15] to the other extreme where the letter is read as showing that Paul and the Corinthians are on good terms with one another.[16] In either extreme and all along the interpretive continuum, no one disputes that the Corinthians are a contentious, carping bunch among themselves. But what is Paul's standing with them at the time of his writing 1 Corinthians? The evidence most often featured to claim that Paul is under heavy attack by the Corinthians is as follows:[17] Chapter 4 is taken to indicate that the Corinthians are making judgments against Paul (4:3); the "puffiness" in 4:6 is construed as "for" Apollos and "against" Paul; and Timothy is sent to reinforce Paul's own ways (4:17) in the supposed struggle. Chapters 5 and 6 are read as Paul's effort to reestablish his authority "to direct their affairs."[18] Chapter 9 is taken as a "fierce defense" of Paul in which he tries to counter their opinion that it is beneath an apostle, a wise man, to work with his own hands. The last bit of evidence on the most extreme reading of Paul as being in strife with the Corinthians is 14:37, a verse in which Paul does, indeed, brandish his authority.

Toward the other end of the continuum, where this commentary stands, one finds a stress on the call for unity among the Corinthians.[19] Rather than Paul's being on the defensive, 1:10–4:21 is Paul's censure of the Corinthians for their divisiveness; his references to himself and judgment (4:1ff.), while no doubt enhancing his own ethos, his character, serve most directly to call the divisive Corinthians to task for their fractious and thoughtless behavior toward one another.[20] The comparisons (*synkrisis*) in 4:1ff. serve the standard function of showing someone who is behaving himself properly, as in the case of Paul and the other apostles, or doing it wrong, as in the case of the Corinthians;[21] and the sending of Timothy is Paul's effort to "strengthen the epistolary appeal by one who represents Paul" and is further support for his call to unity that the rest of the letter amplifies.[22] Finally, chapter 9 is not truly a "defense" but is Paul's setting up of himself as the exemplary person who forgoes the exercise of his rights in the gospel if someone might be harmed or hindered by his use of them.[23] Chapter 9 is Paul's exemplification of Christian freedom tempered by love, as the commentary will show.

Paul does relate to the Corinthians as their father in the faith (4:14) and feels responsible for them. Because he, as their father, sees problems with their conduct, he is at times harsh with them. Accordingly, he alternately warns them (4:14), shames them (6:5; 15:34), cajoles them (14:12), and encourages them (12:31; 14:20). Throughout the letter, however, his concern is to restore them to unity, to refurbish and reshape their concord, their genuine concern (his technical term for this is "love") for one another. We must be scrupulous not to tinge our reading of 1 Corinthians with the acrid atmosphere of 2 Corinthians, where matters on most fronts have deteriorated.

Between the time of 1 Corinthians and the writing of any fragment of 2 Corinthians, Paul's relationship with the Corinthians worsened. He had a "painful visit" with them when things did not go as he or they wanted (2 Cor 2:1-2). He had projected another visit and failed to show up, and some Corinthians were less than impressed (2 Cor 1:15-18). Paul's fiscal management becomes a significant problem in several ways: Some persons want to be Paul's patrons, but he refuses;[24] Paul accepts support from the Macedonians while still refusing support from the Corinthians (2 Cor 11:9); and the Corinthians' zeal for the collection destined for Jerusalem (cf. 1 Cor 16:1-4) waned considerably (2 Corinthians 8–9). But by far the most significant new

15. Gordon D. Fee, *The First Epistle to the Corinthians* (Grand Rapids: Eerdmans, 1987), describes the letter as "combative"; e.g., "Paul is taking them on at every turn" (6); "Paul's authority is eroded" (7).

16. Mitchell, *Paul and the Rhetoric of Reconciliation*, makes a strong case that at the time of writing 1 Corinthians Paul is on good terms with the Corinthians.

17. Following Fee, *The First Epistle to the Corinthians*, 8-10.

18. Fee, *The First Epistle to the Corinthians*, 9.

19. Mitchell, *Paul and the Rhetoric of Reconciliation*, 200, claims that the call to unity in 1:10 is the thesis statement of *"the entire letter"* (emphasis hers) and that everything subsequent serves that overriding purpose.

20. Mitchell, *Paul and the Rhetoric of Reconciliation*, 209-10.

21. Mitchell, *Paul and the Rhetoric of Reconciliation*, 219-22. See also Christopher Forbes, "Comparison, Self-Praise and Irony: Paul's Boasting and the Conventions of Hellenistic Rhetoric," *NTS* 32 (1986) 2-8.

22. Mitchell, *Paul and the Rhetoric of Reconciliation*, 224-25.

23. Mitchell, *Paul and the Rhetoric of Reconciliation*, 244. For the best analysis of the problems with treating chap. 9 as a defense, see Mitchell's careful treatment (245) and her conclusion: "all attempts to analyze 1 Cor 9 as a true defense against actual charges have failed" (244).

24. Peter Marshall, *Enmity in Corinth: Social Conventions in Paul's Relations with the Corinthians*, WUNT 2/23 (Tübingen: Mohr/Siebeck, 1987) 218-58.

development that distinguishes all of Paul's relations with the Corinthians subsequent to the time of 1 Corinthians is the arrival in Corinth of outsiders who challenge his authority (2 Cor 2:17; 3:1-3; 5:11; 10:12-18; 11:2-6, 12-15, 22-23). In 1 Corinthians the problems the Corinthians have are with one another, not with outsiders.

PRIMARY CULTURAL PATTERNS IMPORTANT FOR UNDERSTANDING 1 CORINTHIANS

The Corinthians and their apostle bring certain cultural, social, and literary suppositions to their engagement with one another. Some of these suppositions need to be mentioned as a context for interpretation.

Pater Familias. Paul and his readers share the knowledge that the father of the household is the one responsible for the well-being and comportment of the members of that social unit. It is the father's responsibility to inculcate values, to provide support, to enforce discipline, to train, and to protect all the members of the household. Most fundamental in carrying out these responsibilities is the father's modeling of proper behavior and comportment. The only feature of this social pattern lacking in Paul's letters is that the father trains the family members in a trade. This sweeping sense of responsibility is the proper context for Paul's epistolary efforts to have the Corinthians understand how they should properly behave (4:14-21). It also will help us to understand why it is natural for Paul—and for his readers—to set himself forward so regularly as the one who exemplifies proper life in Christ and who should, therefore, be emulated by his children in the faith.

Honor/Shame; Praise/Blame. The most important cultural norm in Paul's time was the attainment of honor and its equally powerful counterpart, the avoidance, or at least the minimization, of shame. Society was ordered vertically, with all persons concerned with identifying where they stood in the chain of descending power. To be sure, there were the sideward glances to see how others were doing by comparison, but decisions were made and actions were pursued with primary regard for how they would secure honor and avoid shame for oneself, how they would gain praise and limit blame. It was the understood obligation of the subordinate persons to praise and honor their benefactors, the ones on whom they found themselves dependent. The social indicators and patterns played to this structuring and to its attendant maintenance of honor. Seating assignments at social events were carefully arranged in accordance with varying degrees of status (Luke 14:7-11), and great shame was accorded anyone who breached propriety. The right to speak and, when granted, even the order in which persons were expected to speak were structured on the notions of the degree of honor.

Accordingly, when Paul writes that he does not seek to shame the Corinthians (1 Cor 4:14), when he writes something to their shame (1 Cor 6:5; 15:34), or when he mentions neither but in fact casts them in a shameworthy light (1 Cor 11:17-22), he will have hit on a hot-button item.

Patron/Client. In Paul's time everyone had a lord—that is, someone who could rightly be construed as being over someone else, to whom that someone else belonged or was indebted, and to whom that one was responsible. It was not just slaves who belonged to someone. Everyone right up the chain belonged to another person. Even Marcus Aurelius, the Roman emperor, mused that he was responsible to the gods. And one's comportment was understood as being keyed to pleasing one's lord, to whom one was responsible. Great effort was expended in nurturing, cultivating, and even increasing the number of one's patrons; equally prodigious care was given to one's clients to make sure that they remembered their indebtedness and to ensure that they took proper steps to show honor and praise. And so it was up and down the social ladder. One person's client was patron to many below. The power that one received from one's patron was used, by careful distribution of it to one's selected clients, and was subsequently passed on by them to clients who were then in turn indebted to them. Indebtedness and obligation were the fabric of this culture.

An abiding issue before the Corinthians in this letter is the identity of the one to whom they belong—that is Paul's way of tapping this cultural reservoir as a means of expressing the basic and defining relationship in all of life. Paul consistently reminds them that it is the Lord Jesus Christ to whom they are responsible and whom they must please. All are clients of a superior patron, and their actions are to yield honor, not shame, to their Lord. Some Corinthians seek to place themselves in the superior position with regard to other believers and thus to "lord" it over them. Status seeking will be an abiding problem with which Paul is confronted in 1 Corinthians. Paul's countercultural understanding of the gospel runs head-on into this social convention when, with its associated status seeking, it bears on how believers get along with each other.

Stoics. In Paul's time Stoics carried the day. One hardly needed to choose to be a Stoic or even to think of oneself as being a Stoic in certain ways; it was so much in the air that it was a part of the common coinage of life and its exchanges. Accordingly, Paul can and does use Stoic patterns and conceptions as a means of advancing his arguments and of explicating what it means to live the faith. For example, he frequently employs the Stoic conviction that certain matters are indifferent *adiaphora*, and he may even identify, as the Stoics surely did, things preferred and things not preferred from among those indifferent considerations (see 1 Corinthians 7). Another example could be Paul's conviction, expressed in different ways across the letter, that God has allocated or arranged matters as God has chosen (3:5; 7:17; 12:18, 24).

Rhetoric and 1 Corinthians. Rhetoric is the art of persuasion. In Paul's time, rhetoric was the basic form of education for those who could afford it. A growing body of scholarly studies of Paul show that he was indeed well tutored in rhetoric.[25] Even those not trained in rhetoric, as the majority of the Corinthians surely were not, were accustomed to it and knew its conventions by having lived in a rhetorical culture. All written and spoken words were rhetorical, so, in order to understand what was written or said, one always has to consider the rhetoric of what is there. To call something rhetorical is not to be confused with dismissing it as empty, as form prevailing over content. Everything in 1 Corinthians, therefore, is rhetorical, and we as interpreters of it must regularly inquire of its rhetorical force.

There were three types of rhetoric in those days. The first, *judicial rhetoric*, had its focus on the courtroom and generally inquired regarding what had happened in the past in order to make some judgment. The second, *deliberative rhetoric*, concerned itself with deliberations about what one should or should not do in the future, though that future could be quite imminent. The third type, *epideictic rhetoric*, concerned itself with praise and blame either of an individual or of a virtue or vice and had its primary focus on the present, the way things are, or, in the case of a virtue, as things should be. In a general and overall way, documents from that time tend to fall in one of those three categories, though the rhetorical handbooks clearly caution that no rhetorician of any worth sticks to one category, but freely mixes them according to the needs of the occasion.[26] First Corinthians falls primarily into the category of deliberative rhetoric, although there are features of the letter in which Paul employs, as we shall see, some judicial rhetoric and some epideictic rhetoric.[27]

The apostle and letter writer Paul, the Corinthians and some perceived problem or problems with them, and constraints consisting, for example, of shared beliefs and experiences—all three together form the rhetorical situation that must be the context for our evaluation of 1 Corinthians.[28] The dynamic among the three can never be out of sight. In this situation our primary data consists in the letter itself. In the letter we have most directly Paul's efforts to persuade the Corinthians; we can identify Paul's strategy, what he aims for, what he values or affirms, what he considers useless, and what he denies. We have less access and certainty to whether Paul understood his recipients and whether he reflects them and what is going on there accurately. In the letter we can see Paul's assessment of the Corinthians and of what they have been doing;

25. Duane F. Watson, "The New Testament and Greco-Roman Rhetoric: A Bibliography, *JETS* 31 (1988) 465-72, and "The New Testament and Greco-Roman Rhetoric: A Bibliographical Update," *JETS* 33 (1990) 513-24.

26. Although epideictic rhetoric focuses on praise and blame, these topics are also appropriate to and are found in judicial and deliberative rhetoric. See *Ad Herennium* 3.8.15.

27. See Mitchell, *Paul and the Rhetoric of Reconciliation*, 165, where she recognizes that 1 Corinthians 13 is an encomium.

28. See Lloyd F. Bitzer, "The Rhetorical Situation," *Philosophy and Rhetoric* 1 (1968) 1-14, esp. 6-8.

even there, however, in the letter itself we can sense and will actually see evidence that Paul's estimate of the maturity of the Corinthian believers is at dissonance with what they probably thought about themselves (see 3:1ff.). As tempting as it might be, we cannot assume that we can penetrate the thoughts of the persons to whom the letter was written. So, positively put, what we do have greatest access to as we approach the letter are Paul's rhetorical moves and steps, and those will be of great interest in the study that follows.

According to Demetrius of Phalerum (c. 4th cent. BCE), and regardless of which of the three types of rhetoric one used, there were really only three options available to someone, like Paul, who wanted to call upon a person or a group to alter their behavior: flattery, adverse criticism, or figured speech ("indirect speech" or the "covert hint" as it may otherwise be called).[29] In 1 Corinthians we will see that Paul at different times uses each of the three, though in the culture and in the letter the last one, "figured, indirect speech" or the "covert hint," is the most common.[30] In each case we will have to take care to interpret whatever Paul writes within the conventions appropriate to the option he employs in that section.

At points in the commentary it will be noted that Paul uses certain topoi or commonplaces to advance his case. For a first example, much note will be taken of exemplification. Like any good parent in that time, Paul, as the Corinthians' father in the faith, details positive and negative models of the faith and himself patterns the way his children in the faith should behave. In a second example, Paul several times employs synecdoche, a literary device in which reference is made to something by identifying one of its parts, where the part (e.g., wheels) represents and stands for the whole (e.g., car). Third, there will be several occasions to note that Paul uses a ring device called inclusio to tie together a literary unit or to finish a thought. Fourth, maxims, pithy distillations of generally accepted truths, are a feature of rhetoric in antiquity and in Paul's letters.

Paul displays a fundamental ambivalence to culture and the patterns in the world around the Corinthian believers. At times he embraces cultural conventions and patterns. At other times he distances himself and his believers from them. Perhaps such an ambivalence was unavoidable because Paul made the decision not to lead his believers to a Qumran-like isolation; perhaps it was inevitable because human transactions are always couched in culturally transmitted conventions and exchanges. Perhaps it was unavoidable because most persons have blind spots where their convictions have not fully penetrated every nook and cranny of their lives. In Paul's case, perhaps he did not carry his gospel-powered critique through consistently into every facet of his and his congregations' lives. However it happened, Paul's relation to the culture in which he and his followers lived is mixed. A few examples will illustrate the range of Paul's appropriation and critique of cultural patterns.

Beginning with an example of Paul's being critical of cultural patterns, he objects when the Corinthians use their worldly power and status to get their way in the community of believers. He severely chides the wealthy Corinthians for having taken poorer believers to court in order to have their own way (chap. 6) and for abusing their power as hosts of the Lord's supper (11:17-34). For an uncritical appropriation of cultural patterns, consider Paul's blithe assumption that men should have short hair and women should keep theirs long (11:6, 14-15). In between those extremes Paul seems to think that believers can live directly in the world, in the midst of the world's cultural patterns, without the culture's determining their stance or moral choices. We see that sort of reflection most clearly in 1 Corinthians when Paul writes about living ὡς μή (*hōs mē*), "as if not," which closely approximates John's expression of living "in the world" but not "of the world" (7:29-31; John 13:1; 15:19). In that passage and in its context, Paul encourages believers to live "as if not" because "the appointed time has grown short" (7:29 NRSV). Because God's purposes with the world (which include refurbishing it, Romans 8) are drawing to a close, Paul is convinced that the patterns of the world have lost their power, that believers experience a liberation from the definitional influence of social patterns and of participation in the world.

---

29. Demetrius of Phalerum *On Style* 9.2.66.

30. Frederick Ahl, "The Art of Safe Criticism in Greece and Rome," *AJP* 105 (1984) 204: indirect speech was "the normal mode of discourse thoughout much of Greek and Roman antiquity."

Accordingly, Paul thinks that believers live their lives of faith while finding themselves within the world, whose present form is passing away (1 Cor 7:31).

ESPECIALLY PROMINENT CONVICTIONS SEEN IN 1 CORINTHIANS

Occasionally, the commentary will elaborate on what Paul, in a particular passage, either takes for granted or alludes to with the slightest clue. In those circumstances, I will draw on the other Pauline letters as a way of illuminating what Paul and his readers took for granted without saying as much in full detail. Whatever Paul may write to any of his churches, he has a common framework in which he thinks of the gospel. The frame runs from Paul's foundational conviction on the one horizon that Christ's death and resurrection inaugurate the new creation, the redemption of creation, to the other horizon—indeed, to the end of the age at Christ's parousia when God's purposes, begun in Christ's death and resurrection, come to a conclusion.[31] This latter is a time of judgment when all will have to stand (or fall) before God and Christ and give an accounting for the life they have lived and for their actions.

For Paul, the Christian faith is lived in community. The individual is never simply and singly related to God. If "faith" is Paul's code word for right relation to God, then "love" is Paul's code word for right relation to others. Love, the proper caring for another, is the necessary expression of faith, the proper relating to God, because faith expresses itself in love (Gal 5:6). Caring for other believers, building them up, encouraging them, consoling and even warning them, are not options for believers; they are a requirement of faith. We can see this in 1 Corinthians because some of the believers there seem to have focused their attention on themselves and on God and ignored, neglected, or disregarded others; and Paul simply cannot abide it. In this sense, the whole of 1 Corinthians is a study in love.

Paul recognizes that the very constitution of community requires a sort of give-and-receive transaction between the individuals and the community. To be a believer apart from community is inconceivable for Paul. Therefore, believers must be ready to accommodate to the community. That accommodation always entails contributing to the enrichment of the fellowship by putting whatever gifts one has in service to the common good. Perhaps more problematic for modern readers, sometimes integration into the community will cause the individual to override selfishness or the rather natural desire to seek what seems so clearly in one's own self-interest. Paul's assumption is that all individuals in the association will share in the benefits of the affiliation (e.g., security, mutual care and protection, etc.). While Paul's reflections on this balance between individual and community appear at several points in 1 Corinthians, they are expressed most directly in chapter 9.

Paul is so committed to the community as the matrix of the life of faith that when he sees a conflict between the rights of the individual and the rights of the community, he will regularly recommend that the individual eschew the pursuit of individual rights and choose the community's well-being instead. First Corinthians shows this Pauline trait when Paul advises that the ones who speak in tongues withhold expression of them if no one is there to interpret (14:28) and that when one is speaking and another receives a revelation, the speaker should give way (14:30). Paul exemplifies this pattern when he expresses his willingness never to eat meat if it might cause another to stumble (8:13).

We must be careful, however, because in all of his concern for the health of the community, Paul never denigrates the importance of the believer's individuality. Variety and difference are not sacrificed for community. Rather, Paul strives to integrate the distinctiveness of individuals and relishes the importance of difference to the wholesomeness of the fellowship. Accordingly, he acknowledges that different people eat all sorts of different things while others have

---

31. See "The Two Horizons of Paul's Thought World," in J. Paul Sampley, *Walking Between the Times: Paul's Moral Reasoning* (Minneapolis: Fortress, 1991) 7-24.

restrictive diets (8:7-13; 10:25-31); some have homes in which to host the church, and, probably in a rhetorical overstatement, some have nothing (11:18-22); some have a few χαρίσματα (*charismata*), gifts, and others have many (12:4-11; 14:1-5); some live with the law as the defining center of their lives while others do not (9:20-21); some plant, and others water (3:6-9); and every person experiences testing as if it belonged to that person alone (10:13). But each and every one of these quite distinctively individuated persons is welcome, is important, and is even necessary to the body of Christ.

Paul assumes that believers should be responsible moral agents, that their lives are not simply driven from the heart, and that their minds should be integrated with their spirits in all of their moral reasoning. His is the integrated life, at once moral, deliberative, and spiritual—and he models it for those who would follow him. All of life, in every moment and in every situation, must be lived as ready for God's final judgment, not in quaking boots betokening lack of confidence in God's grace active in one's life, but in thankfulness to God for great and abiding mercy, ever present in good and in tough times. Contemplated conduct, therefore, must be weighed with regard to several considerations: how it expresses God's love for us, how appropriate it is to the strength of our faith, and how it affects others.

Different believers are of differing maturity. Some are "babies" in the faith; others are more mature; none are completely mature. As surely as babies learn to crawl and later walk but can carry no additional load, and as more mature persons can not only walk but also carry burdens for themselves and for others, so also Paul thinks it is with believers. Though Paul comes nearest to discussing this problem directly in Gal 6:1-5, it is an issue in 1 Corinthians, where the commentary will show that Paul thinks at least some of the Corinthians are babies in the faith and surely are not as mature as they think they are (3:1-4). Elsewhere in the letter Paul takes their fractiousness as evidence of their immaturity in the faith.

Because of that dissonance between their self-estimation and Paul's, his letter urges them to take careful stock of their standing and of their maturity. Some of the believers at Corinth have (falsely, Paul declares) thought of themselves as having arrived at the fullness of what God can bestow; they have become "arrogant" or "puffed up" as he sometimes puts it. Their arrogance is having deleterious effects on their fellow believers, who seem altogether too ready to accept their compatriots' puffy self-estimate and, with it, too low a self-estimate of themselves. Out of that low self-esteem, the less puffy Corinthians live as if they have less to offer the community of believers. A considerable part of Paul's effort in 1 Corinthians is aimed at bringing all sorts of quite different people back into full and equal participation in the community.

First Corinthians is a case study of several features of the Christian life as it has been experienced through the centuries. First, it is a classic for the problems of unity because, after all, that is one of the major problems across the issues reflected in the letter. Churches, like other social groups, are subject to fractiousness from all sorts of sources, and Corinth certainly has its share. Whether it is wealthy persons treating the poorer with disdain, or especially religiously gifted persons becoming arrogant, prideful, and disdainful of those less gifted, or persons of whatever socioeconomic bracket who think first of themselves and little about the needs of others, or persons who overestimate how strong they are in faith, or persons who have low self-esteem and cower timidly before those they consider more advanced—the list could go on—the church at Corinth has them all.

Likewise, Paul's response to those challenges of the Corinthian believers' unity is a study in distinguishing genuine unity from uniformity. Paul labors to help the Corinthians see that they truly belong to one another in Christ despite the differences of gifts and graces they exhibit. In fact, Paul goes that one better: It is precisely in the differences they bring to the community that he sees the creative, stimulating work of the Holy Spirit. The community's health and growth depend on each person's contributing what the Spirit offers through him or her to the common good of all. Without the variety and distinctiveness that each one brings, the faithful community would be a pale imitation of what it ought to be.

1 CORINTHIANS AS A WINDOW ON EARLY CHRISTIANITY

Paul's letters provide a vista onto the earliest known Christian communities, on churches that existed perhaps as much as a generation ahead of the time the Gospels were written. Paul, the Jew who opposed the earliest Christian movement (2 Cor 11:22; Gal 1:14; Phil 3:3-11), took the gospel to gentiles (non-Jews), who largely populated his churches. In doing so, he did not require circumcision, the traditional mark of belonging to God's people. In its place, as a ritual of admission, Paul required baptism. Even though he did not himself baptize many Corinthians (1 Cor 1:14-17), they *were* baptized. Paul gladly reasons from his convictions about baptism and its significance (1 Cor 12:13; 7:17-24). Though the congregation at Corinth was predominantly gentile (1 Cor 12:2; 8:4-6; 10:6-14), Paul clearly considers them, along with himself, to be God's children (1 Cor 1:3).

Paul's churches, like their synagogue counterparts, regularly gathered in homes. Because the Corinthians' assemblies were so chaotic (1 Cor 14:26-33), and because the Corinthians abused the Lord's supper (1 Cor 11:17-34), we learn a great deal about their practices and about Paul's suggestions of how they ought to comport themselves.

We tend to think of the apocalyptic Paul as making sharp distinctions between his communities, their comportment, and their life-style and that of their neighbors, and from 1 Corinthians 5–6 we will see that, indeed, we should; but the separation is far from absolute. Paul thinks that believers can have dealings with unbelievers (1 Cor 10:27); indeed, some are married to unbelievers (1 Cor 7:12-16), and some unbelievers apparently freely wander into worship occasions. Paul considers none of these exchanges between believers and unbelievers as inappropriate.

PAUL'S LETTERS

Paul's letters—all of them—are situational documents in which he writes concerning the problems he thinks need attention in that particular community of believers. First Corinthians is through and through an argument for unity that honors distinctiveness and diversity; for the believers' proper care of one another, which at the same time is grounded in an accurate self-assessment; and for the formation and upbuilding of maturity of faith that leaves no one out. First Corinthians is a textbook on moral reasoning and on the relation of the individual with the community.

Because we are not privy to what Paul and the Corinthians knew about each other and what the latter knew about Paul's teaching, we are sometimes left with having to take what appears in the letter only as a clue, an allusion, and to figure out what is the larger picture that Paul and the Corinthians may know quite well. We can sometimes reconstruct that larger picture from what we find in the other letters; indeed, we must do so if we are to understand the allusions. So from time to time the commentary will refer to what we can know from the other Pauline letters.

Thirteen New Testament letters name Paul as author, but scholars have long since wondered about the authenticity of that claim with regard to some of the letters. Concerning seven of them, 1 Corinthians included, almost no one doubts the Pauline authorship: Romans, 1 and 2 Corinthians, Galatians, Philippians, 1 Thessalonians, and Philemon.[32] After that group, though, scholarly consensus breaks down. Some scholars deem 2 Thessalonians, Colossians, and Ephesians authentic as well, but some, including me, find these letters to be what we would call Paulinist, indicating that they have come from someone in the Pauline school who writes in Paul's name and represents the Pauline tradition after the apostle has died. A smaller subset of scholars claim authenticity for the Pastoral Epistles, 1 and 2 Timothy, and Titus.[33]

---

32. L. E. Keck, *Paul and His Letters*, 2nd ed. (Philadelphia: Fortress, 1988) 5-6. This judgment also informed the decision of the Pauline Theology Group of the Society of Biblical Literature to focus on the seven mentioned letters. The papers from that seminar were subsequently published as *Pauline Theology*, 3 vols. (Minneapolis: Fortress, 1991–95).

33. See Luke T. Johnson, *The Writings of the New Testament* (Philadelphia: Fortress, 1986) 242-407, who argues for the authenticity of all the letters that bear Paul's name.

This commentary will pay especial attention to the six other letters about which no one has questions of Pauline authorship. Occasionally, I may refer the reader to a passage in the Paulinist tradition (2 Thessalonians, Ephesians, Colossians, 1 and 2 Timothy, and Titus) for further illumination or comparison.

CONCLUDING NOTES

Though we know that chapter designations were added to the biblical texts only in the Middle Ages and that subdivisions into verses came about even later, nevertheless in the commentary I refer to chapters and verses as a means of handy reference. The reader of this commentary will note, however, that I cite occasions where the relatively modern divisions of the text into chapters and paragraphs and verses do not reflect the sections and turning points in Paul's argument.

The translations in the commentary and in the reflections are my own, unless otherwise indicated. In order to make clear to modern readers the semantic range of a given Greek term, I sometimes give additional possible translations of the same term by different English words separated by a slash—for example, Paul's mention of "this authority/freedom of yours" in 8:9. My hope is that such a translation will provide the readers of this commentary with additional information by which they can appreciate the different nuances that ἐξουσία (*exousia*), for example, may have in that verse.

In this commentary the recipients of 1 Corinthians are frequently referred to as "hearers" or "auditors" because the majority of the Corinthians were surely illiterate (1:26) and, therefore, dependent upon someone else to read the letter to them. So most Corinthian believers experienced this letter as a heard communication.

The term "Christian" is lacking in the commentary sections because Paul and his readers did not have this term as a self-description; it was a later development.[34]

---

34. My deepest gratitude goes to my wife, Sally Backus Sampley, for her love, for her careful scrutiny of this entire work, and for her numerous insightful suggestions, and to Suzanne Webber for her helpful editoral recommendations across the commentary.

BIBLIOGRAPHY

(Author's note: Because of publication delays and other publishing commitments, I was unable to take into consideration works published since February 1997.)

Aune, David E. *The New Testament in Its Literary Environment.* Philadelphia: Westminster, 1987. A comprehensive, solid treatment of the literary context for interpreting the New Testament.

Conzelmann, Hans. *A Commentary on the First Epistle to the Corinthians.* Translated by J. W. Leitch. Hermeneia. Philadelphia: Fortress, 1975. Strong in its use of references to the Greco-Roman context for understanding Paul's points.

Fee, Gordon D. *The First Epistle to the Corinthians.* Grand Rapids: Eerdmans, 1987. A resourceful commentary, indicating standard scholarly options throughout, but reading the letter as showing Paul at loggerheads with the Corinthians.

Fitzgerald, John. *Cracks in an Earthern Vessel: An Examination of the Catalogues of Hardships in the Corinthian Correspondence.* SBLDS 99. Atlanta: Scholars Press, 1988. A thoughtful study of hardship lists in the Greco-Roman world; sheds light on Paul's usage.

Forbes, Christopher. "Comparison, Self Praise and Irony: Paul's Boasting and the Conventions of Hellenistic Rhetoric." *NTS* 32 (1986).

Krentz, Edgar M. "Military Language and Metaphors in Philippians." In *Origins and Method: Towards a New Understanding of Judaism and Christianity, Essays in Honour of John C. Hurd.* Edited by B. H. McLean. JSNTSup 88. Sheffield: Academic, 1993.

Lampe, Peter. "Theological Wisdom and the 'Word About the Cross': The Rhetorical Scheme in 1 Corinthians 1-4." *Int* 44 (1990).

Lyons, George. *Pauline Autobiography: Toward a New Understanding.* SBLDS 73. Atlanta: Scholars Press, 1985. A successfully iconoclastic rereading of Paul's autobiographical claims.

MacMullen, Ramsay. *Roman Social Relations 50 B.C. to A.D. 284.* New Haven: Yale University Press, 1974. A readable picture of the social world of that time.

Malherbe, Abraham J. "Determinism and Free Will in Paul: The Argument of 1 Corinthians 8 and 9." In *Paul in His Hellenistic Context.* Edited by T. Engberg-Pedersen. Minneapolis: Fortress, 1995.

Marshall, Peter. *Enmity in Corinth: Social Conventions in Paul's Relations with the Corinthians.* WUNT 2/23. Tübingen: Mohr/Siebeck, 1987. Friendship and enmity as a context for understanding Paul's relations with the Corinthians.

Meeks, Wayne A. *The First Urban Christians: The Social World of the Apostle Paul.* New Haven: Yale University Press, 1983. The best general treatment of Paul's relationship to his social setting.

Mitchell, Margaret M. *Paul and the Rhetoric of Reconciliation.* Louisville: Westminster/John Knox, 1991. An outstanding study of 1 Corinthians in the light of ancient rhetorical practice, social conventions, and norms.

Murphy-O'Connor, Jerome. *St. Paul's Corinth: Texts and Archaeology.* Collegeville, Minn.: Liturgical, 1983. A useful sourcebook on texts and archaeology related to Corinth.

Pogoloff, Stephen. *Logos and Sophia: The Rhetorical Situation of 1 Corinthians.* SBLDS 134. Atlanta: Scholars Press, 1992. Understands the Corinthian divisiveness as having a basis in rhetoric and associated social status, but thinks that the divisions form around Paul and Apollos.

Ramsaran, Rollin A. *Liberating Words: Paul's Use of Rhetorical Maxims in 1 Corinthians 1–10.* Valley Forge, Pa.: Trinity, 1996. Especially helpful in understanding how maxims functioned in the Greco-Roman culture and in 1 Corinthians.

Sampley, J. Paul. *Walking Between the Times: Paul's Moral Reasoning.* Minneapolis: Fortress, 1991. A study of what grounds and shapes Paul's moral reasoning.

Sigountos, J. G. "The Genre of 1 Corinthians 13." *NTS* 40 (1994).

Smit, J. "The Genre of 1 Corinthians 13 in the Light of Classical Rhetoric." *NovT* 33 (1991).

Theissen, Gerd. *The Social Setting of Pauline Christianity: Essays on Corinth.* Edited and translated by J. H. Schütz. Philadelphia: Fortress, 1982. An early and formative study on social considerations as illuminating Paul's relation to the Corinthians.

Tuckett, C. M. "The Corinthians Who Say 'There Is No Resurrection of the Dead' (1 Cor 15,12)." In *The Corinthian Correspondence.* Edited by R. Bieringer. Leuven: Leuven University Press, 1996.

Willis, W. L. *Idol Meat in Corinth: The Pauline Argument in 1 Corinthians 8 and 10.* SBLDS 68. Chico, Calif.: Scholars Press, 1985. A study of Paul's argument against the background of Hellenistic cultic meals.

Winter, B. W. "Civil Litigation in Secular Corinth and the Church. The Forensic Background to 1 Corinthians 6.1-8." *NTS* 37 (1991).

Wuellner, William. "Greek Rhetoric and Pauline Argumentation." In *Early Christian Literature and the Classical Intellectual Tradition: In honorem Robert M. Grant.* Edited by W. R. Schoedel and R. L. Wilken. Théologie Historique 54. Paris: Etudes Beauchesne, 1979.

Zaas, P. S. "Catalogues and Context: 1 Corinthians 5 and 6." *NTS* 34 (1988).

OUTLINE OF 1 CORINTHIANS

I. 1 Corinthians 1:1–4:21, Opening and Appeal

    A. 1:1-9, Letter Opening
        1:1-3, Salutation
        1:4-9, Thanksgiving
    B. 1:10–4:21, Paul's Contextualizing of the Letter
        1:10-17, The Opening Appeal
        1:18-25, Christ, True Power, True Wisdom
        1:26-31, Paul's Application to the Auditors
        2:1-5, Perspective-Keeping via Paul's Exemplary Pattern from the Founding Days
        2:6-16, Two Wisdoms, Two Spirits, Two Representative People
        3:1-4, Not Spiritual People, Babies, Merely Human
        3:5-9, Apollos and Paul: Models
        3:10-15, The Foundation and Each Person's Work
        3:16-17, You Are God's Temple
        3:18-23, Self-Awareness and Proper Perspective
        4:1-5, The Apostles, But Especially Paul, As Exemplary Once More
        4:6-7, The Explicit Key to Paul's Strategy in Chapters 1–4
        4:8-13, The Grand Charade Seen with Evangelical Irony
        4:14-21, Paul Embraces and Warns His Beloved Children

II. 1 Corinthians 5:1–6:20, Community Definition As Seen in Two Related Instances

    A. 5:1-13, The Stain Within: A Threat to the Holiness Appropriate to the Temple of the Holy Spirit
    B. 6:1-11, Wrongfully Crossing the Border in the Other Direction: Taking Community Matters Out into the World
    C. 6:12-20, Summing Up and Looking Ahead

III. 1 Corinthians 7:1-40, Paul's Response to Questions About Relations in Sociosexual Groups

    A. 7:1-7, Husbands and Wives
    B. 7:8-9, Widowers and Widows
    C. 7:10-11, Married Believers and Divorce
    D. 7:12-16, Marriage Between Believers and Unbelievers
    E. 7:17-24, Indifferent Matters: Jew, Greek, Slave, Free
    F. 7:25-28, Counsel for the Unmarried: Paul's Own Maxim
    G. 7:29-35, A Digression Regarding Life Lived Eschatologically
    H. 7:36-38, Betrothed Unmarrieds and the Idealized Responder
    I. 7:39-40, Divorce, Widowhood, and Remarriage

IV. 1 Corinthians 8:1–11:1, Paul's Response to a Corinthian Question About Eating Idol Meat

    A. 8:1-6, Their Question, Their Assumption, Paul's Rehearsal of What They Know
    B. 8:7-13, Persons Differ in Knowledge—An Imaginary and Instructive Scenario
    C. 9:1–10:13, Extended Digression Consisting of Two Examples
        9:1-27, Paul As Exemplar
        9:1-2, Identification of Paul As Free and As Apostle
        9:3-14, Paul, the One of Unexcelled Rights, Chooses Not to Use Them

1 CORINTHIANS 1:1–4:21

OPENING AND APPEAL

OVERVIEW

P aul's undisputed letters share similar structural features. They open with a salutation, which is usually followed by a thanksgiving and the body of the letter. Somewhere in the body of the letter, most often toward the end of the body, Paul makes a direct appeal. Following the body, Paul's letters usually close with a special section of greetings. A grace always concludes Paul's letters. First Corinthians generally accords with these patterns.

1 CORINTHIANS 1:1-9, LETTER OPENING

1 Corinthians 1:1-3, Salutation

COMMENTARY

The salutations of Paul's letters share a common structure with most letters of his time: Person A to Person B, Greetings. However, Paul elaborates each part of this structure in accordance with his particular convictions and purposes. In this letter, he identifies himself as an apostle called by God's will; Sosthenes is "the brother," meaning part of God's family (1:1; cf. Phlm 1, 7, 16, 20). When Paul opens a letter by declaring himself an apostle, we can be certain either that there is some problem in his relationship with the readers or that he wants to reaffirm his apostolic authority as leverage for what he is about to write (see Phil 1:1; Phlm 1). The motif of calling ("election" and "choosing" are semantic alternatives) is echoed in Paul's description of his addressees (1:2) and will reappear for further reflection in 1:26-31. The Corinthians are called to be saints—that is, to live the life of sanctified ones ("saint," "sanctified," "holy" are all from the same Greek root), meaning that they are set apart for or

claimed by God. Paul immediately places the Corinthian church in the larger context of all the other believers (1:2), wherever they may be, who share the trusting dependency that is implied in "calling upon the name of the Lord."

Paul radically reshapes the standard letter "greetings" into what amounts to a blessing, a benediction (1:3). All of his undisputed letters have the identical formula, perhaps because it is so foundational to the Christian life. In this opening, framing statement, grace—God's freely given, unmerited gift or favor—is featured; for Paul, God's grace not only makes possible the beginning of faith but also sustains the believers throughout their lives; grace is the indispensable ground of the life of faith from its beginning to its end. Likewise, peace describes the believers' new relation to God (see Rom 5:1, 10). Can one possibly imagine that when Paul the Jew says "peace" he does not affirm in it the *shalom* of God's proper ordering of the world and human relations within it?

The remainder of 1:3 affirms in a definitional way believers' relation to God and to Christ. God is here depicted as father of the family with both authority and responsibility for the members; implicit is the understanding that those for whom God is father are brothers and sisters of one another. Christ is designated Lord—that is, the one to whom believers belong, who governs the lives of the believers and assures them protection.

REFLECTIONS

1. We share with those Corinthians our having been called and being saints. Paul is "called"; the Corinthians are "called." In our time, we tend to think that only ministers or priests are called, but Paul views all believers as those who have been called by God ("vocation," as distinguished from "career," is a term built from the Latin equivalent of the Greek term). Paul's use of "call" is a way of affirming God's grace (see 1:3) as the ground of new life in Christ, of election (which is literally a "calling out"). All believers are called; sometimes the call has a particular task integral to it (e.g., Paul is to be apostle to the gentiles); typically, the call is to be lived directly in the life context where one is called (see 1 Cor 7:17-24); and at the judgment God will determine whether one has lived faithfully with regard to one's call. Infant baptism is the ultimate expression of God's calling people and claiming them even before they are capable of reaching out to God.

"Saints" is a specialized term in Paul's lexicon. It means "those who have been set apart for God" (Lev 11:44-45). "Called" persons are saints because God has claimed them, because God has set them apart as God's own people. Again, this is an affirmation of God's grace; to be a saint is like a trust, a stewardship, that God gives into a person's care. The same root Greek term for "saint" is found in "sanctification" (see 1:2) and "holy" (see 3:17). Modern uses of the term, so different from Paul's, assume that a person has managed to rise to an extraordinary level of moral performance. So to have someone call us a saint would be an embarrassment of inappropriateness. If we were to appropriate Paul's usage, we would know that each of us is a saint because we belong to God, apart from any question about our moral rectitude. Then we saints should live a life appropriate to our God who has called us.

2. Every one of Paul's letters opens with an affirmation of God's grace, and every letter closes with grace, because grace, God's freely given, unmerited gift, is the alpha and omega of the life of faith. All of life in Christ, at every point (1:4), depends on God's freely bestowed favor and is marked by God's favorable disposition toward believers. Grace is in the call that has already inaugurated our life in Christ; grace is the power of God to support and sustain us in the midst of a broken world; and grace is the assurance that, as Paul puts it, "God is for us" (see Rom 8:31-39) even in times of loss and death (1 Cor 15:57).

3. Though Paul's churches seem to have been house churches, localized gatherings that met in the home of one of the believers, Paul always sees believers everywhere as belonging to one another, as belonging to God's family, as those who are granted the power to call upon the name of their shared Lord. The church becomes our true family. As Jesus said: "Whoever does the will of God is my brother and sister and mother" (Mark 3:35 NRSV).

1 Corinthians 1:4-9, Thanksgiving

COMMENTARY

Like every moment of the life in Christ, Paul grounds his communications in thanksgiving to God ("always," 1:4). The 1 Corinthians thanksgiving lays out the scope of the Christian life, from the inception of God's grace given in Christ to the "day of our Lord," to the "end" when the Lord will be revealed, and within that framework celebrates the way the Corinthian believers have been enriched and amply supplied with χαρίσματα (*charismata*), spiritual gifts (God is the implied and understood provider). Perhaps the mention of "speech and knowledge" in 1:5 is prompted by Paul's recognition that some of the Corinthians have stressed those endowments (see 1:18–2:16) while disparaging other gifts, and he thereby makes common ground with them, even though later in the letter he will attempt to refine their understanding of "speech and knowledge." In this thanksgiving modern readers receive a fundamental clue about the letter's exigence:[35] The Corinthian believers do not lack spiritual gifts, but they do not know how to employ them in service for the community in love. Instead, they ironically create status-oriented cliques based on what was in the first place simply a gift to them (cf. 4:7-8).

In the heart of this passage Paul's affirmation of assurance could not be stronger. The Corinthians' experience of God's enrichment of them "in every way" (1:5 NIV, NRSV) was already a "confirmation" (1:6; βεβαιόω *bebaioō*, "make firm," "establish,"

"confirm") of the testimony about Christ that elicited their faith in the first place. Their response was proof positive of God's calling, but that was only the beginning of their story. From that point, from their having been called and confirmed in their faith, Paul looks forward to the goal toward which God's grace is moving them—namely, "the revelation of our Lord Jesus Christ" (1:7) at the end time. That same Lord, Paul confidently assures them, will "also confirm you until the end" (1:8). What God has begun, God will assuredly bring to completion (cf. the same point in Phil 1:6). The Greek term *bebaioō*, translated here (1:6, 8) as "confirm," functions in papyri as a legal technical term meaning "properly guaranteed security"[36] and has the same stress on assurance in Paul's use of it. The guarantee is grounded in God's faithfulness (1:9)—a motif that Paul surely found grounded across his scriptures (Deut 5:10; 7:9; Pss 89:1-2; 145:13; Isa 49:7; Jer 4:2; Dan 9:4)—but must be matched by faithfulness and proper living on the part of believers. The remainder of 1 Corinthians will show that Paul has serious concerns regarding the latter. Paul's thanksgiving reminds the Corinthians of how richly they have been graced by God and of how God is faithful to carry through on what has been promised. Without saying it here, Paul sets the ground against which he can later say how much the Corinthians risk by their divisiveness and their inconsiderate treatment of each other.

35. Paul Schubert, *Form and Function of the Pauline Thanksgivings* (Berlin: Töpelmann, 1939) 180.

36. BAGD, 138.

REFLECTIONS

1. Because believers are totally dependent on God's transforming grace for their new life in Christ, their basic response must be one of thankfulness to God (1:4); Paul expects thankfulness to God from all persons (Rom 1:21), and here he himself models it. Paul's relationship to other believers and his thankfulness to God for them is based not on whether he likes them or on whether they view issues in the world in the same way, but on the simple and profound fact that God's grace is active in them and in him. Our modern Christian community is founded on God's grace given to all, not on whether we are socially compatible and not on whether we take the same political views.

2. Paul defines the current life of believers by reference to the origin of faith among them ("our testimony about Christ was confirmed in you," 1:6 NIV) and to the "day of our Lord"—that is, to the end time, when Paul expects the Lord to be revealed. Thus the believers' story, our story, is always written into the larger story of what God is ultimately doing in Christ (15:1-2, 24-28); we believers are always pictured as a part of God's cosmic plan. Paul thereby protects against two dangers that are too prevalent in modern renditions of Christianity whereby faith is turned into an internal "attitudinal adjustment" or into an individualistic experience. Our lives in Christ are never just our own but always also involve how we are relating to those around us. Our life in Christ is not manifested simply by a change in attitude but must also make a difference in the choices and decisions we make, the actions we take, and the way we treat not only ourselves but also others.

1 CORINTHIANS 1:10–4:21, PAUL'S CONTEXTUALING OF THE LETTER

OVERVIEW

A primary hermeneutical principle must be affirmed: Within only the broadest constraints of the literary conventions of the times—namely, that letters tended to open with salutations and thanksgivings and to close with greetings and a recognition of the gods—Paul was absolutely free to organize and arrange the contents of 1 Corinthians as he saw fit. So the arrangement of materials within the letter—what comes first, what comes next, what comes last, and so forth—is completely Paul's, and his arrangement sheds light on his purposes and goals. Accordingly, we must pay special attention to matters such as location, sequence, and association.

Roughly one-fourth of the letter, 1:10–4:21, sets the context, the background for Paul's subsequent treatment of particular problems in Corinth, identifies the Corinthian tendency toward divisiveness, and reminds the Corinthians of his exemplary and paternal caring for them. This important passage rehearses Paul's relationship to the Corinthians and theirs to the gospel.

Scholarly interpretation of these opening chapters has been dominated by two issues: (1) What is the identification of the groups that are deduced from 1:12, "Each of you says, 'I belong to Paul,' 'I belong to Apollos,' 'I belong to Cephas [Peter],' 'I belong to Christ'"? and (2) What is the nature and the source of the wisdom teaching that is reflected in 1:18–2:16 and that is assumed to have made an impact on Paul's community? Both of these scholarly traditions have some readily creditable support: (a) Wisdom and knowledge are treated at some length in the opening chapters; (b) by all the evidence the Corinthians were divisive and contentious; (c) Apollos and Paul (and Cephas?) labored with the Corinthians and, therefore, could have been persons of allegiance attachment; (d) Paul admits to having baptized some but not many of the Corinthians, leaving it clear that someone else had baptized the rest of them (1 Cor 12:13, a baptismal tradition, confirms that the Corinthian believers have indeed been baptized); and (e) in that culture, "belonging to" someone was a primary category and one that we will see Paul readily exploit in this letter (see 3:23; 6:20; 7:23).

On the issue of the identification of different "parties" or groups based on 1:12 and its "I belong" statements, scholars have rightly found most difficulty in imagining any one part of Paul's congregations anywhere who might have arrogated to themselves some especial belonging to Christ because a cardinal Pauline assertion is that all believers belong to Christ in a central, defining way (cf. 3:23). That leaves three groups, formed around Paul, Apollos, and Cephas, with perhaps some issue of allegiance to the one who did the baptizing. Since F. C. Baur[37] claimed that there really were only two groups in Corinth and that their allegiance was to Paul (and Apollos) or Cephas (and Christ), some scholars have been tempted to follow Baur's lead.[38] This reconstruction of the dynamics at Corinth supposes that the divisiveness there is between two factions that have formed competitive allegiances, some claiming Paul as their leader and others claiming Cephas (Peter) as theirs. In this construal, not adopted in this commentary, the defining struggle is between Paul and Peter, and their conflict has been reflected onto the undeniable fractiousness at Corinth. Baur's reconstruction has rightly been criticized as having a limited evidential base in Paul's letters.[39] But more tellingly for the interpretation of 1 Corinthians, we must note that Cephas's relationship to the Corinthians is unclear but not monumental in importance; surely, the Corinthians know about Cephas because Paul has taught them about him (15:5), and perhaps Cephas has been through Corinth and, maybe even with his wife, has received their hospitality (9:5). No convincing argument has ever tied particular problems or issues from the rest of the letter to any identifiable groups that could be associated with any of these leaders as distinguished from another.[40]

In fact, what is demonstrable in Corinth is that the Corinthians are given to factions, to cliques, but not that there are identifiable "groups" or "parties." There is no basis for

assuming that the factional tendencies always broke on the same lines with the same people opposing others. As we will see, the church at Corinth has some problems that have clear socioeconomic power and status considerations, but particular, identifiable groups or parties within the church cannot be successfully identified. Accordingly, this commentary will treat not groups but divisions and lack of unity. In so doing we must recognize that our failure to be able to be more precise about the divisiveness may, in fact, be Paul's purposeful "fuzzing" of the specifics as a way of avoiding reifying whatever schisms he knew to be present. In any case, on this issue we cannot penetrate with precision behind our source—namely, Paul's letter.

In these contextualizing chapters Paul does make much of wisdom, first contrasting his gospel with wisdom and then, admitting that he does deal in wisdom with mature persons, he declares that his wisdom is secret and hidden to others. Much scholarly attention has been paid to identifying the source of this wisdom and understanding whether some wisdom speculation has invaded the community.[41] As important as such questions are, if for nothing else than understanding where Paul and the Corinthians might have received or encountered such wisdom traditions, the attention of this study will be placed on the way the wisdom claims function in Paul's argumentation with the Corinthians as an act of persuasion on his part.

Our assessment of the functions of Paul's frequent references to wisdom in chaps. 1–4 must be cognizant of the fact that wisdom seems to play no explicit role in the distinct problems and issues with which chaps. 5–16 are concerned. Status, expressed in terms of boasting, puffiness, comparison, and personal practice, is a concern of the letter throughout. Paul's linking of status concerns and wisdom—which we shall see shortly—reflects the linkage in the culture of the time and allows us to see that Paul's comments about wisdom in the first four chapters set a context for him to deal with status claims throughout

---

37. F. C. Baur, "Die Christuspartei in der korinthischen Gemeinde, der Gegensatz der petrinischen und paulinischen Christenthums in der Altesten Kirche," *Ausgewählte Werke*, ed. K. Scholder (Stuttgart: T. Frommann, 1963) 1:24-76.

38. See Michael D. Goulder, *St. Paul Versus St. Peter: A Tale of Two Missions* (Louisville: Westminster/Knox, 1994).

39. William Baird, " 'One Against the Other'; Intra-church Conflict in 1 Corinthians," in *The Conversation Continues: Studies in Paul and John in Honor of J. Louis Martyn*, ed. R. T. Fortna and B. R. Gaventa (Nashville: Abingdon, 1990) 116-36, carefully assesses and soundly, rightly rejects the line of interpretation that runs from Baur through Schmithals and that Baird identifies as Paul against "one front"—whether that be Baur's Peter or Schmithals's gnostics. The problem of 1 Corinthians is not Paul versus anyone but factions and divisions within and among the Corinthian believers.

40. L. L. Welborn, "On the Discord in Corinth: 1 Corinthians 1–4 and Ancient Politics," *JBL* 106 (1987) 88-89, and esp. n. 16 for some historical perspective on this failed search.

41. A sample of such efforts includes Walter Schmithals, *Gnosticism in Corinth: An Investigation of the Letters to the Corinthians*, 2nd ed., trans. J. E. Steely (Nashville: Abingdon, 1971) 141-55; R. A. Horsley, "Wisdom of Word and Words of Wisdom in Corinth," *CBQ* 39 (1977) 224-39, and "Gnosis in Corinth: 1 Corinthians 8.1-6, *NTS* 27 (1980) 32-51; and Stephen M. Pogoloff, *Logos and Sophia: The Rhetorical Situation of 1 Corinthians*, SBLDS 134 (Atlanta: Scholars Press, 1992).

the letter. There is no reason to doubt that some Corinthians, quite likely responding both to Paul's repeated insistence that believers should consider what they know (more about this pattern as the letter unfolds) and to the culture's identification of sages as ones worthy of status and honor, found themselves identifying their wisdom with status and a right for respect.

While it has been stated that wisdom seems to play no explicit role in the distinct problems or issues of the letter in chaps. 5 and following, we must consider that it may be Paul more than the Corinthians who emphasizes wisdom and expounds on wisdom claims to make his points in the opening four chapters. In what follows, however, we will see that wisdom and status are very directly linked not only in that culture but also in Paul's letter, and concerns with status lace the problems Paul has with the Corinthians in the remainder of the letter. So if wisdom is not one of the Corinthian obsessions, surely status is; in any case, Paul's treatment of wisdom and its associated status lets him establish a basis in these chapters for later reflections about his readers' competitive status concerns.

One other noteworthy feature, and a key to understanding Paul's argumentation, is Paul's frequent employment of what will here be called the rival "two-way" tradition that was so prevalent not only in the wider Greco-Roman world but also among Jews at the turn of the era (Prov 28:18; Wis 5:6-7; cf. *Did.* 1-6).[42] Two rival and opposing ways or paths are depicted, and the auditors are called to take the one and avoid the other (cf. Matt 7:13-14). Much of 1:10–4:21 is constructed on such a frame.

How to Read 1:10–4:21. Previous studies have not taken adequate note of Paul's own clues as to how to interpret these opening four chapters. Two features of 1:10–4:21 frame the section and must provide our primary interpretive keys. First, in keeping with the rhetorical practices of the times, Paul opens and closes—encircles—the whole section with a doubled appeal (1:10; 4:16) and by doing so forms an inclusio, a frame or ring-device within which the surrounded material must be understood. His bracketing

appeals thereby provide a fundamental clue as to what to look for in the intervening chapters and verses. Second, enclosed within the two appeals is Paul's explicit declaration as to his purpose in the intervening sections: He has used himself and Apollos as exemplars in order to make a point (4:6). To understand Paul's purposes in 1:10–4:21, we need to look at the doubled appeal and at the matter of Paul's exemplary treatment of himself and Apollos.

The Doubled Appeal. All of Paul's undisputed letters, 1 Corinthians included, arrive at a point where Paul directly implores his readers for a response (e.g., Rom 12:1; 2 Cor 10:1; Phil 4:2). But in this respect 1 Corinthians is unusual in two ways: (1) The first appeal (1:10) occurs far earlier than in any other Pauline letter, at the beginning of what we might normally call the body of the letter, and (2) it is repeated three chapters later (4:16).

The opening appeal, based on a report from some whom Paul designates as "Chloe's people" that there is discord among the faithful at Corinth, is structured as a contrast between what the Corinthians are now—that is, torn and divided—and what Paul enjoins them to become: one in voice, mind, and opinion (1:10). Although we know nothing about the identity of Chloe and her people, we must suppose that they are in good standing with Paul and with the church at Corinth because Paul cites them as the credible source of his knowledge about the divisiveness (1:11; cf. 3:3).

The second entreaty—"Therefore I appeal to you: Become imitators of me" (4:16)—captures the intervening emphasis on exemplification, links it to Paul's appeal, and draws the opening four chapters to a close. Paul admonishes the Corinthians whose divisiveness demonstrates their lack of maturity. Though he wishes they might behave as "grown-ups" (3:1-2), he calls them his "beloved children" (4:14) and affirms his paternity: "in Christ Jesus, through the gospel, I myself begot you." He alone is their πατήρ (*patēr*), "father" (4:15). In the Roman world, paternity created a reciprocal responsibility between parent and children. The *pater familias* ("head of the household") was responsible for all who lived there; in particular the children's comportment and well-being were

---

42. Aune, *The New Testament in Its Literary Environment*, 197.

in the father's hand. The children learned by modeling after their father, learned whatever trade the household was involved with, but much more fundamentally, learned appropriate conduct. Accordingly, as their father, Paul has written in warning or admonition (4:14) and enjoins them to model after him. They would also do well to emulate Timothy, who like them is a "beloved child" but who, unlike them, understands "Paul's ways" so well that he can come to them as a teacher (4:17).

Both appeals feature contrasts: "Speak with one voice, don't have schisms" (1:10), and "Be like me, your father in the faith, not like babies" who cannot write between the lines (4:6; for this interpretation, see the commentary below). Both appeals acknowledge the disparity between the Corinthians' current discord and the harmony they should have in Christ. The first appeal explicitly urges unity and an end to dissension and divisiveness; the second calls simply for an emulation of Paul, who, by that time, in the intervening sections, has painted himself in his relation to Apollos as the model of cooperation and wholehearted unity in the gospel.

Paul and Apollos As Exemplars. Near the conclusion of 1:10–4:21, Paul baldly states his overriding purpose in the opening chapters and his means of accomplishing it. The purpose: so that the Corinthians might learn not to be puffed up in favor of one and against another. The means: Paul openly declares that, in what has preceded 4:6 ("all this"), he has used a common contemporary rhetorical device, "indirect" or "figured speech," by which he has made a point with reference to himself and Apollos as a roundabout or oblique way of critiquing the Corinthians' predilection for contentions and divisions.[43] Paul's verb in 4:6 is μετασχηματίζω (*metaschēmatizō*), which has a semantic range of "change the form of, transform, change," "disguise," and "say something with the aid of a figure of speech,"[44] so toward the end of the section, Paul explicitly

tells the readers what he has been doing in the previous chapters.

"Frank" or "direct speech" (παρρησία *parrēsia*),[45] the alternative to "indirect speech," was used sparingly in Paul's time; "indirect speech" was the "normal mode of discourse" then.[46] With direct speech the writer or speaker applies the critique directly. Direct speech is argumentative and usually confrontational and leaves the speaker open to reprisal. Indirect speech moves the discussion from the delicate, sensitive issue itself—in this instance, the discord and disharmony among the Corinthian believers—and transfers the discourse to a relatively "safe" topic where what is known or learned there can either in the act of hearing or in later reflection be transposed, ideally by Corinthian self-application, to the touchy issue of their divisiveness.[47] In this letter, the delicate issue is the Corinthians' disharmony with one another, their tendency to take sides; the safe topic is the exemplary relationship of Paul and Apollos. So when we read the references to Paul and Apollos we should recognize that they are not at all the problem. Far from it! In fact, those two leaders, in their work among the Corinthian believers, have embodied the proper harmony and unity despite their considerable dissimilarities. Rather than representing focal points for schisms, as some interpreters have suggested,[48] Paul offers himself and Apollos as models for the way dissimilar Corinthians ought to cooperate and behave in the gospel.

Having recognized Paul's acknowledged strategy of persuasion in 4:6, let us now look at Paul's references to himself and Apollos so that we can see how his "indirect speech" has served to illustrate proper Christian unity in diversity. In 1:12 Paul invites the Corinthians to think of themselves as belonging to

---

43. Benjamin Fiore, "'Covert Allusion' in 1 Corinthians 1–4," *CBQ* 47 (1985) 85-102; David R. Hall, "A Disguise for the Wise: METASCHEMATISMOS in 1 Corinthians 4:6," *NTS* 40 (1994) 143-49; Peter Lampe, "Theological Wisdom and the 'Word About the Cross': The Rhetorical Scheme in 1 Corinthians 1–4," *Int* 44 (1990) 117-31. John Fitzgerald, *Cracks in an Earthern Vessel: An Examination of the Catalogues of Hardships in the Corinthian Correspondence*, SBLDS 99 (Atlanta: Scholars Press, 1988), traces the identification of this as a covert allusion back to J. B. Lightfoot in 1895, 119n. 10.

44. BAGD, 513.

45. See J. Paul Sampley, "Paul's Frank Speech with the Galatians and the Corinthians," in *Philodemus and the New Testament World*, NovTSup, ed. J. T. Fitzgerald, G. S. Holland, and D. Obbink (Leiden: Brill, forthcoming), and Sampley, "Frank Speech," in *Paul in the Greco-Roman World* (Harrisburg, Pa.: Trinity, forthcoming).

46. Frederick Ahl, "The Art of Safe Criticism in Greece and Rome," *AJP* 105 (1984) 204.

47. For more detail on the differences between frank and indirect speech as well as Paul's application of indirect speech to another problem, see J. Paul Sampley, "The Weak and the Strong: Paul's Careful and Crafty Rhetorical Strategy in Romans 14:1–15:13," in *The Social World of the First Christians: Essays in Honor of Wayne A. Meeks*, ed. L. M. White and O. L. Yarbrough (Minneapolis: Augsburg/Fortress, 1995) 43-46.

48. Pogoloff's very suggestive study, *Logos and Sophia*, 189-90, errs in this direction.

him or to Apollos, and right away he signals that these are to be considered as just two "for instances" by adding Cephas (Paul's way of referring to Peter) to the list. Cephas's role in 1 Corinthians is minimal. Outside the opening four chapters (cf. 3:22), Cephas is mentioned only twice (9:5; 15:5), and in no way does either reference, even in the slightest hint, tie Cephas to any group or problem or issue confronting the church at Corinth. If, as I assume, there was not a group at Corinth who held allegiance to Cephas, Paul's readers would have known immediately, with the mention of Cephas, that the entire list, including Paul and Apollos, was simply illustrative and designed to make a point by analogy. Even the modern reader of 4:6 should get that point and take it back as a guideline for reading 1:12.

But in 1:12 Paul does not stop with those belonging to Cephas. As if to ensure that no Corinthian auditors mistakenly take Paul as describing what he thinks are the social realities at Corinth, Paul parodies his own rhetorical enterprise by suggesting the unthinkable possibility that some might fancy that they belong especially to Christ as their group of allegiance. Paul's own follow-up (in 1:13) to his "I belong to Christ" parody once again shows that his purpose is illustrative with respect to himself and Apollos, as he says explicitly in 4:6. When Paul has written "I belong to Christ," he can bear it with a straight face no longer; with irony, he parodies his own parody: "Is Christ divided? Was Paul crucified for you? Or were you baptized into the name of Paul?" (1:13). Each of those questions is clearly structured, as the Greek allows, to signal that Paul expects a negative answer: Of course not!

Does Paul's writing "Each of you says . . ." (1:12) indicate that he thinks everybody in the Corinthian church has, in fact, established such an allegiance with one of the people listed—namely Paul, Apollos, or Cephas? Paul's treatment of chaos in worship in chap. 14 has a similar expression that should guide the interpreter of 1:12. In that context he advises: "Each of you has a psalm, a teaching, a revelation" (14:26). Clearly, the point is that in worship people comport themselves with discipline; the "each" functions in a distributive way to suggest that "different ones"

will recite a psalm, give a teaching, share a revelation, and so forth. So also in 1:12 the "each" is to be understood in an allusive way, not as a dividing up of the congregation with no remainder.

The Paul/Apollos illustrative schema laces through these opening chapters and, following 1:12, next surfaces immediately after Paul has chided the Corinthians for still being babies in Christ when they should be more mature. His evidence that they are babies is a selective reprise of 1:10-12: "as long as there is jealousy and quarreling among you. . . . When one says, 'I belong to Paul,' and another, 'I belong to Apollos,' " that is, as long as there are divisions in the body of Christ, they are still children (3:3-4). Here, just as Paul explicitly and directly tells the reader in 4:6, Paul makes his points simply by referring to himself and Apollos alone. He does in 3:3-4 what later he expressly tells the reader he has intended to do (4:6).

What does Paul expect that the Corinthians should learn from him and Apollos? His answer can be seen in 3:5-9. These two leaders are equally servants of the same Lord who called them (3:5). One planted, the other watered (3:6), they have a common purpose (3:8; lit., "are one"); and each will receive wages for his work. Because God is the one who gives the growth, the ones who plant and water are not in and of themselves anything special at all (3:7); they are simply laborers, "God's servants, working together" (3:9 NRSV); they have nothing about which they should boast or be puffed up. As surely as Paul and Apollos are "one" and should not be puffed up in favor of one or the other, so also the Corinthians should neither be divided nor boastful. Just as Paul and Apollos work together, so also should the Corinthians. Just as Paul and Apollos have individual tasks for which each will receive wages and yet have a common purpose, so also the Corinthians correspond in every detail. The Corinthian believers, as different as they are socioeconomically and as variously gifted as they may be, are all equally and collectively "God's field," "God's building" (3:9).

Later in the same chapter, it is time for perspective-keeping. The Corinthians have lost their way, become confused about basics. In their inclinations to "belong to" certain divisions and thereby achieve a boastable status (3:21), they have lost sight of their true, definitional belonging—namely, to Christ! Because they belong to Christ, who belongs to God (3:23), all partisanship, whether to Paul, to Apollos, to Cephas, or indeed (and this is the real point) to any other human leader or grouping, is inappropriate.

Between the bracketing appeals (1:10; 4:16) that encourage the Corinthians to cease their divisiveness and emulate their father in the gospel, Paul structures his argument around the frame provided by the references to himself and Apollos as exemplary coworkers in the gospel. So the doubled appeal and the indirect speech about himself and Apollos provide fundamental guidelines for interpreting 1:10–4:21. The doubled appeal signals Paul's profound concern, which will undergird the entire letter, that the Corinthians are schismatic—that is, they have lost sight of their true unity in Christ. Their misunderstanding and its resultant divisive behavior cue Paul concerning their immaturity, their childishness, and causes him to play the father who models maturity—and for that Paul turns to indirect speech about himself and Apollos. The Corinthians surely knew how different Paul and Apollos were from each other in so many ways; yet Paul's picture of them, especially as developed in 3:5-9, epitomizes how the Corinthian believers, themselves so different from one another, ought also to work together in the body of Christ.

In the portrait of himself and Apollos, Paul never loses sight that it is he alone who is their father; he is the one who planted. Apollos stands in second place as the one who came into the picture later and who watered what was already planted. But, as different as Paul and Apollos are and as distinct as their contributions, they are one in Christ in an exemplary fashion. The Paul/Apollos lesson is a back-to-basics illustration of Christian unity sketched broadly and consistently across 1:10–4:21 so that the Corinthians, being babies, can learn to "color within the lines," as I interpret Paul's meaning in the cryptic expression "Nothing beyond what is written" (4:6).[49]

49. Fitzgerald, *Cracks in an Earthen Vessel*, 121-28, has the best study of this problem, tracing it from Protagoras forward and indicating "a lesson that is to be learned," 124.

1 Corinthians 1:10-17, The Opening Appeal

COMMENTARY

Paul, calling the Corinthians "brothers and sisters" (ἀδελφοί *adelphoi*, "brethren"; Paul clearly assumes that women are also included, so the suggested translation here and in the NRSV seems appropriate)[50] and thereby claiming common ground with them as children of the same Father, this time God (1:3; cf. v. 11), opens the body of the letter with an appeal that they not be schismatic but speak with one voice, one mind, and one purpose (1:10). Over against their tendency to be schismatic, Paul stacks up an overlapping variety of ways in which he thinks their unity in Christ should express itself. In 1:10 alone, where he first notes their divisiveness,

Paul encases their inclination to divisiveness within three evocations of their unity. In the first, the one that is the immediate object of the appeal, he urges them all to "say the same" (NIV, "agree with one another"; NRSV, "be in agreement"), possibly evoking the reflection about precisely what believers can say together at the very ground of their being. Clearly, from 1 Cor 12:3, Paul thinks that the central and foundational affirmation that "Jesus is Lord" is one such common claim. The second (νοῦς *nous*) and third (γνώμη *gnōmē*) common identifications have so much semantic overlap that they tend to reinforce each other because both could be translated "the same mind or outlook." Paul's point is to be seen in the overlap of the three ways, in their corroboration. His appeal to affirm the same thing and to be of the same

50. Fee, *The First Epistle to the Corinthians*, 52n. 22, notes that "it is clear from the evidence of this letter (11:2-16) and Phil 4:1-3 that women were participants in the worship of the community and would have been included in the 'brothers' being addressed. . . . It is therefore not pedantic, but culturally sound and biblically sensitive, for us to translate this vocative 'brothers and sisters.'"

outlook is Paul's way of declaring that what unites them ought to be far more powerful and comprehensive than what pulls them apart.

As subsequent parts of 1 Corinthians are read, the alert auditors may remember Paul's call for all the Corinthians to be of "the same mind" in 1:10 when they hear his later claim that "we ourselves have the mind of Christ" (2:16). That powerful claim identifies the shared mind that Paul yearns for the Corinthians to have and credits the Holy Spirit as making it possible (2:10-16). Though the notion of having the mind of Christ is not developed much in 1 Corinthians, we can see it elaborated in Phil 2:1-4, a passage directed at another church with dissension. There Paul follows a similar pattern—namely, he stacks up semantic overlaps, even more of them than in 1 Cor 1:10, but to the same point: "Being of the same mind, having the same love, being in full accord and of one mind" (Phil 2:2 NRSV). The unity that believers experience in Christ is supposed to be so profound and so encompassing that they share the demeanor, the outlooks, and the goals that really matter. The remainder of 1 Corinthians will make abundantly clear that Paul does not confuse unity with uniformity; he does not think that believers must all have the identical views on all things (cf. Rom 14:1) or that they must walk in lockstep. On the contrary, he values the distinctiveness of believers, appreciates their differences of gifts and graces (see chap. 12), and expects believers to make a range of acceptable but different moral choices (see chap. 7). The true unity of believers is established by God's grace, by Christ's love, and by the reception of the Holy Spirit. These all believers share, equally and in a constitutive way.

Paul's appeal is made in "the name of our Lord Jesus Christ" (v. 10). As is clear already from 1:2, the Corinthian believers and all the faithful everywhere acknowledge the shared lordship of Christ (cf. 12:3). To appeal "in the name" of that Lord should remind the readers of their baptism, the very rite by which they were brought into this new fellowship. The formula certainly reminds Paul of baptism because he uses it in his parody of their divisiveness: "Or were you baptized in the name of Paul?" Of course not! To appeal "in the name of the Lord" reminds them that Christ is their Lord and invokes his power and his election of them as the proper framework within which the readers should consider Paul's petition.

The term *adelphoi* (NRSV, "brothers and sisters"; NIV, "brothers") occurs thirty-eight times in 1 Corinthians, more than twice as many times as in any other Pauline letter. Its frequency is a subtle testimony to Paul's eagerness to affirm the common, shared ground and the equal standing of all God's children, not only in their relation to Paul but especially to one another. The term depicts the reconciling resocialization of Corinthians from all sorts of social settings into the new family of God and invites them to view each other accordingly.

Divisiveness among those who are in Christ is simply unthinkable for Paul. Paul and Apollos, as important as they have been in the life and growth of the church at Corinth— and even Cephas, whose actual relationship to the Corinthians is relatively obscure—are placed in perspective in this opening passage (1:12). The passage is bracketed by a reference to Christ as Lord on one side (1:10) and the "cross of Christ" on the other (1:17). In one stroke of the pen Paul puts himself (and if himself how much more Apollos and Cephas!) and his importance in perspective: "Paul wasn't crucified for you, was he? And you weren't baptized 'into the name of Paul,' were you?" (1:13*b-c*). There is no need for an answer to these ludicrous questions, whose function is to focus on the real and important issue at hand: "Christ isn't divided, is he?" Of course not. So when "there is jealousy and quarreling among you" (3:3), nothing distinguishes believers from everybody else. The way of the world has become the way of believers. (What is supposed to be outside the assembly of believers has insidiously moved inside; see the Commentary on 5:1–6:20.) The hallmark of Christians is supposed to be unity in Christ (cf. John 13:35); Paul takes anything less than that as a sign of immaturity.

These early verses (vv. 10-17) yield some insights into the church at Corinth and into Paul. First, we learn that certain Corinthian believers were baptized by Paul, though he tries to minimize the importance of his having been the one to do it (vv. 14-16). Crispus (cf. Acts 18:8), Gaius (cf. Acts 19:29; Rom 16:23), and the household of Stephanas—that seems to cover the persons Paul can immediately recall having baptized (1:14, 16). We will learn more about Stephanas and his household at the end of the letter (16:15, 17). Paul's minimizing his role in baptism should not be construed as a depreciation of the rite. All of the Corinthians have been baptized (12:13), and their knowledge of their baptism will be an important consideration in the moral reasoning found in chaps. 7 and 12. Baptism is definitional for all believers; the identity of the baptizer is an indifferent matter. Although the Corinthians seem so concerned about status, their significance lies not in their relation to Paul—or, indeed, to any other person—but in their relation to Christ and, therefore, to God.

Chloe (1:11) seems to have standing with the Corinthian church; she may have been a businessperson whose agents, possibly her slaves, were on the road. Her people are a prime source for Paul's knowledge of the ways the Corinthians have become divisive (v. 11).

Second, we learn how Paul understands his calling: Christ sent him not to baptize but to evangelize (v. 17; cf. 9:19-23). Paul's identity rests not in his function as baptizer but in his preaching of the gospel. The Corinthians surely know this, too, because it was he who, by his proclamation, "planted" the church in Corinth by his preaching (3:6).

Paul's proclaiming of the gospel is not "with eloquent wisdom, so that the cross of Christ might not be emptied of its power" (v. 17). Paul's picture of the Corinthians will become clear as the letter progresses: Some of them are easily swayed by brilliant rhetoric; some have aspirations for wisdom; some are impressed by knowledge; some are awestruck by the faith and gifts of themselves and of others; some place importance in power and status. All of those persons, trading for a counterfeit, lose sight of the only true power, the power of God shown through the cross. The remainder of the letter will distinguish the real power of the cross from contenders, but in v. 17 the counterfeit is rather narrowly identified as sophisticated or cultured speech because that sets up the direction that the letter's next passage will take.

Verse 17 is the foundational statement whose significance is unpacked and refined by Paul in the following verses in which he contrasts "eloquent wisdom" with "the cross of Christ." Each of those phrases is a figure of speech (the rhetorical pattern is called synecdoche) by which the part stands for a larger whole, as, for example, "wheels" may represent or stand for a "car." The "cross of Christ," which Paul subsequently reduces even further to "cross" (v. 18), is a deliberate compression of complex affirmations into a single symbol, chosen here in part no doubt for its inescapably scandalous focus on Christ's death. Here "cross" stands for, signifies, a much larger, pivotal cluster of events so central to Paul's proclamation: the death and resurrection of Jesus Christ. For Paul, the cross, planted squarely in history, stands for the whole story of Christ's death and resurrection as a sign of God's grace and caring for human beings.

A similarly purposeful compression is found in the cryptic expression σοφία λόγου (*sophia logou*; NRSV, "eloquent wisdom"; more lit., wisdom of word or wisdom of speech), which, like "cross of Christ" becoming "cross," is epitomized in the subsequent discussion by the single term "wisdom." The locution's precise meaning has been the subject of controversy. Many commentators, noting the heavy concentration of wisdom terminology in 1:18–2:16, have taken the recurring mention of wisdom as referring to a Greek or Jewish philosophical tradition with which, the supposition goes, some Corinthians are captivated.[51] Such an interpretation understands Paul's opening chapters as trying to free those Corinthians from their fascination with wisdom, but it encounters two difficulties: (1) What is one to make of the relative absence not only of the term "wisdom" (14 times in the first four chaps.; only once thereafter, 12:8) after chap. 4? and (2) How is one to understand the fact that wisdom does not seem to be directly responsible for a single one of the manifold problems that are treated in the rest of the letter? Such an interpretation is not necessary.

It is a feature of the culture in which Paul preached that the persons who were most

---

51. See R. A. Horsley, "Gnosis in Corinth: 1 Corinthians 8.1-6," *NTS* 27 (1988) 32-51.

directly identified with wisdom—namely, the sages—tended to be eloquent, skillful speakers. Cultured speech, eloquently delivered in a refined fashion, was the telltale of high status, of power and wealth, of education and, indeed, of wisdom.[52] In antiquity, the constellation of wealth, high status, cultured speech, and power was fixed; the sighting of any of the major stars allowed one to suppose the whole configuration. Conversely, the lack of "cleverness of speech," cultured or refined speech (possible translations of *sophia logou*, 1:17), was the certain sign of low status and, one might reasonably suppose, a corresponding lack of wisdom, wealth, and power.

Paul pointedly dissociates himself and his proclamation from clever or wise speech, from the kind of wisdom-as-status indicator in which the world, and apparently some Corinthians, put stock. In contrarian fashion, Paul takes his definition from the cross of Christ. In subsequent verses we see that Paul abbreviates these rival constellations into single and opposing terms: wisdom versus cross. To put the same point, but with a flexibility of terminology, there are two types of speech: one emphasizing wisdom and its associated high status, the other featuring the cross and its scandal. Paul sets up rival symbols of the way persons understand and live

their lives: "Eloquent wisdom," pleasant and persuasive as it may be, comes to epitomize culturally accepted connections, associations with important persons or groups as a way of establishing one's own significance, importance, and worth; "cross," Paul's opposing symbol, demolishes all pretensions to status and standing in the world. He writes the Corinthians about his own choice not "to empty the cross of Christ" and, for the first in a long series of instances in 1 Corinthians, sets himself up as a model to be emulated. The implication is that the Corinthians, by their divisiveness, risk emptying the cross, nullifying its power. Cross, alternately, "Christ crucified" (1:23), Paul's opposing symbol, stands in its scandalous starkness for the ultimate in weakness and folly when considered from the standpoint represented by those who would value cultured speech and its associated social status. For the clue that wisdom is not just a matter of knowledge but also a status indicator, note that "power" opens 1:18-25 and that in v. 25 the term is set over against "weakness."

The opening appeal—to cease being divisive—therefore, is structured on the two-way pattern that is so prevalent in Paul's world and in Israel's traditions as well. In the case at hand, Paul sets the way of the cross over against the way of wisdom, the scandalous cross of Christ over against status-indicative cultured speech based on wisdom.

52. See Pogoloff's solid treatment of the strong link between social status and skill at rhetoric in antiquity: *Logos and Sophia*, 129-53.

REFLECTIONS

1. To whom do you belong? As Christians we should answer: "to Christ"; "to God." Other allegiances compete: work, possessions, status, fame, dreams, television, drugs, and so on. The sweeping biblical term for those competing affiliations is "idolatry," a topic that will surface explicitly later in the letter (5:10, 11; 6:9; 10:7), but that means having something else in the governing center of your life besides God or Christ. When you properly belong to Christ or to God, then all the other claimants either take on a proper secondary place or are removed from your life. If you have a friend whom you trust deeply, talk with that person about how you would answer this question: To whom do you belong?

2. With 1:10 we confront one of the problems that prompted 1 Corinthians: divisions within the church. Paul's call for the Corinthians to be "of the same mind and of the same opinion" raises certain questions for modern persons. Does unity preclude differences—differences in actions, in thoughts, in words? Does unity require uniformity of belief and behavior? This touches on an important issue about which Paul has a very sophisticated view. Paul assumes all sorts of differences among people and even credits some of the differences to the Spirit's working to enrich the body (see the argument in 12:4-26). However many differences there may be, or how distinctive the contributions to the body politic, the members of the body must never lose sight of the basis of Christian unity: the shared death with Christ in which God inaugurated their new life in Christ. Christians are united in that they share the same prior indebtedness to sin's power, the same utter need for God's grace, and the same loving redemptive power of God's mercy. Christian unity rests on that shared story, not on the opinions that believers have about issues, and not on the distinctive contributions they are enabled to make to the community of believers. It is not accidental that Paul refers to baptism in this context (1:13-16), because baptism is the ritual expression not only of believers' solidarity with Christ but also of inclusion into Christ, reception of the Spirit, and, therefore, welcome into God's family. This tension, this fundamental exploration of what is and is not Christian unity, will express itself throughout the letter.

3. Baptism is the ritual of admission into Christian community and has been so from the earliest days. Though individuals perform the ritual of baptism, we must be clear that it is God who does the claiming and the welcoming of the baptized persons. So it matters not who does the liturgy of baptism. In the fourth-century Donatist controversy, the issue arose as to whether a baptism done by a sinful priest was to be considered efficacious. The church in its wisdom declared that baptism is warranted by God, whose action is at its heart, not by the priest (or minister) who presides. Paul, in his depreciating of any claim that the baptizer is a status indicator, anticipates the same judgment the church rendered in the Donatist controversy (cf. Phil 1:15-18). For believers today what counts is that God claims us in baptism—each of us, equally. Some will have been immersed. Some will have been sprinkled. Some will have had water poured over them. Some will have been baptized as infants; others will have been baptized as adults. Some will have Jordan River water used. Some will have a bishop do it. But all and every one are equally claimed as God's special people and belong to one another as a result.

1 Corinthians 1:18-25, Christ, True Power, True Wisdom

COMMENTARY

Beginning in 1:18, and indeed running through 2:5, Paul takes the Corinthians "back to basics," back to the crux of the community-founding gospel he first proclaimed to them. The passage is a complex of contrasts in which Paul's purpose seems to be to create the largest possible separation or distinction. Nuance and subtlety give way to hyperbole. Over against the cultured speech, the "eloquent wisdom" of 1:17, and its worldly values, Paul sets the scandalous, folly ridden cross; over against the "wisdom of λόγος [*logos*]" ("speech"; cultured speech symbolizing power as the world views things), Paul offers the *logos* ("word," his preaching) of the cross. Two rival logoi, two competing claims. Here, as in 1:17 (see also Gal 5:11), "cross" simply and boldly stands for the larger complex of affirmations that Paul more frequently carries with "death and resurrection."

In the two-way tradition so widespread in antiquity (cf. Josh 24:14-27; Matt 7:13-14), Paul imagines two distinct groupings of people whom he describes as ἀπολλυμένοι (*apollymenoi*, "those who are perishing") and σωζόμενοι (*sōzomenoi*, "us who are being saved," 1:18). Paul's use of present participles in both these constructions indicates that the "perishing" and the "being saved" are simultaneous, ongoing processes. The way Paul has set it up, the Corinthians would be expected to identify with that part of humanity that is in the process of being saved (though we will see that in subsequent sections of this letter

Paul wonders whether some of the Corinthians may not be in danger of slipping over to become a part of those who are perishing).

The Corinthians already know Paul's gospel and have been formed by it; a modern reader must put together the clues from a passage such as 1:18-25 and see them against a backdrop that we can reconstruct from other Pauline letters. God's decisive action in Christ's death and resurrection has inaugurated the apocalyptic end times. The new creation, the new age (= new aeon), has broken into the old world; the structure of the old world, fraught with the power of sin, is passing away (1 Cor 7:31).[53] Nonbelievers, with mind and heart darkened by the power of sin (Rom 1:21, 28), do not understand or recognize the new creation (cf. 2:8) and God's power at work in it. In fact, talk (or the word) of the cross—the ultimate symbol of shame, humiliation, and rejection—will strike nonbelievers as "folly"; but for believers it is the very power that is transforming their lives.

Paul has abandoned the former divisions of humanity into Jews and Greeks (1:22, 24) because he recognizes that God has called both Jews and Greeks (1:24). But Paul also recognizes that, by their response to the gospel, people have divided themselves into two different categories: "those who are perishing" and "us who are being saved" (cf. the same categories in 2 Cor 2:15), with the latter being understood as "those who are the called" (1:24), in this instance including everyone in the Corinthian church (1:2) and Paul himself (1:1).

As Paul sees it, the fate of each group is not yet set, but for both a process is under way. Salvation is to be completed by God in the future. At present, believers (in 1:21 they are literally described as "the ones who are believing," once again describing the faithful as in a process; cf. 1:18), the ones called by God, are justified; they are reconciled (Rom 5:9-10). Justified, reconciled believers are in the process of moving toward salvation just as unbelievers are in the course of perishing. The "word of the cross," "Christ crucified" (1:23)—that is, the heart of Paul's proclamation—is "folly," "foolishness," even a scandal or offense (1:23) to the latter, but the "power

of God" to the ones being saved (cf. Rom 1:16).

Such a transvaluation of values is what Paul attempts to describe when he calls "Christ crucified" a σκάνδαλον (*skandalon*; NIV and NRSV, "stumbling block," 1:23), from which we surely recognize our English "scandal." The term has a semantic range including "trap," "enticement to false belief," or "something that offends, repulses, elicits opposition."[54] For Paul, "Christ crucified," the very heart of the gospel proclamation, is a profound shock to the hearer. Nothing could be more unlikely than that redemption should come through the humiliating crucifixion of someone. Nothing could be more alien to the culture, its social structures and practices. To hear the scandalous gospel in such a way that one's life is transformed is to experience a *peripeteia*, an utterly shocking and fundamentally transformative turnabout. Elsewhere Paul has resorted to bold claims such as "new creation" (2 Cor 5:17) and "newness of life" (Rom 6:4) in an effort to capture some of the dynamics of the *skandalon*. Admittedly, the gospel is a *skandalon* in that it elicits opposition. Paul, like Jesus (cf. Matt 5:10-12), held that identification with the gospel would inevitably bring opposition (cf. 1 Thess 3:3-4). But the point of Paul's reference in 1:23 is not to account for opposition from outsiders—that does not seem to be a problem at this point in Corinth's life—but to ground the fundamental contrast he is stressing between the gospel and the way of the world.

God's power is not only different from the wisdom of this world, of this age, but is also antithetical to it. Scripture confirms for Paul (note that he assumes that his readers will acknowledge the authority of Scripture) that God "will destroy the wisdom of the wise" (1:19; Isa 29:14; cf. Ps 33:10), which the subsequent rhetorical questions make clear is the wisdom of "this age" or of "the world" (1:20).

Verse 24 shows, however, that Paul does not want to write off wisdom completely, for he claims cryptically "Christ the power of God and the wisdom of God." A positive consideration of what Paul construes as true wisdom will surface for further illumination and

---

53. Sampley, *Walking Between the Times*, 13-17.

54. BAGD, 753.

reflection a little later in the argument (cf. 2:6). In this context, Paul identifies Christ as both the "power of God" and the "wisdom of God" (1:24). This linkage of power and wisdom should be interpreted by Paul's identification of the gospel as "the power of God for salvation" (Rom 1:16) and refers not to Christ as some incarnated wisdom but to Christ's death and resurrection as the locus of God's power effectively working in and for believers. Thus Paul's proclamation can be abbreviated to "Christ crucified" (1:23*a*; cf. 2:2) and even more concentrated as "cross" (1:18). For the present, however, Paul is content to make a hyperbolic contrast between (pretentious, human) wisdom and God's "foolishness" and to declare, "No contest!" In an enlargement of the contrast, Paul extends the metaphor to strength and weakness: "God's weakness is stronger than human strength" (1:25), showing that the wisdom talk is really also about power and status and preparing the way for the next stage of the argument.

Paul's move to attach wisdom talk to power and status is an important key to understanding not only the force of Paul's argumentation but also the internal dynamics of the Corinthian community of believers. Beneath the surface of the text, where the discussion sets one path over against another, lies the ever-present struggle for status and standing that typified Paul's time. The Corinthians are not contending about some intellectual or even theological issue as if such notions could exist in a classroom or debating hall. They are competing for status. Wisdom and its cultured speech earned status in the culture of Paul's time. Peripatetic sages, skilled in rhetoric, claimed status for themselves and exploited others for their own ends. Their teaching drew its power from capitalizing on the social conventions that accorded power and status to a teacher and to what he taught when it was persuasively expressed in eloquence. In such a human transaction, the only power at stake is the power one can evoke from hearers; the hearers generate the power by the very granting of it to a speaker. So there is a circularity in such power. The speaker elicits a willingness on the part of the hearers to credit the speaker with authority and, therefore, status. The speaker, sensing their assent, is buoyed and soars, evoking more consent

from the hearers. Like a bellows-filled balloon whose inflation depends on constant pumping, so the sage and his teaching depend for their authority on constant maintenance and mutual stroking.

Paul sees that the gospel's power depends on nothing but God's own power and not at all on the social and cultural conventions of power. Some of the claims of the gospel crash head-on into such status seeking, and Paul does everything within his rhetorical power to heighten the sense of dissonance and contrast.

What are "the things that are not" (1:28)? The assertion appears in the third "God chose" statement (1:27-28). "God chose the low-born [τὰ ἀγενῆ *ta agenē*; a pointed contrast with the "well-born" of 1:26] and the despised, even the things that are not, in order to make powerless/wipe out the things that are" (1:28). This is densely packed, allusive prose, designed to fit readily within Paul's strong two-way contrast, but now the perspective has shifted from two ways to two ages. In the strongest eschatological categories Paul here describes in a few words what he will refine and expand in 7:29 when he will write of the time being shortened, and in 7:31 when he will describe the schema of this world as passing away. Believers are in transitional times; with Christ's death and resurrection, the new age, the new creation, began. In 1 Cor 1:28 God is described as choosing "the things that are not," the very phrase used of God in Rom 4:17 where God was also depicted as the one who brings life out of death. This is Paul's way of talking about the creative and redemptive power of God that is at work among the Corinthians, bringing God's own future into being at the very same time that "the things that [already] are," like the schema of this world, are passing away, being wiped out, being made powerless. Paul is describing a transitional process as radical as taking what was up and making it down and vice versa. It is a process, a transposition of cosmic proportions, that is under way by God's power; the believers are not causing it, but they surely are its beneficiaries. The prose in this verse may be densely packed, but it is Pauline basics. It should give his auditors perspective because it is clearly rehearsing something that they are supposed to know as elementary.

Paul takes the cultural pulse on another matter in this passage: How does one come to know God (1:21)? Paul's statement, merely adumbrated here but developed further elsewhere, is that in God's wisdom it is not by wisdom that one comes to know God (1:21). In other letters we can observe that Paul prefers to write of God's knowing believers (Gal 4:6). Later in 1 Corinthians Paul will look forward to that eschatological time when he will know as he has already been known (by God, understood; 13:12). Paul's convictions about grace lead him to think that the impetus for relationship with God, whether expressed in terms of faith or knowledge or whatever, moves from God to individuals, not the other way around.

REFLECTIONS

1. Paul's setting of the wisdom of this world over against the wisdom of God risks misunderstanding of both. Across history people have sometimes used this passage to decry human aspirations for wisdom. In so doing, they have set faith over against wisdom, though it should be noted that Paul does not do so. Paul does not disparage wisdom per se. Rather, he casts it as wisdom versus wisdom. The wisdom of God is valued, and Paul does offer that wisdom in his preaching (2:6). At stake is the temptation for us to confuse redemption as coming from possessing the right wisdom, of mistaking salvation for thinking the proper way or having the right ideas. That is the wisdom of the world. Over against the wisdom of having the right ideas and associated status, Paul sets God's power, which has broken into sin's control of the world in the crucifixion of Christ, whom Paul calls "God's power and God's wisdom" (1:24); this power transforms and renews human beings and ultimately all of creation. The concern with wisdom is ultimately an emphasis on status. How do we weigh status in our time? Surely one way is through education, through what we know. Paul devalues the status that we might claim by our knowledge and expertise, but he does not oppose or discredit the use of our God-given minds and wisdom. What counts is not what one knows but by whom one is known.

2. Paul's note about not knowing God by means of wisdom (1:21) raises an important issue that has reverberated down through church history. There has always been the temptation to transform Christianity from a matter of proper relation to God (Paul's code word for that is "faith," meaning a proper trusting dependence on God to do what God has promised) to a question of holding the right ideas or opinions, to assenting to certain propositions. Some churches stress that the real test of belonging to them is on our affirmation of certain doctrinal claims (e.g., the inspiration of the Bible, the transubstantiation of the Communion elements, the virgin birth), in having the right ideas and beliefs. Paul is unfamiliar with such an interest.

3. At the heart of Paul's gospel is a *skandalon*, the cross. When we so frequently wear the cross as an art object, we may find it difficult to think of it as what it was: a scandalous method of capital punishment whose modern counterparts might be the electric chair or the gas chamber. At the center of worship sanctuaries stands the cross, the central symbol of the Christian faith, not a representation of money or a smiley face. We who hold on to the values of the world, whose structure is passing away, will surely stumble over the cross; we who hold on to the cross should be able to find reassurance when the world buffets and persecutes us. The cross as *skandalon* is a challenge to all rival values.

1 Corinthians 1:26-31, Paul's Application to the Auditors

COMMENTARY

In his first effort to make a direct application to his hearers, Paul picks up a link word from the previous section: "call" (κλῆσις *klēsis*). Paul identifies the Corinthian believers as being among those called—that is, as among those people who are being saved (1:2, 24)—and further affirms his bond with them by naming them "brothers and sisters" (v. 26). Here we learn more about the congregation and about Paul's convictions regarding God's present purposes. Some few among the Corinthian believers were "wise" (σοφός *sophos*), "powerful" (δυνατός *dynatos*), and "high born" (εὐγενής *eugenēs*); most were not (1:26).[55] This demography of the Corinthian church mirrors the steep social pyramid of the culture from which the community is called.[56] There was no middle class in the Greco-Roman world. At the top of the pyramid were a few rich persons who were, therefore, automatically persons of power and status. Erastus, apparently Corinth's town treasurer (Rom 16:23), and Gaius, a host of the house church at Corinth (Rom 16:23), were no doubt among such people. The majority of persons in that world, however, and in the church at Corinth as well, were poor and, therefore, lacked social status.

After openly recognizing the social disparity present among the Corinthian believers, Paul, in a finely crafted rhetorical structure, affirms the contrarian scheme of God's grace, introduced with a strong adversative: "nevertheless [ἀλλά *alla*] . . . God chose [ὁ θεός ἐξελέξατο *ho theos exelexato*] . . . God chose . . . God chose" (1:27-28). Similarly, the subjects of God's election are given the same emphasis by repetition of the threefold structure: God chose "the foolish things of the world . . . the weak things of the world . . . the lowborn of the world" (1:27-28) in order to "shame . . . shame . . . reduce to nothing"

(vv. 27-28) their counterparts. God's purposes run counter to the structures and values of the culture; God's actions in Christ have already overturned the worldly status quo.

In a somewhat convoluted but emphatic construction, Paul declares that God's contrarian election has as its ultimate purpose the elimination of boasting: "so that all flesh [πᾶσα σάρξ *pasa sarx*] [semitism = everyone] might not boast before God" (1:29). Like every part of creation (3:21-23; 8:6; 10:26), Paul's auditors are "from God"; they are now "in Christ Jesus" (1:30), who became—note the shift from direct address of the Corinthians to encompass all believers, Paul included—"our wisdom, our righteousness and sanctification and redemption" (v. 30).

Boasting, a problem of considerable proportions in this letter, here emerges for the first time. But the ground for boasting's emergence has already been recognized by Paul when he associates wisdom and power (1:24) and thereby tips his hand regarding his conviction that any concern for wisdom at Corinth was sub rosa and in fact a clutching for power and its inseparable partner, status.

Verses 29 and 31 show that Paul's major concern is to undercut any basis for believers' boasting of their status with God, of their standing in Christ. How can they brag when it is God who has chosen, chosen, chosen them (1:27-28)? When most of them had no worldly prestige? When their "wisdom . . . righteousness and holiness and redemption" are all from God, and when believers have this wisdom, righteousness, holiness, and redemption only because they are in Christ Jesus, whom God has made all these things? The Corinthians hanker after wisdom; Paul does offer true wisdom, namely, Christ (1:24). By his identification of Christ with wisdom, Paul tries to convert their wisdom interests into salvation talk. The source of salvation is not what one knows or the elevated status one can hope to achieve by "having wisdom" as a sort of possession. Paul sees the whole

---

55. Gerd Theissen, *The Social Setting of Pauline Christianity: Essays on Corinth*, ed. and trans. J. H. Schütz (Philadelphia: Fortress, 1982) 69-119.
56. Ramsay MacMullen, *Roman Social Relations 50 B.C. to A.D. 284* (New Haven: Yale University Press, 1974) 89-94.

matter almost completely the other way around. It is not what one possesses (e.g., wisdom) but who has redeemed you, who has become your Lord, that is the question. In that sense "Christ has become our wisdom," and in an effort to distinguish it from any worldly wisdom Paul refines the statement by calling forth a series of terms that are basic for Paul and that Paul more commonly used in preaching the gospel: righteousness, holiness, and redemption. Wisdom may have been a favorite of some Corinthians but Paul arrays alongside it, without apparent need for explanation, the other three: righteousness, holiness, and redemption. Righteousness (δικαιοσύνη *dikaiosynē*), whose root meaning also includes justification and justice *dikaiosynē*, is Paul's code word for the only right relation to God, namely the conferred standing that God freely bestows on those whom God has chosen (Rom 10:3; Phil 3:9). Holiness (ἁγιασμός *hagiasmos*), meaning being set apart for God, another way of talking about being claimed by God, or being called to be a saint, is a reprise of the assertion with which the letter opened (1:2). Redemption (ἀπολύτρωσις *apolytrōsis*) is a term Paul takes from the social world of slavery where slaves were "bought with a price" (cf. ahead, 6:20; 7:23) and, therefore, were claimed by a new lord (κύριος *kyrios*) (cf. 1:31).

Christians' claims, their boasts, are always only derivative. They can boast only because God has claimed them in Christ and in Christ has given them all things, a theme that Paul will announce later (cf. 3:21-23). So, as it is written, the only boasting allowed is boasting in the Lord (v. 31; cf. Jer 9:24, which Paul has creatively altered to make explicit connection with Christ already affirmed in v. 30; see also 1 Cor 15:31).

Two boastings appear in the text. One is unacceptable and improper; the other is appropriate and fitting. This is a typical Pauline move, seen across the corpus. For example, there is a proper and an improper walk (1 Cor 3:3; 2 Cor 10:2; Gal 5:16), a godly grief and a worldly grief (2 Cor 7:8-11), a hope grounded in faith and a hope as the world calculates things (Rom 4:18). In Jer 9:24, Paul sees confirmation that boasting in the Lord is proper (1 Cor 1:31; cf. 2 Cor 10:17 where he quotes the same Jeremiah passage again). Paul discredits self-commendation and lauds the Lord's commendation.[57] To brag about yourself is to lose track that it is God whose work has made you all that you can be. So the only boasting allowed is the one that is equivalent to expressing gratitude to God for what God has accomplished and is doing. To boast in the Lord is to credit the Lord as the source of life. Some Corinthians have lost their way on this issue and have begun to brag about themselves and their accomplishments.

As has been the case from the first appeal (1:10) forward, Paul has set the alternatives in the most hyperbolic fashion. In this passage he has done so as well. Here the alternatives are cast as "chosen" versus "wiped out" (or, as the term καταργέω [*katargeō*] may also mean, "to make powerless" or "to abolish," 1:28). Here the creator God's power to bring into being what does not exist is the same God's redemption of the lowly and the outcast and is the same God's bringing to denouement those who end up on the wrong side of this equation. The auditors would do well to make sure they know for certain which side they are on because the consequences of losing one's place are dire. Paul's rhetoric is designed to remind the Corinthians in whom God has done so much just where they stand and what is their destiny.

57. See Forbes's treatment of self-praise in antiquity: Christopher Forbes, "Comparison, Self Praise and Irony: Paul's Boasting and the Conventions of Hellenistic Rhetoric," *NTS* 32 (1986) 8-10.

REFLECTIONS

1. Boasting has gotten a bad reputation in Christian circles, no doubt because of persons like some of these Corinthians. The NIV corroborates that bad reputation by translating καυχάομαι (*kauchaomai*), when it is used positively, not as "boast" but as "rejoice" (Rom 5:2-3, 11) and as "glory" (Phil 3:3). Proper boasting can be a way of recognizing and celebrating what God has accomplished in one's life so far. Why should all boasting be eliminated just because some boasting can be done improperly?

We Christians have trouble, sometimes, when things go well for us because we get a haughty and independent picture of how we came into such good times. We confuse our blessedness with our own effort, we diminish or eliminate God's hand in it or through it, and we lose perspective. The result can be improper boasting. By contrast, proper boasting would credit God and God's beneficence as the source of everything good and wonderful. It is like the surgeon, who after amazingly successful surgery and upon hearing the patient's expressions of gratitude, declares that it is God who deserves the glory.

2. The descriptions of those whom God chose (1:27-28) have their parallels in the people the four Gospels delight in showing Jesus as having fellowship with: lepers, tax collectors, prostitutes—in short, outsiders. It is ironic that while Jesus welcomed such people and Paul's church at Corinth seems to have been predominantly populated by persons of low social and economic standing, modern churches too often are not even hospitable to such. Some churches even ponder the propriety of having a food kitchen in the church because of the people it might attract. It is safe to wonder how worshipers might respond if such an outcast actually darkened the church door. Perhaps that is why 1 Peter declares that God's judgment must begin with "the household of God" (1 Pet 4:17).

1 Corinthians 2:1-5, Perspective-Keeping via Paul's Exemplary Pattern from the Founding Days

COMMENTARY

Paul's retrospective narrative of the gospel's beginning in Corinth looks back over the three-year period since he left and selectively focuses on what he holds to be central and determinative; it also allows Paul to depict himself as having embodied the gospel to the Corinthians not only in his speech but also in his comportment. Paul's retrospective is not driven by a desire to ensure accuracy of the historical record; rather, his purpose is to be instructive, formative, and even constructive.[58] The gospel calls for proper comportment not only from the evangelist but also from the hearers. Paul's self-depiction features his exemplary and governing determination ("For I decided," 2:2) to be among them as one centered on "Christ Jesus and him crucified." Paul's inadequacies as judged by worldly standards—namely, his weakness, his fear and trembling (2:3), and his lack of flashy rhetorical style (2:4), proved a satisfactory, even fitting, medium for the transmission of the gospel of the cross and for the inauguration of the Corinthians' faith. Paul's limited

eloquence and his determination to focus on the cross assured that the Corinthians' faith would be unmistakably seen for what it is: the Spirit's working as God's power in them. Neither Pauline rhetorical legerdemain nor status conferrable or available by association with Paul accounted for their faith; rather, it was God's power that seized the Corinthians and made them God's people.

For Paul the critical question is what stands at the center of the picture and by which all other parts of the picture gain their meaning and keep their perspective. Paul's answer: He made the careful decision at the beginning of his time with the Corinthians that it would be Christ and the cross, not just at the beginning but throughout. And, by implication, so it should be for the Corinthians in the present. If the crucified Christ is at the center of the picture and all else takes its definition and proportion with reference to that, then a constitutive, formative decision has been made about how the community can distinguish between what is important and what is less important or even indifferent. His statement that "we have this treasure in earthen vessels, to show that the transcendent power belongs

---

58. George Lyons, *Pauline Autobiography: Toward a New Understanding*, SBLDS 73 (Atlanta: Scholars Press, 1985) 226-27.

to God and not to us" (2 Cor 4:7) can be read as a commentary on 1 Cor 2:1-5. Accordingly, boasting and concern with worldly status are out of order.

These verses contain Paul's narrative of community formation. As the apostle who brought the gospel, which he calls in an all-encompassing phrase "the mystery of God" (2:1),[59] to Corinth, Paul is free to recount the story as he sees fit and as serves his purposes in this letter, written some three years later. Note what he chooses to place at the center of the picture: "Christ Jesus and him crucified!" Neither his comportment nor his rhetoric drew attention to Paul; both, however, provided free rein to the Holy Spirit and God's power. It is no surprise, then, that Paul judges his work among the Corinthians as leaving no room for confusion; their faith is grounded on God's power, not on human wisdom or performance or status associated with sophisticated speech.

This passage exemplifies a Pauline tendency and, indeed, a standard rhetorical device known as refinement to use similar phrases to elaborate one another and to paint a rather general picture. While the similar phrases are not synonymous, neither are they technical terms and due to be distinguished by scholarly acumen. The "mystery of God" in 2:1 is identical with "my proclamation," which is the same as "my speech" in 2:4; at its heart is "Christ Jesus and him crucified" (2:2). In similar fashion, the "lofty words or wisdom" of 2:1 has a significant overlap with the "sophisticated, persuasive wisdom" of 2:4 and with the "human wisdom" of 2:5. Paul's refinement, both positively and negatively, makes sure that God's power made present through Christ's crucifixion, rather than Paul himself, stands at the center of the picture.

Paul's humility is exemplary. He who could have lorded it over the Corinthians, he who could have emphasized his role in bringing the gospel as a legitimization for his own status and authority over them, instead denigrates his own importance. He is what he is

describing. In this passage he portrays himself as having embodied the Christ-centered life in his inauguration of the gospel in Corinth. We must assume that his picture had enough verisimilitude to be recognizable to the auditors. His comportment and focus have not changed from the time he first entered Corinth to the time of his writing of 1 Corinthians. Paul presents himself as a radical contrast with those whose association with the gospel provides the ground for enhancement of personal status.

We should not be carried too far toward imagining Paul as an inadequate speaker (2:1). In 2 Cor 11:6 he acknowledges that, somewhat like Moses (Exod 4:10-11), he is unskilled in speaking, but contemporary rhetorical training urged orators to say precisely that about themselves. In that same letter fragment, however, he quotes some as saying that his letters may be powerful enough but "his bodily presence is weak and his speech disdainful" (2 Cor 10:10). While his speech may not have been eloquently delivered, the evidence across the corpus is that it was powerfully effective (cf. Gal 4:13-15; Phil 1:13-14; 1 Thess 2:13). And in the passage before us we have his understanding of why his speech, though not itself powerful, had power—God's power—nonetheless.

The passage is laced with irony. In ironic contrast, Paul reminds the auditors that the gospel focuses on Christ the crucified one, that the one who brought the gospel to them was identified not by the trappings of power and prestige but by frailty, fright, and trembling—and, at the end of these nouns, as if to emphasize his unprepossessing presence, he adds πολύς (*polys*, "much"), which in Greek can be understood to modify each of the preceding. Paul was then and is at the time of his writing the example of the one who, though he could have vaunted himself and called attention to himself, stood aside and pointed ever so clearly at Christ crucified. And the result the Corinthians know full well: The power of God, not human wisdom or cultured speech, produced faith among the Corinthians.

---

59. Other Greek manuscripts read "the testimony of God," which would refer to Paul's own formative preaching to them, his testimony about God to them at the origin of their coming to faith. See 2:7 and 4:1.

REFLECTIONS

1. "I determined to know nothing among you except Jesus Christ and him crucified" (2:2). Paul uses hyperbole, an exaggeration, as a means of focusing on what is central. By so doing, Paul establishes that what brings Christians together and holds them together is the crucified (and risen) Lord. As we observed in 1:26, the Corinthian congregation was socioeconomically diverse, assuring that different social practices and values were represented among them. What could hold such a diverse group together other than a focus on believers' common grounding in Christ expressed in the sharing of Christ's death as represented in baptism? So today Christians of different ethnic and regional backgrounds who differ culturally, politically, and socially, can find unity if they have as their common starting point "Jesus Christ and him crucified." That is no doubt easier to say than to do. Our attention is so readily caught by our differences rather than by what holds us together in its power. If we look for unity in anything other than the cross we will become something other than the church.

2. We must not miss Paul's self-portrait as the stumbling, not-very-gifted speaker. Laypersons today who are asked to share their faith or to talk about the gospel in whatever way, but who are reticent to speak because they feel insecure or inadequate, could take some solace from Paul's self-portrait here. The power of one's own witness, if it is to have any, is ultimately God's power, and God has been pleased to make that power effective through all sorts of cracked, damaged vessels (cf. 2 Cor 4:7). Pastors might also receive some guidance from Paul here if they made certain that their every homiletical effort brought the heart of the gospel into engagement with their hearers.

1 Corinthians 2:6-16, Two Wisdoms, Two Spirits, Two Representative People

COMMENTARY

Whereas 1:18–2:5 contrasted human weakness and human wisdom with God's power in the gospel, the present verses refine that contrast, although Paul now concedes that he does in fact speak a particular wisdom, a wisdom he describes as "not of this age [aeon]," a wisdom that is available to the "mature" and that he has already identified with Christ (1:24). Rhetorical refinement such as this dwells on the same subject but by casting the issue differently seems to be embarking on new territory and ensures the audience's continued attention. Earlier the two-way schema was (human) wisdom versus (God's) power; now it is (God's "secret and hidden") wisdom versus wisdom (of this age, of this age's rulers, and of unspiritual persons). Verses 6-16 are an elaboration, a descanting on the two-way contrast presented in vv. 1-5.

The present passage is framed on an extended opposition: There are two contending wisdoms, two opposed spirits, and, accordingly, two disparate human options, here represented by a single exemplar on each side. The passage pays especial attention to these exemplars, idealizing, on the one side, the "spiritual person" who is taught by the Holy Spirit (2:13), has access to the mysterious, otherwise hidden wisdom of God, and understands "what is truly God's" (2:11) as well as the "gifts bestowed on us by God" (2:12). We must recall that the word "Christian" had not yet been invented as an identifier in Paul's time (cf. Acts 11:26; 26:28, written some decades after Paul); "spiritual person" is probably Paul's own positive construction (cf. Gal 6:1) that properly identifies a believer with the working and inspiration of the Holy Spirit.[60] Over against this person,

---

60. See Richard Horsley, "Pneumatikos vs. Psychikos: Distinctions of Spiritual Status among the Corinthians," *HTR* 69 (1976) 269-88.

Paul sets the negative exemplar, the culturally valued sage, the worldly "wise person" who does not accept or receive (δέχομαι *dechomai*) "the things of the Spirit" (2:14).

We modern readers have one advantage over the Corinthians who first received this letter, who probably heard it read to them: We have the luxury of knowing what comes later in the letter and can read an earlier passage in the light of Paul's purpose as disclosed in a subsequent passage. Verse 6 opens with an invitation for Paul's hearers to include themselves among the mature, the spiritual people, who can receive Paul's not-of-this-age wisdom, and closes by giving them the opportunity to identify themselves with the spiritual person who understands (2:14-15). It even adds the extraordinary claim, "We have the mind of Christ" (2:16). Paul's notoriously ambiguous use of "we" sometimes refers to him alone but, as here, it sometimes leaves an opening for the hearer to identify with Paul. So this passage is framed by an invitation to the Corinthians to think of themselves as mature and also to think of themselves as having the "mind of Christ," which locution in Paul usually means that persons pattern themselves after Christ (cf. Phil 2:1-5).

Imagine the shock in 3:1, however, when Paul tells the Corinthians that he cannot address them as spiritual persons; instead, he must treat them as babies in Christ. An idealized picture of where the Corinthians should be in their maturity, not where they are, is painted in 2:6-16; 3:1-4 describes where they are. In 2:6-16 Paul, like the Cynic choir master before him, sets the pitch a bit high so that more of the singers will come in on note; 3:1-4 is a reality check of some dissonance, but more on that below.

The basic two-way alternative—"those who are perishing" versus "us who are being saved"—was introduced in 1:18. Verses 6-16 elaborate that alternative and once again invite the hearers' identification, on the positive side of the alternative, with "spiritual people." On the one side is the wisdom of this present age and its rulers, who are said, literally, to be passing away (2:6). Like the "unspiritual people" mentioned in 2:14, who "do not receive the gifts of God's Spirit," those rulers, surely the temporal ones (and possibly also the cosmic powers whose ultimate

destiny is expressed in 15:24), did not perceive the secret, hidden wisdom of God, so they "crucified the Lord of glory" (2:8).[61] In Paul's view there is a great, unbridgeable gulf between "those who are perishing" and the ones "who are being saved" (1:18), between the rulers of this age "who are blind to the Lord of glory," "who are passing away," and the Spirit-inspired persons, the "spiritual people," "who discern all things" (2:15).

The "secret and hidden" character of God's wisdom lies not just in its never having been disclosed before but also in its anticipated grandeur. Neither normal eyesight nor human imagination, as they are available to the rulers of this aeon and to unspiritual persons, can grasp "what God has prepared for those who love him" (2:9, a Pauline amalgamation of scriptural echoes; cf. Isa 52:15; 64:3 LXX). "What God has prepared" is both present already and yet not finished (cf. 1:7; 15:20-28). Without God's Spirit no one would have a clue as to the shape or grandeur of God's purpose (2:10; cf. Job 11:7). But "to those who are being saved" God has revealed the Holy Spirit as the means of fathoming "what God has prepared for those who love him" (2:9-11). Only the Spirit knows "the things of God" (2:13), and believers have received that Spirit, not the alternative, opposing spirit of the world (2:12). Believers know and can be expected to know, through the teaching of the Holy Spirit, "even the depths of God" (2:10). The Holy Spirit marks off the ones who are being saved; it enables them to recognize the Lord of glory, not to crucify him; and it helps them understand the "things bestowed . . . by God" (2:12). Only the Spirit-inspired believers, the truly mature, can understand the only true wisdom—namely, the one that Paul speaks (2:6). That is the point of the cryptic clause at the end of 2:13: Only spiritual persons understand spiritual things.

Assumed, but not argued in detail here, is Paul's deep conviction that all believers have received the Spirit (cf. Rom 8:14-17; Gal 3:1), and we have already had occasion to see Paul's reference to baptism (1:14-17), which later in this letter he associates with the reception of the Spirit (12:13). Paul's rich

---

61. Those who would import gnostic concerns into their interpretation of 1 Corinthians seize on 2:7-8, but nothing here or in the opening chapters suggests that Paul has in mind any such mythological construction.

pneumatology is only partially in view in 2:6-16—precisely because his purposes here do not call for anything more. Later in 1 Corinthians we will see Paul's understanding that the Spirit is the provider of charismata for the good of the community (chap. 12). Nowhere in 1 Corinthians, however, would one find Paul's conviction that the Spirit joins with human spirits at the inception of faith and enables people to become God's children (Rom 8:15-16; Gal 4:6); nowhere in this letter would one learn that the Spirit helps in prayer (Rom 8:26), that the Spirit is a down payment of all that God will eschatologically give believers (2 Cor 1:22; 5:5), or that the Spirit produces fruit in the everyday lives of believers (Gal 5:22).

The phrase "those who are unspiritual" (2:14 NRSV) rightly derives its primary definition, via negativa, from Paul's predominant interest in the other group: "those who are spiritual"—that is, those with the Spirit (= all true believers). The Greek term translated "those who are unspiritual" is ψυχικός (*psychikos*), pertaining to the natural, not the spiritual realm. In 15:46 Paul reemploys the same contrast. Throughout 2:6-16 Paul has been concerned to set up alternatives. The spiritual person, taught by the Spirit, understands spiritual things; the natural person, out of that loop, cannot accept "things of the Spirit," indeed takes them as foolishness, and cannot understand them because they are "spiritually discerned"—that is, they can be examined and known only with the assistance of the Spirit (2:14).

Paul has shown two fundamental assumptions about people and life in these verses. First, just as there are two ways, so also all humans can be divided into two groups: those with the Spirit and those without. Second, those with the Spirit can discern (the same Greek verb appears at the end of 2:14 and is repeated twice in 2:15 and has the range of meanings "discern," "examine," and "know") everything that the unspiritual persons can plus all that is disclosed by the Spirit, who, we must recall, fathoms even the depths of God (2:10). For that reason, Paul concludes (2:15) both that the truly spiritual person "examines, knows, discerns" all things and that the truly spiritual person can

claim, with Paul, that "we have the mind of Christ" (2:16).

Spiritual persons, Paul's epitome of the life of faith properly lived, are described in two complementary ways: They have received the Spirit of God (2:11), the Spirit that is from God (2:12), and they have the mind of Christ (2:16). In 1:10 Paul called upon the divisively inclined Corinthians to be united in the same mind but made no specification about which mind that might be; in 2:6-16 he now elaborates the mind both by reference to the Holy Spirit by which believers can know "even the things of God" (2:11) and by reference to Christ, with whom believers can be of one mind (2:16; cf. Phil 2:1-11). When believers are properly guided by the Spirit and have the mind of Christ, they know what is going on, they know what matters, and they are enabled to live in accord with God's purposes.

One more claim about the spiritual person merits closer examination. According to Paul, the spiritual person is subject to the discernment or examination of "no one" (2:15). What does Paul mean here? Does "no one" refer to no one who is from among the unspiritual people? That is the most logical consideration, given his careful, insistent division of humanity into two groups with respect to their access to the Holy Spirit. But one might also ask whether this portrait of the spiritual person who is beyond examination invites any already haughty Corinthians to consider themselves as spiritual persons who are, therefore, (a) able to examine and know all things, and (b) not subject to examination by others. If so, it would seem that Paul has wandered into their camp and bids fair, by rejecting accountability, to heighten the schismatic tendencies of some Corinthians. Such an interpretation would be consistent with Paul's invitation in 2:6 for the Corinthians to think of themselves as "the mature" because Paul readily admits he does impart wisdom to such persons. To see how Paul protects himself from this trap, we will need to study 3:1-4.

Paul's mention of wisdom and rulers "of this age" (τοῦ αἰῶνος τούτου *tou aiōnos toutou*) suggests (rightly) that he thinks of multiple ages. "This age" is always pejorative for Paul (cf. 1:20; 3:18; Rom 12:2); it is an "evil age" (Gal 1:4) dominated by sin, from whose strangling grip God has delivered those who have died with Christ. Those belonging to "this age" are, like the rulers mentioned in 2:8, blinded to what is really going on in God's purpose. In Christ, the new has come, the "new creation" has begun (2 Cor 5:17; Gal 6:15). Those endowed with the Spirit of God can fathom the things of God and so can see that the newness has indeed come in Christ.

So Paul's view is that those who have died with Christ and come to newness of life (Rom 6:4) live in two ages at once. The old age, championed and defined by sin and its power, has been dealt a death blow ("the schema of this world is passing away," 1 Cor 7:31) in Christ's death and resurrection, but the old age continues, holding sway as if it thought itself to have the last word. So believers, those in Christ, live in the old age, but their citizenship is in heaven (Phil 3:20). This evil age has its idolatrous power, its own allure, and its offer of status; it bids for believers' allegiance. Believers live in this evil age—there is no alternative until Christ's parousia and the end of the age—but they walk according to the Holy Spirit (Gal 5:25). This means that believers live in this age "as if not" living in this age; for believers there is a certain eschatological detachment from the age, its values, and its goals (for more on this, see the Commentary on 7:26-31).

As we can see in this passage, Paul sometimes develops his notion of the evil age by making negative claims about "the world" (πνεῦμα τοῦ κόσμου *pneuma tou kosmou*, 2:12). We need to keep clear that Paul writes about the "world" in two very different ways, depending on his purposes. On the one hand, as here, Paul writes (negatively) of a "spirit of this world" as a means of expressing his concern that the Corinthians have brought the values of their culture, their world, into the church. The world has a putative wisdom (1 Cor 1:20), which Paul equates with the world's folly (1:27). On the other hand, for Paul, the world is God's creation, "the earth is the Lord's and its fullness" (10:26; Ps 24:1), God is the world's judge (Rom 3:6, 19), and God's faithful will inherit it (Rom 4:13; cf. Matt 5:5). In Christ's death God was reclaiming the creation, reconciling the world to God's very self (Rom 11:15; 2 Cor 5:19).

In 2:6-16 Paul makes some assumptions about how one knows whatever one knows. Paul assumes that there are two levels of perception: one that is available to everyone and on which some things can be grasped clearly enough; and another whose important insights are available only as a special gift. His understanding is grounded in his apocalyptic viewpoint, which holds that what one can perceive by unassisted human perception is surely limited and possibly distorted. Witness Paul's treatment of what he calls "the rulers of this aeon": (ἄρχοντες τοῦ αἰῶνος τούτου *archontes tou aiōnos toutou*). They did not understand what was before their eyes, deprived as they were of the mysterious and hidden wisdom of God (2:6-8), so they "crucified the Lord of glory" (2:8). Apocalyptic literature always supposes that the true story of what is going on is revealed, uncovered to chosen recipients via a dream, a vision, or, as here, by the working of God's Spirit (2:10). So for Paul it is the Holy Spirit that has disclosed what otherwise would be unknowable—namely, what God is doing in Christ. The very revelation is itself grace, a freely given, unmerited gift from God without which gift believers would be as blind as this aeon's rulers who were clueless as to God's purposes (2:8).

REFLECTIONS

1. One of the great struggles across the history of the church has been how to value creation, the world, and humans' relation to it. In what sense is redemption a deliverance from the world? If one goes to an extreme one can say with docetics and gnostics that the world either was always corrupt and deficient or has become so corroded by sin and evil that salvation must be seen as an extrication of believers from the world and its morass. Paul's view is that the world has, indeed, been corrupted by human sinfulness (Rom 1:18-28) but that God's redemptive purpose in Christ is to restore all of creation to the glory it had before sin caused it to lose its former glory (Rom 8:17-25).

A further step down that same docetic (a form of christology that emphasizes Christ's divinity at the expense of his humanity) and gnostic line has been to claim that human bodies, as part of that creation, are also corrupt and irredeemable—with the inevitable claim that only the soul or spirit of a person is salvageable. But the mainstream of Christian tradition (and Paul himself!) has rejected such extreme claims about bodies (for more on Paul's understanding of body see 1 Cor 6:13; 15:35-41) and about the world as diminishing the richness of our affirmation about God as Creator and about redemption as re-creation.

If the world is not God's good creation, then our choices do not have to respect the world as our habitat. Then the world is ultimately to be escaped. Some discussion about heaven treats the world in that way. Accordingly, if the body and our fleshliness is considered alien to the inner spark or soul that is to be saved from it, then one could cite the antinomian cry, "Let us eat, drink, and be merry, for tomorrow we die." Those who hold with Paul, that the creation is God's and therefore good and that the body is good (cf. Rom 12:1), must make choices and decisions that honor their own bodies and the rest of creation.

2. This is the first of several places in 1 Corinthians in which Paul talks about judging, a very complex topic in this letter and no doubt inspired by a Corinthian readiness to judge one another in ways Paul found unacceptable. First, it must be said that Paul never assumes that believers "play God." It is God who judges (Rom 2:1-2; 14:12-13); it is only the Lord who can discern the secret and hidden purposes of the heart (1 Cor 4:5). A house servant either "stands or falls" (eschato-logical judgment terms in Paul's lexicon) before his or her own master (Rom 14:4). Others have no business meddling in what is divine prerogative, which, in Paul's view, will fully and finally take place at the return of the Lord (Rom 14:10; 2 Cor 5:10). Second, Paul marks off the borders of the community with vice lists (cf. Rom 1:29-32; 1 Cor 5:9-13; 6:9-11; 2 Cor 12:20-21; Gal 5:19-21; see the Commentary and Reflections at 1 Cor 5:9-13). Believers should steer a wide course away from the vices of these lists because such comportment is completely incompatible with membership in the body of Christ. The community has the responsibility to guard the God-given holiness of the congregation, to warn any who stray too near the borders as designated by the vice lists, and to censure anyone, like the man mentioned in 5:1-5, who has violated the sanctity of the borders. This type of judgment, which clearly from 5:5 is not final like divine judgment, but provisional and admonitory, is not only acceptable to Paul but necessary for the health of the community. An important part of community life for Paul is believers' upbuilding, encouragement, consolation, and warning of one another in the daily walk of faith (1 Cor 4:14; 14:3; 1 Thess 5:12, 14).

Modern Christians sometimes find Paul's sense of mutual responsibility trouble-some. In part, also, that is because modern Christianity, in distinction from its Pauline origins, has become so intensely personalized and individualized that someone could say: "The only thing that finally matters is my own personal relation to God." In part it is because community discipline has sometimes been used as a display of power and as a cudgel to enforce a rigid conformity that Paul would not have countenanced (cf. Rom 14:2-5). The dynamics and health of Christian community would probably best be served if Christians could put into practice the delicate balance that Paul tries to achieve between personal, individual differences and distinctions on the one hand and community needs and support on the other. It is no accident that in various letters Paul expresses his concern that when one person stumbles or goes astray all suffer; when one is honored all benefit (Rom 12:15; 1 Cor 12:26; 2 Cor 11:29). Abundant sociologi-cal studies have demonstrated that communities that have no concern with standards and border keeping cannot maintain their sense of being a community.[62] So the issue is how one maintains the standards of Christian community in a way that is wholly in tune with the love and justice that all believers must honor.

3. Paul's letters never use the term "Christian." What moderns would call a "Christian" Paul calls a "spiritual person," that is, one who has received the Holy Spirit. So Paul's primary definition of the believer is by means of the Spirit; likewise, the reception of the Spirit is for Paul the hallmark of entry into the community. Modern Christians ought to wonder from this why so many make so little over the Spirit and its working in the life of faith and in the community. Many modern Christians are Spirit-poor; Paul and his earliest followers were Spirit-rich. It is fair to suppose that the difference lies not in the Spirit's having disappeared but in modern believers' failure to note, appreciate, and cultivate the Spirit's workings. Churches would do well to focus some of their worship life and some of their classes on understanding how the Spirit works and in discerning the Spirit in their communal and individual lives. A good place to start would be Paul's multifaceted picture of the Holy Spirit and its multifarious workings in the life of faith (see 3:16-17).

62. Peter L. Berger and Thomas Luckmann, *The Social Construction of Reality* (Garden City, N.Y.: Doubleday, 1966) 79-82.

1 Corinthians 3:1-4, Not Spiritual People, Babies, Merely Human

COMMENTARY

After 2:6-16, in which Paul painted such a lofty picture of mature, spiritual persons, 3:1-4 had to have a jarring effect upon the Corinthian hearers. Far from being mature or spiritual, Paul calls them "babies in Christ" (νήπιοι ἐν Χριστῷ *nēpioi en Christō*), and, in an effort to stress how disconnected they are from the Spirit, he three times characterizes them as "of the flesh" (3:1, 3). The Pauline alternative to being "of the Spirit" is to be "of the flesh" (σάρκινος *sarkinos*). The spiritual persons, as he just described them in 2:6-16, are the ones who are made privy to the otherwise unfathomable "depths of God" precisely by the work of the Spirit. They are the ones who should know what is going on. Their counterparts, those "of the flesh," are—given Paul's relentless two-way characterizations throughout the letter so far—the "ones who are perishing" (*apollymenoi*, 1:18), the ones who are like the *archontes tou aiōnos* "rulers of this aeon" (2:6-8). They are, as he tells them in 3:3, people without a clue.

Not content to let it go, Paul presses further regarding their immaturity: They should have been ready for solid food but could handle only milk (3:2). What is Paul's evidence

of their immaturity? Their factionalism is emphasized twice over: "jealousy and quarreling" (ζῆλος καὶ ἔρις *zēlos kai eris*) (3:3, an echo of 1:10-11) and factionalism represented by Paul's oblique exemplification, "I belong to Paul," "I belong to Apollos" (3:4, a reprise of 1:12). Regrettably, nothing distinguishes the Corinthians from the persons Paul described as "unspiritual" or "natural" in 2:14: The Corinthians "behave" (περιπατέω *peripateō*) (lit., "walk") like them (3:3); the believers are divisive and contentious just like them (3:3); Corinthians forge partisan allegiances just as they do. Paul is left no other conclusion: "Are you not merely human?" (3:4), meaning, just like persons who have not been claimed by the Holy Spirit.

Later in this letter Paul will celebrate diversity and differences among the believers and credit the Holy Spirit with contributing to it and creating it. The difference is that there Paul affirms that the distinctions are inspired by the Spirit to work for and to enrich the common good (1 Cor 12:7). There the diversity enriches the communion that the community shares; each person brings distinctive gifts to enrich the common, shared life in the community. In the early chapters of 1 Corinthians, Paul sees differences in a very different light. The differences are not Spirit-inspired, and they surely do not enrich the common good. Neither do they enhance the common life. In fact, the divisiveness and factionalism Paul decries destroy community, heighten individualism, and lead to boasting regarding oneself or one's associates and a denigration of others.

Implicit in Paul's chiding identification of the divisive Corinthians as babies and persons who take their cues from the flesh is the unstated counterpart—namely, that Paul has identified the truly spiritual persons as the ones he would also call mature or adult. Other letters allow us to see that Paul does, indeed, think of believers as moving from their starting point as babies in Christ toward greater and greater maturity. The life of faith is a life of growth, of maturing, of growing up. Philemon's slave Onesimus, with his conversion to the faith, has become Paul's child in the faith (Phlm 10). Paul's picture of the entry into the faith is one of a child being able to call God "Daddy" (Rom 8:15; Gal 4:6). From the babylike inception of the faith Paul expects believers to grow toward maturity. The term he uses to express that maturity is τέλειος (*teleios*; Phil 3:15), which can be translated as "perfect," "complete," "mature," "adult," or "fully developed." One who is *teleios* has reached the end or goal (*teleios*) that is appropriate. Paul even understands his own life of faith as exhibiting that same kind of growth toward full adulthood, as he tells the Philippians; though he knows he has not yet reached that goal, has not yet been perfected or become fully mature (τετελείωμαι *teteleiōmai*, Phil 3:12), he nevertheless presses on toward it.

The best that Paul can say about the Corinthians is that their understanding and comportment show that they are merely babies in

the faith. Those who think of themselves as spiritual persons but who contribute to divisions in the community are immature and have an incorrect self-assessment.

Paul escalates the rhetoric: Perhaps they are not even babies in the faith (3:3). When they are schismatic, for whatever reason, the Corinthian believers are as far as possible from maturity and an understanding of what the Spirit produces. Not subtly, Paul tells the Corinthians that they have seriously overestimated themselves and their maturity of faith. Although they are still his "brothers and sisters" (3:1), they are clearly his younger, dependent siblings. The image has yet to surface explicitly in this letter, but Paul in fact considers himself their father in the faith (4:14-15). His relationship to the Corinthian believers is paradoxical. As the one who brought the gospel to the Corinthians and thereby brought them into the family of God, he is *patēr*, father, the one who is ultimately responsible for all the children. On the other hand, for those who are in Christ, for those who have died with Christ, there is no distinction whatsoever (cf. Gal 3:28) because all are equally dependent upon God's grace and, accordingly, they are his brothers and sisters. Both features are true for Paul; like a father, Paul provides his children, who are also his "brothers and sisters" in Christ, some back-to-basics instruction, using himself and Apollos as models.

Throughout the opening two chapters of this letter there have been hints that Paul and at least some of the Corinthians have differing estimates of the maturity of the Corinthian believers. With 3:1-4 the discrepancy in evaluations emerges explicitly. They will not have thought of themselves as marginal babies in the faith, though that is what Paul calls them straight-out. And this will not be the last time that Paul reflects on how much his assessment of them differs from their own.

REFLECTIONS

Paul knows that the Corinthian believers are immature because they bicker and are divisive; in fact, they are acting just like ordinary people, not believers. The Corinthians are the mother church of all subsequent squabbling churches. One of the great shames of the church is that the family of God has so many offspring who will not talk and commune with each other. Christians should find ways to honor the divinely inspired differences that we all bring to the common table without charging one another with being wrong. Different is not necessarily wrong. In the midst of our genuine differences of gifts and graces we should welcome one another in love (Rom 14:1; 15:7).

1 Corinthians 3:5-9, Apollos and Paul: Models

COMMENTARY

Apollos was merely mentioned in 1:12 and in 3:4. Now he receives more attention. All in all, we know relatively little about him. According to Acts, Apollos, an Alexandrian Jew tutored in the faith by Priscilla and Aquila, worked with the Corinthians: "He greatly helped those who through grace had become believers" (Acts 18:27). In this detail the Acts portrait concurs with Paul's claim: Apollos watered what Paul had planted (3:6). Paul differentiates his and Apollos's roles in such a way as to recognize and honor their differences, but what Paul and Apollos did is not so important as (a) that it was God working through their various efforts, and (b) that there was growth. Paul describes himself and Apollos as servants (διάκονοι *diakonoi*, 3:5), fellow workers (3:9) (συνεργοί *synergoi*), who contributed their own labors—one planted, the other watered (3:6)—"as the Lord assigned to each" (3:5). Paul's conviction that God or the Lord makes assignments to each as God or the Lord desires will be repeatedly reaffirmed later in the letter (7:17; 12:11, 18, 24*b*). The force of Paul's argumentation is lost in the NRSV and the NIV renderings of 3:8. More representative of the Greek would be the following: "The planter and the waterer are one; each will receive his own wages according to his own work." Paul and Apollos are presented as united, as one (ἕν

εἰσιν *hen eisin*), though distinct exemplars for the Corinthian believers. The divinely assigned, different functions have the same source (the Lord) and the same end (growth); the individuals retain their differences but are "one," and, Paul extends the metaphor, each will receive a wage based on his own work (cf. Rom 2:6; 2 Cor 5:10). As the letter unfolds, it becomes clear that Paul thinks the Corinthians should be able to see themselves in this mirrored portrait. Implicit in the metaphor is that the Corinthians are "God's field" (3:9); they are the ones who have been the beneficiaries of Paul's planting, Apollos's watering, and God's giving of growth.

It is not surprising that Paul's chief metaphor in this passage is growth because 3:1-4 was founded on the premise that the Corinthians should have grown up more, that they should not still be babies. That passage was structured on the analogy of the family; vv. 5-6 share the presupposition of growth but move the analogy to agriculture, stressing planting and watering.

The passage closes with a refinement. The agrarian imagery gives way to architectural: "You are God's field, God's building." The building metaphor plays a prominent role in the rest of the letter, beginning in the next passage.

REFLECTIONS

1. Paul uses evocative images for the church. Many of them may remind us of Jesus' parables where, for example, fields and buildings also appear. Most of Paul's metaphors feature growth, not so much of numbers as of maturing. A church is always a work-in-progress (the same point of babies who should be growing to maturity; cf. 3:1-2). They can never become satisfied with themselves, but must always be working to improve how well they reflect God's love to the world and among themselves. If we take seriously that we the church are the site where God has chosen to dwell (as Paul will develop that idea in 3:16-17; cf. Gal 2:20), then we will have to live in a way that honors God as host and guest.

Paul's images are rich with implications for the life of faith. The nurture and care of any member of God's family or any planting in God's field requires the attention and tutelage of many others. Believers' lives are always intertwined and interdependent. Accordingly, we should give more attention to the nurturing and supporting roles each person can and should play. Every believer should be both the recipient and donor of nurture and encouragement. If you do not experience both, then you should see what can be done to change the situation. One good starting point could be to make sure that you are supportive and encouraging to others. Another could be a determination to recognize and honor the points at which God's grace is working in your life.

2. Paul uses the Greek term *diakonos* ("servant"; the English word "deacon" comes from this term) to describe himself and Apollos. Clearly, Paul claims no special status or honor by this self-description; rather, he seems to use it as a term to describe someone whose work is a channel for God's working. When you are a conduit for God's work, when service to others is done by you, then you are a *diakonos* whether the church officially designates you as such or not. To be a deacon is not an option but an expectation of the gospel.

1 Corinthians 3:10-15, The Foundation and Each Person's Work

COMMENTARY

Paul planted (3:6). Shifting to the architectural metaphor, he laid the foundation (3:10) upon which others would construct. Paul the father responsible for his children (3:1-4), then Paul the planter who works the field (3:5-9), and now, with the introduction of the architectural image of building, Paul becomes the one who laid the foundation (3:10-15) upon which others must build.

Paul takes the common knowledge that the building can be no better than the foundation, that the building's future rests on the foundation's being properly laid, and declares that, like a builder who knew just how to do it properly and solidly, Paul laid the right foundation, namely, Jesus Christ. This foundation rumination is a refinement of Paul's earlier declaration that when he first came to Corinth he decided to know nothing among them "except Christ and him crucified" (2:2). In the previous image Paul pictured himself as constantly and consistently focused on Christ. Now making the same point but with a building image, Paul starts with the only proper foundation—namely, Christ. But that allows him to develop the notion further:

Others must build on the certified foundation; others' work must be tested; and those whose work stands the test will be rewarded.

Paul, likening himself to a "wise" (σοφός *sophos*, embracing the term for himself; NRSV, "skilled"; NIV, "expert") master builder, laid that foundation by his preaching. Earlier Paul wrote that not many of the Corinthians are wise (1:26), and he will return to that topic in 3:18-20. Will any Corinthians for whom wisdom has become a totem of status fail to notice that Paul here identifies himself as wise? Paul not only imparts wisdom (2:6), he is wise (3:10).

But wisdom is an incidental matter here. One's life, what one builds, one's work, must be appropriate to Jesus Christ, the normative foundation. That is the issue here. As with the exemplification of Paul and Apollos as God's farmworkers, so Paul's depictions of the other builders are informative descriptions of what is expected of all the Corinthians. What is built, how it is built—"Let each watch out how he or she builds" (3:9)— become metaphors for the life of faith. What in 3:1-9 was a matter of growth, whether of babies or of plants, now in 3:10-15 becomes a matter of what one constructs, of what one builds upon the foundation. Paul is convinced that all believers must build (or grow), and all will face a judgment day, "the Day" (3:13; cf. Rom 2:16; Phil 1:6; 1 Thess 5:2), in which their works (or their growth) will be tested. Verses 13-15 refer to this day, characterized in accord with the building image, as a fire, a classical eschatological image of testing (Deut 32:22; Amos 7:4; Mal 3:2). What one builds upon the foundation—"the work of each builder" (3:14), "what sort of work each has done" (3:13)—will be tested by this judgment fire. The passage plays upon the ambivalence of fire, which may destroy or may refine and purify.

Strikingly, this passage focuses on individual responsibility to build upon Jesus Christ as foundation. The possible building materials, carefully arranged in descending value from gold down to straw (3:12), are comprehensively listed because Paul's concern is not so much with which material from among this inclusive list is used but with the structure one builds. Presumably, one uses whatever materials are at hand; the list seems to suggest that any material will do. Everyone has building materials available to them. The focus is on the structure that one builds with whatever is available. "The work of each person" (3:13a, d, 14a, 15a), what one builds, not one's chosen material, is what will be tested by judgment's fire.

The reward or "wage" will be given to the one whose own work "survives" the discerning test of the judgment day's fire (3:14); if someone's work is consumed by the fire, that person suffers loss, though Paul expects that this worker may ultimately be saved "but only as through fire" (3:15). The same notion expressed here in terms of a testing with fire will be expressed later in the letter through a military image of an individual's "standing" or "falling" (10:12).

The being saved "as through fire" (ὡς διὰ πυρός *hōs dia pyros*) (3:15) is Paul's allusive reference not to fire's power to destroy—which has been the focus of most of his attention in this passage—but to fire's capacity to refine. The rich biblical imagery of fire has two nuances, and so does Paul here. Fire consumes and destroys (cf. Deut 32:22; Job 28:5; Ezek 38:22; Amos 7:4), but it also may refine and purify (cf. Ps 66:12; Isa 43:2; Zech 13:9). Paul's abiding conviction that God is known for grace, for giving new chances for redemption, leads Paul to hold out the hope that salvation may ultimately come even to the one whose work is burned up (note the similar point in 5:5; cf. Rom 5:20b). The notion of divine purification by a judgment fire is rooted in Israel's traditions (cf. Isa 1:25-28; 4:3-4). Another biblical image in Paul's scriptures may also be formative here: Israel was "like a brand snatched from the fire" (Amos 4:11; cf. Joshua, who is so described in Zech 3:2).

REFLECTIONS

1. "The day," mentioned already in 1:7-8 and again in 5:5, is the time when Christ returns, when God's purposes are brought to culmination. It is a time of judgment that is mentioned across the Pauline corpus (Rom 2:5, 16; 13:12; 2 Cor 1:14; Phil 1:6, 10; 2:16; 1 Thess 5:2, 4). Paul expects that all people will be judged regarding their works at that time. The life of faith is a trust that is placed in the care of the believers, and their stewardship of this grace will face the scrutiny of divine judgment at the end time (not unlike Jesus' parables of the pounds, Luke 19:11-27, and the talents, Matt 25:14-30).

What will be weighed on judgment day is the work "of each one" (3:13). This is consistent with what Paul says in Rom 2:6 and with his later statement to these same Corinthians: "It is necessary for all of us to appear before the judgment seat of Christ so that each may receive according to what he has done in the body, whether good or bad" (2 Cor 5:10). What one does, how one builds on the foundation of Christ, how one lives up to one's calling, these are the matters on which the judgment will focus. Significantly, one's faith will not be judged; why should God judge what is, after all, a gift from God, a working of the Spirit (1 Cor 12:9)? Paul's primary subject matter in all his letters is understandably the proper comportment of the life of faith because the last judgment will focus on how one has lived the life God has given, on how one has walked in God's grace.

2. Each person is expected to build on the foundation that is Jesus Christ. Note that Paul does not single out any one special pre-approved building material that one has to search for like the holy grail. There is, therefore, no possible excuse for not building or not building much because of a lack of building materials. Paul's image seems to assume that one takes whatever is at hand and uses it to build. Our life of faith, therefore, is not a quest for the "right" material with which to build; instead, the life of faith involves each of us building with the material available to us. Paul's image in 3:11-13 is architectural, but later in this same letter he will make a similar point when he writes about each individual's obligation to place the Spirit-provided gifts (*charismata*), the analogue to available building materials, in service of the common good (12:7). So our building and our using the Spirit's gifts are alternative ways of talking about our responsibility to put what we have and what we are into service of God at all times.

3. Reward is promised here. Paul takes the normal practice of workers being paid for a job well done and projects that the same will be true at the last judgment. After Luther's proper insistence that faith alone and not works is what counts in one's standing before God, Christians have been reticent to talk of works, rewards, and payments. Surely Luther was right that gaining or earning the rewards cannot be the motivation for seeking and doing the good, for working. Gratitude, thankfulness, the glorification of God must remain the prime impulse for all that we do. But we, like Paul before us, should recognize that rewards and wages can function as an encouragment for us and others to stay on track. Paul unabashedly expects that reward, that payoff for himself (9:23).

We must be clear, however, that Paul nowhere even hints that works can make one right with God. On the contrary, only the one who is right with God can (even must), by the assistance of God's own grace, do works that will be viewed favorably at the last day. So, it is always God's grace, that free, unmerited gift, which is at the heart of the life of faith and inspires all that one ever does, which motivates whatever building one constructs on the foundation that is Christ. The circularity of Paul's reasoning needs to be clearly understood. Grace leads to and prompts works, which in turn are recognized by God with favor. The process must spring forth from God's empowering grace—otherwise, Paul's gospel is irrecoverably distorted. Paul can exhort the Philippians to "work out your salvation with fear and trembling" only because, as the rest of the sentence makes abundantly clear, "it is God who works in you to will and to act according to his good purpose" (Phil 2:13 NIV). So rewards talk is important and proper, but is easily distorted or misunderstood.

1 Corinthians 3:16-17, You Are God's Temple

COMMENTARY

Paul refines the notion of the Corinthians' being "God's building" (θεοῦ οἰκοδομή *theou oikodomē*) (3:9). In 3:16-17 he reminds them ("Don't you know?") that they are a very special building, namely, God's temple in which God's Spirit dwells. The idea of God dwelling among the people taps Ezekiel's everlasting covenant of peace in which the Lord God pledges to put the divine sanctuary "among them forevermore" (Ezek 37:26): "My dwelling place will be with them; and I will be their God and they shall be my people"

(37:27). Passage 3:10-15 stressed an individuated message: Each builder's work will be judged on the Day, and rewards will be passed out where appropriate. In his description of them as temple (3:16-17), however, Paul shifts decidedly to plurals: Together, the Corinthian believers are God's special building; they have become the dwelling place of God's Spirit. But there is a warning and a declaration. The warning: If anyone ruins, corrupts, defiles, destroys (φθείρω *phtheirō*) God's temple, then God will ruin or destroy (same verb) that person (3:17). That is the same point Paul pressed just before: The works of each individual will be judged on the last day. Paul closes the passage with his declaration, the reason that proper temple stewardship is so important: God's temple, which they are, is holy, and that temple is not to be defiled.

"Defiling the temple" deserves a further comment. As noted, the verb (*phtheirō*) has a wide semantic range, from corrupting to ruining to destroying. In 3:17*a*, at Paul's introduction of the notion that the Corinthians are God's temple, no effort is made to clarify just what action or thought Paul thinks would either corrupt or destroy God's temple. He offers no example. When the same verb is repeated in 3:17*b* about God's response to human defilement of God's temple, the mind is left to range toward speculation that Paul may anticipate that God will "destroy" such a defiler. Ancient rhetorical handbooks delighted in recommending that the same term be used, occasionally slanted one way first and another way second.[63] Paul does not

63. *Ad Herennium* 4.14.21

have in mind the believers' destroying God's temple; he seems to be much more concerned with their defiling or spoiling the temple. But he seems equally ready to threaten that God will not simply corrupt the one who defiles, but destroy such a one. Any puzzlement that may occur to the reader at this point, however, will evaporate when Paul brings the topic back up under another ruse (yeast and Passover in 5:6-8), when he talks about a particular person, namely the man who "has his father's wife" (5:1), whom Paul views as contaminating the community, which in 3:17 is unambiguously identified as God's temple.

The notion of the Corinthians' sacredness to God, of their being set apart for God, holy to God, has surfaced occasionally in these opening chapters (cf. "saints" in 1:2; "sanctification" in 1:30), is briefly reaffirmed in 3:17, and will become a major focus in chaps. 5 and 6.

The building metaphor has allowed Paul to make several related observations: (1) The Corinthians belong to God (belonging to anyone else, Paul and Apollos included, pales in importance and can in fact be idolatrous). (2) Each believer is expected to be a builder, to produce works. (3) The only foundation upon which any believer can build is that of Jesus Christ. (4) The works of individuals—that is, how they build upon Christ—will be assessed on judgment day with rewards passed out where appropriate. (5) The potential for destruction remains for each individual. (6) The Corinthians are not just any building; rather, they are a temple, a holy place where the Holy One resides, so they must be appropriately holy. And (7) God's Holy Spirit resides in them.

REFLECTIONS

The building image, first introduced in 3:5-9, is here refined so that the readers now are invited to think of themselves as God's dwelling place, indeed, as God's temple. Gentiles and Jews at that time were familiar with the care given to protecting the holiness of temple sites as a fundamental reverence for the deity in charge; remember that ancient Corinth was peppered with temples (see the Introduction). Paul's scriptures contain the pithy claim "You shall be holy, for I the Lord your God am holy" (Lev 19:2 NRSV). In 3:16-17 Paul affirms the same connection because the one dwelling in you is holy, you, that temple, must be holy. If "you are God's temple," then proper temple honoring must require that your self (Paul's word for it would be "body") must be treated with honor. What activities of yours could be counted as dishonoring or defiling yourself, your body, as the temple of God's Holy Spirit?

The modern temptation is to read both of the "you" statements in 3:16 and the last one in 3:17 as if they were in the singular, but in fact Paul has them in the plural. Are the people of God only God's temple when they are in community, as their lives are bound up to others' in the body of Christ? A strong affirmative argument could be made. Or should Paul be understood to speak distributively so that each person can understand that he or she is God's temple? Surely, such an individualization cannot be totally ruled out. In fact, because Paul never anywhere in any of his letters imagines the life of faith as lived in isolation, it is likely that we ought to preserve both sides of the issue, but never the individual realization without that of the community.

If, indeed, "you are God's temple," then your self (Paul's word for it would be "body") must be treated with honor. Some may respond to that assertion by protesting that it is their individual right to treat their bodies as they please. Those people will need to look carefully at 6:19-20 where Paul will elaborate this point and explore further the moral consequences for one's body.

1 Corinthians 3:18-23, Self-Awareness and Proper Perspective

COMMENTARY

Paul expects believers to be self-reflective. Self-deception can be avoided if one's self-estimation is properly based; as we have seen, Paul has structured these opening chapters to suggest that at least some of the Corinthians do not have an accurate self-assessment. The competing wisdoms already explicated in 2:6-7 reemerge here: The path to true wisdom may look like folly (3:18); this world's wisdom is folly with God (3:19). In Paul's view, believers are responsible moral agents; the Corinthians should have been able to keep better perspective on matters and on themselves than some of them have shown themselves able to do. Worldly wisdom and its associated status are a snare; God sees through the presumption, and so should believers; scripture warns believers that the worldly wise are readily deceived and their thoughts are futile (3:19; Job 5:12; 3:20; Ps 94:11). Believers can avoid the snare of false wisdom by maturely aiming for and attaching themselves to the secret and hidden wisdom that Paul imparts to the mature.

Further, believers can keep proper perspective only when they distinguish between what matters and what does not (3:21-23). Paul once again (cf. 1:29) warns against boasting of status gained by association with particular persons (3:21a). Then (3:21b-23), with a clever takeoff from a widespread Cynic formulation, Paul points the Corinthians toward a fuller perspective in the light of the gospel. Cynics have a form of syllogistic argument that runs thus: The wise are friends of the gods, and friends share what they have. The gods own all things; therefore, the wise have full access to all things.[64] Paul runs it the other way around: "All things are yours . . . [quite a list occurs] . . . all belong to you, and you belong to Christ, and Christ belongs to God" (3:21-23). Belonging to Christ and therefore to God means that all things belong to you; therefore, boasting in human associations is out of order, showing as it does a lack of proper understanding and perspective. By extending beyond Paul and Apollos to Cephas, Paul says, in effect, "anyone." In the most sweeping fashion, Paul sketches out the implications of belonging to God in Christ and therefore possessing all things. So to belong and so to possess neutralizes, in a paradoxical way, the importance of all things including (and here Paul draws upon his pattern of listing indifferent matters) the world, life, death, things present, things to come

64. Diogenes Laertius 6.37, 6.72.

(cf. Rom 8:38-39; 14:7-8; Gal 2:20; see also 1 Cor 4:7; 7:29-31).[65] Boasting (3:21) in anything or anyone other than God or the gospel misunderstands and misrepresents where power truly resides. Only God can establish a person's worth. Belonging to God is foundational; that is what matters. All other associations, all other belongings are at best indifferent matters and at worst idolatrous (see 4:7).

Twice in this passage Paul cites scripture as a way of seeing clearly what is important.

65. Sampley, *Walking Between the Times*, 77-82.

Both of the quotations come from the wisdom traditions of Israel (Job 5:13, quoted in 1 Cor 3:19; and Ps 94:11, cited in 3:20) and are employed by Paul as a part of the (true) wisdom that believers ought to know and honor. Paul's association of the two quotations shows that he finds them much to the same point: that God knows what is going on and cuts through human pretensions and posturings. When one knows that about God one knows not to boast on human grounds (3:21). This is not the last piece on "perspective-keeping" in 1 Corinthians.

REFLECTIONS

Paul's first explicit warning of self-deception appears in 1 Cor 3:18 (cf. 6:9; 15:33). Paul's problem with the Corinthians is their overestimation of themselves. Modern believers can experience self-deception in one of two directions, either in an overestimation or in an underestimation of themselves. To aim for too little, to love less than one would be able, would be improper stewardship of one's gifts and graces. Equally problematic, however, is an overestimation, where one thinks oneself capable of more than one's faith and love will allow. Such persons could lose themselves in their efforts to be helpful to others, to "bear one another's burdens" (Gal 6:2), because they did not properly realize their limits. They thus overreach and run the risk not only of causing somebody else harm but also of overextending themselves. Proper self-assessment or perspective-keeping will be treated by Paul at other places later in the letter (see esp. 11:17-34).

1 Corinthians 4:1-5, The Apostles, But Especially Paul, As Exemplary Once More

COMMENTARY

Even apostles who could, with some worldly legitimacy, claim greatness are properly considered "servants/helpers of Christ" and "stewards of God's mysteries" (4:1; cf. 3:5). Chapters 1–4 are an exercise in proportionality, in keeping or regaining proper perspective, and specifically in not overestimating one's importance or standing. Paul shows the way by illustrating that apostles also must keep perspective: They are really only administrators or assistants at best. What may one reasonably ask of such stewards? That they be found trustworthily accountable [to their Lord, understood] (4:2). Once again (4:4c; cf. 3:10-15), the day of judgment puts daily life

and its judgments in perspective. For Paul the only judgment that counts (again, what really matters, cf. 3:21-23) is the Lord's (4:4-5). When it comes to human judgment, whether by fellow Corinthian believers or by some secular court, Paul is like the truly spiritual persons he described in 2:15 who "discern all things, and they are themselves subject to no one else's scrutiny." The Lord will judge. The Lord can judge because only the Lord can penetrate the secrets and know the "purposes of the heart" (4:5). That judgment is appropriately reserved for the time when the Lord comes. Besides, the only commendation or praise that matters is that which, like the wages already mentioned in 3:8, 14, God will give when one's heart (4:5) and work (3:8, 14) are tested and found true.

In 4:1-5 Paul's purposes in chaps. 1–4 emerge for all to see. He has set himself and Apollos forward as exemplars, as models who recognize that (a) they must be trustworthy, and (b) they are accountable to God or to the Lord. Instead of boasting and seeking status from their brothers and sisters in the faith, the Corinthian believers should recognize that the Lord will do the judging and then one's commendation (ἔπαινος *epainos*, "praise," "approval," "recognition"; see the same point made about wages in 3:8, 14) will come from the only source that counts—namely, God.

Once again (cf. 3:10-15), Paul's attention is turned to his individual listener, and he asks, in effect, what reward or gratification one should rightly expect from others and what one can only expect from God. Improper boasting entails the seeking of someone's approval when the only recognition that counts comes from God. Paul's eschatological frame of reference here assures his auditors that they will get recognition, if they deserve it, at the last time, when the Lord comes (3:8; cf. "the Day" in 3:13). In the meantime, believers' energy and attention should be placed on their being regularly and consistently trustworthy servants or assistants as Paul and Apollos have been.

Paul's extraordinary confidence, such that he knows of no charge that can be leveled against him (4:4), positions him as the one not only to serve as model but also, like a father (4:14), to chide the Corinthians as babies whose growth in faith and practice is retarded (3:1-2). This confidence suggests that Paul feels himself blessed as one who has carefully scrutinized his own actions and found "no reason to judge himself" (Rom 14:22 RSV).

Trustworthiness or faithfulness (πιστός *pistos*, "faithfulness," 4:2) is the bottom-line test of a steward or assistant in that time. Significantly in Paul the claim of trustworthiness is made most often about God (same term, 1 Cor 1:9; 10:13; 2 Cor 1:18; 1 Thess 5:24). God can be counted on. That is bedrock. Abraham is depicted as rightly trusting God to do what God has promised (Rom 4:20). Human faithfulness, apostolic faithfulness is derivative and reflective of God's trustworthiness. It should be no surprise that Paul's basic code word for the right relationship one has with God is πίστις (*pistis*, "faith," from the same root as *pistos*). Paul is clear that God is the ultimate judge of one's trustworthiness as a steward. Boasting about one's stewardship is not worth the breath that carries it, and God will not be misled by public relations self-promotions. As we will see when we get to 7:25, Paul does think that faithfulness, trustworthiness can be demonstrated by consistent performance over a period of time, and he thinks he has thus established his trustworthiness with the Corinthians.

REFLECTIONS

1. "I am not aware of anything against myself" (4:4; cf. Job 27:6). Modern believers may read Paul's claim with utter astonishment because who among us can affirm such a clear conscience? Paul has been accurately described as having a "robust conscience."[66] For people in post-Freudian times in which we sense the convolutions of the mind and heart, not to mention a proclivity or profound capacity to self-deceive, it is difficult for us to imagine being able to utter such a claim as Paul does. One may come to terms with this disparity by elevating Paul to some special level of saintly performance, beyond the reach of most mortals—though that certainly would not be Paul's belief about himself and others. Another way may be to realize that modern persons, in part due to advancing studies of the human psyche, have a much more complex picture of the dynamics of willing and intending and interpersonal relationships than Paul had.

66. Krister Stendahl, *Paul Among Jews and Gentiles* (Philadelphia: Fortress, 1976) 80.

2. The central and organizing motif in the culture of Paul's time was praise and blame, another way of describing honor and shame.[67] In the Greco-Roman world, the primary goal around which life was structured and with respect to which one made decisions was the attainment of praise or honor, and its corollary, the avoidance of blame or shame. (See the Introduction for fuller discussion.) Although one may argue that similar motivations of honor and shame were basic in the early part of the twentieth century and, indeed, still function with great power in much of the world, today one can note the decline of such values in the United States and in Europe. Contemporary applications of Paul's gospel must be conscious of the way in which cultural values are shifting or have shifted from those that governed Paul's times. For modern Christians in much of the world, is not acquisition (and in its most exaggerated form, greed) the dominant cultural motif? The point at issue is, Where do persons such as ministers or a group such as a congregation gain leverage as they seek to engage and persuade one another and others? In Paul's time the answer would have been clear: Speak to them about how one gains honor and avoids shame or blame. That is exactly what Paul does across his letters. But if that leverage is lost or at best decreased, and another central totem, namely acquisition or greed, stands at the defining center of our culture, how does the gospel engage persons who are attuned to that totem? One answer could be to struggle to rehabilitate praise and blame. Another could be to begin the creative process of imagining how one can translate Paul's gospel from its earlier praise/blame, honor/shame context into one where acquisition is the governing motif. At its best it will surely be a subversive engagement! And perhaps Paul has already provided a starting point for such reflections in his twice-stated "All things are yours!" (3:21, 22) and in his questions in 4:7. If "All things are yours" means "All the things that matter/are important are yours" as 4:7 suggests, then one does not need to strive for that which God freely gives. Knowing that "all things are yours" should liberate one's energies to be more fully employed in serving others in love.

67. For the significance of honor in Paul's time, see Halvor Moxnes, "The Quest for Honor and the Unity of the Community in Romans 12 and in the Orations of Dio Chrysostom," in T. Engberg-Pedersen, *Paul in His Hellenistic Context* (Minneapolis: Fortress, 1995) 204-13.

1 Corinthians 4:6-7, The Explicit Key to Paul's Strategy in Chapters 1–4

COMMENTARY

Calling them "brothers and sisters" (ἀδελφοί *adelphoi*) and thereby stressing his common ground with his readers, Paul now explicitly discloses the rhetorical strategy that he has been pursuing in the opening section of his letter. As we noted earlier, Paul has used indirect speech, a common mode in his time, to make points to his readers—about themselves and their comportment—by making observations about himself and Apollos. Not only are Paul and Apollos exemplars of different persons being "one" in the gospel and in its life, but they have been the object lessons that Paul hopes the Corinthians will apply to themselves. These opening chapters of the letter are a back-to-basics lesson that Paul hopes to get across so that his hearers can learn "Nothing beyond what is written" (4:6)—that is, not to paint outside the lines.[68] If they learn the most rudimentary lesson then they will not be "puffed up" (φυσιόω *physioō*) (watch for this term to reappear as a negative characterization of misplaced Corinthian zeal in 4:18-19; 5:2) for some and against others. Nothing is more basic to the gospel than to learn the lesson that no matter how different persons may be, they are one in Christ—and there is absolutely no place for schisms, divisiveness, boasting, or judgment. This is the babies' milk of the gospel.

68. Fitzgerald, *Cracks in an Earthern Vessel,* 127.

Then, to drive the point home there is a reprise, with slight modification, of the earlier note that "all things are yours" (3:21-22), this time in a set of powerful questions that insist on the hearers' reflection. Paul walks the auditors through the logic of the gospel: When you are considered in the light of the gospel, what distinguishes you from anyone else? If you have nothing that you did not receive as a gift, then why do you live a lie in your boasting as if you did not receive it?

In 4:6, Paul declares that he has made his Paul-Apollos depiction across the first chapters for two reasons, namely that they may learn from Paul's portrayal of himself and Apollos and the Corinthians may stop their divisiveness. As can readily be seen in the differing translations offered by the NIV and the NRSV, Paul's meaning in the first purpose clause of 4:6 is difficult to know for certain. Some interpretations of the Greek such as the RSV ("not to go beyond what is written") left open the interpretation that Paul is here calling his auditors to live in accord with scripture either in some general sense or in the light of the particular citations he has made (e.g., avoid boasting because of Jer 9:24 as quoted in 1 Cor 1:31, and do not be superficially misled as is affirmed by the quotes of Job and Psalms in 3:19-20). But that runs into two difficulties: (1) What could it have meant "not to go beyond" those texts? and (2) the Greek construction (with the neuter article τό τό) regularly functions to signal the beginning of a quotation such as a maxim or proverb (as the NIV and NRSV have taken it). Taken this way, the question becomes what to make of the "[Do] not [go] beyond what is written." We have seen that Paul takes the Corinthian babies back to basics in these opening chapters of 1 Corinthians. Staying within the rules, within the borders is a way Paul does moral reasoning (see the Commentaries on 5:11 and 6:9-10 for the function of the vice lists) and may, indeed, be the meaning that Paul would have established so well in his teachings earlier that this slight reference in the letter would have been expected to bring Paul's meaning (and the larger instruction) to mind for the auditors. In line with that interpretation is the suggestion that Paul has in mind the ruled slates used in the training of children in writing so that the Corinthian babies were being urged to learn the most basic things once again.[69]

The second purpose clause—"in order that you may not be puffed up in behalf of one and against another"—parallels the first in structure, although the NIV translation veils that fact, and clearly ties Paul's treatment of himself and Apollos into the Corinthian tendency toward divisiveness that was initially raised in the first appeal (1:10). So the Corinthian inclination to puffiness and boasting and to taking sides is noted in 4:6 as precisely what Paul is trying to overcome in this letter.

69. Fitzgerald, *Cracks in an Earthern Vessel,* 121-28.

REFLECTIONS

Grace, the freely given, unmerited gift from God, itself the ground on which all the life of faith stands, is the standard by which all else is gauged. Though the term "grace" does not occur in these verses, that is what the questions in 4:7 are about. Paul's questions aim to establish the common denominator of all of life, they seek to establish or focus upon what is important by ruling some matters out of contention. To those who would vaunt themselves or whom others would lionize, Paul disarms their pretensions by frank questions: "What distinguishes you? What do you have that you have not received [as a gift, understood]? And if you receive, why do you boast as if not receiving?" (4:7). What places all believers, whether in Paul's time or in ours, on common ground is their equal dependence as ones who are the unmeriting recipients of God's grace. So who is anybody trying to fool by boasting as if this common ground of grace were not the most important fact about themselves?

1 Corinthians 4:8-13, The Grand Charade Seen with Evangelical Irony

COMMENTARY

With blistering irony in his every word, Paul now exposes and ridicules those babies who, though they have a shared Lord, would lord it over others. Some in Corinth have gotten ahead of themselves. Real babies in faith, they fancy themselves ruling (which they will, but only eschatologically and equally with all other believers; cf. 6:2-3), they imagine themselves satisfied, even sated. Paul ironically joins them in their imaginings, which he treats as fantasy, and openly yearns for them to reign because, as he allows himself to suppose, he would then share the benefits of their sovereignty. As if to highlight their unreality, Paul lays out a hardship catalog as the realia of apostles. Over against the Corinthian fiction of ruling and being filled, Paul pictures apostles as condemned to death, as what seems to be a theater of the absurd played out before the world, before angels, and before people (4:9). He cannot escape the irony of the contrast: Apostles are fools, some Corinthians wise; apostles are feeble and in disrepute, some Corinthians are strong and honored (4:10). Even in these dire circumstances apostles exemplify the gospel by not returning evil for evil; they bless, endure, and conciliate when people treat them in an opposite fashion (4:12-13). In a shift of image, it is as if apostles have become like the discardable, dirty dishwater by which the world is cleansed (4:13). Paul's hardship lists, a common feature in his letters, serve two basic functions: (1) They affirm that the real power to endure whatever comes one's way (cf. Phil 4:11-13) rests not in one's own grasp but in one's being held securely by Christ in God, and (2) they make eminently clear that the gospel never promises inoculation from distress but rather with every struggle God provides the strength to bear it or the exodus by which to escape it (see the Commentary on 1 Cor 10:1-13).

In these verses Paul opens a little window onto two of his perceptions of what is going on at Corinth. First, their divisiveness is really about power. We have seen their concerns for power in their seeking of status and in their boasting. As Paul has noted, their concerns for status and power show that they have not really gotten the picture of how different their lives in Christ should be from the social and culturally reinforced patterns of the world. They are, indeed, behaving just like children or ordinary people (3:1-4)—in either case, the point is the same. Second, at least some of these divisive Corinthians have collapsed what will truly be theirs—but only in the future—into the present and are comporting themselves as if they have "already arrived."

We have noted that the opening four chapters of 1 Corinthians are designed by Paul to establish a context for dealing with particular problems that they are having. In the verses before us, Paul signals a note that will be played at several points throughout the letter. Its frequency suggests that it is a major and pervasive problem in the Corinthian church: Some believers are claiming for themselves that they are more advanced than other believers. These people, perhaps a minority, think that they already share God's full blessings: What God has begun in Christ is already brought to completion in them. In 4:8-13 Paul tries to shock them into the realization that God's purposes in them are really only begun; the mention of apostles suggests a contrast in that these Corinthian overestimators mistakenly think that they have achieved levels for which apostles have not even dared to reach.

REFLECTIONS

1. This paragraph raises the perennial problem that believers face—namely, how much they already share in the fullness of God's gifts and how much they still await that fulfillment. Some representations of the gospel present it as "pie in the sky by and by" and assume that existence in this world is a drudge only to be endured so that some heavenly reward may be forthcoming. Some of the Corinthians have gone to the opposite extreme and seem to be claiming that in the here and now they have the fullness of all that God will ever give. Paul countenances neither extreme and invites us to consider that life in the world, even when it is beset with suffering and limitation, can be rich with God's grace so that believers can rejoice when they are suffering.

2. Paul depicts himself and the other apostles (4:9-13) as unwilling to respond in kind to rejection by others. They respond by blessing, enduring, and speaking kindly. Our actions should always be governed by our being centered on Christ and should reflect that grace and love. The alternative would be for us to take our cues from those around us and respond to them as they relate to us. Such a course of action has nothing to interrupt it, but, feeding on itself, it could result in a spiral of violence. Grace interrupts and derails anger and its attendant violence.

1 Corinthians 4:14-21, Paul Embraces and Warns His Beloved Children

COMMENTARY

The situation at Corinth is a complex one, for Paul and for the Corinthians. Though absent, Paul knows of the considerable socio-economic differences among the Corinthians (1:26); he hears of the serious schisms and divisiveness among the Corinthians. But Paul is not the only person who has worked with the Corinthians; Paul laid the foundation, Paul planted, but Apollos watered (3:6); and Apollos is still in relationship with the Corinthians, though he, too, is currently absent (16:12). Others were guardians (4:15; cf. 9:5). Sylvanus and Timothy seem to have been involved in establishing the church at Corinth (2 Cor 1:19), though Timothy has been sent or is being sent, depending on how one reads 4:17. At the time of the writing of 1 Corinthians, none of the Pauline leadership is present.

In this circumstance, Paul looks back over his purposes in what he has written so far and positions himself as pre-eminent over all other guardians. He is the Corinthians' father. They are his "beloved children" (τέκνα ἀγαπητά *tekna agapēta*) (4:14) whom he begot in the gospel (4:15). His purpose has been to admonish or warn, not shame them (cf. 4:14); accordingly, he appeals to them (4:16).

In the culture of the time, parents, particularly the pater familias, exemplified proper behavior. Children were expected to learn not only trade but appropriate behavior by modeling after their fathers. Paul draws upon those cultural expectations and appeals to the Corinthians to "be imitators of me" (μιμηταί μου γίνεσθε *mimētai mou ginesthe*, 4:16). This appeal echoes the first one (1:10) in which Paul urged the end of divisions. Let us review first what Paul has established across the opening chapters and second what Paul has suggested is imitable about himself in the first four chapters of this letter.

Through the family metaphor, Paul provides a moral pattern as well as a primary social grouping. All who belong to God are part of God's family and are brothers and sisters (*adelphoi*, occuring 38 times in this letter alone) to one another. On the basis of faith, gentiles are adopted, with full rights of inheritance along with their Jewish brothers and sisters, into God's family (Rom 8:14-23; Gal 4:4-7). The moral pattern is Paul, who thinks of himself as the father of all those who come to faith through his preaching (cf. Phlm 10). The Corinthian children in the faith should model after their father, as Timothy is depicted as doing (4:17). The Corinthians, still too much like babies (3:1-3), need to grow up to be like Paul their father and Timothy their brother.

We cannot ignore the string of clues across these first four chapters that status and pride of place are of great importance to some at Corinth. In the world of Paul's time, status was generally accorded to wealthy persons, and such are some of the members of the Corinthian church (1:26). Over against that cultural standard, Paul positions himself as one who knows several basic things: that true commendation comes only from God (4:5); that human boasting is out while boasting in the Lord is acceptable (1:29-31); that all will be judged solely by the work they have done (3:14); that mutual judgment is out (4:5), and that only the Lord can judge because only the Lord knows the hidden things and the "purposes of the heart" (4:5); that proper self-assessment is crucial (3:18); that, try as they may to make distinctions among themselves, they are all equally dependent on God's grace for their standing in Christ and, indeed, for all they have (3:21-33; 4:7); and that, like a loving father, Paul has broken through their folly laden pretensions and offered them milk—that is, he has taken them by the hand and led them back to the basics of the gospel (3:1). In all these Paul has shown the exemplary care that a father ought to have for his children. But in even more powerful ways he depicted himself as imitable—and to these the commentary now turns.

Paul has laced this entire letter section with references to himself and Apollos as exemplars of the faith. As different as the Corinthians know these two to be, Paul depicts himself and Apollos as persons who work together in harmony for the gospel. They are different people, their work is distinctive, they recognize that their contributions are singular, but in the gospel they are "one" (3:8); there is no boasting, no judgment, no striving for status. Instead, both Paul and Apollos comport themselves in such a way that God can provide the growth in God's own field. They, along with the rest of creation, belong

to the Corinthians, and along with the Corinthians they all together belong to Christ, who belongs to God (3:22-23). Paul eschews status as the world measures it. Instead, he and Apollos are merely servants who, like everyone else, must be found trustworthy (4:2).

In a final exemplification in the opening chapters,[70] Paul stacks up all the apostles over against those people at Corinth who are inclined to make special claims about their importance, and the apostles are depicted, in blistering irony, as the opposites of praise-worthiness, as ones scorned and treated with shame. How do Paul and the other apostles respond? In an exemplary fashion: "When reviled, we bless; when persecuted, we endure; when slandered, we speak kindly" (4:12-13). And this is in the passage immediately prior to his call for imitation of himself. We have no way to know whether the differing groups at Corinth are reviling, persecuting, or slandering one another, but as the pericope in which we find these claims is cast in a hyperbolic style, so also these may be an overstatement. Paul's hyperbolic point could be that even if others were slandering and persecuting, even if they were reviling, he as apostolic exemplar would respond with endurance and a readiness to conciliate (hints already of chap. 13). The basic point is clear: Paul sets himself up as one who does not repay just what he receives, but is enabled to represent the gospel even when he is not treated as he should be. So also, the Corinthians ought to learn from this that they need to be moved by what will later in this letter be called love as they respond to one another.

Paul closes this first section of his letter with a note of warning that puts the Corinthian response directly in the auditors' charge. Some "have become arrogant" (φυσιόω *physioō*, "puffed up"; cf. 4:6), questioning whether Paul is coming—Paul's travel plans do not always seem predictable (cf. 2 Cor 1:15-18)—but he promises not only that he will come but that they can arrange matters so that when he comes he will come as they wish him: either as the father ready to discipline them or the apostle who apparently would rather come "with love in a spirit of gentleness" (4:21). As the opening chapters have made clear, the gospel and the kingdom

70. Mitchell, *Paul and the Rhetoric of Reconciliation*, 39-46.

of God depend not on talk but power; Paul signals himself ready to come in the full power of the gospel (4:19), at which time he will check out these puffed-up, arrogant people who he suggests are long on talk and short on real power (4:19).

Paul's mentions of the kingdom of God are not frequent, but the paucity of references should not be taken as a gauge of its importance. Paul employs kingdom talk in two basic ways in his letters. The first, as reflected here in 4:20, describes what accords with God's reign and what does not. In 4:20 God's reign is positively related to power, negatively related to talk, and functions as a way of cautioning those "arrogant, puffy" people at Corinth not to put themselves in the place of having a confrontation with Paul. This reference to God's reign is formally quite like Rom 14:17, where the kingdom is indifferently related to food and drink but positively and essentially related to "righteousness and peace and joy in the Holy Spirit." Paul's references to "inheriting" God's kingdom (cf. Matt 25:34) function much the same way. Paul has taught the Corinthians and expects them to know that people who do the vices that Paul lists will not inherit God's kingdom or reign; the vices are absolutely disqualifying (1 Cor 6:9; 6:10; Gal 5:21; cf. Eph 5:5). One's conduct in the daily events of life must accord with God's reign or one will not be allowed to enter God's kingdom, and comportment in accord with the kingdom is required if one expects to be a part of the kingdom when

God's plan is brought to its eschatological fulfillment.

Paul's other way of referring to God's reign is eschatological. Much later in 1 Corinthians, Paul depicts how he thinks God's plan, begun in the death and resurrection of Jesus Christ, will come to its full fruition. Paul writes of the end or goal (τέλος *telos*) toward which God has purposed: "Then comes the end, when he [Christ] delivers the kingdom to God, after he [Christ] has made ineffective/wiped out" all opposing powers, and the last enemy to be "made ineffective/wiped out" is death (15:24, 26). This suggests that Christ as risen Lord is in charge of the kingdom—and may we suppose, who is associated with it?—until he hands it over to God at the eschaton, at the conclusion of God's purposes.

Brandishing his authority as the father responsible for his "beloved children," Paul puts the readers on warning that they should imitate him and that they should accommodate to Timothy's representation of "Paul's ways." The reference to Paul's "ways" being those in effect in every church is designed to counter any suggestion that Paul is setting up special, singular requirements for the Corinthians (cf. a similar point in 1 Cor 15:3-11). He can warn, he can appeal—as he has done repeatedly in these opening chapters—but the outcome is totally in the Corinthians' hands. Their response will determine whether Paul has to come with a show of power or, as he seems to suggest he prefers, in a spirit of conciliation (4:21).

REFLECTIONS

1. Strong modern churches foster the resocialization of their members into a recognition of themselves as a new family in Christ, especially as the secular family structure finds itself in such flux. Accordingly, congregants should be encouraged to think of themselves as a family, to care for one another appropriately, and to develop constructive ways of dealing with the inevitable points of conflict among these sisters and brothers. The pastor does not have to be father, though some parishioners will find that an instructive and comforting relationship.

2. Paul's call to imitate him arises out of the cultural matrix in which he and his readers live. Modeling and imitating were venerable socialization patterns that Paul found rich in potential. Paul certainly made good use of them as a way of pointing individuals and communities in the right direction. Timothy, with descriptions affirming his exemplary character, is often highlighted by Paul (16:10-11; Phil 2:19-24; 1 Thess 3:2). Other individuals are affirmed as models (16:15-18; Rom 16:1-2; 2 Cor

8:16-17). Even churches are seen as examples that inspire emulation (1 Thess 1:7-8). Churches today should self-consciously undertake to model the life of faith because their performative witness will often be more profoundly effective than words. Within the church there should also be frequent encouragement not only to live as models for other Christians but also to learn by modeling from others.

3. Paul's observation that the kingdom of God is power, not talk, points to his fundamental conviction that belonging to Christ is not a matter of having the "right" opinions or ideas (Rom 14:1) or of attitudinal adjustment. To be a Christian is to be claimed by the Spirit (Gal 3:1-4). The gospel is power: "It is the power of God for salvation" (Rom 1:16). When the gospel is made out to be ideas to which one assents, then faith is robbed of its power to transform. But a warning is appropriate: Some persons may come to a gradual realization that they have been taken by the Spirit; it does not have to be in a whirlwind of a moment. In fact, some may be reticent to think about the Holy Spirit's function in their lives because they never experienced the whirlwind. Oftentimes the Spirit is quiet and subtle and our hearing may not be attuned. We could try to develop greater sensitivity to the Spirit's gentle and subdued urgings within us. Like Elijah, maybe we expect God to come through with a booming utterance, when sometimes (most often?) it happens that the word comes only through a "still, small" voice (1 Kgs 19:11-12). So it is with the Spirit's workings and promptings, and perhaps we need to learn anew how to listen.

1 CORINTHIANS 5:1–6:20

COMMUNITY DEFINITION AS SEEN IN TWO RELATED INSTANCES

OVERVIEW

With the context provided by chaps. 1–4 Paul is now ready to engage some of the particular issues that concern him regarding the Corinthians. He has learned about the Corinthian believers from oral reports (1:11) and has received a letter of inquiry from them (7:1). The problems and issues are many. Where should Paul begin? Before he turns to their letter, to issues generated by them, he elects to treat two matters of his own choosing: The first centers on a man who "has his father's wife" (chap. 5), the second on the practice of some believers taking their intrachurch disputes before civil courts for adjudication (chap. 6). Before considering the texts themselves, however, some other questions and issues need to be addressed.

Arrangement. Why does Paul choose to start where he does? Paul has the freedom to arrange the rest of the matters in his response to the Corinthians as he sees fit. In that culture, when faced with a string of items, the first and the last are considered to be in the most emphatic positions.[71] Accordingly, what Paul puts first must be taken with seriousness by interpreters. What does his choice tell us about his estimation of the problems in Corinth and about his strategy for dealing with those problems? We will return to these questions at the end of the Commentary on 5:1–6:20.

Literary Unity of Chapters 5 and 6. On a cursory glance, the topics of chaps. 5 and 6 may seem unrelated, but a closer examination shows that they both deal with community definition: The first argues that what should be outside the community—namely, immorality, is wrongly inside it; the second claims that matters that should be dealt with inside the community, disputes that ought to be resolved within the body of believers, are being treated outside it. So in both chapters, the issue is what is appropriate to life in the community and what is more properly left outside the community of faith.[72]

A series of details confirms that chaps. 5 and 6 should be read as a single literary unit. First is an inclusio that ties the opening of chap. 5—"such immorality [πορνεία *porneia*] among you" that even gentiles blush (5:1)—to the conclusion of chap. 6—"Flee from immorality" (*porneia*, 6:18). The term *porneia*, Paul's most comprehensive term for vice and wrongful living within the fellowship, and its semantic relatives lace the two chapters together (5:1, 9-11; 6:9, 13, 16, 18), and in fact provide the link to 7:2 and the next topic, but more about that later. Further, both chapters employ vice lists as a means of rehearsing the border distinctions between behavior appropriate to the community and unacceptable behavior (5:10-11; 6:9-10). Both chapters echo the believers' baptism by use of the phrase that was first mentioned in 1:2: "in the name of the Lord Jesus" (ἐν τῷ ὀνόματι τοῦ κυρίου Ἰησοῦ *en tō onomati tou Kyriou Iēsou*, 5:4; 6:11).

The two chapters conclude (6:19-20) with a reprise on the theme of the temple of the Holy Spirit (from 3:16-17) being holy and with the assertion that the Holy Spirit is residing in the believers ἐν ὑμῖν (*en hymin* "in you"), who are now implored to "Glorify God in your body" (6:20)—a clear lead-in to the subject matter of chap. 7 and, indeed, for all that follows. Though a modern English reader might not notice it, Paul has structured his

---

71. *Ad Herennium* 3.10.17-18.

72. Wayne A. Meeks, *The First Urban Christians: The Social World of the Apostle Paul* (New Haven: Yale University Press, 1983) 129.

opening to the two-chapter section as a striking contrast to his earlier claim that the Holy Spirit dwells (*en hymin*, "in you" or "among you") among the Corinthian believers as the resident power of God's grace (3:16-17). Paul opens chap. 5 with a startling declaration: Where the Holy Spirit is supposed to be dwelling (*en hymin*, "in" or "among you"), there instead, Paul says, *porneia* is *en hymin*, "among you" (5:1). So Paul begins this section with a concern about the absence of the Spirit and its supplantation by *porneia*, and he concludes the two-chapter section with a

return (another inclusio) to the theme of the Holy Spirit dwelling *en hymin*, "in you" or "among you" (6:19-20).

Present as another link between chaps. 5 and 6 is Paul's concern with judging and judgment. Believers are supposed to make certain judgments about those inside the faith community (5:12) and leave other matters of judgment to God (5:13). Another type of judging—the settling of disputes between or among believers—is appropriate within the community (6:1, 5) and is not fittingly taken to unbelievers for adjudication.

1 CORINTHIANS 5:1-13, THE STAIN WITHIN: A THREAT TO THE HOLINESS APPROPRIATE TO THE TEMPLE OF THE HOLY SPIRIT

COMMENTARY

The chapter opens with Paul's forceful "It is actually reported" (Ὅλως ἀκούεται *Holōs akouetai*)—which has the ring of "the word has spread everywhere"—that *porneia* so extraordinarily grievous as to be off the scale is "among you" (ἐν ὑμῖν *en hymin*, 5:1), precisely where instead the Holy Spirit ought to dwell (3:16; 6:19). Nothing could be further from acceptable. Chapter 5 focuses on the situation surely known to all the believers: One of them is living with his father's wife, most likely his stepmother.

Chapter 5 closes with Paul's axiomatic recitation of a deuteronomic refrain, "Drive out the wicked one from among you" (5:13; Deut 19:19; 21:21; 22:24; 24:7). And as one reads the chapter, one can see that this scriptural sentence has shaped Paul's counsel at several points (5:2, 5, 7, 11).

Paul does not address the "man who has done this deed" (5:2), nor does he honor him with the mention of his name. Instead, he turns his attention to the other members of the congregation whom he characterizes as "puffed up" or "arrogant" (φυσιόω *physioō*). For his rebuke of them, Paul looks for some disposition as far from arrogance as possible and suggests a more fitting response would

be grieving (5:2). Paul's concern is with the community and with what their response indicates about their understanding of themselves. The community's response to this man is only the first in what will be a series of problems where the standards of the world and its acceptance of such persons have wrongly come over into the community. The other believers have an obligation to act in a defining way; they need to reaffirm the borders of proper community life and cast the "wicked one" out of their fellowship.[73] Paul's prescription is a radical step, radical in the sense of getting to the root of proper community identity and comportment.

Chapters 1–4 set up the proper contrast between the world and true believers—the rival two-way tradition—and even capitalize on Paul's general depiction of the divisive, boastful believers as behaving just like ordinary non-believers (3:3). In chap. 5 Paul inquires how the believers can tolerate conduct that even the world would find offensive: "not even among the gentiles" (5:1).

Note that Paul chides the ones who are arrogant, puffed up, boastful (5:2; cf. 4:6, 18-19).

---

73. Adela Yarbro Collins, "The Function of 'Excommunication' in Paul," *HTR* 73 (1980) 259-60.

He has had the arrogant and puffy Corinthians in view from early on in this letter. They are the ones who too readily dismiss Paul's coming to Corinth (4:18), and with it challenge his authority; they are likely the same ones who are taking sides and using the gospel as part of a power game (4:6-7); they may even be the same ones whose position Paul has characterized as "already satiated, already rich, already reigning" (4:8).

Paul has undercut the ground for such arrogance by his previously made claims about God's gracious election and call of the Corinthians, most of whom had no social status in the world's eye (1:26-29). God's grace toward undeserving persons—which includes everybody, according to Paul (Rom 3:22b-24)—is the great social leveler so that none of the Corinthians should have been "puffed up in favor of one against another" (4:6 NRSV). "What do you have that you did not receive [as a gift]? And if you received it, why do you boast as if not receiving?" (4:7; cf. 8:1). Understandably for Paul, the only boast that is acceptable is a "boast in the Lord," who has graced the believers—who of course did not deserve the grace (1:31). In unmistakable terms Paul now tells the Corinthians, "Your boast is not good!" (5:6).

Paul's earlier treatment of boasting and puffiness has been somewhat general. In chaps. 1–4 the believers' haughtiness was not identified with any particular actions or expressions of it. Now in chap. 5 Paul encounters the first specific example of how boasting has surely condoned a particular action and thereby challenged the being and identity of the community of believers. In the earlier chapters he has established that boasting is inappropriate; now he confronts a particular action that he explicitly labels πορνεία (*porneia*) and whose perpetrator he identifies with the "wicked one" of the deuteronomic refrain.

Accordingly, Paul thinks the Corinthian believers should not be elated over the man who is living in an immoral way; rather, they should have gone into mourning (5:2). Why? Because that man's action, his *porneia*, is an indictment of the entire community and of their failure to exercise proper care for one another. In 5:3-5 Paul directs them, at their next assembly, to cast him out of the fellowship: "Hand this man over to Satan" (5:5).

At stake is the well-being of the community (Paul turns to this in 5:6ff.) and the future of the one who did the wrong (see the Commentary on 3:15).

The text is allusive. We may suppose that the Corinthians knew Paul's fuller thoughts from his previous discussions with them. We can only take the few clues given here and, with what we know of Paul in his other letters, try to tease out what may be Paul's suppositions embedded within the text. Paul expects to encounter *porneia* out in the world, but not in the church. God's wrath and judgment are currently being manifested in the world against injustice and immorality (Rom 1:18-32). In the final judgment, here called "the day of the Lord" (ἡμέρα τοῦ κυρίου *hēmera tou kyriou*) (5:5; cf. 3:13), God will eradicate all evil, all sin, and those under its throes. In the meanwhile, the believers' job is to maintain proper temple holiness, which means to keep immorality (*porneia*) and injustice from tainting the fellowship of believers.

Paul's instructions to dismiss this man seem to suppose that the only hope for him in "the day of the Lord Jesus" (5:5) is for him to be cast in the meantime into the domain of Satan, where his fleshly pursuits may be unmistakably seen by him as alien to the gospel. If he were allowed to continue in fellowship, he might never, short of the judgment day, be called to account and, therefore, not be challenged to bring his comportment in line with the gospel. By excluding him from fellowship, the community will send a "wake-up call" to the man. No longer would he be able to take their acceptance and perhaps even admiration as an indicator of his being on the right path.

Regarding the man who has his father's wife, Paul develops his argument in stages, like successive transparencies superimposed on one another. Each stage supposes the previous one(s) and adds emphasis, detail, and refinement to the whole picture. In the base portrait (5:1-5), Paul identifies the situation of the man having his stepmother as incontrovertible *porneia*, chides the community not only for their arrogant response but also for their failure to remove the person and, therefore, the *porneia* from their midst; and he directs the community, at their next assembly, to give the man over to Satan—that is, to put him out of the community.

The next transparency (5:6-8) emphasizes their boasting (highlighting 5:2a) and draws upon the common, quotidian experience of yeast leavening dough to insinuate that the man's presence in the community insidiously functions like yeast and affects the whole lump. The note about "cleaning" out the old yeast signals that the common experience of yeast is about to be transformed to the Passover ritual of ridding the house of yeast (Exod 13:7). So the simple act of expunging yeast is transposed into ritual, proper cleansing (the notion will reappear as a link in 6:11, where washing and baptism will be associated with the readers' having been cleansed also) appropriate to Passover where Christ is considered the Passover lamb that has been sacrificed (5:7b-8; cf. Exod 12:21). So just as the man of the first transparency is to be removed from the community, so also the second transparency calls the auditors to "celebrate the festival" by removing the leaven that Paul identifies with two of the most sweeping vices, κακία (kakia, "badness," "depravity") and πονηρία (ponēria, "wickedness," "baseness," 5:8). Paul's replacement virtues will be considered after a look at the third transparency, which Paul superimposes.

Paul's third transparency (5:9-13) allows him not only to reassert his main points but also to demonstrate that his recommendation in the case of this particular man is not an ad hoc opposition to this fellow. His reference to his previous (lost) letter, even though the Corinthians seem to have had some confusion as to its precise meaning, grounds Paul's recommendations to his earlier teaching. By reminding them what he had written he reinforces what he has already sketched in the two previous transparencies. The previous letter not only establishes Paul's consistency but it also serves to show the Corinthians' need for Paul's further tutelage. They should have known not to mingle with "immoral people" (πόρνοι pornoi, an obvious reinforcement of his rejection of porneia in 5:1, 9). Two verses later (5:11) Paul highlights and elaborates his earlier counsel to avoid immoral people: (a) He means immoral people who have the name "brother or sister" in Christ, not all immoral people because avoiding all of them

would be an impossibility—the world is full of them; (b) he reaffirms his strong conviction that vice list conduct is inappropriate to the life of faith and once again, for added emphasis, he leads the vice list of 5:11 with πόρνος (pornos, "immoral person"), one more link to and reinforcement of his spurning of porneia in 5:1. The extended vice list (5:11) elaborates on porneia as symbolizing unacceptable behavior for believers and identifies any believer who does such things as due to be shunned. As if for further emphasis, Paul adds to the twice-mentioned prohibition against "mingling" (συναναμείγνυμι synanameignymi) (5:9, 11a) the injunction not even to eat with such a one (5:11; cf. 11:17-34, where the topic of eating together will be treated again and in more detail).

Paul's two main points in the entire section are consistently affirmed. First, in each of the three transparencies Paul rules out fellowship with believing brothers and sisters who are involved in porneia or other associated vices. Second, in each Paul assumes that it is the community's responsibility to preserve its own God-given integrity by giving to Satan, by cleansing, and by driving out the violator.

Paul's rich Jewish heritage has obviously become his readers' tradition, too, because he does not have to explain his Passover reference. He associates casting this man out of the church with the Jewish practice of cleansing the house of yeast at Passover, rejects their boasting (5:6), and urges them to realize that they are like fresh, unleavened Passover dough. This connection is confirmed by Paul's christological declaration that "our Paschal lamb, Christ, has been sacrificed" (5:7) and by his reckoning that "therefore" they should celebrate the festival by cleaning out the old yeast, which Paul identifies (5:8) with two of the most comprehensive vices that tend to show up in his and similar Stoic lists: κακία (kakia, "badness," "depravity") and (ponēria, "wickedness," "baseness"). Proper celebration of the festival takes its cue from Christ, understood as the Passover lamb, and features as a contrast two virtues as the fitting, unleavened bread (Exod 12:8, 15, 19-20): εἰλικρίνεια (eilikrineia, "sincerity," "purity of motive"; cf. 2 Cor 2:17) and ἀλήθεια (alētheia, "truthfulness," "dependability," "uprightness"). Note that in Paul's scriptures the one who eats leavened bread (= *porneia* in 1 Corinthians) is threatened with being "cut off" from Israel (Exod 12:15), from "the congregation of Israel" (Exod 12:19), a notion fully in line with Paul's use of the deuteronomic refrain explicitly quoted by him in 1 Cor 5:13.

Simply ridding the community of the *porneia* is not sufficient; something positive must be put in its place (cf. Luke 11:24-26). Paul's suggestion of replacement with sincerity and truthfulness is surely a kind of fruit of the Spirit (cf. Gal 5:22), the very Spirit whose dwelling place had been taken by *porneia* (cf. 6:19-20).

Why are these two particular virtues chosen by Paul? We cannot be certain, but Paul's further use of *eilikrineia* with the Corinthians may shed some light on its function here. In 2 Cor 1:12, where Paul writes about his own comportment, he characterizes himself as having acted "in holiness and godly sincerity," which he identifies as being powered by God's grace and which he contrasts with comportment that is based on fleshly (σαρκική *sarkikē*; NRSV, "earthly"; NIV, "worldly; not on Spirit, implied) wisdom. In the 2 Corinthians passage Paul has in mind the same two-way tradition that is already present in 1 Cor 1:21-22 and across the opening chapters: One either lives by worldly wisdom, as some of the Corinthians are inclined to do, or one lives in godly sincerity, with one's motivations pure and open for any to examine. In 2 Cor 1:12 Paul describes himself as living by that godly sincerity; in 1 Cor 5:8 he calls for the Corinthians to live in that same way.

As to why *alētheia* is chosen as the desirable virtue, we may look to the term's other appearance in 1 Corinthians and see that love "rejoices in the truth" (13:6). Paul's strong link between truthfulness and love means that to call for either is to affirm the other. So in Paul's Passover reflection, he urges the Corinthians to celebrate the festival by throwing out the evil (and the immoral person) and by featuring instead what he identifies as the unleavened bread of sincerity and truthfulness (5:8).

Paul's view of Christ's death in 5:7 fits his usual pattern of considering it a past, finished, defining event. He casts it here in Passover garb to sharpen his readers' sense

that the time for cleansing the house of yeast has passed. His rhetoric, therefore, creates a sense of urgency in dealing with the man who has his father's wife. In this context, yeast becomes synonymous with contamination, which must be cast out so that the house (= temple, 3:17) and, in Paul's letter, all who reside there, may be properly holy, a motif that he will explicitly affirm in 6:19-20 as he brings this two-chapter section to a close.[74]

Maintenance of holiness and the avoidance of its counterpart, *porneia*, has been an enduring issue for the Corinthians, and the mark of this problem is visible not only across 1 Corinthians but was featured in the earlier letter (5:9-11). Paul's earlier epistolary effort to address the problem of *porneia* in the believing community did not achieve a resolution, because the matter is still up for consideration not only in 5:1-13 but also across the current letter. Let us attempt to reconstruct, from the evidence in 1 Corinthians, Paul's position on shunning immoral persons and how it has been variously interpreted at Corinth.

Paul reminds the Corinthians that his previous letter had urged them not to "mingle/ associate" (*synanameignymi*) with *pornoi*, immoral people. The repetition of the verb for "mingle" or "mix together" (5:9, 11) could suggest that it was the very term Paul had used in the previous letter. In 5:11 Paul makes clear that the troublesome mingling he had in mind was not, as some had taken it, with the immoral persons of the world. Paul's sense of logic rules out that interpretation, because then one would have had to exit the world, a ludicrous notion for Paul. He then clarifies that he meant for them to avoid nominal believers who, in fact, are immoral people; and to emphasize his point and show that the concern was not narrowly focused only on *porneia*, he elaborates a vice list of totally unacceptable behavior (5:11) that *porneia* has come in this letter to represent.

We can learn from this that for some time, perhaps from the period of their first coming into faith, the Corinthians have had immoral persons in their fellowship; the man who has his stepmother is not at all the first such, though he is acknowledged by Paul to be

74. Collins, "The Function of 'Excommunication' in Paul," 251-63.

an extreme example. We can also learn that Paul's handling of the topic in the previous letter did not solve the matter, though we can surmise that some persons in the believing community actually tried to figure out Paul's advice and follow it. And we can learn that the earliest interpreters of one of Paul's letters, the Corinthians themselves, came up with some radically different understandings of his counsel against mingling with immoral people. Could it not be some of these very readers who concluded that they might do well to divorce their unbelieving spouses (7:12-16)? Is it an even more radical interpretation of Paul's counsel against mingling that leads some married persons to wonder if holiness and human sexuality can coexist and who, therefore, decided to abstain from sexual intercourse (7:5)? And why could not the man with his father's wife be one who took a very different reading on Paul's earlier letter, understanding that two believers could operate on a different and liberated moral code as long as both of them were believers? For such an understanding, *porneia* would be a problem only if one were involved with an unbeliever. And is it not possible that the wealthy believers who adjudicate church matters by taking them to the civil courts (chap. 6) have understood Paul to say that holiness and its appropriate life are possible completely within the structures of the society? This same sort of border question, discerning the way holiness and *porneia* related, could also have contributed to the confusion over whether believers could eat meat offered to idols (cf. their letter's question in 8:1), whether believers could accept dinner invitations from unbelievers (10:27), and how to treat unbelievers when they happen into worship (14:22-25).

The matter is an important and complex one. We know that the Jewish community at Qumran, associated with the Dead Sea Scrolls, resolved the issue of minimizing the contamination of their God-given holiness by fleeing into the desert, the kind of response that Paul rejects in 5:10. But, short of escapism, how can holiness not only be lived but also honored and preserved in the world?

The proper maintenance of holiness, Paul believes, is possible while one lives directly in the world, in contact with immoral people and within the ordinary transactions of human life (cf. 7:29-31). But fellowship within the

community of the faithful is to be measured by another scale: Inside the community absolutely no *porneia* is to be countenanced; immoral people who are nominal brothers and sisters in Christ must not be granted fellowship in the body of Christ. In the community *porneia* has a corrosive, corrupting, contaminating power. This same matter is treated in a different context in Romans 6, where Paul pursues the question of whether faith and sin may coexist, whether the life of faith allows the presence of sin within it. There as here the answer is the same: Faith and sin do not allow any mixture; the one precludes the other. One is either in right relation to God (faith that expresses itself in holiness living) or one is not (then one is under sin, which gains expression in immoral living). There is no middle ground, no third alternative that allows a mix. The people of God, as God's temple, must be completely and purely set apart for God. There can be no admixture of unholiness within God's family; yet God's family can and will live directly in the structures of the world, where sin and unholiness are present.

The problems of distinguishing proper from improper comportment and the holy from the immoral should have been cleared up by Paul's previous letter (5:9). Now in the present letter Paul clarifies that he had been concerned with *pornoi*, immoral persons, in the community and that believers should in fact not even have table fellowship with "someone who bears the name of 'brother' or 'sister'" if they be "immoral, or greedy, or an idolater, or an abusive person, or a drunkard, or a robber" (5:11)—repetitively strung out, as this translation tries to suggest, so as to invite the hearers to extend the list. The vice list here functions in an et cetera fashion to suggest that *porneia* serves to typify the larger problem, another instance of synecdoche; holiness is put in hazard by any comportment that crosses over the border that the vice list represents. In Paul's view, persons whose lives exemplify any of the vices are true outsiders (see the Commentary on 14:16, 23-25); they no more belong in the community than yeast belongs in the house at Passover.[75] The man living with his

75. W. A. Meeks, " 'Since Then You Would Need to Go Out of the World': Group Boundaries in Pauline Christianity," in *Critical History and Biblical Faith: New Testament Perspectives*, ed. T. J. Ryan (Villanova, Pa.: College Theological Society, 1979) 18-19.

stepmother has, by his own comportment, become an outsider whose presence inside the community risks the holiness and well-being of all the members. By community action, the boundaries of the community must be redrawn so that this man is outside where God judges (5:13).

Believers have responsibility for comportment within the community, to monitor it and to call into question any behavior that threatens the health and wholeness, the holiness, of the community; that is what Paul probably has in mind when he asks them, "Is it not you yourselves who judge the ones inside?" (5:12). In 5:3 Paul has modeled this judgment function: He "has pronounced judgment" (reached a decision) regarding the man; he must be expelled. Parenthetically, it may be noted from 2 Cor 2:5-11 that the Corinthians subsequently put Paul's advice about monitoring community behavior into practice; in 2 Cor 2:7-8 Paul suggests that they should restore fellowship to a repentant believer.

Across his correspondence, Paul's vice lists (Rom 1:29-32; 1 Cor 6:9-11; 2 Cor 12:20-21; Gal 5:19-21) function, like a fence around the community of believers, to mark out totally unacceptable behavior. For Paul it is unthinkable that believers might cross over into the actions depicted in the vice lists. When a believer does, as here in chap. 5, Paul considers that the individual no longer belongs; he or she has become like an unbeliever and subject to Satan's rule and to God's direct judgment. Paul fears a contamination of the community by such a presence of *porneia*. Within the fence provided by the vice lists, Paul can embrace a broad range of conduct as long as love is put into practice, but he has no tolerance for any staining of the community's holiness. Why does he reproach the community? Because they have not understood that the wholeness of the community, the health and well-being, indeed, to use Paul's expression, the holiness of the fellowship is at risk.

By clever use of Passover analogies, such as yeast, dough, and unleavened lump, Paul elaborates the theme of believers' being God's temple that must not be corrupted. Should matters get out of hand, as in this instance, and the community find itself defiled, it must urgently move to set matters straight. In 3:17, temple honoring was set over against temple defilement. Now in 5:6-8 the intruding *porneia* is compared to yeast: Even what seems to be a "little bit" leavens the whole lump. Paul likens the believing community to their Jewish forebears who, when the paschal lamb was slain, dared not find even a hint of yeast on the premises. He reminds the believers that, in this analogy, they "really are unleavened" already (5:7), or at least are created and called to be so, and that Christ, the Passover lamb, has indeed already been slain. Accordingly, they have no option but to "clean out the old leaven" that this man represents. Then their lives will be characterized no more by the leaven of "vice and wickedness" but by the more appropriate "purity of motive and truthfulness" (5:8; cf. Rom 11:16).

In 3:17, Paul described the Corinthians as God's holy temple and warned that any threat of defilement, corruption, spoiling (φθείρω *phtheirō*, 3:17) to the temple is itself a peril to the individual who does the corruption (there it was noted that the plural was used). Here in 5:6-8 Paul makes clear that such individual corruption brings the entire community under God's judgment. The same theme will reappear, with the same key verb, in Paul's discussion of resurrection when he quotes the contemporary poetic maxim: "Bad company *corrupts* (*phtheirō*) good character" (15:33 NIV). Paul's final word on the subject of this man's threat to the community's well-being and holiness is the scriptural injunction to "drive out the wicked person from among you" (5:13; cf. Deut 19:19; 22:21, 24; 24:7).

REFLECTIONS

1. Modern Christians often think that to raise questions regarding another person's behavior is a negative thing—and for good reason, because it can too readily be self-righteously and derogatorily delivered. But there is a legitimate question of just how fully love is carried out toward another if one never raises a question about that person's comportment no matter how far out it happens to be. Surely genuine love does not condone all actions done by loved ones. "Tough love" is an expression that suggests that love is not always "yes"; it may and must sometimes be "no" or at the very least "why?" At issue is the difference between meddling and proper responsibility. Clearly, the former is to be avoided, but the latter is an obligation of love. It may be helpful to put meddling and proper mutual responsibility on an imaginary continuum from left to right. On the right is one's clear duty; on the left is what one must avoid. In between is a range of choices, some of which will be more clearly appropriate mutual care and some of which may suggest meddling. Life's moral choices must be made in the gray area of uncertainty where the obligation of love is often clearer than our judgment about the appropriateness of our involvement in a particular gray-area situation. Not to act or to choose to be silent has its own risks—people may be harmed. For example, if one of the clergy abuses someone in the church and nothing is done about it, then the church has failed in its responsibility to care in a loving fashion for all its members. Love to the abused one should take the form of standing over against the clergy and insisting upon restorative therapy; love for the clergyperson should take the form of discipline, removal, and treatment.

2. The problem in all terminations of fellowship, whether in the church or between friends, is one of degree, of determining when the action falls far enough into the gray area to be harmful. Each person needs to be his or her own "gray monitor," but you might find it helpful to have occasional discussions with others about how they make their own decisions about when they think there is too much gray in a situation. Surely, excommunication in a church setting is a radical action whose very need already signals a massive failure of the fellowship to nurture and counsel its members. A church that has done its work of mutual encouragement and mutual checking properly will probably never face the need to withdraw fellowship from an individual. A church that looks the other way at its members' comportment is courting disaster. This is not "throwing the first stone." It is love's obligation for us to reflect with one another about our moral performance.

3. Paul's picture is one that stresses the nurturing and correcting function of the church; when the church functions as it ought, God's judgment need not enter the church. Paul does not treat the question of whether God's judgment is already being experienced by the man, but Paul is convinced that when the man is expelled, he surely comes face-to-face with God's judgment. One other angle is worth considering: Does not the church, when it knows of such vice-listviolating conduct and says nothing, encourage its member to think that the person is perhaps still within the scope of acceptable behavior?

Such a dynamic should raise for modern believers the question of how they signal affirmation and concern about the behavior of others. Surely, one response to that question will be that no one should signal to another at all, but another person might have to wonder whether there can be any real community if people do not care about how each other behaves.

4. Another facet of this issue may be expressed in terms of piety and holiness. For many today, religiousness, holiness is a private matter between the individual and God. But for Paul, holiness and piety, though surely grounded in individuals and in each person's behavior, are community concerns and responsibilities. They are to assemble, to turn this man over to Satan; they are to cleanse out the old leaven; and they are to celebrate the Passover festival with purity of motives and in truth. As will become evident at points across this letter, Christians stand or fall as a community, not as collected individuals. These reflections will cause problems for persons who have privatized their faith and their moral responsibility, for those who think that their moral decisions are theirs alone between themselves and God. Such an individualistic view is totally alien to Paul's picture of how the life of faith ought to be lived.

5. Judgment within the church is not simply a final, leave-it-to-God verdict. Note that the man is turned over to Satan with the hope or expectation that, in some way, he may be "saved on the day of the Lord" (5:5). Paul and the Corinthians may not presume to know the man's ultimate fate because his destiny is God's business, and God's grace works in mysterious ways. Decisions about maintenance of the community, its requisite holiness, and who is allowed full fellowship and participation are not decisions about damnation and salvation because these latter are not the church's dominion; they belong solely to God.

6. Paul's call to the Corinthians is, in effect, to "become what you are in Christ"— that is, to live up to what you have been reconstituted to be in Christ. "You really are unleavened" (5:7); live like it. Much the same point will be made in chap. 6: You really are "washed . . . sanctified . . . justified" (6:11); live like it. Paul paints the picture of what is true in Christ, reminding the believers of what God in Christ has done for them; then he calls the believers to live up to—that is, to live in accord with—their calling.

1 CORINTHIANS 6:1-11, WRONGFULLY CROSSING THE BORDER IN THE OTHER DIRECTION: TAKING COMMUNITY MATTERS OUT INTO THE WORLD

COMMENTARY

Apparently some Corinthian believers are taking other believers to civil courts for the settlement of disputes. It is a logical step for Paul to treat this matter at this point in the letter because, in the just-finished discussion, he has advanced the argument that judgment properly belongs inside the community.

In the Greco-Roman world, who initiated civil court cases? The answer is simple and unmistakable: only the wealthy, only the very powerful few who sat atop the steep social pyramid. We have seen (1:26) that the Corinthian church had a few such people.[76] Those wealthy people must be the ones who conduct business and settle disputes in their accustomed fashion, as they had done regularly in their life before faith came: They turn to the courts, whose verdicts followed wealth. Paul's view of this Corinthian practice is

clear in the way he describes the judges in three places: Worldly judges are the persons who "wrong" others—that is, who do what is not right, not just, not righteous (ἐπὶ τῶν ἀδίκων *epi tōn adikōn*, 6:1); they are the ones who are despised or "have no standing" (NRSV) in the church (6:4); and it follows that they are "unbelievers" (6:6).[77]

Paul thinks that "the saints," his designation for all of the ones who have responded to the call of the gospel and, therefore, are the recipients of this very letter (1:2), are the ones who should be qualified to hear disputes (6:1). Paul's two-way depictions of life's basic alternatives, which he laid out so clearly and distinctively in his opening chapters (1–4), now serve to show how confused the Corinthians are and how wrong is their practice.

When faced with a problem or issue, Paul regularly refers to "what we know" and

---

76. Allan Mitchell, "Rich and Poor in the Courts of Corinth: Litigiousness and Status in 1 Corinthians 6:1-11," *NTS* 39 (1993) 562-63, argues, as does this commentary, that a few wealthy believers were taking "lower status people to court, where the latter were at a disadvantage."

77. For background, see B. W. Winter, "Civil Litigation in Secular Corinth and the Church. The Forensic Background to 1 Corinthians 6.1-8," *NTS* 37 (1991) 559-72.

reasons from that to some advice or resolution. It is a pattern that we will see across 1 Corinthians. In the case at hand, "what we know" is mentioned in rhetorical questions that are so constructed in Greek as to expect a yes answer. "You do know, don't you, that the saints will judge the world?" (6:2). "You do know, don't you, that we will judge angels?" (6:3). Paul finds an irony in the Corinthians' going to worldly courts to settle quarrels when they, the saints, are destined to judge the very world of which those courts are so much a part. How can it be that the Corinthian saints are "incompetent for the most insignificant cases" (6:3)? When believers are destined to judge even angels, how is it possible that they cannot handle "ordinary matters" (βιωτικά *biōtika*, 6:3)? And how can they, who will ultimately judge the world and angels, lay routine day-to-day issues before persons who have no standing in the church? It is too much for Paul: "To your shame I say this!" (6:5).

Paul's rapid-fire questions have the ring of a courtroom. Form follows function. The questions have the effect of placing the auditors, with their fascination with courts, on the witness stand; Paul adopts the stance of the one who with leading questions exposes what he takes to be the shameful conduct of the Corinthian believers.

Lying behind Paul's rebuke is his apocalyptic conviction that, in God's final judgment of sin and its grasp of the world, it is the believers who will form part of the heavenly court (cf. Dan 7:22; 12:3; Wis 3:8; Sir 4:15; 2 Esdr 9:97; *1 Enoch* 104:2; *Testament of Abraham* 1-4; 1QpHab 5:4; Matt 19:28; Rev 3:21; 20:4), who are at least present when God's final judgment takes place (cf. Isa 24:21-22). The notion that angels will face judgment may go back to the story of the sons of God, taken around the turn of the era to be angels (cf. *1 Enoch* 6–19), mentioned in Gen 6:1-6, and their improper conduct; such an interpretation lies behind 2 Pet 2:4 and Jude 6 and probably informs Paul's understanding that is reflected here in 1 Cor 6:3. Paul's questions ("Do you not know," 6:2-3) and the brevity of the discussion show that he expects the Corinthians to know and even to share his sublime picture of the end times. At no single place in the Pauline letters do we see

the whole of Paul's eschatological vision; on some occasions, we see mere hints of it such as these (see 1 Cor 15:24-28). But the way Paul does not have to explain these grand claims indicates that he expects his Corinthian readers to know the assertions and the fuller story of which they are a part.

The sublimity of Paul's eschatological vision, combined with his strong and abiding conviction that judgment will surely take place at the end, mocks the trifling insignificance of the disputes that some Corinthians have dragged before public tribunals. Paul's choice of terms heightens the contrast, to the detriment of those seeking civil resolution of disputes. He uses a superlative: "If the world is to be judged by you, are you not worthy regarding the least cases?" (6:2). He associates their concerns with *biōtika*, what we might call "ordinary" or "day-to-day," "run-of-the-mill" matters that seem rather puny when compared with their anticipated end-time role of judging angels (6:3).

This section is laced with irony. First, with certain ironic rebuke aimed toward those who pride themselves on wisdom and its associated worldly status, Paul inquires, "Is there no wise person among you who could render a [fitting, just, understood] decision?" (6:5). So much for those at Corinth who saw wisdom as an avenue to power but could not see wisdom as applicable to communal strife and differences. According to Paul, lawsuits among the believers are an "utter loss" (6:7) because these very Corinthians recognize neither the nature of community in Christ nor the way believers are to deal with one another.

In parallel constructions that, as an inclusio, explicitly link back to Paul's first description of civil judges as ones who "wrong" others (6:1), Paul seeks to put the believers' strife and contention in perspective: "Why not rather be wronged? Why not rather let yourselves be robbed? Instead you yourselves wrong and rob!" (6:7-8). What characterizes the judgments rendered by unbelieving judges—namely, their wronging of others, is precisely what Paul sees has ironically become operative within the community of believers. The believers at Corinth have become precisely like those outside the faith community—yet another irony and yet one more reason why the community needs to redefine itself as distinct from the world and the latter's patterns of arrangements between and among people.

Chapter 6 and the issue of lawsuits before civil authorities raises once again the questions of community borders, of what is appropriate within the community and of how the community relates to what is going on in the world outside the church. But, in contrast to chap. 5 where *porneia* has crept into the church from the world, now the question of lawsuits raises the issue of matters that should be properly treated precisely within the community. Paul's complaint about Corinthians' going to civil courts to settle disputes is twofold, and both are ironically stated: They who value and vaunt wisdom do not have a wise person to adjudicate disputes, and they whom Paul presumes will be the experts on justice, who will sit in judgment on the world and even on angels (presumably at the end of the ages; 6:2-3), turn to persons outside the community of believers and, therefore, to judges who know nothing about justice and judging.

Paul is convinced that believers should be able to work out their differences with one another amicably and with a sense of fairness and justice; they are, after all, the ones who know the difference between ἀδικία (*adikia*, "wickedness," "injustice") and δικαιοσύνη (*dikaiosynē*, "righteousness," "justice"). But instead they turn to unjust judges for decisions of justice (6:1)! Woefully, the believers, the saints, have shirked their responsibilities to work out disputes among themselves, they have abandoned the standards that should be foundational for their communal life, and they have turned to the standards of the world.

Once again, as in chap. 5, the borders demarcating the community from the world have been breached, and here as there Paul recites a vice list as a means of marking off the distinction (6:9-10; 5:9-11).[78] The "unrighteous," those who do wrong or injustice, such as unbelieving civil judges and some within the community of faith, "will not inherit the kingdom of God" (6:9). Paul expects that the Corinthians should already know that, as the ninth rhetorical question, this one also expecting a yes answer, clearly indicates

(6:9, reprised in 6:10). The listed vices function not only to reprise matters that have preceded but also to hint at those that will follow (e.g., several of the vices mentioned in 6:9-10 echo the list in 5:11; *pornoi*, "immoral ones" ties back to 5:1, 9 and ahead to 6:13-18 and 7:2; idolatry has clear links ahead to chap. 8 and to 10:19).

As in chap. 5, vice lists help Paul to distinguish acceptable behavior from unacceptable and reinforce the proper identity of believers. Paul casts the vice list in 6:9-10 to describe the former lives of some of the believers; it should no longer be descriptive of them. In the strongest contrast allowed in the Greek language (ἀλλά *alla*, "but"), Paul repeatedly dissociates his audience from the vices and the former state of their lives: "But you were washed; but you were sanctified; but you were justified" (6:11). Paul fears that the community border has been breached, that holiness has been contaminated. As a corrective, he tries to distinguish the comportment appropriate to heirs of God's kingdom.

In 6:11 the phrase "in the name of the Lord Jesus Christ" (cf. 1:10; 5:4), combined as it is with the references to the Spirit and to the readers' having been "washed," makes clear that Paul is employing baptismal references as a way of positioning the Corinthians' understandings of themselves and of their new and distinctive calling in Christ. The vice lists conform to the same understanding because Paul's rhetoric is focused here on calling to mind their set-apart status as believers who should live and conduct themselves differently from the world. The same considerations should be in view as we retrospectively interpret the appearance of the identical phrase "in the name of the Lord Jesus" in 5:4. There Paul is urging the community of believers who gather in the Lord's name—that is, under Christ's power and guidance as risen Lord, to turn over to Satan the man who is sleeping with his stepmother. In both places (5:4; 6:11) the phrase serves a fundamental community-definition function; it asks the believers gathered in Christ's name to be reflective about their identity, founded in their baptism, and how they ought to live in order more fully to honor Christ's lordship. So the two appeals to "the name of the Lord" function as yet another inclusio and as

78. P. S. Zaas, "Catalogues and Context: 1 Corinthians 5 and 6," *NTS* 34 (1988) 622-29, esp. 629.

another sign that the topics of chaps. 5 and 6 are interrelated in Paul's purpose.

The appearance of baptismal language— "in the name of the Lord Jesus" (*en tō onomati tou Kyriou Iēsuo*)—signals several important points to the reader. First, and this ties into the earlier interpretation of chaps. 1–4, Paul is taking the auditors back to basics in chaps. 5 and 6. Second, because Paul associates baptism with entry into the faith and believers thus becoming God's children (Rom 8:14-15; Gal 4:6), Paul makes good on his claim in 3:1-2 that he must treat them as babies despite their inclination to more elevated self-estimates. Third, the inclusio of the baptismal formula in 5:4 and in 6:11 ties the content of those sections together despite the superficial sense that they deal with two distinct issues. And finally, the mention of "the Spirit of our God" in 6:11 provides the link, as yet another inclusio, that will bring chap. 6 to a close in the reprise—cast once more in a question expecting a "yes" answer because the Corinthians are supposed to know this and to live by it already—of the claim that the recipients of the letter are the temple of the Holy Spirit (6:19-20; cf. 3:16-17).

Paul has called the Corinthians "babies who are not ready [as he insinuates they should be or as they perhaps think they are] for solid food" (3:1; 4:14);[79] he has characterized them as persons whose humble social origins do not fit with their haughty self-evaluations and pretensions (1:26; 4:8); and he has gone "back to basics" with them, as one can see from the phrase "You do know, don't you . . . ?" repeated eight times—three of them in the upcoming 6:12-20—in the first six chapters (3:16; 5:6; 6:2-3, 9, 15-16, 19).

It has been noted several times since chap. 3 that Paul's estimate of the Corinthians' maturity (really immaturity) in the faith is different from the Corinthians' estimate of themselves. The two linked items in chaps. 5 and 6 are part of Paul's evidence that his estimate, not theirs, is the right one. What they ought to have known—indeed, what Paul

did teach them—from their most juvenile times in the faith would have, should have kept them from the kinds of community-disruptive and destructive actions noted in the man's living with his father's wife and in their taking one another to court. The Corinthian believers have gotten ahead of themselves. They must be taken back to the basics of the life of faith and, together, build from there. As long as the church becomes like the world or the world's ways leach into the communal life of faith, the believers lack understanding and clarity on even the most basic matters.

In one other significant way Paul builds from his conviction that the Corinthians are babies. In the second delineation of vice lists in these two chapters (5:9-13; 6:9-11), Paul inquires of the believers' understandings: "You do know, don't you, that the unrighteous will not inherit God's reign?" (6:9). The talk of "inheriting the kingdom" is not frequent in Paul, but because of its appearance in another letter in a similar connection (Gal 5:21, where even there he also reminds his readers, the Galatians, that he had taught them this point earlier), it must be a traditional teaching of Paul's, and he knows he has already shared it with the Corinthians. The next verse (6:10) elaborates the same point—namely, that persons whose conduct fits the vice list will never inherit God's reign. So we find mention of inheritance alongside baptismal language ("in the name of Jesus," 6:11; 5:4) in the same way that Rom 8:15-17 depicts it, but in Romans the baptismal connection is expressed in terms of receiving the Holy Spirit rather than with the baptismal phrase "in the name of Jesus." In Romans 8 the Spirit enables believers to become God's children, saying "Abba, Pater" ("Father" in Aramaic and in Greek, perhaps a reference to the Lord's Prayer), and then goes ahead to describe them as "heirs" of the full inheritance that God has prepared (Rom 8:17). In 1 Cor 6:9-10 Paul reminds the Corinthians that their association with *porneia* and its related vices places in jeopardy the full inheritance and place in God's reign (cf. 15:24-28) for which the thus-far working of the Spirit has qualified them, if they do not deceive themselves (6:10).

79. Beverly R. Gaventa, "Mother's Milk and Ministry in 1 Corinthians 3," in *Theology and Ethics in Paul and His Interpreters: Essays in Honor of Victor Paul Furnish*, ed. E. H. Lovering, Jr., and J. L. Sumney (Nashville: Abingdon, 1996) 101-13.

REFLECTIONS

1. Disputes, differences of opinions among believers and in a church are not surprising; the way conflicts are resolved says a great deal about the maturity of the believers involved, about the health of a community of believers, about its understanding of itself and its obligations to others, and about its perception of its ultimate destiny and function in God's grand design. Believers are themselves appropriately different from one another (Paul will write about that in detail in chap. 12), so it is entirely to be expected that they will differ in their opinions about things, in their reckoning as to what is important, and in their choices of action or non-action. Fine, but love calls for them to live with one another in a respectful and caring way even when they differ. Believers should discuss with one another how they can achieve the proper respect and care when they do find themselves in a point of difference about belief or practice. Couples and good friends surely have to do this as well.

2. Paul discusses two types of judging in 6:1-8, and both kinds find modern expression. The one judgment is apocalyptic, cosmic, and final and occurs only at the end of the ages when believers can anticipate that they will form a subcourt under God. The other judgment is contingent and corrective. When someone today "damns" another person, we are right to object to the presumption, not only because it arrogates God's prerogative but also because it improperly absolves one from caring. Caring for others is not an option; it is an obligation. Paul assumes a connection between these two judgments: Those who will ultimately be qualified to serve in the cosmic tribunal should surely be able, already in the here and now, to handle what has been translated as "ordinary matters." Both the NIV and the NRSV translate *biōtika* as "trivial cases," which is acceptable insofar as it grasps Paul's intended contrast that has been noted here. But the translation belittles the reality that believers and churches will have differences of opinion, and sometimes quite strong ones, about "ordinary matters"—and perhaps even regarding weighty ordinary matters—that need to be resolved amicably and fairly, which Paul seems to understand.

3. "To have lawsuits with one another is an utter loss for you; why not rather be wronged?" (6:7). Is this Pauline position prescriptive or is it hyperbole? Supporting a Pauline overstatement designed to shock the readers are the following: the intense irony of 6:2-6 and Paul's tendency to overstatement as a means of emphasizing a point (cf. 8:13, where Paul's assertion suggests that he is prepared to become a vegetarian). If one chooses to take it as prescriptive, then one has consequent problems that call for resolution: First, is every Pauline prescription that was made for a particular congregation equally applicable to all other believers and all other congregations across all time? Second, in a litigious culture such as ours, how are believers to avoid being dupes—or, to put it in terms of Jesus' call, how are believers to be as innocent as doves and as wise as serpents (Matt 10:16)?

In either case, it may be helpful to realize that there are striking differences between Pauline churches and the social setting of most modern Christians. Paul's churches were relatively small in number; all of the believers could meet in a patron's home for worship; therefore, they all knew each other and presumably were in frequent contact with one another. In modern churches, the members often do not know one another and sometimes never share the same space with others except at worship. Further, our social structures are so much more complex that one person's involvement in business, for example, may raise liabilities about which that individual may not even be aware.

If we were to take 6:7 as prescriptive, how would we apply it in our modern settings? Clearly, Paul thought conflicts between believers ought to be resolved short of court proceedings, and that is surely still a good guideline for modern believers wherever possible. In fact, churches might do well to set up boards to assist in conflict resolution and thereby use some of the skills that members of the congregation may have, an idea certainly appropriate to Paul (6:5). Churches should aim to minimize the harm to all parties of disputes while maximizing justice. A verse such as the one before us should not be allowed to function in such a way as to ensure injustice; that would be an ultimate irony.

4. Moral reasoning from "what we know" is a vital pattern for Paul and could just as well be so for modern Christians. When faced with a moral choice or dilemma, Paul regularly inquires what believers know and reasons from what is known to an application concerning the issue at hand. For example, how does Paul come to the conclusion that when invited to an unbeliever's home for dinner, you are free to eat whatever is served? He knows his scriptures and remembers that we know "the earth is the Lord's and everything in it" (1 Cor 10:24, quoting Ps 24:1). To take another example, if we know that to love is not an option but an obligation, then we start the deliberation of our moral choices not by deciding whether to love a certain person; rather, we move to weigh how we might express love to this individual.

5. Vice lists, another example of what believers know, function to demarcate behavior that community members agree is beyond the pale. Vice lists serve to define the borders and to mark what believers assiduously must avoid in their comportment. Vice lists are a common feature in Paul's letters (Rom 1:29-32; 13:13-14; 2 Cor 12:20-21; Gal 5:19-21). A glance at the different lists shows that the terms constituting them are not consistent; the contents of the lists seem somewhat tailored toward the circumstances the given letter is addressing. In any case, the lists are not exhaustive but illustrative and are flexible as to content. In no instance is a vice labeled a sin (an important consideration in any case, but perhaps especially in our own time in dealing with matters such as Reflection 6, below, treats). Paul appears to think of sin as a power that bids to take over one's life. He refers to sins in the plural (as if they might be listed) only in materials he takes over from traditional materials that he recites.

It might be a very informative process for a modern church to start with all of Paul's virtue and vice lists and have a lengthy deliberation about what that church would establish for its own vice list; then the congregation—perhaps by highlighting some and by adding new ones—would have ownership of its own self-examination of its borders and, therefore, of its own sense of definition. A modern church could begin with 6:9-11 because there Paul has laid out both sides of the matter: (1) He has offered a vice list that serves to mark off the borders of the community by noting unacceptable behavior (6:9-10), and (2) he has identified, by a series of claims, the positive core of their identity (6:11), of who they have become in the name of Christ and in the Spirit.

6. In modern times two terms from the vice list in 6:9-10 have provoked especial interest. They are μαλακοί (*malakoi*; NIV and NRSV, "male prostitutes") and ἀρσενοκοῖται (*arsenokoitai*; NIV, "homosexual offenders"; NRSV, "sodomites," 6:9). The first term is used, when describing cloth, to mean "soft," but in its more general use it was pejoratively used in the contemporary culture to describe a man who was not adequately "manly" (cf. 16:13); in the cases of homosexual relations, it was used to describe the more passive one. Obviously, it would have been applied to the young boy involved with an older man. The second term was applied to men who engaged in pederasty or were sodomites; accordingly, the term was used to describe the more active male.[80]

If one knows nothing of the cultural practices and prejudices of Paul's time, one can more easily take these ancient terms from that context and make of them what one wishes. In Greek and Roman times, what we would call heterosexual married

80. BDAG 488, 109.

males (and one can suppose the same was true for their female counterparts) might frequently keep a boy (or in the case of wives, a girl) for their pleasure. Sometimes the kept person was a slave, who by definition would have no choice, but there were also boys who solicited sex with elders for pay. For the most part these relationships caught no special attention. Around Paul's time, however, certain prominent moralists had begun to note the more extreme, exploitative cases and to object to them.[81] All of those instances consider abuses; none of those texts concerns itself with relationships in which there is not exploitation.

Clearly, Paul thinks *porneia*, sexual immorality, and his cover-all term for immorality in general, is a characteristic of those outsiders to the faith, of gentiles who have not been converted to the faith (cf. 5:1). From his letters we can tell that Paul was a careful observer of the lives that believers and unbelievers lived. His listing of these two terms in this vice list is probably best understood as part of his general critique of the way non-believers behave. Those two terms cannot be tied to anything else in 1 Corinthians that Paul finds wrong with the Corinthians.[82]

81. See Seneca "On Master and Slave" 7; Plutarch "Dialogue on Love" 751-52; Dio Chrysostom "Envy" 77/78.36-37, and "The Hunter" 151-52, a passage that, like Rom 1:27, decries the way some men have turned away from more socially common sexual patterns in search of increased excitement.

82. Though it is a surprisingly old publication now, Victor P. Furnish's "Homosexuality," in his *The Moral Teaching of Paul: Selected Issues* (Nashville: Abingdon, 1979) 52-82, is still one of the most balanced, thoughtful treatments of the issue.

1 CORINTHIANS 6:12-20, SUMMING UP AND LOOKING AHEAD

COMMENTARY

These verses, the first of two such passages in the letter, function as a hinge, pulling together several points and themes that have preceded and opening out to matters yet to be discussed in detail. This passage, like its parallel text in 10:23–11:1, functions as a staging point, where certain resources previously garnered are marshaled and inventoried in part though not simply to determine where author and readers are, but also to set the context for what follows. Up to this point Paul has dealt with specific actions of the Corinthians—namely, their tolerating the immorality of the man living with his stepmother, and their settling disputes in civil courts, before unbelievers.

Now, for the first time, Paul characterizes and casts up a reflection of their self-estimation: "All things are permissible for me!" (6:12). We cannot be sure what role Paul has had in formulating this maxim, but in its present form, it is probably creditable to the Corinthians. Supporting the contention that some Corinthians formulated the maxim is Paul's twice qualifying the maxim (6:12) and the

individualistic cast of it ("for me"; note that when Paul next rehearses this maxim of theirs, he drops the "for me," 10:23).

Paul has a fondness for maxims and so do the Corinthians (e.g., 8:1, 4); indeed, maxims are a characteristic of Greco-Roman education and culture.[83] No doubt Paul's heavy employment of maxims in 1 Corinthians reflects the society's use of them in moral deliberation and in the education of children. In the Greco-Roman context, maxims (γνῶμαι *gnōmai*; Latin, *sententiae*) were considered epitomes of truth, of commonly shared convictions or perceptions. So they typically function as a "given" from which one argues or builds a case. Also typically, therefore, one does not refute a maxim; one may qualify it or place another maxim over against it for consideration or as a qualification of the first one.

In 6:12 Paul does not reject the Corinthians' maxim. First, he qualifies it with two

83. Rollin Ramsaran, *Liberating Words: Paul's Use of Rhetorical Maxims in 1 Corinthians 1–10* (Valley Forge, Pa.: Trinity, 1996) 5-21.

additions: "but not all things are helpful" and "but I will not be mastered by anything" (6:12). Second, he lodges another maxim, whether of his own composition or not we cannot be sure, alongside theirs—"Food is for the stomach, and the stomach for food"— and, with his forceful declaration that "God will wipe out the one and the other" (6:13), he attempts a bit of perspective-keeping. In effect, he compels the readers to confront the question "Then what really matters?"

What could the Corinthian maxim—"All things are permissible for me" (6:12)—mean, and how could they, as persons standing in the Pauline tradition, have come to embrace or formulate it? Several observations are pertinent. (1) Paul never rejects the maxim (cf. 10:23 where it reappears); he does qualify it in several ways, and when he repeats it (twice) in 10:23 he modifies it by dropping the individualizing "for me," which was surely a part of their formulation of it. From this one must conclude that Paul does not take the maxim as fundamentally alien to his gospel. (2) The NRSV's translation of ἔξεστιν (*exestin*) as "lawful" is misleading; the maxim's contention has nothing to do with the law, but with what is permissible, allowable, or authorized for a believer. (3) We can see elsewhere in Paul's letters that a believer's obligation is to love (Rom 13:8), to put one's faith, that is one's right relation to God, into expression via love (Gal 5:6). And, depending on one's measure of faith, one can make moral decisions within a wider scope if one's faith is stronger or within a narrower scope is one's faith is weaker; when doubts or waverings enter the picture, then one should not undertake the action in question (Rom 14:23).[84]

In the light of these considerations, we can imagine how some Corinthians have understood this maxim to capture their sense of freedom in Christ. First, one like the fellow who has his father's wife (5:1ff.) might in fact misjudge the strength of his faith and think that there are no moral constraints upon him, or at least that the morality of his sleeping with his stepmother is not a problem for his faith. Second, and this is even more likely, some could interpret the maxim in line with Augustine's later expression of the same

sort: "Love and do what thou wilt."[85] In that statement, those who truly and properly love God will and can do as they please because they would never choose to do anything that would prove contrary to their love of God. In a similar way, Paul's Corinthian followers could think themselves thoroughly in line with Paul's teaching when they embraced the maxim in 6:12 and 10:23 as affirming a basic truth about moral reasoning in Christ: "all things [that my relationship to God allows] are permissible for me," or perhaps to take the maxim in a similar way, "all things [that truly matter] are permissible for me." "All [appropriate, fitting] things are permissible for me."

Verses 12-20 are a dense, closely ordered passage that expects some work from its auditors. Rhetorically, it is what was called "figured speech," a type of rhetoric in which rhetorical figures or tropes carry the message like pearls arranged on a string. In order to understand it, we who are not accustomed to figured speech must identify the figures and show how they work. In Paul's time figured speech was much valued and was considered powerful because it invited the hearers or readers to assess the relationship between the different figures and to make self-application of what was heard or read. By employing this kind of address, Paul was perfectly within the normal expectations of his hearers. No signals had to be made; one simply embarked upon figured speech and expected the auditors to make not only the connections between the elements but also the application to themselves. Rhetorical handbooks are regularly insistent that the most effective rhetoric is that which minimizes the rhetor's making of application and maximizes the auditor's self-application.[86]

Let us first lay out the anatomy of 6:12-20:

1. Maxim 1 (twice stated; reflecting the attitude of some of the readers) with Pauline qualifiers (6:12; maxim 1 will be repeated twice in 10:23).

---

84. Sampley, *Walking Between the Times,* 57-60.

85. Augustine, *Tractate on the Epistle of St. John,* trans. H. Browne, rev. and ed. J. H. Myers, in *A Select Library of the Nicene and Post-Nicene Fathers of the Christian Church* (Grand Rapids: Eerdmans, 1956) 7.8.

86. Quintilian *Institutio Oratoria* 9.2.71, LCL, recognizes that "the judge [or any hearer] will be led to . . . believe in that which he thinks he has found out for himself."

---

2. Maxim 2 (for perspective-keeping) with a Pauline qualifier (6:13*a-b*).

3. Maxim 3 (6:13*c*; with an embedded *correctio* [structure: A, not B, but A] mentioning *porneia*, linking it back to the previous discussions of immorality and ahead to 6:18 and 7:2) with a Pauline qualifier (6:14).

4. Maxim 3 opens a structure that is closed several verses later by a refinement (structure: A B, followed by a newly cast A´ B´) whose elements encapsulate, in the intervening space, what we might call "the heart of the matter":

   A: "The body is for the Lord" (6:13*c*)
      B: "God raised the Lord and will raise you" (6:14)
   A´: "You are not your own" (6:19*b*)
      B´: "You were bought with a price" (6:20*a*)

5. "The heart of the matter" (6:15-19*a*), structured around three rhetorical questions in the form of "You do know, don't you . . . ?" which signal that what is discussed in these verses is a "back-to-basics" primer regarding what the Corinthians most certainly should know and should be able to apply to their circumstances that Paul is addressing.

6. Closing injunction (6:20*b*, capping not only 6:12ff. but also chaps. 5–6).

Now that we have its structure laid bare, it is possible to unpack how 6:12-20 functions. By quoting maxim 1, their own saying, Paul establishes common ground with the Corinthians: "All things are permissible for me" (6:12). His attached qualifiers do not question their maxim's general claim but place alongside it another consideration—"not all things are helpful" (to be repeated in 10:23)—and allow Paul to make a personal distinction, "but I will not be mastered by anything" (6:12). What is truly "helpful" is not treated here but will be elaborated later in the letter. Immediately, however, Paul telegraphs the notion that will be developed later—namely, that while mastery by things is ruled out, mastery by the Lord is central to the life of faith (6:20).

Without introduction, maxim 2—"Food is for the stomach and the stomach is for food"—is declared (6:13); the reader is implicitly asked to make some connection of maxim 2 with maxim 1. For the person who would affirm the "no-holds-barred" sentiment of maxim 1, the second maxim would follow with an "of course" certainty: "Surely, I know what the stomach and food are made for!" Somewhat shocking, however, would be the Pauline qualifier: "And God will wipe out both the one and the other" (6:13*b*). God has power over all things (cf. 3:21-23); stomachs and the food they crave are not of enduring value (this is the first reference to eating, which will become the leitmotif of chaps. 8–11).

Again with no introduction, maxim 3 appears. It opens with a disclaimer and then is developed positively: "The body is not for immorality πορνεία [*porneia*] but for the Lord, and the Lord for the body" (6:13*c*).[87] By now the pattern is established. The reader should expect a Pauline qualifier, and there is one: "But God raised the Lord and will raise you through his power" (6:14). What is the reader to make of the dissonance in the claims that God will destroy food and stomach but will raise believers just as he raised the Lord? It is as if two levels of consideration vie with one another. What is important in life? Not food and the stomach. Once again, then what is important? Answer: the close connection between the "body" and its Lord, the Lord whom God has raised from the dead and with whom believers have such an intimate bond. As Paul refines his statement of the affiliation of believers and their Lord (6:20), they are like slaves who have been purchased by a new owner and they are therefore not their own (6:19).

Maxim 3, with its bold claim that "the body is for the Lord and the Lord for the body" (6:13*c*), introduces a major theme of 1 Corinthians, "body" (σῶμα *sōma*) occurs 30 times after these verses; note its appearance already in 5:3). "Body" is not a new concept to the Corinthians: Paul clearly assumes that they know how he uses the term: "You

---

87. The NRSV's inconsistent translation of *porneia* prevents English readers from following Paul's use of the term (cf. 5:1; 6:13, 18; 7:2), and the NRSV's switch to "fornication" for the middle two instances, though it seems to fit the immediate context, narrows Paul's effort to illustrate a broader concern with *porneia* than simply "fornication."

do know, don't you, that your bodies are members of Christ?" (6:15). Modern readers can understand Paul's use of the term *sōma* very readily when they see it used in Rom 12:1: "I appeal to you, therefore, brothers, through the mercies of God, to present your bodies as a living sacrifice, holy and pleasing to God." Many translations rightly render it "present your selves" because for Paul *sōma* is a technical term that refers to one's whole self. Modern people tend to think of "having" a body; Paul thinks of people as being "bodies." *Sōma*, for Paul, stands for one's whole self. Accordingly, maxim 3, in light of its refinement in 6:19-20, really asserts: You, the you who in the Lord do not even own yourself (cf. Gal 2:20), are for the Lord and the Lord is for you. Because believers do not own themselves and are therefore in service of the one who owns them, they must live in a way appropriate to Christ, who became their new owner. The bond between the baptisands and their Lord could not be closer: "The body is for the Lord and the Lord for the body" (6:13c).

Believers belong to the Lord, not to *porneia*, the two mutually exclusive options: "You do know, don't you, that" believers are members of Christ, not members of a prostitute (πόρνη *pornē*, a paranomasia, or wordplay, from the term *porneia*, which one sees just ahead in 6:18). The stark two-way alternatives that structured the opening four chapters of this letter continue in force here. The former style of life and its previously defining relationships have been jettisoned. As Paul has been saying in chaps. 5 and 6, the old patterns and former allegiances cannot be mixed into the new life in Christ.

Paul enlists a powerful metaphor to elaborate the relationship of believers, represented as bodies, to Christ: entering into a relationship with Christ or with a prostitute. "You do know, don't you, that the one who joins himself to a prostitute is one body with her?" (6:16). Paul's fertile mind jumps from the "joining oneself" to Gen 2:24, the text from Israel's scriptures used to authenticate marriage: "A man shall leave his father and mother and join himself to his wife, and the two shall become one flesh" though he quotes only a part of the verse (6:16). The fact that he can switch from "one body" to "one flesh"

suggests that the emphasis is on the oneness, the uniting. This suggestion is reinforced when Paul next develops the same thought regarding "one spirit": "The one who joins himself to the Lord is one spirit with him" (6:17). In vv. 16 and 18 Paul has laid out the two alternatives: One either joins himself to a prostitute (*pornē*; think *porneia*) or one joins himself to the Lord. Because Christians are by definition those who are joined to the Lord, Paul concludes pithily: "[Keep on] flee[ing] *porneia*" (6:18a; cf. 10:14). So Paul likens the relationship of believers to Christ as the proper marriage and the turning to a prostitute (*pornē; porneia*) as harlotry (cf. Jeremiah 2–3; Hosea 2; cf. 2 Cor 11:2). Paul's bottom-line recommendation is unequivocal, clearly stated, and succinct: "Flee *porneia*" (6:18a). Nothing else can proceed until the Corinthians realize that they must at all costs steer clear of any *porneia* contamination.

"The heart of the matter" (6:15-19a). Paul's delineation of "the heart of the matter" is structured around three questions, each of which expects a yes answer, and each of which therefore shows Paul affirming something he expects the Corinthians to understand and also to affirm. All three questions, as distinct as they are, focus on the same topic, "belonging." The first—"You do know, don't you, that your bodies are members of Christ?" (6:15)—affirms that believers as bodies, as whole persons, belong in a special way to Christ—namely, as members of Christ, a metaphor that will be elaborated in much detail in chap. 12. Paul expects the Corinthian auditors to respond to the question, in agreement with him.

The second question—"You do know, don't you, that the one who cleaves to a prostitute is one body with her?" (6:16)—employs a mundane counterpoint but still presses the issue of belonging to another, declaring that the one who clings closely to a prostitute becomes one body, one flesh, with the prostitute. Paul expects the Corinthian auditors to accept that as given. One need not read this as indicating that the Corinthian church is having a problem with believers consorting with prostitutes. Rather, Paul takes something that he can assume every person knows as a reality in Greco-Roman cities—namely, that persons who go to a prostitute become one flesh with that person and therefore belong to the prostitute in a certain and defining sense.

The third question—"You do know, don't you, that your body is the temple of the Holy Spirit?" (6:19)—really refines the first two: The belonging that is at the heart of the issue is a very special one in which the believers are so closely bonded to Christ as to become members of Christ (of Christ's body as 12:12ff. will elaborate it). Only superficially is it like clinging to a prostitute and thus making the two one. The relationship of the believers to Christ, however, is at once more intimate and more profound: intimate because the bond is so strong, so powerful; profound because "the two are" not just "one flesh" but because the "body" has become the residence, indeed the temple, of the Holy Spirit. The Holy Spirit resides in the believers in such a way that their bodies, their very selves, have been transformed into a shrine dedicated to God, who gave them the Holy Spirit and thereby constituted them a temple (cf. 3:16-17). So this two-chapter section opens with what wrongly dwells, *porneia* (5:1), in the Corinthian believers and closes by affirming that it is the Holy Spirit who properly dwells there (6:19-20). And in the intervening verses the same point is considered by asking to whom one belongs. To whom one belongs and who or what dwells in one are the same question, simply addressed in different terms.

The next two maxims (maxim 4, 6:18*b*, and maxim 5, 6:18*c*) have proved difficult for modern interpreters.[88] The sweeping character of the claims in maxim 4, such as "every other sin" being "outside the body," raises confusion as to what is meant: Does the "every other sin," for example, include the immediately mentioned *porneia*? And how does maxim 4 fit with maxim 5, which follows and affirms that sin is indeed related to one's own body?

Maxim 4—"Every sin a person does is outside his body" (6:18*b*)—is widely recognized as being of Corinthian origin[89] and as expressing the view of some in Corinth that, apart from *porneia*, every other sin is one that is "outside the body"—that is, no other sin is so directly related to the body

as *porneia*, which always has some sense of sexual immorality. The NIV translation in fact endorses that understanding of maxim 4 by taking what would otherwise be translated as "all sin" (πᾶν ἁμάρτημα *pan hamartēma*), adding the word "other" and taking the singular noun as plural, "sins." In that way the NIV attempts to minimize the problem with which the interpreter is otherwise faced.

Maxim 5—"The immoral person sins against his own body" (6:18*c*)—is sometimes taken as Paul's critique of maxim 4, lying alongside their maxim as it does.[90] Commending such an interpretation is the strong link in maxim 5 between sin and body, which could be argued as Pauline, but it encounters the difficulty that it privatizes sin, a notion that is difficult to find in Paul's letters.

Here, however, I suggest a different interpretation of these two maxims and of their function. Both 6:18*b* and 6:18*c* are Corinthian maxims that reflect the Corinthian divisiveness even in understanding sin. Some at Corinth say in maxim 4—"All sin which a person does is outside the body"—that sin has no effect upon the body (remember: body can be understood as the self). Their argument goes as follows: If sin does not affect the body, that very body that is the Lord's, then whatever sin one does has no bearing on the body's commitment to the Lord.

Others at Corinth say in maxim 5—"The immoral man sins against his own body" (6:18*c* RSV)—implying that an individual's sin, which these among the Corinthians indeed understand to be against his own body or self, is that person's problem and is not a concern for the community. Both of these interpretations help account for the community's not being aggrieved by the behavior of the man who is sleeping with his stepmother (5:2). Advocates of maxim 4 are convinced that "sin" is of no consequence for the body or for the body's fate; such persons could believe themselves, that is their bodies, delivered beyond what they could construe as extraneous calculations regarding conduct. Champions of maxim 5 could equally well not concern themselves with the man's behavior, but for very different reasons: They could hold that his sin is against

88. Fee, *The First Epistle to the Corinthians*, 261-63, summarizes previous efforts clearly.

89. J. Murphy-O'Connor, "Corinthian Slogans in 1 Cor 6:12-20," *CBQ* 40 (1978) 391-93.

90. See examples of such in Fee, *The First Epistle to the Corinthians*, 261n. 57.

"his own body" only and does not bear upon them in any way; advocates of maxim 5 deny that an individual's sin contaminates or stains other believers. Already in chaps. 5 and 6 Paul has disagreed with both interpretations, and in 6:19, his third "You do know, don't you?" statement in 6:15-19, he tells them in back-to-basics claims just why he stands for something other than what either maxim 4 or maxim 5 reflects.

"You do know, don't you, that your body is the temple of the Holy Spirit, which you have from God, and you are not your own; you were bought with a price?" (6:19-20*a*). This passage is a foundational, definitional declaration of who believers are; it gathers together so much of what he has written to them earlier in the letter and lays the ground for all that he will write to them subsequently. The claim that believers are God's temple in which the Spirit dwells is a reprise of the assertions of 3:16-17, this time linked to "your body" and thereby undercutting the assumptions within both maxim 4 and maxim 5. Likewise, Paul's declaration that they are not their own but have been bought—Paul's analogy is the slave market in the agora or forum—by a new master (6:20, to be reprised in 7:23). In saying that the Corinthians have been "bought with a price" (6:20), Paul has no interest in answering any question as to whom the payment was made. This is not what later came to be called ransom christology in which Christ paid a price with his life so that believers could be free. Paul and his readers would have recognized that this is terminology of the slave market where slaves were regularly traded and, Paul's point, ended up with different lords or masters. Paul's concern is simply and directly to declare that the Corinthians have become subject to—that is, they belong to—a new Lord: Jesus Christ. The Corinthian believers are set apart ("holy"; 3:17) for the one who owns them and whose Spirit dwells in them. Proper "temple maintenance" is therefore a critical obligation of believers, not an option, and much less of no concern to the individual (as in maxim 4) or to the community (as in maxim 5).

Three distinct metaphors coalesce to make the same point: Proper cleaving to the Lord rules out any and all rival cleavings (whether to a prostitute [*pornē*] or to *porneia*); proper

obedience of the slaves to the Lord who owns them obviates all other potential allegiance to other lords; and temple maintenance proper to the Spirit who resides in the temple is obligatory.

Paul frames their maxims with his correctives. A prohibiting command—"Flee *porneia*" (6:18*a*)—introduces the Corinthian maxims, and directly following them (6:19-20) is a reaffirmation of the most important consideration the Corinthian auditors ought to know and understand, and of which Paul has already reminded them earlier—namely, that their body is the temple where the Holy Spirit has chosen to reside (3:16-17). Fleeing the *porneia* (which resides where the Holy Spirit should; 5:1), which would absolutely destroy the holiness appropriate to the Spirit's temple, therefore, is not simply an option; it is a necessity. Like an exclusive sexual commitment, holiness as a sanctum for the resident Holy Spirit requires scrupulous fidelity and stewardship of the self as body properly set aside for the Spirit.

From Paul's reference to his previous letter about *porneia* (5:9) and his clear indication that the Corinthians were confused by it, to Paul's current insistence that the body is special to the Lord and can allow of absolutely no contact with *porneia*, we can see that Paul thinks that the Corinthians themselves continue to be confused and divided regarding how they understand sin and *porneia*, Paul's catchall term for wrongful living.

Believers are one body with the Lord (6:13); they are one spirit with the Lord (6:17); and the Gen 2:24 quotation suggests that they are one flesh as well. Paul goes out of his way to affirm as fully and completely as possible the believers' belonging to Christ as an exclusive and all-embracing identity. It follows as certainly that sin and *porneia* are totally excluded (6:13); their presence cannot be countenanced in any way, by any construal. Belonging to the Lord allows no rival claim, permits no association whatsoever with sin or *porneia*. Once again, Paul capitalizes on his carefully drawn two-way tradition that he laid out so insistently in the opening chapters of this letter.

Paul's "previous letter" (5:9-10) about avoiding immoral persons (πόρνοι *pornoi*) caused confusion among believers in Corinth.

Whether the Corinthians generalize to "all sin" (6:18*b*) or focus on *porneia* (6:18*c*), Paul's earlier letter had left the Corinthians divided concerning what to make of sin in general and *porneia* in particular.

What are believers to do, then? Paul's defining answer concludes this passage and, indeed, brings to a head the concerns of chaps. 5 and 6, and opens out to a consideration of the issues they have raised with Paul in their letter to him: "Therefore, glorify God in your body" (6:20*b*), clearly referring to each one's body, but perhaps also referring to the Corinthians collectively as a body, as the collective body of Christ, in which glorification of God, not backbiting and slander, should be the order of the day.

Chapters 5–6 are a study in definition. There Paul lays down the defining claim for the believers: They are those who were set apart for God, who were "bought for a price," who do not belong to themselves but to their (new) Lord, who will ultimately share with their Lord in resurrection, and whose bodies, their very selves, are members of Christ and the temple in which the Holy Spirit dwells. As persons who have nothing that was not given to them as a gift by God and therefore who are indistinguishable the one from another (4:7), believers should not form cliques as if their baseline stories are not the same but should instead "glorify God in your body" (6:20).

By noting two incidents that have come to his attention, Paul sharpens the community definition in the direction of praxis and comportment. With reference to the *porneia* of the man who "has his father's wife," Paul reflects on community borders—namely, what separates and distinguishes life in the community from that out in the world, and identifies comportment that should not be allowed inside the community. With his mention of some believers' taking others to civil courts to adjudicate disputes, he identifies what should properly stay inside the community and be resolved there. So, whether he looks to distinguish what really should be outside the community, or whether he tries to establish what should remain within and characterize the community, he is in both cases defining Christian community and identifying proper conduct appropriate to the life of faith. His message can be identified in one negative and one positive directive: "Flee *porneia*" and "Glorify God in your body." To avoid *porneia* is requisite to glorifying God in the body; glorifying God in the body necessitates fleeing *porneia*. Merely to avoid the latter does not assure the former, but simply gives proper occasion for the glorification of God to flourish when believers properly pursue it.

How is God glorified in the body? The rest of the letter is an elaboration on that notion and a demonstration of it. As will become evident, glorifying God "in your body" will at once mean (1) that individuals exercise stewardship of their own bodies, their very selves, and (2) that collectively the believers live lovingly and in an edifying fashion with each other as members of the one body that is Christ's.

REFLECTIONS

1. "The body is not for *porneia* but for the Lord and the Lord for the body" (6:13). Without using the term, this is holiness talk. To be set apart for something or for someone is the root meaning of holiness. Today we tend to think of "having a body"; we might even find ourselves talking about "our bodies" as if they were another one of our possessions. For Paul, humans do not have bodies; they are bodies. *Sōma* means body in the sense of one's self—that is, who you are. It was later Christianity, after Paul and no longer dependent upon him, that fell to thinking of human beings as composed of body and some more valuable inner spark that might be termed "soul" or "spirit." Paul's Jewishness comes through handsomely in his understanding of body as who a person is; therefore, it is Paul who, when he wants to talk about God's enduring commitment to individuals, speaks of the phrase that impacted our creeds, "resurrection of the body." Paul's is a lofty and holistic view of the self, lofty because one's present self, as is, is loved and cherished by God and will be preserved by God, and holistic because Paul thinks of the human as a whole integrated being who is not only part of the "new creation" but also the object of God's redeeming love. So redemption is not the salvaging of some inner, perhaps purer essence of the individual; it is the saving of the whole being. *Sōma* is not simply flesh for Paul; one is *sōma*. Paul's profound notion of body as self, as who you are, raises issues for our understanding of how we treat our bodies, that is for how we treat ourselves. Smoking and drugs, like the lack of exercise, are abuses not only of this container that we live in but of our very selves, the selves that God has made us to be.

2. Intimacy with the Lord. Because life in Christ is somatic, Paul daringly writes, as did Hosea 1–3 and Ezekiel 16, of one's relation to one's Lord as like a marriage and contrasts it with a liaison with a prostitute (6:15). If our relationship to Christ is like marriage then we have two distinct angles from which to view the issue. One is to look at our marriages. If they are not in some special way a reflection of what should be an ideal relation with Christ, then it is time to work on our marriages. If our marriage is in better shape than our relation to Christ, then we should be working to improve our relation to Christ. And what can be said about marriages can be extended to other relationships by analogy. In short, how we are with the Lord should find correspondences in the other relationships of our lives.

3. In our individualistic society and culture, Paul's claim that "you are not your own" (6:19) will seem decidedly alien. Are we not in charge of our own lives? Can we not do as we see fit? Our own self-control is a fiction that we struggle to maintain. For Paul, and indeed for everyone in his time, nobody was without a master, a lord to whom they were in some measure responsible. Their culture was in this way a vertical one; even Marcus Aurelius, the emperor, mused about everyone being ultimately derived from and dependent upon deity.[91] Some modern people, giving lip service to equality, find a horizontal image preferable; but in reality modern culture is stratified—and that not just economically—much more severely than we sometimes may want to acknowledge.

Paul's anthropology, his understanding of human nature, emerges here: All people are dependent on some being or some thing beyond themselves to give them meaning and significance (cf. Rom 14:7). So for Paul the issue is not whether one has a lord or not; one simply will have some lord. At stake is what lord one will have. Paul has taken as his model the contemporary practice of buying and selling slaves in the agora (meeting place or marketplace): "you were bought" (ἀγοράζω *agorazō*, 6:20). And, because slaves were supposed to increase their owners' honor, to make their owners look good, Paul transposes the slave's need to honor the owner into his own theological concepts and tells the Corinthians how to honor their new owner: "glorify God in your body" (6:20). In Paul's categories, the chief competing lords are sin, a power that takes over one's life and governs it (and a power that Paul thinks was the former lord of all believers; cf. Rom 3:23), or Christ, whose lordship grants perfect freedom.

One caution: "You are not your own" should not be mistaken to suggest that believers have no responsibility for their actions. In the stratified culture of Paul's time, a slave would know one's master deserved honor, and though slaves were not at their own disposal, they were certainly expected to do everything they could to bring honor to their lord. Paul thinks believers should relate in just such a fashion to Christ as their Lord, seeking his honor in all that they do. Modern Christians, though not likely to think of ourselves as slaves, might still weigh whether a contemplated action might bring honor to our Lord.

---

91. Marcus Aurelius, *Meditations*, 12.26, LCL: "Nothing is a man's very own, but that his babe, his body, his very soul came forth from Him."

1 CORINTHIANS 7:1-40

PAUL'S RESPONSE TO QUESTIONS ABOUT RELATIONS IN SOCIOSEXUAL GROUPS

OVERVIEW

A part from 1 Corinthians, we have no indication in the Pauline corpus that one of Paul's congregations wrote him a letter, though they may have. Some Corinthians, however, have written to Paul (7:1), apparently seeking his guidance and clarification on a range of issues (possibly including the items mentioned in 7:25; 8:1; 12:1; 16:1; cf. 16:12).

By his own arrangement of the topics and material in this letter, Paul has delayed a treatment of the Corinthians' concerns until he has two building blocks in place. The first (chaps. 1–4), by its back-to-basics push, regrounds the Corinthians in the core of the gospel, reminds them of who they are in relation to that gospel and to the world, and calls them to end their fractiousness and, following the example of their apostle, reclaim their unity around the cross. Throughout that first section Paul, their caring father in the gospel, reminds them that they are called, set aside for God in holiness and, in his protracted example of himself and Apollos, exemplifies the proper unity that should prevail among believers, a unity that fully shares the gospel and labors for it, but a unity that also honors the diversity of the participants.

The other building block is chaps. 5–6. It, too, is a lesson in fundamentals, rehearsing as it does the nature of the community, identifying how believers differ from the world and worldly practices, and attempting to clarify what is appropriately treated within the community and what should be left outside it. The unit formed by these two chapters develops a theme already laid down in the first four chapters, namely that people who live by

the gospel walk in a way that is distinct from the world. The believers, as God's children, as God's farm, as God's temple, must make their moral decisions and behave in a way that honors and glorifies the one to whom they belong. The world and its patterns, all of which are entirely familiar to Paul's readers, have leached into the community's internal transactions, and believers have looked to external patterns and practices for negotiating their differences. Paul has cleverly used two related Corinthian situations (the immoral man, chap. 5, and civil court cases, chap. 6) to sharpen their understanding not only of how differently from the world they are to behave but also of how they are to relate to one another as brothers and sisters in Christ.

The starkness of Paul's depictions of the rival two-way traditions in chaps. 1–4—people travel either one way or the other—provides the background for the reflection in chaps. 5–6 of the way the community of faith differs from the world outside. Paul uses the via negativa descriptions—which are frequently cast as depictions of how the world operates—to identify where believers should not look for establishment of their values or for their clues of what is important. To be sure, in its most radical either/or construction, which Paul has featured in the opening six chapters of this letter, to take life's cues not from God, not from the gospel but from the world is properly called "idolatry," a notion that is reflected three times in the vice lists of chaps. 5 and 6 (5:10, 11; 6:9), reappears explicitly in 10:14, and is at issue throughout. Paul's gospel has a strong countercultural critique at its heart, as may be seen in the opening chapters' regular, repeated insistence that there are (only) two ways, one belonging to the gospel and the other belonging to the world. Having carefully established his own context for treating the problems that they have raised in their letter, Paul now turns to their concerns.

From the items in the Corinthians' letter to him, Paul chooses to deal first with marriage and what we modern people might call sexuality. Some Corinthians are confused about how to live the life of faith in the midst of the world, just the sorts of issues that Paul has already been dealing with in the letter so far. From the lengthy treatment of marriage and sexuality issues in chap. 7, we can surmise that the Corinthians are divided in their understandings of how the life of faith bears on sexual matters, and we have every reason to suppose that Paul's previous letter, which addressed how to maintain proper holiness and avoid contamination, is again a part of the Corinthians' deliberations. Some Corinthians seem to have called for sexual abstinence as the proper means of maintaining purity before God; others seem not to share that conviction, perhaps because they may be experiencing difficulty in maintaining abstinence. Their confusion is probably, in part, a direct result of Paul's earlier letter (5:9) in which he had warned them not to mingle or associate, not even to eat, with πόρνοι *pornoi*, "immoral persons," if they are named "brother or sister"—that is, if they are fellow believers (5:9, 11).

Across chapter 7 we see that some Corinthians have taken Paul's counsel to avoid πορνεία *porneia* to extremes, and they have wondered about the purity of their associations, even in marriage. This misapplication of Paul's earlier letter may have been compounded by their noting Paul's celibacy (7:7) and taking it as normative for all believers; Paul's free and frequent offering of himself as an exemplar[92] could easily have contributed to this. So in Corinth some married persons had come to wonder about the propriety of their sexuality (7:5), some marrieds and singles about whether even marriage was appropriate (7:10-11, 28), and some of those married to unbelievers about whether

divorce might not be preferred as a means of maintaining holiness (7:12-15). In chap. 7 we are not confronted with an asceticism that has crept into the congregation, as some have suggested,[93] but a good-faith effort on the part of some to respond to Paul's call for holiness. Some of Paul's followers have tried to apply what they understand of his teachings to the normal sexual practices that have been part of their lives. We see evidence of this perplexity right away when Paul opens this section of the letter by citing a Corinthian maxim: "It is good for a man not to touch a woman," a euphemistic reference to avoiding sexual intercourse (7:1). Some at Corinth have formulated this maxim as a guideline for proper living. Their maxim represents a radical effort—perhaps the most extreme among the believers at Corinth—to maintain holiness, but one that, as we shall see, Paul will find misguided.

The entire passage (7:1-40) is structured by counsels directed toward persons of different marital status: husbands and wives (7:2-7), widowers and widows (7:8-9), marrieds who contemplate divorce (7:10-11), the "rest" (7:12-16), and virgins or unmarrieds (7:25-31). For each sociosexual group Paul maps out a preferred or better course, but for each he also countenances an alternative, concessionary but still acceptable route. Interlaced with those counsels are other components: a rumination about Jews and gentiles, slaves and free (7:17-24), and some reflections about cares (7:32-35), desire and self-control (7:36-38), and the possible remarriage of widows (7:39-40).

Paul's imminent expectation of the end of the ages is fundamental to our understanding of his advice in this chapter. From his oldest extant letter, 1 Thessalonians (see 4:13-18), to the last letter he wrote, Romans (see 13:11-14), Paul is uniformly and steadfastly convinced that God is on the brink of finishing up the creation's restoration, which was begun in Christ's death and resurrection. So also here in 1 Corinthians Paul reminds them of his teaching that "the form of this world is passing away" (7:31). "The time has grown

---

92. Mitchell, *Paul and the Rhetoric of Reconciliation*, 39-60.

93. Will Deming, *Paul on Marriage and Celibacy: The Hellenistic Background of 1 Corinthians 7*, SNTSMS 83 (Cambridge: Cambridge University Press, 1995) 3-4, argues convincingly that Paul's assertions in 1 Corinthians 7 do not support sexual asceticism—as much of the history of interpretation has suggested.

short," he writes (7:29); "the impending crisis" (7:26 NRSV), "the present distress" (7:26 RSV; cf. 1 Thess 3:3) forces believers to act with regard to God's culminating of history. This Pauline conviction leads to the next noteworthy feature of chap. 7.

Because Paul expects the end so directly, he repeatedly counsels the Corinthians to "remain as you are" (7:20, 24, 26, 38, 40). The social structures that they encounter in the world around them are temporally bound and will not survive beyond the parousia; in fact, judging by what Paul says about slavery (7:22), those patterns and structures are already rendered indifferent and powerless. Accordingly, his counsel has an ambivalence about it. On the one side, he recognizes that the life of faith can be lived fully and faithfully in whatever circumstances one encounters (cf. his own hardship lists as examples, 4:10-13; 2 Cor 6:1-10)[94] and that being faithful does not require an overthrow of one's present social setting or status; one can remain as one is. On the other side, precisely because the structures of this age are under an eschatological sentence or verdict that will lead ultimately to their overthrow and which verdict makes them already inconsequential to one's real definition and standing before God, they can be disregarded already or lived in "as if not" living in them (see the Commentary on 7:29-31).

Two other interrelated Pauline principles emerge as the chapter unfolds: Believers should make moral choices with a view to (1) minimizing cares and anxieties, and (2) maximizing devotion to God. These themes appear most clearly in 7:32-35 where Paul's counsel about unmarried men and women opens with his declaration, "I want you to be free from care" (7:32), and closes by encouraging "your appropriate and constant devotion to the Lord, without distraction" (7:35). Paul weighs human relations in the light of these concerns and values and he counsels accordingly.

Our preliminary observations leave untouched the curious passage 7:17-24, which, though in a chapter dedicated to questions of marriage and sexuality, curiously mentions neither. Its location and function will require some accounting.

Finally, two factors must be borne in mind as we read chapter 7: (1) Paul views the life of faith as a walk, as a growth from being a baby to maturity; (2) the whole chapter must be read against the Cynic/Stoic background in which there is a fundamental effort to distinguish what really matters—that is, what really counts—from what does not matter, or from what matters less or not at all. The identification of *adiaphora*, indifferent matters, allowed Stoics to sort through all kinds of things and commitments so as to demarcate and focus upon the most important. At many points in his letters Paul employs this concept of indifferent matters as he relates to his predominantly gentile readership (cf. Rom 8:35-39; 14:8; Phil 1:10, "discern what really matters"; 4:10-13; Gal 3:28). In the passages just referenced one would find quite a list of unimportant matters including one's gender, one's social status, one's ethnic background, the way life comes to be, and even life and death themselves.

One might ask, then, what really matters to Paul. We will find many ways he expresses it: "Jesus Christ and him crucified" (1 Cor 2:2); that his readers will be "blameless at the coming of our Lord Jesus Christ" (1 Thess 5:24); and that his readers maximize their devotion to their Lord.

Among the indifferent matters, Stoics did recognize that there were "preferreds" and "not-preferreds." For example, it mattered not whether one ate sumptuously, but if one were given the opportunity to choose in such a way as not to compromise one's own integrity, then why not eat well?

To be married or not to be married was an indifferent matter to some Stoics and to Paul. Paul did not devalue marriage. But he did recognize that whether one was married or not, marriage did not have any direct or necessary bearing on one's relation to God. A married person or an unmarried person could equally well be in right relation to God or not be in right relation to God. Clearly, Paul considered that the married person has obligations to the spouse (7:1ff., 33-34). In his reflections about marriage, however, Paul freely considers preferred and not-preferred alternatives. Though he reckons marriage as an indifferent matter, Paul does have a "preferred" when he thinks about

94. Fitzgerald, *Cracks in an Earthern Vessel*, 184-201, 203-5.

what minimizes anxiety and maximizes devotion to God (7:32-35) and when he thinks about the last-times afflictions that he is convinced his readers will experience (7:26-31, 36-38). To identify marriage as an indifferent matter is not to diminish its importance, nor is it to declare that it is outside the range of moral consideration. Matters identified as indifferent are simply placed in perspective as of relative but not ultimate importance. So, whereas marriage and nonmarriage are indifferent matters for Paul, he still has preferreds for which he aims.

We must be cautious not to expect in this chapter a full exposition of Paul's understanding of marriage and human sexuality; the chapter is not to be confused with a manual on the family. Almost totally missing, for example, is any counsel regarding children. As is always the case in Paul's letters, he treats matters that he knows bear on his readers. He does not write general treatises and then expect his readers to apply them as they see fit. Rather, he engages the problems that he knows to be theirs, and he engages them in terms to which he has good reason to assume they resonate.

1 CORINTHIANS 7:1-7, HUSBANDS AND WIVES

COMMENTARY

The chapter opens with Paul's recitation of what I have identified as a Corinthian maxim: "It is well for a man not to touch a woman." As noted earlier, maxims, by their very nature, are thought to express truth, shared convictions. The social conventions of Paul's time did not encourage the rejection of another's maxim; instead, one could amplify or qualify a maxim or one could substitute one's own maxim. In the discussion that follows, Paul's citation of the Corinthian maxim (7:1b), he first amplifies their maxim (7:2-7) and later offers his own (7:25).

Note how Paul responds to their maxim that "it is well for a man not to touch a woman." From the previous chapters of his letter, he picks up the thread of the argument cautioning about *porneia* and writes: "Because of *porneia* each man should have his own wife" (7:2a). At first glance Paul's formulation may seem much like their maxim: Both speak to what a man might do; both recognize that a man might have a wife; and the Corinthians who formulated the maxim in 7:1 may think that they, like Paul, are trying to avoid *porneia*—they by not having connubial relations. But there any similarity between Paul's stand and the Corinthian maxim ends.

The counsel that "each man should have his own wife" (7:2a) employs the same verb

Paul used in 5:1 where the man "has his father's wife"; so Paul, unlike the formulators of the maxim in 7:1b, clearly means that sexuality within marriage is a proper way of avoiding *porneia*. The Corinthian maxim commends avoiding conjugal relations altogether. Another, profound difference emerges in Paul's next statement: "and each woman should have her own husband" (7:2b), a verbatim repetition of the same pronouncement he had made regarding the husband in 7:2a, but this time applied to the wife. The Corinthians who formulated the quoted maxim are concerned with men, their rights and practices; Paul is evenhanded about what both men and women should do. Verses 3-4, surely a remarkable passage to modern ears, but perhaps not totally uncommon in Paul's time,[95] clarify Paul's distance from their maxim by depicting marriage as a relationship in which husbands and wives have equal standing and equal authority over the body of the other one.

Only when Paul has distanced himself from their maxim does he directly address (7:5) persons who, by abstaining from sexual intercourse in marriage, seem to be living according to the Corinthian maxim. He

95. See Deming, *Paul on Marriage and Celibacy,* 116-22, for strong Stoic connections for Paul's view in 7:3-4.

grants them what he calls a "concession" (συγγνώμη *syngnōme*)—it pointedly is not to be confused with a command—that they can agree to set aside sex and devote themselves to prayer, but only for a time lest they be overcome by temptation (7:5-6). He is convinced that they should not deprive one another, conceding that they may choose to forgo sexual intercourse for a short time in order to have (more?) time for prayer, but only if there is mutual consent. The danger: Satan will seek to exploit any lack of self-control (7:5).

The passage concludes with Paul's offering his own model of celibacy as indeed preferred, but he is fully aware not only that this is a special charisma, a gift (by God, understood) of abstinence, to him but also not practicable for most. Hence, the concession must be granted (7:6), and the advocates of the maxim would be mistaken to press it (7:1*b*) as if its performance were equally attainable by everyone. Some will have one gift; others will have other gifts; and each must live in accord with and by honoring the gift or gifts that they have. He concludes: "But each has his own gift [charisma] from God, the one in one way, the other in another," a note that will be elaborated and refined in detail in chap. 12.

Paul accomplishes several things here. First, without explicitly attacking their maxim, Paul distances himself from it on several counts and in the process offers a very different picture of marriage: (1) He does not restrict his focus to what men should do; (2) he affirms that sexuality in marriage is not only appropriate but necessary for proper self-control; and (3) he treats men and women evenhandedly and claims that a fundamental reciprocity should be present in their exercise of their sexuality and in their deciding when to have intercourse and when to abstain.

Second, Paul closes this first section by stating what he considers the ideal, which happens to be his own celibate practice, which, as already noted, may well have occasioned their maxim in the first place. But Paul points out that the persons who formulated the maxim of 7:1*b* have erred in several ways: (1) They have taken his own celibacy as a requirement for all men. (2) In so doing, they have not recognized how charismata should function in the community (and he

will have to address that again in more detail in chaps. 12–14; but see in 7:7*b-c* the core of the position he will develop in those later chapters: God disperses the gifts as God sees fit). (3) They have wrongly assumed that husbands are the decision makers with regard to sexuality. (4) They have too narrow a view of acceptable moral decisions and patterns that Paul thinks should properly be open to believers. Theirs may very well have been an effort to enforce uniformity of behavior as a means of achieving unity. In any case, Paul's opening treatment of husbands and wives rejects commanding or supporting one human option (such as their maxim suggests) as the only acceptable practice and offers instead what he readily characterizes as a concession (*syngnōme*, 7:6) that by comparison, with his own charisma taken as the ideal, leaves a wider range of human options possible and acceptable before God.

Third, by his opening engagement of their maxim Paul establishes the notion that believers' moral reasoning may result in a variety of acceptable responses that Paul is pleased enough to range from "better" to "good," from preferable to permissible. The pattern of "ideal" (or "better") plus a concession that is still good and acceptable characterizes Paul's counsel to every group treated in the chapter. In the rest of the chapter, the ideal, the better, the goal is typically presented first, and the concession follows. Here in 7:1-7 it goes the other way around, no doubt because the Corinthian maxim of 7:1*b* is reported in the Corinthian letter to Paul, and he chooses to engage it at the start.

Paul starts with their maxim for two reasons: Some Corinthians have formulated a maxim that is being advocated as applicable to all members of different sociosexual groupings within the church, and their maxim is probably being used to enforce a uniform behavioral pattern that Paul finds too narrowly restrictive and not adequately malleable to the diverse circumstances that different individuals within each group might experience.

The advocates of this maxim quite possibly have thought of themselves as absolutely in line with Paul, his practices, and his teachings. In fact, they may well have taken Paul's previous letter (cf. 5:9) as championing just such a sharp, stringent delineation as their maxim seems to put into practice. And it may be that they were attempting to do what Paul was affirming already in chap. 6—namely, attempting to avoid sin and *porneia* and seeking to honor proper holiness before God. So Paul has the delicate task of delineating his own, more complex moral vision from theirs without rebuking them.

In the material that follows in chap. 7, Paul turns his attention to other sociosexual groupings within the congregation, still using the pattern just identified where an ideal is pictured as the goal but where some action short of the optimum is depicted as acceptable.

REFLECTIONS

1. Across the paragraphs of this literary unit, Paul's presumption is that human beings are sexual creatures for whom sexual passion, expressed in the marital context, is a legitimate and appropriate part of human experience. In our own culture, sex and sexuality are treated in two radically diverse ways. On one hand, sex and sexuality are topics about which people seldom have serious, thoughtful discussions; they are treated in a hush-hush fashion that curiously only serves to mystify them even more and helps to make possible the commercial capitalization on sex and sexuality. In the other treatment of sex and sexuality, they are used everywhere to sell everything from automobiles to toothpaste, and the entertainment media would be at a loss without them. Homes and maybe churches should be places where, in the light of the gospel, we could discuss human sexuality and its drives as a wholesome, even pleasurable part of life. Like anything else that is good, however, sex and sexuality can readily be perverted, but that possibility should neither prevent the discussion nor allow sexuality to be viewed as something intrinsically bad.

2. The assertions about the woman's having authority over the man's body and the man's having authority over the woman's body should give a modern Christian couple an opportunity to discuss and evaluate their practice not only of who is allowed or expected to initiate sexual intercourse but also of how authority is shared in other family decisions and practices. Paul's view of this shared authority honors both the needs and the rights of each sexual partner. And by extrapolation, wives and husbands could work at honoring one another's needs and rights in all aspects of their shared lives.

1 CORINTHIANS 7:8-9, WIDOWERS AND WIDOWS

COMMENTARY

Paul now considers widowers and widows (7:8-9). Although most translations of ἀγάμοις (*agamois*) settle for "unmarried" (NRSV and NIV), it should probably be translated as "widowers" for the following reasons: Biblical Greek does not have a word for "widowers"; Paul addresses single unmarrieds later in the letter (7:25-38); and the other half of the pair addressed in 7:8-9 is clearly widows (χήραι *chērai*).

In his counsel for widowers and widows, Paul adopts the same opening that the Corinthians used for their maxim (καλόν *kalon*) and advises: "It is good/well for them to remain as I am," namely, celibate (7:8; cf. 7:7). As is his pattern throughout, however, Paul offers a concession that if self-control is a problem, they should remarry (7:9). Celibacy is the best course for widows and widowers, but remarriage is preferred over either a loss of self-control or a burning with sexual desire (7:9).

Several connections of 7:8-9 with the preceding verses emerge: Paul expects believers to discern and do the best they can. When self-control is a problem, concessions lead to an accommodating level of performance that, although clearly understood as something less than the best, is still reckoned to be acceptable behavior.

Patterns in Paul's counsel surface here and are replicated throughout his treatment of marriage and human sexuality. Across the chapter Paul establishes what he thinks is the ideal, how he thinks things ought to be, and he depicts that as the goal or paradigm toward which people ought to aim and with regard to which people should order their lives. Yet alongside each such elevated goal-setting, Paul recognizes that, for various reasons, people may not be able to achieve the ideal. And he is careful to make room for full participation in the fellowship of those who, for whatever reason, may not be able to hit the heights.

REFLECTIONS

Paul's is not a rule-based morality. Rather, a range of responses is deemed morally appropriate. Some believers may have problems with this; they may want to assume there is one, right response in every situation. Such a view understands moral reasoning to be involved in figuring out the "right" response among the many options. Paul, however, operates with a notion of what is best and realizes that not everyone will be able to reach that. If we took Paul's view here seriously, then our wrongful judgment of one another would be less easy because we would have to grant that there is more than the one way we have figured out to respond in a given situation.

1 CORINTHIANS 7:10-11, MARRIED BELIEVERS AND DIVORCE

COMMENTARY

In this passage Paul considers whether a marriage between two believers (cf. 7:12-13) can (or should?) end in divorce. Whether this topic is simply Paul's addition or is prompted by circumstances at Corinth, Paul and his auditors know but we never shall. By means of a correctio (structure: A, not A but B), Paul pointedly bases his next counsel not on his own opinion but on a teaching of Jesus: "A wife should not separate from her husband . . . and a husband should not divorce his wife" (7:10-11). Though Paul could not have known any of the Gospels as we do—he was dead before they were written—he assuredly knew enough about the teachings of Jesus and about early Christian claims to have opposed and persecuted Christ's followers (Gal 1:23; 1 Cor 15:9). Among the teachings of Jesus that Paul clearly knew was a statement on divorce (cf. Mark 10:2-5; Matt 5:31-32; 19:9; Luke 16:18).

In Jewish practice and tradition a man could divorce his wife (Deut 24:1-4)—and for almost any reason—but a wife did not have the same right regarding her husband. Roman law and practice allowed either men or women to institute divorce.[96] Corinth, as a Roman colony city, followed Roman law in all matters so that a Corinthian wife or husband could initiate divorce. So Paul's teaching of the higher good as allowing no divorce affirms his understanding of Jesus' teaching and runs counter to the Roman law that most of his Corinthian congregation would have known. His concession, granted in 7:11,

96. Jerome Corcopino, *Daily Life in Ancient Rome: the People and the City at the Height of the Empire*, trans. E. O. Lorimer (New Haven: Yale University Press, 1940) 95-100.

accommodates to the rights of women under Roman colonial law.

Throughout the history of the church much has been made of Paul's choice of words: "divorce" (ἀφίημι *aphiēmi*, 7:11) for the husband, "separation" (χωρίζω *chōrizō*, 7:10) for the wife. In some times and traditions Paul's terminology has been understood to allow a man to divorce his wife, but to allow a woman only to have a legal separation from her husband. This interpretation founders on at least four grounds: (1) It anachronistically forces modern legal categories back onto ancient times; (2) it fails to appreciate that rhetorical training discouraged unnecessary repetition of the same term and encouraged alternate ways of making the same point; (3) it fails to take seriously that Paul counsels any woman who does "separate" to "remain unmarried" (ἄγαμος *agamos*, 7:11), so Paul himself treats *chōrizō* as an actual termination of the marriage; and (4) it overlooks that women are understood a few verses later to have the power to divorce (7:13).

In Paul's time the issue is at once more complex and simpler. First, the semantic ranges of the two terms overlap. In papyri, the term *chōrizō* not only means to leave or separate oneself from someone but also describes the separation that is divorce. *Aphiēmi* means not only "divorce" but also "leave," "abandon," "give up."[97] Second, in Paul's time the line between divorce and separation was often neither a legal distinction nor recorded in public documents. Frequently, in his era, when a marriage failed, the parties simply separated and if they were so inclined, in due time entered into another marriage, but without the modern niceties of legally dissolving the previous marriage. Anachronistic reading not only foists modern sharp distinctions between divorce and separation and modern notions of social practice and legal documentation back onto Paul's time and onto his readers but also subtly endows men with greater rights than women, a position Paul seems dedicated throughout chap. 7 to avoid.

It is much more likely that Paul has simply used two different terms for rhetorical variation, an important rhetorical convention of the times.[98] Clearly, he knows and allows that women can and do divorce—and that they can do so as believers; in 7:13 a believing woman is presumed by Paul to have the right and power to divorce (here the term is *aphiēmi*, the same one used in the end of 7:11) her husband.

If one takes "separate" and "divorce" as the use of different terms to describe the same social reality, then Paul sets the same high standard for both wife and husband. It is better if neither one divorces a spouse, but once again Paul is prepared to make a concession. Within the formulation, however, Paul accommodates to divorce and, indeed, to divorce initiated by a wife, even though he views any divorce as less than the ideal: "If she separates, let her remain unmarried or let her be reconciled to her husband" (7:11).

Quite strikingly, Paul acknowledges that believing behavior may sometimes go counter to an explicit teaching of Jesus. Unmistakably, Paul prefers adherence to Jesus' teaching, but equally beyond question he recognizes that, a contrary teaching of Jesus notwithstanding, there may be times when women and men may need to divorce (see also 7:12-15) and that those who do divorce remain full participants in the fellowship of believers.

The post-divorce options Paul considers are "remain unmarried" and "be reconciled" (7:11). Reconciliation of humans to God and of people to people is at the heart of the gospel for Paul (2 Cor 5:14-21). So as Paul weighs the possible alternatives for divorced people, he quite naturally thinks of reconciliation. We may reasonably wonder whether his counsel to remain unmarried was driven by his conviction that the end of the ages was at hand (cf. 7:26-31; see also the Commentary on 7:25-38). (See Reflections at 7:12-16.)

---

97. BAGD, 125-26.

98. *Ad Herennium* 4.12.18: "We shall avoid the excessive repetition of the same word."

1 CORINTHIANS 7:12-16, MARRIAGE BETWEEN BELIEVERS AND UNBELIEVERS

Commentary

With divorce between believers on his mind, Paul now turns to "the rest" of the married people: those who are married to unbelieving spouses. Admitting that he lacks a pertinent teaching of the Lord (7:12), Paul must draw on other resources and convictions, three in number. First, he seems to extend Jesus' teaching to avoid divorce: Paul advises that believing spouses should not divorce unbelieving spouses if the latter are willing to remain married. Second, he gives another reason, or perhaps it is a hope: "The unbelieving husband is made holy through his wife, and the unbelieving wife is made holy through her husband" (7:14 NRSV). In chap. 5 Paul warned against contamination from the outside world, suggesting that one bit of yeast can leaven the entire lump. In 7:14 Paul affirms a different, even reverse "contagion," but this time a positive one: Sin and *porneia* have a corrosive potential; but sanctification—being claimed and set apart by and for God—also has a rub-off potential that bears on those around, not only on the unbelieving spouse but also on "your children," claiming them also as holy, meaning set apart for and belonging to God (7:14). This is a practical application of what Paul affirmed in Romans when he wrote that although sin abounds, grace abounds the more (Rom 5:20). Paul has a profound conviction that God's power to redeem is active and superabundant, breaking across barriers and through resistance. As surely as sin's power is lethal, even more so is God's power evident in those who belong to God. Not only unbelieving spouses may benefit from God's sanctifying power working through the believing spouse, but Paul assures them that "your children" are holy; they, too, are set apart for and belong to God (7:14). The life of faith is viewed as infectious. Third, he affirms that "God has called us into peace" (7:15), a theme that will emerge again in 14:33. The laconic declaration that "God has called us to peace" (7:15) is given no

defense and no elaboration by Paul, suggesting that this is a foundational claim that he expects them to know and affirm. The fact that the same expression resurfaces in 14:33 and with the same incontrovertible force confirms the reading of it here. Peacemaking, reconciliation are, after all, what Paul sees at the heart of the gospel and therefore of the life of faith (2 Cor 5:14-21; cf. Matt 5:9; Eph 4:1-6). The case of marriage between a believer and an unbeliever is an extreme test of the range of the commitment to peace. The call to peacemaking is not restricted to expression between believers alone, but also is the way believers should relate to unbelievers. This is once again the same commitment to reconciliation that was noted in 7:11. So, when counseling persons whose unbelieving spouses want divorce, Paul finds moral guidance from the conviction that believers who are able to avoid divorce are still called to peace, this time achieved precisely in the divorce itself: Grant divorce to them as a ministration of God's peace.

For two reasons we may surmise that divorce was a matter of great concern among the Corinthians: (1) Paul expends considerable papyri on it (7:10-16), and (2) he breaks into second-person, direct address at two points, when he writes about "your children" in 7:15 and when he lodges the same question to wife and husband as to whether they know that their faith may result in the salvation of their spouses (7:16).

Further, we may wonder whether the Corinthians who formulated their wisdom in the maxim "It is good for a man not to touch a woman" (7:1) may have pressed this view on married persons with the arguments that for married believers divorce would be best but, failing that, abstinence from sexual relations was required and that being married to unbelievers was simply untenable on any grounds. If so, Paul has countered their teaching in several particulars.

Finally, Paul does countenance divorce in such mixed marriages, again as less than the ideal, but only at the instance of the unbelieving spouse (7:15). Also noteworthy is that both statements about the believing husband (7:12, 14*a*) are repeated, verbatim, with regard to the believing wife (7:13, 14*b*); thus Paul continues to reflect the equal care and standing with which he has regarded males and females throughout the first sixteen verses of this chapter.

REFLECTIONS

1. In treating marriages between believers and unbelievers Paul makes two remarkable claims: (1) The children are sanctified by their association with the believer, and (2) he cryptically expresses the possibility that the believing spouse might save the unbelieving spouse, male or female. Nowhere else in the entire Pauline corpus do we find such a statement of salvation being so directly ascribed to human agency. Elsewhere it is God who saves (cf. 1:18, 21); one can surely assume here also that it is God who is understood to save as well, but through the agency of love shown by the believing spouse toward the unbelieving one. What an awesome picture of the power of love between husbands and wives! The assertions that believers may sanctify their spouses and their children (7:14) complement what has been noted about good and bad models and their importance in the communal life of faith. Here we see that one's action, one's comportment is not just a private transaction between the individual and God; what one does and how one lives one's life have the potential to corrode and harm others (cf. 8:10) or to elevate and encourage others (cf. 14:3). Faith and the morality in which it expresses itself, as Paul sees them, are never totally or simply private. That is why one's faith (the right relationship to God) can never be lived without its gaining its expression in love (the right relationship to others; cf. Gal 5:6).

Think about marriage as a mutually sanctifying, mutually upbuilding relationship. Each marriage partner seeks the best for the other, encourages the other, and consoles the other when appropriate; that is love put into action. Also, when we consider our obligations to our children in light of this passage we might think of ourselves as setting them apart as special to God by refracting God's love through us to them. All of our relationships in the family are not just private transactions between us and family members; they are always done in the light of God's care and concern for each person.

2. Divorce is addressed at two points in this chapter: 7:10-11, 12-16. A scan of New Testament views about divorce may provide a context for some reflections about Paul's outlook. According to Mark 10:2-11, Jesus, like Paul, indicates that not-to-divorce had been the ideal but that divorce was allowed as an accommodation, in Mark's case, on account of "hardheartedness." In Matt 19:3-9 Jesus allows divorce (and remarriage) only where unchastity is involved. So when Paul takes care to note that the Lord says the wife should not divorce her husband, he no doubt is referring to the same sorts of Jesus traditions that we see in the Gospels. As indicated in the commentary, Paul's pattern throughout the chapter is to set up the ideal as the goal, but he regularly makes an accommodation to persons who for various reasons cannot attain the goal. So here the goal is conformity with Jesus' teaching that a woman not divorce her husband, but the accommodation follows immediately: "but if she does. . . ." So Paul recognizes and does not forbid divorce, though to divorce is short of the ideal. Further, Paul, in distinction from Deut 24:1-4 but in accord with Roman law, assumes that a wife may institute divorce as well as a husband.

The New Testament shows a persistent commitment to restoring relationships, to affirming peace and reconciliation. In the light of this it is not surprising that Jesus, and Paul in line with him, should counsel against a rush to divorce. Neither is it surprising that each of the noted texts reckons, for different reasons, that divorce is sometimes the chosen course. We should do everything to encourage reconciliation, not just in disputed marriages but in all of life, but we should also recognize that there are times when a marriage ought to be dissolved. Divorce should not be an early step, however, in the treatment of marriage problems.

1 CORINTHIANS 7:17-24, INDIFFERENT MATTERS: JEW, GREEK, SLAVE, FREE

COMMENTARY

These eight verses are a digression. They have no explicit connection with marriage or with sexuality. Husbands and wives, divorce and sexuality—the topics on either side—are simply not mentioned in 7:17-24. After these verses Paul returns to his counsels for another class of individuals in the Corinthian congregation, virgins or unmarrieds (7:25ff.).

Paul clearly expects his original readers to make the connections of vv. 17-24 to what is on either side, and perhaps we modern readers can do the same once we identify what is going on inside the passage. First, we will note the structure of 7:17-24; then we will assess its function. Verses 17-24 have a two-part structure framed within three quite similar statements (7:17, 20, 24). Within that frame one finds a reflection on God's call or election, a theme that has been important in the letter from the start.

The opening sentence, structured as a chiasmus (A B B´ A´), functions like a well-balanced thesis statement for 7:17-24: "Nevertheless, to each [A] as the Lord has apportioned [B], as God has called [B´] each [A´], thus let him walk. I make this rule in all the churches" (7:17). Verse 20, echoing v. 17, says: "Each [A] in the call in which he has been called [B], in this let him remain." Verse 24 resounds and refines the same claim: "Each [A] in the circumstance where he has been called [B], brothers and sisters, in this let him remain with God." The notion of life as a walk, as a way of walking, is a commonplace in Paul's letters (cf. Rom 6:4; 13:13; 2 Cor 5:7; Gal 5:16; Phil 3:17). The theme of "remaining," first exemplified by Paul in 7:8 and reaffirmed in 7:11, emerges in 7:20 and 7:24 as a thread binding together much of his counsel about marriage and sexuality.

Verse 17 and its echoes in v. 20 and v. 24 affirm that Paul expects persons, in all of his churches, to live, specifically to walk, the gospel in the circumstances where they were called, where the grace of God engaged them. Living the gospel is the primary concern. To put it differently, how they "walk"—that is, how they comport themselves—is the key issue. Location and setting are indifferent matters; one's call is not. The gospel can flourish and be walked in any circumstance, and the living of it elevates the person and the circumstance in which the person lives. Paul does not require believers to leave their social setting. As we shall see shortly, this is partly a function of Paul's conviction that the end of the ages is near and, therefore, there is no need of altering social structures, but it also reflects his profound belief that the gospel can be fully lived wherever one is or whatever one's circumstances (cf. 2 Cor 4:7). The three kindred expressions in vv. 17, 20, and 24 frame the passage into two portions, which we now examine.

Verses 17-19 are structured around two questions with appended directions. Circumcision, even though it was a sign of being part of Israel (Gen 17:9-14), and uncircumcision (variant ways of referring to Jew and gentile; cf. Rom 2:28-29) are the first test cases to illustrate how persons should comport themselves when and where they receive their call. Was anyone circumcised—that is, was the person a Jew when called? No need to change that. Was anyone—presumably most of his Corinthian audience—called while a gentile? No need to change that. Unlike the churches in Galatia, the church at Corinth is not having even the slightest problem with circumcision or uncircumcision; the terms are mentioned in the letter only here. So Paul is reciting matters about which the Corinthians have no confusion; he is building a case from something he knows they understand and accept. They realize that they have not been expected to become circumcised when called. Accordingly, the maxim that concludes this section will not surprise them either: "Circumcision is nothing; uncircumcision is nothing; but keeping the commandments of God [that's crucial]" (7:19). Obedience to God matters; circumcision and uncircumcision are indifferent. This clarity on an issue that is purely and simply illustrative, that builds on what they already know, prepares the way for a more complex and immediate issue for some of Paul's readers ahead in 7:20-23. Once again we see a solid Pauline principle at work: Begin with what believers know and build a ground from which to address a problem.

Verses 20-23 deal with slavery and freedom[99] and, like 7:18-19, open with a question, but unlike those previous questions of 7:18, this one is in the second-person singular and is a direct address, suggesting that this is a problem Paul knows is besetting some Corinthians: "Were you a slave when called?" "Don't let it trouble you" (NIV), or "Do not be concerned about it" (NRSV).[100] Paul's justification for why it should be of no concern is not given until a verse later (7:22), but runs as follows: True freedom is found in slavery to the Lord and does not depend on one's social status as reckoned in the world. From the perspective-keeping formulation (7:22), the world's slave is the Lord's free person and the world's free person is the Lord's slave, so, as Paul has already asked the Corinthians in this letter: "Who sees anything different in you?" (4:7 NRSV). Slavery and freedom are indifferent matters "in the Lord." But, as we have seen, the Stoic eagerness to identify "indifferent matters" (*adiaphora*) always also allowed room for distinctions within those *adiaphora* of "preferreds" and "not-preferreds." Though Paul could write to the Philippians, indicating

that he knew how to get along with much and how to get along with plenty (4:12), there is nothing wrong with preferring plenty if one is presented with the choice. So, though Paul is clear that slavery and freedom are in a fundamental sense an *adiaphoron*, an indifferent matter, there is no reason why a believing slave who is given the chance to attain freed person status should not readily take it if he or she so desires. Freedom from slavery can surely be a "preferred."

Near the end of this passage, Paul clearly lays out what he takes to be an unavoidable truth—indeed, one that has already been affirmed in this letter: All believers have been bought by a new Lord, Jesus Christ (v. 23; 6:20). With regard to the world and its values, whether one is a slave should not be a concern; it is not an important matter, but Paul recognizes that one may have the opportunity to gain freedom and he accommodates to that (v. 21). Paul's counsel here has analogies with his advice to the groups noted earlier in chap. 7. In those cases he identified a maximum level, or what he calls "better," performance, but he always allowed for variations from that. Here in the issue of slavery he has no "better" level but instead argues from an indifferent matter (whether one is slave or free) to an allowable, "preferred" course of action.

Paul's congregations seem regularly to have had slaves in them. In the Roman world, slavery was a taken-for-granted institution. Slaves could gain their freedom in certain circumstances such as when their owners bestowed it as a reward or willed it to them at death; at times slaves could purchase their freedom. Corinth had some prominent freedmen who built proud monuments to the worldly success they achieved after they were freed, so we know that social mobility from slavery to freedom was valued by some at Corinth. Perhaps aware of that tangible social pressure, Paul accedes to their desire for freedom as reckoned in the world. This is an important concession because it shows that Paul's continued call to "remain as they are" is not an elevation of the issue of believers' status and circumstance to a level of primary importance, but a call to live, behave, walk in whatever circumstances they find themselves, in accordance with their call. The

---

99. S. S. Bartchy, *MALLON CHRESAI: First-century Slavery and the Interpretation of 1 Corinthians 7:21*, SBLDS 11 (Missoula: University of Montana Press, 1973); Dale B. Martin, *Slavery as Salvation: The Metaphor of Slavery in Pauline Christianity* (New Haven: Yale University Press, 1990).

100. Neil Elliott, *Liberating Paul: The Justice of God and the Politics of the Apostle* (Maryknoll, N.Y.: Orbis, 1994) 32-40, sees in the ambiguity of Paul's cryptic Greek (μᾶλλον χρῆσαι *mallon chrēsai*) in 7:21 a call of liberation, that slaves should take the opportunity of their freedom.

circumstances are not elevated above the life according to the gospel. Rather, the gospel, its call, and its appropriate behavior are the crucial and primary concern; the circumstances in which one finds oneself are indifferent. Here Paul stands in line with venerable Cynic and Stoic convictions that the good life can be lived in any circumstances. So, slaves who see the opportunity to be free must walk in accord with the gospel whether they remain slaves or whether they avail themselves of the chance to be free.

The common ground that all believers, no matter their social status or ethnicity, share is that they are now "owned" by a new master, by Christ as their Lord. The last time Paul wrote in such a way in this letter he also said something else that continues to be true: "You are not your own . . . glorify God in your body" (6:19-20 NRSV). Therefore believers are not free to "become slaves of people" (7:23b; cf. Paul's own self-portrait in the last clause of 6:12).

What is the function of 7:17-24, and how is it accomplished? In part these verses reaffirm common ground between Paul and his readers: He and they know that circumcision and uncircumcision are indifferent matters. So, at the very least, it affirmed what they already knew—namely, that they did not have to alter their ethnicity; they did not have to become Jews, just because they came to believe in the gospel. In part, also, the readers are expected, with Paul's help, to make an analogical application of their understood indifference regarding ethnicity and a supposed indifference regarding other circumstances—these having to do with marital status—that prevailed at the time of their call.

But this explanation does not yet account for Paul's treatment of slaves and free persons. Paul's readers would have understood what Paul was doing in 7:17-24, but it may be more difficult for modern readers to see. They would have known two things that we can learn: (1) In those days it was the standard rhetorical procedure of indirect speech to put some already known, clearly understood matter or principle alongside an issue under deliberation so that the readers could make their own connections and applications. (2) Paul's readers would more readily recognize traditions that Paul had taught

them than we might. As a start, let us see the structure of this passage once more as it fits into its larger context:

7:1-16   discussion of male/female
7:17-20   discussion of Jew/Greek
           (circumcised/uncircumcised)
7:21-24   discussion of slave/free
7:25-40   discussion of male/female

From 1 Cor 12:13–"For in the one Spirit we were all baptized into one body—Jews or Greeks, slaves or free—and we were all made to drink of one Spirit" (NRSV)—we can tell that the Corinthians knew the same baptismal formula—indeed, they may have heard it pronounced over them at the time of their own baptism—that we see reflected in Gal 3:28: "There is no longer Jew or Greek, there is no longer slave or free, there is no longer male or female; for all of you are one in Christ Jesus" (NRSV). The formula, no doubt a tradition composed by others and embraced by Paul, is clearly a favorite of his and is known to be affirmed by his Corinthian readers, because he explicitly argues from it in 12:13 without need for explanation or support.

Now we are in a position to see what Paul is doing by inserting 7:17-24 into the discussion of males, females, and human sexuality. In a chapter where he discusses issues relating to males and females, he has picked up the other two sets from the baptismal formula reflected in Gal 3:28 and in 1 Cor 12:13: Jew and Greek, slave and free. He has reaffirmed that whether an individual is Jew or Greek or slave or free does not matter because all persons are on equal standing and are equally important in Christ. And in so doing, he has shown the Corinthians his fulcrum for moral reasoning throughout the chapter, that is, how he has been deducing his counsels for the various groupings of males and females within the Corinthian congregation. The male/female couplet has not been left out in chap. 7 as some scholars have suggested;[101] that couplet is the subject matter throughout the chapter and so does not need repeating in vv. 17-24.

---

101. Hans Dieter Betz, *Galatians: A Commentary on Paul's Letter to the Churches in Galatia*, Hermeneia (Philadelphia: Fortress, 1979) 200, by reference to 1 Cor 12:13, accounts for the absence of the male/female pair.

Given Paul's profound conviction that in Christ the world's distinctions between male and female no longer prevail, and faced with the Corinthian questions about sexual relations, he has set about to imagine what the relationship between males and females would be if one took seriously that in Christ they have equal standing. As a result, Paul's interpretation throughout the chapter is characterized by an evenhanded, reciprocal, almost verbatim repetition of statements made about husbands and then applied to wives, and vice versa (7:2-4, 12-14, 16, 27, 33-34); further, though Paul does not think divorce is best, wives have just as much right to divorce as do husbands (7:10-11, 13).

Paul's purpose in chap. 7 emerges: He is doing moral reasoning concerning males and females in a way that honors their equal standing as those baptized into Christ. For Paul, those in Christ, whether male or female, are of equal status. He opens the chapter with the Corinthian maxim that radicalizes holiness and elevates men. Without explicitly rejecting the maxim, he envisions life between the sexes in the light of the baptismal formula (Gal 3:28), which is clearly a part of his conviction and, therefore, part of his regular instruction to his followers. It has already been noted that Paul's frequent course of moral reasoning is to go from problem or issue to "what we know" and to reckon from the latter toward a moral stance on the problem or issue. In this instance, Paul is presented with some questions of human sexuality and in particular with a maxim that reflects the efforts of some of his followers to deduce a moral stance appropriate to the gospel. On this occasion Paul moves from some Corinthians' solution as expressed in their maxim (7:1) and, by reference to what believers know, namely the baptismal tradition reflection in Gal 3:28 and 1 Cor 12:13 and 7:17-24, Paul constructs another, quite different picture and expresses it across chapter 7. If in Christ the world's standards and distinctions no longer pertain in any case but particularly in the relationships between male and female, what would a genuinely Christ-based ethic of human sexuality look like? Chapter 7 is a part of Paul's answer.

In 7:17-24 Paul lays down the basis on which he has reasoned in 7:1-16 and by which he will continue to reason in 7:25ff. Before he writes 7:17-24, Paul has already supposed reciprocity and equal standing for each grouping of people he has addressed; only in 7:17-24 does he signal his readers that throughout the chapter he has been operating from the baptismal formula; and with his deliberations about Jews/Greeks and slaves/free he invites his readers not only to perceive the key to his reasoning but also to see that the gospel, though it allows a shift of social setting for its full enactment, does not require it.

The latter is a theme that has surfaced a few times already in this letter. Some Corinthians seem to have taken Paul's call for holiness as a demand for radical breaks with or alterations of all their previous social setting and identification, as if to flee *porneia* were to flee the world and one's social setting. As he elaborates his position, Paul appears to walk a fine line in this chapter; he inclines toward urging all people to stay put, to continue to live in the same context as when they received their call, but he recognizes that some change may be important or necessary (e.g., some may need to divorce, some may have a chance to gain freedom from slavery).

In the passages to which attention now turns, we will see why Paul finds no urgency for believers to alter their social structures or settings and how he thinks believers can live within the world without conforming to its norms. In these passages we will see that Paul continues to examine human relations in the light of the baptismal formula and its equal standing and reciprocity, and it is from this important tradition that he has deduced his maxim, which he offers in the following material.

REFLECTIONS

1. Paul's vision of holiness lived within the world gives us challenges in at least two ways: to understand what holiness means and to imagine how to live it in the world, which in so many ways marches to a different drummer. Maybe it would be helpful to think of holiness as being the center of one's life. Many things vie to become the central, organizing principle of our lives: success, money, prestige, and each person can add to that list. What is at the center governs. So if it is, say, money, then decisions are made with regard to what will make the most money, what will be financially advantageous. Other concerns are ranked out in relation to the central, governing one, or are simply ignored because they do not serve the central concern. Thus it always is, no matter what is at the center of one's life. If God's love and God's purposes are at the center of your life, then all other concerns and values must take their place in rank in relation to that governing commitment. Holiness, being set apart or belonging to God, should be at the center of our lives, according to Paul. If it is and we make our choices and aversions on the basis of the primary consideration that we belong to God, then competing values are put in perspective. Then the first consideration when faced with a moral choice is not how will it affect my finances but how will it honor God's love and God's purposes. Each of us already has something that is a governing principle in the middle of our lives. Or we may have one principle in one kind of circumstance and another in a different situation. A good exercise, best done with others in open discussion, would be to share honestly what is our central, governing principle. Or we can examine a major decision and fruitfully ask what was the central value that was finally determinative in the choice that we made.

2. Paul's relatively quietistic counsel to "remain in the situation where called" (7:24) can be mistaken as a call to inaction, to do nothing, or even to embrace the status quo. There are circumstances that the gospel simply cannot abide and we must be unmistakably clear about that. For example, no one should remain in a physically or emotionally abusive situation. The gospel does not call for one to do that. In a similar way, Paul's counsel to "remain" should not be used as a justification for not seeking better circumstances for oneself and an improvement of one's circumstances.

3. We ought to appreciate and celebrate more fully that it is not just individuals who are changed for the better by their living out the gospel. Their circumstances may also be elevated by the gospel's power; their context and those persons around them may be positively affected by the reverberations of God's grace in and through them. However, there are times when the living of the gospel will set off such a reaction from those around that a believer might do well to leave those circumstances, much as Jesus is portrayed as telling his disciples to shake the dust from their feet as they left those who would ill-treat them (Matt 10:14; Luke 9:5). Even in the passage before us Paul's maxim to "remain as you are" does not become a law; it is a guideline. What an irony if it were to become the basis for a person to become entrapped in harmful or nonviable circumstances.

4. Paul's ready, favorable use of slavery imagery as a means of expressing proper dependence upon God (Rom 1:1; 6:11-23; 1 Cor 3:5; 4:1) should not obscure Paul's real sense of freedom, which he celebrates in Christ (cf. Gal 5:1-14) and which Augustine also affirmed when he said, "My heart is restless until it finds its rest in Thee."[102] Neither can Paul's embracing of slave imagery be transferred without caution to modern times; the use of Paul to endorse slavery in Civil War times in the United States shows those dangers. As in Paul's time, slavery is still a reality in our own time and must be consistently opposed wherever it is happening around this globe. On a more metaphorical level, slaveries are all too present; our yearning for money, for example, can place us in thrall; drug abuse is surely an invidious slavery for many persons. All such slaveries must be exposed, called into question, and the victims of them must, in every possible way, be supported and encouraged to break from them.

102. Augustine *Confessions* 1.1.

1 CORINTHIANS 7:25-28, COUNSEL FOR THE UNMARRIED: PAUL'S OWN MAXIM

COMMENTARY

After Paul's digression (7:17-24), he gives a rather protracted consideration to a last group: the virgins or unmarrieds. The term παρθένος (*parthenos*) means "unmarried" here and does not itself indicate whether the unmarried woman is betrothed, though 7:28 and 7:36-38 suggest that Paul has that reality in mind, at least there. With regard to unmarrieds Paul admits that he has no command of the Lord, but, as one who has been found trustworthy with respect to his calling, he offers his own maxim γνώμη (*gnōmē*, 7:25).[103] Most translations depict Paul as setting forth his "opinion" (NRSV) or "judgment" (NIV, NEB), but, as we have seen, the Corinthians and Paul, like the culture of which they are a part, are very much given to maxims as a ground of moral reasoning.[104] The first section of this chapter was prompted by the Corinthians' maxim (7:1*b*); Paul now offers his own, with a prefixed consideration: "I therefore reckon this to be good, because of the imminent necessity, namely, 'It is good for a person to remain as is'" (7:26). The auditors are left to ponder what Paul may have in mind with the phrase "imminent necessity," and they may think that he once again refers to the burning passion he had mentioned earlier (7:9), but it will become quite clear in vv. 28-31 that no matter how much he may

have passion in view he also has in mind the impending apocalyptic conclusion of God's work already begun in Christ. In his maxim they will hear a theme that has already made its mark on the chapter: "Remain as you are" (7:8, 11, 17-24).

Immediately following his maxim, Paul addresses, directly and in the singular, unmarried persons in the congregation, giving first, as we have come to expect, his counsel concerning the ideal. Verse 27*a* reminds the reader of Paul's earlier counsel to married persons and shows that his advice there was already consistent with his maxim: Those who are married should not seek divorce. Verse 27*b* applies his own, newly announced maxim to the matter at hand, unmarrieds: "Are you free from a wife? Do not seek a wife." Predictably, Paul then directs his counsel to those who cannot attain the ideal, assuring that those who do marry do not sin (7:28*a-b*), but "such ones [as do marry] will have worldly distress [θλῖψις *thlipsis*] which I would spare you" (7:28*c*). *Thlipsis* ("distress," "affliction") refers to distress, whose origin lies in circumstances outside oneself; we can tell from other letters (Rom 8:35; 1 Thess 3:3, 7) that when Paul employs the term he usually thinks of the eschatological distress that all believers inevitably experience as God's purposes come to their conclusion—that distress Paul cannot spare the Corinthians or anyone else and in yet another digression (7:29-35) he attends to its consequences.

103. Rollin A. Ramsaran, "More Than an Opinion: Paul's Rhetorical Maxim in First Corinthians 7:25-26," *CBQ* 57 (1995) 531-41.

104. Ramsaran, *Liberating Words,* 6-7.

REFLECTIONS

1. Paul's justification for marriage is not procreation but the need for acceptable expression of sexuality. Missing altogether in 1 Corinthians 7 is any romanticism; it is nowhere else in that culture either. Some say that notions of romantic love only began in the fourteenth century.[105] But before one dismisses Paul's view of marriage as "minimalist" or "not lofty," one should consider two matters. (1) Based on his deliberation

105. Denis de Rougemont, *Love in the Western World,* trans. M. Belgion (New York: Pantheon, 1956).

(7:17-24) from the baptismal tradition most clearly visible in Gal 3:28, Paul argues for a fundamental reciprocity between husbands and wives (the most striking to modern ears will be that the wife has authority over the husband's body and vice versa, 7:4); and (2) form follows function in such counsel because he repeats almost verbatim his advice to women and to men (cf. 7:2-4, 10-11, 12-16, 27, 32-33).

2. Paul's counsel, expressed in his maxim "remain as you are" (7:26 NIV) and brought to bear on several of the exemplary cases, is powered by his abiding conviction (cf. Rom 13:11-14; 1 Thess 5:1-11) that the "schema of this world is passing away" (7:31), which process of passing creates a "present distress" (7:26) in which "the time [between now and the end] is [mercifully] shortened" (7:29). If Paul had thought differently, say that the end of the world was some distance away as many today do believe, would his counsel in particulars have been different? It is difficult to know because the only Paul we have access to is the one who thought the end was imminent and, therefore, appropriately counseled that people had no need to worry about social structures and their injustice. We do know, however, that he puts leverage on Philemon to accept his former worthless slave Onesimus back, no longer as a slave but as a beloved brother in Christ (Phlm 16). We do know that he has supported slaves who desire freedom (cf. 1 Cor 7:21). It is easy to suppose that, if he had not expected an imminent parousia, he might have more strongly advocated marriage, he might have counseled widows to be more open to the idea of remarriage. Whether Paul would have or not, we must wrestle more fully with the genuine ambiguity of how to maximize our piety and holiness while dealing with the demands and distractions of daily life that we modern people experience. Further, by combining Paul's arguments here for equality and reciprocity with his claims in other places regarding the primacy of love and our obligations to encourage and build one another up, we could construct a rich, thought-provoking, and engaging model of marriage.

1 CORINTHIANS 7:29-35, A DIGRESSION REGARDING LIFE LIVED ESCHATOLOGICALLY

COMMENTARY

The first part of this new digression (7:29-31) is framed by two declarations. One depicts the believers as near the end of the age, near the time of the Lord's return, near the day of judgment: "The appointed time has grown short" (7:29; cf. 4:5). The other isolates the believers from any inclination to live in accordance with the standards of this world: "The *schēma* [σχῆμα, "form," "outward structure"] of this world is passing away" (7:31 *b*). Within those two framing elements Paul evokes, with only the sketchiest adumbrations, a series of snapshots of how to live in the world and yet practice detachment from the values and entanglements the world offers. The statements, all without finite verbs and without full-sentence elaborations, evince life "as if not" (*hōs mē*). The evocations invite the Corinthians to imagine the life of faith as one lived in the world but detached or disengaged from the world's values. With these snapshots or vignettes Paul answers the question of how believers can "remain as they are," namely, still living within the world, without being held captive or conformed to the values and structures of the world. The answer: Live in these structures and in these relationships "as if not," as if the world, its structures, and these relationships did not provide life with its value and meaning because one knows that the defining relationship, and therefore value, comes from one's relation to God, in Christ.

Paul has addressed this same issue, though expressed in different terms, here and there in the current letter: How is one to preserve and honor one's holiness in a world whose structure (*schēma*, 7:31) is passing away? To whom does one belong (1:12; 3:23; 6:20)? As he has done earlier, Paul continues to insist that believers do not have to withdraw from the world and from the social connections that are structured within it; instead, believers can live the life of faith within the social setting where they find themselves called by the gospel. They can "remain as they are" and avoid idolatry while walking appropriately with respect to the gospel.

The second part of the digression (7:32-35) is an amplification of Paul's claim in 7:28 that he would like to spare them worldly distress. This he develops in terms of helping them to be "free from care" (7:32*a*) and in terms of maximizing both the pleasing of the Lord and devotion to the Lord. In this amplification Paul envisions life as a sorting out of competing loyalties and rival cares or concerns. As we would expect, a Pauline ideal does emerge: It is the person, whether male (7:32-33) or female (7:34), who is free from marriage and its attendant concerns (including inevitably and rightly the desire to please one's spouse); it is the person, therefore, who is free to focus on the Lord and on pleasing the Lord. (Earlier in this letter [6:15-16], Paul has shown that he is capable of thinking of one's relation to the Lord in intimate terms of marriage.) As we would also expect, Paul imagines and condones a concession, something less than the ideal: It is the person, whether male or female, who is "divided" (7:34), who is concerned not only about "the things of the Lord" (7:33-34) but also about "the things of the world" (7:33, 34), who is eager not only to please the Lord but also to please a spouse.

The digression concludes with a direct address to all the readers, declaring Paul's

purpose in his counsel and expressing his disposition: He has sought not to put a yoke or noose (βρόχος *brochos*) upon them but to be helpful to them (cf. 6:12; 12:7). And in it all his goal has been to foster "proper, constant devotion to the Lord without distraction" (7:35). Indeed, Paul's self-description of purpose is consonant with what and how he has counseled them. He has avoided yoking them into a singular, uniform performance but has made his suggestions and given his advice with an eye to maximizing their devotion to God no matter their circumstances, all the time recognizing that different abilities and circumstances may call for some performance short of the ideal or goal.

Like the rival two-way tradition that is so prominent throughout the opening chapters of 1 Corinthians, Paul acknowledges two contending schemas (εὔσχημον *euschēmon*, 7:35, versus σχῆμα τοῦ κόσμου *schēma tou kosmou*, 7:31). The latter is the schema of this world, that, on the basis of his apocalyptic confidence, Paul declares is passing away (7:31). With that schema's passing the patterns of the world are being eclipsed. The alternate schema or pattern that Paul understands himself to be promoting in his counsels in chapter 7 is the pattern of proper, appropriate, presentable behavior (ἀλλὰ πρὸς τὸ εὔσχημον *alla pros to euschēmon*, 7:35*c*), which is then elaborated by the remainder of the sentence: "namely, uninterrupted constancy to the Lord." On the one side, the unfavored way, are the patterns of the world, its values, its modes of human relationships; on the other side, the gospel's way, is an undivided devotion to the Lord, which may be expressed in all of life's circumstances and in a range of responses, all of which are acceptable to God, but which operates on very different principles and values from the way of the world. The "proper schema" of 7:35 is the norm—so much so that Paul works from it in the next verse to describe behavior that is inappropriate—that is, not from the proper schema (7:36).

REFLECTIONS

1. Although Paul believes that in some sense individuals find themselves in situations that the Lord has apportioned to them and in which they have been called by

God, Paul shows across this chapter that he assumes that individuals make choices for which they are responsible, that people are capable of self-reflection and can weigh alternative actions and choose the one they deem more appropriate with regard to certain guiding principles or concerns. Persons can override their passions (an ancient concern from the Greeks forward). Self-control/self-mastery is not guaranteed, however (7:5, 8), nor does it have to be maintained in one direction if the cost is too dear (7:36).

2. The curious passage 7:29-32 is an exercise in perspective-keeping from which we modern believers can benefit. Given that "the time has been shortened" (7:29a) and that "the schema of this world is passing away" (7:31), believers relate to every indifferent matter in such a way as not to overvalue it or to confuse it with what is most important. Paul's list in 7:29-31 is illustrative of the sorts of matters that are not ultimate and should not be confused as such: marriage (7:29), mourning and rejoicing (7:30), purchasing/owning (7:30), and, a most sweeping category that functions much as an "et cetera" that includes everyone, "those who use the world" (7:31a). Not to confuse what matters with what does not is a constant human challenge, and one's delineation of the distinction is a road map of one's values and commitments. And all of us "use the world" (7:31a) in a variety of ways. When we use a disproportionate amount of the world's resources, we should have questions of conscience. All of us "use the world" in the sense of living in it, and doing so raises not only the questions of proper stewardship but also the fitting concern not to be entrapped by the world's values. The latter is Paul's concern in this passage and should be ours as well.

3. Paul would spare the Corinthians' "concerns" (NIV) and "anxieties" (NRSV, 7:32) and "worldly tribulations" (7:28) if he were able, but to do so is not in his control. In part the sin-burdened creation waits with eager longing for its deliverance like a woman in labor suffers the birth pangs in the delivery of the child (Rom 8:18-25). Believers are like that: They will not escape those tribulations (1 Thess 3:3). In the context of God's purposes one must honestly acknowledge the pervasive human problem of competing goods and loyalties (dedication to one's beloved and devotion to God), and one soon realizes that one can only hope to minimize, not eliminate, these particular stresses and concerns. So, in fact, Paul finally distinguishes between proper and improper anxieties and concerns. Note that life without concerns is not what the gospel promises; rather, the gospel reminds us that God's grace is always present with us in the midst of our concerns, sustaining and encouraging us (for more on this, see 1 Cor 10:1-13; cf. Rom 8:28).

4. For Paul the effort to please one's spouse is a taken-for-granted obligation of marriage by both husbands and wives. To be sure, it takes energy that might otherwise be placed directly in service of God, but with marriage there is also the need to please one's spouse and, notably, even one's obligations to God do not pre-empt the responsibility to please one's spouse. This is an index of how deeply Paul honors the commitments and responsibilities of marriage partners. How rich is marriage when both spouses place their obligation to please the other ahead of all competing responsibilities.

1 CORINTHIANS 7:36-38, BETHROTHED UNMARRIEDS AND THE IDEALIZED RESPONDER

COMMENTARY

After the digression Paul's focus is clearly and fully on those unmarrieds who are betrothed, engaged. This time, however, the pattern is reversed, with the ideal being reserved for second place, for emphasis and for elaboration, and the concession leads. Building from the picture of the "proper" or "fitting" (*euschēmon*) relation to the Lord just mentioned in 7:35, Paul finds that if an engaged man considers that he is "behaving dishonorably" or "improperly" (ἀσχημονέω *aschēmoneō*) toward his betrothed, if his passions are strong (cf. the same consideration in 7:9), then "let them marry" (7:36). For such a person to marry is not to sin (7:36; cf. 7:28). Following the concession Paul presents the ideal, more fully developed here than anywhere before, which the reader must know will be some form of the guideline: "Remain as you are."

The personification of the ideal responder (7:37) is elaborate, suggesting that this is the model Paul would wish could be found in every group he has addressed in this chapter. Four important assertions identify the idealized person: (1) He or she "stands steadfast in his or her heart"; (2) he or she is not under the sway of necessity, but (3) he or she has control over the passions; and (4) he or she is "convinced in his or her own heart." Items (1) and (4) are so similar as to be an emphatic inclusio.

The detailed picture of the person who makes the ideal response accords well with Paul's own self-discipline as described in Romans and in Philemon. There Paul "knows and is persuaded" (Rom 14:14); he has no doubts or waverings (Rom 14:23); and he recognizes that moral action must not be forced, must not be by compulsion but by choice (Phlm 14). In the case at hand in 1 Cor 7:36, the stalwart-in-faith person will "keep her as his fiancée." Some basics in Paul's understanding of moral reasoning surface in 7:37. At the fore is Paul's consideration that moral decisions are grounded in one's untroubled, unshaken heart (7:37*a, c*). Directly associated is Paul's concern that the individual who is faced with a moral decision not be under compulsion and not be driven by passions (7:37*b*). Although it is not developed by Paul at this point in the letter, an individual who was so free from compulsions and passions, who was so resolved in his or her heart, would be in a position to weigh out what sort of action would be appropriate not only to one's measure of faith but also to love.

Such a person as identified here, Paul claims, "will do well" (7:37). Likewise, the one who marries his own fiancée "will do well" (7:38). So each does "well"; both responses, to marry or not to marry, are within the scope of proper moral comportment for believers. But Paul's predilection for "remaining as you are" as a means of maximizing devotion to the Lord emerges as the "better": "The one who does not marry does better" (7:38). To marry is acceptable, but it is an accommodation to limited self-control and involves a change in social status—and on both counts is devalued compared to "staying as you are."

REFLECTIONS

Paul's idealized portrait of the ideal person merits attention. Not everybody has such an integrated moral life. Sometimes we may find ourselves more whole, sometimes more fractured. The mature believer, as Paul here assumes, is a person whose "head is screwed on straight," or as we might also put it, who is centered around a core of established values. No wind will blow this person off course hither and yon. Neither necessity nor compulsion is a primary factor in the person's moral decision. And the person's choices are not guided by the passions (anger, avarice, lust, etc.). How many of us can recognize ourselves in that portrait? Each of us can take a kind of running inventory of our moral decisions from time to time, examine our choices, and see when we come closer to that portrait and when we seem to have acted in a way alien to it. In those times when we have acted out of passion or compulsively, we can weigh whether we might do differently in another similar situation at another time.

1 CORINTHIANS 7:39-40, DIVORCE, WIDOWHOOD, AND REMARRIAGE

COMMENTARY

Paul concludes his counsel regarding marriage and human sexuality with a word concerning divorce, widowhood, and remarriage. Reaffirming his earlier embrace of the Lord's teaching (7:10) as the ideal, Paul says that as long as the husband lives, the wife is bound to him. His position on that is already clear, but what happens if the husband dies?—an issue he has not addressed heretofore. Paul's concession: "She is free to marry whomever she wishes, but only in the Lord" (7:39)—the last phrase most reasonably being understood to encourage marriage to a believer. Once again,

the ideal emerges: "But she is more blessed (μακαριωτέρα *makariōtera*) if she remains as she is, according to my maxim" (7:40), which he enunciated earlier in 7:26 and from which he has been deliberating right along. He concludes the whole section with what amounts to an enforcement formula: "I think that I have the Spirit of God" (7:40 RSV), an inclusio, or ring device, with 7:25, where he gave the self-estimate that he is "by the Lord's mercy trustworthy" (7:25 NRSV) and immediately introduced his maxim (7:26).

REFLECTIONS

1. The NIV translates *makariōtera* as "happier," the NRSV as "more blessed" (7:40). In biblical traditions, blessedness is a status conferred by God and it always requires, as a fundamental presupposition, that the person blessed be in right relationship with God. So the state of being blessed supposes a proper relation to God requisite to God's blessing being conferred. Such a person—that is, in right relation to God and accordingly conferred to a status of blessedness before God—would have good reason to be happy. But happiness, as it may be understood in modern times, is possible in isolation, as a solitary individual without reference to God, whereas blessedness is not. If happiness is at all construed as one form of pleasure, one can find (momentary?) happiness without God. Because blessedness makes clear God's presence and care for us, blessedness can happen in the midst of distress; happiness never can. Happiness does not by definition declare anything positive or negative about one's relation to God; blessedness does. (Cf. the beatitudes in Matt 5:3-12, where some translations use the unfortunately reductionist translation "Happy are those who . . ." instead of "Blessed are those who. . . .")

2. As we look back across this chapter, we see that Paul's advice about marriage is factored from three concerns and convictions. First, his counsel is grounded in his eschatological conviction that the time before the end is short. Second, he is concerned to maximize devotion to the Lord. Third, throughout his deliberation in chapter 7 he is guided in his counsel by the pre-Pauline baptismal formula that we see so clearly in Gal 3:28, in which distinctions between males and females in the Lord are indifferent matters. The combination of the first two provides the matrix for understanding his maxim to "remain as you are" because the time to the end is presumed to be short. The third—his creative application of the Gal 3:28 tradition—leads Paul to picture marriage as a reciprocal relationship of spouses.

Paul is a realist about human needs and human choices, and about how some of those needs and choices will impinge on one's devotion to the Lord—but his realism helps him grasp that for such a person maximizing devotion to the Lord must take place precisely in the context of those choices and needs.

Paul recognizes the power of sexual passion; he realizes that persons will need to divorce; he understands that slaves may wish freedom; and he concedes that accommodation to such drives and needs, far from being sin, is an appropriate response for believers. Throughout he is guided in his counsel by the pre-Pauline baptismal formula that we see so clearly in Gal 3:28, in which distinctions between males and females in the Lord are overcome as indifferent matters. Like the Stoics in the world and no doubt in the Corinthian church Paul founded, Paul is able to make distinctions among indifferent matters between "preferreds" and "not-preferreds." So Paul's counsel, while affirming that in Christ there is no difference in standing of male and female, nevertheless declares his preferred: In the light of the impending end of the ages, all of them should remain as they are if possible.

3. A realistic view of moral reasoning undergirds this whole chapter. One may know the ideal, the best goal toward which one might aim, but, because of various factors, many of which can be beyond one's control, one may not be able to attain that goal. Paul's presumption is that we should aim as high as we possibly can, without deceiving ourselves into settling for a lesser achievement. Life does not always go as we want; we are not in control of much that happens in and around us, and matters of very different importance bid for our allegiance. Accordingly, it is crucial that we remain clearheaded regarding not only what is in our control but also what is important. Desires must not prevail over self-control (7:37). In times of moral deliberation, believers would do well to ask in scrupulous honesty: What is truly in our control? What is truly important?

1 CORINTHIANS 8:1–11:1

PAUL'S RESPONSE TO A CORINTHIAN QUESTION ABOUT EATING IDOL MEAT

OVERVIEW

With 8:1 Paul turns to a question about eating meat offered to an idol, a matter that comes from the Corinthians' letter to him. Before considering their question and Paul's response, however, a word is in order about how Paul structures his response to their question. Paul takes their rather specific question about a particular practice and uses it as an occasion for a wider elaboration of what constitutes appropriate moral reasoning and community interrelations. In the process, Paul transforms the question from one of eating, purely and simply, as they seem to have asked it, to a view in which eating becomes a metaphor for the larger issue of the proper comportment of all of life. The literary unit in which Paul accomplishes that transformation begins in 8:1 and extends through 11:1.

In this protracted section we see not only the social dynamics of the Corinthian congregation but also Paul's assessment of those dynamics. The picture in these chapters is not so different from what has emerged earlier. Some at Corinth have strong convictions and are accustomed to being heard, to taking—and being given—the lead in moral deliberation, and they seem ready to prescribe moral comportment for others. Others (we may wonder if this is not a majority) seem more accustomed to listening; they find themselves pressured to follow, and, lacking perhaps certainty of conviction and surely their own willingness to stand up and be counted, without voice or power. Perhaps some of them are even responding by trying to live and act like the more vocal and powerful persons, even though Paul considers that it may not be appropriate for them to do so (cf. 8:10-11).

In what he writes, Paul must engage his followers wherever they stand in these social dynamics.

The Corinthians' way of putting the question of 8:1 shows some fundamental affinity with Paul: They have set the issue in terms of "meat offered to an idol" (εἰδωλόθυτος *eidōlothytos*), a Jewish and subsequently Christian way of referring to what others would more simply have called ἱερόθυτος (*hierothytos*), meaning something sacrificed in a temple to a deity.[106] Typically, either of these terms refers to the widespread contemporary practice of sacrificing an animal to a deity, burning some of the flesh on an altar, and eating some of it in a cultic meal, which was always a festive, social occasion. The remainder of the sacrificial animal was sold to the meat market for resale to the public. Believers like the Corinthians, even after they have come over into the faith, may still, therefore, have a range of contact with meat offered to idols: The meat is periodically available in the market for purchase (10:25); unbelieving neighbors may invite believers to dinner and serve such meat (10:27-29); and attendance at some cultic festivals is open to believers as an enviable social occasion (8:10). One might (correctly) surmise that the perennial problem of this letter emerges once again: How does one honor and protect holiness, being set apart for God, while one lives in the world, in the midst of the normal social exchanges that one encounters in Corinth?

---

106. For a detailed study of Paul's argument and concerns here, see W. L. Willis, *Idol Meat in Corinth: The Pauline Argument in 1 Corinthians 8 and 10*, SBLDS 68 (Chico, Calif.: Scholars Press, 1985).

The structure of 8:1–11:1 is as follows: 8:1-6, a clarification regarding what believers think they know and what they should know; 8:7-13, a caution that some are not clear on what they should know, and counsel about how the believers who are clear should relate to such persons; 9:1–10:13, a two-part digression in which Paul offers himself (9:1-27) and historic Israel (10:1-13) as the models of comportment for the community and within the community; 10:14-22, a section in which, through references to baptism and the Lord's supper, Paul returns to the question of eating meat offered to idols, this time considered in a cultic setting; and 10:23–11:1, a summing section, with ties back to 6:12-20, in which the Corinthians' earlier maxim about their freedom in Christ (cf. 6:12) is repeated, refined, and supplemented by Paul's call to imitation of himself and of Christ.

1 CORINTHIANS 8:1-6, THEIR QUESTION, THEIR ASSUMPTION, PAUL'S REHEARSAL OF WHAT THEY KNOW

COMMENTARY

Just as in the treatment of the first item from their letter (7:1), so also here Paul begins by repeating a maxim of some Corinthians: "We know that all of us have knowledge" (8:1*b*). Paul does not oppose or depreciate knowledge (cf. 2:6). As we have seen and will see again numerous times in 1 Corinthians, Paul readily turns to "what we know" as a resource for moral guidance and deliberation. So it is understandable that some of his followers would value and appeal to knowledge as they do here. But Paul's immediate response signals his unhappiness with their claim on two fronts: (1) "Knowledge *puffs up*," and puffiness or arrogance has already emerged as a problem at Corinth; and (2) knowledge is set over against love in such an opposition as to remind one of the rival two-way tradition that has already been such a feature in the letter (see the Commentary on 1:10-17). Paul takes the Corinthians' claim about possessing knowledge as another indication of their eagerness to turn whatever they can toward status, prestige, and rank—which turn Paul has disparaged in 1:18-25; 2:6-13. The Corinthians who have forged this maxim—and it will not have been the whole community—have arrogated to themselves superior status and freedom based on their newfound knowledge in Christ. Of course, Paul shares some responsibility for contributing to such a misunderstanding because he believes that in Christ believers really do understand things differently (cf. his recognition of this in 2:6). But some at Corinth have used this difference to demarcate between the status of themselves and that of other believers in Christ, a stance Paul totally rejects.

Maxims, by nature, are allusive; they invite hearers to engage them and to fill out the larger picture that they evoke only in broad stroke. Let us consider the Corinthian maxim with a view to the larger picture it supposes. Their maxim—"We know that we all have knowledge" (8:1)—reflects a confidence that on its face Paul would appreciate, but Paul's response with three maxims of his own (more on that below) suggests that he finds problems with their maxim. The sweeping inclusiveness, "all of us," affirmed by their maxim simply does not correspond to reality as Paul sees it, as he says directly in 8:7. And one can surmise that their association of this maxim with the question of whether to eat idol meat suggests that they have a freedom to eat, that, as 8:9 will confirm, they have an ἐξουσία (*exousia*), a right, a freedom, and that they hold that all believers should be clear on the freedom to eat, possessing knowledge as they are all supposed to do.

The claim of some Corinthians to possess knowledge (8:1) would not have been strange in Paul's time. Stoics understood that knowledge leads to virtue, that knowledge leads to proper behavior, and that knowledge defines and enhances freedom. So the

Corinthians' claim of knowledge is at the same time their assertion of their freedom, about what is permissible for them (cf. 6:12; 10:23). Paul shares with them the conviction that what one knows has a direct bearing on one's freedom to make consequent choices: For example, if one knows that there is no God but one, then concern about idols diminishes (8:4). His mention of "this authority/ freedom [*exousia*] of yours" (8:9), however, separates him, as does his insistence in 8:7 that not all possess this knowledge, from those Corinthians who simply make their moral decisions from what they themselves know and who show no concern for how the resulting actions might bear on someone who did not have the same knowledge or assurance of what is permissible for them.[107] They are the ones who may have knowledge but not love (8:1).

As noted, in that culture, one usually does not directly reject someone's maxim; instead one adds a qualifier or places another maxim alongside for leverage. In this instance, Paul responds with three of his own maxims (8:1, 4, 4). Paul's first maxim—"Knowledge puffs up, but love builds up" (8:1 NRSV)—is followed by two verses of elaboration (8:2-3). With his first maxim, Paul critiques their placing of knowledge rather than love at the center of either their moral deliberation or their communal life in Christ. Paul has repeatedly been concerned that some of the Corinthians have been puffy and boastful (1:29, 31; 3:21; 4:6-7, 18, 19; 5:2, 6; and note 13:3-4), and the concern emerges here again. Over against knowledge, their definitional marker, Paul sets love. When love is at work, it can only bring about good for others, it can only accomplish or effect edification, upbuilding. Knowledge, while it is indeed important in some ways and though Paul has in fact admitted that he does indeed impart wisdom (2:6), is capable of abuse not only of others, by condescension, but of the one who claims it, by a self-estimate that is inordinate. Put differently, love keeps things in proportion, in perspective better than knowledge; knowledge

without love is sure to come to nothing or even to cause harm. As Paul notes in 8:2, knowledge has a curious capacity to deceive the knower; as he will say eloquently later in this letter, "knowledge passes away" (13:8), knowledge without love reduces one to nothing (13:2) and gains nothing (13:3). Note well that knowledge is not in and of itself bad or worthy of spurn. What is wrong is knowledge that is carried away with itself, knowledge that vaunts itself as giving status, knowledge that may become a stumbling block for another, knowledge that is not put to work in love, and knowledge that eclipses love.

In the Greco-Roman world knowledge was inevitably linked to status, to a concern about where one stands in relation to others. In Paul's communities love is inextricably tied to service, to caring for one another. In 8:3 Paul tries to distinguish wrong knowing, which puts what one knows and its attendant status at the center of life, from the primal and definitional knowing that really counts: being known by God. When one knows oneself to be known by God, then love falls into place and knowing is placed in perspective. When one properly expresses love toward God, then one is known by God (8:3), then one's knowing serves God's love.

Paul touches on an abiding issue here. The problem is how believers can know that knowledge itself does not save them (that is gnosticism's claim) without going to the extreme of claiming that faith and knowledge must be set over against one another. The challenge for a believer is not to become an obscurantist, not to become a know-nothing, in short not to pit knowledge against faith. Faith, indeed, has knowledge that is appropriate to it, as Paul clearly understands (2:6). Paul regularly asks, "What do we know?" as a fundamental operation appropriate to moral reasoning. But, like any other good thing, knowledge can be used to seek status and, indeed, to lord it over others. Knowledge per se is not the problem either for Corinth or for faith; having it function properly in a loving and edifying fashion is the issue and the goal.

Verses 2-3 show that Paul thinks the Corinthians who boast that "all have knowledge" have turned things around backward. They have made themselves the measure of all things as if one's own knowing were

107. For a careful and illuminating discussion of Stoic suppositions between Paul and the Corinthians in chaps. 8 and 9 and how those suppositions lend understanding to the connection of the two chapters in Paul's argumentation, see Abraham J. Malherbe, "Determinism and Free Will in Paul: The Argument of 1 Corinthians 8 and 9," in *Paul in His Hellenistic Context*, ed. T. Engberg-Pedersen (Minneapolis: Fortress, 1995) 231-55.

the defining factor in one's standing or status, as if one were defined and given importance by what one knows. At stake for Paul is proper self-assessment, which for him can never begin with what one knows because that path will always lead to wrongful boasting and to an inflated self-estimate. For Paul the definitive knowing is *God's* knowing of us, which, if love for God is properly in place (cf. Deut 6:5), will result in *our being known*, in our receiving God's love in a way that not only claims us for God but also engages us in love toward others (cf. 13:9, 12).

Although the word does not appear in this context, grace is at issue here. It is not what believers know that sets them right with God and gives them to one another. The flow never runs that way for Paul. God's freely given, unmerited love claims the believers and establishes them. It is a delicate matter in Paul's understanding. One does not come to know God as many Greeks had assumed. Rather, one is known by God (Gal 4:9). All proper knowing proceeds from God and acknowledges that God's knowing precedes and grounds what believers know. God's knowing establishes, constitutes (cf. Exod 33:12, 17) believers, who then must caution themselves that their knowing is derivative and that what they know should function as a guide to love rather than as an index of status and rank.

The Corinthians' maxim in v. 1*a* is, of course, partly right: All believers do have knowledge, and that in two senses. First, all believers who love God have been known by God and so they have the knowledge that is purely a gift of God and that we otherwise call "grace." Second, when love is properly in place, then what believers know can serve well as navigational markers for the travel along the road of faith. What believers know is supposed to help them live the life of love. But their sentential claim that "all possess knowledge" is too sweeping and not discriminating. It allows no specificity, no variation from one believer to the next. Because it is so vague and general, it provides no moral leverage for the question at hand but implies freedom to eat food offered to idols and thereby it seems to claim status. When knowledge is used as a status marker or is used to place others in jeopardy, then perspective has been

lost, things have gotten turned around. And that is what Paul tells the Corinthians in 8:1-3.

With that necessary clarification about knowing and being known (vv. 2-3), Paul picks up once again their question about eating idol meat, and in his next two maxims (which he introduces with "We know" just as they have theirs) lays out the pertinent claims believers should know: "No idol in the world really exists" and "There is no God but one" (v. 4 NRSV). Paul addresses the issue on two fronts, with regard to idols and with regard to God: the first dismissively announced—idols do not truly exist—and the second the occasion for considerable elaboration—there is only the one God (cf. Deut 6:4, the *Shema*, the affirmation that stands at the center of Israel's faith). Paul's point is not just that there is a single deity. Staked out here is one's relation to that deity, the characteristics of that deity, and what we know about that deity—these are what really matter. Life must be lived in light of the deity who is in control (cf. 3:21-23). It is not an option to be unrelated to that God. Life must be lived, moral decisions must be rendered in keeping with what we know about that God. The nature of all being is imaginable only within the scope allowed by and dictated by the nature and purpose of God. A fundamental issue is engaged here: How does what one believes and knows about God bear on the relatively mundane decisions of everyday life? Paul's answer: absolutely critically and definitionally. To whom does one belong? What are the characteristics of the one to whom one belongs? These are recurring issues in 1 Corinthians because they are fundamental to living the life of faith, to understanding one's place in the world, and to moral reasoning.

Both maxims in v. 4 represent part of Paul's rich Jewish heritage that he has inculcated into the Corinthians' faith. Israel's revulsion at idols is clear (Exod 20:4-5, 23; 34:17; Lev 19:4; 26:1; Deut 4:15-20). So is its central claim, best exemplified in the *Shema* of Deut 6:4, that "God is one."

Paul identifies God as Father (echoing 1:3), which sets the context for the intense use of brother/sister concepts in 8:11-13, and, in what begins to sound like a creedal affirmation, God is described as the one who is the source of all things and the one for whom we exist (3:21-23; 8:6*b*; cf. 10:26). Paul identifies Christ as the one "through whom all things and we ourselves exist" (8:6*c*). The assertions about God and Christ reaffirm and refine what Paul already wrote in 3:21-23, that believers ideally should relate to the world and to all things as ones who know they belong to Christ, who belongs to God.

REFLECTIONS

1. "Love builds up" (8:1). Love is Paul's most important concept in describing how believers rightly relate to one another, and it is so critical to his corrective of the Corinthians' interaction that he devotes a whole chapter to its elucidation (chap. 13). Love is not just a sentiment, not just a feeling, not merely a sort of disposition. Love works; it acts; it does things; and the chief thing it does is to edify, build up, cause growth in each of the persons who engages in it and who is engaged by it. Love is not a one-way street; it is more like the proverbial bad penny or like the widow's jar of meal and jug of oil (1 Kgs 17:8-16): You cannot get rid of it; it will not run out. Give it away profligately, prodigally, and it is never exhausted, nor is anyone shorted by the giving away; it does not have to be hoarded; it not only benefits the recipient, it rebounds (in a fuller form than it was sent) to the donor so that donor becomes recipient along with the other. Love works. Love transforms circumstances and people. The loved one is never again the same; the one who loves is never again the same. Love is thus a transaction but not a bartering; it is not susceptible to bargaining. Love, once under way, takes on a life of its own; like the grace on which it is built, it surprises. Love restores, love enlarges, and love makes whole. Most often that is what happens with love. But love is not a magic wand; love can be spurned and rejected; and sometimes love elicits its nearest of kin, hatred.

2. Idolatry is not simply the worship of an object as if it were God. So defined, idolatry would be no significant problem. Paul openly depicts idolatry here as having many gods and lords (8:5) that bid for our allegiance, that in some significant way claim us as belonging to them. The basic question, "To whom do you belong?" therefore, is ultimately a question of proper faithfulness or idolatry. When something takes over your life, begins to run it for you, then you have idolatry. Your false god or lord will be whatever apart from God governs your life. The possibilities are nearly limitless: It could be your work, your health, your desire for a boat, or perhaps a relative, such as a parent or even your children!

1 CORINTHIANS 8:7-13, PERSONS DIFFER IN KNOWLEDGE—AN IMAGINARY AND INSTRUCTIVE SCENARIO

COMMENTARY

Paul indicates a problem, despite the confidence of the Corinthians who formulated the maxim in 8:1: "The knowledge is not shared by all" (8:7). Paul knows that there are believers at Corinth who still have it in their moral consciousness that idols do have some power and that to eat the meat is somehow to continue to show reverence for the deities they all used to recognize. For such persons, for whom the idols continue to represent power, eating causes defilement or staining (8:7; cf. Rom 14:23). In the heart of his deliberation, Paul lays down a defining premise that applies to himself and to all believers: "Food will not commend us to God!" (8:8; cf. Rom 14:10, 17).

In 8:7-13, Paul broadens the discussion from idol meat to all food for two reasons: (1) As noted, eating becomes a metaphor for living, and (2) the issue of eating idol meat is not a separate moral question that needs special, singular treatment. He makes sure that his auditors on either side of this question may understand with utter clarity his claim that *all* food, not just idol meat, is an indifferent matter in one's relation to God: "If we do not eat we are no worse off; if we do eat we are no better off" (8:8). The matter is indifferent. So, Paul thinks it is all right but not better if some, with clear moral consciousness, eat meat offered to idols; and it is all right, yes, even necessary, if others, with what he calls "weak conscience or consciousness," abstain.

Clearly, vv. 7-13 are more directly addressed to the Corinthians who advocate the maxim "We know that all of us possess knowledge" and who accordingly think they have the "warrant" or "power" or "right" ("this liberty of yours," 8:9 NRSV; ἐξουσία [*exousia*], a term that will be the focus of attention in 9:1-18) to behave on the basis of that knowledge. This subgroup may well be the same ones who earlier in the letter were noted as championing their freedom under the maxim "All things are permissible *for me*" (6:12, italics added). The issue becomes palpable when someone with a weaker moral consciousness is tempted (Paul uses the term οἰκοδομέω [*oikodomeō*], "built up"—built up wrongly, understood; 8:10) to emulate the person of (greater) knowledge.

Paul's use of "build up" in 8:10 (NIV, "emboldened"; NRSV, "encouraged") is singular in his undisputed letters because only here he anticipates that believers may "edify," in the sense of encourage, someone to do something that person should not do, to do something that would not be helpful or appropriate to that individual. Love, properly functioning, will not encourage someone to do what is not appropriate, so improper and, therefore, false building up cannot be the work of love (8:1).

Paul refers to a person's moral consciousness (συνείδησις *syneidēsis*) being weak (8:7, 10, 12). Then in 8:11 he shortens the construction by referring to "the weak person." Although he does not directly mention "strong" people or persons with "strong moral consciousness" in vv. 7-13, he seems to be addressing them. First a word about *syneidēsis* in Paul, then some remarks about strong and weak.

Paul's laconic reference to *syneidēsis* here suggests that he has already taught the Corinthians about it and assumes they have it straight, so he feels free to use the term without elaboration. Across the corpus we can see that Paul supposes that a person's *syneidēsis* functions as a sort of moral scanner that is set off only when the contemplated action raises doubts in the mind or heart of the actor as to the act's propriety. It is the moral equivalent of a warning light. It serves the same function (and may be the same thing) as doubts or waverings (διακρίνω *diakrinō*) that one may experience in the face of a contemplated action (Rom 14:23; cf. Rom 4:20).

The reappearance of *syneidēsis* later in 1 Cor 10:23-30 confirms what we have observed and extends it. Paul supposes that each person has an individuated *syneidēsis*, which can be translated as a "moral consciousness" that is specific and pertinent only to that individual. Further, each person is to respect the moral consciousness of others so that, as in Paul's fictional dinner conversation in 10:27-29, when an individual expresses reservations about an action, the hearer must honor that person's scruples even when the contemplated action does not raise similar problems for the hearer.

This is a window onto Paul's anthropology and onto his understanding of moral reasoning. For Paul, each individual has a moral consciousness that allows a given range of actions without setting off any warning bells of impropriety or inappropriateness. Verses 7-13 show that a person's moral consciousness is directly related to one's understanding, in this instance to what one knows—that is, to what one truly understands. Paul holds (8:13) that not everyone has the understanding that idols are nothing. For *those* people, their moral consciousness is limited—that is, it is weak regarding this issue. All persons must act within the scope of their own moral consciousness. And, there is nothing wrong or inadequate about the more limited (weaker) moral consciousness. Just as food will not commend a person to God, so also knowledge does not. The scope or fullness of one's knowledge of that which one understands in such a degree as to be able to act upon it is not what commends to God, but living properly within what one understands and what one views as appropriate.

So the "weak one" is not to be considered inadequate or inferior. That person is merely at one stage or point on the growth continuum, which runs from more limited moral consciousness to a fuller moral consciousness. As the Corinthian babies in faith (3:1) are expected to grow up and mature, so believers are to care for, nurture, and build one another up in love.

Paul's way of describing the dynamics of his imaginary scenario tells us much about his understanding of community. The "weak person" is (a) "brother or sister" (4 times in vv. 11-13), (b) under the same Father (8:6), and (c) is one for "whom Christ died" (8:11). For each of these three reasons the weak person is valuable and deserving of consideration. To act without consideration toward such a brother or sister is labeled by Paul as "sinning against the brethren," and even more powerfully as "sinning against Christ!" (8:12). Christian community is founded on the one fact: Christ died for each person. That, and nothing else, is the common basis of Christian community. Therefore, to cause harm or even stumbling for someone for whom Christ died is to work calumny against Christ, who died for that person and claimed her or him as Christ's own. And because believers are brothers and sisters in Christ, any harm done to another is damaging to the family of God.

Worthy of note here is Paul's notion that sin is not an act that is purely and simply between oneself and Christ (or God). Rather, sin inevitably also affects others. So just as one's faith should always express itself in love to those around one, so sin, that broken relationship with God or Christ, always affects not only the sinner but also those in contact with the sinner (cf. 5:6-7).

Strikingly, Paul does not tell the Corinthians what they ought to do. Instead, he brings this section to a conclusion by saying what *he* would do, or not do (v. 13), and thereby offers himself as a model, as one who is at least as strong in moral consciousness as the strongest of them but who would abstain from meat altogether (probably a resort to hyperbole) rather than to scandalize or cause a brother to fall (v. 13). Paul, the radical model, shows by exemplification what is more important and what is less; and his exemplification in v. 13 paves the way for the protracted exemplification that we call chap. 9.

What began in v. 1 as a question about eating idol meat has become, by the end of the section, a question about eating meat in general—and even abstaining from eating meat when, despite one's own adequate moral consciousness, one sees that one's actions might cause harm to another member of Christ—as an example of proper consideration of others in the exercise of one's freedom in Christ. And for an elaboration of himself as moral exemplar worthy of emulation, he turns to a digression that includes chap. 9 and extends to 10:13, after which he will return to the issues raised by their question regarding meat offered to idols.

REFLECTIONS

1. The Corinthians' question of what one can appropriately eat inescapably raises the question of one's relation to creation and, therefore, ultimately to God. The New Testament often portrays Jesus as giving thanks to God at the breaking of bread or at table fellowship (Mark 6:41; 8:6 and par.; 14:23 and par.; John 6:11), because whatever one eats expresses a dependence of the eater upon some of the remainder of God's creation, and therefore ultimately a dependence upon God as Creator. God of all creation is the source of all things and is the goal of human existence. Humans—and all of creation—are from God and all of human life is lived toward God. So the question of eating, precisely because it is such a perfect metaphor for describing all of life, can be weighed out ultimately and only in relation to God. Therefore, what one knows and believes about God must be factored into any decision or choice about what one eats. And if eating is a metaphor for all of life, as Paul indeed takes it to be in 10:31 at the end of this section of the letter, then whatever one decides or chooses must ultimately be decided and chosen in the light of what one knows and believes about God.

2. Paul describes people as having stronger and weaker moral consciousnesses because he thinks of believers as having different measures of faith (Rom 12:3), as being further along the line of development from babies in the faith (whose moral consciousness is not strongly formed or as fully instructed) to the more mature in faith. And we know from 3:1-2 that Paul thinks the Corinthians have a good many babies in the faith among them. Accordingly, he advises the Corinthians that as they make their choices they must be careful not to harm others among them who may be less mature and, therefore, *more susceptible to influence* to overreach. Wrongful building up must be a concern. Therefore, believers must factor into their moral deliberation notonly how the contemplated action fits them and their relation to God but also how such an action might affect another. Believers are capable of self-control, and they are responsible for their decisions and the actions based upon them. But weaker believers must perforce look to and learn from their stronger-in-faith brothers and sisters who thus inherit a certain added responsibility to choose and to act with the weaker siblings in mind. Believers are not only responsible for themselves and their actions; they are responsible for each other and the way their deeds set examples for others.

With respect to modeling, Paul concludes the chapter by encouraging each of the auditors to model his care, his love for others. But ingredient to the chapter is also a call to the stronger-in-faith believers to take their obligations as models more seriously. Modern believers should be more self-conscious about setting a good example in each and every decision and choice and action. Even if it had no effect on others, it would surely enrich our own faithful response to God. And who knows what use God might make of it in the eyes of someone who observes us?

3. For Paul, sin is never simply a private act between an individual and God or Christ. Such a wrong relation with Christ or with God always inevitably spills over and harms others as well. We hear persons say that what they do with their bodies, for example, is their own business and not anybody else's. Paul would have none of that. If you harm your body, it affects others in ways you do not imagine. Sin in whatever form is corrosive not only of the individual sinner but of those proximate. Paul's notion, therefore, is totally out of joint with the modern inclination to privatize not only our relation to God but also our moral choices, both good and bad.

1 CORINTHIANS 9:1–10:13, EXTENDED DIGRESSION CONSISTING OF TWO EXAMPLES

OVERVIEW

Digressions allow an author to bring a fresh perspective alongside a troublesome deliberative issue.[108] In this case, Paul's digression actually runs through 10:13 and consists of two examples, one largely positive (Paul himself, 9:1-27), one negative (most of those in the exodus, 10:1-13).[109] Paul presents himself

108. Wilhelm Wuellner, "Greek Rhetoric and Pauline Argumentation," *Early Christian Literature and the Classical Intellectual Tradition: In honorem Robert M. Grant,* ed. W. R. Schoedel and R. L. Wilken, Théologie Historique 54 (Paris: Etudes Beauchesne, 1979) 177-88.

109. In agreement with Wuellner, "Greek Rhetoric and Pauline Argumentation," 186-87, that the digression runs from 9:1 through 10:13.

as the example of how a believer who knows he has rights or warrants or powers behaves in love toward others so that they are properly built up (8:1) and not destroyed (8:11). Paul's digression here leaves it for the auditors to make the connection and application to their own situation.

The structure of this digression is rather straightforwardly a chiasmus (A B B´ A´). Paul is established as exemplar, as the model of one who is as free as anyone (item A) and as the Corinthians' apostle possessed of as many rights as anyone (item B) in 9:1-2. Paul's self-depiction as apostle (item B´) in 9:3-18 is of

one who has rights but chooses not to exercise them. His description of his accommodating evangelistic style (9:19-23) shows his undisputed freedom (item A´) to choose for himself an ironic slavery in service of the gospel (cf. 7:21-23). The first part of the digression, that which is focused on Paul, closes with an exhortation that is cast in athletic metaphors (9:24-25) and a final offering of himself as an example (9:26-27). The structure and function of the second part of the digression (the depiction of Israel in 10:1-13) will be discussed later.

1 Corinthians 9:1-27, Paul As Exemplar

1 Corinthians 9:1-2, Identification of Paul As Free and As Apostle

COMMENTARY

The digression opens with two questions stated, as Greek allows, in a form that expects a yes answer. The first question—"I am free, right?"—may invite an explanation (which is at the heart of the digression's purpose) because Paul has just declared that if food causes a brother's fall Paul will simply quit eating meat (8:13). Some of his auditors may well have thought, "Some freedom!" The

second question—"I am apostle, right?"— and its attached comments about seeing Jesus (cf. 15:8) and about his having brought the gospel to them (9:1c-2) sets the stage for Paul's exemplification of apostolic comportment as a textbook study of claimable rights that go unclaimed for a purpose (9:3-18). (See Reflections at 9:24-27.)

1 Corinthians 9:3-14, Paul, the One of Unexcelled Rights, Chooses Not to Use Them

COMMENTARY

Paul sets it forward as a mock defense (ἀπολογία *apologia*) for anyone who would "examine" (cf. 4:3-4) him, and he uses the form to make his points. This is not truly a self-defense,[110] but a rhetorical device

designed to invite hearers to sort through the claims Paul is about to make. Paul uses self-description in order to set himself up as the example the Corinthians should emulate. Because form follows function, we cannot be surprised by the heavy usage of rhetorical questions; in 9:3-12 alone there are twelve. In fact, the rhetorical questions are employed in such a fashion as to put the readers on the stand, so to speak. The readers are placed in the position of being led by the inquisitor,

110. So, convincingly, Wendell Willis, "An Apostolic Apologia? The Form and Function of 1 Cor 9," *JSNT* 24 (1985) 33-48. Mitchell, while acknowledging that scholars have at times read chap. 9 as a self-defense, primarily because Paul uses the term *apologia* in 9:3, has a careful and compelling critique of that reading and instead rightly takes chapter 9 as another Pauline exemplification. See Mitchell, *Paul and the Rhetoric of Reconciliation*, 243-49, esp. 244-55n. 330.

Paul, through a series of questions that in the Greek clearly expect a yes answer. Paul's mock defense functions much as the frequent Matthean parable lead-in—"What do you think?" (Matt 18:12; 21:28)—and engages the auditors.

At issue is not whether Paul is their apostle; even if they wanted to deny that, they could not (9:1*b*-2). The Corinthians are clearly his "work in the Lord" (9:1*b*); they are the seal of his "apostleship in the Lord" (9:2*b*). Even if it were possible for other believing communities to deny Paul's apostleship (cf. paternity, 4:14), the Corinthians simply and surely could not (9:2*a*).

Paul chooses to make his case by depicting himself as the apostle of great rights and great freedom who exercises those rights and freedom (*exousia*, "warrant," "power," "right"; a term he just used in 8:9, "this *exousia* of yours," not at all or at least in a cautionary way; in 9:3-18 the term appears six times as a leitmotif of the passage, 9:4-6, 12, 18) with great care—or not at all if someone might be harmed.

Paul thinks the matter is beyond dispute—and this is the burden of his mock defense: As an apostle he has rights to receive support (9:4-6) as surely as the other apostles do; soldiers, vineyard tenders, and even shepherds have a claim of support from their labors (9:7; cf. Deut 20:6); Scripture upholds it—the law says even oxen are provisioned in return for their labor (9:8-11; Deut 25:4); temple servers eat from the sacrifices (9:13; Deut 18:1-5; Num 18:8ff.), and the Lord declared that those preaching the gospel should get their living from it (9:14; cf. Luke 10:7; Matt 10:10). Into this stack of arguments—which must be counted as rhetorical overkill—whose purpose has been to argue decisively that he has rights that no one among the Corinthians could deny, he inserts the forceful statement: "If others enjoy this *exousia* with you, how much more do we?" (9:12). He follows it with his programmatic exemplary posturing: "We have not used this *exousia*, but we endure all things rather than give some hindrance to the gospel of Christ" (9:12).

It is a curiosity that begs for some explanation: He has spent nine verses (vv. 4-12) establishing beyond question that he has rights and in fact resumes the claim in vv. 13-14—and yet his point is that he has not exercised them. He has rights beyond the scope of anyone in the Corinthian community—"how much more do we?" (v. 12); they must, he thinks, also grant that. Yet, he pointedly reminds them that he has not used those rights. The crucial issue is, Why? The answer is already in v. 12: It is better not to exercise one's rights, even though one does not thereby give them up, than to risk hindrance to the gospel (9:12) or do harm to one of the children of the gospel (8:9), to a brother or sister for whom Christ died (8:11).

The key claim in Paul's mock defense is 9:12*b:* "But we pass over all things in silence [στέγω *stegō*] lest we obscure [lit., "give a hindrance to"] the gospel of Christ." Each part of this dense construction merits examination. The verb in the first clause is *stegō*, which has a semantic range from "endure" or "bear" or "stand" to "pass over in silence," to "keep to oneself," or to "throw a cloak of silence" over.[111] This verb next appears in 13:7, where it describes how love works, which, as it turns out, is exactly what Paul is describing in his mock defense without once using the term: how love bears on the exercise of one's *exousia*. What Paul affirms in 9:12*b* is that he has chosen to look the other way, to disregard his rights, to overlook them across the board, because love calls for—and here he can express it in either of two ways—making sure that no obstacle is placed in the way of the gospel of Christ or in the way of one who has been the recipient of that gospel—namely, a brother or sister in Christ. He of the unexcelled rights has chosen not to employ them because of love. So his lengthy "defense" of his rights has not been made because anyone at Corinth has denied that Paul has them. Rather Paul wants the Corinthians to see that loving means not using whatever rights one has when the employment of those rights might hinder the gospel or harm one of the gospel's children. (See Reflections at 9:24-27.)

111. BAGD, 765-66.

1 Corinthians 9:15-18, Paul, Free Not to Exercise His Rights, Is Bound to Preach the Gospel

Commentary

Paul anticipates a possible misunderstanding of his purpose in his mock defense. Verses 15-18 counter with a flat denial that Paul's purpose in writing all this is to do now what he has never done with the Corinthians before—namely, to cash in on his apostolic rights. A remarkable self-portrait of Paul emerges in these verses: As free as he is in so many ways, he is captive to his call; he has not decided to preach the gospel; he has no choice; he is "entrusted with a commission" (v. 17 NRSV). Therefore, he is not due a "wage" ("reward," vv. 17-18 NRSV); he has no "wage," no payoff, except that in his preaching he makes the gospel of grace properly free of charge (i.e., not something that someone earns!) and that necessarily leaves him free not to take advantage of his *exousia*, his "right."

Paul is a combination of necessity and free will; he is a slave to God, a slave whose heart has been unhardened and whose mind has been renewed, and whose will has been revitalized. As to his preaching the gospel, he has no choice; he must do it or suffer the woes appropriate to his failure to do what he is called to do. Yet he freely enslaves (that is his own strong word and image) himself to all people (9:19) because of the very gospel he freely serves and offers free of charge (9:18).

In chap. 7 Paul had advised the Corinthians of the eschatological way of living "as if not" (7:29-31), and Paul now seems to be modeling before them what it would mean to live "as if not" having *exousia:* It would mean having the right and the freedom that goes with it, but it would mean also not needing to exercise the right or act out the freedom if to do so might cause any "hindrance to the gospel" or harm anyone "for whom Christ died." Paul has offered himself as "exhibit A" of the one who has abundant rights and freedom but chooses not to exercise them out of consideration—"love" is Paul's code word for this proper concern—for others.

Some scholars mistakenly say that Paul "gives up" or "renounces" his rights or freedom here[112] and advocates the same for others, but that is to misunderstand Paul. He does not give up his freedom or his rights; instead, he decides not to exercise his freedom or his rights in certain circumstances—and that involves a very different understanding of freedom. As the letter proceeds he will describe circumstances in which believers would be free to exercise their *exousia* without fear of harming another or hindering the gospel. In fact, in the next chapter Paul will apply the principle he is here enunciating. We will read of his advising the Corinthians that they should feel free to eat whatever is sold in the meat market because, he supposes, to do so in the privacy of one's home causes neither a hindrance to the gospel nor harm to another believer's moral consciousness.

The discussion thus far in chap. 9 requires that Paul, who opened this digression with "I am free" (9:1), address directly just what this curiously abridgeble freedom in Christ means, because someone might say this sounds less like freedom and more like slavery, like being bound by someone else's limited moral consciousness. Paul treats that problem by describing his evangelistic practice (9:19-23), which once again gives the readers not only a window onto his own self-understanding but a picture of how he decides, always in service to the gospel, to accommodate to others. Freedom and slavery are now once again (cf. 7:21-23) the categories in which Paul casts his reflections; in an earlier digression Paul has already said that one's calling in the Lord relativizes not only slavery but also freedom: A slave "is a freedman of the Lord" and the free person "is a slave of Christ" (7:22).

---

112. C. K. Barrett, *A Commentary on the First Epistle to the Corinthians*, 2nd ed. (London: Adam & Charles Black, 1971) 200, writes of "a serious limitation" and a restriction of Paul's liberty. F. F. Bruce, *1 and 2 Corinthians*, NCBC (Grand Rapids: Eerdmans, 1971), expresses it in the following phrases: "curtail his own freedom" (83), "voluntary relinquishing of his right . . . voluntary limitation of his liberty" (86). Roman Garrison, "Paul's Use of the Athletic Metaphor in 1 Corinthians 9," *SR* 22 (1993) 214: "sacrifice of his freedom."

Nevertheless, Paul's claim in 9:19—"I, being free from all people, have made myself a slave to all"—must have been shocking to his contemporaries' ears: Paul, the freest of persons, is bound by the gospel, after all (9:16), and in it and for it he chooses to live the life of service to all so that he "might win the more" (9:19)—that is, so that he could carry out the call with which he is entrusted (9:17).

There is almost a playfulness in Paul's images through the heart of this digression as he uses commercial terms to talk about actions and transactions on a level quite beyond commerce. The proclaimers of the gospel "should get their living by the gospel" (9:14 NRSV; equally possible from the Greek: "should live [i.e., get their life] from the gospel"). Paul is obligated to place before (τίθημι *tithēmi*, a technical term of commerce for "depositing" or "setting aside")[113] people a

113. BAGD, 816.

gospel "free of charge" (9:18); he does not do it for the "wage" but receives a "wage" nevertheless (9:17-18*a*); and he becomes a slave to all so that he can "win" (κερδαίνω *kerdainō*) more people—that is, convert, but the term also has the semantic ring "to gain, make a profit." He does "all things" for the gospel so that he can be a "partner" (συγκοινωνός *synkoinōnos*, the term ordinarily has commercial overtones in the Greco-Roman world) in the gospel (9:23). The language is allusive; it reaches beyond itself, stretching categories, to carry unaccustomed freight, indeed to carry freight that must be expressed in concepts with which he and his hearers have some familiarity. The point never lies either on the level of commerce and transactions or in the playfulness of language, but in the truth toward which it pushes the hearers, a truth about the communal dynamics of the life of faith. (See Reflections at 9:24-27.)

1 Corinthians 9:19-23, Paul's Evangelistic and Exemplary Adaptability

COMMENTARY

In these verses, in which *kerdainō* appears five times, "winning" or "gaining" people for the gospel is the dominant motif; it is the governing focus of Paul's life in response to his call. Irony abounds. The one who most exemplifies freedom in Christ and who has no choice but to preach the gospel as he is called to do has freely chosen to enslave himself to all for the sake of the gospel (9:19, 23). As Paul depicts his evangelistic efforts, his voluntary slavery to all *involves a fundamental and exemplary accommodation to people as and where he finds them.* To Jews, to those "under the law," Paul became as a Jew, as one under the law, though he is quick to remind his readers that he, the one who advocates living "as if not" (7:29-31), is not under the law—but all of this was for the sole purpose of winning, gaining for the gospel, the ones to whom he accommodates (9:20). The same regards gentiles, whom Paul here calls "those outside the law" and to whom he became as one outside the law—though he assures his

readers that he is not outside the law of God but "in the law of Christ," probably meaning under the rule of Christ—to win them. His readers, mostly gentiles, will surely recognize what he here so pithily describes and will no doubt positively identify with him and with their experience of the gospel through him. That identification sets them up rhetorically for the next statement: "I became to the weak as a weak person, so that I might win the weak" (9:22).

As surely as Paul has made common cause with all the Corinthian believers, his explicit identification with the weak must be startling to those who imagine themselves as strong, not weak. In 9:22, Paul's voluntary identification with the weak must remind the readers of his urging them only a chapter earlier (8:10-12) to recognize that some weaker brothers and sisters may not be clear about idols and should, accordingly, not be encouraged, built up, beyond their moral consciousness.

Paul's self-portrait in this digression is complex in proportion to the dilemma he is addressing: On the one hand he pictures himself as superlative in his freedom and in his *exousia*, his "right" that pertains to his high status as an apostle, and he treats it as if he assumes that they recognize this self-portrait and readily identify with his strength and determination. On the other hand, he paints a picture of himself as a voluntary slave who, for the sake of the gospel, identifies with the weak. (This reference must surely hark back to the persons mentioned in 8:7ff. who do not possess the knowledge that idols have no real existence and that there is only one God.) Paul, the exemplary strong, the free person, stands in an imitable way with the weak in the gospel, on account of the gospel, as a requirement of the gospel. As he does, so should every believer.

Then in the formulation—the first part of which most modern people know even if they do not know that Paul is the source of it—"I have become all things to all people in order by all means [or "at least"] to save some" (9:22*b*)—Paul tries to capture his principle of accommodation that he believes so fundamental to life lived in the gospel. His is compressed language, squeezing much into few words. Paul knows that it is not he who saves, but God. Similarly, Paul does not see in this evangelistic accommodation a loss of identity of himself or of the gospel. Intrinsic to it, however, is a fundamental principle that Paul has seized upon and that informs his entire ministry: The gospel, the power of God, always encounters and engages people where they are, where they live, in their social matrix. Inevitably, the gospel moves them and changes them, but it always comes to them, engages them, and nourishes them from that very point, as and where they are. For the concern at hand—the divisiveness of the community and the independent arrogance of some of the believers—Paul's self-portrait as one who accommodates to others, even to the weak, invites his hearers, who readily enough identify with Paul as free person, to identify with him also as voluntary servant who accommodates to the weak and to their needs for the sake of the gospel. (See Reflections at 9:24-27.)

1 Corinthians 9:24-27, Paul, the Athlete Who Takes Care Not to Be Disqualified

COMMENTARY

As Paul draws the first part of the digression to a close, he invites his readers, so familiar with the Athenaic and Isthmian games, the latter probably having been staged no more than eight miles from Corinth and most recently less than a year prior to this writing, to think of themselves as athletes, as indeed he considers himself. In the Greco-Roman world athleticism was highly valued, athletes were honored, and every major city had an arena. The games were analogous to war; the events were often those associated with battle. This association of games and battle fits Paul's notion that God's plan is like a battle and believers must be fit and ready (cf. 2 Cor 6:7; 1 Thess 5:8). To be the very best possible athlete—the function of the "only one wins the prize" argument (9:24)—requires discipline and self-control, self-mastery[114] "in everything" as everyone in that culture surely knew; and it is this point upon which Paul seizes. Craftily using plurals in an inclusive way, Paul reminds the Corinthians that, to paraphrase, "we exercise self-control in all things . . . in order to receive an imperishable wreath or crown" as victors (9:25). Believers are like famous athletes[115] in that believers must exercise self-control "in all things" (πάντα *panta*, 9:25); they are unlike those athletes in that believers are running for imperishable rewards. In 9:25 Paul's emphasis lies on the single term *panta*, "in all things," "in everything." Typically, Paul

114. Stanley K. Stowers, *A Rereading of Romans: Justice, Jews, and Gentiles* (New Haven: Yale University Press, 1994) 45-52, for a treatment of self-mastery in the Greco-Roman world.

115. Garrison, "Paul's Use of the Athletic Metaphor in 1 Corinthians 9," 212-14.

views life as an integrated whole; all of life is to be placed in service to the gospel and others. No compartmentalization. So also here no part of life is exempt from self-control; self-indulgence must be set aside. All of his concern with self-control is Paul's modeling for his auditors the moral life lived with the full discipline and consideration of others. To be sure, some Corinthians may think of themselves as free like Paul. Now in these verses he invites them to be disciplined "in all things" as he is—not only disciplined, but also committed to voluntary slavery and identification with the weak.

So it is with him, Paul says. He runs not aimlessly (unstated but assumed is that he knows the goal toward which he races). He does not simply shadowbox, but he keeps his body (= himself) under the most rigorous, deliberate discipline; indeed (to no one's surprise), he likens it to a sort of self-imposed slavery once again (9:27; cf. 9:19). And so he expects of all his readers not only rigorous, self-imposed discipline but also intentional, voluntary slavery to one another in Christ. This reference to "body" and its proper care surely echoes a similar point made earlier about proper temple maintenance of the body for the resident Holy Spirit (3:16-17). And the slavery Paul here embraces is consonant with the perfect slavery in love that is complete freedom.

Along this line it must not go unnoticed that when Paul describes the proper discipline appropriate to life in the gospel he expresses it in two verbs bearing on τὸ σῶμα (*to sōma*), the body, that is, his own self, understood. The verbs ὑπωπιάζω (*hypōpiazō*, "to treat roughly" or here "to impose discipline") and δουλαγωγέω (*doulagōgeō*, "to enslave or bring into subjection") surround and have as their direct object "the body, the self" (9:27). Paul has already touched on the self-mastery motif in this letter (cf. esp. in 7:38, but implicitly in 8:7-13 and 9:12*b*-14). In 9:26-27 Paul explicitly exemplifies the need and importance of self-mastery as a part of the daily life of the believer this side of the last judgment.

Of equal importance here is Paul's use of *sōma* as his self because his choice of that expression enforces significant links to what he has already written in 1 Corinthians (and will provide a ground for his comments on *sōma* in 1 Cor 15:35-44). As the auditor thinks back to Paul's earlier assumptions about *sōma* in this letter, two passages must come to mind. One is the hinge-passage (6:12-20) where Paul claims that the believing self, the *sōma*, belongs to the Lord in a fundamentally definitional way. The *sōma* is what it is in respect to the Lord, as reckoned in its relation to the Lord (6:13), and the Lord is for the *sōma*, which is related to the self, as in a marriage. The connection is so secure as to be expressible in the striking image: Your *sōma* is the temple of the Holy Spirit (3:16-17). Paul's own exemplary self-portrait in 9:27 shows that, translating from his athletic metaphors employed there, he goes to all lengths to ensure that he practices proper temple maintenance on his own *sōma*.

The first part of the digression closes with an ironic note that may echo Paul's earlier cry of "Woe" if he does not preach the gospel. Would it not be ironic, he says, if after preaching to others he failed to practice what he preached, and, at the judgment, if he were found to be "disqualified" (*adokimos*, a technical term of athletics in which a competitor fails the test or is thrown out of the competition)? The implication is palpable: If Paul, the chosen apostle, can anticipate that he might be found disqualified in the last judgment because he did not exercise a training code and life appropriate to the gospel, then all other athletes in the gospel must reevaluate their discipline and practice and bring themselves into comportment with the gospel. With that, Paul closes the largely positive part of the digression and turns to the story of Israel's exodus out of Egypt (10:1-13) as a means of advancing his argument with a cautionary illustration precisely on this same point.

REFLECTIONS

1. This entire section is a study in exemplification, an offering of models of comportment for the life of faith. Do you look for the ways in which others offer examples of living that would be worth emulating?

2. Paul's opening self-portrait is a study in Christian freedom. His first question, asked in Greek in such a way as to expect a positive answer, "I am free, am I not?" sets the stage for his presentation of himself as an exemplar.

What is freedom? How do we understand it? One of the most popular modern definitions is "free from all constraints and limits." In Paul's time the Stoics thought that one gained freedom by risking less, by placing less of oneself as vulnerable to the actions of Fate or to the doings of others. So one could partially characterize Stoic freedom as a retreat, a withdrawal. Is Paul's decision not to exercise his rights a retreat or withdrawal also? Paul's own discussion of freedom is focused on his right to act, to decide, or to do as he wishes.

A part of freedom is the capacity to choose the very thing that is required. There is a strangeness to the fact that love is commanded of us. How can love, which depends so much on the freedom and spontaneity of the heart, be commanded? Only because the ones commanded to love cannot imagine doing anything else! So they freely embrace what they are ordered and compelled to do. But the difference is the free embrace. Love is perfect slavery; love is perfect freedom.

3. Love requires discipline; it is not an accident that Paul uses boxing as a metaphor for the life of discipline (9:24-27). In order to achieve the goal (the eschatological prize of God's positive judgment), Paul models discipline where one's choices and the actions dependent upon them are not chosen with a view to what might give the most immediate personal pleasure, but are chosen with God's judgment in view—namely, that Paul might avoid being found unworthy or disqualified. So true freedom calls for sorting through the possible courses of action not first with regard to one's rights, no matter how strong or numerous they are, but with regard to what serves the well-being of others and, therefore, the common good.

Paul's final description of his exemplary self here is of the athlete, the boxer, who exercises self-discipline in all things. Paul features an irony: He who would help others by delivering the gospel to them could ironically end up disqualified (like the athlete thrown out of the competition). In this Pauline irony there is a cautionary word for all who, powered by the gospel, busy themselves so much with "helping" and "rescuing" others that they end up not taking proper care with their own self-discipline and thereby risk becoming disqualified. Giving of the self without proper care of the self can be self-destructive (cf. a similar note carried over into 10:12).

4. Paul's assumption throughout 9:1–10:13 is that the Corinthians do not suffer from lack of self-love and self-interest. We do not know what Paul might have said about proper self-love, but his twice-stated embrace of the command to "love your neighbor *as yourself*" (Rom 13:9; Gal 5:14; Lev 19:18) shows that he recognizes self-love as a possible base from which to reckon. In Paul's letters we have access only to his treating the balance tilted the other way, toward improper love of others. One could imagine Paul having critiqued the Corinthians as lacking proper self-love when they seem so desperate to act with no consideration/love of others. A modern Christian might do well to attempt the fashioning of such an argument because in the doing of it one would have to find a way to talk about how loving others is ultimately a form of (proper) self-love.

5. The "as-if-not" quality of life that Paul advocated in 7:29-31 is in chapter 9 put on display. Paul, who is the most free of all, willingly makes himself the servant of all (9:19) in behalf of the gospel. Accordingly, in some respects he lives "as if not" free; in others he lives "as if not" a slave. Put differently, service in the gospel leaves him free to be a slave of others, but in such a way that his freedom is enhanced, not lessened. Also, he relates to his indisputably considerable rights "as if not" having them. Be careful to understand: He has the rights—he and the Corinthians concede that—but he lives with them while being free from having to exercise them. Paul *insists* on his rights, enumerates them at length, and then *forgoes the exercise of his rights*, without giving them up at all. He still has the rights. He simply overrides the use of them with his concern for what serves the gospel and what serves others.

6. "All things to all people." This phrase, taken out of context, has come to mean all sorts of things to all sorts of people. First, the context in the letter. Paul is describing his adaptability in service of evangelism. The function of this statement is identical to that of the "I decided to know nothing among you except Christ" (2:2). Both are hyperboles designed to state unmistakably what is the governing force around which other activities are arrayed. For Paul, whatever advances the gospel is what governs his comportment. But, second, Paul relates one of the secrets of his evangelistic prowess: He goes to people, where they are, on their own terms. He does not require that they come to him or that they meet him on his own ground. He, a Jew, is apostle to gentiles, non-Jews, but they do not have to become Jews in order to be welcomed into the gospel. He knows that the gospel bridges ethnic boundaries and works its power in whatever context. Put in other terms, people do not have to possess authorized, pre-approved dippers before they can drink from the gospel. Paul custom-pours. Paul's is a noteworthy confidence that the gospel does not have to be protected by issuing it only in pre-approved containers.

What is true about the gospel is true about love, its central expression: Love always engages others, precisely where they are; it does not require them to come over or up to one's standards before it can be operative. In fact, one could argue that the only true engagement with others begins with meeting the other persons where they are; otherwise, imperialism sneaks into the picture. The careful reader of 1 Corinthians will have noticed, in the immediately preceding chapter, another illustration of Paul's willingness to adapt to others, when Paul is willing to consider becoming a vegetarian if not doing so would cause a weaker-conscienced brother or sister to stumble (8:13).

But becoming all things to all people does not involve losing or giving up one's own center, becoming gelatin-molded to whatever form appears, or losing track of what is truly important. Quite the contrary, in Paul's case it becomes absolutely critical that he know what really counts. Note Paul's description of his evangelistic strategy. When he became "as one without the law" to gentiles for whom the law was not a part of their knowledge, he knew about himself that he was "not without the law of God." Similarly, when he evangelized Jews, he became "as one under [the authority of] the law," though he knew that he himself was not under the authority of the law—meaning that the law and not God would have been the source of his life. The "as if not" character of the life of faith (see the Commentary on 7:29-35) means not only that allegiance to God is direct and all-encompassing but also that no human institution (the civil government or courts, for example) or distinction (of gender or ethnicity, for example) or practice (even of a religious sort such as keeping certain days or ritual activities) can become a primary filter that can function to separate a person from direct relationship to God. That is radical stuff. Paul is in line with a trajectory that runs from the eighth-century prophets of Israel through Jesus in which nothing, not even or especially religious requirements, stands in the way of one's relation to God. So Paul evangelizes on the principle that by preaching the gospel to all sorts of people, meeting them on their ground, he is affirming that nothing, no human institution or practice or distinction, can be permitted to hinder the communication that God cares passionately about all of God's creatures (not unlike his view in Rom 8:38-39).

1 Corinthians 10:1-13, The Exodus Retold As a Caution

COMMENTARY

The digression begun in chapter 9 continues through 10:1-13 where Paul retells a cautionary version of Israel's exodus from Egypt.[116] His rendition of the exodus story sustains the note of judgment with which his own positive self-portrait ends (9:24-27). By his characterization of some of the Israelites as "idolaters" (10:7) and as ones who "practiced immorality" (10:8), Paul ties together the letter's enduring concern with πορνεία *porneia* as totally unacceptable for the life of faith (5:1; 6:13*b*, 18; 7:2) and the worry about idolatry that has surfaced in the Corinthians' question about eating meat offered to idols (8:1, 4). In his two earlier vice lists, Paul already anticipated his treatment of this topic and named idolatry (5:10, 11; 6:9) and *porneia* as disqualifying persons from inheriting God's reign (6:9-10). Idolatry and *porneia* are explicitly highlighted in Paul's retelling of the exodus and provide the link by which he ultimately exits the digression and makes application (10:14-22) to what was no doubt a specific problem faced by the Corinthian believers: Can they who "partake of the table of the Lord" also share what Paul pejoratively calls the "table of demons" (10:21)?

In 10:23–11:1 Paul sums up not only the argument about eating meat offered to idols (first introduced in 8:1) but links back to 6:12 where he first treated the Corinthians' slogan that "all things are permissible for me" (6:12). This passage (10:23–11:1) serves many functions: It ties together themes and concerns of the letter up to this point; it refines and extends some of the arguments made before; and it makes application to the auditors of the letter.

Typologies take past events, in this case the exodus from Egypt, or former individuals (as Abraham in Romans 4), and *by a selective*

retelling of the old story become a vehicle for guidance in the present. In the retelling the author may make some explicit link to his readers, but typology invites the readers to make their own connections as well. In Paul's typological treatment of the exodus he effectively tells the old story twice, once in 10:1-4, with a warning in 10:5, and with 10:6 Paul begins an explicitly cautionary retelling of the story a second time. Clearly, Paul first tells the old story in ways designed to encourage his auditors to identify with its characters. Those of the original exodus were "Our ancestors" (οἱ πατέρες ἡμῶν *hoi pateres hēmōn*) (10:1 NRSV); they, too, were baptized (10:2); they, too, partook of spiritual food and drink (10:3-4; cf. Exod 16:4, 35; 17:6; Deut 8:3; Num 20:7-11); and they, too, were related in a special way to Christ (10:4). Verse 5, with its doubly emphatic "But not," signals a transition of purpose: "But not with most of them was God pleased."

In 10:6-13 we gain an insight into one way Paul understood Scripture: Its events and characters provide examples, instructions, warnings for contemporary believers (10:6, 11). So what Paul tells about the old event and its characters should have a clear relevance for what he thinks is going on in Corinth. With 10:6, Paul's second telling of the exodus story has a very different spin. Now the persons with whom the readers were encouraged to identify in 10:1-4 turn out to be those who desired evil (v. 6), were idolaters (v. 7; Exod 32:4-6), engaged in sexual immorality (*porneia*; v. 8; Num 25:1-2), tested the Lord (v. 9; Deut 6:16; Ps 78:18; Isa 7:12), and grumbled (v. 10; cf. Num 21:5; Deut 1:26-27). God's judgment is noted in the retelling: Thousands fell in one day (v. 8; Num 25:9), snakes killed others (v. 9; Num 21:6), and others were killed by "the destroyer," that is by an avenging angel (v. 10;

116. William Baird, "1 Corinthians 10:1-13," *Int* 44 (1990) 286-90.

Exod 12:23; cf. 2 Sam 24:16; 1 Chr 21:15; Wis 18:20-25). In effect, Paul says, "Fair warning!"

What are we to make of these characterizations and the light they shed on Paul's view of the Corinthian situation? Were there grumblers or complainers in Corinth? There may well have been, though we have no other text to suggest it directly. Were there those whom Paul considered to be testing the Lord? As surely as there were any idolaters or persons engaged in *porneia*, there were persons Paul considered in danger of God's judgment (cf. 11:29-30). Not every detail of the recounted story needs to fit in a one-for-one fashion.[117] This much is clear: *Porneia* has been an issue in this letter (from chaps. 5 through 7) and idols, idolatry, and idol meat have been a feature as well (5:10, 11; 6:9; 8:1, 4, 7, 10; 10:7-8, 14). The gist of the account is clear: God's people—being chosen by God, being baptized, eating special food and drink—are accountable for their behavior. Neither baptism nor special edibles and potables ensure against God's judgment if the chosen ones stray or "fall" (v. 12). And there can be no mistake about it: God cannot be blamed for any falling because God never tests believers beyond what they can bear; God always graciously provides a way out, an exodus (10:13).

Paul retells the exodus from Egypt in a way that includes and admonishes his predominantly gentile audience ("our fathers," 10:1; "examples for us," 10:6; "for our instruction/warning," 10:11). The recounting of the exodus concludes with Paul's confident assertion that, along with whatever testing may come one's way, God will make "the way of escape" (RSV) or "way out" (NRSV; 10:13).

Paul's telling of the exodus invites his readers to identify with those whom Paul calls their wandering, cloud-guided forebears (10:1; Exod 13:21-22; Ps 105:39); it highlights the connections of his readers with the characters in ancient Israel by retrofitting baptism and Lord's supper motifs onto the old story: "All were baptized into Moses in

the cloud and in the sea and all ate the same spiritual food and all drank the same spiritual drink" (10:2-4a). Even the rock from which they drank (Exod 17:6; Num 20:11) is identified as Christ (10:4b). The ties between Paul's readers and the old story could not be tighter.

Just at the moment when Paul's hearers should have made their most explicit identification, through the christological claim (10:4b), Paul jars his hearers with a radical shift in the trajectory of the story: "Nevertheless, with most of them God was not pleased and they were destroyed in the wilderness" (10:5). With that shocking declaration Paul pursues the downside of the exodus and, by inference, the potential jeopardy for the Corinthian believers: The people of Israel practiced idolatry and immorality; they put God to the test; and they grumbled or murmured against God (10:6-10). Given the emphasis upon idolatry and immorality in Paul's letter up to chap. 10, it is difficult to overemphasize their presence in Paul's retelling of the exodus. Paul's point to the Corinthians is explicitly stated: *Be careful that you know where and how you stand* (10:12).

Paul invites his readers to evaluate or test themselves by making a comparison with the characters in the exodus story. Like their wandering predecessors, they share in the benefits that God has provided and they are guided and nurtured by God. But they must be careful not to comport themselves, like "most" of their forebears, as persons who are tempted to idolatry and immorality and thus put God to the test. *Some* of the Corinthian believers seem to have lost their way. Paul's troubles are not with all of the Corinthians as God's problems were not with all of Israel; we may suppose that a majority of the Corinthians were living according to their faith and in consideration of others, but we do not hear from them directly, though it is safe to suppose that some of them are among those who clued Paul into the divisiveness and other problems among the community.

Paul takes the scriptural story as an example ("warning," 10:6, 11 RSV), as an instruction or warning (10:11) for him and his readers "upon whom the ends of the ages have come" (10:11; cf. 7:26, 31b). The phrase "ends of the ages" (τὰ τέλη τῶν αἰώνων *ta telē tōn aiōnōn*) is Paul's way of writing about Christ's return

---

117. On the dangers of mirror-reading—i.e., on taking every clue in the text to reveal a facet of the situation into which the letter is directed, see J. M. G. Barclay, "Mirror-Reading a Polemical Letter: Galatians as a Test Case," *JSNT* 31 (1987) 73-93, esp. 79-83; and George Lyons, *Pauline Autobiography: Toward a New Understanding*, SBLDS 73 (Atlanta: Scholars Press, 1985) 96-105.

when God's purposes will be finished. The notion is grounded in apocalyptic speculation such as Dan 12:13 and has been mentioned by Paul already in 1 Cor 1:7-8; 7:26, 29-31 (cf. Heb 4:7 and the setting of a certain day). Accordingly, Paul calls upon each of his readers to undertake a careful self-assessment: "For this reason, let the one who thinks that he stands watch out lest he fall" (10:12). The "end of the ages" is a time of judgment when each person faces two alternatives: Either the individual will "fall" (πίπτω *piptō*), as did the twenty-three thousand in the exodus (10:8), or "stand" (ἵστημι *histēmi*; a Pauline technical term for proper grounding and remaining in God's grace; cf. Rom 5:2; 11:20; 1 Cor 15:1; 2 Cor 1:24; cf. Eph 6:13). Self-testing can give an occasion for realignment, for reorientation, in which one can make certain to steer clear of *porneia*, idolatry, and a testing of God. By altering one's course on the basis of self-examination, one can choose to stand (*histēmi*) with the exodus forebears who were faithful rather than fall (*piptō*) like those who tested God.

The passage closes (10:13) with a twist on the warning about putting the Lord to the test (10:9), turning it to a discussion of the tests that befall believers. Here Paul assures his readers that they will not be extraordinarily tested (10:13*a*) and that God, the very God of the exodus, will not let them be tested beyond their powers (10:13*b*), but with every test will provide a "way out," another exodus.

A word about Christ as the rock that followed the people in the wilderness is needed. Paul comes to the notion of the rock "following" them very readily because he notices that the location of the rock, as told in different passages in his scriptures (Ps 78:16 supposes it happened more than once; Exod 17:1-6; Num 20:2-13), is always with God's people but is mentioned first in one place and then in another and so forth. Philo, another Jew who was contemporary with Paul, identified the rock as Wisdom, who, thus personified, never abandoned God's people.[118] As the Lord's supper's food and drink are retrofitted back onto the old story so is Christ. This is easy for Paul because Paul clearly thinks of Christ as having been with God from the very beginning (cf. Phil 2:5-11).

This ends the two-part, massive digression that began in 9:1. Both sections of the digression concluded with a warning about the impending judgment and the need for the auditors to take stock and make sure they discipline themselves as Paul does (9:24-27) and avoid evil, immorality, and idolatry (10:6-13) lest they fall or be destroyed as most of their Israelite forebears were.

Why was this entire digression so long? The answer must lie in Paul's need to move the Corinthians from what they have (partially) understood into a larger and more complex picture. The digression serves two clear functions: (1) to model a proper melding of freedom with love; (2) to warn that being called and included in God's story does not inoculate believers from the responsibility to love one another and therefore to please God. Evidence across the letter shows that the Corinthians have seized onto the truth that in the gospel they are now free; Paul seems to suggest at points that their sense and practice of their new, unrestrained freedom is hazardous to themselves and to each other. Paul's lengthy digression links freedom with a concern— "love" is his code word for it—for one another. Ingredient to this attempted reconfiguration of their thinking is Paul's warning, first about himself as a potentially disqualifiable athlete and then about Israel as ones who, despite eating the special food and drinking the special drink, were struck down because God "was not pleased" with them (10:5).

The digression provides the readers a fresh angle of vision from which they can make their own applications to the questions and issues that beset them. Paul and Israel are safe targets; strong points can be made and applied to them and the readers are left with the opportunity to make self-application. The rhetorical handbooks take special note that persons who apply something to themselves are much more forceful in the application when they seem to come to the point on their own,[119] and this digression offers the auditors such an opportunity.

Taking no chances, Paul moves to make his own applications in 10:14-22 to the issue the Corinthians have raised with him about eating food offered to idols, but Paul broadens the issue to idolatry.

118. Philo *Allegorical Interpretation* 2.86.

119. Quintilian *Institutio de Oratoria* 9.2.71

REFLECTIONS

1. Exemplars can be positive or negative: We can learn how to live appropriately but also how not to. In 10:1-13 some among Israel serve as a negative model. A challenge for modern believers might be to figure out how they might learn from negative models without being non-caring, judgmental, or condescending. To be sure, the Scriptures, in their honest portrayal of humans as ones who stumble or take wrong turns, often provide, as they do for Paul in 10:1-13, a rich resource of such negative examples.

2. Paul's description of Israel as "our ancestors" (10:1 NRSV) to a predominantly gentile congregation is an illustration of what the creeds came to call "the communion of saints." All of God's people, whenever and wherever they were, are, or may be, are jointly and equally part of God's family. The entire biblical story is God's story, and we who have come later are having our stories woven into the ongoing saga of God's people. All of God's saints (see the Commentary on 1:2) belong to one another by God's grace.

3. "God will not let you be tested beyond what you can handle" (10:13). Many people know this Pauline aphorism and shake their heads in bewilderment when they find themselves in awful circumstances. Two features of the text are especially noteworthy. (1) The "yous" in the text are both in the plural, meaning that the experience of the testing and the efforts at handling it are never presumed by Paul to be borne by an individual alone. Paul's assumption is that any testing you experience is never in isolation. A death of a spouse, for example, is also a death experienced by others. And the bearing of the test, the handling of it, is never supposed by Paul to be done by an isolated individual; others will always be bearing it with the one who is tested. So the text supposes that God will not test us beyond what all of us can bear together. Paul's outlook stands in sharp contrast with the modern tendency to privatize and individualize all religious matters and experiences, even including suffering. (2) Note the context in which we find this statement about God's faithfulness not to test too hard. Paul has been writing of God's exodus deliverance of the people of Israel from slavery in Egypt (10:1-11). So the motif of deliverance should be on the reader's mind. Then Paul affirms the faithfulness of God, that God's testing will not be too severe to be borne, and concludes: "But with the testing God will make a way out [an exodus!] so that you can endure" (10:13). With every test, the faithful, dependable God will make sure it is something you collectively can handle, or God will provide an exodus just as in olden times.

4. In the wonders of our retelling it, the exodus has tended to become an all-glorious event, much as the shame and distress of the cross have given way to a jeweled object of beauty, but only in retrospect and only with the benefit of faith's insight. The biblical narratives show that the persons experiencing the exodus found it problematic in the extreme when they were undergoing it, and Paul reflects that in his notice of their grumbling (10:10). Would it not be fair to suggest that most exoduses are not wholeheartedly greeted when they are happening and that most exoduses seem indeed to be deliverance *only* in retrospect? So the promise of a "way out" may in fact be perceived as very troublesome at the time it is happening.

5. Paul's retrofitting of baptism and the Lord's supper images of eating and drinking spiritual food and drink can have a cautionary effect on believers today if they realize that those signs of God's commitment and support did not keep the ancient Israelites from stumbling and from being destroyed. Baptism and the Lord's supper are not insurance against going astray; neither are they excuses for failure to be responsible.

1 CORINTHIANS 10:14-22, PAUL'S APPLICATION: "FLEE IDOLATRY"

COMMENTARY

With the digression (9:1–10:13) ended, Paul resumes the line of his argument from the end of chap. 8, where he had been reflecting about the mutual responsibility believers have for one another as they consider whether to eat meat offered to idols or not. Now in 10:14-20 he addresses the Corinthians regarding their participation in the cultic ceremonies that were a regular feature of the religions that would have been present in Corinth. Obviously, the Corinthian believers still had social contact with their unbelieving neighbors and Paul sees no problem with that (see also 10:27; 14:24). Prior to their conversion, most of the Corinthian believers would have been participants in the cultic festivals—which usually included a festal meal as a high social and religious event—so it is reasonable for them to wonder whether they can continue to take part in the festivals with their unbelieving friends. One can imagine some of the believers, especially the ones who rightly embraced the maxims "An idol is nothing" and "There is no God but one" (8:4), positing that they could indeed take part in the cultic festivals without, as Paul would say it, "putting the Lord to the test" (10:9) or "provoking the Lord to jealousy" (10:22).

Paul's opening line on the topic, however, is not accommodating: "Flee from idolatry" (10:14 NIV). In his moral counsel, Paul, with a better-safe-than-sorry mentality, steers a wide course around perceived ethical problems or obstacles; his readers should recall an example in his own willingness never to eat meat if doing so would cause a brother or sister in Christ to stumble (8:13; see also Rom 14:23). In 10:14-22 Paul refines and particularizes his admonition to "flee from idolatry" by urging his followers to refrain from sharing table with what he dubs "demons" (10:21; cf. Deut 32:17; Ps 106:34-39; Bar 4:7).

For Paul, participation in the Lord's supper (which itself will be a topic for further refinement in 11:17-34) is the fundamental, even defining, community action of believers.

Like no other activity, this fellowship epitomizes believers' relation to Christ and to one another in pristine clarity. Cup and bread are the focal symbols (10:16-17). κοινωνία (*koinōnia*, "association," "partnership," "sharing," "fellowship," and the term from which some people speak of the Lord's supper as "communion") and related terminology ("take part in," "have a share in") lace this pericope and ground Paul's basic supposition that participation and sharing in Christ and the resulting fellowship is exclusively defining. It sets limits and boundaries that exclude any and all other rival participations.

Paul thinks his readers should know enough about Israel's practices to understand that "the ones who eat the sacrifices are partners of the altar" (10:18; cf. 9:13; i.e., they share in the food offered on the altar; cf. Lev 7:6, 15). the same with believers in Christ who drink the cup and eat the bread. And so Paul's logic follows: The same with any cultic participation! Paul thinks ahead and intercepts a possible misunderstanding: It is not that idol sacrifices are anything or that an idol is anything (10:19); he remains clear on that (8:4). The problem for Paul is that what the Corinthians' neighbors sacrifice is offered "to demons and not to God" (10:20; cf. Lev 17:7; Deut 32:17; Ps 106:37), and believers cannot risk being "partners with demons" because that is idolatry and will "provoke the Lord to jealousy" (10:22). The passage closes with an ironic intimation of divine confrontation: "We aren't stronger than the Lord, are we?" (10:22). That is why Paul thinks that fleeing idolatry or any semblance of it—that is, steering a wide course so as to avoid it—is sound advice that "sensible people" should understand (10:14-15).

Paul has reengaged the issue of eating idol meat with a strong link: "For this reason" or "Therefore [διόπερ *dioper*], my beloved, flee from idolatry" (10:14). The Lord's supper, alluded to in Paul's retelling of the exodus story (10:3) and here in 10:15ff. described for the first time in the letter, provides the base from which Paul invites his readers' reflection and assumes their assent by casting his questions in a form that expects a yes answer: Is not partaking in the Lord's supper a partnership, a sharing (*koinōnia*) in the blood and body of Christ (10:16-17)? Precisely in the Lord's supper Paul locates the ground of all believers' being one: Because there is one loaf and because all believers share that one loaf, they, though many, are one body (10:17).

Back to basics once more: Christian unity is grounded in sharing the loaf; it depends on partaking in Christ's death. Paul expects his auditors to know this from their knowledge of Israel's practices to which he has alluded earlier (9:13): It is an inescapable principle that the ones who eat the sacrifices are "partners in the altar" (10:18), just as believers in Christ are partners in his blood and body. Paul is as certain as any of the Corinthians: An idol has no existence (10:19; cf. 8:4), but their cultic participation in Christ rules out cultic participation in pagan sacrifice, which Paul depicts negatively as an honoring of demons (10:20). Believers simply "cannot drink the cup of the Lord and the cup of demons." Just so, they "cannot share the table of the Lord and the table of demons" (10:21); to do so would be to risk provoking the Lord to jealousy (10:22, another echo of Israel's story; Deut 32:21), a turning away from the Lord to demons, a putting of the Lord to the test. Paul's recounting of the exodus from Egypt has already reminded his readers of the destruction that comes upon those who test the Lord (10:9; for more on Paul's understanding of the Lord's supper in particular, see the Commentary on 11:17-34).

Verses 14-22 comprise a remarkable text. In 8:4-13 Paul can imagine a believer's eating meat offered to idols as long as the person of weaker moral consciousness is not destroyed by this exercise of one's freedom. Similarly, just ahead in 10:25-29 he sees no necessary problem in eating idol meat in an unbelieving friend's home. Yet in 10:14-22 he absolutely forbids eating in the pagan cultic setting. Why the difference? Why the different counsel? The answer lies in Paul's

special understanding of the Lord's supper's singular importance in the lives of believers. The Lord's supper is not just another meal; it is not just another get-together of believers. The Lord's supper and its worship setting are for Paul the definitive action that stands at the heart of the life of faith. In the Lord's supper believers can inescapably see that they stand only in and by God's grace; in the supper believers look with confidence toward the future when the end of the ages will come; and in the supper believers see most clearly how they relate to and with each other. The Lord's supper is like a lens through which the most important things about one's new life in Christ are absolutely brought into focus. In this sense worship at the Lord's supper allows no other participation or sharing that could in any way be confused with it. Accordingly, Paul concludes that no one who partakes of the table of the Lord can share the table of demons. Once again, Paul sees matters in rival, two-way form such that belonging to the one forbids participation in the other. And with two questions (10:22) that demand the auditors' participation, Paul echoes not only scripture (Deut 32:21) but more immediately his recent portrayal (10:9) of the ancient Israelites as the ones who tested the Lord, and asks them if they would dare take part in the table of demons and thereby "provoke the Lord to jealousy," pretending to be "stronger than" God. The point cannot be lost on his readers: Their forebears in the exodus (10:1) tested the Lord and "twenty-three thousand fell in a single day" (10:8 NRSV), some were destroyed by serpents (10:9), and others were destroyed by the destroyer; *they* surely were not stronger than God! Now, in his pronouncement that his readers are to steer a wide course around idolatry and not participate in what he derogatorily calls the "table of demons," Paul reaps the harvest of his depiction of the consequences of the Corinthian forebears' having put the Lord to the test in the exodus. Paul's insinuation: Surely the Corinthians will not repeat the folly of their exodus forebears and risk destruction.

REFLECTIONS

In Paul's time, sharing table, dining with someone, was the primary social symbol of acceptance, of belonging, and of mutuality. That is why so many of Jesus' teachings (cf. Luke 14:1, 7, 15) and some parables (cf. Matt 22:1-10; Luke 14:12-14) are set in a dining context. That is also why the book of Revelation depicts Jesus as knocking and asking entry, with the promise that if allowed to enter he will "go inside to him and dine with him and he with me" (Rev 3:20). Has our loss of sharing table affected our participation in the Lord's supper, not to mention our sense of sharing with our families and others for whom Christ died?

1 CORINTHIANS 10:23–11:1, A SECOND SUMMING-UP

COMMENTARY

Like 6:12-20, this passage ties together themes and concerns of the letter up to this point; by recapitulation and refinement, it extends some of the arguments made before and makes application to the auditors of the letter.

Recapitulation. The Corinthian maxim "All things are permissible for me" (2 times in 6:12) is reprised twice to open this passage and Paul echoes his earlier concern for what builds up, for what is advantageous or helpful (6:12; 10:23). In the chapters between the two repeated sets of maxims (6:12; 10:23), Paul suggests or models proper concern for what is helpful and what builds others up by his counsels regarding marriage partners (7:2-5, 12-16), by his hyperbolic pledge to vegetarianism as an avoidance of causing someone to stumble (8:13), and by his self-portrait as the one with unexcelled rights who freely chooses not to use them if the doing so might cause harm or problems for others (chapter 9).

Refinement. Refining requires dwelling on a topic while seeming to move into new material; it usually involves a degree of repetition and a finding of alternate ways to make and elaborate the same point. The passage at hand is structured from their maxim— "All things are permissible"—which is itself already a near replication of 6:12. Noticeably missing—and part of the refinement—from its earlier, Corinthian form, is the individualistic "for me" that was present in 6:12. In the intervening passages Paul has struggled to help the Corinthians see the community base and context of the Christian life; quite recently he has reminded them that they are one body because they share in the one loaf (10:17). Refinement is also present in the phrases Paul adds to their maxim: "But not everything is advantageous/helpful" and "but not everything builds up" (10:23). Their slogan, in its original form (6:12), considers moral choices *from the decision maker's standpoint*; Paul's refining additions (10:23) focus on *the well-being and edification of the community.* In the first of the section that he now brings to a close (8:1–10:22), he already identified love as that which "builds up" (8:1), so his response to their maxim claim that all things are permissible, while not denying it, calls for love to be at the center of reckoning what and how one does what may indeed be allowed. Love will always secure what is advantageous (cf. 13:4-7). In a cryptically worded injunction Paul calls for Corinthian focus on what is advantageous to the others and builds up the others: "Let no one seek his own [advantage] but that of the other one" (10:24). But their maxim—"all things are permissible"—is true also when applied to eating meat offered to idols and subsequently sold in the meat market; without questioning on account of conscience, they may eat anything sold in the meat market because scripture makes it clear that the earth and all its fullness is the Lord's (10:26; Ps 24:1; cf.

1 Cor 3:22-23). The assertion that the earth is the Lord's is an elaboration, a refinement, of Paul's earlier claims that "an idol has no existence," "there is no God but one" (8:4), and all things are from God (8:6; cf. 3:21-23).

Recapitulation, Refinement, and Application (10:23–11:1). With 10:25-30 Paul returns yet again to the issue about eating food offered to idols with which chapter 8 opened. Here Paul offers direct counsel that bears on their individual choices: Corinthian believers should feel conscience-free to eat whatever is sold in the meat market even though much of the meat sold there may have been offered as sacrifice in pagan religions. Paul thinks they should know themselves free to eat because scripture declares that "the earth is the Lord's and its fullness" (10:26; Ps 24:1; cf. also Pss 50:12; 89:11). Scripture accords well with the same sentiment Paul already expressed in a different way in 3:22-23: "The world . . . [and] all things are yours, yours are Christ's, and Christ is God's" (cf. 8:6).

Paul elaborates the same counsel by means of an imaginary circumstance where a believer is invited to dinner by an unbeliever (10:27-30). If the believer is inclined to accept the invitation, Paul sees no problem and, in the same wording used in 10:25 (πᾶν. . . ἐσθίετε *pan . . . esthiete*, "eat everything"—with the "everything" placed first for emphasis—without any problems for your moral consciousness) urges the believer to feel conscience-free to eat whatever is placed before him or her (10:27). The invented scenario allows Paul to explore a most important issue that he had touched upon earlier: How do one's actions impinge on others? Paul's scenario turns on someone's indicating that the entrée meat has previously been offered in sacrifice. It seems to matter little whether one interprets the identifier as a believer or not: Paul counsels respect for that person's conscience and a consequent refusal to eat the meat. This deference to others and a refusal to exercise one's own rights and freedom when it might harm others has become a leitmotif of this letter (a direct application of Paul's own patterning as reflected in 9:1-14), and the motif will continue to appear in later portions of the letter (cf. 11:33; 14:26-33a).

Verses 29b-30 may seem curious, but ultimately must be understood in the light of 10:31–11:1. In what has just preceded Paul has indeed been advocating a caring consideration of others by means of a self-imposed non-exercise of one's freedom when someone else's conscience might be harmed (8:9-13; 10:28-29a), but he recognizes that one's freedom, though not exercised, is not to be "judged" by another's conscience (10:29b). Judgment will indeed be rendered by God (Rom 14:12), but it will be on the basis of what one has done (Rom 2:6-11; 2 Cor 5:10), not on someone else's conscience but on one's own. Believers must be fully convinced (cf. 7:37; Rom 14:5) and without waverings (Rom 14:23) about whatever they, with clear conscience, choose to do. So different believers may do different things and may make distinctive moral choices and may do so quite properly. In Romans Paul makes this point with regard to keeping special days; some honor special days but others do not, and the variation in practice is fine. "Let each be fully convinced in his own mind. The one who sets one's mind on a particular day does so with respect to the Lord. And the one who eats does so with respect to the Lord, for he gives thanks to God. And the one who abstains from eating does so with respect to the Lord, and gives thanks to God" (Rom 14:5c-6). But what they do must be done in love—that is, with respect for others and with a care not to do others harm but to edify them—and to honor God in thankfulness to God. If, in a spirit of thankfulness, one takes part in such a meal as Paul supposes an unbelieving friend might provide, no one should blaspheme one for that in which one partook with thankfulness (10:30).[120]

Paul's basic position emerges: No matter what one does, whether eating or drinking or whatever, "do all things to the glory of God" (10:31). This recapitulation is already an extension because the discussions from chapter 8 forward have focused on eating, but clearly, eating has become a metaphor, another use of synecdoche, for all of one's life and comportment before God.

This section also recapitulates Paul as exemplar. Throughout the letter Paul has offered himself as the model after which his children in the faith should pattern themselves. Now,

---

120. D. F. Watson, "1 Corinthians 10:23-11:1 in Light of Greco-Roman Rhetoric: The Role of Rhetorical Questions," *JBL* 108 (1989) 301-18.

at this point, he positions himself as example in three ways that he holds absolutely fundamental to the life of faith: (1) He tries to give no offense to anyone, here expressed in the intentionally comprehensive triad: Jews, Greeks, and God's church; (2) he tries in all things to please all people because, as he has already told his readers (cf. 9:19-23), he sees exemplary comportment as serving salvation (10:32-33); and (3) he puts into practice what he urged upon his readers in 10:24: that he does not seek his own advantage but that of the many (10:33*b*). And in all of this Paul calls upon his readers to imitate him because he is imitating Christ. To imitate Paul is to recognize that Paul is modeling after Christ.

To the modern reader it may seem that Paul is of several minds about eating meat offered to idols, allowing it in some texts (implicit consent in 8:4-6, explicit approval in 10:25 and 10:27) and prohibiting it in another (10:14-22). What is one to make of this? First, Paul's picture of the moral life is not simply a rules morality—that is, he does not generate one rule that either covers all aspects of life related to a given problem or applies equally to all believers in all circumstances. Second, the moral life is not lived alone but in community, in Christ. Third, the life in Christ is lived in the world where one interacts with unbelievers. Accordingly, Paul thinks that eating sacrificial meat in one circumstance may be fine for one person and not for another. But what may be fine for the person considered alone may not be fine if doing it might harm the other one or wrongly build up the other person. Paul seems to reason that eating meat previously offered to idols is no problem for the persons strong in faith who are clear that there are not rival gods—fine—as long as one's exercise of that freedom does not cause another to stumble (cf. the same stance in Rom 14:21). Likewise, eating sacrificial meat is no problem in an unbeliever's home—as long as no one dining there has a problem of conscience with it. In those two instances there is a consistency in Paul's reckoning.

The exception comes in Paul's ruling out the eating of meat in the cultic setting because Paul's conviction about the Lord's supper—namely, that in it one becomes united with Christ's body, does not allow him room to imagine a similar unification (he has used the daring image of becoming one flesh with a prostitute earlier to make a similar point; cf. 6:15-17) with the demons (he knows there are no other gods so he speaks instead of demons) at an idol's table. His convictions about the Lord's supper as the celebration of unity in Christ cannot logically let him condone believers' participation in the cultic worship of any other religion. "The one who cleaves to the Lord becomes one spirit with him" (6:17). "You have been bought with a price" (6:20; 7:23). At issue is "belonging to the Lord" in a totally inclusive and unmistakable way.

This passage gives access to foundational Pauline ethical considerations. The goal of all actions is to honor the Lord or God; or, in what seems to be a different way of saying the same thing, the goal of all actions is glorifying or giving thanks to God. Love, the careful weighing of how what one does may bear on another and at the same time the mode of one's consideration of others, must be factored into all decisions and into any resultant actions. Fundamental to the full expression of love is Paul's conviction that one does not seek one's own advantage as if what is good for one's self can be separated from the benefit of the others in the body of Christ, but that one must realize that one's own good is inextricably tied up with the good of all the others who are in Christ, a notion that will surface explicitly in 12:26.

We must ask what to make of Paul's two questions in 10:29*b*-30. The editors of the RSV placed a parenthesis marker between vv. 29*a* and 29*b*, no doubt sensing the shift in thought between those two parts. Prior to v. 29*b* Paul has counseled accommodation to others, but the questions of vv. 29*b*-30 indeed raise questions about the limits of such accommodation. As Paul constructs them, the two questions set forward an imaginary questioner's wrestling with the implications of what Paul has said about accommodating to the limitations of others. The questions are evocative and suggestive. They are not answered by Paul. The first question wonders why "my freedom" should be "unfavorably judged"[121]—and thereby limited!—by another's conscience

121. BAGD, 452.

(10:29 b). The second question, though also cast as though it were from the same imaginary questioner about eating the entrée at Paul's fictive meal with the unbeliever, starts with a profoundly Pauline condition—"If I partake with thanks [to God, understood]"—and finishes with a strong Pauline concern, "why am I blasphemed for the very thing for which I give thanks?" We may suppose that Paul asks this question with some passion.

Before pursuing any further the interpretation of the two questions in 10:29 b-30, Paul's ethical counsel needs to be considered. From chapter 8 forward he has advised forgoing the exercise of one's freedom if a brother or sister in Christ might be harmed or caused to stumble by one's contemplated action. Paul is even prepared to become a vegetarian if need be (8:13). In Paul's fictive scenario of dinner in an unbeliever's home (10:27-29 a) we find the same practice, now in view of the conscience of the one who informed that the meat had been "offered in sacrifice" to some deity: Do not eat it out of consideration for the one who raised the issue (10:29 a).

From these two recommendations—do not cause someone to stumble and do be considerate of others' moral consciousness—one can project an imaginary circumstance, not discussed anywhere in Paul's letters, in which each person in a congregation had a problem with some different practice and all the believers honored each of the limitations of all the others, arriving at an ethic of what might be called the "lowest common denominator." Judging from his letters, none of Paul's communities function that way, and nowhere in 1 Corinthians does Paul carry through the logic suggested here. The result would be a quite pallid community, which, rather than growing in its expression of its faith (Paul's code word for this is edification, being built up), would instead look primarily toward cutting back.

In 10:29 b-30 Paul signals to his readers a caution about radicalizing—Paul knows that to be a Corinthian predilection with some of his teachings—his basic moral counsel that the one with the stronger moral consciousness forgoes the exercise of his or her freedom in the face of a weaker consciousness person. In these verses Paul recognizes that harm can happen not only to the one who has the weaker moral consciousness; some consideration also needs to be given to the person of stronger moral consciousness as well. He puts it in the form of two questions so as to prompt the reflection of his auditors. But Paul established himself in 9:1-18 as the exemplary person who never acts without consideration for others. The answer is only suggested by the question. The first question sets up the second one because the latter considers a hypothetical question of someone reviling the person who gives thanks and partakes in food with gratitude. The first question captures the issue as far as Paul has developed it to this point—namely, the limitations of one's freedom by someone with a weaker moral consciousness. The second question takes it a step beyond what Paul has considered before, to weigh the possibility that someone rebukes the person who gives thanks and partakes in food with gratitude.

Once more we need not suppose that this second question mirrors an actual happening at Corinth. More likely it represents Paul's own following through on his own logic to suppose someone who is doing just as he or she should be (giving thanks to God and partaking with gratitude) and yet being criticized. So the matter introduced in 10:29 b-30 is not developed by Paul; it is merely suggested, perhaps to provoke reflection or perhaps even discussion among the Corinthians.

Paul's lengthy and detailed response to the Corinthians' question about meat offered to idols has served not only to give guidance about that particular question, but by Paul's careful shaping and developing of it, has provided him the opportunity to generalize from that issue to all of life lived in Christ together before God. In the process Paul has laid the ground for his treatment of further issues and problems that bear on the Corinthian believers' lives.

Reflections

1. Note Paul's assumption in 10:15-26 about the goodness of all creation. Several points merit pondering. (1) Salvation, redemption is not achieved by extrication from the creation. (2) The creation has always given testimony to God's power and deity (Rom 1:20), but it has been subjected to sin's corruption and finds itself in bondage to decay (Rom 8:20-21). (3) The new creation has begun in Christ (2 Cor 5:16-19). (4) God's redemptive activity will not be complete until the creation is fully restored and shares in the liberty God's children already experience (Rom 8:21). One may freely eat whatever is set before him or her because "the earth belongs to the Lord" (1 Cor 10:26, quoting Ps 24:1). In the same way, one may be sexual because being sexual is a normal feature of divinely created life (1 Corinthians 7).

2. Here and there in Paul's letters one gets glimpses of what he considers the basic reasons for doing things. Why do you do whatever it is that you do? What is your basic motivation for doing anything in life? Of course, there are all sorts of motivations. Some persons are moved by guilt, though nowhere in Paul does one see that. Some do works in the hope that God will find them worthy of reward, but Paul rigorously opposes anything that even smacks of such a notion (e.g., Galatians). Some will do deeds to be seen and praised by others, but Paul does not countenance that. And some will do because they know that without it they will not eat. For Paul there is a basic answer to why anyone should do anything: All of one's doing should come as a grateful response to God's graceful reaching for and loving and claiming us in Jesus Christ before we were worthy, while we were unlovable. Though Paul does not state it so succinctly as John, his sense is the same: We love because God first loved us (1 John 4:19). We do deeds out of thankfulness to God, to glorify God for God's mercy and grace toward us. In that sense the Afro-American spiritual whose words proclaim "My soul is so happy that I cain't set down" captures Paul's sense that there is no way around it: The ones loved by God must reach out, they must do deeds through which love is expressed toward others. Not to do so is unthinkable.

3. First Corinthians 10:24 can be easily misunderstood. Some translations make misunderstanding even more likely: Consider, for example, the NIV's and the RSV's insertion of the word "good," which is totally lacking in the Greek and can be more literally translated: "Let no one seek the [thing] of one's own, but the [thing] of the other." The NRSV logically looks for the unidentified noun, signified here by [thing], in the notion of "advantage" expressed in Paul's elaboration of their maxim in 10:23*a* and echoed in the same formulation as 10:24 in 10:33.

What we actually have here is a pervasive Pauline conviction—namely, that the person who looks after his or her own self first is the person who curiously loses out even on the very goal of securing oneself. Paul learned this in Christ (11:1), who first considered what was good for humans and acted for us rather than for himself (Phil 2:5-11), and God raised him from the dead. Paul modeled that for the Philippians when he would really have preferred to leave the troubles and stresses of life in the world and go be with the Lord full-time but instead chose to stay in the world and work in their behalf (Phil 1:22-26). He urged the same response on the Philippians when he wrote to them: "Each of you should look not only to your own interests, but also to the interests of others" (2:4 NIV). Paul captures the same idea in Rom 15:2: "Let each of you please your neighbor unto the good, to edification." Without using the code word "love," Paul is writing about it. What is at stake is not a denunciation of all concern for one's self; rather it is a matter of priority, a sequencing. Love calls for people to seek the good of another; this is not an option, it is basic faithful living. The love of others should be at the center of one's purpose. Paul's conviction is that when one looks to the interests of others then one's own interests are taken care of in the process. It is almost that one who sets out to secure one's own interests can't get there from here.

But none of this must be confused with having no care for one's self. Paul adopts Jesus' embrace of the Levitical formulation: "Love your neighbor as yourself" (Lev 19:18; Rom 13:9, Gal 5:14). For that formulation to have any viability one must have a certain love for one's self. The problem, of course, is one of proportionality. How does one properly love one's self and also love one's neighbors? What is the difference between proper, proportional love of self and selfishness? The answer is to be found in one's careful self-testing, and the search to distinguish may be assisted by the active, honest, genuine love of friends.

4. Paul imitates Christ (11:1) by not seeking his own advantage but that of the many (10:33). Calls to imitation of Christ are across the Pauline corpus. Paul's counsels to imitation of Christ tend to focus on two areas: (1) what Christ did in giving himself for others, and, (2) the disposition of Christ toward others. Clearly, 11:1 belongs to the former, most prevalent group of references to Christ's caring for others. Other classic examples of that focus are Phil 2:1-11 and Rom 15:1-6 (cf. also texts such as 2 Cor 5:14-21). Belonging to the second type of appeal for imitation would be Paul's call for the Roman believers to welcome one another into mutual fellowship as Christ has welcomed you (Rom 15:7) and Paul's appeal that the Corinthians model Christ's meekness and his clemency, his readiness to forgive (2 Cor 10:1).

Worth noting is what is missing. Christ has already died for us, so believers are not called upon to redeem others. Also, Paul makes no attempt to psychologize Christ by imagining what Christ might have thought; nor does Paul ever write about what Christ might have done in any particular situation.

1 CORINTHIANS 11:2–14:40

THREE WORSHIP PRACTICES OF THE COMMUNITY

OVERVIEW

Text on Paul's agenda in this letter are three items, each of which, taking its cue from 10:14-22, involves the worship practices of the community (women's head covering, 11:2-16; the Lord's supper, 11:17-34; and the use of spiritual gifts, chaps. 12–14). In the structure of the middle of this letter Paul has moved from the Corinthians' question about eating idol meat (8:1) to a discussion of the central, definitive communal act of eating—namely, the Lord's supper (10:14-22). That discussion of the Lord's supper leads Paul very naturally to attach in what we call chap. 11 two other worship matters of concern to him that he links together under the heading of "traditions" (NRSV) or "teachings" (NIV; παράδοσις *paradosis*, 11:2, 23). Both of these worship matters regard traditions or teachings that he acknowledges he has previously conveyed to the Corinthians (11:2, 23). He opens the section with praise for the Corinthians' "holding to the traditions" (11:2) just as he "traditioned" (11:2; using the same root term for the passing of traditions) them, but it turns out that in both matters treated in chap. 11 he objects to certain aspects of their practice.

Traditions play an important role in Paul's gospel. They provide a solid foundation upon which the life of faith may be built and upon which moral reasoning and action may properly be grounded. When Paul confronts a problem in one of his churches he frequently rehearses what "we know" and, from that, reasons toward a solution. The traditions may come from Scripture, from others in the churches before Paul or contemporary with him (cf. 1 Cor 11:23-25; 15:3-8; Phil 2:6-11; Gal 3:28) or, as we have seen, from Paul and even from the churches he established. For Paul, such teachings provide the ground for behavior and for action; they are the navigational markers by which believers set the courses for their lives, both individually and collectively.

In the first passage (11:2-16), directed at a problem that has developed precisely because two of Paul's teachings have come into conflict with each other, much as competing goods sometimes cause problems of moral discernment, Paul tries to build a case for a particular practice that he expects in Corinth and in all of his churches. In the second (11:17-34), Paul critiques and rejects the comportment of some Corinthians at the Lord's supper and attempts to call them back to appropriate understanding and behavior.

1 CORINTHIANS 11:2-16, PROPER COMPORTMENT OF WOMEN IN WORSHIP

COMMENTARY

Women are praying and prophesying in the church at Corinth. Paul takes that practice for granted, and it is no problem (11:5, 13). A later discussion in this letter shows that prophesying is a public mode of discourse that can edify, encourage, console, or lead to conviction in the hearts of others (14:3, 24-25).[122] Clearly, women at Corinth had heard Paul's gospel as welcoming them into full participation in the life of the church.

Even the most casual reading of 11:2-16 will discover Paul's concern: Women in Corinth, at least some of them, had stopped wearing head coverings in worship, and that bothered Paul. These verses are Paul's attempt to bring these women back in line with his teaching and with what is, in fact, the customary practice he has fostered in all of his other churches (11:16). It is reasonable to suppose that the women who had stopped wearing head coverings may have considered themselves in line with Paul's teaching about freedom in Christ, with Paul's embrace of equal standing of the sexes in the Lord (cf. 7:1-24; 12:13; Gal 3:28), with Paul's critique of persons who live according to the patterns and practices of the culture (cf. 6:1ff.), and with Paul's having welcomed women into participation in worship (e.g., praying and prophesying, 11:5).

What are we to make of these head coverings and Paul's dogged insistence that they be worn? At the outset, we must acknowledge that it is not clear just what Paul means by head coverings. The scholarly options range from "something like a shawl" or long hair that might be understood to function much like a shawl, or a more demure hairstyle in place of what might be seen as mantically touseled.[123] The texts simply do not allow a decisive answer. By his treatment of head coverings we can tell that Paul takes them to be customary and expects the Corinthians to have understood them as such. This is another of those instances where Paul and his readers seem to know exactly what is in dispute, but some uncertainty must remain for us.

Even though we cannot with certainty identify the head coverings, we can recognize what Paul is doing in his call for the wearing of head coverings of whatever sort. His insistence that women cover their heads in worship shows that at least on one level—namely, that in Christ there is no male or female—he has not fully carried through the social critique that he elsewhere sees implied so completely in the gospel. But even this observation must be carefully qualified because, as we shall see in what follows, Paul has what for him is an important theological basis for his position.

In these verses, although he assumes women's full participation in worship, he nevertheless wants them to wear some mark that, in fact, distinguishes them from men. His rhetoric stacks up arguments that women should comply.

This passage—in fact, all of chap. 11—is cast in the strong cultural categories of praise/honor and shame. As certainly as modern Western culture is characterized by acquisition and competition, so surely was the Corinthians' ordered around shame and honor. The formative questions that structured the culture and that influenced behavior were: What adds to honor? What avoids or lessens shame? These were the dominant questions in Paul's time, so when Paul speaks of praising or condemning, he is relating in powerful terms of value for himself and his readers.

With this background, let us consider Paul's string of arguments—from claims about God, from culture and nature, and from Scripture—whose underlying force of logic seems to be that if all these indicators or signs point in the same direction, who would presume to go against them? Paul's first and most elaborated argument is a *theological* one (11:3-5) that builds on a claim already made in this letter and is reaffirmed later: God is over all (3:23; cf. 8:6a; 15:24, 28); next is Christ; then human beings. Paul's discussion in 11:3 assumes the same hierarchy but simply runs it in the other direction and starts, where none of his readers would have any objection, with "every man"/"husband" (ἀνδρός *andros* may mean either) having Christ as head (κεφαλή *kephalē*, "source" or "rank," 11:3a). To that claim Paul adds that the head of a "wife"/"woman" (γυνή *gynē* may mean either) is her husband (11:3b), followed directly by "and the head of Christ is God" (11:3c). Paul's readers will have been assimilated to understand that Christ is the head over all people—men and women—and that God is the head over Christ (on this

122. For two studies of prophecy in early Christianity, see David E. Aune, *Prophecy in Early Christianity and the Ancient Mediterranean World* (Grand Rapids: Eerdmans, 1983); Christopher Forbes, *Prophecy and Inspired Speech in Early Christianity and Its Hellenistic Environment* (Tübingen: J. C. B. Mohr, 1995).

123. Fee, *The First Epistle to the Corinthians*, 496-97.

last point see also 15:24, 27-28, where Paul's teaching is laid out in more detail). It is fair to wonder, however, whether the Corinthians would have already known before having heard this letter that Paul also thought that the head of a wife is her husband (11:3). Evidence suggesting that they either have not heard it before or at least have not subscribed to it in their practice is found in Paul's stacking of his arguments to bolster his position.

Culturally, it was considered shameful for a woman to have a shaved or bald head. Paul twice capitalizes on that cultural predisposition, first when he asserts that any woman who prays or prophesies with uncovered head dishonors her head—she might as well have her head shaved, he declares (11:5)—and, second, when he declares that a woman who will not cover her head should have her hair cut (off); the one is as shameful as the other (11:6).

Later in the passage he returns to the argument from the contemporary cultural practice of women, not men, having long hair, which he quite uncritically construes as a reflection of *nature's* own preferences. It is dishonorable for a man to have long hair, but long hair is a woman's mantle of glory (11:14-15). In 11:14-15 Paul caps off his reasoning with what he describes as an argument "from nature." Carefully phrased as a rhetorical question whose Greek supposes a yes answer, Paul asks: "Doesn't nature itself teach you that if a man wears long hair it is a dishonor to him, but if a woman wears long hair, it is her glory?" Rhetoricians agreed that the points of greatest importance should be placed at the beginning and at the end in a sequence such as we have here. So Paul's first argument is one of monumental proportions for him: God is over all (11:2-3). His last proof, which means that he supposes it to be powerful as well, is his argument from nature: Nature teaches that men should not have long hair but that women should. So Paul declares, and his construction of the question shows that he expects the Corinthians to agree with him. The problem, however, is that Paul's argument "from nature" is actually an argument not from nature, but from social convention—indeed, from the social convention that *he* prefers. Might there have been Corinthians who viewed

what was "natural" regarding hair length in a different perspective? Quite possibly. A quotation from Musonius Rufus, a contemporary of Paul and a mentor of Epictetus among others, is instructive because it shows just how self-serving Paul's argumentation is about hair length. In a treatise entitled "On Cutting the Hair," Rufus quotes with approbation Zeno's remark that "it is quite as natural to cut the hair as it is to let it grow long."[124]

Paul calls upon *Scripture* for support, to the effect that man is the "image of God" (Gen 1:27, quoted in 11:7) and that woman was made from man (Gen 2:22, quoted in 11:12*a*). Some modern interpreters have thought that the puzzling "because of angels" comment in 11:10 might reflect Gen 6:1-4;[125] if it does not, then the reference is another of those shared understandings between Paul and his followers that seem beyond our capacity to recover.

All of these Pauline contentions, stacked up one upon another, are designed to convince the Corinthian women that it is proper for them to wear head coverings during worship. Whatever else Paul says in 11:2-16, it remains his hope that the Corinthian women will come over to his understanding of the need for head coverings in the worship setting.

But, curiously, not all of Paul's arguments in 11:2-16 go in the direction just described. Midway through 11:2-16 Paul appears to become self-critical about the implication of his multifaceted but one-sided argument for women to wear head coverings. In his eagerness to bring the Corinthian women into conformity with the practice of women in his other churches (11:16), Paul has distinguished women/wives from and subordinated them to men/husbands—and this in a letter where he has already counterculturally reconstructed the relationship of husbands and wives in marriage (chap. 7) as one of reciprocity and parity. In the process of writing 11:2-16, Paul discovers that two of his own values are in conflict: On the one side, he wants women believers to accommodate to the culturally aligned practice of wearing

---

124. Musonius Rufus "On Cutting the Hair" XXI.10.
125. Hans Conzelmann, *A Commentary on the First Epistle to the Corinthians*, trans. J. W. Leitch, Hermeneia (Philadelphia: Fortress, 1975) 189.

head coverings; on the other side, he believes that in Christ the cultural differentiations between men and women are eschatologically challenged by the gospel.

It is important to note how Paul's argument moves. In the opening verses (11:3-10) he singlemindedly piles up one point after another, all to the end of sustaining his hierarchical distinction in praxis between men/husbands and women/wives. Then, all of a sudden, in 11:11-12 he interrupts his own argument with the particle πλήν (*plēn*, "nevertheless," "however," "but"), which is a standard Greek way to break into a previous discussion and emphasize what is very important, and it introduces what amounts to a strong counterpoint to his own argumentation advanced in 11:2-10. In 11:13*a* he calls for the Corinthians to make their own judgments in this matter, and in 11:13*b*-16 he once again returns to compiling more arguments, whose goal is to encourage the Corinthian women to decide in favor of Paul's view and cover their heads. So the bulk of the argumentation goes in the direction of head coverings, but it is significantly interrupted by Paul's reaffirmation of male/female equality that he sees in the gospel.

Thus 11:2-16 contains two competing arguments based on two distinct pictures of the order of creation. The first, and dominant one, in these verses is structured upon the repeated affirmation that God is the source of all there is, that God is over all and the head of all (3:21-23; 8:6; 15:24-28). No other gods exist; there is no rival Lord. From this basic conviction Paul posits an orderly, hierarchical universe whose structure he details in such a way as to bear on the problem he faces with the women who are not wearing the head coverings. The argument is one of source or head. Beginning with God (for all the right theological reasons), Paul traces the lineage that God is the source or head of Christ, who is the source or head of men, who are the source or head of women—and the woman who does not wear proper head covering dishonors her head, meaning not only her own head but also her husband and, one might wonder, even Christ and God. The claim that man is the source of woman probably draws on the scriptural basis of Gen 2:21-23, which says as much.

Paul knows that this picture or argument is only part of the story; it is one important way of looking at things. But logic *and his other theological convictions* lead him to recognize, counter to his main argument, that every man is, in fact, born of a woman (11:12). Not only that, but Paul has earlier preached to them and can in this letter draw upon it as established tradition that in Christ—"in the Lord" as he puts it in 11:11—there is neither male nor female (Gal 3:28; see the Commentary on 7:17-24; see also 1 Cor 12:13). So his commitment to the tradition that "in the Lord" one finds neither male nor female breaks into his earlier hierarchical argument and shapes and inspires his statement in 11:11: Nevertheless, in the Lord "woman is not independent of man or man independent of woman" (11:11 NRSV). In this portrait of the new creation, men and women are not distinguished, although he knows and reaffirms the truth of the core of the first argument—namely, "All things are from God" (11:12).

In a creative reworking of the same tradition that is found in Gal 3:28 and in 1 Cor 7:17-24 and its context, Paul affirms that "in the Lord there is neither woman apart from man nor man apart from woman" (11:11). While he has suggested in 11:8 (cf. Gen 2:22) that woman came out of man because it served his point there to do so, it is just as surely true that "man is born of woman," as he acknowledges in 11:12*b*. And as if to keep it all in proper perspective, "all that is comes from God" (11:12*c*). Recognizing that he has now presented the Corinthians with very different lines of argument in the same passage and bearing on the same issue, he turns it over to them: "Weigh out these matters among yourselves" (11:13*a*; cf. 6:5). But without waiting for whatever they may decide, Paul stacks up more arguments favoring women wearing head coverings (11:13*b*-16) and clearly hopes the Corinthians will agree with him.

In part we may be dealing with the very nature of theological claims: Each theological assertion is partial; each theological claim is limited and gains certain important points. Not all theological claims fit neatly together without friction. Each important point gained by one theological claim usually causes some conflict with the consequences of some other theological claim. A classic example will illustrate. When one stresses that all power, glory, and honor belong to God—as the Pauline tradition does—one inevitably implies something a bit troublesome about the power of human beings. If God is all-powerful, how can we talk about human beings as having any capacity to make decisions, because choosing this or avoiding that implies not only the exercise of some power of one's own, some freedom of one's will but also inevitably some restriction on God's control? On the other side, if one posits freedom of the human will to choose, what does such an assertion inevitably imply about God's will, about God's power? One may want to hold both positions despite the associated theological ambiguities. Paul surely holds both. Another factor complicates the matter even further: Any theological assertions must take into consideration not only the problems just noted but also the complexity of life and social arrangements that add their own complicating nuances to applied theological claims. Now back to the problem of Paul and Paul's theological claims in 11:2-16.

God is surely over all in Paul's view. Such a claim, right as it is, inevitably contributes to a hierarchical vision. In dealing with idolaters' rival claims, such a conviction might be very helpful and illuminating because it could provide the framework in which one could place oneself in the line of authority and power (Paul used 1 Cor 15:3-11 in such a way; the narrative ties him into the line of divinely appointed authority). But when one is dealing, as Paul is here in 11:2-16, with intimate human exchanges and the social dynamics of his community of believers at Corinth, the conviction that God is over all can lead to stratification.

Another, related issue surfaces in this passage: What is the relation of believers to the culture of which they are a part, and how should believers relate to the norms of the culture? In 1 Corinthians, Paul has established a not altogether consistent pattern on this issue. His two-way teaching in chaps. 1–4 suggests an insurmountable breach between the way of the gospel and the way associated with the culture, but there is an incredible irony even there because in the very making

of his case for separation he uses the categories of the culture to make his point. Further, he expresses astonishment that some Corinthians are resorting to the courts, a typical cultural practice, to settle intracommunal differences. In 11:17-34, Paul criticizes the wealthier Corinthians for carrying their cultural and social practices over into the Lord's supper. And yet in the passage at hand (11:2-16), Paul freely and repeatedly refers to what must be recognized as simply cultural predispositions of his time; for example, women's hair should be long, men's hair should be short, and baldness or shaved heads for women produce culturally endorsed shame.

Short of an effort at complete separation from culture, such as was attempted by the Dead Sea Scrolls community at Qumran and as apparently was pondered by some Corinthians in response to Paul's previous letter (5:9; such complete separation Paul recognizes as impractical, 5:10-11; chap. 8), Paul seems to recognize that there will always be some interaction between gospel and culture, and he even boldly co-opts cultural elements where he thinks they may be helpful to him. Overall, Paul's posture on the matter is eccentric and sporadic. Once one determines not to leave the world, as Paul clearly has decided (cf. Phil 1:23-24), then the issue is joined; then there will always be accommodations to the culture and its practices, and there will be distancing from the culture and its patterns. But in cases like Paul's one has every reason to suppose that his readers will alternately be puzzled by his eccentricity on this matter, and no doubt some will have engaged him precisely on these issues of what could be construed as inconsistency. As we have seen in this very pericope, Paul is himself a bit at loggerheads as he tries to honor two very different convictions.

These verses give us insight into not only Paul's determination but also the acuity of his mind. As to his determination, he wants a practice that the Corinthians could (and perhaps did) argue made an alien demand on them to accommodate to cultural norms of distinction between men and women. Given his lead argument (11:3-5), Paul might respond that his position was based on his theological understanding and not in cultural mores. The acuity of Paul's mind is observed, however, in his capacity to follow the logic of a position, in this instance his own, to its conclusion, to test out the ramifications of his assertions even as he is making them, and to see that his argumentation leads in some sense to a position with which he himself has some problems. We have already seen this same mental facility in Paul's awareness that the inevitable logic of his morality of concessions to weak moral consciousness leads to the problems (see the Commentary on 10:29-30).

One final note is important here. Superficially, the arguments of 1 Cor 9:1-18 and 11:2-16 appear the same because in both Paul scurries around, pulling together all sorts of culturally acknowledged practices in support of single points. In chap. 9, Paul wants to argue that, although nobody is more privileged with rights (9:12a) than he, he lovingly eschews the exercise of those rights because of his love of others; in 11:2-16, he wants to establish the propriety of women wearing head coverings. But the two passages are actually *distinct* in significant ways. The argument in chap. 9 begins from what Paul supposes that *everybody* already knows: that a worker is entitled to some of the fruits of his or her labors. But the argument in chap. 11 begins with what *Paul* knows—namely, that women should wear head coverings. In the former (chap. 9), Paul invites the auditors to apply to him what they already know; in the latter (chap. 11), he wants the auditors to practice what he knows. Further, the first passage uses the cultural assumptions to advocate what turns out ultimately to be countercultural: love triumphing over self-interest; the second passage uses highly selective and even ad hominem interpretations of cultural practices to support cultural conformity of women's wearing head coverings.

REFLECTIONS

1. Paul's complex, convoluted rhetoric in 11:2-16 has as its primary aim getting the women to return to wearing head coverings as he expects in all his churches. In the process, two distinctive arguments, two alternative views, emerge. The primary one in these verses argues from God's primacy, structured hierarchically, and supports Paul's interest in head covering. The other stems from the view that in the Lord there is neither male nor female and is formulated out of a fundamental sense of equality between women and men.

It is tempting to ask which argument, which picture, is the "right" one, and the natural inclination would be to affirm the one that most clearly fits or supports one's own predisposition. Would it not be appropriate to admit that all of our efforts to grasp the whole picture of God's purposes are subject to human limitations of knowledge and expression and that, therefore, each vision, each picture is at best partial and incomplete? Perhaps life does not submit itself to a single story, a single accounting, a single point of moral reckoning. Perhaps that is why Paul is driven, after laying out the second argument, to call for the Corinthians to "judge for yourselves" (11:13).

A nautical metaphor might be helpful as a way of relating to these two very different pictures of "the way things ought to be" that Paul has placed alongside each other. Imagine yourself as sailing in largely unknown waters. You have a chart with certain hazards located on it and must lay out a course that avoids grounding your boat. If you can identify two visible landmarks on the chart, you can, by triangulation, calculate your exact location and navigate in such a way as to be informed by the chart. Paul offers two points on the map with his two pictures of the way things ought to be; the modern believer should be able to benefit from reference to both of them.

2. What could it mean today to consider God or Christ as one's head or source? Such a description must always have within it authority implications and perhaps even fundamentally definitional implications of origin and maybe even significance. With the modern drive toward independence as putatively desirable, how and in what ways can believers think of themselves as having God or Christ as their head or source? What difference would such an affirmation mean for the way one lived, for the way one related to others, for the way one made decisions of choice and aversion?

3. Even if most women will have no problem considering that God or Christ is their "head" or source, many wives will have difficulty thinking of their husbands as their heads or sources. What would it mean for husbands to think of their wives as their heads or sources? Would it be something like Paul's advice that a husband does not have authority over his body but that his wife does (7:4), and that a husband has no right to deny his wife conjugal rights (7:3)? Or would it be something like the Paulinist writing expressed in Ephesians when it calls for both spouses to be "mutually submissive" (Eph 5:21)? Would it be possible for married believers today to work as partners who from time to time take the leadership as head and in other times and in other occasions follow?

1 CORINTHIANS 11:17-34, NOT THE LORD'S SUPPER

COMMENTARY

A second worship practice, which Paul calls the "Lord's supper" and which is also based on traditions, is causing some problems at Corinth. As Paul has instituted it at Corinth, the Lord's supper is part of a full-scale meal, presumably in the home of one of the believers. As distinguished from the head-covering issue in which Paul praises the women for remembering the traditions (11:2), with the Lord's supper Paul finds nothing commendable about their practice. Their coming together for worship should be a good thing; they know the traditions of the supper, and they are observing it (how frequently we cannot know). But concerning the way they comport themselves during the meals, Paul chooses language designed to shock: Yours is not the supper of the Lord (11:20).

This passage concerns the inappropriate behavior on the part of the Corinthians and the tradition as Paul related it to them. It is worth noting that, if the Corinthians had not been making such a mockery of the supper in Paul's view, we would never have known the traditions as Paul received them or even that Paul expected his churches to observe the Lord's supper.

11:17-22. Can it surprise any reader of 1 Corinthians that the Corinthians' observance of the Lord's supper is a highly individualized affair? "Each one takes his own supper;

and one is hungry while another is drunk" (11:21). They may have the requisite cup and bread, but they do not wait for one another before consuming them. The worshipers who arrive early eat and drink early (11:33-34). Paul thinks they "treat the church of God with contempt and put to shame the ones who do not have anything" (11:22).

Put together with what we know of the social conventions and mores of the time, we can suppose what is going on in Corinth at the Lord's supper.[126] One of the members with a large enough house—and this inevitably entails a commensurate servant staff—hosts the dinner in which the Lord's supper is observed. Some persons—this apparently breaks along economic lines also—are free to come early, and they have (the choice?) food and drink. Some get drunk (11:21). Others (Paul characterizes them as "those having nothing") perhaps get there late(r) and find, along with tipsy coworshipers, leftover food at best. (For more on the socioeconomic makeup of the congregation at Corinth, see the Commentary on 1:26-31.)[127]

The Corinthians who are abusing the Lord's supper have minimized or lost the basic Pauline sense that the life of faith is a life of community. The abusers have privatized

---

126. Theissen, *The Social Setting of Pauline Christianity,* 145-74.
127. See Meeks, *The First Urban Christians:,* 69-70.

their faith and their worship in a way that Paul finds totally unacceptable; they have lost any sense that love as the right relation to others is the proper and necessary expression of their faith as the right relation to God.

11:23-26. Paul credits "the Lord" as his source (cf. 1 Cor 7:10; Gal 1:12). The tradition is in the form of a narrative, a story, setting the occasion as the night of Christ's betrayal. Bread, thanksgiving (εὐχαριστέω *eucharisteō*, hence more modern reference to the supper as eucharist; 11:24), dinner, and cup (of wine) frame the narrative. (For the bread-cup sequence, see also Matt 26:26-29 and Mark 14:22-25. See also Luke 22:17-20, where the order is cup-bread-cup.) The particularities within that frame show the richness of Paul's understanding of the supper.

(1) The words of institution—"Do this"—are twice linked to the phrase "in remembrance of me" (11:24-25). The idea of memory and remembering has roots that reach back into Israel and are a part of Paul's Jewish heritage. What is involved in "remembering" in Israel's traditions may be seen, for example, in Deut 26:5-11, where the narrative begins as a story told in the third person, "A wandering Aramean was my ancester; *he* went down into Egypt and lived there as an alien, few in number," and then shifts to the second-person plural "us": "When the Egyptians treated *us* harshly and afflicted *us* . . . *we* cried to the LORD. . . . The LORD brought *us* out of Egypt" (26:5-8 NRSV). The old story becomes the tellers' story; liturgy unites the old story with the current worshipers' story. What happened back then is retold to incorporate the new tellers and hearers as a part of the narrative, as participants in the old and ongoing story. So it is with Paul's understanding of the Lord's supper. When Corinthians tell the story, it becomes *their* story; they "remember" the story in a way that ties their own lives into it in a transforming and illuminating way. As we have already seen in 10:1-13, Paul employs precisely this kind of "remembering" when he recounts the exodus to his Corinthian readers, when he describes the original exodus travelers as "*our* fathers" (10:1), and when he invites the Corinthians to picture themselves as part of the story.

(2) In eating the bread and drinking the cup, "you proclaim the Lord's death until he comes" (11:26). What is meant by "proclaim" (καταγγέλλω *katangellō*)? Although the word can mean "preach," it has a much wider sense in Paul's use of it. When people live fully the new life in Christ, their faith makes itself known, their living of their faith manifests itself to others and makes an impact on them. That is why Paul, in writing to the Thessalonians, remarks: "For the word of the Lord has sounded forth from you not only in Macedonia and Achaia, but your faith in God has gone forth everywhere so that we have no need to say anything" (1 Thess 1:8). The Thessalonians have not sent missionaries; they have lived their faith with profound zeal, and *that* has been so effective a testimony, a proclamation, that Paul has no need to preach. Their story becomes infectious. In the same way, Paul thinks that taking part (in a proper fashion, but more on that later) in the supper is itself a "proclamation."

Paul's particular description of what is proclaimed—"Christ's death until he comes"—fits Paul's purposes at hand and also affirms his basic convictions. This particular phrase is shorthand language, capable of abbreviation among those on the inside who know and remember the whole story as Paul preaches it. The horizons of Paul's vision—indeed, the story he thinks the supper "remembers"—extend from Christ's death, on the one side, to Christ's ultimate return at the end of the ages on the other. In between—and understood—are Christ's resurrection and the association of the members of Christ's body who live in Christ until his return at the end. So Paul thinks that the supper, by what it remembers and proclaims, scans the whole story of redemption in Christ and rehearses for the believers the true scope and setting of the life they are called to live together. Every time believers take part in the supper, they rehearse God's story, who they are and where they are in God's story. If they live it as they should, their very lives will become a fitting proclamation of the gospel to the world.

(3) "This is my body which is for you" (11:24). The identification of the bread with Christ's body is present in all the traditions of the supper (Mark 14:22 and par.). Paul extends the phrase by adding "which is for you," not meaning substitution (as in "in your place") but solidarity of Christ with believers.

In the eating of the bread, believers proclaim Christ as *for* believers, as "on their side," as one sees affirmed about God in Rom 8:31: "If God is *for us*, who can be against us?"

As already noted, "body" is an important term for Paul, both in the Lord's supper traditions and elsewhere in his letters, but in 1 Corinthians its significance has been set since 1 Cor 6:13*b*, where Paul declared that "the body is for the Lord and the Lord for the body" because "our bodies are members of Christ" (6:15). More immediately, Paul's first allusion to the Lord's supper (10:16-17) already made a strong point about "body": "The bread which we break, is it not a sharing κοινωνία [*koinōnia*] in the body of Christ? Because there is one bread, we the many are one body." The supper affirms in its distributing of the bread to the members that Christ's body is for believers; it is as members of Christ's body that Christians have their fundamental identity. The reference to bread is a case of synecdoche (the part stands for the whole); the bread stands for Christ's body, the church, of which all participants are members, a point that Paul develops in chap. 12.

11:27-34. Such an allusive frame of reference as has just been established is also necessary for the understanding of the term "body" (*sōma*) in 11:29: "For the one who eats and drinks *without discerning the body* eats and drinks judgment on himself." The immediate context for understanding "discerning the body" is Paul's concern that some Corinthians are partaking in the supper "unworthily" (11:27-34).

"Discerning the body" (διακρίνων τὸ σῶμα *diakrinōn to sōma*, 11:29) is a densely packed phrase that the Corinthians probably had been prepared to understand and that we may unpack in stages. "Discerning" is a figuring out, a reckoning that a person does or is capable of doing. The body that must be discerned cannot be separated from the just-mentioned "body of the Lord," which was identified with the bread that is eaten in the supper (11:27; on the phrase "body of Christ," see the Commentary and Reflections at 12:12-27). So inevitably discerning the body must in some fundamental sense involve a reckoning or evaluation of how well one is related to Christ, whose body is understood as "for us" in the supper traditions. But

in Paul's thought the body of Christ can never be separated from the members who by God's grace are incorporated into it. So "discerning the body" is Paul's shorthand way of talking about an individual's assessment of two distinguishable but inseparable matters: how well one's life relates to Christ and how well one's love ties one to others who, though many, are one body in Christ. "The one who eats and drinks without discerning the body eats and drinks judgment on himself" (11:29).

Improper or inadequate discernment of the body leaves one vulnerable to judgment (11:29). Paul does not make it explicit here, but we can suppose, in the context of his taking the supper as remembering Christ's death until he comes, that Paul is thinking of the last judgment, God's judgment at the end time. But the reference to self-judging in the present (11:31), along with Paul's construal of Corinthian illness as a sign of present judgment (11:30), makes it clear that Paul also has in mind a present judgment that may be brought upon oneself by improper comportment at the Lord's supper (11:29). Although all this talk about judgment, present and future, may sound threatening, there is good news in Paul's assumption: One can avoid God's present and end-time judgment. How does one elude God's judgment? By using one's self-examination (11:28*a*) in the worship context of the Lord's supper as an occasion, if need be, to redirect one's life. Such persons who by self-examination and self-correction bring themselves more fully into line with God's grace in Jesus Christ will avoid present judgment and, indeed, are already blessed. The ones who do not discern the body are, in Paul's view, already experiencing God's judgment (11:30), an eschatological foretaste of the full and final judgment. Blessing awaits "the one who finds no fault with himself regarding what he discerns" (Rom 14:22). Paul assures the Corinthians that proper selfjudgment, self-assessment, assuming it becomes the occasion for self-correction, is the way to avoid divine judgment (11:31). But failing a contemporary self-correction, one may still benefit from God's presently active judgment that should serve as a wake-up call before the end time, with its final judgment of the world and of those who do not self-correct (11:32).

"Being condemned along with the world" (11:32) is not to be confused with a denigration of the cosmos or of the earth (cf. 10:26). As we saw earlier, Paul thinks that the creation is good, that it, too, has come under the power of sin, and that it, too, is being redeemed. Paul's comment about the world in 11:32 is Paul's shorthand for describing the ways of the world under the sway of sin. Again, as earlier, this is border talk whereby Paul wants to distinguish how people in the body of believers live and relate to one another differently from the way people in the outside world do.

In Paul's picture, blessing and judgment are certain to be meted out at the day of wrath (Rom 2:6-11). But judgment and blessing can also be experienced in life this side of the end. Just as surely as the wrath of God is currently being revealed against all unrighteousness (Rom 1:18), so also the righteousness of God is currently being revealed (Rom 1:17). Paul tells the Corinthians that the illness of some of them is a sign of God's judgment already at work (11:30). Regarding blessing in the present, see Rom 14:22b, where we find the Pauline beatitude "Blessed is the one who is not judging [needing to judge] himself for what he figures out and does" because one's willing and doing are so fully in harmony with God's purposes.

Verses 27-34 fit a recurring pattern in the middle chapters of 1 Corinthians in which descriptions of people's comportment (Paul's, ancient Israel's, and now the Corinthians') culminate in words of warning about judgment. Paul, though called by God as apostle, has kept an athlete's discipline so as to avoid the judgment of disqualification (9:24-27). Israel, though delivered from Egypt, was not exempted from God's judgment just because it was fed and given drink in the wilderness (10:7-13). And now the Corinthians, though privileged to sit at table for the Lord's supper, cannot hope to avoid judgment if they eat and drink "in an unworthy manner" (ἀναξίως anaxiōs), as Paul clearly thinks they are doing.

In 11:27-34 Paul calls for the Corinthians to amend their ways via self-examination in the context of the Lord's supper. "Let a person self-examine" (11:28). Others cannot do it for the individual. In fact, self-examination receives no assistance from others in the community. Paul does not lay out the reasons that the self-evaluation must be individualized and personal, but we can suppose them from his claims elsewhere regarding the hiddenness of the purposes of people's hearts (1 Cor 4:5; 14:25; Rom 2:16). Only the individual person is capable of testing and knowing why he or she did (and avoided) an action.

Paul regularly affirms the vital necessity of self-testing for believers. In 1 Corinthians all of Paul's two-way elaborations have been designed to set a context in which his auditors can see where they stand more clearly. Paul's calling the Corinthians babies (3:1-2) and treating them as such serves the same function, namely to call them to reexamine where they truly stand. In his retelling of the exodus from Egypt in 10:1-13, he already affirmed the importance of self-testing (see esp. 10:12). Elsewhere in his letters Paul urges self-examination upon his readers (cf. 2 Cor 13:5; Gal 6:4). Believers are to test themselves (11:28), their standing in the faith (2 Cor 13:5), their works (Gal 6:4); and always the purpose of such self-evaluation is so that the believers can make a midcourse correction and thereby avoid crashing headlong into God's judgment.

The Lord's supper is the preeminent context in which such self-assessment is appropriate because there the story of God's redemption through Christ is sketched from Christ's death until his return at the end of the ages, which for Paul is ineluctably the ultimate time of judgment. Proper assessment of one's self, and self-correction if need be, is pre-requisite to worthy eating and drinking in the Lord's supper (11:28).

Paul concludes this matter with what seems to be a trademark of his, a practical suggestion or two aimed at helping alleviate the immediate occasion for the problem: "Wait for one another" (11:33); "If someone is hungry, let him eat in his own house" (11:34, echoing 11:22a).

Perhaps the strangest note in 11:17-34, especially for those ancient and modern readers who have followed the frequency of Paul's efforts to minimize splits in the church as the letter has progressed, is his statement: "It is necessary that there be factions so that it may be clear who are the tried and true among you" (11:19). As noted, earlier in this letter Paul tends to invite persons among the Corinthians to identify with lofty rhetorical descriptions, only to find the rug yanked ironically from under them in a kind of shock therapy (cf. 3:1ff.). Paul concedes that there are factions at Corinth; the ideal of unity for which he has argued widely in this letter and which he will continue to advocate (chaps. 12–14) is simply not the reality. The reality is their proclivity to divisions even though not everyone is causing trouble at the Lord's supper; only some haughty (and, in the instance of the supper, likely wealthier) persons are. In 11:19 Paul turns their own thinking back on them: They who reckon themselves better than "those who have nothing" (11:22) are the ones who may ironically discover that they themselves are the ones who are not "genuine" (δόκιμος *dokimos*), 11:19), or "tried and true." For Paul, the term *dokimos* refers to a person who emerges over time as one who has passed the test, who has endured hard times and remained on course in the gospel. The "genuine" persons—or to use another, similarly freighted Pauline category, the "mature" (cf. 1 Cor 2:6; 14:20; Phil 3:15)—emerge as the ones who have continued steadfastly in their life of faith despite buffeting from the world and regardless of

unjust treatment by their brothers and sisters in Christ. With this admission of differentiation, Paul does not renege on his conviction that divisions are inappropriate in the body of Christ; instead he uses the Corinthian factionalism as a means of pointing out that the ones who think themselves to be powerful and better are indeed the ones who may ultimately discover themselves as disqualified, a fate Paul has already told the readers he avoids by rigorous self-discipline (9:27; note there the same Greek term as in 11:19, but with the negating *alpha* prefixed, ἀδόκιμος [*adokimos*; NIV and NRSV, "disqualified," 9:27]). Paul's ultimate concern is to recall all of the Corinthian believers to an appropriate and worthy keeping of the Lord's supper which not only provides the proper foundation for their relation to God's whole plan in Christ but also lays down the fitting relationship between believers who are members of Christ's body that is so prominently featured in the supper ritual. Paul's counsels are driven not by a veneration of the supper properly observed but by the Corinthians' failure to have the supper function among them as it should, namely as a beacon by which to keep their lives on the proper path of faith. As for other matters, Paul assures them he will give further directions when he arrives (11:34*b*).

REFLECTIONS

1. How does one *unworthily* (11:27) take part in the central ritual of the community of faith, in the eating of the bread or drinking of the cup? Paul underlines the matter's importance when he warns that unworthily partaking of the supper leaves one "liable for the body and blood of the Lord" (11:27). For Paul there are two ways one can unworthily take part, and each merits exploration: (1) One can partake without examining oneself (11:28). Or (2) one can participate while failing to "discern the body" (11:29).

Christians have an obligation to know where they stand, and the way to do that is by examining their standing before God and in Christ (7:37; 10:12; cf. 2 Cor 13:5; Gal 6:4). Without proper self-assessment, believers may lose track of where they really are in the life of faith (cf. 1 Cor 4:8-12). One's birth into the faith is associated with Christ's death; one's maturity or completion is identified with Christ's coming to mark the end of the age. The life of faith is lived from new birth to maturity or adulthood and Paul sees it ideally as a progress, as a growth in which one moves along a line between the two horizons of Christ's death on the one side and the parousia on the other.

An up-to-date assessment is crucial because we bear one another's burdens according to the measure of our own faith (Gal 6:2-4) and because each person is to put into God's service whatever degree of maturity each has at a given time. In Paul's view, the Lord's supper is the ideal place where proper self-assessment takes place. So to partake of the Lord's supper "worthily" is not to be confused with *deserving* or *meriting* God's grace (an absurdity and an impossibility on its face), but it is participating in the supper knowing that one stands only because of that grace and knowing just where one stands in one's growth toward maturity. When one properly self-assesses, then that person can take part in the service worthily.

One partakes worthily when one properly "discerns the body" (11:29).[128] No doubt Paul's mention of "body" here is generated by the words of institution (11:24), but a double-sense reference to body is clearly at work. On the one side, Paul thinks of discerning one's relation to Christ. This sense overlaps with the concern in 11:28 that a person's self-test must check out, in effect, how one relates to Christ in the present-day state of one's life. On the other side, though, is the sense already established in Paul's first mention of the Lord's supper, namely that the believers, though many, all constitute "one body" (10:17). Thus to "discern the body" is not only cryptic language for checking out one's relation to Christ, whose body is at the center of the supper, but also "discerning the body" is shorthand for checking out one's relation to all the others who along with one compose the body. So, proper discerning of the body is at once an assessing not only of one's relation to Christ but also of one's relation to all the other members of the body. Ultimately, these two facets of discerning the body are not separable because the believers are so directly and fully associated with Christ and with one another in Christ.

Therefore, the Lord's supper is communion in a double sense: It is the most intimate sharing and participation with Christ, but that communion with Christ is already also the sharing in and with other believers who by definition are also those "in Christ." The Lord's supper is for Paul both personal and communal, inextricably. The Corinthians are a study of those who have forgotten the communal nature of the Lord's supper and have pursued their own interests, perhaps with their special friends, eaten their fill, gotten drunk, and treated their poorer brothers and sisters with disregard if not scorn. So Paul assails them in two ways: First, he says it is not the Lord's supper they eat; second, he warns them that without proper discernment—that is, without recognizing how they all belong equally to one another in Christ—they eat and drink judgment upon themselves.

2. Paul's crediting of some Corinthians with "weakness," "sickness," and even death to God's judgment raises a very serious, fundamental theological problem. Is every illness, every evidence of human frailty a sign of God's judgment? Clearly not for Paul, because he nowhere else makes any such claim in his letters. On the contrary, his letters typically see weakness and frailty as occasions for God's grace and power. Consider some of the evidence. Paul notes Epaphroditus's brush with death and sees that God has worked positively through it (Phil 2:27). The same goes for Paul's own near death reported in 2 Cor 1:8-11. He construes the cracks in these human vessels as showing forth not God's judgment but God's transcendent power working abundantly through human frailties and weaknesses (2 Cor 4:7-12). And he happily relates that his own "thorn in the flesh" becomes to him a sign that God's grace is adequate to whatever is at hand and that God's "power is made perfect in weakness" (2 Cor 12:9). (What that thorn is, though fascinating to ponder, is not important. The important thing is Paul's seeking to be free of it.) What, then, are we to make of Paul's claim in 11:30? It appears to be purely a onetime occurrence in Paul's letters and a function of Paul's (overwrought?) rhetorical effort to drive home a point.

How would Christians be able to discern whether God's judgment was at work in a particular illness or physical problem? I dare suggest that only the individual in question might be able to sort through that issue, and that no one else is *ever* in a

---

128. The phrase has been understood in a variety of ways, from not realizing that the eucharistic bread is different from that of regular meals to not focusing on Christ's death as the bread is taken, but these import foreign concerns.

position to pronounce upon it. A much more important communal effort might be to see how we other believers can join together with the person who is suffering to help him or her bear the burden this side of a God-given exodus-like deliverance that Paul promised in 10:13.

Furthermore, to say that God's judgment was present in a particular illness or problem would not necessarily be the same thing as saying that God caused the illness or the problem. Hearts do give out; immune systems fail or decay; accidents do happen—and all without God having to be considered in any way the cause. But can God work through any and all of these circumstances? Paul's answer to that question is a clear "Yes." Paul shared with the Romans his conviction that, for those who are loving God (the present participle expressing continuing action), God "works unto the good" in all things (Rom 8:28). Our translation "unto the good," though a bit wooden, preserves the sense of the Greek, namely that God, while not at all said to be causing the circumstances, nevertheless actively works in the things that happen, always seeking the good for those who are in right relation with God. If God's blessing can come through the circumstances in which believers find themselves, why should it not also be possible to assert that God's judgment can work through events and situations affecting those persons who live in opposition to God? Noteworthy it is that Paul thinks the end purpose of God's judgment experienced in one's life is self-correction and a reestablishment of one's life on the right track: Chastening—instruction, training, discipline such as a father might do—may occasion a reorientation "in order that we may not be condemned with the world," in the last and final judgment (11:32).

1 CORINTHIANS 12:1–14:40, THE PROPER FUNCTION OF SPIRITUAL GIFTS

OVERVIEW

These chapters are the longest sustained treatment of a problem in the letter, even slightly longer than the section 8:1–11:1. The importance of the issue addressed in chaps. 12–14 is attested not only by its length but also by its position in the letter, coming so late after so many other matters that provide a context. At the heart of the extended treatment lies what is often called "the hymn of love" (chap. 13). While echoing some themes that emerged in his earlier treatment of other problems and issues, the encomium of love provides the base for Paul's counsel in the two chapters that lie on either side. Chapter 12 opens with an item from their letter (12:1; cf. 7:1) and is the third topic in the sequence that relates to worship practices in Corinth (11:2-34).

In the remainder of chap. 12, Paul acknowledges that the Corinthians have problems with spiritual gifts, and, after affirming the basic claim that the Holy Spirit is the power that makes life under Christ's lordship possible, Paul joins with the Corinthians in their recognition of the differences they experience in their Christian life together, appreciates the differences, accounts for them as part of the divine plan, and attempts to reintegrate the differences into what he sees as God's overall purpose. Chapter 14 builds from love's foundational power to refocus the Corinthians' collective life away from competition for status, moves it toward the mutuality of the upbuilding that is the hallmark of love (8:1), and closes, in typical Pauline fashion, with some practical suggestions.

Paul widens the issue from the Corinthians' question about spiritual matters or spiritualists and treats the proper function of "spiritual gifts" (χάρισματα *charismata*) within the community of believers. Toward that end, Paul affirms the constitutive role of the Spirit in allocating the *charismata* in individual believers as the Spirit wishes and for the common good. Such distribution by the Spirit rightly causes the various gifts, each of which is equally important for the enrichment of the community, to appear randomly distributed to the members. The resulting variety has no correlation with status or importance of each recipient but achieves its significance only in respect to what the variety adds to the communal life in Christ. As members of the body of Christ, all individuals have equal standing and importance; and they should use the Spirit-apportioned gifts as a way of caring for and seeking the common good of all.

1 Corinthians 12:1-3, Identification of Topic and Basics About the Spirit

COMMENTARY

The passage begins with what must be a Corinthian question (12:1). Paul responds with a positioning piece, yet another back-to-basics review (12:2-3).

Paul's discussion of *charismata* is probably generated by the Corinthians' letter to him. The section opens with περὶ δὲ τῶν πνευματικῶν (*peri de tōn pneumatikōn*), which can be translated either as "now concerning spiritual things/gifts" or "now concerning spiritual persons." The former translation, favored by the NIV and the NRSV, honors that spiritual gifts do become the chief topic of chaps. 12–14, though the term *charismata* does not occur in 12:1. We know from the thanksgiving (1:4-9) that Paul thinks that the Corinthians were not "lacking in any spiritual gifts" (*charismata,* 1:7 NRSV). The Spirit has generously endowed them with all sorts of gifts. They have abundant evidence of the Spirit's having come among them to dwell (3:16). Now in chaps. 12–14 it becomes clear that this very abundance and the Corinthians' construal of it has become such a problem in their communal life that Paul must address it.

The second translation—"now concerning spiritual persons"—builds from Paul's having set up earlier in the letter the designation "spiritualists" or "those who are spiritual" as a way of referring to mature Christians (2:13-16). This latter translation would then be open to the interpretation that some Corinthians have written inquiring about persons who are making elitist claims on the basis of what they might credit as special or unusually mature Spirit connections. In one sense, all of Paul's followers are properly

called "spiritualists" because the Holy Spirit is the hallmark, the telltale sign of the Christian life (surely Paul's point in 12:3*b*). Given the Corinthians' proclivity for claiming status and for turning most things toward that end, it would not be surprising if some of them had declared themselves to be *more* spiritual than others; with the evidence of chaps. 12–14, they may even have claimed that speaking in tongues was the highest or surest sign of being truly spiritual. Such persons may have thought that to lack the ability to speak in tongues was a sign of spiritual inferiority.

Paul opens his discussion (12:1-3) by taking his auditors back to their origins in the faith, specifically and significantly to their foundational connection with the Holy Spirit. He reminds them of how they had been idolatrous pagans (12:2) and how they came to make the basic Christian confession "Jesus is Lord" (cf. Rom 10:9; Phil 2:11) solely by the working of the Holy Spirit (12:3). Paul's "back-to-basics" move discloses his abiding conviction that the Corinthians' behavior shows them to be babies in the faith (cf. 3:1-2), a note to which he will explicitly return in 14:20.

Commentators have been concerned with what to make of the expression "Cursed be Jesus" (12:3*a*). Some interpreters have supposed that there might even be a group at Corinth who held such a slogan,[129] though if we understand how the rhetoric works, there

---

129. For a sample of efforts to establish a group or situation in which persons might say "Cursed be Jesus," see the opening review in J. D. M. Derrett, "Cursing Jesus (I Cor. XII.3): The Jews as Religious 'Persecutors'" *NTS* 21 (1975) 544-45.

is no need for us to make such a postulation. No one at Corinth champions such a slogan. Instead, Paul here resorts to shock language that is, after all, another, though more dramatic, Pauline move to ask what we know;[130] it is designed to elicit a "we know that" or an "of course not" mode of assent and to get them focused on the basics: "God's Spirit," the Holy Spirit, is the power at the foundation of the Christian life (cf.

Rom 8:15-16, 26; Gal 3:1-2).[131] That Spirit could never allow anyone to curse Jesus; that Spirit properly dwells in the believers (3:16-17), interprets things that are otherwise beyond understanding (2:14), orients the believers to Jesus Christ, and enables believers to make the most fundamental affirmation: "Jesus is Lord." A clearer understanding of how that Spirit works should help the Corinthians come to a better comprehension of the way the Spirit's gifts ought to function within the community of believers.

130. Hans Conzelmann, *A Commentary on the First Epistle to the Corinthians*, trans. J. W. Leitch, Hermeneia (Philadelphia: Fortress, 1975) 204, rightly calls Ἀνάθεμα Ἰησοῦς (*Anathema Iēsous*) "an *ad hoc* construction on Paul's part to form an antithesis."

131. J. M. Bassler, "1 Cor 12:3—Curse and Confession in Context," *JBL* 101 (1982) 415-18.

REFLECTIONS

Although it is the oldest Christian confession, "Jesus is Lord" may ring strange or empty to modern ears. Perhaps it is easier to understand it today in a worship context in which Christians pledge to follow Christ. But the earliest Christians understood it also to be true in their personal lives. In fact, all of life was being dedicated to honoring Christ. Every day. Every decision. Every nook and cranny of one's being and doing. Jesus' lordship is over all of life, or it is properly over none of it. Today we tend to divide up life into sacred and secular, with the sacred being rather restricted to Sundays (and maybe only a part of that) and perhaps to a few times of daily devotion. In a like manner, we may think to restrict Christ's lordship to those sacred times of our lives and figure that in the rest of our time we can operate on a different basis, perhaps the way the rest of the world does. To say that "Jesus is Lord" has meant, from the earliest days, to refuse to have life divided into secular and sacred with two value systems operative in the two areas.

In another important way, to affirm that "Jesus is Lord" has also meant, from earliest times on, that one lived with the expectation that someday—when, we need not know—Christ will return and finish up God's purposes, which include the end of death and the healing of this broken world in which we live. So to affirm Jesus' lordship is to declare that the evil and wrongdoing in the world are unacceptable and inappropriate and that God will ultimately prevail over evil and reclaim all the world, humans and all creation, for God's own self as beloved and dear.

Some may think that they are autonomous beings, that they have no lord. In reality, however, it is often only the young who think that they are in full control of their lives. Persons who "have some miles on them" generally come to realize that, in fact, they control less than they might like to dream. True freedom, as Paul recognized, comes not in abandoning all lordship—because he thought that impossible—but in proper submission in Christ to God, who created us to be in relation. All efforts to live as if we have no lord will be a mirage, a fiction, and will ultimately fall of their own weight.

For Paul, even the most basic affirmation, "Jesus is Lord," is made possible by divine assistance—another affirmation of God's grace. But merely to mouth the formula, "Jesus is Lord," is not of interest to Paul (or to other early Christian communities; cf. Matt 7:21-23) without its marking all of our behavior.

1 Corinthians 12:4-11, Recognition of the Issue of Diversity and Its Significance

COMMENTARY

Paul has a distinctive problem in Corinth, a problem generated by those who misconstrue the riches and abundance manifest in the Spirit's working. Across 1 Corinthians, Paul has been distressed that the congregation of believers is rent with schisms (1:10-11; 3:3; 11:17-18). Partly, this divisiveness may be understood on socioeconomic grounds (1:26-31), as may be seen not only in richer persons' carrying others to court (6:1ff.) but also in the way the Lord's supper is being abused (11:17-22). Ironically, however, their tendency toward divisiveness has also been fueled by the way the Corinthians have perceived the workings of the Holy Spirit among them, and in chaps. 12–14 Paul addresses that problem. Diversity per se is not the problem at Corinth; for Paul, the problem lies in what the Corinthians have made of their diversity on many fronts. So Paul has to distinguish proper diversity from schisms and from divisive subgroups within the community.

In Paul's view, what should persons make of such differences? Paul is not surprised by differences among believers, and he has a variegated picture of what to make of them, as we can see from 1 Corinthians. In most places, Paul sees the differences as being inspired by the Holy Spirit and as enriching the community by God's design. So different persons have different life circumstances, different callings, and thus different *charismata*. Among these differences Paul fails to see a qualitative distinction: All of the differences are appropriate, and God uses them for the common good. That believers are, in fact, different from one another does not trouble Paul. Such differentiation is to be expected. Paul becomes concerned only when those differences (e.g., glossolalia, "speaking in tongues") are taken as status indicators or when they lead to discrimination within the community (e.g., the inconsiderate treatment of "the ones who have nothing" at the Lord's supper).

Paul recognizes that there are apportionments of gifts, of servings, and of workings (12:4-6); therefore, people in the church properly manifest differences in gifts, in service, and in works (12:8-10)—and that is as it should be. To put it more directly, the differences among the Corinthians with regard to *charismata* are not understood by Paul as an accidentally variegated picture. Rather, the Spirit has allocated, dealt out, apportioned the gifts as the Spirit has seen fit for God's purposes.

Rhetorically structured around the word διαιρέσις (*diairesis*, "allocations"), which is repeatedly placed in first position in each of three clauses for emphasis, vv. 4-6 acknowledge that there are differences in *charismata*, in serving, and in working. The translations of *diairesis* by the NRSV ("varieties") and by the NIV ("different kinds") recognize Paul's effort to acknowledge such differences, but they miss the note of *apportionment* or *distribution* that Paul shows he has in mind when he repeats the same basic term once again in v. 11: "The one and same Spirit produces [or works] all of these [*charismata*], distributing [διαιρέω *diaireō*] them to each just as it wishes." By Paul's choice of the term *diairesis* for his description of the diversities among the Corinthians (vv. 4-6), he anticipates the point with which the passage will emphatically conclude: The Spirit is the source of all *charismata* and allocates them to each person as the Spirit chooses.

Equally noteworthy are the conclusions of each of the first three clauses in vv. 4-6. Three different terms appear: *charismata*, "spiritual gifts"; διακονία *diakonia*, "service"; ἐνέργημα *energēma*, "workings." *Diakonia* and *energēma* signal to Paul's auditors that although the central issue of discussion will be spiritual gifts, the same observations are true about all we are granted to do as believers, whether that takes place as some service or ministry or some (more general category) work. Just as Paul took the Corinthians' question about eating (8:1) as an occasion to reflect about drinking and whatever else they do (8:1; 10:31), so also here the issues about *charismata* are placed in the broader context of whatever an individual does, whether serving or any other working.

The opening list of *charismata* (vv. 8-10) is significant. First, the Spirit is credited as the source of each manifestation. Second, the list probably gives some insight into the community at Corinth: Paul's list suggests that there may have been persons there who professed wisdom (v. 8), who healed (v. 9), who performed powerful works, who prophesied, who spoke in tongues, and who interpreted those utterances (v. 10). Furthermore, faith is listed as one of the gifts (v. 9), and, in Paul's view, all believers have been given the gift of faith; accordingly, no one can view himself or herself as being bereft of Spirit-endowed *charismata.*

Speaking in tongues, or glossolalia, is a special problem in the church at Corinth. In every list of gifts (12:10, 28, 30; 14:26; cf. 13:1, 8), tongues and interpretation of tongues are mentioned last, probably a Pauline inversion of the priority affirmed by some Corinthians, and in chap. 14 tongues (mentioned 17 times) become a focus of attention. Although not at all a purely Christian phenomenon, speaking in tongues was surely a feature of Christianity from its earliest days.[132] In the New Testament we find glossolalia in Acts and in 1 Corinthians. Paul's understanding of glossolalia is that it is Spirit-inspired utterance that is "talking with God" (14:2), that upbuilds the individual (14:4), but that without interpretation (by the glossolalist or by another) is not understandable talk and does not edify others (14:5, 19). This view contrasts with the understanding of glossolalia in Acts 2, where the Spirit uses tongues (which can sometimes be translated "languages") as a means of transcending language barriers and thereby assists or works to advance the gospel by overcoming linguistic barriers.

At Corinth some of Paul's followers have received the gift of speaking in tongues and have made the case that, perhaps because it is so obviously present and esoteric, it is the most desirable gift. Accordingly, special status was claimed for those speaking in tongues. For Paul, it is astonishing that what is a *gift* from the Spirit and, furthermore, a gift that is allocated as the Spirit chooses, could become a basis for boasting. Therefore, while recognizing the diverse allocation of gifts, Paul's opening points in vv. 4-11 are that (1) whatever gifts one has are not given to vaunt oneself but are designed to serve the common good of the community (12:7), and that (2) "one and the same Spirit" has allocated the gifts strictly as it pleased the Spirit (12:11). So the gifts are not for our own aggrandizement but are for the community; likewise, no one can boast of having any particular gift because the Spirit has doled them out as it sees fit. Paul, therefore, dissociates gift and status and ties together gift and service to the community. Readers surely recognize that we encounter here an ongoing problem in which Paul struggles to alter the Corinthians' tendencies to individualism and boasting and tries to integrate the believers more fully into community and a sense of belonging to and serving one another in Christ.

Paul's succinct claim that the *charismata* are given "for the common good" (πρὸς τὸ συμφέρον *pros to sympheron*, v. 7) is striking in two ways. First, he claims the *charismata* for the benefit of the community and thus undercuts individual efforts at enhancing status. Second, his auditors, sophisticated rhetorically as they are, will no doubt note the echoes of the root term *sympheron* from its two significantly placed earlier occurrences in the letter (6:12; 10:23). The "common good," or more generally "what is helpful" (to others, understood), has been Paul's gloss on a Corinthian maxim twice before: "All things are permissible." In both of these instances, Paul was addressing a strong Corinthian sense of freedom in Christ: Believers can, indeed, express their faith in a broad and liberating spectrum of choices and situations. But in both 6:12 and 10:23 Paul has tried to increase the scope of consideration of their moral reckoning by saying that believers must also consider whether the projected action is indeed "helpful" (*sympheron*) to others. So against that background Paul bluntly simplifies by saying in v. 7 that *the point* of *charismata* is to help or to serve the

132. Felicitas Goodman, *Speaking in Tongues: A Cross-cultural Study of Glossolalia* (Chicago: University of Chicago Press, 1972).

community. Chapter 14 will be a protracted reflection along the same line—namely, that tongues and giving thanks through them may be quite significant for the one doing it but *will not edify* (another way of describing being helpful or seeking the common good)

the person who does not understand the glossolalia (cf. 14:19). Paul's appeal to "let all be done for edification" is an elaboration of the notion of doing all things, even glossolalia, in such a way as to be helpful, to seek the common good.

1 Corinthians 12:12-13, Introduction of Body-Member Metaphor with Baptismal Tradition

COMMENTARY

To make his case about the interdependency of believers, Paul resorts to a common, contemporary metaphor about parts of the body and their relation to one another, but only after he has once again rehearsed some more "basics" that he thinks the Corinthians should understand (12:12-13). What he writes in these verses is a refinement of what he said in vv. 2-3 about the Spirit's inaugurating his followers' lives as believers and enabling them to turn away from idolatry, but this time the refinement makes the case about the interrelatedness of believers by introducing the extended metaphor of the body. In vv. 12-13 the reference is once again to the Spirit, but this time in its inaugurating connection with baptism. It was in baptism, Paul says, that, by the working of the Spirit, they were made into one body of which they are all the "many members"—that is, every believer's shared story. No matter how many members, and no matter how different they are one from another, there is just one body, just as there is only one Spirit working in all the members. A part of the baptismal liturgy is again reflected here: "whether Jews or Greeks, slaves or free" (v. 13; cf. 7:17-24 for an earlier reflection; see also Gal 3:28). It

is conceivable that Paul is here echoing the very pronouncement that was made as each Corinthian was baptized.

With this refining piece (vv. 12-13) Paul has affirmed their unity, which was grounded in their baptism, has recognized once again their differences (in the expression "whether Jews or Greeks," etc.), and has associated the body/member imagery that carries the same dynamic into the succeeding verses for further development. Paul's implication is that as surely as individual differences, such as ethnicity and social status, were rendered "indifferent" or of no importance by the working of the Spirit in their baptism where they became one, so also any distinctions in terms of being members with distinctive characteristics and functions have no significance.

To inquire whether something is helpful— that is, serves the common good or, as the same point may be alternatively stated, is edifying of others—focuses on the goal of one's actions. Love, which Paul earlier declared "edifies" or "builds up" (8:1), is the way in which the goal is achieved. So love, edification, and common good are all intimately interconnected in Paul's sense of believers' living the proper moral life.

1 Corinthians 12:14-26, The Members' Proper Interrelation Within the Body

COMMENTARY

The remainder of chap. 12 is structured around what amounts to verse-by-verse variations on the twinned themes of distribution/

allocation and common good/helpfulness to others. "To each *is given the manifestation of the Spirit* for the common good" (v. 7). "One and the same *Spirit* who *distributes* to each just as it wishes" (v. 11). "But now *God has arranged* the members, every one of them, in the body as he wanted" (v. 18). But *"God has so composed* [blended, mixed, as of colors] the body" (v. 28, echoing v. 18) "And *God has arranged* in the church." The arrangement of the members, the assignments of the gifts, the composition of the body—all are from God, assigned as the Spirit or God wishes, and all are to be put in the service of others for the common good.

The "one body, many members" metaphor was a commonplace in the Greco-Roman world;[133] one can even find versions of it in which, as here, the different parts of the body argue with one another. The metaphor is aptly chosen for Paul's purposes because it maintains a claim for unity—one body—while recognizing and honoring differences—many, quite different members.

Functioning as a ring device, the one body premise is stated in v. 14 and reprised in v. 20 and thus effectively frames two distinctive treatments of the metaphor. The first metaphor (vv. 15-17) uses the analogy to address persons who have a low self-estimation, who wish they were other than who they are, and seeks to assure them of their importance, even necessity, to the body. The second metaphor (vv. 21-24) addresses those who have a low estimation of others—that is, those who think they have greater importance—and reminds these people, through a more extended elaboration, because the problem is exacerbated at Corinth, that every member is equally important to the well-being of the body. In this section Paul uses the culturally determined practice of dignifying certain parts of the body with clothing to make the case that all parts of the body are necessary, needed, and honored (vv. 22-24). God orders the body in such a way as to ensure that members have proper concern for one

133. Cf. Conzelmann, *1 Corinthians*, 211.

another, sharing not only in honor but also in suffering (vv. 23-26).

Throughout the letter Paul has openly addressed and cautioned against an overly high self-estimation; one can readily deduce that he has a considerable problem with (at least some of) the Corinthians in this regard. Regularly he has chided them for boasting, for being puffed up, for not being as wise as they think, for being babies (3:1-3), for thinking they already reign (4:8), for believing that they stand when they may in fact be falling (10:12), and so forth. Nowhere until 12:15-17 does Paul address low self-estimation. The reason why is not far to find; most of the problems Paul explicitly faces in 1 Corinthians are prompted by persons with too vaunted a self-estimation, by people thinking that they are on the high side of a sharp status gradient, by people puffing themselves up. One may suppose that the majority of the Corinthian believers were not causing the troubles but were instead too regularly on the receiving end of them. The relatively few who boasted, who thought too highly of themselves, paraded their claims before the majority, who, it must be said, at least let them get away with their pretensions or at worst ascribed truth to their posturing. Paul's pastoral problem with the Corinthians thus has a double aspect that is, indeed, explicitly addressed in balanced proportions only here (12:12-24) in the letter: He not only must caution his readers against overestimation (as he has done so regularly throughout the letter), but also here he directly seeks to encourage the others not to think too lowly of themselves and of their importance to the one body. In this connection, it should be noted that in two previous places in the letter Paul has taken the side of the majority, of those who were subjected to the abusive practices of the well-to-do minority: resolving disputes by taking other believers to court (see chap. 6) and their treatment of the "ones who have not" at the Lord's supper (11:17-34).

REFLECTIONS

Here we encounter what is probably Paul's best-known image of the church: The church is the body of Christ. Several observations need to be made. First, the image is not Paul's only one for the church. Many others (building, temple, field) have already been noted in the commentary. Second, this image is used by Paul only when there are problems of disunity (cf. Romans 12), so we should not expect this image to illustrate all that is important to know or consider about the church.

Third, Paul starts with the assumption that the church is the body of Christ. Simply because the believers die with Christ in their baptism and are one with Christ, they are already the body of Christ. Modern Christians sometimes wonder how they might more fully become the body of Christ. That is not Paul's notion. He considers that believers as believers are already the body of Christ, and he exhorts them to relate to one another in a manner appropriate to *what they already are.*

Fourth, chapter 12, with its imagery of the body, is a case study in a conception of unity that still preserves and honors diversity. The unity of the believers is grounded in that each person is an indispensable part of the body and that, though it is unstated here, it is clearly by the grace of God that each one belongs. The individuality is honored in that each believer serves the body in a distinct—neither less nor greater—way. Christian unity neither requires uniformity nor encourages it. In the same way that the gifts are given by the Spirit as the Spirit chooses and in order to serve the common good, the distinctive members are called to be part of the body, and each is to contribute its own special and distinctive work to the well-being of the whole body. For Christians to be different is not only acceptable, but it is expected and even necessary for the richness, wholeness, and vigor of the body. Believers can differ from each other in appearance and function, in what is done (cf. 12:4-11), and even in certain opinions (cf. Rom 14:1, 5-6). Believers' unity lies in their being one in Christ, in the body together; each one of them is a person for whom Christ died, and all of them have that shared death with Christ in common; thus each has been given to the other in Christ.

Fifth, with so many modern Christians having low self-esteem, we might do well to pay special attention to Paul's insistence in 12:15-17 that all the members are *equally* important to the well-being of the body of Christ. No one is less important. No one brings less to the body of Christ.

Finally, note that Christ is not here named as the head of the body. Ephesians and Colossians alter the image of the church as the body of Christ to claim Christ's headship over the church. Paul's purpose and use of the image here in 1 Corinthians affirms the closest possible identification of Christ and the believers. The believers and Christ belong to one another, and the believers are the members of Christ's body.

1 Corinthians 12:27-31, Application of What Has Been Said and Anticipation of the Next Part of the Argument

COMMENTARY

So far in this chapter Paul has been reestablishing "basics," a continuing motif in this letter. In 12:27-31 Paul applies "what we know" about the body to the church and, with another listing of gifts, moves a step closer to the counsel that will be delivered most fully and directly in chap. 14. As surely as God has configured the members of the human body, so it is with the body of Christ (12:27), in which God has arranged that certain gifts be assigned to certain persons. Paul's claim of priority for the apostles (14:28; cf.

9:1) reaffirms his standing, his authority, as did his reference to the Corinthians earlier as babies (3:1) and as did his claim of being their father in the faith (4:14). By listing prophets as second, only behind apostles, Paul tips his hand regarding his laudation of prophecy just ahead (in chap. 14, where we will see what Paul understands by the term).[134] The

---

134. For a detailed consideration of the topic in its broader context, see Aune, *Prophecy in Early Christianity and the Ancient Mediterranean World,* 248-62.

remainder of the items integral to the list should not be of great concern because on some level they no doubt function to make sure that the reader sees prophecy near the top and speaking in tongues at or near the bottom (12:28, 30). The rhetorical questions of 12:29-30, all cast to indicate that they expect a negative answer, invite the hearers to engage themselves in a perspective-giving litany: Not everybody is endowed with all the gifts, but as Paul has said four different ways in this chapter, *the gifts are apportioned as God or the Spirit sees fit* (12:11, 18, 25, 28).

With 12:31, the argument takes a curious turn, surely designed to grasp the auditors' full attention. Paul, who has made a strong case that the gifts are, first, of equal importance, and, second, assigned, apportioned, arranged by divine fiat, now urges the Corinthians to "seek the greater gifts" (χαρίσματα τὰ μείζονα *charismata ta meizona*, 12:31). The focus is on love throughout the next chapter.

REFLECTIONS

1. Paul lists the gifts of the Spirit in 12:4-10, 27-31 and in Rom 12:3-8. How should we understand these lists? Are they intended to be exhaustive? Illustrative? The interpretive landmines related to spiritual gifts are numerous. First, there is the natural human tendency to look at the lists and to check ourselves against them, as we check a part to its template, to see how (or even whether) the Spirit is working one or more of those gifts (*charismata*) in our own lives. Second, we could easily assume that the lists exhaust the possibilities of the Spirit's gifts (see 1 Cor 7:7 for a charisma that is not even in a list); that if one is not an apostle or has not been working miracles or healing recently, we might conclude that this person is not the medium for the Spirit's working. Third, perhaps that one gift more than all the others is *the* gift of choice.

The lists do not agree in content. Speaking in tongues is not even mentioned in the Romans list. Faith, a charisma that, by definition, *every* believer must have, is listed as a gift in 1 Cor 12:9, so no one can look at the lists and not see himself or herself reflected in them somewhere.

Although the lists are somewhat tailored to the circumstances of the letters in which they are found, they are not exhaustive of the ways the Spirit works in believers. Rather, they are *illustrative*. Further, we may conclude that, as Paul is at pains to argue in 1 Corinthians, no one gift is superior to all of the others and that no one gift is the hallmark or telltale sign of one's being a Christian. Likewise, we see that each gift is determined and allocated by the Spirit, as the Spirit wills, as a means of enriching the community life of the believers, and that there is no limit to the number of gifts an individual may exhibit. So modern Christians should view the Pauline lists of gifts as suggestive of the multitude of ways that the Spirit works in and through the lives of individuals to enrich the shared life and the common good of the believers.

One final point: The different kinds of spiritual gifts should not be isolated from the "different kinds of service" and the "different kinds of working" that parallel and overlap in 12:4-6. So as modern believers look for signs of the Spirit's working in them, they should not look simply at the spiritual gifts; that is only one part of the Spirit's working. They should look also at their service as a sign of the Spirit's expression in them; likewise, they should consider also their different ways of working along with and through others as yet another sign of the Spirit's manifesting itself in and through them. Like grace, the Spirit works in lives in surprising ways, some of which bowl us over with their immediate power and obviousness while others may seem more like Elijah's "gentle whisper" (1 Kgs 19:12 NIV), more like silence than a whirlwind. Believers should never underestimate the power or mode of the Spirit's working even if to them its working is neither obvious nor overwhelming. Accordingly, in the shared life of faith even the actions or deeds that seem the most menial and inconsequential may be the medium through which the Holy Spirit works to enrich the common good of the faithful.

2. Some Corinthians have made glossolalia the most important gift, the sign of having made it to the fullness, perhaps even the zenith, of Christian life—and some others in the congregation have let them do so. Evidence may be seen in the way Paul's lists of gifts always put their first-rated gift last (12:10, 30), in the contrast of tongues and love in 13:1, and in the way glossolalia is a continuing topic in chapter 14. For Paul, glossolalia is inspired by God, is edifying of the inspired individual, is not understandable speech without the accompanying gift of interpretation but with interpretation it edifies the whole church, and is just another one of the gifts all of which are equally important for the life of the church and for the common good. Paul surely does not oppose glossolalia and expects that, with interpretation, it will be part of worship (14:26-28).

Some modern Christians, like their Corinthian counterparts before them, have overlooked Paul's arguments to the contrary and have adopted the Corinthians' mistakes: that speaking in tongues is the ultimate gift, that glossolalia signals when a person has *truly* become a full-fledged Christian, and, correspondingly, that the lack of speaking in tongues is taken as a sign of a spiritual deficit. Paul opposes each of these mistakes. In the letter to the Galatians, Paul faces a quite similar problem; there circumcision instead of glossolalia has become the same sort of talisman. In Galatians, Paul argues that the key indicator of whether people are truly believers is whether they have received the Holy Spirit (Galatians 3). What would Paul say to modern Christians who single out one particular indicator (whether it be glossolalia or the "right" ideas on the inspiration of the Bible or abortion, etc.) other than the reception of the Holy Spirit as the key indicator?

1 Corinthians 13:1–14:1*a*, Encomium on Love

OVERVIEW

For a letter that could rightly be called a continuous reflection on love—even Paul's summary injunctions at the end of the letter conclude with "Do everything in love" (16:14 NIV)—the explicit term has been rather infrequent before chap. 13. With its pithy maxim "Love builds up," 8:1 establishes such a close identification of love and edification that subsequently in the letter the appearance of either term, "love" or "edification," should call to mind the other. The way love works or functions in the community is to bring about edification or upbuilding (another translation of the same Greek term, οἰκοδομή *oikodomē*) of others. Likewise, when Paul encourages edification of others he is simply calling for love to be put into action toward them.

Chapter 13, an encomium[135] on love, though not explicitly identifying love as a

charisma, or gift,[136] extols love and thereby sets the stage for the next chapter's specific application of love and its inevitable expression or by-product, upbuilding (14:3-5, 12, 17, 26), to the Corinthians' problematic practices. By the first century, an encomium was a well-established rhetorical device for praising an individual or a virtue. Typically, encomia praise in two ways: by reference to actions as a clue to character (*ethos*) and by comparison and contrast with other virtues or other praiseworthy persons. Usually, encomia open with a prologue and close with an appeal for emulation. Paul's panegyric on love meets all these criteria.

Some scholars have suggested that Paul did not compose chap. 13 but knew it from elsewhere and incorporated it into his argument.[137] Others have posited that one can read from 12:31 to chap. 14 with no

135. J. G. Sigountos, "The Genre of 1 Corinthians 13," *NTS* 40 (1994) 246-60; J. Smit, "The Genre of 1 Corinthians 13 in the Light of Classical Rhetoric," *NovT* 33 (1991) 193-216; Carl R. Holladay, "1 Corinthians 13: Paul as Apostolic Paradigm," in *Rhetoric and the New Testament: Essays from the 1992 Heidelberg Conference*, ed. S. E. Porter and T. H. Olbricht, JSNTSup 90 (Sheffield: JSOT, 1993) 250-64.

136. Note that love is considered by Paul as a "fruit" of the Spirit (Gal 5:22). That is, love is a response, a way of living that is made possible by God's grace through the working of the Holy Spirit. It is, therefore, not simply a gift but a way of being and relating.

137. See Fee, *The First Epistle to the Corinthians*, 626n. 5.

interruption of Paul's argument, that Paul did not compose chap. 13, and that a later redactor of the Pauline corpus put it where it is.[138] Surely one can construe chaps. 12–14 in that fashion, but to do so overlooks some distinct functions of chap. 13. First, the chapter gives perspective and balance to the matter at hand—namely, proper use and understanding of spiritual gifts in the Corinthian church. Second, the chapter has many significant links to the rest of the letter so that it also serves to recapitulate several concerns already registered by Paul. Third, rhetorical handbooks saw such a change of pace and concentration as a powerful way of focusing the auditors' attention. Paul is surely capable of lofty composition, and chap. 13 serves too many of his concerns not to have belonged there from the start.

138. See Fee, *The First Epistle to the Corinthians*, 626n. 5.

1 Corinthians 13:1-3, The Prologue

COMMENTARY

The encomium's prologue (13:1-3), by reference to a series of indisputably important items, establishes love as the sine qua non of the faithful life. It does so by Paul's reminding the Corinthians of his extraordinary gifts, his grandiloquent abilities, and his potential for extravagant deeds. The auditors are asked to survey Paul as being capable of all these; his history with them allows him reasonably to suggest such a range—and yet lacking love. Without love, all his gifts and powers and actions come to naught in the devastatingly pithy declaration, "I am nothing" (13:2).

Imagine the impact of these verses on the original hearers of this letter. First Corinthians has so regularly centered around Paul's offering of himself as a positive example worthy of emulation. In 13:1-3 Paul presents himself once again as a model, but this time as a negative exemplar, as one who, though so very gifted, if lacking love, would be of no worth, no value. This rhetorical device, much like the indirect speech noted in chaps. 1–4, allows Paul to lay out some stern warnings to his auditors without risk of unduly offending them and with the added advantage that his application to himself allows, even subtly commends, that others apply the same test to themselves. The auditors can hear much more forceful and blunt criticism of themselves precisely because it is Paul's critique of his imaginary, contrary-to-fact self.

Not surprisingly, the first item is the highly touted Corinthian favorite: speaking in tongues. Paul invites the hearers to imagine him, richly endowed as they know him to be with the gift of tongues (the reference to "tongues of angels" makes clear we are not dealing with linguistic acumen; cf. 14:18-19; cf. also 7:7), but lacking love (which he assumes they know him in fact not to be): He would be a useless, perhaps even an irritating musical instrument whereas, with love, he would have been helpful and even enriching. Paul's likening his imaginary loveless self to a brassy clanging instrument no doubt anticipates his subsequent development of that image in 14:7-11.

Second is a collection of items (already mentioned, e.g., in 1:18–2:16: prophetic abilities, understanding, and wisdom) with which he assumes some Corinthians have very positive identifications. And in regard to those endowments (which the letter has also been careful to remind the Corinthians Paul certainly does not lack), Paul pictures his imaginary loveless self as "nothing" (13:2). Third are two means of gaining social notoriety and presumably status: a giving away of all one's possessions and some sort of self-immolation (cf. Rom 5:7, where it is said that someone would perhaps die for another; see also Rom 9:3, where Paul imagines himself cut off so that his Jewish brothers and sisters might be included). And without love, neither gains anything. As Paul takes his epistolary walk through their gallery of values, he escalates the shock effect of his own imaginary self-portraits, moving as he does from likening himself to a useless instrument (13:1) to his claim that he is nothing (13:2). Paul's indirect critique of their self-aggrandizement around tongues, wisdom, and understanding is implicit in his imaginary loveless, negative, contrary-to-fact self-portrait.

Extraordinary gifts, grand abilities and skills, extravagant actions—all these, ironically, are emptied of any worth without love. Furthermore, with the mention of each item, the refrains describing lovelessness become more blatantly self-indulgent, more individualistic, and more self-serving. The point, subtly but powerfully made, is that no matter how magnificent the accomplishment, power, or action, when love is missing the exercise in question becomes vain, selfish, fruitless, and individualistic; it does not even serve to accomplish its self-vaunting end. "Without love, I help myself [ὀφελοῦμαι *opheloumai*] not at all" (13:3). As one Scottish translation captures it: "I am nane the better o it."[139] Love's quest can never begin with the question "What's in it for me?" Instead, love

looks first to the other and asks, "What is best for you?" "What would help you?" A few verses into chap. 14, Paul, using the same Greek term ὠφελέω (*ōpheleō*) and modeling love, asks the Corinthians not how they might help *him*, but how he might help *them* (14:6). So within a few verses he does the very thing that he prescribes for them. The proper movement of love begins with attention to the needs of the other person.

Imbedded within the prologue (13:1-3) are two convictions: (1) Love's nature is to seek not one's own needs but the needs of others, and (2) in so doing, love ultimately secures not only the other person but also one's own self. Directly ahead in the encomium Paul will make this same point; he has already made it in 1 Corinthians (10:24, 33), and elsewhere in his letters he is quite regularly insistent on this same dynamic (Phil 2:1-4; cf. Rom 13:8; 15:1-2). (See Reflections at 14:1*a*.)

139. *The New Testament in Scots*, trans. W. L. Lorimer (Edinburgh: Southside, 1983).

1 Corinthians 13:4-7, Recitation of the Acts of Love

COMMENTARY

An encomium of a person recounts past actions worthy of praise; an encomium of a virtue depicts its characteristics and how it functions. In 13:4-7, love's credentials are laid out both positively, with regard for what love does and how it operates, and negatively, with regard to what it avoids and does not do. "Love waits with patience" and while waiting, it is kind and merciful (13:4). Then follows a sequence of declarations of what love is not, declarations that via negativa serve to clarify what is characteristic of love: It is not jealous, not boastful, not puffed up, not behaving disgracefully, not seeking its own purposes, not becoming irritated, not keeping score of wrongs, and not taking pleasure in unrighteousness (13:4-5*a*).

Then with considerable rhetorical flourish Paul concludes the characterization of love by a string of most sweeping claims about love, each beginning with the direct object (πάντα *panta*, "all things"), thereby emphasizing love's all-encompassing scope. The "all

things" list opens and closes with very nearly the same point about how love functions in the present, thus highlighting these two claims: "Love passes over all things in silence" (v. 7*a*) and "Love bears [or endures] all things" (v. 7*d*). On one level these assertions are positive counterparts to the disclaimer that love does not keep track of wrongs; they represent the necessary kind of "running forgiveness" that is ingredient to any sustained relationship. On another level they establish love as the context in which the difficulties and trials of life are met. How do they do so? Because love is never held alone in one's self; love always involves another; love always links one's self to another. This reciprocal character of love has already been acknowledged by Paul in 8:3: "If someone loves God, that person is known by God." Love is a two-way street that provides a context of mutuality, understanding, and relatedness between each person and others, between God and believers, and between believers and believers. And that is the context in which love enables us, with the support of the others who are linked in love, to bear, to endure whatever comes along. This is the same point he already made in 10:13, but this time expressed in terms of love.

The other two claims of v. 7—"love believes all things; hopes all things"—tie faith and hope to love in anticipation of v. 13. It is not surprising that faith (the same Greek term for the verb "believe") and hope should appear here together; they are inextricably tied in Paul's thought (cf. Gal 5:5-6; 1 Thess 1:3; 5:8). Faith, right relationship with God, is the basis on which one has hope regarding the future, because, through faith, one knows God's redemption in the present, one can hope—that is, one can confidently look to the future in anticipation of God's completing the work that God has already begun in the present (cf. Phil 2:12b-13).

Love's believing all things describes neither a willing disregard for reality nor naïveté nor gullibility. It is probably best to take this statement as a posture of openness along the lines of 2 Cor 5:7: "We walk through faith, not through sight." Certainly, to hope all things must be grounded in this confidence in God toward the future, a confidence whose basis is neither visible nor directly knowable, a theme to which Paul returns in 13:12. On the theological level, "walking by faith" describes a way of living in trust upon the God who is "for us" (Rom 8:31; cf. 1 Cor 11:24)—that is, the God who is benevolently disposed toward humans, who brings into being the things that do not exist, and who brings life out of death (Rom 4:17). (See Reflections at 14:1a.)

1 Corinthians 13:8-13, Comparison and Contrast of Love with Other Virtues

COMMENTARY

The next standard feature of an encomium compares the virtue, in Paul's case, love, to others: "Love never ends/fails." Tongues, the favorite of some Corinthians, and prophecy, Paul's alternate favorite, which he is about to advocate in chap. 14, along with knowledge, which will become the topic a few verses later, are limited, even finite; tongues and prophecy are functions that serve the particular needs of a given community within time and history, but whose scope is limited to human performance. Faith and hope are enabled by God's grace, but God does not "believe," and nowhere does Paul say that God "hopes." God does love, however, and so do believers. So love's being and existing is tied to God's very self, and in loving, believers participate with God in a special, unique, even reciprocal way. Love never ends because God's eternal love is the ground and matrix for all human loving.

Paul's eschatological convictions shape what he says here. The present, graced as it is with God's love alive in the community at Corinth, is still only a partial reflection, like that of a mirror whose glass is not clear, of what is yet to come. Paul thinks believers live with a present down payment (2 Cor 1:22; 5:10), with partial insight, or as he will develop it in chap. 15, with the perishable and mortal but in full anticipation of the imperishable and immortal. Paul's vision stretches from his recognition that all believers are somewhere on a pilgrimage from being children in the faith, as he thinks the Corinthians are (3:1), to the time when maturity or the perfect arrives (13:10), to that time when believers no longer walk by faith but by sight, when in the eschaton they see "face to face" (13:12). So Paul anticipates that faith, as important and central as it is, will someday be transcended by the most intimate presence with God. In the meantime, Paul offers himself once again as the model of the person who is no longer a child, who has set aside childish things (13:12). When the perfect arrives, when believers see face-to-face, then Paul expects to exchange his own partial knowledge for a full knowing, then his knowing will correspond to the knowing (God's, assumed but not stated) that has preceded and made possible Paul's partial and proleptic knowing (13:12).

Corinthian interest in "knowing" and "knowledge" is once again put in perspective: Paul, who exceeds them in knowledge as he also excels them in tongues, acknowledges that he knows only "in part" and that the knowledge yet to come, at the end of the ages, so far surpasses present knowledge (note that this same sort of argument will be undertaken in chap. 15 when present glory is contrasted with future glory) as to put present knowing in a modest perspective. But all of this reflection about the partial and the perfect, the present and future knowledge, the now and then, is designed to put love and the "now" in perspective: "But now remain faith, hope, and love, these three, but the greatest of these is love" (13:13). The famous Pauline triad is most clearly present here (cf. Rom 5:1-5; Gal 5:5-6; Col 1:4-5; 1 Thess 1:3; 5:8). At the heart of the Christian life are these three. Paul cannot imagine life in Christ without each part of the triad being in place and fully functioning; all three must remain whatever else may come and go or change or however different one believer is from another.

How is love greater than faith and hope? Faith, the right relation to God, makes love possible (Gal 5:6), so love presupposes faith. Does that suggest that faith is really greater? Paul has already given the cue when he introduced this whole comparative section of the encomium: "Love never fails/ends" (v. 8). Hope, a conviction and a yearning lodged in the heart of the individual, clearly ends when that for which one hopes is finally achieved. Faith, also a human commitment, though not possible without God's grace, may end; one may fall from faith (cf. Gal 3:3-5). By contrast, love, grounded as it is in God and a signal and eternal characteristic of God's commitment toward all creatures, is the one disposition that believers share most fully with God. And that love is eternal.

Love is "greatest" in three senses. First, its eternality, allowing it to be present fully now and yet guaranteed to be present also when the eschatological time brings about that toward which we have believed and hoped, establishes it as superlative. Second, it is greatest when Paul thinks of the Corinthian fascination with gifts, each of which is transient. Faith, hope, and love endure; gifts do not. Gifts are finite; they are given to persons who employ them for a period within the community. Love is the matrix of the life of faith; God's love for people becomes the force that enables them to love others. Third, the "greatest" lack of the Corinthians is love. They are well endowed with gifts, as Paul recognized already in the thanksgiving (1:7). They are quite zealous regarding spiritual matters; Paul acknowledges that, and he urges them to "seek to abound in building up the church"; if one keeps in mind the connection Paul has made in 8:1, that love builds up, one can see that he is in effect saying that they should seek to abound in loving one another (cf. 16:14). They have become too fixated on gifts and have failed to live love toward one another. In that sense, also, the greatest need for them is love. (See Reflections at 14:1*a*.)

1 Corinthians 14:1a, The Encomium's Conclusion, the Appeal for Emulation

COMMENTARY

An encomium typically ends with a call for hearers to be like the person praised or to put in practice the highlighted virtue. Paul follows the expectation: "Pursue love" (14:1*a*). Curiously, the term "love" makes no further appearance until 16:14 and 24, but the Pauline connection between love and upbuilding is so fully established (cf. 8:1) that he no longer needs to use the word "love"; he can (and does) now shift to "building up," "edification" (14:3-5, 12, 17, 26), and he is in fact talking about love without using the term. He can shift his focus to edification not only for rhetorical purposes (the rhetorical handbooks warn about overusing a term and recommend substituting another for it)[140] but also for his paraenetic purposes (he is interested not in lip service to a virtue, but in the real practice of love that by its very nature and function results in the upbuilding of others and in the edification of the church).

140. *Ad Herennium* 4.12.18.

Reflections

1. Paul's encomium of love is one of the loftiest expressions in literature. Its function is to place love, in many of its aspects, in the center of the community's reflection, which location is itself symbolic of love's centrality to the life of faith. Love is the absolutely indispensable feature of the believing life (13:3); without love, no matter how many possessions one has or how prominent one is, one is lost and as good as dead. Some of Paul's assertions about love call for reflection.

(1) "Love always protects" (NIV); "Love bears all things" (NRSV); "Love passes over all things in silence" (13:7*a*). In this pithy statement Paul captures an essential characteristic of love: Not only does love not keep score of past better and worse moments and actions, but it also looks the other way, as it were. When we reflect even about friendship we know that our friendships continue precisely because we are willing to give our friends a break, to give them the benefit of the doubt, and even to overlook slights or inadvertences. If friendship depends on that, then how much more so love.

In extreme circumstances, however, love may not call for passing over something in silence; it may not allow us to look the other way and ignore it. When, for example, a person is abused physically, emotionally, or sexually, this verse cannot be invoked as a reason for the victim to bear it or for the perpetrator to be protected. In matters of fundamental justice and the protection of less powerful persons preyed on by others, love requires that its handmaiden justice be brought to bear. Then, love must protect the victim, not the victimizer. Therefore, love "bears all things" insofar as they do not harm another of God's creatures. Churches have an obligation to be counted foursquare on seeing that love is always hand in hand with justice. There is an irony about love: The very capacity to overlook, not to keep score—which is so vitally important to the functioning of love and to the wholeness of community—leaves love vulnerable to exploitation. And the community of believers, one and all, must be eternally vigilant to avoid or expose that exploitation—in a loving fashion.

(2) There is an ambiguity about love that resists common sense: In seeking the good of the other, one finds one's own good. Intuition would suggest that we take care of ourselves first and if anything or any time is left over, then we turn to others. But Paul supposes that one's good is not achievable apart from the well-being of others in the body of Christ to which all believers equally belong. So there is a circularity to love, starting from God's love of us, which love renews us and remakes us whole, and moving ineluctably until it gains expression toward others as a way of responding in thankfulness to God's love. In that sense, love cannot be held; it cannot be seized; it is realized fully only in its being shared with someone else. We who have been fully loved by God honor and relish that love most completely only in the sharing of it with others. So, to look after the interests of others is inescapably to benefit all persons in the community and therefore to benefit oneself.

This sense of caring for others, however, can become a smoke screen for failing to attend to one's own needs, for hiding one's own desperation and deficiencies. Ideally, Paul supposes that believers ought to have accurate self-assessments, to know where they stand, where their strengths and weaknesses are, and to build upon the strengths and actively work to shore up the weaknesses. As great as it is, love founders when it is used as an excuse either to avoid proper self-care or to cloud proper self-assessment.

Without the proper self-testing that Paul has consistently expected, love cannot properly engage the self one truly is with the needs of another.

There is an analogy in what Paul says about knowing and being known (13:12). God knows us perfectly; what we now know is partial and filled with enigmas, but Paul anticipates that the time is coming when he will know as Paul himself is known already by God. God's knowing, like God's loving, precedes and gives power to our knowing and our loving. Our partial knowing, like our so-far only partial loving, is capable of improvement and growth by God's grace until that end time when we will know as we are known and love as we are loved.

(3) If mountains come and go, but love endures; if love is greater even than faith and hope, then not only does our loving endure beyond us but our loving is our enduring legacy as well. Granted, our loving and its legacy can take many forms. If we took it seriously that our loving was our enduring legacy, then what reorganization would be needed in our lives, in our stewardship of our time, energy, and resources to honor and maximize that legacy?

2. This chapter, or part of it, is read at many wedding ceremonies—and appropriately so, because Paul has recognized some fundamentals about love no matter how it is understood. But it would be a mistake to assume that Paul here has in mind romantic love that is powered by one's yearning for and infatuation with a marriage partner. The love of which Paul writes so eloquently is a love that does not originate in one individual and reach out to another. Rather, the love celebrated in this text comes from God, claims us, and through us reaches out to others, not simply to another person whom we wish for our spouse. The love about which Paul writes, then, can never find its sole object in another single individual but reaches out through and beyond that other person. It is therefore surely appropriate to read this passage at weddings where love is affirmed between two individuals, but never without the sense that the love between those two is first not of their own origination but also that its goal can never be fully realized in its focus on one another. True love, as Paul sees it, always begins with God and always reaches beyond one's self to others. The Pauline notion of love never stops on just one other person, no matter how special, but reaches through the loved one(s) to God's broken world in which this new couple now pledge to make their life together.

3. A commonplace in the history of art depicts Faith, Hope, and Charity (from the Latin *caritas*, for "love") as three women. You can see them, for example, in El Greco's *Modena Triptych*, in which they stand together in the foreground of the crucifixion. In this same painting, El Greco employs a further artistic convention when he depicts Charity (Love) as being surrounded by numerous children clinging to her legs and being carried in her arms. Artists have long understood that love is known by her offspring and characterized by having children too numerous to count.

1 Corinthians 14:1*b*-40, Paul's Affirmation of Edification and Practical Suggestions

OVERVIEW

This large block opens and closes with the same thought: "Seek to prophesy" (14:1*b*, 39). Across the rather extended passage, Paul argues that prophecy is superior to tongues because prophecy "builds up," "edifies" the community, and thereby serves the common good (12:7). Paul has to walk a fine line; he needs to put tongues into their proper perspective without denigrating them. So the closing note of this chapter is designed to ward off the Corinthians' tendency to extremes: "Do not prohibit the speaking in tongues" (14:39). A sort of formula emerges in Paul's reflections: Tongues plus interpretation equals or results in edification for the community; tongues without interpretation builds up only the one speaking in tongues (14:4).

The leitmotif of the section is edification, the fruit of love between and among believers (8:1). The Corinthian church's problem is not a lack of spiritual gifts (1:7), but rather the proper employment of them for the common good (12:7), for mutual upbuilding and enrichment of the communal life of faith. Some in Corinth have privatized and personalized the gifts in an attempt to enhance their own status and well-being. Paul seeks to reincorporate those persons and their gifts into service of the community of believers. His strategy is to stress prophecy, which he apparently thinks not only is available to everyone (14:1*b*, 39) but also builds up others.

This section, thoroughly praxis-oriented and practical in its application throughout and containing a mix of arguments including some exemplification of how things should and should not be, is governed by the question of what most edifies the community. Paul signals his answer in the opening verses: Prophecy is preferred over tongues unless the latter are accompanied by interpretation, in which case the effect is also edification. Once again Paul sets himself as the example of the one whose spirituality integrates the mind and the spirit and whose comportment in worship corresponds to his earlier-described evangelist efforts (9:19-23). He leaves no one out, neither members of the community nor those in the position of novices (see more on this in 14:13-19) nor unbelievers who might happen into the community's worship. The remainder of the chapter gives some practical suggestions, a Pauline hallmark, and closes with an enforcement statement.

1 Corinthians 14:1b-12, Edification Valued Over Glossolalia

COMMENTARY

Throughout the chapter, Paul is careful not to disparage speaking in tongues. Tongues are a language spoken to God (v. 2), a praying of one's spirit (v. 14), a means of thanksgiving (v. 17). Tongues edify the speaker (v. 4). In one respect like all the languages in the world, speaking in tongues is also capable of transmitting meaning, but Paul is convinced the meaning is carried in the interpretation (vv. 5, 11, 13). Speaking in tongues must not be prohibited (v. 39).

But there are limitations and problems with speaking in tongues. Paul uses analogies: If harps and flutes do not play distinctive notes, who will recognize the tune (v. 7)? And more pointedly, because Paul thinks of believers as being a part of God's battle force, if the bugle does not sound a distinct call, who will prepare for battle (v. 8)? It is the same with foreign languages, all of which he credits with power; but they do not convey meaning if the hearer does not understand them (vv. 11, 16).

As laudable as Paul's portrait of tongues is, his argument attempts to transfer the Corinthian high valuation of tongues to an affirmation of the superiority of prophecy—precisely because Paul believes that prophecy edifies the community. Can we discern what Paul means by prophecy?[141] Paul presumes that his auditors know what he means, so we never receive a definition. But we can gain some insight by noting the functions Paul describes. Prophecy edifies others (v. 3), and it edifies the church (vv. 4-5); it consoles and encourages others (vv. 3, 31). It seems to be roughly equivalent, at least in Paul's exemplification and exercise of it, to instruction, to the sharing of some communication, to engagement with someone else's suffering or loss (vv. 19, 31).

141. The best studies that set the background for understanding Paul's use of the term are Aune, *Prophecy in Early Christianity and the Ancient Mediterranean World*; Forbes, *Prophecy and Inspired Speech in Early Christianity and Its Hellenistic Environment.*

In Paul's picture of the way prophecy should actually function in worship, two or three prophets speak, one at a time (14:31), and others weigh out what the prophets have said (14:29). Thus prophecy does not have axiomatic, automatic authority, but may be *granted* authority after community reflection and assent. Paul holds that all persons may prophesy; it is a gift that is available to all (14:24, 31). Finally, prophecy makes sense to novices and unbelievers and may therefore set off a sequence that ultimately could result in the acclamation "Surely God is among you!" (14:25; cf. 3:16; see also the Commentary on 5:1). Prophecy functions to reprove novices and unbelievers, to call them to account, to disclose "the hidden things of their hearts" with the result that they fall on their knees before God, affirming God's presence in the community's worship. So it appears that prophecy, according to Paul, was not to be confused with telling the future; instead, it seems to be a statement intended for and applicable to the community and to those in worship, a declaration that becomes the basis for discussion and assessment—not only of what the prophet has said but also of how it applies to the lives of the auditors. Prophecy is appropriate to a range of human experiences as suggested by edification, consolation, encouragement, and learning (14:3, 31), so it seems able to bear on all aspects of the communal life of the believers.

A potential trap awaits Paul, however, as he pursues his strategy to put speaking in tongues in perspective by stressing the superior importance of prophecy in the life of the church. He faces a congregation among whom some have insisted—and others have conceded—that glossolalia is the preeminent gift, signifying special status and power. Paul's strategy in chap. 14 is to accommodate to the notion that if there is a superior gift, then it must be prophecy. How does Paul avoid having the same status-centered confusion transferred from tongues to prophecy? Several ways: (1) He declares that speaking in tongues, properly accompanied with interpretation, is equivalent to prophecy in that both result in edification of the community (14:5). (2) He describes prophecy as open to all persons equally (14:24, 31) and, therefore, implicitly invites the participation of all believers. (3) Most important, he argues that anyone zealous for spiritual things—and who among the glossalalists would not so describe themselves?—should seek to abound in edifying the church (14:12). Paul's most sweeping goal statement regarding edification is 14:26 (itself a refinement of 14:12): "Let all things be done for building up" (NRSV; the NIV translation chooses the less precise "strengthening" and inserts an unnecessary restriction, "the church"). With Paul's close, early identification of love and edification in 8:1, Paul's prescription in 14:26 could just as well have been formulated as follows: "Let all things be done in love," but he appropriately saves exactly that formulation for the capstone of the entire letter in 16:14.

REFLECTIONS

In chapter 14, edification—that is, "what builds up"—is the test of every contemplated action in the life of the community. The readers who remember Paul's epigram "Love builds up" (8:2) can see the connection with chapter 13 where love is praised. When love works in the community, the community is built up, not necessarily or primarily in numbers, though it would be surprising if the numbers did not also increase, because love has an infectious quality. Love usually brings out the best in the ones loving and in the ones being loved; love usually elicits love in response. And inevitably all who love, are loved, and love in return are built up and encouraged in the most powerful way. Paul's word to those Corinthians who are eager to excel in everything is probably a good word to believers today: "Seek to excel in the edification of the church" (14:12).

1 Corinthians 14:13-19, How to Be Outstanding in Edifying

COMMENTARY

Paul has just urged those who are zealous about spiritual matters (v. 12) to focus their energies on edification. Specifically for glossolalists that would mean praying for the capacity to interpret because tongues plus interpretation leads to edification (v. 13).

Glossolalia is limited in two important respects. First, it does not engage others who might be there when the church meets; without interpretation, tongues will mean nothing to other believers and to any unbelievers who might happen to be present. Second, glossolalia does not engage the whole person; only the spirit, not the mind, is involved.

Paul has to make certain that the Corinthians understand that his critique of their use of tongues does not spring from any jealousy of their gift: He speaks in tongues "more than you all" (v. 18) but, like his emulatable self-portrait in chapter 9, through self-discipline he forgoes the practice of his gift of tongues when he is in church because, reaching for hyperbole to emphasize his point, he would rather speak a few words "with his mind" that make sense to others than a myriad of words in a tongue (v. 19). So his critique of their practice is not grounded in jealousy, because he excels them in tongues, as he expects them to remember.

Individual ancient Greek manuscripts were written entirely in capital letters or entirely in lower case letters, so all translators must decide when capitalization is appropriate and when it is not. Of course, given modern practices, some terms are clearly to be capitalized and others just as surely are not, but sometimes, as here in v. 15, translators and interpreters of the ancient Greek are faced with an ambivalence regarding whether capitalization is appropriate. In 14:15, the issue is how to translate τῷ πνεύματι (tō pneumati)—that is, whether the reference is (simply) to one's own spirit or to the Holy Spirit (which Paul frequently enough calls simply "the Spirit," as this phrase could here be translated; cf. 2:4, 10-11, 13-14). Supporting capitalizing it and understanding that Paul is writing about praying and singing with the assistance of the Holy Spirit is Paul's statement in Rom 8:26 that when we do not know how to pray as necessary, the Spirit intercedes for us in sighs too deep for words. On the other side, that the term "spirit" should not be capitalized and should therefore be taken as referring to the human spirit, is the parallel construction in 14:15-16 with "the mind" (ὁ νοῦς ho nous) where that referent is clearly to the individual's "mind." There is also a third possibility that must be considered here—namely, that the primary referent of πνεῦμα (pneuma, "spirit"), read in the light of its paralleled reference to mind, here is indeed the human spirit as the commitment of one's life, but that for Paul the Holy Spirit's assistance in praying cannot be ruled out of the picture. In this third possibility, then, the reference to pneuma is actually double, both to the human spirit and to the Holy Spirit.

Two patterns of piety are in contention here. The one piety, which stresses what we might call the vertical axis—namely, one's relation to God, and minimizes or treats as secondary the horizontal axis—namely, one's relation to others, is represented by some of the Corinthians. This piety takes primary consideration for one's self and one's relation to God; one's gift is interpreted as a sign of one's importance, of one's recognition by God, and of God's special favor; one's spirit, not one's mind, is seen as the source of one's praying, singing, and blessing; and, most significant, this piety, when it does consider others, always secondarily and sometimes condescendingly takes little cognizance of others because it is so primarily and directly focused on the individual and God. In the portion of the letter at hand, this vertical piety is represented most directly by those who seem to be vaunting their capacity to speak in tongues. The remainder of the letter shows other instances where many among the Corinthian believers, perhaps also driven by such a piety, failed to weigh or perhaps even to be concerned with the way one's actions affect another in the community of believers.

Paul advocates an alternative piety and exemplifies it for them in his self-reflection in chap. 14. Paul's piety embraces the central tenet of the vertical piety: that one's relation to God is fundamental, but goes on to recognize that proper relation to God always already places one in relation to others in Christ. Paul's piety always lovingly integrates all of the believers actively into one's calculations and behavior; it involves the whole self, spirit *and* mind, into one's life as an ongoing act of worship; it views one's gift or gifts as graciously given to serve the common good; and it never acts without consideration for others.

As their father in the faith (cf. v. 20), Paul exemplifies this second piety. In his first portrait of himself in this large section he invites them to imagine his coming to them and speaking only in tongues (v. 6). Of what use would (even) he be to them, he inquires. No edification of others, no building up would take place. He would be useless unless he also spoke to them some revelation, knowledge, prophecy, or teaching (v. 6). His second self-portrait (v. 14) imagines himself being engaged with the community by praying in a tongue and thus engaging only his spirit but not his mind. Praying in tongues, as powerful and important a gift as it is, employs only one's spirit; Paul says one's mind is "unfruitful" when speaking in tongues (v. 14). Unable to condone anything less than full employment of himself or anyone else in service to God (cf. Rom 12:1), Paul resolves to pray, sing, and bless not only with his spirit but also with his mind (vv. 15-16). Here, as in his discussion of what could properly be eaten (chaps. 8–10—to "whatever you eat," Paul added, "whatever you drink or whatever you do" (10:31),

thus extending from one exemplary action to suggest something about the pattern of the entirely integrated and faithful life), Paul moves from the specific issue under discussion, tongues, to the broader practice of one's whole life, here exemplified in "singing" and "blessing." After reminding his auditors that he speaks in tongues "more than all of you" (14:18), Paul concludes his self-portrait with a hyperbolic declaration that, *in church*, he would prefer to speak a few words with his mind rather than myriad words in a tongue (14:19). Why? Because otherwise, others are not engaged, they are not instructed (and one could presumably add the other benefits that have been noted across this chapter: They are not built up, consoled, encouraged; they learn nothing).

Parenthetically and incidentally, we probably gain some insight into Paul's own spirituality in this discussion. When he is alone he readily prays in tongues as a means of speaking with God (14:18, 28). When, however, he is with others in the worshiping community, he wants his life integrated with that of others; no one can be left out; no one can be treated as unimportant. Further, when he is with others in the worshiping community he feels obligated to engage his whole self, his mind and his spirit, in the worship and in its relationship to others. Otherwise, one takes less seriously than one should the obligation to be a channel for edification of others; otherwise, one might miss the edification that others have to offer. And prayer is not the totality of the properly worshipful life: Singing and blessing, to mention just two, are illustrative of the way the whole life ought to be integrated into worship.

REFLECTIONS

1. Paul insists that he prays not only with the spirit (Spirit) but also with the mind, and he sings not only with the spirit (Spirit) but also with the mind. He represents an integration, a wholeness in his life and in his expression of his faith. Because the life of faith is rightly so much a matter of internal disposition, so much a product of the inspiration of the Holy Spirit, as Paul says, joining with our spirits (Rom 8:16), the temptation has been to maximize the spirit-characteristic of the life of faith and minimize if not eliminate the function of the mind. But as we have seen, Paul does not compartmentalize the life of faith into some segment of the person; instead, the whole person, mind and spirit and heart, is renewed and is placed in service of God, its Creator and redeemer. So Paul exemplifies what he hopes his hearers can aspire to: an integrated presentation of their whole selves and their whole lives as a thanksgiving offering, holy and acceptable to God (Rom 12:1). No part of one's being is left out of full employment in service to God; no aspect of life is relegated as outside the scope of God's concern. Paul's is a holistic, integrated view of the individual—and indeed of all of life before God. Put more directly into modern categories, Paul does not separate life into spiritual and secular, religious and the rest of life, Sundays and the remainder of the week. All of life—equally and fully—is under the dominion of God, and every aspect of one's being is placed in service to God.

Paul is radically different from modern persons who compartmentalize their lives into sacred times and secular ones, into spiritual occasions and the rest of life's experience. The connection between worship and all of life is important for Paul. Questions of moral comportment bear as equally on the way one behaves at an unbeliever's home (10:27-29) as on how one conducts one's life in worship. Worship mirrors life as it should be lived and reflects on life as the worshipers have lived it. Ideally, all of life is worship (Rom 12:1). Just as surely as God's grace is the basis of all of life, every day and every moment, so all of life is offered up to God as a thanksgiving for God's grace and bountiful gifts (1 Cor 4:7; 14:16). Understanding this helps interpreters to comprehend how Paul can call upon his followers to "pray without ceasing"—because all of life is an enacted response to and conversation with God.

2. Individual edification is all right, but not the ideal. Paul critiques individualism, even pious individualism, in which an individual "may give thanks well, but the other person is not edified" (14:17). Paul's is a radical affront to the modern tendency to privatize religion, piety, and one's sources of morality. For Paul, the important thing is not just how the individual is with God. Such a privatization of faith is unthinkable and unacceptable for Paul. Faith without community may not be completely bogus, but it is not the real thing, according to Paul. Without community, something so important is missing that the thing itself is called into question. Testifying of one's faith or bearing witness to others is not what Paul is thinking about. He cannot imagine faith of an individualistic piety that thrives without community, without others being positively affected and encouraged by the living of it. Put another way, no proper relation to God is possible without others in support and others who benefit.

1 Corinthians 14:20-40, A Series of Problems in the Corinthians' Fellowship

OVERVIEW

Throughout the last half of chap. 14 a series of issues receive special treatment. Paul's insistence on building up one another and the church provides the immediate context in which he treats the problems.

1 CORINTHIANS 14:20-25, COMPORTMENT AS IT BEARS ON UNBELIEVERS AND NOVICES

COMMENTARY

What about unbelievers and their interchange with believers? Believers and unbelievers in Corinth, in sharp distinction from Thessalonica, have easy and comfortable interaction. In Corinth, some believers are married to unbelievers (7:12-16). Further, Paul can speculate about an invitation to dinner at an unbeliever's home (10:27-29). And unbelievers apparently are sometimes present at worship occasions (14:23-24).

Paul expressed concern that an unbeliever who encounters Corinthian worship, as chaotic as it has been, will mistake the worship of God for the worship in other contemporary temples of hellenistic religions—that is, they will think Paul's followers are simply ecstatically mad (14:23). But even worse, if the unbeliever does not understand what is being said, then he or she will escape the process where such a person's being called to account may ultimately lead to the affirmation of God's presence, in other words to faith. So even in such inadvertant descriptions of worship, Paul holds that believers have an obligation not only to be considerate of unbelievers, but also to expose them to the cutting edge of the gospel.

The text not only comments about unbelievers; it also mentions those "who do not understand" (NIV), "outsiders" (NRSV)—whose identification is a bit more complex (14:16, 23-24). The NRSV translation "outsider" lends itself to be understood as another way—indeed so taken it would be a redundant one—of describing an unbeliever.

The term ἰδιώτης (idiōtēs) describes a person who is "unskilled" (cf. 2 Cor 11:6), who is an amateur, one who is untrained, one who is a non-expert as distinguished from a specialist. That range of meanings does not require that we think of persons so designated as "outsiders" to the believing community; they may simply be less adept, less skilled, less trained than some other believers. In 14:16 the representative person described as an idiōtēs, though set over against an imagined person who is speaking in tongues, is

nevertheless considered able not only to say the "Amen" that Paul and his communities have adopted from Jewish synagogue practice (14:16) but also to be "built up" if only the person could understand what was being said (14:17). Paul consistently reserves the notion of edification as applicable to believers, so the person in "the position of an idiōtēs" is a believer, not an unbeliever.

Paul's introduction of this representative person gives telling clues as to how to understand it. First, the person is not simply declared to be a novice, but ὁ ἀναπληρῶν τὸν τόπον τοῦ ἰδιώτου (ho anaplērōn ton topon tou idiōtou), "one who is in the situation of a novice/beginner." So the phrase can readily be understood to describe someone who, in comparison with others who are more skilled, is in a relatively disadvantaged situation. Second, at other points in Paul's letters, indeed, even in 1 Corinthians (cf. 2:6; 3:1-2), Paul has distinguished between more mature, more advanced spiritual persons and their younger, less mature counterparts, babies in the faith. Third, because this imagined novice believer is mentioned in the context of speaking in tongues, we may suppose that this representative person is *unskilled in tongues and in their interpretation.* So Paul's employment of the phrase "like a novice" here in 14:16 is a reference to a believer who is clearly like a beginner when compared with other believers and their employment of their charismata of speaking in and interpreting tongues. After this rather full picture of the one "in the situation of being a novice," Paul can shorten his subsequent references to idiōtēs (14:23-24) and expect the auditor to remember the cluster of clues identifying the person in the first place (14:16). Therefore, the one "in the position of being an idiōtēs" is an imagined believer who is "untrained, unskilled" in speaking (and in interpreting) tongues.

When the term idiōtēs reappears, it is linked chiastically (A B B′ A′) with the term "unbeliever" (14:23-24) in such a way as to tighten the identification, as if to suggest that to leave a fellow believer, even (or especially?) if that person is "like a novice," out of full participation in worship redefines the border and nature of community so that the person "unskilled" in tongues and in their interpretation is made *equivalent to an unbeliever* and is treated in such a condescending way as to deny the novice's having any standing inside the community. Treated in such a way the one "like a novice" becomes in effect like an unbeliever. In light of such inconsiderate treatment of novices by more-skilled-in-tongues believers, the unbeliever and the *idiōtēs* might as well be one when it comes to their relationship to the community: both may conclude that the tongues speakers are mad; neither will be brought to account. For Paul, such an exclusionary redefinition of the community of believers is scandalously unacceptable and grows from not properly "discerning the body" (11:29). No wonder Paul introduces this paragraph with a warning to grow up and not to be children, but adults (14:20).

The section concludes (14:25) by noting that the chaos of the Corinthians' worship may prevent the unbeliever and the novice from being called to account. Their mistreatment of novices leaches over into a mistreatment of unbelievers so that neither the unbeliever nor the novice will be able to declare what ought to be most obvious: "Surely God is ἐν ὑμῖν [*en hymin*, "among you," "in you"]" (v. 25). To be sure, Paul's actual words may be structured by his recollection of Isa 45:14 or Zech 8:23, but for their meaning here we must be guided by the context where they appear. We need not assume that there is a direct epiphany where God "appears" to the observer. Rather, Paul has given the readers the clues concerning what he means and how to take this expression. The most important clue is that the believers are early said to be God's building or dwelling place (3:9), God's temple (3:16-17) where the Holy Spirit dwells *en hymin*, "among you," "in you." In 14:25 the unbeliever can ideally deduce that God is in the community's midst only when the community lives and worships together in such a way as to reflect God and God's redemptive purposes in having established the community in the first place.

REFLECTIONS

The obligations of worshipers to those who come in from outside is to comport themselves in such a way as to be transparent to God—that is, to behave as people who show God dwelling in or among them (14:25). Though the hearer does not explicitly find the building motif in chapter 14, it is present by implication. "You are God's building" (3:9). "You do know, don't you, that you are the temple of God and that the Spirit of God dwells among you? . . . The temple of God is holy and you yourselves are that temple" (3:16-17). Paul reminds the Corinthians that an outsider should see God reflected in their communal and worship life. In all that it does, the community should mirror its God. In biblical traditions as here in 14:25, when God is truly revealed observers fall to their faces in obeisance. What would it mean for a congregation to fellowship and to worship together in such a way that an outsider would be convinced that God is among them? Paul gives a clue as it relates to the Corinthians' worship: Their worship has become a time of competition, a time when chaos results because each is so eager to show the Spirit's work; God is a God not of unruliness but a God of peace (14:33). Therefore, their worship should reflect the orderliness of God's peace. So, today worshipers should do their "service" to God in such a way that God is honored, so that God's presence, God's identity, God's character shows through. If we took it seriously that all of our actions reflect the God we serve, then some of us would be embarrassed to step back and observe ourselves.

COMMENTARY

We have seen that speaking in tongues has predominated in the worship of the Corinthians, contributing to the sense of chaos and disorder. Much of chap. 14 has argued that prophecy will best serve the community and that tongues are fine as long as there is an interpreter. Now, however, Paul reverts to his habituated response of making practical suggestions. As Paul earlier recommended that instead of defiling the Lord's supper people could eat at home before coming together (11:34), so now he makes sweeping, practical suggestions about their pattern of worship.

Keeping in mind that edification should be the guideline for whatever is done ("Let all things be done for edification," 14:26), Paul first suggests that all persons present should participate in worship. None may be left out or excluded. The skilled ones must be sure that the novices have full participation. When the believers come together for worship, different ones among them offer a psalm, a teaching, a revelation, a tongue, an interpretation (14:26). Second, if there be speaking in tongues (clearly Paul imagines that glossolalia is not a necessary part of worship and just as surely is not to be excluded from worship if an interpreter is available), Paul suggests that it be limited to a couple or three times and then serially and always with interpretation (14:27) so that no unskilled person is made to feel like an outsider. Third, prophecy is treated in the same manner as tongues: Two or three prophets may speak. Fourth, "one at a time" seems to be a pervasive concern (14:27, 31) and its purpose is clear: "so that all may learn and all may be encouraged" (14:31). Paul anticipates a claim that whatever is Spirit-inspired must immediately be granted a sort of *ex cathedra* authority when he says that others present at worship must weigh or pass judgment on what is said (14:29). He also heads off an objection of Spirit-filled persons that they are "beside themselves," captive to the Spirit, and are therefore unable to control themselves: "the spirits of prophets are subject to the prophets" (14:32).

Nowhere in Paul's undisputed letters do we find information on leadership patterns in worship. Clearly, Paul supposes the worshipers to be the significant participants (11:4-5, 26-33*a*). The Spirit, as the giver of the gifts, is understood as the source of inspiration to the participants. Most striking in his worship suggestions, however, is Paul's expectation that when two or three prophets have spoken, then "let the others weigh [pass judgment on] what is said" (14:29). These prophets are not persons who undertake to tell the future, but they are ones whose speech edifies, encourages, and consoles the community (14:3), so prophecy is a word addressed to the gathered people of God about their lives in the present. It is not enough, however, that someone claims to speak in behalf of the Spirit; automatic, unthinking assent is not to be blindly granted by the hearers. Instead, the "others"—because Paul believes that all can prophesy, the "others" probably means all the others—weigh what is said in a given prophetic utterance so as to decide whether to add their affirmative "Amen" to what is said. This is indeed a practical application of his earlier exemplary declaration that he prays and sings not only with his spirit but also with his mind (14:14-15).

Paul's suggestions regarding worship (14:26-33*a*) are not themselves to be confused with a structure or order of worship per se; his comments are very specifically aimed at the particular circumstances at Corinth where tongues have played a disproportionate role. Within his comments, however, are some abiding Pauline themes: Each one participates and contributes; all things are to be done for edification; deference to others is appropriate and fundamental in worship as in all of life; and all should learn and be encouraged.

"The spirits of the prophets are subject to the prophets" (14:32). By this Paul means that prophetic inspiration is to be kept under control by the prophet or prophets who receive it. There is no excuse for using the work of the Spirit as an occasion to override the concern for the needs and well-being of others. In what Paul here writes about prophecy, he makes a practical application of his own boxing metaphor to others (9:24-27), picturing himself as exercising self-control, self-discipline so that he not be disqualified.

Orderly Spirit-inspired worship is properly available to each and every one of the believers. Paul's warrant for his insistence upon orderly worship is stated in maxim form at the end of the paragraph: "For God is not the God of disorder [unruliness] but the God of peace—as in all the churches of the saints" (14:33), taking the last phrase as finishing the preceding paragraph and assuring the Corinthians that Paul's concern to establish orderly worship is not a position imposed only on the Corinthians. We can read the phrase "as in all the churches of the saints" as attached to the Pauline maxim about God because all ancient manuscripts of the New Testament were written one letter immediately after the other, with no spaces, no punctuation marks, no sentence and paragraph markers.

REFLECTIONS

Paul's assumptions about worship services should be considered afresh for today. First, church leadership so often filters down to a few people carrying most of the load, in worship and in other aspects of the church's life. Why is that? In part, it is a natural tendency: Those who do well are deferred to by others. But partly it is also a failure to carry through Paul's assumption that no one should be left out of participation; it is a failure to be ingenious about finding avenues of participation great and small for each and every one. Some will be bashful and reticent and will gladly turn participation over to others; monopoly of participation will harden into habit all around. Second, Paul thinks deference and thoughtfulness of others ought to be the rule when the church comes together. Perhaps those who naturally take leadership ought to put a restraining harness on themselves and have the patience to wait for others—and they surely must be careful not to arrogate to themselves the notion that nothing would happen if they themselves did not do it. Why not put some of that energy into encouraging others to step forward, into making it easier for them to take their first steps? That would be genuinely and fully thoughtful not only of others but also constructive for the community life of faith.

1 CORINTHIANS 14:34-36, WOMEN SPEAKING

COMMENTARY

This harsh passage, urging women's silence in church and subordination to their husbands, with an unspecified reference to "the law" as support, is probably an insertion by an editor who subsequently took this Pauline letter and brought it into conformity with the practices regarding women in his own subsequent-to-Paul time.

Whereas Paul wrote his specific letters to unique churches in different settings, someone, sometime later, collected them and assumed that what Paul wrote to one community might be of value for other communities (cf. an early step along that path in Col 4:16).[142] In the process of bringing the letter collection together, someone edited the correspondence; the degree of alterations is unknowable to us.[143] The results of the editing can easiest be seen in 2 Corinthians where some scholars find fragments

---

142. Nils A. Dahl, "The Particularity of the Pauline Epistles as a Problem in the Ancient Church," in *Neotestamentica et patristica: Eine Freundesgabe, Herrn Prof. Dr. Oscar Cullmann zu seinem 60. Geburtstag ueberreicht*, ed. W. C. van Unnik (Leiden: Brill, 1962) 261-71.

143. Bart D. Ehrman, *The Orthodox Corruption of Scripture: The Effect of Early Christological Controversies on the Text of the New Testament* (New York: Oxford University Press, 1993).

of as many as five letters.[144] For the clearest example, compare the polemical and defensive tone and temper of 2 Corinthians 10–13 with the relatively irenic and reconciled tone of the opening chapters of 2 Corinthians. Other changes such as excisions were also made; for example, the references to "in Rome" in Rom 1:7, 15 were dropped in later manuscripts presumably to make Romans a more universal letter that could be employed in places other than Rome.

Here in 1 Cor 14:34-36 we are probably faced with a later insertion of a text whose posture is at odds not only with Paul's relationships with women in other churches but also with what Paul has said about women earlier in 1 Corinthians. It will be helpful to review the evidence on both counts.

Verses 34-36, with their injunction of women's silence and assertion of their subordination to men, vary from what we have seen in the rest of 1 Corinthians. First, it is clear that women *are* praying and prophesying in the church at Corinth (11:5) and Paul not only makes no effort to stop it, but he seems to assume that it is quite proper; he simply wants women to wear head coverings in the worship setting. Efforts to interpret 11:5 in line with 14:34 may claim that the praying in question was silent prayer and that the women were just speaking among themselves, though there is no hint in 11:5 that such was the case. In fact, the material just treated about prophecy in chap. 14 makes clear that for Paul prophecy is available to everyone and involves speaking in church in such a manner that the "others" may weigh what is said (14:29). So the women at Corinth were in fact speaking, as were the men, during worship. Second, note how Paul used the tradition reflected most clearly in Gal 3:28—"there is neither male nor female"—to reckon the fundamental reciprocity between women and men in marriage and human sexuality (chap. 7). Third, it is Chloe's people who inform Paul of the bickering at Corinth (1:11). We do not know much about Chloe—the Corinthians and Paul knew her very well—but we may suppose that she was a woman of standing with the church (she is named) and a wealthy person whose agents (her servants, perhaps) saw Paul possibly in their pursuit of her business interests.

Further, 14:34-36 is singular when weighed against the picture and roles of women in all of the other undisputed Pauline letters (more on Colossians, Ephesians, and the Pastoral Epistles below). Phoebe, a deacon in the church at Cenchreae, just six miles from Corinth, is praised and commended as Paul's patron (Rom 16:1-2). Euodia and Syntyche, even though they are currently having some personal problems, have "struggled alongside" Paul in the gospel and it appears that their names are in the "book of life" (Phil 4:2-3). Apphia is one of the persons addressed in the letter we call Philemon (Phlm 2). Prisca, dubbed a "fellow worker" (Rom 16:3), and over a half-dozen other women are singled out for greetings and recognition in Romans 16. Clearly, from the way Paul describes the women in his letters they were significant workers in the churches and in the gospel. In the six undisputed letters apart from 1 Corinthians, *no passage suggests any limitation on the roles or functions of women in the Pauline churches.*

Ephesians and Colossians present a different picture; indeed, it is more in line with 1 Cor 14:34-36. Both Ephesians and Colossians, assumed here and by many to be products of Pauline disciples after Paul's death but written in his name, argue for the subordination of wives to their husbands (Eph 5:22-24; Col 3:18).[145] The Pastoral Epistles, 1 and 2 Timothy and Titus, thought here and by some others to be products of yet another, subsequent generation that dates after Ephesians and Colossians in the Pauline tradition, take the matter a step farther, also arguing for submission of women and for the silence of women (1 Tim 2:11-12; cf. Titus 2:5; 1 Pet 3:1) and justify this subordination, as does 1 Cor 14:34, by reference to "the law" (1 Tim 2:13-14).

One might, therefore, describe a trajectory in the early decades of Christianity where Paul, the earliest writer in the New Testament, welcomes women into full participation in the life and work of the gospel and into the worship it generates. As the Pauline

---

144. Furnish, *II Corinthians*, 32-35.

145. See Walter Bujard, *Stilanalytische Untersuchungen zum Kolosserbrief als Beitrag zur Methodik von Sprachvergleichen*, SUNT 11 (Göttingen: Vandenhoeck & Ruprecht, 1973).

tradition was carried on beyond Paul's death (mid 60s CE), and as Paul's assurance of the imminent end of the ages failed to materialize, Paul's followers felt increasing pressure to reaccommodate to the social structures and practices of their unbelieving neighbors.[146] Ephesians and Colossians represent one stage of reaccommodation; the Pastoral Epistles yet another. When one looks at 1 Cor 14:34-36 against that trajectory, one finds that it fits best with the view of women projected in the Pastoral Epistles. If Paul's letters were collected around the turn of the first and second centuries, as is a reasonable assumption, a time sometimes also argued for the writing of the Pastoral Epistles, then the redactor could readily have inserted 1 Cor 14:34-36 to bring the picture of Corinth's worship practices in line with what he thought appropriate in his own time. The result: Women should be silent in church and submissive to their husbands, despite the fact that neither of these positions is sustained by the rest of 1 Corinthians nor by the six other undisputed Pauline letters that we can be sure came from the hand of Paul.

If 14:34-36 was not inserted by a later redactor of the Pauline corpus, then two interpretations merit attention. One, the passage calling for silence from women is in a series of matters where Paul enjoins silence upon a certain subgroup within the church rather than see them intrude on other people's worship (14:28, 30). In the first injunction, he advises glossolalists to keep silent if no interpreters are present (14:29). In the

second, he says that if someone gets a revelation while a prophet is speaking, the prophet should be silent. In all three cases, deference to others, a pattern argued in detail in chap. 9, is urged. These counsels to silence stand as a part of his tendency to offer practical suggestions that are designed to serve the well-being of the community.

Two, the interpretation of 14:34-36 as authentic must account for 14:36, a rather stern rebuke, and identify for what subgroup the reprimand is intended. Generally, it has been assumed to be directed at the women, who are now told to be subordinate (14:34) although it makes limited sense in that way. Alternatively, it could as readily be understood as addressed to some men in the congregation who claim in a maxim that *they* have formulated, in line with much of their culture, that "it is shameful for a woman to speak in church" (14:35*b*).[147] It could be a maxim formulated by the same persons who advocated that "it is good for a man not to touch a woman" (see the Commentary on 7:1) and could be generated by a male-dominated faction that tried in several ways, in opposition to Paul, to relegate women to a lesser role in the life of the community. Read in this way, 14:36 would be Paul's challenge of the men's hybris reflected in their maxim by asking: "Was it from you that the word of God went out? Or, has it arrived at you only?"

146. David L. Balch, *Let Wives Be Submissive: The Domestic Code in 1 Peter*, SBLMS 26 (Chico, Calif.: Scholars Press, 1981) 81.

147. For three very important studies that continue to argue for the authenticity of 1 Cor 14:33*b*-36, see L. A. Jervis, "1 Corinthians 14.34-35: A Reconsideration of Paul's Limitation of the Free Speech of Some Corinthian Women," *JSNT* 58 (1995) 51-74; Elisabeth Schüssler-Fiorenza, *In Memory of Her: A Feminist Theological Reconstruction of Christian Origins* (New York: Crossroad, 1985) 230-33; and Mitchell, *Paul and the Rhetoric of Reconciliation*, 281-82n. 536.

REFLECTIONS

The passage 14:34-36 has attracted much attention, and well it should because it is subject to very different interpretations. Whether one takes these verses as authentic or not, they do stand in the canon. Let us here reflect on the interpretations that consider 14:34-36 as having been written by Paul. All the interpretations that take the passage as authentic share one factor that we modern Christians should not fail to notice: All of them suppose that the verses are Paul's response to a very particular and peculiar situation that has emerged at Corinth. Each of them assumes that Paul is not making church policy de novo or in general, but is reacting to a special problem regarding women at Corinth. Already in this commentary we have seen that where Paul perceives a certain action to be a threat to the health of the community, he will advise a "steer-clear" course and will model such care for his followers. About himself, for example, he has depicted himself as ready to be a vegetarian if his own freedom to eat meat risks harm for any brother or sister for whom Christ died (1 Cor 8:13). So the passage is, first, a response to a particular problem that Paul has encountered only at Corinth. Second, Paul is given to practical suggestions and to counsels that "play it safe," that ask for people to forgo the exercise of their rights when their freedom might otherwise lead them to live and do in a certain way (see the discussion of freedom and one's rights in the Commentary on 9:1-27). It is an irony of the greatest gravity that Paul's counsel in these verses, when taken as authentic, has come to function for some Christians as a polity dictate that keeps modern women from being able to speak in church. As a result, countless numbers of women who are just as clearly called and moved by the Holy Spirit as their male counterparts are kept from placing that calling and movement in service to the community of believers by taking part in some form of ministry. For such people, Paul's particular and situational counsel, written long ago to treat an unusual problem in a church at Corinth, has been reified into church law that is presumed to apply to all women, preventing them from taking full part in the ministry of the church for all time.

The interpretation adopted in this commentary, that 14:34-36 is a later interpolation from a time when Paul's letters were collected and redacted and when women were once again called upon to be submissive as we see in the subsequently written Pastoral Epistles (1 Tim 2:11; 3:4; Titus 2:5; cf. 1 Pet 3:1), is called for by two features already noted in the letter: (1) His counsels about marriage and human sexuality took care to acknowledge that the same rights belong to men and to women, to husbands and to wives (1 Cor 7:2-5); and (2) Paul has already assumed that women are praying and prophesying in church and he treats that activity as quite appropriate (1 Cor 11:5).

1 CORINTHIANS 14:37-40, SECTION CLOSING; ENFORCEMENT STATEMENT

COMMENTARY

With a claim and a suggestion, Paul concludes the whole section that began in 12:1. The claim: Those whose self-assessment inclines them to think of themselves as a prophet or a spiritual person (see the Commentary on 12:1) should recognize the truth of what Paul has written (he accords what he has written the status of a "command of the Lord," 14:37; cf. 7:10). The suggestion: Those who do not recognize, meaning grant authority to, what he has said, should themselves not be recognized (14:38).

Tongues and prophecy surface one last time in a recapitulation: The Corinthians should be zealous to prophesy, and they should not ban tongues (14:39). Paul has a flair for generalizing from the specifics, and he does so once again as he concludes this section. As the question of food offered to idols (8:1) became the occasion for branching

out into several issues regarding eating and ultimately eating became synecdoche (one part stands for a larger whole) for all of life (cf. 10:31), so also here tongues and prophecy lead Paul quite naturally to an all-encompassing assertion: "Let all things be done exemplarily and in order" (14:40). The term translated here "exemplarily" (εὐσχημόνως *euschēmonōs*; "fitting," NIV; "decently," NRSV) is a technical term for Paul, signaling a life lived in such a way that it becomes exemplary—that is, so that it becomes a pattern that informs and inspires others. In a summary appeal in Romans, Paul calls upon the Romans to "walk as models [*euschēmonōs*] as in the daylight" because they have "put on the Lord Jesus Christ" (surely baptismal imagery; see Rom 13:13-14). Likewise, when Paul caps off his admonitions to the Thessalonians, he writes that all his admonitions are so that the Thessalonian believers may "walk as models [*euschēmonōs*] for those outside" the church (1 Thess 4:12). So also the Corinthians are to do "all things . . . as models," which, one can readily see for Paul, includes doing them in good order. Whereas the modeling of the Thessalonians is to be especially for the outsiders, in 1 Corinthians Paul is concerned with believers' modeling not only for those inside the community of faith but also for unbelievers (10:28-29; 14:23-25). So the section concludes on the continuing Pauline concern with the Corinthians to encourage them to care about and for one another, to employ love in all their relations, and, therefore, to edify one another.

REFLECTIONS

If a picture is worth a thousand words, how much more effective is one's life lived in an exemplary way. Often people rightly learn more from us by our actions, by the way we live and by the choices we make than they do from our declarations. Whether we speak or not, we are always writing a script of our values with our deeds, by what we choose to do and by what we avoid. In a way that might challenge us, Paul thinks that believers should reflect the same exemplary walk to persons outside the faith as well as to those within it.

1 CORINTHIANS 15:1-58

Discourse on Resurrection

Overview

Now Paul comes to the last major issue addressed in this letter. Rhetoricians recognized that the first and the last of a series were the places where the most important points should be lodged.[148] So, from his placement of it, we have every reason to expect that Paul considered what we call chapter 15 to be of utmost significance. And Paul does not disappoint us: The topic is nothing less than the gospel itself (15:1). From the first words it is clear that Paul reaches back to his original encounter with the Corinthians, when he initially preached the gospel to them and they believed.

Paul's recitation of the tradition that he passed on to them as the heart of his preaching (15:3-11)—namely, a sort of truncated passion narrative[149] with a special focus on Christ's death, resurrection, and appearance to witnesses, forms an inclusio, a ring construction with his early declaration in this letter that when he came to them he knew "only Jesus Christ and him crucified" (2:1-2). So the letter opens and closes with a reaffirmation that the focus of Paul's gospel with them has been Christ's death and resurrection; that was the core of his founding gospel, and Paul brings his letter to its highest point in a discourse about resurrection and its bearing on the life of faith.

Paul's words in 15:1-2 carefully reconstruct his first contact with them, affirm their reception of his gospel "in which they [still] stand," and point toward their salvation—but this idyllic, panoramic survey crashes head-on into the conditional and cautionary words

148. *Ad Herennium* 3.10.18: "The strongest arguments should be placed at the beginning and at the end. . . . And as for the rest, since what has been said last is easily committed to memory, it is useful, when ceasing to speak, to leave some very strong argument fresh in the hearer's mind."
149. Along with "the motifs of pre-existence and incarnation," according to Richard Hays, *The Faith of Jesus: An Investigation of the Narrative Substructure of Galatians 3:1-4:11*, SBLDS 56 (Chico, Calif.: Scholars, 1983) 256-57.

Paul directly adds: "*If* (εἰ *ei*) you hold fast, *unless* (εἰ μή *ei mē*) you have believed in vain" (15:2).

This entire letter has had a back-to-basics quality where Paul seems ever determined to circle back and pick up the little children who have strayed, become lost, or not grown as much as he had hoped. Prior to chapter 15 it has been particular matters, some more critical, some more peripheral, about which the Corinthians have lost proper focus. Now, however, at stake in Paul's view is the heart of the gospel, their standing in it, and their understanding of it.

Paul gives no clue that this discourse has been prompted by their letter to him. So, precisely what has occasioned it? One can suppose, given that its subject is identified by Paul as the very gospel in which they stand, and given its location at a point of maximum emphasis, that Paul thinks of this matter as *bearing on everything that has preceded it*. As we get into the discourse we will see that one particular misunderstanding about resurrection catches Paul's direct attention.

The major blocks of Paul's argument in chapter 15 are as follows. Paul's early rehearsal of his foundational teaching, based upon and substantiated by received Christian tradition, reminds the Corinthians of the outlines of the gospel he preached to them, the foundation he laid for them (15:3-11). In the next section we can see that some Corinthians appear to be confused about "the resurrection of the dead" (15:12-34). Then, with the help of a fictive interlocutor, Paul is able to make basic affirmations about continuity and contrast of the present life of faith and the yet-to-be-fullness of the life of faith (15:35-57). The discourse closes with a recapitulation and peroration (15:58).

Before proceeding to an examination of the particulars, however, a feature of chapter

15 must be noted. In this section Paul casts his argument, his flow of thought, in extreme language.[150] Nothing is moderated. This is language designed to shock, to call to attention, as we have just noted even in 15:2. Paul not only returns to basics, he shakes the foundations. One can deduce from this that Paul takes the matter at hand with utmost seriousness and expects his hearers to do the same. At stake, in other words, is not some optional or peripheral issue. At issue is nothing less than the heart of the gospel as it can be lived in the world.

Consider how Paul has taken matters to the extreme (as a way of gaining attention and of focusing on what really matters). In the opening nineteen verses he dares to raise the question at three points whether their faith will have amounted to nothing, will have been in vain, or is useless (15:2, 14, 17). He urges them not to be deceived (15:33); he calls them back to their senses (15:34); he conjures up a representative Corinthian spokesman and dubs him "foolish" or "ignorant" (ἄφρων *aphrōn*) (15:36); he speaks of their shame, which we have seen previously in the letter is a hot-button cultural norm (15:34). At the same time that he exposes what he takes to be their folly, he writes just as dramatically of the awesome and unassailable power of God that is working through Jesus Christ to attain the culmination of God's plan: He portrays Christ's ultimate giving over of the kingdom to God when all powers, and among them eventually even death, will be—again the strongest of verbs—set aside, abolished, wiped out (καταργέω *katargeō*, 15:24, 26; cf. 1:28; 6:13). Paul sees a radical dissonance between what God is doing and the Corinthians' life patterns and convictions, and he fears that they are risking their access to sharing in God's redemptive purposes. Nothing less than extremes in rhetoric and in warnings will adequately portray the gravity of what is at stake. Accordingly, Paul lays out his argument so that the Corinthians will not, indeed cannot miss the discrepancy between what they are believing and doing and what God is doing.

Implicit in Paul's understanding is the conviction that once one is in faith—that is, in right relationship with God, once one is justified by or reconciled to God, one can stumble, one can fall (cf. 1 Cor 10:12) from grace, can fall from faith and become once again slaves to sin. For Paul, in the unquestioned letters (see the Introduction), salvation is consistently a future finishing up of what God has already begun in Christ. For Paul believers are not currently saved, they are not already perfected or matured (cf. Phil 3:12-15). As 15:2 suggests, they are on their way toward salvation; and God's grace and power will take them there, "if they hold fast." The letter to the Galatians is good evidence of Paul's belief that reconciled, justified believers can fall from faith (cf. Gal 3:3; 4:8-11; 5:4; 6:9).

At issue between Paul and the Corinthians in chapter 15 is not only their understanding of resurrection, but the way that understanding bears on their behavior. For Paul, what one believes has a direct connection with how one behaves, or at least it ought to, and what one does ought to reflect what one believes. Paul can come at it either way: He can see wrongful conduct and suppose that there is some failure in proper belief, or he can reason from what one believes and reckon what behavior is appropriate to that belief. Chapter 15 starts from the declaration of what he and they believe and only then moves to comportment or to the difference the belief ought to make for one's viewing of human options.[151]

The Corinthians, or at least some among them, have misunderstandings about what Paul and his relayed tradition meant when they spoke of the "resurrection of the dead." Paul puts it in the form of a question, which he lodges after he has recited the foundational teaching seen in 15:3-11: "But if it is preached that 'Christ has been raised from the dead' [15:4], then how can some among you say 'There is no resurrection of the dead'?" (15:12). With these introductory observations, we can now turn to a closer examination of the passages, the flow of the argument, and an elaboration of Paul's rhetorical purposes.

---

150. D. F. Watson, "Paul's Rhetorical Strategy in 1 Corinthians 15," in Porter and Olbricht, *Rhetoric and the New Testament,* 231-49.

151. By contrast, chapter 7, or even chapter 8, moved from questions about proper behavior to concerns about what believers know, and then proceeded with applications to how they should behave.

1 CORINTHIANS 15:1-2, BROAD-BRUSH SCOPE OF THE LIFE OF FAITH

COMMENTARY

Paul's introduction to the expansive discourse on resurrection, indicating as it does that the heart of the gospel is at issue, gives clues of its importance to Paul. Paul rehearses; he reminds them in what amounts to a chain-like argument, each link of which has some special connection to "the gospel": The gospel he preached to them is the gospel they received; the gospel they received is the very one in which they, like supposedly stalwart warriors, stand (cf. Eph 6:14; Rom 14:4); that gospel in and by which they stand is the channel through which they will ultimately be saved. In such a short rhetorical sequence, Paul has sketched their entire Christian biography, from their conversion under Paul's preaching, to their being lifted up and caused to stand so as to take their part in God's great and final conquest of sin and its fruit, death, and he has even sketched their relation to the gospel out to its culmination: "Through the gospel you shall be saved" (15:2a). This fits Paul's picture of the gospel in every detail. Paul has full confidence that, as he wrote the Philippians, the God who has begun such a work in them will surely bring it to completion (Phil 1:6). God is faithful, trustworthy (1:9; 10:13; 2 Cor 1:18; 1 Thess 5:24). Because it depends entirely upon God, Paul is sure that God's plan will be brought to fulfillment. So Paul can confidently write to the Corinthians that they "shall be saved"— that is, that they shall be included in salvation, insofar as it depends on God.

What a shocking thought, then, for Paul to ponder, in his very next words, whether the Corinthians have believed in vain. What if their commitment to the gospel proved pointless and powerless? Attached to these sweeping claims about the gospel are two cautionary notes: One raises the possibility that they might not "hold fast" or "keep in one's memory" (εἰ κατέχετε *ei katechete*, 15:2c) the very gospel on which their life in Christ is founded; the other raises the even more astonishing specter that they might have believed in vain, that all their believing might prove fruitless or end in failure (15:2d). Absolutely nothing in the letter so far has suggested that any of the Corinthian believers have ever entertained the thought that all of this might end in nothing, an ephemeral dream that vanishes like the morning's dew. With 15:2 Paul has moved the question of the Corinthians' destiny to the center of the discussion and will return to it after he reviews "what we know" in 15:3-11.

A minor but significant point is that Paul opens the discourse by calling them "brothers and sisters," thus identifying himself with them and them with him as he undertakes this crucial discussion. The discourse culminates with Paul once again identifying them, this time with emphasis, as "my beloved brothers and sisters" (15:58) and exhorting them to stay the course. (See Reflections at 15:3-11.)

1 CORINTHIANS 15:3-11, THE FOUNDATIONAL TEACHING

COMMENTARY

With a recitation, in traditional form as he received it, Paul reminds them of the gospel they received from him (15:3-10). He suggests it is the same gospel that all the apostles preach (15:11); it is surely the gospel he first preached to them and that they believed (2:1-2). And from Paul's other letters we can see that it is indeed the gospel that he apparently preached in all his churches. Central among its claims is the death and resurrection of Jesus Christ (15:3-4). The actual sequence in the traditional formulation recited in 15:3-11 is: Christ died for "your sins" (though Paul, apart from traditional materials such as these that mention "sins," speaks of sin in the singular and as a power); he was buried; he was raised (the so-called divine passive, indicating that it was God who did the raising) on the third day; and the risen Lord appeared to a sequence of people among whom Paul counts himself as the very last. This is what all churches have as a foundation belief; it is what Paul believes; and it is what he knows the Corinthians believe. Thus the Corinthians are reminded not only of the gospel that they believe, but also that their connection to it is through Paul, enhancing his own ethos and status among them and thereby reinforcing the leverage that he will use with them in what follows.

Paul has written his own story into the tradition that he has received and passed on to them. Most scholars hold that 15:3-5 is the core of the tradition that Paul has received and that he adds other traditions of appearances in the ensuing verses. Those appearances are the occasion for him to weave his own story into the older story. With 15:11 he weaves his auditors' story into the whole.

Paul's self-portrait in his recounting of the traditions is telling. Each detail of it will play an important role in the remainder of the discourse. Paul's own life is paradigmatic for all believers. No previous action of his merits God's favor (Paul's persecution of "the church of God" showed his unworthiness; 15:9), but God's grace is sufficient to transform even such a person as Paul who directly and defiantly opposes God's purpose ("by God's grace I am what I am"; 15:10*a*). Paul confidently asserts that God's grace in him in his preaching the gospel "has not been in vain" (15:10*b*), a potentially striking contrast from his cautionary word to them about their faith possibly being in vain (15:2; cf. his reprise of this concern in 15:14, 58).

Paul goes out of his way to highlight his labors in a hyperbolic fashion: He claims to have labored "harder than all of" the other apostles, but he quickly puts his own works in perspective because they are not really so much his works as God's grace working though him (15:10*c*). Though the Corinthians had never set themselves so directly in opposition to God's plans as Paul did by his persecution of believers, they, too, lived in their sin(s) before the gospel came to them. Also, like Paul, God's grace has demonstratively proved effective in their lives; in a subsequent letter to these same people, Paul will be able to describe what happened in and with them as a "new creation" (2 Cor 5:17).

They and he both know that the transformative power of God has worked effectively in their lives; that is not at issue for even a second. So Paul's labor—read God's grace—among them has already proved effective; that is not in dispute. What *is* at issue is whether the Corinthians will stand firm in their faith and therefore whether they will ultimately be saved (15:2*a*). How are they in danger of falling? The rest of chapter 15 gives us insights and answers.

Paul's discussion of his work (15:10) introduces a theme that will receive attention in this discourse; in fact its importance as a topic is seen in its being a ring device, an *inclusio*, which by appearing also at the close of chapter 15 (15:58), encircles the whole discussion with the significance of what one does. The place and importance of works in relation to faith can cause some confusion. To minimize the confusion, let us put Paul's view in formulaic fashion: Work(s) can never lead to faith, that is, to right relation to God; but faith, when properly functioning, always produces work(s). In 15:10 Paul is very clear that his working is really not his in an independent way, but is "the grace of God [working] with him." The same connection is expressed in Phil 2:12-13 where Paul calls upon the Philippians to work out their own salvation "because God is the one working in you" toward that end (cf. also 1 Thess 2:13). Believers cannot separate their own work from the ongoing work of God (Paul's code word for this is "grace") in them.

REFLECTIONS

1. Basic confessions such as this sketch out the narrative that is at the heart of Paul's preaching. See also Phil 2:1-13 and Galatians 3.[152] In both of these latter passages, just as in 1 Cor 15:3-11, the foundational Christian story is recounted. In Christ's death and resurrection, God has laid claim on God's own creatures, or, to put it differently, God has loved us unlovely people. In the account at hand, Paul laces his own story into the old story. We modern readers can see our own lives linked to the creed in similar ways. Like Paul, we had no special merit—indeed, we may have been living in a way that turned its back on God's grace. Like Paul, we, too, take the tradition that we have received and we transmit it to those who follow us, not only in our retelling of the old story but, from Paul's perspective more importantly, in our living it in an exemplary fashion. As chapter 15 unfolds we will also see that the old story has a direct impact on how we behave and even more fundamentally on why we act or do.

2. Compare the space Paul devotes to the old creedal story prior to his mention of himself with the number of verses he uses to tie his own story into the foundational story. Each of us should be able to tell our own saga as it ties into our collective basic story of Christ's death and resurrection. Some of us will have come to faith through the tender caring of our parents or some other relative. Others will have found our mothers and fathers in the faith outside our biological families. But each of us is indebted to those who carried the faith from the past to the present and mediated it to us. Dare we do less for those who follow us?

152. Hays, *Faith of Jesus*, 247.

1 CORINTHIANS 15:12-34, HOW CAN SOME SAY THERE IS NO RESURRECTION OF THE DEAD?

COMMENTARY

Paul addresses the general issue of the *resurrection of the dead*, which he has heard some Corinthians doubt, using as leverage his and their assumption that Christ was raised from the dead. Paul's argument in chapter 15 confirms this interpretation. The *resurrection of Christ* is not seriously disputed by anyone in Corinth; the resurrection of the dead is. The resurrection of Christ is grounded in Paul's traditionally based preaching that is at the foundation of their belief, as he reminds them (15:3-11). In what follows, Paul does not argue *that* Christ was raised from the dead—they do not dispute that; rather he argues *from* the shared affirmation that Christ was raised from the dead. The contrary-to-fact consideration, "if Christ was not raised from the dead," designed to shock his readers and

to focus their attention, is met with prohibitive and unthinkable consequences for Paul and for the Corinthians: "Then our preaching is empty and your faith is empty; and I am found a false witness of God . . . your faith is useless and you are still in your sins" (15:14-17). After such dismissive rhetoric there is no more mention of any dispute whether Christ has been raised; instead, the discussion shifts to the true topic of dispute, namely the *resurrection of the dead*, and with it the question of when believers will share in a resurrection like Christ's.

How are we to understand the claim of some that "there is no resurrection of the dead"? Just what could they have meant by such an assertion? Resurrection was not a widespread notion in the world at that time. Greek and Roman views of resurrection ranged from assumptions that it was impossible to reckoning that it might happen in an occasional, isolated miraculous event. Some older scriptures of Israel note a few resurrections (1 Kgs 17:17; 2 Kgs 4:18; 13:20) and a few of Israel's later writings expect a future general resurrection (Isa 26:19; Dan 12:2; cf. Job 19:25-27; Ezek 37:1-14). Pharisaic Judaism, whose most notable exemplar in the New Testament is Paul, held, against the Sadducees, for a resurrection.[153] In the light of this information, it is likely that Paul's affirmation of the resurrection of the dead was a striking claim or bit of news for his largely gentile audience in Corinth when he first preached to them. So it is not too surprising that some of Paul's followers in Corinth continued in doubt or came to doubt about resurrection of dead people, though we should note that even those who doubted that dead people might ultimately be raised could have conceded that Christ rose as one of those occasional, isolated miraculous events. Because Paul treats the Corinthians who said "There is no resurrection of the dead" as members of the community, it is safe to suppose that they still hold that Christ was raised from the dead. This interpretation is supported by the fact that Paul, though he briefly entertains the notion, for the sake of argument, that Christ was not raised (15:13-20), simply asserts in 15:21 that *Christ was raised* and builds his case from that fundamental and apparently widespread Corinthian believers' claim.

For Paul, the linkage is indissoluble between the claim that Christ was raised and the assertion that believers likewise will be raised from the dead. The latter follows from the former because Christ was the "firstborn within a large family" (Rom 8:29 NRSV) whose resurrection guarantees the same for all his brothers and sisters; Paul makes the same point to the Corinthians in 15:23 by calling Christ the "first fruits" of the whole resurrection harvest. Indeed, his opening argument assumes and builds from that hinge: If Christ was raised, then believers will also be raised, in due time (15:12-23).

Across the undisputed letters Paul clearly anticipates that believers will be raised, will share a resurrection like Christ's, at the end

time. Believers are not yet raised; they do not yet share in the resurrection (cf. the post-Pauline Eph 2:6 and Col 2:12). Because believers have died with Christ, because they have died to sin, they do already "walk in newness of life" (Rom 6:4) and they are already part of the new creation (2 Cor 5:17). Paul's view about believers not yet sharing the resurrection corresponds to his view noted above that believers are not yet saved. Believers are not yet raised, neither are they yet saved, but God's initial and ongoing work leads them toward that τέλος (*telos*), that goal—if they hold fast (15:2), if they stand firm (15:58).

Evidence from the different parts of 1 Corinthians suggests that while some may have believed that there was no resurrection of the dead, they and/or others may also have transformed the notion of resurrection from what it was for Paul, namely an eschatological, end-of-the-age event, to a spiritualized way of understanding the new life in Christ in the present. Such a transposition of Paul's fundamental preaching not only denies Paul's gospel's claim that death as the final enemy will be destroyed (15:26), but severely alters the way in which persons live and move and have their being in this world, before the parousia. So two, distinguishable problems tie to the Corinthian denial of the resurrection of the dead: First, believers who deny the resurrection of the dead view life in this world, short of the consummation of God's purposes, as the only and total chance they have to find significance and fulfillment for themselves and their lives, as in some way approximating here and now as much as possible (sharing) something of a resurrection vaguely like Christ's own; and second, the *telos* or goal toward which the believing life is directed is lost as a moral guideline to believers.

Paul's scathing sarcasm in 4:8-11 is directed precisely at such persons who have collapsed into the present what for Paul remains future, namely *already* sharing the kingdom: "Already you are satiated, already you have become rich, apart from us you have reigned!" So there are some Corinthian believers who have vaunted that they have already arrived at the fullness of the life of faith that Paul expects only at the parousia. They hold that they have advanced beyond their former peers in the faith. It is such

153. Josephus *The Jewish War* 2.165; *Antiquities of the Jews* 18.16.

persons who may have among them the man "who has his father's wife" (5:1), who are arrogant (5:2), who feel themselves beyond normal moral restraints, who lord it over others at the supper (11:17-34), and perhaps even those who have the highly visible gift of glossolalia (12-14). The persons whom Paul chides as "already" reigning, rich, and filled (4:8-11) could be the same ones who deny the resurrection of the dead *as a future event*, who have transformed Paul's not-until-the-end-of-the-age resurrection of believers and therefore the final defeat of the ultimate enemy, death (15:26) into a spiritualized claim to have achieved *already* some exceptional quality of life that they may very well have called "resurrection." Paul's future expectation of the resurrection of the dead has been transposed by these Corinthians into a present experience.[154]

A dissonance has come to exist between Paul's view of things and their own. Paul's own preaching about sharing Christ's death, dying with Christ, and walking in newness of life (Rom 6:4) lends itself to such a transformation because a hearer could assume that "walking in newness of life" really meant some sort of "resurrection" in the present. It is not difficult to imagine some among the Corinthians taking the newness of life to be what resurrection really means, available as it is already in the present and minimizing or even denying a future resurrection of the dead. Likewise, a few of Paul's other striking claims about the future may have led some to claim that they already enjoyed many or all of the extraordinary powers that Paul envisions in the future. As seen in 1 Corinthians, among those endtime powers that might erroneously be taken as present capacities are: Then believers will judge the world (6:2) and angels (6:3); then believers who have steered clear of the vices will inherit the kingdom (6:9; note that Paul makes clear in 15:50 that inheriting the kingdom is a future event). In fact, until the end time it is Christ, not believers, who reigns "until he has put all his enemies under his feet" (15:25; cf. 4:8).

Because of Paul's strong conviction that Christ is the firstborn of many brothers and sisters, the first fruits of the resurrection, he cannot but see a denial of resurrection of the dead as a denial of Christ's having been raised from the dead. To deny the resurrection of the dead—and therefore also Christ's resurrection—is worse than losing an important claim. It is to believe in vain and thus to remain in one's sins (15:17). That is the force of Paul's rhetoric in 15:12-19. For Paul, the two claims—that Christ has been raised and that others will be raised—are inseparable. The one leads ineluctably, *but only later*, to the other; the latter is simply the yet-to-be finishing of what God has begun in the former. So the future resurrection of the dead is a consequence of Christ's having been raised. God's faithfulness assures that. To question either—the future resurrection of the dead or Christ's resurrection—is to raise questions about the other, and Paul can countenance questioning neither. To put it in different terms, Christ's resurrection was not some unusual event sequestered into the byways of history for Paul; it was the transformative event that marked the turn of history and linked it directly to God's culminating but not yet finished purposes in all of creation. Christ's having been raised by God has as its consequence that others will be raised from the dead, and therefore that death itself will ultimately be defeated—and all of this has credibility because every bit of it rests on God's power and purpose, neither of which can or will be qualified by human reticence, recalcitrance, or failure.

With 15:20-28 Paul elaborates upon the basic teaching that he gave them (15:3-11) and that became the foundation of their faith in which they supposedly stand. Christ, having indeed been raised from among the dead people, is twice designated "first fruits" (ἀπαρχή *aparchē*) (15:20, 23) of those who are sleeping—a euphemism for those who are dead. The mention of "first fruits" refers to the scripturally based practice of sanctifying the whole crop by offering the "first fruits" to God (Exod 23:19). In this way Paul affirms that Christ's resurrection promises or secures the future resurrection of those who belong to Christ. So without using the terms, the "first fruits" claims are language of promise, guarantee, and confidence.

---

154. See C. M. Tuckett, "No Resurrection of the Dead (1 Cor 15,12)," in *The Corinthian Correspondence*, ed. R. Bieringer (Leuven: Leuven University Press, 1996) 274.

Paul's first mention of Christ as "first fruits" (15:20) introduces a double typological elaboration (15:21-23) in which Paul invites the readers to reaffirm their identification with Christ, while Adam is made to symbolize all of those who are destined for death, and Christ is affirmed as the means through which believers are made alive (a theme to which he will return in 15:45-49). The Adam-Christ typology is a commonplace in Paul, appearing in 15:21-22, 45-49 and again in Rom 5:14-21. Biblical typologies work in predictable ways: They always take a person or an event and, by a selective retelling, highlight some point or points that the author wants to make to readers (see another Pauline typology in 10:1-13). When Paul lays out his Adam-Christ comparison and contrast he seeks neither to write history nor to describe some sequence in sacred history, but to call his readers to realize more fully what they have in Christ. So the comments about Adam are backformed from the beliefs about Christ and are used to elaborate, via negativa, not only the significance of Christ for the readers but also the richness of the believers' new life. In 15:22, the point is that the death produced by their solidarity with Adam is ultimately overcome in Christ. (For more on the Adam-Christ typology, see the Commentary on 15:48-50 where Paul returns to it.)

With the second reference to Christ as "first fruits" of the resurrection of all believers (15:23), Paul introduces what was likely a shocking rebuke to those who had spiritualized the resurrection and thereby arrogated such status into the present: "But each in its own turn" (15:23 NIV). The proper order: Christ the first fruits, then only after that those who belong to Christ, at his parousia; in other words, when God's cosmic purposes are brought to fulfillment—and Paul once again elaborates upon his basic teaching by sketching out the final picture of the culmination of God's plan, as follows. Paul drives the "proper order" point home by detailing what will happen at the eschaton and not before. At the end, Christ will give the kingdom, the reign, to God, but only after Christ has laid waste all rule and authority and enemy, including that "last enemy" (θάνατος *thanatos*), death, which God had placed under Christ's feet (a reference to Ps 110:1). Until that time there is no resurrection of the dead and the final defeat of death.

As he sketches the grandeur of God's culminating purposes, Paul's language drifts toward doxology: In the end, even Christ will be made subject to God, who is already in 3:23 credited as being the one to whom all else, including Christ, belongs and who in 8:6 is declared to be the one from whom are all things and for whom people exist (cf. 11:3). The goal: so that "God may be all in all" (NRSV and NIV). How misguided of some of the Corinthians to write themselves into the divine script in an arrogant, previous, and presumptuous way, as if they had already arrived or already reigned (cf. 4:8-13)! To them Paul addresses his comment: "Each in the proper order" (15:23).

Paul then pushes his argument by asking rhetorical questions first about some persons whom he mentions in the third person ("they") and second about himself. Admittedly, Paul's purposes in the rhetorical questions are more certainly accessible than some of the practices to which the questions refer. The questions suggest to the readers the folly of their practices *if the dead are not ever to be raised.* First, the persons Paul describes as "those who are being baptized in behalf of the dead" (15:29). This is another of those matters about which Paul and the Corinthians surely understood one another but which we cannot hope to fathom. The most obvious reading of the text would suggest that there are some at Corinth (note that Paul does not address them directly, but writes about them as an example) who are being baptized in behalf of dead persons, perhaps as representatives of dear ones who either never had a chance to respond to the gospel or who had died while being drawn to the faith. But the truth is that we simply do not know. Most surprising is that Paul did not oppose the practice, which seems to suppose either that grace is transferrable or that one can be a surrogate believer for another. Instead, Paul uses it to expose its folly if there is no resurrection of the dead.

Second, Paul refers to himself and his own labors and struggles (15:30-32a) in a fashion that we can see across the corpus of his letters: He is the one who works against incredible obstacles to proclaim the gospel, whose perdurance in the face of hardships marks him out as trustworthy (cf. 2 Cor 4:7-12; 6:1-10; 11:21*b*-29; Rom 8:31-39),[155] but in this instance his response to hardships gives him the opportunity to focus the question *why* he continues to struggle and work so hard if there is no resurrection of the dead. Paul stacks up phrases to highlight his continuous perils: He is in danger every hour; in effect he dies daily (cf. 2 Cor 6:9 NIV: "dying, and yet we live on"); at the very time of his writing of this letter he is locked in a struggle (wrestling "wild beasts"; see below) in Ephesus. And in the middle of the litany he dares to boast of his work in their behalf, in bringing the gospel to them (cf. 15:10-11), which by its placement pictures his work in their behalf as a part of the whole fabric of his life in service of the gospel and empowered by the grace of God in Christ, who is the Lord of the Corinthians and of Paul. Then, to cap it off, Paul declares, "If the dead are not raised, 'let us eat and drink because tomorrow we die'" (15:32*b-c*), quoting Isa 22:13, and emphasizing the futility and meaninglessness of life if death has the final word.

What does Paul mean when he says "I die daily" (15:31)? The immediate context on either side gives the first clues. "Why are we in danger every hour?" precedes (15:30) and "If, figuratively speaking, I fought wild animals in Ephesus, what good does it do?" follows (15:32). This is hardship talk, which Paul often employs as a sign of his endurance and trustworthiness, but here it is used to highlight the question: Why go to all this apostolic trouble if death has the final word? Paul's answer lies in his deep conviction that in sharing Christ's death believers become one with his suffering, and the powers of the old age vent their anger against the believers so that there is always θλῖψις (*thlipsis*), his technical term for end-times suffering and tribulation (see 1 Cor 7:28). The same point is made when he later writes about "always carrying in the body the death of Jesus" (2 Cor 4:10 NRSV). His dying daily, as indeed his carrying in the body the death of Jesus, is his shorthand way of saying that day-by-day his close identification with Christ's death and his service to his call place him in (hourly and daily) danger. Paul accomplishes one

other point here as well: To those Corinthians who claim already to have "arrived," to have experienced a spiritual sort of resurrection, Paul, the exemplary leader whom no one outperforms, readily identifies himself solely with the death of Jesus and contents himself to wait for the not-yet-realized resurrection of the dead that will only come, in his view, at the end, when Christ returns.

The section concludes with three directives addressed to the Corinthian believers: (1) "Do not be foolish: 'Bad company ruins good morals'" (15:33; quoting the maxim that ultimately may be traced back to the Greek author Menander; cf. another maxim to the same point already in 5:6*b*). (2) "Come to your senses as you ought" (15:34*a*) and (3) "Do not sin" (15:34*b*), with the latter probably surprising the hearers that Paul should construe their actions as in any way representing sin. They have to be warned against sinning; some of them have no knowledge of God; Paul openly declares that he speaks to their shame—all of this is Paul pushing the hearers to the limits, his trying to shock them back to their (better) senses. Why? Because he has come to the heart of the matter: Life in this world, immersed as it is in suffering and brokenness, and work in behalf of the gospel, can all be reduced to folly if there is no resurrection of the dead, if indeed death has the victory, and if indeed death has the last word. Human striving and achieving, even if inspired by the grace of God, is emptied of all its significance if death is the final verdict. How is one's work, indeed one's very essence, one's innermost being more than a whisper if it all ends in death? Paul posits that the resurrection of the dead, which is the logical and necessary outcome of the already-accomplished resurrection of Christ, gives life in the present its meaning, allows and even demands that one enter struggles on behalf of the gospel, and assures that life's struggles and hardships have meaning, a meaning that is ensured by God and that will survive death's sting. Another index that this is indeed the heart of the matter may be seen in Paul's returning to the topic and indeed concluding the discourse on the note that believers know "that in the Lord your labor is not in vain" (15:58). But more on that later.

---

155. Fitzgerald, *Earthen Vessel*, 65-70, 203-5.

REFLECTIONS

1. Whereas most modern understandings of faith focus on *what one believes*, Paul tends to think of faith as the *dynamic, proper relation of people to God*. For Paul, "faith" is his code word for right relation to God; faith is not static, but dynamic, that is, full of power. A deficiency of the English language contributes to the modern understanding because English lacks a verb formed on the same root word as the noun "faith." For the verb, English shifts to "believe," which suggests content or assent to propositions. Not so Greek, where verb and noun are formed on the same root. An important understanding of faith emerges in chapter 15. If Christ has not been raised from the dead, then at stake is not just some wrong belief, some erroneous idea, but faith has lost its *power*—"your faith is ματαία [*mataia*, "empty," "fruitless," "useless," "powerless"]"—and there are disastrous consequences: "You are still in your sins," those who have died in Christ have perished (15:17-18), and the struggles and labor of daily life have no meaning. Faith is the powerfully established, powerfully effective, and productive right relationship to God.

2. A final battle is a typical feature of end-time apocalyptic depictions (cf. Wis 5:17-20; Isa 59:16-19; Rev 19:11-21; Eph 6:10-17) such as Paul's (Rom 8:37-39; 2 Cor 10:3-4; 1 Thess 5:8-9). In the battle God defeats the enemies, variously and somewhat vaguely identified by Paul as the "rulers of this age" (2:6, 8) and "every rule, every authority and power" (15:24). But twice Paul identifies "the last enemy" as yet-to-be-destroyed death (15:26, 54-57). As Paul clearly says, sin, understood as a power, is death's sting; put differently, sin leads to death. Death is effective because it is sin's work, and sin, were it not for God's grace in Jesus Christ, would indeed have the last word. Sin's power was broken in Christ's death and resurrection, though it still stalks about seeking to make a beachhead (Rom 7:8, 11), an offensive landing point from which it can achieve control of one's life by whatever means possible. But believers, having been freed from the lordship of sin and having come under a new Lord, Jesus Christ, are free from the power of sin. And, in Paul's picture most fully elaborated in chapter 15, at the end time when every competing rule and authority and power is finally destroyed, then death also will be destroyed. Then believers will share in Christ's resurrection, death will be no more, and "we shall all be changed."

Anyone who has lost a dear one knows what Paul means when he speaks of the finality of death as an enemy. The utter irretrievability of the lost one sends shock waves of grief. Similarly, those who have faced a terrifying medical diagnosis know death as an ultimate threat. Paul's message, as simple as it is profound, is that death will not have the last word; God will. Paul is not very clear about just how that happens or what it will be like, but he is categorical that God will not allow death to eclipse what we or our loved ones are and the loving that we and they have done.

Sin as a power maneuvering to take advantage of us is one of Paul's great insights. Paul has no truck with the common notion of sin as a wrong deed, as a particular action or set of actions that one should not do. Rather sin is a crafty power that tries to take control of one's life and thereby entice one away from proper dependence upon God. Sin is a primary rival to God and to Christ regarding control over one's life. The deviousness of sin can be seen in its use of even good things, to take some Pauline examples, the law, relations between individuals, and even the practice of one's piety, to take control of our lives.

3. Paul sounds a decidedly future note in these verses. In most of Paul's letters, and indeed in much of 1 Corinthians, Paul is concerned with the present, with how believers live and relate to one another now. To be sure, he thinks they benefit from looking back and from looking forward, but his largest concern is with present comportment.

Part of that focus may come from his concern that his followers can fall away from the grace in which they stand; part of it surely comes with his conviction that the future belongs to God and that God is working it out as pleases God, so that believers do not have the job of securing the future but of living in such a fashion as to be acceptable to God, as to be coordinated with God's plan.

In most of Paul's letters, Paul stresses continuity between the present lives of the believers and God's ultimate plan into which they are being led by the Spirit. Philippians and its "upward call" and "pressing on" (3:13-14) would be a good example. So would 1 Thessalonians with its repeated encouragement to "do so more and more" (4:1, 10). First Corinthians has also made that connection of continuity. But, as we have seen, some at Corinth have collapsed God's future, for Paul, God's yet uncompleted work, into the present. They are the butt of Paul's irony in 4:8-11 where he depicts them as "already" in the kingdom, "already" filled, and "already" rich. Such also are the ones who "deny the resurrection of the dead" (15:12). So in chapter 15 Paul tries to maintain the delicate balance between properly appreciating and celebrating what believers *already* have in Christ and yet clearly recognizing what they have *not yet* received but can with confidence anticipate.

Paul's balance between already and not yet may be difficult for modern Christians to appropriate. Paul was as clear as we that believers were different from non-believers in their comportment of their lives and in the values they affirmed in them. In that sense some believers are like all other believers. But Paul realizes that believers come in all stripes and sizes, ranging from babies in the faith to mature believers. As much joy and assurance as any believers have in their present life, though, they cannot possibly have the fullness of all that God will do for and with them. At present they and all of God's new creation are "works in progress," and that is worth celebrating. But they are not yet complete, not yet finished; God is not yet done with them and with God's purposes with the universe. If we take that to heart, a couple of things should follow: (1) We will continue to press on, to strive to live in accord with God's good and ongoing purposes; and (2) we will be cautious about getting carried away in a boastful way and we will avoid hyperventilating about how wonderful we are.

1 CORINTHIANS 15:35-57, A FICTIVE CHARACTER ALLOWS PAUL TO WRITE ABOUT CONTINUITY AND CHANGE

COMMENTARY

In order to advance his concerns Paul turns to a time-honored rhetorical device of having "a certain person" (τί τι) raise issues that allow Paul the opportunity to include all the Corinthians. In what amounts to a refinement of the matter that capped off the previous section of his argument—namely, how does the future resurrection of the dead bear on actions in the present—Paul uses his interlocutor's queries as an occasion to reflect on two interconnected issues: (1) the continuity between the present and future life in

Christ and (2) the change that will take place between the present and the future.

By personifying the inquisitor, Paul allows the Corinthians to make some identification with the questioner and with the issues, but at the same time it gives him some liberty to be abrasive with the fictive inquisitor without the Corinthians necessarily viewing it as so direct an attack upon them. So they can freely identify with the questions, but when Paul attacks the interlocutor they can distance themselves from the heat of the attack. The character, another example of indirect speech (cf. chaps. 1–4), gives Paul and his hearers some freedom in the exchange and allows for greater clarity to be achieved by bolder comments.

The fictive person's first question "How are the dead raised?" might be of interest to the Corinthians but it is never answered per se; Paul is free to let it go because he has conjured up this fictive person and, like a ventriloquist with his dummy, Paul can have him say what he will and can just as freely ignore what he says once the attention of the hearers is secured. Instead, the second question, "With what bodies do they [the dead] come?" (15:35), with its reference to "body," becomes the focus of Paul's reflections. Paul rebukes the questioner, calling him a "Foolish/ignorant person." The reader is left to wonder whether the fictive person is an ignoramus because he asked the first question or the second. That ambiguity leaves Paul clear to abandon the first question and to undertake an elaborate argument whose burden is that the bodies of things differ, a point Paul will later in the discourse elaborate with regard to resurrection. Paul then takes the interlocutor to the experience of sowing and planting, common enough among persons living in an agrarian culture, and an image he has used already in this letter (3:6-8) with reference to himself.

This fictive person's foolishness lies in not recognizing what everybody is supposed to know, and Paul is at liberty to set him straight. Paul cleverly leaves his audience in the position of going along with him in a knowing way: What one plants does not make life unless it dies, and when one sows one plants not the body that will be but a simple seed to which "God gives a body just as God has chosen" and "each of the seeds has its own body" (15:38). Paul elaborates: The same could be said for flesh, the flesh of folks, of beasts, of birds, and of fish—each is of a distinctive kind of body (15:39). Likewise, when it comes to glory and heavenly and earthly bodies, the sun, the moon, and the stars, all these different bodies have glory, but the glory differs from one to the next. And so it is with all bodies, as Paul is quick to argue (15:42).

Using the most basic analogies and observable phenomena available to every human's experience, Paul makes a very sophisticated set of points. First, what one plants is and is not what grows. Plant a radish seed and one does get a radish, but one plants only a seed and what one harvests is really quite different from the seed, though still a radish. Flesh, bodies, and glory are all variable, distinguishable, and true-to-kind on some sort of dependable pattern[156] that Paul attributes to God just as he earlier in this letter five times affirmed that God arranges matters as God wishes them to be (cf. 3:5; 7:17; 12:18, 24, 28). Second, along with this clarity and dependability there are also mystery and change. To demonstrate this, Paul uses examples that allow him to speak of continuity along with difference. So it is body he writes about, but there are different sorts of bodies, some heavenly, some earthly. And flesh may be flesh, but some of it belongs to people, some to domesticated animals, and some to birds, though it is still all flesh. The same with glory: sun, moon, and stars—and even stars vary in glory. Such a description allows Paul to note commonality but also to honor distinctiveness.

"Thus it is with the resurrection of the dead," Paul asserts (15:42), and by a reprise of his sowing-and-reaping image (last mentioned in 15:36-37) he stresses the *distinctions* between what is sowed and what is reaped but—and this is the genius of his claim—without denying that there is at the same time some fundamental continuity. One can transpose Paul's rhetoric onto a chart:

Sown	*Raised*
corruption	incorruption
dishonor	glory
weakness	power
unspiritual	spiritual body
(ψυχικόν/*psychikon*)	
body	

The list of contrasts draws to a close when Paul reintroduces the "body" concept and says: "If there is a natural body, there is also a spiritual body," stressing that in either case it is body, but a body that is changed—and

156. The Stoics (cf. Seneca, Letter 124, Reason and the True Good) and Epicureans (cf. Lucretius *On the Nature of Things* 2.700-729) would have argued to the same point.

with that the focus shifts to change and "body" becomes the means by which both the change and the continuity are affirmed, but the change is highlighted.

Verses 42-50 are an elaborate and creative development from the humble example of the seed, which is transformed with its planting and sprouting. Paul claims continuity and discontinuity between what we already are and what we shall be and thereby seizes a most complex but important set of factors about the new-but-not-yet-complete life in Christ. The continuity between now and not yet is expressed in that what is planted as a body is a body when raised; those who are of the earth are the very ones who will be the ones who are of heaven; the ones bearing the image of the man of dust will surely bear the image of the man of heaven. The discontinuity is a temporal one, often elsewhere expressed in Paul's frequent categories of "now" and "not yet" but here stated by the use of "first" and "second," "first" and "last," and "sown" and "raised." Both claims—that there is significant continuity and noteworthy discontinuity between the present life of believers and their future, completed life—are important to the richness of the gospel and to Paul's purposes in this chapter.

Paul, knowing that Gen 2:7 (LXX) calls Adam a "living being" (εἰς ψυχὴν ζῶσαν *eis psychēn zōsan*), undertakes a refinement of his Adam-Christ typology, which was introduced in 15:21-22 and calls Christ a "life-giving spirit" (15:45). Once again, a chart may be helpful:

The First Adam	The Last Adam
living being	life-giving spirit
the physical	the spiritual
made of earth	from heaven
those who are of the earth	those who are of heaven
the εἰκών (*eikōn*, "stamp") of the earth	the *eikōn* (stamp) of heaven

The two Adams are clearly types, representing alternative and mutually exclusive identifications or solidarities. This is yet another case of Paul's on-going theme "to whom does one belong?" As in the Sown/Raised chart, so here Paul is eager to mark off two modes of being, two ways of belonging.

Humans can live in the world with one or the other allegiance, one or the other mark of belonging. This is much the same point that he made with the Philippians, but with a very different set of metaphors, when he wrote about living in the world but having their citizenship in heaven (Phil 3:20; cf. 1:27, which would best be translated as "discharge your obligations as citizens worthy of the gospel").

Paul's strongest statement of distinction and separation comes at the end of the two-Adams typology when he affectionately addresses the Corinthians as siblings and uses traditional language to declare, echoing his earlier claim of 6:9, that "flesh and blood cannot inherit the kingdom of God, nor the corruptible inherit the incorruptible" (15:50). The two sides of both charts are not simply to be assimilated to one another; this is yet another expression of his rival two-way mode of thinking that has been manifest from the very first chapters of this letter. Why should he be so pointed in this unless it is his view that some at Corinth are in fact attempting such an inheritance? Just as Paul shocked some of the Corinthians with his earlier blunt declaration "But each in its own order" (15:23*a*), declaring that Christ alone had already experienced resurrection, so here toward the end of this section Paul once again sounds the same theme when he says, with redundancy for emphasis: "But the spiritual is not first, but the physical, then the spiritual" (15:46).

In what we have depicted as two charts, Paul has laid out rich material, not because he has now decided to share some of his theological wisdom that he has earlier admitted to having (2:6), but for the purpose of bringing the Corinthians' thinking into shape so that their behavior will follow properly from it. Paul derides those who think that they already reign (4:8) and declares that "flesh and blood," that is, human beings living in this world, cannot have access to reigning, to the kingdom, not yet, not without radical and fundamental change to which he now turns in 15:51-57.

Usually in his letters Paul labors to lead his readers into a vision that the life already begun in Christ opens out toward God's future in strong continuity and growth so that one "presses on," works for improvement, and matures (cf. Phil 1:25; 3:12-15).

There are two places in the seven undisputedly authentic letters, however, where he highlights a contrast between what believers already have and what they will inherit when the parousia comes: Romans 8 (though affirming continuity as well; e.g., Rom 8:28-39) and here in 1 Corinthians 15. In chap. 15, Paul shares with the Corinthians what he terms a "mystery" (μυστήριον *mystērion*), a disclosure, which, like 15:23*b*-28, depicts what lies ahead, toward the consummation, for all believers. Paul's "we shall not all sleep" (15:51*b*) expresses the conviction that all of his undisputed letters share, namely that the end is imminent, so much so that not all will die before the parousia of Christ.

The important claim, however, is the next: "But we shall all be changed" (15:51*c*, emphatically reaffirmed in 15:52). All believers must be changed; none have arrived, not even Paul (cf. Phil 3:12), who takes backseat to none in terms of growth and strength of faith. And certainly all the Corinthians, including those who have collapsed future into present and claim already to share the resurrection in the present, must be changed.

A trumpet reference (15:52) ties Paul's comments into his larger apocalyptic scenario of a final and determinative battle (cf. 1 Thess 4:16; 5:6-10). Verse 53 opens with a particle (δεῖ *dei*) that would literally be translated "it is necessary," signaling divine action enacting God's plan, extending the picture and once again expressing some continuity between the left and right sides of the charts above: When the dead are raised incorruptible (15:52), then the corruptible will have been cloaked with the incorruptible (cf. the similar image of being further clothed, in 2 Cor 5:4). Then what is mortal will have been cloaked with immortality, and then death, the last enemy (15:26), will finally be destroyed.

Paul's claim of a fundamental continuity makes clear that his view of resurrection does not consist of snatching just a soul or spirit from some to-be-discarded body.

This picture of the last times, designed as it is to give perspective to the Corinthians, moves to closure by identifying the Hosean "sting" of death with sin (Hos 13:14, quoted in 15:55). The connection of "sin leading to death," which is presupposed in 15:56, is such a commonplace as to be formulaic in Paul's letters (cf. Rom 6:16, 21, 23). And, though it seems gratuitous, that is, it appears to have nothing to do with any controversy the Corinthians seem to be having, Paul makes what for him is a ready linkage, that the law provides a fertile setting for sin: namely, that sin delights in the law (though the law itself must not be identified with sin; Rom 7:7-12) and sees in it an unrivaled opportunity to find powerful leverage by which it may bring people under its (sin's) sway (15:56).

Paul brings the main part of the discourse to a close with a "grace," a thanksgiving to God, who, by grace, "is giving us the victory [an echo from the Isa 25:8 quote in 15:54; note also the trumpet in 15:52] through our Lord Jesus Christ" (15:57). The present participle τῷ διδόντι (*tō didonti*) points to God's current and ongoing action in bringing and giving to believers the victory. Paul affirms the process that is under way with Christ's death and that will culminate in the redemption of all of creation. Believers as part of the new creation are already enjoying the benefits of God's redemptive and creative activity. Just as the schema of this world is passing away (1 Cor 7:31) due to God's indictment of sin's sway over creation, so Paul here at the end of this discourse breaks into thankfulness to God for incorporating the believers into God's victorious redemptive work.

REFLECTIONS

1. A fundamental Pauline premise is that everything has a body (σῶμα *sōma*) as God has chosen (this statement is an echo of 12:18, there about spiritual gifts); nothing exists apart from *sōma*. His example of grain serves him well: The grain appears one way before planting and takes on another form after it has been planted (read "dies" 15:36) and comes up sprouted. No surprise in this; all of creation works the same way. Everything has a body as God has chosen and seeds of those bodies come true to form.

In fact, the whole universe, terrestrial and celestial, is composed of distinctive bodies, each with its own particular glory.

Significant dangers attend the overemphasis that Paul here tries to correct. To declare, as some Corinthians have, that the fullness of all that God will give is available in the present, without and before a restoration of all of creation and its accompanying end of suffering and struggle, misleads persons about their present circumstances and about the grandeur of what God is ultimately under way to do: about their present because it caters to the illusory sense that salvation is an individual matter (cf. the "for me" in the Corinthians' maxims in 6:12), which a person can receive fully in the present without the larger social web, and indeed without all of God's broken world being redeemed; and about the final grandeur because it suggests that God's ultimate purposes have concluded with the individual in question, so that a smaller God is presupposed. To think that God's ultimate redemptive purposes are focused in some exclusive way on saving me (or even someone very dear to me) is filled with hubris and arrogance on my side and manifests a failure to see the vastness and the cosmic proportion of God's whole redemptive plan.

Accordingly, Paul's concluding refrain "We shall all be changed" (15:51, 52) is his confident affirmation that God, who has begun this work in believers, will bring it to completion (Phil 1:6), but it is also his sobering caution to those Corinthians who have gotten ahead of themselves by claiming already to have experienced some sort of spiritual resurrection.

2. The element of discontinuity, of surprise or of difference between what is now and what is in God's future, is a natural consequence of Paul's central affirmation that God's grace lies at the outset of the life of faith and undergirds every moment of it from the beginning of faith until God's culminating purposes arrive. Grace has two aspects, the one probably featured more regularly than the other. First, grace is the welcome power of God freely given because God wants to do it, and totally unmerited because we in no sense deserve it. It is what has opened up the life of faith to each of us and therefore is worthy of considerable celebration and thankfulness. The other side of grace, however, is that it turns lives upside down—if we were to speak of grace in terms of baseball, grace would at least be a curveball, and sometimes might appear as a "spitter." Grace can be very unsettling. It changes lives and people often resist and resent change, even if it might be liberating as grace's change always turns out to be. Grace's breaking into lives does not always look on the surface or at first glance even as grace, but more as discombobulation. The time when believers sing God's praises for grace most easily is after it has shaken up their world and after they have come to perceive it for what it is. Grace is frequently visible (sometimes only visible) as grace, for what it *really* is, only in retrospect.

1 CORINTHIANS 15:58, RECAPITULATION AND PERORATION

COMMENTARY

Typically in Paul's time, speakers and writers who came to the end of such an eloquent address as this chapter would highlight and tie together various important themes and call for a response. So it is here. With a forceful "Therefore," Paul addressed the Corinthians very affectionately as "Brothers and sisters, my beloved." His one injunction to them is "Stand firm, immovable," but he then unfolds just how they are to stand fast. Believers stand firm and immovable by "abounding in the work of the Lord always," and they can throw themselves passionately and unreservedly into that work because they should understand the resurrection and what it tells us about life and work in this world: namely, that their labor (note the singular, see below) in the Lord is not in vain, not empty.

Paul's call to them to "be steadfast" (cf. also Col 1:23) is elaborated by three participles that describe how and what they are to do in order to be steadfast. First, they are to be "immovable" (ἀμετακίνητοι *ametakinētoi*), which depicts their ability to stand against whatever winds or experiences buffet them, because of their confidence that God will bring to completion what God has begun in them through Christ (cf. Rom 4:21; Phil 1:6). That is how they can be steadfast. The first participle, "immovable," if it were there alone, might suggest that to "be steadfast" is to hold tight or to stand still. Second, Paul describes what they do to stay steadfast—and interestingly it is not by hunkering down and holding tight. They stand fast by "abounding always in the work of the Lord" (15:58). And they can abound in the work of the Lord because they know, the third participle, "that their labor is not in vain in the Lord" (15:58).

These claims are rich in content, dense in expression and significance, and profound in implication. All these affirmations undergird and explicate Paul's final exhortation: "Stand fast." When transposed to nautical imagery it would be "Stay the course." Paul makes the same argument with the Galatians, there in athletic terminology: You were running well; don't be distracted, lose your way, or turn back (Gal 5:7; 4:9).

So this discourse has moved from its opening where Paul shockingly raised the specter that their faith and his labor might be in vain (15:2), to a clarification about life-in-this-world-in-light-of-the-expected-resurrection, which affirms that actions and struggles and work "in the Lord" are significant and vital.

Special note should be taken that "the work [ἔργον *ergon*] of the Lord" and "your [ὑμῶν *hymōn*, plural] labor [κόπος *kopos*, singular] in the Lord" both employ the singular regarding the Lord's work or labor (two different Greek terms meaning the same thing here) and the believers' collective effort. We must ask why Paul uses the singular here. The answer lies in Paul's fundamental

commitment to the life of faith as a life in community. There is not a list of pre-approved "works" or "labors" of the Lord that individuals must go out and do as solo agents; Paul supposes a much more community-grounded and integrated effort in which all the deeds of the community, and indeed all the actions of all the individuals within it, are coordinated into *a shared work and a common labor* in the Lord. Surely, believers do different things; just as they have different gifts, so also their actions are distinctive. As believers' faith is one and they are therefore united in it (cf. 1 Thess 1:8), so their work, their labor is one because God's singular love is expressed in their varied work.

This reference to labor/work is a critical matter for Paul, for his own thinking, for his actions in behalf of the gospel, and for his communities because it raises the most fundamental of human questions: What do we make of our strivings? What enduring significance do our actions have? Is there meaning to the struggles of our lives? Why does one do anything that one does? These questions are made most poignant by death, which threatens to erase not only the believers themselves but also what the believers have done. Paul's letters show that he and his readers are not immune to such questions. Note how many times he raises the matter of whether he has been "running in vain," a phrase that for him raises the question of the worth of his labor—and even of his life—in behalf of the gospel (Gal 2:2; 4:11; Phil 2:16; 1 Thess 3:5; these references represent rhetorical pressure on the readers of those letters, not self-doubt on Paul's part).

We must now examine the connection Paul sees between life in the present, with its moral dilemmas and choices, with its striving and its yearning, and the finishing up of God's purposes, which still lies in the (imminent) future. The best clues of this interconnection in chapter 15 come in three verses that we now consider in sequence: "If in this life we have hoped in Christ only, we are of all people most to be pitied" (15:19); "If in the way people understand things, I wrestled wild beasts in Ephesus, what good does it do? 'Eat and drink because tomorrow we die'!" (15:32); and the just-noted climax of the discourse, "Therefore, brothers and sisters, my beloved, be firm, immovable, always abounding in the work of the Lord, knowing that your labor in the Lord is not empty" (15:58).

Has God's decisive strike against sin and its power obviated any need for the believers to do anything? Clearly the ultimate power is God's power, in Paul's view. If 2 Thessalonians is any evidence, some of Paul's followers have come to the conclusion that they need not work, that they simply stand idly by and await God's powerful completion of what God has begun. At issue in 1 Corinthians 15 is the question of whether it matters what Paul or they do, whether their labor is in vain.

For an insight, consider what Paul says about himself and his labor. He puts it in the most dramatic of forms, namely, his wrestling of wild beasts—no doubt a figurative reference to the great opposition he is encountering—in Ephesus from whence he writes this letter (16:8-9).[157] Does his laboring in behalf of the gospel in the face of adversaries amount to anything? One answer could be to throw up one's hands in despair at the meaninglessness of life and its struggles and embrace the libertine life because "tomorrow we die." If death has the final word on the meaning of life, then why would one choose wrestling wild beasts over pleasure (eating and drinking)? Paul's life shows that he has chosen the wrestling; his thought expressed in chapter 15 equally testifies that Paul has confidence that "the work of the Lord" and their "labor in the Lord" is not in vain. Why? Because death and its sting of defeat is not the last word. Death, sin's sting and the last enemy, will ultimately be overcome for all believers. Christ's resurrection as "first fruits" (15:20, 23) is the surety that the remainder of the resurrection harvest of believers will be made good. So what one does and what one is in Christ is ultimately valued, valuable, and preserved, beyond death's futile grasp. Thus, one not only can wrestle beasts wherever one is, but one must be part of the great cosmic plan, the battle with evil, in which God is engaged. Engagement, struggle, labor, doing "the work of the Lord" are not an option that believers might choose; they are an obligation. Faith does not have works as simply an option that may or may not be exercised. Faith requires

that works be done. Faith is incomplete—one might even say it is not truly faith—until it expresses itself in deeds. Unwritten in this chapter but supposed is that believers have to exercise moral judgment in the choices that they make, that being in Christ has obligated them, with renewed minds (Rom 12:2), to be responsible moral agents. In the terms of this chapter, moral discernment entails their figuring out what indeed is their proper "labor in the Lord," and then abounding in it always, because they know that their "labor in the Lord is not in vain" (15:58; cf. Paul's exemplary self-portraits in this respect in 3:8ff. and in 15:10).

"If in this life we have hoped in Christ only, we are of all people most to be pitied" (15:19). As Paul has constructed it, this first clause has a certain ambiguity. At issue in its interpretation is what the term "only" modifies. (a) If one takes it to mean "if in this life we have only hoped in Christ," then the question is whether this life, even in Christ, has significance in its own right, that is, whether the life of faith is realized only as a hope whose fulfillment is delayed until a later time. Though Paul does not address that issue directly in chapter 15, elsewhere Paul is clear that the present life in Christ is rich and vibrant; the life of faith is not simply an anticipated life, recognized in the present only or primarily as a hope (cf. 1 Cor 13:13; Rom 5:1). (b) If one takes it to mean "in this life only we have hoped in Christ," then the question is what connection there is between this life and the life to come. Given the way 15:35 introduces a fictive character who asks about the kind of body the dead will have, and Paul's response to the question in 15:36, we must say that Paul is concerned with the significance this bodily life has in light of the renewed and grander bodily life that awaits the believers at the parousia.

The importance of chapter 15 in the letter. By its position as the last major item in the letter chapter 15 caps off the body of the letter. We have seen that it attempts to correct a mistaken assumption among some Corinthians that they already share in some spiritualized resurrection that moves them to what they consider a special plateau, where they deserve honor and where they are no longer bound by certain moral restraints.

---

157. Abraham Malherbe, "The Beasts at Ephesus," *JBL* 87 (1968) 79-80.

And, looking back from this point we have been able to see the several places in the letter where such a mistaken notion of the resurrection may actually have been operative. We must also note that chapter 15, while it deals with resurrection as a topic, nevertheless weaves together some of the themes of the preceding chapters: (1) The opening (15:1-2) has the same comprehensive sweep across the whole of the believing life that is captured in Paul's traditions about the Lord's supper where what one proclaims there is of equal scope: "the Lord's death until he comes" (11:26). (2) The indissoluble linkage between Christ's resurrection, already accomplished, and believers' coming resurrection, which is affirmed in so many ways in chapter 15, was already declared in 6:14. (3) The cosmic portrayal of Christ and his role in God's purpose has been a theme across the letter (3:23; 8:6; 11:3), a theme that is elaborated even more in 15:21-28. (4) The 15:38 claim that God gives a body to different seeds as God chooses is a direct restatement of divine prerogative asserted three times with regard to the distribution of charismata in the congregation (12:11, 18, 24). (5) The declaration that flesh and blood will not be able to inherit the kingdom of God, which provides the basis for the additional formula, "nor the perishable inherit the imperishable" (15:50b), is an echo of 6:9. (6) The reference to one's labor in the Lord not being in vain should call to mind Paul's own self-portrait as a laborer along with Apollos in 3:5-9. Resurrection is the premise on which all of life and all of one's workings or deeds or accomplishments rest. All of one's work in the Lord is not only necessary but also eternally significant.

These thematic and behavioral ties of chapter 15 to the remainder of the letter emphasize the culminating and grounding role this major discussion plays not only in the structure of the letter but also in the understanding and discerning of the moral choices that believers face as they try to live a faithful life of love for one another in a broken world while they await the parousia of their Lord. As the Lord's supper provided the framework within which the believers live the scope of their lives—from Christ's death until he comes—so also the anticipated resurrection endorses, elevates, and sanctifies daily life as a mode of acceptable and thankful offering of themselves to the very God who will faithfully care for them before, in, and beyond death.

REFLECTIONS

1. This grand section ends on a note about work and labor, but that is a theme that showed itself earlier in Paul's comments about being in constant danger for his association with the gospel and about his so-called wrestling with wild beasts in Ephesus. Paul writes 1 Corinthians from Ephesus (16:8) where he notes appreciatively the "wide door" open for his work there. His evidence? Much opposition (16:9). So Paul is wrestling "wild beasts" at Ephesus because of his identification with and presentation of the gospel. The dangers and opposition raise a fundamental question: Why go to all that trouble, effort, and danger? If there is no resurrection, if life is to be lived simply for the value one can tease out of the moment, there is certainly no reason to work, much less to place oneself in harm's way. But, on the other hand, if one's life is truly secure with God, what does that suggest about anxiety brought about by opposition?

As the Corinthians exemplify for us, one's convictions about the resurrection are crucial to the way one handles one's life. If one is convinced that one's salvation is already accomplished, already secure in its fullness, then one might conclude that moral restraints no longer prevail, that one is free to eat, drink, and be merry in whatever way one sees fit, and that one has no need to labor or exert one's self—especially if doing so might land one in difficult circumstances. Such persons, thinking they already had it made, would act as if they deny that Paul's anticipated judgment day has any bearing on their decisions and actions, and might even assume that their works will not be considered at the judgment (cf. Rom 2:6-8; 2 Cor 5:10).

Paul's own life, filled to the brim as it was with work on behalf of the gospel and with that work's attendant risks and opposition, is a resounding answer of another sort, based on his own understanding of the resurrection. (This ties back to the discussion of freedom in the reflections on chapter 9.) Because of Paul's unshakable confidence that God will finish—by vanquishing the last enemy, death—the good work begun in Christ, Paul knows that God will not forsake him, no matter what others may do and no matter what may befall him. This confidence frees Paul from others and frees him for others. This confidence spurs Paul to work, to risk and to brook opposition on behalf of the gospel and his call. Granted, it would not warrant any and every risk; note well that even as Paul did not go right back to Thessalonica when it was apparent that he might be harmed or killed if he did, so we are not describing a blind, unthinking, foolhardy faith. But we would not expect foolhardy faith and unnecessary risk-taking from someone like Paul who insists that his reasonable worship of God (Rom 12:1) involves the regular and full employment of his mind as well as his spirit (14:14-15). When one knows oneself truly secure with God, one is free to serve God with a purity and openness of heart, despite the opposition such a service will surely generate.

No Christian should expect to arrive at that confidence and certainty right away; it is a matter of growth and maturity in faith today, just as it was in Paul's time. Instead of spending one's energies lamenting over not already sharing Paul's confidence, one would do far better to use those energies to build and practice one's faith so that it might grow into such a relationship. It is an effort that other believers and God will support and nourish.

A church convinced of its security in God's grace can therefore be liberated from the social pressures to conform to the culture and can take a public stand where there are matters of justice and human well-being at stake. Such a church can represent the gospel by its public declarations about social issues and by its hands-on involvement with the problems that bedevil our communities. Then the church would be doing the "work" that it is called to do.

2. Note that Paul links one's labors with the "work of God." It is not all labor or work that Paul praises and assures of value, but those labors that attest to God's work in and through one. So Paul's is not a paean of work or busyness for its own sake, but only insofar as one's own labors cohere with the work that God is up to. In fact, though Paul does not do so, one could suggest testing a contemplated action against what one understood about God's work that we see in Christ. One's labors in the Lord endure just as surely as does one's love (1 Cor 13:13); so properly to labor in God's work is at the same time to walk in love. Ours is a world where we seem to have construed our individual worth by reference to our busyness, as if to tell one another how busy we are is an index of our importance and goodness. Next time a friend tells you how busy they are, you might do them a favor to ask them, Why? and To what end? Of course, as surely as you do that work of friendship toward someone else, you should be ready to be asked the same questions.

3. The taunt "Death, where is your sting?" is an awesome one. This childlike standing unabashedly before death and shaking a defiant fist in its face is possible for believers only because they know the rest of the story, namely that death is the "final enemy," yet to be destroyed, but which will be ultimately and finally overcome in God's final triumph. To ask where death's sting is now, as a friend or loved one dies, is not to deny that the person has died, it is not to deny that we have felt and do feel death's sting, and it is not to deny that we feel grief and loss over that death. As Paul uses it, the taunt confidently looks at death and its sting in the present from beyond death, from the standpoint of God's final and completed purposes. *Then* God's power mercifully will have raised the dead; *then* God will have dealt death the sting-removing final blow; and *then* (and now already in confident hope) we may say with Paul that death is overcome by life.

4. We know the grand design of what God is doing in the overall scheme of things because the story moves from Christ's death and resurrection toward the ultimate fulfillment of all of God's promises, toward the redemption of God's creatures and cosmos. We can be part of that story by God's grace and if our lives are conduits for love. Not that we should think of ourselves as bringing God's kingdom. It is God's reign and God is bringing it. At issue for each of us is whether and how fully we will live our lives as a channel through which God's love and mercy can flow to the world and to all of God's creatures.

1 CORINTHIANS 16:1-24

ONE MORE CORINTHIAN QUESTION, PAUL'S PLANS, AND LETTER CLOSING

OVERVIEW

The major points of the letter now having been concluded, Paul turns to a sequence of closing matters, the first of which the Corinthians seem to have raised with him in their letter (cf. 7:1), though it could have come through the Corinthian emissaries.

1 CORINTHIANS 16:1-4, RESPONSE TO A QUERY ABOUT THE COLLECTION

COMMENTARY

The Corinthians have written Paul about the collection. The term "collection" (λογεία *logeia*), suggesting a gathering of funds for a special purpose, appears only here (16:1-4) in the Pauline corpus, but refers to the one-time offering to which he committed himself in Jerusalem (Gal 2:1-10, esp. 2:10). At the Jerusalem conference he promised that he would pull together from his largely gentile churches a goodwill offering as a demonstration, as an affirmation of Christian unity to what he otherwise calls the "saints" or the "poor among the saints in Jerusalem" (Rom 15:26). His letters, apart from 1 Corinthians, show that Paul devotes considerable time and energy to making good on this offering (cf. Rom 15:25-28; 2 Corinthians 8–9) across about a two year span (2 Cor 8:10). We know from 2 Corinthians that the Corinthians initially responded readily to the opportunity to take part in this collection, but that their earlier zeal was lost with the passage of time (8:11). When 1 Corinthians was written, the Corinthian believers were willing participants in this generous undertaking, and Paul's response suggests that their concerns were on the logistics of how to gather it and what its disposition might be. Unlike 2 Corinthians, one finds in 1 Corinthians no hint of contention, confusion, or diminution of zeal about participation in the collection.

Paul, who is in Ephesus and has gone through the Roman province of Galatia to get there, tells the Corinthians that on the matter of the collection he recommends the steps he gave to the Galatian believers on the same topic (16:1). What follows (16:2) is a suggested pattern of regular setting aside so that when Paul arrives they will already have the (presumably substantial) collection ready. A couple of features are noteworthy: (1) The reference in the Greek is to a regular practice of each person setting apart contributions every Sabbath. From such nomenclature of days, we see how completely resocialized these gentiles were to the whole sense that they belonged to the family of God, whose roots are traceable directly to the people of Israel. It is fully understandable that they would embrace a collection aimed to show their solidarity with their believing brothers and sisters in Jerusalem. (2) There is a difficult phrase in 16:2 that the NIV ("set aside a sum . . . income") and the NRSV ("save whatever extra you earn") take distinctively but which generally suggests that each person is to "treasure up" according to how well the person gets along. We probably cannot be more precise as to Paul's meaning than that. Second Corinthians 8:13-15 may be read as an elaboration of his intended meaning here: Equity requires that whatever abundance one has should be put in service of those in need, and he sees scriptural support for this arrangement in Ex 16:18 (NRSV)—"those who gathered much had nothing over, and those who gathered little had no shortage"—which he cites there (2 Cor 8:15).

A similar notion about the collection appears in Romans 15 where Paul expresses a fundamental reciprocity among believers. There, those who have received much (the gentile believers) are indebted to those through whom they received (namely the Jewish believers who preceded them into the faith) and therefore should readily embrace the opportunity to give as they are able (Rom 15:27). On the basis of ability, each is to give to others according to the others' needs. This collection meets the general test of believers' caring for one another in proportion to what they have to offer (cf. 1 Cor 12:7).

At the time of his writing of 1 Corinthians Paul does not anticipate that he will go with the collection to Jerusalem, so he advises them that when he does come to see them next they should have the collection ready and that they can certify certain representatives whom Paul will credentialize with letters; those persons can accompany this "gift" (ἡ χάρις *hē charis,* "grace," "gift") to Jerusalem. Earlier Paul asked, "What do you have that you have not received as a gift?" (4:7). So what the Corinthians offer to the Jerusalem saints is but the grace of God working through them, and the offering then finally is not really only to the Jerusalem saints but ultimately to God, the source of all gifts great and small. Paul closes his comments on the collection by saying that if he does decide to attend to the delivery of the collection to Jerusalem, those designated representatives will go with him. By this means he maintains his own leadership role (16:4).

REFLECTIONS

Paul's comments across the corpus about the collection for the saints in Jerusalem give significant insights into his broader understanding of stewardship. Paul supposes that all believers will be moved to care for others who are in need (cf. the mutuality of Rom 15:27), that each should give in accord with how well one is getting along (16:2; cf. a similar concern in 2 Cor 8:11-15), and that what one contributes is literally a "grace" (16:3). The NIV and NRSV reasonably translate *charis* as "gift" because that is the linguistic center of the concept. But we might do well to think of it as "offering grace" to others because it at once reflects that any giving we do is equivalent to prayerful thankfulness, and is always in response to God's own "grace," which was freely bestowed on us while we were still sinners and which is the ongoing reckoning point by which our lives are lived and nourished day by day. So grace goes around: It comes from God, it is shared by offering such as we have with others, and all that resounds to God's glory. But caution: the grace that we share is not to be confused or identified with any degree of "success" or "prosperity" we have, so that we come to think of ourselves who have more as "more blessed" and those who have less as "less blessed." An identification with "offering grace" might also mean that the thanks over meals would be understood to have connection not only to eating but also to include giving and sharing with others.

1 CORINTHIANS 16:5-9, PROJECTED VISIT PLANS AND PRESENT PURPOSES

COMMENTARY

Most of Paul's letters contain, usually in a closing section, some indication of his plans for the present, and they often project visits to the letter recipients. And 1 Corinthians is no exception, for here he assures the Corinthians that, though he expects to stay at Ephesus through Pentecost, he then looks forward to traveling through Macedonia (a land trip, rather than an Aegean crossing, in other words) on his way for what he hopes may be an extended (across the winter) time with the Corinthians, the Lord willing (16:7). As if it is his normal practice with them, he mentions that at the end of his visit he will expect them to help him along his way wherever he is led to go next (cf. the same treatment expected for Timothy in 16:11; cf. also Rom 15:24; 2 Cor 1:16). His present purposes keep him in Ephesus, the largest city in the Roman Empire after Rome, because he sees what he calls a "great and effective door" opened to him (16:9).

REFLECTIONS

Paul's interpretation of opposition (16:9) as a sign that he is on the right track may seem strange to the modern reader who is concerned with not causing any distress, with not making any waves. Jesus clearly warns that those who pursue righteousness for his sake will experience opposition and affliction, even though they are simultaneously promised blessedness and a share in God's reign (Matt 5:10). Believers should not be surprised by opposition, and at times even by suffering because of identification with the gospel. To be yoked to Jesus by dedication to justice is, as Jesus' words have it, an easy yoke, and his burden is light (Matt 11:30), precisely because he helps carry it. Jesus never said, "Have no enemies." Instead, he told us to relate to our enemies in love (Matt 5:44). So believers will have enemies, will experience opposition for the sake of the gospel. We will have to be careful—and here other believers can no doubt be of service—to distinguish enmity and opposition for the sake of the gospel from that generated in response to our own greed, self-centeredness or peevishness. Knowledge that walking according to the gospel will produce enmity can only be descriptive, never a license, never prescriptive.

1 CORINTHIANS 16:10-12, TRAVEL PLANS OF PAUL'S ASSOCIATES

COMMENTARY

Verses 10-11 are a commendation of Timothy, who along with Titus are Paul's doubles. Are we to suppose that Timothy and the Corinthians have had some troubles? Perhaps. If so, Paul uses his own authority to encourage a proper welcome and support of Timothy. In any case, Paul's characterization of Timothy is significant because it functions exactly as we have seen Paul's own self-descriptions, namely, to set the pattern for others in the community to follow. In fact, Paul's description ties Timothy explicitly and directly to himself: "for he works the work of the Lord just as I do" (16:10). Given that chapter 15 closed with the emphasis on doing the work of the Lord and one's labor in the Lord not being in vain (15:58), the reprise of that model in the portrait of Timothy is not accidental but intended for emulation. Paul's note that he is expecting Timothy (and his entourage) as Timothy comes through Corinth to Ephesus expresses an interest to follow up on the matter of their treatment of Timothy much as Paul's projected visit to Philemon's house (Phlm 22).

Apollos, who throughout this letter seems to be on good terms with Paul (cf. 3:5-9), has been contacted by Paul and urged to go to Corinth. Apollos clearly has his own self-determination, and Paul reports that he has chosen not to go to Corinth at present but will come when the occasion presents itself (16:12). (See Reflections at 16:13-14.)

1 CORINTHIANS 16:13-14, CONCLUDING ADMONITIONS

COMMENTARY

Often at the end of letters Paul has a series of pithy admonitions and quite frequently, as is the case here, the injunctions touch on central or fundamental issues in the letter (2 Cor 13:11; Gal 6:14-16).[158] The first two admonitions—"Be on watch" and "Stand (firm)" are military imagery from Paul's apocalyptic vision that believers are part of God's army who are to be on alert, at their battle stations (cf. 1 Thess 5:6, 10); the second also has the eschatological aspect of standing before the judgment seat and being found worthy, hence the addition "in the faith" (10:12; 15:1; cf. Rom 14:10).[159]

While the third—"Conduct yourselves in a courageous way"—and fourth—"Be strong"—injunctions probably reflect Ps 30:24 LXX (31:25) and may also have battle significance, they also certainly relate to Paul's chiding the Corinthians for being childish, for being babies in the faith, and for not having grown more mature in the faith.

As is typically the case in Greco-Roman rhetoric, the most important injunction is reserved for last, and, appropriately, is the most elaborate in form: "Let all the things that you do be done in love" (16:14). As noted earlier, love is what is most missing in the multifarious transactions of the Corinthians, so Paul's final injunction calls for love to be the guiding presence in *all* that the Corinthians do.

158. Aune, *The New Testament in Its Literary Environment*, 191; J. A. D. Weima, *Neglected Endings: The Significance of the Pauline Letter Closings*, JSNTSup 101 (Sheffield: JSOT, 1994).

159. Edgar M. Krentz, "Military Language and Metaphors in Philippians," in *Origins and Method: Towards a New Understanding of Judaism and Christianity, Essays in Honour of John C. Hurd*, ed. B. H. McLean, JSNTSup 88 (Sheffield: Sheffield Academic Press, 1993) 109. In a yet-unpublished "Notes for a Future Study," circulated on request,

Krentz writes: "The anarthrous use of five imperatives indicates heightened intensity. All fit well into the military semantic field."

REFLECTIONS

Paul's summary call to the Corinthians is an appropriate summary call to all believers everywhere: "Let everything of yours be done in love" (16:14). One never has to apologize for loving, but one may have to distinguish attempts at loving with actually loving. How frustrating and puzzling it is to attempt to love when the intended person or persons do not perceive it as love. Paul Tillich, the theologian, wrote that revelation was not revelation until it was received by someone. So, also, love is not fully love simply in its attempt; it is genuinely love only when it is received as love. Loving is not a science. It must ever be reinvented afresh in every new situation. Oftentimes you will not know whether love has genuinely been received. Loving is a little like Noah on the high seas, sending the dove out day by day. Some days the dove will come home without any sign of its having sighted land; but, fortunately, on other days it just may come home with a branch in its beak, signifying that it has indeed found some fruitfulness. Love's duty is to send the dove, day by day. And perhaps it is best to expect nothing in return because then the love is genuinely given without strings attached. Then when the dove does bring the branch home on occasion, it can be an especial time for rejoicing. How frustrating and puzzling it is to attempt to love when the intended person or persons do not perceive it as love.

1 CORINTHIANS 16:15-18, COMMENDATIONS OF STEPHANAS AND OTHERS

COMMENTARY

Stephanas is one of the pillars of the Corinthian church. His family was the first that Paul baptized there (1:16; 16:15), and he was part of a three-person delegation who visited Paul and no doubt filled him in on what was happening at Corinth. Perhaps they even delivered the letter from the Corinthians to Paul (7:1).

Paul's commendations have exemplary purpose, that is, they, like Paul's autobiographical portraits, highlight model-worthy ways of living: These people "devoted themselves to the service [εἰς διακονίαν *eis diakonian*] of the saints" (16:15 NIV). Paul urges recognition of (16:18) and submission to (16:16) such persons, and, in a sweeping extension, "to all who come together in the work [συνεργοῦντι *synergounti*] and who labor [κοπιῶντι *kopiōnti,* in it, understood]" (16:16). Note well that this extension places Stephanas and all who work like him in line with Paul and his own self-portrait (3:6; 4:12; cf. 15:58). Such persons are exemplary because of their διακονία (*diakonia*), their service, which Paul identifies as refreshing of everyone's spirit (16:18). Parenthetically, one should also note that once again "the work" and "labor" both appear here as they did in 15:58, and both are once again in the singular because all contribute to the "work of the Lord" by their own labors.

REFLECTIONS

Paul commends Stephanas's household because "they have devoted themselves to the service [*diakonia*] of the saints" and sets them forward as the pattern others ought to follow (16:15-16). This is the same circularity noted earlier about love. Persons who have benefited from God's grace must move in love toward others, they must, each and every one of them, engage in service, in ministry toward others. Love received is love that demands to be given, passed along to, shared with others. Service to others is not simply an option; it is the very heart of life according to the gospel.

1 CORINTHIANS 16:19-20, GREETINGS

COMMENTARY

Paul's location at the time of writing, Ephesus, is in the Roman province of Asia (roughly modern Turkey). Aquila and Prisca, the Jewish believers who were expelled from Rome with the other Jews under Claudius's ban in 49 CE (cf. Rom 16:3-4; Acts 18:2), have a house church in Ephesus also. Paul reports greetings from "all the Asian churches" and from Aquila, Prisca, the church in their house, and all the other believers there (16:19). The greetings section closes, as do many of Paul's letters, with his urging the auditors to greet one another with a "holy kiss," obviously another bit of Pauline pressure to have them show the signs of friendship and affection that could genuinely signal the end of their divisiveness (16:20; cf. Rom 16:16; 2 Cor 13:12; 1 Thess 5:26).

1 CORINTHIANS 16:21, AUTOGRAPH

COMMENTARY

In some of his letters Paul takes the pen from his scribe and adds his own personalizing touch (cf. Gal 6:11; Phlm 19). By doing so, Paul adds the full force of his authority to all of the letter and to all that has been written in it.

1 CORINTHIANS 16:22, ENFORCEMENT FORMULA

COMMENTARY

Occasionally Paul closes his letters with a formula of enforcement, warning regarding specific matters (cf. Gal 6:17). Here, Paul makes a foundational affirmation, one which it would be difficult to imagine any Corinthian not sharing: "if anyone does not have friendship with/love the Lord" (16:22; φιλεῖ τὸν κύριον *philei ton kyrion*), but that may, indeed, serve Paul quite well as he has sought at points in this letter to remind the Corinthians of the simple basis of their unity, namely, their relation to the Lord. The consequences of failure to love the Lord are stark: "Let that person be *anathema* (ἀνάθεμα)/ accursed," cut off from the community (cf. 5:1-5; Gal 1:8). Paul concludes this section with the eschatological prayer, preserved in Aramaic, the sister language of Hebrew and probably reflecting a well-established, pre-Pauline prayer of the earliest churches: *Marana tha*, "Our Lord, come." This prayerful call for Christ's parousia echoes the Lord's supper ("you proclaim the Lord's death until he comes," 11:26 NRSV) and the resurrection discourse's introduction (15:3-11), which sketched matters out to the believers' expected but still future salvation.

REFLECTIONS

Paul's call for the Lord to come is his imploring God to bring to conclusion God's redemptive work begun in Jesus Christ. The same sort of response lies behind the cry

"Amen, come Lord Jesus" with which the book of Revelation closes (22:20; cf. the "come," which greets the opening of each of the first four seals in Rev 6:1, 3, 5, 7; cf. Rev 22:17). For Paul, God's foreshortening of the time ("the time [before the end] is shortened"; 1 Cor 7:29*a*) is a sign of God's mercy. Thus, Paul's call and the modern Christian's call for our Lord to come—as we see it in some contemporary liturgies—is at once a recognition that we survive and even thrive in the midst of present tribulations and distress only by the grace of God, and is at the same time an urgent plea for deliverance, for an end to suffering, for a vindication of our faithfulness, and for a complete dawning of God's reign.

1 CORINTHIANS 16:23-24, CONCLUDING GRACE

COMMENTARY

All of Paul's letters open with a call for grace to be upon the readers, and likewise all of his letters close with a standard "grace to you" (Rom 16:20*b*; 2 Cor 13:14; Gal 6:18; Phil 4:23; 1 Thess 5:28; and Phlm 25). Grace is the be-all and end-all of the life of faith; God's grace is not just important at the outset of the life of faith, it is also the very ground of being in all of life, from beginning to end.

As this closing grace starts out in 1 Cor 16:23—"the grace of our Lord Jesus Christ be with you"—nothing is unusual, but the way Paul concludes it ties once again into the problem the letter addresses: "My love be with all of you in Christ Jesus" (16:24). Paul, who has called for love from them to one another (most recently in the summary injunctions; 16:14), now practices what he has preached and affirms his love for *all of them* in Christ Jesus. To the very end of the letter Paul models for them what they most need. And he closes without siding with any group or clique against another. His love is for *all* of them in Christ Jesus. Love for the Lord (16:22) is the sine qua non of belonging in the Christian community, and because all believers are equally in Christ, then love for the Lord calls for, even requires, love of all those who are in Christ. Paul models for them that love as he wishes God's grace upon them.

REFLECTIONS

The letter that opened with grace (1:3) closes with an affirmation of grace (16:23), symbolizing that all the concerns of the letter—and indeed all of life—are enclosed in and supported simply and profoundly by God's grace. Without God's grace we cannot begin the day and face its challenges and opportunities; without God's grace we cannot make the most of the opportunities and find the strength to meet the challenges; and without God's grace we cannot find the peace that allows us to let go of all our unfinished work when the night comes and we must rest.

THE SECOND LETTER TO THE CORINTHIANS

INTRODUCTION, COMMENTARY, AND REFLECTIONS
BY
J. PAUL SAMPLEY

THE SECOND LETTER TO THE

CORINTHIANS

INTRODUCTION

N owhere else in Paul's letters can we observe his enduring relationship with a particular church. In the documents called 1 and 2 Corinthians, Paul relates to the Corinthian believers across a number of years. In those two works scholars have found references to five—and text of at least three—letters Paul wrote to the believers at Corinth and one they wrote to him. When the letters or letter fragments are arranged in a sequence, they portray Paul's relations to the Corinthians as ranging from good times to times not so good. Though we know that Paul had enduring relations with other churches, such as the one at Philippi (Phil 1:5; 4:15-16), we have no such detailed evidence anywhere but with the Corinthians.

In the letters redacted into 2 Corinthians, personal relations, modest goals and purposes, and even what some might consider rather petty matters are the occasion for grand theological reflections. A near-fatal disaster elicits a rumination about the God of consolation and comfort (1:3-11). Paul's poor scheduling and failure to make a promised trip generate a profound reflection on the faithfulness of God (1:15-22). Paul's desire to recement relations with the Corinthians gives him the opportunity to reflect on his ministry to them in three original constructions, depicting himself as minister of the new covenant, as minister through affliction and comfort, and as minister of reconciliation (2:14–6:10). His commitment to the collection for the saints in Jerusalem generates powerful reflections on God's grace and the generosity it inspires (chaps. 8-9). Paul's strife with his opponents in chapters 10–13 provides striking ruminations regarding the Pauline paradox of (divine) strength in (human) weakness.

Discussions of Corinth as a city, its character, the history of Paul's establishing a church there, and the socioethnic makeup of that congregation are all detailed in the Introduction of the Commentary on 1 Corinthians.[1]

---

1. See J. Paul Sampley, "The First Letter to the Corinthians," in this volume.

LITERARY INTEGRITY OF 2 CORINTHIANS

The literary integrity of 2 Corinthians has proved a problem for scholars. Though most agree that the text is made up of more than one letter fragment,[2] much disagreement remains over the number, scope, and even sequence of the fragments. Absolutely no textual variations or manuscript evidence supports any of the partition theories. The lack of such evidence, however, does not necessarily argue against partition; it could simply be that the editing together of available fragments was done before the oldest extant manuscripts were written. Persons who want to pursue varying theses regarding the partition and sequencing of the segments of 2 Corinthians are invited to see the section of this Introduction entitled "Deliberations Concerning Fragmentation and Sequence Within 2 Corinthians."

Events and Circumstances Connecting the Fragments. Before he wrote what we now call 1 Corinthians, Paul had written the Corinthians what has come to be called the "previous" letter (1 Cor 5:9-11), his first to them (*Letter A,* lost). After some time he wrote his second letter to them—now labeled 1 Corinthians (*Letter B*)—in part because of apparent confusion regarding what he meant about holiness in the previous letter.

Sometime after Paul had written and sent 1 Corinthians, he went to Corinth, as 1 Cor 16:5-7 promised. During that visit, one of the Corinthian believers made a verbal attack on Paul, and, to his chagrin, no one came to his defense (2 Cor 2:3; see the Commentary on 2:3 for details of this interpretation). Mortified, Paul left. Although he had promised another visit to the Corinthians, he rethought it (1:23) and instead sent a letter of rather harsh frank speech (*Letter C,* lost; see "Frank Speech," below), calling them to task for the "one who did the wrong," chastizing them for their abandonment of him, and calling them back into "obedience" to him (2 Cor 7:8-16).

The frank speech letter achieved considerable success, as reported by Titus, though it is probably fair to say not quite as much as Paul had wished (2 Cor 6:11-13; 7:2-3*a*). The majority of the Corinthians embraced Paul and disciplined the man who had attacked him (2:6-11; 7:8-16).

When Paul found Titus in Macedonia and got the report on the results of the frank speech letter, he also learned that Titus had been very successful among the Macedonians in gathering the collection for the saints at Jerusalem. The Macedonians had embraced the collection with considerable zeal (8:1-5; 9:2), thinking themselves emulating the Corinthians and the other Achaians. Paul thus found that his earlier plans for the collection (gather it in Macedonia, sweep through Achaia, go to Jerusalem; 2 Cor 1:16) were well under way in Macedonia and that a group was ready to leave for Corinth. Paul was in a bind: The Corinthians, in their recent hithers and fros with Paul, had lost their zeal for the collection. One group, ready and eager (the Macedonians), was about to encounter another group, reticent and unprepared (the Corinthians).

In this context, Paul writes his fourth letter to the Corinthians (*Letter D,* 2 Corinthians 1–9). Several tasks confront him: (1) He must try to build beyond his recently stressed relations with the Corinthians; in particular, he must account for his dependability, even though he broke his promise about a scheduled visit, and he must account for his having resorted to a harsh letter instead of the projected visit. (2) He needs to recognize, and sign off as satisfied by, the Corinthian punishment of the one who did the wrong. (3) He must consolidate his fresh gains with the Corinthians to the point that (4) he can appeal to them for full participation in the collection for the Jerusalem saints. Paul tries to accomplish these goals (1) by accounting for his relatively recent decisions and whereabouts (2 Cor 1:8–2:13; 7:5-16); (2) by an extended initial, *indirect* appeal for a fuller Corinthian embrace of him and his ministry as refracted through a series of powerful, thoughtful lenses (2:14–6:10), followed by a brief, *direct* request for what he has just indirectly sought—namely, more affection—and (3) by moving to an open discussion of his plans for the collection and for their participation in it.

So the letter fragment 2 Corinthians 1–9 reflects complex motives and goals on Paul's part. He has personal incentives: He wants more affection from the Corinthians and thinks that, as the one who was their father in the faith (2 Cor 6:13), he deserves it; and he wants to avoid the

---

2. For the interpretation that 2 Corinthians is one letter, see B. Witherington III, *Conflict and Community in Corinth: A Socio-Rhetorical Commentary on 1 and 2 Corinthians* (Grand Rapids: Eerdmans, 1995).

embarrassment of having bragged about the Corinthians' enthusiasm regarding the collection (9:2), only to have the Macedonians discover, on their projected arrival in Corinth, apathy and perhaps even dissension. He has public motivations as well: The collection is the crown jewel of his ministry because, more than anything else, it demonstrates the unity of believers in the midst of their social and ethnic diversities, and his desire to bring the Corinthians into a more affectionate relationship is not simply self-serving but also accords with his conviction that the Corinthians' destiny depends on their close adherence to his gospel.

A fragment of Paul's fifth letter to the Corinthians is found in 2 Corinthians 10–13 (*Letter E*). Several developments, none of them positive, have muddied the waters for Paul and the Corinthians since his writing of 2 Corinthians 1–9. The letter-commended intruders, whose presence was only a minor matter in 2 Cor 3:1-3, have become a major force because they aligned with some currents of resentment that have been building in Corinth for some time.

The exact dynamics between the outsiders and the Corinthians escape us, but they cannot be ignored because the lines of initiative could have come from disaffected believers or from the rival intruders—but more likely from some combination of the two. Whichever the source, some Corinthians have come to believe that Paul's fiduciary relations are problematic. First, by his refusal to receive support, he has openly shamed some Corinthian believers who bid to become his patrons (12:13). Among this group may be some who had long-standing resentment over his rebuke of their having taken poorer believers to court (1 Cor 6:1-8) and of their having been insensitive to the poor believers who came to the Lord's supper in their houses (1 Cor 11:21-22, 33-34). Second, some Corinthians think he is two-faced, preaching a gospel "free of cost" (1 Cor 9:18) and then drumming up a collection. Third, some Corinthians note Paul's inconsistencies in refusing to accept support from them while receiving help from the Macedonians and raise questions of his probity and motives.[3] Fourth, some Corinthians believe that Paul's insistence on working with his hands is inconsistent with his status as apostle—and they see in the rival intruders the pattern they wish was Paul's. Finally, Paul's letter of frank speech (*Letter C,* the third, lost one) probably also exacerbated some old irritations to which he likely added another when, in his next letter (*Letter D,* 2 Corinthians 1–9), he used frankness as a means of asking for more affection, a culturally problematic use of frank speech (see the Commentary on 2 Cor 6:13).

The ultimate blow comes when (some of) the Corinthians, sensitive about the differences between Paul and his rival intruders, want to "test" Paul, apparently with regard to his apostleship (2 Cor 13:3, 5-10). Paul can no longer avoid confrontation. He projects a third visit, a showdown encounter in which he and they can sort out their differences and he can reassert his authority. The letter fragment 2 Corinthians 10–13 (*Letter E*) announces this visit, warns the Corinthians of the stakes involved, and, by heavy use of irony and under the guise of the fool's weakness, rehearses some of his disputed credentials.

Deliberations Concerning Fragmentation and Sequence Within 2 Corinthians. Possible Fragments Within 2 Corinthians 1–9. With regard to the literary unity of 2 Corinthians 1–9, interpreters have varied widely. Some hold that these chapters all belong to the same letter fragment, but different scholars have posited within those same chapters at least four distinct letter fragments, as listed below.[4]

2 Corinthians 2:14–7:4 Within 2 Corinthians 1–7. Although least convincing on its face, 2 Cor 2:14–7:4 is sometimes argued as a separate letter fragment by scholars who are struck by what they perceive as the lack of a link back to 2:13 and the preceding verses and forward to 7:5-16.[5] The supposed fragment 2:14–7:4 has been placed, on one construction, within a travel narrative, sometimes identified as yet another fragment—beginning in 1:8 (cf. 1:15-17), running through 2:12-13, and finding its completion in 7:5-16—whose travel plans have no

---

3. Though it may have looked to the Corinthians as if the Macedonian support of Paul was patronage, Paul's understanding of it seems quite different. See Sampley, *Pauline Partnership in Christ: Christian Community and Commitment in Light of Roman Law* (Philadelphia: Fortress, 1980) 55-77.

4. D. Georgi, *The Opponents of Paul in Second Corinthians* (Philadelphia: Fortress, 1986) 16-18, holds for five fragments. See M. E. Thrall, *The Second Epistle to the Corinthians* (Edinburgh: T. & T. Clark, 1994) 1:47-49, for a chart of various theories.

5. For the issues and an argument for the continuity of 2 Cor 2:12-13 to the section that opens with 2:14, see A. C. Perriman, "Between Troas and Macedonia: 2 Cor 2:13-14," *ExpTim* 101 (1989) 39-41. D. A. DeSilva, "Measuring Penultimate Against Ultimate Reality: An Investigation of the Integrity and Argumentation of 2 Corinthians," *JSNT* 52 (1993) 57, argues that the "latter section [2:14–7:3] develops themes which are introduced in the former [1:1–2:13]."

clear connection, as these advocates see it, with what they consider the more theological reflections in 2:14–7:4. An alternative construction, but presuming the same intrusion of 2:14–7:4 into chapters 1–7, takes the framing material in 1:1–2:13 and 7:5-16 as a distinct "letter of reconciliation."[6]

2 Corinthians 6:14–7:1. Scholars are divided over whether 6:14–7:1 is a separate Pauline letter fragment that a later redactor has inserted into Paul's appeal for more affection, dividing the latter into two sections (6:11-13; 7:2-4).[7] Further, some declare that these verses are not even authentically Pauline.[8]

2 Corinthians 8 and 2 Corinthians 9. Chapters 8 and 9 both deal with Paul's collection for the saints in Jerusalem, but the opening words of 9:1 (περὶ μὲν γάρ *peri men gar,* "So concerning"; hidden in the NRSV and NIV translations) can be argued to introduce a new item and thereby to suggest that the two chapters once stood alone;[9] 9:2 features the Achaians as models for the Macedonians, while 8:1-5 runs the modeling in the opposite direction, and the accompanying "brothers" in 8:18-20 are a safeguard against accusations against Paul, whereas in 9:3-5 they are supposed to get the donation together before Paul arrives.[10]

2 Corinthians 10–13. Most scholars who admit to any fragmentation recognize that 2 Corinthians 10–13 is a literary unit distinct from what precedes it. If nothing else, its tone is so different, signaling a time of mutual distress between Paul and the Corinthians. Whether this letter fragment should be considered to have originated earlier or later than any other possible fragment is another matter and will receive its treatment below.

Sequence of the Letter Fragments. To compound matters, scholars who hold for the same partition theories do not always agree on the historical sequence of the fragments. Most of the permutations have their advocates. Chapter 9 was written before chapter 8;[11] chapter 8 preceded chapter 9.[12] Chapters 10–13 were written before chapters 1–9 or parts thereof;[13] and chapters 10–13 were written last.[14]

Possible Missing Letter. All of these reckonings are further complicated by Paul's unequivocal declarations (2 Cor 2:9; 7:8-12) that he has earlier written to the Corinthians a letter that has come subsequently to be denominated by scholars as "painful" (so described because of its effect on the Corinthians, 7:8-11) or "tearful" (so named because of Paul's description of his demeanor in writing it, 2:4).

The question naturally arises as to whether any of the letter fragments that reputedly make up 2 Corinthians are part of that painful letter. The most obvious candidate is chapters 10–13 because it is the type of letter—indeed, the only extant candidate—that could aggrieve or bring pain to the recipients (7:8).[15] However, chapters 10–13 fail to qualify as the painful letter on every other count; most important, they make no mention of the one who "did the wrong" (2:3-11; 7:8-12); even though Paul sent the painful letter in place of a visit that he spares them (2 Cor 1:23–2:1), chapters 10–13 allude to no failed visit, but rather invite preparation for an impending visit. Finally, Paul's exuberant description of the Corinthians' change of heart (7:11) does not fit the problem of intruding rivals that pervades chapters 10–13. So we must conclude that the painful letter, though surely written before 2 Corinthians 1–9, is lost in its entirety. Because no fragments of it survive, its content can only be deduced from Paul's description of it in chapters 2 and 7.[16]

---

6. G. Bornkamm, "Die Vorgeschichte des sogennanten Zweiten Korintherbriefes," in *Gesammelte Aufsätze* IV, *BEvT* (München: Evangelischer) 53, 179-90, 192-94.

7. See J. C. Hurd, Jr., *The Origin of I Corinthians* (London: SPCK, 1965) 235-39.

8. See J. Fitzmyer, *Essays on the Semitic Background of the NT,* SBLSBS 5 (Missoula, Mont.: Scholars Press, 1974) 217.

9. So H. D. Betz, *2 Corinthians 8 and 9* (Philadelphia: Fortress, 1985) 90-91; countered decisively by S. K. Stowers, *"Peri men gar* and the Integrity of 2 Corinthians 8 and 9," *NovT* 32 (1990) 340-48.

10. For detailed examination of these and other arguments and their limitations, see V. P. Furnish, *II Corinthians,* AB 33 (Garden City, N.Y.: Doubleday, 1984) 429-33.

11. R. K. Bultmann, *The Second Letter to the Corinthians,* trans. R. A. Harrisville (Minneapolis: Augsburg, 1985) 18.

12. H. Windisch, *Der zweite Korintherbrief* (Göttingen: Vandenhoeck & Ruprecht, 1924) 287.

13. F. Watson, "2 Cor X-XIII and Paul's Painful Letter to the Corinthians," *JTS* (1984) 346.

14. Furnish, *II Corinthians,* 38, 44-46.

15. So Watson, "2 Cor X-XIII and Paul's Painful Letter to the Corinthians," 345-46, and L. L. Welborn, "The Identification of 2 Corinthians 10–13 with the 'Letter of Tears,'" *NovT* 37 (1995) 153.

16. Furnish, *II Corinthians,* 37-38.

The Definition and Sequence of Fragments. This commentary assumes that 2 Corinthians 1–9 is the fragment of one letter, that 2 Corinthians 10–13 is a section of another, and that the sequence in which we find the fragments reflects their actual historical order. The change in tone and in the relation of Paul to the Corinthians in chapters 10–13 indicates that it is a distinct fragment and not a continuation of chapters 1–9. The reasons for adopting this sequence as historical will become clear in the detailed arguments.

The case for further fragmentation of 2 Corinthians 1–9 is not compelling. The purported break between 2 Cor 2:13 and 2:14 is an interpretive failure to see Paul's own connection between details of his travel plans—in particular his having decided not to come when he promised—and 2:14ff., where Paul depicts himself as a prisoner whom God leads around as *God,* not Paul, wills. Scholars' resistance to see 2 Corinthians 8–9 as a continuation of 2 Corinthians 1–7 rests in their failure to comprehend that Paul dare not make explicit mention of the collection, a matter for which they have lost their earlier zeal, until he has recemented his relations with the Corinthians, precisely the initial burden of his efforts in 2 Cor 2:14–7:16. The Commentary will show how well Paul has laid the groundwork in 2:1–7:16 for his treatment of the collection in 2 Corinthians 8–9. As will also be evident in the Commentary, Paul's rhetorical purposes in 2 Corinthians 8–9 tie the two chapters together as a literary unit that caps off 2 Corinthians 1–9 as a single letter.

Methodological Caution. Although all five letters to the Corinthians were written by the same apostle to the same general group of believers in the same city, each letter has a singularly distinctive dynamic that must be honored and not read into or affected by the interpretation of any of the others. For that reason we must exercise great care not to import a conflict or problem from a later letter into an earlier one. The primary clues for determining the relation to Paul in any given letter or fragment must be generated from the document in question.

Taking the Temperature of Paul's Relations with the Corinthians in the Different Letters. The "previous" letter (*Letter A,* lost) leaves us in the dark except for the references to it in 1 Cor 5:9-10. The Corinthians have asked Paul for clarification about holiness and living in the world—a clear indication that they were interested to understand and follow his counsel.

First Corinthians (*Letter B*) manifests the Corinthians in good relations with Paul; they ask his counsel on a series of issues, and he openly seeks to guide and lead them even though their fractiousness with each other shows him that they are nearer being babies in the faith than adults—and are overly engaged in status seeking. Although the Corinthians are in disharmony with one another, they are in good relations with Paul, and no problems or persons impinge from outside the community of believers.

The painful letter (*Letter C,* lost), by the descriptions of it and references to it in 2 Corinthians 1–9, reveals that relations between Paul and the Corinthians have hit some problems. His response in that letter is to call the Corinthians to task; Titus's report reassures Paul that the letter has brought the Corinthians into fidelity to Paul again (2 Cor 7:6-16).

Second Corinthians 1–9 (*Letter D*) tries to build on the success of the painful letter and shows Paul striving to elaborate and to enhance his own ministry for and with them in ways that invite and increase Corinthian allegiance—with the ultimage goal of encouraging and assuring their full participation in the collection for the saints in Jerusalem. Outsiders are noted (2 Cor 3:1-3) but are not considered the threat that they will become by chapters 10–13; Paul's epistolary efforts are focused on the Corinthians and their relationship to him, and not on any intruders.

A ground shift of considerable proportions must be supposed as a context for 2 Corinthians 10–13 (*Letter E*). Paul and the Corinthians have never been in more contentious relations; some of them want to put Paul to the test regarding his apostolic standing and, therefore, authority. The intruders have been established among (at least some of) the Corinthians as rival authorities. Of course, Paul detracts from his rivals, but his attention is focused on the Corinthians and on a final effort to bring them into allegiance. The letter does two things: It addresses some of the differences from the rivals that Paul wants to claim as distinctive for himself, and it lays the groundwork for a personal visit in which the matters may be resolved.

The following table graphs Paul's relations with the Corinthians. The left vertical is a graduated scale depicting the quality of their relationship, ranging from excellent down to poor. Across the bottom is a time line depicting Paul and the Corinthians at the moment of each letter or letter fragment.

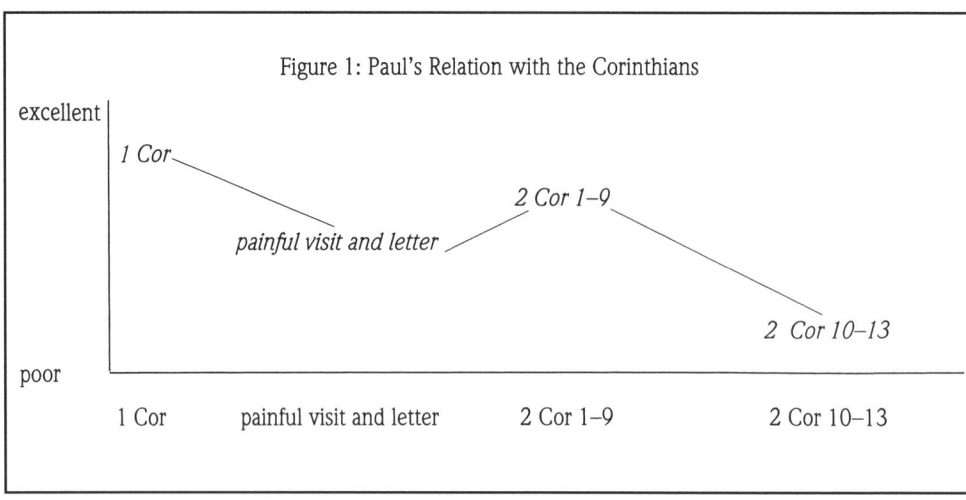

Figure 1: Paul's Relation with the Corinthians

While honoring the methodological caution about keeping Paul's letters and letter fragments from affecting the interpretation of each other, we can observe certain continuities in the Corinthian community of believers. The same socioethnic makeup prevails from letter to letter fragment: A few rich people are part of the community, but most members are not wealthy (1 Cor 1:26); the affluent made a clear impact in taking cobelievers to court (1 Cor 6:1-8) and at the Lord's supper (1 Cor 11:17-34); in 2 Corinthians the wealthy seek to become Paul's patrons, but he refuses them (11:7-10, 20-21; 12:13); and most of the believers are Gentiles (1 Cor 8:1, 7; 12:2). Throughout the Corinthian correspondence, believers have been susceptible to status grasping, envy, fractiousness, and the lure of wisdom and fine speech (1 Cor 1:18-25; 2 Cor 10:10; 11:6).

DATES OF COMPOSITION OF THE LETTERS

The dates of the letters can only be estimated in general terms. The reckoning of dates must be interlaced with Paul's projected and actual visits. Starting from what we can know, Paul wrote 1 Corinthians from Ephesus (1 Cor 16:8) in the fall or winter (53 or 54 CE) and expected to stay there until Pentecost (spring). He promises a visit to Corinth, perhaps to stay for the winter, after he makes the land journey through Macedonia (1 Cor 16:5-6).

When he wrote 2 Corinthians 1–9 from Macedonia, he had only recently made the long-projected visit to Macedonia—but then only because he was desperate to find Titus and to know the Corinthian response to his letter of frank speech (lost to us). Timothy, as the co-author of the current letter fragment (2 Cor 1:1), has returned from Corinth (1 Cor 16:10-11) and accompanied Paul from Asia, where Paul (and Timothy, perhaps, since the plural is used) has recently been spared a threat to his life (2 Cor 1:8-11).

Between the writing of 1 Corinthians and 2 Corinthians 1–9, Paul has made a visit to Corinth that turned bad (with the one who "did the wrong," 2 Cor 2:1-3; 7:12), and, instead of the promised subsequent visit, he wrote them the (lost) letter of harsh frank speech (2 Cor 2:1-4; 7:8-16). What length of time transpired between the writing of 1 Corinthians, which can be dated to the fall or winter of 53 (or at the latest the same period in 54; see the Commentary on 1 Corinthians), and the composition of 2 Corinthians 1–9? We have a clue in Paul's description of the collection for the saints in Jerusalem. Twice he mentions that the Corinthians had begun the collection "a year ago" or "since last year" (πέρυσι *perysi*, 2 Cor 8:10; 9:2). First Corinthians 16:1-4 seems to have been a Pauline response to a Corinthian inquiry regarding the logistics of the collection, so we can presume that in fall 53 or fall 54 they were committed to the collection but not certain how they might best prepare. On this ground, it is possible to project that 2 Corinthians 1–9 was written by the fall of 54 CE (or fall of 55, allowing a year from the range of dates for 1 Corinthians). In the year that passed between the writing of 1 Corinthians and 2 Corinthians 1–9, Paul had time to make the unexpected, fateful return by sea to Corinth (spring or summer), to return to the Roman province of Asia (probably Ephesus), and to write and have Titus deliver his frank speech letter instead of a promised further visit.

Second Corinthians 10–13 requires sufficient time after chapters 1–9 for the following to have occurred: First, the logistics of the collection dictate a certain time lag. As Paul lays it out in 2 Cor 8:16-24, he sends ahead Titus and the two brothers, with the apparent expectation that they will oversee the Corinthians' preparedness before Paul's and some Macedonians' arrival (9:5). Paul's projected visit must have taken on different proportions when he heard for the first time the extent to which the intruders had captured the fancy of at least some of the Corinthians, subverting Paul's authority. The two-stage visit to Achaia would have required some time (during which Paul discovers the seriousness of the threat represented by the intruding rivals). Finally, the itinerary supposes that the sea passages must be opened after the winter and early spring for the projected trip to Judea.

Second, we do not know who informed Paul that matters in Corinth were much worse than he had suspected, but candidates aplenty suggest themselves: Titus, the two selected brothers (8:18, 22), and any of the Macedonians who may have accompanied them with the collection. Each of these people could be expected to be devoted to Paul and sensitively ready to report remonstrations against him. In any case, the writing of 2 Corinthians 10–13—one of whose major burdens is to announce and prepare for Paul's imminent showdown visit to Corinth—need not be more than a few months after the composition of 2 Corinthians 1:1–9. Accordingly, we can posit that 2 Corinthians 10–13 was also written from Macedonia, probably in the spring or early summer of 55 (or of 56, allowing for the same time range noted for 1 Corinthians).

PAUL'S OPPONENTS AT CORINTH

The identification of Paul's opponents has become a growth industry, often with more conjecture and speculation than certainty or substance emerging.[17] Truth be told, we know very little about Paul's opponents in 2 Corinthians. The Corinthians knew their identity; at some point Paul knew enough about them to be or become concerned about them, so he had no need to rehearse it for us as interlopers. Second, we must acknowledge that our primary source for knowing anything about the opponents is Paul, who is biased against them and who has no interest in being fair or what we might call objective in his representations of them. In any search for clues regarding the opponents' identity, we must expect that Paul depicts them in an unfavorable light—that was how opponents were treated in those days[18]—but we can suppose that he did not totally misrepresent them, if not because of his moral values, surely for fear that the Corinthians would dismiss him and all his argumentation if he were too out of line with reality. Exaggeration and distortion cannot be ruled out, however, because Paul's purpose is to overthrow them, to prevail—and to do that he must establish himself as the *sole* legitimate apostle for the Corinthians.

---

17. See J. L. Sumney's laudable methodological caution and circumspection in *Identifying Paul's Opponents: The Question of Method in 2 Corinthians*, JSNTSup 40 (Sheffield: Sheffield Academic, 1990) 15-67. He categorizes the traditional options for identifying Paul's opponents: Judaizers (led by Baur, followed by Barrett, Gunther, Lüdemann), Gnostics (Schmithals), divine men (Georgi and Friedrich), and pneumatics (Käsemann).

18. See J. Paul Sampley, "Paul, His Opponents in 2 Corinthians 10–13, and the Rhetorical Handbooks," in *The Social World of Formative Christianity and Judaism*, ed. J. Neusner, P. Borgen, E. S. Frerichs, R. Horsley (Philadelphia: Fortress, 1988) esp. 165-67.

Third, and along the same line, Paul's knowledge about his opponents is always secondhand (only in 2 Cor 2:5 do we see Paul knowing firsthand a Corinthian opponent). His agents or his other supporters, themselves persons biased in favor of Paul, are the sources of what he knows about the opponents. That means that any knowledge we today have of Paul's opponents in Corinth is thirdhand. Fourth, mirror reading—that is, taking items in the text and assuming that in them Paul is responding to some criticism or to some claim of the opponents—has been overused in the study of Paul's letters.[19] Not every denial or distinction of him can be read as reflecting a charge.[20] Neither is every Pauline theological affirmation a response to something his opponents have said.

Finally, Paul's (indeed, the culture's) predisposition for indirect or figured speech has been underestimated. In such rhetoric one does not take issues head-on but chooses an alternate, less-heated matter, issue, or topic and, by treating it, leaves the hearers to make the application to the question at hand.[21] Paul's original hearers would bring enough information to the hearing of his letters so that they could readily distinguish what we can only surmise—namely, when Paul is speaking directly and when indirectly.

Two Stages of Opposition. For the purpose of identifying Paul's opposition, this commentary distinguishes between two distinct stages of Paul's struggle with the Corinthians as reflected in 2 Corinthians. The two stages correspond to the two letter fragments. The reckoning about Paul's opponents must be different regarding each letter fragment, because Paul's relation to the Corinthians is distinct at the two different times of writing.

When he wrote 2 Corinthians 1–9, intruders were of little consequence. They had come to Corinth with their letters of commendation (3:1-3), but Paul does not treat them as a major problem. Paul is not unaccustomed to having other believers pass through his work sites (Gal 2:4, 11-12; cf. 1 Cor 9:5), so at first the appearance of these people might not have caused him great concern. At that point he has his own special issues with the Corinthians and has just recently heard that his letter of harsh frank speech (*Letter C*) has effected a rapprochement of the Corinthians to him. The lofty theological constructions that he struts before them in 2:14–6:10 are not a reflection of anything his opponents have said, but simply his own creative self-portrayal of his ministry as seen in three grand perspectives.

The exigence of 2 Corinthians 10–13 is starkly different. Now the outsiders, who were merely noted in 3:1-3, have become rivals who have bid with some success for Corinthian allegiance at the expense of Paul's status and authority. So here the central struggle is one of rivalry, of contested authority between Paul and his opponents—and, therefore, of fractured Corinthian allegiance. Much of past scholarship on Paul's Corinthian opponents has assumed, arguably anachronistically, that the central issues between Paul and his opponents were doctrinal—that is, disputes over theological ideas. In Paul's differences with the Corinthians, not ideas but practices, comportment, and standing are in contention.[22] Paul's theological assertions are not at dispute; Paul's authority is.[23] Paul's theological claims are adduced by him as a way of authenticating his authority.

Paul's standing and competence are at issue across all of 2 Corinthians; this fact has led interpreters to bleed what they see and know most clearly from 2 Corinthians 10–13, a distinct and subsequent letter (see elsewhere in the Introduction), back onto 2 Corinthians 1–9. If we resist that simplification and importation, we can distinguish between the way Paul's standing and competence are treated in the two letter fragments.

When the focus is restricted to 2 Corinthians 1–9, then the questions of Paul's adequacy as an apostle, as *their* apostle, are best understood as a Pauline advocacy of himself as the very

19. So G. Lyons, *Pauline Autobiography: Toward a New Understanding* (Atlanta, Scholars Press, 1985).

20. Cf. A. J. Malherbe's compelling interpretation of 1 Thess 2:1-12 not as a denial of a charge against Paul but as Paul's distinguishing of himself from itinerant sages, in "Gentle as a Nurse," *NovT* 12 (1970) 216-17.

21. See Demetrius *On Style* 5.294-296. For a fuller discussion of indirect speech and its canons, see J. Paul Sampley, "The Weak and the Strong: Paul's Careful and Crafty Rhetorical Strategy in Romans 14:1–15:13," in *The Social World of the First Christians: Studies in Honor of Wayne A. Meeks*, ed. L. M. White and O. L. Yarbrough (Minneapolis: Fortress, 1994) 43-46.

22. Theirs was not an "intellectual confrontation." See A. J. Malherbe, "Antisthenes and Odysseus, and Paul at War," *HTR* (1983) 143-73, esp. 168, 172.

23. So C. J. A. Hickling, "Is the Second Epistle to the Corinthians a Source for Early Church History?" *ZNW* 66 (1975) 287, argued powerfully a quarter-century ago.

apostle who brought the gospel to them and who deserves their full adherence by dint of his work with and among them. Paul thus champions himself and his cause as the apostle, as their apostle, whom they should embrace more fully. Paul's rich self-portraits as minister of the new covenant (3:1–4:6), as minister sustained through affliction and mortality (4:7–5:10), and as minister of reconciliation (5:11-21) overlap and reinforce one another, identifying Paul as their apostle who is worthy of their full devotion. Why is Paul led to such a self-promotion? There are two prominent reasons, one directed toward the immediate past, the other targeted toward the immediate future. As to the past, Paul must overcome any residual reticence among the Corinthians not only because of his failure to visit them as he had promised, but also because he had upbraided them harshly with a letter of frank speech (*Letter C*). As to the future, he has to prepare the Corinthians for the Macedonians' imminent and enthusiastic arrival with the collection for the Jerusalem saints when he has learned that the Corinthians have lost their zeal for it. His success with healing the past wounds and with avoiding embarrassment regarding the collection both demand that his ethos, his character and his standing with the Corinthians, be strong—the ultimate goal of 2:14–6:10, the central portion of 2 Corinthians 1–9. Only when his ethos has been sufficiently refurbished can and does he turn explicitly to the touchy question of the collection (2 Corinthians 8–9).

In 2 Corinthians 10–13, Paul's adequacy and standing as an apostle are certainly directly under question and attack. Paul's response is different also—even though some self-commendation continues to be present. Here, in his defense, he is drawn onto the grounds of the opposition: He boasts and references visions and revelations, signs and wonders, but only as a fool. Then he rejects visions and revelations as a basis of authority and puts in their place the standard of day-in-day-out performance—that is, what he has done among them across the years (12:6). Whereas in chapters 1–9 Paul's ethos was burnished by three grand theological ruminations about ministry and how Paul enacted each of them, in chapters 10–13 we see Paul, God's warrior, ironically embracing weakness as his shield and engaging, in turn, in accusation, reproach, apology, and appeal. Finally, in chapters 10–13 we see him declare guidelines for how he and the Corinthians will resolve their differences when he arrives in Corinth.

In order to reconstruct what we can know about Paul's opponents at Corinth, we start from the text, the only evidence we really have, and distinguish three categories: more certain evidence; less certain, but plausible, evidence; and possible evidence.[24] Identification of certain clues regarding the opponents is the more difficult because it is not always easy to tell when Paul is speaking directly and when he is using indirect speech (see the Introduction to 1 Corinthians) as an oblique way of relating to or describing his opponents.

More Certain Indices of Opponents. Nothing is clearer than this: By the time of 2 Corinthians 10–13, the intruders have become Paul's rivals for the leadership of the Corinthian believers. In significant ways they claim to be like Paul, but it is equally important that they distinguish themselves from him. *They* have made the comparison, and Paul finds it odious (10:12); he wants to remove any pretext they have for claiming that they are "just like us" (11:12). But they also move beyond parity, alleging to be superior to Paul (see Paul's mocking designation of them as "super apostles," 11:5; 12:11). This is at the heart of the rivalry.

Inherent in their comparative assessment of Paul is a critique of him at several points. It is impossible to tell just how much or how many of the following points the outsiders generated or how many they simply seized upon and focused sentiments already present among the Corinthians. Either way, however, the Corinthian soil was ready for the planting and harvest.

Paul's bearing and performance are not up to par for a person in such a position of authority, they claim (and appear to have convinced at least some Corinthians). Paul has provided them abundant evidence across the years; the Corinthians will remember that Paul did not come among them with "lofty words of wisdom" but simply preached the cross (1 Cor 2:1-2); that he likened himself, in an ironically self-deprecating way, to leftover dishwater (1 Cor 4:13); that his speech amounts to nothing (2 Cor 10:10); that he has a proclivity to find himself in humble,

24. Sumney, *Identifying Paul's Opponents*, 118, distinguishes "five levels of *certainty of reference*," beginning with "explicit statements" and moving through two levels of "proposed allusions."

if not humiliating, circumstances (1 Cor 4:11-12; cf. 2 Cor 4:7-12; 6:1-10; 11:21b-29); that he made no credible defense when he was with them and that one of their own attacked him (2 Cor 2:1-11); and that he has steadfastly eschewed the perquisites appropriate to his status, insisting instead on supporting himself via demeaning hand work (1 Cor 4:12a; 9:4-14). Further, 2 Cor 10:10 suggests that Paul's opponents have derisively labeled him "weak" in bodily presence.

The intruders, on the other hand, at least by Paul's implications, share the status of being "apostles" in some sense (2 Cor 11:5, 13-15; 12:11), though they, in contrast to Paul, seem ready to relish the entitlements of status and honor (11:20; cf. 11:7-12; 12:17). Accordingly, they do not work to support themselves (11:20; cf., perhaps obliquely, 11:7-12; 12:13-16). Clearly the wealthier Corinthians who were eager to patronize Paul would have found ready recipients in his rivals.

Paul counters on several fronts. With regard to himself, his opening insistence is key: "Look at what is before your eyes" (2 Cor 10:7; 12:6b). The Corinthians' long (and mostly) good history with him should reassure them that he is dependable and faithful. He has never accepted support from them, so why should he start now? On the contrary, he has always worked for their benefit, never his own (12:19; 13:7-9). Absent or present, he has continually been the same Paul (10:11). He brought the gospel all the way to them (10:13-15), and he has stuck by them through thick and thin. Further, he embraces the charge of his weakness as a badge of ironic honor and portrays his weakness over and over as a positive sign of God's abundant power working through him for the gospel and *for them* (2 Cor 11:6a, 23–12:10).

Paul understands that God designated him to take the gospel to the Corinthians, that they are, therefore, part of his divinely appointed "sphere of influence/province" (κανών *kanōn*; see the Commentary on 10:13-16) and that he has paternal responsibilities with the Corinthians because God has given him responsibility for recruiting believers in that area. Others, such as Apollos, may be of assistance to him (1 Cor 3:5-9), but the Corinthians can have only one father (2 Cor 11:2; cf. 1 Cor 4:15). Paul's 2 Corinthians intruders have moved beyond being helpful; they bid to supplant Paul and have wrongly moved into Paul's *kanōn*.

More important, Paul does not directly counsel the Corinthians about what they should do toward the rivals (unless 2 Cor 6:14–7:1 is regarded as authentic and the "unfaithful" in 6:14-16 are dubiously deemed the opponents). Rather, his attention is focused on a call for the Corinthians to reassess their own standing in the faith, to return to their roots in his preaching and to his leadership, and to accord one another the proper attention that love demands.

Less Certain, but Plausible, Indices of Opponents. It is less sure that the opponents are Jewish, though Paul's question, "Are they Hebrews?" and his detailing of his high-caliber Jewish credentials surely point in that direction. Curiously, however, no problems between Paul and the Corinthians are traceable to Jewish issues such as one can see, by contrast, in Galatians, with its concern for circumcision and the place of the law. The two-covenant discussion in 2 Cor 3:1–4:6, which some scholars credit, at least in some measure, to Paul's opponents,[25] is hardly part of a dispute; rather, it is Paul's creative elaboration and enhancement—in a typical Pauline "not this, but that" form—of his own ministry as an appeal for increased Corinthian fidelity.[26] If Paul's adversaries are Jews, allowing for that reading of 11:22, then one can equally argue that Paul credits them with being "ministers of Christ" (διάκονοι Χριστοῦ *diakonoi Christou*, 11:23), though Paul is quick to claim superiority for himself.

We cannot be exactly certain what is behind the letters of recommendation mentioned in 2 Cor 3:1, though the practice is a commonplace in the Greco-Roman world, and it is plausible that the outsiders came to Corinth armed with supporting documents that credited them with a measure of ready-made authority (see 2 Cor 2:17). Whether those letters came from some of the original apostles and/or from some in leadership positions in Jerusalem we simply cannot

25. The most extreme example is D. Georgi, *Paul's Opponents in 2 Corinthians* (Philadelphia: Fortress, 1986) 229-83; cf. J. J. Gunther, *St. Paul's Opponents and Their Background*, NovTSup 35 (1973) 276.

26. Hickling, "Is the Second Epistle to the Corinthians a Source for Early Church History?" 286. L. L. Belleville, "Tradition or Creation? Paul's Use of the Exodus 34 Tradition in 2 Corinthians 3:7-18," in *Paul and the Scriptures of Israel*, ed. C. A. Evans and J. A. Sanders (Sheffield: JSOT, 1993) 185, shows that Paul's creativity comes not in his use of Exodus 34 and his portrait of Moses' fading glory, but in tying the fading glory to the "waning of the covenant."

know.[27] It is attractive to make such connections because the drama is enhanced and we can drift into the timeworn Peter-versus-Paul conundrum—for which there is no other evidence in 2 Corinthians.

Paul resorts to telling about his heavenly transit (12:2-5) as if forced. Did his rivals (or even worse for Paul, some of the Corinthians) credit visions and revelations as an indicator of status and authority? We know that the Corinthians have a long-standing attraction for silver-tongued speech (1 Cor 2:1), but Paul values "knowledge" over "speech" (2 Cor 11:6) as an assessment of apostolic credentials. Curiously, after telling of his extraordinary transport to paradise (12:2-5), Paul effectively rejects visions as an apostolic index, preferring instead what one sees and hears in him (2 Cor 12:6, an echoing refinement of 10:7a). Whether it was the intruders or the Corinthians,[28] visions and revelations bid to play too great a role in estimating status, for Paul's values.

Unclear Indices of Opponents. What are we to make of the reference in 11:4 to "another Jesus," "another spirit," and "another gospel"? Or should that be translated "another Spirit," indicating the Holy Spirit, as the expression could equally well be read? Have the outsiders offered these alternatives, or is this a dramatic rhetorical move on Paul's part? Nowhere in 2 Corinthians is there evidence of a dispute over Jesus or the Spirit (or spirit, for that matter). The Spirit is associated with the second covenant and with Paul's ministry (2 Cor 3:8, 17), as we would fully expect, because Paul sees the Spirit and its reception as the hallmark of the life of faith (see 1 Cor 12:13; Gal 3:2). But Paul does not treat his claims about the Spirit as if they are being defended or advocated over against competing claims about the Spirit.

Paul is given to stark antitheses, especially when he wants to distance an alternative from himself. Paul knows there is only one gospel (Gal 1:7a), but that gospel can be perverted (Gal 1:7b). Paul apparently has a commonplace saying to the effect that anyone who preaches a gospel different from his own is anathema (Gal 1:9: "As I said before, so now again I say"), and he may have recycled that saying here—with elaboration—as a way of setting himself antithetically over against his rivals. In his categories, Paul's rivals represent another gospel if they differ from him—whether the differences are in ideas or in practices. Finally, the Jesus whom Paul proclaims is "Christ Jesus as Lord, with ourselves as your slaves for Jesus' sake" (2 Cor 4:5). Paul's humble, weak demeanor is grounded in the Jesus he preaches, the Jesus who is Lord. So his comportment is, as always, fundamentally christologically based (e.g., 1 Cor 11:1).

Two passages in 2 Corinthians 1–9 have been mirror-read as references to Paul's opponents. Paul's disclaimer that "we are not, like many, hucksters of God's word" in 2:17 may be a reference to opponents. If it is, then we learn nothing in particular about them. Paul's differentiation may, however, be considered a patterned reference to others who preach the gospel out of different (and less noble) motives (see Phil 1:15-18). Interpreters have similarly read 4:2 to mirror Paul's opponents, but it may just as well be Paul's *via negativa* magnification of his own ethos and exemplary comportment (cf. 2:17). Without reinforcement from 2 Corinthians 10–13, a document from a later time and with different dynamics, the two references in 2:17 and 4:2 do not give any certain picture of opponents; accordingly, in the commentary they are not treated as clear indices of opponents.

In sum, we can be sure that Paul's opponents include some intruders who have appeared in Corinth with letters of commendation from some unidentifiable, but putatively powerful, persons. Although the intruders have arrived in Corinth by the time of Paul's writing 2 Corinthians 1–9, their impact is not certain to be major until the time of his composition of chapters 10–13. By then, the intruders have surely found a hearing among some (but we cannot be certain how many) Corinthians and been accorded status and authority by them. When favorable to them, these outsiders claim to be like Paul; but in certain key matters they distinguish themselves from him: They do not act below their station; they do not stoop to menial labor to support themselves; they readily count on patronage from others as part of their apostolic perquisites.

---

27. So also Sumney, *Identifying Paul's Opponents*, 177.
28. C. K. Barrett, "Paul's Opponents in II Corinthians," *NTS* 17 (1971) 244-45, holds it is the latter.

Pauline opposition *among the Corinthians* may no longer be ignored, and the commentary will be assiduous in detailing the sources of Corinthian discontent signaled in the text of 2 Corinthians. At issue between Paul and his opponents (intruders and allied Corinthians alike) is Paul's status and authority with the Corinthians. All else in the contention takes its place around that central pillar. Whether the intruders are also Jews is plausible but is not necessary to determine for the interpretation of any part of 2 Corinthians.

Whatever else one may discern about Paul's opponents, it is clear that he wrote 2 Corinthians 10–13 with the major purpose of setting up the terms and conditions under which he expected to make an imminent, showdown visit to Corinth. He puts the Corinthians, supporters and opponents together, on notice that he expects to bring about Corinthian obedience. In doing so, he must be able to assume that the intruders will have been served a warning as well. In 2 Corinthians, Paul has no direct engagement or contention with his intruding rivals. Like silent third parties as Paul relates to the Corinthians, his rivals are an important part of what amounts to a triangle. And Paul's attention is devoted to regaining the affection and allegiance of the Corinthians; nowhere in 2 Corinthians does he engage the outsiders directly.

For a reasoned estimate of Paul's success or failure in the encounter that 2 Corinthians 10–13 signals, see the Overview to chapters 10–13 in the Commentary.

PAUL'S USE OF "WE" IN 2 CORINTHIANS

Paul employs the plural in self-reference more in 2 Corinthians than in any other letter. Before detailing Paul's goals in doing so, we must note that 2 Cor 1:1 does credit Timothy with co-authorship, so the plural may refer to Timothy as well. Other letters are jointly authored (Gal 1:2; Phil 1:1; 1 Thess 1:1; Phlm 1), however, without such heavy use of plural self-references. So the proliferation of the plural in 2 Corinthians demands an accounting.

By using plural pronouns so often in referring to himself, Paul accomplishes a variety of goals that are important for his rhetorical task of persuading the Corinthians to ally themselves (more fully) with him. First, with the plural self-references, Paul regularly invites the Corinthians to think of themselves as one with him—a major objective in all of 2 Corinthians.

Second, by using plural pronouns Paul encourages the Corinthians to think that Paul does not stand alone, that he has widespread support, and that he is part of a larger group—his rhetoric suggests the mainstream—who advocate the gospel as he does. Among those who can be associated in the plurals are Timothy, the co-author (1:1), the Achaians (i.e., the Corinthians' provincial neighbors, who are also named as addressees; 1:1), the Macedonians (9:2, 4; 11:9), Silvanus (1:19), Titus (2:13; 7:6, 13-14; 8:6, 16, 23; 12:18), and the "brother" praised by all the churches (8:18). All of these people, explicitly mentioned in 2 Corinthians, are allied with Paul.

Third, while some Corinthians might question that Paul was a minister of the gospel, Paul's regular description of his ministry in the plural "we" leaves them no room to deny that God has commissioned ministers such as he and must make it more difficult to deny that Paul is one of them. Fourth, the plural allows Paul to depict himself in rather grand fashion, with diminished risk of his being thought to be boasting inordinately.[29]

Fifth, specifically in regard to the collection for the saints in Jerusalem, Paul's use of plural self-references suggests broad support for him and for the collection while also depicting him as the leader of such a larger movement (with which the Corinthians hopefully will want to ally themselves). Finally, his pervasive use of the plural as a way of referring to himself makes it all the more striking and powerful rhetorically when he explicitly invites the Corinthians into the picture that is otherwise described by the plurals (cf. 3:18; 5:10).

29. See Plutarch *On Praising Oneself Inoffensively* 542B-543F, where speakers can praise and, as in the case at hand, positively associate themselves with others "whose aims and acts are the same as . . . [one's] own and whose general character is similar."

WHAT WE LEARN ABOUT PAUL IN 2 CORINTHIANS

Paul the Person. Paul was a passionate man, given to a wide range of emotions. We observe his anger and distress in 2 Corinthians 10–13 not only as Corinthian opposition hardens against him, but also as some of his beloved drift away under outside influences. Also visible, though, is his heartfelt affection, his sense that he loves the more and is loved less (12:15). Clear as well is his anxiety over whether his painful letter might have proved too painful for the Corinthians (7:6-16); equally clear and powerful are his expressions of relief and joy when he receives Titus's report of their return to filiation with him (7:6-7, 13-14). Professions of his love for them (11:11) fit well with other expressions of friendship, such as his preparedness to spend and be spent for them (12:15), his readiness to live and to die with them (7:3), and his willingness to speak frankly as a friend to them (6:11).

As reflected in 2 Corinthians, Paul's experiences range from the most sublime to the most precarious. What can surpass his being caught up into the third heaven, into paradise (12:2-6)? It is almost as difficult to imagine anyone having more hardships than Paul (4:8-12; 6:4-10; 11:23-27), including his thorn or stake in the flesh (12:7-9) and his Damascus escape (11:30-33). In fact, the letter fragment 2 Corinthians 1–9 opens with Paul's disclosure of a recent experience in Asia (roughly modern western Turkey), where he feared for his life; he refers to it as a virtual death sentence (1:8-11). Even if we allow for some inflation as part of a rhetorical appeal for pity, the experience must have been traumatic.

Paul's self-descriptions are illuminating because they show a Paul not always victorious, not always triumphant, but often vexed, put upon, and, at times, almost overwhelmed. His Asian affliction left him with no resource other than to trust in "God who raises the dead" (1:9). Regarding that situation, he describes himself, in evocative terms, as being utterly, beyond measure weighed down, as despairing of living (1:8). Elsewhere in the same letter he depicts himself as being pushed almost to the brink: afflicted, perplexed, persecuted, and struck down—to each of those powerful verbs he adds a codicil of grace-filled limitations: "but not crushed . . . not driven to despair . . . not forsaken . . . not destroyed" (4:8-9). A similar self-portrait acknowledges a fundamental dissonance between the way he is treated or perceived and how he thinks he truly is: "treated as impostors, and yet are true; as unknown, and yet are well known; as dying, and see—we are alive; as punished, and not yet killed; as sorrowful, yet always rejoicing; as poor, yet making many rich; as having nothing, and yet possessing everything" (6:8c-10 NRSV). Another powerful self-description shows him with "conflicts on the outside, fears within" (7:5 NIV). Some important insights into Paul are available here. First, what one sees and experiences is, thanks be to God, not the whole picture. Second, as strong in faith as Paul was, he never expected his faith or his God to shelter him from the vicissitudes and vagaries of life. He did expect God to be present for him *in whatever circumstance;* indeed, that was Paul's experience.

Paul was a person of incredible theological imagination and resources. Second Corinthians 1–9 is a showcase of his reflections because in those chapters he projects three portraits of his ministry as a means of enhancing his ethos and Corinthian affiliation with him (see the Commentary on 2:14–6:10). Not only does he have his Scriptures as a potent resource and stimulus for his thoughts and for their expression, but he also has pre- and para-Pauline Christian formulations and the conventions of the Greco-Roman world to draw upon and to weave together with his own reflections. Throughout 2 Corinthians, and indeed across all his correspondence, he has no interest in theological notions for their own sake, but only as they engage life, as they bear on the way people comport themselves. His theologizing, therefore, is never abstract or abstruse; instead it is always engaged, always linked to life as real people—he and his hearers—are experiencing it.

Paul's Fiduciary Relations. Paul's flexible financial practices got him into difficulty with some Corinthians—perhaps not early on, but surely by the time 2 Corinthians was written. Although Paul clearly accepted support from the Philippians (Phil 1:5; 2:25; 4:10-16) and even had a Macedonian delivery of support to him while he was at Corinth (2 Cor 11:8-9), he resolutely and stubbornly persisted in his refusal to accept assistance from the Corinthians, even though some Corinthians apparently sought to become his patrons. It is not difficult to imagine, given the cultural suppositions of the time, that Paul refused to become client to some of the wealthy Corinthians because he could not allow himself either to be indebted to them or to be obligated to pay them honor in return for their favor.

Further, Paul regularly expects to be assisted on his journeys by local congregations as he pursues his itinerary (see Rom 15:24), and he does not count that aid as making him a client with its culturally assumed obligations. Even with the Corinthians he distinguishes between accepting their support and their helping him along in his travel (cf. 1 Cor 16:6; 2 Cor 1:16). We may suppose, therefore, that Paul distinguishes clientage from all forms of "hospitality" (see Rom 12:13; 15:24).

Finally, Paul's embrace of the collection for the poor at Jerusalem, an outgrowth of the Jerusalem conference (Gal 2:1-10), may not have created any early Corinthian confusion about his motives (1 Cor 16:1-4), but surely by the time of 2 Corinthians it had become a ground of contention. Witness Paul's extraordinary care to secure reputable representatives to accompany the delivery of the collection (2 Cor 8:18-23) in order to avoid any charges of fiscal abuse.

Unique Information from the Hardship Lists. For the most part, the hardship catalogs detail what we know about Paul from other texts and sources. He often was in danger and experienced great obstacles and problems in his efforts to advance the gospel. We might take special note of how frequently he experienced certain difficulties or the severity of them: "countless floggings, and often near death" (11:23 NRSV) or "afflicted . . . but not crushed . . . struck down" (4:8-9 NRSV).

Two details, however, shed unique light on Paul. First, five times he received the Jewish punishment of thirty-nine lashes (11:24). This discipline, founded on Deut 25:3, was enforced by the synagogues in Paul's time.[30] His submission to this penalty suggests that even after he became an apostle he continued to maintain his ties to Jewish synagogue worship and practice; otherwise, he would neither have been judged out of order or needed to allow himself to be thus chastened. Of course, we cannot tell at what points across his ministry he received the thirty-nine lashes, but five times suggests a longer rather than shorter period. That he kept contact with fellow Jews is also clear from passages like 1 Cor 9:20, but such a passage does not indicate as clearly that he submitted to synagogue authority.

Second, he reports that he was three times beaten with rods (11:25), a Roman punishment (see Acts 16:22-23, 37-39) that was not supposed to be administered to Roman citizens, as Acts 16:37 affirms. Josephus reports, however, that such propriety was not always honored everywhere.[31] Thus Paul's report of having been beaten with rods does not rule out his having been a Roman citizen, as Acts 16:37 declares he was.

PAUL'S THOUGHT WORLD

Although Paul spends much of his time in these letter fragments either commending or defending himself, his way of doing so yields a view of several basic convictions that structure his thought world.

The Cosmic Purposes of God. God is ultimately in control, and, with what has been begun in Christ, God's plan is nearing completion. Paul has been captured and put on display in God's triumphal victory procession as God's power sweeps across the world (2:14-16). The plan and the power belong solely to God. To be sure, Satan has plans (and agents), but he poses no real threat to believers if they stay alert and remember that they have been made privy to Satan's design (2:11). The conclusion of God's purposes is near, so all opposing power is doomed.

Across both letter fragments, Paul uses references to end-time considerations as leverage on the Corinthians. Believers are going to face Christ's judgment for the way they have comported themselves (5:10). The panoply of God's power is marshaled behind Paul as he promises to vanquish all foes and render their defenses useless (10:3-6). God's purpose, in Christ, is the reconciliation of the entire cosmos (5:19), with everyone included, to God; that is why Christ

---

30. See Josephus *Antiquities of the Jews* 4.238; *Mishnah Makkot* 3.
31. Josephus *The Jewish War* 2.308.

"died for all" (5:14-15). This grand portrait of purpose, sketched out across the letter fragments of 2 Corinthians, utterly transcends and renders foolishly impotent any opposition to God, and derivatively to Paul. Captured by and now the agent of this overwhelming divine power, Paul dismisses any rival claims to the Corinthians' fealty and announces himself ready, with God's power, to induce (2:9; 7:15; 10:6; 13:5-10), if not enforce, obedience (13:4).

The Life of Faith as Process, as Growth, as Being Transformed. Paul understands that believers, as a part of God's new creation (5:17), are works in process, that God is working in them to transform them from one degree of glory to another (3:18). The new creation starts when, by God's grace, a person dies with Christ and, in dying, is brought to newness of life (Rom 6:4). At the outset of faith, believers are called babies (1 Cor 3:1-2; Phlm 10) or "weak with respect to faith" (Rom 14:1). As believers progress in the faith, Paul thinks of them as more mature, more like adults (1 Cor 2:6; 14:20; Phil 3:15). Every believer is given a measure of faith by God (Rom 12:3), and they, like their paradigmatic father Abraham, are to grow strong in faith (Rom 4:20). The resurrection at the last day, featured so prominently in 1 Corinthians 15, is confidently expected by Paul to be the capstone, the zenith at which the life of faith is brought to its fulfillment.

Here in 2 Corinthians Paul several times makes clear his anthropological assumption that believers are being transformed, but nowhere clearer or more powerfully than in his declaration: "And all of us . . . are being transformed . . . from one degree of glory to another" (2 Cor 3:18 NRSV; see the Commentary on 3:18). In sharp contrast with "those who are perishing," Paul sees believers—those who are already justified and reconciled (Rom 5:9-10)—as "those who *are being saved,*" who are going "from life to life" (2 Cor 2:15-16, italics added). In a passage where he uses three different terms for "house" as a means of referring to human life, he depicts believers as currently living in what he imaginatively describes as "this tent" and as longing for a transformed, heavenly dwelling (5:1-2). With a shift of metaphor, he again describes the anticipated permutation as an expectation of being "further clothed" (5:4). Believers have died with Christ; God, who "raised the Lord Jesus will raise us also with Jesus" (4:14). Believers have received the Holy Spirit, but that is only a down payment of all that is to come (1:22; 5:5; cf. Rom 8:11). Believers' outer selves are wasting away, but their inner selves are being renewed day by day (4:16). That which is transitory is being replaced by what is eternal (4:18). What is mortal will be swallowed up without remainder by life (5:4). Paul's explicit hope for the Corinthians is that their faith may grow (10:15; cf. 13:9).

Change, growth, and development are presupposed by Paul across the letters. Compare his own self-portrait in 1 Corinthians 13:1, where he looks back to his life as a child and forward to a time not yet here when he will "see face to face . . . and know fully" (1 Cor 13:11-12). He works with the Philippians for their "progress and joy in faith" (Phil 1:25). He labors with the Thessalonians "to complete what is lacking in your faith" (1 Thess 3:10).

Believers' Proper Care for One Another. Although Paul's overriding concern in 2 Corinthians is a return of the Corinthians to full, proper relationship to him, he does not lose sight of their need to be concerned about each other. Ever the model, Paul presents himself as the one who cares in an exemplary way about the Corinthians. In his most dramatic representation of his caring, reserved for the confrontational 2 Corinthians 10–13 fragment, he portrays himself as ready to fail personally if doing so will ensure their doing "what is right" (13:7). He is eager to spend and be spent for them in his effort to secure them in the faith (12:15; cf. similar sacrificial imagery in Phil 2:17). In another instance, he models compassion when he urges the Corinthians to restore to fellowship the one they have dismissed: "pardon and console him, lest he be overwhelmed by excessive grief . . . decide in favor of love for him" (2:7-8). Though the individual had aggrieved Paul and the community (2:5), the communal rebuke must not be so severe or so sustained that the person is permanently lost from the fellowship; even someone who has wronged the community must be cared for in love.

Paul's reflections about the collection provide other windows onto how he thinks believers are or should be related to one another. First, believers should pattern themselves after the best they see in other believers: The Macedonians were spurred to contribute by the reports of the

Corinthians (9:2); now the Corinthians should renew their commitment when they see how readily and fully the Macedonians have embraced the collection (8:1-7). Second, one's bounty provides for the need of another, without anyone's being disadvantaged in the giving or lacking in the receiving (8:12-14). Instead, Paul sees that among believers generosity and need are so correlated that, when proper concern for one another is present, a fundamental equality should result among the believers (ἰσότης *isotēs*, "fairness/equality," 8:13-14; cf. another idealized portrait of believing community in Acts 2:43-47; 4:32–5:11).

Reassessment of Contemporary Values. Profoundly grounded in Paul's gospel and observable across 2 Corinthians are ideas that are at least contrary—and may even be properly deemed subversive—to the culture and to its impact on at least some of the Corinthians. Paul thinks that judgments made simply on what is seen, on what appears, on surface observations, are bound to be wrong. He employs various means to advocate that fundamental skepticism. He distinguishes walking by faith—that is, by trusting God—from walking by sight (5:7); he eschews reckoning from what can be seen in favor of "the things that cannot be seen" (4:18); and he distinguishes what appears on one's face from what is in one's heart (5:12). In embracing this perspective, Paul reaffirms to the Corinthians the same conviction expressed elsewhere in his letters: "Hope that is seen is not hope" (Rom 8:24); "Now we see in a mirror, enigmatically; then face to face; now we know partially; then we shall know completely just as we have been known" (1 Cor 13:12).

Paul acknowledges the same ambiguity in human estimations of other people. To consider another person "according to the flesh" (κατὰ σάρκα *kata sarka*)—that is, according to standard ways of reckoning, is certain to be misleading (5:16). Paul develops the thought christologically, saying that he no longer regards Christ *kata sarka*; to do so would be to view him wrongly, incompletely, without the resurrection that establishes his identity as Lord. Along these same lines, we must understand Paul's later self-description as not walking—that is, comporting himself—*kata sarka* (10:2), and his related assertion that the warfare he is prepared to prosecute against any opposition should not be confused with theoretically defeatable—that is, *kata sarka*—power (10:3).

The same undercutting of traditional cultural values is present in the hardship list of 2 Cor 6:4-10 but is packed especially into the verses at its end. As to the list, Paul's self-commendation comes not in the number of victories he can boast of or in his grand accomplishments or wealth, but is grounded instead in afflictions, hunger, and even disrepute (6:4ff.). The catalog concludes, however, with three couplets, each of which begins with cultural disvalues—"sorrowful," "poor," and "having nothing"—and turns each one of them radically, distinctly on its head—"rejoicing," "enriching many," and "possessing everything" (6:10). By doing this Paul depicts himself, and all those associated with him in the living of the gospel, as being shored up in joy even in the midst of sorrow, as showering riches where poverty seems to prevail, and as possessing everything while others might (wrongly) think the opposite is true. Believers possess everything because, as those who through Christ belong to God, believers share all that God possesses (1 Cor 3:21*b*-23).

Paul's fundamental critique of conventional values in 2 Corinthians should not have come as a surprise to the Corinthians. In an earlier letter to them, Paul had argued that, in the light of God's concluding purposes in reclaiming the cosmos, believers should comport themselves "as-if-not"; that is, they should live in the world so as to practice detachment from the values and entanglements it offers (1 Cor 7:30-31; see the Commentary on 1 Corinthians). As a predominantly Gentile congregation, the Corinthians will have been exposed to such Stoic reflection about "indifferent matters" (ἀδιάφορα *adiaphora*). Paul's inversion of values in 2 Cor 6:10 fits such a context and reinforces a certain distancing from cultural norms.

In a similar way, but focused on the cultural category of rich/poor, Paul's christological claim about Christ's having been rich and submitting himself to poverty for the believers so that by his poverty they might become rich offers a critique of riches and poverty and indirectly provides a model for Paul's relinquishing the accoutrements that some might think appropriate to apostleship (2 Cor 8:9). In this christological formulation, Paul does not offer an escape from poverty to riches as seen in the categories of the world; instead, Paul imparts a perspective that answers the question of what is truly valuable, of where real wealth resides.

Paul's basically contrary-to-culture outlook is also aimed, with great irony, at anyone among the Corinthians who is enamored of the intruders and their values. In focus is the way the intruders have inveigled the Corinthians into according to themselves grand status and support, both of which Paul has assiduously refused. Paul mocks the intruders, their Corinthian allies, and their values with an ironic parody: "You put up with it if someone enslaves you, if someone exploits you, if someone takes advantage of you, if someone is presumptuous, if someone slaps you in the face. With what shame I must say we were too weak to do that!" (11:20-21). Likewise, when acknowledging that, though he accepted support from other churches, he persisted in not burdening the Corinthians, he again feigns shame: "Forgive me this wrong" (12:13 NRSV).

All of Paul's subversion of cultural norms, every bit of his revaluation of values, is grounded in his christological conviction that Christ's resurrection overthrows not only death but also the structures of meaning by which people previously reckoned. If, in Christ, the fundamental antinomy of life and death has been cashiered from its governance of human encounters and significance, then indeed there is a "new creation" and truly "everything has become new" (5:17 NRSV). After Christ's death and resurrection, the norms of conduct have to be revised or newly invented, as the Corinthians have learned already from Paul in 1 Corinthians.

Because Paul's contention with the intruders and their Corinthian adherents comes to focus on his too humble status and demeanor, Paul moves his counter onto the weakness/power antinomy and grounds it in Christ, whom Paul claims "was crucified in weakness but lives by the power of God" (13:4 NRSV). So for Paul crucifixion/life and weakness/power are directly correlated.

By means of the weakness/power doublet, Paul at once defends himself and puts perspective on not only what is truly important, but also where the ultimate power resides. Paul's weakness/power critique has long been known to the Corinthians (see 1 Cor 1:20-25; 15:43), but it probably emerges once again when some unidentified persons are reported to be claiming about Paul that "his letters are weighty and strong, but his bodily presence is weak" (2 Cor 10:10 NRSV). In 11:21, Paul, brimming with irony, embraces the description of himself as "too weak" to take advantage of the Corinthians as the intruders have. From that point in the letter, weakness becomes a major, positive theme of Paul's self-identification; having just recounted a list of hardships and sufferings (11:23-28), he pledges to boast of nothing but his weaknesses (11:30). And so he does, detailing how, in Damascus, he recently managed to escape with his life (11:31-33) and capping it off with a recounting of how he earnestly desired to have the stake or thorn in the flesh removed from him (12:7b-10). Paul depicts his weakness as a perfect avenue for God's power. Although he is not allowed to disclose the message that he received when he was in the third heaven (12:4), he readily recounts the word he received from the Lord in response to his failed petition for the removal of the thorn: "My grace is sufficient; my power is perfected in weakness" (12:9). It is in God's nature to display power in weakness, to place divine treasures in earthen vessels (4:7). God's power is perfectly suited to human weakness. So the culturally generated complaint against Paul, that he does not display the proper perquisites of power and status of a true apostle (12:12), is critiqued and rejected by Paul, who suggests indirectly that the complainers do not understand even the basics regarding the gospel and, by implication, about how God works.

Paul taps a widespread, popular contemporary notion of the inner and outer person and overlays it with a related contrast of temporary and permanent (4:16-18; see the Commentary on 4:16-18), as a part of his sustained argument that what one sees on the surface or outside is not predictably indicative of inner or permanent reality. In so doing he sets the stage for its amplification in the following, kindred antinomies between "face" and "heart" (5:12) and between knowing someone "according to the flesh" and as being related to the new creation (5:16-17).

The Importance of Works. With the classical emphasis on justification by faith we have sometimes lost Paul's perspective on works and their place in the life of faith. Much of

2 Corinthians is directed at the issue of how people behave, at what their conduct is. Paul's own comportment is a continuing topic, sometimes defined positively in terms of what he has done, sometimes delineated negatively as to how he has refrained from behaving (e.g., 2 Cor 1:12, 17; 2:17; 4:2; 11:7-9; 12:6, 14-18).

In 2 Corinthians, Paul is also attentive to the Corinthians' behavior, reminding them that they, like he, will have to face the judgment before Christ at the last day (5:10). Then and there, Paul holds, all believers will be accountable for what they have done (2 Cor 5:10), for their thoughts (Rom 2:16), and for their purposes of heart (1 Cor 4:5). The judgment will be based on "the things done while in the body" (2 Cor 5:10 NIV), whether for good or for bad. Satan's ministers also face an end (τὸ τέλος *to telos*) that will correspond to their works (2 Cor 11:15).

In Romans, Paul develops the final judgment motif more fully. There, using commercial terminology, Paul declares that God will "pay back to each person according to that one's works" (2:6): eternal life, glory, honor, and peace to those who patiently do good and seek immortality; wrath and fury to those who do evil (2:7-10). The repayment is reckoned in terms of the deeds one does (cf. 1 Cor 3:12-15), how one comports oneself in the body, and not whether one has faith, because faith is a gift (χάρισμα *charisma*) given by God to each believer (cf. 1 Cor 12:9-11) and, therefore, not the subject of judgment.

Judgment regarding works has sometimes not been given adequate attention in studies of Paul because interpreters rightly recognize that, for Paul, one does not come to faith by means of works, but by God's grace freely given. Faith—that is, right relation to God—does express itself in works, in deeds of love (Gal 5:6; 1 Thess 1:3). Paul consistently decries any attempt to attain right relation with God by performance of works, by dint of one's own efforts (cf. Rom 3:27-28; 9:30–10:3).

The topic of judgment according to works comes up in 2 Corinthians because Paul feels the need to defend his comportment, his works, among the Corinthians, and he is concerned about their works as expressed in relation to him. At several points in 2 Corinthians 1–9 Paul has reminded the Corinthians that he and they must live and behave in such a way as to be ready for the completion of God's purposes (2 Cor 3:18; 4:17-18; 5:4-5; 6:1-2). The eschatological, end-time references are designed to leverage the Corinthians into closer affiliation with Paul, who, in exemplary fashion, declares himself as aiming to please God in all that he does (5:9) precisely because he knows that "all of us" will have to appear before Christ's tribunal for judgment (5:10).

Continuity/Discontinuity Between Past and Present. On the one side, Paul is convinced that all of God's promises find their "yes," their fulfillment, in Christ (2 Cor 1:20; cf. Rom 1:3; 9:5). Christ is the confirmation of the promises granted the patriarchs (Rom 15:8). Likewise, the gospel was declared already to Abraham (Gal 3:8), and Abraham becomes the type of faithful person whose unconditional trust in God is the model for all believers who follow (Romans 4; Galatians 3). In 2 Corinthians as well, the first covenant shares with the second one, no matter how distinctive they may be in other respects, the fundamental characteristic of "glory," presumably a glory that is in both cases derived or reflected from God, who grants the covenants (2 Cor 3:7-11). So the new covenant is, like the first, still covenant, still made by God, and still manifests the glory from God so that some fundamental continuity between past and present is affirmed.

Driven by a desire to make absolutely clear to the Corinthians that their current relation to God stems from their relation to the gospel through Paul and his ministry, Paul ties his own ministry to a "new" covenant, which he affirms that he represents. To distinguish himself and his ministry from all others, he distances the new covenant from its predecessor in significant ways. He radicalizes the distinction between what he labels as two "ministries" and pictures these ministries as having distinctive covenants. In each instance his ministry and its covenant are distinguished by contrasts or described as surpassing the other one: written on stone/on hearts (3:3), with ink/with the Spirit of the living God (3:3), old/new (3:6, 14), death (stated)/ life (implied; 3:7), letter/spirit (3:6), and fading away/permanent (3:11, 13). Indeed, Paul's eagerness to interpret his own ministry and its covenant as being of singular importance for the Corinthians leads him to an oxymoronic position: He knows that the old covenant had glory, but, being convinced that the new covenant's glory (and, therefore, his ministry) so exceeds the earlier glory, he says that the new glory is so dazzling as to make the earlier glory seem to be no glory at all (3:10).

Reconciliation. Reconciliation as a term presupposes a familial or friendship setting in which, after enmity has been overcome, relationships are restored to amicability. So it is also in Paul. All of creation was made by God for association with God's own self. Sin intervened and led creation, humans included, into alienation and even enmity with God (Rom 5:10). By a freely given gift—that is, grace in Christ—God overcame the enmity and established peace (Rom 5:1), another term for reconciliation.

Among the seven undisputed letters, Paul's most powerful delineation of reconciliation is found in 2 Cor 5:11-21, where the reconciliation is at once cosmic, communal, and personal. It is cosmic in that as surely as the world—that is, all of creation—has been subjected to futility and is in bondage to decay (Rom 8:20-21), in Christ God "was reconciling the world to himself" (2 Cor 5:19 NRSV). In Romans 8:1, Paul describes in more detail how he views God's ultimate rehabilitation of the entire created order: God's newly reclaimed children already experience the "freedom of the glory" for which the rest of creation still longs, much as a pregnant woman experiences her labor pains just prior to delivery (Rom 8:19-23). It is communal in that when Paul describes reconciliation it always has a plural object, "us" or the world in its collectivity (Rom 5:10-11; 2 Cor 5:18-19). Reconciliation is also personal because it takes place "in Christ," precisely the locus where individual believers become members of Christ's body and are given into one another's care (1 Cor 12:12-26). Further, as the commentary shows, in 2 Cor 5:11-21 Paul *explicitly* calls for reconciliation to God, but *the encoded message* is that he wants more filiation from the Corinthians and a heightened sense of reconciliation with them—*to him* as the one who brought the gospel of reconciliation to them in the first place. He is personally concerned that their already established reconciliation to God wash over onto him with new enthusiasm on their part (cf. 2 Cor 6:12-13; 7:2).

SOCIAL AND RHETORICAL CONVENTIONS: EPISTOLARY STYLE

Thoroughly at home in the Greco-Roman world, Paul employs the practices and conventions of the time as a means of engaging with and relating to the Corinthians.

Frank Speech. Frank speech (παρρησία *parrēsia*)[32] was, along with indirect or figured speech and flattery, one of the three ways that a person in Paul's time could attempt to influence deliberation regarding proper behavior. Without ever mentioning it explicitly from 2 Cor 1:3 through 2 Cor 6:10, Paul *indirectly* bids for increased filiation from the Corinthians; in 6:11-13, however, he shifts to frankness and appeals *directly* for increased affection (see also 7:2). Indirect speech treats an issue or problem obliquely, in a roundabout fashion, never head-on, and often without even expressly mentioning the main concern; in 1:3–6:10, Paul strives in a variety of ways to cement his newly restored relations with the Corinthians, though, properly abiding by the canons of indirect speech, he never explicitly states in those verses his concern to do so.

Frankness has friendship as its locus. It is the highest "office of a friend" to call a friend to task, to encourage the friend to reach for the best and to perform at the optimum.[33] Frank speech ranges from "the gentlest sting," on the one extreme, where one pleasantly nudges the friend toward improvement, across a continuum of increasing degrees to the other, harshest extreme: a rebuke. The success of frank speech depends on many considerations, among which are the timing, the proportionality of the severity to the situation, the ethos or character of the frank speaker, and the care to mix in varying, appropriate degrees of praise. In some sense and degree, the friendship is always placed in hazard by the undertaking of frank speech, but true friendship, genuine caring for the other one, sometimes leaves no alternative but to take that risk.

---

32. For the conventions and practice of frank speech, see J. Paul Sampley, "Paul's Frank Speech with the Galatians and the Corinthians," in *Philodemus and the New Testament World,* ed. J. T. Fitzgerald, G. S. Holland, and D. Obbink, NovTSup (Leiden: E.J. Brill, 2001).

33. Philodemus *On Frank Criticism* col. XIXb.

Paul employs a range of frank speech in the correspondence reflected in 2 Corinthians. In the painful letter, he uses harsh frank speech and reports himself appropriately anxious about how the Corinthians have received it (2 Cor 7:5-7, 12-13). In 6:11-13 and 7:2, Paul uses a milder form of frank speech as he calls for the Corinthians to open their hearts to him.

Self-commendation. Modern readers often have great difficulty with Paul's persistent reminders to the Corinthians of his considerable efforts toward them. Similarly, his boasting seems extravagant; he even acknowledges as much in 2 Cor 11:16-17, 21*b;* 12:1. In that culture, friends commended each other, wrote letters of commendation for each other, and put in good words for each other at critical times.

Further, Paul's contemporaries were, as Paul shows himself to be also, not reticent to commend themselves as a part of the self-promotion that was so prevalent culturally. Encomiastic practices regularly expected that a speaker or writer detail, as Paul does here, his deeds that benefited others. Goodwill is earned when one details what one has done for others, when we "refer to our own acts and services without arrogance."[34] *Ad Herennium,* a contemporary rhetorical handbook, wrongly attributed to Cicero, concurs and urges the speaker to reveal "also our past conduct toward the republic, or toward our parents, friends, or the audience."[35] Paul has no interest in the republic; he is totally focused on his audience, the Corinthians, as he recites his good works and diligence in service of the gospel to the Corinthians[36] and hopes thereby to garner their increased goodwill.

Ideally, one should not be totally dependent on self-commendation. One's clients or dependents should rally. In one context where outsiders show up with letters of commendation, Paul assumes that he should not need any such letters of support from his followers (3:1). Later, when his relations with the Corinthians have deteriorated once again, Paul contends that the Corinthians should have met his opponents with commendations, with boasting about him and about what he has meant to them: "You forced me [to be a fool and commend myself], for I ought to have been commended by you" (12:11). When his Corinthian allies failed to commend him, he saw no option other than to commend himself. Therefore, he boasts, but he tempers his boasting with irony and by adopting a fool's pose (11:16, 21*b,* 23; 12:11). Had the Corinthians come to his defense, he would not have felt the need to engage in self-commendation.

Paul openly embraces a certain type of self-commendation: "In every way we commend ourselves as ministers of God" (6:4). The hardship list that follows shows that Paul's self-commendation is grounded in his difficulties and distress, an ironic testimony to the power of God working through and sustaining him in whatever circumstances he encounters. In 6:4-10 irony functions as did the fool's mantle and thus places Paul's self-commendation in perspective.

Epistolary expressions of self-confidence such as we see in 2 Corinthians (1:12-14; 5:11; 11:5; 13:6; cf. Heb 13:18) are an accepted part of persuasion and are necessary when the writer wants "to create or restore a good relationship between" the readers/hearers and himself.[37] In 2 Corinthians 1:1–9, Paul is especially eager to rehearse their grounds for mutual pride, so he mixes praise of them and self-commendation of himself (see 1:13*b*-14). The goal of self-commendation is to shape the way the audience thinks of the speaker. Paul's self-commendation lays out the picture he wants the Corinthians to have of him.[38]

Patron/Client, Honor/Shame. The culturally pervasive categories of patron and client, of honor and shame, continue to make their marks on Paul's communication with the Corinthians. (For a treatment of honor and shame, see the Introduction of 1 Corinthians.)

In the Greco-Roman world a gift or benefaction establishes or maintains a patron/client relationship and places the recipient under obligation. Seneca says it clearly: "The giving of a benefit is a social act, it wins the good will of someone, it lays someone under obligation."[39] For the one who receives a benefit, gratitude is merely the "first installment of his debt."[40] Epictetus deems

---

34. Cicero *De inv.* 1.16.22.
35. Cicero *Ad Herennium* 1.5.8.
36. S. H. Travis, "Paul's Boasting in 2 Cor 10:1–12," *Studia Evangelica,* ed. F. L. Cross (Berlin: Akademie, 1973) 6:529-30; 554-55.
37. S. N. Olson, "Epistolary Uses of Expresssions of Self-Confidence," *JBL* 103 (1984) 588.
38. Olson, "Epistolary Uses of Expresssions of Self-Confidence," 593.
39. Seneca *Of Benefits* 5.11.5.
40. Seneca *Of Benefits* 2.22.1.

the one who "repays a favour without interest" an ingrate.[41] In that world, patronage was the glue that bound every level of society to their benefactors. Not simply a political tool as we know it in modern times, patronage was omnipresent, in all relations, where one person's favor binds the recipient(s) to honor the donors and, in cases of money or possessions, allows the recipients to confer beneficence and, therefore, obligation, on persons beneath them in status.

In 2 Corinthians, patronage is a matter of great importance because some Corinthians seek to become Paul's patrons and thereby support his ministry. These Corinthians, who may reasonably be supposed to include some of the wealthy, are spurred to move in that direction by two forces that we can identify. First, they have seen the Macedonian believers arrive with support for Paul and him accept it (11:9). Given the prevalent cultural patterns, they have every superficial reason to view that transaction as a patron/client relationship between the Macedonians and Paul, exactly the association they seek with him. Second, they seem to have been encouraged by the intruders to think that real apostles did not do menial work (as Paul insisted on doing) as a means of self-support (11:7; 12:16).

Paul, however, rejects their bid of patronage. In strong language he avers that his boast of self-support will not be silenced anywhere in the environs of Corinth (11:10). With an oath as to his truthfulness, he preempts any claim that his refusal of patronage is a sign that he does not love them (11:11). Further, he declares that he is not about to change his long-standing pattern of self-support with them. By refusing their offer of patronage, Paul has avoided being obligated to them, probably an important personal consideration, but, in the categories of the culture, he has rebuked and shamed them by his refusal. In that setting, as in many to this day around the world, patronage and its gifts cannot be refused without shame attaching itself to the would-be donors. Shame produces enmity.[42] No doubt a part of Paul's problems with the Corinthians is attributable to his contravention of the traditional cultural patterns of patronage.

The Types of Rhetoric in 2 Corinthians. In the Greco-Roman world, all rhetoric could be divided into three classes. *Judicial rhetoric,* the most common, addresses questions of culpability regarding the past. *Deliberative rhetoric* attends to questions of what a person or group will do in the (perhaps even imminent) future. *Epideictic rhetoric* focuses on praise and blame, usually of a person, though events may also be the subject. All of Paul's letters are deliberative, at least in part if not completely, because each of them at some point calls for the hearers to reflect on their comportment and to consider emending their current practices. Both letter fragments contained in 2 Corinthians do that, though 2 Corinthians 10–13, with its rehearsal of Paul's past behavior and its preparation for a confrontational showdown, may at times also be judicial. Both letter fragments, insofar as they shower praise or cast blame, engage in some epideictic rhetoric as well.

Epistolary Style. Much attention is properly placed on categorizing the Pauline letters as to type or literary style.[43] For 2 Corinthians, two determinations are necessary, one for chapters 1–9, another for chapters 10–13. Chapters 1–9 are "a letter of apologetic self-commendation."[44] As noted already, the primary burden of 2 Corinthians 1–9 is Paul's recovery of Corinthian filiation after he has subjected them to a frank rebuke.

Chapters 10–13 are an "excellent example of a mixed letter type."[45] Their legal overtones are prompted not only by Paul's eagerness to counter charges made against him, but also by his determination to put the Corinthians on warning of his imminent arrival when he expects to confront his accusers. But the letter is truly a hodgepodge as to style or type, containing as it does not only accusations, self-defense, and reproaches, but also self-commendation and apologies.

Frank speech, discussed above, is, along with indirect speech and flattery, a mode of the speaker's relating to the hearers and can be employed in any of the types of rhetoric noted above and in any epistolary style.

41. Epictetus *Epistles* 81.18; cf. 81.9-10.

42. Peter Marshall, *Enmity in Corinth: Social Conventions in Paul's Relations with the Corinthians,* WUNT 44 (Tübingen: J. C. B. Mohr, 1987) 242-47.

43. See L. L. Belleville, "A Letter of Apologetic Self-recommendation: 2 Cor 1:8–7:16," *NovT* 31 (1989) 150.

44. Belleville establishes this identification quite clearly by comparing 2 Corinthians 1–9 with examples from Sophists. See Belleville, "A Letter of Apologetic Self-recommendation," 158-59.

45. J. T. Fitzgerald, "Paul, the Ancient Epistolary Theorists, and 2 Corinthians 10–13: The Purpose and Literary Genre of a Pauline Letter," in *Greeks, Romans, and Christians: Essays in Honor of Abraham J. Malherbe,* ed. D. L. Balch, E. Ferguson, W. A. Meeks (Minneapolis: Fortress, 1990) 200.

CONCLUDING NOTES

Although we know that chapter designations were added to the biblical texts only in the Middle Ages and that subdivisions into verses came about even later, nevertheless in the Commentary chapters and verses are used as a means of handy reference. The reader of this commentary will note, however, that occasions are cited in which the relatively modern division of the text into chapters and paragraphs and verses does not reflect the sections and turning points in Paul's argument.

The Scripture translations in the Commentary and in the Reflections are my own, unless otherwise indicated. In order to make clear to modern readers the semantic range of a given Greek term, additional possible translations of the same term by different English words separated by a slash are given—for example, Paul's mention of παράκλησις (*paraklēsis*), "so also our encouragement/comfort/consolation abounds through Christ" in 1:5. The hope is that such a translation will provide the readers with additional information by which they can appreciate the different nuances of *paraklēsis* in that verse—and indeed in 1:3-10, where the term or some form of it occurs ten times.

In this commentary the recipients of 2 Corinthians are frequently referred to as "hearers" or "auditors" because the majority of the Corinthians were surely illiterate (1 Cor 1:26) and, therefore, dependent upon someone else to read the letter to them. So most Corinthian believers experienced these letters as a heard communication.

The term "Christian" is lacking in the Commentary sections because Paul and his readers did not employ this term as a self-description. It was a later development.[46]

---

46. Thanks to you, Sally Backus Sampley, love of my life, for your hours of research, for your helpful, insightful critiques, and most of all for your love. Thanks also to Suzanne Webber for her editorial suggestions throughout the commentary.

BIBLIOGRAPHY

Belleville, L. L. "A Letter of Apologetic Self-Commendation: 2 Cor 1:8–7:16." *NovT* 31 (1989). Significant for her classification of the letter and for her understanding of self-commendation.

Danker, F. W. "Paul's Debt to the *De Corona* of Demosthenes: A Study of Rhetorical Techniques in Second Corinthians." In *Persuasive Artistry: Studies in New Testament Rhetoric in Honor of G. A. Kennedy.* Edited by D. F. Watson, JSNTSup 50. Sheffield: Sheffield Academic, 1991. Helpful in understanding Paul's rhetorical techniques.

DeSilva, D. A. "Measuring Penultimate Against Ultimate Reality: An Investigation of the Integrity and Argumentation of 2 Corinthians." *JSNT* 52 (1993). A helpful use of rhetorical traditions for understanding some of Paul's transitions and purposes.

Fitzgerald, J. T. *Cracks in an Earthen Vessel: An Examination of the Catalogues of Hardships in the Corinthian Correspondence.* Atlanta: Scholars Press, 1988. An illuminating window on Paul's adaptation of a social convention.

Furnish, V. P. *II Corinthians.* AB 33. Garden City, N.Y.: Doubleday, 1984. This thoughtful, careful, thorough commentary was a landmark.

Georgi, D. *The Opponents of Paul in Second Corinthians.* Philadelphia: Fortress, 1986. A tendentious study whose methodology and suppositions have carried a disproportionate weight in the study of 2 Corinthians.

Marshall, Peter. *Enmity at Corinth: Social Conventions in Paul's Relations with the Corinthians.* WUNT 44. Tübingen: J. C. B. Mohr, 1987. One of the early looks at Paul's relation to the Corinthians in the light of the way social practices and conventions affected human relations.

Savage, T. B. *Power Through Weakness: Paul's Understanding of the Christian Ministry in 2 Corinthians.* New York: Cambridge University Press, 1996. A competent and suggestive appreciation of Paul's ironic vision.

Sumney, J. L. *Identifying Paul's Opponents: The Question of Method in 2 Corinthians.* JSNTSup 40. Sheffield: Sheffield Academic, 1990. Signal for its cautions about the problems it addresses.

Thrall, M. E. *A Critical and Exegetical Commentary on the Second Epistle to the Corinthians 1–7.* Edinburgh: T. & T. Clark, 1994. Thorough, cognizant of competing interpretations, this commentary exhibits detailed, balanced, insightful illumination of chaps. 1–7.

OUTLINE OF 2 CORINTHIANS

I. 2 Corinthians 1:1–9:15, An Appeal for Affection and for Funds for the Jerusalem Church

    A. 1:1-2, Salutation
    B. 1:3-11, Blessing of God
    C. 1:12-14, Paul's Principled Conduct
    D. 1:15–2:4, Paul's Travel Plans and His Painful Letter
    E. 2:5-11, The One Who Caused the Pain and Paul's Forgiveness
    F. 2:12-13, Paul's Anxiety over Titus the Letter Bearer
    G. 2:14–6:10, A Multifaceted Treatment of Paul's Ministry
        2:14-17, Paul's Place in God's Purposes
        3:1–4:6, Paul's Ministry of a New Covenant
        4:7–5:10, Paul's Ministry Sustained Through Affliction and Mortality
        5:11–6:10, Paul's Ministry of Reconciliation
    H. 6:11–7:4, Paul's Direct Appeal for More Affection
    I. 7:5-16, Reprise of Concern and Reassurances of Confidence
    J. 8:1–9:15, The Macedonians as Models, the Collections, and the Corinthians' Participation
        8:1-7, Macedonia, Ministry, and the Corinthians
        8:8-15, No Command but Advice: Finish What You Began
        8:16-24, Titus and Others as Warrantors of Probity
        9:1-5, Steps to Ensure That the Corinthians Are Ready
        9:6-15, Sowing and Reaping Bountifully

II. 2 Corinthians 10:1–13:13, Paul's Preparation for a Showdown Visit

    A. 10:1-6, Paul's Readiness to Do Battle
    B. 10:7-11, Consider What You Know
    C. 10:12-18, Boasting Within Limit
    D. 11:1-15, Betrothal and Betrayal: Paul and the Opponents
    E. 11:16–12:10, The Fool's Speech: Paul's Boastful Comparison
        11:16-21*a,* Bearing with Fools
        11:21*b*-29, So to Boast
        11:30-33, Boasting and Deliverance Through the Damascus Wall
        12:1-10, The Man in Paradise with a Thorn/Stake in His Flesh
    F. 12:11-13, Apostolic Commendation and Confirmation
    G. 12:14-18, Paul's Final Self-defense
    H. 12:19-21, Preliminary Assessment and Differing Expectations
    I. 13:1-10, Ground Rules and Challenge
    J. 13:11-13, Concluding Admonitions and Grace

2 CORINTHIANS 1:1–9:15

AN APPEAL FOR AFFECTION AND FOR FUNDS FOR THE JERUSALEM CHURCH

OVERVIEW

In 2 Corinthians 1:1–9 Paul has written a powerful letter in which he makes every attempt to put himself forward as the apostle fully worthy of the Corinthians' embrace and obedience. This letter is bracketed on the front by Paul's severe disappointment that the Corinthians did not rally to his side when he was done "wrong" by one of them and by a painful letter of harsh frank speech that he wrote to them subsequent to the "wrong" and prior to what we now call 2 Corinthians 1–9. These chapters were written after Titus's reassurances that the Corinthians had come around and shown themselves ready for a fuller reassociation with Paul. Titus must also have been the one who told Paul that his failure to make a promised trip had generated grumblings among the Corinthians about Paul's dependability; so that becomes one of the first issues treated explicitly in the letter and, we can safely say, referenced indirectly in subsequent defenses of his comportment. The letter is bracketed on the other end by Paul's discovery that the Macedonians have successfully, even cheerfully, gathered the collection and are ready to pursue the itinerary with it that Paul had earlier set out: through Corinth to Jerusalem.

So from the first verse of the letter, Paul knows that he has two overriding concerns to deal with: He must conciliate and reassure the Corinthians that their inclination to realign with him is sound and proper, and he must lay the groundwork—by giving the Corinthians cause to embrace him and by establishing the hooks on which he will hang his final appeal—for persuading the Corinthians to regain their earlier zeal for him *and* to partake wholeheartedly in the collection. Paul cannot settle for just one of the two goals because they are inextricably bound together.

He surely cannot, however, tackle the collection issue until he thinks he has given the Corinthians grounds for full reassociation with him; so the collection is only hinted at in the opening seven chapters. When he does turn explicitly to the collection, he can then capitalize, as he does, on many of the preceding claims and themes that he has so powerfully argued.

That 2 Corinthians 1–9 was not successful on every front will be painfully clear in chapters 10–13. Romans, written after all of the Corinthian correspondence and written from Corinth (Rom 16:23), does depict that Achaia took part in the collection for the saints in Jerusalem (Rom 15:26). "The saints in all of Achaia" were, along with the Corinthians, recipients of 2 Corinthians 1–9 (see 1:1), so Paul's epistolary efforts at encouraging participation in the collection did bear fruit, when seen in the light of Rom 15:26. Whether Achaia's cooperation included Corinthian participation, however, is beyond our capacity to know, but we may ponder that when we take into account the tone of 2 Corinthians 10–13, a subsequent Pauline fragment of a later letter sent to the Corinthians.

2 CORINTHIANS 1:1-2, SALUTATION

COMMENTARY

A comparison of this salutation with that of 1 Corinthians offers some parallels and some significant differences. In both letters Paul describes himself as "apostle of Christ Jesus by God's will" (1:1). In 2 Corinthians, however, Paul names a different person as his co-authoring "brother." Missing is Sosthenes (1 Cor 1:1; cf. Acts 18:17). In his place is Timothy (2 Cor 1:1). Timothy, whom Paul elsewhere describes as his "soul mate" (ἰσόψυχος *isopsychos*, Phil 2:20), has had a long, positive relationship with the Corinthians. He is the one whom Paul had sent to the Corinthians in the early days to teach them "my ways in Christ" (1 Cor 4:17), apparently successfully, and 1 Corinthians closes with Paul, who is detained in Ephesus, sending Timothy once again to work with them (1 Cor 16:10-11). Timothy's continued good standing with the Corinthians is signaled by Paul's inclusion of him (with Silvanus) as one of those who, along with Paul, have faithfully preached Jesus Christ among the Corinthians (2 Cor 1:19). Paul's association of himself with Timothy as co-author bids to co-opt for himself the goodwill Timothy has garnered with the Corinthians over the years. Thus, from the very outset of this letter, Paul works to enhance his own standing with the Corinthians.

The addressees are once again called "the church of God which is in Corinth," as they were in 1 Cor 1:2. Whereas 1 Corinthians stopped with that, the audience for this new letter fragment is significantly widened to include "all the saints who are in the whole of Achaia," the Roman province that includes Corinth and the entire Peloponnese. This enlargement of the audience is a bit like inviting a third party, no doubt favorable to Paul, into the deliberation with the Corinthians. We do not know a great deal about other Pauline churches in Achaia, but we are aware that Phoebe, whom Paul describes to the Romans as one of his patrons and as a deacon of the church at Cenchreae (Rom 16:1), a town at Corinth's eastern shore, is a strong advocate for Paul. It is not unreasonable to suppose that the other believers in her church are also positively related to Paul. If Phoebe is any index, Paul's including other believers in Achaia brings into the circle of letter recipients more people who are favorably attentive to Paul. Already, two details in the salutation—Paul's choosing Timothy as co-author and the inclusion of the Achaians among the addressees—are tilted positively toward enhancing Paul's relations with the Corinthians, a matter of enormous concern throughout 2 Corinthians 1–9.

The salutation concludes exactly as all of Paul's other salutations: with a wish—indeed, a blessing delivered with apostolic bearing—for grace and peace (from God and Jesus Christ; 1:2). Grace, the freely given, unmerited favor of God, is appropriately the greeting among believers because the very life of faith and the basis of their having community together come about as a direct result of God's grace poured into their lives. Grace is not only actively present at the beginning of the life of faith, but it is also the enduring ground of all of life, from start to finish. Peace, no doubt for Paul out of his rich Jewish heritage, is the *shalom* that comes about by God's reclamation and righting of people and their social circumstances. Peace, the end of enmity between people and God (Rom 5:1), is a Pauline code word for the reconciliation that brings alienated persons back into fellowship and into accord with one another and, as we shall see in this letter fragment, between the Corinthians and Paul (2 Cor 5:14-21; cf. 1 Cor 7:15; 14:33; 2 Cor 13:11).

REFLECTIONS

Paul signals an important consideration in these opening verses: Christians are never isolated from one another. They always live their lives of faith in connection with one another. The creedal affirmation "I believe in the communion of the saints" could just as well have derived from Paul, who believes that the saints—that is, all of us whom God has claimed, are given to one another. How matters go for any of God's people is important to all of us. Christian community does not allow any to be left out or behind. The insularity of modern life threatens Christian community and sometimes clouds the visibility of those in need.

2 CORINTHIANS 1:3-11, BLESSING OF GOD

COMMENTARY

Where we might expect to find a thanksgiving in Paul's letters (cf. Rom 1:8-15; 1 Cor 1:4-9; Phil 1:3-11; 1 Thess 1:2-12; Phlm 4-7), we see a "Blessed be God" (NIV, "Praise be") formula, which Paul adopts and adapts from his Jewish heritage. Throughout the literature of Israel and of the early churches the "blessed be" formula is used only of God (1 Kgs 1:48; 2 Chr 2:12; 6:4; Pss 34:1; 72:18[71:18]; Mark 14:61; Luke 1:68; cf. Eph 1:3; 1 Pet 1:3).

A brief look at the formula in Israel's Scriptures is instructive for understanding it in 2 Corinthians 1. David, near his death, uses the expression to praise God's faithfulness in granting that David's son Solomon will sit on the throne God gave to David (1 Kgs 1:48). Even the king of Tyre invokes the formula because the God who made heaven and earth has faithfully granted David a wise son who will build God a temple (2 Chr 2:12). Solomon cites the exodus from Egypt and the selection of Jerusalem as the site for the Temple as the signs that "the LORD has fulfilled his promise that he made" (2 Chr 6:10 NRSV) and on that basis says "Blessed be God" (2 Chr 6:4).

At the heart of one's blessing of God, therefore, is a thankful appreciation of *God's faithfulness,* of God's steadfastness in making good on what God has promised. Even more directly in view for Paul may be the kind of expression exemplified in Psalm 34, where God is blessed explicitly for deliverance from trouble and difficulty, precisely the connection Paul pursues in the verses directly following the "blessed be" formula. The writer of that psalm, like Paul, recognizes that the faithful are beset by distress and afflictions,

but the Blessed One (God) delivers the righteous "out of them all" (Ps 34:19).

Others of Paul's letters show that he has clearly appropriated the expression of God's blessedness and occasionally uses it in doxological settings where he finds himself moved to praise and give thanks to God (Rom 1:25; 9:5), in effect for God's faithfulness, for God's coming through on what has been promised, or in a place where Paul vows his own truthfulness and calls God as his witness (2 Cor 11:31). Blessing God is giving thanks to God; when one believer blesses God, others are expected to join in the affirmation of thanksgiving by saying, "Amen" (1 Cor 14:16). So Paul opens 2 Corinthians with a "blessed be God" formula and thereby anticipates, and indeed sets the context for, his note of the faithfulness of God that explicitly surfaces in 2 Cor 1:18-20 and that associates Paul's faithfulness and dependability with God's. Significantly also, Paul's blessing of God invites the Corinthian auditors to join with him.

Paul's blessing of God opens a passage that begins with God's consolation in the face of afflictions and distress and concludes with a note of hope and thanksgiving. The blessing itself (v. 3) names God as "Father of our Lord Jesus Christ," an echo of the grace that closes the salutation (v. 2; cf. a similar association in 11:31). The sequence "God" and "Father" of vv. 2 and 3*a* is, in v. 3*b,* reversed, forming a small chiasmus (ABB'A'), and allowing Paul an opportunity further to characterize the God who is blessed.

As any proemium or exordium, the classic opening of a speech in Paul's time, was expected to do, vv. 3-10 set the tone and lay down certain themes that will suffuse the passages that follow.[47] The verses are loaded with passion and emotion. Charged rhetoric of extremes flashes before us. The lexicon of difficulties (including θλῖψις *thlipsis*, vv. 4, 8; παθήματα *pathēmata*, vv. 5-7; θλίβω *thlibō*, v. 6; and πάσχω *paschō*, v. 6) contributes to the tone and introduces a major theme of affliction and distress that will lace through the entire letter fragment. A second theme, even more pro nounced in these opening verses, is God's compassion (οἰκτιρμός *oiktirmos*, v. 3) and comfort/consolation (παρακαλέω *parakaleō*, παράκλησις *paraklēsis*, repeated ten times in vv. 3-10 and fourteen times in the remainder of the letter fragment). A third theme, that of abundance, expressed in the term περισσεύω (*perisseuō*), appears twice in the proemium (v. 5) and seven times in the rest of the letter fragment (3:9; 4:15; 8:2, 7; 9:8, 12; cf. 8:2, 14) and ties the two already noted themes together.

These verses depict "suffering/misfortune" (*pathēmata*, vv. 5-6) and "affliction/distress" (*thlipsis*; NIV, "troubles" [v. 4] and "hardships" [v. 8]) as the context in which God's "encouragement/comfort/consolation" (*paraklēsis*) finds its proper expression. Much as in Romans, where Paul said that as sin abounds, grace abounds all the more (Rom 5:20), here in these verses he suggests that God's *paraklēsis* meets human *pathēmata* and *thlipsis* in a superabounding fashion; God's *paraklēsis* overflows people's *pathēmata* and *thlipsis*. Human suffering or misfortune and affliction must not be confused with sin, however—quite the opposite. Identifying with God, with the gospel, assures one of encountering distress and suffering, and that very affliction becomes the locus where God's consolation, comfort, and encouragement find abundant expression.

Paul's use of "we" and "us" throughout this passage invites the Corinthian hearers to picture themselves in solidarity with Paul before their compassionate God, whose comfort meets them in every distress (vv. 3-4). Paul further encourages his listeners to identify with him by his reference to *Christ's* suffering flowing over into "our lives" (v. 5*a* NIV). A christological identification underlies this subpart of his argument (vv. 5, 9). In

quite parallel constructions, Paul ties together the sufferings of Christ, which abound to "our" benefit, with our consolation, which abounds on account of Christ. The two are directly linked for Paul. Paul's eschatological frame of reference and his confidence upon which it is based lead him to affirm that as surely as "we" share Christ's sufferings, "we" are assured that our consolation/comfort abounds because of Christ (v. 5). The Corinthians had heard this confidence in an earlier letter from Paul (cf. 1 Cor 15:1).

In v. 6, however, although the "we" expression continues in the first verb, the hearers will find that Paul now inserts himself and his own experience directly into the picture. For the first time he mentions "your consolation and salvation" and shows by that expression that he has begun to talk primarily about himself, even though he continues to use the plural pronoun "we."

For Paul, association with the gospel guarantees one's being at cross purposes with the world, whose structures are dominated by sin. Witness Paul's telling the Thessalonians that, as they face the opposition of their unbelieving neighbors, they are experiencing precisely what he had forecast for them while he was with them (1 Thess 3:3). Or consider his own self-depiction at the end of 1 Corinthians, where he reports a huge door opened for his evangelizing at Ephesus, "and there are many opponents" (1 Cor 16:9). So affliction, distress, and opposition are expected for those who are claimed by the gospel.

At the heart of Paul's opening engagement of the Corinthians in this letter is his foundational conviction that God comes to the aid of those who are afflicted, who are down-and-out. God dependably meets human suffering with overflowing comfort (cf. the same confidence for those who mourn in Matt 5:4). God faithfully meets the affliction of believers with comfort and with consolation or encouragement.

God, as the source of pity, mercy, and compassion, is known throughout Israel's Scriptures (2 Sam 24:14; Ps 24:6; Isa 63:15; cf. *T. Jos.* 2:3), and we find elsewhere in the letters that Paul affirms God's mercy (cf. Rom 12:1). God is not merely sometimes or occasionally merciful; God is continually and faithfully

47. F. W. Hughes, "The Rhetoric of Reconciliation: 2 Corinthians 1.1–2.13 and 7.5–8.24," in *Persuasive Artistry: Studies in New Testament Rhetoric in Honor of G. A. Kennedy*, ed. D. F. Watson, JSNTSup 50 (Sheffield: Sheffield Academic, 1991) 250-51.

merciful. God's mercy and compassion are attributes that consistently characterize God.

God's comfort and compassion are not given to believers as a personal possession. Recipients of God's merciful encouragement become the channels through whom God's comfort is made available to others who are themselves "in any affliction" (v. 4). Paul finds a certain logic to this: Those who experience the abundance of Christ's sufferings by their exposure to affliction in this world experience a corresponding abundance of comfort (v. 5).

As soon as Paul has established that God's comfort/encouragement/consolation overflows in the face of distress and affliction (vv. 3-5), he tells the Corinthians, in the most general and sweeping way, that any affliction he has suffered has been for their "comfort and salvation"; any comfort he has received is for their comfort, which they experience as they share his sufferings (v. 6). Several important rhetorical moves converge here. First, Paul seeks to secure Corinthian identification with him; his suffering is at once benefiting them, and they should identify with his suffering, as he had already told them in an earlier letter: "If one member suffers, all the members suffer together" (1 Cor 12:26). The form of Paul's formulation is a *sorites*, or chain, each element picking up and reaffirming the previous one: A leads to B; B leads to C; and so forth. Such rhetorical structures are designed to make the strongest connection between the first and the last element in the chain,[48] in this case "afflicted" (v. 6a) and "suffering" (v. 6d). In v. 7 Paul explicitly and powerfully calls them and himself *"partners* in suffering . . . and encouragement" (κοινωνοὶ . . . τῶν παθημάτων . . . τῆς παρακλήσεως *koinōnoi . . . tōn pathēmatōn . . . tēs paraklēseōs*). Second, he seeks to elicit goodwill from the Corinthians toward himself because the rhetorical tradition trained persons to generate goodwill by references to themselves and to their service in behalf of the ones who can return the favor with goodwill.[49] Third, by linking their ultimate "salvation" with "patient endurance" (ὑπομονη *hypomonē*, v. 6), Paul bids them to stay the course even though their relation with Paul has been somewhat stormy of late (see the Introduction).

Because the Corinthians are his partners (he now additionally enforces that identification by calling them ἀδελφοί [*adelphoi*], "brothers and sisters," v. 8)[50] in suffering and comfort (v. 7), and because he has already established that any distress of his is also theirs (v. 6), he makes certain that they learn immediately of the adversity he has recently experienced in Asia, the Roman province that roughly corresponds to the western part of modern Turkey. The Corinthians do not learn what this calamity was, but they surely are told of its enormity. Paul describes his own state in hyperbolic categories: "beyond measure" or "beyond our ability" (καθ' ὑπερβολήν *kath' hyperbolēn*, v. 8; NRSV, "utterly" [ὑπὲρ δύναμιν *hyper dynamin*]). He was so weighed down that he "despaired of life" (v. 8); he felt as if he had received a death sentence (v. 9). Twice more he refers to "the dead" and the "deadly" (vv. 9-10). Clearly, Paul identifies what happened to him in Asia as life threatening. Paul's desperate scenario is surely designed to elicit pity, and therefore support, from his audience.[51]

Stripped of any pretention of personal power, Paul found himself trusting in the God who not only comforts, consoles, and encourages, but also "raises the dead" (v. 9; cf. Rom 4:17, where God is depicted as the one "who raises the dead and calls into being the things that are not"). In his overwhelming distress, Paul relied upon the truth encapsulated in a christological dictum: In raising Christ from the dead, God showed power over death. Paul, despairing of life itself, counted on God, on God's power, a power demonstrated and warranted in Christ's having been raised. If the Corinthians did not know the identity of Paul's Asian crisis from some other source, such as the person who delivered the letter, then they, like we, are left to imagine it.

Paul vests his hope in God because of God's faithfulness in deliverance, the very reason why Paul blessed God at the start of this letter (v. 3). The God who raises the dead (present description, v. 9) is the same God who has delivered Paul (credit from the past, v. 10), presumably from this most

48. H. A. Fischel, *Rabbinic Literature and Greco-Roman Philosophy* (Leiden: Brill, 1973) 77, 151-52n. 126.

49. See *Ad Herennium* 1.5.8, a roughly contemporary rhetorical handbook.

50. Belleville, "A Letter of Apologetic Self-recommendation," 147-48, argues that the body of the letter fragment begins with this verse.

51. Belleville, "A Letter of Apologetic Self-recommendation," 149: "The central concern of the body opening is thus that of reciprocity." See also *Ad Herennium* 2.31.50.

recent, dreadful crisis in Asia, and is the identical God on whom Paul counts (twice, v. 10) to deliver (confidence toward the future) yet again. References to hope have bracketed Paul's report of his brush with death in Asia (vv. 7, 10). Paul's hope is not some wishing against the odds. Hope is based on the very character of God, a steadfast, trustworthy character built across history. Accordingly, Paul looks at the future with confidence that God will bring matters to a fruitful end, and in like fashion, Paul can look death in the face and have confidence that God is the one who delivers/saves/preserves/rescues ($\dot{\rho}\dot{\upsilon}o\mu\alpha\iota$ *ryomai*; 3 times in v. 10).

The passage concludes with Paul's request for intercessory prayer, that the Corinthians join in helping ($\sigma\upsilon\nu\upsilon\pi\upsilon\rho\gamma\dot{\epsilon}\omega$ *synypourgeō*) by their prayers, which Paul construes as thanksgivings for the favor ($\chi\dot{\alpha}\rho\iota\sigma\mu\alpha$ *charisma*; NRSV, "blessing") that has been bestowed upon him—namely, his deliverance. The proemium opens with a blessing of God, who, like the grandest of patrons (on patrons and clients, see the Introduction), has, in the context of abundant intercession of others, done a favor for the distressed client named Paul. It closes with Paul expecting his own deliverance to generate many persons' thanksgivings to that same patron (v. 11; cf. Rom 12:15). Their prayers—and Paul's call for prayers for himself—affirm a reciprocity between Paul and the Corinthians that mirrors the reciprocity that God as divine patron deserves from the believing clientele (v. 11).

Curiously, though many of the openings in Paul's letters *begin* with a thanksgiving (cf. Rom 1:8-15; 1 Cor 1:4-9; Phil 1:3-11; 1 Thess 1:2-10; Phlm 4-7), the opening section of 2 Corinthians *ends* with a thanksgiving that yet once more invites the Corinthians to make common cause with Paul. In vv. 3-11 we have heard only of God's deliverance of Paul from his Asian perils, but this grand thanksgiving for personal deliverance surely serves as a background for Paul's upcoming celebration of his deliverance from tough times with the Corinthians.

REFLECTIONS

1. Blessing God is strange to our ears. We are more likely to think of—or at least to hope for—God's blessing of us. But here Paul has it going the other way. For Paul, blessing God is another way of giving thanks, but the blessing of God is especially to be employed when we hit hard times. It is a way of remembering, a way of reminding ourselves, and one another, that God has delivered us in the past—indeed, that God's nature is to deliver. The God of the exodus is our God. Our recitation of God's faithfulness, via our blessing of God, should not only help us to remember God's deliverance in the past, but also assist our trusting—and even eager—expectation that God's comfort will somehow find us in our present distress. Our God delivers and comforts. The very act of looking for deliverance or comfort is the first faithful response, which itself may help us to see the exodus that is perhaps already graciously before our eyes.

2. We tend to think of comfort as a feeling, as in a comfortable chair or of feeling good about something. In such a conception, the "God of comfort" would help us to feel good. Paul opens a different window onto the understanding of comfort: It is more like a gift that God gives or a door that God opens to us for a way out of affliction.

3. Deep-seated in our culture is the notion that prosperity is a signal of God's favor and that adversity, affliction, or suffering is a sure sign of God's displeasure and judgment. Jesus did not think that suffering or physical problems were a sign of sin (John 9:1-2). Neither does Paul here in this text—or anywhere. Paul's laudation of affliction is not an elevation of suffering for its own sake; neither must it be taken as a prescription so that to be a Christian is to be miserable. Paul thinks distress happens to people along two patterns: in part because people who live by faith are at odds with the world, whose structures are under the power of sin and therefore caustic to Christians, and in part because fragile, finite human beings experience distress and loss as ingredient to life (see 2 Cor 4:16-18).

4. Distress and all the rites of passage that mark great changes or signal the extremities of life (e.g., death, divorce, adverse medical prognoses) provide occasions that may break through human pretense. That is why persons who are dying, or who are around those who are, sometimes find themselves moved to forgive and to overcome previous hostilities and misunderstandings. Just as human distress and change provide occasion for God's abundant comfort, according to Paul, so also we can generously console those we find in adversity. God's comfort is our model and our inspiration. Have you ever been around an older person who, facing death, finds a serenity and peacefulness that is absolutely infectious? That person knows the comfort Paul is describing. Is there any reason why those of us who are not at death's door might not also understand and celebrate that comfort in the junctions of our lives?

5. We may find it easier to show comfort and concern when another person is suffering and more difficult to celebrate his or her deliverance. No jealousy leaches into our thoughts when a friend or acquaintance is experiencing some affliction, but when a friend gets a new, better job, a better car, is admitted into a prestigious college, gets a raise, or has a better harvest, can we be genuinely thankful that person has done well? Another person's deliverance or boon is an occasion for thanksgiving. If we could genuinely rejoice over other people's deliverance and good fortune, then we could contagiously share their joy.

6. Seeing Paul at the end of his rope—indeed, near death—can provide us with a model for dealing with affliction. By all the evidence of his letters, he had innumerable hardships and difficulties (see 2 Cor 6:4-10; 11:23-28; 12:10). As down and out as he was sometimes, he received comfort from God and trusted that God would not let distress have the last word. Too often we romanticize biblical characters, making them distant from us and less like us. Maybe the next time we reflect on our own distresses, failures, and disappointments, we might try to picture ourselves as like Paul and wonder how he found joy in the midst of suffering. Reading some of his passages about joy experienced in the midst of suffering might be a good place to start that reflection (see Romans 8; Phil 1:12-26).

2 CORINTHIANS 1:12-14, PAUL'S PRINCIPLED CONDUCT

COMMENTARY

In the previous section, Paul described the distress he recently experienced in service of the gospel, a conventional move in that time, designed to engender goodwill on the part of auditors. Here he characterizes his conduct, again by reference to a conventional form, an expression of self-confidence.[52] In all of his correspondence, these verses rank as some of his most thorough self-reflections of

how he has conducted his life according to certain principles (ἀναστρέφω *anastrephō*, v. 12). Consistency is the subtext: Paul has comported himself well everywhere (ἐν τῷ κόσμῳ *en tō kosmō*, "in the world," v. 12) as he has with the Corinthians; if anything, he suggests, he has been even more scrupulous with them (περισσοτέρως δὲ πρὸς ὑμᾶς *perissoteros de pros hymas*, v. 12; cf. similar expressions of Paul's superabounding concern for and commitment to the Corinthians, 2 Cor 2:4; 7:15).

---

52. S. N. Olson, "Epistolary Uses of Expresssions of Self-Confidence," *JBL* 103 (1984) 596-97. Cf. 2 Cor 5:11; 11:5; 13:6.

Verse 12, with its declarations of his exemplary comportment and of his commitment to the Corinthians, introduces the twin themes that will ground everything Paul writes through 6:10.

Paul presents his self-portrait as a boast (καύχησις *kauchēsis*, v. 12). Paul writes about boasting in two very distinct ways. If one's boasting is a showing off, a gloating, a suggestion that one's actions are one's own achievement and, therefore, an index of status, then Paul rejects it as inappropriate. (Examples of Paul's view of improper boasting can be seen in 1 Cor 3:21; 4:7; 5:6.) On the contrary, however, one can properly boast of the gospel, of God (Rom 5:11; 1 Cor 1:31; cf. Jer 9:24), and of God's power. In an ancillary fashion, as here, one can boast of one's labors in service of the gospel because that boasting does not simply and unequivocally point to one's own power and accomplishment, but rather places one's own work in the larger picture of God's work (see the discussion of "work" in the Commentary on 1 Cor 15:58). Paul regularly boasts of his preaching the gospel and, as here, of his work in advancing it (Rom 15:17; 1 Cor 9:15; Gal 6:14; Phil 1:26; 2:16; cf. 1 Cor 9:16 for Paul's own sense of the ambiguity of boasting). Proper boasting is always grounded in God's grace-filled, preemptive working and is, therefore, always fundamentally responsive; it points more to God than to oneself.

Boasting and self-commendation do, however, play quite an extensive role in the letter fragments that make up 2 Corinthians and emerge here for first consideration. Self-commendation is used when one wants to recover good relations between the speaker or writer and the audience. This will become an apparent need in the next topic because Paul has failed to make a promised visit to the Corinthians (vv. 15-22). Among the topics that are frequently featured in self-commendations are one's comportment and character, as here in v. 12 (cf. 4:2), one's past efforts in behalf of the hearers, as in 4:5 and 5:13, or the hope that speaker and hearers may be mutually proud of one another, as in 1:14 and 5:12.

Paul introduces his boast with the clause "our conscience bears witness" and thus declares that his accompanying self-commendation has been subjected to the scrutiny of his moral consciousness that confirms its veracity and propriety (v. 12). Thus Paul certifies that what he here declares about his conduct regarding the Corinthians is not lightly or casually advanced. The Corinthians can remember from an earlier letter hearing Paul's view that all believers have moral consciousness or consciences, as the term συνείδησις (*syneidēsis*) may variously be translated, and that some will have weaker and others stronger moral consciousness (1 Cor 8:7, 10, 12). Further, he expects all believers to weigh matters with their consciences (1 Cor 10:23-30), as he has done here in what he now says to them.

He structures his conscience-vetted boast—about how he has conducted himself—in a positive-negative-positive form. Both positive statements give ultimate credit to God as the source of power behind not only Paul's comportment, but also his boast. Paul's frank speech (which the Corinthians have experienced most recently in the no longer extant letter; see the Introduction; reading ἁπλότης [*haplotēs*] instead of ἁγιότης [*hagiotēs*], "holiness," "moral purity") and his sincerity or purity of motive (εἰλικρίνεια *eilikrineia*) are necessarily related. To speak in frankness effectively with friends requires that the speaker have an established ethos founded on sincerity or purity of motive.[53] Paul's choice of words expresses his understanding of his relationship with the Corinthians as one of friendship in which Paul, the friend in question, assures his friends that they have been able to count on him as a dependable, consistent associate whose probity of motive and practiced frankness are indispensable indices of friendship. In v. 12, Paul declares that both his frankness and his sincerity cohere in and ground his conduct. In a classical antithetical construction, Paul declares that his comportment has been guided not by mundane wisdom, but by the grace of God. Paul lays bare his conviction that there are two rival ways of being in the world: One can take primary guidance from what one can figure out about the world on one's own; or one can be guided, and from Paul's perspective energized, by God's grace

---

53. See Plutarch *How to Tell a Flatterer from a Friend* 71E.

(cf. the upcoming alternatives "outer/inner," 4:16; "seen/unseen," 4:18; "face/heart," 5:12).

Paul's reference to what and how he has written to the Corinthians is given as evidence of his sincerity and of his eagerness for them to understand. No doubt the *immediate* focus of the understanding is centered on solidifying the Corinthians' relation to Paul (as expressed by the NIV's insertion of "us" as the object of the understanding Paul hopes for in v. 14). Although the Greek does not explicitly make that connection, Paul's readers are free to do so. Paul does not stop, however, with the immediate. Rather, he transposes the whole question of understanding into an eschatological issue, into whether the Corinthians will *finally* understand as they should so that at the last day, at the judgment, at the return of Christ, they will be found acceptable and that Paul and they can boast of one another (then boasting becomes equivalent once again to thanksgiving) on the day of our Lord Jesus Christ (v. 14). Subtly, Paul elides the Corinthians' understanding of what he writes, and therefore of himself, with their understanding of their place in God's cosmic purposes, which will come to a conclusion in the day of Christ. The ambiguity that resides already in the Greek phrase ἕως τέλους (*heōs telous*), which can mean simply "completely" or "fully" (NIV) or "until the end" (NRSV), is precisely the ambiguity that resides in the entire passage.

REFLECTIONS

1. Boasting has earned a bad reputation—and rightly so when it involves self-puffery and self-service—but we might wonder if boasting is of necessity always to be avoided. It may be difficult for some persons to read Paul, partly because he had a certainty about his faith that many today find beyond their reach, and partly because his boasting sometimes slips beyond what seems to be good taste. When Paul's boasting is clearly in what God is doing, we probably have an easier time. But there is a problem in our reticence to boast: How can we properly celebrate what God is doing in our lives? Must we not tell others about it so that we can celebrate it together? Paul presumes so. Restraint in boasting about God's grace in our lives further privatizes faith and limits community.

2. Consistency of conduct is the foundation of trust in human relations. Friendship can go nowhere if there is not confidence that the other person can be counted on regularly and completely. Trust is built one brick at a time. The structure we build by our day-in/day-out dependability is the house where we live and into which we invite our friends. When it comes to building or destroying trust, there are no little failures of dependability, no little slights of each other. All of our peccadilloes corrode trust. Failing to take the trash out as promised may not seem like such a big thing, but it subtly raises the question of what all our promises mean.

3. Paul's setting of "worldly wisdom" over against the "grace of God" should not be understood as a disparagement of wisdom per se. Neither should it be understood as an advocacy for Christians' not thinking. Clearly, Paul believes the conscience and its moral reflection are important in daily comportment (1:12*b*). Paul probes here the question of where believers begin their reasoning, where they ground it. Paul's answer: Believers start with the grace of God as their reasoning point—that is, they take God's freely given love as the cardinal point, the magnetic north, of their moral compass. Then they reckon from there what shape and direction their own life and loving ought to take. Christians do not start their reckoning from the world and its values.

2 CORINTHIANS 1:15–2:4, PAUL'S TRAVEL PLANS AND HIS PAINFUL LETTER

COMMENTARY

The previous two pericopes have set the context for these verses. In the first passage, Paul established God's faithfulness as the ground for the blessing of God (1:3-11). In the second, Paul pictured himself as a dependable, steadfast friend whose consistent moral probity is his hallmark (1:12-14). Now, in 1:15-22, he has to account for what has no doubt seemed to some Corinthians as a contradiction of his self-portrait in 1:12-14: Paul has not made the visit to Corinth that he had promised (2:1). Instead, he has sent them a letter (2:3), which he (later) describes as "painful" for them and for himself (7:8-12). Paul supposes himself vulnerable to a complaint of vacillation—and he responds to it.

1:15-16. In these verses Paul lays out the itinerary he had wanted (the term βούλομαι [*boulomai*, "wish/want/desire"] appears four times) to follow. The proposed route would have involved two trips through Corinth, which Paul calls a "double favor" (δευτέραν χάριν *deuteran charin*), continuing the language of friendship as well as of patron/client and giving pride of place to Corinth. If this letter fragment was written from Ephesus (see the Introduction), Paul had projected a sea voyage on the Aegean to Corinth, from which he would make his way north overland to Macedonia, the Roman district where Paul had established churches, at least in Thessalonica and in Philippi. From there he had expected to return to Corinth (the doubled favor) and had hoped that they would provide "help on our journey to Judea," the southern part of ancient Palestine where Jerusalem lies (1:16). The Macedonians' plans to go to Corinth with their part of the collection show that they also knew this projected itinerary (9:1-5).

But none of this happened as touted. Paul decided not to go to Corinth. In a refinement, he uses rather formal terminology of rendering a carefully considered choice: "I reached a decision [ἔκρινα δὲ ἐμαυτῷ τοῦτο *ekrina de emautō touto*; 2:1] not to come to you

again painfully [ἐν λύπῃ *en lypē*]" (2:1, italics added).

1:17. A fuller picture of Paul's increasingly troubled relations with the Corinthians is now possible. Since he wrote what we call 1 Corinthians, Paul (1) has made what must have been a disastrous visit to them (Paul describes it as having been "painful," 2:1; more on that follows), (2) has written them what he dubs a "painful" letter instead of making a promised visit (2:2-3), and (3) has thereby left himself open to a charge of vacillation, that he runs hot and cold (1:17-18). Each of these events no doubt caused problems between Paul and the Corinthians, but now they have come together, and Paul addresses them collectively; further, he is concerned for the harm the two events have caused to the Corinthians' relation with him.

The "painful" visit and the "painful" letter are connected to each other in this fashion: Timothy, the co-author of 2 Corinthians 1–9 and who, according to Acts 18:5, was, along with Paul and Silvanus (Silas), present for the founding of the Corinthian church, was first sent back to Corinth by Paul to "explain my ways" (1 Cor 4:17). Next Timothy was dispatched to Corinth, perhaps as bearer of 1 Corinthians to them (1 Cor 16:10-11). From there the matter is not crystal clear, but events seem to have fallen this way: After some time, Timothy apparently returned to Paul in Ephesus with a report that the situation at Corinth had deteriorated. Clearly once again, Paul, in an effort to bring things back into line, went to Corinth for what he now dubs a "painful" visit (2:1); and later, when faced with the prospect of another painful visit, Paul scrubbed his planned trip to Corinth and sent a stern letter instead (7:8). All these problems, addressed first here, will make their impact at later points in the letter fragment as well (cf. 7:8-12).

With that background, we return to Paul's first engagement of this mare's nest of problems: the possible charge that he vacillates, or to put it most directly, that he is not dependably a man of his word in the conduct of his life. This is a serious challenge to the very underpinning not only of Paul's authority, but also of the most essential ingredient to friendship—namely, the dependable, steadfast, trustworthy character of the individual. In two questions formed in the Greek so as to expect a negative answer, Paul tries to distance himself from anyone whose plans and actions are subject to whim and caprice (1:17).[54]

1:18-22. By contrast, Paul is about to present himself—and significantly Silvanus and Timothy—as subject to God. In these verses Paul transposes the challenge of his trustworthiness from the question of his recent change of itinerary, which apparently is an issue with some Corinthians, first, to a claim about God (1:18), then to an assertion about Christ (1:19-20), and then to a longer claim about God (1:21-22). The theological declarations, rich as they are, affirm that it is God, and by implication *not* Paul, who is in charge, a theme that will be explicitly addressed in 2:14-17. Paul takes an oath on God's faithfulness that he, Paul, has not been wishy-washy, "Yes and No," with them regarding his word to them (1:18). In the same way, Christ, God's Son, whom Paul, Silvanus, and Timothy preached among the Corinthians, is not "Yes and No, but always Yes" (1:19). Likewise, God, as seen in connection with past promises, is always faithfully "Yes." Finally, in refinement, Paul has one of his longest descriptions of God, which in the Greek literally reads: "*The* confirming-us-with-you-in-Christ-and-who-sent-us *God.*" This God is not to be denied by Paul (1:21); the implication is that Paul goes as God sends.

Just as quickly as Paul places himself under the shield of God's choosing and sending, he opens up the "we" statement so that each of the Corinthians can understand themselves as also being the recipients of God's claiming and calling action. Paul makes common cause with his Corinthians when he speaks of God's marking "us" with a seal, signifying ownership and protection by God, and giving "us" into "our" hearts the Holy Spirit as a down

payment that ensures the full payment in due time, as earnest money that secures the deal (ἀρραβών *arrabōn*)—another eschatological note, echoing the one of 1:14.

Silvanus (Acts shortens the name to Silas) and Timothy (cf. 1:1) are fittingly mentioned in 1:19 because Paul is taking the Corinthians back to the time when those two and Paul brought the gospel to the Corinthians (cf. Acts 18:5). Silvanus is described by Acts as a prophet, as an authority associated with the Jerusalem Christians (Acts 15:22, 32; cf. 1 Pet 5:12), and as a cohort with Timothy on several occasions (Acts 17:14-15; 18:5; 1 Thess 1:1; 2 Thess 1:1).

Windows onto Paul's theological claims here include, first, his assertion of God's faithfulness (1:18). God's faithfulness and trustworthiness are bedrock Pauline convictions, and the Corinthians have heard this important Pauline claim several times before (1 Cor 1:9; 10:13; cf. 1 Thess 3:3). In its appearance in 1:18, God's fidelity becomes a cloak with which Paul eagerly shrouds himself. Second, Paul's claim that the promises of God find their "Yes" in Christ is a profound interpretation of history. For Paul, God's promises have been made to Abraham (Rom 4:13, 21-22; Gal 3:16-18, 29) and to his offspring (Rom 4:16; Gal 3:16) and to all believers (2 Cor 7:1; Gal 3:21-22). And in Christ, Paul declares, all of God's promises find their exclamatory "yes."

1:23–2:1. Just as Paul's conscience was earlier cited as a witness to his probity of conduct (1:12), so also Paul now escalates his rhetoric and calls God as a witness upon his soul. Paul decided to "spare" (φείδομαι *pheidomai*, "refrain from," 1:23) them another visit from him. His choice of words here suggests that consideration *of them* motivated his decision not to go again to Corinth. Perhaps 1:24 should be understood to represent the two options Paul saw before him: He could either go there and endeavor to force his way with them regarding their faith ("not that we lord it over your faith"), or he could attempt to relate to them as "fellow workers for your joy" (1:24).

In a curiously ironic way, the situation as Paul reflects on it here is somewhat similar and a bit different from the option he gave the Corinthians in 1 Cor 4:21. There he told them he was ready to come to them and that

---

54. L. L. Welborn, "The Dangerous Double Affirmation: Character and Truth in 2 Cor 1,17," *ZNW* 86 (1995) 41-48, argues that the doubled yes and no in 1:17 was recognizable in Paul's time as implying an oath to one's truthfulness.

they could have either the harsh Paul or the gentle Paul, depending on whether they continued as they were or changed their ways. The current situation is similar because Paul, had he come when he had planned, would have been the harsh Paul; there would have been no escaping it, and neither would there have been any joy. It is different because now Paul has decided that he would not go to Corinth because he knew he would find them as he would not like them. In either option, whether he had come to them or not, Paul knows and reaffirms with the Corinthians that "you stand by faith" (1:24). Remembering that "to stand" or "to be confirmed/validated" (ἵστημι *histēmi*) is generally for Paul eschatological, hinting as it does about standing before God's judgment at the end time (cf. Rom 11:20; 1 Cor 10:12), we can see that this little statement at the end of 1:24 is a third in a series of notes hinting that the Corinthians will have to account for themselves before God (1:14, 21-22). And the hearers have just been reminded that the faith by which they do stand and will stand before God is the very faith that Paul brought to them under God's commission (1:19).

Paul pulls together his thoughts, really his defense, on these matters by linking together the aborted visit and the painful letter he sent instead. With the mention of joy in 1:24 and "grief/pain/affliction/sorrow" (λύπη *lypē*) in 2:1, Paul establishes the antithetical frame on which his argument is structured in the opening verses of chap. 2. He has sought to minimize the grief/pain; that consideration ruled out a trip to Corinth ("I reached a decision," 2:1) because, had he come with things as they were, he would have had no alternative but "to come in grief" (ἐν λύπη *en lypē*)—a wonderfully ambivalent expression, available in neither the NRSV or NIV, allowing the hearers to understand that his having come to them as projected would have been painful for both them (developed in 2:2) and him (developed in 2:4).

2:2-4. These verses, an oblique bid for them to gladden him, contain a verbal flow chart mapping grief/pain and joy/gladness between Paul and the Corinthians over the aborted visit and its substituted letter. The Corinthians should be a source of joy for Paul; his joy should be a wellspring of joy for

them—and so it should go round and round. But what if he should aggrieve them? Will it not interrupt the joyous reciprocity that should be in place between himself and the Corinthians? Paul and enough of the Corinthians had drifted into mutual suspicion that some clearing of the air was necessary. Paul's choice of a letter instead of personal presence is depicted in 2:3-4, which describes the letter as being generated not from a desire to cause them distress but to let them know the abundant love he has (ἔχω *echō*, "I have," present tense; 2:4) for them.

Paul's description of this letter makes clear it was an exercise in frank speech (παρρησία *parrēsia*); that is, it took the Corinthians to task for what they had done and the way they had behaved (see the Commentary on 1:12). People in Paul's day often used medical analogies to describe the effects of frank speech:

The true frankness such as a friend displays applies itself to errors that are being committed; the pain which it causes is salutary and benignant, and, like honey, it causes the sore places to smart and cleanses them too.[55]

Accordingly, Paul's use of *lypē* ("pain") to refer to the Corinthians' reception of his frank speech is appropriate. The "cure" sometimes has accompanying "pain."

Paul describes himself as having had no choice but to write a letter he knew would cause pain to the very persons who ought to be cheering up, gladdening him. His decision to administer the painful reproof by letter rather than in person—thereby minimizing his self-exposure—may have been an exercise in wishful thinking as Paul imagines a future visit of real joy beyond the painful frank speech (2:3).

Paul's emotive description of his disposition when he wrote the painful letter overflows with heightened details about his own distress in writing: "Out of much affliction and distress of heart . . . with much weeping" (2:4). Of course, his purpose was not to cause grief or pain—frank speech, properly done, is never undertaken with pain or grief as its goal! Paul was driven to write to

---

55. Plutarch *How to Tell a Flatterer from a Friend* 59D.

them as he did so that they "might know the especial love I have toward you" (2:4; the Greek clause is constructed so that "the love" appears at the start, for even further emphasis). By careful construction of 2:4, Paul assures the Corinthians that he did not lightly decide to write them what turned out to be a painful letter for them. Neither was it easy for him. But his abundant love for them compelled him to undertake it and to hope for an amelioration such as the rest of the letter fragment confirms.

REFLECTIONS

1. God as witness against us (1:23) is a radical way of averring our truthfulness. It would be best if we never had to resort to such a radical claim and if our truthfulness were always obvious. But the complexities of life and, indeed, the post-Freudian capacities we all have for second-guessing ourselves often leave us on less certain ground than Paul vaunts here. Because God is the ultimate judge and alone knows the secrets of the heart (1 Cor 4:5), we can never achieve absolute certainty regarding another person's truthfulness; nor can we expect others simply to take our word regarding our truthfulness. Much more impressive than claims and assertions are a proven track record of being found truthful.

2. In Paul's time, being marked with a seal was a sign of ownership for animals and slaves and of identity for devotees of a cultus (cf. the "mark of the Beast, Satan" in Rev 19:20). The seal not only signified ownership or identity, but also guaranteed safekeeping. Paul declares that believers are sealed by the Holy Spirit. Belonging to the Holy Spirit means receiving one's identity from the Holy Spirit,[56] and the best clue in Paul's letters of what that means is that those sealed would bear what Paul calls "the fruit of the Spirit": love, joy, peace, patience, kindness, generosity, faithfulness, gentleness, and self-control (Gal 5:22). People today may have problems with the notion of "belonging" to or being "owned" by another. In the Greco-Roman world it was a reality for all slaves and a practicality for everyone as they always found themselves somewhere in the patron/client chain that structured society. We might wonder whether our vaunted independence from one another is not a collective illusion.

3. Doors frequently open and close with the "yes" and "no" we hear from those around us. Relations are problematic with persons whose "yes" and "no" seem random and inconsistent. Children whose parents' "no" and "yes" do not dependably stick lose their moorings and often think themselves unloved. Parents' thoughtful "nos" can at times be the surest sign of love for their children. Elsewhere Paul pays attention to God's "no" (2 Cor 12:8-9). Here, however, Paul's picture of God is focused on God's faithfulness, so the issue is God's "yes" and Christ's representation of God's "yes" to all of God's promises.

4. Frankness can be abused. Some take pride in telling whatever is "on their mind" and construe that as a virtue, but the ancients knew better. They understood that the right to use frank speech had to be earned, and only those of high moral character, those who are faithful and dependable, have the right to speak with frankness. Even then, frank speech must be appropriately timed and dispensed in carefully measured doses. Frankness can be overused. Each of us has a finite reservoir of the goodwill necessary to sustain frank speech, and care must be taken not to draw it down too far or too fast. On the other side, however, not to speak frankly to a person with whom we have a special relationship can let the other person down at a significant moment.

---

56. L. L. Belleville, "Paul's Polemic and Theology of the Spirit in Second Corinthians," *CBQ* 58 (1996) 303, concludes: "Enlightenment (3:16-18), regeneration (3:6), and the ongoing and progressive transformation of mortality into immortal existence are attributed to the Spirit (5:1-5; cf. 4:10-11, 16-17)."

Prayerful reflection, a self-examination of whether you are genuinely seeking the good of the other person, and a trust that God will use your efforts creatively should precede any use of frank speech.

5. Just as the genie cannot be put back into the bottle once it has been freed, trust cannot be restored once it is splintered. What might be casually dubbed "a little indiscretion" in a marriage can take years to overcome—and even then may leave a lifelong scar. Trustworthiness, the coin of all relationships (whether marriage, friendship, work, or whatever), is destroyed easier and quicker than it is built. So protecting and caring for trust are not only a priority, but also a day-in/day-out, moment by moment enterprise.

6. In 2 Cor 1:18 Paul takes an oath on God's faithfulness. Clearly what Paul does there has no connection with what we today call cursing or swearing. We are warned against taking oaths in Matt 5:34-37 and Jas 5:12, which argue, as Paul perhaps echoes in 2 Cor 1:18, that one's yes should be simply yes and one's no directly no. Yet Paul is given to calling God as *witness* to his veracity (cf. Rom 1:9; Phil 1:8; 1 Thess 2:5, 10). It is a sure sign of dubiety if one needs to say more than a simple "yes" or "no" in order to be believed. The same may be said for having to repeat ourselves before someone believes us.

2 CORINTHIANS 2:5-11, THE ONE WHO CAUSED THE PAIN AND PAUL'S FORGIVENESS

COMMENTARY

In 2:5-11 we can see what Paul and the Corinthians already know: At Paul's most recent visit, at the meeting he described as "painful" in v. 1, and which he wished not to repeat (1:23), someone distressed him (εἰ δὲ τις λελύπηκεν *ei de tis lelypēken*, "if someone has caused pain") and, therefore, Paul maintains, by indirection, the rest of the Corinthians. We cannot recover the particulars, though this fellow is probably the same one who is mentioned again later in 7:12 as "the one who did the wrong" (τοῦ ἀδικήσαντος *tou adikēsantos*). The importance of this person for Paul and for his relationship with the Corinthians may be observed first in the space devoted to him (2:5-11; 7:5-16) and second in the location of Paul's discussion of him (as an inclusio, as rhetorical bookends, so to speak, for all that falls within). Clearly Paul's chagrin over this person and the Corinthians' failure to take Paul's side played into his travel plans, which are discussed before 2:5-11 (cf. 1:15–2:4) and mentioned after 7:5-16 (cf. 9:4).

What we can know is that the person "who did the wrong" is a man (vv. 5-8; 7:12). Whatever he did was directed primarily at another man ("the one who was wronged," 7:12), but, Paul is at pains to argue, the whole community was grieved in this one occasion (v. 5). Paul acknowledges that he was himself grieved (v. 5). The majority of the believers have punished the man (v. 6), and Paul counsels the community to pardon and console the offender (vv. 6-8). Finally, Paul emphatically reports himself ready to join his pardon to that of the community "for their sake" (v. 10). Of course, the Corinthians and Paul know the details and the identities.

Several observations support the surmise that Paul was the offended one: because he mentions his own personal grief/suffering (v. 5); his visit was so painful that he chose not to return but to write instead (1:23); and he announced his readiness to forgive/pardon (i.e., the person who had wronged him, v. 10). It is Paul's interpretation—with his apologetic "not to overstate"—that enlarges the sense of the wrongdoer's impact from merely himself to the entire community (v. 5). If the offense had been to the Corinthians directly Paul would not have had to venture into such an explanation. That the grief is not just his fits his otherwise commonplace assertion that when one member of the community suffers or stumbles, all do; and its positive counterpart, that when one member rejoices, all share in that joy (Rom 12:15; 1 Cor 12:26; 2 Cor 11:28). His later reference to "the one who was wronged" (7:12) as if it might not be him is a rhetorically delicate self-reference designed, at least in part, to make more emphatic his distancing of his reason for having written from the event of his having been wronged. Finally, Paul's celebration that the Corinthians have reembraced him and his leadership—as reported by Titus, they have experienced godly grief, indignation, and alarm over the event (7:11); have punished the man (2:6); and have recovered their zeal and longing for Paul (7:11)—confirms that Paul had very painfully experienced their abandonment of him in the face of the wrong done him by the man during his painful visit (1:23–2:1).

Some scholars have tried to identify the person who did the wrong with the man who slept with his father's wife (1 Cor 5:1-8), whom Paul encouraged the Corinthians to dismiss from the fellowship. But the match is not compelling on several counts. No concern for a person who was wronged is exhibited in 1 Cor 5:1-8 (cf. 2 Cor 7:12). Further, Paul's rhetoric in 2 Cor 2:5 acknowledges that a person aggrieved Paul directly by something he had done during Paul's visit; that wrong (2 Cor 7:2) hurt Paul. What is worse, the Corinthians did not rally around Paul; they did not defend him as he felt they should have done. His distress over the visit and their failure to come to his support prompted his writing the painful letter: "For this reason, I wrote, so that I might know your being 'tried and true' [δοκιμή dokimē], whether in every respect you are obedient" (sense: "whether . . . you are allied or aligned with me," 2 Cor 2:9; cf. 7:12).

By the time Paul wrote 2 Corinthians 1–9, his sources, among them most assuredly Titus (7:7), had reported that the Corinthians had punished the wrongdoer and reaffirmed their allegiance to Paul. Paul's painful letter had the desired effect, and he is now in the position to practice and to model the reconciliation and forgiveness (2:10) that he so eagerly wants increased between himself and the Corinthians. So he counsels the Corinthians to "forgive" or "pardon" (χαρίζομαι charizomai, 2:7; cf. 12:13) the offender and, picking up the strong theme of the opening verses of this letter fragment, to "comfort/console/encourage" (παρακαλέω parakaleō) the one who was disciplined by their punishment or "censure" (ἐπιτιμία epitimia, 2:6-7). In pardoning one whom they have censured, the believers reflect their God, who, as Paul has already written eloquently in chap. 1, comforts and consoles those who suffer (1:3-11).

"Forgiveness" (χάρις charis) is a term whose understanding is grounded in God's giving freely and graciously to people who do not deserve it. Sometimes Paul expresses that free gift as reconciliation of people to God, a theme that will surface just ahead in 5:14-21. In the context of a community and one of its disciplined members, however, the term functions to describe the restoration of relationships between or among people (see a similar function for μετάνοια [metanoia] in 7:9). Nowhere in the seven undisputed Pauline letters does Paul write about "forgiveness of sins" (cf. Eph 1:7; Col 1:14). Paul's lexicon for restored relations to God includes "justification" and "reconciliation" (cf. Rom 5:6-9; 2 Cor 5:19-20), but not forgiveness of sins. For Paul, forgiveness and pardon are reserved for failed relations between human beings, as here in chap. 2.

Paul's mention of rebuke or punishment "by the majority" suggests that, even when the determination was finally made that the wrongdoer should be punished, not everyone came to Paul's defense against the one who had committed the wrongful act (v. 6). Such a reservoir of resentment against Paul may help to account later for Paul's urging an increase in the Corinthians' affection toward him (6:11-13; 7:2), even in the same letter fragment where he celebrates a restoration of good relations with the Corinthians (7:11-12).

The risk in not forgiving a person is here noted: "lest such a one be swamped/engulfed by extreme sorrow" (v. 7b). In all of Paul's letters we have only two instances of someone's being dismissed from fellowship. In both cases, Paul voices some desire that the person not be totally lost. Paul hopes that at least the spirit of the fellow mentioned in 1 Corinthians 5 "might be saved on the day of the Lord" (1 Cor 5:5). In 2 Cor 2:5-11 Paul wants the man to be restored because he has suffered sufficiently already and Paul does not want to see him lost (vv. 6-7). Paul's summary appeal is succinctly put and may be translated richly in two ways: "Decide in favor of love for him"; "Confirm love for him" (κυρῶσαι εἰς αὐτὸν ἀγάπην *kyrōsai eis auton agapēn*, v. 8). Through his advice to the Corinthians, Paul models love in action. For Paul, believers in the God who comforts, redeems, restores, and reconciles cannot look the other way when one of their brothers or sisters is suffering or has been suffering. They must extend to that person the same love and acceptance and consolation and comfort they have received (cf. Rom 15:7).

In v. 7 Paul encourages them to forgive and console the one who did the wrong. In v. 9 Paul takes the Corinthians into his confidence and identifies with them by telling them, "Whomever you forgive, I also forgive." The statement also assures the Corinthians that when they do grant forgiveness to the one who did the wrong, Paul will join them in it. Paul thereby accomplishes several important things: He shares his authority with the Corinthians, he encourages them to follow through, and he indirectly reassures the one who did the wrong that Paul is ready for him and the community to move beyond the problems they had earlier. "In the face of Christ" (ἐν προσώπῳ Χριστοῦ *en prosōpō Christou*, v. 10; NEB, "as the representative of Christ"; NRSV, "in the presence of Christ") is a metaphorical expression and thus open to several lines of interpretation, but all of them must suggest that Paul's act of forgiving is in some sense appropriate to or generated from Christ. The expression could be Paul's way of saying that, standing before or in the presence of Christ, one could do nothing less than proffer forgiveness. Paul does see a loathsome alternative to forgiveness: He and the Corinthians could let Satan outwit them by robbing them of one of their own. But, using the plural very effectively to incorporate the Corinthians, Paul says, in effect, "That is not about to happen because *we* know Satan's plots" (v. 10, italics added).

REFLECTIONS

1. "Decide in favor of love," Paul's counsel to the Corinthians in 2:8 regarding the man who had been disciplined, is actually a good moral guideline for all of life. When we are torn in our deliberation between two choices, as we often are, one way to weigh out the two alternatives is to explore which one more fully or more directly favors love—love for God, love for others, and even (proper) love for ourselves. The latter may seem very difficult to imagine, but needs to be considered because Jesus' reaffirmation of Lev 19:18—"You shall love your neighbor as yourself" (NRSV)—assumes a proper self-love as the basis for reckoning what will count as love of neighbor.

2. Forgiveness is the indispensable condition of life (before God and with others). No one decides in favor of love each time; sometimes it is even too complex to reckon what favors love the most. Forgiveness is the turning to a clean page, a chance to start afresh, a readiness to let bygones be bygones. Forgiveness is made easier when two things are kept in mind. First, each of us has been forgiven by God—and has needed it! Second, forgiveness without a change in behavior, without subsequent actions and deeds that in fact show a different pattern of life from that which generated the need for repentance, cannot be counted as genuine. Genuine repentance moves beyond words of apology to deeds—indeed, to patterns of performance—that amount to what John the Baptist calls "fruits that befit repentance" (Luke 3:8).

2 CORINTHIANS 2:12-13, PAUL'S ANXIETY OVER TITUS THE LETTER BEARER

COMMENTARY

This letter fragment is laced with accountings of Paul's travels, in part no doubt because Paul's promised, but failed, visit has heightened sensitivity about Paul's plans and how trustworthy he is (1:15-16; 2:1; 7:5). In the text at hand, Paul describes how he went to Troas, the Aegean seaport on northwest Asia. Not incidentally, he says he went there "on account of the gospel of Christ," subtly reaffirming his ethos or character as the one who is regularly focused on the gospel.[57] Also, predictably, Paul reports success: "A door was opened to me in the Lord" (2:12). The metaphor of a door being opened describes for Paul a challenging occasion for preaching the gospel (cf. 1 Cor 16:9). This pattern of Paul's going to a new place and proclaiming the gospel is his signature. The Corinthians know that is who he is. So when they hear his next claim—namely, that he was so anxious to hear from Titus that he picked up and moved to Macedonia, where he would meet Titus (7:6)—they have a clear index of his deep

concern for them. Without Titus to report on how things went with the Corinthians when they received Paul's painful letter, Paul reports that he had no "rest/relief" (ἄνεσις *anesis*), a term the opposite of θλῖψις (*thlipsis*), and a subtle, indirect echo of the affliction with which he opened the letter (2:13). Once again, he depicts himself as the one who is very deeply and properly concerned about the Corinthians. This little detail reinforces all his other claims in this letter to be consistently devoted to them and contributes to his ethos as a dependable friend.

Titus, like Timothy, is one of Paul's doubles who provides crucial liaisons with Pauline communities. Titus, a Gentile convert, was with Paul at the conference at Jerusalem and was not compelled to be circumcised (Gal 2:1, 3). When Paul chose not to make his projected visit to Corinth and sent his harsh letter to the Corinthians, it was probably Titus who actually delivered the letter to the Corinthians. This supposition is supported by Paul's linking Titus so closely to the report of how the Corinthians responded to the letter (7:5-16; cf. 8:6, 16, 23; 12:18).

---

57. For a good treatment of ethos and its importance in relationships in Paul's time, see M. M. DiCicco, *Paul's Use of Ethos, Pathos, and Logos in 2 Corinthians 10–13* (Lewiston: Mellen Biblical, 1995) 36-112.

REFLECTIONS

Should we always take biblical characters to be examples worthy of imitation? Not likely! Cain slays his brother Abel. David has Bathsheba. Judas has his thirty pieces of silver. Peter denies Jesus. It is worth wondering whether Paul is a good example for emulation here. He leaves behind an "open door" to evangelize, which is his calling, and, because of intense anxiety, he seeks word about how the Corinthians have responded to his painful letter. If you had been in Paul's shoes, would you have done that or would you have stayed in Troas? Why?

2 CORINTHIANS 2:14–6:10, A MULTIFACETED TREATMENT OF PAUL'S MINISTRY

OVERVIEW

Although interpreters of this extended section understandably often mine it for its profound and rich theological claims, every portion of it is aimed by Paul not only at enhancing the Corinthians' understanding of his ministry among and for them, but also especially at binding them more closely to himself as their apostle. Given his recent experiences with them and their umbrage over his changed plans, a direct request for increased affection from the Corinthians would be far too risky a rhetorical move at this point. Rather than hazard further alienation of the Corinthians, Paul avails himself of the rhetorical option called *insinuatio,* which features a subtle approach and seeks to lay the ground for an affirmative response to himself that will be sought explicitly and directly only later in the letter (6:12-13; 7:2-4).[58]

The opening section (2:14-17) is rich with imagery that points to one end: Paul is

the agent of God's powerful and triumphant gospel; Paul is part of a victory processional across the Mediterranean world that would make the Romans proud; and Paul is part of a vast sacrifice whose fragrance, though it is being offered up to God, is manifest to everyone around.

Then, in what amounts to a series of three complementary depictions that together make up the heart of this letter fragment, we see (1) Paul's as a ministry of a new covenant (3:1–4:6), (2) Paul's as a ministry sustained through affliction and mortality (4:7–5:10), and (3) Paul's as a ministry of reconciliation (5:11-21). The entire section closes with a primary appeal for the Corinthians not to receive the grace of God in vain (6:1-2) and, once more, a defense of Paul's apostolic probity and an insistence, yet once again, that Paul is worthy of exemplification and honor (6:3-10). The integrity and rectitude of Paul's ministry is *the* issue that laces together everything from 2:14 to 6:10.

---

58. So D. A. DeSilva, "Measuring Penultimate against Ultimate Reality: An Investigation of the Integrity and Argumentation of 2 Corinthians," *JSNT* 52 (1993) 57.

2 CORINTHIANS 2:14-17, PAUL'S PLACE IN GOD'S PURPOSES

COMMENTARY

Shifting to the plural again and employing a formula of thanksgiving (cf. 8:16; 9:15), "Thanks be to God," Paul places himself among the wider group of his colleagues— that is, his coworkers and perhaps even other apostles who, in Christ, are put on display by God in triumph. "Thanks be to God" (τῷ δὲ θεῷ χάρις *tō de theō charis*) is a Pauline expression that he evokes when he wants to honor the great power of God to transform and redeem; so the phrase appears in

passages where Paul is recognizing transformation—that is, where God's own "grace" (χάρις *charis*) toward believers is honored by a reflection of the grace back to God in thankfulness. Accordingly, former "slaves of sin" become, "thanks to God," "slaves of righteousness" (Rom 6:17-18) in Christ Jesus (Rom 6:23) and are delivered from death, "thanks to God," through Jesus Christ (Rom 7:24-25). A similar "thanks be to God" is sounded at the climax of Paul's discourse on resurrection, where he celebrates the gift of God's victory (in 1 Cor 15:57, τὸ νῖκος *to nikos*, a military motif like that of 2:14; cf. Col 2:15) over death through Jesus Christ (1 Cor 15:57). All of these "thanks be to God" formulations, including the one that opens v. 14, are therefore eschatological acknowledgments of God's great power to deliver in Christ.

In v. 14 Paul portrays himself as a vanquished captive who is put on display along with others, as caught up by God's triumphant march of the gospel. Two further textual clues, the one temporal, the other spatial, evince Paul's desire to associate himself with the one and only comprehensive action by God; the claim "always" (πάντοτε *pantote*) stresses God's—and by indirection, Paul's also—faithfulness and dependability; the assertion "in every place" (ἐν παντὶ τόπω *en panti topō*) ties Paul's known travels for the purpose of spreading the gospel prominently into God's overall effort.

All of Paul's communities will have been familiar with the Roman military's victory processions,[59] and Paul's rhetoric in vv. 14-16 would have called to his auditors' minds those processions in which defeated leaders were paraded in shame and disgrace. Just a few years earlier, in 44 CE, Claudius had defeated the southern Britons and came back home to stage a monumental triumph.[60] At least some of the Corinthians, as residents of an official Roman colony city and, therefore, especially attuned to Rome, would have Claudius's triumphal procession in memory. In such processionals, "aromatic substances were also carried."[61]

Paul's use of θριαμβεύω (*thriambeuō*), though it most often is associated with military processions led by the victorious leaders as just suggested, may also call to mind an epiphany procession of deities such as Dionysus and Isis, who were regarded as victors and

were thus honored with processions.[62] Likewise, the fragrance noted in vv. 15-16 may evoke memories of the triumphal incense burned in those very processions.[63] Paul co-opts established conceptions and practices as a way of describing God's awe-inspiring purposes and Paul's place in them.

The imagery of aroma (ὀσμή *osmē*, 2:14, 16) and fragrance (εὐωδία *euōdia*) probably evinces Paul's deep sense of life before God as a sacrifice of thanksgiving, as seen most clearly elsewhere in Rom 12:1: "I appeal to you, therefore, brothers and sisters, on account of the mercies of God, to present your bodies as a living sacrifice [θυσίαν ζῶσαν *thysian zōsan*], holy and pleasing to God." When the Philippians respond in partnership with Paul and send him support via their agent, Epaphroditus, Paul construes their backing as a "fragrant aroma [ὀσμὴν εὐωδίας *osmēn euōdias*], a sacrifice acceptable and pleasing to God" (Phil 4:18). Paul uses this terminology when he contemplates persons who, out of grateful thankfulness to God, consecrate themselves to God and act in loving service to others (see Phil 2:17 as an extreme personal example). Paul understands his own ministry in categories of Israel's sacrifices in Rom 15:16; on account of the grace given to Paul by God, he has become "a minister of Christ Jesus to the Gentiles, with the priestly service to the gospel of God, so that the offering of the Gentiles may be acceptable, sanctified in the Holy Spirit."

In all these instances the sacrifice is a thanksgiving offering to God, but in v. 14 its fragrance makes itself known to all those whom the procession passes as it journeys through the world. In vv. 14-17, Paul views those who represent the gospel, himself included, as the ones who make known the presence of God, much as the fragrance of Wisdom announces her presence in the world (Sir 24:15).

In a refinement of the fragrance imagery, Paul boldly and directly identifies himself as "the fragrance of Christ among the ones who

---

59. Peter Marshall, "A Metaphor of Social Shame: ΘΡΙAMBEYEIN in 2 Cor 2:14," *NovT* 25 (1983) 304, reckons that Greek and Roman literature record some 350 triumphs, many of which recount processionals. See S. J. Hafemann, *Suffering and the Spirit: An Exegetical Study of II Cor. 2:14–3:3 Within the Context of the Corinthian Correspondence* (Tübingen: Mohr, 1986) 22-31, for details of triumphal processions in that time.

60. Suetonius *Life of Claudius* 17.

61. H. S. Versnel, *Triumphus: An Inquiry into the Origin, Development, and Meaning of the Roman Triumph* (Leiden: Brill, 1970) 95.

62. P. B. Duff, "Metaphor, Motif, and Meaning: The Rhetorical Strategy Behind the Image 'Led in Triumph' in 2 Corinthians 2:14," *CBQ* 53 (1991) 83, details literary and pictorial evidence. Duff takes συνέχω (*synechō*) in 2 Cor 5:14 to mean "to take or hold captive" and reads it to mean that the love of Christ, not a deity's vengeance, as 2:14 might wrongly be taken to suggest, has led Paul captive.

63. Incense was also used in epiphany processions as a manifestion of the deity. See Duff, "Metaphor, Motif, and Meaning," 91. See also K. A. Plank, *Paul and the Irony of Affliction* (Atlanta: Scholars Press, 1987) 77.

are being saved and among the ones who are perishing" (v. 15). This antithetical construction is basic to Paul's rival two-way view of how people relate to God (cf. 1 Cor 1:18 and the Commentary there; cf. Matt 7:13-14; 2 Cor 4:3; 2 Thess 2:10). The contrast is stark, allowing no middle ground. One is either counted among the ones who are in process toward salvation or among the ones who are cut off from God and are, therefore, perishing. The Corinthians can hear an encoded message: Paul *is* the aroma of Christ; his gospel is *the* gospel; *they* came to faith—that is, they were included among those who are being saved—through *his* spreading of the gospel, the aroma of Christ; the alternative, stark as it is, awaits them if they turn their backs on Paul.

His even further elaboration of the fragrance imagery—"to the ones an aroma from death to death, to the others, an aroma from life to life" (v. 16)—emphasizes that the ones who are being saved are in process, moving from life to (even more and permanent) life, a thought that will receive confirmation and development in 4:16–5:5. Similarly, those who are perishing have death as their current status, and their future is (permanent) death. Seeing these mutually exclusive alternatives, whose choice dictates not only present status, but also eternal fate, the Corinthians do well to cleave to Paul.

The whole picture is so grand, the choices so final, that Paul throws up his hands in awe at his role in God's eternal purposes, asking, "Who is sufficient/competent [ἱκανός *hikanos*] for these things?" (v. 16c). By this gesture Paul affirms several claims. He has not chosen this role for himself, but has been selected by God, as the Corinthians well know (cf. 1 Cor 1:1, 17; 4:1; 9:16-17); he does not now arrogantly overreach but modestly and beyond his own comprehension finds himself playing this role in God's drama; and he lays the ground for his refinement of this notion a bit later when he will declare that competence or sufficiency rests not on human claims, but on God's graceful pleasure (3:4-6).

What starts out as a contrast between the ones who respond to the gospel positively and negatively (vv. 15-16) concludes with a contrast between "the many who huckster the word of God" and those who, like Paul, speak with moral sincerity and purity of motive

(εἰλικρίνεια *eilikrineia*, v. 17a; this term echoes its earlier appearance in 1:12 as a Pauline attribute) and sets the stage for 3:1–4:6, where the contrast will be elaborated. The Greek of Paul's self-description is dense and powerful: Unlike those people, "the many" (οἱ πολλοί *hoi polloi*), Paul says, "We speak as *from* [ἐκ *ek*] God, *before* [κατέναντι *katenanti*] God, *in* [ἐν *en*] Christ" (v. 17b, italics added). With these prepositions Paul affirms that he is solidly among those commissioned by or sent from God, that he makes his proclamation as one who understands himself to be responsibly standing in God's presence, and finally that he knows himself firmly established in Christ. Though not daring to claim his worthiness to be entrusted with such a responsibility by God, Paul boldly affirms that by God's grace he does stand where he stands and does speak what he says as a part of God's plan. No wonder the next section questions whether Paul is again commending himself (3:1). Paul begins vv. 14-17 with the plural, clearly placing him alongside those others who are (also) God's proper agents. He closes it, still using the plural, but obviously thinking primarily of himself, as 3:1-3 makes clear.

Paul's distinction of himself (and those like him) from the "many who huckster the word of God" is difficult to assess. Has *he* been accused of doing so? He does not credit others with saying that (cf. 10:10a). For someone who has been so scrupulous as Paul at Corinth in insisting on self-support, Paul might be a difficult, hardly credible, target for such a charge. Is Paul deriding some specific people, perhaps the ones just about to be mentioned in 3:1-3, who have shown up in Corinth with letters of commendation? Of course, that is possible, but the sparseness of the evidence gives little ground for certainty. Also possible, and at least as likely, Paul could be using a cultural commonplace about itinerant philosopher types— whom he superficially resembles in some ways, but who were also notorious for bilking their clients and moving on—as a foil for a more elaborate confirmation of his credentials and performance standards.[64]

---

64. A. J. Malherbe, "Gentle as a Nurse," *NovT* 12 (1970) 203-17. Thrall, *The Second Epistle to the Corinthians*, 217, declares: "Paul's aim here is apologetic, not polemical."65. Hafemann states that such a use of θριαμβεύω (*thriambeuō*) "*always* refers to the one having been conquered and subsequently led in the procession, and never to the one having conquered." See Hafemann, *Suffering and the Spirit*, 33.

We may wonder how Paul's self-description as one who by God, in Christ, is "always" being led[65] in triumph accords with his self-portrait in chap. 1, where he reports not only a scrape with death but also the sense of being "so utterly, unbearably crushed that we despaired of life itself" (1:8 NRSV). First, Paul is able to construe the same or similar circumstances in very different lights, depending on what angle of vision he takes on the matter. For example, in 1:8-11, he views his personal distress as something from which he hopes to be delivered; in Gal 4:12-15, he effectively credits illness with causing him to stay still long enough to preach to the Galatians. Second, and probably more germane, Paul's dramatic description of his Asian peril is an indirect appeal for pity and, at the same time, an effort to enhance his ethos with the Corinthians. Accordingly, he paints his distress in sensational proportions ("we despaired of life itself"; "In ourselves we had received the death sentence," 1:8-9). But those descriptions serve the theological point that follows them: "But this happened that we might not rely on ourselves but on God, who raises the dead" (1:9b NIV), a motif that resurfaces later in this letter fragment (cf. 4:7-12).

Finally, the Roman practice of triumphal parades had the victors leading the vanquished, so Paul's picture in vv. 14-17 does not portray him, and the representatives with whom he there counts himself, as *themselves* triumphing always. To the contrary, Paul here describes himself and his fellow ministers of the gospel as the conquered captives who,

in the practices and according to the cultural values of his time, would normally be counted failures, who, at the parade's conclusion, would be slaughtered.

It is *God* who always triumphs; those who are led are not themselves triumphalists—a picture that accords very well with what Paul says about himself and the other apostles in a passage he had earlier written to these Corinthians: "For it seems to me that God has put us apostles on display at the end of the procession, like men condemned to die in the arena" (1 Cor 4:9-13 NIV).[66]

How does this august processional portrait of God's triumphing and leading Paul (and the others represented by the use of plurals) fit into the context of Paul's leaving Troas and going to Macedonia to hear about the Corinthians? Paul pictures himself as the one who, like captives on display, are led along by God in God's processional, captives who nevertheless are the ones through whom God is spreading the fragrance of God's salvific presence across the world. It is at once a humble and an exalted portrait of Paul and his ministry; Paul is not in charge, and yet through him God spreads the gospel. Paul may be so distracted by his concern for the Corinthians that he leaves an open door in Troas, but God does not abandon him or allow any place to miss the fragrance (see v. 14c). In v. 14 Paul celebrates the fact that God is triumphing whether or not Paul is as focused on his evangelizing as he should be.[67]

---

65. Hafemann states that such a use of θριαμβεύω (*thriambeuō*) "*always* refers to the one having been conquered and subsequently led in the procession, and never to the one having conquered." See Hafemann, *Suffering and the Spirit,* 33.

66. P. B. Duff, "Metaphor, Motif, and Meaning: The Rhetorical Strategy Behind the Image 'Led in Triumph' in 2 Corinthians 2:14," *CBQ* 53 (1991) 91, says that Paul's self-portrait as a defeated person embraces the image that his opponents have propagated; it may just as well have played into their hands.

67. So A. C. Perriman, "Between Troas and Macedonia: 2 Cor 2:13-14," *ExpTim* 101 (1989) 40.

REFLECTIONS

1. Life is not static, for Paul or for us. Witness the youth who thinks the world is his oyster, or the older woman who finds herself suddenly alone when her loved one has died. Changes can be for the better or for the worse. In the text before us ("from life to life," 2:16), Paul sees the life of faith as one of progress or growth. When we test our own lives against a pattern of constant enhancement as the desideratum, we are likely to be disappointed and may even become despondent. But Paul nowhere says that this progress is experienced in a straight line. As noted in the Commentary, even Paul's life is not always one of success and progress, but *over time* one's faith, no matter how weak or strong, should grow or improve (Rom 4:20; 14:1; 2 Cor 10:15; 13:9; Phil 1:25).

2. Paul's clear picture of two antithetical groups (one progressing toward salvation and the other in the process of perishing) may seem harsh, and it can even be foolish if we go around trying to sort people into opposing groups. Behind the description of the two groups is a Pauline conviction that one either trusts or believes God or one does not. There is no Pauline middle ground of being just a little bit wicked. Paul probably comes by that understanding from his Scriptures, in which the choice between blessing, life, and prosperity, on the one side, is balanced by curse, death, and adversity on the other side (cf. Deut 30:15-20; Prov 11:19; 14:27; Jer 21:8).

3. It is often said that actions speak louder than words. Paul offers a slight adaptation here: He thinks that the life of faith, in which one offers oneself as a sacrifice of thanksgiving to God (Rom 12:1), has a fragrance that is noticeable and that commends itself to others. For yet another variation on the same theme, see the depiction of believers as letters of commendation written on the hearts and legible by all in 3:2-3. Maybe a helpful way to order things is to worry first about your deeds and whether they are manifestations of love for others and then trust that the proper oral expressions of your convictions or faith will come whenever they are ready.

2 Corinthians 3:1–4:6, Paul's Ministry of a New Covenant

COMMENTARY

Paul must walk a fine line. He is chosen by God to be an apostle, and he is their apostle, as the Corinthians surely realize (cf. 1 Cor 9:2). That divine commission places Paul solidly in God's august plan, which is sweeping the known world. The Corinthians, however, have just been through a time when they did not think very highly of Paul—surely not as highly as he would have preferred. And even now he is working to cement their relation to him. So his boasting about the gospel has built into it the risk that some Corinthians will think he is blowing his own horn.[68]

Paul employs syncresis, the rhetorical mode of comparison, in this section of his letter.[69] He has described most others besides himself as "huckstering" the gospel, an image suggesting that, unlike himself, they are in it for what they can get out of it as they hawk the gospel around the Mediterranean (2:17). Now he further contrasts himself with those few who need letters of recommendation to enhance their status (3:1). In the highly stratified Roman society of Paul's time, letters of commendation were commonplaces.[70] The bearers of such letters came with the stamp of approval of someone of standing whose recommendation the letters' recipients would be expected to honor. Typically such letters praised and endorsed the subject person;[71] sometimes they even requested a favor or the granting of special status to the one named in the letter (see Rom 16:1-2).

Paul does not operate that way. He does not depend on such sycophantic catering. He prefers to have his work speak for itself—and that is exactly what he thinks the Corinthians, who are indisputably his work in the gospel (1 Cor 9:1*d*), should do. So he turns the Roman practice of commendatory letters on its head and avers that the Corinthians

---

68. For a thoughtful reflection on Paul's boasting, see C. K. Barrett, "Boasting (καυχάομαι.κτλ.) in the Pauline Epistles," in *L'Apôtre Paul,* ed. A. Vanhoye (Leuven: University of Leuven Press, 1986) 363-68.

69. C. Forbes, "Comparison, Self-Praise and Irony: Paul's Boasting and the Conventions of Hellenistic Rhetoric," *NTS* 32 (1986) 2-8.

70. Belleville, "A Letter of Apologetic Self-recommendation," 152, treats commendation letters in an informative way. See also J. White, "The Greek Documentary Letter Tradition, Third Century B.C.E. to Third Century C.E.," *Semeia* 22 (1981) 96; S. K. Stowers, *Letter Writing in Greco-Roman Antiquity* (Philadelphia: Westminster, 1986) 154-55; and W. Baird, "Letters of Recommendation: A Study of II Cor 3 1-3," *JBL* 80 (1961) 168.

71. Stowers, *Letter Writing in Greco-Roman Antiquity,* 79-80.

---

themselves are his letters, "written on human hearts" (3:3) and available for all to know and read (3:2). This note will reappear, with more Pauline distress, in 12:11, where Paul will have come to realize that those who have shown up in Corinth with letters of recommendation threaten his standing with the Corinthian believers.

The idea that Paul's commendatory letters have been written on flesh-and-blood hearts (καρδίαις σαρκίναις *kardiais sarkinais*) echoes Jeremiah's prophecy of a new covenant, not like the old one "with their ancestors . . . a covenant that they broke" (Jer 31:31-32 NRSV), but one written "on their hearts" (Jer 31:33; cf. Jer 38:33 LXX). This structures a fundamentally antithetical set of claims that appear from 3:1 through 4:6.

The first antithesis is between letters of commendation that some self-servingly carry with them and letters written on hearts (it matters not much whether the writing is on the Corinthians' hearts or on Paul's; the point is that what is written there can be read and understood by "all people" [ὑπὸ πάντων ἀνθρώπων *hypo panton anthropon*]), which when read reveal that the Corinthian believers are, indeed, "a letter from Christ" (3:3). The contrast is carried even further: The letter has been cared for (one can imagine "written and delivered"; the Greek term is a form of διακονέω [*diakoneo*], which will appear very importantly in the following verses in the nominal form διακονία [*diakonia*], when Paul will characterize his own "ministry") by Paul and was written not with ink, but "by the Spirit of the living God" (cf. 1 Thess 1:9). The Jeremiah echo emerges most clearly in the last contrast: "Not in stone tablets, but in tablets of flesh-and-blood hearts" (3:3; cf. Jer 31:33).

The second antithesis, a refinement of the first, is between competence established by human claim or accomplishment and competence declared by God. God is the ground of Paul's confidence and competence. The claim that Paul's confidence comes through Christ is shorthand for a huge convictional base in Paul. Association with Christ, with his death and suffering, is the ground for Paul's assurance that he will ultimately overcome death and move beyond suffering into joyful, perpetual presence with God, just as Christ, the

firstfruits and the firstborn of many brothers and sisters, has (already) been raised (Rom 8:29; 1 Cor 15:20, 23). It is Christ, himself raised, who makes it possible for Paul to rely not on himself "but on the God who raises the dead" (2 Cor 1:9).

Paul has continued to use plurals throughout the section that deals with his own competence and, therefore, authority. By that choice he has reduced the opportunity for any disgruntled Corinthians to deny that God has commissioned ministers of the gospel such as Paul. Paul's case does not rest on their judgment about him alone, but about all those with whom Paul associates himself as the ones who preach the gospel as it should be, without any personal gain and without any self-aggrandisement. To deny Paul any divinely given competence would require that all other ministers and apostles also be discredited.

Paul credits the Holy Spirit, here called "the Spirit of the living God" (3:3), with having done the writing on human hearts. When he recalls the Roman believers' beginnings of their faith, Paul reminds them that the Spirit joined with their spirits and enabled them to articulate the response of babies calling upon their father: *Abba ho Pater* (ἀββα ὁ πατήρ; Rom 8:15-16).

At the heart of this very complex two-covenant passage (3:1–4:6) lies a quite simple point:[72] Paul's ministry, governed by the Spirit, producing life, and worthy of Corinthian embrace, is radically contrasted with what he dramatically characterizes as the "ministry of death."[73]

To understand what Paul has done in 3:1–4:6, we must know the biblical passages he interlaces, in chain-of-association form,[74]

---

72. B. Wagner, "Alliance de la lettre, alliance de l'esprit: essai d'analyse de 2 Corinthiens 2:14 à 3:18," *ETR* 60 (1985) 65, rightly argues against construing this text as "un exposé doctrinal" where every term must be mined.

73. Once again, Paul's purpose is apologetic, not polemical. See Thrall, *The Second Epistle to the Corinthians*, 237. However, on 297-318, she construes 4:1-6 as a "defence of ministry" and does not see the overarching apologetic purpose argued for in this commentary.

74. E. Richard, "Polemics, Old Testament, and Theology: A Study of II Cor., III,1-IV,6," *RB* 88 (1981) 342-44, affirms Paul's associative flow of thought but questions the appropriateness of using the term "midrash" (cf. his good history of recent research). Fitzmyer states that Paul's argument flows by "the free association of ideas which runs through the entire passage" so that, for example, epistle of recommendation becomes epistles written on the heart, and so on. See J. A. Fitzmyer, "Glory Reflected on the Face of Christ (2 Cor 3:7–4:6) and a Palestinian Jewish Motif," *TS* 42 (1981) 631-32. R. B. Hays, *Echoes of Scripture in the Letters of Paul* (New Haven: Yale University Press, 1989) esp. 125-49, sensitively examines Paul's linking of scriptural passages through 2 Corinthians 3.

into his own text. Although there are allusions to other biblical texts, Paul builds primarily from two, one about Moses and the other about Jeremiah's prophecy of a new covenant.[75] Like his Jewish coreligionist contemporaries, Paul relates to both passages freely, highlights what interests him, ignores what does not, and weaves his own message through the old accounts.[76] The two primary texts are the story of Moses and the stone tablets (Exod 34:29-35) and Jeremiah's new covenant promise (Jer 31:31-34). A rehearsal of both, highlighting Paul's salient interests in them, will aid the interpretation of Paul's own composition.

Central to the first account is Moses' encounter with God, or more particularly with God's glory, in the giving of the commandments and the covenant expressed through them. On Moses' second trip up Mt. Sinai (the first ended in the broken stone tablets [Exod 32:19] when Moses saw that the people were unfaithful while he was gone), Moses is assured that God's "face will go with you," a way of guaranteeing God's presence and favorable disposition (Exod 33:14). Moses beseeches God, "Show me your glory, I pray" (Exod 33:18). God responds by pledging divine presence and graciousness (Exod 33:19), but cautions Moses that "no one shall see my face and live" (Exod 33:20, 23). God then details all the steps that will be taken to protect Moses on the mountaintop while God's fearsome and awe-filled glory passes by (Exod 33:22; cf. 1 Kgs 19:11-12; Hab 3:3-4).

The reader of Exodus has been prepared to understand that God's glory is not to be taken lightly. God's glory is a sign of divine presence in the cloud that led the Israelites in the exodus from Egypt (Exod 16:10; Num 16:42). God's glory is "like a devouring fire" (Exod 24:17 NRSV). When the Lord looked down directly upon the Egyptian army, they were thrown into panic (Exod 14:24); the

splendor of God's face, "no longer veiled by cloud, 'panics' the Egyptians, who recognize him."[77]

When Moses comes down off the mountain with the stone "tablets of the covenant" (Exod 24:12; 31:18; 34:1; Deut 4:13; 5:22; 9:10), he does not realize that his face shines as a reflection of God's glory. But Aaron and the Israelites do, and their response of fear is exactly appropriate as a response to God's glory (Exod 34:30). When Moses has called them to him and finished telling them of the Lord's commands, Moses puts a veil over his face (Exod 34:33), much as the cloud had covered God's glory earlier (Exod 24:16). In the verses that follow, Moses is depicted as alternating between meeting with God ("whenever Moses went in before the LORD," Exod 34:34 NRSV) without a veil and covering his face "again" (Exod 34:35) with a veil when the Israelites again see his face, whose "skin was shining" (Exod 34:34-35).

In two powerful ways, Paul interlaces the Jeremiah passage with the one about Moses. First there is the shared reference to covenant (Exod 34:27-28; Jer 31:32-33). Second, Paul makes an implicit contrast of Jeremiah's "I will write it on their hearts" (Jer 31:33 NRSV) with the old covenant, whose statutes, according to the first passage and widely in Israel's Scriptures, were written or cut into stone (implied, but not stated in Jeremiah 31:1).

Paul weaves these two scriptural accounts throughout his own passage (3:1–4:6), sometimes taking over a detail of the story as is, other times dwelling on one particular, and in other instances changing the detail or taking advantage of it for his particular application. Within Paul's construction, though, he adopts the stance that is present in Jeremiah's depiction of the promised new covenant. In part, the new is described as an alteration of the older, previous covenant.

The passage (3:1–4:6) is like a tapestry that merits close examination first of the most obvious pattern of the weave, the weft, which is cast from one side to the other.[78] This left-to-right fabric is conspicuous because

75. T. B. Savage, *Power Through Weakness: Paul's Understanding of the Christian Ministry in 2 Corinthians* (New York: Cambridge University Press, 1996) 106-10, demonstrates considerable elite and popular contemporary Gentile interest in Moses as well as remarkable contemporary Jewish regard for him.

76. Using the "poetic function of dissimile," Hays rightly suggests that "it becomes unnecessary to postulate a pre-Pauline source for Paul's midrash on Exodus 34 in order to account for the internal tensions of the passage." See Hays, *Echoes of Scripture in the Letters of Paul,* xii.

77. E. L. Greenstein, *The HarperCollins Study Bible,* ed. W. A. Meeks (New York: HarperCollins, 1989) 105.

78. On the literary unity of 3:1–4:6, see E. Richard, "Polemics, Old Testament, and Theology: A Study of II Cor., III,1-IV,6," *RB* 88 (1981) 363-64.

Paul has a fundamentally antithetical message to communicate by it to the Corinthians. Later we will explore the warp, those lines that move vertically down through the passage and express continuity between the old and the new.

The texture across the passage is structured predominantly on an "A, not B" type of argumentation. Paul's primary interest is to depict himself and his ministry (*diakonia*)[79] positively, and he builds, *via negativa,* from that positive depiction to contrast the ministry that is not his. He evinces no genuine concern for any other ministry; his descriptions of the alternate ministry, as indeed of all the contrasts in this passage, are of interest to him solely as they illuminate, elucidate, and enhance his own ministry, *via negativa.* Understandably, he is trumpeting his own ministry and should not be mistaken for advertising an alternative. It is irrelevant, therefore, to wonder if there are people who would embrace Paul's alternative ministry as their own. The negative parts of Paul's rhetoric are not descriptive of anyone but are there simply and solely to amplify himself and his ministry.

The following table features the contrasts that are structured through the passage:

Figure 2: The Two Ministries and Their Consequences

letter versus Spirit

not of letter (3:6)	but new covenant of the Spirit (3:6)
letter kills (3:6)	Spirit gives life (3:6)

rival ministries

diakonia of death (3:7)	*diakonia* of Spirit (3:8)
diakonia of condemnation (3:9)	*diakonia* of righteousness (3:9)
perishing/transitory (3:11)	permanent (which remains [τὸ μένον *to menon*])(3:11)

rival representatives

not like Moses (3:13)	Paul (3:12)

rival consequences

	advantages of Paul's ministry
minds hardened (3:14)	
veil over heart (3:15; "minds," NRSV)	we all with unveiled face, contemplating the glory of the Lord, are being transformed (3:18)

Paul's own comportment illuminated by contrast with its opposite

hidden things of darkness (4:2)	
walking in craftiness	with disclosure of truth not falsifying God's word

reason for this behavior

God of this age blinded the minds of the unbelievers (4:4)	mercifully God has granted this ministry (4:1)

---

79. J. N. Collins, "The Mediatorial Aspect of Paul's Role as *diakonos,*" *AusBR* 40 (1992) 36, takes the term to mean "messenger of the divine" in Paul's self-application.

By the starkest of contrasts, Paul depicts his own ministry, still using the plural as a way of identifying himself with the mainstream, as having been granted by God (4:1),[80] as powered by the Holy Spirit (3:6), as generating righteousness among believers (3:9), as permanent (3:11), and as efficacious (Paul and his adherents are in the process of being transformed, 3:18). Confirmation for the Corinthian believers—and an encouragement for them to identify with Paul as they hear or read this passage—is secured by Paul's radically negative portrayal of the alternative

80. Collins, "The Mediatorial Aspect of Paul's Role as *diakonos,*" 37-41, gives ample evidence that in the Greco-Roman world a *diakonos* was a "go-between" or "message-bearer."

ministry and of its negative results for discernment and moral reasoning. The rival ministry is governed by the concern with the letter, which kills (3:6), and so it is a ministry whose result is death (3:7), in which minds are hardened (3:14) and hearts are veiled over (3:15; "minds," NRSV). Its adherents are counted among the unbelievers who serve the god of this age, Satan,[81] who has blinded their minds (4:4; darkness and blindness characterize Satan's reign: Luke 22:53; Acts 13:4-12; 26:18; 2 Cor 6:14-15; Eph 6:12; Col 1:13; *T. Sim.* 2:7; *T. Levi* 19:1).

Romans 8:2 has the same antinomy and the same rhetorical purpose, striving as it does to depict the "law of the Spirit of life in Christ Jesus" as prevailing over the negatively portrayed alternative, the "law of sin and death." The Spirit always prevails over death for Paul.

It would be misleading, however, to construe the entire passage as being structured simply antithetically. Indeed, 3:1–4:6 does begin with strong adversatives: letter versus Spirit; kills versus gives life; and ministry of death versus ministry of Spirit and righteousness. Translations and other interpretations have taken that set of contrarieties and wrongly transposed them into a sort of schema of history. For example, the RSV translated *diakonia* into "dispensation" and thus encouraged interpreters to read Paul as taking these two contrasts as sequential, supersessionist covenants, with the latter *superseding* and replacing the former.[82] It was then easy for an interpreter to claim that Paul has here a view of history, an *Heilsgeschichte* or sacred history, in which the new covenant and its "dispensation" have replaced the old.[83]

To correct such a view, we need to follow the way Paul has formulated the tapestry of his argument along the warp of the fabric.

What began as a plain contrast, because Paul was justifying his own ministry over against any other ministry—so he set up an opposite that by contrast illuminated and made his own ministry more appealing—moves in 3:7-11 into a threefold use of a widespread Hellenistic and Jewish rhetorical pattern of argument "from the lesser to the greater."[84]

(1) A verse-long protasis, whose condition-of-fact statement affirms that the ministry that ended in death (taking διακονία τοῦ θανάτου [*diakonia tou thanatou*] as a genitive of result or direction, "that brought death," NIV) came, indeed, in "glory/splendor" (δόξα *doxa*, 3:7), sets up an apodosis, or conclusion, that argues, "How much more shall the ministry of Spirit [a genitive of origin or quality] be in glory?" (3:8). So both ministries have glory. Comparison has taken the place of absolute contrast;[85] distinction with a desire to laud the second glory now replaces antithesis.

(2) In the succeeding verse, Paul continues the same reasoning from the lesser to the greater: "If there was glory in the ministry that resulted in condemnation, how much more the ministry of righteousness abounds in glory" (3:9). Once again, Paul assumes that glory is present in *both* ministries, but the glory of the one mentioned second—namely, the one Paul is privileged to be a part of—surpasses the glory of the one mentioned first. Indeed, in the very next verse Paul refines his view of the relationship of the two glories and their respective ministries, arguing that "in this case" the "surpassing glory" associated with Paul's ministry so overwhelms the previous glory as to suggest that the former had no glory at all (3:10).

Paul's oxymoronic construction—"what was glorified has no glory" (καὶ γὰρ οὐ δεδόξασται τὸ δεδοξασμένον *kai gar ou dedoxastai to dedoxasmenon*)—must be considered carefully. With this expression, Paul is trying to provide perspective and proportion that adequately honor the incredible glory associated with God's "new creation," as he will call it just ahead (5:17). Its glory is so prodigious as to reduce to naught anything compared to it. That is not the same as

81. S. R. Garrett, "The God of This World and the Affliction of Paul: 2 Cor 4:1-12," in *Greeks, Romans and Christians: Essays in Honor of A. J. Malherbe*, ed. D. Balch, W. A. Meeks, and E. Ferguson (Minneapolis: Fortress, 1990) 104.

82. See Hays, *Echoes of Scripture in the Letters of Paul*, 156-60, for a thoughtful critique of supersessionist readings of 2 Corinthians 3:1.

83. Another RSV translation facilitated this misinterpretation. Taking γράμμα (*gramma*) in 3:6 not simply as "letter" but as "written code" could mislead one to think of the entirety of Israel's Scriptures as alien to the Spirit, a position Paul nowhere embraces; the problem with the writings of the "old covenant" is simply that they cannot be read and understood apart from the Lord (3:14), not that they should be jettisoned (cf. Rom 7:12; 2 Cor 1:20).

84. Quintillian *Inst.* 5.11.9-12.

85. So E. Richard, "Polemics, Old Testament, and Theology: A Study of II Cor., III,1-IV,6," *RB* 88 (1981) 353.

denying glory to the other ministry.[86] The old ministry is critiqued *by comparison with the ministry of the Spirit* and *for the results that it delivered:* condemnation and ultimately death. In his argument here Paul finds himself very much in a situation similar to that reflected in his argument in Romans 7: The law, even though through it people found death (Rom 7:8-10), is nevertheless holy, and its commandments are "holy, just and good" (Rom 7:12). The thing itself, whether a ministry or the law, can be said to have been good even though people derived negative results from it.

(3) The same general perspective is reflected in Paul's next verse (3:11), where he once again confirms that there was glory before ("For if what is passing away came in glory . . ." 3:11*a*) and avers "how much more has the permanent come in glory" (3:11*b*).

Because "glory" (δόξα *doxa*) is such a major theme in 3:1–4:6 (used 14 times), we must examine Paul's usage of it. From Israel's Scriptures, Paul derives the notion of glorification in two ways: (1) God is known to manifest an awe-inspiring glory, and, in connection with Moses and the mountain (cf. Exod 33:19-22), God assures Moses that he will recognize God because God's glory will pass by and the Lord's name will be called (Exod 33:19). (2) Paul recalls the story about Moses' face glowing with glory after the latter had met with God on the mountain and received the stone tablets of the covenant (Exod 34:29, 35).

Among other confirmations that Paul is primarily focused on his own ministry are these: The rhetorical target is (twice) expressed in the expression "present day" (σήμερον *sēmeron*, 3:14–15), whereby Paul brings his message to bear on his Corinthian hearers; Paul's explicit inclusion of his Corinthian hearers in the expression "we all" (ἡμεῖς δὲ πάντες *hēmeis de pantes*, 3:18); throughout 3:1-4:6 Paul is much more detailed about the new covenant and its characteristics; and Paul's concluding description of his comportment in this new-covenant ministry (4:1-6).

The key to understanding Paul's interest in the two-covenant passage lies in 3:18

where, for the first time, he *explicitly* invites his Corinthian hearers to make a direct identification with what he is writing: "And we all, with unveiled face, looking at the glory of the Lord as in a mirror, are being transformed into his image, from glory to glory, for this comes from the Lord, the Spirit."

As has been noted throughout this commentary, Paul's use of "we" formulations occasionally challenges the interpreter, but in the passage at hand the usage is straightforward. He opens 3:1 with "we" formulations because he wants to depict his own ministry as a part of the one he will magnify by contrasting and comparing it with Moses. From 3:1 until 3:18 Paul's "we" references function primarily as self-descriptions, though secondarily they also cast him as being in the mainline with the others with whom he happily identifies. But with 3:18 and its *hēmeis de pantes* ("we all," "ourselves"), Paul explicitly widens his scope to include the Corinthians (and all believers) and bids them to associate with his multifaceted portrait of them (and of himself), which is contained in this verse.

The verse defines—that is, describes—*who* the believers are, and positions the Corinthians (again, along with Paul) by describing *where* they are in God's unfolding purposes. In good Pauline fashion, the latter always involves depicting where they are now (which Paul elsewhere describes by "already" statements) and where they will be in God's larger plan (which Paul in other places sketches under the rubric "not yet").[87]

The first two items of the verse—"with unveiled face" and "looking at the glory of the Lord as in a mirror"—are woven together out of what has preceded. The notion of veiling goes through three distinguishable phases in this passage. First, the veiling of the face comes from Paul's adaptation of the Moses story in the preceding verses. Paul builds from his recitation of the pattern of Moses' covering his face as it reflects the glory of God (2 Cor 3:7, 13). Moses' facial glory was derived from his being in God's presence, but Paul treats it almost like a tan that, without

86. Contra S. Hafemann, "Paul's Argument from the Old Testament and Christology in 2 Cor 1:1–9," in *The Corinthian Correspondence*, ed. R. Bieringer (Leuven: University of Leuven Press, 1966) 292, in an otherwise insightful interpretation.

87. J. Paul Sampley, *Walking Between the Times: Paul's Moral Reasoning* (Minneapolis: Fortress, 1991) 11-20.

further and renewed exposure, fades.[88] The account in Exod 34:29-35, if it gives a motive for Moses' veiling his face, may suggest that he did it to alleviate the Israelites' fear that he of shiny face looked like a deity (Exod 34:30). Paul provides a very different motive: Moses covers his face "so that the children of Israel should not look intently at the finish of what [the glory, understood] was passing away" (3:13); but this motive rests on Paul's distinctive interpretation that the glory associated with Moses is "passing away" (καταργέω *katargeo*). The term *katargeo* plays a big role in this passage, appearing four times (3:7, 11, 13, 14), and its interpretation is critical. Its semantic range includes "make ineffective, powerless," "nullify," "wipe out, abolish," "set aside"; in the passive, as here, it may mean "cease," "pass away" (3:7, 14), and in the substantive (3:11, 13), "what is transitory."[89]

Second, Paul shifts ground and takes the veiling motif into new, metaphorical territory when he moves the discussion so that it bears on time contemporary with himself and his audience (σήμερον ἡμέρας *sēmeron hēmeras*, "this day/today," 3:14-15) and declares that contemporary, non-believing Jews have hardened minds (τὰ νοήματα αὐτῶν *ta noēmata autōn*) when they read the "old covenant" because "a veil lies over their heart" (3:15)—that is, they do not readily see and understand ("heart" is here a Pauline rhetorical variation for "minds/thoughts" of 3:14; the NRSV translates καρδία [*kardia*] as "minds").[90] "Reading the old covenant" is parallel to "reading Moses" (3:15), which is another way of referring to the Torah, or Pentateuch (the first five books), as having been written by Moses (Acts 15:21; cf. 2 Chr 25:4; Neh 13:1; Mark 12:26).

Until the present day, Paul avers, the veil of non-understanding remains unremoved (3:14), "since only in Christ is it set aside" (3:14 NRSV). This fits Paul's understanding of Scripture and the law elsewhere in his letters. The law and Scripture are brought into focus, are understood clearly only as those "in Christ" look back at it from the standpoint of grace's having claimed them and set them right with God. Apart from one's being "in Christ," the law, which is holy (and its commandments just and good; Rom 7:12, 16) and "spiritual" (Rom 7:14), becomes the vehicle through which sin wreaks havoc and ultimately death (Rom 7:13) so that the very commandment that pointed toward life ends up, courtesy of sin's effective hijacking of it, in death.[91] Paul puts the same argument another way: Israel, seeking a righteousness of their own (for Paul there is no such thing, though its non-existence has not slowed people from living by its fiction) through attempts to perform the law have not found it. Why? Because they have not truly understood the law and accepted righteousness, which is a right relationship as what it can only be: a gift from God (Rom 9:30–10:4; see esp. Rom 9:31 and 10:3).

As Paul depicts it to the Corinthians, Moses put a veil over his face so that the children of Israel would not see the end (τέλος *telos*) of what was fading—namely, the glory reflected on his face (3:13). Paul's affirmation that "in Christ" the veil is set aside (3:14) is shorthand that those who are "in Christ," his favorite expression for those who have already been restored to right relationship to God, are given eyes to see and minds and hearts to understand not only what is going on in God's plan, but also that Moses and all of Scripture still disclose God's purpose and God's will and provide guidance to all God's people. As he put it earlier to the Corinthians, "These things happened as an example for those people, but they are written for our instruction" (1 Cor 10:11).

Third, by contrast with unbelievers (cf. 4:4), Paul describes all believers, but especially featuring himself and his Corinthian

---

88. Belleville, "Tradition or Creation?" 165-84, gives ample evidence to suggest that Paul's interpretation of Moses' fading glory was not unique among contemporary Jews; it need not be understood as having been generated by Paul's opponents. Furnish, *II Corinthians*, 203, rejects the interpretation of fading and prefers annulment, writing of a "glory which, because it is part of the old covenant, is to be annulled as is that covenant." This view is followed by N. T. Wright, "Reflected Glory: 2 Corinthians 3:18," in *The Glory of Christ in the New Testament: Studies in Christology in Memory of George Bradford Caird,* ed. L. D. Hurst and N. T. Wright (Oxford: Clarendon, 1987) 144. M. D. Hooker, "Beyond the Things That Are Written? St. Paul's Use of Scripture," *NTS* 27 (1981) 291, 303-4, dismisses annulment.

89. *BAGD* 417.

90. Rhetorical handbooks advised avoiding the needless repetition of the same term. See *ad Herennium* 4.12.18.

91. See L. E. Keck, "The Absent Good: The Significance of Rom 7:18*a*," in *Text und Geschichte: Facetten theologischer Arbeitens aus dem Freundesund Schülerkreis Dieter Lührmann zum 60. Geburtstag*, ed. S. Maser and E. Schlarb (Marburg: Elwert, 1999) 66-70, who states that sin is the "real culprit."

dependents, as having an "unveiled face" (collectively their hoped-for unity is expressed in their having *one* face, and it unveiled; the NIV and the NRSV change to the plural, "faces") so that they can, indeed, be described as "gazing into the glory of the Lord as in a mirror" (3:18). The identity of "Lord" here as everywhere in Paul's letters must be determined by context and Paul's patterns.[92] When Paul references Scripture, as he does in this passage with its indebtedness to Exodus 33–34, he often adopts κύριος (*kyrios*) as the title for God from his Greek translation of "Yahweh" (cf. Rom 9:28-29; 1 Cor 14:21). The context, from 2:14 (where Paul gives thanks to *God,* who through Christ leads Paul and others), to 3:4 (where Paul's confidence is through Christ to *God*), to 3:5 (where Paul's confidence is from *God*), to the conclusion of the section in 4:6 (where it is *God* who has caused "the light of the glory of God" to shine [φῶς λάμψει *phōs lampsei*; cf. Isa 9:1 LXX] into the hearts of believers)—all of these encourage the reading of "Lord" in 3:18 as referring to God.[93]

Throughout the passage, the references to Christ express means or agency, but the primary relationship is regularly between people and God. Further, the reference in 4:6 is unambiguously to *God's* glory, so that the "glory of the Lord" of 3:18 ought to be taken also as pointing to God. Finally, the image of contemplating the glory of the Lord "as in a mirror" (κατοπτρίζομαι *katoptrizomai*) invites the identification of Christ as the mirror reflecting the glory of God.[94] Taking Christ as the mirror is reinforced at the conclusion of the passage, where once again the glory of God is said to be visible "in the face of Christ," meaning reflected in Christ.[95]

With the notion of gazing indirectly at God's glory, Paul honors his Scriptures' general view, indeed the particular outlook of the Exodus account, that he has employed

as a ground for his two-covenant exposition: Humans cannot bear to look directly at God. In the original story, Moses asks God for assurances (Exod 33:12-16) and is promised by God: "I will pass by before you with my glory [τῇ δόξῃ μου *tē doxē mou*]" (Exod 33:19 LXX). The story goes on to detail the care God takes in protecting Moses from the full effect of God's glory by placing Moses in a hole in the rock and covering him with God's hand (Exod 33:22). God's mercy precludes Moses' looking directly at God's face because God's majesty and power are so great that God declares, "No one shall see me and live" (Exod 33:20 NRSV; see also Judg 6:22-23; 13:22; cf. Isa 6:5).

For Paul, Jesus Christ is the clear, visible reflection of God. Believers, "through Christ" (2 Cor 3:14), experience the removal of the veil, so "with unveiled face" they can gaze intently upon God's glory as in the mirror that Christ provides. With this note, Paul distances the glory of God from direct vision, but at the same time celebrates that believers, in and through Christ, have access to God.

Paul's conception of glory is eschatologically freighted. Because all have sinned, all "have fallen short of the glory of God" (Rom 3:23); but because of God's grace manifested in Christ and because of the from-God redemption of all creation begun in Christ's death and resurrection, those identified with Christ now are confidently assured of the end-time "glory about to be revealed to us" (Rom 8:18)—a glory that in some measure the "children of God" already have received and that the rest of creation longs to achieve (Rom 8:21).

The next part of 3:18 ("being transformed into the same image from glory to glory") parallels and is set contemporaneously with "gazing into the glory of the Lord as in a mirror" so that those who are permitted to contemplate God's glory are the very ones who are being transformed. A well-documented Hellenistic notion holds that to look upon the deity is to be changed and conformed to that deity (or to its image).[96]

For Paul, the beginning of the life of faith is variously described, sometimes using birth or adoption images (Romans 8), other times

---

92. Following Furnish, *II Corinthians,* 211-12.
93. So also S. Hafemann, "Paul's Argument from the Old Testament and Christology in 2 Cor 1:1–9," in *The Corinthian Correspondence,* ed. R. Bieringer (Leuven: University of Leuven Press, 1966) 300.
94. Alan Segal, "Paul and Ecstasy," SBLSP (1986) 574, 575n. 71, interprets the "glory of God" as "the technical term for the *Kābôd* (כבוד), the human form of God appearing in biblical visions" and takes the reference in 3:18 to the "glory of God" as in a mirror as another "mystical theme," which he traces back to Ezekiel 1.
95. N. T. Wright, "Reflected Glory," 145, argues suggestively, if not convincingly, that the "'mirror' in which Christians see reflected the glory of the Lord is . . . *one another"* (italics added).

96. Cf. Furnish, *II Corinthians,* 240, who cites Apuleius *Metamorphoses* XI.15 and *Corpus Hermeticum* IV.11b.XI.15.23-24.

using conversion terminology (ἐπιστρέφω *epistrephō*, "to turn toward," "to turn around"; see Gal 4:9). Here the language of radical change, fundamental transformation, is needed: from death to life, from sin to righteousness. The expression "new creation," which Paul uses in chap. 5, suggests what a fundamental alteration is involved in the inauguration of the new aeon that God has begun in Christ's death and resurrection (5:17; cf. Gal 6:15).

But Paul's interest is not simply focused on what people today might call "the moment of conversion"; he is at least equally profoundly interested in an ongoing transformation that he considers fundamental to and characteristic of the life of faith. Evidence for this view is found widely in the Pauline corpus. Note his critical depiction of the Corinthians as still being babies when they should have been ready for solid food (1 Cor 3:1-2); the positive counterpart is what Paul calls the "spiritual person," who understands and discerns what is important (1 Cor 2:13-15). Onesimus, the runaway slave mentioned in the Letter to Philemon, became Paul's child in the faith (Phlm 10). At the other extreme of the life of faith, Paul imagines the mature, the adult, the person whose faith has grown strong and whose related judgment has correspondingly become more trustworthy—as he states in the first person in the heart of his hymn of love: "When I was a child, I spoke as a child, thought as a child, reasoned as a child; when I became a man, I set aside the things of a child" (1 Cor 13:11). On two other occasions he summons his hearers to identify with adults, with mature people (1 Cor 2:6; Phil 3:15). In another instance, he pictures himself as not having attained maturity, but assiduously seeking it: "Not that I have already received this or am already mature, but I pursue it to make it my own, because Christ Jesus has made me his own" (Phil 3:12). Paul, ever the model of faith for his followers, depicts himself as the ideal: the believer who presses on toward maturity because Christ has claimed him.

Believers are works in progress; they should be moving from their infancy at the beginning of faith toward maturity, toward adulthood in the faith. Paul expresses that conviction in a variety of ways beyond the baby-to-adulthood motif. He writes to the Philippians that he has chosen to stay with them "for your progress [προκοπή *prokopē*, "advancement/furtherance"] and joy in the faith" (Phil 1:25). Using a different Greek term, he makes the same point in his conclusion of the very last letter he writes the Corinthians: "This is what I pray for, your being made complete [κατάρτισις *katartisis*, "completion"]" (2 Cor 13:9). Along this same line, he writes to the Romans about the person who is "weak with respect to faith" (Rom 14:1; see also Rom 15:1; cf. the statements about weaker and stronger consciences, which may reflect the same pattern, 1 Cor 8:7-13). And he expresses his deep wish to visit the Thessalonians so that he may "complete what is lacking in your faith" (1 Thess 3:10).

Another index of Paul's interest in the progress of individuals in the life of faith is his insistence that all things be done for edification, for "building up" (οἰκοδομή *oikodomē*). Granted, sometimes it is the church that is built up (1 Cor 14:4-5, 12), at other times it is clearly individuals (Rom 14:19; 15:2; 1 Cor 14:3, 17). Even where the edification is of the church, Paul clearly is not thinking of growth in numbers of members, but in the growth of members collectively in the faith.[97]

So when Paul writes to the Corinthians about "we all" being "transformed" (μεταμορφούμεγθα *metamorphoumetha*), stated in the passive as a way of crediting God as the transformer, he is expressing, in the tersest scope, a strong conviction about the nature of the believing life. Believers are works in progress; they are being transformed. The rhetorical climax of the Letter to the Romans grounds its appeal for a life appropriate to the gospel by affirming a metamorphosis (using the same Greek term found in 2 Cor 3:18), a transformation, which in this case focuses on a renewal of the mind so that the Roman hearers can make appropriate moral decisions such that God is properly honored (Rom 12:1-2).

---

97. Just as Paul is interested in the growth of invidivual believers' faith, so also he views his congregations collectively and recognizes that some communities are more mature in faith than are others. See J. Paul Sampley, "Reasoning from the Horizons of Paul's Thought World: A Comparison of Galatians and Philippians," in *Theology and Ethics in Paul and His Interpreters; Essays in Honor of Victor Paul Furnish,* ed. E. H. Lovering Jr., and J. L. Sumney (Nashville: Abingdon, 1996) 114-31.

Two particular features of the transformation claim in 2 Cor 3:18, however, are the pithy little expressions τὴν αὐτὴν εἰκόνα (*tēn autēn eikona*, "into the same image") and ἀπὸ δόξης εἰς δόξαν (*apo doxēs eis doxan*, "from glory to glory").[98] The reference to εἰκὼν (*eikōn*; "image/likeness," "icon") functions on at least two levels. First, it is a reflection of the mirror supposed in the construction that has preceded it: "we all . . . gazing upon the glory of the Lord as reflected in a mirror" (2 Cor 3:18*a*; cf. Wis 7:26). Second, interpreting "Lord" to be God and the mirror to be Christ, the *eikōn* as image or reflection continues to be Christ. Paul explicitly confirms this identification four verses later: "Christ, who is the *eikōn* of God" (4:4; cf. Col 1:15). Thus the transformation Paul here celebrates is that all believers are (ideally) becoming ever more Christ-like.

Imitation of Christ is a theme of massive proportions in the Pauline letters and is evinced here. In Paul's view, God's plan includes believers' being "conformed to the image [*eikōn*] of God's son" (Rom 8:29). Paul is convinced that believers will "wear the image of the one from heaven," Christ (1 Cor 15:49). In all these passages, 2 Cor 3:18 included, Paul regularly thinks of believers as being conformed to Christ, but the expression "from glory to glory" indicates, as the NIV translation has rightly rendered it, that this association with Christ involves an "ever-increasing" glorification, or "from one degree of glory to another" (NRSV).[99] The faithful life begins with the restored glory of God from which people had fallen short via sin (Rom 3:23), and it will end in the full, cosmic refurbishment wherein God's glory is once again fully manifest (Rom 8:18-21). So "from glory to glory" expresses, once more, in the most cryptic fashion, Paul's larger picture that the life of the Spirit is a life ever growing and increasing.[100] As believers gaze upon the glory of the Lord, therefore, they actually look to their source and at the same time to their goal

to which, gradually, as they become more like Christ, God's glory reflected, they become more identified with the glory of God.

An enigmatic construction ends 3:18 that may be understood to relate to all the elements in the verse in a most general, correlative way and be translated "as from the Lord, the Spirit" (καθάπερ ἀπὸ κυρίου πνεύματος *kathaper apo kyriou pneumatos*). From the outset, we must acknowledge that Paul does not have a clearly formulated trinitarian view of matters divine;[101] in fact, one could argue that he contributes to the situation that forced the later church to inquire more carefully about the relationship among God, Spirit, and Christ. As already noted, it is sometimes difficult in Paul's letters to know whether "Lord" refers to God or to Christ. In 3:18, κύριος (*kyrios*) is taken to refer to God. At times, however, *kyrios* is applied to Christ (e.g., Rom 1:7 and parallels in the other salutations; Rom 14:9; 1 Cor 12:3; Gal 1:19). At other times, *kyrios*, though standing alone, probably refers to Christ (e.g., 1 Cor 7:10; Gal 5:10; Phil 4:1, 10; 1 Thess 1:6). Again, at times *kyrios* clearly refers to God (e.g., Rom 4:8; 9:28; 10:12). And some references to *kyrios* leave the reader open to think of God or Christ (Rom 12:11; 2 Cor 5:11).

The relation of the Spirit to God and to Christ is even more problematically and variously represented within Paul's letters. Sometimes the Spirit is directly linked to God: Once it is the Spirit from God (1 Cor 2:12); more frequently it is described with the genitive construction, which can denote "source" or "belonging" (πνεῦμα θεοῦ *pneuma theou*) to the Spirit of God (Rom 8:9, 11, 14; 1 Cor 2:11, 14; 3:16; 6:11; 7:40; 12:3). At other times the Spirit is immediately connected to Christ as in the expressions "the Spirit of God's Son" (Gal 4:6), "the Spirit of Jesus Christ" (Phil 1:19), and "the Spirit of Christ" (Rom 8:9). And there are the ambiguous references such as in 2 Cor 3:17-18, where "Spirit of the Lord" requires the hearer to ponder whether "the Lord" refers to God or to Christ.

98. M. D. Hooker, "Adam in Romans 1:1," *NTS* 6 (1960) 305, affirms that Paul frequently associates εἰκὼν (*eikōn*) and δόξα (*doxa*; Rom 8:29-30; 1 Cor 15:42-49; cf. Col 4:4).

99. J. D. G. Dunn, "A Light to the Gentiles: The Significance of the Damascus Road Christophany for Paul," in Hurst and Wright, *The Glory of Christ in the New Testament,* 261, correctly writes of the "process of salvation."

100. J. Lambrecht, "Transformation in 2 Cor 3:18," *Bib* 64 (1983) 246, 251-54, agrees.

101. Though Richard argues that Paul is "developing a trinitarian theme, not on an ontological but on a soteriological and functional level" and rightly observes: "The turning to God is achieved through Christ and remains the work of the Spirit." See E. Richard, "Polemics, Old Testament, and Theology: A Study of II Cor., III,1-IV,6," *RB* 88 (1981) 35.

Perhaps it is our post-Chalcedonian longing for neatness that drives us to distinguish and compartmentalize what obviously for Paul was a more fluid mix. A glance at Rom 8:9-11 may be instructive. The burden of that passage is to stress the immanence of Spirit-Christ-God in the believers. Note the many ways it stresses the indwelling: "dwells in you" (3 times: Rom 8:9, 11); "in you" (once: Rom 8:10); and "has" as in "possesses" (ἔχει *echei*; once: Rom 8:9). A closer look shows that *what* or *who* dwells or is in persons is diversely expressed: It is the "Spirit of God" in Rom 8:9, "the Spirit of the one who raised Jesus from the dead" and "the Spirit of the one who raised from the dead Christ Jesus and who will make alive your mortal bodies" in Rom 8:11; and "Christ" in Rom 8:10. Finally, the Spirit, mentioned so frequently, is three times the Spirit of God (Rom 8:9, 11) and once the "Spirit of Christ" (Rom 8:9). In this Romans passage, Paul's primary interest is to affirm in as many ways as possible the divine presence with believers as that which defines them and gives them meaning. Accordingly, he risks redundancy and even some fuzzing of categories for the larger purpose of accentuating presence and immanence.

In 2 Cor 3:1–4:6, Paul chooses to accentuate the Spirit and its work through him and in the lives of all believers. He cannot simply dwell on the Spirit, however, because he has structured his argument around the story of Moses and God, and his Greek version of the Scriptures has used *kyrios*, "Lord," as the translation for the term "Yahweh." He can and does strengthen the link between Lord and Spirit by an earlier note (2 Cor 3:17, "The Lord [just mentioned] is the Spirit") in which he identifies the Lord of the Exod 34:34 citation in 2 Cor 3:16 with the Spirit, anticipating and setting the stage for the conclusion of 3:18. So Paul has bound up his primary interest—namely, to write about the Spirit's work through him—with his secondary interest: structuring a comparison of himself and Moses that features *kyrios*, "Lord" (meaning "God"). Hence, when he comes to the capstone of his argument in 3:18, he composes a generalizing statement ("as from the Lord, the Spirit") that affirms both "Lord," understood as God, and Spirit as the source, the power behind the ministry of the new covenant that

he has just described and which he personally represents so directly in the lives of the Corinthians, his addressees.

In the two-covenant passage Paul references the Spirit seven times (3:3, 6 [twice], 8, 17 [twice], 18). Rhetorically this mention of a term and a frequent returning to it is called *refining*. Refining requires dwelling on a topic while seeming to move into new material; it usually involves a degree of repetition and a finding of alternate ways to make and elaborate the same point.[102] The first mention of the Spirit ("Spirit of the living God," 3:3), very much in line with Paul's claims in Romans 8 about the Spirit joining with human spirits to enable people to become God's children (Rom 8:15-16), credits the Spirit with working, indeed writing, on human hearts. It is not until a few verses later that the "new covenant" is said to be based on Spirit, not letter (*pneuma*, not γράμμα *gramma*, 3:6); and the rhetorically refining link becomes clear when Paul affirms, in contradistinction from the letter that kills, the "Spirit which makes alive" (3:6c), a clear echo of the "Spirit of the living God" (3:3). The ministry with which Paul readily identifies is characterized by him as ἡ διακονία τοῦ πνεύματος (*hē diakonia tou pneumatos*), "the ministry of the Spirit," which, as in such Greek genitives, can be understood as a ministry driven by the Spirit (genitive of source, origin) and as a ministry that deals in Spirit (and in righteousness, 3:9, and in reconciliation, 5:18; these are genitives of quality).[103] Then, as noted, when the passage moves toward its climax: The Spirit references cluster and ground all of this—ministry, new covenant, freedom—in the Lord God and the Spirit.

Paul's mention of freedom in 3:17 merits attention. The claim that "where the Spirit is, there is freedom" seems gratuitously inserted; but there can be no doubt that Paul very positively associates the Spirit and the life of the Spirit with freedom. Once again Romans 8 is a strong parallel:

Rom 8:2-32	2 Cor 3:1-18
"Spirit of life" (8:2)	"Spirit of the living God" (3:3)

---

102. See *Ad Herennium* 4.42.54.
103. Furnish, *II Corinthians*, 204.

| "has set you free" (8:2) | "the Spirit makes alive" (3:7) "Where the Spirit of the Lord is, there is freedom." (3:17) |

Where the Romans 8 passage sets one νόμος (*nomos*, "law"; in Rom 8:2 signifying a way of being or of living) over against another *nomos* ("the *nomos* of the Spirit of life" versus "the *nomos* of sin and death," Rom 8:2), the 2 Corinthians 3 passage has a similar contrast of life and death, a similar insistence on the work of the Spirit associated with life, and a similar resultant freedom. The focus is not on rival notions of *nomos*, however, but on "old" and "new" covenants (2 Cor 3:6, 14). Likewise, the discussion of freedom in Galatians 5 grounds the peroration that follows: "Let us be in line with the Spirit" (Gal 5:25).

Paul's remark about Spirit-founded freedom, however, is not a call for the Corinthians to celebrate *their* freedom. Paul has had his problems with the Corinthians' zeal for their new freedom in Christ, as a glance over 1 Corinthians readily shows. In fact, his purposes in 2 Cor 3:1-18 are anything but freedom for the Corinthians; he works here assiduously instead to bind them ever more fully to himself. It is *his own* Spirit-inaugurated freedom that he has in view. Paul's assertion of Spirit-grounded freedom is a subtle move on his part because he has used his Spirit-based freedom to upbraid the Corinthians in the "painful" letter of frank speech (παρρησία *parrēsia*) about which Paul will have much more to say later in this letter fragment. In fact, in the passage at hand Paul has adumbrated once before to his use of *parrēsia* in his previous letter: "Having such hope [because he is grounded in the ministry of permanent glory] we have used much frank speech" (3:12),[104] *not like Moses,* who dealt gingerly with the Israelites when he came down off the mountain with his fading glory. Because of Paul's solid grounding in the Spirit and its ministry (3:8), Paul has exercised his freedom—"Where the Spirit of the Lord is, there is freedom"—in his relation

to the Corinthians. Accordingly, he was not "out of line" to have written them using frank speech, even though the letter proved painful to them and to him. In 3:12 and 17 Paul has laid the foundation for further and more explicit reflections about his resort to *parrēsia*, frank speech (2 Cor 7:5-16).

Without the term's being used, Paul has been writing about grace, God's freely given, unmerited disposition working through his ministry. His insistence that his "competence" (ἡ ἱκανότης ἡμῶν *hē hikanotēs hēmōn*) comes not from himself but from God (3:5) affirms that it is God's grace and power, not Paul's own skills or performance, that sustain his association with this ministry of the new covenant. Along this same line, Paul uses passive constructions, a notorious Pauline way of stressing God's grace: In Christ the veil is taken away (3:14, 16), and we are being transformed (3:18).

It is impossible to overstate the importance of the Holy Spirit for Paul's understanding of the life of faith.[105] To be sure, receiving the Spirit is the hallmark of belonging to the new people of God; Spirit reception is associated with the beginning of faith (Rom 8:15-16) and, therefore not surprisingly, with baptism (1 Cor 12:13). When Paul takes the Galatians back to the origin of their faith, he asks about their reception of the Spirit (Gal 3:2). In fact, "spiritualist" or "Spirit-person" (πνευματικός *pneumatikos*) seems to be Paul's basic descriptor for those who today would be called "Christian," a term not available to Paul (1 Cor 2:15; 3:1; Gal 6:1).

In 2 Cor 3:1-18, Paul has attempted two goals. First and most prominent, Paul has tried to overcome any objection that he might have been boasting too much when he identified himself with those whom God, like a victor, always leads around and in whom God manifests life and death (2:14-17). Paul's response lies in his depiction of himself as part of a coterie of especially designated ministers of the new covenant of Spirit, righteousness, and life. His second goal, admittedly quite minor in proportion to the first, is to incorporate his having used *parrēsia* with

---

104. Some scholars, such as Furnish, *II Corinthians,* 206, 230, take *parrēsia* in 3:12 to refer to Paul's psychological demeanor—i.e., Paul acted boldly. John Chrysostom (c. 40–120 CE) knew the rhetorical conventions of frank speech and recognized it as such here. See *Hom.* 7 in 2 Cor. 2. See also J. Migne, *Patrologica graeca* 61.444.104

105. Other functions of the Spirit, not relevant to 2 Corinthians 3, include its producing fruit in the lives of believers (Gal 5:22) and its giving χαρίσματα (*charismata*), "spiritual gifts," to believers (Rom 12:6-8; 1 Cor 12:4-11). See G. D. Fee, *God's Empowering Presence: The Holy Spirit in the Letters of Paul* (Peabody, Mass.: Hendrickson: 1994) 870-95.

the Corinthians in his most recent letter—the lost, "painful" one—as an appropriate action for someone of his standing and ethos. The next segment of 2 Corinthians, 4:1-6, the conclusion to the argument begun in 3:1, elaborates how Paul's performance among and toward the Corinthians is appropriate—to the gospel and, by insinuation, to them.

The passage 4:1-6, addressing Paul's comportment in this very ministry, opens with a strong link to what has just preceded: "because of this" (διὰ τοῦτο *dia touto*), referring to the ministry of the new covenant that Paul has been graced to be a part of (4:1). What follows is a characterization, presented alternately in positive and negative forms and thereby echoing the antithetical structure of the opening of 3:1-18, of the way Paul has comported himself. And 4:1-6 confirms that Paul's primary concern in 3:1-18 was to advance his own standing with the Corinthians. The terminology of the section is charged; strong words provide emphasis to his claims. He has not just "set aside" certain ways of behaving; he has "renounced/disowned" (ἀπεῖπον *apeipon*) them (4:2). He does not "adulterate/falsify" (δολόω *doloō*) the word of God (4:2; perhaps echoing a complaint seen in 2:17). His scrupulousness regarding the way he handles himself and the gospel is of one piece and should serve to commend him not only to the Corinthians, but also to everybody's conscience everywhere (4:2).

In this context, "conscience" (συνείδησις *syneidēsis*, 4:2) functions as a synonym for "minds" (τὰ νοήματα *ta noēmata*), which he uses on either side, in 3:14 and 4:4. Conscience and mind are the human capacities that people must use in moral reasoning as they deliberate how they should live their lives, and in this case as they weigh out how, as Paul hopes for it, they ought to reaffirm their relation to him as the one who has faithfully and truthfully brought them the gospel.

Twice in 4:1-6 Paul, by his careful, and arguably clever, use of rhetoric, leaves the Corinthians no place to turn other than himself. The first is wily; the second is subtle. In the first, Paul picks up on the image of veiling from the previous pericope and takes up what might have been an objection of some Corinthians or even of some outsiders: "If [really, as some believe or perhaps say] our gospel is veiled, it is veiled [only, understood] for those who are perishing" (4:3; cf. 2:15, where Paul divided all human beings into two categories, "those who are being saved" and "those who are perishing"). Paul refines his description of those "who are perishing": "the god of this aeon has blinded the minds of unbelievers so that they do not see the light" (4:4; cf. the "hardened minds" of 3:14). So persons at Corinth who would distance themselves from Paul and his leadership leave themselves open to the charge of being "unbelievers" who really should be counted among "those who are perishing" and that their reasoning capacities are blinded by their deity, the "god of this age" (αἰών *aiōn*, 4:4*a*). Paul, who mentions Satan occasionally (cf. 1 Cor 5:5; 7:5; 2 Cor 2:11; 11:14; 12:7), quite likely has Satan in view, though he pointedly uses the more dramatic "god of this aeon," an expression that neither he nor any other NT writer uses elsewhere (cf. John 14:30; 1 Cor 2:6-8; 8:5; Eph 2:2).

The second rhetorical move is attached to Paul's claim that he preaches not himself but Christ Jesus as Lord: "and ourselves as your slaves for Jesus' sake" (4:5). Already in chaps. 1–9 Paul has anticipated that his lofty claims about himself and his gospel, somewhat muffled as they may be by his insistence on using the plural to include himself with all others who represent the same gospel, may cause some of the Corinthians to bridle (cf. 1:12, 21-22; 3:1-2). In 4:5, therefore, his claim that, no matter how lofty the ministry to which he has been called, he has made himself a slave to the Corinthians—using the term "slave" to translate δοῦλος (*doulos*), for its shock rather than the NIV's milder "servant." The posture of servitude reflects Paul's relation to the Corinthians as expressed elsewhere (e.g., 1 Cor 4:8-13; 9:19) and should help to counteract any Corinthian offense at his lofty self-claims.

But his is not simply a rhetorical strategy to depict himself as a servant or a slave; it accords with his picture of Christ and is, therefore, a Pauline imitation of Christ, who, as the *eikōn* ("image/reflection") of God (4:4), has just been mentioned as the focus of the gospel that Paul propounds. So Paul, like the Christ he proclaims at the heart of his gospel, takes the role of the servant/slave (cf.

"the form of a slave," Phil 2:7) in his relation to the Corinthians.

In this lofty ministry to which, by God's mercy (4:1), Paul has been called, he does not despair (an echo from 1:8-10 and a note that will reappear in 4:16), though the hardship list just ahead in 4:7-12 will suggest that he has had plenty of reasons not only to lose heart but also to lose hope (cf. 3:12). Neither does he resort to shameful, hidden ways. Nor does he walk as one prepared to do just anything (πανουργία *panourgia*, "trickery/[unfavorable] craftiness," 4:2; this will reemerge as a charge with some currency in 12:16). By contrast, he operates with full disclosure of the truth (another oblique reference to his having spoken frankly to them through his "painful" letter) and by so doing expects to "commend himself to everyone's conscience before God" (4:2). This practice of open, truthful disclosure, as Paul views it, "shines forth the light of the gospel, the glory of Christ who is the image of God" (4:4).

Although the discussion earlier has been of the glory of Moses' face (3:7) and of the Lord God (3:18), Paul now identifies the glory as "the glory of Christ" (τῆς δόξης τοῦ Χριστοῦ *tēs doxēs tou Christou*), who, as the "image" or "reflection" (εἰκὼν τοῦ θεοῦ *eikōn tou theou*) of God, reflects the glory that ultimately is God's, just as Paul suggested already in 3:18. The notion of the glory of Christ is refined in 4:6 to be "the light of the knowledge of the glory of God in the face of Christ" (ἐν προσώπῳ Χριστοῦ *en prosōpō Christou*, or "in the presence of Christ"). Ultimately, the glory belongs to God. Glory is known by believers in Christ, whose face, whose presence, reflects that glory like light. The redemptive light, construed as analogous to God's calling forth "light out of darkness" at creation by the powerful and glorious utterance of the word (Gen 1:3), now shines forth (4:4; cf. Gen 1:3; Isa 9:2 LXX) through the luminous gospel Paul preaches and that he has preached from the start in Corinth.

Paul's claims in 4:2*a* about *how he did not act* have been taken by some as an attack on and a denigration of the outsiders who have come into Corinth (see 3:1-3).[106] But they

may just as well be amplifications *via negativa* of Paul's own exemplary comportment, which the rest of 4:2 details quite positively.[107]

Apart from any consideration of Paul's rhetorical goals with the Corinthians in the two-covenant passage (3:1–4:6), we gain some fundamental insight into Paul's convictions. Though engaged with predominantly Gentile audiences in his correspondence, Paul shows clearly here that he thinks covenantally about God's relations to people. Ritually grounded in the Lord's supper, Paul thinks of the renewed relationship made possible through Christ's death ("blood" in 1 Cor 11:25) as a covenant; indeed, it is of that "new covenant" that Paul has been made a minister (3:6).

Scholarship has not always adequately placed Paul's justification/righteousness claims—which are so important to him and to his proclamation of the gospel—within a covenant context. Covenant terminology does not have to be explicit in a given text before we can consider that Paul may have had it as a part of his own framework. Surely Gentiles who were unfamiliar with covenant conceptions could readily have understood that Paul's claim of justification or righteousness suggested a sort of judicial vindication, or, to put it differently, that the charges brought against one had been dropped. This forensic semantic possibility is significant and must be retained regarding Paul's usage. Nevertheless, the richness of detail and interpretive insight reflected in 2 Cor 3:1–4:6 shows that Paul understands his own ministry as a part of God's new covenant, opening full participation to all who are claimed by the Spirit, whether Jew or Gentile.

Because the covenant framework is so pronounced here, our reading of *all of* Paul's claims about justification (or righteousness, which is also based on the same Greek root), no matter where they occur in his letters, must adequately interpret that term within a covenant context. The eighth-century BCE prophets, such as Amos, Hosea, Isaiah, and Micah, take their readers to task for their failure to seek justice, to pursue covenant righteousness, "that quality of life in relationship with others in the community that gives rise to justice"[108] (see Isa 1:17; Hos 10:12;

106. Peter Marshall, *Enmity in Corinth: Social Conventions in Paul's Relations with the Corinthians*, WUNT 44 (Tübingen: J. C. B. Mohr, 1987) 272, 321.

107. Thrall, *The Second Epistle to the Corinthians*, 218, 221-22, also considers this to be apologetic, and not polemical.

108. G. M. Tucker, "Notes on Amos," in *The HarperCollins Study Bible*, 1364.

Amos 5:24; Mic 6:6-8). Paul is quite thoroughly aligned with those prophets when he expects his followers, who are "justified" or "made righteous" with God, by God's grace, to live in love, and to care for others for whom Christ has died. In 3:9 Paul described his work as a "ministry of righteousness," which can readily be understood as a genitive of content or focus: a ministry dedicated to righteousness. For Paul, to live the justified, righteous life is to live in proper (new) covenant relationship to God, to show the appropriate care and concern for others who are also part of that (new) covenant, and to share in the reception of peace and mercy, along with the Israel of God (Gal 6:16).

EXCURSUS: PAUL'S DISCUSSION OF MULTIPLE COVENANTS

Three times in the undisputed Pauline corpus (and also Eph 2:12), Paul refers to more than one covenant. First, 2 Cor 3:1–4:6 mentions more than one covenant, as has been observed. Second, Galatians has the allegorical representation of Abraham's children by the two women, one by the "free woman" (Sarah), and the other by the slave, Hagar (Gal 4:21-31). There the two covenants "correspond . . . to the covenant of promise and the covenant of law,"[109] and in Paul's view the Galatians are "children of the promise, like Isaac" (Gal 4:28 NRSV). Clearly, one of the two covenants in Galatians is positive and is associated with freedom and inheritance; the other is negative and is linked to slavery: The children of the one inherit; the children of the other do not.

The third instance is found in his Letter to the Romans, where Paul acknowledges that the Israelites have many advantages, among which he lists "the covenants" (αἱ διαθῆκαι *hai diathēkai*, Rom 9:4). In Rom 9:4, Paul does not declare how many covenants he has in mind; he simply uses the plural. The textual evidence of that verse suggests that some copyists have thought Paul must have meant "the covenant," and accordingly have reduced it to the singular. But many patristic writers, and even Augustine, know the text as reflecting the plural designation, "the covenants." For one simple reason—namely, that the entire list of the Israelites' advantages in Rom 9:4 is positive, its plural "covenants" cannot be the two covenants depicted in 2 Cor 3:1–4:6; neither can the Rom 9:4 covenants be equated with Paul's Galatians allegorical representation of two rival covenants, one representing the free woman and one representing the slave woman.

Because Rom 9:4 makes positive mention of "the covenants," we cannot import for its interpretation either Galatians' rival covenants or 2 Corinthians' partially contrasted covenants. Scholars have never adequately pursued the issue of how, apart from Paul's dual-covenant construction in 2 Corinthians and the rival covenant depiction in Galatians, a plural of covenants might fit positively within Paul's thinking. An attempt to do so will be made here in an effort to reconstruct the broadest possible backdrop against which modern readers can assess Paul's 2 Corinthians claims about the two covenants. Because Paul nowhere lays out his thought on this matter, the following is admittedly constructive and suggestive and is offered for reflection and deliberation, not as established or completely verifiable.

Israel has two types of covenant: the ברית עולם (*běrît ʿôlām*), or "perpetual covenant," and the suzerainty type, or conditional covenant. The perpetual covenant is exemplified in David and in Abraham and rests solely on God's faithfulness (cf. also the

---

109. R. B. Hays, "Notes on Galatians," in *The HarperCollins Study Bible*, 2189.

covenant with Noah, Genesis 9). It is granted by God, simply out of God's mercy and commitment. No special performance is expected or required by the recipients of this type of covenant. As its name suggests, the perpetual convenant is everlasting. God's covenant with David is a good example. God says of David: "I will establish the throne of his kingdom forever . . . I will not take my steadfast love from him . . . your throne shall be established forever" (2 Sam 7:13-16 NRSV). The warrantee of this covenant is the faithfulness of God. The covenant with Abraham is of this same type. Abraham is simply chosen by God as the one to receive God's commitment of beneficence; he is given God's promise. The covenant is granted not because of something Abraham has done to merit consideration, but simply because God has selected Abraham, and the covenant is for all time (Genesis 15; 17).

The suzerainty type of covenant is granted by the superior, or by analogy God, on the condition of certain performance by the recipients. For example, "These are the statutes and ordinances that you must diligently observe in the land that the LORD, the God of your ancestors, has given you to occupy all the days that you live on the earth" (Deut 12:1 NRSV). This text introduces the conditions on which covenant continuance is predicated. Failure of the covenant recipients to maintain performance can lead to curse rather than blessing (cf. Deuteronomy 27–28); and, if the covenant granter wishes, can lead to termination of the covenant altogether.

Although he never uses the technical term "covenant" to describe it, Paul knows and takes delight in God's special relationship with Abraham (Romans 4; Galatians 3). In fact, Abraham becomes the type of the faithful person, exemplifying complete trust in God's promises, simultaneously glorying in God and growing in faith, and being reckoned righteous by God for his faith. God's commitment to Abraham is unbounded; God's faithfulness grounds that commitment.

Paul creatively incorporates features of both covenant types in his letters and, therefore, in his understanding of the gospel. Central to Paul's connections with the perpetual covenant is his repeated insistence on God's inerrant faithfulness, already affirmed in 2 Cor 1:18 and long since familiar to the Corinthians from 1 Cor 1:9 and 10:13 (cf. 1 Thess 5:24).

The most striking reflection on God's faithfulness, however, comes precisely in Rom 3:1-4, where Paul asks, "What advantage has the Jew?" This is a key passage in the structure of Romans because, although it begins a list of prerogatives ("they were entrusted with God's oracles," Rom 3:2), the list breaks off and is resumed only in the already mentioned Rom 9:4, where he speaks of the Israelites' having the advantage, among other things, of "the covenants." So as to highlight the centrality of God's faithfulness, Paul takes the argument to extremes: "If some were unfaithful, will not their unfaithfulness nullify the faithfulness of God?" (Rom 3:3). Paul's answer is a striking affirmation of God's covenant faithfulness: "No way! Let God be true even if every person is a liar" (3:4, which he supports by citing Ps 51:6). Clearly, God's commitment to the Jews does not rest on *any consideration* of their performance. The worst-case scenario that Paul proposes—let them all be unfaithful—does not unhinge the faithfulness of God. This is unquestionably covenant talk on Paul's part, as the mention of circumcision in 2 Cor 3:1 shows—and of the perpetual covenant type.

At the same time that he affirms God's faithful covenant commitment to people, however, Paul holds that people are responsible to God. Paul declares that believers will be held accountable for their actions (see the Commentary on 5:10). At the end-time judgment, people will be judged regarding their works of obedience (Rom 2:6-10, 16; 14:10). Paul expects believers to be engaged in the labor of love, in behalf of the gospel (1 Cor 15:58; 16:10, 16; 1 Thess 1:3). To do works of love (Gal 5:6) is not merely an option for believers. Those in Christ are expected to experience the love of Christ controlling and extending them toward each other (2 Cor 5:14).

Curiously, like no other early Christian writer, Paul creatively weaves together elements of both types of covenants, the perpetual and the conditional. From the former he grounds his gospel in the unchanging faithfulness of God, and from the latter he expects believers to perform the conditions appropriate to the covenant commitment God has made to them. Romans 9:4, with its mention of "the covenants," lets us see that when Paul thinks of multiple covenants, he does not always set one covenant against another, as in Galatians, nor does he always have a mixed picture of some continuity and some discontinuity, as in 2 Cor 3:1–4:3. In the larger picture, Paul can think of more than one covenant quite positively and embrace elements of both the perpetual and the conditional covenants in his larger understanding of God's purposes.

REFLECTIONS

1. Basic to Paul's construction here is the notion that the glory of God is reflected, not seen directly. How true of life, that God's surprises break out in the most unexpected ways and places: in that little moment where someone reaches out to you in a time of need; where you have joy over being of assistance to someone; or where a baby shows up in a manger and changes lives and history. Maybe God has to surprise us in order to get our attention sometimes. The problem with that, however, is that we might not notice the reflections of God's glory that are happening around us. Part of the task of worship is the rehearsing of how we learn not only to look for God's surprises in life, but also how to recognize them.

2. When our culture uses the term "freedom," it generally means something people achieve through power or cunning or win with luck. Freedom, for Paul, is not something we generate for ourselves, not something we achieve by our own maneuvering or decisions. Freedom is a gift that liberates us to be what God created us to be. Luther had a sense of that when, following Paul, he said that true freedom is found in service to others. Imagine our culture's calling as service of others' freedom! But God's gift of acceptance and love of us as we are affirms who we already are, so we do not need to scrap and fight to earn personal status. God has already given us the only status we need: God's acceptance. With that in mind, we can reach out to others in service.

3. Paul's two-covenant account has prompted both a denigration of Israel as having an inadequate covenant and an accompanying claim of Christian superiority. But Paul's message is at once more complex than inferior/better and at the same time designed to bind the Corinthians to him and his ministry; Paul has no apparent interest here in reflecting on Israel or Jews. Marcion, a second-century heretic who believed there were two Gods and that the God of Jesus was superior to the God of Israel, may be alive in the hearts of some when they read Paul's two-covenant thought here as supersessionist, as replacing the old with the new, without any continuity. In the Middle Ages, cathedral statuary represented this supersessionist view through carved stone figures of two women, "Church" and "Synagogue." On the south transept portal of the Strasbourg Cathedral, for example, lady "Church" stands tall and looks out confidently, carrying a staff topped by a cross and holding a chalice representing Christ's blood. Lady "Synagogue" stands opposite, head bowed and blindfolded, signifying moral ignorance. Often such representations of her also include a crown falling from her head or depict her as dropping the stone tablets of the law. Such characterizations are misrepresentations of Paul's view of the two covenants.

4. Paul's antithesis—what fades versus what persists—is a way for him to distinguish what is important from what is indifferent (for a similar point expressed in other categories, cf. 1 Cor 2:6 and 13:13). In a society so defined by its throwaway character, where items are made not to be repaired but replaced, we are captivated by the latest fashion. Paul, on the other hand, is interested in what remains, what is dependable, what is trustworthy.

5. God is not finished with us as we are. We are works in progress. With its double depiction of the life of faith as being changed into the image of Christ and as moving from one degree of glory to another, 2 Cor 3:18 is a powerful affirmation that the Christian life is one of growth and improvement. That thought, of course, raises for any modern reader the question of whether our faith shows such growth or improvement. Paul thinks one can test oneself in that regard (see the Commentary on 1 Cor 11:28-29 and on 2 Cor 13:5-10).

6. Change is not always a welcome experience; it is at times unsettling. But it is in the nature of grace and of one of its primary expressions, the Holy Spirit, to bring about change, to intercept and interrupt the neat calculus that we like to make between the A's and B's of life by which we attempt to control and understand the way life comes to us. Animosity does not always have to lead to hatred; a wrong step is not always followed by a slap on the wrist. Perhaps we need to discuss with each other how we can embrace change that bids to bring us good or, to put it differently, that moves us to a new place.

7. Paul suggests that a certain comportment is inappropriate to the gospel: The secretive ways of shame and deception are simply ruled out. Jesus' attacks on hypocrites (see Matthew 23) are on the same wavelength. Our English term "hypocrite" is a virtual transliteration of a Greek term (Latin picked it up from the Greek) that refers to a stage actor—that is, someone who puts on a front, who in effect wears a face that is not his or her own, who acts the part of someone else. Dissembling is alien to the gospel.

8. The expression "god of this age" is daring because it risks misunderstanding what Paul knows clearly—namely, that there is only one God (cf. 1 Cor 8:4). But Paul also knows that there are "many gods and many lords" that, in fact, bid to hold sway over our lives (1 Cor 8:5). Whatever is at the center of our lives, whatever governs our decisions and bears on all our actions—that is our god, our true lord. "Idolatry" is the technical term of Israel and of the early churches for putting some thing or purpose other than God at the determining center of our lives. Modern gods/lords that bid for our fealty are legion: job, status, money, happiness, acceptance, and you fill in the blank. Even good things, when our desire for them gets out of proportion, can assume lordship over us and become a "god of this age."

9. In the creation narratives of Israel's traditions, Adam is said to have been created in the image of God (Gen 1:26). All of us, as Adam and Eve's descendants, also share God's image. Paul invites us to think about that christologically: Christ represents and reveals God to us. When we act with love and clemency toward others, we reflect Christ to them (2 Cor 10:1) and, at least in some little measure, re-present Christ to them. The idea behind this notion is that God's love is a powerful agent in every life it engages, so when God's love is imaged or reflected through and beyond us, we reflect not ourselves but Christ through us. When we have to be in the middle of the picture, Christ is not being reflected well (or perhaps at all).

2 Corinthians 4:7–5:10, Paul's Ministry Sustained Through Affliction and Mortality

COMMENTARY

Paradox and incongruity characterize Paul's second of three complementary portraits of his ministry (4:7–5:10). Antinomies are played off against one another throughout, as the following list shows.

not our power	God's power (4:7)
outer	inner (4:16)
seen	not seen (4:18)
temporal	eternal (4:18)
earthly tent	heavenly dwelling (5:1)
be at home	get away (5:6-9)

4:7. Paul's opening metaphor—"We have this treasure in earthenware vessels"—is a powerful cue to what follows in this section, and it will become the theme of "power through weakness," which dominates chaps. 10–13. Continuing to write in the plural, signifying his belonging to the mainstream, Paul adverts to his just-described new-covenant ministry and the glory of God represented within it with his generalizing phrase "this treasure" (θησαυρός *thēsauros*). So grand a treasure borne in such a menial, frail, seemingly inept container makes it unmistakable that the power enabling the whole enterprise is "from God and not from us" (4:7).

4:8-11. The hardship list that follows (4:8-10) is presented as proof that the entire endeavor is from God. Paul wears each of the difficulties as an ironic badge of honor. The verbs are a lexicon of adversity, structured in an "A not B" form. The first, θλίβω (*thlibō*, "hard pressed, afflicted," 4:8) is a repetition of the same verb that inaugurated the *sorites* (form: A leads to B; B leads to C; etc.) in 1:6 and, therefore, invites the hearers to link Paul's early and later delineations of the suffering he has endured for the gospel (and for the Corinthians). The "A not B" form (4:8-9) is designed to paint a picture of considerable, but not totally overwhelming, hardship. The ready conclusion is that the aforementioned "power of God" (4:7) is what has kept the difficulties from being overwhelming so

that Paul does not "lose heart" or "despair" (ἐγκακέω *enkakeō*, 4:1, 16).

Hardship lists (*peristasis* catalogs) are a common feature of the Roman world of Paul's time. Sages often employed such recountings of difficulties to show that they were imperturbable and not governed by externals. Paul does the same.[110] The list in 4:8-9 is but the first of several in 2 Corinthians (cf. 6:4-10; 11:23-29).

At the end of the catalog (4:10), Paul makes a double connection with Jesus: In his own body, Paul carries "hither and yon" (περιφέρω *peripherō*) the death of Jesus (symbolizing Paul's sufferings and afflictions as reflections of Christ's death), so that the life of Jesus (a reference to Jesus Christ's resurrection, which is the very basis of hope) may be shown forth (φανερόω *phaneroō*; an echo of 2:14, where the NIV and the NRSV translate "spreads"), again in his body. The term for "death" here (νέκρωσις *nekrōsis*) is used in contemporary medical writings to describe dead or dying tissue;[111] Paul employs it for dramatic effect (cf. elsewhere in the NT only in Rom 4:19) as a way of emphasizing the difficulties he has experienced for the gospel. Paul's missionizing, despite all his troubles and setbacks, is itself a witness to Christ's resurrection because the perdurance of his mission says nothing more clearly than that the power indeed rests with God. This interpretation is made explicit by Paul when, again using a dramatic term that as a legal technical word has the overtones of being "handed over" or given into the custody of someone, he declares about himself that "we the living are always being bound over [παραδίδωμι *paradidōmi*] to death for Jesus' sake" (4:11; cf. a parallel with Judas's pact to "hand over" Jesus, Matt 26:15;

---

110. J. T. Fitzgerald, *Cracks in an Earthen Vessel: An Examination of the Catalogues of Hardships in the Corinthian Correspondence* (Atlanta: Scholars Press, 1988) 47-116.

111. Fitzgerald, *HarperCollins Study Bible* 2170n. J. Lambrecht, "The Nekrōsis of Jesus' Ministry and Suffering in 2 Cor 4,7-15," in *L'Apôtre Paul: personalité, style et conception du ministère,* ed. A. Vanhoye (Leuven: University of Leuven Press, 1986) 120 and n. 2.

Mark 14:10; note also Paul's receiving a death sentence, 2 Cor 1:9). The expression "for Jesus' sake" (διὰ Ἰησοῦν *dia Iēsoun*) specifies that it is not just any handing over that is being described. It is, instead, a life lived in service of Jesus and in conformity to the gospel;[112] those persons, Paul prominent among them, are the ones who are being given over into the custody of death.

Both 4:10 and 4:11 have opening clauses that identify the death of Jesus with the daily life of new-covenant ministers like Paul; and both sentences conclude with purpose clauses tied up with parallel expressions of "the life of Jesus," once again a reference to the resurrection. Both the death (i.e., crucifixion) and the life (i.e., resurrection) of Jesus are seen in Paul's body, a note to which Paul returns for refinement beginning in 4:16 with a "therefore" (διό *dio*) and with reflections about the "inner" and "outer" person.

4:12. Paul does not resist the temptation to pursue this image for further, personal purposes. Up until 4:12, both the death and the life of Jesus have been present in Paul and in his leadership colleagues (4:10-11). Now, however, Paul turns to a more explicit set of reflections that bear on himself and the Corinthians and alters the picture so that now only *death* is at work *in him* (and in his ubiquitous cohorts) while *life* is at work *in the Corinthians* (4:12). In this direct appeal for sympathy from the Corinthians, Paul seeks to turn his suffering and hardship into a source of increased goodwill from them.

4:13-14. Just as he did in the heart of the two-covenant passage, so also now Paul adverts to the frank speech (see the Introduction) that he employed with the Corinthians in his most recent correspondence with them, the painful letter (4:13). Using a quotation from Ps 115:1 LXX (cf. Ps 116:10), Paul justifies the way he has spoken (harshly) to them in the painful letter, but, at the same time, he accounts for his current self-promotion.

Paul's confidence then and now is grounded in his faith ("Having the same spirit of faith" as the psalmist, 4:13), which contains at its heart the conviction ("we know,"

4:14) of how the rest of the salvation story is going to play out—namely, that God, the understood subject of all the verbs in the declaration, "who raised the Lord Jesus will raise us with Jesus and will present us [before himself, understood] along with you" (4:14). This pithy statement encapsulates the heart of the gospel for Paul, providing the basis for his hope and, indeed, for his perduring in the world (stated in other categories, for his not giving up), where he experiences so much affliction and distress.

In one short sentence Paul scans from the past (4:14*a*) to the future (4:14*b*), affirms that all is based on the character of God (whom Paul aptly describes elsewhere as the one who brings into existence the things that do not exist and who brings life out of death, Rom 4:17), and includes the Corinthians ("along with you") with himself as being destined to be "presented" before God (4:14). The NRSV translation of 4:14 hides what is for Paul a technical term of the judgment day at the parousia: παρίστημι (*paristēmi*), "to present/offer/bring before a judge."

Throughout the corpus of his letters, Paul displays his view that believers will be presented for a last-day accounting of themselves and of their works (see esp. 2 Cor 5:10, where the notion will be reprised and refined). Even later in 2 Corinthians the same idea is garbed in bridal imagery when Paul, depicting himself as the father of the bride, writes of his having betrothed the Corinthians to Christ "in order to *present* you to Christ [ὑμᾶς . . . παραστῆσαι τῷ Χριστῷ *hymas . . . parastēsai tō Christō*] as a pure bride to her one husband" (11:2, italics added; cf. Rom 6:13; 14:10; 1 Cor 8:8). Of course, the death and resurrection of Jesus Christ are at the heart of Paul's gospel. Because Christ was raised from the dead, believers who are one with Christ and who have died with Christ and shared his sufferings already have newness of life and are assured that, at the end times, they will have a resurrection like his (Rom 6:4; Phil 3:10-11). Christ has died and been raised; believers currently share his death and confidently expect to share his resurrection at the end time, at the parousia.[113] At the center of this gospel is Paul's affirmation of

---

112. N. M. Watson, "'The Philosopher Should Bathe and Brush His Teeth': Congruence Between Word and Deed in Graeco-Roman Philosophy and Paul's Letters to the Corinthians," *AusBR* 42 (1994) 12, asserts that this hardship list is not presented to prove "his own fortitude" but as "the sign that his life is being conformed to the pattern of Christ crucified." Cf. 4:11.

113. Cf. Eph 2:5-6 and Col 2:13, letters from the Pauline school that affirm the resurrection in the present, removing the Pauline tension.

God's grace, by which he means God's freely given, unmerited gift of new life in Christ. So it is not surprising that Paul brings this little subsection of his argument to a climax by mentioning grace (4:15), a grace that by its very inner power means that it abounds to more and more people. And how does it do that? The answer is only implied: At least in part, it is by Paul's doing what he is called to do—spread the gospel just as he has done to the Corinthians.

4:15. "All of this is for your sake" (4:15). One may wonder just what the hearers are to include in "all of this" (τὰ πάντα *ta panta*). Immediately in the text it could be that they know, along with Paul, that God is working in them through Christ to present them before God at the end time (4:14). But the "all of this" expression could very well be interpreted not only to mean that immediate affirmation, but also to include Paul's extraordinary experiences of affliction and distress in bringing the gospel to the Corinthians.

"All of this" is also "unto the glory of God." Paul expects "the grace that is reaching more and more people" (4:15 NIV) to "cause thanksgiving to abound, to the glory of God" (4:15, echoing 1:11 in part) because grace, when it transforms a life, generates glorification of God. That is the way grace works, and glorification of God is the fruit of grace at work. The goal of human life, transformed by God's grace, is to glorify God (Rom 1:21; 15:6, 9; 1 Cor 6:20; 2 Cor 9:13), to give thanks to God (Rom 14:6; 1 Thess 5:18), and to bless God (see 1:3 and the Commentary on 1:3-11).

4:16-17. Because of God's grace and the hope founded upon it, Paul reaffirms (διό *dio* "therefore") that he does not "lose heart" (*enkakeō*, "despair/become weary," 4:16), a reprise of 4:1. Using categories no doubt familiar to his predominantly Gentile congregation at Corinth,[114] Paul speaks indirectly about himself by referring to an "inner man" (ὁ ἔσω *ho esō*), as distinguished from an "outer man" (ὁ ἔξω ἄνθρωπος *ho exō anthrōpos*, 4:16). Anyone who goes simply by appearances, by what is seen on the outside, would surely err, Paul argues, because

what they would accurately see is that the "outer man" is indeed "wasting away," being destroyed (διαφθείρω *diaphtheirō*, 4:16). By his repeated references to his afflictions, persecutions, and hardships (1:8-11; 4:7-11), Paul has openly embraced the "external" picture of himself as wasting away, as being destroyed. But the external vista does not disclose the whole story or even the most important part; further, it is not a reliable indicator of the full picture.

By contrast, the internal portrait is the one to be taken seriously, and about that Paul avers: "But our inner self [lit., man] is being renewed day by day" (4:16). The renewal day by day is a clear pointer, once again, toward the eschatological time when days and renewal will reach their goal. From that end-time perspective, Paul takes a third look at his afflictions (θλῖψις *thlipsis*, 1:8-11; 4:7-11, 17) and characterizes them as "momentary" (παραυτίκα *parautika*), "light/insignificant/slight" (ἐλαφρός *elaphros*); seen from this perspective, the afflictions are understood as "producing for us an eternal weight of glory beyond all proportion" (4:17). Elsewhere Paul makes that same association of present affliction or suffering leading to and ensuring a future glory of major proportions (Rom 8:17). Paul has an abiding conviction: Afflictions are part of the life of faith; they are signposts that one is proceeding as should be expected, a claim he made to the Thessalonians (1 Thess 3:3-4; cf. Rom 5:3-5). So his hardship catalogs also serve to document that he is on the right track and, therefore, to enhance his ethos[115] as their proper leader who is due their full adherence.

4:18. There is a slight cautionary note in Paul's development of the idea that appearances can be misleading. He goes ahead to describe himself and the rest of the mainstream as "not looking to the things that are seen, but to the things that are not seen" (4:18). Not only are appearances misleading, but, he says, they are also temporary; they last only for a time (πρόσκαιρα *proskaira*), whereas the unseen things are eternal (αἰώνια *aiōnia*, 4:18). The things that are seen, paralleling his portrayal of his "outer man," are not as reliable a guide as the things that are

---

114. H. D. Betz, "The Concept of the 'Inner Human Being' (ὁ ἔσω ἄνθρωπος *ho esō anthrōpos*) in the Anthropology of Paul," presidential address, *SNTS* (1999). Paul uses Platonic categories but accommodates them to his own non-dualistic anthropology.

115. See Fitzgerald, *Cracks in an Earthen Vessel*, 203; DiCicco, *Paul's Use of Ethos, Pathos, and Logos in 2 Corinthians 10–13*, 60n. 101.

not seen, or as his "inner man." Any Corinthian hearers who might take Paul's sufferings, afflictions, and hardships to be failures are here implicitly put on notice that they could be foolishly misled. Paul, and by implication from the plurals all other ministers like him, take their reckonings from the inner self, from eternals, and from the things that are not seen.

5:1-4. In the verses directly ahead, this same image resurfaces for refinement when Paul writes that "we walk by faith, not by sight" (5:7). This fits also his earlier assertion to these Corinthians that now believers have partial knowledge and will have full knowledge only at the parousia, only at the end of the ages (1 Cor 13:12). The whole section (4:7–5:10) opened with the image of Paul and his associates having divine (and we now know "eternal" as well as "inner") treasures in earthenware vessels (4:7).

The passage concludes in a multiple refinement where the images of inner and outer (4:16), temporal and eternal (4:17), what is seen and what is not seen (4:18), are developed around a series of further, related antinomies: earthly tent/heavenly dwelling (5:1-2), being clothed/being naked (5:3-4), mortal/life, and being at home/taking a journey (5:6-8). Because refinement develops the same points by appearing to be talking about something else, we should not be surprised that twice Paul states, in a slightly different form, that he is "confident/courageous" (5:6, 8; earlier he wrote of "not despairing/losing heart," 4:1, 16).

When Paul introduces a statement with οἴδαμεν (*oidamen*), "we know," he draws on material that he assumes his auditors know and embrace. Therefore, his statement, "If the earthly tent . . . is destroyed, we have a building from God" (5:1 NIV), buttresses what he has previously said about not being misled by externals and appearances (5:1). For emphasis, Paul dwells on the topic. He contrasts an earthly, temporal tent (σκῆνος *skēnos*) with an eternal, heavenly edifice (οἰκοδομή *oikodomē*) and, because his interest is more on the latter, he elaborates it in more detail: It is from God, and not made by hands (5:1). Although the tent is mentioned once more in 5:4, the terminology shifts to vestment with additional clothes (5:3-4).

Recognizing that believers sigh or groan in their earthly existence (5:2), a position thoroughly consonant with Paul's treatment of his hardships and afflictions (4:8-12), and reaffirming that believers groan in this tent (5:4), Paul's choice is not the gnostic one—that is, to escape the body by sloughing it off. Neither is Paul the least bit interested in how people are changed from the tent to the building. On the contrary, his choice is that "we might be further clothed, so that the mortal might be swallowed up without remainder by life" (5:4). For Paul, the alternative is not bodily existence versus life without a body, because life is always bodily. In 1 Cor 15:35-44, Paul makes a similar point by arguing that life now and in God's redemptive future is and will be bodily. Humans do not *have* bodies that can be "taken off," leaving some untarnished inner entity (e.g., the soul, as in much of second-century and some modern versions of Christianity). No, life is bodily. Afflicted, suffering human beings, like earthenware vessels, are the very place where God's treasure is borne.

In 5:4, with his imagery of being further clothed and of life's swallowing up what is mortal, Paul instructs his hearers that his earlier antinomies, such as inner/outer, are not to be taken as completely divorced from one another.[116] In fact, Paul affirms that a process not unlike the transition "from glory unto glory" of 3:18 is under way. Paul has utter confidence that life is "swallowing up" (καταπίνω *katapinō*; the verb is emphatic, "without remainder/completely") what is mortal. What a perspective that gives on what he calls "this slight, momentary affliction" (4:17)! Harking back to 4:17, Paul avers that "the one who is producing [a repeat of the term κατεργάζομαι (*katergazomai*) from 4:17] this very thing [i.e., life's swallowing up of death without remainder] is God who is giving us the down payment of the Spirit" (5:5; cf. 1:22).

5:5. Within this segment of the letter, Paul periodically reaffirms his strong eschatological convictions, which so powerfully inform his view of life in the present. In 5:5, his end-time conviction that death as the last

---

116. P. Grelot, "De la maison terrestre à la maison céleste (2 Corinthiens 4,16-5,10)," 344-45, engagingly argues that throughout this passage Paul sets actual experience over against that for which one hopes.

enemy will be overcome (1 Cor 15:26) is recast as a process that God begins with the granting of the Holy Spirit, which all believers experience at the initiation of their life of faith (Rom 8:15-16). To make his point Paul employs a legal technical term with which his hearers should be acquainted: The Spirit is the ἀρραβῶν (*arrabōn*, "down payment" or "earnest money"), whose initial payment ensures that the one making it (in this case no less than God) will make good on the rest of the obligation (5:5). So the Spirit is here adduced as the guarantee that what God has begun in the afflicted, mortal lives of believers (i.e., life's swallowing up of death) will be finished because God is faithful to do what God has promised (1:20; Phil 1:6).

How could Paul not have "confidence" or "courage" (θαρρέω *tharreō*) when he not only believes God's transforming work is under way but also knows that the Holy Spirit is the down payment of it all? Ever the realist, though, Paul knows that "being at home in the body" inevitably entails, in some measure, "being away from the Lord" (5:6). In other words, the present circumstances, which include suffering and affliction, are not the ideal arrangement or the final picture, the goal. Paul knows that to remain in the world is necessarily to experience distraction and divided devotion. When writing to the Corinthians earlier, he acknowledged that daily concerns of life and the needs of spouses, for example, could divide one's attention and devotion to the Lord (1 Cor 7:32-35).

5:6-10. Verses 6-9 are a complex passage. Using a term sometimes associated with exile (ἐκδημέω *ekdēmeō*),[117] Paul sets up a rhetorical figure (form: ABBAAB) with the A's representing "being at home" (ἐνδημέω *endēmeō*) and the B's meaning "being away from home" (*ekdēmeō*). First, Paul takes "being at home" and "being away from home" in a metaphorical sense and treats that alternative in Stoic categories of *adiaphora*, indifferent matters. Second, he distinguishes being at home in the body from being with the Lord. Finally, the text is framed by two very strongly eschatological claims (5:5, 10).

Being at home/away and adiaphora. To unpack the construction with the "at home" and "away from home" statements, we begin

with 5:9 because there Paul subjugates his preferences with regard to being "at home" or "away" to a matter of infinitely greater importance: that he be one of those "pleasing the Lord" (5:9). In fact, the need to please the Lord trumps any personal preference (5:8) Paul may have. Paul's audience would have understood this deliberation as a Stoic-like sorting out of what is important from what is non-essential (*adiaphora*, "indifferent matters"; cf. 1 Corinthians 7). At many points in his letters, Paul employs this concept of indifferent matters as he relates to his predominantly Gentile audiences (cf. Rom 8:35-39; 14:8; Gal 3:28; Phil 1:10 ["discern what really matters"]; 4:10-13). In the scattered passages just referenced one finds quite a list of unimportant matters, including one's gender, social status, ethnic background, the way life comes to be, and even life and death themselves.

One might ask, then, what really matters to Paul and will find many ways he expresses it: "Jesus Christ, and him crucified" (1 Cor 2:2 NRSV); that his hearers will be "blameless at the coming of our Lord Jesus Christ" (1 Thess 5:23 NRSV); that his auditors maximize their devotion to their Lord (1 Cor 7:32-35); and in the passage at hand that believers "please the Lord" (2 Cor 5:9; cf. 1 Cor 7:19; Gal 5:6; 6:15).

Among the indifferent matters, Stoics did recognize that there were "preferreds" and "not preferreds." For example, it mattered not whether one ate sumptuously, but if one were given the opportunity to choose in such a way as not to compromise one's own integrity, then why not eat well? In 2 Cor 5:6-9, the indifferent matters are whether one is "at home" or "away from home." Clearly, Paul has a preference that would move him beyond his affliction and hardships: "I would prefer rather to be away from the body and at home with the Lord" (5:8). But, like his thorn in the flesh to which he refers in the next letter fragment (12:7*b*-10), his preferences are not always granted to him—or even always chosen by him (Phil 1:23-26).

A similar passage in Philippians is instructive because the same options and assumptions are also present there.[118] Writing to the

---

117. See Plato *Leg.* 9.864E.

118. Thus we are dealing with a Pauline commonplace of being at home and being away, not some slogan of his opponents as J. Murphy-O'Connor argues in "Being at Home in the Body We Are in Exile from the Lord (2 Cor 5:6*b*)," *RB* 93 (1986) 216-17.

Philippians from prison (Phil 1:12-14), Paul declares the options he is considering: "to depart and be with Christ" versus "to remain in the flesh" (Phil 1:23-24 NRSV). The former is "much better" and is what he prefers (1:23); yet, the latter is what he chooses out of consideration for the Philippians and their need for him.

These alternatives, as stated in both passages, do not assume the absence of Christ in one's worldly life. Paul realizes that, for the present, believers cannot escape being in the world, where sin, though its power has been broken in Christ's death and resurrection, controls the structures of the world, and where to be associated with Christ is also to experience tribulation with this aeon and its residual powers. Apart from such negative forces, there are also goals or goods that compete with others for one's time, energies, and commitment; for example, caring for one's spouse properly attenuates one's "undivided devotion to the Lord" (1 Cor 7:35). As long as Paul is at home in the world, he will have anxiety over his churches (2 Cor 11:28); as often as someone in the faith suffers or stumbles, Paul will suffer or be indignant (1 Cor 12:26; 2 Cor 11:29). As long as he represents the gospel in the world, he will experience opposition and suffer affliction. Of course, he would prefer to be delivered from all such distress—and that is what he voices in 2 Cor 5:8. Faith, not sight, enables him to recognize God's power positively at work through these afflictions, bringing about ever-greater glory and having life triumph over the mortal.

The overriding concern in 5:6-9 to "please the Lord" renders "indifferent" whether one is alive (in the earthly body) or beyond life in the earthly body. Paul's rumination that he chooses to transcend his preference and to stay the course with the Corinthians as a way of pleasing the Lord has the added effect of appealing for sympathy and, therefore, stands a chance of winning him some measure of goodwill from them.

Being in the body/away from the Lord. Being in the body is at the same time being with the Lord for Paul. He has no confusion about this; he is being dramatic and forceful. Some modern interpreters have a problem because they do not recognize that Paul is free to set his rhetorical opposites in any way

he chooses. His hearers know that they and Paul are "in Christ," that Christ is even "in them." They are members of Christ. They are part of Christ's body. All that is clear to them and is never a point of dispute in any of Paul's considerable correspondence with the Corinthians. Without any prejudice to any other conviction Paul has, he has simply made a rhetorical decision to write about daily life and has chosen the expression "in the body" to describe that experience; he chooses to write about leaving that daily life and has used going away "to the Lord" to designate that. This interpretation is confirmed when the phrase "in the body" is used to describe the deeds that will be weighed in the final judgment: One's life's works "in the body" will be assessed (5:10).

The eschatological frame. Paul encases 5:6-9 between two strong eschatological assertions (5:5, 10). On the one side is his declaration that receipt of the Holy Spirit is the "earnest money" that, having been "paid," assures God's finishing up of the "contract" (5:5). On the other side, Paul reminds the Corinthians that "all of us" must appear before the "judicial bench" (βῆμα *bēma*) of Christ, where everyone will receive recompense for what he or she has done "in the body" (5:10). So, as curious as the passage is, its interpretation must be guided in every particular by the eschatological framework Paul has given it. For example, Paul's three-time use of *ekdēmeō* (5:6, 8-9), "to leave one's country," "take a journey," "leave home" is surely each time a reference to what happens beyond life in this world, which he twice characterizes in 5:6-9 with the expression "in the body" (5:6, 8), a setup for the phrase's appearance in 5:10. Accordingly, in Paul's stated preference to "be away from the body" and to "be at home with the Lord" (ἐνδημῆσαι πρὸς τὸν κύριον *endēmēsai pros ton kyrion,* 5:8) he is not disclosing any metaphysics of resurrection, but is using "in the body" to express everyday life.

We should not read 1 Corinthians 15 into this discussion. There Paul used the notion of the "resurrection of the body" as a means of countering a *Corinthian* misunderstanding of resurrection, a misunderstanding for which there is no further clue in any of the subsequent Pauline correspondence with the

Corinthians. So here he is not denying "resurrection of the body"; he has no interest in the "how" of resurrection here because his focus is on the way people, specifically himself and the Corinthians, live in their present daily lives. Far from diminishing the importance of "body" in Paul's thought, he carries through the instinct reflected in the opening of 4:1, where he expresses his wonder that God has placed all "this treasure" in such earthenware vessels as humans.

Actually, as 5:10 shows, Paul's attention is focused on the way believers must live their lives in the daily give-and-take of the world so that, when the judgment does come, when the fullness of what the Spirit guaranteed is present, when believers are given the opportunity to be "with the Lord" full-time, then they will pass muster at the judgment seat of Christ. Paul, ever the exemplar, declares in these verses that he has no hesitance to look forward to that day because he knows that he endeavors to live every day of his life in such a fashion that the judgment of "what he has done in the body"—that is, "in his life"—will be found acceptable and that his "recompense" (κομίζω *komizo*, "receive a recompense") will be "good" (ἀγαθός *agathos*), not "worthless" or "bad" (φαῦλος *phaulos*, 5:10).

The picture of the last judgment is intriguing. For the first time since 3:18, Paul explicitly invites the Corinthians ("For we, all of us" [γὰρ πάντας ἡμᾶς *gar pantas hēmas*]) into his frequent use of the plurals by which he for the most part depicts himself in the context of mainstream faith and practice. Not just he, but they also, will have to appear before the tribunal of Christ (cf. Rom 14:10, where it is the βῆμα [*bēma*] of God), so that "each one can receive a recompense for what he or she has done in the body, whether good or evil" (5:10). The term translated as "receive a recompense" (*komizo*) is often used of wages, so the judgment is a sort of payback (cf. the "wages of sin is death," Rom 6:23). This glimpse is supported by other references in the Pauline letters. In 2 Cor 11:15, Paul describes false apostles, whom he associates with Satan, who claim they are Paul's equals;

he dismisses them with the cryptic "their end will be according to their works" (ὧν τὸ τέλος ἔσται κατὰ τὰ ἔργα αὐτῶν *hōn to telos estai kata ta erga autōn*, 11:15). The same outlook is reflected in Romans, where, in part, he cites Prov 24:12 in saying that God "will render to each according to his or her works"; the text goes on to detail not only the types of actions honored and punished but also the ultimate rewards and punishments (Rom 2:6-10).

Paul expects a final assessment regarding what we have done in the day-to-day transactions of life. The judgment will not be on what one believes or on whether one has the right ideas. The judgment will not be levied on one's faith, because faith is the free gift from God of right relationship to God (cf. 1 Cor 12:9). Faith, the right relationship with God, expresses itself, works itself out, in love, in acts of love concretely expressed in daily life (Gal 5:6, πίστις δι' ἀγάπης ἐνεργουμένη *pistis di' agapēs energoumenē*). So justification—being made right with God, which comes on the basis of God's grace freely given—is indeed on the basis of grace through faith. But the judgment Paul expects is focused on the works faith has produced in the individual's life, just as Rom 2:6-10 also indicates.

Taking this insight back to the understanding of the rhetorical transactions Paul is attempting to make with the Corinthians, he stresses human responsibility for daily comportment. His self-portrait throughout chaps. 1–5 has shown him to be exemplary as he has fully lived out his call to be an apostle despite problems, hardships, and afflictions. His stated preference to "be at home with the Lord" (2 Cor 5:8), his acknowledgment that Christ's judicial bench awaits (5:10), and his implied readiness for it all suggest that his repeated avowals of his apostolic probity (1:23-24; 2:17; 4:2, 5, 8-12) are grounded in his understanding that his conduct has, indeed, been appropriate to his call and to the gospel that he proclaims.

REFLECTIONS

1. "Treasure in earthen vessels" is a powerful double metaphor that recognizes the awesome trust God bestows upon each of us and at the same time honors our fragility as bearers of God's grace and might. The image allows Paul and us to celebrate the awesome blessing of life and joy in tribulation, limitation, and difficulty. Because we are God's chosen vessels, we do not need to build cathedrals or make pilgrimages, to engage in extraordinary actions to prove our faith. Instead, we simply need to live our lives each day in ways that love and honor one another. Jesus' parable of the sheep and the goats (Matt 25:31-46) makes the same point: Those who simply and humbly go about each day caring for the ill, visiting the imprisoned, and so forth are so naturally dedicated to caring for one another that there is no room for religious calculation in them. They can honestly ask, "When, Lord, did we see you thus?"

2. Those curious expressions about the death and life of Jesus being in our bodies may help us to reflect on our physical limitations and problems. We are accustomed to thinking of our bodies as having problems, getting fat, or not working as we wish they would. Paul thinks that physical problems are everyday reminders of Christ's death and of our association with it. Likewise, our moments of joy and delight, forgiveness and reconciliation, are windows onto the life of Jesus (i.e., resurrection), making its way into our very corporeal existence. The life of Jesus "in our mortal flesh" (not "body" as in 4:11 NIV) honors the fleshliness of existence as a proper locus for the life of faith. Gnostics denigrated the flesh and fleshliness, and redemption was for them always depicted as an escape from corporeality. Paul embraces human fleshliness and declares, with all its foibles and limitations, that the very life of Jesus comes to expression precisely there. Thus it is not strange that Paul should see in the cross, that earthy, crude instrument, the very ground of hoping and being.

3. We tend to glorify biblical characters and paint them in colors alien to our experiences and lives. It is not one of our better moves. We surmise that they do not suffer, that they have no doubt, that they do not struggle as we do. But note well that Paul describes himself (much as he did in chap. 1) as being near the brink of what he can bear, as about to fall over the edge. Maybe we extol biblical characters out of self-doubt; perhaps, worse, our doing so may be driven by self-loathing or self-pity. As downtrodden and crushed as Paul was, however, he was convinced that God would never let him go.

4. Are you not often taken aback when you meet someone again after several years have passed? "How they have aged!" you might think. Paul takes it for granted that what people see about us, the externals, is wasting away like rust eats into iron. But he also believes that is not the whole story; inside we are being renewed day by day. From inside, the Spirit is working to express its fruit—love, joy, peace, patience, kindness, goodness, faithfulness, gentleness, self-control (Gal 5:22)—in us. Perhaps we should be making every effort to get out of the Spirit's way and let these fruit show through from our inner selves to those around us.

5. "We walk by faith, not by sight" (5:7)—a refinement of Paul's earlier comments about looking to things that are not seen (4:18). This is one of Paul's great pieces of wisdom. Where should we get our clues about purpose and direction, about what to make of what is around us? Fueled by his apocalyptic outlook, Paul knew that to reckon from what is seen, from appearances, is a sure way to be misled about what is really important and about what is truly going on. We all know how easily people can misunderstand when they know just the externals or when they make assumptions from superficial knowledge. Yet, that awareness does not keep us from doing the same thing regarding others. So it is with God's purposes: Imagine how far astray you might go if you made your own decision about Jesus on the basis of his being born out of wedlock; of his keeping company with prostitutes, lepers, and tax collectors; and of his being killed in that culture's most shameful manner (the equivalent of the electric chair or the gas chamber or lethal injection). Paul's care to distinguish between externals and internals should caution us about making superficial, snap judgments regarding the truth about someone. Conclusions and conjectures based on external, superficial information or impressions will more often prove wrong than right—and can do a great disservice, if not injustice, to others.

6. Most popular representations of the final judgment have the smell of sulfur and the sounds of Armageddon about them. Too often the last-day judgment is presented as a fearsome event. Some writers and speakers even use it as a means of frightening their followers into compliance. Note that Paul does not have even the slightest hint of a fearful understanding of the last judgment. It is worth thinking about why Paul does not stoop to fear-mongering when he thinks of the last judgment and of giving an account of his life, of his decisions, of his actions, of his "deeds done in the body." Two reasons for this suggest themselves: First, he knows that the love he is supposed to show toward others is generated by the Holy Spirit (Gal 5:22), so it is quite present if he will simply let the Spirit do its work in his life. Second, in his everyday life Paul always aims for love and seeks to glorify God.

2 Corinthians 5:11–6:10, Paul's Ministry of Reconciliation

COMMENTARY

5:11-12. In the third of his complementary reflections of his ministry, Paul describes himself, along with all the others in the mainstream, as being guided by the "fear of the Lord" as he "persuades" (a euphemism for effectively preaching the gospel and a description of what he is doing as he writes; 5:11). "Fear of the Lord" is a traditional phrase, deeply grounded in Paul's Scriptures (cf. Deut 6:2, 13; 10:20; 28:58; Job 28:28; Ps 111:10; Prov 1:7; Isa 11:2; Jer 32:39). Far from a psychological description or some physical manifestation, "fear of the Lord" in biblical tradition describes post-exilic faithfulness. The ones who "fear the Lord" are the devotees of Yahweh. As Paul has adopted the phrase, it also betokens his sense of the majesty and power, the *mysterium tremendum,* of God, who promotes justice, opposes all wickedness, and expects accountability (cf. Rom 1:18; 3:18-19). Accordingly, appearing before the tribunal of Christ is taken with utmost seriousness, and the "fear of the Lord" means that Paul makes certain that "what he does in the body" is appropriate to the gospel and "pleasing to the Lord" (5:9).

Paul affirms that he is known by God (5:11*b*). God already knows the secrets of peoples' hearts (Rom 2:16; 8:27; 1 Cor 14:25), and at the end time the heart's plans will be revealed (1 Cor 4:5; 1 Thess 2:4). Paul is more confident about God's understanding of him, and less sure about the Corinthians' understanding. His appeal to their consciences is a subtle request that they employ their moral reasoning to bring themselves more fully into conformity with him (5:11).[119] The Corinthians, who should function as letters of commendation for Paul (3:2-3), are now described as those who should be able to boast about Paul because they ought to be competent to distinguish between "appearances" and "realities" (Paul's contrast is literally between "face" ["what is seen," NIV; "outward appearance," NRSV] and "heart," 5:12), harking back to and capitalizing on his earlier differentiation between things seen and not seen and between his "inner" and "outer" self (4:16-18).

119. Sampley, *Walking Between the Times,* 57-58.

5:13. Alongside the contrast between "face" and "heart" (5:12) he lodges another: "out of one's mind" versus "in one's right mind" (5:13). With this pair of enigmatic statements, Paul gives an invaluable, though concise, self-portrait: "If we are out of our mind, it has to do with God; if we are in our right mind, it has to do with you" (5:13). As the Corinthians surely know, Paul is prone to visions and revelations (1 Cor 2:10; 2 Cor 12:7; Gal 1:12; 2:2) and ecstatic speech (glossolalia; 1 Cor 14:18), and they are soon to learn that he was once even transported to paradise (12:1-4). His being "out of his mind" (ἐξίστημι *existēmi*) as between himself and God probably refers to his manifestation of such well-known personal characteristics because his description of glossolalia in 1 Cor 14:2 is congruent; glossolalia, without interpretation, relates the individual to God alone, not to others (1 Cor 14:2).

The verb σωφρονέω (*sōphroneō*), "being in right mind" (5:13), is used one other time in the Pauline corpus in a context where Paul describes balanced, thoughtful, purposeful evaluation of the self that does not overreach the measure of faith meted out by God (Rom 12:3). Applying that sense here, we see that Paul, in effect, says, "When I think in a reasoned, appropriate way about myself, it is for your advantage."

What does Paul's self-portrait in 5:13 reveal about him? It shows that, even though he would delight to depart and be with the Lord unfettered, a part of his life is between himself and God (1 Cor 14:2, 4*a*) and is distinguishable from his relation to believers. When it is just between an individual and God, as in glossolalia, for example, one's own edification benefits from the special relationship to God (cf. 1 Cor 14:4*a*). In that same sphere belong revelations, heavenly transit, and any other such ecstatic experiences; there one is dealing fully and only with God, as Paul says in 5:13*a*.

In the other sphere, where one walks in part by sight, where the outer is wasting away, and where things are transitory, Paul's call as apostle to the Gentiles must be exercised in relation to other believers. There, Paul must honor his relationship with the Corinthians by acting in a reasoned way that serves their interests—which is precisely what he says he is doing (5:13*b*).

Sōphroneō ("to be right-minded," 5:13*b*) and συνείδησις (*syneidēsis*, "moral consciousness," "conscience," 5:11) are both primary terms in Paul's moral reasoning, as one might suspect the Corinthians would already know from their long exposure to him and his teachings. In 5:11 he subtly urges them to use their moral consciousnesses (consciences) in making a proper, not superficial, assessment of him; in 5:13 he describes himself as *continuing* to relate to them with the best of his right-mindedness "for their sakes," just as love always does. Though the term "love" is not mentioned in 5:13, Paul's description of himself as always acting in their interest is tantamount to using the term, which surely is close to his mind, judging from its appearance in the very next verse (5:14).

5:14-21. The terminology and the claims of 5:14-21 are dense and laconically compressed. Much of Paul's richness developed in much more detail in other places is here suggested by the slightest clue. For example, the idea that believers should live not for themselves (5:15) is a tacit reaffirmation of self-commendatory claims that Paul has made about himself previously in this letter (4:2, 12, 15; 5:8-9). But beyond that, the idea of living for Christ (the one "who died and was raised for them," 5:15) subtly suggests the slave market and its practices, which Paul has found so useful in writing elsewhere about how believers are "bought with a price" (1 Cor 6:20; 7:23) and now have a new Lord who deserves their full obedience and service ("You are not your own," 1 Cor 6:19-20; 7:23; Gal 2:20).

5:14-15. In 5:14-21, Paul portrays himself—still using the plural to identify with the mainstream—as the one who has advanced the gospel, whose focus is now depicted as being reconciliation. In fact, 5:14*a*—"for the love of Christ impels us"—is a refinement of 5:13*b*, crediting love as the force that drives Paul's care for the Corinthians. The mention of the love of Christ triggers from Paul a rather set formulation, a Pauline commonplace (signaled by the formulaic κρίναντας τοῦτο ὅτι [*krinantas touto, hoti*, "being convinced of this, that . . ."]) about God's great purpose begun in the death of Christ "for all" (5:14-15).

Paul's employment of the genitive construction ἡ γὰρ ἀγάπη τοῦ Χριστοῦ (*hē gar agapē tou Christou*, "the love of Christ") leaves the hearers and the interpreter to decide whether Paul intends "Christ's love" (for us, understood) or believers' love for Christ. The other place where Paul uses the same Greek expression is Rom 8:35: "Who shall separate us from the love of Christ?" The parallel with Rom 8:39 ("Nothing . . . can separate us from the love of God in Christ") suggests that the phrase in 5:14 ought to be read as subjective, indicating that the direction of the love is from Christ. The flow of love in Paul's thought world seems regularly to be *from* God or Christ *to* human beings. This love establishes, in turn, the right relation to God that Paul calls by the code word "faith." Faith, when it functions as it should, expresses itself in love of others (Gal 5:6).

Most often in the Pauline corpus the term "love" is used to describe how believers relate to one another; less frequently, Paul speaks of God's love for humans (Rom 5:5, 8; 8:39; 2 Cor 13:14). Taking it as Christ's love for believers has the further merit of honoring Paul's deep conviction that, no matter the topic, the initiative, expressed in terms of grace, rests not with people but with God, through Christ.

The verb translated "compels" (NIV) or "urges on" (NRSV; συνέχω *synechō*) has a semantic range from "impels" to "hold within bounds/control." Given the larger context of this letter fragment, Paul can be understood to claim that Christ's love drives him on, affirming what he has repeatedly said earlier in the letter about not despairing (4:1, 16; cf. 2:14-17). In the verses that lie ahead, with the assertions about ambassadorship, for example, further support will be found for the notion that Christ's love impels believers (in particular, Paul) out into the world (5:19).

For Paul elsewhere, however, love just as surely holds a believer within bounds. For example, in a chapter that begins by affirming that love builds up (1 Cor 8:1), Paul writes that he will not eat meat if doing so would cause a brother or sister in Christ to stumble (1 Cor 8:13). On account of love, Paul resists

commanding Philemon what to do about Onesimus, but supposes love will set the borders of Philemon's response (Phlm 8-9).

In the set piece to which Paul adverts (in 5:14-21), the foundational claim is that "one [Christ] has died for all" (5:14). The same assertion is stated in slightly different ways in the corpus: "Christ died for the ungodly" (Rom 5:6 NRSV); "Christ died for us" (Rom 5:8 NRSV; cf. 1 Cor 8:11; 15:3; 1 Thess 5:10). And because he assumes that believers die *with* Christ, which also can be expressed in different fashions (Rom 5:15; 6:3-8), Paul postulates that "therefore all have died" (5:14).

The claim that Christ died "for all" (ὑπὲρ πάντων *hyper pantōn*, 5:14) is repeated for refinement in 5:15 and should be taken, not in a substitutionary manner in the sense of Christ's taking everybody's place at his death, but in the sense of Christ's being for—that is, siding with—people.[120] Christ's death shows that God is "for them," as can be seen unmistakably in Rom 8:31: "If God is for us [ὑπὲρ ἡμῶν *hyper hēmōn*], who can be against us?" (NIV; see the same outlook reflected in Paul's Lord's supper traditions, 1 Cor 11:24). Christ's death broke the power of sin as lord over people's lives (Rom 6:11). People were reconciled to God by Christ's death (Rom 5:10). Jesus' death provides deliverance (1 Thess 1:10). Redemption in Christ's death leads to adoption as God's children (Gal 4:5) and newness of life (Rom 6:4).

The "ones who are living" (οἱ ζῶντες *hoi zōntes*, 5:15) are a subset refinement of the "all" for whom Christ died (5:14; cf. Rom 6:4). So Christ died for everyone (5:14-15). Some of those whom Paul now calls the living ones, have, by sharing his death, been brought to newness of life (cf. Rom 6:4); they are part of what Paul is about to describe as the "new creation" (5:17).

5:16. Christ's death is the transformative event for all of life. Nothing is the same after that. First among the radical changes brought about by Christ's death is the way people should live: no longer for themselves but for the one who died and was raised for them (5:15). The transformations begun in Christ's death and resurrection will be expanded until

---

120. E. P. Sanders, *Paul and Palestinian Judaism: A Comparison of Patterns of Religion* (Philadelphia: Fortress, 1977) 463-72.

they encompass the entire universe (κόσμος *kosmos*, 5:19, which fits the Romans 8 pattern, where the whole of creation longs for the freedom the children of God already experience; see Rom 8:21-23). Another constitutive change involves how believers now view others: no longer κατὰ σάρκα (*kata sarka*), literally, "according to the flesh." Paul's lead up to this passage has established how this phrase must be understood: Believers must look to what is not seen (4:18; 5:7); they must look to the inner person and not take primary clues from the outer person (4:16); they must consider the heart and not the face (5:12).

In this letter, Paul has been practicing what he preaches. Now Christ is set forth as his example: "Even though we once knew Christ *kata sarka*, but now we no longer do so" (5:16). To know Christ *kata sarka* is, in part as Paul recognizes elsewhere, to know him as descended from David according to the flesh (Rom 1:3). "Now"—that is, *this* side of, after, Christ's resurrection—Paul no longer contents himself with that apprehension of Christ. Just as he no longer considers Christ as if he had not been raised from the dead, so also he now asserts that "we can no longer consider anyone" simply from the flesh (*kata sarka*), with that phrase standing now for regarding people from all the misleading, inadequate ways that offer themselves and that Paul has been careful to reject in the previous paragraphs, from 4:7 forward.

To consider anyone simply from the flesh (*kata sarka*) is to view that person as if the fundamentally transformative resurrection of Christ had not taken place—and as if the norms or standards of judgment had not therein been radically altered. Believers are not simply offered a new perspective they may or may not adopt as and when they see fit; rather, something so fundamental has changed in such a profound fashion that the old ways of looking, perceiving, understanding, and, more profoundly, evaluating, have to be let go and replaced with a new way of seeing and understanding.

5:17. Paul accounts for this transformative shift: "If one is in Christ," and all believers by definition are, "he or she is a new creation." Much of Paul's letter before us wrestles with the way people, particularly the Corinthians,

see and understand him, Paul, too much from externals. Those who are part of the new creation can no longer be considered *kata sarka*, according to the standards of the world.

The phrase "new creation" (καινὴ κτίσις *kainē ktisis*) is evocative and enigmatic. It is used only one other time in Paul's letters: "For neither circumcision is anything not uncircumcision, but new creation is" (Gal 6:15). A classic Pauline *adiaphora* (indifferent matters) statement, Gal 6:15 is a refinement of the same general expression found earlier in that very letter: "In Christ Jesus, neither circumcision nor uncircumcision means anything, but faith working through love does" (Gal 5:6). These two Galatians statements, with the same indifferent-matters construction (i.e., neither A nor B matters, but C does), conclude by affirming that what really counts in life is "faith working through love" and "new creation." The similarity of form for the first and second A's and B's suggests that the two C's are in some deep sense mutually interpretive. So "new creation" must allow within it rather definitionally "faith"—that is, the right relationship with God—"expressing itself in love," in the right relationships among those whom God loves. This identification of "new creation" (Gal 5:16) with "faith expressing itself in love" (Gal 5:6) fits equally well with Paul's description elsewhere of believers' "walking in newness of life" (ἐν καινότητι ζωῆς *en kainotēti zōēs*, Rom 6:4).

Finally, Paul's concern with "new creation" in 2 Cor 5:17 parallels the sublime picture in Romans 8, where the whole of creation that was subjected to purposelessness and decay (Rom 8:20-21) because of sin's corrosive power (cf. Rom 1:18-23) is groaning, like a woman in childbirth, toward its own redemption (Rom 8:21-22). Throughout 2 Corinthians 1–5, Paul has shown the capacity to encapsulate in a few sentences, and once even in a single sentence (2 Cor 3:18), much of the gospel—and the life appropriate to it. Here in the two-word construction "new creation," Paul captures the whole of the gospel he represents.

The last part of 2 Cor 5:17 is pithy and subject to very different interpretations, whose viability cannot be judged simply within the immediate context. Where one lands on the hermeneutical issues here depends on how one understands Paul's entire outlook. First, the Greek of the first clause, τὰ ἀρχαῖα παρῆλθεν, ἰδοὺ γέγονεν καινά (*ta archaia parēlthen, idou gegonen kaina*), is readily translatable: "the old things have gone/passed away." The second clause presents the problems. The demonstrative pronoun ἰδου (*idou*) grabs attention by expressing "behold" or "see."

The puzzle rests on how to construe the two terms **gegonen kaina** and on determining their relationship to the rest of the sentence. *Gegonen*, the verb, is the perfect tense, signifying "the *continuance* of *completed action*,"[121] of γίνομαι (*ginomai*), which has the semantic range "come to be," "become," "made." The term *kaina* ("new") with a verb like *ginomai* can be construed as either the subject or the object of the verb. The most prevalent interpretation, as may be seen readily in the NIV and in the RSV, takes *kaina* as the subject: "the new has come." The NRSV achieves its translation, "everything has become new," by honoring, in effect, a variant that specifies the subject as τὰ πάντα (*ta panta*, "all things," "everything") and by assuming, very reasonably, that the singular verb **gegonen** can have a neuter, plural subject.[122] In the NIV and in the RSV, *kaina*, "new," is taken as the subject; in the NRSV it functions as an object or a predicate adjective.

A third interpretation, however, is equally possible, and without resort to any textual variants. The verb **gegonen** can take as its subject τὰ ἀρχαῖα (*ta archaia*, "the old") from the preceding clause, with the resulting translation: "The old things have passed away; see, they [the old things] have become new" (5:17).

The Greek leaves itself open to either translation: "the new has come" or "it [the old] has become new." The consequences of the choice are considerable.[123] The former makes a stronger demarcation between "the old" and "the new," and discontinuity is stressed. The latter recognizes a difference, a transformation, but allows more continuity. We have already seen these issues played out in the two-covenant passage (2 Cor 3:1-18).

And one can see it in a comparison of Romans and Galatians, where, for rhetorical purposes of engaging very different audiences, the former emphasizes continuity and the latter stresses discontinuity.[124]

Paul sometimes accents the continuity of God's purposes. In those places the faithfulness of God is affirmed, and what has happened in Christ is understood as the carrying out of God's plans and promises (see Rom 3:3-4; 15:8-13; 1 Cor 1:9; 10:13; 2 Cor 1:20). When Paul features contrast or discontinuity, however, he usually is trying to help auditors understand how much their lives have changed (see Gal 3:1-5, 22-24) or will yet change before God has finished with them (1 Cor 15:35-50).

What would it mean if Paul were understood to say that "the old things have passed away; see, they have become new" (5:17)? Paul is quite capable of looking at a single phenomenon from two different perspectives and making quite distinctive claims about them. For the most mundane sort of example of this Pauline capacity, Epaphroditus is Paul's "brother, fellow worker, and fellow soldier" and is the Philippians' "apostle and servant" (Phil 2:25). Paul can also abide the complexity in matters where statements in some tension with each other must be made so that the larger picture can be served. Witness the treatment of the two covenants in 2 Cor 3:1–4:6, where Paul employs contrast and antithesis to make his points, but not to the extent of denying value and glory to the first covenant. Paul's picture in the two-covenant passage is much more complex than "out with the old" and "in with the new."

In many of his letters, Paul has an intricate, nuanced view of the relation of past and present, old and new. Paul's choice of the phrase "new creation" (*kainē ktisis*) itself exemplifies the complexity of his thinking. It expresses redemption as a kind of creation renewed, made over. It is a new thing that recaptures, not jettisons, the old, much as Deutero-Isaiah, one of Paul's favorites, projects (see Isa 42:9; 43:19-20).

In some senses, for Paul the old things have passed—especially when Paul wants

121. *BDF* 340, italics added.
122. *BDF* 133.
123. See the reflections on this issue by a variety of authors in *Interpreting 2 Corinthians 5:14-21: An Exercise in Hermeneutics*, ed. J. P. Lewis (Lewiston: Edwin Mellen) 116-18, 136-37, 148-50, 173-74.

124. J. Paul Sampley, "Romans and Galatians: Comparison and Contrast," in *Understanding the Word: Essays in Honor of B. W. Anderson*, ed. J. T. Butler, E. W. Conrad, and B. Ollenberger, JSNTSup 37 (Sheffield: JSOT, 1985) 315-39.

to appreciate the changes faith has wrought. Paul frequently uses "no longer" expressions to describe how things were apart from faith (Rom 6:9; 2 Cor 5:16; Gal 2:20; 3:25; 4:7); believers do walk in "newness of life" (Rom 6:4). Old patterns of living have also passed; believers are not supposed to walk as they formerly did (cf. Gal 4:8-9; Phil 3:13-14).

On other occasions, however, especially when he takes the long view of God's purposes, Paul thinks of continuity. God's promises are finding their fulfillment in Christ (Rom 15:8-13; 2 Cor 1:20). The Scriptures foresaw certain things (Gal 3:8) and were written for the instruction of Paul and his contemporaries (1 Cor 10:6, 11). Christ became a minister to the circumcised in order to confirm the promises given to the patriarchs (Rom 15:8).

5:18-20. "All of this"—the "new creation" that begins in Christ's death—is from God (5:18). Romans 5:6-11 parallels 2 Cor 5:14-21 in instructive ways. Both mention reconciliation as the defining act of God. Both credit love as the defining force (God's, Rom 5:8; Christ's, 2 Cor 5:14). Romans uses the passive as a subtle way of ascribing the reconciliation to God: "For if while we were enemies, we were reconciled to God through the death of his son" (Rom 5:10 NRSV). Here in 2 Corinthians, Paul, in line with his purposes throughout this letter to credit God as working *in him* (cf. 2:17; 3:5; 5:1), openly avers that "all of this is from God who . . . *has given us the ministry of reconciliation*" (5:18, italics added).

Whereas Romans links justification with reconciliation as equivalent and interchangeable terms (Rom 5:9-10), Paul, in 2 Corinthians, lacking any problem with the Corinthians' relationship to the law, does not mention justification (but note 5:21, where the same root term, "righteousness," does cap off the argument). Justification has its social setting in the law or in the courts, and so it does not have any pertinence here in 2 Corinthians; reconciliation has its social setting in a familial or friendship environment where there has been a restoration of a broken relationship, precisely Paul's recent and somewhat continuing problem with the Corinthians.

Paul's statement, still in the plural, that God has "reconciled us to himself through Christ" (5:18) offers a slight invitation to the Corinthians to think of themselves as being included, because that is as true of them as it is of Paul. But as the passage goes on, Paul's plural becomes restrictive to himself once again: "and has given us the ministry of reconciliation" (καὶ δόντος ἡμῖν τὴν διακονίαν τῆς καταλλαγῆς *kai dontos hēmin tēn diakonian tēs katallagēs*, 5:18). Once more he makes an explicit connection between the grand theological tradition and his problems with the Corinthians.

Before he pursues that link with the Corinthians, however, he returns to the tradition yet one more time to affirm that God's work in Christ was cosmic in scope, that it involved a divine forbearance toward human trespasses (which Paul worked hard to communicate as also imitatively operative for him with the Corinthians, 2:5-11; cf. 7:5-12) and, possibly echoing Ps 104:27 LXX, that God has "entrusted to us the word of reconciliation" (5:19).

The twice-stated claim that God selected Paul for this ministry and message of reconciliation (5:18-19) provides him the base to make a not too subtle address to the Corinthians. Paul, who has been made "ambassador for Christ," is now the one through whom God's appeal is made in behalf of Christ: "be reconciled to God" (5:20). The verb πρεσβεύω (*presbeuō*, "to be an ambassador/envoy") places Paul in a lofty position of responsibility, as one who must, in all his activities, represent the one in authority and, as here, speak for him[125] (cf. Paul's use of δοῦλος [*doulos*, "slave"] to the Corinthians as a self-description in 4:5). Paul's call to the Corinthians to "be reconciled to God" is at the same time an encouragement of them to associate themselves more closely with Paul, who is so clearly a major part of God's plan for reconciliation.

Uncharacteristically, 5:20 is the only place in the Pauline corpus where the reconciling is to be done by people. In the other instances, Paul either uses the passive, such as "we were reconciled" (Rom 5:10 NRSV), where God is the understood actor or directly states

---

125. M. M. Mitchell, "New Testament Envoys in the Context of Greco-Roman Diplomatic and Epistolary Conventions: The Example of Timothy and Titus," *JBL* 111 (1992) 649-70. Collins, "The Mediatorial Aspect of Paul's Role as *diakonos*," 36, 44, sees in 5:20 a confirmation that Paul's earlier use of (διακονία *diakonia*) must be read with overtones of "ambassador" and "messenger."

that God is the reconciling one (2 Cor 5:18). We may understand this anomaly because the Corinthians are, at the time of his writing of 2 Corinthians 1–9, the people Paul most needs to reconcile with. The statement explicitly calls for them to "be reconciled to God," but the encoded message is that they should thereby be reconciled to Paul, the ambassador who has brought the reconciliation gospel to them in the first place and thereby been the occasion for the end of their enmity with God (cf. Rom 5:1, 10).

5:21. Rather than let the appeal for reconciliation conclude the tradition and its application, Paul makes a christological development that is very reminiscent of the "story" that structures the Christ hymn in Phil 2:5-11 and that reappears later in the letter fragment before us. The "story" goes like this: (phase 1) The exalted (rich) one assumes lowly (poor) status, becoming like us (phase 2), so that we can become exalted (rich) like him (phase 3). In the other two places in his letters where Paul tells this story (2 Cor 8:9; Phil 2:5-11), his interest resides in the hearers' move with Christ from the second phase to the third. The three phases are represented in 5:21: Phase 1 is the portrait of Christ as the one who did not know sin; phase 2 is Christ's being made (by God) sin on behalf of believers; and phase 3 is expressed in the purpose clause "in order that we might become the righteousness of God in him."

In the Rom 5:6-11 parallel to 2 Cor 5:14-21, Paul puts justification (the same root term as "righteousness" and "justice") alongside reconciliation as a functional synonym. For Paul, to be reconciled to God is to be justified or made righteous or, as Paul puts it elsewhere, to receive the righteousness of God (Rom 9:30–10:4). In Rom 10:3, precisely as in 2 Cor 5:21, the expression "righteousness of God" can be understood as the righteousness that comes from God or that is a characteristic of God. It is no surprise, then, when Paul writes so eloquently of reconciliation as he does in 2 Cor 5:14-21, that the passage should conclude in a claim about righteousness. From the clues one can see widely in the Pauline corpus, being reconciled to God implies some responsibilities to represent the righteousness ("justice" is also in the semantic range of δικαιοσύνη [*dikaiosynē*]) of God

to others. That connection of reconciliation and righteousness/justice manifests itself explicitly in Paul's treatment of the collection for the saints in Jerusalem in 2 Cor 9:9-10.

In 2 Cor 5:21 Paul's chief interests in this particular recasting of the old story lie in getting the hearers to identify with Christ—as Christ identified with them by becoming one with them in their sin—and with the change represented in the purpose clause "our becoming the righteousness of God in [Christ]." Paul is not concerned to get into a theological deliberation about the "sinfulness" or "sinlessness" of Christ. Instead, he is eager to remind the Corinthians of their having been brought from sin to righteousness in Christ by God's grace (this term appears in 6:1) *and by Paul's having been given the ministry of reconciliation.*

Paul's closing tradition celebrates that "in Christ" the believers have been made right with God by God's doing—which is the only way it can happen (cf. Rom 9:30–10:3). This is yet another time in this letter fragment that Paul has brought a section to a climax with what amounts to a concise summary of the gospel (5:21; cf. 3:14, 18).

6:1-3. In 6:1, Paul moves to relate his ministry of reconciliation more explicitly, and he opens with a delightful ambiguity in the participle συνεργοῦντες (*synergountes*, "working together with/cooperating with"). With whom is he cooperating? The Corinthians? God? (Both the NIV, inserting "God's" as the modifier of "fellow workers," and the NRSV, inserting "with him," hide the ambiguity of the Greek.) Paul's history has shown him working together with God; the Corinthians know that about him. What is left open is that the Corinthians could hear this participle as describing themselves as working together with Paul, a goal we have seen Paul pursue by insinuation and innuendo at every possible point in the letter. So Paul, working together at least with God and hoping for the Corinthians' cooperation, appeals to them not to receive the grace of God (which Paul has just been describing and of which Paul was given the ministry of reconciliation) in vain. The formulation "not in vain" (εἰς κενόν *eis kenon*) is a commonplace with Paul that always reckons with whether the person's life has honored the life-governing grace of God

(1 Cor 15:10; Gal 2:2; Phil 2:16; 1 Thess 2:1; 3:5).

Paul's citation of Isa 49:8 provides him with a rallying call for the Corinthians: "Now is the acceptable/favorable time . . . now is the day of salvation" (6:2). It has been Paul's pattern throughout this letter fragment to highlight the eschatology, to emphasize that the Corinthians are near the time of fulfillment and must act accordingly, and he does so here again. Paul's intensity suggests little room for error and later recovery. The Corinthians risk everything if they stray or, as he puts it here, if they receive God's grace in vain.

Paul offers his own self-assessment as to how he, still using the plural and depicting himself as part of the mainstream, has comported himself blamelessly in his ministry (cf. 5:18). Negatively stated, he has given "no one in any way" (μηδεμίαν ἐν μηδενί *mēdemian en mēdeni*) an occasion for making a misstep (6:3). Stated positively, "in everything" he has commended himself as one of God's "ministers" (διάκονοι *diakonoi*, echoes of 3:6–4:1).

6:4-10. To unpack the commendatory "everything," Paul launches into an elaborate hardship list, longer and more stylized than the one in 4:7-12. Its length is designed to overwhelm any remaining opposition and to burnish Paul's ethos. In a list so extensive, overlap and, therefore, intensification must be expected. Also, what comes first and last in a series is always worth special notice because rhetoricians of Paul's time taught that those were the places of supreme emphasis.[126] It can be no surprise that Paul leads off the list with ὑπομονή (*hypomonē*, "patience/endurance/fortitude/perseverence") and θλῖψις (*thlipsis*, "affliction/tribulation/distress," 6:4). To reinforce the *hypomonē* of 6:4, μακροθυμία (*makrothymia*, "steadfastness/forbearance/endurance") shows up two verses later (6:6). Both these terms buttress Paul's self-depiction in this letter as not losing heart, but instead pressing on.

The last two constructions in the list—"as poor, but enriching many" and "as not having, but possessing everything" (6:10)—relate to Paul's economic patterns and to his special

perspective on what really matters. Paul's apostleship has been one of service to others, not self-service and self-aggrandizement, perhaps to the chagrin of some Corinthians who see in him a person of attenuated status, too diminished to be considered a true apostle.

The hardship catalog has an intricate structure. Its repeated elements give it grandeur and suggest a limitless list.[127] The catalog opens with eighteen instances of the preposition ἐν (*en*, "in") constructions that describe (1) situations and circumstances in which Paul has found himself (6:4-5) and (2) his *modus operandi* in those circumstances (6:6). Then Paul shifts prepositions to διά (*dia*, "through") three times, probably to avoid monotony, but he continues through the first *dia* to develop his *modus operandi* (6:7). The other two *dia* constructions (6:8) introduce a section that is finished with seven instances of ὡς (*hōs*, "as") structures (6:9-10), all nine of which (the *dia* and *hōs*) sketch out extremes within which Paul's apostolic ministry has been exercised.

These nine constructions share the outlook that has been developed formerly in this letter fragment where Paul cautions the Corinthians against being deceived by looking simply at the surface and not seeing to the heart of things, and admonishes them not to confuse what is important with what are truly *adiaphora*, "indifferent matters." The other Pauline passage that is most like 6:9-10 in outlook is 1 Cor 7:29-31, where ὡς μή (*hōs mē*, "as-if-not") becomes an eschatological lens through which one sees a way of living within this world without being governed by its values.

The entire hardship list shows Paul exposed to the vagaries of life, to the extremes of shame and honor, from slander to good report, being understood and misunderstood—yet steadfastly dependable through it all. All the quotidian challenges are put in perspective, once again (4:7, 10-12, 16; 5:4), by the ultimate couplet: "as dying, and, see, we live" (6:9).

With this hardship catalog, Paul brings to a conclusion the long section (2:14–6:10) in which he has advanced, along three complementary lines (3:1–4:6; 4:7–5:10; 5:11-21), his apostolic ministry and has attempted to

---

126. See *Ad Herennium* 3.10.17-18; Demetrius, *On Style* 2.63; 5.249.

127. See Demetrius *On Style* 2.63.

give the Corinthians added reasons for adhering to him and for embracing him more fully. The location of the hardship list (6:1-10) at the end of this huge section is fitting; it serves to demonstrate that Paul is tried and true (δόκιμος *dokimos*; see 10:18; 13:7), that he has been and is for the Corinthians through thick and thin, and that he is worthy of their affirmation and affection. So it should not surprise us that Paul turns to press immediately and explicitly (6:11-13) for such an increase of affection.

Apart from Paul's rhetorical purposes with the Corinthians in his sublime affirmations about reconciliation (5:14-21), we should note that the conception is near the heart of his gospel.[128] The term "reconciliation" is a functional equivalent for "justification," as the parallelism of Rom 5:9-10 shows. We have seen in the Commentary on 3:1–4:6 that "justification" and its related term, "righteousness," are for Paul covenant terms that often in the letters have a judicial tone; the provenance of these terms is covenant (where the ones made right with God do what is right) and law court (where the charges formerly lodged against one are dropped). The social setting of reconciliation is distinct; it relates to the restoration of relationships, the end of hostility and enmity, and the overcoming of alienation.

Paul writes of reconciliation in two aspects, one treating of the relation to God and the other detailing relations between human beings. Briefly, Paul's view is that sin, with its lordship power in effect, has alienated people from their proper filiation with God (Rom 1:18–3:20). Enmity has resulted. As Rom 5:1 expresses it, believers have been granted peace with God through Jesus Christ; the enmity between people and God is ended by a decisive act on God's part (Rom 5:10). "Reconciliation" is Paul's term for describing that restored relationship with God.

Equally important to Paul, and a consequence of the divine reconciliation, is the reconciliation of people to each other in Christ. Because God has properly reestablished relations with people, they can no longer carry animosity or grudges or resentments toward one another. The common denominator seen in several letters, and expressed most directly in 2 Cor 5:14-15 ("one has died for all . . . he died for all"), is that in human relations the baseline consideration regarding any human being is that Christ died for that person. Moral deliberation must take care that decisions and choices not harm one for whom Christ has died (Rom 14:15; 1 Cor 8:9-12; cf. Eph 2:11-22; Phil 2:1-5).

128. R. P. Martin, *Reconciliation: A Study of Paul's Theology* (Atlanta: John Knox, 1981), argues that it is the center of Paul's gospel.

REFLECTIONS

1. The most basic fact for Christians is this: People have value because Christ has died for them. People, whoever they are, whether they have responded to Christ or not—Christ died for everyone (2 Cor 5:14-15)—are treasured by God. From the moment of Christ's death, everyone, *everyone,* has value. The problem rests with us. We often want to establish hurdles that others must jump before *we* will grant them value. They must think the way we do, act the way we do, vote the way we do, land on our issues the way we want them to—and the list could go on and on. No, each person's value has *already* been established by Christ's death for them, not by their response to that death. So we do not need to inquire whether persons are fellow Christians before we know that they deserve to be treated with respect. They are valuable because Christ has died for them.

2. Reconciliation is at the heart of life's business. If the most important single factor about any of our lives is God's having reconciled us to God's very self, then the proper celebration of our reconciliation is to share it with others by fostering reconciliation and atonement wherever and whenever we can. (If that is not the most significant single factor in your life, you might consider engaging in some deep reflection about idolatry.) Reconciliation as a ground of life would mean that when your friend makes some negative or judgmental comment about a neighbor, you will resist joining in. Indeed, instead you might respond by noting something you have appreciated about the same neighbor. Thus you may help two of your acquaintances come to understand each other better.

3. Related are Paul's observations that we may experience some difference between our outer and inner selves. Renewal of life can take place in the presence of huge problems that bear externally on us. Paul's is a way of thinking about life as being governed or defined not by what is happening around us—or even to our bodies—but by what God is doing from the inside. Similarly, Paul's contrast between face and heart (5:12) diminishes the definitional power of externals and emphasizes instead what is happening in our hearts.

4. Consider the first time you thought you were in love with someone. Odds are you could not contain yourself—or better yet, you could not contain the love you felt. Christ's love for us is not different in its effect. Christ's love not only claims us for God but also pushes us out toward others. The rubric goes like this: We-who-are-loved love others. Love of others is not an option for which we may or may not decide. Love generates love—that is true among humans most of the time. At the same time that love pushes us toward others, however, it also sets borders on the actions that are fitting or appropriate. Love scrutinizes the options for action and rules out those that are not advantageous or beneficial for others.

5. When Paul contemplates that the Corinthians may have accepted God's grace in vain (6:1), he acknowledges that believers can fall out of faith. You may have heard the expression "Once saved, always saved." It is not Pauline. Paul believed that we can turn away from God (cf. Gal 4:9). It is a powerful testimony to how much God loves us that God's grace at work in our lives frees us to say no to God. There is a delicacy about love: It is fullest and richest when it is freest, when all the trappings of compulsion are gone. Something like that is true also of grace: God's grace does claim us—no mistake about that. But it claims us in a way that enables us fully and freely to embrace it. Grace is perhaps better thought of as a stewardship rather than as a possession.

6. Why do bad things happen to good people? That may be our question, but it is not Paul's. Faith does not function as a protection from hard times or from difficulties. Problems and tribulations are not a sign of God's disfavor. The gospel and its grace do not work as a hermetic seal against difficulties. Paul's hardship lists show that he frequently encounters problems and tribulations. Rather, faith—that is, our trust in God—becomes the assurance that God is "for us," that God is on our side through tough times and good times. Read Rom 8:35-39 and see Paul's powerful assertion that nothing, no matter how bad or how terrifying, can separate us from God's love. Challenging times and situations are occasions for us to trust in "the one who strengthens me" (Phil 4:13); with every predicament, God also provides an exodus (1 Cor 10:13).

7. The last items in the hardship list (6:10) provide what we might describe as an eschatological window on suffering and possessions. Seen from the vantage point of God's ultimate redemptive purposes, sorrow and grief do not have the last word; joy and rejoicing do. Paul's encoded affirmation is that God will not leave us in grief and sorrow (cf. Jesus' beatitude in Matt 5:4; Luke 6:21 b). As to possessions, Paul raises the question as to what makes a person truly rich and what it means to possess something. Paul's view, expressed elsewhere, is that God freely gives us what counts, so boasting about possessions is voided; so also is valuing life based on what we own (1 Cor 4:7). Paul's notion that believers "possess everything" may seem strange to us, but Paul thinks that God, to whom everything belongs by virtue of divine creation and preservation, shares everything with believers (1 Cor 3:21-23).

8. Paul's new perspective that, after Christ's death and resurrection, we regard no one according to the flesh is not applied solely to our brothers and sisters in Christ. Paul's text does not say, "From now on we regard no *fellow believers* according to the flesh." It says *no one.* So even unbelievers must be considered and related to differently now because Christ has died for them, whether they have responded to that death-for-them or not. All of our relationships, with everyone, must be governed by the fact that Christ has died for all; because of that death, they are valued and must be treated accordingly.

2 CORINTHIANS 6:11–7:4, PAUL'S DIRECT APPEAL FOR MORE AFFECTION

COMMENTARY

6:11-13. What was certainly persistent but always subtle, indirect, and encoded in the text before 6:11 is now explicit and direct: Paul yearns for increased affection from the Corinthians. For the first time in the letter since the salutation, he directly addresses them: "you, Corinthians" (6:11). He retains for himself, however, the plural in 6:11-12 and thereby continues to cast himself as part of the larger, mainstream group of believers. Even that ruse breaks down, however, and Paul, expressing his affection, emerges in the singular as he plays the paternal role: "I speak as to children" (6:13; cf. 1 Cor 4:14-16). Paul's address of them as children, as *his* children, is a subtle attempt to recapture some of the familial affection he and they have enjoyed in the past.

Paul is swept up into emotive expressions. He writes of his mouth's being open to them, surely a euphemism for the "frank speech" (παρρησία *parrēsia*), the highest sign of friendship, he has recently used with them in his painful letter (6:11; cf. 3:12; 4:13). He declares that his "heart is open" to them and thus signifies his capacious commitment to them; by contrast, he thinks them restricted in their "affections" (6:12), translating the quite affecting term σπλάγχνα (*splagchna*, "inward parts/entrails/gut") to express the very center of one's being as the locus of the deepest commitment (cf. Phil 1:8; 2:1; Phlm 12, 20). The little subsection 6:11-13 closes with Paul emphatically urging the Corinthians: "You yourselves, open up [your

narrowness, your hearts, understood, as the NIV and NRSV have supplied from 6:11]."

7:2-4. Paul's urgings in 6:11-13 have their reprise in 7:2-4, where, using a different verb (χωρέω *chōreō*), he refines his call for them to open up: "make room [in your hearts, understood] for us" (7:2). Just as in 6:11-12 he began in the plural, so also in 7:2 he starts in the plural and, sounding like he has in earlier sections of this letter, he once again asserts his apostolic probity; so the plural, which pictures him as being in line with other believers, works quite appropriately for him. With the rhetorically repetitive "no one" leading the Greek constructions for heavy emphasis, Paul says the Corinthians have no excuse not to embrace him more openly: "No one have we wronged; no one have we corrupted; no one have we defrauded" (7:2). Unrelenting in his emotional appeal, Paul, exonerating the Corinthians for any doubts along this line, reminds ("I said before," 7:3; cf. 6:11) them that "you are in our hearts."

But the refinement continues significantly: They are in his heart "to live together and to die together," a phrase that has probably been more overinterpreted than many. Paul simply promises that nothing, not even death, can confine his love for them. This is the ultimate pledge of friendship in which Paul sketches out his and the Corinthians' scope of commitment (see similar reflections of love's extent by Paul in Rom 5:7; 9:3). In no sense is Paul here casting any doubt on the resurrection; rather, he is being dramatic and affecting in his depiction of the magnitude of his togetherness with them and, therefore, inscribes related signs of friendship.[129]

As a second index of that devoted friendship, he once again mentions his recent frank speech in the painful letter (7:4a; cf. 6:11; 3:12; 4:13) and, as the refining continues, adds yet another sign of his boasting about them (7:4b). Saying positive things about one's friends is a fundamental duty of friendship; such commendations may redound to the extoller's benefit with the opening of unexpected doors.[130]

The next sentence (7:4c), building from the report of his bragging about them, caps off Paul's request for more affection and telegraphs Paul's final return to the theme of affliction with which he began the letter. Using terms redolent of surfeit, he pictures himself as being sated with encouragement (παράκλησις *paraklēsis*, "comfort/consolation," harking back to the heavy concentration of that term and its root in chap. 1) and as overflowing with joy while he is in the middle of all his afflictions (7:4c). This sentence exhibits once again Paul's ebullient affirmation of life in the midst of suffering, hardship, distress, and affliction, a theme used throughout this letter and, indeed, a hallmark of his gospel (cf. the direct association of joy and suffering in Phil 2:17-18 and 1 Thess 1:6; for the connection of boasting and joy, see Phil 1:25-26).

Given the cultural presuppositions of his time, Paul's direct call for the Corinthians to respond to him with more affection (6:13; 7:2) falls once again under the category of *parrēsia*, "frank speech." Conventionally, frank speech is expected to be used rarely; when employed, it can range from harsh to what Philodemus, a roughly contemporary rhetorician, calls the "slightest sting"[131] from the shouted warning as someone courts disaster, to the gentle urging for a change of decision or behavior. In that culture, any call for an emendation of behavior is understood as frank speech. Paul's painful letter was certainly an example of harsher frank speech (see the Commentary on 2 Cor 7:7-13a).

Now, just a little later and in his very next communication with them, Paul once again employs frank speech in 6:13 and repeats it in 7:2; these two instances are certainly on the "slight sting" end of the scale, but they are frank speech nonetheless.

The material from 2 Cor 1:1–6:10 was not frank speech, though throughout those chapters Paul repeatedly hinted at and indirectly attempted to induce greater allegiance and affection for himself; in those places it was indirect or figured speech.[132] Paul's speech became frank when he directly urged them to "open" their hearts to him (6:12) and "make room for us" (7:2).[133] That he writes, in 2 Corinthians 1–6, *about* his frank speech that he used in the previous, painful letter does not make 2 Corinthians 1–6 frank speech.

When, however, Paul directly asked them to change, to become more affectionate toward him, he violated two canons of frank speech in that culture. Paul's immediate reassurance that what he says is not a condemnation (κατάκρισις *katakrisis*, 7:3) shows that he knows he may have pushed matters too far. First, he followed frank speech in one letter (the painful letter that grieved them into repentance, 7:8-9) with new frank speech in 2 Cor 6:11-13 and 7:2-4. Rhetoricians warn against using frank speech a second time with someone who may be stinging from an earlier "hit," as the Corinthians clearly are. Plutarch, a relatively contemporary moralist, recognizes that persistent hits of frank speech, if not smoothed over, build further and enduring problems in a relationship. Perhaps Paul has now become the recipient of some negative fallout along these lines: "But the man who has been hard hit and scored by frankness, if he be left rough and tumid and uneven, will, owing to the effect of anger, not readily respond to an appeal the next time."[134]

For what amounts to five chapters, Paul seems to have resisted the temptation to be directly frank with them about his desire for more solidarity and affection from them, settling instead for hints and insinuations, a socially acceptable pattern. Then in the sixth

---

129. K. A. Plank, *Paul and the Irony of Affliction* (Atlanta: Scholars Press, 1987) 1-7, depicts Paul as "a kind of poet" of the affections, using emotive and affecting speech powerfully.

130. J. T. Fitzgerald, "Philippians in the Light of Ancient Friendship," in *Friendship, Flattery, and Frankness of Speech,* ed. J. T. Fitzgerald (Brill: Leiden, 1996) 147.

131. See Philodemus *On Frank Criticism.*

132. Sampley, "The Weak and the Strong," 43-46.

133. This is Paul's "response to a lack of reciprocity in a relationship" and therefore a "mild form of censure." See Stowers, "Letters of Praise and Blame," in *Letter Writing in Greco-Roman Antiquity,* 86.

134. Plutarch *How to Tell a Flatterer from a Friend* 74E.

chapter he moves to direct, frank speech. One of the problems with literary frank speech is that its writer is not on hand to see how the recipients are responding. No wonder Paul was "restless" until he heard from Titus's first-hand report regarding his earlier employment of frankness (7:5-7). Paul writes the present letter with only Titus's assessment and word as to how his earlier frank speech was received. Was everyone at Corinth changed by Paul's frank speech in his "painful" letter? Fully? Equally? The odds are that there was some residual sensitivity, if not resentment, among at least some of the Corinthians; frank speech always risks building residual anger.[135] Into that context Paul now launches more frank speech. Granted, it is gentle frankness. At best this is hazardous; at worst, it is foolish. If some people are still irritated, they may experience this gentle frankness as severe even though Paul probably thinks of himself as being affectionate.

The second mistake is Paul's using frank speech in an effort to modify affection or to alter emotions. Frank speech, the rhetoricians know, is designed for deliberative circumstances where an individual (or group) is weighing which direction to go or whether to do something. Frank speech is not to be used in matters of fondness and allegiance. Frank speech employs "the thinking and reasoning powers," not the emotions.[136] A further problem is that love and affection are resistant to command, even the most modest command.

Beyond this, Paul probably did not help his case when he called his auditors "children" (ὡς τέκνοις hōs teknois) when he wrote, "I am speaking as to children" (6:13). Although there is no clue that he intends the reference in 6:13 as anything other than affectionate, some Corinthians may have heard annoying echoes of earlier unpleasantries; Paul had condescendingly addressed them as "babies" (ὡς νηπίοις hōs nēpiois) who were not mature and not ready for meat (1 Cor 3:1-2; though the image is refined to τέκνα [tekna, "children"] in 1 Cor 4:14, 17). And Paul has already said that he writes to them nothing beyond what they can read and understand (2 Cor 1:13), which may have struck some of them as similarly haughty on Paul's part.

The two violations of the culturally accepted guidelines for frank speech and his calling them "children" may have contributed to the breakdown of relations between Paul and the Corinthians that is reflected in nearly every sentence of the letter fragment 2 Corinthians 10-13, which was written subsequently to this frank speech in 6:11-13 and 7:2-4 (see the Introduction). If there was residual resentment toward Paul from the frankness in his painful letter, this new frank speech will have made Paul a ready target for increased animosity and perhaps even enmity such as must be supposed is the context for 2 Corinthians 10–13.

6:14–7:1. Between the two interlocked frank speech passages lies 2 Cor 6:14–7:1, a six-verse conundrum. It does not fit well in its immediate context.[137] Certain of its features do not square well with the rest of the letter fragment. It has some otherwise unknown expressions for Paul. It is about ten degrees off from what we expect from him in several of its claims, but, as we shall see, not alien to Paul in others.

The structure of 6:14–7:1 is rather clear. It opens with a command not to be unevenly yoked (ἑτεροζυγέω heterozygeō, 6:14a)—a term referring to yoking together two unalike draft animals, such as an ox and an ass—with unbelievers[138] and follows with five rhetorical questions (6:14b-16a) that are cast in such direct antithetical form that the hearer is compelled, on the basis of common sense, to answer to each of them with something like, "Nothing whatsoever!" These questions set the ground for the central declaration of the passage, the "for/because" statement that grounds why they should not be yoked with unbelievers: "for we ourselves are the temple of the living God" (6:16b). Immediately following is a catena of scriptural citations that, without using the precise terms of the central declaration, nevertheless affirm and in a multifaceted way extend the truthfulness not only of the central claim but also of the opening command not to be misyoked to unbelievers.

A circular argumentation unpacks the central notion of 6:14–7:1. The hearers are

---

135. See Philodemus *On Frank Criticism* fragment 70.
136. Plutarch *How to Tell a Flatterer from a Friend* 61E.

137. Scott argues that 6:14–7:1 "explains *how they are to open their 'heart.'*" See J. M. Scott, "The Use of Scripture in 2 Corinthians 6:16c-18 and Paul's Restoration Theology," JSNT 56 (1994) 96, italics added.
138. See also Philo *On the Special Laws* 4:204.

God's temple; God does dwell among those who *therefore* become God's people who should *therefore* come out, separate, from those who in 6:14*a* are called unbelievers[139] and not touch anything unclean, and *therefore* God will receive them as God's sons and daughters. The passage concludes with another *therefore* ("having these promises"), which gains expression in the admonition "let us cleanse ourselves" (7:1). Because God dwells among people, they must separate and not touch anything unclean, and the resulting holiness, cleanness, and abstinence prompt God to welcome them as children. God's residence claims, defines, a people who must live and comport themselves appropriately and distinctively; when they do so, God welcomes them as sons and daughters. This circularity of God's claiming a people who then live appropriately and are embraced by God as children is what the author refers to collectively as "these promises" (7:1). The passage concludes with a call for the auditors to join with the writer to "cleanse" themselves "from every defilement of the flesh and spirit" (7:1).

The passage 6:14–7:1 is strange to the immediate context. First, the dynamic in 2 Corinthians 1–9 is between Paul their apostle who, associating himself with a larger group of believers, defends his actions and comportment among and toward the auditors and who for most of the letter implicitly bids for greater esteem and only toward its climax openly asks for greater affection from those to whom he has brought the gospel. Paul's encoded focus is on the Corinthians' relationship to him; prior to 6:14–7:1 there has not been the slightest inkling of concern for *their behavior.* Any attention to behavior has been on Paul, because he has been so determined to show that he has lived and worked in absolute accord with the gospel he has brought to them. Further, though no textual traditions or variants support excising 6:14–7:1, the passage does separate the materials on both sides that, as we have seen, together urge the Corinthians to be more affectionate to Paul. So if the passage were non-Pauline and thus inserted later into the Pauline text, as some

have argued,[140] then it would probably have been done early on, perhaps by the person(s) who edited fragments of more than one letter into the document that we now call 2 Corinthians.

When considered in the light of Paul's earlier correspondence with the Corinthians, 2 Cor 6:14–7:1 appears strange. In these verses, the believers must be on guard against association with unbelievers; they must not be misyoked to them (6:14); they must "come out from them and be separate" (6:17); and they must (protect and) perfect their holiness via a self-cleansing of body and spirit (7:1). The closest Paul comes to such a picture elsewhere in his correspondence with the Corinthians is in the "previous" letter where he warned them about associating with immoral persons (πόρνοι *pornoi*) and later clarifies that he meant immoral persons within the community of believers because, he argues, one simply cannot avoid contact with immoral persons in the world (see the Commentary on 1 Cor 5:9-13).

From many details in 1 Corinthians, however, Paul's hearers will have a dramatically different picture of how holiness is lived in the world. Whether one takes the misyoking in 2 Cor 6:14 to refer to marriage or not, Paul has written quite positively in 1 Corinthians about believers' association with unbelievers. Paul's auditors will know that he condones believers' being married to unbelievers (1 Cor 7:12-16). But 1 Cor 7:12-16 goes beyond condoning marriage to unbelievers; it even speculates that the holiness of the believing spouse may, in fact, positively affect the unbelieving spouse and certainly has affected any children (1 Cor 7:14, 16). In 2 Cor 6:14–7:1, however, Paul expects believers to preserve holiness through separation and withdrawal, a position not unlike what he has *opposed* among some Corinthians (cf. 1 Cor 7:5-7, 12-13, 27-28, 36). In 1 Cor 7:12-16, Paul credits holiness with its own power to cross over the border and influence so as to change unbelievers. The one protects holiness; the other assumes that holiness has its own divinely inspired power. The one fears that holiness may be lost by association with

139. These ἄπιστοι (*apistoi*, "unbelievers") have been identified as Paul's opponents. See N. A. Dahl, *Studies in Paul: Theology for the Early Christian Mission* (Minneapolis: Augsburg, 1977) 69. But Thrall, *The Second Epistle to the Corinthians*, 473, argues against it.

140. For details and propounders of those arguments, see Furnish, *II Corinthians*, 375-83.

unbelievers; the other assumes that holiness may change the unbelievers.

Elsewhere in 1 Corinthians Paul readily condones believers' having social involvement with unbelievers. In an imagined scene, he contemplates that an unbeliever invites a believer to dinner, and he finds absolutely no problem with a believer's going (1 Cor 10:27). Further, Paul anticipates that unbelievers may venture in when the church gathers and is not the least concerned; in fact, he contemplates that such a circumstance may ultimately be the occasion for what we might call a conversion (1 Cor 14:23-25).

In all three instances in 1 Corinthians, associations with unbelievers are viewed quite positively by Paul, and in two of them the relationship is positively infectious. In yet one more passage from 1 Corinthians, Paul depicts believers as living in a world whose structure (σχῆμα *schēma*), tainted by sin, is passing away (1 Cor 7:31; see also Rom 1:18-25); that world is where believers transact their lives. So Paul thinks they live directly in that world, but ὡς μή (*hōs mē*, "as-if-not") doing so (1 Cor 7:29-31). There Paul advocates an eschatological reserve in which believers do not take their clues or values from the world in which they perforce live. They live in that world, but not by it.

The notion that believers can be enjoined to "cleanse themselves" is unfamiliar in the Pauline corpus. For Paul it is God who sanctifies, who washes, who claims people and makes them appropriate as a new creation, for restored relationship. Even the Pauline school, in letters written after Paul's death, maintains the conviction that it is not the believers but Christ who cleanses and purifies (Eph 5:26; Titus 2:14). The temple is *already* made holy (cf. 1 Cor 3:17), and believers honor that holiness as a sort of stewardship given into their care. Writing earlier to these same Corinthians, Paul declares, "But you were washed, you were made holy, you were justified" (1 Cor 6:11). Though the first verb is ἀπολούω (*apolouō*), rather than the καθαρίζω (*katharizō*) of 2 Cor 7:1, the semantic overlap is sufficient to warrant two contrasts: In 1 Cor 6:11 Paul uses the aorist form of the verbs to signify completed, finished action in the past—the Corinthians were washed and made holy, with their baptism probably

being the point of reference (cf. the baptismal phrase "in the name of the Lord Jesus Christ"). Each of the three verbs in 6:11 is in the passive, with God, not the believers, as the one who is understood to have done the washing and the making holy. Also, the term μολυσμός (*molysmos*, "defilement"; NIV, "everything that contaminates," 2 Cor 7:1) occurs nowhere else in Paul, or in the NT for that matter, though Paul uses the verbal form of the term to describe the defilement that he thinks waits for the person who eats meat offered to idols despite his weak conscience, which does not allow it (1 Cor 8:7). The use of the term in 2 Cor 7:1 fits well with the notion of uncleanness mentioned in 6:17.

In other respects, however, 2 Cor 6:14–7:1 is not so alien to Paul's view of things. Paul is quite capable of setting up antithetical pairings as those in 6:14*b*-16. For example, he describes fidelity to Christ with one's body—that is, with one's whole self (cf. Rom 12:1)—as proscribing any rival relationship. He uses an image as old as Israel's prophets, prostitution, to express an alternative, totally unacceptable rival relationship (Jeremiah 2–3; Ezek 16:15-34; Hosea 2): Your bodies, which are members of Christ, cannot also be members of a prostitute (1 Cor 6:15-16). Similarly, while in some circumstances Paul condones eating meat that has been offered to idols (1 Cor 8:4-6; 10:25-27; cf. Rom 14:17), in the cultic setting he cannot and does not approve of it (1 Cor 10:17-21).

Paul readily affirms that Christ, or the Holy Spirit, resides or dwells in or among believers (Christ: Rom 8:10; Gal 2:20; Spirit: Rom 8:9-11; 1 Cor 3:16; 6:19; 1 Thess 4:8; God: 1 Cor 3:16-17 possibly) and even uses the image of the Temple to develop that notion (1 Cor 3:16-17; 6:19), as in 2 Cor 6:16. The expression "the living God" (θεοῦ ζῶντος *theou zōntos*) employs a divine descriptor that, though not frequent in Paul, is represented in the corpus (2 Cor 3:3; 1 Thess 1:9) and is much more widespread in Jewish tradition as a way of describing that God is not subject to death (Deut 5:26; 2 Kgs 19:4, 16; Ps 42:2; Isa 37:4, 17; Jer 10:10; 23:36; Hos 1:2 LXX).[141]

Likewise, the reference to βελιάρ (*Beliar*, or Belial; in Hebrew meaning

---

141. See also Philo *Dec* 67.

"worthlessness"), is a derisive way contemporary Jews referred to Satan[142] or to the antichrist.[143] Satan is mentioned often in the Corinthian correspondence: Satan has power to destroy the flesh of those in sin's thrall (1 Cor 5:5), tests self-control (7:5), has plans (2 Cor 2:11), takes on disguises, and has agents who pretend to be like believers (11:14-15). Satan even tests Paul via the thorn or stake in his flesh (2 Cor 12:7). *Beliar* is the antithesis of Christ (2 Cor 6:15).

The antithetical listing provides a virtual lexicon of Greek synonyms for sharing: "partnership" (μετοχή *metochē*), "fellowship" (κοινωνία *koinōnia*, 6:14 b-c), "agreement" (συμφώνησις *symphōnēsis*), "part/share" (μερίς *meris*), "union" (συγκατάθεσις *sygkatathesis*). All these terms function, in a reinforcing way, to distinguish, to mark off boundaries between the life of faith and its opposite—boundaries that provide the basis for the subsequent call for separation, the avoidance of contact (6:17-18), and ultimately the need for cleansing (7:1).

The use of Scripture citations—"as God said" (6:16), "says the Lord" (6:17), and "says the Lord Almighty" (6:18)—is noteworthy in certain respects. Nowhere else in Paul's works is Scripture introduced with "as God said" (6:16).[144] Nowhere else in Paul is the title "Almighty" (παντοκράτωρ *pantokratōr*) used, though it is found frequently in the Septuagint and in Revelation (e.g., Rev 1:8; 4:8; 11:17). The Scripture citations themselves are at times difficult to identify as to source and occasionally are significantly changed from early manuscripts. The first quotation—"I shall dwell in them," 6:16—is nowhere in the Scriptures of Israel. In fact, nowhere in the Septuagint is God ever the subject of the verb "dwell" (ἐνοικέω *enoikeō*).[145] This citation is probably a free rendition of Lev 26:11 because Lev 26:12 is heavily used in 2 Cor 6:16: (1) "and I will walk about among them" shares with Lev 26:12 LXX, in the same declension, ἐμπεριπατήσω (*emperipatēsō*), and (2) the promise of God, shifted from the direct address of Lev 26:12 to a third-person

declaration, is that God will be their God and they will be God's people. Paul has taken Lev 26:11 LXX, "I shall put my tent among you," and transformed it in 2 Cor 6:16 from direct address and increased the immediacy by dropping the tent and having God dwell directly.

The next quotation (2 Cor 6:17) is introduced with διό (*dio*, "therefore") to link it as a consequence of God's indwelling. The key elements in 6:17 a-c, including "and do not touch the unclean thing," may all be found in Isa 52:11-12 LXX, though in the original text the exiles were called to leave Babylon in a new exodus, whereas in 2 Cor 6:14–7:1 the call is for the hearers to separate themselves from the corrupting influence of unbelievers. By its insertion of "says the Lord," 2 Cor 6:17 gives special emphasis to the call not to touch any unclean thing (Isa 52:11) and to the appended promise, which may well come from Ezek 20:34 LXX, "and I will take you out/receive you," cropping off the rest of the construction that appeared in the Scripture—"from the lands where you have been dispersed"—which does not fit the scope of 6:14–7:1.

Linked to God's promise to receive them (2 Cor 6:17 referencing Ezek 20:34) is another scriptural promise—"and I will be your father" (6:18)—which has been taken from its context of God's promise always to keep a son of David available to Israel (2 Sam 7:14: "I will be a father to him, and he shall be a son to me," NRSV) and has been applied, adaptively and directly, to God's whole people: "and you *yourselves* shall be to me sons *and daughters*" (εἰς υἱούς καὶ θυγατέρας *eis huious kai thygateras*, 6:18, italics added to indicate the alterations the author has made).

The section 2 Cor 6:14–7:1 uses Scripture, two passages that originally had an exodus motif and one text that had to do with Davidic inheritance, for distinctive purposes: to call the hearers to recognize God's dwelling and being among them, to exhort them to separate themselves from contamination, and to promise them that they will be received by God and constituted as sons and daughters before God their Father. Then, focusing on the promises (see 7:1 a), the author urges the hearers to "cleanse themselves," an

---

142. See *T. Reub.* 2, 4, 6; *Jub.* 15:33; CD 6, 9.
143. See *T. Dan* 5; *Sib. Or.* 2.167; 3.63; 73; *Ascension of Isaiah* 4.2.
144. Fitzmyer, *Essays on the Semitic Background of the NT,* 216, notes that the "as God said" formula is absent from Hebrew Scriptures and the Mishnah but has a "Qumran counterpart in CD 6:13; 8:9."
145. Furnish, *II Corinthians,* 363.

exhortation that refines the Isa 52:11 command, "Do not touch an unclean thing" (2 Cor 6:17).

If 6:14–7:1 is neither written by Paul nor inserted where it is by him, we must ask on what principles a redactor might have placed these verses in this place. The question remains a difficult one for many of the reasons cited above. One suggestion, however, merits consideration.[146] In the Greco-Roman world, processions often went through the city and ended at a temple. A herald preceded

the procession, alerted people to prepare the route, and demanded that the temple be readied. Paul's Letter to the Corinthians (chaps. 1–9) has the ingredients for a redactor to connect 6:14–7:1, with its call for preparation of the "temple of the living God," to the triumphal processional mentioned in 2:14-16, with its fragrance "of the knowledge of God." The redactor would have put 6:14–7:1 between the calls for the Corinthians to "open wide" or "make room" (πλατύνω *platynō*, 6:13; χωρέω *chōreō*, 7:2) and would have understood that appeal to be that they prepare themselves as God's temple.

146. The following thesis is propounded by P. B. Duff, "The Mind of the Redactor: 2 Cor 6:14–7:1 in Its Secondary Context," *NovT* 35 (1993) 178-80.

REFLECTIONS

1. Frankness, now as then, is best suited for strong friendship relations. Outside of friendship, frank speech is likely to be perceived as meddlesome at best. But even among friends, speaking frankly is a delicate undertaking that requires caution as well as a sense of timing and proportion. Furthermore, the speaker needs to be of good character and should not have the same log in his or her own eye (cf. Matt 7:1-5). Frank speech can easily slip into abuse, and no excuse can be made for that. There are times, however, when frankness (short of abuse) may be unavoidable, even if the friendship may be lost in the process (cf. Gal 4:16).

2. Open professions of love and affection such as Paul uses are appropriate, even fundamental, to human well-being. Expressions of love are not signs of wimpiness but are absolutely necessary for good rapport among people. Note the number of times when, after someone has suddenly died, the survivors lament that they did not have the chance to say good-bye or "I love you." Simple statements of love are seldom misunderstood.

3. We may be able to resonate with Paul's eagerness for a fuller friendship with the Corinthians. At times we may want or expect more of our friends than they are either willing to give or perhaps even capable of giving. In such circumstances, we might ask whether we are the ones cloaking ourselves and not sharing ourselves fully. If we find that we are doing that, then we might realistically ponder that genuine friendship requires an opening up and a giving from both sides.

4. How should Christians relate to the world around them? Is association with unbelievers inappropriate? There are very different answers in the New Testament. In fact, there are even different answers in Paul's letters. At times Paul knows—and condones—that believers are married to unbelievers (1 Cor 7:12-16). Likewise, he knows that unbelievers may wander into worship (1 Cor 14:24). Yet here in 2 Cor 6:14–7:1 the lines are drawn ever so sharply. These verses emphasize the importance of human responsibility, stressing as they do our obligations to honor our relation to God by examining all other associations in the light of that one, central relationship with God. Any compromise of our being God's temple is inappropriate. Because this passage is not about marriage, these verses probably should not be construed as having any counsel one way or the other about whether a believer should marry an unbeliever.

5. The living God has determined to dwell among us as a temple. People in Paul's world would have known that temple maintenance was a consequence of God's indwelling. The issue would immediately be one of keeping the temple ready and fit for God to dwell there. If we knew that God was bent on living with us, what would we want to change? What associations, what habits, and what patterns of behavior would we need to stop? Temples require cleaning and polishing, and that on a regular and consistent basis.

2 CORINTHIANS 7:5-16, REPRISE OF CONCERN AND REASSURANCES OF CONFIDENCE

COMMENTARY

Like a ring structure or, as rhetoricians would call it, an inclusio, Paul now reaches back to the beginning of the letter to revisit some themes and dwell on them. First, Paul, returning to the plural again as a way of continuing to associate himself with the majority of believers, picks up his journey narrative. Earlier (2:12-13), Paul had detailed his arrival in Troas (northeast shore of the Aegean Sea, in the Roman province of Asia, modern Turkey), his distress because Titus was not there (to inform him about how the Corinthians received his painful letter), and how he was so concerned that he ended his preaching in Troas and went on to Macedonia. As if nothing in the intervening chapters had broken his train of thought, Paul returns to the travel narrative in 7:5: "And, coming into Macedonia, our flesh found no relief" (ἄνεσις *anesis*, "rest," "relief," 7:5; the antonym of θλῖψις *thlipsis*, "affliction," "distress," 7:4).

Second, Paul opened the letter with a self-description grounded on the verb θλίβω (*thlibō*), depicting him as "pressed upon/oppressed/afflicted" (1:6). In 7:5 he uses the same verb and now adds the emphatic and all-encompassing phrase ἐν παντί (*en panti*, "in every way"), which he then elaborates even further with an extension that describes internal and external distress (7:5), an echo of his description of the inner and outer person in 4:16.[147] Paul's portrait (7:5-7) is that of his being so anguished that, once again, he

had to be rescued by God's consolation—this time in the form of Titus, whose message about the Corinthians reassured Paul that his rebuke of the Corinthians had not caused them to turn against him.

Third, Paul's letter-opening rumination about the God who comforts and consoles the afflicted, Paul among them (1:3-11), is reaffirmed in 7:6, where God is poignantly described as "the one who is comforting the downhearted" (using the present participle to denote continued action and a characteristic of God), who now comforts Paul. Just as the theme of consolation/comfort pervaded 1:3-11 (occurring ten times), so also it dominates 7:5-16 (occurring five times).

Finally, only in 7:8-16 do we fully see what was the nature of the painful letter Paul already acknowledged he wrote them (2:3-4) and what connection that had to his distress at not finding Titus at Troas (2:12-13). As noted, adversions to the painful letter and to Paul's use of παρρησία (*parrēsia*, "frank speech") in it have been scattered occasionally within the letter (1:12; 2:4, 17; 3:12; 4:2, 13; 5:11; 6:11). Paul's much-affirmed confidence (1:15; 2:17; 3:4-6; 4:1, 5, 13, 16; 5:6) and his declared affection and signs of friendship for the Corinthians (cf. 1:12-15) are also aspects of frank speech, because the person speaking frankly must have personal integrity and must use frankness in the context of friendship by seeking what is beneficial for the hearers.

The conventional term "painful" has been used in this commentary to refer to the letter

---

147. The mention of inner and outer person here, however, does not serve as the contrast it did in 2 Cor 4:16 but to describe Paul's distress as complete.

of frank speech Paul wrote shortly before he penned what we now call 2 Corinthians 1–9 because it is Paul's own description (2 Cor 7:8-12). The Greek term λύπη (*lypē*) has a semantic range that includes "grief," "sorrow," "pain of mind or spirit," "affliction," "sadness," "distress." But the *lypē* dwelled on in 2 Cor 7:8-12 goes back to Paul's former (i.e., second) visit with the Corinthians when someone caused *lypē* not only to Paul but also, he thinks, to all the Corinthians (2:5). In 7:12 Paul refers to this unnamed person as "the one who acted unjustly/did wrong."

Paul's general use of the term *lypē* refers to the sense of pain or hurt that happens when individuals act harshly or wrongly toward each other. *Lypē* is experienced in community, in the transactions between and among individuals when one is rebuked or hurt. Paul experienced it when someone in the Corinthian community "did wrong" toward him and was not rebuked by his fellow believers (2:1-4). Since Paul's departure and subsequent harsh letter, the Corinthians have punished the man (2:5-11), and Paul expresses his concern that the man be restored lest he become overwhelmed by "overflowing *lypē*" (2:7). Paul's painful (*lypē*) letter caused the Corinthians *lypē*, and the letter itself was written in response to Paul's previous *lypē*.

For Paul, not all *lypē* is bad. There is a *lypē* that can have a positive outcome; it can lead to repentance (εἰς μετάνοιαν *eis metanoian*); it is a *lypē* that is godly (κατὰ θεόν *kata theon*); and it eventuates, without regret, in salvation (7:9-10). In what amounts almost to an aside, Paul ties the grief that the Corinthians have experienced in receiving his painful letter into a reassurance that their "repentance" in response to his letter shows that they are in fact now properly moving toward the ultimate destination of the believing life: salvation (7:10).

In the unquestioned Pauline letters, salvation is not a present reality in the life of believers. Instead, believers who are now justified and reconciled (Rom 5:9-10) look forward with confidence that what God has begun in them will ultimately result in their salvation (Phil 3:12-14).[148] Between the "already" of their having been justified and reconciled

and the "not yet" of their salvation, believers must do their moral reasoning and their own self-assessment to see how fully they are living the faith—that is, how well they are navigating the life of faith. Midcourse corrections are possible, Paul thinks, in the lives of believers (see the Commentary on 1 Cor 11:27-32). Titus reports to Paul that his painful letter became the occasion for the Corinthians to make such a midcourse correction, and Paul now assures them that their godly *lypē* is, therefore, placing them once again in line for salvation.[149]

As a term, "repentance" (μετάνοια *metanoia*) does not occur frequently in Paul's letters (e.g., Acts 2:38; cf. Luke–Acts, where repentance and forgiveness are the chief categories to describe restoration of right relationship with God). Here in 2 Cor 7:9-10, repentance leads to a restoration of right relationship between people: between the Corinthians and Paul. Their repentance, their turning about, their reorienting of themselves places them once again in a collegial relationship with Paul.

The other *lypē*, the one Paul describes as "worldly" (ἡ τοῦ κόσμου λύπη *hē tou kosmou lypē*) and that finds no repentance, brings about death (7:10). Once again, Paul sets up stark alternatives, as he has throughout this letter fragment. This time, according to Paul, the Corinthians have chosen the correct alternative.

Paul has to walk a fine line in his rehearsal of the events surrounding his letter of frank speech. It grieved them. He did not want to grieve them, but, with no choice but to act in their best interests even if it put him and his standing with them at risk, he wrote them a harsh letter designed to elicit repentance, a change of heart and direction. So he has to make clear that the sting or the hurt is not itself his goal and to focus instead on the results that repentance precipitated (7:8-9). Only from the perspective of successfully restored relationships can Paul say that he does not regret having stung them with frank speech—the outcome has made the pain it

---

148. Sampley, *Walking Between the Times,* 20-21.

149. See R. F. Ward, "Pauline Voice and Presence as Strategic Communication," *Semeia* 65 (1994) 102-4, for the importance of the letter carrier, in this instance most likely Titus, in the recitation and interpretation of the contents of the letter he delivers and on the function of the reader as an arbiter of transformation.

caused him and them worth it (7:8). "To live and to die with them," indeed (7:3).

Titus is an important player in these circumstances and times for Paul, and apparently for the Corinthians. His portrait here shows him, like Timothy, who is, along with Paul, designated a writer of the letter, *sympatico* with Paul. In all likelihood, it was Titus who delivered the painful letter. Titus's report of the letter's reception is what Paul first anxiously awaits at Troas and then seeks in Macedonia. Paul had boasted to Titus about the Corinthians (7:14). Titus, Paul's "partner and fellow worker for you" (8:23), is a "double" for Paul because God has given into Titus's heart the "same zeal for you" that Paul has (8:16; cf. the reflection about Titus made a subsequent time by Paul, 12:18).

Apparently, Titus is Paul's source of information about the Corinthians' response to his letter of frank speech. Paul seems satisfied, even overjoyed, with the "goodwill assurances" he hears from Titus.[150] In fact, however, a couple of signs suggest that Paul's response may be a bit overinflated.[151] First, Paul's concluding remark—"I rejoice that in all things I have confidence in you"—while it accords with the social conventions of the time, simply does not jibe with two features of 2 Corinthians 1–7: (1) his repeated, encoded pleading with them throughout the letter fragment to associate more fully with him and his ministry, which is described in such laudatory ways, and (2) his just-completed explicit call for more affection from them. Likewise, his statement that Titus "remembers the obedience of all of you" may be a stretch. It must have been through Titus that Paul learned of some Corinthians' dismay over his canceled visit, and it is most likely especially to them and their distress that Paul addresses his comments about vacillating in making his plans (2 Cor 1:15-22). And is it not likely Titus who informs Paul that the earlier Corinthian zeal for the collection has seriously eroded? Accordingly, we may wonder if Paul has not overstated matters when he extols the Corinthians' zeal, their readiness to clear

themselves, their indignation, fear, longing, and finally their punishment (probably of the one who had done the wrong, 7:11; cf. 2:6). But when these accolades are considered in terms of acceptable, conventional practice in Hellenistic letters of commendation such as this one,[152] one sees that Paul is quite in line with the culturally dictated expectations of placing "expressions of appreciation and confidence" at or near the close of a letter body.[153]

Several possibilities suggest themselves for this modest overinflation. It was a Cynic-Stoic convention for the moralist sage, like a choirmaster, to "pitch the note a bit high" so that the choristers might all come in on the right note. In this instance, Paul might be painting the picture as he would like it to be, hoping that his Corinthian audience would adopt the picture as their own.[154] So it may have been deliberate on Paul's part; he does think in terms of getting things completely right and working toward that. Or it may be that, in his eagerness to get beyond his troubles with the Corinthians, Paul might have glossed over what could have been Titus's more balanced report. Or it might be that Titus himself, because of his own zeal for and hopes in the Corinthians, is the source of the gloss.

Paul's alternation between singular and plural statements regarding himself in 7:5-16 is complex. Verse 2 starts with the plural so that Paul's appeal for more affection pictures himself along with the others whom he has reason to suppose the Corinthians hold in their hearts, but it quickly enough evaporates to the singular as Paul tries to clarify his relation to the Corinthians (7:3-4). Paul's travelogue and his report about hearing from Titus keep him firmly planted among a larger group via plural self-references (7:5-7). The move into his rejoicing finds him predictably in the center of the stage; he rejoices over them as he hears from Titus about their having come

150. See M. M. Mitchell, "New Testament Envoys in the Context of Greco-Roman Diplomatic and Epistolary Conventions: The Example of Timothy and Titus," *JBL* 111 (1992) 660-61, on the conventions of such assurances.

151. Hickling states: "Some element of distortion must be allowed for as a reasonable possibility." C. J. A. Hickling, "Is the Second Epistle to the Corinthians a Source for Early Church History?" *ZNW* 66 (1975) 285.

152. For further studies on the rhetorical power of statements of confidence, see A. J. Malherbe, *Moral Exhortation: A Greco-Roman Sourcebook* (Philadelphia: Westminster, 1986) 125; S. K. Stowers, "*Peri men gar* and the Integrity of 2 Corinthians 8 and 9," 345, and *Letter Writing in Greco-Roman Antiquity*, 96-97, 103-4.

153. Belleville, "A Letter of Apologetic Self-recommendation, 156. See the same pattern in Philemon, where, also near the climax of that argument, Paul expresses his confidence in Philemon's "obedience" and states that he expects that the slaveowner will "do even more than I say" (Phlm 21).

154. So in different terms, S. N. Olson, "Pauline Expressions of Confidence," *CBQ* 47 (1985) 295.

around in their zeal for Paul (7:7-9); indeed, the passage closes with Paul, in the singular, rejoicing because of his great confidence in them (7:16).

His references to the painful letter and to his having written it are all in the singular—he takes full responsibility for the decision to write it, the nature of the writing, and his reason for writing (7:8-9, 12). When it comes to his comportment and to whether he has harmed the Corinthians, Paul uses the plural, just as he has regularly done throughout the letter (7:9*e*, 14*c*). When he writes about his earlier boasting to Titus about the Corinthians, he starts out in the singular, but when he broadens his scope to "everything we said to you," he reverts to his preferred plural whereby he persistently describes his own dependability and faithfulness as being consistent with the mainstream (7:14).

Most telling is his use of the plural in 7:13*b*: "In addition to our consolation, we rejoiced rather more over the joy of Titus." Paul's joy is doubled up with Titus's joy and so is, as it turns out, his consolation because the reference to "our consolation" in 7:13*b* picks up his doubled mention of Titus's consolation in 7:7. So when Paul comes to mention his comfort/consolation over the Corinthians' return to fidelity toward him, Paul joins his own consolation to that of Titus, which Paul first saw when he encountered Titus in Macedonia and initially heard Titus's report. His pairing of himself with Titus in their shared consolation (7:7, 13) previews a subsequent association of them that Paul will make in his next piece of correspondence directed to the Corinthians (12:17-18).

The reference to the Corinthians' "obedience" (ὑπακοη *hypakoē*), "of all of you" (7:15), is Paul's description of their return to agreement with his authority. Earlier, Paul, using the same term, said that he wrote them the painful letter precisely to determine "your character, whether in all things you are obedient" (2 Cor 2:9; cf. 10:6; Phlm 21).

In 7:16, Paul's laudation of his confidence in them sets the context for him to move to the next two chapters, where he treats the Corinthians' participation in the collection he has been orchestrating for delivery to the saints in Jerusalem (chaps. 8–9).

Paul has so much at risk with the Corinthians. As surely as they should have been Paul's letter of recommendation, they should also be his joy and his crown, as the Philippians were (Phil 4:1). Paul knows that he must answer at the judgment regarding how well he has lived out his call to be apostle to the Gentiles, and if the Corinthians turn away from him and, therefore, leave the gospel that he preaches, he will fear that he has "run in vain." He is firmly convinced that their well-being is directly tied to their adherence to his gospel and, therefore, to him; so his efforts to persuade them are critical for their destiny, as he understands matters. As their father in the faith (1 Cor 4:14-15; 9:1), he is directly responsible for them. Harsh frank speech, such as Paul has employed with the Corinthians in his painful letter, risks rejection. Paul has been willing to take that chance because he is convinced that something larger than he is at stake.

Paul's risk potentially ranges beyond the Corinthians, however, because he has learned that the Macedonians (including at least churches in Thessalonica and Philippi) are ready with their enthusiastic contribution to the collection for the saints in Jerusalem. As we shall see in 9:1-5, their projected route of delivery, surely formulated according to Paul's earlier plan (1:16), promises to bring the Macedonians through Corinth to join up with Corinthian representatives and go on to Jerusalem. If Paul's relations with the Corinthians go sour, not only will the Macedonians feel the cold Corinthian chill, but also Paul's collection for Jerusalem, a matter of utmost importance for him, may fall under a cloud.

REFLECTIONS

1. Repentance and forgiveness are complex. Some people withhold forgiveness as a means of maintaining power. Others feign forgiveness but are all too ready to recite the hurtful action later. Some make a habit out of being "sorry" but do not change their behavior. Genuine repentance, such as Paul describes, marks an end to the behavior, and real forgiveness lets the matter go. Perhaps it would be helpful to think of both repentance and forgiveness as work, as a discipline we undertake—really as a transforming of our lives. If we forgive, truly and without strings, then *we* will be different persons afterward. If we repent, we also will become different persons. Repentance and forgiveness cannot be understood as fine-tuning; they are changes from the core of our being. Our repenting and our granting of forgiveness have a better chance of being genuine if we undertake them by asking God both to help us change and to let our forgiveness be total and genuine.

2. Having confidence in another person—being able to depend on someone through thick and thin—is the most valuable asset in human relations. Restored confidence may never be as strong as it was or could have been before a violation. Often we think confidence is built up around the big issues or events—and it may be. But more realistically, confidence and dependability are actually augmented or destroyed in the littlest and most minor situations.

3. Christians care for one another because God cares for each and because God in Christ has given each of us into one another's care. Most of the time our caring for one another is relatively risk free. Sometimes, though, loving a person can lead you to risk your relationship with that person, as Paul did in writing the painful letter of frank speech to the Corinthians. If you think your friend is doing something that will prove ultimately harmful to him or to another person, should you risk the person's enmity by telling him or her the truth (see Gal 4:16)? We may decide to take that step when we realize that we value the person's well-being more than we need his or her friendship.

2 CORINTHIANS 8:1–9:15, THE MACEDONIANS AS MODELS, THE COLLECTIONS, AND THE CORINTHIANS' PARTICIPATION

OVERVIEW

Before examining details in these chapters, we must gain clarity concerning the collection for the saints at Jerusalem, the subject that dominates 2 Corinthians 8–9 and is one of the reasons for Paul's having written 2 Corinthians 1–9. Paul and the Corinthians have a history together around this collection.[155] We know that Paul has been busy—with the Corinthians as with others—setting up the collection for the saints in Jerusalem for at least a year (cf. 2 Cor 8:10). Already in 1 Cor 16:1-4

Paul has dealt with what probably was an earlier question from the Corinthians about the logistics of the collection: How should they gather it? They know Paul is given to practical suggestions, so they ask him for some. Paul provides them with the same instructions he gave to their counterpart churches in Galatia; 1 Cor 16:2-4 details his suggestions and plans as they stood at the time of that writing.

The subject matter of chaps. 8–9 is the collection that Paul variously describes as "for the saints" and "for the poor" in Jerusalem. This offering had its genesis in the conference in Jerusalem as described in Gal 2:1-10 (cf. Acts 15:1) and requires a rehearsal of that event for its understanding.

155. J. L. Martyn, *Galatians,* AB 33A (Garden City, N.Y.: Doubleday, 1997) 222-28, argues that Paul engages in two collections, one with Antioch and this one with the Corinthians and his other "essentially Gentile congregations."

❖   ❖   ❖   ❖

Excursus: The Jerusalem Conference and the Collection for the Poor

Paul recounts to the Galatians his having gone, with Barnabas and the same Titus who figures so prominently in 2 Corinthians 1–9, to Jerusalem in response to a revelation (Gal 2:1-2). The conference had as its focus an issue generated at least in part, and perhaps completely, by Paul's mission to the Gentiles in which he did not insist on circumcision as a rite of entry into God's people. The issue can be put in the form of a question: Do Gentiles have to become Jews in order to be part of God's purpose? Paul's entire mission was a graphic no to that question. In a laconic accounting, Paul suggests that his whole mission might be "in vain" if the Gentile believers were not viewed as acceptable by their Jewish brothers and sisters in the faith (Gal 2:2). Paul reports a good outcome of the Jerusalem deliberation: Titus was not compelled to be circumcised, Paul was not subjugated to the Jerusalem leadership (James, Cephas [Paul's often-used name for Peter], and John); quite the contrary, these Jerusalem pillars "recognized the grace that had been given to" Paul (Gal 2:9 NRSV), gave Paul and Barnabas the "right hand of partnership," and collectively divided the mission among themselves in such a way that Paul and Barnabas should go to the Gentiles while the rest of them should take care of "the circumcised" (Gal 2:9). The pillars requested only that Paul (and Barnabas and Titus?) "remember the poor," which he reports himself eager to do (Gal 2:10). If we had no other Pauline texts we might be baffled about who these poor people were and what remembering them might mean.

By the "right hand of fellowship" (κοινωνία *koinōnia*) the Jerusalem pillars had symbolized that Paul's mission was on equal footing with theirs, an opinion *Paul* already had before he went to the conference. So the conference ratified that Paul's previous missionizing among the Gentiles had not been in vain; the Jewish believers in Jerusalem recognized that the Gentiles whom Paul had evangelized were one with them in Christ. To put the matter differently, Paul's successful efforts at the Jerusalem conference meant that there was indeed just one people of God, not two with one being Jewish and the other Gentile.

Paul variously denominates the recipients of this offering. They are "the poor" (πτωχός *ptochos*, Gal 2:10),[156] "the poor who are among the saints in Jerusalem" (εἰς τοὺς πτωχοὺς τῶν ἁγίων *eis tous ptōchous tōn hagiōn*, Rom 15:26), and simply "the saints" (ἅγιος *hagios*, Paul's technical term for a person set apart for, claimed by God; Rom 15:25; 1 Cor 16:1; 2 Cor 8:4; 9:1, 12).

Similarly, Paul describes the offering using a range of terms. It is a "remembering" (μνημονεύω *mnēmoneuō*, "remember/keep in mind/think of," Gal 2:10), a "collection of money" (λογεία *logeia*, 1 Cor 16:1-2), a "ministry" (διακονέω *diakoneō*; also διακονία *diakonia*, "aid/support/distribution," Rom 15:25; 2 Cor 8:4; 9:1, 12-13), and a "gift" (χάρις *charis*, 1 Cor 16:3; 2 Cor 8:6, 19).

We can develop a general picture of the way Paul's churches responded to the collection. The Macedonian churches at Thessalonica and Philippi, who seem to have had a good history with Paul, have vigorously embraced the offering and generated an astonishing collection (8:1-5). The Galatian churches are not listed in Romans, Paul's last letter, as among those who took part in the collection (Rom 15:26), so we may

---

156. L. E. Keck, "The Poor Among the Saints in Jewish Christianity and Qumran," *ZNW* 57 (1966) 54-78.

suppose that Paul's efforts with them (1 Cor 16:1) failed. The Corinthians started off with great enthusiasm for the collection (2 Cor 8:10); later they had some simply logistical questions and asked Paul for general guidelines about how to proceed (1 Cor 16:1-4), but there was no doubt of their readiness to take part at the time when 1 Corinthians was written.

By the time of the letter fragment 2 Corinthians 1–9, however, at least a year since the Corinthians had made a commitment to the collection (8:10), the Corinthians have lost their earlier enthusiasm for it; some (or all) may even be rebelling at taking part in it. Romans 15:26, written later than 2 Corinthians 8–9, shows that Achaia, the Roman province in which Corinth is located, *did* join with Macedonia in the collection. Whether Corinth was a part of that offering cannot be determined; perhaps Paul's inclusion of "all the saints in the whole of Achaia" among the letter recipients for 2 Corinthians 1–9 was also to increase the base from which he hoped to have participation in the collection even if the Corinthians were recalcitrant on the matter.

Paul's understanding of the collection can be pieced together from snippets of different letters. At its heart, the collection symbolizes for Paul a reciprocal partnership between Jewish and Gentile believers. Paul construes the Gentile believers as being "indebted" (ὀφείλω *opheilō*) to the Jerusalem believers who have preceded them in the faith (Rom 15:27), a picture that is in general supported by Paul's image of the olive tree in Rom 11:17-24. Paul's evangelization has been the occasion for Gentiles to be grafted onto the olive tree; now the roots of that tree nourish the engrafted Gentiles. So, shifting from botanical to business imagery, the Gentiles are indebted to their Jewish brothers and sisters in the faith who have shared spiritual matters. Paul's ready conclusion is thoroughly in line with the Greco-Roman expectations of reciprocity; therefore, the Gentile believers ought to reciprocate by being of service in physical matters (Rom 15:27). Indebtedness necessitates a response.

When the discussion is put in terms of need and abundance, then those who have more are obligated to help those who have less or who are in need. Proportionality and fairness come into play in Paul's reckoning. How much one puts aside is supposed to be commensurate with how well one has prospered during that week (1 Cor 16:2). Those with abundance must share with those with little so that there are reciprocity and equality (ἰσότης *isotēs*, 8:13-14; 9:12). No one is to be "put upon" by this collection (8:13). At the same time, however, everyone "owes" love to others (Rom 13:8), and in this instance love calls for sharing the burden with those who have already shared what was theirs.

The "remembering of the poor"—in its being given and in its being received— becomes for Paul the supreme symbol of the unified people of God in Christ in whom truly there is "neither Jew nor Greek" (Gal 3:28 NIV). Paul construes the collection as a one-time, symbolic act in which the Gentile churches as donors and the Jerusalem believers as recipients each acknowledge that they belong to the other in Christ.[157] Paul sees in the collection a tangible confirmation that his work among the Gentiles is, indeed, recognized for what it is: an integral part of God's overall plan. Gentile believers' participation in the collection is a recognition of their indebtedness to their believing Jewish brothers and sisters (cf. Rom 1:16; 2:9-10).

---

157. Paul's collection is not to be identified with the famine relief of Acts 11:29 because Paul has taken at least one year to collect from the Corinthians (2 Cor 8:10; 9:2). Its symbolic significance for Paul can be seen clearly in the mutuality of Rom 15:27.

Connection of 2 Corinthians 8–9 to 2 Corinthians 1–7. Several factors suggest a strong link between 2 Corinthians 8:1–9 and the preceding chapters.[158] First, in chaps. 1–9 Paul has made a recurring triangulation between himself, the Corinthians, and the Macedonians. For example, the first item of dispute with the Corinthians in this letter fragment concerns Paul's travel plans. He had wanted to visit Corinth first, then go to Macedonia, then return to Corinth and proceed to Judea (1:15-16). Although he does not explicitly state it—and does not need to because they surely already know—he projects a trip to Judea (an example of the rhetorical device called *synecdoche*, a generalizing locution that stands in place of Jerusalem) to deliver the collection that will be the topic of chaps. 8–9. Paul has already been explicit about that in 1 Cor 16:1-4 when he instructs the Corinthians to have the collection ready to send to Jerusalem when he returns (1 Cor 16:3). At the time of that writing, he was not clear whether he personally would go to Jerusalem (1 Cor 16:4), but the indecision seems to have faded by the time he wrote 2 Cor 1:16.

The way matters played out in Paul's life was different from his earlier plans. The earlier, projected itinerary reflected in 1:15-16 (Corinth-Macedonia-Corinth-Judea) gave way to a journey that actually went from Corinth to Ephesus and then through Troas (2 Cor 2:12), in the Roman province of Asia, to Macedonia (2 Cor 2:13; 7:5). Paul suggests that he went from Troas to the Roman province of Macedonia because he was desperate to find Titus and get a firsthand report from him regarding the Corinthians' reception of Paul's painful letter of frank speech, a letter we may suppose Titus delivered to the Corinthians. Paul had to know that Titus was working, representing Paul, in the churches that were prominent in Macedonia, certainly Philippi and Thessalonica, and perhaps also Beroea. Not only was Titus working there, but he also was overseeing the gathering of the collection for the saints in Jerusalem, a follow-up on Titus's own presence at the Jerusalem conference, where the idea of

the collection originated, as 8:16-24 demonstrates. So the collection and Titus and Macedonia and the Corinthians have all been connected to one an other for Paul as a context for the entire letter reflected in 2 Corinthians 1–9. Thus, when Paul desperately wants to know how things went with Corinth, he very logically heads for Macedonia, where he knows Titus is laboring on his behalf regarding the collection.

When Paul arrives in Macedonia and receives Titus's glowing reassurances, Paul is relieved (7:13), but he also discovers another bit of information that places him once again in a curious bind: Titus has been *very* successful with the collection in Macedonia. In fact, everything there seems quite organized, and the Macedonian representatives are ready to move out on the trek that has all along been projected to go through Corinth to join with the Corinthian representatives with their offering and proceed together in a grand processional to Jerusalem to deliver it (8:1-7, 17-19).

Paul has a palpable problem. As a part of his advocacy for the collection in Macedonia, he has boasted about the Corinthians' eagerness for and commitment to the collection (8:11; 9:2-5): "Achaia [the Roman province that includes Corinth; cf. 1:1] has been ready since last year" (9:2). Paul's earlier portrait of the Corinthians appears not to have been too great a stretch; at least a year earlier, they had been quite eager about it and thoroughly committed to it (8:10-12). Spurred on by the example of the Corinthians, the Macedonians had, under Titus's tutelage, outdone themselves (8:2-6), virtually begging to be part of the enterprise.

Meanwhile, Paul's relationship with the Corinthians has been strained, at least with a significant part of that believing community, and he clearly has doubts about whether the Corinthians will be anywhere near as ready as he earlier proudly portrayed them to the Macedonians. Paul clearly imagines a scenario in which the zealous and rightly proud Macedonians arrive in Corinth with their collection and find a church not ready to take part in any collection associated with Paul because of disaffection for him. That is the burden that underlies the entire letter fragment of 2 Corinthians 1–9: If the Corinthians

158. F. W. Danker, "Paul's Debt to the *De Corona* of Demosthenes: A Study of Rhetorical Techniques in Second Corinthians," in Watson, *Persuasive Artistry,* 269, argues that Paul's readers would readily have seen the way chaps. 1–7 set the stage for the discussion of the collection in chaps. 8–9.

are not fully reconciled to Paul, then not only is his relationship to them jeopardized, but also the corrosion may spread to other churches, say in Macedonia, when representatives arrive at Corinth to discover a church and an apostle in disarray. The collection and the Macedonians are a major reason why 2 Corinthians 1–9 had to be written.

Paul's advocacy of one church as a model for another, of one believer as an exemplar for another, is a commonplace in his letters.[159] In fact, this feature of his paraenesis and instruction is grounded in the rhetorical and social pattern of exemplification by which his readers would have experienced most of their learning.[160] Similarly, whereas for Paul boasting about oneself is problematic and to be avoided, boasting about faith, whether it be one's own or someone else's, is positive and important as a way of signifying and affirming how the life of faith ought to be lived. Paul tells the Thessalonians, for example, that by becoming imitators of Paul and Jesus Christ they have become an example for all the believers in Macedonia and Achaia (1 Thess 1:6-7). Likewise, the Romans' faith is said to have made an impact on the whole world (Rom 1:8). Boasting about faith and real-life examples is a basic form of Pauline paraenesis that Paul has used to good effect with the Macedonians.

Now, in 2 Corinthians 1–9, the *Macedonians* become the paradigm. They have warmly and fully associated themselves with Paul's mission and, therefore, with the collection as the most recent example of cooperation. Paul's authority is obviously not challenged by them. They clearly are eager to be associated with Paul and with the collection. Even if one allows for a bit of Pauline rhetorical heightening regarding their contribution, even during difficult times and economic distress, the Macedonians remain exemplary (8:2). In short, Paul offers the Macedonians to the Corinthians as a model of how the latter should behave.[161]

Paul's portrait of the Macedonians in 2 Corinthians 8–9 serves another important rhetorical and epistolary function: Their positive association with Paul legitimates and personifies Paul's heavy employment of the plural throughout so much of chaps. 1–9. Paul is not alone. Paul and Timothy (1:1) are not alone. Paul and "all the saints throughout Achaia" are not alone (1:1). Paul writes his entire letter to the Corinthians with the cloud of fellow witnesses that now clearly includes the Macedonian believers. The Macedonian affiliation with Paul, so solid and enthusiastic, adds considerable rhetorical weight to all he has written prior to 2 Corinthians 8–9.

So we may conclude that there are probably two reasons why chaps. 8–9 occur toward the end. First, Paul needs to confirm and enhance his own rehabilitation with the Corinthians that he thinks his painful letter and Titus's entreaties have begun to secure; only then can he make a specific appeal about the collection to them. Second, the way he handles the collection, depicting the Macedonians so positively as exemplars, adds rhetorical urgency not only to encourage the Corinthians to join in the collection but also to all that has preceded.

Second, the picture and functions of Titus show that the chapters about the collection (chaps. 8–9) are directly related to chaps. 1–7. At the time of the writing of 2 Corinthians 1–9, Titus had become of extraordinary importance for Paul. Along with his delivery of the painful letter, Titus probably facilitated the reorientation of the disgruntled Corinthians back into affiliation with Paul. It was Titus who reported to Paul the Corinthian reception of the letter and their realliance with Paul. Titus received such a welcome that he became emotionally attached to them (2 Cor 7:15); he developed a zeal for them that Paul credits with equalling his own (8:16), and he cares so much for them that he has chosen on his own accord to go to the Corinthians with the Macedonian collection and representatives (8:17).

Titus has become identified with the collection; he was in Macedonia overseeing its completion, its final stages (7:6). Because of Titus's good relations with the Corinthians, founded on his recent success in helping them return to affiliation with Paul, Paul

---

159. Rhetorically this is syncrisis, or comparison. See Betz, *2 Corinthians 8 and 9*, 48 and 49n. 77, who says that it is a *topos* Paul uses again in 2 Corinthians 10–13 about himself and the opponents who have come into Corinth.

160. M. M. Mitchell, *The Rhetoric of Reconciliation: An Exegetical Investigation of the Language and Composition of 1 Corinthians* (Louisville: Westminster/John Knox, 1991) 39-46.

161. Hughes, "The Rhetoric of Reconciliation: 2 Corinthians 1.1–2.13 and 7.5–8.24," 259, rightly argues that Paul's depiction of the Macedonians challenges the Corinthians' sense of honor toward finishing what they had begun.

wisely accepts his offer to return to Corinth and to make ready their participation in the collection before the Macedonians arrive.[162] A further confirmation of Titus's special role is found in a subsequent reflection about him in which Paul, having fallen into more disfavor with the Corinthians, recognizes that Titus still has their respect and links himself tightly to Titus in questions that assume affirmative answers: "I did not take advantage of you through anyone I sent you, right? . . . Titus [surely] did not take advantage of you, did he? We walked in the same spirit, right?" (2 Cor 12:17-18). Paul's stock with the Corinthians is more mercurial than Titus's, but Titus, as the one who is being sent from Macedonia to Corinth with the collection, ties chaps. 8–9 to chaps. 1–7.

Third, some scholars have questioned whether 2 Corinthians 8–9 should be considered as a fragment or fragments of other Pauline letters to the Corinthians. Chief among the arguments for such dissociation is what may seem an abruptness in the introduction of the collection as a topic of consideration; the matter is not presaged, they argue, but simply breaks awkwardly onto the scene.[163] Three considerations, however, argue for affirming that these chapters are part of the original letter fragment that begins in 2 Corinthians 1: (1) The collection must be understood to lie behind Paul's recitation of his travel plans in 2 Cor 1:16; he had projected a return to Corinth and a hope that the Corinthians would grant him help on his journey to Judea, clearly a generalizing reference to Jerusalem. Nowhere in all of Paul's letters does he relate travel plans for Jerusalem or Judea except in connection with the collection (Rom 15:25; 1 Cor 16:3-4), and Paul does not preach where others have already laid a foundation (Rom 15:20). So when he mentions in 2 Cor 1:16 his plans to go to Judea and his hopes that the Corinthians will "speed" him on, he is making an only slightly oblique indication of his hopes and concerns that will be directly addressed in 2 Corinthians 8–9—namely, the collection.

We can ponder why Paul chose the rather general reference to "Judea" at that early stage in the letter instead of more specifically and pointedly mentioning "Jerusalem." The answer may be that, being sensitive from the start that he had to set a proper context for dealing with the collection, which had by now become a galling, problematic matter for at least some of the Corinthians, Paul simply acknowledged that he was headed for Judea and therefore did not fly the Jerusalem-collection flag quite so conspicuously. Precisely because the collection has become a ticklish, sensitive matter between Paul and the Corinthians, as chaps. 8–9 demonstrate, Paul does not turn to it directly until he has labored persistently in the preceding chapters to refurbish his ethos, to encourage a more positive Corinthian embrace of him, and to affirm his own broad affection for them. Only then is he in a position to leverage them for a recovery of their earlier zeal for participating in the collection.

If the Corinthians had been on good relations with Paul right along, then he could have addressed the collection earlier and more directly, but his own relation with them had been through a time of strain in which his moral and persuasive purchase on them was severely diminished. Clearly, Paul's first task is to recement, as much as possible, his relationship with the Corinthians; then and only then can he deal with a derivative issue, the collection.

(2) Paul did not wait until chaps. 8–9, however, to set the stage for treating this now problematic issue. While he has been reaffirming and solidifying his relation to the Corinthians in chaps. 1–7, he has also laid down the themes he uses in chaps. 8–9 to attempt to bring the Corinthians back into participation. For the present purposes, a listing with only a few comments should suffice; more detailed observations about the way the themes serve in 2 Corinthians 8–9 can be reserved for later.

Throughout the opening chapters, Paul has established that his own "ministry" (διακονία *diakonia*) has been the Corinthians' access to the gospel and that his ministry is specifically focused on reconciliation (3:7-11; 5:18-20). Now in chaps. 8–9, Paul identifies the collection as a ministry (*diakonia*) to the saints

162. Sometimes envoys can accomplish what the sender might not be able to do. See M. M. Mitchell, "New Testament Envoys in the Context of Greco-Roman Diplomatic and Epistolary Conventions: The Example of Timothy and Titus," *JBL* 111 (1992) 662.

163. Betz, *2 Corinthians 8 and 9*, 129-34, 139, assumes that 2 Cor 8 is the beginning of a new letter fragment.

in Jerusalem (8:4; 9:1) and that it glorifies the Lord. Corinthian participation demonstrates not only their goodwill (προθυμία *prothymia*, 8:19; 9:2) but also that they identify and share in Paul's ministry of reconciliation because they as Gentiles now signal their identification with their Jewish brothers and sisters in the faith.

Again, in the earlier chapters, Paul in various ways emphasizes that the gospel characteristically overflows in "abundance" (περισσεύω *perisseuō*, 1:5; 3:9). In particular, God's "grace" (χάρις *charis*), a term that will dominate Paul's characterization of the collection and of participation in it (see below), is described as spreading to more people so that it may overflow in thanksgiving to the glory of God (4:15). A Pauline commonplace has it that persons who are the recipients of God's grace are moved to reach out to others. Paul sets up that notion in 4:15 and capitalizes on it in 8:2, 7, 14 and 9:8, 12, where he plays repeatedly on the overflow of abundance that both prompts and characterizes the collection he hopes the Corinthians will once again embrace with zeal.

In 2 Cor 7:11-12 Paul rejoices that Titus's report has reassured him about the Corinthians' reaffirmation of their σπουδή (*spoudē*), "zeal/eagerness/earnestness," for him. In 8:7 Paul characterizes the Corinthians as persons who excel in everything, including *spoudē*, and with that he builds extensively in these two chapters on their newly revitalized zeal and directs it toward their sincere and full participation in the collection (8:7-8, 16-17, 22).

Likewise, "glory" (δόξα *doxa*) is another important link Paul makes between the opening chapters and chaps. 8–9. Though modern readers might most readily remember Paul's heavy elaboration of glory in the two-covenant passage (2 Cor 3:7–4:6), the term makes significant appearance in 4:15, as noted just above, and is eschatologically mentioned in 4:17 before it resurfaces in 8:19, 23 and 9:13.

"Affliction" (θλῖψις *thlipsis*), which opens the letter and is such an enduring theme within it (1:4, 8; 2:4; 4:17; 6:4; 7:4), also inaugurates the discussion of the collection with the report that the Macedonian churches are abundantly ready with their contribution to the collection despite what Paul describes as "a great test of affliction" (8:2). Their dedication to Paul and to the collection not only is exemplary for the Corinthians, but their perduring through affliction also aligns them with Paul and his ministry as reported in the opening chapters of this letter fragment. Further along in the discussion of the collection, the term "affliction" and its counterpart, "rest/relief" (ἄνεσις *anesis*), which appeared together in 7:4-5, are applied to the Corinthians (8:13; cf. 2:13).

Finally, *charis* is the single most frequently used major term in 2 Corinthians 8–9, and Paul uses it here with vast semantic range, from "grace" to "goodwill" to "favor" to "gracious deed or gift" to "thanks or gratitude" (8:1, 4, 6-7, 9, 16, 19; 9:8, 14-15). It opens 2 Cor 1:2 as it does every Pauline letter: "Grace to you." Paul's carrying out of his ministry is credited to God's grace (1:12); all believers have been affected by God's grace (4:15). Paul uses the term in his "thanks be to God" formulation as well (2:14; cf. Rom 6:17; 7:25; 1 Cor 15:57; 2 Cor 8:16; 9:15), and he warns the Corinthians to be cautious that they have not accepted God's grace in vain (6:1). Thus the term *charis* provides a profound link of 2 Corinthians 8–9 to the preceding chapters.

Paul's Understanding of Charis. Much can be learned about Paul's understanding of χάρις (*charis*) in chaps. 8–9. Too often *charis* is understood restrictively as referring to the inauguration of God's redemptive and liberating power that claims a sinner for God—and it surely is that (cf. Rom 5:2; 1 Cor 15:10)—but 2 Corinthians 8–9 will enrich that narrow understanding. In the rhetorical handbooks of Paul's time, speakers are sometimes encouraged, as a means for heightening the attention of their audience, to use the same term in a variety of ways.[164] Paul certainly would have satisfied rhetoricians with his use of *charis*, scattered as it is rather evenly throughout 2 Corinthians 8-9 with a range of semantic functions. In fact, the NIV and the NRSV shield the reader from realizing that the term appears ten times in the two chapters. For the sake of clarity and to honor the importance of this term for Paul, these translations and locations of *charis* are noted here:

164. See *Ad Herennium* 4.14.21.

	NIV	NRSV
8:1	"grace"	"grace"
8:4	"privilege"	"privilege"
8:6	"act of grace"	"generous undertaking"
8:7	"grace of giving"	"generous undertaking"
8:9	"grace"	"generous act"
8:16	"I am glad"	"thanks [to God]"
8:19	"the offering"	"generous undertaking"
9:8	"grace"	"blessing"
9:14	"grace"	"grace"
9:15	"thanks [to God]"	"thanks [to God]"[165]

The variety of English terms and even phrases used to translate the term *charis* is testimony to the richness of Paul's usage here. From the examples in 2 Corinthians 8–9, *charis* is understood to be given by God to people, the Macedonians, in the midst of affliction and poverty (8:1). Not only is the *charis* freely given (by God), but also it is given abundantly, beyond measure (9:14). This quality of overflowing abundance to the

165. Curiously, the same Greek phrase (χάρις τῷ θεῷ *charis tō Theō*) is once translated as "thanks to God" (9:15) and earlier "I am glad" (8:16) by the NIV.

Corinthians—"God is able to overflow *every grace* to you" (9:8)—inexorably prompts them (or at least it should, Paul seems to suggest), since they are provided all they need anyway, to experience that same overflow of abundance into every good work. Put another way, God's grace is powerful and moves the recipients to a reflection of God's abundance so that they respond profusely by doing good works toward others. The NRSV's use of "generous undertaking" reflects the translators' efforts to express that God's grace, once received, generates grace-laden acts to others (8:6-7, 19). And to finish the circle full round, the *charis* that is received as a gift from God can and does properly flow back to God in the form of grateful thanks from the graced recipients: "*Charis* [thanks] be to God" (8:16; 9:15). So, for Paul, *charis* is all at once a gift from God, the good works that *charis* inspires, and the thanks to God for the *charis* and the abundance that it inevitably brings with it. Paul understands the collection for the saints in Jerusalem as a *charis* that represents and produces all of the just identified responses.

2 Corinthians 8:1-7, Macedonia, Ministry, and the Corinthians

COMMENTARY

8:1-5. In his opening statements about the collection, Paul continues his preference for the plural, no doubt to emphasize the larger movement of which he is surely the leader. Once he gets into the discussion, however, he weaves together statements in the singular and in the plural (e.g., plural: 8:18-22, 24; 9:11; 10:3-7, 11-18; singular: 8:23; 9:1-5; 10:1-2, 8-10).

Paul opens his discussion of the collection with one of his formulas of disclosure (1 Cor 12:3; 15:1; Gal 1:11): He wants them to know the grace of God given to the churches of Macedonia. To be sure, all believers know the grace of God in the sense that each is dependent upon God's grace. In this instance, however, Paul wants them to know about the way God's grace has happened in the Macedonian churches. That God's grace is said to

be "given" implies God as the giver and is tautologically emphatic.

Paul's description of the Macedonian churches is striking. They, like Paul, have experienced both the abundance of their joy and the depths of their poverty. Paul combines three things that would not have surprised most of his ancient auditors: The Macedonian churches have experienced at the same time an "abundance of joy," "the depths of poverty," and "a great test of affliction" (8:2).

Affliction and joy within it are a commonplace in Paul. Witness his association of the apocalyptic sufferings of the end time with the pangs of childbirth; the goal toward which the suffering moves is proleptically experienced in the context of affliction (Rom 8:18-25; cf. 1 Thess 5:3). In fact, as recently as 2 Cor 7:4 Paul has declared his own joy in the midst of all his affliction (cf. 6:10; 1 Thess 1:6). "Affliction" (θλῖψις *thlipsis*) has been a topic of considerable attention in chaps. 1–7, including his Asian crisis (1:4, 8); his anguish in writing the painful letter (2:4); human existence, with its outer nature wasting away (4:17); part of his hardship catalog (6:4); and the suffering that all believers share as they live in the world, whose structures have been marred by sin (1:4; cf. 1 Cor 7:31). Likewise, joy and rejoicing in the presence of grief and affliction lace together chaps. 1–9: Believers work to produce and are the source of joy for other believers (1:24; 2:3; 7:7, 9, 13, 16), and they share each other's joy (2:3; 7:13).

In 8:1-5 the Macedonian believers are cast as exemplars.[166] Despite their affliction (8:2), the Macedonians had responded to God's grace in kind—namely, in abundance and beyond their power. Their eagerness to be participants in the collection (8:4) sets up a distinct contrast with the yet to be noted reticence of the Corinthians (8:10-12; 9:3-5). Paul takes care to note that the Macedonians "sought" (αὐθαίρετοι *authairetoi*, "of their own free will," 8:3) partnership in the collection, a note paralleled in Paul's honoring the Corinthians' right of self-determination regarding the collection: "I say this not by command" (8:8).

The Macedonian response was beyond what Paul had hoped for (8:5; cf. a similar sentiment in Phlm 21). Paul describes this amazing reaction first with respect to the Lord and then to himself: "They gave themselves first to the Lord and, in accord with God's will, to us" (8:5). The Macedonians who "gave themselves . . . to the Lord and . . . to us" are already believers when the opportunity to participate in the collection is first presented to them. So the "giving of themselves to the Lord" is not a coming to the faith, but a zealous rededication of themselves in the light of the opportunity presented by the collection. Further, the associated "giving of themselves" to Paul is precisely what he has pleaded, obliquely and then directly, with the Corinthians to do more fully (6:12-13; 7:2-3). This little opening portrait of the Macedonians is

but the first of a series that Paul employs in 2 Corinthians 8–9 as he seeks to inspire the Corinthians not only to embrace him more fully but also to return to their earlier enthusiasm over the collection, which is now coming to fruition.

8:6. The first mention of Titus in chaps. 8–9 ties up the collection's imminent conclusion with its earlier beginning in Corinth (8:6). Here we learn what the Corinthians knew all along: Titus was the one who, as Paul's agent, had also encouraged them about the collection. Now Paul is sending him back to Corinth to finish and states it in a poignant way: Titus is to complete (ἐπιτελέω *epiteleō*, "bring to its conclusion or goal"), literally, "this grace" (τὴν χάριν ταύτην *tēn charin tautēn* 8:6). "This grace," a euphemism for the collection, can be brought to its goal by people because they, as recipients of grace, must share it with others and by so doing return it to God as grace-filled "thanks" (8:16; 9:15).

8:7. Paul's concluding appeal in this opening section lays out the issue that he will pursue in the rest of this chapter and in the next—namely, why and how the Corinthians can take part in the collection—and capitalizes on his understanding of the hallmark of the Corinthians: They are dedicated to, passionately committed to, "excelling." Their zeal for "excelling" has not always been considered a positive attribute by Paul; in fact, much of 1 Corinthians is devoted to countering their tendency to use nearly every occasion to see if they can one-up each other (e.g., who is wise, who has the freedom to eat what, who has which spiritual gift). Whether positive or not, "excelling" is a characteristic of the Corinthians as Paul understands them, and in 8:7 he attempts to turn it to positive ends: "Just as you excel in all things [with a positively stated list of examples following], so we want you to excel in this grace [the collection, understood]." So the stage for further appeal is set by praise of the Macedonians and their commitment to the collection and by Paul's praise of the Corinthians themselves. Note that the last of Paul's examples of their excelling in everything is "your love for us" (8:7 NIV) or "our love for you" (8:7 NRSV). Strong Greek MSS tradition exists for each translation. Sense in context argues for the former, in which case

---

166. See Betz, *2 Corinthians 8 and 9*, 49-53, for illuminating background on the relations between the Roman provinces of Achaia and Macedonia. For the Macedonians as an example, see page 48. See also Stowers, "*Peri men gar* and the Integrity of 2 Cor. 8 and 9," 346.

Paul would here be, like the earlier-noted Cynic choirmaster, pitching the note just a bit high so that the choir, in this case the Corinthians, whom he wishes were more affectionate toward him (6:11-12; 7:2-3), might come in on the right note.

REFLECTIONS

1. Paul is onto something: Believers do and give because they have been done unto and been given to (1 Cor 4:7; 2 Cor 5:14). As 1 John puts it so succinctly: We love because God first loved us (1 John 4:19; cf. John 13:34). Believers cannot fail to love, because love received prompts love in return.

2. In Paul's world, people did most of their learning by modeling after someone, whether it was in a trade, philosophy, sport, household management, moral reasoning, or whatever. As unsettling as the thought may be today, peer pressure often pushes our children to model themselves after other youngsters whose behavioral patterns leave much to be desired. We can dilate about how terrible that is, probably to little effect. Why not instead realize that we underuse exemplification as a way to enhance moral reflection, sieze the opportunity to become better models ourselves, and make public recognition of those whose actions and comportment set a good pattern for us all?

3. Paul's notion that we, recipients of God's grace, must pass it on, that we must finish the circle by redirecting it through us to someone else, is awesome. Think about what it says about human life in its daily routine: It says that every encounter with another person is an opportunity to be a channel of God's grace. In fact, not to think of grace that way is probably to cheat God and certainly to cheat others, because it arrogates grace to us as a sort of possession whose goal and end is us as individuals and not us as community. God's grace is not to be trifled with or to be taken lightly. It comes into the world, finding expression through people. Grace achieves its goal, it becomes the grace it was intended to be, only as it reaches ever more and more people. That is why the collection for the saints was not just an option that the Macedonians or the Achaians might choose to engage in; it was a joyful obligation (as Paul expressed it in Gal 2:10).

4. Paul's description of the Macedonians' giving heartily in the midst of affliction shows his understanding that the life of faith is not an escape. Neither does it hermetically seal us off from distress and difficulty. Grace and joy in the midst of affliction, far from being a sign of God's absence, are instead a sure sign of God's power.

2 Corinthians 8:8-15, No Command but Advice: Finish What You Began

COMMENTARY

8:8. Paul has to walk gingerly with the Corinthians as he tries not only to mend his relation with them but also to reinvigorate and inspire full participation in the collection, so he quickly clarifies that what he writes is not a command (8:8). The Corinthians should operate as fully out of their own free will as the Macedonians have done (8:3). But also like the Macedonians, whose abundant giving in tough times Paul described as a "test" (δοκιμή *dokimē*, 8:2), the Corinthians, through Paul's appeal to them, face a test of their own. What was only implicit in 8:1-7 becomes explicit in 8:8-15: Paul wants the Corinthians to test their own love by comparison with the zeal of the Macedonians (8:8). Paul considers himself and other believers who have been through affliction on behalf of the gospel as δόκιμος (*dokimos*, "tried and true," "approved by test," Rom 16:10; 1 Cor 11:19; cf. its opposite, ἀδόκιμος [*adokimos*, "disqualified"], 1 Cor 9:27). At the Lord's supper, believers examine (δοκιμάζω *dokimazō*), or test, themselves as to how they relate to the body of Christ (1 Cor 11:28-29). Self-assessment is an important and regular Pauline spiritual exercise.[167] Events and situations put individuals to the test as well, in Paul's view. Paul construes as a test what the Corinthians will do about the collection in the light of the Macedonian enthusiasm for it.

Paul leaves the outcome for the Corinthians to decide, but he readily gives his own opinion (γνώμη *gnōmē*), and as these Corinthians already know from one of his earlier letters, Paul thinks his *gnōmē* ought to have weight because of his trustworthiness (1 Cor 7:25).[168] Grace—and how it is responded to—like love, is best not commanded but left to the discretion of the person(s) involved (cf. Phlm 8-9). That is why Paul construes the Corinthian decision about this grace as their test.

8:9. As they face their test in this matter, Paul reminds them of the "big story" in its most cursory form, this time told in categories of wealth and poverty. In Philippians, the same story had been told in grander, probably traditional form by Paul, and there cast in terms of loftiness and humility. The Phil 2:5-11 hymn describes the exalted Christ, who humbled himself, took on the form of a slave, died, and was thereafter exalted once again by God. The story about grace in 2 Cor 8:9 is retrofitted into economic categories appropriate to the topic at hand: the collection. The Lord Jesus Christ, though rich, became poor for the sake of the Corinthians, in this telling of it, so that his poverty might be the occasion for them to become rich (cf. 6:10*b*). As the Corinthians face the test of their love and generosity toward others, Paul reminds them of the big story and of the very grace in which they stand. If they understand that the Lord's abundant grace makes them what they are and gives them all that they have, then how will they possibly be able to stifle grace's overflow or rebound from them to others? Once again in this letter fragment, Paul pulls out the weighty arguments to bolster his appeal to the Corinthians.

8:10-12. The Corinthians will not be surprised that Paul has practical suggestions for them. That is in his character; they have experienced it with him throughout their relationship (cf. 1 Cor 11:22; 14:26-31; 16:2). Accordingly, he first urges them to regain their original enthusiasm for the project (8:7). Paul further argues: Finish what a year ago you started with desire; finish it out of what you have (8:10-12). The latter note, twice sounded and once restated as "not out of what you do not have," shows Paul's careful insistence that he does not now expect them to be put under unreasonable pressure to come up with more funds than is proportionally fitting.

8:13-15. Expanding on this, Paul gives modern readers a window on his sense of fairness and equity in the sharing of goods and proper care among believers. Fairness, equality (ἰσότης *isotēs*, vv. 13-14) seems to be his guideline for an individual's contributions. The principle that "those who have abundance share with those in need" is significantly developed in a reciprocating fashion: The Corinthians' current abundance should meet others' need; others' abundance will meet the Corinthians' need.[169]

In 8:13-15 the ideal seems to be cast primarily in economic categories, but when the collection is treated in Romans where once again Paul addresses his deep conviction of the propriety of reciprocity between believers, he sets it up that "material blessings" are shared by the Gentile believers in appreciation of "spiritual blessings" that the Jewish believers have shared with them (Rom 15:27). Paul finds confirmation, or perhaps the ground for his counsel, in Exod 16:18, which functions here as a maxim: "The one with much did not have too much, and the one with little did not have too little" (8:15; the NIV adds the repeated note of "gathering" in an effort to reflect the exodus story from which the quote comes).

---

167. Sampley, *Walking Between the Times:*, 50-51.
168. See R. A. Ramsaran, *Liberating Words: Paul's Use of Rhetorical Maxims in* 1 Corinthians 1–10 (Valley Forge: Trinity, 1996) 66-68.

169. F. W. Danker, "Paul's Debt to the *De Corona* of Demosthenes: A Study of Rhetorical Techniques in Second Corinthians," in *Persuasive Artistry: Studies in New Testament Rhetoric in Honor of G. A. Kennedy,* ed. D. F. Watson, JSNTSup 50 (Sheffield: Sheffield Academic, 1991) 269-70, identifies this as Paul's emphatic appropriation of the "Hellenic reciprocity structure," but sees it lying behind much of 2 Corinthians 1–7 as well— there between Paul and the Corinthians. For a reading of the collection as strictly "economic mutualism," see J. J. Meggitt, *Paul, Poverty and Survival* (Edinburgh: T. & T. Clark, 1998) 158-61.

REFLECTIONS

1. Reciprocity and care among believers are givens for Paul. Whether it has to do with possessions, as here, or with thoughtfulness about others, as in other places (cf. 1 Corinthians 8), believers are to look after one another. We might readily embrace those sentiments and think that when we have "something extra" we will share it with those less endowed. If we wait to share until we find ourselves with surplus, we may never share because we have been subtly acculturated to think we never have enough. In the process, we readily lose sight of how much is genuinely ample—and accordingly we are sometimes blind as to how much we really have to share. Furthermore, our sharing does not have to be solely or even primarily relegated to our goods or possessions; our time, though we may also feel overdrawn there, is often the dearest giving of ourselves.

2. One church's members decided that, beyond their regular annual financial pledge, they would give to the church's local and international mission budget an additional 10 percent of whatever funds serendipitously happened into their lives. If they found a dollar, they would turn over ten cents of it the next Sunday. If someone paid an old debt that the original lenders had, in effect, written off and expected never to see again, then they would give a tenth of that toward missions. Life is so full of abundance that pops up in our lives in the most unexpected ways. Why not celebrate that by sharing it with persons in need at home and around the world? If nothing else, you and your family might try keeping tabs on that kind of serendipity for a month and see what 10 percent of that figure would be.

3. Paul thinks that believers are rich simply because God, to whom everything belongs, has deigned to share all things with believers (1 Cor 3:21*b*-23). From that assumption Paul derives a powerful critique of the social and cultural values of his and our times. Paul's is a way of asking what is most important, what really counts, and what really matters. The identity of true richness is worthy of reflection. Jesus' parables touched on that issue in various ways (cf. Luke 12:13-21; 14:15-24; 16:19-31).

2 Corinthians 8:16-24, Titus and Others as Warrantors of Probity

COMMENTARY

In an echo of 8:1, Paul opens 8:16 with the claim that the same God whose grace was "given" (δεδομένην *dedomenēn*, 8:1) to the Macedonian churches is the God who "gives [διδόντι *didonti*] the same zeal for you into Titus's heart." Thus Paul ties the Macedonian believers and Titus together with one another and with the Corinthians; and he subtly ties himself with Titus with the claim of "the same zeal," signifying that Titus's zeal for the Corinthians rises to Paul's level.

Commendatory assertions about Titus open and close 8:16-24. Titus, as we have seen, effects a strong, durative connection for Paul with the Corinthians. In fact, Paul

identifies Titus as his own "partner and fellow worker to you" (8:23), a description that will come as no surprise to the Corinthians. Titus, offered as a model for the Corinthians, accepted Paul's appeal, like the Macedonians of his own free will (8:3, 17), and is going to the Corinthians. So, just as Paul has not commanded the Corinthians about the collection (8:8), so also he appeals that Titus devote himself to finishing up this offering. Like Titus, the Corinthians can now accept Paul's appeal and freely embrace participation in the collection.

In this letter fragment, Paul's earlier, repeated sensitivity to possible charges and innuendos that would challenge his integrity (1:12; 2:17; 4:2; 5:11; 6:3; 7:2) provides the background against which to read the series of steps he has taken with the collection to eliminate or at least reduce any chance of accusations of fraud. Paul sends two people for whom he uses the denominator "brother" (ἀδελφός adelphos), his standard way of referring to believers (8:18, 22). Their identities are or will be clear to the Corinthians, but escape modern readers. Reference to one of them, probably the second, will be made in Paul's next letter to the Corinthians (2 Cor 12:18), but nothing there resolves our question of his identity.

The first "brother" is a high-profile person whose fame in the gospel had spread "through all the churches" and who was elected by a show of hands (χειροτονέω cheirotoneō) to be a traveling companion of Paul and the others "in this grace which is being administered by us." This has a dual purpose: for the glory of the Lord and for our "goodwill" (προθυμία prothymia, 8:19). This very respected person, therefore, was handpicked to be the representative of the very churches whose collection was being sent along to Jerusalem via Corinth. Note also that honoring the glory of the Lord precedes any stated concern for securing Paul's reputation.

Between the portrait of the first "brother" and the second, Paul explicitly declares his purpose and standard of care: He seeks to avoid anyone's finding fault with his administration of this lavish gift, and, paraphrasing Prov 3:4 LXX, affirms that he has regard for, "takes into consideration" (προνοέω pronoeō), the good, the "honorable" (καλός kalos), "not only before the Lord but also before people" (8:20-21; cf. Phil 4:8). Note once again that the Lord's assessment is given pride of place over what people think.

The second "brother" is one with whom Paul apparently has quite a history because he says of him, "We have tested him in many ways and many times, finding him zealous." But he is now even more zealous "because of his great confidence in you [the Corinthians]" (8:22). So one brother has special connections with the Macedonian churches and is sent as their representative, and the other one has special connections with Paul—and apparently also with the Corinthians. Both will be traveling with Titus and are dubbed by Paul "representatives of the churches [ἀπόστολοι ἐκκλησιῶν apostoloi ekklēsiōn], the glory of Christ" (8:23).

The section closes (οὖν oun, "therefore") with Paul's challenge to the Corinthians to "give proof" (ἔνδειξις endeixis) before those very churches that are so positively represented in the various persons who make up this delegation, of "your love and our boast about you" (8:24).[170] Paul's "boast" about the Corinthians plays quite a role in this letter: (1) It has spurred the Macedonians to emulate the Corinthians by taking part in the collection (9:2), and (2) Paul's boast about the Corinthians has proved true when Titus sees that the Corinthians are indeed moved to a reaffirmation of Paul by his "painful" letter (7:14).

With the single exception of Paul's identification of Titus as "my partner" (8:23), Paul has used the plural throughout this passage. By using the plural so pervasively, Paul casts as completely aligned and associated with him and with his collection the Macedonian churches, their unnamed representative, Paul's unnamed representative, and Titus. All of them are equally and fully dedicated to seeing the collection through Corinth to Jerusalem. With this resounding portrait of unanimity, Paul is free to turn his attention—and theirs—to the projected arrival of this entourage in Corinth (9:1-5).

---

170. Stowers rightly says that "8:24 is the central exhortation toward which Paul's discourse moves." See Stowers, "*Peri men gar* and the Integrity of 2 Corinthians 8 and 9," 346.

REFLECTIONS

1. The term σπουδή (*spoudē*), which means "zeal/eagerness/earnestness/diligence" (8:16; "concern," NIV) has played quite a role not only here, but elsewhere in 2 Corinthians as well (e.g., 7:11-12; 8:7-8). It is a term Paul uses to describe what he considers proper commitment to something or to someone. *Spoudē* allows no mediocrity or distance, but instead betokens obligation and passion. Thus it fleshes out love so that love's ever-passionate commitment is expressed (note Paul's call for a demonstration of the Corinthians' love in 8:24). In a fashion quite alien to Paul, aloofness and distance, sometimes even a turning in to oneself and one's own interests, are viewed positively in today's culture (cf. Rev 3:15-16).

2. A transaction, a use of personal funds now collected, is viewed as an occasion to glorify the Lord (8:19). The way we allocate our funds every week and every month is a moral statement. Our budgets, whether we actually record them or not, are moral ledgers that depict where our values are. A family could have quite a discussion over where this week's or month's funds are actually going and why.

3. Our patterns of doing and spending are maps of our value systems. At a certain level we know that, because we casually talk about how we "spend" our time. We have only so much time and finite financial resources. Our lives can drift into a style where what appears most pressing at the moment determines what we do. This is to be outer-directed; what is out there (to be done) dictates the organization of our lives. We may even go on to what amounts to autopilot, not even thinking about why we are doing what we do. As with our time, so with our financial assets: Our allocation of each is a logbook of our values put into deeds. Paul's self-analysis on this count is found in 8:21, where he has regard for or takes into consideration the "good/honorable" in all that he does. What a wake-up call it might be for us if we screened our financial and temporal choices—even the smallest of them—for whether they aim for the good and the honorable!

2 Corinthians 9:1-5, Steps to Ensure That the Corinthians Are Ready

COMMENTARY

Moving now predominantly to the singular,[171] Paul puts his relationship to the Corinthians directly into the middle of the picture. As the text shows, he acknowledges just how much *he* has at stake in the Corinthian response. Paul has boasted to the Macedonians about the Corinthians (here the syncresis, or comparison, uses the Corinthians as the model for the Macedonians; cf. 8:1-5), saying that they have been ready since the past year, exactly the time frame he reflected in 8:10. Paul's sending the "brothers" (the two unnamed men and Titus, 8:16-24) as a sort of advance guard is his way of attempting to ensure that the so far recalcitrant Corinthians are prepared by the time Paul (later) arrives in Corinth (9:3).

Paul paints for the Corinthians a worst-case scenario: Imagine some Macedonians coming along with Paul and discovering the Corinthians not ready. Paul, resorting to the plural for just one verb, perhaps because the potential for shame is so overwhelming and pervasive, carries the scenario along: "We ourselves would be humiliated, not to mention you, in this situation" (9:4). In a culture so dominated by shame and honor as is the Roman one of which Paul and his communities are a part,[172] this public humiliation would be devastating—and Paul rightly observes that the shame would be theirs as well as his.

Reverting to the singular again, Paul dwells on his sending of these brothers to "arrange in advance" (προκαταρτίζω *prokatartizō*) what the Corinthians had "promised in advance" (προεπαγγέλλω *proepangellō*, 9:5). Paul acknowledges the range within which

171. Stowers concludes that it is "most implausible to think of chapters 8 and 9 as fragments of two letters." See Stowers, *"Peri men gar* and the Integrity of 2 Corinthians 8 and 9," 348.

172. Stowers, *"Peri men gar* and the Integrity of 2 Corinthians 8 and 9," 347; and S. K. Stowers, *Letter Writing in Greco-Roman Antiquity* (Philadelphia: Westminster, 1986) 27-28, 77-78, 91-94.

the Corinthian response must ultimately fall: From what he most hopes—namely, the "generous gift" produced willingly out of much bounty (εὐλογία *eulogia*)—to its opposite, and what Paul fervently hopes to avoid—namely, "as grudgingly granted" (ὡς πλεονεξίαν *hōs pleonexian*). Paul's rhetoric throughout 2 Corinthians 8–9 is designed to move the Corinthians away from the latter and toward the former.

REFLECTIONS

1. Modeling as ethical instruction and as exhortation is a rich tool that Paul regularly used and that we are far too reticent to employ. Consistent performance and dependability (also known as trustworthiness) are at the heart of any generation's most admired characteristics, but it is easy to discount their importance when it is more convenient for us to do otherwise. There is an infectious quality in failing to keep one's word; when one person defiles the currency of dependability, others also tend to lower the bar on trustworthiness. On the other side, there is a positive infectiousness of faith and zeal.

2. Giving and being responsive to others are best when they flow willingly and not grudgingly. We may wonder how we who are *obliged* to give have any room to talk about giving freely and willingly. If we start with the obligation, we will never understand the freedom. If we begin, instead, with the celebration of what and how much God has done for us and given to us, then the zeal for giving and for responding to others flows freely from it (cf. Luke 12:48; 1 John 4:19).

2 Corinthians 9:6-15, Sowing and Reaping Bountifully

COMMENTARY

9:6-7. Paul, lover of metaphors, expands upon the alternatives with which 9:5 closes— "generous gift" generated out of bounty versus greed, avarice, "grudgingly granted"— and develops his thoughts around the motif of sowing and reaping. His first step is to place the responsibility directly upon each Corinthian. In so doing, he expands his earlier disclaimer that he is not commanding them what to do (8:8) and that the Corinthians need, like the Macedonians and like Titus, to take part in the collection by their own free will (8:3). Laconically, Paul provides three guidelines: (1) "each just as he has decided in his heart," (2) "not reluctantly nor out of necessity," and (3), embracing what Prov 22:8 LXX says as true: "God loves a cheerful/gracious giver" (9:7). Because the claim about God's love is so directly interlaced with personal dispositions, we can conclude that Paul's moral reasoning does not spring simply from internal feelings, reckonings, and calculations. The decisions that are properly lodged in the heart, freely and positively embraced, are nevertheless incited, framed, and defined by God's love.

9:8. This verse has the ring of a finely hewed commonplace that captures much that is important in Paul's reckoning. The sentence has three moments. First is the declaration of a fundamental truth about God: God is able to multiply/increase in abundance (περισσεύω *perissuō*) every grace unto you (9:8*a*). The second moment describes how that divinely inspired abundance affects daily life: "so that you may have *all* sufficiency in *all* things, in *all* time" (9:8*b*, italics added). The rhetorically reinforcing wordplay on "all" in the text (ἐν παντὶ πάντοτε πᾶσαν *en panti pantote pasan*) powerfully elaborates the "abundance" grounded in God's grace as mentioned in 9:8*a* and anticipates a final "all" statement in 9:8*c*. The third moment (9:8*c*) explicitly echoes the "abundance" of the first moment (9:8*a*) and builds from the "so that" (purpose) statement of the second moment

(9:8*b*): "so that you may abound in every [πᾶν *pan*, "all"] good work." Implicit in the distillation of the believer's ethical ground in 9:8 is Paul's assumption that good works are not an option for believers, but a necessity. Believers are free to determine *what* form the good works take, what shape love takes (cf. Phlm 8-14), but they are not free *not* to love; they are not free *not* to do good works. These assumptions emerged already when Paul reminded the Corinthians that "it is necessary for all of us to appear before the tribune of Christ so that each person may receive a recompense for the things done in the body, whether good or bad" (2 Cor 5:10). Believers must do good works. The good works are generated by God's grace, bountifully poured out upon believers.

9:9. Taking an image from one of the psalms and employing the image of God as sower, Paul offers confirmation for his understanding of God as the initiator of grace: God "scatters abroad, he gives to the needy" (9:9; cf. Ps 111:9 LXX). The remainder of the psalm text identifies what is scattered or sown as God's "righteousness/justice" (δικαιοσύνη *dikaiosynē*, which "remains for ever").

9:10. With echoes from Isa 55:10 and Hos 10:12 lending weight to his counsel, Paul elaborates some implications of God's being the source of grace and abundance. God, the understood but unstated subject, who provides "seed to the sower and bread for food" (Isa 55:10 NRSV), "will supply and multiply your store of seed" and "will increase your 'harvest of righteousness'" (Hos 10:12 NRSV). Divinely produced abundance cascades through these rich phrases and clauses, reminding the Corinthians not only of the source of life but also of its bounty with its attendant responsibility to do the aforementioned good work (9:8), which could also be identified as the "righteousness/justice" that Paul, quoting Psalm 111:1, expects (9:9). Grace once received obligates the recipient to the pursuit of justice. In the instance at hand, Paul links taking part in the collection with proper pursuit of righteousness and justice just as he has earlier tied believers' reconciliation to God in Christ with the righteousness/justice that comes from God (2 Cor 5:21).

9:11-15. In the verses that remain about the collection (9:11-15), Paul adopts the plural and thus associates himself with all those who have readily committed to the collection so far, and he looks foward to the immediate future, projecting what he hopes will happen with and through the Corinthians. Because Paul is confident in his knowledge of God, he assures the Corinthians that this God of abundance will enrich them in every generosity, which will bring about "through us" thanksgiving to God (9:11). Widely in the Pauline corpus, the proper and fundamental response to God is quintessentially expressed as resulting in "thanksgiving to God" (cf. Rom 1:21; 1 Cor 14:16; Phil 4:6; Phlm 4). Already in 2 Cor 4:15 Paul has laid the grounds for understanding thanksgiving as the ultimate outcome of God's grace expressed in the lives of people. As God's grace reaches out to more and more people, more and more will respond in thanksgiving to God. Here, in 9:11, Paul recapitulates the same conviction and suggests that if the Corinthians devote their abundance to the collection, then thanksgiving will be generated "through us." Immediately, he expands the frame of reference (9:12): At stake is not merely the saints in Jerusalem and the meeting of their needs, though that is a proper goal, but who knows how many more people may be affected and join in thanksgiving to God?

Throughout these closing verses, Paul is direct about what participation will mean *for the Corinthians.* They will "reap bountifully" if they sow accordingly (9:6 NRSV). God will give them plenty for sowing and will increase their harvest (of righteousness, 9:10). Paul assures them that they will be "enriched in every way" by God for their "generosity/liberality" (ἁπλότης *haplotēs*, 9:11). And not insignificant in Pauline communities, they will be adding to the thanksgivings to God (9:12).

Paul presents it to them as a "testing" (δοκιμή *dokimē*), returning in an inclusio to the testing that the Macedonians faced and passed by their hearty and exemplary participation in the collection (9:13; see also 8:2; cf. 2:9). In between the 8:2 and 9:13 mentions of testing, Paul has explicitly told the Corinthians: "I am testing the genuineness of your own love as compared with the zeal of the others" (8:8).

In 5:14-21 Paul developed the understanding of his ministry as one of reconciliation. There he used the plural, "our ministry." Now, as he concludes his discussion of the collection and his profound hope that the Corinthians will indeed join in it, he twice again (9:12-13) uses the term διακονία (*diakonia*, "ministry/ service") to describe the collection and by so doing invites the Corinthians to make his *diakonia* their own, to identify with it as a ministry of reconciliation (echoing 5:19-20), of uniting them as God's people in Christ, whether Jews or Gentiles. That is why he can conclude his arguments for their participation with a grand portrayal: By taking part in "this ministry" they will be glorifying God (remember all the earlier reflections about glory, 3:7-18) by showing "obedience to your confession of the gospel of Christ" and by "your sharing of your liberality with" the poor in Jerusalem "and with all others" (9:13).

With the last note, Paul places their sharing in the context of the obedience ingredient to their confession, and the sharing is not just with the Jerusalem saints but, like the ministry of reconciliation, is devoted to "all others" because Christ died for all (5:14). So the collection is a special appeal for a *particular* expression of the ministry of reconciliation, but it is only one part of the sharing, caring for others, that is incumbent on persons claimed by the gospel of Jesus Christ, no matter how much or how little they have to contribute. Once again, Paul assumes that the very ones who benefit from the Corinthian generosity will find themselves "longing for" and "praying for you" (9:14)—a hint at the same reciprocity that he expresses so clearly about the collection in Rom 15:27: "If the Gentiles have come to share in their spiritual blessings, they ought also to be of service to them in material things" (NRSV). The prayers and longings of others for the Corinthians are activated by the "surpassing grace of God,"

which is the groundspring of all of faithful life and certainly of faith's generosity.

It is not surprising that Paul's two-chapter appeal about the collection, which began with the defining note of "grace," rises to its conclusion by crediting God's grace as infusing all of life with generosity, with longing, and with prayers one for another. Moved by this grace and its powerful working through the lives of people everywhere, Paul closes with this theme, reworked into a sort of blessing (see the Commentary on 1:3): "Grace be to God for God's indescribable gift" (9:15). Most translations rightly put that as "Thanks be to God" (cf. 8:16 for the same Greek construction).

Grace *from* God comes as a gift. God's grace prompts grace in and among people, and that grace returns to God in the form of thanks. Second Corinthians 8–9 is a case study of all three aspects and of the power of grace. By his formulation of 9:15, Paul has almost redundantly emphasized the "giftiness" of life before God. "Grace" connotes God's free gift, freely given to those whom Paul makes clear in other places do not deserve it (cf. Rom 3:23). But Paul paints God's grace as an "indescribable gift" (ἀνεκδιηγήτῳ δωρεά *anekdiēgētō dōrea*). In doxological form, then, Paul twice highlights the gift quality of life (*charis* and *dōrea*).

With that, the text breaks off. We cannot be certain of how the letter actually concluded. Chapters 10–13 clearly have a startlingly different tone and are part of a distinct subsequent letter (see the Introduction). Subsequent to Paul's time, whoever put these letter fragments together must have edited away the concluding section of the letter that is otherwise complete in 2 Corinthians 1–9. We can only surmise that, given the sublime tone achieved at the end of chapter 9, the rest of the letter would have been collegial and warm.

REFLECTIONS

1. If we think about how hard we worked to arrive where we are, we are likely to become stingy, because there is something innately programmed into us to have us think either that by our hard work we deserve what we have or that we have been shortchanged and do not have enough. If, on the other hand, we think about how many doors have been opened to us, about how we have gotten where we are by the way things have surprisingly opened to or "broken for" us (by God's grace and by the working of the Spirit), then we are more likely to think more generously. No doubt some truth resides on both sides of those arguments. The issue is how we keep perspective. Paul may help us here. God graces. God sows. We do not deserve God's favor, but we receive it. Such beneficence, especially when we know we do not deserve it, takes away some of our control of our lives and places us in a response mode. Grace received demands a response. The grace that comes from God finds its fruition as it flows through us to others.

2. Building on the previous point, God's grace, received by us and expressed through us to another, does not stop in the other, the one to whom we show it. Curiously, that grace binds us to that other person and produces a ready-made chorus of two who should be able to sing quite a song of thanksgiving to God. God's grace cascades and overflows so powerfully that the singing duo will be heard by more—and the circle expands.

3. Giving must not be marked by the slightest degree of reluctance because then it is not freely given. Giving is a delicate transaction. If you put even the tiniest little string on the gift, then it is not truly a gift.

4. How is it that we harvest righteousness/justice (9:10) when we sow and give? We may suppose that Paul, thoroughly consonant with his Jewish heritage, considers caring for those who are in need and giving to those who have less is performing covenant righteousness/justice. In the *shalom*/peace of God, no one can be left out or left behind. To bring them along and to assist them from the abundance of what we have is to keep covenant with God.

5. Following Luther, we tend to affirm the priesthood of all believers, meaning that all of us actually share in ministry. Paul anticipates that outlook when he pictures the Corinthians as taking part in his ministry (9:13). Our giving or not giving out of our abundance, even if those pockets of abundance seem frightfully small to us at times, is a test—of our responsiveness to God's sowing and scattering among us.

2 CORINTHIANS 10:1–13:13

PAUL'S PREPARATION FOR A SHOWDOWN VISIT

OVERVIEW

The remaining chapters of 2 Corinthians (chaps. 10–13) are part of a distinct letter fragment that was written some time after 2 Corinthians 1–9 (see the Introduction). Paul's relationship to the Corinthians has suffered some recent changes, none of which have been beneficial.

First, Corinthian opposition to Paul has broken virulently into the open. As 2 Corinthians shows, subsequent to the time of his writing 1 Corinthians, Paul's relations with the Corinthians have resembled a roller-coaster ride. Before writing 2 Corinthians 1–9, Paul had been offended when the Corinthian believers did not rally to his side after one of their own had done him "wrong." Paul took that as a defection from his authority and an alienation of affection, so he canceled a promised visit and instead wrote them a painful letter of frank speech, calling them to task. As chaps. 1–9 show, Paul understands that, in response to his painful letter, the Corinthians have come about, punished the offender, and rallied to him once more.

Second, of critical importance, outsiders have now intruded into Paul's ongoing problems with the Corinthians. Already when 2 Corinthians 1–9 was written, these persons from outside, accompanied by letters of recommendation, had made contact with members of the Corinthian congregation, but Paul apparently did not then perceive them to be the substantial threat they came to be (3:1-3). We do not know much about these people because Paul follows the canons of his time by which one does not honor opponents with much delineation. Also, we cannot know who might have written the commendatory letters sponsoring the outsiders. We can know how Paul characterizes the intruders; three times

he calls them "apostles" (ἀπόστολοι *apostoloi*), a term that may describe persons who are sent as ambassadors, delegates, or messengers (cf. 8:23; Phil 2:25); but the title does not necessarily indicate that the intruders were among Jesus' earlier disciples. Twice Paul calls them "superapostles" (ὑπερλίαν ἀπόστολοι *hyperlian apostoloi*, 11:5; 12:11). Once he says such persons are "false apostles" (ψευδαπόστολοι *pseudapostoloi*, 11:13). In almost every paragraph of this letter fragment, the opponents' presence is palpable—either in some assertion they have made or in some comparison.

As Paul has indicated throughout 2 Corinthians 1–9, comportment can be a revelatory window on one's true identity. Accordingly, Paul's florid, and perhaps exaggerated, characterization of the outsiders' behavior is designed to show their true colors. Nothing in Paul's claims about them can confidently be taken as an undistorted portrait. Methodologically, we should suppose that, wherever possible, details about them are slanted to make them stand in the worst possible light.[173]

To put it most directly, the heart of the matter is that the outsiders challenge Paul's authority by wanting to be put on a par with him. Further, the outsiders, like Paul, presume that they have rights to support for their preaching of the gospel (cf. 1 Cor 9:4-12), but they, unlike Paul, apparently accept assistance (11:20; 12:13). Paul's most scathing attack centers on the outsiders' "taking advantage" of the Corinthians (11:20); they are said to enslave, devour, take on airs, and

---

173. Paul follows the conventions of his time in this regard. See Sampley, "Paul, His Opponents in 2 Corinthians 10–13, and the Rhetorical Handbooks," 169-71.

even beat the Corinthians in the face (11:20-21)—surely rhetorical hyperbole. At every point, Paul bids to benefit by the comparison.

Third, Paul's fiscal practices, already somewhat problematic for the Corinthians, have emerged as a point of sharp contention between Paul and different groups at Corinth. Although Paul asserts that, as an apostle, he could have demanded support from the Corinthians, he assiduously and persistently avoided doing so (1 Cor 9:3-18; 2 Cor 11:9, 20-21a; 12:13-16). Paul has claimed to preach the gospel "free of charge" (2 Cor 11:7). Some at Corinth apparently think Paul is "robbing churches" because he accepts personal support from other churches, expressly from the Macedonians, precisely while he is in Corinth refusing assistance from the Corinthians—a surefire way to have questions raised by the locals (2 Cor 11:8-9). Some others at Corinth, the wealthy who were accustomed to use their wealth and its status as leverage inside the believing community (cf. 1 Cor 6:1-6; 11:21-22, 33-34), apparently think Paul treats the Corinthians as second-class believers when he refuses to accept their support (2 Cor 12:13). In a culture so vertically structured along patron/client lines as the Greco-Roman world, persons who offer gifts and support bid to be patrons; the recipients, by accepting the beneficence, become clients and are accordingly obliged to honor and laud the patrons.[174] Given those strictures and liabilities, Paul's refusal to accept gifts or support from the Corinthians, especially from the wealthy ones with whom he has had some special problems in the past, is understandable *from Paul's standpoint;* but from the Corinthians' perspective, sharing the culture's view as they do, Paul's refusal to accept a gift and support constitutes a shameful rebuke.[175]

The contrast with Paul's treatment of the Macedonians is palpable: Paul freely accepts support from them, while he is *at Corinth.* How can that be? On the level of interpersonal relationships, doing so has to be the utmost folly because it is virtually guaranteed to ruffle Corinthian sensibilities, though in fairness Paul appears to have no control over when and where the Philippians send him support (Phil 4:10).[176] Paul acknowledges explicitly that his relation to the Philippians, one of the Macedonian churches, is unique, though such an explanation could only fuel Corinthian fires. In his letter to the Philippians, Paul declares that, from the very beginning of his preaching of the gospel to them, he entered into a partnership with them, which he describes in terms of "giving and receiving" (Phil 1:5; 4:15).[177]

Paul's continued advocacy of the collection for the saints in Jerusalem contributes to the problem because the Corinthians flagged in their zeal for participating; yet in 2 Corinthians 8–9 Paul presses them to see it through. In order to avert any last-minute difficulties or criticisms of his handling of the funds generated for the collection by the different churches, Paul arranges for the churches to appoint a representative and adds his own proxies (8:18-23).

Fourth, Paul's relation to the Corinthians, as reflected in the letter fragment 2 Corinthians 10–13, has now clearly become one of contention. The whole document, therefore, must be read in the light of the contemporary conventions for resolving disputes. The full scope of the contention does not become apparent at first. Surely by 13:1-10, however, one can see that Paul anticipates a showdown visit, gives stern warning of his intentions, and makes one last effort to avert a direct, personal confrontation. All of the sections of this letter fragment must be read in that disputatious light. The rhetorical handbooks of Paul's time are the codification of lore and practice regarding how best to make one's case, how to put one's opponents at disadvantage, and how to put the best face on whatever the circumstance. The handbooks were the basic tools of education in antiquity, and Paul shows himself fully aware of the advice and counsel they give.[178]

174. See G. W. Peterman, *Paul's Gift from Philippi: Conventions of Gift-Exchange and Christian Giving* (Cambridge: Cambridge University Press, 1997) 51-89.

175. Peter Marshall, *Enmity in Corinth: Social Conventions in Paul's Relations with the Corinthians,* WUNT44 (Tübingen: J. C. B. Mohr, 1987) 242-47.

176. Twice they sent him help in Thessalonica (Phil 4:16) and the incident of support that in part occasions the writing of the Letter to the Philippians was one that seems to have come unexpectedly (Phil 4:10).

177. J. Paul Sampley, *Pauline Partnership in Christ: Christian Community and Commitment in Light of Roman Law* (Philadelphia: Fortress, 1980) 53-55. Peterman, *Paul's Gift from Philippi,* 55-65, rightly increases the scope to include friendship and social reciprocity.

178. Sampley, "Paul, His Opponents in 2 Corinthians 10–13, and the Rhetorical Handbooks," 162-77.

In a dispute, the handbooks advise that the orator, or in this case the letter writer whose letters become speech when read to recipients, can win goodwill for his case by referring to himself, to his hearers, and to the facts of the case.[179] Paul's rhetorical situation is slightly different from what the handbooks suppose because the people to be persuaded are themselves involved in the case as the auditors of his letter. But the same dynamic remains: Paul needs to make his understanding of the case convincing.

Though we cannot be certain of the outcome of the showdown visit Paul projects in 2 Corinthians 10–13, we can cite several indicators that suggest he likely had success in reclaiming the Corinthians in that encounter: (1) The letter fragment 2 Corinthians 10–13 was preserved; (2) the Achaians (and therefore quite possibly the Corinthians) took part in the collection for the saints in Jerusalem (Rom 15:26); (3) Paul wrote the Letter to the Romans, a subsequent letter, from Corinth, where Gaius, one of Paul's first converts there (see 1 Cor 1:14), is host to Paul "and to the whole church" (Rom 16:23); (4) he sends the Romans greetings from Erastus, Corinth's treasurer (Rom 16:23); and (5) Clement, the second century bishop of Rome, continues to identify the Corinthian church with Paul.[180]

For Paul to have overcome his latest struggle with the Corinthians (as reflected in 2 Corinthians 10–13), he must have had an unfaltering contingent, a dependable and loyal core of believers who stood by him in the hard times at Corinth. We may guess that among those are persons in positions of leadership, such as Gaius (Rom 16:23; 1 Cor 1:14), Stephanas, Fortunatus, and Achaicus (1 Cor 16:15-17). Also possibly instrumental in encouraging fidelity to Paul could be Chloe and her people (1 Cor 1:11)—whether she was a Corinthian or not, Paul's positive mention of her without further identification indicates that she was influential at Corinth— and Phoebe. Phoebe's is perhaps the most interesting case, perhaps partly because we do not know much about her, but what we do know suggests a *much* larger picture of her association and work with Paul. She is from Cenchreae, a town near Corinth, she is a deacon in her local church (Rom 16:1), and surely she is to be counted among those to whom chaps. 1–9 are addressed ("with all the saints in the whole of Achaia," the Roman province where Corinth and Cenchreae are located; 1:1). Paul's description of her in his commendation to the Romans shows that she has been a partner, or more precisely a patron, of him and of many (we may suppose) believers. That she goes to Rome after the writing of 2 Corinthians 10–13, possibly carrying the letter to believers in the proud city of Rome and surely representing Paul, shows that she is a formidable force in her own right. Such a person cannot have played a small role in Paul's successes with the Corinthians, and, though we will never be able to know, she may have been significant in what seems to have been a positive outcome from the final struggle between Paul and the Corinthians (chaps. 10–13).

Paul had another important asset in his relations with the Corinthians: His agents who double for him. Titus and Timothy maintained good connections with the Corinthians across the years—in the commentary we see several occasions on which their relation to the Corinthians may have been stronger than Paul's—and we never see any hint that either Timothy or Titus weakened in his affection and devotion for Paul. Finally, who knows what impact the Macedonians and their fervor for Paul and his mission might have had on the Corinthians?

179. Cicero *On Invention* 1.16.22.
180. See *1 Clem* 47.3.

2 CORINTHIANS 10:1-6, PAUL'S READINESS TO DO BATTLE

COMMENTARY

We cannot tell what or how much of the letter has been lost prior to 10:1. As it stands, this letter fragment opens with an appeal, a feature that sometimes occurs at the later stages in Paul's letters (Rom 12:1; Phil 4:2; 1 Thess 4:1; Phlm 9-10; cf. 1 Cor 1:10). Two factors must be kept in mind throughout chaps. 10–13: (1) Paul is distressed that (some of) the Corinthians have been seduced into fealty to rivals who have infiltrated the believing community, and (2) he is anticipating a showdown visit.

10:1-2. Paul's entreaty to the Corinthians is referenced to Christ's "gentleness/humility" (πραύτης *prautēs*) and "clemency" (ἐπιείχεια *epieikeia*). Christ, in these characteristics, is the model Paul prefers to follow as he anticipates the showdown that will happen with the Corinthians when he makes his projected third visit (13:1, 10)—a confrontation that can be avoided if they change their ways.

Paul's two terms regarding Christ reinforce each other because their semantic fields overlap. Both suggest gentleness, with the former ranging to humility and considerateness toward others and the latter compassing graciousness, clemency, and a disposition to mercy. It is not accidental that, as he anticipates a visit to the Corinthians, Paul uses the very same term he had used earlier when he had projected a visit to the Corinthians, and there also hoped for an alteration of their disposition (1 Cor 4:21). There as here, Paul hopes that the Corinthians will change and become more as he wishes them to be. The earlier alternatives—Paul will come to them with a rod, meaning ready to punish them if they have not modified their behavior, or "in love with a spirit of clemency" (*epieikeia*, 1 Cor 4:21)—are echoed in 2 Cor 10:6. In Galatians, Paul suggests that believers, governed by the Spirit, should always be ready to respond to those who have gone astray by "restoring" them "in a spirit of gentleness"

(*prautēs*, Gal 6:1). In 2 Cor 10:1, Paul practices what he preached to the Galatians.

The Corinthians have the choice of which "Paul" will come to them, whether the one who, like Christ, comes with gentleness and clemency or the one who, like the rod-bearing disciplinarian (1 Cor 4:21) or, as he puts it even more forcefully in 2 Cor 10:2-6, the bold, confident one who, with divine power, destroys all strongholds. If he does not come to them modeling Christ's gentleness and clemency, then he will come as a skilled warrior armed with God's power to wreak devastation on any resistance and obstacle that may be raised against him.

Such a detailed development of the military motif[181] as that in 10:3-6 suggests his underlying assumption that matters with the Corinthians have degenerated so far that a showdown is not likely to be averted. Nevertheless, he "appeals" (παρακαλῶ *parakalō*, 10:1) and "begs" (δέομαι *deomai*, 10:2; effectively doubled for emphasis) them to alter their behavior so that he will not have to use against *them* the arsenal at his disposal (2 Cor 10:1-2). To make certain that the Corinthians are not misled by any mistaken estimates of him, Paul urges them not to gamble on his being "timid/humble/pliant" (ταπεινός *tapeinos*)—as some may well have been suggesting about him (10:1)—when he comes to them.[182]

Paul's behavior surfaced as an abiding topic in 2 Corinthians 1–9, though most of those references functioned as certifications that he is, indeed, a person of high moral character who regularly seeks the advantage of those around him. Now in 2 Corinthians 10–13, however, the references to behavior, though about as frequent, function somewhat differently. Here, the comments about

181. A. J. Malherbe, "Antisthenes and Odysseus, and Paul at War," *HTR* 76 (1983) 143-73.

182. Malherbe, "Antisthenes and Odysseus, and Paul at War," 168-69, argues that the link between ταπεινός (*tapeinos*) in 10:1 and Paul's boldness/confidence is to be understood "in light of the Cynic descriptions of the philosopher's dress as the armament of the gods."

comportment demarcate between Paul and the outsiders, with the latter suggesting that they work on the same terms as Paul and with Paul taking umbrage at any such comparison (cf. 11:12-15).

10:3-6. Verse 3 is crucial for Paul's making certain that the Corinthians understand him. He distinguishes between his comporting himself "in the flesh"—that is, in the world—from the way he is now prepared to wage war: "not according to the flesh"—that is, not in a worldly fashion. Paul's opponents, whether inside the community or outside or both, should understand that "we comport ourselves [περιπατέω *peripateō*, figuratively "walk/behave"] in the flesh" (ἐν σαρκί *en sarki*; NIV, "in the world"; NRSV, "as human beings"; cf. 2 Cor 4:11). The life of faith has no other venue than fleshly, bodily life (cf. 1 Cor 5:10; 2 Cor 5:10). God has seen fit to fill these earthenware vessels with God's own glory (2 Cor 4:7); there is no life that is not in the body (2 Cor 5:6); believers experience life clothed in an earthly tent (2 Cor 5:1). Just so, Paul does walk—that is, comport himself—in the flesh. In that way he is indistinguishable from any other believer.

The function of 10:3*a*, however, is to set the stage for a stark contrast in 10:3*b*: "But we do not wage war according to human standards" (κατὰ σάρκα *kata sarka*; lit., "according to the flesh"), a technical phrase for Paul that often means something to the effect of "as people usually do." By employing paranomasia, a play on words hidden by the NIV and the NRSV, Paul contrasts his walking or behaving *en sarki*, "in the flesh," and therefore appearing just as every other believer, with his not making battle *kata sarka*—that is, like everybody else. A warning is implied, as suggested in this paraphrase: "Sure, we look just like everybody else who is a believer in that we carry out our responsibilities in the fleshliness of life; but do not be deceived, when we (are forced to) engage in battle, we are not like anyone else, but operate with the full panoply of God's power at our beck and call."

To buttress his forewarning, Paul draws upon a range of military images, all of which serve to position him as one of God's primary agents. Note that Paul has shifted to the plural as he places the Corinthians on notice

with this militaristic self-depiction. The plural claims suggest once again that he is not alone; therefore, any opponents must reckon that they engage not just Paul but all those associated with him—and not only that, but the real warning is that they engage, through Paul, the full might of God.

Paul's powerful military imagery (to be examined in detail) sets the dominant tone for the rest of the letter fragment with a *leitmotiv* of weakness associated with Paul and the way the martial power gains expression through him. The militaristic terms are not confined to 10:3-6 because contention and dissension characterize the entire document. Paul's own mission and modus operandi are sometimes cast in military terms. The support Paul receives from other churches is described as "pay," "wages," "rations" (money) paid to a soldier (ὀψώνιον *opsōnion*, 11:8), his "robbing" churches uses a term that can describe plundering the spoils of battle (συλάω *sylaō*),[183] and when he describes the refurbishment he received from the Macedonians, he uses a term common in military literature to describe the replenishing of supplies to troops at the battle front (προσαναπληρόω *prosanaplēroō*, 11:9).[184] Worldly power, no matter how great, arrayed against Paul as God's agent avails nothing. Even the governor under as formidable a king as Aretas, when the former held the city of Damascus under guard in an effort to take Paul into custody, was thwarted by a through-the-wall, basket escape (11:32-33).

In 2 Cor 10:3-6, Paul describes himself as doing military service, as serving in an army (στρατεύω *strateuō*) whose "weaponry" (ὅπλα *hopla*) is not of a "fleshly, worldly" sort (σαρκικά *sarkika*, employing paranomasia by playing off of *kata sarka* from 10:2-3). Rather, his weapons are from God and are of such power as to destroy strongholds, fortresses (10:4). Analogizing from "destroying strongholds," Paul describes his own work as a most effective and thorough military action.

Every aspect of an awesomely efficient military siege is depicted, but now transferred

---

183. For more on Paul's employment of military imagery, see E. M. Krentz, "Military Language and Metaphors in Philippians," in *Origins and Method: Towards a New Understanding of Judaism and Christianity: Essays in Honour of J. C. Hurd*, ed. B. H. McLean, JSNTSup 86 (Sheffield: Sheffield Academic, 1993) 105-27.

184. See Herodotus 5.36; 6.101, 118.

over onto Paul's advocacy of the gospel; not by his own efforts, but by the "knowledge of God," (counter-) arguments are demolished, as is every "rampart offering resistance" (10:5).[185] Every mind is taken captive to obey Christ, and Paul promises to be ready to punish every disobedience whenever their obedience is complete (10:5-6). Paul's picture of military action is modeled from Roman peacekeeping and enforcing operations, which, with vastly superior power, sweep away obstacles, crush resistance, and establish complete compliance.[186] Tacitus, born about the time Paul wrote 2 Corinthians 10–13, captures the Roman sense of making peace that Paul here brandishes toward the Corinthians who might dare to stand against him: "Make a wilderness and call it peace."[187]

Paul's primary message is this: By his association with divine power, he is not just another warrior for the gospel; on the contrary, he personifies the totality of God's force. Obedience to Christ entails association with Paul, and no disobedience will be left unchallenged. His secondary message is: Do not be misled that his being "in the flesh" along with everyone else means that he will battle

185. Malherbe, "Antisthenes and Odysseus, and Paul at War," 171-72, shows that Paul construes his opponents as "self-sufficient, self-confident," like some Stoics of the time who, as Seneca put it, "feel secure in their elevated citadel," not realizing that Paul has the connections and the power (with and from God) to overwhelm every obstacle.

186. See *As the Romans Did: A Sourcebook in Roman Social History*, ed. Jo-Ann Shelton, 2nd ed. (New York: Oxford, 1998) 243.

187. Tacitus *Agricola* 30.5.

as others normally do. This last point is yet another time when Paul warns against judging by externals, not internals (4:16), by face, not by heart (5:12).

Paul's self-portrait here is not unlike his wider picture of the life of faith as described in other letters. All believers live in the world, whose structures are under the power of sin; or as he puts it otherwise, they live in the old aeon even though the new creation has broken into the world in Christ's death and resurrection (1 Cor 7:31). Accordingly, believers live in the world as if they are having no dealings with it, as if their values do not come from it, and as if the norms of their behavior are not dictated by it (cf. 1 Cor 7:29-31). In the case at hand, Paul pictures believers as those whose thoughts are held captive (10:5). In other places, Paul has written about this radical shift as having been effected by a change of lordship, of slaves being bought and brought under the ownership of their new Lord Jesus Christ (1 Cor 6:20; 7:23).

Paul allies himself with all others who forcefully overcome barriers and obstacles to "the knowledge of God," probably a euphemism for the gospel—that is, for "knowledge about God" (2 Cor 10:5). This interpretation is reinforced by Paul's use of the same expression in another military metaphor earlier in his correspondence with these same Corinthians: Through Paul and his associates, God has spread the fragrance of the knowledge of God everywhere (2 Cor 2:14).

REFLECTIONS

1. Gentleness and clemency, when understood in the context of God's power and purposes, are not signs of weakness or wimpiness. We sometimes think that gentleness, compassion, kindheartedness, and a readiness to forgive are symptoms of weakness. In actuality it takes a strong person not to respond in kind to an affront or to a wrong. And it takes a strong person to forgive and to be kind when someone else is not.

2. If God is so powerful and strong that nothing can withstand or prevail against God, we might wonder what place there is for self-determination. We may reflect on two answers. First, if we oppose God and God's plan, then we can expect to be overwhelmed and overcome. God's purposes will be realized whether there is antagonism toward them or not. It is God's kingdom, God's reign, and God is bringing it whether we decide to go along with the plan or not. Second, if we do go along with God's plan, then self-determination comes into play in not only how we steward the resources and gifts God has given us but also in the way we work together with God (cf. 2 Cor 6:1).

3. Paul likes to describe God as the God of order and peace (Rom 15:33; 16:20; 1 Cor 14:33; 2 Cor 13:11; Phil 4:9); yet, in 2 Cor 10:4-6 we have a most martial picture of God and of God's awesome military power at work. How can the two fit together? Should not the God of peace be the one who repudiates such militaristic power? Paul seems to take his cues about peacekeeping from the Romans, who had sufficient military power simply to crush opposition. To maintain peace was to annihilate opposition—by utter and overwhelming force. Paul thinks of God's working the same way: "The God of peace shall soon shatter/smash/crush Satan under your feet" (Rom 16:20). Perhaps we have domesticated "peace" more than Paul has.

4. Show clemency toward others because you have received clemency—that is Paul's current casting of the rule we should adhere to with others as God or Christ has done for us (cf. Rom 15:7 for another form of it). This is a guideline that is represented in the Johannine literature as well: "I give you a new commandment, that you love one another. Just as I have loved you, you also should love one another" (John 13:34; 15:12 NRSV). At the heart of the gospel is the assumption that God's grace has not given us what our rebelliousness deserves, but has given us love instead.

5. Paul's point about walking "in the flesh" but not "according to the flesh" is a fine one. The first expression recognizes that human life is always fleshly, is inescapably part and parcel of life in the world. The second expression relates to taking our cues, our values from the world; this Paul soundly rejects. The Fourth Gospel has its own way of depicting this same phenomenon, with slightly different terminology: We are to be "in the world" but not "of the world" (see John 17:15-18).

2 CORINTHIANS 10:7-11, CONSIDER WHAT YOU KNOW

COMMENTARY

From what the Corinthians know and have seen about Paul, they should not be confused about him or about his purposes with them. Paul's opponents appear in this passage (φησίν *phēsin*, "they say," 10:10), and they have made three claims that surface here: They belong to Christ, perhaps in some special way or to some special degree; they have critiqued Paul's letters as "frightening" the Corinthians and as being βαρύς (*barys*, "weighty") and ἰσχυρός (*ischyros*, "strong"); and Paul's bodily presence is "weak" or "without influence" (ἀσθενής *asthenēs*), and his speech "amounts to nothing" (ἐξουθενέω *exoutheneō*).

Could anything possibly offend Paul more than someone's claiming to belong to Christ in any special way or degree? All believers belong to Christ; Christ is their new Lord. "Belonging to Christ" is so basic to Paul's view of faith that he can use it as a rebuke of the Corinthians' divisiveness (1 Cor 1:12). The genitive construction in question (Χριστοῦ εἶναι *Christou einai*, "to be of Christ") could be taken as a genitive of origin or relationship and, therefore, could have reflected their claim that they, more than Paul, are the ones who genuinely represent Christ. That, too, would be an affront to Paul, but it could play to one of his perpetual vulnerabilities: He did not associate with the historical Jesus, but depends on an appearance of the risen Lord for his call and, therefore, for his authority (1 Cor 9:1; 15:8). He was not one of the original disciples or apostles, but became an apostle only through his specific call (Rom 1:1; Gal 1:15-16).

Some criticisms bear on Paul's letters: They are frightening, weighty, and strong (10:9-10). We know of no other Pauline community that has been treated to so many letters from him as the Corinthians, who by the time of 2 Corinthians 10–13 have received (at least) four earlier letters from Paul. Further, not all the letters have been pleasant. By Paul's own account, one of them was painful and written in tears (2 Cor 2:4); that letter was harsh frank speech. To characterize even a letter of harsh frankness as "frightening," however, possibly reflects Paul's opponents' purposeful misconstrual, because frank speech always supposes a context of friendship and caring.

The other two descriptions of his letters have a wider semantic range and require effort to discern how Paul takes them. The surest point of contact can be made with the contrast between Paul's letters' being weighty and strong compared to Paul's bodily presence ("weak") and his speech ("of no account"). The letters, though they may sometimes frighten, fare relatively well when compared with Paul in person, but only because the personal estimate is so devastatingly negative; note that the backhanded compliment, or at least recognition, that his letters are formidable is eclipsed by the utter weightlessness of the implied personal estimate of Paul. Accordingly, *barys*, whose semantic range is from "heavy/weighty/important" to "burdensome/difficult to fulfill/severe," could by the first three possible translations suggest that Paul's letters are viewed as substantial and significant, claims that have an obvious appropriateness. The last three plausible translations, however, leave room for the opponents to complain that Paul either raises the bar too high or has employed reprimand too often.

The other term applied to Paul's letters, *ischyros* ("strong/mighty/powerful/weighty/effective"), indicates, in contrast to his performance in person, that his letters have substance and command attention. Such a depiction of his letters, especially if one takes the "heavy, weighty, important" range of *barys* in view, would fit 2 Corinthians 1–9 very well. No Pauline letter, with the possible exception of Romans, has more heavyweight theological assertions and constructions per square chapter than 2 Corinthians 1–9. Part of Paul's rhetorical strategy in these chapters surely was to show himself magisterial by his capacity to depict himself and his ministry in compellingly rich

conceptions. Paul does write strong letters, as his opponents charged and as the letters themselves have shown by their survival and impact on history until the present time. The point, however, by the opponents, lies in the contrast between the Paul on the page and the Paul encountered in person.

The charge of a fundamental discrepancy between Paul's impressive letters and his unimpressive presence draws a sharp warning from Paul, saying, in effect, "When I am with you next you will see the same sort of power you credit to my letters" (10:11). Earlier in the passage, Paul makes a concession that perhaps he does boast too much—a signal of what is to come. But he defiantly declares, "I shall not be shamed" (10:8). He will not leave his opponents unanswered, as the remainder of the letter fragment amply demonstrates.

The dissonance between his strong, effective letters and his personal and rhetorical performance has, in its incarnation in Corinth at least, raised questions of his status and, therefore, of his authority. In the culture of that time, honor, and with it authority, was granted when a person's performance and standing reinforced each other. To be considered "weak" was a matter of shame. Paul's opponents have found in him a discordance, a lack of continuity between his comportment, his status, and his powerful letters. Also, Paul's insistence on his own self-support at Corinth can be construed as further evidence of his lack of status, allowing opponents to argue that his authority is clearly overblown.

Paul's double-edged answer: He has a special authority (ἐξουσία *exousia*), granted to him by his Lord, for edification (οἰκοδομή *oikodomē*) of the Corinthians, not for destruction (καθαίρεσις *kathairesis*) of them (10:8). Significantly, the term translated "destruction" (*kathairesis*) is the same root of Paul's claim earlier that he destroys strongholds and arguments (10:4-5); so the Corinthians, and their outsiders, should realize that Paul genuinely brandishes such authority toward them. Edification is at the heart of community care for Paul. It is the fruit of love (1 Cor 8:1); it is every action that encourages growth and improvement in others; nowhere is it the sharing of what might be called devout thoughts. All things among believers should be done in love—that is, for edification (1 Cor 14:26; 16:14). Overall, Paul's care for his communities is probably aptly understood as encapsulated in edification. So Paul's claim that he has the authority to build up and not to destroy covers the full possible range of his exercise of his divinely given power. Finally, the declaration that the Lord has given Paul the authority to edify and not to destroy reappears verbatim as the conclusion of the body of this letter (2 Cor 13:10), thus forming an inclusio, or ring formation, that frames not only the full range of Paul's authority with the Corinthians but also all that Paul writes them in this letter.[188] Paul's stated purpose in his letters is surely not to frighten his recipients (10:9), and not simply to bring them back into solidarity with him, but to edify. Destruction is brandished as a cudgel that he certainly must hope not to use.

188. W. L. Lane, "The Key to Paul's Conflict with Corinth, *TynBul* 33 (1982) 9-10, argued that Paul's authority expressed in "building up" and "tearing down" is prophetic imagery based on passages like Jer 1:10.

REFLECTIONS

1. "Love builds up" (1 Cor 8:1); that is its nature. As Paul's relations with the Corinthians show, however, not everything that one thinks is done in love is perceived by the recipients as such. People can and do harm and destroy one another, and that not always with big or obvious actions. Sometimes people are destroyed bit by bit. Love requires that we oppose harm and destruction in its every instance. Love also requires that we be thoughtfully sensitive when what we intend as a loving action is not perceived as such.

2. Believers belong to Christ (10:7). Nothing is more basic to understand. And all believers belong equally. There is no ranking among believers when it comes to our relation to Christ. Some people create a hierarchy among believers regarding who has some special spiritual gift, such as glossolalia, speaking in tongues; those who have that gift are understood to have arrived at the apex of relations to God; the ones who do not (yet) speak in tongues are thought to be on a lesser plateau. Paul does not share such a distinction. All believers are equally "in Christ," and any gifts they have are granted by the Spirit as the Spirit has chosen for the common good (see the Commentary on 1 Cor 12:4-11).

2 CORINTHIANS 10:12-18, BOASTING WITHIN LIMIT

COMMENTARY

The paragraph opens with comments about comparison (*syncresis*), the rhetorical trope of distinguishing oneself by association and correlation with others. In the vertically arranged Greco-Roman world, *syncresis* sometimes likens oneself to another and at other times uses the comparison to claim advantage over the analogous person. In the paragraphs that follow, Paul uses it both ways, and we will be able to observe that his opponents have employed the same rhetorical device—to Paul's displeasure. The same trope surfaces, not always favorably, as an issue several times in this letter fragment. In 10:12, Paul simply states that he presumes neither to "class" (ἐγκρῖναι *egkrinai*) nor to "compare" (συγκρῖναι *sygkrinai*) himself with others. In fact, he takes it a step further: Those who compare themselves with others show themselves "without understanding" (οὐ συνίημι *ou syniēmi,* 10:12). Paul's is a statement made by a person who gains nothing for himself by association.

Paul views *syncresis* in two very different ways. A positive use of *syncresis* was noted in the discussion of the previous letter fragment where Paul, tapping the culturally driven Corinthian inclination to excel, urges them to participate in the collection (2 Cor 8:7) by modeling themselves after the Macedonians. Likewise, he had previously employed *syncresis* when he had portrayed to the Macedonians the Corinthian enthusiasm for the collection (2 Cor 9:2). Paul readily embraces such instances of *syncresis* because they serve to encourage or spur on others. Paul takes a negative view of it, however, when the comparison is used to denigrate someone or when the comparison is self-serving. It is the latter that we find in 2 Cor 10:12-13.

Parts of this letter fragment reveal that the outsiders readily classed themselves with Paul and made comparisons with him that were favorable to themselves (11:12-15; 12:11). Paul's disparagement of comparison when it is used to gain advantage is not, however, just a strategy employed to aid him in combating his opponents; it is a deep-seated conviction that gains expression at other points in his letters. In his treatment of "spiritual gifts" (χαρίσματα *charismata*) in 1 Corinthians 12, Paul argued that, for the common good, believers should make the most of whatever gift or gifts the Spirit had given, that they should not look covetously at the gifts of others, and that each should realize that the well-being of the body is secured by each member's being different from the others (1 Cor 12:4-11, 14-26).

Any talk of comparison quickly leads Paul to its usual result: boasting, a topic he had already introduced in 10:8. Boast or not, Paul's relation to the Corinthians is special. In a wordplay on limits, divine apportionments, and spheres of influence, Paul reminds the Corinthians of his unique relation to them. His boast is constrained to the measure (μέτρον *metron*) of the sphere of influence (κανών *kanōn*) that God measured out (μερίζω *merizō*) to him: "to reach all the way to you" (10:13).[189] Paul seeks to garner

goodwill by reminding the Corinthians that he is their apostle, their father in the faith; he brought the gospel to them. Paul has not been hesitant to remind them of his paternity (1 Cor 4:14-15; 9:1-2; 2 Cor 1:19, 21; 3:3).

God set the borders. God sent Paul. Paul went. Twice in as many verses Paul declares that he was first to go all the way (ἄχρι *achri*, 10:13-14) to the Corinthians, a clear bid for goodwill, especially as it asks the hearers to reach back to their memories of times when things between themselves and Paul were positive. It also claims Paul's priority over any subsequent intruders.[190] Still remembering the good times, Paul declares that in his coming to them, *he* did not extend beyond the boundaries God had set out for him, as some now have done by coming into his own, God-apportioned field (10:14).

Paul's notion of the proper boast versus the improper boast is important for understanding his claims.[191] Boasting per se is not necessarily bad. Boasting about one another in Christ is absolutely appropriate (2 Cor 1:14; 7:14) because in so doing one does not brag about one's own efforts, but about the efficacy and power of God's grace at work; therefore, ultimately believers' boasting in one another is a way of giving praise and glory to God. Boasting is also viewed positively by Paul when it points to his work in the gospel, and for the same reason—namely, that it is shorthand for boasting about God's work through Paul in the gospel (Rom 15:17-18; 1 Cor 1:31; 2 Cor 1:12). Thus for Paul it is absolutely appropriate for him to boast about the Corinthians: They are the result of God's work in his labors (10:15).

In a play on the notion of limits, Paul declares that he does not "boast beyond limits in the labors of others" as do some—namely, the intruders who have gained some standing among *his* Corinthian followers (10:15). As one can readily see from Romans, Paul is very aware of the borders of his *kanōn*, his "sphere of influence" or his "field." He can boast of his work for God among the Gentiles "from Jerusalem and as far around as

---

189. J. F. Strange, "2 Corinthians 10:13-16: Illuminated By a Recently Published Inscription," *BA* 46 (1983) 168, shows that Paul writes in terms known in the second decade CE when an authority (here God) allocates a κανών (*kanōn*), an apportioned area (here including Corinth). In the light of this interpretation, Paul understands that God has allocated the Roman province of Achaia (among others) to him and that outsiders have no right to enter into what becomes a sort of competition. Paul's self-portrait, then, is that he has exercised proper responsiveness to God's allocation, because he has brought the gospel to Corinth and its environs—and Paul suggests that the Corinthians should recognize this.

190. A. J. Dewey, "A Matter of Honor: A Social-Historical Analysis of 2 Corinthians 10," *HTR* 78 (1985) 215, says the opponents are thus open to the charge of poaching.

191. See the treatment of boasting as self-commendation in J. Lambrecht, "Dangerous Boasting: Paul's Self-Commendation in 2 Cor 10–13," in *The Corinthian Correspondence*, ed. R. Bieringer (Leuven: University of Leuven Press, 1966) 339-46.

Illyricum" (Rom 15:17-20 NRSV), and he can project a mission to Spain (Rom 15:28). But he is very clear that he only hopes for a stopover in Rome and for their support for his mission because he proudly has a policy of not building on another's foundation, but preaching where Christ has not already been named (Rom 15:20; cf. Gal 2:9). Accordingly, he has trouble understanding how others can invade a territory and a people given by God to him for his care.

As if to demonstrate his appropriate caring, Paul expresses his hope for the Corinthians: that their faith may increase, allowing him and his coworkers an increased sphere of influence (*kanōn* again, from 10:13) among them (10:15). In a refinement, Paul has moved from outsiders poaching onto his God-appointed field (*kanōn*, 10:13-14) to his hope for an enlargement of his *kanōn* ("sphere of influence") among the Corinthians. That is an echo of what he wrote to them earlier: They are the ones who have restricted him and constricted themselves in their responsiveness to him (2 Cor 6:12). He implored them then and he appeals to them now to let him once again have fuller sway among them.

In what follows there is the slightest hint that their dalliance with these outsiders is responsible for distracting Paul from what they surely know to be his divinely prompted call to preach the gospel "in other places beyond you" (10:16). With a final mention of *kanōn*, "apportioned territory," Paul indirectly ridicules the intruders by renouncing once more for himself any boasting in "work already done in someone else's sphere of action" (*kanōn*, 10:16; cf. Rom 15:20). So Paul presents himself as the model of boasting and indirectly invites an unfavorable comparison of the Corinthian intruders with himself.

Grounding his reflections in the Jeremiah quote—"The one who boasts, let him boast in the Lord," that he used once before in 1 Cor 1:31—Paul returns to the theme that opened this paragraph: those who commend themselves (10:12, 18). In a cleverly crafted, maxim-like declaration laid down as if beyond dispute, Paul affirms that it is the Lord who commends and, therefore, who determines who is δόκιμος (*dokimos*, "tried and true, "one who has met the test," "approved," NRSV and NIV, 10:18; 1 Cor

11:19; 2 Cor 13:7; cf. ἀδόκιμος [*adokimos*] in 1 Cor 9:27; 2 Cor 13:5-7). At the center of the sentence lies the emphatic declaration "that person is tried and true." On the front is a denial ("Not the one . . ."), and on the end is the claim that functions emphatically as a *correctio* (form: not A but B) with regard to the first, so that the sentence reads, literally: "For not the one commending himself, that one is tried and true, but the one whom the Lord commends" (10:18). Commending oneself, the opening portrait of Paul's opponents in 10:12, is explicitly rejected in 10:18. In its place is the Lord's commendation, which appropriately comes to those who, like Paul, prove themselves through thick and thin as "tried and true" (*dokimos*). The notion of being *dokimos* will return as another inclusio in the peroration that concludes the letter fragment (13:3-10).

Almost hidden in this passage is a genuine Pauline gem: He hopes that their faith will increase (10:15). Nothing more is made of it here, and it does not need explanation because Paul's followers would have recognized that such a hope is fundamental to his view of the life of faith (see the Introduction). Believers start as babies in the faith (cf. 1 Cor 4:15; Gal 4:19; Phlm 10). Earlier, Paul had charged these very Corinthians with being babies too long in regard to faith (1 Cor 3:1). At the other extreme of the life of faith, believers can be mature, can be grown-ups; Paul himself models that growth (Phil 3:12, 15; cf. Abraham, the exemplary faithful person, in Rom 4:19-20). Paul advises the Romans that they have faith measured out to them (by God's grace, understood) and that they should think of themselves appropriately with regard to their measure of faith (Rom 12:3). Finally in this regard, Paul pledges to be with the Philippians for their "progress and joy in the faith" (1:25). So when Paul writes 2 Cor 10:15 he is still hoping that his Corinthian followers will experience growth in faith. Just as their earlier fractiousness among themselves convinced him that they were retarded in their growth in faith (1 Cor 3:1-3), so also now he finds that their being attracted to outsiders who have intruded into the believing community at Corinth is a sign of the still-present need for growth in faith (2 Cor 10:15).

Growth in faith is progress *in* the faith. It is not a matter of believing more today than one did last year; it is not believing something more ardently or fervently. For the Corinthians, immediately, it is being increasingly inured to the attractions and traps that the culture offers, such as status and the worldly signs of prestige; it is distinguishing self-serving apostles from other-serving ones. In the broader picture, progress in the faith means that one's self-estimate of the measure of faith is more accurate (Rom 12:3-8); that one can carry more of another's burden more fully or readily (Gal 6:2-5); that one can aim for and hope to do the higher good (1 Corinthians 7); that one can understand more fully the ramifications of believing that there is only one God and act accordingly (1 Corinthians 8); that, as one's faith grows, one can realize an ever-increasing range of freedom within which one may act faithfully before God (Rom 14:13-23); and that one can freely forgo the exercise of that freedom if doing so might harm another for whom Christ died (1 Cor 10:23–11:1).

REFLECTIONS

1. Self-promotion has become a feature of our culture, and many are attracted to it. But some are repulsed by it, and many Christians think any positive statement about oneself is excessive, dangerous, and wrong, and they cringe at the thought of saying anything positive about their "measure of faith." Perhaps a way to start thinking about the issue is to make a distinction between bragging—where the attention focuses on us—and giving thanks to God—where the recognition rests with God. What are the hazards and limits of self-promotion? Nothing is socially more painful than listening to someone who does nothing but talk about himself.

2. Perhaps we could recover boasting about God's work in our private and collective lives. If we fail to bring to the level of consciousness the ways and places God is working, we risk becoming less observant. Think how much joy we might miss, personally and collectively. The Spirit sometimes nudges or prompts us ever so slightly regarding something. If we fall out of the pattern of openly taking note of such noodlings, then those quiet movements of the Spirit may be unnoticed and that instance of God's grace lies fallow.

3. Where do you find your own value? Paul pictures that some people try to "sell" themselves to others; they push themselves and try to inflate their own personal stock. Paul and most of the world in his time (and in ours, too) think that is a dead end. Although he does not develop it, Paul differentiates those whom the Lord commends and says that they are the ones who are really "tried and true" or "approved" (10:18).

4. Comparing ourselves with others; measuring ourselves by others—it may be possible to imagine some good coming out of doing this, but it is so much more likely to be detrimental to everyone and derogatory to some. You can always find someone who is better at something or who is worse at it, but what have you truly learned about yourself in the process? If you make a series of comparisons with persons who are much better at something than you, you may begin to feel quite inadequate. If the comparisons are with persons who are much worse at something than you, then your chances of self-deception are dangerously high. Paul, building on a strong Corinthian tendency to compete among themselves, encourages the Corinthians to turn that energy toward a positive end: Outdo one another in edifying one another (1 Cor 14:12). A sweet irony attends the notion of people's trying to outdo one another in loving each other (cf. "love builds up," 1 Cor 8:1).

5. Paul believes that faith increases (10:15). What does that mean, and how does it happen? It means that one's relation to God grows, that you do not have the same "measure of faith" (Rom 12:3) today that you had when you first came to faith. Just as our love for another surely can grow, so also our trust in God can grow. An analogy with physical fitness is not awry. If you do not use your muscles, they will atrophy. If your faith is not employed on a regular basis in the decisions you make and in your choices, then it is likely to diminish rather than grow. Faith's increase is only possible through its regular employment in more and more of the decisions of life. Particularly on matters where you wonder which of two choices you should make, ask yourself what course of action would most fully express your relation to God.

6. The boasting we hear in some circles today goes like this: "I just did it for Jesus" or "The glory goes to God (or Jesus)." Such a boast may be genuine and heartfelt. Only the speaker knows that. But this practice can become a religiously sanctioned way of calling positive attention to oneself and, therefore, to one's virtue—and insofar as it does, it has its own dangers. Compare Jesus' critique of public shows of piety and righteousness (Matthew 6).

2 CORINTHIANS 11:1-15, BETROTHAL AND BETRAYAL: PAUL AND THE OPPONENTS

COMMENTARY

11:1-3. Twice in 11:1 Paul bids the Corinthians to put up with a little foolishness from him. With that he retells their foundational story from the perspective of the Jewish father of the betrothed, whose responsibility it is to see that his daughter is kept pure for the occasion of her marriage. His description, though laconic, is rich in its historical and literary reverberations and in its imagery. Paul enhances the reach into the past by going all the way to the story of the first couple and expresses his fear that, just as the serpent deceived Eve (Gen 3:1-7, 13; cf. 1 Tim 2:14) by its "readiness to do anything/cunning/craftiness/trickery" (πανουργία *panourgia*, 11:3; a mode of operation Paul has already renounced for himself, 2 Cor 4:2), so the Corinthians' thoughts—instead of being led captive to Christ (2 Cor 10:5) as they should be—will be led astray from a sincere and pure devotion to Christ.

Christ as bridegroom and the church as bride is a widespread image among the early believers (cf. Eph 5:23-27; Rev 19:7-9; 21:2, 9), as is the association of Jesus with an eschatological marriage feast (cf. Matt 9:15; 25:1-13). The image draws on a daring ancient Israelite portrait of God and Israel as lovers (Isa 49:18; 61:10; 62:5; Song of Songs), which almost always has as a part of the story that the beloved betrays the loved one and turns to adultery and harlotry, a note Paul echoes here (2 Cor 11:3; cf. Jeremiah 2:1–3; Ezek 16:1-22; Hosea 2:1).

As depicted by Paul, the marriage has not been consummated. Corinth remains the betrothed virgin daughter whose purity and devotion to Christ, her one husband, Paul fears, are in crisis. Paul, singularly responsible to deliver the daughter unblemished to her husband, worries that the Corinthians are in danger of being deceived. In order to fulfill his responsibilities, Paul must present (παρίστημι *paristēmi*) the Corinthians as a pure bride to Christ (11:2). *Paristēmi* is an eschatological technical term for Paul, describing the appearance, the presentation of the person or persons before God or Christ as judge; the term may also have overtones of a sacrifice presented in thanksgiving to God (cf. Rom 6:13; 12:1; 2 Cor 4:14). The notion of judgment was part of Paul's argument in a former letter (2 Cor 5:10) and is not alien to the bridal context.

11:4. Paul chides the Corinthians about how readily they, like ancient Israel, turn from their appointed lover, Christ. The claims about someone preaching "another Jesus" or the Corinthians receiving a spirit (or Spirit) different from the one they received or receiving another gospel have generated nearly endless commentary and debate about which of the three terms gets the major stress.[192] Some scholars think Paul's rhetoric here provides snapshots of what is going on in Corinth by which we can detail the profile of the controversy.[193] But this is highly unlikely because nowhere else in the letter is there any clue about a different picture of Jesus—in other words, a christological controversy—being disputed (cf. 2 Cor 4:5),[194] and nowhere is there any evidence that claims about the spirit (or Spirit) are in contention (cf. the other instances of πνεῦμα [pneuma] in the letter fragment, 12:18; 13:13). Neither is there any clue in the simple mention of "Jesus," without any other name or title, because elsewhere in the corpus Paul shows himself comfortable in reducing any longer formation to the single name Jesus (Rom 3:26; 2 Cor 4:10-11, 14; Gal 6:17; Phil 2:10; 1 Thess 1:10; 4:14).[195]

A "different gospel" in the most general way is, of course, at issue. Paul knows there is no other gospel than his, but he sometimes mentions, as here (11:4), a reputed gospel (cf. Gal 1:6-9). That gospel is sometimes designated as Paul's (Rom 2:16; 16:25; 2 Cor 4:3). No one else in the early churches has such a complete identification of himself and the gospel he preaches. An attack on Paul's gospel can be construed by Paul as an attack on him; conversely, an attack on Paul is sometimes taken by him as an attack on his gospel. Similarly, a critique of his gospel can lead Paul to respond in defense of himself, and an attack on him can be challenged by a defense of his gospel. We may surmise at least one reason for Paul's close identification of himself and

his gospel. For him, gospel is not fundamentally or even primarily about ideas; if it were, preaching (and teaching the gospel) would become a sort of dispensing of properly vetted ideas and claims. Rather, for Paul the gospel is God's power working to save (Rom 1:16) and is never disincarnated from a life lived. Put in different terms, the gospel is a way of living and being in the world and before God. Paul thought it incumbent on him, as the father of all the faithful who follow him, to model the life of faith for and with them. Gospel and life are always intricately interlaced for Paul. Thus an attack on his gospel is equivalent to an attack on his life, and vice versa.

"Another Jesus" is most likely Paul's own construction. He is given to such patterns of thought. In 1 Cor 8:5-6 he has already pondered other "gods" and "lords" (cf. 2 Thess 2:4); in other letters we find "another gospel" (Gal 1:7-9) and "have another view [than mine]" (Gal 5:10).

Most likely, these sweeping mentions of another Jesus, another S(s)pirit, and another gospel are prime examples of indirect speech in which the actual issues are supplanted by obviously different ones that none of the readers would be able to attach in a one-for-one relation to the real problems.[196] Paul has chosen to mention items known by everyone to be at the heart of his preaching—Jesus, Spirit, and gospel—and thereby given his hearers the perfect opportunity to think back to the origin of their faith—namely, to Paul's proclamation. Thus Paul has once again implicitly invited them to identify and affirm their alignment with Paul, with the *Jesus* he preached *to them* when he first brought the gospel to them, with the *Spirit* that came *to them* when his preaching was first effective, and with his *gospel* to which *they,* from their origins in the faith, have subscribed.

Note the context in which Paul presents these supposed alternative Jesuses, Spirits, and gospels: They are in a foundational narrative about his having preached the gospel to them as the point of origin of their faith. So in accord with his basic, foundational preaching, he mentions the Jesus that he preached among them at the beginning, the Spirit, which is, in Paul's letters, the hallmark of

192. G. D. Fee, "'Another Gospel Which You Did Not Embrace': 2 Corinthians 11:1.4 and the Theology of 1 and 2 Corinthians," in *Gospel in Paul,* ed. L. A. Jervis and P. Richardson (Sheffield: Sheffield Academic, 1994) 117-22, evaluates the traditional options.

193. J. Murphy-O'Connor, "Another Jesus (2 Cor 11:4)," *RB* 97 (1990) 248-51, following Windisch and Georgi in making no differentiation between the opponents' identity and role in 2 Corinthians 1–9 and chaps. 10–13, asserts that "the issue that continues to divide them [Paul and his opponents] is 'Jesus.'" Barrett, "Paul's Opponents in II Corinthians," 242, declares that "the intruders proclaim another Jesus . . . by the kind of behaviour described in II Cor. xi. 20," but Paul does not express it if he thinks so.

194. Thrall, *The Second Epistle to the Corinthians,* 296-97, denies that 3:1–4:6 has within it any christological controversy. As his title suggests (Fee, "'Another Gospel Which You Did Not Embrace,'" 119), Fee sees "another gospel"—not another Jesus or another Spirit—as the key issue. T. B. Savage, *Power Through Weakness: Paul's Understanding of the Christian Ministry in 2 Corinthians* (New York: Cambridge University Press, 1996) 155-58, has a powerful reflection regarding "another Jesus," claiming, in effect, that Paul's opponents have substituted for Paul's Jesus as Lord (2 Cor 4:5) a portrait that has no shame and weakness in it.

195. Barrett, "Paul's Opponents in II Corinthians," 241.

196. For the way indirect, figured speech worked, see Sampley, "The Weak and the Strong," 43-46.

the origin of faith, and the gospel, which is his collective way of referring to all that he has proclaimed among them from the very first. This rhetoric is designed to elicit from his auditors an "of course" kind of response in which they affirm that there can be no other Jesus, Spirit, or gospel than that which came with Paul's original betrothal of them to Christ.

He opened this paragraph by asking them to "bear with" (ἀνέχω *anechō*) a little foolishness from him; in 11:4 he comes full round to say that they "bear with" (*anechō*) it readily enough when others represent a gospel different from his. Paul's criticism is not on the ones who preach (cf. Phil 1:15-18), but on the Corinthians' readiness to "bear with" anything and, by implication, without discernment.

11:5. Paul turns his attention to these "others." Paul probably coins the expression "super apostles" (ὑπερλίαν ἀπόστολοι *hyperlian apostoloi*) for them. The appellation "super apostles" is Paul's own sarcastic way of indirectly acknowledging their claims to be superior to him (in whatever way). The hearers know who these people are, but we are left to surmise. Paul uses the term ἀπόστολος (*apostolos*) in a variety of ways. *He* is one, as he designated himself in 1 Cor 1:1 and 2 Cor 1:1, called by God and given a ministry to the Gentiles (Rom 15:15-16). He received his call through a revelation of Jesus Christ (1 Cor 15:8-11; Gal 1:11-12, 15-16). Paul does, however, use the same term, tapping into its basic sense, to describe a person who is sent on a mission (2 Cor 8:23; Phil 2:25) and who is in no way to be confused with what some gospel writers call "the twelve." Accordingly, we simply lack sufficient evidence to tell if these persons whom Paul dubs "super apostles" are from among the original disciples of Jesus or if, as may be more likely, they are persons who, like Paul, were not members of that group.[197]

Paul has always been vulnerable to the charge that he did not associate with Jesus as an original follower. Surely this complaint is part of his predicament with the Galatians, where we see his testiness in his description of the other apostles as "supposed to be acknowledged leaders (what they actually were makes no difference to me; God shows no partiality)" (Gal 2:6 NRSV). Also, when he reminds the Corinthians of the gospel he preached, Paul recounts his creedal form of the core narrative, and onto it he weaves his own story in a classic, but telling, understatement:

Last of all, as to one born in a miscarriage, he appeared even to me. For I myself am the least of the apostles and not worthy to be called apostle because I persecuted the church of God. But by the grace of God, I am what I am, and God's grace to me was not in vain; to the contrary, I worked more than any of them—not I but the grace of God in me. (1 Cor 15:8-10 NRSV)

Paul is zealous for, one might even say jealous of, the churches that have emerged because of his preaching. He thinks of them as his responsibility and often strikes an athletic note of hoping not to have run in vain as he tries to ready these communities for the parousia, the impending end of the aeon (1 Cor 15:58; Gal 2:2; Phil 2:16; 1 Thess 3:5). In the same spirit, but in rather direct and considered speech (λογίζομαι *logizomai*, "I reckon"), Paul insists to his Corinthian readers that he is not the least bit inferior to "these super apostles" (2 Cor 11:5).

11:6. Contemporary rhetorical training counseled would-be orators to say something like, "Unaccustomed as I am to public speaking . . ." as a means of rousing some pity, and therefore goodwill, from their hearers.[198] Accordingly Paul concedes that he is not skilled in oratory, that he is an "amateur in speech" but certainly not in knowledge, as should be clear to them "in everything and in all ways" (11:6). In keeping with contemporaneous rhetorical strategies of defense, Paul not only seeks pity, but he also is ready to concede that a possible charge levied against him is *partially* true:[199] He may not be the best

197. Following Barrett and Käsemann, R. P. Martin, noting 11:5 and 12:11, conjures up two distinct groups and takes the first to be the Jerusalem authorities and the second to be emissaries of the former. See R. P. Martin, "The Opponents of Paul in 2 Corinthians: An Old Issue Revisited," in *Tradition and Interpretation in the New Testament: Essays in Honor of E. E. Ellis,* ed. G. F. Hawthorne and O. Betz (Grand Rapids: Eerdmans, 1987) 285.

198. E. A. Judge, "Paul's Boasting in Relation to Contemporary Professional Practice," *AusBR* 16 (1968) 37.

199. Sampley, "Paul, His Opponents in 2 Corinthians 10–13, and the Rhetorical Handbooks," 166-67.

orator. But the concession sets the context for a strong denial on a related front: He is not an "amateur" or "untrained" (ἰδιώτης *idiōtēs*) when it comes to what he knows—and that should be abundantly clear (cf. "Look at what is before your eyes," 2 Cor 10:7).

11:7. Paul is stung by criticism of his consistent practice of supporting himself while he is with the Corinthians. The matter has taken on increased proportions in Paul's history with the Corinthians. At first, his care not to be a burden to the Corinthians must have been commendatory, especially in the light of the widespread pattern of wandering sages who made a living from fleecing those with whom they shared their wisdom.[200] Now, however, the matter has reached new and unpleasant proportions because Paul treats it or adverts to it a total of three times in this letter fragment (2 Cor 11:7-11, 20; 12:13-17).

In the first treatment, he ratchets up his rhetoric to hyperbolic levels as he responds, in the isolation of the first person, to Corinthian criticism with highly loaded speech, which may even echo his portrait of Christ in 2 Cor 8:9. Paul humbled himself so that they might be exalted, he preached the gospel to them "at no cost" (δωρεάν *dōrean*), and in the heaviest of Pauline theological categories, he asks sardonically whether it was a "sin" (ἁμαρτία *hamartia*) to do so.

11:8-11. Next he reflects what must have been a charge against him: The support he received from the Macedonian believers was tantamount to robbery of those churches (11:8-9). Paul does not even attempt to refute that accusation directly, but turns it to a question of his using the Macedonian support "for ministry/service to you" (διακονία *diakonia*, 11:8). When Paul doubles up verbs, as he does in 11:9—"I have guarded myself and I shall guard myself"—he displays a clearly thought-out decision that is his incontrovertible policy, in this case, not to burden them in any way. He declares, in effect, "The case is closed" by vowing what he thinks is beyond dispute: "The truth of Christ is in me: This boast of mine [to resist burdening you] will not be silenced in the whole region of Achaia" (11:10). The reference to all of Achaia, in a passage consistently in the singular, once

again serves to remind the Corinthians that, even though Paul is speaking in the singular, he in effect calls to witness all his supporters in the entire region. Paul openly ponders: Could the Corinthians possibly be confused that his refusal to accept their support means that he does not love them? In one of his most poignant, briefest, and therefore most powerful statements, Paul answers his own query: "*God* knows [that I do, understood]" (11:11, italics added).

11:12. As if he needed to be more emphatic, Paul once again doubles verbs, though this time the scope of his emphasis is broadened beyond resisting their support, to the way he does his ministry, to the entire profile of how he operates: "That which I do, thus shall I do" (11:12). The very succinctness of the declaration heightens the emphasis, as does the choice of verb, which very simply, but powerfully, refers to everything he does. The claim of consistency is of great importance for ethos enhancement, for the declaration of his dependable, unchangeable character that is the cornerstone of faithfulness and trustworthiness.[201] Paul pledges that the consistency of his patterns among the Corinthians will undercut the claims and pretensions of his opponents, will "cut down the pretext of those wanting a pretext that in what they boast they may be found just like us" (11:12).

He thinks the Corinthians should "look at what is before their eyes" indeed (10:7). Paul has been faithfully dependable and consistent; that is the ethos his entire work with them has manifested. Now he finds himself besieged by intruders who would present themselves as working on the same terms as he.

11:13-15. Certainly, one distinguishing mark between Paul and them is that, unlike them, Paul continues to refuse to live off the Corinthians. That realization alone should prompt the Corinthians to the fuller understanding that these intruders are frauds. Paul says so directly and in rhetoric that, as it advances, increases in vitriol. He brings heavy rhetorical artillery to bear on them; refining his earlier reference to them as "super apostles" (11:5),[202] they are "false apostles,

---

200. R. F. Hock, *The Social Context of Paul's Ministry: Tentmaking and Apostleship* (Philadelphia: Fortress, 1980) 48-49.

201. See Cicero *Of Oratory* 2.43.178-84; Quintillian *Institutes of Oratory* 6.2.18-19.

202. And not distinguishing two groups, as Barrett, "Paul's Opponents in II Corinthians," 252-53.

deceitful workers, masquerading/disguising [μετασχηματίζομαι *metaschēmatizomai*] themselves as apostles of Christ" (11:13).[203] Stripping off their disguise, Paul identifies them as Satan's "agents/ministers" (διάκονοι *diakonoi*) who can only pretend to be what Paul and his kind are in fact: ministers of righteousness (διάκονοι δικαιοσύνης *diakonoi dikaiosynēs*). These pretenders have followed, true to form, their leader, Satan, who disguises himself as an "angel of light" (11:14). In what amounts, by implication, to a verdict, Paul concludes his invective against the intruders: "Their end shall be according to their works" (11:15), a position his followers in general and the Corinthians in particular know Paul believes about everyone (1 Cor 3:14; 2 Cor 5:10; cf. Rom 2:6-11).

In that culture, Paul's practice of self-support is vulnerable to several criticisms, all of which may in some form and degree be present in the Corinthians' responses. First, some may think that Paul's failure to take support puts him on a lower social plane than other apostles because he stoops to menial labor for self-support. Paul is quick to point out that the intruders have "taken advantage" of the Corinthians (11:20). Turn the rhetoric around, however, and we may suppose that the intruders relish the perquisites that come with status (cf. 1 Cor 9:4-6, which assumes exactly such prerogatives as appropriate) and deride Paul's refusal as reflecting poorly on him.

Second, in the patron/client culture that pervades every level of the social structures, patronage was a substantial way of wielding influence and creating a subset of persons indebted to the patron. Some of the Corinthians are wealthy (cf. 1 Cor 1:26). It is difficult to imagine that they were not aware that Paul accepted the patronage of Phoebe, a deacon of the church at Cenchreae, a town just a handful of miles from Corinth (Rom 16:1-2). Therefore, when Paul persisted in his pattern of refusing support from Corinthian believers, he rejected any efforts at patronage from them. To refuse gifts and support was unheard of in that culture and inevitably resulted in a shaming of those who would patronize him.[204] The consequences of shame reverberate through this letter fragment in passages such as 12:14-15, where Paul appears to be justifying his decision not to become a client of any of the Corinthians. Third, some of the Corinthians—possibly the same persons as in the previous point—may have thought that Paul's refusal of support from them made them, in effect, second-class citizens among Pauline communities because they knew that Paul accepted support from some others (cf. 12:13).

It is true that nowhere in the Pauline letters do we find an example of Paul accepting support from believers while he is working with them, so his refusal to do so with the Corinthians may fit that pattern. But more seems to be at stake here. For instance, Paul never tells the Corinthians, who seem eager to support him, that it is not his pattern "in all the churches," a response the Corinthians and we know he can make (cf. 1 Cor 7:17; 11:16; 14:33*b*). That would have been an easy argument for him to have made, and it might have been much more compelling to them than the justifications he offers in the letter fragment.

203. For more on the way people derided their opponents, see L. T. Johnson, "The New Testament's Anti-Jewish Slander and the Conventions of Ancient Rhetoric," *JBL* 108 (1989) 419-41.

204. Seneca *Of Benefits* 1.10.3-4 holds that no crime exceeds ingratitude. See G. W. Peterman, *Paul's Gift from Philippi: Conventions of Gift-Exchange and Christian Giving* (Cambridge: Cambridge University Press, 1997) 69.

REFLECTIONS

1. Paul's opponents disguise themselves as "apostles of Christ" (11:13). Across the biblical traditions, there is a problem: It is possible to cry, "Lord, Lord," and not be a true follower of Christ (cf. Matt 7:21-23). Similarly, prophets like Amos were distressed that people did all the religious ceremonies and rituals and failed to take care of one another (Amos 4:1-5). Neither the prophets nor Jesus nor Paul could contemplate that life could be divided into categories where parts were devoted to God and the rest left it open to do as one pleased. Put another way, what one believes and how one behaves must be intricately and fundamentally interconnected. The true life of faith reaches beyond the formulas and rituals so that every aspect of life, all of one's behavior, is seen as an expression of one's devotion to God.

2. The expression "God knows" (11:1) expresses a Pauline confidence (cf. Rom 2:16; 1 Cor 14:25). Unlike us humans, God does not confuse externals with internals, face with heart. This is both good news and (potentially) bad news. It can be bad news if we think we hide our actions or motives from God or if we stand in judgment of one another. But it can be good news when our contemporaries misunderstand us because we can know that we are perfectly understood by God (1 Cor 13:12).

3. The "bride of Christ" image, as powerful as it has been throughout history, may be troublesome to some today. It lauds virginity and extols purity. Paul's use of the image is not designed to set standards for women—or men—who want to marry today, but instead serves him as a way of arguing, from the religious and cultural norms of his time, for a certain standard of behavior from the Corinthians. On the positive side, then and now, however, the image expresses a presupposed intimacy of believers with Christ.

4. Paul accepts support from the Macedonians, but not from the Corinthians, because the latter want to have him become their client. If giving has a string attached to it, then that string mars the giving and the receiving. If you find yourself being edgy that somebody has not "recognized" some gift or act that you gave or did, then you may find that you did not give absolutely freely. Of course, when a gift or deed is appreciated and the recipient's joy overflows in return, your joy is redoubled.

5. How many different gospels are there? Paul thinks there is only one true gospel. There are many forms of the gospel. Each of the first four books of the New Testament is called a Gospel, but each one has a superscription that says, "The gospel [or good news, as the term means] according to" Matthew, Mark, Luke, or John. So the persons who put the New Testament together wanted to affirm that there was just one gospel that came in many forms. Today, we might do well to ask what gospel, what "good news" is being represented by our churches, by what is preached, and by the programs that are endorsed. In the same way, however, note how corporations and political groups try to co-opt religion as a means of advancing their causes.

2 CORINTHIANS 11:16–12:10, THE FOOL'S SPEECH: PAUL'S BOASTFUL COMPARISON

Overview

Paul's arrangement of passages that compose the fool's speech resembles a roller coaster, moving dramatically from the lows to the highs to the lows again. Or, described differently, Paul moves the reader from hardships (11:21*b*-29), through a story of deliverance from adversity (11:30-33), to the pinnacle of a heavenly journey (12:1-6), to adversity or hardship from which there is no extrication (12:7-10). These accounts, all strung together, amount to Paul's own exemplification of his statement to the Philippians: "I have learned in whatever situation I am to be content; I know how to be humbled and I know how to abound. . . . I can handle all things in the one who strengthens me" (Phil 4:11-13).

This entire section begins with Paul's appeal to be accepted as foolish (ἄφρων, *aphrōn*; 11:16, a development from 11:1). and when the next section opens, Paul confirms that, in the intervening verses, he knows that he has indeed been foolish (12:11). Key to the whole section, however, is the concept of weakness, which, once introduced in 11:21, forms an *inclusio,* or ring device, that reaches beyond the next hardship catalog (11:21*b*-29), which demonstrates that Paul, in his service of the gospel, and despite his noteworthy religious pedigree, has been buffeted by the vagaries of life. Who can compare with such a set of hardships? No one can be weaker, he argues (11:29). Weakness becomes an ironic badge of honor. In a curiously circuitous fashion, Paul has found a way to boast (11:30), but this time about who has lived the life of greater adversity and affliction. As in the earlier hardship catalogs, Paul shows himself, like a sage, able to abide the vicissitudes of life (albeit with a new note of irony to be examined later) and stay steadily focused on and faithful in his commitment to God and to the gospel.

From the lowest reaches to which experience can lead, as exemplified in the hardship list (11:21*b*-29), to the loftiest exposure for which one in that world could aspire—namely, transport into the heavens, Paul's fool's speech ranges (12:1-6). Then, immediately after the heavenly transit, Paul reverts to the first-person singular and describes a persistent impediment, his "thorn/stake in the flesh" (12:7-10). He openly boasts about his hardships and even employs the first-person singular—because it is an ironic boast and therefore has a certain buffer from offending the auditors. The transit to the third heaven, however, is another matter. No irony protects there. Accordingly, Paul takes the rhetorically viable route of casting the experience in the third person, as if it were about someone else whom Paul knows.[205]

205. H. D. Betz, *Der Apostel Paulus und die sokratische Tradition; eine exegetische Untersuchung zu seiner Apologie 2 Korinther 10–13* (Tübingen: Mohr, 1972), 91, 95. A. T. Lincoln, *Paradise Now and Not Yet: Studies in the Role of the Heavenly Dimension in Paul's Thought with Special Reference to His Eschatology* (Cambridge: Cambridge University Press, 1981) 75, finds Paul here in line with apologetic conventions in the Socratic tradition.

2 Corinthians 11:16-21*a*, Bearing with Fools

COMMENTARY

11:16-19. Paul employs the fool's mode as a cover for some self-commendation. He realizes he is pressing beyond the limits he should honor. He cautions his auditors that he himself speaks (expressed in the singular) with no authority from the Lord, but as in foolishness (2 Cor 11:17; cf. 1 Cor 7:10, 12). Gone are the mainstream, the others who stand with him. In effect, he seems drawn onto his opponents' turf; others boast of worldly accomplishments (κατὰ σάρκα *kata sarka*), so Paul will boast as well (11:18).

Paul establishes the theme of the Corinthians' "putting up" or "bearing with" him, which amounts to a request for them to give him the benefit of the doubt. Already in 11:1, as he finds himself being drawn more and more to self-defense and self-promotion, he asks them to "bear with" him in "a little foolishness." They are ready enough to "bear with" apostles who intrude. Varying the terminology the slightest, Paul asks them to "accept" him "as foolish" (11:16). Reverting to the terminology of "bearing with," Paul ironically chides them as having already demonstrated that they, indeed, "bear with fools" because they put up with all kinds of extreme, wrongful treatment from the intruders (11:19).

11:20-21a. Just as he described the intruders in strikingly vivid and negative terms in 11:13, so also in 11:20 Paul characterizes the extremes the Corinthians are willing to bear from outsiders: "If someone reduces you to slavery, if someone exploits you, if someone takes advantage of you, if someone takes on airs, if someone strikes you in the face"—Paul thinks the Corinthians will "bear with" it (11:20). The list of abuses is itself foolish; we cannot take the descriptions as reflecting exactly what the opponents are doing, because the "striking in the face" is probably a hyperbolic extension of the rhetoric toward an extreme "what will they do and you abide next?" Paul paints a satirical characterization of the Corinthians in

11:20 as people who will put up with almost anything from the outsiders. Now he wants his moment of forbearance from them. Irony becomes his mode, and he portrays himself as being ashamed that he was too weak to have prevailed over them in such a fashion, and he almost asks their forgiveness (11:21).

Note that he embraces "weakness" (11:21) and thereby introduces a theme that will permeate much of the remaining letter fragment (a root form of ἀσθενέω *astheneō*, 11 times).[206] At different points in the Corinthian correspondence, Paul has employed an ironic self-portrait.[207] Already in 1 Cor 4:10-13 he tied the weak and fool themes together and ironically applied them to himself (cf. 1 Cor 1:25). Human pretensions to strength fall of their own weight in the face of God's true power. So Paul ironically credits to his weakness his "failure" to enslave the Corinthians, as he suggests the intruders have done. The notion of weakness, once introduced here, is featured in the fool's speech and is a *leitmotiv* in all that follows.

206. J. L. Sumney, "Paul's 'Weakness': An Integral Part of His Conception of Apostleship," *JSNT* 52 (1993) 89-90, traces Paul's self-identification as apostle of weakness back to 1 Thessalonians.

207. K. A. Plank, *Paul and the Irony of Affliction* (Atlanta: Scholars Press, 1987); A. B. Spencer, "The Wise Fool (and the Foolish Wise): A Study of Irony in Paul," *NovT* 23 (1981) 349-60.

REFLECTIONS

Our bearing with others and they with us is the currency of any relationship. Try as we may to be consistently loving and thoughtful, we inevitably fall short of our ideals. So bearing with us is a necessity that we ask of our friends and loved ones. But putting up with us must have its limits. Abuse, whether physical or emotional, simply must not be borne because the damage is too severe and protracted. It is no longer Christian love that bears with abuse.

2 Corinthians 11:21*b*-29, So to Boast

COMMENTARY

Paul's distraction with the intruders leads him into the very comparison that he so much derided just a while earlier as he wrote: "When these people measure themselves by one another and compare themselves with one another, they do not understand" (10:12). Paul's is the classical and eternal problem that when setting oneself over against one's opponents, one can be drawn onto the adversaries' grounds. Strangely, one becomes like one's enemies. Here, Paul is drawn into the very *syncresis* that he so opposes.

Lest we be too harsh, we note that Paul is in a predicament. Remember that outsiders have encroached on what Paul considers to be his own territory and that some Corinthians who really owe their coming into the faith to Paul now seem drawn to this alien leadership. Paul thinks that the Corinthians should have honored their longstanding filiation to him. What is more, they should have defended him from the intruders' charges and innuendos and sent them packing. Then Paul would not have perceived the need to defend himself.

When the most evident avenue—namely, Corinthian defense of Paul—fails, what alternatives are left to him? Rhetorical handbooks and practice advise that he must aim for goodwill (*benevolentia*) by making reference (a) to himself and to his service toward the state or the community, (b) to his opponents, (c) to the jury (in the case of a letter, the recipient for whom the letter is intended), and (d) to the case or situation itself.[208] The first three are primary, according to Cicero, but (c), the jury (in this case, the Corinthians), is not very responsive to Paul, and (d), the case itself, is not directly or fully discernible in the way Paul treats it in 2 Corinthians 10–13. So Paul, for whatever reasons, has not availed

208. See Cicero *De inv.* 1.16.22.

himself of (d). Therefore, Paul is really left with two avenues of approach toward recovery of goodwill in chaps. 10–13: references to himself and to his opponents (a and b).

With regard to oneself, one recites, as Paul does, one's own previous efforts for the "Corinthians,"[209] from bringing the gospel to them through to the present; one references one's own credentials and generally enhances one's own ethos, or character. Regarding the opponents, one questions their motives, exposes their ethos and comportment as inappropriate or inconsiderate, and suggests their selfishness and luxurious idleness. Paul's attacks on his adversaries have been peppered across chaps. 10–11, and they will continue. But in 11:21b–12:10, the heart of the fool's speech, Paul works (sometimes ironically) to enhance his own ethos and thereby attempts to win goodwill.

To the modern ear, Paul's heavy focus on himself may grate, but in his own culture it was in the very nature of what was expected. In his letters, Paul is a good cultural example of a person who knows the importance of an enhanced ethos for his leadership role and style, and he accordingly makes certain that his letters cultivate and enrich his ethos regularly. Usually, however, Paul is not so blatant in using syncrisis, comparison, as he is in the text at hand. *Paul's opponents* have apparently used syncrisis by claiming to be different from him in certain details (e.g., readily taking support, 11:20; 12:13) and by declaring themselves like Paul in certain particulars (apostleship, authority, and having a διακονία [*diakonia*], "ministry," like his, 11:12-15). Paul is convinced of how different the intruders are, and in 11:21b-29. he undertakes syncrisis to demonstrate the difference.[210]

We have seen that it is difficult, and perhaps even doubtful, to be sure whether every detail in a given passage of 2 Corinthians is a one-for-one counter to something the opponents are saying or doing (cf. 11:4 and the

Introduction).[211] So it is here in the opening part of Paul's comparison—presented in a barrage of rhetorical questions sounding like an interrogation of a witness—when he boasts, somewhat redundantly, that if the intruders are Hebrews, Israelites, and offspring of Abraham, so is he, emphatically (κἀγώ *kagō*, "I too!" 11:22). This triple insistence supports the interpretation that the outsiders are, like Paul, Jewish and lends some general support to speculation whether they may have connections with Jerusalem.

Paul's query whether the intruders are "ministers/servants of Christ" (διάκονοι *Cristou' diakonoi Christou*, 11:23; cf. 11:15 and Paul's own self-depiction as διάκονος [*diakonos*] in 3:1–4:6) moves Paul from comparison ("So am I," 11:22) to superlative, framed by the iterative disclaimers that he is speaking "in foolishness" (11:21b) and "irrationally" (11:23b). He and they may be Jews, but when it comes to being ministers of Christ, Paul goes over the edge: "I am more" (ὑπὲρ ἐγώ *hyper egō*, 11:23).

His evidence for being a better minister of Christ begins with his labors ("with regard to labors, far more") and immediately merges into a hardship list of great proportions (11:23-28). Once again, Paul's ministry is ironically best measured by the difficulties, adversities, afflictions, and setbacks he has encountered and surmounted in his representation of the gospel (see also 1:3-11; 4:7-10; 6:4-10). Once again, hardships endured in the service of the gospel are Paul's best evidence and confirmation of his faithfulness and dependability with regard to the gospel and to the call to service. *Nothing* deters Paul. The longer and more detailed the list— and this is the longest in all of Paul's letters—the more attestation that Paul has placed the gospel first and has pursued its propagation with a singleness of purpose that cannot be thwarted and that should not be underestimated.

This hardship catalog is impressive on several counts. First is its structure. The list opens with four parallel prepositional phrases, each beginning with the preposition "in/with" (ἐν *en*): "in labors," "in imprisonments," "in floggings," and "in [that is, near] death." Each of these phrases ends with some modifier that suggests inordinate numbers. Next in the list

---

209. Encomiastic tradition expected a recounting or cataloging of one's deeds (*res gestae*) that benefit others. See Belleville, "A Letter of Apologetic Self-recommendation," 154-55; Travis, "Paul's Boasting in 2 Cor 10-12," 6:529-30.

210. Plutarch (*On Praising Oneself Inoffensively* 540C-D, 541C) repeatedly acknowledges that self-praise will be viewed as appropriate when "defending your good name or answering a charge."

211. See G. Lyons, *Pauline Autobiography: Toward a New Understanding* (Atlanta: Scholars Press, 1985) 78, for his rather devastating critique of "mirror reading," in which every detail in a passage is read as a cue to the opponents' real position.

are events defined and linked by numbers of times or length of duration: "five times," "three times," "once," "three times," "a night and day," and "many" (11:24-26*a*). Next is a litany of troubles introduced by eight "in danger from" constructions (11:26*b* to the end of the verse) and is followed by a little summarizing phrase of rhetorical doubling, "in toil and in hardship" (11:27*a*), before the list concludes, as it began, with (four) prepositional phrases, each beginning with *en*: "with sleepless nights," "in hunger and cold," "with much fasting," and "in the cold and destitute" (11:27*b* to the end of the verse).

Second, this hardship catalog confirms some details already known about Paul and gives new information not otherwise known. Paul's imprisonments are numerous (Rom 16:7; 2 Cor 6:5; Phil 1:12-14; Phlm 1, 9-10, 13, 23; cf. Acts 16:23-40; 24:27; 28:16; Eph 3:1; 4:1; Col 4:10), though the location of them remains problematic. His having been shipwrecked we know from Acts 27:9-44. Journeys are certainly troublesome issues with the Corinthians (cf. 2 Cor 1:15-18, 23–2:3; 7:5; 9:3-4; 10:2; 12:20–13:1, 10). Danger experienced by Paul was the subject of much attention in 2 Cor 1:3-11.

The beatings mentioned in 11:24-25 (cf. 6:5) provide new information, unavailable elsewhere in his letters. The first type of beating, Paul acknowledges, is a synagogue-based Jewish punishment[212] via lashes and is grounded in Deut 25:3, which provides for a maximum of forty lashes. Contemporary Judaism, scrupulous to make certain that punishments not exceed the biblical limit, practiced a flogging that was described as "forty less one." Though it would be interesting to know what Paul did on each occasion to be judged worthy of these punishments, we are at a loss to know.[213] The other mentioned punishment, the beating with rods, is Roman (Acts 16:22-23; cf. 1 Thess 2:2) and is inappropriate treatment of Roman citizens (Acts 16:37-39), though Josephus reports that on occasion Roman citizens were subjected

to such discipline.[214] Thus Paul's having received the Roman flogging with rods cannot be used with confidence to comment on the veracity of Acts regarding Paul's Roman citizenship, but Paul's reference to having been beaten with rods three times does suggest that he may have had run-ins with Roman authorities about which we otherwise know nothing.

Third, the list embraces shameful circumstances. Here is Paul as fool, "boasting" about having been in jails, punished by Jews and Romans, in danger from more and varied circumstances than one is likely to imagine, and deprived of food, clothing, and comfort. If the irony were not already apparent in the list, Paul's tag line—"If anyone is weak, am I not also weak?"—makes it clear. Neither the Corinthians nor apparently the intruders are reflected as casting any doubt that Paul has been a very successful advocate for the gospel around much of the eastern Mediterranean basin. And what does he here choose to boast about? His weakness. Despite his perils and predicaments, the gospel is powerfully present through his weakness. The only conclusion he can imagine is that it is God's doing. The gist: How can anyone deny Paul is a genuine apostle when, despite the way his life looks through the prism of his problems, the gospel he preached is powerfully present in the lives of people like the Corinthians? With this extended hardship list, Paul has documented that his life has been one long demonstration of weakness. And this weakness and his problems show unmistakably that the undeniable success of his missionizing rests solely and powerfully in God (cf. the same point made already in 1 Cor 2:5).

The Corinthians will not know at this point what we modern readers can know by reading ahead, but they will learn when Paul's folly narrative finally discloses the key to understanding it all: the Lord's own statement, "My grace is sufficient; my power is made perfect in weakness" (12:9). Before the recipients of this letter hear the just-noted key, though, they will hear Paul cap off the hardship list (11:28-29), exemplify his weakness with a description of an escape from Damascus (11:30-33), and, completing his fool's speech, tell of his transit to paradise and his thorn/spike in the flesh (12:1-8).

212. This beating is not to be confused with persecution. See E. P. Sanders, "Paul on the Law, His Opponents, and the Jewish People in Philippians 3 and 2 Corinthians 11," in *Anti-Judaism in Early Christianity,* ed. P. Richardson and D. Granskou (Waterloo: Wilfrid Laurier University, 1986) 1:88; A. J. Hultgren, "Paul's Pre-Christian Persecutions of the Church: Their Purpose, Locale, and Nature," *JBL* 95 (1976) 104.

213. Sanders, "Paul on the Law, His Opponents, and the Jewish People in Philippians 3 and 2 Corinthians 11," 89, sees evidence here that Paul continued synagogue attendance and submitted to its discipline.

214. Josephus *The Jewish War* 2.308.

Though formally the list may be said to conclude with 11:27, Paul extends it with a statement that functions as a sort of "et cetera": "apart from the unmentioned things" (11:28*a*). Suggesting he could go on, that the list as supplied only scratches the surface, Paul finally focuses instead on the "daily pressure" he finds in his "anxiety for all the churches" (11:28), a pressure of which the recipients of the Corinthian letter are clearly part.

Paul concludes the first part of his fool's speech, most of which is composed of the hardship catalog, with an affirmation of the underlying message of the entire hardship list—namely, his theme of weakness (11:29, reprised from 11:21*a*) as the key to understanding not only Paul and his ministry, but also the gospel and what it reports God is doing. Through rhetorical questions designed to draw the hearers into his deliberation, Paul suggests that if anyone is weak, so is he (11:29*a*); *that* is what the list of hardships and difficulties has had as its subtext.

The genius of fools has always been in their freedom from convention, in their holding a lens through which we see what is not otherwise clear. In a subversion of the culture's value system—and perhaps also that of at least some Corinthians—weakness becomes Paul's badge of honor, for reasons that will become clearer at the end of the fool's speech (12:7-10). The Corinthians, and perhaps even more their intruding new leaders, ought not to be confused by this "weakness," though, because it is not powerlessness; neither does it lead to Paul's withdrawal, as the second rhetorical question in 11:29 shows: "Who is caused to stumble, and I am not burned up?" By such a comment Paul signals to one and all that any causing to stumble or sin (σκανδαλίζω *skandalizō*) will bring Paul's ire. That puts the Corinthians on notice with regard to their proper concern for one another and surely warns them that they need to scrutinize the impact the outsiders—indeed, any filiation the Corinthians may have with them—may have on each of their brothers and sisters in the faith.

If we return to the first question of 11:29*a*—"Who is weak and I am not weak?"—we can now see its function. There Paul models the way in which believers, whether weak or strong, ought to identify with one another and with their well-being. Paul's last rhetorical question (11:29*b*) is, therefore, a call to vigilance and responsibility on the part of all believers and certainly neither a Pauline pledge always to be for the ones who are harmed nor some little personal detail about himself that Paul now (of all times!) decides to share with his followers. Rather, it is Paul applying to himself and modeling what he passionately holds: No believer can stand by with impunity when another believer is made to stumble or sin, that is, go wrong.

REFLECTIONS

1. What should a believer make of hardships and afflictions? As is popularly asked, Why do bad things happen to good people? Perhaps we should declare outright that bizarre and apparently absurd things do happen, that not all things make sense. Sometimes immune systems fail, hearts give out, and other organs fail. We are finite creatures with a limited life span. But the word of faith says, with Paul, that God works *in* and *through* all things to bring about good for those who love God (Rom 8:28). Often the good that God works through something is visible only later and in retrospect. The affirmation of God working good through an occasion is not to say that the event was itself good (the death of a loved one, for example, is unabashedly an awesome loss); nor is it to be confused with saying that God "caused" it. An important function of hardships, as Paul understands them, is to help distinguish what is truly important or powerful from those things that are not.

2. What should we say about Paul's being carried away a bit? He acknowledges it; so should we. No doubt his opponents will have noticed it. Paul is indeed drawn onto his opponents' ground and, even though it fits the social conventions of the time, is boasting like a foolish person. Paul's inversion of his boast so that it focuses on his weakness goes to the heart of his gospel—namely, that the power belongs to God. Nevertheless, in his foolish boasting, Paul's frailty and humanity show through. As much as he understood and as much as he accomplished, he is still frail in some ways—like us. Biblical characters from Adam and Eve forward have always had their foibles and problems; yet, God stays committed to them—and to us. Perfection of performance is not a prerequisite to God's love, fortunately.

3. Pretentions to power often have a puffiness about them. People who are weak or who have low self-esteem sometimes bluster about, pretending to be powerful persons, apparently hoping that others may be (more) convinced by their posturing. Real power can genuinely express itself in gentleness and even in weakness. The biblical story throughout history affirms this. The Hebrews, weak and servile, were delivered from powerful Egypt. Jericho's walls were no match for Joshua. Little David bested Goliath. Jesus had a manger for a crib.

4. It is not just because Paul was an apostle that he said, "When anyone falls, I burn" (11:29). It is the duty of every believer to be troubled by failed love, by injustice, to "burn" when anyone falls, and to stand against anyone who has led to another's distress or downfall.

2 Corinthians 11:30-33, Boasting and Deliverance Through the Damascus Wall

COMMENTARY

Still aware of its folly, Paul refines his boasting, saying that if forced to it, as he feels he is, he will focus on his weakness (11:30), a weakness already delineated in the preceding hardship catalog (11:23-29). Paul seals that determination with an oath as to his truthfulness (11:31); the particular form of the oath certifies, as it did when Paul employed it in 1:3, the faithfulness of God to deliver.[215] Paul swears on God's faithfulness that he does not lie; when Paul boasts of his weakness, it is the same as boasting about God's power to deliver and is an affirmation that Paul, knowingly weak in many ways, represents the God of power whose forces against opposition and wrong have been described as overwhelming in 10:3-6.

Paul's resort to boasting in his weakness is not simply a strategical move in his struggle with the Corinthians; it is also and more profoundly his tapping of a fundamental truth of his life—indeed, of the life of faith

everywhere and in all time. When Paul is in difficulty, beset by affliction or even by a threat to his life (1:3-11)—and, in this context, we may add, opposition—Paul trusts in God's faithfulness and mercy and expects God to deliver. That is the story of Paul's life and of the life of faith.

In 11:30-33, Paul makes exactly the same connections that he does in the opening of 2 Corinthians 1–9. There Paul began with the "blessed be God" formulation, went on to describe the endangerment of his life in Asia, and acknowledged God's faithful deliverance of him (see the Commentary on 1:3-11). In 11:30-33, it is the work of God "who is blessed forever" (NIV, "praised") that prevents Aretas IV (the Nabatean king [9 BCE–c. 40 CE] who ruled over Damascus) from capturing Paul, even though Aretas held the city under guard because he wanted to take Paul into custody (cf. Acts 9:24-25). Such power was arrayed—ineffectively—against Paul, who is weak in and of himself to prevail. In Israel's traditions, God is blessed because God keeps promises and preserves, guards,

215. Danker calls it "strongest reinforcement . . . an oath." See Danker, "Paul's Debt to the *De Corona* of Demosthenes," 279-80.

the faithful. So here also, Paul blesses God for his own deliverance because he was let down from a wall window in a rope basket and fled Aretas's hand. Strikingly absent from the story is a single detail of anything Paul did or had to do in order to be delivered. There is no word of any plan or of specific co-conspirators, just the simple, powerful detail: "Through a window, in a rope basket, I was let down and fled his hand" (11:33).

Paul's weakness, as reflected in the Damascus basket story, is the occasion for God's power, though that point is not explicitly made in the account. Paul depicts himself as the one who trusts God and God's power to deliver him; the blessed-be formula shows that. So his boasting in this instance is covertly a boasting about God, as the "blessed be God" (11:31) formulation indicates. So Paul's weakness is an occasion for God's power. Encoded for the Corinthian audience and their intruders is the suggestion that they ought to reckon carefully before they take Paul and his boasted weakness lightly. Harking back to 11:29, the Corinthians are once again placed on warning, much as they were when Paul reminded them that he is burned up when anyone is made to fall.

REFLECTIONS

1. It may be difficult to affirm in every challenging or problematic situation, but the God we believe in is the God of the exodus, the God who delivers. It is God's character to do so, as Paul knows and expresses in 1 Cor 10:13. God will always provide an exodus, a way out. Memory and hope position us with regard to understanding the situations that bid to overwhelm us—memory, because we recite our history of God's having delivered us in the past; and hope, because we look forward confidently to the future, to a time and situation that we may not yet be able to envisage, when "the God who delivers" will do so once again (2 Cor 1:10).

2. Paul's encoded assumption should be ours: There is no circumstance, no matter how apparently stacked against us, in which God is not there with us and for us. If God is for us, Paul declaimed, then nothing can separate us from the love of God in Christ Jesus our Lord (Rom 8:38-39). Such an affirmation is no guarantee that the city governors of life will not pursue us; rather, it is a declaration that even then and there God will be for us and will ultimately deliver us. In such situations we, too, can affirm: "Blessed be God."

3. Paul's story contains within it an implicit critique of the political structures of his time and thereby raises the question of when believers should relate positively and when they should relate critically (and perhaps even subversively) to the political, social, and economic structures of their own times. Christianity is not owned by any political system or by any given social or economic framework. The Christian faith can be lived within any situation. Often religion in general and Christianity in particular have been used to lend moral authority to governing and social structures, occasionally even when the structures were oppressive to some of its citizens.

4. Paul fled from Damascus. He fled from Thessalonica when a threat to his life arose (1 Thess 2:2, 17-20; see also Acts 16:19-40). Why not stay and be flogged or killed? When should one flee? When should one stand and be counted, even at one's peril? It is clear, from Paul's recounted hardships, that he certainly was caught at times, whether inadvertently or not. Every day we face small versions of those grand challenges; discerning when to stand and when to go away to await another day is part of the daily moral calculus that is required of us. Christians have found that collective assessment, where believers communally reflect on past performance, can be a positive encouragement to improvement, to what Paul calls "edification."

2 Corinthians 12:1-10, The Man in Paradise with a Thorn/Stake in His Flesh

COMMENTARY

This double-faceted passage concludes the fool's speech, combining the loftiest of experiences, a transport into the third heaven, with the lowliest, a persistent, unavoidable "thorn/stake in the flesh." The two stories belong to and interpret each other as demonstrating the extremes a person may experience in life.

12:1-7a. The first story, that of a man transported to paradise,[216] is set in the ongoing context of the fool's boast, which has been under way since 11:16. In 11:30, Paul had written, "If it is necessary to boast . . ."; in 12:1 he declares, "It is necessary to boast." But quickly acknowledging that there is no advantage in doing so, he declares his intent to proceed to "visions and revelations of the Lord." We may wonder whether the intruders have boasted of their own visions; if so, Paul answers with a considerable "one-up" here. If the Corinthians have embraced the notion that visions and revelations are important indices of genuine apostolic standing, then Paul signs in impressively. Paul suffered in comparison with the original disciples in that he never saw Jesus in the flesh, but depended on visions, on the call of Christ for his authority. In any case, Paul here enhances his ethos.

Paul chooses to cast the story of his own translation into heaven[217] in the third person and to describe it as having happend to "a man," but there can be no doubt that the man is Paul. Rhetorical conventions of the time suggested that there might be occasions when a speaker could advantageously tell a personal story as if it were about someone else.[218] One

such time would be when the telling of a story so self-aggrandizing might cause the auditors to cringe with resentment over the vainglorying. Paul has already pushed beyond modesty in his boasting; now he wants to tell the Corinthians about an event so grand as to sound too self-commending, even in the categories of Paul's time.

The story is structured around what Paul knows in contrast to what God knows. Paul knows "a man in Christ" who fourteen years earlier was snatched up into the third heaven (12:2). Paul does not know whether the transit was "in the body or out of the body," but "God knows" (12:2; we cannot determine, or rule out, whether Paul's disavowal of knowledge is sarcasm directed at some position taken by the opponents). Two verses later, Paul repeats that he knows a certain man who was snatched up into paradise and heard "unspeakable words which it is not permitted for the man to speak" (12:3-4). Repeating for emphasis, God knows (in the Greek the reader is left to imply the related "Paul does not know") whether the journey to paradise was "in the body or apart from the body" (12:3). That is the whole of the story.

Allusive in the extreme, the account fairly begs for the audience to clamor for more details, but the story carries its own antidote to that with its built-in reference to "unspeakable words" and to the prohibition on speaking. Paul has crafted the story in such a way as to attract and to hold off the audience at the same time.

Fourteen years earlier, at the time of this transit, what was happening in Paul's life? If a date of 54–56 CE is accepted for the parts of 2 Corinthians (see the Introduction), then the vision took place sometime around 40–42, some seven years after Paul had been called or converted near Damascus (Gal 1:17c). If we take the Galatians framework of Paul's chronology, then seven years after his call Paul would have been some three years into the time when he was in the "regions of Syria

---

216. Third heaven (12:2) and paradise (12:4) are not two distinct destinations but probably rhetorical variations for effect. See Lincoln, *Paradise,* 79.

217. P. Schäfer, "New Testament and Hekhalot Literature: The Journey into Heaven in Paul and in Merkavah Mysticism," trans. P. Vermes, *JJS* 35 (1984) 33-34, rejects the assertions that 2 Cor 12:2-4 can be understood in the light of Merkavah mysticism.

218. See Plutarch, *On Praising Oneself Inoffensively* 542C, on praising another; 539A-547F, on safe self-praise. See also Quintilian 11.1.21. In intertestamental literature, the heavenly ascent accounts are, with the exception of *T. Abraham,* in the first person. See M. Dean Otting, *Heavenly Journeys: A Study of the Motif in Hellenistic Jewish Literature* (Frankfurt: Peter Lang, 1984). M. Goulder, "Vision and Knowledge," *JSNT* 56 (1994) 53-71, argues that, given Paul's disparagement of visions, the man in 12:2 cannot be Paul.

and Cilicia," the areas around Antioch and his hometown, Tarsus (Gal 1:18-21; cf. Acts 15:23, 41). That would be after his Jerusalem visit of a fortnight with Cephas and James (Gal 1:18-19). Therefore, this heavenly voyage is not to be confused with any revelation or vision that occurred in conjunction with his call or conversion. Paul, however, is given to visions and revelations (12:1; 1 Cor 9:1; 15:8; Gal 1:12; 2:1-2), so a later time presents no problem.

In Paul's culture, heavenly journeys often functioned to confirm divine approval and authentication.[219] This story counts as a boast on that basis. By telling it, Paul obliquely claims special status for himself, a status so grand that his opponents might not be able to compete.

"Paradise" ($\pi\alpha\rho\acute{\alpha}\delta\epsilon\iota\sigma\sigma\varsigma$ *paradeisos*), in times before Paul, referred to an enclosure like a formal garden or a park.[220] In some Jewish literature of Paul's time, paradise was understood to refer to the Garden of Eden.[221] It was also understood as an irenic place above the earth.[222] Elsewhere in the NT the term refers to the place where God presides and cares for those who are chosen (cf. Luke 23:43; Rev 2:7).

The notion of heaven's having layers or levels or of there being more than one heaven is well attested in other NT writings (Luke 21:26; Eph 4:10; Col 1:16, 20; 2 Pet 3:5, 7, 10, 12-13).[223] The plural is lacking in Philo and Josephus.[224] The idea of a third heaven is known from other literature.[225] The combination of third heaven and paradise, as found here in 12:2-3, is also found in other ancient literature.[226]

It is curious that, throughout his ministry with them, Paul has not said a word to the Corinthians about this event. Along with his use of the third person, his well-maintained silence to this point may further mitigate against any Corinthian aversion to his boast. His breaking of his long-standing silence on the matter does, however, indicate the degree to which the Corinthian defection distresses him; his long silence shows how little public value he credits to visions, revelations, and transports. Further, that it is a transport of some time ago reduces the chance that some critic could claim that Paul conveniently came up with a vision when he needed one.

Paul also uses the heavenly transport story to secure a comfort zone on boasting. The third-heaven man allows Paul to continue his own boast in his weakness, a theme that now stretches back through 11:29-30 to 11:21, and to add to it his boasting "in behalf of such a one" (12:5). Paul's claim in 12:6 is revealing: Such a vision and transit, he suggests, would be a solid basis for boasting, and it is the truth, as difficult as it might be to believe the recounted details. Paul could boast about "such a one"; he would not be a fool in doing so, and he would be speaking the truth if he did. But he expressly refrains from boasting about that event. He can have it both ways. By telling the story, he indirectly vaunts himself; by not boasting about it (telling it in the third person and now explicitly refusing to structure a boast on it), he subtly renounces power and authority built on claims of visions. In fact, he can have it the way he wants them to relate to him—namely, on the basis of his consistent performance and behavior among them: "lest someone think of me more than they see in me or hear from me" (12:6).

Paul is content to let the record of his relation to them stand on its own; as he wrote near the start of this letter fragment, "Look at what is before your eyes" (10:7). Paul will not use any vision or revelation, no matter how grand, to trump his own day-to-day performance—that is, what they see in him or hear from him. If the intruders are boasting of their visions and revelations, Paul one-ups them with this extraordinary heavenly journey and then, irony of ironies, refuses to build a case for his authority upon that, choosing instead to let the matter be decided by what they have seen and heard in him. What they have encountered in him all along is the gospel lived in their midst, with the power clearly

219. Andrew T. Lincoln, *Paradise Now and Not Yet: Studies in the Role of the Heavenly Dimension of Paul's Thought with Special Reference to His Eschatology* (Cambridge: Cambridge University Press, 1981) 83-84.

220. On heaven, heavenly ascents, and paradise as reflected in Jewish and Hellenistic traditions, see Lincoln, *Paradise Now and Not Yet*, 77-85.

221. See Josephus *Antiquities of the Jews* 1.37; *Sib. Or.* 1.24, 26, 30; *Pss. Sol.* 14:3; Diognetus 12:3.

222. See En 32:3; 20:7; *T. Levi* 18:10; *Sib. Or.* frag. 3, 48.

223. Dean-Otting, *Heavenly Journeys*, 275. For other Jewish treatments of heavenly ascent, see C. R. A. Morray-Jones, "Paradise Revisited (2 Cor 12:1-12): The Jewish Mystical Background of Paul's Apostolate (the Jewish Sources and Paul's Heavenly Ascent and Its Siginificance)," *HTR* 86 (1993) 177-217, 265-92.

224. *BAGD* 598.

225. Philopatris 12; *T. Levi* 3:3.

226. See *Apoc. Mos.* 37:5; *2 Enoch 8:1* (B) and *2 Enoch* 31:1-2 (A). See also Lincoln, *Paradise*, 79.

being God's and with Paul being the menial earthenware vessel through which God has made this treasure present (4:7). Once again, Paul argues that his having been "tried and true" with them should be his strongest commendation; he has a history with them that shows him trustworthy through good times and bad—and the following verses (12:7b-10) illustrate a persistent adverse situation for Paul that, in contrast to the heavenly transport story, is no doubt well known to them.

Paul's treatment of his heavenly transport has implications for the grounding of religious authority. As Paul has set up the issue, it may be characterized as authority based on visions and revelations versus authority based on performance. The former invites allegiance for persons who themselves alone can vouch for what they report. They have the visions or revelations; they report them; and the hearers can credit them with as much authority as they see fit. That relationship makes the audience dependent on the visionaries. By nature, visions cannot be subjected to scrutiny; they happen in a given moment and can be shared only in the telling, and they rest on the experience of the individual who has received them. Sheer reception of the vision vests the recipient with some status.

On the other side, Paul in effect renounces authority built on "visions and revelations," though he is quick to make clear that his renunciation is not a cover for his lack of them. On the contrary. In contrast, Paul prefers to rest the case for his own authority with the Corinthians, and with anyone else, on his performance day in and day out. His work with them has not been a "flash in the pan" but has constituted a consistent, dependable, "tried and true" history. Such conduct holds up under scrutiny and evaluation. Furthermore, the Corinthians have been the beneficiaries of Paul's performance throughout the years. They can judge from what they have seen in him and heard from him (12:6).

12:7b-10. Forming the ultimate contrast, Paul moves from heavenly transport to a discussion of his σκόλοψ (*skolops*, "thorn/stake") in the flesh, which he says was given to him to keep him from being too elated by "an abundance of revelations" (2 Cor 12:7). He needs no explanation for the Corinthians about this *skolops*, on two counts: He

expects the Corinthians to know the term as he uses it, and he seems to expect that they know well what it refers to in his life. For Paul, his *skolops* in the flesh is a perspective keeper; the passive "given me" is usually a way for Paul to designate God, and it may be so here, even though Paul identifies the *skolops* as a "messenger/agent/angel of Satan" (ἄγγελος σατανᾶ *angelos satana*, 12:7). Could he be using the passive to suggest that Satan is the one who has given him the *skolops*? In any case, Paul describes his handling by the satanic agent as a "beating or rough treatment" (κολαφίζω *kolaphizō*, "torment," the NIV and NRSV choice, regrettably encourages modern readers to make a psychological interpretation) that obviously was of such duration for Paul to appeal at three distinct times for its removal (12:8).

The *skolops* "in the flesh" (τῇ σαρκί *tē sarki*) has inspired all sorts of speculation that Paul refers to some illness or physical problem that plagued him for some time, though anyone like Paul who can have survived all the hardships he reports (Rom 8:35-39; 1 Cor 4:11-12; 2 Cor 1:8-10; 4:7-10; 6:4-10; 11:21b-29) and traveled so widely around and across the Mediterranean would not have had overwhelming physical problems or weakness.[227] The candidates for identification of his *skolops* in the flesh have been of two sorts: either his opponents or a physical problem such as epilepsy, hysteria, depression, headaches, or eye problems—even leprosy and malaria have had their advocates, as have stuttering, spiritual temptations (from opponents or generated from his own conscience).[228] Of identifications there is no end.[229] Truth be told, we do not have a clue. Nor can we. Nor need we. *What* the problem is—that is not a concern for Paul.

The term *skolops* refers to a pointed stake or to a thorn and is most often used in English translations to mean the latter. According to certain texts,[230] the term refers to sharpened wooden stakes (1) that form a palisade for

---

227. L. Woods, "Opposition to a Man and His Message: Paul's 'Thorn in the Flesh' (2 Cor 12:7)," *AusBR* 39 (1991) 52, argues persuasively that the hardship catalog in 2 Cor 11:23-29 suggests that any physical limitation of Paul must have been minimal.

228. *BAGD*, 441.

229. See C. K. Barrett, *A Commentary on the Second Epistle to the Corinthians* (London: Black, 1973) 314-16.

230. D. M. Park, "Paul's *skolops tē sarki*: Thorn or Stake (2 Cor 12:7)" *NovT* 22 (1980) 180n. 6, details a series of pertinent texts.

defensive purposes, (2) that are placed in a pit or depression on the hopes that opposing soldiers might fall upon them to their great distress, or (3) that are used to impale an enemy as a means of torture.[231] Paul, who thinks of God's grand purposes as a battle (cf. 2:14; 10:3-6) and of Satan as having plans (2:11), strategies, and agents (11:14-15), ties this "stake" to Satan as one of his messengers or agents (ἄγγελος *angelos*, can also be "angel," for "angel of Satan").[232] Whatever this stake actually was, Paul here interprets it as a trap, a palisade, a torture prepared by a clever enemy to take him out of the battle plan. But it has only partial effect, and that unintended: It simply keeps him from being overly elated by his many revelations, some of which are obviously grand, as can be seen in the instance of the heavenly transit just reported.

Paul's appeal to the Lord, three times, that the stake "should leave him" (12:8; not, as the NIV would have it, that the Lord should "take it away from me"), once again could suggest that the stake is something planted by Satan as a "messenger" and Paul wishes it removed. Paul does not address why the stake was not removed. Clearly it was not (cf. Mark 14:36).

The problematic description that the thorn/stake is in some sense from Satan has traditionally been resolved by claiming that there is a sort of teamwork between God and Satan such that God "allows" Satan (cf. Rev 13:5, 7, 15) to impose this impediment on Paul or that Satan unwittingly carries out God's will.[233] Surely, Paul trusts that he can seek redress by petitioning the Lord (12:8), and that God's grace can be said to work in the thorn/stake supports the same notion (12:9).

If as a "messenger of Satan" the stake is not something that *God* has given Paul, but that Satan has in some sense given him, then provocative considerations emerge. Given Paul's statements elsewhere about Satan, and given the understandings of warfare in Paul's time, we may make the following observations:[234] Paul believes that Satan is on the prowl (in at least one instance even depicted in military terms, Rom 16:20), has his own ministers (just as Paul is a minister of God, 2 Cor 11:13-15), and has a scheme that obviously is designed to thwart God's plan.

Paul thinks believers are cued in to Satan's plans and modus operandi (2:11), which is to foil matters for believers whenever possible (1 Cor 7:5). How natural for Paul, considering God's plan to be a battle against cosmic powers, to think of the military trap of his time whereby a pit is dug and filled with pointed stakes as a surprise to the enemy, who would fall unwittingly into it, or as more nearly fits Paul, would have the stake driven into the enemy's flesh as an excruciating torture. Given such a context, God has not given the *skolops* to him; Satan's agent has.

Paul's biblical sources inform him, on a "model of affliction" patterned on Job,[235] that Satan zeros in on exemplary righteous people in hopes of leading them astray so that they will fall in status before God. In his self-depiction in 12:7-9, Paul embraces this picture. He, as the apostle of unequaled probity and standing with God, has been identified by Satan as a prime enemy. As in a military move designed to trap Paul, Satan has employed a messenger, an ἄγγελος (*angelos*, "angel") of Satan. To the Corinthians, then, Paul subtly portrays himself as the one who, more effectively than others, understands and opposes Satan's plan.

Paul nowhere says that God *causes* all things to happen, though he does say elsewhere what would fit very well here: Though God does not cause all things, God does *work in* all things for good unto those who love God (Rom 8:28). So, with the stake, though God did not cause it, God can work through it to keep Paul from being too elated regarding his extraordinary revelations (12:7; cf. Rom 9:17 for God's power shown through Pharaoh). Then in this case, God has co-opted Satan's stake as a means of helping Paul keep perspective and, incidentally, showing that God is ultimately in control. It follows that

---

231. Park, "Paul's *skolops tē sarki*," 181.

232. Paul holds that Satan disguises himself as an "angel" (2 Cor 11:14). Later Judaism tied Satan to an angel of death. See W. Foerster, "Σατανᾶς," *TDNT* 7:162.

233. Cf. J. C. Thomas, "'An Angel from Satan': Paul's Thorn in the Flesh," *Journal of Pentecostal Theology* 9 (1996) 44-45.

234. See Garrett, "The God of This World and the Affliction of Paul: 2 Cor 4:1-12," 104-7, who gives "Paul's view of Satan."

235. In what follows I am indebted to S. R. Garrett, "Paul's Thorn and Cultural Models of Affliction," in Whitei and Yarbrough, *The Social World of the First Christians*, esp. 97: "an oblique but positive assertion about himself."

Paul's prayers to the Lord that it be removed credit God with the power to remove it, but the answers to his requests show God's refusal and give Paul the occasion to understand once again the paradoxical relationship of power and weakness that he now interprets for the Corinthians.

Rhetorically, the mention of Paul's "stake in the flesh" is most assuredly not a confession of a less than exemplary life. Such a self-disclosure would not fit his needs or purposes here. Neither is it an admission that Satan or sin has insinuated itself into Paul's life. Nowhere in the Pauline corpus has Satan or sin affected Paul's life of faith.[236] Paul is clearly in a defensive mode in 2 Corinthians 10–13 because relations between him and the Corinthians have eroded to dangerous levels. Nothing would be served by an admission of failure or inadequacy. On the contrary, his "stake" must be interpreted in the light of all the hardships that have been detailed in this letter fragment; they show that he is so properly dedicated to the work of the gospel that *nothing* can distract him—not even his well-known "stake in the flesh." Accordingly, the stake must be interpreted the same as any of the hardships or difficulties: as an *impediment*—granted, one of unavoidable proportion—but not as a moral flaw.

What Paul got in the Lord's response to his appeal, though not a removal of the stake as he had requested, was instead a twofold assurance: that the Lord's grace is sufficient and that the Lord's power is perfected in weakness (12:9). The sufficiency of God's grace is a basic conviction for Paul. Romans may state it most directly: As much as sin may abound, God's grace abounds even more (Rom 5:20). It is a part of the grand contention that ultimately eventuates in God's victory, that grace, not sin, that righteousness, not death, will have the last word (Rom 5:21). Recycling the story of the exodus from

Egypt in his earlier writing to the Corinthians, Paul made the same point about God's grace without using the term: Nothing, no matter how severe, can happen for which God does not also provide a way out, a new exodus (1 Cor 10:13). No simpler formulation of the good news is possible: God's grace is sufficient. Period.

God's power and human weakness also have a strong association in Paul's thought. Already in an earlier letter to the Corinthians, Paul took the related antinomy of wisdom and folly and allied it with power/weakness (1 Cor 1:26-30; 4:10). Indeed, human redemption is available only through God's grace and power; humans, weak and helpless because of sin, are unable to extricate themselves from sin's power without divine help (Rom 5:6; 8:26). More immediately, in 2 Corinthians 10–13 Paul has been focused on his own weakness as an avenue of God's power, and now in 12:8-10 that thought reaches its apex.

The notion of God's power being perfected or brought to its fullness (τελέω *teleō*) in weakness is also a fundamental Pauline conviction, though nowhere else said so poignantly or forcefully. Faith's beginning is precisely an exercise of God's power in weakness (Rom 5:6); what people cannot achieve is given to them freely as a gift—in other words, as grace. The gospel is defined as "God's power" to those who believe (Rom 1:16; cf. 1 Cor 1:18). Without using the term "weakness," Paul's depiction of human beings as earthenware vessels into which God has poured such treasure is "in order to show that the overwhelming power is from God and not from us" (2 Cor 4:7).

The paradoxical (God's) power through (human) weakness frees, even compels, Paul to boast of his weaknesses. Now, to boast of his weakness gives the glory to God, whose power after all is the only and effective power in his life—indeed, in the world. Paul focuses on "the power of *Christ*" (12:9), probably because it is Christ, in Paul's gospel, who suffers the ultimate helplessness in his crucifixion and is himself the hallmark of God's power, effective in his being raised from the dead. The Greek phrase ἡ δύναμις τοῦ Χριστοῦ (*hē dynamis tou Christou*, "the power of Christ") probably refers to power that comes

---

236. For Paul, faith and sin are mutually exclusive (Rom 14:23). One cannot serve two masters, the Lord and sin (Rom 6:1-14; 1 Cor 6:20; 7:23). Even Romans 7:1, which used to be regularly interpreted along the lines of faith and sin mixed into Paul's life, despite the evidence to the contrary in Romans, has in modern times been powerfully argued not to be auto-biographical, but exemplary. P. W. Meyer, "The Worm at the Core of the Apple," in *The Conversation Continues: Studies in Paul and John in Honor of J. Louis Martyn*, ed. R. T. Fortna and B. R. Gaventa (Nashville: Abingdon, 1990) 64-65. On the specific rhetoric of Romans 7:1, see S. K. Stowers, "Romans 7:7-25 as a Speech-in-Character (προσωποποιία)," in *Paul in His Hellenistic Context*, ed. T. Engberg-Pedersen (Minneapolis: Fortress, 1995) 180-202.

from Christ, that is granted by and through Christ. In wishing, therefore, for the power of Christ to "take up residence" in him, Paul in effect prays that he may be a locus of God's power being perfected in weakness. The notion of "taking up residence" (ἐπισκηνόω *episkēnoō*, 12:9) has a slight echo back to the passage where Paul was describing human nature as like an "earthly tent" (οἰκία τοῦ σκήνους *oikia tou skēnous*, 5:1); now he wants the "power of Christ" to tent itself upon him.

In two beautifully crafted statements (12:10), Paul brings his fool's speech to a conclusion (διό *dio*, "therefore"). The first suspends a mini-hardship list between the opening verb (εὐδοκέω *eudokeō*, "I delight in/approve of") and the concluding phrase "for the sake of Christ," in last place for dramatic emphasis. The mini-list leads, of course, with weakness, the featured topic at hand, and moves in an ever more severe gradation through insults (a reference to claims against him), to hardships, to the Pauline combination of persecutions and calamities (cf. Rom 8:35)—all "for the sake of Christ," affirming Paul's solidarity with and focus upon Christ as the model of the life of faith (12:10). The second statement is the most sweeping: "For whenever I am weak, then strong I am" (this translation honors Paul's ending with the emphatic εἰμι [*eimi*, "I am"], 12:10).

REFLECTIONS

1. Christians, following Paul, have chosen the cross as the central symbol of faith because it, better than any other, seizes upon the proclamation that the power, indeed, resides with God. The story did not end with the death of Jesus, but the cross stands empty by God's power, by God's grace, by God's goodwill toward all humankind. Christ, as the perfect representation of true power, the power of God, embodies a certain ambiguity about life. On the one hand, he is crucified in weakness, subject as we are to the power of oppression and death. If the story ended there we would be most pitiable (1 Cor 15:19) and there would be no basis for hope. As the resurrected one, on the other hand, Christ becomes the epitome of power, because God, the all-powerful one, raised him from the dead and promises the same to us.

2. Believers cannot expect to be like Paul in every respect; he really was extraordinary—and that not just in his own time. The grandeur of his religious life, with its spectacular visions and numerous revelations, need not be the litmus test of our own faith. We are more likely to identify with Paul in his weakness, but if we see in that weakness, as he did, the way for God's power to be vigorously at work, then we, like Paul, can be God's agents.

3. We should reflect about what "boasting of weakness" does not mean. It should not become, as it easily could, an occasion for a cop-out, for doing very little or even nothing. In the same fashion, it could become a justification of the status quo, for not making an effort to change things, because we are so weak.

4. Paul's fool's speech, with its highs and its lows, might serve as a help in our daily perspective keeping. When we weigh out our life at the end of each day, we might use Paul's roller-coaster fool's speech as a framework for thinking that allows us to acknowledge our accomplishments without getting carried away and thinking too highly of ourselves and to admit our failures, insults, and difficulties without losing perspective and falling into despair.

2 CORINTHIANS 12:11-13, APOSTOLIC COMMENDATION AND CONFIRMATION

COMMENTARY

Paul admits to being the fool, but places the responsibility for that on the Corinthians, who should have been commending him, an echo of 3:1-3. He knows—and believes they should realize also, if they merely "looked at what is before their eyes" (2 Cor 10:7)—that he is not inferior to these superlative apostles, "even if nothing I am" (12:11), playing *ad absurdum* off of his "then powerful I am," which closed the fool's speech in 12:10. Even if he is *nothing,* he is not inferior to them. He offers evidence that provides a window on what he thought were the credentials of apostles: All the distinguishing marks of an apostle have been produced among the Corinthians—and that with "all patience."

The three terms in Paul's list all interpret one reality: the working of wondrous deeds. The first two, "signs" (σημεῖον *sēmeion,* "sign," "distinguishing mark") and "wonders" (τέρας *teras,* "prodigy/portent/omen"), are often, as here, linked together in Scripture (Matt 24:24; John 4:48; Acts 2:22; Heb 2:4). The third, "mighty works" (δύναμις *dynamis*), is a common term used to describe miracles or other demonstrations of power (Mark 6:5; Acts 2:22). Paul as wonder-worker is a figure not depicted in his letters, but the way he writes about himself in 12:12 leaves no doubt that he expects the Corinthians to know him in this way. Perhaps 1 Cor 2:4 alludes to such performance.

As Paul surveys his completed work for the gospel when he writes to the Romans, he offers a self-portrait that confirms the 2 Cor 12:12 picture. The parallels are striking. In Rom 15:18, Paul declines to boast except in the work that God or Christ has done through him. Christ worked through Paul "by word and deed, by the power of signs and wonders, by the power of the Spirit of God" (Rom 15:18-19 NRSV).

It is worth pondering why we do not see Paul the worker of mighty deeds in his letters. Several reasons probably account for it. Foremost is that in Paul's letters we have his

wrestling with particular problems or issues that have arisen in his absence, and in every case except Romans his readers know the kinds of works he has done; so repetition of them would be pointless or perhaps even self-serving. Acts is a good comparison; it was written by someone else and depicts Paul as an apostle doing mighty works and preaching. In Acts we have no clue that Paul ever wrote a letter; in the letters we have no depiction of Paul as a miracle worker.

The evidence is before the Corinthians both in Paul's history with them and in his representation of it in the declaration of 12:12. The Corinthians have in no way been deprived, Paul claims, by his ministry among them. In a loaded question that probably touches on sensitive matters between Paul and the Corinthians, he asks: "In what way have you been treated less well than the other churches, except that *I myself* did not burden you?" (12:13, italics added).

Once again, the persistent problem of Paul's refusal of Corinthian support is manifest. Already in this letter fragment, the issue has surfaced in 11:7-12 and again in 11:20; it will continue to be a controversy through much of the remaining verses of 12:14-18. Paul's refusal to accept support from the Corinthians for his work among them has gone from being a positive badge of honor, as it was in his early days with them, to a sign of his treating them as second-class citizens among all the churches ("How have you been treated less well?"). Paul's opponents have probably seized on this issue as a powerful critique of him and have found a sensitive hearing for it at Corinth. The argument by Paul's intruding opponents probably went something like this:

As Paul knows and earlier even wrote to you, apostles, like soldiers and even shepherds (1 Cor 9:4-7), have the right to support for their work in behalf of the gospel. They should put their time and energies into the gospel and its proclamation; besides, it is beneath them to work in self-support (as Paul so stubbornly does). If Paul is truly an apostle, he should gladly welcome your offers of support; he clearly does from the Macedonians. Paul's refusal of support by you Corinthians shows that he does not honor you. In fact, it is worse than that: His rejection of your efforts to help him is a shameful slap in your faces; it is, as everybody knows, an act of enmity, not of friendship. We, on the other hand. . . .

Paul's response, in a nutshell, is that the Corinthians have not been deprived of any of the signs and wonders that apostles do and that they have not missed out on anything with Paul, except that he doggedly insists on continuing not to accept support from them. The tone of this letter fragment suggests that Paul has gotten himself into deep water, in part because of this practice, and his determined perdurance in it does not bode well for the future of a very troubled relationship. But persist he does. In fact, he resorts to burning irony and escalated rhetoric about his not having been willing to "burden" them: "Forgive me this injustice!" (12:13).

REFLECTIONS

1. One ought to weigh the wisdom of stubborn persistence in an action that is clearly offensive to others, even when the act may be defended on the highest moral grounds. Input from others is an important consideration in our moral reflection. When we receive signals from others that our actions are not appreciated, it is an occasion for us to review those actions. Is continuing that action worth the concern, distress, or even pain caused to others? Ordinarily, not. The given action must be very important in order to justify its continuance. At some point, however, one may have to decide what is right and proper, not guided solely by what others think, and take a stand for what is deemed crucial. The two extremes outlined here are the moral range within which we often find ourselves: faithfulness to our own consciences and genuine respect for others.

2. Though Paul clearly made the decision to boast, he places responsibility for his boasting on the Corinthians. All of us have been let down by our friends sometimes. When we thought they should have come through for us, they did not. How to deal with that disappointment can be a problem. Should it be mentioned? Only if it can be done in a loving, nonjudgmental way. Should we simply ignore it? Only if we can let it forever be a bygone; if it will haunt us, then it probably is better to bring it up for discussion, but only if we can do it in a constructive way.

2 CORINTHIANS 12:14-18, PAUL'S FINAL SELF-DEFENSE

COMMENTARY

Stung by Corinthian disaffection, Paul projects a third visit to Corinth and alerts them that when he gets there he will not be moved on the matter of self-support. He will do then as he has always done ("I shall not burden you," 12:14); Paul's consistency has been a subtle theme of this letter fragment (cf. 2 Cor 10:11; 11:6c, 12; 12:12). Availing himself, and indirectly reminding them, of his paternal relationship to them, Paul resorts to a commonplace of that world: Parents should not take their offsprings' possessions but should store up treasures for their children; that is the way it is supposed to be, and that is all Paul is trying to do.[237]

237. O. L. Yarbrough, "Parents and Children in the Letters of Paul," in *The Social World of Formative Christianity and Judaism,* ed. J. Neusner, P. Borgen, E. S. Frerichs, R. Horsley (Philadelphia: Fortress, 1988) 131, 136-38.

Three poignant claims gain expression in this paragraph. Paul does not want their goods; he wants the Corinthians: "For I don't seek your things but *you*" (12:14, emphasis added to honor the rhetorical force of last position in the Greek).[238] Then, using the terminology of commerce and transferring it over into the realm of friendship, he emphatically affirms, "But I myself would gladly spend [δαπανήσω *dapanēsō*] and be spent [ἐκδαπανηθήσομαι *ekdapanēthēsomai*] for the good of your souls" (12:15). The second verb intensifies the first and extends it to the very giving of one-self in sacrifice for another, a dramatic and not unfamiliar notion in Paul's thinking about love (cf. Rom 9:3; 1 Cor 13:3; Phil 2:17).

Paul presents himself as baffled. How can it be that, when he loves them more, they might love him less (12:15)? Already in 2 Cor 6:11-13 and 7:2 Paul has noted with some sadness the asymmetry of his affection for them, which excels over theirs for him. That problem continues in chaps. 10–13.

Paul pursues the argument about his "burdening" them because he has been accused not only of treating them as second-class citizens (12:13), but also of craftily wheedling money out of them—of feathering his own nest—under the ruse of the collection for the saints in Jerusalem (cf. chaps. 8–9). In effect, Paul is charged with being duplicitous and craftily deceptive.

Paul's defense is a rehearsal of his recent history with the Corinthians and focuses on

whether he or any representative of him has "taken advantage" (πλεονεκτέω *pleonekteō*, also "defraud/cheat/outwit," 12:17-18) of the Corinthians. Already in an earlier statement of affection, Paul declared that he has not taken advantage of anyone (7:2). By the time of chaps. 10–13, his claim of not having defrauded the Corinthians is not readily granted, so he extends the defense to include his emissary Titus, a person whom the Corinthians continue to love and respect. Paul rehearses his having sent Titus and the unnamed "brother" to pursue the finishing of the collection (8:16-23); Paul chose and sent just such persons of sound character and standing so that there would be no confusion about his handling of the collection.

In a series of three rhetorical questions, each of which is structured in the Greek to lead the hearers toward the answer Paul thinks they must necessarily grant, he grills the Corinthians regarding their specious suspicions that he has defrauded them in the collection. The last two questions adopt Paul's preferred image for living the life of faith—namely, walking—and affirm, via questions expecting yes answers, that he and Titus walked "in the same spirit" and "in the same footsteps" (12:18; cf. Rom 13:13; 14:15; Gal 5:16; Phil 3:17). Paul bargains from their appreciation of Titus and claims that there is not a hair's breadth of difference between Titus and himself; accordingly, the implication is that the Corinthians should be just as ready to embrace Paul.

238. See Demetrius *On Style* 5.249.

REFLECTIONS

1. Paul makes an important distinction between possessions and having the love and affection—indeed, the very self—of another. For him, compared with personal relationships, possessions are distinctly secondary. How many families get lost in this one? Family feuds sometimes begin over the slightest amount of money or over some thing. Once under way such squabbles take on a life of their own that is totally disproportionate to the thing or money in question. In that context, we have lost the truth that relationships between people are paramount. Lamentably, money and possessions often are the cement in relationships, as wills and their being contested often painfully demonstrate.

2. It is painful to love more and be loved less. Ideally, the love you express would be met in equal return, but, as Paul knew with the Corinthians, life does not always work that way. An important issue is how you respond when the love you feel you give is not reciprocated in measure. Do you (always, sometimes, never) withdraw or cut back your loving commensurately? Realism would suggest that you surely must alter your expectations, though you may continue to show love without a price tag attached. To be sure, when your loving efforts are met with physical or emotional abuse, proper self-love requires extrication of yourself from the situation.

2 CORINTHIANS 12:19-21, PRELIMINARY ASSESSMENT AND DIFFERING EXPECTATIONS

COMMENTARY

12:19. Paul is now focused on his impending visit with the Corinthians, and he thinks back over not only this letter, but also his long-term relationship with them. As to this letter, Paul once again addresses his posture in writing this time. He imagines them considering this letter that he now is writing, and he wonders if they will take his letter simply as a self-defense, as if the *big* issue might be what they think of what he has done in this letter, for better or for worse. With apodeictic confidence, Paul describes his speaking that constitutes this letter on two levels: (1) He implies that what he has written is not tailored to fit the audience and does not take its cues from them, but (2) what he speaks, he declares "before God, in Christ" (12:19). Succinctly, Paul affirms that his speaking (and surely his writing because his letters are simply written speech) takes its cues from God and is spoken from Paul's secure standing in Christ (cf. the identical formulation in 2:17 and the Commentary there).

With the only explicitly expressed affection in the entire letter fragment, Paul addresses the Corinthians as "beloved" and declares sweepingly that all he has said and done (significantly there is no verb in the sentence, so the hearers are left to supply verbs as we have done here, taking the clue from τὰ δὲ πάντα [*ta de panta*, "everything"]) is for their "building up" (12:19). Remember that this letter fragment is framed by Paul's affirmation of his authority from the Lord to "build up, not destroy" the Corinthians (10:8; 13:10; cf. 10:4). Paul claims that he is using that authority for its intended purpose: for the edification of the Corinthians—and

he has always worked toward that goal, "in everything" (12:19).

12:20-21. This section of the letter closes with Paul's imagining his estimate of the Corinthians and their assessment of him when he and they are finally together again in the impending visit. In an ABA´B´A pattern, Paul expresses a series of fears: (A) that when he comes to them, he will find them not as he wishes; (B) that he will be found by them to be what they do not wish; (A´) that a vice list will characterize them; (B´) that, on his coming, "my God may humiliate me before you"; and (A) that "I may have to mourn over many" who sinned and have not repented.

In these fears, Paul recognizes that his projected appearance in Corinth will not necessarily terminate his problems with the Corinthians. Relations between him and the Corinthians have come to sorry straits. He may well recall that one such earlier visit ended in failure (2:1; 7:12) and may now wonder whether his projected visit will be any better. He has good reason to be concerned also whether the Corinthians will now finally have got over their long-standing tendencies toward quarreling, jealousy, selfishness, and disorder, to mention just a few of the vices listed in 12:20. The Corinthians have been quarrelsome and disputatious since the second letter Paul wrote them (1 Cor 1:10-12; 3:1-3; 4:6; 14:23-25, 40). And πορνεία (*porneia*, "immorality"), with its related challenge of impurity (12:21), has been a problem for them since the very first letter Paul wrote to them (1 Cor 5:9-11). With his vice list, Paul dares to dig up old bones of contention with them and seems to suggest that his much-vaunted consistency in working for their edification is matched, admittedly in reverse, by their consistent tendency to stray into the vices about which he has warned them vigorously many times (1 Cor 5:9-11; 6:9-10).

Vice lists were a commonplace in Jewish and Roman circles in Paul's time, and he employs them freely and often in his letters as part of his basic moral instruction (Rom 1:29-31; 1 Cor 5:10-11; 6:9-10; Gal 5:19-21). Vice lists function for Paul to describe behavior that is beyond the pale, that believers simply cannot do. He uses them like a fence around the life of faith and treats vices as actions that must be avoided.[239] The lists vary and seem somewhat tailored to each special situation to which they are addressed. So here the first part of the list (12:20) reflects the fractiousness that Paul believes characterizes the Corinthians. Incidentally, Clement, the second-century bishop of Rome, agreed, saying in effect that Paul really got them right when he noted they were contentious and resistant to authority.[240]

The second part of the vice list (12:21) is a less certain window onto what is happening at Corinth at the time of Paul's writing 2 Corinthians 10–13. Paul's dramatics, depicting himself as needing to go into mourning over the Corinthians, suggests that he is reaching a bit, as do his challenge to their purity and his accusations of *porneia* and debauchery. These latter dredge up long-standing complaints of Paul against the Corinthians and are a way for him once again to assert his authority as the one responsible for the purity of the

bride that he as father has betrothed to Christ (11:2). Just how descriptive these images are to the situation at the time of this writing only the original hearers could assess.

Paul cashes in a cultural chip of considerable prevalence and power when he tells the Corinthians that their wandering into the nonviable territory of vice may expose him to shame. The Mediterranean culture of Paul's time was governed by the central dyad of shame and honor.[241] One always did whatever one could to enhance the latter and minimize the former. Although Paul recognized that ultimately praise and honor come only from God (Rom 2:29; 1 Cor 4:5), he also clearly realized that commendation and honor were a normal and proper part of the life of faith (6:8). The Corinthians should have commended Paul (3:1-3); the brother praised by the churches is sent along with the collection to assure the donors that their gifts are being handled properly (8:18); Paul assumes that there are people and things worthy of praise (Phil 4:8).

Paul's projected peril of Corinthian-induced shame and its associated mourning must also be understood in the context of Paul's end-time judgment convictions. As noted in 5:5 (see the Commentary), Paul thinks that all believers, himself included, must appear before the tribunal of Christ or God (cf. Rom 14:10) and give accounting for their lives. Paul expects to be held accountable at the last judgment for the way he has lived his call to be apostle to the Gentiles. Those churches that respond well and live appropriately to the gospel are Paul's "joy and crown" (Phil 4:1; 1 Thess 2:19).

239. J. Paul Sampley, "Faith and Its Moral Life: A Study of Individuation in the Thought World of the Apostle Paul," in *Faith and History: Essays in Honor of P. W. Meyer*, ed. J. T. Carroll, C. H. Cosgrove, E. E. Johnson (Atlanta: Scholars Press, 1990) 230-31.

240. See *1 Clem* 47.3.

241. A. J. Dewey, "A Matter of Honor: a Social-historical Analysis of 2 Corinthians 10:1," *HTR* 78 (1985) 210-16, sets up the cultural force of honor as a context for understanding Paul's argument.

REFLECTIONS

1. Paul assumes that we do assess one another, that friendship involves an occasional reckoning. The dissonance of finding a friend not as we wish can become a crisis in the relationship. How does one deal with the difference between the reality and what one yearns for in the other person? In courtship and marriage, psychologists suggest, we should love the other person for who he or she is, not for what we imagine that person can become. People, and therefore their relationships, do change, and sometimes at different paces; so the matter is of continuing importance in all relationships.

2. Paul pictures himself as always working for the Corinthians' edification. In Paul's categories, therefore, he thinks of himself as consistently loving them. Being consistently loving toward others is an awesome performance measure. While most of us may think Paul's level of performance is beyond us, his example could inspire us to aim higher.

2 CORINTHIANS 13:1-10, GROUND RULES AND CHALLENGE

COMMENTARY

13:1. Echoing 12:14, Paul announces once again his impending third visit. Paul's trips to Corinth can be logged as follows: When he wrote 1 Corinthians, from Ephesus (1 Cor 16:8), he projected a visit to Corinth (1 Cor 4:18-21; 11:34; 16:3-9); in 2 Cor 2:1-3 he mentions his second visit to them and describes it as a "painful" one where, as we have seen, he was wronged by a certain unnamed Corinthian and the rest of the believers did not come to his aid; he planned another visit to them but did not go and wrote them a letter instead (2 Cor 1:17, 23; 2:1); he plans a visit to Corinth with those Macedonians who have gathered their contribution to the collection for the saints in Jerusalem (2 Cor 9:1-5) but does not get to go before turmoil prompts his writing of 2 Corinthians 10–13. Now, finally, he plans his third visit to them.

He knows that his relationship with the Corinthians is at an all-time low and anticipates that the impending visit will be fraught with controversy and confrontation. Accordingly, he details ground rules for the way he expects them to resolve their disputes—they with him and he with them—when he arrives. Not surprisingly, he resorts to tried-and-true practices predicated on Israel's Scriptures: Two or three witnesses must corroborate any charge (Deut 19:15; cf. Matt 18:16; 1 Tim 5:19). Through the practice of multiple attestation to a charge, Paul reduces the chances of a recurrence of any single individual's wronging him (2 Cor 2:5-11; 7:12).

13:2. By careful choice of tough-sounding words, Paul labors to depict his imminent arrival in Corinth as worthy of dread. Perhaps he needs to counter the image that some at Corinth have fostered of

him as a relative wimp in personal presence (10:10). First, he doubles strong verbs: "I said beforehand in warning and I tell before it happens" (προείρηκα καὶ προλέγω *proeirēka kai prolegō*). Second, he paints a picture of consistency by reminding them that when he was with them in his second visit, he told them that if he ever paid them another visit he would not "spare" (φείσομαι *pheisomai*) any of them. Third, he specifies those whom he is prepared to withstand: They are the ones who have sinned previously (an echo of 12:21), including, no doubt, the one who did the previous wrong (2:5; 7:12), but extending in the most sweeping fashion: "and all the others," whoever they may be.

Now we are in a position to understand why Paul introduced a vice list and wrote about people sinning in 12:20-21. He has taken the stringent step of identifying those who might oppose him as persons who by their opposition demonstrate that they no longer belong to the (true, understood) community of believers (cf. 4:3-4). Their rejection of Paul is tantamount to their crossing the forbidden border into vice-list territory, into a status of sin. That is heavy language. Paul effectively ties any current opposition to the "ones who sinned before," to those whom the community has since reproved and reinstated (2:5-11). His rhetoric is designed to disadvantage those at Corinth who would deign to mount opposition to him when he arrives.

13:3. Understandably, he expects challengers because he already has word that some Corinthians "seek a demonstration [δοκιμή *dokimē*, "test/ordeal/proof"] that Christ is speaking" in him. Paul is up against some clever people who in this charge have taken what they know is a fundamental

Pauline concept and turned it against him. Paul believes and has taught the Corinthians that self-testing and self-assessment are part of the discipline of the life of faith.[242] The primary and repeated locus of that self-testing is in the Lord's supper (1 Cor 11:27-32) but is in no way restricted to that occasion. The same *dokim* root term shows up in Paul's descriptions of persons who have demonstrated character through trials and the vagaries of life (1 Cor 16:3; 2 Cor 8:8, 22) and in his wanting to know the character of the Corinthians (2 Cor 2:9; 9:13). Now they turn it against him and challenge whether there is any proof (*dokimē*) that Christ is speaking in him. He turns the notion of self-testing back on them, beginning in 13:5, and uses forms of the term *dokim* five times in three verses (13:5-7).

The very notion of Christ's being in a person is foundational for Paul; it is unthinkable that a believer would not have Christ resident (Rom 8:10; Gal 2:20; cf. Col 1:27). No wonder Paul has evoked boundary talk about sinners and vice lists (12:20-21; 13:2); he is responding in kind to their questioning of whether Christ is in him and speaking through him. Not only do some at Corinth question Paul's authority to speak, but they also express doubts about his standing in Christ.

Paul takes the question of his status in Christ and deftly attempts to move the controversy to *Christ's* power. Rather than defend himself, Paul brings the already developed paradox of strength and weakness to bear on *Christ's* relationship to the Corinthians. What Paul packs into the next couple of verses is compressed and laconic. His premise is stated first: Whatever anyone may say about Christ in Paul, they cannot deny that Christ is powerful in and among themselves. They have experienced that power of Christ, no matter their judgment about Paul. Stated negatively and then positively for emphasis: "Christ is not weak to you but powerful in/among you" (13:3b).

13:4. Two crucial affirmations follow from the Corinthians' incontrovertible experience (note the two occurrences of γάρ [*gar*] that open and correlate v. 4a and v. 4b). First is a christological elaboration of the Pauline

242. Sampley, *Walking Between the Times,* 50-51.

connection between weakness and power, with Christ's crucifixion on the one side and Christ's resurrection on the other. In 13:4b Paul identifies his own weakness with Christ's crucifixion, with which, in the Pauline tradition, *every* believer must identify. That allows Paul to elevate his own weakness, which some at Corinth seem determined to accentuate, by identifying it with Christ's crucifixion "in weakness." So, second, Paul is weak in Christ, granted, but that shared weakness unambiguously attests to Paul's own status in Christ and gives Paul the grounds to warn any opponents at Corinth that he, and those who stand with him, currently share proleptically in "*God's power,*" which has already been expressed authoritatively in Christ's resurrection. Paul announces himself ready to express that power authoritatively on his arrival in Corinth. Christ's resurrection thus becomes a warrant for Paul's authority (really for God's power expressed in Paul).

Paul's return to the plural in 13:4b serves him well because it portrays him as enjoying the collegiality of all those who have shared weakness in Christ's death and been adorned with God's power in the new life that has resulted (cf. Rom 6:4). From death to life, from weakness to power—those are the matrixes in which Paul's own special calling, authority, and power must be understood. With this christological and even theological identification, Paul attempts to convert a charge of weakness into a badge of honor.

13:5. From this position of reaffirmed authority, Paul turns the tables on the auditors. Those who would demand proof or a test of Paul are called by him, through a powerful doubling of verbs with considerable semantic overlap, to "test" (πειράζω *peirazō*) and to "examine" (δοκιμάζω *dokimazō*) *themselves* (13:5a) whether they "are in the faith" (13:5b), whether Christ is indeed "in/among them" (13:5c, the very charge they had lodged against Paul in 13:3a). Clearly, the test Paul proposes employs boundary language, echoing again the same concerns that have come to dominate the letter fragment since 12:20. Paul could not resort to more basic criteria for identity: Are you still in the faith, and is Christ really in/among you?

Paul presses them with a question formed in the Greek to expect a positive answer, and no doubt evoking a curious irony because it employs a verb of recognition intensified with a prefixed preposition: "You are certain, aren't you, that Christ is in/among you?" (ἐπιγινώσκω *epiginōskō*). The intentionality of the irony is confirmed by his immediately providing an extreme alternative: "unless perhaps you are disqualified" (ἀδόκιμος *adokimos*, "not standing the test, worthless"). Once again, Paul takes their indictment of him, that they want proof (δοκιμή *dokimē*) that Christ is speaking in him (13:3), turns the notion against them by urging that they test or show proof (*dokimazō*) regarding themselves (13:5), and with yet one more turn insinuates that they may fail the test (the same root term [*adokimos*] but with the alpha-privative negating it).

To understand how the term *adokimos* functions in Paul's lexicon, consider his athletic self-portrait presented in 1 Cor 9:24-27, where he earlier wrote to the Corinthians that he—and they in emulation of him—must run in such a way as to win the prize and *so as not to be* disqualified (*adokimos*). In 2 Cor 13:5 he uses the same term to suggest that those Corinthians who would test him may themselves ironically "fail the test" or "be disqualified" from the life of faith, which, as is apparent throughout 2 Corinthians 10–13, Paul considers as analogous with a contest or a battle (cf. 10:3-6).

13:6. In keeping with his recognition (12:20) that his arrival in Corinth will occasion his assessment of them ("I fear . . . I may find you not as I wish") and their assessment of him ("you may find me not as you wish"), Paul now turns to *their* assessment of *him*: "And I hope that you know that we ourselves are not disqualified" (*adokimos*).

13:7-8. Lest the Corinthians think that he is out to win them over at any cost, Paul openly reflects about their and his final destinies. Ultimately Paul hopes that the Corinthians will do "the good" (τὸ καλόν *to kalon*) rather than "anything bad" (κακόν *kakon*, 13:7), because without *re*stating it (see 5:10; cf. Rom 2:6-10), Paul confidently expects and has taught the Corinthians that God repays people according to what they have done in the body. So if the Corinthians do "the good/right," Paul knows their outcome with God will also be good. If he could secure their

doing the right, then he could imagine and even countenance his being found "disqualified" (*adokimos*, 13:7; cf. 12:15).

Without the explicit terminology here, Paul thinks sacrificially and presents himself as being prepared to give himself up for their well-being, a notion found between Paul and other groups of persons as well (cf. Rom 9:3; 1 Cor 13:3; Phil 2:17), a profound Pauline affirmation of continuing friendship with the Corinthians. Paul depicts himself as weighing their prosperity ahead of his own; for them to meet the test is more important than for him to do so. Paul's prayer is *for them,* not that he may have some Pyhrric victory of appearing to be qualified, to have passed the test and yet find them lost (13:7). Just as he earlier said that he could not take advantage of the Corinthians (11:20-21), so now he declares that he cannot push matters to his own benefit because, as he puts it, he and those associated with him, can do "nothing against the truth but [only] in behalf of the truth" (13:8). Resorting once again to his identification with weakness over against strength, Paul joyfully embraces weakness if it means that the Corinthians can be strong (and therefore not fall away from the faith; 13:9).

13:9. Paul concludes this section with another prayer, this one so succinct as to be the more powerful, for their κατάρτισις (*katartisis*, "being made complete/completion"), a term that appears again as his second appeal in his closing petitions (καταρτίζω *katartizō*, 13:11). What he prays (to God) for here he appeals (to the Corinthians) for in 13:11: their restoration to their former, proper condition, their being made complete, for them to mend their ways. Very simply put, Paul wishes and prays that the Corinthians would return to the way they used to be.

13:10. Paul is not spoiling for a fight. He closes by saying that he has written in this harsh frankness from a distance because he would prefer, when he does come to them, not to have to deal sharply (ἀποτόμως *apotomōs*) with them, though he readily reminds them of the Lord-given power he mentioned to them at the beginning of this letter fragment (10:8), an authority for building them up rather than destroying them. Edification is what love at work does; the Corinthians learned that from Paul long ago in his teaching (1 Cor 8:1) and in his comportment toward them. Paul calls them "beloved" and declares that "everything we do . . . is for the sake of building you up" (12:19). Edification and love are Paul's choices for the Corinthians, and his adherence to them is the ultimate sign of his honoring of his Lord-given authority. Destruction or tearing down (καθαίρεσις *kathairesis*), though mentioned, is the farthest thing from his wishes for the Corinthians.

REFLECTIONS

1. Self-sacrifice, the giving of oneself for another, is a deep-seated Christian notion. Love considers the other person and seeks the good for that person. When love for another causes self-harm, however, then love threatens to become self-hatred and, therefore, not the love that truly loves the neighbor *as oneself* (Rom 13:9; Gal 5:14). Discernment must be employed to realize when proper giving way to others drifts over the line and becomes improper treatment of oneself.

2. Differences of opinion, different notions of what ought to be done, and even disputes may be inevitable. It is not wrong in church or among friends to have differences of opinion and to find ways to adjudicate them. The critical issue becomes *how* you live with those with whom you differ, and *how* you adjudicate differences. Though arrogance and disregard for others may lead us to think otherwise, virtue and truth seldom reside on one side alone.

3. Calling on one another to make a self-test is important, even basic, to the life of faith because self-testing can become the occasion not only for repentance, for a change of one's ways, but also for improvement or growth. Worship services are a prime, regular time for such self-assessment, but nothing should prevent anyone from taking stock of oneself at any time. Believers have a responsibility to care for and about one another. The call for self-testing is not to be confused with sitting in judgment on someone else; that would be inappropriate poaching on God's turf. A good rule of thumb might be to require self-scrutiny before you ask someone else to examine his or her own life. It is always *self*-testing that is to be done; the most you can do regarding another person is to request a self-test.

2 CORINTHIANS 13:11-13, CONCLUDING ADMONITIONS AND GRACE

COMMENTARY

Regularly, Paul closes his letters with pithy admonitions that very often give a real insight into his sense of what is most needed in the community. For example, 1 Corinthians closes with a string of admonitions, the last of which is, "Let everything you do be done in love" (1 Cor 16:14). Nothing could have been more apt there.

In 2 Corinthians 13:1, Paul concludes with a series of very pointed exhortations addressed to the Corinthians as "brothers and sisters" (ἀδελφοί *adelphoi*). The first, χαίρετε (*chairete*), could be translated "rejoice," but as a closing greeting such as this, it can readily be translated "farewell" (NRSV) or "goodbye" (NIV). Beyond that first greeting, we find a series of trenchant commands. Heading the list is the καταρτίζεσθε (*katartizesthe*) that was mentioned in connection with the related notion in 13:9: "Restore things to the proper condition/order." Next, παρακαλεῖσθε (*parakaleisthe*): "Be comforted through a favorable change in the situation."[243] Τὸ αὐτὸ φρονεῖτε (*to auto phroneite*) is a phrase that functions, as here, in Paul's letters to urge unity or an end to dissension, or both (Phil 2:2; 4:2).[244]

The last in the series, εἰρηνεύετε (*eirēneuete*), calls upon the Corinthians to "be at peace" and extends with a related promise: "and the God of love and peace will be with you" (13:11). God is regularly associated with peace and reconciliation in Paul's letters (peace: Rom 1:7 and par.; Rom 5:1; 15:33; 16:20; 1 Cor 7:15; 14:33; 2 Cor 1:2; Phil 4:7, 9; 1 Thess 5:23; reconciliation: Rom 5:10; 2 Cor 5:18-20). Paul's appeal for the Corinthians to be at peace with one another (and with Paul when he arrives on his projected visit?) is sanctioned by its identification with God as the one who champions love and peace.

The Corinthians can enact their being God's people of peace and love by greeting one another with a "holy kiss" (13:12a). This kiss is obviously a known social convention that Paul has inculcated as a practice in his churches (1 Thess 5:26; cf. Rom 16:16), and the Corinthians clearly know of it (1 Cor 16:20). Calling this kiss "holy" suggests that it is a social convention taken over from the larger culture and made acceptable for believers as an intimate greeting, one person of another.[245] Paul urges them to address one another with the "holy kiss" and from this we may suppose that he wants the love and peace to be affirmed first among the Corinthians, on the receipt of his letter, and ahead of his arrival there. We may suppose that, even though there are obviously critics of Paul among the believers, there are surely also persons still devoted to him. Thus it is possible to imagine that the troubles with Paul that we see reflected in 2 Corinthians 10–13 have riven the community of believers at Corinth once again. So Paul here urges the start of

reconciliation that he may have faint hopes will prepare a better reception than he has heretofore had reason to expect.

Paul's letters generally feature greetings, from Paul and often from those with him, just in advance of the closing grace. Typically, Paul names some people or churches who join in the greeting (1 Cor 16:19; Phil 4:21; Phlm 23-24), but he also sometimes includes, as here, a sweeping reference to "all the saints" (1 Cor 16:20; Phil 4:22). The mention of "all the saints" as greeting the Corinthians bids to have a special meaning in 2 Corinthians 10–13, though, because Paul's frequent resort to the plural as a self-reference has surely been used to show that, despite opposition at Corinth, he has vast support from other Mediterranean-basin believers about whom the Corinthians surely know.

Grace opens and closes every undisputed Pauline letter, just as grace encompasses every moment of the life of faith for all believers. The life of faith is totally dependent from beginning to end on God's unmerited, freely bestowed gift. Sometimes Paul associates grace directly with God; other times, as here, he associates it with Christ. The letters typically close by affirming the grace of Christ—that is, grace from Christ, which is understood to be present for each believer who is addressed in the letter. The love of God is a reprise of that characteristic just sound-ed two verses before (13:11, 13). The κοινωνία (*koinōnia*), "association," "communion," "fellowship," of the Holy Spirit is powerfully ambiguous here, and both aspects fit Paul's convictions very well. The term can refer to a close personal relationship of each auditor with the Holy Spirit; or it can refer to the fellowship *among* believers that is fostered by the Holy Spirit that produces, for example, all the spiritual gifts to enrich the common good of the community (1 Cor 12:7; cf. Gal 5:22). The two interpretations are not mutually exclusive. Given Paul's struggle with the Corinthians, it is easy to imagine that both aspects are possible but that the latter is surely important for Paul's rhetorical purposes. Paul often uses the term *koinōnia* to refer to the association of believers (cf. 1 Cor 1:9; Phil 1:5) that in other places is called the ἐκκλησία (*ekklēsia*), "church." The Spirit, by its joining with the human spirit, brings people into relation to God in Christ (Rom 8:16). What people came to call

243. *BAGD*, 623.

244. J. Paul Sampley, *Pauline Partnership in Christ: Christian Community and Commitment in Light of Roman Law* (Philadelphia: Fortress, 1980) 62-68; G. W. Peterman, *Paul's Gift from Philippi: Con;entions of Gift-Exchange and Christian Giving* (Cambridge: Cambridge University Press, 1997) 131-32.

245. W. Klassen, "The Sacred Kiss in the New Testament: An Example of Social Boundary Lines," *NTS* 39 (1993) 130-33, reasonably claims it is "a public declaration of the affirmation of faith" expressed in Gal 3:28 (p. 135).

a trinitarian formulation is appropriate to Paul, who, though he clearly does not have a well-formulated trinitarianism, nevertheless uses references to all three—God, Christ, and Holy Spirit—to express the complex and rich divine engagement of people that Paul calls grace.

Paul's extension "be with all of you" once again affirms that all the Corinthians stand on the same ground and belong to one another because of God's love, the grace in and from Christ, and the fellowship generated by the Holy Spirit.

REFLECTIONS

It is worth pondering how those admonitions, although directed to cantankerous Corinthians, might bear on our lives today. For example, how can we "live in peace" when there is so much strife and suffering in the world today? Surely God's love and peace have always been depicted as being present even in the midst of violence. Consider the Matthean form of the birth and infancy accounts of Jesus (Matt 1:18–2:23), and notice how much violence permeates those stories; precisely in that context God's Son is born as the hope of the world. Surely, also, that is why the cross, that emblem of shame and violence, has become for us the sign of God's being "for us" (Rom 8:38-39).

THE LETTER TO THE GALATIANS

INTRODUCTION, COMMENTARY, AND REFLECTIONS
BY
RICHARD B. HAYS

THE LETTER TO THE
GALATIANS

INTRODUCTION

P aul's angry, passionate letter to the churches of Galatia provides a glimpse of the controversy that surrounded the expansion of the Christian movement into Gentile communities in the ancient Mediterranean world. The identity of the newly established mission churches was up for grabs: Were they to be understood as branches on the tree of Judaism, or were they to be understood as belonging to a new and distinctive community, neither Jewish nor pagan? Were Gentile converts bound to accept Jewish practices and values? In what ways were they free to maintain their former ways of life? By the middle of the first century CE the struggle over such questions had burst into open conflict. Paul visualizes the struggle for identity formation of the Galatian churches in a vivid image: As the apostle whose preaching had brought these communities into being, he is like a mother in the throes of labor until they are fully formed according to the image of Christ (Gal 4:19).

The Letter to the Galatians is important not only as a primary source document for reconstructing formative Christianity but also for its theological message. Paul responded to the Galatian crisis with a trenchant theological analysis of the issues at stake. This analysis, and the proclamation of the gospel that follows from it, have exercised a powerful influence on subsequent Christian theology and preaching. Both Augustine and Martin Luther, for example, took their bearings from Paul's message of radical grace, apart from works of the Law. Thus the Letter to the Galatians is the fountainhead for all subsequent Christian theological reflection about justification by faith, the cross, the power of the Spirit, and the meaning of Christian freedom. The letter was preserved and cherished in the church because it offers a compelling model for how to think theologically about challenges faced in the community's life.

As we read this letter, we find that we have entered an argument already under way. Galatians is not a general theological treatise; it is an urgent pastoral letter written to a specific cluster of churches at a moment of crisis. Consequently, it is full of allusions to persons, events, and issues known well to the original readers and, therefore, not fully explained. To interpret the letter, then, we must do a certain amount of reconstructive guesswork about the circumstances Paul was addressing.

WHY DID PAUL WRITE THE LETTER?

Paul had founded the churches of Galatia during his missionary travels in Asia Minor, sometime after the Jerusalem meeting described in 2:1-10. Everything in this letter indicates that Paul's Galatian converts were formerly Gentile pagans (4:8-9). Paul came to them unexpectedly as a result of some sort of personal affliction (4:13-14) and preached to them the message of "Jesus Christ crucified" (3:1) as God's transformative deed to deliver humankind from "the present evil age" (1:4). The Galatians accepted the message joyfully (4:14-15), were baptized (3:26-28), and experienced dramatic manifestations of the Holy Spirit (3:2-5; 4:6). We do not know how long Paul spent in Galatia, but he left his fledgling churches there confident that they were "running well" (5:7).

At the time of the composition of the letter, however, Paul had received word that his apostolic work in Galatia was being undermined by Jewish-Christian missionaries who had arrived on the scene preaching "a different gospel" (1:6) and seeking to persuade the Gentile Galatians to be circumcised (5:2-4; 6:12-13). It is important to recognize that these missionaries were not non-Christian Jews trying to induce the Galatians to abandon their newfound Christian faith; rather, the conflict portrayed in Paul's letter is an *intra-Christian* dispute. The newly arrived missionaries in Galatia were arguing that Gentiles who had believed in Jesus should take the next step into full covenant membership by being circumcised. Apparently these Jewish-Christian preachers, telling the Galatians that Paul had failed to instruct them properly in God's Law, were finding a receptive audience among the Galatians (1:6; 3:1; 4:21; 5:4; 5:7), who were already adopting at least some aspects of Jewish Law observance (4:10-11). Outraged by this development, Paul fired off his letter to dissuade the Galatian churches from accepting this revision—Paul calls it a perversion (1:7)—of the gospel.

The identity of the rival missionaries is unknown. Paul does not identify them by name (this is perhaps a studied rhetorical tactic on his part), and we have no other sources of information about their activities or teachings. Thus we are forced to reconstruct their message from the evidence provided by Paul's polemical rebuttal. A few New Testament scholars have speculatively identified these Pauline opponents as Gnostics or as Gentile leaders indigenous to the Galatian churches, but such theories have not proved persuasive. The evidence indicates overwhelmingly that the rival missionaries were Jewish Christians, and all recent scholarly commentators have viewed them as such.

The term "Judaizers," once widely used to describe these missionaries, has recently fallen into disfavor for two reasons. First, it wrongly implies that the conflict in Galatia was between Jewish and anti-Jewish factions. In fact, Paul himself was a Jewish-Christian apostle, and the argument in this letter is between two different Jewish-Christian interpretations of the gospel. Second, the verb "to Judaize" (ἰουδαΐζω *ioudaizō*), which appears in 2:14, does not mean "to make someone else into a Jew"; rather, it means "to adopt Jewish practices." Thus the label "Judaizers" would aptly be applied to Gentiles who accepted the circumcision gospel, but it will not do to describe the rival missionaries themselves. Consequently, recent interpreters have sought other terms. The term "agitators," based on Paul's pejorative characterization of his opponents (1:7; 5:10, 12), has been widely adopted, but it, too, quickly skews our perception toward an unsympathetic interpretation of their motives. Certainly, they did not think of themselves as agitators, nor would they have defined themselves primarily as Paul's opponents. They saw themselves as preachers of the gospel and advocates of the Law. We will arrive at a deeper and more sympathetic reading of the situation if we choose a designation that does not prematurely dismiss them as troublemakers. J. Louis Martyn has dubbed them "the Teachers,"[1] and J. D. G. Dunn refers to them in his commentary as "missionaries."[2] The latter term seems most clearly to describe their activity, and it will be employed throughout this commentary (capitalized to indicate that Paul is referring to a specific group of adversaries).

---

1. J. L. Martyn, *Galatians*, AB 33A (New York: Doubleday, 1997) 117-26. Martyn's reconstruction of their teachings provides the basis for the description given below.

2. J. D. G. Dunn, *The Epistle to the Galatians*, Black's NT Commentary (Peabody, Mass.: Hendrickson, 1993) 11.

The basic elements of the Missionaries' message are reasonably clear: They believed Jesus to be the Messiah of Israel and saw themselves as summoning Gentiles in the name of Jesus to come under obedience to the Law revealed to Moses at Mount Sinai. They probably regarded Jesus as the authoritative interpreter of the Law. (Throughout this commentary the word *Law* is capitalized whenever it refers to the Torah, the holy Law of Israel.) From the way that Paul constructs his counterargument against them (3:1–5:1), we may draw the following inferences with some confidence:

(1) The Missionaries preached the necessity of circumcision as a means of entering covenant relationship with the God of Israel.

(2) They called for observance of Jewish sabbaths and feast days (4:8-11) and presumably advocated obedience to everything written in the Law (3:10), promising that those who kept the commandments would find life (3:12).

(3) They taught that the Law of Moses was divinely ordained to provide moral order and restrain human fleshly impulses (5:16, 24).

(4) They claimed to represent more faithfully than Paul the teachings of the "mother"church in Jerusalem.

(5) They based their message on Scripture, particularly on the story of Abraham and God's institution of the covenant of circumcision (Genesis 17). In accordance with Jewish tradition, they regarded Abraham as the father of proselytes, and they urged the Galatians to follow his example by being circumcised. We may infer that Deut 27:26 and Lev 18:5 also featured prominently in their preaching (see the Commentary on 3:10-14).

In short, they represented a form of traditional Jewish teaching that called for Law observance, and they sought, in the name of Jesus, to extend the good news about the Law of God to the Gentiles.

Why did Paul object so fiercely to this message? Why did he not view the Missionaries' preaching as a variant of the gospel that could be tolerated within a pluralistic early Christian movement?[3] The answer to this question must be provided through a careful reading of the letter, but we may summarize, by way of preview, some of the main lines of Paul's argument.

According to Paul's diagnosis, the Missionaries were preaching a false gospel despite their use of Christian language. We may identify four interlocking motifs in Paul's radical critique of their message.

(1) The Missionaries' emphasis on circumcision and Law observance as the *conditional* grounds for covenant membership negates the sufficiency of God's grace, which was shown through the death of Jesus for our sake (2:20-21). The cross, not the Law, is the basis of our relationship to God. In short, the Missionaries have a deficient christology.

(2) The Missionaries underestimate the power of the Spirit to animate and guide the life of the faithful community. Where God's Spirit has been poured out on the church, Paul claims, there is no more need for a written code of Law to direct and restrain the community. We need only to follow the life-giving Spirit to resist the desires of the flesh (5:16-26). In short, the Missionaries have a deficient pneumatology.

(3) The Missionaries deny "the truth of the gospel" (2:5, 14) by undermining the unity of Jews and Gentiles in Christ. The reconciling power of God is to be demonstrated not by forcing Gentiles to become Jews but by bringing circumcised and uncircumcised believers together at one common table. Thus the spread of the gospel requires a Law-free mission to the Gentiles. In short, the Missionaries have a deficient ecclesiology.

(4) The Missionaries act as though the death of God's Son on the cross had not changed the world irrevocably. They think that things can go on just as before, with the Law providing the fundamental structure for the identity of the people of God. But, in fact, the gospel is the

---

3. Cf. his appeal for tolerance of differences in Rom 14:1–15:13.

revelation of God's apocalyptic action that has undone and transformed the world (6:14-15). In short, the Missionaries have a deficient eschatology.

Taken together, these four deficiencies constitute, in Paul's eyes, a fundamental betrayal of the gospel, a reversion to life under the Law before Christ came to set us free. That is why Paul so vehemently seeks to persuade the Galatians to reject the overtures of the Missionaries.

THEOLOGICAL THEMES

As the constructive alternative to the Missionaries' message, Paul reproclaims his gospel of grace. The central themes of that gospel may be summarized briefly.

1. Human beings are "rectified" (set in right relation to God) not through obeying the Law but through the faithfulness of Jesus Christ (see the Commentary on 2:16), who gave himself for us (2:20). Using a different metaphor, Paul proclaims that we are adopted as God's children solely as a result of Christ's redemptive death (4:4-7), not because of anything we have done or could do. As these examples show, Paul uses various images to describe God's saving action, but the message is consistent: We are included in God's covenant people ("the Israel of God," 6:16) solely by God's gracious action in Christ for our sake.

2. Paul's proclamation focuses on the cross as a liberating event (2:20-21; 3:1, 13-14; 6:14-15). In Galatians, the cross is interpreted not primarily as an atoning sacrifice for forgiveness of sins but as a cataclysmic event that has broken the power of forces that held humanity captive, brought the old world to an end, and inaugurated a new creation. Throughout the letter Paul is reflecting upon the story of Jesus' loving self-donation to rescue us from enslavement (1:3-4).

3. As a result of Christ's death on a cross, the Spirit is given to all who are in Christ (3:13-14). The Spirit gives us life (5:25), confirms our status as God's children (4:6-7), and transforms the character of our community life so that we produce fruit pleasing to God (5:22-25). Because of the transformative power of the Spirit, there can be no artificial division between the gospel and "ethics." God's redemptive work necessarily includes the reshaping of the community's life together.

4. In the new community created by the Spirit, the markers that once separated Jews from Gentiles have been invalidated—or, speaking more precisely, annihilated (3:28; 5:6; 6:15). God's purpose is to create a single new people who are "one in Christ Jesus," bound together in faith and love.

5. Those who recognize the saving work of God in Christ and live in the power of the Spirit experience *freedom*. They are no longer constrained, enslaved, or separated from one another. The climactic exhortation of the letter, therefore, urges the Galatians to stand firm in the freedom won for them by Christ (5:1).

EPISTOLARY, RHETORICAL, AND HOMILETICAL STRUCTURE

1. Galatians as a Letter. Galatians is a real letter, not a treatise or an essay composed in the fictive literary form of an epistle. Formally, the letter contains many features characteristic of Hellenistic letters of its time.[4] Most of these formal stylistic features have relatively little importance for our interpretation of the text. More significant is a comparison of the structure of Galatians to the structure of Paul's other letters. These usually contain the following components: opening salutation, thanksgiving or blessing, body, moral exhortation, closing (greetings, doxology, benediction). The letter to the Galatians noticeably lacks two of these characteristic elements: the thanksgiving and the closing greetings to individuals in the churches to whom the letter is addressed. These striking omissions are an indicator of the strained relationship between Paul and the Galatian churches.

The letter was composed to be read aloud to each of the assembled Galatian congregations. There is no indication in the letter itself of the identity of the person authorized to deliver and

---

4. For an extensive list of such elements, see Richard N. Longenecker, *Galatians*, WBC 41 (Dallas: Word, 1990) cv-cix.

read it. The letter serves as a substitute for Paul's personal presence—a substitute recognized by Paul as frustratingly inadequate (4:20)—and seeks to reestablish his authority in the community.

2. Galatians as Deliberative Rhetoric. Because the letter was composed for public hearing, it has many structural and stylistic characteristics in common with the forms of rhetoric that were taught and practiced in the Hellenistic world. Any educated person in Hellenistic antiquity would have received training in how to structure a speech and influence an audience, and Paul's letter shows that he was well versed in such matters.

In 1979, Hans Dieter Betz made an important contribution to our understanding of Galatians by publishing a learned critical commentary arguing the thesis that Galatians was an "apologetic letter" structured in accordance with the conventions of ancient judicial rhetoric.[5] That is, Paul writes as though he were on trial before a jury, speaking in his own defense and in defense of the Spirit. The present commentary will highlight some places where Betz's proposals prove particularly illuminating. Subsequent reviewers and commentators have observed that Galatians does not fit the apologetic letter genre as neatly as Betz argued;[6] nonetheless, Betz's work catalyzed numerous other studies of the rhetorical strategies embodied in Paul's letters.[7] Out of these studies, there is an emergent consensus that the rhetorical genre of Galatians is not primarily judicial but rather *deliberative*; it belongs to a category of rhetoric whose aim is to persuade the audience to follow a certain course of action.[8] In the case of Galatians, the persuasion is primarily negative in character: Paul is trying to persuade his Galatian readers not to be circumcised and not to become Law observers. (One can also discern in the letter positive statements of the action Paul urges; the Galatians should imitate him in abandoning Torah observance [4:12], drive out the Missionaries [4:30], and stand firm in their freedom [5:1].) Paul was not slavishly following a rhetorical handbook on how to write a deliberative speech, but he was employing rhetorical strategies that were simply in the air in his culture. A knowledge of how such strategies worked may occasionally help us to see how the argument is put together. For example, the rhetoricians taught that a good persuasive speech should employ arguments appealing to *ethos* (the trustworthiness of the speaker), to *pathos* (emotive impact on the audience), and to *logos* (reasoned argumentation).[9] We see Paul deploying his argument in a way that honors this recommendation. For example, the account of his own apostolic credentials in chapters 1 and 2 functions as an *ethos* argument, the lengthy exegetical discussion in 3:6-29 is clearly a *logos* argument, and his otherwise puzzling shift to a relational appeal in 4:12-20 is a classic illustration of a *pathos* argument.[10]

Perhaps the most important function of rhetorical analysis is to remind us that Paul's original readers and hearers were shaped by a culture in which rhetorical performance was cultivated and prized. Their ways of listening and judging were shaped by the prevailing conventions of oratory—a fact that became a problem for Paul at Corinth, where his opponents and some of his own converts judged him deficient in the rhetorical arts (2 Cor 10:10; cf. 1 Cor 1:18–2:5).[11] Consequently, when we hear Paul pulling out all the rhetorical stops in Galatians, we should recognize that he is arguing in a manner conventional for his time and necessary if he was to persuade his hearers to hold fast to the gospel he had preached to them.

3. Galatians as a Sermon. Without excluding either the epistolary or the rhetorical mode of analysis, Martyn has highlighted one other important way of viewing the Letter to the Galatians: It is above all "an argumentative sermon" composed to be delivered "in the context of a service of worship—and thus in the acknowledged presence of God—not a speech made by a

---

5. H. D. Betz, *Galatians: A Commentary on Paul's Letter to the Churches in Galatia,* Hermeneia (Philadelphia: Fortress, 1979).

6. Particularly telling is the fact that 5:1–6:10, which Betz calls the *exhortatio,* has no parallel in actual apologetic speeches or in the instructions in rhetorical handbooks about how such speeches should be composed.

7. Among more recent Galatians commentaries, see especially Longenecker, *Galatians;* and Ben Witherington III, *Grace in Galatia: A Commentary on St. Paul's Letter to the Galatians* (Grand Rapids: Eerdmans, 1998).

8. G. A. Kennedy, *New Testament Interpretation Through Rhetorical Criticism* (Chapel Hill: University of North Carolina Press, 1984) 144-52; Witherington, *Grace in Galatia,* 25-36. Longenecker's analysis is more complicated; he sees Galatians as a mixed type, showing both forensic and deliberative characteristics. Martyn dissents from the consensus; see below on "Galatians as a Sermon."

9. Aristotle *Rhetoric* 1.2.

10. For further discussion of these rhetorical modes, see Longenecker, *Galatians,* cxiv-cxix.

11. See D. A. Litfin, *St. Paul's Theology of Proclamation:* 1 Corinthians 1:1–4 and Greco-Roman Rhetoric, SNTSMS 79 (Cambridge: Cambridge University Press, 1994).

rhetorician in a courtroom."[12] As Martyn insists, the purpose of the letter is "reproclamation of the gospel," and for that reason it is not so much an argument as an *announcement.*[13] Paul is not merely trying to persuade the Galatians to agree with his opinions; rather, he is seeking to unleash the power of the gospel once again in their midst. The effectiveness of the letter will ultimately depend not on Paul's literary or rhetorical skill but on the activity of God's Spirit when the Galatians hear the letter read.

THE INTERPRETATION OF SCRIPTURE

As has been noted, the Missionaries based their preaching partly on scriptural texts, particularly the story of Abraham. An important part of Paul's strategy is to refute their interpretations and to reclaim the biblical story (i.e., the OT) as a witness to the gospel. Paul's determination not to abandon the Bible into the hands of the Law-observant Missionaries was a crucial strategic decision that ultimately helped to preserve the OT as part of the Scripture of the Christian church. According to his reading, anyone who really listens to the Law will find that it supports his proclamation, not that of his adversaries (e.g., 4:21).[14] Indeed, he claims that Scripture "preached the gospel beforehand" to Abraham by declaring that all nations (i.e., Gentiles) would be blessed in him (3:8). This shows, among other things, that Paul saw Scripture not just as a repository of proof texts about Jesus as the Messiah but as a *story*—a story focused on God's promise to bless and redeem all nations.[15]

Paul's portrayal of Scripture as a living, speaking agent plays a significant role in his argument, not only in 3:6-9 but also in his account of how Scripture "imprisoned all things under the power of sin" (3:22) and in his argument that Scripture commands the Galatians to expel the Missionaries (4:30). Because Paul believed that Scripture was a living voice through which God spoke to the church, he dared to propose startling new readings, such as his allegorical interpretation of the Sarah/Hagar story (4:21–5:1), claiming that the Gentile believers, not the Law-observant Jewish Christians, are the true children promised to Abraham. This bold revisionary reading stands at the climax of the central argumentative section of the letter.

While the Abraham stories are the most prominent scriptural texts in Galatians, Paul's language from start to finish is salted with scriptural imagery and allusions, such as his echoing of prophetic call narratives in the account of his own call (1:15); his citations of Deuteronomy, Leviticus, and Habakkuk in 3:10-14; his artful contrapuntal evocation of Isa 54:1 in Gal 4:27; his appeal to the love commandment of Lev 19:18 (Gal 5:14); and his echoing of Isaiah's "new creation" imagery (Gal 6:15). A careful reading of the letter, then, must attend to Paul's use of Scripture throughout the argument. He produces revisionary imaginative readings of the texts in service of his preaching of the gospel. Yet, at the same time, he claims with full seriousness that only the gospel truly discloses the meaning that remained latent in these texts prior to the coming of Christ.

EARLY CHRISTIAN CONFESSIONAL TRADITIONS

In addition to scriptural quotations and allusions, Paul weaves into his argument several early Christian confessional and liturgical traditions.[16] The most widely recognized of these traditions is the baptismal affirmation of the unity of the church in Christ (3:27-28). A number of other passages also appear to draw on early christological confessions (see, e.g., 1:3-4; 2:16, 20; 3:13-14; 4:4-5). These citations anchor Paul's arguments in a deep layer of early Christian tradition that would have been acknowledged not only by the Galatians but also by the rival Missionaries

---

12. Martyn, *Galatians,* 21.

13. Martyn, *Galatians,* 22-23.

14. Paul is able to sustain this position by ignoring the narrative about Abraham's circumcision in Genesis 17. How might Paul have responded if pressed to deal with this text? His later treatment of Abraham in Romans 4 provides some clues; see esp. Rom 4:9-12.

15. On Paul's hermeneutical strategies, see Richard B. Hays, *Echoes of Scripture in the Letters of Paul* (New Haven: Yale University Press, 1989); "The Conversion of the Imagination: Scripture and Eschatology in 1 Corinthians," *NTS* 45 (1999) 391-412.

16. For a detailed list, see Betz, *Galatians,* 26-28.

as authoritative. Paul's case will be made more persuasive if he can show how these confessional statements reinforce his gospel rather than the Law-observant anti-gospel he is combating. Here Paul stands on very solid ground, indeed, for these early confessions consistently narrate the initiative of God and/or Christ in bringing about the redemption of humankind; thus the narrative plot of the confessions supports Paul's insistence that it is Christ's grace—not the Law—that brings about rectification. Our reading of the letter will be enriched if we attend closely to Paul's deft use of these traditional materials.

Thus we see that Paul's Letter to the Galatians is a complex and rhetorically artful performance. He makes a formidable case for his gospel by linking the Galatians' experience of the Spirit with extended arguments based on Scripture and on early Christian tradition. Like a good orator, he also attempts to enlist their sympathies and to bolster their confidence in him as an authoritative interpreter of the gospel.

HISTORICAL PROBLEMS

Where were the Galatian churches located? This question is surprisingly difficult to answer. The Roman province of Galatia in Paul's time included a large area of central Asia Minor (modern Turkey). The province was named after the Galatian people, a tribe of Celtic origin that had migrated from Europe in the third century BCE and settled in the central highlands of Anatolia, the region around Ancyra (modern Ankara). In 25 BCE, Augustus created the *Provinicia Galatia,* which included not only the traditional territory of the Galatians but also a stretch of territory extending south to encompass the city of Iconium, as well as the towns of Lystra and Derbe; these places are mentioned in the Acts of the Apostles as sites of missionary activity by Paul and Barnabas (Acts 14:1-23).

Because Paul nowhere in the letter mentions any particular towns or cities, it is impossible to be sure whether "the churches of Galatia" (1:2) were located in the traditional territory of the ethnic Galatians ("North Galatia") or in the places mentioned in Acts 14, in Roman provincial Galatia ("South Galatia"). Likewise, we have no idea how many "churches of Galatia" there were.

As is so often the case in historical inquiry, scholarly argument has tended to focus on the problems for which we have the least evidence. Thus there is a massive quantity of secondary literature debating the North Galatian/South Galatian question. The debate remains inconclusive and almost entirely irrelevant for interpreting Paul's letter.

The issues that are primarily at stake in this debate are how to connect Paul's Letter to the Galatians with Luke's narrative in the Acts of the Apostles and how to date the composition of the letter. When Paul wrote to "the churches of Galatia," was he addressing churches in "South Galatia" founded during his "first missionary journey" in the Lukan schema (Acts 13–14)? Or was he writing to churches he had founded in "North Galatia" during the "second missionary journey" (Acts 16:6) and later visited once again (Acts 18:23)? Since Luke's account is highly schematized and not a comprehensive account of Paul's activity (for example, Acts never mentions the fact that Paul wrote letters to his churches), the question remains unresolvable.

In favor of the North Galatian theory is the fact that Paul addresses his readers as "Galatians" (3:1), a designation more naturally applied to ethnic Galatians than to "South Galatian" dwellers in the Roman province, who might not have referred to themselves in this way. It should also be noted that Luke never uses the designation "Galatia" for the areas mentioned in Acts 13–14; he uses it only in Acts 16:6 and 18:23. Thus, in the history of the interpretation of the letter, from the patristic era up until modern times, it was almost unanimously held that Paul was writing to churches in central Asia Minor composed of the descendants of the Celtic tribe.[17]

In favor of the South Galatian theory is the fact that it enables a reconstruction of Paul's activity that minimizes contradictions between Galatians 2 and Acts 15 (see below on the date of composition). As already noted, however, the nature of Luke's epic narrative about

17. See Longenecker, *Galatians,* lxiii-lxiv. Longenecker nonetheless subscribes to the South Galatian hypothesis.

the expansion of the early Christian mission is such that it should not be pressed for precision about matters of detail. (E.g., Acts 9:26-30 has Paul introduced by Barnabas to the church in Jerusalem shortly after his conversion experience and preaching publicly there; by contrast, in Gal 1:18-24 Paul emphatically insists that he was "unknown by sight to the churches of Judea" for at least fourteen years after his initial call.) Thus avoidance of contradiction between Acts and Galatians 2:1 should not be a decisive factor in determining the addressees and date of Paul's letter.

If Acts does not provide a precise chronology of Paul's life, and if even the location of the Galatian churches cannot be determined with confidence, it becomes difficult to ascertain a precise date for the composition of the letter. It must follow by some significant length of time Paul's meeting with the Jerusalem church leaders (2:1-10), which is probably to be dated about 48 or 49 CE. After the Jerusalem meeting, we have to allow time for the following events to occur: the confrontation at Antioch and Paul's falling-out with the Antioch church (2:11-21); Paul's preaching to the Galatians and their reception of the gospel; Paul's departure; the arrival in Galatia of the rival Missionaries; and the report to Paul of the changed situation. Some commentators date Galatians as early as 49 CE, while others place the letter as late as 56 CE, in close proximity to the writing of Romans. The thematic similarities between Galatians and Romans appear to favor the later date, but several recent commentators have argued for an earlier dating of 50–51 CE.[18] One advantage of this earlier dating is that it allows more time between Galatians and Romans for the refinement of Paul's position concerning the Law and the fate of Israel.

As Moises Silva has pointed out, although proponents of the South Galatian hypothesis tend to date the letter early, there is no necessary logical connection between this theory about the geographical destination of the letter and its dating. If one assumes the historical reliability of Acts, then the North Galatian hypothesis requires a date for the letter after the Jerusalem Council of Acts 15, since only afterward did Paul go to Galatia (Acts 16:6). But if one accepts the South Galatian hypothesis, the letter could have been written at any time after Paul's initial founding of the churches in Galatia.[19] In view of the paucity of hard evidence, the best we can do is to say that Galatians was written sometime in the period of 50–56 CE.[20]

One crucial question for interpretation concerns the relationship between Galatians 2 and Acts 15. Does Acts 15 describe the same meeting to which Paul refers in Galatians 2? The similarities between the accounts make it virtually certain that they are variant narratives of the same event. In both texts, Paul and Barnabas go to Jerusalem to meet with the leaders of the church and debate whether Gentile converts must be circumcised (see the Commentary on 2:1-10). There are, however, two significant discrepancies between the accounts: (1) Luke seems to describe the council as a public assembly, including all the apostles and elders of the church, whereas Paul insists that he met privately with a handful of Jerusalem leaders (Gal 2:2); (2) according to Luke's account, the council issued a statement approving admission of Gentiles but asking them "to abstain from what has been sacrificed to idols and from blood and from what is strangled and from fornication" (Acts 15:29). This latter account seems in tension with Paul's claim that the Jerusalem leaders added nothing to his Law-free gospel for the uncircumcised, except a reminder to remember the poor (Gal 2:6-10). The first of these discrepancies does not present a major difficulty; Paul could be referring to a behind-the-scenes meeting with James and Cephas and John in the context of a larger public conference. The second discrepancy is more puzzling: If the "pillar" apostles had made a public decree that Gentile converts did not need to be circumcised, why did Paul not refer to it in support of his argument in Galatians? And why did Paul not instruct the Galatians that all the apostles had agreed that Gentiles need not observe the Law save for the restrictions of the apostolic decree (Acts 15:23-29)?[21] There are several possible explanations, but the likeliest one is that Paul knew of no such declaration of

---

18. E.g., Dunn, *The Epistle to the Galatians*, 19, argues for 50–51 CE, and Martyn, *Galatians*, 19-20, for about 50 CE.

19. Moises Silva, *Explorations in Exegetical Method: Galatians as a Test Case* (Grand Rapids: Baker, 1996) 129-39. If one posits a longer interval between Paul's evangelization of the Galatians and the writing of the letter, some explanation is required for Paul's statement that the Galatians are "so quickly" deserting the gospel (1:6).

20. Betz, *Galatians*, 12, identifies the years between 50 and 55 CE as "a reasonable guess" for the date of composition.

21. These restrictions are based on the requirements imposed by the holiness code (Leviticus 18–20) not only on Israel but also on non-Israelites who are resident aliens in the land.

the apostolic council; his letters nowhere give evidence of the existence of such an agreement. It appears that Luke has telescoped events and read back into this meeting an agreement that emerged somewhat later in the development of early Christianity.[22] In this commentary, then, it will be assumed that Galatians 2 and Acts 15 refer to the same meeting in Jerusalem and that Paul's Letter to the Galatians, therefore, was written sometime after that meeting.

GALATIANS AS SCRIPTURE

Paul treated Scripture (by which he meant the collection of writings that Christians later came to call the Old Testament) as a living voice that had the power to speak to the church in his own time (Gal 4:30). By so doing, he set a precedent that has instructed Christians ever since about how to approach Scripture with an ear tuned expectantly to listen for the Word of God. What happens, then, when Galatians itself becomes incorporated into the canon of texts that the believing community confesses to be Scripture? Can we expect to hear in Galatians a living voice that will speak to our time, just as Genesis and Isaiah spoke to Paul's situation?

Martin Luther's reading of Galatians offers a classic illustration. He read Paul's polemic against the Torah-observant Missionaries as an attack on the abuses of the Roman church of his own day, for he believed Rome was teaching justification by works in a way just as destructive of the gospel as were the teachings of Paul's opponents. Luther knew, of course, that there was a difference between the ancient Jewish-Christian preachers of circumcision and the Christian sellers of indulgences in Europe 1,500 years later, but the analogy between the situations was so strong that the text of Galatians became a medium through which Luther heard God speaking directly to the struggles that he confronted.[23]

What would it mean for us to listen to Galatians for a similar word targeted to the church today? This question will be posed in the Reflections sections throughout the commentary, but it may be useful to summarize in advance some of the key themes that emerge again and again as we seek to listen to this text speaking to our time.

1. Rectification Through the Faithfulness of Jesus Christ. Much Christian preaching, particularly in some Protestant traditions, has fallen into the trap of celebrating the subjective faith experience of individuals as though religious experience were an end in itself, or as though we could somehow secure God's acceptance by the device of our believing. Indeed, Galatians has often been exploited for proof texts defending exactly such a message. Careful reading of the text, however, shows that Paul's Letter to the Galatians is a powerful attack on such self-referential accounts of salvation. From start to finish, Paul proclaims that *God* has acted to set the world right and to rescue us from slavery to human religious programs. God did this not merely through some mysterious change of feelings in the hearts of individuals, but through the faithfulness of Jesus Christ, whose love and fidelity culminated in his giving up his life on the cross for our sake. Our trust in him is a response to this saving deed. Reading Galatians in the light of this fundamental insight will require us to rethink the meaning of "faith" and "justification." It will also require us to examine critically the individualistic sentimentality that often surrounds talk in the church about "faith."

2. The Gospel and Judaism. Galatians is not an anti-Jewish text. It is, rather, a manifesto against distortions of the gospel introduced by *Christian* preachers who subordinate Christ to the Law. Reading Galatians after the Holocaust forces us to rethink how we have twisted Paul's good news into a pretext for violence. The Christian community, gathered as "the Israel of God" (6:16), as Abraham's children, must rediscover the ways in which Paul was a profoundly Jewish thinker, despite his ambiguous assessment of the Law. In order to think through this question fully, we will find ourselves moving beyond Galatians into the issues that Paul was inexorably drawn to address in Romans 9–11. As a part of the canon of Christian Scripture, Galatians

---

22. On the question of the relation between Acts 15 and Galatians 2, see esp. Craig C. Hill, *Hellenists and Hebrews: Reappraising Division in the Earliest Church* (Philadelphia: Fortress, 1991) 103-47.

23. Martin Luther, *Lectures on Galatians (1535)*, translated by Jaroslav Pelikan in *Luther's Works*, vols. 26-27 (Saint Louis: Concordia, 1963–64).

should never be read in isolation from Paul's further reflections on the ultimate salvation of Israel.

3. A Church United at One Table. Paul holds forth the vision of a community of faith in which all are one in Christ (2:11-21; 3:26-29). This is not merely a matter of an isolated slogan in Gal 3:28; it is a central theme of the letter as a whole. Jews and Gentiles are no longer to be divided, because Christ's death has brought us together. Therefore, all manifestations of racial and ethnic divisiveness are betrayals of "the truth of the gospel." Galatians is one of the canon's most powerful witnesses against a cultural imperialism that excludes anyone from fellowship on the basis of criteria not rooted in the gospel.

4. Freedom, Not Autonomy. We live in an age obsessed with personal freedom. In such a time, it is far too easy to hear Paul's proclamation of freedom (5:1) as a license for the indulgence of individual desires and interests. Galatians will teach us, to the contrary, that the freedom for which Christ has set us free is a freedom to serve one another in love (5:6, 13-14). The freedom of which Paul speaks is not autonomy. It is freedom for life together in community under God (6:1-10).

5. The Crucified World and the New Creation. Galatians proclaims an apocalyptic gospel. Christ came to defeat the oppressive powers that held us captive and to "rescue us from the present evil age" (1:4). As Paul develops the implications of this confession, he discloses to his readers that the entire world of orderly religious norms that he had once zealously defended has been "crucified" (6:14); it no longer has any claim upon him. The real world in which we now live is the "new creation" brought into being by Christ, in which we are given new life and are guided by the Spirit. As the church reads Galatians, then, we are constantly challenged to reject the wisdom of business as usual—including the business of religion—and to see reality as redefined by the cross. Those who live by this rule will no longer be manipulated by the popular culture's images of security and respectability. We will live, instead, manifesting the fruit of the Spirit, and our life together will be a sign of the world to come.

BIBLIOGRAPHY

Commentaries:

Betz, Hans Dieter. *Galatians: A Commentary on Paul's Letter to the Churches in Galatia.* Hermeneia. Philadelphia: Fortress, 1979. This landmark commentary analyzes the structure of the letter in terms of Greco-Roman rhetoric and offers numerous parallels from Hellenistic literary and philosophical texts.

Bruce, F. F. *The Epistle to the Galatians: A Commentary on the Greek Text.* NIGTC. Grand Rapids: Eerdmans, 1982. Careful, philologically precise interpretation of Galatians according to the traditional Protestant paradigm.

Cousar, Charles B. *Galatians.* Interpretation. Atlanta: John Knox, 1982. Expository commentary for teachers and preachers, offering discerning theological reflections on each paragraph of the text.

Dunn, James D. G. *The Epistle to the Galatians.* Black's NT Commentary. Peabody, Mass.: Hendrickson, 1993. A sustained reading of the letter in the light of Dunn's advocacy of "the new perspective on Paul"; Dunn sees Paul arguing not against Judaism but against the inappropriate use of circumcision and food laws as exclusionary boundary markers for the covenant community. Dunn offers a wealth of parallels from ancient Jewish texts.

Edwards, Mark J., ed. *Galatians, Ephesians, Philippians.* Ancient Christian Commentary on Scripture. Volume 8. Downers Grove, Ill.: InterVarsity, 1999. Anthology of brief excerpts from patristic commentaries (Jerome, John Chrysostom, Augustine, and others).

Longenecker, Richard N. *Galatians.* WBC 41. Dallas: Word, 1990. Exhaustive critical commentary on the Greek text, attending both to ancient Hellenistic rhetoric and to Jewish exegetical traditions.

Martyn, J. Louis. *Galatians*. AB 33A. New York: Doubleday, 1997. Theologically penetrating reading of the letter as Paul's reproclamation of an apocalyptic gospel. Martyn provides detailed reconstruction of the situation in Galatia and the message of the rival Jewish-Christian Missionaries. A brilliantly cohesive interpretation of Galatians, to which the present commentary is heavily indebted.

Matera, Frank J. *Galatians*. Sacra Pagina 9. Collegeville, Minn.: Liturgical, 1992. A clear and careful exposition in a Roman Catholic commentary series that seeks to combine critical analysis with sensitivity to religious meaning. Matera argues for "the faith of Jesus Christ" (Gal 2:16) and follows Dunn in interpreting "works of the Law" as symbols of Jewish identity.

Williams, Sam K. *Galatians*. ANTC. Nashville: Abingdon, 1997. In a series aimed at modeling exegesis for theological students, Williams unpacks the letter's argument in an engaging essay style that illuminates the text theologically.

Witherington, Ben III. *Grace in Galatia: A Commentary on St. Paul's Letter to the Galatians*. Grand Rapids: Eerdmans, 1998. Taking a "socio-rhetorical" approach, Witherington argues that Galatians must be read as deliberative rhetoric, seeking to persuade the readers to turn away from circumcision. Helpfully traces recent scholarly debates about the letter.

Specialized Studies:

Baker, Mark D. *Religious No More: Building Communities of Grace and Freedom*. Downers Grove, Ill.: InterVarsity, 1999. Fascinating study showing how Paul's gospel has been read and misread in evangelical Protestant communities in Honduras. Shows how careful exegesis of Galatians yields a liberating message for Christians in the barrio.

Barclay, John M. G. *Obeying the Truth: A Study of Paul's Ethics in Galatians*. Studies of the New Testament and Its World. Edinburgh: T. & T. Clark, 1988. This fine exegetical study of Galatians 5–6 demonstrates the inner logic of these chapters and their place within the overall argument of the letter.

Bassler, Jouette, ed. *Pauline Theology*, Vol. 1: *Thessalonians, Philippians, Galatians, Philemon*. Minneapolis: Fortress, 1991. Collection of essays from the Pauline Theology Group of the Society of Biblical Literature. Includes significant essays on Galatians and on the overall shape of Paul's theology.

Beker, J. Christiaan. *Paul the Apostle: The Triumph of God in Life and Thought*. Philadelphia: Fortress, 1980. Major study of Pauline theology, arguing that the apocalyptic message of the triumph of God grounds the coherence of Paul's thought amid his varied responses to contingent pastoral problems.

Boyarin, Daniel. *A Radical Jew: Paul and the Politics of Identity*. Contraversions: Critical Studies in Jewish Literature, Culture, and Society 1. Berkeley: University of California Press, 1994. Boyarin, whose primary scholarly expertise is in the field of rabbinic Judaism, offers an original and provocative reading of Paul as a Jewish cultural critic wrestling with the tension between the universal reign of the one God and the particularity of Jewish election and ethnic difference.

Cousar, Charles B. *A Theology of the Cross: The Death of Jesus in the Pauline Letters*. OBT. Minneapolis: Fortress, 1990. Well-crafted study that draws on recent advances in research to delineate Paul's interpretation of the cross.

Dahl, Nils A. *Studies in Paul: Theology for the Early Christian Mission*. Minneapolis: Augsburg, 1977. Collection of Dahl's classic essays on Paul.

Donaldson, Terence L. *Paul and the Gentiles: Remapping the Apostle's Convictional World*. Minneapolis: Fortress, 1997. Major study of Paul's understanding of the Gentile mission.

Dunn, James D. G. *The Theology of Paul's Letter to the Galatians*. New Testament Theology. Cambridge: Cambridge University Press, 1993. Concise summary of the theology of the letter; complementary to Dunn's commentary.

Hays, Richard B. *The Faith of Jesus Christ: An Investigation of the Narrative Substructure of Galatians 3:1-4:11.* SBLDS 56. Chico, Calif.: Scholars Press, 1983. Argues for "the faithfulness of Jesus Christ" as an integral element of the gospel narrative that undergirds Paul's argument in Galatians.

————. *Echoes of Scripture in the Letters of Paul.* New Haven: Yale University Press, 1989. A study of Paul's readings of, and allusions to, the OT.

Hill, Craig C. *Hellenists and Hebrews: Reappraising Division Within the Earliest Church.* Minneapolis: Fortress, 1991. Important historical study giving a nuanced account of the relations between the Jerusalem church and the emergent Gentile mission in the Hellenistic world; particularly valuable for understanding the Jerusalem council (Gal 2:1-10) and the conflict at Antioch (Gal 2:11-21).

Käsemann, Ernst. *New Testament Questions of Today.* Translated by W. J. Montague. Philadelphia: Fortress, 1969. Contains Käsemann's seminal essay "The Righteousness of God in Paul."

————. *Perspectives on Paul.* Translated by Margaret Kohl. Philadelphia: Westminster, 1971. Collected essays. Käsemann's work continues to define many of the issues debated in the study of Pauline theology.

Martyn, J. Louis. *Theological Issues in the Letters of Paul.* Nashville: Abingdon, 1997. Collection of Martyn's essays; overlaps with and complements his commentary.

Sanders, E. P. *Paul and Palestinian Judaism: A Comparison of Patterns of Religion.* Philadelphia: Fortress, 1977. Watershed study that exposed and discredited widely held Christian caricatures of ancient Judaism, giving well-developed readings of Jewish "covenantal nomism" and of Paul's belief in salvation through participation in Christ.

————. *Paul, the Law, and the Jewish People.* Philadelphia: Fortress, 1983. Extends and nuances the account of Paul's thought given in *Paul and Palestinian Judaism.*

Segal, Alan F. *Paul the Convert: The Apostolate and Apostasy of Saul the Pharisee.* New Haven: Yale University Press, 1990. Partly in reaction against Stendahl (see below), Segal examines the way in which Paul's abandonment of Torah observance constituted a break with his Jewish heritage. Helpful on the exegesis of Paul's statements about law.

Silva, Moises. *Explorations in Exegetical Method: Galatians as a Test Case.* Grand Rapids: Baker, 1996. A series of thoughtful exegetical probes into Galatians, designed to introduce students to proper exegetical methodology. Contains good discussion of date and addressees of the letter.

Stendahl, Krister. *Paul Among Jews and Gentiles and Other Essays.* Philadelphia: Fortress, 1976. Contains Stendahl's famous essay "The Apostle Paul and the Introspective Conscience of the West" and other essays challenging the traditional "Lutheran" reading of Paul, refocusing attention on the acceptance of Gentiles as the key issue driving Paul's arguments about justification.

Tamez, Elsa. *The Amnesty of Grace: Justification by Faith from a Latin American Perspective.* Nashville: Abingdon, 1993. Develops a liberationist reading of Paul's teaching on justification.

Westerholm, Stephen. *Israel's Law and the Church's Faith.* Grand Rapids: Eerdmans, 1988. The most articulate recent defense (against Stendahl, Sanders, and Dunn) of the traditional Protestant reading of Paul's teaching on justification. Also contains useful summaries of major developments in Pauline studies in the twentieth century.

Witherington, Ben III. *Paul's Narrative Thought World: The Tapestry of Tragedy and Triumph.* Louisville: Westminster/John Knox, 1994. A wide-ranging account of the large dramatic themes of Paul's gospel.

Wright, N. T. *The Climax of the Covenant: Christ and the Law in Pauline Theology.* Edinburgh: T. & T. Clark, 1991. Collection of exegetical essays, especially valuable for interpretation of the "curse" theme in Galatians 3.

OUTLINE OF GALATIANS

I. Galatians 1:1-10, The Letter Opening

    A. 1:1-5, Salutation
    B. 1:6-10, Rebuke and Curse

II. Galatians 1:11–2:21, A Narrative Defense of Paul's Gospel

    A. 1:11-12, Thesis Statement: The Divine Origin of Paul's Gospel
    B. 1:13-24, Paul's Apostolic Call and Independence from Jerusalem
    C. 2:1-10, Paul's Meeting with the Jerusalem Leaders
    D. 2:11-21, Two Tables or One? Confrontation at Antioch
        2:11-14, Paul's Rebuke of Cephas
        2:15-21, Jews and Gentiles Alike Are Rectified Through Christ's Death

III. Galatians 3:1–5:1, Counterarguments Against the Rival Missionaries

    A. 3:1-5, The Experience of the Spirit
    B. 3:6-29, The Promise to Abraham
        3:6-9, The Blessing of Abraham Included the Gentiles
        3:10-14, Christ's Death Liberates Israel from the Law's Curse
        3:15-18, The Covenant Promise Predated the Law
        3:19-25, The Law as Temporary Custodian
        3:26-29, In Christ We Are Abraham's Seed
    C. 4:1-11, The Fullness of Time Has Come
        4:1-7, We Are Heirs and Children of God
        4:8-11, No Turning Back
    D. 4:12-20, An Appeal to Restore a Ruptured Relationship
    E. 4:21–5:1, An Allegory of Slavery and Freedom

IV. Galatians 5:2–6:10, Pastoral Counsel to the Galatians

    A. 5:2-12, A Call to Reject Circumcision
    B. 5:13-15, Freedom for Love
    C. 5:16-26, The Works of the Flesh and the Fruit of the Spirit
    D. 6:1-10, Life Together in the Church

V. Galatians 6:11-18, Postscript: The Cross and New Creation

GALATIANS 1:1-10

THE LETTER OPENING

GALATIANS 1:1-5, SALUTATION

COMMENTARY

1:1. The strong claim made by the opening words of his letter to the Galatians is that God has authorized Paul's mission and his message. He identifies himself as an "apostle" (ἀπόστολος *apostolos*), one who is sent, and he emphatically asserts that the sender is not any human person or institution, but "Jesus Christ and God the Father, who raised him from the dead" (v. 1*b*). Thus, from its very first line, the letter asserts Paul's authority to proclaim the gospel and to speak for God.

Paul's greetings always follow the standard pattern of epistolary salutations in Greco-Roman letters: sender to receiver, greetings.[24] Paul characteristically expands the greeting format by adding a paragraph of thanksgiving (e.g., Rom 1:8-15; 1 Cor 1:4-9; Phil 1:3-11; Col 1:3-14; 1 Thess 1:2-10; 2 Thess 1:3-12; Phlm 4-7; cf. 2 Tim 1:3-5) or a prayer of blessing (2 Cor 1:3-7; cf. Eph 1:3-14).[25] These greeting and thanksgiving sections often foreshadow concerns that Paul will develop in the body of the letter. (For example, the opening of 1 Corinthians emphasizes that the Corinthians are "sanctified in Christ Jesus," gives thanks for their rich gifts of speech and knowledge, and reminds them that they are called into the fellowship [κοινωνία *koinōnia*] of Jesus Christ [1 Cor 1:1-9]. As the letter unfolds, we discover that these themes are prominent among the matters that Paul wants to discuss with the Corinthians: the call to sanctification, the proper use of knowledge and spiritual gifts, and the importance

of love within the community.)[26] Precisely because the standard letter structure provides a framework for comparison, the distinctive features of Paul's salutation in Galatians stand out clearly.

Elsewhere Paul begins his letters by describing himself as an apostle (Rom 1:1; 1 Cor 1:1; 2 Cor 1:1; Col 1:1; cf. Eph 1:1; 1 Tim 1:1; 2 Tim 1:1; Titus 1:1), but nowhere else is that self-description set in opposition, as it is in Galatians, to a false conception about the source of his authority: "sent not from men nor by man" (NIV; the NRSV's rendering, "sent neither by human commission nor from human authorities," is a paraphrase). This suggests immediately that in the Letter to the Galatians Paul is defending his apostleship against questions or accusations (see the Commentary on 1:11-12). Paul insists that his apostleship is not an office conferred by human agency; rather, it is a divine commission, resting upon no lesser authority than the power of God, the power that raised Jesus from the dead. This is, incidentally, the only explicit reference to the resurrection of Jesus in Galatians.

1:2. While other Pauline letters explicitly name co-senders (e.g., Sosthenes in 1 Cor 1:1; Timothy in 2 Cor 1:1; Phil 1:1; and Col 1:1; Silvanus and Timothy in 1 Thess 1:1 and 2 Thess 1:1), Galatians is said to be sent by Paul and certain unnamed associates: "all the brothers with me" (NIV). The NRSV again paraphrases, in the interest of inclusive language, by rendering ἀδελφοί (*adelphoi,* "brothers") as "members of God's family"; certainly Paul's practice of calling members of the church *adelphoi* was intended to include

24. On the formal structure of letters in Paul's time, see S. K. Stowers, *Letter Writing in Greco-Roman Antiquity* (Philadelphia: Westminster, 1986).

25. Cross-references in this commentary will treat Colossians as an authentic Pauline letter, while assuming that Ephesians and the Pastoral Epistles are products of a subsequent Pauline school.

26. See Richard B. Hays, *First Corinthians,* Interpretation (Louisville: John Knox, 1997) 15-21.

both male and female members of the community (cf. Gal 3:28). The phrase as used here probably does not refer to all the Christians in the (unknown) location where Paul composed the letter, but specifically to Paul's missionary coworkers (cf. Phil 4:21), some of whom were women (Rom 16:1-7; Phil 4:2-3). Presumably, these colleagues were not known personally to the Galatians; if they had been, Paul would certainly have named them, since their names would lend additional weight of authority to Paul's argument. The rhetorical effect of mentioning a group of co-senders is to suggest that Paul is not an isolated preacher but that his work enjoys the support of others.

Each of Paul's other letters is addressed to a church in a specific city (e.g., Rome, Corinth, Philippi, Thessalonica; Philemon is addressed to an individual family and the church that meets in their house). Galatians is distinctive in being directed to "the churches" of a wider geographical area or province (but see also 2 Cor 1:1; on the interpretation of "Galatia" and the location of these churches, see the Introduction). Apparently, it was written as a circular letter to be read in several churches. This may explain the surprising absence of specific greetings to individuals at the end of the letter. We do not know the name of a single Galatian Christian. Also noteworthy—in contrast to other letters that address the readers as "saints"—is the fact that Paul omits any laudatory description of the Galatians.

1:3. Paul characteristically replaces the standard greeting of Hellenistic letters ("greetings," χαίρειν *chairein*) with a grace-and-peace wish: "Grace [χάρις *charis*] and peace [εἰρήνη *eirēnē*; cf. Hebrew שלום *šālôm*] from God our Father and the Lord Jesus Christ." This may be understood either as a prayer for the readers or as a performative utterance that actually conveys the blessing of God's grace to them. Either way, it highlights a truth fundamental to Paul's gospel: God has graciously taken the initiative to bring peace and reconciliation. The grace-and-peace formula stands as a reminder of this truth, even at the beginning of a letter as severe as this one.

1:4. Only in Galatians, however, is the formula expanded by the addition of a confessional tradition that explicates the meaning of "grace and peace" through a compact

narrative summary of the gospel Paul proclaimed: The Lord Jesus Christ "gave himself for our sins to rescue us from the present evil age" (v. 4; J. Louis Martyn vividly translates, "so that he might snatch us out of the grasp of the present evil age").[27] Why does Paul add this elaboration of the grace-and-peace formula? We may be sure that he was not wasting words. In the very beginning of the letter, Paul wants to underscore two themes of fundamental importance: The gospel is about *Jesus Christ's gracious self-giving* (i.e., his death) for our sake (cf. 2:20), and that self-giving must be understood as *an apocalyptic rescue operation.* Paul's gospel declares God's gracious invasion of the world, not merely a new human "religious" possibility. The expression "the present evil age" signals the apocalyptic frame of reference in which Paul thinks. In Jewish apocalyptic traditions, the history of the world is divided into two ages: the present age of corruption and the age to come, when God's justice will finally be established (see, e.g., Isaiah 60:1; 65:17-25; 2 Esdr 7:50, 113; *1 Enoch* 91:15-17, *2 Apoc. Bar.* 15:8; 44:8-15). As a result of Christ's death, Paul proclaims, we have been liberated from the destructive power of the world as we have known it. These convictions provide the foundation for Paul's response to the problem in Galatia.

Jesus carried out his rescue operation "according to the will of our God and Father." In the opening verses of this letter, Paul places heavy emphasis on the description of God as "Father" (vv. 1, 3-4). Why so? We see here a foreshadowing of a theme that will be of crucial importance for Paul's argument later: Those who are rescued by Jesus are given the Spirit and thereby made God's children, so that they can cry to God, "Abba, Father" (4:4-7). Paul wants to convince the Galatians that in Christ they are already God's children; for that reason they do not need to undergo circumcision in order to become children of Abraham (on the issue of addressing God as "Father," see the Reflections at 4:4-7). The threefold naming of God as Father in the salutation reinforces this truth about the readers' relation to God.

In v. 4 Paul is probably quoting an early Jewish-Christian christological confession,

27. Martyn, *Galatians,* 90.

perhaps based on Isa 53:12 LXX: "And he bore the sins of many, and on account of their sins he was handed over." The allusion in v. 4 to Jesus' death as an expiatory sacrifice for *sins* (plural) is often taken as a sign of the pre-Pauline origin of the formula, because Paul, rather than focusing on discrete transgressions of Torah, characteristically thinks of *sin* in the singular as an oppressing power (see, e.g., Rom 3:9; 6:12-14; Rom 3:25-26, which likewise treats the death of Jesus as an atoning sacrifice for "sins previously committed," is also generally regarded as Paul's citation of a similar tradition; see also Rom 4:25; 5:8; 8:3; 2 Cor 5:21). If the reference to Jesus' death "for our sins" (v. 4*a*) is traditional, then Paul's account of the results of this death in v. 4*b* represents his own further interpretation of this tradition; the death of Jesus marks the end of the power of the old age (cf. 6:14-15). It would be wrong to regard this interpretation as a rejection of the Jewish-Christian atonement tradition; here, as in Rom 3:21-26, Paul adopts and endorses the view of Jesus' death as an atoning sacrifice, but he insists at the same time on defining the meaning of this event so that it is shown to be the turning point of the ages. Jesus' death does not simply procure the forgiveness of sins; rather, it transposes us into an entirely new reality by liberating us from the power of "the present evil age."

1:5. Alone among Paul's letters, Galatians concludes its salutation with a doxology (v. 5). Martyn has suggested that the purpose of this doxology is to evoke the setting of worship and to draw the Galatian hearers of the letter into affirming Paul's reproclamation of the gospel by saying the "Amen" along with him.[28] Thus, by the end of v. 5, Paul has completed his salutation and laid the theological groundwork for his response to the Galatians. If the Galatians did, indeed, join with Paul in the "Amen," they were in for a rude shock when they heard his next words.

28. Martyn, *Galatians*, 87.

GALATIANS 1:6-10, REBUKE AND CURSE

COMMENTARY

1:6. Immediately following the salutation, we expect to find a thanksgiving section, as in most of Paul's other letters, in which he gives God thanks for the church to which he is writing and expresses his confidence that God is at work in their midst. In this letter, however, Paul is far too upset with the Galatians to give thanks.[29] Instead, he confronts them abruptly with a strong rebuke, charging them with abandoning God: "I am astonished that you are so quickly deserting the one who called you in the grace of Christ and are turning to a different gospel" (v. 6). "The one who called you" refers not to Paul, but to God. Elsewhere in Paul's writings, including 1:15 and 5:8, it is consistently God who "calls"; the verb καλέω (*kaleō*) describes God's gracious action of summoning people into special covenantal relation (see, e.g., Rom 8:30; 9:11-12; 1 Cor 1:9; 1 Thess 2:12; 5:24). Thus Paul is rebuking the Galatians for defection not merely from the Pauline mission movement but also, more fundamentally, from God's grace (cf. 5:4: "You who want to be justified by the law have cut yourselves off *from Christ*: you have fallen away *from grace*" [NRSV, italics added]). The "grace of Christ" is closely linked with Christ's death (2:20-21).[30] "Grace," therefore, is not to be understood merely as God's kindly disposition; rather, grace is embodied in God's powerful and costly action for the salvation of the world through Christ's self-giving on the cross. God's calling of the Galatians took place through the event of Christ's death and through Paul's proclamation of that death to them (3:1). Insofar as they have now turned their backs on that proclamation, they have turned themselves against God.

29. The absence of an explicit thanksgiving section in 2 Corinthians may be similarly explained. The opening of the letter reflects a strained moment in Paul's relationship with the Corinthian church.

30. The point stands even if the reading of some ancient MSS that lack "of Christ" in this verse is the original one.

The verb "you are deserting" (μετατίθεσθε *metatithesthe*) is sometimes used in Greek literature to describe the conversion of a person from one philosophical school to another. The same verb is used in 2 Maccabees to describe defection from Torah observance: "Antiochus not only appealed to him in words but promised with oaths that he would make him rich and enviable if he would turn [μεταθέμενον *metathemenon*] from the ways of his ancestors" (2 Macc 7:24 NRSV). Ironically, Paul sees the Galatians' act of turning *toward* law observance as a similar act of defection.[31] Their defection is said to have occurred quickly, but we do not know whether this means soon after Paul's departure or in a relatively short time after the coming of the rival Missionaries to Galatia. Either way, Paul is upset with them for failing to stay the course by holding fast to what he had taught them.

The Galatians have turned "to another gospel" (cf. 2 Cor 11:4). This is one important piece of evidence showing that the rival Missionaries were Jewish *Christians*; they were not urging Paul's Galatian converts to renounce their newfound Christian faith. Instead, they were preaching a version of the gospel that invited Gentiles to be circumcised as a sign of their membership in the people of God (see 5:2-12; 6:12). In all likelihood, they understood this as a completion of the gospel that Paul had preached, which was in their view partial and defective. Paul's formulation in vv. 6-7*a* acknowledges that the Missionaries represent their message as a "gospel" but then immediately revokes the legitimacy of that designation. It is a so-called gospel, but not really the gospel, because there can be only one true gospel—and that is the gospel already preached to the Galatians by Paul, which did not require Gentiles to become Jews.

What does the term "gospel" (εὐαγγέλιον *euangelion*) mean? It certainly does not refer to a text that tells the story of Jesus; at the time Paul wrote this letter, there were no written texts called "gospels." The use of the term to describe such stories was a later development in early Christianity. In the ancient Roman world, the plural form of this term was often used in the propaganda of the imperial cult

to describe proclamations of military victories or honors accorded to the emperor. An excellent example of this use of the term has been preserved in an inscription from Priene, in Asia Minor, dating from 9 BCE. The inscription extolls the emperor Augustus as a god and proclaims that his birthday should mark the beginning of the calendar year, because "the birthday of the god [Augustus] was for the world the beginning of the glad tidings [εὐαγγέλια *euangelia*] which have gone forth because of him."[32] The early Christian use of the term "gospel" or "glad tiding" (always in the singular)[33] may have been formulated in conscious contrast to the use of this noun in the imperial cult as a way of declaring that Jesus, not Caesar, is Lord.

At the same time, Paul's usage is certainly influenced by the OT's use of the cognate verb, which appears twice in the Greek text of Isa 52:7:

. . . as the feet of the one who *proclaims* [εὐαγγελιζομένου *euangelizomenou*] a message of peace,
as one who *proclaims* [εὐαγγελιζόμενος *euangelizomenos*] good things,
for I shall announce your salvation,
saying "O Zion, your God will reign." (author's trans.)

(For Paul's explicit citation of this passage, with minor differences, see Rom 10:15; for other passages in Isaiah using the same verb, see Isa 40:9; 60:6; 61:1; cf. Joel 2:32 LXX.) The message announced by the bearer of good news in Isaiah is the joyous news of the end of Israel's exile and oppression, the news of the reign of God.

1:7. Against this background, we should understand that the gospel is the triumphantly proclaimed message that God has at last taken control and begun to reign. That helps to explain why Paul regards the Missionaries' message as a non-gospel; in his view, it merely extends the status quo that pertained under the Law prior to the coming

---

31. Dunn, *The Epistle to the Galatians*, 39-40.

32. For the Greek text and secondary literature, see C. Friedrich, "εὐαγγελίζομαι," *TDNT*, 2:724.
33. Martyn, *Galatians*, 128-32. See also B. R. Gaventa, "The Singularity of the Gospel: A Reading of Galatians," in J. M. Bassler, ed., *Pauline Theology* (Minneapolis: Fortress, 1991) 1:147-59.

of Jesus. Their "gospel" does not reflect the world-transforming effect of his death and resurrection.

Paul speaks of the Missionaries as those who "confuse" (οἱ ταράσσοντες *hoi tarassontes*, better translated as "disturb") the Galatians. This description, taken in conjunction with Acts 15, provides further evidence that the newly arrived Missionaries were pressing the Galatians to be circumcised. According to Acts, some individuals came to Antioch from Jerusalem, teaching that "unless you are circumcised according to the custom of Moses, you cannot be saved" (Acts 15:1*b*). Luke then summarizes the response of the leaders of the Jerusalem church in terms very similar to the language Paul uses in Galatians. They write to the church at Antioch, saying, "We have heard that certain persons who have gone out from us, though with no instructions from us, have said things to disturb [ἐτάραξαν *etaraxan*] you and have unsettled your minds" (Acts 15:24). The verb "disturb" here is precisely the same one Paul uses in Gal 1:7. Perhaps Luke's description of the Judean agitators is influenced by the language of Paul's Letter to the Galatians. Be that as it may, the "disturbers" in Galatia are certainly preaching a message very much like the one summarized in Acts 15:1.

Paul sees such a non-gospel as a reversion to "the present evil age" from which Jesus' death has rescued us (v. 4); therefore, he is adamant that it cannot be accepted as a legitimate form of the Christian message. The Missionaries are trying to "pervert [μεταστρέψαι *metastrepsai*] the gospel of Christ" (the verb carries connotations of turning the message upside down).[34] Therefore, there can be no compromise or dialogue with them. They are to be excluded and cursed.

1:8-9. Paul twice pronounces the curse: "Let them be accursed [ἀνάθεμα *anathema*]." The term refers to something or someone delivered over (sometimes as an offering) for divine destruction. Significantly, these curses are conditional; that is, they are not pronounced on specified individuals but are left open, applicable to anyone who might proclaim a false gospel. The Greek language allows Paul to make a subtle but important distinction between the two conditions in

these verses. The first conditional sentence (v. 8), constructed with ἐάν (*ean*, "if") and a verb in the subjunctive mood, points to a hypothetical future possibility: "Even if it ever should happen that we or an angel from heaven should proclaim to you a gospel contrary to what we proclaimed to you, let that one be accursed." The second conditional sentence (v. 9), however, is constructed with εἰ (*ei*, "if") and a present indicative verb, pointing to a situation that is, in fact, likely to exist in the present: "If anyone is preaching to you a gospel contrary to what you received [as it seems *is* indeed happening], let that one be accursed."

Paul certainly does not anticipate proclaiming a different gospel, but by including himself hypothetically under the threat of curse, he makes an important point. He is not asking for the Galatians' personal allegiance to him; rather, what matters is their allegiance to the gospel message. Even if Paul should ever stray and begin preaching something different, the Galatians should reject him and cling to the gospel. The reference here to "an angel from heaven" has sparked speculation that the rival Missionaries were claiming that their own message was based on an angelic revelation, especially since later in the letter Paul refers to the Mosaic Law as "ordained through angels" (3:19). This is a possible inference, for Jewish apocalyptic literature of this period frequently features an angelic figure who interprets revelatory visions.[35] On the other hand, the reference to an angel may be rhetorical hyperbole, suggesting that if the Galatians should ignore even a celestial messenger with a false gospel, they should all the more ignore the Missionaries' purely human urgings. After v. 8 provides the theoretical frame of reference (*anybody* who distorts the gospel is under a curse), v. 9 zeroes in precisely on the actual situation that Paul has heard about in the Galatian churches. (He gives no explanation of how he received this information; the letter makes no reference either to a letter from the Galatians or to messengers bearing reports about them.) Paul does not name the perverters of the gospel—if indeed he knows their names—but the artful rhetoric of vv. 6-9 will leave the readers with little doubt whom he has in mind. Paul has scored a direct hit on the rival Missionaries.

34. Betz, *Galatians*, 50.

35. Dunn, *The Epistle to the Galatians*, 45.

1:10. The forcefulness of Paul's language causes him to pause and reflect ruefully on a charge that was leveled against him. The Missionaries have accused him of being a sophist who tells people just what they want to hear. That, they say, is why he did not tell the Galatians about God's inconvenient and painful requirement of circumcision. In their view, Paul was offering his gentile converts a cheap, watered-down facsimile of God's truth, rather than explaining the full and salutary discipline offered in the Law of Moses.[36] In short, they charged that Paul was a "people pleaser," playing to the crowd. But now, having made the stern, uncompromising curse of v. 9 at his rivals, in v. 10 he asks the Galatians, in effect, "So does that sound like I'm a waffler seeking human approval? Am I seeking to please human beings or God?" Some commentators have argued that "trying to win the approval" of God is a bad thing, related to magic or sorcery that seeks to manipulate God.[37] In the light, however, of the strong antitheses between human and divine in the opening verses of this letter (vv. 1, 11-12), it makes better sense to understand "seeking God's approval" as the positive opposite of "seeking human approval." The latter charge is the one Paul is concerned to refute, as shown by his restatement of the question: "Or am I trying

to please people?" The bitterly ironic tone of the questions in v. 10 shows that this is still a part of the rebuke section. Paul is chiding the Galatians for giving credence to the Missionaries' unflattering characterization of his motives.

Against such charges, Paul has a convincing rebuttal: "If I were still pleasing people, I would not be a servant of Christ." The word translated "servant" here is δοῦλος (*doulos*), which really means "slave." To be Christ's slave entails persecution, suffering, and conformity to the way of the cross. Paul can describe the scars that he bears (see 2 Cor 6:4-5; 11:23-25) as "the marks of Jesus branded on my body" (6:17)—that is, the identifying brand showing that he is a slave owned by Christ. He has hardly chosen an easy or popular life. Under such circumstances, it is patently ridiculous for his adversaries to accuse him of flattery and preaching a mini-gospel to solicit human approval.

Almost hidden away in this rejoinder is the key word "still." By inserting this word, Paul implies that he formerly was a people pleaser; his days of people pleasing were his time as a zealous Torah-observer (see 1:13-14). Thus he turns the charge around and points it back at his critics. Since he will later accuse the Missionaries of promoting circumcision in order to avoid persecution (6:12), the inference lies at hand that it is actually they, not he, who are seeking human approval (cf. 4:17).

36. Dunn, *The Epistle to the Galatians*, 49-50.
37. E.g., Betz, *Galatians*, 55.

REFLECTIONS

Sometimes we are called upon to draw the line and to pronounce anathema upon distortions of the gospel. For many comfortable, educated Christians in Western culture, this is a distinctly uncomfortable truth; we are wary of dogmatic certainty. Mindful of the harm done by overzealous "true believers," some of them Christians, we tend to prefer tolerance, dialogue, and compromise. We value a plurality of perspectives, and we believe that we can be enriched by the witness of others whose experience of God seems different from our own. Elsewhere in his letters, Paul works hard to build Christian community across boundaries formed by different understandings of God's will (Rom 14:1–15:13). Yet Paul's Letter to the Galatians stands in the New Testament canon as an urgent reminder that some versions of the gospel are perversions. The opening verses of the letter throw down the gauntlet and call the readers to reaffirm their allegiance to the singular gospel of Jesus Christ and to reject counterfeit "gospels."

A few historical examples can illustrate the point. When Martin Luther nailed his ninety-five theses to the door of the castle church in Wittenberg in 1517, protesting the sale of indulgences, he was confronting the distortion of the truth by Christian leaders who had lost sight of the gospel of God's free, unmerited grace. (It is no coincidence that Luther found in Galatians the clearest articulation of Christian freedom.) When Karl Barth and members of the Confessing Church in Germany drafted the Barmen Declaration in 1934, they said no to the Nazis' usurpation of the church. In this way, they defined the truth of the gospel against a false gospel of nationalism and ethnicity. Likewise, when in 1982 the World Alliance of Reformed Churches denounced the acceptance of racial apartheid by the Dutch Reformed Church of South Africa as a heresy, they were following Paul's example of pronouncing a curse on a dangerous perversion of the gospel. If the church is to bear witness to the gospel with integrity in "the present evil age," it must have the courage to make such discernments and to speak prophetically against destructive teachings that deny the grace of God.

These examples are instructive because each one involves a discernment about perversions of the gospel through specific social practices within the church. Paul was not cursing pagan outsiders for their unbelief; rather, he was warning Christian believers against a danger presented by preachers who spoke the language of Christian faith. Just as the Missionaries in Galatia did not understand themselves to be opposing God, so also the Roman Catholic hierarchy in the sixteenth century, the German Christians of the 1930s, and the Dutch Reformed Afrikaaners in South Africa believed themselves to be theologically justified in their actions and interpretations of the Christian message. With the wisdom of hindsight, these cases—especially the last two—look like clear instances of perversion of the gospel. (And these racial/ethnic definitions of the gospel in Germany and South Africa are closely analogous to the abuse against which Paul was fighting in his day.) One of the urgent tasks of Christian preaching, however, is to make such discernments *prospectively,* to identify ways in which the church is *now* in danger of being misled by persuasive disturbers who have repackaged the gospel and assimilated it wrongly to cultural norms of the present age. Thus the preacher working from the opening verses of Paul's letter will want to look with a critical eye at popular contemporary forms of Christian teaching and practice and weigh them against the gospel of the grace of Christ.

At the same time, we must be sure that it is really the *gospel* that provides the standards for critical evaluation. For some Christians, Paul's curse against false teaching may appear to justify harsh judgments against any ideas of which they happen to disapprove. But this is to misappropriate Paul; elsewhere, we see that he champions tolerance of diversity within the Christian community on nonessential matters (e.g., Romans 14–15; 1 Cor 8:1–11:1). It is crucial to recognize that Paul curses the rival Missionaries for promulgating a teaching that compromises the heart of the gospel. Consequently, in order to apply Gal 1:6-9 analogically to our contemporary setting, we must first delineate carefully the character of the gospel. Although Paul's opening salvo does not yet offer a specific diagnosis of the problem with the "different gospel" (1:6) that was tempting the Galatians, it does offer some crucial definitions of the standard against which all formulations of the gospel must be measured:

(1) The gospel is not a human construction; it comes from God, who has taken the initiative to rescue us (1:1, 3-4). This divine initiative can be understood only as "grace" (1:3, 6), the freely given love of God.

(2) The grace of God is embodied and made effective in the self-giving of Jesus on the cross (1:4; cf. 2:20-21; 3:1, 13; 6:14). Jesus' death somehow atones for our sins and releases us from the oppressive power of "the present evil age." (Paul's compact formulation in 1:4 does not yet explain how the death of Jesus achieves these effects.)

(3) The self-giving of Jesus is in accordance with the will of God (1:4); indeed, the fact that "grace and peace" come from "God our Father and the Lord Jesus Christ" (1:3) suggests that the death of Jesus is in some mysterious sense the act of God (cf.

Rom 5:8: "God proves his love for us in that while we still were sinners Christ died for us," NRSV).

(4) The gracious God who has thus acted to liberate us is known as "God our Father" (1:1, 3-4). This implies that we are God's children, members of God's family.

(5) God raised Jesus from the dead (1:1). The resurrection shows God's power over death. Thus, as Christ delivers us from the grip of the present age, he also sets us free from the power of death.

(6) Implied in all of this is an apocalyptic analysis of the human plight and its solution. God's grace has broken into an otherwise hopeless situation and changed everything. Later in the letter, Paul will describe this apocalyptic transformation as "new creation" (6:15). The provocative choice of the word εὐαγγέλιον (*euangelion*, 1:6-9) to encapsulate the message suggests that God's invasive grace stands in opposition to the political powers of this world.

Of course, Paul develops none of these points at any length in Gal 1:1-10, but when we reread these opening sentences in the light of the rest of the letter, we can see how clearly Paul has sketched out the convictions that undergird his challenge to the Galatians. Any representation of the gospel that denies any of the six points listed above must be judged as a corrupt counterfeit.

Paul's apostolic authority is grounded in the truth of these affirmations. He is accountable to proclaim this message and no other. Because he is a slave of Christ (1:10), he is accountable to one master only, and he is no longer concerned about human approval (cf. 1 Cor 4:1-5). This text provides a stimulus to consider how our own actions may be driven by the need for human approval. In subtle and pervasive ways, our character is formed—or malformed—by our desire for applause. The congregation that wrestles with Galatians will find itself summoned to a life in which the only approval that matters is God's.

GALATIANS 1:11–2:21

A NARRATIVE DEFENSE OF PAUL'S GOSPEL

GALATIANS 1:11-12, THESIS STATEMENT: THE DIVINE ORIGIN OF PAUL'S GOSPEL

COMMENTARY

Having opened the letter with a sharp rebuke of the Galatians for their defection from the gospel he had preached to them, Paul now forcefully asserts the thesis that he will defend in the first major section of the letter (1:11–2:21): His gospel is of divine origin, and his apostleship, therefore, is not dependent on any human authority. As we have seen, this theme was already introduced in 1:1, but Paul now sets it forth emphatically in two negations and one positive assertion (note the structural similarity to 1:1):

(1) The gospel that Paul preaches is not of human origin.
(2) Paul did not receive it from a human source, nor was he taught it.
(3) It came through (God's) revelation of Jesus Christ.

Why does Paul begin with two denials rather than with the positive thesis? As the argument unfolds, it becomes clear that he is responding to charges made by the rival Missionaries.[38] Presumably, they have told the Galatians something like this: "Paul was originally taught the gospel by the apostles in Jerusalem. But now he has deviated from the Jerusalem-authorized version of the gospel by preaching a watered-down gospel of merely

human devising, a gospel that disregards the divinely given commandments of the Law."

Paul indignantly declares that this is a complete misrepresentation of the true situation. The Law-free gospel for the Gentiles was given to him—against all his natural human training and inclination—by God. The initiative belonged entirely to God, as does the content of his message. Paul was never discipled by the Jerusalem authorities, nor has he ever been under their jurisdiction.

In v. 11, Paul addresses the Galatians for the first time as "brothers [and sisters]" (ἀδελφοί *adelphoi*; cf. 3:15; 4:12, 28; 5:11, 13; 6:1, 18). This manner of address shows that Paul still regards them as members of God's family; rather than denouncing and excommunicating them, he is appealing to them to recognize their true identity in Christ.

The somewhat unwieldy expression in v. 11, τὸ εὐαγγέλιον τὸ εὐαγγελισθέν ὑπ᾽ ἐμοῦ (*to euangelion to euangelisthen hyp᾽ emou*), is impossible to render exactly into idiomatic English; literally, it means "the gospel that was gospeled by me." This slightly cumbersome locution suggests that Paul himself is an instrument of the gospel's power rather than an agent responsible for its content. This gospel is "not something that man made up" (the NIV's helpful paraphrase of the phrase κατὰ ἄνθρωπον [*kata anthrōpon*, "according to a human being"]). The warrant for this claim is given in v. 12. Paul did not receive the gospel message secondhand as something passed along by other firsthand witnesses (cf. Luke

---

38. A historical memory of anti-Pauline polemic by some Jewish Christians is preserved in the third-century Pseudo-Clementine literature. For full texts and discussion, see J. Irmscher and G. Strecker, "The Pseudo-Clementines," *New Testament Apocrypha*, ed. W. Schneemelcher, English trans. ed. R. McL. Wilson (Louisville: Westminster/John Knox, 1992) 2:483-541. Relevant excerpts are given by Betz in an appendix to his commentary. See Betz, *Galatians*, 331-33.

1:1-2); rather, he received it directly through "a revelation of Jesus Christ." This formulation stands in sharp contrast to conceptions of the authoritative transmission of religious tradition in the Judaism of Paul's time. Consider, for purposes of comparison, the opening of the tractate *'Abot* in the Mishnah:

Moses received the Law from Sinai and committed it to Joshua, and Joshua to the elders, and the elders to the Prophets, and the Prophets committed it to the men of the Great Synagogue.[39]

While the rabbis found religious confidence in such a conception of an authoritative chain of tradition (closely analogous to what Christian theologians, such as Irenaeus, would later claim for apostolic tradition), Paul, by contrast, claims *unmediated* access to God's revelation.

Paul can also speak elsewhere—using precisely the same vocabulary of "handing down" and "receiving"—of the gospel as mediated through a process of tradition (notably in 1 Cor 11:23-25 and 15:3-7, but see also Gal 1:8-9). Does Paul contradict himself? It is important to remember that his point in Gal 1:11-12 is that his own commission as an apostle is not dependent on any such process of tradition. Even though he can pass on traditional kerygmatic and liturgical formulas to his churches as authoritative summaries of the gospel, these formulas must be understood as particular "performances" of an underlying story that Paul has learned directly from God. When the matter is understood in this way, there is no contradiction between Gal 1:11-12 and 1 Cor 15:3-7. These two statements serve very different rhetorical functions within the arguments in which they appear. The first, rebutting an accusation that Paul has invented his own gospel, asserts that his apostolic message has a divine origin; the second recalls for the Corinthians the specific terms in which that message was presented to them originally.

The phrase "a revelation of Jesus Christ" is grammatically ambiguous. Does it mean that Jesus Christ is the one who gives the revelation (subjective genitive) or that he is the one who is revealed by God (objective genitive)?

Paul's usage elsewhere settles the question clearly in favor of the latter interpretation; for example, just a few sentences later in Galatians, Paul writes that God was pleased "to reveal his Son" (v. 16; for discussion of the specific form and content of the revelation, see the Commentary on 1:16).

The last clause of v. 12 is elliptical, lacking a verb. The NRSV and the NIV both supply "I received it," repeating the main verb from v. 12*a,* resulting in the following reading of the sentence:

For I did not receive it from a human source, nor was I taught it, but [I received it] through a revelation of Jesus Christ.

This is certainly a possible interpretation, but we could equally well complete the sentence by supplying the words "it came." This would be entirely in keeping with Paul's understanding of the gospel as a dynamic power that has broken into the present time. The gospel is "the power of God for salvation" (Rom 1:16 NRSV), and Paul can speak of it as something that "comes" to those who hear it, as in 1 Thess 1:5: "Our message of the gospel came to you not in word only, but also in power and in the Holy Spirit" (NRSV; see also Gal 3:23-25, in which Paul speaks of "faith"—a virtual synonym for "the gospel"—as something that "came" into the sphere of human history). In line with this understanding, we could translate as follows:

For I did not receive it from a human source, nor was I taught it, but [it came] through a revelation of Jesus Christ.

This picture of the gospel as a powerful, inbreaking word is consonant with the meaning of "revelation" (ἀποκάλυψις *apokalypsis*). Revelation is God's activity, an act of disclosure initiated from the divine side that reorients all human perception and knowledge (see Rom 1:17, where Paul declares that in the gospel "the righteousness of God is being revealed [ἀποκαλύπτεται *apokalyptetai*]"). Paul characteristically speaks of the revealing of Jesus Christ as an eschatological event connected with final judgment and the consummation of God's purposes for

---

39. See *m. Abot* 1:1. This comparison is noted by Martyn, *Galatians,* 143.

all creation (Rom 8:19; 1 Cor 1:7; 2 Thess 1:7). Paul's bold claim, then, is that he has been given, in advance of the last day, a privileged preview of the glory of Christ and that this revelation has determined the shape and content of the gospel that he preaches. This claim sets the agenda for Gal 1:13–2:21. (See Reflections at 1:13-24.)

GALATIANS 1:13-24, PAUL'S APOSTOLIC CALL AND INDEPENDENCE FROM JERUSALEM

COMMENTARY

Paul begins a lengthy defense of his thesis by retelling his own history, some of which he had told the Galatians previously. The narrative here is certainly not a comprehensive autobiography; it is tailored to emphasize a few key facts that support Paul's present case. Two themes run through the narrative: (1) the divine origin of Paul's call to preach the gospel and (2) Paul's independence from the Jerusalem church. On both points, he is defending himself against misrepresentations by the Missionaries.

At the same time, if we read this narrative solely as a defense speech, we will miss one of its important functions. Paul is also offering himself as a model, an authoritative pattern for the Galatians as they seek to understand how to live faithfully before God (see the Commentary on 4:12).[40] Paul was once a zealous observer of the Law of Moses, but now he has been seized by God for a new mission and redirected into a new life. He has, in fact, "died to the Law" (2:19). Thus the Galatians, who are being urged to become subject to the Law, should instead emulate Paul's example of freedom from it. Paul's own life story shows that life in Christ is life in a sphere of freedom beyond the Law; thus, to come under the Law is not to advance—as the Missionaries are trying to persuade the Galatians—but to go backward into bondage. None of these points are yet explicit in the letter, but Paul is laying the groundwork for them by retelling his story in chapters 1 and 2.

1:13-14. "For you have heard,"[41] he reminds the Galatians, "of my earlier life in Judaism." Surprisingly, the word "Judaism" (Ἰουδαϊσμός *Ioudaismos*) appears in the NT only in these verses. (For earlier occurrences, see 2 Macc 2:21; 8:1; 14:38; 4 Macc 4:26; the term appears also in the letters of Ignatius of Antioch early in the second century CE.) Its usage here, as also in the Maccabean literature, strongly suggests that it designates a body of practices that distinguish Jews from Gentiles, particularly with reference to circumcision, dietary laws, sabbath observance, and the system of sacrifices and feasts.[42] That is to say, "Judaism" refers not so much to a set of beliefs or doctrines as to a culture; it designates a network of habitual observances that characterize the Jewish people as members of a distinctive society set apart for God in the midst of the pagan world. Within that cultural network of practices, Paul used to live; indeed, he "advanced" in it beyond his contemporaries among his own people (v. 14). The verb "advanced" (προέκοπτον *proekopton*) was a word widely used by Greco-Roman moral philosophers, particularly Stoics, to describe their progress in the disciplines of living a wise life. Paul's use of this term here sheds light on his retrospective understanding of his former life; "Judaism" was for him a kind of moral culture in which one could seek to excel. Indeed, it was possible to compare one's own attained level of excellence to the level attained by others pursuing the same set of practices.

One of the ways in which Paul excelled in the practice of Judaism was—as he now ruefully observes—by "violently persecuting

40. See B. R. Gaventa, "Galatians 1 and 2: Autobiography as Paradigm," *NovT* 28 (1986) 309-26.
41. The word "for" (γάρ *gar*), oddly translated in the NRSV as "no doubt," shows that Paul will now begin the task of producing evidence for the thesis of 1:11-12.

42. Dunn, *The Epistle to the Galatians,* 56.

the church of God and trying to destroy it." Why would such hostile action be cited as evidence of excellence in the practice of Judaism? The key to understanding Paul's point here lies in a term he uses in the last clause of v. 14: "I was exceedingly zealous [ζηλωτής zēlōtēs] for the traditions of my ancestors." As Martin Hengel has argued, the terms "zealous" and "zeal" had assumed in Second Temple Judaism a very specific meaning related to the preservation of Jewish religious and ethnic purity by whatever means necessary, including violence.[43] The great OT exemplar of such zeal was Phinehas, who had averted a plague afflicting Israel through an act of vigilante violence by killing an Israelite man and his foreign Midianite wife, impaling both of them (apparently during the act of sexual intercourse) with a single spear (Num 25:6-18). According to the story in Numbers, the reaction of the Lord to this deed was one of glowing approbation:

The LORD spoke to Moses, saying, "Phinehas son of Eleazar, son of Aaron the priest, has turned back my wrath from the Israelites by manifesting such zeal among them on my behalf that in my jealousy I did not consume the Israelites. Therefore say, 'I grant him my covenant of peace. It shall be for him and for his descendants after him a covenant of perpetual priesthood, because he was zealous for his God, and made atonement for the Israelites.'" (Num 25:10-13 NRSV, italics added)

The story is remembered and celebrated in Sir 45:23-24; 1 Macc 2:54; and 4 Macc 18:12, each time repeating the key word "zeal."

The story of Phinehas is evoked explicitly in the account of the beginning of the Maccabean revolt in 1 Macc 2:15-28. Seeing a fellow Jew preparing to offer pagan sacrifice in accordance with the command of Antiochus IV Epiphanes, Mattathias kills him on the altar. The narrator of 1 Maccabees then comments, "Thus he burned with zeal for the Law, just as Phinehas did against Zimri son of Salu" (1 Macc 2:26 NRSV, italics added). Following this pivotal event, Mattathias issues a general call to resistance: "Let everyone who

is zealous for the Law and supports the covenant come out with me" (1 Macc 2:27 NRSV, italics added).

The prophet Elijah is also remembered as a hero exemplifying "zeal" (Sir 48:2; 1 Macc 2:58) because he took the sword and slaughtered the prophets of Baal (1 Kgs 18:40), in accordance with the commandment of Deut 13:1-5 that the prophets of false gods are to be put to death. Later, giving God an account of his actions, Elijah declares, "I have been very zealous for the LORD, the God of hosts" (1 Kgs 19:10).

With such precedents as Phinehas, Elijah, and the Maccabean heroes, it is not surprising that Saul the zealous Pharisee was willing to employ violence against the early Jewish Christians. He saw himself as the defender of the faith of Israel, even making atonement for Israel by persecuting these apostates who were, in his view, speaking treason against the one God (Deut 13:5). The linkage between "zeal" and persecution of the church is made once more in Paul's Letter to the Philippians, where he affirms that he was "circumcised on the eighth day, a member of the people of Israel, of the tribe of Benjamin, a Hebrew born of Hebrews; as to the law, a Pharisee; as to zeal, a persecutor of the church; as to righteousness under the law, blameless" (Phil 3:5-6 NRSV, italics added).

Thus, when Paul speaks of his "zeal for the traditions of my ancestors" (v. 14), he is not merely speaking of a punctilious personal piety; he put his zeal into action by using force against those whom he considered enemies of the Law. (This does not mean that Paul was a member of an organized Zealot party engaged in armed resistance against Roman authority; as the examples of Phinehas and Mattathias suggest, zealot reprisals were usually targeted internally at members of the Jewish community who were perceived to be traitors.)[44]

Paul does not say where his persecuting activity occurred. Acts 8:1-3 gives an account of his "ravaging the church" in Jerusalem, but Paul's own statements in Gal 1:17 and 22 seem to imply that his activity was based in Damascus rather than Jerusalem. Nor does he narrate exactly how he persecuted

---

43. M. Hengel, *The Zealots: Investigations into the Jewish Freedom Movement in the Period from Herod I Until 70* A.D. (Edinburgh: T. & T. Clark, 1961).

44. For further discussion of ζηλωτής (*zēlōtēs*) and its importance for interpreting Paul's persecuting activity, see Dunn, *The Epistle to the Galatians*, 60-62; N. T. Wright, "Paul, Arabia, and Galatians," *JBL* 115 (1996) 683-92.

the church. Despite the story of the stoning of Stephen in Acts 7, early Jewish Christians were not ordinarily subject to capital punishment in the synagogues; more likely, we should imagine that Paul was administering the penalty of disciplinary flogging of offenders, a penalty that Paul himself later suffered from synagogue authorities (2 Cor 11:24).[45]

1:15-17. In any case, Paul relates this unhappy history of persecution in order to emphasize that God brought it to an end. Paul's zeal for the Law led him to seek to destroy "the church of God," the eschatological community that God was raising up in the world. But God had other plans for Paul. And so, in a long temporal clause stretching through vv. 15-16*b,* Paul alludes to his experience of apostolic calling. Most interpreters have read these words as a reference to the "Damascus Road experience," narrated three times by Luke in Acts (9:1-19; 22:1-21, and 26:2-23). In interpreting Galatians, however, it is necessary to attend carefully to what Paul says and does not say here, for his Galatian addressees certainly had no access to the Lukan narrative. Paul says nothing about being on the road to Damascus or about a blinding light or a voice from heaven. He is interested neither in telling a vivid conversion story nor in talking about his own experience; instead, he wants to describe what God did. God, he says—the one who had "set me apart from my mother's womb"[46] and "called me through his grace"—was pleased "to reveal his Son in me so that I might proclaim him among the Gentiles." This densely formulated description of his calling demands close scrutiny.

Paul describes his call by using language and imagery taken from Jeremiah and Isaiah. Consequently, Paul's call must be understood on the pattern of the OT prophetic call narratives. In other words, Paul saw this event not as a conversion from one religion to another, but as a summons by the God of Israel to undertake a special prophetic mission.[47] Both

of the texts that Paul echoes here foreshadow a ministry of proclamation to the Gentiles:

Now the word of the LORD came to me saying:
    "Before I formed you in the womb I knew you,
    and before you were born I consecrated you;
    I appointed you a prophet to the nations
        [LXX: ἔθνη *ethnē,* "Gentiles"]."
    (Jer 1:4-5 NRSV, italics added)

Listen to me, O coastlands,
    pay attention, you peoples from far away!
The LORD called me before I was born,
    while I was in my mother's womb he named me.
.   .   .   .
And now the LORD says,
    who formed me in the womb to be his servant,
to bring Jacob back to him,
    and that Israel might be gathered to him,
.   .   .   .
he says,
    "It is too light a thing that you should be
        my servant
    to raise up the tribes of Jacob
    and to restore the survivors of Israel;
I will give you as a light to the nations
        [LXX: ἐθνῶν *ethnōn,* "Gentiles"],
    that my salvation may reach to the end of
        the earth."
    (Isa 49:1, 5-6 NRSV, italics added)

We may be sure that Paul did not randomly allude to these particular texts; he finds in the figures of Jeremiah and Isaiah a prefiguration of his own apostolic calling to proclaim the gospel to the nations/Gentiles.

This is the purpose for which Paul was "set apart" by God (cf. Rom 1:1) before he was born, though he did not come to realize that until much later, when he was "called through [God's] grace" (v. 15; on God's "calling," see the Commentary on 1:6). As was noted in the discussion of 1:3-4, God's "grace" is God's powerful unmerited love that reaches out to rescue those who are trapped in the destructive grip of the present evil age. Paul recognizes that only by grace can he, the former persecutor of the church, be called and embraced by God and entrusted with a crucial apostolic mission to the Gentiles (cf. 1 Cor 15:8-10*a*).

That mission is the major emphasis of v. 16. Two interpretations of v. 16*a* are possible,

45. Paula Fredriksen, "Judaism, the Circumcision of Gentiles, and Apocalyptic Hope: Another Look at Galatians 1 and 2," *JTS* NS 42 (1991) 549, 556.

46. It is unclear why the NRSV and the NIV both replace the vivid image of the Greek text with a pallid paraphrase (NRSV, "before I was born"; NIV, "from birth"). The NIV places the more literal translation in a footnote as an alternative rendering.

47. See K. Stendahl, *Paul Among Jews and Gentiles* (Philadelphia: Fortress, 1976) 7-23.

one emphasizing Paul's *reception* of revelation and the other emphasizing his *proclamation* of it. Reading this passage through the lens of the Acts narrative, many interpreters have translated the passage as in the NRSV: God chose "to reveal his Son *to* me." Paul would thus be referring to some experience like the Damascus Road story in which he encountered a revelation of the Son of God. That is a possible reading, and it is consistent with v. 12 (see also 1 Cor 9:1; 15:8). The Greek text here, however, reads ἐν ἐμοί (*en emoi*), which would more naturally yield the translation given by the NIV as well as in the NRSV footnote: God chose "to reveal his Son *in* me." The prepositional phrase would then be instrumental in function: Paul is saying that it was God's purpose to reveal his Son in and through Paul's own person. (The phrase "in me" does not refer to "the inward reality of Christian experience,"[48] as though Paul were locating the event of revelation within his own heart. This sort of introspective individualism is foreign to Paul's thought world; he is describing the dynamic outreach of the gospel to the Gentiles through him.) That may sound like an extravagant claim, but it is consistent with Paul's conception of his identity and ministry. He can say, "It is no longer I who live, but it is Christ who lives in me" (2:20 NRSV). He can urge his Corinthian readers to imitate him as he imitates Christ (1 Cor 11:1). He can even say that all who see the glory of the Lord are transformed into the divine image (2 Cor 3:18). In view of these convictions, it is not surprising to find Paul in v. 16 affirming that it was God's purpose to make Christ manifest *in* him in order that he might effectively proclaim Christ to the Gentiles.

On either interpretation, the disclosure of God's Son[49] is a transformative apocalyptic event. The verb "to reveal" (ἀποκαλύπτω *apokalyptō*) signals a manifestation of Christ that has transformed Paul's life from a life of zeal for the ancestral traditions to a life of "gospeling" Christ (the same verb as in vv. 8-9, 11) among the Gentiles. We should not draw a distinction between Paul's first experience of coming to believe in Christ and a later

experience of commissioning for apostleship; rather, the two are one and the same. The gracious call of God was, according to Paul's account, precisely the call to become an apostle to the Gentile world. This is not merely a significant event in Paul's own spiritual journey; he presents it as a decisive moment in the unfolding of God's cosmic plan for spreading the gospel.

All of the theologically important material in vv. 15-16*b*, however, belongs to a subordinate clause in this sentence. Paul's main affirmations are contained in the independent clauses of vv. 16*c*-17: "[After my call], I did not confer with any human being, nor did I go up to Jerusalem to those who were already apostles before me, but I went away at once into Arabia, and afterwards I returned to Damascus." We see here that Paul is still producing evidence in support of the thesis stated in vv. 11-12: His gospel is dependent on no human source. This is proved by the fact that he did not take counsel with anyone—especially the Jerusalem apostles—after receiving his apostolic call. Instead, he "immediately" went away to Arabia. The verb in v. 16*c* (προσανεθέμην *prosanethemēn*) is rightly translated by the NIV as "consult"; J. D. G. Dunn has suggested that its meaning may be specified as "consult in order to be given a skilled or authoritative interpretation."[50] That is precisely what Paul insists he did *not* do; he did not consult with "flesh and blood" (both the NRSV and the NIV use paraphrases here rather than reproducing Paul's concrete language). Paul does not dispute that the Jerusalem apostles are, in fact, legitimate apostles; indeed, he concedes that they preceded him on the scene as preachers of the gospel (cf. 1 Cor 15:5-9). His point is, however, that he did not seek them out to receive instruction in the faith; having received a commission directly from God, he went his own way. He portrays himself, as J. L. Martyn puts it, as a "lone-wolf apostle."[51]

Why did Paul go to Arabia, and what did he do there? The sketchy narrative of v. 17 gives us no answers to these questions. Most commentators suppose that he went to the cities of the kingdom of Nabatea, to the south

48. Longenecker, *Galatians*, 32.
49. This is the first reference in Galatians to Christ as God's Son. For further discussion of this title, see the Commentary on 2:20 and 4:4-7.

50. Dunn, *The Epistle to the Galatians*, 67.
51. Martyn, *Galatians*, 170.

and east of Damascus,[52] in order to preach the gospel there. This supposition is supported by Paul's passing reminiscence in 2 Cor 11:32-33 of an unpleasant brush with the authority of the Nabatean king Aretas IV (8 BCE–40 CE) in Damascus. Certainly, going to preach the gospel would be a natural sequel to the call described in vv. 15-16. The difficulty, however, is that there is no extant tradition of a Pauline mission in Nabatea. A different proposal, offered by N. T. Wright, builds on the fact that Paul's only other reference to Arabia (Gal 4:25) identifies it as the site of Mt. Sinai. Wright speculates that Paul, who had previously identified with the zealous Elijah, followed Elijah's footsteps by going off into the wilderness to Mt. Horeb (= Sinai; see 1 Kgs 19:1-18), there to seek God and to come to grips with his new prophetic commission.[53] This interesting suggestion is reinforced not only by the fact that Paul elsewhere explicitly links his own ministry with that of Elijah (Rom 11:1-6) but also by the fact that he ended his mysterious sojourn in Arabia by returning to Damascus, just as Elijah had done (1 Kgs 19:15). None of this, however, is pertinent to Paul's immediate argument, and so he says nothing more about it in v. 17.

1:18-20. Only after three years (probably after his call rather than after his return to Damascus) did Paul go to Jerusalem. The cautious discussion in vv. 18-24 looks very much like an exercise in damage control. Paul cannot deny—however much he might like to—that he spent time in Jerusalem, but he is concerned to emphasize the brevity of his stay and his limited contact with members of the Jerusalem church. He spent two weeks staying with Cephas (= Peter; see 2:7-8; John 1:42) and saw none of the other apostles except James, the brother of the Lord.

This James, the brother of Jesus (Mark 6:3), is to be distinguished from James the son of Zebedee and James the son of Alphaeus, both of whom appear in the lists of Jesus' twelve disciples (e.g., Mark 3:17-18). Although there is no evidence that he was a follower of his brother prior to the crucifixion, James became a witness of the resurrection of Jesus (1 Cor 15:7) and ultimately assumed a role of authority in the early Jerusalem church (Acts 15:13-21; 21:18; cf. Gal 2:9, 12).

Paul's tantalizing narrative frustrates our curiosity to know what he discussed with Peter and James. It is sometimes suggested that Peter must have instructed Paul specifically about Jesus, so that this visit provides the basis for Paul's knowledge of Jesus' life and teachings. In fact, however, Paul seems eager to deny any such inference, and the scarcity of specific references to such traditions in Paul's letters would seem to corroborate his denial.[54] Paul tells us nothing about the content of his conversations with Peter, but he presents the visit as a matter of casual contact and emphasizes that (in contrast to the account given by Acts 9:26-30) he had no public contact with the gathered Christian community. This seems so improbable that Paul feels compelled to back up his statements with an emphatic oath that he is not lying (v. 20). This is one of the clearest signs that Paul is responding to allegations, and not merely telling his own story. The rival Missionaries in Galatia must have claimed that Paul had been taught and commissioned by the Jerusalem church. Paul emphatically denies this report.

1:21-24. After his two-week visit, Paul went away to "the regions of Syria and Cilicia." These are, respectively, the territories of Antioch (his base of mission for a time, Acts 13–14) and Tarsus (his hometown, Acts 9:11; 21:39). He mentions his area of operations once again to stress his distance from Jerusalem, as shown by vv. 22-24. The churches of Judea, including Jerusalem, had still not laid eyes upon him. This establishes once again the independence of his apostolic mission from their authority.

Of special interest here is Paul's account of what the Judean churches said about him during this period. He reports that they enthusiastically approved of his preaching, for he was "proclaiming [εὐαγγελίζεται *euangelizetai*] the faith he once tried to destroy." Indeed, they praised God for his work (v. 24). Paul thus looks back to an earlier period of independence and harmony between his mission and the Jerusalem community. At this stage,

---

52. See Betz, *Galatians*, 73-74, and literature cited there.

53. N. T. Wright, "Paul, Arabia, and Galatians," *JBL* 115 (1996).

54. For his few direct references to Jesus tradition, see 1 Cor 7:10-11; 11:23-26; and perhaps 1 Thess 4:15-17. On the whole question, see V. P. Furnish, *Jesus According to Paul* (Cambridge: Cambridge University Press, 1993).

there was no dispute about the Law and no suggestion that Paul's gospel was in any sense deficient. The Judean churches understood him to be preaching the same "faith" that they shared. All of this is important because it implies that all the recent trouble and conflict had been caused not by a change in Paul's preaching, as the Missionaries alleged, but by a change of mind in the churches of Judea and Jerusalem that has created new pressure for circumcision and Law observance among the Gentiles (cf. 2:12).[55]

The expression "proclaiming the faith" in v. 23 also shows that "the faith" can function for Paul as a synonym for "the gospel." "The faith" is not just a matter of inward attitudes of the heart; it alludes to the substantive content of Christian preaching, as summarized in kerygmatic formulas such as Gal 1:3-4 and 1 Cor 15:3-5. This observation will prove important in interpreting other references to "faith" (πίστις *pistis*) later in the letter.

55. On this whole problem, see Fredriksen, "Judaism, the Circumcision of Gentiles, and Apocalyptic Hope"; R. Jewett, "The Agitators and the Galatian Congregation," *NTS* 17 (1970–71) 198-212.

REFLECTIONS

1. Galatians 1:11-24 raises the pressing issue of the relationship between tradition and revelation. Paul juxtaposes his gospel against all religious tradition handed on by human authorities. This poses two urgent problems for those who preach the gospel in our time. First, can the Christian message be formulated as a tradition, or is there something about the gospel that resists fixed traditional formulation? If the latter, is it possible for a community to build its life on the basis of the gospel? Second, should preachers of the Word continue to claim the same sort of unmediated authority that Paul asserted for himself? If so, are they in danger of grounding their message in an appeal to their own private experience?

The Christian church has historically accepted Paul's claim to be a witness to the risen Jesus in a way that set him apart from other Christians who have subsequently experienced the presence of Christ. Accordingly, Paul's claim to be a special apostle to the Gentiles has been acknowledged in the church, and his few extant writings have been collected and canonized as authoritative guides to Christian faith and practice. Yet, there is a certain irony about this development: Paul the lone-wolf apostle, whose message was neither conveyed nor authorized by any church, becomes the source of a body of binding ecclesiastical tradition! Paul, of course, encouraged this development; he commended his churches for keeping the traditions he had taught them (1 Cor 11:2) and scolded them when they failed to do so. In the Pastoral Epistles, we see a later and fuller development of this conception of tradition in the Pauline churches. Even in Galatians, Paul emphatically expects his readers to hold fast to the form of the gospel that they had received from him (Gal 1:8-9). Thus Paul's letters give ample evidence that the gospel can be expressed in fixed formulations that command the confessional assent of the community.

It should be clear, then, that Paul is no advocate of a free-form spirituality in which each person listens individualistically for messages from God and in effect invents his or her private religion. Paul would have been appalled by the story of Sheila Larson, who told interviewers that her religion was "Sheilaism."[56] He certainly did not think of his own message as "Paulinism." On the contrary, his ministry makes sense if and only if it really is true that his message was given him by the God who created the universe and chose to rescue fallen humanity through the death and resurrection of

56. R. N. Bellah et al., *Habits of the Heart: Individualism and Commitment in American Life* (Berkeley: University of California Press, 1985) 220-21, 235.

Jesus Christ. That is the singular, apocalyptic message that Paul was entrusted with at the time of his call, a message so clear and compelling that it required no corroboration from those who had been apostles before him.

It is, therefore, an abuse of this passage to treat it as a proof text for the sanctity of individual conscience, or private religious experience, in opposition to entrenched tradition. The bumper sticker that reads "Question Authority" does not express a Pauline perspective. The dichotomy posed in Gal 1:11-24 is not between the individual and tradition but between *God's* gospel and *human* tradition. True authority resides in preaching that gives expression to the apocalyptic gospel message.

Of course, Paul believed that this message has a way of unsettling the stable structures of the present age, because it constantly calls the community to measure its life against the eschatological truth of the gospel. Every practice, every institution, must be measured in relation to the eschatological vision of freedom and unity in Christ (see, e.g., Gal 3:28). It is not easy to build stable community structures in the church. One of the reasons why the Galatians found the message of the Missionaries tempting is that it offered the apparent security of fixed rules and structures. These issues will be addressed more specifically later in the letter, but it is important to recognize from the beginning that Paul resists the teaching of the Missionaries precisely because he sees it as turning the gospel into a domesticated human tradition and thereby making the church into another cultural community in which we might "advance" zealously if we play by the rules. He insists that the gospel is something wholly different: a message from God that breaks in on us from outside our religious culture and transforms everything.

But what, then, of the second question? What should we make of people who claim direct access to God's revelation, unmediated by any tradition? Can Christian preachers claim privileged access to revelation? The answer is both no and yes. No, we cannot say that we are among the original roster of witnesses to the resurrection, as Paul was (1 Cor 15:3-8; note that Paul describes the appearance of the risen Christ to him as "last of all"). Paul, standing close to the apocalyptic event of Christ's death and resurrection, was given a special commission to take the extraordinary news to the Gentiles, proclaiming that Israel's God had now acted for the salvation of the whole world. In that sense, Paul's position is unique, and our calling to proclaim the gospel is only analogous to his, not identical. But, on the other hand, the analogies are real; we continue to believe and proclaim that God has broken the power of the present evil age (Gal 1:4) and that the story of God's Son, Jesus Christ, is the revelation of God's purpose for creation. So we do not replicate Paul's experience of revelation, but we do continue to see the world in the light of the same revelation that he announced. The distinction is crucial: Those who lust after experiences of continuing revelation easily fall into fantasy and delusion, but those who attend steadily to the singular once-for-all revelation of Jesus Christ are given a truthful vision of reality as it is in God's new creation (Gal 6:15).

2. The connection between zeal and persecution is another theme worth pondering in this passage. Religious conviction and passion can have an ugly side. Paul sadly recognizes in his own past that his zeal for the traditions of his ancestors led him to sanction and commit acts of violence (see 1 Cor 15:9; Phil 3:6; 1 Tim 1:12-16; cf. Rom 10:1-3). The preacher who takes up this matter will want to keep two points clearly in focus.

First of all, the link between zeal and violence is not distinctive to Judaism. From time to time one encounters claims that Judaism is inherently a religion of violence and that Christianity is inherently immune to this problem.[57] The bare facts of history

---

57. See, e.g., R. Hamerton-Kelly, *Sacred Violence: Paul's Hermeneutic of the Cross* (Minneapolis: Fortress, 1992). For a critique of Hamerton-Kelly, see D. Boyarin, *A Radical Jew: Paul and the Politics of Identity* (Berkeley: University of California Press, 1994) 214-19.

disconfirm this caricature: Christians have a tragic, bloody history of inquisition and persecution against dissenters, including preeminently the Jewish people. Thus we must take care not to point the finger at "Judaism" as the cause of Paul's persecuting impulse. All three of the great monotheistic religions (Judaism, Christianity, Islam) have shown the tendency to engender persecution and violence. The reasons for this are not hard to understand; those who take seriously the holiness of the one God find it difficult to tolerate people who blasphemously deny that God or transgress God's revealed law. Of course, each of these great traditions also contains its own theological checks and balances to constrain the persecuting impulse and to enjoin humility and mercy. The urgent tasks of the preacher are to warn that the laudable desire to defend the truth can contain the seeds of violence and to show how that desire must be disciplined by the deeper wisdom of the tradition.

In the case of the Christian gospel, the cross is the central symbol that short-circuits justifications of violence: God's way of dealing with dissenters and adversaries was not to destroy them but to give his Son to die *for* them. Thus when Paul received his call, he did not turn around and start persecuting Jews who failed to believe the gospel; rather, in conformity with the example of Jesus, Paul became the persecuted (Gal 5:11; 6:17) rather than the persecutor. The second point to be kept in focus, then, is that Paul's own life history provides an example that should cause Christians to turn away from zealous persecution. Paul's story models the way in which the gospel calls us to renounce violence as an instrument of God's righteousness. Our responsibility is not to eradicate the enemies of God but to announce God's reconciling power in the world (see 2 Cor 5:17-20).

3. This leads to the final major theme that emerges from reflection on this text: the transforming power of God's surprising call. Paul was transformed from persecutor to apostle, leaving the churches in Judea marveling and giving glory to God. Paul does not tell this story as a testimony of "what Jesus did for me," as though the important thing were how Paul's sins were forgiven or his needs met. Rather, this passage is a testimony about how the *apokalypsis* of Jesus Christ turned Paul's world upside down and made him into an instrument of God's reconciling grace, reaching out to those who had previously been "strangers to the covenants of promise, having no hope and without God in the world" (Eph 2:12 NRSV). If we are to do justice to Paul's testimony, our preaching on this passage must not dwell on the inner, personal experience of conversion; we should dwell, instead, on God's act of seizing us and empowering us for tasks we never could have imagined.

GALATIANS 2:1-10, PAUL'S MEETING WITH THE JERUSALEM LEADERS

COMMENTARY

Paul next gives a brief account of his summit meeting with the leaders of the Jerusalem church. This account continues his defense of the thesis stated in 1:11-12: Paul received his gospel by revelation, not from any human source. Thus, even in telling the story of his concord with the Jerusalem leaders, he is careful to maintain independence from their direction. This is a delicate rhetorical and political balancing act; Paul wants to claim the endorsement of the Jerusalem apostles (who had, in fact, recognized the validity of his mission to the Gentiles) without conceding undue authority to them. This double political agenda makes Gal 2:1-10 a complex passage whose nuances must be considered carefully.

In order to follow the strategy of Paul's argument, we must keep two points clearly in mind:

(1) There are not two but three parties involved in the dispute described here: Paul and Barnabas as representatives of the Antioch church, the "pillar" apostles of the Jerusalem church, and the "false brothers" (i.e., the party within the Jerusalem church demanding circumcision of Gentile converts).[58] Paul depicts the last group as the source of the conflict, and he conspicuously does not describe them as endorsing the agreement between the first two groups.

(2) The whole narrative prefigures the conflict currently being played out in Galatia, and Paul's recounting of the matter is shaped by the debate over circumcision in the Galatian churches. It is possible that there is some direct link between the "false brothers" and the rival Missionaries who have come to Galatia; whether that is so or not, Paul tells the story in a way that makes the parallels obvious.

This much is clear. Nonetheless, 2:1-10 leaves us with many unanswered questions. Parts of the passage are difficult to follow, for Paul is so agitated that he has written convoluted and incomplete sentences. We can virtually hear him spluttering with anger as he writes; his butchered syntax reflects the strong passions that still swirl around the controversy. Any interpretation of the passage requires some filling of syntactical gaps and some hypotheses about the uncertain chronology of events briefly alluded to here.

More difficult still is the question of how Paul's account of this Jerusalem meeting is to be coordinated with the narrative of the Acts of the Apostles. Because Paul solemnly swears that this meeting took place during his second visit to Jerusalem after his call, some critics have attempted to link Gal 2:1-10 with the "famine relief visit" of Acts 11:27-30, thereby preserving the historical accuracy of the Lukan narrative.[59] The more natural reading of the evidence, however, identifies Gal 2:1-10 with Luke's story of the apostolic council in Acts 15.[60] This commentary assumes that

the meeting described in Gal 2:1-10 is the same meeting described in Acts 15. There are, of course, discrepancies between the two accounts. This is not surprising, for Luke is piecing together traditional sources from an earlier period, whereas Paul is giving a first-hand account—which also, to be sure, has an apologetic agenda. Readers interested in a full explanation of the problem may refer to the standard critical commentaries and NT introductions.

2:1-2. The continuation of Paul's retrospective narrative is marked by the third occurrence of the adverb ἔπειτα (*epeita*, "then," v. 1; also in 1:18, 21). It is impossible to be sure whether the fourteen-year interval mentioned in v. 1 includes or follows the three years between Paul's call and his first visit to Jerusalem (1:18). The important point for Paul's argument is that during this lengthy period he had no direct dealings with Jerusalem; presumably he was engaged in preaching to Gentiles in Syria and Cilicia (1:21) and perhaps elsewhere in Asia Minor, working from a base in the Antioch church (cf. Acts 13–14).

This Gentile mission work, however, provoked controversy among Jewish Christians (see Acts 15:1-5), and a decision was made that Paul and Barnabas should go to Jerusalem to discuss the matter with the church there. Paul, in distinction from Acts, does not say explicitly that he and Barnabas went as representatives of the Antioch church; it is possible that Paul avoids mentioning this fact because of his subsequent falling out with that community (2:11-14). The present narrative is crafted to create the impression that Paul was operating as a freelance apostle under the guidance of revelation (v. 2), and the role of Barnabas in the Jerusalem meeting is minimized in Paul's account. Nonetheless, there are good reasons to think that Paul and Barnabas were, in fact, sent by the church at Antioch. Verse 1 corresponds closely to Acts 15:1-2, and Luke's report of opposition by Pharisaic Jewish Christians tallies well with Paul's references to the "false brothers"; they were saying, "It is necessary for [Gentile converts] to be circumcised and ordered to keep the law of Moses" (Acts 15:5 NRSV).

58. Betz, *Galatians*, 81-83.

59. This view is defended by Longenecker, *Galatians*, lxxiii-lxxxiii.

60. For defenses of this view, see C. C. Hill, *Hellenists and Hebrews: Reappraising Division in the Earliest Church* (Philadelphia: Fortress, 1991) 103-47; M. Silva, *Explorations in Exegetical Method: Galatians as a Test Case* (Grand Rapids: Eerdmans, 1996) 129-39.

The composition of the delegation from Antioch to Jerusalem was significant. Barnabas, a prominent Jewish Christian, had worked closely with Paul in the Gentile mission (see Acts 13–14; 1 Cor 9:6; Col 4:10). According to Luke's account, he was "a Levite, a native of Cyprus," who became a leading member of the earliest Jerusalem church (Acts 4:36-37). Luke also portrays him as Paul's early supporter and mentor who interceded for him and introduced him to the fearful and skeptical members of the Jerusalem church shortly after his call experience (Acts 9:26-27). Since Paul vehemently denies having been anywhere near Jerusalem during this period of his life (Gal 1:17-24), the accuracy of this biographical detail about Barnabas is doubtful. According to Acts 11:19-26, Barnabas was also sent by the Jerusalem church as an emissary to Antioch, where he witnessed and warmly approved the beginnings of the Gentile mission and even recruited Paul to come from Tarsus to Antioch to participate in this work. Thus Barnabas was a natural choice to represent the Antiochene church in its negotiations with Jerusalem; he was a Jew of impeccable hereditary credentials who had strong personal ties to the Jerusalem church. He also had a reputation for living up to his name ("son of encouragement") by acting as a conciliator (unlike Paul, who was a more abrasive character).

Titus, on the other hand, was an uncircumcised Greek (v. 3), presumably a convert of Paul (cf. Titus 1:4). Although he is never mentioned in Acts, he plays a large role in 2 Corinthians as Paul's emissary to Corinth (see 2 Cor 2:13; 7:6-7, 13-15; 8:6, 16-24; 12:18). The decision to take him to Jerusalem (a decision for which Paul implicitly claims responsibility) was a deliberately provocative move. The presence of the uncircumcised Titus would place the Jerusalem authorities face-to-face with a test case: Their decision about the validity of a Law-free mission to the Gentiles could not be treated as a theoretical halakhic problem, for it would have immediate impact on a particular Gentile who stood before them as evidence of the fruits of Paul's preaching.

The effect of this multicultural delegation to Jerusalem was described aptly by Martin Luther:

By presenting himself with both of them [sc. Barnabas and Titus] he [Paul] intended to make it clear that he was at liberty to be a Gentile with Titus and a Jew with Barnabas. Thus he would prove the freedom of the gospel in each case, namely that is is permissible to be circumcised and yet that circumcision is not necessary, and that this is the way one should think of the entire law.[61]

In other words, the very composition of the delegation bore witness to the gospel, as encapsulated in Gal 5:6 and 6:15. The gospel creates a new community in which circumcision no longer erects social barriers.

Paul declares that he made this trip to Jerusalem "according to revelation" (κατὰ ἀποκάλυψιν *kata apokalypsin*; translated by both the NRSV and the NIV as "in response to a revelation"). This statement is sometimes thought to contradict Acts 15:2, in which Paul and Barnabas are "appointed" by the Antioch church to go to Jerusalem. In fact, however, there is no real tension between these statements. The story told in Acts 13:2-3 provides an instructive parallel. Paul and Barnabas received a missionary commissioning from Antioch through a prophetic word from the Holy Spirit that came to the community during worship. This revelation was then confirmed by the community's action of sending them out after fasting, prayer, and the laying on of hands. When Paul says that he went to Jerusalem "according to revelation," he probably has something similar in mind: a prophetic word received in the worshiping assembly at Antioch and acted upon by the church (note esp. Acts 15:3: "So they were sent on their way by the church"). In 1 Cor 14:26, 30, for example, Paul speaks of prophets in the church as receiving "a revelation" from God.[62] Thus the reference to "revelation" in Gal 2:2 should merely remind us that Paul and the other early Christians believed that the Holy Spirit was powerfully at work in the church, continuing to act and speak through revelatory prophetic gifts.

Upon his arrival in Jerusalem, Paul expounded his gospel. His language describing this event is carefully chosen. He "set before them" (ἀναθέμην *anethemēn*) the

---

61. Martin Luther, cited in Betz, *Galatians* 84n.252.
62. These comments are in agreement with F. J. Matera, *Galatians,* Sacra Pagina 9 (Collegeville, Minn.: Liturgical Press) 72.

gospel that he was proclaiming among the Gentiles. This verb in no way implies that he submitted his gospel to the Jerusalem leaders hoping meekly for their approval; instead, it simply means that he placed his gospel on the table before them. As the opening chapter of the letter has emphatically stated, Paul was in no doubt about the truth or divine origin of his message.

Why, then, does he say he did this "to make sure that I was not running, or had not run, in vain"? The answer to this question lies in the theology of election that Paul expounds fully in Romans 11. He sees the Gentile mission as an unexpected initiative of God to make Israel jealous and ultimately to bring them to recognize the truth of the gospel (Rom 11:11-12). His own preaching to Gentiles was a necessary part of that plan (Rom 11:13-14). God's ultimate purpose was to raise up a new eschatological people composed of Jews and Gentiles together praising the one God through Jesus Christ (Rom 15:7-13; cf. the expression "Israel of God" in Gal 6:16). God's plan requires, then, that the Jerusalem community hear Paul's account of the Gentile mission and its fruits. If they reject the legitimacy of this mission, it will indeed make Paul's work futile in one sense, for their rejection will thwart God's intent to bring Jew and Gentile together as one in Christ.[63] In fact, however, Paul did not anticipate any such failure; he believed that the gospel was the power of God at work in the world and that it would efficaciously bring the Jerusalem leaders to recognize the validity of his work. As he tells the story, that is precisely what did happen.

Paul is careful to emphasize, however, that not everyone in the Jerusalem church participated in this meeting.[64] He set forth his gospel "privately to those who seemed to be leaders" (v. 2). This is the first appearance of an expression that occurs four times in this passage: "those who seem [to be something]" (οἱ δοκοῦντες *hoi dokountes*; also twice in v. 6 and again in v. 9). The term expresses

some degree of ironic distance from claims being made for the authority of the Jerusalem leaders; in Plato's *Apology,* Socrates uses the same expression to speak with withering disdain of those who "seem to be wise." In the context of Galatians, Paul's reference to the "seeming" or "reputed" leaders allows him "to recognize the *de facto* role which 'the men of reputation' play, without compromising his theological stance that God and Christ are the only authority behind his gospel."[65]

2:3-5. In any case, Paul presented his case only to these eminent persons in the Jerusalem church. Despite pressure from the circumcision group, Titus was not compelled by these leaders to be circumcised. (This certainly does not mean that he freely chose to be circumcised; that would undercut Paul's whole argument. The point is that he remained uncircumcised.)[66] This simple fact was a great victory for Paul's position, for it symbolized Jerusalem's acceptance of Antioch's Gentile mission, with its practice of receiving uncircumcised Gentiles into the church.

This decision by the Jerusalem leaders, however, was reached in the face of heavy pressure from those whom Paul calls the "false brothers" (v. 4). Who were these people? It is important to observe that they were Jewish Christians (i.e., not non-Christian Jewish undercover agents seeking to sow dissension in the church). Luke's narrative describes them as "believers who belonged to the sect of the Pharisees" (Acts 15:5), as did Paul himself (Acts 23:6; Phil 3:5). Paul, however, labels them as "false brothers" because they hold to a gospel that he regards as false (see Gal 1:6-9); the implication is that they, therefore, do not have a rightful claim to be members of Christ's family.

Despite Paul's scorn, the position of the "false brothers" is understandable. Given the clear teaching of the Law of Moses about circumcision—a teaching that Jesus had certainly never challenged or revoked—they believed that circumcision was the divinely

63. Here I am in agreement with C. B. Cousar, *Galatians,* Interpretation (Atlanta: John Knox, 1982) 39; Dunn, *The Epistle to the Galatians,* 94; Martyn, *Galatians,* 193.

64. This is one of the differences from Acts 15, which describes a public consultation. Again, the difference is not difficult to understand. No doubt the really important conversation, from Paul's point of view, may have occurred in private negotiating sessions with the Jerusalem leaders.

65. Betz, *Galatians,* 87.

66. The circumcision of Timothy (Acts 16:1-3) was a different matter, for his mother was Jewish. Under Jewish law, that made him a Jew rather than a Gentile. Therefore, according to Acts at least, Paul decided that Timothy should be circumcised. This report obviously stands in tension with the policy that Paul elsewhere describes as "my rule in all the churches," that all should remain in the condition in which they were called, whether circumcised or uncircumcised (1 Cor 7:17-20).

appointed sign of covenant membership in the people of God. J. D. G. Dunn suggests that their arguments may have been similar to those attributed by Josephus to the Jew Eleazar, who sought to persuade Izates, king of Adiabene, to be circumcised after he had become an adherent of Judaism:

In your ignorance, O king, you are guilty of the greatest offence against the law and thereby against God. For you ought not merely to read the law but also, and even more, to do what is commanded in it. How long will you continue to be uncircumcised? If you have not yet read the law concerning this matter, read it now, so that you may know what an impiety it is that you commit.[67]

Interestingly, this same passage in Josephus shows that Eleazar's opinion was not necessarily held by all Jews in the same way. Ananias, the merchant who had instructed Izates in the practices of Judaism, thought it politically dangerous for the king to accept circumcision and actually advised against it.[68] A good case can be made that Jewish thinkers of Paul's day did not necessarily pressure Gentiles to be circumcised; we know that Hellenistic synagogues attracted circles of "godfearers," Gentiles who followed Jewish worship practices without undergoing circumcision. The prevailing Jewish eschatological hope was that Gentiles would abandon their idolatry and worship the living God of Israel, but this did not necessarily entail their converting to Judaism and being circumcised. Paula Fredriksen explains this line of thinking: "When God establishes his Kingdom . . . these two groups will together constitute 'his people': Israel, redeemed from exile, and the Gentiles, redeemed from idolatry. Gentiles are saved as Gentiles: they do not, eschatologically, become Jews."[69]

The disagreement between Paul and the "false brothers," then, may have turned on the issue of eschatology. What time was it? Was the Gentile mission a sign of the new eschatological age, in which Gentiles were granted a full place in God's kingdom? Or, alternatively, were the rules of the old age

still in force, so that full participation in God's people was possible only for those who were marked by circumcision as members of the covenant?

When Paul testifies that Titus was not "compelled" to be circumcised, he uses the same verb (ἀναγκάζω anagkazō) that appears in 2:14 ("How can you *compel* the Gentiles to live like Jews?") and again in 6:12 ("It is those who want to make a good showing in the flesh that try to *compel* you to be circumcised"). This threefold occurrence of the verb links together three different historical settings: the meeting in Jerusalem (2:1-10), the controversy at Antioch (2:11-21), and the situation in Galatia (6:12-13). In all three cases, the "compulsion" in view is not some sort of violent coercion (circumcision at knifepoint, as it were), but rather a matter of argument and social pressure, as the example of Cephas at Antioch shows (vv. 11-14). Paul projects these three situations simultaneously on the same screen, as manifestations of a single underlying conflict.

This conflict is a serious struggle, as Paul's use of military metaphors in vv. 4-5 shows. He portrays the "false brothers" as spies who have "infiltrated our ranks" in order to "enslave" the free citizens. When Paul speaks of infiltration, he must be thinking not of their spying on his meeting with the Jerusalem leaders but of their previous stealthy surveillance of the mixed church of Jews and Gentiles in Antioch. This would explain what he means by saying that they "slipped in to spy on the freedom we have in Christ Jesus"; they were suspiciously observing the freedom with which Jews and Gentiles associated and worshiped together, including the celebration of the Lord's supper. The military imagery is not accidental; Paul really does see a war in progress (see Rom 6:12-14; 2 Cor 10:3-6; Phil 1:27-30; cf. Eph 6:12-20). These "false brothers" are enemy agents, partisans of the power of the "present evil age" (Gal 1:4). That is why Paul refuses any compromise or negotiation with them. Using battlefield imagery, he insists that he and Barnabas "did not give in to them for a moment" (lit., "did not yield in submission to them for one hour").

For the first time in the letter to the Galatians, Paul introduces in vv. 4-5 the antithetically paired categories of freedom and slavery.

---

67. Josephus *Antiquities of the Jews* 20.44-45. Cited by Dunn, *The Epistle to the Galatians,* 99-100.

68. Josephus *Antiquities of the Jews* 20.40-41.

69. Fredriksen, "Judaism, The Circumcision of Gentiles, and Apocalyptic Hope," 547.

These terms will reappear as a major theme of the epistle in 3:28; 4:1-11; 4:21–5:1; and 5:13. It is of more than passing interest, then, that in the first appearance of these words, "freedom" refers to the unqualified association of Jewish and Gentile Christians, while "enslavement" refers to the attempted imposition of circumcision on Gentile believers. Of course, the circumcision advocates did not think of themselves as trying to enslave Gentile Christians; to the contrary, circumcision was understood among Jews as a sign of freedom from the passions of the flesh, a freedom created by the secure order of the divine law.

When Paul says that he and Barnabas took this stand against circumcision of Gentiles "so that the truth of the gospel might remain with you" (thus the NIV; "always" in the NRSV has no basis in the Greek text), he does not mean that they were thinking specifically of the Galatians at that time; indeed, the Galatian churches almost surely were not even founded at the time of the meeting in Jerusalem. He means that this stand was necessary to preserve the gospel for the Gentiles as a whole, both present and future, among whom the Galatians constitute a subset. Here again we see Paul weaving his narrative about the past together with the present controversy in Galatia. "The truth of the gospel" is closely tied here (as also in v. 14) to Paul's insistence on preaching a gospel free from legal and cultural prerequisites, a gospel that focuses on God's liberating initiative.

2:6-10. In these verses, the false brothers disappear from view, and Paul focuses now on the responses of James, Cephas, and John—apparently the key leaders in the Jerusalem Christian community—to his private presentation of the gospel he proclaimed. Paul hints even more broadly about his misgivings concerning their authority, or at least concerning the reverence in which they were held by some others. He cites the OT maxim that "God shows no partiality" (lit., "God does not take the face"; see, e.g., Deut 10:17; 2 Chr 19:7; Sir 35:13)[70] in order to indicate once again that he was not overawed by these reputed pillars of the church. Having been authorized directly by God's call, Paul looked them in the eyes as their equal. Nonetheless,

for the purposes of his present argument, it is useful for him to be able to state that they added nothing to his articulation of the gospel. In other words, they did not instruct Paul to add something about circumcision and law observance to his preaching.

How is Paul's report related to the outcome of the apostolic council as recounted in Acts 15? In Acts, Luke says that the conference reached a formal decision—under the guidance of James—that Gentile converts were not required to be circumcised, but that they should "abstain from what has been sacrificed to idols and from blood and from what is strangled and from fornication" (Acts 15:28-29 NRSV). In other words, they were required to observe those prohibitions of the holiness code that apply to aliens residing in Israel (Leviticus 17–18). This certainly would constitute an addendum to Paul's gospel. If Paul knew anything about this "apostolic decree" described in Acts 15, he offers no hint of it in precisely the places where we would expect it—in Romans 14–15 and 1 Corinthians 8–10. The likeliest hypothesis is that Luke, writing a generation later, has retrojected a later church agreement back into the period of Paul's lifetime. Paul's emphatic denial in Gal 2:6 suggests that no such understanding was reached at the Jerusalem meeting.

The theological basis for the concord that was, in fact, reached between Paul and the Jerusalem apostles is explained in vv. 7-8: It is the same God who has worked in both Peter and Paul, the same God who has "entrusted" the gospel to each. Thus, despite the fact that they are called to work in different cultural spheres, each recognizes the grace of God at work in the other's ministry. Does the formulation of v. 7 mean that there actually are two different gospels, a "gospel of the uncircumcision" and a "gospel of the circumcision"? This would seem to contradict Paul's emphatic assertion that there can be only one gospel (1:6-9). Thus Paul's formulation in v. 7 should be understood to mean that Peter and Paul are complementary instruments of the one gospel (cf. 1 Cor 3:5-9), commissioned to speak primarily to different ethnic constituencies. Thus there are "two missions in which the one gospel is making its way into the whole of the cosmos."[71]

---

70. See J. M. Bassler, *Divine Impartiality: Paul and a Theological Axiom*, SBLDS 59 (Chico, Calif.: Scholars Press, 1982) 171-74.

71. Martyn, *Galatians*, 202.

New Testament scholars have sometimes speculated that vv. 7-8 actually contain the wording of a formal agreement reached in the Jerusalem meeting, because only in these two verses does Paul use the Greek name "Peter" rather than the Aramaic "Cephas" and because the reference to the two gospels in v. 7 is not precisely paralleled elsewhere in Paul's letters. A corollary of this theory is that the wording of v. 8 (as reflected more precisely in the NRSV) may imply a subtle status distinction between Peter, who is recognized as an apostle, and Paul, to whom this title is not explicitly applied. Despite the ingenuity of such speculations, they are finally unpersuasive. Paul gives no indication that he is quoting the text of a formal agreement; he is merely summarizing in his own words (as he does again in v. 9) what the Jerusalem apostles recognized about his ministry. And we should not make too much of the omission of the term "apostleship" (ἀποστολή *apostolē*) with reference to Paul's mission in v. 8. As Frank Matera has pointed out, in the Greek both v. 7 and v. 8 are elliptical: "Paul entrusted with *the gospel to the uncircumcised,* Peter *to the circumcised;* Peter entrusted with *apostleship to the circumcised,* Paul *to the uncircumcised.*"[72] The non-repetition of "apostleship" in v. 8 is no more significant than the non-repetition of "gospel" in v. 7.

Far more important exegetically is the fact that v. 8 describes the ministries of both apostles as the work of God's power. The verb "to work in" (ἐνεργέω *energeō*), used twice here, is a characteristic Pauline word that appears in other contexts where God's effective power through human instruments is described (e.g., Gal 3:5; 5:6; Phil 2:13; Col 1:29; 1 Thess 2:13; cf. Eph 3:20). The best parallel to v. 8 is found in Paul's discussion of the complementarity of different gifts within the one body of Christ in 1 Corinthians 12:

There are varieties of activities [ἐνεργημάτων *energēmatōn*] but it is the same God who activates [ἐνεργῶν *energōn*] all of them in everyone. . . . All these are activated [ἐνεργεῖ *energei*] by one and the same Spirit, who allots to each one individually just as the Spirit chooses. (1 Cor 12:6, 11 NRSV)

Paul's use of the same verb in v. 8 suggests that the complementarity of the two missions to the Jews and to the Gentiles is grounded in this same truth: Both missions are the work of God's Spirit. This language is not a compromise agreement worked out in a negotiation between power brokers; rather, it reflects their common recognition of a power bigger than any of the human agents involved.

Recognizing this, James and Cephas and John gave to Paul and Barnabas "the right hand of fellowship [κοινωνία *koinōnia*]," signifying that they were engaged in a common venture. (On James and Cephas, see the Commentary on 1:18-19.) John is probably the son of Zebedee, one of the Twelve who, along with Peter and his brother James (not the same James mentioned in v. 9), had been part of an inner circle of Jesus' followers; for example, the tradition says John was present with Jesus at the transfiguration (Mark 9:1 par.) and in the Garden of Gethsemane (Mark 14:33 par.). He appears in the early chapters of Acts as a preaching companion of Peter (e.g., Acts 3–4), and he is later identified by the tradition as the Beloved Disciple who stands behind the tradition of the Fourth Gospel. Paul mentions him only here. The mention of this threesome indicates that they were recognized as the leading authority figures in the early Christian community in Jerusalem. The metaphorical reference to them as "pillars" is reminiscent of the Jewish tradition of calling Abraham, Isaac, and Jacob the "pillars" of Israel.[73] Paul is clearly dubious about this title, for he once again employs the distancing locution, "those *reputed* to be pillars."[74]

The important point for the purpose of Paul's argument is that these three pillar apostles "recognized the grace that had been given to me" (see Rom 1:5; 12:3; 15:15; 1 Cor 3:10; cf. Eph 3:2, 7). Paul represents this not merely as their acknowledgment of Antioch's Gentile mission but as a special confirmation of his own particular graced calling.[75] This is a critical move in Paul's argument. It enables him to claim that the

72. Matera, *Galatians,* 77.

73. R. D. Aus, "Three Pillars and Three Patriarchs: A Proposal Concerning Gal 2:9," *ZNW* 70 (1979) 252-61.

74. Interestingly, by the end of the first century, *1 Clement* applies this same title to Peter and to Paul. See *1 Clem* 5:2-7.

75. Dunn observes that "at this point 'grace' (*charis*) approaches the sense of 'charism' (*charisma*)—charism as the expression and embodiment of grace in word and action." See Dunn, *The Epistle to the Galatians,* 108.

Jerusalem leaders had once given their blessing to his Law-free preaching of the gospel. If now the Missionaries in Galatia were appealing to the authority of Jerusalem to overrule Paul, this could only mean one of two things: Either the Missionaries were perpetrating a lie or—as vv. 11-14 suggest—there had been a failure of nerve on the part of the Jerusalem leaders, a turning back from what God had revealed. Once upon a time, there had been a clear understanding, and they had shaken hands on it: Paul and Barnabas would preach to the Gentiles, and the Jerusalem apostles would preach to "the circumcision" (v. 9). As sad experience would soon prove, however, this formulation was neither unambiguous nor sufficient to clarify the relations between Jews and Gentiles in mixed worshiping communities.

At the time of the Jerusalem meeting, the only stipulation added by the Jerusalem leaders was that Paul and Barnabas should "remember the poor" (v. 10), meaning that they should provide financial support for those in need. The obligation of supporting the poor and the oppressed was a deeply ingrained element of Jewish piety, a fundamental element of Israel's covenant obligations (see, e.g., Deut 15:7-11),[76] and Paul readily affirmed his eagerness to be responsive to this concern. This exhortation by the Jerusalem pillars was a primary impetus for Paul's decision to raise money from his Gentile mission congregations for "the poor among the saints at Jerusalem" (Rom 15:26). Several references in Paul's letters show that

this collection became a major project of his ministry (Rom 15:25-27; 1 Cor 16:1-4; 2 Corinthians 8–9)—a project in which the Galatians themselves participated at some point (1 Cor 16:1).[77] Paul understood the collection as a gesture of solidarity between the Gentile congregations and the Jerusalem church (Rom 15:26-27); perhaps he even saw it as symbolizing the eschatological tribute of the nations to Israel's God on Mt. Zion (Isa 2:2-3; 60:1-16). As the time drew near for him to take the collected offering to Jerusalem, however, Paul was worried that it would not be accepted by the Jerusalem community (Rom 15:30-32) because of his deteriorating relations with the representatives of the church there.

When Paul wrote Galatians, however, he could point to the Jerusalem leaders' request, confident that he had kept his end of the bargain. As the Galatians knew, he was collecting money for the poor in Jerusalem.[78] It was the others, particularly Cephas, who had in Paul's judgment reneged on the agreement. Thus Paul's meeting with the Jerusalem leaders marked a high-water point of unity in the early Christian mission (though we must remember that the circumcision party was not included in the fragile unity achieved at the Jerusalem meeting). After this, as we shall see, the understanding that the Antioch and Jerusalem representatives had reached started to unravel.

76. For an extended discussion with references, see Dunn, *The Epistle to the Galatians,* 112-13.

77. The absence of any reference to the churches of Galatia in Rom 15:26 is striking. Had the Galatians withdrawn their support for the collection?

78. Martyn, *Galatians,* 225, challenges this view, suggesting that Paul began organizing his collection later, after the writing of Galatians.

REFLECTIONS

For many Christian congregations, the early church's debate over circumcision may seem like a strange matter belonging to another time and place. Today, the only debates about circumcision have to do not with Christian identity, but with the health benefits or disadvantages of this surgical procedure for male infants. Why did the issue of circumcision matter so much to Paul and to the "false brothers"? Why did it pose a stern challenge to the unity of the church in the first generation of Christians?

The answer is that circumcision symbolized Jewish identity in a pagan world; consequently, it became a symbolic hot-button issue for early Christian communities struggling with the problem of how to define their identity. Were the emergent Gentile churches an extension of Judaism into pagan culture? Or did they represent a new phenomenon that could not be fully accommodated to the categories and cultural forms of Jewish tradition? When we understand Paul's meeting with the Jerusalem leaders within its historical context, we see that it defines a number of problems that remain with us today.

1. The meeting of Paul, Barnabas, and Titus with the pillar apostles of the Jerusalem church was a crucial event in the process of clarifying the identity of the church. The event should not be interpreted anachronistically, as though it were the first ecumenical council of the church catholic; it was, after all, simply a conference involving representatives of two key churches. Nonetheless, its historical significance was weighty, because it marked Jerusalem's acceptance in principle of the validity of a Gentile mission that did not require converts to become proselytes to Judaism in order to be recognized as followers of Jesus. This meant that the participants in this meeting were defining the church not as a sectarian variant of Judaism, but as a wholly new eschatological community in which Jews and Gentiles together acknowledged a common Lord.

Although this development, viewed in retrospect, might look inevitable, the outcome of the debate was by no means self-evident in the first Christian generation. The circumcision party among the Jewish Christians clearly saw adherence to Torah as the entryway and primary identity marker for the early Jesus movement: "Unless you are circumcised according to the custom of Moses, you cannot be saved" (Acts 15:1 NRSV). They may have seen Jesus as the new and definitive interpreter of the Law, but they still understood themselves—not surprisingly—as living and moving within the symbolic world of the cultural reality that Paul calls *Ioudaismos* ("Judaism"). Paul and Barnabas, on the other hand, were pressing for a radical innovation, a community whose identity was grounded solely in the story of Christ's death and resurrection.

It is not clear whether James, Cephas, and John understood the full implications of what they were agreeing to in the way that Paul did. (Indeed, subsequent developments suggest that they did not.) They may have thought they were merely acknowledging that uncircumcised Gentiles could participate in the life of the Christian community in precisely the same way that Gentile "godfearers" had previously participated in the life of the synagogue—as adherents on the periphery of the community who were not required to adopt full Torah observance, but who were also in some sense not yet full members of the people of God.

How does all this inform our reflection about Christian identity in our time? The crucial point of analogy is this: Whenever we allow the identity of our community to be fundamentally defined by any sort of national or cultural or even religious marker other than the gospel, we are repeating the error of the "false brothers." Paul insists that we must not allow the dominant culture to set the boundaries of "religion" or to define the character of our community. Instead, Paul's vision for the identity of the Christian community demands that we define ourselves exclusively in the light of the cross and resurrection (see Gal 6:14-15; cf. 1 Cor 1:18–2:5).

The dominant symbolic world in relation to which the church in Western culture must define its identity is no longer Jewish culture; rather, it is the culture of public secular rationality.[79] Wherever we find that people have begun to think of themselves as Americans first and Christians second or to meld these identities uncritically together, we are in the presence of a false gospel. Wherever we encounter pressure to allow our identity to be shaped fundamentally by market forces or by allegiance to racial or ethnic identity, we should remember the examples of Paul and Barnabas, who refused to yield even for a moment to the pressure to conform to prevailing expectations about what normal "religious" behavior looks like.

2. A minor theme of the passage is Paul's indifference to authority and reputation. He refused to regard his meeting with the "pillars" as an awe-inspiring occasion

<hr />

79. See D. S. Yeago, "Messiah's People: The Culture of the Church in the Midst of the Nations," *Pro Ecclesia* 6 (1997) 146-71.

(Gal 2:6); he did not go to Jerusalem to ask for their autographs. This text, therefore, might provoke reflection on the ways we become intimidated by or inappropriately deferential to authority figures, even within the church. The gospel calls us to stand up, as Paul and Barnabas did, and bear witness clearly to what God is doing in the world. We may hope that those who are reputedly leaders in the church will listen; but whether they listen or not, our witness-bearing task is the same.

3. The central message of Gal 2:1-10 is that the progress of the gospel in the world is God's activity. That is especially clear in 2:7-8, where we are told that the conference participants recognized that God was working in both Peter and Paul and that both of them had been entrusted with a message. The same is true today: All who serve in the church's various ministries are the vehicles of God's Word. (This passage can fruitfully be linked with Paul's portrayal in 1 Corinthians 12 of the Holy Spirit working through the distribution of diverse gifts to different members of the body of Christ.) We are instruments, not entrepreneurs. The implications of this truth are wide-ranging. On the one hand, it means that we are accountable to exercise faithfully the trust we have been given; on the other hand, it means that we need not be anxious, because we can trust that God's purposes will be accomplished. Our decision is whether to cooperate with those purposes (as the participants in the Jerusalem meeting did) or to stand in the way (as the "false brothers" did).

4. The military metaphors of 2:4-5 suggest that God's activity will often encounter opposition and conflict. When that happens, we should not be surprised. As long as we live in the "present evil age" on this side of the day of the Lord, the proclamation of the gospel will call forth the opposition of enemy powers. (See the Commentary and Reflections at 1:6-10.)

5. The mutual recognition of two distinct gospel missions to Jews and Gentiles raises fascinating questions about the church's mission strategy. Should we promote particular ethnic missionary initiatives aimed at separate cultural-linguistic communities? Should the church sponsor one mission for Hispanics, one for African Americans, one for persons of Korean ancestry, and another for Anglo-Americans? Common sense would appear to commend this strategy, and the Jerusalem agreement of Gal 2:1-10 might be taken as a precedent for it. Yet, as the sequel in 2:11-21 shows, this strategy is not without its problems. The danger is that these communities will define themselves primarily in relation to ethnicity rather than in relation to the gospel and that the church will become splintered into cultural factions. In order to prevent this unhappy outcome, if there are to be special ethnically defined ministries, frequent face-to-face meetings like the Jerusalem conference are essential, so that the circumcised will have to encounter the uncircumcised face-to-face, so that we can bear witness to the diverse works being done through us by the one Spirit, and so that we can extend to one another "the right hand of fellowship" (2:9).

6. Finally, 2:10 should not be neglected as a mere throwaway line. Authentic fellowship across cultural lines in the church requires us to take seriously the covenant obligation of concern for the poor. Where such concern is not put into action, the solidarity sealed by the handshake of 2:9 will be in serious jeopardy. One could imagine a sermon on Gal 2:1-10 that would treat v. 10 as the climax of the passage, challenging members of the congregation to demonstrate their commitment to "the truth of the gospel" (v. 4) through their eagerness to fulfill the mandate to "remember the poor."

GALATIANS 2:11-21, TWO TABLES OR ONE?
CONFRONTATION AT ANTIOCH

OVERVIEW

Up through 2:10, it looks as though all is well. Paul has emphatically claimed the authority of divine revelation as the source of his preaching, and he has recounted a major triumph in the Jerusalem meeting: The "false brothers" were defeated, and the leaders of the Jerusalem church affirmed their approval of Paul's mission to the Gentiles. In the next section of the letter, however, the plot of Paul's narrative takes a sharp turn; the unity achieved at Jerusalem was shattered by a subsequent conflict at Antioch. The account of this conflict (vv. 11-21) is the climax toward which Paul's story has been building.

Paul highlights his confrontation with Cephas (Peter) because it provides the background against which he views the present controversy in Galatia. The issues in the two situations are not identical, but they are closely parallel. Thus Paul can frame his account of his speech to Peter on the former occasion (vv. 14b-21) as a programmatic statement that speaks indirectly to the Galatians as well. Indeed, this speech can be seen as a concise summary of the themes of the letter as a whole.[80]

Translations and commentaries often place the termination of Paul's address to Peter at the end of v. 14 (as in the NRSV) and treat vv. 15-21 as a separate unit. It must be remembered that ancient Greek manuscripts did not employ the convention of placing quotation marks around quoted direct discourse; therefore, the question of where Paul's speech ends is a matter of interpretive judgment. This commentary will argue that the speech extends through v. 21 (as in the NIV; cf. NRSV footnote). There is no indication in the text of a change of addressee until 3:1, and the first-person plural pronouns in vv. 15-17 show that Paul is continuing to address a Jewish audience (i.e., the Jewish Christians

at Antioch), not the Gentile Galatians. Consequently, vv. 11-21 should be treated as a single coherent unit. Indeed, several obscurities in Paul's highly compressed language in vv. 15-21 can be clarified if they are understood in relation to the dispute over table fellowship in Antioch.

At the same time, Paul artfully narrates this story in such a way that it serves as a transition into his direct address to the Galatians in 3:1. A movie director making a film of this text might reproduce the effect in the following way: The scene opens in a public meeting of the church at Antioch with Paul confronting Peter; as Paul speaks (vv. 14b-21), the camera pans in on his face so that the members of the Antiochene church gradually disappear from view after v. 18. Then, at 3:1, as Paul says, "O foolish Galatians," the camera pans back again to reveal Paul in an entirely different setting, pacing the floor and dictating the letter to his secretary. The desired effect is that the Galatians will hear the speech to Peter as being addressed to their situation as well.[81]

One result of this rhetorical technique is that Paul never finishes the story of the Antioch controversy; we do not find out how Peter responded to Paul's challenge, and we do not hear how the Antiochene church decided to resolve the dispute. Almost certainly this means that Paul lost. If he had, in fact, convinced Peter and the other Jewish Christians to accept his arguments, he surely would have said so in this letter, just as he did in the preceding narrative of the Jerusalem meeting (vv. 1-10). Regardless of the outcome, however, the telling of this story allows Paul to articulate the theological principles that undergird his present response to the Galatians.

---

80. Betz, *Galatians,* 113-27, followed by Longenecker, *Galatians,* 80-96, describes Gal 2:15-21 as the *propositio* of the letter, the statement of the case to be defended.

81. Martyn suggests that Paul's speech becomes "a speech addressed to the Teachers [Missionaries] in Galatia," rather than to the Galatians themselves. While this suggestion may be correct, there is no direct indication of it in the text, and it underestimates the partial rhetorical parallel between Cephas and the Galatians; both parties are being swayed by outside emissaries to adopt Jewish practices. See Martyn, *Galatians,* 230.

The major theme of the unit is that the gospel mandates the formation of a new community in which there is no division between Jew and Gentile, a community in which Jews and Gentiles eat at one table together, not two separate tables.[82] The speech of vv. 14*b*-21 supports this claim by arguing that right relation to God depends

fundamentally on "the grace of God" (2:21), and not on observance of the ethnically particular signs of covenant membership (circumcision and food laws). This grace has been made effective through the death of Jesus Christ, which avails for Jew and Gentile without distinction (cf. Rom 3:21-31). Consequently, Peter's withdrawal from table fellowship with Gentile believers at Antioch was, as Paul sees it, a symbolic rejection of God's reconciling grace.

82. For the image of two tables, see M. Baker, *Religious No More: Building Communities of Grace and Freedom* (Downers Grove, Ill.: InterVarsity, 1999) 79-84, 96.

Galatians 2:11-14, Paul's Rebuke of Cephas

COMMENTARY

2:11-13. The coming of Cephas to Antioch (v. 11) marks a major complication in the story. Antioch was a great and prosperous city in northern Syria, the third largest city in the Roman Empire (after Rome and Alexandria).[83] According to Josephus, its large Jewish population mixed freely with the Gentiles there.

The Jewish race, densely interspersed among the native populations of every portion of the world, is particularly numerous in Syria, where intermingling is due to the proximity of the two countries. But it was at Antioch that they especially congregated. . . . Moreover, they were constantly attracting to their religious ceremonies multitudes of Greeks, and these they had in some measure incorporated with themselves.[84]

Even allowing for Josephus's penchant for hyperbole, we may safely conclude that Antioch was home to a substantial Jewish community that had attracted a large number of "godfearers," Gentiles who were drawn to the worship of the one God in the synagogue. Thus it is not surprising that as the early Jewish Christians began to spread the gospel message, it was at Antioch that they first began to preach extensively to Gentiles. Indeed, Antioch became a major base of operations

for the mission to the Gentiles (see Acts 11:19-26; 13:1-3).

The multicultural Antiochene Christian community presented new challenges that had been neither anticipated nor resolved by the agreement at the Jerusalem meeting, which had dealt only with the issue of circumcision (vv. 6-10).[85] Paul understood the agreement to imply a comprehensive recognition of the equality and fellowship of Jews and Gentiles in Christ (cf. 3:28), but some of the strictly Torah-observant Jewish Christians at Jerusalem interpreted the agreement less liberally. In effect, the Jerusalem agreement had acknowledged a separate-but-equal Gentile mission, but it had not addressed the problem of social relations and table fellowship between Jewish and Gentile Christians. The Christians at Antioch, recognizing the grace of God in their midst (Acts 11:21-24), made a practice of eating together, Jews at table with Gentiles (v. 12*a*). Some Jewish Christians from Jerusalem, however, found this practice objectionable. Why?

The Law of Moses contains no prohibition of eating with Gentiles. The people of Israel were commanded to abstain from unclean foods and from meat or wine tainted by association with idolatry; but as long as certain fundamental dietary precautions were observed, there was no reason why even

83. Longenecker, *Galatians*, 65. For more information on the city, see W. A. Meeks and R. L. Wilken, *Jews and Christians in Antioch in the First Four Centuries of the Common Era*, SBLSBS 13 (Missoula, Mont.: Scholars Press, 1978).

84. Josephus, *The Jewish War* 7.43, 45.

85. As already noted in the Commentary on 2:6-10, Luke's narrative of the "apostolic decree" in Acts 15:22-29 is almost surely an anachronistic account. There is no evidence in Paul's letters for the existence of such an agreement on food laws.

strictly Torah-observant Jews could not share table fellowship with Gentiles.[86]

What, then, was the nature of the issue at Antioch, and why did the "men from James" pressure Peter to stop eating with Gentile believers? Paul gives no explanation of their reasoning; therefore, we can only make guesses. It is possible that the food at the common meals was not kosher, that Peter and other Jewish Christians were disregarding basic Jewish dietary laws by eating meat with blood in it, or pork and shellfish. If so, this would explain Paul's remark that Peter had been living "like a Gentile" (v. 14). On the other hand, it seems unlikely that such flagrant violations of Jewish norms would have been practiced at Antioch, particularly if the Gentile converts were drawn primarily from the ranks of the "godfearers," who presumably would have already assimilated to Jewish dietary practices. It is more probable that the "men from James" were objecting to the practice of associating with Gentiles at table. This seems to be the implication of Paul's language in v. 12, which says nothing about the food as such but speaks of eating "with the Gentiles." Such association was not forbidden by Jewish Law, but it would have been perceived, in certain circles, as risky and impolitic: "Close association might lead to contact with idolatry or transgression of one of the biblical food laws. . . . James worried that too much fraternization with Gentiles would have bad results, and that Peter's mission [to the circumcised, 2:8] would be discredited if he were known to engage in it himself."[87]

It is possible that the pressure to shun such associations may have come from a faction in the Jerusalem church that wanted to make the emergent Christian movement look good in the eyes of their fervent Jewish countrymen. Robert Jewett has proposed that both the Antioch incident and the controversy in Galatia should be understood against the historical background of a rising Zealot movement in Palestine that advocated radical separation from Gentiles; in such an atmosphere,

Gentile sympathizers among the Jewish people might have been targeted for reprisals. The early church was a movement within Judaism, but the Gentile-friendly form it took in Antioch posed difficulties for Judean Jewish Christians who wanted "to avert the suspicion that they were in communion with lawless Gentiles."[88] Consequently, the response of this faction at Jerusalem was to urge Peter, with the blessing of James, to avoid contact with Gentiles, perhaps in hopes of pressuring the Gentile converts into accepting circumcision and full Torah-observance. Jewett argues that similar motives lay behind the pressure for circumcision of the Galatian Christians: "If they could succeed in circumcising the Gentile Christians, this might effectively thwart any Zealot purification campaign against the Judean church."[89] (Note how well this hypothesis explains Paul's otherwise puzzling statements in Gal 6:12-13.)

In any case, whatever political pressures may have been exerted on Peter, Paul had no tolerance for his waffling actions. Paul "opposed him to his face" (v. 12) in a public showdown ("before them all," v. 14) at Antioch. In Paul's view, God's verdict was already pronounced upon Peter's behavior: "he stood condemned." The renderings of the NIV ("in the wrong") and the NRSV ("self-condemned") both soften the severity of Paul's judgment; because Peter's action was a betrayal of the gospel, Paul saw him as standing under *God's* condemnation.

Who were the "people from James"? Paul does not identify them, but he indicates that they were a delegation from Jerusalem seeking, with the approval of James, to urge Peter to eschew fraternization with Gentiles. We do not know why Peter was in Antioch or how long he had been there, but the imperfect tense of the verb "used to eat" (συνήσθιεν *synēsthien*) implies that his sharing table fellowship with Gentiles had been a habitual practice over some period of time, not merely an isolated incident. When confronted by the messengers from Jerusalem, however, Peter "drew back and kept himself separate." The verb "draw back" (ὑποστέλλω *hypostellō*)

86. E. P. Sanders, "Jewish Association with Gentiles and Galatians 2:11-14," in *The Conversation Continues: Studies in Paul and John in Honor of J. Louis Martyn,* ed. R. T. Fortna and B. R. Gaventa (Nashville: Abingdon, 1990) 170-88.

87. Sanders, "Jewish Association with Gentiles and Galatians 2:11-14,"186.

88. Jewett, "The Agitators and the Galatian Congregation," 205. Jewett's argument is followed by Longenecker, *Galatians,* xciii-xcvi.

89. Jewett, "The Agitators and the Galatian Congregation," 206.

suggests a tactical retreat, like an army pulling back from an exposed position.[90]

By "separating himself," Peter was accommodating his actions to a well-established Jewish belief that the people of God should keep themselves free from defiling contact with the evil and idolatrous Gentile world. As already noted, eating with Gentiles was not a technical violation of Torah, but many Jews may have preferred to separate themselves from Gentiles as much as possible, out of a general sense that Gentiles were unclean and distasteful. The *Letter of Aristeas,* a Jewish apologetic work of the second century BCE, articulates the reason for such separation:

To prevent our being perverted by contact with others or by mixing with bad influences, [Moses] hedged us in on all sides with strict observances connected with meat and drink and touch and hearing and sight, after the manner of the Law.[91]

Such an interpretation of the purpose of the Torah could readily lead, in some circles, to a generalized attitude of wariness toward Gentiles, as we see in *Jub.* 22:16: "Eat not with them . . . for their works are unclean."[92] A similar indication of Jewish aversion for Gentiles is found in the Acts of the Apostles, in the story of Peter's vision and commission to preach to the household of the Gentile centurion Cornelius. Peter begins his conversation with them by saying, "You yourselves know how unlawful it is for a Jew to associate with or to visit any one of another nation" (Acts 10:28 RSV).[93] The Roman historian Tacitus confirms the stereotypical impression of Jews as a misanthropic people who "eat separately" from others.[94] Even if such statements are

exaggerated, they offer a broad sketch of a general perception that relations between Jews and Gentiles were fraught with tension, a tension focused particularly on eating practices.

Nothing in Paul's language suggests that the dispute focused specifically on eucharistic fellowship between Jewish and Gentile believers; the issue seems to have been whether they could eat together under any circumstance. If, however, Peter and the other Jewish Christians were avoiding all table fellowship, this would have included the Lord's supper, which at this early time seems ordinarily to have been celebrated in the context of a communal meal (see 1 Cor 11:17-34). In 1 Corinthians, Paul insists on interpreting the Lord's supper as a powerful symbol of communal unity, but he makes no such argument in Galatians. This suggests that the manner of celebrating the Lord's supper was not a central issue at Antioch. At the same time, it also suggests that Paul could not assume the experience of sharing the eucharist as a basis for his broader argument about table fellowship. It would have been a powerful argument for Paul to say, "If you share the bread and wine with Gentiles at the table of the Lord, how can you refuse to eat ordinary meals together?" Paul's silence on this point suggests that Peter, Barnabas, and other Jewish Christians were not celebrating the Lord's supper with the Gentile Christians in Antioch.

Paul charges that Peter separated himself from the common table because he feared "the circumcision faction" (οἱ ἐκ περιτομῆς *hoi ek peritomēs*). It is not precisely clear what group Paul has in mind here. Does he mean Jewish people in general, or does the term refer to a specific group of Jewish Christians? In view of Paul's use of this expression elsewhere (Rom 4:12; cf. Acts 10:45), it seems that he is referring not to Jews in general but to members of the early Christian movement who have Jewish ancestry. Furthermore, Luke's use of the same terminology in Acts 11:2 suggests that it could sometimes designate members of a particular party or faction within the Jerusalem church that focused on maintaining clear Jewish group boundaries.[95] Thus it appears that Paul is

90. Betz, *Galatians,* 108.

91. Letter of Aristeas, 142.

92. Philip F. Esler, *Galatians* (London: Routledge, 1998) 93-116, argues, based on passages such as the ones cited here, that Jews during the late Second Temple period universally eschewed table fellowship with Gentiles. For a more nuanced account of the evidence on this question, see Sanders, "Jewish Association with Gentiles and Galatians 2:11-14."

93. Of course, Peter follows this statement by declaring that God has shown him to observe a different policy toward Gentiles: "But God has shown me that I should not call anyone profane or unclean" (Acts 10:28*b*). If Peter had indeed held such views at an earlier stage, as his eating with Gentiles at Antioch would suggest (Gal 2:12*a*), his subsequent withdrawal from association with Gentile Christians would be all the more reprehensible.

94. Tacitus *Histories* 5.5.1-2. Dunn also calls attention to the recurrent motif, in Jewish literature from the Maccabean period to the first century CE, of the glorification of heroes and heroines whose fidelity to the law is demonstrated by refusal to eat "the food of Gentiles" (Dan 1:8-16; Tob 1:10-13; Jdt 10:5; 12:1-20; Additions to Esther 14:17; *Joseph and Aseneth* 7:1; 8:5). See Dunn, *The Epistle to the Galatians,* 118.

95. For this interpretation of οἱ ἐκ περιτομῆς (*hoi ek peritomēs*), see Martyn, *Galatians,* 236-40.

accusing Peter of fearing other Jewish *Christians;* the problem is intra-ecclesial.

Even though the messengers from James may have focused their suasion on Peter alone, his withdrawal from the common table predictably influenced others, so that the other Jewish Christians, including even Paul's close associate Barnabas, followed his lead (v. 13). From Paul's perspective, this was a disaster. The previously unified Antioch community was now split into two different ethnic communities, with Torah observance as the dividing wall between them. In place of one common table, there were now two separate tables.

Paul describes this mass withdrawal from the one table as "hypocrisy" (ὑπόκρισις *hypokrisis*, v. 13). The Greek word does not have quite the same connotation of malicious duplicity that is present in the English. In Greek, the ὑποκριτής (*hypokritēs*) is an actor, someone who wears a mask and plays a role. Thus *hypokrisis* is the act of playing out a scripted role. Paul's point is that Peter and the other Jewish Christians at Antioch are caught up in playing a part that does not represent their own considered convictions; they are caving in to external pressure, carrying out someone else's agenda. This is another way of expressing the charge of people pleasing (see the Commentary on 1:10).

The fact that Barnabas joined in this role playing must have been especially galling to Paul.[96] It was Barnabas who had stood with him at Jerusalem in resisting the "false brothers" (vv. 1-5). According to Luke's account in Acts, Barnabas had originally rejoiced when he came to Antioch and found Gentile believers experiencing the grace of God along with Jewish believers (Acts 11:19-26). Now, however, as Paul saw it, Barnabas had been "carried away" (v. 13) by group pressure, and Paul was left to stand alone as an advocate for God's new creation of a community in which Jews and Gentiles could eat at one table.

2:14. Paul's sharp public rebuke of Peter may seem excessive, particularly if Peter was acting out of a concern to protect Jewish Christians in Jerusalem from persecution by fervent Jewish nationalists. Paul seems to give him no credit for good motives or to make any attempt to talk the matter out privately (cf. Matt 18:15-17) or even to correct Peter "in a spirit of gentleness" (Gal 6:1). What accounts for Paul's vehement response? The answer can only be that he saw in Peter's action "the effective preaching of an anti-gospel in the midst of the Antioch church."[97] Consequently, Paul did not hesitate to take an uncompromising stand, because "the truth of the gospel" was at stake (v. 14; cf. 1:6-9). Paul had used the same phrase in 2:5 to describe what was at issue in the controversy over circumcision in Jerusalem. In both cases, "the truth of the gospel" is linked directly with the fellowship of Gentile and Jewish believers on equal terms: Neither circumcision nor observance of dietary laws should divide the church. "The truth of the gospel," therefore, is not merely a doctrine but a social reality, a truth that must be embodied in the practices of a community. This truth was being violated by the exclusionary social practices of Peter and those who joined him in a policy of separate tables. Paul saw in their withdrawal a failure to "walk straight" (ὀρθοποδέω *orthopodeō*) toward the truth of the gospel. (The NRSV's "not acting consistently" is a pallid paraphrase; better is the NIV's "not acting in line with the truth of the gospel.") Thus he addressed to Peter a passionate speech seeking to re-call him and the other Jewish Christians to the one table with the Gentiles.

Paul opens fire with an ad hominem argument charging Peter personally with bad faith and gross inconsistency: "If you, though a Jew, live like a Gentile and not like a Jew, how can you compel the Gentiles to live like Jews?" (v. 14*b*). To "live like a Jew" means, in this case, to observe Jewish dietary restrictions. The question presupposes that Peter does not ordinarily live a strictly Torah-observant life—and that he would make no pretense of doing so. This would be consistent with his custom of eating with Gentiles at Antioch before the arrival of the delegation from James. Paul charges that by caving in to the pressure from the Jerusalem delegation, Peter is in effect requiring the Gentile converts at Antioch to adopt a higher standard of Torah observance than he himself would normally follow.

---

96. Was the Antioch incident the fundamental cause of the split between Paul and Barnabas, attributed to other causes in Acts 15:36-41?

97. Martyn, *Galatians,* 235.

As noted earlier, the "compulsion" in view here is not a matter of violent coercion but of manipulative group pressure; Peter and the other Jewish Christians at Antioch were in effect "compelling" Gentiles to adopt Jewish observances by boycotting the common table. There is no indication here that the delegation from James was pressing for Gentiles to be circumcised; that issue had already been clearly settled—with the approval of James—by the meeting in Jerusalem (vv. 1-10). The verb ἰουδαΐζειν (*ioudaizein*), translated here as "live like Jews" (v. 14), does not necessarily denote converting to Judaism;[98] rather, it means to adopt Jewish practices.[99] Presumably, the Gentile Christians could have overcome any objection to table fellowship by conforming their diets to the dictates of Jewish Law. This might appear harmless enough, but in this outside pressure for Gentile Christians to conform to Jewish dietary standards, Paul sees a betrayal of the gospel. (See Reflections at 2:15-21.)

98. It does apparently have this meaning in Josephus *Jewish War* 2.454. Martyn, *Galatians*, 236, however, suggests that this example, like Esth 8:17 LXX, carries connotations of superficiality and insincerity in the adoption of the Jewish way of life.

99. See, e.g., Ign. *Magn.* 10.3: "It is monstrous to talk of Jesus Christ and to practice Judaism [ἰουδαΐζειν *ioudaizein*]."

Galatians 2:15-21, Jews and Gentiles Alike Are Rectified Through Christ's Death

COMMENTARY

The reasons for this judgment follow in the highly compressed argument of vv. 15-21, which serves as a *précis* of the argument of the entire letter. As noted, Paul has composed his account of this speech with the Galatians in view. Thus the theological argument of vv. 15-21 applies equally to the conflict at Antioch and to the Galatians' present quandary over circumcision. The interpreter's task is to see how the argument functions at each of these levels.

2:15-16. Still addressing Peter, Paul affirms (v. 15) his own participation in the hereditary Jewish tradition that defines its identity sharply against Gentile outsiders: "We ourselves are Jews by birth [lit., "by nature"] and not Gentile sinners." In this traditional Jewish frame of reference, the Gentiles are categorized as "sinners" (ἁμαρτωλοί *hamartōloi*) simply by virtue of their being outsiders to the covenant people. Given the more receptive attitude toward Gentiles that Paul has come to hold as the apostle to the Gentiles, we may assume that he employs this categorical label with some degree of irony. Nonetheless, the point is a serious one: He, along with Peter and the delegation from Jerusalem—and, it must be noted, along with the rival Missionaries in Galatia—is a Jew, a sharer in the heritage of Israel (see Phil 3:4-6). His purpose for emphasizing this common ethnic identity emerges as the rest of the sentence unfolds; even those Jewish Christians who are most conscious of their ethnic identity share a common confession about justification through Christ. Paul points to this shared confessional tradition in order to use it as the foundation of his argument that Torah observance is not necessary for Gentiles in the new situation that God has brought into being.

The confession articulated in v. 16—which Paul presents as the common belief of Jewish Christians—is the heart of the message of Galatians, the gospel in a nutshell. This confession is so concisely formulated, however, that it presents numerous exegetical problems. Paul writes here in a theological shorthand, and each phrase must be unpacked carefully.[100] Consequently, we must make several crucial interpretative decisions here that will determine our reading of the letter as a whole.

The issues that demand attention are (a) the structure of the sentence in vv. 15-16; (b) the meaning of the verb "to justify"; (c) the meaning of the phrase "by works of the Law"; (d) the meaning of the expression "through the faith of [or in] Jesus Christ" (διὰ πίστεως

100. Betz describes this unit as consisting of "dogmatic abbreviations, i.e., very short formulaic summaries of doctrines." See Betz, *Galatians*, 114.

Ἰησοῦ Χριστοῦ *dia pisteōs Iēsou Christou*); (e) the allusion to Psalm 143 in the last clause of v. 16.

(a) The Structure of the Sentence. The NRSV produces a simpler and more readable English text of vv. 15-16 by turning the participial phrase at the beginning of v. 16 into an independent clause and starting a new sentence in the middle of the verse:

We ourselves are Jews by birth and not Gentile sinners; yet we know that a person is justified not by the works of the law but through faith in Jesus Christ. And we have come to believe in Christ Jesus.

Unfortunately, this translation loses some important nuances of the Greek syntax. The verb "know" in v. 16*a* is actually a participle (εἰδότες *eidotes*); thus a more literal translation would read as follows:

We ourselves are Jews by birth and not Gentile sinners; yet, knowing that a person is justified not by the works of the law but[101] through the faith of Jesus Christ, even we have trusted in Christ Jesus.

The emphasis here falls on the words "even we" (καὶ ἡμεῖς *kai hēmeis*), with the *kai* understood as explicative (not a conjunction introducing an independent clause, as in the NRSV), reminding the reader that the "we" of v. 16 is precisely the same Jewish constituency signaled in v. 15. Paul's point is that "even we Jews by birth" (i.e., not just Gentiles) have placed trust in Christ *instead of* in works of the law as the ground of justification.

(b) The Meaning of the Verb "to Justify." The crucial verb "to justify" (δικαιόω *dikaioō*), which occurs three times in this

verse, appears here for the first time in Galatians. To be "justified" is to be declared in the right or placed in right relationship to God.[102] The term has its origins in the language of the law court, but in Israel's prophetic literature and psalms the term takes on a distinct eschatological connotation: Even though the present may be a time of suffering and oppression, the prophets and the psalmists look to God as the source of future vindication. God will ultimately act to "justify" the covenant people by rescuing them and overthrowing their enemies and oppressors. In many OT contexts, the best English translation of the verb is "to vindicate." For example, in Isa 50:7-8*a* the mysterious "Servant" figure declares:

The LORD God helps me;
  therefore, I have not been disgraced;
therefore I have set my face like flint,
  and I know that I shall not be put to shame;
  he who *vindicates* me [ὁ δικαιώσας με
  ho dikaiōsas me] is near. (NRSV, italics added)

Thus the verb "justify" points not merely to a forensic declaration of acquittal from guilt but also to God's ultimate action of powerfully setting right all that has gone wrong.

Consequently, when Paul speaks here of "being justified," he repeatedly uses the passive voice. The implied agent of "justification" is God; it is God alone who has the power to set things right. That is why—virtually by definition—no human being can be justified by works of the Law; such works, even if undertaken in obedience to God, remain limited human acts. "Justification," however, is the eschatological act of God. Thus, when he refers in v. 16 to being "justified," Paul is speaking of God's world-transforming eschatological verdict as it pertains to individual human beings. Because this verdict effectively sets right all that had gone wrong, the best English translation of the verb *dikaioō* is "to rectify" (see the excursus: "The Language of Righteousness").

---

101. The Greek here is ἐὰν μή (*ean mē*), which would usually be translated as "except." Dunn (*The Epistle to the Galatians*, 137-38) finds here an ambiguity deliberately calculated by Paul to win Peter's assent to the formulation; the hearer or reader could understand the sentence to mean, "A person is not justified by the works of the Law *except* through faith in Jesus Christ." On this reading, the formula would not exclude works of the Law but promote faith in Christ as the one way through which one could attain justification by (also?) doing what the Law requires. Virtually all other commentators, however, interpret *ean mē* here as adversative ("but rather") or, if read as exceptive, as applying only to the verb rather than to the appended prepositional phrase "by works of the Law." This would yield the translation "A person is not justified by works of the Law; (a person is not justified) except through faith in/of Jesus Christ." This is a more cumbersome rendering that is essentially equivalent to the adversative sense. For discussion of the translation issue, see Longenecker, *Galatians*, 83-84; Martyn, *Galatians*, 251.

102. For a full discussion, see R. B. Hays, "Justification," *ABD* 3.1129-33. See also S. K. Williams, *Galatians*, ANTC (Nashville: Abingdon, 1997) 62-65.

EXCURSUS: THE LANGUAGE OF RIGHTEOUSNESS

The verb δικαιόω *dikaioō* bears a very close relation to the adjective δίκαιος (*dikaios*) and the noun δικαιοσύνη (*dikaiosyne*). These words are often translated into English as "righteous" (as in 3:11 NRSV) and "righteousness" (as in 3:6, 21; 5:5 NRSV; 2:21 NIV), while *dikaioō* is usually translated as "justify." Such translations run the risk of obscuring for the English reader many of the inner connections in Paul's thought. The following chart illustrates the relationships between these terms:

Greek	English (Latin root)	English (Anglo-Saxon root)
δικαιόω	justify	rectify
δίκαιος	just	righteous
δικαιοσύνη	justice	righteousness *or* rectification

The coherence of Paul's argument becomes clearer if the English translation consistently employs one or the other of these systems of related terms.[103] Accordingly, subsequent discussion in this commentary will ordinarily employ the terms "rectify," "righteous," and "righteousness/rectification."

---

103. Martyn, *Galatians*, which consistently translates δικαιόω (*dikaioō*) as "rectify" and δικαιοσύνη (*dikaiosyne*) as "rectification," represents a constructive solution to this linguistic difficulty.

Although "rectification" is an important motif in Paul's theology, there is nothing about his use of the verb that is unusual in the context of first-century Judaism. (To be sure, his understanding of *how* God acts to bring about rectification is sharply distinctive; see the section "The Faith of Jesus Christ," below.) His usage is thoroughly consonant with the OT examples noted above, and it is closely paralleled by the language of grateful thanksgiving found in the Dead Sea Scrolls:

As for me, my judgment is with God.
In his hand are the perfection of my way
and the uprightness of my heart.
He will wipe out my transgression through his
   righteousness. . . .
As for me, if I stumble, the mercies of God
shall be my eternal salvation.
If I stagger because of the sin of my flesh,
my judgment shall be
by the *righteousness* of God which endures
forever. (1QS 11:2-3, 12)

Thus, when Paul asserts that Peter and other Jewish Christians share his fundamental understanding of "rectification" as God's action made effective through Christ, there is no reason to doubt his claim. The controversy arises only when we seek further clarification about the roles of "works of Law" and "the faith of Jesus Christ" in relation to the process of rectification.

(c) Works of the Law. Martin Luther found in Paul's dichotomy between "faith" and "works of the law" a hermeneutical principle that provided the theological impetus for the Reformation. Luther interpreted "works of the law" as a metaphor for all human striving for God's approval. Thus, he saw in Gal 2:16 a contrast between earning salvation through meritorious performance of good deeds and receiving salvation through faith alone (*sola fide*).[104] This doctrine provided him with a powerful polemical weapon against the practices

---

104. Martin Luther, *Lectures on Galatians (1535)*, *Luther's Works*, vol. 26, trans. Jaroslav Pelikan (St. Louis: Concordia, 1963) 122-41.

and teachings of the sixteenth-century Roman Catholic Church. Luther's reading of Paul exercised widespread influence on subsequent Christian interpreters, who associated the attempt to earn salvation through good works with Pharisaic Judaism and, therefore, saw Paul as announcing a radical break with the Jewish understanding of God and salvation.

The difficulty with this account of the matter is that it rests upon a caricature of Judaism, as E. P. Sanders has demonstrated in his watershed study *Paul and Palestinian Judaism*.[105] Judaism has never taught that individuals must earn God's favor by performing meritorious works; members of the covenant people are already embraced by God's gracious election and mercy. Obedience to the Law is not a condition for getting in; rather, it is a means of staying in the covenant community. Sanders describes this Jewish pattern of religion as "covenantal nomism." Nearly all scholars who study early Judaism and Christianity now acknowledge that Sanders's description of Palestinian Judaism is basically correct.

How, then, are we to understand the contrast that Paul draws in 2:16 between being rectified by faith and being rectified by works of the Law? Is Paul setting up an artificial foil, a false depiction of his own Jewish heritage? A solution to this problem has been offered by J. D. G. Dunn, who has proposed that the expression "works of Law" (ἔργα νόμου *erga nomou*) refers not to meritorious deeds in general but specifically to those practices that stand as outward symbols of Jewish ethnic distinctiveness: circumcision, dietary observances, and sabbath keeping.[106] If that is right, we could paraphrase Paul as follows:

We ourselves are Jews by birth and not Gentile sinners; yet, knowing that a person is rectified not by wearing the badges of ethnic identity but through the faith of Jesus Christ, even we have trusted in Christ Jesus.

Thus Paul's critique would be targeted not at "Pelagianism" (seeking to earn salvation

through good works) but at ethnic exclusivity (claiming soteriological privilege on the basis of racial or sociocultural distinctiveness). One advantage of this interpretation of "works of the Law" is that it so clearly fits the situation Paul is addressing at Antioch.[107] By withdrawing from table fellowship with Gentiles, Peter was not seeking to earn salvation through good deeds; rather, he was seeking to maintain the boundary between the ethnic Jewish-Christian community and its Gentile neighbors. For this reason alone, Dunn's explanation is to be strongly preferred to the traditional "Lutheran" reading of the passage.

To be sure, the phrase *erga nomou* does not refer only to markers of ethnic identity; in principle, it refers—as Dunn has acknowledged—to the comprehensive range of actions required by the Torah.[108] (Martyn translates it as "observance of the Law.")[109] Still, the immediate context in Galatians suggests that the expression "works of Law" points especially to the few litmus-test practices where Jewish identity was symbolically at stake. (Indeed, it is probable that the phrase *erga nomou* was being used by the rival Missionaries in Galatia to characterize the obedience they sought to impose upon Paul's Gentile converts.)

(d) The Faith of Jesus Christ. If, then, Paul's confessional formula declares that no one is rectified through Law observance or adherence to the identity-marking practices of Judaism, what is the positive alternative? Here once again we must consider whether Luther and the Reformers were informed by an adequate exegesis of Paul. The Western Christian tradition has generally understood the phrase διὰ πίστεως Ἰησου Χριστοῦ (*dia pisteōs Iēsou Christou*) to mean "through believing in Jesus Christ." This suited Luther's theology well: In place of human striving for acceptance, salvation is conditioned solely upon believing the proclaimed gospel message. But is this what Paul meant to say? There are reasons to think that he had something different in mind; the phrase *dia pisteōs Iēsou Christou* points not primarily

---

105. E. P. Sanders, *Paul and Palestinian Judaism: A Comparison of Patterns of Religion* (Philadelphia: Fortress, 1977).

106. Dunn, *The Epistle to the Galatians*, 135-37. See also Dunn's essays, "The New Perspective on Paul" and "Works of the Law and the Curse of the Law (Gal. iii.10-14)," in *Jesus, Paul and the Law* (Louisville: Westminster/John Knox, 1990) 183-214, 215-41.

107. Dunn, *The Epistle to the Galatians*, 136-37, observes that the immediately preceding discussion in Galatians has focused precisely on two of these markers of ethnic identity: circumcision (2:1-10) and eating practices (2:11-14).

108. J. D. G. Dunn, "4QMMT and Galatians," *NTS* 43 (1997) 147-53.

109. Martyn, *Galatians*, 250.

to our cognitive response to the preached gospel but to Jesus Christ's act of fidelity in undergoing death for our sake.

Paul's prepositional phrase is semantically ambiguous. The genitive case (*Iēsou Christou*) could be either objective or subjective—i.e., gramatically speaking, Jesus could be either the object or the subject of the action implied in the noun πίστις (*pistis*, "faith"). It is impossible to reproduce the ambiguity exactly in an English translation of the phrase, but we can illustrate the point by constructing a parallel expression: "We are rectified by the love of Jesus." Does that mean that we are rectified because we love Jesus (objective genitive) or because Jesus loves us (subjective genitive)?[110] The ambiguity can be resolved only by situating the sentence in a larger discourse or structure of thought.

Furthermore, the noun *pistis* offers a range of semantic possibilities for English translators. It can be rendered as "faith," "faithfulness," "fidelity," or "trust." It probably does not, however, mean "belief" in the sense of cognitive assent to a doctrine; rather it refers to placing trust or confidence in a person. The cognate verb πιστεύω (*pisteuō*) can be translated as "believe" or "trust." English, regrettably, lacks a verb form from the same root as the noun "faith." All of this contributes to the uncertainty over how to interpret Paul's statements in v. 16.

Paul uses similar expressions about the faith of/in Jesus Christ in Gal 2:20 and 3:22 and again in Rom 3:22, 26, as well as in Phil 3:9.[111] The interpretation of all these passages has been extensively debated in recent critical literature,[112] and recent English-language commentators on Galatians have lined up rather evenly divided on both sides of the question.[113] While acknowledging the lack

of scholarly consensus, the commentary that follows here will develop a reading of Galatians that understands *pistis Iēsou Christou* to mean "the faithfulness of Jesus Christ" as manifested in his self-sacrificial death.[114] As v. 16 suggests, this formulation does not originate with Paul; it is the common property of early Jewish Christianity. But what does it mean? The phrase "the faithfulness of Jesus Christ" makes sense only if we read it as an allusion to a *story* about Jesus, "who gave himself for our sins to set us free from the present evil age, according to the will of our God and Father" (1:4). His self-giving was interpreted by early Christians as an act of *pistis*, faithfulness. When all humanity had fallen away into unfaithfulness, he alone was faithful to God. At the same time, his death was an act that showed forth *God's* faithfulness (cf. Rom 3:3), God's determination not to abandon his people to slavery and death. Thus, when Paul writes that a person is rectified only *dia pisteōs Iēsou Christou*, he is thinking of Christ's faithfulness as embodied in his death on a cross, which was the event through which God acted to rescue us (cf. Rom 5:8: "God proves his love for us in that while we were still sinners Christ died for us").

In the light of this understanding, we can paraphrase vv. 15-16*a* once again to clarify their sense:

We ourselves are Jews by birth and not Gentile sinners; yet, knowing that a person is rectified not by observance of the Law but through Jesus Christ's faithful death for our sake, even we have trusted in Christ Jesus in order that we might be rectified through the faithfulness of Christ and not through observance of the Law.

This interpretation is confirmed by Paul's last sentence in this paragraph (v. 21), where he sums up his argument by insisting that rectification comes not "through the Law" but through "Christ's death."[115]

(e) Paul's Allusion to Psalm 143. The last clause of v. 16 ("because no one will be rectified by works of the Law") appears redundant, but it is actually Paul's appeal to a

110. A third possibility is that the sentence means that we are rectified by having Jesus-like love, a quality of love that has its origin in Jesus (genitive of author). Williams opts for understanding "faith of Jesus Christ" along these lines. See Williams, *Galatians*, 67-70.

111. Relevant for purposes of comparison are also Col 3:5 and Eph 3:12. See also Rom 4:16, where τῷ ἐκ πίστεως Ἀβραάμ (*tō ek pisteōs Abraam*) certainly does *not* mean "to the one who has faith *in* Abraham"; it means "to the one who shares the faith *of* Abraham."

112. For a full discussion of the options, see R. B. Hays, "ΠΙΣΤΙΣ and Pauline Christology: What Is at Stake?"; J. D. G. Dunn, "Once More, ΠΙΣΤΙΣ ΧΡΙΣΤΟΥ"; and P. J. Achtemeier, "Apropos the Faith of/in Christ: A Response to Hays and Dunn," in *Pauline Theology, Vol. 4: Looking Back, Pressing On*, ed. E. E. Johnson and D. M. Hay (Atlanta: Scholars Press, 1997) 35-92.

113. In support of "faith in Jesus Christ": Betz, Dunn. In support of "the faithfulness of Jesus Christ": Longenecker, Matera, Martyn. Williams adopts the "authorial genitive" solution and translates the phrase as "Christ-faith."

114. In addition to the arguments set forth in Hays, "ΠΙΣΤΙΣ and Pauline Christology," see Martyn, *Galatians*, 270-71.

115. Martyn, *Galatians*, 271.

scriptural proof to clinch his point.[116] His language here echoes Ps 143:2: "Do not enter into judgment with your servant, for no one living is righteous before you" (NRSV). The parallel is more clearly evident in the Greek texts than in most English translations:

Ps 142:2 LXX	
(= Ps 143:2 MT	Gal 2:16d
And do not enter into judgment with your slave	
Because before you	Because by works of the Law
no living being	no flesh
will be justified	will be justified
(δικαιωθήσεται	(δικαιωθήσεται
dikaiōthēsetai)	*dikaiōthēsetaî)*

The psalm does not include the phrase "by works of the Law" (Paul has added this phrase to highlight the point he is making), but the psalmist does affirm that no human being can stand before God's judgment and that all hope for deliverance rests in the power and righteousness of God. Twice in Psalm 143 the speaker invokes God's righteousness (δικαιοσύνη *dikaiosynē*):

Hear my prayer, O LORD;
Give ear to my supplication in your truthfulness;
Answer me *in your righteousness.*

. . . .

For your name's sake, O LORD, you will make me alive.
In your righteousness you will bring my soul out of tribulation.
(Ps 143:1, 11[142:1, 11] NRSV)

By alluding to this psalm Paul underscores his claim that the gospel of justification/rectification through God's act in Christ is entirely consistent with what those who are "Jews by birth" already know—or should know—through the witness of Scripture: We are set in right relationship to God only through God's own act of grace. The ground of our hope is the righteousness of God, not any human "works" or ethnic status. When Paul changes the wording of the psalm from "no

one living will be justified" to "no *flesh* will be justified," he is perhaps subtly anticipating the argument he will make later in the letter against "those who want to make a good showing *in the flesh*" by compelling the Galatians to be circumcised (6:12).[117]

Thus, in vv. 15-16, Paul has set forth his grounds for challenging Peter in Antioch—grounds that serve also as the theological basis for his challenge to the Galatians to reject the pressure to be circumcised. In the sentences that follow (vv. 17-21), Paul answers some anticipated objections and elaborates his position.

2:17-18. In v. 17, Paul dramatically articulates the objection that the emissaries from James (v. 12) had raised against the Jewish Christians at Antioch who were eating with Gentiles (and perhaps also the objection raised by the Missionaries in Galatia against Paul): Those who eat with Gentiles thereby become "sinners" (the same word as in v. 15) just like the Gentiles and thereby drag the name of Christ through the mud, making him an accomplice in sinful actions—and therefore, in effect, the table-waiter[118] of sin! The conditional sentence in v. 17 is formulated not as a contrary-to-fact condition but as a real condition: Paul and others who join him at table with Gentiles *are* "seeking to be rectified in Christ" (v. 16), and they *are* in fact being perceived as sinners by those who disapprove of their actions. The protasis of the sentence reflects the evaluative perspective of those who condemn the practice of the common table. For the sake of argument, Paul momentarily grants their point of view, saying, in effect, "All right, then, so eating with Gentiles means that we (Jewish Christians) ourselves are sinners." If that is the consequence of solidarity with the Gentiles, so be it! But then Paul asks whether it follows that Christ, by bringing together Jews and Gentiles, is thereby aiding and abetting sinful behavior: "Is Christ then a servant [διάκονος *diakonos*] of Sin? Certainly not!" Paul conjures up and then emphatically rejects an absurd image of Christ waiting upon Sin as a personified power; the term *diakonos* ("servant," often used of table servants) links the

---

116. For a more detailed exposition, see R. B. Hays, "Psalm 143 and the Logic of Romans 3," *JBL* 99 (1980) 107-15.

117. Martyn, *Galatians,* 253.
118. Dunn, *The Epistle to the Galatians,* 141. Dunn suggests that Paul here may be alluding ironically to traditions of Jesus' table fellowship with sinners and his self-description as a *diakonos* (Mark 10:42-45).

objection vividly to the scene of Jews and Gentiles eating at one table. It is impossible to say whether this image was already suggested by Paul's detractors or whether Paul has formulated it as a rhetorical strategem to show the absurdity of the objection.

Paul next explains why he regards it as a mistake for Peter and Barnabas and other Jewish Christians to withdraw and separate themselves (v. 12) from eating with Gentiles: "For if I build up again the very things that I once tore down, then I demonstrate that I am a transgressor" (v. 18). Paul shifts here from the first-person plural pronouns and verbs that he employed in vv. 15-17 to the first-person singular, which he uses throughout vv. 18-21. It is sometimes suggested that he does this for reasons of rhetorical tact. By using himself as an example, he makes the point more gently than if he directly confronted Peter with the accusation of transgression. In view of the confrontational tone of vv. 11-14, however, this explanation is not very satisfying. A better explanation is that Paul is already beginning the mental transition from the situation at Antioch to the situation in Galatia, no longer addressing Peter directly but beginning to address the issues raised against him personally by the Missionaries in another setting. (In terms of the cinematic analogy suggested above, in v. 18 the camera now pans in for the close-up shot of Paul's face.)

The language of tearing down and rebuilding something suggests the image of the Torah as a wall that separates Israel from the Gentiles.[119] Paul's gospel declares that Jesus Christ has torn down this wall. The image is powerfully developed in Eph 2:14-16:

For he is our peace; in his flesh he has made both groups into one and has broken down the dividing wall, that is the hostility between us. He has abolished the Law with its commandments and ordinances, that he might create in himself one new humanity in place of the two, thus making peace, and might reconcile both groups to God in one body through the cross, thus putting to death that hostility through it. (NRSV)

This passage, probably the work of one of Paul's immediate followers, expresses well Paul's understanding of his apostolic commission as the outworking of God's design to bring Jews and Gentiles together into one new people. By pressuring Paul to separate himself from eating with Gentiles, Peter and the emissaries from Jerusalem are asking him to build up again the wall of separation that he had previously torn down not just at Antioch but throughout his mission to the Gentiles.

If he does rebuild that wall, Paul insists, he will establish that he is a transgressor. There are two possible readings of this statement. Paul could mean that the very act of rebuilding the wall of commandments and ordinances would itself be an act of transgression against God's will. This would be a radical and ironic inversion of what the term "transgression" had meant in Paul's "former life in Judaism" (1:13), in which transgression referred to violations of the Law's boundaries, not to reestablishing them.[120] On the other hand, Paul could mean that rebuilding the wall of separation would show that his entire apostolic labor of preaching the Law-free gospel to Gentiles had not been a fulfillment of the will of God but a flagrant violation of God's holiness; to follow Peter in leaving the common table would show that Paul's whole apostleship had been in vain (cf. 2:2), an extended defiance of God. His practice of disregarding dietary restrictions and bringing Jews and Gentiles together in the church would have been, from this point of view, nothing but transgression against God.[121] This latter interpretation is the one that Paul's original hearers would have been more likely to grasp.

2:19-21. The issue is not left long in doubt, however. Paul moves quickly to declare that the old frame of reference, in which the Law must separate Jews and Gentiles, no longer applies. It has been abolished by the crucifixion of Jesus. Paul understands this crucifixion as a cosmic event in which he participates, with the result that he has "died to the Law" (v. 19). Because he has died to the Law, going back to it is impossible; rebuilding the wall is impossible for Paul, because, having been

---

119. For the use of this image within Hellenistic Judaism, see the *Letter of Aristeas* 139: "In his wisdom the legislator [Moses] . . . surrounded us with unbroken palisades and iron walls to prevent our mixing with any of the other peoples in any matter, being thus kept pure in body and soul, preserved from false beliefs, and worshiping the only God omnipotent over all creation."

120. This interpretation is favored by Martyn, *Galatians*, 256.

121. For this reading of 2:18, see A. F. Segal, *Paul the Convert: The Apostolate and Apostasy of Saul the Pharisee* (New Haven: Yale University Press, 1990) 202-3.

crucified with Christ, he has come into an entirely new life animated by Christ.

One puzzling feature of v. 19 is Paul's statement that "*through the Law*" he died to the Law. If he had written, "through the *cross* I died to the Law," his line of argument would be clear. But why does he say instead, "through the *Law*"? Nothing in the immediate context offers an explanation of what Paul means by this opaque formulation. Certainly Paul is not thinking of "dying to the Law" through discovering the futility of his own attempts to observe it; according to his own self-description, he was "as to righteousness under the Law, blameless" (Phil 3:6). (The inappropriateness of the popular picture of Paul prior to his conversion as laboring under the burden of a guilt-ridden conscience was eloquently demonstrated by Krister Stendahl in his classic essay, "The Apostle Paul and the Introspective Conscience of the West.")[122] Commentators sometimes refer to Rom 7:11, which says that Sin working "in the commandment, deceived me and through it killed me" (NRSV). In fact, however, this passage sheds no light on Gal 2:19; in Romans, it is clear that one dies to the Law not "through the Law" but "through the body of Christ" (Rom 7:4 NRSV)—i.e., through union with his death in baptism (Rom 6:1-11). Dunn proposes that when Paul says "through the Law" he is referring to his activity as a persecutor of the church, motivated by zeal for the Law.[123] This interpretation leaves unexplained how this activity caused Paul to die to the Law; apart from God's intervention and call, he could have gone right on persecuting the church. The explanation that finds the greatest support within the text of Galatians itself is that the Law played an active role in the death of Jesus and pronounced a curse upon him (Gal 3:13). Thus, since Paul's death to the Law came about through his being "crucified with Christ" (v. 19; cf. 6:14), the Law played an instrumental role in this process. In fact, however, Paul does not offer any explicit explanation of this point, and we may be well advised to concede that we do not know exactly what Paul meant by the aphoristic statement "through the Law I died to the Law."

The point that matters for Paul is that he *has* passed through this death, leaving the Law behind, "so that I might live to God." This extraordinary assertion—driving a wedge between the Law and God—would be scandalous to the ears of Jews zealous for the Law.[124] The more usual Jewish perspective on the relation between the Law and life before God is illustrated by two passages in 4 Maccabees (4 Macc 7:19; 16:25) that apply the expression "to live to God" to those who undergo martyrdom precisely for the sake of the Law. The latter passage states the matter concisely:

By these words the mother of the seven encouraged and persuaded each of her sons to die *rather than violate God's commandment.* They knew also that those who die for the sake of God *live to God,* as do Abraham and Isaac and Jacob and all the patriarchs. (4 Macc 16:24-25 NRSV, italics added)

Unlike the Maccabean martyrs, Paul has died not *for* the Law but *to* it, and he claims thereby to have found life before God. This new life includes, of course, the fellowship of Jews and Gentiles together in a single worshiping congregation gathered in the name of Jesus. Those who are calling for a retreat from this radical new form of community are simply, in Paul's view, living on the wrong side of the cross, in the old age.

When Paul says that he has been "crucified with Christ," he is not referring merely to some sort of private mystical experience. (The "I" throughout vv. 18-21 is a paradigmatic "I," rhetorically inviting readers of the letter to join with Paul in these confessional statements.) Union with Christ's death is the common experience of all who are "in Christ." This is articulated most clearly in Rom 6:3-6 (see also Rom 7:6; 2 Cor 4:10; Phil 3:10; Col 2:20; 3:3):

Do you not know that all of us who have been baptized into Christ Jesus were baptized into his death? Therefore we have been buried with him

---

122. See Krister Stendahl, "The Apostle Paul and the Introspective Conscience of the West," *HTR* 56 (1963) 199-215; reprinted in Stendahl, *Paul Among Jews and Gentiles*, 78-96.

123. Dunn, *The Epistle to the Galatians*, 143.

124. Martyn, *Galatians*, 257, comments: "It is not an exercise in mere fantasy to imagine that, as Paul's messenger finished reading v. 19, the Teachers jumped to their feet, loudly charging Paul with blasphemy."

by baptism into death, so that, just as Christ was raised from the dead by the glory of the Father, so we too might walk in newness of life. For if we have been united with him in a death like his, we will certainly be united with him in a resurrection like his. We know that our old self *was crucified with him* so that the body of sin might be destroyed, and we might no longer be enslaved to sin. (NRSV, italics added)

The cross is a transformative event that has changed the world and incorporated Paul— along with all who receive the gospel—into a new sphere of power. It is noteworthy that the verb "crucified with" (συνεσταύρωμαι *synestaurōmai*) is in the perfect tense, signifying a completed past action whose effects continue into the present; Paul's union with Christ's crucifixion is not merely a once-upon-a-time event but a reality that continues to determine his present existence.

That is why he goes on to say, "It is no longer I who live but Christ who lives in me."[125] Having died to his old identity, and to the Law that shaped that identity, Paul lives in the mysterious power of the risen Christ. This means that all his values and practices are reshaped in accordance with the identity of the crucified one. The character of that identity is sketched by the latter part of v. 20: "The life I now live in the flesh I live by faith—that is, by the faith of the Son of God who loved me and gave himself for me."[126] The hallmarks of this new identity are love and self-giving, rather than circumcision and Law observance. All of this has obvious implications for the debate over table fellowship with Gentiles.

The two participles in v. 20*b* that are translated "loved" (ἀγαπήσαντος *agapēsantos*) and "gave" (παραδόντος *paradontos*) are both aorist participles, pointing to the singular past event of the cross as the locus of Jesus' love and self-donation. In other words, the love of which Paul speaks here is not Jesus' warm feeling of affection toward humanity; rather, it is an *enacted* love, a love that was made manifest in action and in suffering. Precisely that

action gives content to the expression "the faith of the Son of God." Here, once again as in v. 16, we face the question of whether to translate *pistis*, followed by the genitive case, as "faith in" or "faith of." Here in v. 20, the balance of probability tips strongly toward the latter. Paul is not claiming that he lives now by "believing in" the Son of God; he has, in fact, just (rhetorically) denied any continuing personal agency at all. Instead, it is now the *pistis* of the Son of God, Jesus Christ's own self-giving faithfulness, that moves in and through him.[127] The life that he now lives "in the flesh" (i.e., in embodied historical existence) is both animated and determined by Jesus Christ's faithfulness. As J. Louis Martyn articulates it, "Christ's faith constitutes the space in which the one crucified with Christ can live and does live."[128] Here the function of *pistis* parallels the role of "grace" (χάρις *charis*) in Paul's story of salvation, as a comparison to Rom 5:15 shows:[129]

Rom 5:15	Gal 2:20
. . . the free gift in grace,	. . . I live in faith,
namely the grace of the one man Jesus Christ	namely the faith of the Son of God

It is, therefore, no coincidence that Paul's next sentence (v. 21) refers to the theme of grace: Grace is embodied in Christ's faithful death for our sake.

With 2:21, Paul summarizes what he has been saying in the whole of this compact but powerful speech in vv. 15-21: Righteousness/rectification comes *not* through the Law but through Christ's death on a cross. The implication of this is that those who continue to insist on Law observance as a necessary condition for Gentiles' full participation in the people of God are in effect declaring Christ's death null and void and returning to social and religious norms that defined the status quo *before* Christ's death. They may be accusing Paul of nullifying the grace of God by ignoring the

---

125. Paul often refers to being "in Christ"; for other references to the less common idea of Christ dwelling in the believer, see Rom 8:10; 2 Cor 13:5; Col 1:27; Eph 3:17.

126. In the expression "gave himself for me," Paul may be echoing the language of Isa 53:12. See also Gal 1:4; Rom 5:7-8; Mark 10:42-45; John 15:12-13.

127. Here we may well identify the grammatical construction as an "authorial genitive," pointing to Jesus Christ as the source or origin of the *pistis* that now animates Paul's life.

128. Martyn, *Galatians*, 259.

129. For an analysis of the syntactical parallelism of these texts, see R. B. Hays, *The Faith of Jesus Christ: An Investigation of the Narrative Substructure of Galatians 3:1-4:11*, SBLDS 56 (Chico, Calif.: Scholars Press, 1983) 168.

requirements of God's graciously given Law, but Paul turns the tables on this accusation. "I do not nullify the grace of God," he says. Unspoken but strongly implied is the counter-accusation: "It is *you* who nullify the grace of God by acting as though Christ's death was of no importance."

We may put Paul's point in the form of a question: If righteousness were available through the Law, why was it necessary for Jesus to die? Here we see how Paul's pattern of confessional logic begins with the kerygma and then works toward resolution of disputed points. The foundational truth is that Jesus Christ died "to set us free from the present evil age" (1:4). It follows that the Law was powerless to achieve that end. Thus rectification cannot be achieved through the Law. Verse 21 illustrates the truth of Sanders's dictum that Paul's thought moves "from solution to plight."[130] That is, Paul does not begin with an analysis of the human predicament under the Law and then offer the gospel as a solution; instead, he begins with the confession that Christ died for us and then works out the implications of that confession for diagnosing the human plight and determining the role of the Law.

Paul's formulation in v. 21 contains a deft wordplay that is difficult to translate. The word translated by the NRSV as "for nothing"

is δωρεάν (*dōrean*), an adverb formed from the accusative case of the noun δωρεά (*dōrea*), which means "gift," as in Rom 5:15. We can come close to capturing the ambiguity of Paul's sentence by translating, "If rectification comes through the Law, then Christ died *gratuitously.*" The Son of God did in fact "give himself" as a gift, but those who think rectification comes through Law have turned this gracious gift into a gratuitous superfluity.

That is the bottom line of Paul's charge against Peter at Antioch (and by implication against the rival Missionaries in Galatia). As Paul sees it, by caving in to the pressure of the emissaries from James, Peter has "set aside the grace of God." Their insistence on Law observance as the necessary hallmark of the identity of the people of God turns out to nullify the grace of God and render Christ's death meaningless. Paul proclaims that God has chosen to set things right in the world through the cross and through bringing into being a new people in which the old barrier between Jew and Gentile is broken down and made irrelevant. The cross cuts away all the systems of distinction by which we set ourselves apart from others, including the distinction between Jew and Gentile. Thus, when Peter refuses to eat with Gentiles, he is living as though the cross were of no effect. Those who have been crucifed with Christ will no longer separate themselves from one another but will gather around one table.

130. Sanders, *Paul and Palestinian Judaism,* 443.

REFLECTIONS

At the end of the day, was there to be one church or two "separate but equal" churches? That is the issue brought sharply into focus by Paul's confrontation with Peter at Antioch. Was there to be one table where Jews and Gentiles could eat together as brothers and sisters in Christ, or was it necessary to maintain two separate tables, symbolizing the separate cultural identity of the Jewish Christians? The issue was a difficult one, because the Jewish Christians who separated themselves from the common table believed that they were acting in obedience to the revealed Law of God. It was one thing to accept—as the "pillar" apostles had done at the conference in Jerusalem (2:1-10)—that Paul had a legitimate mission to preach the gospel to Gentiles; however, it was quite another thing for Jewish Christians to share table fellowship with the Gentiles who became believers. Would this not lead inevitably to compromising the distinctive identity of God's people? The actions of Peter—and the other Jewish Christians such as Barnabas who followed him in withdrawing from table fellowship with Gentiles—pointed toward the formation of two permanently separated churches, divided along ethnic lines. (And inevitably such a division implied the superiority and greater purity of the Jewish-Christian church.) This concrete social and political setting must always be kept in mind by the interpreter of Gal 2:11-21.

Preaching on this passage can be difficult because Paul's account of his passionate response to Peter (2:14-21) is compressed into an unusually dense discourse, prefiguring the major themes of the remainder of Galatians. The themes are weighty, and Paul sketches them so concisely that the congregation may struggle to grasp what he is saying. In order to keep the major issues in focus, the interpreter of Gal 2:11-21 will find it helpful to bear in mind four questions:

1. Who sets things right?
2. What role has Jesus played in setting things right?
3. What is the character of the new life that the death and resurrection of Jesus have inaugurated?
4. How is the truth of the gospel embodied in social practices?

The following reflections are keyed to these four central questions.

1. *Rectification as God's Doing.* Who sets things right? As the exegetical discussion above has emphasized, "rectification" refers to *God's* action of setting things right. God "rectifies" his people by coming to their rescue and instituting right order in a world gone wrong. The noun δικαιοσύνη (*dikaiosynē*), usually translated as "righteousness," is closely linked to the idea of God's covenant faithfulness: Those who are "rectified" are claimed by God's grace as belonging to the people of God; thus "righteousness" (the status of being rectified) is virtually equivalent to covenant membership. Paul's gospel shakes the world by disconnecting this status of belonging to the people of God from observance of the Law and attributing it instead solely to the gracious action of God, through the faithfulness of Jesus Christ. Thus rectification is God's doing from start to finish. Only God can set things right, and God has chosen to do that through the death of Jesus rather than through the Law. One of the world-transforming implications of this message is that the Law no longer defines or limits the boundaries of God's grace.

The full implications of this paradigm shift in understanding "righteousness" are difficult to grasp. Paul protests that most of his Jewish-Christian contemporaries failed to understand the logic of their own confession (2:15-16) about rectification through Christ and, therefore, inappropriately sought to police the boundaries of the covenant community. Once we understand that rectification is *God's* doing, not ours, important consequences follow. First of all, this truth sets us free from fear and anxiety. As Paul writes elsewhere, "It is God who justifies. Who is to condemn?" (Rom 8:33*b*-34*a* NRSV). Realizing that rectification cannot be a human attainment sets us free to rely fully on the boundless grace of God, disclosed in Christ's death for us. We can let go of our anxious need to make things come out right, our anxious need to ensure the "purity" of the church.

Another important consequence of this teaching is that "righteousness"—understood as "rectification"—is never a present possession, because God's final verdict lies in the future. God has not yet set all things right. That is why Paul speaks in Gal 5:5 of *awaiting* "the hope of righteousness." When we recognize that rectification is God's doing, we will find ourselves looking to the future for God to fulfill that hope, rather than supposing that we can forcibly set everything right in the present. Thus learning who sets things right is the great antidote to violence and intolerance.

2. *The Faithfulness of Jesus Christ.* What role has Jesus played in setting things right? Consistent with the message that rectification is God's doing, not ours, is Paul's proclamation that we are rectified only "through the faithfulness of Jesus Christ." We are not rectified by the strength or purity of our own believing. If Paul had meant that, then "faith" would be a new kind of "work," a human achievement by which we place ourselves into right relation with God. As was pointed out in the Commentary, when Paul says that "a person is rectified not through Law-observance but through the faithfulness of Jesus Christ," he is pointing to Jesus' act of loving self-giving on the cross. The shorthand expression "the faithfulness of Jesus Christ" refers to Jesus' death for our sake. The phrase interprets Jesus' death both as his act of radical trust in the God who gives life to the dead (cf. Rom 4:17) and, at the same time, as God's act of faithfulness toward a humanity that needed to be rescued from the grasp of sin and death. As Paul declares in Rom 5:8, "God proves his love for us in that while we still were sinners Christ died for us" (NRSV). That is why Paul can proclaim that "the righteousness of God" (i.e., God's faithful covenant love) is disclosed "through the faithfulness of Jesus Christ" (Rom 3:21-22).[131]

This interpretation does not deny that Paul saw Jesus as the object of faith; Gal 2:16 goes on to say explicitly that "we placed our trust in Christ Jesus." But the whole emphasis of Paul's message shifts, on this reading, from the subjective state of the believer to the proclamation of what God has done for us in the event of the cross. The difference is subtle but important. Those who preach on Galatians need to drive the point home forcefully: The gospel that Paul preaches is the story of Jesus Christ, "who gave himself to deliver us from the present evil age" (1:4); it is the story of "the faithfulness of the Son of God who loved me and gave himself for me" (2:20). This means that preaching on this text should invite us not to introspective assessment of our own believing but rather to grateful acknowledgment of what Jesus Christ has done for us.

What he has done for us is not merely to enable us to believe and thereby find individual forgiveness of sins. Instead, his faithful death has created a whole new world and liberated us from bondage to powers that once held us captive. Preaching that attends to this aspect of the message of Galatians will have a narrative character, and the narrative will not be just the story of our journey from unbelief to belief; rather, such preaching will recount the story of Jesus' death as the destruction of the old regime and the inauguration of the new creation. It is unintelligible to preach Gal 2:11-21 apart from the passion and resurrection narratives.

3. *Crucified with Christ/Christ Lives in Me.* What is the character of the new life that the death and resurrection of Jesus have inaugurated? Despite the previous observations, the gospel narrative will also address the individual hearer. In 2:19-21, Paul does speak of his own experience in this new creation. What he reports, however, is nothing less than the annihilation of his old identity through the cross. He has entered into union with Christ's death in such a way that he can make the remarkable statement, "It is no longer I who live, but Christ who lives in me." What are we to make of this decentering of the personality, this replacement of the ego by the presence of the living, risen Christ? Sam K. Williams wisely remarks, "Here (vv. 19-20), as so often elsewhere, Paul is at least as much poet as theologian as he searches for language and reaches for images appropriate to his experience of Christ."[132] Paul is describing the experience of having his former life-world terminated and entering a new sphere of reality where he is no longer in charge. This is not merely a matter of having his sins forgiven (indeed, Paul never mentions "forgiveness" in this letter); instead, it is a matter of being transformed for service. Paul finds himself—to his own great surprise—the instrument of Christ's reconciling love, the agent of Christ's mission to a world of Gentiles whom he previously regarded as unclean "dogs."

Over time, Christians have found in Paul's words an apt description of the mystery of being caught up into God's transformation of the world in such a way that the very core of the self is claimed and transmuted by the power of the living God. Paul is not speaking of some sort of momentary mystical "high"; rather, he is describing the ongoing experience of living "in the flesh" as the embodiment of "the faithfulness of the Son of God who loved me and gave himself for me." By the power of that faithfulness he

---

131. This passage shows conclusively the correctness of the translation "faithfulness of Jesus Christ." What sense would it make to claim that God's righteousness is disclosed through *our believing* in Jesus Christ?

132. Williams, *Galatians,* 81-82.

finds himself living a new high-risk existence, leaving behind the securities of Law and ethnic affiliation, proclaiming the message of God's love and embodying that message by sitting at one table with those whose way of life he once counted unclean. This involves concrete and costly political choices; it may mean initiating contacts with the poor in Third World countries or serving the homeless in our own cities. Christians who find themselves crossing cultural boundaries to do the work of God in ways that they never could have imagined will often find themselves explaining what has happened by echoing Paul's words: "It is no longer I who live, but it is Christ who lives in me."

4. *The Truth of the Gospel: One Table.* How is the gospel embodied in social practices? Paul insists that "the truth of the gospel" (2:14) is a social reality: The gospel must be embodied in the practices of a community that shares a common life. One can betray the truth of the gospel not only by preaching false doctrine but also by engaging in false practices—particularly practices that fracture the unity of the church. The foundation of Paul's opposition to Peter is his conviction that, through the death and resurrection of Jesus, God has brought into being a new community that embraces Jews and Gentiles together as God's people. This is not merely an implication of the gospel or an inference from the gospel; rather, it is an integral part of the gospel itself. Wherever we see Christians trying to rebuild walls of separation in the church, walls that separate people along ethnic or cultural lines, we can be sure that the integrity of the gospel is being violated, and, like Paul, we should feel compelled to speak out against such practices.

As noted in the Reflections on 1:1-10, systems of apartheid or racial segregation offer particularly clear contemporary analogies to the abuses that Paul opposed in Antioch and Galatia. But it may be far too easy to pronounce condemnations on apartheid-era South Africa, while ignoring equally insidious abuses closer to home. The Jewish Christians at Antioch were not passing legislation to restrict the activity of Gentiles; they were merely withdrawing into private, privileged enclaves for their meals and worship. When the problem is stated that way, we are forced to ask whether in fact many of our churches practice a de facto ethnic and cultural exclusivity, reflecting the ethnic and socioeconomic exclusivity of our residential neighborhoods. When that happens, our assemblies deny in fact, if not in principle, the truth of the gospel.

On the other hand, the history of the church provides numerous impressive testimonies of the power of the gospel to break down the wall of separation between different races and cultures. One of the most remarkable stories of this kind from recent history emerged from the bloody conflict in Rwanda, where in 1994 members of the Hutu tribe carried out mass murders of the Tutsi tribe. At the town of Ruhanga, fifteen kilometers outside Kigali, a group of 13,500 Christians had gathered for refuge. They were of various denominations: Anglicans, Roman Catholics, Pentecostals, Baptists, and others. According to the account of a witness to the scene, "When the militias came, they ordered the Hutus and Tutsis to separate themselves by tribe. The people refused and declared that they were all one in Christ, and for that they were all killed," gunned down en masse and dumped into mass graves.[133] It is a disturbing story, but it is also a compelling witness to the power of the gospel to overcome ethnic division. Paul would have regarded these Rwandan martyrs as faithful witnesses to the truth of the gospel. Having been "crucified with Christ," they preferred to die rather than to deny the grace of God that had made them one in Christ.

133. E. Thomas, "Can These Bones Live?" *SOMA (Sharing of Ministries Abroad) Newsletter* (October 15, 1996) 1-15.

GALATIANS 3:1–5:1

COUNTERARGUMENTS AGAINST THE RIVAL MISSIONARIES

OVERVIEW

Paul has amply defended the integrity of his own proclamation. He now turns abruptly to confront his readers, addressing the specific situation in Galatia that provoked him to write the letter. After rebuking the Galatians once again for their fickle susceptibility to the preaching of the rival Missionaries (3:1), he launches a series of arguments against their teachings. The Missionaries are urging the Gentile Galatians to accept circumcision and to observe at least some of the distinctive practices of the Jewish Law. They have pressed their agenda by appealing to scriptural texts that teach the importance of circumcision—particularly the story of Abraham, who was regarded in Jewish tradition as "the father of proselytes." Paul sets forth a string of counterarguments that constitute the central section of the letter (3:1–5:1).

The line of argument in these chapters is complex, dense, and sometimes difficult to follow. The following brief summary provides a preview and overview of the discussion.

Paul begins with an appeal to the Galatians' experience of the Spirit (3:1-5) and then turns to a complicated exegetical argument (3:6-29), seeking to show that Scripture defines "Abraham's offspring" in a way very different from what the Missionaries have claimed. In 4:1-11, Paul returns to the experiential argument, asserting that the experience of the Spirit confirms his interpretation of Scripture: The "fullness of time" has come, and the Galatians are God's children apart from any observance of the Torah. Their failure to recognize this is leading them to consider turning back the eschatological clock and returning to a state of slavery (4:8-11). The next section (4:12-20) is a brief interlude in which Paul reminds the Galatians of their past affection for him and urges them not to be swayed into infidelity by the blandishments of the Missionaries. Finally, Paul concludes his counterarguments by returning to the Abraham story and proposing a provocative interpretation of the figures of Hagar and Sarah as symbols for two different ecclesial communities characterized by slavery and freedom (4:21-31). The argument builds to a climax in 5:1 with Paul's urgent appeal to the Galatians: "Stand firm, therefore, and do not submit again to a yoke of slavery."

Underlying this battery of arguments is Paul's conviction that Christ's death and resurrection have inaugurated a new age in which the old laws and norms no longer apply. "Christ has set us free" (5:1), and that has changed everything, including the markers of covenant membership that formerly distinguished Jews from Gentiles. Those who are children of God in Christ Jesus now participate in a new creation, signified by baptism (3:27-28). In this new creation, circumcision is no longer relevant.

GALATIANS 3:1-5, THE EXPERIENCE OF THE SPIRIT

COMMENTARY

3:1. Paul's reference to his experience of Christ's transforming grace (2:20-21) leads him to remind the Galatians of their own initial experience of hearing the gospel. Paul is astonished (cf. 1:6) that they have been led astray by the Missionaries. Indeed, he finds this so remarkable that he attributes it metaphorically to witchcraft. The verb "bewitch" (βασκαίνω *baskainō*), which occurs only here in the NT, is often used to refer to spells cast by "the evil eye." By using this term Paul characterizes the preachers of the anti-gospel as malevolent sorcerors and the Galatians as their dupes or victims. The Galatians, who had seen Paul's vivid portrayal of Jesus Christ before their own eyes, now have their eyes glazed over as if by magic. Paul tries to break the spell by forcefully scolding them to snap them out of it: "O foolish Galatians!"

What does Paul mean when he says that "Jesus Christ was clearly portrayed as crucified" before the eyes of the Galatians? Certainly he is not referring to the actual event of Jesus' crucifixion, which the Galatians did not literally witness. Most commentators have concluded that Paul is speaking of his vivid narration of the passion story in his preaching; he told the story of Jesus' death so compellingly that it was as though the Galatians had seen it with their own eyes.[134] This interpretation could also be related to Paul's claim to "carry the marks of Jesus branded on my body" (6:17). Paul's scars, incurred in his mission, are signs of his suffering with Christ in a way that makes the crucifixion palpably present to all with eyes to see. (Cf. his reference in 2 Cor 4:10-11 to "carrying in the body the death of Jesus, so that the life of Jesus may also be made visible in our bodies," NRSV). In that case, Paul's own physical scars would serve as a powerful visual aid for his preaching of the cross.

One other possibility, however, deserves attention. The verb προγράφω (*prographō*, translated as "clearly portrayed" by the NIV

and as "publicly exhibited" by NRSV) is used elsewhere by Paul to mean "written beforehand" in Scripture (Rom 15:4). Is it possible that by selecting this verb Paul implies that his story of Christ crucified was told through interpretation of scriptural texts? If so, the reference would be not to the gospel passion narratives—which had not yet been written at this time—but to the lament psalms, interpreted as prefigurations of Christ's crucifixion.[135]

In any case, Paul's point is that the Galatians have had firsthand experience of Jesus Christ as the crucified one. The perfect participle "crucified" (ἐσταυρωμένος *estaurōmenos*) refers to a past action whose effects continue into the present. Paul portrayed Jesus as one whose identity was marked definitively and permanently by his death on a cross (cf. 1 Cor 2:1-2). Because the Galatians first heard the gospel in this way, Paul implies, they ought to have been immune to the message of the Missionaries, which plays down the world-changing character of Christ's death.

3:2. Following this reminder of his earlier cross-centered preaching, Paul brings the issue to a head. He poses a loaded rhetorical question that he regards as decisive for the whole dispute: "The only thing I want to learn from you is this: Did you receive the Spirit by observing the Torah [ἐξ ἔργων νόμου *ex ergōn nomou*] or from the message that elicits faith [ἐξ ἀκοῆς πίστεως *ex akoēs pisteōs*]?" (On the interpretation of the former Greek phrase, see the Commentary on 2:16; on the latter, see below.) In Paul's view, if the Galatians give a truthful answer to this question, the debate is over. They already have received the Spirit of God entirely apart from circumcision, apart from any observances of the Jewish Law.

This is Paul's first reference to the Spirit, which now will become a major theme of

---

134. Betz, *Galatians*, 131.

135. In Rom 15:4 the reference to things "written beforehand" points to Ps 69:9, quoted by Paul in the previous verse. On Paul's christological interpretation of the psalms, see R. B. Hays, "Christ Prays the Psalms," in *The Future of Christology: Essays in Honor of Leander E. Keck*, ed. A. J. Malherbe and W. A. Meeks (Minneapolis: Fortress, 1993) 122-36.

the letter, often in dichotomous opposition to "flesh" (4:29; 5:16-26; 6:8). As Paul will go on to argue (4:6-7), the Spirit is the single sufficient sign that the Galatians already have been adopted into God's family; therefore, the Missionaries' demand for circumcision is superfluous.

The logic of Paul's argument here closely parallels the story of the conversion of Cornelius and his household in Acts 10–11: Gentiles hear the gospel preached, and the Spirit falls upon them. The only appropriate response to this act of God is articulated in Peter's question, "Can anyone withhold the water for baptizing these people who have received the Holy Spirit just as we have?" (Acts 10:47). Through baptism, those who have received the Spirit are received into the community of God's people. Both in Acts and in Gal 3:2, it is presupposed that receiving the Spirit is a palpable experience, a datum so vivid as to be undeniable. Paul does not seek to convince the Galatians that they really have received the Spirit; the argument works the other way around. He argues from the indisputable empirical fact that they have received the Spirit in order to convince them that no further validating action is required to ensure their status as God's children.

We have already seen in the discussion of 2:16 that *ex ergōn nomou* refers to the practice of keeping the commandments of Torah, particularly those commandments that were seen as "litmus-test" indicators of Jewish ethnic identity: circumcision, food laws, and sabbath observance. Paul has argued emphatically that no one is rectified (set in right relation to God) by such practices. Now he asks rhetorically whether the Galatians received the Spirit through such actions (knowing perfectly well that they did not).[136]

What, then, is the positive alternative? In Paul's forced-choice multiple-choice quiz, the right answer is that the Galatians received the Spirit *ex akoēs pisteōs*. What does this phrase mean? The NIV and the NRSV agree in translating the phrase as "by believing what you heard." This is, however, only one possible interpretation of an ambiguous expression. Indeed, it is an improbable interpretation because it takes the genitive noun *akoēs* as the object of the verbal noun *pisteōs*. Since the cognate verb *pisteuō* takes objects in the dative or accusative case, this is not a likely reading of the text. It is more likely that *akoēs*, not *pisteōs*, is the object of the preposition *ex*. The resulting translation possibilities are summarized in Fig. 1:

The noun ἀκοή (*akoē*) can sometimes mean "hearing," but Paul's use of it in a similar context in Rom 10:16-17 suggests that he understands it to mean "what is heard"—in other words, the proclaimed message. Thus Martyn translates the phrase as "the proclamation that has the power to elicit faith" (i.e., option c).[137] On the other hand, Dunn argues that "the phrase is more obviously to be taken as describing an action of the Galatians (in antithesis to 'works of the law'): the hearing which stimulated and expressed itself in the faith by which . . . they received the Spirit" (i.e., option a).[138] Here the interpreter of the letter is faced with a crucial fork in the road. Does Paul attribute the receiving of

136. The question, which links the Galatian situation directly to the Antioch controversy through the catchphrase "by observing the Law," also suggests that there is a close link between being justified/rectified (2:16) and receiving the Spirit (3:2).
137. Martyn, *Galatians*, 281, 286-89.
138. Dunn, *The Epistle to the Galatians*, 154.

Figure 1: The Meaning of ἐξ ἀκοῆς πίστεως (*ex akoēs pisteōs*)*

If *akoē* means "hearing":
    (a) *pistis* = "believing": "by hearing with faith"
    (b) *pistis* = "the faith": "by hearing the faith" (i.e., "by hearing the gospel").
If *akoē* means "message":
    (c) *pistis* = "believing": "from the message that elicits faith"
    (d) *pistis* – "the faith": "from the message of the faith" (i.e., "from the gospel message").

*For discussion of these options, see R. B. Hayes, *The Faith of Jesus Christ*, SBLDS 56 (Chico, Calif.: Scholars Press, 1983) 143-49.

the Spirit to a human action ("hearing with faith") or to divine initiative ("the message that elicits faith")? Paul's consistent emphasis elsewhere on the gospel as a word of divine power that transforms human beings (e.g., 1 Thess 2:13) strongly suggests the latter interpretation. This is confirmed by Paul's reprise of the question in v. 5, where he speaks of God as the one who supplies the Spirit and works miracles *ex akoēs pisteōs*.

3:3. Paul's next question implies that the Missionaries are telling the Galatians that they must undergo circumcision in order to be "completed." This idea may well have derived from their interpretation of the story of Abraham. Later rabbinic teaching in the Mishnah links circumcision explicitly to perfection in the light of Genesis 17: "Great is circumcision, for in spite of all the virtues that Abraham our father fulfilled, he was not called perfect, until he was circumcised, as it is said, 'Walk before me, and be thou perfect'" (Gen 17:1).[139] Paul, however, scoffs at the idea that, having begun with the Spirit (through the proclaimed message), the Galatians would now seek to be perfected "in the flesh" (i.e., by cutting off their foreskins). (The NIV's paraphrase, "by human effort," catches one implication of Paul's question but loses the ironic double entendre of his reference to "the flesh.") The very idea, he insists, is "foolish."

3:4. Paul asks another question that contains an ambiguity, reflected in the differing translations of the NIV ("Have you *suffered* so much for nothing?") and the NRSV ("Did you *experience* so much for nothing?"). The verb πάσχω (*paschō*) is capable of carrying either meaning. Because the immediate context speaks only of apparently positive experiences of the Spirit and miracles, most modern commentators have settled on the latter interpretation, reflected in the NRSV. On the other hand, the letter does contain a number of references to persecution and suffering as the lot of those who are in Christ (4:29; 5:11; 6:12, 17), and Paul elsewhere links the joyful experience of the Spirit directly with the experience of suffering (e.g., Rom 8:14-30; 1 Thess 1:6). It is possible, therefore, that he is alluding to some experience of the Galatians, unknown to us, in which they suffered for

the gospel (cf. Rom 8:35-36; 1 Thess 2:14). Most patristic interpreters understood the passage as a reference to the Galatians' suffering.[140] Either way, Paul's point is that the Galatians' own experience will have been "in vain" if they now discount their own earlier reception of the Spirit by accepting the requirement of circumcision (cf. 4:11; 1 Cor 15:2). Paul qualifies his own question by adding "if it really was for nothing"; this clause has the rhetorical effect of holding open the possibility that the Galatians will, after all, heed Paul's appeal and reject the influence of the rival Missionaries.

3:5. The question in this verse repeats the initial question of v. 2, this time adding a reminder of the powerful manifestations of God's Spirit that the Galatians had witnessed in their midst. Indeed, Paul's wording suggests that they continue to experience these signs of the Spirit (note the present tense of the participles "supplies" and "works" in describing God's action). English translations unavoidably expand and paraphrase the highly elliptical Greek sentence, which reads literally, "Therefore, the one who supplies the Spirit to you and works miracles in your midst—from works of Law or from the message of faith?" Once again, Paul's emphasis lies on *God's* agency and initiative: It is God who gives the Spirit freely. The idea that God's action must be somehow prompted by Torah observance is presented as self-evidently ridiculous, since the Galatians had already experienced these evidences of God's working long before the rival Missionaries arrived on the scene with their gospel of circumcision.

The reference to "miracles" (δυνάμεις *dynameis*; more lit., "works of power") reminds us that Paul lived and moved in a symbolic world like the one that we see in the Gospels and the Acts of the Apostles, a world in which God was powerfully at work to perform healings and signs. For example, in reasserting his authority over the Corinthian church, Paul declares that when he was present with them, "The signs of a true apostle were performed among you with

---

139. See *m. Ned.* 3:11.

140. For citations from the commentaries of Marius Victorinus (BT 1972:31 [1167D-1168A]) and Ambrosiaster (CSEL 81.3:32), see M. J. Edwards, ed., *Galatians, Ephesians, Philippians,* Ancient Christian Commentary on Scripture, vol. 8 (Downers Grove, Ill.: InterVarsity, 1999) 37.

utmost patience, signs and wonders and mighty works [δυνάμεσιν *dynamesin*]" (2 Cor 12:12 NRSV). In the Corinthian correspondence, Paul seeks to counterbalance the Corinthians' excessive enthusiasm for such manifestations of power. Here in Galatians, however, Paul gives these manifestations full weight as evidence of the working of God's Spirit, prior to and apart from the practices of Torah observance.

The force, then, of Gal 3:1-5 is to call the Galatians to reflect back on their own initial experience of coming to faith and on their continuing experience of living in the power of the Spirit. Such experiences, Paul contends, should prove beyond all question that they need no fleshly marker to certify the authenticity of their conversion.

REFLECTIONS

1. Galatians 3:1-5 highlights the experience of the Holy Spirit as the sign and proof of the new life in Christ. As we shall see in the rest of chapter 3, Paul is concerned to show that this experience is confirmed by the testimony of Scripture. Nonetheless, the rhetoric of 3:1-5 suggests that the experience ought to be independently self-validating. The formerly pagan Galatians have been caught up by the power of the proclaimed gospel into a new life in which they continually experience the outpouring of God's Spirit and see the Spirit's mighty works in their community (3:5). In the face of this experience, the arguments for requiring circumcision simply lose their force.

Paul's line of argument here should be startling to Christians who insist on going strictly "by the book" of traditional teaching—as startling as it was to conscientious Jewish Christians of Paul's day. Where the Spirit breaks in and brings new life, we should acknowledge it gratefully as God's doing and not worry too much about whether all the proper rules and ecclesiastical proprieties are being observed. The preacher who follows the message of this passage will call the congregation to remember and reclaim their identity as God's people solely on the basis of their living experience of God's grace and power; no one should "bewitch" them into thinking of themselves as second-class Christians or as spiritually deficient because they have not undergone some discipline or ritual (all elitist "second blessing" theologies must stumble over this passage) or because they have not obtained the approval of some ecclesiastical bureaucracy.

2. The difficulty, however, is that this argument presupposes that the experience of the Holy Spirit is a concrete and powerful life-transforming experience that leaves no room for doubt. Paul assumes that such an experience of the Spirit characterized the members of his churches (cf. 1 Cor 12:1-13). The Acts of the Apostles, using the same language Paul employs in Gal 3:2, offers several narratives of individuals who "receive the Spirit." In virtually every case, there are clear signs of transformation: They speak in tongues and prophesy, they offer up enthusiastic praise to God, or they find themselves caught up into a new life of sharing and service (e.g., Acts 2:38; 8:17; 10:44-48). For many Christians today, the same claim could be made; for them, Gal 3:1-5 is a powerful reminder that their life depends on the Spirit and not on any "fleshly" standards. But what of churches in which most members would not claim such direct experience of the Spirit in their lives? The unavoidable conclusion is that for such communities Paul's argument from experience will fall on deaf ears. Unless they have a living experience of the power of the Spirit, they are likely to be acutely susceptible to various non-gospels that seek to define their identity on the basis of race or nation or gender or economic class or some other marker of social status. For such communities, the text of Gal 3:1-5 can only stand as a tantalizing glimpse of a living spiritual experience to which the gospel beckons them.

3. Once again in this passage, as in 2:16-21, Paul places strong emphasis on the priority of God's gracious action. The gospel message (ἀκοὴ πίστεως *akoē pisteōs*) is the instrument through which God supplies the Spirit and does mighty works. "Observing the Law" as a human action is set in opposition to "the message that elicits faith" (3:2, 5). The latter, which is God's doing, not ours, is alone responsible for the outpouring of the Spirit. The preacher who deals with this text will have to take great care to correct or qualify English translations, such as the NIV and the NRSV, that interpret *akoē pisteōs* as an action of the Galatians, something that *they* did instead of doing "works of the Law" in order to receive the Spirit. This interpretation, as argued in the Commentary, misreads the passage and, in fact, repeats the error of the rival Missionaries by failing to acknowledge the priority and sufficiency of God's action.

GALATIANS 3:6-29, THE PROMISE TO ABRAHAM

OVERVIEW

Although the argument from experience (3:1-5) might seem decisive on its own terms, Paul moves next into a much lengthier engagement with the interpretation of Scripture (3:6-29). His aim is to show (1) that the Galatians' spiritual experience is consonant with Scripture, rather than contradictory, and (2) that the rival Missionaries' interpretation of Scripture is incorrect—or, more precisely, inapplicable to the new eschatological situation created by Jesus' crucifixion. The unit is bracketed by references to God's promise to Abraham (vv. 6-9, 29). The overall purpose of this complex argument is to demonstrate—against the urging of the Missionaries, who

teach that Gentiles must be circumcised in order to be children of Abraham—that God's original blessing of Abraham included Gentile believers (vv. 6-9) and that the Galatians, who are "in Christ" via their baptism, are already Abraham's rightful heirs (vv. 26-29). Since the Missionaries were extolling the glories of the Law, the question inevitably arises, Where does the Law fit into Paul's narration of the Gospel? Therefore, in order to make his case, Paul must develop an account of the relation between Law and faith (vv. 10-14), between Law and promise (vv. 15-18), and the role of the Law within God's design to bring rectification only through Christ (vv. 19-25).

Galatians 3:6-9, The Blessing of Abraham Included the Gentiles

COMMENTARY

3:6-7. The NRSV of these verses stays closer to the Greek syntax than does the NIV. The conjunction "just as" (καθώς *kathōs*) creates a link between the Galatians' experience of the Spirit and the retelling of the Abraham story that Paul will now undertake.[141] He wants them to see their experience prefigured

in the story of Abraham; in both cases the blessing of God comes as sheer grace.

Paul begins his treatment of Abraham with a quotation of Gen 15:6, a thematic keynote for all that will follow (cf. Rom 4:3, where Paul introduces an even lengthier exposition of the significance of Abraham with the same quotation). The passage is crucial for Paul, not only because it links the verb "believed" and the noun "righteousness" but also because it

---

141. Martyn, *Galatians*, 294, translates, "Things were the same with Abraham."

focuses attention on a point in the story of Abraham *prior to his circumcision* where he is said to be accounted[142] righteous—i.e., in right covenant relationship with God (cf. Rom 4:9-12).

For that reason, Gen 15:6 provides Paul with crucial hermeneutical leverage against the Missionaries, who have almost certainly drawn the attention of the Galatians to Genesis 17, in which Abraham receives and obeys the commandment to circumcise himself and all the males of his household. By zeroing in instead on Gen 15:6, Paul, in effect, says, "No, the story of Abraham is not fundamentally about circumcision and obeying the Law; it is about trusting God's promise."

In v. 7, Paul offers a striking commentary on the passage he has just quoted. Genesis 15:6, of course, says nothing about Abraham's children or how their identity is to be determined (but see Gen 15:5). The inference lies readily at hand, therefore, that Paul is countering something the Missionaries have told the Galatians: that only those who are circumcised can be Abraham's true children. That is why Paul's rejoinder places particular emphasis on the demonstrative pronoun "these" (οὗτοι *houtoi*), which is unfortunately left untranslated by most English versions. It is as though Paul is saying, "No, it is not the circumcised who are Abraham's children; rather, those whose identity is derived from faith, *these* are Abraham's children."

These comments have followed Martyn's translation of οἱ ἐκ πίστεως (*hoi ek pisteōs*) as "those whose identity is derived from faith."[143] This is a helpful paraphrase of Paul's compact expression "the ones from faith." It is not entirely satisfactory to translate this odd expression as "those who believe" (NIV, NRSV). Paul has probably formulated the term in conscious opposition to "the ones from circumcision" (οἱ ἐκ περιτομῆς *hoi ek peritomēs*), his description of the emissaries from James who precipitated the Antioch incident (2:12). In both cases, the preposition *ek* serves to suggest that the object of the preposition ("faith" or "circumcision") is the source of being—or key identity marker—for

the people in question. They are "faith people"[144] or "circumcision people."

3:8-9. Paul is not content, however, merely to argue for an analogy between Abraham's faith and the faith of those who now have placed their trust in Christ; instead, he goes on to quote another text from Genesis (actually a conflation of Gen 12:3 with Gen 18:18/22:18) that portrays Abraham as the conduit of blessing for the Gentile world: "All the Gentiles [ἔθνη *ethnē*] will be blessed in you." Remarkably, Paul treats this statement as something that Scripture *said to* Abraham. Scripture (ἡ γραφή *hē graphē*), personified here as a speaking character in Paul's retelling of the story, is said to have spoken prophetically, actually "foreseeing" long ago that God "is [now] justifying the Gentiles on the basis of faith" and therefore pre-preaching the gospel (προευηγγελίσατο *proeuēngelisato*) to Abraham! Strikingly, the "gospel" that Scripture announced beforehand is focused on the promise that Gentiles will be blessed in Abraham. Paul says nothing yet about Jesus; instead, the meaning of "gospel" is articulated in terms of a blessing to Gentiles in or through Abraham. The blessing pronounced on Abraham filters down, or out, to the whole world.

The implication of all this is explained clearly in another exegetical comment by Paul in v. 9: "So, faith people [*hoi ek pisteōs*] are blessed with the faithful [πιστῷ *pistō*] Abraham." It is noteworthy that Paul describes Abraham with the simple adjective "faithful." Many English translations paraphrase to make the sentence conform more closely to preconceived notions about Pauline theology, as in the NRSV: "Abraham who believed." Dunn rightly sees that Paul "saw no danger in speaking of Abraham's faithfulness," but this accurate assessment undercuts his earlier claim that Paul is seeking to "drive a wedge between the two senses of πίστις (*pistis*; faith, faithfulness)."[145] In fact, the Greek language will not permit such a wedge to be driven. The single noun *pistis* includes in its semantic range the meanings "trust," "faithfulness," "fidelity," "faith." Therefore, Paul can read the scriptural statement "Abraham believed [ἐπίστευσεν *episteusen*] God" and

---

142. The NIV's "credited" is a good translation of ἐλογίσθη (*elogisthē*), a verb whose semantic field is primarily that of commerce and finance.
143. Martyn, *Galatians*, 299.

144. Williams, *Galatians*, 86-87.
145. Dunn, *The Epistle to the Galatians*, 163, 167.

conclude that Abraham is rightly to be called faithful (πιστός *pistos*). The root idea in both expressions is that Abraham placed his trust in God; that, for Paul, is the meaning of faithfulness. Thus Paul's summary remark in v. 9 links together the conclusions he has drawn

from his citations of Genesis: The blessing of Abraham is ultimately intended for the whole world (not just for Jews), and Abraham's true children are those whose identity is rooted in trusting God's promise. (See Reflections at 3:26-29.)

Galatians 3:10-14, Christ's Death Liberates Israel from the Law's Curse

COMMENTARY

Although Paul's line of argument in vv. 6-9 is clear, the next section (vv. 10-14) is one of the most difficult passages anywhere in his letters. Paul seems to be reading the OT texts he cites in strange ways. He makes the astonishing claim that Scripture itself pronounces a curse on "those who rely on the Law" (v. 10). He also seems to set Scripture against Scripture (vv. 11-12). Furthermore, he quotes Deuteronomy in support of the startling assertion that the crucified Christ became a curse (v. 13). What is going on in this confusing paragraph?

Some interpreters think that Paul is asserting the unfulfillability of the Law; those who try to keep the Law are under a curse because they are bound to fall short of perfect obedience and, therefore, incur God's wrath. This is such a ridiculous caricature of Judaism, however, that it could hardly have been taken seriously as a persuasive argument in Paul's time. If Paul had made such claims, the rival Missionaries could easily have refuted him by pointing out that the Law makes ample provision for forgiveness of transgressions through repentance, through the sacrificial system, and through the solemn annual celebration of the Day of Atonement. In fact, however, Paul does *not* say that it is impossible to obey the Law, although this supposition has been read into the text by many generations of Christian interpreters. Paul, reflecting on his own former life as a Pharisee, can say that he was, "as to righteousness under the Law, blameless" (Phil 3:6 NRSV). This certainly does not mean that he never sinned; it simply indicates that his transgressions were dealt with according to the Law's provisions and that he, therefore, was in no way wracked by a guilty

introspective conscience.[146] If Paul did not regard the Law as unfulfillable, then, how are we to understand the logic of his exposition?

It is important to bear in mind that Paul's argument drives toward the confessional affirmation of vv. 13-14: Christ's redemptive work removed the curse from Israel so that the blessing of Abraham (v. 8) can come to Gentiles and so that "we" (= all God's people, Jews and Gentiles together) can receive the promise of the Spirit. The reference to the blessing of Abraham in v. 14 links vv. 10-14 firmly to vv. 6-9; Paul is still answering the question of how Gentiles can now receive the blessing first promised to Abraham. With this in mind, we must read vv. 10-14 carefully to see how they fit into Paul's argument.

3:10. Paul coins a compressed expression, "those who are from works of Law" (ὅσοι ἐξ ἔργων νόμου *hosoi ex ergōn nomou*), which stands in antithetical contrast to οἱ ἐκ πίστεως (*hoi ek pisteōs*; v. 7). If, as we have seen, that expression means "those whose identity is derived from faith," then the phrase in this verse must mean "those whose identity is derived from works of Law." (The paraphrases of the NIV and the NRSV offer a similar interpretation.) This description of the Torah-observant faction is already, from Paul's point of view, a decisive indictment, since he insists that those who are in Christ derive their identity from Christ and Christ alone (2:20; 3:26-28). By framing the discussion in these terms, Paul already implies that "faith" and "works of Law" are opposite and incompatible sources of identity.

146. Stendahl, "The Apostle Paul and the Introspective Conscience of the West," 78-96.

These people whose identity is derived from keeping the commandments of Torah are, Paul now claims, "under a curse." The polarity between curse and blessing has already been subliminally suggested by Paul's citation of Gen 12:3 in v. 8: "I will bless those who bless you, and the one who curses you I will curse; and in you all the families of the earth shall be blessed." In v. 8, Paul quoted only the last part of the verse, but now he picks up the latent "curse" theme and turns the claim of his adversaries upside down. They were contending that the blessing of Abraham is for those who are circumcised, but Paul now provocatively assigns the blessing to uncircumcised Gentiles and the curse to the circumcised advocates of Torah observance.

He supports this scandalous claim by quoting Deut 27:26, though his wording differs slightly from both the MT and the LXX.

Deut 27:26 MT: Cursed be anyone
  who does not uphold
  the words of this law
  by observing them. (NRSV)

Deut 27:26 LXX: Cursed is anyone
  who does not remain in
  all the words of this law,
  to do them.

Gal 3:10: Cursed is anyone
  who does not remain in
  all the things that are written in the book of
    the Law,
  to do them.

Paul's citation follows the LXX closely, except that he has replaced the phrase "all the words of *this law*" (i.e., the specific covenant law of Deuteronomy 26–28) with a phrase imported from Deut 28:58 or 30:10: "all the things *that are written in the book of the Law*." The change in wording has the effect of expanding the reference to the canonical Law of Moses as a whole.

Many readers have found Paul's appeal to this text surprising, because it seems to say exactly the opposite of what Paul claims. In Deuteronomy the curse is pronounced on those who do *not* do what the Law requires, but v. 10*a* seems to say—so many interpreters

have thought—that those who conscientiously *do* what the Law requires are cursed.

To understand Paul's point, we must recognize two things. First, those who are said to be under a curse are not "those who do the Law," but rather "those whose identity is derived from works of Law." It is those who still live within the sphere of the deuteronomic covenant who are said to be subject to the curse, living under the jurisdiction of the threatening words of Deuteronomy 27.[147] Thus Paul is simply informing the Galatians of a point repeatedly emphasized in Deuteronomy: Those who enter the covenant are subject to its sanctions and curses. Paul's citation of Deut 27:26 reminds the reader of the whole structure of Israel's covenant obligations, including the solemn curses and blessings that attend the covenant in Deuteronomy 27–28.[148] Thus to be "under a curse" (v. 10) is to live under Deuteronomy's dispensation of *conditional* curses and blessings, to be subject to strict judgment contingent upon obedience.

Second, these curses apply to Israel as a whole, not merely to individual Jews living under the Law. The book of Deuteronomy is emphatic in its warning that the punishment for disobedience will be inflicted upon the nation as a whole and that the whole people will be carried away into exile before God finally intervenes to rescue and restore them. In Deut 31:29, Moses explicitly predicts that after his death the people will turn aside from God's commandments and that God's anger will fall upon them. This prediction is then given a hymnic elaboration in the Song of Moses (Deuteronomy 32), a passage of great importance for Paul's interpretation of Scripture.[149] Thus, when Paul warns the Galatians that those whose identity is grounded in the Law are under a curse, he is in effect saying to them, "If you affiliate yourself with those who place their hope in obeying the Law (i.e., the Missionaries), you are joining a losing team"—not because obedience is theoretically impossible, but because Israel historically has failed and has in fact incurred

---

147. C. D. Stanley, "'Under a Curse': A Fresh Reading of Galatians 3:1.10-14," *NTS* 36 (1990) 481-511.

148. For this point and for much of what follows, see N. T. Wright, *The Climax of the Covenant: Christ and the Law in Pauline Theology* (Edinburgh: T. & T. Clark, 1991) 137-56.

149. See R. H. Bell, *Provoked to Jealousy: The Origin and Purpose of the Jealousy Motif in Romans 9–11*, WUNT (Tübingen: Mohr, 1994).

the judgment of which Deuteronomy solemnly warns. That is, Israel was sent away into exile, and, despite the return from exile, has never recovered the blessings promised in Deut 28:1-14.

3:11-12. In these verses, the logic of the argument becomes clearer if we make a minor change in punctuation of the Greek text (the oldest Greek MSS have no punctuation), yielding the translation, "Now because no one is rectified by the Law, it is clear that 'The righteous one will live by faith.'" The first clause provides the warrant for the second, not (as in the NRSV and the NIV) the other way around.[150] Paul takes it as a given—as he had done earlier in 2:16—that the Law does not have the power to set people in right relation to God. From that fact—confirmed by Israel's historical experience of disobedience and exile—Paul concludes that there must be some other way to be rectified. Therefore, he finds another scriptural text that bears witness to the way in which "the righteous" will at last encounter God's rectifying power.

The text to which Paul points is Hab 2:4, the same text that he later employs as the keynote of his Letter to the Romans (Rom 1:17). This passage is the source of the catch-phrase *ek pisteōs* ("from/by faith"), which Paul has already used in 2:16 and 3:7-9, and which he will use again in 3:12, 22, 24 and 5:5 (see also Rom 1:17; 3:26, 30; 4:16; 5:1; 9:30, 32; 10:6; 14:23). This unusual turn of phrase appears nowhere else in the OT, and Paul uses it only in Galatians and Romans—the two letters where he quotes Hab 2:4.[151] Thus the phrase *ek pisteōs* becomes in these two letters a slogan alluding to Hab 2:4 as the revelatory hermeneutical lens through which Scripture must be read.

Habakkuk 2:2-4 is God's answer to the prophet's anguished complaint that God has allowed injustice to prevail in the world by allowing foreign rulers to oppress Israel. This passage was seen by many ancient Jewish interpreters, including the Qumran community, as an important eschatological prophecy;[152] the LXX translators read the passage as a messianic text, as did the author of the Letter to the Hebrews (Heb 10:37-38). The title "The Righteous One" (ὁ δίκαιος *ho dikaios*) appears elsewhere in the NT as an honorific title for Jesus (Acts 3:14; 7:52; 22:14; 1 Pet 3:18; 1 John 2:1) and elsewhere in Jewish sources (e.g., *1 Enoch* 38:2; 58:6) as a title for the long-awaited eschatological deliverer.[153] It is probable, therefore, that Paul is playing subtly on this background of messianic expectation. At this stage of the argument, however, Paul does not explicitly refer to Jesus; his argument can be understood non-messianically, as an assertion that Hab 2:4 provides the key to understanding how God has chosen to bring about rectification and life: through faith, not through the Law. The link created in v. 11 between the verbs "to be rectified" and "to live," which he seems to use synonymously, reflects Paul's conviction that true "life," eschatological life, is accessible only for those who are restored by faith (*ek pisteōs*) to right covenant relationship with God.

But what then of those portions of the Law of Moses that do not speak of faith and seem to make life and blessing contingent upon doing what the Law requires? Paul cannot avoid this problem, because the Missionaries who held up Abraham to the Galatians as a model for undergoing circumcision no doubt also pointed out passages such as Lev 18:5, which promises that "the one who does these things [ὁ ποιήσας αὐτά *ho poiēsas auta*; exactly the same language found in Deut 27:26] will live by them." Paul faces the issue head-on. He cites Lev 18:5 in stark juxtaposition to Hab 2:4 and declares that "the Law is not *ek pisteōs*." The conclusion is compelling that Paul portrays Lev 18:5 as an empty promise, a part of the ineffectual scheme of salvation centered on works of Torah, a scheme now rendered inoperative by the death of Jesus.[154] To live within the Law's sphere of power is

---

150. Wright, *The Climax of the Covenant,* 149n. 42, crediting his student Christopher Palmer. For further defense of this reading, see A. Wakefield, "The Hermeneutical Significance of Paul's Use of Citations in Galatians 3:6-14" (Ph.D. diss., Duke University, 2000).

151. D. A. Campbell, "Romans 1:17—A Crux Interpretum for the *Pistis Christou* Debate," *JBL* 113 (1994) 265-85.

152. A. Strobel, *Untersuchungen zum eschatologischen Verzögerungsproblem auf Grund der spätjudisch-urchristlichen Geschichte von* Habakkuk 2:1,2 ff., NovTSup 2 (Leiden: Brill, 1961).

153. For discussion of this motif, see R. B. Hays, "'The Righteous One' as Eschatological Deliverer: A Case Study in Paul's Apocalyptic Hermeneutics," in *Apocalyptic and the New Testament: Essays in Honor of J. Louis Martyn,* ed. J. Marcus and M. L. Soards, JSNTSup 24 (Sheffield: JSOT, 1989) 191-215.

154. In Rom 10:6, Paul interprets Lev 18:5 in a different and far more positive way. See Hays, *Echoes of Scripture in the Letters of Paul,* 73-83; Wright, *The Climax of the Covenant,* 149.

to live in the world narrated by Leviticus and Deuteronomy, a world in which the Law promises life but cannot deliver it, a world in which a curse hangs over Israel (see also Lev 18:24-30, which threatens that "the land will vomit you out" if the Law is violated). In that world, no one can be justified before God (v. 11), because Israel has tragically gone the way that Deuteronomy prophesied, into infidelity and bondage (see, e.g., Deut 28:45-51). But, according to Paul's proclamation, that world no longer exists.

3:13-14. The curse pronounced by the Law has been broken by Christ's death. Paul's verb "redeemed" (ἐξηγόρασεν *exēgorasen*) is the word used to describe the emancipation of a slave. This language introduces a metaphor to which Paul will return repeatedly: Life under the Law is a form of slavery (4:1-11, 21–5:1). The result of Jesus' crucifixion, however, is to set the enslaved people of Israel free at last from the curse pronounced by Deuteronomy. Given the ugly history of Christian attitudes toward Judaism, it is important to recognize that the expression "the curse of the Law" does not mean that the Torah is a curse; rather, it refers specifically to the curse *pronounced by* the Law, as Paul has just quoted it in v. 10. It is this curse that Jesus has now nullified by his self-sacrificial death.

Paul says that "Christ redeemed us from the curse of the Law *by becoming a curse* for us." Paul's language here is deliberately paradoxical and provocative. Jesus entered so fully into Israel's enslaved condition that he absorbed and exhausted the curse fully in his own innocent death. The thought is exactly paralleled in a similarly pregnant confessional statement in 2 Cor 5:21: "For our sake [God] made him to be sin who knew no sin, so that in him we might become the righteousness of God" (NRSV). In Jesus' death a mysterious pattern of exchange was enacted, so that for our sake he took upon himself all the consequences of the world's sin. Such an awesome mystery can only be proclaimed, not explained. This mystery stands at the heart of Paul's gospel: The Son of God died an ignominious death for our sake. Jesus' death on a cross not only defines the meaning of love but also transforms everything, ending the old world under the Law and opening up a new world of grace, freedom, and blessing. That is why Paul regards a return to life under the Law as an absurd denial of God's grace.

The shocking claim that Jesus became a curse is supported by another quotation from Deuteronomy: "cursed [ἐπικατάρατος *epikataratos*] is everyone who is hung on a tree" (Deut 21:23). Paul has slightly modified the LXX, which reads, "cursed [κεκατηραμένος *kekatēramenos*] *by God* is everyone who is hung on a tree." Paul omits "by God," leaving the source of the curse unspecified, and uses the same word for "cursed" that appears in Deut 27:26, ensuring that the reader will link the passages together; the curse that Jesus took upon himself is precisely the curse already mentioned in v. 10. In its original context, Deut 21:23 provides the rationale for the deuteronomic law prohibiting Israel from leaving the dead body of a hanged criminal dangling on a tree overnight, for the dead body would "defile the land." By provocatively applying this saying to the crucified Jesus, Paul has given the text a twist, rereading it in the light of the story of Jesus' crucifixion (cf. v. 1). As Dunn notes, by Paul's time the passage had also been read by some other Jewish interpreters as a reference to the Roman punishment of crucifixion.[155]

It has sometimes been suggested that in Paul's earlier days as a persecutor of the church (1:13, 23) he would have brandished this very verse, Deut 21:23, against his Christian opponents to prove that the crucified Jesus had died under God's curse and, therefore, could not possibly have been the Messiah. If so, then when he experienced his transforming call to apostleship and became convinced that God had vindicated Jesus by raising him from the dead, he would have recognized that the Law that cursed Jesus must have been utterly wrong. This in turn would explain how Paul came to hold the view that the Law was abrogated by Christ's death. All this is, however, highly speculative, for Paul never hints at any such process in the development of his thought. It is far likelier that v. 13 reflects an early Jewish-Christian confessional tradition that explained the saving effects of Jesus' death by interpreting the crucifixion as Jesus' vicarious sacrifice, in which

---

155. 4QpNah 1:7-8; 11QTemple 64:6-13. See also Dunn, *The Epistle to the Galatians*, 178.

he took the effects of the deuteronomic curse upon himself. Whether Paul is the author of that tradition or whether vv. 13-14 are his citation of a tradition is impossible to determine with confidence.

In any case, the purpose of Jesus' taking the curse upon himself is explained in v. 14; the blessing of Abraham, long ago promised to the Gentiles (cf. vv. 8-9), can at last flow to them (cf. Rom 15:8-12), and the Spirit can be received by all God's people, through faith. Here again we find an ambiguity: Does Paul mean through their own faith or through the faith(fulness) of Jesus? The flow of logic in vv. 13-14 would suggest the latter: Christ redeemed Israel from the consequences of its unfaithfulness through his faithful death in order that we might receive the Spirit through Christ's faithfulness.[156] Paul, however, lets the ambiguity stand, perhaps for deliberate rhetorical purposes. The sentence could also be understood to mean that we receive the Spirit "through the faith that is elicited by Christ's faithful death in our behalf."[157]

In the previous paragraph (vv. 6-9), Paul has explicitly linked the blessing of Abraham with the rectification of the Gentiles—i.e., their acceptance into right covenant relationship with God. How is this outcome dependent on Christ's redemption of *Israel* from Deuteronomy's curse? Paul does not explain the connection (this is one reason for supposing that vv. 13-14 might be a pre-existing confessional formula), but we can make some guesses. The prophetic text that most powerfully shapes Paul's vision of the eschatological inclusion of the Gentiles is the book of Isaiah.[158] Isaiah holds forth the vision of God's final redemption and restoration of Israel as a prelude to the gathering of the Gentiles to worship the one true God on Mt. Zion (e.g., Isa 2:2-4; 60:1-22). So long as the people of Israel remain in bondage under the curse, this eschatological scenario cannot come to pass. The confessional formula of vv. 13-14 appears to assume that at last through Christ's death the curse has been lifted, Israel has been set

free, the exile has ended, so that the ingathering of the Gentiles can now begin.

This interpretation also explains how Paul can equate the "promise" with the reception of the Spirit. This is a somewhat puzzling move, because the passages in Genesis that speak of the blessing of Abraham make no reference at all to the Spirit. Thus it appears that Paul has creatively expanded the actual content of the promise; whereas Genesis speaks of God's gift of land and numerous descendants, Paul regards the promise to Abraham as being fulfilled in the church's experience of the Holy Spirit. The explanation for this inferential leap lies once again in the prophetic texts that promise Israel's ultimate restoration from exile. In Isaiah and Ezekiel, God's promise of restoration is repeatedly depicted through the image of the outpouring of God's Spirit (Isa 32:15-17; 44:1-5; 59:21; Ezek 11:14-21; 36:22-27; 37:1-14). Particularly noteworthy is Isa 44:3, in which the terms "spirit" and "blessing" are used in synonymous parallelism:

For I will pour water on the thirsty land,
    and streams on the dry ground;
I will pour my *spirit* upon your descendants [LXX:
    σπέρμα *sperma*],
    and my *blessing* upon your offspring. (NRSV)

Although Paul does not cite this passage, it probably underlies and surely illuminates Gal 3:1-14. Indeed, it helps us to see how Paul's argument from Scripture is constructively linked with his earlier argument from experience (vv 1-5); the experience of the Spirit in the church is a sign that God's eschatological restoration of Israel has begun. The fact that Gentiles such as the Galatians have also experienced this outpouring of the Spirit is consistent with the prophetic vision, which in turn was already "pre-proclaimed" in the promise to Abraham (vv. 6-9).

Dunn goes so far as to describe vv. 10-14 as "a midrash on Deuteronomy's three-stage schema of salvation-history": covenant, exile, and restoration.[159] That is a fundamentally correct observation, but we must also reckon with the radically revisionary character of this "midrash"; it is an interpretation that leads

156. Matera, *Galatians*, , 121, 124-25. Paul's use of the definite article in the phrase διὰ τῆς πίστεως (*dia tēs pisteōs*) might lend support to this interpretation.

157. Martyn, *Galatians*, 323.

158. F. Wilk, *Die Bedeutung des Jesajabuches für Paulus*, FRLANT 179 (Göttingen: Vandenhoeck & Ruprecht, 1998); J. R. Wagner, *Heralds of the Good News: Paul and Isaiah 'In Concert' in the Letter to the Romans*, NovTSup (Leiden: Brill, 2001).

159. Dunn, *The Epistle to the Galatians*, 180.

to the conclusion that the Torah's promise of life for those who remain within its structure of commandments is a false promise. Indeed, those who persist in trying to live under the Law after Christ has done away with its curse are, in fact, reverting to life under the curse. Hence, the urgency of Paul's argument against the Missionaries. Abraham is to be read not as a model of circumcision and Torah observance but as a prefiguration of the gospel: He simply trusts God and receives God's promise. Paul sees this same story being re-enacted in his Gentile churches.

This interpretation helps us to resolve two long-debated exegetical problems in vv. 13-14: (1) To whom do the pronouns "us" and "we" refer? (2) How are the two purpose clauses in v. 14 related to each other? According to the reading given here, "us" in v. 13 refers specifically to the Jewish people (including Jewish Christians, like Paul), who had incurred the curse of the Law through disobedience. On the other hand, the "we" in v. 14*b* must refer to the whole new community of God's people, transcending the Jew/Gentile distinction, on whom God is now pouring the Spirit. This means that both of the purpose clauses in v. 14 follow directly as consequences of Christ's redemptive death (v. 13). The logic of the clauses is as follows:

(a) Christ's death redeemed "us" [*Jews*] from the curse pronounced by the Law.

This has two effects:

(b¹) in Christ Jesus, the blessing of Abraham comes to the *Gentiles,*

(b²) and "we" [*Jews and Gentiles together*] receive the Spirit.

Whether this is a traditional formula or Paul's own fresh coinage, it reflects a fundamental shift of perspective that underscores the socially inclusive gospel for which Paul is battling. The speaker of such a confession moves from an initial identification with ethnic Israel (a), through an acknowledgment of God's blessing of the Gentiles (b¹), to a final declaration that through Christ's death Jews and Gentiles alike are united in receiving the Spirit (b²). Thus the experience of the Spirit is interpreted as the fulfillment of what Scripture has promised: the blessing of all nations. (See Reflections at 3:26-29.)

Galatians 3:15-18, The Covenant Promise Predated the Law

COMMENTARY

Paul now takes another tack. In vv. 15-18 he compares God's covenantal promise, spoken to Abraham, to a human last will and testament, which cannot be annulled by the subsequent action of a third party. This last will promised an inheritance to Abraham and to his "seed," which Paul identifies exclusively with Christ. The analogy has serious risks and limitations, because it compares God's promise to a human legal instrument that would become effective only upon the death of the testator, and because it seems to imply (wrongly) that the Law was instituted not by God but by some other party. These are scandalous implications; nonetheless, for the sake of argument, Paul is willing to press this analogy a long way, because it allows him to highlight two points: The Law came much later than the promise to Abraham and is, therefore, secondary, and the blessing of Abraham must be understood as an *inheritance* that rightly belongs to Gentiles as well as to Jews. From this point of view, the Missionaries' insistence that only Torah observers are Abraham's heirs appears to be a legal ploy to steal the inheritance from the Gentiles to whom God had promised it.

This line of argument, however, raises fundamental questions about the Law. If it had no saving efficacy and cannot be understood as a further specification of the covenant with Abraham, why did it come into existence? Is it to be understood as an evil entity set in opposition to God's promises? In vv. 19-24, Paul addresses these issues and contends that the Law had a limited, temporary purpose in God's design to save the world ultimately through Christ's faithfulness. Now that Christ, the Seed who is the true inheritor of the promise, has come, the Law no longer has any constructive purpose in God's economy.

In the final paragraph of this unit (vv. 25-29), Paul explains that the Galatians and all who are "in Christ" through baptism have entered a whole new world where all the old human divisions—including the distinction between Jew and Gentile symbolized by circumcision—no longer have the power to separate us from one another. All who are incorporated into Christ are thereby given an identity as "Abraham's seed"; therefore, they are all legitimate heirs whether they are circumcised or not.

The unity of the argument is sometimes obscured when this section is broken down into short, discrete paragraphs (e.g., vv. 15-18, 19-22, 23-25, and 26-29). The key to the overall logic of the section is found in the link between v. 16 and v. 29: The promise is given to Abraham and his seed, who is Christ (v. 16), and all who are in Christ are therefore Abraham's seed (v. 29).

3:15. Paul realizes that he is about to undertake a high-risk argument fraught with the possibility of misinterpretation; therefore, he prefaces this section with a disclaimer. The Greek text of v. 15*a* says, literally, "Brothers, I speak in a human way," indicating that he is aware of the limitations of the figurative analogy he is about to propose: God's dealing with humanity can be only indirectly grasped by means of such illustrations.[160] (The NRSV and the NIV give a paraphrase rather than a translation at this point.) By addressing the Galatians as "brothers" (for the first time since 1:11), Paul signals a transition, modulating his voice into a warmer tone after the scolding address of 3:1.

The term "will" (διαθήκη *diathēkē*) is semantically ambiguous, and Paul makes the ambiguity serve his daring analogy. *Diathēkē* is the ordinary term in Greek for a last will and testament, but the LXX translators also employed it to translate the Hebrew word for "covenant" (ברית *bĕrît* with Abraham as though this "covenant" were a human "will."

Once the will has been ratified by the testator, no one else can add a codicil to it or annul it. The language here is technical legal terminology,[161] but Paul has selected his words carefully to echo and prefigure other language in his argument. The term "annul" (ἀθετέω *atheteō*) is the same verb used in 2:21 ("I do not *nullify* the grace of God"); thus he subtly suggests that to annul God's *diathēkē* by superimposing the Law upon it is a way of negating God's grace. Also, the verb "adds to" (ἐπιδιατάσσεται *epidiatassetai*) subtly prepares the way for the etymologically related participle "ordained/put into effect" (διαταγείς *diatageis*) in v. 19. This verbal connection between v. 15 and v. 19 implies that the angelic administration of the Law (v. 19) was an addition that cannot supersede the promise made by God to Abraham.

3:16. Having set up the analogy between God's covenant and a human will, Paul now takes the role of probate judge, interpreting the language of the original *diathēkē* as precisely as possible. He observes that the promises (Gen 12:1-3, 7; 13:14-17; 15:5; 17:4-8; 22:16-18; 26:2-5) were addressed to Abraham "*and to his seed*." (Probably the reference is particularly to Gen 17:8, in view of the repeated use of the term *diathēkē* in that context.) Paul drives home the point that the noun "seed" (σπέρμα *sperma*) is singular, not plural, and then offers a startling interpretation: The singular seed is Christ. Thus he reads the promises in Genesis as direct prophetic figurations of Christ, who is the ultimate heir designated by God's promissory testament.

This remarkable reading of Genesis has often been regarded as an instance of Paul's exegetical sleight of hand, lifting a proof text completely out of context and disregarding the obvious fact that "seed" is a collective noun that refers to Abraham's numerous descendants, more numerous than the stars of heaven (Gen 15:5). We must not, however, hastily dismiss Paul's interpretative strategy. He is certainly aware that Abraham has many children, not just one (Gal 3:7), and—most important—his exposition drives toward the climactic affirmation in v. 29: "If you [pl.] belong to Christ then you [pl.] are Abraham's seed [*sperma*], heirs according to

---

160. See the parallels in Rom 3:5; 6:19; and 1 Cor 9:8. Rom 6:19 is especially helpful in illuminating the sense of Gal 3:15*a:* "I am speaking in human terms because of your natural limitations" (NRSV).

161. See references in Betz, *Galatians*, 155-56.

promise." This shows that Paul knows perfectly well that *sperma* is a collective noun and that the Genesis texts point toward multiple progeny for Abraham. In v. 16, however, he plays on the grammatically singular form of the word, in a style formally reminiscent of rabbinic exegesis, to register the claim that it is only in and through Christ that the promises find fulfillment. Christ is the one true heir of the inheritance promised to Abraham, and Christ's people share in this inheritance only by becoming incorporated into his life (cf. 2:20; 3:26-28).

Paul's exegesis looks strange by modern critical canons, but he is building upon a Jewish tradition that the messianic "seed" (*sperma*) of David will inherit a kingdom established forever, in accordance with God's covenant promise (2 Sam 7:12-14; Ps 89:3-4). Thus, in v. 16, Paul implicitly links the promise to Abraham with the promises to a "seed" that will come forth from David, the Messiah (Χριστός *Christos*). This sort of catchword linkage, known as *gezerah shawah*, was commonly employed by Jewish interpreters in Paul's day. Whether this technique would have made Paul's argument persuasive to the Missionaries, however, is doubtful. Paul's exposition of the *diathēkē* ignores the salient fact that God's covenant with Abraham expressly mandates circumcision: "This is my covenant, which you shall keep, between me and you and your seed after you: every male among you shall be circumcised" (Gen 17:10; cf. the whole context in Gen 17:9-14, 23-27). The Missionaries might well protest that Paul's adjudication of the "will" has omitted one of its central stipulations and that it is he, not they, who should be accused of trying to alter the terms of the *diathēkē*. How Paul would have answered this objection we do not know, for in the present passage he simply ignores the commandment of circumcision in Genesis 17. At this point, we have come up against one of the limitations of Paul's analogy; perhaps this explains why, when he reformulates his exegesis of the Abraham story in Romans 4, he no longer employs this particular line of argument.

3:17. Paul now drives home the point of his analogy: The Law came 430 years after the promise to Abraham (the figure is based on Exod 12:40-41) and, therefore, cannot possibly render the promise to Abraham void. The *diathēkē* was ratified directly by God, long before the Law came into being. Thus the Law must be regarded as a secondary and inferior arrangement. (It should be kept in mind that to people in the ancient world, novelty was not a virtue; the new was suspect, whereas old ideas and customs were accorded dignity and authority.) Anyone who tries to use this late and secondary codicil to invalidate the covenant with Abraham or to prevent his rightful heirs from receiving what was promised to them should, therefore, be ruled out of court.

It is probably significant that Paul attributes the establishment of the covenant/will directly to God's action but uses a much vaguer expression for the advent of the Law: The Law "came into being" somehow.[162] Paul avoids saying that God gave the Law (cf. vv. 19-20, which distance God from the Law by emphasizing the intermediary roles of Moses and the angels). This omission is necessary for the extended metaphor of vv. 15-18 to work. The covenant with Abraham trumps the Law both because of its temporal priority and because of God's direct initiative in establishing it.

3:18. Paul concludes his development of the "testament" analogy by invoking for the first time the word "inheritance" (κληρονομία *klēronomia*), which will become a key theme in several later passages (3:29; 4:1-7, 30). Using a contrary-to-fact condition, he demonstrates the absurdity of claiming that Abraham's inheritance could possibly come through the Law. The structure of v. 18*a* parallels a pattern already encountered in 2:21*b*:

Gal 2:21*b*: For if rectification were through the Law, then Christ died for nothing.

Gal 3:18*a*: For if the inheritance were from the Law, it is no longer from the promise.

This parallelism highlights the virtual synonymity of "rectification/righteousness" and "inheritance" in Paul's symbolic world; both terms refer to the status of sharing in the blessing of Abraham, in right covenant relation to

162. Martyn, *Galatians*, 341-42.

God, as symbolized and confirmed by the gift of the Holy Spirit. Could anyone claim that such benefits were available through the Law? Paul dismisses such a notion as contrary to everything he has said about the story of God's promise to Abraham.

In vv. 11-12, Paul set "Law" and πίστις (*pistis*, "faith[fulness])" in opposition to one another; here in v. 18, the latter term of the polarity is replaced by "promise," emphasizing yet again that *God* is the active agent who gives the promised inheritance to Abraham and his heirs. Lest there be any remaining doubt on this point, Paul hammers home his point in v. 18*b:* "But God graced Abraham through promise." The perfect tense verb "graced" (κεχάρισται *kecharistai*) indicates an action anchored in the past (the Genesis story) with effects flowing into the present. The statement may be taken as a summary of everything Paul has said so far about Abraham, pointing back not only to v. 16, but to vv. 6-9 and 14 as well. God acts freely to give grace and blessing through promise, not through Law. The interposition of the Law, therefore, can only be a hindrance to this freely promised grace. (See Reflections at 3:26-29.)

Galatians 3:19-25, The Law as Temporary Custodian

COMMENTARY

3:19. This whole train of thought, however, leads inescapably to a crucial question, which Paul at last voices in this verse. If the Law of Moses cannot confer the Spirit (vv. 2-5), pronounces a curse on its adherents (v. 10), cannot bring rectification and makes empty promises of life (vv. 11-12), and cannot add anything valid to the Abrahamic covenant (vv. 15-18), "Why then the Law?" Why has God permitted the Law to come into being? What possible purpose can it serve?

Paul gives a direct answer, but unfortunately the answer is notoriously obscure. The Law, he says, "was added because of [χάριν *charin*] transgressions [παραβάσεων *parabaseōn*]." This statement has been interpreted in widely varying ways. At least five options should be considered:

(1) The Law was added to *produce* or provoke transgressions.[163] This interpretation reads v. 19 in the light of Rom 5:20: "But Law came in, with the result that the trespass multiplied; but where sin increased, grace abounded all the more" (NRSV).

(2) The Law was added to *identify* humanity's inchoate sinfulness as conscious trangression, explicit violation of the revealed divine will.[164] Compare Rom 4:15: "For the Law brings wrath; but where there is no Law, neither is there transgression [*parabasis*]."

(3) The Law was added to *restrain* transgressions, to pose a constraint on human sin. This reading points forward to Paul's image of the Law as "disciplinarian" in vv. 23-25.

(4) The Law was added to *provide a remedy* for transgressions in the interim before the coming of Christ.[165]

(5) The Law was added by God because of the transgressions of Israel in worshiping the golden calf (Exodus 32). Jerome comments: "It was after the offense of the people in the wilderness, after the adoration of the calf and their murmurings against God, that the Law came to forbid transgressions."[166] On this reading, Paul is still commenting, in line with v. 17, on the OT story of how the Law came into existence. As the citation from Jerome indicates, this explanation may be combined with number 3.

Of these explanations, the first and fourth are almost certainly to be rejected, because they do not fit intelligibly into Paul's argument here. Nothing else that Paul says in Galatians offers any hint that he has either the provocation of transgressions or the merciful remediation of transgressions in mind. The fifth option is possible, because Paul clearly is thinking in vv. 19-20 about the Exodus narrative of the giving of the Law; however,

---

163. Betz, *Galatians*, 165; Martyn, *Galatians*, 354-55.
164. Matera, *Galatians*, 128; Longenecker, *Galatians*, 138-39 (with some qualification).

165. Dunn, *The Epistle to the Galatians*, 189-90.
166. Jerome, *Epistle to the Galatians* 2.3.19-20 (PL 26:391C [440]), cited incorrectly as 26:366A [440] in Edwards, *Galatians, Ephesians, Philippians*, 45.

if Paul intends to allude to the golden calf incident, he has given his readers no clues to that effect.

The best options are the second and third, because each fits understandably into the line of argument in Galatians 3. Given the brevity of Paul's statement, it is impossible to decide between these two interpretations; indeed, he may have had both things in mind, as his unpacking of the Law's function in the succeeding verses (vv. 21-25) indicates. The idea that Paul is pointing to the Law's disclosive function of identifying sin as transgression against God's will is supported by v. 22a, which highlights Scripture's revelatory function of disclosing the universality of human sin (cf. Rom 3:9-20). Furthermore, the parallel in Rom 4:15 occurs in a passage very similar to Galatians 3, dealing with the promise to Abraham, and the key term παράβασις (*parabasis*) appears in both passages. At the same time, there is also a good case to be made for the third interpretation (the Law as a restraint on sin), because Paul goes on in vv. 23-25 to explicate the Law's function as one of restrictive but protective custody, using the metaphor of the παιδαγωγός *paidagōgos* (see the Commentary on 3:24-25). It is probably best, then, to read these successive depictions of the Law's identifying and restraining functions as a twofold explanation of what Paul means by saying that the Law was "added because of transgressions."

In any case, the Law was designed as a temporary expedient, "until the Seed should come to whom the promise had been made." The NIV's capitalization of the word "Seed" correctly links this statement back to v. 16, which declared that the "seed" is to be identified as Christ. The Law, whatever its purpose, was designed to be in effect only until Christ's coming (see also vv. 24-25). Once the inheritance has been given and received, the Law becomes superfluous.

Who was responsible for adding the Law? The preceding discussion assumes that the Law was instituted by God and that the passive verb, προσετέθη (*prosetethē* was added") points to the action of God. It has occasionally been suggested, however, that Paul is implying that the Law was introduced by angelic powers acting apart from God.[167] Such an assertion

would be virtually blasphemous in the eyes of Paul's Jewish contemporaries, including the rival Missionaries in Galatia. Paul avoids making any such explicit statement; nonetheless, the wording of v. 19 is curiously indirect. Paul says, literally, that the Law was "ordained through angels by the hand of a mediator." As has been already noted, the participle διαταγείς *diatageis* ("ordained," from the verb διατάσσω *diatassō*) might be understood to echo the verb ἐπιδιατάσσεται (*epidiatassetai*) in v. 15, which referred to the illicit attempt by someone to add a codicil to a duly ratified will. This echo would cast a shadow of doubt on the motives of the angels in v. 19. The prepositional phrase "through angels" suggests, however, that the angels are God's instruments rather than the initiators of the giving of the Law. In the OT, only Deut 33:2 speaks directly of the presence of angels in the giving of the Law at Sinai (see also Ps 68:17); in this passage, they serve to enhance the glorious manifestation of God's power. Similarly, in Acts 7:53 (whose phrasing is very close to Gal 3:19) and Heb 2:2 we find depictions of the angels as agents of God's revelation to Israel, and the tradition that angels were present at Sinai was common in Second Temple Jewish texts.[168]

Paul takes this pious midrashic elaboration of the exodus story and gives it a different twist. Rather than enhancing the awesome revelatory character of the Law, the presence of angels shows that God was not acting directly at Sinai, as when God spoke to Abraham. Rather, the Law was administered through intermediary figures, thus distancing God from the Law.

3:20. The phrase "by the hand of a mediator" refers to the role of Moses in receiving the Law and transmitting it to the people (for the expression "by the hand of Moses," see Lev 26:46; Num 36:13). Philo's *Life of Moses* explicitly gives Moses the title of "mediator and reconciler."[169] This much is clear, but Paul's further statement about the mediator

---

167. H. Hübner, *Law in Paul's Thought* (Edinburgh: T. & T. Clark, 1984) 24-36; Martyn, *Galatians*, 356-57.

168. For a list of references, see Longenecker, *Galatians*, 139-40.

169. Philo *Life of Moses* 2.166; see also *Assumption of Moses* 1.14. The reference to Jesus Christ as the "one mediator between God and humankind" in 1 Tim 2:5 led many patristic interpreters to see in Gal 3:19 a reference to Christ's mediatorial work. Because Paul is speaking here of the giving of the Law at Sinai, this interpretation is certainly incorrect. In Heb 8:6; 9:15; 12:24, Jesus is described as the mediator of a new covenant; here there is an explicit contrast to Moses as mediator of the old covenant, which the author of Hebrews regards as superseded by the new.

in this verse is another maddeningly opaque sentence. The confession that "God is one" evokes the *Shema* (Deut 6:4), the fundamental confession of Israel's faith. This confession is itself part of the very Law that Paul is now paradoxically distancing from God! The oneness of God in v. 20 *b* is to be linked with the singularity of the "seed" in v. 16 and the oneness of the people of God in v. 28. The deficiency of the Law, therefore, may be related to its divisive character, its inability to bring Jews and Gentiles together into a single new people. The oneness of God can be rightly reflected only in a community unified by the fulfillment of God's promise in Christ.[170] Notwithstanding these observations, there is no scholarly consensus about the meaning of v. 20. Its general sense seems to be that because the Law was delivered through an intermediary figure, it does not convey God's grace directly, as did the promise to Abraham (v. 18).

3:21. In light of these remarks about the Law, Paul raises rhetorically the scandalous inference that might be drawn from everything he has said in vv. 1-20: "Is the Law then opposed to the promises of God?" Paul's detractors would accuse him of having constructed a position that leads exactly to this horrifying conclusion (cf. Rom 7:7, 13). Elsewhere he writes, in a more measured discussion of the role of the Law, that the Law is "holy and righteous and good" (Rom 7:12). In Galatians, however, he has made no such laudatory remarks about the Law; so far, he has portrayed it only as a source of the curse. His opponents might understandably portray Paul as a renegade Jew in rebellion against God's Law—a proto-Marcionite theologian who paints the Law as an evil power working against God. But he spits out a forceful denial: "Certainly not!" (μὴ γένοιτο *mē genoito*). Paul frequently employs this rhetorical device of formulating a false inference, and then emphatically denying it, to head off misinterpretations of his thought, particularly with reference to the sensitive topic of the Law. The closest parallel is Rom 3:31: "Do we then abolish the Law by this faith? By no means! On the contrary, we uphold the Law."

In this verse, Paul declares the inference— that the Law is opposed to the promise—to

170. Wright, *The Climax of the Covenant,* 168-72.

be false. Why? Because the Law would be in opposition to the promise only if it had been intended by God to be the agent of life and righteousness. Paul, however, denies that premise. The Law, he argues, was given for a very different reason, which he will explain in vv. 22-24. Here we encounter another contrary-to-fact condition: "If a Law had been given which had the power to give life, then rectification/righteousness would indeed have been from the Law" (cf. 2:21; 3:18). In that case, the Law would offer a rival system of salvation as an alternative to the promise. Paul insists, however, that the Law had no such power (cf. Rom 8:3) and was never intended for such a purpose. He has already argued emphatically that righteousness is ἐκ πίστεως (*ek pisteōs*), not ἐν νόμῳ (*en nomō*, vv. 11-12). Consequently—and this is the point of v. 21—the Law, understood rightly, is not in a relation of competition or opposition to the promise. Thus, by denying the lifegiving power of the Law, Paul is not opposing the Law but affirming its true purpose.

What, then, is that true purpose? In vv. 22-24 Paul gives a twofold answer: The purpose of the Law was to "imprison all things under the power of sin" and to keep Israel in protective custody until the coming of Christ into the world.

3:22. Paul continues to use metaphors. Here he personifies the Law (actually "Scripture" in this formulation) as a jailkeeper that locks "all things" up together under the power of sin. The fact that Paul can use "Scripture" in this way as a virtual synonym for "Law" (see the parallel statement about being imprisoned under Law in v. 23) shows that he maintains a significant role for the Law as an actor in the divine redemptive drama. (Note the positive proclamatory role assigned to Scripture in v. 8.) In its role as jailer, the Scripture performs exactly the same role assigned to the Law in Rom 3:9-20: It declares all human beings, Jew and Greek alike, to be "under the power of sin" (Rom 3:9; Gal 3:23; the NIV's broad paraphrase accurately conveys the sense: "the Scripture declares that the whole world is a prisoner of sin"). In Romans, Paul explains that the Law performs this function "so that every mouth may be silenced, and the whole world may be held accountable to God." How does the Law achieve this end?

"Through the Law comes the knowledge of sin" (Rom 3:19-20). In other words, the Law discloses the truth about our human condition: We are alienated from God and stand under God's righteous judgment. That is the meaning of Paul's jailkeeper metaphor in v. 22a. Paul attributes this "locking up" function to God's intentional design, as demonstrated by the close parallel in Rom 11:32, where Paul uses exactly the same verb, this time with God as the subject: "God has locked up all in disobedience so that he may be merciful to all." In the light of Rom 11:32, we can see more clearly what Paul is saying in Gal 3:19-22. The Law is not an adversary of God's redemptive purpose; rather, God has used the Law to illuminate Israel's condition—and therefore, *a fortiori,* the universal human condition—of bondage to the power of Sin (cf. Rom 7:7). Thus the Law forecloses all human attempts at saving ourselves. The reason for this confinement under the power of Sin is explained in vv. 22b-24: It was a necessary step in God's design to rectify the world through Jesus Christ.

Thus in this verse as in Romans, the function of the Law in disclosing human sinfulness is part of a larger divine purpose. The reason why God used the Law to lock all things up under sin was "so that what was promised might be given through the faithfulness of Jesus Christ to those who believe" (see the reading in the NRSV footnote). The thought here is closely parallel to 2:16, but Paul has now substituted the "promise" language of 3:14-18 for the "rectification" terminology found in the earlier passage. This suggests that the two semantic fields are generally synonymous in Paul's mind; both "promise" and "rectification" point to our inclusion in the eschatological people of God, who share in the blessing promised to Abraham.

In both passages, this blessing is made effective "through the faithfulness of Jesus Christ" (see the Commentary on 2:16). The NIV and the NRSV both reflect the awkwardness of attempting to interpret ἐκ πίστεως Ἰησοῦ Χριστοῦ (*ek pisteōs Iēsou Christou*) to mean "through faith in Jesus Christ." The NRSV reads the phrase as a modifier of the noun "promise" (ἐπαγγελία *epangelia*), producing the peculiar rendering, "what was promised through faith in Jesus Christ." This makes no sense, since

neither the Genesis text nor Paul's exposition of it has referred to anything being promised through faith in Jesus Christ. The NIV, on the other hand, recognizing that the prepositional phrase *ek pisteōs Iēsou Christou* is properly to be read as modifying the verb "given" (δοθῇ *dothē*), is forced to insert a redundant passive participle "being given," which does not appear in the Greek text. These problems are avoided if we adopt the straightforward translation given above: "so that what was promised might be given through the faithfulness of Jesus Christ to those who believe." The long-awaited promise is brought to fulfillment through "Christ's trustful obedience to God in the giving up of his own life for us."[171]

Paul's point is that the Law teaches us to discern the depth of human sin and need, thereby locking up even God's elect people Israel in the same bondage to sin that was shared by the pagan world. In such a desperate situation, the only hope is for God to act. That was precisely God's design, and God did act through Christ's faithful death to liberate us from the power of sin and the present evil age (cf. 1:4; 2:20; 3:13).

3:23-25. Paul repeats and elaborates what he has just said, but now he develops a different metaphor that suggests the Law's functions of restraint and protection: The law was our παιδαγωγός (*paidagōgos*) until Christ came. The noun, despite the English cognate "pedagogue," does not mean "teacher." The *paidagōgos* (lit., "child-leader") was a slave in the Greco-Roman household who supervised and guarded children. His responsibility was to walk them to and from school, to see that they behaved properly and stayed out of harm's way.[172] The *paidagōgos*, however, was not a member of the family, and when the child grew to a certain age, his services were no longer required. The Law was like that for Israel, Paul proposes. It had a certain necessary role in confining, guarding, and disciplining God's people during the interval between Moses and Christ,[173] but that

171. Martyn, *Galatians,* 361.

172. For a helpful summary of the functions of the pedagogue, see Williams, *Galatians,* 102-3. For fuller accounts, see D. J. Lull, "'The Law Was Our Pedagogue': A Study of Gal 3:19-25," *JBL* 105 (1986) 481-98; N. H. Young, "*Paidagogos:* The Social Setting of a Pauline Metaphor," *NovT* 29 (1987) 150-76.

173. This view of the Law as providing a protective confinement is closely parallel to explanations of the role of the Law in Josephus, *Ap.* 3.173-74 and the *Letter of Aristeas* 142. See the helpful discussion in Matera, *Galatians,* 139-40.

interval has now come to an end (v. 25). This metaphor allows Paul to affirm that the Law once had a constructive role to play in God's overall plan, while at the same time insisting that its role is now at an end.

In sketching out this analogy, Paul uses the language of "faith" again in a way that calls for comment. The period of confinement was "until [εἰς *eis*] the faith [τὴν πίστιν *tēn pistin*] would be revealed [ἀποκαλυφθῆναι *apokalyphthēnai*]." Here, "the faith" cannot possibly refer to human subjective believing, because it is something that comes by revelation, and Paul has insisted from the beginning of the letter that revelation is not a matter of human possibility; rather, it is a matter of divine action and divine disclosure (see, e.g., 1:11-12). Taken by itself, "the faith" could mean "that which is believed," but in the present context, the best interpretation is that the definite article refers the reader back to the faith mentioned in the previous sentence: the faith of Jesus Christ. The correctness of this reading is confirmed by v. 24, in which Paul formulates a synonymous idea: We were under the *paidagōgos* "until Christ came" (taking *eis* again as temporal, as in v. 23). In other words, Paul sets the revelation of "the faith" in v. 23 in synonymous parallelism with the coming of Christ in v. 24. The coming of Christ "reveals" faith because "he loved me and gave himself for me" (2:20); God's faithfulness (cf. Rom 3:3) is disclosed to the world through the cross, which is God's saving action for our sake.

In the light of this exegesis, the NIV's translation of v. 24 must be judged seriously misleading. It paraphrases *paidagōgos*, ignores the parallelism with v. 23, and therefore takes *eis* in a spatial, rather than temporal, sense ("to," rather than "until"). As a result, it attributes to Paul the claim that the purpose of the Law was "to lead us to Christ." This is completely incongruous with the way Paul has developed the *paidagōgos* metaphor. Nowhere in Galatians, or in any of his other letters, does Paul argue for a progressive educative function of the Law; its purpose, according to these verses, is protective custody. The point is critical: According to Paul, we did not make our way, under the tutelage of the Law, progressively to Christ; instead, Christ came to us. In no other way could we have been released from our confinement.

The purpose of Christ's coming was "in order that we might be rectified *ek pisteōs*" (v. 24*b*). In view of the way Paul has used πίστις (*pistis*) in vv. 22-23, the most natural interpretation is that v. 24*b* refers again to Christ's faithful death for our sake (as also in 2:16). The Law kept us locked up until that event, which was God's intended means of setting us free. Now that this liberating event has broken into our world, Paul proclaims, "we are no longer subject to a *paidagōgos*" (v. 25).

With that, Paul brings his discussion of the purpose of the Law to a decisive conclusion. Living on this side of Christ's death, he tells the Galatians, we are in a new eschatological age. Thus we need not entertain the idea of coming under the supervision of the Law. The Law has served its purpose, and its commission is at an end. Its confining role was ordained by God during the period before Christ; consequently, it was neither evil nor in opposition to God. Neither, however, should it be understood as a means to rectification and life. Least of all should it be allowed to restrict the access of Gentile Christians to receiving the inheritance that God promised to Abraham. (See Reflections at 3:26-29.)

Galatians 3:26-29, In Christ We Are Abraham's Seed

COMMENTARY

3:26. Paul now begins to draw the conclusions that follow from his lengthy discussion of the promise to Abraham. The conjunction "for" (γάρ *gar*) forges a close logical connection between this verse and the foregoing context; this connection is more clearly represented by the NRSV than by the NIV. The reason why we are no longer subject to the disciplinary constraint of the Law (v. 25) is provided here. The NRSV also more accurately represents the sense of the sentence by placing "in Christ Jesus" at the beginning as an adverbial modifier of the main verb, rather than connecting it with the noun "faith," as in the NIV. This is the characteristic Pauline "in Christ" formula (see, e.g., 1:22; 2:4, 17; 3:14; 5:6), which he uses repeatedly to characterize Christian existence as a state of corporate unity with Christ.

The emphasis here falls heavily on the word "all" (πάντες *pantes*), the first word in the sentence in the Greek text. *All* the Galatian believers, without distinction, are already children (lit., "sons") of God in Christ Jesus via "the faith." No further action of circumcision or religious observance is required to secure this status. The noun πίστις (*pistis*), again used here with the definite article, carries forward the line of thought from vv. 22-25, referring to the faith(fulness) of Christ. It is through his gracious act of faithful self-giving that the Galatians have been brought into God's family as children. At the same time, since the noun is not limited by any pronoun or genitive phrase, it is slightly ambiguous; it can be understood as referring either to Christ's faith or to ours (cf. the similar ambiguity in vv. 11, 14, 24).

Paul's main point, however, is that all who are in Christ are now God's "sons." In order to see what Paul is claiming here, it is crucial to recognize that the epithet "sons of God" was employed in the OT and in Jewish tradition as a designation for Israel as God's elect people.

You are sons of the LORD your God. . . . For you are a people holy to the LORD your God; it is you the Lord has chosen out of all the peoples on earth to be his people, his treasured possession. (Deut 14:1-2 NRSV)

And the LORD said to Moses, "I know their contrariness and their thoughts and their stubbornness. And they will not obey until they acknowledge their sin and the sins of their fathers. But after this they will return to me in all uprightness and with all of (their) heart and soul. And I shall cut off the foreskin of their heart and the foreskin of the heart of their descendants. And I shall create for them a holy spirit, and I shall purify them so that they will not turn away from following me from that day and forever. And their souls will cleave to me and to all my commandments. And they will do my commandments. *And I shall be a father to*

them, and they will be sons to me. And they will all be called 'sons of the living God.' And every angel and spirit will know and acknowledge that they are my sons and I am their father in uprightness and righteousness. And I shall love them." (*Jub* 1:23-25)[174]

Against this background, we see that Paul is telling the Gentile Galatians that, in Christ, they are now given the honorific name "sons of God" that was once reserved for the Jewish people alone. (This is a theme that he will develop further in 4:4-7; cf. Rom 8:14-16.) Thus this verse closely parallels Paul's earlier affirmation (v. 7) that all who are ἐκ πίστεως *ek pisteōs* are "Abraham's children." In both cases, he has taken a title that originally asserted Israel's special privilege and extended it to include Gentile believers.

3:27. Paul offers a further warrant for this claim by pointing to the practice of baptism. Presumably all the members of the Galatian churches had undergone baptism as adult believers, since all were converts from paganism. Paul now reminds them of this experience of initiation, a marker of their passage into a new life. They had been baptized "into Christ." The wording here is probably not a direct quotation of a liturgical formula, since early Christian baptism was performed "in the name of Jesus Christ" or some variant thereof (cf. Matt 28:19; Acts 2:38; 1 Cor 6:11). Rather than a quotation, Paul's wording here represents an interpretation of the significance of baptism. As in Rom 6:3-11, Paul interprets baptism as signifying union with Christ (highlighted by the NIV), which entails death to one's old life and entry into a new world. The character of this new world will be spelled out further in v. 28.

The reference to being "clothed with Christ" is probably an allusion to a feature of early Christian baptismal liturgies. Persons being baptized removed their garments, were baptized naked, and then put on a new white garment, signifying the new life they were entering.[175] Other allusions to this practice may be found in Rom 13:14; Eph 4:22-24;

---

174. In addition to these examples, see also Exod 4:22-23; Hos 1:10; 11:1; Sir 36:17; 3 Macc 6:28; 4 Ezra 6:55-59; *Pss Sol* 17:26-27. For discussion of this motif, see B. Byrne, *"Sons of God"—"Seed of Abraham": A Study of the Idea of the Sonship of God of all Christians in Paul Againstthe Jewish Background*, AnBib 83 (Rome: Pontifical Biblical Institute, 1979).

175. W. A. Meeks, *The First Urban Christians: The Social World of the Apostle Paul* (New Haven: Yale University Press, 1983) 151.

and Col 3:9-10. As Williams has pointed out, the language of being "clothed with" some attribute is pervasive in the OT. To take a single example, the psalmist prays that Israel's priests might be "clothed with righteousness," and later in the same psalm God declares, "Its priests I will clothe with salvation" (Ps 132:9, 16 NRSV). To be "clothed" with some quality or attribute is to take on the characteristics of that in which one is clothed.[176] None of the many OT examples adduced by Williams, however, refer to being "clothed in" a *person.* Paul's language of "putting on Christ" is another figurative way of describing the mysterious personal union with Christ to which he referred in 2:20. In such a union, those who are "in Christ" share in his divine sonship and take on his character. The baptismal imagery here, then, points to the transformation of identity that the Galatians have undergone.

3:28. The full implications of that transformation are spelled out with reference to the abolition of social distinctions. At this point, in contrast to v. 27, Paul is probably quoting an early Christian baptismal formula (cf. 1 Cor 12:13; Col 3:11). If so, he is calling to mind the words that had been pronounced over each of the Galatian believers at the time of their baptism, words that declared unmistakably the obsolescence of the Jew/ Greek boundary that the Missionaries were trying to reestablish through their advocacy of circumcision. The radical vision set forth in this formula reflects the new creation that God has brought into being (cf. 6:15). In this new world in Christ, three binary oppositions that characterized all human existence in the old age have been dissolved.[177] Each of these oppositions should be examined carefully.

(1) There Is No Longer Jew or Greek. This is the element of the formula that Paul particularly wants to emphasize in the present context. In the old age, the Law protected the religious and cultural separateness of the Jewish people, setting them apart from all other peoples (collectively categorized as "the nations" [= Gentiles]). In Christ, however, this separateness is abolished, because Jews and Gentiles are constituted together as

one new people of God (see 6:16; Rom 3:29-30; 15:7-13; cf. Eph 2:11-20). In the light of this new reality, ethnic distinctions no longer matter. The implication of this is, of course, that circumcision as a marker separating Jews from Gentiles no longer matters (5:6).

(2) There Is No Longer Slave or Free. Distinctions of social class are negated in the new creation. The identity of Christians as "children of God" (v. 26) is given to them by their participation in Christ; consequently, they are now related to one another as brothers and sisters, no longer in a social hierarchy that distinguishes slave and free (cf. Phlm 15-16). The baptismal formula declares that social class and power have been delegitimated in Christ.

Admittedly, the "already/not yet" tension in Paul's thought leaves room for uncertainty about the extent to which this eschatological vision of equality is to be embodied in social practice. The key to understanding Paul's thought on this question is to recognize that he sees the church as an alternative community that prefigures the new creation in the midst of a world that continues to resist God's justice. Thus Paul is not calling for a revolution in which slaves rise up and demand freedom; rather, in this verse he is declaring that God *has* created a new community, the church, in which the baptized *already* share equality. To the extent that vv. 26-29 have hortatory force, they call the Galatians to "get in line with the Spirit" (5:25) and manifest in their common life the κοινωνία (*koinōnia*) of the new creation, in which these binary social distinctions no longer count for anything. Yet, because the present sociopolitical realities of this world are soon to pass away, Paul elsewhere counsels members of his churches to remain in the social station in which they found themselves at the time of their conversion (1 Cor 7:17-24, 29-31). (The rule of thumb that believers should "remain in the condition in which you were called," applied to the circumcision controversy, suggests that uncircumcised Gentiles should remain uncircumcised; see 1 Cor 7:18-20.) This is not a matter of social conservatism; rather, it is a matter of eschatological patience while eagerly awaiting God's coming new order. In chap. 4, Paul will take up the slavery/freedom opposition and develop its implications

176. Williams, *Galatians,* 105.
177. For an extensive discussion of parallels to the formula in ancient religion, philosophy, and political thought, see Betz, *Galatians,* 189-201.

by urging the Galatians to stand firm in their new freedom in Christ. This demonstrates once again that Paul expects the church to move toward the practical realization of the baptismal formula's vision.

(3) There Is No Longer Male and Female. Paul makes no use of this opposition in the argument of Galatians; this is one piece of evidence that suggests he is quoting a formula. Attentive readers of the NRSV will note that this third element breaks the formal pattern of the previous oppositions: there is no longer a *or* b; there is no longer c *or* d; there is no longer male *and* female. (The NIV misses this crucial shift.) What is the reason for this change? Paul is echoing the language of Gen 1:27: "*male and female* he created them." To say that this created distinction is no longer in force is to declare that the new creation has come upon us, a new creation in which even gender roles no longer pertain. (Paul omits this third element when he alludes to the formula in 1 Cor 12:13, perhaps because of the difficulties and controversies in Corinth over issues of sexual conduct and marriage; see 1 Cor 5:1-13; 6:12-20; 7:1-40.)

The fact that the Letter to the Galatians is not concerned with gender roles does not diminish the force or importance of this element of Paul's vision for the church as a transformed community. If the church is to be a sign and foretaste of the new creation, it must be a community in which gender distinctions—like the ethnic and social distinctions noted in the first two parts of the formula—have lost their power to divide and oppress. This does not mean that those who are in Christ cease to be men or women, any more than the male members of the community cease to be circumcised or uncircumcised. Rather, it means that these distinctions are no longer the determinative identity markers, no longer a ground for status or exclusion. It should be noted that circumcision is an identity marker applicable only to males; therefore, a community that singles out circumcision as its key sign of covenant membership will inevitably privilege male identity as normative. There is no evidence in Paul's letters that he ever consciously considered this point, but the ritual of baptism, identical for both sexes, is distinctly appropriate as the sign of inclusion within a community in which the old distinction between "male and female" has ceased to separate those who are in Christ.

The implications of Paul's extraordinary baptismal declaration of the new creation are summed up in the final clause of v. 28: "for you are all one in Christ Jesus." The new world into which the Galatians have been initiated through baptism is a world in which the most salient feature of their identity is their unity in Christ. Because all participate in this unity, they should firmly reject invidious appeals from the Missionaries to reinstantiate the ethnic and status distinctions that characterized the world before the faith of Christ invaded the world and changed everything.

3:29. The concluding sentence of the paragraph wraps up the entire argument of vv. 6-29, particularly recalling the language of vv. 15-18. Those who are Christ's people are de facto "Abraham's seed." With this affirmation, Paul has laid all his cards on the table. In v. 16, he had asserted that only Christ was the Seed, the single true heir of the promise made to Abraham. But this was only the first move in a more complex argument. Because the baptized have entered into union with Christ, they are one new person in him and with him; therefore, they all participate equally in the same privileged status as joint "heirs according to the promise" (cf. Rom 8:14-17). The last phrase picks up again the language of v. 18, thus emphasizing that the inheritance now given to Gentile believers comes through God's free, gracious promise to Abraham, not through the Law. This is also the fulfillment of the gospel that Scripture had proclaimed to Abraham, that all the Gentiles would be blessed in him (v. 8).

REFLECTIONS

Galatians 3:6-29 must be read as a continuous block of argument in order to grasp its overall import. When it is subdivided—as it usually is for liturgical or homiletical purposes—it tends to fall apart into enigmatic fragments. When we read Paul's argument whole, however, its themes come powerfully into focus. Paul is urging the Galatians to understand themselves as heirs of God's promise to Abraham, by virtue of their union with Christ. If they stand firm in a clear-eyed recognition of the blessing they have already received, they will not be seduced into pursuing circumcision as though it were necessary to secure their place among the people of God. In the course of his richly textured argument, Paul develops a number of themes that can stimulate fundamental theological reflection.

1. *The Source of Our Identity.* Our identity is given to us fundamentally through our union with Christ. Paul saw this union as figured forth and enacted in baptism. In baptism we "put on" Christ; we enter into union with him in such a way that all other markers of status and identity fall away into insignificance (3:27-29). Centuries of the practice of infant baptism in the culture of christendom have obscured the dramatic symbolism that the early Christians saw in baptismal initiation. In baptism, the person being baptized confessed the lordship of Jesus Christ over all creation, disrobed to signify the putting off of an entire way of life, was immersed below the water as if undergoing burial (Rom 6:3-5), was raised to a new life, and was clothed in new garments symbolizing the transformation that had occurred. Baptism was a symbolic participation in Christ's death and resurrection, and no one could undergo it without realizing that one life had ended and a new one had begun.

Paul saved his appeal to baptism for the climactic place in the argument of Gal 3:6-29 because it so powerfully embodied what he wanted to say to the Galatians: They were to find their identity in Jesus Christ alone. For one who has been "clothed" with Christ, no further religious observances (such as circumcision or food laws) are necessary in order to be in right standing with God. Our human religious impulse tirelessly seeks new signs and ceremonies that we can use to set ourselves apart from others or to court God's favor. Paul insists that all of that has been put to an end in Christ.

Paul saw the rival Missionaries as pursuing a policy of cultural imperialism—that is, as he saw it, they were trying to impose specifically Jewish identity markers on Gentiles who had already been given a decisive new identity as God's people in Christ. He disapprovingly called the circumcision faction "those whose identity is derived from works of Law" (see the Commentary on 3:10).

Paul's passionate rejection of this kind of ethnic/religious "identity politics" should lead us to reflect carefully on the ground of our own identity. To what extent is our sense of who we are grounded in the gospel of Christ, and to what extent is it determined by other factors? Such questions may lead us to uncomfortable conclusions. In our time there are many movements, even within the church, that seek to define an identity based on race, on national origin, on gender, or on sexual orientation. Such movements are the contemporary analogues of the "circumcision party" within the early church, against which Paul so passionately fought. Against all such determinations of identity, Paul reminds us that we are one with Christ through baptism.

Someone might object that baptism is simply one more religious ritual and that to elevate this one above all other identity-defining practices is just one more manifestation of religious imperialism. Of course, human sinfulness can distort even baptism into a new basis for perverse pride and division, as Paul learned all too well in his dealings with the church at Corinth (1 Cor 1:10-17). The point is, however, that Paul sees baptism not as an end in itself, but as a signifier of our union with Christ, through faith. Galatians 3:26-29 should not be read apart from 3:6-9, in which Paul declares that those whose identity is rooted in faith are Abraham's children. To be rooted in faith and to be "in Christ" are, in Paul's theological vision, synonymous (3:26).

Identity derived from faith is different from all others if and only if the death and resurrection of Jesus really are—as Paul proclaimed—the singular event through which God has chosen to redeem the world. Otherwise, the gospel is merely one more religious system that will serve human pride and ambition. The character of our faith is determined by that decisive event to which it looks.

2. *The Meaning of Faith.* Galatians was Martin Luther's favorite epistle, because he saw in it a compelling expression of the doctrine of justification by faith alone. When we speak of "faith" as a central theme of this letter, however, we must observe carefully how Paul actually uses this concept. The root meaning of πίστις (*pistis*) is "trust" (see the Commentary on 2:16). Abraham is the paradigm of faith because he *trusted* in God's promise. Abraham's faith was not a matter of believing a list of propositions or a system of doctrines about God; rather, it was a matter of primal trust in the bare, direct promise of God to bless him and to give him many descendants. Paul develops this interpretation of Abraham's faith at greater length in Romans 4:

> Hoping against hope, he believed that he would become "the father of many nations." . . . No distrust made him waver concerning the promise of God, but he grew strong in his faith as he gave glory to God, being fully convinced that God was able to do what he had promised. Therefore his faith "was reckoned to him as righteousness." (Rom 4:18, 20-22)

Abraham heard God's word and trusted it. That is the picture of faith that Paul evokes in Gal 3:6-9. This sort of trust is the model for the trust that the Galatians also demonstrated when they believed Paul's proclamation of the good news of the gospel, God's blessing upon them as Gentiles outside the Law, by sheer grace. That is the faith that receives rectification and life, a kind of life that the Law was unable to give (3:11-12). Faith is not a matter of mustering a heroic capacity to believe the odd or the miraculous; it is simply a matter of receiving gratefully a gift that God has chosen to give us, completely without regard to our deserving. It is a matter of reliance on the Word of God as the one truth upon which we stake our lives.

We must beware of becoming infatuated with faith as an aspect of our own subjectivity or religious experience. Protestant preaching has often fallen into the trap of treating faith as a new kind of "work," a human achievement that somehow merits God's approval. On such a distortion, the judgment of William Law is apt: "Suppose one man to rely on his own faith and another to rely on his own works, then the faith of the one and the works of the other are equally the same worthless filthy rags."[178] A careful reading of Gal 3:6-29 provides the corrective for this error. Paul is not interested here in a phenomenological description of faith as a human disposition. Instead, he is interested in telling the story of how faith "came," breaking into the prison of human experience to set us free (3:23-25). Faith is something "revealed" to us as God's deed; it is not merely the illumination of a new human possibility. Karl Barth comments:

> The fact that I live in the faith of the Son of God, in my faith in him, has its basis in the fact that He Himself, the Son of God, first believed for me. . . . the great work of faith has already been done by the One whom I follow in my faith, even before I believe, even if I no longer believe, in such a way that He is always, as Heb 12:2 puts it, the originator and completer (ἀρχηγός καὶ τελειωτής *archēgos kai teleiotēs*) of our faith. . . . His faith is the victory which has overcome the world.[179]

In Gal 3:22-26, *pistis* ("faith") is used by metonymy to refer to the faith(fulness) of Jesus Christ. It refers not primarily to Jesus' own subjective trust in God but rather to the act by which his fidelity to God was embodied: his self-giving death on the cross (2:20), which was the fulfillment of his mission to set humanity free from bondage (3:13, 23 25). Until this revelation of faith through Christ's death, we were imprisoned

178. William Law, cited in A. G. Hebert, "'Faithfulness' and 'Faith,'" *Theology* 58 (1955) 379.
179. K. Barth, *Church Dogmatics* II/2 (Edinburgh: T. & T. Clark, 1957) 559.

under the power of sin. Christ's act for our sake has broken that power, so that God's promised blessing has now been given to us "through the faith(fulness) of Jesus Christ" (3:22; cf. 3:14). To be sure, we who receive that blessing can and should be described as "those who believe" (3:22) or "those whose identity is derived from faith" (3:7, 9) because we look to Christ's crucifixion with the same grateful trust that Abraham displayed toward God's covenant promise. All our talk and preaching about "faith," therefore, must take care to respect the focus of Paul's proclamation on what Jesus has done. Otherwise, faith-talk will turn into one more subtle attempt at human self-affirmation.

3. *Christ Has Liberated Us from Captivity.* It is noteworthy that Paul says nothing at all in Galatians 3 about "forgiveness of sins." The effect of Christ's death is described not in terms of forgiveness but in terms of liberation from captivity. Paul uses two different metaphors to describe the bondage from which Christ has liberated us: Israel's condition of being in exile under the curse pronounced by Deuteronomy (Gal 3:10, 13) and the more general human condition of being imprisoned under the power of Sin (3:22-23). Through his death on a cross, Jesus has set both Jews and Gentiles free from these states of bondage.

For Israel, the exile is ended and the time of God's deliverance has arrived, as shown by the outpouring of the Spirit that God had promised (see the Commentary on 3:14). But Paul has dramatically reworked the meaning of this prophetic vision. In standard Jewish expectation, the time of eschatological deliverance was expected to create an Israel in which the authority of the Law would be restored and honored; indeed, something like this may have been exactly what the rival Missionaries were teaching the Galatians. In Paul's vision, however, there is no question of a return to Torah observance. With the lifting of the Law's curse, the Law's whole system of conditional blessings and curses is consigned to the past. The freedom that Christ gives is the freedom for a community that lives under the Spirit (5:16-26), no longer under the threat of the Law's curse.

For the Gentiles, the power of Sin—pictured in 3:22 as a hostile cosmic power (cf. Rom 6:12-23; 7:13-25)—is broken. Rather than living as captives in a state of ignorance and alienation from God, the Gentiles are now released to a state of freedom and are taken into God's family as children (3:26) who are rectified—that is, received as God's own people, Abraham's children (3:6-9, 26-29).

Paul will develop the implications of this liberation image more fully in chapters 4–5. With regard to the present passage, however, the implication is that our preaching should stress Christ's victory that sets us free. Christians are constantly tempted to slip into new legalisms, rigid systems of law or morality that define—and thus confine—us. Whether the confining system is first-century Pharisaic Judaism, Roman imperial ideology, pre-Reformation Catholic hierarchy, Victorian codes of propriety, capitalist consumerism, patriarchal privilege, or late modern "political correctness," the liberating message of Galatians is the same. Christ's victory is not merely a substitutionary atonement for the forgiveness of sins; rather, Christ's apocalyptic victory breaks the old systems of confinement.

4. *The Spirit as God's Promised Blessing.* Closely related to the previous point is the fact that the promised blessing given to the new community in Christ is "the promise of the Spirit" (3:14; cf. 3:2-5; 4:6-7). In place of the expectation of a promised land (Gen 17:8), Paul speaks of the Spirit as the fulfillment of God's promise to Abraham. (This fact shows that Paul is using the story of Israel's exile and restoration metaphorically.) The "inheritance" now given to the new community of Jews and Gentiles in Christ (3:18, 29) is redefined in terms of the presence of the Spirit that makes them one and assures their status as God's children. In a similar way, our proclamation of the gospel should continue to point to the ways in which we see the Spirit of God at work in our churches as a sign of the inheritance that God has graciously given us.

Although claims about the Spirit's presence are necessarily elusive, Paul's example should embolden us to recognize and celebrate the Spirit's work in our midst.

5. *The Law's Place in the Christian Story.* Paul has developed an argument about the Law that sounds like sheer heresy, if not blasphemy, to devout Jewish ears. In Jewish tradition, the Law was viewed as God's gracious gift, a source of wisdom and life. The interpreter of Galatians should always remember to read this chapter against the backdrop of Ps 19:7-11, which declares that "the law of the LORD is perfect, reviving the soul" and cherishes God's ordinances as "more to be desired . . . than gold, even much fine gold" (NRSV). By contrast, Paul speaks of the Law only as a source of curse or, at best, as a temporary jailkeeper until the coming of Christ. He explicitly denies the lifegiving power of the Law (3:11-12), which the psalmist had extolled. Of all the texts in the New Testament canon, Galatians appears to be the most relentlessly negative in its evaluation of Old Testament Law. Thus this letter can easily give rise to Marcionite teachings that caricature Judaism as a harsh religion of legalism and, therefore, radically reject the Law and the Old Testament.

It is important, therefore, to realize that Paul goes right to the brink of rejecting the Law, but then pulls back decisively (3:21). The Law is not seen as a direct manifestation of God's grace, like the promise to Abraham, but it is assigned an important role in the unfolding of the story of God's redemption of the world through Christ. Even in this most anti-Law letter, Paul is not denying that God gave the Law; rather, he is resisting the demand that Gentile converts be forced to come under the Law's requirement of circumcision. Everything that Paul says must be interpreted within the framework of this specific situation. In Romans, he seeks to give a more diplomatic and balanced account of his understanding of the Law—perhaps in response to some of the criticism and controversy that this earlier polemical letter evoked. Because Christianity has a long and tragic history of violence against Jews and ignorant disparagement of Judaism, the interpreter of Galatians should take care to set Paul's statements about the Law within their proper historical setting as an *intra-Christian* argument about the ways in which the Law should or should not continue to provide direct norms for the life of the church.

We have seen that Paul identifies two purposes for which the Law was given: identifying sin as transgression and restraining sinful behavior in the era prior to the coming of Christ. To what extent do these functions remain valid now that we are no longer subject to the power of the Law? A good case can be made that the Law's diagnostic function remains valuable for the church; the Law continues to teach us that we are in rebellion against a loving God who desires our wholeness. Our sinful behavior, therefore, is to be understood not merely as destructive to human communities but also as transgression against a holy God. Without the Law, we would not have known that. On the other hand, the Law's role as disciplinarian is now decisively revoked by the coming of Christ. We are in a new situation where, according to Paul, we are to live under the guidance of the Spirit, apart from Law (5:13-26). The specific "do's" and "don'ts" of the Torah are no longer regulative for the Christian community. This claim, of course, raises its own problems, which Paul will discuss later in the letter.

Finally, Galatians 3 emphatically excludes two roles that have sometimes been assigned to the Law. First, the Law cannot confer life and righteousness. It was never designed by God for that purpose (3:10-12, 21). It can point toward these ends, but it lacks the power to confer the goals to which it bears witness (cf. Rom 8:1-4). Second, the Law does not "lead us to Christ" (see the Commentary on 3:23-25). There is a venerable history of Christian teaching on the Law as an educative preparation for the gospel, but that teaching is entirely contrary to what Paul says here. The Law does not lead us to Christ; rather, Christ came to us in our imprisonment. The difference is crucial for Christian preaching.

6. *New Creation: Unity in Christ Transforms Social Divisions.* The baptismal formula of Gal 3:28 has been widely cited as a charter for movements seeking social justice and equality. Yet, the use of Paul's words to support egalitarian social programs has been challenged by many interpreters because of evidence elsewhere in Paul's writings that he countenanced the institution of slavery within the church (1 Cor 7:17-24; Col 4:1; and the ambiguous case of the Letter to Philemon) and the subordination of women (1 Cor 11:3-16; 14:34-35; cf. Eph 5:21-33; 1 Tim 2:8-15).[180] Rarely has it been sufficiently appreciated, however, that Paul passionately argues for putting into social practice the abolition of the distinction between Jew and Gentile (see the Commentary on 2:11-21). This suggests that he did not understand the baptismal formula to prescribe merely a spiritual equality before God in a way that had no social implications. Furthermore, the evidence on the other two issues (slavery and male/female relations) is sufficiently ambiguous to suggest that Paul's vision did, in fact, destabilize traditional assumptions about power in a way that had practical implications in his communities. For example, he counseled mutuality in marital sexual relations (1 Cor 7:3-4), and women did prophesy (1 Cor 11:5) and exercise roles of leadership in the mission (Rom 16:1-7; Phil 4:2-3).[181] Whatever we may think in retrospect about the adequacy of Paul's implementation of the vision articulated in the formula, it is hard to deny that he believed the church to be a new community brought into being by the power of God's grace in which old social inequalities were being overturned and transformed (see also 1 Cor 1:18-31).[182]

In interpreting Gal 3:28, we should bear in mind its place within the argument of the letter. Paul is passionately insisting that uncircumcised Gentile Christians are not second-class citizens in the kingdom of God and that they should recognize themselves, just as they are, as "children of God" on an equal footing with Jewish Christians who equally owe their status as rectified children of God to the faithfulness of Jesus Christ. As Paul puts the case in Rom 10:12, "There is no distinction between Jew and Greek; the same Lord is Lord of all and is generous to all who call on him" (NRSV). In support of this argument, Paul appeals to the baptismal formula as the basis on which the Galatians should be acknowledged to share full equality with Jewish Christians as Abraham's heirs. Thus we see clearly that Paul regards the formula as having practical social implications for the life of the church.

In our time, then, our task is analogous to the one that Paul faced. Most of our churches do not face pressure for Gentiles to be circumcised, but we do confront numerous divisions and hostilities between different racial and ethnic groups. Our preaching and our practices must encourage the same reconciliation between (say) black and white Christians that Paul envisioned between "Jew and Greek."

Likewise, we confront continuing controversies about the full participation of women in the "inheritance" and in the life of the church. As we deal with this issue, we may take our cues from Paul and look back also to the formula of Gal 3:28 as an important starting point for our theological reflection. If we do that, it is not hard to see where our reflection will lead. Those who resist the ordination and leadership of women in the church's ministry stand in a role analogous to the rival Missionaries, who sought to reinstitute the distinctions and requirements of the old age before Christ's coming. In the community of the new creation, our oneness in Christ overcomes and delegitimates the distinctions of race, social class, and gender that divided

---

180. For the history of the debates over the use of Paul's letters to address these issues, see W. M. Swartley, *Slavery, Sabbath, War, and Women: Case Issues in Biblical Interpretation* (Scottdale, Pa.: Herald, 1983).

181. For discussion of the evidence, see V. P. Furnish, *The Moral Teaching of Paul: Selected Issues,* rev. ed. (Nashville: Abingdon, 1985) 83-114; E. Schüssler Fiorenza, *In Memory of Her: A Feminist Theological Reconstruction of Christian Origins* (New York: Crossroad, 1983) 205-41; B. Witherington III, *Women in the Earliest Churches,* SNTSMS 59 (Cambridge: Cambridge University Press, 1980); R. B. Hays, *The Moral Vision of the New Testament: Community, Cross, New Creation* (San Francisco: HarperSanFrancisco, 1996) 46-56.

182. Betz comments: "There can be no doubt that Paul's statements have social and political implications of even a revolutionary dimension. The claim is made that very old and decisive ideals and hopes of the ancient world have come true in the Christian community." See Betz, *Galatians,* 190.

us when we were prisoners under the power of Sin. Of course, the practical outworking of this vision of the new creation remains the ongoing task of the church in history as we "eagerly wait for the hope of righteousness" (5:5).

7. *Hearing the Voice of Scripture.* The conviction that the Law's role as a temporary guardian has now ended does not lead Paul to a rejection of the authority of Scripture in the community of faith. Instead, he rereads Scripture with new eyes in the light of God's revelation in Christ and produces fresh and startling interpretations. This is not merely a pragmatic debate strategy, as though he were compelled to answer the Missionaries' arguments by debating them on their own turf. As we see from Paul's other letters, the ongoing dialogue with Scripture is a regular feature of his theological reflection.[183]

In Gal 3:6-29, Paul uses seven explicit quotations from Scripture, and, as we have seen, there are several other important allusions in the background of his argument (an obvious example is Deut 6:4 in Gal 3:20). Some of these passages may have been originally injected into the debate by the Missionaries (Gen 17:8; Lev 18:5; Deut 27:26), but others are surely Paul's own contribution (Gen 12:3; 15:6; Hab 2:4). Two features of Paul's use of Scripture in this section of the letter are particularly noteworthy.

First, Paul reads Scripture as a narrative with a plotline. It is not simply a respository of rules and wise sayings; rather, it tells a story of what God was doing in his dealings with Israel. The promise to Abraham anticipated God's future intention to bless all nations; this promise predated the Law by 430 years; the giving of the Law through the mediation of Moses had the effect of imprisoning everyone under Sin, setting the stage for the advent of Christ; now that Christ has come we have received the inheritance, and it makes no sense to go backward by reinstating the Law. *In order to understand our proper identity and calling, we have to understand this plotline and where we fit into it.* These observations may seem fairly elementary, but in Paul's time it was by no means a foregone conclusion that Scripture should be read in this narrative fashion. Other Jewish interpreters, such as Philo, for example, read these stories as timeless allegories of the soul's quest for transcendence.[184] Paul, by contrast, exemplifies a concern for reading Scripture as a story rooted in history, a story in which we are to find our place. In the church today, we have too often lost this larger view of Scripture's narrative coherence. We read it as a fragmented collection of pericopes or as snippets that turn up in the lectionary, or we open it at random, looking for moral rules or ad hoc spiritual illumination. Paul's example encourages us to see the larger narrative framework.

The second striking feature of Paul's reading of Scripture is that he treats it as a living voice, an agent that speaks and acts. Scripture pre-preached the gospel to Abraham (3:8), Scripture curses (3:10, 13) and blesses (3:8-9), Scripture speaks promises (3:11, 16), and Scripture locked up all things under the power of Sin (3:22). In short, Scripture for Paul is living and active. It has played a key role in God's plan, and its voice continues to be heard in the community of faith. Of course, such descriptions of Scripture's speech and action are metaphorical, but that does not mean that they are not to be taken seriously. For Paul, Scripture forms the matrix within which theological debate and reflection must be conducted, and the crucial task for the community is to hear Scripture's voice rightly. That remains true for the church today, no less than in Paul's time.

---

183. See Hays, *Echoes of Scripture in the Letters of Paul*; "The Conversion of the Imagination: Scripture and Eschatology in 1 Corinthians," *NTS* 45 (1999) 391-412.

184. See, for example, Philo, *On the Migration of Abraham* and *Who Is the Heir of Divine Things?* LCL, trans. F. H. Colson and G. H. Whitaker (Cambridge, Mass.: Harvard University Press, 1932); see also *On Abraham*, LCL, trans. F. H. Colson (Cambridge, Mass.: Harvard University Press, 1935).

GALATIANS 4:1-11, THE FULLNESS OF TIME HAS COME

OVERVIEW

As we have seen, Paul opened his counter-arguments in 3:1-5 with a direct appeal to the Galatians' own experience of receiving the Spirit in response to his proclamation of the gospel. He then turned to an argument from Scripture in 3:6-29, demonstrating that by virtue of their participation in Christ the Galatians are already "Abraham's seed" and, therefore, legitimate heirs of God's promise (which is also identified with the Spirit in 3:14, the only reference to the Spirit in that section of the letter). Now in 4:1-7 he refers

again to their experience of the Spirit as proof that they are children, not just of Abraham, but of God. The Spirit is the sign that they have been adopted into God's family. Paul contrasts this experience of familial relation to God to the Galatians' former state as slaves of cosmic powers and makes the astonishing assertion that, should they place themselves under the Jewish Law, they would be returning to the same state of slavery they had previously known as pagans (4:8-11).

Galatians 4:1-7, We Are Heirs and Children of God

COMMENTARY

Using the image of the Galatians as "heirs" in 3:29 as a point of departure, Paul picks up this imagery again and develops it with specific application to the present situation of the Galatians—and all believers, Jewish and

Gentile alike—now that Christ has come. In some ways, 4:1-7 can be read as a recapitulation of 3:23-29, as Dunn demonstrates:[185]

185. Dunn, *The Epistle to the Galatians*, 210. His table is reproduced here with minor changes.

Figure 2: Parallels Between Gal 3:23-29 and 4:1-7*

3:23-29
(23) Before the coming of faith
    we were held in custody under the Law
    confined until the coming faith should be revealed
(24) The Law was our custodian until
    Christ came . . .
(25) But now that faith has come

we are no longer under a custodian.
(26) For all of you are sons of God . . .
(27) You all were baptized into Christ . . .
(29) So then you are Abraham's seed,
    heirs in accordance with promise.

4:1-7
(1) As long as the heir is a child . . .
(2) he is under guardians and stewards
    until the time set by the father.
(3) As children we were enslaved
    under the elemental forces
(4) But when the fullness of time came,
    God sent his Son . . .
(5) in order to redeem those under the Law.
    in order that we might receive adoption.
(6) God sent the Spirit of his Son . . .
(7) So that you are no longer a slave but a son,
    and if a son, then an heir through God.

* Adapted from Dunn, *The Epistle to the Galatians.* Used by permission of A & C Black.

Paul is not merely repeating himself. He introduces several new elements that apply the inheritance analogy directly to the situation the Galatians now face, and he more explicitly describes the sending of God's Son as a cosmic rescue operation.

4:1-2. Paul continues to set forth a picture based on the metaphor of inheritance. In these verses he describes the situation of a minor (male) heir whose father's will has made provision for his estate to be managed by "guardians and trustees" during the period of the heir's minority. In vv. 3-5, Paul will explain how this picture applies to the situation of the Galatians. The term "heir" (κληρονόμος *klēronomos*) in v. 1 is singular, as in the NIV; the NRSV has made it plural in the interest of inclusive language. These comments will follow the NIV's usage, in order to stay closer to the imagery Paul actually employs.[186]

When Paul says that the minor heir is "no different from a slave," he is employing rhetorical exaggeration, with a view to the application he will develop in vv. 3-5. The heir is, of course, in a very different position from a slave because he is the rightful owner of the property, and he will eventually take charge of it. During the period of his minority, however, he does not have authority over the management of the property, which is in the hands of "guardians and trustees." There has been much scholarly discussion of the precise legal background for Paul's terminology.[187] The former term refers to a legally appointed guardian or tutor, whereas the latter is a general term for "steward" or "administrator." This word, which appears, for example, in a number of Jesus' parables (e.g., Luke 16:1-9), regularly designates a slave charged with oversight and management of a household's affairs. Paul applies the same word metaphorically to himself, as a steward charged by God with responsibility for the church, in 1 Cor 4:1-2. Paul is speaking in general terms here for the purpose of illustration, and there is no point in seeking to pin down precise legal details presupposed by the analogy, which works only loosely in any case. The salient point is that the young heir is "under"

(ὑπό *hypo*) the authority of these guardians; this is the same preposition used in 3:22-25 and in 4:3-5 to refer to being under Sin, under the Law, under the (*paidagōgos*), and under the "elements of the world" (see the Commentary on 4:3, 9).

In Paul's illustration, as in these other cases, the heir's subjection is only temporary. He is subject to the guardians and trustees only "until the time set by the father." The "time set" is a fixed day on which the heir's minority ends and he receives control of the estate. In Roman law, this date was not determined at the discretion of the individual testator. It was fixed by law; the minor was under a tutor until the age of fourteen and then under a "curator" until age twenty-five. Again, however, whether this detail corresponds precisely to the provisions of inheritance law in Paul's culture is beside the point; he is already looking ahead to his application in v. 4, thinking of the fact that it is God who appoints the time for the state of subjection to come to an end. The crucial word here is the preposition "until," which recalls 3:19, 23 and anticipates 4:4. Paul is highlighting the temporary character of the heir's subjection.

4:3. Now Paul applies his illustration. The little parable of the enslaved heir is a figurative depiction of the experience of Paul and his readers. Immediately, we face a crucial question: To whom do the first-person plural pronouns here and in v. 5 refer? Is Paul referring to "we Jews" (as in 2:15-16; 3:13*a*, and probably 3:23-25), or is he now speaking from a perspective that includes his Gentile converts (as in 3:14)? The parallel between v. 3 and vv. 8-9 requires the latter: All humanity was "enslaved" prior to the coming of the Son of God. Paul's inclusion of himself in the class of persons enslaved under the elements may in the first instance be understood as an example of his identification with his Gentile addressees, as in 1 Cor 9:21*a;* however, as we shall see in vv. 8-11, Paul has in mind a more radical analysis of the human plight. The Law itself is among the enslaving "elements"; thus he as Jew shared with the pagan Galatians a condition of slavery from which he needed to be liberated (see the Commentary on 4:8-11).

But this analysis leads to the second crucial problem in v. 3: the meaning of Paul's expression τὰ στοιχεῖα τοῦ κόσμου (*ta stoicheia*

---

186. Paul's extended metaphor presupposes the inheritance customs of his day, in which property would ordinarily be inherited by male offspring.
187. See Betz, *Galatians*, 203-4; Longenecker, *Galatians*, 162-64.

tou kosmou). The NRSV's "the elemental spirits of the world" and the NIV's "the basic principles of the world" represent two different interpretations of this much-contested expression.[188]

The term *stoicheia* can mean "the basics" or "rudimentary principles" of any field of knowledge (see Heb 5:12). If Paul has this meaning in mind here, he is saying, "We were enslaved to basic principles of religion (whether pagan religion or Jewish Law) that we have now outgrown or transcended." On this reading, Paul is saying that the human problem is one of ignorance, and its solution would be a revelation that brings higher knowledge, enabling us to move to maturity. This interpretation, represented by the NIV, has received the support of several recent commentators.[189] There are, however, two serious objections to this reading. First, none of the ancient parallels in which *stoicheia* has the meaning "basic principles" speak of "the basic principles *of the world*." Second, and most telling, Paul does not speak in Gal 4:1-7 of a gradual growth or progression beyond an elementary stage of religion to a more advanced one. He speaks, rather, of an invasion of the world by God's Son to rescue us from a state of slavery to the *stoicheia*.

By far the most common meaning of *stoicheia* in the first century was "the elemental substances from which everything in the natural world is composed"—that is, according to the traditional view, earth, air, fire, and water (e.g., 2 Pet 3:10, 12). Indeed, this is the only meaning attested outside the Pauline letters in this period for the expression *ta stoicheia tou kosmou*.[190] It is not immediately evident how this meaning would be pertinent in Gal 4:3, 9 (but see Martyn's proposal, below).

Later texts, from the second century CE onward, begin to use the expression to refer to "elemental spirits" associated with these four elements. Developing out of this meaning was a tendency to associate these elemental spirits with the heavenly bodies (sun, moon, and stars), whose movements were thought to exercise determinative—and sometimes hostile—control over human life. This is the interpretation represented by the NRSV and supported by some important commentaries.[191] Thus, on this reading, the *stoicheia* can be closely linked with "the cosmic powers of this present darkness . . . the spiritual forces of evil in the heavenly places" (Eph 6:4 NRSV). It is not hard to see how Paul could associate the worship of pagan deities, in the Galatians' former life, with slavery to such celestial powers. The difficulty for this reading, however, emerges in vv. 9-10, when Paul describes the Galatians' turning to observance of Jewish Law as a return to slavery under the *stoicheia*. How could Law-observant worship of the God of Israel possibly be categorized as slavery to the principalities and powers?

In the light of the evidence, Martyn has argued persuasively that the rival Missionaries in Galatia may have sought to convince the Galatians that their worship of pagan divinities was an ill-informed worship of the natural elements (the second meaning of *stoicheia*) that ought to point them to a truer form of religion, exemplified by Abraham, who moved through the contemplation of the heavenly bodies to discern the God who made and ordered them. In support of this suggestion, Martyn cites several impressive parallels from Hellenistic Jewish texts.[192] The point of the Missionaries' evangelistic strategy, then, would be to persuade the Galatians that the Law provided the true understanding of the natural world and the heavenly bodies and, therefore, regulated the calendar of human religious observance in a manner that enabled correct celebration of holy feasts at the proper times; hence, Paul's disparaging reference to observing "special days and months and seasons and years" (v. 10). This would explain why Paul could make the otherwise puzzling claim that coming under the Law would constitute a resubjection to the *stoicheia* (see the Commentary on 4:8-10).

In any case, Paul portrays all humanity as existing in a condition of slavery prior to God's dramatic intervention. That intervention is the theme of vv. 4-7.

4:4-5. The expression "when the fullness of time had come" indicates the apocalyptic

---

188. The definitive discussion of the term is now that of Martyn, *Galatians*, 393-406, on which much of the following interpretation is based.

189. Longenecker, *Galatians*, 165-66; Matera, *Galatians*, 149-50; Williams, *Galatians*, 109-11.

190. See also Col 2:8, 20. The use of the expression there would fit nicely into Martyn's analysis, though Martyn does not treat Colossians in his discussion. See Martyn, *Galatians*, 400-406.

191. E.g., Betz, *Galatians*, 205.

192. See esp. Wis 13:1-5; Philo *On Abraham* 69-70; Josephus *Antiquities of the Jews* 1.155-56.

frame of reference for Paul's thought. God is conceived as having a cosmic timetable and an appointed day (cf. v. 2) to break into humanity's history of misery to bring the promised redemption. (For other such apocalyptic conceptions of the appointed fulfillment of time, see Dan 8:19; 11:35; 1 QpHab 7:2; Mark 1:15; Luke 21:24; Acts 1:7; 3:21; Eph 1:10.) The decision to intervene is God's alone, and the timing is God's alone (cf. Mark 13:32, where it is only the Father who knows the time of appointed deliverance).

This passage shares with Rom 8:3-4 the motif of God's sending the Son to redeem humanity from a state of powerlessness; furthermore, both passages move to a climactic affirmation of the Spirit as a transforming power in the community of those whom the Son has redeemed (see also Rom 8:15-17). The similarity of these passages to John 3:16-17 and 1 John 4:9-10 has encouraged the hypothesis that in Gal 4:4-5 Paul is quoting a confessional "sending formula" that was current in early Christian communities.[193] Several commentators have questioned whether this formula presupposes the heavenly pre-existence of the Son.[194] It is true that the idea of "sending" by itself can be used with reference to God's commissioning of prophets or apostles (e.g., Jer 7:25; Acts 22:21) and need not imply pre-existence. Nonetheless, regardless of the hypothetical origins of the formula, in the light of Phil 2:5-11 (also much debated) and other Pauline expressions of exalted christology (e.g., 1 Cor 8:6), it seems likely that Paul did think of the Son as pre-existent, sent forth from heaven on a rescue mission.

At the same time, two participial phrases give expression to the full humanity of the Son, who is the protagonist in this narrative of redemption. He was "born of a woman, born under Law." The expression "born of a woman" indicates simply that he was human (cf. Job 14:1; Matt 11:11). There is no indication here, or anywhere else, that Paul knew the name of Jesus' mother or that he knew a tradition of Jesus' virgin birth. The fact that Jesus was "born under Law" means that he was a Jew. Further, it means that he found

himself under the same confining custody of the Law that Paul has already described in 3:23—just as the heir in 4:2 was under guardians and trustees.

It is tempting to read Paul's narrative in counterpoint with the parable of the wicked tenants (Mark 12:1-12), in which the vineyard owner sends a beloved son to reclaim an inheritance that is being badly managed by abusive administrators, who say of the son, "This is the heir; come, let us kill him" (NRSV). Almost certainly Paul is not referring to this parable, but—if he is quoting a confessional tradition in vv. 4-5—the motif of God's sending the Son may have its roots in Jesus' parable, as remembered and interpreted by the community after his death and resurrection. Whatever one might make of these parallels, however, it is clear that Paul does not have a christological allegory in mind in vv. 1-2, as v. 3 makes clear; the heir in his analogy stands not for Christ (despite 3:16) but for humanity enslaved under the *stoicheia.*

The fact that God's Son was born under subjection to the Law is crucial to his mission, which was to "redeem [ἐξαγοράσῃ/ *exagorasē*] those under Law." The verb refers to emancipation from slavery, with overtones of paying the price to purchase the slave's freedom (cf. 1 Cor 6:19*b*-20). This is the same verb that Paul used in 3:13, the only other place in his letters that the word occurs. The link makes it clear that the Son achieved his rescue mission by taking the Law's curse on himself in his death on the cross; in order for him to do that, it was necessary that he be born as one of the people of Israel, under the Law. Although the cross is not explicitly mentioned in v. 5, it would be misleading to suppose that Paul here thinks of a redemption achieved solely through the incarnation of the Son as opposed to through his death.[195] Paul did not compartmentalize confessional statements in that fashion. Galatians 3:13 and 4:4-5 are two summarizations of the same story, and the action of "redemption" alluded to in 4:5 has already been more fully narrated in the earlier passage.

If v. 5*a* refers to Christ's redemption of Israel from the Law's curse, then the second clause of the verse refers to the rectification of Gentiles, made possible by Christ's

193. Betz, *Galatians: A Commentary on Paul's Letter to the Churches in Galatia,* 205-9, with other literature cited there.

194. E.g., Dunn, *The Epistle to the Galatians,* 215; see also Dunn's *Christology in the Making: A New Testament Inquiry into the Origins of the Doctrine of the Incarnation* (Philadelphia: Westminster, 1980) 38-44.

195. Betz, *Galatians,* 207-8.

redemptive death.[196] They are now adopted into God's family. (This is the simple meaning of the noun υἱοθεσία [*huiothesia*], rightly translated as "adoption" by the NRSV but given a needlessly complicated paraphrase in the NIV; for other uses of the term, see Rom 8:15, 23; 9:4; Eph 1:5.) This clause is closely parallel to 3:14*a*, "in order that in Christ Jesus the blessing of Abraham might come to the Gentiles." The fact that Paul now speaks of "adoption" shows that he has moved beyond the framework of his analogy in vv. 1-2, where he spoke of one who stands to receive an inheritance by birth. The Gentiles, by contrast, are embraced within God's grace as adopted children. The idea is similar to the point Paul makes in Rom 11:17-24, using the metaphor of the Gentiles as wild olive branches grafted onto a cultivated olive tree. God's mercy has called a people "not from the Jews only but also from the Gentiles" (Rom 9:24 NRSV). The vision of the Gentiles as adopted into God's family through the death of Christ is elegantly articulated in a passage in Ephesians that can be read as a commentary on Gal 4:5*b*:

So then, remember that at one time you Gentiles by birth, called "the uncircumcision" by those who are called "the circumcision"—a physical circumcision made in the flesh by human hands—remember that you were at that time without Christ, being aliens from the commonwealth of Israel, and strangers to the covenants of promise, having no hope and without God in the world. But now in Christ Jesus you who once were far off have been brought near by the blood of Christ. . . . So then you are no longer strangers and aliens, but you are citizens with the saints and also members of the household of God. (Eph 2:11-13, 19 NRSV)

At the same time, Paul's adoption metaphor may have another nuance as well. In contrast to God's own Son, all other human beings, including Jewish believers, enter God's family only by adoption. Augustine saw this point clearly in commenting on this passage: "He says *adoption* so that we may clearly understand that the Son of God is unique. For we are sons of God through his generosity and the condescension of his mercy, whereas he is Son by nature, sharing the same divinity with the Father."[197] Thus, even if the adoption metaphor initially envisions God's acceptance of Gentiles, it must be expanded to include God's adoption of Jewish believers as well, as suggested by the parallel with 3:26: "in Christ Jesus, you are *all* children of God *through faith*," i.e., not through the Law.

Thus by the end of v. 5 Paul has completed the first phase of his explanation of the inheritance analogy: God has liberated us from slavery to the *stoicheia* by sending the Son to invade our prison and set us free, thus bringing Jews and Gentiles alike into God's family.

4:6. But Paul is not quite finished developing his theme. He points again to the Galatians' experience of receiving the Spirit, just as he had done at the beginning of his counter-argument in 3:1-5. This time, however, he does not just point to the experience; he gives it a fuller theological interpretation within the story of God's mission of rescue and adoption. The adoption was in one sense "legally" accomplished in Jesus' death and resurrection, but that is not the end of the story. God has provided experiential confirmation of our adoption by pouring out the Spirit (see the Commentary on 3:14). God not only sent the Son into the world, but also "because you are sons, God sent the Spirit of his Son into our hearts." This is the sign and pledge of our new status as God's children. (The NRSV, by opting for the inclusive-language translation "children" in v. 6*a*, loses the connection in the Greek text between "sons" and "Spirit of his Son"; the sense of the sentence is better conveyed in the NIV, so long as we understand, in the light of 3:28, that "sons" is a metaphor that includes both men and women in God's family.) The shift from second to first person ("*you* are sons . . . into *our* hearts") in this verse is awkward, and it has predictably created problems in the manuscript tradition (see the NRSV footnote). Williams is probably right that by shifting momentarily into the second person Paul "pointedly singles out the recipients of the letter, the Gentiles of Galatia,"[198] since it is their status as "sons" that is under dispute.

196. If Paul is quoting a confessional formula, was it originally coined in a Gentile congregation? This would explain the shift from "those under the Law" to "we" in this verse.

197. Augustine *Epistle to the Galatians* 30 [1B.4.4-5], PL 35:2126. Cited in Edwards, *Galatians, Ephesians, Philippians*, 56.

198. Williams, *Galatians*, 111.

Christian interpreters have long struggled over the narrative sequence implied in this verse, which seems to make the sending of the Spirit a second action subsequent to adoption as children. It is important to realize that Paul is not describing here the life history of the individual believer; instead, he is narrating God's redemptive invasion of an enslaved world. Within the narrative, the sending of the Son must come first; once he has completed his mission through his death on the cross, then the Spirit can be sent to those who are adopted by virtue of this liberating death that demolished the prison walls. In terms, however, of the experience of individual believers, the sending of the Spirit into our hearts is a fundamental aspect of conversion/initiation, as the parallel to 3:26-29 shows (see Fig. 2, p. 1108). In other words, Paul is in no way describing a "second blessing" experience for those who earlier had experienced justification. The sending of the Spirit is God's action that both effects and confirms our entrance into God's family.

The motif of God's sending forth the Spirit is reminiscent of some Jewish traditions about the sending of divine wisdom from the throne of God. For instance, in Wis 9:17, Solomon inquires of God, "Who has learned your counsel, unless you have given wisdom and sent your holy spirit from on high?" (NRSV; see also Wis 9:10). In this verse, however, Paul is speaking of the Spirit not as a source for understanding God's will and wisdom but as an intensely experienced confimation of God's gracious embrace. When the Spirit is sent into our hearts, Paul says, it cries out, "Abba, Father." We should not understand this as a reference to recitation of the Lord's prayer; rather, this is the language of ecstasy, as we can see from Paul's use of the vivid participle "crying out" (κρᾶζον *krazon*). It is sometimes suggested that the Aramaic word "Abba" was uttered by "baptizands as they rise from the water,"[199] as a grateful acknowledgment of their new status as God's children. On the other hand, it is also suggested that the use of "Abba" in spirit-inspired prayer was conscisly modeled after the prayer language of Jesus, "an echo of Jesus' own prayer style" (cf. Mark 14:36).[200] Either way, Paul's point is that the Spirit is a powerful presence in the hearts of the Galatians, enabling or impelling them to cry out to the Father of Jesus Christ as their own Father.

4:7. Paul draws this narrative of inheritance to a climactic and triumphant conclusion, assuring the Galatians of their new status in Christ. By sending the Son into the world, God has liberated them and transformed them from slaves into sons. Since they are now sons of God (cf. 3:26), they are surely now heirs (cf. 3:29). Of this truth, the presence of the Spirit in their midst is the decisive confirmation. The expression "an heir, through God" (NRSV, translating literally) is odd, because God is elsewhere described as

199. Martyn, *Galatians*, 391-92.
200. Dunn, *The Epistle to the Galatians*, 221.

Figure 3: Parallels Between Gal 4:4-6 and 3:13-14*

Gal 4:3-6	*Gal 3:13-14*

(4) God sent forth his Son,
     born of a woman,
     born under Law,	

(5) in order that he might redeem
     those under Law,
     in order that we might receive adoption.
	(13) Christ redeemed
	     us from the curse of the Law
	     by becoming a curse for us . . .

	(14) in order that the blessing of Abraham
	     might come to the
	     Gentiles through Christ Jesus,
	     in order that we might receive the

(6) God sent forth the Spirit of his Son into our hearts. . . .	promise of the Spirit through the faith.

*Adapted from R. B. Hays, *The Faith of Jesus*, SBLDS 56 (Chico, Calif.: Scholars Press, 1983) 118.

the source, not the medium, of the inheritance (the NIV again tries to avoid the awkwardness by paraphrasing). Some copyists, feeling the difficulty here, produced various theological corrections, including the reading "an heir of God through Christ" (NRSV note).

The sequence of thought in vv. 6-7 is exactly paralleled by Rom 8:15-17: Starting from slavery (and fear), we have received the Spirit that enables us to cry, "Abba, Father!"

This Spirit bears witness of our new status as children of God and heirs. The fact that Paul repeats this argument in Romans shows that it is not merely a contingent response to the situation in Galatia—or, more precisely, that if it was a contingent response to that situation, he retained it as a central element in his account of the gospel. (See Reflections at 4:8-11.)

Galatians 4:8-11, No Turning Back

COMMENTARY

4:8. After the jubilant rhetorical climax of v. 7, Paul adopts a more sober tone again as he broods over the present peril of the Galatians. During their years of living as pagans, they "did not know God"—a typical Jewish judgment of Gentiles (see Ps 79:6). Paul repeats the reminder that during this period of ignorance they were enslaved to "beings that by nature are not gods" (cf. v. 3). This expression shows that Paul does not think of the στοιχεῖα (*stoicheia*) merely as rudimentary religious principles that have now been superseded. Instead, they are personified forces that once exercised hostile dominion over the lives of his readers. Paul elsewhere acknowledges the reality and presence of spiritual powers in the world, called by various names, such as "gods," "lords," "demons," and "rulers of this age" (1 Cor 2:8; 8:5-6; 10:20-21). Such powers are no threat to the sovereignty of the one God; indeed, through Christ, God will ultimately destroy or subdue them (1 Cor 15:23-28; Phil 2:10-11; cf. Col 1:15-20; 2:15). But, because we live in the time between the times, when all things are not yet made subject to God, these not-gods continue to exercise power and to oppress and enslave those who will serve them. Gentiles who worship idols, therefore, are under the domain of these enslaving powers.

4:9. Consequently, Paul poses an incredulous question designed to expose the absurdity of the Galatians' present infatuation with the Law, by linking the Law-observant life to their former state of slavery. The artful wording of v. 9*a* illuminates the deep theological syntax of Paul's gospel: "Now, however, that

you have come to know God—or rather to be known by God. . . ." The self-correction is an artful way of calling attention to the theological "ungrammaticality" of any claim that we as finite creatures can save ourselves by attaining a higher knowledge of God. (Perhaps the Missionaries were offering the Galatians a non-gospel along these lines; cf. 1:6-7.) The Galatians have entered a new world not because of some epistemological advance of their own, but because God, in elective love, has now "known" them (see the close parallel in 1 Cor 8:2-3; cf. 1 Cor 13:12). For the OT background of God's "knowing" of Israel, see, e.g., Amos 3:2: "You only have I known of all the families of the earth."

Having been known by God, Paul asks them, "How can you turn back again to the weak and beggarly *stoicheia*?" Their turning to observe the Law would be a conversion, to be sure, but a wrongheaded one. The verb "turn" (ἐπιστρέφω *epistrephō*) is the same word characteristically used to describe a repentant person turning back to God or the conversion of Gentiles to serve the one true God of Israel. Paul uses this verb, for instance, of the pagan Thessalonians' response to his preaching of the gospel: "You turned [ἐπεστρέψατε *epestrepsate*] to God from idols to serve a living and true God" (1 Thess 1:9). Thus the action that the Galatians are contemplating would be a conversion in reverse—a reversion to their former state of slavery.

This is perhaps the most stunning sentence in this entire confrontational letter. Paul is suggesting that Judaism's holy observances are, in effect, no different from paganism's worship of earthly elements. He could hardly have said anything more calculated to arouse the outrage of the Missionaries, but the rhetorical shock value of his question is surely calculated. He is trying to jolt the Galatians out of the hypnotic spell of the Law-gospel.

Paul refers to the *stoicheia* as "weak and beggarly." This is a paradox, for he also attributes to them the power to enslave their adherents. Why, then, does he also call them weak? It is a stock theme of Jewish polemic against idolatry that idols are lifeless and impotent (e.g., Isa 46:3-5). Martyn cites the satirical depiction of the idolator in Wis 13:18-19:[201]

For health he appeals to a thing that is weak;
for life he prays to a thing that is dead;

.   .   .   .

he asks strength of a thing whose
hands have no strength. (NRSV)

This passage may be particularly significant if, indeed, Wis 13:1-5 supplies the link in Paul's mind between pagan worship and "the elements." This may be part of the explanation for Paul's disparaging reference to the weakness of the *stoicheia*. Insofar as they have any power at all, it is the power of illusion. They have already been defeated by the Son of God's victorious incursion. But Paul may also be thinking of the Law in particular as "weak." He has already noted that the Law does not have the power to give life (3:21). This is a consistent motif in Paul's critique of the Law. Particularly pertinent is Rom 8:3, in which he describes the Law as powerless because "it was weak through the flesh," and then goes on to say that God, by sending the Son, has solved the problem that the weak Law failed to solve. The connection of ideas here is very close to Gal 4:4-9.

4:10. Paul goes on with a descriptive statement about practices that the Galatians have adopted in his absence; this description provides the key to understanding the apparently outrageous implications of Paul's equating of Law with the *stoicheia*. The Galatians show themselves to be coming back under the sway of the *stoicheia* by adopting a pattern of life

governed by fixed calendrical observances. The observances of the Jewish liturgical calendar were calibrated to the motions of the sun and moon (sabbath, new-moon festivals, the Day of Atonement, Passover, and other festivals). Jewish sources from the Second Temple period show that there was heated controversy between advocates of lunar and solar calendrical systems over the proper way of keeping times and seasons. For example, *Jubilees,* a text championing the solar calendar, insists that "the Lord set the sun as a great sign upon the earth for days, sabbaths, months, feast (days), years, sabbaths of years, jubilees, and for all the (appointed) times of the years" (*Jub.* 2:9). Equally interesting as background to this verse is a passage from *1 Enoch:*

True is the matter of the exact computation of that which has been recorded . . . concerning the luminaries, the months, the festivals, the years and the days. . . . He has the power in the heaven both day and night so that he may cause the light to shine over the people—sun, moon, and stars, and all the principalities of heaven which revolve in their (respective) circuits. These are the orders of the stars which set in their (respective) places seasons, festivals and months. (*1 Enoch* 82:7-9)[202]

Thus it is quite likely that the Missionaries would have impressed on the Galatians the importance not only of being circumcised but also of keeping the sabbaths and feasts at the proper astronomically determined times. If so, it would make sense for Paul to assert that the Galatians' newfound interest in observing Jewish festivals was leading them back into bondage under the power of the astral elements.

If that is the case, why does Paul not refer explicitly to "festivals, new moons, or sabbaths" as in Col 2:16? Why, instead of these specific references to Jewish observances, does he use the generic description, "days and months and seasons and years"? He may be alluding to the biblical creation story, which says that the lights were placed in the dome of the sky on the fourth day of creation "for signs and for seasons and for days and years"

---

201. Martyn, *Galatians,* 411.

202. These passages are cited by Dunn, whose entire discussion of Gal 4:10 is to be consulted for much helpful information. See Dunn, *The Epistle to the Galatians,* 227-29. Cf. Martyn, *Galatians,* 412-18.

(Gen 1:14 NRSV). If this text no longer provides a warrant, as it did in Judaism, for observing special times and seasons, it can only be for the same reason that there is no longer "male and female" in Christ: The new creation has broken in. By using these generic terms, however, rather than the specific terminology of the Jewish liturgical calendar, Paul facilitates his provocative linking of the Law with the *stoicheia*. When one strips away the specific terminology of the Jewish festivals, Paul suggests, one sees that they are in essence just another kind of nature religion! He is saying, in effect, "You used to be in slavery to the cosmic elements; if you come under the Law, you will be back under the control of these same cosmic forces." Here again we see Paul using skillful, explosive, high-risk rhetoric.

4:11. Finally, after expressing his puzzlement that the Galatians could want to return to enslavement, Paul throws up his hands in anxious exasperation. He is afraid that all his work of preaching and teaching in their midst will, in fact, be subverted and come to nothing. A literal translation of his words here reads, "I am afraid for you, lest somehow I have labored in vain for you." The verb "labored" (κοπιάω *kopiaō*) is a term that Paul often uses to describe his work in spreading the gospel (1 Cor 4:12; 15:10; Col 1:29; cf. 1 Tim 4:10). For an especially close parallel, see Phil 2:16: "It is by your holding fast to the word of life that I can boast on the day of Christ that I did not run in vain or labor in vain" (NRSV). The word "in vain" (εἰκῇ *eikē*) also reminds us of Gal 3:4. Paul contemplates the distressing prospect that the churches he founded in Galatia might abandon the gospel and that his work will be wasted. The reference to his work among the Galatians provides a transition to the next section (4:12-20), in which he recalls his earlier time with them and appeals to them to remember their special relationship with him.

REFLECTIONS

1. Enslavement as the fundamental human condition: Is it true? Paul characterizes life outside the sphere of Christ's power as a condition of bondage to powers that hold us captive. For many readers of Galatians, the description will seem apt: Those who suffer from addiction to drugs, alcohol, or compulsive behaviors often confess that they are in the clutches of a destructive force that overpowers them. Those who live in poverty or under political oppression know all too well that they are pawns of a system that is too powerful to fight. For all who live in such circumstances, Paul's proclamation comes as joyous good news: God has sent Jesus to share our plight and to loose our chains. Likewise, many who have lived under the grip of empty secular philosophies have found in the gospel a release from the enslaving power of materialism and hedonism—the usual forms that paganism takes in our time. For those who have experienced a transformation from darkness into light, Paul's metaphor of being redeemed from slavery will seem apt, indeed.

But what of those who live ordinary, respectable lives in conditions of prosperity in a free democratic political order? They have never knowingly worshiped false gods, nor have they known overt oppression. Will they find Paul's talk of enslavement to be either exaggerated or irrelevant? Like Jesus' interlocutors in the Fourth Gospel, they may say, "We are descendants of Abraham and have never been slaves to anyone" (John 8:33 NRSV). How does Paul's message speak to such hearers? The interpreter of this text may find an important clue in Paul's identification with the previously pagan Galatians. He insists that he—along with his Jewish compatriots—was enslaved under the στοιχεῖα (*stoicheia*) just as they were. All humanity, apart from Christ, is bound together in a solidarity of servitude. Even the most religiously devout—indeed, perhaps especially they—are entangled in subtle forms of bondage. One sees this only in retrospect, only in the light of the cross. This is a sweeping proclamation that levels all the distinctions we love to make between ourselves and others.

Thus the single message that we were all slaves and that all are now equally redeemed through Christ's death will come to different hearers with quite different impacts. For those who know their need, it is a word of hope and comfort; for those who fancy themselves free and autonomous, it is an offense and a challenge to reevaluate their true condition. Just as the Missionaries were no doubt riled by Paul's words, so also the contemporary religious reader may find a stumbling block in Paul's apocalyptic picture of redemption.

2. An apocalyptic picture it is, for according to this passage—which aptly summarizes the overall message of the letter—we are rescued from bondage by a divine act of intervention. In the fullness of time, God sent the Son into the world to redeem us. Everything, therefore, depends on God's timing, God's initiative, and God's powerful act of deliverance. The Son did not come to give us better information about God and thereby to lead us progressively to a knowledge of the truth; rather, the Son came to die for us and set us free (cf. 3:13-14). Consequently, any preaching that trumpets "humanity come of age" or implies an evolutionary view of Christianity as a more advanced form of religion has totally misconstrued Paul's message. The misunderstanding is perhaps encouraged by Paul's figurative illustration about a minor heir who eventually receives an inheritance. As we have seen, however, the illustration is being used to make two points: The Galatians used to be in slavery, and that slavery was only a temporary state, abolished by God's act of deliverance at a time appointed by God. There is actually some tension between the figurative story and Paul's application of it; therefore, the emphasis in preaching on the text should be on Paul's application (4:3-7) rather than on the illustration (4:1-2). Anyone who starts with 4:1-2 and interprets the passage to speak of a human development toward higher knowledge or faith has twisted the text.

3. The rhetorical climax of the passage comes in 4:6-7, as Paul describes the experience of the Spirit in the hearts of the Galatians. The Spirit-inspired utterance acclaiming God as "Abba" is the sign confirming that they now enjoy an intimacy with God that comes only through being part of God's family. They have been adopted by God and, therefore, enjoy all that rightfully belongs to God's children.

Once again, as in 3:1-5, we see that Paul does not try to convince the Galatians that they possess the Spirit; rather, the Spirit is the datum from which Paul argues. The Spirit is palpably, audibly present in their midst, and it serves as proof of their identity as "sons of God." Since this designation was reserved in the Old Testament for Israel (see the Commentary on 3:26), Paul is affirming that the Gentile Galatians have now entered covenant relation with God as members of God's family. (Here as throughout 3:1–5:1 he is arguing that they need not undergo circumcision to secure this status.) At the same time, in view of Paul's radical analysis of universal human bondage, it should be clearly understood that 4:6-7 does not suggest any privileged status for Jewish believers. They, like the Gentile Galatians, are adopted children. Augustine perceptively suggests that it is precisely for this reason that Paul has reported the spirit-inspired cry "Abba, Father" in both Aramaic and Greek: "Now we see that he has elegantly, and not without reason, put together words from two languages signifying the same thing because of the whole people, which has been called from Jews and Gentiles into the unity of faith."[203] If we are right in seeing this cry to God the Father as a baptismal experience, then it is the common ground for all believers; their identity as God's children and their unity in Christ are both confirmed by the Spirit in their hearts.

4. In our time, it is necessary to reflect carefully on the image of God as "Father" in this passage,[204] for some theologians have argued that this image reinforces

---

203. Augustine *Galatians* 31 [IB.4.6], cited in Edwards, *Galatians, Ephesians, Philippians,* 57.
204. For a full, theologically perceptive discussion of the issues, see Marianne Meye Thompson, *The Promise of the Father: Jesus and God in the New Testament* (Louisville: Westminster/John Knox, 2000).

oppressive patriarchal social structures. Furthermore, it is sometimes suggested that Paul's "Father" language excludes or alienates those whose own human fathers have been cruel or absent. In response to these concerns, three points should be kept clearly in mind by the interpreter of Gal 4:6.

First, the Jewish and Christian theological traditions, interpreted rightly, have not understood God as gendered: God, who dwells in unapproachable light, transcends such anthropomorphic categories. One consequence of Israel's prohibition of making idols and artistic depictions of God is that God cannot be crudely rendered as male or female. The New Testament's "Father" imagery must be interpreted with deference to this fundamental rule of theological grammar. God—contrary to the theories of Freud and Feuerbach—is not merely a projection of our human fathers, real or fantasized. Instead, human fatherhood is a distant and broken approximation of the true fatherhood that we learn about in Scripture's story of God's creative and loving care for us. Thus the image of God as Father provides the norm by which all human conceptions of fatherhood may be judged and healed.

Second, the consistent function of Paul's use of the image of God as Father is to emphasize that God is the giver of a promised inheritance. Thus the "Father" language highlights God's generous and loving provision for a beloved people. As Marianne Meye Thompson writes, "Father will become a dysfunctional metaphor if we insist on the form of the term without lodging it in the biblical narrative of God's faithfulness, care and provision and if we abstract it from the particular promises made to and through Jesus, the Son, in whom and through whom the faithful have their inheritance."[205]

Third, because the promised inheritance provided by God the Father has now been graciously extended to Gentiles in Christ, the "fatherhood" of God serves as a basis for Paul to assert our common belonging to God's family. Jews and Gentiles alike have been "adopted" by God's elective grace and, therefore, can now address the one God as Father. In Gal 4:6, the cry, "Abba, Father," serves to confirm our status as God's children and thereby to bring reassurance of the freedom and blessings that we enjoy. Thus there is no distinction within God's adoptive family, and we should receive one another as brothers and sisters.

These are the central themes that should be developed in any homiletical reflection on the Father image in this passage. Paul is not reinforcing some authoritarian claim about God or about church hierarchy. Rather, he is assuring the Galatians that they can resist the authoritarian claims of the Missionaries precisely because their status as God's children is already confirmed by the Spirit.

All of this suggests that interpretation of the passage should celebrate a joyous confidence in our relation with God and with one another. This is not a relation grounded merely in our common humanity; it is a relationship created by the Spirit of Christ (4:6) in the community of baptized believers who have now been "known by God" (4:9). Within that community, to address God as "Father" is not to claim sentimental intimacy, but rather to acknowledge God as the giver of blessings and the ground of our unity.

5. The trouble is that even those who have received the Spirit can—perplexingly—fall back into slavery. We can make choices that turn us away from the grace of God to embrace once again our former state of bondage. We may forget that we are living in the fullness of time and relapse into living as though God had not sent the Son to set us free. Therefore, Paul ends this section of the letter with a rebuke (4:8-11). Interpreters who seek to hear the text's message will not fail to hear a word of warning for the church in our time also.

The full force of Paul's message comes through when we realize that the Galatians were not relapsing into paganism as such. They were considering a step that was

205. Thompson, *The Promise of the Father*, 132.

presented to them as a higher and more spiritual form of the gospel that they had already accepted through Paul's preaching. They were not rejecting the gospel but seeking to improve upon it. But Paul diagnoses the circumcision gospel as a step back into human religiosity. There is no way, he insists, to add more deluxe or advanced features to the gospel of the cross. In 4:10, therefore, he links Judaism to pagan religion by positing a phenomenological parallelism between Judaism's observance of a calendar of holy feasts and the pagan veneration of the natural and celestial worlds. (This is Paul in his most "radical Protestant" mode. Elsewhere he is less unremitting on the question of feasts; see Rom 14:5-6 and the reference to Pentecost in 1 Cor 16:8.)

In our time, few Christians will be inclined to regard Christian faith as a preliminary step toward the keeping of Jewish Law and festivals, but there are many other forms of "spirituality" being marketed as more refined understandings of religion that somehow go beyond the primitive particularity of Paul's gospel. Some of these spiritualities claim to be Christian, and others do not. Many books on "New Age" religion now flooding popular bookstores exemplify this tendency. From the prophetic Pauline point of view, these "New Age" approaches to spirituality are "weak and beggarly" attempts to manipulate God or to find God within oneself; therefore, all of them would simply lead back into slavery to the elements of the natural world. That world is God's good creation, but when human beings worship the creation—including the human self— rather than the Creator, they fall into blindness (Rom 1:18-25) and slavery. Most of all, such false worship leads into pathetic fixation on our own spirituality rather than on what God has done once and for all through Jesus Christ.

Paul looks at the Galatians with incredulity. They have been rescued from slavery to the elements of nature by Jesus Christ, and now they are "turning back" to slavery again (4:9). It is as though he is watching a bizarre and tragic film in which an abused adolescent, having been rescued from the clutches of the villain, spurns the rescuer and falls into another abusive relationship. Paul implores the Galatians to recognize what time it is: The fullness of time for redemption has come. Therefore, they must not run the film backward, not retrogress to an earlier sequence; instead, they should accept the freedom God has given them.

The task of the preacher working with this text is to reflect deeply on the ways in which our congregations today unaccountably reject God's gift of adoption and liberation, choosing instead familiar destructive patterns of life and religiosity. Then, after identifying such analogies and patterns, our next task is to reproclaim the good news of 4:3-7: God has sent the Son to set us free and has given us the Spirit as a sign that we are children and heirs of God.

GALATIANS 4:12-20, AN APPEAL TO RESTORE A RUPTURED RELATIONSHIP

COMMENTARY

Paul now makes an appeal of a different kind by reminding the Galatians of their earlier warm relationship with him. He passionately urges them not to forsake the bond that they once shared. In the course of this argument, he unfavorably characterizes the motives of the rival Missionaries and employs a striking metaphor, comparing himself to a mother in childbirth. He concludes the section with a wish that he could be present with the Galatians in person, not merely through the medium of a letter.

This unit is notoriously difficult to interpret. There are three reasons for its difficulty: (1) Paul is emotionally agitated as he writes, and the discussion is somewhat disjointed;

(2) he alludes briefly to events well known to the Galatians but unknown to us; (3) he employs rhetorical *topoi* and conventional expressions that are unfamiliar to us. Taken together, these factors—especially the second—require us to do some guesswork in order to read the passage. Some questions here can never be resolved with certainty. Still, the overall point is clear: Paul, like an aggrieved mother, sees his children going astray and implores them to remember their birth and early upbringing.

4:12. For the first time in the letter, Paul addresses the Galatians with a direct imperative. This imperative is, however, enigmatic. In what way does Paul want the Galatians to be like him? Paul has deliberately formulated his directive as a paradox: Because he has previously become like the Galatians, they should now become like him.

Elsewhere, Paul frequently presents himself as an example to be imitated (1 Cor 4:16; 11:1; Phil 3:17; 1 Thess 1:6; 2:14; 2 Thess 3:7, 9). This may strike some readers today as strangely immodest, but in the ancient world it was commonplace. The philosopher or moral teacher was expected to provide a model for followers to emulate, because wisdom was embodied in a way of life. In most of Paul's imitation passages, he urges his readers to be conformed to Christ's example of self-sacrificial suffering for the sake of others, as reflected in the apostle's own conduct.

In 4:12, though, Paul gives the imitation motif a different twist. When he says, "I have become as you are," he is referring to his own decision to reject the practices of Torah observance and live like a Gentile. His reason for this decision is explained in 1 Cor 9:21: "To those outside the Law I became as one outside the Law . . . so that I might win those outside the Law" (NRSV). For the sake of his mission as apostle to the Gentiles, he "tore down" the barriers between Jew and Gentile (2:18) and adopted, in effect, a Gentile way of life. Earlier in the letter he has narrated the outworking of this decision in his account of the controversy at Antioch; he ate with Gentiles and took a stand against other Jewish Christians who refused to do so (2:11-14).

Ironically, the Galatians—the Gentiles whose non-Law-observant way of life Paul had adopted—were now starting to take

on Jewish Law observance. Paul, therefore, appeals to them passionately ("I beg you") to halt this course of action and to imitate him in living a life that is not subject to the Law.

If the Galatians persist in coming under the Law, not only will they be returning to slavery, but also they will inflict a wrong on Paul by undoing his apostolic work (v. 11). In the past, the Galatians never inflicted injury on him, as he reminds them in v. 12*b*. This reminder belongs, as Betz has suggested, to a cluster of motifs in the passage that echo common Hellenistic ideas about friendship.[206] It was a commonplace maxim of Hellenistic philosophy that friends can have confidence that they will do no harm to one another.

4:13-14. In fact, when Paul first came to the Galatians' communities, they had received him gladly, even though he was enduring physical suffering. Far from wronging him, they took him in and accepted the gospel that he brought them.

The events to which Paul alludes in this verse remain concealed in the mists of history. He says that it was because of "weakness of the flesh" that he first proclaimed the gospel to them. This has usually been interpreted (as in the NIV) as a reference to some sort of illness, but the NRSV's more general translation is closer to the meaning of the Greek text. A good case can be made that Paul is referring to the scars and injuries that he sustained through persecution (cf. 6:17; Acts 14:19; 2 Cor 6:4-5; 11:23-25).[207] This hypothesis fits well with the suggestion that the visible portrayal of the crucifixion to which Paul refers in 3:1 may have been in fact a display of his own wounds, which he later calls "the marks of Jesus" (6:17). Verse 13 may be correlated in some way with Paul's reference in 2 Cor 12:7 to a "thorn in the flesh," through which he came to learn that God's power is "made perfect in *weakness*" (ἀσθένεια *astheneia*, 2 Cor 12:9)—the same word that appears here. Contrary to popular supposition, this "thorn in the flesh," rather than referring to some sort of chronic illness, may also be

206. Betz, *Galatians,* 220-37.

207. A. J. Goddard and S. A. Cummins, "Ill or Ill-Treated? Conflict and Persecution as the Context of Paul's Original Ministry in Galatia (Galatians 4:1.12-20)," *JSNT* 52 (1993) 93-126. In support of this interpretation they cite a number of the Church Fathers, such as Chrysostom, Theodore of Mopsuestia, Theodoret of Cyrus, and Augustine, as well as Thomas Aquinas and Martin Luther (95n. 7).

directly linked to the effects of persecution, as 2 Cor 12:10 suggests.

Whatever the reason, Paul's physical condition required him to travel to Galatia (to recuperate from being flogged, beaten, or stoned?), with the result that he brought the gospel to the Galatians for the first time. Others may have beaten him up, but the Galatians received him graciously. Indeed, despite the repugnance of his physical condition—whatever it was—they received him as though he were a heavenly messenger (cf. 1:8), as though he were Jesus Christ himself. This last detail may suggest once again that the apostle's wounds marked him as Christ's messenger, "carrying in the body the death of Jesus, so that the life of Jesus may also be made visible in our bodies" (2 Cor 4:10 NRSV). The Galatians could easily have been repelled by Paul's fleshly affliction (it was a "trial" to them), but they did not "scorn or despise" him. The first of these verbs (ἐξουθενέω *exoutheneō*) is, interestingly, used several times in the NT to refer to the contemptuous treatment Jesus received during his passion (Mark 9:12; Luke 23:11; Acts 4:11; cf. 1 Cor 1:28). Perhaps more significantly, the same verb is also used in Paul's account of what his detractors at Corinth said about him: "his bodily presence is *weak* and his speech *contemptible* [ἐξουθενημένος *exouthenēmenos*]" (2 Cor 10:10 NRSV, italics added). The second verb in v. 14*a*, ἐκπτύω (*ekptyō*), refers literally to the act of spitting at someone. It can be understood metaphorically to mean "to despise," or it could have its literal sense here. In antiquity, it was commonly thought that one could ward off the effects of the "evil eye" or of demonic influence by spitting three times.[208] It is impossible to tell from Paul's brief reference whether he intends the verb literally or metaphorically. In either case, he is describing something that the Galatians did *not* do; rather than despising Paul, they saw through the outward affliction and received him with joy.

4:15. In the light of this memory of his former warm reception in Galatia, Paul now asks them a pointed question, literally, "Where then is your blessing?" (not, as in the NIV, "joy"). Despite the opinion of many commentators to the contrary, the term μακαρισμός

(*makarismos*) does not refer to a state of blessedness, but to a concretely pronounced blessing, as it does in Rom 4:6, 9, the only other place where Paul uses the word. Paul is not asking the Galatians what happened to the feeling of blessedness they used to have; rather, he is asking what happened to the word of blessing they once pronounced on him. Why are they now speaking criticism of him rather than blessing him? (The NRSV's paraphrase gets closer to this sense.) This is completely in line with the thought of the passage, which focuses on how the Galatians' attitudes toward Paul have changed.

Once they held Paul in such high esteem that they would have torn out their own eyes for his sake. This gruesome image has given rise to speculation that Paul's "weakness of the flesh" was some sort of eye disease. Betz has argued persuasively, however, that Paul "alludes to a literary motif which must have been almost proverbial in his time." He cites a story from Lucian's *Toxaris* in which Dandamis negotiates the release of his friend Amizoces from captivity by sacrificing his own eyes.[209] The point is not that Paul is alluding specifically to this story but that he is employing a proverbial motif. It is as though he had said—to employ an idiom more familiar in our culture—"You would have given your right arm for me." This would not, of course, necessarily indicate that there was anything wrong with the speaker's arm; it is simply a figurative way of describing a deep and committed friendship.

4:16. All of that has now changed, however. As a result of the teaching of the Missionaries, the Galatians have begun to see Paul not as a friend but as an "enemy."[210] Whether this is really what they thought or whether this is what Paul expects them to think after reading this confrontational letter is impossible to say. Most significant is the last phrase of his sentence: "by telling you the truth." Paul portrays himself as a straight-shooting truth teller. He has insisted that his Law-free gospel is God's truth. It came by revelation (1:11-12), and Paul will not compromise the truth for any reason (2:5). The "truth of the gospel" is inextricably bound up with the vision of one table where Jews and

208. Dunn, *The Epistle to the Galatians*, 234.

209. Betz, *Galatians*, 228, referring to Lucian *Toxaris* 40-41.
210. The term "enemy" is explicitly applied to Paul in the later Pseudo-Clementine literature. See *Ep. Petr.* 2.3.

Gentiles sit together in Christ without being divided by the barriers of the Law (2:14). Perhaps the Missionaries, on the other hand, have persuaded the Galatians that Paul has betrayed them by preaching a watered-down gospel that lacked the full benefit of circumcision and Torah observance. If so, Paul now challenges the Missionaries' motives for alienating the affections of the Galatians away from him. He, Paul, tells the truth, whereas they are manipulators and flatterers who are preventing the Galatians from living in the truth (5:7).

4:17-18. That v. 16 reflects a direct accusation of the Missionaries is suggested by the way Paul moves seamlessly into v. 17 without even naming his adversaries. It was clear enough to the Galatians whom he meant. The verb ζηλόω (*zēloō*), which appears three times in these verses, is ambiguous. It can mean "to desire earnestly"; therefore, it can be used with connotations of eagerly courting someone's favor, as in a romantic relationship.[211] Alternatively, it can have a religious sense, "to be zealous for God" (cf. 1:14). Finally, it can have a pejorative sense, "to be jealous or envious." The last of these meanings makes no sense in the present context, but it is likely that Paul is making a clever play on the first two. The primary meaning is the first sense: The Missionaries are "courting" the Galatians to win them over (the NIV supplies this idea). At the same time, Paul's choice of the verb *zēloō* is ironically appropriate, because the Missionaries pride themselves on their zeal for the Law, as Paul did also during his former life in Judaism (1:13-14). They would probably describe their courtship of the Galatians as an expression of their religious zeal.

Paul asserts, however, that this courting is a form of flattery and a devious exercise of power. Their ulterior motive, as Paul sees it, is to shut the Galatians out in order that the Galatians in turn might court them. This seems like a puzzling claim on the surface. Some commentators, followed by the NIV, suppose that the motive ascribed to the Missionaries is to lock the Galatians away from Paul, so as to have all the attention for themselves. This interpretation, however, requires an odd translation of the verb "to shut out" (ἐκκλείω *ekkleiō*; rendered "alienate" by the NIV),

and it also requires the insertion of the words "from us," which are not in the Greek text. A better explanation is provided by the scenario Paul has already described at Antioch: The Jewish Christians withdraw from fellowship with Gentile Christians, shutting them out in order to put pressure on them to "Judaize" (2:11-14). As already suggested, Paul saw in that situation an analogy to the present crisis in Galatia (see the Commentary on 2:11-21). Paul looks at the Galatian situation with psychological realism and sees that the exclusivity of the Jewish-Christian Missionaries makes their religious "club" seem highly desirable to those who are on the outside. If the Galatians want to join the in group, they must come under the Missionaries' sphere of influence by accepting circumcision.[212]

Thus the Missionaries' "zeal" for the Galatians is "for no good purpose." In principle, Paul has no objection to other teachers coming on the scene for a good cause (v. 18; cf. the case of Apollos in Corinth, 1 Cor 3:5-9); he need not monitor everything that happens in his absence. As Betz notes, it is one of the conventions of the friendship *topos* that "true friendship does not change even when the friends are separated."[213] In this case, however, Paul thinks that the Galatians are falling for a false courtship by seducers who will lead them away not only from their relationship with him, but also from the gospel altogether.

4:19. This line of thought leads to Paul's anguished outcry. He addresses the Galatians fondly as his "children." In other letters, Paul speaks of his relation to his communities as being like that of a father to his children (e.g., 1 Cor 4:14-15; 1 Thess 2:11-12). But here he gives the parental metaphor a surprising spin. As he sees the Galatians turning back into their former state of slavery, he fears that he will have to start all over with them. It is as though they had never been born into their new life in Christ, or as though the birth process was somehow incomplete. Thus Paul pictures himself as a mother again in labor pains, struggling to give birth to the Galatians once again.[214] The image suggests both the futility

---

211. Betz, *Galatians*, 229, suggests that the term can also be used "to describe the sincere and deep concern one friend has for another."

212. For a helpful discussion, see Dunn, *The Epistle to the Galatians*, 238.

213. Betz, *Galatians*, 232.

214. On this metaphor and the implications that follow from it, see B. R. Gaventa, "The Maternity of Paul: An Exegetical Study of Galatians 4:19," in Fortna and Gaventa, *The Conversation Continues*, 189-201.

of the Galatians' reversion to life under the στοιχεῖα (*stoicheia*) and the pain that Paul experiences as he tries to wrest them back into the sphere of Christ's lordship.

Beverly Gaventa, observing that "birth pangs" is a stock image in Jewish and Christian apocalyptic texts for the suffering that accompanies God's eschatological action of bringing the new age into being (e.g., *1 Enoch* 62:4; *2 Apoc Bar* 56:6; 4 Ezra 4:2; 1QH 3.7-10; Mark 13:8; Rom 8:22; 1 Thess 5:3; Rev 12:2), has proposed that Paul sees his "birthing" of the Galatians as a part of the cosmic travail at the turn of the ages: "Paul's anguish . . . reflects the anguish of the whole created order as it awaits the fulfillment of God's action in Jesus Christ."[215] The apostolic "labor" is part of the eschatological conflict whereby God is claiming and redeeming the world. The Galatians find themselves in the push and pull of this cosmic struggle.

In v. 19*b*, however, as Gaventa also shows, Paul mutates the metaphor into something else: "until Christ is formed in you." If he had wanted to carry the birthing image through consistently, he would have had to say something like "until you are born anew in Christ." The fact that Paul transmutes his own metaphor in midsentence suggests that he has something else in view here. He is not merely concerned about the rebirth of the Galatians as individuals; rather, his vision is for the community as a whole to take on the character of Christ. The pronoun "you" is plural, and the phrase ἐν ὑμῖν (*en hymin*) is best translated not as "in (each one of) you" but rather as "among you, in your midst."[216] The apostle's apocalyptic birth pangs are bringing forth a new community formed in the image of Jesus Christ; Christ will live in the community just as he lives in Paul (2:20; cf. the idea of conformity to Christ in Rom 8:29). Elsewhere, Paul will express this idea by using the image of the "body of Christ" (Rom 12:4-5; 1 Cor 12:12, 27). The dynamic equation between Christ and community has already anchored the exegetical argument that Paul makes in 3:16, 29: The christologically defined "seed" turns out to include all who belong to Christ.

In 4:19, however, Paul runs the equation the other way: As the eschatological community is birthed into the world, it takes the form of Christ. These metaphors are bold and fantastic, but Paul finds no other way to make his radical claim with its full force.

4:20. For the present, however, Paul feels powerless, at such a distance, to help the Galatians in the midst of this struggle. He longs to be with them, but he cannot be. (In contrast to other letters, he makes no mention of a planned future visit; the comparison to 1 Cor 4:14-21 is particularly striking.) The expression translated "change my tone" is literally "change my voice." This might refer to Paul's wish to modulate his tone of voice into a gentler sound in contrast to the harsh rebuke of the present letter (1:6-9; 3:1-5; 4:8-11; cf. 5:12). Another possible interpretation is that he wishes to exchange the merely written language of the letter for a live personal conversation with the Galatians, preferring oral encounter to written text.

Paul brings the unit to an end on a note of helpless puzzlement, recapitulating the attitude of v. 11. The Galatians' rejection of the previously warm relationship with their apostle has left him stunned and perplexed. "Paul acts as if he has run out of arguments."[217] Of course, that is not the case. This is a rhetorical device to convey Paul's shock at the Galatians' abandonment of the relationship with the apostle who had previously given them birth.

The central idea of vv. 12-20, then, is that the Galatians have ruptured their relationship with Paul. They have been led astray by the false and deceptive tactics of the Missionaries, and they have abandoned their first loyalty. Paul appeals to them to reaffirm their original bond with him by becoming as he is: free from the Law. In the course of making this argument, he employs both traditional friendship motifs and the familial metaphor of a mother giving birth to children. This appeal is designed to renew their personal adherence to the relationship with him. If Paul's personal appeal succeeds, then the other arguments in the letter—based on experience (3:1-5; 4:1-11) and Scripture (3:6-29; 4:21–5:1)—can do their work in due course.

---

215. Gaventa, "The Maternity of Paul," 194. Martyn suggests that Isa 45:7-11 is the source behind Paul's use of the childbirth imagery. See Martyn, *Galatians*, 427-29.

216. Gaventa, "The Maternity of Paul," 196. Martyn, *Galatians*, 424, translates it, for emphasis, "until Christ is formed in your congregations."

217. Betz, *Galatians*, 237. This rhetorical device is known as *dubitatio*.

REFLECTIONS

1. The most striking feature of this passage is its personal pathos. After lengthy rational argumentation, Paul plays the card of an appeal to emotion. In addition to all the reasons he has given the Galatians for rejecting circumcision, Paul now makes a heartfelt appeal to personal loyalty. If they have any decency, Paul implies—if they are not fickle friends—they will stand with Paul in this controversy.

What are we to make of this sort of argument? The first reaction of many readers will be to see it as shameless manipulation, a kind of emotional blackmail. Could a preacher today legitimately confront a polarizing issue in the church by appealing in a similar way to the personal loyalty of his or her congregation? Would this not be seen as desperate special pleading?

Probably so. We must recognize first of all that the sort of argument Paul makes in 4:12-20, an argument from pathos, was a familiar type of rhetoric in the ancient Mediterranean world. Audiences and readers expected this sort of appeal, and it would not have grated on their sensibilities in the same way it would on the sensibilities of a congregation in our time. Paul was artfully employing conventions of discourse in his culture. We must do the same thing in ours. We should not slavishly imitate Paul's rhetoric; rather, we must find ways of making our appeal for the gospel within genres that are rhetorically persuasive for our culture.

Second, we should note that this appeal to pathos is only a brief interlude embedded within an extended theological argument. It is not the whole argument; rather, it provides an affective appeal for the readers to weigh seriously what Paul is saying in the rest of the letter.

Finally, with these due cautions, it is worth observing that Paul did believe passionately that the gospel created deep personal relationships between believers. The Galatians, to whom Paul writes, are not merely an audience to be manipulated, not a "market" for a commodity he is selling. Rather, they are his brothers and sisters. Their earlier gratitude to him for bringing them the gospel forged a bond of love between them. Paul is genuinely distraught over the prospect of seeing that bond broken, and he cares urgently about the fate of his "children." All of this provides us with an appealing model for relationships in Christ. Are we a people whose common joy in the gospel would lead us to tear out our eyes for one another—or, if we prefer, give our right arms for one another? Or have we been courted and seduced, for no good purpose, by missionaries of a consumerism that would prefer to keep us apart and aloof?

2. Paul's appeal to the Galatians to imitate his example (4:12) should provoke sustained reflection. The ancient Mediterranean world took role modeling very seriously. To assess the meaning or truth of any philosophy, it was necessary to examine the lives of its exponents. This cultural assumption was carried over into the early church; the meaning of the gospel was to be embodied in the lives of the community's leaders. For that reason, Paul's self-depiction in the first two chapters of Galatians provides the crucial background to the exhortation of 4:12; Paul has modeled a life set free from the Law, a life willing to sacrifice all claims of racial or ethnic privilege for the truth of a gospel that calls Jews and Gentiles together at one table. That is the example he holds before the Galatians' eyes.

All of this poses an acute question for us: To whom do we look for role models who exemplify the truth of the gospel? To be sure, the canonical New Testament narrates the stories of apostles and saints who stand as permanent models for us. But we also need living embodiments of the gospel in our own time, real people in our communities to whom we can point and say, "*There* is what a life lived faithfully in Christ looks like." It will not do simply to point to faraway saints like Mother Teresa; one task of the church's ministry is to identify and acknowledge those women and men in our midst who embody the gospel. This may appear disturbingly antidemocratic, because it necessarily implies that some people among us know better than others how to practice the faith. Christian fidelity is not just a matter of untutored intuition so that everybody's opinion about it is of equal worth; rather, discipleship is a craft that must be learned from others with superior knowledge and experience. Like the Galatians, who were faced with a choice between Paul's example and the teaching of the Missionaries, we must learn to choose our role models wisely.

3. The need for such discernment leads us into reflection about the criteria we employ to identify role models who embody the gospel. The question was posed sharply in a famous essay by Plutarch: How do we tell a flatterer from a friend?[218] Paul's assertion that he tells the truth (4:16) is of no help, since both parties would make similar claims. The present passage, being an emotional appeal, does not explicitly address this problem, but it does contain a couple of hints.

First, if it is true that Paul's "weakness of the flesh" is an allusion to injuries inflicted upon him as a result of his preaching the gospel, then there is a correspondence between suffering and truth (see the Commentary on 4:13-14). The one who comes as an authentic messenger of Jesus Christ is likely to share in Christ's suffering. This is not an explicit theme of Gal 4:12-20, but it is characteristic of Paul's thought (see, e.g., Rom 8:17, 22-23; 1 Cor 4:9-13; 2 Cor 4:7-12; 6:1-12; 11:16–12:10; Phil 1:27-30). This is a paradox, but it is grounded in the proclamation of a crucified messiah.

Second, one attribute of false friends is described in 4:17: The Missionaries simultaneously court the Galatians and exclude them from the circle of the Torah-observant in group. Thus they appeal to the upwardly mobile vanity that is satirized by Groucho Marx's well-known quip: "I wouldn't join any club that would have me as a member." True friends and true messengers of the gospel do not play such exclusive games. The good news of Jesus Christ comes to us as we are, without entrance requirements and strings attached, without playing on our vanity.

4. Finally, Paul's use of the apocalyptic metaphor of "birth pangs" (4:19) suggests that something more than a ruptured friendship is at stake here. The "birthing" of the Galatian congregations was a part of God's plan to bring a new world into being, a "new creation" in which neither circumcision nor uncircumcision matters (3:28; 6:15). This puts the personal appeal of this passage in its proper cosmic context. Whatever we may feel about personal ties and loyalties, we must see the birth and life of our congregations within God's eschatological design for the redemption of the world. The aim of Paul's missionary labors was to see Christ formed in human communities of love that transcended old cultural boundaries. Wherever the church acts in ways that reinstate such cultural and ethnic boundaries, the new creation is blocked and denied, but God will continue to find ways to bring it to birth, perhaps painfully, in our midst.

---

218. Plutarch, *How to Tell a Flatterer from a Friend*, in *Plutarch's Moralia I*, trans. F. C. Babbitt, LCL (Cambridge, Mass.: Harvard University Press, 1927).

GALATIANS 4:21–5:1, AN ALLEGORY OF SLAVERY AND FREEDOM

COMMENTARY

Paul now brings his counterarguments against the rival Missionaries to a rhetorical climax. As we have seen, the central section of Galatians (3:1–5:1) consists of a series of arguments designed to negate the influence of these interlopers and to recall the Galatians to the Law-free gospel Paul had orginally preached to them. The personal appeal of 4:12-20 creates an emotional change of pace and invites the Galatians to reaffirm their intimate tie with Paul. The final argument of this section (4:21–5:1), then, is the *pièce de résistance,* designed to win the readers over decisively by demonstrating that the Law-free mission to the Gentiles is in fact prefigured in the Torah itself—indeed, prefigured by the very narrative on which the Missionaries have based their teaching. In the light of this demonstration, Paul concludes with a rallying cry, summoning the Galatians to stand fast in the freedom that Christ has given them (5:1).

In reading 4:21–5:1, it is of utmost importance to recognize that Paul's polemic is not directed against Jews or Judaism as such. Rather, the targets are the Jewish-*Christian* Missionaries who are disrupting his Gentile churches. This has important implications for the interpretation of the "two covenants" in this passage.

4:21. Paul goes on the offensive, taking the battle to the Missionaries' home turf. "All right," he says, "you Galatians want to be under the Law? I can play that game. Listen to what the Law says." The expression "under the Law" has appeared earlier in the argument with decidedly negative connotations. To be "under the Law" is to be in a state of confinement (3:23) from which one needs to be liberated (4:5; cf. 5:18). Thus Paul's choice of words here is laden with sarcasm. The Galatians are showing, by their susceptibility to the Missionaries' message, that they find the Law attractive and want to come under its control (4:8-11). Paul, therefore, announces his intention to show them that even the Law supports his gospel rather than the one offered by the Missionaries.

In the Greek, v. 21*b* says, literally, "Do you not hear the Law?" (thus the NRSV is closer than the NIV to the original sense of the verse: It is a matter of attentive listening). There may be an ironic echo here of the Shema (Deut 6:4): "*Hear,* O Israel. . . ." In the OT, hearing and obedience are closely linked. In the present passage, Paul wants to force the Galatians to hear the story afresh; if they do, they will receive direction about what to do. His opening question (v. 21) points toward the climactic Scripture quotation in v. 30,

which is introduced by the formula, "What does the Scripture say?" If the Galatians listen to what the Law actually says, they will hear it speaking the words "Throw out the slave woman and her child." The purpose of this paragraph is to prepare them to interpret this directive properly.

The fact that Paul can refer to the story of Abraham's two sons (Genesis 16–21) as "the Law" shows that he uses the term broadly; it includes OT narrative as well as the commandments of the Sinaitic covenant (cf. 1 Cor 14:21, where Paul introduces a quotation from Isaiah as something written in the Law). In vv. 21 and 30, the terms "Law" and "Scripture" appear to be used synonymously.

4:22. Rather than actually quoting the text of Genesis at this point, Paul gives a concise summary of the narrative. The allusive manner in which he does so suggests that the Galatians must be familiar with the story already. He names neither Ishmael nor Isaac, and he does not explain anything about the plot of the tale. Paul's use of the definite article in this verse is rightly represented by the NIV: "one by the slave woman and the other by the free woman." Again, this suggests that he is referring to characters already known to the readers, Hagar and Sarah, though he does not give their names here. C. K. Barrett has argued persuasively that the stories of Genesis 16 and 21 were being used by Paul's opponents as a primary basis for their teaching.[219] According to their telling of the story, the true descendants of Abraham, through Isaac, should be circumcised; Gentiles converted by Paul who remain uncircumcised would be in the position of Ishmael, illegitimate sons who would eventually be sent away without inheriting what was promised to Abraham. The Missionaries' interpretation of the story must have been similar to that found in *Jubilees,* giving a place of special privilege to Abraham's physical descendants through Isaac—i.e., the Jewish people:

And through Isaac a name and a seed would be named for [Abraham]. And all of the seed of his sons would become nations. And they would be counted with the nations. But from the sons of

---

219. C. K. Barrett, "The Allegory of Abraham, Sarah, and Hagar in the Argument of Galatians," in J. Friedrich et al., eds., *Rechfertigung: Festschrift für Ernst Käsemann zum 70. Geburtstag* (Tübingen: Mohr, 1976) 1-16.

Isaac one would become a holy seed and he would not be counted among the nations because he would become the portion of the Most High . . . so that he might become a people (belonging) to the Lord, a (special) possession from all people, and so that he might become a kingdom of priests and a holy people. (*Jub.* 16:17-18)[220]

If that is what the Galatians had been told about the story, then Paul is executing a bold counterreading, reversing the polarity of the story by claiming that it is the uncircumcised Gentile converts who correspond to Isaac, the child of promise (v. 28).

It is also noteworthy that Paul refers to Sarah not by name but as "the free woman." In fact, in Genesis, while Hagar is repeatedly called "the slave woman," Sarah is never explicitly called "the free woman." Paul's use of this epithet subliminally sets up the interpretation that he wants to give, by highlighting the opposition between "slave" and "free."

4:23. Paul's initial summary of the story about Abraham's two sons[221] in v. 22 is uncontroversial. In this verse, however, Paul begins to introduce his own reading of the story; that is probably why the adversative conjunction "but" (ἀλλά *alla*, untranslated by the NIV and the NRSV) introduces this verse.[222] Abraham's fathering of one son was performed "according to the flesh," whereas the fathering of the other was performed "through promise." (This does not mean that Isaac was conceived without sexual intercourse; it refers to the fact that he was born through the power of God's promise after Sarah was past the normal age of childbearing; Gen 18:11.) Ishmael, on the other hand, was conceived apart from God's promise through the "fleshly" stratagem of having Abraham impregnate Hagar, Sarah's Egyptian slave woman (Gen 16:1-16). (The NIV omits the word "flesh" and thereby loses the key word that allows Paul to link Ishmael with the fleshly rite of circumcision.)

The opposition between "flesh" and "promise" is at first surprising; we expect the juxtaposition of "flesh" and "spirit," as in

v. 29. Presumably, in v. 23 Paul is keeping his initial narration as close as possible to the Genesis story, where there is no reference to the Spirit. The mention of "promise" also reminds the reader of Paul's earlier insistence that God granted the inheritance to Abraham "through promise" (3:18, exactly the same phrase found in 4:23) and that the Gentile Galatians are "heirs according to the promise" (3:29). Thus Paul sets the stage for his claim (v. 28) that Isaac, who was begotten "through promise," prefigures the Galatians themselves.

4:24. Having quickly sketched the story of Abraham's two sons in terms implicitly favorable to his own theological reading, Paul now starts to lead the Galatians through an explicit interpretation of the story's details. He announces his program in v. 24*a*: "These things are to be interpreted allegorically." The passive participle "interpreted allegorically" (ἀλληγορούμενα *allēgoroumena*) refers not to the symbolic character of the text but to the character of the interpretation given by the reader. Allegory was a well-known method for interpreting ancient stories of gods and heroes—such as Homer's epic tales—as containers of higher philosophical truths. Paul's contemporary, Philo of Alexandria, was a highly educated Jewish philosopher who applied allegorical methods to the interpretation of Israel's Scripture. For example, Philo read the story of Abraham's two sons as a symbolic portrayal of how the soul (Abraham) must transcend the realm of sense perception and sophistry (Hagar/Ishmael) and ascend to a higher knowledge of wisdom and virtue (Sarah/Isaac).[223]

Many modern interpreters, uncomfortable with the allegorical method of interpretation, have contended that Paul's interpretative strategy is actually typological rather than allegorical. Insofar as this distinction differentiates Paul's reading from the Alexandrian propensity to interpret narratives as coded vehicles of timeless philosophical truths, the distinction may be useful.[224] The verb "to interpret allegorically," however, simply

220. For an extensive survey of the history of interpretation of the story of Hagar and Sarah in Jewish sources, see Longenecker, *Galatians*, 200-6.

221. The fact that Abraham later had more sons by Keturah (Gen 25:1-6) is irrelevant to Paul's allegory.

222. Martyn, *Galatians*, 434.

223. Philo, *Cher.* 8-9; *Sob.* 7-9.

224. In fact, it is more helpful to recognize that typology is nothing other than a particular type of allegory, in which the latent sense of a narrative is to be found in later events rather than in "higher" spiritual concepts. On this question, see Hays, *Echoes of Scripture in the Letters of Paul*, 115-16, 160-64.

suggests that the narrative is to be read as having a latent sense, a figurative meaning that is to be distinguished from its overt literal sense. By this definition, Paul's reading is certainly allegorical. Accordingly, the NIV translation ("These things may be taken figuratively") conveys the proper meaning. Paul is not worried about a technical method of allegory; he is merely saying that the story has a hidden significance, which he will now explain.

The two women are "two covenants." Here is a potential pitfall for Christian interpreters, who are likely to leap to the conclusion that Paul means the old covenant (Law) and the new covenant (gospel). We must remember, however, that Paul has emphatically insisted that the covenant of promise is God's covenant with Abraham, which is much older than the Sinaitic covenant (3:15-18). This means—and the point is crucial—that the two covenants do *not* represent "Judaism" and "Christianity." Rather, Paul claims that the covenant of promise and freedom is what the Law itself, rightly understood, teaches (see the Reflections). It is a matter of two rival interpretations of Israel's heritage—and both interpretations are being promulgated by Jewish *Christians* (Paul and the Missionaries). The salient difference between the two covenants in the present context is not their respective ages but their results: One bears children for slavery, the other for freedom.

The NIV's rendering of v. 24c is clearer than the NRSV's: "one *covenant* [not "one woman"] is from Mount Sinai." That covenant, the Law of Moses, is "bearing children for slavery." The connection of the Law with slavery has already been strongly implied in vv. 1-11; now Paul asserts it overtly. Furthermore, he asserts that Hagar, the slave woman, represents the Law. This is such an astounding claim that he must digress in vv. 25-27 to explain it. Regrettably, the digression leads him away from his exposition of the two covenants, and he never completes the comparison, although it is not too difficult to fill in the blanks in the light of the interpretive clues he has provided (see Fig. 4).

J. Louis Martyn has suggested that "bearing children" is a metaphor for gaining

converts through missionary preaching.[225] This suggestion has considerable pertinence in view of Paul's use of the childbearing metaphor in v. 19 to describe his own "birthing" of the Galatian churches. The metaphor of "birth pangs" in v. 19 leads smoothly into the allegorical treatment of childbearing in vv. 22-31. If Martyn is right, then Hagar represents the covenant proclaimed by the Jewish-Christian missionaries, whose work has provoked Paul to write the letter. They are "bearing children for slavery" through their evangelistic work of preaching a Law-observant gospel, which Paul regards as a formula for bondage to the στοιχεῖα (*stoicheia,* vv. 9-10). This proposal helps us to see how 4:21–5:1 powerfully advances the argument of the letter as a whole.

4:25. Paul elaborates on his allegorical interpretation of the figure of Hagar, but his elaboration has baffled generations of interpreters. Some ancient scribes, puzzled by the sentence, deleted the name "Hagar," leaving the clear (but pointless) statement, "For Sinai is a mountain in Arabia" (NRSV textual note). Some modern interpreters have proposed that Paul's identification of Hagar with Mt. Sinai rests on a far-fetched pun exploiting the similarity between her name and the Arabic word for "rock." It is impossible here to recount all the proposals that have been advanced to emend or interpret v. 25a.[226] The following explanation tries to make sense out of the text before us with a minimum of conjecture, bearing in mind that Paul must have intended his sentence to be intelligible to the Galatians.

One important clue does not come through in translation: Paul uses the neuter definite article (το *to*) before Hagar's name. This shows that he is referring to "Hagar" as a word appearing in a text, an item in a field of elements to be allegorically interpreted. This would be best represented in English translation by putting the word in quotation marks: "Now 'Hagar' is Mount Sinai in Arabia." There is no explicit basis in the text of Genesis for this assertion. It is impossible to know

---

225. Martyn, *Galatians,* 451-54. This interpretation is supported by the observation that, whereas the LXX consistently uses the verb "to bear" (τίκτω *tiktō*) to describe the childbearing activity of Hagar and Sarah, Paul substitutes in 4:23-24, and 29 the verb γεννάω (*gennaō*), which can mean either "beget" or "bear." Note Paul's use of the latter verb to speak of his own generative apostolic work in 1 Cor 4:15.

226. See Betz, *Galatians,* 244-45; Longenecker, *Galatians,* 211-12.

with certainty why Paul posits this symbolic equation, though it may have something to do with the fact that Hagar is the mother of Ishmael, regarded in Jewish lore as the progenitor of the Arab people. An equally good explanation, however, is that the equation is simply required by the allegory that Paul is propounding. Hagar has already been identified in v. 24 with the covenant from Mt. Sinai; what Paul is doing in v. 25 is justifying a further symbolic linkage between Mt. Sinai and Jerusalem.

The verb "corresponds" ($\sigma\upsilon\sigma\tau\upsilon\iota\chi\acute{\epsilon}\omega$ *systoicheō*) in v. 25*b* is a key to reading the whole passage. It does not mean "represents." Its root meaning is "to stand in line with" something. As many commentators have recognized, this term recalls the Pythagorean tables of opposites, which order pairs of elemental categories into opposing columns (male vs. female, hot vs. cold, etc.).[227] In an analogous way, Paul's allegory lines up the symbolic elements of the Genesis story in two oppositional columns. All of the elements in a single column are closely associated with one another.

227. See the discussion in Aristotle *Metaphysics* I.v.6-17 [986a-987a].

Figure 4: Oppositional Columns in Paul's Allegory	
slave	**free**
Hagar	Sarah
Ishmael	Isaac
flesh	promise/spirit
Mr. Sinai	――――
the present Jerusalem	the Jerusalem above

In the light of this pattern, Paul's statement in v. 25*b* makes more sense. He is saying that, within his allegory, "Mt. Sinai" stands in the same column with "the present Jerusalem." This enables him to link the Sinai covenant with the empirical city of Jerusalem; both are associated with rigorous adherence to the Law. In the light of these observations, we may now offer a fresh translation of vv. 24-26:

(24) These things are to be interpreted allegorically, for these two women are two covenants. One covenant is from Mt. Sinai, bearing children into slavery: This is Hagar.
(25) Now "Hagar" is Mt. Sinai in Arabia, but she/it stands in the same column with the present Jerusalem, for (Jerusalem) is in slavery with her children.
(26) But the Jerusalem above is the free woman (Sarah); this is our mother.

On this reading, the function of v. 25*a* is to smooth the transition between the assertions made in vv. 24*b* and 25*b*. Despite the apparent geographical incongruity, Paul is explaining how "Hagar" can symbolize both the Sinai covenant (associated with a mountain in Arabia) and the present Jerusalem. The link works, he claims, because Hagar, Sinai, and Jerusalem are all in the "slavery" column.

This still leaves the question of why Paul says the present Jerusalem is in slavery with her children (v. 25*b*). On one level, this is merely a more vivid repetition of the picture already sketched in 3:23; 4:4-5; and 4:8-10: Living under obedience to the Law is in itself a state of slavery, Paul asserts, in contrast to the freedom won for us by Christ. This picture would have particular force if we understand "the present Jerusalem" as a veiled reference to the Jerusalem church, which has been the source of many conflicts and troubles for Paul (cf. 2:12).[228] The Jerusalem church, along with the children begotten through its Law-observant mission to Gentiles, remains in bondage to the Law.

A second level of meaning is possible, however, in the light of 3:10-14 (see the Commentary on 3:10-14). We should not be surprised to find multiple levels of meaning in an allegorical interpretation. The city of Jerusalem symbolizes Israel, which is, empirically

228. Martyn, *Galatians*, 439, 457-66.

speaking, in slavery under the dominion of Rome. The curse pronounced by the Law has brought "a nation from far away, from the end of the earth, to swoop down on you like an eagle" (Deut 28:49 NRSV), so that Jerusalem is under the heel of Caesar. Was the present Jerusalem in slavery? A contemporary observer would have needed to look no further for confirmation than the Antonia Fortress, where Roman troops were stationed immediately adjacent to the Temple Mount. This is not Paul's primary point in Gal 4:25, but the political captivity of Jerusalem provides the immediate real-world background for Paul's symbolic identification of Jerusalem with the slave Hagar. To speak of the present Jerusalem as living under slavery was hardly a far-fetched fantasy. By contrast, Paul believes, those who are in Christ are now free citizens of a heavenly commonwealth (v. 26; cf. Phil 3:20), are no longer under the curse, and, therefore, are no longer in bondage to the worldly authorities. That such a vision might underlie Paul's words is suggested also by the fact that he quotes Isa 54:1—a prophecy of the liberation and restoration of Jerusalem—in v. 27.

4:26. In contrast to the present Jerusalem in slavery, Paul links himself and the Galatians to "the Jerusalem above," which is identified with "the free woman," Sarah. (Here the NIV gives an accurate translation, the NRSV a paraphrase.) The term "free woman" (ἐλευθέρα *eleuthera*) refers, of course, to vv. 22-23, where Sarah was introduced, in opposition to Hagar, as "the free woman." Paul is still explicating his allegorical reading of the Genesis story. The image of an eschatological "Jerusalem above" is suggested in OT texts such as Isaiah 54 and Ezekiel 40–48 and more fully elaborated in later Jewish apocalyptic texts (e.g., 2 Esdr 7:26; 10:25-28; 13:36; *1 Enoch* 90:28-29; *2 Apoc. Bar.* 4:2-6). The same image appears also in Heb 12:22; 13:14; Rev 3:12; and in particularly clear form in Revelation 21.[229] The metaphor of Jerusalem as "mother" is found, e.g., in Ps 86:5 LXX and 2 Esdr 10:7, and it is pervasively presupposed by the recurrent motif of Jerusalem as a barren woman ultimately to

be restored and blessed by God with many children.[230] All of this suggests that Paul is drawing on a well-established apocalyptic theme: The people of God, despite suffering and adversity in the present, are children of a heavenly Jerusalem that will be eschatologically revealed. The novelty is that he now includes his Gentile readers among the children of this heavenly Jerusalem.

4:27. In support of this assertion, Paul cites a scriptural text, Isa 54:1. On the surface, it is not immediately apparent how the quotation functions in the argument. Close examination, however, shows that Paul has selected this quotation carefully. The reference to a "barren woman" recalls the story of Sarah's barrenness before the birth of Isaac. In the context of Isaiah 54, this traditional motif of Sarah the barren woman has been metaphorically juxtaposed with the condition of Jerusalem during the exile. The prophet uses the metaphor of God's miraculous blessing of Sarah (cf. Isa 51:1-3, the only reference to Sarah in the OT outside of Genesis) to proclaim God's miraculous restoration of the fortunes of Zion. Where the city had previously lain empty and desolate, there will now be numerous children, numerous inhabitants. (Thus the author of Isaiah 54 is already reading the Genesis narrative typologically to point to the hope of Jerusalem's restoration.) Important for Paul's use of the text, Deutero-Isaiah associates the miraculous increase of Zion's children with the gathering of the Gentiles to acknowledge the justice of the God of Israel (e.g., Isa 49:6; 51:4-5; 52:10; 54:2-3; 55:5). Thus Sarah, the free woman—the allegorical figure for the heavenly city—will cry out joyfully at the "birth" of many children, including Gentile converts. This, as Paul reads it, is the ultimate fulfillment of God's promise to Abraham and Sarah (cf. 3:8-9, 14, 29). Paul's major purpose for citing Isa 54:1 is to evoke Deutero-Isaiah's central theme of God's gracious eschatological restoration of Israel and a universal embrace of the nations.

The final line of the quotation is a little confusing, because, in the context of vv. 21-31, it appears to identify "the one who has a husband" with Hagar. This detail does not

229. For further references, see Longenecker, *Galatians*, 214.

230. On the history of this motif, see M. Callaway, *Sing, O Barren One: A Study in Comparative Midrash*, SBLDS 91 (Atlanta: Scholars Press, 1986); K. Blessing, "The Background of the Barren Woman Motif in Galatians 4:27" (Ph.D. diss., Duke University, 1996).

fit easily with the narrative of Genesis 16–21, but Paul probably does intend precisely this comparison. His own Gentile mission, symbolized by the figure of Sarah, has been blessed by God with remarkable fruitfulness in contrast to the Law-observant Jewish mission to Gentiles, symbolized here by Hagar, which (despite her fleshly union with Abraham) has not met with the same success.

4:28. Paul has now completed his exposition of the allegory, and he spells out its specific application to his readers. From this crucial turn, the discourse moves toward the imperative of v. 30. The direct address to the Galatians ("Now *you,* brothers") recalls earlier points in the argument where Paul shifts into the mode of second-person address to drive home the implications of his argument:

3:26: In Christ Jesus *you* are all sons of God through faith.
4:6: And because *you* are sons, God has sent the Spirit . . .
4:28: Now *you,* brothers and sisters, are children of promise. . . .

In this case, their status as children and heirs of the promise is bound up with their relation to Isaac. The Greek κατα Ἰσαάκ (*kata Isaak*) does not merely mean "like Isaac" (NRSV, NIV) but "in the line of Isaac"[231] or "in the pattern of Isaac."[232] Their correspondence to Isaac rests not merely on analogy; it is more substantial than that. They are the heirs for whom the promise was destined from the first (cf. 3:8). Paul spells out this crucial concept more fully in Rom 9:7*b*-8, quoting Gen 21:12: "'It is through Isaac that σπέρμα *sperma* [seed] shall be called for you.' This means that it is not the children of the flesh who are the children of God, but the children of the promise are counted as *sperma* [seed]" (author's trans.). Note here the same antithesis between "flesh" and "promise" that appears in Gal 4:23.

The crucial identity claim in Paul's reading of the allegory is this: "You Gentile believers are the children that God promised to Abraham." He annexes the "Isaac" role for his Gentile converts and thereby confiscates it from the Missionaries, who claim

circumcision as a prerequisite for this status. Once Paul has made this hermeneutical shift, the consequences follow quickly in vv. 29-30.

4:29. Paul draws a parallel between Ishmael's persecution of Isaac and the present time, in which he sees the representatives of the Law-observant covenant persecuting Law-free believers. Both sides of the comparison require some clarification.

The text of Genesis says nothing about Ishmael's persecution of Isaac. If anything, in Genesis 21 it is the other way around: Sarah's jealousy on behalf of Isaac leads her to persecute the innocent victims Hagar and Ishmael. Where does Paul get the idea of Ishmael as persecutor? Paul is interpreting Gen 21:9 in the light of a Jewish exegetical tradition that interpreted Ishmael's "playing with" Isaac as some sort of malicious activity, such as mocking, idolatry, or child molestation.[233] This tradition allows Paul to cast Ishmael, the child begotten according to the flesh, as the persecutor of Isaac—here described for the first time as begotten "according to the Spirit." Isaac thus becomes an allegorical figure for believers who receive the Spirit and cry "Abba, Father" (4:6-7).

But how does the allegory work for Paul's own time? Who is persecuting whom? We know from Paul's own testimony that, prior to his apostolic call, he persecuted the church and tried to destroy it (1:13, 23). This might suggest that this verse alludes to Jewish persecution of Christians. If, however, we have been right to read the allegory of vv. 21-31 as a figurative contrast between two different early Christian evangelistic missions, a slightly different interpretation of v. 29 is required. For Paul's analogy to work, the Torah-observant Jewish Christians must be characterized as persecutors of Paul and his Gentile converts. Would such a claim make any sense to Paul's readers? Perhaps it would. Certainly, Paul suffered considerable opposition from Jewish Christians; in 5:11 he implies that he is "still being persecuted" because he refuses to preach circumcision. Furthermore, the Missionaries are excluding uncircumcised Gentiles from fellowship (2:11-14; 4:17); the exclusion may have been

231. Matera, *Galatians,* 171.
232. Martyn, *Galatians,* 432.

233. The rabbinic evidence is gathered by W. A. Meeks, "'And Rose Up to Play': Midrash and Paraenesis in 1 Cor 10:1-22," *JSNT* 16 (1982) 64-78, see 69-70.

accompanied by solemn threats of God's curse and judgment on those who remained uncircumcised. This sort of "harrassment and pressure tactics" could readily be characterized as persecution.[234] (Note the reference in 5:12 to "those who unsettle you.") Finally, we should not dismiss lightly Paul's cryptic reference to the Galatians' having "suffered so much" (3:4 NIV). Whatever that may mean, v. 29 assumes that the Galatians will be able to fill in the blanks; their own knowledge of contemporary persecution of Law-free believers by the advocates of the Law-observant mission will allow them to make sense of Paul's charge.

4:30. The stage is now set for the dramatic climax of this passage. Paul has reversed the traditional polarities of the Genesis narrative so that now the Law-observant Missionaries are, shockingly, placed in the same "column" with Hagar and Ishmael, while the Gentile Galatians are identified as Sarah's free children. Paul had begun the passage by asking provocatively, "Do you not hear the Law?" In fact, however, except for the quotation of Isa 54:1 in v. 27, we have not yet heard the voice of the Law in this passage. Paul has given summaries but not quotations. Now at last he gives the cue for Scripture to speak directly to the Galatians (cf. the active role assigned to Scripture in 3:8, 22). The words he quotes from Gen 21:10 are actually Sarah's demand to Abraham, but Paul lifts them out of that context and treats them as a command spoken by Scripture directly to the hearers of this letter: "Throw out the slave woman and her son, for the slave woman's son will never share in the inheritance with the son of the free woman."[235] It is a stunning rhetorical moment. Paul has saved his ace, his most dramatic argument, for the end. If the Galatians have followed Paul's exposition of the allegory, they will not miss the import of this command: *Scripture* is speaking directly to them, telling them to throw out the rival Missionaries and their converts. The inheritance belongs rightly to the children of the free woman, and they should not tolerate the presence of troublemakers who are trying to

lure them into slavery (cf. 1:8-9). They should expel the Missionaries from their churches.

4:31. This summarizing sentence recapitulates what Paul has already said in vv. 26 and 28. This time, however, he reverts to a first-person plural formulation, gathering the Galatians to his side of the argument.

5:1. This sentence stands as the hortatory conclusion to the whole train of argument thus far, particularly the counterarguments of 3:1–4:31. The NIV and some other translations and commentaries treat this verse as the beginning of a new unit; this division of the text obscures the role of this verse as the culmination of the freedom/slavery antithesis that has dominated chap. 4.

Galatians 5:1 encapsulates the message of the letter in a single powerful slogan. It is a standard around which Paul hopes to rally the readers. Here, as throughout the central section of the letter, the primary emphasis falls on the indicative declaration of what Christ has done. Christ has set us free (cf. 3:13; 4:4-5). Christ has liberated us into the realm of freedom.[236] The indicative declaration is immediately followed by a corollary summons: Because Christ has set us free, we are to take a firm stand in the freedom we have been given. Paul has already narrated his action in Jerusalem as a model of standing firm in freedom (2:4-5), and he urges the Galatians to take their stand also. In the situation at hand, this would mean that they would stand firm against the teaching of the Missionaries. The verb "stand" ($\sigma\tau\acute{\eta}\kappa\omega$ *stēkō*)—particularly when taken in combination with the last clause ("and do not submit again to a yoke of slavery")—almost surely invokes a military image, with apocalyptic overtones (as in 1 Cor 16:13; Phil 1:27; 4:1; 2 Thess 2:15). In a time of cosmic struggle and opposition, the Galatians are exhorted to hold their ground without being frightened away by the enemy.

The image of the "yoke" is often used elsewhere in a positive sense to describe the discipline provided by teaching, particularly the teaching of Torah.[237] In this sense, the yoke provides stability and guidance, rather

234. Williams, *Galatians*, 131.

235. In order to achieve this effect, he has to modify the wording of the quotation just slightly, most notably by replacing "my son Isaac" (Gen 21:10) with "the son of the freewoman." This change is necessary if Scripture, rather than Sarah, is to be heard as the speaker.

236. This interpretation follows Martyn, *Galatians*, 447, in reading the dative case of the noun "freedom" as having a locative function: Freedom is figuratively conceptualized as a space into which Christ has placed us.

237. See *m. Abot* 3.5.

than being something to chafe against (cf. the Matthean adaptation of this theme to the teaching of Jesus, Matt 11:29-30). The Missionaries may have spoken of the Law as a yoke in these terms, as a gracious divine gift. If so, Paul once more reverses the valence of their language. By shifting the metaphor from the context of benign instruction to the field of military conflict, he depicts the yoke as a symbol of enslavement. Here the Missionaries are implicitly portrayed not as kindly instructors, but as insidious slavemasters, seeking to bring the Galatians under the constraint of a new religio-cultural system of domination (cf. Acts 15:10).[238] Because Christ has delivered the Galatian churches from slavery, they should never, under any circumstances, tolerate being subjected to it again (cf. 4:8-9). With that ringing cry, the central section of Paul's letter comes to a close.

238. See Dunn, *The Epistle to the Galatians,* 263.

REFLECTIONS

1. *Claiming the Law as a Witness to the Gospel.* It is easy to imagine that in mounting his argument against the Missionaries, Paul could have rejected the Law altogether. Angered by the efforts of these Jewish-Christian evangelists, he might have declared a moratorium on Bible reading and announced a new covenant, under the guidance of the Spirit, that had no use any longer for Israel's sacred texts. He might have conceded that the Missionaries were right about the Law's requirements, including circumcision, and concluded that Israel's Scripture therefore had no place in shaping the thought and practice of the church. In short, he might have taken the position adopted by the twentieth-century New Testament scholar Rudolf Bultmann:

> To the Christian faith the Old Testament is no longer revelation as it has been, and still is, for the Jews. . . . The events which meant something for Israel, which were God's Word, mean nothing more to us. . . . To the Christian faith the Old Testament is not in the true sense God's Word.[239]

In Gal 4:21–5:1, however, Paul takes a very different line. He is not content to abandon Israel's Torah into the hands of his adversaries. Instead he argues passionately that the story of Abraham's two sons speaks directly to his Gentile readers. Israel's Law is not somebody else's book, for the Galatians themselves are Abraham's children, children of the promise in the pattern of Isaac. In order to receive guidance about what to do in their present time of controversy, they should listen to what Scripture says (4:1, 30). The whole passage claims that Scripture, rightly read, bears witness to the Law-free gospel for Gentiles.

Paul's strategy of argument is all the more striking if, as seems likely, the Missionaries were using the story of Isaac and Ishmael as a key text in support of their preaching of circumcision. By challenging them on the ground of their interpretation of the text, Paul set a crucial precedent for all subsequent Christian theology, preaching, and pastoral care: Scripture is foundational for the faith of the church. Normative proposals about Christian practices must be adjudicated through debating the interpretation of Scripture. As the Letter to the Galatians shows, the appeal to Scripture does not settle issues in a simple, straightforward way. The right reading of Scripture may be bitterly contested, as it was in Galatia. Still, Scripture defines the arena in which the contest must take place.

When Paul asks of the Galatians, "Do you not hear the Law?" we might well ask what he expects them to hear. On the basis of his entire argument in 3:1–5:1, we are

239. R. Bultmann, "The Significance of the Old Testament for Christian Faith," in *The Old Testament and Christian Faith,* ed. B. W. Anderson (New York: Harper and Bros., 1963) 31-32.

able to give some answers. He expects them to hear in the "Law" the encompassing narrative of the Old Testament, not just rules about ritual and behavior. He expects them to hear a word of gracious promise from God, a word that predates all human striving for righteousness. He expects them to hear a call to rejoice in the unimaginable superabundance of God's grace toward those who were formerly enslaved and deprived (4:27). Most of all, he expects them to hear themselves named as God's children, heirs of the promise.

After they have heard all that in the Law, there is one more thing Paul wants them to hear: an uncompromising command to "drive out" those who would enslave them by reading the Law as a package of rules or as a charter of ethnic privilege. This will sound harsh to many readers—as no doubt it did to the Galatians when they first read the letter. But on this point, Paul insists, there can be no compromise, for compromise will lead back to slavery.

All of this provides an important model for the church's continuing relation to Scripture. The text of the Old Testament cannot be dismissed as irrelevant or antiquated, nor can it be labeled as somebody else's book. The Old Testament is the Scripture of the Christian church. In the death and resurrection of Jesus Christ, the righteousness of God is disclosed apart from Law, but it is also attested by the Law and the prophets (Rom 3:21). We must learn to read the Old Testament as Paul read it, as a narrative of promise and grace.

To put the matter this way, however, raises at least two thorny issues. First, by claiming the Old Testament as Scripture, does Paul set the church on a path of supersessionism that leads to anti-Jewish attitudes? Second, are the methods Paul uses to reclaim the Old Testament narrative (allegory, in this case) legitimate methods? Let us address each of these issues in turn.

2. *The Problem of Supersessionism.* In the history of interpretation, Paul's allegory of the two covenants has often been read as an argument for the superiority of Christianity over Judaism. On this reading, Paul is trying to take the Bible away from the Jewish people and claim it for the Christian church. As we have seen in the Commentary section, however, this is a misreading of the passage. Paul is not rejecting Judaism as such; rather, writing as a Jewish Christian, he is contesting the interpretation of Israel's heritage offered by a rival group of Jewish-Christian missionaries who are disrupting his congregations in Galatia by seeking to impose their interpretation on a group of Gentiles. The bitter conflict played out in the Letter to the Galatians, then, is an argument between rival Jewish-Christian interpreters, all of whom share the conviction that the right interpretation of Scripture is a matter of great urgency.

Paul believed that the death of Jesus had initiated a "new covenant" (1 Cor 11:25) and that his own task as a missionary was to proclaim that new covenant to Jews and Gentiles alike (2 Cor 3:6). But we should bear in mind the way in which the "new covenant" image functions in Jer 31:31-34, a passage to which Paul alludes several times in his letters (e.g., Rom 2:15; 2 Cor 3:3). The new covenant does not overturn and renounce the old; rather, in the new covenant God writes the Law on the hearts of the people and restores them to a relationship with him that they had broken through their unfaithfulness. It constitutes an internalizing and renewal of the old covenant.

Paul's view of the matter is complex, because in his judgment the Sinaitic covenant had severe limitations. It did not have the power to give life, only the power to curse and imprison its adherents. Yet, when facing the prospect of declaring the Law antithetical to God's purposes, Paul backs away emphatically (3:21). The Law is not superseded so much as it is assigned a temporary role in God's larger purposes. Furthermore, in addition to the Law's confining function, it also has a witness-bearing function, which continues unabated. That is why Paul repeatedly cites Scripture as an authoritative point of reference for his congregations. At the same time, however, his reading of Scripture—as in the present passage—is daringly revisionary and transformative. He reads Israel's holy texts in previously unforeseen ways, always through the lens of the gospel.

Where does all this leave the Jewish people who remain faithful adherents of the Law and reject the gospel that Paul preaches? The question does not arise in the Letter to the Galatians, which is concerned primarily with the issue of whether Gentile converts must come under the Law. When Paul does finally address the issue of the fate of the Jewish people in relation to the gospel, he gives a lengthy dialectical response, insisting that God has not abandoned Israel and that they will be saved eschatologically (Romans 9–11).

Thus it would be wrong to characterize Paul as a supersessionist.[240] The interpreter of Gal 4:21–5:1 should take care not to use this text as a launching platform for hostile generalizations about Judaism. The best reading of the text will insist on seeing it as an intra-Christian argument championing the freedom of Gentile converts from Law observance.

3. *The Validity of Allegory.* Paul achieves his triumphant hermeneutical transformation of the Sarah and Hagar story by employing allegorical interpretation. This method enjoyed great popularity among patristic and medieval theologians, was sharply challenged by the Reformers, and fell into serious disrepute among critical scholars in the modern era, because it seemed to disregard the original literal sense of the texts it purported to interpret. How, then, are we to evaluate Paul's practice of allegorical reading? Should we repudiate it or emulate it?

Paul's figurative reading strategy depends from start to finish on delineating correspondences between the scriptural story and the events of his own time. The *dramatis personae* of Genesis 21 become correlated with the players on the stage of the Galatian churches. The Galatians are to envision themselves in the role of Isaac, the child of promise, and they are to see the Missionaries and their converts in the roles of Hagar and Ishmael. This sort of imaginative discernment of parallels between past narrative and present situation is very different from Philo's allegories that demythologize the biblical narrative into abstract spiritual truths. In fact, Paul's method of discerning parallels between the biblical narrative and the crisis facing his readers is invariably employed whenever preachers see the circumstances of their own day illumined or prefigured by the stories of Scripture. Thus all Christian preaching is inescapably allegorical, in the Pauline sense. The function of preaching is not to give factual historical reports; rather, it is to make metaphors, linking the ancient text with the present life of the congregation in fresh imaginative ways so that the text reshapes the congregation's vision of its life before God.

By that criterion, Paul's allegory in Gal 4:21–5:1 is a brilliantly successful piece of preaching, enabling his readers to envision themselves as free children of Abraham and as children of an eschatologically restored Jerusalem caught up in joyous songs of praise to God. It moves them from fearful uncertainty about their identity to celebratory determination to stand fast in the graciously given gift of freedom. When allegory functions like that, in service of proclaiming the gospel, who can withhold the water for baptizing it? The key question is whether the allegorical reading is governed by the larger shape of the biblical story—as it is here in Galatians—or whether the method is drafted into the service of other conceptualities. Any interpretative method can be abused, including historical criticism. The tests of validity are finally theological rather than methodological.

Of course, whenever we read the text with metaphorical freedom, we must do so with a certain ironic distance from our own interpretation. Allegory is a playful method; its best practitioners, like Paul, know perfectly well that their allegorical interpretations are not identical with the literal sense of the text. Nonetheless, they dare

---

240. For a fuller discussion of the problem, see Hays, *The Moral Vision of the New Testament,* 411-17.

to believe that their fresh interpretative performances are done through the lens of the gospel story with the guidance of the Holy Spirit. If so, such interpretations will disclose meanings previously hidden but now brought forth as the community needs them. Allegorical interpretation of this sort is a species of prophecy. Paul "hears" the text of Gen 21:10 speaking directly to the churches of Galatia, and his figurative reading helps them to hear the word also.

4. *The Meaning of Freedom.* Above all, Gal 4:21–5:1—the rhetorical climax of the letter—is a clarion call to stand fast in the freedom won by Christ. Any and all preaching on this text must highlight its summons to freedom. Interpreters of the text must beware of confusing the freedom of which Paul speaks with nationalistic discourses about freedom; this is not Fourth of July oratory. On the other hand, neither is Paul speaking merely about rugged individualism or an inner liberty of the conscience or the will. The crucial indicator of that fact is that freedom in Christ manifests itself through the formation of concrete communities where the old barriers of nation, race, class, and gender are overcome in communion at the one table (cf. 3:26-29; 5:13-15). In short, the freedom Paul proclaims is an *ecclesial* freedom; it is to be embodied in the corporate life of the church, as Gal 5:13–6:10 will make clear.

This freedom is to be sharply distinguished from "autonomy," a word that means literally "self-law." To be autonomous is to be, paradoxically, at the mercy of ourselves. By contrast, the freedom of which Paul speaks is freedom in Christ, a freedom that says, "It is no longer I who live, but it is Christ who lives in me" (2:20). It is not a freedom that chants, as did the Corinthians, "All things are lawful for me" (1 Cor 6:12; 10:23). Rather, it is a freedom for life in community, a freedom for mutual service in love.

What would it mean to "stand firm" in this place of freedom? It would mean, minimally, to form communities in which we resist the pressure to conform to standards imposed by the Law for covenant membership—or other analogous standards. We know ourselves to be free solely because of Christ's liberating invasion of the slave camp in which we all were confined prior to his coming. Thus, freedom is a gift, not an achievement. Where freedom is so understood, it leaves room for genuine diversity. We need not be bound by anxiety about pleasing others (1:10) or meeting expectations imposed on us by those who fancy themselves the guardians of order. We are accountable only to God, "in whose service is perfect freedom."

By standing firm, a community of true freedom gives the creation—which now groans in bondage—a glimpse of "the freedom of the glory of the children of God" (Rom 8:21). The freedom that we know now in Christ is a future-oriented sign, a foretaste, a pointer to the new creation.

GALATIANS 5:2–6:10

PASTORAL COUNSEL TO THE GALATIANS

OVERVIEW

In chaps. 5–6, Paul at last addresses the issue of circumcision explicitly, warning the Galatians of the dire consequences of following the Missionaries' teaching (5:2-12). He then offers them an alternative vision for a community that lives in love (5:13-15) under the guidance of the Spirit. Implied, but not stated, is a comparison between the Spirit and the Law, which the Missionaries have presented as a necessary antidote to the flesh. Paul, by contrast, commends the Spirit as the one power able to counteract the desires of the flesh (5:16-26). Finally, he instructs the Galatians on how to relate to one another as a community, including practices of mutual correction, sharing, and doing good to one another (6:1-10). Throughout this section we see Paul's pastoral concern for the Galatian churches, which have been disrupted by the incursion of the Missionaries, apparently with the result that they are experiencing dissension and conflict (5:15, 26; 6:1-4).

GALATIANS 5:2-12, A CALL TO REJECT CIRCUMCISION

COMMENTARY

5:2-4. For the first time in the letter, Paul names the specific issue that has evoked his impassioned response: circumcision. (This was foreshadowed by his earlier reference to resisting pressure to circumcise Titus [2:3], but now for the first time we learn that circumcision is the primary issue confronting the Galatian churches.) The Galatians are considering being circumcised, and Paul regards the prospect as a disaster. Paul's words give us no clue about why pressure for circumcision is now being brought upon the Galatian churches despite the agreement that he had earlier worked out with the "pillars" in the Jerusalem church (2:1-10). It is likely, in the light of the subsequent controversy at Antioch (2:11-14), that at least some factions within the Jerusalem church no longer regarded that agreement as binding. We must also remember that the faction Paul calls the "false brothers" (2:4) had never been party to the agreement in the first place.

The opening of a new section is punctuated by Paul's emphatic interjection of his own authoritative persona into the discourse: "Look! I, Paul, am telling you. . . ." He has laid out a lengthy theological argument to support his position (3:1–5:1); now he arrives at the practical application of all he has said so far, and he throws the full weight of his personal authority behind his blunt declaration that circumcision will negate any benefit the Galatians might have received from Christ.

This is an extraordinarily strong claim. Does Paul mean that Jews cannot be believers, cannot receive Christ's benefits? Clearly he cannot mean that; Paul himself, as a Jew, was circumcised (Phil 3:5). What he is saying is that Gentile converts to the Christian faith must not allow themselves to be circumcised.

Why? Some of the reasons are to be found in the arguments of chaps. 3 and 4: Circumcision, as an entry to living under the Law, is a backward step to an earlier stage of the story, a step that leads into slavery. But in 5:2-4, he articulates his position in even stronger terms. He posits a fundamental incompatibility between Law and Christ; they represent separate spheres of power, such that anyone who chooses to enter the Law's sphere of power has been cut off from access to Christ. One's allegiance must rest in one sphere or the other; no compromise is possible. To choose circumcision voluntarily is to deem Christ insufficient and thereby to abandon his sphere of influence.

That, perhaps, explains Paul's reminder in v. 3 that circumcision creates an obligation to obey the whole Law. As we saw in the discussion of 3:10-14, his point cannot be that the Law requires sinless perfection, for the Law contains extensive provisions to provide atonement and forgiveness of sins. Rather, he is telling the Galatians that if they choose to be circumcised, they are crossing a guarded border into an occupied territory where the Law rules. The Law is a total way of life, a religious system that makes a total demand on one's life. To come under the Law (3:23; 4:4-5, 21) is to enter a sphere where the Law is sovereign. One cannot then pick and choose which commandments to follow; it is a total package. One must either get in or get out. (Here we no doubt hear an echo of Paul the rigorous Pharisee, who well understood the comprehensive demand of the Law during his earlier period of surpassing zeal for the traditions of his ancestors; see 1:13-14.)

Scholars have sometimes speculated on the basis of v. 3 that the Missionaries in Galatia were urging circumcision merely as a token identity marker, without actually calling for total Law observance. In view of Paul's overall argument, however, that seems improbable. The Galatians, Paul says, "desire to be subject to the Law" (4:21), and they are already adopting the observance of sabbaths and Jewish festivals (4:10). Furthermore, as part of their case for circumcision, the Missionaries were ominously quoting Deuteronomy: "Cursed is everyone who does not observe and obey all the things written in the book of the Law" (3:10). Thus, when Paul

writes that circumcision creates an obligation to do the whole Law, he cannot be telling the Galatians something they do not already know. The warning takes its force from the way Paul poses Christ and Law as mutually exclusive options, in stark contrast to the Missionaries' desire to blend them together.

The consequence of this exclusivity is spelled out in v. 4: Those who seek to be rectified through the Law have made Christ of no effect and have fallen out of grace. "Grace" is conceived here (like "freedom" in v. 1) as a location, a sphere from which the Galatians will exile themselves if they go forward with the action they are contemplating. The thought is a more pointed restatement of the conclusion of Paul's sharp challenge to Peter: "I do not nullify the grace of God; for if rectification comes through the Law, then Christ died for nothing" (2:21). Nullifying the grace of God is precisely what the Galatians will do, Paul warns, if they undergo circumcision. (The NRSV rendering of v. 4, "cut yourselves off from Christ," conveys the right idea but suggests a pun on "cutting" the flesh that is not present in the Greek text; the NIV is preferable.)

Paul's formulation of the warning carries a note of irony. He writes, literally, "You who are being rectified by the Law. . . ." Since he has already unconditionally asserted that no one *can* be rectified by the Law (2:16; 3:11), Paul is ironically suggesting that the attempt to seek rectification through circumcision is not only futile but also illusory. His use of the verb "justify/rectify" (δικαιόω *dikaioō*) in this sentence reinforces our finding that "rectification" refers in the first instance to inclusion within the covenant people of God (see the Commentary on 2:16). That is the end the Galatians would seek through circumcision. As the apostle has affirmed repeatedly, however, the Galatians have already been embraced into God's people through the faithfulness of Jesus Christ, entirely apart from any action on their part. Thus their seeking covenant membership in some other way constitutes a tragic rejection of God's grace in Christ.

5:5-6. In contrast to those who seek rectification/righteousness (δικαιοσύνη *dikaiosynē*) through the Law, "*We* [the position of the pronoun is emphatic] by the Spirit eagerly await, through faith, the [eschatological] hope of righteousness." The contrast between v. 4 and v. 5 is to be noted: Those who seek righteousness through the Law claim covenant membership as a present possession, whereas Paul and those who share his vision look to a future eschatological verdict of God. While Paul can sometimes speak of rectification as having occurred already through the death and resurrection of Jesus (e.g., Rom 5:1), his dialectical eschatology continues to insist that *dikaiosynē* is a future state of affairs. Insofar as "rectification" refers to being included within God's people, Paul's congregations have already experienced it, and they bear witness to it through fellowship between Jews and Gentiles at one table; nevertheless, insofar as "rectification" refers to God's final establishment of justice, it remains a future hope.[241]

The futurity of rectification is not a prominent theme of Galatians, but it is a deep and consistent emphasis of Paul's theology. The language of v. 5 prefigures the much fuller development of the same ideas in Rom 8:18-25: Those who have the Spirit groan along with a creation still in bondage while eagerly awaiting the fulfillment of our hope. Important here is not only the noun "hope" (ἐλπίς *elpis*), but also the verb "await eagerly" (ἀπεκδέχομαι *apekdechomai*, v. 5; Rom 8:19, 23, 25), which depicts the joyous longing with which believers expect the ultimate disclosure of God's glory and grace. The same verb appears in 1 Cor 1:7 and Phil 3:20; in both cases, it refers to the expectation of Christ's glorious coming again to transform us into his glory and to rule over creation. These passages help us to see more fully what Paul means by "the hope of righteousness."

The capacity to wait in eager expectation is sustained, Paul says, by the Spirit and by faith. These terms carry with them in v. 5 the full weight they have acquired through his earlier exposition (2:16; 3:1-14, 22-26; 4:6-7). The Spirit is the promised blessing given to Jew and Gentile alike through Christ's faithful death; it cries out and testifies, even in this time of waiting, that we are God's children. Paul's use of the phrase "by faith"

(ἐκ πίστεως *ek pisteōs*) takes on special pertinence here. It is derived from Hab 2:4 (cited in Gal 3:11), where it supplies the answer to the prophet's complaint about the suffering endured by God's people. God's answer to Habakkuk—which becomes a keynote for Paul's preaching of the gospel—is that the righteous one will live ἐκ πίστεως *ek pisteōs*. In other words, the righteous will live in a posture of trustful expectation, waiting for God to bring the promised deliverance. That is precisely the stance Paul describes in v. 5.

The apocalyptic character of the hope to which Paul refers is highlighted in v. 6, which strongly recalls the "new creation" theme hinted at in 3:28 and made fully explicit in 6:15. Those who are "in Christ Jesus" have entered a sphere that anticipates the eschatological redemption, a sphere in which the very categories of "circumcision" and "uncircumcision" have become utterly null and void. Paul says (literally) that they no longer "have strength." In this situation, the Missionaries' urging the Galatians to be circumcised appears ridiculous; it is a retrogression to a world of categories that have been abolished by the cross.

In place of these old categories now vitiated, there appears one new reality that does have strength and validity: "faith working through love." The expression "faith *working*" might have struck the first-time readers of this letter as an oxymoron. Has not Paul set "faith" and "works" in absolute opposition to each other (3:10-12)? Verse 6*b* forces us to reexamine what Paul means by both terms. His polemic against "works" is not meant to disparage the doing of good deeds (see also 6:9-10). Rather, he is targeting "works of the *Law*," the specific acts of obedience that define membership in the Jewish people as determined under the Law of Moses. This was the issue faced by the Galatians, not the issue of whether they could earn their salvation by good works (see the Commentary on 3:10). At the same time, "faith" is not merely a subjective mental attitude or an inventory of doctrinal beliefs; it refers—as it did in the case of Abraham—to trust lived out in practice. This is nowhere clearer than in v. 6. Faith is not a state of passive quiescence. In Christ, faith becomes effectively enacted through love.[242]

---

241. The phrase "hope of righteousness" is ambiguous. Does it mean "that for which righteousness hopes" (subjective genitive) or "the hope which consists in righteousness" (epexegetical genitive)? The latter interpretation is to be preferred. See Martyn, *Galatians*, 472.

242. Dunn comments: "Here Paul comes as close as he ever does to James (James ii.18)." Dunn, *The Epistle to the Galatians*, 272.

The word "love" (ἀγάπη *agapē*) is a favorite Pauline theme that makes its first appearance within the letter here in v. 6. More precisely, this is the first appearance of the noun. Paul used the verb once previously in the letter, in a context that defines its meaning with considerable precision. Paul now lives "by the *faith* of the Son of God, who *loved* me and gave himself for me" (2:20). The love of the Son of God is shown by his action of self-giving for our sake; this self-giving in turn is understood as the enactment of his faith. Thus Gal 2:20 provides a paradigmatic picture of "faith working through love." What does it look like? It looks like Jesus on the cross. That, Paul says, is the only thing that matters in the new creation. The church is called to embody this faith working through love in a way that corresponds to the story of the cross. The demand for circumcision is completely irrelevant to this calling.

5:7-10. In vv. 5-6 Paul portrays his positive vision of the community of faith, awaiting rectification through Christ and animated by faith working through love. In v. 7, however, his thoughts turn sadly once again to the Galatians, who have stumbled and are in danger of losing the vision. He employs the athletic metaphor of running a race (cf. 1 Cor 9:24-27; Phil 3:12-14; 2 Tim 4:7). The Galatians "were running well"; the verb is in the imperfect tense, indicating that for some time after Paul's departure they had continued to make progress, like a runner striding forward smoothly. But now something has happened to trip them up. The NIV ("Who cut in on you?") represents the Greek text precisely, while the NRSV loses the metaphor. The Galatians are now like runners thrown off stride by another runner cutting into their path and shoving them off balance. At the same time, Paul's choice of verb almost certainly carries a witty double entendre: The Missionaries have "cut in" on them by demanding to cut the flesh of their foreskins.

The effect of the Missionaries' interference has been to divert the Galatians from "obeying the truth."[243] Again, as in 2:5, 14, we see that "the truth" entails certain behaviors, or perhaps better, certain forms of community

life. The truth is not merely an idea to be acknowledged; it is a body of practices to be followed. The truth demands not just intellectual assent but practical obedience. The verb translated as "obeying" also carries the sense of "being persuaded." The Missionaries have knocked the Galatians off balance by undercutting their confidence about the gospel Paul had preached to them, so that they are no longer fully persuaded of the truth they had been taught before.

Rhetorical persuasion has played a major role in the Missionaries' strategy. But Paul asserts that this persuasion—however superficially appealing—does not come from God ("the one who called you"; cf. 1:6). The Galatians have been diverted from their original calling by someone who is not an agent of God, someone employing manipulative rhetoric. The sequence of thought recalls 1:6-9, where Paul pronounces anathema on anyone who promotes confusion by preaching a message that does not come from God. Commentators sometimes suggest that v. 8 implies that Satan is the source of the Missionaries' false persuasive power (cf. 2 Cor 12:7; 1 Thess 2:18), but that inference goes beyond what Paul says here. His main point is to deny any divine authorization for his rivals' persuasive rhetoric. The question, "Who cut in on you?" does not require an answer; Paul and his Galatian readers know perfectly well whom he is talking about.

The transition of thought in vv. 9-10 seems abrupt and puzzling, but there is more coherence here than meets the eye initially. The key to understanding the flow of thought is to recognize that, just as in 4:30–5:1, Paul is calling for the Galatian churches to expel the Missionaries from their communities.[244] That is why he quotes the proverb, "A little leaven leavens the whole batch of dough" (v. 10). This is a word of warning about the subtle corrupting power of false teaching and behavior. In 1 Cor 5:6, Paul quotes precisely the same proverb to support his order that the Corinthians expel a flagrant sexual offender from the church. Here in vv. 9-10 the issue is different, but the point is the same: The church should take action to preserve its integrity by excising the cancer before it can

---

243. On this whole topic, see J. M. G. Barclay, *Obeying the Truth: A Study of Paul's Ethics in Galatians*, Studies of the NT and Its World (Edinburgh: T. & T. Clark, 1988).

244. Williams, *Galatians*, 140-41.

spread. The Missionaries' teaching is not from God (v. 8), and it must be rooted out before it corrupts the community. Paul does not repeat the directive of 4:30, but the point is clear: The proverb of v. 9 is a warrant for them to take strong exclusionary action.

Verse 10 follows logically from this reading of v. 9. Paul is confident that the Galatians will take his view of the matter and act accordingly—i.e., that they will throw out the rival Missionaries. Of course, this expression of confidence is itself an exaggeration, a rhetorical ploy designed to enlist their support; for a less sanguine view of the situation, see 4:11, 20. Nevertheless, Paul is confident "in the Lord" (v. 10) that the Galatians will see the truth; he cannot believe that God will allow his work to be destroyed.

The latter part of v. 10 also fits with this train of thought. He writes, literally, "The one who is confusing you will bear the judgment." In the last analysis, the judgment of which Paul speaks is surely God's judgment, but, in a more proximate sense, he may be speaking also of the community's act of exclusionary judgment on the troublemaker. In the light of this interpretation, we can paraphrase vv. 7-10 as follows, with explanatory expansions in italics:

You were running well. Who cut in on you *and knocked you off balance,* to keep you from obeying the truth? Their elaborate rhetoric does not come from God who calls you; *if you listen to them they will lead you astray. Therefore, you must drive them out of your community,* because a little leaven leavens the whole lump of dough. *If you let them stay in your midst, they will corrupt the entire church.* I am confident in the Lord that you will not think otherwise, *and that you will do as I say. Even if this sounds harsh, it is a matter of God's judgment.* Anyone who tries to confuse you will bear the judgment, whoever he may be.

Why does Paul formulate the word of warning in v. 10b in the singular, in contrast to the plural depiction of the opponents in 1:7 and 5:12? Three explanations are possible: (1) Paul is thinking of a single person, the leader of the Missionaries' efforts; (2) since there are multiple Galatian churches, perhaps there is only a single rival Missionary at work in each one;[245]

(3) the warning is formulated in general terms to apply to any individual who may trouble the Galatian churches. The simplest explanation, and therefore probably the best, is the third. If Paul had in mind a single adversary, there is no reason to think that he would shrink from naming him, as he named Cephas in 2:11-14. At the same time, the indefinite expression "whoever he may be" communicates a studied disregard for the authority the Missionaries claimed, just as Paul's ironic reference to "those who were reputed to be pillars" in 2:6, 9 suggests that he was not impressed by their reputation. (The NIV captures this nuance better than does the NRSV.)

5:11. Abruptly Paul—perhaps provoked by his reference in v. 10b to his rivals' work of sowing confusion in the Galatian churches—responds to an ad hominem accusation. His response is so brief and cryptic that it is difficult to be sure what he is responding to. For some reason, the Missionaries were claiming that Paul sometimes preached circumcision. In the light of our knowledge of Paul's letters, the claim seems bizarre. What could Paul's rivals have meant? There have been numerous conjectures,[246] but the likeliest construction is that the troublemakers were telling the Galatians that Paul did, in fact, advocate circumcision on other occasions in other communities, but that he had kept this crucial knowledge of God's covenant seal back from the Galatians, perhaps because he was a "people pleaser," afraid to risk incurring their disfavor (cf. 1:10). The story reported in Acts 16:1-3 would provide grist for this rumor mill: Paul had, in fact, supported the circumcision of Timothy, who was well known to the believers in Lystra and Iconium (i.e., "South Galatia").[247] In short, the Missionaries alleged, Paul had waffled and failed to tell the Galatians the whole truth about God's requirements, although he showed by his actions elsewhere that he really did recognize the importance of circumcision.

To refute this accusation, Paul points to his own experience of persecution at the hands

---

245. Dunn, *The Epistle to the Galatians,* 278.

246. For a helpful list of six options, see Dunn, *The Epistle to the Galatians,* 278-80.

247. Luke is careful to point out that Timothy's mother was Jewish (Acts 16:1). Under Jewish tradition, this made him a Jew rather than a Gentile.

of Jewish believers. "If I were preaching circumcision," he says in effect, "these zealous Jews would not be giving me trouble all the time." But in fact, since Paul is regularly persecuted by the circumcision faction, that proves he is not a supporter of their position. If he had given up preaching his Law-free gospel for Gentiles, there would be no point of conflict. (For references to the persecution of Christians, and of Paul in particular, see 1:13, 23; 4:29; 6:12, 17; perhaps also 4:13-14.) It may be debated whether the persecution Paul refers to originates specifically from Jewish-Christian authorities (as 4:29 would suggest) or from non-Christian synagogues (1:13-14; Acts 14:19; 17:5-14).

Paul also gives a theological reason for his refusal to "preach circumcision" (the phrase is probably his own capsule summary of the Missionaries' Law-observant gospel): If he preached circumcision, then "the offense [lit., "stumbling block" (σκάνδαλον *skandalon*)] of the cross has been abolished." The logic of the sentence requires that the *skandalon* be understood as a good thing. Paul throws this phrase out as though he expects his Galatian readers to understand what he means. Perhaps in his earlier preaching to them he had used this terminology, but there is no prior explanation for it in this letter. Presupposed is the line of thought that Paul develops in 1 Cor 1:18–2:5: The proclamation of the cross is "a *skandalon* to Jews and foolishness to Gentiles, but to those who are the called, both Jews and Greeks, Christ the power of God and the wisdom of God" (1 Cor 1:23-24 NRSV). The cross confounds all human religion and philosophy, all human wisdom. It is the strange instrument by which God has shattered the old world and brought a new one into being (cf. 2:19-21; 3:13-14; 6:14-15). Thus, in the compressed formula of v. 11*b,* Paul is saying that he could not go back to preaching circumcision (as he did in his former life, 1:13-14), because to do so would be to negate the world-transforming power of the gospel that had been divinely revealed to him. It would be to go back to business as usual in a world where circumcision served to mark the Jewish people off from the rest of the world. For the religious worldview of that former life, the cross is a stumbling block because it delegitimates the distinctions between Jew and Gentile, between sacred and

profane, that structure the whole meaning of that world.

Thus, in v. 11 Paul rebuts the insinuation that he has advocated circumcision in other churches with a brief two-pronged response. The empirical evidence of his continued harassment from the circumcision party shows that the accusation is false, and, in any case, if he started advocating circumcision, it would constitute nothing less than a repudiation of the gospel—just as the Galatians will now be repudiating the gospel if they allow themselves to undergo circumcision.

5:12. The thought of the Missionaries' outrageous misrepresentation of his true position causes Paul to boil over with anger. He fires a ferocious gibe at his adversaries. It is a crude joke: "If they are so eager to start cutting on the male sexual organ, I wish they would just castrate themselves." One imagines that when the letter was read in the Galatian churches, this bold swipe would have elicited a few gasps from the congregation, followed by laughter from Paul's partisans and outrage from his detractors. We may feel that this sort of coarse humor hardly commends Paul's argument, but here, as elsewhere in the letter, Paul is exploiting the rhetorical techniques available to him to persuade his readers to take his side of the argument.[248]

The fact that Paul goes to such a rhetorical extreme to attack his opponents demonstrates how strongly he felt about the issues under debate and how furious he was about the Missionaries' misleading account of his own convictions and about their "unsettling" of his congregations. On the other hand, Paul's sarcastic linkage of circumcision with castration might justly be regarded by the Missionaries as a scurrilous libel. The argument has, by any measure, turned ugly.

248. Betz notes that "the ridiculing of eunuchs was a standby of the diatribe preacher." That is hardly what Paul is doing here, but the analogy may be relevant. Commentators have long observed that the pagan cult of Cybele, which had a prominent temple in the "North Galatian" city of Pessinus, was well-known for its castrated priests. See Betz, *Galatians,* 270. Paul's vicious joke may be intended to link the Missionaries' emphasis on circumcision with this sort of pagan ritual, in which case 5:12 would provide another example of Paul's provocative portrayal of Judaism as just one more variant of pagan religion under the *stoicheia.* See 4:8-11; Martyn, *Galatians,* 478. Within Jewish tradition, however, practices of sexual mutilation were regarded with horror. As Paul well knew, the Law that the Missionaries championed lays down a stern rule: "No one whose testicles are crushed or whose penis is cut off shall be admitted to the assembly of the Lord" (Deut 23:1 NRSV). If Paul's gruesome wish were granted, then the circumcision advocates would thereby be cut off from their own people.

REFLECTIONS

1. *No Packages of Membership Requirements.* It takes no great leap of imagination to see how Paul's comments on the issue of circumcision might be applied to other issues that arise from time to time in the life of the church. We face an analogous challenge whenever the preaching of the gospel is accompanied by some further proviso that says, "Of course you must trust in God's grace through Jesus Christ, *but* if you really want to belong to God's people, you must do one more thing. . . ." It is the "but" clause that is fatal, no matter what the "one more thing" may be. The analogy to the Galatian situation is particularly strong when the "but" clause includes some stipulation about national or ethnic identity. Paul is the eternal enemy of all efforts to bundle the gospel as part of a package deal that includes additional membership requirements. All such attempts at bundling turn out to be rejections of the grace of God.

2. A corollary of the previous point is that Christ makes a comprehensive claim on our lives. There can be no divided loyalties, no compromises, no areas where we remain autonomous agents. Karl Barth expresses the point powerfully:

> For by this covenant we are not only embraced by the fact of the death and resurrection of Jesus Christ. . . . We are also embraced (and closely so, without any empty or neutral zones) by His living command through which He wills to sanctify us, attract us to Himself, and therefore awaken us to obedience, as partners in His covenant.[249]

Our life is totally embraced by Christ without any "neutral zones." The Law constitutes a rival symbolic universe, and precisely for that reason it must be categorically rejected. There can be no other symbolic universe, for we are encompassed by the sphere of Christ's power and grace. If we recognize that and live accordingly, we will—paradoxically—learn the meaning of freedom.

3. *The Hope of Righteousness.* Galatians 5:5 is the clearest statement in the letter that the rectification in which we trust remains a future hope. We look to the future, trusting that God will set all things right in the end. The apocalyptic language of "eager expectation" characterizes our longing for God's new world, a world that we hope for but do not yet see (cf. Rom 8:24-25). And yet, at the same time, we already find ourselves living into that new world, for in Christ circumcision and uncircumcision have ceased to be valid categories (5:6). The tension between 5:5 and 5:6 is the dialectical tension between the "not yet" and the "already." This tension is a fundamental truth about life in Christ, as we live in the strange time between his resurrection and his coming again in glory, the anomalous time that T. S. Eliot called "the time of tension between dying and birth."[250] One of the problems with the Missionaries' message was that it sought to dissolve this tension by making rectification immediately available in life under the Law, symbolized by the concrete act of circumcision. Paul's gospel resists such closure and calls us to live in a world destabilized by the cross, while looking to the future with hope.

4. *Faith Working Through Love.* In place of the fixed categories of circumcision and uncircumcision, categories that divide Jew and Gentile, the new life in Christ is characterized by the dynamic reality of "faith working through love." Faith that is kindled by God will necessarily issue forth in action. The character of faith's action is defined by "the faith of the Son of God who loved me and gave himself for me" (2:20). Thus love-empowered faith will manifest itself in sacrificial service for others (cf. 5:13-14).

---

249. Barth, *Church Dogmatics* II/2, 708.
250. T. S. Eliot, "Ash Wednesday," in *The Complete Poems and Plays, 1909–1950* (New York: Harcourt, Brace & World, n.d.) 66.

The participle Paul uses in the expression "faith *working* through love" comes from the verb ἐνεργέω (*energeō*; cf. the English cognate "energy"), which Paul almost always uses to describe an external power working in and through human beings. Sometimes the external power is evil—such as passions (Rom 7:5) or death (2 Cor 4:12) or "the mystery of lawlessness" (2 Thess 2:7)—but more often it is the power of God through the Holy Spirit (1 Cor 12:6, 11; Gal 2:8; 3:5; Col 1:29; 1 Thess 2:13; cf. Eph 1:11, 20; 3:20). Emblematic of this latter cluster of passages is Phil 2:13: "For it is God who is at work [ἐνεργῶν *energōn*] in you, enabling you both to will and to work [ἐνεργεῖν *energein*] for his good pleasure" (NRSV). The "faith working through love" that human beings experience, then, is nothing less than the power of God working, through us, effectually in the world. Those who experience God's power in their lives will say with Paul that "it is no longer I who live but Christ who lives in me." The faith we experience is "the faith of Jesus Christ" not only because he is its exemplar, but also because he is its active source. Thus the faith of Christ will always manifest itself in love (see 1 Cor 12:31*b*–13:13). Doctrinal orthodoxy without the active manifestation of love is not the faith of which Paul speaks.

5. *Paul's Polemic.* Paul's passionate resistance to the rival Missionaries leads him to utter, in the heat of debate, a violent wish that they would castrate themselves (5:12). Does this text provide a model for discourse in the church today, in a time when we have our own bitter controversies? In one sense, the answer is, "Of course not." Mudslinging and obscene jokes are not likely to promote peaceful resolution of disputes; Paul's outburst sits oddly alongside his call for "faith working through love" in 5:6. One doubts that Paul would defend, in retrospect, his choice of words. Yet it is important to see the larger context in which this hostile remark is made. Paul is unequivocally calling for the Galatians to expel from their churches a group of outside agitators who are, in his view, subverting the gospel and leading people away from Christ. They are causing the Galatians to fall away from grace. This is serious business.

Paul's invective is reminiscent of the psalms that pray for harm to befall the enemies of God and of God's people (Ps 137:8-9 is the most notorious example). Discernment is called for here.

On the one hand, the presence of such texts in the canon of Scripture does not necessarily commend the hostility of the speakers' voices; the Bible is full of texts that show human beings, even God's beloved elect human beings, in the light of sober reality. Paul, like Abraham and Jacob and David, had his rough side. In that sense, he is no better than the rest of us, and Gal 5:12 offers a glimpse of Paul's unsanctified pique. In a strange way, we may find such displays of fallibility comforting, knowing that even apostles can have lapses of judgment.

On the other hand, Paul's anger has a deep and serious cause, and we should not too quickly pass over this point. The underlying anger is not isolated to this one verse; from 1:6-9 onward, controlled anger sets the tone of the whole letter. And, if one grants Paul's conviction that the Missionaries are in fact leading his churches to fall away from the grace of God, the anger would be fully justified, like Jesus' anger at the Temple money changers or like God's anger toward hard-hearted and unfaithful Israel (e.g., Deut 32:15-22). If we believe that there are times when lines must be drawn and evil named as evil (see the Commentary and Reflections on 1:6-9), then there is a time for anger (cf. Eccl 3:8). Christian faith does not mandate bland tolerance of destructive powers. Indeed, Gal 5:12 may cause us to pause to reflect on whether we have failed to be as angry as we should be toward those who corrupt and disrupt the church's faith in the gospel.

6. Finally, Paul's reference to "the stumbling block of the cross" (v. 11) reminds us of the fundamental message of the gospel, the story of the crucified Jesus Christ (3:1, 13). Invariably we encounter subtle temptations to repackage the message in ways that obscure or minimize the cross. We would dearly love to move the cross out of the center of the story, because then we could work out some sort of accommodation and coordination with other religious and philosophical worldviews; we could preach circumcision and Jesus, too—perhaps a Jesus who was an enlightened teacher of wisdom. But that would be unfaithful. There is no gospel without the offense of the cross, for the cross puts an end to all our human projects of self-justification. Paul will return to the point in his postscript (6:12-14). Our preaching, like his, must return to it again and again.

GALATIANS 5:13-15, FREEDOM FOR LOVE

COMMENTARY

5:13. Many commentators consider this verse to be the beginning of the final major section of the letter, taking vv. 2-11 as the conclusion of the letter's central argument (3:1–5:11) and treating 5:13–6:10 as a unit of paraenesis (moral exhortation) appended to the main body of the discussion. There are some good reasons for this analysis; the most important factor is that only in 5:13–6:10 do we find a concentration of verbs in the imperative and hortatory subjunctive moods. By contrast, vv. 2-12 consist of warnings and reproaches. Nevertheless, the structural markers in the Greek text suggest a different division, which is followed in this commentary. The clear break point comes in v. 2 with Paul's emphatic interjection, "Look, I, Paul, am telling you. . . ." There is no such clear new beginning at this verse, which is introduced simply with the conjunction "for" (γάρ *gar*), implying that the content of v. 13*a* supplies the logical warrant for the preceding statements. (The NRSV translates the conjunction, while the NIV does not.) Verses 11-12 are a slight digression, as Paul rebuts a false accusation, and the *gar* of v. 13 should be understood to resume and support the argument of vv. 2-10, with vv. 7-10 interpreted as an implicit call for the Galatians to expel the rival Missionaries (see the Commentary on 5:7-10). The line of thought leading from v. 2 into v. 13 can be paraphrased, then, as follows:

If you let yourself be circumcised, you will be separated from Christ (vv. 2-4). Circumcision is irrelevant in the new creation brought by Christ (vv. 5-6). Therefore, you should reject circumcision

and drive out the Missionaries who demand it; I am confident that you will do as I say (vv. 7-10). The reason that you should take this action is that you were called to freedom (v. 13*a*).

Thus it makes better sense to treat 5:2–6:10 as the final major unit of the letter. This section is unified by Paul's pastoral concern to show the Galatians how to conduct their lives together as a community.

Despite the fact that, structurally speaking, v. 13 does not mark the beginning of a new unit, it does serve an important transitional function. The first part of the sentence sums up the central thesis of the letter ("For you were called to freedom"), reminding the readers of the climactic manifesto of 5:1. It is God who has done the calling (1:6; 5:8), and the freedom has been won by Christ (1:4; 2:20; 3:13; 4:4-5; 5:1). Having summarized the gospel proclamation, however, Paul now confronts a new challenge: Does the freedom given by Christ leave us without moral guidance? That is the problem introduced and addressed by v. 13*bc*: "Only do not use your freedom as an opportunity for the flesh, but through love become slaves to one another."

If the Law was a temporary custodian that has now been dismissed from service by Christ, and if the Law no longer functions to regulate human life, then are we adrift on a sea of moral confusion? No doubt this was one of the major arguments put forward by the Missionaries. They sought to convince the Galatians that Paul had irresponsibly baptized them without giving them the appropriate instruction in the Law, which, they asserted, was necessary to hold humanity's sinful impulses ("the flesh") in check. The Law provides guidance (cf. the metaphor of the "yoke" in 5:1) to keep us from going astray into sin and error. This was one of the glorious benefits of the Law in standard Jewish teaching.[251] In the light of this challenge, Paul must provide an alternative account of how his gospel provides sufficient moral direction for the daily life of the community of faith. Betz explains the logic behind the transition to moral exhortation that occurs in v. 13:

Paul realizes that mere polemic against circumcision and law (5:2-12 . . .) does not do justice to the Galatian trouble. There has to be a positive and viable proposal as to how to deal effectively with misconduct and failure, that is, with the "flesh."[252]

The entire unit of 5:13–6:10, then, provides Paul's positive proposal about how the community is to deal with the problem of "the flesh": They are called to live in love, under the guidance of God's Spirit, not of the Law. The precise language that Paul uses in v. 13 should be noted carefully. The verb "use" is supplied by the NRSV and the NIV to complete an elliptical sentence that lacks a verb; Martyn's suggestion is an equally viable way of filling out the thought: "only do not *allow* freedom *to be turned into.* . . ."[253] (The Greek does not say "*your* freedom"; this possessive pronoun, too, has been supplied by the translations.) The thing that freedom must not be turned into is an ἀφορμὴν τῇ σαρκί (*aphormēn tē sarki*). The difference between the NIV ("to indulge the sinful nature") and the NRSV ("as an opportunity for self-indulgence") at this point is an indicator of the challenge of translating this phrase properly. The noun ἀφορμή (*aphormē*) means literally a staging area or base of operations for a military campaign.[254] It came to be used metaphorically in Hellenistic Greek to mean "opportunity" (NRSV), but Paul may very

well be using it here with some conscious resonance of its original literal sense. The Galatians have been caught up in a cosmic conflict, and they must take care not to let the territory won for them by Christ become a staging ground for a counterattack by the hostile power of the flesh.

"Flesh" (σάρξ *sarx*) is the other key word in the expression. The paraphrases of the NIV and the NRSV convey only part of its range of connotations. It can be used in a neutral sense to mean the physical body or the stuff of which it is made (2:20; 6:13), usually with the nuance of mortality or mortal limitation (1:16; 4:13-14; cf. Rom 8:3). On the other hand, it can be used, as it is throughout 5:13-26, to refer to a sinful power resident in human existence that opposes God. In Galatians, Paul sometimes plays artfully on this ambiguity, as in 3:3 and 4:23, 29. In some contexts it is difficult to tell whether Paul is using the term metonymically to describe the fallen human creature in the state of alienation from God, or whether he is thinking of "Flesh" as a hostile power (like "Sin" and "Death"), external to the individual human self. Indeed, this ambiguity is particularly acute throughout 5:13-26. Paul's use of military metaphors throughout the passage (vv. 13, 17, 25) suggests that—at least for the dramatic imagery of his exhortation—he is employing the image of Flesh as a quasi-personified hostile power. The message of v. 13*b*, then, is, "Do not allow freedom to become a base of operations for the hostile power of the Flesh."

The positive recommendation that Paul offers as an antidote to allowing Flesh to take control comes as a surprise. We might expect him to say, "Do not allow freedom to become a base of operations for the hostile power of the Flesh, but resist sinful desires with all your might," or some such. Instead, he writes: "Through love become slaves to one another." After his forceful repudiation of slavery (4:8-9, 25-26; 5:1), this formulation comes as a shocking paradox. The Galatians are to use their freedom to become slaves! (By translating the verb δουλεύω [*douleuō*] as "serve," the NIV minimizes the paradox and loses the clear link to the foregoing imagery of slavery.) Paul does not speak of becoming slaves to God or Christ, or even of

---

251. Barclay, *Obeying the Truth* 107, gives numerous references. A single example will suffice: "[Moses] did not leave practical training in morals inarticulate; nor did he permit the letter of the law to remain inoperative. . . . He left nothing, however insignificant, to the discretion and caprice of the individual. What meats a man should abstain from, and what he may enjoy; with what persons he should associate; what period should be devoted respectively to strenuous labor and to rest—for all this our leader made the law the standard and rule, that we might live under it as under a father and master, and be guilty of no sin through wilfulness or ignorance" (Josephus *Against Apion* 2.174).

252. Betz, Galatians, 273.

253. Martyn, *Galatians*, 479.

254. BAGD, 127.

"righteousness" (cf. Rom 6:15-23). Instead, he says, they are to serve *one another* as slaves. If the way to keep Flesh from gaining a base of operations is through loving, mutual service, this suggests that the power of Flesh will try to manifest itself through pride, rivalry, and autonomy. Thus Paul's prescription has shifted the conversation into the realm of relationships within the community, as the rest of the hortatory section (5:13–6:10) will confirm.

Paul's paradoxical prescription for mutual slavery would have sounded strange and offensive to Greek ears; the ideal of Hellenistic philosophy, particularly Stoicism, was to attain a position of autonomous detachment. A classic definition of freedom is given by Epictetus:

He is free who lives as he wills, who is subject neither to compulsion, nor hindrance, nor force, whose choices are unhampered, whose desires attain their end, whose aversions do not fall into what they would avoid.[255]

In the context of such a prevailing ideology, Paul's call for the Galatians to enslave themselves would have seemed bizarre. His counterintuitive advice, however, oddly transforms the meaning and context of slavery. Becoming "slaves to one another," where the acts of service are conceived as mutual, redefines the concept of slavery, which is necessarily hierarchical in character.[256]

The other major element in Paul's prescription for resisting the Flesh is "love." This clearly links v. 13 back to "faith working through love" (v. 6), which is the one effective power that has replaced the Law's emphasis on circumcision. Paul will next show how his counsel of love as the antidote to Flesh is related to the rival Missionaries' favored solution.

5:14. Another rhetorical shock follows hard upon the first. If we were shocked to find Paul speaking in a paradoxically positive way about slavery, we will be equally surprised to discover in this verse that the Law suddenly assumes a positive valence. Up to this point in the letter, the Law has been depicted primarily as the instrument of curse, confinement,

and slavery. But now, suddenly, Paul declares that the Law finds its central meaning in a single verse from Leviticus: "You shall love your neighbor as yourself" (Lev 19:18). This remarkable reversal of field requires careful examination. How can Paul say that "the whole law" is fulfilled in loving the neighbor?

First, we should remember that in 4:21–5:1 Paul had refused to leave the Law in the possession of the circumcision party. He argued that if the Galatians will, in fact, "hear the Law," they will hear it proclaiming them to be children of the promise. Indeed, they will hear it calling for the expulsion of those who demand circumcision! This suggests that Paul has already staked a claim on a new and different reading of the Law, a dramatic hermeneutical revision in the light of the gospel. Reading the Law through the lens provided by the cross and the resurrection of Jesus—as well as through the experience of the Holy Spirit in communities of Gentile believers—Paul now sees in it a meaning very different from anything he could have grasped during his former life as a zealous Pharisee. The Law has undergone a hermeneutical transformation, so that it now becomes a witness to the gospel (cf. Rom 1:2; 3:21; 10:5-13; 15:4; 1 Cor 10:11; 2 Cor 3:12-18).

Second, the verb translated by both the NIV and the NRSV as "summed up" (πεπλήρωται *peplērōtai*) requires careful attention. The usual meaning of πληρόω (*plēroō*) is to "fill up" or "fulfill." This term must be distinguished from the common Jewish expressions "doing the Law" (cf. 3:12) and "keeping the commandments," both of which refer to concrete obedience to the Law's specific requirements.[257] By contrast, the expression "fulfill the Law" never occurs in Jewish texts; it is, so far as we can tell from surviving sources, a distinctively Christian locution. When Paul employs this terminology, he is "using vocabulary unprecedented in Jewish tradition."[258] The NIV and the NRSV translators may have chosen "summed up" in order to avoid the impression that Paul is speaking here of "fulfilling" the Law's requirements in the sense of "doing" them all. As Martyn points out, however, the translators

255. Epictetus, *Diss.* 4.1.1.
256. Barclay, *Obeying the Truth,* 109.

257. Betz, *Galatians,* 275; S. Westerholm, "On Fulfilling the Whole Law (Gal 5:1.14)," *SEÅ* 51-52 (1986-87) 229-37.
258. Barclay, *Obeying the Truth,* 138.

are reading v. 14 in the light of the close parallel in Rom 13:9, where Paul uses a different verb that does mean "summed up."[259]

Furthermore, Paul has placed this verb in Gal 5:14 in the perfect tense. Most commentators treat the perfect tense here as an instance of the rare "gnomic perfect," expressing a general maxim.[260] The possibility must be at least considered, however, that Paul is using the perfect tense in the more usual way: to narrate a past action whose effects continue into the present. The most straightforward translation of the verse, then, would yield the reading, "For the whole Law *has been brought to fulfillment* in one saying [λόγῳ *logō*; not "commandment"]."

Finally, we should observe that the scriptural text in which Paul says that the Law has been brought to fulfillment is Lev 19:18, a passage cited in Mark and Matthew, in combination with Deut 6:4-5, as *Jesus'* summary of the meaning of the Law (Matt 22:34-40; Mark 12:28-34; cf. Matt 19:19; Luke 10:25-28; Jas 2:8). Paul's citation formula implies that the quotation is already familiar to the Galatians (lit., "For the whole Law has been brought to fulfillment in one word, in the [saying]: 'You shall love your neighbor as yourself'"). It seems probable that Paul knew the widely circulated early Christian tradition of Jesus' teaching on this point and had passed it along to the Galatian churches during his founding of these communities.[261]

Later rabbinic sources reflect various debates among the rabbis about how to sum up or organize the Law under a small number of commandments or fundamental principles,[262] but these texts differ from Gal 5:14 in one crucial way: The rabbis never entertain the idea that their summarizing categories could replace the specific commandments of the Law or make it unnecessary to obey commandments such as circumcision, food laws, or the sabbath.[263] Thus these texts, even if the traditions they preserve could be traced back to the first century, would be of little use for understanding what Paul means in this verse.

In the light of all this evidence, how should we understand what Paul is claiming in Gal 5:14? The Missionaries were urging the Galatians to be circumcised and to do what the Law required in order to bring order and moral security to their lives. Paul proclaims, however, that a new reality has come on the scene "in Christ Jesus" (cf. 5:6): The Law has been brought to fulfillment. By whom? For Paul there can be only one answer: by Jesus, "the Son of God who loved me and gave himself for me" (2:20). Paul believes that the full meaning of the Law, which was previously hidden from Israel (2 Cor 3:14-15), has now been eschatologically disclosed and brought to completion by Jesus. How did Jesus bring the Law to fulfillment? The question can be answered on two levels. First, in his teaching, he disclosed that the Law's deepest sense is brought to expression in Lev 19:18. Second, through his loving death for the sake of others, he embodied the meaning of that teaching, as Gal 2:20 indicates. By the combination of his teaching and his sacrificial death, Jesus reshaped the Law and thus brought it to fulfillment. That explains why Paul uses the perfect tense in v. 14*a*.

Does this interpretation mean that v. 14 is not, after all, a behavioral directive for the Galatians? By no means. Verse 14 provides the warrant (note γάρ *gar* again) for the imperative of v. 13. To paraphrase: "Through love become slaves to one another. Why? Because Jesus has brought the Law to fulfillment by teaching and embodying neighbor-love, thus spotlighting Lev 19:18 as the Law's true aim." The Galatians are exhorted to participate in this fulfilling of the Law through their own loving service (v. 13), which corresponds to and mirrors the love of Jesus. The logic of this exhortation runs parallel to 3:16, 29, in which, because Christ is first of all Abraham's seed, all who belong to Christ turn out to be Abraham's seed. Or again, in 3:22, the promise is given on the basis of Jesus Christ's faithfulness to all who believe.

259. Martyn, *Galatians*, 519-23.

260. BDF #344 (p. 177) remarks that the perfect is "rarely used" in this sense. In fact, the only two examples given of the "gnomic" use of the perfect tense (Matt 13:46 and Jas 1:24) are explained as mistakes of usage: "There is a strong suspicion that the aor. . . . and the perf. are incorrectly mixed." Gal. 5:14 is not cited here.

261. Dunn, *The Epistle to the Galatians*, 291-92.

262. See especially *b. Sabb.* 31a: "On another occasion it happened that a certain Gentile came before Shammai and said to him, 'Make me a proselyte, on condition that you teach me the whole Torah while I stand on one foot.' Thereupon he [Shammai] repulsed him with the builder's cubit which was in his hand. When he went before Hillel he [Hillel] said to him, 'What is hateful to you do not to your neighbor; that is the whole Torah, while the rest is commentary thereof. Go and learn it.'" For further references, see Longenecker, *Galatians*, 243-44.

263. Martyn, *Galatians*, 515-18.

In each of these parallel cases, believers participate in Christ's faith and inheritance and love and, therefore, manifest the correlate of these blessings in their own lives and character. They are "conformed to the image of [God's] Son, in order that he might be the firstborn within a large family" (Rom 8:29).

The theological logic underlying vv. 13-14 is spelled out more fully in Rom 8:3-4:

For God has done what the Law, weakened by the flesh, could not do: by sending his own Son in the likeness of sinful flesh, and as a sin offering,[264] he condemned sin in the flesh so that the just requirement of the Law might be fulfilled [πληρωθῇ *plērōthē*] in us, who walk not according to the flesh but according to the Spirit.

Thus, insofar as the Galatians walk according to the Spirit, they will not allow the Flesh to pervert Christ's gift of freedom. They will instead be conformed to Christ in becoming slaves to one another, just as he became a slave for our sake (cf. Phil 2:3-8). In this way they will embody the meaning of love.

This interpretation leads us to make one more tentative exegetical suggestion. Is it possible that Paul read Lev 19:18 not as a commandment, but as a word of prophetic promise? We must recall, first of all, that Paul does not use the word "commandment" or "command" in Gal v. 14. These terms are supplied by the translators to interpret the simple word λόγος (*logos*), meaning "word," "sentence," "saying." Furthermore, the verb "love" in the Greek quotation of Lev 19:18 follows the LXX in using the future indicative form ἀγαπήσεις (*agapēseis*), rather than the imperative. This is a regular feature of the LXX's idiom; Hebrew imperatives are often rendered by Greek future indicatives. Paul was no doubt well aware of this idiosyncrasy of LXX style. That would not stop him, however, from hearing in this text an inspired prediction of a reality that would be

264. Here following the NRSV alternate translation.

newly brought into being by the Spirit in the community of the new creation: "The whole Law has been brought to fulfillment [by Jesus Christ] in a single [prophetic] word: 'You *will* love your neighbor as yourself.'" That is what the Greek text appears to say. Just as he saw the rectification of the Gentiles prefigured in Scripture's blessing of Abraham (3:8-9), so also Paul sees Christ's community of loving mutual service prefigured in the Law.

5:15. From this eschatological vision of neighbor-love, Paul turns his gaze back to the depressing present reality of the Galatian churches. This verse is our first clear indication that these churches were struggling with internal problems of rivalry and dissension. There is no reason to suppose that Paul is speaking here of a purely theoretical possibility. The fact that he returns in v. 26 to a similar warning against competitiveness and envy suggests that he is addressing a real situation "on the ground" in Galatia. It is impossible to tell for certain from these references whether the dissension was already brewing before the arrival of the Missionaries—in which case they might have presented the Law as a solution to the Galatians' internal struggles—or whether the infighting had actually been provoked by the Missionaries' message, with some of the Galatians opting for circumcision and law observance and claiming spiritual superiority over others who did not follow their lead. Paul's comment in v. 7 might favor the latter hypothesis; the Galatians were "running well" before the Missionaries came on the scene, but now they were facing conflict within their churches. This scenario would precisely parallel Paul's narrative about what happened in the church at Antioch (2:11-14).

The image in this verse is that of a vicious dogfight, in which the Galatians are depicted as snapping at one another with bared fangs. The verbs portray an escalating conflict, ending with their destruction of one another. The contrast to v. 13 could hardly be more stark. Paul fears that the Flesh will gain the upper hand in Galatia. (See Reflections at 5:16-26.)

GALATIANS 5:16-26, THE WORKS OF THE FLESH AND THE FRUIT OF THE SPIRIT

COMMENTARY

5:16-18. Paul now addresses the question of how the community can receive moral guidance in the absence of the Law. As we have seen, the Missionaries have argued that only the Law can curb and discipline the unruly human impulses that lead to moral chaos. In v. 16, Paul sets forth his own opposing view in the form of a thesis: "But *I* say [in distinction to what the Missionaries are saying] walk by the Spirit and you will never carry out the desire of the flesh."

The first verb in the thesis is an imperative directing the Galatians to "walk" (περιπατεῖτε *peripateite*) by the guidance of the Spirit. (Both the NIV and the NRSV translate this metaphorical verb by the more colorless "live.") Paul's metaphor of "walking"—a figure for conducting one's life in a certain manner—is based on a common Hebrew idiom; the verb הלך (*hālak*, "walk") is regularly used in this sense in the OT. This verb is the root of the noun הלכה (*hălākâ*), the body of Jewish didactic tradition about how to comply with the Law in one's daily life.

The more crucial point of translation concerns the verb in the second clause, "gratify" (τελέω *teleō*; more lit., "carry out," "bring to completion"). The NRSV has interpreted it as though it were an imperative, coordinate with the first verb in the sentence: "Live by the Spirit and do not gratify . . ." while the NIV has read it, correctly, as an aorist subjunctive, spelling out the consequences that will follow from obeying the imperative of the first clause: "Live by the Spirit, and you *will not* gratify. . . ." These are two significantly different interpretations: the first a command, the second a promise. On grounds both grammatical and theological, the NIV is to be strongly preferred. The double negative οὐ μὴ (*ou mē*), which regularly occurs with the aorist subjunctive, expresses emphatic negation of a future possibility. On this reading, the sentence is a conditional promise: "If you walk by the Spirit, you will never carry out the desire of the flesh."

The expression "the desire of the flesh" ("desire" [ἐπιθυμία *epithymia*] is singular, not plural, in the Greek text) is probably a Greek rendering of an underlying Hebrew expression יצר בשר (*yēṣer bāśār*), which describes the fleshly evil impulse that underlies and empowers human sin.[265] It is important to recognize that "desire of the flesh" does not refer only to sexual passions. Indeed, the list of "works of the flesh" in vv. 19-21, though it begins with three terms designating sexual misconduct, gives far more emphasis to other offenses. "The flesh" is a comprehensive term for the sphere of autonomous fallen humanity, conceived as standing in opposition to God. "Flesh" asserts itself anywhere that self-seeking human desire opposes itself to the divine will and the wholeness of the community. It is likely that the Missionaries had waxed eloquent about the fearsome power of this evil impulse and about the necessity of obeying the Law to overcome it. In contrast to their claims, Paul reassures the Galatians that they do not need the Law to resist this impulse. (Indeed, as he argues more extensively in Romans 7, the Law is actually ineffectual against the problem of fleshly desire.) The Spirit of God is the only agent powerful enough to overcome the desire of the flesh.

Why is walking by the Spirit the effective way to hold the desire of the flesh in check? Paul goes on to explain that the Spirit and the flesh are fundamentally opposed. The singular desire of the Flesh (here still, as in v. 13, imagined as a malevolent power) is to oppose the Spirit of God, while the Spirit is fundamentally set against the Flesh. The two are, as Paul explains, set in opposition to each other, like soldiers lined up in opposing ranks on a battlefield. Given this opposition, there is no doubt in Paul's mind about the eventual victor: God will finally overcome all enemies (cf. 1 Cor 15:20-28). Those who walk by the power of God's Spirit will receive the

265. J. Marcus, "The Evil Inclination in the Letters of Paul," *IBS* 8 (1986) 8-21.

empowerment necessary to subdue the Flesh. That is why Paul can express such confidence about the outcome of the struggle.

The whole passage will be badly misinterpreted if one understands Spirit and Flesh as anthropological terms for a perennial duality within the individual human personality. "Flesh" may be in some sense an anthropological term, though it should be noted that the human self remains intact as a moral agent after the "flesh" has been crucifed (v. 24). The Spirit, on the other hand, is not the human spirit; it is God's Spirit, sent into the human sphere only after Christ's death and resurrection (3:13-14; 4:6). This means that the opposition between Flesh and Spirit came into being only through Christ; the war between them, described in v. 17, is part of the eschatological rescue mission through which God is bringing redemption to an enslaved world.[266]

The last clause of v. 17 is difficult to interpret, because it seems to undercut what Paul has just asserted in v. 16. If Flesh can frustrate the aims of the Spirit, or if Flesh and Spirit are locked in a standoff, then how can Paul make the confident claim that walking by the Spirit will overcome the desire of the flesh? John Barclay has convincingly argued that the metaphor of warfare provides the crucial clue to interpreting the conclusion of v. 17:

Warfare excludes some options and necessitates others. If they walk in the Spirit they are caught up into this conflict, which means that they are not free to do whatever they want—ἵνα μὴ ἃ ἐὰν θέλητε ταῦτα ποιῆτε (5:17). Such conflict ensures that their freedom is not absolute, for their walk in the Spirit will set them against the flesh and thus define the moral choices they must make.[267]

This interpretation would yield a slightly different translation, as follows: "for these are opposed to each other, so that you might not [just] do whatever you want." The advantage of this interpretation is that it shows how v. 17 advances Paul's argument. He is rebutting the charge that he has left the Galatians with no moral guidance. He responds by insisting that those who walk by the Spirit will in no way carry out the desire of the Flesh (v. 16),

because Flesh and Spirit are at war, so that the Spirit "provides a counteracting force which motivates and directs them to *exclude* the flesh."[268] Consequently they are not, as the Missionaries charge, left in a position where they are simply free to follow their own whims and do whatever they want. They are, in fact, given very clear marching orders.

That affirmation leads nicely into v. 18. As they walk, even though they are not under the Law, they nonetheless have clarity of purpose, because they are led by the Spirit. The expression "under Law" (see 3:23-25; 4:4-5; cf. Rom 6:14) refers to the state of slavery from which Christ has set his people free. The concept of being led by the Spirit of God also appears in Rom 8:14, where it is part of a much longer discussion (Rom 8:1-17) about living according to the Spirit rather than according to the flesh. That whole passage may be taken as an expansion of ideas developed more briefly here.

The central point of vv. 16-18, then, is that the Spirit provides strong leadership and direction in a world that is described as an eschatological war zone. Those who say the Law is sufficient to overcome the Flesh do not recognize the time of crisis in which the church walks; those who charge that without the Law the Galatians will be left undisciplined and confused do not know the power of the Spirit.

5:19-21. Indeed, Paul continues, there is no reason at all for anyone to be confused about what is going on in the world, because "the works of the flesh are obvious." In other words, we do not need the Law to identify them. He then gives a list of fifteen such works. The list, of course, is not comprehensive; it is merely an illustrative catalog of the human behaviors that result when the flesh is given a base of operation (for similar vice lists, see Mark 7:21-22; Rom 1:29-31; 1 Cor 6:9-10; 2 Cor 12:20). The list is in some respects conventional. It begins with three terms identifying sexual offenses, continues with two words for idolatry and occult magical practices, and concludes with two terms for self-indulgent partying. The most interesting feature, however, occurs in the middle of the list: a lengthy catalog of eight words that highlight dissension and offenses against

266. Martyn, *Galatians*, 494.
267. Barclay, *Obeying the Truth*, 112.

268. Barclay, *Obeying the Truth*, 115.

the unity of the community—enmities, strife, jealousy, anger, quarrels, dissensions, factions, and envy. Paul's concentration on these community-destroying behaviors shows that his primary concern is for the unity and peace of the Galatian churches (cf. vv. 15, 26). It also reinforces the point that "works of the flesh" are not just sensual vices. The meaning of walking according to the flesh is articulated by Paul's question to the divided Christians at Corinth: "As long as there is jealousy and quarreling among you, are you not of the flesh and behaving [lit., "walking"] according to human inclinations?" (1 Cor 3:3 NRSV).

The NIV's translation in v. 21, "those who live like this," is an attempt to render the linear aspect of the present participle πράσσοντες (*prassontes*); it refers to continuing action over time, not to a single violation. Paul is not saying, for example, that a single outburst of anger will result in exclusion from the kingdom of God.

This is not the first time, Paul indicates, that he has warned the Galatians about these nasty competitive behaviors. Presumably he warned them already during the time that he was present with them, for the reference cannot be to anything he has written earlier in this letter.

Unlike the vice lists in popular Hellenistic philosophical texts, Paul's list does not simply serve the purpose of advising the readers about how to develop a virtuous character and avoid bad habits.[269] Instead, the list functions as an eschatological warning: Those who practice the works of the flesh "will not inherit the kingdom of God."[270] Paul only occasionally refers to the "kingdom of God" (Rom 14:17; 1 Cor 4:20; 15:24; Col 4:11; 2 Thess 1:5; cf. Eph 5:5; Col 1:13; 1 Thess 2:12; 2 Tim 4:1, 18), which was a major theme of Jesus' teaching. To "inherit" the kingdom means to receive the eschatological blessings promised to those who are God's children (see Matt 5:5; 25:34; 1 Cor 6:9-10; 15:50; Rev 21:7). In the context of Galatians, where the metaphor of inheritance has played a central role in the argument of chaps. 3–4 (esp. 3:15-18; 3:29–4:7), Paul's choice of language is highly significant. The

Missionaries have taught that circumcision is necessary to inherit the kingdom. Paul, by contrast, indicates that one is excluded from the inheritance by these flesh-driven, community-splitting behaviors—precisely the outcomes produced, in his view, by the politics of the circumcision faction (2:11-14; 4:17; 5:15, 26; 6:13).

5:22-23. In contrast to the multiple and various "works" of the flesh, the Spirit produces the singular "fruit" of a community characterized by the gracious qualities listed in these verses. We should not interpret this fruit as referring only to character qualities of the individual; Paul is primarily concerned with the way in which the Spirit's work is made manifest in community. This catalog, like the foregoing list of fleshly works, should be understood as illustrative rather than comprehensive. Paul offers different lists of gifts and workings of the Spirit in Rom 12:6-8 and 1 Cor 12:7-11. Here in Galatians, his emphasis is on the peaceful and community-building character of the Spirit's work.

We should observe that Paul is not directly exhorting the Galatians to cultivate these qualities. Rather, he is speaking descriptively, painting a picture of the harvest the Spirit produces. The metaphor of fruit suggests one of Paul's primary points. Fruit cannot be humanly manufactured; it can grow only organically, as God gives the growth—in this case, through the life-giving energy of the Spirit (cf. Rom 8:9-11).

Not every item in Paul's catalog of fruit requires comment, but it is noteworthy that the list begins with "love" and ends with "self-control." Love, produced by the Spirit, should set the tone for all that occurs in the community's life together (cf. 5:6, 13; 1 Corinthians 13). "Self-control" (ἐγκράτεια *egkrateia*), a term that appears only here in Paul's letters, is set in deliberate contrast to the drunken revelry that concludes the list of works of the flesh. Paul concludes the list of fruit of the Spirit by asserting that the Spirit produces peaceful and orderly self-discipline. This is particularly significant as a response to the Missionaries' claim that only the Law could provide a means of controlling the fleshly evil impulse.[271]

---

269. Matera, *Galatians*, 207-10.

270. Matera, *Galatians*, 208-9, notes several parallels between Gal 5:19-23 and the exposition of "the Two Ways" in 1QS 3:13–4:26.

271. On the importance of self-mastery in Greco-Roman thought, see S. K. Stowers, *A Rereading of Romans: Justice, Jews, and Gentiles* (New Haven: Yale University Press, 1994) 42-82.

Finally, we should note that amid the fruit of the Spirit, we find "faithfulness" (πίστις *pistis*). This is the same word translated elsewhere in the letter as "faith." By rendering it in v. 22 as "faithfulness," the translators of the NIV and the NRSV recognize its proper semantic range. This faithfulness granted to the church as a fruit of the Spirit is no different from the *pistis* by which the Gentiles are rectified (3:8), no different from the *pistis* of Jesus Christ (2:16, 20; 3:22). Faith(fulness) is a sign of the Spirit's presence and work.

Paul concludes his list of the Spirit's fruit with the slightly acerbic remark that "there is no Law against such things." The force of this comment may best be understood against the background of the common Jewish characterization of Gentiles as "lawless" sinners. The Galatians may have been warned by the Missionaries that unless they are circumcised they will fall into moral confusion, doing things contrary to God's Law. In response, Paul describes the gracious behavior that flows from the Spirit even among uncircumcised Gentile believers, and then comments, with gentle irony, that there is no Law against this kind of conduct. The effect is comparable to the argument that Paul makes in Rom 2:25-29, where he comments that "those who are physically uncircumcised but keep the Law will condemn you that have the written code and circumcision but break the Law" (Rom 2:27).

5:24-26. In the summarizing sentences of this unit, Paul returns explicitly to the problem raised in vv. 13 and 16. "Those who belong to Christ" (cf. 3:29) will not, despite the Missionaries' warnings, be overwhelmed by the impulses of the Flesh, because they have "*crucified* the Flesh with its passions and desires." This strange formulation seems to violate the usual syntax of Paul's theology. Ordinarily, Paul speaks of Jesus Christ as the primary agent who overcomes God's adversaries, and he speaks of other human beings as the recipients of Christ's grace-giving actions. They participate mysteriously with Christ in his crucifixion and death (2:19; 6:14; Rom 6:6) and thereby are set free from sin, whose power is destroyed in Christ's crucifixion. Here, however, it is Christ's people who are said to be the agents that do the crucifying

of the Flesh (cf. Rom 8:13). What does Paul mean by this? The likeliest interpretation is that v. 24 is a reference to baptism; by choosing to undergo baptism, believers willingly put to death their old fleshly identity. They actively identify with Christ's crucifixion and death. In this way they "crucify" the Flesh, putting its divisive desires behind them.

This baptismal interpretation is supported by the next turn in Paul's argument in v. 25, where he refers to the Spirit's life-giving role, also strongly associated with baptism. The verse is closely parallel to v. 16, but unlike v. 16 it is clearly hortatory. The NIV rendering in this verse is helpful. Paul takes it as a given that he and his readers share together in the experience of new life brought by the Spirit (3:2; 4:6-7). If that is so—if the Spirit is the power that gives life—Paul exhorts the Galatians to "keep in step with the Spirit." The verb here is στοιχέω (*stoicheō*), perhaps used here in playful counterpoint to the earlier references to the oppressive στοιχεῖα (*stoicheia*, 4:3, 9). Rather than being regimented under the confining *stoicheia*, those who belong to Christ now "walk in line" with the Spirit. The Spirit gives freedom without aimlessness and order without repression.

In v. 26, Paul once again urges the Galatians to abandon their infighting. In v. 15, he made the appeal by comparing them to snarling wild animals; here in v. 26 he speaks literally, exhorting them to forswear arrogant, envious, and competitive behavior. As noted in v. 15, this warning may have become particularly necessary because of the activities of the Missionaries, whose message and *modus operandi* resulted in sharply defined group barriers, separating Law-observant Christians from those who did not keep the Law. Their strategy, as Paul sees it, is to foster envy (4:17). Paul's vision for his churches, by contrast, is that they should embody the love of Christ in ways characterized by the fruit of the Spirit. The dissension in Galatia, brought on the scene by Missionaries who championed a flesh-marked covenant, was a palpable sign that the power of the Flesh was at work to disrupt the church. Paul urgently calls them, therefore, to recover their humility and unity under the guidance of the Spirit.

REFLECTIONS

1. Galatians 5:13-26 is the most impassioned defense anywhere in Scripture of the sufficiency of the Spirit to guide the community of faith. The Missionaries' message that the Law must provide ordered governance for the community was powerfully appealing to the Galatians because it tapped into a deep and persistent human need for rules and structure. We fear that without firm guidelines we will fall into chaos. The Missionaries brought a gospel that answered this felt need. They could offer an entirely persuasive interpretation of Scripture, and they offered clear guidance about how the Galatians should conduct their lives. Their Law-observant version of the gospel could claim to be rooted in an ancient and holy tradition. It is no wonder that their message found a hearing among a group of recent converts struggling to work out how to reorder their lives in response to the gospel.

Paul insists, however, that the security offered by the Law is false security and that the gospel summons those who belong to Christ to live in freedom. (*The Revised Common Lectionary* helpfully attaches 5:1 to the reading of 5:13-25; however, it also omits 5:26, thus ending the lection on the upbeat hortatory note of 5:25 and deleting Paul's specific warnings against rivalry and envy.) Paul's counsel is a daring summons, urging the church to trust that it can live without being subject to the Law of Moses as long as the Spirit guides and shapes the community, for the community will organically produce fruit formed by the Spirit. A church guided by Paul's hopeful word would cultivate a community of flexibility and freedom, living with openness toward the unpredictable liberating movement of God's Spirit. It is a radical and inspiring vision. The church at its best has been willing to take the gamble that Paul recommends, wagering its future on the guidance of the Spirit, trusting God and performing without a safety net. One thinks of the stories of the earliest church in the Acts of the Apostles, of John Wesley going into the fields to preach to coal miners, or of the Spirit-led African American church during the civil rights movement.

But is Paul right? Can we really trust the Spirit to guide the community, or is Paul's vision of the church an ideal that cannot stand up to the pragmatic tests of human experience? Is it, therefore—as Paul's adversaries charged—a prescription for disaster? Everyone knows that there are dangers, as Paul himself saw in the Corinthian church, in communities that throw away rules and traditions and seek to live in pure spiritual spontaneity. It is all too easy for talk about the Spirit to grow careless and to serve as a cover for sexual misconduct, financial irresponsibility, and manipulative abuses by the community's leaders. In the absence of Israel's Torah as a guide to life, then, must the Spirit-led church inevitably settle into a new law of some sort, a system of rule-governed institutions? (This tendency is already exemplified within the New Testament canon by the Pastoral Epistles.) Is "the institutionalization of charisma" a necessary and unavoidable development?

Our answer to these questions will depend upon whether we believe in the real presence and activity of the Spirit in our midst. Paul is not making a theoretical appeal for human moral intuition and spontaneity over written law codes. When Paul counsels the Galatians to keep in step with the Spirit (5:25), he is not thinking of the Spirit as a theological abstraction or as an inference from human subjectivity; rather, he is thinking of the Spirit as the active presence of God that does mighty deeds in the community (3:5) and cries out audibly in the church's worship (4:6). Only a church that knows the presence of the Spirit in this way can regard Paul's counsel as credible. At the same time, Paul affirms clearly that the guidance of the Spirit will have a recognizable character (5:22-23) that distinguishes it from the works inspired by the flesh. All things considered, the dangers of seeking to follow the guidance of the Spirit are fewer than the dangers of living under the stifling and divisive regulation of the Law.

2. The opposition between Spirit and Flesh (5:17) is not an anthropological dualism, not a conflict in the human individual between the sinful lower nature and the higher, better self. Rather, the opposition is a cosmic conflict between the redemptive power of God and the rebellious fallen creation. This conflict may play itself out partly in the arena of the divided self (Rom 7:14-15), but the warfare of which Gal 5:13-26 speaks cannot be reduced to a battle within the human psyche. The arena that draws Paul's special interest is the corporate life of the church, in which the Flesh seeks to produce factions and strife (5:20), while the Spirit brings peace (5:22). But we need not limit our field of vision to ecclesiological concerns. Wherever there is violence in the world, the Flesh is rampant. Those who belong to Christ will oppose violence not by counterviolence—that would be to succumb to the deception of the Flesh—but by manifesting the fruit of the Spirit even in the face of murderous opposition, keeping in step with the Spirit of Christ.

3. A corollary of the preceding point is that sex is not the only problem. The power of the Flesh is not confined to sexual misconduct. The problem with the Flesh is much bigger, and sexual misbehavior is only one of its manifestations. It is noteworthy that in the Letter to the Galatians Paul mentions sexual offenses only in passing in his conventional vice list (5:19*b*), but devotes no further discussion to them. His warning against the Flesh's works focuses instead on envy, backbiting, and competitiveness (5:15, 20, 26). Many hearers of this letter—especially in our sexually overstimulated culture—will hear the term "flesh" and think immediately of sexual scandal. An important part of the interpreter's task, then, is to recover the fuller meaning of Paul's theological vocabulary. "Flesh" is the realm of autonomous fallen humanity, living at odds with God.

4. In addition to the call to walk by the Spirit, the other major imperative sounded in these verses is found in 5:13. The way we avoid giving the Flesh a base of operations is by becoming slaves of one another, through love. That is what Paul calls his readers to do. The freedom won by Christ must be employed as Christ employed his freedom in the act of winning ours. The antidote to fleshly rivalry is self-emptying love. According to Paul, it is through such love that Christ brought the Law to fulfillment, and it is such love that should govern our relations to one another.

GALATIANS 6:1-10, LIFE TOGETHER IN THE CHURCH

COMMENTARY

In the final section of Paul's pastoral counsel to the Galatian churches (6:1-10), he offers them a few brief directives about what it might mean for a community to walk by the Spirit. The specific practices he commends to them are mutual correction of one another (v. 1-2), self-examination (vv. 3-5), and financial support of the community's teachers (v. 6). In vv. 7-8, Paul places this advice in the context of God's eschatological judgment and recapitulates the contrast between Flesh and Spirit. Finally, he concludes the hortatory material

with a general admonition to do good, both to everyone and specifically to others within the community (vv. 9-10).

6:1-2. Paul thinks of the church as an extended family (v. 10), in which members should take responsibility for one another. He wants the members of the Galatian churches to see themselves not as rivals competing to see who can be the most devout (5:26), but rather as brothers and sisters (ἀδελφοί *adelphoi*, v. 1) supporting one another as they walk through perilous times of spiritual warfare. Because they bear responsibility for one another, they cannot casually allow other members of the family to go astray; they have an obligation to hold one another accountable to live as faithful followers of Jesus. At the same time, the responsibility for correcting erring members must be exercised with great gentleness and humility, so that the community's discipline will reflect the character of the Lord that the community serves.

The situation envisioned in v. 1 is hypothetical and general in character. If any member of the church is "caught" (NIV) in a transgression (rightly NRSV, not "sin" as in the NIV), other members should take action. This directive shows that Paul has a realistic assessment of the human fallibility of his congregations. Despite the assurance of 5:16, he knows that believers will in fact fall into misconduct. The church must therefore have guidelines for how to respond to such situations. They must cultivate the practice of mutual correction.

The phrase "you who are spiritual" (NIV) refers to all members of the community, not to a select group of spiritual leaders. (NRSV tries to clarify this point by offering the paraphrase "you who have received the Spirit.") By addressing the Galatians in this way, Paul gently challenges them to accept and live up to the description: They are to be people whose identity is shaped by the Spirit. In this case, to be "spiritual" means to act for the mending of the community, the recovery of order and peace; it is precisely the opposite of being "fleshly," which leads to conflict. The verb translated "restore" (καταρτίζω, *katartizō*) is used, e.g., in Mark 1:19 to describe the mending of fishing nets, and Paul uses it to speak of the restoration of unity within the community (1 Cor 1:10).

While there are many passages in contemporary Greco-Roman literature that speak of the philosopher's responsibility to rebuke and correct others,[272] the closest extracanonical parallel to v. 1 is to be found in the Dead Sea Scrolls, in the Rule of the Community:

They shall rebuke one another in truth, humility, and charity. Let no man address his companion with anger, or ill-temper, or obduracy, or with envy prompted by the spirit of wickedness [cf.

Gal 5:26]. . . . but let him rebuke him on the very same day lest he incur guilt because of him. And furthermore, let no man accuse his companion before the congregation without having first admonished him in the presence of witnesses. (1QS 5:24–6:1)

Because this passage envisions rebuke and correction within the common life of a community devoted to the worship and service of the God of Israel, it is strikingly close to the picture presented by Gal 6:1.[273] That Paul generally advocated such practices within his churches is suggested by 2 Cor 2:5-11. Passages such as Matt 18:15-18; Luke 17:3-4; and Jas 5:19-20 bear witness to similar disciplinary procedures in other early Christian communities. Underlying all of these texts is Lev 19:17: "You shall not hate in your heart anyone of your kin; you shall reprove your neighbor, or you will incur guilt yourself" (NRSV). It is hardly coincidental that this admonition immediately precedes the command to "love your neighbor as yourself" (Lev 19:18), which Paul takes as the epitome of the Law. The rebuke of the neighbor is an expression of loving the neighbor.

Paul is concerned not only *that* the word of correction be spoken; he is equally concerned about *how* it is spoken. The rebuke must be offered "in a spirit of gentleness"— i.e., in accordance with the fruit produced by the Spirit ("gentleness," 5:23). Furthermore, Paul issues a warning to the one who speaks the word of admonition—and here he sharpens the point by shifting from the second-person plural to the second-person singular: "watch yourself, lest you also be tempted." The possible temptation could take either of two forms: Either the admonisher could be tempted to fall into the same sin as the erring member, or the admonisher could be tempted to an attitude of pride and condescension. Paul does not specify which of these possible problems he has in view. There is no need for us to decide between them; it is sufficient to recognize that the practice of mutual correction is fraught with dangers of prideful abuse, and, at the same time, that all of us share in a common human frailty. Indeed, Paul's warning here implies an astute psychological insight: We may be most harshly condemning

---

272. For references, see Betz, *Galatians*, 297.

273. Barclay, *Obeying the Truth*, 174.

of those failings to which we ourselves are the most susceptible.

Verse 2 should be taken specifically in conjunction with v. 1: If the Galatians take on the responsibility for correcting one another in this way, they will in fact be "bearing one another's burdens." (Paul uses the verb "bear" [βαστάζω bastazō] in a similar way in Rom 15:1-2: "We, the powerful, ought *to bear* the weaknesses of the powerless and not to please ourselves. Let each of us please the neighbor for the good, for the purpose of building up [the church].") To live under the guidance of the Spirit is to live in a relationship of interdependence. This can be a costly matter, because our common sinfulness gives us the capacity to inflict pain upon one another and place heavy loads upon each other. It would be far easier to live as autonomous individuals without having to worry about responsibility for the conduct of others. But that would not be life in Christ. Of course, burden-bearing entails far more than the practice of mutual admonition; it also entails the sharing of stresses and sorrows, the practice of economic sharing, and all kinds of imaginative ways of becoming slaves to one another (5:13).

What is the source of the daunting mandate to bear one another's burdens?[274] Paul leaves no doubt about the answer to that important question. If the Galatians bear the burdens of their brothers and sisters, they will "fulfill the Law of Christ." That Law is the source of the obligation to carry the weight imposed by the sin of others.

But what can Paul possibly mean by speaking of "the Law of Christ"?[275] Like "faith working" in 5:6, this expression appears at first to be an oxymoron. Through most of the letter, Paul has set "Law" and "Christ" in sharp opposition to one another (2:16, 21; 3:13; 5:4). The Law is portrayed as the confining power from which Christ has liberated us. How can Paul now suddenly speak of a "Law of Christ"?

An important clue is given by the verb "fulfill" (ἀναπληρόω *anaplēroō*), which echoes the verb employed in 5:14, where Christ is said to have brought the Law to fulfillment in the one word (Lev 19:18) that foretells love of neighbor as the Law's central message. Christ "fulfilled" the Law through his self-sacrificial death (1:4; 2:20), which definitively embodied the meaning of love—and therefore also the Law's true meaning (cf. Rom 13:8-10; 15:1-4; see the Commentary on 5:13-14). In this way, Christ took possession of the Law and transformed it hermeneutically. From the point of his death onward, the Law can be understood anew as the Law of Christ, the Law defined by and belonging to him.[276]

The Galatians, then, are being summoned to re-enact the event by which Christ brought the Law to fulfillment. The idea of repetition may be conveyed by the prefix *ana* in the verb *anaplēroō*. Martyn paraphrases: "Bear one another's burdens, and in this way you yourselves will repeat Christ's deed, bringing to completion in your communities the Law that Christ has already brought to completion in the sentence about loving the neighbor."[277] To fulfill the Law of Christ, then, is to play out over and over again in the life of the community the pattern of self-sacrificial love that he revealed in his death.

The syntax of 6:2 is parallel to 5:16: The sentence begins with a present imperative verb (prescribing the community's continuing action) and ends with a clause whose verb is in the future indicative (describing the results that will follow if the imperative is heeded).[278] Fulfilling the Law of Christ will follow as a consequence of the church's simple daily acts of assuming responsibility for one another.

To be sure, Paul's startling phrase "the Law of Christ" may have an ironic polemical edge. The rival Missionaries—whether or not they used precisely this expression—linked Christ with the Law and perhaps even preached about Jesus as the authoritative interpreter of

---

274. Betz, *Galatians*, 299, has argued that Paul derives this mandate from conventional maxims of "the Hellenistic philsophical tradition" (e.g., Xenophon *Memorabilia* 2.7.1-14; Aristotle *Nicomachean Ethics* 9.11.1-6). For an alternative view that the logic of Paul's mandate is ultimately grounded in the example of Christ, see R. B. Hays, "Christology and Ethics in Galatians: The Law of Christ," *CBQ* 49 (1987) 268-90.

275. For a summary of various scholarly proposals, see Matera, *Galatians*, 219-21.

276. Barclay, *Obeying the Truth*, 132-35; Martyn, *Galatians*, 554-58. This interpretation represents a modification of my position in Hays, "Christology and Ethics," which contended that "the law of Christ" refers not at all to the Torah, but rather to a principle or pattern exemplified by Christ's gracious self-giving.

277. Martyn, *Galatians*, 547-48.

278. As the NRSV footnote indicates, some Greek manuscripts have a reading in which the verb of the second clause is also an imperative: "Bear one another's burdens and, in this way, fulfill the Law of Christ." The future indicative, represented in both the NRSV and the NIV, is to be preferred.

the Mosaic Torah.[279] In 6:2, then—just as in 4:21 and 5:14—Paul initiatiates a counteroffensive by claiming that his gospel articulates the true positive relation between Christ and the Law. The force of 6:2 can then be explained in the following paraphrase:

The rival Missionaries are telling you that in order to be Christ's people, authentic children of Abraham, you must be circumcised and obey the commandments of the Sinaitic Law. But I say to you, by contrast, that if you bear one another's burdens, becoming slaves of one another through love—correcting one another gently instead of competing viciously as the Missionaries have led you to do—you will fulfill the Law as Christ has redefined it.

This is analogous to the ironic rhetorical inversion that Paul employs in 1 Cor 9:21: "To those outside the Law I became as one outside the Law (though I am not free from God's Law but am under Christ's Law) so that I might win those outside the Law" (NRSV).[280] In both cases, Christ dramatically redefines the meaning of "Law" so that it is precisely those outside the Law, as traditionally interpreted, who turn out to exemplify the Law's meaning.

6:3-5. The connection of these verses to the foregoing context is not immediately evident. Paul's advice here is best understood as a continuation of the warnings expressed in 5:26 and 6:1b. The Galatians had found themselves drawn into serious conflict with one another over the question of the necessity of observing the Jewish Law. Perhaps some individuals who had started to observe the Law fancied themselves better or more spiritually advanced than the other members of the Galatian churches, and they were tempted to adopt censorious attitudes toward the others (cf. 6:13b). In 5:26, Paul directly exhorts them to abandon this attitude. In 6:1-2, he offers a different model, based on the pattern of Christ, in which mutual correction would be done in a Spirit of gentleness. Then, in vv. 3-5, he addresses individuals in the community and warns them against boasting; rather than comparing themselves with each other and boasting to each other, they should

conduct a sober self-assessment and keep their boasting to themselves.

The advice that each person should test his own "work" [singular] seems surprising in a letter that has disparaged "works [plural] of Law" in opposition to "faith." But this challenge to self-examination is a common Pauline theme. A close parallel in 2 Corinthians is especially illuminating: "Examine yourselves to see whether you are living in the faith. Test yourselves. Do you not realize that Jesus Christ is in you?—unless, indeed, you fail to meet the test!" (2 Cor 13:5 NRSV; cf. Rom 12:3; 1 Cor 11:28). Paul is convinced that authentic faith manifests itself in action (Gal 5:6), and that Christ and the Spirit empower such faithful action (2:20; 5:22-25). Thus to test one's "work" is to examine whether it really embodies the loving character of Christ.

It is Paul's firm conviction that God will subject our actions to eschatological judgment (e.g., 1 Cor 3:10-15), and he speaks on more than one occasion about having grounds for "boasting" in his own apostolic work (Rom 15:17; 1 Cor 9:16; 2 Cor 1:12-14; Phil 2:16). Each person will receive commendation from God, as appropriate, in the end (1 Cor 4:3-5). In the present time, however, we should keep our self-evaluation to ourselves. That is the meaning of v. 4, which would be better translated, "Each one must test his own work, and then he will direct his boast to himself alone and not to his neighbor."[281] On this interpretation, vv. 3-4 fit easily together with Paul's warning against competitiveness in 5:26. This admonition would also follow logically from the cautionary note of 6:1b: The person who corrects another must scrutinize his or her own motivations carefully. If correcting one's brother or sister is actually a subtle device for self-aggrandizement, comparing others unfavorably to one's own high moral character, then the practice of mutual correction will become an insidious form of spiritual "one-upmanship."

This still leaves, however, the problem of how to understand v. 5, which appears to be a flat contradiction to v. 2. After telling the Galatians to bear one another's burdens, how can Paul turn around and write, "for all must carry their own loads"? Both verses employ the same verb (*bastazō*, "bear," "carry"), but

---

279. Betz, *Galatians*, 300-301.
280. For similar rhetorical inversions of "the Law," see Rom 3:27; 8:2.
281. Barclay, *Obeying the Truth*, 160.

the second appears to reverse what was said in the first. Is Paul simply stringing together conventional maxims linked by catchwords, so that there is no coherent line of thought in the passage? Is he just blathering in a sententious but contradictory manner, like a first-century Polonius? Or is the juxtaposition of these sentences an artful paradox, designed to provoke thought? There are two keys to understanding how vv. 2 and 5 fit together in a coherent manner.

First, we must recognize the different functions of these two sentences within the discourse. Verse 2 is an imperative, calling the community as a whole to exercise mutual responsibility through loving restoration of a transgressor. Verse 5, on the other hand, functions as a warrant for the advice that each individual should examine his or her own actions; thus, it affirms a basic truth that is foundational to Paul's theology: God will judge the world and hold each person accountable (cf. Rom 2:6-10; 3:19). When the two statements are placed in context, they are complementary rather than contradictory. Paul is saying that we are all personally accountable to God, *and* that we are called to form communities in which we help one another through mutual corrective admonition.[282]

Second, the saying of v. 5 should be interpreted as an allusion to God's eschatological judgment.[283] Verse 5 belongs to the same tradition of Jewish apocalyptic thought that is more fully articulated in 4 Ezra, written a generation later than Paul's letters:

The day of judgment is decisive and displays to all the seal of truth. Just as now a father does not send his son, or a son his father, or a master his servant, or a friend his dearest friend, to be ill or sleep or eat or be healed in his place, so no one shall ever pray for another on that day, *neither shall anyone lay a burden on another; for all then shall bear their own righteousness and unrighteousness.* (4 Ezra 7:104-105, italics added)

Paul's concise expression in v. 5 points in the same direction. The "work" of each of us will

be presented individually before God at the final judgment, at which time no one else can take our place or bear our load. Thus, the future tense of the verb "will bear" is a real temporal future, not the timeless gnomic future of a proverb. This conclusion is reinforced by the clear references to eschatological judgment in vv. 7-9, as well as 5:10, which uses the same verb *bastazō* to speak of incurring God's judgment.

Accordingly, the logic of Gal 6:1-5 runs as follows:

(1-2) In the present time we are called to help and support one another in the church through mutual counsel and admonition; by bearing each other's burdens in this way we embody Christ's reconfigured Law.

(3-4) In correcting one another, we must exercise appropriate humility and scrutinize our own work,

(5) for at the final judgment each of us must bear our own load; that is, we will be called to account not just by one another, but by God.

The tension between v. 2 and v. 5, then, serves the rhetorical purpose of highlighting Paul's paired themes of mutual responsibility and individual accountability.

6:6. This commandment for the person who is taught (ὁ κατηχούμενος *ho katēchoumenos*—the source for the English cognate "catechumen") to "share in all good things with the teacher" is to be understood as a directive to provide financial support for those who carry out the ministry of teaching in the community. There is no reason to suppose that Paul is referring to an institutionalized "catechumenate" or to restrict the application of this verse to pre-baptismal instruction. Paul can use the verb in a non-technical way to refer to the instruction given through prophecy in the church (1 Cor 14:19) or to the instruction that Jews received in the Law (Rom 2:18; for other uses of the term in the NT, see Luke 1:4; Acts 18:25; 21:21, 24). It does appear, however, that Paul recognizes the presence of some persons in the churches of Galatia who are designated as teachers of "the word." This could refer to instruction either in the interpretation of Scripture or in the emergent body of early Christian

---

282. Barclay, *Obeying the Truth*, 162.
283. D. Kuck, "Each Will Bear His Own Burden: Paul's Creative Use of an Apocalyptic Motif," *NTS* 40 (1994) 289-97; Matera, *Galatians*, 215. Contra Betz, *Galatians*, 304.

tradition; in all likelihood, Paul would have made no sharp distinction. His own writings bear witness that the teaching of Scripture was a fundamental part of his apostolic work of founding churches.[284] The sort of teaching that Paul has in mind is not an academic exercise; it is a gift of the Holy Spirit, given by God for building up the body of Christ for its work of service (Rom 12:7; 1 Cor 12:28).

Martyn has hypothesized that the instructors mentioned in v. 6 were persons whom Paul had authorized to continue teaching the gospel in the Galatian churches after his departure and that the rival Missionaries were trying to discredit and displace these Pauline teachers.[285] If so, that would explain why Paul brings up this topic in his pastoral advice to the community. On the other hand, if the situation were as Martyn imagines it, it is difficult to understand why Paul would devote only one isolated, non-polemical sentence to the problem. It is perhaps more likely that Paul mentions the support of teachers simply because it belongs to his overall vision of a community walking under the guidance of the Spirit: The members admonish one another, examine themselves in humility, and share in ordered teaching and learning to grow toward greater maturity in the faith.

6:7-8. Paul now moves toward summarizing and concluding the hortatory part of his letter. The statements of v. 7 are bits of proverbial wisdom that he applies to the Galatian situation. Both proverbs point to the certainty of God's final judgment. God cannot be "mocked"—that is, scornfully disregarded—because his judgment of the world is comprehensive and just. Paul is in effect saying to the Galatians, "Remember, this is *God* you are dealing with here, not some image of your own construction. Don't think you can get away with anything, for God judges everything in the end." The proverb about sowing and reaping is a nearly universal maxim warning that actions have consequences; for example, "Whoever sows injustice will reap calamity" (Prov 22:8 NRSV; cf. Job 4:8).[286] Paul adapts the proverb here to speak of what we will "reap" on the day of God's ultimate judgment.

Why are these warnings necessary? There is no evidence in the letter that the Galatian churches were particularly plagued by libertine behavior or by careless attitudes about the will of God. If anything, they have been conscientiously concerned to do what God requires. That is why the Missionaries have made inroads in Galatia. The best explanation is that Paul sees the Galatians as standing in danger of "mocking God" by devaluing God's gracious gift in Jesus Christ and seeking justification through other means (cf. 2:21; 5:4). Paul, therefore, warns that God's grace cannot be spurned without dire consequences (cf. Heb 12:25). The agricultural imagery of the second proverb provides a transition into a specific warning about the perilous prospect faced by the Galatians if they follow the counsel of the Missionaries.

What does Paul mean by sowing "to the flesh"? (The NIV's translation of v. 8, adding the words "to please" and rendering σάρξ *sarx* as "sinful nature," implies that Paul is concerned primarily about physical or sexual lusts; however, this interpretation distorts Paul's meaning. The NRSV is a more literal translation, though the translators have converted the sentence into a conditional formulation couched in the second person in order to achieve a gender-inclusive reading.) The meaning of "flesh" has already been shaped by Paul's previous use of the term in 3:3 and 5:13-26. He has already performed the rhetorical feat of packaging circumcision together with self-indulgence under the rubric of "the flesh," and he has associated both with the envious self-asserting desire that fractures the community (see the Commentary on 5:13-26). To sow to "the flesh," then, would mean to place one's confidence and hope for the future in the mundane expedient of cutting the flesh, i.e., circumcision.

Given the fact that Paul has presented circumcision as a package deal with other connotations of "flesh," the conclusion that he draws in 6:8 comes as no surprise: Those who sow to the flesh by relying on circumcision are giving the flesh a base of operations (5:13), and they will therefore reap from the flesh only corruption—that is, only decay and death. (For similar use of the word "corruption" [φθορά *phthora*] see 1 Cor 15:42, 50,

284. Hays, "The Conversion of the Imagination," 391-412.
285. Martyn, *Galatians,* 552.
286. For other parallels, see Dunn, *The Epistle to the Galatians,* 329-30; Barclay, *Obeying the Truth,* 164.

where both the NIV and the NRSV translate it as "that which is perishable.")

By way of contrast, "sowing to the Spirit" means placing one's confidence and hope in the working of God's Spirit. Because Paul has already used the image of "fruit" to characterize the product of the Spirit's activity in the community, he can easily continue the harvest metaphor. The harvest associated with the Spirit is "eternal life." Paul does not often use this terminology, but on the other occasions that he does use it, he sets it in opposition to death, and it clearly has eschatological connotations (Rom 2:7; 5:21; 6:22-23); thus we should probably understand v. 8*b* as an allusion to the resurrection of the body, as elsewhere in Jewish apocalyptic traditions (e.g., Dan 12:2; 2 Macc 7:9; *Pss Sol* 3:12).[287] The opposition in v. 8 between "corruption" and "eternal life" (cf. 1 Cor 15:42-58) also encourages the inference that Paul is thinking of the resurrection of the dead. We see a similar chain of ideas in Rom 8:9-13: Paul opposes the death-producing power of the flesh to the life-giving power of the Spirit, which is linked to the resurrection of the body.

Understood in this way, v. 8 encapsulates the message of the letter as a whole. It is not a moralistic warning against sensual self-indulgence; instead, it is a warning against placing confidence in anything that belongs to the realm of the merely human—particularly circumcision. Paul insists that only the Spirit of God has the power to confer life.

6:9-10. Paul now draws his exhortation to a close with a word of general encouragement to persist in doing good. In light of the promise that we will reap eternal life from the Spirit, he urges the Galatians not to grow weary or give up, even in the face of opposition, but to endure faithfully to the end (cf. Luke 18:1; 2 Cor 4:1, 16-18). The motif of being spurred on to faithful labor by the promise of eschatological reward and the hope of resurrection is a recurrent one in Paul's thought (see, e.g., Rom 8:18-39; 1 Cor 15:58; Phil 3:10-14; 3:20–4:1; 2 Thess 3:13). The reference to "the proper time" (NIV) is, again, an allusion to the day of eschatological judgment.

The emphasis on "doing good" in these concluding verses demonstrates clearly that

Paul is not opposed in principle to human efforts to do the right thing; therefore, his earlier polemic against "works of the Law" must be understood as targeted particularly against the Mosaic Law and its signs of ethnically defined covenant membership (see the Commentary on 2:11-21 and 3:10-14). Of course, as shown by 5:22-25, our efforts to do good are to be understood as Spirit-empowered manifestations of God's working in us (cf. 2:20), not as autonomous performances. The doing of the good in 6:9-10, then, is synonymous with "faith working through love" (5:6).

We should hear an eschatological nuance in Paul's phrase "as we have opportunity" (lit., "as we have time" [καιρός *kairos*]). He is saying, "While the opportunity remains, let us seize the moment to do the good" (cf. Rom 13:11-14; 1 Cor 7:29; 2 Cor 6:2; Col 4:5; cf. Eph 5:16). Thus the NRSV's "whenever we have an opportunity" is misleading, because it mutes the note of eschatological urgency.

Verse 10 delineates the scope of the community's efforts in terms both general and particular. Paul exhorts his readers to do good works "for all," thus expanding the sphere of moral concern to the world at large. On this passage, Chrysostom comments: "The way of life that comes from grace takes the whole land and sea as the table of mercy."[288] At the same time, Paul recognizes the human limitation of the Galatians' efforts to do good to others, particularly in light of the eschatological qualifier posed by the opening words of v. 10; consequently, he counsels them to focus their energies particularly on doing good to those who belong to "the household of faith" (cf. Eph 2:19; 1 Tim 3:15). The "household" in Greco-Roman antiquity was not restricted to blood relatives, but the NIV and the NRSV have both chosen to replace Paul's word by the term "family," which has more connotative resonance for readers in our time. As we interpret "family," we must remember Paul's insistence that all belong to God's family only by virtue of gracious adoption (4:4-7); if we do that, the metaphor will not mislead us.

Dunn suggests that Paul's phrase "the household of faith" may be coined by Paul

---

287. Dunn, *The Epistle to the Galatians*, 331.

288. John Chrysostom, "Homily on Galatians 6:9-10," *Interpretatio Omnium Epistularum*, ed. F. Field (Oxford: Clarendon, 1849–62) 4.97, cited in Edwards, *Galatians, Ephesians, Philippians*, 98.

in conscious juxtaposition to the common OT expression "the house of Israel." That is doubtful, because Paul's wording here does not correspond precisely to the LXX's rendering of the phrase "house of Israel." If Paul had meant to evoke this echo, he could have written, "and especially to the house of faith" (τὸν οἶκον τῆς πίστεως *ton oikon tēs pisteōs*). Nonetheless, Dunn is correct to observe that in Paul's description of the church, "the bonding characteristic of this household is faith, and not membership of ethnic Israel, and not the Torah."[289] By characterizing the community in this way, Paul's final exhortation reminds the Galatians one more time that their membership in the community of God's people depends from first to last on faith, and that they therefore share a common bond with one another.

Verse 10 also shows that we cannot make a facile distinction between the particularism of Judaism and the universalism of Pauline Christianity. Paul, no less than his Jewish-Christian opponents, believed that God had elected a particular community as special recipients of God's grace and messengers of God's word. The major difference between Paul and the Missionaries lay in the question of how that community was demarcated. For the Missionaries, the key identity markers were circumcision and Law-observance; for Paul, the decisive identity markers were faith and the Spirit. On Paul's view, the Spirit-powered community was given the task of doing good and offering the message of reconciliation to the whole world (cf. 2 Cor 5:18-21), but that reconciling work had to begin at home within the community of believers. As long as rivalry and envy prevailed because of the antagonism stirred up by the circumcision advocates (5:15, 26), the work of God was being hindered. Therefore, Paul's final appeal to the Galatians to work for the good of the household of faith constitutes another plea, in a different key, to reject the divisive message of circumcision.

289. Dunn, *The Epistle to the Galatians*, 333.

REFLECTIONS

If the Galatians were looking for a detailed blueprint of how to order their lives, they might have found Paul's letter considerably less satisfying than the teachings of the Missionaries, who could point to the elaborately detailed Law of Moses as a guide to life.[290] By contrast, Paul sketches only a few short strokes in his portrayal of a community guided by the Spirit. He could hardly have done otherwise: If it is the Spirit that provides the guidance, it is impossible to be narrowly prescriptive in advance. Had Paul given the sort of comprehensive instruction manual that at least some of the Galatians desired, he would have been offering a new law code and undercutting his own argument. Nonetheless, in Paul's few short strokes in 6:1-10 he has given a remarkably rich and suggestive account of themes that might characterize the common life of a Spirit-led community.

1. *The Church as an Extended Family of Mutual Responsibility.* Paul insists that the church is to be a community in which believers share responsibility for one another's lives. Life in the Spirit is not a life of lonely striving, not a life restricted to a zone of privacy; rather, it is a life lived in community. The church, like an extended family of brothers and sisters, is characterized by the interdependence of its members. This interdependence entails not only mutual support in times of need, but also the willingness to confront one another, when necessary, with a word of admonition. Within the individualistic culture of the modern West, Paul's counsel seems strange, and many Christians would find it offensive to be held accountable by their brothers and sisters in the faith. But we should recognize that mutual support and mutual accountability are two sides of the same coin; both are rooted in the conviction that we are a people with a shared calling and a shared identity. Because we are members of one body in

290. Barclay, *Obeying the Truth*, 170.

Christ, our common welfare depends on the spiritual health of each member, and we have a stake in helping one another walk faithfully. (As Lev 19:17-18 implies, mutual reproof and love of neighbor belong together.) A church that takes Paul's pastoral guidance seriously will seek to develop patterns of life together that enable us to profit from gentle and timely corrections offered by other members of the community. Furthermore, Paul's vision of a church that practices mutual correction is by no means isolated within the New Testament; Gal 6:1 should always be read alongside Matt 18:15-22, where Jesus teaches his disciples to confront one another openly when wrongs are committed within the fellowship—and to forgive one another freely when they are acknowledged.

2. *The Law of Christ and the Imitation of Christ.* By urging the Galatians to bear one another's burdens, Paul calls them to conform their lives to the self-sacrificial pattern of Jesus' life. Although he does not explicitly use the language of "imitation of Christ" in Galatians, Paul is operating within the same theological paradigm that informs his counsel in passages such as 1 Cor 11:1; Phil 2:1-13; and 1 Thess 1:6-7. Jesus' self-sacrificial death provides a model that illuminates the meaning of love; therefore, those who are "in Christ" participate in a form of life that is conformed to the crucified Lord. When we look not to our own interests but to the interests of others (Phil 2:4), we are faithfully mirroring the character of the Son of God who loved us and gave himself for us (Gal 2:20). Any interpretation of Gal 6:1-10 should highlight the transformative insight of Gal 6:2; it is through loving service (cf. 5:13-14) that Christ has brought the Law to its intended fulfillment; consequently, we participate in that fulfillment by our loving service of one another. There is always an insidious temptation to turn the Law into a barrier against our neighbors or a ladder for our own self-aggrandizing aspirations. Only when the Law is read through the lens provided by the cross does it become the Law of Christ.

3. *Renouncing Rivalry and Conflict in the Church.* Paul's concentration on the problem of discord and rivalry in the community (5:15, 20-21, 26; 6:1-5) suggests that this is one of the central issues addressed by the letter. At this point, there are obvious parallels between the Galatian churches and the churches of our own time. Paul's diagnosis of the roots of conflict is therefore of considerable interest. He suggests that boasting and strife result from "sowing to the flesh." As we have seen, in its original context, this phrase referred to placing confidence in circumcision and the merely human works of the Law. In our own time, however, one of the besetting temptations for the church is to "sow to the flesh" by investing our identity in various theories and accounts of human sexuality. The result, Paul would say, is thoroughly predictable: Wherever the church grounds its identity in fleshly practices—and particularly wherever commitment to an orthodox "party line" concerning such practices becomes an exclusionary criterion for membership in the community—we can expect to reap corruption. Indeed, we will see brothers and sisters in the church biting and devouring one another (5:15). A community that sows to the Spirit will invest its hopes not in any identity defined by sexuality but in the common identity given to us in Christ by the Spirit (cf. 3:26-29; 4:6-7).

4. *Personal Accountability and Self-examination.* The admonition that each one of us should examine ourselves and keep our boasting to ourselves (6:3-4) is a sound piece of counsel too rarely heard or heeded in the church. We live in an image-conscious age that encourages us constantly to compare ourselves with others and to worry over how we appear in the eyes of others. If we truly tested our own work (6:4) only with a view to pleasing God and maintaining the integrity of our life with God, it would go a long way toward eliminating the defensive posturing that corrupts our relationships with one another.

5. *The Community Under God's Eschatological Judgment.* The standard that counts in our self-examination is not merely our self-defined values; it is God's standard, for it is to God that we are ultimately accountable (6:5, 7-9; cf. 1 Cor 4:3-5). No matter how successfully we project an image of integrity or religiousness in the world, there is no fooling God, who knows our hearts and the real quality of our work. Only work that is the fruit of the Spirit will be of value at the time of the eschatological harvest. One of the major functions of Paul's concluding exhortation is to place all our doings under the scrutiny of God's final judgment. This has two immediate consequences: It inculcates humility (6:3-5), and it sustains our vision and hope in the midst of hard labor and adversity (6:9-10). One problem with much Christian preaching—at least in mainline Protestantism—is that it has lost sight of the eschatological horizon of God's judgment. It has therefore allowed the church to lose direction and take its bearings from "the present evil age" (1:4). The interpreter of Gal 6:1-10 must seek to reclaim the conviction that God will judge us and finally vindicate us.

This way of putting the matter immediately raises a problem: How is the warning of 6:5 related to Paul's claim that we are rectified solely through participation in Christ's triumph for us? The maxim of 6:5 makes it sound as though we are to be judged solely on the basis of our own works (cf. Rom 2:6-11; 2 Cor 5:10). This complicated theological problem requires a longer response than can be given here, but we can offer some hint of the lines along which an answer might develop. The key is to recognize that our "work" (6:4) is not an independent achievement; rather, it is the fruit of the Spirit's working in and through us (5:22-23), as suggested by the paradox of Phil 2:12*b*-13: "Work out your own salvation with fear and trembling; for it is God who is at work in you, enabling you both to will and to work for his good pleasure" (NRSV). Because the Spirit has already given us life, the Spirit will also direct our lives in ways consonant with God's will (5:25). We are not autonomous moral agents but instruments of God's working in the world. Or, to use a different image, it is only by virtue of Christ living in us (Gal 2:20) that we can fulfill the Law of Christ and thereby stand before God's judgment not in fear, but in hope of inheriting the kingdom of God.

6. *The Importance of Teaching.* A minor, but still significant, note in the passage is the emphasis placed on teaching in 6:6. The church needs the ministry of those who do the work of instructing others in the Word, and it should share its resources in a way that makes the ministry of teaching possible. One suspects that Paul thought the Galatians' need for proper teaching was particularly acute. There is always the temptation to think that other needs are more pressing or practical, and that teaching is an optional luxury for the church. In the absence of faithful instruction, however, the church quickly goes astray—as the Galatians were doing—and loses its sense of direction. "The Word" provides the indispensable point of orientation for the community's life.

7. *"Sowing" Our Trust in the Spirit.* Finally, Paul wraps up his exhortation by posing a stark alternative. We "sow" either to the flesh or to the Spirit. For Paul, the apocalyptic thinker, there is no middle ground. The seeds that we cast will fall either on one ground or the other. This means that we are always confronted by the choice of where to commit our hopes, our energy, and our resources; in this choice, we place our lives on the line.

The Galatians were confronted by the choice between committing themselves to a gospel of circumcision ("sowing to the flesh") and trusting in a Law-free gospel ("sowing to the Spirit"). Given subsequent historical developments, few Christian preachers today will find themselves addressing congregations that are tempted to regard the Christian gospel as a deficient, stripped-down version of Judaism. Still, Paul's warning against trusting in the flesh remains relevant, if we bear in mind the scope of the term "flesh" in his theological lexicon; it refers to all self-asserting activity that seeks security in anything other than the promise of God. When "flesh" is defined in this way, we can see that our congregations face the temptation to "sow to the flesh" whenever they are tempted to define or defend themselves through ethnic exlusivity, through material possessions, or through violence. These are the insidious dangers that we face. To allow Paul's gospel to speak to our time, then, we must proclaim boldly that from ethnic exclusivity we will reap hatred; from acquisitiveness we will reap corruption; and from violence we will reap violence. Against all of these things, if we place our trust in the Spirit, we will discover a more excellent way.

GALATIANS 6:11-18

POSTSCRIPT: THE CROSS AND NEW CREATION

COMMENTARY

To conclude the letter, Paul adds a postscript written in his own hand. This was a common practice in Hellenistic letters: An amanuensis or scribe would write out the body of the text, and the sender would add a final word of greeting or summary. In the case of Galatians this concluding paragraph is far more than a perfunctory sign-off; it functions as the *peroratio* of the letter, a carefully crafted distillation of the message designed to drive home the central points one more time.[291] For this reason the postscript provides a key to understanding the central concerns of the letter. Paul pens the final sentences with urgency and passion, offering a last glimpse of the heart of his gospel: the cross and new creation.

Usually, Paul's letter closings contain greetings and good wishes to various individuals in the community of the addressees. The absence of such friendly words in the last paragraph of Galatians corresponds to the absence of a thanksgiving in the letter's opening: Both are signs of the strained relationship between the apostle and his churches in Galatia.

6:11. The "large letters" signify that Paul has now taken the pen and begun to compose his closing word. Some have speculated that Paul writes in large characters because of a physical disability or poor eyesight (see the Commentary on 4:13-15, above). There is, however, no indication in the text at this point that Paul is calling attention to his physical condition. It is more likely that the large letters simply serve to give special emphasis to what he will write in this paragraph. It is as though he were writing his postscript in a

larger font, with boldface type, to command the special attention of his readers.

For other passages in which Paul writes a concluding personal postscript, see 1 Cor 16:21; Col 4:18; Phlm 19; cf. 2 Thess 3:17. Romans 16:22 contains a word of greeting from the scribe, Tertius.

6:12-13. Paul immediately launches an ad hominem attack on the rival Missionaries, characterizing their motives in highly derogatory terms. He alleges that they are urging the Galatians to be circumcised only in order to make themselves look good, to avoid persecution, and to have a basis for boasting. Of course, the Missionaries themselves would have given a very different account of their motives. The Galatians must decide who is to be trusted.

The focus on circumcision in vv. 12-13 is a crucial piece of evidence disclosing the issue that triggered Paul's angry letter. Paul says that the Missionaries are trying "to compel you to be circumcised." Tellingly, "compel" (ἀναγκάζω *anagkazō*) is the same verb he used of the "false brothers" in 2:4 and of Peter in 2:14; in each case Paul speaks of rigorously Law-observant Jews trying to manipulate or coerce Gentiles into coming under the Law. Their reason for this, Paul asserts, is "to make a good showing in the flesh." Paul is once again making a play on the word *flesh,* evoking its unfavorable connotation (the sphere of the merely human, as opposed to the sphere of the divine Spirit) while at the same time alluding to the physical act of circumcision. By translating the phrase as "make a good impression outwardly," the NIV loses these connotations. The good physical impression would be good only in the eyes of Jews; Greeks and Romans tended to

291. Betz, *Galatians,* 313.

regard circumcision as a repugnant practice of disfigurement.

Paul also alleges that the Missionaries' advocacy of circumcision is a strategy for avoiding persecution "for the cross of Christ." The persecution in question is persecution at the hands of Jews or Jewish Christians. During this historical period there was no official Roman persecution of Christians, and, in any case, the Romans would hardly have persecuted anyone for the crime of being uncircumcised![292] Earlier in the letter Paul has referred to his own activity as a persecutor of the church (1:13, 23), and he has implied that in the present time Law-observant Jewish Christians are engaged in persecuting non-Law-observant Christians (4:29; 5:11). The motive for such persecuting activity remains a matter of conjecture. Robert Jewett has proposed that the church in Jerusalem during this period was under pressure from a rising movement of Zealot-inspired nationalism that regarded the emergent Jewish-Christian groups as suspect because of their close affiliation with Gentiles. These Judean Jewish Christians, in turn, might have sought to persuade Gentile Christians to undergo circumcision in order to defuse criticism from their zealous Jewish compatriots[293] (see the Commentary on 2:11-14). This theory has the virtue of explaining the otherwise puzzling statement by Paul in 6:12: The Missionaries want to compel the *Gentile Galatians* to be circumcised in order that *they, the Jewish Christians,* might avoid persecution.

At the same time, the reference to persecution might be understood in a more general way: All who preach the cross, as Paul does, can expect to encounter opposition and persecution from a world offended by a gospel that proclaims the end of all ethnic, social, and religious privilege and distinction. The cross has put an end to all such systems (vv. 14-15). By domesticating the gospel, however, and turning it into a minor refinement of the religion of the Sinaitic Law, the Missionaries would avoid the gospel's radical implications and thereby fit more comfortably into recognized religious categories. This would enable them to escape the sort of persecution that Paul himself constantly encountered (see on v. 17, below). This does not mean that they did not speak of the crucifixion of Jesus in their preaching; presumably they did, but they did not interpret the cross, in Paul's fashion, as the apocalyptic termination of the old world of religious symbolism and obligation.

The charge raised in v. 13a is puzzling for two reasons: There is a question about the meaning of the participle that is translated "those who are circumcised" (οἱ περιτεμνόμενοι *hoi peritemnomenoi*), and it is not clear what Paul means by accusing "those who are circumcised" of not keeping the Law. Because the participle is a present middle/passive form, some interpreters have suggested that it should be translated "those who are being circumcised" and understood as a reference to the Gentile Galatians who were accepting the Missionaries' call for circumcision without yet adopting comprehensive observance of the Jewish Law. Alternatively, it could simply mean "the circumcised" (NRSV) and function as a blanket term for the Jewish-Christian Missionaries who were unsettling the Galatians. The latter interpretation makes better sense in the present context, where vv. 12 and 13b certainly refer to the Jewish-Christian Missionaries.

But if that is right, why does Paul say that they do not keep the Law?[294] We should not read into the text the idea that the Law is impossible to keep (see the Commentary on 3:10-12). Nor can we accept Dunn's suggestion that they fail to keep the Law precisely by relying on "their practice as Jews" (= "works of the Law")—thereby abusing their covenantal privilege and becoming prideful. According to this reading Paul's claim is that only those who recognize that the Law teaches faith as the ground of relation to God really obey it rightly.[295] This subtle interpretation runs aground on the verb that Paul uses in v. 13: "to keep" (φυλάσσω *phylassō*); this verb characteristically refers to performing

---

292. It is sometimes suggested that Gentile Christians might have wanted to adopt Jewish practices because Judaism was a *religio licita*, a legally recognized religion. According to this theory, by presenting themselves to Roman authorities as Jews, Christians could be excused from pressure to participate in the cult of emperor worship, thereby escaping persecution. There is, however, no evidence of such a scenario in Galatians. Nothing is said about the imperial cult, and all the letter's references to persecution suggest that the persecution of Christians came from Jewish sources.

293. Jewett, "The Agitators and the Galatian Congregation," 198-212.

294. For a list of possible interpretive options, see Dunn, *The Epistle to the Galatians*, 338-39.

295. Dunn, *The Epistle to the Galatians*, 338-39.

the specific commandments of the Law. Paul does not say that they do not "fulfill" the Law (cf. 5:14; 6:2), but simply that they do not do what it requires. What, then, could Paul mean by this accusation?

The best clue we have within Galatians is the similar charge that Paul levels against Peter in 2:14: If he himself is not a scrupulous observer of the Law, why is he trying to compel the Gentiles at Antioch to live like Jews? In other words, 6:13*a*, like 2:14, should be understood as a charge of hypocrisy. Paul is saying that the circumcision advocates are only dabblers in the Law, not really carrying out its comprehensive requirements. This accusation reflects Paul's rigoristic interpretation of the total demand of the Law (see his self-description in 1:14 as having been "more zealous" than his Jewish contemporaries). In the eyes of Paul, the former zealous Pharisee (Phil 3:6), those who merely practice circumcision and observe some of the feasts cannot claim to be living fully in accord with everything the Law requires. There can be no partial or selective observance of the Law (see the Commentary on 5:2-4).

This interpretation is supported by Paul's final comment about the Missionaries in v. 13*b*. They are not really interested in keeping the Law, he asserts, for their real motive for wanting to circumcise the Galatians is "so that they may boast about your flesh" (cf. the warning against boasting in 6:3-4). In effect, he is saying that his rivals want to display the foreskins of the Galatians as trophies of their own triumphant persuasive power. This accusation of self-centered vanity is consistent with Paul's earlier warning that the Missionaries want to exclude the Galatians in order to gain influence over them (4:17).

The prohibition of boasting is a recurrent theme of Paul's correspondence. In Romans he particularly identifies boasting with the Jews' presumption of their moral or religious superiority by virtue of their knowledge of God's Law (Rom 2:17-18); Paul insists that such boasting is excluded by "the Law of faith" (cf. Gal 6:2), the teaching that Jew and Gentile alike are justified only through faith (Rom 3:27-30). Something similar is in view in Paul's accusation in Gal 6:13*b:* He is warning that the Missionaries want to assert the superiority of Jewish religious

tradition through compelling uncircumcised Gentiles to accept circumcision. The newly circumcised flesh of the Galatians would then become the ground for these Jewish-Christian Missionaries to boast about their conquest of Gentile disobedience. In short, Paul is labeling the Missionaries' push for circumcision as a form of chauvinistic religious self-assertion.

6:14-15. Contrasting himself to these boastful proselytizers, Paul declares that he wishes never to boast about anything—except "the cross of our Lord Jesus Christ." It is an acute paradox to speak of boasting in the cross, for the cross is precisely the place where all human effort and pride come to an end. The cross is God's deed, not ours. To "boast" in the cross, then, is to acknowledge that our efforts lead only to death and that our confidence can rest only in God's grace, which rescues us from the present evil age. Elsewhere, Paul makes the same point by quoting Jer 9:24: "Let the one who boasts, boast in the Lord" (1 Cor 1:31; 2 Cor 10:17 NRSV). That kind of boasting precludes self-aggrandizement, for it focuses exclusively on "Jesus Christ, and him crucified" (1 Cor 2:2 NRSV) and on our hope of sharing in his sufferings and glory (Rom 5:2-3, 11).

The cross, in Paul's narrative world, is the transformative event that ended the old order of things, the event through which "the world has been crucified to me, and I to the world." This startling imagery expresses God's violent and irrevocable termination of everything that Paul had previously believed and cherished. In light of the cross he has come to count all his ethnic pride and personal achievements as a complete loss (Phil 3:4-11). His previous identity has disappeared altogether, and his new identity is given him only through his participation in Christ, who animates the life he now lives (Gal 2:19-20). That is why he can also say that the flesh has been crucified for those who belong to Christ. They participate, not just symbolically but actually, in his death; therefore, they have entered the new eschatological world where his life empowers the community to "walk in newness of life" and consider themselves "dead to sin and alive to God" (Rom 6:4, 11 NRSV).

This language of the world's crucifixion should not be understood merely as an event within the psyche of the individual believer. It is the κόσμος (*kosmos*) that has been crucified, not merely Paul's perception of the *kosmos*. The στοιχεῖα τοῦ κόσμου (*stoicheia tou kosmou*) have been overthrown and abolished by Christ's death and resurrection (cf. Col 2:13-15). A new reality has been brought into being that determines the destiny of the whole creation. That is why Paul moves on in the next sentence (v. 15) to speak of "new creation." In the new creation, the old order's categories have been dissolved into nothingness. It is not merely that circumcision is of lesser importance in the new scheme of things; rather, the whole binary opposition between circumcision and uncircumcision has been literally nullified. Thus "the world that is now passé is not Judaism as such, but rather the world of *all* religious differentiation."[296]

Paul has made this point earlier in the letter with his sweeping declaration that in Christ the categories of Jew/Greek, slave/free, and male/female have ceased to have validity (3:28), and he has drawn out the pastoral implications of this truth for the circumcision question (5:6). The implications of this message for the relation of Jews and Gentiles in the church are aptly interpreted in Eph 2:15-16:

He has abolished the Law with its commandments and ordinances, that he might create in himself one new humanity in place of the two, thus making peace, and might reconcile both groups to God in one body through the cross. (NRSV)

Now, in his climactic summary of the letter's message, he divulges the fundamental reason underlying these remarkable claims: "For neither circumcision nor uncircumcision is anything, but—*new creation*!" The broken syntax of the sentence expresses the utter discontinuity between the abolished cosmos and the new world. There is no way to finish the sentence; Paul can only blurt "new creation!" (Unfortunately, both NIV and NRSV mute the literary effect by filling the gap and smoothing Paul's exclamation into a tamer complete sentence.) We see a parallel

movement of thought in the one other place that Paul speaks of new creation:

So if anyone is in Christ—new creation! Everything old has passed away; see, everything has become new! (2 Cor 5:17, author's trans.)

Paul is not speaking here about "the establishment of a new religion"[297] or the spiritual rebirth of an individual. He is claiming that the God who created the world has come to reclaim and transform it.

The ground of this hope lies in Israel's Scripture, with its prophetic visions of God's ultimate transformative justice. Particularly important is Isa 65:17-25, which begins with an extraordinary promise:

For I am about to create new heavens
and a new earth;
the former things shall not be remembered
or come to mind. (Isa 65:17 NRSV)

This vision of God's new creation is fundamental to Paul's theology; he proclaims not just the salvation of souls, but also God's eschatological redemption of the creation (see Rom 8:19-23; cf. Rev 21:1-5).[298]

In this new creation, the Missionaries' pressure for the practice of circumcision simply makes no sense. It is a reversion to the *status quo ante,* an attempt to reenter a symbolic world that has been obliterated by the cross. Thus with Gal 6:14-15 Paul has completed his forceful recapitulation of his argument.

6:16. Having begun the letter with a curse on the perverters of the gospel (1:8-9), Paul chooses to end it with a blessing on his readers in the hope that they will have been persuaded by his arguments to renounce circumcision and live as Gentiles under the direction of the Spirit. Since he does not know the effect that his letter will achieve, however, he formulates the blessing in conditional terms. The blessing is pronounced not on the Galatian churches generally, but specifically on "those who will follow this rule" (note the future tense). The verb "will follow" (στοιχήσουσιν *stoichēsousin*) is the

---

296. Martyn, *Galatians,* 565, emphasis in original; see also pp. 570-74; Williams, *Galatians,* 165.

297. Betz, *Galatians,* 320.
298. For references to the motif of new creation in other Jewish texts, see *Jub.* 4:26; *1 Enoch* 72:1; *4 Ezra* 7:75; *2 Apoc. Bar.* 32:6; 1QS 4:25; 1QH 11:10-14; 13:11-12. See also Martyn, *Galatians,* 565n. 64.

same word used in the exhortation of 5:25: "Since we live by the Spirit, let us *keep in step* with the Spirit." These two sentences certainly interpret one another: To keep in step with the Spirit is to follow the "rule" of 6:14-15, and to follow this rule is to be guided by the Spirit to discern the new creation. Only those readers who heed this rule are the recipients of the "peace and mercy" invoked by the apostle.

The word "rule" (χανών *kanōn*) refers literally to a measuring stick. Paul employs it metaphorically here to speak of the measure of truth and conduct articulated in v. 15 (and perhaps v. 14 as well): Boast only in the cross, for the old world is abolished and we live in the presence and hope of the new creation. Paul's frequent warnings elsewhere against boasting support the interpretation that v. 14 belongs to the rule to which Paul refers.

The blessing that Paul pronounces is deeply traditional and Jewish in character (cf. Ps 125:5; 128:6; *Pss Sol* 9:11; 11:9). "Peace" and "mercy" correspond to שלום (*šālôm*) and חסד (*ḥesed*), deeply resonant Hebrew words for God's blessing and grace. The most striking parallel to Gal 6:16 appears in the nineteenth benediction, the "Blessing of Peace" of the *Shemoneh Esreh* (Babylonian recension), a liturgy used regularly in the synagogue: "Bestow *peace,* happiness and blessing, grace and loving-kindness and *mercy upon us and upon all Israel,* your people" (italics added).[299] It is impossible to document the use of this specific benediction in the synagogues of Paul's day, but it is likely that he did know such a prayer and that he formed his benediction to the Galatians by analogy to it. It is important to observe that in this prayer "us" refers to the congregation praying the prayer, while "all Israel" is not a separate second group; rather, "all Israel" is the larger covenant community, the people of God to which the praying community ("us") belongs.

The potentially ambiguous wording of Gal 6:16 has generated much controversy about the meaning of the distinctive expression "the Israel of God," an expression that never occurs elsewhere in Paul's letters, in the extant literature of Second Temple Judaism, or in rabbinic literature.[300] From a purely syntactical point of view, there are two ways of reading the blessing. The question is whether Paul is referring to a single group (as in the NIV) or to two different groups (as in the NRSV). The possibilities are as follows:

(a) As for those who follow this rule, peace and mercy be upon them
—that is, upon the Israel of God.
(b[1]) As for those who follow this rule, peace and mercy be upon them
—and (also) upon the Israel of God.

A variation on the second option is to read the peace benediction as applying to Christians who accept Paul's line of argument and the mercy benediction as a second separate word of blessing on non-Christian Jews who may still, Paul hopes, experience God's mercy. This would yield the translation:

(b[2]) As for those who follow this rule, peace be upon them
—and mercy upon the Israel of God.

Those scholars who argue for b[1] or b[2] appeal for support to the argument of Romans 9-11, especially Rom 11:25-32, where the word *mercy* appears prominently in conjunction with Paul's affirmation that "all Israel will be saved."

If Paul meant to refer, however, to the ultimate salvation of the Jewish people, including those who in the present time reject the preaching of the gospel, he has provided no clues of this sort for his readers in Galatia. He had not yet written the Letter to the Romans, and Galatians nowhere touches upon the problem of God's faithfulness to Israel or the ultimate salvation of the Jewish people. The apostle is concerned with an entirely different set of problems posed by the demand that his Gentile congregations become Law observant. In the course of his argument he has asserted in the strongest possible terms that the Gentile members of his churches in Galatia are children of Abraham, heirs of God's promised blessing (3:6-9, 29), rightful heirs of the promise through Isaac (4:28, 31), Sarah's children. It is they who fulfill the Law (5:14; 6:2). In light of these claims there is only one possible way that the original readers could have understood the blessing of Gal 6:16: The Israel of

299. Betz, *Galatians*, 321.
300. Longenecker, *Galatians*, 299.

God refers to all who are in Christ (i.e., translation *a*).[301] It is a description of the elect eschatological community of faith composed of Jews and Gentiles alike. It is equivalent in meaning to "the household of faith" (6:10). The Israel of God, then, is another name for those who follow the rule of the new creation.[302]

For Paul to use the term "Israel" in this way is a bold move indeed, but certainly no bolder than his claim that the Gentile Galatians are Abraham's seed, children of promise in Isaac's line—indeed, it is substantively identical to that claim. Thus the blessing that Paul pronounces at the end of the letter forcefully restates the letter's central thesis.

6:17. In a final rhetorical gesture Paul demonstrates dismay at having to put up with the hassle of answering the Missionaries' arguments and rebutting their charges. He gives a surprising reason for his request that no one trouble him further with these matters: Because he bears the marks (στίγματα *stigmata*) of Jesus on his body. This expression refers to the scars that he has incurred in the course of his apostolic labors. By his own testimony Paul suffered numerous floggings and beatings, and he was once stoned (2 Cor 11:23-25; cf. 2 Cor 6:4-5; Acts 14:19). Such abuse would no doubt have left his body battered and marked by scars. Experiences such as these may lie behind Paul's reference to some sort of physical affliction that occasioned his first visit to Galatia (Gal 4:13-14).

Paul interprets these bodily scars as signs of his identification with his crucified Lord. Indeed, his battered body becomes for him a visible depiction of the gospel of the cross. This is probably what he has in mind when he describes himself as "carrying in the body the putting to death (νέκρωσις *nekrōsis*) of Jesus, so that the life of Jesus may also be made visible in our bodies" (2 Cor 4:10). The wounded apostle becomes a walking exhibit of the message of "Jesus Christ, and him crucified."[303] In all likelihood this conviction

explains what Paul means when he says that in his original preaching to the Galatians "Jesus Christ was publicly exhibited as crucified" (3:1 NRSV).

The point of Gal 6:17 is that Paul's battle scars demonstrate his integrity and the truth of his message. Unlike the rival Missionaries, who seek to dodge persecution (v. 12), Paul has undergone it gladly and repeatedly for the sake of the gospel. Therefore, the Galatians should listen to him and not to a group of slick interlopers who have not paid the price of following a crucified Lord.

One additional nuance might be suggested by Paul's reference to "the marks of Jesus." In ancient Mediterranean culture slaves were characteristically branded with a mark to show to whom they belonged. Because Paul regards himself as Christ's slave (1:10), he may be suggesting that his physical scars mark him as the possession of the crucified Lord, Jesus. In that case 6:17 would imply that the Missionaries should desist from bothering him because he is working under the orders and authority of his master. Their attempt to interfere with his apostolic work is, in fact, an interference not just with him, but also with Jesus.

6:18. The final sentence of the postscript, after all the distress and anger of this letter, pronounces a simple benediction on the readers. "The grace of our Lord Jesus Christ" surrounds and embraces this entire turbulent argument (1:3; 6:18). Grace refers to the loving favor of God, made effective in the world through Christ's death. (For other mentions of grace in Galatians, see 1:6, 15; 2:9, 21; 3:18; 5:4.) After stern warnings to the Galatian churches not to fall away from grace, in the end the apostle utters a prayer that Christ's grace will remain with their spirit. Here and only here in the letter, "spirit" is used as an anthropological term rather than as a reference to the Spirit of God.

Nearly identical benedictions are found in Phil 4:23 and Phlm 25. In Gal 6:18, however, Paul adds one word that does not appear in the others: ἀδελφοί (*adelphoi*). It is the last word before the "amen," the penultimate word before the silence into which the Galatians will have to speak their response to Paul's appeal. By poignantly addressing his readers in this last breath of the postscript as

---

301. Thus Betz, *Galatians*, 322-23; Longenecker, *Galatians*, 298-99; Martyn, *Galatians*, 574-77.

302. This inclusion of Gentile believers within "Israel" is commensurate with Paul's pastoral strategy in 1 Corinthians. In writing to a predominantly Gentile church in Corinth, he describes Israel in the wilderness as "our fathers" (1 Cor 10:1) and refers to his readers' past as the time "when you were Gentiles" (1 Cor 12:2). In short, he narrates the Gentile Corinthians into the people Israel.

303. See S. Kraftchick, "Death in Us, Life in You: The Apostolic Medium," in *Pauline Theology*, vol. 2: *1 & 2 Corinthians*, ed. D. M. Hay (Minneapolis: Fortress, 1993) 156-81.

brothers and sisters, Paul affirms a continuing hope that they will not turn away from the gospel, that they will remain his brothers and sisters within the family of faith.

REFLECTIONS

1. *The Problem of Cultural Imperialism.* From a historical point of view we are in no position to assess the fairness of Paul's harsh critique of the Missionaries. We have no access to their writings and no other documents to provide information on the situation of the Galatian churches. We have only Paul's account of the matter. Were they really as chauvinistic and self-interested as Paul contends? Perhaps so, but human motivations are complex. Presumably they believed themselves to be promoting the cause of obedience to God's will. In our reflection on the text, we will not make much progress through speculative psychologizing about the Missionaries and their motives. We will do better to concentrate on the effects of their actions on the Gentile believers in Galatia.

Paul's chief objection to the Missionaries' message was that it sought to superimpose their Jewish religious culture upon Gentiles who had already encountered the gospel through Paul's Law-free preaching. Their insistence on circumcision had the effect of making Gentiles jump through a Jewish hoop in order to participate fully in the new community of the people of God. This sort of cultural imperialism was anathema to Paul.

We need to think carefully about the reason why Paul found this cultural imperialism so objectionable. It was not because he believed that there was some intrinsic value to Gentile cultural practices, not because he believed that each person had a right to make private choices about religious preference, and certainly not because he believed that proselytizing was wrong *a priori.* Paul was, after all, engaged in a lifelong project of seeking to win converts for the gospel and to transform the cultures of the Gentile communities where he established churches. Paul's objection to the Missionaries' cultural imperialism was that it had the effect of nullifying the grace of God. In communities where Gentiles had already received the Spirit, they were now being told that their experience was somehow deficient and that they had to conform themselves to Jewish religious practices in order to participate fully in God's promise of life. Thus they were being led subtly to discount the redemptive work of Jesus Christ as their one ground of hope and to substitute for it a program of human religious observances. That is why Paul put his foot down in opposition to the circumcision party.

Therefore, as we reflect on Galatians as Scripture, we must ask ourselves at what points we are in danger of superimposing our religious culture—even the cultures of particular church traditions—on communities that are responding to the gospel in fresh, indigenous ways under the guidance of the Spirit. This can happen not only when Christian missionaries encounter non-Western cultures, but also when established churches frown on charismatic churches or independent churches outside the usual denominational structure. It can happen when older Christians object to the musical and artistic forms of worship among younger Christians. It most certainly happens in every case where ethnic pride or nationalism co-opts the gospel. After reading Galatians carefully we will find ourselves prompted to scrutinize our churches to see whether we may be unintentionally nullifying the grace of God through explicit or implicit membership requirements unrelated to the heart of the gospel.

2. *Boasting in the Cross.* Paul's postscript reminds us that the cross is at the heart of the Christian message. It destroys all pride, for through the cross the whole world has been crucified. This astounding metaphor requires sustained reflection. If we are tempted to boast in our wealth or intelligence or accomplishments, we are pursuing a path that leads nowhere. The most insidious temptation—the one faced in Galatia—is the temptation to boast in moral or religious superiority. The cross destroys all such boasting and focuses our eyes upon Jesus, whose loving self-donation discloses the one truth that can be trusted, the truth of God's love for us. That is why we can boast only in "the cross of our Lord Jesus Christ." To "boast" of the cross is of course not boasting at all: The paradox redefines the verb, so that boasting becomes worship and acclamation of the crucified Jesus. Furthermore, as we focus our attention on the cross, we learn that we render true honor to the crucified Lord only by becoming conformed to him so that we become servants to one another in love (5:13). Truly to boast in the cross is to put our own lives on the line in acts of service that declare in deed as well as in word that the cross is the revelation of God's love.

3. *New Creation.* Paul's gospel is not only a negative word that proclaims the demolition of our old world of religion, value, and morality. The gospel also proclaims that God is making all things new. As the marks of Jesus on Paul's body testify, the coming of the new creation is neither easy nor complete in the present time. The breaking in of God's redemptive power has triggered costly conflict with the powers that have a vested interest in the old order. The calling of the apostle—and of the church—is to bear witness steadfastly to the coming new order of God's justice. The new creation is not, however, merely a dream or a vision; it takes on empirical reality in the community of God's people, whose life together already testifies to the reconciling power of the gospel. That is one reason why Paul was so insistent that Gentiles not be circumcised. The policy of circumcision made it look as though the Gentile converts were simply being absorbed into Judaism, but Paul was insistent that "the Israel of God" was a new eschatological reality, a community in which the circumcision/uncircumcision distinction no longer functioned to divide humanity. That is the rule that Paul invokes as the identifying standard for walking under the guidance of the Spirit: no more fleshly divisions. As we have seen earlier in the letter, where the grace of Jesus Christ is at work, God's people will find themselves united around one table, not divided at separate tables. The one table where circumcised and uncircumcised sit together in love is a sign and foretaste of the new creation.

For many readers in our time, the deepest ethnic divisions will not be those between Jew and Gentile, but between different racial groups, even within the church. Sadly, it remains true, as Martin Luther King, Jr., observed a generation ago, that 11:00 A.M. Sunday is the most segregated hour of the week in the United States. If we hear Paul's letter as a message spoken not just to ancient Galatians, but also to us, we will hear it as a call to racial reconciliation. If we can read Gal 6:15 and echo it in our hearts by confessing, "Neither whiteness nor blackness is anything, but—new creation!" then peace and mercy will be upon us indeed.

ABBREVIATIONS

BCE	before the Common Era
ca.	circa
CE	Common Era
cent.	century
cf.	compare
chap(s).	chapter(s)
d.	died
Dtr	Deuteronomistic historian
esp.	especially
fem.	feminine
HB	Hebrew Bible
l(l).	line(s)
lit.	literally
LXX	Septuagint
masc.	masculine
MS(S)	manuscript(s)
MT	Masoretic Text
n(n).	note(s)
neut.	neuter
NT	New Testament
OG	Old Greek
OL	Old Latin
OT	Old Testament
par(r).	parallel(s)
pl(s).	plate(s)
SP	Samaritan Pentateuch
v(v).	verse(s)
Vg	Vulgate
\\	between Scripture references indicates parallelism

Names of Pseudepigraphical and Early Patristic Books

Apoc. Abr.	*Apocalypse of Abraham*
2–3 Apoc. Bar.	Syriac, Greek *Apocalypse of Baruch*
Apoc. Mos.	*Apocalypse of Moses*

Ascen. Isa.	*Ascension of Isaiah*
As. Mos.	*Assumption of Moses*
Barn.	*Barnabas*
Bib. Ant.	Pseudo-Philo, *Biblical Antiquities*
1–2 Clem.	*1–2 Clement*
Did.	*Didache*
1–2–3 Enoch	Ethiopic, Slavonic, Hebrew *Enoch*
Ep. Arist.	*Epistle of Aristeas*
Gos. Pet.	*Gospel of Peter*
Herm. Sim.	Hermas, *Similitude(s)*
Ign. Eph.	Ignatius, *Letter to the Ephesians*
Ign. Magn.	Ignatius, *Letter to the Magnesians*
Ign. Phld.	Ignatius, *Letter to the Philadelphians*
Ign. Pol.	Ignatius, *Letter to Polycarp*
Ign. Rom.	Ignatius, *Letter to the Romans*
Ign. Smyrn.	Ignatius, *Letter to the Smyrnaeans*
Ign. Trall.	Ignatius, *Letter to the Trallians*
Jub.	*Jubilees*
POxy	B. P. Grenfell and A. S. Hunt (eds.), *Oxyrhynchus Papyri*
Pss. Sol.	*Psalms of Solomon*
Sib. Or.	*Sibylline Oracles*
T. Benj.	*Testament of Benjamin*
T. Dan	*Testament of Dan*
T. Iss.	*Testament of Issachar*
T. Job	*Testament of Job*
T. Jud.	*Testament of Judah*
T. Levi	*Testament of Levi*
T. Naph.	*Testament of Naphtali*
T. Reub.	*Testament of Reuben*
T. Sim.	*Testament of Simeon*

Names of Dead Sea Scrolls and Related Texts

CD	Cairo (Genizah text of the) Damascus Document
DSS	Dead Sea Scrolls
8HevXII gr	Greek scroll of the Minor Prophets from Naḥal Ḥever
Q	Qumran
1Q, 2Q, etc.	numbered caves of Qumran, yielding written material; followed by abbreviation of biblical or apocryphal book
1Q28b	Rule of the Blessings (Appendix b to 1QS)
1QH	Thanksgiving Hymns (Qumran Cave 1)
1QM	War Scroll (Qumran Cave 1)
1QpHab	Pesher on Habakkuk (Qumran Cave 1)
1QpPs	Pesher on Psalms (Qumran Cave 1)
1QS	Rule of the Community (Qumran Cave 1)
1QSa	Rule of the Congregation (Appendix a to 1QS)
1QSb	Rule of the Blessings (Appendix b to 1QS)
4Q175	Testimonia text (Qumran Cave 4)
4Q246	Apocryphon of Daniel (Qumran Cave 4)
4Q298	Words of the Sage to the Sons of Dawn (Qumran Cave 4)
4Q385b	fragmentary remains of Pseudo-Jeremiah that implies that Jeremiah went into Babylonian exile. Also known as ApocJer[c] or 4Q385 16. (Qumran Cave 4)

4Q389a	several scroll fragments now thought to contain portions of three pseudepigraphical works including Pseudo-Jeremiah. Also known as 4QApocJer[e]. (Qumran Cave 4)
4Q390	contains a schematized history of Israel's sin and divine punishment. Also known as psMos[e]. (Qumran Cave 4)
4Q394–399	Halakhic Letter (Qumran Cave 4)
4Q416	Instruction[b] (Qumran Cave 4)
4Q521	Messianic Apocalypse (Qumran Cave 4)
4Q550	Proto-Esther [a-f] (Qumran Cave 4)
4QFlor	Florilegium (or Eschatological Midrashim) (Qumran Cave 4)
4QMMT	Halakhic Letter (Qumran Cave 4)
4QpaleoDeutr	copy of Deuteronomy in paleo-Hebrew script (Qumran Cave 4)
4QpaleoExod	copy of Exodus in paleo-Hebrew script (Qumran Cave 4)
4QpNah	Pesher on Nahum (Qumran Cave 4)
4QpPs	Psalm Pesher A (Qumran Cave 4)
4QPrNab	Prayer of Nabonidus (Qumran Cave 4)
4QPs37	Psalm Scroll (Qumran Cave 4)
4QpsDan	Pseudo-Daniel (Qumran Cave 4)
4QSam	First copy of Samuel (Qumran Cave 4)
4QTestim	Testimonia text (Qumran Cave 4)
4QTob	Copy of Tobit (Qumran Cave 4)
11QMelch	Melchizedek text (Qumran Cave 11)
11QPs[a]	Psalms Scroll (Qumran Cave 11)
11QT	Temple Scroll (Qumran Cave 11)
11QtgJob	Targum of Job (Qumran Cave 11)

Targumic Material

Tg. Esth. I, II	First or Second Targum of Esther
Tg. Neb.	Targum of the Prophets
Tg. Neof.	Targum Neofiti

Orders and Tractates in Mishnaic and Related Literature

To distinguish the same-named tractates in the Mishnah, Tosefta, Babylonian Talmud, and Jerusalem Talmud, *m., t., b.,* or *y.* precedes the title of the tractate.

ʾAbot	ʾAbot
ʿArak.	ʿArakin
B. Bat.	Baba Batra
B. Meṣ.	Baba Meṣiʿa
B. Qam.	Baba Qamma
Ber.	Berakot
Dem.	Demai
Giṭ.	Giṭṭin
Ḥag.	Ḥagigah
Hor.	Horayot
Ḥul.	Ḥullin
Ket.	Ketubbot
Maʿaś.	Maʿaśerot
Meg.	Megilla
Menaḥ.	Menaḥot

Mid.	Middot
Moʿed Qaṭ.	Moʿed Qaṭan
Nazir	Nazir
Ned.	Nedarim
p. Šeqal.	pesachim Šeqalim
Pesaḥ.	Pesaḥim
Qidd.	Quddušin
Šabb.	Šabbat
Sanh.	Sanhedrin
Soṭah	Soṭah
Sukk.	Sukkah
Taʿan.	Taʿanit
Tamid	Tamid
Yad.	Yadayim
Yoma	Yoma (=Kippurim)

Other Rabbinic Works

ʾAbot R. Nat.	ʾAbot de Rabbi Nathan
Pesiq. R.	Pesiqta Rabbati
Rab.	Rabbah (following abbreviation of biblical book—e.g., Gen. Rab. = Genesis Rabbah)
Sipra	Sipra

Greek Manuscripts and Ancient Versions

<u>Papyrus Manuscripts</u>

$\mathfrak{P}^1$	third-century Greek papyrus manuscript of the Gospels
$\mathfrak{P}^{29}$	third- or fourth-century Greek papyrus manuscript
$\mathfrak{P}^{33}$	sixth-century Greek papyrus manuscript of Acts
$\mathfrak{P}^{37}$	third- or fourth-century Greek papyrus manuscript of the Gospels
$\mathfrak{P}^{38}$	fourth-century Greek papyrus manuscript of Acts
$\mathfrak{P}^{45}$	third-century Greek papyrus manuscript of the Gospels
$\mathfrak{P}^{46}$	third-century Greek papyrus manuscript of the letters
$\mathfrak{P}^{47}$	third-century Greek papyrus manuscript of Revelation
$\mathfrak{P}^{48}$	third-century Greek papyrus manuscript of Acts
$\mathfrak{P}^{52}$	second-century Greek papyrus manuscript of John 18:31-33, 37-38
$\mathfrak{P}^{58}$	sixth-century Greek papyrus manuscript of Acts
$\mathfrak{P}^{64}$	third-century Greek papyrus fragment of Matthew
$\mathfrak{P}^{66}$	second- or third-century Greek papyrus manuscript of John (incomplete)
$\mathfrak{P}^{67}$	third-century Greek papyrus fragment of Matthew
$\mathfrak{P}^{69}$	third-century Greek papyrus manuscript of the Gospel of Luke
$\mathfrak{P}^{75}$	third-century Greek papyrus manuscript of the Gospels

<u>Lettered Uncials</u>

ℵ	Codex Sinaiticus, fourth-century manuscript of LXX, NT, Epistle of Barnabas, and Shepherd of Hermas
A	Codex Alexandrinus, fifth-century manuscript of LXX, NT, 1 and 2 Clement, and Psalms of Solomon
B	Codex Vaticanus, fourth-century manuscript of LXX and parts of the NT

C	Codex Ephraemi, fifth-century manuscript of parts of LXX and NT
D	Codex Bezae, fifth-century bilingual (Greek and Latin) manuscript of the Gospels and Acts
G	ninth-century manuscript of the Gospels
K	ninth-century manuscript of the Gospels
L	eighth-century manuscript of the Gospels
W	Washington Codex, fifth-century manuscript of the Gospels
X	Codex Monacensis, ninth- or tenth-century manuscript of the Gospels
Z	sixth-century manuscript of Matthew
Θ	Koridethi Codex, ninth-century manuscript of the Gospels
Ψ	Athous Laurae Codex, eighth- or ninth-century manuscript of the Gospels (incomplete), Acts, the Catholic and Pauline Epistles, and Hebrews

Numbered Uncials

058	fourth-century fragment of Matthew 18
074	sixth-century fragment of Matthew
078	sixth-century fragment of Matthew, Luke, and John
0170	fifth- or sixth-century manuscript of Matthew
0181	fourth- or fifth-century partial manuscript of Luke 9:59–10:14

Numbered Minuscules

33	tenth-century manuscript of the Gospels
75	eleventh-century manuscript of the Gospels
565	ninth-century manuscript of the Gospels
700	eleventh-century manuscript of the Gospels
892	ninth-century manuscript of the Gospels

Names of Nag Hammadi Tractates

Ap. John	Apocryphon of John (also called the Secret Book of John)
Apoc. Adam	Apocalypse of Adam (also called the Revelation of Adam)
Ep. Pet.	Letter of Peter to Philip
Exeg. Soul	Exegesis on the Soul
Gos. Phil.	Gospel of Philip
Gos. Truth	Gospel of Truth

Ancient Versions

bo	the Bohairic (Memphitic) Coptic version
bo[mss]	some manuscripts in the Bohairic tradition
d	the Latin text of Codex Bezae
e	Codex Palatinus, fifth-century Latin manuscript of the Gospels
ff^2	Old Latin manuscript, fifth-century translation of the Gospels
Ir[lat]	the Latin translation of Irenaeus
latt	the whole Latin tradition (including the Vulgate)
mae	Middle Egyptian
sa	the Sahidic (Thebaic) Coptic version
sy	the Syriac version
sy[s]	the Sinaitic Syriac version

<u>Other Abbreviations</u>

700*	the original reading of manuscript 700
$\aleph^*$	the original reading of Codex Sinaiticus
$\aleph^1$	the first corrector of Codex Sinaiticus
$\aleph^2$	the second corrector of Codex Sinaiticus
$\mathfrak{M}$	the Majority text (the mass of later manuscripts)
C^2	the corrected text of Codex Ephraemi
D^*	the original reading of Codex Bezae
D^2	the second corrector (c. fifth century) of Codex Bezae
f^1	Family 1: minuscule manuscripts belonging to the Lake Group (1, 118, 131, 209, 1582)
f^{13}	Family 13: minuscule manuscripts belonging to the Ferrar Group (13, 69, 124, 174, 230, 346, 543, 788, 826, 828, 983, 1689, 1709)
pc	a few other manuscripts

Commonly Used Periodicals, Reference Works, and Serials

AAR	American Academy of Religion
AASOR	Annual of the American Schools of Oriental Research
AB	Anchor Bible
ABD	*Anchor Bible Dictionary*
ABR	*Australian Biblical Review*
ABRL	Anchor Bible Reference Library
ACNT	Augsburg Commentaries on the New Testament
AcOr	*Acta Orientalia*
AfO	*Archiv für Orientforschung*
AfOB	Archiv für Orientforschung: Beiheft
AGJU	Arbeiten zur Geschichte des antiken Judentums und des Urchristentums
AJP	*American Journal of Philology*
AJSL	*American Journal of Semitic Languages and Literature*
AJT	*American Journal of Theology*
AnBib	Analecta Biblica
ANEP	J. B. Pritchard (ed.), *The Ancient Near East in Pictures Relating to the Old Testament*
ANET	J. B. Pritchard (ed.), *Ancient Near Eastern Texts Relating to the Old Testament*
ANF	*Ante-Nicene Fathers*
ANRW	*Aufstieg und Niedergang der römischen Welt*
ANTC	Abingdon New Testament Commentaries
ANTJ	Arbeiten zum Neuen Testament und Judentum
APOT	R. H. Charles (ed.), *The Apocrypha and Pseudepigrapha of the Old Testament*
ASNU	Acta Seminarii Neotestamentici Upsaliensis
ATANT	Abhandlungen zur Theologie des Alten und Neuen Testaments
ATD	Das Alte Testament Deutsch
ATDan	Acta Theologica Danica
Aug	*Augustinianum*
AusBR	*Australian Biblical Review*
BA	*Biblical Archaeologist*

BAGD	W. Bauer, W. F. Arndt, F. W. Gingrich, and F. W. Danker, *Greek-English Lexicon of the New Testament and Other Early Christian Literature*, 2nd ed. (Bauer-Arndt-Gingrich-Danker)
BAR	*Biblical Archaeology Review*
BASOR	*Bulletin of the American Schools of Oriental Research*
BBB	Bonner biblische Beiträge
BBET	Beiträge zur biblischen Exegese und Theologie
BBR	*Bulletin for Biblical Research*
BDAG	W. Bauer, W. F. Arndt, F. W. Gingrich, and F. W. Danker, *Greek-English Lexicon of the New Testament and Other Early Christian Literature,* 3rd ed. (Bauer-Danker-Arndt-Gingrich)
BDB	F. Brown, S. R. Driver, and C. A. Briggs, *A Hebrew and English Lexicon of the Old Testament*
BDF	F. Blass, A. Debrunner, and R. W. Funk, *A Greek Grammar of the New Testament and Other Early Christian Literature*
BEATAJ	Beiträge zur Erforschung des Alten Testaments und des antiken Judentum
BETL	Bibliotheca Ephemeridum Theologicarum Lovaniensium
BEvT	Beiträge zur evangelischen Theologie
BHS	*Biblia Hebraica Stuttgartensia*
BHT	Beiträge zur historischen Theologie
Bib	*Biblica*
BibInt	*Biblical Interpretation*
BibOr	Biblica et Orientalia
BJRL	*Bulletin of the John Rylands University Library of Manchester*
BJS	Brown Judaic Studies
BK	*Bibel und Kirche*
BKAT	Biblischer Kommentar, Altes Testament
BLS	Bible and Literature Series
BN	*Biblische Notizen*
BNTC	Black's New Testament Commentaries
BR	*Biblical Research*
BSac	*Bibliotheca Sacra*
BSOAS	*Bulletin of the School of Oriental and African Studies*
BT	*The Bible Translator*
BTB	*Biblical Theology Bulletin*
BVC	*Bible et vie chrétienne*
BWA(N)T	Beiträge zur Wissenschaft vom Alten (und Neuen) Testament
BZ	*Biblische Zeitschrift*
BZAW	Beihefte zur Zeitschrift für die alttestamentliche Wissenschaft
BZNW	Beihefte zur Zeitschrift für die neutestamentliche Wissenschaft
CAD	*The Assyrian Dictionary of the Oriental Institute of the University of Chicago*
CB	*Cultura Bíblica*
CBC	Cambridge Bible Commentary
CBOTS	Coniectanea Biblica: Old Testament Series
CBQ	*Catholic Biblical Quarterly*
CBQMS	Catholic Biblical Quarterly Monograph Series
ConBNT	Coniectanea Neotestamentica or Coniectanea Biblica: New Testament Series
ConBOT	Coniectanea Biblica: Old Testament Series
CP	*Classical Philology*
CRAI	Comptes rendus de l'Académie des inscriptions et belles-lettres

CRINT	Compendia Rerum Iudaicarum ad Novum Testamentum
CTM	*Concordia Theological Monthly*
DJD	Discoveries in the Judaean Desert
EB	Echter Bibel
EI	*Encyclopaedia of Islam*
EKKNT	Evangelisch-katholischer Kommentar zum Neuen Testament
Enc	*Encounter*
EncJud	C. Roth and G. Wigoder (eds.), *Encyclopedia Judaica*
EPRO	Etudes préliminaires aux religions orientales dans l'empire romain
ErIsr	*Eretz-Israel*
EstBib	*Estudios bíblicos*
ETL	*Ephemerides Theologicae Lovanienses*
ETS	Erfurter theologische Studien
EvQ	*Evangelical Quarterly*
EvT	*Evangelische Theologie*
ExAud	*Ex Auditu*
ExpTim	*Expository Times*
FAT	Forschungen zum Alten Testament
FB	Forschung zur Bibel
FBBS	Facet Books, Biblical Series
FFNT	Foundations and Facets: New Testament
FOTL	Forms of the Old Testament Literature
FRLANT	Forschungen zur Religion und Literatur des Alten und Neuen Testaments
FTS	Frankfurter Theologische Studien
GBS.OTS	Guides to Biblical Scholarship. Old Testament Series
GCS	Die griechischen christlichen Schriftsteller der ersten [drei] Jahrhunderte
GKC	Emil Kautzsch (ed.), *Gesenius' Hebrew Grammar*, trans. A. E. Cowley, 2nd ed.
GNS	*Good News Studies*
GTA	Göttinger theologischer Arbeiten
HALAT	*Hebräisches und aramäisches Lexikon zum Alten Testament*
HAR	*Hebrew Annual Review*
HAT	Handbuch zum Alten Testament
HBC	*Harper's Bible Commentary*
HBT	*Horizons in Biblical Theology*
HDB	*Hastings' Dictionary of the Bible*
HDR	Harvard Dissertations in Religion
HeyJ	Heythrop Journal
HNT	Handbuch zum Neuen Testament
HNTC	Harper's New Testament Commentaries
HR	*History of Religions*
HSM	Harvard Semitic Monographs
HSS	Harvard Semitic Studies
HTKNT	Herders Theologischer Kommentar zum Neuen Testament
HTR	*Harvard Theological Review*
HTS	Harvard Theological Studies
HUCA	*Hebrew Union College Annual*
IB	*Interpreter's Bible*
IBC	Interpretation: A Bible Commentary for Teaching and Preaching
IBS	*Irish Biblical Studies*
ICC	International Critical Commentary

IDB	*The Interpreter's Dictionary of the Bible*
IDBSup	supplementary volume to *The Interpreter's Dictionary of the Bible*
IEJ	*Israel Exploration Journal*
Int	*Interpretation*
IRT	Issues in Religion and Theology
ITC	International Theological Commentary
JAAR	*Journal of the American Academy of Religion*
JAL	Jewish Apocryphal Literature Series
JANESCU	*Journal of the Ancient Near Eastern Society of Columbia University*
JAOS	*Journal of the American Oriental Society*
JBL	*Journal of Biblical Literature*
JETS	*Journal of the Evangelical Theological Society*
JJS	*Journal of Jewish Studies*
JNES	*Journal of Near Eastern Studies*
JNSL	*Journal of Northwest Semitic Languages*
JPS	Jewish Publication Society
JQR	*Jewish Quarterly Review*
JR	*Journal of Religion*
JRH	*Journal of Religious History*
JSJ	*Journal for the Study of Judaism in the Persian, Hellenistic, and Roman Periods*
JSNT	*Journal for the Study of the New Testament*
JSNTSup	Journal for the Study of the New Testament Supplement Series
JSOT	*Journal for the Study of the Old Testament*
JSOTSup	Journal for the Study of the Old Testament Supplement Series
JSP	*Journal for the Study of the Pseudepigrapha*
JSS	*Journal of Semitic Studies*
JTC	*Journal for Theology and the Church*
JTS	*Journal of Theological Studies*
KAT	Kommentar zum Alten Testament
KB	L. Koehler and W. Baumgartner, *Lexicon in Veteris Testamenti libros*
KEK	Kritisch-exegetischer Kommentar über das Neue Testament (Meyer-Kommentar)
KPG	Knox Preaching Guides
LCL	Loeb Classical Library
LTQ	Lexington Theological Quarterly
MNTC	*Moffatt New Testament Commentary*
NCBC	New Century Bible Commentary
NHS	*Nag Hammadi Studies*
NIB	*The New Interpreter's Bible*
NIBC	*The New Interpreter's Bible Commentary*
NICNT	New International Commentary on the New Testament
NICOT	New International Commentary on the Old Testament
NIGTC	The New International Greek Testament Commentary
NJBC	*The New Jerome Biblical Commentary*
NovT	*Novum Testamentum*
NovTSup	Supplements to Novum Testamentum
NPNF	*Nicene and Post-Nicene Fathers*
NTC	New Testament in Context
NTG	New Testament Guides
NTS	*New Testament Studies*
NTT	*Norsk Teologisk Tidsskrift*

OBC	*The Oxford Bible Commentary*
OBO	Orbis Biblicus et Orientalis
OBT	Overtures to Biblical Theology
OIP	Oriental Institute Publications
Or	*Orientalia* (NS)
OTG	Old Testament Guides
OTL	Old Testament Library
OTM	Old Testament Message
OTP	*Old Testament Pseudepigrapha*
OTS	*Oudtestamentische Studiën*
PAAJR	*Proceedings of the American Academy of Jewish Research*
PEFQS	Palestine Exploration Fund Quarterly Statement
PEQ	*Palestine Exploration Quarterly*
PGM	K. Preisendanz (ed.), *Papyri Graecae Magicae*
PTMS	Pittsburgh Theological Monograph Series
QD	Quaestiones Disputatae
RANE	Records of the Ancient Near East
RB	*Revue biblique*
ResQ	*Restoration Quarterly*
RevExp	*Review and Expositor*
RevQ	*Revue de Qumran*
RSRel	*Recherches de science religieuse*
RTL	*Revue théologique de Louvain*
SAA	State Archives of Assyria
SB	H. L. Strack and P. Billerbeck, *Kommentar zum Neuen Testament aus Talmud und Midrasch,* 6 vols. 1922–61
SBAB	Stuttgarter biblische Aufsatzbände
SBB	Stuttgarter biblische Beiträge
SBL	Society of Biblical Literature
SBLDS	SBL Dissertation Series
SBLMS	SBL Monograph Series
SBLRBS	SBL Resources for Biblical Study
SBLSCS	SBL Septuagint and Cognate Studies
SBLSP	SBL Seminar Papers
SBLSS	SBL *Semeia* Studies
SBLSymS	SBL Symposium Series
SBLWAW	SBL Writings from the Ancient World
SBM	Stuttgarter biblische Monographien
SBS	Stuttgarter Bibelstudien
SBT	Studies in Biblical Theology
SEÅ	*Svensk exegetisk årsbok*
SJLA	Studies in Judaism in Late Antiquity
SJOT	*Scandinavian Journal of the Old Testament*
SJT	*Scottish Journal of Theology*
SKK	Stuttgarter kleiner Kommentar
SNTSMS	Society for New Testament Studies Monograph Series
SOTSMS	Society for Old Testament Studies Monograph Series
SP	Sacra Pagina
SR	*Studies in Religion/Sciences religieuses*
SSN	Studia Semitica Neerlandica
ST	*Studia Theologica*
SUNT	Studien zur Umwelt des Neuen Testaments
SVT	Supplements to Vetus Testamentum

SVTP	Studia in Veteris Testamenti Pseudepigraphica
SWBA	Social World of Biblical Antiquity
TB	Theologische Bücherei: Neudrucke und Berichte aus dem 20. Jahrhundert
TD	*Theology Digest*
TDNT	*Theological Dictionary of the New Testament*
TDOT	*Theological Dictionary of the Old Testament*
TextS	Texts and Studies
THKNT	Theologischer Handkommentar zum Neuen Testament
TLZ	*Theologische Literaturzeitung*
TOTC	Tyndale Old Testament Commentaries
TQ	*Theologische Quartalschrift*
TSK	*Theologische Studien und Kritiken*
TSSI	*Textbook of Syrian Semitic Inscriptions*
TToday	*Theology Today*
TynBul	*Tyndale Bulletin*
TZ	*Theologische Zeitschrift*
UBS	United Bible Societies
UBSGNT	*United Bible Societies Greek New Testament*
UF	*Ugarit-Forschungen*
USQR	*Union Seminary Quarterly Review*
UUÅ	Uppsala Universitetsårsskrift
VC	*Vigiliae Christianae*
VT	*Vetus Testamentum*
VTSup	Supplements to Vetus Testamentum
WA	M. Luther, *Kritische Gesamtausgabe* (= "Weimar" edition)
WBC	Word Biblical Commentary
WBT	Word Biblical Themes
WMANT	Wissenschaftliche Monographien zum Alten und Neuen Testament
WTJ	*Westminster Theological Journal*
WUNT	Wissenschaftliche Untersuchungen zum Neuen Testament
ZAH	*Zeitschrift für Althebräistik*
ZAW	*Zeitschrift für die alttestamentliche Wissenschaft*
ZNW	*Zeitschrift für die neutestamentliche Wissenschaft und die Kunde der älteren Kirche*
ZTK	*Zeitschrift für Theologie und Kirche*